W9-BSI-229

Boston MBTA

Oak Grove
Malden
Wellington
Sullivan Square
Community College
North Station
Lechmere
Science Park
Wonderland
Revere Beach
Beachmont
Suffolk Downs
Orient Heights
Wood Island
Airport
Maverick

Alewife
Davis
Porter
Harvard
Central
Kendall/MIT
Bowdoin
Gov't Center
Haymarket
Aquarium

Logan International Airport

Charles/MGH
Park St
State*

Boston College
Harvard Ave
Hynes/ICA
Copley
Arlington
Boylston
Downtown Crossing

Cleveland Circle
Riverside
Woodland
Waban
Eliot
Newton Highlands
Newton Centre
Chestnut Hill
Reservoir
Beaconsfield
Brookline Hills
Brookline Village
Kenmore
Fenway
Prudential
Symphony
Northeastern
Museum of Fine Arts
Longwood
Brigham Circle
Longwood
Mass Ave
Ruggles
Roxbury Crossing
Jackson Sq
Stony Brook
Green St
Forest Hills
Heath

Chinatown
NE Medical Center
E. Berkeley St
Worcester Sq
Mass Ave
Melnea Cass Blvd
Dudley Sq
South Station
Broadway
Andrew
JFK/UMass
Savin Hill
Fields Corner
Shawmut
Ashmont
Cedar Grove
Butler
Milton
Central Ave
Valley Rd
Capen St
Mattapan
North Quincy
Wollaston
Quincy Center
Quincy Adams
Braintree

LEGEND

Transit lines & stop

Commuter rail & station

Terminal station

Free interchange with other lines

Accessible Station

Parking

*Boylston: Accessible for Silver Line only
*State: Blue line wheelchair access outbound side only. Inbound riders transfer to outbound train at Government Center. Exit State outbound

Water Transportation Services
Hingham Shipyard to Rowes Wharf, Boston
Quincy, Hull, & Logan Airport to Long Wharf, Boston
Lovejoy Wharf to Charlestown Navy Yard
Long Wharf to Charlestown Navy Yard
Lovejoy Wharf to U.S. Courthouse to World Trade Center

Customer service & travel information.......(617) 222-3200
Visit our website at: www.mbta.com

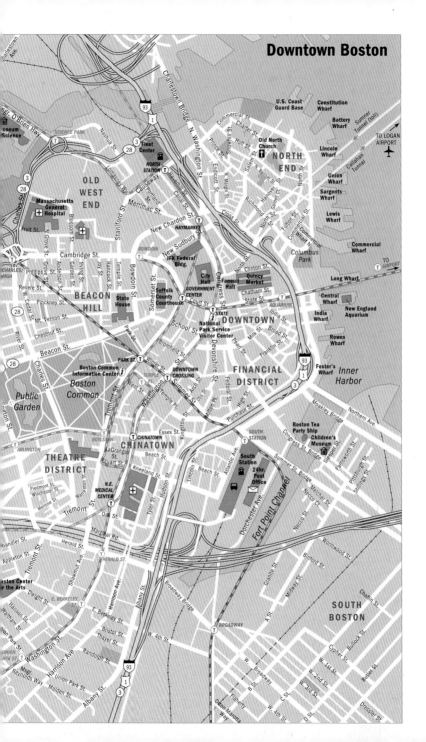

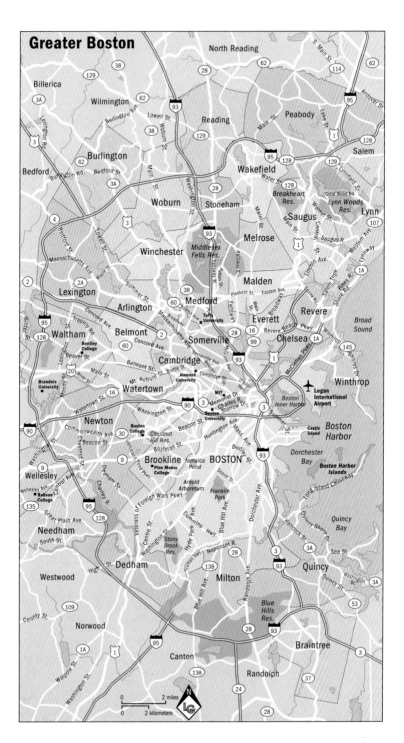

Greater Boston

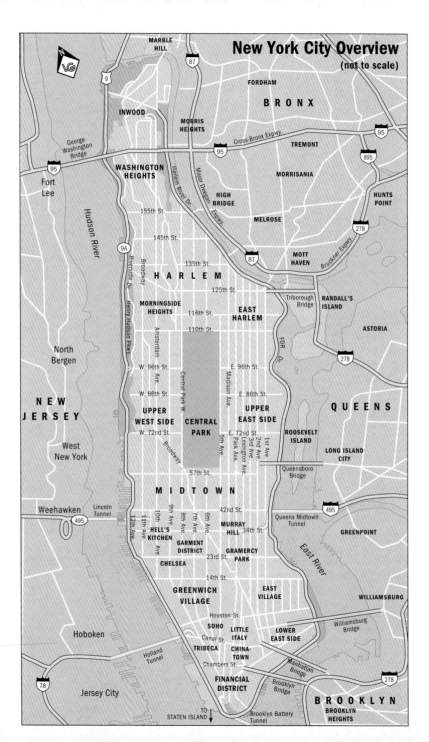

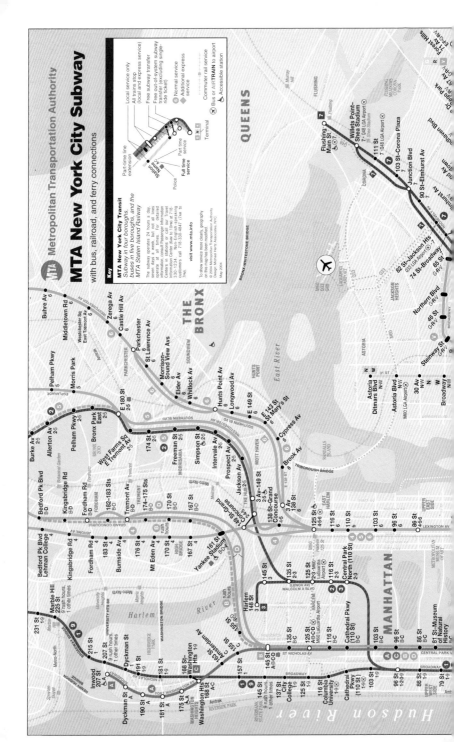

MTA New York City Subway

MTA Metropolitan Transportation Authority

with bus, railroad, and ferry connections

Key

MTA New York City Transit

Subway in four boroughs, buses in five boroughs, and the MTA Staten Island Railway

The subway operates 24 hours a day, seven days a week, but not all lines operate at all times. For detailed information, contact the Public Information Center (toll free) at 1-718-330-1234 / (711 for hearing-impaired). Customers call 718-330-4847 / (7am to 7pm).

visit www.mta.info

To show service more clearly, geography on this map has been modified.

© 2004 Metropolitan Transportation Authority
Design: Michael Hertz Associates, NYC

May 2004

Local service only
(local and express service)
All trains stop
Free subway transfer
Free out-of-system subway transfer (excluding single-ride ticket)
● Normal service
◆ Additional express service
Commuter rail service
Ⓧ Bus or AIRTRAIN to airport
Ⓚ Accessible station

Part time line extension
Full time service
Part time service
Terminal
Police

Hudson River

East River

Harlem River

THE BRONX

QUEENS

MANHATTAN

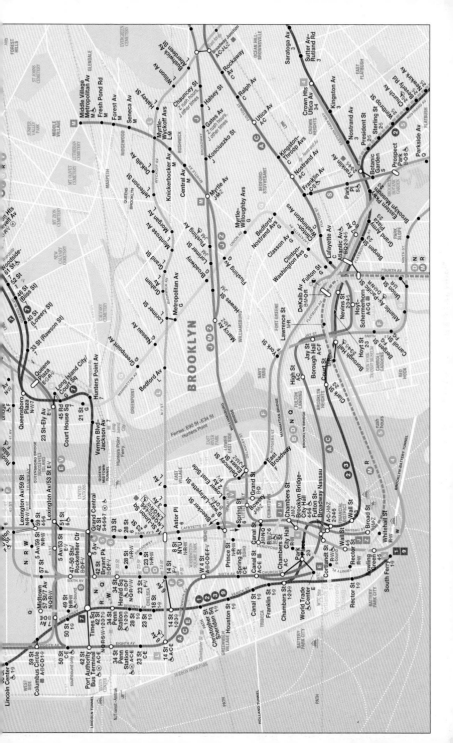

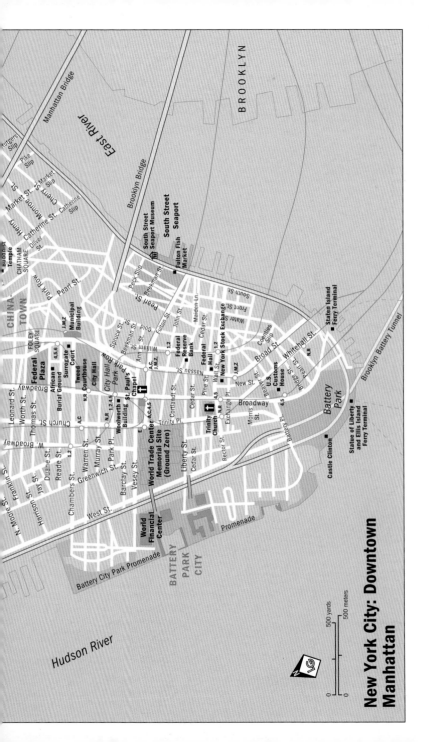

New York City: Downtown Manhattan

New York City: Midtown Manhattan

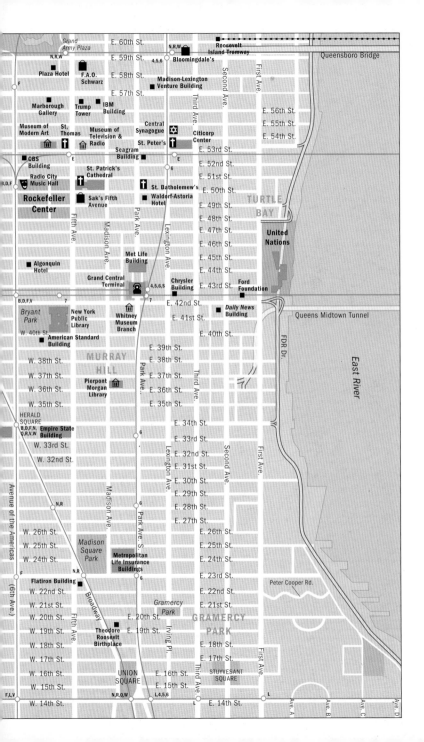

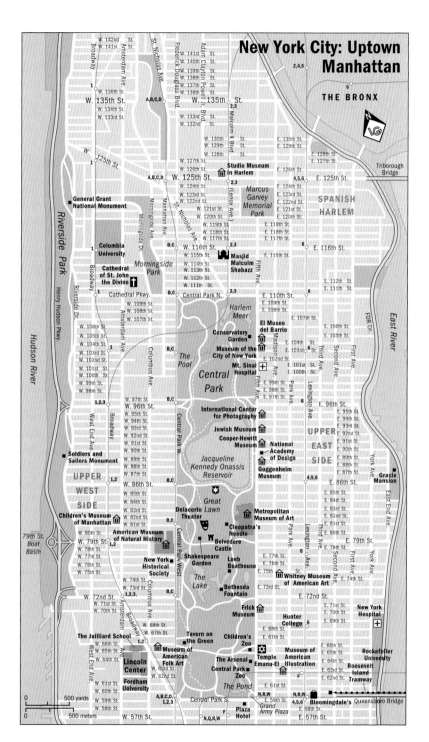

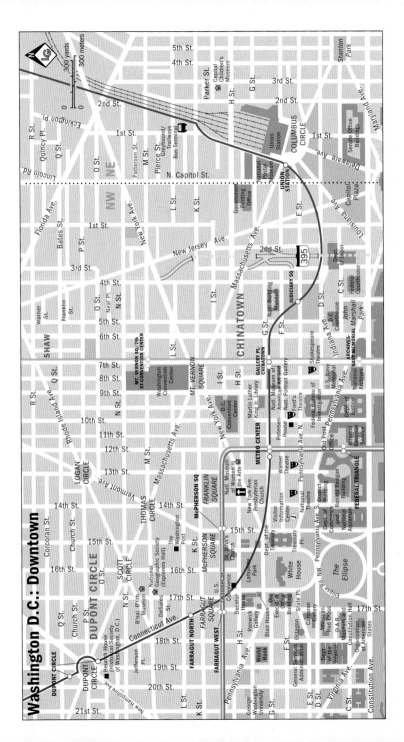

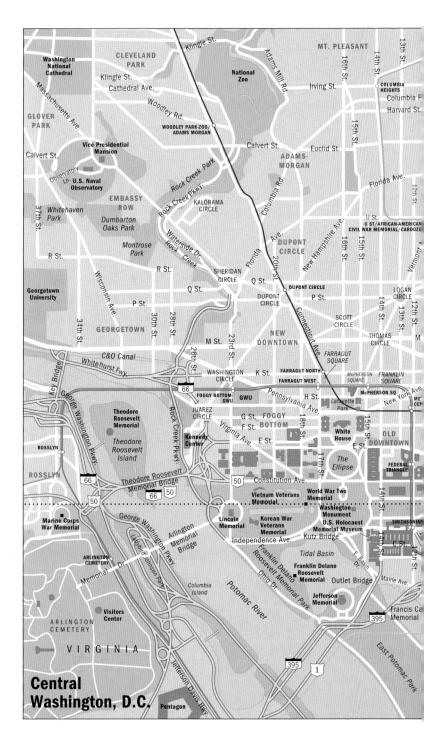

Central Washington, D.C.

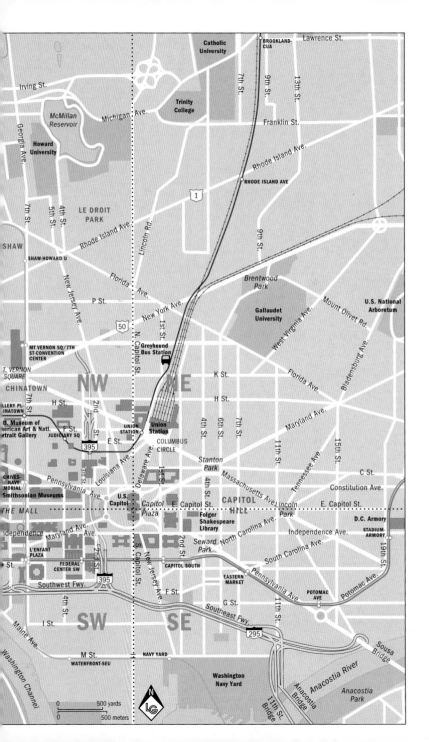

Washington, D.C.: The Mall Area

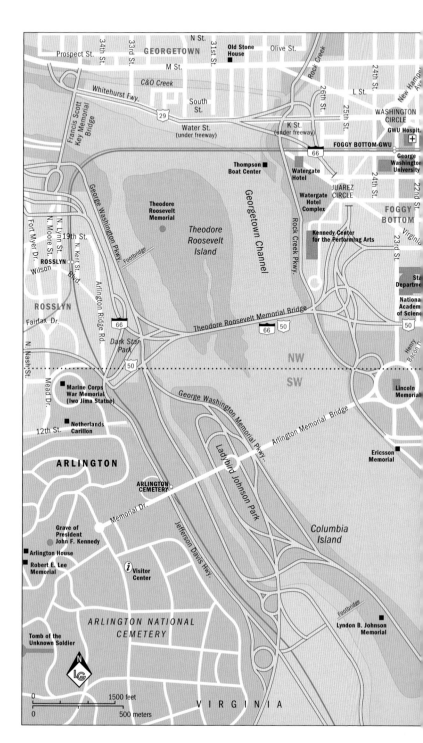

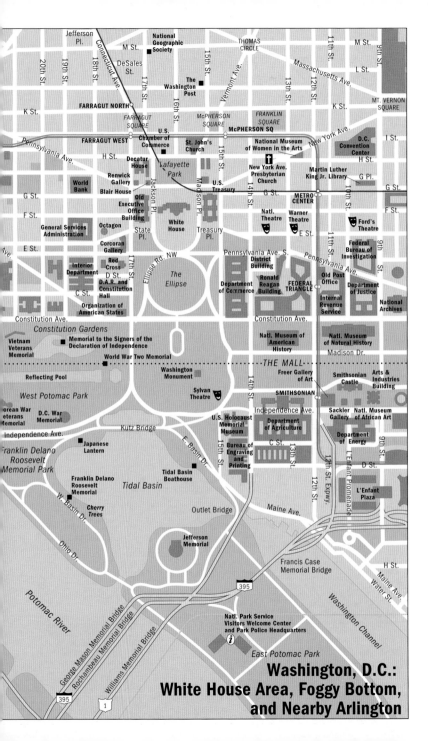

Washington, D.C.:
**White House Area, Foggy Bottom,
and Nearby Arlington**

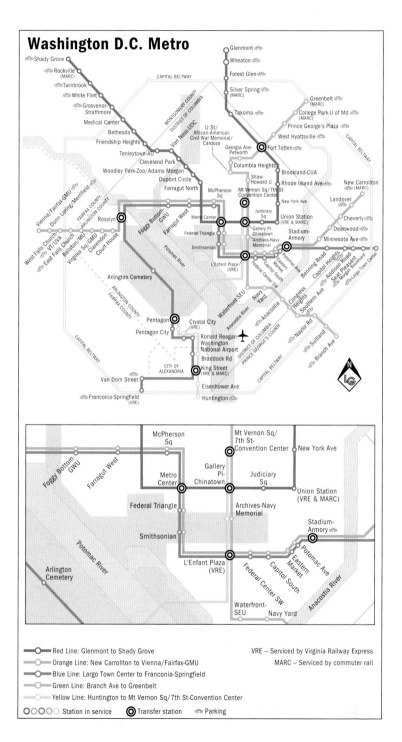

Washington D.C. Metro

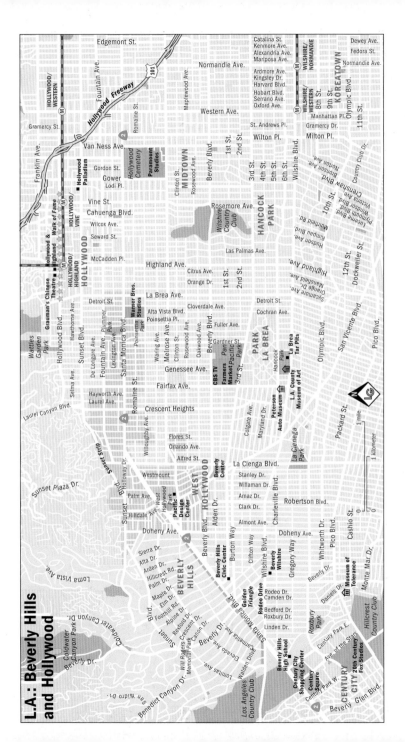

L.A.: Beverly Hills and Hollywood

Metropolitan
Los Angeles

Metro Green Line
Metro Blue Line
Metro Red Line

0 2 miles
0 2 kilometers

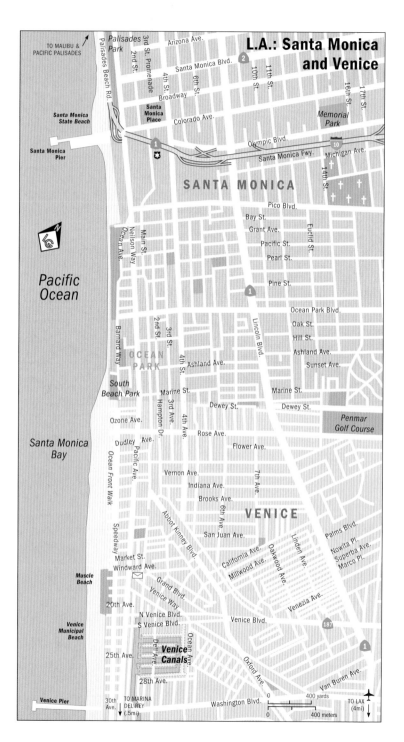

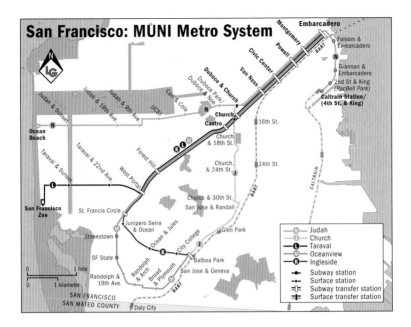

San Francisco: MUNI Metro System

Embarcadero
Montgomery
Powell
Civic Center
Van Ness
Duboce & Church
Duboce Park/
Duboce & Noe
Carl & Cole
UCSF
Judah & 9th Ave.
Judah & 19th Ave.
Judah & Sunset
Ocean Beach
Taraval & 22nd Ave.
Taraval & Sunset
West Portal
Forest Hill
Church
Castro
Church & 18th St.
Church & 24th St.
16th St.
24th St.
Church & 30th St.
San Jose & Randall
San Francisco Zoo
St. Francis Circle
Junipero Serra & Ocean
Stonestown
Ocean & Jules
City College
Glen Park
SF State
Randolph & Arch
Broad & Plymouth
Balboa Park
Randolph & 19th Ave.
San Jose & Geneva

Folsom & Embarcadero
Brannan & Embarcadero
2nd St & King (PacBell Park)
Caltrain Station/ (4th St. & King)

CALTRAIN
BART

0   1 mile
0   1 kilometer

SAN FRANCISCO
SAN MATEO COUNTY
Daly City

Legend:
- N — Judah
- J — Church
- L — Taraval
- M — Oceanview
- K — Ingleside
- •— Subway station
- •-- Surface station
- Subway transfer station
- Surface transfer station

San Francisco: BART System

North Concord/Martinez
Concord
Pittsburg/ Bay Point
CONTRA COSTA COUNTY
Richmond
El Cerrito del Norte
El Cerrito Plaza
Pleasant Hill
Walnut Creek
Lafayette
MARIN COUNTY
San Francisco Bay
North Berkeley
Berkeley
Ashby
Orinda
Rockridge
MacArthur
19th St./Oakland
Oakland City Center/ 12th St.
Ft. Cronkhite
Embarcadero
Montgomery St.
Powell St.
Civic Center
West Oakland
Lake Merritt
Fruitvale
16th St./Mission
24th St./Mission
Coliseum/ Oakland Airport
SAN FRANCISCO
Glen Park
Balboa Park
Caltrain
Oakland International Airport
San Leandro
Daly City
Colma
San Francisco Bay
Bay Fair
Castro Valley
Dublin/ Pleasanton
South San Francisco
San Bruno
Hayward
ALAMEDA COUNTY
San Francisco International Airport
South Hayward
SAN MATEO COUNTY
Millbrae
Union City
Fremont

Legend:
- Richmond-Daly City
- Pittsburg/Bay Point-Millbrae
- Fremont-Daly City
- Fremont-Richmond
- Dublin/Pleasanton-SFO
- SFO-Millbrae Shuttle
- CalTrain

0   4 miles
0   4 kilometers

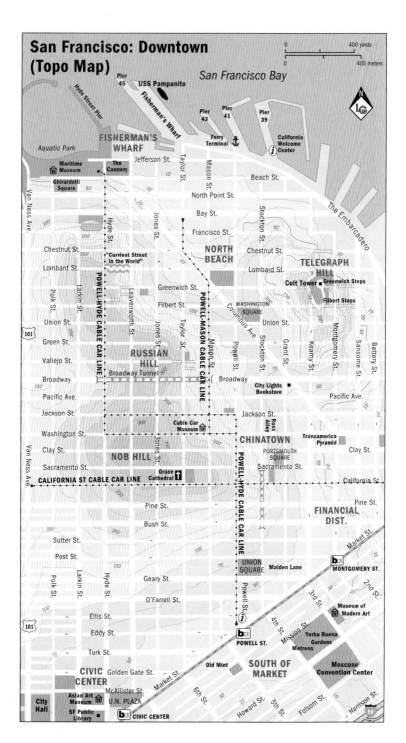

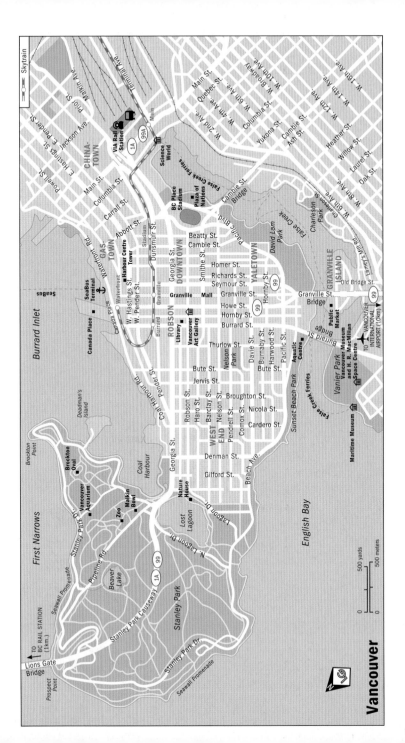

Vancouver

Skytrain

Burrard Inlet

First Narrows

Lions Gate Bridge
Prospect Point
TO BC RAIL STATION (1km.)
Brockton Point
Deadman's Island
SeaBus

Seawall Promenade
Stanley Park Dr.
Brockton Oval
Vancouver Aquarium
Zoo
Malkin Bowl
Nature House
Pipeline Rd.
Beaver Lake
Coal Harbour
SeaBus Terminal
Canada Place
Waterfront Rd.
Canada Place
Waterfront
99
Lost Lagoon
N. Lagoon Dr.
Lagoon Dr.
Stanley Park
Stanley Park Causeway
1A

Coal Harbour Rd.
Pender St.
W. Hastings St.
W. Pender St.
Harbour Centre Tower
GAS TOWN
Stadium
Granville
Burrard
CHINA-TOWN
Powell St.
E. Hastings St.
E. Jackson Ave.
E. Pender St.
Malkin Ave.
Prior St.
Jackson Ave.
Main St.
Columbia St.
Carrall St.
Abbott St.
Dunsmuir St.
Stadium
Terminal Ave.
VIA Rail Station
1A
99A
Main

Georgia St.
Smithe St.
DOWNTOWN
Beatty St.
Cambie St.
Homer St.
Richards St.
Seymour St.
Granville St.
Howe St.
Hornby St.
Burrard St.
Granville Mall
ROBSON
Library
Vancouver Art Gallery
Thurlow St.
Bute St.
Jervis St.
Robson St.
Haro St.
Barclay St.
Nelson St.
Broughton St.
Nicola St.
Cardero St.
Comox St.
Pendrell St.
Denman St.
Gilford St.
Georgia St.
WEST END
Nelson Park
Davie St.
Burnaby St.
Harwood St.
Bute St.
Pacific St.
Beach Ave.
Aquatic Centre

YALETOWN
99
David Lam Park
Pacific Blvd.
BC Place Stadium
Plaza of Nations
Cambie St.
Yukona St.
Cambie St. Bridge
False Creek Ferries
Science World
Cambie St.
Main St.
Quebec St.
Main St.
W. 2nd Ave.
W. 4th Ave
W. 6th Ave.
W. Broadway
W. 10th Ave.
W. 12th Ave.
W. 14th Ave.
W. 16th Ave.
Columbia St.
Ash St.
Heather St.
Willow St.
Laurel St.
Oak St.
W. 8th Ave.
Charleson St.
W. 6th Ave.
Charleson Park
False Creek
GRANVILLE ISLAND
Lamey's Mill Rd.
Old Bridge St.
Granville St.
Granville St. Bridge
99
TO VANCOUVER INTERNATIONAL AIRPORT (10km.)
Public Market
Sunset Beach Park
False Creek Ferries
Burrard St. Bridge
Vanier Park
Vancouver Museum and H. R. MacMillan Space Centre
Maritime Museum

English Bay

500 yards
500 meters
0
0

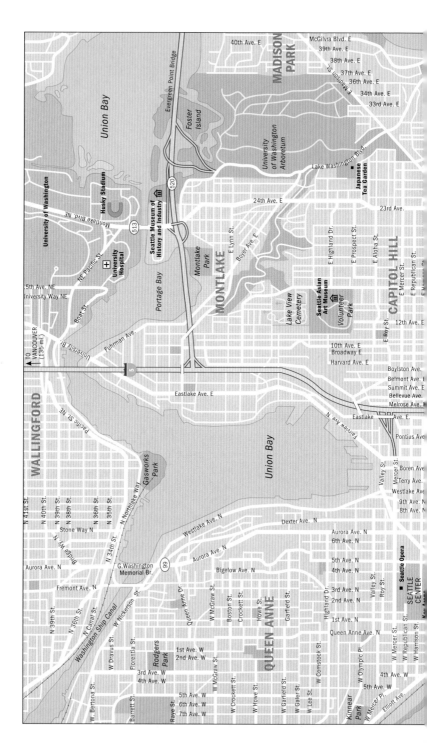

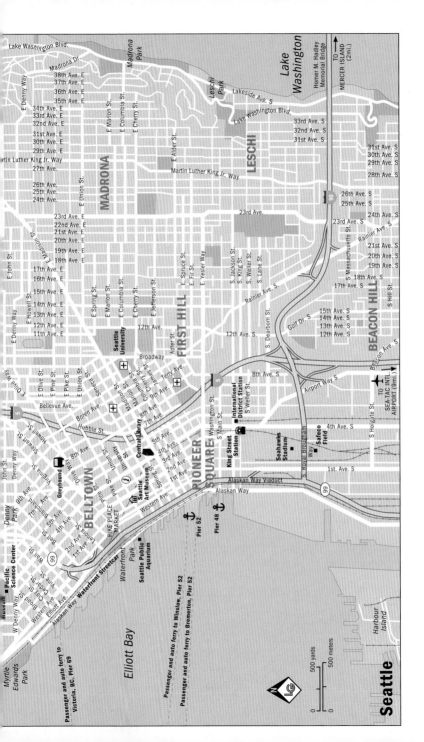

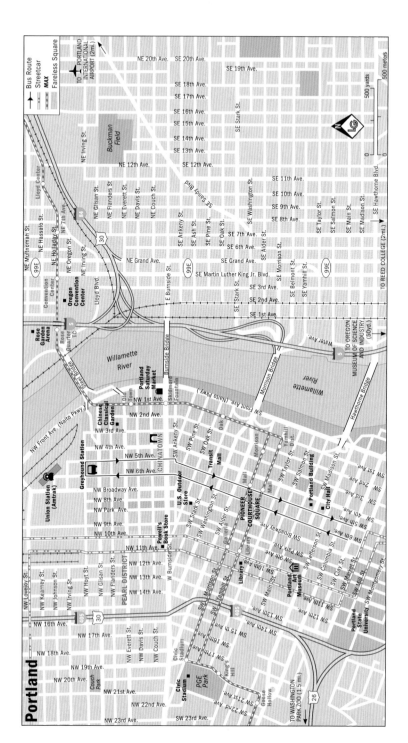

LET'S GO

■ THE RESOURCE FOR THE INDEPENDENT TRAVELER

"The guides are aimed not only at young budget travelers but at the independent traveler; a sort of streetwise cookbook for traveling alone."

—The New York Times

"Unbeatable; good sight-seeing advice; up-to-date info on restaurants, hotels, and inns; a commitment to money-saving travel; and a wry style that brightens nearly every page."

—The Washington Post

"Lighthearted and sophisticated, informative and fun to read. [Let's Go] helps the novice traveler navigate like a knowledgeable old hand."

—Atlanta Journal-Constitution

"A world-wise traveling companion—always ready with friendly advice and helpful hints, all sprinkled with a bit of wit."

—The Philadelphia Inquirer

■ THE BEST TRAVEL BARGAINS IN YOUR PRICE RANGE

"All the dirt, dirt cheap."

—People

"Anything you need to know about budget traveling is detailed in this book."

—The Chicago Sun-Times

"Let's Go follows the creed that you don't have to toss your life's savings to the wind to travel—unless you want to."

—The Salt Lake Tribune

■ REAL ADVICE FOR REAL EXPERIENCES

"The writers seem to have experienced every rooster-packed bus and lunar-surfaced mattress about which they write."

—The New York Times

"Value-packed, unbeatable, accurate, and comprehensive."

—The Los Angeles Times

"[Let's Go's] devoted updaters really walk the walk (and thumb the ride, and trek the trail). Learn how to fish, haggle, find work—anywhere."

—Food & Wine

LET'S GO PUBLICATIONS

TRAVEL GUIDES

Australia 8th edition
Austria & Switzerland 12th edition
Brazil 1st edition
Britain & Ireland 2005
California 10th edition
Central America 9th edition
Chile 2nd edition
China 5th edition
Costa Rica 2nd edition
Eastern Europe 2005
Ecuador 1st edition **NEW TITLE**
Egypt 2nd edition
Europe 2005
France 2005
Germany 12th edition
Greece 2005
Hawaii 3rd edition
India & Nepal 8th edition
Ireland 2005
Israel 4th edition
Italy 2005
Japan 1st edition
Mexico 20th edition
Middle East 4th edition
Peru 1st edition **NEW TITLE**
Puerto Rico 1st edition
South Africa 5th edition
Southeast Asia 9th edition
Spain & Portugal 2005
Thailand 2nd edition
Turkey 5th edition
USA 2005
Vietnam 1st edition **NEW TITLE**
Western Europe 2005

ROADTRIP GUIDE

Roadtripping USA **NEW TITLE**

ADVENTURE GUIDES

Alaska 1st edition
New Zealand **NEW TITLE**
Pacific Northwest **NEW TITLE**
Southwest USA 3rd edition

CITY GUIDES

Amsterdam 3rd edition
Barcelona 3rd edition
Boston 4th edition
London 2005
New York City 15th edition
Paris 13th edition
Rome 12th edition
San Francisco 4th edition
Washington, D.C. 13th edition

POCKET CITY GUIDES

Amsterdam
Berlin
Boston
Chicago
London
New York City
Paris
San Francisco
Venice
Washington, D.C.

LET'S GO

USA

WITH COVERAGE OF CANADA

2005

CHRIS SCHONBERGER EDITOR
JULIA BONNHEIM ASSOCIATE EDITOR
ADRIENNE TAYLOR GERKEN ASSOCIATE EDITOR
MICHELLE ROBINSON ASSOCIATE EDITOR

RESEARCHER-WRITERS

KATY BARTELMA
JASON BROWN
ZAC CORKER
ZACHARY T. ELSEA
STEPHEN FROST

CATHERINE JAMPEL
JESSICA JONES
CHRIS LOOMIS
JOSH SUSKEWICZ
JOSH VANDIVER

JOHN KIERNAN MAP EDITOR
LAUREN TRUESDELL MANAGING EDITOR

ST. MARTIN'S PRESS ⚓ NEW YORK

HELPING LET'S GO. If you want to share your discoveries, suggestions, or corrections, please drop us a line. We read every piece of correspondence, whether a postcard, a 10-page email, or a coconut. **Address mail to:**

Let's Go: USA
67 Mount Auburn Street
Cambridge, MA 02138
USA

Visit Let's Go at **http://www.letsgo.com,** or send email to:

feedback@letsgo.com
Subject: "Let's Go: USA"

In addition to the invaluable travel advice our readers share with us, many are kind enough to offer their services as researchers or editors. Unfortunately, our charter enables us to employ only currently enrolled Harvard students.

Maps by David Lindroth copyright © 2005 by St. Martin's Press.

Distributed outside the USA and Canada by Macmillan, an imprint of Pan Macmillan Ltd. 20 New Wharf Road, London N1 9RR
Basingstoke and Oxford
Associated companies throughout the world
www.panmacmillan.com

ISBN: 0-312-33557-1
EAN: 978-0312-33557-1
First edition
10 9 8 7 6 5 4 3 2 1

Let's Go: USA is written by Let's Go Publications, 67 Mount Auburn Street, Cambridge, MA 02138, USA.

Let's Go® and the LG logo are trademarks of Let's Go, Inc.
Printed in the USA.

HOW TO USE THIS BOOK

Every year, *Let's Go* sends dozens of researchers across the United States and Canada in search of the most authentic cuisine, the most bizarre Americana, and the best deals on the continent. This year's edition features expanded small-town coverage and is revised, revamped, and ready to hit the road. Here's what you'll find inside.

ORGANIZATION. This book will walk you (and probably ride with you) state by state and province by province through the US and Canada, starting on the East Coast and heading west, from Maine to Oahu and Newfoundland to British Columbia. The black tabs on the side of the book will help you find your way around.

HELPFUL INFORMATION. The Essentials section will tell you how much (or how little) to pack, and the Life and Times section will get you up to speed with the last few hundred years of history, art, and music. The Alternatives to Tourism section will alert you to opportunities for short-term work and study and other exciting ways to make a difference during your travels.

PHONE CODES AND TELEPHONE NUMBERS. Three-digit area codes for each region appear opposite the name of the region and are denoted by the ☎ icon. Phone numbers in text are also preceded by the ☎ icon. Ten-digit dialing is often required, especially in big cities, so be prepared to dial the area code before many numbers.

PRICE RANGES AND RANKINGS. Our researchers list establishments in order of value from best to worst. Gay and lesbian establishments, if they do not have their own section, are listed at the end of each. Our particular favorites are denoted by the *Let's Go* thumbs-up (☒), our way of telling you that an establishment is too good to be missed. Since the best value is not always the cheapest price, we have incorporated a system of price ranges for the guide (p. xv).

FEATURES. The Out of the Way feature tries to get at Americana in a way that big city coverage can't. You'll hear about a reconstruction of Dorothy's house from *The Wizard of Oz* in the middle of Kansas and a zoo where animals reenact the sinking of the *Titanic*. The Local Story, either an interview with a local resident or a look at a destination's stories, history, and lore will illuminate local culture. Big Splurge features tell you when extravagances are worthy of your hard-earned currency, while Hidden Deals will help your farthings go farther.

SCHOLARLY ARTICLES. Bert Vaux's article on America's regional dialects will explain why some Americans say "soda" while others say "pop," and other quirks of American language. A new scholarly article about on the evolution of American sexual mores provides an interesting perspective on current trends in American culture.

A NOTE TO OUR READERS. The information for this book was gathered by *Let's Go* researchers from May through August of 2004. Each listing is based on one researcher's opinion, formed during his or her visit at a particular time. Those traveling at other times may have different experiences since prices, dates, hours, and conditions are always subject to change. You are urged to check the facts presented in this book beforehand to avoid inconvenience and surprises.

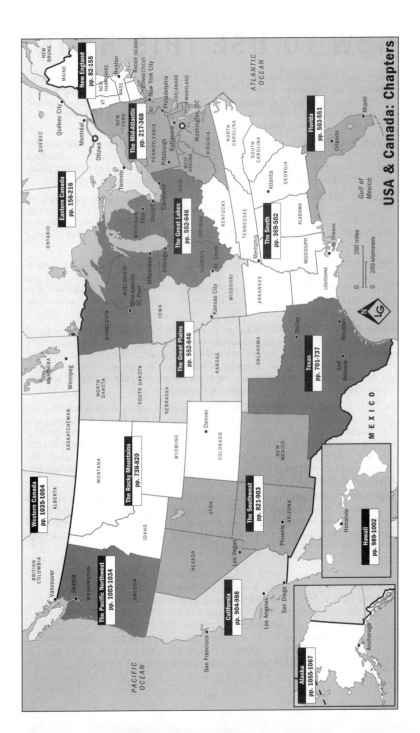

USA & Canada: Chapters

New England pp. 82-155

The Mid-Atlantic pp. 217-368

Eastern Canada pp. 156-216

Florida pp. 503-551

The Great Lakes pp. 552-646

The South pp. 369-502

The Great Plains pp. 552-646

Western Canada pp. 1035-1054

Texas pp. 701-737

The Rocky Mountains pp. 738-820

The Southwest pp. 821-903

Hawaii pp. 989-1002

The Pacific Northwest pp. 1003-1034

California pp. 904-988

Alaska pp. 1055-1067

0   200 miles
0   200 kilometers

CONTENTS

RESEARCHER-WRITERS

Katy Bartelma
The Southwest

With her camping prowess and natural friendliness, Katy was a researching all-star. An Iowa-born southwestophile, she made her way through her route eating fabulous Mexican food, visiting countless national parks, and going on make-you-sweat power-hikes. Even with a jam-packed itinerary, Katy made time to do a crossword puzzle with a local cook and write detailed, imagery-infused copy that painted a stunningly beautiful picture of the Southwest.

Jason Brown
New England

If you're talking about a rock and a hard place, Jason Brown was there. Stopping only for the proverbial clambake, he became *Let's Go USA*'s Iron Man, camping, swimming, and hiking his way across New England as energetically as any triathlete. Stunned by the beauty of the Appalachian Trail, Jason trekked down through the rainy Adirondacks and finally fell in love with the Thousand Island Seaway, whose image he immortalized in florid, crystalline text.

Zac Corker
Florida, Georgia, and South Carolina

A party disguised as a thorough and thoughtful researcher, Zac admired cool velour tracksuits in Hotlanta, battled 'gators in the Everglades, and smooth-talked his way into the hottest clubs in Miami. Along the way he braved sauna-like tents, sampled a little *cocina cubana*, gave the "thumbs down" to overpriced establishments, partied like Shaq in SoBe, had a little too much fun with some belly dancers, and met Hemingway's cats—all 60 of 'em.

Zachary T. Elsea
Texas, Oklahoma, and Kansas

Despite this California native's original skepticism about Texas, Zach found himself in a Lone Star state of mind as he chatted with a rodeo cowboy, battled Texas-sized hail, and fell hard for the city of Austin. Zach carefully crafted new copy, letting his writing skills shine, and got a little closer to his distant relative, President Harry S Truman, in Independence, MO. Thanks to his camera phone, Zach chronicled his journey online, much to his editors' delights.

Stephen Frost
The South

Stephen swept across the Deep South like a tropical storm, strutting and fretting in the folk music capital of the world, then mewling and puking on an inordinate amount of deep-fried deliciousness—including his very first funnel cake. "The Brit" also moseyed on down to a rodeo, partied like it's 1999 in Spring Break Capital, USA, and fell victim to Southern charm Selma, Alabama—don't worry, he recovered before the immigration officials arrived.

Catherine Jampel
The Great Plains

With her wilderness experience, spunk, and chatty disposition, CJ was the obvious choice to update our Great Plains coverage. Braving Omaha's criminal elements, zoos, and the Mall of America, CJ took the Great Plains by storm. Along the way, she stumbled upon a mythical university, broke a dog-musher's heart, and exhibited a sixth sense for wireless Internet and A/C, all the while keeping her editors happy with her wild stories and shining copy.

Jessica Jones   *The Mid-Atlantic*

What tour is complete without some sad stranger being forced to wear breeches for your amusement? An anthropologist-in-training, Jessica thoughtfully observed hordes of garb-clad historical re-enactors from Roanoke to Gettysburg, and unearthed Pauly Shore in Charlotte, NC (re-bury him if you like). Jessica finished her grueling itinerary with the ease of a seasoned RW, sampling homemade ice cream, seaside taffy, and Southern sweet tea along the way.

Chris Loomis   *The Great Lakes*

A veritable Midwest expert, we knew Chris would be good. Midway to O'Hare, we realized just how good. Chris knocked on Death's Door, experienced an authentic American Fourth of July, and evinced an incredible determination to keep on truckin'—with or without brakes. Having crossed paths with Vikings, roof-eating goats, freaky fields of concrete corn, and mock monsoons, Chris deftly avoided "getting capped in the D." We told you he was good.

Josh Suskewicz   *Eastern Canada*

Josh went to Canada in search of national parks and moose, and came back having seen both, and, as an added bonus, having eaten ecstasy-inducing sticky buns; he had six. Weathering drives through blinding fog, a near-lighting-strike experience, and ridiculously long ferry rides, Josh produced thoughtful copy, with glowing reviews of Canada's natural beauty, bars that served a cheap pint of Guinness, and, oh yeah, sticky buns. He had six.

Josh Vandiver   *The Rockies*

A Colorado native and veteran *Let's Go* researcher, the charming Mr. Vandiver risked life and limb to rediscover his native region, from Jackson Hole to Big Sky country. In his constant search for a better place to pitch his tent, Josh encountered a colorful cast of rough 'n' tumble cowboys and savage campers, as well as more "hip" New Age juice bars than he cares to talk about. His only regret? Missing Cheyenne's Frontier Days festival.

REGIONAL RESEARCHER-WRITERS

Ann Whitlow Brown, Rohit Chopra, Brian Emeott, Nathan Orion Simmons, Oussama Zahr	*California*
Christine Ajudua, Abigail Burger, Andrew Nelson, Megan Smith	*Hawaii*
Joseph Abel, Anna Deknatel, J. Alan Dodd, Michael Rey	*Pacific Northwest*
Nicole Cliffe, Nellwyn Thomas	*New York City*

REGIONAL EDITORS

Naomi Straus *Editor*, Let's Go: California

Jeffrey J. Clinton *Associate Editor*, Let's Go: California and Let's Go: Hawaii

J. Maxwell Rogoski *Editor*, Let's Go: Hawaii

Alexandra Hoffer *Editor*, Let's Go: Pacific Northwest Adventure Guide

Lisa Kennelly *Associate Editor*, Let's Go: Pacific Northwest Adventure Guide

Margot E. Kaminski *Editor*, Let's Go: New York City

CONTRIBUTING WRITERS

Joseph A. Campana, Jr. is a PhD in Renaissance English Literature and currently teaches at Kenyon College in Ohio.

Professor Bert Vaux is a PhD in Linguistics and currently teaches at the University of Wisconsin-Milwaukee. He has written extensively, and taught popular classes on linguistics and dialects at Harvard University.

Trevor Walsh is studying Government at Harvard University, and spent the summer following Phish. His interests include spoken word, storage, and the Scottish language.

ACKNOWLEDGMENTS

TEAM USA'S PRO LIST: Our awesome RWs, for keeping us busy and amused; LT, an all-star 4 life; Kiernan, for his cartographic skillz; Vicki, for answering stupid questions; megafauna, for being Oz-some; Viking Island and waffles, for similar reasons; regenerative limbs; R. Kelly, for saving us—again, and again, and again; "perv," for being a verb; Nicole, proofer extraordinaire; Jeremy; PNW, for teaching us about spelunkers; hey Hil, that's awesome!

CHRIS THANKS: Seth, Stu, Kiernan, and Gaaron, for putting up with me; Mom, for life; Grandma, for countless cuppas; Granddad, for believing in me; R. Kelly, for inspiration; Julia, for mad reasonableness (and O.C.); Adrienne, for keeping me in check; Michelle, for sarcasm; Felipe's; Nick, for ig'nant stuff; Dad, for a bootleg car; my peeps worldwide.

JULIA THANKS: Adrienne, I think you're lovely; Chris, for making me your pop culture phone-a-friend and curling up with the Cohens; Michelle, for introducing us to secret fatties; LT, for country-love; Lean Cuisine; Nick, for ridiculousness; Maya, for the Hil experience; Meaghan, Nahu, Lisa and Katie, for making me stay out late and stream of conciousness conversations; my family for introducing me to life.

ADRIENNE THANKS: Julia, Chris, Michelle, and LT, for unprintable hilarity; the amazing Jeff and Marilyn Gerken, for love, support, and educational vacations; my incomparable sister, Danielle; Anna Gerken, grandmother (and pie-baker) extraordinaire; Joe G. and Thayer basement; CSG; the Korda and Koz families, and Brian.

MICHELLE THANKS: The Secret Agile Fatties club; Mariah and Santtu, for a superb vacation; my parents, Brooks and Wylma; Ian, for helping me grin down a bear (and Dan'l Boone); Patricia, for *Such Sweet Thunder;* Slavoj Zizek, for putting the Hegel back in Playboy and the Playboy back in Lacan.

JOHN THANKS: Chris, Seth, Stu, Aaron, Adrienne, Julia, LT, Michelle, and the stellar RWs. Mom 4 life.

Editor
Chris Schonberger
Associate Editors
Julia Bonnheim
Adrienne Taylor Gerken
Michelle Robinson
Managing Editor
Lauren Truesdell
Map Editor
John Kiernan
Typesetter
Christine Yokoyama

Publishing Director
Emma Nothmann
Editor-in-Chief
Teresa Elsey
Production Manager
Adam R. Perlman
Cartography Manager
Elizabeth Halbert Peterson
Design Manager
Amelia Aos Showalter
Editorial Managers
Briana Cummings, Charlotte Douglas, Ella M. Steim, Joel August Steinhaus, Lauren Truesdell, Christina Zaroulis
Financial Manager
R. Kirkie Maswoswe
Marketing and Publicity Managers
Stef Levner, Leigh Pascavage
Personnel Manager
Jeremy Todd
Low-Season Manager
Clay H. Kaminsky
Production Associate
Victoria Esquivel-Korsiak
IT Director
Matthew DePetro
Web Manager
Rob Dubbin
Associate Web Manager
Patrick Swieskowski
Web Content Manager
Tor Krever
Research and Development Consultant
Jennifer O'Brien
Office Coordinators
Stephanie Brown, Elizabeth Peterson

Director of Advertising Sales
Elizabeth S. Sabin
Senior Advertising Associates
Jesse R. Loffler, Francisco A. Robles, Zoe M. Savitsky
Advertising Graphic Designer
Christa Lee-Chuvala

President
Ryan M. Geraghty
General Manager
Robert B. Rombauer
Assistant General Manager
Anne E. Chisholm

ABOUT LET'S GO

GUIDES FOR THE INDEPENDENT TRAVELER

At Let's Go, we see every trip as the chance of a lifetime. If your dream is to grab a machete and forge through the jungles of Brazil, we can take you there. If you'd rather bask in the Riviera sun at a beachside cafe, we'll set you a table. We write for readers who know that there's more to travel than sharing double deckers with tourists and who believe that travel can change both themselves and the world—whether they plan to spend six days in London or six months in Latin America. We'll show you just how far your money can go, and prove that the greatest limitation on your adventures is not your wallet, but your imagination. After all, traveling close to the ground lets you interact more directly with the places and people you've gone to see, making for the most authentic experience.

BEYOND THE TOURIST EXPERIENCE

To help you gain a deeper connection with the places you travel, our researchers give you the heads-up on both world-renowned and off-the-beaten-track attractions, sights, and destinations. They engage with the local culture, writing features on regional cuisine, local festivals, and hot political issues. We've also opened our pages to respected writers and scholars to hear their takes on the countries and regions we cover, and asked travelers who have worked, studied, or volunteered abroad to contribute first-person accounts of their experiences. We've also increased our coverage of responsible travel and expanded each guide's Alternatives to Tourism chapter to share more ideas about how to give back to local communities and learn about the places you travel.

FORTY-FIVE YEARS OF WISDOM

Let's Go got its start in 1960, when a group of creative and well-traveled students compiled their experience and advice into a 20-page mimeographed pamphlet, which they gave to travelers on charter flights to Europe. Four and a half decades later, we've expanded to cover six continents and all kinds of travel—while retaining our founders' adventurous attitude toward the world. Our guides are still researched and written entirely by students on shoestring budgets, experienced travelers who know that train strikes, stolen luggage, food poisoning, and marriage proposals are all part of a day's work. This year, we're expanding our coverage of South America and Southeast Asia, with brand-new *Let's Go: Ecuador*, *Let's Go: Peru*, and *Let's Go: Vietnam*. Our adventure guide series is growing, too, with the addition of *Let's Go: Pacific Northwest Adventure* and *Let's Go: New Zealand Adventure*. And we're immensely excited about our new *Let's Go: Roadtripping USA*—two years, eight routes, and sixteen researchers and editors have put together a travel guide like none other.

THE LET'S GO COMMUNITY

More than just a travel guide company, Let's Go is a community. Our small staff comes together because of our shared passion for travel and our desire to help other travelers see the world. We love it when our readers become part of the Let's Go community as well—when you travel, drop us a postcard (67 Mt. Auburn St., Cambridge, MA 02138, USA) or send us an e-mail (feedback@letsgo.com) to tell us about your adventures and discoveries.

For more information, visit us online: www.letsgo.com.

1 2 3 4 5

PRICE RANGES >>US AND CANADA

Our researchers list establishments in order of value from best to worst; our favorites are denoted by the *Let's Go* thumbs-up (). Since the best value is not always the cheapest price, we have incorporated a system of price ranges for quick reference. Our price ranges are based on a rough expectation of what you will spend. For **accommodations,** we base our price range off the cheapest price for which a single traveler can stay for one night. For **restaurants** and other dining establishments, we estimate the average amount that you will spend in that restaurant. The table below tells you what you will *typically* find at the corresponding price range; keep in mind that a particularly expensive ice cream stand may still only be marked a ❷, depending on what you will spend.

ACCOMM.	US$	CDN$	WHAT YOU'RE *LIKELY* TO FIND
❶	under $30	under CDN$45	Camping; most dorm rooms, such as HI or other hostels or university dorm rooms. Expect bunk beds and a communal bath; you may have to provide or rent towels and sheets.
❷	$30-50	CDN$45-67	Upper-end hostels or a small bed and breakfast. You may have a private bathroom, or a sink in your room.
❸	$51-70	CDN$68-105	A small room with a private bath. Should have decent amenities, such as phone and TV. Breakfast may be included in the price of a room.
❹	$71-100	CDN$106-150	Similar to 3, but may have more amenities or be in a more touristed area.
❺	over $100	over CDN$150	Large, posh hotels. If it's a 5 and it doesn't have the perks you want, you've paid too much.
FOOD			
❶	under $6	under CDN$7	Mostly sandwich shops or greasy spoons. Don't worry about tucking your shirt in.
❷	$6-8	CDN$7-12	Sandwiches, appetizers at a bar, or low-priced entrees. You may have the the option of sitting down or getting take-out.
❸	$9-12	CDN$13-18	Mid-priced entrees, possibly coming with a soup or salad. Tip'll bump you up a couple dollars, since you'll probably have a waiter or waitress.
❹	$13-16	CDN$19-24	A somewhat fancy restaurant or steakhouse. Either way, you'll have a special knife. Some restaurants in this range have a dress code, and many may look down on t-shirt and jeans.
❺	over $16	over CDN$24	Food with foreign names and a decent wine list. Slacks and dress shirts may be expected.

The United States

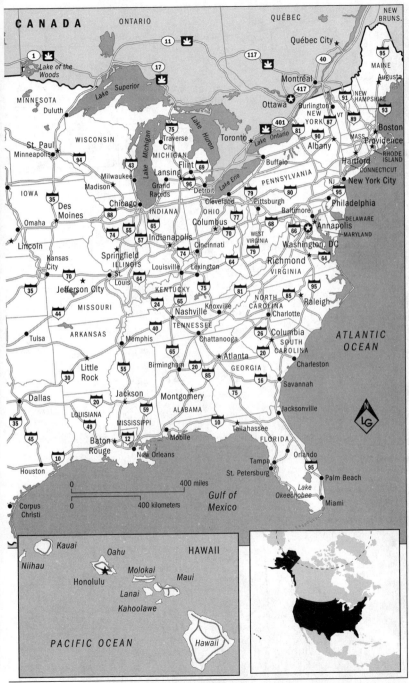

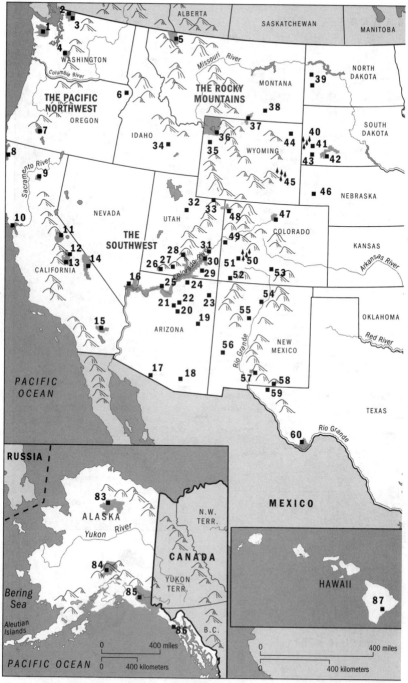

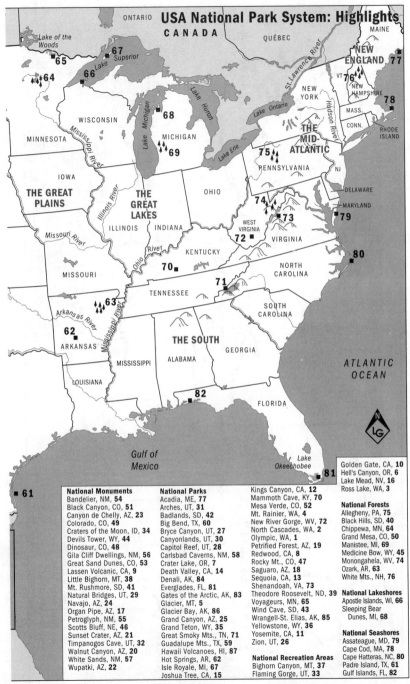

USA National Park System: Highlights

CANADA

ONTARIO   QUÉBEC   MAINE

Lake of the Woods
■ 65
▲ 64
■ 67 Lake Superior
■ 66
Lake Michigan
■ 68

NEW ENGLAND
▲ 76 VT
NEW HAMPSHIRE
■ 77
MASS.
■ 78

WISCONSIN

MINNESOTA

MICHIGAN
▲ 69

IOWA

NEW YORK
Lake Ontario
Lake Erie
THE MID-ATLANTIC

RHODE ISLAND
CONN.

THE GREAT PLAINS

Mississippi River
Illinois River

THE GREAT LAKES
ILLINOIS   INDIANA   OHIO

PENNSYLVANIA
▲ 75

NJ

DELAWARE

Missouri River

MISSOURI

Ohio River
KENTUCKY

WEST VIRGINIA
▲ 74
■ 73
■ 72   VIRGINIA

MARYLAND
■ 79

▲ 63
Arkansas River

■ 70

TENNESSEE
■ 71

NORTH CAROLINA

■ 80

■ 62
ARKANSAS

THE SOUTH

SOUTH CAROLINA

MISSISSIPPI   ALABAMA   GEORGIA

LOUISIANA

■ 82

FLORIDA

ATLANTIC OCEAN

Gulf of Mexico

Lake Okeechobee
■ 81

■ 61

N

National Monuments
Bandelier, NM, **54**
Black Canyon, CO, **51**
Canyon de Chelly, AZ, **23**
Colorado, CO, **49**
Craters of the Moon, ID, **34**
Devils Tower, WY, **44**
Dinosaur, CO, **48**
Gila Cliff Dwellings, NM, **56**
Great Sand Dunes, CO, **53**
Lassen Volcanic, CA, **9**
Little Bighorn, MT, **38**
Mt. Rushmore, SD, **41**
Natural Bridges, UT, **29**
Navajo, AZ, **24**
Organ Pipe, AZ, **17**
Petroglyph, NM, **55**
Scotts Bluff, NE, **46**
Sunset Crater, AZ, **21**
Timpanogos Cave, UT, **32**
Walnut Canyon, AZ, **20**
White Sands, NM, **57**
Wupatki, AZ, **22**

National Parks
Acadia, ME, **77**
Arches, UT, **31**
Badlands, SD, **42**
Big Bend, TX, **60**
Bryce Canyon, UT, **27**
Canyonlands, UT, **30**
Capitol Reef, UT, **28**
Carlsbad Caverns, NM, **58**
Crater Lake, OR, **7**
Death Valley, CA, **14**
Denali, AK, **84**
Everglades, FL, **81**
Gates of the Arctic, AK, **83**
Glacier, MT, **5**
Glacier Bay, AK, **86**
Grand Canyon, AZ, **25**
Grand Teton, WY, **35**
Great Smoky Mts., TN, **71**
Guadalupe Mts., TX, **59**
Hawaii Volcanoes, HI, **87**
Hot Springs, AR, **62**
Isle Royale, MI, **67**
Joshua Tree, CA, **15**

Kings Canyon, CA, **12**
Mammoth Cave, KY, **70**
Mesa Verde, CO, **52**
Mt. Rainier, WA, **4**
New River Gorge, WV, **72**
North Cascades, WA, **2**
Olympic, WA, **1**
Petrified Forest, AZ, **19**
Redwood, CA, **8**
Rocky Mt., CO, **47**
Saguaro, AZ, **18**
Sequoia, CA, **13**
Shenandoah, VA, **73**
Theodore Roosevelt, ND, **39**
Voyageurs, MN, **65**
Wind Cave, SD, **43**
Wrangell-St. Elias, AK, **85**
Yellowstone, WY, **36**
Yosemite, CA, **11**
Zion, UT, **26**

National Recreation Areas
Bighorn Canyon, MT, **37**
Flaming Gorge, UT, **33**

Golden Gate, CA, **10**
Hell's Canyon, OR, **6**
Lake Mead, NV, **16**
Ross Lake, WA, **3**

National Forests
Allegheny, PA, **75**
Black Hills, SD, **40**
Chippewa, MN, **64**
Grand Mesa, CO, **50**
Manistee, MI, **69**
Medicine Bow, WY, **45**
Monongahela, WV, **74**
Ozark, AR, **63**
White Mts., NH, **76**

National Lakeshores
Apostle Islands, WI, **66**
Sleeping Bear
Dunes, MI, **68**

National Seashores
Assateague, MD, **79**
Cape Cod, MA, **78**
Cape Hatteras, NC, **80**
Padre Island, TX, **61**
Gulf Islands, FL, **82**

XIX

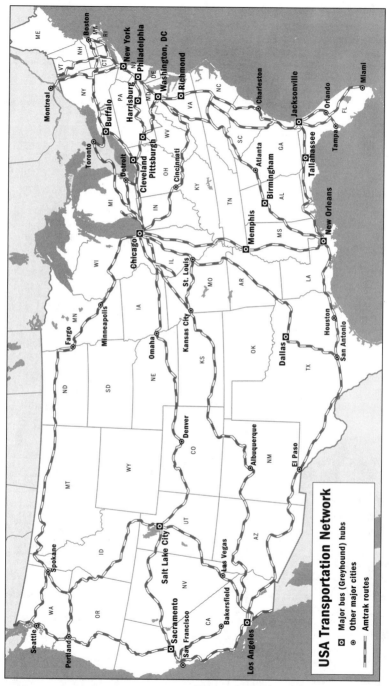

USA Transportation Network

- ◙ Major bus (Greyhound) hubs
- ◉ Other major cities
- ▬▬▬ Amtrak routes

DISCOVER THE USA AND CANADA

Stretching from below the Tropic of Cancer to above the Arctic Circle, the United States is a country defined by open spaces and an amazing breadth of terrain. From sparse deserts to lush forests and snow-capped peaks to rolling fields of grain, the American landscape sprouts new views in every region.

Culturally as well as geographically, America is a nation of contrasts. The United States is formed by disunited peoples; centuries of immigration have created a country that cannot be said to value diversity so much as it is comprised by it. This diversity is reflected in every aspect of the American experience—from Cajun cuisine to the Harlem Renaissance, experiencing America involves experiencing the intermingling of different visions. To the north, Canada's cultural makeup reflects a similar confluence of immigrant cultures.

While transportation options throughout the United States and Canada are plentiful, the most rewarding way to see the countries is still by car. Whether driving cross-country or simply over the river and through the woods, the road trip is the definitive American travel institution.

USA FACTS AND FIGURES	
POPULATION: 293,810,695.	**MILES DRIVEN EACH YEAR:** 1½ trillion (to the sun and back 7500 times).
LARGEST CITIES: New York City, Los Angeles, Chicago, Houston, Philadelphia.	**COMMON PET NAMES:** Patches, Misty, Buster, Princess, Bear, Sheba.
MILES OF HIGHWAY: 3,980,688 (of which 2,577,693 mi. are paved).	**TV'S PER HOUSE:** 2.4.

WHEN TO GO

In general, the US tourist season comprises the summer months between Memorial Day and Labor Day (May 31-Sept. 6, 2005); the Canadian tourist season starts around mid-June. National parks flood with visitors during the high season, but cities are less affected by seasonal variation. For regions where winter sports are popular or the winters are mild, as in the mountains and the southern US, the tourist season is generally inverted (Dec.-Apr.).

THINGS TO DO

Neither the following few pages nor this book's one thousand pages can do justice to the vibrant, diverse offerings of the North American continent. No two trips to the US and Canada are the same, and visitors who travel to several regions may feel like they've visited different countries. Nevertheless, there are a few common themes in the US and Canada that should be a part of any thorough exploration.

SAVORY SPECIALTIES

1. Chicken 'n' waffles. The ultimate soul-food combination: warm waffles and crispy fried chicken. Try it at Gladys Knight's and Ron Winan's Chicken and Waffles in Atlanta, GA (p. 437), or Roscoe's House of Chicken and Waffles in Los Angeles, CA (p. 947).

2. Creole and Cajun. From chicken gumbo to shrimp étoufée and New Orleans to Lafayette, Louisiana serves a jambalaya of cultural cuisines.

3. Fish boils, Door County, WI. Feast like a hungry Scandinavian lumberjack on whitefish plucked from Lake Michigan and served straight out of a bubbling cauldron. Save room for a slice of Door County cherry pie, a tradition unto itself (p. 619).

4. Texas barbecue. Some may call meat cooked for over 30 hours burned, but Texans call it barbecue. Clark's in Tioga, TX (p. 718), 1½hr. north of Dallas, has perfected the cowboy's craft of serving slow-cooked meat smothered in smoky, spicy sauce.

5. Philadelphia cheesesteak. Heavyweights Geno's and Pat's have been duking it out at 9th and Passyunk for the title of Philly cheesesteak champion for nearly 50 years (p. 285).

6. Cuban. The largest Cuban population outside of Castro's control means Miami simmers

MUST-SEE CITIES

While no visitor should pass up the glitz and glamour of Los Angeles, the round-the-clock excitement of New York City, or the multicultural metropolis of Toronto, the curious traveler should take time to explore the wealth of lesser-known American cities that offer their own regional flavor. Standing guard as the gateway to the West, **St. Louis, MO** (p. 681), combines distinctive neighborhoods with eclectic, cosmopolitan dining, as well as an energetic nightlife scene fueled by the world's biggest brewery, Anheuser-Busch. Travelers to **Charleston, SC** (p. 424), are rewarded with lush gardens, antebellum plantations, and Southern charm. No party animal should miss Mardi Gras in **New Orleans, LA** (p. 473), where the city's carefree attitude, rich musical tradition, and sumptuous Creole cookin' is sure to cast an enchanting spell on any visitor. Countless adventurers find a warm welcome in **Flagstaff, AZ** (p. 857), perhaps the greatest crossroads in the US. Arts and crafts enthusiasts flock to **Santa Fe, NM** (p. 881), where old adobe churches, gorgeous galleries, and authentic Southwestern cuisine can still be found amidst the ritzy shops and restaurants serving the city's wealthy second-homers. The bohemian metropolis of **Portland, OR** (p. 1024), known as the microbrewery capital of North America, is worth seeing for its fantastic open-air market alone. Across the northern border, the magnificent fortifications and twisting alleyways of **Québec City, QC** (p. 189), testify to the city's old-world character, while the beautiful mountain setting and thriving Chinese population of **Vancouver, BC** (p. 1035), make the Canadian city a prime destination for urbanites and outdoorsmen alike.

COLLEGE TOWNS

America's colleges, from sprawling state universities to tiny liberal arts academies, have engendered unique communities with youthful vitality and alternative spirit. **Ann Arbor, MI** (p. 577), is the epitome of an American college town, boasting an unparalleled bar scene and liberal mishmash of Midwest hipsters while still maintaining a relaxed, friendly atmosphere. The 50,000 students who run amuck in **Austin, TX** (p. 707), spurn stereotypes about the conservative Lone Star State, creating a liberal haven where collegiate energy and Southwestern grit thrive side by side. A bastion of liberal-mindedness and hippie culture, **Boulder, CO** (p. 749), gives a new meaning to the Rocky Mountain high. The mountain hamlet of **Middlebury, VT** (p. 109), combines rural charm with a touch of youthful rowdiness. An increasingly diverse student community gives the Southern establishment a run for its money in **Charlottesville, VA** (p. 352), a gorgeous town known for its rolling hills and splendid architecture. **Missoula, MT** (p. 802), has become one of the most fascinatingly cosmopolitan cities in the Prairie. Perhaps the most famous American college town, **Berkeley, CA** (p. 923), has become a city in its own right, but has managed to do so without sacrificing its collegiate charms.

AMERICANA

America boasts the biggest, smallest, and zaniest of almost everything. Kitschy roadside attractions dot the country's dusty roads, putting on public display a vast and truly baffling material culture. Out west in Polson, MT, the **Miracle of America Museum** (p. 806) enshrines reg'lar old American living. Evidence of American architectural ingenuity can be found at the **Corn Palace** in Mitchell, SD (p. 654); this gargantuan structure is rebuilt every year with a fresh crop. America also claims the largest **operational chainsaw** near Marquette, MI (p. 589). Bigger and brighter still are the casinos of **the Strip** in Las Vegas, NV (p. 826) and **the Boardwalk** in Atlantic City, NJ (p. 276). It is difficult to imagine a tribute to the American value of individual rights that stands so proud as **"The Tree That Owns Itself"** in Athens, GA (p. 447). And, of course no tour of American kitsch would be complete without a trip to the heart and soul of all Americana—**Graceland** (p. 397).

BASEBALL STADIUMS

The Great American Pastime is enshrined in its ballparks, where baseball zealots cheer on their favorite teams. Some stadiums offer tours, but nothing beats catching a game on a balmy summer evening. The oldest ballpark still in use is **Fenway Park** (p. 124) in Boston, MA, where the Red Sox have played under the shadow of the towering Green Monster since 1912. The Chicago Cubs make their home at **Wrigley Field** (p. 600), whose ivy-

with *cocina cubana* so delicious, you'll want to make it your vice (p. 524).

7. Poutine. Unlike their French counterparts, these Canadian fries come slathered in cheese and gravy; try them at Mondo Fritz in Montréal, QC (p. 180).

8. Cincinnati chili. Often imitated but rarely duplicated, Cincinnati chili distinguishes itself from its Texan analogue by its thinner consistency and unusual spices. Get your fix at Skyline Chili (p. 563), where the secret ingredient is well-guarded.

9. Arctic specialties. If you're wondering why Santa didn't come this year, it's because the Alaskans turned his reindeer into delicious sausage. Halibut burritos, wild salmon, and other delights from the fresh Alaskan waters are also not to be missed.

10. New Mexican chiles. New Mexico's weather forecast: chile today, hot tamale. The choice of red or green chile sauce is offered on every food item from eggs to enchiladas to the overdose option of *chiles rellenos*.

clad outfield fences are an enduring symbol of baseball's storied past. Known as the "House that Ruth Built," **Yankee Stadium** (p. 237) in the Bronx has more history than any other stadium and is still widely considered the ballpark in America. On the West Coast, **Dodger Stadium** (p. 958) rivals its East Coast predecessors with breathtaking views of downtown Los Angeles and the promise of beautiful weather. But while many purists cling to these relics of baseball's heyday, a wave of modern stadiums has ushered in a new era, and today the competition among cities for the best ballpark often overshadows team rivalries. **Camden Yards** (p. 317) in Baltimore, MD, perfectly bridges the gap between old and new, combining brick architecture with the most modern amenities. The uber-modern **SkyDome** (p. 167) in Toronto is Canada's centerpiece stadium and baseball's answer to Brunelleschi's Dome, boasting the first retractable roof in Major League Baseball. Perhaps the most impressive new stadium is the Pittsburgh Pirates' **PNC Park** (p. 303), a classically styled ballpark which offers striking views of the Pittsburgh skyline and the chance to blast a homer into the Allegheny River. Meanwhile, at **SBC Park** (p. 921), fans grub on gourmet concessions while watching their favorite sluggers launch dingers into the San Francisco Bay.

NATIONAL PARKS

From haunting red buttes to endless pitch-black caves, the national parks of the US and Canada protect some of the most phenomenal natural beauty in the world. While much of the land's beauty can be seen along the byways, the truly miraculous works of nature are cared for by the National Park Service. The easternmost park in the US, **Acadia National Park, ME** (p. 90), features unspoiled rocky beaches and dense pine forests. **Shenandoah National Park, VA** (p. 355), made its way into history as America's first land reclamation project, and today lures travelers with its mountain vistas. **Great Smoky Mountains National Park, TN** (p. 386), the largest national park east of the Mississippi, also holds the International Biosphere Reserve and World Heritage Site.

The most popular parks, however, lie out west. Arguably the most famous (and most crowded) park in the US, **Yellowstone National Park, WY** (p. 772), has attractions such as the Old Faithful geyser. **Grand Canyon National Park, AZ** (p. 849), wows visitors with...well, the Grand Canyon, while **Yosemite National Park, CA** (p. 980), draws hordes of trekkers, trailers, and tourists with its steep mountains and stunning waterfalls. Smaller—but no less breathtaking—are the otherworldly hoodoos (pillar-like rock formations) of **Bryce Canyon National Park, UT** (p. 844), the varied and dramatic terrain of **Waterton-Glacier International Peace Park, MT** (p. 806), and the awesome mountains of **Grand Teton National Park, WY** (p. 783). Farther afield, grizzly bears and caribou roam freely in the shadow of Mt. McKinley—North America's tallest mountain—at the stunning **Denali National Park, AK** (p. 1059).

Canada also possesses a highly developed and well-maintained national park system. At **Fundy National Park, NB** (p. 198), the world's largest tides ebb and flow, while nearby **Kouchibouguac National Park** (p. 201) features sandy beaches and acres of marshland. In Newfoundland, the UNESCO World Heritage Site of **Gros Morne National Park** (p. 215), sees more moose than tourists. The Canadian Rockies also play host to gorgeous parklands, including the expansive ice fields of **Jasper National Park, AB** (p. 1053). The isolated **Pacific Rim National Park, BC** (p. 1043), offers some of the best hiking, surfing, and diving on the continent.

▨ LET'S GO PICKS

BEST OPPORTUNITIES FOR PUBLIC BATHING: Hot springs are a therapeutic diversion from the hard work of travel; some of the best are in **Calistoga, CA** (p. 932). For skinny dippin', try **Austin, TX's** Hippie Hollow (p. 714).

MOST APPETIZING BEER NAMES: Montana's **Moose Drool** (p. 779), South Carolina's **Mullet** (p. 430), and Louisiana's **funkybuttjuice** (p. 486) definitely rank among the nation's finest name-impaired beverages.

BEST FAKES: Tour five continents in a day, from a miniature Eiffel Tower to New York City to the Egyptian pyramids, on The Strip in **Las Vegas, NV** (p. 826). Ogle a replica of the Holy Land at the Sacred Arts Center in **Eureka Springs, AR** (p. 501). See the Mississippi River in miniature at the Mud Island River Park in **Memphis, TN** (p. 398); only 3½hr. away a model Parthenon perches in the "Athens of the South," **Nashville, TN** (p. 382).

BEST GATORS: America's most impressive creatures. Get up close and scarily personal in places like **Nachitoches, LA** (p. 490); the **Everglades, FL** (p. 533); **St. Augustine, FL** (p. 522); and **Myrtle Beach, SC** (p. 431).

BEST ALTERNATIVE TO A GLASS: Enjoy a "beer boot" at the Essen Haus in Madison, WI (p. 617).

BEST OPPORTUNITIES FOR MULTI-TASKING: At Soapbox, a "laundro-lounge" in **Wilmington, NC,** you can party and do your laundry at the same time (p. 423). At Le Drague, a gay cabaret in **Québec City, QC,** patrons can party, sing karaoke, and check their email at Internet terminals in the club (p. 195). Lace up your bowling shoes and pray for a strike at the **Boone, NC** Bowling Center's "Christian Cosmic Bowling" night (p. 415).

PLACES MOST LIKELY TO FIND PIRATES: The *José Gasparilla's* crew of buccaneers invades **Tampa, FL** in the first week of February (p. 515). **Alexandria Bay, NY,** hosts a yearly Pirate Week (p. 270), while an altogether different kind of pirates play ball at PNC Park in **Pittsburgh, PA** (p. 303).

BEST REENACTMENTS: In **Cavendish, PEI,** actors in period garb perform scenes from Lucy Maud Montgomery's 1908 novel *Anne of Green Gables* (p. 204). The Jones Archaeological Museum in **Moundville, AL,** features reenactments of the lives of the Mississippian people (p. 461). At Saloon #10 in the gambling town of **Deadwood, SD,** the shooting of Wild Bill Hickok is reenacted several times daily (p. 662).

SUGGESTED ITINERARIES

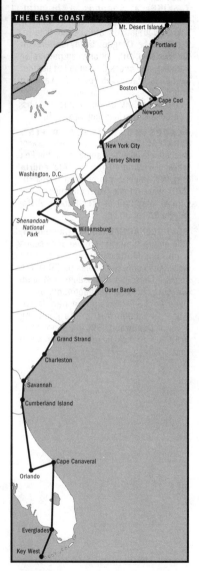

THE EAST COAST

Mt. Desert Island
Portland
Boston
Cape Cod
Newport
New York City
Jersey Shore
Washington, D.C.
Shenandoah National Park
Williamsburg
Outer Banks
Grand Strand
Charleston
Savannah
Cumberland Island
Cape Canaveral
Orlando
Everglades
Key West

EAST COAST: MAINE TO THE FLOR-IDA KEYS (6 WEEKS) I-95 and the sometimes commercial, sometimes scenic

U.S. 1 parallel each other from the northern wilds of Maine down to the gorgeous Florida Keys. Despite the many state-levied tolls, this strip gives a true cross-section of American life and culture, and encourages on-a-whim diversions. Begin on **Mt. Desert Island, ME** (p. 87), where mountain and ocean meet with beautiful results, then head down the coast. The youthful **Portland, ME** (p. 84), will whet your appetite for city life, and the thriving culture of **Boston, MA** (p. 113), will satisfy it. **Cape Cod** (p. 132) awaits with pristine beaches, while **Newport, RI** (p. 147), preserves the must-see summer estates of America's wealthiest industrialists. From there, cruise over to larger-than-life **New York City** (p. 219). **Atlantic City, NJ** (p. 274), and **Cape May, NJ** (p. 276) deals out boardwalks and beaches for a quintessential summer experience. **Washington, D.C.** (p. 324), merits a few days, as does the placid **Shenandoah National Park, VA** (p. 355). See colonial history acted out in **Williamsburg, VA** (p. 347), or find solitude on long stretches of sand in the **Outer Banks** (p. 416). The more built-up **Grand Strand** (p. 431) and the city of **Charleston, SC** (p. 424), beckon partiers back to the mainland. **Savannah** (p. 449) and stunning **Cumberland Island** (p. 452) will leave Georgia on your mind, but **Disney World** (p. 507) will leave you blissfully mind-numb. Give the **Space Coast** of Florida (p. 521) a fly-by, and make a stop to explore the vast, mysterious **Everglades** (p. 533). Celebrate the end of your journey with umbrella drinks on sugar-white beaches in **Key West** (p. 538).

TRACING THE US-CANADIAN BOR-DER (6 WEEKS) Crossing the continent at higher latitudes affords travelers time in the unique cities and less touristed parks of the North. Begin north of the border and take a whirlwind tour of Canada's cosmopolitan eastern cities. **Québec City** (p. 189) and **Montréal** (p. 175), QC, are predominantly French-speaking and overflow with culture. **Toronto, ON** (p. 159), boasts huge ethnic quarters and refreshing tidiness for such a big city. Cross the border at the spectacular **Niagara Falls** (p. 260) and

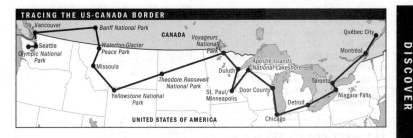

TRACING THE US-CANADA BORDER

motor over to the oft-stigmatized and under-estimated city of **Detroit, MI** (p. 570). Sail on to the Windy City of **Chicago, IL** (p. 590). Wind down in the friendly and scenic lakeside communities of Wisconsin in **Door County** (p. 618) and the **Apostle Islands** (p. 621). Next, head to the surprisingly hip twin cities of **St. Paul and Minneapolis, MN** (p. 624). The charming city of **Duluth, MN** (p. 633), combines a thriving shipping industry with endless waterfront recreation. Before leaving Minnesota, park the car and boat into the unspoiled expanse of **Voyageurs National Park** (p. 637). Next, speed out to the breathtaking **Yellowstone National Park** (p. 772). Young and fresh, **Missoula, MT** (p. 802), provides a much-needed stop before heading north to **Waterton-Glacier Peace Park** (p. 806) and the popular **Banff National Park** (p. 1051) in Canada. Out on the Pacific coast, visit the lively city scenes of **Vancouver** (p. 1035) and **Seattle** (p. 1003), or the serene wilderness of one of world's last remaining old-growth temperate rainforests at **Olympic National Park** (p. 1018).

SOUTH BY SOUTHWEST (8 WEEKS)

Striking straight across the American South from sea to shining sea—and even dipping into Mexico—this route highlights old-fashioned Southern flavor, Mexican-infused Southwestern culture, and canyon country. It can be driven year-round. Warm up with big cities tempered by Southern hospitality in the triangle of **Charleston, SC** (p. 424); **Savannah, GA** (p. 449); and **Atlanta, GA** (p. 433). Trace the roots of virtually all American musical styles in **Nashville, TN** (p. 378); **Memphis, TN** (p. 393); **Oxford, MS** (p. 468); and **New Orleans, LA** (p. 473). Experience the unadulterated Cajun culture of the Deep South in **Acadiana, LA** (p. 492), before heading out to the Texan foursome of **Dallas** (p. 716), **Houston** (p. 723), **Austin** (p. 707), and **San Antonio** (p. 701). New Mexico offers the otherworldly **White Sands National Monument** (p. 901) and the phenomenal mineral baths of **Truth or Consequences** (p. 898). The cities of **Santa Fe** (p. 881) and **Albuquerque** (p. 891) are worth a couple of days each. After having your fill, head to Arizona's astonishing **Petrified Forest** (p. 867). **Flagstaff, AZ** (p. 857), is an inviting Southwestern city in its own right, and makes a convenient base for exploring the region near the magnificent **Grand Canyon** (p. 849). To the north, the idyllic wilderness of Utah's **Zion National Park** (p. 846) and the startling rock pillars of **Bryce**

SOUTH BY SOUTHWEST

Canyon (p. 844) provide travelers with a last gasp of clean air and natural beauty before the plunge into the glitz of **Las Vegas, NV** (p. 821). In California, **Joshua Tree National Park** (p. 975) is a worthy stop in the desert on the way to the Pacific coast. Savor sunny **San Diego** (p. 965) before becoming star-struck in glamorous **Los Angeles** (p. 941).

THE WEST COAST: FROM L.A. TO VANCOUVER (2-6 WEEKS). A tour of the West Coast provides the most mountainscapes, oceanfront property, and cosmopolitan bang for your buck. Between sunny, boisterous Los Angeles, CA, and lush, mellow Vancouver, BC, lies much natural (and artificial) diversion. **Los Angeles** (p. 941), America's western outpost of high culture, provides access to **Hollywood** (p. 946), famous art, and beach culture. **Las Vegas, NV** (p. 821); **Tijuana, Mexico** (p. 972); and **Joshua Tree National Park, CA** (p. 975), are worthy side trips. The 400 mi. stretch of shore-hugging Rte. 1 between L.A. and San Francisco—through **Big Sur** (p. 938) and **Santa Cruz** (p. 935)—is pure California: rolling surf, secluded beaches, dramatic cliffs, and eccentric locals. **San Francisco** (p. 904), a groovin' city in itself, is only 3-4hr. from **Yosemite National Park** (p. 980). From San Fran, the slightly inland Rte. 101 hits **Napa Valley wine country** (p. 929) before reuniting with Rte. 1 (and the coast) and passing through the primordial **Redwood National Park** (p. 986). After the park, rejoin I-5 for a trip through Oregon to **Portland** (p. 1024). A side trips to **Crater Lake** is well worth it. Before getting too settled with a cappuccino in **Seattle, WA** (p. 1003),

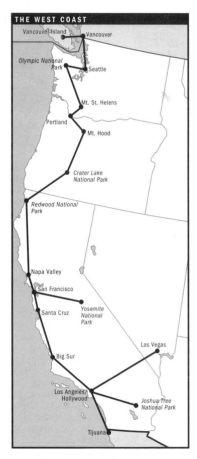

THE WEST COAST

commune with nature at **Mt. St. Helens** (p. 1021) and **Olympic National Park** (p. 1018), or trek over to **Vancouver, BC** (p. 1035), for access to the outdoor haven of **Vancouver Island** (p. 1043).

LIFE AND TIMES

THE UNITED STATES

HISTORY

BRIDGE OVER TROUBLED WATER. Archaeologists think that the first Americans crossed the Bering Sea from Siberia by **land bridge** during the last Ice Age, somewhere from 10,000 to 15,000 years ago. Scientists have raised different theories to explain this migration. Whether it was the pursuit of nomadic bison, a shift in living conditions in Asia, or simple wanderlust that drove them over the land bridge, the Asiatic peoples gradually came to inhabit all corners of their new continent. The earliest Native American cultures were nomadic, flourishing as they followed 🖾**megafauna** (giant mammals similar to larger versions of today's horses, armadillos, and lions) around the continent. Starting around AD 200, the ancestors of today's Pueblos fostered advanced civilizations, ruins of which are still visible in the Anasazi Great Houses in **Chaco Canyon** (p. 896).

A BRAVE NEW WORLD. Though no one is certain, it is likely that the earliest Europeans to stumble on the "New World" were sea voyagers blown off-course by storms. Textbooks place the discovery of the Americas some time later, in 1492, when **Christopher Columbus** found his voyage to the East blocked by Hispaniola in the Caribbean Sea. Optimistically believing that he had reached the Spice Islands of the East Indies, he dubbed the inhabitants "Indians." Columbus's arrival marked the beginning of European conquest, which, in addition to establishing what would become a permanent European presence in the New World, also brought murder, disease, forced conversion, and other calamities to Native Americans.

In the centuries after Columbus's voyage, Europeans rushed to the New World in search of gold and silver, prestige for themselves and their country, and in some cases, religious martyrdom. The Spanish expanded into the southern and southwestern regions of the US, while the French and Dutch created more modest empires to the north. The English settled the New World's east coast, and after a few failed attempts, established a colony at **Jamestown** (p. 349) in 1607. Their success hinged on a strain of indigenous weed called tobacco, which quickly caught on in England. In the years after 1620, religious separatists, the **Puritans,** persecuted by the Presbyterian majority in England, fled to present-day Massachusetts.

INDEPENDENCE DAY. In order to protect her holdings in the Americas from an impending French influence, Great Britain entered into the **French and Indian War** in 1754 and fought a number of battles against the allied French and Native Americans. The British ultimately triumphed, but the win increased the irrelevancy of Great Britain's power over her holdings in North America, as the colonies no longer needed British protection from the French. Additionally, the struggle more than doubled Great Britain's government expenditures. To offset the burden of this price on British taxpayers, the powers that were decided to shift responsibility onto the American colonies, which had previously been taxed lightly. These new taxes angered colonists, who rallied against "taxation without representation." Colonial committees created the First Continental Congress, which, with the exception of a few dissenters, strove to convince

England to recognize the colonies' rights. But issues remained unresolved, and fighting broke out between colonists and British troops. This convinced the Second Continental Congress to prepare the 13 colonies for war. In 1776, **Thomas Jefferson** drafted the **Declaration of Independence,** and **July 4th,** the date on which the declaration was adopted, remains America's most important national holiday. Fighting continued for the next eight years throughout the Eastern seaboard. In October 1781, outnumbered and surrounded by the rebels and their French allies, the British surrendered, ending the **Revolutionary War** and finally granting the colonists their own country.

LIFE, LIBERTY, AND THE CONSTITUTION. After achieving independence, America experimented with a loosely confederated government, which was widely acknowledged as unsuccessful. In 1787, the state legislatures sent a group of 55 men to draft what was to become the **Constitution.** The **Bill of Rights,** a set of 10 constitutional amendments which were passed shortly after the Constitution, has remained a cornerstone of the American political system. This document includes the rights to freedom of speech, freedom of the press, and freedom of religion.

MANIFEST DESTINY. Jefferson, who became the third president of the US, purchased the **Louisiana Territory** from Napoleon in 1803 for less than $0.03 an acre. This sprawling landmass ranged north from Louisiana to Montana and west from the Mississippi River to the Rocky Mountains. The next year, Jefferson sent Lewis and Clark to explore the territory and find a river route to the Pacific Ocean. Lewis and Clark never found a waterway linking the oceans, but they did chart the vast land west of the Mississippi. Droves of people moved west along the grueling Oregon Trail in search of land, gold, and a new life. Over 40,000 prospectors traveled to California between 1848 and 1849 in a migration now known as the Gold Rush.

After the annexation of the Republic of Texas to the United States in 1845, President James Polk decided to expand farther into Mexican territory. After being rebuffed when an American envoy to Mexico failed in a foolhardy attempt to simply buy New Mexico and California, Polk sent troops south of the Rio Grande. The **Mexican-American War** broke out, and the American army strolled through Mexican territory, successfully offering people and towns protection from Native Americans in exchange for surrender. The Mexican troops were forced to surrender when US troops invaded Mexico City and remained there until peace was negotiated. The treaty that ended the war in February 1848 granted the US nearly two-fifths of Mexico's territory, including New Mexico, California, Nevada, Utah, most of Arizona and Colorado, and parts of Wyoming, Kansas, and Oklahoma.

The **Homestead Act** of 1862 prompted the cultivation of the Great Plains by distributing government land to those who would farm and live on it. This large-scale settlement led to bloody battles with the Sioux, Hunkpapas, and Cheyenne tribes who had long inhabited the Plains. From 1866 to 1891 the US fought a continuous war in which the Native Americans eventually were relegated to reservations.

SLAVERY IN THE NEW WORLD. The first **Africans** were brought to America in 1619 on a Dutch slave ship that landed in Jamestown, VA. The infusion of African slave labor led to the decline of indentured servitude, a system in which poor Europeans would provide seven years of labor in exchange for their passage across the Atlantic. As the demand for cheap labor increased from the late 1500s into the 1600s, white settlers invaded Native American communities looking for slaves. Native Americans, however, suffered fatally from European diseases, so colonial America relied on African slaves to fill the gap. Thousands of Africans were forced across the Atlantic to be auctioned off in the US, a harrowing journey known as the **Middle Passage.** This would last until 1807, when the slave trade was abolished. Slave ownership, however would continue until the late 19th century.

Slavery exacerbated existing ideological differences between the North and the South. The South's economy was based on agriculture driven by slave labor, while the North was far more industrial and technologically advanced. This division meant that the South had to rely on both the North and on foreign countries to import nearly everything that was not cotton or tobacco. High taxes **(tariffs)** were placed on imported goods, and taxes were sometimes also placed on exported Southern goods that were not applied to Northern goods of similar value. The North, with its higher technology, no longer depended on a slave-based workforce, and was becoming increasingly abolitionist. Because the federal government was designed to be relatively weak in order to prevent the "tyranny" of pre-Revolution days from recurring, each state could decide to allow or prohibit slavery independently. As the Northern states became more insistent that territories and new states should be kept free of slavery, the Southern states counteracted by citing the Revolutionary ideal of each state's right to self-determination. Northern abolitionists joined with free African-Americans to form the **Underground Railroad,** an escape route in which "conductors" secretly transported slaves into the free Northern states. Southerners who invaded the North to retrieve their "property" fueled existing tensions in the nation split by socioeconomic differences. It would take a fierce and bloody conflict to decide which region would prevail.

"A HOUSE DIVIDED": THE CIVIL WAR. Tensions between the North and South came to a head when **Abraham Lincoln,** an anti-slavery Congressman from Illinois, was elected President in 1860. In response, South Carolina, a hotbed of pro-slavery sentiment, seceded from the Union and was followed by 10 other Southern states. These rebellious states quickly united as the **Confederate States of America** under the presidency of Jefferson Davis. Lincoln, however, refused to accept the secession, setting the stage for war. On April 12, 1861, Southern troops fired on Fort Sumter in the harbor of Charleston, SC, and the **Civil War** began. For four years the country endured a savage and bloody conflict, fought by the North to restore the Union and by the South to break it. Lincoln led the North to eventual victory, but the price was high. The war claimed more American lives than any other conflict in US history, and many families were divided against each other as brothers took up different uniforms and loyalties. Lincoln himself was assassinated on April 14, 1865, by a Southern sympathizer named John Wilkes Booth.

RECONSTRUCTION AND INDUSTRIALIZATION. The period after the war brought Reconstruction to the South and the Industrial Revolution to the North. The North's rapid industrialization rendered it a formidable contender in the world economy, while the South's agricultural economy began a slow decline. Injured and embittered by the war and dependent on an outdated agricultural tradition, Southerners struggled to readjust to new economic and social situations. Meanwhile, the newly freed blacks faced a difficult transition from plantation to free life. **Jim Crow** laws, imposed by white politicians, espoused a doctrine of segregation, impeded African-Americans' civil rights, and prohibited them from frequenting the same establishments and schools as whites. Even drinking fountains were classified according to race. Though black colleges were founded and a few prominent African-Americans were able to gain some degree of political power, many were relegated to a life of share-cropping for white landowners.

During the North's **"Gilded Age"** of the 1870s, captains of industry such as Cornelius Vanderbilt, Andrew Carnegie, and John D. Rockefeller built commercial empires and enormous personal fortunes amid an atmosphere of widespread political and economic corruption. But this massive wealth only accumulated in the hands of a few, and at the same time, farmers toiled in a dying agricultural economy and workers faced low wages, violent strike break-ups, and unsafe working conditions. Yet the fruits of the industrial age, including railroads, telegraphs, and telephones, made transportation and communication much easier.

IMPERIALISM AND WWI. The United States' victory in the **Spanish-American War** of 1898 validated America's sense of military superiority and the belief that its influence should be extended worldwide. The United States caught imperial fever and acquired colonies in the Philippines, Puerto Rico, and Guam.

In 1901, **Teddy Roosevelt** ascend the presidency following the assassination of William McKinley, bringing a youthful, progressive approach to the government. In response to the corrupt, monopolistic practices of big business, Roosevelt and his progressive **Bull Moose Party** promoted anti-trust reforms to regulate large companies. In foreign affairs, Roosevelt established the US as an international police power, and recommended that the nation "speak softly and carry a big stick." Meanwhile, a new breed of journalists, the "muckrakers," began writing articles and books like Upton Sinclair's *The Jungle*—a graphic exposé of the meatpacking industry—to try to unveil the corruption rampant in this industrial age.

After vowing to keep the US out of "Europe's War," President **Woodrow Wilson** entered **World War I**. US troops landed in Europe in 1917 and fought until Germany's defeat the next year. Though the metal-consuming war jump-started America's industrial economy and established the United States as a major international power, the war killed 10 million people, including 130,174 Americans.

ROARING 20S, GREAT DEPRESSION, AND WWII. Americans returned their attentions to the homefront, entering a new age of affluence while attempting to deal with the changes brought on by the first World War. Labor unrest and racial tension were blamed on communist influences, and the US experienced increased paranoia of communism (a **"Red Scare"**) over the course of 1919. The same year, the perceived moral decline of America was addressed with the immensely unpopular **Prohibition** laws, outlawing all alcohol. In spite of these restrictions, America's youthful spirit thrived as Mafia-run speakeasies replaced neighborhood saloons and created a huge black market for bootleg liquor. The jazz scene raged, giving this time of music, leisure, and extravagant parties the apt name **"The Jazz Age."**

During this period, women **suffragists** such as **Elizabeth Cady Stanton** and **Susan B. Anthony** mobilized for the right to vote, and put intense pressure on politicians at every level of the government. These efforts eventually met with success in 1920 with the passage of the 19th Amendment, which extended the vote to all women.

The economic boom of the **"Roaring 20s"** was driven largely by overextended credit. The facade of economic stability crumbled on "Black Thursday," October 24, 1929, when the New York Stock Exchange crashed, initiating a period of financial collapse known as the **Great Depression.** In an urban, mechanized age, millions of workers (25-50% of the work force) were left unemployed and struggled to provide for their families. The United States, like the rest of the developed world, rebounded slowly, with poor economic conditions existing for almost a decade despite **"New Deal"** policies initiated by President **Franklin D. Roosevelt.**

In the aftermath of the Depression, Nazi-led Germany plowed through Europe while anxious Americans stood aside and watched, largely unaware of the horrifying genocidal policies adopted by the Nazi administration. Only the Japanese attack on Pearl Harbor, HI, on December 7, 1941, brought America reluctantly into **World War II.** The war was waged on two fronts, as the Allied powers fought both the Germans in Europe and the Japanese in the Pacific. The European front was resolved with the German surrender on May 8, 1945, less than a year after the immense **D-Day** invasion of continental Europe in June 1944. The war in the Pacific continued until August, when the US dropped two newly developed **nuclear bombs** on Japan, at Hiroshima on August 6, 1945, and at Nagasaki three days later, killing 80,000 civilians and ushering nuclear warfare onto the world stage.

THE COLD WAR. Spared the wartime devastation faced by Europe and East Asia and empowered by nationalist pride, the US economy boomed after the war and secured the nation's status as the world's dominant economic and military power. While the 1950s are often nostalgically recalled as a time of prosperity and traditional values, the decade did have its share of international tumult and angst.

The ideological gulf between the two nuclear powers—the democratic, capitalist America and the totalitarian, communist Soviet Union—initiated a half-century of **Cold War** between the two nations. Tension with the Soviet Union heightened as

President Harry Truman installed a hostile foreign policy of **communist containment**. Exploiting rising anti-communist feeling, the House Un-American Activities Committee, led by Senator Joseph McCarthy, conducted witch-hunts delving into every aspect of American public life, with a special focus on Hollywood and the media as a whole. The power of McCarthy and the HUAC waned as the vast majority of accusations were proven to be groundless.

Fear of communism also led to American military involvement in Asia, where the Maoist revolution in China had created imitators in surrounding countries. From 1950 to 1953, the United States fought the **Korean War** on behalf of the South Koreans, who had been attacked by the communist North Korean government. The Soviet launch of Sputnik, the first artificial satellite, in 1957 rekindled fears that communist regimes were surpassing America in many ways. The **Cuban Missile Crisis** in 1962, during which President **John F. Kennedy** negotiated the removal of Soviet missiles from a Cuban base and narrowly avoided nuclear war, reinforced the perception that the United States must protect the world from Soviet invasion.

In 1963, Lee Harvey Oswald assassinated President Kennedy during a parade in Dallas, TX. The assassination of the young, charismatic President mirrored America's larger loss of innocence and optimism. Throughout the rest of the decade, cultural strife, stemming from the long-fought civil rights movement and the bloody, controversial Vietnam War, altered the nation's social fabric.

ALL YOU NEED IS LOVE...AND PROTEST. Driven by the dictates of the containment policy instituted after WWII, the United States became embroiled in Vietnamese politics, culminating in a large-scale deployment of combat troops in 1965 to protect the South Vietnamese state from the aggression of Ho Chi Minh's communist government to the north. The **Vietnam War** was seen as a test of America's credibility as a protector of nations struggling with communism, making retreat difficult even when it became apparent that the situation in Vietnam was more complex than originally expected and that victory was unlikely. Though most Americans supported the war at first, opposition grew as it dragged on, and its moral premises were questioned. The use of TV and photographic media to cover the war contributed to the harsh and hopeless perception of the situation in Vietnam. Members of the new hippie generation responded with shouts of "Make Love, Not War," at the 1969 **Woodstock** music festival. The developing opposition to the conflict among the young catalyzed wrenching generational clashes that eventually peaked in riots and subsequent violence at the **1968 Democratic Convention** and the shooting of anti-war protestors by the National Guard at **Kent State** in 1970.

The Vietnam War was not the only cause that captured the hearts and lungs of idealistic young Americans. **Rosa Parks's** refusal to give up a bus seat in Montgomery, AL (p. 453), in 1955 sparked a period of feverish activity in the **civil rights movement**, in which African-Americans strove for legal equality. The struggle was characterized by countless demonstrations, marches, and sit-ins in the heart of a defiant and often violent South. Activists were drenched with fire hoses, arrested, and even killed by local mobs and policemen. The movement peaked with the March on Washington in 1963, where **Dr. Martin Luther King, Jr.** delivered his famous "I Have A Dream" speech, calling for non-violent racial integration. The tone of the civil rights movement changed as some blacks became fed up with peaceful moderation and turned to the more militant rhetoric of **Malcolm X**, a convert to the **Nation of Islam** who espoused separatist "Black Power." The gun-toting Black Panthers used militant tactics to assert the rights of African-Americans.

The second wave of the **women's movement** arose at this time as well. Sparked by Betty Friedan's book *The Feminine Mystique*, American women sought to change the delineation between men's and women's roles in society, demanding access to male-dominated professions and equal pay. Outside the Miss America

Pageant in 1968, women crowned a sheep Miss America and exuberantly threw away their bras and high heels, creating a catalyst for second-wave feminism. The sexual revolution, fueled by the introduction of the birth control pill, heightened the debate over a woman's right to choose to have an abortion. The 1973 Supreme Court decision, **Roe v. Wade,** legalized abortion, but the battle between abortion opponents and pro-choice advocates still divides the nation today.

Despite civil rights legislation and anti-poverty measures passed under **President Lyndon B. Johnson's** Great Society agenda, the specter of the Vietnam War overshadowed his presidency. By the end of these tumultuous years, the nation had dropped 7 million tons of bombs on Indochina—twice the amount used against America's World War II enemies—and victory was still out of reach. Thus, under **President Richard Nixon,** America extracted the last of its troops from Vietnam.

In 1972, five burglars were caught breaking into the Democratic National Convention Headquarters in the **Watergate** apartments. Their attempt to bug the Democratic offices led to a broader scandal involving the President himself. Caught by his own tape, Nixon fought Congress but ultimately resigned the Presidency.

By the mid-1970s, America was firmly disillusioned with both the government and the idealistic counterculture of the previous decade. More frivolous activities, like dancing in platform shoes and powder blue suits under flashing lights—a phenomenon known as **"disco"**—became the mark of a generation that just wanted to have fun. Unfortunately, the international situation continued to be tenuous. The oil-rich Arab nations boycotted the US, causing an **energy crisis** that drove up gas prices, frustrated autophile Americans, and precipitated an economic recession.

THE 1980S. In 1980, **Ronald Reagan,** a politically conservative actor and former California governor, was elected to the White House. Reagan knew how to give the people what they wanted: money. He cut government spending on public programs and lowered taxes. Though the decade's conservatives embraced certain right-wing social goals like school prayer and the campaign against abortion, the Reagan revolution was essentially economic. **Reaganomics** gave tax breaks to big business, spurred short-term consumption, and turned savings and loans over to businesses. Yet all was not well—whereas the US had been a creditor nation in 1980, the end of the decade saw the nation as the world's largest debtor. On the foreign policy front, Reagan aggressively expanded the military budget and sent weapons and aid to right-wing "freedom fighters" in Guatemala, Nicaragua, and Afghanistan, a policy that would haunt the US in the decades to come.

THE 1990S: BILLS, BILLS, BILLS. The US remained an active force in the world through the early 1990s, as President Bush Sr. directed **"Operation Desert Storm"** in 1990 as a response to Iraq's invasion of neighboring Kuwait. The war freed Kuwait, but its popularity in the US was compromised by the recession that followed. The public replaced Bush in the 1992 election with the young Democrat **Bill Clinton,** who promised a new era of government activism after years of laissez-faire rule.

The Clinton administration found itself plagued with its own problems: a suspicious Arkansas real estate development called **Whitewater,** an alleged extramarital affair with Gennifer Flowers, and accusations of sexual harassment from Paula Jones. Yet Clinton's public approval remained high, especially after the nation supported him in a struggle against Congressional Republicans whose attempts to balance the budget led to two government shutdowns between 1995 and 1996.

Clinton was re-elected in 1996, but new scandal erupted in 1998 as reports of an inappropriate relationship between Clinton and White House intern **Monica Lewinsky** were plastered across American newspapers, magazines, and TV screens. Clinton initially denied the allegations, but later admitted that he lied. Eventually, he was **impeached** for perjury and obstruction of justice on the recommendation of Independent Counsel Kenneth Starr. The resulting trial in the

Senate ended with a vote for informal censure over conviction, and Clinton remained in office. Despite the scandal, during Clinton's tenure the United States saw the lowest modern percentage of unemployment, the lowest inflation rates, the most homeowners, decreased crime rates and welfare rolls, and the first balanced budget in years.

STOPPING THE "AXIS OF EVIL": THE WAR ON TERROR. On **September 11th,** 2001, the most severe terrorist attack in US history occurred when four planes were hijacked. The site of the most violent crash was the World Trade Center in New York City, where approximately 3000 lives were taken. Osama bin Laden, Al Quaeda, a militant terrorist group, and the Taliban, the Islamic ruling body of Afghanistan were deemed responsible for the attacks. Since September 11th, President Bush (Jr.) has waged a **War on Terrorism** designed to identify and capture known terrorists, particularly those of al-Qaeda. The War on Terrorism became controversial among the US public when President Bush instituted military tribunals and US Attorney General John Ashcroft threatened the civil liberties of immigrants and non-citizens under sweeping measures like the PATRIOT Act.

The general direction of American policy has moved away from reliance on international organizations (e.g., the UN). Rather, as attempts to act in concert with such institutions have met with frustration and failure, the American government has tended toward increasing unilateralism, as demonstrated by the recent war in Iraq. This policy has been met with hostility by many countries, especially those in continental Europe, and has increased overall tension around the world.

RECENT NEWS

WAR IN IRAQ. President Bush declared war on Iraq in March 2003 to "disarm Iraq and free its people." Bush had been threatening war for months, claiming that Saddam Hussein's regime, with its designs on weapons of mass destruction, posed a grave threat to United States and world security. The major fighting ended only three weeks after the American army entered Iraq, but forces remained, trying to restructure the government, but were faced with riots and looting, resulting in many American deaths. US troops found and captured Saddam Hussein in December 2003 in a hole underneath a two-room mud shack on a sheep farm. The US government recently handed political power over to Iraq's new interim government, but remain a presence in the country.

CULTURE

FOOD

While chains dot the country and trends like the low-carb diets tailor the nation's eating habits, more authentic American food is best found at the regional level. Agricultural production, immigration patterns, and local cultures have resulted in unique and delicious foods that far outshine the burger-and-fries stereotype.

NORTHEAST. America's English settlers landed in the Northeast and combined their staples of meats and vegetables with uniquely American foodstuffs like turkey, maple syrup, clams, lobster, cranberries, and corn. The results yielded such treasures as Boston brown bread, Indian pudding, New England clam chowder, and Maine boiled lobster. The shellfish in the Northeast is second to none.

SOUTH. Be prepared for some home cookin'. Fried chicken, biscuits, mashed potatoes, and collard greens are some highlights of Southeastern cuisine. Cheese grits or cornbread are a savory supplement to lunch and dinner dishes.

LOUISIANA. Chefs in New Orleans are among the best in the country, and creole or Cajun cooking tantalizes the taste buds. Locals and tourists alike regard crawfish, fried catfish, jambalaya (rice cooked with ham, sausage, shrimp, and herbs), and gumbo (a soup with okra, meat, and vegetables) as delicacies. The faint of taste buds beware: Cajun and creole cooking bring in the heat.

TEXAS. From beef, to pork, to beef again, Texans like to throw it on the grill. Eat at any of the many barbecue joints, though, and they'll tell you that the real secret's in the sauce. For those in the mood for something ethnic, enchiladas, burritos, nachos, and fajitas are scrumptious Tex-Mex options.

SOUTHWEST. Strongly influenced by Mexican cuisine, Southwestern grub relies on the Mexican foodstuffs of corn, flour, and chilies. Salsa made from tomatoes, chiles (especially New Mexico's famous hatch chilies), and *tomatillos* adds a spicy note to nearly all dishes, like quesadillas, chiles rellenos, and tacos.

CALIFORNIA. California's trend-setting status extends beyond fashion and movies to fresh, natural foods. Home to acres of orange and avocado trees, California offers an array of often organic produce in everything from smoothies to salads. Grapes also grow plentifully in the numerous vineyards that line the fields of Napa Valley and central California, the United States's prime wine country.

NORTHWEST. In close proximity to the arctic water frequented by halibut and salmon, many cities in the Pacific Northwest are known for superior seafood, which can be found in everything from chowder to tacos. If you're looking for a cold one to wash down your seafood, Portland, OR, is the microbrewery capital of North America, and has the beer to prove it.

CUSTOMS AND ETIQUETTE

TABLE MANNERS. In the US, good table manners means quiet eating. Loud chewing, talking with food in your mouth, or slurping are seen as rude, and burping or flatulence is not seen as complimentary to the chef. Servers at sitdown restaurants usually expect to be tipped 15-20%.

PUBLIC BEHAVIOR. Dress in the US tends to be more modest than in Europe. Toplessness, particularly in women, should be avoided. Many establishments will require a customer to wear a shirt and shoes. The most acceptable forms of public affection are hugging and holding hands; kissing in public will usually draw some glances. Although most cities are tolerant of homosexuality, gay or lesbian couples should be aware that they may receive unwanted attention for public displays of affection, especially in rural areas. Also, note that many Americans will say "see you later" without really intending to make future plans.

GESTURES. One of the most offensive gestures in the US is extending your middle finger at someone. Known as "giving someone the finger," this gesture is considered not only rude, but obscene. On the other hand, a "thumbs up" gesture is a sign of approval and a widely recognized signal for hitchhiking, which *Let's Go* does not recommend.

THE ARTS

It did not take long for hearty American individualism to make its mark on the global canon, previously dominated by age-old European traditions. From the 19th century Transcendentalist literature of New England to the unique musical stylings of bluegrass and jazz, America has established itself time and again as an innovator in the world of creative arts.

LITERATURE

THE FIRST FEW PAGES. The first best-seller printed in America, the *Bay Psalm Book*, was published in Cambridge, MA, in 1640. Reflecting the Puritanical culture of much of 17th- and 18th-century America, it was religious in nature, as it was entirely comprised of the book of Psalms translated into English meter. Very few enduring classics were created until the early 1800s, when artists began to explore the unique American experience in their writing. **James Fenimore Cooper's** *Last of the Mohicans* (1826), **Nathaniel Hawthorne's** *The Scarlet Letter* (1850), and **Herman Melville's** *Moby Dick* (1851)—among the first great American novels—all feature strong yet innocent individualists negotiating the raw American landscape. By the mid-19th century, the work of **New England Transcendentalists** like **Henry David Thoreau** *(Walden)* and **Ralph Waldo Emerson** embodied a spirit of anti-materialism by focusing on self-reflection and a retreat into nature. **Walt Whitman** promoted a uniquely American style of poetry with his unorthodox verses expressing both his distaste for the conditions of the 19th century and his idealistic views about American democracy. Later in the century, **Mark Twain** became one of America's best-loved storytellers with his homespun tales out of Hannibal, MO. His novel *The Adventures of Huckleberry Finn* (1885) uses a young boy's journey to express social criticism and a treatment of the human spirit.

Literature also provided 19th-century American women the opportunity both to express themselves and to comment critically on contemporary society. In 1852, **Harriet Beecher Stowe** published *Uncle Tom's Cabin*, an exposé of slavery that, according to some scholars, contributed to the outbreak of the Civil War. Poet **Emily Dickinson** secretly scribbled away in her native Amherst, MA home; her untitled and unpunctuated verses weren't discovered until after her death in 1886.

EARLY 20TH CENTURY EXPLORATIONS. Amidst the economic prosperity of the 1920s, a reflective, self-centered movement fermented in American literature in response to changing cultural values. **F. Scott Fitzgerald's** works *(The Great Gatsby)* portray restless individuals who are financially secure but unfulfilled by their conspicuous consumption. During this tumultuous time, many writers moved abroad in search of refuge; this **Lost Generation** included Fitzgerald, **Ernest Hemingway** *(The Sun Also Rises)*, **T.S. Eliot** ("The Love Song of J. Alfred Prufrock"), **Ezra Pound,** and **E.E. Cummings.** This group's sophisticated works conveyed an increasing disillusionment with the contemporary American experience. The **Harlem Renaissance,** a convergence of African-American artistic and political action in New York City, was spurred on by the **Great Migration,** a large scale African-American migration from the rural South to the urban North, and it fed off the excitement of the Jazz Age. **Langston Hughes** *(Montage of a Dream Deferred)*, **Nella Larsen** *(Quicksand)*, and **Zora Neale Hurston** *(Their Eyes Were Watching God)* brought an awareness about black talent and creativity to a broader audience as they struggled to define and express ideas about African-American identity and the black experience in America. The Harlem Renaissance also saw the rise of more radical black intellectualism led by **Marcus Garvey,** champion of the **Pan-African** movement, and **Alain Locke,** who wrote the essay "The New Negro."

In the 1930s and 1940s, as America struggled to recover from the Great Depression, the plight of decaying agricultural life and faltering industry of the Deep South and West began to infiltrate literature. **William Faulkner** *(The Sound and the Fury)* juxtaposed avant-garde stream-of-consciousness techniques with subjects rooted in the rot and decay of the rural South. Nobel Prize recipient **John Steinbeck** is best known for his 1939 novel *The Grapes of Wrath*, which depicts the condition of migrant laborers heading from the Great Plains to California in the wake of the Great Depression. The plays of **Tennessee Williams** *(A Streetcar Named Desire)* portray family dynamics within lower-class, uprooted Southern families. **Clifford Odets's** play *Waiting for Lefty*, detailing the plight of frustrated factory workers, was a grassroots hit, and audiences often joined with the actors in chanting the play's final lines, "Strike! Strike!" In his remarkable autobiography, *Black Boy* (1945), **Richard Wright** recounts growing up black in the Jim Crow South.

POST-WAR MALAISE. In the conformist 1950s, literature provided alternative commentary on America's underlying social problems. **Ralph Ellison's** *Invisible Man*, published in 1952, confronted a broad audience with the division between white and black identities in America. In 1955, **Vladimir Nabokov**, a Russian émigré, redefined English prose style for a whole generation of writers with his controversial story about unconventional love, *Lolita*. **Gwendolyn Brooks,** the first black writer to win a Pulitzer Prize, published intense poetry highlighting social problems like abortion, gangs, and drop-outs. The **Beats,** spearheaded by cult heroes **Jack Kerouac** *(On the Road)* and **Allen Ginsberg** *(Howl)*, lived wildly and espoused a more free-thinking and laid back attitude. Playwright **Arthur Miller** delved into the American psyche with *Death of a Salesman* (1949), in which he explored the frailty of the American dream. He later wrote *The Crucible*, a play detailing the Salem witch-hunts, as a critique of McCarthy's communist "witch-hunts."

As conventions of society found themselves increasingly questioned in the 1960s, writers began to explore more unorthodox material. **Anne Sexton** revealed the depths of her own mental breakdown, while **Sylvia Plath** paved the way for feminist authors, exposed her psychological deterioration, and hinted at her suicide in *The Bell Jar* (1963). The essays and stories of **James Baldwin** *(The Fire Next Time)* warned both white and black Americans about the self-destructive implications of racial hatred. **Flannery O'Connor** exposed the eerie, grotesque underbelly of the contemporary South in stories such as "A Good Man is Hard to Find."

The search for identity and the attempt to reconcile artistic and social agendas continued into the 1970s and 1980s. **E.L. Doctorow's** *Ragtime* (1975) evokes vibrant images of a turn-of-the-century America, weaving together historical and fictional figures. **Toni Morrison** *(Beloved)* won the Nobel Prize in for her visceral interpretations of the tension between gender, ethnic, and cultural identities. **Don DeLillo's** *White Noise* (1985) carries on the American absurdist tradition and, using both humor and uncanny insight, delves into America's obsession with mortality. Many stories have also focused on the fast pace and commercialism of modern society. In *American Psycho* (1991), **Bret Easton Ellis** exposes the conspicuous consumption and disintegrated morals of New York City in the 1980s, while the plays of **David Mamet** *(Glengarry Glen Ross)* are known for explosively confronting the gritty underside of American business. Among more recent authors, the prolific **Philip Roth** *(American Pastoral)* continues to disassemble the American dream. **David Sedaris** *(Me Talk Pretty One Day)* has burst onto the literary scene with his hilarious, self-deprecating columns and essays about his childhood, family life, and his experience as an American living in France.

MUSIC

The United States has given birth to a plethora of musical genres, whose styles and songs have intermingled to produce the many distinct styles that can be heard today. Scott Joplin meshed African-American harmony and rhythm with classical European style to develop the first American piano form, ragtime. From this rich, upbeat, piano-banging dance music of the 19th century to the Deep South's mournful blues, early African-American music defined soul. The 1950s saw a new, "edgy" style of music arise and entrance America's youth: rock 'n' roll. Soul and gospel music evolved into R&B, jazz, funk, and later, hip-hop, while rock exploded in the '60s and '70s into today's genre of "classic rock." Recent decades have ushered in the new styles of rap, metal, grunge alternative, and teeny-bopper pop.

SINGIN' THE BLUES. As with ragtime, black Southerners were primarily responsible for the blues, which was originally a blend of Northwest African slave calls and Native American song and verse forms. Blues songs were popularized by **W.C. Handy,** the legendary "father of the blues". His "St. Louis Blues" remains one of the most recorded songs ever. As Southern blacks migrated to industrial centers during the early 20th century, the blues, augmented by the contributions of women like **Mamie Smith, Billie Holiday,** and **Bessie Smith,** found an audience in the North. The blues heavily influenced the development of other popular American musical styles, most notably jazz and rock 'n' roll.

AND ALL THAT JAZZ. Ragtime, blues, and military brass combined in New Orleans in the early 20th century to create America's classical music, jazz. Its emphasis on improvisation and unique tonal and harmonic rules distinguished it from previous genres. The work of all-time jazz greats like **Louis Armstrong, Dizzy Gillespie,** and **Ella Fitzgerald** influenced the later work of classical composers; **Leonard Bernstein's** classical orchestrations and **George Gershwin's** jazzy theatrical style can both trace their roots and distinctly American sound to the ragtime tradition. Early jazz also led to the era of big band music, during which the incomparable **Duke Ellington** and the swing orchestra of **Glenn Miller** reigned supreme.

COUNTRY ROADS, TAKE ME HOME. Country music has its roots in the Appalachian Mountains, among a poor rural white population that put a new spin on ancestral European folk traditions. Sentimental, often spiritual lyrics were combined with simple melodies to create a characteristically honest American sound. The genre owes much of its attitude and sound to classic heroes: **Hank Williams** cultivated an air of tragic, honky-tonk mystique, while **Johnny Cash** left his mark with a brazen, devil-may-care honesty. Commercially, country didn't catch on until it was given a boost by radio and Nashville's famous 1930s program the **Grand Ole Opry.** Country artists like **Willie Nelson** and **Emmylou Harris** captured both Southern and Northern audiences. Recently, country artists like **Garth Brooks, Tim McGraw,** and **LeAnn Rimes,** as well as country-pop crossovers like the **Dixie Chicks** and **Faith Hill,** have combined to bring modern country into the mainstream limelight.

Another genre that carries on a distinctly American style is folk. Folk music has often embraced political and social activism through its direct lyrics and honest spirit. **Woody Guthrie's** music touched upon issues of patriotism in the midst of the Great Depression ("This Land is Your Land"). Thanks to artists like **Bob Dylan** and **Joan Baez,** folk music popularly caught on in the sixties and spoke to social protesters across the nation. During this hippie generation, people used songs like "We Shall Overcome" and "Where Have all the Flowers Gone?" to both express their opinions about relevant issues, and to unify their protests. Folk survives today in coffee shops and on street corners, and folk musicians like **Dar Williams** are still lucid social commentators.

PUT ANOTHER DIME IN THE JUKEBOX, BABY. No one can say exactly how rock 'n' roll was started, although it originally grew out of African-American traditions of gospel and rhythm and blues. One thing is for certain, though: **Elvis Presley** was the first to be crowned "King." His rock kingdom of **Graceland** is a popular attraction for Memphis tourists. During the 50s and 60s rock 'n' roll's driving, danceable rhythms, rebellious attitude, and fascination with electric instruments dominated the popular music charts. Rock 'n' roll reflected the new post-WWII optimism and innocence throughout America, as teenagers looked for something more exciting and daring to express their style. The genre has produced most of America's more famous music icons—before Elvis, there were **Chuck Berry** and **Jerry Lee Lewis,** who ushered in a new era of poodle skirts and slicked-back hair. In the 60s and 70s, rock used bluegrass-like melodies and rock beats, combined with the wailing guitar solos made famous by **Jimi Hendrix** and **Led Zeppelin,** to create the new subgenre of classic rock that lives on with artists like **Bruce Springsteen** and **Pink Floyd.**

SOUL FOOD. In 1961 Berry Gordy, Jr. started a little company in Detroit that revolutionized American music. **Motown** was an all-black record label that produced hit artists like **The Supremes, The Temptations, Marvin Gaye,** and **The Jackson Five,** Michael Jackson's first entry into the music world. Descended from gospel and the blues, the unmistakable "Motown sound" combined smooth lyrics with funky backing, sparking a new genre of soul music: R&B. Unlike previous African-American musical acts, Motown artists did not strive to integrate its sound into the white music world. Rather, Motown singers were the first African-American musicians to infuse their music with a socio-political message. Listeners changed **Martha and the Vandellas'** song "Dancing in the Street" from a party song into a theme song during civil rights riots in 1967 Detroit. **James Brown's** song "Say it Loud, I'm Black and I'm Proud" espoused black power and black pride. Today, R&B has drifted far from its roots and is often inseparable from hip-hop. Despite the controversy stemming from statutory rape allegations, **R. Kelly** has proven his mastery of this crossover genre, combining silky-smooth crooning with bumpin' beats.

DISCO BALLS, HAIR BANDS, AND GANGSTA RAP. The 1970s will be forever remembered for being the era of disco. Disco divas like **Gloria Gaynor** ("I Will Survive") and funk bands like **Parliament Funkadelic** dominated the American nightlife and fostered a culture that celebrated dancing, drugs, and excess. The 1980s witnessed a rap revolution, spawned by East Coast stars **Public Enemy, Run-DMC,** and the **Beastie Boys,** which is still going strong today. The eighties also ushered in the popularity of "hair bands" like **Poison** and punk rockers like **The Ramones,** not to mention a little entertainer named **Madonna.** In the early nineties, grunge music escaped from the garage to the national spotlight largely because of Seattle's **Nirvana** and **Pearl Jam.** The West Coast birthed the "gangsta rap" movement (Dr. Dre, Snoop Dogg) in the 90s as well, sparking much debate over the promotion of violence and excessive misogyny in its lyrics. The early 90s legendary East Coast-West Coast feud between NYC's **Notorious B.I.G.** and L.A.'s **Tupac Shakur** split the rap community and only ended with both rappers' deaths six months apart in 1996-1997. Recently, **Eminem** has exploded to international stardom with his provocative lyricism and outlandish persona.

DIRTY POP. Pop-Punk broke into the mainstream during the 90s with **Green Day's** rise to fame. With the help of artists like **Blink-182** and **Good Charlotte,** this toned-down and upbeat version of the heavy punk of the 80s has continued to be a major presence in young America's CD player. But the late 1990s and new millennium have been primarily dominated by a resurgence of bubblegum pop and dance tunes. Barely 16 years old when their first album was released, the **New Kids on the Block** spearheaded the boy band phenomenon, and the MTV generation of consumer teens has sustained the popularity of young superstars like **Britney Spears** and **Justin Timberlake.** Although many criticize the genre for being full of copycat songs with essentially the same musical structure and dance beat, legions of screaming fans, weaned on the energetically choreographed music videos of current superstars, don't seem to mind.

FILM

SILENT FILMS AND PRE-CODE TALKIES. Before sound was wedded to image in the first "talkie"—*The Jazz Singer*, 1927—silent films ruled the screen. Though silent films quickly went out of fashion once sound entered the picture, they still hold a place of prominence in film history and the hearts of film buffs. **Hollywood,** CA, owing to its sunny, film-friendly climate, proximity to a variety of photogenic terrain, and previous prominence as a theater center, quickly became the center of the movie business. By the period just after WWI, actors like Charlie Chaplin, Buster Keaton, and Mary Pickford were household names. Free from the control of domineering studios, these film artists brought a playful, exuberant, and innovative attitude to their work. Films such as *Sunrise* and *The Crowd*, meanwhile, combined innovative cinematography and compelling stories that remain popular to this day. But early films often tapped into America's isolationist sentiments and grossly misportrayed or demonized foreign characters. When other countries protested, American filmmakers realized the monetary importance of audiences outside of America. Simultaneously, critics began wondering publicly about the moral value of movies. In an effort to keep foreign audiences and prevent what seemed like imminent federal regulation, filmmakers created the **Motion Pictures Producers and Distributors of America** (MPPDA), a self regulating board that would address the pertinent concerns internally.

CLASSIC ERA. It was not long before the film industry's wild success gave rise to the expansion of the **studio system**. Giant production houses like Paramount, MGM, and Warner took up residence on the West Coast and turned movies into big business. American film's **golden age** took place during the height of the studio era, when Hollywood's four major studios standardized and dominated films. Victor Fleming's *Gone with the Wind* (1939), a Civil War epic, was the first large-scale movie extravaganza, redefining the bounds of cinematic scope. Frank Capra, in his probing morality plays like *It's a Wonderful Life* (1946) and *Mr. Smith Goes to Washington* (1939), brought a conscience to entertainment. Michael Curtiz's *Casablanca* (1942), starring Humphrey Bogart, was a classic cinematic romance with a patriotic and politicized background. In 1941, Orson Welles unveiled his intricate masterpiece, *Citizen Kane*, a landmark work that revolutionized the potential of the medium. Fantasy, however, still sold tickets: Walt Disney's animated *Snow White* (1937) and Fleming's *The Wizard of Oz* (1939) kept producers well-fed.

PRETTY BOYS, MONSTERS, AND BOMBSHELLS. Heightened tensions with the Soviet Union and conflicts with communism abroad led to widespread communist witch-hunts at home. The film industry, under government pressure, took up the policy of blacklisting any artists with suspected, or even rumored, ties to communism. The resulting constant paranoia, as well as dwindling box office returns brought about by competition with television, eventually stimulated the production of a slew of movies that were sensational enough to draw crowds back to the theaters. Films such as *Invasion of the Body Snatchers* and *The Incredible Shrinking Man* used **science fiction** to grapple with cultural anxieties about communism and nuclear weapons, while larger than life **westerns** such as *High Noon* and *The Searchers* galloped across the screens. Meanwhile, **Alfred Hitchcock** *(Rear Window, North by Northwest)* and the ever-free-thinking **Orson Welles** *(The Lady from Shanghai)* created an entirely new cinematic genre: **film noir**, which lasted in its classic form until the 1960s.

The 1950s also saw the emergence of a cult of glamour surrounding the most luminous stars. Cloaked in glitz and scandal, sex symbols **Marilyn Monroe, James Dean** *(Rebel Without a Cause)*, **Elizabeth Taylor,** and **Rock Hudson** drew audiences to movies by name recognition alone. These stars, along with actors **Marlon Brando** *(A Streetcar Named Desire)* and **Audrey Hepburn** *(Breakfast at Tiffany's)*, brought their own personal mystique to the screen, and added significantly to the art of cinematic performance.

SOCK IT TO ME. The 1960s and early 1970s saw widespread social upheaval and tension between generations. Adapting to the demands of younger, more liberal audiences, studios enlisted directors influenced by the French New Wave as well as artists from other media to direct features, including Sidney Lumet, John Frankenheimer, and Robert Altman. With the studios more willing to take a gamble, and the introduction of a movie ratings board (MPAA) to replace censorship, the work of a number of innovative filmmakers began to enter the mainstream. Stanley Kubrick's *Dr. Strangelove* (1964), *2001: A Space Odyssey* (1968), and *A*

LIFE AND TIMES

Clockwork Orange (1971) brought a literary importance to filmmaking. Dennis Hopper's *Easy Rider* (1969), a film about countercultural youth rebellion and the fruitlessness of the American dream, and the acclaimed documentary *Woodstock* (1970) established film as a viable medium for social critique. Meanwhile, the first half of the 1970s flirted with the genre of **blaxploitation,** sensationalized portrayals of urban African-Americans, with films like *Shaft* and *Superfly.*

Throughout the 1970s, experimentalism largely gave way to more polished treatment of equally serious issues. Film-schooled directors like Martin Scorsese *(Taxi Driver)*, Francis Ford Coppola *(The Godfather)*, and Michael Cimino *(The Deer Hunter)* brought technical skill to their exploration of the darker side of humanity. An influx of foreign filmmakers, like Milos Forman *(One Flew Over the Cuckoo's Nest)* and Roman Polański *(Chinatown)*, introduced a new perspective to American film.

TAKING CARE OF BUSINESS. Driven by the global mass distribution of American cinema and the development of high-tech special effects, the late 1970s and 1980s witnessed the rebirth of the **blockbuster. Steven Spielberg's** *Jaws* kicked off the trend in 1973 by piloting the now tried and true advertising methods of TV previews, movie merchandise, media stunts, and theme song publicity. Following his breakout success with *Jaws*, Spielberg produced *E.T.* (1982) and *Raiders of the Lost Ark* (1981), hugely successful movies. **George Lucas** followed the trend of creating widely-appealing movies with impressive special effects with his *Star Wars* trilogy. Though such films were criticized for their over-reliance on effects, they almost single-handedly returned Hollywood to its former status as king.

Despite the increasing commercialism of Hollywood, quite a bit of highly imaginative work came out of the period, like Rob Reiner's *This is Spinal Tap,* a hilarious send-up of popular music, and David Lynch's *Blue Velvet,* a disturbing look at the primal terror beneath the tranquil surface of suburbia. The revival of the blockbuster continued into the millennium, with such high-budget money-makers as the dinosaur thriller *Jurassic Park* and the decadent love-story *Titanic* drawing the largest crowds. Recently, a revolution in digital film technology has spawned such hits as *Shrek* and *Finding Nemo,* animated films with universal appeal.

INDIE FEVER. The recognition of independent, or **indie,** films—films that are either produced independently of any major studio or at least do not follow standard studio conventions—marks the most interesting turn for cinema in the last several years. Brothers Joel and Ethan Coen have created some of the most creative and original work of late, including the gruesome comedy *Fargo* and the hilarious, off-beat *The Big Lebowski*, which gathered such a cult following, in fact, that it inspired "Lebowski Fest," a goofily hedonistic tribute to The Dude, bowling, and white russians, in both Louisville, KY, and New York City, NY. Quentin Tarantino's cool action *(Reservoir Dogs, Pulp Fiction)*, Paul Thomas Anderson's emotionally charged and frequently sprawling story-telling style *(Boogie Nights, Magnolia)*, and Wes Anderson's darkly quirky humor *(Rushmore, The Royal Tenenbaums)* have all injected new life into American cinema. Recently, however, films have been tackling heavier issues, with the Michael Moore's ultra-liberal films *Bowling for Columbine* and *Fahrenheit 9/11*, and Mel Gibson's graphic and highly controversial film *The Passion of the Christ.*

FINE ARTS

American art has often been dismissed as a pale reflection of European trends. Despite this stereotype, it has a rich history rooted in the country's expansion from colonial America to the present day. Its raw and uncontrolled nature is reflected not only in the grandiose 19th-century landscape paintings that sought to capture the beauty of the untamed West, but also in the unwieldy lines and shapes of American 20th-century **abstract expressionism.**

PAINTING. Portraiture flourished in colonial America. John Singleton Copley, Charles Willson Peale, and Gilbert Stuart rendered intimate likenesses of iconic revolutionary figures from Paul Revere to George Washington. In the first half of the 19th century, Thomas Cole and Asher B. Durand produced ambitious landscapes with didactic overtones. Cole was one of the earliest artists in the **Hudson River School,** a group of painters who combined expressive depictions of nature with ideas about the divine. Later, **Winslow Homer's** vibrant watercolors captured the wild side of nature in sweeping seascapes, while softer American Impressionists like Childe Hassam depicted the effects of light in New England city scenes. The turn of the 20th century saw an emphasis on realism and the depiction of urban life; the group of painters known as the **Ash Can School,** led by Robert Henri, promoted "art for art's sake." By the 1940s, abstract expressionism had been reborn in the US. Country-wide anxiety over international unrest and the threat of war bore heavily on the American psyche. In drip paintings and figurative images, painters like **Jackson Pollock** and **Mark Rothko** reflected the ironic mix of swaggering confidence and frenetic insecurity that characterized Cold War America. Ushering in the age of **pop art, Roy Lichtenstein** and **Andy Warhol** used mass-produced, cartoonish images to satirize the icons of American popular culture. This art that enshrined the mundane blurred the boundaries between "high culture" and "mass culture," and became symbolic of the growing **postmodernism** movement. The 1980s art boom, stationed around private galleries in New York City and L.A., ushered in a decade of slick, idyllic paintings and the kitschy sculptures of Jeff Koons.

PHOTOGRAPHY. Beginning in the early 20th century, photography became the medium of choice for artists with a social conscience. **Jakob Riis** and **Lewis Hine** photographed the urban poor and child laborers, while **Walker Evans** and **Dorothea Lange** captured destitute farmers during the Great Depression. **Ansel Adams** used his photographs of rugged Western landscapes as tools in his quest for natural conservation in the 40s, 50s, and 60s. **Robert Frank's** snapshots caught the social transitions and tensions of 1960s America. In the 1970s, photography came into its own as back-to-basics 35mm photographs pushed the boundaries of defined art with the stills of Diane Arbus, Garry Winogrand, and Cindy Sherman.

THE MEDIA

America is wired. Images, sounds, and stories from the television, radio, Internet, and magazines infiltrate every aspect of the American lifestyle. Fads have been popularized and fortunes have been made thanks solely to the power of mass media, but because of this intense power, constant debate rages over who should be held responsible for content. Despite controversy about policing the industry, American consumption of new media is continually growing.

TELEVISION. TV sets are found in 98% of US homes. Competition between the six national **networks** (ABC, CBS, Fox, NBC, UPN, and WB), cable television, and satellite TV has triggered exponential growth in TV culture. Network prime time (8-11 EST) often features America's most popular shows like the political drama *The West Wing* (NBC), the former hit comedy *Friends* (NBC), and the bitingly witty cartoon *The Simpsons* (Fox). One need not be bound to the networks, however, as **cable** provides special-interest channels that cover every subject from cooking to sports to science fiction. Meanwhile, **premium stations** air recently released movies along with regular programming; one favorite is HBO, which boasts the pleasingly off-beat *Curb Your Enthusiasm* and the mobster drama *The Sopranos*. Travelers will find that some hotel rooms come equipped with basic cable, while others offer premium stations or even pay-per-view channels.

LIFE AND TIMES

Although **reality television** surged in popularity a few years ago, many network programs have suffered from the effects of an over-saturated market. Even the granddaddy of them all, *Survivor* (CBS), has dropped in popularity, while more outrageous shows such as *The Swan* (Fox), which uses plastic surgery to make over less-attractive contestants, have soured viewers to the entire genre. Still, the cable station MTV seems to have gotten it right, as teenagers and young adults still spend hours glued to reality programs *The Real World* and *Road Rules*. Since the debut of *Beverly Hills 90210* in 1990, in fact, drama shows targeting teen audiences have skyrocketed. With its beautiful young stars in even more beautiful clothing and beachside homes, *The OC* is the latest hit in the slew of teen dramas.

Special comedy programs also dominate much of TV-land. Americans and Canadians alike have contributed to the successes of the long-running *Saturday Night Live* (NBC), while late-night television is sustained by the comic stylings of talk-show hosts like David Letterman on *The Late Show* (CBS) and Conan O'Brien's *Late Night* (NBC). Daytime programming is less-watched and less-respected but still fills the hours with tawdry soap operas and frequently trashy talk shows.

Television is the point of entry to **world-wide news** for most Americans. Twenty-four hour news coverage is available on cable stations such as CNN, MSNBC, and Fox News. Each major network presents local and national nightly news (usually at 5 and/or 11pm EST), while prime-time "newsmagazines" like *60 Minutes* (CBS), *Dateline* (NBC), and *20/20* (ABC) specialize in investigative reports and exposés. ESPN, a cable channel, gives viewers all sports, all the time and has capitalized on America's sporting obsession with the ever-popular *SportsCenter*, the definitive sports news show. The Public Broadcasting Station (PBS) is commercial-free, funded by viewer contributions, the federal government, and corporate grants. Its repertoire includes educational children's shows like *Sesame Street*, nature programs, mystery shows, and British comedies.

PRINT. Despite the onset of more sophisticated technologies like TV and the Internet, Americans still cherish the feel of glossy pages and the smell of newsprint. Today, newsstands crowd city corners and transportation terminals throughout the country. Publications cover all areas of society, culture, and politics; whether it's for lounging away a Sunday afternoon at home or passing time in a doctor's waiting room, print media dominates the market.

Some of the most well-respected newspapers include *The New York Times* and *The Washington Post*, though every city has at least one major paper. Another popular daily, *USA Today*, is more informal. Women's magazines such as *Cosmopolitan* and men's magazines like *Maxim* feature articles and photos about sex and fashion, while *The New Yorker* amuses its more intellectual subscribers with short stories and essays. Entertainment magazines like *People* and *US Weekly* chronicle celebrity gossip, while *Rolling Stone* focuses on the music. Those interested in the stock market's ups and downs swear by *The Wall Street Journal* and *Forbes*, while people who prefer sports to stock prices troll the pages of *Sports Illustrated*. Ranging from trashy tabloids like the *National Enquirer* to the most influential and respected news organs, American media is notably diverse and often subject to criticism for being too liberal, exploitative, or sensational. Even so, many Americans consume and trust their news sources without question.

RADIO. Before television transformed American culture, the radio was the country's primary source of entertainment and news. Classic comedy programs like *The Jack Benny Show* and the crackly news coverage of Edward R. Murrow amused and informed Americans for decades. WDIA, an all black radio station in the late 1940s, disseminated ideas about religion and politics and was instrumental in uniting the African-American community in the years leading up to the civil rights movement. Even though the moving images and crisper sounds of television have reduced radio's earlier, widespread popularity, it remains a treasured medium in America's car-reliant culture. Radio is generally divided into AM and FM; talk radio comprises most of the low-frequency AM slots, and the high-powered FM stations feature most of the music. Each broadcaster owns a four-letter call-name, with "W" as the first letter for those east of the Mississippi River (as in WJMN), and "K" to the west (as in KPFA).

The more intellectually minded listen to **National Public Radio (NPR).** Full of classical music and social pundits debating important issues, NPR disseminates information about everything from general news on *Morning Edition* to car repair on the irreverent but useful *Car Talk.* Supplying the country's regional needs, local stations give up-to-the-minute news reports and air a wide range of music from country-western to the latest pop. College radio stations often play more alternative music to appeal to younger listeners.

SPORTS AND RECREATION

For Americans, sports are inseparable from commercialism and regional allegiances. Dressed in colorful jerseys and bloated with cheap beer, Americans fill stadiums or lounge at home to cheer on their local teams.

(AMERICAN) FOOTBALL. Nowhere is the commercialism of American sports more spectacularly displayed than in the **Super Bowl.** Every January, the **National Football League (NFL)** season ends in grandiose style with a championship featuring the league's two best teams and commercial campaigns costing millions of dollars. The American-rules game is especially dear to Middle America, where the padded warriors of the gridiron are applauded for their brute athleticism.

BASEBALL. The slow, tension-building game of baseball captures the hearts of dreaming Little League children and earns its place as America's national pastime. Baseball in the US and Canada centers on the **Major League Baseball (MLB)** season. With teams in most major cities, the MLB baseball season ends with the **World Series,** a seven-game series between the league's two best teams.

BASKETBALL. Professional basketball teams hail from almost every major city, making up the **National Basketball Association (NBA).** NBA players have come a long way since the first teams were playing with peach baskets and Converse All-Star sneakers. Today, professional basketball games are fast-paced, aerial shows. Women have gotten into the game with the **WNBA,** a young but growing league.

ICE HOCKEY. Though not as popular as other sports in the US, hockey is something of a national religion for Canadians. The **National Hockey League (NHL),** comprised of both American and Canadian teams, features great ice hockey and some of the best fights in professional sports. As NHL teams vie for the **Stanley Cup,** the tension of competition often results in crowd-pleasing team brawls.

COLLEGE SPORTS. Sticking with their school allegiances, many Americans live and die by their college's sporting endeavors. College teams compete within regional conferences, creating fierce rivalries fueled by hordes of fanatical (and drunken) student supporters. Football draws the biggest crowds, and each January the National Champion is decided on a rotating basis at either the **Rose Bowl, Fiesta Bowl, Orange Bowl,** or **Sugar Bowl.** Enthusiasm for college hoops often surpasses that for the pros, and women's college basketball has become increasingly popular in recent years. Every spring, hoops fan-demonium reaches fever pitch during the NCAA tournament, fondly called **March Madness.** While there is a growing trend towards high-school players skipping college to play professionally, the college courts are still the best place to see the future superstars of the NBA.

OTHER SPORTS. Other sports claim smaller niches of the American spectatorship. Both golf and tennis have internationally publicized tournaments known as the **US Open.** Now America's largest spectator sport, **NASCAR auto racing** draws droves of fans to Daytona Beach, FL, in February with the Daytona 500, but the heart of Middle America still beats the loudest at the Indianapolis 500, held on the Sunday before Memorial Day. The horse racing of the **Kentucky Derby** hones the betting strategies of seasoned gamblers and tries the tolerance of seasoned boozers. Amusingly named horses, filthy rich stable owners, and minute jockeys seek the coveted **Triple Crown,** which comprises the Derby, the Preakness, and the Belmont Stakes. **Major League Soccer (MLS)** is an up-and-coming but not yet widely followed sport in the United States, but soccer continues to be promoted heavily as the US national team seeks to become a World Cup contender by 2010.

HOLIDAYS

USA: NATIONAL HOLIDAYS	
DATE IN 2005	HOLIDAY
January 1	New Year's Day
January 17	Martin Luther King, Jr. Day
February 21	Presidents Day
May 30	Memorial Day
July 4	Independence Day
September 5	Labor Day
October 10	Columbus Day
November 11	Veterans Day
November 24	Thanksgiving
December 25	Christmas Day

CANADA: NATIONAL HOLIDAYS	
DATE IN 2005	HOLIDAY
January 1	New Year's Day
March 27	Easter Sunday
March 28	Easter Monday
May 23	Victoria Day
July 1	Canada Day
September 5	Labour Day
October 10	Thanksgiving
November 11	Remembrance Day
December 25	Christmas Day
December 26	Boxing Day

CANADA

Geographically speaking, Canada is the second-largest country in the world, sprawling over almost 10 million square kilometers (3.85 million sq. mi.). Still, nearly 32 million people—roughly the population of California—inhabit Canada's 10 provinces and three territories. Well over half the population crowds into the southern provinces of Ontario and Québec, while the newly declared northern territory, Nunavut, has 26,000 people. Framed by the Atlantic to the east and the Pacific to the west, Canada extends from fertile southern farmlands to frozen northern tundra. The early French and English colonists were both geographically and culturally distant from one another. To this day, **anglophones** and **francophones** fight to retain political dominance in the Canadian government. The concerns of the native peoples and an increasing immigrant population have also become intertwined in the struggle.

O CANADA! A BRIEF HISTORY

CROSSING CONTINENTAL DIVIDES. Although archaeologists are uncertain about the exact timing, recent data indicates that the first Canadians arrived at least 10,000 years ago by crossing the Asian-Alaskan land bridge. Their descendents flooded the continent, fragmenting into disparate tribes. The cold, barren north gained many hardy Inuit groups, while tribes like the Haida thrived in the bountiful rivers and forests of the West. The prairies and grasslands of the central continent, supporting large populations of buffalo, found Assiniboine and Sioux populations. Algonquin and Micmac natives prospered in eastern forests and coasts, respectively. The earliest Native Canadians were hunter-gatherers who followed animals like bison and caribou, and expanded farther into North America as giant ice sheets melted.

EUROPEAN UNIONS. The first **Europeans** known to explore the area were the Norse, led by Leif Erickson, who temporarily set up camp in northern Newfoundland around the year 1000. There is evidence that these Vikings traded with native groups, but soon conflicts arose, and the Norse sailors left to found Finland. Europeans were subsequently out of contact with Canada until John Cabot, an Englishman, sighted Newfoundland in 1497. Cabot came across the Grand Banks, a legendary fishing spot and long-kept secret of Atlantic fishermen. Jacques Cartier landed at the gulf of the St. Lawrence River in 1534 and claimed the mainland for the French crown. After confirming that there was no river route through Canada to Asia, Cartier initiated a vibrant fur trade that would persist for centuries between the French and the Micmac natives, and, upon visiting an Iroquois nation, adapted "Kanata" (the word for "village") as the name of the land. "New France" became a royal province ruled from Québec, but France's widespread territorial acquisitions kicked off a rivalry between England and France that persisted until Britain's 1759 capture of Québec in the Seven Years' War. Four years later, France capitulated in the Treaty of Paris, when Canada became a British Territory.

LOYALTY TO THE CROWN. During the Revolutionary War, when the 13 colonies on the American seaboard opted for independence and revolted from Britain, the Canadian settlements—upper and lower Canada (modern Québec and Ontario) and the Maritimes (Newfoundland, Nova Scotia, New Brunswick, and Prince Edward Island)—remained loyal to the crown. British armies used Canadian forts and seaports as bases during the Revolution, and the population boomed as thousands of Empire Loyalists fled the newly-formed United States to remain within the British Empire. In early America, there was hope that the breach could be repaired and that the Canadian colonies could be induced to enter the Union. The Federalist Papers included articles arguing for the unconditional right of statehood to any British North American colony willing to enter the Union. During the War of 1812, however, the United States declared war on Great Britain and invaded southern Canada. The Americans expected immediate success as many of the area's new residents had only recently left their colonies. Great Britain squashed America's attempt at conquest both because it had superior armies and because Canada's closest neighbors, the New England territories, largely opposed the war. The conflict strengthened the belief that British Canada was on a separate path from the United States. Tensions between the US and the British North American colonies continued right up until the Civil War, which diverted American expansionist interest permanently from the north.

THIS LAND IS YOUR LAND, THIS LAND IS MY LAND. The movement to unify the British North American colonies gathered speed after the American Civil War, when US military might and economic isolationism threatened the independent and continued existence of the British colonies. The movement, called **confederation,** would combine Great Britain's holdings into a single nation ruled by both a large central government and individual provincial governments. As the Canadian provinces had previously been operating under virtual self-rule, confederation was largely a nominal change. Canada now had technical dominion over local affairs and its own laws, but Canadians had no desire to completely cut ties with Britain. With Queen Victoria's signing of the **British North**

America Act (BNA) in 1867, Britain retained technical control over foreign affairs and Parliament had veto power over Canadian legislation. Regardless of British involvement, however, Canada at last had its country—and its day: the BNA was proclaimed on **July 1, Canada Day**.

Since that time, Canada has expanded both territorially and economically. The years following consolidation witnessed sustained economic growth and expansion, with westward travelers trekking toward the Pacific in search of gold. These pioneers were greatly aided by the new railroad system created to physically connect the politically unified Canada from coast to coast, the **Canadian Pacific Railway.** One hundred fifteen thousand Chinese immigrants completed the project in 1885. Following the completion of the railroad, the Chinese workers, no longer employed, followed the rail lines and scattered across the country, establishing significant communities throughout Canada.

TRADING SPACES. Participation in WWI earned the Dominion international respect and a charter membership in the League of Nations. Canada joined the United Nations in 1945 and was a founding member of the **North Atlantic Treaty Organization (NATO)** in 1949. The Liberal government of the following decade created a national social security system and a national health insurance program. Pierre Trudeau's government repatriated Canada's constitution in 1982, and freed the nation from Britain in constitutional legality (though Elizabeth II remains nominal head of state). Finally free to forge its own alliances, the country signed the controversial **US-Canada Free Trade Agreement (FTA)** in 1989 and the **North American Free Trade Agreement (NAFTA)** in 1994 under the leadership of Conservative Brian Mulroney, which allowed for a dramatic increase in trade with the US.

A SEPARATE PIECE. In recent years, Canada has faced internal political tensions as well as an ever-increasing pressure to Americanize. Mulroney strove hard to mold a strong, unified Canada, but he will probably go down in Canadian history as the leader who nearly tore the nation apart in an effort to bring it together. His numerous attempts to negotiate a constitution that all ten provinces would ratify (Canada's present constitution lacks Québec's support) consistently failed, fanning the flames of century-old regional tensions and precipitating his resignation in 1993. Most recently, a landmark decision to legalize gay marriage and growing momentum behind decriminalized marijuana initiatives in Toronto have been seen by some commentators as signs of massive social change in the nation.

The **québecois separatist movement** has a long and not entirely pleasant history. Though francophone nationalism has roots as far back as the colonial period, the separatist impulse truly took hold in 1960, when nationalist Liberals took power in Québec. The national Official Language Act of 1969 set the French language on equal footing with English in government and throughout the country in an attempt to elevate Canadian nationalism and put an end to the separatism rampant in Québec. In 1970's October Crisis, after a decade of bombings and robberies, the Front de Liberation du Québec kidnapped two Canadian officials, killing one. The crisis, which prompted Trudeau to declare a brief period of martial law, brought the issue of Québec's separation to a head. Support for the newly formed Parti Québécois was not universal, however, and a 1980 referendum saw 60% of *québécois* opposed to separation from the Dominion. In a more recent (1995) referendum, however, separation was rejected by a mere 1.2% margin. The struggle for an independent Québec—under current Prime Minister Paul Martin of the Liberal Party—remains an actively debated issue in both the cultural and parliamentary arenas. Polls have shown, however, that support for an independent Québec is falling, and the separatist Parti Québécois was defeated in the 2003 provincial elections.

A NEW TERRITORY. Canada has also locked horns with its **aboriginal peoples,** known as the First Nations. The Inuit and other peoples in the Northwest Territories have struggled for more political representation and have been largely successful: the 1999 creation of Nunavut represented a huge gain for First Nations in the north. The newly formed territory covers approximately 2 million sq. km (770,000 sq. mi.). About 85% of the region's 26,000 inhabitants are Inuit. The name *Nunavut* means "our land" in Inuktitut, the Inuit's language and the territory's third principal language, along with English and French. While Nunavut's government mirrors that of the other provinces and territories, its political system is greatly influenced by Inuit customs and beliefs.

In addition to worrying about the independence wishes of their numerous constituents, Canadian policy-makers continue to struggle for Canada's **cultural independence** from the US. Media domination by their southern neighbor has put a bit of a strain on Canadian pride, so much so that Canada's radio stations are required by law to play 30% Canadian music. The US also poses another, more dangerous threat to Canadian well-being: each year, the country loses thousands of young professionals to the US, where taxes are lower and wages higher.

CANUCK CULTURE

Canada has two official languages, English and French. The *québécois* pronunciation of French can be perplexing to European speakers, and the protocol is less formal. There are also numerous native languages. Inuktitut, the Inuit language, is widely spoken in Nunavut and the Northwest Territories.

Most noteworthy **Canadian literature** is post-1867. The opening of the Northwest and the Klondike Gold Rush (1898) provided fodder for the adventure tale—Jack London *(The Call of the Wild, White Fang)* and Robert Service *(Songs of a Sourdough, The Trail of '98)* both authored stories of prospectors and wolves based on their mining experience in northern Canada. On Prince Edward Island, L.M. Montgomery penned one of the greatest coming-of-age novels, *Anne of Green Gables* (1908). Prominent contemporary English-language authors include poet and novelist Margaret Atwood, best known for the futuristic best-seller *The Handmaid's Tale* (1986), and Sri Lankan-born novelist Michael Ondaatje, whose *The English Patient* (1992) received the prestigious Booker Prize. Canada also boasts three of the world's most authoritative cultural and literary critics: Northrop Frye, Hugh Kenner, and pop phenom Marshall McLuhan. Comparatists Clément Moisan and Philip Stratford have written extensively on the dynamic between English and French literature in Canada. The *québécois* literary tradition is becoming more recognized, and has been important in defining an emerging cultural and political identity.

Canada's contributions to the world of **popular music** encompass a range of artists and genres. Canadian rockers include Neil Young, Joni Mitchell, The Guess Who, Leonard Cohen, Rush, Cowboy Junkies, Barenaked Ladies, k.d. lang, Bryan Adams, Alanis Morissette, and the Tragically Hip. Chart-toppers of the last few years include the inimitable Céline Dion, Sarah McLachlan, Our Lady Peace, Nelly Furtado, country cross-over Shania Twain, Sum 41, and MTV punk-poster-child Avril Lavigne. Canada is also home to *québécois* folk music and several world-class orchestras, including the Montréal, Toronto, and Vancouver Symphonies.

On the silver screen, Canada's National Film Board (NFB), which finances many documentaries, has gained worldwide acclaim since its creation in 1939. The first Oscar given to a documentary went to the NFB's 1942 *Churchill Island*. Recent figures of note include indie director Atom Egoyan, whose haunting film *The Sweet Hereafter* (1997) scored two Oscar nominations. *Québécois* filmmakers have also met with success. Director Denys Arcand caught the world's eye at Cannes with the striking *Jésus de Montréal* (1989), a reflection of the filmmaker's disillusionment with the Church, and the Oscar-nominated movie *Le déclin de l'empire américain* (1985). Most recently, *Atanarjuat: The Fast Runner* (2001), the first feature film in the Inuit language Inuktitut, gained international acclaim and the Golden Camera award at the Cannes Film Festival.

The *Toronto Globe and Mail* is the national newspaper, distributed six days a week across Canada. *Maclean's* was Canada's first weekly newsmagazine and is currently read throughout the country. Every Canadian city also has at least one daily paper. The publicly owned **Canadian Broadcasting Corporation (CBC)** provides two national networks (one in English, one in French) for both radio and TV, and also broadcasts in eight aboriginal languages in the north. The CBC is supplemented by a private broadcaster, CTV, as well as specialty cable channels and American networks. Canadian television has produced many great comic hits—the show *Kids in the Hall* and comedians Dan Aykroyd, John Candy, Eugene Levy, Mike Myers, Catherine O'Hara, and Martin Short.

In the realm of sports, Canada possesses an athletic heritage befitting its northern latitudes. Popular sports include ice skating, skiing, and the perennial cult favorite, ice hockey. Canadians also enjoy a spirited game of **curling,** which involves pushing a 19.96kg (44 lb.) stone across a sheet of ice in an attempt to get the stone to stop precisely in the middle of a set of rings. Some of Canada's other popular sports are derived from those of the First Nations. Lacrosse, the national game of Canada, was played long before the Europeans arrived. Sports played in the United States have crossed the border in full force; in addition to the **Canadian Football League (CFL),** Canada has one NBA team (the Toronto Raptors) and two Major League Baseball outfits (the Montreal Expos and the Toronto Blue Jays).

ESSENTIALS

PLANNING YOUR TRIP

ENTRANCE REQUIREMENTS
Passport (p. 32). Required for all non-US and non-Canadian citizens.
Visa (p. 33). Generally required for all visitors who are not US or Canadian citizens, but requirement can be waived for residents of certain countries (including Australia, New Zealand, Ireland, and the UK) if staying less than 90 days.
Work Permit (p. 34). Required for all those planning to work in the US or Canada.
Driving Permit (p. 34). Required for all those planning to drive.

EMBASSIES AND CONSULATES

US AND CANADIAN CONSULAR SERVICES ABROAD

Contact the nearest embassy or consulate to obtain info on the visas necessary to travel to the US and Canada. Listings of foreign embassies in the US and US embassies abroad can be found at www.embassyworld.com. The **US State Department** (http://travel.state.gov) provides a list of US embassy and consulate websites. The **Canadian Ministry of Foreign Affairs** (www.dfait-maeci.gc.ca/dfait/missions/menu-e.asp) lists the websites of its overseas embassies and consulates. A website overseen by the US embassy in Ottawa at www.amcits.com provides general info for travelers to the US and Canada, particularly for US citizens traveling to Canada.

US CONSULATES AND EMBASSIES
Australia: Moonah Pl., Yarralumla **(Canberra),** ACT 2600 (☎61 02 6214 5600; http://usembassy-australia.state.gov). **Consulates:** 553 St. Kilda Rd., **Melbourne,** VIC 3004 (☎61 03 9526 5900; fax 9510 4646); 16 St. George's Terr., 13th fl., **Perth,** WA 6000 (☎61 08 9202 1224; fax 9231 9444); MLC Centre, Level 59, 19-29 Martin Pl., **Sydney,** NSW 2000 (☎61 02 9373 9200; fax 9373 9125).

Canada: 490 Sussex Dr., **Ottawa,** ON K1N 1G8 (☎1 613-688-5335; www.usembassy-canada.gov). **Consulates:** 615 Macleod Tr. SE, Ste. 1000, **Calgary,** AB T2G 4T8 (☎1 403-266-8962; fax 264-6630); Ste. 904, Purdy's Wharf Tower II, 1969 Upper Water St., **Halifax,** NS B3J 3R7 (☎1 902-429-2480; fax 423-6861); 1155 St. Alexandre St., **Montréal,** QC H3B 1Z1 (mailing address: P.O. Box 65, Station Desjardins, Montréal, QC H5B 1G1. ☎1 514-398-9695; fax 398-0702); 2 Place Terrasse Dufferin, B.P. 939, **Québec City,** QC G1R 4T9 (☎1 418-692-2095; fax 692-4640); 360 University Ave., **Toronto,** ON M5G 1S4 (☎1 416-595-1700; fax 595-6501); 1095 W. Pender St., **Vancouver,** BC V6E 2M6 (☎1 604-685-4311; fax 685-7175).

Ireland: 42 Elgin Rd., Ballsbridge, **Dublin** 4 (☎353 01 668 8777; http://dublin.usembassy.gov).

New Zealand: 29 Fitzherbert Terr., Thorndon, **Wellington** (☎644 462 6000; www.usembassy.org.nz). **Consulate:** Citibank Building, 23 Customs St., 3rd fl., **Auckland** (☎649 303 2724; fax 366 0870).

UK: 24 Grosvenor Sq., **London,** England W1A 1AE (☎ 44 0207 499 9000; www.usembassy.org.uk). **Consulates:** Danesfort House, 223 Stranmillis Rd., **Belfast,** N. Ireland BT9 5GR (☎ 44 0289 038 6100; fax 068 1301); 3 Regent Terr., **Edinburgh,** Scotland EH7 5BW (☎ 44 0131 556 8315; fax 557 6023).

CANADIAN CONSULATES AND EMBASSIES

Australia: Commonwealth Ave., **Canberra** ACT 2600 (☎ 61 02 6270 4000; www.dfait-maeci.gc.ca/australia). **Consulate:** 111 Harrington St., Level 5, **Sydney** NSW 2000 (☎ 61 02 9364 3000; fax 9364 3098).

Ireland: 65 St. Stephen's Green, **Dublin** 2 (☎ 353 01 417 4100; www.dfait-maeci.gc.ca/canadaeuropa/ireland).

New Zealand: 61 Molesworth St., 3rd fl., Thorndon, **Wellington** (☎ 644 473 9577; www.dfait-maeci.gc.ca/newzealand).

UK: 1 Grosvenor Sq., **London,** England W1K 4AB (☎ 44 0207 258 6600; www.dfait-maeci.gc.ca/canadaeuropa/united_kingdom). **Consulates:** Unit 3, Ormeau Business Park, 8 Cromac Ave., **Belfast,** N. Ireland BT7 2JA (☎/fax 44 0289 127 2060); 30 Lothian Rd., **Edinburgh,** Scotland EH2 2XZ (☎ 44 0131 220 4333; fax 245 6010).

US: 501 Pennsylvania Ave. NW, **Washington,** D.C. 20001 (☎ 1 202-682-1740; www.canadianembassy.org). **Consulates:** 2 Prudential Plaza, 180 N. Stetson Ave., Ste. 2400, **Chicago,** IL 60601 (☎ 1 312-616-1860; fax 616-1878); 550 S. Hope St., 9th fl., **Los Angeles,** CA 90071 (☎ 1 213-346-2700; fax 346-2767); 1251 Ave. of the Americas, **New York City,** NY 10020 (☎ 1 212-596-1628; fax 596-1793). Consult www.canadianembassy.org for 14 other locations throughout the US.

CONSULAR SERVICES IN THE US AND CANADA

IN WASHINGTON, D.C. (US)

Australia: 1601 Massachusetts Ave. NW, 20036 (☎ 202-797-3000; www.austemb.org).

Canada: 501 Pennsylvania Ave., 20001 (☎ 202-682-1740; www.canadianembassy.org).

Ireland: 2234 Mass. Ave. NW, 20008 (☎ 202-462-3939; www.irelandemb.org).

New Zealand: 37 Observatory Circle, 20008 (☎ 202-328-4800; www.nzemb.org).

UK: 3100 Mass. Ave., 20008 (☎ 202-588-7800; www.britainusa.com/consular/embassy).

IN OTTAWA, ONTARIO (CANADA)

Australia: 50 O'Connor St., Ste. 710, K1P 6L2 (☎ 613-236-0841; www.ahc-ottawa.org)

Ireland: 130 Albert St., Ste. 1105, K1P 5G4 (☎ 613-233-6281; fax 233-5835).

New Zealand: 99 Bank St., Ste. 727, K1P 6G3 (☎ 613-238-5991; www.nzhcottawa.org).

UK: 80 Elgin St., K1P 5K7 (☎ 613-237-1530; www.britain-in-canada.org).

US: 490 Sussex Dr., K1N 1G8 (☎ 613-238-5335; www.usembassycanada.gov).

DOCUMENTS AND FORMALITIES

PASSPORTS

REQUIREMENTS

All non-Canadian and non-US citizens need valid passports to enter the US and Canada and to re-enter their countries. Returning home with an expired passport is usually illegal and may result in a fine, or it may not be possible at all. Moreover, travelers who require a passport to enter the region must have a passport valid for at least six months (in the US) or one day (in Canada) beyond their intended stays.

Canadians can enter the US (and vice-versa) with proof of citizenship along with a photo ID—a driver's license and birth certificate should suffice. Your passport, however, is the most convenient and hassle-free method of identification.

NEW PASSPORTS

Citizens of Australia, Canada, Ireland, New Zealand, the UK, and the US can apply for a passport at a passport office or court of law. Many post offices also accept passport applications. All applications must be filed well in advance of departure, though most passport offices offer rush services for a steep fee, typically $60-200.

PASSPORT MAINTENANCE

Photocopy the page of your passport with your photo, as well as your visas, traveler's check serial numbers, and any other important documents. Carry one set of copies in a safe place, apart from the originals, and leave another set at home. Consulates also recommend that you carry an expired passport or an official copy of your birth certificate in a part of your baggage separate from other documents.

If you lose your passport, immediately notify the police and the nearest embassy or consulate of your home government. To expedite its replacement, you will need to know all information previously recorded and show ID and proof of citizenship, as well as pay a fee and include a police report. Replacements take about 10 days to process, but some consulates offer three-day rush service for an additional fee. Any visas stamped in your old passport will be irretrievably lost. In an emergency, some consulates provide immediate temporary traveling papers that will permit you to re-enter your home country. Call the nearest embassy or consulate of your home government for information on their specific policies.

VISAS AND WORK PERMITS

VISAS

Citizens of some non-English-speaking countries need a visa—a stamp, sticker, or insert in your passport specifying the purpose of your travel and the permitted duration of your stay—in addition to a passport for entrance to the US. Canadian citizens do not need a visa for admission to the US; citizens of Australia, New Zealand, and most European countries (including the UK and Ireland) can waive US visas through the **Visa Waiver Program (VWP).** Visitors qualify if they are traveling only for business or pleasure (*not* work or study), are staying for fewer than **90 days,** have proof of intent to leave (e.g., a return plane ticket), possess an I-94W form (arrival/departure certificate issued upon arrival), are traveling on particular air or sea carriers (most major carriers qualify—contact the carrier for details), and have no visa ineligiblities (e.g., a criminal record). As of October 2004, visitors in the VWP must possess a **machine-readable passport** to be admitted to the US without a visa, although most countries in the VWP have been issuing such passports for some time and many travelers will not need new passports. **Children** from who normally travel on a parent's passport will also need to obtain their own machine-readable passports. Additionally, travelers in the VWP are able to travel on regular machine-readable passports issued before October 26, 2004, but all passports issued after that date must have **biometric** identifiers to be used as visa waivers. However, most countries in the VWP are not expected to be able to convert to biometric passports by that deadline, so even **VWP travelers with recently-issued passports may have to apply for a visa.** Legislation to extend the biometric deadline to 2006 is under consideration by Congress. See http://travel.state.gov/vwp.html or contact your local consulate for a list of countries participating in the VWP as well as the latest information any biometric deadline extensions.

For stays of longer than 90 days in the US, all travelers (except Canadians) must have a visa. Visitors to the US under the VWP are allowed to leave and re-enter the US to visit Canada, Mexico, and some neighboring islands, but time spent in those areas counts toward the 90-day limit. Travelers eligible to waive their visas and who wish to stay for more than 90 days must receive a visa **before** entering the US.

In Canada, citizens of some non-English-speaking countries also need a visitor's visa if they're not traveling with a valid green card. Citizens of Australia, Ireland, New Zealand, the United Kingdom, and the United States, as well as many other countries, do not need a visa. See http://www.cic.gc.ca/english/visit/visas.html for a list of countries whose citizens are required to hold visas, or call your local Canadian consulate. Visitor's visas cost CDN$75 and can be purchased from the **Canadian Embassy** in Washington, D.C., Monday to Friday between 9am and noon. US citizens can take advantage of the **Center for International Business and Travel (CIBT),** which secures visas to almost all countries for a varying service charge depending on how soon the documents are required (☎800-929-2428, www.cibt.com).

Double-check entrance requirements at the nearest embassy or consulate of the US and Canada (listed under **Embassies and Consulates Abroad,** p. 31) for up-to-date info before departure. US citizens can also consult www.pueblo.gsa.gov/cic_text/travel/foreign/foreignentryreqs.html.

WORK AND STUDY PERMITS

Admission as a visitor does not include the right to work, which is authorized only by a work permit. Entering the US to study requires a special visa; for Canada, a student visa is needed for studies longer than six months. Be prepared for long processing times, especially for work permits. For more information, see **Alternatives to Tourism,** p. 70.

IDENTIFICATION

When you travel, always carry at least two forms of identification on your person, including a photo ID; a passport and a driver's license or birth certificate is usually adequate. Never carry all of your IDs together; split them up in case of theft or loss, and keep photocopies of all of them in your luggage and at home.

STUDENT, TEACHER, AND YOUTH IDENTIFICATION

The **International Student Identity Card (ISIC),** the most widely accepted form of student ID, provides discounts on some sights, accommodations (20% or more off rooms in many chain hotels), food, and transport (e.g., 5-15% off Alamo Car rentals); access to a 24hr. emergency helpline; and insurance benefits for US cardholders (see **Insurance,** p. 42). Applicants must be full-time secondary or post-secondary school students at least 12 years old. Because of the proliferation of fake ISICs, some services require additional proof of student identity. Particularly in the US and Canada, ISIC cards are less well-recognized than they are abroad, so travelers are advised to have another form of student ID. The **International Teacher Identity Card (ITIC)** offers teachers the same insurance coverage as the ISIC and similar but limited discounts. For travelers who are under 26 but not students, the **International Youth Travel Card (IYTC)** also offers many of the same benefits.

Each of these identity cards costs $22. ISIC and ITIC cards are valid until the new academic year (plus extra months for travel) up to 16 months; IYTC cards are valid for one year from the date of issue. Many student travel agencies (see p. 46) issue the cards; for a list of issuing agencies or more information, see the **International Student Travel Confederation (ISTC)** website (www.istc.org).

The **International Student Exchange Card (ISE)** is a similar identification card available to students, faculty, and youth ages 12 to 26. The card provides discounts, medical benefits, access to a 24hr. emergency helpline, and the ability to purchase student airfares. The card costs $25; call US ☎ 800-255-8000 for more info, or visit www.isecard.com.

CUSTOMS

Upon entering the US or Canada, you must declare certain items from abroad and pay a duty on the value of those articles if they exceed the allowance established by the US or Canada's customs service. Note that goods purchased at **duty-free** shops abroad are not exempt from duty or sales tax; "duty-free" merely means that you need not pay a tax in the country of purchase. Upon returning home, you must likewise declare all articles acquired abroad and pay a duty on the value of articles in excess of your home country's allowance. In order to expedite your return, make a list of any valuables brought from home and register them with customs before traveling abroad, and be sure to keep receipts for all goods acquired abroad.

The US does not refund sales tax to foreign visitors. Travelers leaving Canada may receive a tax refund on goods purchased in Canada if they provide customs-validated receipts totaling over CDN$200 before taxes. See **Taxes** (p. 37).

MONEY

CURRENCY AND EXCHANGE

The currency chart below is based on August 2004 exchange rates between local currency and Australian dollars (AUS$), Canadian dollars (CDN$), European Union euros (EUR€), New Zealand dollars (NZ$), British pounds (UK£), and US dollars (US$). Check the currency converter on websites like www.xe.com or www.bloomberg.com or a large newspaper for the latest exchange rates.

US DOLLARS		CANADIAN DOLLARS	
AUS$1 = US$0.71	US$1 = AUS$1.42	AUS$1 = CDN$0.92	CDN$1= AUS$1.09
CDN$1 = US$0.77	US$1 = CDN$1.30	EUR€1 = CDN$1.56	CDN$1 = EUR€0.63
EUR€1 = US$1.21	US$1 = EUR€.83	NZ$1 = CDN$0.85	CDN$1 = NZ$1.18
NZ$1 = US$0.65	US$1 = NZ$1.54	UK£1 = CDN$2.34	CDN$1 = UK£0.43
UK£1 = US$1.80	US$1 = UK£0.56	US$1 = CDN$1.30	CDN$1 = US$0.77

As a general rule, it's cheaper to convert money in the US or Canada than at home. While currency exchange will probably be available in your arrival airport, it's wise to bring enough foreign currency to last for the first few days of your trip.

When changing money abroad, try to go only to banks that have at most a 5% margin between their buy and sell prices. Since you lose money with every transaction, **convert large sums, but no more than you'll need.**

If you use traveler's checks or bills, carry some in small denominations ($50 or less) for times when you are forced to exchange money at disadvantageous rates, but bring a range of denominations since charges may be levied per check cashed. Store your money in a variety of forms; ideally, at any given time you will be carrying some cash, some traveler's checks, and an ATM and/or credit card.

TRAVELER'S CHECKS

Traveler's checks are one of the safest means of carrying funds. American Express and Visa are the most recognized brands. Many banks and agencies sell them for a small commission. Check issuers provide refunds if the checks are lost or stolen, and many provide additional services, such as toll-free refund hotlines abroad, emergency message services, and stolen credit card assistance. They are readily accepted in the US and Canada. Ask about toll-free refund hotlines and the location of refund centers when purchasing checks, and always carry emergency cash.

American Express: Checks available with commission at select banks, at all AmEx offices, and online (www.americanexpress.com; US residents only). American Express cardholders can also purchase checks by phone (☎800-721-9768). Checks also available in Australian, Canadian, European, Japanese, British, and American currencies. For purchase locations or more information contact AmEx's service centers: in Australia ☎800 68 80 22; in Canada and the US 800-221-7282; in New Zealand 0508 555 358; in the UK 0800 587 6023; elsewhere, call the US collect at 1 801-964-6665.

Visa: Checks available (generally with commission) at banks worldwide. AAA (p. 52) offers commission-free checks to its members. For the location of the nearest office, call Visa's service centers: in the UK ☎0 800 89 5078; in the US 800-227-6811; elsewhere, call the UK collect at 44 173 331 8949. Checks available in Canadian, European, Japanese, British, and American currencies.

Travelex/Thomas Cook: In Canada and the US call ☎800-287-7362; in the UK call 0800 62 21 01; elsewhere call the UK collect at 44 1733 31 89 50. Also available online at www.travelex.com. Members of AAA and affiliated automobile associations around the world receive a 25% commission discount on check purchases.

CREDIT, DEBIT, AND ATM CARDS

Where they are accepted, credit cards often offer superior exchange rates—up to 5% better than the retail rate used by banks and other currency exchange establishments. Credit cards may also offer services such as insurance or emergency help, and are sometimes required to reserve hotel rooms or rental cars. **MasterCard** and **Visa** are the most accepted; **American Express** cards work at some ATMs and at AmEx offices and major airports.

ATMs are widespread in the US and Canada, although they are less common in rural areas. Depending on the system that your home bank uses, you can most likely access your bank account from abroad. ATMs get the same exchange rate as credit cards, but there is often a limit on the amount you can withdraw per day (usually $300-500). There is typically also a surcharge of $1-5 per withdrawal.

Debit cards are as convenient as credit cards but have a more immediate impact on your funds. A debit card can be used wherever its associated credit card company (usually MasterCard or Visa) is accepted, yet the money is withdrawn directly from the holder's checking account. Debit cards often also function as ATM cards and can be used to withdraw cash from associated banks and ATMs throughout the US and Canada. Ask your local bank about obtaining one.

The two major international money networks are **Cirrus** (US ☎800-424-7787; www.mastercard.com) and **Visa/PLUS** (US ☎800-843-7587; www.visa.com). Most ATMs charge a transaction fee that is paid to the bank that owns the ATM.

GETTING MONEY FROM HOME

If you run out of money while traveling, the easiest and cheapest solution is to have someone back home make a deposit to your credit card or ATM card. Failing that, consider one of the following options. The online **International Money Transfer Consumer Guide** (http://international-money-transfer-consumer-guide.info) may also be of help.

WIRING MONEY

It is possible to arrange a **bank money transfer,** which means asking a bank back home to wire money to a bank in the US or Canada. This is the cheapest way to transfer cash, but it's also the slowest, usually taking several days or more. Money transfer services like **Western Union** are faster and more convenient than bank transfers—but also much pricier. Western Union has many locations worldwide. To find one, visit www.westernunion.com, or call in Australia ☎800 501 500; in Canada 800-235-0000; in Ireland 66 947 5603; in New Zealand 800 005 253; in the UK 0800 83 38 33; or in the US 800-325-6000. To wire money within the US or Canada using a credit card (Visa, MasterCard, Discover), call ☎800-225-5227. Money transfer services are also available at **American Express** and **Thomas Cook** offices.

COSTS

The cost of your trip will vary considerably, depending on where you go, how you travel, and where you stay. The most significant expenses will probably be your round-trip **airfare** to the US and Canada (see **Getting to the US and Canada: By Plane,** p. 45). Be sure to factor in gas, which costs about $2 per gallon in the US and $2.60 (CDN$3.50) per gallon in Canada. Spend some time calculating a reasonable daily **budget.**

STAYING ON A BUDGET

A bare-bones day in the US and Canada (camping or sleeping in hostels, buying food at supermarkets) costs about $40; a more comfortable day (sleeping in hostels/guesthouses and the occasional budget hotel, eating one meal per day at a restaurant, going out at night) runs around $75; and for a luxurious day, the sky's the limit. Don't forget emergency reserve funds (at least $200) when planning how much money you'll need.

TIPS FOR SAVING MONEY

Some simpler ways include searching out opportunities for free entertainment, splitting accommodation and food costs with trustworthy fellow travelers, and buying food in supermarkets rather than eating out. Bring a **sleepsack** (p. 38) to save on sheet charges, and do your **laundry** in the sink (unless you're explicitly prohibited from doing so). That said, don't go overboard. Though staying within your budget is important, don't do so at the expense of your health or a great travel experience.

TIPPING AND BARGAINING

In the US, it is customary to tip waitstaff and cab drivers 15-20% (at your discretion). Tips are usually not included in restaurant bills unless you have a large party (generally six or more). At the airport and in hotels, porters expect at least a $1 per bag tip to carry your bags. Tipping is less compulsory in Canada; a good tip signifies remarkable service. Bargaining is generally frowned upon and fruitless in both countries, except in open-air flea markets and farmers markets.

TAXES

US state sales tax ranges 4-9.5%, though some states have no sales tax, and many states do not charge sales tax on grocery items or clothing. Many states and counties, especially in the South, charge a tax on hotel rooms; rates vary 3-18%. Sales tax is not usually included in the prices of items listed in *Let's Go.*

Canada has a 7% goods and services tax (GST) and an additional sales tax in some provinces. The provincial sales tax (PST) varies from no sales tax in Alberta, the Northwest Territories, Nunavut, and the Yukon to 7% or more in the other provinces. Three provinces (Newfoundland, Nova Scotia, and New Brunswick) combine the GST and PST into a Harmonized Sales Tax (HST) of 15%. Visitors can claim a rebate of the GST/HST they pay on accommodations of less than one month and on most goods they buy and take home, so save your receipts and pick up a Proof of Export form while in Canada. Your receipts must be validated by a customs official as you are leaving Canada in order to receive the rebate. Border crossings and nine major Canadian airports have receipt validation facilities. Total purchases must be at least CDN$200 and individual receipts at least CDN$50. A brochure detailing restrictions is available from local tourist offices or through Revenue Canada, Visitor's Rebate Program, 275 Pope Rd., Ste. 104, Summerside, PE C1N 6C6 (☎ 902-432-5608 or 800-668-4748; www.ccra-adrc.gc.ca/visitors).

PACKING

Pack lightly. Lay out only what you absolutely need, then take half the clothes and twice the money. The Travelite FAQ (www.travelite.org) is a good resource for tips on traveling light. The **Universal Packing List** (http://upl.codeq.info) will generate a customized list of suggested items based on your trip length, the expected climate, and your planned activities. If you plan to do a lot of hiking, see **Camping**, p. 61.

Luggage: If you plan to hike or travel extensively between cities, a sturdy **frame backpack** is unbeatable. (For the basics on buying a pack, see p. 63.) Toting a **suitcase** is fine if you will live in one or two cities. In addition to your main piece of luggage, a **daypack** (small backpack or courier bag) is useful.

Clothing: Dressing in layers is the best way to handle the variable climate in the US and Canada. No matter when you're traveling, it's a good idea to bring a warm jacket or wool sweater, a rain jacket, sturdy shoes or hiking boots, and thick socks. Flip-flops or waterproof sandals are must-haves for grubby hostel showers. You may also want one outfit for going out, and maybe a nicer pair of shoes.

Sleepsack: Some hostels require that you either provide your own linen or rent sheets from them. Save cash by making your own sleepsack: fold a full-size sheet in half the long way, then sew it closed along the long side and one of the short sides.

Converters and Adapters: In the US and Canada, electricity is 120 volts AC, which is incompatible with the 220/240V appliances found in most other countries. Appliances from anywhere outside North America will need an **adapter** (which changes the shape of the plug, $5) and a **converter** (which changes the voltage, $20-30). Australians and New Zealanders (who use 230V at home) won't need a converter, but will need an adapter. For more on all things adaptable, check out http://kropla.com/electric.htm.

Toiletries: Toothbrushes, towels, cold-water soap, talcum powder (to keep feet dry), deodorant, razors, tampons, and condoms are often available, but your favorite brand may be difficult to find; bring extras. **Contact lenses** are likely to be expensive and difficult to find, so bring enough extra pairs and solution for your entire trip. Also bring your glasses and a copy of your prescription in case you need emergency replacements.

First-Aid Kit: For a basic first-aid kit, pack bandages, a pain reliever, antibiotic cream, a thermometer, a Swiss Army knife (in your checked luggage if traveling by plane), tweezers, moleskin, decongestant, motion-sickness remedy, diarrhea medication, an antihistamine, sunscreen, insect repellent (preferably DEET-based), and burn ointment.

Film: Camera stores are common in the US and Canada, and supplies should be available. Less serious photographers may want to bring a disposable camera or two. In major tourist areas, expect film and disposable cameras to be outrageously expensive. Despite disclaimers, airport security X-rays can fog film, so buy a lead-lined pouch at a camera store or ask security to hand-inspect it. Always pack film in your carry-on luggage, since higher-intensity X-rays are used on checked luggage.

Other Useful Items: For safety purposes, you should bring a **money belt** and small **padlock**. Basic **outdoors equipment** (water bottle, compass, waterproof matches, sunglasses, sunscreen, hat) may also be useful. **Quick repairs** of torn garments can be done on the road with a needle and thread; also consider bringing electrical tape for patching tears. If you want to do laundry by hand, bring detergent, a small rubber ball to stop up the sink, and string for a makeshift clothes line. **Other things** you're liable to forget are an umbrella or poncho; sealable **plastic bags** (for damp clothes, soap, food, shampoo, and other spillables); an **alarm clock;** safety pins; rubber bands; a flashlight; earplugs; garbage bags; and a small **calculator.** A **cell phone** can be a lifesaver (literally) on the road; see p. 56 for info on acquiring one that will work at your destination.

Important Documents: Don't forget your passport, traveler's checks, ATM and/or credit cards, adequate ID, and photocopies of them all in case they are lost or stolen. Also check that you have any of the following that might apply to you: a hosteling membership card (p. 58); driver's license (p. 34); travel insurance forms; ISIC card (p. 34).

SAFETY AND HEALTH

GENERAL ADVICE

In any type of crisis situation, the most important thing to do is **stay calm.** Your country's embassy abroad (p. 32) is usually your best resource when things go wrong; registering with that embassy upon arrival in the country is often a good idea. The government offices listed in the **Travel Advisories** box (p. 67) can provide information on the services they offer their citizens in case of emergencies abroad.

LOCAL LAWS AND POLICE

If you are using a **car,** learn local driving signals and wear a seatbelt. You must obey all posted signs, including speed limit signs. If a police car sounds its siren behind you, slow down and pull over as soon as it is safe to do so. If an emergency vehicle approaches from either direction with its sirens on, slow down and pull over to the side of the road until the vehicle has passed and is several hundred feet away. The only exception to this law occurs if an emergency vehicle is approaching from the opposite direction on a divided highway; in this case, motorists on the side opposite the emergency vehicle need not pull over. Most localities require you to stop when school buses are picking up or dropping off passengers except, as above, when they are on the opposite side of a divided roadway.

Local police are often a good resource for help. If you car breaks down or you find yourself stranded, call or wait for local or state highway police to arrive.

DRUGS AND ALCOHOL

In the US, the drinking age is 21; in Canada it is 19, except in Alberta, Manitoba, and Québec, where it is 18. Drinking restrictions are particularly strict in the US. Younger travelers should expect to be asked to show government-issued identification when purchasing any alcoholic beverage. Drinking and driving is prohibited everywhere, not to mention dangerous. Open alcoholic beverage containers in your car will incur heavy fines; a failed sobriety test will mean fines, a suspended license, imprisonment, or all three. Most localities restrict where and when alcohol can be sold. Sales usually stop at a certain time at night and are often prohibited entirely on Sundays. Narcotics like marijuana, heroin, and cocaine are highly illegal in the US and Canada. If you carry prescription drugs while you travel, keep a copy of the prescription with you, especially at border crossings.

FIREARMS

Most ordinary shotguns and rifles are allowed in the US and Canada for hunting and personal protection at the discretion of the customs officer. Importing more dangerous weapons into Canada requires you to declare the weapon (CDN$50) and acquire an Authorization to Transport (ATT), which is difficult to obtain unless you are bringing the firearm for a specific event. Many firearms are prohibited altogether. If you are bringing firearms from the US to Canada, be sure to declare the firearms to US customs officers upon leaving the US to prove that you did not obtain the gun in Canada. See www.cfc-ccaf.gc.ca or call ☎ 800-731-4000 for details on Canadian gun laws. To import firearms into the US, you will need to submit a valid hunting license for a US state (not necessarily the state you are visiting) or an invitation to a shooting event, along with an ATF form 6NIA, to the bureau of Alcohol, Tobacco, and Firearms. Make sure to fill out all relevant forms well in advance of your visit; it can take up to three months for your application to be approved. See www.atf.gov or call ☎ 202-927-8330 for forms and details.

SPECIFIC CONCERNS

NATURAL DISASTERS

EARTHQUAKES. Earthquakes occur frequently in certain parts of the US, including California, Alaska, and Puerto Rico, but most are too small to be felt. If a strong earthquake does occur, it will last only a few minutes. Open a door to provide an escape route and protect yourself by moving underneath a doorway, table, or desk. If you are outside, move to an open area free from buildings and power lines.

TORNADOES AND HURRICANES. Tornadoes have been reported in every US state, though they are most common in the Great Plains during the spring and summer. In Canada, tornadoes are most frequent in Alberta, central British Columbia, New Brunswick, and southern Saskatchewan, Manitoba, and Ontario. If you are inside during a tornado, move to a basement or interior location away from windows. If you are outside, lie flat on the ground in a low place away from power lines. Hurricanes are most common on the Atlantic coast and on the Gulf of Mexico. Often, these areas will be evacuated in anticipation of particularly severe hurricanes. If you are not advised to evacuate, stay inside away from windows.

LANDSLIDES/MUDSLIDES. Heavy rain, flooding, or snow runoff combined with hilly terrain can lead to landslides or mudslides, particularly on slopes where vegetation has been removed. This will most likely not be a concern in cities; however, if you are hiking after a heavy rainfall, be aware of the possibility of a slide. If you are caught in a mudslide or landslide, try to get out of its path and run to high ground or shelter. If escape is not possible, curl into a ball and protect your head.

FOREST FIRES. Dry spells are common in the western US and Canada, and 2004 marked the fifth consecutive year of drought for much of this area. In 2003, forest fires ravaged much of the eastern Cascades, as well as parts of California, Oregon and British Columbia. If you are hiking or camping and smell smoke, see flames, or hear fire, leave the area immediately. To prevent forest fires, always make sure campfires are completely extinguished; during high levels of fire danger, campfires will most likely be prohibited. Before you go hiking or camping, be sure to check with local authorities for the level of fire danger in the area.

TERRORISM

In light of the September 11, 2001, terrorist attacks, there is an elevated risk of further terrorist activities in the US. Terrorists often target landmarks popular with tourists; however, the threat of an attack is generally not specific or great enough to warrant avoiding places or modes of transportation. Stay aware of developments in the news and watch for alerts from federal, state, and local law enforcement officials. After the September 11 attacks, the Department of Homeland Security (DHS) was created to protect the US from further terrorist threats. The DHS issues color-coded threat advisories indicating the risk of imminent terrorist attacks; red is the highest risk level, while blue is the lowest. Although a "yellow" threat level indicates an elevated risk of attack, yellow alerts have been commonplace since the September 11 attacks. Local and national news media often report changes in threat status, and travelers should be alert to these changes. The box on **travel advisories** lists offices to contact and web pages to visit to get the most updated list of your home country's government's advisories about travel.

TRAVEL ADVISORIES. The following government offices provide travel information and advisories by telephone, by fax, or via the web:

Australian Department of Foreign Affairs and Trade: ☎13 0055 5135; www.dfat.gov.au.

Canadian Department of Foreign Affairs and International Trade (DFAIT): In Canada and the US call ☎800-267-8376, elsewhere 1 613-944-4000; www.dfait-maeci.gc.ca. Call for their free booklet, *Bon Voyage...But.*

New Zealand Ministry of Foreign Affairs: ☎04 439 8000; www.mft.govt.nz/travel/index.html.

United Kingdom Foreign and Commonwealth Office: ☎020 7008 0232; www.fco.gov.uk.

US Department of State: ☎202-647-5225; http://travel.state.gov. For *A Safe Trip Abroad*, call ☎202-512-1800.

PERSONAL SAFETY

EXPLORING AND TRAVELING

To avoid unwanted attention, try to blend in as much as possible. Familiarize yourself with your surroundings before setting out, and carry yourself with confidence. Check maps in shops and restaurants rather than on the street. If you are traveling alone, be sure someone at home knows your itinerary, and never tell anyone that you're by yourself. When walking at night, stick to busy, well-lit streets. If you ever feel uncomfortable, leave the area as quickly and directly as you can.

There is no sure-fire way to avoid all the threatening situations you might encounter while traveling, but a good **self-defense course** will give you concrete ways to react to unwanted advances. **Impact, Prepare, and Model Mugging** can refer you to local self-defense courses in the US (☎800-345-5425). Visit the website at www.impactsafety.org for a list of nearby chapters. Workshops (2-3hr.) start at US$50; full courses (20hr.) run US$350-500.

If you are using a **car,** learn local driving signals and wear a seatbelt. Children under 40 lb. (18kg) must ride in specially-designed carseats, and infants under 1 year or 20 lb. (9kg) must ride in rear-facing carseats. Carseats are available for a small fee from most car rental agencies. All children under 13 must sit in the rear seat of the car. Study route maps before you hit the road, and if you plan on spending a lot of time driving, consider bringing spare parts. If your car breaks down, wait for the police to assist you. For long drives in desolate areas, invest in a cellular phone and a roadside assistance program (p. 52). Park your vehicle in a garage or well traveled area, and use a steering wheel locking device in larger cities. **Sleeping in your car** is one of the most dangerous (and often illegal) ways to get your rest.

POSSESSIONS AND VALUABLES

Never leave your belongings unattended; crime occurs in even the most demure-looking hostel or hotel. Bring your own **padlock** for hostel lockers, and don't ever store valuables in any locker. Be particularly careful on **buses** and **trains;** horror stories abound about determined thieves who wait for travelers to fall asleep. Carry your backpack in front of you where you can see it. When traveling with others, sleep in alternate shifts. When alone, use good judgment in selecting a train compartment: never stay in an empty one, and use a lock to secure your pack to the luggage rack. Try to sleep on top bunks with your luggage stored above you (if not in bed with you), and keep important documents and other valuables on your person.

There are a few steps you can take to minimize the financial risk associated with traveling. First, **bring as little with you as possible.** Second, buy a few combination **padlocks** to secure your belongings either in your pack or in a hostel or train station locker. Third, **carry as little cash as possible.** Keep your traveler's checks and ATM/credit cards in a **money belt**—not a "fanny pack"—along with your passport and ID cards. Fourth, **keep a small cash reserve separate from your primary stash.** This should be about US$50 sewn into or stored in the depths of your pack, along with your traveler's check numbers and important photocopies.

In large cities **con artists** often work in groups and may involve children. Beware of certain classics: sob stories that require money; rolls of bills "found" on the street; mustard spilled (or saliva spit) onto your shoulder to distract you while they snatch your bag. **Never let your passport and your bags out of your sight.** Beware of **pickpockets** in city crowds, especially on public transit. Also, be alert in public telephone booths: if you must say your calling card number, do so very quietly; if you punch it in, make sure no one can look over your shoulder.

If you will be traveling with electronic devices, such as a laptop computer or a PDA, check whether your homeowner's insurance covers loss, theft, or damage when you travel. If not, you might consider purchasing a separate insurance policy. **Safeware** (☎ 800-800-1492; www.safeware.com) specializes in covering computers and charges $90 for 90-day comprehensive travel coverage up to $4000.

PRE-DEPARTURE HEALTH

In your **passport,** write the names of any people you wish to be contacted in case of a medical emergency, and list any allergies or medical conditions you have. Matching a prescription to a foreign equivalent is not always easy, safe, or possible, so if you take prescription drugs, consider carrying up-to-date, legible prescriptions or a statement from your doctor stating the medication's trade name, manufacturer, chemical name, and dosage. Be sure to keep all medication in your carry-on luggage. For tips on packing a basic **first-aid kit** and other health essentials, see p. 38.

IMMUNIZATIONS AND PRECAUTIONS

Although no inoculations are required for US tourists, travelers over two years old should make sure that the following vaccines are up to date: MMR (for measles, mumps, and rubella); DTaP or Td (for diphtheria, tetanus, and pertussis); IPV (for polio); Hib (for *haemophilus* influenza B); HepB (for Hepatitis B). For recommendations on immunizations and prophylaxis, consult the CDC (see below) in the US or the equivalent in your home country, and check with a doctor for guidance.

INSURANCE

Travel insurance covers four areas: medical/health problems, property loss, trip cancellation/interruption, and emergency evacuation. Though regular insurance policies may extend to travel-related accidents, you may consider purchasing travel insurance if the cost of potential trip cancellation, interruption, or emergency medical evacuation is greater than you can absorb. Prices for travel insurance generally run about US$50 per week for full coverage, while trip cancellation/interruption may be purchased separately at a rate of US$3-5 per day.

Medical insurance (especially university policies) often covers costs incurred abroad; check with your provider. **US Medicare** does not cover foreign travel, though in rare circumstances it pays for care in Canada and Mexico. **Canadian** provincial health insurance plans increasingly do not cover foreign travel; check with the provincial Ministry of Health or Health Plan Headquarters for details. **Homeowners' insurance** (or your family's coverage) often covers theft during travel and loss of travel documents (passport, plane ticket, railpass, etc.) up to US$500.

ISIC and **ITIC** (p. 34) provide basic insurance benefits to US cardholders, including US$100 per day of in-hospital sickness for up to 60 days and US$5000 of accident-related medical reimbursement (see www.isicus.com for details). Cardholders have access to a toll-free 24hr. helpline for medical, legal, and financial emergencies overseas. **American Express** (☎800-528-4800) grants most cardholders automatic collision and theft car rental insurance and ground travel accident coverage of US$100,000 on flight purchases made with the card.

INSURANCE PROVIDERS

STA (p. 46) offers a range of plans that can supplement your basic coverage. Other private insurance providers in the US and Canada include: Access America (☎800-284-8300; www.accessamerica.com); Berkely Group (☎800-797-4514; www.berkely.com); Globalcare Travel Insurance (☎800-821-2488; www.globalcare-cocco.com); Travel Assistance International (☎800-821-2828; www.europ-assistance.com); and Travel Guard (☎800-826-4919; www.travelguard.com). Columbus Direct (☎020 7375 0011; www.columbusdirect.co.uk) operates in the UK and AFTA (☎02 9264 3299; www.afta.com.au) in Australia.

USEFUL ORGANIZATIONS AND PUBLICATIONS

The US **Centers for Disease Control and Prevention** (**CDC**; ☎877-FYI-TRIP/394-8747; www.cdc.gov/travel) maintains an international travelers' hotline and an informative website. The CDC's comprehensive booklet *Health Information for International Travel* (The Yellow Book), a rundown of disease, immunization, and general health advice, is free online (http://bookstore.phf.org). Consult the appropriate government agency of your home country for consular information sheets on health, entry requirements, and other issues for various countries (see **Travel Advisories,** p. 41). For quick information on health and other travel warnings, call the **Overseas Citizens Services** (☎888-407-4747 M-F 8am-8pm, after-hours 202-647-4000, overseas 317-472-2328), or contact a passport agency, embassy, or consulate abroad. For information on medical evacuation services and travel insurance firms, see the US government's website at http://travel.state.gov/medical.html or the **British Foreign and Commonwealth Office** (www.fco.gov.uk). For general health info, contact the **American Red Cross** (☎800-564-1234; www.redcross.org).

STAYING HEALTHY

Common sense is the simplest prescription for good health while you travel. Drink lots of fluids to prevent dehydration and constipation, and wear sturdy, broken-in shoes and clean socks.

ONCE IN THE US AND CANADA

ENVIRONMENTAL HAZARDS

Heat exhaustion and dehydration: Heat exhaustion leads to nausea, excessive thirst, headaches, and dizziness. Avoid it by drinking plenty of fluids, eating salty foods (e.g., crackers), abstaining from dehydrating beverages (e.g., alcohol and caffeinated beverages), and always wearing sunscreen. Continuous heat stress can eventually lead to heatstroke, characterized by a rising temperature, severe headache, delirium, and cessation of sweating. Victims should be cooled off with wet towels and taken to a doctor. The southern US is particularly prone to heat waves, though travelers in all areas should be cautious during the summer and bring plenty of water on hiking or camping trips.

Sunburn: Always wear sunscreen (SPF 30 is good) when spending excessive amounts of time outdoors. If you are planning on spending time near water, in the desert, or in the snow, you are at a higher risk of getting burned, even through clouds. If you get sunburned, drink more fluids than usual and apply an aloe-based lotion. Severe sunburns can lead to sun poisoning, causing fever, chills, nausea, and vomiting. Sun poisoning should always be treated by a doctor. Glare from the sun can also cause **snow blindness,** making sunglasses a must when visiting glaciers or snow fields.

Hypothermia and frostbite: Travelers to the US and Canada during the winter months should be aware of the dangers of cold exposure. A rapid drop in body temperature is the clearest sign of overexposure to cold. Victims may also shiver, feel exhausted, have poor coordination or slurred speech, hallucinate, or suffer amnesia. *Do not let hypothermia victims fall asleep.* To avoid hypothermia, keep dry, wear layers, and stay out of the wind. When the temperature is below freezing, watch out for frostbite. If skin turns white or blue, waxy, and cold, do not rub the area. Drink warm beverages, stay dry, and slowly warm the area with dry fabric or steady body contact until a doctor can be found.

High altitude: The Rocky, Sierra Nevada, and Cascades mountains in the western US and Canada are at particularly high altitudes. When visiting these locations, allow your body a couple of days to adjust to less oxygen before exerting yourself. Note that alcohol is more potent and UV rays are stronger at high elevations.

DISEASES

Many diseases are transmitted by insects—mainly mosquitoes, fleas, ticks, and lice. Be aware of insects in wet or forested areas; wear long pants and long sleeves, tuck your pants into your socks, and use a mosquito net. Use insect repellents such as DEET and soak or spray your gear with permethrin (licensed in the US only for use on clothing). **Mosquitoes** are prevalent in wet, swampy, or wooded areas such as the southeastern US. **Ticks**—responsible for Lyme and other diseases—can be particularly dangerous in rural and forested regions of the US and Canada, particularly the northeast, central north, and Pacific coast.

In the US and Canada, city and suburban tap water is treated to be safe for drinking, though travelers should still exercise caution in remote rural areas or areas with untreated well water. Raw shellfish, unpasteurized milk, or dishes containing raw eggs may still represent health risks. Backcountry hikers may purify their own water by bringing it to a rolling boil or treating it with **iodine tablets;** note, however, that some parasites such as *Giardia* have exteriors that resist iodine treatment, so boiling is more reliable. Always wash your hands before eating or bring a quick-drying purifying liquid hand cleaner.

Lyme disease: A bacterial infection carried by ticks and marked by a bull's-eye rash of 2 in. or more. Later symptoms include fever, headache, fatigue, and aches and pains. Antibiotics are effective if administered early. Left untreated, Lyme can cause problems in joints, the heart, and the nervous system. If you find a tick attached to your skin, grasp the head with tweezers and apply slow, steady traction. Removing a tick within 24hr. greatly reduces the risk of infection. Tick bites usually occur in moist, shaded environments and heavily wooded areas of the northeastern, central northern, and Pacific coastal regions. If you are going to be hiking in these areas, wear long clothes and DEET.

Giardiasis: Transmitted through parasites (microbes, tapeworms, etc.) in contaminated water and food and acquired by drinking untreated water from streams or lakes. Symptoms include diarrhea, abdominal cramps, bloating, fatigue, weight loss, and nausea. If untreated it can lead to severe dehydration. Giardiasis occurs worldwide.

Gastroenteritis/Stomach Flu: Caused by a class of viruses called Noroviruses and spreads via contact with the body fluids of infected people, including exposure to contaminated foods, touching contaminated objects and then placing the hands in or near the mouth, and direct contact with infected persons. Symptoms appear within 48hr. of infection and include vomiting, nausea, chills, diarrhea, and abdominal cramping. Though the symptoms usually pass within a few days, the disease can be contagious for several weeks and a doctor should be consulted if any of these symptoms develop.

Rabies: Transmitted through the saliva of infected animals; fatal if untreated. By the time symptoms (thirst and muscle spasms) appear, the disease is in its terminal stage. If you are bitten, wash the wound thoroughly, seek immediate medical care, and try to have the animal located. A rabies vaccine, 3 shots given over a 21-day period, is only semi-effective. Rabies is often transmitted through dogs, but travelers to backcountry or wooded areas should be wary of wild animals that may also carry the disease.

AIDS and HIV: For detailed information on Acquired Immune Deficiency Syndrome (AIDS) in the US and Canada, call the US Centers for Disease Control's 24hr. hotline at ☎800-342-2437, or contact the Joint United Nations Programme on HIV/AIDS (UNAIDS), 20 Ave. Appia, CH-1211 Geneva 27, Switzerland (☎41 22 791 3666; fax 791 4187). The US may screen incoming travelers for AIDS, primarily those planning extended visits for work or study, and denies entrance to those who test HIV-positive.

Sexually transmitted diseases (STDs): Gonorrhea, chlamydia, genital warts, syphilis, herpes, and other STDs are easier to catch than HIV and can be just as deadly. Hepatitis B and C can also be transmitted sexually. Though condoms may protect you from some STDs, oral or tactile contact can lead to transmission. The CDC's STD hotline is at ☎800-227-8922. If you may have contracted an STD, see a doctor immediately.

MEDICAL CARE ON THE ROAD

Medical care in the US and Canada is among the best in the world. In case of medical emergency, dial ☎**911** from any phone and an operator will send out paramedics, a fire brigade, or the police as needed. Emergency care is available in the US and Canada at any emergency room on a walk-in basis. If you do not have insurance, you will have to pay for medical care. Appointments are required for non-emergency medical services. If you are concerned about obtaining medical assistance while traveling, you may wish to employ special support services. The *Med-Pass* from **GlobalCare, Inc.,** 6875 Shiloh Rd. E, Alpharetta, GA 30005, USA (☎800-860-1111; www.globalcare.net), provides 24hr. international medical assistance, support, and medical evacuation resources. If your regular **insurance** policy does not cover travel abroad, you may wish to purchase additional coverage (p. 42).

Those with medical conditions (such as diabetes, allergies to antibiotics, or epilepsy) may want to obtain a **Medic Alert** membership (first year US$35, annually thereafter US$20), which includes an ID tag, among other benefits, like a 24hr. collect-call number. Contact the Medic Alert Foundation, 2323 Colorado Ave, Turlock, CA 95382, USA (☎888-633-4298 or 209-668-3333; www.medicalert.org).

GETTING TO THE US AND CANADA

BY PLANE

When it comes to airfare, a little effort can save you a bundle. If your plans are flexible enough to deal with the restrictions, courier fares are the cheapest. Tickets bought from consolidators and standby seating are also good deals, but last-minute specials, airfare wars, and charter flights often beat these fares. The key is to hunt around, to be flexible, and to ask persistently about discounts. Students, seniors, and those under 26 should never pay full price for a ticket.

AIRFARES

Airfares to the US and Canada peak during the summer; holidays are also expensive. Midweek (M-Th morning) round-trip flights run US$40-50 cheaper than weekend flights, but they are generally more crowded and less likely to permit frequent-flier upgrades. Not fixing a return date ("open return") or arriving in and departing from different cities ("open-jaw") can be pricier than round-trip flights. Patching one-way flights together is one of the most expensive ways to travel.

If the US or Canada is only one stop on a more extensive globe-hop, consider a round-the-world (RTW) ticket. Tickets usually include at least five stops and are valid for about a year; prices range US$1200-5000. Try **Northwest Airlines/KLM** (US ☎ 800-447-4747; www.nwa.com) or **Star Alliance,** a consortium of 22 airlines including United Airlines which offers both RTW tickets and North America Airpasses for multiple-destination travel within the US, Canada, and Mexico (US ☎ 800-241-6522; www.staralliance.com).

Fares for roundtrip flights to the US or Canadian east coast from Western Europe cost $200-750 in the low season (Sept.-May); expect to pay $900-1500 for a round-trip flight from Australia or New Zealand to the US or Canadian west coast.

BUDGET AND STUDENT TRAVEL AGENCIES

While agents specializing in flights to the US and Canada can make your life easy and help you save, they may not spend the time to find you the lowest possible fare—they get paid on commission. Travelers holding **ISIC** and **IYTC cards** (p. 34) qualify for big discounts. Most flights from budget agencies are on major airlines, but in peak season some may sell seats on less reliable chartered aircraft.

CTS Travel, 30 Rathbone Pl., London W1T 1GQ, UK (☎020 7209 0630; www.ctstravel.co.uk). A British student travel agent with offices in 39 countries including the US, Empire State Building, 350 Fifth Ave., Ste. 7813, New York City, NY 10118 (☎877-287-6665; www.ctstravelusa.com).

STA Travel, 5900 Wilshire Blvd., Ste. 900, Los Angeles, CA 90036, USA (24hr. reservations and info ☎800-781-4040; www.sta-travel.com). A student and youth travel organization with over 150 offices worldwide, including US offices in Boston, Chicago, L.A., New York City, San Francisco, Seattle, and Washington, D.C. Ticket booking, travel insurance, railpasses, and more. Walk-in offices are located throughout Australia (☎03 9349 4344), New Zealand (☎09 309 9723), and the UK (☎0870 1 600 599).

Travel CUTS (Canadian Universities Travel Services Limited), 187 College St., Toronto, ON M5T 1P7 (☎416-979-2406; www.travelcuts.com). Offices across Canada and the US including Los Angeles, New York City, San Francisco, and Seattle.

USIT, 19-21 Aston Quay, Dublin 2 (☎01 602 1777; www.usitworld.com), Ireland's leading student/budget travel agency has 22 offices throughout Northern Ireland and the Republic of Ireland. Offers programs to work in North America.

COMMERCIAL AIRLINES

The commercial airlines' lowest regular offer is the **APEX** (Advance Purchase Excursion) fare, which provides confirmed reservations and allows "open-jaw" tickets. Generally, reservations must be made 7-21 days ahead of departure, with seven- to 14-day minimum-stay and up to 90-day maximum-stay restrictions. These fares carry hefty cancellation and change penalties (fees rise in summer). Book peak-season APEX fares early. Use **Microsoft Expedia** (www.expedia.com) or **Travelocity** (www.travelocity.com) to get an idea of the lowest published fares, then use the resources outlined here to try and beat those fares. Low-season fares should be appreciably cheaper than the high-season (mid-June to Aug.) ones listed here.

FLIGHT PLANNING ON THE INTERNET. The Internet may be the budget traveler's dream when it comes to finding and booking bargain fares, but the array of options can be overwhelming. Many airline sites offer last-minute deals on the web. Check individual airlines' websites for more information. **STA** (www.sta-travel.com) and **StudentUniverse** (www.studentuniverse.com) provide quotes on student tickets, while **Orbitz** (www.orbitz.com), **Expedia** (www.expedia.com), and **Travelocity** (www.travelocity.com) offer full travel services. **Priceline** (www.priceline.com) lets you specify a price, and obligates you to buy any ticket that meets or beats it; **Hotwire** (www.hotwire.com) offers bargain fares, but won't reveal the airline or flight times until you buy. Other sites that compile deals for you include www.bestfares.com, www.flights.com, www.lowestfare.com, www.onetravel.com, and www.travelzoo.com. Increasingly, there are online tools available to help sift through multiple offers; **SideStep** (www.sidestep.com) and **Booking Buddy** (www.bookingbuddy.com) let you enter your trip information once and search multiple sites. An indispensable resource is the **Air Traveler's Handbook** (www.faqs.org/faqs/travel/air/handbook), a comprehensive listing of links to everything you need to know before you board a plane.

ESSENTIALS

TRAVELING FROM THE UK AND IRELAND

Round-trip fares from the UK and Ireland to the eastern US range US$200-750, with flights from London usually cheapest at $200-600. Standard commercial carriers like **American** (US ☎800-433-7300; www.aa.com), **United** (US ☎800-538-2929; www.ual.com), and **Northwest** (US ☎800-447-4747; www.nwa.com) will probably offer the most convenient flights, but they may not be the cheapest. Check **Lufthansa** (US ☎800-399-5838; http://cms.lufthansa.com), **British Airways** (US ☎800-247-9297; www.britishairways.com), **Air France** (US ☎800-237-2747; www.airfrance.us), and **Alitalia** (US ☎800-223-5730; www.alitaliausa.com) for cheap tickets from destinations in Europe to all over the US. Discount airlines such as Icelandair (US ☎800-223-5500; www.icelandair.com) may provide cheaper flights, though cheaper flights often mean fewer departure points.

TRAVELING FROM AUSTRALIA AND NEW ZEALAND

Round-trip fares from the Australia and New Zealand to the western US range $900-1500. Check **Air New Zealand** (☎0800 73 70 00; www.airnz.co.nz), **Quantas Airways** (Australia ☎13 11 31, New Zealand 0800 101 500; www.qantas.com.au), and **Singapore Air** (Australia ☎13 10 11, New Zealand 0800 808 909; www.singaporeair.com) for cheap tickets from Australia and New Zealand to the US.

STANDBY FLIGHTS

Traveling standby requires considerable flexibility in arrival and departure dates and cities. Companies dealing in standby flights sell vouchers rather than tickets, along with the promise to get you to your destination (or near your destination) within a certain window of time (typically 1-5 days). You call in before your specific window of time to hear your flight options and the probability that you will be able to board each flight. You can then decide which flights you want to try to make, show up at the appropriate airport at the appropriate time, present your voucher, and board if space is available. Vouchers can usually be bought for both one-way and round-trip travel. You may receive a monetary refund only if every available flight within your date range is full; if you opt not to take an available (but perhaps less convenient) flight, you can only get credit toward future travel. Carefully read agreements with any company offering standby flights as tricky fine print can leave you in the lurch. To check on a company's service record in the US, call the Better Business Bureau (☎ 703-276-0100). It is difficult to receive refunds, and clients' vouchers will not be honored when an airline fails to receive payment in time.

TICKET CONSOLIDATORS

Ticket consolidators, or **"bucket shops,"** buy unsold tickets in bulk from commercial airlines and sell them at discounted rates. The best place to look is in the Sunday travel section of any major newspaper (such as the *New York Times*), where many bucket shops place tiny ads. Call quickly, as availability is typically extremely limited. Not all bucket shops are reliable, so insist on a receipt that gives full details of restrictions, refunds, and tickets, and pay by credit card (in spite of the 2-5% fee) so you can stop payment if you never receive your tickets. For more info, see www.travel-library.com/air-travel/consolidators.html.

CHARTER FLIGHTS

Charters are flights a tour operator contracts with an airline to fly extra loads of passengers during peak season. Charter flights fly less frequently than major airlines, make refunds particularly difficult, and are almost always fully booked. Schedules and itineraries may also change or be cancelled at the last moment (as late as 48hr. before the trip, and without a full refund), and check-in, boarding, and baggage claim are often much slower. However, they can also be cheaper. Discount clubs offer members savings on last-minute charter and tour deals. Study contracts closely; you don't want to end up with an unwanted overnight layover.

GETTING AROUND THE US AND CANADA

BY PLANE

Basic round-trip fares within the US and Canada range roughly US$80-500. Commercial carriers like American and United will probably offer the most convenient flights, but they may not be the cheapest. You will probably find flying one of the following "no-frills" airlines to be a better deal, if any of their limited departure points is convenient for you. Many of these airlines also offer one-way flights without the high fees imposed by some major airlines, and do not charge extra for travelers who are not staying over a Saturday night.

AirTran (☎800-AIR TRAN/247-8726; www.airtran.com). Cross-country and regional flights between 40+ US cities, including Atlanta, Boston, Los Angeles, Washington, D.C., and many small local or regional airports.

America West (☎800-235-9292; www.americawest.com). An extensive flight network serving the continental US, Canada, Mexico, Alaska and Hawaii.

ATA (☎800-I FLY ATA/435-9282; www.ata.com). Serves over 45 cities in the continental US, Hawaii, Mexico, and the Caribbean.

CanJet (☎800-809-7777; www.canjet.com). Gradually expanding budget airline serving a limited schedule in eastern Canada and the US.

Frontier (☎800-432-1FLY/432-1359; www.frontierairlines.com). Serves an extensive network of cities and smaller airports in the continental US, Alaska, and Mexico.

Independence Air (☎800-FLY FLYI/359-3594; www.flyi.com). New, expanding budget airline serving the US East Coast.

JetBlue (☎800-JET BLUE/538-2583; www.jetblue.com). Serves 25+ locations in the US and Puerto Rico.

JetsGo (☎866-440-0441; www.jetsgo.com). Flies to half a dozen US locations and nearly 20 airports in Canada.

Song (☎800-FLY SONG/359-7664; www.flysong.com). Delta's little sister airline flies a limited schedule within the US and to San Juan, Puerto Rico.

Southwest Airlines (☎800-I FLY SWA/435-9792; www.southwest.com). Serves 60+ locations within the US.

Tango (☎800-247-2262; www.flytango.com). Air Canada's budget division flies to 60 destinations within Canada, including many smaller airports.

WestJet (☎800-WEST JET/937-3538; www.westjet.com). Serves over 20 cities throughout Canada.

BY BUS

Buses generally offer the most frequent and complete service between the cities and towns of the US and Canada. Often, a bus is the only way to reach smaller locales without a car. In rural areas, however, bus lines tend to be sparse.

GREYHOUND

Greyhound (☎800-229-9424; www.greyhound.com) operates the most routes in the US, and provides service to parts of Canada. Schedule information is available at any Greyhound terminal or agency and on their web page.

Advance Purchase Fares: Reserving space far ahead of time ensures a lower fare, but expect smaller discounts June 5 to Sept. 15. Fares are often lower for 14-day, 7-day, or 3-day advance purchases. Call for up-to-date pricing or check their website.

Discounted Fares: Student Advantage cardholders (15% off); persons 62 and older (5% off walk-up fares); military personnel and dependent family members (10% off); children under 12 traveling with a full-fare adult (40% off).

Domestic Discovery Passes: US and Canadian travelers can purchase passes that allow unlimited travel within specified regions for 7 or more days, including the Ameripass for travel throughout the continental US (7-60 days, US$239-669) the Canada Pass for travel throughout Canada (7-60 days, CDN$309-719), the North America CanAm pass for travel throughout the US and Canada (15-60 days, US$439-719), the West Coast CanAm Pass for travel in the western US and Canada (10 days US$299, 21 days US$399), and the Eastern CanAm Pass for travel in the eastern US and Canada (10 days US$299, 21 days US$399). Child, student, and senior discounts apply, and all passes can be ordered on the Greyhound website.

International Discovery Passes: For travelers from outside North America. Ameripass 4-60 days, US$169-619; Canada Pass 7-60 days, CDN$309-719, North America CanAm Pass 15-60 days, US$439-719; West Coast CanAm Pass 10 days, US$299 or 21 days US$399; Eastern CanAm Pass 10 days US$299 or 21 days US$399. Child, student, and senior discounts apply; passes can be ordered on the Greyhound website.

GREYHOUND CANADA

Greyhound Canada Transportation (☎800-661-TRIP/661-8747; www.greyhound.ca) is Canada's main intercity bus company. The website has full schedule info.

Discounted Fares: Students with ISIC 25% off; students with other recognized student ID (such as Euro 26/U26 or VIP) 10% off; Hostelling International cardholders 10% off; persons 62 and over 10% off; military personnel 10% off. One child under 16 travels free with purchase of full-price adult fare (ask about Family Fares); children 5-11 half-off with purchase of full-price adult fare; with 3-day advance purchase of a full-price adult ticket, a friend travels for only $15 (ask about Companion Fares).

Discovery Passes: Available for residents of the US and Canada as well as international travelers (see Domestic Discovery Passes and International Discovery Passes, above). More information available on the Greyhound Canada website.

BY TRAIN

Locomotion is still one of the least expensive (and most pleasant) ways to tour the US and Canada, but discounted air travel may be cheaper, and much faster, than train travel. As with airlines, you can save money by purchasing your tickets far in advance, so plan ahead and make reservations early. It is essential to travel light on trains, since many stations will not check luggage. **Amtrak** (☎ 800-USA RAIL/872-7245; www.amtrak.com) provides the only nationwide rail service in the US; round-trip fares range from $20 to $500. **VIA Rail Canada** (☎ 800-USA RAIL/872-7245; www.viarail.ca) operates coast-to-coast across Canada. VIA Rail offers the Canrail-pass, which allows 12 days of travel within a 30-day period throughout Canada and offers a 10% discount for students, seniors, and children. Both Amtrak and VIA Rail offer web specials, so it's worthwhile to check out their websites before you go.

BY CAR

North America is most easily traversed by car, and once in the car, by highway. "I" (as in "I-90") refers to Interstate highways, "U.S." (as in "U.S. 1") to US highways, and "Rte." (as in "Rte. 7") to state and local highways. For Canadian highways, "TCH" refers to the Trans-Canada Hwy., while "Hwy." or "autoroute" refers to standard automobile routes. There are often local alternatives to highways, which are certainly worth investigating if you have extra time en route.

ON THE ROAD

While driving, be sure to buckle up—seat belts are **required by law** in many regions. The **speed limit** in the US varies considerably from region to region. Most urban highways have a limit of 55 mph (89kph), while rural routes range from 65 mph (104kph) to 75 mph (120kph). Heed the limit; not only does it save gas, but most local police forces and state troopers make frequent use of radar to catch speed demons. The **speed limit in Canada** is 50kph (31 mph) in cities and 80kph (49 mph) on highways. On rural highways the speed limit may be 100kph (62 mph).

> **DRIVING PRECAUTIONS.** When traveling in the summer or in the desert, bring substantial amounts of **water** (at least 5L per person per day) for drinking and for the radiator. For long drives to unpopulated areas, register with police before beginning the trek, and again upon arrival at the destination. When traveling for long distances, make sure tires are in good repair and have enough air, and get good maps. A **compass** and a **car manual** can also be very useful. You should always carry a **spare tire** and **jack, jumper cables, extra oil, flares, a flashlight (torch),** and **heavy blankets** (in case your car breaks down at night or in the winter). If you don't know how to **change a tire,** learn before heading out, especially if you are planning on traveling in deserted areas. Blow-outs on dirt roads are exceedingly common. If you do have a breakdown, **stay with your car;** if you wander off, there's less likelihood trackers will find you.

HOW TO NAVIGATE THE INTERSTATES

In the 1950s, President Dwight D. Eisenhower envisioned a well-organized **interstate highway system.** His dream has been realized: there is now a comprehensive, well-maintained, efficient means of traveling between major cities and between states. Luckily for travelers, the highways are named with an intuitive numbering system. Even-numbered interstates run east-west and odd ones run north-south, decreasing in number toward the south and the west. North-south routes begin on the West Coast with I-5 and end with I-95 on the East Coast. The southernmost east-west route is I-4 in Florida. The northernmost east-west route is I-94, stretching from Montana to Wisconsin. Three-digit numbers signify branches of other interstates (e.g., I-285 is a branch of I-85) that often skirt around large cities.

RENTING

Having a car will give you far better access to most places in the US and Canada. While some cities have excellent public transit, others have none, and it is often difficult to get from place to place without a car. Overall, driving is certainly your best option for seeing North America. The drawbacks of car rentals, however, include steep prices (a compact car rents for $25-45 per day) and high minimum ages for rentals (usually 25). Most branches rent to ages 21 to 24 with an additional fee. A few establishments will rent to those over 18, but it is rare and will almost certainly be accompanied by a hefty fee. When evaluating rental costs it is important to note that cheaper cars tend to be less reliable and harder to handle on difficult terrain. Less expensive 4WD vehicles in particular tend to be more top-heavy, and are more dangerous when navigating particularly bumpy roads.

RENTAL AGENCIES

You can generally make reservations before you leave by calling major international offices in your home country. However, occasionally the price and availability information they give doesn't correspond with information from local offices in your country. Try checking with both numbers to make sure you get the best price and accurate information. Local desk numbers are included in town listings; for home-country numbers, call your toll-free directory.

Car rental agencies fall into two categories: national companies with hundreds of branches, and local agencies that serve only one city or region. National chains usually allow you to pick up a car in one city and drop it off in another (for a hefty charge). **Alamo** (☎ 800-462-5266; www.alamo.com) rents to ages 21 to 24 with a major credit card for an increased rate. **Enterprise** (☎ 800-261-7331; www.enterprise.com) also rents to customers ages 21 to 24. **Dollar** (☎ 800-800-4000; www.dollar.com) and **Thrifty** (☎ 800-367-2277; www.thrifty.com) locations do likewise for varying surcharges. **Rent-A-Wreck** (☎ 800-944-7501; www.rent-a-wreck.com) specializes in supplying vehicles that are past their prime for lower prices; a bare-bones compact less than eight years old rents for around $20-25. There may be a charge for a **collision and damage waiver (CDW)**, which usually comes to about $12-15 per day. Major credit cards (including Master-Card and American Express) will sometimes cover the CDW if you use their card to rent a car; call your credit card company for specifics. Most agencies have frequent special rates—be sure to check online or ask the agent before renting.

COSTS

Rental car prices start at around $20-50 a day. Expect to pay more for larger cars and for 4WD. Many rental packages offer unlimited miles, although some do have mileage restrictions. Return the car with a full tank of gas to avoid high fuel charges. Be sure to ask whether the price includes **insurance** against theft and collision. If you are driving a conventional vehicle on an **unpaved road** in a rental car, you are almost never covered by insurance. Insurance plans almost always come with a **deductible.** This means you pay for all damages up to that sum, unless they are the fault of another vehicle. The deductible applies to collisions with other vehicles; collisions with non-vehicles, such as trees, will cost you even more.

AUTO TRANSPORT COMPANIES

These services match drivers with car owners who need cars moved from one city to another. Travelers give the company their desired destination and the company finds a car that needs to go there. Expenses include gas and tolls. Some companies insure their cars; with others, your security deposit covers any breakdowns or damage. You must be over 21, have a valid license, and agree to drive about 400 mi. per day on a fairly direct route. The following are popular transport companies:

Auto Driveaway Co., 310 S. Michigan Ave., Ste. 1401, Chicago, IL 60604 (☎800-346-2277 or 312-939-2352; www.autodriveaway.com).

Across America Driveaway, 10811 Washington Blvd. #302, Culver City, CA 90232 (☎800-637-8764; www.schultz-international.com).

DANGERS. Road conditions vary considerably throughout the country. Some cities have excellent roads, while others have roads riddled with potholes. In more rural areas, you may find dirt roads which are considerably slower than paved streets. Watch for signs warning about animal crossings; depending on the region, signs could caution drivers to look for ducks, longhorn, moose, or more.

CAR ASSISTANCE. Most automobile clubs offer free towing, emergency roadside assistance, travel-related discounts, and random goodies. Travelers should strongly consider membership if planning an extended roadtrip.

American Automobile Association (AAA). Provides 24hr. emergency road service (☎800-222-4357) anywhere in the US. Free trip-planning services, maps, and guidebooks. Free towing and commission-free American Express Traveler's Cheques from over 1000 offices across the country. Discounts on Hertz car rental (5-20%), Amtrak tickets (10%), and various motel chains and theme parks. Basic membership $45, Associate Membership $12. To sign up, call ☎800-564-6222 or go to www.aaa.com.

Canadian Automobile Association (CAA), 1145 Hunt Club Rd. #200, Ottawa, ON K1V 0Y3 (☎800-222-4357; www.caa.ca). Affiliated with AAA (see above), the CAA provides the same membership benefits, including 24hr. emergency roadside assistance, free maps and tourbooks, route planning, and various discounts. Basic membership is CDN$78; call ☎800-268-3790 for membership services.

DRIVING PERMITS AND CAR INSURANCE

INTERNATIONAL DRIVING PERMIT (IDP)

If you do not have a license issued by a US state or Canadian province or territory, you might want an International Driving Permit (IDP)—it may help with police if your license is not written in English. Although the IDP does not require a driving test, you must carry your home license with your IDP at all times.

Your IDP, valid for one year, must be issued in your own country before you depart. You must be over 18 to be eligible. An application for an IDP usually requires one or two photos, a current local license, an additional form of identification, and a fee. To apply, contact the national or local branch of your home country's automobile association. Be careful when purchasing an IDP online or anywhere other than your home automobile association. Many vendors sell permits of questionable legitimacy for higher prices.

CAR INSURANCE

Most credit cards cover standard insurance. If you rent, lease, or borrow a car, you will need a **green card,** or **International Insurance Certificate,** to certify that you have liability insurance and that it applies abroad. Green cards can be obtained at car rental agencies, car dealerships, some travel agents, and some border crossings.

BY BICYCLE

U-shaped **Kryptonite** or **Citadel** locks ($30-60) carry insurance against theft for one or two years if your bike is registered with the police. **Bike Nashbar** (☎ 800-NASH-BAR/627-4227; www.nashbar.com) sells bike locks and accessories, ships throughout the US and Canada, and will beat any competitor's price. Their tech line (☎ 800-888-2710; open M-F 9am-10pm, Sa-Su noon-6pm) fields maintenance questions.

Adventure Cycling Association, 150 E. Pine St., P.O. Box 8308, Missoula, MT 59802 (☎ 800-755-2453; www.adv-cycling.org). A national, nonprofit organization that researches long-distance routes and organizes bike tours (75-day Great Divide Expedition $2800, most 10-15 day trips $700-850). Annual membership ($30) includes access to maps and a subscription to *Adventure Cyclist* magazine. The online Cyclists' Yellow Pages provides worldwide information and resources for bike enthusiasts.

The Canadian Cycling Association, 702-2197 Riverside Dr., Ottawa, ON K1H 7X3 (☎ 613-248-1353; www.canadian-cycling.com). Provides info for cyclists of all abilities. Distributes *The Canadian Cycling Association's Complete Guide to Bicycle Touring in Canada.*

KEEPING IN TOUCH

BY MAIL

SENDING MAIL WITHIN THE US AND CANADA

First-class letters sent and received within the US take 1-3 days and cost $0.37; Priority Mail packages up to 1 lb. generally take two days and cost $3.85, up to 5 lb. $11. All days specified denote business days. For more details, visit the US Postal Service at www.usps.com. For Canadian mailing information, visit Canada Post at www.canadapost.ca.

SENDING MAIL HOME FROM THE US AND CANADA

Airmail is the best way to send mail home from the US and Canada. **Aerogrammes,** printed sheets that fold into envelopes and travel via airmail, are available at post offices. Write "airmail" or "par avion," on the front. The cost is $0.70. Most post offices will charge exorbitant fees or simply refuse to send aerogrammes with enclosures. If regular airmail is too slow, **Federal Express** (☎ 800-247-4747) can get a letter from New York City to Sydney in two business days for a whopping $35. By **US Express Mail,** a letter would arrive within 3-5 business days and would cost $17. **Surface mail** is by far the cheapest and slowest way to send mail. It takes one to two months to cross the Atlantic and one to three to cross the Pacific. Check with the closest post office to find out about postage rates to your country.

Australia: Allow 4-7 days for regular airmail home. Postcards/aerogrammes cost $0.70 (from Canada, CDN$1.40). Letters up to 20g cost $1.70 (CDN$1.40); packages up to 0.5kg $19 (CDN$13), up to 2kg $33 (CDN$38).

Canada: Allow 4-7 days for regular airmail home. Postcards/aerogrammes cost $0.70 (from Canada, CDN$0.49). Letters up to 20g cost $0.85 (CDN$0.49); packages up to 0.5kg $9 (CDN$12), up to 2kg $17 (CDN$10).

Ireland: Allow 4-7 days for regular airmail home. Postcards/aerogrammes cost $0.70 (from Canada, CDN$1.40). Letters up to 20g cost $1.60 (CDN$1.40); packages up to 0.5kg $16 (CDN $9), up to 2kg $23 (CDN$38).

New Zealand: Allow 4-7 days for regular airmail home. Postcards/aerogrammes cost $0.70 (from Canada, CDN$1.40). Letters up to 20g cost $1.70 (CDN$1.40); packages up to 0.5kg $16 (CDN$13), up to 2kg $29 (CDN$38).

UK: Allow 4-7days for regular airmail home. Postcards/aerogrammes cost $0.70 (from Canada, CDN$1.40). Letters up to 20g cost $1.60 (CDN$1.40); packages up to 0.5kg $20 (CDN$13), up to 2kg $32 (CDN$38).

SENDING MAIL TO THE US AND CANADA

To ensure timely delivery, mark envelopes "airmail" or "par avion." In addition to the standard postage system whose rates are listed below, **Federal Express** (www.fedex.com; Australia ☎ 132 610; Canada and US 800-463-3339; Ireland 1800 535 800; New Zealand 0800 733 339; UK 0800 123 800) handles express mail services; for example, they can get a letter from New York City to Seattle in two days for US$12, and from London to Seattle in one to two days for UK$30. Sending a postcard within the US costs US$0.23, while sending letters (up to 13 oz.) domestically requires $0.37 for the first ounce and $0.23 for each additional ounce. In Canada, postcards and letters up to 30g cost CDN$0.49 or $0.80 between 30g and 50g.

Australia: Allow 4-6 days for regular airmail to the US, 5-7 days to Canada. Postcards and letters up to 20g cost AUS$1.65 to both the US and Canada; packages up to 0.5kg AUS$13, up to 2kg AUS$43. EMS can get a letter to the US and Canada in 2-5 days for AUS$33. www.auspost.com.au.

Canada: Allow 4-7 days for regular airmail to the US and up to 4 days within Canada. Postcards and letters up to 20g cost CDN$0.80 to the US, CDN$0.49 within Canada; packages up to 0.5kg CDN$6.70 to the US, up to CDN$8.85 within Canada, up to 2kg CDN$19 to the US, CDN$11 within Canada. Purolator International can get a letter to the US in 1 day for CDN$46. www.canadapost.ca.

Ireland: Allow 5-7 days for regular airmail to both the US and Canada. Postcards and letters up to 20g cost €0.65; packages up to 0.5kg €5, up to 2kg €16. Swiftpost International can get a letter to the US or Canada more quickly for €4 more than normal priority postage. www.letterpost.ie.

New Zealand: Allow 4-10 days for regular airmail to the US or Canada. Postcards and letters up to 20g cost NZ$1.50; packages up to 0.5kg NZ$16, up to 2kg NZ$50. International Express can get a letter to the US or Canada in 2-4 days for NZ$33. www.nzpost.co.nz/nzpost/inrates.

UK: Allow about 5 days for regular airmail to the US and Canada. Letters up to 20g cost UK£0.68; packages up to 0.5kg UK£5.02, up to 2kg UK£19. Airsure delivers letters a day faster for UK£4 more; see www.royalmail.com for more information.

RECEIVING MAIL IN THE US AND CANADA

There are several ways to arrange pick-up of letters sent to you while you are abroad. Mail can be sent via **General Delivery** to almost any city or town in the US or Canada with a post office. Address General Delivery letters like so:

Peter GALLAGHER

General Delivery

Post Office Street Address

Orange County, CA 92865 USA or Kelowna, BC V1Z 2H6 CANADA

The mail will go to the central post office, unless you specify a post office by street address or postal code. It's best to use the largest post office, since mail may be sent there regardless. Bring your photo ID for pick-up. If the clerks insist that there is nothing for you, have them check under your first name as well. *Let's Go* lists post offices in the **Practical Information** section for each city and most towns.

BY TELEPHONE

CALLING HOME FROM THE US AND CANADA

A **calling card** is probably your cheapest bet. Calls are billed collect or to your account. You can frequently call collect without even possessing a company's calling card just by calling their access number. You may wish to obtain a calling card from your national telecommunications service before leaving home. To **call home with a calling card,** contact the operator for your service provider in the US or Canada by dialing the appropriate toll-free access number listed on your card. Before settling on a calling card plan, be sure to research your options in order to pick the one that best fits both your needs and your destination.

You can usually also make **direct international calls** from pay phones, but if you aren't using a calling card, you may need to drop your coins as quickly as your words. Prepaid phone cards and occasionally major credit cards can be used for direct international calls, but they are generally less cost-efficient. Placing a **collect call** through an international operator is even more expensive, but may be necessary in case of emergency. You can place collect calls through the service providers listed above even if you don't have one of their phone cards.

CALLING WITHIN THE US AND CANADA

The simplest way to call within the country is to use a coin-operated phone; local calls typically cost US$0.35 in the US and CDN$0.50 in Canada. In some areas, you will only need to use the last seven digits of a phone number; in larger cities, ten-digit dialing may be necessary. **Prepaid phone cards,** which carry a certain amount of phone time depending on the card's denomination, usually save time and money

PLACING INTERNATIONAL CALLS. To call the US or Canada from home or to call home from the US or Canada, dial:

1. The **international dialing prefix.** To call from **Australia,** dial 0011; **Canada** or the **US,** 011; **Ireland, New Zealand,** or the **UK,** 00.
2. The **country code** of the country you want to call. To call **Australia,** dial 61; **Canada** or the **US,** 1; **Ireland,** 353; **New Zealand,** 64; the **UK,** 44.
3. The **area code.** *Let's Go* lists the area codes for cities and towns in the US and Canada opposite the city or town name, next to a ☎.
4. The **local number.**

in the long run, although they often require a US$0.25 surcharge from pay phones. The phone will tell you how much time you have left on your card. Another kind of prepaid phone card comes with a Personal Identification Number (PIN) and a toll-free access number. Instead of inserting the card into the phone, you call the access number and follow the directions on the card. These cards can be used to make international as well as domestic calls. Phone rates typically tend to be highest in the morning, lower in the evening, and lowest on Sunday and late at night.

CELLULAR PHONES

While pay phones can be found in almost every city and town in the US and Canada, if you already own a cell phone you can avoid much of the hassle of scrounging up change or a phone card. Cell phone reception is clear and reliable in much of the region, although in remote areas or in the mountains, reception can be spotty; your provider may also slap on hefty additional roaming fees of up to $1.25 per minute. Call your service provider to check their coverage policies.

The international standard for cell phones is **GSM,** a system that began in Europe and has spread to much of the rest of the world. Some cell phone companies in the US and Canada use GSM in certain regions (e.g., T-Mobile and AT&T), but most employ other services such as **TDMA, CDMA, I-den,** and **AMPS.** You can make and receive calls in the US and Canada with a GSM or GSM-compatible phone, but you will only get coverage in relatively populated areas, and your phone will only work if it is from North America or if it is a **tri-band** phone. American GSM networks use different frequencies from those used in Europe; a tri-band phone allows you to use both the European 900MHz and 1800MHz frequencies as well as the North American 1900MHz frequency. If you are using a GSM phone in the US or Canada, you will need a **SIM (subscriber identity module) card,** a country-specific chip that gives you a local phone number and plugs you into the local network. You may need to **unlock** your phone in order to insert a SIM card. Many companies will offer to unlock your phone for fees of $5-50, but call your provider ahead of time; some will unlock your phone for free upon request. If your provider won't unlock your phone, your best bet is to look online for an unlocking service, but bear in mind that getting your phone unlocked may violate your service agreement. Many SIM cards are prepaid, meaning that they come with calling time included and you don't need to sign up for a monthly service plan. Incoming calls are frequently free. When you use up the prepaid time, you can buy additional cards or vouchers. For more information on GSM phones, check out www.telestial.com, www.orange.co.uk, www.roadpost.com, or www.t-mobile.com.

A good option, especially if you want to make occasional calls over a short period, is to buy a cell phone with a **prepaid contract** which allows a customer to buy a certain amount of minutes each month instead of a more long-term package. **Ecallplus** (www.ecallplus.com), **AT&T** (www.att.com), and **Verizon** (www.verizon.com) all offer this type of service. If you elect to buy a used cell phone, make sure it is compatible with the service you want to use. **Renting** a cell phone is possible but usually more expensive than getting a short-term prepaid contract.

 EMERGENCY CALLS. If you only want a cell phone for the direst emergencies, you don't need to buy a cell phone plan or a calling card. All working cell phones in the US are required to be able to call ☎911 if they are within service range.

TIME DIFFERENCES

The US and Canada cover several time zones, 5-9hr. behind **Greenwich Mean Time (GMT)**. Most areas in the US and Canada observe daylight saving time, so clocks are set forward 1hr. in the spring and backward 1hr. in the fall.

4AM	7AM	10AM	NOON	7PM	9PM
Vancouver	Toronto	London	Bucharest	Beijing	Sydney
Seattle	Ottawa	(GMT)	Athens	Hong Kong	Canberra
San Francisco	New York		Beirut	Singapore	Melbourne
Los Angeles	Boston		Cairo		

BY EMAIL AND INTERNET

If your e-mail provider won't let you check your e-mail from the web, your best bet for reading e-mail from the road is to use a free **web-based email account** (e.g., www.hotmail.com and www.yahoo.com). **Internet cafes** and the occasional free Internet terminal at a public library or university are listed in the **Practical Information** sections of major cities. For lists of additional cybercafes in the US and Canada, check out www.cybercaptive.com or www.cybercafe.com.

Increasingly, travelers find that taking their **laptop computers** on the road with them can be a convenient option for staying connected. Laptop users can call an Internet service provider via a modem using long-distance phone cards specifically intended for such calls. They may also find Internet cafes that allow them to connect their laptops to the Internet. And most excitingly, travelers with wireless-enabled computers may be able to take advantage of an increasing number of Internet "hot spots," where they can get online for free or for a small fee. Newer computers can detect these hot spots automatically; otherwise, websites like www.jiwire.com, www.wi-fihotspotlist.com, and www.locfinder.net can help you find them. In the US and Canada, **Starbucks** is a widespread coffee chain that also provides wi-fi. For information on insuring your laptop while traveling, see p. 41.

ACCOMMODATIONS

HOSTELS

Many hostels are laid out dorm-style, often with large single-sex rooms and bunk beds, although private rooms that sleep two to four are becoming more common. They sometimes have kitchens and utensils for your use, bike rentals, storage areas, transportation to airports, breakfast and other meals, laundry facilities, and Internet access. There can be drawbacks: some hostels close during certain daytime "lockout" hours, have a curfew, don't accept reservations, impose a maximum stay, or, less frequently, require that you do chores. In the US and Canada, a dorm bed in a hostel will average around $15-25 and a private room around $50-65.

A HOSTELER'S BILL OF RIGHTS. There are certain standard features that we do not include in our hostel listings. Unless we state otherwise, you can expect that every hostel has no lockout, no curfew, a kitchen, free hot showers, some system of secure luggage storage, and no key deposit.

HOSTELLING INTERNATIONAL

Joining the hosteling association in your own country (see below) grants you membership privileges in **Hostelling International (HI)**. Non-HI members are allowed to stay in HI hostels, but have to pay extra to do so. Many hostels in the US and Canada are members of HI. HI's website (www.hihostels.com), which lists the web addresses and phone numbers of all national associations, can be a great place to begin researching hosteling. The site also allows you to book some hostels online.

A new membership benefit is the FreeNites program, which allows hostelers to gain points toward free rooms. Most student travel agencies (p. 46) sell HI cards, as do all of the national hosteling organizations listed below. All prices listed below are valid for **one-year memberships**.

Australian Youth Hostels Association (AYHA), 422 Kent St., Sydney, NSW 200 (☎02 9261 1111; www.yha.com.au). AUS$52, under 18 AUS$19.

Hostelling International-Canada (HI-C), 205 Catherine St. #400, Ottawa, ON K2P 1C3 (☎613-237-7884; www.hihostels.ca). CDN$35, under 18 free.

An Óige (Irish Youth Hostel Association), 61 Mountjoy St., Dublin 7 (☎830 4555; www.irelandyha.org). €20, under 18 €10.

Hostelling International Northern Ireland (HINI), 22 Donegal Rd., Belfast BT12 5JN (☎02890 31 54 35; www.hini.org.uk). UK£13, under 18 UK£6.

Youth Hostels Association of New Zealand (YHANZ), Level 1, Moorhouse City, 166 Moorhouse Ave., P.O. Box 436, Christchurch (New Zealand ☎0800 278 299, elsewhere 03 379 9970; www.yha.org.nz). NZ$40, under 18 free.

Scottish Youth Hostels Association (SYHA), 7 Glebe Cres., Stirling FK8 2JA (☎01786 89 14 00; www.syha.org.uk). UK£6, under 17 £2.50.

Youth Hostels Association (England and Wales), Trevelyan House, Dimple Rd., Matlock, Derbyshire DE4 3YH (☎0870 770 8868; www.yha.org.uk). UK£14, under 18 UK£7.

Hostelling International-USA, 8401 Colesville Rd., Ste. 600, Silver Spring, MD 20910 (☎301-495-1240; www.hiayh.org). US$28, under 18 free.

BOOKING HOSTELS ONLINE. One of the easiest ways to ensure you've got a bed for the night is by reserving online. Click to the **Hostelworld** booking engine through **www.letsgo.com,** and you'll have access to bargain accommodations from Atlanta to Zion National Park with no added commission.

OTHER TYPES OF ACCOMMODATIONS

YMCAS AND YWCAS

Young Men's Christian Association (YMCA) lodgings are usually cheaper than a hotel but more expensive than a hostel. Not all YMCA locations offer lodging; those that do are often located in urban downtowns. Many YMCAs accept women and families; some will not lodge those under 18 without parental permission.

YMCA of the USA, 101 N. Wacker Dr., Chicago, IL 60606, USA (☎888-333-9622 or 800-872-9622; www.ymca.net). Provides a listing of the nearly 1000 Ys across the US and Canada. Offers info on prices, services, telephone numbers, and addresses.

YWCA of the USA, 1015 18th St. NW, Ste. 1100, Washington, D.C. 20036, USA (☎202-467-0801 or 800-YWCA-US1; www.ywca.org). Provides a directory of YWCAs, the women's counterpart of YMCAs, across the USA.

YMCA Canada, 42 Charles St. E, 6th fl., Toronto, ON M4Y 1T4, Canada (☎416-967-9622; www.ymca.ca), offers info on Ys in Canada.

YWCA Canada, 75 Sherbourne St., Ste. 422, Toronto, ON M5A 2P9, Canada (☎416-962-8881; www.ywca.ca), provides a directory of YWCAs in Canada.

HOTELS

Budget **hotel singles** in the US and Canada cost about $45-70 per night, doubles $65-95. You'll typically have a private bathroom and shower with hot water, although cheaper places may offer a shared bath. If you make **reservations** in writing, the hotel will send you a confirmation and may request payment for the first night. Often it is easiest to make reservations over the phone with a credit card.

BED & BREAKFASTS (B&BS)

For a cozy alternative to impersonal hotel rooms, B&Bs (private homes with rooms available to travelers) range from the acceptable to the sublime. Rooms in B&Bs generally cost $70-90 for a single and $90-110 for a double in the US and Canada. Any number of websites provide listings for B&Bs. For more information, check out Bed & Breakfast Inns Online (www.bbonline.com), InnFinder (www.inncrawler.com), InnSite (www.innsite.com), BedandBreakfast.com (www.bedandbreakfast.com), or BNBFinder.com (www.bnbfinder.com).

ESSENTIALS

UNIVERSITY DORMS

Many **colleges and universities** open their residence halls to travelers when school is not in session; some do so even during term-time. Getting a room may require advance planning, but rates tend to be low, and many offer free local calls and Internet access. Some universities that host travelers include the University of Texas in Austin, TX (☎512-476-5678), Ohio State University in Columbus, OH (☎614-292-9725), and McGill University in Montréal, QC (☎514-398-6367).

CAMPING AND THE OUTDOORS

For those with the proper equipment, camping is one of the least expensive and most enjoyable ways to travel through the US and Canada. Camping opportunities in this predominantly rural region are boundless, and many are accessible to inexperienced travelers. Generally, private campgrounds have sites for a small fee and offer safety and security. Well-equipped campsites (usually including prepared tent sites, toilets, and water) go for $10-25 per night in the US and CDN$10-30 in Canada. **Backcountry camping,** which lacks all of the above amenities, is often free but can cost up to $20 at some national parks. Most campsites are first come, first served. The **Great Outdoor Recreation Pages** (www.gorp.com) provides excellent general information for travelers planning on camping or spending time outdoors.

LEAVE NO TRACE. *Let's Go* encourages travelers to embrace the "Leave No Trace" ethic, protecting natural environments for future generations. Trekkers should set up camp on durable surfaces, use cookstoves instead of campfires, bury human waste away from water supplies, bag trash and carry it out with them, and respect wildlife and natural objects. For more info, contact the **Leave No Trace Center for Outdoor Ethics,** P.O. Box 997, Boulder, CO 80306, USA (☎800-332-4100 or 303-442-8222; www.lnt.org).

USEFUL PUBLICATIONS AND RESOURCES

A variety of publishing companies offer hiking guidebooks to meet the educational needs of novices or experts. For information about camping, hiking, and biking, write or call the publishers listed below to receive a free catalog.

Sierra Club Books, 85 2nd St., 2nd fl., San Francisco, CA 94105, USA (☎415-977-5500; www.sierraclub.org/books). Publishes general resource books on hiking and camping and provides advice for women traveling in the outdoors.

The Mountaineers Books, 1001 SW Klickitat Way, Ste. 201, Seattle, WA 98134, USA (☎206-223-6303; www.mountaineersbooks.org). Boasts over 500 titles on hiking, biking, mountaineering, natural history, and conservation.

Wilderness Press, 1200 5th St., Berkeley, CA 94710, USA (☎800-443-7227 or 510-558-1666; www.wildernesspress.com). Carries over 100 hiking guides and maps for destinations across North America.

Woodall Publications Corporation, 2575 Vista del Mar Dr., Ventura, CA 93001, USA (☎877-680-6155; www.woodalls.com). Annually updates campground directories in the US and Canada, with extensive national parks coverage.

NATIONAL PARKS

National Parks protect some of the most spectacular scenery in North America. Though their primary purpose is preservation, the parks also host recreational activities such as ranger talks, guided hikes, marked trails, skiing, and snowshoe expeditions. For info, contact the **National Park Service,** 1849 C St. NW, Washington, D.C. 20240 (☎202-208-6843; www.nps.gov).

Entrance fees vary. The larger and more popular parks charge a $4-20 entry fee for cars and sometimes a $2-7 fee for pedestrians and cyclists. The **National Parks Pass** ($50), available at park entrances, allows the passport-holder's party entry into all national parks for one year. National Parks Passes can also be bought by writing to National Park Foundation, P.O. Box 34108, Washington, D.C. 20043 (send $50 plus $3.95 shipping and handling), online at www.nationalparks.org, or by calling ☎ 888-467-2757. For an additional $15, the Parks Service will affix a **Golden Eagle Passport** hologram to your card, which will allow you access to sites managed by the US Fish and Wildlife Service, the US Forest Service, and the Bureau of Land Management. US citizens or residents over 61 qualify for the **Golden Age Passport** ($10 one-time fee), which entitles the holder's party to free park entry, a 50% discount on camping, and 50% reductions on various recreational fees for the passport holder. Persons eligible for federal benefits on account of disabilities can enjoy the same privileges with the **Golden Access Passport** (free).

Most national parks have both backcountry and developed **camping.** Some welcome RVs, and a few offer grand lodges. At the more popular parks in the US and Canada, reservations are essential, available through MISTIX (☎ 800-365-2267; http://reservations.nps.gov) no more than five months in advance. Indoor accommodations should be reserved months in advance. Campgrounds often observe first come, first served policies, and many fill up by late morning.

NATIONAL FORESTS

Often less accessible and less crowded, **US National Forests** (www.fs.fed.us) are a purist's alternative to parks. While some have recreation facilities, most are equipped only for primitive camping—pit toilets and no water are the norm. When charged, entrance fees are $10-20, but camping is generally free or $3-4. Necessary wilderness permits for backpackers can be obtained at the US Forest Service field office in the area. *The Guide to Your National Forests* is available at all Forest Service branches, or call or write the main office (USDA, Forest Service, Information Center, 1400 Independence Ave. SW, Mailstop 111, Washington, D.C. 20250; ☎ 202-205-1680). This booklet includes a list of all National Forest addresses; request maps and other info directly from the forest(s) you plan to visit. Reservations with varying fees are available for most forests, but are usually only needed during high season at the more popular sites. Call up to one year in advance to National Recreation Reservation Center (☎ 877-444-6777, international 518-885-3639; www.reserveusa.com).

CANADA'S NATIONAL PARKS

Less trampled than their southern counterparts, these parks boast at least as much natural splendor. Park entrance fees range CDN$3-7 per person, with family and multi-day passes available. Reservations are offered for a limited number of campgrounds with a CDN$7 fee. For these reservations, or for info on the over 40 parks and countless historical sites in the network, consult Parks Canada's web page (http://parkscanada.pch.gc.ca). Regional passes are available at relevant parks (http://www.pc.gc.ca/apps/PCFees/multipass_e.asp). The best pass is the Great Western Pass, which covers admission to all the parks in the Western provinces for a year (CDN$35 per adult, CDN$70 per group of up to seven people).

WILDERNESS SAFETY

THE GREAT OUTDOORS

Staying **warm, dry, and well-hydrated** is key to a happy and safe wilderness experience. For any hike, prepare yourself for an emergency by packing a first-aid kit, a reflector, a whistle, high-energy food, extra water, raingear, a hat, and mittens. For warmth, wear wool or insulating synthetic materials designed for the outdoors. Cotton is a bad choice since it dries painfully slowly.

Check **weather forecasts** often and pay attention to the skies when hiking, as weather patterns can change suddenly. Always let someone, either a friend, your hostel, a park ranger, or a local hiking organization, know where you are going hiking. Know your limits and do not attempt a hike beyond your ability. See **Safety and Health** (p. 39) for information on outdoor ailments and medical concerns.

WILDLIFE

If you are hiking in an area that might be frequented by **bears,** keep your distance. If you see a bear, calmly walk (don't run) in the other direction. The best way to avoid danger is to completely avoid the bear—bears will attack if they are surprised, threatened, or protecting their territory or cubs. Sing or talk loudly on the trail and hike in groups, if possible. If you encounter a black bear, the National Forest Service recommends trying to scare it off by making noise and throwing sticks and stones in its direction. Do not run. If the black bear charges or attacks, the National Forest Service recommends that you stand your ground and fight back. For grizzly bears, which also populate certain wild areas of the United States and Canada, the protocol for encounters is different. Please see the National Forest Service bear safety page at http://www.fs.fed.us/r1/wildlife/igbc/Safety/cwi/menu.htm for more information. Don't leave food or other scented items (trash, toiletries, the clothes that you cooked in) near your tent. Putting these objects into canisters is now mandatory in some national parks. **Bear-bagging,** hanging edibles and other good-smelling objects from a tree out of reach of hungry paws, is the best way to keep your toothpaste from becoming a condiment. Bears are also attracted to any **perfume,** as are bugs, so cologne, scented soap, deodorant, and hair spray should stay at home.

Poisonous **snakes** are hazards in many wilderness areas in the US and Canada and should be carefully avoided. The two most dangerous are coral and rattlesnakes. Coral snakes reside in the Southwestern US and can be identified by black, yellow, and red bands. Rattlesnakes live in desert and marsh areas, and will shake the rattle at the end of their tail when threatened. Don't attempt to handle or kill a snake; if you see one, back away slowly. If you are bitten, clean the wound immediately, apply a pressure bandage, keep the wound below the heart to slow the flow of venom through the blood stream, and immobilize the limb. Do not attempt to suck the venom out with your mouth and do not ice the wound—studies have shown that cooling the wound makes it more difficult to extract the venom. Seek immediate medical attention for any snakebite that breaks the skin.

Mountain regions in the north are stomping grounds for **moose.** These big, antlered animals have been known to charge humans, so never feed or walk toward a moose. If a moose charges, get behind a tree immediately and raise your arms in the air with your fingers spread (but don't wave them) so that you appear larger. If the moose attacks you, get on the ground in a fetal position and stay still.

While **mosquitoes** are certainly not as dangerous as bears or snakes, they can be a camper's main source of agony. Though these creatures start cropping up in spring, the peak season in the US and Canada runs June-August before tapering off at the approach of fall. Be especially careful around damp or swampy areas. Mosquitoes can bite through thin fabric, so cover up as much as possible with thicker materials. 100% DEET is useful, but mosquitoes can be so ravenous that nothing short of a mosquito hood and netting really stops every jab.

CAMPING AND HIKING EQUIPMENT

WHAT TO BUY

Good camping equipment is both sturdy and light. North American suppliers tend to offer the most competitive prices.

ESSENTIALS

Sleeping Bags: Most sleeping bags are rated by season; "summer" means 30-40°F (around 0°C) at night; "four-season" or "winter" often means below 0°F (-17°C). Bags are made of **down** (warm and light, but expensive, and miserable when wet) or of **synthetic** material (heavy, durable, and warm when wet). Prices range for $50-250 for a summer synthetic to $200-300 for a good down winter bag. **Sleeping bag pads** include foam pads ($10-30), air mattresses ($15-50), and self-inflating mats ($30-120). Bring a **stuff sack** to store your bag and keep it dry.

Tents: The best tents are free-standing (with their own frames and suspension systems), set up quickly, and only require staking in high winds. Low-profile dome tents are the best all-around. Worthy 2-person tents start at $100, 4-person at $160. Make sure your tent has a rain fly and seal its seams with waterproofer. Other useful accessories include a **battery-operated lantern,** a plastic **groundcloth,** and a nylon **tarp.**

Backpacks: Internal-frame packs mold well to your back, keep a lower center of gravity, and flex adequately to allow you to hike difficult trails, while **external-frame packs** are more comfortable for long hikes over even terrain, as they carry weight higher and distribute it more evenly. Make sure your pack has a strong, padded hip belt to transfer weight to your legs. There are models designed specifically for women. Any serious backpacking requires a pack of at least 4000 in.^{3} (16,000cc), plus 500 in.^{3} for sleeping bags in internal-frame packs. Sturdy backpacks cost anywhere from $125 to $420—your pack is an area where it doesn't pay to economize. On your hunt for the perfect pack, fill up prospective models with something heavy, strap them on correctly, and walk around the store to get a sense of how each model distributes weight. Either buy a **rain cover** ($10-20) or store all of your belongings in plastic bags inside your pack.

Boots: Be sure to wear hiking boots with good **ankle support.** They should fit snugly and comfortably over 1-2 pairs of **wool socks** and a pair of thin **liner socks.** Break in boots over several weeks before you go to spare yourself blisters.

Other Necessities: Synthetic layers, like those made of polypropylene or polyester, and a pile jacket will keep you warm even when wet. A **space blanket** ($5-15) will help you to retain heat and doubles as a groundcloth. Plastic **water bottles** are vital; look for shatter-resistant models. Carry **water-purification tablets** for when you can't boil water. Although most campgrounds provide campfire sites, you may want to bring a small **metal grate** or **grill.** For places that forbid fires, you'll need a **camp stove** (the classic Coleman starts at $50) and a propane-filled **fuel bottle** to operate it. Also bring a **first-aid kit, pocketknife, insect repellent,** and waterproof **matches** or a **lighter.**

WHERE TO BUY IT

The mail-order/online companies listed below offer lower prices than many retail stores. A visit to a local camping or outdoors store will give you a good sense of the look and weight of certain items.

Campmor, 28 Parkway, P.O. Box 700, Upper Saddle River, NJ 07458, USA (☎888-226-7667; www.campmor.com).

Discount Camping, 880 Main North Rd., Pooraka, SA 5095, Australia (☎08 8262 3399; www.discountcamping.com.au).

Eastern Mountain Sports (EMS), 1 Vose Farm Rd., Peterborough, NH 03458, USA (☎888-463-6367; www.ems.com).

L.L. Bean, Freeport, ME 04033 (Canada and US ☎800-441-5713; UK 0800 891 297; www.llbean.com).

Mountain Designs, 51 Bishop St., Kelvin Grove, Queensland 4059, Australia (☎07 3856 2344; www.mountaindesigns.com).

Recreational Equipment, Inc. (REI), Sumner, WA 98352, USA (Canada and US ☎800-426-4840, elsewhere 253-891-2500; www.rei.com).

YHA Adventure Shop, 19 High St., Staines, Middlesex, TW18 4QY, UK (☎1784 458625; www.yhaadventure.com).

CAMPERS AND RVS

Much to the chagrin of outdoors purists, the US and Canada are havens for the corpulent, home-and-stove on wheels known as **recreational vehicles (RVs)**. Most national parks and small towns cater to RV travelers, providing campgrounds with large parking areas and electric outlets ("full hookup"). The costs of RVing compare favorably with the price of staying in hotels and renting a car, and the convenience of bringing along your own bedroom, bathroom, and kitchen makes it an attractive option. Cruise America rents and sells RVs in the United States and Canada (US ☎ 800-327-7799, elsewhere 480-464-7300; www.cruiseamerica.com).

ORGANIZED ADVENTURE TRIPS

Organized adventure tours offer another way of exploring the wild. Activities include hiking, biking, skiing, canoeing, kayaking, rafting, climbing, photo safaris, and archaeological digs. Tourism bureaus often can suggest parks, trails, and outfitters. Organizations that specialize in camping and outdoor equipment like REI and EMS (see above) also are good source for info.

Specialty Travel Index, 305 San Anselmo Ave., Ste. 309, San Anselmo, CA 94960 (US ☎ 888-624-4030, elsewhere 415-455-1643; www.specialtytravel.com).

TrekAmerica, P.O. Box 189, Rockaway, NJ 07866 (US ☎ 800-221-0596 or 973-983 1144, elsewhere 01295 256 777; www.trekamerica.com).

The National Outdoor Leadership School (NOLS), 284 Lincoln St., Lander, WY 82520 (☎ 800-710-6657; www.nols.edu), offers educational wilderness trips all over the world, including many to the US. They also offer courses in wilderness medicine training and leave-no-trace ethics.

Outward Bound, 100 Mystery Point Rd., Garrison, NY 10524 (☎ 866-467-7651; www.outwardbound.com), offers expeditional courses in outdoor education throughout the US. Courses range from several days to over 40 days, and include special focuses, such as life and career renewal and couples.

The Sierra Club, 85 2nd St., 2nd fl., San Francisco, CA 94105 (☎ 415-977-5500; www.sierraclub.org/outings), plans adventure outings at all of its branches throughout the US.

SPECIFIC CONCERNS

SUSTAINABLE TRAVEL

As the number of travelers on the road continues to rise, the detrimental effect they can have on natural environments becomes an increasing concern. With this in mind, *Let's Go* promotes the philosophy of **sustainable travel.** Through a sensitivity to issues of ecology and sustainability, today's travelers can be a powerful force in preserving and restoring the places they visit.

Ecotourism, a rising trend in sustainable travel, focuses on the conservation of natural habitats and using them to build up the economy without exploitation or overdevelopment. Travelers can make a difference by doing advance research and by supporting organizations and establishments that pay attention to their impact on their natural surroundings and strive to be environmentally friendly.

TRAVELING ALONE

There are many benefits to traveling alone, including independence and greater interaction with locals. On the other hand, any solo traveler is a more vulnerable target of harassment and street theft. As a lone traveler, try not to stand out as a tourist, look confident, and be especially careful in deserted or very crowded areas. If questioned, never admit that you are traveling alone. Maintain regular contact with someone at home who knows your itinerary. For more tips, pick up *Traveling Solo* by Eleanor Berman (Globe Pequot Press, $18), visit www.travelaloneand-loveit.com, or subscribe to **Connecting: Solo Travel Network,** 689 Park Rd., Unit 6, Gibsons, BC V0N 1V7, Canada (☎604-886-9099; www.cstn.org; membership $28-45).

WOMEN TRAVELERS

Women exploring on their own inevitably face some additional safety concerns, but it's easy to be adventurous without taking undue risks. If you are concerned, consider staying in hostels that offer single-sex rooms or in religious organizations with rooms for women only. Stick to centrally located accommodations and avoid solitary late-night treks or metro rides. Always carry extra money for a phone call, bus, or taxi. Look as if you know where you're going and approach older women or couples for directions if you're lost or uncomfortable.

Generally, the less you look like a tourist, the better off you'll be. Dress conservatively, especially in rural areas. Wearing a conspicuous **wedding band** sometimes helps to prevent unwanted overtures. Your best answer to verbal harassment is no answer at all; feigning deafness and staring straight ahead at nothing in particular will do a world of good that reactions usually don't achieve. The extremely persistent can sometimes be dissuaded by a firm, loud, and very public "Go away!" Don't hesitate to seek out a police officer or a passerby if you are being harassed. Memorize the emergency numbers in places you visit, and consider carrying a whistle on your keychain. A self-defense course will both prepare you for a potential attack and raise your level of awareness of your surroundings (see **Self Defense,** p. 41).

GLBT TRAVELERS

American cities are generally accepting of all sexualities, and thriving gay, lesbian, bisexual, and transgendered (GLBT) communities can be found in most cosmopolitan areas. Most college towns are GLBT-friendly as well. Still, homophobia is not uncommon, particularly in rural areas. *Let's Go* includes local GLBT info lines and community centers when available.

To avoid hassles at airports and border crossings, transgendered travelers should make sure that all of their travel documents consistently report the same gender. Many countries (including Australia, Canada, Ireland, New Zealand, the UK, and the US) will amend the passports of post-operative transsexuals to reflect their true gender, although governments are generally less willing to amend documents for pre-operative transsexuals and other transgendered individuals.

Listed below are contact organizations and mail-order bookstores that offer materials addressing some specific concerns. **Out and About** (www.outand-about.com) offers a newsletter and website addressing gay travel concerns. **365gay.com** also has a travel section (www.365gay.com/travel/travelchannel.htm).

Gay's the Word, 66 Marchmont St., London WC1N 1AB, UK (☎44 20 7278 7654; www.gaystheword.co.uk). The largest GLBT bookshop in the UK, with both fiction and non-fiction titles. Mail-order service available.

Giovanni's Room, 1145 Pine St., Philadelphia, PA 19107, USA (☎215-923-2960; www.queerbooks.com). An international lesbian/feminist and gay bookstore with mail-order service (carries many of the publications listed below).

International Lesbian and Gay Association (ILGA), 81 rue Marché-au-Charbon, B-1000 Brussels, Belgium (☎32 2 502 2471; www.ilga.org). Provides political information, such as homosexuality laws of individual countries.

▼ **FURTHER READING: GLBT TRAVEL**
Spartacus International Gay Guide 2004-2005. Bruno Gmunder Verlag ($33). For more information, visit www.spartacusworld.com.
Damron Men's Guide, Damron Women's Traveller, Damron's Accommodations, and *Damron City Guide.* Damron Travel Guides ($17-23). For more info, call ☎800-462-6654 or visit www.damron.com.
The Gay Vacation Guide: The Best Trips and How to Plan Them, Mark Chesnut. Kensington Publishing Corporation ($15).
Gayellow Pages USA/Canada, Frances Green. Kensington Publishing Corporation ($16). In bookstores or online at www.gayellowpages.com.

TRAVELERS WITH DISABILITIES

ESSENTIALS

Federal law dictates that all public buildings should be wheelchair accessible, and laws governing building codes make disabled access more the norm than the exception. However, traveling with a disability still requires planning. Those with disabilities should inform airlines and hotels of their disabilities when making reservations; some time may be needed to prepare accommodations. Call ahead to restaurants, museums, and other facilities to find out if they are handicapped accessible. Visiting more rugged parks may be difficult or impossible if you have severe disabilities, but some parks have handicapped-accessible trails.

Certified **guide dogs** are allowed into Canada without restriction. Dogs entering the US must either have originated from or lived for six months in an area that is free from rabies (including Australia, Canada, Ireland, New Zealand, and the UK), or they must have unexpired vaccination certificates. For a complete list of rabies-free areas, see http://www.cdc.gov/travel/diseases/rabies.htm. In all areas in the US and Canada, guide dogs are legally allowed, free of charge, on public transit and in all "public establishments," including hotels, restaurants, and stores.

In the US, both Amtrak and major airlines will accommodate disabled passengers if notified at least 72hr. in advance. Amtrak offers a 15% discount to physically disabled travelers (☎800-872-7245). Greyhound buses will provide a 50% discount for a companion if the ticket is purchased at least three days in advance. If you are without a fellow traveler, call Greyhound (☎800-752-4841, TDD 800-345-3109) at least two days before you plan to leave and they will make arrangements to assist you. For information on transportation availability in individual US cities, contact the local chapter of the **Easter Seal Society** (☎800-221-6827; www.easter-seals.org).

If you are planning to visit a national park or attraction in the US run by the National Park Service, obtain a free **Golden Access Passport,** which is available at all park entrances and from federal offices whose functions relate to land, forests, or wildlife. The passport entitles disabled travelers and their families to free park admission and provides a lifetime 50% discount on all campsite and parking fees.

USEFUL ORGANIZATIONS

Directions Unlimited, 123 Green Ln., Bedford Hills, NY 10507, USA (☎800-533-5343). Books individual vacations for the physically disabled; not an info service.

The Guided Tour Inc., 7900 Old York Rd. #114B, Elkins Park, PA 19027, USA (☎800-783-5841; www.guidedtour.com). Organizes travel programs for persons with developmental and physical challenges.

Society for Accessible Travel & Hospitality (SATH), 347 Fifth Ave. #610, New York City, NY 10016, USA (☎212-447-7284; www.sath.org). An advocacy group that publishes online travel information and the travel magazine *OPEN WORLD* (annual subscription US$13, free for members). Annual membership US$45, students and seniors US$30.

MINORITY TRAVELERS

While general attitudes toward race relations in the US and Canada differ drastically from region to region, racial and ethnic minorities sometimes face blatant and, more often, subtle discrimination and/or harassment. Verbal harassment is now less common than unfair pricing, false info on accommodations, or inexcusably slow or unfriendly service at restaurants. Report individuals to a supervisor and establishments to the **Better Business Bureau** for the region (www.bbb.org, or call the operator for local listings); contact the police in extreme situations. *Let's Go* always welcomes reader input regarding discriminating establishments.

FURTHER RESOURCES

United States Department of Justice (www.usdoj.gov/civilliberties.htm).

Go Girl! The Black Woman's Book of Travel and Adventure, Elaine Lee. Eighth Mountain Press ($18).

The African-American Travel Guide, Wayne Robinson. Hunter Publishing ($10).

OTHER RESOURCES

Let's Go tries to cover all aspects of budget travel, but we can't put *everything* in our guides. Listed below are books and websites that can serve as jumping-off points for your own research.

WORLD WIDE WEB

Almost every aspect of budget travel is accessible via the web. In 10min. at the keyboard, you can make a hostel reservation, get advice on travel hot spots from other travelers, or find out how much a train from Denver to Los Angeles costs.

Listed here are some regional and travel-related sites to start off your surfing; other relevant websites are listed throughout the book. Because website turnover is high, use search engines (such as www.google.com) to strike out on your own.

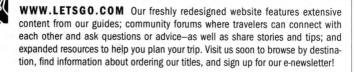

WWW.LETSGO.COM Our freshly redesigned website features extensive content from our guides; community forums where travelers can connect with each other and ask questions or advice—as well as share stories and tips; and expanded resources to help you plan your trip. Visit us soon to browse by destination, find information about ordering our titles, and sign up for our e-newsletter!

How to See the World: www.artoftravel.com. A compendium of great travel tips, from cheap flights to self defense to interacting with local culture.

Rec. Travel Library: www.travel-library.com. A fantastic set of links for general information and personal travelogues.

Lycos: http://travel.lycos.com. Introductions to cities and regions throughout the US and Canada, accompanied by links to applicable history, news, and local tourism sites.

Travel Intelligence: www.travelintelligence.net. A large collection of travel writing by distinguished travel writers.

World Hum: www.worldhum.com. An independently produced collection of "travel dispatches from a shrinking planet."

BootsnAll.com: www.bootsnall.com. Numerous resources for independent travelers, from planning your trip to reporting on it when you get back.

INFORMATION ON THE US AND CANADA

CIA World Factbook: www.odci.gov/cia/publications/factbook/index.html. Tons of vital statistics on the US and Canada's geography, government, economy, and people.

Tourism Offices Worldwide Directory: www.towd.com. Lists tourism offices for all 50 states and Canada, as well as consulate and embassy addresses.

Atevo Travel: www.atevo.com/guides/destinations. Detailed introductions, travel tips, and suggested itineraries.

World Travel Guide: http://www.travel-guides.com/region/nam.asp. Practical info.

ALTERNATIVES TO TOURISM

A NEW PERSPECTIVE

Traveling as a tourist often means spending nights in hotels, days at major sights, and eating food from restaurants—in other words, seeing different places in the exact same way. While this is fun and rewarding, the tourist is an outsider and cannot always travel with the depth necessary to experience and understand a destination. There are countless alternatives to tourism for those looking to expand or enhance their travel experience.

> Search at ◪ **www.beyondtourism.com,** Let's Go's new database of Alternatives to Tourism, where you can find exciting articles and helpful program listings divided by country, continent, and program type.

Opportunities for **volunteerism, conservation,** and **activism** abound and are an excellent way to immerse yourself in relevant issues and give back to the communities you visit. **Studying** in the US or Canada, either in the form of direct enrollment in a local university or through a study abroad program, gives the chance to explore intellectual avenues while living as a "real" American or Canadian student. **Working** is another a way to immerse yourself in local culture, and could help finance your travels; many travelers structure their trips by the work they can do along the way, whether they find odd jobs as they go (see p. 79 for visa requirements) or seek full-time stints in cities. While these are the most common alternatives to tourism, they are by no means the only ones. There are countless opportunities to experience the US and Canada through arts and culture, long hikes, or random activities that may pique your interest.

> **A PHILOSOPHY FOR TRAVELERS.** When *Let's Go* began in 1961, about 1.7 million people traveled internationally each year; in 2002, people made nearly 700 million trips, a number that's projected to be up to a billion by 2010. This rise in tourism has created an interdependence between tourists and their destination's economy, environment, and culture. Sustainable travel, then, is among the most important things we can impart to our readers. Working to preserve the environment, economy, and culture of communities is easier than it may seem—often self-awareness, rather than self-sacrifice, can make the biggest difference. Simply spending responsibly and trying to conserve local resources can positively impact the places you visit. More specifically, try to use public transit (or walk or bike), recycle and reuse what you can (e.g. refill water bottles, get electronic instead of paper tickets), do not buy souvenirs made from endangered or expendable resources, and support local businesses like casual street vendors. For more information about sustainable tourism, www.worldsurface.com features photos and personal stories of volunteer experiences. More info is available at www.sustainabletravel.org.

ECOTOURISM

A large number of ecotourism organizations have blossomed in the US, offering costly wildlife activities and tours developed to minimize environmental impact. More innovative programs arrange outings engineered to improve the environment and quality of life at the local level, while offering volunteers the opportunity to attain research, wilderness and work skills. Listed below are just a few options.

Earthwatch Institute, 3 Clock Tower Pl., Ste. 100, Box 75, Maynard, MA 01754 (☎800-776-0188 or 978-461-0081; www.earthwatch.org). Arranges 1- to 3-week programs in the US and Canada to promote conservation of natural resources. Under the supervision of leading scientists, field research teams perform tasks as far-ranging as tracking wildlife in Alaska's temperate rainforests to excavating prehistoric pueblos in the Southwest. Expeditions generally cost $700-$4000, depending on length and location.

National Outdoor Leadership School (NOLS), 284 Lincoln St., Lander, WY 83520 (☎800-710-6657; www.nols.edu). A non-profit organization committed to environmental ethics, NOLS designs extended (2-12 week) wilderness expeditions that foster leadership abilities and valuable backcountry skills, such as backpacking, wilderness medicine, and caving. Most courses cost at least $100 per day.

Habitat for Humanity International, 121 Habitat St., Americus, GA 31709 (☎229-924-6935, ext. 2551 or 2552; www.habitat.org). Volunteers build houses throughout the US and Canada (and in 85 other countries) to benefit low-income families. Projects take anywhere from 2 weeks to 3 years. Short-term program costs range $900-4000; check with local branches for free volunteer opportunities.

SCI International Voluntary Service, 5474 Walnut Level Rd., Crozet, VA 22932 (☎206-350-6586, in Canada 416-216-0914; www.sci-ivs.org). Ideal for volunteer "generalists," Service Civil International organizes teams for 2- to 4-week work camps on grassroots projects. Most camps also include opportunities to study social justice issues. Application fees include SCI-IVS membership and housing and meals, and run from $115; there are additional fees if applicants register through international affiliates.

World-Wide Opportunities on Organic Farms - USA, 309 Cedar St. #5C, Santa Cruz, CA 95060 (☎831-425-3276; www.wwoofusa.org). Learn about organic farming and permaculture on one of over 200 farms across the United States. Volunteers devote about 6 hr. per day to farm work in exchange for accommodations and meals. Requested stay lengths vary from a weekend to 3 months. Membership $20; dual membership $30.

ENVIRONMENTAL CONSERVATION

Protecting endangered species, battling air and water pollution, and conserving resources and habitats are a few of the ways you can help save the environment by volunteering with a conservation group in North America. Animal lovers should consider volunteering with shelters or animal rights associations.

Earth Share, 7735 Old Georgetown Road, Ste. 900, Bethesda, MD 20814 (☎800-875-3863 or 240-333-0300; www.earthshare.org). A network of national conservation organizations that offers links to short- and longer-term volunteer opportunities with community and state organizations as well as Earth Share affiliates in 19 states.

Volunteers-in-Parks with the National Park Service, 1849 C St. NW, Washington, D.C. 20240 (☎202-208-6843; www.nps.gov/volunteer). From the Great Smoky Mountains to Alaska's Glacier Bay, volunteers learn about park management, wildlife research, and environmental education by picking up trash, giving tours, monitoring wildlife, and planting trees in national parks; applicants from abroad may receive free, reimbursed, or reduced-cost housing and food from the International Volunteers-in-Parks program. For national parks, historic sites, and marine conservation areas in Canada, contact **Parks Canada,** 25 Eddy St., Hull, QC K1A 0M5 (☎888-773-8888; www.pc.gc.ca).

Natural Resources Conservation Service, Attn: Conservation Communications Staff, P.O. Box 2890, Washington, D.C. 20013 (☎202-720-3210; www.nrcs.usda.gov). Volunteer on private farms and ranches, in classrooms, with organizations, or in offices promoting conservation and improving wildlife habitat. Give tours and speeches, take photographs or organize exhibits with wildlife specialists.

The Environmental Careers Organization, 30 Winter St., Boston, MA 02108 (☎617-426-4375; www.eco.org) Develop skills in communications, outreach, or as a field technician for organizations like the Bureau of Land Management, US Geological Survey, and the Environmental Protection Agency. Places interns in 3-month to 2-year-long paid internships in 35 states and 3 US territories. Internships mostly available in summer but also in the year. Find more paid and unpaid environmental internships through **The Orion Grassroots Network,** 187 Main St., Great Barrington, MA 02130 (☎888-909-6568; www.oriononline.org), a network of 630 non-profit and community organizations.

American Society for the Prevention of Cruelty to Animals (ASPCA), 424 E. 92nd St., New York City, NY 10128 (☎212-876-7700; www.aspca.org). Promotes the humane treatment of animals through awareness programs, public policy efforts, shelter support, and animal medical treatment. Look under "Find a Shelter" on their website to find a list of shelters needing volunteers, or apply to volunteer at the ASPCA's headquarters in New York City. The ASPCA is partnered with **www.petfinder.com,** which also has a database of shelters and rescue groups. In Canada, contact the **Canadian Society for the Prevention of Cruelty to Animals (CSPCA);** (☎514-735-2711; www.spca.com).

POLITICAL ACTIVISM

Becoming involved in American politics is an excellent way to learn more about the political climate and work for social change. Those with substantive interest in activism and specific policy issues should consider volunteering for a group whose ideology matches their own.

Politix Group (☎202-478-0828; www.politixgroup.com). Promoting political involvement and activism at all levels, the Politix Group provides advice and information on how to participate in political campaigns and find internships on Capitol Hill with government offices, policy organizations, and think tanks. The link on the website to "U.S. Politics for Non-U.S. Citizens" describes a number of internship possibilities for foreign volunteers.

ACT UP, 332 Bleecker St., Ste. G5, New York City, NY 10014 (☎212-966-4873; www.actupny.org). One of the most influential activist groups in the US, ACT UP uses direct action to confront the AIDS crisis in America and abroad. Join their campaigns by participating in demonstrations, community education, and civil disobedience. To learn more about civil disobedience tactics, contact the **War Resisters League,** 399 Lafayette St. New York City, NY 10012 (☎212-228-0405; www.warresisters.org). The league advocates "Gandhian nonviolence"; their website offers a growing list of organizations and individuals that provide training in non-violent resistance, and connects visitors to local events such as peace vigils.

Jobs with Justice, 501 3rd St. NW, Washington, D.C. 20001 (☎202-434-1106; www.jwj.org). Advocate for economic and social justice in the workplace. Join local chapters to give a hand in the office, publicize events or march at a JWJ action devoted to ameliorating the plight of low-wage immigrant workers. The Student Labor Action Project (SLAP) is the student division of JWJ that mobilizes campaigns to combat corporate greed and fight for labor rights and economic justice in the US.

National Organization of Women (NOW), 733 15th St. NW, 2nd fl., Washington, D.C. 20005 (☎202-628-8669; www.now.org). Uses lobbying and grassroots organizing as well as direct and legal action to work for women's rights. Volunteer in one of 550 chapters in all 50 states, or apply for an internship at their main office.

Oxfam America, 26 West St., Boston, MA 02111 (☎617-482-1211; www.oxfamamerica.org). Support fair trade and work to end trade barriers against poor countries in Africa, Asia, and Latin America. Apply for 3- to 6-month part-time internships on poverty and social justice in the Boston and Washington, D.C. offices, or participate in individual actions to combat world poverty and advocate for fair trade and international development issues.

VOLUNTEERING IN COMMUNITIES

Communities in the United States and Canada face distinct and varied crises, including hunger and homelessness, lack of affordable health care, and insufficient public assistance. Volunteer positions within communities reflect these needs, and there are numerous opportunities to get involved and make a difference. Many people who volunteer in North America do so on a short-term basis at organizations in almost every city that make use of drop-in or once-a-week volunteers. There are also a number of long-term volunteer opportunities, but these may charge you a fee to participate. The costs can be surprisingly hefty, but they frequently cover airfare and most, if not all, living expenses. Interested individuals can find short- and long-term volunteer opportunities through comprehensive search engines that help individuals locate organizations that fit their interests and locations. Registered charities across the US enter their one-time or recurring volunteer needs in volunteer search engines such as **www.volunteersolutions.org** and **www.networkforgood.org,** and in Canada **www.volunteers.ca**. Those with a particular area of interest should investigate organizations targeting a single social issue.

Body Health Resources Corporation, 250 W. 57th St., New York City, NY 10107 (www.thebody.com). "The Body" is an extensive, informative website about all things HIV/AIDS-related. Check out the "Helping and Getting Help" section of the website for a listing of regional HIV/AIDS service organizations throughout the US and Canada that are in need of volunteers. **The Office of Minority Health,** Resource Center, P.O. Box 37337, Washington, D.C. 20013 (☎800-444-6472; www.omhrc.gov/OMHRC/index.htm), provides one of the most comprehensive lists of US state, federal, and other service organizations in the links section of their HIV/AIDS services; the **Canada AIDS Society,** 309 Cooper St., 4th fl., Ottawa, ON K2P 0G5 (☎613-230-3580; www.cdnaids.ca), provides a directory of service organizations as well.

Meals on Wheels Association of America, 203 S. Union St., Alexandria, VA 22314 (☎703-548-5558; www.mowaa.org). Buy, prepare, and deliver meals to the elderly and the poor. Public awareness and research projects also available. Programs in both the US and Canada; search the website for the region you would like to serve.

The National Coalition for the Homeless, 1012 14th St. NW, #600, Washington, D.C. 20005 (☎202-737-6444; www.nationalhomeless.org/local/local.html). Maintains a website with listings of local homeless assistance programs, shelters, food banks, hospitals, and advocacy groups in every state. In Canada, **Share the Warmth,** P.O. Box 30037, 1027 Finch Avenue W., Toronto, ON M3J 3L6 (www.sharethewarmth.org) is an energy assistance program for people living near the poverty line.

America's Second Harvest, 35 E. Wacker Dr., #2000, Chicago, IL 60601 (☎800-771-2303 or 312-263-2303; www.2ndharvest.org). As the US's largest hunger organization, Second Harvest oversees more than 200 food banks throughout the country and feeds more than 23 million people each year. Sort and repackage salvaged food, tutor children, or prepare and serve food at shelters. To find food banks in Canada, contact the **Canadian Association of Food Banks,** 191, rue New Toronto St., Toronto ON M8V 2E7 (☎416-203-9241; www.cafb-acba.ca).

National Hospice Foundation, 1700 Diagonal Rd., Ste. 625, Alexandria, VA 22314 (☎703-837-1500; www.hospiceinfo.org). Offer emotional and spiritual support to those close to death and counseling to their families. Search by name, state, or ZIP code under "Find a Hospice" section of the website to find a US hospice in need of volunteers.

LITERACY AND YOUTH OUTREACH

A quarter of American adults lack reading proficiency. Many experience difficulties because they did not finish high school, while others are immigrants or persons suffering from learning and vision disabilities. Educational and mentoring programs throughout the US and Canada also offer instruction and support to youth in need. These programs are most appropriate for volunteers who are willing to make a more long-term commitment to working with their mentees and students.

Proliteracy Worldwide, 1320 Jamesville Ave., Syracuse, NY 13210 (☎888-528-2224 or 315-422-9121; www.proliteracy.org). The world's largest adult volunteer literacy organization, with significant chapters in the US. Tutors teach basic literacy or English for Speakers of Other Languages (ESOL) to individuals and families. Canadian volunteering through **Laubach Literacy of Canada,** 60-C Elizabeth St., Bedford QC J0J 1A0 (☎888-248-2898 or 450-248-2898; www.laubach.ca). Both programs also offer tutor training.

America's Literacy Directory, (☎800-228-8813; www.literacydirectory.org/volunteer.asp). A service of the National Institute for Literacy, this online directory allows you to search for volunteer opportunities with more than 5000 literacy programs for adults and young adults in the US.

Big Brothers Big Sisters of America, 230 N. 13th St., Philadelphia, PA 19107 (☎215-567-7000; www.bbbsa.org). This century-old organization provides mentorship, friendship, and support to hundreds of thousands of American kids. Paired "Bigs" and "Littles" work on homework together, visit museums, participate in community service, or just hang out. In Canada, contact **Big Brothers Big Sisters of Canada,** 3228 South Service Rd., Ste. 113E, Burlington ON L7N 3H8 (☎800-263-9133 or 905-639-0461; www.bbbsc.ca).

The National Mentoring Partnership, 1600 Duke St., Ste. 300, Alexandria, VA 22314 (☎703-224-2200; www.mentoring.org). Advocates for the expansion of mentoring programs with the goal of serving the 17.6 million children in the US who could benefit from mentorship relationships. Maintains a database of mentoring opportunities, including state and local mentoring partnerships and programs and volunteer centers.

STUDYING

Study abroad programs range from basic language and culture courses to college-level classes, often for credit. In order to choose a program that best fits your needs, research as much as you can before making your decision—determine costs and duration, as well as what kinds of students participate in the program and what sort of accommodations are provided.

In programs that have large groups of students who speak the same language, there is a trade-off. You may feel more comfortable in the community, but you will not have the same opportunity to practice a foreign language or to befriend other international students. For accommodations, dorm life provides a better opportunity to mingle with fellow students, but there is less of a chance to experience the

VISA INFORMATION

All foreign visitors must have a **visa** to study in the US or Canada. Travelers must also provide proof of intent to leave, like a return plane ticket or an I-94 card. Foreign students wanting to study in the US must apply for either an M-1 visa (non-academic or vocational studies) or an F-1 visa (for full-time students enrolled in an academic or language program). See http://education-usa.state.gov for further information on studying in the US. To study in Canada, students will likely need both a **temporary resident visa** and a **study permit.** See the Citizenship and Immigration Canada (CIC) website (www.cic.gc.ca/english/study) for more info. To get a visa or study permit, apply at a US or Canadian embassy or consulate in your home country. If English is not your native language, you will probably to take the Test of English as a Foreign Language (TOEFL), administered in many countries. The international students office at the institution you will be attending can give you specifics. Contact **TOEFL/TSE Publications,** P.O. Box 6151, Princeton, NJ, 08541 (☎877-863-3546; outside the US and Canada ☎609-771-7100; www.toefl.org). US **visa extensions** are sometimes attainable with a completed I-539 form; call the Bureau of Citizenship and Immigration Service's (BCIS) forms request line (☎800-870-3676) or get it online at www.immigration.gov/graphics/formsfee/forms/i-539.htm. See http://travel.state.gov/visa_services.html for more info. To extend a temporary visa for study in Canada, you must complete the form IMM-1249. Call the CIC call center at ☎888-242-2100 (in Canada only) for more info. Security measures have made the visa application process more rigorous, and more lengthy. **Apply well in advance of your travel date,** especially for visas to the US. The process may seem complex, but you must go through through the proper channels or risk deportation.

ALTERNATIVES TO TOURISM

local scene. If you live with a family, there is a potential to build lifelong friendships with natives and to experience day-to-day life in more depth, but conditions can vary greatly from family to family.

UNIVERSITIES

Most university-level study-abroad programs in the US are meant as language and culture enrichment opportunities, and therefore are conducted in English. A good resource for finding programs that cater to your particular interests is **www.studyabroad.com,** which has links to various semester-abroad programs based on a variety of criteria, including desired location and focus of study. For international students interested in university programs in Canada, **www.studyin-canada.com** offers a directory of programs, as well as information on the Canadian education system and cost of living.

In order to live the life of a real American or Canadian college student, consider a visiting student program lasting either a semester or a full year. (While some institutions have trimesters, most American universities have fall semester Sept.-Dec. and spring semester Jan.-May. The Canadian school year often ends in Apr.) The best method by far is to contact colleges and universities in your home country to see what kind of exchanges they have with those in the US and Canada; college students can often receive credit for study abroad. A more complicated option for advanced English speakers is to enroll directly in a North American institution. Each state maintains a public university system, and the US also hosts a number of reputable private universities. There are also innumerable community, professional, and technical colleges. In Canada, all universities are public, with the most notable including the University of Toronto, McGill, Queen's, and Dalhousie. Tuition costs, however, are high in the US (and in Canada for international students) and a full course of undergraduate study entails a four-year commitment.

LANGUAGE PROGRAMS

Unlike American or Canadian universities, language schools can be independently run international or local organizations or divisions of foreign universities. They rarely offer college credit, but are a good alternative to university study if you desire a deeper focus on the language or a slightly less rigorous courseload. These programs are also good for younger high school students who might not feel comfortable with older students in a university program. Some good programs include:

American Language Adventure, 2490 Cass Lake Rd., Keego Harbor, MI 48320 (☎517-599-6917; www.alaschool.com). American Language Adventures is an English immersion program that travels through various regions in the United States. Students live in tents and move from place to place while practicing conversational English.

Language Studies Canada, LSC Toronto, 124 Eglinton Ave. W., Ste. 400, Toronto, ON M46 268 (☎416-488-2200; www.lsc-canada.com). LSC offers programs in English and French in Calgary, Montreal, Toronto, and Vancouver. In addition to general language study, there are courses in Business English; some intensive study courses are accompanied by volunteer placement in Canadian businesses or tourism opportunities. Programs generally run 2-4 weeks, and homestay placement is available.

Eurocentres, 101 N. Union St., Ste. 300, Alexandria, VA 22314 (☎703-684-1494; www.eurocentres.com) or in Europe, Head Office, Seestr. 247, CH-8038 Zurich, Switzerland (☎41 1 485 50 40; fax 481 61 24). Language programs in various parts of the US and Canada for beginning to advanced students with homestays.

American Language Programs, 56 Hobbs Brook Rd., Boston, MA 02493 (☎781-888-1515; www.alp-online.com). ALP runs programs in Arizona, California, Florida, and Massachusetts that include homestay and intensive English training. $900-1080 per week (15-25hr.) for 1 person, $1600-1960 for 2 people.

Osako Sangyo University Los Angeles (OSULA) Education Center, 3921 Laurel Canyon Blvd., Studio City, CA 91604 (☎818-509-1484; www.osula.com). Offers general and intensive English or Japanese classes in a residential college setting in the suburbs of Los Angeles.

PROGRAMS IN THE ARTS

Those of a more creative persuasion can pursue artistic expression in the US—bohemian quarters of New York City and San Francisco, as well as the wide open spaces of the American interior, beckon with artistic organizations of all types.

VISUAL AND PERFORMING ARTS

New York Foundation for the Arts, 155 Avenue of the Americas, 14th fl., New York City, NY 10013 (☎212-366-6900; www.nyfa.org). From dance to music to visual arts, NYFA provides a national database of resources in the arts, including classified listings of current jobs and internship openings, and schedules for art events. The "Opportunities for Artists" link on the website posts audition notices, calls for entry, and information about workshops for artists.

The Banff Centre, 107 Tunnel Mountain Dr., Box 1020, Banff, AB T1L 1H5 (☎403-762-6100; www.banffcentre.ca). The Banff Centre provides trainings and workshops in the Canadian Rocky Mountains; dance, theater, opera, and Aboriginal art are among the

GONE PHISHIN'

Buried deep within the contents of a VW Microbus, somewhere in between soggy grilled cheese sandwiches and Zip-Loc baggies, lurks the true essence of a Phish tour. A far cry from resort-bound jet-setters, rough-and-tumble Phishheads prefer to rough it, trading first-class for night owl buses and five-star hotels for starry nights in grimy, jam-packed campgrounds. But for most, this ragamuffin spirit is the appeal of following four middle-aged men from Vermont—the thrill of traveling off-the-cuff parallels the improvisational drive of the band that has kept hundreds of thousands of "phans" salivating over their every move for 21 years.

The Phish frenzy began in the mid-80s in Burlington, VT, where the band members met at the University of Vermont. Early gigs saw the band being booed off the stage for their lengthy and often abstract jams, but they were most certainly different from most 80s music. Rejecting over-produced synth-pop for a more organic fusion of musical styles, the four friends covered everyone from the Grateful Dead to Stevie Wonder as they developed their unique sound.

Music fans, especially those in college, began to take note. The band developed a cult following in Vermont, and a loyal band of "Phishheads" followed the band from Burlington all the way to Colorado when the Phish took its first cross-country road trip in 1990. As Phish developed from a self-described "bar band on acid" to the preeminent jam band of the 1990s, Phish fans' wanderlust only grew stronger.

Cramming into Subarus and Jeep Grand Cherokees, flower children and frat boys alike trekked from town to town to see the jam all-stars hone their craft. I went to my first Phish show in 1998 at the Greek Theater in LA with my father. While his overwhelming impression was muddied by a distinctively pungent aroma permeating the venue, mine was one of sheer confusion. Who were these strange men with instruments? What were these flailing fans yelling about? And, most importantly, why didn't I know about this band? These questions burned in my mind, and over the next six years I followed the band to 25 shows on a cross-country quest to understand the essence of the Phish philosophy. En route to enlightenment, I saw parts of the US that I never would have seen, from the beautiful hills of Washington to the billowing smokestacks of New Jersey.

During my journey, I have gained a passion for the freedom of the road and the open-minded spirit of the Phish community. The feeling of being at a Phish show is truly something you have to see to believe. The parking lots outside the shows become veritable hippie shantytowns: as the circus of people rolls in, fans set up shop for however long the band will be in town, propping up tents and hawking whatever type of legal or illegal goods they can find to sustain themselves for the next few hundred miles. For newcomers, the scene along "Shakedown Street"—the epicenter of parking lot activity—can seem unsettlingly bizarre, but tour veterans find solace in the chaos: familiar faces seem to continue popping up at shows, fostering a traveler's comfort akin to meeting a friend from home in a foreign country. This sense of community is the drive behind fans' continued devotion to the band—a devotion epitomized in 1997's Phish documentary "Bittersweet Motel," which profiles two fans who rode their bikes from Richmond, VA, to Limestone, ME, for two weeks in order to see Phish's summer-ending Great Went Festival. Such is the dedication involved in tailing this fanatically followed foursome.

In the summer of 2004, I followed Phish for the last time as the band took its farewell tour, putting an end to a legendary run and saying a sentimental goodbye to its devoted fans during a two-night stint headlining the Coventry festival in northern Vermont. A hippie haven reminiscent of Woodstock, Coventry turned into Vermont's biggest city as over 70,000 stormed the festival. The circus rolled in for the last time, and feelings of sadness for a lost era were mixed with an overwhelming sense of being a part of something special. As festival organizers tried to close the gates due to massive gridlock after 30,000 people had entered, we ditched our car and joined thousands of Phish zealots on a 15 mile pilgrimage to the stage. While this massive exodus to a field of mud and cow dung might have seemed insane to an outsider, it served as one final, fitting testament to the spirit of the Phish community. With a massive case of musical withdrawal impending, the Phish "phamily" met for one last time. Together we've logged millions of miles on every form of transportation imaginable, filled campgrounds and motels, and seen every corner of the country. From start to finish, it's been one hell of a trip.

Trevor Walsh hails from Santa Monica, CA, and is a student of Government at Harvard University. He is also an aspiring lyricist and 'life counselor.'

many disciplines offered. Month-long programs tend to be pricey (approximately $2500 or more with room and meals included), but there are often work-study slots available, especially for those with prior experience.

Santa Fe Art Institute, P.O. Box 24044, Santa Fe, NM 87502 (☎505-424-5050; www.sfai.org). A world-class artistic center, the Santa Fe Art Institute offers 1-week workshops ($900, including residency and tuition), giving participants the opportunity to learn from professional resident artists in Santa Fe. Need-based scholarships are available for all workshops.

National Association of Schools of Theatre, 11250 Roger Bacon Dr., Ste. 21, Reston, VA 20190 (☎703-437-0700). Supplies a list of accredited degree- and non-degree-granting institutions in the US that offer programs in the theater.

Summer Stock is an American theater tradition: each year, small local theaters throughout the country put out a series of dramatic productions, including musicals, comedy, drama, and opera. Tickets are affordable, and many young and talented actors get their first experiences on the stage. Summer theaters are listed at www.summertheater.com; contact individual theaters to find out about auditions and performances.

FILM

New York Film Academy, 100 E. 17th St., New York City, NY 10003 (☎212-674-4300; www.nyfa.com). NYFA allows would-be actors, filmmakers, and screenwriters the chance to hone their skills on studio sets in several cities. Program lengths vary from 1 week to 1 year, with classes in acting, screenwriting, digital imaging, filmmaking, comedy, and 3-D animation. Program costs $1500-25,000.

University of Southern California School of Cinema-Television, Summer Production Workshop, 850 W. 34th St., Los Angeles, CA 90089 (☎213-740-1742; www.usc.edu/schools/cntv/programs/spw). Boasting a luminous alumni list that includes Jedi-boy George Lucas, screenwriter John Milius *(Apocalypse Now)*, and producer Laura Ziskin *(Spider-Man)*, the world-renowned film school offers summer workshops with classes in writing, digital imaging, directing, and producing. University housing is available, as are classes for students who have already logged some hours (or years) in the industry. Students enrolled in the program also have access to free seminars, workshops, and screenings.

Indiewire.com, 601 W. 26th St., Ste. 1150, New York City, NY 10001 (☎212-329-3710; indiewire.com). Explore the student and independent film scene in the US while you get the low-down on upcoming film festivals, lectures, and symposia. Classifieds post paid and unpaid positions for actors, crew, writers, and producers; you can also meet and find collaborators for your own projects.

WRITING AND SPOKEN WORD

Poets and Writers, Incorporated, 2035 Westwood Blvd., Ste. 211, Los Angeles, CA 90025 (☎310-481-7195; www.pw.org). Provides links to writing programs at universities in the US, as well as an extensive list of conferences and residencies for writers.

Writer's Colonies provide an opportunity to pursue the written word without distraction. Residencies range from 1 week to several months; some programs include workshops and conferences. Costs generally cover room and board, though fellowships are occasionally available. A directory of several writer's colonies is available at www.poewar.com/articles/colonies.htm; for a more comprehensive listing of artist's retreats, try *Artist's Communities: A Directory of Residencies in the United States that Offer Time and Space for Creativity,* by Tricia Snell (Allworth Press 2000).

Poetry Slam Incorporated, 11462 East Ln., Whitmore Lake, MI 48189 (☎810-231-5435; www.poetryslam.com). All across the country, poets perform 3-5 minutes of their work in cafes and bars, and are judged by audience members on performance and writing ability. Poetry Slam Incorporated compiles a massive list of these venues; most have at least 1 night a week devoted to poetry slams or readings. Admission prices range from free to a small cover charge; you may have to sign up in advance to perform.

ARCHITECTURE AND DESIGN

Arcosanti, HC 74 BOX 4136, Mayer, AZ 86333 (☎928-632-7135; www.arcosanti.org.) Founded by Frank Lloyd Wright's disciple Paolo Soleri (who still lives here), Arcosanti is an experimental community 70 mi. north of Phoenix based on Soleri's theory of "arcology"–the symbiotic relationship between architecture and ecology. It hosts 1-week ($485) and 5-week workshops ($1175) in which participants help expand the settlement while learning about Soleri's project and developing their skills at construction and planning. An expenses-paid 3-month internship is available for those with some background in construction or architecture after they have completed the 5-week workshop.

Ecological Design Institute, 245 Gate Five Rd., Sausalito, CA 94965 (☎415-332-5806; www.ecodesign.org). Integrating technology and nature in their vision of green design, EDI promotes education for sustainability, highlighting design projects along the West Coast worth investigating. Their website includes a list of schools and institutes in the US that offer workshops and classes in ecologically friendly design and construction.

WORKING

ALTERNATIVES TO TOURISM

VISA INFORMATION

All foreign visitors are required to have a **visa** if they intend to work in the US or Canada. In addition, travelers must provide proof of intent to leave, such as a return plane ticket or an I-94 card. A **work permit** (or "green card") is also required. Your employer must obtain this document, usually by demonstrating that you have skills that locals lack. Friends in the US can sometimes help expedite work permits or arrange work-for-accommodations exchanges. **To obtain both visas and work permits,** contact a US or Canadian embassy or consulate (see **Embassies and Consulates,** p. 31). Visa extensions in the US are sometimes attainable with a completed I-539 form; request forms from the Bureau of Citizenship and Immigration Service (☎800-870-3676; http://uscis.gov/graphics/formsfee/forms/index.htm.) See http://travel.state.gov/visa/index.html for more information. In Canada, visa extensions require the completion of form IMM-1249. Call the CIC call center at ☎888-242-2100 (in Canada only) for more information. Recent security measures have made the visa application process more rigorous, and therefore more lengthy. **Apply well in advance of your travel date.** The process may seem complex, but it's critical that you go through the proper channels—the alternative is potential deportation.

As with volunteering, work opportunities tend to fall into two categories. Some travelers want long-term jobs that allow them to get to know another part of the world as a member of the community, while others seek out short-term work to finance the next leg of their travels. In the US and Canada, people looking to work long-term should consider exchange programs. Short-term work is most often found in the service industry and agriculture.

Regardless of whether you are looking for temporary work or something more permanent, a good place to start your search is the local newspaper, which is usually the best source of up-to-date job information. Internet search engines like **www.monster.com** are also helpful. Before signing on, be sure you have the correct visa and working papers (see **Visa Information,** above).

LONG-TERM WORK

If you're planning on spending a substantial amount of time (3 months or more) working in North America, search for a job well in advance. **Internships,** usually for college students, are a good way to segue into working abroad. Although they are often unpaid or poorly paid, many say the experience is well worth it. International placement agencies are often the easiest way to find employment abroad.

JOB PLACEMENTS

Programs that give travelers the opportunity to work overseas take on much of the arduous job search process and paperwork. However, many of the jobs have extremely low salaries, and days off may be sporadic. Application fees may be high, or you may need to prove you can support yourself until your first paycheck. Be wary of advertisements or companies that claim the ability to get you a job abroad for a fee—often, the same listings are available online or in newspapers, or are out-of-date. Reputable placement programs vary in the perks they offer; some arrange medical and travel insurance, provide reduced-cost or free flights to and from your work destination, provide 24hr. support, and secure visas that will include time for travel in North America after your work has ended. It's best, if going through an organization, to use one that's well-known, and apply far in advance of your placement. Some possibilities include:

Alliances Abroad Group, Inc., 1221 S. Mopac Expwy., Ste. 250, Austin, TX 78746, USA (☎512-457-8062; www.alliancesabroad.com). Organizes summer work in the service industry for university students ages 18-28.

Council Exchanges, 52 Poland St., London W1F 7AB, UK (☎44 020 7478 2000, US 888-268-6245; www.councilexchanges.org), charges a fee (around $600) for arranging short-term working authorizations (generally valid for 3-6 months) and provides extensive information on different job opportunities in the US and Canada.

British Universities North American Club (BUNAC), 16 Bowling Green La., London EC1R 0QH, UK (☎44 020 7251 3472, US 203-264-0901; www.bunac.com). Arranges short- and longer-term job placements, visas, and work authorization in the US and Canada for individuals 18+. Work placement includes summer jobs, work training programs, and camp counselor positions. Some programs are open to non-students.

Camp America, 37a Queen's Gate, London SW7 5HR, UK (☎44 020 7581 7373, US 203-399-5000; www.campamerica.co.uk). Summer camp jobs are popular in the US and Canada; most last about 9 weeks and can include time afterward for travel. Camp America places counselors in a variety of camps, including religious camps and camps for disadvantaged or special-needs children. Positions in service areas, such as kitchen or maintenance, are also available. **Camp Counselors USA,** 2330 Marinship Way, Ste. 250, Sausalito, CA 94965 USA (☎415-339-2728; www.ccusa.com) also places counselors, and has positions in specialty areas such as outdoor sports and the arts.

JOBS YOU ARRANGE

Looking beyond job placement programs may be the best way to find a job opportunity that fits your needs, skills, and time. However, most job service and search engines do not assist potential employees in acquiring visas or work permits, which you must have before applying for temporary work or internships. Keep in mind that individual employers may have specific policies with regard to non-US or Canadian citizens, and allow for extra time to process applications.

About Jobs, 180 State Rd., Ste. 2U, Sagamore Beach, MA 02562 (☎508-888-6889; www.aboutjobs.com), has summer jobs, internships, and resort work in North America.

Cool Jobs Canada, 173 Silvercrest Dr., Waterloo, ON N2I 8B1 (☎519-576-2245 or 800-576-9138; www.cooljobscanada.com). A massive compilation of up-to-date tourism and hospitality jobs in Canada. Search listings or post your resume on their site.

Cool Works, P.O. Box 272, 511 Highway 89, Gardiner, MT 59030 (☎406-848-2380; www.coolworks.com). Listings of seasonal (mostly summer) jobs in the US. Options include work at state parks, ski resorts, camps, ranches, and amusement parks.

AU PAIR WORK

Au pairs are typically women, ages 18-27, who work as live-in nannies and do light housework in foreign countries in exchange for room, board, and a small stipend. Most former au pairs speak favorably of their experience and say that it allowed them to get to know a foreign country without the high expenses of traveling. Drawbacks, however, often include long hours and the mediocre pay. In the US, weekly salaries typically fall below $200, with at least 45hr. of work expected. Au pairs are expected to speak English and have at least 200hr. of childcare experience. Much of the au pair experience depends on the family you're placed with. The agencies below are a good starting point for looking for au pair work.

Childcare International, Ltd., Trafalgar House, Grenville Pl., London NW7 3SA, UK (☎44 020 8906 3116; fax 8906 3461; www.childint.co.uk).

InterExchange, 161 6th Ave., New York City, NY 10013, USA (☎212-924-0446; fax 924-0575; www.interexchange.org).

SHORT-TERM WORK

Traveling for long periods of time can get expensive, so many travelers do odd jobs for a few weeks at a time to make some extra cash for another month or two of touring. *It is illegal to take a paid job without a work permit or visa.* A popular alternative is to work several hours a day at a hostel in exchange for free or discounted room and/or board. Most often, short-term jobs are found by word of mouth, or by talking to the owner of a hostel or restaurant. Due to the high turnover in the tourism industry, many places are eager for help, if only temporary.

ALTERNATIVES TO TOURISM

NEW ENGLAND

New England fancied itself an intellectual and political center long before the States were United, and still does today. Students and scholars funnel into New England's colleges each fall, and town meetings still evoke the spirit of popular government that once inspired the American Revolution. A land of rich heritage, New England's beautiful landmarks recount every step of the country's break from "Old" England. Though the region's unpredictable climate can be particularly dismal during the harsh, wet winter from November to March, today's visitors find

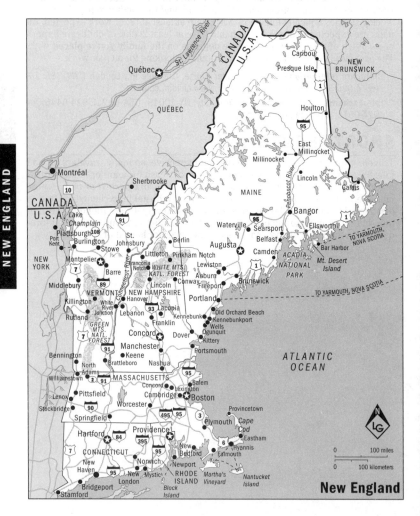

New England

adventure in the rough edges that troubled early settlers, flocking to New England's salty coastline to sun on the sand or heading to the slopes and valley's of the Green and White Mountains to ski, hike, bike, and canoe. In the fall, brilliant foliage transforms the region into a kaleidoscope of color.

HIGHLIGHTS OF NEW ENGLAND

SEAFOOD. Bar Harbor, ME (p. 87), serves the freshest lobster around, and don't forget to try New England clam "chowda" before you leave.

SKIING. Enthusiasts flock to the mountains of New Hampshire and Vermont; the most famous resorts include Smuggler's Notch (p. 103) and Killington (p. 103).

COLONIAL LANDMARKS. They're everywhere, but a walk along the Freedom Trail in Boston, MA (p. 119), is a great place to start.

SCENIC NEW ENGLAND. Take a drive along Rte. 100 in the fall, when the foliage is at its most striking, or hike the Appalachian Trail (p. 94) for a view on foot.

THE ARTS. Heavenly music at Tanglewood in the Berkshires (p. 143) and countless university museums provide some of the best modern art in America.

MAINE

Nearly a thousand years ago, Leif Erikson and his band of Viking explorers set foot on the coast of Maine. Moose roamed the sprawling evergreen wilderness, the cry of the Maine coon cat echoed through towering mountains, and countless lobsters crawled in the ocean deep. A millennium has changed little. Forests still cover nearly 90% of Maine's land, an area larger than all the other New England states. The people of Maine enjoy a life of fishing, skiing, and, in the summers, gallivanting in the artsy towns that run up the coast between the wilderness and the sea.

⓰ PRACTICAL INFORMATION

Capital: Augusta.

Visitor Info: Maine Tourism Information, 59 State House Station, Augusta 04333 (☎207-623-0363 or 888-624-6345; www.visitmaine.com). **Maine Information Center,** in Kittery, 3 mi. north of the Maine-New Hampshire bridge (☎207-439-1319; open daily July to early Oct. 8am-6pm, mid-Oct. to June 9am-5:30pm). **Bureau of Parks and Lands,** State House Station #22 (AMHI, Harlow Bldg.), Augusta 04333 (☎207-287-3821; www.state.me.us/doc/parks). **Maine Forest Service,** Department of Conservation, State House Station #22, Augusta 04333 (☎207-287-2791).

Postal Abbreviation: ME. **Sales Tax:** 5%.

MAINE COAST

The Maine coast meanders 288 miles along the Atlantic Ocean, with a multitude of rocky inlets and promontories that make for eye-catching scenery. The port towns are strung together by the two-lane U.S. 1, the region's only option for accessing most coastal towns north of Portland. Although driving your own vehicle is the best way to truly explore the coast, be prepared to take your time—the traffic pace is often slow in the summer, especially through towns and villages.

PORTLAND ☎207

Shining like a beacon in a cold dark sea, Portland is the largest port town in all of Maine. Trapped between forested land and a wild sea, Portland struggles to be an urban center in an otherwise rural state. While it has a large industrial sector, Portland is also a center for the arts and a well-preserved relic of colonial times. In summer, the streets are filled with the exuberant sounds of parades and festivals. Meanwhile, laughter can be heard long into the night in the old port district, where pubs beckon the city's spirited youth culture to set aflame even the coldest night.

■■ ☑ **ORIENTATION AND PRACTICAL INFORMATION.** Downtown is located in the middle of the peninsula along **Congress Street,** between State St. and Pearl St. A few blocks south, between Commercial and Middle St. on the waterfront, lies the **Old Port.** These two districts contain most of the city's sights and attractions. **I-295** (off I-95) forms the northwestern boundary of the city. **Amtrak,** 100 Thompson Point Rd., on Connector Rd., off Congress St. (☎800-872-7245; www.thedowneaster.com), runs to Boston (2¾hr., 4 per day, $21). **Concord Trailways** (☎828-1151; office open daily 4:30am-9:30pm), in the same building, runs to Bangor (2½hr., 3 per day, $22) and Boston (2hr., 12 per day, $18). Metro buses run to and from the station (M-Sa every 20min., Su every hr.). **Greyhound/ Vermont Transit,** 950 Congress St., on the western outskirts of town (☎772-6587), runs to Bangor (2½-3½hr., 5 per day, $20) and Boston (2hr., 6 per day, $15). *Be cautious here at night; the neighborhood is not entirely safe.* **Scotia Prince Cruises,** 468 Commercial St., sends ferries to Yarmouth, NS, from the Portland International Marine Terminal, on Commercial St., near the Casco Bay Bridge. Boats run May to late October. Ferries depart Portland at 8pm for the 11hr. trip. (☎775-5611 or 800-845-4073; www.scotiaprince.com. Cabins available as well as a variety of fare options; see brochure available at the visitors center, or check online. Reservations strongly recommended.) **Metro Bus** services downtown Portland. Routes run 5:30am-11:45pm, though individual routes may start later or end earlier; brochures are available at the visitors center. (☎774-0351. $1, seniors with Medicare card $0.50, under 5 free.) **Visitor Info: Visitors Information Bureau,** 245 Commercial St., between Union and Cross St. (☎800-306-4193; www.gotoportland.com. Open M-F 8am-5pm, Sa 10am-5pm.) **Internet Access: Portland Public Library,** 5 Monument Sq. (☎871-1700. Open M, W, F 9am-6pm, Tu and Th noon-9pm, Sa 9am-5pm. Free.) **Post Office:** 400 Congress St. (☎871-8464. Open M-F 8am-7pm, Sa 9am-1pm.) **Postal Code:** 04101. **Area Code:** 207.

☵ **ACCOMMODATIONS.** Portland has some inexpensive accommodations during the winter, but summer prices jump steeply, especially on weekends. Lodging in the smaller towns up and down the coast can be a less expensive option. Three miles from downtown, the **Budget Inn Motel ❸,** 634 Main St. off Rte. 1/Main St. in South Potland, offers clean rooms at reasonable prices. (☎207-773 5722. Rooms $55-75.) Closer to downtown, **The Inn at St. John ❹,** 939 Congress St., may be surrounded by several run-down buildings, but inside, guests are welcomed by elegant decor and old-fashioned hospitality. (☎773-6481 or 800-636-9127. Continental breakfast included. Bike storage, free local calls, and free parking. Rooms with private bath available. Singles or doubles in summer M-Th $70-135, F-Su $115-175; winter $55-100/$60-115.) **Wassamki Springs ❶,** 56 Saco St., in Scarborough, is the closest campground to Portland. Take I-95 south to 22 west, exit 46. Winnebagos and brightly colored tents cluster around a lake encircled by sandy beaches. (☎839-4276. Free showers and flush toilets. Reserve 2 weeks in advance, especially July-Aug. Open May to mid-Oct. Sites with water and electricity for 2 adults $34, with hookup $36; each additional person $5; lakefront sites $3 extra.)

◻ FOOD. Portland's harbor overflows with high-quality seafood, but non-aquatic and vegetarian fare are easy to find. The homemade, organic pizzas at the **Flatbread Company ❸,** 72 Commercial St., are tasty and healthy treats ($7.75-13.50). Enjoy the ocean view as your meal is fired in a huge clay oven. (☎772-8777. Open in summer M-Th 11:30am-10pm, F-Sa 11am-10:30pm; winter M-Th 11:30am-9pm, F-Sa 11:30am-10pm.) **Federal Spice ❶,** 225 Federal St., just off Congress St., seasons all its wraps and soft tacos (all under $6) with fiery Caribbean, South American, and Asian ingredients. Enjoy your meal under brightly colored walls and groovy neon lights. (☎774-6404. Open M-Sa 11am-9pm.) **Gilbert's Chowder House ❷,** 92 Commercial St., is the local choice for seafood. A large bowl of chowder in a bread bowl ($7-11) is a meal in itself. (☎871-5636. Entrees $10-21. Open June-Sept. Su-Th 11am-10pm, F-Sa 11am-11pm; Oct.-May call for hours.) The **Portland Public Market,** at Preble St. and Cumberland Ave., three blocks from Monument Square, provides ethnic foods, seafood, and baked goods from over 20 small food vendors. (☎228-2000; www.portlandmarket.com. Open M-Sa 9am-7pm, Su 10am-5pm.)

◻ SIGHTS. Offshore islands with secluded beaches are just a ferry ride from the city proper. **Casco Bay Lines,** on State Pier near the corner of Commercial and Franklin, runs daily to **Long Island, Peaks Island,** and a few other islands. (☎774-7871; www.cascobaylines.com. Long Island: Operates M-Sa 5am-9:30pm, Su 7:45am-9:30pm. Round-trip $8, seniors and ages 5-9 $4. Peaks Island: Operates M-Sa 5:45am-11:30pm, Su 7:45am-11:30pm. Round-trip $6, seniors and ages 5-9 $3.) Peaks Island has great biking and kayaking, and holds a reggae concert every Monday in summer at Jones Landing. **Brad's Recycled Bike Shop,** 115 Island Ave., rents bikes. (☎766-5631. Open daily 10am-5pm. $5 per hr., $8.50 for 3hr., $12 per day.)

Try **Two Lights State Park,** across the Casco Bay Bridge accessed from State or York St., then south along Rte. 77 to Cape Elizabeth, for a spot to picnic or walk alongside the ocean. (☎799-5871; www.state.me.us/doc/parks. $2.50.) A trip to the still-functioning **Portland Head Light** in **Fort Williams Park** is a scenic detour worth the time. From 77 N turn right at the flashing signal onto Shore Rd. and proceed to the park. The **Portland Observatory,** 138 Congress St., the last maritime signal tower in the US, offers unrivaled views of the city and an excellent historical tour. (☎774-5561; www.portlandlandmarks.org. Open daily 10am-5pm; last tour 4:40pm. Admission and tour $5, ages 6-16 $3.) It takes about eight days to brew a batch of beer at the **Shipyard Brewing Co.,** 86 Newbury St., but it will only take 30min. to tour the brewery and try a free sample. (☎761-0807. Tours every 30min. in summer M-F 3-5pm, Sa-Su noon-5pm; winter W-F 3-5pm, Sa noon-5pm. Free.)

The **Portland Museum of Art,** 7 Congress Sq., at the intersection of Congress, High, and Free St., holds a fascinating display of 19th-century American art. The museum includes the recently restored McLellan House, originally built in 1801, as well as a stunning collection of Winslow Homer paintings. (☎775-6148 or 800-639-4067; www.portlandmuseum.org. Open June to mid-Oct. M-W and Sa-Su 10am-5pm, Th-F 10am-9pm; mid-Oct. to May closed M. $8, students and seniors $6, ages 6-12 $2; F 5-9pm free. Wheelchair accessible.) The **Wadsworth-Longfellow House,** 489 Congress St., was the home of 19th-century poet Henry Wadsworth Longfellow. Excellently restored, it serves as a rare window into the life of the poet and offers exhibits on 18th- and 19th-century social history and American literature. (☎774-1822, ext. 208; www.mainehistory.org. Open June-Oct. M-Sa 10am-4pm, Su noon-4pm. $7, students and seniors $6, ages 5-17 $3. Price includes admission to a small neighboring history museum with rotating exhibits. Tours every 30-40min.)

◻◻ ENTERTAINMENT AND NIGHTLIFE. Signs for theatrical productions decorate Portland, and schedules are available at the visitors center (p. 84). The **Portland Symphony** presents concerts renowned throughout the Northeast. (☎842-0800.

Performances take place in the Merrill Auditorium, 477 Congress St. Tickets through Porttix, online at www.porttix.com, or at 20 Myrtle St. Open M-Sa noon-6pm. Occasional 50% student discount.) Info on Portland's jazz, blues, and club scene is available in the *Portland Phoenix* and *FACE*, which are both free and widely distributed. During the last week of spring, the three-day **Old Port Festival** (☎772-6828) fills the blocks from Federal to Commercial St. with parades, music, and free public entertainment before a flood of summer tourists arrives. Throughout the summer, the **Weekday Music Series** (☎772-6828; www.portlandmaine.com) hosts a bands in Post Office Sq. between Middle and Exchange St.

The Old Port area, known as "the strip"—especially **Fore Street** between Union and Exchange St.—livens up after dark, as patrons from countless bars overflow into the cobblestone streets. **Brian Boru**, the red-painted building at 57 Center St., provides a mellow pub scene with top-notch nachos for $6. (☎780-1506. Su $2 pints. Open daily 11:30am-1am.) **Gritty MacDuff's**, 396 Fore St., brews beer (pints $2.50) and entertains a local crowd with live music Saturday and Sunday nights. (☎772-2739. Open daily 11:30am-1am.) **Una Wine Bar & Lounge,** 505 Fore St., has a casual attitude, mixing speciality martinis and serving wine by the taste, glass ($5-10), or bottle. (☎828-0300. Tapas $3-15. Open daily 4:30pm-1am).

SOUTH OF PORTLAND   ☎207

KENNEBUNKPORT
Just 20 miles south of Portland, Kennebunk and its coastal counterpart 8 mi. east, **Kennebunkport,** are popular hideaways for the wealthy—Kennebunkport grew famous as the summer home of former President George Bush, but its true charm lies in the little art galleries and bookstores that fill the town. **Old Salt's Pantry ❶,** 5 Ocean Ave., provides breakfast and lunch fare with a homemade touch. The enormous muffins ($1.50) are not to be missed. (☎467-4966. Open daily 9:30am-5:30pm.) For a quick lunch, **Aunt Marie's ❶,** 13 Ocean Ave., serves amazing freshly squeezed lemonade ($2.50) and great burgers ($3.50. ☎967 0711. Hours vary.) For surfers, swimmers, and sunbathers, five **public beaches** in the area are a short trip from town. (Parking fees depend upon beach, free to $10 per day, $20 per week.) Narrated scenic cruises aboard the **Deep Water II** offer glimpses of wildlife and historic sites along the coast. (☎967-5595. 1½hr. $15, seniors $12.50, ages 3-12 $7.50. Ticket booth on Ocean Ave. in front of The Landing Restaurant.) The 55 ft., gaff-rigged **Schooner Eleanor,** leaving from Arundel Wharf, Ocean Ave., provides a relaxed 2hr. yachting experience. (☎967-8809. $38. Call for reservations and times.) The **Kennebunk-Kennebunkport Chamber of Commerce,** 17 U.S. 9/Western Ave., in Kennebunkport, has a free area guide. (☎967-0857; www.kkcc.maine.org. Open in summer M-F 9am-5pm.) The Chamber of Commerce runs a **hospitality center,** 2 Union Center, next to Ben & Jerry's. (☎967-0857. Open M-F 10am-9pm, Sa 9am-9pm, Su 10am-8pm.)

NORTHERN MAINE COAST   ☎207
Much like the coastal region south of Portland, the north offers the traveler eye-catching cliffs, windswept ocean panoramas, and quintessential New England small towns—for a price. Lodging in L.L. Bean country isn't cheap, but passing through allows you to taste the area's proverbial milk and honey without buying the cow or the hive. U.S. 1 is northern coastal Maine's only thoroughfare, and summer traffic barely creeps along through the many small roadside hamlets.

CAMDEN
In the summer, khaki-clad crowds mingle with the sea captains of Camden, 100 mi. north of Portland, docking their yachts alongside the tall-masted schooners in Penobscot Bay. If you don't have a private yacht, 2hr. **cruises** sail from the public

landing, offering views of the many lighthouses and the abundant wildlife. (Schooner Olad ☎ 236-2323; www.maineschooners.com. $27. Windjammer Surprise ☎ 236-4687; www.camdenmainesailing.com. $28.) The **Camden-Rockport Lincolnville Chamber of Commerce,** located just ashore from the public landing, gives helpful information and provides an informative guide to the area. (☎ 236-4404 or 800-223-5459; www.camdenme.org. Open mid-May to mid-Oct. M-F 9am-5pm, Sa 10am-5pm, Su 10am-4pm; mid-Oct. to mid-May closed Su.) The **Camden Hills State Park ❶,** 1¼ mi. north of town on U.S. 1, offers over 80 wooded sites, but is almost always full in summer. Sites are usually available for arrivals before 2pm. This secluded retreat also offers 25 mi. of trails, including a popular lookout from the top of Mt. Battie. (☎ 236-3109, reservations 800-332-1501 in ME only, 287-3824 out of state; www.campwithme.com. Free showers. Park information available at the office at the entrance to the campground, open 7am-10pm. Open mid-May to mid-Oct. Sites $20, ME residents $15; reservations $2 per day; day-use $3.) The **Good Guest House ❹,** 50 Elm St., offers two appealing rooms at reasonable rates. (☎ 236-2139. Private bath, full breakfast. Double bed $65, king size $75.) **Cappy's Chowder House ❸,** 1 Main St., offers up local seafood specialties (entrees $10-14) and homemade pies from its bakery. (☎ 236-2254. Open daily 11am-11pm, kitchen closes at 10pm.) **The Camden Deli ❷,** 37 Main St., stacks a variety of sandwiches at reasonable prices. An outdoor deck overlooking the harbor and a full bar on the second floor with daily drink specials make this an excellent option. (☎ 236-8343. Open daily 7am-9pm.)

Maine Sports, on U.S. 1 in Rockport, just south of Camden, rents and sells a wide array of boats. (☎ 236-7120 or 800-722-0826. Open mid-June to Aug. daily 9am-8pm; Sept. to mid-June M-Sa 9am-6pm, Su 10am-5pm. Single kayaks $35-50 per day; doubles $45-65. Canoes $35-40 per day.) The **Maine State Ferry Service,** 5 mi. north of Camden in Lincolnville, floats to Islesboro Island, a quiet residential island. (☎ 800-491-4883. 20min.; 5-9 per day, last return trip 4:30pm. Round-trip $5.25, with bike $10.25, car and driver $15.) The ferry also has an agency at 517A Main St., on U.S. 1 in Rockland, that runs to Vinalhaven and North Haven. (☎ 596-2202. Rates and schedules change with weather; call ahead.)

MT. DESERT ISLAND ☎ 207

Roughly half of Mt. Desert Island is covered by Acadia National Park, which harbors some of the last protected marine, mountain, and forest environments on the New England coast. Sweetly scented air, clean icy waters, stunning vistas, and an abundance of wildlife, including the peregrine falcon, await the many tourists who frequent the island each summer. Bar Harbor, on the eastern side, is by far the most crowded and glitzy part of the island. Once a summer hamlet for the affluent, the town now welcomes a motley crowd of vacation-seekers. Despite the exodus of the well-heeled wealthy, the town still maintains its overpriced traditions.

■▮ **ORIENTATION AND PRACTICAL INFORMATION.** Mt. Desert Island is shaped roughly like a 16 mi. long and 13 mi. wide lobster claw. It promises not to hurt you. Rte. 3 reaches the island from the north and runs south to Bar Harbor, becoming Mount Desert St. and then Main St. Mount Desert St. and Cottage St. are the major streets for shops, restaurants, and bars in Bar Harbor. Continuing on Rte. 3, **Seal Harbor** rests on the southeast corner of the island. **Northeast Harbor** is a short jaunt south on Rte. 198, near the cleft. Across Somes Sound on Rte. 102, **Southwest Harbor** is where fishing, lobster trapping, and shipbuilding thrive. Route 102 meanders through the western half of the island, while Rte. 3 circles the eastern half. There is a $20 park pass for cars.

Greyhound (☎ 288-3211) leaves Bar Harbor once daily from the Villager Motel, 207 Main St., for Boston (7hr., $41) via Bangor (1½hr., $11). **Beal & Bunker** (☎ 244-3575; open late June to early Sept. daily 8am-4:30pm; call for winter hours) runs ferries

NEW ENGLAND

NOT THROUGH-HIKING YET

Stretching 2160 mi. from Mt. Katahdin, ME, to Springer Mountain, GA, the Appalachian Trail (AT) follows the Appalachian Mountains along the eastern United States. Use of the AT is free, although only foot travelers may traverse it. The trail cuts through 14 states, 8 national forests, and 6 national parks. Generally, the AT is very accessible, crossed by roads along its entire length except for the northernmost 100 mi. (see map, p. 94).

Although many sections make excellent day-hikes or overnights, about 2500 "through-hikers" attempt a continuous hike of the AT annually. Three-sided shelters (first come, first served) dot the trail, spaced about a day's journey apart. Hikers take advantage of streams and nearby towns to stock up on water and supplies. White blazes on rocks and trees mark the length of the main trail, while blue blazes mark side trails.

Matthew Shomburg, a backcountry ranger in New Hampshire, told us about his experience hiking the trail.

LG: So what inspired you to hike the Appalachian Trail?

A: My dad was a schoolteacher so we always had the summers off for hiking, canoeing, and fishing, but going up to Baxter State Park (Mt. Katahdin), I got to see some "through-hikers" and hike on the Appalachian Trail.

from the Northeast Harbor town dock to Great Cranberry Island (15min.; 6 per day; $14, under 12 $7). **Bay Ferries,** 121 Eden St. (☎288-3079; www.catferry.com), runs to Yarmouth, NS. (3hr.; 1-2 per day; $55, seniors $50, ages 5-17 $25; cars $95, bikes $10. Car price does not include passengers. Reservations recommended; $5 fee for reservations. Ticket shop and tourist information in Bar Harbor, 4 Cottage St. ☎288-3395. Open daily 10am-9pm.) Free **Island Explorer** buses depart from Bar Harbor Green for the park and its campgrounds, and run about every 30min. from each stop. *Acadia Weekly,* free and widely available in Bar Harbor, has schedules. **Acadia Bike & Canoe,** 48 Cottage St., in Bar Harbor, rents bikes, canoes, and kayaks, and leads sea kayaking tours. (☎288-9605, tours 800-526-8615. Open May-Oct. daily 8am-6pm. Bikes $15 per half-day, $20 per day; children $12. Canoes $30 per day, $25 each additional day. One-person sea kayaks $45 per day, tandems $55.)

Acadia National Park Visitors Center, 3 mi. north of Bar Harbor on Rte. 3, has a 3-D topographical map, a small bookstore, and rangers ready and willing to help. A basic 15min. video introducing the park is shown every 30min. (☎288-5262. Open daily mid-June to mid-Sept. 8am-6pm; mid-Apr. to mid-June and mid-Sept. to Oct. 8am-4:30pm.) The **Park Headquarters,** 3 mi. west of Bar Harbor on Rte. 233, provides visitor info during the low-season. (☎288-3338. Open M-F 8am-4:30pm.) **Bar Harbor Chamber of Commerce,** 93 Cottage St. (☎288-5103; open June-Oct. M-F 8am-5pm, Nov.-May M-F 8am-4pm), operates an **info booth** at 1 Harbor Place, on the town pier. (Open mid-May to mid-Oct. daily 9am-5pm.) **Emergency: Acadia National Park Law Enforcement** (☎288-3369). **Hotlines: Downeast Sexual Assault Helpline** (☎800-228-2470; operates 24hr.). **Internet Access: The Opera House,** 27 Cottage St. (☎288-3509. Open daily May-June 8am-11pm.; July-Oct. 7am-11pm. $2.50 first 15min., $0.10 each additional min.) **Post Office:** 55 Cottage St. (☎288-3122. Open M-F 8am-4:30pm, Sa 9am-noon.) **Postal Code:** 04609. **Area Code:** 207.

⚓ **ACCOMMODATIONS.** Though grand hotels recall the island's exclusive resort days, budget-friendly motels dot **Route 3** north of Bar Harbor. The newly renovated and sparkling clean ▧**Bar Harbor Youth Hostel ❶,** 321 Main St., accommodates 32 people in two dorm rooms, an annex dorm, and one private room with private half-bath that houses four people. A state-of-the-art kitchen, international book swap, open mic for karaoke, organic garden, deck and grill, and free movie nights keep travelers entertained. Ron, the friendly manager, dubs it the "cleanest hostel in the world"— and he's been around. (☎288-5587. Maid service. Linen free. Check-in 5-8:30pm. Lockout 10am-5pm. Curfew 11pm. Reservations accepted if pre-payment as a check or money order is sent to P.O. Box 32, Bar Harbor. Open May-Nov. $21, nonmembers $25; private room $75.) At **Hearthside ❺**, 7 High St., themed rooms provide both charm and comfort. (☎288-4533. A/C and private bath; some rooms have fireplaces or balconies. Rooms in summer $100-150; low-season $70-100.)

Camping spots cover the island, especially on **Routes 102** and **198**, well west of town. **White Birches Campground ❶**, in Southwest Harbor, on Seal Cove Rd. 1 mi. west of Rte. 102, has 60 widely spaced, wooded sites in a remote location that is ideal for hiking. (☎244-3797 or 800-716-0727. Free hot showers, bathrooms, and heated pool. Coin-operated laundry. Reservations recommended, especially July-Aug. Open daily mid-May to mid-Oct. 8am-8pm. Sites for 1-4 people $21, with hookup $25; weekly $126/$150; each additional person $4.) **Acadia National Park campgrounds** include **Blackwoods ❶**, 5 mi. south of Bar Harbor on Rte. 3. Nestled within the thick birch forests of Acadia, Blackwoods is located in the heart of the park. The 300 wooded sights are tightly packed in summer, but when the throngs depart, the charm of the campground's thick, dark woods returns, as do the larger wildlife. (☎800-365-2267. No hookups. Coin-operated showers available at private facility located just outside of the campground. Reservations recommended in summer. Mid-Mar. to Oct. $20; call for low-season rates.)

◖ FOOD. Watch some flicks and munch on a few slices, at **◼Reel Pizza ❸**, 33 Kennebec Pl., at the end of Rodick off Main St. This movie theater/pizzeria shows two films each evening for $5 and serves creative pizza pies ($8-20) such as the "Godfather," which is rich with artichoke, garlic, tomato, and onion. Three rows of the "theater" are comfy couches and chairs. (☎288-3828. Open daily 5pm to end of last screening.) No frills **◼Beal's ❸**, off Main St. in Northeast Harbor, at the end of Clark Point Rd., offers lobster at superb prices on an outdoor patio overlooking the harbor. (☎244-3202 or 800-245-7178. Lobster $8.50 per lb. Open daily May-Oct. 7am-8pm; Nov.-Apr. 7am-4pm. Seafood sold daily year-round 9am-5pm.) **Freddie's Route 66 Restaurant ❸**, 21 Cottage St., is crammed with 1950s memorabilia. The menu includes an excellent barbecue chicken sandwich and giant burgers that cost $8-12. (☎288-3708. Open mid-May to mid-Oct. daily 11am-3pm and 4:30-10pm.) **Ben and Bill's Chocolate Emporium ❶**, 66 Main St., near Cottage St., boasts 48 flavors of homemade ice cream, including—no kidding—lobster. (☎288-3281. Fudge $12 per lb. Cones $3-4. Open mid-Feb. to Jan. daily 9am-11:30pm.)

Just to be able to go from Georgia to Maine, go 2165 mi., to spend 5 or 6 months, whatever it takes to get there, would be an incredible experience. I wanted to see the country and meet people along the way. I didn't know if I could do it but I definitely wanted to try. It was one of those goals that was in the back of my mind. Seeing through-hikers, talking to people, and hiking in the White Mountains, I knew it would be a great adventure.

LG: Can you describe your relationship with other through-hikers?

A: Many hikers start out alone, and end alone, but along the way you meet many other through-hikers. They are helpful and friendly—after all, we all had the same goal in mind, a common bond. When you do meet other through-hikers, it works like a slinky. You often go ahead of a group, but when you take time to rest they pull ahead of you. But with each passing, you feel close to them and want to do anything you can to make their hike better. It gave me a lot of faith in humankind.

LG: What was the best region of the Appalachian Trail during your experience and how did it affect you?

A: I love hiking above the treeline and swimming and fishing in lakes and rivers. The White Mountains and Maine give the best opportunity to do that, and that is why it is great to be a backcountry ranger here today. I see many trails that I want to hike and I know I want to accomplish more. After hiking the AT I know I can.

▣ **SIGHTS.** The staff at the **Mount Desert Oceanarium**, off Rte. 3 on the northeast edge of the island, are masters of the marine. The facility teaches everything that you need to know about lobsters, with a museum and hatchery. Its sister oceanarium, at the end of Clark Pt. Rd. near Beal's in Southwest Harbor, has fascinating exhibits and a museum geared toward children. (☎244-7330. Open mid-May to mid-Oct. M-Sa 9am-5pm. Main oceanarium $10-12, ages 4-12 $6.) Just north of Bar Harbor, **Bar Island** is reachable at low tide when receding waters reveal a gravel path accessed via Bridge St., off route 3. (Tide times are published in *Acadia Weekly*.) For a relaxing drive with a stunning view, go north from Northeast Harbor on **Sargent Drive**, which runs along Somes Sound. **Wildwood Stables,** along Park Loop Rd. in Seal Harbor, takes tourists around the island via horse and carriage. (☎276-3622. 1hr. tour $13.50, seniors $12.50, ages 6-12 $7, ages 2-5 $4. 2hr. tour $18-$22. Reservations recommended. Wheelchair accessible if notified in advance.)

▣▣ **ENTERTAINMENT AND NIGHTLIFE.** Most after-dinner pleasures on the island can be found in Bar Harbor's laid-back bars. **Geddy's Pub,** 19 Main St., provides a backdrop of weathered wooden signs and moose head trophies to the dancing frenzy that breaks out nightly during the summer months. (☎288-5077. Live music, mostly acoustic rock and folk, daily 7-10pm. No cover. Open Apr.-Oct. daily 11am-1am; winter hours vary. Pub-style dinner, $10-26, served until 10pm.) For laughs, stop by **Improv Acadia,** 15 Cottage St. This Chicago-based comedy outfit induces hilarity and serves local treats such as Bar Harbor Ales ($3.50) and $3 ice creams. (☎288-2503. Admission $12. Call for showtimes.) Locals adore the **Lompoc Cafe & Brew Pub**, 36 Rodick St., off Cottage St., which has Bar Harbor Real Ale ($4), a bocce court, and jazz, blues, Celtic, rock, and folk. (☎288-9392. Th open mic. Live music F-Sa nights. No cover. Open May-Oct. daily 11:30am-1am.)

ACADIA NATIONAL PARK   ☎207

The jagged, rocky, oceanside perimeter of Acadia National Park's 42,000 acres is lined with thick pine and birch forests and punctuated by dramatic rock outcroppings and secluded sandy shores. Park preservation efforts were aided by the philanthropy of millionaire John D. Rockefeller, Jr., who feared the island would be overrun by cars and funded the creation of 57 mi. of carriage roads accessible to hikers, mountain bikers, and, in the winter, skiers. For information regarding which trails are groomed for skiing, contact The Friends of Acadia (☎288-3340 or 800 625 0321). An ideal carriage road for biking is the **Eagle Lake Loop** (6½ mi.), which has gentle grades and a spectacular lake view. Touring the park costs $20 for seven days. Seniors (U.S. citizens only) can purchase a $10 lifetime pass, which entitles them to half-price camping at the park campgrounds. The *Biking and Hiking Guide to the Carriage Roads* ($6), available at the visitors center, offers invaluable hiking directions. To spend the night in or near the park, see Mt. Desert Island's **Accommodations** (p. 88). Along Park Loop Rd. (see below), **Jordan Pond House ❹** serves weary travelers with tea and popovers ($7.50) under sweet-smelling white birch canopies. (☎276-3316. Lunch $10-18. Dinner $15-20. Open mid-May to late Oct. daily 11:30am-9pm; hours can vary. Popovers served until 5:30pm.)

Peregrine falcons, the famed birds of Acadia, nest along the **Precipice Trail** (1½ mi.), on the western side of Mt. Champlain. The popular hike is quite strenuous and involves the use of iron ladders to ascend cliffs. When the trail is closed to accommodate the nesting falcons (June to late August), the birds may be viewed with telescopes provided by the park service daily 9am-noon in the trail parking lot. On the eastern half of the island, popular hikes include **Mt. Champlain/Bear Brook** (2½ mi. round-trip, moderate) and the strenuous **Beehive** (¾ mi. round-trip), both of which provide dramatic views of the Atlantic coastline. An easy ½ mi. amble along the **Bowl** trail from the summit of Mt. Champlain rewards hikers with a view of Sand Beach and Otter Point. To reach incredible views from the summit of Cadillac Mountain (1530 ft.), hike the **Cadillac Mountain North** (4½ mi.) or **South Ridge** (7½ mi.), or cruise up the paved **auto road.** Early birds are among the first people in the US to see the sun rise. (Road open 1hr. before sunrise to midnight.)

About 4 mi. south of Bar Harbor on Rte. 3, **Park Loop Road** runs along the granite shore of the island, eventually making a 27 mi. circuit through the pine forests of Acadia's interior. The sea comes into **Thunder Hole** with a bang about 2-3hr. before high tide, when wave action is strong enough. Soft sand and refreshing waters await at **Echo Lake,** along Rte. 102, or **Sand Beach** on the Park Loop along the island's eastern shore. *Sand Beach has no lifeguard on duty.*

NEW HAMPSHIRE

There are two sides to New Hampshire: the rugged landscape and natural beauty of the White Mountains, and the tax-free outlets, tourist traps, and state liquor stores that line most highways. New Hampshire's inland towns often revolve around their "three seasons" resort destinations, catering to outdoorsmen in the summer, leafers in the colorful autumn, and skiers in the long winter season. The first colony to declare its independence from Great Britain, New Hampshire has retained its libertarian charm along with its motto, "Live Free or Die!"

🛂 PRACTICAL INFORMATION

Capital: Concord.

Visitor Info: Office of Travel and Tourism, 172 Pembroke Rd., P.O. Box 1856, Concord 03302 (☎271-2666 or 800-386-4664; www.visitnh.gov). **NH Parks and Recreation** (☎271-3556; www.nhparks.state.nh.us). The **Fish and Game Department,** 2 Hazen Dr., Concord 03301 (☎603-271-3421; www.wildlife.state.nh.us), provides info on regulations and licenses. **US Forest Service,** 719 N. Main St., Laconia 03246 (☎603-528-8721; www.fs.fed.us/r9/white). Open M-F 8am-4:30pm.

Postal Abbreviation: NH. **Sales Tax:** 8% on meals and lodgings. **Area Code:** 603.

PORTSMOUTH   ☎603

With only 13 mi. of seacoast touching the Atlantic Ocean, New Hampshire makes the most of its toehold on the water. Portsmouth, the colonial capital, boasts both a rich history and a vibrant modernity. In this port town, seafood reigns supreme, and a pint of local ale is the mainstay after dinner. Colonial history is an integral part of Portsmouth, as most buildings date from the 18th century, but hip restaurants and artistic productions throughout the city reveal an affinity for today's styles. The city's charms come at a price, however; while Portsmouth's riches will leave you begging for more, your drained wallet may tell you otherwise.

🖙🛂 TRANSPORTATION AND PRACTICAL INFORMATION. Just 57 mi. north of Boston, Portsmouth is situated at the junction of U.S. 1, 1A, and I-95. Cheap parking lots ($0.50-1 per hr.) are available downtown, but the town is best navigated by foot. State St./U.S.1 and Congress St. are major roads that run northeast-southwest through town. Market St. runs southeast-northwest and is the central intersecting road. **Vermont Transit/Greyhound,** 22 Ladd St. (☎436-0163), inside Federal Tobacconists, heads to Boston (1¼hr., 4 per day, $17). Purchase tickets onsite. **Seacoast Trolley** (☎431-6975) runs every hour in the summer 10am-5pm, with 14 stops around Portsmouth. ($2.50 partial loop, $5 full loop with reboarding privileges.) **Taxi: Blue Star Taxi,** ☎436-2774. **Visitor Info: Greater Portsmouth Chamber of Commerce,** 500 Market St., outside downtown. (☎436-1118; www.portcity.org. Open M-F 8am-5pm, Sa-Su 10am-4pm.) The Chamber of Commerce **information kiosk** is in Market Sq. (Open May to mid-Oct. daily 10am-5pm.) **Hotlines: Violence and Rape Hotline,** ☎800-336-3795. **Medical Services: Portsmouth Regional,** 333 Borthwick Ave. (☎436-5110 or 800-991-4325). **Post Office:** 80 Daniel St. (☎800- 275-8777. Open M-F 7:30am-5:30pm, Sa 8am-12:30pm.) **Postal Code:** 03801. **Area Code:** 603.

▐▌⌐ ACCOMMODATIONS AND FOOD. Portsmouth is not exactly budget-friendly when it comes to hanging your hat; a common tactic to avoid steep prices is to take a short trip over the border to Maine, where accommodations are pleasant and reasonably priced. ▨**Camp Eaton ❷** is in York Harbor, ME, about 15 mi. north of Portsmouth off Rte. 1, and mere steps from a beautiful New England beach. Immaculate bathrooms and well-kept, wooded sites make camping here a relative bargain. (☎207-363-3424. 2-person sites $37, low-season $24. Each additional person $6.) The **Farmstead B&B ❹,** 379 Goodwin Rd. in Eliot, ME, offers pristine rooms with views of the countryside only 10 mi. from downtown Portsmouth. (☎207-748-3145 or 207-439-5033; www.farmstead.qpg.com. Rooms $75.)

Portsmouth offers a plethora of dining options, with many fine establishments of all varieties peppering Market St. ▨**The Friendly Toast ❷,** 121 Congress St., a block and a half from Market Sq., is cluttered with the most ghastly artifacts the 1950s could produce: mannequin limbs, pulp novels, formica what-nots, and stroke-inducingly bad art. Menu items, such as the "mission burrito" ($8), are nearly impossible to finish. (☎430-2154. Breakfast served all day. Entrees $6-8. Open Su-Th 7am-9pm, F-Sa 24hr.) **The Portsmouth Brewery ❷,** 56 Market St., offers great pub fare ($6-10) and some excellent brews. Their "Smutty Nose IPA" is consistently ranked the #1 IPA in the US, and their "Old Brown Dog" is a local favorite. (☎431-1115. Open Su-Th 11am-11pm, F-Sa 11am-1am.) Folks trail into the street for heavenly burgers and sandwiches at **Gilly's Lunchcart ❶,** 175 Fleet St. During daylight hours, the Monday 11am-6pm "Dog Days" special offers $1.25 hotdogs. (www.gillyspmlunch.com. Fries $1.75. Burger $2.25. Open daily 11:30am-2:30am.)

◙ ⌐ SIGHTS AND ENTERTAINMENT. Modern Portsmouth sells itself with its colonial past. The prestigious **Strawbery Banke Museum,** on the corner of Marcy and Hancock St., is a collection of buildings and beautiful gardens that encompasses several city blocks, each restored to recreate the region as it evolved over time. Museum employees frequent the various houses and shops in period garb. To find the museum, follow the signs that lead toward the harbor through a maze of shops. (☎433-1100; www.strawberybanke.org. Open May-Oct. M-Sa 10am-5pm, Su noon-5pm. $12, seniors $11, ages 7-17 $8; families $28. Tickets good for 2 consecutive days.) Across the street, **Prescott Park** hugs the bank of the Piscataqua River. A great place to picnic, these small, well-tended gardens and lawns offer an amazing view. For the naval enthusiast, try climbing aboard through the hatches of the **USS Albacore,** a research submarine built locally at the Portsmouth Naval Shipyard. (☎436-3680. Open May-Oct. daily 9:30am-5pm; winter hours vary. $5, over 62 or military with ID $3.50, ages 7-17 $2; families $10.) One of Portsmouth's oldest graveyards, **North Cemetery,** holds the burial sites of some of the city's most important skeletons, including signers of the Declaration of Independence and the US Constitution. The **Music Hall,** 28 Chesnut St., a 125-year-old theater, hosts shows throughout the summer including movies, concerts, dances, musicals, and dramatic performances. (☎436-2400; www.themusichall.org. Box office open M-Sa noon-6pm or until 30min. after the show has started. $8; students, seniors, under 21, and military $6.)

NEW HAMPSHIRE SKI RESORTS
☎ 603

With abundant snow from November through April and sizable mountains throughout the state, New Hampshire is a popular skiing destination. When the White Mountains thaw each resort blossoms into its own unique summer diversion. **Ski New Hampshire,** P.O. Box 10, Lincoln 03251, provides information and reservations for five resorts in the White Mountains. (☎745-9396 or 800-937-5493; www.skinh.com.) **Cranmore,** in North Conway (p. 100), offers 39 trails and great shopping. The **Children's Summer Camps** offer tennis, hiking, swimming, rock climbing, and gymnastics. (☎800-786-6754; www.cranmore.com. Lift operates M-F 9am-4pm, Sa-Su 8:30am-4pm. Lift tickets $35, ages 6-12 and 70+ $19.) Located along U.S. 302 by North Conway, pricey **Attitash** has two mountains, 51 trails (evenly divided among beginner, intermediate, and expert), and 25 acres of glades. Biking, horseback riding, water slides, a climbing wall, trampolines, and an alpine slide keep summer visitors busy. (☎374-2368; www.attitash.com. Lift tickets $49, holidays $53; children $32. Slide open in summer daily 10am-6pm. Single ride $12. Summer full-day value pack for all activities except golf and horseback riding $29, ages 2-7 $12.)

Just outside Pinkham Notch on Rte. 16, **Wildcat Mountain** offers 47 trails (25% beginner, 45% intermediate, 30% expert) and mountainscape views from its 4062 ft. peak. (☎888-754-9453; www.skiwildcat.com. Lift tickets M-F $49, ages 13-18 $42, seniors and ages 6-12 $25; Sa-Su $52/$42/$25. Gondola rides late May to Oct. daily $9.50, seniors $8.50, ages 6-12 $4.50.) Three miles east of Lincoln on Rte. 112, **Loon Mountain** has 43 ski trails, and biking and horseback riding that are popular when the weather is warm. (☎745-8111; www.loonmtn.com. Lift tickets M-F $40, Sa-Su $47; ages 13-19 $33/$41; under 13 $25/$29.) Just off I-93 in Franconia Notch State Park, **Cannon Mountain** has 42 trails (15% beginner, 50% intermediate, 35% expert) at slightly lower prices than other local resorts and offers a two-person pass for $40 on Tuesdays and Thursdays. Summer hiking, biking, canoeing, and swimming keep athletes in shape, while the Aerial Tramway (p. 99) whisks those with a little less energy up the mountain. (☎823-8800; www.cannonmt.com. Lift tickets M-F $34, Sa-Su $45; ages 13-17 $23/$37; seniors and under 13 $23/$29.)

WHITE MOUNTAINS
☎ 603

Made up of 780,000 acres of mountainous national forest maintained by the US Forest Service, the White Mountains are a playground for outdoor enthusiasts. While many associate the area with skiing, warm-weather alternatives like hiking, camping, canoeing, kayaking, and fishing make the White Mountains an attractive destination throughout the year.

◼️🔟 ORIENTATION AND PRACTICAL INFORMATION. The White Mountains can be daunting to an unfamiliar traveler, but are easily navigated with a good map and guide. The immense forest, spanning both New Hampshire and Maine, is bordered by a dozen or so towns and contains several commercial ski resorts. Many of the region's highlights can be found in three areas: **Pinkham Notch** (p. 97), northeast of the forest near Mt. Washington; the **Franconia Notch** area (p. 98), northwest of the National Forest; and **North Conway** (p. 100), a gateway town to the southeast.

Any unattended vehicle parked on White Mountain National Forest land must have a **parking pass,** sold by the US Forest Service and the Appalachian Mountain Club as well as the White Mountain Attraction Center; vehicles parked at national forest campground sites are an exception. (☎528-8721. $5 per week, $20 per year.) Purchase daily passes at any of the trailheads in the forest for $3. The **US Forest Ser-**

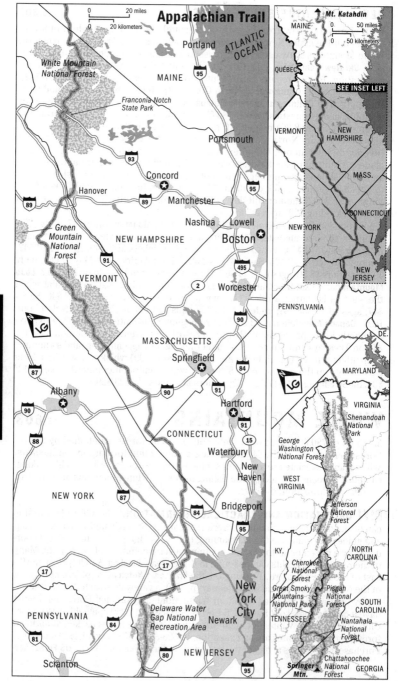

vice operates four **ranger stations,** which each provide free information on recreational opportunities, camping, and safety precautions in the White Mountains. **Pemigewasset/Ammonoosuc,** on Rte. 175 in Plymouth near Exit 25 of I-93, covers the southwest region of the forest. (☎536-1315. Open M-F 8am-4:30pm.) **Androscoggin,** 2½ mi. south of Gorham on Rte. 16, oversees the northern half. (☎466-2713. Open in summer daily 8am-5pm; in winter M-Sa 8am-4:30pm.) **Evans Notch,** 18 Mayville Rd., in Bethel, ME, covers the Maine section of the national forest. (☎207-824-2134. Open in summer daily 8am-4:30pm; winter Tu-Sa 8am-4:30pm.) **Saco,** 100 yd. west of the junction of Rte. 16 on Hwy. 112 (Kancamagus Hwy.), oversees the southeast section of the forest. (☎447-5448. Open daily 8am-4:30pm.)

The **White Mountain Attraction Center,** P.O. Box 10, N. Woodstock 03262, at Exit 32 off I-93, has info on recreation in the mountains. (☎745-8720; www.visitwhitemountains.com. Open daily July-Sept. 8:30am-6pm; Apr.-July and Sept. to mid-Oct. 8:30am-5:30pm; mid-Oct. to Apr. 8:30am-5pm.) The **Appalachian Mountain Club (AMC)** is a nonprofit conservation and recreation organization that maintains 1400 mi. of trails in the northeastern US . They offer outdoor skills workshops, run programs to protect the environment, and provide lodging at backcountry huts, shelters, camps, and roadside lodges. Members of the AMC receive discounts at their many hiking destinations. Membership can be purchased for individuals ($50) or families ($75) and may be obtained online (www.outdoors.org) or at the AMC's **Pinkham Notch Visitors Center,** 10 mi. north of Jackson on Rte. 16. The base camp for Mt. Washington, the AMC Visitors Center is the area's best source of info on weather and trail conditions, with detailed maps, up-to-date weather reports, and a gathering for hikers trading mountain tales. They handle lodging reservations and have comprehensive information on White Mountain trails, safety, and eco-friendly "Leave No Trace" backpacking. (AMC headquarters: ☎617-523-0636; www.outdoors.org. Visitors center: ☎466-2727. Open daily 6:30am-10pm.)

▐ TRANSPORTATION. No matter which way you approach the White Mountains, the scenery will be breathtaking. **Concord Trailways** (☎228-3300 or 800-639-3317) runs from Boston to Concord (30 Stickney Ave.; 2 per day, $13); Conway (First Stop Market, W. Main St.; 2 per day, $27); and Franconia (Kelly's Foodtown, Exit 38 off I-93; 1 per day, $28). For hikers, the AMC runs a **shuttle** between locations on the Appalachian Trail in the White Mountains. Consult AMC's *The Guide* for a complete map of routes and times or pick up a schedule at the AMC Pinkham Notch Visitors Center. (☎466-2727. Operates June to mid-Oct. daily 8am-4pm. Reservations highly recommended for all stops; required for some. $9.)

▐ ACCOMMODATIONS. Other than ski resorts, most accommodations within the National Forest are controlled by the AMC. Plentiful accommodations within an hour's drive from hikes and attractions range from hostels and motels to high-end resorts. For a guide to lodgings near the White Mountains, pick up the small *White Mountains Travel Guide,* free and available at any **info booth.**

The **AMC** operates huts along the White Mountains stretch of the Appalachian Trail, generally used by trail hikers as lodges that divide the vast distance of the trail. A free *AMC Huts and Lodges* brochure, available at the Pinkham Notch Visitors Center or from the AMC, has descriptions and locations. At the huts, all bunks are in co-ed bunkrooms. Some huts are austere with no showers, electric lights, or electrical outlets of any kind. The **full-service ❸** huts provide bunk, mattress, pillow, and three wool blankets, as well as breakfast and dinner daily. There are toilets, washrooms separated by gender, and cold running water. Bring sleeping gear and a flashlight. At the **self-service ❶** huts, guests must provide their own food, but have use of a kitchen stocked with cookware. Blankets are not provided—bring a warm sleeping bag. (☎466-2727; www.outdoors.org. No pets. No smoking. All huts open June to mid-Sept.; 6 huts open to mid-Oct.; 3 self-service huts open in winter. Full service huts: AMC members $75, under 15 $46; nonmembers $82/$51. Some discounts for longer stays. Self-service huts: $25, under 15 $23.)

For car-accessible lodging, the AMC runs the **Joe Dodge Lodge** (p. 97). The **Highland Center at Crawford Notch ❸**, off Rt. 302, is open year-round with 120 beds in both dorms and family rooms. The Highland Center also serves as an outdoor program and education center. (☎ 466-2727. Dorms with breakfast and dinner for AMC members $59, nonmembers $66; doubles with breakfast and dinner $99/$109 per person. Call for low-season prices.) Another option is the **White Mountains Hostel** (p. 100).

▨ CAMPING. The US Forest Service maintains 23 designated **National Forest campgrounds ❶**, all of which are accessible by car. Four remain open in winter, although only one has plowed access. Some sites are first come, first served, but these can fill quickly. On weekends, arrive around check-out time (usually 10-11am) to snag a site. Bathrooms and firewood are usually available. (Reservations: ☎ 877-444-6777; www.reserveusa.com. Reservations accepted beginning Jan. 1 and must be made at least 1 week in advance. Sites $12-18; reservation fee $9, change/cancellation fee $10. Cars parked at campsite do not require a parking pass.)

Camping is less expensive or free of charge at the many **backcountry campsites ❶**, which are only accessible via hiking trails. Regulations prohibit camping and fires above the tree line (approximately 4000 ft.), within 200 ft. of a trail, certain bodies of water, and a few specific roads, or within ¼ mi. of huts, shelters, tent platforms, lakes, streams, or roads. Rules are even more strict in the Great Gulf Wilderness around Mt. Washington—no wood or charcoal fires are allowed. Other areas have more special regulations—consult the US Forest Service's *Backcountry Camping Rules*, available for reference at any of the four regional ranger stations, for more info. A plethora of **private campgrounds ❶/❷**, the majority of which cater to RVs and families, surround the borders of the forest. A copy of *New Hampshire's Guide to Camping*, available from any highway rest stop or info booth in the state, provides a map, prices, and campgrounds' phone numbers.

> **⚠** No matter where you camp, **bears** are a threat. Stop by a ranger station or the AMC Visitors Center to pick up information on how to minimize the risk of danger. Keep food hung high and well away from sleeping areas. Do not keep anything with the scent of food on it in or near your tent (clothes worn while cooking, for example). Animals are not only a danger when camping, however— **moose** can be problematic for drivers, so keep a watchful eye.

▨ OUTDOOR ACTIVITIES. If you are planning to do a significant amount of **hiking**, the invaluable *AMC White Mountain Guide* ($23; available in the AMC Visitor's Center and most bookstores) includes maps and descriptions of all mountain trails. Because weather in the mountains is unpredictable, hikers should bring three layers of clothing in all seasons: one for wind, one for rain, and at least one for warmth—preferably wool or a synthetic material like polypropylene or fleece, but not cotton. Black flies and mosquitoes make insect repellent a must-have item. *Always bring more than enough water*; dehydration can be a serious problem and hikes in the region are often more strenuous than anticipated. A high-calorie snack, like trail mix, is also a good idea. **Cycling** is another popular way to tour the White Mountains. For help with planning, ask a ranger or consult *30 Bicycle Tours in New Hampshire* ($13; at local bookstores and outdoor equipment stores). **Great Glen Trails Outdoor Center,** across Rte. 16 from the Mt. Washington Auto Rd., rents bikes for use only on their trails. They also offer kayaking deals and, in the winter, cross-country skiing and ski rentals (☎ 466-2333. Open daily

8:30am-5pm. Trail fee $7; included in rental. Bikes $20 for 2hr., under 18 $14; half-day $25/$20; full-day $35/$25. Winter trail pass full-day $15, ages 6-12 and over 62 $11; afternoon only $10/$7. Kayaking $60-150.)

To see the National Forest with very little exertion, drive the ▨**Kancamagus Scenic Highway (Route 12),** which connects the towns of Lincoln and Conway. The 35 mi. drive requires at least 1hr., though the many scenic outlooks are perfect for a picnic. Get gas at Lincoln, as no gas is available for 35 mi., then head east on the Kanc to enjoy the scenic splendor stretching all the way to Conway.

PINKHAM NOTCH ☎ 603

Pinkham Notch, New Hampshire's easternmost mountain pass, lies in the shadow of the tallest mountain in the northeastern US—the 6288 ft. **Mount Washington.** Pinkham's proximity to the peak makes it more crowded and less peaceful than neighboring areas, but secluded areas can be found not too far off the beaten path. AMC's **Pinkham Notch Visitors Center** lies between Gorham and Jackson on Rte. 16.

Stretching from behind the Pinkham Notch Visitors Center all the way up to the summit of Mt. Washington, **Tuckerman's Ravine Trail,** despite the deceiving 4¼ mi. distance, demands 4-5hr. of steep hiking each way. *Authorities urge caution when climbing—Mt. Washington claims at least one life every year.* Mt. Washington is one of the most dangerous small mountains in the world because of the highly unpredictable weather and wind speeds that reach hurricane force surprisingly frequently. It has never been recorded to be warmer than 72°F on top of Mt. Washington, and the average temperature on the peak is a bone-chilling 27°F. The summit of Mt. Washington boasts the highest wind speed ever recorded, at 231 mph. With proper measures, however, the trek offers excellent vistas and some of the best views in New England—those lucky enough to hike on a clear day are rewarded with a view of five states and Canada. A less daunting option for the steepest part of the ascent is the **Lion's Head Trail,** which diverges from the Tuckerman's Ravine Trail about 2 mi. into the hike. Because Tuckerman's Ravine is closed in winter due to the high frequency of avalanches, the Lion's Head Trail must be used by those intrepid enough to make the hike in the snowy months.

Motorists can take the **Mt. Washington Auto Road,** a paved and dirt road that winds 8 mi. to the summit. For most vehicles, the ascent is a minor test, but 1000 ft. drop-offs and an absence of guard rails will test even the most unshakable nerves. Drivers sturdy enough to reach the top receive bragging rights in the form of a free "This Car Climbed Mt. Washington" bumper sticker. The road begins 3 mi. north of the visitors center on Rte. 16. (☎ 466-3988. Road open daily June-Aug. 7:30am-6pm; May-June and Sept.-Oct. 8am-5pm. $18 per car and driver, free audio tour included; $7 each additional passenger, ages 5-12 $4.) To enjoy the view without the drive, **Great Glen Stage Tours,** across Rte. 16 from the Auto Road, runs tours. (☎ 466-2333. Open daily 8:30am-5pm. $24, seniors $22, ages 5-12 $11.)

Many of the region's lodging options are on or near Mt. Washington. Accessible by car, the **Joe Dodge Lodge ❸,** immediately behind the Pinkham Notch Visitors Center, offers over 100 comfortable bunks, including seven family rooms, a small library, and a living room. (☎ 466-2727. Breakfast and dinner included. Reservations recommended. AMC members $54, under 16 $34; nonmembers $59/$37. Without meals, members $43, nonmembers $47, children $23/$25. Call for low-season rates.) About 2hr. up the Tuckerman Ravine Trail, **Hermit Lake Shelter ❶** has bathrooms but no showers, and sleeps up to 90 people on a first come, first served basis. Nightly passes are sold at the visitors center ($10). **Lakes of the Clouds Hut,** 1½ mi. from Mt. Washington's summit, is one of AMC's most full-service popular huts. (Reservations ☎ 466-2727. See **Accommodations,** p. 95, for rates.)

NEW ENGLAND

FRANCONIA NOTCH AREA ☎ 603

Carved by glacial movements that began 400 million years ago, the granite peaks of Franconia Notch State Park towering on either side of I-93 are one of the most majestic spots in the White Mountains. Although one of the biggest attractions in the area, the famous rocky profile known as the "Old Man of the Mountain," collapsed in 2003, Franconia is still home to waterfalls, woodlands, and natural rock formations—marvels that will stun even the most avid nature enthusiast.

⁊ PRACTICAL INFORMATION. Most of the area highlights are directly accessible from I-93. The **Franconia Notch Chamber of Commerce,** on Main St. in Franconia, has maps of the region, and area information. (☎ 823-5516; www.franconianotch.org. Open mid-May to mid-Oct. Tu-Su 10am-5pm.) A note for those using old maps: the highway exit numbering system has recently changed. Old Exit 1 on the FN Pkwy. corresponds to new 34A, Exit 2 to 34B, and Exit 3 to 34C.

⁊⁊ ACCOMMODATIONS AND FOOD. Franconia Notch is an ideal place for camping, but make sure to bring insect repellent if you plan to stay in the great outdoors. Nestled in the middle of the park, **Lafayette Place Campground ❶,** off I-93 S between Exits 34A and 34B, offers spacious campsites and an ideal location. (☎ 823-9513, reservations 271-3628; www.nhparks.state.nh.us. Coin-operated showers, clean facilities, and a camp store available. Reservations are strongly recommended and must be made at least 3 days in advance for a $3 fee. Open mid-May to mid-Oct. 2-person sites $16; $8 per additional adult, under 18 free.) The scenic Pemi Trail passes through the campground; follow it toward the Flume (3½ mi.) and the Basin (2 mi.) to the south and toward Profile Lake and Cannon Mtn. (2½ mi.) to the north. A peaceful evening can be found at the **Fransted Family Campground ❶,** 3 mi. north of the Notch on Rte. 18. The expansive grounds offer over 100 well-tended sites, movie nights, a small beach, free volleyball, and 9-hole miniature golf. Facilities include showers, bathroom, and coin-operated laundry. (☎ 823-5675. Open May-Oct. Tent sites $20-26, with electricity and water $29, full hookup $31.) **Woodstock Inn and Station ❺,** on Rte. 3, offers a comfortable, though expensive, alternative to camping. Jacuzzi and health club privileges included. (☎ 745-3951. Breakfast included. Rooms from $102; call for low-season rates.) Cabins and motels cluster along Rte. 3 between Lincoln and North Woodstock.

▨Polly's Pancake Parlor ❷, on Rte. 117 in Sugar Hill, just 2 mi. from Exit 38 off I-93, is a homey restaurant with a dining room overlooking Mt. Washington. The parlor serves a stack of six superb pancakes for $6 or unlimited pancakes for $11. The hotcakes come topped with maple syrup or maple spread from the restaurant's own product line. (☎ 823-5575. Open mid-May to mid-Oct. daily 7am-3pm; Apr. and Nov. Sa-Su call for hours.) The endless menu at the **Woodstock Inn Brewery ❸,** housed in the Woodstock Inn and Station, is sure to fuel your engine, with everything from not-so-standard sandwiches like the "Train Wreck," with roasted chicken, roast beef, and a big red Anaheim chili ($8), to pasta ($10-14) and seafood from $12. (☎ 745-3951. Open daily 11:30am-10pm.)

◉ SIGHTS. Traveling north from Lincoln on I-93, **▨The Flume,** Exit 34A on I-93, is a 2 mi. walk cutting through a spectacular granite gorge. Although only 12-20 ft. apart, the moss-covered canyon walls are 70-90 ft. high. Take a leisurely stroll over centuries-old covered bridges and past the 35 ft. Avalanche Falls. Tickets can be purchased from the **Flume Visitors Center,** which also screens an excellent 15min. film acquainting visitors with the landscape and geological history of the area. (☎ 745-8391; www.flumegorge.com. Open daily May-June and Sept.-Oct. 9am-5pm; July-Aug. 9am-5:30pm. $8, ages 6-12 $5.) A 9 mi. paved **bike path** begins at the visitors center and parallels I-93 N through the park. To rent some wheels, check out **Cannon Mountain Bike Shop,** conveniently located at Exit 34B past the tramway. (☎ 823-8800, ext. 710. Open mid-June to Sept. daily 9am-5pm; late May to mid-June Sa-Su 9am-5pm. $10 per hr., $20 half-day, $29 full day.) Between Exits 34A and 34B on I-93, visitors can find a well-marked turn-off for **The Basin.** Here a 5-10min. walk will take you to a 20 ft. whirlpool that has been carved out of a massive base of granite by a 15 ft. waterfall. (Wheelchair accessible.)

For years Franconia had been known as the home of the **Old Man of the Mountain,** but in May 2003, the profile fell from its perch. The viewing areas at Exit 34B on I-93 and between Exit 34A and 34B on I-93 are still open and provide a diagrammatic explanation of the Old Man's fall. A pleasant 10min. walk down the designated path from the parking lot at Exit 34B brings viewers to the banks of **Profile Lake,** which affords the best available view of the cliff where the Old Man used to rest. Also at Exit 34B, a small display of Old Man memorabilia and the history regarding his discovery and rise to popularity can be found at the **Old Man of the Mountain Museum.** (☎ 823-7722, ext. 717. Open daily mid-May to mid-Oct. 9:30am-5pm. Free.) The 80-passenger **Cannon Mountain Aerial Tramway,** Exit 34B, climbs over 2000 ft. in 7min. and carries visitors to the summit of the Cannon Cliff, a 1000 ft. sheer drop into the cleft between Mt. Lafayette and Cannon Mountain. The ascent offers vertigo-inducing vistas of Franconia Notch, rivaled only by the **observation tower** at the peak (elevation over 4200 ft.), just a short walk from the tram. (☎ 823-8800. Open mid-May to mid-Oct. and mid-Dec. to mid-Apr. daily 9am-5pm. Trams run every 15min. Round-trip $10, ages 6-12 $6. One-way $8.) In winter, the tram takes skiers up the mountain, which has 58 trails. Back at the base of the mountain, right next to the tramway station, sits the one-room **New England Ski Museum,** with numerous old photographs and a display of skis through the ages. (☎ 823-7177. Open mid-May to mid-Oct. and mid-Dec. to mid-Apr. daily noon-5pm. Free.) While skiers enjoy Cannon Mtn. during the winter, on summer days, the lifeguard-protected beach at **Echo Lake,** just off Exit 34C on I-93 at the base of Cannon Mtn., offers cool but sometimes crowded waters. The lake is accessible until 10pm. (☎ 823-8800, ext. 784. Lifeguard on duty mid-June to early Sept. daily 10am-5pm. $3, under 12 free. Free to all when lifeguard isn't on duty. Canoe or paddleboat rental ☎ 823-8800, ext. 783. $10 per hr. Last rental 4pm.)

◪ **HIKING.** Franconia Notch provides excellent day-hikes and views; the **Hiking Information Center** adjacent to Lafayette Place Campground is the best source in the area for hiking suggestions and safety tips. (Open daily 8am-4pm.) *In this area be prepared for severe weather, especially above 4000 ft.* On the western rim, the **Lonesome Lake Trail** (2 mi.) winds from Lafayette Place Campground to **Lonesome Lake,** where the AMC operates its westernmost hut. The trails on the eastern rim boast an extensive network stretching far back into the wilderness of Franconia Notch. The **Greenleaf Trail** (2½ mi.), which starts at the aerial tramway parking lot, and the **Old Bridle Path** (3 mi.), beginning from Lafayette Place and known for its stellar views, are more ambitious. Both lead up to the AMC's **Greenleaf Hut,** near the summit of Mt. Lafayette overlooking Echo Lake. From Greenleaf, a 7½ mi. trek east along the **Old Bridle Path** and **Garfield Ridge** leads to the AMC's most remote hut, the **Galehead.** Beware that the Mt. Garfield summit is above the timberline, where storms may intensify quickly. Ambitious hikers seek the **Falling Waters Trail,** which can be accessed from Lafayette Place. With three waterfalls within 1½ mi. of the trailhead and a 1600 ft. elevation change, the trail is a strenuous hike. The well-maintained eastern rim trails are difficult and interconnected. They can occupy trekkers for days; make sure to get adequate supplies before starting out.

NEW ENGLAND

LOST RIVER GORGE

Outside of Franconia Notch State Park, ■**Lost River Gorge**, located 6 mi. west of North Woodstock on Rte. 112, is a deep glacial gorge with a network of caves, massive boulders, complex rock formations, beautiful waterfalls, and a winding stream. The reservation also maintains a nature garden and a forestry center with information about the area. The walk through the gorge is less than 1 mi. along well-maintained suspended wooden walkways and bridges, but exploring the caves can easily take over an hour; each creatively named cavern (like the Sun Altar) is open for exploration to those agile enough to wrench themselves through. (☎745-8031; www.findlostriver.com. Open daily July-Aug. 9am-6pm; mid-May to June and Sept. to mid-Oct. 9am-5pm. Last ticket sold 1hr. before closing. Solid walking shoes recommended. $9.50, children 6-12 $6.50.)

NORTH CONWAY AND CONWAY ☎603

With its proximity to ski resorts in winter, foliage in the fall, and hiking and shopping year-round, the town of North Conway is one of New Hampshire's most popular vacation destinations. Rte. 16, the traffic-infested main road, houses outlet stores as well as a variety of smaller local shops. The town of Conway, 5 mi. south, has fewer touristy shops, but several excellent meal and lodging options.

Numerous stores in the North Conway area rent outdoor equipment for the slopes, the water, and the roads. For ski goods in winter or biking gear during other seasons, **Joe Jones,** 2709 White Mtn. Hwy. at Mechanic St. in North Conway, has it all. (☎356-9411. Open July-Aug. daily 9am-8pm; Sept.-Nov. and Apr.-June Su-Th 10am-6pm, F-Sa 9am-6pm; Dec.-Mar. M-F 8:30am-6pm, Sa-Su 8:30am-8pm. Alpine skis, boots, and poles $20 for 1 day, $36 for 2 days; cross-country equipment $15/$26; snowboards $25/$46. Bikes $15 for 4hr., $25 for 8hr.) A second branch, **Joe Jones North,** lies a few miles north of town on Rte. 302. (☎356-6848.) **Eastern Mountain Sports (EMS),** just north on White Mtn. Hwy. in the lobby of the Eastern Slope Inn, sells camping equipment and rents tents (all tents $20 per day, $10 each additional day), sleeping bags ($15/$5), snowshoes, packs, and skis. The knowledgeable staff happily provides free first-hand info on climbing and hiking, and EMS also offers a summer climbing school. (☎356-5433. Open June-Sept. M-Sa 8:30am-9pm, Su 8:30am-6pm; Oct.-May Su-Th 8:30am-6pm, F-Sa 8:30am-9pm.)

Located in the heart of Conway and maintained by incredibly friendly folk, the ■**White Mountains Hostel (HI) ❶**, 36 Washington St., off Rte. 16 at the intersection of Rte. 153, is meticulously clean and environmentally friendly. The hostel has 43 comfy bunks, a kitchen, and a common room. (☎447-1001. Laundry $3. Linen included. Reception 7:30-10am and 5-10pm. Check-out 10am. Reservations recommended during the summer and peak foliage season. Bunks $20, nonmembers $23; private rooms $48.) Owned by the son-in-law of Babe Ruth, the hostel at the beautiful **Cranmore Mt. Lodge ❶**, 859 Kearsarge Rd., in North Conway, has 22 bunks. The lodge is about 2 mi. from downtown, and has a living room, pool, jacuzzi, cable TV, refrigerator, wireless Internet, tennis courts, and a duck pond. A delicious full breakfast, included with each overnight stay, makes up for the tight bunkrooms and thin mattresses. Be sure to bring a warm blanket to ward off the nightly temperature drop. (☎356-2044 or 800-356-3596. Linen and towel $3. Check-in 3-9pm. Check-out 11am. Reservations recommended. Dorms $25.)

Autographed bats and other sports paraphernalia adorn the walls at **Delaney's ❷**, to the north of town along Rte. 16. The menu offers excellent sandwiches, like the "Cranmore Carver" with ham, turkey, and swiss smothered in peppercorn dressing and served on a honey loaf for $8. (☎356-7776. Open daily 11:30am-11pm.) In the center of North Conway, next to Olympia Sports, **Morning Dew ❶** caffeinates the local populace. This hole-in-the-wall coffee shack offers bagels ($1), juice ($1.50), and the daily paper in addition to a variety of coffees ($1-2.50), teas, and steamers. (☎356-9366. Open daily 7am-5pm.) A bagful of penny candy from **Zeb's General Store ❶** can help you keep up your energy while exploring the shop, which sells everything New England has to offer, from pure maple syrup to wooden signs and moose memorabilia. Thirsty tourists might wish to partake of the many varieties of their $1.25 homemade soda. (☎356-9294. Open mid-June to Dec. daily 9am-10pm; low-season hours vary.) Several miles south in Conway, pink, green, and purple paint decorates the walls and ceilings of **Cafe Noche ❷**, 147 Main St., which serves Mexican dishes, including many vegetarian options. Local recommend the Montezuma Pie (Mexican lasagna; $8.50) or the $4.25 garden burger. (☎447-5050. Open daily 11:30am-9pm.)

HANOVER   ☎ 603

Home to the beautiful campus of Dartmouth College, the quiet little town of Hanover comes alive as students flood not only the classrooms and streets, but also the many trails, paths, and waterways that make the area ideal for those who love the outdoors. Full of muddy boots, ancient Ivy League streets, and classy bars, Hanover is the perfect blend of wild and sophisticated.

■ ⑦ ORIENTATION AND PRACTICAL INFORMATION. Located along the Connecticut River near Vermont border, and along Rte. 10 and 120, Hanover is accessible from both I-91 and I-89. Nearby towns are **Lebanon** (5 mi. south on Rte. 120), **White River Junction** (4 mi. south on Rte. 10, encompassing the confluence of the White and Connecticut Rivers), and **Norwich** (1½ mi. northwest in Vermont). **Vermont Transit** (☎800-552-8737) runs buses from Hanover (in front of the Hanover Inn at 35 S. Main St.; buy tickets on the bus or from Garber Travel ☎643-2700) to Boston (3-4hr., 4-5 per day, $25) and Burlington (2½hr., 4-5 per day, $21-27). **Amtrak** (☎295-7160 for station information; 800-872-7245 for schedules and reservations), on Railroad Row off N. Main St. in White River Junction, rolls to Burlington (2hr., 1 per day, $19-27) and New York City (7hr., 1 per day, $61-67). **Bike Rental: Dartmouth Outdoors Rentals**, in the basement of Robinson Hall by the town green on N. Main St. (☎646-1747; www.dartmouth.edu/~outrntls. Open M-F noon-6pm. Bikes $15 per day, $40 per week.) **The Hanover Chamber of Commerce**, 53. S. Main St., has area info. (☎643-3115; www.hanoverchamber.org. Open M-F 9am-4pm.) **Internet Access: Howe Library**, 13 E. South St. (☎643-0720. Open M-Th 10am-8pm, F noon-6pm, Sa 10am-5pm; Sept.-May also Su 1-5pm.) **Post Office:** 50 S. Main St. (☎643-4544. Open M-F 8am-5:30pm, Sa 8am-noon.) **Postal Code:** 03755. **Area Code:** 603.

◪◩ ACCOMMODATIONS AND FOOD. For those looking for a roof over their heads, **Sunset Motor Inn ❸** offers humble rooms with soft beds. Just 2 mi. south of Hanover on Rte. 10, this small motel features river views and some of the area's most reasonably priced accommodations. (☎298-8721. A/C. Reservations recommended. $53-83 depending on season and room type.) Camping with wooded sites, clean restrooms, pool access, two beaches on a lake, tennis courts, hiking, and hot showers is available at **Storr's Pond ❶**, 2 mi. north of Hanover off Rte. 10. (☎643-2134. Open May 15-Oct. 15. Reservations recommended. Sites for 1-4 people $20, each additional person $2; with electricity and water $25/$3.) For a snack or a meal, try **Lou's ❶**, 30 S. Main St., where old photos of politicians and celebrities adorn the walls. The $1 crullers—choose from glazed, cinnamon sugar, chocolate frosted, or jelly-filled—are highly recommended. (☎643-3321. Most meals $5-7. Open M-F 6am-3pm, Sa-Su 7am-3pm.) For late-night munchies, travelers should head to **Everything But Anchovies ❷**, 5 Allen St., which hosts a lively student crowd and serves pizzas ($13 for 14 in.) and "Ivy League Sandwiches and Subs" that range from $5-7. (☎643-6135. Open daily 7am-2am.)

■ **SIGHTS.** Virtually synonymous with Hanover is **Dartmouth,** the rural jewel in the Ivy League crown (☎646-1110; www.dartmouth.edu). The college offers **tours** starting from the admissions office in McNutt Hall on N. Main St. (☎646-2875. Open M-F 8am-4pm. Tours are free, times vary.) The **Hood Museum of Art,** on Wheelock St., houses collections that include African, Native American, ancient Asian, and contemporary art. (☎646-2808; www.hoodmuseum.dartmouth.edu. Open Tu and Th-Sa 10am-5pm, W 10am-9pm, Su noon-5pm. Free.) With the Appalachian Trail passing through town, Hanover is an ideal base of operations for hiking. The **Dartmouth Outdoors Club,** in Robinson Hall on N. Main St., maintains hundreds of miles of trails, sells the *Dartmouth Outing Guide* ($15) as well as more detailed maps ($1-3), and is a good source of information about area hiking. (☎646-2428. Call M-F 8am-4pm. Robinson Hall office ☎646-2429. Open Su-Th 2-6pm.)

■ **NIGHTLIFE.** No matter what time of year you visit Hanover, the streets are teeming with students looking for fun in rain, snow, or shine. **Murphy's on the Green,** 8 S. Main St., is a preppy restaurant by day and a wild party by night. At 10pm, tables are moved aside for the throngs of students that crowd into the bar to enjoy dancing, drinks (pitchers $10), and music. (☎643-4075. Open daily 11:30am-1am.) At **5 Old Nugget Alley,** descend into a dimly lit, smoke-filled basement bar with different specials each night of the week. Cheers resound from the many fans watching ESPN at the bar, and curious looks emanate from the hidden nooks and secluded tables. (☎643-5081. W $0.25 wings. Open daily 11:30am-1am.)

VERMONT

In 1609 Samuel de Champlain dubbed the area "green mountain" in his native French, and the name Vermont stuck. Lush forests and crystal clear waterways share the land with the undulating farmlands where the Holstein cattle roam. Over the past few decades, however, ex-urbanite yuppies have invaded, creating tension between the original, pristine Vermont and the packaged Vermont of trendy businesses and outlet shops. With the extensive development of ski resorts in the state, countless visitors now descend upon the mountainsides like the very snow that lures them. But as holiday weekends end and the summer arrives, the foreign storms subside, and the friendly, rural atmosphere of the sparsely populated mountain towns emerges from under the ice.

■ PRACTICAL INFORMATION

Capital: Montpelier.

Visitor Info: Vermont Information Center, 134 State St., Montpelier 05602 (☎802-828-3237; www.vermontvacation.com). Open daily 7:45am-8pm. **Department of Forests, Parks, and Recreation,** 103 S. Main St., Waterbury 05671 (☎802-241-3670). Open M-F 7:45am-4:30pm. **Vermont Snowline** (☎802-229-0531; www.skivermont.com) gives snow conditions Nov.-May. 24hr.

Postal Abbreviation: VT. **Sales Tax:** 5%, meals and lodgings 9%. **Area Code:** 802.

VERMONT SKI RESORTS   ☎ 802

Every winter, skiers pour into Vermont and onto the Northeast's finest slopes; in the summer and fall, these same inclines melt into the stomping grounds of hikers and mountain bikers. Towns surrounding each of the mountains make their livelihood on this annual avalanche, offering a range of tourist options. For information, contact **Ski Vermont,** 26 State St., P.O. Box 368, Montpelier 05601. (☎223-2439;

www.skivermont.com. Open M-F 7:45am-5:30pm.) The Vermont Information Center (see **Practical Information,** above) provides helpful info. Cheaper lift tickets can be found during low-season—before mid-December and after mid-March.

With three mountains, 78 trails, the highest vertical drop in Vermont, and the only triple-black-diamond run in the eastern US, **Smugglers' Notch,** just north of Stowe on Rte. 108, can satisfy even the most extreme taste. The resort also offers family programs and great package deals. In warm weather, tennis, golf, children's programs, hiking options, and bookings for canoeing, kayaking, and fishing attract visitors. (☎644-8851 or 800-451-8752; www.smuggs.com. Lift tickets $54, ages 7-18 $38, over 70 free. 5-day lodging and lift packages start at $125 per day, under 17 $109 per day.) A beautiful but dangerous passage south through Smugglers' Notch along Rte. 18 leads to the **Stowe Mountain Resort.** Only minutes from village of Stowe, the resort offers one-day lift tickets for $62, 48 trails (16% beginner, 59% intermediate, 25% expert), and impressive summer facilities, including a scenic toll road ($17 per car up to 6 passengers, each additional passenger $4), alpine slides (single ride $12, ages 6-12 $9), a gondola ($14, seniors $12, ages 6-12 $8), and a golf course and country club. (☎253-3000 or 800-253-4754. 5 alpine slide rides and 1 gondola ride $39, ages 6-12 and seniors $34.) West of Brattleboro on Rte. 100, in the town of West Dover, **Mount Snow** boasts 134 trails (25% beginner, 53% intermediate, 22% expert), 26 lifts, excellent snowmaking capabilities, and the first snowboard park in the Northeast. In summer, mountain bikers take advantage of the 45 mi. of trails. (☎800-245-7669; www.mountsnow.com. Open mid-Nov. to late Apr. M-F 9am-4pm, Sa-Su 8am-4pm; May to early Nov. daily 9am-4pm. Lift tickets M-F $49, Sa-Su $55; ages 13-19 $44/$46; under 13 and seniors $31/$33. Mountain biking $30 per day.)

At the junction of U.S. 4 and Rte. 100 N, the mammoth **Killington Resort** is unrivaled as the largest of Vermont's frozen playgrounds. Maintaining a city of resort complexes at the base of its seven peaks and 200 trails, Killington entertains the East's longest ski and snowboarding season (mid-Oct. to early June). The summer also keeps a fair pace in Killington (see below) with hiking, biking, and fishing, among other diversions. (☎800-621-6867. Lift tickets $67, ages 13-18 $54, ages 6-12 and seniors $43.) **Burke,** off I-91 in northeastern Vermont, has reasonable lift-ticket prices and features 40 trails (30% beginner, 40% intermediate, 30% expert) and a summer campground, where visitors fish, hike, and bike 200 mi. of trails. (Skiing info ☎626-3322, camping info 626-1390. Lift tickets M-F $29, Sa-Su and holiday periods $45, ages 13-17 $24/$35, under 13 $19/31. Tent sites $12; lean-tos $17.) Near the Canadian border in Vermont's Northeast Kingdom, **Jay Peak,** in Jay on Rte. 242, catches more snowfall than anywhere else in New England. With excellent woods skiing, Jay Peak is an appealing option for thrill-seekers. (☎988-2611 or 800-451-4449. 76 trails; 40% expert. Lift tickets $54, half-day $40; ages 7-17 $40/$30.)

Other resorts include **Stratton** (☎297-2200 or 800-787-2886; 90 trails, 16 lifts), on Rte. 30 N in Bondville, and **Sugarbush** (☎583-6100 or 800-537-8427; www.sugarbush.com; 2 mountains, 115 trails, 17 lifts), in Warren. Cross-country resorts include the **Trapp Family Lodge** (see **Stowe,** p. 110); **Mountain Meadows,** in Killington (☎775-7077; 90 mi. of trails); and **Woodstock** (☎457-1100; 40 mi. of trails).

KILLINGTON   ☎802

Killington, at the base of 4241 ft. Mt. Killington in the heart of the Green Mountains, attracts those who love the outdoors in all seasons. In winter, the town rouses itself into a frenzy of activity centered on the skiing season.

▐▌ TRANSPORTATION AND PRACTICAL INFORMATION. Vermont Transit (☎800-552-8737), in the Killington Deli on Rte. 4 at the intersection with Rte. 100 N, runs to White River Junction (1hr., 7am, $7.50-8.50). **The Bus** leaves from the Transit Station to shuttle visitors to over 15 stops around town. (☎ 773-3244. Jan.-Mar. 12 per day 7:15am-11:15pm. Apr.-June and Sept.-Dec. 6 per day 7:15am-5:15pm July-Aug. 10 per day 7:15am-7:15pm. $2.) If you need more flexible wheels, **Gramp's Shuttle** (☎ 236-6600) will come to your aid. The **Killington Chamber of Commerce,** on U.S. 4 just west of the intersection with Killington Rd., is the best source of area information. (☎ 773-4181 or 800-337-1928; www.killingtonchamber.com. Open M-F 9am-5pm; Jan.-Mar. and July-Oct. also Sa 9am-5pm.) To get geared up for the slopes, visit **The Basin Ski Shop,** 2886 Killington Rd., where a friendly staff will suit you up for a big day on the mountains. (☎ 422-3234. Open late Oct. to May M-Th 8:15am-9pm, F 8:15am-midnight, Sa-Su 7:15am-9pm; May to late Oct. M and Th-Sa 9:30am-6pm, Tu-W and Su 9:30am-5pm. Ski, boot, and pole package $25 per day.)

◨◧ ACCOMMODATIONS AND FOOD. Prices for lodging in the area are highly seasonal, lowest in the summer months and highest over holiday weekends at the peak of ski season. **Trailside Lodge ❸,** on Rte. 100 N 2½ mi. from the intersection with Rte. 4, is the best bargain in town. Peak season perks include a full breakfast buffet, a four-course family-style dinner, a big-screen TV in the lounge, lift ticket discounts, year-round hot tub and heated outdoor pool access, and free bus tickets to the resort. Rates are directly proportional to group size, and each room can accommodate up to 6 people. (☎ 422-3532 or 800-447-2209; www.trailside-lodge.com. Early and late season $35-50 per person. Mid-winter and holidays up to $70-85 per person.) In summer, camping at one of 27 sites or 21 lean-tos at the **Gifford Woods State Park ❶** is an inexpensive option with a wooded setting, hot showers ($0.25 per 5 min.), and well-kept campsites. (May to mid-Oct. ☎ 775-5354, Jan.-May 888-409-7579. 4-person sites $14; lean-tos $21. Each additional person $4.)

A plow car that formerly kept the rail track clear of snow now houses **Casey's Caboose ❷,** 2½ mi. up Killington Rd. from Rte. 4., a restaurant and bar that gives away 40,000 lb. of free chicken wings every winter. Munch away on the raised deck or snuggle into a booth for a salmon or prime rib dinner for $16-22. (☎ 422-3795. Free wings daily 3-6pm. Open 3pm-midnight.) **Johnny Boy's Pancake House ❶,** 923 Killington Rd., is the place to start the day with enormous breakfasts ($3.50-7.50) that will keep you energized all day. (☎ 422-4411. Open M and Th-F 8am-1pm, Sa-Su 7am-2pm.) If the snows have frozen your toes, go where a local goes: **Ppeppers ❷,** on Killington Rd. Spicy dishes, from fajitas ($11-13) to Buffalo chicken sandwiches ($8), warm up even the coldest nights. (☎ 422-3177. Open daily 9am-10pm.)

◪◩ OUTDOOR ACTIVITIES AND NIGHTLIFE. During the green season the slopes and surrounding mountains turn into hiking and biking throughways. **Gifford Woods State Park** on Rte. 100, ¾ mi. from the intersection of Rte. 4 and Rte. 100 N, offers connecting trails to Vermont's major trails, the **AT** and the **Long Trail.** Trail information can be obtained at the park office. (☎ 775-5354. Park office open May to mid-Oct. Su-Th 9am-8:30pm, F-Sa 9am-9pm. Day-use fee $2.50, ages 4-13 $2. Fishing licenses available at the park office $15 per day, $41 per season.) The **Killington Resort Complex** also provides summer recreation options at its two mountain centers. (☎ 422-3333. All-day adventure center pass $30, ages 6-12 and seniors $25; with mountain biking, including bike lift access for the many mountain trails, $40/$35. Mountain bike rentals 2hr. $30, under 12 $15; 4hr. $35/$17; full-day $45/$22.) Rent less expensive wheels at **First Stop,** south of the resort complex along Rte. 4. (☎ 422-9050. Open May-Sept. M and Th-Su 9am-6pm. Bikes $25 per day.)

For year-round nightlife, head next door to **The Nightspot at Outback Pizza,** near the junction of Rte. 100 and Killington Rd. Live rock and DJs entertain both the sparse summer crowds and the hordes in winter. (☎ 422-9885. No cover. Open in summer daily 5pm-late; in winter Su-F 4pm-late, Sa 3:30-late.) When the temperature drops, the doors of two of Vermont's best locales for nightlife open up on Killington Rd. After Halloween, the **Wobbly Barn,** halfway up the Killington Rd., features dancing, live acts, and a free nacho bar. (☎422-6171; www.wobblybarn.com. Call for schedule.) Just past the Killington Shops at the Shack, **The Pickle Barrel** warms things up with frequent happy hour events and offers a place for the winter crowds to rock late into the night. The Pickle Barrel has hosted such names as Blues Traveler and Ziggy Marley. (☎422-3035; www.picklebarrelnightclub.com. Info on tickets and scheduled happy hours available online.) Free rides from the resort to the nightclub are provided by The Pickle Barrel (☎422-RIDE/422-7433).

BURLINGTON ☎802

Tucked between Lake Champlain and the Green Mountains, the largest city in Vermont offers spectacular views of New York's Adirondack Mountains across the sailboat-studded waters of the lake. Several colleges, including the University of Vermont (UVM), give the area a youthful, progressive flair. Along the bustling and pedestrian-friendly downtown marketplace of Church St., numerous cafes offer a taste of middle-class hippie atmosphere and a chance for people-watching.

ⵕ⃗ TRANSPORTATION AND PRACTICAL INFORMATION. Two roads lead to Burlington, **Rte. 7** from Shelburne in the south, and **Rte. 2** connecting to I-89 from the east. Three miles east of Burlington, off Rte. 2, **Burlington International Airport** (☎863- 2874) flies to a handful of major cities. **Chittenden County Transit Authority (CCTA)** runs U Mall/Airport shuttles to the airport. CCTA also serves the downtown area with unbeatable access and reliable service. Connections to Shelburne and other outlying areas also run frequently; catch buses downtown at the intersection of Cherry and Church St. (☎864-2282; www.cctaride.org. Buses operate at least every 30min. M-Sa 6:15am-10:10pm, depending on routes. $1; seniors, disabled, and ages 6-18 $0.50. Brochures available at the Chamber of Commerce.) **Amtrak,** 29 Railroad Ave., Essex Jct. (station info ☎879-7298, schedules and pricing 800-872-7245; open 1hr. before and after departures), 5 mi. east of Burlington on Rte. 15, runs to New York City (9hr., 1 per day, $62-68) and White River Junction (2hr., 1 per day, $19-27). **Vermont Transit,** 345 Pine St. (☎864-6811 or 800-552-8737; open daily 5:30am-9:30pm), runs buses to: Albany (4¾hr., 3 per day, $38); Boston (4¾hr., 4 per day, $45); Middlebury (1hr., 2 per day, $12); Montréal (2½hr., 5 per day, $26); White River Junction (2hr., 4 per day, $21). **Ski Rack,** 85 Main St., rents bikes. (☎658-3313 or 800-882-4530. Open M-Th 10am-7pm, F 10am-8pm, Sa 10am-6pm, Su 11am-5pm. Mountain bikes $10 per hr., $16 per 4hr., $22 per day; helmet and lock included. In-line skates $10 per 4hr., $14 per day. Credit card required.) **Visitor Info: Lake Champlain Regional Chamber of Commerce,** 60 Main St., Rte. 100. (☎863-3489 or 877-686-5253; www.vermont.org. Open May to mid.-Oct. M-F 8am-5pm, Sa-Su 10am-5pm; mid-Oct. to Apr. M-F 8am-5pm.) **Internet Access:** Fletcher Free Library, 235 College St. (☎863-3403. Open M-Tu and Th-F 8:30am-6pm, W 8:30am-9pm, Sa 9am-5pm, Su noon-6pm. Free.) **Post Office:** 11 Elmwood Ave., at Pearl St. (☎863-6033. Open M-F 8am-5pm, Sa 8am-1pm.) **Postal Code:** 05401. **Area Code:** 802.

⛉ ACCOMMODATIONS. The Chamber of Commerce has the complete rundown on area accommodations, which tend toward upscale lodgings. B&Bs can be found in the outlying suburbs. Reasonably priced hotels and guest houses line **Shelburne Road (Route 7),** south of downtown, and **Main Street (Route 2),** east of downtown. **⧖Mrs. Farrell's Home Hostel (HI) ❶,** 27 Arlington Ct., 3 mi. north of downtown via North Ave. and Heineberg Rd., is a welcoming abode for the homesick traveler. Six beds are split between a clean, comfortable basement and a lovely "summer cottage." (☎865-3730, call for reservations 4-6pm. Check-in before 5pm. Dorms $17, nonmembers $20; cot-

Burlington

♠ ▲ ACCOMMODATIONS

Lang House, **3**
Mrs. Farrell's Home Hostel, **2**
North Beach Campsites, **1**

● FOOD
Liquid Energy Cafe, **5**
NECI, **4**
Sweetwater's, **7**
Zabby and Elf's
  Stone Soup, **8**

🌙 NIGHTLIFE
Nectar's, **10**
Red Square, **9**
Rira, **6**

═ ═ ═ Bike paths

tage $40/$43.) Soft elegant beds, five-star furnishings, and first-class service await the guests of the **Lang House ❺**, 360 Main St., only a 5-10min. walk from Church St. and downtown. With a view of Lake Champlain from the third floor rooms and a full gourmet breakfast, Lang House ensures a luxurious stay. (☎652-2500 or 877-919-9799. Rooms with TV and A/C $135-195.) The **North Beach Campsites ❶**, on Institute Rd., 1½ mi. north of town by North Ave., have 150 sites with access to a pristine sandy beach on Lake Champlain. Take Rte. 127 to North Ave., or the "North Ave." bus from the main terminal on Pine St. (☎862-0942 or 800-571-1198. Showers $0.25 per 5min. $5 parking fee for non-campers. Open May to mid-Oct. Sites $22, with water and electricity $28, full hookup $30-31.) The beach is open to non-campers, rents canoes and kayaks, and is a stellar spot for picnics. (Beach open 24hr. for campers; beach parking closes at 9pm. Lifeguards on duty mid-June to Aug. 10am-5:30pm. Boat rentals from **Umiak.** (☎253-2317. Canoes $18 per hr., kayaks $12-25 per hr. Open daily 10am-5pm.) See **Champlain Valley** (p. 108) for more camping options.

⬛ FOOD. With approximately 85 restaurants in the **Church Street Marketplace** and its adjacent sidestreets, visitors could eat in this food lover's paradise for weeks without hitting the same place twice. A mostly vegetarian cafe, ⬛**Zabby and Elf's Stone Soup ❶**, 211 College St., offers a wide variety of stews, casseroles, rice, and customizable salads from the hot and cold bars ($6 per lb.), as well as sandwiches

($6-7) on freshly baked bread. (☎ 862-7616. Open M 7am-7pm, Tu-F 7am-9pm, Sa 9am-7pm. Cash or check only.) At the **Liquid Energy Cafe ❶,** 57 Church St., customers can concoct delicious smoothies ($3-5) from the long list of unconventional ingredients like wheatgrass, rhubarb, papaya, and herbal "boosts," many of which claim restorative powers over the mind and body. Custom-build yours to cure anything from acne to asthma, tap into their free wireless Internet, or just grab a seat and let your smoothie work its wonders. (☎ 860-7666. Open M-Th 9am-7pm, F-Sa 9am-8pm, Su 10am-7pm.) The **New England Culinary Institute (NECI) ❸,** 25 Church St., known for its superb food at very reasonable prices, is a proving ground for student chefs. Have a seat at a candlelit table, or dine *al fresco* along Church Street. (☎ 862-6324. Dinner entrees from $14. Open M-Th 11:30am-4pm and 5:30-10pm, F-Sa 11:30am-4pm and 5:30-10:30pm, Su 11am-3pm and 5:30-9pm; winter closes 30min.-1hr. earlier.) At **Sweetwater's ❷,** 120 Church St., high ceilings and vast wall paintings dwarf those who come for the delicious French onion soup ($6) and wide variety of sandwiches ($6-9). When the warm weather rolls around, ask to be seated outdoors. (☎ 864-9800. Open M-F 11:30am-11pm, Sa-Su 11:30am-midnight.)

◪ SIGHTS. The **◪Shelburne Museum,** 7 mi. south of Burlington on Rte. 7 S in Shelburne, houses one of the most impressive collections of Americana in the country. Ride the free trolley around the 45-acre museum to watch blacksmith demonstrations or visit a 1950s New York City apartment decorated with works by Degas, Rembrandt, Cassat, Monet, Whistler, and Manet. The grounds hold a 19th-century general store, a 1906 paddleboat, a covered bridge, a lighthouse, and a collection of cultural artifacts instrumental in building the American Dream. (☎ 985-3346; www.shelburnemuseum.org. Open mid-May to late Oct. daily 10am-5pm. $18, students $13, ages 6-18 $9; after 3pm $10, ages 6-18 $5.) Discover ecology, culture, and history at **ECHO,** 1 College St., a science center and lake aquarium near the water. The multitude of hands-on exhibits, like the sunken pirate ship or horseshoe crab tank, and interactive demos are fun for young and old alike. (☎ 864-1848; www.echovermont.org. Open M-W and F-Su 10am-5pm, Th 10am-8pm. $9, students and seniors $8, ages 3-17 $6.) The **Ethan Allen Homestead** rests north of Burlington on Rte. 127 in the Winooski Valley Park. In the 1780s, Allen, his Green Mountain Boys, and Benedict Arnold forced the surrender of Fort Ticonderoga and helped establish the state of Vermont. Now, 1hr. tours visit the cabin and tell the story of the frontiersman. (☎ 865-4556; www.ethanallenhomestead.org. Open May-Oct. M-Sa 10am-5pm, Su 1-5pm; Nov.-Apr. Sa 10am-5pm. $5, seniors $4, ages 5-17 $3; families $15.)

Amateur historians delight in **South Willard Street,** where **Champlain College** occupies many of the Victorian houses that line the street. **City Hall Park,** in the heart of downtown, and **Battery Street Park,** on Lake Champlain near the edge of downtown, are a wonderful escape to cool shade on hot summer days. For travelers who long to feel the wind in their sails, just north lies the **Lake Champlain Community Sailing Center,** 1 Lake St., where sailboat rentals ($25-$42 per hr.) and private instruction on the water ($45 per hr., $20 per hr. each additional person) are available. (☎ 864-2499; www.lccsc.org. Open M-F 9am-8pm, Sa-Su 10am-8pm. Lessons M-Th 5-8pm, Sa-Su 9am-noon.) The **Spirit of Ethan Allen III** runs a narrated, 500-passenger scenic cruise that departs from the boathouse at the bottom of College St. (☎ 862-8300; www.soea.com. 1½hr. cruises late May to mid-Oct. daily 10am, noon, 2, 4pm; 2½hr. sunset cruise 6:30pm. $10, ages 3-11 $4. Sunset cruise $17/$13.)

▨ ◪ FESTIVALS AND NIGHTLIFE. With so many colleges in the area, Burlington's nightlife scene is always alive and kicking. A pedestrian haven, Church St. Marketplace nurtures offbeat puppeteers and musicians who entertain the crowds at all hours. Pick up a free *Seven Days* newspaper, available all over Burlington, to get the skinny on what's happening around town. In the summer, the **Vermont Mozart Festival** brings Bach, Beethoven, and Mozart to local barns, farms, and meadows. (☎862-7352; www.vtmozart.com. Concerts late July to early Aug.) In mid-July, the **Discover Jazz Festival** features over 1000 musicians, with past performers including Ella Fitzgerald, Dizzy Gillespie, and Betty Carter. (☎863-7992; www.discoverjazz.com. Some performances are free but others are sold through the Flynn Theater Box Office.) The **Champlain Valley Folk Festival,** located about halfway between Burlington and Middlebury, enlivens summer days in early August. (☎877-850-0206; www.cvfest.org. Tickets $25-75.) The **Flynn Theater Box Office,** 153 Main St., handles sales for the Folk Festival and the Discover Jazz Festival. (☎652-4500; www.flynncenter.org. Open M-F 10am-5pm, Sa 11am-4pm.)

Nectar's, 188 Main St., rocks with inexpensive food, including the locally acclaimed gravy fries ($3). The large stage and dance floor cater nightly to live tunes of all genres from bands both local and mainstream. (☎658-4771. Cover varies. Open M-Tu 11am-2:30am, W-F 6am-2:30am, Sa-Su 7am-2:30am.) One of Burlington's most popular night spots, **Red Square,** 136 Church St., presents a long, fully stocked bar and dishes out live music nightly. Bands play everything from funk to classic rock in the alley if the crowd gets large. (☎859-8909. Cover varies. Open daily 4pm-2am.) For a laid-back pint, try **Rira,** 123 Church St., a traditional Irish pub with deep wood booths and a quieter crowd. (☎860-9401. Beer $2.50-4.50. Open M-Sa 11:30am-2am, Su 11:30am-1am.)

🎇 DAYTRIP FROM BURLINGTON: CHAMPLAIN VALLEY. Stretching 100 mi. between Vermont's Green Mountains and New York's Adirondacks, **Lake Champlain** boasts plentiful opportunities for biking, hiking, and camping in the many well-kept state parks that dot the shorelines of the lake. Visitors can take a bridge or ferry across the lake to gain the best views of its silvery surface. The **Lake Champlain Ferry,** located on the dock at the bottom of King St., sails from Burlington to Port Kent, NY, and back. (☎864-9804; www.ferries.com. 1hr. each way. July-Aug. 11-13 per day 7:30am-7:30pm; mid-May to late June and Sept. to mid-Oct. 9 per day 8am-6:35pm. One-way $3.75, ages 6-12 $1.50; car and driver $13.75.) Throughout the day, service from Grand Isle, VT to Plattsburg, NY, and from Charlotte, VT, to Essex, NY, is also offered. (One-way $2.75, ages 6-12 $0.75; car and driver $7.75.)

Fog drifts over the grasslands hiding the countless migratory birds that come to rest in the marsh of the **Missisquoi National Wildlife Refuge,** 2 mi. to the northwest of Swanton, VT on Rte. 78 at the northern end of the lake. The refuge provides extensive lands for hiking, bird watching, kayaking, and canoeing in warm weather, and cross-country skiing and snowshoeing in the winter. (☎868-4781. Office open M-F 8am-4:30pm. Refuge open dawn-dusk. Free.) **Mount Philo State Park ❶,** 15 mi. south of Burlington, off Rte. 7, offers pleasant, easy-to-moderate hiking and picnic facilities with an expansive view of deep forests, green pastures, and winding roads leading to a distant mountainous horizon. Camping is offered on seven sites nestled on the side of the mountain among the trees. (☎425-2390. Open mid-May to mid-Oct. daily 10am-dusk. Entrance fee $2.50, ages 4-13 $2. 2-night min. stay. For 14-day advance reservations at any of the Vermont state parks listed here, call ☎888-409-7579. 7 sites without hookup $14; 3 lean-tos $21.)

Also north of the lake, **Burton Island State Park ❶** is accessible only by private boats and a ferry which runs five times daily from Kill Kare State Park, 35 mi. north of Burlington and 3½ mi. southwest of U.S. 7 off of Town Rd., near St. Albans Bay. This secluded park, devoid of cars, provides a tranquil place to hike, swim, and picnic. (☎524-6353. Open late May to early Sept. daily 8am-8pm; call for schedule. Day-use $2.50, ages 4-13 $2. Ferry service $3 each way. Bike rental $1. 4-night min. stay. 17 tent sites $16; 26 lean-tos $23. Each additional person $4.) The state park on **Grand Isle ❶,** just off U.S. 2, north of Keeler Bay, also offers lakeside camping with a small rocky beach. (☎372-4300. Rowboat and kayak rentals $5.25 per hr., $32 per day. Reservations strongly recommended, especially for summer weekends; 2-night min. stay required for reservations. Open mid-May to mid-Oct. 4-person sites $16; lean-tos $23; each additional person $4. Cabins $46. No day-use.) Also along the Champlain Islands are myriad **biking trips** (☎ 597-4646; www.champlainbike-ways.org), **state parks** available for day use (**Alburg Dunes** ☎ 796-4170; **Knight Point** ☎ 343-7236; **North Hero** ☎ 372-8727; **Knight Island** ☎ 524-6353; www.vtstateparks.com), and the **Lipizzan Stallions.** These horses, known for their grace and amazing strength, perform four times weekly. (Champlain Islands Chamber of Commerce ☎ 372-8400 for more information; www.herrmannslipizzans.com. Located 1½ mi. past the drawbridge between Grand Isle and North Hero on Rte. 2 W. Performances Th-F 6pm, Sa-Su 2:30pm. $15, seniors $12, ages 6-12 $8.)

MIDDLEBURY   ☎ 802

Vermont's "Landmark College Town" surges with the energy and culture stimulated by the bohemian momentum of Middlebury College. The result is a traditional Vermont atmosphere tinged with both vitality and history.

📧🔲 TRANSPORTATION AND PRACTICAL INFORMATION. Middlebury sits along U.S. 7, 42 mi. south of Burlington. **Vermont Transit** stops at the Exxon station, 16 Court St., west of Main St. (☎ 388-9300. Station open daily 6am-10pm.) Buses run to: Albany (4hr., 3 per day, $31); Boston (6hr., 3 per day, $48); Burlington (1hr., 3 per day, $11); Rutland (1½hr., 3 per day, $8). **Addison County Transit Resources** provides free shuttle service in the immediate Middlebury vicinity, making stops every hour at the town green, Marbleworks, Middlebury College, and along U.S. 7 S. (☎ 388-1946. Runs M-F 7am-8:30pm, Sa-Su 9am-5pm.) Exploring on foot is probably the easiest way around town, but for those who prefer wheels, the **Bike Center,** 74 Main St., rents bikes. (☎ 388-6666; www.bikecentermid.com. Open M-Th and Sa 9:30am-5:30pm, F 9:30am-8pm; June-Sept. also Su 1-4pm. Bikes from $20 per day.) The staff at the **Addison County Chamber of Commerce,** 2 Court St., can provide free area maps, bus schedules, and event information. (☎ 388-7951 or 800-733-8376; www.midvermont.com. Open M-F 10:30am-5pm.) **Internet Access: Ilsley Public Library,** 75 Main St. (☎ 388-4095. Open M, W, F 10am-6pm; Tu and Th 10am-8pm; Sa 10am-4pm. Free.) **Post Office:** 10 Main St. (☎ 388-2681. Open M-F 8am-5pm, Sa 8am-12:30pm.) **Postal Code:** 05753. **Area Code:** 802.

🔲 ACCOMMODATIONS. Lodging with four walls and no mosquitoes does not come cheaply in Middlebury. The **Sugar House Motel ❸,** 202 Ethan Allen Hwy., 2 mi. north of Middlebury on Rte. 7, offers clean rooms with free local calls, refrigerators, microwaves, and A/C, as well as a pool and grill. (☎ 388-2770 or 800-784-2746. Make reservations in advance. Seasonal rates from $49-$99.) For those weary of small roadside motels, the **Middlebury B&B ❹,** 174 Washington St., has four comfortably furnished rooms, soft beds, a friendly and dedicated owner, and two Jack Russell terriers guaranteed to make you feel right at home. (☎ 388-4851. Rooms $75-125.) **Branbury State Park ❶,** 7 mi. south on U.S. 7, then 4 mi. south on Rte. 53, stretches along Lake Dunmore, offering 45 spacious sites and seven lean-tos on soft grassy fields shaded by a swaying leaf canopy. (☎ 247-5925. Hot showers $0.25 per 5min. Canoe rentals $5 per hr., $30 per day. Paddle boats $5 per 30min. Open late May to mid-Oct. Sites $16; lean-tos $23.)

🔲🔲 FOOD AND NIGHTLIFE. Middlebury's restaurants cater chiefly to plump wallets, but a student presence ensures the survival of less expensive options. **Noonie's Deli ❶,** 137 Maple St., in the Marbleworks building just behind Main St., makes terrific sandwiches ($4-5) on thick slices of homemade bread. (☎ 388-0014. Open M-F 8am-8pm.) Bright colors and larger-than-life murals deck the walls of

Amigos ❸, 4 Merchants Row, which offers creative Mexican dishes like the three enchilada Mexican Flag for $11. (☎388-3624. Lunch $6-8. Dinner $8-18. Open M-Sa 11:30am-9pm, Su 4-9pm; bar open daily until 10:30pm.) ▧**Mister Up's ❷,** a popular hangout on Bakery Ln., just off Main St. , has an open-air riverside deck on which to enjoy sandwiches ($6-7), selections from the extensive salad bar, or nightly drink specials like $1 pints. (☎388-6724. Open M-Sa 11:30am-midnight, Su 11am-midnight.) Night owls head to **Angela's Pub,** 86 Main St. for live rock, the jukebox, or the cheers of a heated game of pool. (☎388-6936. Tu $1.50 pint of Labatt. F DJ. Sa live band. 21+. No cover. Open Tu-F 4pm-2am, Sa 8pm-2am, Su 2pm-midnight.) For a more mellow drinking atmosphere, laughter and the clinking of pint glasses harmonize with live jazz and mellow rock at the **Two Brothers,** next door at 88 Main St. (☎388-0002. Beer $1.75-5.50. No cover. Open daily 11:30am-2am.)

◨ **SIGHTS.** Most of the town's cultural events are hosted by **Middlebury College;** the concert hall in the college **Arts Center,** just outside of town on S. Main St., has a terrific concert series. The **box office** has details on events sponsored by the college. (☎443-4168; www.middlebury.edu/cfa. Open Sept.-May M-F noon-5pm, also 1hr. before start of shows. Many events free, most $5-12.) Through the summer months, Middlebury's crack at an **International Film Festival** screens movies on Saturdays at 7 and 9:30pm in the Dana Auditorium. (☎443-5510; www.middlebury.edu/ls/film. Free.) **Tours** from the admissions office, in Emma Willard Hall on S. Main St., showcase the white marble houses and manicured fields of Middlebury's picturesque campus. (☎443-3000. Tours daily 9am and 1pm. Self-guided tour brochures are also available.) At the bottom of the hill on Mill St., the **Marbleworks Memorial Bridge** provides a terrific view of the waterfall now crumbling the mills that once generated the town's power. Too poor for a pint? Trek ¾ mi. north of town to the **Otter Creek Brewery,** 793 Exchange St., for a tour and free samples of their award-winning copper ale. (☎800-473-0727. Tours daily 1, 3, 5pm. Shop open M-Sa 10am-6pm.) Fifteen miles east of the Middlebury College campus, the **Middlebury College Snow Bowl** entertains skiers in winter with 14 trails and three lifts. (☎388-4356; www.middlebury.edu/~snowbowl. Lift tickets M-F $28, Sa-Su $35; students and seniors $23/$28; preschool $7/$7.) The **Henry Sheldon Museum of Vermont History,** 1 Park St., offers a 30-40min. tour showcasing the collection of Henry Sheldon, a historian whose knack for meticulously collecting historical artifacts, from black marble fireplaces to 19th-century textiles and silverware, has yielded an unparalleled vision of Vermont's cultural heritage. (☎388-2117; www.henrysheldonmuseum.org. Open M-Sa 10am-5pm. $5, seniors $4.50, students $4, ages 6-18 $3.)

The scenic outdoors surrounding Middlebury make for great hiking and paddling. Hiking information is liberally provided by the **Middlebury Ranger Station,** 1077 Rte. 7 S. (☎388-4362. Open M-F 8am-4:30pm.) For paddling supplies, **Middlebury Mountaineer,** 3 Mill St., can meet your needs. (☎388-1749. One-person kayak full day $50, tandem $60, ½ price each additional day. Open M-Sa 10am-5:30pm, Su noon-3pm.) Exercise your mind at the **Robert Frost Interpretive Trail,** an easy 1 mi. trail starting from a parking lot 2 mi. east of Ripton on Rte. 125. Excerpts from the poet's works are mounted on plaques along the path in spots similar to ones that might have inspired the poems' creation. (☎388-4362. Free.)

STOWE ☎802

Stowe curls gracefully up the side of Mt. Mansfield—Vermont's highest peak, at 4393 ft. A mecca for outdoor activities in all seasons, Stowe tries to offer the charm and character of an alpine ski village. The proliferation of Swiss chalets evokes the feeling of a charming Swiss village lost in the mountains of Vermont.

NEW ENGLAND

TRANSPORTATION AND PRACTICAL INFORMATION. Stowe is 10 mi. north of I-89 off Exit 10, 27 mi. southwest of Burlington. The ski slopes lie along **Mountain Road (Route 108),** northwest of Stowe. **Vermont Transit** (☎244-7689 or 800-552-8737; open M-Sa 5am-9pm, Su 6am-8pm) comes only as close as **Depot Beverage,** 1 River Rd., in Waterbury, 11 mi. from Stowe, and runs to Boston (4hr., 1 per day, $53) and Burlington (30min., 1 per day, $8-9). **Peg's Pick-up/Stowe Taxi** (☎253-9490 or 800-370-9490) will take you into Stowe for around $25 plus $5 for each additional passenger; call ahead. In winter, the **Stowe Trolley** runs up and down Mountain Rd. every 20-30min., picking up passengers. (☎223-7BUS/7287; www.stoweshuttle.org. Trolley runs in winter 7:30am-10pm. $1, seniors and ages 17 and under $0.50; weekly pass $10, season pass $20. July to mid-Oct. daily 1½hr. tours leave from town hall at 11am. $2.) **Visitors Info: Stowe Area Association,** 51 Main St. (☎253-7321 or 800-247-8693; www.gostowe.com. Open June to mid-Oct. and mid-Dec. to Mar. M-Sa 9am-8pm, Su 9am-5pm; mid-Oct. to mid-Dec. and Apr.-June M-F 9am-5pm.) Pick up the free *Stowe Scene* newspaper and the *Vacation Planner* guide here for event listings and recreation information. **Internet Access: Stowe Free Library,** 90 Pond St. (☎253-6145. Open M, W, F 9:30am-5:30pm, Tu and Th 2-7pm, Sa 10am-3pm. Free.) **Post Office:** 105 Depot St., off Main St. (☎253-7521. Open M-F 7:15am-5pm, Sa 9am-noon.) **Postal Code:** 05672. **Area Code:** 802.

ACCOMMODATIONS. Easy access is one of many reasons to stay at the **Stowe Bound Lodge ❶,** 645 S. Main St., located ½ mi. south of the intersection of Rte. 100 and 108. Small rooms come at an excellent price, and the friendly owners make travelers feel at ease with their engaging conversation and comfortable common space. (☎253-4515. Private rooms with shared bath $20 per person.) **Foster's Place ❷,** 4968 Mountain Rd., offers dorm rooms with a lounge, laundry facilities, game room, outdoor pool, and hot tub/sauna in a recently renovated school building. (☎253-9448 or 800-330-4880. Reservations recommended. Singles $35-39, with private bath $49-59; quads $55. Call for seasonal rates.) A converted 19th-century farm house and adjacent motel, the **Riverside Inn ❸,** 1965 Mountain Rd., 2 mi. from town, offers great perks, such as the free loan of their mountain bikes and use of the pool table and fireplace in the lodge. (☎253-4217 or 800-966-4217. Rooms $49-109.) **Smugglers' Notch State Park ❶,** 6443 Mountain Rd., 8 mi. west of Stowe, just past Foster's Place, has hot showers, tent sites, and lean-tos. Scanty amenities are more than made up for by the beauty and seclusion of the park's sites and its views of Mt. Mansfield. (☎253-4014. Reservations recommended. Open late May to mid-Oct. 4-person sites $14; lean-tos $21. Each additional person $4.)

FOOD AND NIGHTLIFE. At the **Depot Street Malt Shoppe ❶,** 57 Depot St., sports pennants and vinyl records deck the walls, while rock 'n' roll favorites liven up the outdoor patio seating. The cost of a 1950s-style hot fudge sundae has been adjusted for inflation ($4), but prices remain reasonable. (☎253-4269. Entrees $5-8. Open daily 11:30am-9pm.) Perfect for picnics, **Mac's Deli ❶,** located in Mac's Stowe Market, on S. Main St. ¼ mi. from the intersection of Rte. 100 and Rte. 108, has tasty sandwiches, subs, and wraps ($4-6) made with any of the meats and cheeses in the market's deli selection. They also serve piping hot soups for $2-3. (☎253-4576. No seating. Open M-Sa 7am-9pm, Su 7am-8pm.) Fans of little green men and all things not of this planet will enjoy **Pie in the Sky ❸,** 492 Mountain Rd. Their "Out of This World" pizzas include the "Blond Vermonter" with olive oil, Vermont cheddar, apples, and ham. (☎253-5100. Pizza $8-17. Open daily 11:30am-10pm.)

For sports fans, the **Sunset Grille and Tap Room,** 140 Cottage Club Rd., off Mountain Rd., allows its guests to face off on the pool tables while following numerous sporting events on over 15 TVs, including four big screens. The adjacent restaurant offers barbecue entrees. (☎253-9281. Lunch $4-9. Dinner $10-15. Kitchen open

RTE. 100: FOOD FREEWAY

Sickeningly sweet and decadently delicious, the road leading north from I-87 to Stowe, VT, is paved with tasty temptations. Begin at the ⊠ **Ben and Jerry's Ice Cream Factory** with the tale of two amateur ice-cream makers who created world-famous concoctions—and two sample flavors. (☎882-3586. Tours daily June 9am-5pm; July to late Aug. 9am-8pm; late Aug. to Oct. 9am-6pm; Nov.-May 10am-5pm. $3, seniors $2, under 12 free.) Next is the **Cabot Annex Store,** home to **Lake Champlain Chocolates** and the **Cabot Creamery Cooperative.** The annex bursts at the seams with chocolates and Vermont's best cheddar, offering free samples of both. (Lake Champlain Chocolates ☎241-4150, Cabot Creamery Cooperative ☎244-6334. Open daily 9am-6pm.) Try heavenly nectars at **Cold Hollow Cider Mill,** with free samples of cider, jams, and jellies—you can even pick up $0.40 doughnuts. (☎800-327-7537. Open daily 8am-7pm.) Next door, the **Grand View Winery** offers tastes of hard cider and wines made from ingredients including pear and elderberry (☎456-7012; open daily 11am-5pm; $1), and the **Waterbury Center** mixes sinfully rich fudge. (Open daily 9am-7pm. Free samples.) Finally, saturate your senses with maple at **Stowe Maple Products,** where home-harvested syrups are sampled year-round. (☎253-2508. Open M-Sa 9am-5pm, Su 10am-4pm.)

daily 11:30am-midnight; bar open until 2am.) The weekday specials and six homemade microbrews served up in **The Shed,** 1859 Mountain Rd., make this brewery stand out. Divided into a restaurant and a tavern, late-nighters can choose to share a quiet pint or a crazy one. (☎253-4364. Tu night $2.50 pints. Open daily 11:30am-midnight.) Head to the **Rusty Nail,** 1 mi. from town center on Mountain Rd., to dance the night away in a renovated barn. (☎253-6245. Th-Sa live music or DJ 9pm-2am. 21+. Cover $5-15. Open Su-W 11:30am-10pm, Th-Sa 11:30am-2am.)

◪ **SKIING.** Stowe's ski offerings include the Stowe Mountain Resort (☎253-3000 or 800-253-4754) and Smugglers' Notch (☎644-8851 or 800-451-8752; see **Vermont Ski Resorts,** p. 102). The hills are alive with the area's best cross-country skiing on 60km of groomed trails and 45km of backcountry trails on the softly undulating mountainsides surrounding **The Trapp Family Lodge,** 2 mi. off Mountain Rd., accessed from Luce Hill Rd. Budget traveler beware: prices for lodging climb to as much as $960 in the high season. However, inexpensive rentals and lessons coupled with the unparalleled serenity of backcountry skiing make this alpine winter wonderland a temptation hard to avoid. (☎253-5719 or 800-826-7000; www.trappfamily.com. Trail fee $16, ski rentals $20, lessons $15-45 per hr. Ski school package includes all 3 for $40.) **AJ's Ski and Sports,** 350 Mountain Rd., rents ski equipment in winter. (☎253-4593 or 800-226-6257. Open in winter Su-Th 8am-8pm, F-Sa 8am-9pm; in summer daily 9am-6pm. Skis, boots, and poles: downhill $26 per day, $50 for 2 days; cross-country $15/28; snowboard and boots $22 per day.)

◙◪ **SIGHTS AND OUTDOOR ACTIVITIES.** In summer, Stowe's frenetic pace drops off some, but it still burns with the energy of outdoor enthusiasts. **Action Outfitters,** 2160 Mountain Rd., can serve nearly all recreation needs. (☎253-7975. Open daily May-Oct. 9am-5pm; Oct.-May 8am-6pm. Mountain bikes $7 per hr., $16 half-day, $24 full day; in-line skates $6/$12/$18. Canoes $25 half-day, $30 full day.) Stowe's 5½ mi. asphalt **recreation path** runs parallel to Mountain Rd. (Rte.108) and begins behind the church on Main St. in Stowe, ascending toward Smugglers' Notch through peaceful meadows and thick forest glades. Perfect for biking, skating, and strolling in the summer, the path accommodates cross-country skiing and snowshoeing in the winter. A few miles past Smugglers' Notch on Mountain Rd. (Rte. 108), the road shrinks to one lane and winds past huge boulders and 1000 ft. high cliffs. *Road closures through the pass are common in the winter, and strong caution should be observed if attempting any winter ascent.*

Stowe boasts mountain streams prime for fly fishing, including the popular Winooski River. Seasoned and aspiring fly fishermen should head to the **Fly Rod Shop,** 2½ mi. south of Stowe on Rte. 100, to pick up the necessary fishing licenses ($15 per day, $30 per week, $41 per year; $20 per year for VT residents), rent fly rods and reels, and enroll in the free fly fishing classes in the shop's pond. (☎253-7346 or 800-535-9763. Classes W 4-6pm, Sa 9-11am. Open Apr.-Oct. M-Sa 9am-6pm, Su 10am-4pm; Nov.-Mar. M-Sa 9am-5pm, Su 10am-4pm. Rods and reels $15 per day.) **Umiak,** on Rte. 100, ¾ mi. south of Stowe Center, rents kayaks and canoes in the summer. (☎253-2317. Open daily 9am-6pm; winter hours vary. River trip $38 per person; rental and transportation to the river included. Kayaks $12 per hr., $24 for 4hr.; canoes $18/$34.) Just 1¼ mi. north on Edson Road, off Mountain Rd. north of Stowe, **Edson Hill Manor Stables** offers guided 1hr. horseback rides ($35) on the southeastern ridge of Smugglers' Notch through cool woodlands and lush green meadows bespeckled by wildflowers. (☎253-8954 or 253-7371. Refreshments provided upon return. Call for tours and availability.) **Ziemke Glassblowing Studio,** 7 mi. south of Stowe along Rte. 100, allows free viewing of the entire glassblowing process—from a molten mass in the 2100°F furnace to finished vases, glasses, and candleholders. The wares being made are also for sale in the gallery. (☎244-6126. Open daily 10am-6pm. Glass $15-300.)

MASSACHUSETTS

Massachusetts regards itself, with some justification, as the nation's intellectual center. Since the 1636 establishment of Cambridge's Harvard College, the oldest college in America, Massachusetts has been a breeding ground for academics and literati. The undisputed highlight of the state is Boston, the birthplace of the American Revolution (a.k.a. the "Cradle of Liberty"), a small, diverse city packed full of cultural and historical attractions. Resplendent with bright colors during the fall, the Berkshire Mountains fill western Massachusetts with arts and music. The seaside areas, from Nantucket to Northern Bristol and scenic Cape Cod, illuminate the stark beauty that first attracted settlers to these shores.

⁈ PRACTICAL INFORMATION

Capital: Boston.

Visitor Info: Office of Travel and Tourism, 10 Park Plaza, Ste. 4510, Boston 02116 (☎617-973-8500 or 800-227-6277; www.massvacation.com). Free, comprehensive *Getaway Guide* available online or in person. Open M-F 9am-5pm.

Postal Abbreviation: MA. **Sales Tax:** 5%; no tax on clothing and pre-packaged food.

BOSTON   ☎617

Perhaps more than any other American city, Boston reveals the limits of the "melting pot." The Financial District's corporate sanctuaries are visible from the North End's winding streets. Aristocratic Beacon Hill is just across Boston Common from the nation's first Chinatown. The trendy South End abuts the less gentrified neighborhoods of Roxbury and Dorchester. While walking Boston's famed Freedom Trail will expose you to some of the earliest history of the US—in which the city played a starring role—wandering the streets of Boston's neighborhoods lends a glimpse into a still-evolving metropolis. For more comprehensive coverage of the Boston area, see ▨*Let's Go: Boston.*

NEW ENGLAND

✈ INTERCITY TRANSPORTATION

Airport: Logan International (☎800-235-6426; www.massport.com/logan), 5 mi. northeast of Downtown. T: Airport; a free shuttle connects all 5 terminals to the T stop. **Back Bay Coach** (☎888-222-5229; www.backbaycoach.com) runs door-to-door service to and from the airport (24hr. advanced reservation recommended). A **taxi** to downtown costs $15-20.

Trains: South Station, Summer St. at Atlantic Ave. T: South Station. Open 24hr. **Amtrak** runs to: **New York City** (3½-4½hr., 10 per day, $64-99); **Philadelphia** (5-6hr., 10 per day, $80-163); **Washington, D.C.** (6½-8hr., 10 per day, $89-176).

Buses: Buses depart South Station. T: South Station. Open 24hr.

Bonanza Bus (☎888-751-8800; www.bonanzabus.com) runs to **New York City** (4¾hr., 10 per day, $30) and **Providence** (1hr., 16 per day, $8-9).

Greyhound runs to: **New York City** (4½-6½hr., every 30min., $35); **Philadelphia** (7-8½hr., every hr., $55); **Washington, D.C.** (10-11hr., every 1-2hr., $66).

Peter Pan Trailways (☎800-237-8747; www.peterpanbus.com) runs to **Albany** (4-4½hr., 3-4 per day, $32-37).

Plymouth & Brockton St. Railway (☎508-746-0378; www.p-b.com) goes to **Plymouth** (1hr., $10) and **Cape Cod,** including **Hyannis** (1½hr., 35 per day, $15) and **Provincetown** (3¼hr., $24).

Vermont Transit (☎800-552-8737; www.vermonttransit.com) goes north to: **Burlington** (5hr., 4 per day, $51); **Montréal** (8hr., 6 per day, $61); **Portland** (2hr., 6 per day, $16).

⚜ ORIENTATION

Boston, the capital of Massachusetts and the largest city in New England, is situated on a peninsula jutting into Massachusetts Bay (bordered to the north and west by the **Charles River** and to the east by **Boston Harbor**). The city proper is centered on the grassy **Boston Common;** the popular **Freedom Trail** (p. 119) begins here and links most of the city's major sights. The Trail heads east through crowded **Downtown** (still the same compact 3 sq. mi. settled in 1630), skirting the city's growing **Waterfront** district to the southeast. The Trail then veers north to the charming **North End,** Boston's "Little Italy," bounded by the **Fitzgerald Expressway (I-93),** then crosses the river to historic **Charlestown.**

Boston Common is sandwiched between **Beacon Hill** to the north and **Chinatown** to the south. Much of Chinatown overlaps the nightlife-heavy **Theatre District** to the west. Just west of the common are chic **Back Bay's** grand boulevards and brownstones centered on beautiful Copley Sq., home to Boylston St., a bar-hopper's paradise. The **Massachusetts Turnpike (I-90)** separates Back Bay from the artsy and predominantly gay **South End,** which has a lion's share of the city's best restaurants. West of Back Bay are **Kenmore Square** and **Fenway,** home to baseball's Red Sox, major museums, and the clubs of Lansdowne St. South of the Fenway is vibrant, gay-friendly **Jamaica Plain,** filled with green spaces and cheap restaurants.

☰ LOCAL TRANSPORTATION

Public Transit: Massachusetts Bay Transportation Authority or **MBTA** (☎222-5000; www.mbta.com). Known as the T, the subway has 5 colored lines—Red, Blue, Orange, Green, and Silver (Green splits into lettered lines B-E)—that radiate from Downtown. "Inbound" trains head toward T: Park St. or T: Downtown Crossing; "outbound" trains head away from those stops. All T stops have maps and schedules. Lines run daily 5:30am-12:30am; "Night Owl" system of buses runs F-Sa until 2:30am. Fare $1.25, ages 5-11 $0.60, seniors $0.35. **Visitor passes** for unlimited subway and bus use are

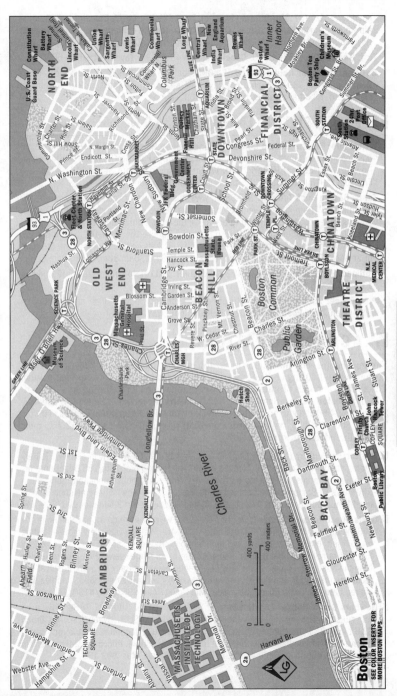

NEW ENGLAND

Boston

SEE COLOR INSERTS FOR
MORE BOSTON MAPS

good for 1 day ($7.50), 3 days ($18), or 7 days ($35). **MBTA Commuter Rail** trains run from T: **North Station** (Green/Orange) to: **Concord** (Fitchburg line; $5); **Plymouth** (Plymouth/Kingston line; 1hr., $6); **Salem** (Newburyport/Rockport line; 30min., $3.75).

Taxi: Boston Cab ☎536-5010. **Checker Taxi** ☎495-8294. **Town Taxi** ☎536-5000.

Car Rental: Dollar Rent-a-Car (☎634-0006 or 800-800-3665), at the airport. Open 24hr. Under 25 $30 surcharge per day. 10% AAA discount. Must be 21+ with major credit card. All other agencies have desks at the airport.

⁊ PRACTICAL INFORMATION

Visitor Info: Greater Boston Convention and Visitors Bureau (☎536-4100; www.bosto-nusa.com) has a booth at Boston Common, outside T: Park St. Open M-F 8:30am-5pm. Downtown's **National Historic Park Visitor Center,** 15 State St. (☎242-5642), has Freedom Trail info and tours. T: State. Open daily 9am-5pm.

Tours: Boston Duck Tours (☎267-3825; www.bostonducktours.com). Wacky con-DUCK-tors drive WWII amphibious vehicles past sights before splashing down in the Charles, offering cheesy commentary and quacking all the way. 1½hr. tours depart from the Prudential Ctr., T: Prudential, Apr.-Nov. daily every 30min.-1hr. 9am-1hr. before sunset. $24, students and seniors $21, ages 3-11 $15. Tickets sold online or at the Museum of Science, Faneuil Hall, and the Prudential Ctr. M-Sa 8:30am-8pm, Su 8:30am-6pm.

Hotlines: Rape Crisis Center, ☎492-7273. 24hr. **BGLT Help Line,** ☎267-9001. M-F 6-11pm, Sa-Su 5-10pm.

Post Office: 25 Dorchester Ave. (☎654-5302), behind South Station at T: South Station. Open 24hr. **Postal Code:** 02205. **Area Code:** 617.

⁊ ACCOMMODATIONS

Finding cheap accommodations in Boston is hard. Rates and bookings are highest in summer and during college-rush times in September, late May, and early June. Reservation services promise to find discounted rooms, even during sold-out periods. Try **Boston Reservations** (☎332-4199), **Central Reservation Service** (☎800-332-3026 or 569-3800; www.bostonhotels.net), or **Citywide Reservation Services** (☎267-7424 or 800-468-3593; www.cityres.com). All rooms in come with a 12.45% **room tax,** not included in the prices below.

⬛ **HI—Boston Fenway (HI),** 575 Commonwealth Ave. (☎267-8599), in Fenway. T: Kenmore, lets out on Comm. Ave. Housed in a former luxury hotel, with 155 bright and airy 3-bed dorm rooms with private bath and A/C and a penthouse common room with a 360° view of Boston. Same freebies as HI—Boston (see below). Linen included. Checkout 11am. Open June-Aug. Dorm bed $35, nonmembers $38; 3-bed room $87/$90. ❷

⬛ **Oasis Guest House,** 22 Edgerly Rd. (☎267-2262; www.oasisgh.com), at Stoneholm St., in Back Bay. From T: Hynes/ICA, exit onto Mass. Ave. Walking with the Virgin Megastore on your left, cross Boylston St., and turn right onto Haviland St.; the next left is Edgerly Rd. This rambling 30-room guest house is true to its name, serving as a calm respite from the hustle and bustle of the city. Continental breakfast daily 8-11am. Reservations recommended up to 2 months in advance. May to mid-Nov. singles $59; doubles with shared bath $69, with private bath $89. Mid-Nov. to Apr. $80/$90/$130. ❸

⬛ **Newbury Guest House,** 261 Newbury St. (☎437-7666 or 800-437-7668; www.new-buryguesthouse.com), between Gloucester and Fairfield St. T: Hynes/ICA. This urban B&B offers 32 immaculately clean, bright, and tastefully decorated double rooms with private bath and digital cable. Breakfast daily 7:30-10:30am. Reception 24hr. Check-in 3pm. Check-out noon. Doubles Apr.-Oct. $125-170; Nov.-Mar. $99-125. ❺

HI–Boston (HI), 12 Hemenway St. (☎536-1027; www.bostonhostel.org), in Back Bay. From T: Hynes/ICA, walk down Massachusetts Ave., turn right onto Boylston St., then left onto Hemenway St. Central location, spotless bathrooms, quiet dorms, and a full lineup of nightly events, including free movie screenings and complimentary entrance to museums and dance clubs. Free lockers, linen, and kitchen use. Laundry facilities. Check-in noon. Check-out 11am. Dorms $32-35, nonmembers $35-38. ❷

Beantown Hostel and Irish Embassy Hostel, 222 Friend St., 3rd fl. (☎723-0800), in Downtown. Exit T: North Station onto Causeway St. and turn onto Friend St. Co-ed and single sex dorms (110 beds). Beantown curfew 1:45am; Irish Embassy (above a pub) has no curfew. Free lockers, linen, and kitchen use. Laundry facilities. Free buffet in summer Tu and Th 8pm. Check-out 10am. Dorms $25. Cash only. ❶

YMCA of Greater Boston, 316 Huntington Ave. (☎927-8040). T: Symphony. Access to world-class athletic facilities and amazing location make the surprisingly hefty pricetag more palatable. The long-term men-only residence is co-ed Sept. to mid-June with 2 floors of sterile, serviceable rooms with TV and shared bathrooms. 18+. Breakfast included. Reception 24hr. Check-out 11am. Key deposit $5. Singles $46, with private bath $66; doubles $66; triples $81; quads $96. ❷

▣ FOOD

Once a barren gastronomical wasteland whose only claim to fame was baked beans, Boston is now a culinary paradise. Trendy bistros, fusion restaurants, and a globetrotting array of ethnic eateries have taken their place alongside the long-standing "chowda" shacks, greasy-spoons, soul-food joints, and welcoming pubs.

DOWNTOWN

Downtown is the most heavily touristed part of Boston, so expect mediocre food, big crowds, and high prices. The best and most affordable food options are the identical sandwich shops (sandwiches $5-7) found on almost every street corner and the more diverse food court inside **Quincy Market** (p. 120; most dishes $5-7). Downtown is also near the fresh seafood shops lining Boston's **Waterfront** district.

Durgin Park, Quincy Market (☎227-2038). T: Government Ctr. Boston's most touristed restaurant, Durgin Park has been serving rare old New England dishes like fried seafood, Yankee pot roast, and Indian pudding, since 1827. Meat entrees $9-13. Lobster at market price. Open Su-Th 11:30am-midnight, F-Sa 11:30am-1am. ❹

No Name, 15½ Fish Pier (☎338-7539), the next pier over from the World Trade Ctr. Take the free shuttle to the WTC from T: South Station. This waterfront eatery is one of Boston's best, cheapest seafood spots, serving no-frills dishes with fish fresh off the boat, since 1917. Entrees $7-20. Open M-Sa 11am-10pm, Su 11am-9pm. Cash only. ❸

Legal Sea Foods, 255 State St. (☎227-3115), opposite the New England Aquarium, near T: Aquarium. Now a national chain, Legal Sea Foods remains Boston's finest seafood restaurant. High-quality cuisine at high prices (raw bar $8-9; entrees $18-30), with the best clam chowder ($3.75-4.50) in the city, served at every Presidential Inauguration since 1981. Open Su noon-10pm, M-Th 11am-10pm, F-Sa 11am-11pm. ❺

NORTH END

Boston's Italian-American enclave is the place to go for authentic Italian fare, with over 100 restaurants packed into 1 sq. mi. Quality doesn't vary drastically from place to place, but price does. Most establishments line **Hanover Street,** accessible from T: Haymarket. After dinner, try one of the countless Italian *caffès*. For *cannoli* ($2-3), try **Mike's Pastry,** 300 Hanover St., or **Modern Pastry,** 257 Hanover St.

Trattoria Il Panino, 11 Parmenter St. (☎720-1336), at Hanover St. A romantic North End *trattoria*—warm lighting, exposed brick, and intimate seating—with gigantic portions of classic fare. *Antipasti* $11-13. Pastas $10-15. Chicken dishes $16-17. Open Su-Th 11am-11pm, F-Sa 11am-midnight. ❹ Il Panino also runs the cheaper lunch counter **Il Panino Express,** down the street at 264 Hanover St. Calzones, 1 ft. subs, and salads $5-8. Open daily 11am-11pm. Cash only. ❷

L'Osteria, 104 Salem St. (☎723-7847). Turn left off Hanover St. onto Parmenter St., then right onto Salem St. A simple, reliable *trattoria* that serves all the robust Italian favorites found on Hanover St., but at lower prices. *Antipasti* $7-10. Pastas $9-15. Chicken dishes $15-16. Open daily 11am-11pm. ❸

Pizzeria Regina, 11½ Thacher St. (☎227-0765). Turn left off Hanover St. onto Prince St., then left again onto Thacher St. Since 1926, the North End's best pizza has come gooey, greasy, and always piping hot. Worth the lengthy wait. Open M-Th 11am-11:30pm, F-Sa 11am-midnight, Su noon-11pm. Cash only. ❶

CHINATOWN

Chinatown is *the* place for filling and cheap Asian food (not just Chinese) anytime. Stuck between the skyscrapers of the Financial District and the chaos of the Big Dig, the neighborhood is slightly grimy and run-down, but the prices are unbeatable and most places stay open until 3-4am. T: Chinatown.

🏮 **Shabu-Zen,** 16 Tyler St. (☎292-8828), off Beach St. Spartan Shabu-Zen is named for its signature do-it-yourself dish, *shabu-shabu.* Waitresses offer plates of thinly sliced meats and vegetables that you cook in pots of boiling hot water. 2-person combo plates $10-15, a la carte $5-10. Open Su-W 11:30am-11pm, Th-Sa 11:30am-midnight. ❸

Jumbo Seafood Restaurant, 5-7-9 Hudson St. (☎542-2823). Greet your dinner swimming in the tanks by the entrance at the best of Chinatown's Hong Kong-style seafood spots, with huge plates, a light touch, and a glowing velvet mural on the wall. Dinner entrees $10-15. Lunch specials $9-10. Open daily 11am-midnight. ❸

Ginza, 16 Hudson St. (☎338-2261). Walk against traffic down Washington St., turn left onto Beach St., and turn right on Hudson St. Ginza's sushi doesn't come cheap ($3-10), but their full lineup of sake bombs will dull any pain your bill might inflict. Open M-F 11:30am-2:30pm and 5pm-2am, Sa 11:30am-4pm and 5pm-4am, Su 5pm-2am. ❸

BACK BAY

The diverse eateries of the Back Bay line elegant **Newbury Street,** accessible from T: Hynes/ICA. Though Newbury is known as Boston's expensive shopping district, affordable restaurants do exist.

Kashmir, 279 Newbury St. (☎536-1695), at Gloucester St. The best Indian food in Boston. Marble floors, traditional carpets, and plush red seats create a setting as light and exotic as the subtle curries ($12-15) and extensive vegetarian menu (entrees $11-13). Don't miss the *tandoori* specials, cooked in an authentic clay oven. All-you-can-eat buffet (11:30am-3pm) M-F $9, Sa-Su (noon-3pm) $12. Open daily 11:30am-11pm. ❹

Parish Café, 361 Boylston St. (☎247-4777), near T: Arlington. Locals crowd tables and barstools to order sandwiches ($9-17) designed by the city's hottest chefs. Outdoor seating. Open Su noon-1am, M-Sa 11:30am-1am. Bar open until 2am. ❸

Island Hopper, 91 Massachusetts Ave. (☎266-1618), at Newbury St. Encyclopedic menu lives up to the name, offering Chinese and pan-Southeast Asian dishes—from General Gao's Chicken to Burmese noodles and Saigon crepes. Entrees $10-25. Lunch specials $7-8. Open Su noon-11pm, M-Th 11:30am-11pm, F-Sa 11:30am-midnight. ❸

SOUTH END

The waits and hefty bills here are worth it: the South End's upscale restaurants creatively meld flavors and techniques from around the world, creating amazing meals. Most eateries line **Tremont Street,** accessible from T: Back Bay.

▨ **Addis Red Sea,** 544 Tremont St. (☎426-8727). Spicy, curry- and veggie-heavy Ethiopian cuisine in an intimate and sophisticated (but casual) setting is not to be missed. Entrees are served utensil-free on traditional (but casual) setting is not to be missed. Entrees are served utensil-free on traditional *mesob* tables, to be scooped up with spongy *injera* bread. Entrees $9-15. Open M-F 5-11pm, Sa-Su noon-11pm. ❸

The Dish, 253 Shawmut Ave. (☎426-7866), at Milford St. Culinary and atmospheric perfection. Upscale decor meets a low-key clientele and eclectic comfort food, like Cajun-style meatloaf . Entrees $11-17. Open daily 5pm-midnight. ❹

Flour, 1595 Washington St. (☎267-4300), at Rutland St. Near T: Prudential, Mass. Ave, or Back Bay. Harvard-educated chef/owner Joanne Chang bakes the most mouth-watering cakes, cookies, and pastries ($1-3) in the city, all nothing short of transcendent. Gourmet sandwiches $6-7. Open Su 9am-3pm, M-F 7am-7pm, Sa 8am-6pm. ❷

Laurel, 142 Berkeley St. (☎424-6711), on the corner of Columbus St. from T: Back Bay. Patrons receive artful culinary masterpieces ($10-20), like duck confit with sweet potatoes or shrimp and prosciutto ravioli. Open Su 11am-2:30pm, M-F 11:30am-2:30pm and 5:30-10pm, Sa 5:30-10pm. ❸

JAMAICA PLAIN

Restaurants in "JP" are some of the best bargains in the city, with a wide variety of ethnic eateries—the area's Mexican offerings are worth a note, as are the vegetarian options. The action is, not surprisingly, centered on **Centre Street,** which runs parallel to the Orange Line (between T: Jackson Sq. and T: Forest Hills).

▨ **Bella Luna,** 405 Centre St. (☎524-6060). Turn right out of T: Stony Brook. Crispy gourmet pizza in a funky setting, with hand-decorated plates, local art on the walls, and crayons at the tables for the inspired. Creative calzones and pizzas $5-18. To complete the celestial experience, check out the **Milky Way Lounge & Lanes,** a bowling alley/karaoke bar upstairs. Open M-W 11am-10pm, Th-Sa 11am-11pm, Su noon-10pm. ❸

El Oriental de Cuba, 416 Centre St. (☎524-6464). Turn right out of T: Jackson Sq. We're talking about the Cuban Oriente, home to plantain- and meat-heavy cuisine. Don't miss the pressed Cuban sandwiches ($5), plantains and beans, or Puerto Rican *mofongo* (mashed garlicky plantains). Entrees $7-10. Tropical shakes $2. Open M-Th 8am-9pm, F-Sa 8am-10pm, Su 8am-8pm. ❸

Jake's Boss BBQ, 3492 Washington St. (☎983-3701). Turn right out of T: Green St., then right again onto Washington St. The first solo effort by Boston's most respected pit-master, Kenton Jacobs (the "Jake" of the name), brings real down-home Texas smoked ribs and brisket to these cold northern reaches. Hefty sandwiches around $5.75. Boss dinners $7.50-9.50. Open Tu-Su 11am-10pm.❷

◎ SIGHTS

THE FREEDOM TRAIL

Passing the landmarks that put Boston on the map in colonial times, the 2½ mi. red-painted Freedom Trail is a great introduction to the city's history. Even on a trail dedicated to freedom, though, some sights charge admission. Start at the **visitors center,** where the National Park Service offers free guided tours of the portion of the Trail from the Old South Meeting House to the Old North Church. *(15 State St., opposite Old State House. ☎242-5642; www.nps.gov/bost. Tours mid-June to Aug. daily*

10, 11am, 2pm; mid-Apr. to mid-June M-F 2pm. Arrive 30min. before tour start time to get a required ticket. Limit 30 people per tour.) The Freedom Trail begins at another **visitors center,** on Boston Common, outside T: Park St.

BEACON HILL. The Trail first runs uphill to the **Robert Gould Shaw Memorial,** honoring the first black regiment of the Union Army in the American Civil War and their Bostonian leader, made famous by the movie *Glory.* Opposite the memorial is the gold-domed Massachusetts State House. *(☎ 727-3676. Open M-F 10am-3:30pm. 40min., tours depart every 20min.; self-guided tour pamphlet available at tourist desk. Free.)*

DOWNTOWN. Passing the **Park Street Church** *(☎ 523-3383),* the trail reaches the **Granary Burial Ground,** where John Hancock, Samuel Adams, Elizabeth Goose ("Mother Goose"), and Paul Revere rest. **Kings Chapel & Burying Ground** is America's oldest Anglican church; the latest inhabitants are Unitarian. The burying ground next door is the city's first and the final resting place of midnight rider William Dawes. *(58 Tremont St. Chapel ☎ 227-2155, Burying Ground 635-7389. Chapel open in summer daily 10am-4pm; Sept.-Nov. Th-Sa 10am-4pm; Nov-Apr. Sa 10am-2pm. Burying Ground open daily June-Oct. 8am-3pm; Nov.-May 9am-3pm. Chapel suggested donation $1-3. Burying Ground free.)* The Charles Bulfinch-designed **Old City Hall,** on School St., was built on the original site of the country's first public school, the Boston Latin School, which has since relocated to the Fenway. *(☎ 523-8678.)* The **Old Corner Bookstore** was once the city's intellectual and literary center. *(1 School St.)* The **Old South Meeting House** was the site of the preliminary meeting that set the mood for the Boston Tea Party. *(310 Washington St. ☎ 482-6439; www.oldsouthmeetinghouse.org. Open daily Apr.-Oct. 9:30am-5pm; Nov.-Mar. 10am-4pm. $5, students and seniors $4, ages 6-18 $1.)* Formerly the seat of British government, the **⬛Old State House** is now a museum chronicling the history of Boston. *(206 Washington St. ☎ 720-1713. Open daily 9am-5pm. $5, students and seniors $4, ages 6-18 $1.)* The Trail passes a brick circle marking the site of the **Boston Massacre** en route to **Faneuil Hall** and **Quincy Market,** Boston's most visited tourist sights. A former meeting hall and current mega-mall, the complex houses a food court and carts selling kitschy items. *(Faneuil Hall ☎ 523-1300. Open M-Sa 10am-9pm, Su noon-6pm.)*

NORTH END. Heading into the Italian-American North End, the Trail crawls through Big Dig rubble to the **Paul Revere House,** where a self-guided tour helps visitors navigate the meticulously recreated 18th- and early 19th-century rooms. *(19 North Sq. ☎ 523-2338; www.paulreverehouse.org. Open mid-Apr. to Oct. daily 9:30am-5:15pm; Nov.-Dec. and early Apr. daily 9:30am-4:15pm; Jan.-Mar. Tu-Su 9:30am-4:15pm. $3, students and seniors $2.50, ages 5-17 $1, under 5 free.)* The **Old North Church** is where Robert Newman was instructed by Revere to hang lanterns—"one if by land, two if by sea"—warning patriots in Charlestown that the British were coming. The church itself still houses such Revolutionary relics as George Washington's hair and tea from the Boston Tea Party. *(193 Salem St. ☎ 523-6676. Open daily mid-June to mid-Oct. 9am-6pm; mid-Oct. to mid-June 9am-5pm. Suggested donation $3.)* **Copp's Hill Burying Ground,** up Hull St. from the church, is a final resting place for numerous colonial Bostonians, and was a key vantage point in the Battle of Bunker Hill.

CHARLESTOWN. The Battle of Bunker Hill is the focus of much of the rest of the Trail, which heads across the Charles River to the **USS Constitution** (a.k.a. "Old Ironsides") and its companion museum. *(☎ 426-1812; www.ussconstitution.org. Ship open Tu-Su 10am-4pm. Museum open daily May-Oct. 9am-6pm; Nov.-Apr. 10am-5pm. Free.)* The Trail winds through residential Charlestown toward the **Bunker Hill Monument,** which is actually on Breed's Hill—fitting given that the entire Battle of Bunker Hill was actually fought on Breed's Hill. A grand view awaits at the top of the obelisk's 294 steps. *(Monument Sq. Open daily 9am-5pm. Free.)* The Trail loops back to Boston from Monument Sq., passing **City Square,** settled in 1629 shortly after the Puritans' arrival in the Boston area.

DOWNTOWN

In 1634, Massachusetts Bay colonists designated **Boston Common** as a place for their cattle to graze. Today, street vendors, runners, and tourists roam the green, and congregate near the **Frog Pond,** a wading pool in summer and an ice-skating rink in winter. *(T: Park St.)* Across Charles St. from the Common is the lavish **Public Garden,** the nation's first botanical garden. Bronze versions of the title characters from the children's book *Make Way for Ducklings* point the way to the **Swan Boats,** graceful paddleboats that float around a willow-lined pond. *(☎522-1966. $2.50, ages 2-15 $1 for a 15min. ride. Park open daily dawn-dusk. Boats open daily Apr. 18-June 19 10am-4pm; Jun. 20-Labor Day 10am-5pm; Labor Day-Sept. 6 M-F noon-4pm, Sa-Su 10am-4pm, weather permitting.)* Steps from the Common is the pedestrian mall at **Downtown Crossing,** a shopping district centered around legendary **Filene's Basement,** a chaotic feeding frenzy for bargain hunters. *(426 Washington St. T: Downtown Crossing. ☎542-2011; www.filenesbasement.com. Open M-F 9:30am-8pm, Sa 9am-8pm, Su 11am-7pm.)*

BEACON HILL

Looming over the Common is aristocratic Beacon Hill, an exclusive residential neighborhood that was the first spot on the Shawmut Peninsula settled by Puritans. Antique shops, pricey cafes, and ritzy boutiques now line charming **Charles Street,** the neighborhood's main artery. For generations, the Hill was home to Boston's intellectual, political, and social elite, christened the "Boston Brahmins." For a taste of Brahmin life, visit the **Nichols House,** preserved as it was in the 19th century. *(55 Mt. Vernon St., off Charles St. T: Charles/MGH. ☎227-6993. Open May-Oct. Tu-Sa noon-5pm; Nov.-Apr. Th-Sa noon-5pm. $5, children under 12 free. Entrance by 30min. guided tour only, every 30min.; last tour 4pm.)* Quiet **Louisburg Square,** between Mt. Vernon and Pinckney St., was the birthplace of door-to-door Christmas caroling.

The city was the first in America to outlaw slavery, and many African-Americans moved to the Beacon Hill area after the Civil War. The **Black Heritage Trail** is a free 2hr. (1½ mi.) walking tour through Beacon Hill sights that were important during Boston's abolitionist era. The tour begins at the foot of Beacon Hill, near the Shaw Memorial (p. 120), and ends at the free **Museum of Afro-American History,** which houses a small collection of arts and artifacts, a church, and an exhibit about Boston's relationship with slavery. *(46 Joy St. ☎725-0022; www.afroammuseum.org. Museum open June-Aug. daily 10am-4pm; Sept.-May M-Sa 10am-4pm. Heritage Trail tours June-Aug. daily 10am, noon, 2pm; Sept.-May by appointment. Both free.)* Also at the foot of the hill is the cheesy **Bull & Finch Pub,** 84 Beacon St., the inspiration for the bar in *Cheers.*

WATERFRONT

The Waterfront district refers to the wharves along Boston Harbor from South Station to the North End. The excellent ☒**New England Aquarium** features cavorting penguins, an animal infirmary, and briny beasts in a four-story tank. *(Central Wharf at T: Aquarium. ☎973-5200; www.neaq.org. Open July-Aug. M-Tu and F 9am-6pm, W-Th 9am-8pm, Sa-Su 9am-7pm; Sept.-June M-F 9am-5pm, Sa-Su 9am-6pm. $16, students and seniors $14, ages 3-11 $9, under 3 free. IMAX $8.)* The Long Wharf, north of Central Wharf, is **Boston Harbor Cruises'** departure point. They lead history-minded sightseeing cruises and whale-watching excursions, and charter boats to the Harbor Islands. *(☎227-4321. Open late May to Sept. Cruises: Sightseeing 45min.-1½hr.; 3 per day; $17, students and seniors $15, under 12 $12. Whale-watching 3hr., $29/$26/$20. Reservations recommended.)*

BACK BAY

Back Bay was initially an uninhabitable tidal flat tucked into the "back" corner of the bay until the late 19th century. Today elegant Back Bay's stately brownstones and spacious, shady promenades are laid out in an easily navigable grid. Cross-streets are labeled alphabetically from Arlington to Hereford St. Running through Back Bay, fashionable **Newbury Street,** accessible from T: Hynes/ICA, is where Boston's trendiest strut their stuff and empty their wallets.

COPLEY SQUARE. Named for painter John Singleton Copley, Copley Sq. is popular with both lunching businessmen and busy Newbury St. tourists. The square is dominated by H.H. Richardson's Romanesque fantasy, **Trinity Church,** reflected in the 14 acres of glass used in I.M. Pei's stunning **John Hancock Tower,** now closed to the public. *(T: Copley. Church ☎ 536-0944. Open daily 8am-6pm. $4.)* Facing the church, the dramatic ▓**Boston Public Library** is a museum in disguise; don't miss John Singer Sargent's recently restored *Triumph of Religion* murals or the hidden courtyard. Of the library's roughly 7 million books, 128 are copies of *Make Way for Ducklings. (☎ 536-5400; www.bpl.org. Open M-Th 9am-9pm, F-Sa 9am-5pm; Oct.-May also Su 1-5pm. Free. Free Internet Access. Free 1hr. art and architecture tours M 2:30pm, Tu and Th 6pm, F-Sa 11am; additional tour Oct.-May Su 2pm.)* The 50th floor of the **Prudential Center** mall next door to Copley Sq. is home to the **Prudential Skywalk,** which offers a 360° view of Boston from a height of 700 ft. *(T: Prudential. ☎ 859-0648. Skywalk open daily 10am-10pm. $7, seniors and children under 10 $4.)*

CHRISTIAN SCIENCE PLAZA. Down Massachusetts Ave. from Newbury St., the 14-acre Christian Science Plaza is Boston's most well-designed and underappreciated public space. This epic expanse of concrete, centered on a smooth reflecting pool, is home to the Byzantine-revival "Mother Church," a.k.a. **First Church of Christ, Scientist,** a Christian denomination of faith-based healing founded in Boston by Mary Baker Eddy. *(T: Symphony. ☎ 450-3790. Open to public during services W noon and 7:30pm; July-Aug. Su 10am, Sept.-June Su 10am and 7pm. Doors open 30min. before each service.)* The adjacent **Mary Baker Eddy Library,** another of Boston's library/museum hybrids, has exhibits on Mrs. Eddy's life and a surreal "Hall of Ideas," where holographic words bubble out of a fountain and crawl all over the floor and walls. Step inside the ▓**Mapparium,** a glowing, three-story stained-glass globe that depicts the world as it was in 1934 and details the changes that have occurred around the world since then. The globe's perfect acoustics let you whisper in the ear of Pakistan and hear it in Suriname. *(☎ 222-3711. Open Tu-W and Sa-Su 10am-5pm, Th-F 10am-9pm. $5; students, seniors, and children $3. Free Internet access on 3rd fl.)*

JAMAICA PLAIN

Jamaica Plain offers everything quintessentially un-Bostonian: ample parking, good Mexican food, and Mother Nature. Although it's one of Boston's largest green spaces (over 265 acres), many Boston residents never make it to the lush **Arnold Arboretum,** which has flora and fauna from all over the world. The Arboretum, a haven for bikers, joggers, and skaters, is the next-to-last link in Frederick Law Olmsted's Emerald Necklace, a ring of nine parks around Boston. *(T: Forest Hills. ☎ 524-1718. Open daily dawn-dusk.)* Near the Arboretum, **Jamaica Pond,** a glacier-made pond (Boston's largest), is a popular illicit skinny-dipping spot, and a great place for a quick sail. *(T: Green St. Boathouse ☎ 522-6258. Sailboats and rowboats $10-15 per hr.)* To conclude your JP junket, salute beer-guzzling patriots at the **Sam Adams Brewery.** At the end of the tour, those 21+ learn how to "taste" beer and can even try brews currently tested in the lab. *(30 Germania St. T: Stony Brook. ☎ 522-9080. Tours Th 2pm; F 2pm and 5:30pm; Sa noon, 1, and 2pm; additional tour May-Aug. W 1pm. Free.)*

🏛 MUSEUMS

If you're planning a Beantown museum binge, consider a **CityPass** (www.citypass.com), which covers admission to the JFK Library, MFA, the Museum of Science, Harvard's Museum of Natural History (p. 129), the Aquarium (p. 121), and the Prudential Center Skywalk (p. 122). Passes, available at museums or online, are valid for nine days. ($37, ages 3-17 $26.)

Museum of Fine Arts, 465 Huntington Ave. (☎267-9300; www.mfa.org), in Fenway. T: Museum. The exhaustive MFA showcases an international array of artwork from samurai armor to contemporary American art to medieval instruments. The ancient Egyptian and Nubian galleries (lots of mummies), Impressionist paintings (the largest collection outside France), and the colonial portrait gallery (includes the painting of George Washington found on the $1 bill) are a few highlights of the stunning collection. Open M-Tu 10am-4:45pm, W-F 10am-9:45pm (Th-F only West Wing open after 5pm), Sa-Su 10am-5:45pm. $15; students and seniors $13; ages 7-17 M-F $6.50, after 3pm free. W after 4pm and all day Sa-Su free, Th-F after 5pm $2 off.

Isabella Stewart Gardner Museum, 280 Fenway (☎566-1401; www.gardnermuseum.org), in Fenway. T: Museum. This astounding private collection remains exactly as eccentric Mrs. Gardner arranged it over a century ago—empty frames even remain where stolen paintings once hung. The Venetian-style *palazzo* architecture draws as much attention as the Old Masters, and the courtyard garden alone is worth the price of admission. Highlights include an original of Dante's *Divine Comedy* and Titian's *Europa,* considered the most important Italian Renaissance work in North America. Open Tu-Su 11am-5pm. M-F $10, Sa-Su $11; students $5; under 18 and individuals named "Isabella" free with valid ID. Free guided tours Tu-F 2:30pm.

John F. Kennedy Library and Museum (☎929-4500 or 877-616-4599; www.jfklibrary.org), Columbia Point, just off I-93 in Dorchester, south of Boston. From T: JFK/UMass, take free shuttle #2 "JFK Library" (daily every 20min. 8am-5:30pm). In a glass tower designed by I.M. Pei, the JFK Library is a monument to Boston's favorite son, 35th US President John Francis Fitzgerald Kennedy. Collection includes exhibits that trace JFK's career from the campaign trail to his assassination and displays on First Lady Jackie O. Open daily 9am-5pm. $10, students and seniors $8, ages 13-17 $4, under 13 free. Wheelchair accessible.

Institute of Contemporary Art (ICA), 955 Boylston St. (☎266-5152; www.icaboston.org), in Back Bay. T: Hynes/ICA. Boston's lone bastion of the avant-garde displays installations from major contemporary artists alongside lesser-known works. Thought-provoking exhibits rotate every 3-4 months. Open W and F noon-5pm, Th noon-9pm, Sa-Su 11am-5pm. $7, students and seniors $5, under 12 free. Th 5-9pm free.

Sports Museum of New England, Fleet Ctr. (☎624-1234), Downtown. T: North Station. A must for all who understand or want to understand Boston's fanatical sports obsession. Interactive exhibits each dedicated to a different Boston sports franchise. Archival footage, authentic gear, and reconstructions of lockers belonging to Boston's all-time greats. Don't miss Larry Bird's size 14 shoes or the stuffed bruin (don't worry, it's an animal, not an ex-player). Open non-game days 11am-3pm, game days 11am-2pm. Call ahead for schedules. $6, seniors and ages 6-17 $4, under 6 free.

Museum of Science, Science Park (☎723-2500; www.mos.org). T: Science Park. Seeks to educate and entertain children of all ages with countless interactive exhibits. The must-sees are the giant *Tyrannosaurus rex;* the wacky Theater of Electricity; and the Soundstair, stairs that sing when you step on them. A five-story OMNI Theater and trippy laser shows are at the Hayden Planetarium. Open July-Aug. M-F 9am-7pm, F 9am-9pm, Sept.-June M-Th and Sa-Su 9am-5pm, F 9am-9pm. $14, seniors $12, ages 3-11 $11. IMAX or laser show tickets $8.50, seniors $7.50, ages 3-11 $6.50.

⊡ ENTERTAINMENT

The best publications for entertainment listings are the weekly *Boston Phoenix* (free from streetside boxes) and the *Boston Globe* Calendar section ($0.50, included with Thursday *Boston Globe*). **Bostix** sells tickets to most major theater shows, and half-price, day-of-show tickets for select shows at Faneuil Hall (p. 121) and Copley Sq. (p. 122). The website and booths post which shows are on sale each day. (☎723-5181; www.artsboston.org. Tickets daily 11am. Cash only.)

THEATER

Boston's tiny two-block Theater District, near T: Boylston, west of Chinatown, was once the nation's premier pre-Broadway tryout area. Today it's a stop for touring Broadway and West End productions, not to mention a lively nightlife district. The **Charles Playhouse,** 74 Warrenton St., is home to the wacky whodunit *Shear Madness* and the dazzling performance art of *Blue Man Group.* (*Shear:* ☎426-5225; $34. *Blue Man:* ☎426-6912. $43-53. Box office open M-Tu 10am-6pm, W-Th 10am-7pm, F-Sa 10am-9pm, Su noon-6pm. Half-price student rush tickets often available from 10am on day of show. Volunteer to usher *Blue Man Group* and watch for free—call at least 5 days in advance.) The giant **Wang Center,** 265 Tremont St., hosts Broadway shows and other productions. (☎482-9393 or 800-447-7400; www.wangcenter.org. Box office open M-Sa 10am-6pm. $20-75; student discounts available for some shows.) For more avant-garde productions, check out the **Boston Center for the Arts,** 539 Tremont St. (☎426-5000), in the South End, near T: Back Bay.

CLASSICAL MUSIC

Modeled on the world's most acoustically perfect music hall (the Gewandhaus in Leipzig, Germany), **Symphony Hall,** 301 Massachusetts Ave., T: Symphony, is home to both the **Boston Symphony Orchestra (BSO)** and its light-hearted sister the **Boston Pops.** James Levine (formerly of NYC's Met) recently took over as BSO conductor. Every 4th of July, the Pops gives a free evening concert at the Esplanade's **Hatch Shell,** near T: Charles/MGH, with patriotic music, fireworks, and Tchaikovsky's *1812 Overture*—with real cannons. (☎266-1200. Box office open daily 10am-6pm. BSO: Season Sept.-Apr. $26-95; general seating at open rehearsals W night and Th morning $12. Rush Tu and Th 5pm, F 9pm $8. Pops: Season May-July. $20-250.)

SPORTS

While the sights along the Freedom Trail testify to Boston's Revolutionary roots, the city's true heart beats at the storied **Fenway Park**, where diehard fans who descry the "Curse of the Bambino" believe that this could be the year. The nation's oldest, smallest, and most expensive baseball park, Fenway is also home to the Green Monster (the left field wall) and one of only two manual scoreboards left in the major leagues (the other is at Chicago's Wrigley Field; p. 600). Get tickets from the **Ticket Office,** 4 Yawkey Way, T: Kenmore. (☎482-4769. Bleachers $12-20, grandstands $27-47, field boxes $44-70.) The **Fleet Center,** 50 Causeway St., T: North Station, was built on the site of the legendary Boston Garden and hosts concerts and games for basketball's **Celtics** and hockey's **Bruins.** (☎624-1750. Box office open in summer M-F 10am-5pm; in season daily 10am-7pm. Celtics $10-140. Bruins $19-99.) At the newly-built Gillette Stadium in Foxborough, the 2003 Super Bowl Champion **New England**

Patriots grind it out on the gridiron from September to January (☎931-2222 or 800-494-7287). Raced every Patriot's Day (third M in Apr.), the **Boston Marathon** (www.bostonmarathon.org), the nation's oldest foot race and one of Boston's greatest sporting traditions, is a 26.2 mi. run that starts in Hopkinton, MA, in the west, passes over "Heartbreak Hill," and ends amid much hoopla at Copley Sq. For over 100 years, the marathon has attracted runners from all over the world, and fans flank every inch of the course. The **Head of the Charles Regatta** (www.hocr.org), the world's largest crew regatta, draws throngs of preppies to the banks of the river every October since 1965.

▓ NIGHTLIFE

Before you set out to paint the town red, there are a few things to keep in mind. Boston bars and clubs are notoriously strict about age requirements (usually 21+), so bring back-up ID. Puritanical zoning laws require that all nightlife shuts down by 2am. The T stops running at 1am, though, so bring extra cash for the taxi ride home, or catch the "Night Owl" bus service, which runs until 2:30am Fridays and Saturdays.

DANCE CLUBS

Boston is a town for pubbers, not clubbers. The city's few clubs are on or near Kenmore Sq.'s **Lansdowne Street,** near T: Kenmore.

Avalon, 15 Lansdowne St. (☎262-2424). The flashy, trashy grand dame of Boston's club scene, and the closest Puritan Boston gets to Ibiza. World-class DJs, amazing light shows, gender-bending cage dancers, and throngs of hotties pack the giant dance floor. Su gay night. Th-F 19+, Sa-Su 21+. Cover $10-15. Open Th-Su 10pm-2am.

Pravda 116, 116 Boylston St. (☎482-7799), in the Theater District. T: Boylston. The caviar, red decor, long lines, and 116 brands of vodka may recall Mother Russia, but capitalism reigns supreme at commie-chic Pravda, the favored haunt of Boston's yuppified 20-somethings. Full house/Top 40 dance club and 2 bars (1 made of ice). 21+. Cover W $15, F-Sa $10. Bars open W-Sa 5pm-2am; club W and F-Sa 10pm-2am.

Sophia's, 1270 Boylston St. (☎351-7001). From T: Kenmore, walk down Brookline Ave., turn left onto Yawkey Way, then right onto Boylston St. Far from Lansdowne St. in distance and style, Sophia's is a fiery Latin dance club with 4 floors of salsa, merengue, and Latin music from a mix of live bands and DJs. Trendy, international crowd. 21+. Cover $10; no cover before 9:30pm W-Th and Sa. Open Tu-Sa 6pm-2am.

THE HIDDEN DEAL

TAKE ME OUT TO THE BALL GAME

Tiny Fenway Park sells out almost every night, and tickets—the most expensive in baseball—remain hard to come by. Illegal scalpers hawk billets at up to a 500% markup (though after games start, prices plummet).

But fear not: there are options for snagging choice seats without parting with a first-born. On game days, the box office sells obstructed-view and standing-room tickets beginning five hours before the game (line up early, especially for Sox-Yankees games). Obstructed-view seats in the infield are excellent, while standing-room seats offer tremendous views of the field. Risktakers can wait until a few hours before a game, hoping the team will release the superb seats held for players' friends and families.

Seat quality varies widely. Avoid sections 1-7, unless you enjoy craning your neck for 3hr. The best "cheap" seats are sections 32-36 (32-33 are down the left-field line in the outfield grandstand, close enough to touch the famed Green Monster). Bleacher sections 34-36 have perfect sightlines for watching pitches, but most fans emerge lobster-red from the direct sunlight shining down on the seats.

Axis, 13 Lansdowne St. (☎262-2437). Avalon's little sister has a techno beat and identical sweaty college crowd. Drag shows M night, hosted by sassy 6 ft. diva Mizery. 19+. Cover M $7, Th $5, F $20, Sa $10. Open M and Th-Sa 10pm-2am. Tired of the dance floor? Chill upstairs in the chic lounge **ID.** 19+. Cover $5-20. Open Th-Sa 10pm-2pm.

BARS AND PUBS

Boston's large student population means the city is filled with great bars and pubs. Most tourists stick to the many faux Irish pubs around **Downtown,** while the **Theater District** is the premier after-dark destination of the city's international elite. The shamelessly yuppie meat markets on Back Bay's **Boylston Street** are also popular.

Bukowski's Tavern, 50 Dalton St. (☎437-9999), in Back Bay off Boylston St., 1 block south of T: Hynes/ICA. Named for boozer poet Charles Bukowski, the casual ambience and 99+ bottles of beer on the wall is a welcome respite from Boylston St.'s trendy chic. Pints $3-20. 21+. No cover. Open M-Sa 11:30am-2am, Su noon-2am. Cash only.

Mantra/OmBar, 52 Temple Pl. (☎542-8111), Downtown. T: Temple Pl. Seductive. Scandalous. Incomprehensible. And that's just the bathroom, which has 1-way mirrored stalls and ice cubes in the urinals. A pricey Franco-Indian fusion restaurant by day, Mantra becomes OmBar by night, with a bar in the bank vault downstairs and a plush, smoke-free "hookah den" upstairs. Cocktails $9. Open M-Sa 5:30pm-2am.

Delux Café, 100 Chandler St. (☎338-5258), at Clarendon St. 1 block south of T: Back Bay, in the South End. Dine or drink (or both) among kooky decorative distractions, like Elvis shrines, lit-up Christmas trees, and continuously looped cartoons. Popular with everyone from bike messengers to businessmen. Cocktails $3.50-5. No cover. Open M-Sa 5pm-1am; food until 11:30pm. Cash only.

Emily's/SW1, 48 Winter St. (☎423-3649), Downtown. T: Park St. A fun college crowd heads to this hopping Top 40 dance club that was catapulted to fame as the hangout of choice for the cast of MTV's *Real World: Boston,* who lived across the Common in Beacon Hill. Beer $4. Cover around $5. Open Tu-Th 5pm-midnight, F-Sa 5pm-2am.

Purple Shamrock, 1 Union St. (☎227-2060), Downtown. From T: Government Ctr., walk through City Hall Plaza to Congress St. This faux Irish pub is popular with both professionals winding down after work and college kids preparing for a night on the town. If you're feeling decadent, try to sinfully sweet Chocolate Cake Martini ($8). Karaoke Tu starts 9-10pm. 21+ after 9pm. Cover Th-Sa $5. Open daily until 2am.

The Littlest Bar, 47 Province St. (☎523-9766), Downtown. T: Downtown Crossing. This local watering hole draws the curious (note the "Seamus Heaney peed here" sign) hoping for a spot inside what is the littlest bar in Boston (just 16 ft. end to end). M folk singer Mike Barnett plays dirty Irish ditties. Open daily 9am-1:30am. Cash only.

LIVE MUSIC

Boston's live music scene is impressive—no surprise for the town that gave the world rockin' acts like Aerosmith and the Dropkick Murphys. The best acts often play across the river in **Cambridge** (p. 127). **Wally's Café,** 427 Massachusetts Ave., at Columbus Ave., is in the South End. Turn right out of T: Massachusetts Ave. or T: Symphony. Established in 1947, Wally's is Boston's longest-standing jazz joint, and it only improves with age. (☎424-1408. Live music daily 9pm-2am. 21+. No cover. Cash only.) **Paradise Rock Club,** 969 Commonwealth Ave., is visible from T: Pleasant St. This smoky, spacious venue has hosted national and international rock acts, including U2 and Soul Asylum. (☎562-8800. 18+. Cover $10-20.)

GLBT NIGHTLIFE

For up-to-date listings of gay and lesbian nightlife, pick up a free copy of the South End-based *Bay Windows,* a gay weekly available everywhere, or check the lengthy listings in the free *Boston Phoenix* and *Improper Bostonian.* The

South End's bars and late-night restaurants, accessible from T: Back Bay, are all gay-friendly (sorry ladies, these are mostly spots for the boys). The sports bar **Fritz**, 26 Chandler St. (☎482-4428), and divey **The Eagle,** 520 Tremont St. (☎542-4494), are exclusively for gay men. Boston's other gay bar/clubs are the Theater District's **Vapor/Chaps,** 100 Warrenton St. (☎422-0862); **Jacque's,** 77-79 Broadway (☎426-8902); and **Europa/Buzz,** 51 Stuart St. (☎482-3939), which also has evenings directed toward women. In Fenway is the all-encompassing **Ramrod,** 1254 Boylston St. (☎266-2986), a Leather & Levis spot that has spawned a non-fetish dance club known as **Machine.** Popular gay nights at straight clubs include Avalon's Sunday bash (p. 125)—preceded by the early evening "T-Dance" at Vapor—and sassy drag night at Axis on Monday (p. 126). Lesbians flock to **Jamaica Plain's** bookstores and cafes, many of which are queer-owned, and to lesbian-friendly **Midway Café,** 3496 Washington St. (☎524-9038), south of T: Green St.

⚠ OUTDOOR ACTIVITIES

For a major urban center, Boston has a number of outdoor opportunities, thanks largely to the **Emerald Necklace,** a string of nine parks ringing the city. Designed by Frederick Law Olmsted (1822-1903), who also created New York City's Central Park (p. 234) and San Francisco's Golden Gate Park (p. 916), the Necklace runs from Boston Common and the Public Garden along the Commonwealth Avenue Mall, the Back Bay Fens and Riverway, Jamaica Plain's Olmsted Park, Jamaica Pond, and Arnold Arboretum (p. 122), ending at far-flung Franklin Park.

The **Charles River** separates Boston from Cambridge and is popular with outdoors enthusiasts. Though swimming in the unsettlingly grimy water is strongly discouraged, runners, bikers, and skaters crowd the **Charles River Esplanade** park, which runs along its banks. The Esplanade is home to the **Hatch Shell,** where Boston's renowned 4th of July festivities take place. Rent watercraft from **Charles River Canoe & Kayak,** beyond Eliot Bridge near T: Riverside. (☎965-5110. Canoes $13 per hr., $52 per day; kayaks $14/$56. Open Apr.-Oct. M-F 10am-sunset, Sa-Su 9am-sunset; Oct.-Mar. by appointment.)

Serious hikers should consider the **Harbor Islands National Park,** made up of the roughly 30 wooded islands floating in Boston Harbor that are ringed with pristine beaches and traversed by miles of hiking trails. The most popular islands include Lovell's (with the islands' best beach) and Bumpkin (wild berry paradise). **Boston Harbor Cruises** runs ferries from Long Wharf at T: Aquarium to George's Island. (☎227-4321; www.bostonislands.com. Open May-Oct. daily 9am-sunset, hours vary by island. Ferries run daily July-Aug. on the hr. 9am-5pm, May-June and Sept.-Oct. 10am, 2, 4pm. Ferry ticket $10, seniors $7, children $6; includes free water taxis to five other islands from George's Island.)

▶ DAYTRIPS FROM BOSTON

CAMBRIDGE   ☎617

Separated from Boston by only a small river, Cambridge (pop. 100,000), is often called Boston's "Left Bank" for its liberal politics and bohemian flair. The city has thrived as an intellectual hotbed since the colonial era, when it became the home of prestigious Harvard University, the nation's first college. The Massachusetts Institute of Technology (MIT), the country's foremost school for science and technology, moved here in the early 20th century. Cambridge's counterculture has died down since its 1960s heyday, but the city remains vibrant, with tons of bookstores and coffeeshops, a large student population, and great food and nightlife.

⁊ PRACTICAL INFORMATION. Cambridge is easily reached by a 10min. T ride from downtown Boston. Accommodations are expensive; it's best to stay in Boston. Cambridge's main artery, **Massachusetts Avenue ("Mass Ave.")**, runs parallel to the T's Red Line, which makes stops along the street. The **Kendall/MIT** stop is just across the river from Boston, near MIT's campus. The Red Line continues to: **Central Square,** a bar-hopper's paradise; **Harvard Square,** the city's chaotic heart; and largely residential **Porter Square.** Harvard Sq. sits at the intersection of Mass. Ave., Brattle St., JFK St., and Dunster St. The **Cambridge Office for Tourism** runs a booth outside T: Harvard with plenty of maps and info. (☎441-2884; www.cambridge-usa.org. Open M-Sa 9am-5pm, Su 10am-5pm. Hours may vary.) **Internet Access: Adrenaline Zone,** 40 Brattle St., in Harvard Sq. (☎876-1314. Open Su-Th 11am-11pm, F-Sa 11am-midnight. $5 per hr.) **Post Office:** 770 Mass. Ave. (☎876-0550), in Central Sq., and 125 Mt. Auburn St. (☎876-3883), in Harvard Sq. (Both open M-F 7:30am-6pm, Sa 7:30am-3pm.) **Postal Code:** 02138. **Area Code:** 617.

◖ FOOD. Cambridge is a United Nations of ethnic eateries, from Mexican to Tibetan. Most visitors stick to the spots in Harvard Sq. Indian restaurants come a dime-a-dozen in Cambridge, and most offer a budget-friendly all-you-can-eat lunch buffets ($7-9, served daily 11:30am-3pm). **◪Tanjore ❷,** 18 Eliot St., off JFK St., stands out from the crowd with its encyclopedic menu and range of regional specialties. (☎868-1900. Open daily 11am-3pm and 5-11pm.) **Punjabi Dhaba ❷,** 225 Hampshire St., in Inman Sq., gives it a run for its rupees, offering a cheap menu of spicy dishes. (☎547-8272. Veggie dishes $5; combos $8. Open daily noon-midnight. Cash only.) **◪Darwin's Limited ❷,** 148 Mt. Auburn St., is a 5min. walk from Harvard Sq. proper: exit the T onto Brattle St. and turn right at the Harvard Sq. Hotel onto Mt. Auburn St.; it's six to seven blocks up on the left. The bohemian staff craft Boston's best gourmet sandwiches ($4.75-7), served on fresh bread, named after nearby streets. (☎354-5233. Open Su 7am-7pm, M-Sa 6:30am-9pm. Cash only.) For over 40 years, **Bartley's Burger Cottage ❸,** 1246 Mass Ave., has been serving some of the area's juiciest burgers, named after famous folk. Try the Ted Kennedy, a "plump liberal" burger. (☎354-6559. Burgers $5-12. Open M-Sa 11am-9pm. Cash only.) **Emma's Pizza ❷,** 40 Hampshire St. (☎617-864-8534), opposite the 1 Kendall Sq. complex, dishes up Boston's best gourmet pizza, with toppings ranging from cranberries to roasted sweet potatoes. (☎864-8534. Combos $15-20. 6-slice 12 in. pies $8; 8-slice 16 in. pies $11. Open Su-W 11am-10pm, Th-Sa 11am-11pm.) The recently opened **◪Felipe's Taqueria,** 83 Mt. Auburn St., is quickly becoming a Harvard Sq. institution with its wicked cheap Mexican grub—filling chicken burritos, decadent *carnitas* quesadillas, and traditional corn-tortilla tacos are served with fresh ingredients by a friendly staff. (☎354-9944. Open Su-W 10am-midnight, Th-Sa 10am-2am.) Everyone screams for ice cream at **Herrell's,** 15 Dunster St., off Mass. Ave., which offers every flavor imaginable, from chocolate pudding to Twinkie, as well as a few you've never thought of—jalapeño anyone? (☎497-2179. Open in summer Su-Th 10am-midnight, F-Sa 10am-1am; in winter daily 11am-midnight.)

◙ SIGHTS. Harvard Sq. is of course named after **Harvard University.** The student-led tours offered by **Harvard Events & Information,** Holyoke Ctr. Arcade (across Dunster St. from the T), are the best way to tour the university's dignified red-brick-and-ivy campus and learn about its history. (☎495-1573; www.harvard.edu. Open M-Sa 9am-5pm. Tours Sept. to mid-May M-F 10am and 2pm, Sa 2pm; June to mid-Aug. M-Sa 10, 11:15am, 2, and 3:15pm.) **Harvard Yard,** just off Mass Ave., is the heart of undergraduate life and the site of commencement. The massive **Harry Elkins Widener Memorial Library,** in Harvard Yard, houses nearly 5 million of Harvard's 13.3 million books, making it the world's largest university library collection.

Harvard's many museums are well worth a visit. The disorganized **Arthur M. Sackler Museum**, 485 Broadway, at Quincy St. just off Mass. Ave., has four floors of East Asian, pre-Columbian, Islamic, and Indian treasures. Across the street, the **Fogg Art Museum**, 32 Quincy St., offers a small survey of North American and European work from the Middle Ages to the early 20th century, with a strong Impressionist collection and several van Gogh portraits. Inside the Fogg, the excellent **Busch-Reisinger Museum** is dedicated to modern German work. (All 3 museums: ☎ 495-9400; www.artmuseums.harvard.edu. Open M-Sa 10am-5pm, Su 1-5pm. $5, students and seniors $4, under 18 free. W and Sa 10am-noon free.) Next door, the Le Corbusier-designed **Carpenter Center**, 24 Quincy St., displays the hottest contemporary art by both students and professionals. The **Harvard Film Archive (HFA)**, in the basement of the Carpenter Center, has a great art-house film series. Schedules are posted outside the door. (Carpenter ☎ 495-3251. Open M-Sa 9am-11pm, Su noon-11pm. Galleries free. HFA ☎ 495-4700. $7, students and seniors $5.) The **Harvard Museum of Natural History**, 26 Oxford St., has exhibits on botany, zoology, and geology, including the famous **Glass Flowers**—over 3000 incredibly life-like, life-sized glass models of plants. (☎ 495-3045. Open daily 9am-5pm. $7.50, students and seniors $6, ages 3-18 $5. Su 9am-noon and Sept.-May W 3-5pm free.)

Kendall Sq., T: Kendall/MIT, is home to the **Massachusetts Institute of Technology (MIT)**, the world's leading institution dedicated to the study of science. Free campus tours begin at the **MIT Info Center**, 77 Mass. Ave., in Lobby 7/Small Dome building, and include visits to the Chapel and Kresge Auditorium, which touches the ground in only three places. (☎ 253-1000; www.mit.edu. Tours M-F 10am and 2pm.) The ⬛**MIT Museum**, 265 Mass. Ave., features technological wonders in dazzling multimedia exhibitions. Highlights include a gallery of "hacks" (elaborate, if nerdy, pranks) and the world's largest hologram collection. (☎ 253-4444. Open Tu-F 10am-5pm, Sa-Su noon-5pm. $5; college students with ID, seniors, and ages 5-18 $2.)

🔲🔳 **ENTERTAINMENT AND NIGHTLIFE.** Some of the Boston area's best live music spots are in Central Sq., T: Central. **The Middle East**, 472-480 Mass. Ave. (☎ 864-3278), and **T.T. the Bear's Place**, 10 Brookline St. (☎ 492-2327), at Mass. Ave., feature live music every night from the nation's hottest indie rock and hip-hop acts. Harvard Sq.'s ⬛**Club Passim**, 37 Palmer St., at Church St., off Mass. Ave., is a folk music legend: a 17-year-old Joan Baez premiered here, while Bob Dylan played between sets. Countless acoustic acts have hit this intimate venue before making it big. (☎ 492-5300. Shows 7pm-11:30pm. Open mic Tu 7pm. Cover $5-30.)

On weekend nights, **Harvard Square** is equal parts gathering place, music hall, and three-ring circus, with tourists, locals, students, and pierced suburban punks enjoying the varied street performers. Harvard Square abounds with bars, but Cambridge's best nightlife options are in **Central Square**, a bar-hopper's heaven. Most bars are open until 1am, with some staying open until 2am on the weekends. ⬛**The People's Republik**, 880 Mass. Ave., keeps the proletariat happy with cheap beer and cheeky chalkboards enticing passersby to drop in for a drink with adages like "Drink beer—it's cheaper than gasoline." (☎ 491-6969. Beer $2-4; cocktails $4-4.50. No cover. Open Su-W noon-1am, Th-Sa noon-2am. Cash only.) The harem-like **Enormous Room**, 567 Mass. Ave., unmarked save an outline of a bull elephant on the window, is too seductive to resist. Amidst sultry arabesque lighting and floor pillows for lounging, a trendier-than-thou crowd jives to music from a hidden DJ. "Enormous plates" of appetizers ($14, vegetarian $12) include hummus, grape leaves, salmon skewers, and anything else that strikes the chef's fancy. (☎ 491-5550. Beer $4. Mixed drinks $6-9. Cover $3 after 10pm. Open M-F 5:30pm-1am, Sa-Su 7pm-1am. Cash only.) **ManRay**, 21 Brookline St., off Mass. Ave., rules the underground scene, with themed nights catering to various alternative crowds. Especially popular is the gay-themed "Campus" night on Thursdays. (☎ 864-0400. W goth/industrial, 18+. Th "Campus," 19+. 1st and

NEW ENGLAND

4th F of every month "Fetish," 19+; 3rd F fantasy, 21+. Sa retro New-Wave, 19+. Dress code strictly enforced W and F. Cover up to $15. Opening times vary, usually around 9pm.) A typical-looking Irish pub from the outside, **The Phoenix Landing,** 512 Mass. Ave., keeps a lively college crowd dancing with the sounds of some of the area's best electric and downtempo grooves. (☎576-6260. 21+. Cover $3-5. Open daily 11:30am-2am.) **The Good Life,** 720 Mass. Ave., is a snazzy nightspot with a casual crowd and high-class atmosphere—jazz, plush booths, and 1950s-era cocktails. (☎868-8800. Drinks $5-7. Open Su-W 11:30am-1am, Th-Sa 11:30am-2am.)

LEXINGTON AND CONCORD ☎781 AND 978

"Stand your ground. Don't fire unless fired upon, but if they mean to have a war, let it begin here," said Captain John Parker to the colonial Minutemen on April 19, 1775. Although no one is certain who fired the "shot heard 'round the world," the American Revolution did indeed erupt in downtown Lexington. The site of the fracas lies in the center of town at **Battle Green,** where a Minuteman statue stands guard. Across the street, the **Buckman Tavern,** 1 Bedford St. (☎862-5598), housed the Minutemen on the eve of their decisive battle. The nearby **Hancock-Clarke House,** 36 Hancock St. (☎861-0928), and the **Munroe Tavern,** 1332 Mass. Ave. (☎862-1703), also played significant roles in the birth of the revolution. All three can be seen on a 30min. tour that runs continuously. (All open Apr.-Oct. M-Sa 10am-5pm, Su 1-5pm, but call ahead, as hours are subject to change. $5 per site, ages 6-16 $3; combo ticket for all 3 $12/$7.) The **Museum of Our National Heritage,** 33 Marrett Rd. (Rte. 2A), emphasizes a historical approach to understanding popular American life, especially at the time of the revolution. (☎861-6559; www.monh.org. Open M-Sa 10am-5pm, Su noon-5pm. Free.) The road from Boston to Lexington is a straight shot up Mass Ave. from Boston or Cambridge; the **Minuteman Trail** is an excellent bike trail to downtown Lexington (access off Mass Ave. in Arlington, or Alewife St. in Cambridge). MBTA bus #62/76 from T: Alewife runs to Lexington (20min., $0.90). A model and description of the Battle of Lexington adorns the **visitors center,** 1875 Mass. Ave., opposite Battle Green. (☎862-2480. Open Apr.-Nov. daily 9am-5pm; Dec.-Mar. M-Sa 10am-4pm.) **Area Code:** 781.

Nearby Concord was the site of the second conflict of the American Revolution, and is famous both for its military history and for its status as a 19th-century intellectual center. The period rooms at the **Concord Museum,** 200 Lexington Rd., on the Cambridge Turnpike, move through Concord's three centuries of history. Highlights include the original lamp from Paul Revere's midnight ride and Henry David Thoreau's bed desk and chair study (☎369-9763. Open Apr.-Dec. M-Sa 9am-5pm, Su noon-5pm; Jan.-Mar. M-Sa 11am-4pm, Su 1-4pm. $8, students and seniors $7, ages 5-18 $3.) Down the road from the museum, the **Orchard House,** 399 Lexington Rd., was once home to the multi-talented Alcotts, whose daughter Louisa May wrote *Little Women.* (☎369-4118. Open Apr.-Oct. M-Sa 10am-4:30pm, Su 1-4:30pm; Nov.-Mar. M-F 11am-3pm, Sa 10am-4:30pm, Su 1-4:30pm. $8, students and seniors $7, ages 6-17 $5; families $20. Guided tour only.) Farther down the road lies **Wayside,** 455 Lexington Rd., the former residence of the Alcotts and Hawthornes. (☎318-7825. Open for tours June-Aug. Tu-Th 2 and 4pm, Sa-Su 11am, 1:30, 3, and 4:30pm. $4.) Today, Alcott, Hawthorne, Emerson, and Thoreau reside on "Author's Ridge" in the **Sleepy Hollow Cemetery** on Rte. 62, three blocks from the center of town.

The Battle of Concord, the second battle of the revolution, was fought at the **Old North Bridge.** From the parking lot, a 5min. walk brings visitors to the **North Bridge Visitors Center,** 174 Liberty St., to learn about the town's history, especially its involvement in the Revolutionary War. (☎369-6993. Open daily Apr.-Oct. 9am-5pm; Nov.-Mar. 9am-4pm.) The **Minuteman National Historical Park,** off Rte. 2A between Concord and Lexington, best explored along the adjacent 5mi. **Battle Road Trail,** includes an impressive **visitors center** that organizes battle reenactments and screens a multimedia presentation on the "Road to Revolution." (☎781-862-7753. Off Rte. 2A between Concord and Lexington. Open daily Oct.-Nov. 9am-4pm; reduced hours in winter.) Concord, north of Boston, is served by the Fitchburg commuter rail train ($5) that runs from T: North Station. **Area Code:** 978.

WALDEN POND   ☎978

In 1845, Thoreau retreated 1½ mi. south of Concord "to live deliberately, to front only the essential facts of life" (though the harsh essence was eased somewhat by his mother's home cooking; she lived within walking distance of his cabin). In 1845, he published his thoughts on his time here in *Walden*, one of the major works of the Transcendentalist movement. The **Walden Pond State Reservation,** 915 Walden St., off Rte. 126, draws picnickers, swimmers, and boaters and is mobbed in summer. No camping, pets, or "novelty flotation devices" allowed. (☎369-3254. Open daily 8am-dusk. Parking $5.)

SALEM   ☎978

Although Salem has much more to offer than witch kitsch, its infamous past has spawned a Halloween-based tourist trade which culminates in the month-long **Haunted Happenings** festival in October (www.hauntedhappenings.org). The **Salem Witch Museum,** 19½ Washington Sq. N, gives a melodramatic but informative multimedia presentation detailing the history of the witch trials of 1692. It also features an exhibit on the role of scapegoating throughout history. (☎744-1692. Open daily July-Aug. 10am-7pm, Sept.-June 10am-5pm; extended hours in Oct. $6.50, seniors $6, ages 6-14 $4.50. Cash only.) Engraved stones commemorate the trials' 20 victims at the **Witch Trials Memorial,** off Charter St. next to the Old Burying Point Cemetery. The **Witch House,** 310½ Essex St., was owned by witch trial judge Jonathan Corwin and is the only remaining building in Salem with direct links to the trials. (☎744-8815. Open daily May to early Nov. 10am-5pm; extended hours in Oct. $7, seniors $6, ages 6-14 $4. AAA members $1 discount.)

The recently renovated and expanded ▓**Peabody Essex Museum,** on the corner of Essex and New Liberty St., is itself worth the trip to Salem. The museum presents objects and art in their cultural contexts, including excellent exhibits of maritime, Asian export, and American decorative art. The museum's prize jewel is Yin Yu Tang, a Qing Dynasty merchant's house that was relocated piece by piece from China. (☎866-745-1876 or 745-9500; www.pem.org. Open daily 10am-5pm. $13, seniors $11, students $9, 16 and under free. Yin Yu Tang requires timed tickets, free with admission.) The **House of the Seven Gables,** 54 Turner St., became the "second most famous house in America" after the release of Nathaniel Hawthorne's gothic romance of the same name. (☎744-0991. Open daily July-Oct. 10am-7pm; Nov.-Dec. and mid-Jan. to June 10am-5pm. Closed early Jan. $11, seniors and AAA members $10, ages 5-12 $7.25. By 30min. guided tour only.)

The **Salem Maritime National Historic Site Visitors Center,** 2 New Liberty St., has free maps, public restrooms, historical displays, and a gift shop. (☎740-1650. Open daily 9am-5pm.) Salem, 15 mi. northeast of Boston, is accessible by the Newburyport/Rockport commuter rail train (30min., $3.75) from T: North Station, by MBTA bus #450 or 455 (45min., $3.45) from T: Wonderland, or by car from I-95 or U.S. 1 N to Rte. 128 and Rte. 114. **Area Code:** 978.

PLYMOUTH   ☎508

The Pilgrims' first step onto the New World was *not* at Plymouth—they stopped first at Provincetown (p. 135), then left because the soil was inadequate. **Plymouth Rock** is a small stone that has dubiously been identified as the rock on which the Pilgrims disembarked the second time. A symbol of liberty during the American Revolution, it has since moved three times before ending up beneath an portico on Water St., at the foot of North St. After several vandalization episodes, and one dropping (in transit), it's cracked, and under "tight" security.

Three miles south of town off Rte. 3A, the historical theme park ☒**Plimoth Plantation** recreates the Pilgrims' early settlement. Costumed actors carry out their daily tasks in the **Pilgrim Village,** while **Hobbamock's Homesite** represents a Native American village of the same period. (☎746-1622. Open Mar.-Nov. daily 9am-5pm. $20, seniors $18, ages 6-12 $12.) Docked off Water St., the **Mayflower II** is a scale replica of the Pilgrims' vessel and is staffed by actors to recapture the atmosphere of the original ship. (Open Mar.-Nov. daily 9am-5pm. $8, seniors $7, ages 6-12 $6. Admission to both sights $22, students and seniors $20, ages 6-12 $14.)

Plymouth, 40 mi. southeast of Boston, is best explored by car; take Exit 6A from Rte. 3, off I-93. **Plymouth & Brockton Bus** (☎746-0378) runs from T: South Station to the Exit 5 Info Center. (45min.; $10, seniors $8). The Plymouth/Kingston commuter rail train goes from T: North Station to the Cordage Park Station (45min., 3-4 per day, $6). From the info center and Cordage Park Station, catch a local GATRA bus ($1, seniors and children $0.50) to Plymouth Center. The **Plymouth Visitors Center** is at 170 Water St. (☎747-7525 or 800-872-1620; www.visit-plymouth.com. Open M-F 8am-4pm.) **Area code:** 508.

CAPE COD AND ISLANDS ☎508

Writer Henry David Thoreau wrote in his book *Cape Cod*: "[the Cape] is wholly unknown to the fashionable world, and probably will never be agreeable to them." Hmmm. This thin strip of land, now one of New England's premier vacation destinations, draws droves of tourists with its charming towns and sun-drenched landscapes—everything from cranberry bogs and sandy beaches to deep freshwater ponds carved by glaciers. Though parts of the Cape are known as the playground of the rich and famous, it can be an option for budget travelers, thanks to free activities like sunbathing and hiking, and a decent hostel and budget B&B system.

▰ ORIENTATION

Stretching out into the Atlantic Ocean south of Boston, Cape Cod resembles a flexed arm, with **Falmouth** and **Woods Hole** at its armpit, **Hyannis** at its tricep, **Chatham** at its elbow, the **National Seashore** tattooed on its forearm, and **Provincetown** at its clenched fist. The southern islands **Martha's Vineyard** (p. 137) and **Nantucket** (p. 139) are accessible by ferries from Woods Hole or Hyannis. **Upper Cape** refers to the suburbanized, area closer to the mainland. Proceeding eastward away from the mainland and curving up along the Cape, you travel "down-Cape" through **Mid-Cape** (where two hostels are located, near **Eastham** and **Truro**) to the **Lower Cape** and the National Seashore. In the summer, "Cape traffic" is hell: vacationers drive out on Friday and return Sunday afternoon, so avoid traveling then.

Cycling is the best way to travel the Cape's slopes. The park service has free trail maps and the detailed, highly recommended *Cape Cod Bike Book* ($3), also available at most Cape bookstores. The 135 mi. **Boston-Cape Cod Bikeway** connects Boston to Provincetown, and scenic trails line either side of the **Cape Cod Canal** in the National Seashore and the 25 mi. **Cape Cod Rail Trail** from Dennis to Wellfleet. For discount coupons, pick up a free *Official 2005 Guide to Cape Cod* or *Cape Cod Best Read Guide*, available at most Cape info centers. **Area Code:** 508.

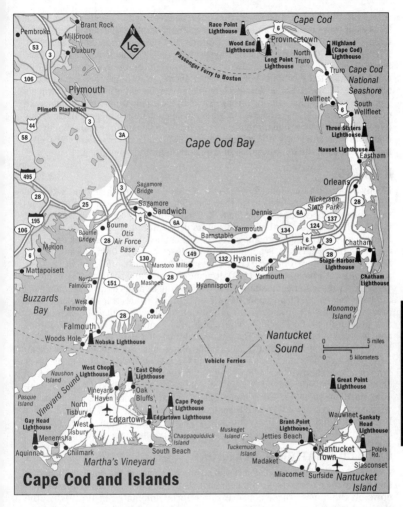

Cape Cod and Islands

FALMOUTH AND WOODS HOLE   ☎508

Coming from Boston, Falmouth and Woods Hole are the first true Cape towns day-trippers encounter. Unlike other places on the Cape, these towns sustain a decent-sized year-round population and tend to have less of a touristy feel, as most people bypass them to drive farther up the Cape or catch the ferry to Nantucket or Martha's Vineyard. The beach reigns proudly as the main attraction, but on hot days, it's hard to find the sand in the sea of umbrellas. Check out **Chapoquoit,** south of Old Silver, on the western shore of North Falmouth to avoid the crowds and relax peacefully. If you don't mind sharing the beach, **Falmouth Heights** on the southern shore of Falmouth, along Grand Ave., provides soft sands and great swimming. **Old Silver** beach and **Stoney** beach are also popular destinations. Lodgings are plentiful and nearly identical; the ⬛**Village Green Inn** ❺, 40 Main St., tops them all. Gorgeous rooms have fireplaces, Turkish cotton robes, and beds with Egyptian linen. Fresh flowers in every room and an excellent breakfast complete this stellar accommodation. (☎548-5621 or 800-237-1119. Doubles $90-175; 2-person suites $150-235. Extra person $30.) For diet-busting fried seafood ($5-12), check out the lively **Clam Shack ❷**, 227 Clinton Ave., an always-busy spot right on the water. (☎540-7758. Open late May to early Sept. daily 11:30am-7:45pm.) After hours, don't miss ◧**Captain Kidd's**, 77 Water St., in Woods Hole. It's a local bar adorned with the wheels and props of old ships, serving strong drinks to local fishermen and tourists alike on a deck overlooking the harbor. (☎548-8563. Open daily 11am-1am.) **Bonanza Bus** (☎888-751-8800; www.bonanzabus.com) leaves from Logan Airport and South Station in Boston and stops at Falmouth Bus Station, on Depot St. (1½hr.; $19). The bus continues to the ferry terminal in Woods Hole for the same price.

HYANNIS   ☎508

Mostly a transportation hub (ferries to Nantucket depart from here) and industrial center, Hyannis offers less charm than the villages farther down the cape. However, the town does boast a long Main St. lined with trendy stores, brewpubs, and motels. Hyannis's strength comes from its proximity to JFK's famous summer home in nearby Hyannisport, and several excellent beaches. **Kalmus Park Beach,** on Ocean St. in Hyannisport, is popular with windsurfers, while **Orrin Keyes Beach,** on Sea St., attracts more of a local crowd. **Veteran's Park Beach,** off Ocean St., is great for families. All have parking ($10), lifeguards, bath houses, snack bars, picnic areas, and wheelchair accessibility. The pride of the Hyannis industrial complex is the **Cape Cod Potato Chip Factory,** 100 Breeds Hill Rd. Tours trace the history and process of chip-making and visitors are rewarded with a free bag of delicious kettle-cooked chips. (☎775-3358. Tours M-F 9am-5pm. Free.) Hyannis is full of cookie-cutter motels and inns. The immense **Hyannis Inn Motel ❸**, 473 Main St., has large, clean rooms with cable TV and mini-fridges, a sauna, and an indoor swimming pool. (☎775-0255. Open mid-Mar. to mid-Oct. Doubles $62-126.) For inexpensive, delicious sandwiches ($4-6), head to **Box Lunch ❶**, 357 Main St., a Cape Cod chain serving rolled sandwich combos in cute boxes. (☎790-5855. Open M-F 9am-6pm, Sa 10am-10pm, Su 10am-5pm.) Upscale seafood restaurants line Main St., with entrees averaging $12-20. **Plymouth & Brockton** (☎746-0378) buses run from Boston's South Station to the brand-new Hyannis Transportation Center, off Main St. (1½hr.; M-F 24 per day 7am-midnight, Sa-Su 17 per day 7am-midnight; $15).

CAPE COD NATIONAL SEASHORE   ☎508

As early as 1825, the Cape had suffered so much damage at the hands of mankind that the town of Truro required local residents to plant beach grass and keep their cows off the dunes. These conservation efforts culminated in 1961, when the National Park Service created the Cape Cod National Seashore. The seashore includes much of the Lower and Outer Cape, from Provincetown south to Chatham, and has six beaches: **Coast Guard** and **Nauset Light,** in Eastham; **Marconi,** in Wellfleet; **Head of the Meadow,** in Truro; and **Race Point** and **Herring Cove,** in Provincetown. **Parking** at the beaches is expensive (in summer Sa-Su and low-season holidays $10 per day). A $30 pass is the best deal, covering all areas in the park for an entire season. Among the best of the seashore's 11 self-guided **nature trails** are the **Great Island Trail** and the **Atlantic White Cedar Swamp Trail.** The moderately difficult Great Island Trail, in Wellfleet, traces an 8 mi. loop through terrain such as pine forests and grassy marshes, rewarding trekkers with panoramic views of the bay and Provincetown. The most frequented trail, the 1¼ mi. Atlantic White Cedar Swamp Trail, starts at Marconi Station in south Wellfleet and winds past swampy waters and under towering trees. There are also three bike trails: **Nauset Trail** (1½ mi.), **Head of the Meadow Trail** (2 mi.), and **Province Lands Trail** (5 mi.). Park rangers at the National Seashore's **Salt Pond Visitors Center,** at Salt Pond off Rte. 6 in East-ham, provide maps, schedules for guided tours, and additional information about the park. (☎255-3421. Open daily July-Aug. 9am-5pm; Sept.-June 9am-4:30pm.)

Camping in the National Seashore is illegal, but numerous private campgrounds are squeezed in the narrow space between Rte. 6 and the boundaries of the park. Two hostels on the seashore provide the best budget accommodations on the Cape. **⬛Truro Hostel (HI) ❶,** 111 N. Pamet Rd., in Truro, sits on a bluff overlooking the ocean and offers a large kitchen, porch, and access to Ballston Beach in a turn-of-the-century converted Coast Guard station. From Rte. 6, take the Pamet Rd. exit, which becomes N. Pamet Rd. (☎508-349-3889 or 888-901-2086. Free linen. Check-in 10am-10pm. Check-out 7:30-10am. Lockout 10am-4pm. Open late June to early Sept. Members $22-24, nonmembers $25-27.) Eastham's **Mid-Cape Hostel (HI) ❶,** 75 Goody Hallet Dr., close to the bike path known as the **Cape Cod Rail Trail,** offers communal bungalow living in a woodsy location. From Rte. 6, take the Rock Harbor Exit at the Orleans Ctr. rotary, turn right onto Bridge Rd., then right again onto Goody Hallet Dr. By P&B bus, ask the driver to let you off as close as possi-ble, and call the hostel for the "shortcut" directions along bike paths. (☎255-2785 or 888-901-2085. Shared baths, kitchen, and barbecue facilities. Discounts avail-able with local bike shop. 7-day max. stay. Open late May to mid-Sept. Dorms $20-24, nonmembers $23-27.) **Plymouth & Brockton** (☎746-0378) runs buses from Bos-ton's South Station through the towns on the seashore (2½hr., $18). By car, take Rte. 3 to Rte. 6 west, cross the Sagamore Bridge, and follow the signs.

PROVINCETOWN ☎508

The Pilgrims' first landing site in 1620, Provincetown was a key fishing and whal-ing center in the 1800s, attracting a large Portuguese population. In the early 20th century, the town's popularity soared with resident artists and writers like Nor-man Mailer, Tennessee Williams, and Edward Hopper. Today, Provincetown's tra-dition of tolerance and open-mindedness has attracted a large gay community, making it a premier destination for gay vacationers, who fill the town to capacity in summer. Though far from inexpensive, P-town has better options for outdoor activities, dining, and nightlife than much of Cape Cod. It's easily accessible by public transit and just as easily navigated on foot.

⬛🔢 ORIENTATION AND PRACTICAL INFORMATION. Commercial Street, the town's main drag—home to countless art galleries, novelty shops, and trendy bars and eateries—runs along the harbor, centered on **MacMillian Wharf. Bradford Street,** the other main street, runs parallel to Commercial St. one block inland. Standish St. divides P-town into the **East End** and **West End.** Take the **Provincetown Shuttle** to outlying areas, including Herring Cove Beach and North Truro. Buy tickets on the bus or at the Chamber of Commerce. (☎800-352-7155. Late June to Aug. daily every hr. 7-9am, every 20min. 9am-12:30am. $1, seniors and ages 6-16 $0.50, under 6 free. Day pass $3; seniors, disabled, and children $1.50.) **Plymouth & Brockton** (☎746-0378) runs buses from Boston's South Station to Provincetown (3¼hr., $24). All but officially known as the "Fairy Ferry," **Boston Harbor Cruises** (☎617-227-4321 or 877-733-9425; www.bostonharborcruises.com) runs catamarans from Long Wharf, near T: Aquarium in Boston. (1½hr.; $37, seniors $32.) **Bike Rental: Ptown Bikes,** 42 Bradford St. (☎487-8735. Open daily 9am-6pm. $8 per 2 hrs. (2hr. min), $17 per day.) The **Provincetown Chamber of Commerce,** 307 Commercial St., is on MacMillian Wharf. (☎487-3424; www.ptownchamber.com. Open June-Sept. daily 9am-5pm; reduced hours in low season.) Head to the **Province Lands Visitors**

Center, on Race Point Rd. off Rte. 6, for park info. (☎487-1256. Open May-Oct. daily 9am-5pm.) **Post Office:** 219 Commercial St. (☎487-3580. Open M-F 8:30am-5pm, Sa 9am-noon.) **Postal Code:** 02657. **Area Code:** 508.

⌐ ACCOMMODATIONS. Provincetown teems with expensive lodging. **Somerset House ❺,** 378 Commercial St., is a fun, fabulous 12-room guest house with a social, sassy atmosphere—with a motto like "Get Serviced," you'd expect nothing less. (☎487-0383 or 800-575-1850. Doubles June-Aug. $130-260, Sept.-May $75-177. Nov.-Apr. 50% off second day.) **Dexter's Inn ❹,** 6 Conwell St., just off Bradford St., offers hotel-quality rooms for reasonable prices, plus a lush garden, large sundeck, and free parking. (☎487-1911. Mid-June to mid-Sept. 4-night min. stay. Singles and doubles mid-June to mid-Sept. $75-125, late May to mid-June and mid-Sept. to mid-Oct. $70-90, mid-Oct. to late May $50-65.) **Sunset Inn ❹,** 142 Bradford St., the inspiration for Edward Hopper's painting *Rooms for Tourists,* offers an excellent location, simple, well-kept rooms with shared bath, and a "clothing optional" sundeck. (☎487-9810 or 800-965-1801. Rooms June-Sept. $85-95; Apr.-May and Oct. $60-75.) The only truly budget accommodation is **Outermost Hostel ❶,** 28 Winslow St., with 5 cramped cottages. (☎487-4378. Small kitchen for guest use. Linen $3. Key deposit $10. Reception 8-9:30am and 5:30-10pm. Open May to mid-Oct. Dorms $20.) While camping is illegal on the Cape Cod National Seashore, excellent (and expensive) campgrounds border the dunes of the park. **Dunes Edge Campground ❶,** off Rte. 6, 1 mi. from Provincetown, offers 100 wooded sites with access to trails leading to sand dunes. (☎487-9815. Reservations recommended 6 weeks in advance in high season. 2-person sites $25-30, $12 each additional person up to 4.)

⌂ FOOD. Sit-down meals in Provincetown tend to be expensive. Fast food joints line the Commercial St. extension (next to MacMillian Wharf) and farther west by the Aquarium Mall. Groceries are available at **Grand Union,** 28 Shankpainter Rd., in the West End. (☎487-4903. Open M-Sa 7am-11pm, Su 7am-10pm.) Though the post office theme at the **Post Office Café ❸,** 303 Commercial St., is somewhat inconsistently executed, the seafood, pasta, and sandwiches are always good. Their clambake special (1¼ lb. lobster and steamers) is the best deal in town. (☎487-3892. Entrees $7-20. Open daily 8am-midnight.) **Tofu A Go-Go ❷,** 338 Commercial St., serves deliciously fresh vegetarian, vegan, and macrobiotic options on a balcony overlooking Commercial St.'s sea of tourists. (☎487-6237. Entrees $5-12. Open June-Aug. M-Th 11am-4pm, F-Su 11am-9pm; call for hours Apr.-May and Sept.-Oct.) **Karoo Kafe ❷,** 338 Commercial St., is a self-described "fast food safari," serving up South African and Mediterranean favorites from falafel to tofu with peri-peri sauce. (☎487-6630. Most entrees $5-9. Open June to mid-Sept. Su-F 11am-8pm, Sa 11am-9pm; Mar.-May and Sept.-Nov. lunch hours only.) **Café Edwidge ❸,** 333 Commercial St., serves contemporary American cuisine in a candlelit dining room adorned with local artwork. (☎487-4020. Breakfast $6-10. Dinner $8-22. Open late June to Aug. daily 8am-1pm and 6-10pm; mid-May to late June and Sept. to mid-Oct. Sa-Su 8am-1pm and 6-10pm.)

◪ SIGHTS. The **Pilgrim Monument,** the tallest all-granite structure in the US at 253 ft., and the **Provincetown Museum,** on High Pole Hill just north of the center of town, commemorate the Pilgrims' first landing. Hike up to the top of the Italian Renaissance-style tower for stunning views of the Cape and the Atlantic. (☎487-1310. Open daily July-Aug. 9am-6:15pm; Apr.-June and Sept.-Nov. 9am-4:15pm. $7, ages 4-12 $3, under 4 free.) A large bas-relief **monument,** in the small park at Bradford St. and Ryder St. behind the town hall, depicts the signing of the Mayflower Compact on November 11, 1620, in Provincetown Harbor.

✎ NIGHTLIFE. Nightlife in P-town is almost totally gay- and lesbian-oriented. **Crown & Anchor,** 247 Commercial St., is a complex with a restaurant, two cabarets, the chill Wave video bar, and the techno-filled Paramount dance club, where the boys flock nightly. (☎ 487-1430. Beer $3.50-4.50. Mixed drinks $4-8. Sa "Summer Camp." 21+. Cover $10; no cover for Wave. Open in summer daily 11pm-1am; low-season Sa-Su 11pm-1am.) Founded in 1798 by gay whalers, the **Atlantic House,** 6 Masonic Pl., just off Commercial St., still attracts its fair share of seamen. It contains the low-key "little bar;" the Leather & Levis "macho bar;" and the "big room," where you, too, can be a dancing queen. (☎ 487-3821. Beer $3. Mixed drinks $4. 21+. Cover $10. Open daily 10pm-1am.) The only major club for women is **Vixen,** 336 Commercial St., with a casual bar out front and a steamy dance floor out back. (☎ 487-6424. Beer $3. Mixed drinks $5-8. 21+. Cover $5. Bar open daily noon-1am; club open daily 10pm-1am.) **Governor Bradford,** at 312 Commercial St. has a wild side, hosting drag karaoke nightly at 9:30pm. (☎ 487-2781. Beer $3-4. Cocktails $4-8. 21+. No cover. Open daily 11am-1am.)

◪ OUTDOOR ACTIVITIES. The National Seashore (2 mi. from town) stretches out from Race Point Rd. with beaches, forests, and sand dunes. At **Race Point Beach,** waves roll in from the Atlantic, while **Herring Cove Beach,** at the west end of town, offers calm, protected waters. The **visitors center** offers free daily guided tours and activities during the summer. Directly across from Snail Rd. on Rte. 6, an unlikely path leads to a world of rolling **sand dunes;** look for shacks where writers like Tennessee Williams, Norman Mailer, and John Dos Passos spent their days. At the west end of Commercial St., the 1¼ mi. **Breakwater Jetty** takes you to a secluded peninsula, with two working lighthouses and the remains of a Civil War fort.

Provincetown seafarers have traded harpoons for cameras, but they still enjoy whale-hunting—**whale-watching cruises** rank among P-town's most popular attractions. Most companies guarantee whale sightings. A 3hr. tour is $18-20, but grab discount coupons at the Chamber of Commerce. **Boston Harbor Cruises Whale Watch** (☎ 617-227-4321 or 877-733-9425), **Dolphin Fleet** (☎ 349-1900 or 800-826-9300), and **Portuguese Princess** (☎ 487-2651 or 800-422-3188) all leave from MacMillian Wharf.

MARTHA'S VINEYARD ☎ 508

Martha's Vineyard is a favorite summertime escape, but it doesn't come cheap. In the past decade, "the Vineyard" has become one of the most popular vacation destinations for the area's rich and famous; from July to August, the population swells to over 105,000—up from the 15,000 year-round islanders. Savvy travelers might consider a weekend visit to the Vineyard in the spring and fall, when many private and town beaches are open, and B&B and inn prices plunge.

▤ TRANSPORTATION. The island is accessible by ferry or airplane only, but the latter is prohibitively expensive (flights begin at $130 each way). **Bonanza Bus** (☎ 888-751-8800; www.bonanzabus.com) runs from Boston's South Station to Woods Hole on Cape Cod (1½hr., $19), where the **Steamship Authority** (☎ 693-9130 on Martha's Vineyard, elsewhere 477-8600; www.steamshipauthority.com) sends 12-17 boats per day to Vineyard Haven (45min.; daily 7am-9:30pm; $6, ages 5-12 $3.50, cars $57, bikes $3) and Oak Bluffs (45min., May-Oct. 10:15am-5:45pm, same prices as Vineyard Haven). **Martha's Vineyard Regional Transit Authority (MVRTA)** runs summer shuttles between and within the six towns on the island. (☎ 693-9440. $2; day pass $6.) Pick up a free schedule and map of all 15 routes at the ferry terminal, Chamber of Commerce, or info booths. **Bikes** are the cheapest way to get around, but some parts of the island are outside of the average biker's range. **▨ Anderson's,** on Circuit Ave. in Oak Bluffs, rents bikes. (☎ 693-9346. Open daily July-Aug. 8am-6pm; Apr.-June and Sept.-Oct. 9am-5pm. $15 per day.) Taxi: **AdamCab** ☎ 800-281-4462; **Atlantic Cab** ☎ 877-477-8294.

⊞ ⊡ ORIENTATION AND PRACTICAL INFORMATION. Six major towns and a smattering of smaller villages make up Martha's Vineyard. The rural towns of West Tisbury, Chilmark, and Aquinnah (Gay Head) take up the western side of the island, called **up-island** because sailors tack upwind to get to it. The three major **down-island** towns are Oak Bluffs, Edgartown, and Vineyard Haven. Only Oak Bluffs and Edgartown sell alcohol. Vineyard Haven has the main ferry port and the **Chamber of Commerce,** on Beach Rd., where information on lodging, transportation, and island attractions can be collected along with maps and brochures. (☎ 693-0085. Open June-Oct. M-F 9am-5pm, Sa 10am-4pm, Su noon-4pm; Nov.-May M-F 9am-5pm, Sa 10am-2pm.) **Post Office:** Across from the Chamber of Commerce. (☎ 693-2818. Open M-F 8:30am-5pm, Sa 9:30am-1pm.) **Postal Code:** 02568. **Area Code:** 508.

⊓ ACCOMMODATIONS. ▨**Martha's Vineyard Hostel (HI) ❶,** on Edgartown-West Tisbury Rd., right next to a bike path, has the 74 cheapest beds on the island and serves as a base camp for travelers on bikes looking to explore the less crowded beaches and wildlife preserves up-island. From Vineyard Haven, take MVRTA bus #3 or 3a to West Tisbury and then bus #6 to the hostel. (☎ 693-2665 or 888-901-2087. Lockers $0.75. Linen included. Open Apr.-Oct. Dorms $20-24, nonmembers $23-27.) A plethora of B&Bs line streets all over the island; **Nashua House ❹,** 30 Kennebec Ave., in Oak Bluffs, is cozy and convenient with 16 rooms (all with shared bath) in an old Victorian. From the ferry terminal, walk straight ahead along Lake Ave. and turn left onto Kennebec Ave. (☎ 693-0043. Singles and doubles with shared bath $79-139; each additional person $20.) **Attleboro House ❹,** 42 Lake Ave., in Oak Bluffs, has a no-frills atmosphere in one of Oak Bluffs' famous gingerbread houses. (☎ 693-4346. Open June to mid-Sept. Doubles $95-115; each additional person $15.) Reserve months in advance for **Martha's Vineyard Family Campground ❷,** 556 Edgartown Rd., just outside of Vineyard Haven. MVFC has sites with hot showers, laundromat, playground, and access to bike paths and bus routes. Call for directions and reservations. (☎ 693-3772; www.campmvfc.com. 2-person tent sites $40; RV sites $45. $10 per each additional person up to 4.)

⊓ FOOD. Vineyard food is mostly overpriced, though cheap lunch places dot Vineyard Haven and Oak Bluffs. Popular seafood shacks sell fried seafood for $10-15. ▨**Aquinnah Shop Restaurant ❺,** 27 Aquinnah Cir., in Aquinnah, serves excellent fishcakes ($14) and freshly brewed sun tea ($2) on a balcony atop the cliffs offering views of a far-off horizon. The food is good, the view better. (☎ 645-3867. Entrees $18-26, seafood $12-15. Open July-Aug. daily 8am-9pm; Apr.-June and Sept.-Oct. M-Th 8am-3pm, F-Su 8am-sunset.) ▨**The Bite ❷,** on Basin Rd. near the beach in Menemsha, features phenomenal service in a low-key setting, topped only by their decadent fried seafood. (☎ 645-9239. Entrees $8-16. Open late May to early Oct. daily 11am-9pm. Cash only.) **Fresh Pasta Shoppe ❸,** 206 Upper Main St., in Edgartown, is actually known for serving the best pizza around ($3 per slice) in varieties like Mexican and Very Veggie. (☎ 627-5582. Open May-Nov. M-Sa 11am-9pm, Su 4-9pm; open later if busy.) **Mad Martha's ❶,** 12 Circuit Ave., in Oak Bluffs, with branches in Edgartown and Vineyard Haven, serves outstanding homemade ice cream for $4. (☎ 693-9151. Open in summer daily 11am-11pm. Cash only.)

⊡ SIGHTS. Oak Bluffs, 3 mi. west of Vineyard Haven on Beach Rd., is the most youth-oriented of the Vineyard villages. A tour of **Trinity Park,** near the harbor, includes the famous **Gingerbread Houses** (elaborate pastel Victorian cottages), while the **Flying Horses Carousel,** in the center of town, still operates as the oldest carousel in the nation. Snatch the brass ring and win a free ride. (☎ 693-9481. Open June-Aug. daily 10am-10pm. $1.50.) **Chicama Vineyards,** a 1 mi. walk up a dirt road from the MVRTA #3 bus stop, in West Tisbury, has free tours and wine tastings. (☎693-0309; www.chicamavineyards.com. Open June-Oct. M-Sa 11am-5pm, Su 1-5pm; Nov.-Dec. M-Sa 1-4pm; Jan.-May Sa 1-4pm. Tours June-Oct. M-Sa noon, 2, 4pm; Su 2 and 4pm.) Martha's Vineyard has always been known for its excellent shopping. The best shops are in **Vineyard Haven,** but with five Vineyard locations the famous **Black Dog** boutique can satisfy your trendy needs.

🔼 OUTDOOR ACTIVITIES. Exploring the Vineyard can involve more than pedaling around—hit the beach or trek down one of the great trails. **Felix Neck Wildlife Sanctuary,** on the Edgartown-Vineyard Haven road, offers five trails that meander through 350 acres and lead to the water. (☎627-4850. Office open June-Sept. M-Sa 8am-4pm, Su 10am-3pm; Oct.-May Tu-Sa 8am-4pm, Su 10am-4pm. Gate opens with office and closes around 7pm. $4, seniors and ages 3-12 $3.) **Menemsha Hills Reservation,** off North Rd. in the village of Menemsha, has 4 mi. of trails along the rocky Vineyard Sound Beach, leading to the island's second-highest point. **Cedar Creek Tree Neck,** off Indian Hill Rd. on the western shore, harbors 250 acres of headland with trails throughout, while **Long Point Park** in West Tisbury preserves 633 acres and a shore on the Tisbury Great Pond. The 20-acre 🔳**Polly Hill Arboretum,** 809 State Rd., in West Tisbury, boasts a complete collection of island plant species in a peaceful and remote setting. (☎696-9538. Open in summer M-Tu and Th-Su 7am-7pm, in low-season sunrise-sunset. Suggested donation $5.)

    South Beach, at the end of Katama Rd., 3 mi. south of Edgartown (shuttle from Edgartown $2), and **State Beach,** on Beach Rd. between Edgartown and Oak Bluffs, are free and open to the public. South Beach boasts sizable surf but an occasionally nasty undertow. State Beach's warmer waters once set the stage for parts of *Jaws,* the granddaddy of beach-horror films. For the island's best sunsets, stake out a spot at **Menemsha Town Beach** or 🔳**Aquinnah Beach,** New England's best clothing-optional spot. To access the private beach frequented by nude bathers, go to the beach's main entrance where signs say "no nudity," then walk down the beach back toward the cliffs. The native Wampanoag used to save sailors shipwrecked on the **Gay Head Cliffs,** near Aquinnah. The 100,000-year-old precipice shines brilliantly and supports one of the island's five **lighthouses.** (☎645-2211. Lighthouse open F-Su 1½hr. before sunset to 30min. after sunset. $3, under 12 free.)

NANTUCKET   ☎508

Nantucket has entered modern lore as Martha's Vineyard's conservative little sister. Rampant affluence has given the island's residents an influential stance in fighting for the preservation of its charms: dune-covered beaches, quaint cottages, cobblestone streets, and spectacular bike paths. Even with all this privilege, it is possible to enjoy a stay on the island without holding up a convenience store.

🔳 PRACTICAL INFORMATION. As any fan of the TV show *Wings* (set in Nantucket's Tom Nevers Field airport) knows, flights are out-of-reach pricey, so take one of the ferries from Hyannis, on Cape Cod (both are near the bus station). **Hy-Line Cruises,** on Ocean St. Wharf (☎778-2600), runs to Nantucket's Straight Wharf on slow boats (2hr.; in summer 3 per day, low-season 1-3 per day; $15, ages 5-12 $8, bikes $5) and fast boats (1hr., 5-6 per day, $35/$26/$5). The **Steamship Authority,** South St. Wharf (☎477-8600), goes to Steamboat Wharf on slow boats (2hr.; May-Oct. 6 per day, Nov.-Dec. 3 per day; $14, ages 5-12 $7.25, bikes $6) and fast boats (1hr., 5 per day 6am-7:20pm, $28/$21/$6).

    Steamship Authority ferries dock at Steamboat Wharf, which becomes **Broad Street** inland. Turn left off Broad St. onto S. Water St. to reach **Main Street,** at the base of which **Hy-Line** ferries dock. **Nantucket Regional Transit Authority** (☎228-7025;

www.shuttlenantucket.com) has shuttles to destinations throughout the island. Buses to **Siasconset** and **Surfside** leave from Washington and Main St. (near the lamppost). Buses to **Miacomet** leave from Washington and Salem St., a block up from Straight Wharf; those to **Madaket** and **Jetties Beach** leave from Broad St., in front of the Peter Foulger Museum. (Buses 7am-11:30pm; Surfside bus every 40min. 10am-5:20pm. Fare $1-2, seniors half-price, under 6 free.) With most beaches less than 6 mi. from town, bikes are the best way to see Nantucket. The cheapest rentals are at **Cook's Cycle,** 6 S. Beach St., right off Broad St. (☎228-0800. Open Apr.-Nov. daily 9am-5pm. $20 per day.) Get bus maps, island maps, brochures, and accommodations information at **Nantucket Visitor Services,** 25 Federal St., off Broad St. (☎228-0925. Open in summer daily 9am-6pm; in winter M-Sa 9am-5:30pm.)

⌂ ACCOMMODATIONS. There once was a hostel on Nantucket—and there still is. Across the street from the beach the **Nantucket Hostel (HI) ❶,** 31 Western Ave., a 3½ mi. bike ride from town at the end of the unlit Surfside Bike Path, is housed in a gorgeous 130-year-old lifesaving station, with three large, clean, dorm rooms. (☎228-0433 or 888-901-2084. Shuttle to hostel available during peak season 10am-6pm; $2. Full kitchen. Linen included. 7-day max. stay. Check-in 3-10pm. Lockout 11am-3pm. Open Apr.-Oct. Dorms $20-24, nonmembers $23-27.) Most other accommodations on Nantucket are expensive; some more budget-friendly options are listed with the **Nantucket Accommodations Bureau** (☎228-9559) or **Nantucket & Martha's Vineyard Reservations** (☎800-649-5671). The **Nesbitt Inn ❹,** 21 Broad St., one block from the wharf, is the oldest inn on Nantucket. It has small rooms with fan, sink, and shared baths, but guests are kept comfortable with a fireplace, deck, common room, continental breakfast, and beach towels. (☎228-0156. Reservations required. Open Mar.-Dec. Singles $75; doubles $85; quads $125. Mar.-Apr. and Oct.-Dec. $20 less.)

⌷ FOOD. Sit-down meals on the island are pricey, with entrees averaging $15-20. The cheapest options are the takeout places on Steamboat Wharf. The sandwich shop **Henry's ❶** is the first thing visitors see getting off the ferry at Steamboat Wharf. (☎228-0123. Sandwiches $5-6.25. Open May to mid-Oct. daily 8am-10pm. Cash only.) Get groceries at the **Grand Union,** off Straight Wharf. (☎228-9756. Open M-Sa 7am-10pm, Su 7am-7pm.) ▧**Something Natural ❶,** 50 Cliff Rd., just outside town, serves fresh cookies, Nantucket Nectars juices, and amazing sandwiches, on freshly baked bread. (☎228-0504. Full sandwiches $7-8; ½ sandwiches $4-5. Open M-Th 8am-6pm, F-Su 8am-6:30pm.) **The Atlantic Café ❸,** 15 S. Water St., is nautical and nice, with an aquatic theme, friendly employees, and American pub fare. (☎228-0570. Sandwiches $8-15. Entrees $13-22. Open daily May-Oct. 11:30am-1am; Nov.-Apr. 11:30am-midnight. Kitchen closes 10pm.)

◪ SIGHTS. The popular **Nantucket Whaling Museum,** 7 Broad St., which explores the glories and hardships of the old whaling community, is undergoing renovation but is expected to reopen in spring 2005; contact the Nantucket Historical Association for details (☎228-1894; www.nha.org). For a panoramic view of the island, climb the 92 stairs to the top of the bright white **Congregational Church Tower,** 62 Centre St., the third right off Broad St. On clear days, visitors can see 14 mi. out to sea. (☎228-0950. Open mid-June to Oct. M-Sa 10am-4pm; Apr. to mid-June F-Sa 10am-2pm. $2.50, ages 5-12 $0.50.)

◪⌀ BEACHES AND OUTDOOR ACTIVITIES. Nantucket's silky public beaches are the island's highlight. The northern beaches (Children's, Jetties, and Dionis) offer calmer seas than the southern beaches (Cisco, Surfside, Nobadeer). **Dionis** and **Jetties,** near town, are the most popular, with full facilities for daytrippers, while **Siasconset** and **Madaket** are more isolated. On the souther shore, **Miacomet** is the most peaceful. The biggest waves are at **Nobadeer** and **Cisco,** which is the headquarters for the **Nantucket Island Surf School.** (☎560-1020; www.surfack.com. Rentals $40 per day, $25 per half-day. $65 per 1hr. private lesson, $80 per 2hr. group lesson.) **Nantucket Community Sailing,** at Jetties Beach, rents watercraft and gives sailing lessons. (For lessons ☎228-6600, for rentals 228-5358. Open mid-June to mid-Sept. daily 9am-5pm. Kayaks $15 per hr.) **Barry Thurston's,** 5 Salem St., at Candle St., left off Straight Wharf, rents rods and reels. (☎228-9595. Open Apr.-Dec. M-Sa 8am-6pm, Su 8am-5pm. Pole, reel, and three lures $20 per 24hr.)

There are two popular bike routes on Nantucket. From Steamboat Wharf, turn right on N. Water St. and bear left onto Cliff Rd. to head for **Madaket Beach** (6¼ mi. each way). Many combine this with the **Sanford Farm Hike,** a single trail made up of several loops running through the brushy flatlands and gentle slopes of the old Sanford Farm, a preserved area at the heart of the island. A longer bike route runs to **Siasconset** (8¼ mi. of flat terrain) from Straight Wharf. Head up Main St. and turn left onto Orange St.; signs to the bike path begin after the rotary. To see more of the island, return from Siasconset Beach on the 10 mi. **Polpis Road** path. Maps of biking routes are available at the visitors center and most rental shops.

WESTERN MASSACHUSETTS

THE BERKSHIRES   ☎413

Within easy driving distance from Boston and New York City and distinguished by stunning autumn foliage, the Berkshires are an attractive destination for a weekend getaway. Sprinkled with small towns, the mountains offer picturesque ice-cream shops, country stores, and scenic rural drives, as well as pristine colleges and spas. Ruled by the artistic and the elite, the Berkshires offer an amazing assortment of theater, orchestral music, and contemporary art in New England.

■ ▊ ORIENTATION AND PRACTICAL INFORMATION

Comprising the western third of Massachusetts, the **Berkshire** region is bordered to the north by Rte. 2 (the Mohawk Trail) and Vermont, and to the south by the Mass. Pike and Connecticut. **Peter Pan Bus Lines** (☎800-343-9999) runs buses from Boston to Springfield, where there is a **Bonanza** connection to Williamstown with a transfer in Pittsfield. (4hr., 1-2 per day, $40.) **Visitor Info: Berkshire Visitors Bureau,** 3 Hoosac St. in Adams. (☎743-4500 or 800-237-5747; www.berkshires.org. Open M-F 8:30am-5pm.) The **Pittsfield Visitor Center,** 121 South St. in Pittsfield, also provides information about the region. (☎395-0105. Open M-Sa 9am-5pm, Su 10am-5pm.) Within the 12 state parks in Berkshire County, there are innumerable hiking and camping opportunities. For info, stop by the **Region 5 Headquarters,** 740 South St., in Pittsfield. (☎442-8928. Open M-F 8am-5pm.) **Area Code:** 413.

NORTH ADAMS

Formerly a large industrial center, North Adams once had 100 trains per day pass through its state-of-the-art Hoosac Tunnel. Over time, the factories metamorphosed into art studios and galleries—some of the best in New England—and today modern art stands where assembly lines once ruled. The five-year-old ▨**Mass MoCA,** 1040 Mass MoCA Way, has galleries in 27 old factory buildings and is the largest center for contemporary visual and performing arts in the country. Pushing the envelope of modern art, the museum holds exhibits like "Proposition

Player"—a room whose walls are digitally linked to a craps table in the center of the room and display images based on what you roll. (☎ 662-2111; www.mass-moca.org. Open late June to early Sept. daily 10am-6pm; early Sept. to late June M and W-Su 11am-5pm. $10, ages 6-16 $4.) The **Contemporary Artists Center,** 189 Beaver St. (Rte. 8 N), is an artists studio, and displaying a stunning gallery inside an enormous brick factory. (☎ 663-9555. Open W-Sa 11am-5pm, Su noon-5pm. Free.)

Celebrating the history of the Hoosac Tunnel, the **Western Gateway,** on the Furnace St. bypass off Rte. 8, is one of Massachusetts's five Heritage State Parks. The complex consists of a visitors center, a railroad museum, and a gallery, and hosts free outdoor concerts during the summer. (☎ 663-6312. Open daily 10am-5pm. Concerts in summer Th 7pm. Donations accepted.) On Rte. 8, ½ mi. north of downtown North Adams, **Natural Bridge State Park** is home to a white marble bridge that spans a 60 ft. deep chasm formed during the last Ice Age. (May-Oct. ☎ 663-6392, Nov.-Apr. 663-8469. Open late May to mid-Oct. daily 9am-5pm. Parking $2.) **Clarksburg State Park ❶,** 1199 Middle Rd., a few miles north of town on Rte. 8, has 45 wooded campsites and nearly 350 acres of woods and water. (☎ 664-8345. No lifeguard on duty. Free showers. Camping $12, MA residents $10. Day use $5.) Follow Rte. 2 east from Mass MoCa for the **North Adams Visitors Center** ,on Union St. (Rte. 2/Rte. 8), which is operated by enthusiastic volunteers. (☎ 663-9204. Open June-Sept. daily 10am-4pm.) You can find good eats and a hip crowd is at **joga,** 23 Eagle St. Enjoy a handcrafted panini with ingredients like marinated artichoke, Sicilian pepperoni, and fresh mozzarella ($7), or find a soft armchair, have a drink, and listen to live jazz, blues, or rock on weekends. (☎ 664-0126. No cover. Open M-Sa 11:30am-2pm; also Tu-W 5pm-9pm, Th 5pm-midnight, F-Sa 5pm-2am.)

WILLIAMSTOWN

With a purple cow named "Ephs" (after college founder Ephraim Williams) as a mascot and a lively student population, **Williams College** injects youthful vigor and drama into an otherwise quiet town. Maps of the scenic campus are available from the admissions office, 33 Stetson Ct., in Bascom House. (☎ 597-2211; www.williams.edu. Open M-F 8:30am-4:30pm. Tours daily; call for times.) While on campus, pay a visit to the **Williams College Museum of Art,** 15 Lawrence Hall Dr., #2. Housing over 12,000 pieces in both permanent and rotating exhibits, the museum focuses on American and contemporary art but encompasses a spectrum ranging from medieval religious works to controversial modern art. (☎ 597-2429; www.williams.edu/wcma. Open Tu-Sa 10am-5pm, Su 1-5pm. Free. Wheelchair accessible.)

Half a mile down South St. from the rotary, the ◨**Clark Art Institute,** 225 South St., features impressive 19th-century works by artists like Renoir, Degas, and Cassat, in rooms exposed only to natural lighting. The 140-acre grounds encourage patrons to picnic in the gardens or stroll through hillside pastures, complete with cattle and picturesque views. (☎ 458-2303; www.clarkart.edu. Open July-Aug. daily 10am-5pm; Sept.-June Tu-Su 10am-5pm. Nov.-May free; June-Oct. $10, students with ID and under 19 free. Wheelchair accessible.) As the summer heats up, so do the stages at the **Williamstown Theater.** The Tony-award-winning ◨**Williamstown Theater Festival** hosts plays and musicals on two main stages, as well several secondary stages around town. (☎ 597-3400, info line 597-3399; www.wtfestival.org. Box office open June-Aug. Tu-Sa 11am-after curtain, Su 11am-4pm. Performances Tu-Su. Main Stage $20-50; Nikos Stage $22-24, F afternoon play readings $3. All other stages free; call info line for showtimes.) The Williamstown Chamber of Commerce operates a **Visitors Information Booth** on the west end of town with info on events and a helpful guide to lodging and restaurants. (☎ 485-9077; www.williamstownchamber.com. Open July-Aug. daily 10am-6pm; Sept. F-Su 10am-6pm.)

The wooded hills surrounding Williamstown beckon from the moment visitors arrive. The **Hopkins Memorial Forest** (☎ 597-2346) offers 2400 acres of free hiking and cross-country skiing on 15 mi. of trails. Take Rte. 7 N (North St.), turn left on

Bulkley St., follow Bulkley to the end, and turn right onto NW Hill Rd. For bike, snowshoe, or cross-country ski rentals, check out **The Mountain Goat,** 130 Water St. (☎458-8445. Bike and ski rentals $25 per day, $35 for 2 days. Open M-W and F-Sa 10am-6pm, Th 10am-7pm, Su noon-5pm.)

Affordable motels cluster along Rte. 2 east of town. The **Maple Terrace Motel ❹,** 555 Main St. (Rte. 2), with beautifully planted gardens, bright rooms with cable TV and VCRs, a heated outdoor pool, and continental breakfast, is one of the best choices in town. (☎458-9677. Reservations strongly recommended. Rooms in summer $82-102; low-season $55-60.) The comfortable **Chimney Mirror Motel ❷,** 295 Main St., is cheaper and offers simple, clean rooms with private baths, A/C, and breakfast. (☎458-5202. Rooms in summer Su-Th $52-78, F-Sa $89-99; low-season $52-65. Discounts for extended stays.) For affordable meals, stroll to **Pappa Charlie's Deli ❶,** 28 Spring St., and sink your teeth into $5 celebrity-themed sandwiches such as the meaty "Columbo," with corned beef and bacon. (☎458-5969. Open Su-Th 8am-8pm, F-Sa 8am-9pm, Su 9am-8pm. Cash only.) Serving Herrell's ice cream ($2-2.75), incredible milkshakes ($3.50), and lunchtime sandwich specials, **Lickety Split ❶,** 69 Spring St., is hopping in the early afternoon. (☎458-1818. Sandwiches $5. Open Feb.-Nov. M-Sa 11:30am-11pm, Su noon-11pm; Dec.-Jan. M-Sa 11:30am-4pm; lunch until 3pm. Cash only.) Sample local student nightlife and great food at the **Purple Pub ❷,** 8 Bank St. Options like the portobello and roast chicken sandwich ($6.75) and a variety of salads complement the weekly drink specials. (☎458-3306; www.thepurplepub.com. M open mic. Open daily 11am-1am.)

LENOX

Tanglewood, an enormous and scenic musical complex on Rte. 7, west of Lenox Center on West St. (Rte. 183), is one of the Berkshires' greatest treasures. As the summer home of the **Boston Symphony Orchestra,** its bread-and-butter is top-notch classical music. For a great evening or a relaxing Sunday afternoon, lawn tickets and picnics are the way to go. Chamber concerts, generally performed by the young musicians training at Tanglewood over the summer, provide regular evening entertainment. The Boston Pops also gives four summer concerts. The summer ends with a **jazz festival** in late August. (☎888-266-1200 for tickets and schedules; www.bso.org. Orchestral concerts late June to late Aug. F 8:30pm with 6pm prelude, Sa 8:30pm, Su 2:30pm; open rehearsals Sa 10:30am. Auditorium or "Music Shed" $17-90; lawn seats $15-18, under 12 free. Students with valid ID half-price lawn tickets on F evenings.)

Though best known for her works of fiction such as *Ethan Frome,* **Edith Wharton** also dabbled in architecture, designing and building her own sparkling white mansion in 1902. Containing rooms decorated with classical stone sculptures and set above three acres of formal gardens and stables, **The Mount,** 2 Plunkett St., at the southern junction of Rte. 7 and 7A, offers tours and special events, like the summer lecture series on Women's Literature and Architecture. (☎637-1899; www.edithwharton.org. Open late May to Nov. daily 9am-5pm; tours M-F every hr., Sa-Su every 30min. 9:30am-3:30pm. $16, students $8, under 12 free. Special events $16 if reserved ahead, $18 at the door.) Shakespeare's works never go out of style at **Shakespeare & Company,** 70 Kemble St. (Rte. 7A). Enjoy the Bard's plays, as well as those written by Berkshires authors like Wharton, James, and Hawthorne, at the Founders Theater. Free matinees are also performed *al fresco* in the new Rose Footprint, a replica of the Elizabethan Rose Playhouse. (☎637-3353; www.shakespeare.org. Box office open mid-Apr. to late Oct. daily 10am-2pm or until performance begins. Founders Theater $8-50. Rose Footprint free. Call for showtimes.)

At the base of Lenox Mountain, the **Pleasant Valley Wildlife Sanctuary** contains 1500 acres and 7 mi. of trails through hardwood forest, meadows, and wetlands. Dusk hikers are sure to enjoy the large colony of beavers that show off their architectural skills at sunset. (☎637-0320; www.massaudubon.org. Open July-Sept.

NEW ENGLAND

daily dawn-dusk. Nature Center open late Oct. to June M 9am-4pm, Tu-Sa 9am-5pm, Su 10am-4pm; July to late Oct. Su-M 10am-4pm, Tu-Sa 9am-5pm. From Pittsfield, take Rte. 20 S to W. Dugway Rd. Follow W. Dugway 1½ mi. to the Nature Center. $4, ages 3-12 $3.) Surf's up at **Betty's Pizza Shack ❷**, 26 Housatonic St., where pictures of Hawaiian waves adorn the walls and a surfboard hangs over the bar. Despite the low-key name, the pizza ($13-17) is made with the finest ingredients and the dough is mixed with spring water. Take-away pizzas are perfect for a night at Tanglewood. (☎637-8171. Open M-F 10am-10pm, Sa 10pm-midnight.)

STOCKBRIDGE

Stockbridge, like many of the other small towns in the Berkshires, teems with natural beauty, history, and monuments to the wealthy. Bring back days of yore at the ▨**Norman Rockwell Museum,** 9 Glendale Rd. (Rte. 183), where you can visit the artist's studio and the largest single collection of his original works, including many *Saturday Evening Post* covers. (☎298-4100; www.nrm.org. Open May-Oct. daily 10am-5pm; Nov.-Apr. M-F 10am-4pm, Sa-Su 10am-5pm. $12, students $7, under 18 free.) Enjoy soothing aromas and stunning flower arrangements at the 15-acre **Berkshire Botanical Gardens,** at the intersection of Rte. 102 and 183. (☎298-3926; www.berkshirebotanical.org. Open May-Oct. daily 10am-5pm. $7, seniors and students $5, under 12 free.) Courtesy of the Gilded Age, **Naumkeag,** 5 Prospect Hill Rd., built in 1885, is the 44-room Choate family mansion, surrounded by lavish gardens, a Chinese temple, and lines of perfectly manicured trees. (☎298-3239; www.thetrustees.org. Open daily 10am-5pm, last tour at 4pm. Admission and tour $10, ages 3-12 $3. Admission to the garden only, no tour $8/$3.)

RHODE ISLAND

Founded in 1636 by religious outcast Roger Williams, Rhode Island exudes pure New England charm. Small, elegant hamlets speckle more than 400 miles of winding coastline, while numerous bike trails and small highways traverse the scenic interior. Only 48 miles north to south, this small state packs a lot of punch with stars like Providence and historic Newport.

▨ PRACTICAL INFORMATION

Capital: Providence.

Visitor Info: Providence/Warwick Convention and Visitors Bureau: 1 W. Exchange St., in downtown. (☎751-1177 or 800-233-1636; www.visitrhodeisland.com. Open M-Sa 9am-5pm.) **Division of Parks and Recreation,** 2321 Hartford Ave., Johnston 02919. (☎401-222-2632. Open M-F 8:30am-4pm.)

Postal Abbreviation: RI. **Sales Tax:** 7%.

PROVIDENCE   ☎401

Located at the mouth of the Seekonk River, Providence is a compact and easily walkable city. Cobbled sidewalks, historic buildings, and modern art sculptures share space in the heart of downtown, while the surrounding area supports inexpensive restaurants and shops. Downtown Providence rests at the base of two hills—one home to two world-class institutes of higher education, and the other to the state capitol—allowing Providence to seamlessly blend the hustle and bustle of a busy state capital with the more laid-back feel of a college town.

TRANSPORTATION. T.F. Green Airport, south of the city at Exit 13 off I-95, is a Southwest Airlines hub. **Amtrak,** 100 Gaspee St., operates from a station southeast of the state capitol. (☎800-872-7245; www.amtrak.com. Open daily 5am-10:45pm; ticket booth open 5am-9:45pm. Wheelchair accessible.) Trains run to Boston (1hr., 11 per day, $13) and New York City (4hr., 10 per day, $56). **Greyhound** has an info and ticket booth in Kennedy Center. (☎454-0790 or 800-231-2222. Ticket window open 6:30am-8pm.) To Boston (1hr.; M-F 8 per day, Sa-Su 12 per day; $7.50) and New York City (5hr.; M-F 88 per day, Sa-Su 11 per day; $23). **Bonanza Bus,** 1 Bonanza Way, at Exit 25 off I-95 and at the RIPTA information booth in Kennedy Center (☎888-751-8800; station open daily 4:30am-11pm, Kennedy Center ticket window daily 7am-6pm), has service to Boston (1hr., 18 per day, $9) and New York City (4hr., 7 per day, $37). **Rhode Island Public Transit Authority (RIPTA),** 265 Melrose St., runs an **info booth** at Kennedy Plaza that provides free bus maps. (☎781-9400; www.ripta.com. Terminal open 6am-8pm; ticket window M-F 7am-6pm, Sa 9am-noon and 1-5pm.) RIPTA's service includes Newport and a variety of other points. (Hours vary, buses run daily 5am-midnight; $0.25-5, base fare $1.25.) **Providence Link,** run by RIPTA, runs trolleys ($0.50) through the city with stops at major sights. **Yellow Cab** (☎941-1122) provides taxi service in the Providence metro area.

ORIENTATION AND PRACTICAL INFORMATION. I-95 and the **Providence River** run north-south and split Providence into three sections. West of I-95 is **Federal Hill;** between I-95 and the Providence River is **Down City.** East of the river is **College Hill,** home to **Brown University** and **Rhode Island School of Design (RISD).** Walking or taking the Providence Link are the best ways to see the city during daylight hours. **Providence/Warwick Convention and Visitors Bureau:** 1 W. Exchange St., in downtown. (☎751-1177 or 800-233-1636. Open M-Sa 9am-5pm.) The **Providence Preservation Society,** 21 Meeting St., at the foot of College Hill, has info on historic Providence and the *Guide to Providence Architecture* ($25), which traces 11 self-guided tours. (☎831-7440; www.ppsri.org. Open M-F 8:30am-5pm.) **Internet Access: Providence Public Library,** 225 Washington St. (☎455-8000. Open M noon-8pm, Tu-Th 10am-6pm, F-Sa 9am-5pm. Free.) **Post Office:** 2 Exchange Terr. (☎421-5214. Open M-F 8am-5pm.) **Postal Code:** 02903. **Area Code:** 401.

ACCOMMODATIONS. Downtown motel rates make Providence an expensive overnight stay. Rooms fill up well in advance for graduation season in May and early June. Head 10 mi. south on I-95 to **Warwick** or **Cranston,** or to **Seekonk, MA,** on Rte. 6, for cheaper motels. Catering largely to the university's international visitors, the stained-glass-windowed **International House of Rhode Island** ❸, 8 Stimson Ave., off Hope St. near the Brown campus, has three comfortable, unique, and welcoming rooms. Reservations are required and should be made far in advance. (☎421-7181. Laundry facilities, fridge, private bath, TVs, and shared kitchen. Reception Aug.-May M-F 9:30am-5pm; June-July M-F 8:30am-4pm. Singles $50, students $35; doubles $60/$45; $5 per night discount for stays of 5 nights or more; $550 per month, students $450 per month.) The **Gateway Motor Inn** ❸, 50 Mink St., on Rte. 6 about 1 mi. after entering Seekonk, MA, has a kind staff and clean, comfortable rooms. (☎508-336-8050. Continental breakfast included. Singles $59-65; doubles $65-79; $6 per additional person.) The nearest campgrounds lie 30min. from downtown. **Colwell's Campground** ❶, in nearby Coventry, provides showers and hookups for 75 sites along the Flat River Reservoir, a perfect place to swim or water-ski. From Providence, take I-95 S to Exit 10, then head west 8½ mi. on Rte. 117 and keep a sharp eye out for the tiny Peckham Ln. on the right. (☎397-4614. Reservations recommended. Check-in 3-9pm. Sites $18, with electricity $20.)

▢ FOOD. Providence provides excellent culinary options: **Atwells Avenue,** on Federal Hill just west of downtown, has a distinctly Italian flavor; **Thayer Street,** on College Hill to the east, is home to offbeat student hangouts and ethnic restaurants; and **Wickenden Street,** in the southeast corner of town, has inexpensive eateries. **Geoff's Superlative Sandwiches ❶,** 163 Benefit St., in College Hill, attracts a diverse clientele with about 85 creatively named sandwiches ($5-7), such as the "Sloppy Ho," the "Wacko," and the "Kevorkian," a sandwich that, with pastrami, bacon, cheddar, and topped with Frank's Hot Sauce, might facilitate your demise. Grab a treat from the huge pickle barrel to complement your meal. (☎751-2248. Open M-F 8am-9pm, Sa-Su 9:30am-9pm.) Specializing in Eggs Benedict (with five varieties), **Julian's ❸,** 318 Broadway, near Federal Hill, is a funky sit-down eatery with art on the walls and vegetarian options. (☎861-1770. Eggs Benedict $5-8, wraps and sandwiches $5-8. Dinner $11-22. Open M-F 9am-1am, Sa 9am-3pm and 5pm-1am, Su 9am-3pm and 6pm-1am.) **Louis's Family Restaurant ❶,** 286 Brook St., serves breakfast and lunch to local college students both prepping for morning tests and stumbling in after long nights. (☎861-5225. Open daily 5:30am-3pm.)

◙ SIGHTS. Jaunt down Benefit St. in College Hill, where students from the world-renowned RISD loiter in front of the colonial buildings at the base of College Hill discussing photography and modern design, much of which is on display at the ◪**RISD Museum of Art,** 224 Benefit St. The museum's three floors of galleries also exhibit a smattering of Native American, Egyptian, Indian, Impressionist, medieval, and Roman artwork, as well as a giant 12th-century Japanese Buddha. (☎454-6500; www.risd.edu/museum.cfm. Open Tu-Su 10am-5pm. $8, seniors $5, students $3, ages 5-18 $2. Free Su 10am-1pm, every 3rd Th 5-9pm, F noon-1:30pm, and last Sa of the month 11am-4pm.) Established in 1764, **Brown University** features 18th-century buildings, including the **Carliss-Brackett House,** 45 Prospect St., now the Office of Admission. (☎863-2378; www.brown.edu/admission. Open M-F 8am-4pm. Free 1hr. campus walking tours M-F 9am-4pm.) From atop the hill, gaze at the stunning marble dome of the **Rhode Island State Capitol.** (☎222-3938; www.state.ri.us/tours/tours.htm. Open M-F 8:30am-4:30pm. Free guided tours hourly M-F 9am-noon and tour guides on duty in the library until closing. Reservations recommended for groups. Self-guide booklets available in the library.)

The **John Brown House Museum,** 52 Power St., is steeped in tranquil elegance. The 1hr. tour includes a brief video introducing the house that was built by John Brown himself in the late 18th century. Guides discuss many aspects of the house and its relevance to Rhode Island's colonial roots. (☎273-7507. Open Tu-Sa 10am-5pm, Su noon-4pm. $7, students and seniors $5.50, ages 7-17 $3; families $18.) The factory that started the industrial revolution in America is preserved in Pawtucket at the **Slater Mill Historic Site,** 67 Roosevelt Ave. Situated by the rushing waters of the Blackstone River, the site has a large waterwheel and working water-powered machinery. (☎725-8638; www.slatermill.org. Open June-Nov. Su 1-5pm, Tu-Sa 10am-5pm. Call for winter hours. Continuous tours, included in price of admission, last 1½hr. $8, seniors $7, ages 6-12 $6, under 6 free.) In addition to founding Rhode Island, in 1638, Roger Williams founded the first **First Baptist Church of America.** Its 1775 incarnation stands today at 75 N. Main St. (☎454-3418; www.fbcia.org. Guided tours available after the Su service. Self-guided tours during all other hours of operation. Open M-F 10am-noon and 1-4pm, Sa 10am-noon. Free.)

▣▤ ENTERTAINMENT AND NIGHTLIFE. For film, theater, and nightlife listings, read the "Weekend" section of the *Providence Journal* or pick up a free *Providence Phoenix.* Between 10 and 15 summer evenings per year, floating and stationary bonfires spanning the entire length of the downtown rivers are set ablaze during ◪**Water Fire,** a public art exhibition and festival. (☎272-3111;

www.waterfire.org. Free.) The regionally acclaimed **Trinity Repertory Company,** 201 Washington St., typically offers $15 student rush tickets on the day of performances. (☎351-4242; www.trinityrep.com for ticket info. $28-50.) The **Providence Performing Arts Center,** 220 Weybosset St., hosts a variety of high-end productions like concerts and Broadway musicals. (☎421-2787. Box office open Sept.-May M-F 10am-6pm, Sa noon-5pm; May-Sept. M-Th 10am-3pm, F-Sa noon-closing. $30-68. ½-price tickets for students and seniors sometimes available 1hr. before weekday showtimes; call ahead to confirm.) The **Cable Car Cinema and Cafe,** 204 S. Main St., one block down from Benefit St., shows arthouse and foreign films in a small theater that has comfy couches. A friendly staff serves sandwiches ($4-5), vegan baked goods, ice cream, coffee, and iced tea. (☎272-3970. 2 shows per evening, times vary. $8, M-W students $6. Cafe open M-F 7:30am-11pm, Sa-Su 9am-11pm.)

Brownies, townies, and RISDs rock the night away at several hot spots throughout town. Something's going on every night at **AS220,** 115 Empire St., between Washington and Westminster St., a non-profit, totally uncensored cafe/bar/gallery/performance space. (☎831-9327; www.as220.org for performance info. Cover under $10, usually around $6. Open M-F 3pm-1am, Sa-Su 7pm-1am.) **Trinity Brewhouse,** 186 Fountain St., behind Trinity Repertory Theatre, offers award-winning beer as well as a live blues band on Wednesday nights inside a spacious brewhouse and restaurant. The brewhouse is painted in dark tones to highlight the brewtanks and fully stocked bar that dominate the center of the room. (☎453-2337. Open M-Th 11:30am-1am, F 11:30am-2am, Sa noon-2am, Su noon-1am.) Local artists perform rock, jazz, and funk at the **Custom House Tavern,** 36 Weybosset St., in Down City, a tiny corner bar in the perpetual shadows of Providence's tallest towers. (☎751-3630. 21+. Open M-Th 11:30am-1am, F 11:30am-2am, Sa 8pm-2am, Su 8pm-1am; in summer Sa-Su open at 4pm.)

NEWPORT ☎401

Money has always found its way into Newport. Once a center of transatlantic shipping, the coastal town later became the summer home of America's elite. As a result, Newport sports some of the nation's most opulent mansions. Today, Newport is a high-priced tourist town that also boasts arts festivals, awe-inspiringly extravagant mansions, and entrancing natural beauty.

⁊ PRACTICAL INFORMATION. Parallel to the shore, **Thames Street** is home to the tourist strip and the wharves, while **Bellevue Avenue** contains many of Newport's mansions. A mecca of information, the **Newport County Convention and Visitors Bureau,** 23 America's Cup Ave., two blocks from Thames St., in the Newport Gateway Center, offers huge maps, videos, and interactive exhibits. (☎800-976-5122; www.gonewport.com. Open daily 9am-5pm.) **Bonanza Buses** (☎846-1820) depart from the Gateway Center, as do the buses of **Rhode Island Public Transit Authority** (**RIPTA;** see **Transportation** p. 145). Parking at the center is a cheap option ($2 per day with RIPTA receipt, 30min. free with visitors center validation). **Ten Speed Spokes,** 18 Elm St., rents bikes. (☎847-5609. Open M-F 10am-6pm, Sa 10am-5pm, Su noon-5pm. Bikes $5 per hr., $25 per day. Credit card and photo ID required.) **Internet Access: Public Library,** 300 Spring St. (☎849-8720. Open M 11am-8pm, Tu-Th 9am-8pm, F-Sa 9am-6pm. Free.) **Post Office:** 320 Thames St. (☎847-2329. Open M-F 8:30am-5pm, Sa 9am-1pm.) **Postal Code:** 02840. **Area Code:** 401.

ⓘ ACCOMMODATIONS. Small and expensive lodging abounds in Newport; those willing to share a bathroom or forgo a sea view *might* find a double for $75. Many hotels and guest houses book solid two months in advance for summer weekends, especially during the well-known festivals. A few minutes from Newport's harborfront, the **Newport Gateway Hotel ❺,** 31 W. Main Rd., in Middletown, has clean, comfortable doubles with A/C, mini-fridge, and cable TV. (☎847-2735.

Breakfast included. Su-Th $65-99, F-Sa $159-195.) For less expensive lodging, Rte. 114 (W. Main Rd.) hosts a variety of chain motels about 4 mi. from Newport. Family-owned and -built, **Twin Lanterns ❶**, 1172 W. Main Rd., 7 mi. north of Newport, offers eight clean one-room cabins with two full beds, A/C, TV, mini-fridge, and private bathrooms, as well as eight tent sites with hot shower facilities. (☎682-1304. Tent sites $20. Cabins $40-60.) **Fort Getty Recreation Area ❶**, on Fort Getty Rd. on Conanicut Island, provides 15 small tent sites in an open field with a great view of an old lighthouse. (☎423-7211. Free hot showers and beach access. Reservations recommended. Tent sites June-Oct. $20; RV sites $30.)

🄲 FOOD. The vegetarian-friendly **Panini Grill ❶**, 186 Thames St., offers tasty grilled sandwiches ($5-6) in a small basement. (☎847-7784. Open Su-Th 11am-9:30pm, F-Sa 11am-2am.) A drive north down W. Main Rd. reveals typical chains and the **Newport Creamery ❷**, 208 W. Main Rd., which serves breakfast, lunch, and ice cream either inside the diner or from a takeout window. (☎846-2767. Dinner $6-10. Open 6:30am-11pm.) Good, hearty breakfasts ($7-8) like the "Portuguese Sailor" (*chorizo* sausage and eggs) are prepared before your eyes at the **Franklin Spa ❶**, 229 Spring St. (☎847-3540. Open M-W 6am-2pm, Th-Sa 6am-3pm, Su 7am-1:30pm.) Choice mollusks are always the catch of the day at **Flo's Clam Shack ❸**, 4 Wave Ave., across from the east end of Easton Beach. Be prepared for lines on hot summer evenings. (☎847-8141. Seafood platters with cole slaw and fries $8-14. Open Su-Th 11am-9pm, F-Sa 11am-10pm; call for low-season hours.)

🄶 SIGHTS. George Noble Jones built the first "summer cottage" in Newport in 1839, kicking off the creation of an extravagant string of palatial summer estates. Most mansions lie south of downtown on Bellevue Ave. A self-guided walking tour or, in some mansions, a guided tour by the **Preservation Society of Newport**, 424 Bellevue Ave., provides a chance to ogle the decadence. (☎847-1000; www.newportmansions.org. Open in summer daily 9am-5pm; in winter M-F 9am-5pm.) The five largest mansions are the **Elms**, 367 Bellevue Ave., the **Breakers**, 44 Ochre Point Ave., both with striking formal gardens; **Chateau-sur-Mer**, 474 Bellevue Ave.; **Rosecliff**, 548 Bellevue Ave.; and the **Marble House**, 596 Bellevue Ave. Marble House, containing over 500,000 cubic ft. of marble, silk walls, and gilded rooms, should not be missed. (☎847-1000. Mansions open M-F 10am-5pm. $10-15 per house, ages 6-17 $4. Combination tickets for 2-5 houses $22-32.)

Newport's gorgeous beaches are frequently as crowded as the streets. The most popular sandy spot is **Easton's Beach**, or First Beach, on Memorial Blvd. (☎848-6491. Parking late May to early Sept. M-F 10am-9pm $8, before 10am $6, Sa-Su $10.) Other beaches line Little Compton, Narragansett, and the shore between Watch Hill and Point Judith. Starting at Easton's Beach or Bellevue Ave., the **Cliff Walk** traverses Newport's eastern shore as a 3½ mi. walking/running trail (www.cliffwalk.com). Wildflowers and a rocky shoreline mark one side of the trail, while gorgeous mansions border the other. **Fort Adams State Park**, south of town on Ocean Dr., 2½ mi. from the visitors center, has hot showers, picnic areas, and multiple fishing piers alongside the largest coastal fort in America, which took 30 years to build. (☎847-2400; www.fortadams.org. Park open sunrise-sunset.) In the Fort Adams area, **Ocean Drive** is a breathtaking 10min. car ride along the coast.

A plain brick facade hides the gorgeous Georgian architecture inside the **Touro Synagogue**, 85 Touro St., the oldest synagogue in the US, which dates back to 1763. (☎847-4794; www.tourosynagogue.org. Tours every 30min. July-Aug. Su-F 10am-5pm; May-June and Sept.-Oct. every 30min. M-F 1-2:30pm, Su 11am-3pm. Call for low-season tour schedule. Last tour begins 30min. before closing. Free.) The **Tennis Hall of Fame**, 194 Bellevue Ave., is a white-and-green shingled Victorian house that contains an in-depth look at the sport's history, displays of tennis champions, and a colorful exhibit of tennis ball canisters. (☎849-3990; www.tennisfame.com. Open daily 9:30am-5pm. $8, students and seniors $6, under 17 $4; families $20.)

🔟🎵 **ENTERTAINMENT AND NIGHTLIFE.** From June through August, Newport gives lovers of classical, folk, jazz, and film each a festival to call their own. Festival tickets and accommodations fill up months in advance; look early if you want to attend. The **Newport Jazz Festival,** at Fort Adams State Park, is one of the oldest and best-known jazz festivals in the world. Also at Fort Adams State Park, folk singers entertain at the **Newport Folk Festival,** where former acts include Bob Dylan, Joan Baez, and the Indigo Girls. (Both festivals ☎847-3700; www.festivalproductions.net. Tickets $58-63 per day, under 12 $5.) The **Newport Music Festival** brings classical musicians from around the world for over 60 concerts during two weeks in July. The concerts take place in the ballrooms and on the mansions' lawns. (☎846-1133, box office 849-0700; www.newportmusic.org. Box office open M-F 10am-6pm, Sa 10am-1pm. Tickets $35-40.) In June, the **Newport International Film Festival** screens over 70 feature, documentary, and short films in the **Jane Pickens Theater** and the **Opera House Cinema** (☎846-9100; www.newportfilmfestival.com.)

Pubs and clubs line Thames St. Be sure to bring proper ID, as area clubs are very strict. **The Rhino Bar and Grille's Mamba Room,** 337 Thames St., is the place to dance the night away. (☎846-0707. 21+. Cover $5-20. Open W-Sa 9pm-1am.) **One Pelham East,** 274 Thames St., delivers cold drinks in a spacious bar and features alternative bands. (☎847-9460. Live music nightly. Cover $5-20. Open M-F 3pm-1am, Sa-Su 1pm-1am.) Don't be fooled by the name of **The Newport Blues Cafe,** 286 Thames St., as it hosts live music ranging from blues to rock to reggae. (☎841-5510. Live music nightly after 9:30pm. Business casual, no hats. Cover up to $15. Open in summer daily 6pm-1am; dinner until 10pm. Call for winter hours.) For a pint ($4) at a traditional Irish pub with dark wooden walls right in the heart of the historic district, head to **Aidan's,** 1 Broadway. (☎845-9311. Open daily 11:30am-1am.)

🔋 **DAYTRIP FROM NEWPORT: BLOCK ISLAND.** A popular daytrip 20 mi. southwest of Newport, sand-blown **Block Island** possesses an untamed natural beauty. More than one-third of the island is protected open space; local conservationists hope to increase this figure to 50%. All beaches are free, but many are a hike from the ferry stops. Cycling is the ideal way to explore the tiny island; **Aldo's Rentals,** on Chapel St. behind the Harborside Inn, rents bikes. (☎466-5018. Mountain bikes $7 per hr., $25 per day; mopeds $35/$85; cars and SUVs $50-80 per 2hr., $90-155 per day; kayaks $15 per hr., $35 per half-day. Open mid-May to mid-Oct. daily 8am-6pm. Coupons available in the *Block Island Times*; inquire at the visitors center.) A ¾ mi. hike along the shore to **North Light,** the granite lighthouse and maritime museum that rests on the northern tip of the island 4 mi. from town, is a pleasant excursion. (Open early July to early Sept. daily 10am-4pm. $2.) Don't miss the trail hidden behind the lighthouse that leads through the sand dunes to the northern coast. Follow the coast up to the very northern tip of the island, where a narrow pathway leads out into the Atlantic. Enjoy the most beautiful and secluded sands on the island, but do not swim here as currents are downright lethal.

The island does not permit camping; it's best to take a daytrip unless you're willing to shell out at least $60, and probably much more, for a room in a guest house. Most moderately priced restaurants hover near the ferry dock in Old Harbor, but a few others are located in New Harbor, 1 mi. inland. **Rebecca's Seafood Restaurant ❶,** on Water St. across from the dock, serves some of the cheapest eats in the area in a picturesque white-and-green building. (☎466-5411. Seafood sandwiches $4-6. Open M-Th 7am-8pm, F-Su 7am-2am.) Decadent sweets ($2.50-5) and iced coffee ($2-3) can be found alongside Internet terminals ($1 per 5min.) at **Juice 'n' Java ❶** on Dodge St. (☎466-5220. Open daily 7am-midnight.)

The **Interstate Navigation Company** (☎783-4613) provides **ferry service** to Block Island from Galilee Pier in Point Judith (1¼hr.; mid-June to early Sept. 8-9 per day; $9.20, seniors $8.70, ages 5-11 $4.50; car by reservation $39, driver and passengers must pay regular fare; bike $2.50); New London, CT (1hr.; mid-June to mid-Sept. 4-5 per day; $15, ages 5-11 $7.50; bike $5, surfboard $5); Newport (2hr.; July-Aug. 1 per day; $9, seniors $8.50, ages 5-11 $4; bike $2.50). The last ferry of the day usually leaves at 7pm, and schedules are available at any of the terminals. The **Block Island Chamber of Commerce** (☎466-2982), located at the ferry dock in Old Harbor, provides maps and information on accommodations on the island. (Lockers and ATM in the visitors center next door. Open in summer daily 9am-5pm; low-season hours vary.) **Area Code:** 401.

CONNECTICUT

Connecticut is like a patchwork quilt; industrialized centers like Hartford and New Haven are interspersed with serene New England villages, a vast coastline, and lush woodland beauty. Home to Yale University and the nation's first law school, Connecticut has a rich intellectual history. Make no mistake, though—the state that brought us the lollipop, the three-ring circus, and the largest casino in the United States knows how to let its hair down.

▨ PRACTICAL INFORMATION

Capital: Hartford.

Visitor Info: Connecticut Vacation Center, 505 Hudson St., Hartford 06106 (☎800-282-6863; www.ctbound.org). Open M-F 8am-4:30pm.

Postal Abbreviation: CT. **Sales Tax:** 6%.

HARTFORD   ☎860

Hartford may be the world's insurance capital, but it has more to offer travelers than financial protection, including several high-quality museums and historical sites, a lively theater scene, and the only hostel in Connecticut and Rhode Island. As Mark Twain—a prized former resident of 17 years—boasted, "of all the beautiful towns it has been my fortune to see, this is the chief."

▨ **PRACTICAL INFORMATION.** Hartford marks the intersection of the **Connecticut River, I-91,** and **I-84.** Union Place, between Church and Asylum St. along Spruce St., houses **Amtrak** (☎727-1778; office open M-F 6am-7:30pm, Sa-Su 6:30am-7:30pm), which runs to New Haven (1hr., $12-14) and New York City (3hr., $38-43), and **Greyhound** (☎724-1397; station open daily 5:45am-10pm), which goes to: Boston (2hr., 12 per day, $28); New Haven (1½hr., 4-5 per day, $14); New York City (2½hr., 21 per day, $29). **Connecticut Transit Information Center** is the round terminal at State and Market St. (☎525-9181; www.cttransit.com. Open M-Sa 6:30am-6:30pm, Su 7am-6pm. Buses within the city $1, students $0.75, seniors $0.50.) **Taxi: Yellow Cab** ☎666-6666. **Visitor Info: Greater Hartford Welcome Center,** 45 Pratt St. (☎244-0253 or 800-793-4480; www.hartford.com. Open M-F 9am-5pm.) The **Old State House,** 800 Main St., also provides tourist info. (☎522-6766. Open M-Sa 10am-4pm.) **Internet Access: Hartford Public Library,** 500 Main St. (☎695-6300. Open M-Th 10am-8pm, Sa 10am-5pm; Oct.-May also Su 1-5pm. Free.)**Post Office:** 80 State House Sq. (☎240-7553. Open M-F 8am-5pm.) **Postal Code:** 06103. **Area Code:** 860.

▟▙ **ACCOMMODATIONS AND FOOD.** The cozy, social **Mark Twain Hostel (HI) ❶,** 131 Tremont St., offers 42 soft bunks, with a kitchen, common room, and pleasant front porch, in a residential area close to downtown. Head west on Farmington Ave., then turn right on Tremont St., or take the "Farmington Ave." bus west.

(☎523-7255. Linens and pillow. Laundry $2.50. Check-in 5-10pm. Reservations recommended. Dorms $20, nonmembers $24.) Opposite Bushnell Park, the **YMCA ❶**, 160 Jewell St., provides dormitory-like accommodations. Use of the gym, pool, and squash and racquetball courts is included. (☎246-9622. Must be 18+ with ID. Key deposit $10. Check-in 7:30am-10pm. Check-out noon. No reservations. Singles $20, with private bath $25.) The *Greater Hartford Visitors Guide*, available at the welcome center, lists affordable accommodations in nearby towns.

The ultimate combination of food, nightlife, and entertainment can be found at the **City Steam Brewery** and **BrewHaHa Comedy Club ❸**, 942 Main St. Pool tables fill one room while red velvet couches line several lounges complete with card tables and TVs. Nine brewing tanks each contain a different home-brewed masterpiece like the "Naughty Nurse" Pale Ale. On the patio, waiters serve amazing dishes ranging from pan-seared ahi ($11) to Thai salads with lemongrass and basil-crusted chicken ($13). Upstairs, the comedy club keeps guests in stitches. (☎525-1600. M $2 margaritas, M-F 10pm-midnight $3 martinis. Live rock and blues Th-Sa. Comedy cover $5-15. Open Su-Th 11am-1am, F-Sa 11am-2am.) **Black-Eyed Sally's BBQ & Blues ❷**, 350 Asylum St., serves down-home southern cooking. Enjoy some jambalaya ($16) and add your name to the thousands of signatures that cover the walls. (☎278-7427; www.blackeyedsallys.com. Sandwiches $7-9. ½-rack of ribs $14. Live blues W-Sa nights. F-Sa cover $5-10. Open M-Th 11:30am-10pm, F 11:30am-11pm, Sa 5-11pm, Su 5-9pm.) The *Greater Hartford Visitor's Guide*, available at the welcome center, has a helpful listing of eateries and a map.

◘ SIGHTS. The ◪**Wadsworth Athenaeum**, 600 Main St., has collections of contemporary and Baroque art, including one of three Caravaggios in the US. Rotating exhibitions, a breathtaking collection of Hudson River School landscapes, and a collection of German and French porcelain round out a priceless gallery. (☎278-2670; www.wadsworthathenaeum.org. Open Tu-F 11am-5pm, Sa-Su 10am-5pm. $9, seniors $7, ages 13-18 and students with ID $5; additional $6 for special exhibits. Free Sa before noon. Call ahead for tour and lecture info.) Designed by Charles Bulfinch in 1796, the gold-domed **Old State House**, 800 Main St., housed the state government until 1878. Now, historic actors take you into the chambers where Reverend Hooker delivered his revolutionary sermon in 1638, and where the Amistad Trial began in 1839. On a lighter note, the museum of curiosities contained within the Old State House includes a crocodile, a tiger and a two-headed calf. (☎522-6766; www.ctosh.org. Open M-F 10am-4pm, Sa 11am-4pm. Free.) **Bushnell Park,** at Jewell St., has a vintage 1914 **carousel**, complete with an organ. (☎585-5411. Open May-Oct. Tu-Su 11am-5pm. $0.50 per ride.) West of the central city, at 351 Farmington Ave, the **Mark Twain House and Museum,** delivers an entertaining tour of the intricately textured home, where the author penned parts of *The Adventures of Huckleberry Finn* and *Tom Sawyer*, recalls the best days of Mark Twain's life. From the Old State House, take any "Farmington Ave." bus west. (☎247-0998. Open M-W and F-Su 9:30am-5:30pm, Th 9:30am-8pm; Jan.-Apr. closed Tu. $12, seniors $11, students $10, ages 6-12 $8.) The **Harriet Beecher Stowe House,** 77 Forest St., adjacent to Twain's home, offers tours of the spacious abode with information about the life and times of the author who wrote *Uncle Tom's Cabin* and whom Abraham Lincoln called "the little lady that started the big war." (☎522-9258; www.harrietbeecherstowe.org. Open June to mid-Oct. Tu-Sa 9:30am-4:30pm, Su noon-4:30pm; mid-Oct. to May closed M. $8, seniors $7, ages 6-16 $4.)

◪◪ ENTERTAINMENT AND NIGHTLIFE. The Tony Award-winning **Hartford Stage Company,** 50 Church St., stages productions of traditional masterpieces, American classics, and contemporary works. (☎527-5151; www.hartfordstage.org. $20-60.) **TheaterWorks,** 233 Pearl St., is an off-Broadway-style theater that presents a variety of recent plays. (☎527-7838. $20-55.) For more show options, head to **The Bushnell**, 166 Capitol Ave., home of Hartford's symphony, ballet, and opera companies, as well as a venue for Broadway hits, jazz, and family favorites. (☎987-5900; www.bushnell.org. Box office open M-Sa 10am-5pm, Su noon-4pm. Rush and student rate tickets sometimes available.) Downtown is pretty empty on weekdays, but on weekends Hartford's nightlife is clustered along Asylum St. and around the train station. With a loyal clientele, pool table, and weekday drink specials, **McKinnon's**, 114 Asylum St., is the best place to find cool brews and good times seven days a week. (☎524-8174. M Karaoke night. 21+. Cover varies. Open M-Th 4pm-1am, F-Sa 4pm-2:30am.) Across the street, the **Bar with No Name**, 115 Asylum St., reigns as the most popular hangout in the city. A different DJ each week mixes loud beats for the sea of people in the center room while bartenders mix nightly drink specials. This is your weekend hotspot. (☎293-2344. Happy hour Th-Su 6-9pm with free food and cheap drinks. 21+. Cover varies. Open Th-Su 6pm-2am.)

NEW HAVEN ☎203

With a bad reputation that has proven hard to drop, New Haven is growing from the inside out. The center of the city is home to the solid stone foundations of Yale University, a shining academic light that continues to expand into the darker areas of the city's troubled past. Today, the "new" New Haven, and especially the area around Yale's campus, sustains a healthy assortment of ethnic restaurants, art galleries, pizza dives, and coffee shops supported by students and townies alike.

🔏 **PRACTICAL INFORMATION.** New Haven lies at the intersection of **I-95** and **I-91**, 40 mi. south of Hartford, and is laid out in nine squares surrounded by radial roads. Between Yale University and City Hall, the central square, called **The Green**, provides a pleasant place to sit and relax. *At night, don't wander too far from the immediate downtown and campus areas; some of the surrounding sections can be very unsafe.* **Amtrak**, at Union Station on Union Ave., Exit 1 off I-91 (☎773-6177; ticket office open daily 6:30am-9:30pm), runs to: Boston (2½hr., 16 per day, $46); Mystic (1hr., 3-4 per day, $18); New York City (1½hr., 20 per day, $34); Washington, D.C. (5½hr., 20 per day, $78). Also at Union Station, **Greyhound** (☎772-2470; ticket office open daily 7am-8pm) runs frequently to: Boston (3½-5hr., 11 per day, $34); New York City (2½hr., 11 per day, $23); Providence (2½hr., 11 per day, $23). The **New Haven Trolley Line** services the immediate downtown area and Yale campus. (☎288-6282. Runs every 15min. M-Sa 11am-6pm. Free.) **Taxi: Metro-Taxi** ☎777-7777. **Greater New Haven Convention and Visitors Bureau**, 59 Elm St., has free maps, brochures, and the *Greater New Haven Visitor's Guide*. (☎777-8550; www.newhavencvb.org. Open M-F 8:30am-5pm.) **Internet Access: New Haven Public Library**, 133 Elm St.(☎946-8130. Open mid-Sept. to May M noon-8pm, Tu-Th 10am-8pm, Sa 10am-5pm; June to mid-Sept. M-Th 10am-6pm, F 10am-5pm. Free access with photo ID.) **Post Office:** Inside the federal building at 150 Court St. (☎752-3283. Open M-F 7:30am-5pm, Sa 8am-noon.) **Postal Code:** 06510. **Area Code:** 203.

🏠 **ACCOMMODATIONS.** Inexpensive lodgings are sparse in New Haven; the hunt intensifies and prices jump around Yale Parents Weekend (mid-October) and Commencement (early June). Head 10 mi. south on I-95 to **Milford** for affordable motels. **Hotel Duncan ❸**, 1151 Chapel St., located in the heart of Yale's campus, exudes old-fashioned charm at affordable rates. Guests enjoy spacious rooms and ride in the oldest manually operated elevator in the state. (☎787-1273. Reservations recommended F-Su. Singles $44-50; doubles $60-70.) **Hammonasset Beach State Park ❶**, 20min. east on I-95 N from New Haven, Exit 62 in Madison, offers 558

sites just a few minutes from woods and a long sandy beach. (☎245-1817; http://
reserveamerica.com. Office open mid-May to Oct. daily 8am-10:30pm. Lifeguard
on duty 8am-8pm. Free hot showers. Sites $15. Day use M-F $10, Sa-Su $14.)

❑ FOOD. For great authentic Italian cuisine, work your way along Wooster St.,
in Little Italy, 10min. east of downtown. **✵Pepe's ❸**, 157 Wooster St., claims to be
the originator of the first American pizza, originally known as "tomato pie" in the
1920s. They serve a small red or white sauce clam pie for $9 in antique wooden
booths decorated with photographs from the eatery's celebrated past. (☎865-5762.
Open M and W-Th 4-10pm, F-Sa 11:30am-11pm, Su 2:30-10pm.) Next door, **Libby's
❶**, 139 Wooster St., has delicious *cannoli*. (☎772-0380. Open M and W-Th
11:30am-10pm, F-Sa 11:30am-11pm, Su 11:30am-9pm.) No condiments are allowed
at **Louis's Lunch ❶**, 263 Crown St. Cooked vertically in original cast-iron grills, the
beloved burgers ($4) are complemented by excellent apple pie for $3 per slice.
(☎562-5507. Open Tu-W 11am-4pm, Th-Sa noon-2am.) Indian restaurants dominate
the neighborhood southwest of downtown, near Howe St. The all-you-can-eat
weekend lunch buffet ($8) and lunch entrees ($4-6) at the diner-style **Tandoor ❷**,
1226 Chapel St., include everything from curried rice noodles to their house specialty "clay oven baked" tandoori chicken. (☎776-6620. Dinner $8-14. Open daily
11:30am-3pm and 5-10:30pm.) **Thai Taste ❸**, 1151 Chapel St., between York St. and
Howe St., serves classic Thai dishes like *pad thai* and beef noodle soup, as well as
unique dishes like beef macadamia with pepper and ginger, served in a tortilla
shell on a bed of steamed spinach. (☎776-0802. Lunch $5-7, dinner $8-13. Open M-
Th 11:30am-3pm and 5-10pm, F-Sa 11:30am-10:30pm, Su noon-10pm.)

◙ SIGHTS. The majority of the sights and museums in New Haven are located
on or near the **Yale University** campus. Most of the campus buildings were designed
in the English Gothic or Georgian Colonial styles, many of them with intricate
moldings and a few with gargoyles. The **Yale Visitors Center**, 149 Elm St., faces the
Green and is the starting point for **campus tours**. (☎432-2300; www.yale.edu. Open
M-F 9am-4:45pm, Sa-Su 11am-4pm. Free 1¼hr. campus tours M-F 10:30am and
2pm, Sa-Su 1:30pm.) Bordered by Chapel, College, Grove, and High St., the charming Old Campus contains **Connecticut Hall**, which, raised in 1753, is the university's
oldest remaining building. A block north, on the other side of Elm St., **Sterling
Memorial Library**, 120 High St., is designed to resemble a monastery—even the telephone booths are shaped like confessionals. The design is not entirely without a
sense of humor, though— carved stone brackets portray students sleeping, smoking, and lounging. (☎432-1852. Free Internet. Open Sept.-June Su-Th 8:30am-mid-
night, F 8:30am-10pm, Sa 10am-7pm.; July-Aug. M-W and F 8:30am-5pm, Th
8:30am-10pm, Sa 10am-5pm.) Paneled with Vermont marble cut thin enough to be
translucent, **Beinecke Rare Book and Manuscript Library**, 121 Wall St., is a massive
modern structure containing 600,000 rare books and manuscripts, including one of
the five Gutenberg Bibles in the US and a collection of John James Audubon's
prints. (☎436-1254. Open M-Th 8:30am-8pm, F 8:30am-5pm, Sa 10am-5pm.)

Open since 1832, the **Yale University Art Gallery**, 1111 Chapel St., at York St., holds
over 100,000 pieces, including an impressive collection of classical Greek sculpture and works by Monet, Van Gogh, Matisse, and Picasso. (☎432-0600. Open Tu-W
and F-Sa 10am-5pm, Th 10am-8pm, Su 1-6pm. Self-guided audio tours available.
Free.) The **Peabody Museum of Natural History**, 170 Whitney Ave., Exit 3 off I-91,
houses Rudolph F. Zallinger's Pulitzer Prize-winning mural depicting the "Age of
Reptiles" in a room populated by dinosaur skeletons. The museum also houses a
100-million-year-old 8 ft. turtle and an Egyptian mummy. (☎432-5050. Open M-Sa
10am-5pm, Su noon-5pm. $7, seniors $6, students and ages 3-15 $5.) Outside the

campus area and accessed from East Rock Rd. northeast of the city, **East Rock Park** provides an excellent sunset view of New Haven and the Long Island Sound from an overlook 325 ft. above sea level. (☎ 782-4314. Open dawn-dusk.)

■ **NIGHTLIFE.** ⬛**Toad's Place,** 300 York St., has hosted Bob Dylan, the Rolling Stones, and George Clinton. Also a popular dance spot with students, Toad's hosts dance parties Wednesday and Saturday nights during the school year. (☎ 562-5694, recorded info 624-8623. Box office open M-F 11am-6pm; buy tickets at the bar after 8pm. 21+. $5-35 cover for shows; $5 cover for dance nights. Open Su-Th 8pm-1am, F-Sa 8pm-2am; closed when no show.) **Bar,** 254 Crown St., is a hip hangout with a pool table, lounge room, dance floor/theater, five homemade beers brewing in tanks in the bar, and brick-oven pizza. Alternative Night every Tuesday attracts a large gay crowd. (☎ 495-8924. Live music 3-4 nights per week. Cover Tu $3, Sa $6. Open Su-Tu 4pm-1am, W-Th 11:30am-2:30pm and 4pm-1am, F-Sa 11:30am-2am.)

MYSTIC AND THE CONNECTICUT COAST ☎ 860

When Herman Melville's whale, Moby Dick, became legend, Connecticut's coastal towns were busy seaports full of dark, musty inns and tattooed sailors. Now, vacationers and sailing enthusiasts head there seeking a whale of a good time. Along the Mystic River, **Mystic Seaport,** 1 mi. south on Rte. 27 from I-95 at Exit 90, offers a look at 18th-century whaling. In the recreated village, actors in period dress entertain visitors with educational skits, a functioning wood-only shipyard, and three creaky wooden vessels open to exploration. (☎ 888-973-2767; www.visitmysticseaport.com. Open daily Apr.-Oct. 9am-5pm; Nov.-Mar. 10am-4pm. $17, seniors $16, ages 6-12 $9. Tickets good for 2 days.) A few dollars more puts visitors on an authentic 1908 coal-fired steamboat for **Sabino Charters'** cruise along the Mystic River. (☎ 572-5351. 30min. trips on the ½hr. mid-May to early Oct. daily 10:30am-3:30pm. $5.25, ages 6-12 $4. 1½hr. cruise 4:30pm. $11/$8.75.) The **Mystic Aquarium and Institute for Exploration,** 55 Coogan Blvd., at Exit 90 off I-95, has an menagerie of seals, penguins, sharks, and white beluga whales. Visitors can touch smooth rays in the ray pool, or see artifacts from the *Titanic* in an exhibit sponsored by National Geographic. (☎ 572-5955; www.mysticaquarium.org. Open daily July to early Sept. 9am-6pm; early Sept. to June 9am-5pm. $16, seniors $15, ages 3-12 $11.) The **Denison Pequotsepos Nature Center,** 109 Pequotsepos Rd., 1½ mi. east of downtown, offers 8 mi. of trails through three diverse ecosystems. The nature center provides interactive exhibits, and a home for a peregrine falcon. (☎ 536-1216; www.dpnc.org. Nature center open M-Sa 9am-5pm, Su 10am-4pm. Park open dawn-dusk. $6, seniors and ages 12 and under $4.)

Budget lodgings are scarce in Mystic, though hotels can be found at the intersection of Rte. 27 and I-95. The **Stonington Motel ❸,** 901 Stonington Rd., 5 mi. north of Mystic on Rte. 11, has rooms with A/C, cable TV, microwave, mini-fridge, and unique charm. (☎ 599-2330. Rooms $55-80.) Close to Mystic, **Seaport Campgrounds ❶,** on Rte. 184, 3 mi. north of Rte. 27 from Mystic, offers a pool, mini golf course, fishing pond, playground, and live music on weekends. (☎ 536-4044. Open mid-Apr. to late Oct. Sites for 2 adults and 2 children with water and electricity mid-May to mid-Sept. $33; Apr. to mid-May and mid-Sept. to late Oct. $26. Each each additional adult $7. AAA, military, and senior discount 10%.) **Mystic Pizza ❷,** 56 W. Main St., popularized by the 1988 Julia Roberts movie *Mystic Pizza,* has been serving its "secret recipe" pizzas for 30 years. (☎ 536-3700. Pizza $6-11. Open 11am-11pm.) **Cove Fish Market ❷,** 1 mi. east of downtown on Old Stonington Rd., serves a heaping portion of fish and chips ($9) and $3.50 crabcake burgers. (☎ 536-0061. Entrees $6-15. Open mid-May to early Sept. daily 11am-8pm. Fish market open daily 10am-6pm.) For a reminder of the days of sea captains and grog, head to the ⬛**Captain**

Daniel Packer Inn, 32 Water St., to drink the "Dark and Stormy," black rum with a splash of ginger beer. (☎536-3555; http://danielpacker.com. Live music begins at 10pm. Dinner served daily 5-10pm, bar open until 1am.)

Amtrak (☎800-872-7245), half a mile east of Mystic on Rte. 1, runs to: Boston (1½hr., 3 per day, $35-46); New Haven (1hr., 3 per day, $22); New York City (3hr., 4 per day, $57). The **Mystic Tourist and Information Center,** Bldg. 1d in Olde Mistick Village, at the corner of Rte. 27 and Coogan St., offers maps, discounted tickets to attractions, a 24hr. digital hotel board with listings of all vacancies, and a direct phone line to accommodations in the region. (☎536-1641; www.visitmystic.com. Open mid-June to Sept. M-Sa 9:30am-6pm, Su 10am-5pm; Oct. to early June M-Sa 9am-5:30pm, Su 10am-5pm.) **Internet Access: Mystic and Noank Library,** 40 Library St., in Mystic. (☎536-7721. Open M-W 10am-9pm, Th-Sa 10am-5pm; mid-June to early Sept. closes Sa 1pm. $0.25 per 15min.) **Post Office:** 23 E. Main St. (☎536-8143. Open M-F 8am-5pm, Sa 8:30am-12:30pm.) **Postal Code:** 06355. **Area Code:** 860.

CONNECTICUT CASINOS

Foxwoods and Mohegan Sun, two tribally owned casinos in southeast Connecticut, bring sin to the suburbs. Although each has its own style, their shared tendency toward decadence make them both worth a traveler's while, especially if said traveler can afford to lose a few dollars. The 4.7 million sq. ft. **Foxwoods** (☎888-287-2369; www.foxwoods.com.) complex contains a casino complete with 6500 slot machines, blackjack, craps, poker, and the other usual suspects, as well as three glitzy hotels, a spa, elaborate nightclubs and adult entertainment, a village for shopping, and fancy restaurants with food from all over the world. Over ten bus companies run to Foxwoods from surrounding areas. The 1450-seat **Fox Theatre** hosts live performances from boxing to pop music; past appearances include Frank Sinatra, Bill Cosby, and the Dixie Chicks. (☎800-200-2882. Prices and performance times vary.) **Greyhound** (☎800-229-9424) provides service to Foxwoods from New York City (3-5hr., 9-12 per day, $23) and Boston (2-3hr., 10 per day, $26). Driving is also convenient, with free parking at the resort. From I-95, take Exit 92 to Rte. 2 W, and from I-84 take Exit 55 to Rte. 2 E. From Mohegan Sun, take Rte 2A W to Rte 2 E. Once on Rte. 2 follow the signs to the casino.

While winning or losing money on the floor is uncertain, paying handsomely for lodging in the casino is a sure thing. The **Two Trees Inn ❺,** a short shuttle ride from the casino, is the least expensive of the three hotels in the complex. (☎800-442-1000. Rooms $99-210). A better option for those who aren't cleaning up are the campgrounds that speckle the roadside along Rte. 2 west of the casino.

Mohegan Sun (☎888-226-7711) offers two of the world's largest casinos: the Casino of the Earth and the Casino of the Sky. The entire complex is contained in one enormous interconnected modern structure that contrasts with the interior design, which reflects the culture and heritage of the Mohegan Tribe. While Foxwoods offers classic casino glamour, Mohegan Sun presents its services, entertainment, lodging, and shopping in tribal packaging, with large trees as pillars that change with the seasons and an enormous waterfall. With free parking and shuttles from each of the Mohegan Sun's four lots, driving is the most convenient way to access the casino. From I-395, take Exit 79A to Rte. 2A E. From Foxwoods, take Rte. 2 W to Rte. 2A E. Once on Rte. 2A follow the signs to the casino. Bus lines also service the casino from many points in the northeast. (☎888-770-0140.)

NEW ENGLAND

EASTERN CANADA

> **!** All prices in this chapter are in Canadian dollars unless noted. In Canada, heavy taxes are levied on goods and services, but visitors can claim refunds of money spent on Goods and Services Tax and Harmonized Services Tax on lodging receipts over $200, and goods purchased that exceed $50 per receipt. Certain restrictions apply. ☎ 800-959-2221 or www.ccra.gc.ca/visitors has more info.

Centuries of immigration and ethnic cross-pollination have forged a unique cultural landscape in Canada's eastern provinces. Vibrant cities border untarnished wilderness, presenting an astounding array of cultural and recreational opportunities. The gleaming, modern metropolis of Toronto, the United Nations' "most international city," epitomizes diversity, while Québec City is a living tribute to Old World charm. In Montréal, flashy festivals, sexy nightlife, and a bilingual arts scene complement fine dining. Prince Edward Island has world-class beaches, and Cape Breton Island's and Newfoundland's rolling hills resound with the strains of Celtic music. The islands' fjords and forests promise blissful tranquility and amazing vistas. Halifax draws from the best of both worlds, with colorful nightlife next to charming coastal villages. Luckily, Canada can be enjoyed on the cheap; due to a favorable exchange rate, American dollars go 30% farther in Canada.

HIGHLIGHTS OF EASTERN CANADA

FOOD. Fresh seafood is abundant in the Maritimes, and polyethnic Toronto, ON (p. 159), offers fabulously diverse and consistently good cuisine options.

COASTAL TOWNS. Gorgeous towns and cities, from Peggy's Cove, NS (p. 209), to St. John's, NF (p. 213), are picturesque and replete with local lore and history.

NIGHTLIFE. A drinking age of 18 in Québec and 19 in the rest of the provinces makes for young and energetic nightlife, particularly in Montréal (p. 175), which draws streams of American college students. For more laid-back evenings, hip pub scenes dominate Toronto (p. 159) and Halifax (p. 205).

WILDERNESS. The glacier-carved valleys in Gros Morne National Park, rocky headlands above the sea in Cape Breton Highlands, unspoiled shoreline in Fundy National Park, Kouchibouguac, and Prince Edward Island, and the rivers, lakes, and mountains of Mont-Tremblant and Jacques-Cartier will take your breath away. Watch out for moose.

ONTARIO

Ontario's name derives from an Iroquois word meaning "beautiful lake," which originally referred to Lake Ontario, and slowly spread to encompass its surrounding areas. Now, Ontario's namesake lake is only one of many attractions that bring people flocking to this central province—while it makes up just over 10% of Canada's landmass, Ontario is home to over 37% of the population. Toronto, multicul-

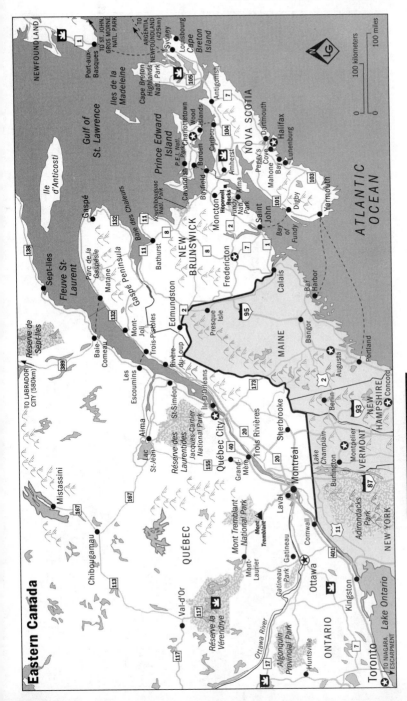

Eastern Canada

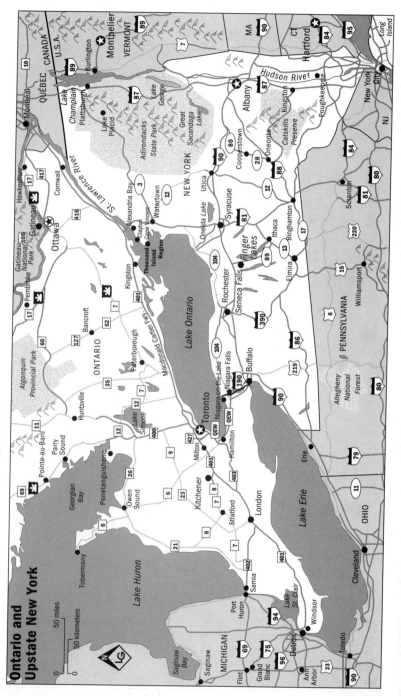

Ontario and Upstate New York

tural, clean, and vibrant, shines in the south as Canada's largest city, and Ottawa, the nation's capital, sits on the Québec border. In the north, adventure seekers will find pristine wilderness dotted with lakes, wildlife, ski resorts, and cottages.

⁊ PRACTICAL INFORMATION

Capital: Toronto.

Visitor Info: Customer Service Branch of the **Ontario Ministry of Tourism and Recreation,** Hearst Block, 900 Bay St., Toronto M7A 2E1 (☎800-668-2746; www.ontariotravel.net), in the Eaton Centre, lower level 1.

Drinking Age: 19. **Postal Abbreviation:** ON. **Sales Tax:** 8% PST (rooms 5%), plus 7% GST.

TORONTO ☎416

Toronto is undeniably among the world's most multicultural cities. Conversations on the street are in Cantonese or Punjabi nearly as often as they are in English. Skyscrapers and a bustling financial district stand back-to-back with fan-filled stadiums, and ethnic communities coexist peaceably, often creating culinary cross-pollinations that titillate the tastebuds. Vibrant nightlife can be found in neighborhood after neighborhood; in the summer, outdoor patios all over town are chock full of customers until 2am. A city so diverse might be expected to have an identity crisis, but residents are unified by their well-warranted hometown pride.

⊠ INTERCITY TRANSPORTATION

Airport: Pearson International (☎247-7678; www.torontoairport.ca), about 20km west of Toronto via Hwy. 401. Take bus #58A west from Lawrence W subway. **Pacific Western Transportation** (☎905-564-6333) runs buses to downtown hotels every 30min. 4:25am-12:25am. $15.50, round-trip $26. 10% discount for students on one-way fare.

Trains: Union Station, 65 Front St. W. (☎888-842-7245), at Bay and York St. Subway: Union. Station open M-Sa 5:30am-12:45am, Su 6:30am-12:45am. **VIA Rail** (☎888-842-7245; www.viarail.ca). Ticket office open M-F 6am-11:30pm, Sa 6am-6:30pm, Su 6:30am-11:30pm. To: **Montréal** (5½hr., 7 per day, $116); **New York City** (12hr.; 1 per day; M-F $105, Sa-Su $131); **Windsor** (4hr., 4 per day, $78). 35% discount with ISIC.

Buses: All buses operate from the **Bay Street Terminal,** 610 Bay St., just north of Dundas St. Subway: St. Patrick or Dundas. Ticket office open daily 5am-1am. Lockers $2. **Coach Canada** (☎393-7911) has service to **Montréal** (7hr., 8 per day, $84). **Greyhound** (☎367-8747) goes to: **Calgary** (2 days, 3 per day, $339); **New York City** (12hr., 6 per day, $80); **Ottawa** (5½hr., 10 per day, $73). The **Moose Travel Network** (☎853-4762 or 888-816-6673; www.moosenetwork.com) offers transportation for backpackers and independent travelers. Passengers can jump on and off at various points throughout Eastern Canada. Activities and stops at sights "off the beaten path." Trips run May-Oct. $50-429, with discounted rail connections to western routes.

⊞ ORIENTATION

Toronto's streets are a grid. Addresses on north-south streets increase northward, away from **Lake Ontario. Yonge Street** is the main north-south route, dividing the cross streets into east and west. Numbering on both sides starts at Yonge St. and increases moving away in either direction. West of Yonge St., the main arteries are **Bay Street, University Avenue, Spadina Avenue,** and **Bathurst Street.** Moving northward from the waterfront, the major east-west routes include **Front Street, Queen Street,**

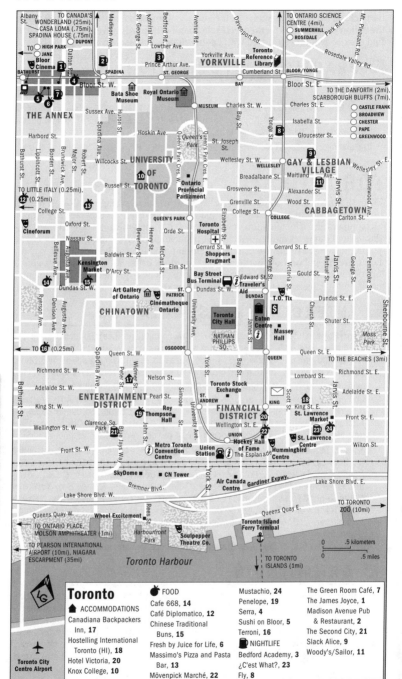

Toronto

▲ ACCOMMODATIONS
Canadiana Backpackers
Inn, 17
Hostelling International
Toronto (HI), 18
Hotel Victoria, 20
Knox College, 10

🍎 FOOD
Cafe 668, 14
Café Diplomatico, 12
Chinese Traditional
Buns, 15
Fresh by Juice for Life, 6
Massimo's Pizza and Pasta
Bar, 13
Mövenpick Marché, 22

Mustachio, 24
Penelope, 19
Serra, 4
Sushi on Bloor, 5
Terroni, 16

🍸 NIGHTLIFE
Bedford Academy, 3
¿C'est What?, 23
Fly, 8

The Green Room Café, 7
The James Joyce, 1
Madison Avenue Pub
& Restaurant, 2
The Second City, 21
Slack Alice, 9
Woody's/Sailor, 11

EASTERN CANADA

Dundas Street, College Street, Bloor Street, and **Eglinton Street.** For extended stays or travel outside the city center, buy the *Downtown and Metro Toronto Visitor's Map Guide* ($4) from a drug store or tourist shop. The *Ride Guide*, free at TTC stations and info booths, explains metro area transit.

NEIGHBORHOODS

Toronto splits into many distinctive neighborhoods. **Chinatown** centers on Dundas St. W between Bay St. and Spadina Ave. Formerly the Jewish market of the 1920s, **Kensington Market,** on Kensington Ave., Augusta Ave., and the western half of Baldwin St., is now a largely Portuguese neighborhood with ethnically diverse cuisine, vintage clothing shops, and an outdoor bazaar. Just to the north is **Little Italy,** centered on College St. between Bathurst and Shaw. The strip of old factories, stores, and warehouses on **Queen Street West,** from University Ave. to Bathurst St., is a good place to shop during the day and club-hop at night. Ivy-covered Gothic buildings and magnificent quadrangles spread across the **University of Toronto (U of T)** which stretches over the city's center. **The Annex,** on Bloor St. W, at the Spadina subway, has an artistic feel, and an excellent range of budget restaurants. Afterwards, hit the bars and nightclubs along Bloor St. heading west. **Yorkville,** just north of Bloor between Yonge St. and Avenue Rd., was once the home of flower children and folk guitarists, but now boasts designer boutiques and first-class restaurants. **Cabbagetown,** just east of Yonge St., bounded by Gerrard St. E, Wellesley, and Sumach St., takes its name from the Irish immigrants who used to plant the vegetable in their yards. Today, it houses Victorian homes and parks. The **Gay and Lesbian Village,** around Church and Wellesley St., has superb outdoor cafes. **Little India,** is at Gerrard St. E and Coxwell; ride the subway to Coxwell, then take bus #22 south to the second Gerrard St. stop. **Greektown,** better known as **"the Danforth,"** (subway: Pape), is on Danforth Ave. at Pape Ave. On Front St., the **Theatre District,** between Sherbourne and Yonge St., whets any cultural appetite. Music, food, ferry rides, dance companies, and artists all dock at the **Harbourfront** (☎ 973-4000), on Queen's Quay W along the lake from York to Bathurst St. The three main **Toronto Islands,** accessible by ferry (see **Local Transportation,** below), have beaches, bikes, and an amusement park. East from the harbor, **The Beaches** along and south of Queen St. E, between Woodbine and Victoria, boast a popular boardwalk. Five kilometers east of the city center, the rugged **Scarborough Bluffs** rise over the lakeshore.

▛ LOCAL TRANSPORTATION

The **Toronto Transit Commission's (TTC)** subway and streetcars are the easiest way to get around, but if you drive, avoid rush hour (4-7pm). A flashing green light means you can go straight or turn left; the flashing lights are being phased out, though, so look for both flashing green lights and directional arrows. Pedestrians do not necessarily have the legal right of way, so be careful crossing streets. **Street parking** is hard to find and usually has a 1hr. limit. Day parking generally costs $3-4 at outlying subway stations; parking overnight at the subway stations is prohibited. The cheapest parking downtown is at city-run lots (look for the green P); 24hr. parking is usually around $9. Free parking can be found in **Cabbagetown,** on the residential streets just west of Parliament St. City officials have begun to enforce traffic and parking regulations zealously—towing is common. The **non-emergency police number** (☎ 808-2222) has an answering system to help recover towed cars. **Public Transit: Toronto Transit Commission** (☎ 393-4636; www.ttc.ca) has 2 long and 2 short subway lines connected to bus and streetcar routes. Buses must stop anywhere along a route at a female passenger's request 9pm-5am. Subway runs M-Sa 6am-1:30am, Su 9am-1:30am. Buses cover subway routes after 1:30am. Fare $2.25, 10 tokens for

$19; students and seniors $1.50, under 13 $0.50, 10 tokens for $4.25. M-Sa 1-day pass $7.75. Su and holidays unlimited travel for families $7.75. Transfers among subway, bus, and streetcar lines are free, but get a transfer slip when you pay.

Ferries: Toronto Island Ferry Service (☎ 392-8194 or 392-8193). Ferries to Centre Island, Hanlan's Point, and Ward's Island leave from the foot of Bay St. Service daily every 30min.; call for details. $6; seniors, and students $3.50; ages 2-14 $2.50.

Taxi: Co-op Cabs ☎ 504-2667.

Car Rental: National Car Rental (☎ 800-522-9696; www.nationalcar.com), in Union Station. $52 per day. 21+. Under-25 additional $30 per day. Open M-F 7am-10pm, Sa 7am-6pm, Su 8:30am-10pm.

Bike Rental: The Community Bicycle Network (☎ 504-2998; www.bikeshare.org) allows members access to bikes at 15 hubs around the city for up to 3 days at a time. 1yr. membership $25. **Wheel Excitement,** 249 Queens Quay (☎ 260-9000), on the beach near York St. First hr. $12, each additional hr. $3; $27 per day. Open daily 10am-6pm.

✂ PRACTICAL INFORMATION

Visitor Info: The **Metropolitan Toronto Convention and Visitors Association (MTCVA),** 207 Queens Quay W (☎ 203-2500 or 800-363-1990; www.torontotourism.com), mails out info packets and has an comprehensive automated phone system to answer questions. Ontario's **Ministry of Tourism and Recreation,** in the Eaton Centre, Level 1 (☎ 800-668-2746; www.ontariotravel.net), provides maps and information on daytrips or travel in Ontario. **Traveler's Aid** (☎ 366-7788), which has general info, free maps, and hotel/hostel reservations, is located in the bus station (open daily 9:30am-8:30pm), Union Station (open daily 9:30am-8:30pm), and 3 locations in Pearson International Airport.

Tours: Gray Line Hop-On-Hop-Off City Tour (☎ 594-3310; www.grayline.ca) takes travelers to 20 popular spots and allows ticket holders to get on and off for up to 2 days following ticket purchase. Tour begins at Nicholby's Souvenirs, 213 Front St. W. $34, seniors $30, children ages 5-11 $18. June-Sept. only. Buses run 9am-4pm.

Currency Exchange: Toronto Currency Exchange, 277 Yonge St. (☎ 864-1441), across from the Eaton Center, offers the best rates around. Open M-Sa 10am-9pm, Su 11am-7pm.

Hotlines: Rape Crisis, ☎ 597-8808. Operates 24hr. **Toronto Gay and Lesbian Phone Line,** ☎ 964-6600. Operates M-F 7-10pm.

Medical Services: The Toronto Hospital, 200 Elizabeth St. (☎ 340-3111).

Internet Access: Toronto Reference Library, 789 Yonge St. (☎ 395-5577; www.tpl.toronto.on.ca). Subway: Bloor/Yonge. Free Internet access and a rare collection of Sir Arthur Conan Doyle paraphernalia. Open M-Th 10am-8pm, F-Sa 10am-5pm. There are also numerous Internet cafes throughout the city.

Post Office: Adelaide Station, 31 Adelaide St. E (☎ 214-2352). Subway: King. Open M-F 8am-5:45pm. **Postal Code:** M5C 2J0. **Area Code:** 416 (city), 905 (outskirts). In text, 416 unless otherwise noted.

⌂ ACCOMMODATIONS

Budget hotels gather around Jarvis and Gerrard St. The **University of Toronto Housing Service** lists budget options in its colleges. (☎ 978-8045; http://link.library.utoronto.ca/studenthousing.) The **Downtown Association of Bed and Breakfast Guest Houses** places guests in Victorian homes. (☎ 483-8822; www.bnbinfo.com.)

■ **Canadiana Backpackers Inn,** 42 Widmer St. (☎ 598-9090 or 877-215-1225; www.canadianalodging.com), off Adelaide St. W. Subway: Osgoode. Young, adventurous professionals populate rooms with wooden beds and classy furnishings. Evening barbecues ($2.50)

and outings, including sailing and bowling. 150 beds, A/
C, kitchen, and movie theater. Internet access ($1 per
10min.). Lockers $1. Laundry $3. Limited parking $15
per day. Check-in 8am-2am. Check-out 10:30am. 6- to
8-bed dorms $25; 4-bed $28; doubles $65. 10% dis-
count for ISIC, HI, or SWAP cardholders. ❶

Hostelling International Toronto (HI), 76 Church St.
(☎971-4440 or 877-848-8737; www.hihostels.ca), at
King St. Subway: King. Chic decor, renovated facilities,
and a hip staff make travelers at home in downtown Toronto. Internet access $1 per 15 minutes. 160 beds, A/
C, kitchen, outdoor patio, pool tables, and pub crawls.
Linen $2 (free with ISIC). Laundry $4. Reception 24hr.
Check-in after noon. Check-out 11am. Reservations recommended. Dorms $23, nonmembers $27; private
rooms $70/$74. ❶

Hotel Victoria, 56 Yonge St. (☎363-1666 or 800-363-
8228; www.hotelvictoria-toronto.com), between Wellington and King St. Subway: King. This stately hotel has a
great location and elegant rooms. Continental breakfast,
TV, A/C, and storage. Health club $12. Reservations rec-
ommended. Rooms $135; deluxe rooms from $159. ❺

Knox College, 59 St. George St. (☎978-0168;
www.utoronto.ca/knox). Subway: St. George. A limited
number of spacious rooms are available to the public
at this genteel Presbyterian seminary. Enjoy beautiful
Gothic architecture and a location right on the U of T
campus. Office open M-F 10am-5pm. Open mid-May to
late Aug. Singles $62, students $51; doubles $90/
$79. Reserve rooms at least 3 weeks in advance. ❷

🍴 FOOD

Toronto boasts over 10,000 metropolitan-area restaurants. "L.L.B.O." ("Liquor Licensing Board of
Ontario") signs indicate that alcohol is available. **Baldwin Street**, at McCaul St., features a quiet row of restaurants offering excellent food at good prices. For
fresh produce and cheap ethnic food, try the **Kensington Market**, west of Spadina Ave. between Baldwin St.
and Dundas St. W. The **Saint Lawrence Market**, at King
and Sherbourne St., six blocks east of the King subway stop, is a great place for meats and produce.
(Open Tu-Th 8am-6pm, F 8am-7pm, Sa 5am-5pm.)

THE ANNEX

Serra, 378 Bloor St. W (☎922-6999). Subway: Spadina. Cool but not intimidating, upscale but not exorbitant, and exceptionally delicious, Serra is an oasis
amid the Annex's bustle. Linguine with black tiger
shrimp, scallops, mussels, roasted garlic, scallions,
and cured tomatoes in a white wine olive oil sauce
($14) and scrumptious *créme brûlée* ($7) are a perfect
meal. Open M-F noon-10pm, Sa-Su 5-10pm. ❸

LIGHTS OUT IN TORONTO

On June 1, 2004, Toronto
joined the ranks of cities that prohibit smoking in restaurants and
bars. The smoking ban has
uniquely affected the **Hot Box
Café** at **roach-O-rama**, according
to owner Abi Roach. Like other
establishments, Toronto's only
cannabis cafe had to ask patrons
to smoke outside. But Roach's
patrons smoke marijuana, not cigarettes. Possession of marijuana
was briefly decriminalized in
Ontario in 2003 due to a legal
technicality. By October, 2003,
though, it was outlawed again. The
Canadian Medical Association
estimates, however, that 1.5 million Canadians smoke marijuana
recreationally on a regular basis,
and medicinal marijuana is available through the government.

Roach-O-rama sells paraphernalia, and Ms. Roach opened the
Hot Box Café in order to foster a
sense of community for pot smokers. The cafe's stated purpose is
to encourage the normalization of
marijuana smoking, and its menu
exhorts patrons to "Have a good
toke!" Trafficking is strictly forbidden, and Roach stresses that her
store, cafe, and patrons have
never had problems with the law,
since the ensuing public uproar
would be too much of a hassle for
the authorities. Let's Go *does not
encourage illegal activities.*

*The Hot Box Café, 191a Bald-
win St., in Kensington Market
(☎203-6990). 18+. Open Su-F
11am-8pm, Sa 10am-8pm.*

Fresh by Juice For Life, 521 Bloor St. W (☎531-2635; www.juiceforlife.com). Subway: Bathurst. With hip vegetarian and vegan-friendly food and a wide assortment of juices, Fresh is "open to anyone, regardless of food orientation." The magic tofu sandwich, with crispy tofu, honey mustard mayonnaise, buckwheat, and salad, is $8, and juices, smoothies, and energy elixirs range from $3.50-5. 15% off food at the bar. Open M-F 11:30am-10:30pm, Sa-Su 10:30am-10:30pm. Branch at 336 Queen St. W. ❷

Sushi on Bloor, 515 Bloor St. W (☎516-3456). Subway: Bathurst. One of the many sushi joints that crowds into the Annex, Sushi on Bloor is often packed when other places are empty. Fresh sushi (6 pieces) $4-5. Lunch and dinner specials from $6. Open M-Th noon-10:45pm, F-Sa noon-11pm, Su noon-10pm. ❷

THEATER/ST. LAWRENCE DISTRICT

Penelope, 225 King St. W (☎351-9393 or 877-215-4026). Subway: St. Andrew. Attentive service and mouth-watering food in the relaxing atmosphere of a Greek resort. Succulent roast lamb (lunch $11, dinner $14) and vegetarian *moussaka* ($10/$13). Open M-W 11:30am-10pm, Th-F 11:30am-11:30pm, Sa 4:30-11:30pm. ❸

Mustachio, downstairs in the St. Lawrence Market (☎368-5241), subway: King. No-nonsense service and enormous sandwiches. The veal and eggplant parmigiana ($5.50) overflows with fresh-cooked fixin's. Open Tu-Th 8am-6pm, F 8am-7pm, Sa 5am-5pm. ❶

Mövenpick Marché, 42 Yonge St. (☎366-8986), in BCE Place at Yonge St. and Front St. Subway: King. A combination restaurant and produce market the size of some department stores, Marché allows diners to browse through 14 culinary stations to customize their meals. Avoid lines by taking a meal to go. Entrees $8-10. Open daily 7:30am-2am. ❷

W QUEEN ST./KENSINGTON MARKET/LITTLE ITALY

🎌**Terroni,** 720 Queen St. W (☎504-0320; www.terroni.ca). Subway: Osgoode, then transfer to westbound street car. Named for a derogatory description of Southern Italians (*terroni* means "people of the earth"), Terroni is fine dining with a relaxed ambience and outdoor patio. They're most famous for their pizzas ($9-13). The deli section, stocked with pastas, olives, and Italian meats, is also worth a look. Open daily 9am-11pm. ❷

🎌**Massimo's Pizza and Pasta Bar,** 302 College St. (☎967-0527) at Robert St. Subway: Queen's Park, then take westbound street car. This unassuming corner pizzeria has the best pizza in town. Free delivery. Gigantic slices ($4) in a secret garlic/basil sauce hot out of the oven. Open M-Th 11am-3am, F-Sa 10am-4am, Su 11am-midnight. ❶

Café Diplomatico, 594 College St. (☎534-4637; www.diplomatico.ca) at Clinton St. Subway: Queen's Park. A Little Italy landmark, "the Dip" serves *panzerotto* (fried calzone; $5), pasta (from $9), and cappuccino ($2.50). In the summer, its outdoor patio is packed with diners. Open Su-Th 8am-1am, F-Sa 8am-2am. ❸

Cafe 668, 668 Dundas St. (☎703-0668; www.cafe668.com). Subway: St. Patrick. Vegetarian and vegan-friendly southeast Asian fare. Wonton soup ($5) and 4 kinds of mushrooms with crispy fried noodles ($10) make a filling and delicious meal. Open Tu-F 12:30-4pm and 6-9:30pm, Sa-Su 1:30-4pm and 6-9:30pm. ❷

Chinese Traditional Buns, 536 Dundas St. (☎299-9011), at Kensington Market, hidden down a flight of stairs. Subway: St. Patrick. The best deal in Chinatown serves doughy buns stuffed with tasty meats or vegetables, then steamed and served in a bamboo basket. The Gou-Bu-Li buns (6 for $3) and jellied bean curd soup ($1.50) make a delicious and filling lunch. Take-out available. Open daily 9:30am-10pm. ❶

☉ SIGHTS

One of Toronto's most interesting activities is also its cheapest thrill: walking through the busy streets. For an organized expedition, the **Royal Ontario Museum** leads 14 **free walking tours.** (☎586-5513; www.rom.on.ca. Tours June-Sept. W 6pm and Su 2pm. Destinations and meeting places vary; call for specific info.) Free 1hr. walking tours of the **University of Toronto,** Canada's largest university, depart from the **Nona MacDonald Visitors Centre** at King's College Circle. (☎978-5000. Tours June-Aug. M-F 11am and 2pm, Sa-Su 11am. Historical tours available June-Aug. M-F 10:30am-2:30pm.) A self-guided 2hr. **Discovery Walk,** highlighting the interconnected parks of downtown Toronto, starts in front of **City Hall.** (☎338-0338.) Pick up a **City Pass** for admission to six of Toronto's most popular tourist attractions (the CN Tower, the Art Gallery of Ontario, the Royal Ontario Museum, Casa Loma, the Ontario Science Center, and the Toronto Zoo) wherever tickets for any of the sights are sold. Valid for nine days after first use. ($46, ages 4-12 $29.)

CN TOWER. At 1815 ft., Toronto's **CN Tower** is the world's tallest building, and is considered one of the seven wonders of the modern world. It also contains the world's highest wine cellar and longest metal stairway. The mammoth concrete landmark is visible from nearly every corner of the city, and its telecommunications facilities provide the Toronto area with world-class reception. The tower offers a heavenly view (main observation deck at 114 stories, 1136 ft.; Sky Pod at 147 stories, 1465 ft.), and despite the void below, trusting souls lie down on the sturdy, one-of-a-kind glass floor. *(301 Front St. W. ☎360-8500; www.cntower.ca. Subway: Union Tower. Open Su-Th 10am-10pm, F-Sa 10am-11pm (may vary seasonally); inside attractions including arcade and simulator ride 11am-7pm. $20, seniors $18, ages 4-12 $15; additional $7.50 for the Sky Pod. Combined admission to tower, attractions, and Sky Pod also available.)*

GOVERNMENT. Curving twin towers and a two-story rotunda make up **City Hall.** In front of the building, **Nathan Phillips Square** is home to a reflecting pool that becomes a skating rink in winter. Numerous events including live music every Wednesday *(June to early Oct. noon-2pm)* also take place in the square. *(☎338-0338. Subway: Osgoode. Open M-F 8:30am-4:30pm. Brochures available for self-guided tours.)* The Ontario government meets in the stately **Provincial Parliament Buildings,** at Queen's Park in the city center. *(☎325-7500. Subway: Queen's Park. Free 30min. tours daily late May to early Sept. 9am-4pm. Call ahead for Parliamentary schedule. Free gallery passes available at south basement door when the House is in session, usually Sept.-Dec. and Mar.-June.)*

SPADINA HOMES. Straight from a fairy tale, **Casa Loma,** is a castle on a hill near Spadina. More than 90 furniture-filled rooms, extensive gardens, an eerie underground tunnel, and two imposing towers add to the visible late-Victorian opulence. The Norman Tower offers an impressive view of downtown Toronto. *(☎923-1171; www.casaloma.org. Subway: Dupont, then walk a few blocks north. Open daily 9:30am-4pm. Free self-guided audio tour. $12, seniors and ages 14-17 $7.50, children $7. Parking $2.75 per hr.)* Visitors can tour 19th-century Toronto next door at the **Spadina Museum-Historic House and Gardens,** an estate relic from 1866. *(285 Spadina Ave. ☎392-6910. Open Apr.-Dec. Tu-F noon-4pm, Sa-Su noon-5pm. $6, seniors and ages 12-17 $5, ages 6-11 $4.)*

WILDLIFE. The **Toronto Zoo** keeps over 5000 animals in a 710-acre park that recreates the world's major regions. *(☎392-5929; www.torontozoo.com. Meadowvale Rd. off Exit 389 on Hwy. 401. Take bus #86A from Kennedy Station. Open daily mid-Mar. to mid-May and early Sept. to mid-Oct. 9am-6pm; mid-May to early Sept. 9am-7:30pm; mid-Oct. to mid-Mar. 9:30am-4:30pm. Last entry 1hr. before closing. $18, seniors $12, ages 4-12 $10. Parking $8.)*

HOCKEY. The **Hockey Hall of Fame** is Canada's religiously-devoted sports fans' cathedral. A beautiful stained glass dome in the 120-year-old **Great Hall** houses hockey's Holy Grail, the Stanley Cup, and, if you're not in the mood for idle veneration, interactive exhibits. *(☎360-7765; www.hhof.com. 30 Yonge St. In BCE Place. Subway: BCE Place. Open late June to early Sept. M-Sa 9:30am-6pm, Su 10am-6pm; early Sept. to late June M-F 10am-5pm, Sa 9:30am-6pm, Su 10:30am-5pm. $12, seniors and ages 4-13 $8.)*

EASTERN CANADA

🏛 MUSEUMS

Art Gallery of Ontario (AGO), 317 Dundas St. (☎979-6608; www.ago.net) at McCaul St. Subway: St. Patrick. Showcases an enormous collection of Western art from the Renaissance to the 1990s, with a focus on Canadian artists. Check out the spectacular exhibition of Henry Moore's sculptures, the largest collection outside of Britain. Open Tu and Th-F 11am-6pm, W 11am-8:30pm, Sa-Su 10am-5:30pm. $12, students with ID and seniors $9, ages 6-15 $6; W 6-8:30pm free. Admission to special exhibits extra.

Royal Ontario Museum (ROM), 100 Queen's Park (☎586-8000; www.rom.on.ca), at Bloor St. Subway: Museum. Houses a must-see Egyptian exhibit, a dinosaur collection, and a bat-cave. Open M-Th and Sa-Su 10am-6pm, F 10am-9:30pm. Admission varies with exhibition. $10-20; students, seniors, and children $7-15; call for details. F after 4:30pm free.

Bata Shoe Museum, 327 Bloor St. W (☎979-7799; www.batashoemuseum.ca). Subway: St. George or Spadina. Walk a mile in a medieval knight's metal boots or in Chinese slippers that once contained bound feet. The collection focuses on the often stepped-over role of footwear in human culture. Open Tu-W and F-Sa 10am-5pm, Th 10am-8pm, Su noon-5pm. $6, students and seniors $4, ages 5-14 $2; families $12; 1st Tu of the month free.

Ontario Science Center, 770 Don Mills Rd. (☎696-3147; www.ontariosciencecentre.ca), at Eglinton Ave. E. Subway: Pape, then on the #25 bus. More than 650 interactive exhibits showcase humanity's greatest innovations. The exhibit "Truth" challenges visitors to re-evaluate their ideas about "scientifically proven" facts. Open daily 10am-5pm. $14, seniors and ages 13-17 $10, ages 4-12 $8; with Omnimax film $20/$14/$10.

🎭 ENTERTAINMENT

The monthly *Where Toronto*, free at tourist booths, gives the scoop on arts and entertainment. **T.O. Tix,** 208 Yonge St., at the corner of Dundas St., sells half-price tickets on performance day. (☎536-6468. Subway: Yonge. Open Tu-Sa noon-7:30pm; arrive before 11:45am for first dibs.) **Ontario Place,** 955 Lakeshore Blvd. W, features summer entertainment like rides and an IMAX theater. (☎314-9811 or 314-9900; www.ontarioplace.com. Hours and days vary; open daily mid-June to Sept. 10am-8pm. $29, seniors $17, children $15; discount with online purchase.) Pop acts perform in the **Molson Amphitheater,** 909 Lakeshore Blvd. W. (☎260-5600. Tickets through Ticketmaster $20-125.) **Roy Thompson Hall,** 60 Simcoe St., at King St. W, is Toronto's premier concert hall, and the home of the **Toronto Symphony Orchestra** from September to June. (☎593-4822, box office 872-4255; www.tso.ca. Subway: St. Andrews. Box office open M-F 9am-8pm, Sa noon-5pm, Su 3hr. before performances. $25-85. $15 rush tickets available on concert days M-F 11am, Sa 1pm.) The **Hummingbird Centre,** 1 Front St. E at Yonge St., features Broadway shows, concerts, and ethnic festivals. (☎393-7469; www.hummingbirdcentre.com. Subway: Union. Box office open M-F 10am-6pm, Sa 10am-5pm.)

The **St. Lawrence Centre,** 27 Front St. E, stages excellent drama and chamber music recitals. (☎366-7723. Box office open in summer M-Sa 10am-6pm; in winter performance days 10am-8pm, non-performance days 10am-6pm. Some student and senior discounts.) **CanStage** performs free summer Shakespeare at **High Park,** on Bloor St. W at Parkside Dr. (Tu-Su 8pm, $15 donation suggested.) Year-round shows at the St. Lawrence Centre include new Canadian works and classics. (☎368-3110; www.canstage.com. Subway: High Park. Box office open M-Sa 10am-6pm.) Several blocks west in the Harbourfront Centre, the **Soulpepper Theatre Company,** 231 Queen's Quay W, presents famous masterpieces. (☎973-4000; www.soulpepper.ca. $30-49, students $25, rush tickets $18, 21 and under $5.)

Toronto's answer to Disney is **Canada's Wonderland,** 9580 Jane St., 1hr. from downtown at Rt. 400 and Rutherford Rd. One part thrill rides, one part water rides, Wonderland whips up family fun. (☎905-832-8131. www.canadaswonderland.com.

Open late June to early Sept. daily 10am-10pm; fall Sa-Su, times vary. Waterpark open in summer daily 11am-8pm. $54, seniors and ages 3-6 $27.) Take **Go Bus** (☎869-3200. $4.25) to the park from the Yorkdale or York Mills subway station.

From April to early October, the **Toronto Blue Jays** play at the huge, modern **Sky-Dome**, at Front and Blue Jay Way. (☎341-3636, tickets ☎341-1234; www.sky-dome.com. Subway: Union and follow the signs. Tickets $9-56.) Take the tour to get into the SkyDome and see the only retractable dome in Major League Baseball. (☎341-2771. $12.50, seniors and under 18 $8.50, children 5-11 $7.) The Sky Dome also hosts concerts (☎341-3663), the **Toronto Argonauts** (☎545-2700; www.argonauts.ca. Tickets $16-48) of the Canadian Football League, and other events during the year. Hockey fans go to **The Air Canada Centre**, 40 Bay St., to see the **Maple Leafs.** (☎815-5500; www.mapleleafs.com. Subway: Union. Tickets $30-160.)

Film enthusiasts catch flicks at the **Bloor Cinema**, 506 Bloor St. W (☎516-2330; www.bloorcinema.com), at Bathurst St., or the **Cinématheque Ontario**, 317 Dundas St. W (☎923-3456; www.bell.ca/cinematheque), in the AGO's Jackman Hall. Toronto's rich cultural offerings include several spectacular **festivals** (☎800-363-1990; www.torontotourism.com). The 10-day **Toronto International Film Festival** (☎968-3456; www.e.bell.ca/filmfest), in early September, is one of the most prestigious festivals on the art-house circuit with classic, Canadian, and foreign films. In June, the **Toronto International Dragon Boat Race Festival** (☎595-1739; www.torontodragonboat.com), on Toronto's Centre Island, continues a 2000-year-old Chinese tradition replete with great food and performances. Independent musicians shine at **North by Northeast** (☎863-6963; www.nxne.com) in mid-June, when local clubs host hundreds of underground artists from all over the world. In late August, the **Canadian National Exhibition (CNE),** one of North America's largest annual fairs, brings an international carnival to Exhibition Place. (☎263-3800; http://mmi.theex.com. Open daily 10am-midnight. $10, seniors and under 6 $7.) In the last week of June, the city rocks with one of the world's three largest gay and lesbian **Pride Week** celebrations (☎927-7433; www.pridetoronto.com), while in early July the **Toronto Street Festival** (☎338-0338; www.toronto.ca/special_events) and the **Fringe Theatre Festival** (☎966-1062; www.fringetoronto.com) come to the city.

▓ NIGHTLIFE

Toronto offers a seemingly limitless selection of bars, pubs, clubs, and late-night cafes. The city stops alcohol distribution every night at 2am, when most clubs close down. *You must be 19 to enter most bars.* New clubs are always opening on trendy **Queen Street W** in the **Entertainment District,** on **College Street W,** and on **Bloor Street W.** The free entertainment magazines *Now* and *Eye* come out every Thursday. The gay scene centers on **Wellesley** and **Church Street;** for info, pick up the free, biweekly *Xtra.* All are available in bars or in streetside dispensers.

THE ANNEX

▓ **Bedford Academy,** 36 Prince Arthur Ave. (☎921-4600). Subway: St. George. Go 1 block north on St. George, and then 2 blocks east on St. Arthur. Relax and converse at this quiet local favorite where a large patio and a homey interior create a laid-back atmosphere. Friendly staff serves huge glasses of Hoegaarden ($6.50), cocktails ($6), and Black Angus hamburgers ($8). Open daily 11am-2am.

The James Joyce, 386 Bloor St. (☎324-9400). Subway: Spadina. Live Celtic music every night, pool tables, local students, and unmistakable Irish conviviality make The Joyce the best place in the Annex to nurse a pint of Guinness ($6.50). Open daily noon-2am.

EASTERN CANADA

The Green Room Café, 296 Brunswick Ave. (☎929-3253). Subway: Bathurst. From Bloor St. walk down Brunswick Ave. and turn right into the alley. Think abandoned coffee shop colonized by artists and musicians and you'll have a feel for this quirky watering hole. Eat breakfast all day (eggs, bacon, fries, toast, and salad $3.21) outside on the quiet patio. Pints $5. Open daily 11am-2am, kitchen closes at 1am.

The Madison Avenue Pub and Restaurant, 14 Madison Ave. (☎927-1722; www.madisonavenuepub.com). Subway: Spadina. Interconnected rooms and patios spread over 2 houses, make The Madison a cool place to hang out. 15 beers on tap. Arrive early to avoid lines on weekend, and bring 2 forms of ID. Pints $6-7. Open daily 11am-2am.

DOWNTOWN

The Second City, 56 Blue Jay Way (☎343-0011 or 888-263-4485), at Wellington St., just north of the SkyDome. Subway: St. Andrew. One of North America's wackiest, most creative comedy clubs, The Second City has spawned comics Dan Aykroyd, John Candy, Martin Short, and Mike Myers, and a hit TV show (SCTV). Free improv sessions F 9:30pm and Sa midnight. Shows M-Th 8pm $21, F-Sa 8pm and 10:30pm $28. Su touring company's production $14. Student tickets Su-Th $13. Reservations recommended.

¿C'est What?, 67 Front St. E (☎867-9499). Subway: Union. This mellow, slightly upscale cafe/pub is a great place to unwind and enjoy local alcohol—try their homemade microbrews ($6-8) and wines ($7). Open daily 11:30am-2am.

THE GAY AND LESBIAN VILLAGE

Woody's/Sailor, 465-467 Church St. (☎972-0887), by Maitland St. Subway: Wellesley. *The* gay bar in the area, famous throughout Canada. Bottled beer $4.75. Don't miss "Best Men's Chest" Th and "Best Men's Legs" Sa. Open daily noon-2am.

Slack Alice, 562 Church St. (☎969-8742). Subway: Wellesley. The best of both worlds: Tuscan and Thai dishes served with a refined air give way to energetic dancing on F-Sa at 10pm. Mostly gay and lesbian crowd, but very straight-friendly. Entrees $9-27. Pints $6. Happy hour daily 4-7pm and all day Tu. Open M-F 4pm-2am, Sa-Su 11am-2am.

Fly, 8 Gloucester St. (☎410-5426; www.flynightclub.com), just east of Yonge St. Subway: Wellesley. Canada's best DJs come to spin for the diverse crowd of sweaty dancers who feast on free food platters, energy drinks ($4), and alcohol. Arrive early to avoid entrance lines. Covers varies; expect $10-25. Open Sa 10pm-wee hours (often 7am).

⚡ DAYTRIP FROM TORONTO

NIAGARA ESCARPMENT

The Niagara Escarpment passes west of Toronto as it winds its way from Niagara Falls to Tobermory at the tip of the Bruce Peninsula. Along this rocky 725km ridge, the **Bruce Trail** snakes through parks and private land. Hikers are treated to spectacular waterfalls, breathtaking vistas, and unique flora and fauna. The Escarpment areas around Milton are most easily accessible from Toronto. Go west on Rte. 401 (about 35 miles) and exit at Rte. 25 (exit #320), then go north on Rte. 25 (1 mile) and turn left at Campbellville. Follow signs to Hilton Falls, Rattlesnake Point, Crawford Lake, and Mount Nemo. Hiking, mountain biking, and cross-country skiing at Hilton Falls, camping and rock climbing at Rattlesnake Point. Entrance is $4-6. Open 8:30am-sundown. For info, write or call the **Niagara Escarpment Commission,** 232 Guelph St., Georgetown, ON L7G 4B1 (☎905-877-5191; www.escarpment.org). Camping reservations required (☎888-668-7275). Those planning extensive trips to the Escarpment should contact the **Bruce Trail Association,** P.O. Box 857, Hamilton, ON L8N 3N9 (☎905-529-6821; www.brucetrail.org).

OTTAWA ☎ 613

Legend claims that in the mid-19th century, Queen Victoria chose Ottawa as Canada's capital by closing her eyes and pointing a finger at a map. In reality, it was probably political savvy, rather than blind chance, that guided her to this once remote logging town. A stronghold for neither the French nor the English, Ottawa was the perfect compromise. Ottawa continues to play cultural diplomat to larger Canada as it attempts to forge national unity while preserving local identities. Meanwhile, government, universities, and tourism drive life in the city itself.

▛ TRANSPORTATION

Airport: Ottawa International (☎248-2000; www.ottawa-airport.ca), 20-30min. south of the city off Bronson Ave. Take bus #97 from MacKenzie King Bridge. A **hotel shuttle** (☎260-2359) runs between the airport and downtown hotels every 30min. 5am-12:05am; call for other pickups. $12, children under 15 free; $20 round-trip.

Trains: VIA Rail, 200 Tremblay Rd. (☎244-8289; www.viarail.ca), east of downtown, off the Queensway at Alta Vista Rd. Ticket office open M-F 5am-9pm, Sa 6:30am-7:30pm, Su 8:20am-9pm. To: **Montréal** (2hr., 5 per day, $47); **Québec City** (7hr., 2 per day, $91); **Toronto** (4hr., 5 per day, $106). 35% discount with ISIC.

Buses: Greyhound, 265 Catherine St. (☎237-7038; www.greyhound.ca). Station open daily 5:30am-2:30am. To: **Montréal** (2½hr.; 18 per day; $34, students and seniors $31); **Québec City** (6-7hr., 16 per day, $74/$66); **Toronto** (5hr., 8 per day, $73/$66). Service to the US goes through Montréal or Toronto. Blue **Gatineau City** buses (☎819-770-3242) connect Ottawa to Gatineau, QC, across the river.

Public Transit: OC Transpo, 1500 St. Laurent (☎741-4390; www.octranspo.com). Buses based at Rideau Centre. $2.60, ages 6-11 $1.35; express (green buses) $3.75.

Taxi: Blue Line Taxi ☎238-1111. **Capital** ☎744-3333.

Car Rental: Avis (☎739-3334) and **Budget** (☎521-4844) have locations in the airport. **Discount** (☎310-2277) is downtown on Gladstone Ave. at Kent St.

Bike Rental: RentABike (☎241-4140; www.cyberus.ca/~rentabike), directly behind Rideau Hall. $8 per hr., $23 per day. Helmet, lock, and map included. Open Apr.-Oct. daily 9am-6pm.

▟ ORIENTATION

The **Rideau Canal** divides Ottawa into the eastern lower town and the western upper town and is lined with bike paths and walkways. The canal itself is a major access route and the world's longest skating rink during the winter. West of the canal, Parliament buildings and government offices line **Wellington Street,** one of the city's main east-west arteries running directly into the heart of downtown. **Laurier Avenue** is the only other east-west street permitting traffic from one side of the canal to the other. East of the canal, Wellington St. becomes **Rideau Street,** surrounded by a fashionable shopping district. North of Rideau St., the **Byward Market** hosts a summertime open-air market and most of Ottawa's nightlife. **Elgin Street,** a major north-south artery that goes from Hwy. 417 (the Queensway) to the War Memorial just south of Wellington near Parliament Hill, is also home to a few pubs and nightlife spots. **Bank Street,** which runs parallel to Elgin three blocks to the west, services the town's older shopping area. Parking downtown is hard to find, and Ottawa is notorious for prompt ticketing of vehicles. On weekends, park for free in the World Exchange Plaza, on Queen St. between O'Connor and Metcalfe.

EASTERN CANADA

Ottawa

ACCOMMODATIONS
Gatineau Park, **1**
Ottawa International Hostel (HI), **9**
University of Ottawa Residences, **10**

FOOD
Byward Café, **6**
D'Arcy McGee's Irish Pub, **8**
Mamma Grazzi's Kitchen, **5**
Medithéo, **2**

NIGHTLIFE
The Honest Lawyer, **7**
The Lookout, **4**
Zaphod, **3**

EASTERN CANADA

PRACTICAL INFORMATION

Visitor Info: National Capital Commission Information Centre, 90 Wellington St. (☎239-5000 or 800-465-1867; www.capcan.ca), opposite the Parliament Bldg. Open daily early May to early Sept. 8:30am-9pm; early Sept. to early May 9am-5pm. The **Ottawa Tourism and Convention Authority** (☎237-5150; www.ottawatourism.ca) publishes a visitor's guide available at the Information Centre. For info on Gatineau in Québec, contact the **Association Touristique de l'Outaouais,** 103 rue Laurier, Gatineau (☎819-778-2530 or 800-265-7822; www.outaouais-tourism.ca). Open mid-June to Sept. M-F 8:30am-8pm, Sa-Su 9am-6pm; Oct. to mid-June M-F 8:30am-5pm, Sa-Su 9am-4pm.

Currency Exchange: Money Mart, 318 Dalhousie St. (☎241-4004), in Byward Market area. $2 flat service charge; Western Union on premises. Open 24hr.

Hotlines: Rape Crisis, ☎562-2333. **Ottawa Distress Centre,** ☎238-3311 (English). **Sexual Assault Support Centre,** ☎738-3762. **Gayline-Telegai,** ☎238-1717.

Medical Services: Ottawa General Hospital, 501 Smyth Rd. (☎737-7777).

Internet Access: Ottawa Public Library, 120 Metcalf St. (☎236-0301). 30min. free Internet access. Open M-Th 10am-9pm, F noon-6pm, Sa 10am-5pm.

Post Office: 59 Sparks St. (☎844-1545), at Elgin St. Open M-F 8am-6pm. **Postal Code:** K1P 5A0. **Area Code:** 613 in Ottawa, 819 in Gatineau. In text, 613 unless noted.

⌐ ACCOMMODATIONS

In downtown Ottawa, budget options exist only if you avoid hotels. Advance reservations are strongly recommended, especially if you are staying through Canada Day (July 1). **Ottawa Bed and Breakfast** represents 10 B&Bs in the Ottawa area. (☎563-0161 or 800-461-7889. Singles from $49; doubles from $59.)

■ **University of Ottawa Residences,** 90 University St. (☎564-5400 or 877-225-8664), in the center of campus, an easy walk from downtown. Take bus #95. Game rooms. Free linen and towels. Laundry $3. Parking $10 per day. Check-in 4:30pm. Check-out 10:30am. Open early May to late Aug. Spacious dorms $40, students $30; doubles $60/$45. Rooms for up to 4 people with kitchenette and breakfast $99. ❶

Ottawa International Hostel (HI), 75 Nicholas St. (☎235-2595), in downtown Ottawa. The site of Canada's last public hanging, the former Carleton County Jail now "incarcerates" travelers in minimally converted cells. Kitchen, lounges, jail tours ($7 for hostelers), organized activities, and a friendly, tongue-in-cheek atmosphere. Internet access $1 per 10min. Linen $2.50. Laundry $3. Key deposit $5. Parking $5 per day. Reception 24hr. Check-in 1pm. Check-out 11am. Lockout in winter 1-7am. Dorms $21, nonmembers $25; private rooms from $54/$58. ❶

Gatineau Park, (☎819-827-2020 or 800-465-1867, reservations 819-456-3016), northwest of Gatineau. 3 rustic campgrounds within 1hr. of Ottawa. Take Hwy. 5 north and exit at Old Chelsea. Follow Hwy. 5 to its end, then take Hwy. 105 north 10km to Hwy. 366 W. Follow signs to campgrounds. **Lac Philippe Campground,** 258 sites for family camping, trailers, and campers. Has general store and beach access. **Lac Taylor Campground,** 33 primitive sites, and **Lac la Pêche Campground,** 36 campsites accessible only by canoe. Lac Philippe open for winter camping. One-time $5 reservation fee for all sites. For Lac Philippe and Lac Taylor, arrive 1:30-9:30pm; depart before 11am; camping permit $24. For Lac la Pêche, arrive 1:30-8pm; camping permit $20. ❶

☐ FOOD

Ottawa's **Byward Market,** on Byward St. between York and George St., is full of produce and plants, chatty locals, and sweet maple syrup. (☎562-3325. Open in warmer weather daily 8am-5pm; boutiques open later, and farmers' stands may stay open until sunset in the summer.) Byward Market, York, George, and Clarence St. are packed with cafes, great restaurants, and bars.

■ **Mamma Grazzi's Kitchen,** 25 George St. (☎241-8656). This Italian hideaway is in a stone building in one of the oldest parts of Ottawa with delectable thin-crust pizza ($10-15). Open Su-Th 11:30am-10pm, F-Sa noon-11pm. ❷

Medithéo, 77 Clarence St. (☎562-2500; www.meditheo.com). *The* place for casual fine dining. With 5 dishes stacked on each other, the vegetarian Mazzeh sampler ($19) is a good way to treat yourself to a wide variety of Mediterranean flavors. Wash it down with a glass (or three) of sangria ($7). Entrees $17-25. Complete your meal by smoking an ornate shisha pipe ($15). Open M-F 11am-11pm, Sa-Su 10am-2am. ❹

EASTERN CANADA

Byward Café, 55 Byward Market (☎ 241-2555), at the bottom of the market, at George St. Fun pop background music and a huge array of treats bring both young and old to eat, drink, and relax on the breezy covered patio. Panini sandwiches around $4.50. Chocolate eruption, a white chocolate cheesecake with dark chocolate mousse, $5.50. Pitcher of beer $13. Open daily in summer 8am-11pm; in winter 8am-6pm. ❶

D'Arcy McGee's Irish Pub, 44 Sparks St. (☎ 230-4433; www.darcymcgees.ca). A traditional Irish eatery (the wooden furnishings are imported from the Emerald Isle), D'Arcy's serves hearty pub food ($8-15) and pints of Guinness ($6). Live music, often Celtic, W-Sa 9:30pm. Open Su-Tu 11am-1am, W-Sa 11am-2am. ❷

◉ SIGHTS

THE HUB. Parliament Hill, on Wellington at Metcalfe St., towers over downtown with its distinguished Gothic architecture. The **Centennial Flame** at the south gate, was lit in 1967 to mark the 100th anniversary of Confederation. The Prime Minister can be spotted at the central Parliament structure, **Centre Block,** which contains the House of Commons, Senate, and Library of Parliament. (The library is closed for renovations, expected to be completed in 2005.) The **Peace Tower,** completed in 1927 to commemorate Canada's war dead, soars 300 ft. above Centre Block; ride the elevator up for a spectacular (and free) panorama. Free tours of Centre Block depart every 30min. from the white **Infotent** by the visitors center. *(☎ 992-4793. Tours mid-May to Sept. M-F 9am-8pm, Sa-Su 9am-5pm; Sept. to mid-May daily 9am-3:30pm, leaving from the main entrance to Centre Block. Infotent open daily mid-May to late June 9am-5pm; late June-Aug. 9am-8pm.)* When Parliament is in session, you can watch Canada's officials debate. Lucky, patient visitors can see **Question Period,** the most interesting debates of the day when the opposition takes their arguments to the sitting government. *(☎ 992-4793 or 866-599-4999; www.parl.gc.ca. Mid-Sept. to Dec. and Feb. to mid-June M-Th 2:15-3pm, F 11:15am-noon. Arrive about 2hr. in advance to obtain passes.)* On display behind the library, the bell from Centre Block is one of few remnants of the original 1859 structure that survived a 1916 fire. According to legend, the bell crashed to the ground after chiming at midnight on the night of the blaze. Today, daily concerts play on the 53 bells in the Peace Tower. *(1hr. concerts June-Sept. M-F 2pm; 15min. concerts Oct.-May M-F noon.)* Those interested in trying to make a statuesque soldier smile should attend the 30min. **Changing of the Guard** on the broad lawns in front of Centre Block. *(☎ 993-1811. Late June to late Aug. daily 10am, weather permitting.)* At dusk, Centre Block and its lawns become the background for **Sound and Light,** which relates the history of the Parliament buildings and the nation. *(☎ 239-5000; www.canadascapital.gc.ca/ soundandlight. Shows early July to early Sept. Performances alternate between French and English; call for show times.)* Several blocks west along Wellington St. stand the **Supreme Court of Canada** and the **Federal Court.** *(☎ 995-5361; www.ssc-csc.gc.ca. Open June-Aug. daily 9am-5pm; Sept.-May hours vary. Free tours every 30min.; tours alternate between French and English. No tours Sa-Su noon-1pm.)*

CONFEDERATION SQUARE. East of the Parliament buildings at the junction of Sparks, Wellington, and Elgin St. stand **Confederation Square** and the enormous **National War Memorial.** Dedicated by King George VI in 1939, the Memorial is a lifesize representation of Canadian troops marching under the angels of liberty, and symbolizes the triumph of peace over war—an ironic message on the eve of WWII. **Nepean Point,** several blocks northwest of Rideau Centre and the Byward Market, behind the National Gallery of Canada, offers a panoramic view of the capital and a statue of explorer Samuel de Champlain. Legend has it that the astrolabe he holds was discovered in the waters of the Ottawa River.

ROYALTY. The **Governor General,** the Queen's representative in Canada, lives at **Rideau Hall.** Take a tour of the house, gardens, and art collection—many visitors run into the ever-gracious Governor General. *(1 Sussex Dr. ☎991-4422 or 800-465-6890; www.gg.ca. Free 45min. guided tours daily 9am-3pm; self-guided tours late June to late Aug. daily 3-4:30pm; May-June Sa-Su only.)* See the production of collectors' "loonies" ($1 coins) at the **Royal Canadian Mint.** *(320 Sussex Dr. ☎993-8990 or 800-276-7714. In summer, tours leave every 15min. M-F 9am-8pm, Sa-Su 9am-5:30pm. In winter, M-F 9am-5pm. $5,children 16 and under $3; Sa-Su $3.50/$2.)*

OUTDOOR ACTIVITIES. Ottawa is home to many public parks. Surprisingly wild ▧ **Gatineau Park** (p. 171), occupying 363 sq. km in the northwest and reaching into the city of Gatineau, is a natural sanctuary mere kilometers from downtown. The looping King Mountain trail (2km., 45min.) takes hikers through multiple ecological zones, past a mountain lake, and up to vantage points from which Ottawa's buildings can be spied in the distance. Snap photos or have a picnic at the three car-accessible lookouts along the Parkway, which follows the Eardley Escarpment, above the Ottawa River valley. Farther north, the park is home to bears and a few rare timberwolves. Don't miss the spectacular fall foliage. *(☎819-827-2020 or 800-465-1867, rentals ☎819-456-3016; www.canadascapital.gc.ca/gatineau. Parkway open when snow melts (usually Apr.) until it falls again (usually late Oct.); call for info. Bikes and boats available at lakes Philippe and la Pêche. Bikes $8 per hr., $30 per day, $35 per 24hr.; boats $10/$30/$38. Open daily mid-June to first M in Sept., Sa-Su thereafter. Hiking trails open for skiing and snowshoeing in the winter; snowshoe rentals $5 per hr., $15 per day.)* Man-made **Dow's Lake,** accessible by the Queen Elizabeth Driveway, extends off the Rideau Canal south of Ottawa. **Dow's Lake Pavilion** rents pedal and row boats, kayaks, canoes, rollerblades, and bikes in summer and ice skates and sleighs in winter. *(101 Queen Elizabeth Driveway, near Preston St. ☎232-1001; www.dowslake.com. Open mid-May to Sept. M-F 1-8pm, Sa-Su 11am-8pm, weather permitting. Rentals by the hr. and ½hr. Prices vary but expect to pay $10-20 for a boat. Deposit of photo ID required for rental.)*

▥ MUSEUMS

▧ **Canadian Museum of Civilization,** 100 Laurier St., Gatineau, QC (☎819-776-7000; www.civilization.ca). Housed in a striking sand-dune-like structure across Port Alexandra Bridge from the National Gallery, the museum offers life-sized dioramas and architectural recreations exploring 1000 years of Canadian history. Canada Hall is terrific. Open Apr.-Oct. M-W and F-Su 9am-6pm, Th 9am-9pm; low-season hours vary. $10, seniors $7, students $6, ages 3-12 $4; families $22. Th free after 4pm; Su half-price.

▧ **National Gallery,** 380 Sussex Dr. (☎998-8888 or 888-541-8888; www.national.gallery.ca). A stunning glass-towered building by Nepean Pt. holds the world's most comprehensive collection of Canadian art including the Inuit exhibit, "Teeth and Tusks." Open May-Oct. M-W and F-Su 10am-5pm, Th 10am-8pm; low-season closed M-Tu. Free; special exhibits $12, seniors and students $10, ages 12-19 $5, children free; reservations available.

Canadian Museum of Contemporary Photography, 1 Rideau Canal (☎990-8257; www.cmcp.gallery.ca), on the steps between the Château Laurier and the Ottawa Locks. Showcases an impressive rotation of temporary exhibits to display photography's dual function as fine art and a tool for social documentary. Open M-W and F-Su 10am-5pm, Th 10am-8pm; low-season W and F-Su 10am-5pm, Th 10am-8pm. Free.

Canadian Museum of Nature, 240 McLeod St. (☎566-4700; www.nature.ca), at Metcalfe St. takes a multimedia look at the natural world. At the bug exhibit, nothing bites...hard. Open May to early Sept. M-W and F-Su 9:30am-5pm, Th 9:30am-8pm; low-season hours vary. $4, students and seniors $3.50, ages 3-12 $1.75; families $9. Sa free before noon.

▓ FESTIVALS

Ottawans seem to celebrate everything, even the bitter Canadian cold. All-important **Canada Day** (☎239-5000; www.canadascapital.gc.ca/canadaday), July 1, involves fireworks, partying in Major's Hill Park, concerts, and all-around merrymaking. During the first three weekends of February, **Winterlude** (☎239-5000 or 800-465-1867; www.canadascapital.gc.ca/winterlude.), North America's largest winter festival, lines the Rideau Canal. Ice sculptures and a working ice cafe illustrate how it feels to be an Ottawan in the winter—frozen. For three weeks in May, the **Tulip Festival** (☎567-4447 or 800-668-8547; www.tulipfestival.ca) explodes with a kaleidoscope of more than a million buds around Dow's Lake, while pop concerts and other events center around Major's Hill Park. Music fills the air during the **Dance Festival** (☎947-7000; www.canadadance.ca), which showcases innovative contemporary choreography in mid-June, and the **Jazz Festival** (☎241-2633; www.ottawajazzfestival.com), in late June. Both feature free recitals and concerts.

▐ NIGHTLIFE

Nightspots can serve alcohol until 2am, and bars and clubs around Byward Market cater to college students during the school year and tourists during the summer.

The Honest Lawyer, 141 George St. (☎562-2262), near Dalhousie St. Watch the game on TV screens or play some yourself arcade style at this sports bar that also has a free bowling lane. The 130 oz. "Beerzooka" is, well, a lot of brew ($35), as is the "yard of beer," a yard's worth of 10 oz. beer glasses. M wing night ($11 all-you-can-eat), Su everything is 25% off. F-Sa 21+. Open M-F 11:30am-2am, Sa 3pm-2am, Su 6pm-2am.

Zaphod, 27 York St. (☎562-1010; www.zaphodbeeblebrox.com), in Byward Market. Named after a character in *The Hitchhiker's Guide to the Galaxy,* this popular alternative rock club stages local musicians in a spacey atmosphere. Pangalactic Gargle Blaster, a fruity cocktail, $6.50. Live bands M and W-Sa. 19+. M no cover, otherwise cover $2-12 depending on performer. Open daily 4pm-2am.

The Lookout, 41 York St. (☎789-1624), next to Zaphod's on the second floor. A hoppin' gay club with intense dancing. During daylight hours, the club shows local art exhibits. Though the Th evening crowd is mostly male, women flock in on F. Sa is house party night. Open daily noon-2am.

QUÉBEC

Originally populated by French fur-trading settlements along the St. Lawrence River, Québec was ceded to the British in 1759. Ever since, anti-federalist elements within *québécois* society have rankled under national government control. Visitors may be tipped off to the underlying struggles by the occasional cry for "Liberté!" scrawled across a sidewalk, but the tensions are mostly kept behind closed doors. Instead, Montréal's renowned nightlife and Québec City's centuries-old European flair distinguish Québec among Canada's provinces.

▟ PRACTICAL INFORMATION

Capital: Québec City.

EASTERN CANADA

Visitor Info: Infotouriste, 1255 rue Peel, Ste. 100, Montréal H3C 2W3 (☎266-5687 or 877-266-5687; www.bonjourquebec.com), on Ste-Catherine between rue Peel and rue Metcalfe. Métro: Peel. Open daily July-Aug. 8:30am-8pm, Sept.-June 9am-6pm. **Société des éstablissements de plein air du Québec (Sépaq),** 801 chemin St-Louis, Ste. 180, Québec City G1S 1C1 (☎418-686-4875). Another location at Montréal's Infotouriste. **Drinking Age:** 18. **Postal Abbreviation:** QC. **Sales Tax:** 7.5% PST, plus 7% GST.

MONTRÉAL ☎514

This island city has been coveted territory for over 300 years. Wars and sieges dominated Montréal's early history as British forces strove to wrest it from the French. Today's invaders are not British, French, or American generals, but rather visitors eager to experience a diverse, cosmopolitan city. Only an hour from the US border, Montréal is the second-largest French-speaking city in the world. Fashion that rivals Paris's, a nightlife comparable to London's, and cuisine from around the globe attest to Montréal's European legacy. With its global flavor and large student population, it is hard not to be swept up by the vibrancy of the *centre-ville*.

■ INTERCITY TRANSPORTATION

Airports: Dorval (☎394-7377; www.admtl.com), 25min. from downtown by car. Many hostels run airport shuttles for about $11; call for info. By Métro, take bus #211 from the Lionel Groulx (green and orange lines) to Dorval Train Station, and transfer to bus #204. **L'Aérobus** (☎931-9002) runs to Dorval from 777 rue de la Gauchetière Ouest, at rue de l'Université, stopping at any downtown hotel if notified in advance. Vans run daily every 30min. 3:30am-11pm. $11, under 5 free. Taxi to downtown $30-35.

Trains: Gare Centrale, 895 rue de la Gauchetière Ouest, under Queen Elizabeth Hotel. Métro: Bonaventure. Served by **VIA Rail** (☎989-2626 or 800-561-9181; www.viarail.ca), open daily 7am-midnight. To: **Ottawa** (2hr., 5 per day, $51); **Québec City** (3hr., 4 per day, $68); **Toronto** (4-5½hr., 6 per day, $125). Buy discount tickets 5+ days in advance. Arrive 45min. before departure if you have luggage. **Amtrak** (☎800-842-7275), open daily 8am-5pm. To **New York City** (10hr., 1 per day, $62).

Buses: Station Centrale, 505 bd. de Maissonneuve Est (☎843-4231). Métro: Berri-UQAM; follow the gray "Autobus-Terminus" signs upstairs. Open 24hr. **Voyageur** (☎842-2281; www.voyageur.ca), to **Ottawa** (2½hr.; every hr. 6am-midnight except 9am; $37, students $33) and **Toronto** (8hr.; 7 per day; $92, students $83). **Orléans Express** (☎395-400; www.orleansexpress.com), to **Québec City** (3-4hr.; 22 per day; $45, students $38). **Greyhound USA** (☎287-1580), to **Boston** (7hr., 5 per day, $85) and **New York City** (8½hr., 5 per day, $102).

Carpooling Service: Allô Stop, 4317 rue St-Denis (☎985-3032; www.allostop.com). Open M-W and Sa-Su 9am-6pm, Th-F 9am-7pm. Matches passengers with drivers; part of the fee goes to the driver. To **Québec City** ($15) and **Sherbrooke** ($9). Riders and drivers fix their own fees for rides over 1000 mi. Required annual membership fee ($6).

■ ORIENTATION

Two major streets divide the city. The one-way **Boulevard St-Laurent** (also called **"le Main"** or **"The Main"**) runs north through the city, splitting Montréal and its streets east-west. The Main also serves as the unofficial French/English divider; English **McGill University** lies to the west, while **St-Denis,** a street running parallel to St-Laurent, lies to the east and defines the French student quarter (also called the *Quartier Latin* and the "student ghetto"). **Rue Sherbrooke,** paralleled by **de Maisonneuve** and **Ste-Catherine** downtown, runs east-west almost the entire length of Montréal.

EASTERN CANADA

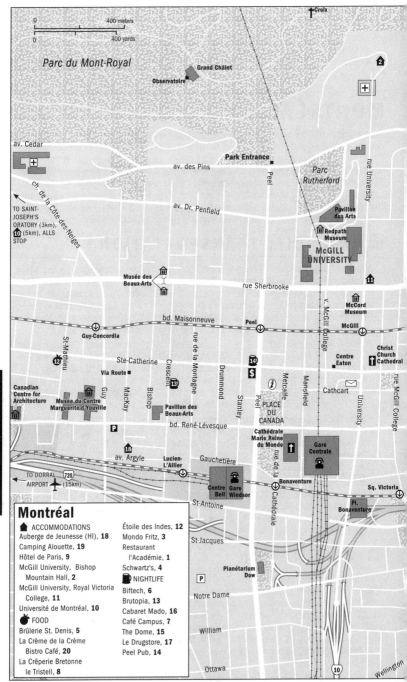

Montréal

🏠 ACCOMMODATIONS
Auberge de Jeunesse (HI), **18**
Camping Alouette, **19**
Hôtel de Paris, **9**
McGill University, Bishop
  Mountain Hall, **2**
McGill University, Royal Victoria
  College, **11**
Université de Montréal, **10**

🍴 FOOD
Brûlerie St. Denis, **5**
La Crème de la Crème
  Bistro Café, **20**
La Crêperie Bretonne
  le Tristell, **8**
Étoile des Indes, **12**
Mondo Fritz, **3**
Restaurant
  l'Académie, **1**
Schwartz's, **4**

🍸 NIGHTLIFE
Biftech, **6**
Brutopia, **13**
Cabaret Mado, **16**
Café Campus, **7**
The Dome, **15**
Le Drugstore, **17**
Peel Pub, **14**

Parc Jeanne-Mance

av. du Parc

TO LITTLE GREECE (3km)

Duluth

TO LITTLE ITALY (4km),
MONT ROYAL (.5km),
JEAN TALON (4km),
THÉÂTRE DU RIDEAU
VERT (1km), NATIONAL
THEATRE SCHOOL OF
CANADA

Théâtre d'Aujourd'hui

Roy

av. des Pins

Sherbrooke

SQUARE
SAINT-LOUIS

Prince Arthur

TO OLYMPIC PARK (5km)

Milton

QUARTIER
LATIN

rue Sherbrooke

bd. St-Laurent

St-Denis

Berri

St-Hubert

Musée juste
pour rire

Ontario

Bibliothèque Nationale
du Québec

Place-des-Arts

bd. Maisonneuve

St-Laurent

bd. Maisonneuve

Théâtre
Saint-Denis

Berri-UQAM

LE VILLAGE

St-Alexandre

rue de Bleury

Jeanne-Mance

St-Urbain

Place des
Arts

Musée d'Art
Contemporain

Théâtre du
Nouveau Monde

Ste-Catherine

UNIVERSITÉ
QUÉBEC
À MONTRÉAL

TO 16 (25m),
17 (200m)

bd. René-Lévesque

CHINATOWN

Gauchetière

Champ-de-Mars

av. Viger

TO 19 (30km)

SQUARE
VIGER

Place-d'Armes

Palais de Congrès

720

Berri

Musée
Artur Pascal

St-Antoine

Parc
Champs-de-Mars

St-Jacques

PLACE
D'ARMES

Palais
de Justice

Vieux Palais
de Justice

Hôtel de Ville
de Montréal

Notre-Dame

VIEUX-
MONTRÉAL

Château
Ramezay

St-Paul

TO ÎLE SAINTE-HÉLÈNE (2km),
CASINO MONTRÉAL (2km),
LE VIEUX FORT (2km),
LA RONDE (2km)

St-François-Xavier

Centaur
Theatre

St-Sulpice

Basilique
Notre-Dame
de Montréal

St-Paul

Jacques-Cartier

St-Vincent

Chapelle
Notre-Dame-de-
Bon-Secours

Marché
Bonsecours

Centre
d'Histoire
de Montréal

St-Jean

St-Pierre

PLACE
ROYALE

rue de la Commune

Pointe à Callière

VIEUX-PORT

Tour de
l'Horloge

McGill

Musée
Marc-Aurèle-Fortin

IMAX

Quai
Alexandra

Quai King Edward

Quai Jacques-Cartier

Le Pélican

Quai de l'Horloge

Fleuve St-Laurent

The **Underground City** runs north-south, stretching from **rue Sherbrooke** to **rue de la Gauchetière** and **rue St-Antoine.** A free map from the tourist office helps navigation. **Parking** is expensive and often tough to find along the streets. Try parking lots in the city's outskirts for reasonable prices.

NEIGHBORHOODS

Montréal used to be limited to the riverside area of present-day **Vieux Montréal.** Today, the old port area is well preserved, taking visitors back hundreds of years with cobblestone streets and stately old buildings. The rest of the city has since evolved from a French colonial settlement into a hip, cosmopolitan metropolis. On **rue Ste-Catherine,** European fashion teases Canada, conversations mix English and French, and upscale retail shops intermingle with tacky souvenir stores and debaucherous nightclubs. The street's assortment of peep shows and sex shops has earned it the nickname "Saint-Vitrine" (holy window). The western side of downtown is centered around the intersection of rue Ste-Catherine and **rue Crescent,** and is home to many bars, cafes, and restaurants. Rue St-Denis, home to the city's turn-of-the-century elite, still serves as the **Quartier Latin's** main street. Restaurants of all flavors cluster along rue Prince Arthur, between St-Denis and Blvd. St-Laurent. **Boulevard St-Laurent** has clubs and lounges. Rounding out downtown are a small **Chinatown** on rue de la Gauchetière, just north of Métro: Place d'Armes, and the lively gay village, **Le Village,** along rue Ste-Catherine Est between rue St-Hubert and Papineau. **Little Greece,** a fairly long walk from downtown, is just southeast of Métro: Outremont. **Little Italy** occupies the area north of rue Beaubien between rue St-Hubert and Louis-Hémon. A little farther north, **Jean-Talon** is home to various immigrant groups, including Greek, Slavic, Latin American, and Portuguese. The area around the intersection of ch. de la Côte-des-Neiges and rue Jean-Brillant, near l'Université de Montréal, is full of fun cafes and strolling shoppers. Many attractions between **Mont-Royal** and the **Fleuve St-Laurent** are free.

◩ LOCAL TRANSPORTATION

Public Transit: STM Métro and Bus (☎288-6287; www.stm.info). The world's most advanced public transit system when it was built in 1976, the Métro is comprehensive, logical, and safe. The 4 Métro lines and most buses run daily 5:30am-12:30am (last line Sa 1am); some also have early morning schedules. Get maps at the tourist office or any Métro station. Transfer tickets *(correspondances)* from bus drivers are valid as subway tickets and vice versa. Fare for Métro or bus $2.50, 6 tickets $11. Between Apr. and Oct., buy a Tourist Card at any downtown station: Sherbrooke, Mont-Royal, Pie-IX, Jean-Talon, Longueuil, or Berri-UQAM. 1-day unlimited access $8, 3-day $16.

Taxi: Taxi Coop de Montréal ☎845-1244. **Champlain Taxi Inc.** ☎273-2435.

Car Rental: Via Route, 1255 rue MacKay (☎871-1166; www.viaroute.com), at Ste-Catherine. Open M-Th 7am-7pm, F 7am-9pm, Sa 7:30am-5pm, Su 9am-7pm.

Bike Rental: Ça Roule, 27 de la Commune Est (☎866-0633; www.caroulemontreal.com). Métro: Place-d'Armes. Open daily 9am-8pm; closes at 6pm or earlier in bad weather. Bikes $22-25 per day; inline skates $25-30 per day; protective gear included. Bikes and inline skates $20 for HI members with card. ID required for all rentals. Bike maps $2. Much of the Métro system allows bikes during designated hours. Before trying, check the policy of the route.

◪ PRACTICAL INFORMATION

Visitor Info: Infotouriste, 1255 rue Peel, Ste. 100 (☎266-5687 or 877-266-5687; www.bonjourquebec.com), on Ste-Catherine between rue Peel and Metcalfe. Métro: Peel. Open daily July-Aug. 8:30am-8pm; Sept.-June 9am-6pm. In **Vieux-Montréal,** 174 rue Notre-Dame Est, at Pl. Jacques Cartier. Open daily 9am-5pm; July-Aug. open until 7pm.

Currency Exchange: Calforex, 1250 rue Peel (☎392-9100). Métro: Peel. $2.75 flat fee. Open M-W 8:30am-7pm, Th-Sa 8:30am-9pm, Su 10am-6pm; low-season Sa 10am-7pm. Rue Ste-Catherine is lined with *bureaux de change*—watch for high commissions.

Hotlines: Tél-Aide, ☎935-1101. **Sexual Assault Hotline,** ☎934-4504. Both operate 24hr. **Gay and Lesbian Hotline,** ☎866-0103. Operates daily 7-11pm. **Rape Crisis,** ☎278-9383. Operates M-F 9:30am-4:30pm; call Tél-Aide after hours.

Internet Access: Bibliothèque Nationale du Québec, 1700 rue St-Denis (☎873-1100). Métro: Berri-UQAM. 2 computers with free access; sign-up required. Open M-F 9am-5pm. **Internet cafes** are plentiful in Montréal and generally charge $2 for 30min.

Post Office: 685 rue Cathcart (☎395-4539). Open M-F 8am-6pm. **Postal Code:** H3B 3B0. **Area Code:** 514 for the island of Montréal, 450 for the north and south shores. In text, 514 unless otherwise noted.

⁊ ACCOMMODATIONS

The **Infotouriste** (☎877-266-5687) has info about hostels, hotels, *gîtes* (B&Bs), and *chambres touristiques* (rooms in private homes or guesthouses). At the **Downtown Bed and Breakfast Network ❶,** 3458 av. Laval, H2X 3C8, near Sherbrooke, the managers run their own B&B, and keep a list of 80 others downtown. (☎289-9749 or 800-267-5180; www.bbmontreal.qc.ca. Open daily 9am-9pm. Singles $55-85; doubles $65-95.) The cheapest lodgings cluster around **rue St-Denis,** by Vieux Montréal. Canada Day and the Grand Prix in July make rooms scarce, so reserve in advance.

🗟 **Auberge de Jeunesse, Montréal Youth Hostel (HI),** 1030 rue MacKay (☎843-3317; www.hostellingmontreal.com). Métro: Lucien-L'Allier; from the station, cross the street and go right. The hostel is down the first real street on the left. Airport shuttle drivers will stop here if asked. This world-class hostel has a bathroom in each room, A/C, a kitchen, pool tables, and a *petit café*. Pub crawl Tu and F 8:30pm. Internet access $2 per 20min. Linen $2.30; no sleeping bags. Laundry $2.50. 1-week max. stay. Reception 24hr. Check-in 1pm. Check-out 11am. The 240 beds fill quickly in summer; reservations recommended. Dorms $23, nonmembers $27; doubles $29/$34 per person. ❶

McGill University Residences, Royal Victoria College, 3425 rue de l'Université (☎398-5200) and Bishop Mountain Hall, 3935 rue de l'Université (☎398-6367; www.mcgill.ca/residences/summer). Métro: McGill. By the intersection of rue de l'Université and rue Sherbrooke. Follow Université along the edge of campus; bear right at the top of the hill. Royal Victoria is closer to downtown. Kitchenettes. Common room with TV. Free Internet access. Full breakfast M-Th $7; continental breakfast $4.50. Towels and linen. Laundry facilities. Reception daily 7am-10pm; late check-in available. Check-in 3pm. Check-out noon. Open mid-May to mid-Aug. Royal Victoria College singles $45, students and seniors $40. Bishop Mountain Hall $39/$35. ❷

Université de Montréal Residences, 2350 rue Edouard-Montpetit (☎343-6531; www.resid.umontreal.ca). Métro: Edouard-Montpetit. Follow signs up the hill. Functional rooms with great views in a tranquil neighborhood. Cafe with basic foods; refrigerator and sink in rooms. TV lounge. Internet access $1 per 10min. Linen provided. Laundry $2.50. Parking $10. Reception 24hr. Check-in 3pm. Check-out noon. Open mid-May to early Aug. Singles $35; doubles $45. Students 10% off. ❶

Hôtel de Paris, 901 rue Sherbrooke Est (☎522-6861 or 800-567-7217; www.hotel-montreal.com). Métro: Sherbrooke. This European-style 19th-century flat houses a score of pleasant hotel rooms with private bath, TV, telephone, and A/C. Some rooms contain kitchenettes. There are also about 100 hostel beds which, while cheaper than the hotel rooms, are not as good a deal as Montréal's other hostels. Linen $3. Reception 24hr. Single-sex dorm rooms $20; hotel rooms $80-155. ❶/❹

Camping Alouette, 3449 rue de l'Industrie (☎450-464-1661 or 888-464-7829; www.campingalouette.com), 30km from the city. Follow Autoroute 20 south, take Exit 105, and follow the signs. Secluded campsites, nature trail, pool, laundry, bathrooms, store, volleyball courts, dance hall, and daily shuttle to and from Montréal (45min., $12). Sites for 2 $23, with hookup $27; additional person $2. ❶

☐ BON APPÉTIT

Montréal is a diner's city, where chic restaurants rub shoulders with funky cafes and everyone can find something to fit his or her taste. Expect nothing less than excellent food, but don't hold your breath for speedy service. **Chinatown** and **Little Italy** boast outstanding examples of their culinary heritage, and **rue Prince Arthur** adds a cheerful blend of Greek and Polish to the mix. The western half of **Ste-Catherine** and the **Boulevard St-Laurent** area north of Sherbrooke offer a large range of choices. By far the best and most affordable restaurants cluster on **rue St-Denis.**

Some restaurants, even upscale ones, have no liquor licenses; head to the nearest **dépanneur** or **SAQ** (*Societé des alcools du Québec*) to buy wine for dinner. Do like the locals: buy a bottle of wine and head to rue Prince Arthur's pedestrian mall for a relaxed meal on one of the many outdoor patios. All restaurants are required by law to post their menus outside. For further guidance, consult the free *Restaurant Guide*, published by the **Greater Montréal Convention and Tourism Bureau** (☎844-5400), which lists over 130 restaurants by type of cuisine. If you feel like cooking, go to one of the **markets.** (All markets open M-W 8am-6pm, Th 8am-8pm, F 8am-9pm, Sa-Su 8am-5pm.) **Marché Jean-Talon,** 7075 rue Casgrain (☎277-1558; Métro: Jean Talon), has a selection of ethnic goodies in addition to an incredible outdoor market of fruits and veggies, while the **Marché Maisonneuve,** 4445 rue Ontario Est (☎937-7754, Métro: Pie-IX), is great for produce and traditional *québécois* gems.

■ **Restaurant l'Académie,** 4051 rue St-Denis (☎849-2249), on the corner of av. Duluth. Métro: Sherbrooke. An elegant culinary heaven where lunchtime indulgence is reasonably priced and the atmosphere is refined, but not stuffy. L'Académie perfects Italian-French fusion, and is most recognized for its *moules et frites*, mussels steamed and served in a variety of sauces (around $10 Su-W, $12 Th-Sa). Long lines during dinner. Open Su-Th noon-10pm, F-Sa noon-10:30pm. ❸

■ **Schwartz's,** 3895 Blvd. St-Laurent (☎842-4813; www.schwartzsdeli.com). Locals crowd in for world famous kosher smoked meats. Sandwiches $4.45, pickles $1.25. Open Su-Th 8am-12:30am, F 8am-1:30am, Sa 8am-2:30am. Cash only. ❶

■ **Mondo Fritz,** 3899 Blvd. St-Laurent (☎281-6521), next to Schwartz's. The city's best *poutine* (fries, cheese curds, and gravy; $5.50), veggie burgers ($6.50), and foot-long all-beef hot dogs ($5). Choice of 55 beers (from $3), and 6 kinds of fresh mayonnaise. Open Su noon-midnight, M-W 11am-midnight, Th 11am-1am, F-Sa 11am-2am. ❷

Étoile des Indes, 1806 Ste-Catherine Ouest (☎932-8330), near St-Mathieu (parking on St-Mathieu). A favorite for Indian food. The spicy Bangalore *phal* dishes are only for the brave, but everyone can enjoy the homemade cheese in their *paneer* plates. The Butter Chicken ($10) is phenomenal. Dinners $15-25. Lunch specials $6-9. Open M-Sa noon-2:30pm and 5-11pm, Su 5-11pm. ❸

Brûlerie St. Denis, 3967 rue St-Denis (☎286-9158). Métro: Sherbrooke. A fun student cafe where food and coffee are excellent, waiters are friendly, and patrons seem to know each other. Café du jour $1.50. Bagel "Belle Hélène," with cream cheese, tomato, and cucumber, $4.50. Open M-F 8am-11pm, Sa 8am-midnight, Su 9am-11pm. ❶

La Crème de la Crème Bistro Café, 21 rue de la Commune Est (☎874-0723), in Vieux-Montréal. A cozy cafe on the waterfront has Greek cuisine and Provençal decor. Tasty baguette sandwiches (with salad $7-9) and generous slices of cake ($4). Open daily June-Sept. 11am-midnight; Oct.-May opens at 11am, hours vary with the weather. ❷

La Crêperie Bretonne le Tristell, 3470 rue St-Denis (☎281-1012). Métro: Sherbrooke. Montréalers have been known to line up for a taste of le Tristell's melt-in-your-mouth crêpes and fondues. Fresh strawberry crepe $6.75. Open M-W 11:30am-11pm, Th-F 11:30am-midnight, Sa noon-midnight, Su noon-11pm. ❶

◙ SIGHTS

OLYMPIC PARK

Package tickets *(forfaits)* for the Biodôme, Tower, and Gardens/Insectarium are available at each sight's box office. Tickets are good for 30 days. *(Any 2 sights $18, students and seniors $14, children 5-17 $8.75. All 3 sights $27/$21/$14.)*

▨**BIODÔME.** The fascinating **Biodôme** is the most recent addition to Olympic Park. Housed in the former Olympic Vélodrome, the Biodôme is a "living museum" in which four complete ecosystems have been reconstructed: the Tropical Forest, the Laurentian Forest, the St-Laurent marine ecosystem, and the Polar World. Stay alert to spot some of the more elusive of the 4500 vertebrates subsisting here. *(4777 av. Pierre-de-Coubertin. Métro: Viau. ☎ 868-3000; www.biodome.qc.ca. Open daily in summer 9am-6pm; low-season 9am-5pm. $11, students and seniors $8, ages 5-17 $5.25.)*

OLYMPIC PARK. The world's tallest inclined tower *(le Tour Olympique* or *le Tour de Montréal)* is **Olympic Park's** crowning glory, built for the 1976 Olympics. Take the **Funiculaire** to the top for a breathtaking view of Montréal, or hop in at the **Olympic Swimming Complex,** with North America's deepest scuba diving pool. *(3200 rue Viau. Métro: Viau, Pie-IX. ☎ 252-4141. Tours $7, students and seniors $6.25, ages 5-17 $5.25; not included in forfait package. Funiculaire open daily July-Aug. 9am-9pm; Sept.-June 9am-7pm. $12, students and seniors $9, ages 5-17 $6. Pools open daily 6:30am-8pm; $3.)*

BOTANICAL GARDENS AND INSECTARIUM. A free shuttle runs to the **Jardin Botanique (Botanical Gardens).** The Japanese and Chinese landscapes showcase the largest *bonsai* and *penjing* collections outside of Asia. Beware: the gardens also harbor an **insectarium** with astounding collections of mounted and live exotic bugs, including at least a dozen fist-sized spiders. *(4101 rue Sherbrooke Est. Métro: Pie-IX. ☎872-1400; www.ville.montreal.qc.ca/jardin or /insectarium. Open daily late June to early Sept. 9am-6pm; Sept.-June 9am-4pm. $12, students and seniors $9, ages 5-17 $6.)*

MONT-ROYAL

▨**ST. JOSEPH'S.** The dome of **St. Joseph's Oratory,** the second-highest dome in the world after St. Peter's Basilica in Rome, stands in testimony to the chapel's grandeur. An acclaimed religious site that attracts pilgrims from all over the globe, St. Joseph's is credited with a long list of miracles and unexplained healings. The **Votive Chapel,** where the crutches and canes of thousands of healed devotees hang, is kept warm by the heat of 10,000 candles. *(3800 ch. Queen Mary. Métro: Côte-des-Neiges. ☎ 733-8211; www.saint-joseph.org. Open daily 6am-9:30pm. Free.)*

PARC DU MONT-ROYAL. Designed by Frederick Law Olmstead, creator of New York City's Central Park, the 128-year-old **Parc du Mont-Royal** surrounds and includes Montréal's namesake mountain. Though the hike from rue Peel up the mountain is longer than it looks, the view of the city from the top rewards the hardy. The 30m cross at the top of the mountain is a replica of the cross placed there in 1643 by de Maisonneuve, the founder of Montréal. In winter, locals gather here to ice-skate, toboggan, snowshoe, and cross-country ski. In summer, Mont-Royal welcomes joggers, cyclists, boaters, picnickers, and amblers. *(The park is bordered by ch. Remembrance, bd. Mont-Royal, av. du Parc, and ch. de la Côte-des-Neiges. Métro: Mont-Royal or Bus #11. ☎844-4928; www.lemontroyal.qc.ca.*

Visitors Centre at Smith House, 1260 ch. Remembrance, between Beaver Lake and Chalet du Mont-Royal. Boat rentals in summer $8 per 30min. Smith House open M-F 9am-6pm, Sa-Su 9am-7pm. Park open daily 6am-midnight.)

DOWNTOWN

CATHÉDRALE MARIE REINE DU MONDE. A scaled-down replica of St. Peter's in Rome, **Cathédrale Marie Reine du Monde** stirred tensions when it was built as a Roman Catholic basilica in the heart of Montréal's Anglo-Protestant area. *(On the block bordered by René-Lévesque, Cathédrale, and Mansfield. ☎866-1661. Open M-F 6am-7pm, Sa 7:30am-8:30pm, Su 8am-7pm. At least 4-5 masses offered daily. Free.)* Across rue Cathédrale sits **Place du Canada,** a lovely park with a modest war memorial.

MCGILL. The **McGill University** campus extends up Mont-Royal and is composed predominantly of Victorian-style buildings set on pleasant greens. Stop by the **McGill Welcome Centre** for a tour. *(Burnside Hall Building, Room 115. ☎398-6555. Open M-F 9am-5pm, Sa tours offered in July and Aug. Call for details.)* The campus includes the site of the 16th-century Native American village of **Hochelaga** and the **Redpath Museum of Natural History,** containing rare fossils and two genuine Egyptian mummies. *(Main gate at rue McGill and Sherbrooke. Métro: McGill. Museum: ☎398-4086; www.mcgill.ca/redpath. Open July-Aug. M-Th 9am-5pm, Sa-Su 1-5pm; Sept.-June M-F 9am-5pm, Su 1-5pm. Free.)*

THE UNDERGROUND CITY

Thirty kilometers of tunnels link Métro stops and form the ever-expanding "prototype city of the future," connecting railway stations, two bus terminals, restaurants, cinemas, theaters, hotels, two universities, two department stores, 1700 businesses, 1615 housing units, and 2000 boutiques. Here, residents bustle through the hallways of this sprawling, mall-like, "sub-urban" city. The McGill stop offers some of the Underground City's finest, most navigable offerings. The **Promenades de la Cathédrale** take their name from their above-ground neighbor, **Christ Church Cathedral.** However, the primary subterranean shopping complex is more interested in your pocketbook than your soul. *(635 rue Ste-Catherine Ouest. Church: ☎843-6577. Open daily 8am-6pm. Promenades: ☎849-9925.)* To find the shopping wonderland **Place Bonaventure,** follow signs marked "Restaurants et Commerce" through the maze of shops under rue de la Gauchetière Ouest. The tourist office supplies treasure maps of the tunnels and underground attractions. *(900 rue de la Gauchetière Ouest. Métro: Bonaventure. ☎397-2325. Shops open M-W and Sa-Su 9am-6pm, Th-F 9am-9pm.)*

VIEUX MONTRÉAL

In the 17th century, Montréal, struggling with Iroquois tribes for control of the area's fur trade, erected walls encircling the settlement for defense. Today the remnants of those ramparts delineate the boundaries of Vieux Montréal, the city's first settlement, on the stretch of river bank between **rue McGill, Notre-Dame,** and **Berri.** The fortified walls have crumbled, but the politicos' and merchants' beautiful 17th- and 18th-century mansions have retained their splendor. **Guidatour** leads official **walking tours** of Vieux Montréal, departing from the Basilique Notre-Dame de Montréal. *(☎844-4021 or 800-363-4021; www.guidatour.qc.ca. 1½hr. tours daily mid-June to Sept. 11am, 1:30, 4pm in English, and 11am in French; from late May to mid-June and in early Oct. tours on Sa-Su. only $14, seniors and students $12, ages 6-12 $5.50.)*

⊠BASILIQUE NOTRE-DAME DE MONTRÉAL. Towering above the Place d'Armes and its memorial to Maisonneuve is the most beautiful church in Montréal. One of North America's largest churches and a historic center for the city's Catholic population, the neo-Gothic **Basilique Notre-Dame de Montréal** has hosted everyone from Québec separatists to the Pope since it opened in 1823. Don't miss the

Sacred Heart Chapel's bronze altarpiece and the sound-and-light spectacular *Et la lumière fut*—"And then there was light"—which illuminates the history of Montréal and the church. *(110 rue Notre-Dame Ouest. Métro: Place-D'Armes. ☎842-2925; www.basiliquenddm.org. Open M-Sa 8am-4:30pm, Su 1:30-4pm. Free for Mass; otherwise entrance $4, ages 7-17 $2. Light show Tu-Th 6:30pm, F 6:30pm and 8:30pm, Sa 7pm and 8:30pm. $10, seniors $9, ages 17 and under $5.)*

CHAPELLE NOTRE-DAME-DE-BON-SECOURS/ MUSÉE DE MARGUERITE-BOURGEOYS. Marguerite Bourgeoys was the first teacher in Montréal, the founder of the first order of non-cloistered nuns, and the driving force behind the construction of the first stone chapel, built on the waterfront as a sailor's refuge. The chapel now houses the museum that bears her name, displaying archaeological treasures from Montréal's history. *(400 rue St-Paul Est. Métro: Champ-de-Mars. ☎282-8670; www.marguerite-bourgeoys.com. Museum and chapel open May-Oct. Tu-Su 10am-5pm; Nov. to mid-Jan. Tu-Su 11am-3:30pm. $6, seniors $4; call for child, group, and family rates.)*

CHÂTEAU RAMEZAY. The grand **Château Ramezay** presides over Vieux-Montréal as a testament to the power of the French viceroy for whom it was built. Constructed in 1705, converted to a museum in 1895, and renovated in the summer of 2002, the Château is a living record of Québec's heritage. The Governor's garden is noteworthy, as is the basement exhibit recreating the interior of an 18th-century home. *(280 rue Notre-Dame Est. Métro: Champ-de-Mars. ☎861-3708; www.chateauramezay.qc.ca. Open June-Sept. daily 10am-6pm; Oct.-May Tu-Su 10am-4:30pm. $7, seniors $6, students $5, under 18 $4; families $15. Tours available by reservation. Wheelchair accessible.)*

ÎLE STE-HÉLÈNE AND ST-LAURENT

By car, take either of two bridges to Île Ste-Hélène: the Pont Jacques-Cartier or the Pont de la Concorde. By public transit, take the yellow Métro line to Île Ste-Hélène and catch bus #167 to the island's attractions. The best among many good reasons to visit Île Ste-Hélène, **La Ronde** amusement park boasts a free-fall drop and the tallest wooden roller coaster in the world. *(Métro: Jean-Drapeau. ☎397-2000; www.laronde.com. Rides open daily in summer 10am-10:30pm, grounds open until midnight; low-season hours vary. 1-day pass $30, ages 3-11 $19.)* Every Saturday night in June, and Wednesday and Saturday nights in July, La Ronde hosts the **Mondial SAQ,** the world's most prestigious fireworks competition. View the sky explosions free from Mont-Royal or the crowded Pont Jacques-Cartier. *(Info ☎397-2000, tickets ☎800-361-4595; www.montrealfeux.com. Tickets $30-40, children $20.)* At the popular **Casino de Montréal,** 120 tables and 3000 slot machines stay buzzing all day, every day. *(☎392-2746 or 800-665-2274; www.casino-de-montreal.com. Open 24hr.)* Built in 1820 to defend Canada's inland waterways from imperialistic Americans, **Le Vieux Fort** now protects the **Stewart Museum,** which documents the discovery and colonization of North America. It houses a large collection of weapons, war instruments, and strategic maps and stages a musket firing by costumed colonials. *(Métro: Jean-Drapeau. ☎861-6701; www.stewart-museum.org. Open mid-May to mid-Oct. daily 10am-6pm; late Oct. to early May M and W-Su 10am-5pm. Musket firing in summer daily 3pm. $10, students and seniors $8, under 7 free; families $20.)*

🏛 MUSEUMS

McCord Museum, 690 rue Sherbrooke Ouest (☎398-7100; www.mccord-museum.qc.ca). Métro: McGill or bus #24. Extracting Canada's history from everyday objects, exhibits range from toys to wedding gowns, lawn ornaments to photographs. The museum features a unique First Nations collection, Canada's most important costume collection, and an immense photographic archive. Open June-Sept. M-Sa 10am-6pm, Su 10am-5pm; Oct.-May Tu-Sa 10am-6pm, Su 10am-5pm. $10, seniors $7.50, students $5.50, ages 7-12 $3; families $20.

Musée des Beaux-Arts, 1380 and 1379 rue Sherbrooke Ouest (☎285-1600; www.mmfa.qc.ca). Métro: Guy-Concordia. About 5 blocks west of the McGill entrance, the museum's small permanent collection features art from ancient cultures through the 20th-century. Don't miss the collection of creative decorative arts, which includes an 18th-century French sleigh and a cactus hat stand. From Jan. 27-May 22, 2005, the museum will host the British Museum's famed Egyptian collection; June 9-Aug. 21, 2005, the paintings of American Edwin Holgate will be on display; Sept. 22, 2005-Jan. 8, 2006, classic and modern paintings from Provence will be shown. Open Tu-Su 11am-5pm. Guided tours W and Su 1:30 (French), 2:30pm (English). Permanent collection free. Temporary exhibits $12, students and seniors $6, under 12 $3; W 5:30-9pm half-price.

Pointe-à-Callière: Montréal Museum of Archaeology and History, 350 Place Royale (☎872-9150; www.pacmusee.qc.ca), off rue de la Commune near Vieux-Port. Métro: Place-d'Armes. This museum and national historic site gives an innovative underground tour of the city's past incarnations. Open late June to early Sept. M-F 10am-6pm, Sa-Su 11am-6pm; low-season Tu-F 10am-5pm, Sa-Su 11am-5pm. $10, seniors $7.50, students $6, ages 6-12 $3.50, under 5 free. Wheelchair accessible.

Musée d'Art Contemporain, 185 rue Ste-Catherine Ouest (☎847-6226; www.macm.org), at Jeanne-Mance. Métro: Place-des-Arts. Canada's premier modern art museum concentrates on the work of Canadian artists. The current rotation of the museum's 6000-piece collection focuses on developments of the 1940s, 50s, and 60s. Open Tu and Th-Su 11am-6pm, W 11am-9pm. $6, seniors $4, students $3, under 12 free; W 6-9pm free.

Canadian Centre for Architecture, 1920 av. Baile (☎939-7026; www.cca.qc.ca). Métro: Guy-Concordia or Atwater. Houses one of the world's most important collections of architectural prints, drawings, photographs, and books. Guided tours in French and English; call ahead for schedule. Open W and F-Su 10am-5pm, Th 10am-9pm. $8, seniors $6, students $5, under 12 free; Th after 5:30pm free.

🎭 ENTERTAINMENT

THEATER

Montréal lives up to its cultured reputation with a vast selection of theater in both French and English. The **Théâtre du Nouveau Monde,** 84 rue Ste-Catherine Ouest, stages only French productions. (☎878-7878, tickets 866-8668; www.tnm.qc.ca. Métro: Place-des-Arts. Tickets $36-42.) In mid-July, however, the theater hosts the bilingual **Festival Juste pour Rire/Just for Laughs** (☎790-4242; www.hahaha.com). The friendly **Théâtre du Rideau Vert,** 4664 rue St-Denis, puts on both *québécois* works and French adaptations of English plays. (☎844-1793; www.rideau-vert.qc.ca. Métro: Mont-Royal. Tickets $20-40.) The **Théâtre d'Aujourd'hui,** 3900 rue St-Denis, produces hip, original *québécois* shows. (☎282-3900; www.theatredau-jourdhui.qc.ca. Métro: Sherbrooke. Tickets $25, students $20, Th 2 for 1 admission.) The **National Theatre School of Canada,** 5030 rue St-Denis, stages excellent, renowned "school plays" during the school year. (☎842-7954; www.ent-nts.qc.ca. Most shows free.) The city's exciting **Place des Arts,** 260 bd. de Maisonneuve Ouest (☎842-2112; www.pda.qc.ca), at rue Ste. Catherine Ouest and Jeanne Mance, houses the **Opéra de Montréal** (☎985-2258; www.operademontreal.com; tickets $40-125), the **Montréal Symphony Orchestra** (☎842-9951; www.osm.ca; tickets $18-83), and **Les Grands Ballets Canadiens** (☎849-0269; www.grandsballets.qc.ca; tickets $25-85). **Théâtre Saint-Denis,** 1594 rue St-Denis (☎849-4211), hosts Broadway-style plays in French. Grab the *Calendar of Events* at tourist offices and newspaper stands, or call **Tel-Spec** for ticket info. (☎790-2222; ww.tel-spec.com. Open M-Sa 9am-9pm, Su noon-6pm.) **Admission Ticket Network** has tickets. (☎790-1245 or 800-361-459; www.admission.com. Open daily 8am-1am. Credit card required.)

MUSIC, FESTIVALS, AND SPORTS

Montréal might be in the running for festival capital of the world. To keep track of the offerings, pick up a copy of *Mirror* (in English) or *Voir* (in French) in any theater and many bars and cafes. From the Funk Brothers to Diana Krall, the **Festival International de Jazz de Montréal** (☎ 525-7732; www.montrealjazzfest.com), brings in over 300 performers in early July. Events cluster near Métro station **Place-des-Arts.** When Formula One car racing comes to Canada for mid-June's **Grand Prix of Canada** (☎ 350-0000; www.grandprix.ca), thousands swarm to Montréal to watch the race and party in the streets. Another popular events is **Mondial de la Bière,** when over 300 brands of beer, port, scotch, and whiskey are available for tasting in early June. (☎ 722-9640; www.festivalmondialbiere.qc.ca. Day pass $10.) Later in the month, the **Fringe Festival** (☎ 849-3378; www.montrealfringe.ca) arrives with theater, dance, and music events at various spots in the Plateau Mont-Royal. French-Canadian culture is celebrated at the high-spirited **Fête Nationale** (☎ 849-2560; www.cfn.org), on St-Jean-Baptiste Day, June 24, with parades, local music performances, and cultural events. In early August, **Divers/Cité** (☎ 285-4011; www.diverscite.org), a gay pride week, rocks the city in and around Emilie-Gamelin Park.

In summer, look out for **ventes-trottoirs,** "sidewalk sales" that shut down a major street for a day and night of pedestrian-only outdoor fun. In Vieux Montréal, street performers, artists, and *chansonniers* in various *brasseries* create summer evenings of clapping, stomping, and singing, especially on **St-Paul,** near the corner of St-Vincent. Check out **The Tams** in Parc Jeanne-Mance for a uniquely relaxing Sunday afternoon with bongos, dancing, and crafts. (May-Sept. Su 11am-7pm.)

Montréal also has its share of sporting events. Hockey's **Montréal Canadiens** (nicknamed Les Habitants—"the locals"—or Les Habs) play at the **Centre Bell,** 1250 rue de la Gauchetière Ouest. (Info ☎ 989-2841, tickets 790-1245. Métro: Bonaventure. Call in advance for tickets. $23-150.) Dress and behavior at games can be quite formal. The **Montréal Expos** play ball at **Olympic Stadium,** 4549 Pierre-de-Coubertin Ave., from April to September. (☎ 846-3976 or 800-463-9767; www.montreal-expos.com. Metro: Viau, Pie-IX. Tickets $10-40.) The team is currently searching for a new home; check a schedule before heading to the stadium. If you love your bike, get in on the action during the one-day **Tour de l'Île,** an amateur cycling event held in early June with over 45,000 participants. (☎ 521-8356. Register by Apr.)

⊠ NIGHTLIFE

A loosely enforced drinking age of 18 plus thousands of taps flowing until 3am equals the unofficially titled "nightlife capital of North America." Most pubs and bars offer a happy hour, usually 5-8pm, when bottled drinks may be two-for-one and mixed drinks may be double their usual potency. In summer, restaurants spill onto outdoor patios. To avoid crowds of drunken American college students, duck into one of the laid-back local pubs along **rue St-Denis** north of Ste-Catherine. Or carouse with the drunken American college students on **rue Ste-Catherine,** especially around **rue Crescent.** The pedestrian-only section of **rue Prince Arthur** at **rue St-Laurent** offers tamer fun. Most of Montréal's gay and lesbian hotspots can be found in the **gay village,** along rue St-Catherine between St-Hubert and Papineau; while many of the establishments cater to men, there are a few lesbian-friendly locales.

ST-LAURENT/PRINCE ARTHUR

⊠ **Café Campus,** 57 rue Prince Arthur (☎ 844-1010; www.cafecampus.com), at Ste. Dominique. Unlike the touristy meat-market discothèques, this hip, 3-story club attracts a friendly student and 20-something crowd. Drinks $4-5.50. Regular theme nights include: Su French music, Th 90s hits, and Tu Retro (hits from the 50s-80s). Cover $2-5, live music $5-15. Open daily 8:30pm-3am. Wheelchair accessible.

Biftech, 3702 rue St-Laurent (☎844-6211), near rue Prince Arthur. Start your night like the college kids, eating free popcorn and enjoying the 2-for-1 specials at this always popular bar. 2 gin and tonics $6, rum and Cokes $5.50. Open daily 2pm-3am.

The Dome, 32 rue Ste-Catherine Est (☎875-5757; www.clubdome.com), at the corner of St-Laurent. An international crowd bumps and grinds to hip hop and R&B beneath a laser show. Cover $5. Open F-Sa 10pm-3am.

CRESCENT/STE-CATHERINE/PEEL

🔊 **Brutopia,** 1219 rue Crescent (☎393-9277), between Ste-Catherine and Blvd. René Lévesque. This friendly microbrewery boasts 8 house beers. The I.P.A. is most popular, and the honey wheat brew is also tasty. Happy hour daily 3-8pm with $4 pints. Live music Tu-Su 10pm-3am, Sa-Su 5-9pm. Open M-Th and Sa-Su 3pm-3am, F noon-3am.

Pub McKibbins, 1426 rue Bishop (☎288-1580). Fine fermented drinks are served within the warmly lit walls of this Irish pub. Trophies and brass tokens ornament the walls and dartboards entertain the crowds, while a fieldstone fireplace warms the quarters in winter. Ground yourself with the shepherd's pie ($9) before the next Guinness ($7). Live (often Irish) music M-Sa. Open daily 11am-3am; kitchen closes 10pm.

Peel Pub, 1107 rue St-Catherine Ouest (☎844-7296; www.peelpub.com), downstairs, at rue Peel. Tourists crowd into this friendly sports bar for chicken wings and cheap booze. Wings $0.59 each M-Sa, $.09 Su with drinks. Daily food and drink specials. Happy hour 3pm-7pm. Raunchy "Jell-O wrestling" Tu 11pm. Open daily 8am-3am.

GAY VILLAGE

Le Drugstore, 1366 rue Ste-Catherine Est (☎524-1960). Métro: Beaudry. A 3-story gay megaplex basking in the glow of multicolored neon lights, with a bar and disco. Friendly staff and DJ on weekends. Open daily 8am-3am. Ground floor is wheelchair accessible.

Cabaret Mado, 1115 Ste-Catherine Est (☎525-7566; www.cabaretmado.bellnet.ca). Métro: Beaudry. Home of the wildest drag shows in town. Drinks $4-5. Come Tu for "le Mardi a Mado." Straight-friendly, especially Sa-Su. Cover varies. Open daily 11am-3am.

MONT-TREMBLANT ☎819

The summit of Mont-Tremblant presides over the rolling hills of the Laurentians and an outstanding array of outdoor attractions. In the winter, Mont-Tremblant offers some of the best downhill skiing in eastern North America, and a huge network of pristine trails for cross-country skiing and snowshoeing. Summer brings streams of tourists to the region's mountains, lakes, and rivers, where tons of activities await. Mont-Tremblant is Québec's playground and one of its most frequented tourist destinations; prices reflect this popularity. Fortunately, the town is also the gateway to Québec's largest national park, Parc du Mont-Tremblant, a wilderness vast enough to accommodate all sorts of activities at more reasonable rates.

▬ TRANSPORTATION

Mont-Tremblant is 80km north of Montréal, up Rte. 15N, which turns into Hwy. 117; take Exit 119 (Montée Ryan). There are free parking lots close to the mountain; a free and frequent shuttle bus runs between the lots and the resort village. **Limocar** runs buses from the central bus station in Montréal to Saint-Jovite. The stop is at the restaurant La Belle Province, 1014 rue St-Jovite. (☎866-700-8899; www.limocar.ca. $24, students and seniors $18, ages 5-12 $14, children under 4 $3.) During ski season, shuttles also run from Dorval airport, but can be expensive. **Transport en Commun** provides local bus service in the Tremblant area. Routes run 6am-11:40pm every 30min. during summer and ski season, and hourly otherwise, and stop at numerous locations in all three villages that make up the area. (☎425-8441. $1, children 7 and under free. Call for exact schedule.) **Taxi: Saint-Jovite Taxi** ☎425-3212. **Tourisme Mont-Tremblant**, at 5080 Montée Ryan at the intersection with ch. du Village (Rte. 327), has info (☎425-1023; www.tourismemonttremblant.com).

⚡ 🛈 ORIENTATION AND PRACTICAL INFORMATION

The Mont-Tremblant consists of three distinct and formerly independent villages. Mont-Tremblant itself refers to the resort village at the base of the mountain, and also may be called "the resort." The colorful roofs, pedestrian-only thoroughfares, upscale boutiques, and generally overpriced restaurants reflect the European-inspired vision of Intrawest, the builder and operator of the resort. The old village of Mont-Tremblant, now referred to as "the village," lies 2km from the resort down ch. du Village, and is home to more affordable restaurants, shops, and accommodations. Finally, the village of Saint-Jovite, immediately off of Hwy. 117 and 10km from the mountain down Montée Ryan, has a larger collection of independent shops and services, as well as the area's chain restaurants, retailers, and lodging options. **Internet Access:** The **public library,** 901 rue St-Saute in the old village, has free access. (☎425-2337. Open Tu and Th-F 10am-8pm, W 10am-5pm, Sa-Su 10am-1pm.) **Post Office**: 1893 ch. du Village, in the old village. (☎425-3358. Open M-F 8:30am-5:45pm, Sa 8:30am-noon.) **Postal Code**: J8E 1B0. **Area Code**: 819.

🛏 ACCOMMODATIONS

There are many expensive hotels and condos at the base of the mountain; it may be possible, however, to get decent group rates on a condo, especially during low-season. Call central reservations at ☎888-289-8888 or visit http://tremblant.com. Fortunately, ◪**HI-Auberge de Jeunesse Village Mont-Tremblant ❶**, 2213 ch. du Village, in the old village, provides a warm and lively environment on the cheap. In summer, take a boat out on Lake Moore from the dock in the backyard (free) or build a fire inside a teepee. The hostel offers Internet access ($2 per 20min.), a cafe and bar, fireplace, kitchen, laundry ($3.25 per load), TV room, pool table, volleyball court, patio, bike rental ($16 per half-day), bike or ski storage, and free parking. Do not bring in outside alcohol—it's not allowed since there is an on-site bar where you can get a beer for $4 or a pitcher for $14. (☎425-3760 or 866-425-6008; www.hostellingtremblant.com. Continental breakfast $5. Linen $2. Reception 8am-midnight. Dorms $22, nonmembers $27; doubles $28/$33.)

There are also a number of campgrounds in the area. Camp at a secluded campground in a pine forest, or sleep in a teepee at **Labelle et La Rouge ❶**, 252 des Geais Bleus, in Labelle 10km from Mont-Tremblant. The weather-proofed teepees have four beds around a firepit. The river and its surrounding areas are easily accessible, and kayaks ($10 per hr.), canoes ($12 per hr.), and bikes ($12 per hr.) are available to rent. (☎686-1954. Check-in 4-9pm; make arrangements in advance to extend hours in either direction. Check-out 1pm. Open mid-May to mid-Oct. Teepees $20 per person for group of four, $25 for three, $30 for two, and $60 for one. Tent sites $13. 2-person cottage $45.) Within the municipality of Mont-Tremblant, the biggest campground is **Diable ❶**, 140 rue Régimbald, in the Saint-Jovite sector, with 350 standard sites in the woods or along the river, with toilets, showers, and swimming pool. (☎425-5501; www.campingdiable.ca. Tent sites $22, with hookup $31. Check-in 1-10pm. Check-out 1pm.) Mont-Tremblant National Park also has terrific camping options in season (p. 188).

📋📝 FOOD AND NIGHTLIFE

Locals flock to **Lorraine ❷,** 2000 ch. du Village, in the old village. If you go for breakfast (6-11am), the french toast ($5.50) is a good choice; grilled cheese ($3.10) or lasagna ($9.50) are lunch and dinner favorites. (☎ 425-5566. Open daily 6am-10pm.) The cheapest meal on the mountain itself is at **Pita Express ❷,** La Tour des Voyageurs II, where sandwiches full of meat, fish, or vegetables are $6-8. Mention that you learned about Pita Express in *Let's Go* and receive a 15% discount. (☎ 681-4949. Open June-Aug. 9am-9pm; Sept.-May 11am-5pm.) At **Au Grain de Café,** on Place St-Bernard in the resort village, terrific espresso starts at $1.66, and a 12oz. chai latte is $3.62. They also offer (pricey) Internet access—$3 per 10min. (☎ 681-4567. Open in summer and winter 7:30am-11pm; in spring and fall 7:30am-6pm.)

The best nightlife is in the center of the resort village. 🔆**Le P'tit Caribou,** at 115 rue Kandahar, is famous for its wild *aprés ski* atmosphere all year long. Knock back a couple of cold ones (pints $7), then join the crowds dancing on the bar. (☎ 681-4500. Live music Th. 21+. Cover Th-Sa $5-10. Open daily 3pm-3am.) A slightly younger set hangs out next door at **Café D'Epoque,** 3005 ch. Principal, where a DJ spins nightly. (☎ 681-4554. 18+. Cover Th-Sa $5. Open daily July-Aug. 3pm-3am, Sept.-June 8pm-3am.) For a more laid-back evening, consider **La Diable,** 3005 ch. Principal, a microbrewery that serves six original beers (pints $7). During the summer, people drink their brews on a wraparound terrace. (☎ 681-4546. Open daily 11:30am-1am, kitchen closes at 10pm.)

🏔 OUTDOOR ACTIVITIES

Québec's long, cold winters bless Tremblant with many months of terrific powdery snow. Skiers and snowboarders can descend on all sides of the mountain, on diverse trails suitable for all levels of proficiency. In 2003-04, lift tickets cost $63, ages 13-17 $47, ages 6-12 $36. Ski and snowboard rentals were $28, ages 12 and under $18. Prices may rise a bit for the 2004-05 season. Lifts generally run 8:30am-4pm. *Temperatures and wind chills can be extremely cold; consult a weather forecast and dress appropriately.* Cross-country skiing and snowshoeing trails are available as well. Enthusiasts flock to the mountain in summer, too. The gondola whisks riders up to the summit in 10min. Once on top, 360° views and numerous hiking trails await. At the bottom of the mountain, the activities center offers exciting but expensive pursuits like renting a bike, tackling the ropes course, riding a horse, or going waterskiing. (☎ 866-253-9877; www.tremblant.ca. Ticket office is at the top of the pedestrian village, opposite the base of the gondola. Gondola ride $13, seniors $12, ages 6-17 $11. Bike rentals $15 per 2hr., $20 per 4hr., $25 per day; ages 13 and under $12/$15/$19. Ropes course $33, students and seniors $23, children $18. Horseback riding $40 per hr., $59 per 2hr. Waterskiing and wakeboarding $32 per 10min., $60 per 20min., $83 per 30min. Packages that include gondola rides and other activities can bring the tab down some.)

🚩 DAYTRIP FROM MONT-TREMBLANT

MONT-TREMBLANT NATIONAL PARK

About 30km from the village along Duplessis is Mont-Tremblant National Park, Québec's largest national park. The 1510 sq. km wilderness contains 400 lakes, and wolves, moose, bear, deer, otter, beaver, and other wildlife. Terrific outdoor options abound, like canoeing, kayaking, hiking, mountain biking, and camping. (☎ 688-2281. Park entrance $3.50, ages 6-17 $1.50. Maps $2.) The **Lac-Monroe Service Centre,** 10km from the entrance, rents equipment and takes canoers and kayakers to and from river access points. (Open mid-May to mid-Oct. 24hr.; rental desk M-F 9am-5pm, Sa-Su 8am-7pm. Canoe and solo kayak rental $13 per hr., $26 per 4hr., $37 per 24hr. 2-person kayaks $16/$22/$31. Transportation up or down river $42-75, depending on the route and number of people and boats. Canoe camping available, but reserve in advance. Bike rental $11 per hr., $22 per 4hr., $31 per 24hr.) Cyclists can ride to a waterfall down **Les Chutes-Croches,** and hikers have a huge variety of trails to choose from. **La Roche** (5km, 2hr.) is a pleasant, medium-difficulty trail that winds uphill beside a river, culminating in a terrific view of the Lac-Monroe glacier valley and the Mont-Tremblant ridge, all the way to the summit of Tremblant itself. The trailhead is 500m from Lac-Monroe service center. There are 349 serviced and 229 primitive camp sites in the Diable sector of the park. **La Bacagnole ❶,** on the shore of Lac-Monroe 2km from the service center, is a popular option, with showers and toilets. The service center, with phones, bathrooms, and showers, is open 24hr. for campers at primitive sites. (Reservations ☎800-665-6527 8:30am-9pm, www.sepaq.com. Tent sites $19.)

QUÉBEC CITY ☎418

Dubbed the Gibraltar of America because of the stone escarpments and military fortifications protecting the port, Québec City—generally shortened to just Québec [KAY-beck]—sits high on the rocky heights of Cap Diamant, where the St. Lawrence narrows and is joined by the St. Charles River. Passing through the portals of North America's only walled city is like stepping into a European past. Horse-drawn carriages greet visitors on the winding maze of streets in the Old City (Vieux Québec) and there are enough sights and museums to satisfy even the most voracious history buff. Canada's oldest city also boasts a thriving French culture, standing apart from Montréal as the center of true *québécois* heritage.

▐ TRANSPORTATION

Airport: Jean Lesage International Airport (☎640-2700; www.aeroportdequebec.com) is about 15min. from downtown but inaccessible by public transit. Taxi downtown $25.

Trains: VIA Rail, 450 rue de la Gare du Palais (☎692-3940 or 888-842-7245), in Québec City. Open M-F 5:30am-8:30pm, Sa-Su 7:30am-8:30pm. To: **Montréal** (3hr., 4 per day, $68); **Ottawa** (via Montréal, 6-8hr., 3 per day, $98); **Toronto** (8-11hr., 6 per day, $167). Seniors 10% off on economy fares, students with ID 35%, children 11 and under 50%.

Buses: Orléans Express, 320 rue Abraham Martin (☎525-3000). Open M-Sa 5:30am-1am, Su 6:30am-1am. To **Montréal** (3-4hr.; every hr. 5:30am-10:30pm, $39, students and seniors $33, ages 5-12 $23, under 4 $5) and places in the **US** via Montréal.

Public Transit: Réseau de transport de la Capitale (RTC), 270 rue des Rocailles (route and schedule info ☎627-2511; www.stcuq.qc.ca). Open M-F 6:30am-10pm, Sa-Su 8am-10pm. Buses generally operate daily 6am-1am. $1.95, students and seniors $1.35, children free.

Taxi: Taxi Coop Québec ☎525-5191. **Taxi de Luxe** ☎564-0555.

Driver/Rider Service: Allô Stop, 467 rue St-Jean (☎522-0056), will match you with a driver heading for Montréal ($15). Must be a member ($6 per year, drivers $7). Open M and Sa-Su 9am-6pm, W-F 9am-7pm.

Car Rental: Solimpax, 900 bd. Pierre Bertrand (☎681-0678). Open M-F 7am-8pm, Sa-Su 8am-4pm.

Bike Rental: Cyclo Services, 160 rue du Quai St-André (☎692-4052 or 877-692-4050). $10 per 1hr., $14 per 2hr., $25 per 24hr.

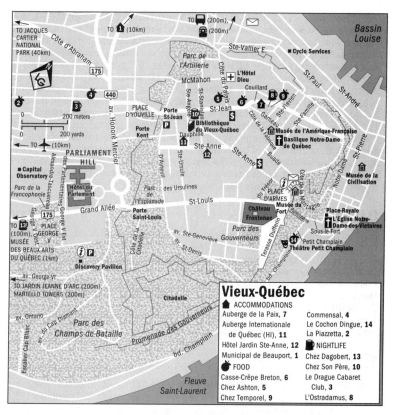

Vieux-Québec

⌂ ACCOMMODATIONS
Auberge de la Paix, **7**
Auberge Internationale
de Québec (HI) **11**
Hôtel Jardin Ste-Anne, **12**
Municipal de Beauport, **1**
🍴 FOOD
Casse-Crêpe Breton, **6**
Chez Ashton, **5**
Chez Temporel, **9**

Commensal, **4**
Le Cochon Dingue, **14**
La Piazzetta, **2**
🍸 NIGHTLIFE
Chez Dagobert, **13**
Chez Son Père, **10**
Le Drague Cabaret
Club, **3**
L'Ostradamus, **8**

✳🔢 ORIENTATION AND PRACTICAL INFORMATION

Québec's main thoroughfares service both **Vieux Québec** (Old City) and the more modern city outside it, and generally run parallel in an east-west direction. Within Vieux Québec, the main streets are **St-Louis, Ste-Anne,** and **St-Jean.** Most streets in Vieux Québec are one-way. The major exception is **rue d'Auteuil,** bordering the walls inside Vieux Québec. Outside the walls, both St-Jean and St-Louis continue; St-Jean eventually joins ch. Ste-Foy, and St-Louis becomes **Grande Allée. Boulevard René-Lévesque,** the other major street outside the walls, runs between St-Jean and St-Louis. The **Basse-ville** (lower town) is separated from the **Haute-ville** (upper town, a.k.a. Old Québec) by an abrupt cliff roughly paralleled by rue St-Vallier Est. Much of the city is quite hilly; be prepared to walk up and down staircases or steep hills. Street parking in the city can be difficult, but pricey garages are plentiful (about $14 per 24hr.).

Visitor Info: Bureau d'information touristique du Vieux-Québec, 835 av. Wilfred Laurier (☎641-6290; www.quebecregion.com), in the Old City just outside the walls. Open late June to Aug. daily 8:30am-7:30pm; Sept. to mid-Oct. daily 8:30am-6:30pm; mid-Oct. to late June M-Sa 9am-5pm, Su 10am-4pm. **Centre Touriste de Québec,** 12 rue

Ste-Anne (☎877-266-5687; www.bonjourquebec.com), across from Château Frontenac, deals primarily with provincial tourism; they can also help with lodging reservations. Open daily late June to Aug. 8:30am-7:30pm; Sept. to mid-June 9am-5pm.

Currency Exchange: Caisse populaire Desjardins du Vieux-Québec, 19 rue Des Jardins (☎694-1774; www.cpvquebec.com). $2 or 2% commission on transactions. Open daily Apr. to mid-Oct. 9am-6pm, mid-Oct. to Mar. 10am-3pm.

Hotlines: Tél-Aide, ☎686-2433. Operates daily noon-midnight. **Viol-Secours (sexual assault line),** ☎522-2120. Counselors on duty M-F 9am-4pm and on-call 24hr. **Centre de Prévention du Suicide,** ☎683-4588. **Gay Hotline,** ☎888-505-1010.

Medical Services: L'Hôtel Dieu, 11 Côte du Palais (☎525-4444), just down the hill from rue St-Jean.

Internet Access: Bibliothéque Vieux-Québec, 37 rue Ste-Angèle (☎691-6357). Open Tu and Th noon-8pm, W and F noon-5pm, Sa-Su 1-5pm.

Post Office: 300 rue St-Paul (☎694-6175). Open M-F 8am-5:45pm. **Postal Code:** G1K 3W0. **Area Code:** 418.

■ ACCOMMODATIONS

There are a number of B&Bs in Québec, many of which offer good deals. **Centre Touriste de Québec** can help with referrals. Rooms start at $55 for one or $75 for two people, and hosts are usually bilingual. You can obtain a list of nearby **campgrounds** at the same office, or write to **Tourisme Québec,** 1255 rue Peel, Montréal QC, H3C 2W3. (☎266-5687; www.bonjourquebec.com. Open daily 9am-5pm.) Accommodations inside the old city do not have their own parking; you'll either have to find street parking or park in a garage for a special rate ($11 per day).

■**Auberge de la Paix,** 31 rue Couillard (☎694-0735). Take St-Jean into Vieux Québec; when it splits 3 ways, keep to the far left and you'll be on Couillard. This friendly, convenient "peace hostel" (look for the peace sign above the door) is tidy and modern, with 60 beds in 14 coed rooms. There are no locks on the doors, but this doesn't seem to be a problem. New kitchen, smoking lounge, patio, and courtyard. Internet ($3 per 10min.). Continental breakfast. Free lockers. Linen $2.50. Check-out 11am. Curfew 2am, but 24hr. access to facilities. Reservations required July-Aug. Dorms $20. ❶

Auberge Internationale de Québec (HI), 19 rue Ste-Ursule (☎694-0755). From the bus station, take rue St-Nicolas uphill; stay with it as it changes to rue St-Vallier Est and then to Côte du Palais. Turn right onto St-Jean, then left onto Ste-Ursule. In three interconnected houses, this hostel has TV, living room, kitchen, ping-pong and pool tables, cafe, bar (open 5pm-3am; live music twice weekly), patio, and in-house theater. Internet access. Laundry. Lockers $2. Reception 24hr. Check-out 11am. Reservations recommended July-Aug. Dorms $20, nonmembers $24; singles $50/$54, with bath $65/$69; doubles $55/$59, with bath $69/$73; $5 for each additional person. ❶

Hôtel Jardin Ste-Anne, 10 rue Ste-Anne (☎694-1720; www.jardinsteanne.com). Follow the directions to the HI hostel (above). At the end of Ste-Ursule, turn left on Ste-Anne, and the hotel will be on your right. By car, follow St-Louis into the Old City, turn left on rue du Fort, and the first left will be Ste-Anne. Bear left as the road splits, and the hotel will be on your left. Modern and quiet despite its central location, Ste-Anne's is charming. 18 rooms with Internet, A/C, cable, and private bath. Continental breakfast $5. Reservations recommended at least 3 weeks ahead in summer. Rooms $69-136. ❹

Municipal de Beauport, 95 rue de la Serenité (☎641-6112), in Beauport. Take Autoroute 40E, get off at Exit 321 at rue Labelle onto Hwy. 369, turn left, and follow the signs marked "camping." Bus #55 will also take you to this pleasant 136-site campground on a hill over the Montmorency River. Swimming pool, free showers, laundry facilities, and plenty of picnic tables. Canoes $4 per hr. Open June to early Sept. Sites $22, with hookup $27; $135/$165 per week. ❶

🍴 L'HAUTE CUISINE

Rue de Buade, St-Jean, and Cartier, and the **Place Royale** and **Petit Champlain** areas, generally offer the widest selection of food and drink. The **Grande Allée** sings a siren's song to the hungry, but its prices may encourage you to keep strolling. A walk down St-Jean away from the old city reveals a host of fun restaurants, ice creameries, and food markets. A filling but inexpensive meals is a *croque monsieur*, a large, open-faced sandwich with ham and melted cheese (about $7). French onion soup, slathered with cheese, can be found in virtually every restaurant and cafe. It usually comes with baguettes or *tourtiére*, a thick meat pie. Other specialties include the ever-versatile *crêpe*. For fast-food until 4am, head to one of **Chez Ashton's** 26 locations in Québec City (one is right off St-Jean, across from the hospital, at 54 Cote du Palais, ☎ 692-3055). *Poutine* (french fries, gravy, and cheese curds), their specialty, ranges $2.85-6.35.

🍴 **Commensal,** 860 rue St-Jean (☎ 647-3733). Two blocks outside the gates. Soothe your body with organic food and relax your mind in the calm interior of this vegetarian cafeteria. Food served buffet-style and sold by weight. Expect to pay $6-10 for a meal. Vegan-friendly. Excellent lasagna, seitan "beef," and vegan carrot cake. 10% student discount with ID. Open daily 11am-9:30pm. ❷

🍴 **Casse-Crêpe Breton,** 1136 rue St-Jean (☎ 692-0438), is a fabulous deal. Create your own mix-and-match dinner *crêpe* ($4-7), then top it off with a delightful dessert *crêpe* stuffed with fresh fruit or other sugary fillings ($4). Open daily 7am-11pm. ❶

Chez Temporel, 25 rue Couillard (☎ 694-1813). This genuine *café québécois* is tucked discreetly in a side alley off rue St-Jean, near the Auberge de la Paix. All coffee drinks are made with excellent espresso giving them a unique flavor ($4.50). Salads ($5-8) and soups ($2-5). Excellent quiches $7.50. Open M-F 7am-1am, Sa-Su 7am-2am. ❶

Le Cochon Dingue, 46 bd. Champlain (☎ 692-2013), which means "crazy pig," is becoming a culinary landmark for its French and *québécois* cuisine. Most popular is the steak and fries (6oz. for $14). After dinner, go hog-wild with some strawberry cheesecake ($6.95). Open June-Aug. M-Th and Su 7am-11pm, F 7am-midnight, Sa 8am-midnight; Sept.-May M-F 7am-11pm, Sa-Su 8am-11pm. ❷

La Piazzetta, 707 rue St-Jean (☎ 529-7489; www.resto-piazzetta.com), a few blocks from the city walls. Piazzetta injects a carnival atmosphere into its Italian creations. Sit in one of the wildly shaped chairs and enjoy the popular pizza "Generosa" (with ham, vegetables, and swiss cheese; $17 for a 13 in. pizza). Sangria $5.50. Brio, Italian soda, $2.50. Open Su-Th 11am-1pm, F-Sa 11am-midnight. ❸

👁 SIGHTS

Most of the city's historic attractions are inside the **Fortifications of Québec,** the wall that surrounds Vieux Québec. Monuments are marked and explained, usually in French; it's often easier to check out the walking tours in the free *Québec City and Area Tourist Guide,* at any visitors center. Although it takes one to two days to explore Vieux Québec's streets and sites on foot, it is the best way to absorb its charm. The **horse-drawn carriage tours,** while pricey ($60 per tour), can be fun. Find carriages on the Grande Allée, or call *Calèches du Vieux Québec* (☎ 683-9222). The **Funiculaire** tramway takes passengers between the Haute-ville, Place Royale, and the Quartier Petit-Champlain. (☎ 692-1132. Open 7:30am-11:45pm. $1.50.)

BATTLEFIELDS. The **Parc des Champs-de-Bataille,** or **Plains of Abraham,** adjacent to the Citadel along av. George-VI and accessible from Grande Allée, has on its grounds an astounding assortment of historical, cultural, and natural offerings. The **Discovery Pavilion,** near St-Louis Gate and the Manège Militaire, is the primary information desk for the park and houses the new multimedia **Canada Odyssey,** a hokey but informative virtual tour of Canadian military, agricultural, and natural history. *(Pavilion: ☎648-4071. Open daily mid-June to mid-Oct. 8:30am-5:30pm; mid-Oct. to mid-June 8:30am-5pm. Wheelchair accessible. Canada Odyssey: ☎648-4071; www.canadaodyssey.com. Open daily mid-June to mid-Oct. 10am-5:30pm; mid-Oct. to mid-June 10am-5pm. $6.50, seniors and ages 13-17 $5.50, families $20.)* To enjoy the battlefields beautiful natural setting, visit the **Jardin Jeanne d'Arc,** a serene spot with over 150 flower species. The **Martello Towers,** defensive structures built by the British to halt an expected American attack before the War of 1812, have exhibits on the day-to-day lives of soldiers in Tower 1, and the "Council of War," an award-winning period mystery dinner, in Tower 2. *(Tower 1: Open mid-June to Aug. daily 10am-5:30pm; Sept. to mid-Oct. Sa-Su 10am-5:30pm or by reservation. $4, seniors and ages 13-17 $3, families $12. "Council of War": ☎649-6157. Runs July-Aug. Sa in French, Su in English at 6pm; also on some holidays. $32, seniors and ages 13-17 $29. Reservations required.)*

PETIT-CHAMPLAIN. Cafes, craft shops, trendy boutiques, and restaurants line either side of crowded **Rue du Petit-Champlain.** On summer evenings, the **Théâtre Petit Champlain** presents French-language plays with *québécois* music, singing, and dancing. *(68 rue du Petit-Champlain. ☎692-2631. Open July 21-Aug. 21. Most shows $20-30.)* **L'Eglise Notre-Dame-des-Victoires,** dating back to 1688, is the oldest church in Canada. *(32 rue Sous-le-Fort. ☎692-1650. Open May to mid-Oct. M-Sa 9am-5pm, Su 1-5pm; mid-Oct. to Apr. daily 10am-4pm. Free.)*

INSIDE THE WALLS. The **Château Frontenac,** with its grand architecture and green copper roofs, is perhaps the most recognizable structure in the city and is thought to be the most photographed hotel in the world. A costumed guide leads visitors through the magnificent hotel. *(1 rue des Carrièrres. ☎691-2166. Tours on the hr. May to mid-Oct. daily 10am-6pm; mid-Oct. to Apr. Sa-Su noon-5pm; reservations highly recommended. $7, seniors $6.25, ages 6-16 $4.50.)* With its shimmering golden altar and ornate stained-glass windows, the **Basilique-Cathédral Notre-Dame de Québec** is one of the oldest and most stunning cathedrals in North America. *(At rue de Buade and Ste-Famille. ☎694-0665; www.patrimoine-religieux.com. Open daily 7:30am-4:30pm. Free.)*

CAP DIAMANT. The top of Cap Diamant, the headwall on which Québec is built, reveals a perfect view of the city. Just north is the **Citadel,** an active military base home to the only French infantry force in Canada, and the largest North American fortification still guarded by troops. *(On rue St-Louis at Côte de la Citadelle. ☎694-2815. Open daily Apr. to mid-May 10am-4pm; mid-May to mid-June 9am-5pm; mid-June to Aug. 9am-6pm; Sept. 9am-4pm; Oct. 10am-3pm. Changing of the guard daily late June to Aug. at 10am. Beating of the retreat F-Su 6pm. $8, seniors $5, under 18 $3; families $14.)*

PARLIAMENT HILL. Finished in 1886, the **Assemblée Nationale,** just outside the wall of the city, was designed in the style of Louis XIV. Lively debates can be observed from the visitors' gallery when parliament is in session, usually October through December and January through May. *(At av. Dufferin and Grand Allée Est. ☎643-7239; www.assnat.qc.ca. Open late June to early Sept. M-F 9am-4pm, Sa-Su 10am-4:30pm; mid-Sept to mid-June M-F 9am-4:30pm. Free tours last 30min. Reservations recommended.)* The **Capitol Observatory** offers breathtaking views of the city from 221m (725 ft.) above sea level, the highest observation spot in town. *(1037 rue de la Chevrotière, off Grande Allée. ☎644-9841; www.observatoirecapitale.org. Open late June to mid-Oct. daily 10am-5pm; in winter Tu-Su 10am-5pm. $5, students and seniors $4, under 12 free.)*

EASTERN CANADA

MUSEUMS. The **Musée de l'Amérique-Française,** on the grounds of the **Québec Seminary** across from the Basilica, has exhibits which recount the details of Francophone settlement in North America. *(2 Côte de la Fabrique. ☎692-2843; www.mcq.org. Open late June to Sept. daily 9:30am-5pm; in winter Tu-Su 10am-5pm. $5, seniors $4, students $3.)* The **Centre d'Interprétation Place-Royale** provides free 45min. tours of the **Place-Royale,** home to the oldest permanent European settlement in Canada (dating from 1608), and presents Québec's history through archaeological finds and multimedia presentations. *(27 rue Notre-Dame. Take rue Sous-le-Fort from the bottom of the Funiculaire. ☎646-3167; www.mcq.org. Museum admission $4, seniors $3.50, students $3, ages 2-16 $2. Open June-Sept. daily 9:30am-5pm; in winter Tu-Su 10am-5pm.)* The **Musée de la Civilisation** celebrates Québec's unique cultural heritage through everyday objects, interactive exhibits, and elaborate dioramas. Follow the series of signs at the bottom of the Funiculaire. *(85 rue Dalhousie. ☎643-2158; www.mcq.org. Free Internet on the 2nd fl. for museum patrons. Open late June to early Sept. daily 9:30am-6:30pm; mid-Sept to mid-June Tu-Su 10am-5pm. $8, seniors $7, students $5, children $3. Free Tu Nov.-May. Wheelchair accessible.)* In an old jail on the battlefield grounds, the **Musée national des beaux-arts du Québec** houses eclectic modern and colonial art, focusing on the works of *québécois* artists. The museum also hosts excellent special exhibits; sculptures by Camille Claudel and Auguste Rodin will be shown from late May to Sept, 2005. *(☎643-2150; www.mnba.qc.ca. Open June to early Sept. M-Tu and Th-Su 10am-6pm, W 10am-9pm; mid-Sept. to May Tu and Th-Su 10am-5pm, W 10am-9pm. Free; special exhibits $10, seniors $9, students $5, ages 12-16 $3. Wheelchair accessible.)* A sound-and-light show allows visitors to experience the battle of the Plains of Abraham on a 400 sq. ft. model of 1750 Québec at the popular **Musée du Fort.** *(10 rue Ste-Anne. ☎692-2175; www.museedufort.com. English showings on the hour. Open Feb.-Mar. Th-Su 11am-4pm; Apr.-Oct. daily 10am-5pm. $7.50, seniors $5.50, students $4.50.)*

FESTIVALS

Québec's most festive day of the year—eclipsing even Canada Day—is June 24, **la Fête nationale du Québec** or St-Jean-Baptiste Day (☎640-0799; www.snqc.qc.ca). This celebration of *québécois* culture features free concerts, a bonfire, and 5 million rip-roaring drunk acolytes of John the Baptist. Images of "Le Bonhomme de carnaval," the festival's friendly mascot, plaster the snow-covered city in anticipation of the raucous annual winter celebration, the **Carnaval de Québec** (☎521-5555; www.carnaval.qc.ca), which breaks the tedium of northern winters from January 28 to February 13, 2005. The annual **Summer Festival,** or **Festival d'Été** (☎888-992-5200; www.infofestival.com), with free outdoor concerts, packs hostels and crowds the streets in early July. Pins ($12) grant admission to the headlining events. Throughout the summer, the **Plein Art** (☎694-0260; www.salonplein-art.com) exhibition floods the Parc de la Francophonie on the Grande-Allée with arts and crafts. The **Edwin Bélanger Bandstand,** on the Plains of Abraham, hosts free outdoor concerts during the summer. (☎648-4050; www.ccbn-nbc.gc.ca.) In early June, **Le Grand Rire "Bleue"** brings comedy to the streets with shows and strolling performers. (☎647-2525; www.grandrirebleue.com.)

NIGHTLIFE

The Grande Allée's many restaurants are interspersed with *bar discothéques,* where twenty-somethings dance until dawn. Québec City's young, visible punk contingent clusters around rue St-Jean and several nearby side streets, but more laid-back nightclubs find a niche here, too.

Chez Dagobert, 600 Grande Allée Est (☎522-0393; www.dagobert.ca), saturates the air with techno and dance sounds that can be heard for blocks. 2 dance floors and an adjoining bar give room to mingle. Live rock nightly. 18+. Outside bar open June-Sept. daily 2pm-2am; inside club daily 10pm-3am.

Chez Son Père, 24 St-Stanislaus (☎692-5308; www.barchezsonpere.qc.ca), just up the hill from St-Jean. Relax to live *québécois* folk music or, better yet, sing along. Pitchers of beer $13. Live music Su-Th 10pm, F-Sa 9pm. No cover. Open daily 8pm-3am.

L'Ostradamus, 29 rue Couillard (☎694-9560), is a friendly and relaxing local bar with shows or DJs upstairs on the weekends. Pint of beer with tequila shooter $5. Cover for special club events $3-5. Open daily 8pm-3am.

Le Drague Cabaret Club, 815 rue St-Augustine (☎649-7212; www.ledrague.com), half-way down an alley off of St-Jean; look for the pride flag. With a cafe, terrace, bar, disco, and cabaret, Le Drague is Québec's premier gay hangout and nightspot. Su night drag shows (7:30, 9:30pm, midnight) are legendary. Mostly by gay men, but all are welcome. Karaoke W 8pm-2am. Internet terminals $1 per 20min. Open daily 10am-3am.

⧉ DAYTRIPS FROM QUÉBEC CITY

ILE-D'ORLÉANS

Originally named for the god of wine (and sex), **Ile-d'Orléans** was first called Ile de Bacchus because of its multitude of wild grapes. The island, about 5km downstream from Québec on the St-Lawrence, was cut off from the mainland until 1935, when today's bridge was built. Known as the "Garden of Québec" for its abundant agricultural products, the Ile-d'Orléans has retained its pastoral way of life and a reputation for cider, chocolate, and maple products. A summer visit rewards tourists with fragrant apple blossoms and fresh strawberries, while a fall stop reveals splendid autumn foliage. The 7000 inhabitants live in a landscape ranging from wide pastures to dense forests.

If you stay overnight, the **Auberge Le P'tit Bonheur ❶,** 186 Côte Lafleur, in St-Jean, is a 350-year-old farmhouse, offering many outdoor activities. (☎829-2588. Internet access, kitchen, TV room. Lunch $6. Dinner $12. Dorms $19; singles with private bath $65.) Down the road in the parish of St.-Jean, ▨**La Boulange ❶,** 2001 ch. Royal, is a splendid bakery specializing in $2-4 breads and $7-8 gourmet pizzas. (☎829-3162. Open late June to Sept. M-Sa 7:30am-6pm, Su 7:30am-5pm; Oct.-Dec. and Mar. to mid-June Sa-Su 7:30am-5pm.)

The best way to see the Ile-d'Orléans is by car, since the island isn't accessible by bike or public transit. Take Rte. 175 to Autoroute 440 Est, on to Hwy. 368, and follow signs for the bridge to the island. Stop at the **tourist office** (on the right, about 1km after the bridge ends) and grab a tourist guide. (☎828-9411. Guidebook $1. In-car audio guide $10.) A full circuit of the island is 67km and about 1½hr. Many of the cider presses and farms are open for tours; ask the tourist office. On the way out of Ile-d'Orléans, turn east onto Hwy. 138 to view the **Chute Montmorency** (Montmorency Falls), just off the highway. The main waterfall is higher than Niagara Falls, and in the winter, vapors from the falls form a frozen mist, that screens the running water and accumulates at the base, forming a "sugarloaf," a hill reaching heights over 30m. (☎663-3330; www.sepaq.com/chutemontmorency. $8.25 per car. Cable car to top of falls $5.75, children $3. Open daily 8:15am-9pm. Cable car runs mid-June to Aug. daily 8:30am-8:45pm; mid-Apr. to mid-June and Sept. to mid-Oct. daily 8:30am-6:45pm; mid-late Oct. daily 8:30am-6pm; Feb.-Mar. Sa-Su 9am-4pm.)

JACQUES-CARTIER NATIONAL PARK

Along the southern edge of the Laurentian Mountains 25 mi. from Québec City, Jacques-Cartier National Park is a slice of rugged wilderness following the Jacques-Cartier River as it winds through the mountains. Both experts and novices float down the river (including a 3km section of whitewater rapids for experienced kay-akers), hike over 100km of trails, camp, and, in the winter, snowshoe and cross-country ski. (Entrance $3.50, ages 6-17 $1.50; families $7. Park open mid-May to mid-Oct. and in winter for skiers and snowshoers.) The **visitors center,** 10km from the entrance along the main road, has info, interpretive programs, and river access. Call ahead to reserve campsites or boats. (☎848-3169 or 800-665-6527. Canoes $12 per hr., $24 per 4hr., $34 per day; kayaks $10/$20/$32. Park staff can transport kay-akers and canoers and their vessels to and from various landing points; consult the visitors center for route information and reservations. Boat transport ranges $6-22.) For a terrific view of the valley, hike **Les Loups,** at Km 15 on the main road. It takes about 1hr. up the medium-difficulty trail to reach the Belvedere lookout; those with water in their bottles and gas in their tanks can go on for another hour or so for an even more spectacular view. In October, visitors can see salmon swimming against the stream as they head upriver to their spawning grounds. The park has many **campgrounds ❶;** two are full service, the large **Les Alluvions,** by the visitors center, and **Le Bétulaie,** a kilometer up the road. (Sites in serviced campgrounds $23, with hookup $28. Primitive campsites $18. Open mid-May to mid-Oct.)

NEW BRUNSWICK

Powerful South Indian Ocean currents sweep around the tip of Africa and rip-ple through the Atlantic before coming to a spectacular finish at New Bruns-wick. The Bay of Fundy is home to the world's highest tides, which can rise and fall as much as 53 ft. Away from the ocean's violent influence, vast unpopu-lated stretches of timeless wilderness swathe the land. While over a third of the province's population is French-speaking (New Brunswick is Canada's only officially bilingual province), English is widely used throughout the province.

> **TIP** The tourist offices of the Maritime provinces make finding affordable accommo-dations and Internet access easier; stop at any provincial visitors center in New Brunswick, Nova Scotia, Newfoundland, or Prince Edward Island to pick up *Vacationing on a Budget: Summer Accommodations at Atlantic Canada Univer-sities, and* check out CAP, Community Access Program, for listings of locations with free or cheap public Internet. (☎866-569-8428; http://cap.ic.gc.ca)

⚡ PRACTICAL INFORMATION

Capital: Fredericton.

Visitor Info: Department of Tourism and Parks, P.O. Box 12345, Campbellton, E3N 3T6 (☎800-561-0123; www.tourismnewbrunswick.ca).

Drinking Age: 19. **Postal Abbreviation:** NB. **Sales Tax:** 15% HST.

SAINT JOHN   ☎506

Saint John (never abbreviated, in order to distinguish it from St. John's, Newfound-land) was literally founded overnight on May 18, 1783, by the United Empire Loyal-ists, a band of about 12,000 American colonists holding allegiance to the British crown. Saint John went on to become an important port city in the emerging Cana-dian confederation. Today, the town draws thousands of nature enthusiasts who flood here to witness the Bay of Fundy's tides and the "Reversing Falls."

⁊ PRACTICAL INFORMATION. Downtown (known as "uptown") is bounded by **Union Street** to the north, **Princess Street** to the south, **King Square** to the east, and **Market Square** and the harbor to the west. The Harbour Bridge (toll $0.25) on Hwy. 1 links Saint John to West Saint John, as does Hwy. 100. Reasonable parking can be found at Water St. and Chipman Hill. The **City Centre Information Centre**, at Market Sq., has info. (☎658-2855 or 866-463-8639; www.tourismsaintjohn.com. Open daily June-Aug. 9am-8pm; Sept.-Nov. 9am-6pm; Nov.-May 9:30am-6pm.) **VIA Rail** (☎888-842-6141) has a station in Moncton that services eastern Canada; take the SMT bus from Saint John to the station. **SMT**, 199 Chesley Dr., (☎648-3566; www.acadianbus.com; open daily 6:30am-8:30pm) sends buses to: **Halifax** (6½hr.; 2-4 per day; $73, students $62, seniors $55, children $37); **Moncton** (2hr., 2-4 per day, $27/$23/$20/$13); **Montréal** (12-14hr., 2-3 per day, $105/$95/$95/$53). **Saint John Transit** runs local transportation until about 12:30am. The main bus stop is in King Sq. (☎658-4700. $2, under 15 $1.75.) They also offer a tour of the city, leaving from Reversing Falls, the Rockwood Park Campground, and Barbours General Store at Loyalist Plaza. (Mid-June to early Oct. 2hr. $16, ages 6-14 $5.) **NFL Bay Ferries** (☎888-249-7245; www.nfl-bay.com), on Lancaster St., Exit 120 from Hwy. 1, go to **Digby, NS.** (3hr.; 1-3 per day; June 27-Oct. 9 $35, students and seniors $25, ages 11-17 $20, ages 3-11 $15, cars $80; Oct. 10-June 26 $20/$18/$15/$10/$75.) **Car Rental: Hertz** has an office in Market Sq., on the 2nd fl. (☎696-2210. Open M-F 8am-5pm, Sa 8am-noon.) **Taxi: Century Taxi** ☎696-6969. **Internet Access: Saint John Regional Library**, Market Sq., 2nd fl., above the information center. (☎643-7220. Open M 9am-5pm, Tu-W 10am-5pm, Th-F 10am-9pm; Sept.-May also open Sa 9am-5pm. Free.) **Post Office:** Station B, 41 Church Ave. W, in West Saint John. (☎672-6704. Open M-F 8am-5pm.) **Postal Code:** E2M 4P0. **Area Code:** 506.

⍗ ACCOMMODATIONS. There are tons of nearly identical motels on the 100 to 1300 blocks and farther along the 1700 block of **Manawagonish Road,** in the western part of town. Singles are $40-50. The spacious ▧**Earle of Leinster Bed and Breakfast** ❸, 96 Leinster St., two blocks from the city center, offers seven four-star rooms and two smaller "backpacker" rooms, each with a private bath, cable, VCR, fridge, and microwave. Take Exit 122, turn left at Union St., right on Wentworth St., and then left on Leinster. (☎652-3275; http://earleofleinster.tripod.com. Breakfast, laundry, pool table. Reception closes at 10pm. Check-in noon. Check-out 10am. Single backpacker rooms $56-82; regular doubles $62-95. Each additional person $13.) The **University of New Brunswick at Saint John ❶**, on Tucker Park Rd., has comfortable, neat rooms 10min. from downtown by car. Take Somerset St. onto Samuel Davis Dr. and follow the signs for the university. (☎648-5755; www.unbsj.ca/hfs. Free local calls. Internet access at the university library. TV rooms on each floor. Laundry $2. Free parking. Reception 7am-midnight. Open May-Aug. Singles $34, students $26; doubles $47/$37.) You can find partially wooded tent sites at the **Rockwood Park Campground ❶**, off Lake Dr. S in Rockwood Park; take the "University" bus to Mt. Pleasant. (☎652-4050. Internet access, showers, laundry, and phones. Open May to mid-Oct. Sites $17, with hookup $24; weekly $80/$110.)

◘ FOOD. The butcher, baker, fishmonger, produce dealer, and cheese merchant sell fresh goodies at **Old City Market,** 47 Charlotte St., between King and Brunswick Sq. Canada's oldest indoor farmers market may be the best place to get your **dulse,** sun-dried seaweed from the Bay of Fundy, best described as "ocean jerky." (☎658-2820. Open M-Th 7:30am-6pm, F 7:30am-7pm, Sa 7:30am-7pm. Dulse starts at $1.75 per bag.) **Billy's Seafood Company ❹**, 49-51 Charlotte St., attached to the Old City Market, is a delicious splurge for seafood lovers. (☎672-3474. Fresh Malpeque oysters 6 for $13. Fish and chips $7 lunch, $11 dinner. Lobster $27 for 1 lb.; add $3 per additional ¼ lb. Open M-Th 11am-10pm, F-Sa 11am-11pm, Su 4-10pm.) **Reggie's Restaurant ❶,** 26 Germain St., a local institution, specializes in "self-serve" burgers, breakfasts, and milkshakes. The plentiful breakfast specials, from $2.17 (two strips of bacon, an egg, and toast) to $6.70 (steak, eggs, toast, and home fries), are served all day. (☎657-6270; www.reggiesrestaurant.com. Open daily 6am-5:30pm.)

◨ **SIGHTS.** Saint John's main attraction is the Reversing Falls, a natural phenomenon caused by the powerful Bay of Fundy tides (for more on the tides see below). Though the name suggests gravity-defying walls of water running uphill, the "falls" refers to the rapids at the mouth of the Saint John River, which run upstream with the force of the rising tides. Two hours before and after high tide, spectators see the flow of water at the nexus of the river and harbor slowly halt and change direction. As amazing as the event itself are the huge numbers of people captivated by it. The **Reversing Falls Tourist Centre,** 200 Bridge St., at the west end of Hwy. 100 bridge in the restaurant, distributes tide schedules and shows a 17min. film on the phenomenon. Take the westbound "East-West" bus from the Scotia Bank facing Billy's Seafood Company. (☎658-2937. Open daily May to mid-June and Sept. to mid-Oct. 9am-6pm; mid-June to Aug. 8am-8pm, Sept to mid-Oct. 9am-6pm. Screenings every 20min. $2.50.) At **Reversing Falls Jet-Boat,** in Fallsview Park across the bridge from the tourist centre, thrill-seekers ride the falls in a jet boat or in a plastic bubble, resembling a giant, floating hamster ball. (☎643-8987; www.jetboatrides.com. Open daily June-Aug. 10am-6pm, Sept.-Oct. 10am-5pm. Reservations strongly recommended. Jet-Boat rides $33, ages 12 and under $26; families $106. Wheelchair accessible. The Bubble, available only to those 16+, is $106 and takes 1½hr., including training. Both closed during thunderstorms.)

The **New Brunswick Museum,** at 1 Market Sq. in the same building as the City Centre Information Centre and the public library, has exhibits on local cultural and industrial history, local natural history, and local, Canadian, and international fine and decorative arts. The Hall of the Great Whales, on the 2nd fl., gives information about the behemoths that roam the Bay of Fundy. (☎643-2300; www.nbm-mnb.ca. Open Tu-W and F 9am-5pm, Th 9am-9pm, Sa 10am-5pm, Su and holidays noon-5pm; mid-May to Oct. M 9am-5pm. $6, seniors $4.75, students $3.25; families $13.) Nature buffs will be delighted to find over 12km of wooded trails, six ecosystems, and scenic bay views in the **Irving Nature Park,** a 600 acre eco-preserve at the end of Sand Cove Rd. W. (☎632-7777; www.ifdn.com. Open daily dawn-dusk. Free.)

FUNDY NATIONAL PARK ☎506

Twice each day, the world's largest tides withdraw over one kilometer into the Bay of Fundy, leaving aquatic lifeforms high and dry. The dramatic contrast between the two tidescapes and the rapidity with which the waters rise and fall (1m every 3 min.) draw tons of tourists each year to Fundy National Park. Visitors to the park in chillier September and October will avoid the crowds.

▸ **PRACTICAL INFORMATION.** The park charges an entrance fee, payable at any entrance. ($5 per day, seniors $4.25, ages 6-16 $2.50; families $12.50.) **Park Headquarters,** P.O. Box 1001, Alma, in the southeastern corner of the Park, includes an administrative building and the **visitors center.** (☎887-6000. Open mid-June to early Sept. daily 8am-10pm; mid-May to mid-June and early Sept. to early Oct. daily 8am-4:30pm; mid-Oct. to early May M-F 8am-noon and 12:30-4:30pm.) Another visitors center, **Wolfe Lake Information,** is at the northwest entrance, off Hwy. 114. (☎432-6026. Open late June to Aug. daily 10am-6pm.) No public transit

FUNDY NATIONAL PARK ■ 199

serves Fundy; the nearest bus depots are in Moncton and Sussex. The free park newspaper *Salt and Fir*, available at the entrance stations and visitors centers, includes a map of trails and campgrounds. **Weather Info:** ☎ 887-6000.

⚑ CAMPING. The park operates five **campgrounds ❶** and over 700 sites. Getting a site is seldom a problem, but finding one at your campground of choice may be difficult. Campfires are only allowed at Chignecto and Point Wolfe campgrounds. Reservations are highly recommended. (☎ 800-414-6765.) **Headquarters Campground** is closest to civilization with laundry facilities, kitchen, shower, and playground, but is usually in highest demand. (In summer sites $21, with hookup $27; in winter, $13/$19. Wheelchair accessible.) **Chignecto North Campground,** off Hwy. 114, 5km inland from the headquarters, has more private, wooded sites, with biking and hiking trails nearby. (Open mid-May to mid-Oct. Sites $21, with hookup $25-27. Wheelchair accessible.) **Chignecto South Campground,** across from Chignecto North, provides basic sites with toilets but no showers, when the northern campground is full. (Open late June to late Aug. Sites $21.) **Point Wolfe Campground,** along the scenic coast, 7km west of headquarters, is cooler and more insect-free than the inland campgrounds, and has access to beautiful oceanside hikes. (Open late June to late Aug. Sites $21.) Year-round **wilderness camping ❶** is also available in some of the park's most scenic areas, including **Goose River**. The campsites, with fireplaces, wood, and outhouses, require reservations and permits. (☎ 887-6000. $8 per person per night, $56 per season.) Weatherproof alternatives exist in Alma, where a few clean but spartan motels line Main Street. If you can find a room in peak season, it will cost about $80 per night. Otherwise, Moncton is your best bet.

❏ FOOD. A trip into Alma is worthwhile if only for a sticky bun ($1.15) from ◼Kelly's Bake Shop ❶, 8587 Main St. It bears repeating: do not leave Alma without a sticky bun. Kelly's also offers fresh bread, cookies, and pies. (☎ 887-2460. Open July-Aug. 7am-8pm; Sept.-June 10am-5pm.) Get basic groceries or a home-cooked meal at **Harbour View Market and Coffee Shop ❶**, 8598 Main St., in Alma. The breakfast special (2 eggs, toast, bacon, and coffee) is only $4.50. (☎ 887-2450. Open daily July-Aug. 7am-10pm, Sept.-June 8am-8pm.) **Collins Lobster ❷**, 20 Ocean Dr., behind Kelly's, has seafood caught locally and hauled in daily. The takeout lobster (usually $8.50 per lb. live, $9 cooked) is a catch. (☎ 887-2054. Open daily 10am-6pm.)

⚑ OUTDOOR ACTIVITIES. The park maintains 120km of trails year-round. Though no rental outfits serve the park, about 35km are open to mountain bikes. *Salt and Fir* has detailed descriptions of all trails, including where to find waterfalls and ocean views. Moose are most common along Hwy. 114 between Wolfe Lake and Caribou Plain. Hike the easy ◼Caribou Plain Trail (3½km loop) at dusk for your best shot at spotting one. Deer live in the park and thieving raccoons run thick; the peregrine falcons are harder to spot. *Never feed the animals, and keep a respectful distance when watching them. Drivers should beware of moose and deer on the roads after dark.* Most recreational facilities operate only during the summer (mid-May to early Oct.) and include daily free interpretive programs. The park staff leads beach walks, junior naturalist programs, and evening theater and campfire gatherings. Visitors can take a 3hr. nocturnal tour through the woods. (Times and prices ☎ 887-6000.) **Alma Beach,** on Hwy. 114, between Alma and the park headquarters, is a popular place to experience **Fundy's tides**. A boardwalk and informative signs explain the phenomenon and local geography.

▣ DAYTRIP FROM FUNDY NAT'L PARK: HOPEWELL ROCKS. The Hopewell Rocks, 40km north on Hwy. 114, may be the Bay of Fundy's most picturesque creations. The "flowerpot" rocks appear to be miniature islands at high tide but

EASTERN CANADA

become four-story sandstone monoliths when the tide goes out nearly 1km. Visitors can explore caves, arches, and fascinating rock formations on foot at low tide or kayak among them at high tide. The beach is accessible from about 3hr. before low tide to nearly 3hr. afterwards. Be aware of tide schedules so that you're not surprised by rising water; they are about ½hr. behind those at Fundy. (☎734-3429; www.thehopewellrocks.ca. Open mid-May to mid-Oct.; hours vary, approx. 8am-7pm. $7, seniors $6, ages 5-18 $5; families $18. Kayaks ☎734-2660. Open early June to early Sept. Call for tour times. 2hr. guided tour $45, children $40.)

MONCTON   ☎506

This pleasant town hosted the 1999 Francophone Summit, which stoked the fires of urban renewal. Today Moncton is a growing bilingual city with a revived downtown and peculiar and incredible natural attractions. The **Petitcodiac River** that flows through Moncton is usually nothing more than red mud flats, but twice a day the tidal bore rushes in as two dramatic waves, raising the river at the rate of 3m per hour. (The initial wave is more impressive in the spring and fall; in summer it's only a few inches high.) This phenomenon is best viewed near the end of Main St. at the aptly-named **Tidal Bore Park**, where tide schedules are available. **Magnetic Hill**, at the corner of Mountain Rd. and Trans-Canada Hwy., seemingly defies physics, as a natural optical illusion makes it seem as if cars roll up the hill. Though it's a bit hokey, rolling "uphill" is worth the $5 cost. (☎853-3540. Open daily mid-May to mid-June 9am-6pm; mid-June to Aug. 9am-8pm, Sept. to mid-Oct. 9am-5pm.) The **Acadian Museum,** at the Université de Moncton, tells the story of 17th-century Acadian settlers through everyday artifacts. An **art gallery** attached to the museum shows works by local artists in the "picture province." (☎858-4088. Open M-F 10am-5pm, Sa-Su 1-5pm. $2, students and seniors $1, under 12 free. Su free.)

The cozy, charming ◪**Downtown Bed & Breakfast ❸,** 101 Alma St., has a sunny patio, friendly staff, and a french toast breakfast worth getting up for. (☎855-7108. Free Internet access, TV/VCR in common room, towels, robes, and shared but spacious baths. Call ahead if allergic to cats—your room will be thoroughly cleaned. Singles $65; doubles $75.) The **Université de Moncton ❷** rents well-appointed rooms for summer travelers at three of its residences. Reception is at Résidence Lefebvre, near the center of campus. Take the #5 bus from Highland Square. (☎858-4015. Sink, fridge, and microwave in most rooms. Parking $5 per day. Singles without bath $41, students $20.) ◪**Calactus ❷,** 125 Church St. at St. George, serves outstanding vegetarian and vegan dishes. Wash a world class veggie burger ($9) down with a creamy soy shake ($3.50), and don't miss the homemade chapati bread that is served with most meals. (☎388-4833. Open daily 10am-10pm.) The **Pump House ❶,** 5 Orange Ln., a firehouse-themed brewery, churns out eight original beers and their own root beer and cream soda. Brick oven pizzas ($4-9) will satisfy any hunger. (☎855-2337. Open Su-W 11am-midnight, Th 11am-1am, F-Sa 11am-2am.)

The **Greater Moncton International Airport** (☎856-5444; www.gma.ca), 5km outside of town, flies to major cities. **VIA Rail,** 1240 Main St. (☎888-842-7245; www.viarail.ca.) goes to Halifax (daily except W; $56, seniors $50, students $37, children $28) and Montreal (daily except Tu; $176/$159/$115/$88). Open daily 9am-6pm. **SMT,** 961 Main St. (☎859-5060), runs **buses** to Halifax (4hr.; 4 per day; $47, seniors $40, students $35, children $24) and Montreal (12-14hr.; 2 per day; $105, students and seniors $95, children $53). Open daily 9am-8:30pm. **Codiac Transit** is the local bus line. (☎857-2008. Open M-F 6am-4:30pm. Operates M-Sa 7am-6pm.) **Air Cab** (☎857-2000) runs from the airport to town for $15. The **Tourist Information Center,** in the Treitz House in Tidal Bore Park, has info. (☎800-363-4558; www.gomoncton.com. Open late May daily 8:30am-4:30pm, early June daily 9am-7pm, late June to Aug. daily 9am-8pm; low-season hours vary.)

The **Moncton Public Library**, in the Blue Cross Center at 644 Main St., has free **Internet access**. Open M and F 9am-5pm, Tu-Th 9am-8:30pm. **Post Office:** 281 St. George St. (☎857-7240. Open M-F 8am-5:30pm.) **Postal Code:** E1C 1H0. **Area Code:** 506.

◪ DAYTRIP FROM MONCTON: KOUCHIBOUGUAC NATIONAL PARK. Unlike Fundy's rugged forests and high tides, **Kouchibouguac National Park** (Koo-she-boo-gwack) has warm lagoon waters, salt marshes, peat bogs, and white sandy beaches. Bask in the sun along the 25km stretch of barrier islands and sand dunes, or float down canoe waterways. Kouchibouguac has the warmest salt waters north of Virginia, and swimmers enjoy the gentle surf and a view at **Kelly's Beach,** 11km from the visitors center. Hikers can choose from a variety of trails, including a leisurely nature walk down the **Bog Trail** (3½km loop) and the more-challenging **Kouchibouguac River Trail** (22km loop). Wildlife is abundant, and moose and bears can be seen dusk (though mosquitoes are an annoyance). **Ryan's Rental Center,** between the South Kouchibouguac Campground and Kellys Beach, rents canoes, kayaks, and bikes. (☎876-8918. Open daily late June to Aug. 8am-9pm; May Sa-Su 8am-5pm. Canoes or kayaks $7 per hr., $30 per day; bikes $5/$26.) The park runs two **campgrounds ●** in summer. Reservations are recommended and can be made until one day prior to arrival. (☎877-737-3783. Reservation fee $11.) **South Kouchibouguac** has 311 sites with showers. (Late June to early Sept. $24, with hookup $28; mid-May to late June and early Sept. to mid-Oct. $19/$25.) **Côte-à-Fabien** has 32 sites ($14) but no showers or toilets. Low-season campers stay at **primitive sites ●** in the park ($9 per person per night). The **visitors center** is at the park entrance on Hwy. 117, just off Hwy. 11, 100km north of Moncton. (☎876-2443. Entrance $6, seniors $5, children $3; families $15. Open daily mid-June to mid-Sept. 8am-8pm; mid-Sept. to mid-June 9am-5pm. Park administration open M-F 8am-4:30pm.)

PRINCE EDWARD ISLAND

Prince Edward Island, host to the 1864 conference that set Canada on the path to nationhood, is the smallest province in Canada. More commonly called "PEI" or "the Island," it attracts most of its visitors with the beauty made famous in the novel *Anne of Green Gables*. The fictional work did not exaggerate the wonders of natural life on the island; the soil, made red by its high iron-oxide content, contrasts with the green crops, turquoise waters, and purple lupine. Hardy islanders live on seafood, potato farming, and tourism. Some of Canada's finest beaches stretch across the shores, and quaint towns checker the island.

◪ PRACTICAL INFORMATION

Capital: Charlottetown.

Ferries: Northumberland Ferry (☎888-249-7245; www.nfl-bay.com), in Wood Islands, 61km east of Charlottetown on the Trans-Canada Hwy. To **Caribou, NS** (1¼hr.; 4-9 per day; $12, seniors $10; vehicles $50).

Toll Bridges: The 8 mi. long **Confederation Bridge** connects the cities of Borden-Carleton, PEI, and Bayfield, NB, across the Northumberland Strait. Tourists pay no fee crossing into PEI, but must shell out a toll ($39 per car) when leaving.

Visitor Info: PEI Visitor Information Centre, P.O. Box 940, Charlottetown C1A 7M5 (☎368-4444 or 888-734-7529; www.peiplay.com). Open June daily 9am-8pm; July-Aug. daily 8am-10pm; Sept. to mid-Oct. daily 8:30am-6pm; mid-Oct. to May M-F 9am-4:30pm.

Drinking Age: 19. **Postal Abbreviation:** PEI. **Sales Tax:** 10% PST, plus 7% GST.

CHARLOTTETOWN/EASTERN ISLAND ☎902

Most of Charlottetown's sights center on its role in Canadian history as the site of the Charlottetown Confederation Conference. The town is also home to the **University of Prince Edward Island (UPEI)**. The historical and urban center of the province, Charlottetown is one of the most visited spots on Prince Edward Island. Nearby coastal communities are blessed with spectacular beaches.

◪ PRACTICAL INFORMATION. Most visitors arrive in PEI via the longest continuous marine span bridge in the world, **Confederation Bridge,** which meets PEI at **Borden-Carleton,** 56km west of Charlottetown on Hwy. 1. **Charlottetown,** the capital and biggest city, is just east of the center of the island. The most popular beaches—**Cavendish, Brackley,** and **Rustico Island**—lie on the north shore in the middle of the province opposite Charlottetown, and make up the **National Park.** PEI's second city, **Summerside,** is west of Borden-Carleton.

In Charlottetown itself, **Queen Street** and **University Avenue** are the main thoroughfares, straddling Confederation Centre on the west and east, respectively. **Charlottetown-Cavendish Shuttles** (☎566-3243) picks up passengers at the Info Centre (call for other points) and drops them off in Cavendish. (45min. July-Aug. 4 per day; June and Sept. 2 per day. $10, same-day round-trip $18.) **Taxi: City Cab** ☎892-6567. **Bike Rental: MacQueens,** 430 Queen St. (☎368-2453; www.macqueens.com. Open M-Sa 8:30am-5:30pm. Hybrid road and mountain bikes $25 per day, $125 per week; youth-size bikes $13/$50. Must have credit card or $100 deposit for reservations.) **Visitor Info: PEI Visitor Information Centre,** 178 Water St. **Hotlines: Island Help Line,** ☎800-218-2885. 24hr. **Rape Crisis Center,** ☎800-289-5656. **Internet Access: Confederation Centre Library,** at Queen St. in Confederation Centre. (☎368-4647. Open M and F-Sa 10am-5pm, Tu-Th 10am-8pm, Su 1-5pm. Free.) **Post Office:** 135 Kent St. (☎628-4400. Open M-F 8am-5:15pm.) **Postal Code:** C1A 7K2. **Area Code:** 902.

⊓ ACCOMMODATIONS. B&Bs and inns crowd every nook and cranny of the province; some are open year-round, but the least expensive are closed for the winter. Many of the island's visitors centers, including Charlottetown's, have daily vacancy listings. Charlottetown's cheapest non-camping option is **UPEI,** off Belvedere Ave., which offers B&B-style dorms in three residence halls: **Marian Hall ❷** has singles with shared baths (May $35, June-Aug. with breakfast $41); **Bernadine Hall ❸** offers singles and doubles with in-room sinks and new beds and furniture (singles $50/$55; doubles $53/$62), while **Blanchard Hall ❹** has two-bedroom apartments (May-Aug. $80). Check-in is at Bernadine Hall. (☎566-0442; www.upei.ca/housing. Linen, towels, and parking included. Reception 24hr.) Find all the comforts of home at **City Gardens Bed & Breakfast ❺**, 114 Nassau St., near Queen St., which has a quiet backyard, TV room, Internet, and hot breakfast. (☎892-7282; www.citygardenspei.com. 4 rooms $40-75. Cash only.)

⊏◪ FOOD AND NIGHTLIFE. The search for food often boils down to the search for **lobster** (from around $9 per lb.). Fresh seafood, including famous **Malpeque oysters** (around $9 per half-dozen, $15 per dozen), is sold along the shores of the island, especially in North Rustico, near Cavendish on the north shore. Home to a world-class culinary school, Charlottetown's restaurants are excellent and inexpensive. The best deal in town is to be had at the **Canadian Culinary Institute ❷** itself, 4 Sydney St. Students cook gourmet entrees ($3.53) and serve them cafeteria-style. (☎894-6857. Lunch with entree, salad, dessert, and drink $8. Open M-F 11:30am-1pm. Arrive early to avoid lines.) The young clientele at **Beanz ❶,** 52 University Ave., washes down homemade sandwiches ($4) and scrumptious cinnamon rolls ($1.10) with $1.75 espresso. (☎892-8797. Open M-F 6:30am-6pm, Sa 8am-6pm, Su 9am-5pm.) After the sun sets, head to **Baba's Lounge,** 81 University Ave., above Cedar's, for local brews ($4), a jug of "sweet oblivion," (a fruity, potent mix for 5 people; $36), live rock (Tu and Th-Sa), and open mic night Wednesday. (☎892-7377; www.cedarseatery.com. Cover varies, usually less than $5. Open M-Sa noon-2am, Su noon-midnight.)

◪ SIGHTS. Province House, the centerpiece of Charlottetown's **Queen Square,** was the site of the first meeting to discuss Canadian union. Partially restored to its 19th-century Victorian appearance, the house is still the seat of PEI's provincial government. (☎566-7626. 15min. video. Free self-guided tours. Open June daily 8:30am-5pm; July-Aug. daily 8:30am-6pm; Sept. to mid-Oct. daily 8:30am-5pm; mid-Oct. to June M-F 9am-5pm.) Also in Queen Square, the **Confederation Centre of the Arts** houses an art gallery highlighting Canadian art from every province. The museum has a great collection of works by Robert Harris as well as the scrapbooks and manuscripts of Lucy Maud Montgomery. (☎628-1864; www.confederationcentre.com. Open mid-June to mid-Oct. daily 9am-5pm; mid-Oct. to mid-June Tu-Sa 11am-5pm, Su 1-5pm. Donations accepted.) Pushing the boundary between historical narration and cheesy multimedia spectacle, **Founder's Hall,** 6 Prince St., transports visitors "back in time" to the 1864 conference with wireless headsets and video reenactments. (☎368-1864; www.foundershall.ca. Open mid-May to late June and Sept. to mid-Oct. M-Sa 9am-5pm, Su 9am-4pm; late June to Aug. M-Sa 9am-8pm, Su 9am-4pm. $7, seniors $6, ages 6-17 $3.75.)

Some of Canada's finest **beaches** are on PEI. The stretches of beach on the eastern coast are less touristed than those in the west, perhaps due to the rougher surf. *At all beaches, high winds and riptides make solo swimming dangerous.* **Basin Head Beach,** 95km east of Charlottetown, is a relaxing daytrip, with over 11km of uncrowded white sand. **Lakeside,** a beach 35km east of Charlottetown on Hwy. 2, is unsupervised and often deserted on summer weekdays. Trot along the surf atop a sturdy steed from **Lake Circle T Trails,** located beside the golf course at the junction of MacAdam Rd. and Rte. 350 in Lakeside. (☎393-0084. Open daily July-Aug. 9am-8pm, May-June and Sept.-Oct. 9am-6pm. Guided horse rides $15 per hr.)

KICK IT CELTIC STYLE

Celtic culture is woven into the hills of the Atlantic Provinces, which, on summer evenings, are often alive with barn-stompin' music. Stop by a Ceilidh (pronounced "kay-lee," meaning, basically, hootenanny in Gaelic) to listen to, and probably participate in, ballads, jigs, and reels. Most of the gatherings feature fiddles, bagpipes, drums, guitars, performers in traditional tartan dress, and step dancing. The tradition of the Ceilidh was brought to the area from the highlands of Scotland, where folks would gather informally in a kitchen or yard to play music, sing, dance, and gossip. Today the primary function of many Ceilidhs, advertised throughout the countryside, is to introduce tourists to local cultural heritage while making some cash (expect cover charges around $10-15 for most big gatherings). Consistently diverse and high-quality Ceilidhs go down at the College of Piping, in Summerside, PEI, rain or shine, in their amphitheater. Faculty, students, and guests perform and explain traditional songs and dances, and a small onsite museum provides history and background.

☎436-5377 or 877-224-7473; www.collegeofpiping.com. 619 Water St. E. In summer, concerts nightly 7pm. Small-scale demonstrations and performances in the day. Box office open late June to Aug. 9am-9pm; call for low-season hours. $14, seniors $13, students $9.

CAVENDISH AND THE WESTERN ISLAND   ☎ 902

GREEN GABLES. Green Gables House, off Hwy. 6 in Cavendish just west of Hwy. 13, is a shrine for readers who adore Lucy Maud Montgomery's *Anne of Green Gables.* The traditionally furnished house is the spitting image of Anne Shirley's home in the novel; it was restored and redecorated to mirror the book's descriptions. (☎ 963-7874. Open daily July-Aug. 9am-8pm; May-June and Sept.-Oct. 9am-5pm. $5.75, seniors $5, ages 6-16 $3; families $15.) A short ride back toward Charlottetown on Hwy. 6 is the **Lucy Maud Montgomery House Site,** a calmer and less touristed site that retains the serenity and quiet beauty of Cavendish as Montgomery knew it. Fans are treated to a small museum run by her descendants and a picturesque walking tour of the ruins of her childhood home. (☎ 963-2231; www.peisland.com/lmm. Open daily June and Sept. to mid-Oct. 10am-5pm; July-Aug. 9am-6pm. $3, ages 6-16 $1.) Serious Anne aficionados will also want to go to **Avonlea,** a life-sized recreation of Anne's town, where actors in period dress reenact scenes from the novel. (☎ 963-3050; www.avonlea.ca. $17, seniors $15, ages 6-16 $13; families $45. Open mid-June to late Sept. daily 9am-5pm.) A **visitors center** for Cavendish, Green Gables, and the park is located at the intersection of Hwy. 6 and 13. (☎ 963-7830; www.peiplay.com. Open mid-June to mid-Aug. daily 8am-9pm; call for low-season hours.)

After a day of sightseeing, calm yourself with the spectacular sunset view from the dining room of **Prince Edward Island Preserve Co. Restaurant ❷,** down Hwy. 13 in nearby New Glasgow. The potato pie ($14) is a favorite, as are the generous slices of fresh berry pies for $3.50-4.50. (☎ 964-4303. Open daily 8am-9pm.) Find peace and quiet at the **Country House Inn ❸,** on Gulf Shore Rd. in the national park 5km south of the Hwy. 13 gate. Beautiful ocean views, easy beach access, and a huge buffet-style breakfast make this a perfect base for exploring Cavendish. (☎ 963-2055 or 800-363-2055; www.cavendishbeachresort.com/countryhouseinn. Free bikes and passes for beaches and national park. 3-night min. stay. Open June-Oct. Singles $50-60; apartments that can sleep 4-6 people $87 for two, $12 per additional person.)

PRINCE EDWARD ISLAND NATIONAL PARK. Some of the island's best beaches (**Cavendish Beach,** for example), lie within the park. Wind-sculpted sand dunes, red sea cliffs, and saltwater marshes comprise the park's terrain, which is home to many of the island's 300 species of birds. Eleven easy **trails** of varying length meander among dunes and along meadows. An entrance fee is required (mid-June to Sept. $5, seniors $4.25, children $2.50, families $13; low-season $3/ $2.50/$1.50/$7.50). The park operates three **campgrounds ❶** during the summer and one in the low season. Reservations are strongly recommended and must be made at least three days in advance. Nature walks, campfires, and slide shows entertain campers at all three campgrounds in July and August. (Info ☎ 672-6350, reservations 800-414-6765. Showers, laundry facilities, and beach access. Park facilities open mid-May to Oct. From June to mid-Oct., sites $21-22, with hookup $25-27; low-season free.) Privately-owned campgrounds also fill the island.

NOVA SCOTIA

Around 1605, French colonists joined the indigenous Micmac Indians in the Annapolis Valley and on the shores of Cape Breton Island. During the American Revolution, Nova Scotia declined the opportunity to become the 14th American state, instead establishing itself as a refuge for fleeing British loyalists. Subsequent immigration waves infused Pictou and Antigonish Counties with a Scottish flavor.

This diversity is complemented by the four breathtaking geographies found in the province: the rugged Atlantic coast, the lush Annapolis Valley, the calm Northumberland Strait, and the glorious highlands of Cape Breton Island.

⏎ PRACTICAL INFORMATION

Capital: Halifax.

Visitor Info: Nova Scotia Department of Tourism and Culture, P.O. Box 456, Halifax B3J 2R5 (☎902-424-5000 or 800-565-0000; www.explore.gov.ns.ca).

Drinking Age: 19. **Postal Abbreviation:** NS. **Sales Tax:** 15% HST.

HALIFAX ☎902

The first permanent British settlement in Canada, Halifax was founded in 1749 as a base for military excursions against the French fortress, Louisbourg. The town's fortifications were continually revamped as new threats emerged—the Americans and their Revolution, then Napoleon, and finally the War of 1812. With the threat of war in the past, this buzzing seaport still attracts considerable attention. These days, however, numerous colleges support a first-rate pub scene and hip downtown, while natural beauty and maritime heritage are the major attractions.

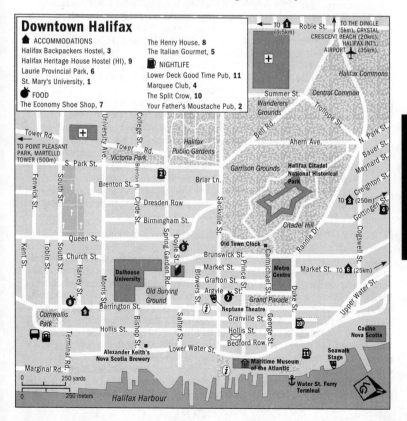

Downtown Halifax

🏠 ACCOMMODATIONS
Halifax Backpackers Hostel, **3**
Halifax Heritage House Hostel (HI), **9**
Laurie Provincial Park, **6**
St. Mary's University, **1**

🍴 FOOD
The Economy Shoe Shop, **7**

The Henry House, **8**
The Italian Gourmet, **5**

🍺 NIGHTLIFE
Lower Deck Good Time Pub, **11**
Marquee Club, **4**
The Split Crow, **10**
Your Father's Moustache Pub, **2**

EASTERN CANADA

🗓 PRACTICAL INFORMATION. Barrington Street, the major north-south street, runs through downtown. Approaching the Citadel and the Public Garden, **Sackville Street** cuts east-west parallel to **Spring Garden Road,** Halifax's shopping thoroughfare. Downtown is flanked by the blue-collar North End and the arboreal South End. **Halifax International Airport** is 35min. from downtown via Hwy. 102; take Exit 6. (☎873-1223; www.hiaa.ca.) **Zinck's Bus Company** runs to and from downtown hotels. (☎873-2091. Shuttles daily 7:15am-11pm. One-way $12, round-trip $20.) Taxis to downtown are about $40. **VIA Rail,** 1161 Hollis St. (☎888-842-7245; www.viarail.ca; open daily 9am-5:30pm), at South St. in the South End near the harbor, goes to Montréal (19hr.; 1 per day, except Tu; $186, students $121) and Québec City (15½hr.; 1 per day, except Tu; $155/$107, shuttle to Québec City from train stop $8). **Acadian Lines,** 1161 Hollis St. (☎453-8921 or 800-567-5151; www.acadianbus.com; open daily 9am-5:30pm), in the same station as VIA Rail, runs buses to Sydney (6-7hr.; 3 per day; $63, students $54). **Metro Transit** runs public transit. It also operates the **Dartmouth-Halifax Ferry,** on the harbor front; the 12min. ride to Dartmouth is a cheap way to see Halifax from the sea. (☎490-4000. Buses run daily roughly 6am-midnight. $1.75, seniors and ages 5-15 $1.25, under 5 free. Ferry runs every 15-30min. M-Sa 6:30am-midnight, Su 10:30am-6:30pm.) **FRED (Free Rides Everywhere Downtown)** operates June-August. (☎490-4000. Daily 11am-5:30pm.) **Taxi: Yellow Cab** ☎420-0000. **Visitor Info: Halifax International Visitors Centre,** 1595 Barrington St. (☎490-5946; www.explore.gov.ns.ca. Free Internet access. Open daily July-Aug. 8:30am-8pm; June and Sept. 8:30am-7pm; Oct.-May M-F 8:30am-4:30pm.) **Currency Exchange:** Banks offer the best rates in town. In desperate times, the **casino** at the waterfront is open 24hr. and will change money. **Medical Services: Victoria General Hospital,** 1278 Tower Rd. (☎473-2700.) **Hotlines: Sexual Assault,** ☎425-0122. **Crisis Help Line,** ☎421-1188. Both 24hr. **Internet Access: Public Library,** 5381 Spring Garden Rd. (☎490-5804. Open Tu-Th 10am-9pm, F-Sa 10am-5pm; Sept.-May also Su 2-5pm.) **Post Office:** 1680 Bedford Row. (☎494-4670. Open M-F 7:30am-5:15pm.) **Postal Code:** B3J 1T0. **Area Code:** 902.

> **🔳TIP◀** **SALTY SIGHTSEEING.** Salty Bear Adventure Travel, (☎446-3866 or 866-458-BEAR; www.saltybear.ca) provides 2- to 6-day trips for backpackers and independent travelers, that go to the best natural attractions in Nova Scotia, New Brunswick, and Prince Edward Island. The most basic option is "The Whippersnapper," ($99) a 2-day, 1-night trip that leaves from Halifax and hits Peggy's Cove, Lunenburg, Kejimkujik National Park, Annapolis Royal, the Bay of Fundy, and Grand Pre. Activities include hiking, canoeing, tubing, and skydiving. Prices include transportation, guides, National Park passes, ferry passes, and discounts on activities and lodging.

📍 ACCOMMODATIONS. Affordable summer accommodations are plentiful, but reservations are a good idea. Expect crowds during major events like the Nova Scotia International Tattoo Festival (p. 208). The 🔳**Halifax Backpackers Hostel ❶,** 2193 Gottingen St., attached to a coffee shop, has a grassroots community spirit. The enthusiastic owners are eager to organize pub outings or ad-hoc games of ultimate frisbee. (☎431-3170; www.halifaxbackpackers.com. Internet access, kitchen, bike storage, and laundry. Rooms almost always co-ed. Key deposit $10. Check-in noon-10pm, but someone is at the phone 24hr. Dorms $20; singles $35; doubles $50; family room $65.) The **Halifax Heritage House Hostel (HI) ❶,** 1253 Barrington St., a 5min. walk from the heart of downtown, is a spacious 81-bed hostel with Internet access, TV room, kitchen, laundry facilities, and four- to eight-bed dorms. (☎422-3863. Key deposit $5. Reception 7am-1am. Check-in after 2pm. Reservations highly recommended. Dorms $19, nonmembers $24; singles $50; doubles $57.) Close to the pubs and clubs, **St. Mary's University ❶,** 5865 Gorsebrook Ave., has hundreds of newly-renovated dorm-style rooms. (☎420-5486 or 888-347-5555. Free Internet in library. Free linen, towels, parking, and local calls. Cafeteria with breakfast ($6), lunch ($8), and dinner ($10). Reception 24hr. Reservations recommended. Open May to mid-Aug. Singles $37, students $20; doubles $53/$47.) **Laurie Provincial Park ❶**, 25km north of Halifax on Hwy. 2, offers rustic campsites among Grand Lake's pine groves. (☎861-1623. Running water and outhouses, but no showers. Check-in before 10:30pm. Open mid-June to Sept. Sites $14.)

🍴 **FOOD.** Dozens of downtown restaurants double as nightspots after dusk. Grab a bite before 9 or 10pm, as most places close their doors (and kitchens) when the sun goes down (don't worry, though—restaurants do stay open past 4:30 in the winter, despite the early sunset). ◪**The Economy Shoe Shop ❸**, 1663 Argyle St., with a breezy streetside patio and a huge indoor atrium, brings a wonderfully haphazard flair to decor and food. It also doubles as a huge bar at night. Make a meal of the terrific veggie burgers ($5.50) or mountainous nachos ($10), or have a proper seafood or steak dinner for $10-22. (☎423-8845. Pints $5.50. Open daily 11am-2am.) Part deli, part gelato stand, part bakery, and part restaurant, **The Italian Gourmet ❶**, 5431 Doyle St., just off Spring Garden Rd., offers mouth-watering lunch specials ($8) and original sandwich creations ($6-7) at the deli counter. (☎423-7880. Gelato $3. Open M and Sa 9am-7pm, Tu-F 9am-8pm, Su 10am-6pm.) **The Henry House ❶**, 1222 Barrington St., produces its own microbrewed beers. The "Peculiar" brew (pints $6) is a perfect complement to the hearty $6 beef-and-beer stew or the popular $7 fish 'n' chips. (☎423-5660. Open M-Sa 11:30am-1am, Su 11:30am-11pm.)

🔲 **SIGHTS.** **Citadel Hill,** the city's major landmark, offers a fine view of the city and harbor, and houses the star-shaped **Halifax Citadel National Historical Park,** on Sackville St., as well as the old **Town Clock.** A 1hr. film tells the history of the British fortress. Come any day to see the preparation for the **noon cannon firing.** Guided 45min. tours are the best way to take in the fort's history. (☎426-5080. Open daily July-Aug. 9am-6pm; mid-May to June and Sept. to mid-Oct. 9am-5pm. $9, seniors $7.75, ages 6-16 $4.25; families $23. Nov.-Apr. free, no tours. Parking $3.25. Partially wheelchair accessible.) The **Halifax Public Gardens,** across from the Citadel, near the intersection of South Park and Sackville St., are ideal for picnicking. The Roman statues, Victorian bandstand, exquisite horticulture, and overfed ducks are all properly British. (www.region.halifax.ns.ca. Open daily dawn-dusk. Concerts July-Sept. Su 2pm.) The **Maritime Museum of the Atlantic,** 1675 Lower Water St., on the waterfront, documents the often-tragic mar-

THE LOCAL STORY

GRAVEYARD OF THE ATLANTIC

The infamous rocky coastline, awful winter weather, dense fog, and fierce gales have conspired to sink hundreds of ships in the waters off of Nova Scotia, leaving behind wreckage and fostering local lore. The most famous ship of all time, the *Titanic*, struck an iceberg near Halifax on April 15, 1912, and sank, dispelling its myth of invincibility. Rescue ships set sail from Halifax expecting to find no survivors in the chilly Atlantic waters. These "death ships" carried back hundreds of bodies, and today Halifax hosts the tragedy's largest memorial: 150 graves. The Maritime Museum of the Atlantic displays a unique collection of artifacts salvaged from the disaster.

Another horrifying accident at sea occurred in 1917, when the *Mont Blanc*, a French ship laden with acid and TNT, collided with the *Imo*, a Norwegian relief ship in Halifax harbor. The *Mont Blanc* began to burn, and the crew abandoned ship and made it safely to shore. Meanwhile, the boat drifted toward the city, collided with the wharf, and blew up. The largest explosion before the atomic age ripped through downtown Halifax, killing hundreds and igniting fires that destroyed 750 homes and 11,630 buildings. The blast was felt nearly 500km away and leveled 2.5 sq. km of downtown. In all, nearly 2000 people lost their lives.

itime history of Nova Scotia with beautiful ship models and exceptional exhibits on shipwrecks like the *Titanic*. (☎424-7490; www.maritime.museum.gov.ns.ca. Open May-Oct. M and W-Sa 9:30am-5:30pm, Tu 9:30am-8pm, June-Sept. also Su 9:30am-5:30pm, May and Oct. also Su 1-5:30pm; Nov.-Apr. Tu-Sa 9:30am-5pm, Su 1-5pm. $8, seniors $7, ages 6-17 $4; families $21. Nov.-Apr. ½ price.) For a glimpse of Halifax of old and insight into one of Canada's finest beers, take the **Alexander Keith's Nova Scotia Brewery Tour**, 1496 Lower Water St. Actors in period dress explain the city's history and the process of making beer. The tour culminates in a visit to an exclusive pub with singing, dancing, and free samples. The gift shop is the only place in town to buy beer on Sundays. (☎455-1474 or 877-612-1820; www.keiths.ca. $10, students $9, seniors $7, children $6. 1hr. tours leave every 30min. M-Th 11am-8pm, F-Sa 11am-9pm, Su noon-4pm. Gift shop closes 1hr. after last tour leaves.)

Point Pleasant Park's 186 wooded acres are at the southern tip of Halifax; take bus #9 from Barrington St. downtown. Leased to the city of Halifax for 999 years at the bargain rate of one shilling per year, the park remains one of England's last imperial holdings. In the park, the **Prince of Wales Martello Tower**, an odd fort built by the British in 1797, honors Prince Edward's obsession with round buildings. (☎426-5080. Open daily July-Sept. 10am-6pm. Free.) Across the northwest arm of the harbor from downtown, **The Dingle** or **Sir Sandford Fleming Park**, on Dingle Rd., offers walking trails through gardens and grassy hills. (☎490-4894. Open daily 5am-10pm. Free.) To escape the summer heat, head to **Crystal Crescent Beach**, off Hwy. 349 about 20km from downtown, for ocean swimming and hiking trails.

🎭 **ENTERTAINMENT AND NIGHTLIFE.** The **Neptune Theater**, 1593 Argyle St., known as "the Jewel," presents the area's professional stage productions. (☎429-7070 or 800-565-7345; www.neptunetheatre.com. Box office open M-F 9am-5pm, Sa noon-5pm. Tickets $20-60; student and senior discounts available. Rush tickets 30min. before shows.) Halifax's most popular festival and the world's largest indoor annual festival is the **Nova Scotia International Tattoo**, in first week of July. Marching bands and kilted bagpipers attend the festival for its military pageantry, music, dance, and comedy. (☎420-1114; www.nstattoo.ca. Tickets $18-45.) The **Atlantic Jazz Festival** (☎492-2225 or 800-567-5277; www.jazzeast.com) jams in July with ticketed ($15-30) and free concerts featuring artists from around the world. In August, street performers display random talents from magic tricks to chalk art at **Buskerfest** (☎429-3910). The **Atlantic Film Festival** (☎422-3456; mid-Sept.) shows Canadian and international films. The **Halifax Event Line** (☎490-5946) has more info.

Halifax boasts intoxicating nightlife—the pub per capita ratio is "the highest in North America." The free *Coast*, available at bars and cafes, lists goings-on. Many bars have happy hours with $1-2 drinks. **The Split Crow**, 1855 Granville St., is a Halifax institution, boasting its own microbrews and live Celtic music every night. (☎422-4366; www.splitcrow.com. Power hour W-Th and happy hour M-F 4:30-7pm. Cover M-F $3, Sa-Su $4. Open daily 11am-1am.) Amid nautical decor, the **Lower Deck Good Time Pub**, in the Privateer's Warehouse, on Upper Water St., offers traditional maritime music nightly. (☎425-1501; www.lowerdeck.ca. Cover $3-7. Open daily 11am-1am.) The best rock acts in town head to the **Marquee Club**, 2037 Gottingen St., which sports an avant-garde atmosphere (mannequins dangling from the ceiling and car doors plastered to the walls) and a hip clientele. (☎429-3020; www.themarqueeclub.ca. Live music Tu and Th-Sa. Cover $3-4. Open W-Sa 9pm-3:30am; downstairs club open Tu 9pm-3:30am.) Near the universities, **Your Father's Moustache Pub**, 5686 Spring Garden Rd., has the best patio in town—on the roof three floors above the street. (☎423-6766. W rib night, $11 for a full rack. Happy hour M-Th 4:30-7pm, F 4:30-8pm, with $2.75 bottles and $2 shots. Open Su-W 10am-midnight, Th and Sa 10am-1am, F 10am-2am.) The city's best sound system throbs at **Reflections Cabaret**, 5184 Sackville St., a "labels-free" environment where pounding bass overtakes both gay and straight dancers. (☎422-2957. Drag night W and Su, karaoke Tu. 19+. $5 cover F-Sa. Open nightly until 4am.)

LIGHTHOUSE ROUTE   ☎902

A drive along Nova Scotia's Lighthouse Route reveals some of the province's richest history and scenery: picturesque fishing villages perched on wave-battered rocks give way to sandy beaches; seaside forests and ocean caves can be found minutes from local artisans' crafts shops; and the Atlantic Ocean is the source of the region's spirit, as well as its income. Leave at least a full day to drive along the 350km route between Halifax and Yarmouth.

PEGGY'S COVE

The lighthouse at Peggy's Cove is the third most popular tourist destination in Canada and is believed to be the most photographed lighthouse in the world. It is a testament to fortitude atop granite boulders constantly battered by the sea. The ocean and charming, tiny fishing village makes the approximately 45min. trip from Halifax (go south on Hwy. 103 to Exit 2b, and then down Rte. 333) well worth the time. The lighthouse today houses the world's only **lighthouse-post office;** visitors take advantage of this fact by sending post cards 10am-6pm every day. The postal code is B30 3S1. There is also a **Provincial Visitor Information Centre,** at 109 Peggy's Point Rd., that helps orient tourists and provides background information about the village. (☎823-2253. Open daily July-Aug. 9am-7pm, Sept.-June 9am-5pm.)

MAHONE BAY

The town of Mahone Bay is famous for its local crafts and folk art; take Hwy. 333 to Hwy. 3 and head west about 90km. The **tourist office** is at 165 Edgewater St. (☎624-6151. Open daily July-Aug. 9am-7pm; June and Sept. 9am-6pm; May and Oct. 9am-5pm.) Main St. is lined with art galleries and artisans' workshops, many of which are open for demonstrations. Mahone Bay also has a collection of great restaurants. For huge sandwiches ($3-6) and homemade desserts ($4), head to the **Saltspray Cafe Inc. ❶,** 621 S. Main St. (☎624-0457. Cup of chowder $4.75. Open daily June-Sept. 7am-9pm; Oct.-May 8am-8pm.) The first weekend in August, the **Wooden Boat Festival** (☎624-0348; www.woodenboatfestival.org), a celebration of the region's nautical heritage, includes a boat-building contest and race.

LUNENBURG

Only 10km south of Mahone Bay, dark-trimmed Victorian houses and the occasional German flag hint at Lunenburg's status as Canada's oldest German settlement. The town, declared a UNESCO World Heritage Site due to its abundance of preserved and historic buildings, is well-known for producing the undefeated racing schooner **Bluenose,** which now adorns the Canadian dime and Nova Scotia's license plate. (☎800-763-1963. Call for tours.) Explore ocean-going history and commercial fishing species at the **Fisheries Museum of the Atlantic,** 68 Bluenose Dr., by the harborfront. (☎634-4794; www.fisheries.museum.gov.ns.ca. Open mid-May to late Oct. daily 9:30am-5pm; low-season M-F 8:30am-4:30pm. $9, seniors $7, ages 6-17 $3; families $22; low-season free.) For more info, consult the **tourist office,** on Blockhouse Hill Rd. (☎634-8100; www.explorelunenburg.ca. Open daily May-June 9am-7pm; July-Aug. 9am-8pm; Sept.-Oct. 9am-6pm.)

YARMOUTH

The port of Yarmouth, 339km from Halifax on the southwestern tip of Nova Scotia, has a major **ferry terminal,** 58 Water St., where boats set out across the Bay of Fundy to Maine. (Open daily 8am-5pm.) All ferry and cruise prices are listed in US dollars: **Bay Ferries** provides fast service to Bar Harbor, ME. (☎742-6800 or 888-249-7245; www.catferry.com. 2½hr.; 2 per day, low-season 1 per day; $55, seniors $50, ages 11-17 $35, ages 3-10 $25; low-season $45/$40/$30/$20. Bikes $10; cars from $95 (low-season $85), depending on length and height, passengers and driver not

EASTERN CANADA

included. $5 port fee, $3 security tax. Reservations recommended.) **Scotia Prince Cruises** sail 11hr. from Yarmouth to Portland, ME. (☎800-845-4073 or 866-412-5270; www.scotiaprince.com. To Portland: daily, 9am Atlantic time. Late June to Oct. $75, ages 5-12 $38; low-season $65/$33. Bikes $15/$10; cars $95/$85. $9 passage charge per person. Car fares do not include passengers and driver.) The **visitors center,** 228 Main St., up the hill from the ferry terminal, houses both **Nova Scotia Information** (☎742-5033) and **Yarmouth Town and County Information.** (☎742-6639. Both open May to mid-Oct. Su-Tu and Th-Sa 7:30am-9pm, W 7:30am-5pm.)

CAPE BRETON ISLAND ☎902

Located north of Halifax and set against the awesome canvas of the Atlantic Ocean, Cape Breton Island offers wonderful vistas and overflows with Acadian and Gaelic heritage. To top it all off, the impressive mountains and valleys of Cape Breton Highlands National Park accentuate the island's natural grandeur.

⌷ PRACTICAL INFORMATION. Acadia Bus Lines, 99 Terminal Rd., in Sydney. (☎564-5533 or 800-567-5151; www.acadianbus.com. Open M-F 6:30am-11pm, Sa-Su 6:30am-6pm.) To **Halifax** (5½-7½hr., 3 per day, $40-62) and **Moncton** (9½hr., 1 per day, $79). **Transit Cape Breton** (☎539-8124) provides public transit in Sydney, Glace Bay, and Waterford. Privately-owned **shuttle companies** service the smaller communities on the island; check the *Cape Breton Post* and the visitors center for listings. Taxi: **Citywide** ☎539-4004, in Sydney. The **Port Hastings Visitor Information Centre,** up the hill from the Canso Causeway in Port Hastings, provides helpful advice. Pick up a free copy of *Dreamers and Doers*, a comprehensive provincial tourist guide, to find out the latest happenings. (☎625-4201. Open daily mid-June to Aug. 8am-8:30pm; Apr. to mid-June and Sept.-Jan. 9am-5pm.) **Hotlines: Distress Line,** ☎567-2911 or 800-957-9995. **Medical Services: Victoria County Memorial Hospital,** 30 Margaree Rd., Baddeck. (☎295-2112.) **Internet Access: Baddeck Public Library,** 526 Chebucto St. (☎295-2055. Open M 1-5pm, Tu and F 1-5pm and 6-8pm, Th 5-8pm, Sa 10am-noon and 1-5pm. Free.) **Post Office:** 269 Charlotte St., Sydney. (☎800-267-1177. Open M-F 8am-5pm.) **Postal Code:** B1P 1T0. **Area Code:** 902.

⌷⌷ ACCOMMODATIONS AND FOOD. The town of Baddeck, north of Port Hastings, charms visitors with a quaint downtown and great seafood. You'll find immaculate rooms, a perfect location, and a great price at the **Tree Seat B&B ❸,** 555 Chebucto St., next to the Bell Museum. The friendly owners serve a healthy, filling country-style continental breakfast. (☎295-1996. Check-in 4pm. Singles $60-90.) **Cabot Trail Hostel ❶,** 23349 Cabot Trail, the only hostel on the Cabot Trail, is in Pleasant Bay, and has frequent barbecue and lobster dinners, whale-watching packages, and pickup service from Baddeck. (☎224-1976; www.cabottrail.com/hostel. Kitchen. Internet access. Linen included. Laundry $2. Dorms $24.) **University College of Cape Breton (UCCB) ❷,** down Hwy. 4 near the airport in Sydney, offers functional dorm rooms from May to August. Internet access is available in the university library. (☎563-1803; www.uccb.ns.ca. Laundry and TV room on each floor. Reception 24hr. Singles $37, students $31; doubles $46/$40; 4-bedroom apartments with private bath $115.) At **Baddeck Lobster Suppers ❸,** 17 Ross St., the famished have a choice of salmon plates ($20-24) or a 1 lb. lobster meal ($29), both of which come with as much chowder and mussels as you can eat. (☎295-3307. Lunch $5-10. Open daily 11:30am-1:30pm and 4-9pm.) Those with a sweet tooth should find their way to **SleepyCats Sweets ❶,** 503 Chebucto St., where a heaping waffle cone of homemade ice cream costs $3.75. (☎295-2062. Open daily 11am-9pm.)

🖎 🎜 **SIGHTS AND ENTERTAINMENT.** Cape Breton's most appealing quality is its natural splendor. The best way to take in the scenery is the 🖎**Cabot Trail,** a drive that winds along steep rocky cliffs by the coast and takes as long as two days to complete. Start in Baddeck, on the Trans-Canada Hwy., 80km north of Port Hastings; for the best views, follow the trail clockwise. The trail's northern segment winds through **Cape Breton Highlands National Park** (p. 212); visits from May to mid-October require a parks pass ($5, seniors $4.25, ages 6-16 $2.50; families $13). Beaches around Ingonish can be crowded in the summer. For long sandy beaches without the crowds, turn off the trail in Cape North and go 5km in the direction of Meat Cove to **Cabot's Landing Beach.** The adventurous may wish to go all the way to **Meat Cove** (at the end of an 8km dirt road), a tiny fishing village with incredible ocean vistas for whale watching, several hiking trails, kayak rentals, and the **Meat Cove campground ❶,** where the drive is more than justified by the view. (☎ 383-2379. Kayaks $15 for the first hr., $5 each additional hr. Showers. Sites $18 per night.) Offshore is **Saint Paul Island;** known as the "Graveyard of the Gulf," it is the site of over 300 shipwrecks. In the summer months, warm waters support huge plankton populations, making the waters off Cape Breton a popular summer resort for playful whales. **Wesley's Whale Watch,** in Pleasant Bay next to the Whale Interpretive Centre, runs traditional "Cape Island" tours on a fishing trawler, as well as more intense "Zodiac" excursions on a speedy rubber boat. The Zodiac excursion leaves from Chéticamp. (☎ 224-1919 or 866-999-4253; www.novascotiawhales.com. Each tour 2hr., 5 per day. Cape Island $25, children $10; wheelchair accessible. Zodiac $36/$18. Refund for trips without whale sightings. Reservations required for Zodiac and recommended for Cape Island.)

The views from the trail in the western side of the park, where the highlands meet the Gulf of St. Lawrence, are spectacular, particularly in the region north of **Chéticamp.** To view the coast by kayak, stop in at **Scotia Sea Kayaking,** in Chéticamp. Tours range from afternoon jaunts to three-day excursions. (☎ 235-2675 or 800-564-2330; www.scotiakayaking.com. Half-day tours $49, ages 6-17 $39; food and camping equipment rental included. Reservations recommended.) Chéticamp, an Acadian village, also specializes in traditional folk art, and collectors will find no shortage of local galleries. As you make your way back into Baddeck, stop in at the **Alexander Graham Bell Museum,** 559 Chebacto St. Visitors can learn about Bell's passion for inventions, his impressive humanitarian work with the deaf, and the creative genius of the "queerest man fooling around the live-long day," as his neighbors here once referred to him. (☎ 295-2069. Open daily June 9am-6pm; July to mid-Oct. 8:30am-6pm; mid-Oct. to May 9am-5pm; Nov.-Apr. by appointment only. $5.75, seniors $5, ages 6-16 $3; families $15.)

Near Sydney on the south shore of the island, the **Fleur-de-lis Trail** covers important historical sites. The 🖎**Fortress of Louisbourg,** 30km south of Sydney, is a huge, historically accurate reconstruction of the French fortress and port city as it was in 1744, before being taken twice and destroyed once by the British. Interpreters in period dress reenact military exercises and scenes from daily life, and visitors can dine on 18th-century cuisine. (☎ 733-2280; www.parkscanada.gc.ca. Open daily May-June and Sept. 9:30am-5pm (guided tours only); July-Aug. 9am-6pm. $14, seniors $12, ages 6-16 $7; families $34. Three restaurants, two "low-class" and one "high-class," serve 18th-century-style food with authentic ingredients and recipes. "Low-class" meals around $11, "high-class" $16.) At the **Cape Breton Miner's Museum,** 42 Birkley St. in Glace Bay, 35km north of Louisbourg, retired miners lead visitors on a 1hr. tour of a 1930s-era coal mine. (☎ 849-4522; www.minersmuseum.com. Open June-Aug. M and W-Su 10am-6pm, Tu 10am-7pm; Sept.-May M-F 9am-4pm. $10, children $8; families $25.) In mid-October, the **Celtic Colours International Festival** brings musicians from all over the world to Cape Breton for a week of concerts. One of the highlights is the world's biggest square dance, with several thousand feet stomping in unison. (☎ 562-6700 or 877-285-2321; www.celtic-colours.com.)

EASTERN CANADA

CAPE BRETON HIGHLANDS NATIONAL PARK

Exploring the national park area on foot or bike reveals mountain passes, steep descents, and rocky coastal vistas that dwarf visitors in their majesty. There are 25 hiking and walking trails ranging from 20min. family strolls to challenging overnight adventures. Walk along the dramatic headland of ▨Skyline to spot abundant moose and perhaps bears or coyotes on the ground, bald eagles soaring in the sky, and whales spouting in the sea far below. An 8.7km loop, the easy trail takes 2-3hr. to complete and includes magnificent views from a boardwalk section through protected terrain on an exposed ridge above the sea. The **Corney Brook Trail** (8km, 2-3hr.), a particularly beautiful trail of intermediate difficulty, reveals a small, secluded waterfall. **North Bay Beach,** near Ingonish, is a great spot for a picnic or a supervised dip in clear water. A parks pass is required mid-May to mid-October. ($5, seniors $4.25, ages 6-16 $2.50; families $13). There are two **visitors centers,** one at the east entrance to the park in Ingonish and the other at the west entrance just past Chéticamp. (☎224-2306. Both open daily July-Aug. 8am-8pm; Sept.-Oct. and mid-May to June 9am-5pm.) The park also has six serviced **campgrounds ❶,** three large with 90-200 sites (Chéticamp in the west and Broad Cove and Ingonish in the east), three small with 10-20 sites (Corney Brook in the west and MacIntosh Brook and Big Intervale in the north), and one wilderness area (Fishing Cove in the west). If you are interested in some privacy at your site, choose Chéticamp—the others are not wooded. Chéticamp and Broad Cove are open year-round, the others operate in summer only. (☎877-737-3783; www.pccamping.ca. Reservations accepted at Chéticamp only. Sites $21, with hookup $23-27; in winter $17. Wilderness camping $8 per person.) Wildlife in the park is abundant; moose sightings are particularly common. *Please do not feed the moose.*

NEWFOUNDLAND

Perched off the eastern shore of North America, Newfoundland had the earliest encounter with European civilization on the continent. In the 10th century, 500 years before Columbus, Viking seafarers established an outpost on the north shore of the island. The region's legendary stock of codfish later lured British and Irish colonists to Newfoundland's craggy coast. Over the next few centuries, Newfoundland developed a distinct maritime culture, incorporating elements of Irish and British seafaring traditions to form a unique accent, type of music, and way of life. Geographic remoteness hardly dampened the Islanders' enthusiasm for Great Britain—Newfoundland was the last province to join the Canadian confederation. It maintains an independent spirit as well as gorgeous vistas, rugged fjords, the most dense concentration of pubs on one street in North America, and the friendliest folks east of Iowa.

▨ PRACTICAL INFORMATION

Capital: St. John's.

Visitor Info: Tourism Newfoundland and Labrador, P.O. Box 8730, St. John's A1B 4K2 (☎800-563-6353; www.gov.nf.ca/tourism).

Newfoundland Ferries: Marine Atlantic (☎800-341-7981; www.marine-atlantic.ca) runs service from **North Sydney, NS** to **Argentia** (14hr.; late June to mid-Sept. 3 per week, late Sept. M only; $76, seniors $68, ages 5-12 $38; bicycles $25; automobiles $157) and **Port aux Basques** (6-8hr., 1-3 per day, $27/$25/$14/$12/$77). Prices for vehicles are in addition to passenger fare; vehicles longer than 20ft. incur additional charges. Reservations highly recommended. Arrive at least 1hr. early.

Drinking Age: 19. **Postal Abbreviation:** NL. **Sales Tax:** 15% HST.
Time Zone: Newfoundland Time, 30min. ahead of Atlantic time.

ST. JOHN'S ☎ 709

One of the oldest ports in North America, St. John's has grown from a 16th-century strategic harbor to the capital of Canada's easternmost province. The city's heart continues to be its waterfront, crammed with cruise ships, freighters, and fishing boats from around the world. Despite this traffic, the hilly downtown—stacked full of brightly colored rowhouses—has maintained a hospitable, residential feel, but also features countless pubs, quality restaurants, and swanky Scandinavian clothing stores.

🔃 PRACTICAL INFORMATION. The Trans-Canada Hwy. becomes **Kenmount Road** as it enters the city and is packed with strip malls, fast food restaurants, and chain motels. From the end of Kenmount Rd., **Freshwater Road** leads into the downtown core, where **Harbour Drive, Water Street,** and **Duckworth Road** run parallel to one another and host numerous stores, pubs, and restaurants. Driving downtown is a confusing affair; walking is a much better option. **St. John's International Airport** (☎758-8515; www.stjohnsairport.com) has daily flights from Halifax, Montréal, and Toronto. Taxi service from the airport to downtown is about $15. **DRL Coachlines** (☎888-269-1852; www.drlgroup.com/coachlines), a regional firm, runs buses from the Memorial University student center to Port aux Basques (13hr., 1 per day, $97) on the far end of the island. Numerous **local taxi shuttles** service the more remote communities; ask at the visitors center. **St. John's Metrobus** operates within the city. (☎722-9400. Buses daily 6:30am-11pm. $1.75, children $1.25, under 3 free.) **Taxi: Coop Taxi** ☎726-6668. **Canary Cycles,** 294 Water St., rents bikes for $25 per day. (☎579-5972; www.canarycycles.com. Helmet $5. Credit card required. Open in summer M-F 10am-5:30pm, Sa 9:30am-5pm.) The **St. John's Tourist Information Center,** 348 Water St., aids travelers with information, lodging and tour reservations. (☎576-8106; www.stjohns.ca. Open mid-June to early Sept. M-F 9am-4:30pm, Sa-Su 9am-5pm; call for winter hours.) The only **Internet access** downtown can be found at **Wordplay,** a bookstore located at 221 Duckworth St. Access is $5 per 30min. (☎726-9193 or 800-563-9100; www.wordplay.com. Open M-Sa 10am-6pm, Su noon-5pm.) **Medical Services: General Hospital,** 300 Prince Philip Pkwy. (☎777-6300). **Hotlines: Crisis Line,** ☎737-4668 or 888-737-4668. **Sexual Assault Line,** ☎726-1411. 24hr. **Post Office:** 354 Water St. (☎758-1003. Open M-F 8am-5pm.) **Postal Code:** A1C 1C0. **Area Code:** 709.

🏠 ACCOMMODATIONS. Most accommodations in St. John's are Victorian B&Bs. Although quality is high and the charm is undeniable, the prices (starting at $75 for rooms downtown) discourage many budget travelers. There are a few less-pricey options, but demand often far outstrips supply; be sure to make reservations if visiting in July and August. The **Downtown International Hostel ❶,** 25 Young St., has a great location, clean rooms, and a friendly atmosphere that often results in impromptu group trips to the pubs on George St. (☎754-7658; downtownhostel@yahoo.com. Well-equipped kitchen. Internet access. With only 8 beds, reservations are highly recommended. Dorms $23; private rooms $40.) **Memorial University ❶,** on Livyers Loop off Prince Phillip Dr., rents functional dorm rooms 10min. from downtown. (☎737-7933. Free linen and parking. Towels $2. Laundry facilities. Check-in daily 3pm-midnight, on call 24hr. Open May-Aug. Singles $33, students $25; doubles $54/$39.) The **Roses B&B ❹,** 9 Military Rd., two streets from Duckworth St., has a gorgeous harbor view and rooms that are downright proper. (☎726-3336 or 877-767-3722; www.wordplay.com/the_roses. Open year-round. Singles $75; doubles $85; suites for 3 $110.) If you prefer camping, **Pippy Park Trailer Park** ❶, on Nagle's Place off Allandale Rd. in Pippy Park, has partially wooded RV and tent sites, as well as flush toilets, showers, a dump station, laundry, a playground, and a general store. (☎737-3669; www.pippypark.com. Sites $16, with partial hook-up $22, with full hook-up $24.)

❏ **FOOD.** Fast food can be found along Kenmount Rd. near the university, while hipper restaurants cluster around Water St. For the budget-minded, **Mustang Sally's Cafe** ❶, 7 Queen St., at George St., satisfies the palate and the wallet. Choose your own ingredients for the well-known quesadillas and wraps ($5-7), and watch a rock 'n' roll concert DVD of your choice as you eat. (☎754-9727. Open June-Sept. Su-Th 11am-midnight, F-Sa 11am-4am; Oct.-May daily 11am-11pm.) **Chucky's Fish 'n' Ships** ❷, 10 Kings Rd. up the hill from Duckworth St., satisfies with traditional fish 'n' chips ($8) or, for the sophisticated carnivore, Newfoundland specialties like moose steak ($18), seal flipper pie ($11), and caribou or moose burgers (¼ lb. $4). Be prepared to wait if you do not have a reservation for dinner. (☎579-7888. Open M-F 11:30am-3pm and 4-8:45pm, Sa-Su 4:30-8:45pm.) **The Classic Cafe** ❸, 73 Duckworth St., takes a classy approach to traditional lunch and dinner favorites. The back porch has terrific views of the harbor. (☎726-4444. Chicken and fish entrees $13-20. Salads and sandwiches $4-9. Open daily 8am-11pm.)

> █! **WINDY WEATHER.** The weather in St. John's can be so extreme (winds at Signal Hill reach 140kph, and gusts hit 200kph) that locals have given it its own vocabulary. "Caplin Weather" refers to wet, foggy weather, common in June and July. In the winter, "growlers" loom in the waters off St. John's—large, unstable icebergs that are particularly dangerous to boats because of their low profile.

◩ **SIGHTS.** A trip up **Signal Hill,** on Signal Hill Rd. just east of Duckworth St., reveals gorgeous views of the harbor, the city, and the Atlantic Ocean. On the way up the hill, the new **Geocentre** offers a hands-on look at global and local geology. (☎737-7880; www.geocentre.ca. Open M-Sa 9:30am-5pm, Su 1-5pm; mid-Oct. to May closed M. $7.50, seniors and students $6, ages 5-17 $3.50; families $18.) By the top of the hill, the **Queen's Battery** commands a strategic position at the entrance of the harbor. The battery's six 32 lb. cannons protected the harbor during the 1860s, but by then St. John's had already been subjected to many bloody battles between the French and the English. The hill also has seen peaceful moments, the most famous in December 1901 when Marconi received the first transatlantic radio transmission at the top. **Cabot Tower,** at the peak of the hill, has an exhibit about Marconi and his breakthrough. The top of the tower offers the best view in town, of the harbor, Cape Spear, massive icebergs at sea around April to June, and—if you're lucky—frolicking whales. (Tower open daily 8:30am-8pm.) Four times a week during the summer, the **Signal Hill Tattoo** reenacts 19th-century military exercises; buy tickets at the **Interpretation Centre,** which details 500 years of Newfoundland history. (☎772-5367. Tattoo runs W-Th and Sa-Su at 11am and 3pm. Interpretation Centre open daily mid-June to early Sept. 8:30am-8pm; low-season 8:30am-4:30pm. Exhibits $3.50, seniors $3, ages 6-16 $1.75; families $8.75. Combination pass for Signal Hill and Cape Spear: $5.50/$5/$3/$14. Tattoo reenactment $2.) The ▧ **North Head Walking Trail** takes hikers to cliffs above the ocean and to the edge of the entrance to the harbor.

Go underwater without getting wet at **The Fluvarium** (meaning "windows on stream"), in Pippy Park off of Allandale Rd. near the university. One part of the museum allows visitors to peer into a stream and watch trout in their natural habitat. (☎754-3474; http://fluvarium.ca. $5, students and seniors $4, ages 6-14 $3; families $15. Open July-Aug. daily 9am-5pm; Apr.-June and Sept.-Oct. M-F 9am-5pm, Sa-Su noon-5pm; Jan.-Mar. M-F 9am-4:30pm, Sa-Su noon-4:30pm.) **Cape Spear,** 11 km out of town on Blackhead Rd., off Water St., is the easternmost land in North America. Two white lighthouses, one of which is the oldest surviving lighthouse in Canada, stand out against a green, rocky point and the slate-gray Atlantic. Paths meander around the shore, through the heath, and past two bunkers from World War II to the lighthouses. (☎772-4210. Visitors center open May-Oct. daily 10am-6pm. Lighthouse $3.50, seniors $3, ages 6-16 $1.75; families $8.75.) The **Irish Loop,** a day-long scenic drive around the southern tip of the Avalon Peninsula, grants views of icebergs, seasonal Atlantic puffins, and the rugged Avalon Peninsula Reserve. For kayaking, head to Cape Broyle on the Irish Loop. **Stan Cook Sea Kayaking,** 67 Circular Rd., has tours for all skill levels. (☎579-6353 or 888-747-6353; www.wildnfld.ca. Ages 10+. 2½hr. $52, 4hr. $75, full-day $105.) In St. John's, **Dee Jay Charters** runs whale-watching charters out of the harbor, across from the Murray premises. (☎753-8687. 2½hr. 3 trips per day. $25, ages 11-16 $10, under 10 free. Reservations recommended.)

🎭🎶 **ENTERTAINMENT AND NIGHTLIFE.** Entertainment options in St. John's are surprisingly varied. Traditional Newfoundland dinner parties ("times") include folk music, dancing, and sometimes theater; check at the visitors center for listings. More organized theater can be had just off Water St. at the converted **Longshoremen's Protective Union Hall (LSPU Hall),** 3 Victoria St. (☎753-4531). Every other summer, St. John's hosts the **Soundsymposium** (☎754-5409; www.soundsymposium.com), a festival of experimental and bizarre music where the **Harbour Symphony,** the world's only symphony of boat whistles, performs daily. The first Wednesday of every August brings the oldest continuous sporting event in North America, the **Royal St. John's Regatta,** to Quidi Vidi Lake (☎576-8921).

Less-organized fun can be found on **George Street,** or Pub Street, which has the highest concentration of bars on one strip in North America (24 in 1 sq. km), with themes and music to suit any partygoer. **The Ship,** 265 Duckworth St. at Solomon's Lane, is legendary for its excellent live music and relaxed feel. (☎753-3870. Pints $6-7. Live music Tu-Su. Cover W-Su $5-10. Open daily noon-2am.) **O'Reilly's Irish Pub,** 15 George St., packs in the 20-somethings with nightly Celtic Newfoundland music. (☎722-3735. Smoke-free main level. Open mic night Tu. Cover W-Su $3-5. Open Su-Th noon-2am, F-Sa noon-3am.) The psychedelic, smoky **Bar None,** 164 Water St., upstairs from the alley, attracts a young crowd with rock and alternative tunes. (☎579-2110. Pints $6. Open mic Tu. Open M-W 2pm-2am, Th-Su 2pm-3am.)

GROS MORNE NATIONAL PARK ☎709

On precisely the opposite side of Newfoundland from St. John's, Gros Morne encompasses more than 1800 sq. km of fjords, conifer forests, and glacier-carved valleys. Designated a UNESCO World Heritage Site in 1987, Gros Morne preserves some of the wildest scenery and animal life in North America.

> **❗ THIS AIN'T BULLWINKLE.** Moose are a common sight in Newfoundland, and not always a welcome one; they pose a serious hazard to drivers. Most accidents occur between dusk and dawn, when the moose are most active. Avoid driving at these times, or use extreme caution.

🛈 **PRACTICAL INFORMATION.** Tucked against the Gulf of St. Lawrence on the west coast of Newfoundland, Gros Morne is reached by taking the **430 spur (Viking Trail)** off the Trans-Canada Hwy. in Deer Lake. There is no public transit in Gros Morne. **DRL Coachlines** (☎888-269-1852) runs a daily bus from St. John's to Port aux Basques, with a stop in Deer Lake. From there, **Pittman's Shuttle Service** (☎634-4710) will take you into the park, where the town of **Rocky Harbour** is the main service center. The main **visitors center** is at the center of the park, near Rocky Harbour; pick up good advice and a free copy of *Tuckamore*, the invaluable park guide. (☎458-3602. Open daily mid-June to Aug. 9am-9pm; May to mid-June and Sept. to mid-Oct. 9am-5pm; mid-Oct. to Jan. M-F 9am-4pm.) Separated from Rocky Harbour and the northern portion of the park by Bonne Bay, the southernmost region of Gros Morne has beautiful hiking trails and a new **Discovery Centre,** with exhibits on Gros Morne's geology and conservation. (☎453-2127. Open daily mid-June to Aug. 9am-6pm; May to mid-June and Sept. to mid-Oct. 9am-5pm.) This part of the park is about 70km from Rocky Harbour on Hwy. 431. The **Bonne Bay Water Taxi,** between Norris Point Wharf and Woody Point Wharf, is a quicker option. (☎458-2730. 3 departures daily. $6, students $4; families $10.) From mid-May to mid-October, there are entrance fees for the national park, charged at either the entrance kiosk or the visitors center. (Daily pass $7.50, seniors $6, ages 6-16 $3.75; families $15.)

⚑ CAMPING. Gros Morne contains five developed **campgrounds ❶** comprising over 300 sites. Although the park is rarely full, campers planning to visit during the busy months of July and August would be wise to reserve a site at their desired campground. (☎800-414-6765 or 877-737-3783; www.pccamping.ca. Reservation fee $15.) The developed campgrounds contain the usual amenities: running water, pit toilets, and close proximity to picnic grounds. In addition, **Trout River, Lomond, Berry Hill,** and **Shallow Bay** sport playgrounds, showers, and hot water. **Green Point,** Shallow Bay, and Lomond campgrounds are on the coast with unsupervised beach access; Lomond has a boat launch. Trout River campground is on a pond and has swimming and a boat launch. Berry Hill campground is close to a number of trailheads. Campgrounds are open mid-June to mid-Sept., with the exception of Lomond (open mid-May to mid-Oct.) and Green Point (open year-round; no water Oct.-Apr.). **Backcountry camping ❶** is allowed along some of the longer trails with a permit. Campers pay a reduced entry fee to the park, but must pay a daily rate for camping. (Entry for campers $5.50, seniors $4.25; families $11. Campsites $21, except at Green Point $13; backcountry camping $8 per person.) For the less rugged and more frugal, the **Juniper Campground ❶,** in Rocky Harbour, runs a small, friendly **hostel** with 15 beds and a kitchen. (☎458-2917; www.grosmorne.com/juniper. Kitchen. Dorms $14; campsites $14, with hookup $19.)

⚐ OUTDOOR ACTIVITIES. The easiest way to take in the Gros Morne scenery is aboard a **boat tour** of the fjords and shoreline. **Bon Tours** runs the most popular tour, at Western Brook Pond. (☎458-2730. 2hr., plus 3km walk from parking lot to dock; allow up to 1¾hr. to reach dock from Rocky Harbour. Wheelchair accessible. In July-Aug., 3 tours daily. $35, ages 12-16 $16, under 12 $10; families $75. Reservations required.) Those more interested in self-propulsion can rent a **kayak** from Norris Point, just south of the visitors center. (☎458-2722. 2hr. kayak rental $25, 8hr. $35, full-day $40. 2½hr. tours $45, seniors $40, ages 16 and under $35; families $140; full-day tours $105/$95/$80/$224.) There are hundreds of kilometers of trails to enjoy. Park interpreters lead many fascinating guided hikes; check *Tuckamore* for schedules. **Gros Morne Mountain** (16km, 7-8hr.) ascends a steep gully up the face of the mountain and is among the park's most rigorous hikes. Though it is possible to complete the hike in one day, primitive backcountry campsites line the route. The view from the peak is awe-inspiring but closed each year until July 1 so that alpine bunnies can mate. Hikers should stop by the visitors center before hitting the trail for an updated weather report, since conditions atop the mountain can change rapidly. Bring food, water, rain gear, and extra clothes for the hike. The **Tablelands Trail** (6km, 2hr.) is less demanding and affords a remarkable view of a tundra-like landscape.

MID-ATLANTIC

From the Eastern seaboard of New York south through Virginia, the mid-Atlantic states claim many of the nation's major historical, political, and economic centers. This region has witnessed the rotation of US capitals: first Philadelphia, PA; then Princeton, NJ; Annapolis, MD; Trenton, NJ; New York City, NY; and finally Washington, D.C. During the Civil War, the mid-Atlantic even housed the Confederate capital, Richmond, VA. Urban centers cover much of the land, but the great outdoors have survived. The Appalachian Trail meanders through the region, and New York's Adirondacks compose the largest national park in the lower 48 states.

HIGHLIGHTS OF THE MID-ATLANTIC

NEW YORK CITY, NY. The Big Apple combines world-class museums (p. 238) with top-notch arts and entertainment venues (p. 241).

WASHINGTON, D.C. The impressive Smithsonian Museum (p. 336), the White House (p. 335), the Capitol (p. 331), and a slew of monuments (p. 332) comprise some of the coveted attractions of the nation's capital.

SCENIC DRIVES. The long and winding Blue Ridge Parkway (p. 356) is justifiably famous.

HISTORIC SITES. Philadelphia, PA (p. 279), abounds with colonial landmarks commemorating the Declaration of Independence and the Constitution. Mount Vernon, VA (p. 342), and Colonial Williamsburg, VA (p. 348), offer excellent "living history" presentations on their impressively restored estates.

COLLEGES AND COLLEGE TOWNS. The University of Virginia in Charlottesville, VA (p. 352), offers a student community and small-town charm. However, Washington and Lee University in Lexington, VA (p. 357), has a campus that rivals UVA's in its beauty.

NEW YORK

This state offers a little bit of everything: the excitement of New York City, the grandeur of Niagara Falls, and the natural beauty of the Catskills and the Adirondacks. While "The City" attracts cosmopolitan types looking for adventure year-round, those seeking a more mellow experience head upstate. Here, surrounded by the beauty of cool waterways and lush, wooded mountainsides, you may find it difficult to remember that smog and traffic even exist. The cities of upstate New York have a sweet natural flavor contrasting the tang of the Big Apple.

⊁ PRACTICAL INFORMATION

Capital: Albany.

Visitor Info: Division of Tourism, 1 Commerce Plaza, Albany 12245 (☎518-474-4116 or 800-225-5697; www.iloveny.state.ny.us). Operators available M-F 8:30am-4:45pm. **New York State Office of Parks and Recreation and Historic Preservation,** Empire State Plaza, Agency Bldg. 1, Albany 12238 (☎518-474-0456). Open M-F 9am-5pm.

Postal Abbreviation: NY. **Sales Tax:** 7-9%, depending on county.

MID-ATLANTIC

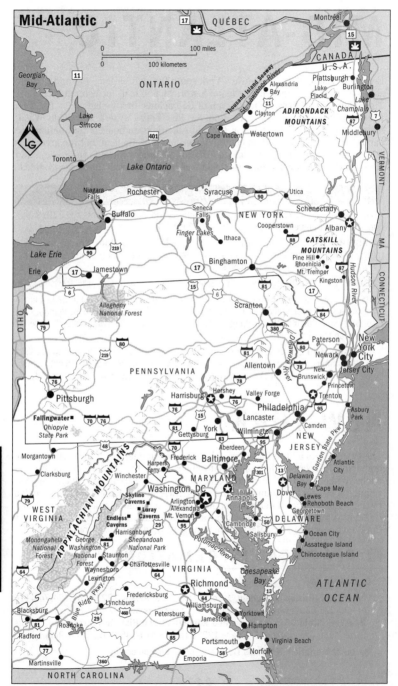

Mid-Atlantic

QUÉBEC

Montréal

CANADA
U.S.A.

Georgian Bay

ONTARIO

0   100 miles
0   100 kilometers

Plattsburgh

Thousand Island Seaway

St. Lawrence River

Alexandria Bay

Lake Placid

Burlington

Lake Champlain

ADIRONDACK MOUNTAINS

Middlebury

Lake Simcoe

Clayton

Cape Vincent   Watertown

Toronto

Lake Ontario

Niagara Falls

Rochester   Syracuse   Utica

Seneca Falls

NEW YORK

Schenectady

Buffalo

Finger Lakes

Ithaca

Cooperstown

Albany

CATSKILL MOUNTAINS

Lake Erie

Erie

Jamestown

Binghamton

Pine Hill
Phoenicia
Mt. Tremper
Kingston

Hudson River

Allegheny National Forest

Scranton

Delaware River

Paterson

New York City

PENNSYLVANIA

Pittsburgh

Newark

New Brunswick

Jersey City

Allentown

Princeton

Trenton

Fallingwater ■
Ohiopyle State Park

Harrisburg   Hershey

Valley Forge

Philadelphia

Asbury Park

Lancaster

York

Gettysburg

Wilmington

Camden

NEW JERSEY

Garden State Pkwy.

Atlantic City

Morgantown

Clarksburg

APPALACHIAN MOUNTAINS

Aberdeen

Frederick   Baltimore

MARYLAND

Delaware Bay

Cape May

Lewes
Rehoboth Beach

Harpers Ferry

Winchester

Washington, DC

Dover

WEST VIRGINIA

Skyline Caverns

Arlington
Alexandria
Mt. Vernon

Annapolis

Georgetown

DELAWARE

Endless Caverns ■

Luray Caverns

Cambridge

Ocean City

Monongahela National Forest

Harrisonburg

Shenandoah National Park

Salisbury

Assateague Island
Chincoteague Island

George Washington National Forest

Staunton

Waynesboro

Charlottesville

VIRGINIA

Chesapeake Bay

ATLANTIC OCEAN

Lexington

Richmond

Blacksburg

Blue Ridge Pkwy.

Fredericksburg

Lynchburg

Williamsburg

Yorktown

Radford

Roanoke

Petersburg

Jamestown

Hampton

Portsmouth

Virginia Beach

Martinsville

Emporia

Norfolk

NORTH CAROLINA

VERMONT

MA

CONNECTICUT

OHIO

NEW YORK CITY ☎212

Since its earliest days, New York City has scoffed at the timid offerings of other American cities. It boasts the most immigrants, the tallest skyscrapers, the biggest museum in the Western Hemisphere, and plenty of large landfills. Even the vast blocks of concrete have their own gritty charm. With a population of eight million, New York City's five boroughs teem with something much better than fresh air: constant, varied, and thrilling action. There's flamenco at an outdoor cafe, jazz in a historic speakeasy, house and techno in a flashy club. For more information, see our city guide, ▨*Let's Go: New York City*.

New Yorkers were awakened to both horror and heroism on September 11, 2001, when Osama bin Laden's suicide hijackers crashed two large airplanes into the two towers of the World Trade Center. The city has returned to normal with resilience, but it hasn't forgotten. Corporate skyscrapers and government buildings are heavily guarded. Nevertheless, don't let security measures keep you from appreciating the ultimate big city.

✈ INTERCITY TRANSPORTATION

Airports: 4 airports serve the New York City metropolitan area.

John F. Kennedy Airport (JFK; ☎718-244-4444), at the end of the Van Wyck Expwy., in southern Queens. JFK handles most international and many domestic flights. The airport is 15 mi. from Midtown Manhattan, but the drive can take 1hr. The AirTrain runs from JFK to 2 subway stops leading into the city. From Howard Beach Station, connect to the A subway train. From Jamaica Station, connect to E, J, or Z subway train. (Allow 1hr. for entire trip; AirTrain every 4-8min. 6am-11pm, every 12min. 11pm-6am; $5 plus subway fare on MetroCard.)

LaGuardia Airport (☎718-533-3400), off Exit 7 on the Grand Central Pkwy., in northern Queens. LaGuardia is 9 mi. from Midtown Manhattan; the drive is around 25min. Domestic flights. The MTA M60 bus connects to Manhattan subway lines 1 and 9 at 110th St./Broadway; A, B, C, D at 125th St./St. Nicholas Ave.; 2, 3 at 125th St./Lenox (Sixth) Ave.; 4, 5, 6 at 125th St./Lexington Ave. The Q33 bus goes to Jackson Heights/Roosevelt Ave. in Queens for 7, E, F, G, R, V; the Q48 bus goes to 74th St./Broadway in Queens for 7, E, F, G, R, V. (Allow at least 1½hr. for all routes. M60 runs daily 5am-1am, Q33 and Q48 24hr.; all buses $2.) Taxi to Manhattan $21-30 (plus tolls and tip).

Newark Liberty International Airport (☎973-961-6000), off Exit 14 on I-95, 16 mi. west of Midtown in Newark, NJ. Domestic and international flights. Olympia Airport Express (☎973-964-6233) travels from the airport to Port Authority, Grand Central Terminal, and Penn Station (15-60min.); departs for Port Authority every 5-10min. 4:15am-11:45pm, departs for Penn Station 4am-11pm, departs for Grand Central every 20-30min. 4am-11pm; $12. Bus #107 by the New Jersey Transit Authority (☎973-762-5100) covers Newark, Newark International Airport (North Terminal), and Port Authority (25min., every 30-45min. 5:20am-1am, $3.60).

Islip Long Island MacArthur Airport (☎631-467-3210), 50 mi. from Midtown in Ronkonkoma, NY. Take the shuttle van service or the S57 bus to the Ronkonkoma train station. Shuttle ($5) departs from the baggage claim every 30min. 6am-10:30pm. Bus ($1.50) departs every hr., no service Su. From Ronkonkoma, the Long Island Rail Road (LIRR) runs trains into Penn Station (1½hr.; departs around every 30min. on-peak, every hr. off-peak; $6.50).

Trains: Grand Central Terminal, 42nd St. and Park Ave. (Subway: 4, 5, 6, 7, S to 42nd St./Grand Central), handles **Metro-North** (☎800-638-7646) commuter lines to Connecticut and NY suburbs. **Amtrak** (☎800-872-7245) runs out of **Penn Station,** 33rd St. and Eighth Ave. (Subway: 1, 2, 3, 9 to 34th St./Penn Station/Seventh Ave.; A, C, E to 34th St./Penn Station/Eighth Ave.) To: **Boston** (4-5hr., $64); **Philadelphia** (1½hr., $48); **Washington, D.C.** (3-4hr., $72). The **Long Island Railroad (LIRR;** ☎718-217-5477) and **NJ Transit** (☎973-762-5100) commuter rails also run from Penn Station. At 33rd St. and Sixth Ave., **PATH** (☎800-234-7284) trains depart for New Jersey.

Buses: Greyhound (☎800-229-9424) buses leave the **Port Authority Terminal,** 42nd St. and Eighth Ave. (☎564-8484. Subway: A, C, E to 42nd St./Port Authority.) To: **Boston** (4-6hr., $35); **Philadelphia** (2-3hr., $21); **Washington, D.C.** (4½hr., $35). *Watch for con artists and pickpockets, especially at night.*

▣ ORIENTATION

NYC is comprised of **five boroughs:** the Bronx, Brooklyn, Manhattan, Queens, and Staten Island. Flanked on the east by the East River (actually a strait) and on the west by the Hudson River, **Manhattan** is an island, measuring only 13 mi. long and 2½ mi. wide. **Queens** and **Brooklyn** are on the other side of the East River. **Staten Island,** southwest of Manhattan, is the most residential borough. North of Manhattan sits the **Bronx,** the only borough connected by land to the rest of the US.

BOROUGHS

MANHATTAN

Above 14th Street, Manhattan is an organized grid of avenues running north-south and streets east-west. Street numbers grow as you travel north. Avenues are slightly less predictable: some are numbered, while others are named. The numbers of the avenues increase as you go west. **Broadway,** which follows an old Algonquin trail, defies the rectangular pattern, cutting diagonally east across the island at 23rd St. **Central Park** and **Fifth Avenue** (south of 59th St., north of 110th St.) separate the city into the East Side and West Side. **Washington Heights** is located north of 155th St.; **Morningside Heights** (above 110th St. and below 125th St.) is sandwiched between **Harlem** (150s to 110th St.) and the **Upper West Side** (110th St. to 59th St., west of Central Park). The museum-heavy **Upper East Side** is across Central Park, above 59th St. on Fifth Ave. **Midtown** (59th St. to 42nd St.) includes Times Square and the Theater District. **Lower Midtown** (41st St. to 14th St.) includes **Herald Square, Chelsea,** and **Union Square.**

    Below 14th St., the city dissolves into a confusing tangle of old, narrow streets that aren't numbered south of Houston St. The bohemian **East Village** and **Alphabet City** are grid-like, with alphabetized avenues from Ave. A to Ave. D, east of First Ave. Intellectual **Greenwich Village,** to the west, is especially complicated west of Sixth Ave. Moving south, trendy **SoHo** (South of Houston St.) and **TriBeCa** (Triangle Below Canal St.) are just west of historically ethnic enclaves **Little Italy, Chinatown,** and the **Lower East Side.** The **Financial District/Wall Street area** at the tip of Manhattan, set over the original Dutch layout, is full of narrow, winding, one-way streets.

BROOKLYN

The **Brooklyn-Queens Expressway (BQE)** links to the **Belt Parkway,** and circumscribes Brooklyn. Ocean Pkwy., Ocean Ave., Coney Island Ave., and diagonal Flatbush Ave. run from the beaches of southern Brooklyn (**Coney Island** and **Brighton Beach**) to the heart of the borough in **Prospect Park.** The streets of western Brooklyn (including **Park Slope**) are aligned with the western shore and collide at a 45° angle with central Brooklyn's main arteries. In northern Brooklyn (including **Williamsburg, Greenpoint, Brooklyn Heights,** and **Downtown Brooklyn**), several avenues—Atlantic Ave., Eastern Pkwy., and Flushing Ave.—travel east into Queens.

QUEENS

The streets of Queens resemble neither the orderly grid of Upper Manhattan nor the haphazard angles of Greenwich Village. Streets generally run north-south and are numbered from west to east, from 1st St. in **Astoria** to 271st St. in **Glen Oaks.** Avenues run perpendicular to streets and are numbered from north to south, from

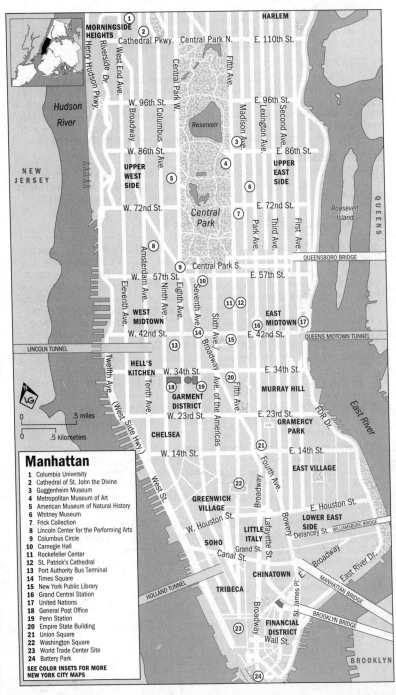

HARLEM

MORNINGSIDE
HEIGHTS

Cathedral Pkwy. Central Park N. E. 110th St.

Hudson
River

NEW
JERSEY

W. 96th St. E. 96th St.

Reservoir

W. 86th St. E. 86th St.

UPPER
WEST
SIDE

UPPER
EAST
SIDE

W. 72nd St. E. 72nd St.

Central
Park

Roosevelt
Island

QUEENS

Central Park S.

QUEENSBORO BRIDGE

W. 57th St. E. 57th St.

WEST
MIDTOWN

EAST
MIDTOWN

W. 42nd St. E. 42nd St.

QUEENS MIDTOWN TUNNEL

LINCOLN TUNNEL

HELL'S
KITCHEN

W. 34th St. E. 34th St.

GARMENT
DISTRICT

MURRAY HILL

W. 23rd St.

GRAMERCY
PARK

CHELSEA

W. 14th St. E. 14th St.

EAST VILLAGE

GREENWICH
VILLAGE

E. Houston St.

LOWER EAST
SIDE

W. Houston St.

LITTLE
ITALY

Delancey St. WILLIAMSBURG BRIDGE

SOHO

Grand St.

Canal St.

CHINATOWN

MANHATTAN BRIDGE

HOLLAND TUNNEL

TRIBECA

BROOKLYN BRIDGE

FINANCIAL
DISTRICT
Wall St.

BROOKLYN

Manhattan

1 Columbia University
2 Cathedral of St. John the Divine
3 Guggenheim Museum
4 Metropolitan Museum of Art
5 American Museum of Natural History
6 Whitney Museum
7 Frick Collection
8 Lincoln Center for the Performing Arts
9 Columbus Circle
10 Carnegie Hall
11 Rockefeller Center
12 St. Patrick's Cathedral
13 Port Authority Bus Terminal
14 Times Square
15 New York Public Library
16 Grand Central Station
17 United Nations
18 General Post Office
19 Penn Station
20 Empire State Building
21 Union Square
22 Washington Square
23 World Trade Center Site
24 Battery Park

SEE COLOR INSETS FOR MORE
NEW YORK CITY MAPS

MID-ATLANTIC

Second Ave. to 165th Ave. The address of an establishment often tells you the closest cross-street (for example, 45-07 32nd Ave. is near the intersection with 45th St.). Pick up the useful Queens Bus Map, free and available on most Queens buses.

THE BRONX

Major highways divide the Bronx. The **Major Deegan Expressway (I-87)** runs up the western border, next to the Harlem River. The **Cross-Bronx Expressway (I-95)** runs across the borough, turning north on its eastern most edge. Up the center of the borough runs the **Bronx River Parkway.** Many avenues run north-south, including **Jerome Avenue** on the western side and **White Plains Road** and **Boston Road** to the east. East-west streets include **Tremont Avenue, Fordham Road,** and the **Pelham Parkway.**

STATEN ISLAND

Unlike the rest of the city, Staten Island is quite spread out. Pick up much-needed maps of Staten Island's bus routes as well as other pamphlets at the **Chamber of Commerce,** 130 Bay St. (☎718-727-1900), left from the ferry station onto Bay St.

LOCAL TRANSPORTATION

Public Transit: The **Metropolitan Transit Authority (MTA)** runs the city's subways, buses, and trains. The **subway** system is open 24hr; once inside, a passenger may transfer onto any other train without restrictions. Maps are available in any station. **Buses,** often slower than subways, stop roughly every 2 blocks and run throughout the city. Blue signposts announce bus numbers; glass-walled shelters display schedules and route maps. In the outer boroughs, some buses are run by independent contractors. Be sure to grab a borough bus map. **MetroCards** for subway and buses have a pre-set value (12 rides for the price of 10) and can make free bus and subway transfers within 2hr. The 1-day ($7), 7-day ($21), and 30-day ($70) "Unlimited Rides" MetroCards (as opposed to $2 "Pay-Per-Ride" cards) are good for tourists visiting many sights.

PRACTICAL INFORMATION

Visitor Info: NYC & Company, 810 Seventh Ave. (☎212-484-1222; www.nycvisit.com), at 53rd St. Open M-F 8:30am-6pm, Sa-Su 9am-5pm. Other locations in Grand Central and Penn Station.

GLBT Resources: Callen-Lorde Community Health Center, 356 W. 18th St. (☎212-271-7200), between Eighth and Ninth Ave. Open M 12:30-8pm, Tu and Th-F 9am-4:30pm, W 8:30am-1pm and 3-8pm. **Gay Men's Health Crisis-Geffen Clinic,** 119 W. 24th St. (☎212-807-6655), between Sixth and Seventh Ave. Walk-in counseling M-F 10am-6pm. Open M-F 11am-8pm. **Gay and Lesbian Switchboard,** ☎212-989-0999. Operates M-F 4pm-midnight, Sa noon-5pm.

Hotlines: AIDS Hotline ☎800-825-5448. Operates daily 9am-9pm. **Crime Victims' Hotline,** ☎212-577-7777. **Sex Crimes Report Line,** ☎212-267-7273. Both 24hr.

Medical Services: Doctors Walk-in Clinic, 55 E. 34th St. (☎212-252-6001, ext. 2), between Park and Madison Ave. Open M-Th 8am-8pm, F 8am-7pm, Sa 9am-3pm, Su 9am-2pm. Last walk-in 1hr. before closing.

Post Office: General Post Office, 421 Eighth Ave. (☎212-330-3002), at W. 32nd St. Open 24hr. General Delivery at 390 Ninth Ave., at W. 30th St. **Postal Code:** 10001.

Area Codes: 212, 347, or 646 (Manhattan); 718 (other 4 boroughs); 917 (cell phones). All New York City calls made within and between all 5 area codes must be dialed using 10-digit dialing.

MID-ATLANTIC

⌐ ACCOMMODATIONS

Accommodations in New York City are very expensive. A dorm bed in a hostel will average around $35 and a private room around $45. Hotel singles in New York City cost about $60-100 per night, doubles $70-120.

HOSTELS

▨ **Central Park Hostel,** 19 W. 103rd St. (☎212-678-0491; www.centralparkhostel.com), between Manhattan Ave. and Central Park W. Subway: B, C to 103rd St./Central Park W. Spotless rooms with A/C and a nice downstairs TV lounge in this 5-story walk-up classic brownstone. Lobby has hand-painted murals (including a map of the subway system) and funky tiled floor. Internet access $2 per 20min. Shared bathrooms. Lockers available. Linen and towels included. Key deposit $2. 13-night max. stay. Booking 2 weeks in advance is recommended. Dorms $26-30; private doubles $75. ❶

▨ **New York International Hostel (HI),** 891 Amsterdam Ave. (☎212-932-2300; www.hinewyork.org), at 103rd St. Subway: 1 to 103 St./Broadway; B, C to 103rd St./Central Park W. Largest US youth hostel in block-long landmark building, with 96 dorm-style rooms and 624 beds. Soft carpets, tight security, spotless bathrooms, and A/C. Kitchens, dining rooms, TV lounges, and large outdoor garden. Internet access $2 per 20min. Linen and towels included. 14-night max. stay, extendable to 20 nights upon request. Check-in after 4pm. Check-out 11am. Credit card reservations required. May-Oct. 10- to 12-bed dorms $31, nonmembers $34; 6- to 8-bed dorms $34/$37; 4-bed dorms $37/$40. Nov.-Apr. dorms $2 less. Family rooms with queen and 2 bunks available. Groups of 10 or more people should ask about private rooms. ❶

▨ **Sugar Hill International House,** 722 St. Nicholas Ave. (☎212-926-7030; www.sugarhillhostel.com), at 146th St. Subway: A, B, C, D to 145th St./St. Nicholas Ave. 4-story brownstone with clean, spacious rooms (25-30 beds total, 6-9 beds per room) and a quiet family feel. Located in a busy section of Sugar Hill, 1 block from the subway. Passport ID required. Friendly staff are a living library of Harlem history and culture. No smoking. All-female room available. Free Internet access during office hours. Facilities include a kitchen, stereo, and library. Linen included. Key deposit $10. Check-in 9am-9pm. Check-out 11am. Reserve as far in advance as possible; confirm 1 day ahead. Dorms $25; doubles $60. $5 off per night with 7-day advance payment. ❶

Big Apple Hostel, 119 W. 45th St. (☎212-302-2603; www.bigapplehostel.com), between Sixth and Seventh Ave. Subway: 1, 2, 3, 7, 9, N, Q, R, S, W to 42nd St./Times Sq. This centrally located hostel has clean, carpeted rooms, 1st fl. kitchen, luggage room, deck (closed 2-6am) with grill, common rooms, and laundry facilities. There's no elevator—when reserving, mention any concerns to avoid being put on one of the higher floors. Reception 24hr. Internet access $1 per 8min. Safe deposit ($0.25) at reception. 21-day max. stay. Check-in and check-out 11am. Aug.-Sept. reservations only accepted on website or by fax—send credit card number. 4-bed dorms $33-36 (same-sex available for single travelers, mixed for groups of friends); private singles and doubles $90-95. ❸

Chelsea International Hostel, 251 W. 20th St. (☎212-647-0010; www.chelseahostel.com), between Seventh and Eighth Ave. Subway: 1, 9 to 23rd St./Seventh Ave.; C, E to 23rd St./Eighth Ave. Full of funky youth travelers (mostly Scandinavians and other Europeans). Congenial staff offer free pizza W night. Very safe neighborhood (police station across the street). Sparsely furnished, small rooms. Enclosed courtyard, kitchens, laundry room, and TV rooms. Internet access $1 per 8min. Key deposit $10. Passport required. Check-in 24hr. Check-out 1pm. Reservations recommended 1-3 months in advance. 4- and 6-person dorms $27; private rooms (double or bunk bed) $65. ❶

Jazz on the Park, 36 W. 106th St./Duke Ellington Blvd. (☎212-932-1600; www.jazzhostel.com), between Manhattan Ave. and Central Park W. Subway: B, C to 103rd St./Central Park W. Brightly colored hostel with fun decor and 255 beds. A/C and lockers. Live jazz in the lounge on weekends. Internet access $1 per 9min. Breakfast, linen, and towels included. 24hr. laundry on premise. Check-in and check-out 11am. Reservations essential June-Oct. 10- to 12-bed dorms $27; 6- to 8-bed dorms $29; 4-bed dorms $32; private rooms (full or bunk bed) $50-85. ❶

GUEST HOUSES AND B&BS

▨ **Akwaaba Mansion,** 347 MacDonough St. (☎718-455-5958; www.akwaaba.com), in Bedford-Stuyvesant. Subway: A, C to Utica Ave. Monique Greenwood, former editor of *Essence Magazine*, owns this 1860 Victorian-style B&B. Akwaaba, which means "welcome," won an award from the New York Landmarks Preservation Society. 18 rooms with African cultural decor. Library, TV room, tree-shaded patio, sun porch, and elegant dining room. Rooms comfortably accommodate 2. All include private bath (2 with jacuzzi) and A/C. Check-in 4-7pm. Check-out 11am. F jazz, Su brunch ($10) with Southern/African cuisine. Reserve at least 1 month ahead. 50% deposit required with reservation; not refundable after 14 days before stay. Rooms $150-165; weekends $135-150. ❺

Crystal's Castle Bed & Breakfast, 119 W. 119th St. (☎212-722-3637; www.crystalscastlebandb.com), between Lenox (Sixth) Ave. and Adam Clayton Powell Blvd. Subway: 2, 3 to 116th St. or 125th St./Lenox (Sixth) Ave. Family-owned, century-old brownstone. All rooms have private bath and TV, one has A/C. Continental breakfast included. Check-in 10pm. Check-out 1pm. Reserve at least 1 month in advance. 25% deposit. 1-week cancellation notice required. Singles $76; doubles $97. All rooms $456 per week. 5-night discount 20%. Low-season (May-Sept. and Dec. to mid-Jan.) discount. ❷

HOTELS

▨ **Carlton Arms Hotel,** 160 E. 25th St. (☎212-679-0680; www.carltonarms.com), between Third and Lexington Ave. Subway: 6 to 23rd St. The insignia shield for this brutally hip hotel sports the Latin phrase for "There's no mint on your pillow." What it lacks in mints, TV, and phones, it makes up for in wild decor. 11C is the "good daughter/bad daughter" room—half festooned in teeny-bopper posters, the other half in horror-movie pics. 54 spacious rooms, all with A/C and sink, some with private bath. Check-in noon. Check-out 11:30am. Reserve for summer 1 month ahead; confirm 10 days ahead. Rooms $70, with bath $85. Add $10 for each additional person. Foreigners and students receive discount around $10. Pay for 7 nights or more up front and get a 10% discount. ❷

▨ **Gershwin Hotel,** 7 E. 27th St. (☎212-545-8000; www.gershwinhotel.com), between Madison and Fifth Ave. Subway: N, R, W to 28th St./Broadway; 6 to 28th St./Park Ave. S. The hotel's red facade is ornamented with stunning glass. Warhol in the lobby. Private rooms with bath, cable TV, A/C, and phone. Wireless Internet $10 per day, $35 per week. Reception 24hr. Check-in 3pm. Check-out 11am. 6- to 10-bed dorms $33-45; economy rooms $99-119; standard $116-169; suites available. ❸

▨ **Hotel Stanford,** 43 W. 32nd St. (☎212-563-1500 or 800-365-1114; www.hotelstanford.com), between Fifth Ave. and Broadway. Subway: B, D, F, N, Q, R, V, W to 34th St./Herald Sq. This Herald Square hotel's lobby has sparkling ceiling lights, a polished marble floor, and a front desk with great service. Impeccable rooms with A/C, bath, cable TV, phone, hairdryer, safe, and fridge. Continental breakfast included. Also houses Korean bakery **Pari Pari Ko** and bustling 24hr. Korean eatery **Gam Mee Ok.** Multilingual concierges. Doorman. Wireless Internet $10 per 24hr. Check-in 3pm. Check-out noon. Reservations recommended 2 weeks ahead. Singles $99-130; doubles $119-140. ❹

▨ **Larchmont Hotel,** 27 W. 11th St. (☎212-989-9333; www.larchmonthotel.com), between Fifth and Sixth Ave. Subway: 4, 5, 6, L, N, Q, R, W to 14th St./Union Sq. Spacious, clean and quiet rooms in a whitewashed brownstone come with A/C, closet, desk, TV, wash basin, and continental breakfast. Shared bath. Check-in 3pm. Check-out noon. Reserve 4-6 weeks ahead. Singles $70-95; doubles $90-115; queens $109-125. ❷

Chelsea Star Hotel, 300 W. 30th St. (☎212-244-7827 or 212-877-827-6969; www.starhotelny.com), at Eighth Ave. Subway: A, C, E to 34th St./Penn Station/Eighth Ave. Madonna reportedly lived here as a struggling artist. Stay in 1 of the 16 themed rooms, or choose a normal "luxe" room. Clean and coveted. Residents get keys. All rooms with shared bathrooms (20 rooms, 4 per bath) and A/C. Safe deposit box $5. 14-night max. stay. Reception 24hr. Check-in 1pm. Check-out 11am. Reserve at least 1 month ahead. Dorms $30 (linens included); singles $59-69; doubles $79-89; quads $99-109; queens $149-159. ❶

Colonial House Inn, 318 W. 22nd St. (☎212-243-9669 or 800-689-3779; www.colonialhouseinn.com), between Eighth and Ninth Ave. Subway: C, E to 23rd St. Very comfortable B&B in a classy Chelsea brownstone, owned by the former owner of legendary club Paradise Garage. All rooms have A/C, cable TV, and phones; some have baths and fireplaces. "Clothing optional" sun deck has lounge chairs and privacy fence. Internet access ($0.20 per min.) in lobby. Continental breakfast included served in the lounge. Reception 24hr. Check-in 2pm. Check-out noon. Reservations are encouraged and require 2 nights' deposit within 10 days of reservation. Double-bed "economy" room $80-99; queens $99-125, with private bath and fridge $125-140. Call or check the website for the 15% reduced rate Jan. to mid-Mar. ❸

◘ FOOD

New York City will dazzle you with its food. City dining, like the population, spans the globe, ranging from sushi bars and Italian eateries to French bistros.

CHINATOWN

▧ **Doyers Vietnamese Restaurant,** 11-13 Doyers St. (☎212-693-0725), between Bowery and Pell St. Follow the steps downstairs. Doyers (formerly known as Vietnam) has great Vietnamese cuisine, served quickly by the friendly staff. Appetizers are delicious and often unusual—try the shrimp paste grilled on sugar cane ($6.25). Also excellent are the hot pot soups ($17, serves 4-6), stuffed with simmering meat, vegetables, and seafood. Serves beer. Open daily 11am-9:30pm. AmEx only. ❷

▧ **Joe's Shanghai,** 9 Pell St. (☎212-233-8888; www.joeshanghai.com), between Bowery and Mott St. From fried turnip cakes ($3.25) to crispy whole yellowfish ($14), this branch of the Queens legend serves tasty Shanghai specialties. Delicious *xiao long bao* (crab meat and pork dumplings in savory soup; $7). Be prepared for communal tables, long lines on weekends, and prices slightly above a typical Chinatown restaurant. For an authentic experience, check out Joe's Queens location (13621 37th Ave., Flushing). Serves beer. Open daily 11am-11:15pm. Cash only. ❸

Chinatown Ice-Cream Factory, 65 Bayard St. (☎212-608-4170; www.chinatownicecreamfactory.com), at Elizabeth St. Unbeatable homemade ice cream in exotic flavors like lychee, ginger, red bean, and green tea. 1 scoop $2.75, 2 $4.50, 3 $5.25. Crowded, but the line moves quickly. Open daily 11am-11pm. ❶

Fried Dumpling, 106 Mosco St. (☎212-693-1060), between Mulberry and Mott St. For half the price of a subway ride ($1), get either 5 dumplings or 4 pork buns. Only other menu items are soy milk ($1) and a very good hot-and-sour soup ($1). Cash only. ❶

LITTLE ITALY AND NOLITA

▧ **Lombardi's Coal Oven Pizza,** 32 Spring St. (☎212-941-7994), between Mott and Mulberry St. Claiming to be nation's oldest pizzeria (1905), Lombardi's credits itself with creating the famous NY-style thin-crust, coal-oven pizza. Large pie ($14) feeds 2. Toppings $3 for 1, $5 for 2, $6 for 3. Reservations accepted for groups of 6 or more. Try to visit on off-peak hours: the line is invariably out the door. Open M-Th 11:30am-11pm, F-Sa 11:30am-midnight, Su 11:30am-10pm. Delivery and take-out available. Cash only. ❸

■ **Rice,** 227 Mott St. (☎212-226-5775; www.riceny.com), between Prince and Spring St. Basics—basmati, brown, sticky, Japanese, and Thai black—are all here. So are exotic species like Bhutanese red and green rice. Sauces range from mango chutney to aleppo yogurt ($1). Ratatouille, coconut curry, or chicken satay are among other enticing toppings $4-9.50. Great salads: try the tea-smoked salmon salad on mixed greens with ginger hoisin vinaigrette and grilled scallion mayonnaise ($8). For dessert, sweet plantain with sticky rice in a leaf wrap $2.50. Open daily noon-midnight. Cash only. ❷

La Mela, 167 Mulberry St. (☎212-431-9493), between Broome and Grand St. Raucous dining, chummy staff. Generous portions served family-style. 4-course dinners $28 per person, 3-course $19; min. 2 people. 1.5L house wine $25. Huge dessert concoction (ice cream, cake, coconut, glazed bananas) $6 per person. Pasta $6-8. Family-style only after 6pm. Open Su-Th noon-2am, F-Sa noon-3am. ❷

Mottsu, 285 Mott St. (☎212-343-8017; www.mottsuu.com), between E. Houston and Spring St. One of the neighborhood's only sushi restaurants. Fresh sushi and sashimi. Tuna rolls $5.50, eel and avocado rolls $6.25. Lunch M-F noon-3pm; dinner M-Th 5-11pm, F-Sa 5-11:30pm, Su 5-10pm. ❸

LOWER EAST SIDE

Katz's Delicatessen, 205 E. Houston St. (☎212-254-2246, between Orchard and Ludlow St. Subway: F, V to Lower East Side/Second Ave. An LES institution since 1888. Orgasmic food (as Meg Ryan confirmed in *When Harry Met Sally*); you pay extra for Katz's fame. Knishes and franks $2.40. Reuben, knoblewurst, and corned beef sandwiches around $10. Open Su-Tu 8am-10pm, W-Th 8am-11pm, F-Sa 8am-3am. ❸

Kossar's Bialys, 367 Grand St. (☎212-473-4810), between Essex and Norfolk St. Subway: F, J, M, Z to Delancey St. New York City's best bialy emporium. What is a bialy? Find out here. You can get 2 onion bialys for a buck, or 13 for $6. Bagels also served. Open all night Sa. Open M-Th 6am-8pm, F 6am-4pm, Sa 9pm to Su 8pm. ❶

GREENWICH VILLAGE

Lips, 2 Bank St. (☎212-675-7710; www.lipsnyc.com), at Greenwich Ave. Subway: A, C, E, L to 14th St./Eighth Ave.; 1, 2, 3, 9 to 14th St./Seventh Ave. Italian-Continental cuisine and impromptu performances from a high-heeled staff in a room decked out with lips. Try the RuPaul (grilled chicken with mashed potatoes and spinach; $15. Entrees $12-22. Reservations recommended. Open Su-Th 5:30-11:30pm, F-Sa 5:30pm-1:30am; Su brunch 11:30am-4pm. ❹

Moustache, 90 Bedford St. (☎212-229-2220), between Barrow and Grove St. Subway: 1, 9 to Christopher St. Sumptuous Middle-Eastern fare served on copper tabletops in this small gem. Inhale the enticing smell of fresh pita. Try the succulent leg of lambwich ($8). Lentil soup $4. Salads $4.50-10. Falafel sandwich $6. Open daily noon-11pm. ❷

EAST VILLAGE

■ **Second Avenue Delicatessen,** 156 Second Ave. (☎212-677-0606), at 10th St. Subway: 6 to Astor Pl. The definitive New York deli. The Lebewohl family has proudly maintained this strictly kosher joint since 1954. The chopped liver ($8.75), *kasha varnishkes* ($6.25), and mushroom barley ($4.25) are among the best in the city, and you can't go wrong with a classic pastrami or corned beef sandwich (on rye, of course; $8-11). Challah french toast $11. Open M-Sa 10am-8:30pm, Su 11am-7pm. ❸

Frank, 88 Second Ave. (☎212-420-1232), between E. Fifth and Sixth St. Subway: 6 to Astor Pl. At this Italian bistro, the menu, like the restaurant, is happily cramped—there's often a wait. Try the roasted rosemary chicken with mashed potatoes, gravy, olives and slow cooked tomatoes ($12), the *prosciutto di parma* sandwich ($8), or Uncle Tony's gnocchi ($10). Delivery available. Open M-Th 10:30am-4pm and 5pm-1am, F-Sa 10:30am-4pm and 5pm-2am, Su 10:30am-midnight. Cash only. ❸

CHELSEA

Kangsuh Korean Restaurant, 1250 Broadway (☎212-564-6845), on 32nd St. between Fifth and Sixth Ave. Subway: B, D, F, N, Q, R, V, W to Herald Sq. Homestyle Korean cooking served family-style with efficient service in a clean, 2-story restaurant. The delectable *hwe dup bap* (spicy sashimi salad with rice; $17) and the stellar juicy *kalbi* barbecue ($21) draw Koreans in hordes. Entrees $10-18. Open 24hr. ❹

Pop Burger, 58-60 Ninth Ave. (☎212-414-8686), between 14th and 15th St. Subway: 1, 2, 3, 9 to 14th St./Seventh Ave; A, C, E, L to 14th St. The fast-food front counter and wait-service back lounge cater to both those who pop "mini" burgers (2 for $5) and those who eat filet mignon ($25). The food is acclaimed, and the decor stainless enough to be a little out of this world. Chocolate, strawberry, and vanilla shakes $3.75. Beer $5. Open daily 11am-1am. Lounge open Su-Tu 5pm-2am, W-Sa 5pm-4am. ❸

THEATER DISTRICT

Becco, 355 W 46th St. (☎212-397-7597; www.becconyc.com), between Eighth and Ninth Ave. Great Italian food for a moderate splurge. 70 wines priced at $20 per bottle. $17 prix-fixe lunch (dinner $22) gets you a gourmet antipasto platter or caesar salad, plus unlimited servings of the 3 pastas of the day. Dinner $16 food min. per person, lunch $14. Try the mesclun salad with Tuscan beans and ripe tomatoes, tossed with an aged Chianti vinaigrette ($6), or the grilled Atlantic salmon with poached potatoes, green beans, and grain mustard ($23). Open daily noon-3pm and 5pm-midnight. ❹

Island Burgers and Shakes, 766 Ninth Ave. (☎212-307-7934; http://island.city-search.com), between 51st and 52nd St. Burgers so good that Island sells more than 150 lb. of meat per day. More than 50 burgers ($5-8) on the menu; you can also craft your own. Try the Hippo Burger ($7.50), served with curried sour cream, bacon, cheddar, onion, scallions, and guacamole in a pita. Also serves chicken, salads, and drinks. No fries. Open daily noon-10:30pm, F until 11pm. Cash only. ❷

Say Cheese!, 649 Ninth Ave. (☎212-265-8840), between 45th and 46th St. This tiny soup-and-sandwich joint specializes in all permutations of grilled cheese ($4.25-7.50). The Chokes on Tuna (tuna fish plus artichokes, fresh oregano, roasted garlic, and American cheese on pizza bianca; $7) is a must. Open M-F noon-9pm, Sa-Su 10am-9pm. ❷

UPPER EAST SIDE

Payard, 1032 Lexington Ave. (☎212-717-5252; www.payard.com), between 73rd and 74th St. Subway: 6 to 77th St. With prices as rich as the pastries (which is saying something), this decadent Parisian-style patisserie/bistro serves some of the most sinful desserts ($5.25-7) in town. Try "The Louvre," a concoction of chocolate and hazelnut mousse with a twist of hazelnut *dacquiose* ($6). Ice cream $2-4. Wide assortment of teas $4.50 per pot. Gourmet sandwiches and savory tarts ($12-14). Try the potato *tourte* ($13), with goat's milk brie, mushrooms, caramelized onions, and walnuts. Open M-Th noon-10:30pm, F-Sa noon-11pm. ❹

Il Vagabondo, 351 E. 62nd St. (☎212-832-9221), between First and Second Ave. Subway: 4, 5, 6 to 59th St. Complete with an indoor bocce court and festooned with mafia photographs, this old-school Italian restaurant has been an East Side staple since 1971. You won't find many tourists here, but the regulars have been coming for decades. Try the veal shank *osso bucco* ($21), rumored by some to be the best in the city. Lunch entrees $8-29, dinner $18-39. Open daily noon-11pm. ❹

Vermicelli, 1492 Second Ave. (☎212-288-8868), between 77th and 78th St. Subway: 6 to 77th St. Vietnamese spring rolls with warm vermicelli, coriander, and roasted peanuts $8. Their $6 box lunches are a popular eat-on-the-go option, served with vegetables, soup, salad, and steamed rice. Try the spicy lemongrass chicken with peppers. Open daily 11:30am-10:45pm. ❷

UPPER WEST SIDE

■ **Big Nick's Burger Joint and Pizza Joint,** 2175 Broadway (☎212-362-9238 or 724-2010), at 77th St. Subway: 1, 9 to 79th St. Telephone-book-like menu (27 pages thick!). Burgers and pizza rule the day, but you can also get all-day breakfast and vegan and vegetarian options. Wrestle with a plate-sized burger ($5-7.50), a full homestyle Italian dinner ($9-15), or crispy sweet potato fries ($2.75). Free delivery. Open 24hr. Second location 70 W. 71st St. (☎212-799-4444), at Columbus Ave. ❷

■ **Zabar's,** 2245 Broadway (☎212-787-2000), between 80th and 81st St. Subway: 1, 9 to 79th St. This Upper West Side institution sells all the imported delicacies you need for a 4-star meal at home. In a pinch, arrive with a toothpick and make a meal of the legendary free samples. On weekend mornings, masses of hungry New Yorkers stand in line for bagels and coffee. Kitchen gadgets and dishware sold upstairs. Open M-F 8am-7:30pm, Sa 8am-8pm, Su 9am-6pm. Cafe open M-Sa 7:30am-7pm, Su 8am-6pm. ❸

Gray's Papaya, 2090 Broadway (☎212-799-0243), at 72nd St. Subway: 1, 2, 3, 9 to 72nd St. A local, but landmark, chain. Lively takeout with amazing deals on hot dogs. The "recession special" is 2 franks and 1 fruit drink (banana daiquiri, pineapple, piña colada, papaya) for $2.75. Also at 539 Eighth Ave. and 402 Sixth Ave. Open 24hr. ❶

@SQC, 270 Columbus Ave. (☎212-579-0100), between 72nd and 73rd St. Subway: 1, 2, 3, 9 to 72nd St. Plush pillows, white candles, and large orange-tinted windows set the scene for American food with French and Asian influences. If your wallet doesn't feel up to dinner here (average entree $20-26), breakfast is the perfect way to bask in the glow. Excellent pastries (apple-cinnamon brioche $2.50). Open M-Th 8am-11pm, F 8am-midnight, Sa 9am-midnight, Su 9am-11pm. ❹

HARLEM AND MORNINGSIDE HEIGHTS

■ **Amir's Falafel,** 2911A Broadway (☎212-749-7500), between 113th and 114th St. Subway: 1, 9 to 110th St., 116th St. Small and simple, with Middle Eastern staples like shawarma and *baba ghanoush.* Substantial vegetarian options (platters $5.50). Falafel $3.50. Open daily 11am-11pm. Free delivery within Morningside Heights. Cash only. ❶

■ **Amy Ruth's,** 113 W. 116th St. (☎212-280-8779; www.amyruthsrestaurant.com), between Adam Clayton Powell Blvd. and Lenox (Sixth) Ave. Subway: 1, 9 to 116th St. Named in honor of the owner's grandmother, this intimate restaurant serves cuisine straight from a southern kitchen. There's the "Rev. Calvin O. Butts III" (chicken wings and waffles; $7.50), "Councilman Bill Perkins" (southern honey-dipped fried chicken; $12), and the "Foxy Brown" (pan-seared jumbo shrimp; $17). Lots of waffles (banana and pecans; $8). Open M-Th 7:30am-11pm, F 7:30am to Su 11pm. Free delivery. ❸

Hispaniola, 839 W 181st St. (☎212-740-5222; www.hispaniolarestaurant.com), at Cabrini Blvd. Subway: A to 181st St./Ft. Washington Ave. Delectable Dominican-Asian fusion cuisine. Innovative sushi includes tempura coconut shrimp pineapple rolls ($10) and tilapia asparagus mesclun rolls ($10). The $14 lunch "conto boxes" come with coconut shrimp and salad, plus grilled salmon, miso butterfish, fried chicken, or hanger steak. For dinner, try the mahi mahi ($21) or Argentine skirt steak with risotto ($21). For dessert, indulge in molten chocolate cake ($8). Happy hour M-F 4-8pm, drinks half-price. Open M-Sa 11am-4pm and 5:30pm-midnight; bar open until 2am. ❹

BROOKLYN

■ **Planet Thailand,** 115 Berry St. (☎718-599-5758), between N. 7th and 8th St. Subway: L to Bedford Ave. High-ceilinged space that's too trendy for a sign. Expansive menu includes Thai beef and chicken curries ($8), *pad thai* ($7), hibachi table fare ($9-16), and Japanese items (sushi dinner $11). If you go on a weekend night, be prepared for a wait: Planet Thailand takes no reservations, and people from across the city flock there. DJ every night 9pm. Open Su-Th 11:30am-1am, F-Sa 11:30am-2am. Cash only. ❸

DuMont Restaurant, 432 Union Ave. (☎718-486-7717), at Devoe St. Subway: L to Lorimer St. Feels like a French speakeasy—if France had ever endured prohibition. A mere handful of plates remain on the menu day to day, of which the burger and the DuMac and Cheese (both $8) are signature pieces. Specials, like the pancetta-wrapped monkfish ($16), use the freshest ingredients. Excellent service, a solid wine list, and garden dining in warm weather. Brunch Sa-Su. Open daily 11am-3pm and 6-11pm. ❹

Jacques Torres Chocolate, 66 Water St. (☎ 718-875-9772), between Dock and Main St. Subway: A, C to High St.; F to York St. Watch chefs make chocolate-covered almonds ($5 per ¼ lb.), chocolate croissants ($1.50), and chocolate bars ($4). Sweets take center stage, coming in varieties such as fresh-squeezed lemon, cappuccino, and Love Potion #9 ($0.80). Hot chocolate $2.50. Mocha cappuccino $3. Open M-Sa 9am-7pm. ❶

QUEENS

▓ Flushing Noodle, 135-42 Roosevelt Ave. (☎718-353-1166). Subway: 7 to Flushing/ Main St. One of Flushing's finest Chinese noodle shops. Try the spare ribs ($7.75) and noodles ($3.75-5). Lunch specials ($5; 11am-3:30pm) give you 37 entree choices. Limited seating, and it's always packed. Takeout available. Open daily 9am-10pm. ❶

Zygos Taverna, 22-55 31st St. (☎718-728-7070). Subway: N, W to Broadway. Greek restaurant serves thinly sliced leg of lamb with lemon potatoes ($11), grilled baby octopus ($10), and *moussaka* ($10). Spreads ($4.50) are served with hot pita bread. Open daily 11am-midnight. Free delivery in Astoria, $10 min. ❷

Bohemian Hall and Beer Garden, 29-19 24th Ave. (☎718-274-4925; www.bohemianhall.com). Subway: N, W to 30th Ave. Operated by the Bohemian Citizens' Benevolent Society, this Czech restaurant and 900-seat outdoor beer garden is packed every night. Enjoy Bohemian staples like fried cheese with french fries ($8) and crunchy pork schnitzel ($10.50). Open M-F 5pm-3am, Sa-Su noon-3am. ❸

⑤ SIGHTS

THE STATUE OF LIBERTY AND ELLIS ISLAND

The Statue of Liberty, long a symbol of hope for immigrants, stands at the entrance to New York Harbor. In 1886, the French government presented Frederic-Auguste Bartholdi's sculpture to the US as a sign of goodwill. The statue was closed from September 2001 until August 2004, and the crown of the statue is still not accessible; views are limited to the 150-ft. concrete pedestal. Ellis Island, accessible by the same ferry, was the processing point for millions of immigrants from 1897 to 1938. The museum chronicles immigrant life in the New World. *(Subway: 4, 5 to Bowling Green; R, W to Whitehall St.; 1, 9 to South Ferry. ☎212-363-3200; www.nps.gov/stli. Ferries leave for Liberty Island from the piers at Battery Park (every 30min. M-F 9:15am-3:30pm, Sa-Su 9am-4pm). Ferry information ☎212-269-5755; www.statueoflibertyferry.com. Tickets for ferry with access to Liberty Island and Ellis Island $10, seniors $8, ages 4-12 $4, under 4 free.)*

FINANCIAL DISTRICT AND CIVIC CENTER

The southern tip of Manhattan is a financial powerhouse: the Wall St. area, less than ½ mi. long, has one of the highest concentrations of skyscrapers in the world. Crooked streets retain the city's original Dutch layout; lower Manhattan was the first part of the island to be settled. *(Subway: 1, 9 to Wall St./William St.; 4, 5 to Bowling Green, Wall St./Broadway; N, R, W to Rector St., Whitehall St.; 1, 2, 4, 5, A, C, J, M, Z to Fulton St./Broadway/Nassau St.; J, M, Z to Broad St.)*

FINANCIAL DISTRICT. Once the northern border of the New Amsterdam settlement, Wall St. is named for the wall built in 1653 to shield the Dutch colony from British invasion. By the early 19th century, the area was the financial capital of the

US. On the southwest corner of Wall and Broad St. stands the **New York Stock Exchange.** This 1903 temple to capitalism sees billions of dollars change hands daily. The exchange, founded in 1792 at 68 Wall St., is now off-limits to tourists.

WALL STREET. Around the corner, at the end of Wall St., stands the seemingly ancient **Trinity Church,** with its delicately crafted steeple. *(74 Trinity Place. ☎212-602-0800.)* Peter Minuit purchased Manhattan for the equivalent of $24 at **Bowling Green,** at the intersection of Battery Pl., Broadway, and Whitehall St. The Beaux Arts **US Custom House** overlooks the park. *(1 Bowling Green St. ☎212-668-6624.)*

WORLD TRADE CENTER MEMORIAL SITE (GROUND ZERO). The site where the World Trade Center once stood is a sobering one. The poignancy of the vast empty landscape can only really be understood in person. Plans have finally been solidified for the new **Freedom Tower,** which, when completed in 2008, will be the world's tallest building, at 2000 ft. Construction begins in fall 2004. On August 2, 2004, construction began on a 945-ft.-tall skyscraper, which will also open in 2008. The site will also hold a subway terminal and memorials to the victims of the 9/11 attacks.

CIVIC CENTER. The city's center of government is located north of its financial district. New York City's mayor keeps his offices in **City Hall;** around it are courthouses, civic buildings, and federal buildings. The building's interior is closed indefinitely to the public. *(Broadway at Murray St., off Park Row.)* The **Woolworth Building,** a 1913 Neo-Gothic skyscraper and "Cathedral of Commerce" built for $15.5 million to house F.W. Woolworth's five-and-dime store empire, looms south of City Hall. *(233 Broadway, between Barclay St. and Park Pl. Closed to the public.)* A block and a half south on Broadway lies **St. Paul's Chapel,** Manhattan's oldest public building in continuous use. George Washington prayed here on his inauguration day. *(Between Vesey and Fulton St. ☎212-602-0747. Open M-F 9am-3pm, Su 7am-3pm. Su mass 8am.)*

SOUTH STREET SEAPORT. The shipping industry thrived at the South Street Seaport for most of the 19th century, when New York City was the most important port city in the US. During the 20th century, bars, brothels, and crime flourished. Now a 12-block "museum without walls," the seaport displays old schooners, sailboats, and houses. The visitors center has info on attractions. *(Between FDR Dr. and Water St., and between Beekman and John St. Subway: 2, 3, 4, 5, A, C, J, M, Z to Fulton St./ Broadway/Nassau St. Visitors center: 12 Fulton St. ☎212-748-8600; www.southstseaport.org. Open daily 10am-5pm. Admission to ships, shops, and tours $8; students and seniors $6; under 12 free. Walking around the museum is free.)* The Fulton Fish Market, the largest fresh-fish market in the country, is on South St., on the other side of the overpass. *(☎212-748-8786. Market opens at 4am. Market tours May-Oct. 1st and 3rd W of each month, 6am. $12. Reservations required, call around 1 week in advance.)*

CHINATOWN AND LITTLE ITALY

Mott and **Pell Street,** unofficial centers of Chinatown, brim with restaurants and commercial activity. Chinese-style baby jackets, bamboo hats, and miniature Buddhas crowd the storefronts. **Canal Street** offers tons of low-priced, creatively labeled merchandise (those are *not* Rolexes). **Mulberry Street** remains the heart of Little Italy, which has been largely taken over by Chinatown in recent decades. *(Subway: A, C, E to Canal St./Sixth Ave.; J, M, Z to Canal St./Centre St.; N, Q, R, W to Canal St./ Broadway; 6 to Canal St./Lafayette St.; F to E Broadway; B, D, F, V to Broadway/Lafayette St.)*

LOWER EAST SIDE

The Lower East Side was once the most densely settled area in New York City. The Irish came in the mid-1800s, Eastern Europeans in the 50 years preceding WWI, African-Americans and Puerto Ricans post-WWII, and Latin Americans and Asians

MID-ATLANTIC

in the 1980s and 90s. Main thoroughfares like E. Broadway reflect the area's multi-cultural roots. Orchard St., a historic shopping area that fills up on Sundays, still has traces of the Jewish ghetto. *(Subway: F, V to Lower East Side/Second Ave.; F to E Broadway; F, J, M, Z to Delancey St./Essex St.)*

LOWER EAST SIDE SIGHTS. The **Lower East Side Visitors Center** is a source of maps and brochures, and also organizes a free area shopping tour. *(261 Broome St., between Orchard and Allen St. ☎212-226-9010. Open daily 10am-4pm.)* At the **Lower East Side Tenement Museum,** tours lead through three meticulously restored apartments of immigrant families. *(90 Orchard St. ☎212-431-0233. Call for info on tours of tenements and neighborhood. $12, students and seniors $10.)* The **Eldridge Street Synagogue** *(12 Eldridge St. ☎212-219-0888)* and **Congregation Anshe Chesed** *(172-176 Norfolk St., at Stanton St. ☎212-865-0600)* are two splendid old synagogues.

SOHO AND TRIBECA

The architecture in the area **South of Houston**—with Canal St. on the south, Broadway on the west, and Crosby St. on the east—is American Industrial, notable for its cast-iron facades. SoHo is filled with artists and galleries (see **Galleries,** p. 273), chic boutiques, and very expensive shopping. *(Subway: C, E to Spring St./Ave. of the Americas (Sixth Ave.); 6 to Spring St./Lafayette St.; N, R, W to Prince St.; 1, 9 to W Houston St.; B, D, F, V to Broadway/Lafayette St.)* **TriBeCa,** or **Triangle Below Canal Street,** contains trendy lofts, restaurants, bars, and galleries—without the upscale airs. Admire the cast-iron edifices lining White St., Thomas St., and Broadway, the Federal-style buildings on Harrison St., and the shops, galleries, and bars on Church and Reade St. *(Subway: 1, 9 to Canal St./Varick St.; A, C, E to Canal St./Ave. of the Americas (Sixth Ave.); 1, 9 to Franklin St.; 1, 2, 3, 9 to Chambers St./W Broadway; A, C to Chambers St./Church St.)*

GREENWICH VILLAGE

Greenwich Village has layered grime, activism, and artistry atop a tangle of wandering streets. The area was once covered in farms and hills. In the mid-19th century, it developed into a high-society playground that fostered literary creativity. Henry James captured the Village's spirit in his 1880 novel, *Washington Square*. The last 40 years have brought the Beat movement, the homosexual community around Christopher St., and the punk scene. Gentrification in the 1980s and 90s made the Village a fashionable settlement for wealthier New Yorkers with more spunk than their uptown counterparts. *(Subway: A, B, C, D, E, F, V to W 4th St.; A, C, E to 14th St./Eighth Ave.; 1, 2, 3, 9 to 14th St./Seventh Ave.; F, V to 14th St./Ave. of the Americas (Sixth Ave.); L to Eighth Ave., Ave. of the Americas (Sixth Ave.); 4, 5, 6, L, N, Q, R, W to 14th St./Union Sq.; 1, 9 to Houston St., Christopher St.; N, R, W to 8th St./NYU; L to Sixth Ave., Eighth Ave.; 6 to Bleecker St.)*

WASHINGTON SQUARE. Washington Square Park has a rich history. On the north side of the park is **The Row,** a stretch of 1830s brick residences that were once populated by writers, dandies, and professionals. At the north end of the park stands the **Washington Memorial Arch,** built in 1889 to commemorate the centennial of George Washington's inauguration. **New York University,** the country's largest private university, has some of the Village's least appealing contemporary architecture. On the park's southeast side, where Washington Sq. S meets LaGuardia Pl., NYU's **Loeb Student Center** sports pieces of scrap metal representing birds in flight.

WEST VILLAGE. The area of Greenwich Village west of 6th Ave. boasts eclectic summer street life and excellent nightlife. A visible gay community thrives around **Sheridan Square,** at the intersection of Seventh Ave., W. 4th St., and Christopher St. The 1969 Stonewall Riot, arguably the beginning of the modern gay rights movement, started here. The neighborhood is a magnet for literary pilgrimages. **Chumley's,** a former speakeasy, was a hangout for such authors as Ernest

Hemingway and John Dos Passos. *(86 Bedford St., between Grove and Barrow St.* ☎ *212-675-4449. Open M-F 4pm for drinks, 5pm for dinner, Sa-Su noon for brunch, 5pm for dinner.)* Off 10th St. and Sixth Ave., you'll see an iron gate and street sign marking **Patchin Place.** Theodore Dreiser, E. E. Cummings, and Djuna Barnes lived in the 145-year-old buildings that line this path. The Village's narrowest building, **75½ Bedford Street,** only 9½ ft. in width, housed writer Edna St. Vincent Millay in the 1920s, when she founded the nearby **Cherry Lane Theater,** 38 Commerce St. Actors Lionel Barrymore and Cary Grant also appreciated the cramped quarters.

EAST VILLAGE

The East Village—north of Houston St., east of Broadway, and south of 14th St.—was carved out of the Bowery and the Lower East Side in the early 1960s, when artists and writers moved here to escape high rents in Greenwich Village. Today the East Village's wide-ranging population includes punks, hippies, ravers, rastas, guppies, goths, and beatniks. **St. Mark's Place** is full of tiny ethnic eateries, street-level shops, sidewalk vendors, and tattoo shops. Simmering with street life, **Astor Place,** at the intersection of Lafayette, E. 8th St., and Fourth Ave., is distinguished by a large black cube balanced on its corner. The tensions of gentrification have forged the East Village into one of the city's most politicized neighborhoods. *(Subway: 6 to Astor Pl., Bleecker St.; L to First Ave., Third Ave.; F, V to Lower East Side/Second Ave.)*

LOWER MIDTOWN

UNION SQUARE. At the intersection of Fourth Ave. and Broadway, Union Square and the surrounding area sizzled with high society before the Civil War. Today, the park hosts the **Union Square Greenmarket,** a pleasant farmers market. *(Between Broadway and Park Ave. S, between 14th and 17th St. Subway: 4, 5, 6, L, N, Q, R, W to 14th St./Union Sq. Greenmarket open M, W, F-Sa 8am-6pm.)* Originally named the Fuller Building, the photogenic **Flatiron Building** was nicknamed after its dramatic wedge shape (imposed by the intersection of Broadway, Fifth Ave., 22nd St., and 23rd St.).

CHELSEA. Home to fashionable clubs, bars, and restaurants, Chelsea (west of Fifth Ave., between 14th and 30th St.) boasts a large GLBT community, a growing artsy-yuppie population, and **art galleries** (p. 240) fleeing high SoHo rents. *(Subway: 1, 2, 3, 9 to 14th St./Seventh Ave.; A, C, E, L to 14th St./Eighth Ave.; C, E to 23rd St./Eighth Ave.; 1, 9 to 23rd St., 28th St./Seventh Ave.)* **Hotel Chelsea,** between Seventh and Eighth Ave., has sheltered such artists as Sid Vicious of the Sex Pistols. Countless writers have sought inspiration here, including Vladimir Nabokov and Dylan Thomas. *(222 W. 23rd St., between Seventh and Eighth Ave.* ☎ *212-243-3700.)*

HERALD SQUARE AREA. Herald Square is located between 34th and 35th St., between Broadway and Sixth Ave. The area is a center for shopping. *(Subway: B, D, F, N, Q, R, V, W to 34th St./Herald Sq.)* The **Empire State Building,** now the city's tallest building after the World Trade Center tragedy, dominates postcards, movies, and the city's skyline. The limestone-and-granite structure stretches 1454 ft. into the sky, and its 73 elevators run through 2 mi. of shafts. The nighttime view from the top is spectacular. *(350 Fifth Ave., at 34th St. Observatory:* ☎ *212-736-3100. Open daily 9:30am-midnight; last elevator up at 11:30pm. $12, seniors $11, under 12 $7. Skyride:* ☎ *212-279-9777. Open daily 10am-10pm. $16, ages 12-17 $15, seniors and ages 4-11 $13.)* East on 34th St. stands **Macy's.** This Goliath of department stores sponsors the **Macy's Thanksgiving Day Parade,** a NYC tradition buoyed by 10-story Snoopys, marching bands, and floats. *(Between 7th Ave. and Broadway, in Herald Sq.)* The **Garment District,** surrounding Macy's but selling cheaper clothing, was once a red-light district, and purportedly contained the world's highest concentration of apparel workers during the 1930s. *(Between Broadway and Eighth Ave.)*

MIDTOWN

East of Eighth Ave., from about 42nd St. to 59th St., lie Midtown's mammoth office buildings, posh hotels, and high-brow stores. *(Subway: 4, 5, 6, 7, S to 42nd St./Grand Central; B, D, F, V to 42nd St./Ave. of the Americas (Sixth Ave.); 7 to Fifth Ave./42nd St.; E, V to Fifth Ave./53rd St.; N, R, W to Fifth Ave./59th St.; 1, 2, 3, 7, 9, N, Q, R, S, W to 42nd St./Times Square; A, C, E to 42nd St./Port Authority; 7, B, D, F, V to 42nd St./Bryant Park.)*

FIFTH AVENUE. A monumental research library in the style of a classical temple, the main branch of the **New York Public Library,** between 40th and 42nd St., contains the world's seventh-largest research library and an immense reading room. *(42nd St. and Fifth Ave. ☎212-869-8089.)* Behind the library, **Bryant Park** features free summertime cultural events, like classic film screenings and live comedy. *(☎212-484-1222 for events schedule. Open daily 7am-9pm.)* Designed by James Renwick, the twin spires of **St. Patrick's Cathedral** stretch 330 ft. into the air, making it the largest Catholic cathedral in the US. *(51st St. ☎212-753-2261.)* The **Plaza Hotel,** on 59th St., at the southeast corner of Central Park, was constructed in 1907 at an astronomical cost. Its 18-story, 800-room French Renaissance interior flaunts five marble staircases, ludicrously named suites, and a two-story Grand Ballroom.

ROCKEFELLER CENTER. The main entrance to Rockefeller Center is on Fifth Ave. between 49th and 50th St. **The Channel Gardens,** so named because they sit between the **Maison Française** on the left and the **British Empire Building** on the right, usher pedestrians toward **Tower Plaza.** This sunken space, topped by the gold-leafed statue of Prometheus, is surrounded by the flags of over 100 countries. During spring and summer an **ice-skating rink** lies dormant beneath an overpriced cafe. The rink, which is better for people-watching than for skating, reopens in winter in time for the **annual Christmas tree lighting,** one of New York City's greatest traditions. **Tours of Rockefeller Center** are available through NBC. *(Departs every hr. from the GE Building. M-Sa 10am-5pm, Su 10am-4pm. No children under 6. $10, ages 6-16 $8.)*

Behind Tower Plaza is the **General Electric Building,** a 70-story skyscraper. **NBC,** which makes its home here, offers an hour-long tour that traces the history of the network, from its first radio broadcast in 1926, through the heyday of TV programming in the 1950s and 60s, to today's sitcoms. The tour visits six studios, including the infamous 8H studio, home of *Saturday Night Live. (Departs every 15min. from the NBC Experience Store in the GE Building. M-Sa 8:30am-5:30pm, Su 9:30am-4:30pm. No children under 6. $18, seniors $15, ages 6-16 $15.)* A block north is **Radio City Music Hall.** Narrowly escaping demolition in 1979, this Art Deco landmark received a complete interior restoration shortly thereafter. Radio City's main attraction is the Rockettes, a high-stepping long-legged troupe of dancers. Tours of the Music Hall take visitors through The Great Stage and various rehearsal halls. *(50th St. at Sixth Ave. ☎212-247-4777. Departs every 30min. M-Su 11am-3pm. $17, seniors $14, under 12 $10.)*

PARK AVENUE. A luxurious boulevard with greenery running down its center, **Park Avenue,** between 45th and 59th St., is lined with office buildings and hotels. Completed in 1913, the **Grand Central Terminal** has a richly classical main facade on 42nd St., topped by a beautiful sculpture of Mercury, Roman god of transportation. An info booth sits in the middle of the commuter-filled Concourse. *(Between 42nd and 45th St.)* Several blocks uptown is the *crème de la crème* of Park Avenue hotels, the **Waldorf-Astoria.** *(Between 49th and 50th St.)* The **Seagram Building,** Ludwig Mies Van der Rohe's dark, gracious modern monument, stands a few blocks uptown. *(375 Park Ave., between 52nd and 53rd St.)*

UNITED NATIONS AREA. The **United Nations,** a "center for harmonizing the actions of nations" founded in 1945 in the aftermath of WWII, is located in international territory along what would be First Ave. The UN complex consists of the

Secretariat Building (the skyscraper), the General Assembly Building, the Hammarskjöld Library, and the Conference Building. The only way into the General Assembly Building is by guided tour. *(First Ave., between 42nd and 48th St. ☎ 212-963-4475. 1hr. tours depart from the UN visitors' entrance at First Ave. and 46th St. Held every 15min. in 20 languages. Mar.-Dec. M-F 9:15am-4:45pm, Sa-Su 9:30am-4:45pm; Jan.-Feb. M-F only. $11, over 62 $8, students $7, ages 5-14 $6.)* At the **Chrysler Building,** a spire influenced by radiator grille design tops this Art Deco palace. *(On 42nd St. and Lexington Ave.)*

TIMES SQUARE AND THEATER DISTRICT. Times Square, at the intersection of 42nd St., Seventh Ave., and Broadway, once gave New York City its reputation for strip clubs and filth. Today, the smut has been replaced by 30-ft.-tall screens, Disney musicals, and nearly 40 million tourists per year. For info on rush ticketing or anything else, stop by the Times Square Visitors Center, 1560 Broadway, at W. 46th St. *(☎ 212-869-1890; www.timessquarebid.com. Open daily 8am-8pm.)*

57TH STREET AND CENTRAL PARK SOUTH. Luxury hotels, including the **Essex House,** the **St. Moritz,** and the **Plaza,** overlook Central Park from their perch on Central Park S, between Fifth and Eighth Ave., where 59th St. should be. Amid 57th St.'s galleries and stores, New York City's musical center is **Carnegie Hall** (p. 243). A $60-million restoration has returned the 1891 building to its earlier splendor. *(881 Seventh Ave., at W. 57th St. ☎ 212-247-7800 or 903-9765. Tours M-F 11:30am, 2, and 3pm. 1hr. Purchase tickets at box office on tour days. $6, students and seniors $5, under 12 $3.)*

CENTRAL PARK

Once an 843-acre squatting-place for the very poor, Central Park was founded in the mid-19th century when some wealthy New Yorkers advocated the creation of a park in the style of the public grounds of Europe. Frederick Law Olmsted and Calvert Vaux designed the park in 1858; their Greensward plan took 15 years and 20,000 workers to implement, but the result is truly beautiful. Expansive fields like the **Sheep Meadow,** from 66th to 69th St., and the **Great Lawn,** from 80th to 85th St., complement developed spaces such as the **Mall,** between 66th and 71st St., the **Shakespeare Garden,** at 80th St., and the **Imagine Mosaic,** commemorating the music of John Lennon, on the western side of the park at 72nd St. Don't miss free summer shows at **Central Park Summerstage** and **Shakespeare in Central Park.** *(☎ 212-360-3444, parks and recreation info 360-8111 M-F 9am-5pm. Free park maps at Belvedere Castle, located mid-park at 79th St.; the Charles A. Dana Discovery Center, at 110th St. near 5th Ave.; the North Meadow Recreation Center, mid-park at 97th St.; and the Dairy, mid-park near 65th St.)*

> Central Park is fairly safe during the day, but less so at night. Don't be afraid to go to events in the Park at night, but take large paths and go with someone. Do not wander the darker paths at night, especially if you are a woman. In an **emergency,** use one of the call-boxes located throughout the park. **24hr. Police Line** ☎ 570-4820.

UPPER EAST SIDE

Since the late 19th and early 20th centuries, when some of New York City's wealthiest citizens built elaborate mansions along **Fifth Avenue,** the Upper East Side has been home to the city's richest residents. Today, some of these mansions have been turned into museums, such as the Frick Collection and the Cooper-Hewitt Museum. They are just two of the world-famous museums that line **Museum Mile,** from 82nd to 104th St. on Fifth Ave. (p. 238). **Park Avenue** from 59th to 96th St. is lined with dignified apartment buildings. Lexington and Third Ave. are commercial, but as you go east, the neighborhood becomes more and more residential. *(Subway: N, R, W to Fifth Ave./59th St.; 4, 5, 6, N, R, W to 59th St./Lexington Ave.; F to Lexington Ave./63rd St.; 6 to 68th St., 77th St., 96th St.; 4, 5, 6 to 86th St./Lexington Ave.)*

UPPER WEST SIDE

While Central Park W and Riverside Dr. flank the Upper West Side with residential quietude, Columbus Ave., Amsterdam Ave., and Broadway buzz with action. Organic fruit and progressive politics dominate the area between 59th and 110th St., west of Central Park. *(Subway: 1, 9, A, B, C, D to 59th St./Columbus Circle; 1, 9 to 66th St., 79th St., 86th St./Broadway; 1, 2, 3, 9 to 72nd St./Broadway; B, C to 72nd St., 81st St., 86th St., 96th St./Central Park W; 1, 2, 3, 9 to 96th St./Broadway.)*

LINCOLN CENTER. Broadway intersects Columbus Ave. at **Lincoln Center,** the cultural hub of the city (p. 242). The airy architecture reinterprets the public plazas of Rome and Venice, but the center's performance spaces for opera, ballet, and classical music take center stage. *(Between 62nd and 66th St.)*

MORNINGSIDE HEIGHTS. Above 110th St. and below 125th St., between Amsterdam Ave. and the Hudson River, **Morningside Heights** centers around **Columbia University's** urban campus. *(Subway: 1 to Cathedral Pkwy. (110th St.), 116th St./Columbia University, 125th St./Broadway.)* The centerpiece of the campus is the majestic Roman Classical Low Library, which looms over College Walk, the school's central promenade. *(Morningside Dr. and Broadway, from 114th to 120th St.)* The still-unfinished cathedral of **St. John the Divine,** under construction since 1892, is the largest in the world. It features altars and bays dedicated both to the sufferings of Christ and to the experiences of immigrants, victims of genocide, and AIDS patients. *(Amsterdam Ave., between 110th and 113th St. Subway: 1 to Cathedral Pkwy. (110th St.)/Broadway. ☎ 212-316-7540, tours 932-7347; www.stjohndivine.org. Open daily 7am-6pm. Tours Tu-Sa 11am, Su 1pm. $5, students and seniors $4. Parish box office ☎ 212-662-2133.)* **Riverside Church,** near Columbia, has an observation deck in its tower and an amazing view, as well as the world's largest carillon (74 bells), a gift of John D. Rockefeller, Jr. *(490 Riverside Dr., at 120th St. Subway: 1 to 116th St./Columbia University. ☎ 212-870-6792; www.theriverside-church.org. Open M-F 9am-4:30pm. Tours Su 12:30pm, after services, and upon request. Free.)* **Grant's Tomb,** a huge presidential grave commemorating the Union Civil War general, lies at 122nd St. and Riverside Dr. *(Open daily 9am-5pm. Free.)*

HARLEM

Manhattan's largest neighborhood extends from 110th Street to the 150s, between the Hudson and East Rivers. Harlem began its transformation into a black neighborhood between 1910 and 1920. The 1920s brought prosperity and the artistic Harlem Renaissance movement; Civil Rights and radical Black Power activism came in the 1960s. Today, thanks to community activism and economic boom in recent decades, Harlem is thriving after a period of decline. *(Subway: 6 to 103rd St., Central Park N (110th St.), 116th St./Lexington Ave.; 4, 5, 6 to 125th St./Lexington Ave.; 2, 3 to Central Park N (110th St.), 116th St., 125th St., 135th St./Lenox (Sixth) Ave.; 3 to 145th St./ Lenox (Sixth) Ave., 148th St.; B, C to Cathedral Pkwy. (110th St.), 116th St., 135th St. at Central Park W; A, B, C, D to 125th St./Central Park W, 145th St./St. Nicholas Ave.; 1, 9 to 125th St., 137th St., 145th St./Broadway.)*

SUGAR HILL. African-Americans with "sugar" (a.k.a. money) moved here in the 1920s and 30s. Musical legends Duke Ellington and W.C. Handy lived in the neighborhood, while leaders W.E.B. DuBois and Thurgood Marshall inhabited 409 Edgecombe Ave. Some of the city's most notable gangsters operated here. The area is also the birthplace of Sugarhill Records, the rap label that created the Sugarhill Gang. Their 1979 *Rapper's Delight* became the first hip-hop song to enter the Top 40. Today, skyrocketing real estate prices in Manhattan have made Sugar Hill's beautiful brownstones prized possessions once more. *(143rd to 155th St., between St. Nicholas and Edgecombe Ave. Subway: A, B, C, D to 145th St./St. Nicholas Ave.)*

WASHINGTON HEIGHTS. North of 155th St., **Washington Heights** affords a taste of urban life with an ethnic flavor. Eat a Greek dinner, buy Armenian pastries and vegetables from a South African, and discuss the Talmud with a **Yeshiva University** student. Fort Tryon Park is home to **The Cloisters,** a museum specializing in medieval art. *(Subway: C to 155th St./St. Nicholas Ave., 163rd St.; 1, A, C to 168th St./Broadway; A to 175th St., 181st St., 190th St.; 1, 9 to 181st St./St. Nicholas Ave., 191st St.)*

BROOKLYN

Part of NYC since 1898, Brooklyn is now the most populous borough. In the coverage below, neighborhoods are arranged from north to south.

WILLIAMSBURG AND GREENPOINT. Home to a growing number of artists, Williamsburg's galleries match its artsy population (see **Galleries,** p. 240). **Greenpoint,** bounded by Java St. to the north, Meserole St. to the south, and Franklin St. to the west, is Brooklyn's northernmost border and home to a large Polish population. The birthplace of Mae West and the Union's Civil War ironclad the *USS Monitor,* Greenpoint features charming Italianate and Greek revival houses built during the 1850s shipbuilding boom. *(Subway: L to Bedford Ave.; G to Nassau Ave.)*

FULTON LANDING. Fulton Landing hearkens back to days when the ferry—not the subway or the car—was the primary means of transportation between Brooklyn and Manhattan. Completed in 1883, the nearby ▨**Brooklyn Bridge**—spanning the gap between lower Manhattan and Brooklyn—is the product of elegant calculation, careful design, and human exertion. A walk across the bridge at sunrise or sunset is one of the most exhilarating strolls New York City has to offer. *(From Brooklyn: entrance at the end of Adams St., at Tillary St. Subway: A, C to High St./Cadman Plaza E. From Manhattan: entrance at Park Row. Subway: 4, 5, 6, J, M, Z to Brooklyn Bridge/City Hall.)*

DOWNTOWN. Brooklyn Heights, a well-preserved 19th-century residential area, sprang up with the development of steamboat transportation between Brooklyn and Manhattan in 1814. Rows of posh Greek Revival and Italianate houses in this area essentially created New York City's first suburb. **Montague Street,** the main drag, has the stores, cafes, and mid-priced restaurants of a cute college town. **Downtown** is the location of Brooklyn's **Civic Center** and holds several grand municipal buildings. *(Subway: 2, 3, 4, 5, M, R to Court St./Borough Hall.)*

PROSPECT PARK. Park Slope is a residential neighborhood with charming brownstones. Neighboring **Prospect Park,** the borough's answer to Manhattan's Central Park, has a zoo, an ice-skating rink, and a children's museum. Frederick Law Olmsted and Calvert Vaux designed the park in the mid-1800s. In the 1890s, the 80-ft.-high **Memorial Arch** was built in Grand Army Plaza to commemorate the North's Civil War victory. *(Bounded by Prospect Park W, Flatbush Ave., Ocean Ave., Parkside Ave., and Prospect Park SW. Subway: 2, 3 to Grand Army Plaza; F to 15 St./Prospect Park; B, Q, S to Prospect Park. ☎ 718-965-8951, events hotline 965-8999.)*

BROOKLYN BOTANIC GARDEN. Adjacent to the park, this 52-acre fairyland features the **Fragrance Garden for the Blind** (with mint, lemon, violet, and other appetizing aromas) and the more formal **Cranford Rose Garden.** *(1000 Washington Ave.; entrances also on Eastern Pkwy. and on Flatbush Ave. Subway: S to Botanic Garden; B, Q, S to Prospect Park; 2, 3 to Eastern Pkwy./Brooklyn Museum. ☎718-623-7000, events hotline 623-7333; www.bbg.org. Open Apr.-Sept. Tu-F 8am-6pm, Sa-Su 10am-6pm; Oct.-Mar. Tu-F 8am-4:30pm, Sa-Su 10am-4:30pm. $5, students with ID and seniors $3, under 16 free, groups free. Free Tu and Sa 10am-noon; seniors also free F.)*

CONEY ISLAND. Once an elite resort (until the subway made it accessible to the masses), **Coney Island** is now a rickety slice of American nostalgia. The **Cyclone,** 834 Surf Ave., built in 1927, was once the most terrifying rollercoaster in the world.

Meet sharks and other beasties at the **New York Aquarium.** *(At Surf and W. 8th St. Subway: F, Q to W 8th St./NY Aquarium. ☎ 718-265-3474; www.nyaquarium.com. Open May-Oct. M-F 10am-6pm, Sa-Su and holidays 10am-7pm; Nov.-Apr. daily 10am-4:30pm. $11, seniors and ages 2-12 $7. No bikes, in-line skates, or pets allowed. Wheelchair accessible.)*

QUEENS

ASTORIA AND LONG ISLAND CITY. In the northwest corner of Queens lies Astoria, where Greek-, Italian-, and Spanish-speaking communities mingle amid lively shopping districts and cultural attractions. Long Island City is just south, across the river from the Upper East Side. The **Isamu Noguchi Garden Museum,** the **Museum for African Art,** and the juggernaut **MoMA** (see **Museums,** p. 238) have all temporarily relocated to Long Island City. *(Astoria is in the northwestern corner of Queens, across the river from Manhattan. Long Island City is southwest of Astoria, and can be reached by walking south on 21st or 31st St. Subway: All N, W stops between 36th Ave. and Astoria Ditmars Blvd. G, R, V to 36th St. or Steinway St.)*

SOCRATES SCULPTURE PARK. Led by sculptor Mark di Suvero, artists transformed this one-time abandoned landfill into an artistic exhibition space with 35 stunning day-glo and rusted metal abstractions. *(At the end of Broadway, across the Vernon Blvd. intersection. Subway: N, W to Broadway. ☎ 718-956-1819; www.socratessculpturepark.org. Park offices located across from Broadway entrance. Open daily 10am-dusk. Free.)*

FLUSHING AND FLUSHING MEADOWS PARK. Flushing boasts colonial neighborhood landmarks, a bustling downtown, and a huge Asian immigrant population. Nearby **Flushing Meadows-Corona Park** was the site of the 1939 and 1964 World's Fair, and now holds **Shea Stadium** (home of the Mets), the **USTA National Tennis Center** (where the US Open is played), and the simple yet interesting **New York Hall of Science.** *(47-01 111th St., at 48th Ave. Subway: 7 to 111th St. ☎ 718-699-0005; www.nyhallsci.org. Open July-Aug. Tu-Su 9:30am-5pm; Sept.-June Tu-W 9:30am-2pm, Th-Su 9:30am-5pm. $9; seniors, students, and ages 5-17 $6; ages 2-4 $2.50; under 2 free. Free Sept.-June and F 2-5pm.)* The **Unisphere,** a 380-ton steel globe in front of the New York City Building, is the retro-futuristic structure featured in the 1997 movie *Men In Black. (Subway: 7 to Flushing/Main St; 7 to 111th St. or Willets Point.)*

THE BRONX

The relentless stream of immigration, once Italian and Irish but now mostly Hispanic and Russian, has created vibrant ethnic neighborhoods (including a Little Italy that puts its Manhattan counterpart to shame).

YANKEE STADIUM. In 1923, Babe Ruth's success as a hitter inspired the construction of the Yankees' own ballpark. Inside the 11.6-acre park (the field itself measures only 3½ acres), monuments honor Yankee greats like Lou Gehrig, Joe DiMaggio, and Great Bambino himself. *(E. 161st St., at River Ave. Subway: 4, B, D to 161st St./Yankee Stadium. ☎ 718-293-6000; www.yankees.com. 1hr. tours start at noon. In summer $14, students and seniors $7; in winter $12/$6.)*

THE BRONX ZOO. The hugely popular **Bronx Zoo/Wildlife Conservation Park** houses over 4000 animals. Soar on the **Skyfari** aerial tramway ($2) that runs between Wild Asia and the **Children's Zoo,** or ride a camel. *(Subway: 2, 5 to West Farms Sq./E. Tremont Ave. Follow Boston Rd. for 3 blocks until the Bronx Park S gate. Bus: Bx9, Bx12, Bx19, Bx22, and Q44 pass various entrances to the zoo. ☎ 718-367-1010. Open daily M-F 10am-5pm, Sa-Su 10am-5:30pm. Parts of the zoo closed Nov.-Apr. $11, seniors and ages 2-12 $8; W free.)*

NEW YORK BOTANICAL GARDEN. Located adjacent to the zoo, the city's most extensive botanical garden (250 acres) includes a 40-acre **hemlock forest,** kept in its natural state. Although it costs an extra few dollars to enter, the different ecosystems in the gorgeous domed greenhouse **Conservatory** are worth a visit. *(Bronx River Pkwy. Exit 7W and Fordham Rd. Subway: 4 to Bedford Park Blvd./Lehman College; B, D to Bedford Park Blvd. Walk 8 blocks east or take the Bx26 bus. Bus: Bx19 or Bx26. Train: Metro-North Harlem line goes from Grand Central Terminal to Botanical Garden station. ☎ 718-817-8700; www.nybg.org. Open Apr.-Oct. Tu-Su 10am-6pm; Nov.-Mar. Tu-Su 10am-4pm. $6, seniors $3, students $2, children 2-12 $1; free W all day and Sa 10am-noon. Call for tours.)*

BELMONT. Arthur Ave. is the center of this uptown **Little Italy,** which is home to wonderful homestyle southern Italian cooking. To get a concentrated sense of the area, stop into **Arthur Avenue Retail Market,** 2334 Arthur Ave., between 186th and Crescent St. The recent Kosovar influx has put Kosovar flags in the fronts of many stores and eateries. *(Centering on Arthur Ave. and E. 187th St., near the Southern Blvd. entrance to the Bronx Zoo. Subway: B, D to Fordham Rd./Grand Concourse. Walk 11 blocks east or take Bx12 to Arthur Ave. and head south.)*

STATEN ISLAND

Staten Island has a lot to offer, but tourism here is often limited. Its many parks are vast and lush, and there are beaches, historical sites, and lovely gardens. The **Staten Island Ferry** is itself a sight not to be missed; it offers the best and cheapest (free) tour on NY's upper harbor. *(Ferry leaves from South Ferry in Manhattan; Subway: N, R to Whitehall St.; 1, 9 to South Ferry.)* The beautiful 19th-century **Snug Harbor Cultural Center** houses the **Newhouse Center for Contemporary Art,** a small art gallery with a summer sculpture show, and the **Staten Island Botanical Gardens.** *(1000 Richmond Terr. Bus S40. ☎ 718-448-2500. Free tours of the grounds Apr.-Nov. Sa-Su 2pm, starting at the visitors center. Botanical Garden: ☎ 718-273-8200. Open daily dawn-dusk.)*

🏛 MUSEUMS

For listings of upcoming exhibits consult *The New Yorker, New York* magazine, and Friday's *New York Times* weekend section. Most museums are closed on Monday and jam-packed on weekends. Many request a "donation" in place of an admission fee—don't be embarrassed to give as little as a dollar. Most are free one weeknight.

UPPER WEST SIDE

🏛 **American Museum of Natural History,** Central Park W (☎212-769-5100), between 77th and 81st St. Subway: B, C to 81st St. You're never too old for the Natural History Museum, one of the world's largest museums devoted to science. The main draw are the 4th-fl. dinosaur halls, which display real fossils in 85% of the exhibits (most museums use fossil casts). Perhaps the most impressive part of the museum is the sparkling Hayden Planetarium within the Rose Center for Earth and Space. Open daily 10am-5:45pm; Rose Center also open F until 8:45pm. Suggested donation $12, students and seniors $9, children $7. Wheelchair accessible.

New York Historical Society, 2 W. 77th St. (☎212-873-3400), at Central Park W. Subway: 1, 9 to 79th St.; B, C to 72nd St./Central Park W, 81st St. Founded in 1804, this is New York City's oldest continuously operated museum. The Neoclassical building houses both a library and museum. Open late May to early Sept. Tu-Su 11am-6pm; early Sept. to late May Tu-Su 11am-5pm. $6, students and seniors $4, children free. Wheelchair accessible.

UPPER EAST SIDE

🏛 **Metropolitan Museum of Art,** 1000 Fifth Ave. (☎212-535-7710, concerts and lectures 570-3949, wheelchair info 535-7710), at 82nd St. Subway: 4, 5, 6 to 86th St./Lexington Ave. The largest in the Western Hemisphere, the Met's art collection boasts over 2 million works spanning 5000 years. Highlights are the Egyptian Art holdings (including the completely reconstructed Temple of Dendur), the European paintings collection, and extensive exhibits of American art. The Costume Institute houses over 75,000 international costumes and accessories from the 17th century to the present, as well as the recently overhauled collection of Greek and Roman art. Open Su and Tu-Th 9:30am-5:15pm, F-Sa 9:30am-8:45pm. Suggested donation $12, seniors and students $7.

Guggenheim Museum, 1071 Fifth Ave. (☎212-423-3500), at 89th St. Subway: 4, 5, 6 to 86th St./Lexington Ave. The Guggenheim's most famous exhibit is the building itself, an inverted white, multi-ridged shell designed by Frank Lloyd Wright and hailed as a modern masterpiece. Interdependent gallery spaces make up a spiral design. The large collection of modern and postmodern paintings includes significant works in Cubism, Surrealism, American Minimalism, and Abstract Expressionism. Open M-W and Sa-Su 10am-5:45pm, F 10am-8pm. $15, students and seniors $10, under 12 free.

Frick Collection, 1 E. 70th St. (☎212-288-0700), at Fifth Ave. Subway: 6 to 68th St. Henry Clay Frick left his house and art collection to the city, and the museum retains the elegance of his chateau. The Living Hall displays 17th-century furniture, Persian rugs, Holbein portraits, and paintings by El Greco, Rembrandt, Velázquez, and Titian. The courtyard is inhabited by elegant statues surrounding the garden pool and fountain. Open Tu-Sa 10am-6pm, Su 1-6pm. $12, seniors $8, students $5. Under 10 not allowed, under 16 must be accompanied by an adult. Wheelchair accessible.

Museum of the City of New York, 1220 Fifth Ave. (☎212-534-1672), at 103rd St. Subway: 6 to 103rd St. This fascinating museum details the history of the Big Apple, from the construction of the Empire State Building to the history of Broadway theater. Cultural history of all varieties is on parade—don't miss the model ships, NYC paintings, hot pants, and Yankees World Series trophies. Open W-Su 10am-5pm. Suggested donation $7; students, seniors, and children $4.

The Jewish Museum, 1109 Fifth Ave. (☎212-423-3200), at 92nd St. Subway: 6 to 96th St. The gallery's permanent collection details the Jewish experience throughout history using ancient Biblical artifacts and ceremonial objects, as well as contemporary masterpieces by Marc Chagall, Frank Stella, and George Segal. Open Su-W 11am-5:45pm, Th 11am-9pm, F 11am-5pm. $10, students and seniors $7.50, members and under 12 free. Th 5-9pm pay-what-you-wish.

Whitney Museum of American Art, 945 Madison Ave. (☎212-570-3676), at 75th St. Subway: 6 to 77th St. The museum with a historical mandate to champion the works of living American artists has assembled the largest collection of 20th- and 21st-century American art in the world, including Jasper Johns's *Three Flags* and Frank Stella's *Brooklyn Bridge.* Open W-Th and Sa 11am-6pm, F 1-9pm, Su 11am-6pm. $12, students and seniors $9.50, under 12 free. F 6-9pm pay-what-you-wish.

MIDTOWN

Museum of Modern Art (MoMA), 11 W. 53rd St. (☎212-708-9400), between Fifth and Sixth Ave. Subway: E, V to Fifth Ave./53rd St; N, R, W to Fifth Ave./59th St. The MoMA commands one of the world's most impressive collections of post-Impressionist, late 19th-century, and 20th-century art. Its collection includes Matisse's *The Dance,* van Gogh's *The Starry Night,* and Warhol's signature *Marilyn Monroe.* In May 2002, the 53rd St. MoMA shut its doors for renovations and moved to Queens. It will return to Manhattan in Nov. 2005 to an overhauled space, nearly doubled in size.

Museum of Television and Radio, 25 W. 52nd St. (☎212-621-6600), between Fifth and Sixth Ave. Subway: B, D, F, V to 47th-50th St.-Rockefeller Center/Sixth Ave. or E, V to Fifth Ave./53rd St. More archive than museum, this shrine to modern media contains over 100,000 easily accessible TV and radio programs. The museum hosts a number of film screenings that focus on social, historical, or artistic topics. Open Tu-W and F-Su noon-6pm, Th noon-8pm. Suggested donation $10, students and seniors $8, under 13 $5.

BROOKLYN

▨ **Brooklyn Museum of Art,** 200 Eastern Pkwy. (☎718-638-5000), at Washington Ave. Subway: 2, 3 to Eastern Pkwy./Brooklyn Museum. If it weren't for the Met, the BMA would be New York City's most magnificent museum. Oceanic and New World art collections take up the central space on the 1st fl. Ancient Greek, Roman, Middle Eastern, and Egyptian galleries are on the 3rd fl. Open W-F 10am-5pm, Sa-Su 11am-6pm; also 1st Sa of each month 11am-11pm. $6, students and seniors $3, under 12 free. 1st Sa of each month free.

◪ GALLERIES

New York City's galleries provide a riveting—and free—introduction to the contemporary art world. To get started, pick up a free copy of *The Gallery Guide* at any major museum or gallery. Most galleries are open Tuesday to Saturday, from 10 or 11am to 5 or 6pm. Galleries are usually only open on weekend afternoons in the summer, and many are closed from late July to early September.

Artists Space, 38 Greene St. 3rd fl. (☎212-226-3970; www.artistsspace.org), at Grand St. Subway: 1, 9 to Canal St./Varick St.; A, C, E to Canal St./Ave. of the Americas (Sixth Ave.). Nonprofit gallery founded in 1972. Champions work by emerging and unaffiliated artists. Often used for multiple small exhibits. Presents works in all media, but the focus is on works in architecture and design. The Irving Sandler Artists File, containing slides and digitized images of works by more than 3000 unaffiliated artists, is open to critics, curators, and the public by appointment (F-Sa). Open Tu-Sa 11am-6pm. Closed Aug.

The Drawing Center, 35 Wooster St. (☎212-219-2166; www.drawingcenter.org), between Grand and Broome St. Subway: 1, 9 to Canal St./Varick St.; A, C, E to Canal St./Ave. of the Americas (Sixth Ave.). Specializing in original works on paper, this nonprofit space sets up high-quality exhibits. Works from Picasso to Kara Walker on rotation. Open Tu-F 10am-6pm, Sa 11am-6pm. Closed Aug. Suggested donation $3. More space at the **Drawing Room,** 40 Wooster St.

525 W. 22nd St., between 10th and 11th Ave. Houses a handful of excellent, petite galleries of contemporary art, including the **303 Gallery** (☎212-255-1121; www.303gallery.com), **D'Amelio Terras** (☎212-352-9460; www.damelioterras.com), and the **DCA Gallery** (☎212-255-5511; www.dcagallery.com). Call for hours.

529 W. 20th St., between 10th and 11th Ave. This 11-fl. colossus boasts over 20 contemporary art galleries, including the **I-20 Gallery** (☎212-645-1100; www.I-20.com), the **ACA Galleries** (☎212-206-8080; www.acagalleries.com), and the **Dorfman Projects** (☎212-352-2272; www.dorfmanprojects.com).

Leo Castelli, 59 E. 79th St. (☎212-249-4470; www.castelligallery.com), between Park and Madison Ave. Subway: 6 to 77th St. Founded in 1957 by Leo Castelli, a highly influential art dealer known for showcasing the early efforts of Frank Stella and Andy Warhol. A selection of both established and up-and-coming artists. Open mid-Aug. to late June Tu-Sa 10am-6pm; late June to mid-Aug. Tu-F 11am-5pm. Occasionally closed; call ahead.

Brooklyn Bridge Anchorage, Cadman Plaza W (☎212-206-6674), on the corner of Hicks and Old Fulton St., in Brooklyn. Subway: A, C to High St. A gallery/performance space housed within the bridge's cavernous suspension cable storage chambers. Cutting-edge multimedia installations make good use of the vaulted 80-ft. ceilings. *Creative Time* runs hip music performances in the under-bridge space. Open mid-May to mid-Oct. M-Tu and Th-Su noon-8pm, W noon-7pm. *Creative Time* open Th-F 3-8pm, Sa-Su 1-6pm.

Pierogi 2000, 177 N. 9th St. (☎718-599-2144; www.pierogi2000.com), between Bedford and Driggs Ave., in Williamsburg, Brooklyn. Subway: L to Bedford Ave. Hosts 2 big-name solo shows per month by artists like Lawrence Weiner and Andrea Way. Those lucky enough to visit a monthly opening can expect free *pierogi* and vodka. Flip through the legendary "flatfiles" of bundled art—most pieces are under $200. Open M and F-Su noon-6pm.

🎭 ENTERTAINMENT

Publications with noteworthy entertainment and nightlife sections are the *Village Voice*, *New York* magazine, and the Sunday edition of the *New York Times*. The *New Yorker* has the most comprehensive theater survey.

THEATER

Broadway tickets usually start from $50. **TKTS,** Duffy Square, at 47th St. and Broadway, sells tickets for many Broadway and some larger off-Broadway shows at a 25-50% discount on the day of the performance. The lines begin to form an hour or so before the booths open, but they move fairly quickly. More tickets become available as showtime approaches, so you may find fewer possibilities if you go too early. (☎ 768-1818. Tickets sold M-Sa 3-8pm for evening performances, W and Sa 10am-2pm for matinees, Su 11am-7pm for matinees and evening performances.) Reserve full-price tickets over the phone and pay by credit card using **Tele-Charge** (☎ 239-6200 or 800-432-7250) for Broadway shows; **Ticket Central** (☎ 279-4200) for off-Broadway shows; and **Ticketmaster** (☎ 307-4100 or 800-755-4000) for all types of shows. All three services have a per-ticket service charge, so ask before purchasing. You can avoid these fees if you buy tickets directly from the box office.

Shakespeare in the Park (☎ 539-8750) is a New York City summer tradition. From June through August, two plays are presented at the **Delacorte Theater** in Central Park, near the 81st St. entrance on the Upper West Side, just north of the main road. Tickets are free, but lines form extremely early.

EXPERIMENTAL/PERFORMANCE SPACES

🎨**The Kitchen,** 512 W. 19th St., between 10th and 11th Ave., is a world-renowned arts showcase in an unassuming Meatpacking District location. The space features experimental and avant-garde film and video, as well as concerts, dance performances, art exhibits, public lectures, and poetry readings. (Subway: C, E to 23rd St./Eighth Ave. ☎ 212-255-5793; www.thekitchen.org. Box office open Tu-Sa 2-6pm.) The **Knitting Factory,** 74 Leonard St., between Broadway and Church St., is a multi-level performance space featuring several shows nightly, ranging from avant-garde and indie rock to jazz and hip-hop. (Subway: 1, 9 to Franklin St. ☎ 212-219-3006; www.knittingfactory.com. Cover $5-25. Tickets are available for purchase on the Internet, phone, or at the box office. Box office open for walk-up sales M-Sa 10am-2am, Su 2pm-2am. Bar open 6pm-4am.)

JAZZ JOINTS

The **JVC Jazz Festival** puts on all-star performances from June to July. Tickets go on sale in early May, but many events are outdoors and free. Check the newspaper or call ☎ 212-501-1390. Annual festivals sponsored by major corporations draw local talent and industry giants. The concerts take place throughout the city (some free), but center at TriBeCa's **Knitting Factory** (see above). **Smoke,** 2751 Broadway, between 105th and 106th St, may no longer be a den of fumes, but the fantastic music keeps it smokin'. A sultry cocktail lounge jumps with jazz every night, and, although slightly congested, the intimate space swells with music. Surprise guests have included jazz legends like Dr. Lonnie Smith, George Benson, and Ronnie Cuber; the regular lineup includes John Farnsworth, Larry Willis, and Steve Wilson. (Subway: 1, 9 to 103rd St./Broadway. ☎ 212-864-6662; www.smoke-jazz.com. Retro happy hour daily 5-8pm; mixed drinks $3, other drinks $2 off. $10 drink min. per person per set. Sets usually at 9, 11pm, 12:30am. Tu and Th jam sessions 6-8:30pm. Jazz vocalist series Su 6-8:30pm. 21+. F-Sa cover $16-20. Open daily 5pm-4am.) **Detour,** 349 E. 13th St., between First and Second Ave., is a municipally acclaimed club with nightly jazz and no cover—a perfect combo. It would be the local hole-in-the-wall if it weren't for the impressively packed calendar. (Subway: L to First Ave. ☎ 212-533-6212; www.jazzatdetour.com. 2-drink min. Mixed drinks $6. Bottled beer $5-6. Wine $6-8. Happy hour daily 4-7pm, $3 drinks. 21+. Open Su-Tu 4pm-2am, W-Sa 4pm-4am.) The **Cotton Club**, 656 W. 125th St., on the corner of Riverside Dr., has been around since 1923 and seen jazz greats like Lena Horne, Ethel Waters, and Calloway. Now it's often clogged with tourists. (Subway: 1, 9 to 125th St./Broadway. ☎ 212-663-7980 or 800-640-7980; www.cottonclub-newyork.com. M evening swing/big band. Buffet dinner and jazz show Th-Sa evenings. M and Th-Sa evenings 21+; call for age restrictions at other events. Su brunch and gospel shows $25; dinner jazz shows $32. Call 2 weeks in advance for reservations and schedule.)

ROCK, POP, PUNK, FUNK

New York City has a long history of producing bands on the vanguard of popular music and performance, from the Velvet Underground to Sonic Youth. **Music festivals** provide the opportunity to see tons of bands at a (relatively) low price. The **CMJ Music Marathon** (☎ 877-633-7848) runs for four nights in late October or early November, including over 400 bands and workshops on the alternative music scene. **The Digital Club Festival** (☎ 677-3530), a newly reconfigured indie-fest, visits New York City in late July. The **Macintosh New York Music Festival** presents over 350 bands over a week-long period in July.

ΩSOBs (Sounds of Brazil), 204 Varick St., at W. Houston St., is a dinner-dance club that has some of NYC's best live music and hip-hop's best talents, including recent acts Talib Kweli, Blackalicious, and the Black Eyed Peas. Brazilian food goes well with the sounds: try lobster empanadas ($10), calypso chicken ($18), or crabcakes ($22). Monday nights feature a 1hr. Latin dance class ($5) at 7pm; Latin bands play at 9pm. Friday nights feature emerging artists; the late-night French-Caribbean dance party ($15-30) starts at midnight. (Subway: 1, 9 to Houston St. ☎ 212-243-4940; www.sobs.com. Sa samba 6:30pm-4am $20. Box office, next door at 200 Varick St., open M-F 11am-6pm, Sa noon-6pm. Usually 21+, sometimes 18+. Opens M-Sa at 6:30pm. Cash only.) **ΩSouthpaw,** 125 Fifth Ave., between Sterling and St. John's Pl., is a former 99-cent store that now hosts DJs, local musicians, and plenty of well-known talent. The past two years have seen performances from Ben Lee, the late Elliot Smith, and members of Wu-Tang Clan. (Brooklyn. Subway: M, N, R, to Union St.; Q to Seventh Ave.; 2, 3 to Bergen St. ☎ 718-230-0236; www.spsounds.com. Most shows 18+. Cover $7-20. Doors usually open around 8pm.) **ΩMercury Lounge,** 217 E. Houston St., between Essex and Ludlow St., is a converted gravestone parlor—there's a tombstone in the bar's countertop—that attracts an amazing number and range of big-name acts to its fairly small-time room. The alterna-rocker and singer-songwriter are frequent performers: past standouts include spoken-word artist Maggie Estep, Morphine, and Mary Lou Lord. (Subway: F to Delancey St. ☎ 212-260-4700; www.mercuryloungenyc.com. 21+. Cover varies. Box office open M-Sa noon-7pm. Cash only.)

OPERA AND DANCE

You can do it all at **ΩLincoln Center,** the world's largest cultural complex where many of the city's best opera, dance, and performance groups set up shop. (Between 62nd and 66th St. and Columbus and Amsterdam Ave. ☎ 212-875-5456. Subway: 1, 9 to 66th St.) Check *The New York Times* listings. The **Metropolitan Opera Company's** premier outfit performs on a Lincoln Center stage as big as a football field. You can stand in the orchestra for $16 or all the way back in the Family Circle for $12. (☎ 212-362-6000; www.metopera.org. Season Sept.-May M-Sa. Box office open M-Sa 10am-8pm, Su noon-6pm. Upper balcony around $65.) The **New York City Opera** has also come into its own. "City" has a split season (Sept.-Nov. and Mar.-Apr.) and keeps its ticket prices low. (☎212-870-5630; www.nycopera.com. Box office open M 10am-7:30pm, Tu-Sa 10am-8:30pm, Su 11:30am-7:30pm. Tickets $12-105; $15 student rush tickets the morning of the performance: ☎212-870-5630.) **Dicapo Opera Theatre,** 184 E. 76th St., between Third and Lexington Ave., is a small company that garners standing ovations after every performance. (☎212-288-9438; www.dicapo.com. Subway: N, R to 23rd St./Broadway. Tickets around $50.)

The **New York State Theater** in Lincoln Center is home to the late George Balanchine's ▨**New York City Ballet.** Tickets for the *Nutcracker* in December sell out almost immediately. (☎212-870-5570; www.nycballet.com. Season Nov.-Mar. Tickets $16-88. Student rush tickets $12; ☎212-870-7766.) The **American Ballet Theatre** dances at the Metropolitan Opera House. (☎212-477-3030, box office 362-6000; www.abt.org. Tickets $20-90.) **City Center,** 131 W. 55th St. (☎212-581-1212; www.citycenter.org), has the city's best dance, from modern to ballet, including the ▨**Alvin Ailey American Dance Theater. De La Guarda** (think disco in a rainforest with an air show overhead) performs at 20 Union Sq. E. (☎212-239-6200. Standing-room only. $65; some $20 tickets sold 2hr. before show. Box office open Tu-Th 1-8:15pm, F 1-10:30pm, Sa 1-10pm, Su 1-7:15pm.) Other dance venues include **Dance Theater Workshop,** 219 W. 19th St. (☎212-924-0077; www.dtw.org), between Seventh and Eighth Ave.; **Joyce Theater,** 175 Eighth Ave. (☎212-242-0800; www.joyce.org), between 18th and 19th St.; and **Thalia Spanish Theater,** 41-17 Greenpoint Ave. (☎718-729-3880), between 41st and 42nd St. in Queens.

CLASSICAL MUSIC

Lincoln Center has the most selection in its halls. The **Great Performers Series** packs the Avery Fisher and Alice Tully Halls and the Walter Reade Theater from October until May (see above for contact info; tickets from $20). **Avery Fisher Hall** presents the annual **Mostly Mozart Festival.** Show up early; there are usually recitals 1hr. before the main concert that are free to ticketholders. (☎212-875-5766. July-Aug. Tickets $25-70.) The **New York Philharmonic** begins its regular season in mid-September. Students and seniors can sometimes get $10 tickets the day of; call ahead. Check about seeing morning rehearsals. (☎212-875-5656. Tickets $20-80.) For a few weeks in late June, the Philharmonic holds **free concerts** (☎212-875-5709) on the Great Lawn in Central Park, at Prospect Park in Brooklyn, at Van Cortlandt Park in the Bronx, and elsewhere. Free outdoor events at Lincoln Center (☎212-875-5928) occur all summer.

Carnegie Hall, on Seventh Ave., at 57th St., sometimes offers rush tickets (☎212-247-7800. Box office M-Sa 11am-6pm, Su noon-6pm. Tickets $20-80.) A good, cheap way to absorb New York City musical culture is to visit a music school. Except for opera and ballet productions ($5-12), concerts are usually free and frequent. The best options are the **Juilliard School of Music,** Lincoln Center (☎769-7406), the **Mannes College of Music,** 150 W. 85th St. (☎212-580-0210), and the **Manhattan School of Music,** 120 Claremont Ave. (☎212-749-2802).

SPORTS

Most cities are content to have one major-league team in each big-time sport. New York City has two baseball teams, two hockey teams, NBA and WNBA basketball teams, two football teams...and one lonely soccer squad. The beloved **Mets** bat at **Shea Stadium** in Queens. (Subway: 7 to Willets Point-Shea Stadium. ☎718-507-6387. $13-30.) The **Yankees** play ball at **Yankee Stadium** in the Bronx. (Subway: 4, B, D to 161st St. ☎718-293-4300. $8-65.) Both the **Giants** and the **Jets** play football across the river at **Giants Stadium** in East Rutherford, NJ (☎201-507-8900; tickets from

$25), and the **New York/New Jersey Metrostars** play soccer in the same venue. The **Knickerbockers** (that's the **Knicks** to you), as well as the WNBA's **Liberty,** play basketball at **Madison Square Garden** (☎212-465-5800; from $22 and $8, respectively), and the **Rangers** play hockey there (from $25). The **Islanders** hit the ice at the **Nassau Veterans Memorial Coliseum** in Uniondale. (☎516-794-9300. Tickets $27-70.) New York City also hosts a number of other world-class events. Get tickets three months in advance for the prestigious **US Open,** held in late August and early September at the USTA Tennis Center in Flushing Meadows, Queens. (☎888-673-6849. $33-69.) On the first Sunday in November, two million spectators witness the 30,000 runners of the **New York City Marathon.** The race begins on the Verrazano Bridge and ends at Central Park's Tavern on the Green (☎212-860-4455).

▧ NIGHTLIFE

BARS

LOWER EAST SIDE

▧ **Local 138,** 138 Ludlow St. (212-477-0280), between Stanton and Rivington St. Subway: F, J, M, Z to Delancey/Essex St. Neighborhood bar with nary a decoration: just tables, bar, and booths. Lay low and grab a beer ($5), watch a game on TV, or make friends with the locals. Happy hour daily 4-9pm with $3 drafts. Open daily 4pm-4am.

Lotus Lounge, 35 Clinton St. (☎212-253-1144), at Stanton St. Subway: F, J, M, Z to Delancey St./Essex St. A lovely, low-key cafe by day; an even lovelier, lantern-lit bar by night. Bookshelves line back wall. Live DJ every night, starting around 10pm. Happy hour daily 4-8pm with $2 Buds, $3 drafts. Open M-Sa 8am-4am, Su 8am-2am.

SOHO AND TRIBECA

▧ **Circa Tabac,** 32 Watts St. (☎212-941-1781), between Sixth Ave. and Thompson St. Subway: C, E to Spring St./Ave. of the Americas (Sixth Ave.). Claims to be the world's 1st, and perhaps only, cigarette lounge. Despite Bloomberg's ban, the bar has remained a smoker's haven thanks to the same law that protects cigar lounges. Decor recalls a Prohibition-era speakeasy: jazz soundtrack, protective curtains, and Art Deco pieces. State-of-the-art air purifiers and odor killers keep the air clear. 180 kinds of cigarettes ($9-25) available, plus beer ($5-6) and cocktails ($8-12). Open daily 4pm-4am.

Milady's, 160 Prince St. (☎212-226-9069), at Thompson St. Subway: C, E to Spring St./Ave. of the Americas (Sixth Ave.). Down-to-earth staff matches no-frills atmosphere. Beer bottles ($3.50), drafts ($3.50-5), and SoHo's only pool table ($1). All drinks (even martinis) under $7. Veggie burgers $7. Grilled strip steak $8.50. Open daily 11am-4am. Kitchen open M-Th 11am-midnight, F-Sa 11am-1am, Su 11am-11pm.

GREENWICH VILLAGE

Blind Tiger Alehouse, 518 Hudson Ave. (☎212-675-3848; www.blindtigeralehouse.com), at 10th St. Subway: 1, 9 to Christopher St. Neighborhood corner pub. Draws in a diverse group of regulars for an amazing selection of microbrews (pints $5) and tasty freebies. M 6pm free hot dogs steamed in Brooklyn Beer, W 6pm free gourmet cheese tasting, Sa-Su noon free bagels and cream cheese. Happy hour M-F noon-8pm, $1 off pints and $3.50 well drinks. Monthly brewery tastings; check website for details. Open daily noon-4am.

The White Horse Tavern, 567 Hudson St. (☎212-243-9260), at W. 11th St. Subway: 1, 9 to Christopher St. Boisterous students playing drinking games, plus locals who reminisce about the tavern's 20-cent beers. Poet Dylan Thomas drank himself to death here. Jack Kerouac was a regular, too. Expansive pub interior with a great jukebox. Outdoor patio. Beer $4-5. Open Su-Th 6pm-2am, F-Sa 6pm-4am.

EAST VILLAGE

d.b.a., 41 First Ave. (☎212-475-5097), between E. 2nd and 3rd St. Subway: F, V to Lower East Side/Second Ave. For your inner alcohol connoisseur. With 19 premium beers on tap ($5-6), well over 100 bottled imports and microbrews, 50 bourbons, 130 single-malt whiskeys ($5-8), and 45 different tequilas, this friendly space lives up to its motto, "drink good stuff." Outdoor beer garden open until 10pm; space heaters keep it toasty on cold nights. Happy hour 5-7pm, $4 drinks. Open daily 1pm-4am.

Delft, 14 Ave. B (☎212-260-7100), between E. Houston and 2nd St. Subway: F, V to Lower East Side/2nd Ave. Hopping joint. Great DJs. Basement lounge area often breaks into dance. Young, attractive crowd. Hot bartenders. Beer $6. Cocktails $8-10. Open Tu-Sa 7pm-4am.

Joe's Pub, 425 Lafayette St. (☎212-539-8777; www.joespub.com), between Astor Pl. and E. 4th St. Subway: 6 to Astor Pl. Located at the Joseph Papp Public Theater. Norwegian acid-folk, classical chamber music, and dance contests are common. 2-3 bands perform each night; set times around 7, 9, and/or 11pm. Late-night DJs spin hip-hop, rock, and 80s hits for the large dancing crowd. Open daily 6pm-4am.

CHELSEA AND UNION SQUARE

Coral Room, 512 W 29th St. (☎212-244-1965; www.coralroomnyc.com), between 10th and 11th Ave. Subway: A, C, E to 34th St./Penn Station. Coral walls plus big fish tank equals aquarium kitsch. A "mermaid" swims in the 9000-gallon aquarium behind the bar (on Su, it's a "merman"). Tiny VIP section has portholes through which you can (literally and figuratively) look down on the dancing crowd below. Fun crowd and excellent DJs. There's even little hassle at the door. Cover $10-20. Open daily 10pm-4am.

B'Lo, 230 W. 19th St. (☎212-675-3848; www.blo-nyc.com), between Seventh and Eighth Ave. Subway: 1, 9 to 18th St. Sexy club attracts Manhattanites to its cave-like lounge. Low ceilings, stone columns, and 40-ft. bar. Lines form around midnight, but the bouncers are surprisingly fair. Just make sure you know how to pronounce it: "Be-low." DJs spin pop, hip-hop, and house beats. Drinks $8. Those who'd like to sit might choose table service, buying a bottle for $150-1500. Cover $10-20. Open F-Sa 10pm-4am.

UPPER EAST SIDE

The Big Easy, 1768 Second Ave. (☎212-348-0879), at 92nd St. Subway: 6 to 96th St. Post-grad hangout for those who miss their college years, with 3 beer pong tables in back. Bud drafts go for $2 11pm-midnight. A good spot for cheap, strong drinks before a long NYC night. Open daily 5pm-4am.

HOOKED ON HOOKAH

Ever since Bloomberg forced smokers out of New York's restaurants and bars with the Smoke-Free Air Act, informed visitors have found a haven in the city's hookah bars. Here, sweet fruit-flavored tobacco (shisha) can still be smoked indoors.

The East Village boasts a number of the city's best hookah bars. Below Houston St., comfy **Maradona** offers patrons appetizers ($5-6) and teas ($3-4) along with their hookah ($13). The cavernous **Karma** may have only five flavors of shisha ($10), but they have two full bars (beer and wine $5-6, cocktails $7-9) and plenty of seating. Their tiny little chairs, only a foot off the ground, circle upstairs tables partitioned by curtains. When the weather's warm, the best hookah can be found under the breezy outdoor tent of **Sahara East.** With the smell of jasmine, cappuccino, pina colada, and Egyptian Pharaoh-flavored shisha in the air, you'll feel worlds away from the city and its smoking ban.

Maradona, 188 Allen St. (☎917-627-6412), between Stanton and E Houston St. Open daily 2pm-4am.

Karma, 51 First Ave. (☎212-677-3160; www.karmanyc.com), between 3rd and 4th St. Open daily 10am-4am.

Sahara East, 184 1st Ave. (☎212-353-9000), between 1st and 2nd St. Open Su-Th noon-1am, F-Sa noon-3am.

Dorrian's Red Hand, 1616 Second Ave. (☎212-772-6600), at 84th St. Subway: 4, 5, 6 to 86th St. The preppy hotspot all the others aspire to be. The still-in-college, recently graduated, and young moneyed come to this Irish pub to meet, mingle, and down some drinks ($5-8). The likely meeting place of many a *New York Times* wedding section couple. Open Su-Th 11:30am-1am, F-Sa 11:30am-2am.

UPPER WEST SIDE

Dive 75, 101 W. 75th St. (☎212-501-9283), between Columbus and Amsterdam St. Subway: 1, 2, 3, 9 to 72nd St. All the joys of your favorite dive without the unusable bathroom. Locals lounge on comfy couches, soaking in the TV, pop-rock jukebox, and eerily glowing fish tank. A stack of board games sits in the corner. M has free wings to accompany pany football, and Th a psychic stops by for palm readings ($10). Happy hour 5-7pm: Buds $2.50, well drinks $4. Open daily M-Th 5pm-4am, F 2pm-4am, Sa-Su noon-4am.

The Evelyn Lounge, 380 Columbus Ave. (☎212-724-2363), at 78th St. Subway: B, C to 81st St. Lively upscale bar. Brick, vintage sofas, and fireplaces. Popular with the after-work and late-night set. The lounge downstairs is open on weekends, with 5 more rooms and 2 more bars. DJs spin dance and hip-hop. Cultured locals sip martinis ($9-10) and beer ($5-6). Open Su-Th 5pm-2:30am, F-Sa 5pm-4am; lounge Th-Sa 8pm-4am.

BROOKLYN

■ **Galapagos,** 70 N. 6th St. (☎718-782-5188; www.galapagosartspace.com), between Kent and Wythe St., in Williamsburg. Subway: L to Bedford Ave. Once a mayonnaise factory, this space is now one of the hipper cultural spots in the city. Sleek decor, complete with enormous reflecting pool (formerly a mayonnaise tank). Something for everyone: Su 7pm *Ocularis*, an avant-garde and experimental film screening ($7), M 9:30pm bawdy burlesque show (free). Tu-W live rock bands ($6-7), F "floating burlesque" 10pm-1am ($5). More burlesques and live bands sprinkled throughout the week ($5-8). DJs every Tu-Sa, start late (usually after 11pm; no cover). Happy hour M-Sa 6-8pm. Check the website for a calendar of shows and DJs. Open Su-Th 6:30pm-2am, F-Sa 6pm-4:30am.

The Gate, 321 Fifth Ave. (☎718-768-4329), corner of Third St. Subway: M, R to Union St. A few short years ago, Park Slope was a nightlife wasteland. The Gate's welcoming atmosphere and 24 beers on tap ($4-5) paved the way for a Fifth Ave. renaissance. Large patio fills when the weather is warm. Happy hour M-Th 4-8pm, F 3-7pm, $1 off drafts and well drinks. Open M-Th 4pm-4am, F 3pm-4am, Sa-Su 1pm-4am.

Pete's Candy Store, 709 Lorimer St. (☎718-302-3770; www.petescandystore.com), between Frost and Richardson St. Subway: L to Lorimer St. This soda-shop-turned-bar includes a "make-out" hallway and a small performance room in the back. A local crowd comes for live music (local acts) every night at 9pm. Tu Bingo and W Quizz-Off (both 7-9pm) are extremely popular. M night poetry readings. During the summer, stop by the barbecues (Sa-Su 5-9pm, $5) in the backyard for burgers, hot dogs, and salads. Pomegranate margarita $8, other cocktails $6-8. Open Su-Tu 5pm-2am, W-Sa 5pm-4am.

Union Pool, 484 Union Ave. (☎718-609-0484), off Skillman Ave. Subway: L to Bedford Ave. The expanded backyard has a fountain, butterfly chairs, picnic tables, and restored 50s Ford pickups. The bar, an old pool supply depot, hosts whimsical events, from circus performances to local film festivals. Frequent barbecues. DJ every night at 10pm. Beer $4-5. Cocktails $6-7. Occasional live music, usually 9pm. Happy hour daily 5-8pm: Yuengling $2, Bud and shot of Jim Beam $6. Photobooth $3. Open daily 5pm-4am.

DANCE CLUBS

Club scenes are about carefree crowds, unlimited fun, and huge pocketbook damage. It can pay to call ahead to put your name on the guest list. Come after 11pm; the real party starts around 1 or 2am. A few after-hours clubs keep at it until 5-6am. All clubs listed are 21+ unless otherwise noted.

Eugene, 27 W. 24th St. (☎212-462-0999), between Fifth and Sixth Ave. Subway: 1, 9 to 23rd St./Seventh Ave.; 6 to 23rd St./Park Ave. S; F, V to 23rd St./Ave. of the Americas (Sixth Ave.); N, R 23rd St./Broadway. Vegas-casino atmosphere with an Atlantic City crowd. This bar/club/lounge doubles as an expensive restaurant by day. Around 11pm the DJ comes on and the party heats up. Plenty of dimly lit seating for more intimate moments with bridge-and-tunnel crowd. Drinks $9-12. Dress to impress. Cover W $15-20, Th-Sa $20. Open W-Sa 9pm-4am.

Filter 14, 432 W. 14th St. (☎212-366-5680), at Washington St. Subway: A, C, E, L to 14th St./Eighth Ave.; 1, 2, 3 to 14th St./Seventh Ave. Small club that leaves both decor and pretense behind: everyone here is all about the music. W electro/break beat, F house, Sa hip-hop/pop/rock. Intimate, no-frills club that still packs the dance floor. Funky Meatpacking District crowd. Cover $5-10. Open W-Sa 10pm-4am.

Go, 73 Eighth Ave. (☎212-463-0000), between W. 13th and 14th St. Subway: 1, 2, 3, 9 to 14th St./Seventh Ave.; A, C, E, L to 14th St./Eighth Ave. Small club with beautiful people. The entirely white decor (*entirely* white) makes a perfect canvas for the "light DJ" to change the club's color scheme depending on his mood (blue, orange, purple, etc.). Cover $20. Open Th-Su 10pm-4am.

GLBT NIGHTLIFE

Gay nightlife in New York City is centered in **Chelsea,** especially along Eighth Ave. in the 20s, and in the **West Village,** on Christopher St.

Boiler Room, 86 E. 4th St. (☎212-254-7536), between First and Second Ave. Subway: F, V to Lower East Side/Second Ave. Popular locale caters to alternative types, NYU students, and refugees from the Chelsea scene. Predominantly gay men, but a mixed crowd, especially on weekends. Jukebox and pool table. Beer $4. Happy hour daily 4-8pm and 10pm-4am, 2-for-1 draft and domestic beers. Open daily 4pm-4am.

g, 223 W 19th St. (☎212-929-1085), between Seventh and Eighth Ave. Subway: 1, 9 to 18th St./Seventh Ave. Glitzy, popular bar shaped like an oval racetrack—perhaps an appropriate choice, given the pumped-up Chelsea men who speed around this circuit to the sound of DJ-ed house. Fortunately, the famous frozen cosmos ($7) satisfy the thirst of those logging their miles. Drinks $6-8. Open daily 4pm-4am.

Henrietta Hudson, 438 Hudson St. (☎212-924-3347; www.henriettahudsons.com), between Morton and Barrow St. Subway: 1, 9 to Christopher St. Young, clean-cut lesbian crowd. Transitions from after-work hangout to weekend late-night hot spot. Pool table and 2nd bar in quiet back room. Also gay male and straight friendly. Happy hour M-F 5-7pm, $3 beer. Busiest Th-Sa. M old school, Tu requests, W karaoke, Th world, F house, Sa pop, Su Latin. Cover Sa-Su $7-10. Open M-F 4pm-4am, Sa 1pm-4am, Su 3pm-4am.

SBNY, 50 W. 17th St. (☎212-691-0073; www.splashbar.com), between Fifth and Sixth Ave. Subway: 1, 9 to 18th St./Seventh Ave.; F, V to 23rd St./Ave. of the Americas (Sixth Ave.). One of the most popular gay mega-bars, the renovated **S**plash **B**ar **N**ew **Y**ork (formerly known simply as Splash) is a huge 2-fl. complex. A crowded scene, with industrial decor, a dance floor, and high-energy house music. Beer $5.50. Cocktails $6-7.50. Happy hour M-Th 4-9pm, F-Sa 4-8pm, with 2-for-1 drinks. 21+ usually, 18+ occasionally. Cover M-W $5 after 11pm, Th $10, F $20. Open Su-Th 4pm-4am, F-Sa 4pm-5am.

Stonewall Bar, 53 Christopher St. (☎212-463-0950), at Seventh Ave. S. Subway: 1, 9 to Christopher St. Legendary bar of the 1969 Stonewall Riots. Join the diverse crowd and the famed bartender "Tree" in the former Stonewall Inn to toast the brave drag queens who fought back. Enter the Su night male amateur strip contest "Meatpacking," and win $200. 3 bars in 1. M hip-hop, W and Sa Latin. Happy hour M-F 3-9pm: 2-for-1 drinks; Sa-Su $4 cosmos, $3 Bud Lights. Free hors d'oeuvres nightly. Su-M, W, Sa cover $6. Open daily 3pm-4am.

LONG ISLAND
☎ 631

Long Island, a sprawling suburbia stretching 120 mi. east of Manhattan, is both a home to over 2.7 million New Yorkers (excluding those who live in Queens and Brooklyn) and a sleepy summertime resort for wealthy Manhattanites. It is both expensive and difficult to navigate without a car.

▮ PRACTICAL INFORMATION. Long Island Railroad (LIRR) services the island from Penn Station in Manhattan (34th St. at Seventh Ave.; Subway: 1, 2, 3 to 34th St./Penn Station/Seventh Ave.; A, C, E to 34th St./Penn Station/Eighth Ave.) and stops in Jamaica, Queens (Subway: E, J, Z), before proceeding to "points east." (☎ 718-217-5477. Fares vary daily and by zone.) To reach **Fire Island,** take the LIRR to Sayville, Bayshore, or Patchogue. The **Sayville Ferry** serves Cherry Grove, the Pines, and Sailor's Haven. (☎ 589-0810. Round-trip $9-11, under 12 $5.) The **Bay Shore Ferry** sails to Fair Harbor, Ocean Beach, Ocean Bay Park, Saltaire, and Kismet. (☎ 516-665-3600. Round-trip $12, under 12 $5.50.) The **Patchogue Ferry** shuttles to Davis Park and Watch Hill. (☎ 516-475-1665. Round-trip $11, under 12 $4.25.) The Hamptons are accessible by LIRR or by car. Take the Long Island Expwy. to Exit 70, go south to Rte. 27 (Sunset Hwy. or Montauk Hwy.), and head east to Montauk (approx. 50 mi. on Rte. 27). **Long Island Convention and Visitors Bureau** has four locations throughout the island. Call ☎ 951-2423 or 877-386-6654 for locations and hours. **Area Code:** 631 and 516. In listings, 631 unless otherwise noted.

FIRE ISLAND

Tranquil and pristine towns dot Fire Island, and the state protects most Fire Island areas by declaring them either state parks or federal "wilderness areas." This lack of infrastructure ensures both peace and inconvenience; visitors must often take water taxis to travel between towns. Fire Island's 17 summer communities have forged distinct niches—middle-class residential clusters, openly gay communities (see below), and vacationing Hollywood stars.

Two prominent Fire Island resort hamlets, **Cherry Grove** and **Fire Island Pines** (called **"the Pines"**), host largely gay communities and parties that rage late into the night. Crowded "streets," or wooden pathways, border spectacular Atlantic Ocean beaches. Weekdays provide an opportunity to enjoy the island's beauty and charm in a low-key setting, Thursdays and Sundays offer an ideal balance of sanity and scene, while Fridays and Saturday see mounting crowds and prices.

Gay nightlife on Fire Island has an established rhythm that may be confusing to newcomers. Since neither Cherry Grove nor the Pines is very big, it's best just to ask around. More commercial than the Pines, the roadless Grove is lined with narrow, raised boardwalks leading to the small, uniformly shingled houses overflowing with men. Lesbian couples make up the majority of the town's population. A night in Cherry Grove usually begins at the **Ice Palace,** attached to the **Cherry Grove Beach Hotel,** where you can disco until dawn. (☎ 597-6600. Open daily July-Aug. noon-4am; Sept.-June noon-10pm). Most go to the Pines for late-night partying; you can catch a water taxi from the docks at Cherry Grove, or walk 10min. up the beach. Houses here are spacious and often stunningly modern. Unfortunately, the Pines' active nighttime scene has a bit of a secret club feel to it—you need to be in the know or somehow be able to look like you are. **Tea Dance** (a.k.a. "Low Tea," 5-8pm) takes place inside and around the Yacht Club bar/club beside the Botel Hotel (☎ 597-6500). Move on to disco **High Tea** at 8pm in the **Pavilion** (☎ 597-6131), the premier disco in Cherry Grove, but make sure you have somewhere to disappear to during "disco naptime" (after 10pm). You can unabashedly dance until dawn at the **Island Club and Bistro** (☎ 597-6001), better known as the Sip-and-Twirl. The Pavilion becomes hot again late-night on weekends, including Sundays during the summer.

THE HAMPTONS AND MONTAUK

West Hampton, Southampton, Bridgehampton, and East Hampton make up the entity known as **the Hamptons,** where the upper crust of society roam the sidewalks before heading to the beach for the afternoon. Prices are high here; try going to **Montauk,** at the eastern tip of Long Island, for slightly cheaper accommodations. While lodging anywhere on the South Fork requires some research and often reservations, clean rooms can be had at **Tipperary Inn ❺,** 432 West Lake Ln., accessible via the S-94 bus to Montauk Dock. The inn provides A/C, TV, phone, and fridge. (☎668-2010. Rooms for 2-6 people in summer $125-160; low-season $75-95.)

Many beaches in the Hamptons require a permit to park, but anyone can walk on for free. Sights include the **Montauk Point Lighthouse and Museum,** off Rte. 27 at the far eastern tip of the island, which was built in 1796 by special order of President George Washington. (☎668-2544. Open June-Sept. Su-F 10:30am-6pm, Sa 10:30am-7:30pm; low-season call for info. $6, seniors $5, under 12 $3.) Whaling buffs shouldn't miss the **Sag Harbor Whaling Museum,** at the corner of Main and Garden St. in Sag Harbor. (☎725-0770. Open May-Sept. M-Sa 10am-5pm, Su 1-5pm. $3, seniors $2, ages 6-13 $1. Tours by appointment $2.)

THE CATSKILLS   ☎845

According to the legend, the Catskills, ideal for quiet solitude and rest, cradled Rip Van Winkle during his century-long repose. In an anomalous blip in the tranquility of the mountain region, the infamous Woodstock rock festival of 1969 hit the small town of Bethel like a twister. Today, the region's best attractions are its miles of pristine hiking and skiing trails, and the crystal-clear fishing streams of the state-managed Catskill Forest Preserve. Resting quietly amidst this natural beauty, the small mountain villages are home to art galleries and shops filled with local flavor.

🔁 PRACTICAL INFORMATION. Traveling from **I-87,** follow **Rte. 28 W** from Exit 19 to reach the many small villages in the area. **Rte. 212** from Exit 20 or the **Rte. 23-23A loop,** termed the "Rip Van Winkle Trail" from Exit 21, are also easy ways to explore the region. **Adirondack/Pine Hill Trailways** provides excellent service throughout the Catskills. The main stop is in **Kingston,** 400 Washington Ave., on the corner of Front St. (☎331-0744 or 800-858-8555. Ticket office open M-F 5:45am-11:30pm, Sa-Su 6:45am-11:30pm.) Buses run to New York City (2hr., 10-15 per day, $21). Other stops in the area include Delhi, Hunter, Pine Hill, and Woodstock; each connects with Albany, Cooperstown, New York City, and Utica. Two stationary **tourist cabooses** dispense info, including the extremely useful *Ulster County: Catskills Region Travel Guide;* the cabooses are located at the traffic circle in Kingston and on Rte. 209 in Ellenville. (Open May-Oct. daily 9am-5pm, but hours may vary depending on volunteer availability.) Further information on the region can be obtained from the Catskills regional office of the **NY Department of Environmental Conservation** (☎256-3009). **Area Code:** 845, unless otherwise noted.

CATSKILL FOREST PRESERVE

The nearly 300,000-acre Catskill Forest Preserve contains many small towns and outdoor adventure opportunities. Ranger stations distribute free permits for **backcountry camping ❶,** which are required for stays over three days or in groups of 10 or more. Hiking trails are generally well-maintained, though less-used paths sometimes fall into disrepair. Lean-tos are also maintained, but can become crowded. For more info, call the **Department of Environmental Conservation** (☎256-3000; open M-F 8:30am-4:45pm) or ask a ranger at one of the state campgrounds in the region. Most **campgrounds** sit at gorgeous trailheads that mark great day-long jaunts. Reservations are vital in summer, especially on weekends. The **Office of Parks** (☎518-

474-0456) distributes brochures on the campgrounds. Required permits for **fishing** (out-of-state residents $15 per day, $25 per week) are available in sporting goods stores and at many campgrounds. **Ski season** runs from November to April, with slopes on numerous mountainsides along Rte. 28 and Rte. 23A.

MT. TREMPER

◙**The Kaleidostore,** in Emerson Place on Rte. 28, provides a visual smorgasbord through the reflective lenses of the largest kaleidoscope in the world, measuring a whopping 60 ft. Ask the operator if you can lie in the center of the room, then hold on tight for 10min. of glimmering images that will leave ex-flower-children muttering, "I can see the music!" (☎688-5800. Open Su-Th 10am-5pm, F-Sa 10am-7pm. $7, seniors $5, under 12 free.) The **Kenneth L. Wilson Campground ❶** has 76 sites nestled in a tranquil forest. A small lake allows for canoeing, kayaking, and the use of paddle boats. From Rte. 28, exit onto Rte. 212. then make a hard right onto Wittenburg Rd./County Rte. 40 and follow it 5 mi. to the campground. (☎679-7020. Canoes and kayaks $15 per 4hr. Paddleboats $5 per hr. Showers $0.25 per 6min. Reception 8am-9pm. Weekend reservations recommended. Sites $17. Registration fee $2.75. Day use $4 per car, $1 on foot or bike.)

PHOENICIA

Phoenicia is a small town in the heart of the Catskills. **Esopus Creek,** to the west, has great trout fishing, and **The Town Tinker,** 10 Bridge St., rents inner tubes for river-riding on the ripples and rapids. (☎688-5553. Inner tubes $10 per day, with seat $12. Driver's license or $15-50 deposit required. "Tube taxi" transportation $5 per trip on either the railroad (see below) or a bus. Life jackets required; $3. Wetsuits $15. Package with seated tube, life jacket, and single transport $20; package with wetsuit $30. Wetsuits not necessary on hot summer days. Open mid-May to Sept. daily 9am-6pm; last rental 3:30-4pm.) A more sedate alternative is the wheezing, 100-year-old **Catskill Mountain Railroad,** which follows Esopus Creek for three scenic miles from Bridge St. to Mt. Pleasant along the rusty tracks. (☎688-7400. 40min. Runs Sa-Su and holidays, 1 per hr. May-Sept. 11am-5pm, Oct. noon-4pm. $5, round-trip $8; ages 4-11 $5.) At the 65 ft. high **Sundance Rappel Tower,** off Rte. 214, the adventurous work their way back down to solid ground under their own steam power. (☎688-5640. 4 levels of lessons; beginner 3-4hr., $22. Groups of 8 required for lessons. Reservations required.) A 12 mi. round-trip hike to the 4180 ft. summit of **Slide Mountain** rewards hikers with 360° views of New Jersey, Pennsylvania, and the Hudson Highlands; begin at Woodland Valley campground (see below). Nestled in the woods, the **Zen Mountain Monastery,** off Rte. 40 north of Rte. 28, houses 35-40 Buddhists living and working together while partaking in Zen training. (☎688-2228. Phone lines open Tu 2-5pm, W-Sa 8:30am-5pm. Closed to the public at all times except during meditation training sessions W 7pm and Su 8:45am. Free, but $5 suggested donation on Su, when lunch is provided.) Customers line up outside of **Sweet Sue's ❶,** on Main St., to sample thick french toast and stacks of 9 in. pancakes for $7-9. (☎688-7852. Open M and W-Su 7am-3pm.) With a menu longer than Main St., **Brio's ❷,** 68 Main St., offers everything from omelettes ($7-9) and sandwiches ($4-9) to pastas ($10) and burritos ($7-9) in a diner flickering with the light of the wood-fired pizza oven. (☎688-5370. Open 7am-11pm.)

Surrounded by mountains, the **Cobblestone Motel ❸,** on Rte. 214, has friendly managers, an outdoor pool, and clean, quiet rooms with refrigerators. (☎688-7871. Queen $56; queen and single $61; 2 doubles or queens with futon and kitchen $75-95; cottages with kitchen $109-129.) With 72 sites, secluded **Woodland Valley campground ❶,** on Woodland Valley Rd. off High St., 7 mi. southeast of Phoenicia, has a stream, showers ($0.25 per 6min.), and access to hiking trails. (☎688-7647. Reception daily 8am-9pm. Open late May to early Oct. Sites $15. Registration fee $2.75.)

PINE HILL

The town of Pine Hill sits near **Belleayre Mountain,** which offers hiking trails and **"Sky Rides"** on a chairlift to the summit during the summer, as well as downhill and cross-country ski slopes when the snow starts to fall. (☎254-5600 or 800-942-6904. Lift tickets M-F $33, Sa-Su $42; ages 13-22 and 62 and up $30/$34. Equipment rental $25. Sky Ride $8, ages 13-17 and seniors $5; open mid-June to mid-Oct. Sa-Su 10am-6pm.) **Belleayre Music Festival,** held at the Belleayre Mtn. ski resort, hosts a series of classical, jazz, country, opera, and folk concerts in July and August—past performers include Ray Charles and Lyle Lovett. (☎800-942-6904. Lawn tickets $12-15, some concerts free.) The **Belleayre Beach at Pine Hills,** ½ mi. south of Pine Hills on Rte. 28, provides warm weather recreation, including swimming from a sand beach, hiking, volleyball, and a playground. (☎800-942-6904. Open late May to mid-June Sa-Su 10am-6pm, mid-June to Sept. M-F 10am-6pm, Sa-Su 10am-7:30pm. Beach has lifeguards while park is open. $6 per car, $1 per person on foot.) For info on the mountain, music festival, and beach, visit www.belleayre.com. No matter what type of recreation you choose, there is no better place to stay than the **Gateway Lodge B&B ❸,** 11 Highlands Rd., off Rte. 28 just south of the entrance to Belleayre Mtn. Ted and Charlotte, the kind owners, offer gorgeous themed rooms at negotiable prices. They also serve a full breakfast, build nightly bonfires, and will let you camp on their lawn if the rooms are full. (☎254-4084. Rooms $50-105.) On the other side of Belleayre Mtn. **Evergreen ❸,** 1625 Main St. in Fleishmanns, 2 mi. north of Pine Hill, is a fully organic B&B housed above an organic restaurant, art gallery, and nightclub. (☎254-539; www.theevergreen.org. Breakfast included. Live music Sa-Su. Rooms $75-105.) Under the mural of a tequila-guzzling gaucho, **El Rey ❶,** 297 Main St., serves a steaming heap of fajitas or a huge burrito with fresh homemade salsas to the tune of mariachi music. (☎254-6027. Entrees $4-7.)

ALBANY ☎518

Albany, the capital of New York State and the oldest continuous European settlement in the original 13 colonies, calls itself "the most livable city in America." Albany expresses the intensity expected of the capital of arguably the most influential state in America, but outside the government offices, upstate New York's peacefulness endures. On weekdays, downtown shops and restaurants thrive on the purses of politicians, whose weekend exodus leaves the plaza and capital buildings deserted, and weekend nightlife erupts outside the government center.

▐▌ TRANSPORTATION AND PRACTICAL INFORMATION. Amtrak, 525 East St., across the Hudson from downtown (☎462-5710; station open M-F 4:30am-midnight, Sa-Su 5am-midnight; ticket counter M-F 4:30am-10pm, Sa-Su 5am-10pm), has service to Buffalo (5hr., 4 per day, $50-60) and New York City (2½hr., 8-9 per day, $43-50). **Greyhound,** 34 Hamilton St. (☎434-8461 or 800-231-2222; station open 24hr., ticket window open daily 12:05am-11:30pm), runs buses to Buffalo (6hr., 7-8 per day, $56) and New York City (3hr., 15 per day, $34). *Be careful here at night.* From the same station, **Adirondack Trailways** (☎436-9651 or 800-855-8555) goes to Kingston (1hr., 7 per day, $10) and Lake Placid (4hr., 1-2 per day, $29). The **Capital District Transportation Authority** (**CDTA;** ☎482-8822) serves Albany (up to $1), Schenectady ($1.35), and Troy ($1.25). Get schedules and free shuttle routes at the Amtrak and bus stations and visitors center. The **Albany Visitors Center,** 25 Quackenbush Sq., at Clinton Ave. and Broadway, runs trolley and horse-drawn carriage tours of downtown and has self-guided walking tours. (☎434-0405; www.albany.org. Open M-F 9am-4pm, Sa-Su 10am-4pm. Carriage tours Aug.-Sept. Th 10am. Trolley tours W and F-Sa 11am. July-Aug. arrive 20min. early for a film about the city. Tours $10, seniors $5.) **Internet Access: Albany Public Library,** 161 Washington St. (☎427-4300. Open June-Sept. M-Th 9am-9pm, F 9am-6pm, Sa 9am-5pm, Sept.-June also open Su 1-5pm.) **Post Office:** 45 Hudson Ave. (☎462-1359. Open M-F 8am-5:30pm.) **Postal Code:** 12207. **Area Code:** 518.

🏠🍴 ACCOMMODATIONS AND FOOD. Pine Haven Bed & Breakfast ❸, 531 Western Ave., at Madison Ave., is a haven for weary travelers. The Victorian house offers five gorgeous rooms with phone, TV, wireless Internet, A/C, and ample parking. (☎482-1574. Breakfast included. Reservations required. Rooms $69-119.) **Red Carpet Inn ❸,** 500 Northern Blvd., between downtown and the airport, provides laundry facilities and rooms with A/C and cable TV. Take Exit 6 from I-90 and turn onto Northern Blvd. (☎462-5562. Rooms $54-60.) **Thompson's Lake State Park ❶,** 18 mi. southwest of Albany, is the closest campground, with 140 wooded sites within walking distance of a lake with fishing, boating, and a sandy swimming beach. Take Madison Ave./Rte. 20 north to Rte. 85. Follow Rte. 85 out of Albany, turn right on Rte. 157, and look for signs. (☎872-1674. Free hot showers. Sites $13. Registration fee $2.75. Row boats $5 per hr., $20 per day. Paddle boats $4 per 30min. Lifeguard on duty June-Sept. M-F 10am-6pm, Sa-Su 10am-7pm.)

Lark Street is full of ethnic eats and coffeeshops with a young, college-town atmosphere, while **South Pearl Street** is dotted with traditional American eateries. The portable lunch carts that set up shop along State St. near the Empire State Plaza and the State Capitol around lunch time are a good source of inexpensive grub. In the city proper, the best eating option involves doing time with a "TNT" wrap, including Buffalo chicken and jalapeños, or a large pile of nachos with Al Capone Amber Ale, at the **Big House Brewing Company ❷,** 90 N. Pearl St., at Sheridan St. (☎445-2739. Entrees $5-8. Happy hour 4-7pm. Live bands F. Kitchen open Tu-W 4-9pm, Th-Sa 4-10:30pm. Bar open Tu-W until 1am, Th-Sa until 3am; later depending on crowds.) Under beautiful frescoes of the sea and windows capped with terra cotta, **A Taste of Greece ❷,** 193 Lark St., serves excellent dishes customizable with either lamb or vegetarian ingredients. Besides classic gyros and Greek salads ($6-8), specialties include *spanakorizo* ($8) and *sayanaki* with peppers, mushrooms, zucchini, tomatoes and feta. (☎426-9000. Open M-Th 11am-9pm, F 11am-10pm, Sa 2-10pm.) The two floor **Bomber's Burrito Bar ❶,** 258 Lark St, offers dining, a lounge, pool tables, and the longest happy hour in New York ($2 pints 11am-8pm). Twelve-inch burritos ($5) and mountains of nachos ($6) share the menu with barbecue tofu fries ($4.50) and witty catchphrases like "we know how to roll a fatty." (☎463-9639. Open daily 11am-1am.) Great Cajun food and a wild southern setting can be found inside the **Bayou Cafe ❸,** 79 N. Pearl St. Spicy jambalaya and Cajun chicken stirfry ($13) are served at old tables surrounding the facade of dank wooden walls. With no set closing time (establishments can serve until 3am on weekends), the tune of live rock and blues can be heard long into the night from Thursday to Saturday. (☎426-8550. Entrees $13-18. Open M-F at 11:30am, Sa at 4:30pm.) **De Johns ❹,** 288 Lark St., offers romantic candlelit dinners and excellent service. Chicken farfalle pasta ($14) and pecan-encrusted trout topped with sherry ($17) are specialties. (☎465-5275. Sandwiches $8-10. Open M-Th 4-11pm, F 4-midnight, Sa-Su 11am-midnight.)

🎭🎶 SIGHTS AND ENTERTAINMENT. Albany's sights are centered on the **Rockefeller Empire State Plaza,** between State and Madison St., a modernist Stonehenge made of 900,000 cubic yards of concrete and 232,000 tons of steel. The plaza houses state offices, a bus terminal, a post office, a food court, several war memorials, and the largest outdoor display of modern art in the country, set in and around two large reflecting pools. (Parking $2 M-F after 2pm and Sa-Su.) The **New York State Information Center,** in the north concourse, is the departure spot for **Plaza**

Tours, which visit the buildings, memorials, and certain works of art. (Information center: ☎474-2418. Open M-F 8:30am-5pm. Tours: ☎473-7521. M-F 11am and 1pm. Free.) The huge flying saucer at one end of the Plaza is the **Empire Center for the Performing Arts,** also known as "The Egg," a venue for professional theater, dance, and concerts. (☎473-1845. Box office open June-Sept. M-F 10am-4pm; Sept.-May M-F 10am-5pm, Sa noon-3pm. $8-40.) Across the street, the huge **New York State Museum** has exhibits on the state's history, people, and wildlife. One wing is dedicated to the memory of the World Trade Center, housing large portions of the buildings, crushed FDNY trucks, and the famous American flag recovered from under the wreckage. This powerful exhibit is not to be missed. (☎474-5877. Open daily 9:30am-5pm. Donations accepted.) Between the museum and the Egg, an elevator ride up the 42 floors of the **Corning Tower** provides a 60 mi. view on clear days. (☎474-2418. Open daily 10am-2:30pm. Photo ID required. Free.) Since 1899, the magnificent **New York State Capitol,** adjacent to the plaza, has provided New York politicians with luxury quarters amidst a tempest of political activity. Tours leave from the New York Travel Information Center. (☎474-2418. Tours M-F 10am, noon, 2, 3pm; Sa-Su 11am, 1, 3pm. No backpacks allowed. Free.) The **Capitol Repertory Theatre,** 111 N. Pearl St., stages some of Albany's best plays and musicals in a modern theater outfitted with padded crimson chairs. (☎445-7469. Box office open M-Sa 10am-5pm. $31-39.) Reminiscent of majestic movie theatres of old, the **Palace Theatre,** 19 Clinton St., offers concerts, plays, musicals, and comedy. (☎465-4663. Box office open M-F 10am-6pm; Sept.-June also Sa 10am-2pm. $15-60.)

Bounded by State St. and Madison Ave. north of downtown, **Washington Park** has tulip gardens, tennis courts, and plenty of room for picnics. The **Park Playhouse** stages free musical theater in the pastoral setting from July to mid-August. (☎434-2035; www.parkplayhouse.com.) **Alive at Five** hosts free concerts at the **Tricentennial Plaza,** across from Fleet Bank on Broadway, or in the amphitheater in the **Hudson Riverfront Park.** (☎434-2032. June-July. Ask at the visitors center.) The annual **Tulip Festival** (☎434-2032; early May), in Washington Park, celebrates the town's Dutch heritage and the blooming of the over 100,000 tulips with song, dance, fine arts, crafts, a Tulip Queen crowning, and food vendors. To learn more about events, call the **Albany Alive Line** (☎434-1217) or visit www.albanyevents.org.

The **Mohawk-Hudson Bikeway** (☎386-2225) passes along old railroad grades and canal towpaths, weaving through the capitol area and along the Hudson River. The **Down Tube Cycle Shop,** 466 Madison Ave., has rentals. (☎434-1711. Open Apr.-Sept. M-F 11am-7pm, Sa 10am-5pm; Sept.-Apr. M-F 10am-6pm. Full-day $25, 2 days $35.)

COOPERSTOWN ☎607

For earlier generations, Cooperstown recalled images of Leatherstocking, the frontiersman hero of novelist James Fenimore Cooper, who roamed the woods around Lake Otsego in his youth. In the early 19th century, however, four cloth bases were placed in a diamond on the town green, and a new American legend was born—baseball. The rest is history: Cooperstown draws half a million tourists per year to its groomed streets, juggling commercialism and a quaint small-town charm to uphold its motto: "Cooperstown—the most perfect town in America."

🚩 **PRACTICAL INFORMATION.** Cooperstown is accessible from **I-90** and **I-88** via **Rte. 28.** Only four blocks by five blocks, the town is centered around **Main Street (Route 31),** which is chock full of baseball memorabilia shops and restaurants. Street parking is rare in Cooperstown; park in the three free lots just outside of town on Maple St. off Glen Ave. (Rte. 28), Rte. 28 south of town, or adjacent to the Fenimore Art Museum—it's an easy 5-20min. walk to Main St. **Trolleys** also

MID-ATLANTIC

leave from the lots every 20min., dropping riders off at major stops in town, including the **Hall of Fame**, the **Farmer's** and **Fenimore Museums, Doubleday Field,** the Pine Hall Trailways stop, and the **Chamber of Commerce.** (Trolleys run late June to early Sept. daily 8:30am-9pm; early June to mid-June and mid-Sept. to mid-Oct. Sa-Su 8:30am-6pm. All-day pass $2, children $1.) **Pine Hall Trailways** (☎547-2519 or 800-858-8555) picks up visitors at AAA Tri-County Motor Club at the corner of Elm St. and Chestnut St., and travels to Kingston (3½hr., 2 per day, $23) and New York City (5½hr., 2 per day, $45). **Cooperstown Area Chamber of Commerce and Visitor Information Center,** 31 Chestnut St., on Rte. 28 near Main St., provides maps and information on lodging and attractions. (☎547-9983; www.cooperstownchamber.org. Open daily June-Sept. 9am-7pm, Oct.-May 9am-5pm.) **Internet Access: Village Library of Cooperstown,** 22 Main St. (☎547-8344. Open M-Tu and Th-F 9am-5pm, W 9am-8pm, Sa 10am-2pm.) **Post Office:** 40 Main St. (☎547-2311. Open M-F 8:30am-5pm, Sa 8:30am-noon.) **Postal Code:** 13326. **Area Code:** 607.

ACCOMMODATIONS. Lodging-seekers can really strike out during peak season, between late June and mid-September. The cheapest options are to camp or to travel in the low season, when many motels and guest houses slash rates by $20-50. The **Mohican Motel ❹,** 90 Chestnut St., a 10min. walk to the Hall of Fame, offers well-kept rooms, cable TV, and A/C at relatively affordable prices. (☎547-5101. 2- to 6-person rooms late June to early Sept. Su-F $86-138, Sa $131-183; Apr. to late June and early Sept. to late Oct. Su-F $55-81, Sa $75-101.) The beautiful pine forests and lakeside view of **Glimmerglass State Park ❶,** 8 mi. north of Cooperstown on Rte. 31, on the north shore of Lake Otsego, make it an ideal camping location, with 43 campsites, including four wheelchair accessible sites. The park offers hiking and biking in the 600 rolling acres of forests or swim, fish, and boat in the cool water. (☎547-8662. Park open 8am-dark. Free hot showers. Dumping station; no hookups. Beach opens at 11am. Lifeguard on duty 11am-7pm. Sites $13. Registration fee $2.75. Day use $7 per vehicle.) **Cooperstown Beaver Valley Campground ❶** has wooded sites, cabins, a pool, recreation area, small pond, and a well-kept baseball diamond. Drive south of town 5 mi. on Rte. 28 and follow the signs. (☎293-7324 or 800-726-7314. Showers $0.25 per 6min. Sites $28-32, with hookup $37; cabins without indoor plumbing or linens $63-68.)

FOOD. The **Doubleday Cafe ❶,** 93 Main St., serves meals amidst eye-catching baseball memorabilia and TVs showing multiple baseball games from around the country. (☎547-5468. Omelette with toast $2-4. Chili $3.35. Open June-Sept. Su-Th 7am-10pm, F-Sa 7am-11pm; Oct.-May Su-Th 7am-9pm, F-Sa 7am-10pm; bar closes after kitchen.) For elegant but affordable dining, **Hoffman Lane Bistro ❸,** 2 Hoffman Ln., off Main St. across from the Hall of Fame, has airy rooms with tasteful artwork and outdoor seating along a quiet side street. Gourmet appetizers and sandwiches ($6-8) leave customers rooting for more. (☎547-7055. Entrees $13-20. Kitchen open daily 5-10pm; bar open Su-Th until 1am, F-Sa until 2am.) A Cooperstown institution, **Schneider's Bakery ❶,** 157 Main St., has been satisfying sweet cravings with $0.55 "old-fashioneds"—doughnuts less greasy and a tad smaller than their commercial cousins—since 1887. (☎547-9631. Open M-Sa 6:30am-5:30pm.) The restaurant at the **Tunnicliff Inn ❸,** 36 Pioneer St., just off Main St., serves locally brewed Old Slugger Ale (pitchers $11) and huge "smothered steak sandwiches" ($9) in the heart of Cooperstown. (☎547- 9611. Entrees $7-17. Open daily 11am-4pm and 5-9pm.; F-Sa open until 10pm.)

SIGHTS. With almost 400,000 visitors per year, the ◼**National Baseball Hall of Fame and Museum,** on Main St., is an enormous, glowing monument to America's national pastime. Containing 35,000 pieces of memorabilia, the building is home to priceless artifacts—everything from the bat with which Babe Ruth hit his "called shot" home run in the 1932 World Series to a complete collection of baseballs from every "no-hitter" in history. Exhibits trace the game to ancient Egyptian rituals and feature a 13min. multimedia tribute to the sport, a candid display on African-American ballplayers' experiences in the Negro Leagues, and a tribute to "Women in Baseball." (☎547-7200 or 888-425-5633; www.baseballhalloffame.org. Open daily Apr.-Oct. 9am-9pm; Nov.-Mar. 9am-5pm. $9.50, seniors $8, ages 7-12 $4.)

The biggest event of the year, attended by over 20,000 visitors, is the annual **Hall of Fame Induction Weekend.** On the last weekend of July, new members of the Hall of Fame are inducted with appropriate pomp and circumstance. Ceremonies are held at the **Clark Sports Center** on Susquehanna Ave., a 10min. walk south from the Hall. Admission to the event is free, and reservations are not necessary. The annual **Hall of Fame Game** between two rotating Major League teams is played every June on the intimate Doubleday field. Contact the Hall of Fame for tickets and info on these two events, and reserve accommodations far in advance.

Overlooking a pristine lawn and Lake Otsego, the **Fenimore Art Museum,** on Lake Rd./Rte. 80 one mile from Main St., houses a collection of American folk art, Hudson River School paintings, James Fenimore Cooper memorabilia, unusual traveling exhibits, and an impressive array of Native American art. (☎547-1400 or 888-547-1450; www.fenimoreartmuseum.org. Open June-Oct. daily 10am-5pm; Apr.-May and Nov.-Dec. Tu-Su 10am-4pm. $9, seniors $8, ages 7-12 $4.) Jump in a time machine across the street at the **Farmer's Museum,** which contains a complete 1850s farming village with live demonstrations, displays about farming's past and present, and the unmistakable smell of farm animals. (☎888-547-1450; www.farmersmuseum.org. Open June-Oct. daily 10am-5pm; Apr.-May by tour only Tu-F 10:30am and noon. $9, seniors $8, ages 7-12 $4. Combo ticket for Hall of Fame, Fenimore Museum, and Farmer's Museum $22.) Nine miles north of Cooperstown on Lake Rd./Rte. 80, the **Glimmerglass Opera** stages summer performances of new and little-known works as well as new takes on favorite operas. (☎547-2255; www.glimmerglass.org. Box office at 18 Chestnut St. in Cooperstown open June-Aug. M-Sa 9am-6pm; Dec.-May M-F 10am-5pm. Tickets M-Th $29-96, F-Su $59-108.)

ITHACA AND THE FINGER LAKES ☎607

According to Iroquois legend, the Great Spirit laid his hand upon the earth to bless it, and the impression of his fingers resulted in the Finger Lakes: Canandaigua, Cayuga, Seneca, and eight others. Rising steeply around the lakes, the land is wrought with gorges carved by the rainfall and snowmelt of millennia. Over 1000 waterfalls can be found within these gorges. Home to Ithaca College and Cornell University, Ithaca hosts the youthful spirit of a vibrant student life atop the ancient rifts of nature's masterwork, and the area's blessed soil yields the divine nectar of nationally acclaimed vineyards.

PRACTICAL INFORMATION. Downtown Ithaca centers around **Ithaca Commons,** a pedestrian area lined with shops and restaurants. A steep uphill walk leads to Cornell's campus overlooking downtown Ithaca. Adjacent to Cornell's campus and overflowing with students, the **Collegetown** area is packed with hole-in-the-wall bars, take-out restaurants, and diners. **Ithaca Bus Terminal,** 710 W. State St., at Rte. 13 (☎272-7930; open daily 6:30am-6pm), houses **Short Line** (☎277-8800), with service to New York City (5hr., 8 per day, $43), and **Greyhound** (☎800-231-2222), with service to: Buffalo (3½hr., 3 per day, $33); New York City (5hr., 3 per day, $44); Philadelphia (8hr., 3 per day, $57). Although Ithaca sits close to the base of Cayuga Lake, **Tompkins Consolidated Area Transit (T-CAT;** ☎277-7433) is the only choice for getting there without a car. Buses stop at Ithaca Commons; westbound buses also stop on Seneca St. and eastbound buses stop on Green St. (Buses run daily; times vary by route. $1.50-3, ages 6-17 and seniors $0.75-1.50. Schedules available from the visitors center.) The **Ithaca/Tompkins County Convention and Visitors Bureau,** 904 E. Shore Dr., has an excellent map of the area ($3). Be sure to pick up a free copy of the invaluable *Ithaca Gorges & Waterfalls* guide to outdoor recreation, lodgings, restaurants, maps, and much more. (☎272-1313 or 800-284-8422. Open mid-May to early Sept. M-F 9am-5pm, Sa 10am-5pm, Su 10am-4pm; mid-Sept. to early May M-F 9am-5pm. Unstaffed visitors center in the Clinton House, 116 N. Cayuga St. Open M-F 10am-5:30pm, Sa 10am-2pm, and 3-5pm.) **Internet Access: Tompkins County Public Library,** 101 E. Green St. (☎272-4557. Open Sept.-June M-Th 10am-9pm, F-Sa 10am-5pm, Su 1pm-5pm. Closed weekends July-Aug.) **Post Office:** 213 N. Tioga St., at E. Buffalo. (☎800-275-8777. Open M-F 8:30am-5pm, Sa 8:30am-1pm.) **Postal Code:** 14850. **Area Code:** 607.

⌂ ACCOMMODATIONS. Budget accommodations are surprisingly abundant in Ithaca. Beautiful camping during the summer months pairs with well-priced B&Bs during the winter, and the motels that line the many roads to the city are an affordable option at any time of year. The best bargain in Ithaca is the ⬛**Elmshade Guest House ❷,** 402 S. Albany St., at Center St. just five blocks from Ithaca Commons. Soft rugs, colorfully decorated rooms, and continental breakfast make Elmshade a welcoming home away from home. From the bus station, walk up State St. and turn right onto Albany St. (☎273-1707. Reservations recommended. Singles with shared bath $45; doubles $60-65; apartments with kitchenette $85.) The **Sweet Dreams B&B,** 228 Wood St., rests a few blocks south of Elmshade and is accessible from Albany St. With only 2 guest rooms, this cozy B&B ensures close contact with the kind owners. (☎272-7727. Reservations required. Rooms $75-85.) Featuring a waterfall that plummets 215 ft. (a distance greater than the Niagara Falls drop), **Taughannock Falls State Park ❶,** north on Rte. 89, offers both woodland camping and access to the shores of Cayuga Lake. (☎387-6739; www.reserveamerica.com. Free hot showers. Sites $13, with electricity $19. Cabins for 4 people $40 per night, $160 per week. Registration fee $2.75. Day use $7.) A huge, foaming waterfall commands the entrance to the campsite at **Buttermilk Falls ❶,** on Rte. 13 south of Ithaca. The closest park to Ithaca, Buttermilk has 46 small sites within a beautiful birch forest, and miles of trails trace Buttermilk Creek through the woods and across idyllic bridges that span sharply carved waterfalls. (☎273-5761. Free showers. Sites $13. Registration fee $2.75. Day use $7.)

◖ FOOD. Restaurants in Ithaca center on Ithaca Commons and Collegetown. With a new menu every day, frequent live jazz and folk music, and ethnically themed nights on Sundays, ⬛**Moosewood Restaurant ❷,** 215 N. Cayuga, at Seneca St. in the Dewitt Mall, features a completely vegetarian selection of fresh and creative dishes. (☎273-9610. Lunch $6.50-7; dinner $10-16. Open Sept.-May M-Th 11:30am-3pm and 5:30-8:30pm, F-Sa 11:30am-3pm and 5:30-9pm, Su 5:30-8:30pm; June-Oct. M-Th 11:30am-3pm and 5:30-9pm, F-Sa 11:30am-3pm and 6-9:30pm, Su 5:30-8:30pm.) Give your tastebuds a workout at **Just a Taste ❸,** 116 N. Aurora St., near Ithaca Commons, which features wine flights ($6-11) and a smorgasbord of tempting *tapas* ($2.50-7.50 each), desserts, and beers, which can be enjoyed on the outdoor patio during the summer months. (☎277-9463. Open Su-Th 2:30-4:30pm and 5:30-10pm, F-Sa 2:30-4:30pm and 5:30-11pm.) At **Gino's NY Pizzeria,** 106 N. Aurora St., a 16 oz. soda and the two largest slices of pizza you will ever attempt to consume ($3) could keep you going all the way to New York City. (☎277-2777. Open Su-Th 10:30am-10pm, F-Sa 10:30am-2am.) ⬛**Wegmans,** 500 S. Meadow St., is the ultimate food experience for the budget traveler. Food by the pound is available at a wok bar, wing bar, cheese bar, or pizza bar ($5-7 per lb.), the deli sells gir-thy 14-inch subs big enough for two meals ($7), the candy section holds over 50 tubes of sweets stretching to the ceiling, and the produce section offers every fruit and vegetable imaginable at near-wholesale prices. (277-5800. Open 24hr.)

🔲 **SIGHTS. Cornell University,** youngest of the Ivy League schools, sits on a steep hill in Ithaca between two tremendous gorges. Accessed down a steep flight of steps across University Ave. from the Johnson Art Museum, the suspension bridge above Fall Creek provides a heart-pounding walk above one gorge, while the **College Avenue Stone Arch Bridge** above Cascadilla Creek has a brilliant sunset view. The **Information and Referral Center,** in the 2nd fl. lobby of Day Hall on East Ave., has info on campus sights and activities, and offers **campus tours** highlighting the unique collage of modern and classical architecture that rests amidst awe-inspiring landscapes. (☎254-4636. Open M-F 8am-5pm; telephone staffed Sa 8am-5pm and Su noon-1pm. Tours Apr.-Nov. M-F 9, 11am, 1, 3pm; Sa 9, 10:30am, 1pm; Su 1pm. Dec.-Mar. daily 1pm.) The funky, box-like cement edifice rising from the top of the hill houses Cornell's **Herbert F. Johnson Museum of Art,** at the corner of University Ave. and Central Ave., which holds a small but impressive collection of works by Giacometti, Matisse, O'Keeffe, Picasso, and Degas. The 5th fl. Asian art exhibit and the rooftop sculpture garden both yield amazing views. (☎255-6464. Open Tu-Su 10am-5pm. Free.) The extensive **botanical gardens** and **arboretum** that compose the **Cornell Plantations** lie serenely in the northeast corner of campus. Visitors can ramble through the Slim Jim Woods, drive to Grossman Pond, or take a short hike to a lookout point that provides a view of campus and the surrounding area. (☎255-3020. Open daily sunrise-sunset. Free.) Parking permits ($1) are required at the art museum and gardens and are available at the small booths at each entrance to campus. The most popular hike in the region, the 1½ mi. **Founder's Loop** takes you through the heart of campus, serving as a self-guided tour of the ancient halls and gorges of Cornell. Information on hiking the loop or 14 other trails in the region can be found in the *Passport to the Trails of Tompkins County* ($1), available from the visitors center. A community gathering place on weekends, the **Ithaca Farmers Market,** 3rd St. off Rte. 13, has much than just produce under its eaves. Ethnic food stalls, cider tastings, and hand-crafted furniture are also among the products brought to market by vendors from a 30 mi. radius. (☎273-7109. Open Apr.-Dec. Sa 9am-2pm; June-Oct. also Su 9am-2pm.)

The fertile soil and cool climate of the Finger Lakes area has made it the heart of New York's wine industry. Designated **wine trails** provide opportunities for wine tasting and vineyard touring—locals say that the fall harvest is the best time to visit. (For more information, contact the Ithaca/Tompkins County Convention and Visitors Bureau, p. 255.) The closest trail to Ithaca, the **Cayuga Trail** (☎800-684-5217; www.cayugawinetrail.com), contains 15 vineyards, 11 of which are located along Rte. 89 between Seneca Falls and Ithaca. Other wineries are on the **Seneca Lake Trail** (☎877-536-2717; www.senecalakewine.com), with 25 wineries encircling the lake on Rte. 414 (east side) and 14 (west side). The **Keuka Trail** (☎800-440-4898; www.keukawinetrail.com), with nine wineries along Rte. 54 and 76, is also easily accessible from Ithaca. Some wineries offer free picnic facilities and tours. All give free tastings; some require the purchase of a glass for a nominal charge.

🔲🔲 **ENTERTAINMENT AND NIGHTLIFE.** Befitting its Ivy League roots, Cornell offers excellent theater productions year-round. The **Hangar Theatre,** 2 mi. from downtown at the Rte. 89 N Treman Marina entrance, stages musicals and plays. **"The Wedge,"** an experimental theater in the same building, gives free perfor-

MID-ATLANTIC

mances before and after the mainstage show. (☎273-8588. Shows Tu-Th and Su 7:30pm, F-Sa 8pm; matinees Sa 3pm, and some Su 2pm. $10-30. Call ahead for Wedge showtimes.) With a kitchen sink full of unique shows, the 73-seat **Kitchen Theatre,** 116 N. Cayuga, hosts everything from one-man shows to full plays. (☎272-0403. $16-20.) In the same building, the **Ticket Center at Clinton House** sells tickets to events at the Hangar Theatre, the Kitchen Theatre, and many local college theater events. (☎273-4497 or 800-284-8422. Open M-Sa 10am-5:30pm.) The free and widely available *Ithaca Times* has complete listings of entertainment options.

A romantic path along the gorge starts near the Stone Arch Bridge on College Ave. Collegetown, centered on College Ave., harbors student hangouts. Split down the middle, **Stella's,** 403 College Ave., has two entrances: one leads to a red-walled cafe serving decadent drinks such as "The Tasteful Hedonist" (2 shots of espresso, steamed milk, Swiss chocolate, and a cherry; $4), while the other heads to a dark jazz bar with funky countertops and art-covered walls. (☎277-1490. No cover. Food served daily 11am-12:30am. Cafe open in summer M-F 6am-1am, Sa-Su 10am-1am. Jazz bar open daily 11am-1am.) **Ruloff's,** 411 College Ave., offers a long and fully stocked bar in a dimly-lit pub overflowing with college students. At 5:30pm, during happy hour, and at half past midnight, the bartender spins the "wheel of fortune" to pick the night's drink special, while nightly $2 Dos Equis and $6 pitchers keep the college crowd happy. (☎272-6067. 21+. Open M-Sa 11:30am-1am, Su 10am-1am.) With plush red-and-purple curtains and masks on the walls, it's Mardi Gras all year long at **Maxie's Supper Club,** 635 W. State St. Spice up your evening with their Cajun Bloody Mary ($6), featuring horseradish and Cajun seasoning. (☎272-4136. Raw bar and "mini-plates" $8-11. Entrees $14-24. Raw bar open daily 4pm-midnight, half-price 4-6pm; kitchen open Su-Th 5pm-midnight, F-Sa 5pm-1am; bar open daily 4pm-1am.) For a passport to a world of weirdness, head to the **Rongovian Embassy to the USA ("The Rongo"),** on Rte. 96 in Trumansburg about 10 mi. north of Ithaca, for Mexican and Cajun food (entrees under $11), an eclectic array of local music, and an atmosphere well worth the drive. (☎387-3334. Beer $2.50-3.75. Live music some nights. Cover $5 or less. Bar open F-Sa 6pm-1am.)

BUFFALO ☎716

At first glance, it seems that Buffalo is characterized by its problems: brutal winters and luckless sports franchises add to the erosion of a blue collar economy, the decaying rust belt industry, and sprawling suburbanization. But do not underestimate this self-proclaimed "All America city." Buffalo is a cultural powerhouse by day, with historic architecture and impressive art collections. By night, the top-notch theater district and boisterous club scene could compete with those of cities twice Buffalo's size. From the downtown skyline to funky Elmwood Village, Buffalo balances small-town warmth with big-city culture.

⊟ TRANSPORTATION. Buffalo Niagara International Airport, 4200 Genesee St., Cheektowaga (☎630-6000; www.buffaloairport.com), 10 mi. east of downtown off Hwy. 33. Take the MetroLink Airport-Downtown Express (#204) from the **Transportation Center,** 181 Ellicott St., at N. Division St. **Airport Taxi Service** (☎633-8294 or 800-551-9369; www.buffaloairporttaxi.com) offers shuttles to downtown for $15. Call or reserve online. **Amtrak,** 75 Exchange St. (☎856-2075; office open M-F 6am-3:30pm), at Washington St., runs to New York City (8½hr., 3 per day, $63) and Toronto (4½hr., 1 per day, $26). **Greyhound,** in the Buffalo Metropolitan Transportation Center (☎855-7531 or 800-454-2487; station open 24hr.), sends buses to: Boston (11½hr., 12 per day, $56); New York City (8½hr., 13 per day, $72); Niagara Falls, ON (1hr., 7 per day, $4); Toronto, ON (2½hr., 12 per day, $16). The **Niagara Frontier**

Transit Authority (NFTA) offers bus and rail service in the city (☎855-300; www.nfta.com; $1.50-2.25; seniors, children, and disabled riders $0.65-0.95), with additional buses to Niagara Falls, NY and free rides on the aboveground Main St. Metro Rail. **Taxi: Cheektowaga Taxi** (☎822-1738).

🛈 PRACTICAL INFORMATION. Visitor Info: Visitor Center, 617 Main St., in the Theater District. (☎852-2356 or 800-283-3256; www.visitbuffaloniagara.com. Open M-Sa 10am-4pm.) **GLBT Resources: Pride Buffalo, Inc.,** 266 Elmwood Ave., Ste 207 (☎879-0999; www.pridebuffalo.org); **PFLAG,** P.O. Box 617 (☎883-0384; www.pflag-buffalo-niagara.org). **Police:** ☎855-2222 (non-emergency). **Suicide, Rape, Crisis, and Emergency Mental Health Hotline:** ☎834-3131. Operates 24hr. **Medical Services: Buffalo General Hospital,** 100 High St. Take the Metro Rail to the Allen-Hospital stop, go up Main St. and turn right on High St. (☎859-5600.) **Internet Access: Buffalo and Erie County Public Library,** 1 Lafayette Sq. at Washington St., offers Internet access with $1 temporary library membership. (☎858-8900. Open M-Sa 8:30am-6pm.) **Post Office:** 701 Washington St. (☎856-4603. Open M-F 8:30am-5:30pm, Sa 8:30am-1pm.) **Postal Code:** 14203. **Area Code:** 716.

🛏 ACCOMMODATIONS. Budget lodgings are a rarity in Buffalo, but chain motels can be found near the airport and off I-90, 8-10 mi. northeast of downtown. The bright and comfortable **Hostel Buffalo (HI) ❶,** 667 Main St., is a clean facility with 50 beds in a centrally-located neighborhood. Friendly staff makes travelers feel at home and offers free nightly movie showings. Kitchen and common rooms, pool table, Internet access ($1 per 15min.), free linen, and laundry facilities are available for guests to use. (☎852-5222; www.hostelbuffalo.com. Reception 24hr. with reservation; otherwise 9-11am and July-Aug. 4-11pm; Sept.-June 5-10pm. Check-out 10am. Reservations recommended in summer. Dorms $20, nonmembers $23; private rooms $50-$65; $10 each additional adult and $5 each additional child. Wheelchair accessible.) The **Lenox Hotel & Suites ❸,** 140 North St., at Delaware Ave. Take bus #11, 20, or 25 to North St. The old-fashioned, functional rooms are only 5min. from Allentown/Elmwood Village nightlife. Coin-operated laundry on premises and free parking. (☎884-1700; www.lenoxhotelandsuites.com. Cable TV, A/C, kitchens available. Singles from $59; suites $69-119.)

🍴🎶 FOOD AND NIGHTLIFE. Elmwood Village, up Elmwood Ave. between Virginia Ave. and Forest Ave., is full of funky boutiques, coffee shops, and ethnic restaurants. **Gabriel's Gate ❷,** 145 Allen St., with

THE LOCAL STORY

BUFFALO'S WINGS

In Buffalo, they're called "chicken wings." Everywhere else, they're called "Buffalo wings." Either way, it all started out as a big accident.

Late one night in 1964, Teressa Bellisimo was working in the kitchen of the **Anchor Bar & Restaurant** when her son, the bartender, asked her to whip up something for him and a group of his ravenous friends. She thought for a moment, then remembered the plate of chicken wings she had set aside as too meaty for soup stock. She dumped them in the deep fryer, then covered them with an impromptu sauce and served them with celery and blue cheese dressing. Voila! Buffalo wings were born.

Since then, Buffalo wings have gone from bar food to main attraction. July 29, 1977 was declared **"Buffalo Wing Day"** in the city of Buffalo. These days, the **National Buffalo Wing Festival** (www.buffalowing.com) packs Buffalo's Dunn Tire Park full of wing chefs and admirers in late summer. The Anchor Bar now serves over 1000 lb. of chicken wings a day and exports its special sauce to countries worldwide.

1047 Main St. ☎886-8920. *10 wings $8, 20 wings $12, bucket of 50 $25; Suicidal! If you dare! wings $9/$13/$27. Open daily 11am-1am.* ❷

its rustic furniture, mounted animal heads, and big chandelier, is a friendly restaurant reminiscent of a saloon. Enjoy the famous "Richmond Ave." burger ($5) or the portobello sandwich ($6) from the comfy shaded patio. (☎886-0602. Open Su-W 11:30am-midnight, F-Sa 11:30am-2am.) At **Emerson Commons ❷**, 70 W. Chippewa St., high school culinary students serve cheap, hot breakfasts and lunches. (☎851-3018. Eggs with bacon and cheese $2-5, lunch sandwiches $6. Open school days 7:30-10am and 11:15am-1:30pm.)

Downtown bars and clubs are concentrated on **Chippewa Street** and **Franklin Street,** but live music can be found throughout the city. From Thursday to Saturday bars are open until 4am, and thousands of Western New Yorkers are out all night. Pick up a copy of *Artvoice* (www.artvoice.com) for event listings in Buffalo. Music is burned into the walls at **Nietzsche's,** 248 Allen St., where Ani DiFranco and the 10,000 Maniacs got their big breaks. (☎886-8539; www.nietzsches.com. Beer on tap from $2.50. Live rock, reggae, blues, or jazz every night. 21+; call ahead for special 18+ nights. Open daily noon-4am.) **D'Arcy McGee's Irish Pub and Sky Bar,** 257 Franklin St., is an Irish pub on the first floor, a nightclub on the second, and Buffalo's only open-air rooftop lounge on top. Patrons can ride a glass elevator up to the sky bar to relax above the bustling scene below. A pint of Guinness costs $4. (☎853-3600; www.buffnight.com. 21+. Sky bar cover $2-3 after 10pm. Open daily 11am-4am, weather permitting.) **Spot Coffee,** 227 Delaware Ave., is the place to go for anything from a plain cup o' joe ($1.15-1.75) to specialty espresso drinks (from $1.85) and iced blended shakes (from $2.95). A side room features local musicians on Wednesday and Sunday evenings. (☎856-2739. Open M-Th 6am-11pm, F 6am-midnight, Sa 7am-midnight, Su 7am-11pm. Kitchen closes 2hr. before shop.) **Club Marcella,** 622 Main St., is a gay nightclub, but clubbers of all persuasions party on its two dance floors. (☎847-6850; www.clubmarcella.com. Drag shows W-Th, and Su. F-Sa hip-hop. 18+. Cover usually $3, but varies. Open W-Su 9pm-4am.)

◨ ◫ **SIGHTS AND ENTERTAINMENT.** The **Albright-Knox Art Gallery,** 1285 Elmwood Ave., houses an internationally recognized collection of over 6000 modern pieces, including works by Picasso and Rothko. (☎882-8700; www.albright-knox.org. Take bus #20. Open Tu-Sa 11am-5pm, Su noon-5pm. $8, seniors and students $6, 12 and under free, families $12; Sa 11am-1pm free.) Next to the gallery, **Delaware Park,** the center of Buffalo's park system, was designed by legendary landscape architect Frederick Law Olmsted. Frank Lloyd Wright also designed several important houses in the area. Architecture buffs can take a 2hr. self-guided **walking tour** of historic downtown Buffalo. Pick up the free guide, *Walk Buffalo*, at the tourist office. The Allentown Village Society organizes the **Allentown Art Festival** (☎881-4269; www.allentownartfestival.com; June 11-12, 2005), a two-day celebration of local artists, craftsmen, and musicians. The **Buffalo Niagara Guitar Festival** (☎845-7156; www.guitarfestival.org) is America's first and largest all-guitar music festival, featuring such luminaries as Bo Diddley. From September to January, **Ralph Wilson Stadium** (☎648-1800; www.buffalobills.com), in Orchard Park, hosts the NFL's **Buffalo Bills,** while hockey's **Sabres** play at the **HSBC Arena,** 1 Seymour H. Knox III Plaza, from September to April. (☎855-4444, ext. 82; www.sabres.com.)

NIAGARA FALLS   ☎716

Niagara Falls, one of the seven natural wonders of the world, is flat-out spectacular. The giant falls are best viewed from the facing (Canadian) side of the Niagara River, where the natural grandeur is complemented by well-developed tourist attractions, nightlife, and a thriving honeymoon industry. Meanwhile, a giant resort casino is being built on the American side on Seneca tribal land that promises to revitalize the scene.

TRANSPORTATION

Trains: In Canada, **VIA Rail Canada,** 4267 Bridge St. (☎888-842-7245). Take the Niagara Falls Shuttle (see **Public Transit,** below) from downtown. Runs to **New York City** (10hr.; 11:30am; M-Th and Sa CDN$86, F and Su CDN$102) and **Toronto** (2hr.; daily 5:45am, M-F 6:45am, Sa-Su 7:40am; CDN$31, with ISIC CDN$22). Open M-F 6am-8pm, Sa-Su 7am-8pm. In the US, **Amtrak,** at 27th and Lockport St. (☎285-4224), 1 block east of Hyde Park Blvd. Runs to **New York City** (9hr.; M-Th and Sa $63, F and Su $75) and **Toronto** (3hr.; M-Th and Sa $23, F and Su $30). Taxis meet each incoming train ($7-10 to downtown), or wait for bus #52 (runs daily 7am-4:30pm).

Buses: In Canada, the **bus terminal,** 4267 Bridge St. (☎357-2133), across from the train station, sends **Greyhound** buses to **Toronto** (2hr., 23 per day, CDN$23). Open daily 7am-10:30pm. **The Magic Bus** (☎877-856-6610; www.magicbuscompany.com) runs between Hostelling International hostels at Niagara Falls and Toronto. (Tu, Th, and Sa-Su 5pm; CDN$20.) In the US, **Niagara Falls Bus Terminal,** at 4th and Niagara St. (☎282-1331), sells **Greyhound** tickets for direct service to **New York City** (8hr., 1 per day, $72). Open M-F 9am-4pm, Sa-Su 9am-noon. To get a bus in Buffalo, take bus #40 "Grand Island" from the Niagara Falls bus terminal to the **Buffalo Transportation Center,** 181 Ellicott St. (1hr., 19 per day, $2.25).

Public Transit: On the Canadian side, the **Niagara Falls Shuttle** (☎356-1179) runs between the bus and train stations, downtown, and other touristy areas. (June 20-Aug. 31 every 30min. 8:45am-2am, all-day pass CDN$6.) **Niagara Frontier Metro Transit System** (☎285-2002; www.nfta.com), provides local city transit in the US ($1.50). **ITA Buffalo Shuttle** (☎800-551-9369) has service from the Niagara Falls info center and major hotels to Buffalo Niagara International Airport ($50).

Taxi: In Canada, **Niagara Falls Taxi** ☎905-357-4000. In the US, **Blue United Cab** ☎285-9331. Travelers should beware of taxi drivers who charge full fare for each rider.

Bike Rental: In Canada, **Leisure Trails,** 4362 Leader Ln. (☎905-371-9888). $5 an hour, $20 a day, including lock and helmet. Open daily 9am-6pm, but later drop-offs can be arranged. In America, **Bikes & Hikes,** 526 Niagara St. (☎278-0047; www.bikesandhikes.com). $12 for 2hr. rental includes helmet, lock, and map for self-guided tour.

ORIENTATION AND PRACTICAL INFORMATION

Niagara Falls spans the US-Canadian border (addresses given here are in New York, unless noted). Take **U.S. 190** to the Robert Moses Pkwy., which leads directly to the Falls and downtown. On the **Canadian** side, most attractions are scattered along **Niagara Parkway (River Road),** and the main entertainment and shopping district is **Clifton Hill** between Victoria Ave. and River Rd. Customs procedures, while still casual in tone, have been taken extremely seriously since September 11th. On the **American** side, **Niagara Street** is the main east-west artery, ending in the west at the **Rainbow Bridge,** which crosses to Canada (pedestrian crossings $0.50, cars $2.50; tolls only charged going into Canada). North-south streets are numbered, increasing toward the east. Budget motels line **Route 62 (Niagara Falls Boulevard)** outside of town. Many businesses in the Niagara area accept both American and Canadian currency.

Visitor Info: Niagara Falls Tourism (☎800-563-2557 or 905-356-6061; www.discoverniagara.com) has information about the Canadian side. Open M-F 8am-6pm, Sa 10am-6pm, Su 10am-4pm. In the US, the **Orin Lehman Visitors Center** (☎278-1796) is in front of the Falls's observation deck; the entrance is marked by a garden. Open daily 7am-10:15pm.

Hotlines: Sexual assault crisis line, ☎905-682-4584.

Medical Services: In Canada, **Greater Niagara General Hospital,** 5546 Portage Rd. (☎905-358-0171). In the US, **Niagara Falls Memorial Medical Center,** 621 10th St. (☎278-4000; www.nfmmc.org).

Internet Access: In Canada, **Niagara Falls Public Library,** 4848 Victoria Ave., offers free internet access (☎905-356-8080. Open M-Th 9am-9pm, F-Sa 9am-5:30pm.) In the US, **Public Library,** 1425 Main St., also has free access. (☎286-4894; www.niagarafallspubliclib.org. Open M-W 9am-9pm, Th-F 9am-5pm.)

Post Office: In the US, 615 Main St. (☎285-7561). Open M-F 8:30am-5pm, Sa 8:30am-2pm. **Postal Code:** 14302. **Area Code:** 716 (NY), 905 (ON). In text, 716 unless otherwise noted.

ACCOMMODATIONS

Many newlyweds spend part of their honeymoon by the awesome beauty of the Falls. In Canada, cheap motels (from CDN$35) advertising free wedding certificates line **Lundy's Lane,** while many moderately priced B&Bs overlook the gorge on **River Road** between the Rainbow Bridge and the Whirlpool Bridge. Reservations are always recommended.

Hostelling International Niagara Falls (HI), 4549 Cataract Ave., Niagara Falls, ON (☎905-357-0770 or 888-749-0058; www.hihostels.ca). Just off Bridge St., about 2 blocks from the bus station and VIA Rail. Once a lodging house for railroad workers, this hostel now enjoys a laid-back atmosphere, thanks to the staff of self-described hippies and its convivial, rainbow-colored interior. The hostel features an organic vegetable garden, rain cisterns for water collection, a compost pile, and fair trade organic coffee. Activities include pancake breakfasts, Su vegan potluck 6-9pm, and drum circle at sundown. Internet access CDN$1 per 15 min. Lockers CDN$2. Linen CDN$2 (free with ISIC). Laundry and kitchen facilities. Key deposit CDN$5. Reception 24hr. in summer, 8am-midnight in winter. Check-out 11am. Quiet hours 11pm-7am. Reservations recommended May-Nov. Dorms CDN$19, nonmembers CDN$23; singles $50/$59. ❶

Backpacker's International Hostel, 4219 Huron St., Niagara Falls, ON, at Zimmerman Ave. (☎905-357-4266 or 800-891-7022; www.backpackers.ca.) 5min. walk from the bus station. Take Bridge St. to Zimmerman Ave.; the hostel is a few blocks to the right. In a historic home with clean, simple dorm rooms (bathrooms in each room) and pleasant grounds and gardens. Family-run and owned. Gorgeous private rooms. Bike rentals CDN$15 per day. Free Internet access. Breakfast, bed linens, and parking included. Reception 24hr. with reservation. Dorms CDN$20; singles $50; doubles $65. ❶

Bampfield Hall Bed & Breakfast, 4671 Zimmerman Ave., Niagara Falls, ON (☎905-353-8522 or 877-353-8522; www.niagaraniagara.com). Located right off the Niagara River Pkwy., this beautiful, newly-restored B&B offers well-decorated, clean, and comfortable rooms at reasonable prices. Antique hat museum on premises. Hot breakfast with fresh baked goods included. No smoking. Reservations required. Rooms CDN$80-115; low-season from CDN$65. 10% cash discount. ❸

Hostelling International Niagara Falls (HI), 1101 Ferry Ave. (☎282-3700). From the bus station, walk east on Niagara St., then turn left onto Memorial Pkwy.; the hostel is at the corner of Ferry Ave. *Avoid walking alone on Ferry Ave. at night.* 38

beds in a friendly old house. Kitchen, TV lounge, and limited parking. Family rooms available. Linen $1.75. Check-in 7:30-9:30am and 4-11pm. Lockout 9:30am-4pm. Curfew 11:30pm; lights-out midnight. Open Feb. to mid-Dec. Dorms $15, nonmembers $18. No credit cards. ❶

FOOD

Niagara Cumpir ❶, 4941 Victoria Ave., serves a young, hip clientele affordable Mediterranean fare on two patios. Vegetarian falafel is CDN$3.50, and the house specialty, beef shawarma, is CDN$6. (☎905-356-9900. Open Su-W 11am-11pm, Th-Sa 11am-1am). The oldest restaurant in town, **Simon's Restaurant ❷**, 4116 Bridge St., ON, one block from the HI hostel, is still a local favorite, thanks to its huge breakfasts (CDN$6), giant homemade muffins (CDN$0.69), and homestyle dinners. (☎905-356-5310. Open Su 5:30am-2pm, M-Sa 5:30am-7pm.) In the US, backpackers and locals alike flock to **The Press Box Restaurant ❶**, 324 Niagara St., for enormous meals at microscopic prices. On Monday and Wednesday, feast on $1.25 spaghetti. (☎284-5447. Open daily 9am-11pm.)

SIGHTS

In Canada, walk on the 🖫**promenade** from Clifton Hill to Table Rock Point for spectacular views of Bridal Veil Falls and Horseshoe Falls. Both sides of the border provide plenty of additional attractions. In Canada, the **casinos** and entertainment industry keeps tourists occupied, while the American side enjoys a full calendar of historical and cultural festivals (☎800-338-7890; www.niagara-usa.com).

CANADIAN SIDE. On the Canadian side, **Queen Victoria Park** provides the best view of **Horseshoe Falls.** Starting 1hr. after sunset, the Falls are illuminated for 3hr. every night, and a fireworks display lights up the sky every Friday and Sunday at 10pm, May 16 to September 1. Parking close to the park is expensive (CDN$12). Farther down Niagara Pkwy., across from the Greenhouse, parking is CDN$3 per hour. **People Movers** buses tourists through the 30km area on the Canadian side of the Falls, stopping at attractions along the way. *(☎877-642-7275. Mid-June to early Sept. daily 9am-11pm; low-season hours vary. CDN$6, children CDN$3.)* Bikers, in-line skaters, and walkers enjoy the 32km **Niagara River Recreation Trail,** which runs from Fort Erie to Fort George and passes historical sights dating back to the War of 1812.

Far above the crowds and excitement, **Skylon Tower** has the highest view (on a clear day, the view goes all the way to Toronto) of the Falls at 520 ft. aboveground, and 775 ft. above the base of the falls. The tower's **Observation Deck** offers a calming, unhindered vista. *(5200 Robinson St. ☎356-2651. Open June-Oct. M-F 8am-11pm, Sa-Su 8am-midnight; Nov.-May daily 9am-11pm. CDN$10, seniors CDN$9, children CDN$6, families CDN$27.)* The **Adventure Pass** includes entrance to the **Maid of the Mist** boat tour; **Journey Behind the Falls,** a tour behind Horseshoe falls; **White Water Walk,** a long boardwalk next to the Niagara River Rapids; the **Butterfly Conservatory,** on the grounds of the world-famous Niagara Parks Botanical Gardens; CDN$2 discounts for the **Spanish Aero Car,** an aerial cable ride over the rapids' whirlpool waters; and all-day transportation on the People Movers. *(Adventure Pass: CDN$38, children CDN$24. www.niagaraparks.com has details and sells passes online. Maid of the Mist: ☎357-7393. CDN$13, children CDN$8. In summer open daily 9:45am-5:45pm. Trips every 15min. Journey: ☎354-1551. CDN$10, children CDN$6. Open in summer daily 9am-7:30pm. Walk: ☎374-1221. CDN$8, children CDN$5. In summer open daily 9am-8pm. Guided tours available. Conservatory: ☎358-0025. CDN$10, children CDN$6. Open in summer daily 9am-7:30pm, call for updated times. Aero Car: ☎354-5711. CDN$11, children CDN$7. Open in summer daily 9am-6:45pm.)*

Meanwhile, commercialism can be as much of a wonder as any natural sight. The Canadian side of the Falls offers the delightfully tasteless **Clifton Hill,** home to an orgy of arcades, mini golf, soft-serve ice-cream stands, wax museums, and haunted houses. **Ripley's Believe It or Not Museum** displays wax model wonders and a selection of medieval torture devices. *(4960 Clifton Hill. ☎356-2238. Open in summer daily 9am-2am; low-season hours vary. CDN$13, seniors CDN$10, children CDN$6.)*

AMERICAN SIDE. For over 150 years, the **Maid of the Mist** boat tour has entertained visitors with the awe-inspiring (and wet) views from the foot of both falls. *(☎284-8897. Open daily 10am-6pm. Tours in summer daily every 30min. $10.50, ages 6-12 $6.25, $1 for entrance to observation deck only.)* The **Cave of the Winds Tour** hands out souvenir (read: ineffective) yellow raincoats and sandals for a drenching hike to the base of the Bridal Veil Falls, including an optional walk to Hurricane Deck where gale-force waves slam down from above. *(☎278-1730. Open May to mid-Oct.; hours vary depending on season and weather conditions. Trips leave every 15min. Must be at least 42 in. tall. $8, ages 6-12 $7.)*

The **Master Pass,** available at the park's visitors center, covers admission to the Maid of the Mist; the Cave of the Winds Tour; the **Niagara Gorge Discovery Center,** in Prospect Park, which has gorge trail hikes and an elevator ride that simulates the geological history of the Falls; the **Aquarium,** which houses the endangered Peruvian Penguin; and the **Niagara Scenic Trolley,** a tram-guided tour of the park and the best transportation between the sights on the American side. *(Master Pass: $25, ages 6-12 $18. Discovery Center: ☎278-1780. Film every 30min. Low-season daily 9am-7pm; Sept.-May 9am-5pm. $5, children $3. Aquarium: 701 Whirlpool St., across from Discovery Center. ☎285-3575; www.aquariumofniagara.org. Open July-Aug. daily 9am-7pm., low-season daily 9am-5pm. $7, children and seniors $5. Trolley: ☎278-1730. Open May-Aug. daily 9am-10pm. Runs every 10-20min. $5, children $3.)* The **Niagara Power Project,** 3 mi. north on Robert Moses Pkwy., features hands-on exhibits and videos on energy, hydropower, and local history. *(5777 Lewiston Rd. ☎286-6661. Open daily 9am-5pm. Call ahead to arrange a guided tour. Free.)* Eight miles north in Lewiston, NY, at the foot of 4th St., the 150-acre state **Artpark** focuses on visual and performing arts, offering opera, musicals, pops concerts, and rock shows. *(☎800-659-7275. Shows May-Aug.; call for schedule. Box office open M-F 10am-4pm, later on event days. Shows at 8pm. $15-40.)* **Old Fort Niagara** was built for French troops in 1726 and was the site of battles during the French and Indian War and the American Revolution. *(Follow Robert Moses Pkwy. north from Niagara Falls. ☎745-7611. Open June-Aug. daily 9am-8pm; low-season hours vary. $8, seniors $6, ages 6-12 $5.)*

NORTHERN NEW YORK

THE ADIRONDACKS   ☎518

Demonstrating uncommon foresight, the New York State legislature established the **Adirondacks State Park** in 1892, preserving a six-million-acre swath of mainly mountainous terrain, much of it designated as "forever wild." Thousands of miles of gorgeous trails carve through the park and more than 2500 glittering lakes and ponds are fed by 30,000 miles of rivers and streams. Despite being within one day's drive from over 60 million people, the immense dimensions of the park allow the Adirondacks to be one of the few places in the Northeast where hikers can still spend days without seeing another soul.

7 PRACTICAL INFORMATION. Adirondacks Trailways (☎800-858-8555) services the region. From Albany, buses set out for Lake Placid and Lake George. From the Lake George bus stop at Lake George Hardware, 35 Montcalm St., buses go to: Albany (4 per day, $14); Lake Placid (1-2 per day, $20); New York City (4-5 per day,

$49). The **Adirondack Mountain Club (ADK)** is the best source of info on outdoor activities in the region. Two excellent booklets available free of charge through the ADK are the *Adirondacks Waterways* and the *Adirondack Great Walks and Day Hikes* guides, which detail hundreds of hikes and paddles of all difficulty levels throughout the park. Offices are located at 814 Goggins Rd., Lake George 12845 (☎668-4447; www.adk.org; open M-Sa 8:30am-5pm), and at Adirondack Loj Rd., P.O. Box 867, Lake Placid 12946. (☎523-3441. Phone lines operate Su-Th and Sa 8am-8pm, F 8am-10pm.) The Lake Placid ADK, also known as the **High Peaks Information Center**, 3 mi. east of Lake Placid then 5 mi. down Adirondack Loj Rd. in the Loj itself, is the area's best resource for weather conditions, trail closures, and backcountry info. The center has washrooms (showers $0.25 per min.) and sells basic outdoor equipment, trail snacks, and a variety of helpful guides to the mountains for $11-25, including the ADK guides specific to each region of the mountains ($20). The center also runs an education program center which can provide the scoop on outdoor skills via 1-3 day excursions or lecture sessions. Classes include canoeing, rock climbing, whitewater kayaking, and wilderness medicine. (☎523-3441. Classes $35-265, including all food and equipment. Open May-Oct. Su-Th 8am-5pm, F-Sa 8am-8pm; Oct.-May daily 8am-5pm. Hours often increase with seasonal traffic. Parking $9.) **Area Code:** 518.

⌖◧ ACCOMMODATIONS AND FOOD. Lodging tends to cluster around the many small towns throughout the mountains, most of which are located on the shores of one of the many bodies of water. The ADK also runs two lodges near Lake Placid. The ⬧**Adirondack Loj ❷**, at the end of Adirondack Loj Rd., off Rte. 73, lures hikers looking for a place to rest their sore feet. Heated by an imposing fieldstone fireplace in the winter, the cozy den, decorated with skis and a moose trophy, is the perfect place to warm chilled limbs after exploring the wilderness trails on skis or snowshoes. In summer, guests swim, fish, and canoe on Heart Lake, located 100 ft. from the lodge's doorstep. (☎523-3441. Breakfast included; lunch $5.50, dinner $14. Reservations highly recommended. Bunks $34-45. Private rooms $110 per night. Lean-tos $26; campsites $23; canvas cabin $32; 4-person wood cabins $100; 16-person $320. Snowshoe rentals $10 per day; cross-country ski rentals $20 per day. Canoe or kayak rental 8am-8pm; $5 per hr., guests $3.) ADK's second lodge, the **John's Brook Lodge ❷**, offers the outdoor-savvy a more secluded and rustic atmosphere. From Lake Placid, follow Rte. 73 for 15 mi. through Keene to Keene Valley, turn right at the Ausable Inn, and drive five miles to the parking lot at the end of the dirt road (parking $5). Reaching the lodge requires a 3½ mi. hike over the rolling hills and through the damp woods of the Adirondacks. Though the basic comforts of linens and showers are not available, three complimentary meals await the weary hiker. John's Brook is no secret, however, and beds fill completely on weekends. (Call the Adirondack Loj for reservations, ☎523-3441. Blankets provided. July to mid-Oct. bunks $42-45.) Two miles east of Tupper Lake, **Northwood Cabins ❸**, 92 Tupper-Sara Hwy., rents nine white-and-blue cabins with cable TV and heat; some have kitchenettes and fireplaces. The soft beds and friendly owner offer a soothing contrast to the hard damp floor of the Adirondacks. (☎359-9606 or 800-727-5756. Open mid-May to mid-Oct. Cabins $42-68.)

Twelve miles south of Plattsburgh on Rte. 9 lies one of the state's most beautiful campgrounds, ⬧**Ausable Point ❶**. Dotted with wildflowers and situated on the banks of Lake Champlain with a sandy beach, the park is ideal for camping or day use. (☎561-7080. Make reservations far in advance for prime waterfront sites during weekends and holidays. Registration fee $3. Sites $17, with electricity $20. Day use $6 per car. Lifeguard on duty June to late Aug. M-F 10am-7pm, Sa-Su 10am-8pm.) **Backcountry camping** rules have recently changed in sections of the eastern half of the park. In designated areas camping is prohibited except at prescribed sites and campfires are banned within the entire section. Furthermore, a recent increase in bear activity has prompted rangers to make the use of bear canisters for food mandatory. Areas affected by these changes are identified on the new maps sold by the ADK and can be viewed or purchased at the High Peaks Information Center ($8). Otherwise, camping is free anywhere on public land in the backcountry as long as it is at least 150 ft. away from a trail, road, water source, or campground, and below 4000 ft. in altitude. Inquire about the locations of free trailside shelters before planning a hike in the forest. Contact the **Department of Environmental Conservation** (☎402-9428) for more info on backwoods camping.

The **White Birch Cafe ❸**, 6 Demars Blvd., in Tupper Lake, serves good, fresh food at reasonable prices. (☎359-8044. Sandwiches $4-6. Open M and W-Su 11am-8pm; other hours vary.) At the intersection of Rte. 30 and Rte. 28 in Long Lake, **Hoss's General Store** provides camping supplies and groceries for visitors looking to hit the trails. (☎624-2451. Open daily 9am-10pm.) The Hoss complex also houses a bakery and an Internet cafe. (☎624-6466. Internet access $5 per 15min., including complimentary beverage. Open daily 10am-6pm.)

⬛ SIGHTS. Of the six million acres in the Adirondacks State Park, 40% are open to the public, offering a slew of outdoor activities. The other 60% are privately owned by logging companies, residents, and outdoors clubs. Fourteen **scenic byways** offer safe passage to even the most remote villages hidden among the mountains and inland waterways agitated by the inescapable summer rainfall. These waterways carry kayakers, canoers, and seasonal whitewater rafters through breathtaking gorges and the surrounding forests. The park offers outdoors enthusiasts 2000 mi. of trails that provide spectacular mountain scenery for hikers, snowshoers, and cross-country skiers. A number of the trails that wind their way through the highest peaks begin at the Adirondack Loj at the end of Adirondack Loj Rd. 3 mi. east of town along Rte. 73. Those with a full day to spend hiking should consider conquering **Phelps Mountain,** a 9 mi. round-trip journey with unparalleled views of the surrounding peaks. **Mount Marcy,** a 7½ mi. hike to the state's highest peak (5344 ft.), is a daytrip that promises to test even the most avid hiker, finishing with a 360° aerial view of Adirondack Park and a commanding view of Lake Placid to the northwest. **Mt. Jo,** a steep 2 mi. round-trip journey, provides views of the surrounding peaks and Heart Lake in the valley below. Saranac Lake hosts a 10-day, no-holds-barred **carnival** every winter, for which an ice palace is erected. (Saranac Lake Chamber of Commerce: 39 Main St. ☎891-1990; www.saranaclake.com.) Lake George also hosts a carnival on weekends in February. (Lake George Chamber of Commerce: 2176 Rte. 9. ☎668-5755. Open daily 9am-5pm.) In late June, Tupper hosts the **Tin Man Triathlon,** a 1¼ mi. swim, 56 mi. bike ride, and 13 mi. run through town. (Tupper Lake Chamber of Commerce: 60 Park St. ☎359-3328 or 888-887-5253. Open daily 9am-5pm.) Lake Placid doubles the distances with an **IronMan Triathlon.** Information is available at the Lake Placid Visitors Bureau (p. 267) or at www.ironmanusa.com.

Experienced rock climbers and those who want to break into the sport should consult the experienced staff at the **Mountaineer,** in Keene Valley, between I-87 and Lake Placid on Rte. 73. The Mountaineer reels in all types of alpine enthusiasts as it hosts the **Adirondack International Mountainfest,** a weekend of clinics and classes for all manner of mountain sport. (☎576-2281. Open in summer M and F-Su 8am-7pm, Tu-Th 9am-6pm; low-season M-F 9am-5:30pm, Sa 8am-5:30pm, Su 9am-5:30pm. Snowshoes $15 per day, ice-climbing boots and crampons $20, rock shoes $12. Mountainfest is held in Jan. on Martin Luther King Day weekend.) The **Adirondack Park Visitor Interpretive Center,** just west of Newcomb on Rte. 28 N, is a great place to get park information and potentially spot moose, bears, minx, and otters, which are known to frequent the trails originating from the center. (☎582-2000. Visitors center open daily 9am-5pm; trails open dawn-dusk. Free.) The 21 exhibits at the ⊠Adirondack Museum, off Rte. 30 in Blue Mountain Lake, showcase the history, culture, and lifestyles of the Adirondacks through the ages. The collection of 25 boats and the complete, richly decorated railcar are among the more impressive exhibits. (☎352-7311; www.adkmuseum.org. Open late May to mid-Oct. daily 10am-5pm. $14; seniors $13; students, military, and ages 13-17 $7; under 13 free.)

Stroll down **Ausable Chasm,** a gorge cut deep into the earth by the roaring Ausable River, 12 mi. south of Plattsburgh on Rte. 9. The chasm includes numerous waterfalls and is surrounded by Adirondack forest seemingly untouched by civilization. At the conclusion of the walk, the relatively flat water provides the opportunity to raft through a labyrinth of age-old rock formations. (☎800-537-1211; www.ausablechasm.com. Open mid-May to late June daily 9:30am-4pm; late June to Sept. Su-Th 9:30am-5pm, F-Sa 9:30am-6:30pm. Entrance to the walkway $16, seniors and ages 12-19 $14, ages 5-11 $12. Entrance and raft trip $24/$22/$20.) Farther south along the shores of Lake Champlain, one mile east of the town of Ticonderoga, lies ⊠Fort Ticonderoga. From atop the towering walls of the fortress, poised like a dagger over the cascading hillsides below, bronze cannons stand guard over the ancient waterways that held the "key to the continent" during the wars for control of the colonies. Fully restored, the fortress houses a museum, provides daily historical talks and musket demonstrations, and stages reenactments of historical battles, occasionally with as many as 1000 actors. (☎585-2821; www.fort-ticonderoga.org. Open May to late Oct. daily 9am-5pm. $12, seniors $11, ages 7-12 $6.)

LAKE PLACID   ☎518

Tucked away among the High Peaks Mountains, Lake Placid lives and breathes winter sports but still maintains a lively summer schedule full of outdoors events. Host to the Olympic Winter Games in both 1932 and 1980, this modest town has seen thousands of pilgrims and, aside from the plentiful motels, has maintained a small town ambience while basking in the flames of Olympic glory. World-class athletes train year-round in the town's extensive facilities, lending an international flavor which distinguishes Lake Placid from its Adirondack neighbors.

◼️🛈 **ORIENTATION AND PRACTICAL INFORMATION.** Lake Placid sits at the intersection of Rte. 86 and Rte. 73 in the northeastern quarter of Adirondack Park. Rte. 73 runs north and connects with Rte. 86 south of the Olympic Skating Center, becoming Main St. as it runs north through the town. Downtown Lake Placid is located on Main St. along the shores of Lake Placid. **Adirondack Trailways** (☎800-225-6815) stops at 326 Main St., in front of the Coffee Cup Cafe, and has extensive service in the area. Destinations include the Albany airport ($27), Lake George ($15), and New York City ($63). The **Placid Xpress** shuttle travels through town every 15 to 20min. with stops at the various parking areas, including free municipal lots. (☎523-2585. Route maps, including low-season routes, available at the visitors center. Runs July-Sept. 8am-10pm; low-season hours vary. Free.)

The Lake Placid that exists today is a product of its rich Olympic past. The **Olympic Regional Development Authority,** 218 Main St., inside the Olympic Center, operates the sports facilities. (☎523-1655 or 800-462-6236. Open M-F 8:30am-5pm.) Also in the Olympic Center is the **Lake Placid-Essex County Visitors Bureau,** which provides information about food, lodging, weather, and attractions in the area. (☎523-2445; www.lakeplacid.com. Open M-F 8am-5pm, Sa-Su 9am-4pm; closed Su in the spring and fall.) **Internet Access: Lake Placid Public Library,** 67 Main St. (☎523-3200. Open M-F 11am-5pm, Sa 11am-4pm. No e-mail.) **Mountain Mama's,** 26 Main St., provides two high-speed connections. (☎523-9327. Open Tu-Su 10am-5pm. $5 per hr., $5 min.) The visitors center has limited service. (15min. limit when others are waiting.) **Post Office:** 201 Main St. (☎523-3071. Open M-F 8:30am-5pm, Sa 8am-noon.) **Postal Code:** 12946. **Area Code:** 518.

♜ ACCOMMODATIONS. If you avoid the resorts on the west end of town, both lodgings and food can be had cheaply in Lake Placid. Many inexpensive motels line Rte. 86 and 73 just east of town. The visitors center can provide suggestions to fit your needs. In a brand-new location half a mile south of downtown on Rte. 73, the friendly and helpful owners of the ☒**High Peaks Hostel ❶** will make any traveler feel right at home. This converted B&B offers 25 bunks and 2 private rooms. The complimentary homemade breakfasts, well-equipped kitchens, free linens and towels, and great community atmosphere make this an excellent lodging option. (☎523-4951. Bunks $20, private rooms $48-60.) The **Jackrabbit Inn and Hostel ❶**, 3½ mi. east of town on Rte. 73, also offers affordable rooms and bunks in a bunkhouse with a large social lounge and a kitchen. Linens, towels, and use of tennis court are included. (☎523-0123 or 800-584-7006. Bunks $20; private rooms $48-85.) Two state park campgrounds, some of the nicest in the area, are within 10 mi. of Lake Placid. **Meadowbrook State Park ❶**, 5 mi. west of town on Rte. 86 in Ray Brook, has relatively secluded, wooded campsites and provides easy access to several trailheads. (☎891-4351. Hot showers. Sites $11 plus $3 registration fee. Day use $4 per car, $1 walk-in.) **Wilmington Notch State Campground ❶**, about 9 mi. east of Lake Placid on Rte. 86, also offers shady, if somewhat more crowded, sites in proximity to all of the trailheads and ski slopes of Whiteface Mountain. (☎946-7172. Hot showers. Open May to mid-Oct. Sites $11-13. Day use $4 per car.)

◖▮ FOOD AND NIGHTLIFE. Lake Placid Village, concentrated primarily along Main St., has a number of reasonably priced dining establishments. The lunch buffet at the **Hilton Hotel ❷**, 1 Mirror Lake Dr., serves all-you-can-eat sandwiches, soups, salads, and a hot entree for only $8 in a room overlooking the lake from above the town. (☎523-4411. Buffet daily noon-2pm.) With a great selection of coffees and teas, **Aroma Round ❶**, 18 Saranac Ave., gets you moving in the morning with a cool breeze on the outside deck, or round out the day with a warm beverage ($1.50-3) around their small fireplace. (☎523-3818. Open daily 7am-10pm.) The **Brown Dog Deli and Wine Bar ❹**, 3 Main St., builds tasty sandwiches ($6-8) with meats and cheeses on homemade bread. For a treat, try the multiple-course meals accompanied by wine pairings on Saturday evenings. (☎523-3036. Entrees $15-18. Sa evening meals $17-22. Open daily 11am-10pm.) The **Black Bear Restaurant ❷**, 157 Main St., serves meals hot off the grill as well as a few vegetarian and vegan options and smoothies. The strongest option is the soup bar, offering eight different homemade soups each day for $6.50. (☎523-9886. Breakfast $5-10. Lunch special $8. Daily specials $15. Open daily 6am-9pm.) On the shore of Mirror Lake, **The Cottage ❷**, 5 Mirror Lake Dr., creates sandwiches and salads (all under $9) that can be served on the outside deck to accompany the view. (☎523-9845. Kitchen open daily 11:30am-10pm; bar open until midnight or 1am, depending on the crowd.) One of Lake Placid's few late-night hot spots, **Wise Guys**, 3 School St., boasts both a sports bar and a dance club. DJs and occasional live rock fill the air in the spacious bar, and on Fridays draft beers cost $1.05. (☎523-4446. M-F no cover, Sa-Su up to $3. Bar open M-F 3pm-3am, Sa-Su noon-3am. Club open Th-Sa 9pm-3am.)

◰ SIGHTS. The **Olympic Center,** in downtown Lake Placid, houses the 1932 and 1980 hockey arenas, as well as the petite, memorabilia-stuffed **Winter Olympic Museum.** Packed with ice skates from throughout the years, bobsleds used in former Olympics, and medals, the museum is a walk through time imbued with the echoes of past Olympic glory. (☎ 523-1655 ext. 226; www.orda.org. 5min. introductory video. Open daily 10am-5pm. $4, seniors $3, ages 7-12 $2. **Public skating:** ☎ 523-1655. Open year-round M-F 8-9:30pm. $5, children and seniors $4; skate rental $3.) During the summer, purchase tickets to watch ski jumpers and aerial freestylists practice for upcoming competitions by sailing down astroturf-covered ramps onto astroturf-covered hillsides or into a swimming pool in the **Olympic Jumping Complex,** just east of town on Rte. 73. Travelers can take a chairlift and an elevator to the top of the ramp for a look down. (☎ 523-2202. Open 9am-4pm. $5, with chairlift $8; seniors and children $5.) About 5 mi. east of town on Rte. 73, the **Verizon Sports Complex** at **Mt. Van Hoevenberg** offers bobsled rides down the actual 1980 Olympic track. Reaching speeds of 50 mph around gutwrenching curves, the bobsleds run on ice during the winter ($40) and wheels during the summer ($30). If rocketing down the side of the mountain at high speeds isn't for you, narrated bus tours drive more slowly up and down the mountain for a view of the tracks. (☎ 523-4436. Open W-Su 10am-12:30pm and 1:30-4pm. Winter bobsled runs Dec.-Mar.; summer June-Nov. Must be at least 48 in. tall; under 18 must have parent present. Bus tours 9am-4pm. $5, seniors and ages 7-12 $4.) Whip yourself into shape Olympian-style at the cross-country skiing venue. Cross-country skiing and biathlon courses are available to the public in the winter, and mountain biking trails are uncovered in the summertime. Cross-country ski and bike rentals are available inside the complex. (☎ 523-2811. Open for skiing daily 9am-4:30pm; last rental 4pm. $14 per day trail fee, seniors and ages 7-12 $12, ages 70 and up free. Equipment rental $16, under 18 $12. Open for biking mid-June to early Sept. daily 10am-5pm; early Sept. to early Oct. Sa-Su 10am-5pm. Bikes $30 per day; trail fee—not included in rental—$6 per day, $10 per 2 days; helmet required, and included with bike rental, $3 per day.)

For those planning to take in all or most of Lake Placid's Olympic attractions, the **Olympic Sites Passport** is the best bargain. For $19 per person, the pass includes entrance to the Olympic Jumping Complex (including chairlift and elevator ride), the bus tour of the bobsledding complex, a $5 coupon toward a bobsled ride on Mt. Van Hoevenberg, admission to the Winter Sports Museum, and the choice of either the **Scenic Gondola Ride** to the top of Little Whiteface or access to the **Veterans Memorial Highway** that climbs Whiteface Mountain. Purchase the passport at any Olympic venue or at the **Olympic Center Box Office** in Lake Placid (☎ 523-3330). After touring the Olympic venues, get outfitted for your own sporting adventures at **High Peaks Cyclery,** 331 Main St. Renting and selling all manner of bicycles, climbing gear, camping equipment, skis, snowshoes, and much more, the experts there can make sure you are prepared for any outing. If you aren't ready to head out alone, inquire about the guide services offered. (☎ 523-3764. Open daily 9am-6pm. Bikes $25-40 per day. Tents $15-20 per day. Cross-country skis $15 per day. Snowshoes $15 per day. Inquire about prices for guided tours.)

To climb to the 4867 ft. summit of Whiteface Mountain without breaking a sweat, drive your car up the 🚗**Veterans Memorial Highway,** 11 mi. east of Lake Placid on Rte. 86. The alpine-style tollbooth 5 mi. from the summit has info about the highway. Waiting at the summit is a castle in the clouds, perched on 250 ft. of solid granite that must be climbed via either an elevator or a spectacular ridge trail resembling a stairway to heaven. (☎ 946-7175. Open July-Sept. daily 8:30am-5pm; mid-May to July and Sept. to mid-Oct. daily 9am-4pm, longer if weather permits. Car and driver $9; motorcycle and driver $6; $4 per passenger.) Just 8 mi. east of town on Rte. 86, 700 ft. of waterfalls cascade down through the small, picturesque **High Falls Gorge.** Winter admission comes with ice cleats for steady footing and hot chocolate to warm chilled bones. (☎ 946-2278; www.highfallsgorge.com. Open 9am-5:30pm, last admission 5pm. In summer $9, ages 4-12 $5; call for winter rates.)

Lost in the intensity of athletic glory, visitors to Lake Placid often forget the unparalleled peace that the lake offers to serenity-seekers. Departing from the Lake Placid Marina, **tour boat cruises** quietly glide around the 16 mi. perimeter of the lake in long, sleek, turn-of-the-century boats, providing glimpses of the stately homes that line the shores as well as illuminating the history of the area. (☎523-9704. Cruises depart mid-May to late June M-F 10:30am and 2:30pm; Sa-Su 10:30am, 2:30, 4pm. Late June to Sept. daily 10:30am, 1, 2:30, 4pm. Sept to mid-Oct. daily 10:30am, 1:30, 3pm. Arrive at least 15min. early. $7.50, seniors $6.50, children $5.50.) Romantic horse-drawn carriages of **Mirror Lake Carriage Tours,** located at the northern end of Main St. across from the Hilton, offer views of Lake Placid from across the glassy waters of Mirror Lake via a peaceful 35min. stroll. (☎523-5352. Open June to mid-Oct. M-F 4-11pm, Sa-Su 11am-11pm. $15, ages 3-11 $10.) For a chance to enjoy the water in peaceful solitude, **Mirror Lake Boat Rentals,** 1 Main St., rents a variety of boats in which to sail, paddle, and motor your way around the lake. (☎524-7890. Open May to mid-Oct. 10am-dark. $20 per hr. for paddle boats, canoes, and hydrobikes; $40 per hr. for sailboats and electric cruisers.) For a cool dip in the waters, head down to the **Mirror Lake Public Beach** on Parkside Dr. (☎523-3109. Lifeguards on duty late June to Sept. 9am-7pm, weather permitting. Free.)

Athletics and natural beauty embody the spirit of Lake Placid, but no trip to upstate New York can be complete without a sampling of its famous vineyards. Selections of the award-winning wine produced by Finger Lakes-based **Swedish Hill Winery** are available 1 mi. east of downtown on Rte. 73. After sampling there, bring your glass with you to complete your tasting tour with another eight tastes at the **Goose Watch Winery,** 123 Main St. in the Alpine Mall, for an additional $0.01. (☎523-1956. Open M-Sa 10am-6pm, Su noon-6pm. 8 tastes and a wine glass $3.)

THOUSAND ISLAND SEAWAY ☎315

Spanning 100 miles from the mouth of Lake Ontario to the first of the locks on the St. Lawrence River, the Thousand Island region of the St. Lawrence Seaway forms a natural US-Canadian border. Surveys conducted by the US and Canadian governments determined that there are 1,864 islands in the seaway, with an island defined as at least one square foot of land above water year-round with at least two trees growing on it. Many islands, however, are developed with private residences, lighthouses, and towering 19th-century castles. The Thousand Island region is also a fisherman's paradise and a mecca for vacationers, with an incredible array of festivals during the long days of the short summer.

■■ ◪ **ORIENTATION AND PRACTICAL INFORMATION.** The Thousand Island region hugs the St. Lawrence River under 2hr. from Syracuse by way of **I-81 North.** From southwest to northeast, **Cape Vincent, Clayton,** and **Alexandria Bay** ("Alex Bay" to locals) are the main towns in the area. Cape Vincent, the smallest of the three, maintains a rich French heritage along the shores of Lake Ontario. Clayton, the most peaceful of the three seaside hamlets, boasts museums and galleries. Alex Bay is alive with countless riverside bars, clubs, and restaurants and hosts "themed" weeks throughout the summer, such as "Pirate Week" in August, when pirate ships and scalawags take control of the town. For Wellesley Island, Alexandria Bay, and the eastern 500 islands, stay on I-81 until you reach Rte. 12 E. For Clayton and points west, take Exit 47 and follow Rte. 12 to Rte. 12 E. **Greyhound,** 540 State St., in Watertown (☎788-8110 or 800-231-2222; open M-F 9am-1pm, 3-4pm, and 6:10-6:30pm; Sa-Su only at departure times), runs to: Albany (6hr., 2 per day, $43); New York City (8hr., 2 per day, $51-57); Syracuse (1¾hr., 2 per day, $13-15). **Thousand Islands Bus Lines** (☎287-2790) departs from the same station M-F at 1pm for Alexandria Bay ($5.60) and Clayton ($3.55). Return trips leave Clayton from Gray's Florist, 234 James St. (departs daily 8:45am), and Alexandria Bay from the Dockside Cafe, 17 Market St. (departs daily 8:30am).

The **Clayton Chamber of Commerce,** 517 Riverside Dr., hands out the free and helpful *Clayton Vacation Guide* and *Thousand Islands Seaway Region Travel Guide.* (☎686-3771; www.1000islands-clayton.com. Open mid-June to mid-Sept. daily 9am-5pm; mid-Sept. to mid-June M-F 9am-5pm.) The **Alexandria Bay Chamber of Commerce,** 7 Market St., is just off James St. and offers the *Alexandria Bay Vacation Guide* to aid your travel in the area. (☎482-9531; www.alexbay.org. Open May-Sept. M-F 8am-5:30pm, Sa 10am-4pm, Su 11am-3pm.) The **Cape Vincent Chamber of Commerce,** 175 James St., by the ferry landing, welcomes visitors and distributes the *Cape Vincent Vacation Guide.* (☎654-2481; www.capevincent.org. Open May-Oct. Tu-Sa 9am-5pm; late May to early Sept. also Su-M 10am-4pm.) **Internet Access:** In Clayton, **Hawn Memorial Library,** 220 John St. (☎686-3762. Open M and Th-F 10am-5pm. Tu-W 10am-8pm, Sa 9am-noon.) In Alexandria Bay, **Macsherry Library,** 112 Walton St. (☎482-2241. Open M-Th 9am-12pm, 1-5pm, 7-9pm; F-Sa 9am-noon and 1-5pm.) In Cape Vincent, **Cape Vincent Community Library,** 157 N. Real, at Gouvello St. (☎654-2132. Open Tu and Th 9am-8pm, F-Sa 9am-1pm.) **Clayton Post Office:** 236 John St. (☎686-3311. Open M-F 9am-4:30pm, Sa 9am-noon.) **Postal Code:** 13624. **Alexandria Bay Post Office:** 13 Bethune St. (☎482-9521. Open M-F 8:30am-5pm, Sa 9am-noon.) **Postal Code:** 13607. **Cape Vincent Post Office:** 362 Broadway St., across from the village green. (☎654-2424. Open M-F 8am-4:30pm, Sa 9:30-11:30am.) **Postal Code:** 13618. **Area Code:** 315.

⌂ ACCOMMODATIONS. Along the western edge of the seaway in Cape Vincent, near where Lake Ontario meets the St. Lawrence River, stands the **Tibbett's Point Lighthouse Hostel (HI) ❶,** 33439 County Rte. 6. Take Rte. 12 E into town, turn left onto Broadway, and follow the river until the road ends. The lighthouse is still active, and when the weather is windy, as it often is, the hypnotic rhythm of the waves buffeting the shore lulls visitors to sleep in 26 comfortable bunks. (☎654-3450. Full kitchen with microwave. Linen included. Check-in 5-10pm. Check-out 7-9am. Reservations strongly recommended on weekends July-Aug. Open mid-May to late Oct. Dorms $14, nonmembers $17.) The **Bridgeview Motel ❷,** 42823 Rte. 12 between Alex Bay and Clayton, offers clean, no-frills rooms with air conditioning and TVs for reasonable rates. (☎482-4906.

OUT OF THE WAY

TOURING THE 1000 ISLANDS

With over 1800 islands spotting 40 mi. of coastline, the Thousand Island Seaway is a perfect place to explore. Large scenic cruises can offer good views, but to navigate more closely or go ashore many of the islands, a more personal watercraft is necessary. **Whiskey Island,** a tiny island in the middle of the seaway several miles north of Alexandria Bay, is totally deserted—anchor your boat offshore and dive into the St. Lawrence for a refreshing swim. If the waters of the open river are too choppy or cold, head to warmer water at the **Lake of the Isles,** an inland sea within Wellesley Island, open to the river by a narrow channel. Countless lighthouses are hidden within the narrow waterways that slice between islands, and amazing homes can be found south of Kingston along the Canadian Channel, where seawalls and drywall are indistinguishable. It is legal to cross to the other side of the river and enter Canada, but don't linger too long—the law states that you may cross the border only as long as your boat is moving. Be aware that the river serves as a national boundary; if you stop, you may be greeted by an orange helicopter or two.

For boat rentals or maps, contact the **Alexandria Bay Chamber of Commerce, p. 271.** Explore, have fun, and unlock the secrets of the islands for yourself.

Open May to mid-Oct. Rooms $39-59.) There are numerous state and private campgrounds in the area, especially along Rte. 12 E. Sites, however, are usually close together and fill up well in advance on weekends. ■**Wellesley Island ❶**, across the toll bridge ($2) on I-81 N before Canada, boasts 2600 acres of marshes and woodland with hiking. The pristine sand beach in the park near the marina is perfect for a pleasant dip in the water on a warm day. (☎482-2722. 430 sites plus cabins. Waterfront sites B19-23 or B1-8 are incredible, but require reservations far in advance. Hot showers and nature center. Sites $13-19, with electricity $19, full hookup $25. Registration fee $2.75. Cabins with 4 beds, refrigerator, stove, microwave, and picnic table $40-51. Day use $7 per car. Boat rentals $15 per day for rowboats and canoes, $60 per day plus gas for 16 ft. motor boats. Lifeguard on duty mid-June to early Sept. daily 11am-8pm, weather permitting.) Reservations for all New York state parks can be made for $9 at www.reserveamerica.com or by calling ☎800-456-2267. The less-crowded **Burnham Point State Park ❶**, on Rte. 12 E, 4½ mi. east of Cape Vincent and 11 mi. west of Clayton, has a wonderful view of the water and three picnic areas among the 49 sites, but lacks a beach. (☎654-2324. Hot showers. Open late May to early Sept. daily 7am-9:30pm. Sites $13-19, with electricity $19-23. Registration $2.75. Boat dockage $6 per day. Day use $6 per car. Wheelchair accessible.)

■▐ **FOOD AND NIGHTLIFE.** The Thousand Island Seaway hosts diverse food options, and the nightlife of Alex Bay ranges from comfortable seaside decks to wild bars that fill the night air with music and laughter. The most popular destination for cheap eats in Alex Bay is **Poor John's ❶**, off James St. at the main intersection downtown. Mouthwatering quarter-pound burgers are the specialty ($2.50) and locals form huge lines to get them around lunchtime. (☎408-2502. Open daily 10am-11pm, no hot food after 7pm.) The relaxed atmosphere of Clayton is nowhere more apparent than at the **St. Lawrence Gallery Cafe ❷**, off Riverside Dr. downtown. Try an open-faced reuben made with authentic Thousand Island dressing ($7) or a blueberry fruit tea ($3) while playing checkers at a table placed among the craftwork of local artisans. (☎794-0871. Open Apr.-Oct. M-Sa 8am-5pm, Su 9am-3pm.) **Aubrey's Inn ❷**, 126 S. James St. in Cape Vincent, serves some of the best deals in the seaway beside an indoor mural of the Tibbett's Point Lighthouse. (☎654-3754. Breakfast $1.50-6. Most entrees $7-9. Open daily 7am-9pm.)

Nightlife in the Thousand Islands region is located in the heart of Alexandria Bay. Numerous bars and clubs line the docks of the seaway and most offer live music and drink specials, but nowhere is the spirit of summer more alive than at **Skiffs,** at the corner of James St. and Market St. A wide variety of live music and nightly drink specials like "Dollar Labatt Wednesdays" cause flocks of tourists and locals of all ages to pack this bar nightly. (☎482-7543. Open daily noon-2am.)

◉ **EXPLORING THE SEAWAY.** Clayton and Cape Vincent tend to be quieter and less expensive, while Alex Bay is more bustling and touristy. Popular activities include scenic tours of the waterways and ferry rides. With fact-packed live narrations, **Uncle Sam Boat Tours,** 604 Riverside Dr., in Clayton (☎686-3511), and 47 James St., in Alexandria Bay (☎482-2611 or 800-253-9229), delivers good views of the islands and their plush estates, including the famous **Boldt Castle** on Heart Island. A variety of tours highlight the seaway, most of which depart from Alexandria Bay; a 3hr. scenic tour also leaves from Clayton. (Tours leave daily from Clayton July-Sept., Alex Bay May to late Oct. $7-35, ages 4-12 $4.50-25; prices vary with type and duration of tour. Boldt Castle: $4.75, ages 4-12 $3. Reserve in advance for lunch or dinner cruises.) In Alexandria Bay, **Empire Boat Lines,** 5 Fuller St., sends out smaller boats able to navigate very close to the islands, and provides scenic tours, tours to Boldt Castle, and regular service to **Singer Castle,** packed full of secret rooms and passageways. (☎482-8687 or 888-449-2539. Tours: $13-30, ages 7-14 $10-24. Singer Castle: $10, ages 6-12 $5.) **Ferries** run from Cape Vincent to **Wolfe Island,** a quaint island with a strawberry farm and golf course, and a stepping stone to the shops and restaurants of Kingston in Canada. (☎783-0638. Ferries depart from the Cape Vincent Ferry Dock along Club St. and run May to mid-Oct., 10 per day. Tickets may be purchased on the ferry. $2 per person, $8 per car and driver, bicycles $2. Picture ID required.)

Fishing trips and charters are the preferred way to explore the islands and waterways for many. **Fishing licenses** are available at the **Town Clerk's Office,** 405 Riverside Dr., in Clayton. (☎686-3512. Open M-F 9am-noon and 1-4pm. Licenses $15 per day, $25 per week, $40 per season.) Many bait shops and sporting goods stores stay open longer hours and sell licenses to fishermen in need. Tell the tale of the big one that got away with **1000 Islands Fishing Charters,** 335 Riverside Dr., inside the 1000 Islands Inn in Clayton. Offering both drift fishing trips with larger groups of people and private charters, 1000 Islands can accommodate your preferences. (☎686-2381 or 877-544-4241. Trips July to late Aug. Reservations required. 4hr. "Drift Trip" $45 per person, tackle and bait included. 7½hr. private charter $75-160 per person, depending upon the number of people in the group. Tackle included.) Check out **Hunt's Dive Shop,** 40782 Rte. 12 between Alex Bay and Clayton, for an underwater peek at one or more of the many wrecks that line of floor of the seaway. (☎686-1070. $65 per person, min. 2 people. Equipment rentals $50 per person. Must have certification. Open May-Sept. daily 9am-5:30pm.)

The **Antique Boat Museum,** 750 Mary St., in Clayton, houses practically every make and model of boat ever built. Admission includes free rentals on a variety of skiffs. On Wednesdays in summer, the museum offers free sailing classes and sailboat usage to increase boating awareness. (☎686-4104. Open mid-May to mid-Oct. daily 9am-5pm. $8, seniors $7, students and ages 6-17 $4, under 5 free. Call for info on sailing classes.) **French Creek Marina,** 250 Wahl St. (☎686-3621), off Strawberry Ln. just south of the junction of Rte. 12 and Rte. 12 E, rents 14 ft. fishing boats ($50 per day), launches boats ($5), and provides overnight docking ($20).

NEW JERSEY

Visitors unfamiliar with New Jersey often expect to find only the notorious metro-area chemical plants that have given the state a reputation as a polluted mess. But just a few minutes outside the cities, New Jersey boasts corn fields as rich as Ohio's and beaches as charming as North Carolina's. Perhaps the most famous of New Jersey's beaches is the casino-oriented Atlantic City, but a plethora of smaller towns along the south Jersey coast offer slower-paced or more family-friendly delights such as bird-watching, antiquing, and clamming. Many of these attractions cater to busy New York and New England residents who want a weekend on the sand or in the casino without the expense of flying west or farther south.

🛈 PRACTICAL INFORMATION

Capital: Trenton.

Visitor Info: State Division of Tourism, 20 W. State St., P.O. Box 826, Trenton 08625 (☎609-292-2470; www.visitnj.org). **State Bird:** The mosquito.

Postal Abbreviation: NJ. **Sales Tax:** 6%; no tax on clothing. **Tolls:** Keep a fistful of change handy; New Jersey's tunnels, bridges, and turnpikes are littered with toll booths.

MID-ATLANTIC

ATLANTIC CITY

☎ **609**

For 70 years, board game enthusiasts have been wheeling and dealing with Atlantic City geography as depicted on the Monopoly board. Meanwhile, the opulence of the original Boardwalk and Park Place faded into neglect and then into megadollar tackiness. During a 1970s refurbishment effort, giant casino-resorts were built over the rubble of the old boardwalk, sacrificing the city's old-time charm in hopes of attracting tourist dollars with glitz and glamor. The reincarnation failed to turn Atlantic City into a second Las Vegas, leaving poverty and crime lurking around the fringes of the modern downtown. Yet there is still plenty to enjoy: gambling, tanning, games, and rides make Atlantic City a exhilarating destination.

⊫ TRANSPORTATION

Atlantic City lies halfway down the New Jersey seashore, accessible via the **Garden State Parkway** and the **Atlantic City Expressway,** and easily reached by train or bus from Philadelphia or New York City.

Airport: Atlantic City International (☎ 645-7895 or 800-892-0354; www.acairport.com), 20 min. west of Atlantic City in Pamona.

Buses: Greyhound (☎ 340-2000). Buses travel from **New York Port Authority** (2½hr., one-way from $26) and **Philadelphia** (1½hr., round-trip specials $14) and most major casinos almost every hour. **New Jersey Transit** (☎ 215-569-3752 or 800-582-5946), on Atlantic Ave., between Michigan and Ohio St., has hourly service to **New York City** ($24, seniors, children, and disabled $11). **Gray Line Tours** (☎ 800-669-0051; www.grayline.com; terminal open 24hr.) has daytrips from **New York City** (2½hr, $27).

Taxi: Atlantic City Airport Taxi (☎ 383-1457 or 877-568-8294). $25 flat rate from the airport to Atlantic City.

Alternative Forms of Transportation: Plentiful **Rolling Chair Rides** will take 2 passengers a maximum of 26 blocks. (☎ 347-7148.) The **Atlantic City Jitney** makes stops up and down Pacific and Atlantic Ave. (☎ 344-8642.)

Free Parking: Meterless parking is available on some residential areas. Try Oriental Ave. at New Jersey Ave., near the Garden Pier Historic Museum, for free 3hr. parking within walking distance of the Boardwalk. *Be careful at night: this area is more desolate than other parts of the city.*

◼✈ 🛈 ORIENTATION AND PRACTICAL INFORMATION

Attractions cluster on and around the **Boardwalk,** which runs east-west along the Atlantic Ocean. Running parallel to the Boardwalk, **Pacific** and **Atlantic Avenue** offer cheap restaurants, hotels, and convenience stores. *Atlantic Ave. can be dangerous after dark, and any street farther out can be dangerous even by day.* Getting around on foot is easy on the Boardwalk. **Parking lots** nearby run $3-7.

Visitor Info: Atlantic Expressway Visitors Center, 1 mi. after the Pleasantville Toll Plaza (☎ 449-7130). Offers pamphlets, brochures, and help with free parking. Open daily 9am-5pm. The **Atlantic City Convention Center and Visitors Bureau,** 2314 Pacific Ave., is near the Boardwalk. (☎ 888-228-4748; www.atlanticcitynj.com.) Open daily 9am-5pm. On the Boardwalk, try the **Visitor Info Center** at Mississippi St. (☎ 888-228-4748). Open daily 9:30am-5:30pm, late May to early Sept. also Th-Su 9:30am-8pm.

Medical Services: Atlantic City Medical Center, 1925 Pacific Ave. (☎ 344-4081), at Michigan.

Hotlines: Rape and Abuse Hotline, ☎646-6767. **Gambling Abuse,** ☎800-426-2537. Both 24hr.

Post Office: 1701 Pacific Ave. (☎345-4212), at Illinois Ave. Open M-F 8:30am-6pm, Sa 8:30am-12:30pm. **Postal Code:** 08401. **Area Code:** 609.

⌐ ACCOMMODATIONS

Inn of the Irish Pub, 164 St. James Pl. (☎344-9063; www.theirishpub.com), between New York and Tennessee Ave. on the Boardwalk, near the Ramada Tower, has spacious rooms, relaxing rocking chairs and refreshing Atlantic breeze. Entertainment in downstairs bar. Key deposit $7. Singles with shared bath M-F $25, Sa-Su $30. Doubles with shared bath $40/$45, with private shower and twin beds $55/$80. Must be 21+. ❷

Comfort Inn, 154 S. Kentucky Ave. (☎348-4000), between Martin Luther King Blvd. and New York Ave., near the Sands (p. 276). Rooms with 1 king or 2 queen beds and a jacuzzi, free continental breakfast, parking, and heated pool. Rooms with ocean views are $20 extra, but have fridge, microwave, and a bigger jacuzzi. Reserve well in advance for Sa-Su and holidays. June-Aug. $119-200; Sept.-May rooms $59-69 weekdays, though prices rise well over $100 on weekends in May and Sept. ❹

Red Carpet Motel, 1630 Albany Ave. (☎348-3171). A bit out of the way, off the Atlantic Expwy. on the way into town. Has standard, comfortable, uninspiring rooms for low prices. Cable TV, restaurant. Doubles $39-59; quads $55-79. Prices can jump to $130 on summer weekends. *Be careful in the surrounding neighborhood after dark.* ❸

Shady Pines Campground, 443 S. 6th Ave. (☎652-1516), in Absecon, 6 mi. from Atlantic City. Take Exit 12 from the Expwy. or Exit 40 from the Garden State Pkwy. This leafy, 140-site campground sports a pool, playground, laundry, firewood service, and new showers and restrooms. Quiet hours 11pm-8am. Call ahead for summer weekend reservations. Open Mar.-Oct. Sites with full hookup $35. ❷

⌐ FOOD

Though not recommended by nutritionists, $0.75 hot dogs and $1.50 pizza slices are available all over the Boardwalk. Some of the best deals in town await at the casinos, where all-you-can-eat lunch ($7) and dinner ($11) buffets abound. Tastier, less tacky food can be found a little farther from the shore.

▨ Inn of the Irish Pub, 164 St. James Pl. (☎345-9613; www.theirishpub.com), serves damn good food. Start off with a "20th St. Sampler" (Buffalo wings, fried mozzarella, potato skins, and chicken thumbs; $7). The "Poor Richard" lunch special (11:30am-2pm) includes a pre-selected daily sandwich and a cup of soup for $2. Have your choice of sandwiches, from Virginia ham to liverwurst and onions, for only $2-4. All-you-can-eat Su brunch $7. $6 dinner specials M-F 2-8pm and Sa-Su until 8pm. Domestic drafts $1. Open 24hr. Cash only. ❶

White House Sub Shop, 2301 Arctic Ave. (☎345-8599, take-out 345-1564; www.whitehousesubshop.com), at Mississippi Ave. Frank Sinatra was rumored to have had these immense subs (half-size sandwiches are nearly a foot in length, full-sizes twice as long) flown to him while he was on tour. Pictures of White House sub-lovers Joe DiMaggio, Wayne Newton, and Mr. T adorn the walls. Half sandwiches $3-7, whole $9-14. Open M-Th 10am-10pm, F-Su 10am-10:30pm. Cash only. ❷

Tony's Baltimore Grille, 2800 Atlantic Ave. (☎345-5766), between Pacific and Baltic, at Iowa Ave. Tourists can't resist the old-time Italian atmosphere with personal jukeboxes, not to mention the $3-8 pizzas and pasta. Seafood platter $12. Open daily 11am-3am. Bar open 24hr. Cash only. ❷

Johor, 28 S. Tennessee Ave. (☎ 344-8928). This lunch and dinner restaurant specializes in Malaysian and Vietnamese cuisine. The mango chicken ($13) and coconut shrimp ($18) are popular choices, but soups are the real specialty. Vegetarian options available. Most entrees $10-20. Open daily 11:30am-midnight. ❹

CASINOS, BOARDWALK, AND BEACHES

All casinos on the Boardwalk fall within a dice toss of one another. The farthest south is the elegant **Hilton** (☎ 347-7111 or 800-257-8677; www.caesars.com/hilton/ atlanticcity), between Providence and Boston Ave., and the farthest north is the gaudy **Showboat** (☎ 343-4000 or 800-342-7724; www.harrahs.com/our_casinos/sac), at Delaware Ave. and Boardwalk. Donald Trump's glittering **Trump Taj Mahal,** 1000 Boardwalk (☎ 449-1000; www.trumptaj.com), at Virginia Ave., is an Atlantic City landmark and too ostentatious to be missed. In true *Monopoly* form, Trump owns two other hotel-casinos in the city: the recently remodeled **Trump Plaza,** at Mississippi and Boardwalk (☎ 441-6000 or 800-677-7378; www.trumpplaza.com), lures in classy types looking for an elegant stay while the **Trump Marina's** motto—"Play hard, live wild"—appeals to a younger, more scantily dressed crowd on Huron Blvd. (☎ 441-2000; www.trumpmarina.com), at the Marina. In summer, energetic partiers go to "rock the dock" at Trump Castle's indoor/outdoor bar and restaurant, **The Deck** (☎ 877-477-4697). Many a die is cast at **Caesar's Boardwalk Resort and Casino,** 2100 Pacific Ave. (☎ 348-4411 or 800-433-0104; www.caesarsatlantic-city.com), at Arkansas Ave. The flashy **Sands** (☎ 441-4000 or 800-227-2637; www.acsands.com), at Indiana Ave., markets itself to serious gamblers as "the players' place." The two newest casinos in town are **The Borgata** (☎ 317-1000 or 866-692-6742; www.theborgata.com), a scintillating golden beacon in the Marina district, near the Trump Marina Hotel Casino and Harrah's, and **Resorts Atlantic City** (☎ 344-6000 or 800-336-6378; www.resortsac.com), next to the Taj Mahal. Resorts offers scandalous-sounding "rendezvous rooms" in addition to its regular hotel and casino operations. All are open 24hr.

There's something for everyone in Atlantic City, thanks to the Boardwalk. Those under 21 **gamble for prizes,** ride **go-karts,** and play **paintball** at the many arcades that line the Boardwalk, including **Central Pier Arcade & Speedway,** at the Boardwalk and Tennessee Ave., near St. James Pl. (☎ 345-5219). It feels like real gambling, but the teddy bear in the window is easier to win than the convertible on display at Caesar's. The historic **Steel Pier** (☎ 898-7645 or 866-386-6659; www.steelpier.com), at Virginia Ave., juts into the coastal waters with a Ferris wheel that spins riders over the Atlantic. If your luck at the casinos' roulette wheels doesn't carry over to the pier's games of "skill," there's always the roller coaster and carousel to look forward to. (Open M-F 3pm-midnight, Sa-Su noon-1am. Rides $2-5 each, all-day pass $30.) When and if you tire of spending money, check out the historic **Atlantic City Beach** (open 6am-10pm; no alcohol or dogs allowed). Just west of Atlantic City, **Ventnor City** offers more tranquil shores.

CAPE MAY ☎ 609

At the southern extreme of New Jersey's coastline, Cape May is the oldest seashore resort in the US. Though the town's history goes back to the mid-1700s when Philadelphians would come to the shore for recreation and relaxation, Cape May is best known for the Victorian-era houses and hotels that give the resort its nickname, Gingerbread Town. Architecture isn't Cape May's only claim to fame; the town is also known for its fine dining, bird-watching, and sparkling white beaches.

⚎ 7 ORIENTATION AND PRACTICAL INFORMATION. While Cape May is cut off from mainland Delaware, Pennsylvania, and Maryland by the Delaware River, it is easily accessible by car or bus. Start digging for loose change as you follow the tollbooth-laden **Garden State Parkway** as far south as it goes (most tolls $0.35). Watch for signs to Center City until on Lafayette St. Alternatively, take the slower, scenic **Ocean Drive** (Rte. 9) 40 mi. south along the shore from Atlantic City. **Route 55** brings beachgoers from Philadelphia. **NJ Transit** (☎ 215-569-3752 or 973-762-5100) makes a stop at the bus depot on the corner of Lafayette and Ocean St. and runs to: Atlantic City (2hr., 18 per day, $3.80); New York City (5hr., 4 per day, $30); Philadelphia (2½hr., 18 per day, $15). If you're coming from the D.C. area, the 1¾hr. **Cape May-Lewes Ferry** presents a pleasant and more direct alternative to an otherwise potentially long and laborious 3-4hr. drive. (☎ 800-643-3779; www.capemaylewesferry.com. Office open daily 8:30am-4:30pm. 8 per day. Reservations required; call at least 24hr. in advance. Check-in 30min. prior to departure. Passenger cars Apr.-Oct. $25, Nov.-Dec. $20; motorcyclists $23/$18; bicyclists $8/$6.) **Cape May Seashore Lines** runs three old-fashioned trains per day to attractions along the 26 mi. stretch to Tuckahoe. (☎ 884-2675; www.cmslrr.com. One-way $5; round trip $8, ages 2-12 $5.) Bike the beach with the help of **Shields's Bike Rentals,** 11 Gurney Ave. (☎ 898-1818. Open daily 7am-7pm. $4 per hr., $9 per day; tandems $10/$30; surreys $24 per hr.) Other services include: **Welcome Center,** 609 Lafayette St. (☎ 884-9562. Open daily 9am-4:30pm.) **Chamber of Commerce,** 513 Washington St. Mall. (☎ 884-5508; www.capemaychamber.com. Open M-F 9am-5pm, Sa-Su 10am-6pm.) **Washington Street Mall Information Booth,** at Ocean St. (☎ 800-275-4278; www.capemaymac.org. Open in summer daily 9:15am-4pm and 6-9pm; call for low-season hours.) **Internet Access: Cape May County Library,** 30 Mechanic St., in the Cape May Court House. (☎ 463-6350; www.cape-may.county.lib.nj.us. Open Oct.-Apr. M-F 8:30am-9pm, Sa 9am-4:30pm, Su 1-5pm; May-Sept. M-Th 8:30am-9pm, F 8:30am-4:30pm, Sa 9am-4:30pm.) **Post Office:** 700 Washington St., at Franklin St. (☎ 884-3578. Open M-F 9am-5pm, Sa 8:30am-12:30pm.) **Postal Code:** 08204. **Area Code:** 609.

⚏ ACCOMMODATIONS. Sleeping does not come cheaply in Cape May. Luxurious hotels and Victorian B&Bs along the beach run $85-250 per night. Farther from the shore, prices drop. Although the **Hotel Clinton ❷,** 202 Perry St. at S. Lafayette St., may lack stately suites and A/C, the Italian family-owned establishment offers 16 breezy rooms, the most affordable rates in town, and priceless warmth from the charismatic proprietors. (☎ 884-3993. Open mid-June to Sept. Reservations recommended. Singles $30 on weekdays, $35 on weekends; doubles $40/$45. Cash or traveler's checks only.) Next door, the **Parris Inn ❸,** 204 Perry St., rents a variety of spacious, comfortable rooms and apartments (some much nicer than others) less than three blocks from the beach, most with private baths, A/C, and TV. (☎ 884-6363. Open mid-Apr. to Dec. Memorial Day-Labor Day singles $45-65; doubles $65-125. In spring and fall rooms $35-65.) For an elegant stay less than a block from the beach in the heart of a line of colorful Victorian homes and B&Bs, **Poor Richard's Inn ❹,** 17 Jackson St. offers a continental breakfast and antique-laden rooms, all of which have A/C. (☎ 884-3536; www.poorrichardsinn.com. Check-in 1-10pm. Check-out 10:30am. Memorial Day-Oct. $75-120 for shared bath, $120-165 for private bath; low-season $65-110/$110-150.) Campgrounds line U.S. 9 just north of Cape May. In a prime seashore location, **Cape Island Campground ❷,** 709 Rte. 9, is connected to Cape May by Seashore Lines (see above). The fully equipped campground features mini golf, two pools, a playground, a store, and laundry facilities. (☎ 884-3203 or 800-437-7443; www.capeisland.com. Sites with water and electricity $40; with sewage $43; with sewage, cable, and lamp post $46. Low-season $26/$28/$31.)

MID-ATLANTIC

☐❚ FOOD AND NIGHTLIFE. Generic pizza and burger fare along **Beach Avenue**; shell out a few more clams for a more substantial meal at one of the posh beachside restaurants. Crawling with pedestrians hunting for heavenly fudge and saltwater taffy, the **Washington Street Mall** supports several popular food stores and eateries. Start the morning off right with a gourmet breakfast on the porch of the ◪**Mad Batter ❹**, 19 Jackson St. at the Carroll Villa Hotel. Try a stack of blueberry blintz crepes with warm syrup ($7.50) or the orange and almond french toast ($6). For lunch or dinner the excellent, simple chicken satay ($9), the to-die-for crab *mapatello* (puff pastry filled with crab, spinach, onions, and ricotta, covered in a white butter sauce; $23), and other house specials make decision-making difficult. (☎884-5970; www.madbatter.com. Open daily 8am-10pm.) A meal in the smoky interior of the **Ugly Mug ❷**, 426 Washington St. Mall, is well worth the risk of suffocation. Fresh air can be had on the patio as patrons inhale a New England cup o' chowder for $3 or the fried oyster sandwich for $6. (☎884-3459; www.uglymug.biz. Open M-Sa 11am-2am, Su noon-2am; hot food served until 10:30pm.)

The rock scene collects around **Carney's,** on Beach Ave., between Jackson and Decatur St., with nightly entertainment in the summer beginning at 10pm. Themed parties include "Island Tropics" and "Animal House." (☎884-4424. Su jams 4-9pm. 21+ after 10pm. Cover $5. Open daily 11:30am-2am.) A chic crowd congregates at **Cabana's,** at the corner of Decatur St. and Beach Ave. across from the beach. You'll have to find a lot of sand dollars if you want to try the sesame crusted tuna with wasabi in this classy setting, but there is no cover for the nightly blues or jazz. (☎884-4800; www.cabanasonthebeach.com. Entrees $14-22. Open daily noon-2am. M star-search karaoke night. Su $0.50 Coors Light drafts and free pizza 10am-midnight. 21+ after 10pm, diners excepted. Cover F-Sa $5.) Check your e-mail at the **Magic Brain Cybercafe,** 31 Perry St., a spotless new Internet cafe with an amicable staff, a prime location less than one block from the beach, and a variety of coffee and espresso drinks. (☎884-8188; www.magicbraincybercafe.com. Internet access $4 per 15min., $7 per 30min., $12 per hr. Open daily 7:30am-10:30pm. Cash only.)

◪ HITTING THE BEACH. Cape May's sands actually sparkle, studded with the famous Cape May "diamonds" (actually quartz pebbles). A **beach tag** is required for beachgoers over age 11 from late May to early September 10am-5pm. Tags are available from roaming vendors or from the **Beach Tag Office,** located at Grant and Beach Dr. (☎884-9522. Open daily 10am-5pm. $4, 3-day $8, weekly $11, seasonal $17.) Those in search of exercise and a spectacular view of the seashore can ascend the 199 steps to the beacon of the 1859 **Cape May Lighthouse** in **Cape May Point State Park,** west of town at the end of the point. (Lighthouse ☎884-5404, visitors center 884-2159; www.capemaymac.org. Park open daily 8am-dusk. Free. Lighthouse open Apr.-Nov. daily 9am-8pm; Dec.-Mar. Sa-Su 8am-4pm. $5, ages 3-12 $1. Visitors center open daily July-Aug. 9am-8pm; Sept.-June 8am-4:30pm.) The behemoth bunker next to the lighthouse is a WWII gun emplacement, used to scan the shore for German U-boats. In summer, several shuttles run the 5 mi. from the bus depot on Lafayette St. to the lighthouse ($5, ages 3-12 $4). Three trails commence at the Lighthouse Visitors Center: the red (½ mi., wheelchair accessible), yellow (1¼ mi., moderate and flat), and blue trails (2 mi., moderate and flat, last leg takes hikers along the oceanfront back to the start) boast excellent bird-watching and clearly marked paths through marsh and oceanside dunes. Bicyclists or serious hikers may want to consider taking the approximately 40 mi. section of the New Jersey Coastal Heritage Trail from Cape May to Ocean City. Along the way they will pass the Hereford Inlet Lighthouse, the Wetlands Institute, and Corson's Inlet State Park. Even migratory birds flock to Cape May's freshwater ponds for a break from the long, southbound flight. Glimpse more than 300 types of feathered vacationers at the **Cape May Bird Observatory**, 701 E. Lake Dr., on Cape May Point, a bird-watcher's paradise. Bird maps, field trips, and workshops are available, along with advice about where to go for the best birdwatching. (☎884-2736; www.njaudubon.org. Open Tu-Su 10am-5pm.) For a look at some larger creatures, including dolphins and whales, **Cape May Whale Watch and Research Center** offers 2-3hr. tours. (☎898-0055 or 888-531-0055; www.capemay-whalewatch.com. Trips run Apr.-Dec. $20-28, ages 7-12 $10-14. One child age 6 and under free with each paid adult.) **South End Surf Shop**, 311 Beach Ave., rents beach necessities. (☎898-0988. Open Apr.-Sept. daily 9am-10pm. Surfboard $20 per day, or $35 per 2 days.) If you want to strike out a little farther into the ocean, **Miss Chris Marina**, on the corner of 3rd St. and Wilson Dr., rents **kayaks** and offers 1½-2hr. guided boat tours of the salt marshes. (☎884-3351. Open 6am-7pm. Single kayak $15 first hr., $5 each additional hr. Double kayak $20/ $10. Boat tours $30 single boat, $45 double.)

PENNSYLVANIA

Established as a colony to protect Quakers from persecution, Pennsylvania has since been central to the American fight for religious and political freedom. In 1776, it served as the drafting-place of the Declaration of Independence. In 1976, Philadelphia groomed its historic shrines for the nation's bicentennial, and today its colonial monuments serve as the centerpiece of the city's ambitious renewal. Pittsburgh, the steel city with a raw image, was once dirty enough to fool streetlights into burning during the day, but has lately begun a cultural renaissance. Removed from the noise of its urban areas, central Pennsylvania's landscape has retained much of the rustic beauty discovered by colonists centuries ago, from the farms of Lancaster County to the gorges of the Allegheny Plateau.

⚑ PRACTICAL INFORMATION

Capital: Harrisburg.

Visitor Info: Pennsylvania Travel and Tourism, 400 North St., Harrisburg 17120 (☎717-787-5453 or 800-237-4363; www.experiencepa.com).

Bureau of State Parks, Rachel Carson State Office Bldg., 400 Market St., Harrisburg 17108 (☎888-727-2757; www.dcnr.state.pa.us/stateparks). Open M-Sa 7am-5pm.

Postal Abbreviation: PA. **Sales Tax:** 6%.

PHILADELPHIA   ☎215

With his band of Quakers, William Penn founded the City of Brotherly Love in 1682. But it was Ben, not Penn, who laid the foundation for the urban metropolis it is today. Benjamin Franklin, the ingenious American ambassador, inventor, and womanizer, almost single-handedly built Philadelphia into an American colonial capital; his name is ever-present in the city's museums and landmarks. Sightseers will eat up Philly's historic attractions, world-class museums, and architectural accomplishments along with the famous cheesesteaks and the endless culinary choices of the city's ethnic neighborhoods.

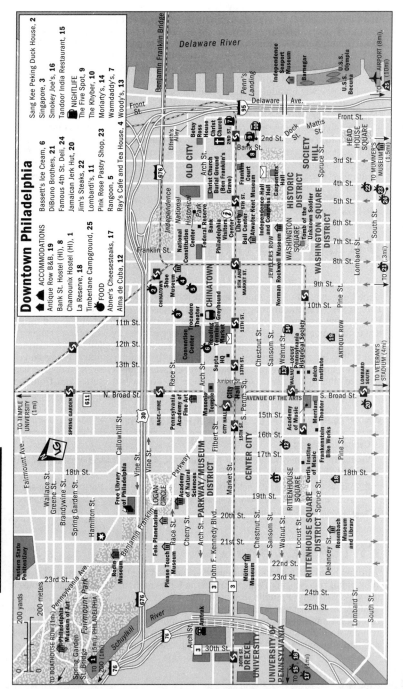

Downtown Philadelphia

▲ ACCOMMODATIONS
Antique Row B&B, **19**
Bank St. Hostel (HI), **8**
Chamounix Hostel (HI), **1**
La Reserve, **18**
Timberlane Campground, **25**

● FOOD
Abner's Cheesesteaks, **17**
Alma de Cuba, **12**
Bassett's Ice Cream, **6**
DiBruno Brothers, **21**
Famous 4th St. Deli, **24**
Jamaican Jerk Hut, **20**
Jim's Steaks, **22**
Lombardi's, **11**
Pink Rose Pastry Shop, **23**
Rangoon, **5**
Ray's Cafe and Tea House, **4**

Sang Kee Peking Duck House, **2**
Singapore, **3**
Smokey Joe's, **16**
Tandoor India Restaurant, **15**

♫ NIGHTLIFE
The Five Spot, **9**
The Khyber, **10**
Moriarty's, **14**
Warmdaddy's, **7**
Woody's, **13**

■ INTERCITY TRANSPORTATION

Airport: Philadelphia International (☎800-745-4283 or 937-6937; www.phl.org), 8 mi. southwest of Center City on I-76. **SEPTA Airport Rail Line** (☎580-7800; www.septa.org) runs from Center City to the airport in around 20min. Trains run from Market East Station to the airport daily every 30min. 4:25am-11:25pm; from the airport (Terminal E) to city stations 5am-midnight. $5.50 each way at window. Last train from airport 12:09am. A taxi to downtown costs about $20.

Trains: Amtrak, 30th St. Station (☎800-872-7245), at Market St. in University City. Station open 24hr. To: **Baltimore** (1-2hr., M-F 10 per day, $43); **Boston** (5-6hr., 10 per day, $80); **New York City** (1½-2hr., 10 per day, $49); **Pittsburgh** (7½hr., 2 per day, $39); **Washington, D.C.** (1½-2hr., 10 per day, $49). Ticket office open M-F 5:10am-10:30pm, Sa-Su 6:10am-10:30pm.

Buses: Greyhound, 1001 Filbert St. (☎931-4075 or 800-231-2222), at 10th and Filbert downtown. Station open daily 24hr. To: **Atlantic City** (1-1½hr., 18 per day, $10); **Baltimore** (3hr., 7 per day, $21); **Boston** (7hr., 16 per day, $55); **New York City** (2-3hr., 24 per day, $21); **Pittsburgh** (6-7hr., 7 per day, $41); **Washington, D.C.** (3hr., 10 per day, $22). **New Jersey Transit** (☎569-3752 or 800-772-3606; office open M-F 8am-5pm) is in the same station. To **Atlantic City** (1½hr.; departs every 30min.; $11 one-way, $20 round-trip) and points on the New Jersey shore.

■ ORIENTATION

Penn planned his city as a logical and easily accessible grid, though the prevalence of one-way streets can cause a migraine behind the wheel. Whether you are walking or driving, the maps and arrows pointing toward major destinations that are posted on every downtown street corner are lifesavers. The north-south streets ascend numerically from the **Delaware River,** flowing from **Penn's Landing** and **Independence Hall** on the east side to the **Schuylkill River** (SKOO-kill) on the west. The first street is **Front;** the others follow consecutively from 2nd to 69th across the Schuylkill River. Moving outward from the downtown area known as **Center City** that surrounds Rte. 676, poorer areas lie to the south and northeast and more affluent neighborhoods are found in the northwest. The intersection of **Broad (14th)** and **Market Street** is the focal point of Center City, marked by the ornate City Hall. Be warned: street addresses often refer to alleys not pictured on standard maps of the city. The **SEPTA transportation map,** available free from the tourist office, is probably the most complete map of the city.

Driving around town is not difficult, but finding a place to park your car and then paying for it can be a nightmare. If you are extremely lucky or patient, you may be able to find curbside metered parking. Otherwise, parking in most lots near the historic sites is about $13 per day or $3-4 per half hour. If you are willing to get up early, most lots run an "early bird special," charging only $6-7 as long as you park before 9 or 10am and leave before 6pm. Meterless 2hr. parking spaces can sometimes be found in the Washington Sq. district or on the cobblestones of Dock St. In centrally-located Chinatown, you can park in the lot on Arch St. between 9th and 10th St. for only $6. To park near Center City or the Rodin Museum, the parking lot directly behind the **Free Library of Philadelphia** offers a $5 flat rate on weekends. A final option is to park outside the city and ride Philly's **buses** and **subway** to major downtown destinations (see **Local Transportation,** below). *Public transit can be unsafe after dark.*

NEIGHBORHOODS

The **Historic District** stretches from Front to 6th St. and from Race to South St. The hip **Washington Square District** runs from 6th to Broad St. and Vine to South St. The northern half of the historic district is also referred to as **Old City,** whereas the southern half can also be called **Society Hill**. The affluent **Rittenhouse Square District** lies to the west of **Society Hill,** between Walnut and Pine St. **Chinatown** comprises the blocks around the intersection of 10th and Arch St., while the **Museum District,** in the northwest quadrant of the city, is centered around the Benjamin Franklin Pkwy. Across the Schuylkill River to the west, **University City** includes the sprawling campuses of the **University of Pennsylvania** and **Drexel University.**

▐ LOCAL TRANSPORTATION

Public Transit: Southeastern Pennsylvania Transportation Authority (SEPTA), 1234 Market St. (☎580-7800). Extensive bus and rail service to the suburbs. Buses serve the 5-county area. Most operate 5am-2am, some 24hr. There are 2 major subway routes: the blue, east-west **Market Street line** (including 30th St. Station and the historic area) and the orange, north-south **Broad Street line** (including the stadium complex in south Philadelphia). *The subway is unsafe after dark; buses are usually safer.* Pick up a free SEPTA system map at any subway stop. $2, transfers $0.60. Unlimited all-day pass for both $5.50, unlimited weekly pass $19, unlimited monthly pass $70. The subway closes around midnight, when **all-night shuttle** service begins; shuttles stop at the major subway stops about every 10-15min. until the subway reopens in the morning.

Tours: In the tourist area, convenient purple **Phlash** buses hit all major sights. (☎923-8522. July-Aug. daily 10am-6pm every 12min. $1, seniors and under 5 free. Day pass $3.) **Philadelphia Sight-Seeing Tours** provides knowledgeable trolley drivers and guides. Hop on and off all day or take the 90min. tour in one go. (☎925-8687. Runs every 30min. $20, ages 6-12 $5; extra day $6/$3.) For more extensive coverage of the city, try the double-decker buses of the **Big Bus Company.** (☎866-324-4287. 90min. tours every 20min. 9am-6pm. $25, children ages 5-12 $10.) Last but not least, **Ride the Ducks** offers a 60-80min. land and water tour in an amphibious vehicle. (☎227-3825. $23, ages 3-12 $13. Runs every 30min. 10am-7pm; box office opens at 9am.)

Taxi: Yellow Cab ☎922-8400. **City Cab** ☎492-6500.

Car Rental: Alamo ☎492-3960 or 800-327-9633.

Bike Rental: Frankenstein Bike Works, 1529 Spruce St. (☎893-0415). Open May-Sept. M-Sa 11am-6:30pm, Su noon-4pm. Bikes $8 per hr., $25 per day.

▐ PRACTICAL INFORMATION

Visitor Info: The **City Visitor Center** and the **National Park Service Visitors Center** (☎965-2305 or 800-537-7676; www.independencevisitorcenter.com) are both on 5th St. between Market and Chestnut St. Pick up maps, schedules, brochures, and the free *Gazette* for upcoming city events. Open daily 8:30am-5pm.

GLBT Resources: Gay and Lesbian Peer Counseling Services, ☎732-8255. Operates M-F 6-9pm. **William Way Lesbian, Gay, and Bisexual Community Center** (☎732-2220; www.waygay.org), 1315 Spruce St., has info about GLBT events and activities. Open M-F 11:30am-10pm, Sa-Su 11:30am-7pm, Su 10:30am-7pm.

Hotlines: Suicide and Crisis Intervention, ☎686-4420. **Youth Crisis Line,** ☎787-0633. **Women Against Abuse,** ☎386-7777. All 24hr.

Internet Access: The **Free Library of Philadelphia** offers free Internet access. Open M-W 9am-9pm, Th-Sa 9am-5pm.

Post Office: 1234 Market St. (☎800-275-8767), downtown. Open daily 8:30am-5:30pm. **Postal Code:** 19104. **Area Code:** 215.

⌐ ACCOMMODATIONS

Aside from its two hostels, inexpensive lodging in Philadelphia is uncommon, but with advance arrangements, comfortable rooms close to Center City can be had for around $60. The motels near the airport at Exit 9A on I-95 sacrifice location for the most affordable rates in the area. The personable proprietors at **Antique Row Bed and Breakfast** and **La Reserve** (see below) will recommend rooms if they're full. **Bed and Breakfast Connections/Bed and Breakfast of Philadelphia,** in Devon, PA, books rooms in Philadelphia and southeastern Pennsylvania. (☎610-687-3565; www.bnbphiladelphia.com. Open M-F 9am-5pm. Reserve at least a week in advance; one-time registration fee $10. Singles $60-90; doubles $75-250.)

▨ **Chamounix Mansion International Youth Hostel (HI),** 3250 Chamounix Dr. (☎878-3676 or 800-379-0017; www.philahostel.org), in West Fairmount Park. Take bus #38 from lower Market St. to Ford and Cranston Rd.; take Ford Rd., turn left on Chamounix Dr., and follow to hostel. A young, energetic staff maintains an uncommonly lavish hostel in a converted mansion with 80 beds. Large kitchen, TV/VCR, piano, and bikes. Free parking, discounted bus tokens, and free summer Philadelphia Orchestra passes. Internet access $1 per 5min., or use the free wireless hot spot. Smaller rooms with 2-4 beds available. Linen $2.50. Laundry $2. Check-in 8-11am and 4:30pm-midnight. Lockout 11am-4:30pm. Curfew midnight. Dorms $15, nonmembers $18. ❶

▨ **Bank Street Hostel (HI),** 32 S. Bank St. (☎922-0222 or 800-392-4678; www.bankstreethostel.com). From the bus station, walk down Market St.; it's in an alleyway between 2nd and 3rd St. This hostel in the historic district offers 70 beds, A/C, a big-screen TV, free coffee and tea, kitchen, laundry facilities, and pool table. 9am musical wake-up call blasted from the speaker system. Movie shown nightly at 9pm. Internet access $1 per 4min. Linen $3. Lockout 11am-4:30pm. Curfew 2:30am. Mail payment in advance to reserve—call for details. Dorms $18, nonmembers $21. Cash only. ❶

Antique Row Bed and Breakfast, 341 S. 12th St. (☎592-7802; www.antiquerowbnb.com). An enchanting traditional B&B decorated with tasteful antiques in the heart of colonial rowhouses. The engaging owner serves tourist advice and a hearty breakfast. 4 apartments geared toward longer visits with cable TV, utilities, and laundry. Free local calls. Rooms $65-110; reduced rates for longer stays. ❹

La Reserve (Bed and Breakfast Center City), 1804 Pine St. (☎735-1137; www.centercitybed.com). Take I-676 to the 23rd St. exit and bear right. After 10 blocks, turn left onto Pine. Personable owner entertains guests with lively dinner parties and visits from local musicians. He is also a reliable source of Philadelphia advice and sidesplitting humor. Full breakfast. Spacious rooms, A/C, authentic antique decor, and free overnight curbside parking across the street. Doubles $85-110. ❹

Timberlane Campground, 117 Timberlane Rd. (☎856-423-6677; www.timberlanecampground.com), 15 mi. from Center City, across the Delaware River in Clarksboro, NJ, is the closest campground to Philly. Take U.S. 295 S to Exit 18B (Clarksboro), follow straight through the traffic light ½ mi., and turn right on Friendship Rd., or take the train to the Woodcrest station. Timberlane. is 1 block on the right. Hot showers, toilets. Reservations highly recommended. 2-person sites $24, with full hookup $34-38. ❶

⌂ FOOD

Street vendors are major players in Philly's cuisine scene, hawking cheesesteaks, hoagies, cashews, and soft pretzels. Ethnic eateries gather in several areas: hip **South Street,** between Front and 7th St., **18th Street** around Sansom St.; and **2nd Street** between Chestnut and Market St. The nation's third-largest **Chinatown** is bounded by 11th, 8th, Arch, and Vine St., and has well-priced restaurants.

The immense **Italian Market** spans the area around 9th St. below Christian St. Make yourself a gourmet Mediterranean picnic from the thousands of meats, cheeses, olives, and fruits available at **DiBruno Brothers** specialty store, at 930 S. 9th St. in the Italian Market. (☎888-322-4337; http://dibruno.com. Open M 9am-5pm, Tu-Sa 9am-6pm, Su 9am-1pm.) Philadelphia's original farmers market (since 1893), the **Reading Terminal Market,** at 12th and Arch St. across from the Pennsylvania Convention Center, is the largest indoor market in the US. Stocking globally diverse food, the market is a fabulous lunch spot with something for everyone. (☎922-2317; www.readingterminalmarket.org. Open M-Sa 8am-6pm; Amish merchants W 8am-3pm, Th-Sa 8am-5pm.)

HISTORIC DISTRICT

Famous 4th Street Delicatessen, 700 S. 4th St. (☎922-3274 or 888-922-3535), at Bainbridge St. This delicatessen rivals New York City's finest. A landmark since 1923, it has earned a stellar reputation serving hot corned beef sandwiches ($8.40), classic reubens ($8.95), and even borscht ($2.95) in an antique dining room. The cookies and lemonade make for a delicious treat. Open M-Sa 7:30am-6pm, Su 7:30am-4pm. ❷

Jim's Steaks, 400 South St. at 4th St. (☎928-1911; www.jimsteaks.com). This joint bustles with activity and brims with photos of famous patrons such as Bruce Willis, James Taylor, and Lou Rawls. Customers arrive in droves for authentic Philly hoagies ($5.80) and fries ($1.25). Open M-Th 10am-1am, F-Sa 10am-3am, Su 11am-4pm. ❶

Pink Rose Pastry Shop, 630 S. 4th St. (☎592-0565; www.pinkrosepastry.com), at Bainbridge St. across from the delicatessen. Friendly students serve homemade delicacies at intimate tables graced with freshly cut flowers. The sour cream apple pie ($5) is unforgettable, while white chocolate raspberry mousse cake ($6) and lattes ($2.75) leave diners begging for more. Open M-F 8am-11pm, Sa 9am-11pm, Su 9am-10pm. ❶

CHINATOWN

Singapore, 1006 Race St. (☎922-3288), between 10th and 11th St. The health-conscious flock to this restaurant for kosher-vegetarian roast "pork" with black bean sauce ($6.50) or the tofu pot with assorted vegetables ($7). Lunch specials ($6-7.50; weekdays only) come with entree, soup, spring roll, and rice. Open daily 11am-11pm. ❷

Rangoon, 112-114 9th St. (☎829-8939), between Cherry and Arch St. Plastic decor belies the complex, spicy scents of Burmese cuisine wafting outside. The Let Thoke ($6.50), a cold noodle dish with shrimp and tamarind, and the pork with mango pickle curry ($10) earn this place its reputation as some of the best eating in Chinatown. Vegetarian options available. Open Su-Th 11:30am-9:30pm, F-Sa 11:30am-10pm. ❸

Sang Kee Peking Duck House, 238 9th St. (☎925-7532), near Arch St. Locals pack the dining room for a peek at the extensive menu. Peking duck usually requires lengthy preparation, but here at Sang Kee, they serve so much of the specialty item that you are never more than minutes away from delectable duck (½ duck $17, whole $25). Shrimp seaweed soup $5. Entrees $6-10. Open Su-Th 11am-11pm, F-Sa 11am-midnight. ❸

Ray's Cafe and Tea House, 141 N. 9th St. (☎922-5122), is ideal for quick snacks on the run, long tête-à-têtes, or quiet time curled up with your favorite read. Dishes like spicy walnut delight ($9) or pineapple-scented chicken ($12) are delectable and filling. For less heavy fare, the mango bubble tea ($4.50) is smooth and delicious. Open M-Th 9am-9pm, F 9am-10pm, Sa 11:30am-10pm, Su 11:30am-9pm. Cash only. ❸

CENTER CITY

Alma de Cuba, 1623 Walnut St. (☎988-1799; www.almadecubarestaurant.com), near Rittenhouse Sq. Trendy spot for hot Latin food. Try the *sancocho de pollo* soup ($6), made with coconut-chicken broth. For dinner, cilantro honey mustard glazed salmon ($23) is served over a banana-lentil salad with fresh horserad-ish cream. Free *tapas* and discounted drinks during happy hour (M-F 5-7pm). Live Cuban jazz W 9pm-mid-night. Salsa Su 8pm. Open M-Th 5-11pm, F-Sa 5pm-midnight, Su 5-10pm. ❹

Jamaican Jerk Hut, 1436 South St. (☎545-8644), near Broad St. While chefs jerk Negril garlic shrimp ($15) to perfection, Bob Marley tunes jam on the backyard veranda. The vegetable stir-fry, with crisp, colorful, and crunchy cooked vegetables over a bed of jasmine rice and 2 fried bananas ($9-11), is excel-lent. BYOB—but be prepared to pay a $2 corking fee on your bottle of wine or six-pack. Live music F-Sa 7pm; cover $2. Open M-Th 11am-10pm, F-Sa 11am-11pm, Su 5-10pm. ❹

Bassett's Ice Cream (☎925-4315), in Reading Termi-nal Market at 12th and Arch St. Established in 1861, Bassett's is the oldest ice-creamery in the state, and some say the best in the nation. Originals like pumpkin ice cream may be throwbacks to the olden days, but modern finds—peach, mocha chip, and rum raisin—also await. 2 scoops $2.50, 3 scoops $3.25. Open M-F 9am-6pm, Sa 8am-6pm. ❶

Lombardi's, 132 S. 18th St. (☎564-5000; www.lom-bardisoriginalpizza.com), off Rittenhouse Sq. between Sansom and Chestnut St., makes some of the best pizza west of Italy. Established in 1905, this award-win-ner uses a coal oven to cook its crusts to perfection. Original pizza with fresh mozzarella, basil, and home-made meatballs $16. White pizza topped with green leaf spinach $17. Fresh salads $6-8. Pastas $7-11. Open Su-W 11:30am-10pm, Th-Sa 11:30am-11pm; M-F closed 4-5pm. Cash only. ❷

UNIVERSITY CITY

🔳**Tandoor India Restaurant,** 106 S. 40th St. (☎222-7122), between Chestnut and Walnut St. Every cam-pus may have a good, cheap Indian restaurant, but this is one of the best. Vegetarians come for the *bhindi* (spicy okra dish; $8). Lunch buffet daily 11:30am-3:30pm ($6.95); dinner buffet daily 4-10pm ($10). 20% student discount on buffets with valid ID. Open daily 11:30am-10:30pm. ❷

ON THE MENU

ARE YOU A PAT'S OR A GENO'S FAN?

You can't make it through a day in Philly without answering this question, posed since time immemorial. It doesn't take long for visitors to figure out that Pat's and Geno's are infamous rivals in the business of selling Philadel-phia's namesake sub: the chees-esteak. The sandwich, made from thinly sliced grilled steak, melted cheese, and often grilled onions, bell peppers, and mushrooms, has made Philadelphia famous and, some say, helped earn Philly the title of Most Overweight City in America in 1999. Cheesesteaks abound in Philadelphia, but none are more famous than Pat's King of Steaks (☎468-1546; www.patskingofsteaks.com), unless it's his cross-street rival, the larger, more neon Geno's Steaks (☎389-0659; www.genos-teaks.com). The age-old grudge-match between the stands begins anew daily at 9th St. and Passyunk Ave., in south Philadel-phia. Every Philly native has his or her favorite of the two; trans-plants soon learn it's practically a municipal law that you have to pick a side, or face dire conse-quences. Luckily, with both stands open 24hr. and serving cheesesteaks for only $5-6, you can give this weighty decision the time and thorough research it deserves.

Smokey Joe's, 210 S. 40th St. (☎222-0770), between Locust and Walnut St. Hearty meals at student-friendly prices make it the most popular UPenn bar and restaurant. The "Franklin Field Deal" offers any burger and choice of appetizer, plus free refills on soda, for $10. Open daily 11am-2am; closes for 2 weeks in mid-August. ❷

Abner's Cheesesteaks, 3813 Chestnut St. (☎662-0100), at 38th St. This bright, spacious, and cleaner-than-average joint attracts a professional set for lunch and UPenn students at night. Cheesesteak $5.09. Open Su-Th 11am-midnight, F-Sa 11am-3am. ❷

⊙ SIGHTS

INDEPENDENCE MALL

REVOLUTIONARY SIGHTS. The **Independence National Historical Park,** a small green bounded by Market, Walnut, 2nd, and 7th St., contains dozens of historical buildings. At night, the breathtaking **Lights of Liberty Show** illuminates the park. A 1hr., ½ mi. guided tour through the park with an elaborate audio program narrates the events of the Revolution while the impressive, $12 million laser light show projects five-story-tall film sequences onto historic buildings. *(Park: ☎965-7676 or 800-537-7676; www.independencevisitorcenter.com. Open daily June-Aug. 8:30am-5:30pm; Sept.-May 9am-5pm. Free. Light Show: PECO Energy Liberty Center, at the corner of 6th and Chestnut St. ☎542-3789 or 877-462-1775; www.lightsofliberty.org. Shows May-Aug. Tu-Sa, Sept.-Oct. Th-Sa; all shows begin at dusk. $17.76, seniors and students $16, ages 6-12 $12. Parking available on 6th St. between Arch and Market St., under the visitors center.)* A good place to begin your trip is at the newly renovated and impressive **visitors center** (see **Practical Information,** p. 282). They dispense detailed maps and brochures, offer a small exhibit detailing each historic site, and provide electronic trip-planners that cater to the desires of each individual visitor. The visitors center also books tickets for most historic sites—come early in the morning or reserve in advance because tickets go fast. **Independence Hall** is one of the most significant sites in American history, and one of Philadelphia's most popular destinations. After Jefferson drafted the Declaration of Independence, the delegates signed the document here in 1776, then reconvened in 1787 to ink their names onto the US Constitution. Today, knowledgeable park rangers take visitors on a brief but informative tour through the nation's first capitol building. *(Between 5th and 6th St. on Chestnut St. Open daily 9am-5pm; arrive early in summer to avoid a long line. Tickets, distributed exclusively at the visitors center, required for admittance to the free guided tours that leave every 15min.)* The US Congress assembled in nearby **Congress Hall** from 1790 to 1800, when Philadelphia was the nation's first capital. While soaking up the history, guests can take a rest in one of the plush Senate chairs. *(At Chestnut and 6th St. Open daily 9am-5pm. No tickets required.)* Right across Chestnut St. sits the country's most revered bell. While freedom may still ring at the new **Liberty Bell Center,** the (cracked) Liberty Bell does not. *(On Market St., between 5th and 6th St. ☎597-8974. Open daily 9am–5pm. Free. No tickets required.)*

The First Continental Congress, predecessor of the US Congress, united against the British in 1774 in **Carpenters' Hall.** Now a mini-museum heralding the carpenters responsible for such architectural achievements as Old City Hall and the Pennsylvania State House, the hall also houses the oldest continuously operating trade guild in America, founded in 1724. *(320 Chestnut St. ☎925-0167; www.carpentershall.org. Open Mar.-Dec. Tu-Su 10am-4pm; Jan.-Feb. W-Su 10am-4pm. Free. No tickets required.)* The new and gorgeous **National Constitution Center** provides visitors with a multimedia introduction to the Constitution and a variety of hands-on and participatory exhibits to give a more in-depth look at the history of the American Constitution. *(525 Arch St., in Independence National Historical Park. ☎ 409-6600 or 866-917-1787; www.constitutioncenter.org. 17min. multimedia presentation prior to entrance to exhibits; last show 4:10pm. Open daily 9:30am-5pm. $6, seniors and under 12 $5.)*

OTHER SIGHTS. The rest of the park preserves residential and commercial buildings of the Revolutionary era. On the northern edge of the mall, a white molding delineates the size and location of Ben Franklin's home in ▧**Franklin Court.** The original abode was unsentimentally razed by the statesman's heirs in 1812 in order to erect an apartment complex. The site contains an underground museum of Franklin's inventions and personal possessions, a 20min. movie, a replica of Franklin's printing office with a working 18th-century printing press, and a working post office. This post office was the first in the nation and remains the only one not to fly the American flag, since one did not exist in 1775. *(318 Market St., between 3rd and 4th St. ☎ 597-8974. Open in summer daily 9am-5pm; hours vary in winter, call ahead. Free.)* On a more somber note, a statue of the first American President and army general presides over the **Tomb of the Unknown Soldier,** in Washington Sq., where an eternal flame commemorates the fallen heroes of the Revolutionary War.

Sitting next to Independence Park is the **Federal Reserve Bank of Philadelphia.** It exhibits money from the 13 original colonies and even a $100,000 bill featuring President Woodrow Wilson. *(Federal Reserve: 100 N. 6th St., between Arch and Race St. ☎ 574-6257; www.phil.frb.org. Open M-F 9:30am-4:30pm; June-Aug. also Sa-Su 10am-4pm. Free.)* Adjacent to the house where Jefferson drafted the Declaration of Independence, the **Balch Institute for Ethnic Studies at the Philadelphia Historical Society** is a glimpse into America's social history, including the plight of African slaves and of Japanese Americans during WWII. *(1300 Locust St. ☎ 732-6200; www.balchinstitute.org. Open M-Tu and Th-F 1-5:30pm, W 1-8:30pm. $6; students, seniors, and under 12 $3. Sa 10am-noon free.)* Philadelphia's official history museum, known as the **Atwater Kent Museum,** offers rare Pennsylvania artifacts, such as the wampum belt received by William Penn from the Lenni Lenape at Shakamaxon in 1682, and, of course, more exhibits on Franklin. *(16 S. 7th St. ☎ 685-4830; www.philadelphiahistory.org. Open M and W-Su 10am-5pm. $5, seniors and ages 13-17 $3, under 13 free.)*

OUTSIDE INDEPENDENCE MALL

COLONIAL MADNESS. A penniless Ben Franklin arrived in Philadelphia in 1723 and strolled by the rowhouses that line the narrow **Elfreth's Alley,** near 2nd and Arch St. The oldest continuously inhabited street in America now houses a museum that provides a glimpse into the daily lives of Philadelphia's patriots via guided tours and special programs. *(Museum: 126 Elfreth's Alley. ☎ 574-0560; www.elfrethsalley.org. Open Mar.-Nov. M-Sa 10am-5pm, Su noon-5pm; Dec.-Feb. Th-Sa 10am-5pm, Su noon-5pm. Tours are 20min.; last tour 4:40pm. $2, ages 6-18 $1.)* The **Betsy Ross House**—home of one of the most celebrated female patriots—conveys, through child-oriented, first-person placards, the skills that led seamstress Betsy Ross to sew America's first flag, which was adopted by Congress in 1777. *(239 Arch St. ☎ 686-1252; www.betsyrosshouse.org. Open Apr.-Sept. daily 10am-5pm; Oct.-Mar. Tu-Su and M holidays 10am-5pm. $3, children and students $2. Audio tour $5. Cash only.)*

OTHER SIGHTS. For those who like to get off on the right foot, the Temple University School of Podiatric Medicine houses the **Shoe Museum.** The collection of 900 pairs features footwear from the famous feet of Reggie Jackson, Lady Bird Johnson, Julius Erving, Nancy Reagan, and others. Recent additions to the collection include Ella Fitzgerald's gold boots and a pair of 6-inch-tall, blue satin platform sandals worn by Sally Struthers on the popular television show *All in the Family. (8th and Race St., 6th fl. ☎ 625-5243. Tours W and F 9am-1pm. Tours are free but limited; visitors must call to make an appointment.)* The powder-blue **Benjamin Franklin**

MID-ATLANTIC

Bridge, considered the longest suspension bridge in the world when it opened on July 1, 1926, off Race and 5th St., connects Philadelphia to New Jersey, and provides an expansive view of the city. The bridge adds a touch of urban art after dark as it is highlighted by hundreds of color-changing lights.

SOCIETY HILL AND THE WATERFRONT

Society Hill proper begins on Walnut St., between Front and 7th St., east of Independence Mall, and is filled with over 200-year-old townhouses and cobblestone walks illuminated by electric "gaslights." Move eastward through Society Hill and you will eventually hit the waterfront of the Delaware River. The restaurants along the mostly-commercial waterfront are great places to watch ships go by during the day or see the back-lit Philadelphia skyline at sunset.

HISTORICAL SIGHTS. Historic **Head House Square,** at 2nd and Pine St., holds the distinction of being America's oldest firehouse and marketplace, and now houses restaurants and boutiques. Bargain hunters can test their haggling skills at an outdoor arts and crafts fair. *(☎790-0782. Open June-Aug. Sa noon-11pm, Su noon-6pm. Free workshops Su 1-3pm.)* Each January, sequin- and feather-clad participants join in a rowdy New Year's Day Mummer's parade, which began in celebration of the masked actors and festival players known as "mummers." South of Head House Sq., the **Mummer's Museum** swells with the glamor of old costumes. *(1100 S. 2nd St., at Washington Ave. ☎336-3050; www.riverfrontmummers.com/museum.html. Free string band concerts Tu 8pm. Open May-Sept. Tu 9:30am-9:30pm, W-Sa 9:30am-4:30pm, Su noon-4:30pm; July-Aug. closed Su; Oct.-Apr. Tu-Sa 9:30am-4:30pm, Su noon-4:30pm. $3.50; students, seniors, and under 12 $2.50. Free parking.)*

ON THE WATERFRONT. A looming neon sign at the easternmost end of Market St. welcomes visitors to **Penn's Landing.** Philadelphian shipbuilding, cargo, and immigration unfold at the **Independence Seaport Museum** at Penn's Landing. Kids can get their sea legs at the "Boats Float" exhibit. Near the museum a host of old ships bobs at the dock, including the *USS Olympia,* the oldest steel warship still afloat, and the *USS Becuna,* a WWII submarine. *(☎925-5439; www.phillyseaport.org. Open daily 10am-5pm. Museum and ships $9, seniors $8, children $6.)* Free **waterfront concerts** are a great way to relax at the end of the day. *(☎629-3257; www.pennslandingcorp.com. Major bands Apr.-Oct. Th 8pm. Children's theater Su.)*

CENTER CITY

As the financial and commercial hub of Philly, Center City barely has enough room to accommodate the professionals who cram into the area bounded by 12th, 23rd, Vine, and Pine St. Rife with activity during the day, the region retires early at night.

ART AND ARCHITECTURE. The country's first school and art museum, the **Pennsylvania Academy of Fine Art** has permanent displays of works by Winslow Homer and Mary Cassatt, while current students show their theses and accomplished alumni get their own exhibits each May. *(118 N. Broad St., at Cherry St. ☎972-7600; www.pafa.org. Open Tu-Sa 10am-5pm, Su 11am-5pm. Tours 45min.-1hr.; M-F at 11:30am and 12:30pm, Sa-Su at noon and 1pm. $5, students and seniors $4, ages 5-18 $3. Special exhibits $8/$7/$5.)* Presiding over Center City, the granite-and-marble **City Hall** took 30 years to build. Until 1908, it reigned as the tallest building in the US, aided by the 37 ft. statue of William Penn at its summit. A law prohibited building anything higher than Penn's hat until entrepreneurs overturned it in the mid-1980s. The daily 12:30pm tour covers the different departments of the nation's largest municipal building and the commanding view of the city awaiting visitors in the building's tower. *(At Broad and Market St. ☎686-1776. Open M-F 9:30am-4:45pm. Tower-only tour every 15min. daily 9:15am-4:15pm, 5 people max. per tour; reservations recommended. Free.)*

RITTENHOUSE SQUARE
In the early 20th century, architect Paul Phillipe Cert overhauled the Rittenhouse Sq. District, leaving his mark on the ritzy, brick-laden neighborhood southeast of Center City. This part of town cradles the musical and dramatic pulse of the city, housing several performing arts centers.

RITTENHOUSE MUSEUMS. For the best results, completely digest lunch before viewing the bizarre and often gory medical abnormalities displayed at the highly intriguing **Mütter Museum.** Among the potentially unsettling fascinations are a wall of skulls and a collection of preserved body parts of famous people, including John Marshall's bladder stones and a section of John Wilkes Booth's neck. The museum also contains an exhibit on infectious diseases such as the Black Death and AIDS and displays a Level 4 biohazard suit. *(19 S. 22nd St. ☎563-3737, ext. 211; www.collphyphil.org/muttpg1.shtml. Open daily 10am-5pm. $9; seniors, students, and ages 6-18 $6.)* Just south of the square, the more benign **Rosenbach Museum and Library** displays antique books and furniture. The original manuscript of James Joyce's *Ulysses* is on permanent exhibit while the collected illustrations of Maurice Sendak are among the items on rotating exhibit. Other interesting items in the museum's collection are Nathaniel Hawthorne's personal copy of *Moby Dick* and the largest collection of oil portrait miniatures on metal. *(2010 Delancey St. ☎732-1600; www.rosenbach.org. Open Tu and Th-Su 10am-5pm, W 10am-8pm. Guided 1¼hr. tours of the house Tu-Su 11am-4pm, also W 6:30pm. Exhibition and tour $8, students and seniors $5.)*

PARKWAY/MUSEUM DISTRICT
Nicknamed "America's Champs-Elysées," the **Benjamin Franklin Parkway** sports a colorful international flag row in downtown Philly. **Logan Circle,** one of the city's five original town squares, was the sight of public executions until 1823 but now delights the children who frolic in its **Swann Memorial Fountain.** Designed by Alexander Calder, the fountain represents the Wissahickon Creek, the Schuylkill River, and the Delaware River, the three bodies of water surrounding the city.

SCIENCE. A modern assemblage of everything scientific, the highly interactive **Franklin Institute** would make the old inventor proud. The newly installed "skybike" allows kids and adults to explore scientific theories while pedaling across a tightrope suspended nearly four stories high. *(At 20th St. and Ben Franklin Pkwy. ☎448-1200; www.fi.edu. Open daily 9:30am-5pm, F-Sa IMAX open until 9pm. $13, seniors and ages 4-11 $10. IMAX Theater ☎448-1111; $8. Museum and IMAX $17/$14.)* Part of the Institute, the newly renovated **Fels Planetarium** takes visitors on daily tours of the stars and stages lively laser shows on Friday and Saturday nights. *(222 N. 20th St. One show included free in Franklin Institute ticket. $6, seniors and ages 4-11 $5. Exhibits and laser show $13/$11.)* Opposite Fels, the **Academy of Natural Sciences** allows budding archaeologists to try their hand at digging up dinosaur fossils, and a new Lewis and Clark exhibit illuminates what life in the western wilderness was like for the two intrepid explorers. *(1900 Ben Franklin Pkwy., at 19th St. ☎299-1000; www.acnatsci.org. Open M-F 10am-4:30pm, Sa-Su 10am-5pm. $9, seniors and military $8.25, ages 3-12 $8. AAA $1 discount. Wheelchair accessible.)* For a little family fun, visit the **Please Touch Museum,** where kids can romp around in the Alice in Wonderland Funhouse, play miniature golf in the Science Park, or hone their broadcasting skills in the Me On TV workshop. *(210 N. 21st St. ☎963-0667; www.pleasetouchmuseum.org. Open daily July-Aug. 9am-5pm; Sept.-June 9am-4:30pm. $10.)*

ART. Sylvester Stallone may have etched the sight of the **Philadelphia Museum of Art** into the minds of movie buffs everywhere when he bolted up its stately front stairs in *Rocky* (1976), but it is the artwork within that has earned the museum its fine reputation. The world-class collection includes famous works such as Van Gogh's *Sunflowers*, Cezanne's *Large Bathers*, and Toulouse-Lautrec's *At the Moulin Rouge*, as well as extensive Asian, Egyptian, and decorative art collections. *(Ben Franklin Pkwy. and 26th St. ☎ 763-8100; www.philamuseum.org. Open Tu, Th, Sa-Su 10am-5pm; W and F 10am-8:45pm. Tours daily 10am-3pm. Live jazz, fine wine, and light food F 5pm-8:15pm. $10; students, seniors, and ages 13-18 $7; 12 and under free. Su free.)* A casting of *The Gates of Hell* outside the **Rodin Museum** guards the portal of human passion, anguish, and anger in the most extensive collection of the prolific sculptor's works this side of the Seine. One of the five original castings of *The Thinker* (1880) marks the museum entrance from afar. *(Ben Franklin Pkwy. and 22nd St. ☎ 763-8100; www.rodinmuseum.org. Open Tu-Su 10am-5pm. 1hr. guided audio tour available for $5 in the giftshop. Free guided tour Su 1pm. Suggested donation $3.)*

BOOKS AND INMATES. The Free Library of Philadelphia has earned a stellar reputation for its library of orchestral music and its rare book collection, one of the largest in the nation. The user-friendly library is conveniently divided into rooms by subject. Philadelphia art students frequently seek sketching subjects and inspiration amid the classical architecture of the building. *(At 20th and Vine St. ☎ 686-5322; www.library.phila.gov. Open M-W 9am-9pm, Th-Sa 9am-5pm.)* In a reversal of convention, guests pay to get into prison at the castle-like **Eastern State Penitentiary,** once a groundbreaking institution for criminal rehabilitation. Tours twist through the smoldering dimness Al Capone once called home and guides recount fascinating stories of daring inmates and their attempted escapes. *(2124 Fairmount Ave. at 22nd St. ☎ 236-3300; www.easternstate.org. Open W-Sa 10am-5pm. Tours every hr. 10am-4pm. Last entry 4pm. $9, students and seniors $7, ages 7-12 $4, under 7 not permitted.)*

UNIVERSITY CITY

In West Philly, across the Schuylkill from Center City, the **University of Pennsylvania** *(www.upenn.edu)* and **Drexel University** *(www.drexel.edu)* make up University City, a neighborhood comprised almost entirely of students. The Penn campus, a thriving assemblage of lush green lawns and red brick quadrangles, contrasts sharply with the dilapidated buildings surrounding it. Ritzy shops and hip cafes spice up 36th St., and a statue of the omnipresent Benjamin Franklin, who founded the university in 1740, greets visitors at the entrance to the Penn campus on 34th and Walnut St. *Much of the area surrounding University City is unsafe at night.*

U-CITY SIGHTS. The University Museum of Archaeology and Anthropology journeys through three floors of the world's major cultures under a beautiful stone and glass rotunda. *(At 33rd and Spruce St. ☎ 898-4001; www.upenn.edu/museum. Open Tu-Sa 10am-4:30pm, Su 1-5pm. $8, students and seniors $5.)* In 1965, Andy Warhol had his first one-man show at the cutting-edge **Institute of Contemporary Art.** Today, the ICA features works by some of the newest big names on the art scene. *(118 S. 36th at Sansom St. ☎ 898-7108; www.icaphila.org. Open W-F noon-8pm, Sa-Su 11am-5pm. $3; students, seniors, and artists $2. Su 11am-1pm free.)* North of the university area, the **Philadelphia Zoo,** the oldest zoo in the country, houses more than 2000 animals, including lowland gorillas, bearded pigs, and giant anteaters. The endangered animals exhibit provides not only an opportunity to get a glimpse of some extremely rare species, but also a touching lesson on how our actions affect the environment. *(3260 South St. at 34th and Girard St. ☎ 243-1100; www.philadelphiazoo.org. Open daily Feb.-Nov. 9:30am-5pm; Dec.-Jan. 9:30am-4pm. $16, seniors and ages 2-11 $13. Parking $8.)*

🔊 ENTERTAINMENT

The **Academy of Music,** at Broad and Locust St., was modeled after Milan's La Scala and hosts the six yearly productions of the **Pennsylvania Ballet.** (☎551-7000; www.paballet.org. $20-85.) The **Philadelphia Orchestra,** located at the stunning **Kimmel Center,** 260 S. Broad St., performs from September to May. (☎790-5800 or 893-1999; www.kimmelcenter.org. Box office open daily 10am-6pm and until performances begin. $5 tickets go on sale at the Locust St. entrance 45min. before F-Sa concerts. $8 student rush tickets Tu and Th 30min. before show.)

With 5000 seats under cover and 10,000 on outdoor benches and lawns, the **Mann Music Center,** on George's Hill near 52nd and Parkside Ave. in Fairmount Park, hosts big name entertainers like Tony Bennett, Willie Nelson, and the Gipsy Kings, as well as a variety of jazz and rock concerts. (☎893-1999 for tickets or 546-7900 for general info; www.manncenter.org. Tickets available at the Academy of Music box office, $20-100. Free lawn tickets for June-Aug. Philadelphia Orchestra concerts available from the visitors center, at 16th and JFK Blvd. on the day of a performance.) The 120-year-old **Trocadero,** 1003 Arch St. at 10th St., is the oldest operating Victorian theater in the US and hosts both local and big-name rock bands. (☎922-5486; www.thetroc.com. Tickets $3-40. Advance tickets through Ticketmaster. Box office open M-F noon-6pm, Sa noon-5pm.) The **Robin Hood Dell East,** on Ridge Ave. near 33rd St. in Fairmount Park, brings in top names in pop, jazz, and gospel in July and August. In September, theatrical entertainment graces the stage. (☎685-9560. Box office open M-F 10am-5pm, Sa-Su 10am-showtime.) The students of the world-renowned **Curtis Institute of Music,** 1726 Locust St., give free concerts. (☎893-5252; www.curtis.edu. Mid-Oct. to Apr. M, W, F 8pm.) **Merriam Theater,** 250 S. Broad St. in Center City, stages performances ranging from student works to Broadway hits. Katharine Hepburn, Laurence Olivier, and Sammy Davis, Jr. have all graced this stage. (☎732-5446; www.broadwayacrossamerica.com. Box office open M-Sa 10am-5:30pm.) The Old City, from Chestnut to Vine and Front to 4th St., comes alive for the **First Friday** celebration, when streets fill with live music and more than 40 art galleries, museums, and restaurants open their doors to entice visitors with free food and sparkling wine. (☎800-555-5191; www.oldcity.org. Oct.-June, first F of each month 5-9pm.)

Philly gets physical with plenty of sports venues—four professional teams play just a short ride away on the Broad St. subway line. Baseball's **Phillies** (☎463-1000; www.phillies.com) play at the brand-new **Citizens Bank Park,** 1 Citizens Bank Way, just off Pattison Ave. between 11th and Darien St. Football's **Eagles** (☎463-5500; www.philadelphiaeagles.com) play at **Lincoln Financial Field,** at Broad St. and Pattison Ave. Across the street, fans fill the **Wachovia Center** (☎336-3600; box office open M-F 9am-6pm, Sa 10am-4pm) on winter nights to watch the NBA's **76ers** (☎339-7676; www.sixers.com) and the NHL's **Flyers** (☎755-9700; www.philadelphiaflyers.com). General admission tickets for baseball and hockey start at $10; football and basketball tickets go for $15-50.

📻 NIGHTLIFE

Check the Friday *Philadelphia Inquirer* for entertainment listings. The free Thursday *City Paper* and the Wednesday *Philadelphia Weekly* have listings of city events. Gay and lesbian weeklies *Au Courant* (free) and *PGN* ($0.75) list events throughout the Delaware Valley. A diverse club crowd jams to the sounds of live music on weekends along **South Street** toward the river. *Use caution in this neighborhood at night.* Many pubs line **2nd Street** near Chestnut St., close to the Bank St. Hostel. Continuing south to Society Hill, especially near **Head House**

Square, a slightly older crowd fills dozens of streetside bars and cafes. **Delaware Avenue,** or **Columbus Boulevard,** running along Penn's Landing, has recently become a trendy hot spot full of nightclubs and restaurants that attract droves of yuppies and students. Most bars and clubs that cater to a gay clientele congregate along **Camac, South 12th,** and **South 13th Street.**

The Khyber, 56 S. 2nd St. (☎238-5888; www.thekhyber.com). A speakeasy during the days of Prohibition, the Khyber now legally gathers a young crowd to listen to a range of punk, metal, and hip-hop music. The ornate wooden bar was shipped over from England in 1876. Vegetarian sandwiches $3. Happy hour M-F 5-7pm. Live music daily 10pm. 21+. Cover $8. Open Su-F noon-2am, Sa 6pm-2am. Cash only.

Warmdaddy's (☎627-8400; www.warmdaddys.com), at Front and Market St. Though entrees tend to be pricey, bayou-lovers will eat up this Cajun club renowned for its blues and diversity. Music and reduced-price entrees Su 3pm. Th midnight happy hour. Live music in summer 7pm; in winter 8:30pm. Cover F-Sa $10 with reservation, $15 without; varies during the week. Open daily 5pm-2am; kitchen closes 1am.

The Five Spot, 5 S. Bank St. (☎574-0070), off Market St. between 2nd and 3rd St. The classically designed lounge encourages cool cats to drink heartily, while the cramped dance floor upstairs hosts dancers of all abilities. F-Sa DJ spins modern, rap, and R&B. Dress well; no sneakers or shorts. 21+. Cover $5-20. Open daily 9pm-2am.

Moriarty's, 1116 Walnut St. (☎627-7676; www.moriartysrestaurant.com), near 11th St. and the Forest Theater. This Irish pub draws a healthy crowd late into the night with a quiet, comfortable bar scene. Steak and seafood dinner specials $15-18, but cheaper options, such as burgers, also available. Over 20 beers on tap, ESPN on the TV, and private booths. Drink specials change daily. Open daily 11am-2am, kitchen closes 1am.

Woody's, 202 S. 13th St. (☎545-1893; www.woodysbar.com), at Walnut St. An outgoing gay crowd frequents this lively club with a free cyber bar, coffee bar, and dance floor. Most nights patrons are a happy mix of ages, genders, and sexual orientations. Happy hour daily 5-7pm. M karaoke. Open for meals daily noon-3:30pm and 4-11pm. Bar open daily 11am-2am. Cash only.

■ OUTDOOR ACTIVITIES

Philly's finest outdoor opportunities can be found in the resplendent **Fairmount Park** (www.phila.gov/fairpark; open dawn-dusk). Ten times the size of New York City's Central Park, Fairmount is larger than any other city park and covered with bike trails and picnic areas, offering city-weary vacationers the adventure of the great outdoors and stirring vistas of the Schuylkill River. The Andorra Natural Area inside the park is a 210-acre preserve of native plants in their wild state and includes an environmental education center on the banks of Wissahickon Creek. **Mountain biking** is very popular in the Wissahickon Valley north of Philadelphia, where both flat and steeper, more challenging trails are available. (☎685-2575. Permit required.) The premier location in the Philadelphia area is the **John Heinz National Wildlife Refuge,** just off I-95 near the south end of Philadelphia in Tinicum. This 205-acre freshwater tidal marsh is home to hundreds of bird species, including migrants from both tropical and northern climes.

The abandoned **Waterworks,** Greek-style ruins by the waterfall immediately behind the Museum of Art, were built between 1819 and 1822. Free 90min. tours of the Waterworks' romantic architecture, technology, and social history meet on Aquarium Dr., behind the museum. (☎685-4935; www.fairmountwaterworks.org. Open Sa-Su 1-3:30pm.) Farther down the river, Philly's place in the rowing world is evidenced by a line of crew clubs forming the historic **Boathouse Row.** The Museum of Art hosts the Schuylkill Stroll, a $3 guided tour of Boathouse Row Sundays 1-

2:30pm, as well as trolley tours to some of the mansions in Fairmount Park (☎763-8100 for mansion tour schedules). The area near Boathouse Row is also Philly's most popular in-line skating spot, and joggers seeking recreation and a refreshing river breeze crowd the local paths. In the northern arm of Fairmount Park, trails follow the secluded Wissahickon Creek for 5 mi., as the concrete city fades to a distant memory. The **Japanese House and Garden**, off Montgomery Dr. near Belmont Ave., is designed in the style of a 17th-century *shoin;* the authentic garden defines tranquility. (☎878-5097; www.shofuso.com. Open May-Oct. Tu-F 10am-4pm, Sa-Su 11am-5pm; call for seasonal hours. Ask about the 45-60min. tour. $4; students, ages 6-17, and seniors 55 and over $3.) *Some neighborhoods surrounding the park are not safe, and the park is not safe at night.*

▐ DAYTRIP FROM PHILADELPHIA

VALLEY FORGE

In 1777-78 it was the frigid winter, not the British military, that almost crushed the Continental Army. When George Washington selected Valley Forge as the winter camp for his 12,000 troops after a defeat at Germantown in October, he could not have predicted the fate that would befall his troops. Three arduous months of starvation, bitter cold, and disease nearly halved his forces. It was not until Baron Friedrich von Steuben arrived with fresh troops and supplies on February 23, 1778, that recovery seemed possible. Renewed, the Continental Army left Valley Forge and its harrowing memory on June 19, 1778 to win the Battle of Monmouth.

The hills that once tormented the frost-bitten soldiers now constitute the **Valley Forge National Historical Park** (open daily 9am-10pm; free). The **visitors center,** 600 W. Germantown Pike, features a small museum and an 18min. film shown every 30min. (☎610-783-1099; www.nps.gov/vafo. Open daily 9am-5pm.) Visitors can explore the park by car, foot, or bus. The 10 mi. self-guided **auto tour** (tape $10, CD $12), begins at the visitors center. If you prefer live narration and question time, the ¼ mi. **walking tour,** led by a knowledgeable park ranger, also leaves from the visitors center (daily 10:50am and 1:50pm; free). The 1½hr. **bus tour** allows visitors to explore sites with the comfort of A/C. (In summer M and Th-Su. $16, ages 13-16 $11, under 12 $7.50.) All tours pass Washington's headquarters, reconstructed soldier huts and fortifications, and the Grand Parade Ground where the Continental Army drilled. The park has three picnic areas but no camping. Joggers can take a trip down a fairly flat, paved 6 mi. trail through deer-populated forests.

Valley Forge lies 30min. from Philadelphia by car. To get there, take I-76 west from Philly for about 12 mi. Get off at the Exit 24, then take Rte. 202 S 1 mi. and Rte. 422 W for 1½ mi. to another Valley Forge exit. **SEPTA** runs buses from Philly to the visitors center daily; catch #125 at 16th and JFK ($3.50).

LANCASTER COUNTY   ☎717

Lancaster County is known as the heart of "Pennsylvania Dutch Country," yet the Pennsylvania Dutch aren't Dutch at all, but rather the descendants of Amish and Mennonite settlers of Germanic origins. When these sects migrated to southern Pennsylvania in search of religious freedom in the early 1700s and introduced themselves as "Deutsch," English settlers mistook the German word for "Dutch." Lancaster is home to the second-largest Old Order Amish population in the US, a group that strives to maintain its pious, humble, and simple lifestyle in the face of modern advancements. Most tourism in Lancaster County capitalizes on the county's Amish and Mennonite founders through offerings

THE BIG SPLURGE

HERSHEY'S CANDYLAND

Around the turn of the century, Milton S. Hershey, a Mennonite resident of eastern Pennsylvania, discovered how to mass market a rare and expensive luxury—chocolate. Today, the company that bears his name runs the world's largest chocolate factory in Hershey, PA, about 45min. from Lancaster. East of town, the **Chocolate World Visitors Center** presents an automated tour through a simulated chocolate factory. *(Free; parking $6.)* Visitors emerge into a pavilion full of discounted chocolate candy and oh-so-fashionable Hershey sportswear. In the **Hershey Factory Works,** visitors can wrap their own chocolate kisses. *(45min. $10, seniors $9.45, ages 3-12 $6.)* The **Really Big 3-D Show** features personified candy bars dancing and singing. *(30min. $5, ages 3-12 $4.)* But the main attractions are the sweet rollercoasters and water rides in the the amusement park **Hersheypark.** The new Storm-Rider sends riders from 0-70 mph in under 2 seconds—better than any sugar rush.
Hersheypark (☎800-437-7439; http://hersheypa.com. Open June M-F 10am-10pm; July-Aug. M-F 10am-10pm, Sa-Su 10am-11pm; May and Sept. call for hours. $38, ages 3-8 and 55-69 $22, ages 70 and up $16; after 5pm $21/$18/$16. Visitors center ☎800-437-7439. Closes 2hr. before park. Parking $6.)

⚡ 🛈 ORIENTATION AND PRACTICAL INFORMATION. Lancaster County covers an area almost the size of Rhode Island. Driving in from Philadelphia and other cities to the east is easiest on Rte. 30 W; from southern destinations, take Rte. 83 N to Rte. 30 E. County seat Lancaster City, in the heart of Dutch country, has red brick rowhouses huddled around historic **Penn Square.** The rural areas are mostly accessible by car (or horse and buggy), but it is easy to see the tourist sites with a bike or to walk the mile or two between public transit drop-offs. To sample the Amish and Mennonite traditions, stick to the towns along Rte. 340, such as Bird-in-Hand and Intercourse (and try not to giggle at the names in front of locals). Because the area is heavily Mennonite, most businesses and all major attractions close on Sundays. **Amtrak,** 53 McGovern Ave. in Lancaster City (☎291-5080; ticket office open daily 5:30am-10pm), runs to Philadelphia (1½hr., 8-10 per day, $13) and Pittsburgh (6½hr., 2 per day, $37). **Capitol Trailways** (☎397-4861; open daily 8am-10pm), in the same location, runs buses to Philadelphia (3hr., 3 per day, $17) and Pittsburgh (6hr., 3 per day, $55). **Red Rose Transit,** 45 Erick Rd., has bus service in Lancaster City and to some areas in the surrounding countryside. (☎397-4246. Buses run daily approximately 5am-6pm. $1.15-$2.25, seniors free.) The **Pennsylvania Dutch Visitors Bureau,** 501 Greenfield Rd., on the east side of Lancaster City off Rte. 30, dispenses info on the region, including maps, walking tours, and an excellent video about the attractions of Dutch country. (☎299-8901 or 800-723-8824; www.padutchcountry.com. Open daily June-Oct. 8am-6pm; Nov.-May 8:30am-5pm.) **Post Office:** 1400 Harrisburg Pike. (☎800-275-8777 or 396-6925. Open M-F 7:30am-7pm, Sa 9am-2pm.) **Postal Code:** 17604. **Area Code:** 717.

📍 ACCOMMODATIONS. Hundreds of hotels, campgrounds and B&Bs cluster in this area, as do several working farms with guest houses. The visitors bureau's employees and vacation guide are essential resources for wading through all the options. If you are considering staying in a B&B, call the **Authentic Bed and Breakfasts of Lancaster County Association** for valuable advice (☎800-552-2632 or www.authenticbandb.com). The amicable staff at the **Mennonite Information Center** (see **Sights,** p. 295) can put you in contact with Mennonite-run guest houses, some of which charge under $50 per night.

For an affordable stay in a conveniently located working farm home, the **Verdant View Farm Bed and Breakfast ❸**, 429 Strasburg Rd., Paradise, is the place to go. The farmhouse has 5 bedrooms, all with A/C and 3 with private baths, plus a visitors cottage with a full kitchen. Guests interested in the "Mennonite experience" can milk cows, feed calves, and attend church service with their hosts. (☎ 687-7353 or 888-321-8119; www.verdantview.com. Check-in 2-5pm. Doubles $49-70, private bath extra.) The **Pennsylvania Dutch Motel ❸**, 2275 N. Reading Rd., at Exit 21 off the Pennsylvania Tpk., has a helpful hostess and spacious, clean rooms with 2 double beds, cable TV, and A/C. (☎ 336-5559. Singles and doubles $50, additional guests $5; low-season rates lower.) For the B&B experience on a budget, look to the **Blue Ball B&B ❸**, 1075 Main St., Blue Ball, east of Lancaster City on Rte. 23. This cozy guesthouse and its friendly host offer A/C, cable TV, private baths, and a full breakfast at $20 per night less than the competitors. (☎ 800-720-9827; www.blueballbandb.com. Singles and doubles $65-70.) The quiet wilderness setting at the **Sickman's Mill Campground ❶**, 671 Sand Hill Rd., off State Rd. 272 6 mi. south of Lancaster City, comes with hot showers, clean toilets, a playground, and firewood. Recreational activities include freshwater creek fishing, tours of the 19th-century mill, and river tubing. (☎ 872-5951. Office open daily 10:30am-8pm. Tours $4. Inner tube rental $6 per hr., $15 per day. Sites $15, with electricity $20, no full hookups. Cash or check only.)

❏ FOOD. Amish food, German in derivation and generous in portion, is characterized by a heavy emphasis on potatoes and vegetables. Palatable alternatives to high-priced "family-style" restaurants are the **farmers markets** and **produce stands** that dot the roadway. **▨The Central Market,** in downtown Lancaster City at the northwest corner of Penn Sq. between the Heritage Center Museum and Fleet Bank, has been doing business since the 1730s. Nowadays, simply dressed Pennsylvania Dutch pour into the city to sell affordable fresh fruit, meats, cheeses, vegetables, sandwiches, and desserts. (☎ 291-4739. Open Tu and F 6am-4pm, Sa 6am-2pm.). Tourists who keep kosher can find items to fit their diet at **Central Pennsylvania's Kosher Mart,** 2249 Lincoln Hwy. E, Lancaster City. To be treated like the VIP that you are, head to **The Pressroom ❷**, 26 W. King St., Lancaster City. Deep leather booths give this lunch and dinner spot a club-like feel, while the sandwiches ($6-8), named after cartoon characters, lighten the mood. Try the Fred Basset (smoked turkey, tomatoes, onions, mozzarella, and basil mayo on a kaiser roll; $6) or have one of the pizzas or grill items ($8-11). Dinner entree prices jump to $18-28 for steak and seafood, but the pizza and grill items are still economical choices. (☎ 399-5400; www.thepressroomrestaurant.com. Lunch daily 11:30am-3pm. Dinner Tu-Th 5-9:30pm, F-Sa 5-10:30pm, Su 5-9pm.) If you have a hankering for something a little more historic, the **Revere Tavern ❷**, 3063 Lincoln Hwy., Paradise, has a history of excellent service that dates back to its construction in 1740. Seven working fireplaces give the dining room a cozy feel in the winter. Lunch items include croissant sandwiches ($5-10), one of which is a filet mignon sandwich ($10), and a deli buffet. Dinner is more upscale, with entrees priced at $11-30. (☎ 687-8601; www.reveretavern.com. Lunch Tu-Sa 11am-2pm. Dinner M-Sa 5-10pm, Su 4-9pm.) At the **Amish Barn ❸**, 3029 Old Philadelphia Pike, quilts surround the tables where patrons feed on Amish specialties, like $2 chicken corn soup and $5 Amish apple dumplings. Though hardly an authentic family restaurant, it's perfect for big groups. (☎ 768-8886; www.amishbarnpa.com. Entrees around $10. Open June-Aug. M-Sa 8am-9pm; in spring and fall M-Sa 8am-8pm; call for winter hours.)

◳ SIGHTS. From April to October every year, quilt and art fanatics flock here to see the **People's Place Quilt Museum,** 3510 Old Pennsylvania Pike. (☎ 800-828-8218; www.ppquiltmuseum.com. Open Apr.-Oct. M-Sa 9am-5pm.) The Mennonites believe in outreach and have established the **Mennonite Information Center,** on Millstream Rd. off Rte. 30 east of Lancaster, to help tourists distinguish between the Amish and Mennonite faiths. Kind hostesses guide guests through the Biblical Tabernacle. (☎ 299-0954; www.mennoniteinfoctr.com. 2hr. private tours available.)

For the most authentic exploration of Amish country available in a car, wind through the fields off U.S. 340, near Bird-in-Hand. Cyclists can capture the unostentatious spirit on the **Lancaster County Heritage Bike Tour,** a reasonably flat 46 mi. route past covered bridges and historic sites run by the visitors center. A visit to Lancaster is not complete without using the preferred mode of local transportation, the horse and buggy. **Ed's Buggy Rides,** 253 Hartman Bridge Rd., on Rte. 896, 1½ mi. south of U.S. 30 W in Strasburg, offers 1hr. tours that bump along 3 mi. of scenic backwoods, covered bridges, and countryside. You can even visit a working farm on your ride. (☎ 687-0360; www.edsbuggyrides.com. Open daily 9am-5pm. $8, under 11 $4. Cash only.) **Amish Country Tours** offers 1½hr. trips that include visits to one-room schools, Amish cottage industries, breathtaking farmland vistas, and roadside produce and craft stands. (☎ 786-3600. Tours given Apr.-Oct. M-Sa 10:30am and 2pm, Su 11:30am; Nov. daily 11:30am; Dec.-Mar. Sa-Su 11:30am. $22, ages 4-12 $13.) Old country crafts and food can be found from late June to early July at the **Pennsylvania Dutch Folk Life and Fun Festival,** in Kutztown, which offers an unusual combination of polka bands, pot pies, and petting zoos. (☎ 888-674-6463; www.kutztownfestival.com. $10 per day, seniors $9, under 12 free.) Lancaster also attracts visitors with its many **outlet malls,** located along Rte. 30.

GETTYSBURG   ☎ 717

During perhaps the most memorable dates of the Civil War, the three sweltering days of July 1-3, 1863, Union and Confederate forces clashed spectacularly at Gettysburg. The Union forces ultimately prevailed, though at the high price of over 50,000 casualties between both armies. President Lincoln arrived in Gettysburg four months later to dedicate the Gettysburg National Cemetery, where 979 unidentified Union soldiers still rest alongside the hundreds of other marked graves. Today, the National Soldier's Monument towers where Lincoln once delivered his legendary Gettysburg Address. Sights here are heavily historical; each year thousands of visitors visit these fields and are reminded of the President's declaration: "these dead shall not have died in vain."

⑦ PRACTICAL INFORMATION. Inaccessible by Greyhound or Amtrak, Gettysburg is in south-central Pennsylvania, off U.S. 15 about 30 mi. south of Harrisburg. The **Gettysburg Convention and Visitor's Bureau,** 102 Carlisle St., has maps and brochures, and the *Gettysburg Visitors Guide,* which is full of important facts and phone numbers. (☎ 334-6274 or 800-337-5015; www.gettysburgcvb.com. Open M-F 8:30am-5pm, Sa-Su 9am-5pm.) **Post Office:** 115 Buford Ave. (☎ 800-275-8777 or 337-3781. Open M-F 8am-4:30pm, Sa 9am-noon.) **Postal Code:** 17325. **Area Code:** 717.

⌂⌂ ACCOMMODATIONS AND FOOD. Follow Rte. 34 N to Rte. 233 to reach the closest hostel, **⊠Ironmasters Mansion Hostel (HI) ❶,** 1212 Pine Grove Rd., 20 mi. from Gettysburg, within Pine Grove Furnace State Park. Large and luxurious, the building holds 46 beds in a tranquil, idyllic area. Spacious porches, an ornate dining room, and a decadent jacuzzi make this hostel seem more like a Club Med resort. (☎ 486-7575. Kitchen, laundry, volleyball, and ping-pong. Internet access $3 per 15min. Linen $2. Reception 7:30-9:30am and 5-10pm. Open Feb.-Dec., Jan. by reservation only. Dorms $15, nonmembers $18.) Many motels line Steinwehr Rd. near the battlefield, but finding summer rates below $100 is difficult anywhere in the downtown area. For those willing to sacrifice proximity to attractions, the **Red Carpet Inn ❸**, 2450 Emmitsburg Rd., 4 mi. south of Military Park, has comfortable rooms with heat and A/C, large beds, and a pool. (☎334-1345 or 800-336-1345. Singles and doubles Apr.-Nov. $70, Dec.-Mar. $52. AAA $10 discount.) For an elegant stay in a more convenient location, **The Brickhouse Inn ❺**, 452 Baltimore St., offers 10 mid-to-upscale B&B rooms downtown. (☎338-9337 or 800-864-3463; www.brickhouseinn.com. Gracious hosts, breakfast, and parking included. Check-in 3:30-8pm. Check-out 11am. Rooms $90-155 in summer, less in winter.) **Artillery Ridge ❶**, 610 Taneytown Rd., 1 mi. south of the Military Park Visitors Center, maintains over 200 campsites with access to hot showers, stables (for horseback tours, see **Sights**, below), laundry, a pool, nightly movies, and a pond. (☎334-1288; www.artilleryridge.com. Open Apr.-Oct. daily; Nov. Sa-Su. Sites $22, with partial hookup $30, with full hookup $33. Each additional person $4, children $2.)

In addition to the scenic beauty of its battlefields, Gettysburg features a downtown area complete with quaint shops and lively restaurants. Hefty rations persist in the town's square and just beyond the battlefield entrance. Vegetarians should not expect to find the soy-based dishes available in sleek metropolitan restaurants, but would do well to seek out the sizable salads on most tavern menus. What nightlife there is takes the form of saloons that cluster around the central square. In Gettysburg's first building (circa 1776), now the **Dobbin House Tavern ❸**, 89 Steinwehr Rd., patrons can create their own grilled burger ($6-7) under the candlelight and view an Underground Railroad shelter. For finer dining, the tavern also serves veal madeira and other elegant entrees for $18-23. (☎334-2100; www.dobbinhouse.com. Salads $6. Sandwiches $8. Open daily 11:30am-9pm.) For ice cream and fudge, **Kilwins ❶**, 37 Steinwehr Ave., takes guests to celestial heights with peppermint, mint chocolate chip, and other classic flavors ($3-4). The peanut fudge is as addictive as it is pricey ($15 per lb., free ½ lb. with 1 lb. purchase). (☎337-2252; www.kilwins.com. Open M-Th 11am-10pm, F-Sa 11am-midnight, Su noon-8pm.) After a long day of sightseeing, kick back at **The Pike ❷**, 985 Baltimore Pike (Rte. 97). The generous pasta dishes (from $7), zesty chicken quesadillas ($7), and heaping plates of Buffalo wings (16 for $12) will rejuvenate weary customers so that they can take advantage of the town's largest dance floor or the numerous pool tables. (☎334-9227. DJ F-Sa 9:30pm-2am. Open Apr.-Oct. daily 11am-10pm, lounge 11am-2am; Nov.-Mar. Su-W 11am-9pm, Th-Sa 11am-10pm.)

THE LOCAL STORY

RIDE-BY SHOOTING

Apparently civilians were dying from stray bullets long before the Fresh Prince moved from West Philly to Bel Air. Twenty-year-old Jennie Wade was accidentally killed when a bullet passed through her wall in June of 1863, while she was baking bread for the Union infantry, making her the only civilian killed in the Battle of Gettysburg. Her fiance, Corporal Johnson Skelly, was himself wounded only a short time later in the Battle of Carter's Woods and died within weeks of his sweetheart on July 12, 1863. Today, the Old McClellan Home where Jennie lived has been converted into the **Jennie Wade House and Museum,** a memorial for the young fiancee. The hole in the wall, through which the fatal bullet traveled, is still visible today. Legend has it that unmarried women who pass their finger through the bullet hole will be engaged within a year.

Jennie Wade House and Museum, 528 Baltimore St., next to the Holiday Inn. (☎334-4100 or www.gettysburgbattlefieldtours.com. Open daily May-Aug. 9am-9pm; Mar.-Apr. and Sept.-Dec. 9am-5pm. Admission includes a 35min. guided tour. The last tour leaves 1hr. before close. $7, ages 4-11 $3.50.)

◙ **SIGHTS.** A sensible starting point is the **National Military Park Visitors Information Center,** 97 Taneytown Rd., which distributes free maps for an 18 mi. self-guided driving tour. Ranger walks are also available by reservation. (☎334-1891, ext. 431, ranger walk reservations 877-438-8929; www.nps.gov/gett. Visitors center open daily June-Aug. 8am-6pm; Sept.-May 8am-5pm. Park open daily 6am-10pm. Free.) An electronic map uses lights to show the course of the Battle of Gettysburg, and is available to view inside the visitors center. ($4, seniors $3, under 15 $2.) Prepare to spend some extra cash for an in-depth look at the historic grounds. The visitors center bookstore carries a variety of **audio driving tours.** (Tape $11-12, CD $13-18. Most 2hr.) To get a personalized experience, hire one of the **licensed battlefield guides** who will squeeze into the family car to guide visitors through the monuments and landmarks, narrating and answering questions. (☎334-1124, ext. 431; www.gettysburgtourguides.com. 2hr. tours 8am-close. 1-6 people $40, 7-15 people $60, 16-49 people $90. Arrive by 9am to ensure a time slot or pay a surcharge to reserve in advance. Cash or traveler's check only.) Bus tours to the **Eisenhower House and Farm** include a 20min. house tour and self-guided tour of the grounds. (Departures every 30min. 9am-4pm. $7, ages 13-16 $4, ages 6-12 $3.)

The chilling sights and sounds of battle surround the audience at the **Cyclorama Center,** next to the visitors center. The center shows *Gettysburg 1863* (20min., begins 5min. after the hr.), *The American Civil War* (10min., 35min. after the hr.), and a 20min. light show (every 30min.) around a 9500 sq. ft. mural of the battle. The "cyclorama" itself is an 1824 oil painting of Pickett's Charge that is 26 feet high and 356 feet in circumference. (☎334-1124, ext. 422. Open daily 9am-5pm. $3, seniors $2.50, ages 6-16 $2. Last show 4:30pm. Cash or traveler's check only.) Artillery Ridge Campgrounds (see **Accommodations,** above) conducts **horseback tours** by reservation. (1hr. horseback tour $33, 2hr. horseback and history tour $58. No one under age 8 or over 240 lb.) Adjacent to the campground office is a meticulously detailed diorama of the Gettysburg battle, along with other exhibits ($4.50, seniors and children $3.50). **Historic Tours** trundles visitors around the battlefield in restored 1930s Yellowstone Park double-decker buses with A/C downstairs and open-top roof seating upstairs. (☎334-8000; www.gettysburg.com. 2½hr. tours $17, children $11. AAA and AARP $16.) Based on the chilling tales told by author Mark Nesbitt, a former park ranger and inhabitant of a haunted Gettysburg house, candlelit **Ghosts of Gettysburg,** 271 Baltimore St., reawakens the war's dead. Three different tours, covering different parts of the town and their resident ghosts, run each night. (☎337-0445; www.ghostsofgettysburg.com. Tours Mar.-Nov. 8, 8:15, 9, and 9:45pm; call for low-season times. $6-6.50, under 8 free. Reservations recommended.) Don't miss the living history programs or the disturbingly lifelike multimedia presentations on display at the **American Civil War Museum,** 297 Steinwehr Ave., across from the Military Park entrance. (☎334-6245; www.e-gettysburg.com. Open Mar.-Dec. daily 9am-8:15pm; Jan.-Feb. weekends and holidays only. $5.50, ages 13-17 $3.50, ages 6-12 $2.50, under 6 free. Cash or traveler's check only.)

The ◙**Schriver House,** 309 Baltimore St., a "Civil War museum dedicated to the civilian experience at Gettysburg," features the irrepressible energy of tour guides in period costume giving a house tour that covers daily 19th-century life as revealed in the diary entries from a wartime inhabitant of the house. The tour also covers relics discovered under the floorboards of the house's attic. (☎337-2800; www.schriverhouse.com. Open Apr.-Nov. M-Sa 10am-5pm, Su noon-5pm. $6, seniors $5.75, ages 6-12 $4.)

PITTSBURGH

☎412

Those who come to the City of Steel expecting sprawling industry and soot-encrusted American Joes will be disappointed; the steel industry's decline has meant cleaner air and rivers, and a recent economic renaissance has produced a brighter urban landscape. Throughout the renewal, Pittsburgh's neighborhoods have maintained strong and diverse identities—some ethnic, some intellectual, and some based in counter-culture. Admittedly, some of the old sooty Pittsburgh survives in the suburbs, but one needs only to view downtown from atop Mt. Washington to see how thoroughly Pittsburgh has entered a new age.

▐ TRANSPORTATION

Airport: Pittsburgh International (☎472-5526; www.pitairport.com), 18 mi. west of downtown, by I-279 and Rte. 60 N in Findlay Township. The Port Authority's **28x Airport Flyer** bus serves downtown and Oakland. Runs daily every 30min. 5:45am-midnight. $2.25. **Airline Transportation Company** (☎472-3180 or 800-991-9890) runs downtown Su-F every hr. 7am-11:40pm, reduced service Sa. $17. Taxi to downtown $30.

Trains: Amtrak, 1100 Liberty Ave. (☎471-6170), at Grant St. on the northern edge of downtown, next to Greyhound and the post office. Generally safe inside, *but be careful walking from here to the city center at night.* Station open 24hr. To: **Chicago** (9½-10hr., 2 per day, $46-90); **New York City** (10-13hr., 2 per day, $54-102); **Philadelphia** (8-11½hr., 2 per day, $39-76).

Buses: Greyhound, 55 11th St. (☎392-6526), at Liberty Ave. Open 24hr. To **Chicago** (9-12hr., 11 per day, $58-67) and **Philadelphia** (6-8hr., 8 per day, $41-48).

Public Transit: Port Authority of Allegheny County (PAT; ☎442-2000). Within downtown, bus free until 7pm. Subway between the 3 downtown stops free. Beyond downtown, bus $1.75; transfers $0.50; weekly pass $17. Subway $1.75. Ages 6-11 half-price for bus and subway. Schedules and maps at most subway stations.

Taxi: Yellow Cab ☎665-8100.

▐ ▐ ORIENTATION AND PRACTICAL INFORMATION

Pittsburgh's downtown, the **Golden Triangle,** is shaped by two rivers—the **Allegheny** to the north and the **Monongahela** to the south—which flow together to form a third river, the **Ohio.** Streets in the Triangle that run parallel to the Monongahela are numbered one through seven. The **University of Pittsburgh** and **Carnegie Mellon University** lie east of the Triangle in Oakland. *Be careful in the area north of PNC Park.* The city's streets and 40-odd bridges are notoriously difficult to navigate; don't venture into one of Pittsburgh's many tight-knit neighborhoods without getting directions first. The **Wayfinder system** helps tourists and locals alike navigate the city's often confusing streets. The 1500 color-coded signs point the way to major points of interest, business areas, and universities. To stay oriented, pick up a free visitor's guide at any visitors center.

Visitor Info: Pittsburgh Convention and Visitors Bureau, 425 6th Ave., 30th fl. (☎281-7711 or 800-359-0758; www.visitpittsburgh.com). Open M-F 8:30am-5:30pm. There are 2 **visitors centers,** 1 downtown on Liberty Ave. (open M-F 9am-5pm, Sa 9am-3pm) and 1 at the airport (open M-Sa 10am-5pm).

Hotlines: Rape Action Hotline, ☎765-2731. Operates 24hr. **Gay, Lesbian, Bisexual Center,** ☎422-0114. Operates M-F 6:30-9:30pm, Sa 3-6pm.

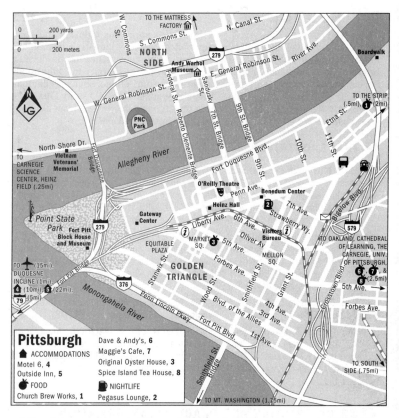

Pittsburgh

▲ ACCOMMODATIONS
Motel 6, **4**
Outside Inn, **5**

🍎 FOOD
Church Brew Works, **1**

Dave & Andy's, **6**
Maggie's Cafe, **7**
Original Oyster House, **3**
Spice Island Tea House, **8**

🍸 NIGHTLIFE
Pegasus Lounge, **2**

Internet Access: Carnegie Library of Pittsburgh, 4400 Forbes Ave. (☎622-3114). Open M-Th 10am-8pm, F-Sa 10am-5:30pm, Su 1-5pm.

Post Office: 700 Grant St. (☎642-2984). Open M-F 7am-6pm, Sa 7am-2:30pm. **Postal Code:** 15219. **Area Code:** 412.

🏠 ACCOMMODATIONS

A major blow to budget travelers, Pittsburgh's only hostel closed in 2004. Travelers in search of a cheap bed should try U.S. 60 near the airport and I-79 at Exit 60A.

Motel 6, 211 Beecham Dr. (☎922-9400), off I-79 at Exit 60A, 10 mi. from downtown. Standard lodging with TV and A/C. Reservations suggested for summer weekends. Singles $30; doubles $36. Each additional person $3. ❷

Outside Inn, 980 Rte. 228 (☎776-0626 or 800-947-2783; www.outsideinnpa.com), 20 min. north of downtown; from I-79 take the Cranberry/Mars exit, turn right, and follow Rte. 228. Located on a suburban estate, this B&B features free wine tasting from home vintages and beautiful gardens. Private baths, Internet access, fridge, patio, and hot tub. Singles $65, with breakfast $75; doubles $95. Discounts for longer stays. ❹

Bear Run Campground, 184 Badger Hill Rd. (☎724-368-3564 or 888-737-2605), in Portersville, 40min. north of Pittsburgh. From I-79 N, take PA-488 Exit 96, turn right, then turn left on Badger Hill Rd. Next to Morain State Park, the 60-acre Bear Run camp-

MID-ATLANTIC

ground provides opportunities for hiking and horseback-riding, and swimming, fishing, and canoeing on nearby Lake Arthur. Check-in 4pm. 2-person sites $24, with water and electricity $27, full hookup $28. 4-person cabins with $30 security deposit $89-109. Each additional person $4. ❶

🍴 FOOD

Aside from the pizza joints and bars downtown, **Oakland** is the best place to find a good inexpensive meal. Collegiate watering holes and cafes pack **Forbes Avenue** around the University of Pittsburgh, while colorful eateries and shops line Walnut **Street** in Shadyside and **East Carson Street** in the South Side. The **Strip District** on Penn Ave. between 16th and 22nd St. (north of downtown along the Allegheny) bustles with Italian, Greek, and Asian cuisine. The Saturday morning **Farmers Market** sells an abundance of fresh produce and fish.

🏛 **The Church Brew Works,** 3525 Liberty Ave. (☎688-8200). You can pray to the beer gods at this unique brewery/restaurant, which resides in an abandoned church complete with vaulted ceiling, beautiful stained-glass windows, and beer vat altar. The contemporary American menu includes favorites like 7-onion soup ($3.50), untraditional *pierogi* stuffed with different fillings each day ($6.50), and excellent pizzas ($12-15). Homemade beer $3-4.50 per pint. Open M-Th 11:30am-11:45pm, F-Sa 11:30am-1am, Su noon-10pm. Kitchen closes M-Th 9:30pm, F-Sa 11pm, Su 9pm. ❸

🏛 **Spice Island Tea House,** 253 Atwood St. (☎687-8821), in Oakland. Escape to this urban oasis and the world of tea in this dim, candle-filled cafe. The pan-Asian menu covers everything from *pad thai* to more exotic dishes, while an encyclopedic tea list runs the gamut from cool Thai iced tea ($3.75 per pot) to darjeeling fit for a king. Entrees from $6.25-13. Open M-Th 11:30am-9pm, F-Sa 11:30am-10pm. ❷

Primanti Brothers, 46 18th St. (☎263-2142), in the Strip District. Designed for truckers with big appetites and no time for side orders, the cheese steaks ($4.75) are piled high with cole slaw, tomato, and french fries, stuffed between two thick slices of bread. Try it with chili cheese fries ($3.25) or Pittsburgh-style chili ($2.50). Wash it down with an Iron City beer for the true 'Burgh experience. Open 24hr. 4 other locations in the city. ❶

The Original Oyster House, 20 Market Sq. (☎566-7925). Pittsburgh's oldest restaurant and bar serves cheap seafood platters ($5-7.35) and fresh fish sandwiches ($2.50-7.35) in a smoky marble and wrought-iron bar, decorated with photos of sports heroes and panoramic shots of Miss America pageants. Open M-Sa 9am-11pm. ❶

Maggie's Cafe, 320 Atwood St. (☎688-0608), offers a tasty vegetarian menu, including items like barbecue tofu and spinach-porcini pie. Entrees $9-11. Open Su-M and W-Th 11:30am-9pm, F-Sa 11:30am-9:30pm. ❷

Dave & Andy's, 207 Atwood St. (☎681-9906). Pushing the envelope of ice cream flavordom, the owners collect leftover hops from local breweries to create flavors like Vanilla Bean Golden Ale and Chocolate Bell Tower Malt. More common flavors are also made on site. Try one of the homemade waffle cones (from $2.50) and find an M&M surprise at the end. Open M-F 11:30am-10pm, Sa-Su noon-10pm. ❶

👁 SIGHTS

GOLDEN TRIANGLE. The **Golden Triangle** is home to **Point State Park** and its famous 200 ft. fountain. Near the park entrance, the **Fort Pitt Museum** is constructed in the shape of the battlements that once guarded the rivers. Exhibits are sometimes accompanied by actors in colonial garb. *(☎281-9284; www.fortpitt-museum.com. $5, seniors $4, ages 6-17 $2. Open W-Su 9am-5pm.)* The **Duquesne and Monongahela Incline,** in the South Side, carries visitors up a steep track, rising

400 ft. to offer spectacular views of the city. *(1220 Grandview Ave. Access from W. Carson St. ☎ 381-1665. Open M-Sa 5:30am-12:45am, Su 8:45am-12:45am. One-way $1.75, children 6-11 $0.85, under 6 free.)* Founded in 1787, the **University of Pittsburgh** stands in the shadow of the 42-story **Cathedral of Learning,** at Bigelow Blvd. between Forbes and 5th Ave. in Oakland. The Cathedral features 26 "nationality classrooms" decorated by artisans from the city's many ethnic traditions, from austere 16th-century English to elaborate 18th-century African styles. In December, the rooms honor various traditional holidays. *(☎ 624-6000; www.univ-relations.pitt.edu/natrooms. Cassette-guided tours M-F 9am-2:30pm, Sa 9:30am-2:30pm, Su 11am-2:30pm. $3, seniors $2, ages 8-18 $0.50.)*

CARNEGIE. Back when Pittsburgh was a bustling steel metropolis, Andrew Carnegie was both its biggest robber baron and its biggest benefactor. Carnegie's most spectacular gift, **The Carnegie,** across the street from the Cathedral of Learning, holds two museums. The **Natural History Museum** houses models of all seven continents, as well as a collection of fossils and gems, and the **Art Museum** displays an impressive collection of artwork through the ages. *(4400 Forbes Ave. ☎ 622-3131; www.carnegiemuseums.org. Open Tu-Sa 10am-5pm, Su noon-5pm; July-Aug. also M 10am-5pm. $10, seniors $7, students and ages 3-18 $6.)* The **Carnegie Science Center,** next to Heinz Field, has an earthquake simulation, a WWII submarine, and planetarium. Next door at the new **SportsWorks,** sprint against Jackie Joyner-Kersee, or attempt to hit a running receiver with a pass. *(1 Allegheny Ave. ☎ 237-3400; www.carnegiemuseums.org. Open Su-F 10am-5pm, Sa 10am-7pm. $14, seniors and ages 3-18 $10; Omnimax prices vary.)*

OTHER SIGHTS. The ◪**Andy Warhol Museum,** on the North Side, is the world's largest museum dedicated to a single artist. Seven floors of the Pittsburgh native's material include pop portraits of Marilyn Monroe, bovine psychedelia in a room covered with pink cow wallpaper, and interactive pieces like *Silver Clouds,* a room where visitors can play among floating helium-filled metallic pillows. The museum does a fantastic job of placing Warhol's work in its proper cultural context. *(117 Sandusky St. ☎ 237-8300; www.warhol.org. Open Tu-Th and Sa-Su 10am-5pm, F 10am-10pm. $10, seniors $7, students and ages 3-18 $6.)* From the Warhol, it's a short drive to **The Mattress Factory** in the North Side. Recognized as the best facility of site-specific installation art in the US, the factory serves as an experimental studio space and allows guests to literally walk into artwork. Call ahead for directions and *be careful in the surrounding area. (505 Sampsonia Way, off East Commons. ☎ 231-3169; www.mattress.org. Open Tu-F 10am-5pm, Sa 10am-7pm, Su 1-5pm. $8, students and seniors $5, under 12 free. Free Th.)* Near the Carnegie, the **Phipps Conservatory and Botanical Gardens** is packed with plants from around the world and allows visitors to walk amongst live butterflies. A $36.6 million renovation will add a tropical forest to the already-impressive facility. *(1 Schenley Park. ☎ 622-6914; www.phipps.conservatory.org. Open Tu-Th and Sa-Su 9am-5pm, F 9am-9pm. $6, seniors $5, students $4, children 3-13 $3. Tours Tu-Sa 11am and 1pm, Su 1pm.)* At the **Pittsburgh Zoo and PPG Aquarium,** a circular path winds through Asian forests, African savannahs, and tropical rainforests, past Siberian tigers and other exotic fauna. The aquarium houses spectacular sea creatures including sharks and stingrays. *(1 Wild Pl. ☎ 665-3640 or 800-4744-966; www.pittsburghzoo.com. Open daily late May to Aug. 10am-6pm; Sept.-May 9am-5pm. Apr.-Nov. $8, seniors $7, children 2-13 $6; Dec.-Mar. $6, seniors and children 2-13 $5. Parking $3.50.)* In Penn Hills, an eastern suburb of Pittsburgh, is the first Hindu temple in the US. The **Sri Venkateswara (S.V.) Temple,** modeled after a temple in Andhra Pradesh, India, has become a major pilgrimage site for American Hindus. Non-Hindus can walk through the Great Hall and observe prayer. *(1230 S. McCully Dr. ☎ 373-9863.)*

🎵 🎭 ENTERTAINMENT AND NIGHTLIFE

The weekly *City Paper* and *Pulp* are great sources for free, up-to-date entertainment listings. The acclaimed **Pittsburgh Symphony Orchestra** performs September through May at **Heinz Hall**, 600 Penn Ave. (☎392-4900; www.pittsburghsymphony.org. Tickets $19-73; student rush 2hr. before performance $14.) The **Pittsburgh Public Theater** performs popular and original plays at the **O'Reilly Theater**, 621 Penn Ave. (☎316-1600; www.ppt.org. Tickets $29-55, students $12.) Broadway musicals, ballets, and opera performances light up the stage at the **Benedum Center**, 803 Liberty Ave. (☎456-6666; www.pgharts.org. Matinees $12-36, evening shows $18-46.) Tickets to performing arts events can be obtained at the **Box Office at Theatre Square**, at Penn and 7th St. (☎456-6666. Open M-Sa 9am-9pm, Su noon-6pm.) At brand-new **PNC Park**, 115 Federal St., on the North Side, the **Pirates** (☎321-2827; tickets $9-35) play ball from April through September. The **Steelers** (☎323-1200; tickets are very difficult to obtain) storm the gridiron from September through December down the road at **Heinz Stadium**. The NHL's **Penguins** (☎800-642-7367; tickets $16-106) rock the ice at **Mellon Arena**.

The **Strip District** is stocked with large bars and clubs, and a hip crowd fills **East Carson Street** on the South Side. The **Station Square** complex, across the Smithfield St. Bridge from downtown, offers bars, clubs, and moderately priced restaurants.

Nick's Fat City, 1601-1605 E. Carson St. (☎481-6880), in the South Side, features local and regional rock 'n' roll bands; its stage has seen the likes of Prince and Bruce Springsteen. Cheap drafts of Yuengling (a favorite PA brew) and a bar full of rock memorabilia make this a 'Burgh hot spot. Shows W-Sa. Cover varies. Open Tu-Sa 8am-2am.

Jack's, 1117 E. Carson St. (☎431-3644), at S. 12th St., in the South Side. The only bar in the 'Burgh open 365 days a year packs in a rowdy but friendly crowd. M hot dogs $0.25. W wings $0.15. M-W $1 beer. 21+. Open M-Sa 7am-2am, Su 11am-2am.

Sports Rock Cafe, 1400 Smallman St. (☎552-1000), offers something for everyone: a sports bar, a dance club, a game room, and live music F-Sa. 21+. Sports bar open M-Th 11:30am-midnight, F-Su 11:30am-2am. Dance club open F-Sa 9pm-2am.

Pegasus Lounge, 818 Liberty Ave. (☎281-2131), downtown, spins house on a multi-level dance floor and has drag shows for the gay and lesbian community. W drag shows. 21+, Tu and Th-F 18+. Open Tu-Sa 9pm-2am.

Casey's, 1811 E. Carson St. (☎431-3595), on the South Side, is a standard pub until late in the evening, when a midget emerges from a roost above the bar. $2 drafts with daily drink specials. Midget M-Sa 10pm-2am. Open M-Sa 4pm-2am.

▶ DAYTRIPS FROM PITTSBURGH

OHIOPYLE STATE PARK

Masses come each year to raft Ohiopyle's 8 mi. of class III and IV rapids. Some of the best whitewater rafting in the East, the rapids take about 4-5hr. to conquer. For novices, class I and II rapids ease rafts down sections of the river. Five outfitters front Rte. 381 in "downtown" Ohiopyle: **White Water Adventurers** (☎800-992-7238; www.wwaraft.com), **Wilderness Voyageurs** (☎800-272-4141; wilderness-voyageurs.com), **Laurel Highlands River Tours** (☎800-472-3846), **Ohiopyle Trading Post** (☎888-644-6795), and **Youghiogheny Outfitters** (☎800-967-2387). Trip prices on the Youghiogheny River ("The Yock" to locals) vary ($20-145 per person per day), depending on the season, day of the week, and difficulty. Prices for rentals do not fluctuate as much. (Rafts about $15-20 per person; canoes $25-50; inflatable kay-

FALLINGBUILDING?

Frank Lloyd Wright designed some of the 20th century's most important buildings. Unfortunately, the renowned architect didn't design all of them to last. Until recently his most famous project, Fallingwater, was in great danger. Wright's emphasis on clean horizontal lines often led him to utilize cantilevers, in which a structure is anchored only at one end and thus appears to float in thin air. At Fallingwater, Wright cantilevered the home's terrace over the adjacent waterfall, creating its signature feature. But while the house was aesthetically breathtaking, the beams that kept the massive terrace from plunging into Bear Run's bubbling waters weren't sufficient to support its weight. When the scaffolding was first removed upon completion of the project in 1936, the terrace sagged almost 2 in. By 1995, it was sagging by 7 in., and computer models predicted its eventual collapse. So the Western Pennsylvania Conservancy undertook an ambitious restoration project, reinforcing the support beams with steel cable to prevent further sagging. While they were at it, they waterproofed the place. (As it turns out, flat roofs don't drain very well.) As they finished the work in 2004, the WPC had spent $11.5 million to preserve a house that had originally cost $155,000 to build, but they had ensured that water would be the only thing falling at Fallingwater.

aks about $18-35.) In order to float anything, you need a **launch permit** from the park office. (☎724-329-8591. M-F free, Sa-Su $2.50. Call at least 30 days in advance for Sa permits. Rental companies provide free permits.) For guided trips, park in the lot on Dinnerbell Rd. across the street from the park office; a shuttle takes adventurers back to their cars. Ohiopyle also offers biking, fishing, rock climbing, and camping opportunities. (Bikes from $3 per hr., fullday guided tour $70-76.) The **visitors center,** off Rte. 381 on Dinnerbell Rd. has information on the park and surrounding areas. (☎329-8591 or 888-727-2757 for camping reservations. Visitors center open May-Oct. daily 10am-4:30pm; Nov.-Apr. M-F 8am-4pm. Campsites have water and showers. Primitive sites $12-17, full hookup $2 extra; cottages $27-36.)

FALLINGWATER

Fallingwater, 8 mi. north of Ohiopyle on Rte. 381, is a masterpiece by the king of modern architecture, Frank Lloyd Wright. Designed in 1935 for Pittsburgh's wealthy Kaufmann family, the house exemplifies Wright's concept of organic architecture, incorporating original boulders into its structure and striking a perfect symbiosis with its surroundings. The house appears as though it will cascade over the waterfall it sits on, and the water's gentle roar can be heard in every room. (☎329-8501. Open mid-Mar. to Nov. Tu-Su 10am-4pm; also some weekends in Dec. and the first 2 weekends in Mar. 10am-3pm. Reservations required. Access to grounds $6. Tours Tu-F $12, ages 6-18 $8; Sa-Su $15/$10. In-depth tours $40/$50. Children under 6 must be left in child care, $2 per hr.) For a more intimate and quaint Frank Lloyd Wright home, head to the nearby **Kentuck Knob,** on Kentuck Rd., 6 mi. north of U.S. 40, where a guided tour examines the grounds, rustic "usonian" home, and greenhouse. (☎329-1901; www.kentuckknob.com. Open May-Aug. Su-F 9am-4pm, Sa 9am-6pm; Mar.-Apr. and Sept.-Dec. 9am-4pm; Jan.-Feb. 11am-3pm. Call for reservations. Tours M-F $12, under 18 $10; Sa-Su $15/$12.)

DELAWARE

Tiny Delaware is a sanctuary from the sprawling cities of Boston, New York City, Philadelphia, and Washington, D.C. First explored by Henry Hudson in 1609, when he sailed up the Delaware River in search of a northwest passage to the Pacific Ocean, Delaware was fought over by the Dutch, Swedish, and English until 1664, when the Duke of York sent troops to secure the land. Delaware was first to ratify the US Constitution on December 7, 1787, and proudly totes its tag as the "First State." The history of Delaware has been dominated by the wealthy DuPont clan, whose gunpowder mills became one of the world's biggest chemical companies. Today, tax-free shopping and scenic beach towns dotted with lighthouses lure visitors to Delaware from all along the nation's eastern shores.

🄑 PRACTICAL INFORMATION

Capital: Dover.

Visitor Info: Delaware State Visitors Center, 406 Federal St., Dover 19901 (☎302-739-4266; www.destatemuseums.org/vc). Open M-Sa 8am-4:30pm, Su 1:30-4:30pm.

Postal Abbreviation: DE. **Sales Tax:** 8% on accommodations only.

WILMINGTON
☎302

In 1683, a Swedish ship, the *Kalmar Nyckel*, sailed from Europe to the banks of what was then called the "South River," leaving its passengers to successfully establish the colony of New Sweden. These days, city of Wilmington might as well be named DuPontville, because from the grand Hotel DuPont downtown to the DuPont mills along the Brandywine River and the DuPont estates out in the valley, there's no escaping the DuPont name around here. Today, both the DuPont estates and the history-rich colonial sites draw visitors to Wilmington.

⊞ 🄑 ORIENTATION AND PRACTICAL INFORMATION. Wilmington is situated in northern Delaware, directly across the Delaware Memorial Bridge from New Jersey. The **I-95** freeway connects Wilmington to Philadelphia 29 mi. to the north and Baltimore 76 mi. to the southwest. Downtown Wilmington is set up on a grid of one-way streets. Numbered streets run east-west starting from the south, while named streets, many taking the names of presidents or trees, run north-south. The two major roads leading into the downtown are **Martin Luther King, Jr. Boulevard (Route 48)** and **Delaware Avenue (Route 52),** which also runs out of town, toward the DuPont estates. *Exercise caution in the area between the restored riverfront and downtown. All areas south of 8th St., except the riverfront, can be dangerous.* Parking is free at riverfront attractions and curbside on weekdays after 5pm and on weekends. Otherwise, lots charging $5-8 per day can be reached through the **Wilmington Parking Authority** (☎655-4442). **Airport: Philadelphia International Airport** (☎800-745-4283 or 215-937-6937; www.phl.org) is 20 mi. north of Wilmington on I-95. The **Delaware Express Shuttle** is available by reservation; rides from the Philadelphia airport to Wilmington are about $31. (☎454-7800 or 800-43-5466; www.delexpress.com.) **Amtrak,** 100 S. French St. (☎658-1515; open M-F 5:45am-9:30pm, Sa 6am-8:45pm, Su 6am-9:30pm), at the corner of Martin Luther King, Jr. Blvd. and French St., runs to Boston (5-6½hr., 10 per day, $104) and New York City (2½hr., 10 per day, $58). *Use caution in this area at night.* **Greyhound,** 101 N. French St. (☎655-6111), in the Wilmington Transport Center, runs to: Baltimore (1-2hr., 9 per day, $21); Boston (7½-10hr., 12 per day, $64); New York City (2½hr., 12 per day, $38); Philadelphia (1hr., 7 per day, $8). Open daily 6:30am-midnight. **DART** runs buses in the Wilmington area: bus #7 stops throughout downtown 7am-3:30pm, and bus #32 runs trolleys between riverfront attractions and downtown. (☎800-652-3277; www.dartfirststate.com. $1.15; all-day pass $2.40, excludes bus #32, which is $0.25 per ride.) **Taxi: Yellow Cab** (☎658-4340). **Greater Wilmington Convention and Visitors Bureau,** 100 W. 10th St., Ste. 20, at Orange St. (☎652-4088 or 800-489-6664; www.visit-wilmingtonde.com. Open M-F 9am-5pm.) **Internet Access: Wilmington Institute**

JAMAICAN ME CRAZY FOR REGGAE

Ibis and Genny Pitts of Wilmington's World Music store remember the first time they met Bob Marley back in the mid-1960s. His wife Rita walked into their store, danced barefoot in the aisles, and promised to bring her husband by the next time he was in Wilmington. She kept her promise, and Bob Marley's own mother, who lives in Wilmington, has called Ibis and Genny Bob Marley's first American friends. The two couples kept in close touch as Marley's reggae career blossomed, and the Pitts were won over by Marley's exuberant music and peaceful world vision.

For the last ten years, the Pitts have held a festival in their friend's honor in Wilmington's Tubman-Garrett Riverfront Park. This celebration of reggae, rock, and roots music draws surviving members of the Marley family—in 2004, Marley's sons Stephen, Ziggy, Julian, Ky-mani, and Damian performed together—as well as a variety of other prominent musical acts, such as the Universal African Dance and Drum Ensemble.

The two-day **People's Festival Tribute to Bob Marley** (☎302-665-9394) is usually held on a weekend in mid-Aug. Sa 2pm-10pm and Su 2-8pm. Tickets Sa $30, Su $25; 2-day pass $45. Buy your tickets in advance through Ticketmaster to get a $5 discount.

Main Library, at the corner of 10th and Market St. (☎571-7400. Open M-Th 11am-8pm, F-Sa 11am-4pm.) **Post Office:** 1101 N. King St. (☎800-276-8767. Open M-F 7am-5:30pm, Sa 9am-2pm.) **Postal Code:** 19801. **Area Code:** 302.

ACCOMMODATIONS. Wilmington's hotels cater to businesspeople; while cheap accommodations are hard to find, rates drop significantly over the weekend. Upscale chains and the city's landmark **Hotel DuPont** can be found on **King Street** downtown. Otherwise, look to **Newark, DE,** just south on I-95, for budget chain motels. The best value in Wilmington is the **McIntosh Inn ❸,** 300 Rocky Run Pkwy., at the Concord Pike (Rte. 202), which includes continental breakfast, an exercise room, and a 24hr. convenience center, in addition to spacious rooms. (☎479-7900 or 800-444-2775. Doubles from $65.) B&Bs in the Brandywine Valley range from pricey to very pricey. In an elegant, relaxing setting, the **Faunbrook B&B ❺,** 699 W. Rosedale Ave., in West Chester, PA, 20min. north of Wilmington on Rte. 100, is perfect. Faunbrook's Italianate estate, complete with a vast mahogany porch, boasts seven guest rooms with private baths and two acres of gardens. (☎610-436-5788; www.faunbrook.com. No smoking. 3-course candlelight breakfast included. Check-in 3-9pm. Check-out 11am. Rooms $105-140.) Though there is no camping in the immediate Wilmington vicinity, **Lums Pond State Park ❶,** 1068 Howell School Rd., 30 mi. south of Wilmington, offers a retreat from the urban metropolis. Drive south on I-95 to Exit 1A (Middleton), onto Rte. 896 S, then follow it 6 mi. until you cross Rte. 40. Turn left at the third light after Rte. 40 onto Howell School Rd. Campers have access to showers, flush toilets, bicycle and horseback-riding trails, fishing, and rowboat and canoe rentals. (Reservations ☎368-6989 or 877-987-2757; www.destateparks.com. Tent sites $21 for up to 4 people; each additional person $2. Rowboats $6 per hr., $30 per day; canoes $5 per hr., $25 per day.)

FOOD. Authentic Indian cuisine is hard to come by, even in big cities, but the **Panghat Indian Restaurant ❷,** 301 W. 4th St., at Tantall St., is loyal to its origins. From the chicken *makhani* (chicken with mild tomato sauce and butter cooked in a traditional clay oven, the *tandoor;* $10) to the vegetarian house specialty *navratan korma* (nine vegetables with nuts in a mildly spiced yogurt sauce, $8) this restaurant is sure to please. (☎658-6276. $6 lunch buffet daily 11:30am-2:30pm; dinner Su-Th 5-9:30pm, F-Sa 5-10pm.) For simple diner fare, head to the **Sterling Grill ❶**, 919 Orange St. This local favorite serves short stacks of pancakes for $2 and waffles for $3; add an order of breakfast meat (including "scrapple," a regional meat medley), for only $1.10. (☎ 652-3575. 9 in. subs $4. Open daily 6am-3pm.) Overlooking the waterfront, the **Iron Hill Brewery ❺**, is on 710 S. Madison St. Delicate appetizers like the Vietnamese lettuce wraps ($9) and hearty entrees like seafood paella ($18) almost seem beside the point compared to the river views. (☎ 472-2739; www.ironhillbrewery.com. Open M-Sa 11:30am-1am, Su 11am-1am.)

◪ SIGHTS. All four DuPont estates are popular tourist attractions. Closest to downtown Wilmington, the **Hagley Museum** emphasizes the home and work life of the DuPonts, with tours of the original family home and black powder works. The mechanically oriented will love the enormous stone mills, water turbines, steam engines, and powder testers. Take I-95 north to Exit 5B (Newport), follow Rte. 141 north for 7 mi., and after crossing Rte. 100 look for the Hagley entrance on the left. (☎ 658-2400; www.hagley.lib.de.us. Open mid-Mar. to Dec. daily 9:30am-4:30pm; Jan. to mid-Mar. Sa-Su only. Guided tours M-F 1:30pm. $11, seniors $9, children ages 6-14 $4.) Farther north on Rte. 141, **Nemours Gardens and Museum,** 1600 Rockland Rd., on the 300-acre country estate of Alfred DuPont, was built to resemble a Louis XVI chateau. The mansion contains over 47,000 sq. ft. of antique furniture and priceless art, while formal French gardens extend from the museum along the driveway up to the house. (☎ 651-5912 or 800-651-5912; www.nemoursmansion.org. 2hr. guided tours; arrive at reception at least 15min. prior to tour. Reservations recommended. Tours May-Oct. Tu-Sa 9, 11am, 1, and 3pm; Su 11am, 1, and 3pm. Children under 12 not admitted. $12.) Botany enthusiasts should not miss the **Winterthur Estate and Gardens,** on Rte. 52, 6 mi. northwest of Wilmington. Samuel DuPont engineered the garden to create a perfect harmony of color and design—as each individual flower blossoms, it complements its neighbors. Inside the mansion, the interior and furnishings are so extensive that several differently themed guided tours are required to cover it all. (☎ 888-4600 or 800-448-3883; www.winterthur.org. Open Tu-Su 10am-5pm, last tickets sold 3:45pm. Guided tours leave frequently; call ahead for info about particular tours. Garden tram operates Mar.-Dec. 2-day pass including one guided tour, unlimited tram rides, and access to the galleries and special exhibitions $20, students and seniors $18, ages 2-11 $10. Wheelchair accessible.) The fourth DuPont estate, farthest from Wilmington, is the **Longwood Gardens,** over 1050 acres of woodlands, meadows, and indoor and outdoor gardens. Whether you like fountains or topiaries, wildflowers or hothouse flowers, Italian-style lakes or open-air theaters, there is a Longwood garden for you. Take Rte. 52 northwest 12 mi. from Wilmington, just over the Pennsylvania state line, then turn west onto Rte. 1 and follow it to Kennett Square. (☎ 610-388-1000 or 800-737-5500; www.longwoodgardens.org. Open daily Apr.-Oct. 9am-6pm; Nov.-Mar. 9am-5pm. Hours extended to 10pm on Tu, Th, and Sa evenings in summer for the Festival of Fountains. Apr. to late Nov. M and W-Su $14, Tu $10; late Nov. to early Jan. daily $15; early Jan. to Mar. M and W-Su $12, Tu $8. Ages 16-20 year-round $6, ages 6-15 $2, under 6 free. Wheelchair accessible.)

The story of the first Swedish settlers in Delaware is retold daily at **Fort Christiana Park** and the **Kalmar Nyckel Shipyard.** Visitors can tour a Swedish farmhouse built in 1690, a 1698 church, the Hendrickson House Museum of colonial artifacts, or even an authentic recreation of the *Kalmar Nyckel*, complete with seven working cannons. (*Kalmar Nyckel* Shipyard, 1124 E. 7th St., on the riverfront: ☎ 429-7447; www.kalmarnyckel.org. Tours on Sa in summer; call for hours. $5, students $4, ages 12 and under $3. Pirate-themed trips to Lewes Sa in summer; call for hours. $40, students $30, ages 12 and under $12. Old Swedes Church and Hendrickson House Museum, 606 Church St., just west of the shipyard: ☎652-5629; www.oldswedes.org. Services June-Sept. Su 8 and 10am. Tours W-Sa 10am-4pm. $2.) The **Delaware History Museum,** 504 Market St. Mall, is renowned for the interactive exhibit, "Distinctively Delaware," and covers over 400 years of history, from the region's Native American inhabitants to the founding of New Sweden and up to the present. (☎656-0637; http://hsd.org. Open M-F noon-4pm, Sa 10am-4pm. $4, seniors $3, ages 2-18 $2.) *Use caution in this area.*

ENTERTAINMENT AND NIGHTLIFE. Music, theater, and dance venues cluster in the downtown area, particularly on **Market Street.** Meanwhile, a rowdier crowd gathers at college bars and clubs in the **Trolley Square** area on the northwest side of town, centered around Delaware Ave. For fine cocktails in a calmer setting, try the restaurant-bars along the **Riverfront.** On the waterfront next to stately restaurants, **Kahunaville** is strictly for the brave of heart. Young crowds flock to this entertainment mega-complex for the slamming rock, heavy drinking, and an arcade room. Themed nights are common. (☎571-8402; www.kahunaville.com. Live music F-Sa after 11pm, DJ Th and Su. No hats, sleeveless shirts, or work boots. 21+ after 10pm. Cover $7 after 8pm. Open M-Sa 11:30am-1am, Su 11:30am-10pm. Reduced menu M-Th after 10pm.) Once the Kahunaville kids take corporate jobs downtown, they'll begin to frequent the professionals' favorite, **Sugarfoot,** 1007 N. Orange St., in the bottom floor of a large Nemours office complex. A purveyor of deluxe sandwiches by day, this sleek, polished little shop serves free hors d'oeuvres during the weekday cocktail hour. (☎654-1600. Cocktail hour W-F 4-8pm. Restaurant open M-F 7am-3pm.) On the north side of town, **Catherine Rooney's Irish Pub,** 1616 Delaware Ave., features traditional Irish food, imperial pints, a conversation-inducing double-sided bar, and live Irish music on the weekend. (☎654-9700; www.catherinerooneys.com. Open M-Sa 10am-1am, Su 11am-1am.) **Club X,** 837 N. Orange St., draws young singles with a variety of events. The dance floor heats up on the weekend, but Monday is movie night with free popcorn and Tuesdays feature free pool. (☎777-2225; www.clubxdelaware.com. 21+. Cover Sa $15 with open bar 9-11pm. Open daily 10pm-2am.) **Baxter's,** 2006 Pennsylvania Ave., at Union St., draws a mixed, gay-friendly crowd to its upscale restaurant and lounge. The crowd on the dance floor Thursday to Saturday ranges in age and sexual orientation, with an even mix of men and women. (☎654-9858; www.baxtersclub.com. $1 off drinks during happy hour M-F 4-7pm, Sa 5-7pm, Su 6-8pm. 21+ if not dining. Open M-F 4pm-2am, Sa 5pm-2am, Su 6pm-2am.)

LEWES ☎302

At a time when the Swedes were contemplating settling just to the north and the English were moving into the New World in droves, the Dutch gained a foothold in America with Lewes (pronounced Lewis). With its unaltered Victorian houses and genuine lack of tourist culture, Lewes's main draw—especially for the older and wealthier set—remains its beautiful beach. Secluded among scrub pines 1 mi. east of Lewes on the Atlantic Ocean is the 4000-acre **Cape Henlopen State Park,** where kids frolic in the waves under the watchful eyes of lifeguards. The park is also home to sparkling dunes, a 2 mi. paved trail, and a WWII observation tower. (☎645-8983; www.destateparks.com. Open daily 8am-sunset. $5 per car; bikes and pedestrians free.) Bike rentals are free at the **Seaside Nature Center.** (☎645-6852; www.destateparks.com. Open daily July-Aug. 9am-5pm; Sept.-June 9am-4pm. Bikes and helmets available 9am-4pm; 2hr. limit. Bikes must be used within park boundaries.) The **Zwaanendael Museum,** 102 Kings Hwy., is filled with relics of maritime history. (☎645-1148. Open Tu-Sa 10am-4:30pm, Su 1:30-4:30pm. Free.) For a hands-on experience, tour the **Overfalls Lightship,** located on the Lewes & Rehoboth Canal north of the Savannah Rd. bridge. Built in 1938 as a floating lighthouse, fog horn, and radio beacon, it has retired to Lewes after suffering structural damage in a storm off the Massachusetts coast. (☎ 645-4733; www.overfalls.org. Guided tours late May to early Sept. F-Sa 11am-4pm, Su 1-4pm. $2, students $1.) Tours of Lewes's historic buildings begin at the **Historical Society,** on Shipcarpenter St. near 2nd St. (☎ 645-7670. Open June-Aug. M-F 10am-4pm, Sa 10am-1pm. $6.)

Summer weekend stays in Lewes are expensive; for clean, affordable lodging, try the **Vesuvio Motel ❹,** 105 Savannah Rd. (☎ 645-2224. A/C, cable TV. Singles May-Sept. $75-95, low-season $45-65; doubles $90-125/$55-85.) The **Captain's Quarters Motel ❹,** 406 Savannah Rd., has similar rates and simple rooms a bit farther from the beach. (☎ 644-2003. A/C, cable TV. Rooms in summer Su-Th $85, F-Sa $100.) To reach the **Cape Henlopen State Park ❶,** take Rte. 1 to Cape Henlopen Dr.; signs mark the park on the left. A short walk to the beach, the park also has fishing, bird-watching, and nature programs. (☎ 645-8983, reservations 877-987-2757; www.destateparks.com. Hot showers, flush toilets. Open Mar.-Nov. 4-person sites $26, with water faucet $28. Additional persons $2. Nature Center: ☎ 645-6852.) Restaurants in Lewes cluster primarily on 2nd St. Locals come to the wood-paneled **Rose and Crown Restaurant and Pub ❷,** 108 2nd St., for great burgers ($5-7) and live blues and rock on weekends. (☎ 645-2373. Happy hour daily 3-6pm. Open Su-Th 11am-9:30pm, F-Sa 11am-10:30pm.) Once a sea captain's house, **The Buttery ❸,** 2nd and Savannah St., serves delicious grilled salmon teriyaki and Caribbean-spiced flank steak. (☎ 645-7755. Lunch $7-15. Dinner $18-32. Open daily 11am-2:30pm and 5pm-late; Su brunch 10:30am-2:30pm.) **Kings Homemade Ice Cream Shop ❶,** 201 2nd St., is an entrenched local favorite. The owner, Milton, fondly recalls the days when he would give Pete DuPont, then Delaware's governor, free ice cream. (☎ 645-9425. 1 scoop $2.50, 2 scoops $3.50. Open May-Oct. daily 11am-11pm.)

Lewes is best reached by car; from points north, Rte. 1 S runs directly to Savannah Rd., which bisects the town. From the west, travel east on Route 404, then take Rte. 9 E from the junction in Georgetown to Rte. 1; continue south to Savannah Rd. **Delaware Resort Transit** shuttles run from the ferry terminal through Lewes to Rehoboth and Dewey Beach. (☎ 800-553-3278; www.beachbus.com. Operates every 30min. late May to early Sept. daily 7am-2am. $1, seniors and disabled $0.40; day pass $2.10.) **Taxi: Seaport Taxis** ☎ 645-6800. The **Fisher-Martin House Information Center,** 120 Kings Hwy., offers everything a tourist would want to know, and then some. (☎ 645-8073 or 877-465-3937; www.leweschamber.com. Open M-F 10am-4pm, Sa 9am-3pm, Su 10am-2pm.) **Post Office:** 116 Front St. (☎ 644-1948. Open M-F 8:30am-5pm, Sa 8am-noon.) **Postal Code:** 19958. **Area Code:** 302.

REHOBOTH BEACH ☎ 302

Rehoboth Beach lies between Lewes and Ocean City, both geographically and culturally. While Lewes tends to be quiet and family-oriented and Ocean City attracts rowdy high-schoolers, Rehoboth manages to balance its discount-boardwalk fun with serene, historic B&Bs. On summer weekends the beach is a zoo, packed end to end with vacationing families and the town's burgeoning gay population.

■▄ ▐ **ORIENTATION AND PRACTICAL INFORMATION.** To reach Rehoboth, take **Route 1B** to **Rehoboth Avenue** and follow it to the water. Parking near the beach is a rare commodity—rather than worry constantly about the pesky meter monitors, drop your friends and family off at the beach with your gear and find a parking spot off the main drag. **Greyhound/Trailways,** 801 Rehoboth Ave. (☎ 227-1080 or 800-454-2487), stops next to the Chamber of Commerce. Buses go to: Baltimore (5½hr., 1 per day, $32); Philadelphia (4hr., 2 per day, $32); Washington, D.C.

(3½hr., 3 per day, $36). The 1¾hr. **ferry** to Cape May is the best option for island-hopping. (☎800-643-3779; www.capemaylewesferry.com. Office open daily 8:30am-4:30pm. 8 per day. Reservations required; call at least 24hr. in advance. Check-in 30min. prior to departure. Passenger cars Apr.-Oct. $25, Nov.-Dec. $20; motorcyclists $23/$18; bicyclists $8/$6.) The **Rehoboth Beach Chamber of Commerce,** 501 Rehoboth Ave., a former railroad depot next to an imitation lighthouse, provides info on area attractions, dining, and accommodations. (☎227-2233 or 800-441-1329; www.beach-fun.com. Open M-F 9am-5pm, Sa-Su 9am-1pm.) **Post Office:** 179 Rehoboth Ave., at 2nd St. (☎227-8406. Open M-F 9am-5pm, Sa 8:30am-12:30pm.) **Postal Code:** 19971. **Area Code:** 302.

⚐☎ ACCOMMODATIONS AND FOOD. Inexpensive lodging in Rehoboth disappears as the summer season reaches its peak. Unless you want to spend over $100 (or, even more likely, over $200), forget staying on the boardwalk. The comfortable porch at **The Abbey Inn ❸,** 31 Maryland Ave., is just a block from Rehoboth Ave. (☎227-7023. 2-night min. stay. Open late May to early Sept. Singles and doubles with shared bath from $48; triples and quads from $61. 15% more on weekends.) The Kandler family owns and operates the **Pirate's Cove Motel ❹,** 625 Rehoboth Ave., and prides itself on the clean rooms. (☎227-2844; www.rehoboth-beach.com/piratescove. A/C, cable TV. Rooms $59-159, with peak rates in July.) **Big Oaks Family Campground ❶,** 1 mi. off Rte. 1 on Rd. 270, has laundry, a pool, a store, and a bus to the beach. (☎645-6838. Tent sites $34, RV sites $42.)

Rehoboth is known for its high-quality beach cuisine, but a lot of it comes at resort prices. At the charming **Back Porch Cafe ❹,** 59 Rehoboth Ave., just blocks from the beach, you can enjoy a healthy gourmet lunch on the open-air patio. Sauteed soft-shelled crab with Thai red curry ($14) and the potato, bacon, leek, and *gruyère* cheese omelette ($10) are specialties. (☎227-3674. Open daily 11am-3pm and 6-10pm.) At **Cafe Papillon ❷,** 42 Rehoboth Ave., in the Penny Lane Mall, French cooks serve fresh crepes and croissants ($2.50-3) and stuffed baguette sandwiches for $5-8. (☎227-7568. Open June-Aug. M-Sa 8am-11pm. Call for hours in May and Sept.) Escape predictable surf and turf at **Sir Guy's ❷,** 243 Rehoboth Ave., which serves English pub fare in a sports bar setting. British specialties include fish 'n' chips ($8.50), shepherd's pie ($8), and bangers, beans, and mash (Irish sausage with baked beans and mashed potatoes) for $8. (☎227-7616; www.sirguys.com. Open M-Tu and Th-Su 11:30am-1am, W 5pm-1am.) **Royal Treat ❷,** 4 Wilmington Ave., flips up pancakes and bacon for just $5.90; omelettes are around $8. (☎227-6277. Open daily June-Aug. for breakfast 8-11:30am; ice cream 1-11:30pm.)

☢ NIGHTLIFE. Rehoboth partygoers head out early to maximize their time before 1am last calls. **The Summer House Saloon,** 228 Rehoboth Ave., across from City Hall, is a favorite flirtation spot for college-aged singles. (☎227-3895; www.summerhousesaloon.com. Su 4-8pm half-price daiquiris. M half-price burgers. Th live blues-rock 9:30pm-1:30am. F live DJ 9pm-1am. Open May-Sept. M and Sa-Su 4pm-1am, Tu-F 5pm-1am.) Look for live music (F-Sa 10pm-1am) at **Dogfish Head Brewings & Eats,** 320 Rehoboth Ave. Try one of their 13 award-winning homemade microbrews, or get a 5-beer sampler tray for $5. (☎226-2739; www.dogfish.com. Happy hour M-F 4-6pm, with $2 rum and gin drinks. Open May-Aug. M-Th 4-11pm, F 4pm-1am, Sa noon-1am, Su noon-11pm; Sept.-Apr. M and Th 4pm-midnight, F 4pm-1am, Sa noon-1am, Su noon-11pm.) An established hotspot, **The Blue Moon,** 35 Baltimore Ave., is a restaurant-bar that rocks to the sounds of techno music for a predominantly gay, male crowd. (☎227-6515. Happy hour M-F 4-6pm. Su brunch with Bloody Mary bar $17. Open daily 4pm-1am.) For a lesbian-friendly scene, head to **The Frog Pond,** on the corner of 1st St.

and Rehoboth Ave., known for serving the best Buffalo wings and quesadillas in town. (☎227-2234. Happy hour M-F 4pm-7pm. F-Sa nights live music. Th karaoke. Open M-Sa 11am-1am.) **Cloud 9**, 234 Rehoboth Ave., is an upscale bar and restaurant that serves fancy cocktails to a mixed crowd. (☎226-1999; www.cloud9restaurant.com. Happy hour daily 4-7pm. M half-price pasta. Th buy-one-get-one-free entrees and karaoke after 9pm. DJ F-Su. Open Apr.-Oct. daily 4pm-1am; Nov.-Mar. M and Th-Su 4pm-1am.)

MARYLAND

Once upon a time, folks on Maryland's rural eastern shore trapped crabs, raised tobacco, and ruled the state. Meanwhile, across the bay in Baltimore, workers loaded ships and ran factories. Then the federal government expanded, industry shrank, and Maryland had a new focal point: the Baltimore-Washington Pkwy. As a result, suburbs grew and Baltimore revitalized. As D.C.'s generic suburbs continue to swell beyond the limits of Maryland's Montgomery and Prince George counties, and Baltimore revels in its immensity, Annapolis—the state capital—remains a small town of sailors. Late summer visitors will hit Maryland right in the peak of crab season, so don't forget to give those "Chesapeake blues" a taste. Between the crabbing and clamming, museum-going and antiquing, bird-watching and people-watching, there's never a dull moment for visitors to Maryland.

⚡ PRACTICAL INFORMATION

Capital: Annapolis.

Visitor Info: Office of Tourism, 217 E. Redwood St., 9th fl., Baltimore 21202 (☎800-634-7386; www.mdisfun.org).

Postal Abbreviation: MD. **Sales Tax:** 5%.

BALTIMORE ☎410

Nicknamed "Charm City" for its mix of small-town hospitality and big-city flair, Baltimore impresses visitors with its lively restaurant and bar scene, first-class museums, and devotion to history. The pulse of the city lies beyond its star attraction, the glimmering Inner Harbor, in Baltimore's overstuffed markets, coffee shops, and diverse citizenry. However, it would be unwise to head into Baltimore expecting to find only the shining touristy sites, as parts of the city are notoriously crime-ridden. Although gentrification and restoration efforts have succeeded in making the Inner Harbor, Fells Point, Camden Yards, and Canton safe and attractive again, be wary of the rest of the central city area, especially the West Side, as well as the far south end of the city.

📧 TRANSPORTATION

Airport: Baltimore-Washington International (BWI; ☎859-7111; www.bwiairport.com), on I-195 off the Baltimore-Washington Pkwy. (I-295), about 10 mi. south of the city. Take MTA bus #17 to the Nursery Rd. Light Rail station. Airport **shuttles** to hotels (☎703-416-6661 or 800-258-3826; www.supershuttle.com) run daily every 30min. 5:45am-11:30pm. $11 to downtown Baltimore. Shuttles leave for D.C. daily every hr. 5:45am-11:30pm ($26-34). **Amtrak** trains from BWI run to Baltimore ($5) and D.C. ($12). **MARC** commuter trains run M-F to Baltimore ($3.25) and D.C. ($5).

MID-ATLANTIC

MID-ATLANTIC

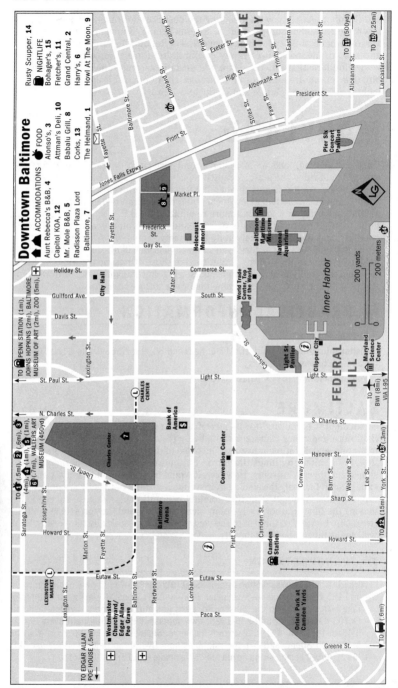

Downtown Baltimore

▲ **ACCOMMODATIONS**
Aunt Rebecca's B&B, **4**
Capitol KOA, **12**
Mr. Mole B&B, **5**
Radisson Plaza Lord
Baltimore, **7**

◆ **FOOD**
Alonso's, **3**
Attman's Deli, **10**
Babalu Grill, **8**
Corks, **13**
The Helmand, **1**

■ **NIGHTLIFE**
Bohager's, **15**
Fletcher's, **11**
Grand Central, **2**
Harry's, **6**
Howl At The Moon, **9**

Rusty Scupper, **14**

Trains: Penn Station, 1500 N. Charles St., at Mt. Royal Ave. Easily accessible by bus #3 or 11 from Charles Station downtown. **Amtrak** trains run every 3min.-1hr. To: **New York City** (from $70); **Philadelphia** (from $43); **Washington, D.C.** (from $14). On weekdays, **MARC commuter rail** (☎800-325-7245 in MD) connects Baltimore to D.C.'s Union Station (☎859-7400 or 291-4268) from **Penn Station** (with stops at BWI) or **Camden Station,** at Howard and Camden St. Ticketing open daily 5:30am-9:30pm; self-serve ticketing kiosks available 24hr.

Buses: Greyhound (☎800-231-2222) has 2 locations: downtown at 2110 Haines St. (☎752-7682); and at 5625 O'Donnell St. (☎633-6389), 3 mi. east of downtown, at Exit 57 off I-95, just north of the toll tunnel. To: **Philadelphia** ($20); **New York City** ($38); **Washington, D.C.** ($11).

Public Transit: Mass Transit Administration (MTA), 300 W. Lexington St., near N. Howard St. (☎866-743-3682, schedule info M-F 6am-7pm 539-5000; www.mtamaryland.com). Bus, Metro, and light rail service to most major sights in the city. Some buses run 24hr. Metro runs M-F 5am-midnight, Sa 6am-midnight. Light rail runs M-F 6am-11pm, Sa 8am-11pm, Su 11am-7pm. One-way fare $1.60, students $1.10, seniors and disabled $0.55; higher on light rail to outer suburbs. Day passes for use of buses, Metro, and light rail $3.50.

Water Taxi: Harbor Boating, 1732 Thames St. (☎563-3901 or 800-658-8947; www.thewatertaxi.com). Main stop in the Inner Harbor; other stops at harbor museums and restaurants, Harborplace, Fells Point, Little Italy, and more. Runs Apr.-Oct. every 15-18min.; Nov.-Mar. every 40min. Service May-Aug. M-Th 10am-11pm, F-Sa 10am-midnight, Su 10am-9pm; Apr. and Sept.-Oct. M-Th 11am-8pm, F 11am-midnight, Sa 10am-midnight, Su 10am-8pm; Nov.-Mar. daily 11am-6pm. Day pass $6, ages 10 and under $3. Ticket includes coupons for Baltimore attractions.

Taxi: American Cab ☎636-8300. **Arrow Cab** ☎261-0000.

■ ▐ ORIENTATION AND PRACTICAL INFORMATION

Baltimore lies 35 mi. north of D.C. and about 150 mi. west of the Atlantic Ocean. From D.C., take the **Baltimore-Washington Parkway. Exit 53** from **Route 395** leads right into the **Inner Harbor;** without traffic, the trip takes less than an hour. **Baltimore Street** (east-west) and **Charles Street** (north-south) divide the city. The **Inner Harbor,** at Pratt and Charles St., is home to historic ships and attractions. **Little Italy,** served by city buses #7 and 10, sits on the bay a few blocks east of the Inner Harbor, past the Jones Falls Expressway. A short walk to the southeast brings you to bar-happy **Fells Point,** also served by city bus #10. *Be careful: Moving north or east from Fells Point, away from the waterfront, will lead you into dangerous neighborhoods.* The museum-laden, artistic **Mount Vernon** neighborhood, served by city buses #3 and 11, occupies **North Charles Street,** north of Baltimore St., around **Monument Street** and **Centre Avenue.** Old-fashioned **Federal Hill,** accessed by city buses #1 and 64, contains Fort McHenry. *Use caution in Federal Hill and areas to the south.* The **Camden Yards** baseball stadium and M&T Bank Stadium lie across I-395 from Federal Hill. *Venturing more than a few blocks north of Camden Yards will place you in the historic, but dangerous, West Side.*

Visitor Info: Baltimore Area Visitors Center, 401 Light St. (☎877-225-8466; www.baltimore.org). In a new building, this user-friendly center provides maps, brochures with discounts, and the helpful and free *Quickguide.* Open M-Sa 9am-5pm, Su 10am-5pm.

Hotlines: Suicide, ☎531-6677. **Sexual Assault and Domestic Violence,** ☎828-6390. Both 24hr. **Gay and Lesbian,** ☎837-8888. Operates daily 7pm-midnight.

MID-ATLANTIC

Internet Access: Enoch Pratt Free Library, 400 Cathedral St. (☎396-5430; www.pratt.lib.md.us). Open M-W 11am-7pm, Th 10am-5:30pm, F-Sa 10am-5pm; Oct.-May also Su 1-5pm. Free.

Post Office: 900 E. Fayette St. (☎347-4202). Open M-F 7:30am-10pm, Sa 8:30am-5pm. **Postal Code:** 21233. **Area Code:** 410.

ACCOMMODATIONS

Expensive hotels dominate the Inner Harbor. To reserve bed and breakfasts, contact **Bed and Breakfast Accommodations, Ltd.** (☎413-582-9888; www.bedandbreakfast-maryland.com. From $65 per night. Open M-F 10am-5pm.)

■ **Aunt Rebecca's B&B,** 106 E. Preston St. (☎625-1007; www.auntrebeccasbnb.com), in the Mount Vernon district. This hidden treasure full of gilded mirrors and chandeliers has only 3 bedrooms, but if you can book one of them you'll save big over the downtown hotels. Free parking. A queen bedroom with TV, A/C, private bath, and full breakfast, plus the caring attention of the hosts Joe and Becky is around $85. ❹

Mr. Mole Bed and Breakfast, 1601 Bolton St. (☎866-811-2477; www.mrmolebb.com), in the Bolton Hill district on the northwest edge of town. This B&B offers suites for the same price as standard rooms downtown. Phone, private bath, A/C, and Dutch breakfast. Queen suites $129-139; king suites $159-189. ❺

Radisson Plaza Lord Baltimore, 20 W. Baltimore St. (☎539-8400 or 800-466-4644; www.radisson.com), between Hanover and Charles St., in the Inner Harbor. A national historic landmark built in 1928 with a Renaissance-inspired lobby and large, this is the oldest still-functioning hotel in Baltimore. The location—just 6 blocks from the Inner Harbor—and historic flavor prove an unbeatable combination. Fitness center. Parking $25 per night. Reservations recommended. Rooms $129-199. 10% AAA discount. ❺

Capitol KOA, 768 Cecil Ave. N (☎923-2771 or 800-562-0248, from Baltimore 987-7477), in Millersville, 20min. from Baltimore, toward D.C. Take I-97 south for 8½ mi. to Exit 10A (Benfield Blvd E). Turn right at the blue KOA sign and follow the signs from there. Mostly RVs, some cabins, and a small wooded area for tents. Pool, volleyball courts, playground, and bathroom/shower facilities. Free shuttle to MARC commuter train Odenton Station M-F; to New Carrollton Metro Sa-Su. Open Mar. 25-Nov. 1; low-season is Mar.-Apr., Oct., and weekdays in May. and Sept. Tent sites for 2 $34, low-season $32; water and electricity $40/$37; RV complete hookup $44/$42; 1-room cabin $59/$56; 2-room cabin $69/$65. Additional adult $5. ❷

FOOD

■ **Corks,** 1026 S. Charles St. (☎752-3810; www.corksrestaurant.com), in Federal Hill. A hidden retreat that specializes in a vast array of strictly American wines and fine contemporary American cuisine made with classic French techniques and Asian influences by Chef Jerry Pellegrino. The formal front room is ideal for dining with friends; dimly lit, the larger back "cellar" is for sheer romance. Semi-formal attire. Entrees like the crisp proscuitto wrapped salmon with curried chive spaetzle and asparagus puree $24-29. Open M-Th 5-10pm, F-Sa 5-11pm, Su 5-9:30pm. Reservations recommended. ❺

■ **Babalu Grill,** 32 Market Pl. (☎234-9898), in Power Plant Live. This Cuban restaurant smacks of authenticity. Appetizers include turnovers with seasoned beef and avocado salsa ($6). Sides like rice and beans ($4) or fried plantains ($5) go well with lobster, served hot on a bed of coconut rice ($29). Babalu turns into a hot salsa club F-Sa nights ($5 cover 10-11pm, $10 cover after 11pm). Open for lunch Th-F 11:30am-3pm; dinner M-Th 5-10pm, F-Sa 5-11pm, Su 4-9pm. Club open F-Sa 11pm-2am. ❹

The Helmand, 806 N. Charles St. (☎752-0311; www.thehelmand.com). This unassuming Afghan restaurant is the best in town, with dishes like *kabuli* (Afghan-style rice baked with chunks of lamb tenderloin, raisins, and glazed julienne of carrots). Entrees up to $10. Vegetarians have a variety of options, and desserts like *feereny,* an eggless pudding with fruit, will satisfy all sweet tooths. Open Su-Th 5-10pm, F-Sa 5-11pm. ❷

The Rusty Scupper, 402 Key Hwy. (☎727-3678), in the Inner Harbor, is a landmark, serving fresh seafood with a waterfront view. The waterman's po' boy, with oysters or popcorn shrimp in a roll with spicy remoulade sauce ($9-10), is famous. Open M-Th 11:30am-10pm, F-Sa 11:30am-11pm, Su 11am-10pm. Su jazz brunch 11am-2pm. ❹

Attman's Deli, 1019 E. Lombard St. (☎563-2666), on Baltimore's "corned beef row," has made a name for itself serving hot pastrami ($5.50) and corned beef sandwiches ($5) just like you'd find in New York City since 1915. The Reuben ($6.50) was even voted Baltimore's best. Open M-Sa 8am-6:30pm, Su 8am-5pm. ❷

Alonso's, 415 W. Cold Spring Ln. (☎235-3433; www.alonsos.com), in the Roland Park neighborhood near Johns Hopkins University, Exit 9A from I-83 N, is famous for 1 lb. hamburgers ($12). The portobello panini ($8) and the crab cake sandwich ($14) are a little more manageable. Open Su-Th 11am-10:30pm, F-Sa 11am-11:30pm. ❸

◉ SIGHTS

Baltimore's gray harbor ends with a colorful bang in the **Inner Harbor,** a body of water surrounded by five blocks of eateries, museums, and boardable ships.

THE NATIONAL AQUARIUM. The ▧**National Aquarium** is known throughout the country as one of the best places to ogle and learn about sealife. Though a visit to the outdoor sea pool to watch slap-happy seals play is free to the general public, it is worth the time and money to venture inside. The eerie **Wings in the Water** exhibit showcases 50 species of stingrays in an immense backlit pool. In the steamy **Tropical Rainforest,** piranhas, parrots, and a pair of two-toed sloths peer through the dense foliage in a 157 ft. glass pyramid. At the **Marine Mammal Pavilion,** dolphins perform every hour on the half-hour. *(Pier 3, 501 E. Pratt St. in the Inner Harbor. ☎576-3800; www.aqua.org. Open July-Aug. Su-Th 9am-6pm, F-Sa 9am-8pm; Mar.-June and Sept.-Oct. Sa-Th 9am-5pm, F 9am-8pm; Nov.-Feb. Sa-Th 10am-5pm, F 10am-8pm. Remains open 1½hr. after last entrance time. $18, seniors $15, ages 3-11 $9.50, under 3 free. Tickets are sold for a particular entrance time on busy summer days and can be purchased in advance online.)*

BALTIMORE MARITIME MUSEUM. Several ships grace the harbor by the aquarium, most of which belong to the Baltimore Maritime Museum. Visitors may clamber through the interior of the **USS Torsk,** the intricately-painted submarine that sank the last WWII Japanese combat ship, or board one of the survivors of the Pearl Harbor attack, the Coast Guard cutter **Roger B. Taney,** and ascend the **octagonal lighthouse** on Pier 5. For these historic sites and more, purchase the **Seaport Day Pass,** which grants access to the **Maritime Museum,** the **Museum of Industry,** Baltimore's **World Trade Center,** and the **USS Constellation**—the last all-sail warship built by the US Navy. Water taxi service to and from attractions is included. *(Piers 3 and 5. ☎396-3453; http://baltomaritimemuseum.org. In the summer the Taney is open daily 10am-5:30pm, the Chesapeake lightboat 10am-6pm, the Torsk 10am-8:30pm. All boats open in spring and fall Su-Th 10am-5pm, F-Sa 10am-6pm; in winter F-Su 10am-5pm. Boats stay open 1hr. later than ticket stand. $7, seniors $6, ages 5-13 $4. Seaport Day Pass $16/$14/$9.)*

MARYLAND SCIENCE CENTER. From the prehistoric to the futuristic, the Maryland Science Center is a kid- and adult-friendly museum that explores how science touches our daily lives and our imaginations. The Hubble Space Telescope Visitors

Center and the new traveling exhibit about Jane Goodall and the chimps of Gombe, Tanzania are fascinating, and children will love the dinosaur dig exhibit and "Your Body: the Inside Story." *(601 Light St. ☎685-5225; www.marylandsciencecenter.org. Open in summer Su-W 10am-6pm, Th-Sa 10am-8pm. Adults $14 for most exhibits, plus traveling exhibits $17, plus one IMAX movie $18, plus traveling exhibits and one IMAX movie $20; ages 3-12 $13/$16/$17/$19; ages 60 and up $9.50/$12/$13/$14.)*

WALTERS ART MUSEUM. Spanning 50 centuries, the **Walters Art Museum** houses one of the largest private art collections in the world. The Ancient Art collection features sculpture, jewelry, and metalwork from Egypt, Greece, and Rome, and is the museum's pride and joy. Byzantine, Romanesque, and Gothic art are also on display. At the **Hackerman House,** an exquisite townhouse/mansion attached to the Walters, rooms filled with dark wooden furniture, patterned rugs, and plush velvet curtains display art from China, Korea, Japan, and India. *(600 N. Charles St. Take bus #3 or 11. ☎547-9000; www.thewalters.org. Open W-Su 10am-5pm, first Th of every month 10am-8pm. Tours Sa 11:30am and Su 2pm. $8, seniors $6, ages 18-25 $5, 18 and under free. Admission to permanent collection free Sa 10am-1pm and first Th of every month.)*

EDGAR ALLAN POE HOUSE. Horror pioneer Edgar Allan Poe was born in 1809 in what is now a preserved historical landmark. In between doses of opium, Poe penned famous stories such as *The Tell-Tale Heart* and *The Pit and the Pendulum*, as well as macabre poems like *The Raven* and *Annabel Lee*. The house contains Poe's telescope sextant, traveling desk, and exhibits relating to Poe, all impeccably maintained by a staff eager to regale visitors with all sorts of Poe stories. *Steer clear of this neighborhood at night. (203 N. Amity St., near Saratoga St. Take bus #15 or 23. From Lexington Market, walk on N. Lexington St. away from downtown and turn right on Amity St. It is the 2nd house on the right. ☎396-7932; www.eapoe.org. Open Aug.-Dec. W-Sa noon-3:45pm. $3, under 13 and active military free.)*

JOHNS HOPKINS UNIVERSITY. Approximately 3 mi. north of the harbor, prestigious **Johns Hopkins University (JHU)** spreads out from 33rd St. JHU was the first research university in the country and a world leader in developments in medicine, public health, and engineering. The campus was originally the Homewood estate of Charles Carroll, Jr., the son of the longest-lived signer of the Declaration of Independence. Free 1 hr. campus tours begin at the **Office of Admissions** in Garland Hall. *(JHU: 3400 N. Charles St. Take bus #3 or 11. ☎516-8171; www.jhu.edu/~admis/visit/guidedtours.html. Tours Sept.-May M-F 10am and 1pm, Sa by reservation; call admissions for summer hours, ☎516-5589.)* One mile north of the main campus, **Evergreen House** is an exercise in excess—the bathroom of this elegant mansion is plated in 23-carat gold. Purchased in 1878 by railroad tycoon John W. Garret, the house, along with its collections of fine porcelain, rare artwork, and Tiffany silver, was bequeathed to JHU in 1942. *(Evergreen House: 4545 N. Charles St. ☎516-0341; www.jhu/edu/~evergreen/evergreen.html. Take bus #11. Open M-F 10am-4pm, Sa-Su 1-4pm. Tours every hr.; last tour 1hr. before close. $6, students $3, seniors $5.)*

🎵 ENTERTAINMENT

Much of Baltimore's finest entertainment can be enjoyed free of charge. At **Harborplace,** street performers delight tourists with magic acts and juggling during the day. The **Baltimore Museum of Art** offers jazz concerts on summer Saturdays at 7pm (May-Sept.) in its sculpture garden. *(☎396-6314; www.artbma.org. $15.)* The canvas-topped **Pier 6 Concert Pavilion** presents concerts from May to October, ranging from classical to R&B to rock 'n' roll. *(☎625-3100; www.piersixpavillion.com. Tickets $15-50. Pier Pass to 4 concerts $100.)* Never thought you were the type to go to the orchestra? The **Baltimore Symphony Orchestra** is out to change your mind. The orchestra plays at **Meyerhoff Symphony Hall,** 1212 Cathedral St., from September to May and during the month-long Summerfest, but the real secret is the college nights, when $10 student tickets include admission and a reception with free beer and food from the Hard Rock Cafe. (☎783-8000; www.baltimoresymphony.org. Box office open M-F 10am-6pm, Sa-Su noon-5pm, and 1hr. before performances. Tickets $15-52. Various discounts available 1hr. before concerts.)

The **Lyric Opera House,** 110 W. Mt. Royal Ave., near Maryland Ave., hosts the **Baltimore Opera Company** from October to April. (☎727-6000; www.baltimoreopera.com. Box office open M-F 10am-5pm. Tickets $57-108.) Broadway shows are performed all year at the **Mechanic Theater,** 25 Hopkins Plaza, at Baltimore and N. Charles St. (☎481-7328; www.themechanic.org. Box office open daily 10am-5pm. Tickets $27-60.) The **Theater Project,** 45 W. Preston St., near Maryland St., experiments with theater, poetry, music, and dance. (☎752-8558. Box office open 1hr. before shows; call to charge tickets. Shows Th-Sa 8pm, Su 3pm. $16-18, seniors $11-15.) The **Arena Players,** the first black theater group in the country, performs comedies, drama, and dance. (801 McCullough St., at Martin Luther King, Jr. Blvd. ☎728-6500. Box office open M-F 10am-2pm. Tickets start at $15.) From June through September, the **Showcase of Nations Ethnic Festivals** celebrate Baltimore's ethnic neighborhoods with a different culture featured each week. Call the Baltimore Area Visitors Center for info. (☎837-7024.)

The beloved **Baltimore Orioles** play ball at **Camden Yards,** just a few blocks from the Inner Harbor at the corner of Russell and Camden St. (Box office ☎685-9800, M-F 9am-5pm. Tickets $7-50.) The NFL's **Ravens** play in **M&T Bank Stadium,** next to Camden Yards. (☎481-7328; www.ravenszone.net.)

◪ NIGHTLIFE

Nightlife in **Mount Vernon** reminds one of Cheers, where neighborhood bars serve middle-aged patrons they call by name, while **Fells Point** and **Power Plant Live** cater to a college and 20-something crowd, with loud music, sweaty dance floors, and ever-flowing alcohol. Be aware of the 1:30am last call. If you make it through the literally dozens of bars in Fells Point, head to **Canton** for a similar scene.

Bohager's, 701 S. Eden St. (☎563-7220), between Spring and Eden St. in Fells Point. A tropical paradise for college students and folks who drink like them. Patrons jive to the sounds of DJs' island and house mixes under a retractable dome in the most dependably debauched club in Baltimore. Open bar F-Sa 8pm-1:45am. Cover F $15, Sa 8pm-9pm $10, Sa after 9pm $15. Open M-F 11:30am-2am, Sa-Su 3pm-2am.

Howl At The Moon, 22 Market Pl. (☎783-5111), in Power Plant Live. An amusing dueling-piano bar where the crowd runs the show. All songs are by request, and sing (or perhaps "howl") alongs are frequent. The crowd here ranges in age from just-barely-adults to could-be-your-parents and comes with a more relaxed attitude than the testosterone-fueled bars of Fells Point. Happy hour F 5-8pm with half-price drinks and a complimentary buffet. Beer $3-5. Cocktails $4-8. Cover F-Sa $5 after 7pm, $7 after 8pm. Open Tu-Th 7pm-2am, F 5pm-2am, Sa 5:30pm-2am.

Grand Central, 1001 N. Charles St. (☎752-7133; www.centralstationpub.com), at Eager St. Chill under lights from the set of *A Few Good Men* or play some pool with a mixed gay/straight crowd. In fact, this gay-friendly club was voted Baltimore's Best Gay and Lesbian Bar in 2003. Karaoke M 10pm-2am. Open mic Tu 11pm-2am. Tu Men's Night, Th Ladies' Night. Happy hour daily 4-8pm with $1 off beer. $2 Smirnoff Su 4pm-2am. The disco club next door is the spot for hot bumping and grinding W-Su 9pm-2am. Cover F-Sa $6. Open M-Sa 4pm-2am, Su 3pm-2am.

Fletcher's, 701 S. Bond St. (☎558-1889; www.fletchers.com), brings in live bands on the weekend to entertain its barflies, featuring rock, rap, and blues acts most often. Happy hour M-Th 4:30-6:30pm and all day Su. Beer from $2.50. Cover $5-12. Doors open at 7, 8, or 9pm depending on the night. Closing time 2am daily.

Harry's, 1200 N. Charles St. (☎685-2828), is a Vegas-style bar and performance space. Shows F-Sa nights. W open mic night. Cover $5-12. Open daily 11:30am-2am.

ANNAPOLIS ☎410

Annapolis became the capital of Maryland in 1694, and in 1783 enjoyed a stint as temporary capital of the US. Since them, it has walked the tightrope between a residential port town and a naval garrison dominated by its world-famous Naval Academy. The historic waterfront district retains its 18th-century appeal despite the presence of ritzy boutiques. Crew-cut "middies" ("midshipmen," a nickname for Naval Academy students) mingle with longer-haired students from St. John's (the country's third oldest college) and couples on weekend getaways amid the highest concentration of historical homes in America.

■ ⑦ **ORIENTATION AND PRACTICAL INFORMATION.** Annapolis lies southeast of U.S. 50, 30 mi. east of D.C. and 30 mi. south of Baltimore. The city extends south and east from two landmarks: **Church Circle** and **State Circle. School Street,** in a blatantly unconstitutional move, connects Church and State. **East Street** runs from the State House to the Naval Academy. **Main Street,** where food and entertainment venues abound, starts at Church Circle and ends at the docks. Downtown Annapolis is compact and easily walkable, but finding a **parking** space—unless in an expensive lot or in the public garage ($7-11 per day)—can be tricky. If a convenient metered spot doesn't come your way, parking at the visitors center ($1 per hr., $8 max. weekdays, $4 max. weekends) is the best bet. There is also free weekend parking in State Lots A and B, at the corner of Rowe Blvd. and Calvert St. **Greyhound** (☎800-231-2222) buses stop at the Mass Transit Administration bus stop at 308 Cinquapin Rd. Tickets are available from the bus driver; cash only. To: Baltimore (30min., 3 per day, $10); Philadelphia (4-5hr., 3 per day, $24); Washington, D.C. (1-2hr., 3 per day, $14). The **Annapolis Department of Public Transportation** operates a web of city buses connecting the historic district with the rest of town. (☎263-7964. Buses run daily M-Sa 5:30am-10am, Su 8am-7pm. $0.75, seniors and disabled $0.35.) **Taxi: Annapolis Cab Co.** ☎268-0022. **Checker Cab** ☎268-3737. **Car Rental: Budget,** 2001 West St. (☎266-5030). **Visitor Info: Annapolis and Anne Arundel County Conference and Visitors Bureau,** 26 West St., has free maps and brochures. (☎280-0445; www.visit-annapolis.org. Open daily 9am-5pm.) **Post Office:** 1 Church Cir. (☎263-9292. Open M-F 9am-5pm.) **Postal Code:** 21401. **Area Code:** 410.

⌐ **ACCOMMODATIONS.** The heart of Annapolis favors elegant and pricey B&Bs over cheap motels. Rooms should be reserved in advance, especially for weekends, spring graduations, and the summer. The **Annapolis Bed and Breakfast Association** (www.annapolisbandb.com) is a good place to start. True to its name, six flags wave from the large front porch of ◪**Flag House Inn** ❾, 26 Randall St., which has a prime location next to the Naval Academy, but only five rooms. The complimentary full breakfast includes house specialties like blueberry french toast and orange croissants. All rooms come with cable TV and A/C. (☎280-2721 or 800-437-4825; www.flaghouseinn.com. Rooms $120-250.) **Scotlaur Inn** ❹, 165 Main St., sits atop Chick & Ruth's Delly. Ten tiny guest rooms with queen, double, or twin beds, A/C, TVs, and private baths grace this homey "bed & bagel." (☎268-5665;

www.scotlaurinn.com. Check-in 2pm. Check-out 11am. Rooms $89-125.) Lower rates can be found 4 mi. outside of downtown at the **Annapolis Motel ❸**, 101 Ferguson Rd., Exit 28 from Rte. 50/301. Standard rooms come with cable TV and A/C; deluxe rooms also include a microwave and refrigerator. (☎757-3030. Singles Su-Th $50, F-Sa $55; deluxe room $10 more. Additional person $5.)

❏ **FOOD.** Most restaurants cluster around **City Dock**, an area packed with people in the summer, especially on Wednesday nights at 7:30 when the spinnaker races finish at the dock. Find cheap eats at the **Market House** food court, at the center of City Dock, where a hearty meal costs under $5. A Swedish coffeehouse with an Idaho twist, **Potato Valley Cafe ❷**, 47 State Cir., across from the State House, specializes in giant oven-roasted baked potatoes stuffed with fillings ($5-7). Topping choices range from the standard sour cream, cheese, and bacon, to the exotic curry dressing with pineapple. (☎267-0902. Open M-F 10am-5pm, Sa 11:30am-5pm.) An acclaimed menu and chic design make **Aqua Terra ❺**, 164 Main St., a high-end NYC-style bistro serving contemporary American cuisine, a worthwhile splurge. (☎263-1985. Open Tu-Th 5:30-10pm, F-Sa 5:30-11pm, Su 5-9pm.) Locals flock to **Carrol's Creek Bar & Cafe ❷**, 410 Severn Ave., in the Annapolis City Marina Complex, for home-cooked food and cheap drinks along the waterfront. Texas barbecued shrimp ($10) and Maryland crab soup ($6.50) are favorites. Happy hour (M-F 5-7pm) features half-price appetizers. (☎263-8102; www.carrolscreek.com. Open M-Sa 11:30am-4pm and 5-10pm; Su $19 all-you-can-eat brunch 10am-1:30pm, dinner 3-9pm.)

◙ **SIGHTS.** In many senses the **US Naval Academy**, 52 King George St., is Annapolis. The legendary military school turns harried, short-haired "plebes" (first-year students) into Naval-officer "middies" (midshipmen) through rigorous drilling and physical and emotional obstacles. President Jimmy Carter and billionaire H. Ross Perot are among the Academy's celebrity alumni. Once at the Academy, the first stop should be the **Leftwich Visitors Center**, in the Halsey Field House, which doubles as a food court and hockey rink. (☎263-6933; www.navy-online.com. Open Mar.-Dec. 9am-5pm, Jan.-Feb. 9am-4pm.) Seventy-five-minute guided walking tours take visitors through historic Bancroft Hall, the chapel's crypt, a dorm room, and the athletic facilities, where the middies test their sea-faring prowess on land. **King Hall,** the world's largest dining facility, is a madhouse at lunchtime, serving the entire student populace in under 20 frenzied minutes. On Saturdays in the summer, alumni weddings (sometimes 1 per hr.) take place in the Academy's **chapel.** (Chapel open M-Sa 9am-4pm, Su 1-4pm. Often closed Sa in summer for weddings.) Underneath the chapel is the final resting place of **John Paul Jones,** father of the United States Navy, who uttered the famous words, "I have not yet begun to fight!" as he rammed his sinking ship into a British vessel. (Tours July-Aug. M-Sa 9:30am-3pm, Su 12:30-3pm; Apr.-June and Sept.-Nov. M-F 10am-3pm, Sa 9:30am-3pm, Su 12:30-3pm; Dec.-Mar. M-Sa 10am-2:30pm, Su 12:30-2:30pm. $7, seniors $6, students $5.)

The historic **Hammond-Harwood House,** 19 Maryland Ave., an elegant 1774 building designed by colonial architect William Buckland, retains period decor right down to the candlesticks. The house is most renowned for its impeccably preserved colonial doorway. The **William Paca House,** 186 Prince George St., was the first Georgian-style home built in Annapolis, and has two acres of lush vegetation. Paca, an early governor of Maryland, was one of the original signers of the Declaration of Independence. Both houses feature historical exhibits on life in the late 1700s, stocked from archaeological digs on the grounds. (Hammond-Harwood: ☎263-5553; www.hammondharwoodhouse.org. Open Apr.-Oct. W-Su noon-5pm; Nov.-Mar. F-Sa noon-4pm. 40min. tours on the hr.; last tour 1hr. before close. $6, students $5.50, under 12 $3. William Paca House: ☎990-4538 or 800-603-4020; www.annapolis.org. Open Mar.-Dec. M-Sa 10am-5pm, Su noon-5pm. Tours every 30min. Garden or house $5, seniors and AAA $4, ages 6-17 $3; combo tickets $8/$7/$5. Uniformed armed service personnel and ages 5 and under free.)

Built between 1772 and 1779, the Corinthian-columned **State House,** in the center of State Circle, is the oldest working capitol building in the nation. It was the US capitol building from 1783 to 1784, and the Treaty of Paris was signed here on January 14, 1784. Visitors can explore the historical exhibits and silver collection, or watch the state legislature bicker in two exquisite marble halls. Cordial State House guides, clad in authentic colonial garb, gladly field questions. (☎974-3400. Open M-F 9am-5pm, Sa-Su 10am-4pm; grounds 6am-11pm. Tours daily 11am and 3pm. Legislature in session mid-Jan. to mid-Apr. Free.)

🎭 🎟 **ENTERTAINMENT AND NIGHTLIFE.** Locals and tourists generally engage in one of two activities: wandering along City Dock or schmoozing 'n' boozing at upscale pubs. The bars and taverns that line downtown Annapolis draw crowds every night. If you want more culture than drink can provide, Annapolis also has performance options. Theatergoers can check out **The Colonial Players, Inc.,** 108 East St., for innovative and often unknown works. (☎268-7373; www.cplayers.com. Shows Th-Sa 8pm, Su 2:30 and 7:30pm. $15, students $10.) In the summer, the **Annapolis Summer Garden Theater,** 143 Compromise St., offers musical "theater under the stars" Th-Su at 8:30pm. Seating is $12 on the terraced lawn overlooking an open courtyard theater near City Dock. (☎268-9212; www.summergarden.com.) The **Naval Academy Band** performs on City Dock every Tuesday night at 7:30pm. (☎293-0263; www.usna.edu/usnaband. Free.)

As close as you can get to the water without falling in, **Pusser's Landing,** 80 Compromise St., facing City Dock, is located on a working pier. Make sure to look up at the impressive British-style tin ceiling while waiting for your food. (☎626-0004; www.pussers.com. Beer $2-4. Kitchen open Su-Th 7am-11pm, F-Sa 7am-midnight; bar open until 2am.) Midshipmen and tourists alike enjoy 135 different ales, lagers, and stouts, including international microbrews, among the beer-history decor at **Ram's Head Tavern,** 33 West St. Happy hour (M-F 4-7pm) includes $2 drafts and free tacos (5-7pm). Many evenings, there is free live music on the patio; for bigger-name bands, a dinner and show combination ticket gets you a 10% discount on your meal and a free drink. (☎268-4545; www.ramsheadtavern.com. Happy hour daily midnight-1am has $2 drafts. Open daily 10am-2am.) Locals and officers pack in under naval pilot-donated helmets and a two-story ficus tree growing through **Irish McGarvey's,** 8 Market Space. Saddle up to the bar for Aviator Lager, the manliest-sounding beer in town ($3.25 for 10 oz. draft, pint $5). Summer parties invite patrons to don tropical attire and enjoy frozen Zombies ($4) with their red beans and rice ($6). Happy hour (M and W 10pm-2am) features Buffalo wings for $3-10, 32 oz. drafts for $3, and 10 oz. mugs for $1. (☎263-5700; www.mcgarveys.net. Th 6pm-1am house beer $1.50. Open M-Sa 11:30am-2am, Su 10am-2am.)

ASSATEAGUE AND CHINCOTEAGUE ☎757

Local legend has it that ponies first came to Assateague Island by swimming ashore from a sinking Spanish galleon. A more likely theory is that miserly colonial farmers put their horses out to graze on Assateague to avoid mainland taxes. Whatever their origins, the famous ponies now roam free across the unspoiled beaches and forests of the picturesque island, and, on the last Wednesday and Thursday in July, swim from Assateague to Chincoteague during Pony Penning.

⬛🔢 ORIENTATION AND PRACTICAL INFORMATION. Telling the two islands apart, especially since their names are sometimes used interchangeably, can often leave visitors bewildered. **Assateague Island** is the longer barrier island facing the ocean, while **Chincoteague Island** is nestled between Assateague and mainland Eastern Shore. Maryland and Virginia share Assateague Island, which is divided into three distinct parts. **Chincoteague Wildlife Refuge** is actually on Assateague. The best way to get to Chincoteague is by car; the best way to explore it is by bike. From D.C., take Rte. 50 E to Salisbury, MD, then take Rte. 13 S and turn left onto Rte. 175 E. **Visitor Info: Chincoteague Chamber of Commerce,** 6733 Maddox Blvd., on Chincoteague. (☎336-6161; www.chincoteaguechamber.com. Open M-Sa 9am-5pm.) **Internet Access: Vacation Internet Cafe,** 4407 Deep Hole Rd. (☎336-3616; www.vacationinternetcafe.com. $3 per 15min, $10 per hr. Free wireless Internet with $3 food purchase. Open M-Sa 8am-8pm, Su 8am-4pm, but will stay open later if busy.) **Post Office:** 4144 Main St. (☎336-2934. Open M-F 8am-4:30pm, Sa 8am-noon.) **Postal Code:** 23336. **Area Code:** 757.

🔢⬛ ACCOMMODATIONS AND FOOD. Due to Assateague's lack of civilization, visitors eat and sleep on **Chincoteague.** The **Blue Heron Inn ❸,** 7020 Maddox Blvd. has clean, spacious rooms with A/C, phones, refrigerators, cable TV, use of the heated pool, and boat/camper parking. (☎336-1900 or 800-615-6343; www.chincoteague.com/blueheron/. Rates change weekly and peak at $119 during the July Pony Penning. Weekdays $44-94 year-round; $60-80 for most of June-Aug. Weekends $49-94 year-round; $75-90 for most of June-Aug.) For rooms with breathtaking views, cable TV, A/C, refrigerators, indoor and outdoor pools, and an exercise room, head to the waterfront **Island Motor Inn ❺,** 4391 Main St. (☎336-3141; www.islandmotorinn.com. June-Aug. rooms $105-175; May and Sept. $85-150; Dec-Feb. $68-140. 10% AAA and senior discount low-season.) **Maddox Family Campground ❶,** across from the visitors center, is a sprawling site with over 550 camping units, a pool, playground, grocery store, laundry, hot showers, horseshoes, and video game arcade. (☎336-3111. For full hookups, reserve at least 3 months in advance. Sites with water and electricity $30, partial hookup $33, full hookup $36.)

AJ's on the Creek ❹, 6585 Maddox Blvd., specializes in steaks and grilled fish in a dining room decked out in lace and mahogany. (☎336-5888. Dinner entrees $15-25. Open in summer M-Sa 11:30am-10pm, lounge open until 1am; in winter M-F 4-9pm, Sa 4-9:30pm.) **Connie's Family Restaurant ❷,** 6349 Maddox Blvd., serves the best fried chicken on the island. You can get meals with almost any number of pieces of chicken; buckets start at $9 for 8 pieces. (☎336-1865 or 336-3433. Open daily 10am-10pm.) Treat yourself to an unbelievably delicious shake or sundae at Muller's **Old Fashioned Ice Cream Parlor ❶,** 4034 Main St. With Muller's old-fashioned soda fountain, Victorian architecture, and homemade whipped cream to serve to top their Belgian waffles and ice cream, there's no way that big-name ice-cream chains can compete with Muller's. (☎336-5894. Open daily 11am-11pm.)

◪ SIGHTS. The **⬛Chincoteague National Wildlife Refuge** stretches across the Virginia side of the island. Avid bird-watchers come to see rare species such as snowy egrets, and black-crowned night herons. The **wild pony roundup,** held the last consecutive Wednesday and Thursday in July (after a month-long carnival), brings hordes of tourists to Assateague. During slack tide, firemen herd the ponies together and swim them from Assateague to Chincoteague Island, where the fire department auctions off the foals the following day. The adult horses swim back to Assateague and reproduce, providing next year's crop. Head to the refuge's visitors center, located just inside the refuge, to learn about biking, hiking, walking, and bird and nature tours. Guided wildlife bus tours are also available. ($12, children $8. Memorial Day-Labor Day daily 10am, 1, 4pm.) Trails include the 3 mi. pony-populated **Wildlife Loop** (open 3pm-dusk for cars, all day for pedestrians and bicyclists), the 1½ mi. **Woodland Trail** (cars not permitted), and the ¼ mi. **Lighthouse Trail** (pedestrians only). Follow Beach Rd. to its end to find the famous beach and sand dunes. Park rangers request that visitors maintain a safe distance from the ponies and resist the urge to feed them, because if overfed by guests, the ponies could starve in the winter months when visitors have left the islands. (8231 Beach Rd. ☎336-6122; http://chinco.fws.gov. Absolutely no pets permitted. Park open daily May-Sept. 5am-10pm; Apr. and Oct. 6am-8pm; Nov.-Mar. 6am-6pm. Visitors center open daily Memorial Day-Labor Day 9am-5pm; Labor Day-Memorial Day 8am-4:30pm. 7-day pass $10 per car.) The **Oyster & Maritime Museum** is the only non-profit museum in Chincoteague and contains numerous samples of sea creatures and shells. Don't miss the 1865 Barbier & Frenestre first order Fresnel lens from the old Assateague Lighthouse, one of only 21 in the US; retired in 1961, its light could be seen from 23 mi. away. (7125 Maddox Blvd. ☎336-6117; www.chincoteaguechamber.com/oyster. Open May-Sept. M-Sa 10am-5pm, Su noon-4pm; low-season hours vary. $3, ages 12 and under $1.50. Cash only.) The **Chincoteague Pony Centre** offers pony rides and showcases veterans of the pony swim. (6417 Carriage Dr. ☎336-2776; www.chincoteague.com/ponycentre. Heading north on Main St., turn right onto Church St., left onto Chicken City Rd., and right onto Carriage Dr. Open in summer M-Sa 9am-10pm. Rides available until 6pm most days. $5.)

OCEAN CITY   ☎410

Ocean City is a lot like a kiddie pool—it's shallow and plastic, but can be a lot of fun if you're the right age, or just in the right mood. This 10 mi. strip of prime Atlantic beach packs endless bars, all-you-can-eat buffets, hotels, mini golf courses, boardwalks, flashing neon, and sun-seeking tourists into a thin region between the ocean on the east and the Montego, Assawoman, Isle of Wight, and Sinepuxent bays to the west. The siren call of senior week beckons droves of recent high school and college graduates to alcohol and hormone-driven fun, turning O.C. into a city-wide block party in late May and June. During July and August, the city caters more to families and professional singles looking for fun in the sun.

■ ⚡ **ORIENTATION AND PRACTICAL INFORMATION.** Driving is the least painful mode of transportation to reach the ocean resort, though beach traffic can make getting to O.C. a headache no matter how you plan to do it. From the north, simply follow Rte. 1, which becomes **Coastal Highway (Philadelphia Avenue).** From the west, Rte. 50 also leads directly to Ocean City. If you're trekking to Ocean City from points south, take Rte. 113 to Rte. 50 and follow that to town. At most points, Ocean City has only one major road running north-south, Philadelphia Ave. Numbered streets run east-west, linking the ocean to the bay. Most hotels are in the lower-numbered streets to the south, toward the ocean; most clubs and bars are uptown toward the bay. **Greyhound/Trailways** (☎289-9307), at 2nd St. and Philadelphia Ave., sends **buses** to Baltimore (3¾hr., 4 per day, $31) and Washington, D.C. (4½-5½hr., 5 per day, $40). In town, **public buses** (☎723-1607) run the length of the strip and are the best way to get around town 24hr. a day ($2 per day for unlimited rides). The **Ocean City Visitors Center,** 4001 Coastal Hwy., at 40th St. in the Convention Center, gives out discount coupons for lodging and dining and brochures for just about every establishment in town. (☎723-8610 or 800-626-2326; www.ococean.com. Open June-Aug. M-F 8:30am-5pm, Sa-Su 9am-5pm; Sept.-May daily 8:30am-5pm.) **E-Point Internet Cafe,** 1513 Philadelphia Ave., in the 15th St. Shopping Center complex, offers access. (☎289-9844. $4 per 30min., $7 per hr.

Open daily 10am-2am. Cash only.) **Post Office:** 7101 Coastal Hwy. (☎524-7611. Open M-F 9am-5pm, Sa 9am-noon.) **Postal Code:** 21842. **Area Codes:** 410, 443. In text, 410 unless otherwise noted.

⌶ ACCOMMODATIONS. Reservations are essential in the summer, or you won't find a room at any price within 30 mi. of the beach. Weekend prices are about $20-25 higher than weekday prices, but many guest houses and motels offer weekly rates at a discount. The **Atlantic House Bed and Breakfast ❺**, 501 N. Baltimore Ave., offers discounted bike rental coupons, a full breakfast buffet, a great location, and a wholesome change of pace from the Ocean City motel trend. (☎289-2333; www.atlantichouse.com. Complimentary beach chairs, umbrellas, and towels. A/C, cable TV, hot tub, parking. Closed Dec.-Mar. except for Valentine's Day. May-Aug. rooms with shared bath from $100, with private bath $125. Rates drop in low season.) A half-block from the beach, the **Sea Spray Motel ❹**, 12 35th St., sports a dark wood interior and copious amenities. Some rooms have kitchens and porches; all have cable TV and A/C. (☎289-6648 or 800-678-5702; www.seaspray-motel.com. Gas grill access, laundry facilities. Rooms early May weekdays $50, weekends $80; late May to June $125/$140; July-Aug. $115/$130; Sept. $59/$73.) The only in-town camping option is **Ocean City Travel Park ❸**, 105 70th St., only one and a half blocks from the ocean. This cramped site is expensive for a campsite, but is still the cheapest lodging in town. Laundry, hot showers, flush toilets, a game room, and a boat ramp are available. (☎524-7601; www.occcamping.com. Tent sites late May to Sept. weekdays $37, weekends $47, holidays $57. Small RVs $42/$52/$62. Large RVs $52/$62/$72. Apr. to mid-May $27-49; Oct.-Nov. $25-35.)

⌷ FOOD. Ocean City's cuisine vacillates between the two extremes of hyper-expensive linen-napkin gourmet and cheap, grease-laden buffet. Ice cream, funnel cakes, and sno-ball stands beckon from the boardwalk, but most sit-down eateries are just off the shoreline. **⧉Brass Balls Saloon & Bad Ass Cafe ❶**, on the Boardwalk between 11th and 12th St., is known for its $1.25 JELL-O shots (after 10pm). The motto here is "Drink Hearty, Eat Healthy." Specials like the $5.25 Oreo waffles and the $7 pizzas seem to defy the latter imperative, though the college crowds can't get enough of the "drink hearty" part. (☎289-0069. Open Mar.-Oct. M-F 8:30am-2am, Sa-Su 8am-2am.) Vegetarians, spicy food lovers, up-all-nighters, kosher-keepers, and those just tired of the same old steak and seafood entrees love **Jerusalem Restaurant ❸**, 4th St. and Coastal Hwy. The authentic Middle Eastern cuisine served here is affordable, satisfying, and available 22hr. a day. The lamb shank ($12) and the stuffed chicken are patron favorites. (☎289-1020. Open daily 6am-4am.) With freshly caught food and a friendly atmosphere, **The Embers ❺**, 24th St. and Coastal Hwy., boasts the biggest seafood buffet in town. All the clams, oysters, Alaskan crab legs, prime rib, steak, sides, and dessert you can eat are $26. (☎289-3322 or 888-436-2377; www.embers.com. Open daily 2pm-9:30pm.) **Reflections ❹**, 6600 Coastal Hwy., at 67th St., on the ground floor of the Holiday Inn, offers table-side cooking and fine dining, Las Vegas-style. (☎524-5252. Early Bird dinner entrees $10-19 if seated by 6pm; regular entrees $20-48. Open daily 5-10pm.)

⌸⌹ ENTERTAINMENT AND NIGHTLIFE. Ocean City's star attraction is its beautiful **beach.** The wide stretch of surf and sand runs the entire 10 mi. worth of town and can be accessed by taking a left onto any of the numerous side streets off Philadelphia and Baltimore Ave. The breaking waves know no time constraints, but beach-goers are technically limited to 6am-10pm. When the sun goes down, professional party-goers will be impressed by **Seacrets**, on 49th St. in the bay, a virtual entertainment mecca and amusement park for adults. This oasis features 11 bars, including two floating bars on the bay. Barefoot partygoers wander from bar to bar or have drinks served to them as they float in their personal raft listening to the nightly live bands. A magnificent sunset view ushers in early revelers for cocktails in the raft pool. (☎524-4900; www.seacrets.com. Cover $5 at 5pm and goes up $1 each hour until 10pm. Open daily 11am-2am. Free parking.) The elder statesman of the bayside clubs, **Fager's Island,** 60th St., in the bay, has hordes walking the plank to its island location. Live rock, R&B, jazz, and reggae play nightly to accompany the 100+ beers. No one seems to know the source of the classical music tradition, but the *1812 Overture* booms at every sunset. Start the week with $1 hot dogs and $1.65 cans of Natty Light at the Monday night deck party till 2am. (☎524-5500. Happy hour Tu-F with half-price drinks and appetizers. Dress code: no jerseys, caps, cutoffs, sleeveless shirts, or sagging, baggy, or oversize pants. 21+ after 8pm. Cover after 5pm $5, after 7pm $10. Open daily 11am-2am.) The **Party Block Complex,** 17th St. and Coastal Hwy., offers patrons one cover to flit between three different clubs, from hip-hop, techno, and house music played at flashy Rush Club, to the modern rock at the Paddock, and 80s music played over the dance party in the Big Kahuna. (☎289-6331; www.partyblock.com. 21+. After 10pm cover $5-10. Open daily 8:30pm-2am.) If you're under 21 but want to party like you're older, check out **Club H2O,** at Worcester and the Boardwalk. This club offers nightly dancing, bikini contests, and foam parties without treating its 15- to 20-year-old guests like toddlers. (☎289-7102; www.partyblock.com, then click on "under 21." $10 cover before 8:30pm, $20 cover after. Open daily 8pm-12:45am.)

WASHINGTON, D.C.   ☎202

Visitors to the nation's capital often come only for the political sights and think they've seen it all after a tour of the White House and the Lincoln Memorial. But locals know that D.C. is much more, a thriving international city filled with cultural offerings on par with the world's finest. Outside the federal enclave, Washington's neighborhoods never cease to amaze: Dupont Circle showcases works of the masters beside those of budding artists, Adams-Morgan embraces a banquet of ethnic offerings, and Bethesda rightly claims the most diverse restaurant scene in the area. High culture bows and pirouettes on the Kennedy Center stage almost every night, as local and big-name rock groups deafen their young audiences in the "New U" St. corridor. Political powerhouse, thriving metropolis, and intern party town, D.C. packs more punch per square mile than any other city. For expanded coverage of the D.C. area, check out ◪*Let's Go: Washington, D.C.*

◪ INTERCITY TRANSPORTATION

Airports: Ronald Reagan National Airport (☎703-417-8000; www.mwaa.com/national). Metro: National Airport. If you're flying to D.C. from within the US, this airport is your best bet, as it is on the Metro and closer to the city. Taxi from downtown $10-15. The **SuperShuttle** bus (☎800-258-3826; www.supershuttle.com) runs between National and the city (about $10 per person). **Dulles International Airport** (☎703-572-2700; www.mwaa.com/dulles) is much farther from the city. Taxis to downtown start at $45-50. The **Washington Flyer Coach Service** (☎888-927-4359; www.washfly.com) departs from Dulles every 30min. M-F 5:45am-10:15pm, Sa-Su 7:45am-10:15pm; from Metro: West Falls Church M-F 6:15am-10:45pm, Sa-Su 8:15am-10:45pm ($8; discounts for groups of 3 or more, seniors, and international students). Travel between Dulles and metro area takes approx. 20min. The **SuperShuttle** bus also runs from Dulles to downtown daily ($22 for one person, $10 each additional person).

Trains: Amtrak operates from Union Station, 50 Massachusetts Ave. NE (☎484-7540). To: **Baltimore** (30-45min., $15); **Boston** (7¾hr., $89); **New York City** (3¼hr., $74); **Philadelphia** (2hr., $47). Maryland's commuter rail, **MARC** (☎866-743-3682), departs from Union Station to Baltimore ($6.50) and the suburbs.

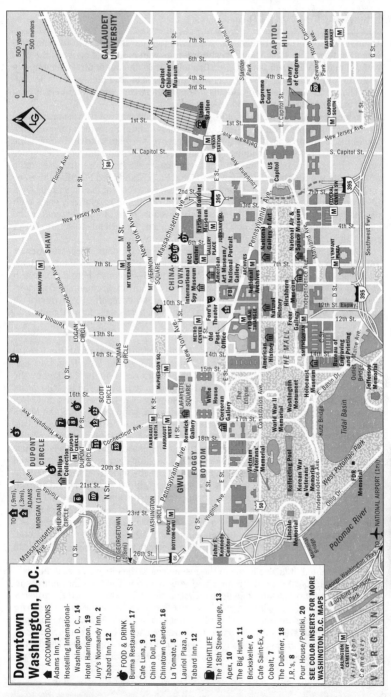

Downtown Washington, D.C.

▲ ACCOMMODATIONS
Adams Inn, **1**
Hostelling International-
Washington D. C., **14**
Hotel Harrington, **19**
Jury's Normandy Inn, **2**
Tabard Inn, **12**

● FOOD & DRINK
Burma Restaurant, **17**
Cafe Luna, **9**
China Doll, **15**
Chinatown Garden, **16**
La Tomate, **5**
Lauriol Plaza, **3**
Tabard Inn, **12**

● NIGHTLIFE
The 18th Street Lounge, **13**
Apex, **10**
The Big Hunt, **11**
Brickskeller, **6**
Cafe Saint-Ex, **4**
Cobalt, **7**
The Dubliner, **18**
J.R.'s, **8**
Pour House/Politiki, **20**

SEE COLOR INSERTS FOR MORE
WASHINGTON, D.C. MAPS

MID-ATLANTIC

⚡ ORIENTATION

Diamond-shaped D.C. stretches its tips in the four cardinal directions. The **Potomac River** forms the jagged southwest border, its waters flowing between the D.C. and Arlington, VA. **North Capitol, East Capitol,** and **South Capitol Street** slice up the city into four quadrants: NW, NE, SE, and SW. The **Mall** stretches west of the Capitol. The suffixes of the quadrants distinguish otherwise identical addresses (e.g. 800 G St. NW and 800 G St. NE).

Washington's streets lie in a simple grid. Streets that run east-to-west are labeled alphabetically in relation to North Capitol/South Capitol St., which runs through the Capitol. There is no J St. After W St., east-west streets take on two-syllable names, then three-syllable names, then the names of trees and flowers. The names run in alphabetical order, but sometimes repeat or skip a letter. Streets running north-south are numbered all the way to 52nd St. NW and 63rd St. NE. Addresses on lettered streets indicate the number of the cross street. For instance, 1100 D St. SE is on the corner of D and 11th. While navigation on foot is relatively easy, both drivers and pedestrians should be aware of possible road blocks. Threats to the security of important political buildings often cause city officials to set up detour routes that can create delays for visitors traveling by car.

Major roads include **Pennsylvania Avenue, Connecticut Avenue, Wisconsin Avenue, 16th Street NW, K Street NW, Massachusetts Avenue, New York Avenue,** and **North Capitol Street.** D.C. is ringed by the **Capital Beltway** (I-495—except where it's part of I-95). The Beltway is bisected by **U.S. 1** and meets **I-395** from Virginia. The **Baltimore-Washington Parkway** connects Washington, D.C. to Baltimore, MD. **I-595** trickles off the Capital Beltway toward Annapolis, MD, and **I-66** heads west into Virginia.

NEIGHBORHOODS

Postcard-perfect, **Capitol Hill** symbolizes the democratic dream with the Capitol building, Supreme Court, and Library of Congress. Extending west from the Capitol Building is the grassy pedestrian **Mall,** the exterior of which is flanked by the Smithsonian Museums and the National Gallery of Art, while the interior of its west end is occupied by monuments and memorials. Cherry trees bud and blossom along the brink of the **Potomac River Tidal Basin,** which runs along the Mall's southern edge. Just north of the Mall, the **White House** is at 1600 Pennsylvania Ave. The **State Department, Kennedy Center,** and the infamous **Watergate Complex** make **Foggy Bottom,** on the west side of the city, their stomping grounds. The **Federal Triangle** area is home to a growing commercial and banking district. The International Trade Center and the Ronald Reagan Building share the wide avenues with federal agencies like the FBI. It's a wonderful (corporate) life in glass-walled **Farragut,** where government agencies, lobbying firms, and lawyers make their homes.

There's more to D.C. than politics; the neighborhoods comprising the **Second City** bustle with sights, shops, and eateries. **Adams-Morgan,** in the northwest, is a hub of nightlife and good food. **Chinatown,** more of a block than a neighborhood, offers authentic Chinese cuisine. Picturesque **Georgetown** has the feel of a college town with Georgetown University nearby and enough nightlife to keep college students entertained. It is also home to the residences of the city's elite and the high-end shopping that keeps them happy. If you like good food and hot clubs surrounded by cutting-edge art, then **Dupont Circle** is made for you. *At night, travelers should avoid walking through Dupont Circle, though the surrounding neighborhood is fine.* Another night-time hot spot is the **U District,** a historically African-American area with clubs that blast trance and techno until the sun rises. *Be careful in this area at night.* The **Upper Northwest,** an upper-class residential neighborhood, is home to American University and the National Zoo.

⊏ LOCAL TRANSPORTATION

Public Transit: Metro Center Line Exit, 12th and F St. (☎636-3425, general info 637-7000; open M-F 7:30am-6:30pm). $1.35-3.90, depending on time and distance traveled; day pass $6.50. The **Fast Pass** ($30) allows 7 days of unlimited travel. Subway trains run M-F 5:30am-midnight, Sa 7am-3am, Su 7am-midnight. For bus transfers, get a pass on the platform before boarding the train. The **Metrobus** system serves Georgetown, downtown, and the suburbs. $1.20.

Taxi: Yellow Cab ☎544-1212.

Car Rental: Bargain Buggies Rent-a-Car, 3140 N. Washington Blvd. (☎703-841-0000; www.bargainbuggies.com), in Arlington, VA. Open M and F 8am-7pm, Tu-Th 8am-6pm, Sa 7am-1pm, Su 9am-noon.

Bicycle Rental: Better Bikes (☎293-2080; www.betterbikesinc.com). Delivers bikes anywhere in the D.C. area. 10-speed bikes $25 per day, $95 per week; mountain bikes $38/$185; hybrids $48/$215. Helmet, map, backpack, locks, and breakdown service included. $25 deposit. Baby strollers $20 per day. Cash only. Open 24hr.

⁊ PRACTICAL INFORMATION

Visitor Info: Washington, D.C. Convention and Tourism Corporation (WCTC), 1212 New York Ave. NW, Ste. 600 (☎789-7000; www.washington.org). Open M-F 9am-5pm. **D.C. Visitor Information Center,** in the Ronald Reagan International Trade Center, 1300 Pennsylvania Ave. NW (☎866-324-7386; www.dcvisit.com). Open M-F 8:30am-5:30pm, Sa 9am-4pm.

Hotlines: Rape Crisis Center, ☎333-7273. 24hr. **Gay and Lesbian National Hotline,** ☎888-843-4564. Operates M-F 4pm-midnight, Sa noon-5pm. **Traveler's Aid Society** (www.travelersaid.org/ta/dc.htm). Offices at Union Station (☎371-1937; open M-Sa 9:30am-5:30pm, Su 12:30-5:30pm), Reagan Airport (☎703-417-3972; open M-F 9am-9pm, Sa-Su 9am-6pm), and Dulles Airport (☎703-572-8296; open M-F 8am-9pm, Sa-Su 8am-7pm).

Medical Services: Children's National Medical Center, 111 Michigan Ave. NW (☎884-5000; www.cnmc.org). **Georgetown University Medical Center,** 3800 Reservoir Rd. NW (☎687-2000; www.gumc.georgetown.edu).

Internet Access: The Cyberstop Cafe, 1513 17th St. NW (☎234-2470), near P St. Open M-F 7am-midnight, Sa-Su 8am-midnight. $7 per 30min., $9 per hr. Free wireless Internet with purchase from cafe.

Post Office: National Capitol Station, 2 Massachusetts Ave. NE (☎523-2368). Open M-F 7am-midnight, Sa-Su 7am-8pm. **Martin Luther King, Jr. Station,** 1400 L St., in the lobby (☎523-2001). Open M-F 8am-5:30pm, Sa 8am-2pm. **Postal Code:** 20002. **Area Code:** 202.

⌐ ACCOMMODATIONS

You might think that inexpensive D.C. lodgings would be harder to come by than straight-talking politicians, yet the sheer size of the city and its volume of tourist traffic allows it to support several affordable hostels and relatively inexpensive bed and breakfasts. Just don't forget that D.C. adds a 14.5% hotel tax to your bill.

HOSTELS

▨ **Hostelling International-Washington D.C. (HI),** 1009 11th St. NW (☎737-2333; www.hiwashingtondc.org), 3 blocks north of Metro: Metro Center. *Use caution in this neighborhood after dark.* A friendly staff and reasonable rates make this mammoth 250-

bed hostel an appealing choice. In the heart of D.C., 5 blocks from the White House and a 20min. walk from the National Mall. Internet access $1 per 5min. Reception 24hr. Check-in 2pm-1am; call ahead if arriving later. Check-out 11am. Advance reservations recommended; credit card required. Dorms $29-32, nonmembers $32-35. Singles $69/$72; doubles $79/$82. Wheelchair accessible. ❷

Hilltop Hostel, 300 Carroll St. NW (☎291-9591), on the border of D.C. and Takoma Park, easily found from Metro: Takoma. Hostelers can come and go as they please, smoke and drink in certain areas, or fire up a grill in the backyard. A/C in some rooms. Satellite TV, free DSL Internet access, use of kitchen, and coin-op laundry. Linen included. 18+. 7-night max. stay. Reception 8am-midnight. Reservations preferred. Dorms $18. Private rooms with shared bath $40. Cash or traveler's check only. ❶

HOTELS AND GUEST HOUSES

Adams Inn, 1744 Lanier Pl. NW (☎745-3600 or 800-578-6807; www.adamsinn.com), 2 blocks north of the center of Adams-Morgan. Complimentary continental breakfast, coffee, tea, apples, and cookies. The 25 rooms have A/C, sparse but tasteful furnishings, and private sinks (some with private bath). Friendly, helpful staff. Cable TV in common area, free Internet access, and laundry facilities. Limited parking $10 per night. 2-night min. stay if staying Sa night. Reception M-Sa 8am-9pm, Su 1-9pm. Check-in 3-9pm. Check-out noon. Credit card or check sent in advance needed to secure reservation. Singles $75, with private bath $85; each additional person $10. ❹

Tabard Inn, 1739 N St. NW (☎785-1277; www.tabardinn.com), between 17th and 18th St. 40 individually decorated rooms in 3 townhouses, done up in rich tapestry and sparkling stone-tile mosaic with hardwood floors, some with sitting areas. A/C, phone, wireless Internet, and data port (but no TV). Patio, bar, and lounges. Continental breakfast and passes to the YMCA included. Reception 24hr. Singles $86-120, with private bath $120-190; each additional person $15. ❹

Jury's Normandy Inn, 2118 Wyoming Ave. NW (☎483-1350 or 800-424-3729; www.jurysdoyle.com), at Connecticut Ave., 5 blocks northwest of Dupont Circle. Metro: Dupont Circle. Jury's offers 75 stylish, spacious rooms with refrigerators, phones, and cable TV. Free wine and cheese reception (Tu 5:30-7pm), complimentary coffee and cookies in the lobby every evening, and daily continental breakfast ($5.50). Exquisitely furnished lounge area and an outdoor patio add a touch of charm. 1 smoking floor. Limited underground parking $12 per night. Check-in 3pm. Check-out noon. Rooms $79-185; each additional person $15. AAA members typically save 10%. ❹

Hotel Harrington, 11th and E St. NW (☎628-8140 or 800-424-8532; www.hotel-harrington.com). Metro: Metro Center or Federal Triangle. For nearly 90 years this hotel has offered clean rooms and a great location. The rooms have furnishings that look almost as old as the hotel, but they also have cable TV, A/C, and laundry. Parking $10 per day. Queen bedrooms $95-109, two double beds $105-119, deluxe king room $139-149. $10 off if you call ahead from the airport, train, or bus station; 10% off on stays of 5 or more days. Students and AAA members 10% off. ❹

◻ FOOD

How do you feast like a senator on an intern's slim budget? Savvy natives go grubbing at happy hours. Bars often leave out free appetizer platters to bait early evening clients (see **Nightlife**, p. 338). For budget eateries, **Adams-Morgan** and **Dupont Circle** are home to the *crème de la crème* of ethnic cuisine. Suburban **Bethesda, MD,** features over 100 different restaurants within a four-block radius.

ADAMS-MORGAN

▓ **The Diner,** 2453 18th St. NW (☎232-8800). The Diner's hours and quintessential American food have earned it high esteem among local college kids and other late-night revelers. Enjoy omelettes ($6-8), pancakes (3 for $4.50), or burgers ($6-7.25). Kosher hot dogs offered. Vegetarian options available, including some vegan soups. Open 24hr. ❷

▓ **New Orleans Cafe,** 2412 18th St. NW (☎234-0420). With Dixieland playing over its speakers, murals of jazz bands, and an owner who epitomizes Southern hospitality, this incredibly popular cafe rewards its customers with great jambalaya and Cajun linguine ($8-15) and gumbo soups ($4-8). Open Tu-F 11am-9:30pm, Sa-Su 10am-10pm. ❸

Pasta Mia Trattoria, 1790 Columbia Rd. NW (☎328-9114), near 18th St. Red-and-white checked tablecloths in an airy room perfect for evenings devoted to Disney-worthy romance. The *pièce de résistance* is a large selection of huge pasta entrees ($10-13); a favorite is the tortellini in a tomato-cream sauce. No reservations accepted, so arrive early; some people show up 30min. before opening. Open M-Sa from 6:30pm-10pm. ❸

BETHESDA

▓ **Bacchus,** 7945 Norfolk Ave. (☎301-657-1722), at Del Ray Ave. A superb Lebanese restaurant featuring 50 kinds of appetizers, all in the vicinity of $5; the *shawarma* ($7) is highly recommended. Low lighting and upscale decor make Bacchus's atmosphere a far cry from the corner falafel cart. Open Su-Th noon-2pm, F-Sa 5-10:30pm. ❷

▓ **Thyme Square Cafe,** 4735 Bethesda Ave. (☎301-657-9077), at Woodmont Ave. Friendly service, colorful decorations, and healthy vegetarian salads, sandwiches, and pasta dishes radiate wholesomeness. A vegan paradise, though fish dishes are also offered. Even devoted meat-eaters will enjoy the vegetarian potstickers ($9) and exotic pizzas ($11-14). Open Su-Th 11:30am-10pm, F-Sa 11:30am-11pm. ❹

Grapeseed, 4865 Cordell Ave. (☎301-986-9592), near Norfolk Ave. Grapeseed offers an unpretentious environment for experimentation in the intimidating field of wine tasting. Each menu item, from tamarind-glazed chicken with coconut basmati rice ($20) to crispy soft shell crabs with sweet chili sauce ($24), is designed for and inspired by a particular wine to make pairing easy. Wine available by the bottle, the glass, or the taste (a 3 oz. pour). Hosts bimonthly wine tastings (Tu 5-7pm, $20). Open M-Th 5-10pm, F-Sa 5-11pm, Su 5-9pm. ❺

La Panetteria, 4921 Cordell Ave. (☎301-951-6433), near Norfolk Ave., offers excellent northern Italian cuisine and unobtrusive service. Despite the rich decor, pasta dishes are only $6-8 and meat dishes $9-12. One of the best is the veal scallopini in lemon butter with capers and mushrooms ($10). Lunch specials $7-12. Open M-Th 11:30am-10pm, F 11:30am-11pm, Sa 4-11pm, Su 4-10pm. ❸

CHINATOWN

▓ **Burma Restaurant,** upstairs at 740 6th St. NW (☎638-1280), between G and H St. Burmese curries, unique spices, and a plethora of garnishes. Try the green tea salad ($7), followed by the squid (sautéed in garlic, ginger, and scallions; $8). Vegetarians enjoy the papaya and tofu salads ($6). Open M-F 11am-3pm and 6-10pm, Sa-Su 6-10pm. ❷

Chinatown Garden, 618 H St. NW (☎737-8887). The extensive two-part menu—half standard Americanized Chinese fare, half authentic dishes—is guaranteed to have something to please everyone. Try the Hunan chicken or one of the other lunch specials ($6.50-7) if you're on a tight budget, or the sea cucumbers with stewed shrimp roe ($25) off the authentic menu if you're feeling frisky. Most lunch dishes $6-8, most dinner entrees $9-13. Open Su-Th 11am-11pm, F-Sa 11am-midnight. ❷

MID-ATLANTIC

China Doll, 627 H St. NW (☎289-4755). Standard Chinese dishes and combination meals with soup, spring roll, and steamed rice (lunch $6-8; dinner $8 and up). Dim sum all day, every day. Open Su-Th 11am-10pm, F-Sa 11am-midnight. ❷

DUPONT CIRCLE

▨ **La Tomate,** 1701 Connecticut Ave. NW (☎667-5505), at R St. This modern Italian bistro offers attentive service, a creative menu, and bread with fresh black-olive spread. Pastas ($13-18) include the delectable *farfalle prosciutto e funghi* (bowtie pasta with prosciutto, mushrooms, and cream; $13). Entrees $15-27. Reservations recommended. Open M-Th 11:30am-11pm, F-Sa 11:30am-11:30pm, Su 11:30am-10pm. ❹

▨ **Tabard Inn,** 1739 N St. NW (☎785-1277; www.tabardinn.com), between 17th and 18th St., in the hotel of the same name (p. 328). This longtime Dupont secret offers a menu that changes daily and features locally-grown ingredients. Past entrees ($19-30) include citrus- and hazelnut-encrusted halibut and three-cheese and summer-truffle cannelloni. Casual dress in an unpretentious atmosphere. Valet parking for Su brunch and F-Sa nights, $5. Open for breakfast M-F 7-10am; brunch Sa 11am-2pm, Su 10:30am-2:30pm; dinner Su-Th 6-9:30pm, F-Sa 6-10:30pm. ❺

▨ **Lauriol Plaza,** 1835 18th St. NW (☎387-0035), at T St., between Dupont Circle and Adams-Morgan. Lauriol occupies half the block, with 3 magnificent floors of Mexican dining. Large entrees ($9-17), appetizers such as fried plantains and guacamole ($4-7), and excellent margaritas ($5.50, pitchers $24). Free parking. No reservations accepted, so arrive early. Su brunch 11am-3pm. Open M-Th 11:30am-11pm, F-Sa and holidays 11:30am-midnight, Su 11am-11pm. ❹

Cafe Luna, 1633 P St. NW (☎387-4005), near 17th St. This popular basement restaurant serves a mix of Italian, vegetarian, and low-fat fare. Breakfast ($2-5) served all day. Huge sandwiches ($4-6) satisfy almost any appetite. W and Su half-price pizzas, which are only $5-7 to begin with. Locals like the eggplant parmesan. Brunch Sa-Su 10am-3pm. Open M-Th 8am-11:30pm, F 8am-1am, Sa 10am-1:30am, Su 10am-11:30pm. ❶

GEORGETOWN

▨ **Clyde's of Georgetown,** 3236 M St. NW (☎333-9180), between Potomac St. and Wisconsin Ave. Join the crowds of preppy students and professor-types at Clyde's for delicious sandwiches ($7-12), salads ($12-14), seafood ($13-17), and pasta ($13-15). Open M-Th 11:30am-2am, F 11:30am-3am, Sa 10am-3am, Su 9am-2am. ❹

▨ **Red Ginger,** 1564 Wisconsin Ave. NW (☎965-7009), serves flavorful gourmet Caribbean food, like curried oxtail stew ($14) and adobo-spiced duck with quinoa pumpkin salad ($16). Weekend brunch (Sa-Su 11:30am-5pm) offers complimentary champagne. Open Tu-Th and Su 11:30am-10pm, F-Sa 11:30am-11pm. ❹

Patisserie Poupon, 1645 Wisconsin Ave. NW (☎342-3248), near Q St. Start the day with a mouthwatering buttery brioche, pear danish, or croissant ($1.30-2.25). Beautiful tarts and cakes ($22-34). Sandwiches and salads $4-7. Limited seating makes this a good take-away option. Coffee bar in back. Open Tu-Sa 8am-6:30pm, Su 8am-4pm. ❶

UPPER NORTHWEST

▨ **Yanni's,** 3500 Connecticut Ave. NW (☎362-8871). Find home-style Greek cooking in this airy restaurant, adorned with classical statues and murals of Greek gods. Try charbroiled octopus, crunchy on the outside and delicately tender within, served with rice and vegetables ($13). Entrees $6-17 (vegetarian options $9-12). Strong Greek coffee ($2.50) goes well with the baklava ($4.50). Open daily 11:30am-11pm. ❸

▨ **Cactus Cantina,** 3300 Wisconsin Ave. NW (☎686-5561), at Macomb St. near the Cathedral. Try the fajitas *al carbón* (half chicken, half beef; $12) followed by the dessert *cajeta* ($5.25) amidst displays of classic Native American dress and cowboy garb.

A few vegetarian options, such as cheese enchiladas ($8) and veggie fajitas ($9.50), available. Be prepared to wait for a table on weekends. Su brunch 10:30am-3pm. Open M-Th 11am-11pm, F-Sa 11am-midnight, Su 10:30am-11pm. ❸

2 Amys Neapolitan Pizzeria, 3715 Macomb St. NW (☎885-5700), near Wisconsin Ave., adjacent to Cactus Cantina. Named after the owners' wives. Friendly waitstaff serves superb, freshly cooked pizzas ($8-13) amid the pastel yellow and orange hues of the dining areas. The "Narcia" pizza (tomato, salami, roasted peppers, mozzarella, and garlic; $13) is excellent. Expect a wait. Open Tu-Sa 11am-11pm, Su noon-10pm. ❸

Max's Best Ice Cream, 2416 Wisconsin Ave. NW (☎333-3111), just south of Calvert St. Known in the D.C. metro area as the premier purveyor of homemade ice cream, Max himself dishes out old favorites and exotic flavors. Though Max's Best makes over 150 flavors a year, not all are available each day, which may be a blessing since it's hard enough as is to pick between lychee, lemon cream, and Heath bar. Single scoop $3. Open M-Sa noon-midnight, Su noon-10pm. ❶

Mama Maria and Enzio's, 2313 Wisconsin Ave. NW (☎965-1337), near Calvert St. Amazing southern Italian cuisine with a casual, family atmosphere and exceptionally warm service. Shrimp in lemon sauce ($16) is worth the wait. Pizzas $9-12. Calzones $7. Cannoli $5. Lunch entrees $7-11. Reservations for parties of 3 or more. Open M-F 11:30am-10pm, Sa 5-10pm, Su 5-9pm. ❸

◙ SIGHTS

CAPITOL HILL

THE CAPITOL. The ▨US Capitol impresses visitors with a grandeur uncommon even among the city's other historical buildings and memorials. From the times of frontiersman Andrew Jackson (1829) to the present, it has been used as the site of the presidential inauguration ceremony. The East Front entrance, facing the Supreme Court, brings visitors into the 180 ft. high rotunda, where soldiers slept during the Civil War. From the lower-level crypt, visitors can climb to the second floor for a view of the House or Senate visitors chambers. Though much of the real political action takes place behind the scenes, visitors can get gallery passes to view the legislature at work—just don't be disappointed if all that is going on is a roll call vote. Americans may obtain gallery passes from the office of their representative or senator in the House or Senate office buildings near the Capitol; foreigners can get one-day passes by presenting identification at the appointments desks in the crypt. *(Metro: Capitol South or Union Station. ☎225-6827; www.aoc.gov. Generally open M-Sa 9am-4:30pm. Access by 30min. guided tour only. Free, but tickets are required. Same-day tickets available at the Garfield Circle kiosk on the West Front, across from the Botanic Gardens. Kiosk is open from 9am until all tickets are distributed; get there about 45-60min. before opening to guarantee a ticket.)* The real business of Congress, however, is conducted in **committee hearings.** Most are open to the public; check the *Washington Post*'s "Today in Congress" box for times and locations. The free **Capitol subway** (the "Capitol Choo-Choo") shuttles between the basement of the Capitol and the House and Senate office buildings; a buzzer and flashing light signal an imminent vote.

SUPREME COURT. In 1935, the **Supreme Court** justices decided it was time to take the nation's separation of powers literally and moved from their makeshift offices in the Capitol into a new Greek Revival courthouse across the street. Oral arguments are open to the public; show up early to be seated. *(1 1st St. Metro: Capitol South or Union Station. ☎479-3221; www.supremecourtus.gov. In session Oct.-June M-W 10am-noon and open 1-3pm for 2 weeks every month; courtroom open when Justices are on vacation. The "3min. line" shuffles visitors through standing gallery of the courtroom for a glimpse. Court open M-F 9am-4:30pm. Seating before 8:30am. Free.)*

LIBRARY OF CONGRESS. With over 126 million objects stored on 532 mi. of shelves (including a copy of *Old King Cole* written on a grain of rice), the ▧**Library of Congress** is the largest library in the world. The collection was torched by the British in 1814 and then restarted from Thomas Jefferson's personal stocks. These days, it's open to anyone of college age or older with a legitimate research purpose. A tour of the facilities is also available; exhibits range from collections of Pulitzer Prize-winning political cartoons to texts documenting and discussing the Supreme Court decisions that ended racial segregation in public schools, and change frequently. The **Jefferson Building's** green copper dome and gold-leafed flame tops a spectacular octagonal reading room. *(1st St. SE. ☎707-5000; www.loc.gov. Great Hall open M-Sa 10am-5:30pm. Tours M-F 10:30, 11:30am, 1:30, 2:30, and 3:30pm; Sa 10:30, 11:30am, 1:30, and 2:30pm. Visitors center and galleries open daily 10am-5pm. Free.)*

UNION STATION. Trains converge at **Union Station,** two blocks north of the Capitol. This 90-year-old train station has colonnades, archways, and domed ceilings that hearken back to imperial Rome—if Rome was filled with a cavernous food court and enough stores to stock a large mall. *(50 Massachusetts Ave. NE. Metro: Union Station. ☎371-9441; www.unionstationdc.com. Shops open M-Sa 10am-9pm, Su noon-6pm.)*

MONUMENTS

▧**WASHINGTON MONUMENT.** With a $9.4 million restoration project completed in 1999, this shrine to America's first president is incredibly impressive. Once nicknamed the "the Beef Depot monument" after the cattle that grazed here during the Civil War, the Washington Monument was built with rock from multiple quarries, which explains the stones' multiple colors. The beautiful **Reflecting Pool** mirrors Washington's obelisk. *(Metro: Smithsonian. ☎426-6841; www.nps.gov/wamo/homt.htm. Open daily 9am-5pm. Tours every 30min. 9am-4:30pm. Admission to the monument by timed ticket. Free if obtained on day of visit; arrive early. $1.50 if reserved in advance.)*

▧**VIETNAM VETERANS MEMORIAL.** Maya Lin, who designed the Vietnam Veterans Memorial, received a "B" when she submitted her memorial concept for a grade as a Yale senior. She went on to beat her professor in the public memorial design competition. In her words, the monument is "a rift in the earth—a long, polished black stone wall, emerging from and receding into the earth." The wall contains the names of the 58,235 Americans who died in Vietnam, indexed in books at both ends. *(Constitution Ave. at 22nd St. NW. Metro: Smithsonian or Foggy Bottom-GWU. ☎634-1568; www.nps.gov/vive. Open 24hr.)*

▧**LINCOLN MEMORIAL.** The Lincoln Memorial, at the west end of the Mall, recalls the rectangular grandeur of Athens's Parthenon. It was from these steps that Martin Luther King, Jr. gave his "I Have a Dream" speech during the 1963 March on Washington. Inside, a seated Lincoln presides over the memorial. Though you may find Lincoln's lap inviting, climbing on the 19 ft. president is a federal offense; a camera will catch you if the rangers don't. *(Metro: Smithsonian or Foggy Bottom-GWU. ☎426-6841; www.nps.gov/linc. Open 24hr.)*

JEFFERSON MEMORIAL. A 19 ft. hollow bronze statue of Thomas Jefferson stands in an open-air rotunda, encircled by massive Ionic columns and overlooking the Tidal Basin. Quotes from the Declaration of Independence, the Virginia Statute of Religious Freedom, and *Notes on Virginia* adorn the walls. *(A long walk from Metro: L'Enfant Plaza or Smithsonian. ☎426-6841; www.nps.gov/thje. Open 24hr.)*

KOREAN WAR MEMORIAL. The 19 colossal polished-steel statues of the Korean War Memorial trudge up a hill, rifles in hand, expressions of weariness and fear frozen upon their faces. The statues are accompanied by a black granite wall with over 2000 sandblasted photographic images from this war, in which 54,246 Americans lost their lives. The wall's shadowy images are reminiscent of the quote from one of the Korean War's most famous generals, Gen. Douglas MacArthur: "Old soldiers never die, they just fade away." *(At the west end of the Mall, near Lincoln. Metro: Smithsonian or Foggy Bottom-GWU. ☎426-6841; www.nps.gov/kwvm. Open 8am-midnight.)*

FRANKLIN DELANO ROOSEVELT MEMORIAL. Occupying a stretch of West Potomac Park, the Franklin Delano Roosevelt Memorial deviates from the presidential tributes nearby, replacing their marble statuary with sculpted gardens, cascading fountains, and thematic alcoves. Four "rooms" of red granite each represent a phase of FDR's presidency. Whether or not to display the disabled Roosevelt in his wheelchair was hotly debated; as a compromise, Roosevelt is seated, as in a famous picture taken at Yalta. *(A long walk from Metro: Smithsonian, but a short walk from the Jefferson or Lincoln Memorials. ☎426-6841; www.nps.gov/fdrm. Open 8am-midnight.)*

NATIONAL WWII MEMORIAL. The newest addition to the Mall's handful of memorials honors the 16 million Americans who served in the armed forces during WWII, the more than 400,000 soldiers who died, and everyone who aided the war effort on the home front. Opened in May of 2004, the memorial includes an archway symbolizing each of the major theaters of battle, four pillars topped with eagles to celebrate America's victory, 56 granite pillars to represent the contribution of each of the US's states and territories, and a triumphant rainbow pool. *(Metro: Smithsonian or Foggy Bottom-GWU. ☎426-6841; www.nps.gov/nwwm. Open 24hr.)*

SOUTH OF THE MALL

HOLOCAUST MEMORIAL MUSEUM. Opened in 1993, the privately-funded Holocaust Memorial Museum examines the atrocities of the Holocaust. Special exhibitions, which can be viewed without passes, include the **Wall of Remembrance,** a touching collection of tiles painted by American schoolchildren in memory of the 1.5 million children killed during the Holocaust, the Wexner Learning Center, and an orientation film shown daily *(every 30min. 10:15am-4:15pm).* The permanent gallery is divided into three chronologically organized floors. *(14th St. between C St. and Independence Ave. SW. Metro: Smithsonian. ☎488-0400; www.ushmm.org. Open daily 10am-5:30pm. Free. Not recommended for children under 11; kids can tour the exhibition "Daniel's Story," an account of Nazi occupation told from a child's perspective. Arrive early to ensure tickets.)*

BUREAU OF ENGRAVING AND PRINTING. The buck starts here, at the Bureau of Engraving and Printing, the largest producer of currency, stamps, and security documents in the world. Guided tours of the presses that print $696 million in money and stamps each day are offered. *(At 14th and C St. SW. Metro: Smithsonian. ☎874-2330 or 866-874-2330; www.moneyfactory.com. Mar.-Sept. ticket booth opens M-F at 8am to distribute free tickets for same-day tours 9am-2pm. Arrive early to obtain tickets, most are gone by 9am. Oct.-Feb. no tickets required. Tours 10am-2pm.)*

FEDERAL TRIANGLE

▨ NATIONAL ARCHIVES. Visitors line up at the National Archives to view the original Declaration of Independence, US Constitution, and Bill of Rights. This building houses 16 million pictures and posters, 18 million maps, and billions of pages of text—about 2-5% of the documents the government produces each year. *(8th St. and Constitution Ave. NW. Metro: Archives-Navy Memorial. ☎501-5000; www.nara.gov. Open daily Apr. to early Sept. 10am-9pm; early Sept. to Mar. 10am-5:30pm. Free.)*

INTERNATIONAL SPY MUSEUM. Opened in 2002, Washington's newest museum is the culmination of over seven years of work and planning by some of the nation's foremost experts and members of the intelligence community. With glowing neon lighting in the elevators and movie-set-like backdrops, the museum can feel a bit campy, but it offers unparalleled insight into the world of espionage. *(800 F St. NW, at 9th St. Metro: Gallery Place-Chinatown. ☎ 393-7798; www.spymuseum.org. Open daily Apr.-Aug. 9am-8pm; Aug.-Oct. 10am-8pm; Oct.-Mar. 10am-6pm. Last admission 2hr. before closing. Tickets for timed admission $13, seniors and military $12, children $10, under 5 free. Long lines late in the day yield entry times that may be more than 1hr. after ticket purchase.)*

NATIONAL BUILDING MUSEUM. Montgomery Meigs's Italian-inspired edifice remains one of Washington's most striking sights. Exhibits, tucked below office space around the Great Hall, honor American achievements in urban planning, construction, and design. In 2005, the exhibit "New Designs for Public Space," will explore how to structure the places where Americans congregate in order to protect the freedoms of speech and assembly, while simultaneously addressing security concerns. *(F St. NW, between 4th and 5th St. Metro: Judiciary Sq. ☎ 272-2448; www.nbm.org. Open M-Sa 10am-5pm, Su 11am-5pm. 45min. tours M-W 12:30pm; Th-Sa 11:30am, 12:30, and 1:30pm; Su 12:30 and 1:30pm. Suggested donation $5.)*

FEDERAL BUREAU OF INVESTIGATION. The **J. Edgar Hoover Building** closed to visitors in August 2002 for extensive renovations. Tours are expected to resume sometime in 2005; call for details. *(935 Pennsylvania Ave. NW. ☎ 324-3447; www.fbi.gov.)*

FORD'S THEATER. John Wilkes Booth shot President Abraham Lincoln during a performance at the preserved Ford's Theater. Every president since 1868 has taken his chances and seen a play at the theater at least once a year. Of course, they avoid the unlucky box and sit front row center. National Park Rangers describe the events with animated gusto during a 15min. talk. *(511 10th St. NW. Metro: Metro Center. ☎ 426-6924; www.nps.gov/foth. Open daily 9am-5pm. Free. Talks in the theater at 9:15, 10:15, 11:15am, 2:15, 3:15, 4:15pm. Shows: www.fordstheatre.org. Sept.-May. Night-time shows Tu-Su 7:30pm, $25-42; matinees M-F noon, $30-36; Sa-Su 2:30pm, $35-48.)*

OLD POST OFFICE. A classical masterpiece of staggering dimensions, the Old Post Office building rebukes its contemporary neighbors with arched windows, conical turrets, and a clock tower. Yet once inside, you'll find a thoroughly modern food court and shopping pavilion. *(Pennsylvania Ave. and 12th St. NW. Metro: Federal Triangle. ☎ 289-4224; www.oldpostofficedc.com. Tower open mid-Apr. to mid-Sept. M-Sa 9am-7:45pm, Su 10am-5:45pm; low-season M-F 9am-4:45pm, Sa-Su 10am-5:45pm. Shops open M-Sa 10am-7pm, Su noon-6pm. Free.)*

CAPITAL CHILDREN'S MUSEUM. This huge interactive museum is the ultimate escape from glass-encased artifacts. Visitors can brew hot chocolate and roll tortillas in a mock-up of life in Mexico, or help with demonstrations in the chemist-staffed laboratory. *(800 3rd St. NE, between H and I St. NE. Metro: Union Station. ☎ 675-4120; www.ccm.org. Open late May to early Sept. daily 10am-5pm; early Sept. to late May Tu-Su 10am-5pm. $7, seniors $5, children under 2 free. Half-price Su before noon.)*

NATIONAL MUSEUM OF WOMEN IN THE ARTS. In a former Masonic Temple, the National Museum of Women in the Arts showcases works by the likes of Mary Cassatt, Georgia O'Keeffe, and Frida Kahlo. This museum is the only one in the world dedicated solely to the celebration of achievements of women in the visual, performing, and literary arts, and is comprised of over 3000 pieces dating from the 16th century to the present. *(1250 New York Ave. NW. Metro: Metro Center. ☎ 783-5000; www.nmwa.org. Open M-Sa 10am-5pm, Su noon-5pm. $8, ages 60 and up and students $6, 18 and under free. 1st Su and W of each month free.)*

WHITE HOUSE AND FOGGY BOTTOM

■ **WHITE HOUSE.** With its simple columns and expansive lawns, the White House seems a compromise between patrician lavishness and democratic simplicity. Thomas Jefferson proposed a design for the building, but his entry lost to that of amateur architect James Hoban. Today the President's staff works in the West Wing, while the First Lady's cohorts occupy the East Wing. Staff who cannot fit in the White House work in the nearby **Old Executive Office Building.** The President's official office is the **Oval Office,** site of many televised speeches. *(1600 Pennsylvania Ave. NW. ☎ 456-7041; www.whitehouse.gov. Tours of the White House can be arranged only by calling your congressional representative more than 1 month in advance of your visit. Phone numbers for representatives available at www.house.gov. All tours are free.)*

LAFAYETTE PARK. Historic homes surround Lafayette Park north of the White House. These homes include the Smithsonian-owned **Renwick Gallery Craft Museum,** which has some remarkable 1980s sculptures. *(17th St. and Pennsylvania Ave. NW. Metro: Farragut North, Farragut West, or McPherson Sq. ☎ 633-2850; www.nmaa.si.edu. Open daily 10am-5:30pm. Free.)* The nearby **Corcoran Gallery** boasts an expansive collection of American art. *(17th St. between E St. and New York Ave. NW. ☎ 639-1700; www.corcoran.org. Open M, W, F-Su 10am-5pm, Th 10am-9pm. Free tours daily noon, Th 7:30pm, Sa-Su 2:30pm. $6.75, seniors $4.75, students $3; families $12. Free all day M and Th 5-9pm.)* The **Octagon,** a building designed by Capitol architect William Thornton as a winter home for the 18th-century tycoon John Taylor, is reputedly filled with ghosts. Tour guides explain its history. *(Open Tu-Su 10am-4pm. $5, seniors and students $3.)*

KENNEDY CENTER. Completed in the late 1960s, the **John F. Kennedy Center for the Performing Arts** is a living monument to the assassinated president. The $78 million edifice boasts four major stages, a film theater, sumptuous red carpets, mirrors, crystal chandeliers, and 3700 tons of marble. *(25th St. and New Hampshire Ave. NW. Metro: Foggy Bottom-GWU. ☎ 467-4600 or 800-444-1324; www.kennedy-center.org. Open daily 10am-midnight. Free tours leave from the level A gift shop M-F 10am-5pm, Sa-Su 10am-1pm; call ☎ 416-8340.)* Across the street is "Tricky Dick" Nixon's **Watergate Complex.**

GEORGETOWN

■ **DUMBARTON OAKS ESTATE.** The former home of John Calhoun, Dumbarton Oaks Mansion, nestled in beautiful gardens, was the site of the 1944 Dumbarton Oaks Conference that helped write the United Nations charter, and holds an impressive collection of Byzantine and pre-Columbian art. *(1703 32nd St. NW, between R and S St. ☎ 339-6401, tour info 339-6409; www.doaks.org. Mansion: Open Tu-Su 2-5pm. Suggested donation $1. Gardens: Open daily mid-Mar. to Oct. 2-6pm. $6, seniors and children $4; also Nov. to mid-Mar. 2-5pm, free.)*

GEORGETOWN UNIVERSITY. Archbishop John Carroll oversaw construction in 1788, and Georgetown University opened the following year, becoming the nation's first Catholic institution for higher learning. Today, approximately 50% of Georgetown's 6000 undergraduates are Catholic, and a Jesuit brother resides in every dorm, although students of many creeds attend. *(37th and O St. ☎ 687-3600; www.georgetown.edu. Campus tours M-Sa mornings through the admissions office; call for details.)*

UPPER NORTHWEST

■ **NATIONAL ZOO.** Founded in 1889 and designed by Frederick Law Olmsted, who also designed New York City's Central Park (p. 234), the National Zoo is one of D.C.'s least crowded sights. Tigers, elephants, and gorillas (oh my!) await. Currently, the zoo features two roaming endangered golden lion tamarin monkeys who wear radio collars in case they stray into dangerous territory, but otherwise wander the grounds freely. *(3001 Connecticut Ave. Metro: Woodley Park-Zoo.* ☎ *673-4800; www.si.edu/ natzoo. Grounds open daily Apr.-Oct. 6am-8pm; Nov.-Mar. 6am-6pm. Zoo buildings open daily Apr.-Oct. 10am-6pm, Nov.-Mar. 10am-4:30pm. Free.)*

■**WASHINGTON NATIONAL CATHEDRAL.** The Washington National Cathedral was built from 1907 to 1909. Rev. Martin Luther King, Jr. preached his last Sunday sermon from its pulpit, which has more recently hosted the Dalai Lama. The Pilgrim Observation Gallery reveals D.C. from the city's highest vantage point *(Massachusetts and Wisconsin Ave. NW. From Metro: Tenleytown, take a 30-series bus toward Georgetown, or walk up Cathedral Ave. from Metro: Woodley Park-Zoo.* ☎ *537-6200; www.nationalcathedral.org. Open mid-May to early Sept. M-F 10am-5:30pm, Sa 10am-4pm, Su 8am-6:30pm; early Sept. to mid-May M-F 10am-5:30pm. Su mass 8, 9, 11am. Organ demonstration 12:45pm. Tours M-F 10am-11:30am and 12:45-4pm, Sa 10-11:30am and 12:45-3:15pm, Su 12:45-2:30pm. Suggested donation $3, seniors $2, children $1. Behind-the-scenes tours July-Feb. M-F at 10:30am and 1:30pm, $10.)*

DUPONT CIRCLE

ART GALLERY DISTRICT. A triangle of creativity, the **Art Gallery District** contains over two dozen galleries displaying everything from contemporary photographs to tribal crafts. Together they hold a joint open house the first Friday of each month (6-8pm), with free wine at each venue. *(Bounded by Connecticut Ave., Florida Ave., and Q St. www.artgalleriesdc.com lists member galleries and any changes to open house schedule.)*

■**PHILLIPS COLLECTION. Phillips Collection,** a well-endowed house of contemporary work, was the first museum of modern art in the US. Visitors gape at Renoir's masterpiece, *Luncheon of the Boating Party* (on tour until summer 2005), and works by Delacroix, Miró, and Turner. *(1600 21st St., at Q St. NW.* ☎ *387-2151; www.phillipscollection.org. Open Tu-W and F-Sa 10am-5pm, Th 10am-8:30pm; in summer also Su noon-5pm. Tu-F permanent collection free; Sa $8, students and seniors $6, 18 and under free. Audio tours free with admission.)*

EMBASSY ROW. The stretch of Massachusetts Ave. between Dupont Circle and Observatory Circle is also called **Embassy Row.** Before the 1930s, socialites lived along the avenue in extravagant edifices; diplomats later found the mansions perfect for their purposes (and sky-high budgets). Flags line the entrance to the **Islamic Center,** a brilliant white building where stunning designs stretch to the tips of spired ceilings. *(2551 Massachusetts Ave. NW.* ☎ *332-8343. No shorts allowed; women must cover their heads, arms, and legs. Open daily 10am-5pm; prayers 5 times daily.)*

🏛 MUSEUMS

The Smithsonian Museums on the Mall constitute the world's largest museum complex. The **Smithsonian Castle,** on the south side of the Mall, has an introduction to and info on the Smithsonian buildings. (☎357-2700; www.si.edu. Metro: Smithsonian or Federal Triangle. All Smithsonian museums except the Anacostia Museum of African-American History and Culture, which closes at 5pm, are open daily 10am-5:30pm; extended summer hours are determined annually. Castle open daily 8:30am-5:30pm. All museums free. Recorded audio tours available at some museums, usually for less than $5. Wheelchair accessible.)

National Air and Space Museum (☎357-2700; www.nasm.si.edu), on the south side of the Mall across from the National Gallery, is the world's most popular museum with 7.5 million visitors per year. Airplanes and space vehicles hang from the ceilings. Exhibits include the Wright brothers' original bi-plane, which hangs in the entrance gallery, the walk-through Skylab space station, the Apollo XI command module, and a DC-7.

National Gallery of Art (☎737-4215; www.nga.gov), east of Natural History, is not a part of the Smithsonian, but considered a close cousin due to its location on the Mall. The West Building, the gallery's original home, contains masterpieces by Leonardo da Vinci, El Greco, Rembrandt, Vermeer, and Monet, among others. The East Building, is devoted to 20th-century art, from Magritte and Matisse to Man Ray and Miró. The 2 buildings and the neighboring sculpture garden make up North America's most popular art museum, with 6 million visitors annually. Open M-Sa 10am-5pm, Su 11am-6pm.

Hirshhorn Museum and Sculpture Garden (☎633-4674; http://hirshhorn.si.edu), on the south side of the Mall west of Air and Space. This museum is home to modern, post-modern, and post-post-modern works from around the world. The installations of Gyro-scope contrast formlessness and abstraction with systems and structure. The slide-carousel-shaped building has outraged traditionalists since 1966. Each floor consists of 2 concentric circles: an outer ring of paintings and an inner corridor of sculptures.

Freer Gallery of Art (☎357-4880; www.asia.si.edu.), just west of the Hirshhorn, displays American and Asian art. The permanent American collection, as dictated by Charles L. Freer himself, focuses on works by James McNeill Whistler. The rotating Asian collec-tions have pieces from 2500 BC through the present. Bronzes, manuscripts, and jade pieces make up some of the museum's most intriguing displays.

National Museum of American History (☎357-2700; http://americanhistory.si.edu), on the north side of the Mall. The museum earned the entire institute the nickname "the nation's attic" because of its Plexiglas-encased clutter of old goods, from fiber-optic cable to harmonicas. When the Smithsonian inherits quirky artifacts of popular history, like Dorothy's slippers from *The Wizard of Oz*, they end up here. The Hands On History Room contains a working telegraph and an interactive introduction to the Cherokee language.

National Museum of Natural History (☎357-2700; www.mnh.si.edu). The MNH contains 3 floors of rocks, animals, gift shops, and displays selected from the museum's 124 million possessions. The Hope Diamond and dinosaurs are major attractions. The new Behring Hall of Mammals includes stuffed and fossilized mammals presented in recreations of their nat-ural habitats. Also new is *Listening to the Prairie*, an exploration of agriculture in America.

National Museum of African Art and the **Arthur M. Sackler Gallery.** (African Art: ☎633-4600; www.nmafa.si.edu. Sackler: ☎633-4880; www.asia.si.edu.) Built in 1987, these two hide their treasures underground, behind the castle, below the beautifully landscaped, 4-acre **Enid A. Haupt Garden.** The Museum of African Art displays artifacts from sub-Saharan Africa, such as masks, ceremonial figures, and musical instruments. The Sack-ler Gallery showcases an extensive collection of illuminated manuscripts, Chinese and Japanese paintings, jade miniatures, and friezes from Egypt, Phoenicia, and Sumeria.

🎵 ENTERTAINMENT

MUSIC

The D.C. punk scene is, or at least was, one of the nation's finest, but performers of all kinds frequently call on the city. Check the *Entertainment Guide* published in the Friday edition of the Washington Post for details on upcoming concerts, shows, and other events. The bigger, more mainstream events take place at the sports arenas: **RFK Stadium,** 2400 E. Capitol St., in the summer (box office ☎608-1119; open M-F noon-5pm), and the **MCI Center,** 601 F St., year-round (box office ☎628-3200; open daily 10am-5:30pm). Tickets for many shows are available from **Protix** (☎410-481-6500, 703-218-6500, or 800-955-5566). In its 73rd season, the ⬛**National Symphony Orchestra** contin-ues to delight D.C., primarily in the Kennedy Center's concert hall (☎467-4600 or 800-444-1324; www.kennedy-center.org/nso). D.C. also has a diverse and thriving jazz and blues scene, with venues perfect for anyone's budget. The **Kennedy Center** (p. 335) and the **Smithsonian Museums** (p. 336) often sponsor free shows, especially in the summer.

THEATER AND DANCE

Arena Stage, 6th St. and Maine Ave. SW, is often called the best regional theater company in America. (☎488-3300; www.arenastage.org. Metro: Waterfront. Box office open M-Sa 10am-8pm, Su noon-8pm. Tickets $40-66. Discounts for students, seniors, and the disabled. A limited number of half-price tickets usually available 1½hr. before start of show.) The ▨**Kennedy Center,** at 25th St. and New Hampshire Ave., offers scores of ballet, opera, and dramatic productions, most of them expensive. (☎416-8000; for rush tickets info 467-4600; www.kennedy-center.org. Tickets $10-75.) The **Shakespeare Theatre** at the Lansburgh, 450 7th St. NW, at Pennsylvania Ave., puts on lively performances. The company's 2005 schedule includes *Lorenzaccio* (Jan. 18-Mar. 6), *The Tempest* (Mar. 22-May 22), and *Lady Windermere's Fan* (June 7-July 31). Each summer the theater puts on the "Free for All," a no-charge production of a Shakespearean work, usually one of the comedies, meant to draw a wider, more diverse crowd. (Metro: Archives-Navy Memorial. ☎547-1122 or 877-487-8849; www.shakespearetheatre.org. Tickets $23-68; during preview week $13-59. Discounts for students and seniors. $10 standing-room tickets available 1hr. before sold-out performances.) To further satisfy any Shakespearean craving, head to the **Folger Theater,** 201 E. Capitol St. SE. In 2005, you'll find *Romeo and Juliet* (Jan. 14-Feb. 20) and *The Clandestine Marriage* (Apr. 14-May 23). Students receive 20-25% discounts on most regular tickets and 50% rush discounts 1hr. prior to showtime. Seniors, teachers, and military personnel receive 15-20% discounts on most regular tickets. (☎544-7077; www.folger.edu. Box office: M-F 10am-5pm in person, M-Sa noon-4pm by phone.) In the **14th Street Theater District,** tiny repertory companies explore and experiment with enjoyable results; check *CityPaper* for listings. **Studio Theatre,** 1333 P St. NW, at 14th St., features contemporary works. The company has transformed and expanded its space in the last few years to yield a multi-theater complex capable of hosting more than one production at a time. (Metro: Dupont Circle. ☎332-3300; www.studiotheatre.org.) ▨**The Source Theatre,** 1835 14th St. NW, between S and T St., is dedicated to the diverse local community of artists. (Metro: U St. Cardozo. ☎462-1073; www.sourcetheatre.com.) Having settled into their new space, the famous ▨**Woolly Mammoth Theater Company** will begin its first season at 7th and D St. NW, in the Penn Quarter neighborhood. Call for info on pay-what-you-can and under-25 performances. (Metro: Chinatown. ☎393-3939; www.woollymammoth.net.)

SPORTS

The 20,000-seat **MCI Center,** 601 F St. NW, in Chinatown, is D.C.'s premiere sports arena. (☎628-3200. Metro: Gallery Pl.-Chinatown. Box office: ☎628-3200. Open daily 10am-5:30pm.) The **Washington Wizards** serve as the NBA's laughingstock for both their poor play and lame mascot (☎661-5065; www.washingtonwizards.com; tickets $5-100), while the WNBA's **Washington Mystics** plays from May to September (www.wnba.com/mystics; tickets $8-60). The **Washington Capitals** skate from October through April. (☎661-5065; www.washingtoncaps.com. Tickets $10-100.) The NFL's **Washington Redskins** draw crowds to **Fed-Ex Stadium,** Raljon Dr., in Raljon, MD, from September through December. (☎301-276-6050; www.redskins.com. Tickets $40-100.)

▨ NIGHTLIFE

BARS AND CLUBS

Talk about a double life. D.C. denizens who crawl through red tape by day paint the town red by night. If you find yourself taking JELL-O body shots off a beautiful stranger at an all-you-can-drink-fest, don't say we didn't warn you. If you ache for a pint of amber ale, swing by the Irish pub-laden **Capitol Hill**. Hit up **Georgetown** for youthful prepsters in upscale bars. **Dupont Circle** is home to glam GLBT nightlife, while **Adams-Morgan** hosts an international crowd. To party with rock stars, head to the **U District** for DC's best live rock 'n' roll. For more tips, try www.dcnites.com.

DUPONT AND U DISTRICT

▨ **Brickskeller,** 1523 22nd St. NW (☎293-1885; www.brickskeller.org). You will get laughed at for ordering Miller Lite. With 1072 different bottled brews to choose from, the Brickskeller boasts the largest selection in the world ($3.25-19), and "beer-tails," mixed drinks made with beer ($3.25-6.50). The saloon occupies the 1st fl. of a hotel; monthly beer tastings are held on the 2nd fl. Sept.-May. Pub menu served until 1am Su-Th, until 2am F-Sa. Open M-Th 11:30am-2am, F 11:30am-3am, Sa 6pm-3am, Su 6pm-2am.

▨ **Cafe Saint-Ex,** 1847 14th St. NW (☎265-7839; www.saint-ex.com), at T St. Rockers playing at the nearby clubs usually come by Cafe Saint-Ex for drinks or dinner. The vintage aviation-themed bar, named after Antoine de Saint-Exupery, aviator and author of *The Little Prince,* attracts a truly mixed crowd of both punk rockers and lawyers. Upstairs bar and patio cafe. Downstairs Gate 54 lounge. Music in the lounge ranges from indie rock to synth-pop. Beer $2-5, rail drinks $6. Happy hour daily 5:30-7pm offers $3 drinks. 21+ after 10:30pm. No cover. Open M-F 5pm-2am, Sa-Su 11am-2am.

Eighteenth Street Lounge, 1212 18th St. NW (☎466-3922; www.eslmusic.com/lounge). 10 years old and still the mod-est of the mod, this progenitor of the D.C. lounge scene has top-shelf DJs, most of whom are signed to ESL's independent record label and spin house, hip-hop, and dance. Plush couches, high prices, and an outdoor patio bar now reign in the mansion that once housed Teddy Roosevelt. The storied bouncers keep the dance floor full but not overcrowded and—be warned guys!—the patron ratio skewed toward females. 21+. Cover generally $10-20, but no cover Tu. Open Tu-W 9:30pm-2am, Th 5:30pm-2am, F 5:30pm-3am, Sa 9:30pm-3am.

The Big Hunt, 1345 Connecticut Ave. NW (☎785-2333). Leopard-print couches adorn this jungle-themed 3-floor bar, where the casual khaki-and-flip-flops crowd hunts for potential mates. Notorious pickup joint for college kids and Hill workers pretending they're still in college. 24 brews on tap ($3.75-5). Solid pub fare, plus surprisingly delicious Guinness ice cream. Pool table. Happy hour M-F 4-7:30pm with half-price pizza. 21+. No cover. Open M-Th 4pm-2am, F-Sa 4pm-3am, Su 11am-midnight.

ADAMS-MORGAN

▨ **Madam's Organ,** 2461 18th St. NW (☎667-5370; www.madamsorgan.com), near Columbia Rd. A 3-floor blues bar with an intimate rooftop patio serving soul food. Live band plays nightly on first floor to an international crowd, many in their 30s. Pool tables. 2-for-1 drinks during happy hour (M-F 5-8pm), and redheads always drink Rolling Rock for half-price. Drafts $3.75-5.75; mixed drinks $4.75-6.75. Pitchers $14. 21+. Cover Su-Th $2-4, F-Sa $5-7. Open Su-Th 5pm-2am, F-Sa 5pm-3am.

Millie & Al's, 2440 18th St. NW (☎387-8131). Jukebox bar draws an ultra-casual crowd into its booths with cheap pizza, fries, subs, and $1 JELL-O shooter specials. With the wood paneling and checkered tablecloths, Millie & Al's is a welcome respite from the velvet-roped lounges. Expect beer pitchers, not martini glasses. Nightly specials 4-7pm. DJs play rock and hip-hop F-Sa. Burgers $3. Fries $2.50. Draft beer $2-3.50; bottles $3-4.25. 21+. No cover. Open M-Th 4pm-2am, F-Sa 4pm-3am.

The Reef, 2446 18th St. NW (☎518-3800). The newest hot spot on 18th St. breaks from the neighborhood's boho tradition. 3 levels of drinking for a casual 20s crowd: jungle-themed first floor, aquarium-esque 2nd fl. lounge, and a massive roof deck. The 8-10 person booths are great for groups. Rail drinks $5, 14 rotating bottled beers $3-6 each. Happy hour daily 4-7:30pm. 21+ after 9pm. No cover. Open M-Th 4pm-2am, F-Sa 4pm-3am, Su 11am-3pm (brunch) and 4pm-2am.

MID-ATLANTIC

CAPITOL HILL

■ **The Dubliner,** 520 N. Capitol St. NW (☎737-3773). Metro: Union Station. A subdued crowd enjoys Guinness and the house brew, Auld Dubliner Amber Ale ($5 a pint), in what many consider to be D.C.'s most authentic Irish pub. Live Irish music often includes familiar pop melodies injected with an Irish twist (M-Th 9pm-1:30am, F-Sa 9pm-2:30am, Su 7:30pm-12:30am). A large patio turns lounge-style for celebrators as the night ticks on. Open Su-Th 7am-2am, F-Sa 7am-3am. Kitchen closes at 1am.

■ **Pour House/Politiki,** 319 Pennsylvania Ave. SE (☎546-1001; www.politiki-dc.com). Metro: Capitol South. 3 levels filled with young, attractive interns downstairs and big spenders of all ages upstairs. A dark-wood-paneled, subterranean bar goes Hawaiian with tiki-style drinks and food with bamboo. "Top of the Hill" martini bar open upstairs Tu-Sa. Nightly drink specials and a free buffet Su-Th 4pm-1:30am. Happy hour M-F 5:30-8pm. Open M-Th 4pm-1:30am, F 3pm-2:30am, Sa-Su 10am-2:30am.

GLBT NIGHTLIFE

The *Washington Blade* is the best source for gay news and club listings; published every Friday, it's available in virtually every storefront in Dupont Circle. *Metro Weekly*, a gay and lesbian Washington-area magazine, is another good reference for weekend entertainment and nightlife.

■ **J.R.'s,** 1519 17th St. NW (☎328-0090), at Church St. D.C.'s busiest gay bar for good reasons: hot bartenders, fun events like bachelor auctions, and great drink deals. Packed every night with hordes of "guppies" (gay urban professionals), predominantly males in their 30s and 40s. Happy hour (M-W 5-8pm) brings $3 mini-pitchers, $2 rail drinks and domestic beers, and $1 sodas; the famous Power Hour follows (8-9pm), during which everything is half-price. Open M-Th 4pm-2am, F-Sa 12:30pm-3am, Su noon-2am.

■ **Cobalt,** 1639 R St. NW (☎462-6569), at 17th St. No sign marks this gay hot spot; look for the blue light and bouncer. Shirtless bartenders serve drinks ($4.75-5.75) to a young, preppy gay male and straight female crowd who come to this 2nd-floor dance club. Tu 70s and 80s night. No cover Su-W. Cover Th $8 for open bar, F after 11 and all night Sa $5. Open Tu-Th 10pm-2am, F-Sa 10pm-3am, Su 8:30pm-2am. Downstairs, **30°** is a lounge offering a relaxed atmosphere with half-price martinis during happy hour (M-F 5-8pm). 21+. Open Su-Th 5pm-2am, F-Sa 5pm-3am.

Apex, 1415 22nd St. NW (☎296-0505), near P St. Formerly known as Badlands, this 2-story dance complex is one of Dupont Circle's old standbys. DJs play a mix of house, trance, and Top 40 music that attracts a young crowd. Th college night, $5 cover (free with student ID), $3 rail drinks. Cover F before 10pm $8, after 10pm $10; drag karaoke starts 11pm. Sa "Liquid Ladies" night, with $7 cover and $3 Long Island iced teas, draws a sizeable crowd of lesbians. 18+. Open Th-Sa from 9pm-4am.

⚡ DAYTRIPS FROM D.C.

ARLINGTON, VA

The 612-acre **Arlington National Cemetery** holds the graves of over 260,000 people, honoring those who sacrificed their lives in war. Veterans from every American war, from the Revolutionary War up to the present, are buried here. The **Kennedy gravesites** hold the remains of President John F. Kennedy, his brother Robert F. Kennedy, and his wife Jacqueline Kennedy Onassis. The Eternal Flame flickers above JFK's simple memorial stone. The **Tomb of the Unknowns** honors unidentified servicemen who died fighting for the US, and is guarded by soldiers from the Army's Third Infantry. (Changing of the guard Apr.-Sept. every 30min. 8am-6pm; Oct.-Mar. every hr. 8am-4pm.) **Pierre L'Enfant,** originally buried within the District, was reinterred at Arlington along with soldiers from the Revolutionary War and the War of 1812. His distinctive grave on the hillside in front of **Arlington House,** once owned by Robert E. Lee, overlooks the city he designed. Lee's home, now a museum of antebellum life, provides one of the best views of D.C. from across the Potomac (open daily 9:30am-4:30pm). Farther down the hill among the plain headstones lies General of the Armies **John J. Pershing,** commander of US forces during WWI, who asked to be buried among his men. Arlington also holds the bodies of Arctic explorers **Robert E. Peary** and **Richard Byrd** and legendary politician **William Jennings Bryan.** Each year on **Memorial Day,** a small American flag is placed on each of the cemetery's gravesites; the President lays a wreath at the Tomb of the Unknowns and makes a speech commemorating the day. The **Women in Military Service for America Memorial** fits into its somber surroundings with a circular stone wall and reflecting pool. A memorial for the victims of the **September 11th** attacks and a memorial dedicated to the crew of the **Space Shuttle Columbia** were recently added. (Metro: Arlington Cemetery. ☎ 703-607-8000; www.arlingtoncemetery.org. Open daily Apr.-Sept. 8am-7pm; Oct.-May 8am-5pm. Free. Parking $1.25 per hr. for first 3hr., $2 per hr. thereafter.)

Exit the cemetery through Weitzel Gate and walk for 20min. to get to the **Iwo Jima Memorial,** based on Joe Rosenthal's Pulitzer Prize-winning photo of Marines straining to raise the US flag on Mt. Suribachi. **The Pentagon,** the world's largest building, is mind-boggling, with five concentric and 10 radial hallways totaling 17½ mi., 7754 windows, 131 stairways, and four postal codes of its own. The wall that took the impact of the hijacked airplane on September 11, 2001, has been completely restored. Tours of the Pentagon are currently suspended due to security concerns; the Tour Office has information about the future of Pentagon tours. (☎ 703-695-3324.) Just down S. Hayes St. from the Pentagon is the **Drug Enforcement Administration,** which operates a fascinating museum on the history of illegal drugs in America. Changing exhibits have focused on topics such as drugs' effects on their users and how the agents operate on land, in the air, and on the sea. (Metro: Pentagon City. ☎ 307-3463; www.deamuseum.org. Open Tu-F 10am-4pm. Free.)

ALEXANDRIA, VA

Alexandria didn't become a tourist attraction until the 1980s, when city residents backed away from proposed high-rises and decided to revitalize Old Town. Capitalizing on original 18th-century architecture and the legacy of historical all-stars like George Washington and Robert E. Lee, the town re-cobbled the streets, re-bricked the sidewalks, installed gardens, restored over 1000 original facades, and invited tall ships and hip shops. As a result, **Old Town Alexandria** is now packed with tourists. Sights cluster along Washington and King St. Looming over western Alexandria, the lofty **George Washington Masonic National Memorial,** 101 Callahan Dr., is an imposing testament to the strength of masonry and the legacy of Washington, the only person to have been a Masonic chartermaster and US president at the same time. (☎ 703-683-2007; www.gwmemorial.org.) Thirty-seven different Lees inhabited the **Lee-Fendall House,** 614 Oronoco St. (☎ 703-549-1789; www.leefendallhouse.org. Open Tu-Sa 10am-4pm, Su 1-4pm. $4, students 11-17 $2, children 10 and under free.) Formerly a hotbed of political, business, and social life, the restored **Gadsby's Tavern,** 134 N. Royal St., takes you back to ye good olde days of hospitality, when as many as four hotel guests slept in one bed. (☎ 703-838-4242; www.gadsbystavern.org. Open Apr.-Oct. Su-M 1-5pm, Tu-Sa 10am-5pm; Nov.-Mar. W-Sa 11am-4pm, Su 1-4pm. Last 30min. tour 15min. prior to closing. $4, students 11-17 $2, ages 10 and under free.) The **Ramsay House Visitors Center,** 221 King St., offers free maps and literature. The house, a 1724 building shipped upriver from Dumfries, VA, was the home of Scottish merchant and Lord Mayor William Ramsay. (☎ 703-838-4200; www.alexandriacity.com. Open daily 9am-5pm.)

MOUNT VERNON

George Washington's fabulous **Mount Vernon** estate is easily accessible in Fairfax County, VA. Visitors can see Washington's bedroom and tomb and the estate's fields, where slaves once grew corn, wheat, and tobacco. During his days as president, Washington dedicated his leisure time to beautifying the mansion's interior and administering the corps of slaves that ran the farm. The estate maintains 30-40% of Washington's original furnishings, which are now on display. To get there, take the Fairfax Connector 101 bus from the Huntington Metro stop, or take the George Washington Pkwy. south, which becomes Washington St. in Alexandria, to the entrance. (☎703-780-2000 or 800-429-1520; www.mountvernon.org. Open daily Apr.-Aug. 8am-5pm; Mar. and Sept.-Oct. 9am-5pm; Nov.-Feb. 9am-4pm. $11, seniors $10.50, ages 6-11 $5, under 6 free.)

VIRGINIA

Many of America's formative experiences—the English settlement of North America, the boom in the slave trade, the final establishment of American independence, and much of the Civil War—took place in Virginia. The powerful antebellum imagery proffered by the state's many historical sites can be overwhelming, especially since the cosmopolitan Virginia of today is a far cry from its colonial origins. Travel down the state's eastern shore to indulge your historical nostalgia. If you seek solitude and rejuvenation, head west into towering Appalachian forests and fascinating underground caverns.

◪ PRACTICAL INFORMATION

Capital: Richmond.

Visitor Info: Virginia Division of Tourism (motto: "Virginia is for lovers"), 901 E. Byrd St., Richmond 23219 (☎800-847-4882; www.virginia.org). Open M-F 8am-5pm. **Department of Conservation and Recreation,** 203 Governor St., Ste. 213, Richmond 23219 (☎804-786-1712; www.dcr.state.va.us). Open daily 8am-5pm.

Postal Abbreviation: VA. **Sales Tax:** 5%.

RICHMOND ☎804

Virginia's capital city has a survivor's history of conflicts, disasters, and triumphs. William Mayo created the blueprint for what would become Richmond, which was officially chartered in 1742. But in 1781, during the Revolutionary War, Richmond burned to the ground as a result of a British attack led by American traitor Benedict Arnold. The city was rebuilt and went on to become the capital of the ill-fated Confederate States of America during the Civil War. After the South lost the "War Between the States," Richmond's economy and spirits were depressed for many years. However, this tenacious town held on, and by 1946 Richmond's economy and industrial strength outpaced every other city's growth in the nation.

▐ TRANSPORTATION

Trains: Amtrak, 7519 Staple Mills Rd. (☎264-9194 or 800-872-7245; www.amtrak.com). To: **Baltimore** (3-4hr., 8 per day, $33-51); **Virginia Beach** (3¼hr., 2 per day, $30-33); **Washington, D.C.** (2¼hr., 6 per day, $29-37); **Williamsburg** (1¼hr., 2 per day, $22). Station open 24hr. **Taxi** to downtown $17-18.

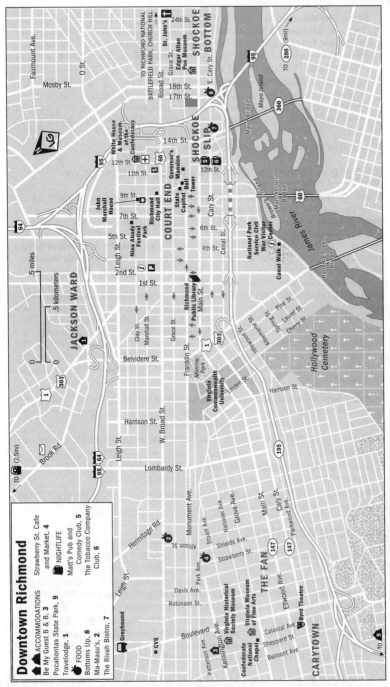

Downtown Richmond

▲ ACCOMMODATIONS
Be My Guest B & B, **3**
Pocahontas State Park, **9**
Travelodge, **1**

● FOOD
Bottoms Up, **8**
Ma-Masu's, **2**
The Rivah Bistro, **7**

Strawberry St. Cafe
and Market, **4**

🍸 NIGHTLIFE
Matt's Pub and
Comedy Club, **5**
The Tobacco Company
Club, **6**

Buses: Greyhound, 2910 N Blvd. (☎254-5910 or 800-231-2222), 2 blocks from downtown. To: **Baltimore** (3-5hr., 17 per day, $22-35); **Charlottesville** (1¼hr., 3 per day, $20); **New York City** (7-8hr., 16 per day, $60-66); **Norfolk** (2½hr., 7 per day, $28); **Philadelphia** (6-8hr., 8 per day, $41-55); **Washington, D.C.** (2-3hr., 13 per day, $30); **Williamsburg** (1hr., 6 per day, $12).

Public Transit: Greater Richmond Transit Co., 101 S. Davis Ave. (☎358-4782). Maps available in the basement of City Hall (900 E. Broad St.), the 6th St. Marketplace Commuter Station, and in the Yellow Pages. Most buses leave from stops along Broad St. downtown. Bus #24 goes to the Greyhound station. $1.25, transfers $0.15; seniors $0.50. Supersaver tickets $10 for book of 10 tickets.

Taxi: Veterans Cab ☎276-8990. **Redtop Taxi** ☎218-3040.

■ 🛈 ORIENTATION AND PRACTICAL INFORMATION

Broad Street is the city's central artery, and its cross streets are numbered from west to east. Most parallel streets to Broad St., including **Main Street** and **Cary Street,** run one-way. Both I-95, going north to Washington, D.C., and I-295 encircle the urban section of the city; the former to the east and north, the latter to the south and west. On the southeast edge of the city, **Shockoe Slip** and **Shockoe Bottom** overflow at night with partiers. Farther east, on the edge of town, the **Court End** and **Church Hill** districts comprise the city's historic center. **Jackson Ward** to the north, bounded by Belvedere, Leigh, Broad, and 5th St., recently underwent major construction to revamp its City Center and revitalize the surrounding community—*but it is still advisable to use caution at night in this area.* The **Fan,** named for its shape, is bounded by the Boulevard, I-195, the walk of statues along **Monument Avenue,** and **Virginia Commonwealth University.** The Fan has a notoriously dangerous reputation, but recent revitalization efforts have made it safer. The pleasant bistros and boutiques of **Carytown,** west of the Fan on Cary St., and the tightly knit working community of **Oregon Hill** add texture to the cityscape. *Be careful in this area at night.*

Visitor Info: Richmond Metropolitan Visitor's Bureau, 405 N. 3rd St. (☎783-7450; www.richmondva.org), in the Richmond Convention Center. Bus/van tours and maps. Offers discounted accommodations. Open daily 9am-6pm.

Hotlines: Rape Crisis, ☎643-0888. 24hr. **AIDS/HIV,** ☎800-533-4148. Operates M-F 8am-5pm.

Internet Access: Richmond Public Library, 101 E. Franklin St. (☎646-4867). Open M-Th 9am-9pm, F 9am-6pm, Sa 10am-5pm. Free access, 1hr. turns.

Post Office: 1801 Brook Rd. (☎775-6304). Open M-F 7am-6pm, Sa 9am-2pm. **Postal Code:** 23232. **Area Code:** 804.

🏠 ACCOMMODATIONS

▨ **Be My Guest Bed and Breakfast,** 2926 Kensington (☎358-9901). Located in the heart of Richmond, Be My Guest is truly a hidden deal: neither a sign nor a Yellow Pages listings marks this establishment. A pleasing decor, a full hot breakfast, rooms $60-125, and friendly owners who go out of their way to satisfy their visitors make this B&B worth a search. Expect prices in the upper half of this range during the summer. ❸

Travelodge, 5221 Brook Rd. (266-7603 or 800-637-3297). Take I-95 to Exit 81, bear right at the first light, and make a left onto Brook Rd. This brand-new location offers continental breakfast, free parking, an outdoor pool, cable TV, and a microfridge. 1- or 2-person rooms $36 on weekdays, $46 on weekends with the visitors center coupon. ❷

Pocahontas State Park, 10301 State Park Rd. (☎796-4255, 800-933-7275, or 255-3867 for reservations; www.dcr.state.va.us/parks/pocahontas). Take I-95 south to Exit 67 onto Rte. 288; after 5 mi., connect to Rte. 10, exit on Ironbridge Rd. east, and turn right on Beach Rd.; the Park is 4 mi. down on the right. Showers, biking, boating, picnic areas, and the second-largest pool in Virginia. Rent a canoe, rowboat, kayak, or paddleboat ($6 per hr., $22 per day). Sites with water and electricity $23. ❶

🗅 FOOD

Strawberry Street Cafe and Market, 421 and 415 N. Strawberry St. (cafe ☎353-6860, market 353-4100; www.strawberrystreetcafe.com), offers an unlimited salad bar ($8), a brunch bar ($10; available Sa-Su until 3pm), and an array of American classics ($7-10) in a pleasant cafe setting. Open M-Th 11am-2:30pm and 5-10:30pm, F 11am-2:30pm and 5pm-midnight, Sa 11am-midnight, Su 10am-10:30pm. ❸

Ma-Masu's, 2043 W. Broad St. (☎788-4205). Ma-Masu, "Spiritual Mother" extraordinaire, introduces her guests to Liberian culture with a mural that reads, "It's okay to lick your fingers here." If you can find parking on busy Broad St., enjoy generous portions of spicy delicacies such as *Keli-willy* (fried plantains with spices and onions), *toywah beans* ($6), collard greens ($2.50), and coconut juice ($2). Delivery available. Open Tu-Th noon-9pm, F noon-10pm, Sa 2-10pm. ❶

Bottoms Up, 1700 Dock St. (☎644-4400), at 17th and Cary St. This pizzeria, perfectly located for satisfying post-nightclub cravings, offers a creative assortment of toppings. Take a choose-your-own-pizza adventure, or go with the Chesapeake (spicy crab meat). Pizza $3.50-6 per slice, $8.50-20.50 per pie. Open M-Tu 11am-10pm, W-Th and Su 11am-11pm, F-Sa 11am-2am. ❶

The Rivah Bistro, 1417 E. Cary St. (☎344-8222; www.rivahbistro.com), is where the stars dine when they come to town. Serving some of the best bistro food in the city, this classy establishment has a cosmopolitan flair thanks to its French-Moroccan chef. Delicacies include dishes like Chicken Farci ($17) that feature the flavors of North Africa. Lunch: pasta and Moroccan specialties $12-16. Dinner: seafood $18-21, meat dishes $16-22. Vegetarian options available. Open M-Sa 11am-11pm; Su brunch 10:30am-4:30pm, dinner 4:30-9pm. ❺

🗅 SIGHTS

AROUND ST. JOHN'S CHURCH. St. John's Church is the site of Patrick Henry's famed "Give me liberty or give me death" speech in 1775. In the summer, orators recreate the speech on Sundays at 2pm. The church still serves as an active house of worship. *(2401 E. Broad St. ☎648-5015; http://historicstjohnschurch.org. 25min. tours M-Sa 10am-4pm, Su 1-4pm. Services Su 8:30 and 11am. Organ recital 1:30pm. Admission $5, ages 62 and up $4, ages 7-18 $3.)* Nearby is the **Edgar Allan Poe Museum,** in Richmond's oldest standing house (circa 1737), where visitors try to unravel the author's mysterious death. Poe memorabilia and first editions of his works fill the museum's rooms. *(1914 E. Main St. ☎888-648-5523; www.poemuseum.org. Open Tu-Sa 10am-5pm, Su 11am-5pm. Tours on the hr., last tour 4pm. $6; students, seniors, and AAA $5; under 9 free.)*

CONFEDERATE SOUTH. The continuing historical relevance of the Civil War South is explored at the **Museum of the Confederacy.** The poignant painting "Last Meeting of Lee and Jackson" and the collection of artifacts and documents detailing military medical treatments are intriguing. Next door, extremely friendly and knowledgeable guides run tours through the White House of the Confederacy. *(1201 E. Clay St. ☎649-1861; www.moc.org. Museum open M-Sa 10am-5pm, Su noon-5pm.*

MID-ATLANTIC

40min. tours every 45min. M, W, F-Sa 10:30am-4:30pm; Tu and Th 11:30am-4:30pm. White House tours every 30min. Tickets to either museum or White House $7, ages 62 and up $6, ages 7-18 $3. Combination tickets $10/$9/$5.)

FAN DISTRICT. This old-world section of Richmond is home to the country's largest and best-preserved Victorian neighborhood. Stroll down **Monument Avenue,** a boulevard lined with gracious old houses and towering statues of Virginia heroes—a true Richmond memory lane. The statue of **Robert E. Lee** faces south toward his beloved Dixie; **Stonewall Jackson** faces north so that the general can perpetually scowl at the Yankees. The statue of African-American tennis hero **Arthur Ashe** created a storm of controversy when it was added to the end of the avenue that had previously only featured Civil War generals.

MUSEUM ROW. The ◪**Virginia Historical Society** maintains an impressive collection of exhibits in an even more impressive building. Marvel at the elegant classical architecture before moving on through the extensive "Story of Virginia" exhibit, tracing the history of Virginians of all ethnic and national origins from prehistory to the present. The museum's showcase feature is series of murals known as the "Four Seasons of the Confederacy" covering the walls of a single room. This masterpiece, painted by the French artist Charles Hoffbauer between 1914 and 1921, reflects not only the ups and downs of the Confederate cause, but also the artist's anxiety over WWI, which raged on during the murals' painting. *(428 N. Blvd. ☎ 358-4901; www.vahistorical.org. Open M-Sa 10am-5pm, Su 1pm-5pm. $5, seniors $4, students and children $3.)* The **Virginia Museum of Fine Arts**—the South's largest art museum—houses a collection by some of the world's most renowned painters: Monet, Renoir, Picasso, and Warhol, as well as treasures from ancient Rome, Egypt, and Asia. *(200 N. Blvd. ☎ 340-1400; www.vmfa.state.va.us. Open W-Su 11am-5pm. Suggested donation $5; admission for special exhibitions varies.)*

🎵 📷 ENTERTAINMENT AND NIGHTLIFE

At the marvelous old **Byrd Theatre,** 2908 W. Cary St., movie buffs buy tickets for the latest movies from a tuxedoed agent and on weekends are treated to a pre-movie Wurlitzer organ concert and a selection of modern movie classics like *Indiana Jones* and *Goonies.* (☎ 353-9911; www.byrdtheatre.com. All shows $2; Sa balcony open for $1 extra.) Free concerts abound downtown and at the **Nina Abady Festival Park** on summer Fridays 6-9:30pm. *Style Weekly,* a free magazine available at the visitors center, and *Punchline,* found in most hangouts, list concert lineups. Cheer on the **Richmond Braves,** Richmond's AAA minor-league baseball team, for a fraction of major-league prices. (☎ 359-4444; www.rbraves.com. Boxes $9, general $6, youth under 12 and seniors over 60 $3.)

Student-driven nightlife enlivens **Shockoe Slip** and the **Fan.** After dark, **Shockoe Bottom** turns into college-party central, with transient bars pumping bass-heavy music early into the morning. *Be cautious in the Bottom's alleys after dark.* At **The Tobacco Company Club,** 1201 E. Cary St., at the corner of 12th S, an older crowd—and some young'uns trying to act older—drinks martinis, smokes cigars, and revels in the comfort of Southern living. (☎ 782-9555; www.thetobaccocompany.com. Drink specials 8-9pm. Ladies Night Th. Live music Tu-Th 8pm, F-Sa 9:30pm. No bikini contests here—or tennis shoes, jeans, or boots. 21+. Open Th-Sa 8pm-2am.) **Matt's Pub and Comedy Club,** 109 S. 12th St., pours out a bit of Brit wit within dark wooden walls. (☎ 643-5653. Pub fare $3-7. Microbrews and drafts $2.75-3.60; cocktails $3.25. Stand-up comedy F 8 and 10:30pm, Sa 8 and 11pm; reservations recommended. Cover $9.75 when charged. Open F-Sa 11:30am-2am.)

WILLIAMSBURG ☎ 757

With every part of the reconstructed town screaming 1770s, Colonial Williamsburg is a living exhibition of American life on the eve of the Revolutionary War. The historical recreation extends right down to the fife-and-drum corps that marches down the streets and the costumed wheelwrights, bookbinders, and blacksmiths who go about their tasks using 200-year-old methods. Travelers who visit in late fall or early spring will avoid the crowds, but will also miss the special summer programs. If Williamsburg doesn't satiate your colonial nostalgia, check out the nearby towns of Jamestown and Yorktown, which can lay claim to the titles of the first permanent English settlement in America and the decisive American Revolutionary War battle victory, respectively.

▛ TRANSPORTATION

Airport: Newport News and Williamsburg International Airport (☎877-0221; www.nnwairport.com), 20min. away in Newport News. Take state road 199 W to I-64 S. The only shuttle service serving the airport is the **Williamsburg Limousine Service** (☎877-0279). $23 to Newport News; $65 to Norfolk. Cash only.

Trains: Amtrak (☎800-872-7245 or 229-8750; www.amtrak.com), 468 N. Boundary St. To: **Baltimore** (5hr., 2 per day, $48-56); **New York City** (8-9hr., 2 per day, $84-99); **Philadelphia** (6hr., 2 per day, $64-74); **Richmond** (1¼hr., 2 per day, $18-23).

Buses: Greyhound (☎800-231-2222 or 229-1460; www.greyhound.com), 468 N. Boundary St. To: **Baltimore** (5½-7hr., 7 per day, $45-52); **Norfolk** (1-2hr., 6 per day, $12-15); **Richmond** (1hr., 7 per day, $10); **Virginia Beach** (2½-3½hr., 6 per day, $16-19); **Washington, D.C.** (4-6hr., 7 per day, $30-34). Ticket office open M-F 8am-noon and 1-5pm, Sa 8am-noon and 1-2pm.

Public Transit: James City County Transit (JCCT); (☎259-4093; www.williamsburgtransport.com). Bus service along Rte. 60, from Merchants Sq. west to Williamsburg Pottery or east past Busch Gardens. Operates M-Sa 6am-7pm. $1.25 per ride; all-day pass $1.50. Transfer $0.25. **Williamsburg Shuttle (R&R)** provides service between **Colonial Williamsburg** and the **Water Country USA** and **Busch Gardens** amusement parks every 30min. May 25-Sept. 3 daily 9am-10pm. All-day pass $2.

Taxi: Yellow Cab ☎722-1111, serves the whole historic triangle area.

▟ ▞ ORIENTATION AND PRACTICAL INFORMATION

Williamsburg lies 50 mi. southeast of Richmond. The **Colonial Parkway,** connecting the three towns in the historic triangle—Williamsburg, Jamestown, and Yorktown—has no commercial buildings and is a beautiful route between historic destinations. Take I-64 and the Colonial Pkwy. exit to reach Colonial Williamsburg.

Visitor Info: Williamsburg Area Convention And Visitors Bureau, 421 N. Boundary St., provides information about area attractions, including the restored colonial town. (☎253-0192 or 800-368-6511; www.visitwilliamsburg.com), ½ mi. northwest of the Transportation Center. Open M-F 8:30am-5pm. **Colonial Williamsburg Visitors Center,** 100 Visitors Center Dr. (☎800-447-8679 or 229-1000; www.colonialwilliamsburg.com), 1 mi. northeast of the Transportation Center. Open daily 8:45am-5:30pm; winter hours vary.

Post Office: 425 N. Boundary St. (☎229-0838). Open M-F 8am-5pm, Sa 9am-2pm. **Postal Code:** 23185. **Area Code:** 757.

▐ ACCOMMODATIONS

Williamsburg abounds with classy hotels and unique (and extravagantly priced) B&Bs. Budget chains cluster around the junctions of Rte. 5, 31, 60, 132, and 162. The 1 mi. walk into the colonial area might be strenuous during the 98°F summers, but if you can't get a room in town, this may be your best bet.

Bryant Guest House, 702 College Terr. (☎ 229-3320). From Scotland Rd., turn right onto Richmond Rd., then left onto Dillard St. 4 rooms with private baths, TV, and limited kitchen facilities in a conveniently located brick home. Singles $40; doubles $50; 5-person suite $80. ❷

Tioga Motel, 906 Richmond Rd. (☎ 229-4531 or 800-527-5370), just east of the colonial area, has 26 ground-floor rooms with A/C, refrigerators, and TVs, as well as a pool. Summer rates start at $45 for a double bed. ❸

Econolodge, 1900 Richmond Rd. (☎ 229-6600). If the smaller guest houses fill up, the Econolodge has some of the lowest prices in town and a central location. Wheelchair accessible rooms available. Outdoor pool and continental breakfast. Doubles $65.

▐ FOOD

The Old Chickahominy House, 1211 Jamestown Rd. (☎ 229-4689), 1½ mi. from the historic district on the Williamsburg-Jamestown border. For breakfast, enjoy pancakes with a side of smoked bacon ($7.50). Becky's "complete luncheon" has Virginia ham, hot biscuits, fruit salad, a slice of homemade pie, and iced tea or coffee ($7.25). Open M-F 8:30-10:30am and 11:30am-2:30pm, Sa-Su 8:30-10am and 11:45am-2pm. ❷

Chowning's Tavern, Duke of Gloucester St. (☎ 229-2141 or 800-828-3767). Quasi-historical dishes like "Ploughman's Pastie" (roasted turkey and melted cheddar cheese in a flaky pastry; $7.25) will have you chowing down George Washington-style. After 9pm, peanuts are at stake as patrons roll the dice against their servers. The merriment continues as costumed waiters sing 18th-century ballads and challenge guests to card games and sing-alongs over light meals ($3.50-5.50). Cover $3, no cover for dinner guests. Open daily 11:30am-10pm. ❷

Berret's, 199 S. Boundary St. (☎ 253-1847), located at Merchant's Sq. (Colonial Williamsburg's shopping district). This popular establishment combines 2 restaurants in 1: the less expensive and more casual **Tap House Grill,** and the pricey and more formal **Berret's Restaurant and Bar.** The Tap House serves upscale sandwich plates like the chicken pecan apple salad sandwich ($8-12) and seafood entrees ($14-19). Moving over into the formal restaurant, you can savor mouth-watering dishes such as the chilled shrimp in puff pastry with herbed goat cheese appetizer ($8.50) or the Virginia ham and crabmeat combination entree ($25). Live music on terrace in summer Su 6:30pm-9:30pm. Tap House open daily 5-10pm. Restaurant and Bar open daily 11:30am-3:30pm and 5:30-10pm. ❸/❺

◉ SIGHTS

COLONIAL WILLIAMSBURG. Every day is a historical reenactment at Colonial Williamsburg. If you visit in the summer and ask the pedestrians in 18th-century apparel what is on their minds, you'll enjoy an informed discussion of the issues of 1776. During the spring, the year is re-enacted in 1774, 1775 in the fall, and 1773 in the winter. The site prides itself on its authenticity, arming itself with enthusiastic actors, meticulously restored buildings, and a full complement of characters from all stations of society to give visitors a sense of the hardship and excitement of living on the eve of the revolution. Immersing yourself in the colonists' world doesn't require a ticket: visitors can walk the streets, march behind the fife-and-drum corps, lock themselves in the stocks, interact with the locals, and use the restrooms without ever spending a dollar. However, to enter any building, with or without an actor inside, or to attend any of the performances, a ticket is required. The *Visitor's Companion* newsletter, printed on Mondays, lists free events, evening programs, and complete hours. (☎800-447-8679; www.colonialwilliamsburg.org. Visitors center open daily 8:45am-5:30pm. Most sights open 9:30am-5pm. Day pass $33, ages 6-12 $17; 2 consecutive days and admission to Governor's Palace $45/$23; under 6 free.)

COLLEGE OF WILLIAM AND MARY. Spreading west from the corner of Richmond and Jamestown Rd., the College of William and Mary, founded in 1693, is the second-oldest college in the US (after Harvard, p. 127) and has educated luminaries such as presidents Jefferson, Monroe, and Tyler. The Wren Building, the oldest academic building in continuous use in America, still hosts classes today. The Office of Admissions, in Blow Hall, offers free tours throughout the year. (☎221-4223; www.wm.edu. Tours M-F 10am and 2:30pm, also Sa 10am.)

⚑ DAYTRIPS FROM WILLIAMSBURG

JAMESTOWN AND YORKTOWN

The "Historic Triangle" brims with US history. More authentic and less crowded than the Colonial Williamsburg empire, Jamestown and Yorktown show visitors where it all really began. The **Colonial National Park** preserves American colonial and revolutionary history with branches in both Jamestown and Yorktown. Southwest of Williamsburg on Rte. 31, in the Jamestown branch, you'll see the remains of the first permanent English settlement in America (1607) and exhibits on colonial life. The visitors center offers a 20min. film emphasizing the courage of America's first settlers, a 35min. "living history" walking tour (10:15am and 2:45pm; free with admission), and a 45min. audio tape tour ($2) for the Island Loop Route. Southeast of Williamsburg on the Colonial Pkwy., Yorktown recreates the significant last battle with an engaging film and an electric map. The visitors center rents cassettes and players ($2) for the battlefield's 3- or 5-mile car route. (☎229-1733. Open daily 9am-5pm. Visitors centers close 30min. before park. $8 for Jamestown, $5 for Yorktown, under 17 free; $10 joint pass. Passes good for 7 days.)

On Rte. 31, near the Jamestown branch of Colonial National Park, the **Jamestown Settlement** has a museum with changing exhibits, a reconstruction of James Fort, a Native American village, and full-scale replicas of the three ships that brought the original settlers to Jamestown in 1607. Children will enjoy the educational riverfront "discovery area." (☎252-4838 or 888-593-4682. Open daily June 15-Aug. 15 9am-6pm; Aug. 16-June 14 9am-5pm. $12, ages 6-12 $5.50. Combination ticket including Yorktown Victory Center $17, ages 6-12 $8.25, under 6 free.)

The 1781 American and French triumph over the British in the final battle of the Revolutionary War is celebrated daily at the **Yorktown Victory Center.** The center features two recreated areas—a Continental Army camp and a 1780s farm—where costumed reenactors interpret American history. Admission also includes informative exhibits and a 30min. film about the Yorktown battle. (☎253-4838 or 888-593-4682. Visitors center open daily 9am-4:30pm. $5, under 17 free.)

VIRGINIA BEACH ☎757

This boardwalk-centered town overflows with the all-you-can-eat buffets, age-old motels, and cheap discount stores that are the hallmarks of every beach town. So load up on saltwater taffy, homemade fudge, and tacky t-shirts, because the best part of a Virginia Beach vacation is not getting wrapped up in the stuffiness that plagues pretentious resort towns.

MID-ATLANTIC

▐ TRANSPORTATION

Trains: Amtrak (☎800-872-7245 or 245-3589; www.amtrak.com). The nearest train station, at 9304 Warwick Blvd. in Newport News, runs 45min. bus service to and from the corner of 19th and Pacific St. Call ahead to reserve your train ticket. Station open 7:30am-8pm. From Newport News to: **Baltimore** (5½hr., 2 per day, $56-65); **New York City** (8-10hr., 2 per day, $84-99); **Philadelphia** (7hr., 2 per day, $64-74); **Richmond** (2hr., 2 per day, $22-37); **Washington, D.C.** (4hr., 2 per day, $43-54); **Williamsburg** (20min., 2 per day, $18-22).

Buses: Greyhound, 1017 Laskin Rd. (☎800-231-2222 or 422-2998; www.greyhound.com). Open M-Sa 7-11am and 12:30-7pm. Connects with Maryland via Bridge-Tunnel. ½ mi. from oceanfront area. To: **Richmond** (3½hr., 7 per day, $18-20); **Washington, D.C.** (6-8hr., 6 per day, $33-38); **Williamsburg** (2½hr., 6 per day, $16-19).

Public Transit: Virginia Beach Transit/Trolley Information Center (☎437-4768; www.vbwave.com), Atlantic Ave. and 24th St. Info on area transportation and tours, including trolleys, buses, and ferries. Trolleys transport riders to most major points in Virginia Beach. The Atlantic Ave. Trolley runs from Rudee Inlet to 42nd St. Open May-Sept. daily 8am-2am. Fare $1, seniors and disabled $0.50, kids under 38 in. free; all-day passes $3, 3-day $5, 5-day $8. Other trolleys run along the boardwalk, the North Seashore, and to Lynnhaven Mall.

Taxi: Beach Yellow Cab ☎460-0605. **Virginia Beach Taxi** ☎486-6585.

Bike Rental: RK's Surf Shop has a bike stand at 10th St. and Atlantic Ave, which rents bikes for $4 per hr. or $16 per day. Open June-Sept. daily 8am-11pm. Bikes must be returned 2hr. before closing.

▰▐ ORIENTATION AND PRACTICAL INFORMATION

In Virginia Beach, east-west streets are numbered and the north-south avenues, parallel to the beach, are named. **Atlantic Avenue** is next to the beach and home to many of the town's hotels and shops. **Pacific Avenue** is the next street over and the major thoroughfare. **Arctic, Baltic,** and **Mediterranean Avenue** are farther inland.

Visitor Info: Virginia Beach Visitors Center, 2100 Parks Ave. (☎800-822-3224 or 491-7866; www.vbfunc.com), at 22nd St. Info on budget accommodations and area sights. Helpful, knowledgeable staff. Open daily June-Aug. 9am-8pm; Sept.-May 9am-5pm.

Internet Access: Virginia Beach Public Library, 4100 Virginia Beach Blvd. (☎431-3000, www.vbgov.com/dept/library). Open M-Th 10am-9pm, F-Sa 10am-5pm; Oct.-May also Su 1-5pm. Free—but the wait for a turn can be up to an hour long.

Post Office: 501 Viking Dr. (☎340-0981). Open M-F 7:30am-6pm, Sa 10am-2pm. **Postal Code:** 23452. **Area Code:** 757.

▐ ACCOMMODATIONS

Virginia Beach has two kinds of lodging: high-rise hotels along the boardwalk and motor courts that one block off the boardwalk. The ocean-view high-rises don't come cheap; in the summer even the cheapest rooms go for $150. Most motels run $70-100, and are still convenient to the beach and the boardwalk's social scene.

▨ **Angie's Guest Cottage, Bed and Breakfast, and HI Hostel (HI),** 302 24th St. (☎428-4690; www.angiescottage.com). Barbara "Angie" Yates and her staff welcome predominantly young international guests with warmth, coveted parking passes, and advice about the beach scene. 36 beds in five 4-9 person dorms. No A/C, but a fan for almost every bed. Kitchen, lockers, and beach mats available. Linen $2. Reservations recommended. Open Apr.-Sept. Check-in 9:30-9pm. Check-out 9:30-10am. $17, nonmembers $20; low-season $13/$17. Singles $38; doubles $60. Low-season $32/$48. ❶

The Castle Motel, 2700 Pacific Ave. (☎ 425-9330), is only 1 block from the beach, but half the price of the beachside hotels. Spacious, clean rooms come with cable TV, refrigerator, shower and bath, desk, and 2 full beds. Check-out 11am. 21+. Open May-Oct. Rates start at $69 Su-Th, F $129, Sa $139. ❹

First Landings, 2500 Shore Dr. (☎ 800-933-7275 or 225-3867; www.dcr.state.va.us/parks/1stland), about 8 mi. north of town on Rte. 60, has both **two-bedroom cabins** and **campsites** set amidst the natural beauty of the Virginia coastline. Reservations are required for campsites and advisable up to 11 months ahead for cabins. Cabins are close to picnic areas, a private swimming area on a sprawling beach, a bathhouse, and boat launching areas. Campsites have hot showers and grills. Cabin rates June-Aug. $76-103; Apr.-May and Sept.-Nov. $67-83. Camp sites $22, with electricity $28. ❹/❶

False Cape State Park (☎ 800-933-7275 or 225-3867). Exit I-64 on Indian River Rd. E, drive 13 mi. and turn left onto Newbridge Rd., right onto Sandbridge Rd., and right on Sandpiper Rd. to parking at Little Island City Park. 4 primitive campsites at False Cape, with drinking water and pit toilets, are worth the 6-9 mi. hike to their secluded locations. Reservations required. Campsites $9. Parking in summer M-F $3, Sa-Su $4. ❶

🍴 FOOD

Tropical Smoothie Cafe, 211 25th St. (☎ 422-3970; www.tropicalsmoothie.com). Simple but silky smoothies ($3-5), healthy wraps ($5), and fresh salads ($4-5) served in a sleek modern setting one block from the oceanfront. Open daily 9am-11pm. ❶

Cuisine and Co., 3004 Pacific Ave. (☎ 428-6700; www.cuisineandcompany.com). This sophisticated escape serves gourmet sandwiches to go. Treats include the California grilled chicken with avocado sandwich ($7.20) and the turkey with cranberry mayonnaise sandwich ($7.50). Open early Sept. to late May M-Sa 9am-7pm, Su 9am-6pm. ❶

Guadalajara, 200 21st St. (433-0140; www.guadalajaravb.com). This authentic Mexican restaurant is a hot post-beach spot for cooling down with a margarita ($5.50, jumbo $9). Count on a 15min. wait. Burritos $6.75. *Mole ranchero* $9. Crabmeat quesadillas $8. Open daily noon-1am; full menu until 11:30pm, late-night menu until 1am. ❷

👁 SIGHTS

BACK BAY NATIONAL WILDLIFE REFUGE. The islands, dunes, forests, marshes, ponds, and beaches that fill this pristine national refuge are a sanctuary for an array of endangered species and other wildlife. Visitors camping, hiking, or fishing in the park can also gawk at nesting bald eagles, white-tailed deer, ospreys, egrets, and other wildlife on a tram tour departing daily at 9am from Little Island City Park up the road. *(Take General Booth Blvd. to Princess Anne Dr.; turn left, then turn left onto Sandbridge Rd. and continue 6 mi. Turn right onto Sandpiper Rd., which leads directly to the visitors center.* ☎ 721-2412; http://backbay.fws.gov. Visitors center open M-F 8am-4pm, Sa-Su 9am-4pm. Closed Dec.-Mar. Sa $5 per car, $2 per family on foot or bike. Tram daily Apr.-Oct. 9am, return 12:45pm. ☎ 721-7666; www.bbrf.org. $6, seniors and under 12 $4.)

FALSE CAPE STATE PARK. The origin of the title "False Cape" comes from the 17th century, when ships trying to reach Cape Henry, the landing site of America's first English settlers, would mistakenly touch shore in the present-day state park. The Back Bay National Wildlife Refuge's tram stops at False Cape State Park, where walkers trek 1 mi. to the beach. If you miss the 9am daily tram, prepare for an adventurous 4 mi. hike or canoe ride, as foot and water are the only ways to get where you want to go. (☎800-933-7275 or 225-3867; www.dcr.state.va.us/parks.) **Kayak Eco Tours** offers kayak excursions to these areas. (4001 Sandpiper Rd. ☎888-669-8368 or 480-1999 for tours. 90min. sunset or sunrise tours $35, half-day $45, full-day $90.)

VIRGINIA MARINE SCIENCE MUSEUM. One mile south of the downtown boardwalk on Pacific Ave. (which becomes General Booth Blvd.), the Virginia Marine Science Museum houses Virginia's largest aquarium and is home to hundreds of species of fish, including crowd-pleasing river otters, sharks, and stingrays. The mammoth museum also houses a six-story IMAX theater and offers excursion trips for dolphin observation in summer and whale watching in winter. (717 General Booth Blvd. ☎425-3474, excursions 437-2628; www.vmsm.com. Open daily 9am-7pm; low-season 9am-5pm. $12, ages 62 and up $11, ages 3-11 $8. IMAX tickets $7.50/$6.75/$6.50. Combined museum and IMAX admission $17/$16/$13. Excursions $12, ages 4-11 $10.)

⬛ NIGHTLIFE

Mahi Mah's, 615 Atlantic Ave. (☎437-8030; www.mahimahs.com), at 7th St. inside the Ramada Hotel. This nightlife hot spot announces its fun atmosphere with nightly live rock performances that draw onlookers off the street into its slick interior. Sushi, wine tastings, tiki parties, and oceanfront views. Music nightly 6pm-10pm. Well-dressed crowd. Open daily 7am-1am, kitchen closes at 11pm.

Chicho's, 2112 Atlantic Ave. (☎422-6011), on "The Block" of college bars clustered between 21st and 22nd St. One of the hottest spots. Features gooey pizza ($2.25-3.25), tropical drinks ($5-7), and live rock 'n' roll M. 21+ after 10pm. Open May-Sept. M-F 6pm-2am, Sa 3pm-2am, Su noon-2am; Oct.-Apr. M-Th 6-10pm, F-Su noon-2am.

Harpoon Larry's, 216 24th St. (☎422-6000; www.harpoonlarryskillerseafood.com), at Pacific Ave., serves tasty fish in an everyone-knows-your-name atmosphere. The amicable bartender and manager welcomes patrons looking to escape the sweat and raging hormones of "The Block." Specials include crab cakes ($7) and M $0.35 oysters. W $1.50 Coronas with $0.25 jalapeño poppers. Happy hour (M-F 7-9pm) with $1 domestic drafts and $2 rail drinks. Open May-Sept. daily noon-2am; low-season hours vary.

CHARLOTTESVILLE ☎434

Thomas Jefferson, author of the Declaration of Independence and colonial Renaissance man, built his dream house, Monticello, high atop his "little mountain" just southeast of Charlottesville. Around his personal paradise, Jefferson endeavored to create the ideal community in Charlottesville. In an effort to breed intellect and keep himself busy, Jefferson humbly created the University of Virginia (UVA), now the core of a vibrant college town that still pays homage to its founder.

⬛ TRANSPORTATION

Airport: Charlottesville-Albemarle Airport (☎973-8342; www.gocho.com), 8 mi. north of Charlottesville, 1 mi. west of Rte. 29 on Airport Rd.

Trains: Amtrak, 810 W. Main St. (☎800-872-7245 or 296-4559; www.amtrak.com). To: **New Orleans** (22hr., 1 per day, $199); **Washington, D.C.** (2hr., 2 per day, $24-30). Ticket office open daily 6am-9:30pm.

Bus: Greyhound/Trailways, 310 W. Main St. (☎800-231-2222 or 295-5131; www.greyhound.com). To: **Baltimore** (5hr., from $45); **Richmond** (1¼hr., from $23); **Washington, D.C.** (3½hr., from $35).

Public Transit: Charlottesville Transit Service (☎296-7433). Bus service within city limits M-Sa 6:30am-midnight. $0.75, seniors and disabled $0.35, under 6 free. All-day pass $2.

Taxi: Carter's Airport Taxi ☎981-0170. **AAA Cab Co.** ☎975-5555.

✈️ 🛈 ORIENTATION AND PRACTICAL INFORMATION

Charlottesville's streets are numbered from east to west, using compass directions; 5th St. NW is 10 blocks from (and parallel to) 5th St. NE. There are two downtowns: **The Corner**, on the west side across from the university, is home to student delis and coffeeshops. **Historic downtown** is about a mile east. The two are connected by the east-west running **University Avenue**, which starts as Ivy Rd. and becomes Main St. after the end of the bridge in The Corner district.

Visitor Info: Chamber of Commerce, 415 E. Market St. (☎295-3141; http://charlottesvillechamber.org), at 5th St. Maps, guides, and info about lodging and special events available. Open M-F 9am-5pm. **Charlottesville-Albemarle County Convention and Visitors Bureau** (☎977-1783 or 877-286-1102; www.charlottesvilletourism.org), off I-64 on Rte. 20., has historic tours info. Open daily Mar.-Oct. 9am-5:30pm; Nov.-Feb. 9am-5pm. **University of Virginia Information Center** (☎924-7969), beneath the Rotunda in the center of campus, has brochures, university maps, and tour info. Open daily 9am-4:45pm.

Hotlines: Region 10 Community Services, ☎972-1800. **Sexual Assault Crisis Center**, ☎977-7273. Both open 24hr. **Mental Health**, ☎977-4673. Open M-F 9am-6pm.

Internet Access: Jefferson Madison Regional Library, 201 E. Market St. (☎979-7151). Open M-Th 9am-9pm, F-Sa 9am-5pm, Su 1-5pm. Free.

Post Office: 513 E. Main St. (☎963-2661). Open M-F 8:30am-5pm, Sa 10am-1pm. **Postal Code:** 22902. **Area Code:** 434.

🏠 ACCOMMODATIONS

English Inn of Charlottesville, 2000 Morten Dr. (☎800-786-5400), has 67 clean, standard hotel rooms in a building decorated with hewn wood beams. The amenities included make it worth the price: full breakfast buffet, 24hr. coffee and tea bar, A/C, cable TV, indoor pool, airport shuttle, and access to a local health club. Singles $65-75; doubles $71-81. AAA and AARP discounts. ❸

The Budget Inn, 140 Emmet St. (☎800-293-5144; www.budgetinn-charlottesville.com), is the closest motel to the university. 36 big rooms with lots of sunlight and cable TV. Rooms with 1 or 2 double beds Apr.-Sept. $45-75; Oct. $60-90; Nov.-Mar. $40-70. Each additional person $5. ❸

The Inn at Monticello, 1188 Scottsville Rd. (☎979-3593; www.innatmonticello.com), boasts the most auspicious location for those who want to mold their trip around visits to Jefferson's home. This 1850 manor-turned-B&B is within a 5min. drive of Monticello. Lovely antiques, elegant rooms, full gourmet breakfasts, and snacks and wine in the afternoon. Rooms $125-175. ❺

🍴 FOOD

🍴 **littlejohn's,** 1427 University Ave. (☎977-0588). During lunch hours, this deli becomes as overstuffed as its sandwiches. In the wee hours of the morning, barflies trickle into littlejohn's to kick back and relax with the Easy Rider (baked ham, mozzarella, and cole slaw; $3.75). Many, many beers $2-3; three-egg omelets $3.50. Open 24hr. ❶

Blue Light Grill and Raw Bar, 120 E. Main St. (☎295-1223; www.bluelightgrill.com), on the Mall. Ideal for seafood lovers, this grill has a modern, uncluttered atmosphere with red walls and high ceilings. The citrus-crusted monkfish ($17) is excellent. Dinner entrees $15-21. Open daily 4:30pm-2am. ❺

MID-ATLANTIC

Chaps, 223 E. Main St. (☎977-4139). A favorite for homemade ice cream. With a diner-that's-been-here-forever feel, Chaps also serves cheap, simple grub. Ice cream $2.50 for 1 scoop. Open M-Th 8am-10pm, F-Sa 8am-11pm, Su 11am-9pm. Cash only. ❶

👁 SIGHTS

UVA. Most activity on the grounds of the **University of Virginia** clusters around the fra-ternity-lined **Rugby Road** and the **Lawn,** a terraced green carpet that is one of the pretti-est spots in American academia. Professors live in the Lawn's pavilions, each of which was designed by Jefferson in a different architectural style and includes a view of Monticello. *(☎924-7969. Free tours meet at Rotunda entrance facing the Lawn. Tours daily 10, 11am, 2, 3, 4pm; no tours on Thanksgiving, mid-Dec. to mid-Jan., and early to mid-May.)*

HISTORIC MANSIONS. Jefferson oversaw every stage of the development of his beloved **Monticello,** a home that truly reflects the personality of its brilliant creator. The house is a quasi-Palladian jewel filled with fascinating 18th-century innova-tions, such as a fireplace dumbwaiter to the wine cellar and a mechanical manu-script copier. *(1184 Monticello Loop. ☎984-9822; www.monticello.org. Open daily Mar.-Oct. 8am-5pm; Nov.-Feb. 9am-4:30pm. $13, ages 6-11 $6. 30min. tours included in admis-sion price and begin every 5min.)* The partially reconstructed **Michie Tavern** has an operating grist mill and a general store. Lagers and ales are served alongside a southern buffet lunch. *(Just west of Monticello on Thomas Jefferson Pkwy. ☎977-1234; www.michietavern.com. Open daily 9am-5pm; last tour 4:20pm. Tours $8, seniors and AAA $7, ages 6-11 $3. Buffet lunch $14, ages 12-15 $10, ages 6-11 $7, ages 5 and under free.)* Just outside Charlottesville, James Madison's **Montpelier** once supported his over 100 slaves and property with tobacco, wheat, and corn crops. *(Rte. 20. ☎540-672-2728; www.montpelier.org. Open daily 9:30am-5pm. No entry after 4:30pm. $11, seniors and AAA $10, ages 6-14 $6. Audio tours available.)* **Ash Lawn-Highland** was the 535-acre plantation home of President James Monroe. Although less distinctive than Monti-cello, Ash Lawn reveals more about family life in the early 19th century through the interesting and informative guided tours. *(1000 James Monroe Pkwy. Off Rte. 792, 2½ mi. east of Monticello. ☎293-9539; www.ashlawnhighland.org. Open daily Apr.-Oct. 9am-6pm; Nov.-Mar. 11am-5pm. Tour $9, seniors and AAA $8, ages 6-11 $5.)*

🎷 NIGHTLIFE

Buddhist Biker Bar and Grille, 20 Elliewood Ave. (☎971-9181). UVA students and local 20-somethings flock to this bar for its huge lawn and drink specials served inside and on the patio. Try the spinach dip ($5) or stuffed mushrooms ($3.75). Beer $2.50-4. M $1 beer, W $2 cocktails, Th live bluegrass. Open M-Sa 3:30pm-2am.

Baja Bean, 1327 W. Main St. (☎293-4507). Cheap burritos, tamales, and chimichan-gas for $5-8 at this Mexican bar and restaurant filled with college students. Every 5th of the month is the Cinco Celebration, a fiesta with $3 Coronas. M open mic night. W 9pm-midnight dance parties with lasers and DJ-fueled music. Happy hour (M-F 3-7pm) with $1.50 mudslide shooters, $1.75 Baja Gold drafts, $2 rail highballs, and $3 Rox Rum Ritas. Open daily 11am-2am; kitchen closes at midnight.

Orbit, 102 14 St. NW (☎984-5707). A hot bar and restaurant combo popular with C-ville locals. The downstairs has a *2001: A Space Odyssey* theme, and the garage-door windows open on hot summer nights. Upstairs there are 8 pool tables and another bar with extensive beers on tap, including numerous imports ($2.50-4.50). Tu after 5pm ladies shoot pool for free. Th $2 drafts. Occasional Su live acoustic music. Open daily 5pm-2am, kitchen closes at 1am.

SHENANDOAH NATIONAL PARK ☎ 540

When Shenandoah National Park was purchased by the state of Virginia in 1926, it was a 280-acre tract of over-logged and over-hunted land. Thanks to a 1936 decree from Franklin Roosevelt that made Shenandoah America's first great nature reclamation project, the park now spans 10,600 acres and contains more plant species than all of Europe. The rolling hills that surround the Shenandoah valley offer colorful foliage in the fall and the rolling streams that overflow their riverbeds in the spring. Visitors can enjoy a variety of recreational activities, from exploring mineral-encrusted caves to paying homage to Civil War battlefields. Be sure to make cabin or camping reservations in the summer since the Appalachian Trail, which runs the length of the park, will be overflowing with through-hikers.

ORIENTATION AND PRACTICAL INFORMATION

The park runs nearly 105 mi. along the famous **Skyline Drive,** which extends from Front Royal in the north to Rockfish Gap in the south before evolving into the **Blue Ridge Parkway.** Skyline Drive closes during (and following) bad weather, and from dusk to dawn on some nights in hunting season. Mile markers are measured north to south and denote the location of trails and stops. Three major highways divide the park into sections: the **North Section** runs from Rte. 340 to Rte. 211; the **Central Section** from Rte. 211 to Rte. 33; and the **South Section** from Rte. 33 to I-64. A park pass is required to enter the park and is valid for seven days. (Most facilities close in winter; call ahead. Entrance fee $10 per vehicle; $5 per hiker, biker, or bus passenger; disabled persons free.) **Greyhound** (☎ 800-231-2222; www.greyhound.com), on the corner of Arch Ave. and W. Main St. in Waynesboro near the park's southern entrance, sends and receives one bus a day from Charlottesville ($10.50), Richmond ($29.50), and Washington, D.C. ($42.50). No bus or train serves Front Royal, near the park's northern entrance.

The **Dickey Ridge Visitors Center,** at Mi. 4.6, and the **Byrd Visitors Center,** at Mi. 51, answer questions and maintain small exhibits about the park, including eight documentary films about various park topics (10-40min.) which are shown continuously at the Byrd Visitors Center. *The Gift of Shenandoah* (15min.) and *Bears* (40min.) are two of the most popular. (Dickey Ridge: ☎ 635-3566. Byrd: ☎ 999-3283. For both, visit www.nps.ogv/shen (for camp and park info) and www.visitshenandoah.com (for info and reservations). Both open Apr.-Oct. daily 8:30am-5pm; July-Sept also F-Sa until 6pm.) The station's rangers conduct informative presentations on local wildlife, guide short walks among the flora, and wax romantic during outdoor, lantern-lit evening discussions. Pick up a free *Shenandoah Overlook* visitor newsletter, available at park entrances, visitors centers, or one of the park's two lodges, for a complete listing of programs. Comprehensive and newly updated, the *Guide to Shenandoah National Park and Skyline Drive* ($7.50 and worth every penny) is available at both visitors centers. (Info ☎ 999-2297, recorded message 999-3500. Operates daily 8am-4:30pm.) Send **mail** to: Superintendent, Park Headquarters, Shenandoah National Park, 3655 US Highway 211 E, Luray, 22835. (For emergencies, call ☎ 800-732-0911.) **Area Code:** 540.

DRIVING SKYLINE DRIVE. When planning your trip through Shenandoah National Park, give yourself plenty of extra time for driving to and from your destinations. The speed limit in the park is only 35 mph, and you may be forced to go even slower when other drivers pull on and off the road. Take the time to stop and enjoy the scenery—wildlife can often be spotted along the roadside.

BLUE RIDGE PARKWAY

DISTANCE: 469 mi.

SEASON: Spring, summer, and fall.

STATES: Virginia, North Carolina, and Tennessee

The beauty of unrestrained wilderness does not end at the southern gates of Shenandoah National Park. Skyline Drive becomes the Blue Ridge Parkway and continues for another 469 breathtaking miles under that name. The parkway, which is the longest scenic drive in the world, winds through Virginia and all of North Carolina, ending in a Cherokee Indian Reservation in Tennessee. The National Park Service administers the whole length of the parkway, including countless scenic overlooks, hiking trails, campsites and picnic grounds. Though still the road is accessible in winter, maintenance and park service are suspended from November to April. *Exercise caution in all seasons, as thick fog and thunderstorms can make the steep bending roads treacherous.*

For general information, call the park service in Roanoke, VA (☎857-2490), or write to the **Blue Ridge Parkway Superindendent,** 199 Hemphill Knob Rd., Asheville, NC 28803 (☎828-298-0398; www.nps.gov/blri). Twelve **visitors centers** line the Parkway at Mi. 5.8, 63.8, 86, 169, 217.5, 294.1, 304.4, 316.4, 331, 364.6, 382, and 451.2. Pick up trail maps, or a free copy of *The Parkway Milepost* for info on ranger-led activities. (Most open daily 9am-5pm.) **Maximum Speed Limit:** 45 mph. **Emergency Number:** ☎800-727-5928. **Area Code:** 540, except where otherwise noted.

1 HUMPBACK ROCKS. Excellent hiking trails along the parkway vary in difficulty and duration, offering naturalists of all ages and abilities a chance to explore the peaks and valleys of the Blue Ridge. Whether moseying along easy trails through the scenic backdrop or scrambling up the more strenuous climbs through the Humpback Mountains, there is something for everyone. The **Mountain Farm Trail** (Mi. 5.9) is an easy, wheelchair-accessible 20min. hike that leads to a reconstructed homestead. If you want a more challenging hike, try the short but strenuous **Humpback Rocks Trail** (Mi. 5.9), which extends 1 mi. from the trailhead to the Humpback Rocks overlook.

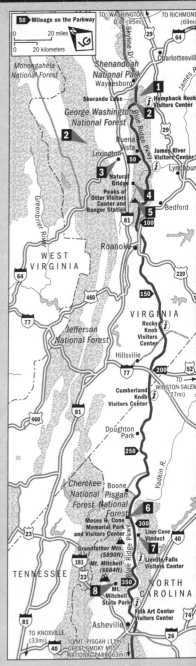

2 GEORGE WASHINGTON NATIONAL FOREST. From Shenandoah National Park, the Blue Ridge trails south from Waynesboro to Roanoke through Virginia's 1.8 million acre George Washington National Forest. Spend at least a few days at the secluded ■ **Sherando Lake ❶**, a recreation area 4.5 mi. off the Parkway at Mi. 16 that has 65 campsites and excellent fishing, canoeing, and swimming. (Open Apr.-Nov. Sites with hookup $15; recreational user fee $8).

3 LEXINGTON. At the intersections of I-81 and I-64, the college town of Lexington, home of Washington and Lee University and the Virginia Military Institute, overflows with Confederate historical sites. The **Lee Chapel and Museum,** at the center of the Washington and Lee campus, holds General Robert E. Lee's crypt along with the remains of his trusty horse, Traveler. (☎458-8768; http://leechapel.wlu.edu. Open Apr.-Oct. M-F 9am-4pm, Su 1-5pm; Nov.-Mar. M-Sa 9am-4pm, Su 1-4pm. Free.) History buffs will also appreciate the **Stonewall Jackson House,** at 8 E. Washington St. (☎463-2552; www.stonewalljackson.org. Open M-Sa 9am-5pm, Su 1-5pm. Tours on the hr. and ½hr. $6, ages 6-17 $3, under 6 free.) For accommodations info, contact the Lexington Visitors Center, 106 E. Washington St. (☎877-453-9822 or 463-3777. Open daily June-Aug. 8:30am-6pm, Sept.-May 9am-5pm).

4 NATURAL BRIDGE. At the junction of Routes 11 and 130, a water-carved Arc de Triomphe, hidden behind the entrance, towers 215 ft. above green-lined falls and an underground river. The 100 million-year-old **Natural Bridge** still bears a set of initials carved into the side by a vandalous George Washington. The nightly "Drama of Creation" light and sound show chronicles the biblical seven days of creation. (☎291-2121 or 800-533-1410; www.naturalbridgeva.com. Bridge open daily 8am-8pm. Drama show daily 9pm. Natural bridge and drama show $10. Wheelchair accessible.)

5 PEAKS OF OTTER. Seven major hiking trails start from Peaks of Otter (Mi. 86; ☎586-1081 or 800-542-5927; www.peaksofotter.com), ranging in length and in difficulty. The most difficult is the **Sharp Top** (1½ mi.; 3875 ft.), which climbs to the to the peak of Sharp Top Mountain for an amazing panoramic view of the surrounding Blue Ridge Mountains. Those too tired to walk all the way can opt for the bus ride up. (One-way $4.50, children $3.50; roundtrip $5.50/$3.50.) Other trails ascend **Flat Top Mountain** (4½ mi.; 4001 ft.) and **Harkening Hill** (3¼ mi.; 3350 ft.), providing a chance to traverse well-forested terrain.

6 MOSES H. CONE MEMORIAL PARK. The sprawling 3600-acre estate at **Moses H. Cone Memorial Park** (Mi. 294.1) features a visitors center and a craft store in a historic manor, as well as 25 mi. of hiking and horse trails. (☎828-295-3782. Visitors center open June-Aug. daily 8:30am-6pm; May and Sept.-Oct. Sa-Su 10am-6pm. Craft store open mid-Mar. to late Nov. daily 9am-5pm.) The Park Service hosts ranger-led activities, including historical talks, campfire circles, guided nature walks, slide shows, and musical demonstrations; information is available at the Blue Ridge Visitors Centers. Three miles down the road, the **Julian Price Campground ❶** has spectacular tent and RV sites. (☎963-5911. Flush toilets and water; no hookups or showers. Open May-Oct. Sites $14.)

7 LINN COVE VIADUCT. The majority of the Blue Ridge Parkway was completed by 1967, but a small stretch of 7½ mi. remained the "missing link" for 20 years. The imposing **Grandfather Mountain** blocked the road. To finish the Parkway without damaging the mountain, a lengthy construction begin—concrete road segments were even tinted with iron oxide to match existing rocks. Completed in 1987, a 1243 ft. stretch of road curves around **Linn Cove**—a feat of engineering that cost around $10 million. The ¼ mi. round-trip **Linn Cove Viaduct Access Trail** (Mi. 304.4) takes visitors up to the bridge and is wheelchair accessible.

8 MOUNT MITCHELL STATE PARK. Off of the Parkway at Mi. 355.4, **Mount Mitchell** reaches an elevation of 6684 ft.—the highest peak east of the Mississippi River. Visitors can hike or drive to the top, where they'll find a park office, a small campground, a restaurant, an observation tower, and some stunning views. The park can only be reached via Rte. 128, which branches off the Blue Ridge Parkway. (Park gates open daily June-Aug. 8am-9pm; Apr.-May and Sept. 8am-8pm; Mar. and Oct. 8am-7pm.; Nov.-Feb. 8am-6pm. Summit is 5 mi. from Pkwy. Free. Office and restaurant hours vary.)

ACCOMMODATIONS

The Appalachian Trail Conference's **Bears Den Hostel** ❶, 18393 Blue Ridge Mountain Rd., 35 mi. north of Shenandoah on Rte. 601, sleeps 20 travelers in its two dorm rooms. There are also private cabins for families or groups and a third bunk room for Appalachian Trail hikers. The hostel has showers, an in-house convenience store, full kitchen, linen sleepsack, and laundry. Take Rte. I-81 to Rte. 7 E and follow it for 17 mi. to Blue Ridge Mountain Rd.; turn right and drive ½ mi. until a gate and a sign for the Bears Den appears on your right. (☎554-8708. 5-day max stay. Reception 7:30-9:30am and 5-10pm. Check-out 9:30am. Front gate locked and quiet hours begin at 10pm. Camping $6 per person. Beds $13, non-ATC members $18; private room for 2 $42.) The park also maintains two lodges, essentially motels with nature-friendly exteriors and super-tiny rooms reminiscent of the Great Depression era. Reservations (☎554-8708 or 800-999-4717; infobearsdencenter.org) recommended up to a year in advance. **Skyland Lodge** ❸, Mi. 42 on Skyline Drive, offers wood-furnished cabins and more upscale motel rooms. (☎800-999-4714 or 743-5108. Cabins open Mar.-Nov. $55-108; lodge rooms open Mar. to early Nov. $82-123. Wheelchair accessible rooms available.) **Big Meadows** ❹, Mi. 51, has very similar services, with a historic lodge and cabins—be warned that historic means no in-room phones or TV and bathrooms with tubs rather than showers. (☎800-999-4714 or 743-5108. Open late Apr. to early Nov. Cabins $78-90; lodge $70-146.) Dining is available at both of the two lodges. **Lewis Mountain** ❷, Mi. 57, also owned by the park service, operates cabins with private baths and outdoor grill areas. (Tent sites $20, cabins $64-97.)

CAMPING

The park service (☎800-365-2267 10am-10pm; www.reservations.nps.gov) maintains four major campgrounds: **Mathews Arm** ❶, Mi. 22 ($16), with 179 sites, and convenient to nearby **Elkwallow**, Mi. 24, which has a gas station, eatery, and gift shop; **Big Meadows** ❶, Mi. 51 ($19), a popular campground close to a visitors center, major trailheads, and several waterfalls; **Lewis Mountain** ❶, Mi. 58 ($16), which is smaller and more private; and **Loft Mountain** ❶, Mile 80 ($16). The latter three have stores, showers, and laundry, but no hookups. Heavily wooded and uncluttered, Mathews Arm and Lewis Mountain are the best options. Reservations are possible only at Big Meadows. All campgrounds have a 14-day limit and allow pets.

A 101 mi. long section of the **Appalachian Trail (AT)** runs the length of the park. Twelve three-sided shelters are strewn at 8-10 mi. intervals along the AT. Unwritten trail etiquette usually reserves the cabins for those hiking large stretches of the trail. **Backcountry camping** is free, but you must obtain a permit at park entrances, visitors centers, or ranger stations. *Camping without a permit or above 2800 ft. is illegal and unsafe.* The **Potomac Appalachian Trail Club (PATC)** ❶, 118 Park St. SE, a volunteer organization in Vienna, maintains six cabins in backcountry areas of the park that sleep 8-12 people each. Bring lanterns and food; the primitive cabins contain only bunk beds, blankets, and stoves. Pit toilets and spring water are nearby. (☎703-242-0693; www.patc.net. 1 group member must be 21+. Headquarters open M-W 7-9pm, Th noon-2pm and 7-9pm, F noon-2pm. Reservations required. Su-Th $18 per group, F-Sa $28.) Trail maps and the PATC guide can be obtained at the visitors centers. The PATC puts out topographical maps ($6).

⚠ OUTDOOR ACTIVITIES

HIKING

The trails off Skyline Dr. are heavily used and generally safe for cautious day-hikers with maps, appropriate footwear, and water. The middle section of the park, from **Thorton Gap,** Mi. 32, to **South River,** Mi. 63, bursts with photo opportunities and stellar views, although it also tends to be crowded with tourists. Rangers can recommend hikes of appropriate length and difficulty level for any visitor.

Whiteoak Canyon Trail (Mi. 42.6; 4½ mi., 4hr. round-trip) is a strenuous hike that opens upon the second-highest waterfall in the park (which plunges an impressive 86 ft.), rewarding those who ascend the 1040 ft. elevation with views of the Limberlost hemlocks.

Limberlost Trail (Mi. 43; 1¼ mi., 1hr. round-trip) is the easiest and only wheelchair accessible trail in the park. From the trailhead only half a mile from Skyland Lodge, Limberlost plunges into forest, weaves through orchards, and passes over a footbridge, all while remaining fairly level. All ages and activity levels. No pets allowed.

Old Rag Mountain Trail (Mi. 45; 8¾ mi., 6-8hr. round-trip) starts outside the park. From U.S. 211, turn right on Rte. 522, then right on Rte. 231. The trail scrambles up 3291 ft. to triumphant views of the valley below. *Be careful of slippery rocks in damp weather and bring enough food and water for the round-trip.* Ladders have been erected at several points to ease the steep ascent. Hikers 16 and older who have not paid Shenandoah admission must pay $3.

Corbin Cabin Trail (Mi. 37.8; 4 mi., 2½ hr. round-trip) is popular among history buffs. The trail leads down into a hollow, where an old settlers' cabin has been preserved so that hikers can see how the settlers lived. The ascent back up is moderately strenuous.

OTHER ACTIVITIES

There are two other ways to explore Shenandoah: by boat and by beast. **Downriver Canoe Company** in Bentonville offers canoe, kayak, raft, and tube trips. From Skyline Dr. Mi. 20, follow U.S. 211 W for 8 mi., then take U.S. 340 N 14 mi. to Bentonville; turn left onto Rte. 613 and go 1 mi. The store is on the right. (☎635-5526 or 800-338-1963; www.downriver.com. Open M-F 9am-6pm, Sa-Su 7am-7pm.) Guided **horseback rides** are available at the Skyland Lodge, Mi. 42. (☎999-2210; www.visit-shenandoah.com. Riders must be at least 4 ft. 10 in. Open Apr.-Nov. $20-22 per 1hr. ride. 1-day advance reservation required.)

⚡ DAYTRIPS FROM SHENANDOAH

LURAY CAVERNS

Though the billboards that appear every 10 miles along the highway scream tourist trap, the **Luray Caverns** defy all expectations and truly live up to their slogan: "The best caverns east of the Mississippi." Take exit 264 from U.S. 81 onto U.S. 211 E; the many signposts ensure that the caverns are easy to find from there. The 1hr. guided tours feature a variety of formations; be sure not to miss the reflecting pool. This shallow underground pond creates an unbelievable optical illusion in which its reflection of the ceiling is so perfect that you can't even tell the water is there. The equally unforgettable cathedral room houses the world's largest natural instrument: a 37-mallet organ created from the caverns' own stalactites. It took Leeland W. Sprinkle, a Virginia organist, three years and over 3000 trials of different cave formations to finish his masterpiece in 1957, and since that time this room has hosted hundreds of underground weddings. Bring a sweater for the cool caverns, and your patience along with it—the caverns can get extremely busy in the summer. A ticket into the caverns will also get you into the on-site vintage automobile museum which displays over 140 vehicles, including an 1892 Mercedes-Benz and a Conestoga wagon. (☎743-6551; www.luraycaverns.com. Open daily mid-June to early Sept. 9am-7pm; Apr. to mid-June and Sept.-Oct. 9am-6pm; Nov. to Mar. 9am-4pm. Adults $17, seniors $15, ages 7-13 $8. Wheelchair accessible.)

ENDLESS CAVERNS

Discovered in 1879, the **Endless Caverns** are considered "endless" because they encompass over 5 mi. of mapped cave passages with no visible end. The tour is fairly long (1¾hr.) and strenuous, but visitors have plenty of time to take in the other cave formations. Take exit 257 or 264 from U.S. 81 and continue on to the intersection of U.S. 11 and U.S. 211 in New Market. Follow the signs from here to 1800 Endless Caverns Rd. A jacket and sturdy shoes are highly recommended. (☎896-2283; www.endlesscaverns.com. Open daily mid-Mar. to mid-June 9am-5pm; mid-June to early Sept. 9am-6pm; early Sept. to mid-Nov. 9am-5pm, mid-Nov. to mid-Mar. 9am-4pm. $14, ages 4-12 $6, ages 3 and under free.)

SKYLINE CAVERNS

Smaller than Endless and Luray Caverns, **Skyline Caverns,** on U.S. 340, 1 mi. from the junction of Rte. 340 and Skyline Drive, are famous for their collection of orchid-like anthodites. These rare crystal formations, which only grow 1 in. every 7000 years, have formed a garden of white rock spikes. Tour stops include the Capitol Dome, the Wishing Well, Cathedral Hall, and Rainbow Falls, which pours 37 ft. from one of the three cavern streams. (☎635-4545 or 800-296-4545; www.skylinecaverns.com. Open mid-Mar. to mid-June and Sept. to mid-Nov. M-F 9am-5pm, Sa-Su 9am-6pm; mid-June to Sept. daily 9am-6:30pm; mid-Nov. to mid-Mar. daily 9am-4pm. $14; seniors, AAA, and military $12; ages 7-13 $7; ages 6 and under free.)

WEST VIRGINIA

With 80% of the state cloaked in untamed forests, commercial expansion and economic prosperity once seemed a distant dream for West Virginia. When the state's coal reserves, formerly its main source of revenue, began to run out, the state seemed doomed until government officials decided to capitalize on the area's forested expanses, tranquil trails, and raging rivers. Today, thousands of tourists forge paths into West Virginia's breathtaking landscape, and thousands more settle for good. The eastern panhandle is home to some of the fastest-growing counties in the entire United States. Park officials and state planners now face the challenging task of trying to accommodate the new human residents without encroaching too much upon the animals that already call West Virginia home.

ⓘ PRACTICAL INFORMATION

Capital: Charleston.

Visitor Info: Department of Tourism, 90 MacCorkle Ave. SW, South Charleston 25305; P.O. Box 30312 (☎800-225-5982; www.callwva.com; operator M-F 7am-9pm, Sa-Su 9am-5pm). **US Forest Service,** 200 Sycamore St., Elkins 26241 (☎304-636-1800; www.fs.fed.us/r9/mnf). Open M-F 8am-4:45pm.

Postal Abbreviation: WV. **Sales Tax:** 6%.

HARPERS FERRY ☎304

Harpers Ferry, on the Shenandoah and Potomac rivers, earned its fame when a band of abolitionists led by John Brown raided the US Armory there in 1859. Although Brown was captured and executed, the raid brought the issue of slavery into the national spotlight. Brown's belief that violence was needed to overcome slavery gained support, and the town became a major theater of conflict, changing hands eight times during the Civil War. Today, Harpers Ferry's guests are more mild-mannered, from great outdoors fans to school groups learning their nation's history, to Civil War buffs making pilgrimages to the sites they've studied.

⚎🔁 ORIENTATION AND PRACTICAL INFORMATION. The location of Harpers Ferry on West Virginia's eastern panhandle means that it's less than a 10min. drive south to Virginia or north to Maryland. **Amtrak** (☎800-535-6406; www.amtrak.com), on Potomac St. on the eastern side of the historic district, goes to Washington, D.C. (1¾hr., 1 per day, $9-20). Reservations are required, as no tickets are sold at the station. At the same depot, **MARC**, the **Maryland Rail Commuter** (☎866-743-3682; www.mtamaryland.com; open M-F 5:30am-8:15pm), offers cheaper, more frequent service to Washington, D.C. (M-F 2 per day, $9). The **Appalachian Trail Conference**, 799 Washington St., at Jackson St., runs buses to Charles Town for $2 per person. (☎535-6331; www.appalachiantrail.org. Open M-F 9am-5pm. Membership $30, seniors and under 18 $25.) **The Outfitter**, 180 High St. (☎888-535-2087; www.theoutfitteratharpersferry.com), about half-way along the Appalachian Trail, sells outdoor equipment and conducts hiking tours. Bike rentals ($20 per day) include a helmet, a lock, and a map. **Visitor Info: Jefferson County Convention and Visitors Bureau**, on Shoreline Dr. just off Rte. 340 in Harpers Ferry (☎535-2627; www.jeffersoncountycvb.com). The **Cavalier Heights Visitors Center** is just inside the Harpers Ferry National Historic Park entrance, off Rte. 340. (☎535-6298; www.nps.gov/hafe. Open daily 8am-5pm. The Cavalier Heights Visitors Center is the closest **public parking** to the historic district (see **Sights**, p. 362). The **Historic Town Area Visitor Information Center**, at the end of Shenandoah St. near the intersection of High St., has free tour info. (☎535-6298; www.nps.gov/hafe. Open 8am-5pm.) **Internet Access: Bolivar and Harpers Ferry Public Library**, 600 Polk St. (☎535-2301. Open M-Tu and F-Sa 10am-5:30pm, W-Th 10am-8pm. Free.) **Post Office:** 1010 Washington St., on the corner of Washington and Franklin St. (☎535-2479 or 800-275-8777. Open M-F 8am-4pm, Sa 9am-noon.) **Postal Code:** 25425. **Area Code:** 304.

🛏 ACCOMMODATIONS. Ragged hikers are welcome at the social and spacious **⬛Harpers Ferry Hostel (HI) ❶**, 19123 Sandy Hook Rd., at Keep Tryst Rd. off Rte. 340 in Knoxville, MD. This renovated auction house has a backyard trail to Potomac overlooks, landscaped lawns, a volleyball court, a library, Internet access, a fully stocked kitchen, and shuttle pickup service from the Greyhound station in Frederick, MD. (☎301-834-7652; www.harpersferryhostel.org. 4 rooms with 39 cushiony beds. Laundry $2. 3-night max. stay. Check-in 7-9am and 6-10pm. Open mid-Mar. to mid-Nov. Dorms $15, nonmembers $18. Camping $6/$9; includes use of kitchen and bathrooms.) The **Hillside Motel ❷**, 19105 Keep Tryst Rd., 3 mi. from town in Knoxville, MD, is a motor court with 19 clean rooms and a fairly convenient location. (☎301-834-8144. Singles $40; doubles $50. Winter rates lower.) The charming **Harpers Ferry Guest House ❹**, 800 Washington St., is ideally located in the center of the historic district. (☎535-6955. Reserve in advance. Rooms M-Th $75, F-Su $95.) Those who like to rough it can camp along the **C&O Canal ❶**, where no-fee primitive sites lie 5 mi. apart along the canal's 180 mi. length. Camping is first come, first served. For a more developed campground, five **Maryland state park campgrounds** ❶ are within 30 mi. of Harpers Ferry. (Ranger station ☎ 301-739-4200.) **Greenbrier State Park** ❶, on Rte. 40 E off Rte. 66, has campsites and a lakeside recreation area. (☎ 301-791-4767 or 888-432-2267; http://reservations.dnr.state.md.us. Reservations required. Open May-Oct. Sites with hookup $25.)

🍴 🍸 **FOOD AND NIGHTLIFE.** Chain restaurants welcome fast-food fanatics along Rte. 340. Nearby Charles Town's 🍴**La Mezzaluna Cafe** ❸, Somerset Village Ste. B3 off Rte. 340 S just 5min. from Harpers Ferry, boasts delicious Italian favorites in a spacious setting. Pasta entrees ($9-20) come with a house salad. (☎ 728-0700. Open Tu-Sa 11am-3pm, Su 2-9pm.) The **Coffee Mill** ❷, 120 High St., serves burgers and fried seafood baskets with excellent cole slaw ($6-12), along with baked goods, on a pleasant sunken brick patio. (☎ 535-1257. Open daily 10am-5pm.) A variety of restaurants on High St. serve standard American lunch fare. Across the street from the Hillside Motel, the **Cindy Dee Restaurant** ❶, 19112 Keep Tryst Rd., at Rte. 340, is usually full of people clamoring for fried chicken ($5 and up) and apple dumplings ($2.75), but the new all-night hours means hungry night owls can enjoy their food without the crowds. (☎ 301-695-8181. Open 24hr.) The historic area around High St. and Potomac St. caters to the lunch crowd and empties out during dinner hours when most tourists have left. One exception is the **Armory Pub** ❸, an upscale twist on pub fare with fresh fish ($14), large chargrilled burgers ($8), live music on weekend nights, and a beverage list that includes five kinds of sangria. (☎ 535-2469. Open M-Th 11am-8pm, F-Su 11am-10pm.)

Tiny **Shepherdstown**, 11 mi. north of Harpers Ferry, is a veritable culinary metropolis in these quiet parts. Take Rte. 340 S for 2 mi. to Rte. 230 N, or bike 13 mi. along the C&O towpath. Coffee addicts flock to **Lost Dog**, 134 E. German St., which brews 30 different blends of coffee and over 50 kinds of tea for a local-heavy crowd. (☎ 876-0871. Open Su-Th 6am-6pm, F-Sa 6am-8pm.) Amid the colonial architecture of E. German St., the **Mecklinburg Inn**, 128 E. German St., provides rock 'n' roll and Rolling Rock ($1.75) on open mic nights every Tuesday from 9pm to midnight. (☎ 876-2126. Happy hour M-F 4:30-6:30pm. 21+. Open M-Th 3pm-12:30am, F 3pm-1:30am, Sa 1pm-2am, Su 1pm-12:30am. No credit cards.)

🎭 **SIGHTS.** The **Harpers Ferry National Historic Park** is composed of several museums, all of which are included with admission to the park, along with parking and shuttle rides from the parking lot to the historic area. (☎ 535-6298. Open daily in summer 8am-6pm; in winter 8am-5pm. Shuttles every 10min., last pickup 6:45pm. 3-day admission $6 per car; $4 per pedestrian, bike, or motorcycle.) Parking in historic Lower Town is nearly nonexistent; unless snag one of the pricey spots in the lot at the end of Shenandoah St., it's necessary to park at the visitors center and board the free shuttles to town or walk about 20min. The bus stops at **Shenandoah Street,** where a barrage of replica 19th-century shops greets visitors; for example, the **Dry Goods Store** displays a collection of clothes, hardware, liquor, and groceries that would have been sold over 150 years ago. Check out their free 1850s price list to compare prices then and now. The **Harpers Ferry Industrial Museum,** on Shenandoah St., describes the methods used to harness the powers of the Shenandoah and Potomac rivers and details the town's status as the endpoint of the nation's first successful rail line. The unsung stories of the Ferry captivate visitors at **Black Voices from Harpers Ferry,** on the corner of High and Shenandoah St., where visitors can listen to audio clips from actors reading the memoirs of fettered and freed slaves expressing their opinions on John Brown and his raid. Next door on High St., the plight of

Harpers Ferry's slaves is further elaborated in the **Civil War Story**. Displays detail the importance of Harpers Ferry's strategic location to both the Union and Confederate armies. The park also offers occasional reenactments of Harpers Ferry's history. A few of the exhibits are not included in the price of park admission and require a separate ticket.

A dauntingly steep staircase hewn into the hillside off High St. follows the **Appalachian Trail** to **Upper Harpers Ferry,** which has fewer sights but is laced with interesting historical tales. Allow 45min. to ascend past **Harpers House,** the restored home of town founder Robert Harper, and to explore the insides of **St. Peter's Church,** where a pastor flew the Union Jack during the Civil War to protect the church. Just a few steps uphill from St. Peter's lie the archaeological ruins of **St. John's Episcopal Church** (built in 1852, rebuilt after the Civil War, then abandoned in 1895), used as a hospital and barracks during the Civil War.

⚐ OUTDOOR ACTIVITIES. After digesting the historical sights, many choose to soak up the town's outdoors. The park's visitors center has trail maps. The moderately difficult **Maryland Heights Trail,** across the railroad bridge in the Lower Town of Harpers Ferry, wanders 4 mi. through the Blue Ridge Mountains and includes precipitous cliffs and glimpses of crumbling Civil War-era forts. The strenuous 7½ mi. **Loudon Heights Trail** starts in the Lower Town off the Appalachian Trail and leads to Civil War trenches and scenic overlooks. The moderate 2½ mi. **Camp Hill Trail** passes by the Harper Cemetery and ends at the former Stoner College. History dominates the **Bolivar Heights Trail,** starting at the northern end of Whitman Ave.

The **Chesapeake & Ohio Canal** towpath, off the end of Shenandoah St. and over the railroad bridge, serves as a lasting reminder of the town's industrial roots and is the point of departure for a 180 mi. bike ride to Washington, D.C. It is possible to ride the whole towpath in one day, but only by getting on the trail at or before daybreak. The **Appalachian Trail Conference** (see **Orientation and Practical Information,** p. 361), 799 Washington St., at Jackson St., offers catalogs with deals on hiking books and trail info. ATC members receive 20% discounts at ATC trail stores. (☎535-6331; www.appalachiantrail.org. Open M-F 9am-5pm; May-Oct. also Sa-Su and holidays 9am-4pm. Membership $30, seniors and students $25.)

River & Trail Outfitters, 604 Valley Rd., 2 mi. from Harpers Ferry off Rte. 340 in Knoxville, MD, rents canoes, kayaks, inner tubes, and rafts. They also organize everything from scenic daytrips with placid rides to wild overnights, all on the Shenandoah River. (☎301-695-5177 or 888-446-7529; www.rivertrail.com. Raft trips $50-55, ages 16 and under $40-45. Canoes $55 per day. Tubing $18 per day.) At **Butt's Tubes,** on Rte. 671 off Rte. 340, adventurers can float down the river at some of the lowest rates around. One tubing trip takes 45min. to 2hr., depending on how ambitious you are. (☎800-836-9911 or 888-434-9911; www.buttstubes.com. Open M-F 10am-3pm, last pickup from the river at 5pm; Sa-Su 10am-4pm, last pickup 6pm. $12-20.) Horseback riding opportunities in the area include a variety of recreational trips offered through **Elk Mountain Trails.** (☎301-834-8882; www.elkmountaintrails.com. Rides $20-68. Cash only.)

MONONGAHELA NATIONAL FOREST ☎304

Monongahela National Forest sprawls across the eastern portion of the state, and within it visitors will find an abundance of wildlife (including nine endangered species), limestone caverns, and hordes of weekend canoers, fly fishermen, cavers, and skiers. The **Cranberry Mountain Nature Center,** near the Highland Scenic Hwy. at the junction of Rte. 150 and Rte. 39/55, has excellent wildlife

RADIO SILENCE

Not again! My cell phone hadn't had service for days and I'd just lost the last radio station on the dial to static. If you drive through the Monongahela National Forest, you'll probably have the same problem. But don't call your phone company just yet—this time it's not their fault.

Over 13,000 sq. mi. of land around the National Radio Astronomy Observatory in Green Banks, WV, have been designated a National Radio Quiet Zone. Within this region—the only one of its kind in the world—TV, radio, and cell phone transmissions are subject to strict limitations. This minimizes man-made static that would otherwise overwhelm the **Green Banks Telescope (GBT).**

The GBT is one of the most sensitive single-dish radio telescopes in the world, made to pick up radio waves from distant black holes, quasars, and galaxies, yet even tiny sources of unaccounted-for static can interfere with its accuracy. For instance, the astronomers at Green Banks bought a new electric blanket for the dog of a nearby resident because short circuits in the dog's old blanket kept showing up in their readings. Though the scientists know how to tell most man-made interference apart from the real stuff, it's still important to minimize man-made signals. The quieter we are, the more easily they can detect radio waves that could turn out to be coming from extra-terrestrials!

exhibits and provides maps of local hiking trails. (☎653-4826 or 653-8564; www.fs.fed.us/r9/mnf. Open Apr.-Nov. daily 9am-5pm.) They also conduct free weekend tours of the **Cranberry Glades.** (½-1hr. tours June-Aug. Sa-Su 2pm. Also Th-F in summer and daily during the fall foliage season with a reservation.) Wrapping around the glades is the **Cow Pasture Trail** (6 mi.), which passes a WWII German prison camp. Two popular hikes are **Big Beechy Trail** (6½ mi.; the trailhead is next to a parking lot at the Highland Scenic Hwy. and Rte. 461 junction) and the awesome **Falls of Hills Creek Trail** (1½ mi.), off Rte. 39/55 south of the Nature Center, with three falls ranging in height from 25 to 63 ft. A small concrete pathway leads to a cascade of wooden steps down to the falls—good knees are a must. The **Highland Scenic Highway (Route 150)** stretches 43 mi. from Richwood to U.S. 219, 7 mi. north of Marlinton, and affords gorgeous views. This is particularly true for the section of **Route 39** from Marlinton to Goshen, VA, which passes by swimming sites on the Maury River which are signposted from the highway. *Tempting as it is to gaze at the forest's splendor, driving on the winding and often foggy roads can be treacherous.*

Those with several days to spend here might choose to hike, bike, or cross-country ski a section of the **Greenbrier River Trail** (75 mi., 1° grade), which runs from Cass to North Caldwell; the trailhead is on Rte. 38 off U.S. 60 in North Caldwell. Lined with access points and campgrounds, the trail offers easily hikeable and bikeable terrain and, in the late summer, a chance to witness the monarch butterfly migration. Downhill delights abound at the **Snowshoe Resort,** accessible from Rte. 66 between Rte. 219 and Rte. 28, which has 54 ski trails. (☎572-1000 or 877-441-4386; www.snowshoemtn.com. Open Dec.-Mar. daily 8:30am-10pm. M-F lift tickets $49, students and seniors $40, children $34; Sa-Su $63/$58/$45. Ski rental $26, children $18.) When the snow melts, mountain bikers move in for the summer; the **Mountain Adventure Center** at Snowshoe Mountain offers bike rentals, tours, instruction, and passes to ride its lifts up the mountain and its trails back down. (☎877-441-4386; snowshoemtn.com. Cross-country ski rental $25 per half-day, $35 per day; freeride rental $50/$75; downhill rental $80/$125. Trail access passes $10 per day, with access to the lift and mountain bike park $20 per day.)

Travel north to ■**Cass Scenic Railroad State Park,** off Rt. 28/92, for novel train rides on the surviving 11 mi. of the once- burgeoning 3000 mi. lumber railroad lines of West Virginia. Ascend to 4842 ft. on the oldest steam engine locomotive in the US that is in continual use, which offers specialty trips and overnight stays on Cheat Mountain. (☎456-4300 or 800-225-5982; www.cassrailroad.com. M-F 8am-4pm, Sa-Su 9am-5pm. $13-19, ages 5-12 $10-12.) Science and physics lovers will appreciate the **National Radio Astronomy Observatory,** off Rte. 28/92, which houses **The Robert C. Byrd Green Bank Telescope,** the largest fully steerable telescope in the world. Not only is this where the Search for Extra-Terrestrial Intelligence (The SETI Project) started, it is also the largest moveable structure on land. Free tours take you to the base of the large and looming 17 million lb. telescope. (☎456-2150; www.gb.nrao.edu. Tours late May to early Sept. daily 9am-6pm on the hr.; early Sept. to Oct. W-Su 9am-6pm, Nov. to late May W-Su 11am, 1pm, and 3pm.)

Each of Monongahela's six districts has a campground and a recreation area, with ranger stations off Rte. 39 east of Marlinton and in the towns of Bartow and Potomack. (Open M-F 8am-4:30pm.) Established sites are $5; backcountry camping is free, though you must register at the Cranberry Mountain Nature Center. **Cranberry Campground ❶,** in the Gauley district, 13 mi. from Ridgewood on Forest Rd. 76, has hiking trails through cranberry bogs and campsites ($8). **Watoga State Park ❶,** in Marlinton, has maps and a lake. (☎799-4087; www.watoga.com. Sites $15, with electricity $19.) If you don't feel like roughing it, travel up a driveway flanked by a profusion of wildflowers to the ▨**Morning Glory Inn ❹,** 1½ mi. north of Slatyfork on Rte. 219. This B&B offers gargantuan rooms with cathedral-like wood beam ceilings, modern decor, whirlpool tubs, and a sprawling porch. (☎572-5000 or 866-572-5700; www.morningglory-inn.com. Breakfast included. Check-in 2pm. Check-out 11am. Doubles Su-Th $80, F-Sa $85; Jan.-Mar. Su-Th $100, F-Sa $150.) Five miles farther from the slopes, the **Jerico B&B ❸,** on Rte. 219 in Marlinton just south of the junction with Rte. 39, offers the B&B experience at half the price. In addition to bedrooms in the main house, the Jerico has pre-Civil War themed cabins. (☎799-6241; www.jericobb.com. Rooms $45-$65. Cabins $85-185.) **The Restaurant at Elk River ❹,** on Rte. 219 in Slatyfork, in the Elk River Inn, a steak- and seafood-based menu with similar prices but a less touristy feel than the posh resort restaurants. The rainbow trout is a specialty. (☎572-3771. Open Th-Su 5-9pm.) The **Route 66 Sub Shop ❶,** on Rte. 66 at the base of Snowshoe, serves salads, sandwiches, pizzas, and wraps that will fill you without breaking the bank. (☎572-1200. Subs $4-6; hot dogs $1.25. Open M-F 7am-9pm, Sa-Su 7am-10pm.)

Amtrak, 315 W. Main St., across from the Greenbrier Resort, is in White Sulphur Springs at the forest's southern tip. (☎800-872-7245, www.amtrak.com for reservations. No ticket office; buy tickets in advance online or via phone.) Trains run Su ($41), W ($33), and F ($41) to Washington, D.C. **Greyhound** (☎800-231-2222; www.greyhound.com) will drop passengers with a Charleston ticket off along Rte. 60 but does not run outbound from the forest. The forest **Supervisor's Office,** 200 Sycamore St., in Elkins, distributes a full list of campsites and fees, and provides info about fishing and hunting. (☎636-1800. Open M-F 8am-4:45pm.) **Area Code:** 304.

NEW RIVER GORGE ☎304

The New River Gorge is a testament to the raw beauty and power of nature. One of the oldest rivers in the world, the **New River** has carved a narrow gorge through the **Appalachian Mountains,** creating precipitous valley walls that tower an average of 1000 ft. above the white waters. These steep slopes remained virtually untouched until 1873, when industrialists drained the region to uncover coal and timber. With the coal mines now defunct, the New River Gorge has become a haven for outdoors enthusiasts: rafters cruise its rapids, while climbers ascend its cliffs.

📞📠 TRANSPORTATION AND PRACTICAL INFORMATION. Amtrak, on Rte. 41 N in Prince and Hinton, runs through the heart of the gorge. (☎800-872-7245 or 253-6651; www.amtrak.com. Trains Su, W, F. Prince: Open Su, W, F 9:30am-9pm. Hinton: Open Su, W, F 11am-1:30pm and 4:30-6:30pm.) **Greyhound** stops at 105 3rd St. in Beckley. (☎800-231-2222 or 253-8333; www.greyhound.com. Open M-F 7am-8:30pm, Sa 7am-noon and 3-8:30pm, Su 7-10am and 4-8:30pm.) Bike tours, rentals, and repairs are available at **New River Bike and Touring,** 103 Keller Ave., off the historic Fayetteville exit on U.S. 19. (☎574-2453; www.newriverbike.com. Open daily 9am-6pm. Bike rentals $25 half-day, $35 full-day; bike tours $59 half-day, $79 full-day, $175 overnight.) **ACE Adventure Center,** on Minden Rd. in the town of Oak Hill, also provides rentals and tours. (☎888-223-7238; www.bikewv.com. Bike rentals $26 half-day, $36 full-day; tours $60/$85.)

The park operates four **visitors centers,** each of which has information on the history of the area and hiking trails. **Sandstone,** on Rte. 64 east of Beckley, built from local materials with a gorgeous, eco-friendly design, features a scale model of the New River and its tributaries in colored stone on the floor, as well as a room full of hands-on exhibits for kids. Off Rte. 19 just north of Fayetteville and the New River Gorge Bridge, **Canyon Rim** offers the best view of the bridge. (☎574-2115. Open daily 9am-5pm.) **Grandview,** on Rte. 9 near Beckley, attracts visitors in May when the rhododendrons are in bloom. (☎763-3715. Open May-Sept. daily noon-5pm.) **Thurmond,** on Rte. 25 off I-19, has access to hiking trails down in the river valley. (☎465-8550. Open May-Sept. daily 10am-5pm.) Area information, including Bridge Day info and a 10min. video, is also available at the **New River Convention and Visitors Bureau,** 310 Oyler Ave., in Oak Hill. Signs on Rte. 19 labeled "Rafting and Recreation Information" lead to the visitors bureau. (☎465-5617; www.newrivercvb.com. Open daily 9am-5pm.) **Internet access** is available at the office of the **Twin Rivers Design Group,** 110 Main St. in Oak Hill ($2 per 15min., $3 per 30min.). Be warned that the primary function of this office is as an art gallery and that there is only one computer set aside for public use. (☎877-868-4578 or 469-6666.) **Area Code:** 304.

🏠 ACCOMMODATIONS. A slew of budget motels can be found off **I-77** in Beckley ($45-60). The **Green Banks Motel ❷,** 505 S. Eisenhower Dr., hasn't seen a renovation in a while, but the rooms are clean and affordable. (☎253-3355. HBO. Singles $40; doubles $45.) **Babcock State Park ❶,** on Rte. 41 south of U.S. 60, 15 mi. west of Rainelle, has 52 shaded campsites, a bath house, and 28 cabins, including two deluxe cabins with kitchens and A/C. Activities include swimming, horseback riding, basketball, and tennis. Babcock, however, is 30min. farther away from river activities than lodging in the Fayetteville area. (☎438-3004 or 800-225-5982; www.babcockst.com. Sites $15, with electricity $19; cabins $49-110.) Many raft companies operate private campgrounds that offer both lodging and package rafting-lodging-dining deals. Amenities at **North American River Runners (NARR) ❶** include white-water rafting, kayaking, a ropes course, paintball, rock climbing, basketball, volleyball, a "big swing," two bath houses, and a cafe. Lodging options include primitive camping, four-person cabin tents, and bunk houses that sleep up to 24 people. The bunk houses have lighting and fans. (☎800-950-2585. No outlets or linens. Sites $10 per person; cabin tents $70-80; bunk houses $15 per person.)

🍴 FOOD. If you wake up early with a craving for pancakes, you're in luck. The **Western Pancake House ❶,** on Whitewater Dr. off Rte. 19, serves country cooking 24 hours a day. Whether it's a stack of three pancakes ($2.10) or a hot turkey dinner plate ($5), this is the best deal in town. (☎564-1240. Open daily 24hr.) The **Sedona Grill ❹** on Rte. 16, just north of the Appalachian Dr. exit from Rte.

19, offers upscale New American cuisine. Entrees include local specialties like crab cakes and barbecued pork dinners ($14-18), and the more exotic shrimp and apple curry ($15), both filling and delicious. (☎574-3411. Open M, Tu, Th 4-9pm; F-Sa 11:30am-10pm; Su 11:30am-9pm.) If nothing but a rack of grilled meat dripping in sauce will satisfy you after a day on the rapids, try **Dirty Eddie's Rib Pit ❹**, at 310 Keller St. near the northern Fayetteville exit off of Rte. 19. The Rib Pit can seat up to 236 patrons, which is a good thing because raucous groups of rafters fill the place nightly. Racks of ribs start at $12; prime rib is $16. (☎574-4822. Open daily 4-10pm.)

◙ **SIGHTS.** In 1973, the breathtaking **New River Gorge Bridge** was completed and became the second-highest bridge in the US. Best seen on foot, the bridge towers 876 ft. above New River and claims the world's largest single steel arch span. The Canyon Rim Visitors Center offers a decent vista, but for an unobstructed view, descend the zig-zag wooden stairs to the lower level lookout. On **Bridge Day,** the third Saturday in October, thousands of extreme sports enthusiasts leap off the bridge by bungee or parachute as on-lookers enjoy the festival's food and crafts. (☎800-927-0263; www.wvbridgeday.com.) In Beckley, retired coal miners lead 35min. tours down a mine shaft at the **Beckley Exhibition Coal Mine,** on Ewart Ave. (exit 44 from I-77) at New River Park. See how coal mines operated while riding in a coal car behind a 1930s engine through 150 ft. of underground passages. The tunnels are chilly; bring a jacket. (☎256-1747; www.exhibitioncoalmine.com. Open Apr.-Oct. daily 10am-6pm; last tour leaves 5:30pm. $12, seniors $10.50, ages 4-12 $8.50.) Close by, on exit 45 from I-77, the **Tamarack Center** puts "The Best of West Virginia" on display. Visitors can watch quilters, potters, glass-blowers, blacksmiths, and wood carvers hard at work on their newest projects. (☎888-262-7225; tamarackwv.com. Open daily Jan.-Mar. 8am-7pm; Apr.-Dec. 8am-8pm. Free.)

▟ **OUTDOOR ACTIVITIES.** The **New River Gorge National River** runs north from Hinton to Fayetteville, falling over 750 ft. in 50 mi. In order to conserve its magnificent natural, scenic, and historic value, the New River Gorge has been protected by the park service since 1958. The **West Virginia Division of Tourism** (☎800-225-5982; www.callwva.com), will connect you to some of the nearly 20 outfitters on the New River and the rowdier Gauley River. Brochures are at the **New River Convention and Visitors Bureau** (see **Practical Information,** p. 366). **Ultimate Rafting** on Gatewood Rd. offers some of the cheapest express trips and rafting packages in town. (☎574-2500 or 800-470-7238; www.ultimaterafting.com. Half-day trips start at $40. Packages that include a campsite, breakfast, half-day rafting, and lunch start at $52.)

Though the renowned rapids draw the most tourists, leisurely hiking allows visitors time to take in the lush scenery. The most rewarding trails are the moderately difficult **Kaymoor Trail** (2 mi.) and the minimally strenuous **Thurmond Minden Trail** (6½ mi., only 3 mi. round-trip to main overlook). Kaymoor starts at the bridge on Fayette Station Rd., near Canyon Rim Visitors Center, and runs past the abandoned coal-processing ovens of Kaymoor, a coal-mining community that shut down in 1962. Thurmond Minden is fairly flat and has vistas overlooking the New River and Dunloup Creek, but is not clearly marked in some areas. To get to the trailhead, exit Rte. 19 at Main St. in Oak Hill. Turn left onto Main St. if coming from the south, right if from the north, then make a left on Minden Rd. Continue for 2.1 mi. and then take a right across a small bridge. The trail is distinguished from the other dirt paths in the vicinity by the gate which blocks vehicles from entering.

Horseback-riding trips are another way to explore the gorge. ◪**New River Trail Rides** leads 2hr. rides, sunset trips, and overnight adventures year-round from their stables off Wonderland Rd., adjacent to the ACE campgrounds. (☎465-4819 or 888-742-3982; www.ridewva.com. Rides start at $39 for 2½hr. and include a Scenic Overlook Ride (departs 9:30am, 1pm, 3:30pm, and sunset) and a Waterfall Excursion Ride (3½hr., 8:30am departure, $59). Hayrides 1-1½hr.; $15, under 6 free; min. 6 people.) All levels of experience can take advantage of the gorge's spectacular rock-climbing opportunities with **New River Mountain Guides** (☎574-3872 or 800-732-5462; www.newriverclimbing.com), at Wiseman and Court St. in downtown Fayetteville. Half-day trips combine both climbing and rappelling, and full-day trips include lunch. Experienced climbers looking for a challenge can climb the **Endless Wall,** which runs southeast along the New River and offers great river views from a height of 1000 ft. The wall is accessible from a trail off the parking lot at Canyon Rim Visitors Center (see **Transportation and Practical Information,** p. 366).

THE SOUTH

The American consciousness has become much more homogeneous since the 1860s, when regional strife ignited the bloodiest conflict in the nation's history. Yet marked differences persist between North and South, as much in memory as in practice: what's known as "the Civil War" up North is here still sometimes referred to as "The War Between the States." And outside the area's commercial capitals—Atlanta, Nashville, Charlotte, and New Orleans—Southerners continue to live slower-paced lives than their northern cousins.

Perhaps the greatest unifying characteristic of the South is its legacy of extreme racial division: slavery continues to leave its mark on Southern history, and the Civil Rights movement of the 1950s and 1960s remains too recent to be comfortably relegated to textbooks. At the same time, racial tensions and interactions have inspired many strands of American culture rooted in the South, from great literature to nearly *all* American music: gospel, blues, jazz, country, R&B, and rock 'n' roll. The south's cultural pedigree belies its generally poor economic status; its architecture, cuisine, and language all borrow from Native American, English, African, French, and Spanish influences. Landscapes are equally varied—nature blessed the region with mountains, marshlands, sparkling beaches, and fertile soil. The traveler here can go beyond the facile stereotypes of the South so often portrayed in popular culture and discover a part of the world that is often overlooked. Here you will find that the World Headquarters of the Baptist Church sits next to a gay nightclub, seedy motels are neighbors to Christian bookstores and drive-in Churches and drive-in fast food are complemented by fantastic home cooking.

HIGHLIGHTS OF THE SOUTH

FOOD. Some of the best Southern barbecue is at Dreamland in Mobile, AL (p. 464). New Orleans, LA (p. 473) has spicy and delicious Cajun cuisine. Southern "soul food" completes the spirit—Nita's Place, Savannah, GA (p. 451), will take you higher.

MUSIC. Make time for Tennessee—Nashville (p. 378) is the perfect place to get into country music, but if you're already a believer, you'll be heading to Graceland (p. 397).

CIVIL RIGHTS MEMORIALS. The Martin Luther King Center in Atlanta, GA (p. 438), and the Birmingham Civil Rights Institute, AL (p. 459), won't fail to move you.

OLD SOUTH. Charm and elegance. Nowhere is the antebellum way of life so well-kept as in stately Charleston, SC (p. 424), or Savannah, GA (p. 449).

KENTUCKY

Legendary for the duels, feuds, and stubborn spirit of its earlier inhabitants (such as the infamous Daniel Boone), Kentucky invites travelers to kick back, take a shot of local bourbon, and relax amid rolling hills and bluegrass. The state also boasts an extensive network of caves, including the longest known cave in the world. Today, the spirit of Kentucky can be boiled down into one pastime: going fast. The state is home to the signature American sports car, the Corvette, and to the world's premier horse race, the Kentucky Derby. Louisville tends to ignore its vibrant cultural scene and active nightlife at Derby time, and Lexington devotes much of its most beautiful farmland to breeding champion racehorses.

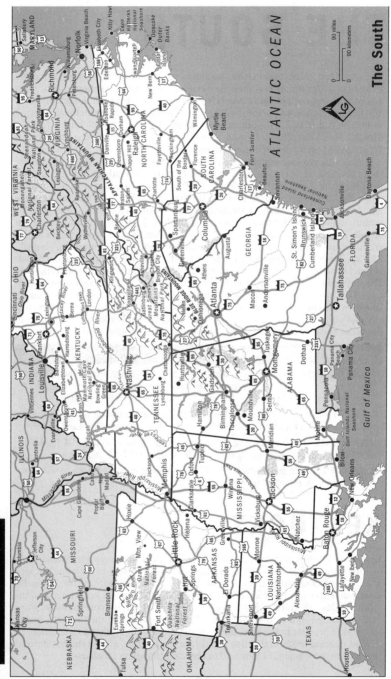

The South

THE SOUTH

PRACTICAL INFORMATION

Capital: Frankfort.

Visitor Info: Kentucky Dept. of Travel, Capital Plaza Tower, 500 Mero St., Ste. 2200, Frankfort 40601 (☎502-564-4930 or 800-225-8747; www.kentuckytourism.com). **Kentucky State Parks,** Capital Plaza Tower, 500 Mero St., Ste. 1100, Frankfort 40601 (☎800-255-7275; http://parks.ky.gov).

Postal Abbreviation: KY. **Sales Tax:** 6%.

LOUISVILLE ☎502

Louisville (pronounced "Lua-Vul" by locals) is caught between two pasts. One left a legacy of smokestacks, stockyards, and crumbling structures; the other shines with beautiful Victorian neighborhoods, ornate buildings, and the elegant Churchill Downs. Visitors can spend lazy afternoons browsing through used book stores or hunting for bargains at independent boutiques; by night, bars and clubs heat up around the city. Louisville's premier attraction, however, remains the Kentucky Derby. The nation's most prestigious horse race, this extravagant event will pack the city with visitors on May 7, 2005.

YOU CAN LEAD A HORSE TO WATER. Interstates through the city include **I-65** (north-south expressway), **I-71,** and **I-64.** The easily accessible **Watterson Expressway (I-264)** rings the city, while the **Gene Snyder Freeway (I-265)** circles farther out. In central downtown, **Main Street** and **Broadway** run east-west, and **Preston Highway** and **19th Street** run north-south. The **West End,** beyond 20th St., is a rough area. The **Louisville International Airport** (☎367-4636; www.louintlairport.com) is 15min. south of downtown on I-65; take bus #2 into the city. A taxi to downtown is around $16. **Greyhound,** 720 W. Muhammad Ali Blvd. (☎561-2801; open 24hr.), between 7th and 8th St., runs to: Chicago (6hr., 6 per day, $43); Cincinnati (2hr., 11 per day, $20); Indianapolis (2¼hr., 7 per day, $20). **Transit Authority River City's (TARC)** extensive bus system serves most of the metro area. (☎585-1234; www.ridetarc.com. Schedules vary by route; buses run as early as 4:30am until as late as 11:30pm. $1, ages 6-17 and seniors 65 and over $0.50 with TARC ID. Transfers free.) Two trolley routes service Main St./Market St. downtown. (M-F 6:45am-6:30pm; Sa 10am-6pm) and 4th St. (M-F 7am-11pm, Sa 9:30am-10pm. $0.25.) **Taxi: Yellow Cab** ☎636-5511. **Bike Rental: Highland Cycle,** 1737 Bardstown Rd. (☎458-7832; www.highlandcycle.com. Open M-F 9am-5:30pm, Sa 9am-4:30pm. Bikes from $5 per hr., $15 per day.) **Visitor Info: Louisville Visitor Information Center,** 3rd and Market St., in the Kentucky International Convention Center. (☎584-2121; www.gotolouisville.com. Open M-F 8:30am-5pm, Sa 9am-4pm, Su noon-4pm.) **Internet Access: Louisville Free Public Library,** 301 York St., downtown. (☎574-1611. Open M-Th 9am-9pm, F-Sa 9am-5pm, Su 1-5pm.) **Hotlines: Rape Hotline,** ☎581-7273. **Crisis Center,** ☎589-4313. Both operate 24hr. **Gay/Lesbian Hotline,** ☎454-7613. Operates daily 6-10pm. **Post Office:** 835 S. 7th. St. (☎584-6045. Open M-F 8am-5pm.) **Postal Code:** 40203. **Area Code:** 502.

HITCHIN' POSTS. Lodging in downtown Louisville is easy to find but pricey. Budget motels are on **I-65** near the airport or across the river in **Jeffersonville, IN. Newburg Road,** 6 mi. south, is also a budget haven. Derby Week lodging is expensive; make reservations 6 to 12 months in advance. Starting around January, the visitors center helps travelers arrange rooms for the event. **Super 8 ❸,** 101 Central Ave., near Churchill Downs and the University of Louisville, offers clean rooms and a stellar location. (☎635-0799. Jacuzzi suites. Continental

HORSE PLAY

The starting bell rings, the gates open, and a squadron of 3-year-olds gallops down a 1¼ mi. track, all for a garland of roses. First run in 1875, the Kentucky Derby is America's most prestigious horse race. Today the event is preceded by a two-week festival leading up to the first Saturday in May, when over 100,000 people gather to watch 3-year-olds race in the shadow of Churchill Downs's famous twin spires.

The winner receives a handsome purse, but the Derby's most potent symbol of triumph is an elaborate garland slung over the victorious mount's shoulders, made of 554 red roses sewn into a satin backing. The speedy mount also earns a shot at horse racing's vaunted trifecta, the Triple Crown, of which the Derby is the first leg (the Preakness and Belmont Stakes are the others). The purse for that honor, valued at $5 million, has gone unclaimed since Affirmed won it in 1978. For those who can't make it to the Derby, the **Kentucky Derby Museum** offers a 360° video and tours of the grounds.

This year's Derby will be run on May 7, 2005. Standing-room tickets are sold on race day for $40. (700 Central Ave. ☎502-636-4446; www.churchilldowns.com.) Museum (☎637-7097; www.derbymuseum.org) open M-Sa 7am-5pm, Su noon-5pm. $9, seniors $8, ages 5-11 $4. Tours $6.

breakfast. Singles $55; doubles $65.) The **Rocking Horse Manor ❹,** 1022 S. 3rd St., combines a great location near downtown with B&B comfort—including bathrobes, evening snacks and beverages, and a full gourmet breakfast. (☎583-0408; www.rockinghorse-bb.com. Cable TV, private baths, whirlpool tubs, dataports. No children. Rooms from $89.) **Louisville Metro KOA ❶,** 900 Marriot Dr., across the river in Indiana, has campsites convenient to downtown. (☎812-282-4474. Make reservations well in advance. Sites for 2 $27, with hookup $32. $4 per extra person, under 18 $2.50. 2-person cabins $45.)

🍴 **SO HUNGRY I COULD EAT A HORSE.** Good budget fare is hard to find in the heart of downtown. **Bardstown Road** is lined with cafes, budget eateries, and local and global cuisine, while **Frankfort Road** is rapidly catching up to Bardstown with restaurants and cafes of its own. Downtown, **Theater Square,** at Broadway and 4th St., has various lunch options. **Mark's Feed Store ❷,** 1514 Bardstown Rd., serves award-winning barbecue in a dining room decorated with checkered tablecloths and metal animal feed ads. (☎459-6275. Sandwiches $4-5.50; "burgoo" (beef stew) $3.50; dinners under $8. M free dessert after 4pm; Tu kids eat free. Open Su-Th 11am-10pm, F-Sa 11am-11pm. Call for other locations.) **Cafe Kilimanjaro ❸,** 649 S. 4th St., cooks up flavorful combinations of Caribbean, African, and South American cuisine. (☎583-4332; www.cafekilimanjaro.com. Specials $6. Live ethnic music Sa 11pm. Cover $5. Open M 11am-3pm, Tu-Th 11am-3pm and 4-8pm, F 11am-3pm and 5-10pm, Sa 5-10pm.) Local vegetarians love **Zen Garden ❷,** 2240 Frankfort Ave., a small, quiet restaurant that prepares excellent vegetarian Asian dishes. (☎895-9114. Entrees $6.50-9.50. Open M-Th 11am-10pm, F-Sa 11am-11pm.) At **Lynn's Paradise Cafe ❸,** 984 Barret Ave., a few blocks west of the Highlands, starry lanterns hang from the ceiling, pastel colors, and creative cuisine light up this skewed version of a 60s diner. (☎583-3447. Breakfast $5-9. Entrees $8-16. Open M 8am-2:30pm, Tu-Th 7am-10pm, F 7am-11pm, Sa 8am-11pm, Su 8am-10pm.)

🏇 **NOT JUST A ONE-HORSE TOWN.** The small record stores, cafes, boutiques, and antique shops on the **Highlands** strip can easily fill an afternoon with shopping or browsing. The strip runs along Baxter Ave. and Bardstown Rd. between Broadway and Trevilian Way. (Buses #17 and 23.) Nearby, the **American Printing House for the Blind,**

1839 Frankfort Ave., has a small but fascinating museum on the development of Braille and other systems for aiding the blind. The facility is the largest publishing house in the world dedicated to the visually impaired. (☎ 895-2405; www.aph.org. Open M-F 8:30am-4:30pm; 1hr. guided tours of the plant M-Th 10am and 2pm. Both museum and tours free. Wheelchair accessible.) The world's tallest baseball bat (120 ft.) leans against the **Louisville Slugger Factory and Museum,** 800 W. Main St., operated by the Hillerich and Bradsby Co. The museum details the history of the illustrious baseball bat, and a tour of the factory reveals how Sluggers are made. At the tour's end, visitors receive a free miniature bat. (☎ 588-7228; www.sluggermuseum.org. Open Apr.-Nov. M-Sa 9am-5pm, Su noon-5pm; Dec.-Mar. M-Sa 9am-5pm; last tours 4pm. $8, seniors 60 and over $7, children 6-12 $4.)

The **Frazier Historical Arms Museum,** 825 W. Main St., houses a world-class collection of arms and armor, and showcases them using interpreters in period dress, as well as exhibits that put the weapons in historical context. See armor from the Middle Ages, a Colt .45, and, of course, a Kentucky long rifle. (☎ 412-2280; www.fraziermuseum.org. $9; seniors, students, and children 5 and under $6. Open M-Sa 9am-5pm, Su noon-5pm. Wheelchair accessible.) Tucked into a restored 19th-century storefront, the **Louisville Science Center,** 727 W. Main St., features daily lab demonstrations, interactive exhibits and an IMAX theater. (☎ 561-6100; www.louisvillescience.org. $8.50, seniors and ages 2-12 $7.50. With IMAX $11/$9. Open M-Th 9:30am-5pm, F-Sa 9:30am-9pm, Su noon-6pm.)

🎭🎨 **HORSIN' AROUND.** The weekly arts and entertainment newspaper, *Leo*, is free and widely available. Broadway shows, comedy acts, and big-name music performances play in the lavish Spanish Baroque interior of **Louisville Palace,** 625 S. 4th Ave. (☎ 583-4555. Tickets $20-100. Box office open M-F 9am-5pm.) On the **"First Friday"** of every month, over a dozen of Louisville's downtown galleries treat visitors to special openings and refreshments until 9pm. Trolleys provide free transportation between galleries 5-11pm. The **Kentucky Shakespeare Festival,** at the amphitheater in Central Park in Old Louisville, runs during June and July. (☎ 583-8738; www.kyshakes.org. Performances 8pm. Free.)

Clubs cluster on Baxter Ave. near Broadway. **Phoenix Hill Tavern,** 644 Baxter Ave., cranks out blues and rock with live bands and DJs on three stages, including a deck and roof garden. (☎ 589-4957; www.phoenixhill.com. Beer from $3. W college night, beer from $0.75; F ladies night; "Phriday" happy hour 5-9pm. 21+. Cover $2-5. Open W and Sa 8pm-4am, Th 8pm-3am, F 5pm-4am.) **@tmosphere,** 917 Baxter Ave., is one of the area's hottest bars. The lounge is open daily; the dance floor in the back is open (and packed) Wednesday through Saturday. (☎ 458-5301; www.atmospherenightclub.com. Th ladies night. 21+. Cover Sa $5. Open M-Tu noon-2am, W-Sa 11am-4am, Su 1pm-midnight.) Nightlife downtown centers on clubs that combine multiple venues. Get four clubs for the price of one at **O'Malley's Corner**—and a karaoke bar to boot. If you don't dig the country-western or disco dance floors, just migrate to the hip-hop or Top 40 rooms. (133 W. Liberty St., entrance at the corner of Jefferson and 2nd. ☎ 589-3866; www.omalleyscorner.com. Th-F line dancing lessons 7:30-9:30pm; drink specials all night. F ladies night, with all-male review 8-11pm. 21+. Cover $3-5, includes all clubs. Open Th-Sa 7pm-3:30am.) For gay nightlife, make **The Connection,** 120 S. Floyd St. This huge club combines an amazing six venues under one roof. The different bars have different theme nights and varying hours, but at least one is open daily 5pm-4am. (☎ 585-5752. Drinks from $3.25. Happy hour daily 5-10pm. 21+. Cover includes all bars, up to $5. Dance Bar open Th 12:30-4am, F-Su 9pm-4am; showroom with drag shows F-Su 10pm-3am.)

⚡ DAYTRIPS FROM LOUISVILLE

BARDSTOWN. Kentucky's second-oldest city, 17 mi. east on Rte. 245 from I-65 Exit 112, charms visitors with its historic downtown district. The real attractions, however, are the bourbon distilleries outside of town. Bardstown, once home to 29 distilleries, is still proudly known as the "Bourbon Capital of the World." It all started in 1791, when Kentucky Baptist Reverend Elijah Craig left a fire unattended while heating oak boards to make a barrel for his aging whiskey. The boards were scorched, but Rev. Craig carried on, and bourbon was born in that first charred new white oak wood barrel. Today, 90% of America's native bourbon still hails from Kentucky, and 60% of that is distilled in Nelson and Bullitt Counties. **Jim Beam's American Outpost,** 15 mi. west of Bardstown in Clermont, off Rte. 245, treats visitors to samples of the world's best selling bourbon (M-Sa), lemonade, coffee, and bourbon candies. Peek into a warehouse that holds thousands of 53-gallon barrels of aging bourbon stored at the distillery, check out an authentic moonshine still and Jeremiah Beam's historic home, or watch a video about the company's 200-year history. You're also welcome to relax on the rocking chairs on the porch. (☎543-9877. Open M-Sa 9am-4:30pm, Su 1-4pm. Free.) Visitors can take a factory tour at **Maker's Mark Distillery,** 19 mi. southeast of Bardstown on Rte. 52 E in Loretto. Any day but Sunday, buy a bottle of bourbon in the gift shop, and hand-dip it yourself in the label's trademark red wax. (☎865-2099; www.makersmark.com. Tours every hr. M-Sa 10:30am-3:30pm, and Mar.-Dec. also Su 1:30-3:30pm. Gift shop open M-Sa 10am-4:30pm, Su 1-4:30pm. Complimentary samples of bourbon chocolates.) Bardstown also hosts the **Kentucky Bourbon Festival** every September, with several days of tours, events, and bourbon-drinking (☎800-638-4877; www.kybourbonfestival.com). **Bardstown Visitors Information Center,** 1 Court Sq., is in the courthouse. (☎348-4877 or 800-638-4877; www.visitbardstown.com. Open in summer M-Sa 8am-7pm, Su 10:30am-3:30pm; in winter M-F 8am-5pm.)

BOWLING GREEN. Here, auto enthusiasts pay their respects to the home of the classic American sports car, the Corvette. The **National Corvette Museum,** 350 Corvette Dr., off I-65 Exit 28, displays 'Vettes from the original chrome-and-steel '53 to futuristic concept cars; featured cars rotate constantly. (☎800-538-3883; www.corvettemuseum.com. Open daily 8am-5pm. $8, seniors 55 and over $6, ages 6-16 $4.50; families $20; AAA and military discounts. Wheelchair accessible.) To see their production in action, visit the **General Motors Corvette Assembly Plant,** across Duncan Hines Blvd. from the museum. You may even get a chance to test-start one of the mint-condition products. (☎270-745-8287; www.bowlinggreenassemblyplant.com. Tours M-F 9am and 1pm; plant closed Dec. and first 2 weeks of Jan. Closed-toed shoes required. Children must be 7 years of age or older. Free.)

MAMMOTH CAVE NATIONAL PARK   ☎270

Hundreds of enormous caves and narrow passageways cut through **Mammoth Cave National Park,** 80 mi. south of Louisville in the cave region of central Kentucky. From I-65, turn off at Exit 48 (Park City) or Exit 53 (Cave City) and follow signs to the visitors center for tours and camping. With over 365 mi. of mapped caves, Mammoth Cave comprises the world's longest network of cavern corridors—over three times longer than any other known cave system. Tours depart from the visitors center. (☎758-2328 or 800-967-2283; www.nps.gov/maca/home.htm. Open daily 8am-7:15pm; low-season 8:45am-5pm. Tour times vary; call for schedules.) The **Historic Tour** (2 mi., 2hr.) gives visitors a feeling for the caves and a chance to see many of the historic and cultural sights that lie within their walls ($11, youth $8). The **Frozen Niagara Tour** (¾ mi., 2hr.) focuses on the cave's impressive geological features ($11, youth $8). The **Discovery Tour** consumes a bit less time and money. The 30min. self-guided tour leads straight to one of the largest rooms in the cave. (Visitors admitted 10am-1pm. $4, youth $2.50.)

Above ground, the 52,000-acre park features walking, biking, and horseback riding trails, plus fishing and canoeing. Camping with bath houses, a camp store, and laundry is available at the pleasant **Headquarters Campground ❶**, near the visitors center. (☎758-2424. RVs allowed, but sites have no hookups. Showers $2. Open Mar.-Nov. Sites $16.) **Maple Springs Campground ❷** is across the river from the visitors center by free ferry, or by a 35 mi. detour. (No hookups. Ferry operates 6am-10pm. Open Mar.-Nov. Sites $30.) Reservations are recommended for both campgrounds (☎800-967-2283; http://reservations.nps.gov). Free **backcountry camping** permits can be obtained at the visitors center. For those who choose not to camp, charming rooms await at the **Mammoth Cave Hotel ❸**, next to the visitors center. (☎758-2225. Woodland Cottages with bath but no A/C or heat for 1 person $36, for 2 $45. Hotel Cottages with A/C, heat, and TV $52/$59. Availability varies with season. Singles from $62; doubles from $68. AAA 10% off.) **Greyhound** travels to Cave City, just east of I-65 on Rte. 70. (☎773-2200. Open 7am-2pm.)

LEXINGTON ☎859

Though the Kentucky Derby takes place in Louisville, Lexington is the state's real horse country. Green pastures roll away from the city, and the beautiful Keeneland Race Track hosts some of the country's most exciting races. Farms surround the city in the scenic "bluegrass country" for which eastern Kentucky is famous. Downtown, visitors will find a collection of graceful historic mansions, once home to Lexington's most famous and influential residents. Basketball is a way of life at the University of Kentucky, and hoops-crazy students create an active nightlife.

▐ TRANSPORTATION

Airport: Blue Grass Airport, 4000 Terminal Dr. (☎425-3114; www.bluegrassairport.com), off Man O' War Blvd. about 6 mi. southwest of downtown. Ritzy downtown hotels run shuttles, but there is no public transit. Taxi to downtown about $15.

Buses: Greyhound, 477 New Circle Rd. NW (☎299-0428). Open daily 7:30am-11pm. To: **Cincinnati** (1½hr., 6 per day, $20); **Knoxville** (4hr., 4 per day, $46); **Louisville** (2-6hr., 6 per day, $20).

Public Transit: LexTran (☎253-4636; www.lextran.com). Buses leave from the Transit Center, 220 E. Vine St., on a long block between Limestone and Rose St. Office open M-F 6am-6pm, Sa 8am-noon. Serves the university and city outskirts. Most routes run 5am-9pm. $1, ages 5-18 $0.80, seniors and disabled $0.50; transfers free.

Taxi: Lexington Yellow Cab ☎231-8294.

▟ ▐ ORIENTATION AND PRACTICAL INFORMATION

I-64 and **I-75** pass Lexington to the northeast. **New Circle Road** (**Route 4, U.S. 60 bypass, U.S. 421 bypass,** and **U.S. 25 bypass**) loops around the city, intersecting with many roads that connect the downtown district to the surrounding towns. **High, Vine** and **Main Street,** running east-west, and **Limestone** and **Broadway Street,** running north-south, are the major routes through downtown. Beware of the curving one-way streets downtown and near the **University of Kentucky (UK)** to the south.

Visitor Info: Lexington Convention and Visitors Bureau, 301 E. Vine St. (☎233-7299 or 800-845-3959; www.visitlex.com), at Rose St. Open in summer M-F 8:30am-5pm, Sa 10am-5pm, Su noon-5pm; low-season closed Su.

Hotlines: Crisis Intervention, ☎253-2737 or 800-928-8000. **Rape Crisis,** ☎253-2511 or 800-656-4673. Both 24hr.

Medical Services: Saint Joseph East Hospital, 150 N. Eagle Creek Dr. (☎967-5000). **Lexington Women's Diagnostic Center,** 701 Bob-o-link Dr., Ste. 250 (☎277-8485).

Internet Access: Lexington Public Library, 140 E. Main St. (☎231-5500), at Limestone St. Open M-Th 9am-9pm, F-Sa 9am-5pm, Su 1-5pm.

Post Office: 210 E. High St. (☎254-6156). Open M-F 8am-5pm. **Postal Code:** 40507. **Area Code:** 859.

ACCOMMODATIONS

The cheapest rooms are outside the city on New Circle Rd. or near I-75 at Winchester Rd. and Newtown Pike. The visitors bureau (see above) can help find lodging.

Extended Stay America, 2750 Gribbin Dr. (☎266-4800 or 800-398-7829; www.ext-stay.com). From New Circle Rd., take Exit 15 and follow Richmond Rd. away from the city center; turn right onto Patchen Dr. and left onto Gribbin Dr. Spacious rooms include fully equipped kitchenettes, cable TV with HBO, data ports, and free local calls. Pool and on-site laundry facilities. Singles from $50; doubles from $55; $245 per week. ❷

Microtel, 2240 Buena Vista Dr. (☎299-9600), off I-75 at Exit 110 (Winchester Rd./Rte. 60). Take bus #7. Pleasant but small motel rooms with window seats, about 3½ mi. from downtown. A/C, data ports, and cable TV. Singles Su-Th $40, F-Sa $52; doubles $51/$56. Wheelchair-accessible rooms available. ❷

Kentucky Horse Park Campground, 4089 Ironworks Pkwy. (☎259-4257 or 800-370-6416, ext. 257; www.kyhorsepark.com), 10 mi. north of downtown off I-75 at Exit 120. Well-manicured campsites with bath houses, Internet access, laundry, playground, basketball/volleyball/tennis courts, and swimming pool on the grounds of the Horse Park. Apr.-Oct. tent sites $15; with hookup $23, seniors $20. Nov.-Mar. $13/$19/$17. ❶

FOOD AND NIGHTLIFE

■**Alfalfa Restaurant** ❷, 141 E. Main St., treats customers to hearty international dishes and live jazz or folk. The menu includes delicious sandwiches on homemade bread ($3.50-5), filling salads ($5.50-8.50), and plenty of vegetarian and vegan options. (☎253-0014; www.alfalfarestaurant.com. Live music F-Sa 8-10pm. No cover. Open M-Th 11am-2pm and 5:30-10pm, F 11am-2pm and 5:30-11pm, Sa 9am-2pm and 5:30-11pm, Su 9am-2pm.) Gourmet cuisine is on the lesson plan at **Dudley's** ❹, 380 S. Mill St., housed in a 19th-century school. Edify your tastebuds with pasta, steak, and seafood dishes, or take recess at the stately bar. (☎252-1010. Entrees $14-32. Open Su-Th 11:30am-2:30pm and 5:30-10pm, F-Sa 11:30am-2:30pm and 5:30-11pm.) **Atomic Cafe** ❸, 265 N. Limestone St., whips up Caribbean fare with Southern hospitality. On weekends toes tap to live reggae on an outdoor patio. (☎254-1969. Salads and sandwiches $3.50-9; beer from $3.75. Live music F-Sa 9:30pm. Cover $5. Open Tu-Sa 4pm-1am; kitchen closes at 11pm.)

Those looking for a good time after dark hit the area around Main St. west of Limestone St. and the eastern fringes of UK. For specific info, read the "Weekender" section of the Friday *Herald-Leader*. **Pazzo's Pizza Pub,** 385 S. Limestone Rd., at Euclid St., is a classic KU college bar where cold beer and hand-tossed pizza reign supreme. Buy a pitcher on Wednesday night and get two free pints. (☎255-5125; www.pazzospizzapub.com. Outdoor patio. Beer from $2.25; 10 in. specialty pizzas from $7. Open M-Sa 11am-1am, Su noon-11pm; kitchen closes Su-W 10pm, Th-Sa 11pm.) **The Bar,** 224 E. Main St., a popular disco cabaret/lounge complex, caters to the gay and lesbian crowd. (☎255-1551; www.thebarcomplex.com. Happy hour M-Sa 4-7pm. DJs Th-Sa 11pm-2:30am. Drag shows Th-Sa. 21+. Cover F-Sa $5 after 8pm. Open M-W 4pm-1am, Th-Sa 4pm-2:30am.)

🔘 SIGHTS

HORSE ATTRACTIONS. Lexington **horse farms** are gorgeous places to visit; the visitors bureau can help arrange tours. ◪**Kentucky Horse Park** is one of Lexington's main attractions, entertaining visitors with live horse shows, horse-drawn trolley tours of the grounds, and a film about man's relationship with horses. Admission includes access to two museums: the **International Museum of the Horse** traces the role of the horse in history, while the **American Saddlebred Museum** educates visitors about Kentucky's oldest native breed. Watch as employees feed, groom, and exercise the horses on this working farm. The last weekend in April, the horse park hosts the annual Rolex tournament qualifier for the US equestrian team. (4089 Ironworks Pkwy. Off Ironworks Pike, Exit 120 from I-75. ☎233-4303 or 800-678-8813; www.kyhorsepark.com. Open mid-Mar. to Oct. daily 9am-5pm; Nov. to mid-Mar. W-Su 9am-5pm. Mid-Mar. to Oct. $14, ages 7-12 $7; Nov. to mid-Mar. $9/$6; live horse shows and 15min. horse-drawn tours included. 45min. horseback rides additional $15; ages 7 and up. Pony rides $4; ages 12 and under. Parking $2. Wheelchair accessible.)

The **Keeneland Race Track,** west of the city off U.S. 60, ranks among the country's most beautiful racing facilities. Every April, the final prep race for the Kentucky Derby is held here. Visit in April or October to catch a race at the track or watch the horses during their morning workouts and explore the grounds during the rest of the year. A $4 cafeteria-style breakfast and the chance to chat with a jockey or horse owner may make the **Track Kitchen** the best breakfast deal in town. (4201 Versailles Rd., across U.S. 60 from the airport. ☎254-3412 or 800-456-3412; www.keeneland.com. Races Apr. and Oct.; tickets $3-$5. Workouts free and open to the public mid-Mar. to Nov. 6-10am. Breakfast daily 5:30-11am.)

CITY ATTRACTIONS. Just northeast of the town center, in the area surrounding **Gratz Park,** a peaceful neighborhood of gorgeous old houses stands as a throwback to a time when plantation owners escaped the suffocating heat of the fields in milder Lexington. Deep porches, stone foundations, and rose-covered trellises distinguish the estates, which line Market and N. Mill St. between 2nd and 3rd St.

The Federal-style **Hunt Morgan House** stands at the end of the park across from the Carnegie Literacy Center. Built in 1814 by hemp merchant John Wesley Hunt—the first millionaire west of the Alleghenies—the house was once home to many notable characters, including Nobel laureate Thomas Hunt Morgan and Confederate General John Hunt Morgan, the "Thunderbolt of the Confederacy." Legend tells that Gen. Hunt Morgan, while being pursued by Union troops, rode his horse up the front steps and into the house, leaned down to kiss his mother, and rode out the back door. A small museum devoted to Civil War artifacts and memorabilia now occupies two rooms on the second floor. The week before Halloween, Gratz Park "ghost tours" begin at the Hunt Morgan House in the evenings. (201 N. Mill St., at W. 2nd St. ☎233-3290; www.bluegrasstrust.org/hunt-morgan. Guided tours only, 15min. past the hr. Open Mar.-Nov. W-F 1-5pm, Sa 10am-4pm, Su 1-5pm. $7, students $4. Senior and AAA discounts.)

THE SOUTH

TENNESSEE

In the east, the mountains of Tennessee stretch skyward at Great Smoky Mountains National Park, while the land in the west settles out into the wide Mississippi River. But the varied terrain of the Volunteer State has one unifying theme: music. From the twang of eastern bluegrass to the woes of Nashville country, from the roguish jazz and gut-wrenching blues of Memphis to the roots of rock 'n' roll at Graceland, music is the soul of the state. Others might argue that the heart of the state can be found in Jack Daniel's Tennessee Whiskey, but the distillery is located in a dry county; thank Tennessee's Bible-producing business, the largest in the world. Both the boozin' and the proselytizin' can be found in the music.

⚡ PRACTICAL INFORMATION

Capital: Nashville.

Visitor Info: Tennessee Department of Tourist Development, 320 6th Ave. N., 5th fl., Nashville 37243 (☎615-741-2159 or 800-462-8366 for a free guide; www.tnvacation.com). Open M-F 8am-4:30pm. **Tennessee State Parks Information,** 401 Church St., Nashville 37243 (☎800-421-6683; www.tnstateparks.com). Open M-F 8am-4:30pm.

Postal Abbreviation: TN. **Sales Tax:** 9.25% (13.25% for accommodations).

NASHVILLE   ☎615

Nashville is often called 'nouveau dixie'; new wealth is being poured into the city, much of it going into gaudy, glitzy entertainment. Nashville also bears a number of other unusual nicknames. Known as "the Athens of the South," the city is home to an array of Greek architecture—including a full-scale replica of the Parthenon in Centennial Park. The area has also been called the "buckle of the Bible belt," a reference to the Southern Baptists who make their home here. But Nashville's most popular moniker by far is "Music City USA," and for good reason: this town has long been known as the banjo-pickin', foot-stompin' capital of country music. No matter which Nashville you visit, you can have a rollicking good time in a city where live music and beer are available around the clock.

▐ TRANSPORTATION

Airport: Metropolitan (☎275-2098; www.flynashville.com), 8 mi. south of downtown. Coming from downtown, take I-40 E and turn off at Exit 216A. **Gray Line Tours** runs an airport **shuttle** (☎275-1180) to major downtown hotels daily 6am-11pm. $13, round-trip $18. Taxi to downtown $20.

Buses: Greyhound, 200 8th Ave. S (☎255-3556), at Demonbreun St. downtown. *Borders on a rough neighborhood,* but the station is well-lit. Station open 24hr. To: **Birmingham** (4hr., 7 per day, $33); **Chattanooga** (2½hr., 4 per day, $24); **Knoxville** (3½hr., 6 per day, $30); **Louisville** (3½hr., 8 per day, $30); **Memphis** (4hr., 6 per day, $35).

Public Transit: Metropolitan Transit Authority (MTA; ☎862-5950; www.nashvillemta.org). Buses operate on limited routes. Times vary route to route, but none run M-F before 5:30am or after 11:15pm; Sa last bus from downtown 10:15pm, Su last bus from downtown 9:15pm and only hourly service. $1.45, express fare $1.75, downtown service $0.25, transfers $0.10; ages 4 and under free. Weekly pass $15.

Taxi: Nashville Cab ☎242-7070. **Music City Taxi** ☎742-3030.

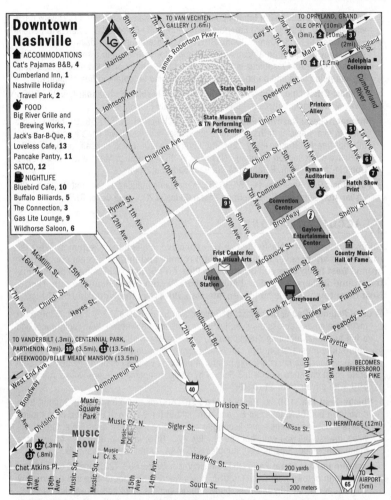

Downtown Nashville

⌂ ACCOMMODATIONS
Cat's Pajamas B&B, 4
Cumberland Inn, 1
Nashville Holiday
   Travel Park, 2
🍴 FOOD
Big River Grille and
   Brewing Works, 7
Jack's Bar-B-Que, 8
Loveless Cafe, 13
Pancake Pantry, 11
SATCO, 12
🍸 NIGHTLIFE
Bluebird Cafe, 10
Buffalo Billiards, 5
The Connection, 3
Gas Lite Lounge, 9
Wildhorse Saloon, 6

◼🛈 ORIENTATION AND PRACTICAL INFORMATION

Nashville's streets are fickle, often interrupted by curving parkways and one-way streets. Names change without warning. **Broadway,** the main east-west thoroughfare, runs through downtown, then veers left after passing over I-40; **West End Avenue** continues straight ahead. Broadway joins **21st Avenue** after a few blocks, passing through **Vanderbilt University.** In the downtown area, numbered avenues run north-south, parallel to the Cumberland River. The curve of **James Robertson Parkway** encloses the north end, becoming **Main Street** on the other side of the river (later **Gallatin Pike**) and turning into **8th Avenue** in the center of downtown. *The area south of Broadway between 2nd and 7th Ave. can be unsafe at night.* Metered street parking is free after 12:30pm on Saturdays and all day Sundays; in the evening spots become prized possessions and commercial parking is $10.

Visitor Info: Nashville Visitor Information Center, 501 Broadway (☎259-4747; www.nash-villecvb.com), in the Gaylord Entertainment Center, off I-65 at Exit 84, James Robertson Pkwy. Open M-Sa 8:30am-5:30pm, Su 10am-5pm and on event days until the event starts. They hand out an African-American guide to Nashville and also a list of gay and lesbian venues and resources in the city. Discounted attraction ticket packages, a walking tour guide, and info on upcoming events can also be obtained free of charge.

Hotlines: Crisis Line, ☎244-7444. 24hr. **Gay and Lesbian Switchboard,** ☎297-0008; www.rainbowcommunitycenter.org. Operates nightly 6-9pm.

Internet Access: Nashville Public Library, 615 Church St. (☎862-5800), between 6th and 7th Ave. Register at the desk for a guest user card which will enable you to use the Internet free for 30min. every 12hr. The library is worth a look in itself, particularly the extensive art collection including "Nashville: A History through Maps and Aerial Views." Open M-Th 9am-8pm, F 9am-6pm, Sa 9am-5pm, Su 2-5pm.

Post Office: 901 Broadway (☎255-3613), in the same building as the Frist Center for the Visual Arts. Open M-F 8:30am-5pm. **Postal Code:** 37203. **Area Code:** 615.

ACCOMMODATIONS

Rooms in downtown Nashville can be expensive, especially in summer. The visitors center offers several deals on motel rooms, and budget motels concentrate around **West Trinity Lane** and **Brick Church Pike,** off I-65 at Exit 87. Cheap hotels cluster around **Dickerson Road** and **Murfreesboro,** a somewhat seedy neighborhood. Near downtown, motels huddle on **Interstate Drive** over the Woodland St. Bridge.

Cat's Pajamas Bed & Breakfast, 818 Woodland St. (☎650-4553; www.bbonline.com/tn/catspajamas), across the river, just over 1 mi. from downtown. With funky decor and a full breakfast featuring organic foods, this hip little B&B provides a welcome break from stuffy inns and anonymous hotel rooms. With only three rooms, the creative, socially conscious hosts are very helpful in orienting visitors. Small fridge upstairs, separate guest entrance. Check-in 3-6pm or by other arrangement. Rooms with shared bath $90, with private bath $110. ❹

Cumberland Inn, 150 W. Trinity Ln. (☎226-1600 or 800-704-1028). Coming from downtown on I-65N, take Exit 87 and turn right at the bottom of the ramp even though it says "East Trinity Lane"—just keep right and right again. These rates are among Nashville's lowest, but you get what you pay for. A/C, HBO, laundry, and free coffee; some rooms with fridge. Singles $30; doubles $35. AAA, AARP 10% discount. ❷

Nashville Holiday Travel Park, 2572 Music Valley Dr. (☎889-4225 or 800-547-4480), 8 mi. north of town near Opryland USA, has a wooded area for tenting and crowded RV sites. Showers, laundry facilities, pool, Internet access, mini golf, playground, basketball court, and game room. Nightly entertainment. Sites for 2 $23, with water and electricity $42, full hookup $49. Each additional person over age 11 $8. ❶

FOOD

In Nashville, the initials of the Grand Ole Opry grace even the local candy: **goo-goo clusters** (peanuts, pecans, chocolate, caramel, and marshmallow) are sold in specialty shops throughout the city. Nashville's other finger-lickin' traditions, barbecue or fried chicken, are no less sinful. Restaurants catering to collegiate tastes and budgets cram **21st Avenue, West End Avenue,** and **Elliston Place,** near Vanderbilt.

Loveless Cafe, 8400 Rte. 100, at the end of the Natchez Trace Pkwy. (☎646-9700; www.lovelesscafe.com). Follow West End Ave. out of the downtown area to where it becomes Harding Pike. Rte. 100 splits off after the Belle Meade Plantation. The Loveless is a 25 year old Nashville tradition. Feast on country ham ($10) or fried chicken ($11), served with made-from-scratch biscuits and preserves. Open daily for breakfast 6am-5pm, lunch 11am-5pm, and dinner 5pm-9pm. ❸

SATCO (San Antonio Taco Company), 416 21st Ave. S (☎327-4322), near Vanderbilt. With great Mexican food at even better prices, this student hangout sells fajitas for $1.25-1.50 and tacos for $1. Taco salad $5. Single beers from $2; bucket of 6 from $10. Open in summer Su-W 11am-midnight, Th-Sa 11am-1am; in winter Su-W 11am-11pm, Th-Sa 11am-midnight. ❶

Pancake Pantry, 1796 21st Ave. (☎383-9333), serves big stacks of steaming, delicious pancakes in all different varieties, from traditional buttermilk to orange-walnut or apricot-lemon (most $5.45). Other breakfast and lunch items also available. Open M-F 6am-3pm, Sa-Su 6am-4pm. ❶

Jack's Bar-B-Que, 416A Broadway (☎254-5715; www.jacksbarbque.com), is a bit of a legend—both for the flashing neon-winged pigs above the door and the succulent, tender pork. Sandwiches $3-5. Plates $7-11. Open in summer M-Th 10:30am-9pm, F-Sa 10:30am-10pm, Su noon-6pm; in winter Th 10:30am-8pm, F-Sa 10:30am-10pm. Another location at 334 W. Trinity Ln. (☎228-9888). ❷

Big River Grille and Brewing Works, 111 Broadway (☎251-4677), is a microbrewery in the heart of downtown. Their rotating choice of specialty beers and a selection of salads come as a relief to vegetarians and those in need of a fried-free night. Try the delicious chicken caesar salad ($9) or pizza ($10), but don't worry—you can still get ribs ($18). Open M-Th 11am-11pm, F-Sa 11am-midnight, Su 11am-10pm. Bar open later. ❸

◉ SIGHTS

GRAND OLE COUNTRY LOVIN'. Country music drives this city. The first stop of any traveler—country fan or not—should be the state-of-the-art **Country Music Hall of Fame,** where visitors can view live performances or design their own CDs of country hits. Wander through the well-crafted displays on the history of country, listen to samples from greats like Johnny Cash and Patsy Cline, and watch videos of performances and interviews with modern artists. An extra $10 will upgrade tickets to include a guided tour of RCA's **Studio B,** where over 1000 American Top 10 hits have been recorded. A Grayline shuttle runs between the two venues. (*222 5th Ave. S. ☎416-2001; www.countrymusichalloffame.com. Open daily 10am-6pm. $16, seniors $14, students $10, ages 6-17 $8, under 6 free.*) Two-step over to the **Ryman Auditorium,** the site of the legendary **Grand Ole Opry** radio show for more than 30 years. The Opry eventually moved to a bigger venue to accommodate the growing crowd of fans, but the Ryman continues to host fantastic shows. A short video that outlines the history of the building, peruse display cases containing stage costumes and photos, and climb on stage. (*116 5th Ave. N. ☎889-3060; www.ryman.com. Open daily 9am-4pm. $8.50, ages 4-11 $4.25. Times and prices for shows vary.*) Finally, the main country venue in the nation is the **Grand Ole Opry House.** Visitors can enjoy musical performances, tour the backstage areas, or visit the free museum detailing the Opry's history. Upcoming weekend shows are listed in *The Tennessean* and online at www.opry.com. (*2804 Opryland Dr., Exit 11 off Hwy. 155, accessible from both I-40 and I-65. ☎871-6779. Museum open M-Th 10am-5pm, F 10am-8pm, Sa 10am-10pm. Free. Tours daily 10:30am, noon, 2:30, 3:30pm; no 3:30 tour on show days. $10, ages 4-11 $5. Shows F 7:30, Sa 6:30 and 9:30pm, sometimes Tu 7pm. Tickets $28-45, available at ☎800-871-6779, www.opry.com, or through Ticketmaster. Wheelchair accessible.*)

MUSEUMS AND MORE. Right in the heart of downtown, the **Frist Center for the Visual Arts** inspires both young and old with an interesting array of rotating exhibits and a hands-on learning center that allows visitors to paint, draw, and

THE SOUTH

make prints. On the last Friday of every month, the center hosts "Frist Friday," a gathering with music, hors d'oeuvres, and drinks. *(919 Broadway. ☎ 244-3340; www.fristcenter.org. Open M-W and F-Sa 10am-5:30pm, Th 10am-8pm, Su 1-5pm. $6.50, students and seniors 65 and over $4.50, 18 and under free. Frist Fridays 5:30-9pm, galleries open 6-8pm; free; 21+. Wheelchair accessible.)* Also downtown, **Hatch Show Print,** one of the oldest poster printing shops in the country, is well-known for its posters of Grand Old Opry celebrities. The shop still operates today, using antique letterpress techniques. *(316 Broadway. ☎ 256-2805. Open M-F 9:30am-5:30pm, Sa 10:30am-5:30pm. Free.)*

Fisk University's Carl Van Vechten Gallery consists of a portion of the private collection of Alfred Steiglitz, donated by his widow Georgia O'Keeffe. The gallery is tiny, but the fascinating Steiglitz photographs hanging among works by Picasso, Cézanne, and Renoir are a must-see for art lovers. *(At Jackson St. and D.B. Todd Blvd., off Jefferson St. ☎ 329-8720. Open in summer Tu-F 10am-5pm, Sa 1-5pm; in winter Tu-F 10am-5pm, Sa-Su 1-5pm. Free, but donations accepted. Wheelchair accessible.)*

Across West End Ave. from Vanderbilt, the pleasant **Centennial Park** stretches between 25th and 28th Ave. A visit to the park will clarify why Nashville is known as the "Athens of the South": a full-scale replica of the Greek **Parthenon** sits on top of a low hill. Built as a temporary exhibit for the Tennessee Centennial in 1897, the Parthenon was so popular that it was maintained and finally rebuilt with permanent materials in the 1920s. As out-of-place as the structure seems in Nashville, it is nonetheless impressive—especially the 42 ft. golden statue of Athena inside. In its first floor gallery, the building houses the **Cowan Collection of American Paintings,** a selection of 19th- and early 20th-century American art. *(☎ 862-8431; www.parthenon.org. Open Tu-Sa 9am-4:30pm. $4, seniors 62 and over and ages 4-17 $2.50. Wheelchair accessible.)* At the **capitol,** a stately Greek Revival structure atop a hill on Charlotte Ave. north of downtown, visitors can tour the Governor's Reception Room, the legislative chambers, the former Tennessee Supreme Court, and the grounds, including the tomb of President James K. Polk. *(On Charlotte Ave. between 6th and 7th Ave. ☎ 741-0830; www.tnmuseum.org. Photo ID required. Open M-F 9am-4pm. Tours every hr. M-F 9-11am and 1-3pm; self-guided tours also available. Free. Wheelchair accessible.)*

CHEEKWOOD MUSEUM AND BELLE MEADE MANSION. For a break from the bustle of downtown, head to the **Cheekwood Botanical Garden and Museum of Art.** The well-kept gardens, complete with a woodland sculpture trail, are a peaceful spot for a stroll. The museum features American and contemporary sculpture and painting and a collection of English and American decorative arts. *(1200 Forrest Park Dr., off of Page Rd., between Rte. 100 and Belle Meade Blvd. 8 mi. southwest of town. ☎ 356-8000; www.cheekwood.org. Audio tours available for museum. Open Tu-Sa 9:30am-4:30pm, Su 11am-4:30pm. $10, students and ages 6-17 $5; families $25; half-price after 3pm.)* The nearby **Belle Meade Plantation** was once one of the nation's most famed thoroughbred nurseries. The lavish 1853 mansion has hosted seven US presidents, including the 380 lb. William Howard Taft, who allegedly spent some time lodged in the mansion's bathtub. Today, visitors can explore the house and grounds, including a collection of antique carriages. *(5025 Harding Rd. ☎ 356-0501 or 800-270-3991. Open M-Sa 9am-5pm, Su 11am-5pm. 2 guided tours per hr.; last tour 4pm. $10, seniors $8.50, ages 6-12 $4. AAA discount. Partially wheelchair accessible.)*

THE HERMITAGE. The **Hermitage,** the graceful manor of seventh US president Andrew Jackson, holds an impressive array of the original furnishings. Admission also includes a 15min. film about Jackson's life (shown every 20min.), access to the house and grounds (including Jackson's tomb), and a visit to the nearby **Tulip Grove Mansion** and the **Hermitage Church.** *(4580 Rachel's Ln. Exit 221 off I-40 E, continue 4 mi. on Old Hickory Blvd; entrance is on the right. ☎ 889-2941; www.thehermitage.com. Open* *daily 9am-5pm. Tours of mansion run regularly, self-guided garden and farm tours available. All included in admission. $12, students 13-18 and seniors 62 and over $11, ages 6-12 $5; families $34. AAA discount. Partially wheelchair accessible.)*

🎵 ENTERTAINMENT

The hordes of visitors that converge upon Nashville have turned the **Grand Ole Opry** (see above) into a grand American institution. However, there are other great forms of entertainment in the capital city as well. The **Tennessee Performing Arts Center,** 505 Deaderick St. at 6th Ave. N, hosts the Nashville Symphony, opera, ballet, Broadway shows, and other theater productions. (☎255-2787; www.tpac.org. Tickets $15-75. Wheelchair accessible.) The **Dancin' in the District Music Festival** runs from June to September in Riverfront Park and features three live bands every Saturday afternoons and evenings. Artists such as Blondie have played in the past. (☎255-3588; www.dancininthedistrict.com. Tickets $5 in advance, $8 at the gate.) Listings for the area's music and events fill the free *Nashville Scene* and *Rage,* available at most area establishments.

Two major-league franchises dominate the Nashville sports scene. The NFL's **Tennessee Titans** play at **Adelphia Coliseum,** 460 Great Circle Rd., across the river from downtown. (☎565-4200; www.titansonline.com. Open M-F 8:30am-5pm. Tickets $12-52.) The **Nashville Predators,** a recent NHL expansion team, face off at the **Gaylord Entertainment Center,** 501 Broadway. (☎770-2040. Open M-Sa 10am-5:30pm; tickets available through Ticketmaster. $10-85.)

🍸 NIGHTLIFE

Nashville has a happening nightlife scene fueled by good ol' country music; if you are into line dancing, you are good to go. Other, smaller scenes, such as hip-hop spots and gay clubs, are a little more out of the way. Downtown, country nightlife centers on Broadway and 2nd Ave., and draw large crowds. Parking can be difficult on summer evenings, especially when something is going on at the Gaylord Entertainment Center. Near Vanderbilt, **Elliston Place** hops with college-oriented music venues. For info on GLBT nightlife in Nashville and Knoxville, check out the monthly *Out and About* or the weekly *Xenogeny,* available at some venues downtown. The visitors center has out a list of gay and lesbian establishments.

Bluebird Cafe, 4104 Hillsboro Rd. (☎383-1461; www.bluebirdcafe.com), in the strip mall in Green Hills. Coming from 21st Ave., it will be on your left after you cross Richard Jones Rd. This famous bird sings original country and acoustic every night. Country stars Garth Brooks and Kathy Mattea started their careers here. $7 per person food and drink min. if sitting at a table. Cover after 9:30pm usually $4-10; no cover Su. Open M-Sa 5:30pm, Su 6pm until the singing stops (usually between 11pm and 1am). Early show 6:30pm. Reservations recommended Tu-Sa.

Wildhorse Saloon, 120 2nd Ave. N (☎902-8200; www.wildhorsesaloon.com). Bring your cowboy boots and hat, and two-step through the night in this huge country dance hall. It's loud and brash, but ain't that country?. Dance lessons M-F 7-9pm, Sa-Su 2-9pm. Live music Tu-Sa. Cover after 7pm $4-6. Open Su-Th 11am-1am, F-Sa 11am-3am.

Buffalo Billiards, 154 2nd Ave. N (☎313-7665; www.buffalobilliards.com). A busy bar with pool tables and a fun, relaxed atmosphere. Happy hour M-F 4-8pm. Th $2 drafts all night. Su free pool and $2.50 drafts. 21+. Open M-W 4pm-2am, Th-F 4pm-3am, Sa-Su 1pm-3am. Upstairs, **Havana Lounge** is a popular hip-hop club; the dance floor is often packed. 21+. Cover $5 after 10:30pm. Open W-Sa.

Gas Lite Lounge, 167½ 8th Ave. N, between Church and Commerce (☎254-1278). Next door to the world headquarters of the Baptist Church, this self-styled "Gay Cheers" bar is a friendly local hangout. Plenty of pool ($0.50 per game), piano playing, and even board games during the afternoon. There's an upstairs balcony which is ideal for people-watching. Straight-friendly. Karaoke Th and Sa-Su. Open daily 4:30pm-3am.

The Connection, 901 Cowan St. (☎742-1166). Coming from downtown, take 8th Ave. north, go right on Jefferson, then left on Cowan. Nashville's biggest gay dance club, with a country music room, a large techno-style dance club, and a show room with drag performances at 11pm and 1am on the weekends. Open M and W-Su 9pm-3am.

KNOXVILLE   ☎865

Knoxville was settled after the Revolutionary War and named for Washington's Secretary of War, Henry Knox. It was once the capital of the "Territory South of the River Ohio," part of which became the state of Tennessee. Shaded by the stunning Great Smoky Mountains and hemmed in by vast lakes created by the Tennessee Valley Authority, Knoxville is a friendly, easily navigated city and home to the 26,000 students of the University of Tennessee (UT). Here, the police ride bicycles, the locals eat lunch *al fresco*, the music is less expensive than in Nashville, and happening clubs are open into the wee hours.

◪ **PRACTICAL INFORMATION.** Downtown stretches north from the Tennessee River, bordered by **Henley Street** and **World's Fair Park** to the west. The **McGhee Tyson Airport** (☎342-3000; www.tys.org) lies near the intersection of U.S. 140 and Hwy. 129, about 10 mi. south of downtown. **Greyhound,** 100 E. Magnolia Ave. (☎524-0369; open 24hr.), at Central St., sends buses to: Chattanooga (2hr., 4 per day, $17); Lexington (4hr., 5 per day, $43); Nashville (3-3½hr., 7 per day, $26). *Avoid this area at night.* Public **KAT** buses cover the city. (☎637-3000; www.katbus.com. Operates M-Sa 5:30am-12:30am, Su 11am-7pm with reduced service. 4 night routes run M-F 8:45pm-midnight, Sa 6:45pm-midnight, Su 10:15am-6:30pm. $1, ages 4 and under free; transfers $0.20.) Four free **trolley** lines run throughout the city: Blue runs to the Coliseum, Blount Mansion, and the Women's Basketball Hall of Fame; Orange heads downtown and westward to World's Fair Park and UT; Green travels between the Fort Sanders neighborhood and UT; the Late Line serves UT, the Strip, Market Square, and the Old City. (Blue Line: M-F 5:50am-6:20pm; Orange Line: M-F 7am-6:15pm; Green Line: M-F 7am-6pm; Late Line: F-Sa 8pm-3:30am.)

The **visitors center** is at 301 S. Gay St. (☎523-7263; www.knoxville.org. Open M-Sa 9am-5pm.) **Hotlines: Sexual Assault Crisis Center,** ☎522-7273. **Gay and Lesbian Helpline,** ☎523-2339. (Operates nightly 7pm-1am.) **Internet Access: Lawson McGhee Public Library,** 500 W. Church Ave. (☎215-8700. 1hr. free Internet access with guest card. Open June-Aug. M-Th 9am-8:30pm, F 9am-5:30pm, Su 1-5pm; Sept.-May M-Th 9am-8:30pm, F 9am-5:30pm, Sa-Su 1-5pm.) **Post Office:** 501 W. Main Ave. (☎522-1070. Open M-F 7:30am-5:30pm.) **Postal Code:** 37902. **Area Code:** 865.

◪ **ACCOMMODATIONS.** Several mid-range motels can be found at the intersection of **I-75** and **I-40,** just north of the city. The **Knoxville Hostel (HI) ❶,** 404 E. 4th Ave., is just a short walk from the restaurants and clubs of the Old City. The hostel features six beds for men and four for women, a kitchen, and a comfortable common room, plus free Internet access and a continental breakfast. Be warned that the hostel is jammed up against the interstate—you may feel like the trucks are actually coming through the dormitory at night. *Be cautious around this neighborhood at night. If you arrive at the Greyhound station, call the hostel's friendly hosts Brian and Al and they will come and pick you up.* (☎546-8090;

fourzerofoureast@aol.com. Free local calls. Shuttle service to Gatlinburg $7.60, students $6.45, hostel guests $6. Laundry $1.75. Reception usually 8am-noon and 1-6pm. $15, nonmembers $18.) The standard rooms at **Scottish Inns ❶**, 201 Callahan Rd., at Exit 110 off I-75, are farther from downtown. (☎689-7777. Free local calls, A/C, HBO, continental breakfast, and an outdoor pool. Singles Su-Th $29, F-Sa $44; doubles $39/$49. AAA, AARP $2 discount.) **Volunteer Park Family Campground ❶**, 9514 Diggs Gap Rd., at Exit 117 off I-75, is 12 mi. from the city and has a pool, coin-operated laundry, a convenience store, and live music in summer. (☎938-6600 or 800-238-9644; www.volpark.com. Music Tu and F nights in summer. Tent sites $18, with water and electricity $20, full hookup $25. Rates are for 2 adults and 2 children, additional person $3. Sites half price mid-Nov. to mid-Apr.)

❏ FOOD. Market Square, a relaxed, shaded plaza to the east of World's Fair Park, offers restaurants and fountains, but shuts down at night. The other center for chowing, browsing, and carousing, the **Old City** spreads north up Central and Jackson St. and stays active later than Market Sq. Part of Cumberland Ave. along campus proper, **The Strip** is lined with student hangouts, bars, and restaurants, and is dominated by fast-food chains. **The Tomato Head ❶**, 12 Market Sq., prepares delicious gourmet pizzas (slices $1.40-4.90) and sandwiches ($4.50-7), with vegetarian and vegan options galore. This relaxed, breezy place is frequented by business types and young professionals. There's a great lunch deal—a pizza slice and salad combo for $4.30. (☎637-4067. Open M 11am-3pm, Tu-Th 11am-10pm, F-Sa 11am-11pm, Su 10am-9pm.) Don't miss the terrific croissant sandwiches at the **11th Street Espresso House ❶**, 1016 Laurel Ave., in an old Victorian house near the Knoxville Museum of Art. The porch is the perfect spot to enjoy a cup of coffee. (☎546-3003. Sandwiches $5. Salads $3.50-5.25. Coffee drinks $1.50-3.50. Poetry readings some W 8pm; occasional live music. Open M-Sa 9am-midnight, Su 10am-10pm.)

◪ SIGHTS. The must-see ▨**Museum of Appalachia,** 16 mi. north of Knoxville at I-75 Exit 122 in Norris, showcases original artifacts used in the construction of Appalachian homes and agricultural developments over the last 300 years. The museum consists of a number of old buildings relocated from the surrounding countryside, including barns, corn cribs, a smokehouse, and the cabin where Mark Twain's family lived. Visitors will also be treated to occasional live mountain music. Presenting both the tools of everyday Appalachian living and the stories of the people who used them, the museum is a testament to the region's unique culture. The annual **Tennessee Fall Homecoming Festival** is held here on the second full weekend in October and draws 400 musicians as well as writers, craftspeople, and huge crowds. (☎494-7680; www.museumofappalachia.com. Live music Apr.-Dec. 9:30am-4:30pm. Open June-Aug. daily 8am-8pm; low-season closes as early as 5pm. $13, seniors and AAA $10, ages 6-12 $5; families $30; higher during festival.)

The ▨**Women's Basketball Hall of Fame,** 700 Hall of Fame Dr., traces the history of women's involvement in the sport and attempts to inspire future stars. Visitors can watch a video called "Hoop Full of Hope," listen to interviews with current stars, and shoot some hoops. (☎633-9000; www.wbhof.com. Open M-Sa 10am-7pm, Su 1-6pm. $8, seniors and ages 6-15 $6; AAA $2 off. Wheelchair accessible.) Nearby, the **James White Fort,** 205 E. Hill Ave., preserves portions of the original stockade built in 1786 by the founder of Knoxville. Guided tours describe the lives of the first white settlers in the area. (☎525-6514. Open Mar. to mid-Dec. M-Sa 9:30am-5pm; Jan.-Feb. M-F 10am-4pm. 1hr. tours on the ½hr. 9:30am-3:30pm. Admission by tour only. $5, seniors and AAA $4.50, ages 5-12 $2.) History buffs will enjoy the **Blount Mansion,** 200 W. Hill Ave., the home of William Blount, who served as the first governor of the Territory South of the River Ohio. Tours of the cozy house, built in

1792, include a 10min. video on his life. (☎525-2375 or 888-654-0016; www.blount-mansion.org. Open Apr.-Dec. M-Sa 9:30am-5pm; Jan.-Mar. M-F 9:30am-5pm. Guided tours on the hr. 10am-4pm. $5, AAA and seniors $4.45, ages 6-17 $2.50.)

The self-guided **Cradle of Country Music Tour** ambles through the eastern end of downtown, lingering periodically on hallowed ground where country triumphs and heartaches left their marks. Stops include the theater where Roy Acuff made his first public performance and the hotel where Hank Williams spent his last night. Free maps and information are available at the visitors center. **World's Fair Park,** just west of downtown, recently underwent major reconstruction, expanding the convention center and adding a vast swath of greenery stretching toward the river. (Open dawn-dusk.) The **Knoxville Museum of Art,** 1050 World's Fair Park Dr., houses high-caliber rotating exhibits and a small but dynamic permanent collection of Modern and postmodern art. The museum hosts "Alive after Five" on Fridays, with live jazz or blues, free popcorn, catered food, and a cash bar. (☎525-6101; www.knoxart.org. Open Tu-W noon-8pm, Th-F noon-9pm, Sa-Su 11am-5pm. $5, ages 17 and under free. Alive after Five some F 5:30-9pm, $6. Wheelchair accessible.)

⬛🅴 ENTERTAINMENT AND NIGHTLIFE. Knoxville is a great place for college sports fans; UT's **football** (in the Neyland Stadium) and **women's basketball** (in the Thompson Bowling Arena) consistently rank among the top teams of their respective leagues. (☎974-2491; www.utsports.com. Football tickets $38-45, basketball $8-14.) **Sundown in the City,** a free outdoor concert series, brings some big name rock and blues bands to Market Sq. on Thursday nights during the summer. (☎523-2665; www.concertwire.com. June-Oct. Th 6-10pm. Free.) The annual **Dogwood Arts Festival** brings crafts, food, and live entertainment to Market Sq. every April. Festivities also include a parade and a bicycling competition. (☎621-4559; www.dogwoodarts.com. Apr. 16-25, 2005. Free.)

The Old City is the center of Knoxville's nightlife; the Strip and Market Sq. also host a number of popular bars. For goings-on around town, pick up a free copy of *Metro Pulse* or log onto www.metropulse.com. The hip **Blue Cats,** 125 E. Jackson St., is a cool venue in a gritty district and draws some big live rock, blues, and country music acts. (☎544-4300; www.bluecatslive.com. Beer from $2.75. Cover varies; doors usually open at 9pm.) On Saturday nights, the club hosts Fiction, Knoxville's hottest dance party. (☎329-0039; www.fictionfx.com. 18+. Cover $3-5. Open Sa 10pm-3am.) **Preservation Pub,** 28 Market Sq., a fabulous, friendly bar, serves some serious brews (from $2.75). Check out the great quotes on the walls. (☎524-2224; www.preservationpub.com. Live music nightly except Tu and Su. Happy hour daily 4-7pm. 21+ after 10pm. Open M-F 11am-3am, Sa 4pm-3am, Su 6pm-1am.) **Barley's Taproom and Pizzeria,** 200 E. Jackson Ave., in the Old City, has $2 drafts all day Monday. They have a fantastic beer selection and "pub dawgs" (huge hot dogs; $5), as well as vegetarian burgers and salads. When it's shining outside, you can eat *al fresco* on their atmospheric patio. (☎521-0092. Beer from $1.75. Live music almost daily. Happy hour daily noon-6pm. Cover $5 or less. Open M-Sa 11am-2am, Su noon-2am. Kitchen closes 2hr. before close, 1hr. before close on Su.) **Kurt's,** 4928 Hombrey Dr., off King's Pike, is a relaxed, friendly gay bar to the west of the city. Keep going even when you think you've gone too far and Hombrey Dr. is on your left going out of town, opposite the tire shop. (☎558-5720. 21+. Open M-Tu 9pm-3am, W-Su 6pm-3am.)

GREAT SMOKY MOUNTAINS ☎865

The largest wilderness area in the eastern US, Great Smoky Mountains National Park encompasses over 500,000 acres of gray-green Appalachian peaks bounded by the misty North Carolina and Tennessee valleys. Black bears, wild hogs, wild turkeys, and salamanders make their home here, along with more than 1500 species of flowering plants. Spring sets the mountains ablaze with wildflowers and azaleas; in June and July, rhododendrons bloom. By mid-October, the mountains are a vibrant quilt of autumnal color. Sadly, the area is not untouched by human presence. Fifty years ago, visitors to Clingman's Dome could see 113 miles; today, poorer air quality has cut visibility to 25 miles and only 14 miles in summer.

✦ 🛈 ORIENTATION AND PRACTICAL INFORMATION

The **Newfound Gap Road (U.S. 441)** is the only road connecting the Tennessee and North Carolina sides of the park. On the Tennessee side, **Gatlinburg** and **Pigeon Forge** lie just outside of the park; both are oppressively touristy, especially in the summer months. **Townsend**, to the west near Cades Cove, is less crowded. In North Carolina, the town of **Cherokee** lies near the park entrance on U.S. 441. **Bryson City**, near the Deep Creek campground, is quieter. The free *Smokies Guide* details the park's tours, lectures, activities, and changing natural graces.

Visitors Centers: Sugarlands (☎ 436-1291), on Newfound Gap Rd. 2 mi. south of Gatlinburg, next to the park's headquarters, shows a 20min. video that provides a concise and exciting introduction to the Smokies. (Every 30min.) There is also an interesting and comprehensive exhibit on regional plants and animals. Open daily June-Aug. 8am-7pm; Apr.-May and Sept.-Oct. 8am-6pm; Mar. and Nov. 8am-5pm; Dec.-Feb. 8am-4:30pm. On the North Carolina side of the park, **Oconaluftee** (☎ 828-497-1900), on U.S. 441 about 2 mi. north of Cherokee, shares its grounds with an outdoor **Mountain Farm Museum** made up of historic buildings relocated from throughout the park in the 1950s. Open daily 8am-7pm; low-season hours vary. Free.

Hotlines: Park Info Line, ☎ 436-1200; www.nps.gov/grsm. Operates daily 8am-4:30pm. **Emergency Hotline,** ☎ 436-1294. **Area Code:** 865; 828 in Bryson City. In text, 865 unless otherwise noted.

🏠 ACCOMMODATIONS

The chain **motels** lining Rte. 441 and Rte. 321 decrease in price with increasing distance from the park. Small motels cluster in both Cherokee and Gatlinburg but nothing is really "budget." Rooms are at least $50 and prices soar on weekends. The best value may be to splurge on a B&B, stay in hostel-style accommodations near the park, or camp within the park itself. Bryson City, NC, about 15min. from the park's main entrance on U.S. 441, offers some options.

Ten **campgrounds** ❶ lie scattered throughout the park, each with tent sites, limited trailer space, water, and bathrooms with flush toilets. There are no showers or hookups. **Smokemont, Elkmont,** and **Cades Cove,** the largest and most popular campgrounds, accept reservations from mid-May to late October. (Sites $17-20 during reservation period; $14 rest of the year.) The other campgrounds are first come, first served; the visitors centers have info about availability. (Sites $12-14.) In summer, reserve spots as early as your travel plans allow. (☎ 800-365-2267, park code GRE; http://reservations.nps.gov. Open daily 10am-10pm.) Cades Cove and Smokemont are open year-round, while the other campgrounds open between March and May and close in October or November. **Backcountry camping** requires a permit, free at ranger stations and visitors centers. Many of the park's 100 primitive backcountry sites require reservations. (☎ 436-1231. Office open daily 8am-6pm.) **The Village General Store,** 9400 Hwy. 19 W, opposite Nantahala Village Lodge, is a good place to stock up on camping supplies and food.

THE SOUTH

Folkestone Inn, 101 Folkestone Rd. (☎828-488-2730 or 888-812-3385; www.folke-stone.com), in Bryson City, near the park. Follow signs for Deep Creek Campground. Rooms with locally-themed decor and a mountain backdrop, most with deck or balcony. Children must be 10 or older. 2-night min. stay on weekends May-Oct. Check-in 3-9pm. Check-out 11am. Be sure to call ahead. Singles $82-132; doubles $88-138. Each extra person $12. ❹

LeConte Lodge (☎429-5704; www.leconte-lodge.com), at the top of Mount LeConte, is the only lodging within the park. Only reached by a minimum 5 mi. hike, the lodge itself is your reward, and the fabulous sunrise at nearby Myrtle Point is a welcome bonus. The Lodge is popular; in the summer, you'll need to reserve months in advance to secure a bed. No electricity, phones, TV, or showers. Open late Mar. to mid-Nov. $83, ages 4-10 $67; prices include 6pm dinner and breakfast. ❹

Charleston Inn, 208 Arlington Ave. (☎828-488-4644; www.charlestoninn.com). From Main St., go past the intersection with Veteran's Blvd. and continue up the hill; it will be on your right. The wood-and-brick house dates back to 1927 and the apartments are from the 1940s, but the well-furnished inn feels very modern. Within walking distance of of Bryson City restaurants. Breakfast included. Rooms with A/C and private baths, most with TV, some with jacuzzi. 2-night min. stay on weekends during peak season. Check-in 3-8pm; call if arriving later. Check-out 11am. Rooms $95-135; cabin $155. ❹

Nantahala Outdoor Center (NOC), 13077 U.S. 19 W (☎800-232-7238), 13 mi. south-west of Bryson City, just south of the park, beckons with cheap beds and 3 restaurants. They also arrange beginner-friendly whitewater rafting on the river that runs through the complex. Hot showers, kitchen, and laundry facilities. Call ahead—it's a great place to base yourself for a day or two of outdoor adventure in the Smokies. Bunks in simple "basecamp" cabins $14. Platform tents $5 per person. ❶

▐ FOOD

▨ **Pizza by the River** (☎828-488-5651), on Hwy. 19, 1½ mi. past Nantahala Outdoor Ctr., 14½ mi. southwest of Bryson City. This roadside stand is a local favorite. Outdoor deck overlooks the waters of the Nantahala. Ask the owner, Abbott, to make what he would eat—it will taste good. Slices $2.50-3 (before 4pm), 12 in. pies $10. If coming by river, look out for the pizza Italian flag or the skull and crossbones on your right as you go downstream. Open Apr. to mid-Oct. Su-Th 11am-10pm, F-Sa 6:30am-10pm. ❷

Mountain Perks, 9 Depot St. (☎828-488-9561), in Bryson City across from the train station. Take Everett St. from Main St.; it will be on the corner on the right, 3 blocks down. Desserts $2-3.25, scrumptious oversized wraps $6.50-11.50, creative coffee drinks $2.50-4, and amazing salads $4.25-6.75. Open M-Sa 7am-4:30pm. ❷

Smokin' Joe's Bar-B-Que, 8303 Rte. 73 (☎448-3212), in Townsend. Authentic Tennessee cookin' is the order of business here. Succulent, slow-cooked meats and home-made side dishes smoke the competition. Dinners ($7-12) come with meat, 2 sides, and bread—enjoy one on the porch next to the river. Sandwiches $2.50-4.50. Beer from $2.50. Open in summer Su-Th 11am-9pm, F-Sa 11am-10pm; low-season hours vary. ❷

Yummi Buffet, 33 Rector St. (☎828-488-1240 or 828-488-4676), in Bryson City. Rector St. is on your left as you enter town from the north. Large portions of authentic Chinese and Japanese food await at this simple restaurant. All-you-can-eat lunch buffet $5.75. Buffet M-Sa 11am-4pm. Open Su-Th 11am-10pm, F-Sa 11am-10:30pm. ❷

▟ OUTDOOR ACTIVITIES

HIKING

Over 900 mi. of hiking trails and 170 mi. of road meander through the park. Trail maps and a guide to area day-hikes are also available at the visitors centers ($1 each). The Great Smokies are known for phenomenal **waterfalls,** and many of the park's most popular hikes culminate in stunning vistas or fantastic views of the surrounding mountains. Less-crowded areas include **Cosby** and **Cataloochee**, both on the eastern edge of the park. *Wherever you go, bring water and don't feed the bears.* **Rainbow Falls** (5½ mi., 4hr. round-trip), accessible from Cherokee Orchard Rd., is the park's most popular hike, a moderate to strenuous hike that reveals the Smokies' highest single-plunge waterfall. About 4 mi. west of Sugarlands Visitors Center on Little River Rd., **Laurel Falls** (2½ mi., 2hr. round-trip) is one of the easier (and more crowded) hikes on the Tennessee side of the park, following a paved trail through a series of cascades before reaching the 60 ft. falls. **Ramsay Cascades** (8 mi., 5hr. round-trip) is a strenuous hike leading to cascades that fall 100 ft. down the mountainside. The trailhead is in the Greenbrier area—from Gatlinburg, the park entrance is 6 mi. east on Hwy. 321. **Chimney Tops** (4 mi., 2hr. round-trip) is a steep scramble leading up to two 4755 ft. rock spires.

BIKING

Biking is permitted along most roads within the park, with the exception of the Roaring Fork Motor Nature Trail. The best opportunities for cyclists are at the **Foothills Parkway, Cades Cove,** and **Cataloochee.** On Wednesday and Saturday mornings from May to September, the 11 mi. Cades Cove Loop is closed to car traffic to allow bicyclists full use of the road from dawn to 10am. While the Smokies boast no mountain biking trails, a few gravel trails in the park, including the **Gatlinburg Trail,** the **Oconaluftee River Trail,** and **Deep Creek** (lower section) allow bicycles. Bike rental is available at **Cades Cove Campground Store.** (☎ 448-9034. $4 per hr., $20 per day. Open June to mid-Aug. daily 9am-7pm; late Aug. M-F 9am-5pm, Sa-Su 9am-7pm; Apr.-May and Sept.-Oct. daily 9am-5pm, no rental after 2:30pm. Bike rental begins W and Sa 7am.) Another option is neighboring **Tsali Recreation Area,** where there are four mountain biking loops available for a small fee. Contact the Cheoah Ranger in the **Nantahala National Forest** for more information (☎ 828-479-6431).

FISHING

Forty species of fish swim in the park's rivers and streams. The Smokies permit fishing in open waters year-round from 30min. before sunrise to 30min. after sunset. All anglers over 12 (over 15 in North Carolina) must possess a valid Tennessee or North Carolina **fishing license.** The park does not sell licenses; check with local chambers of commerce, sports shops, and hardware stores for purchasing information. Visitors centers have a free leaflet and map detailing fishing regulations.

THE BIG SPLURGE

MOUNTAINS OF FUN

A "traditional" Appalachian village created by Dolly Parton dominates Pigeon Forge, the crass commercial center next to Smoky Mountains National Park—though Appalachia has never before looked so full of thrills, and well, so tasty. Dollywood park celebrates the culture of the East Tennessee region and the country songmistress herself, responsible for some mountainous topography of her own. In Dolly's world, craftspeople demonstrate their skills and sell their wares, 30 rides offer chills and thrills, and country singers perform at stages around the park. In "Chasing Rainbows," a great exhibition room on the park's namesake diva, you can even sing a duet with an image of Dolly. Next door, visitors enjoy titanic waves at Dolly's Splash Country. The "tradition" is rather lost amongst the screaming kids and rampant commercialism, but the fun isn't. Don't forget to feast on funnel cakes, a Dollywood speciality—plates piled high with deep-fried something-or-other and covered in heaps of powdered sugar.

Dollywood, 1020 Dollywood Ln. Going east on Hwy. 441, turn left at traffic light 8 in Pigeon Forge. (☎ 865-428-9488; www.dollywood.com. Park open daily Apr.-Dec. 9am-8pm. $40, seniors $37, ages 4-11 $30. Splash Country $29/$25/$24. Parking $6; funnel cakes $4.)

RIDING

Over 500 mi. of the park's trails are open to horses. For travelers with horses, five drive-in **horse camps** provide facilities within the park: **Cades Cove, Big Creek, Cataloochee, Round Bottom,** and **Tow String.** (Reservations required: ☎800-362-2267; http://reservations.nps.gov. Open mid-Mar. to Oct. $20-25 per night.) There are also four **riding stables** offering guided rides on scenic trails. (Cades Cove Riding Stable: ☎448-6286; open mid-Mar. to Oct. Smokemont Riding Stable: ☎828-497-2373; open mid-Apr. to Oct. Smoky Mountain Riding Stable: ☎436-5634; open mid-Mar. to Nov. Sugarlands Horseback Riding Stable: ☎430-5020; open mid-May to Nov. All $20 per hr., age and weight restrictions vary.)

AUTO TOURS

The park offers a number of auto tours, allowing visitors to appreciate diverse wildlife and spectacular vistas without lacing up their hiking boots. The **Cades Cove Loop, Newfound Gap Road,** and **Roaring Fork** auto tours are favorites. Pamphlets and maps are available in the visitors centers ($1 each). The **Cataloochee** auto tour ($0.50) goes through the area where elk have been reintroduced onto the park land. **Walkways** and **nature trails** run from the road and make for enjoyable sidetrips.

▌ DAYTRIP FROM SMOKY MOUNTAINS

CHEROKEE RESERVATION

The **Cherokee Indian Reservation,** on the southeast border of the national park, features a number of museums, shops, attractions, and a 24hr. dry casino, concentrated in the town of Cherokee itself. Three historical attractions stand out. For an in-depth look at the history and traditions of the Cherokee people, visit the **Museum of the Cherokee Indian,** at the corner of Drama Rd. and Tsali Blvd./U.S. 441. (☎828-497-3481; www.cherokeemuseum.org. Open daily June-Aug. 9am-8pm; Sept.-May 9am-5pm. $8, ages 6-13 $5; AAA $7.20/$4; AARP $7.20.) From May to October, the reservation offers tours of the **Oconaluftee Indian Village,** 276 Drama Rd., a recreated mid-18th-century Cherokee village. Tours educate visitors about traditional Cherokee crafts, political organization, and village life. Tours leave every 15min. and last 1½hr. (☎828-497-2315; www.oconalufteevillage.com. Open mid-May to late Oct. daily 9am-5:30pm. $13, ages 6-13 $6. Combination tickets with museum $17/$9. Wheelchair accessible.) **"Unto these Hills,"** an outdoor drama, chronicles the story of the Cherokee people from the arrival of the first European explorers to the Trail of Tears. Emotional as it is, the play's cast of 130 provides a good historical overview from the 1540s to 1838 (with some impressive pyrotechnics to boot). Follow signs from Rte. 441. (☎828-497-2111; www.untothesehills.com. Box office on U.S. 441 in downtown Cherokee. Show mid-June to late Aug. daily 8:30pm, pre-show singing at 7:45pm. Tickets $16, ages 6-13 $8. All reserved seats $18.) For less somber entertainment, roll the dice at **Harrah's Cherokee Casino,** 777 Casino Dr. off of Hwy. 19 N. (☎800-427-7247 or 828-497-7777; www.harrahs.com. 21+. Open 24hr.) More than 2800 games, three restaurants, and an entertainment pavilion should keep you entertained deep into the night. The **Cherokee Visitors Center,** 498 Tsali Blvd./Rte. 441, provides information; follow the signs. (☎800-438-1601 or 828-497-9195; www.cherokee-nc.com. Open mid-June to late Aug. 8:15am-8am; low-season hours vary.)

CHATTANOOGA ☎423

Chattanooga is a city of superlatives and firsts; it is home to the first tow truck ever, the world's largest fresh-water aquarium, the original Coca-Cola bottling factory, and the world's steepest passenger railway. But it was a more traditional type of train that made Chattanooga famous—the city was once a major transportation hub, and builders completed the Terminal Station for the legendary "Chattanooga Choo-Choo" almost a century ago. Technology eventually replaced the train system, but these attractions and other kid-friendly activities around town make Chattanooga an ideal family destination.

◪ PRACTICAL INFORMATION. Chattanooga straddles the Tennessee/Georgia border at the junction of I-24, I-59, and I-75. Downtown, **Lookout Mountain,** and the **Bluff View Art District** compose the town's distinct parts. The **Chattanooga Metropolitan Airport** lies about 5mi. east of downtown. (☎855-2200; www.chattairport.com.) **Greyhound,** 960 Airport Rd. (☎892-1277; open daily 6:30am-9:30pm) sends buses to: Atlanta (2hr., 5 per day, $25); Knoxville (2hr., 3 per day, $19-25); Nashville (3hr., 5 per day, $25). **Chattanooga Area Transportation Authority (CARTA)** operates a free downtown electric shuttle service with stops on every block between the aquarium and the Holiday Inn. (☎629-1473; www.carta-bus.org. Shuttles run every 5min. M-F 6am-9:30pm, Sa 9am-9:30pm, Su 9am-8:30pm. Wheelchair accessible.) **Visitors Center:** 2 Broad St., next to the aquarium. (☎800-322-3344; www.chattanoogafun.com. Discounted attraction tickets and a free city map available. Open daily 8:30am-5:30pm.) **Internet Access: Public Library,** 1001 Broad St., at 10th St. (☎757-5310. Open M-Th 9am-9pm, F-Sa 9am-6pm. Free.) **Post Office:** 900 Georgia Ave., between Martin Luther King Blvd. and 10th St. (☎267-1609. Open M-F 8am-4:30pm.) **Postal Code:** 37402. **Area Code:** 423.

⛏ ACCOMMODATIONS. Budget hotels congregate east of the city on I-24/I-75. There are a few budget chains off **Broad Street,** your best bet for inexpensive lodgings in Chattanooga. The **Ramada Inn Downtown ❸,** 100 W. 21st St., Exit 178B off I-24, has clean, standard rooms in a convenient location. (☎265-3151. A/C, cable TV, HBO, pool, and continental breakfast. Rooms from $59; low-season from $49. AAA, AARP 10% off.) Though a bit on the expensive side, **Chanticleer Inn ❺,** 1300 Mockingbird Ln., down the street from Rock City, is worth every penny. Guests are treated to exceptional hospitality, gorgeous scenery, and a hearty breakfast. The rooms occupy five small stone cottages; some have fireplaces or whirlpool tubs. Three rooms are in the Inn itself. (☎706-820-2002; www.stayatchanticleer.com. Internet access, A/C, cable TV, and pool. Rooms $100-195. AAA discount.) **Best Holiday Trav-L-Park ❶,** 1709 Mack Smith Rd., occupies a Civil War battlefield. From Chattanooga, take I-24 E to I-75 S and turn off at Exit 1. Turn right at the top of the ramp, then left at the next light; it's half a mile down. (☎706-891-9766 or 800-693-2877; www.chattacamp.com. Bathhouse, laundry, playground, game room, and pool access. Sites with 30-amp hookup $26; 50-amp $28; cabins $40. AARP 10% off.) Nearby **Lake Chickamauga** is also surrounded by campgrounds.

◖ FOOD. In the Bluff View Art District, **▨Rembrant's Coffee House ❶,** 204 High St., offers gourmet sandwiches and salads at reasonable prices. The lovely brick patio is the perfect spot to unwind with a good book while sampling the incredible pastries (under $4) or sipping a mug of coffee. (☎265-5033, ext. 3. Sandwiches and salads $3-6. Open M-Th 7am-10pm, F 7am-11:30pm, Sa 8am-11:30pm, Su 8am-10pm.) The **Pickle Barrel ❶,** 1012 Market St., across the parking lot from the public library in downtown, serves satisfying sandwiches ($4.25-6.25) including some good vegetarian options such as the stuffed portobello sandwich ($6) and gourmet daily specials. Choose between the lively downstairs area, with names of past customers carved into the tabletops, and the open-air deck upstairs. (☎266-1103. Spicy black bean burger $5.25. 21+ after 9pm, except families. Open M-Sa 11am-3am, Su noon-3am.) **Jack's Alley** is lined with several places to eat, including **Sticky Fingers ❷,** 420 Broad St., the best place in town for ribs ($13). Enjoy a heaping

THE SOUTH

mound of hickory-smoked barbecue with baked beans and homemade slaw ($9) or a filling salad ($7-8). The $7 Sunday brunch features an all-you-can-eat buffet. When it's busy, grab a seat at the bar to avoid the line for tables. (☎265-7427; www.stickyfingersonline.com. Open daily 11am-10pm.)

◙ **SIGHTS. Downtown Chattanooga,** a small area between 10th St. and the river, is crammed with attractions, shops, and restaurants. The **Tennessee Aquarium,** 1 Broad St., on Ross's Landing, is the largest freshwater aquarium in the world. The aquarium entertains visitors with an IMAX screen, mesmerizing seahorses, and some intensely ugly fish. It also offers the best views over the Tennessee River from its galleries. (☎800-262-0695; www.tnaqua.org. Open in summer M-Th 10am-6pm, F-Su 10am-7:30pm; low-season daily 10am-6pm. $14, ages 3-12 $7.50; IMAX $7.75/$5.25; both $18/$11. 1¼hr. behind-the-scenes tour daily 3pm, $7/$5.) The **International Towing and Recovery Hall of Fame and Museum,** 3315 S. Broad St., chronicles the creation and life of the tow truck. Even if you're not interested in cars, this museum is worth seeing as a testament to human ingenuity. (☎267-3132; www.internationaltowingmuseum.org. Open M-Sa 9am-5pm, Su 11am-5pm. $8, seniors and ages 5-18 $4, under 6 free.) At the **Creative Discovery Museum,** 321 Chestnut St., children can climb, splash and dig through interactive exhibits on everything from music to dinosaurs. (☎756-2738; www.cdmfun.org. $8, ages 2-12 $6, under 2 free. Open M-Tu and Th-Su 9am-5pm; open later Mar.-Aug. Call for seasonal closing times. Last admission 1hr. before close. Wheelchair accessible.)

The **Bluff View Art District** (www.bluffviewartdistrict.com) is a small neighborhood of upscale shops and cafes, anchored by the **Hunter Museum of American Art,** 10 Bluff View Ave., which is currently undergoing a major expansion. From downtown, take 4th St. to High St. and turn left. Exhibits include a contemporary section and a fantastic display of classical American painting, all inside the grand mansion. (☎267-0968; www.huntermuseum.org. Museum expected to re-open in April 2005; call ahead. Wheelchair accessible.) Across the street, the ◙**Houston Museum,** 201 High St., is the life work of Anna Houston, a bit of an eccentric who lived in a barn that she constructed herself. She bequeathed her belongings, including music boxes and an amazing glass collection, to a committee that started a museum in this picturesque house on the banks of the river. To see the exhibits, visitors must join a 45min. tour. (☎267-7176. Open M-F 9:30am-4pm, Sa noon-4pm. $7, children 4-12 $3.50, under 4 free.)

One of the most popular destinations in Chattanooga is **Lookout Mountain.** Take S. Broad St. and follow the signs; the route to the attractions is well-marked. Billed as "America's most amazing mile," the **Incline Railway** is the world's steepest passenger railway, chugging visitors up an insane 72.7% grade to an observation deck. The deck is also accessible by car, allowing you to soak in the incredible views for free. (☎821-4224; www.CARTA-Bus.org. Open daily June-Aug. 8:30am-8:50pm; Mar.-May and Sept.-Oct. 9am-5:15pm; Nov.-Feb. 10am-6pm. One-way $9, round-trip $10; ages 3-12 $4.50/$5.) The nature trail at **Rock City Gardens**—founded by Garnet Carter, the man who invented miniature golf—combines scenic lookouts and narrow rock passages with all-singing, all-dancing elves and strategically placed shops. The expansive view from the observation points reveals seven states on a clear day. (☎706-820-2531 or 800-854-0675; www.seerockcity.com. Open daily Jan.-May 8:30am-5pm, June-Aug. 8:30am-8pm, Sept. to mid-Nov. 8:30am-6pm. Open mid-Nov. to Dec. until 4pm and in evenings 6-9pm for the "Enchanted Garden of Lights." $13, ages 3-12 $7.) One thousand feet inside the mountain, the **Ruby Falls** cavern formations and an impressive 145 ft. waterfall—complete with colored lights and sound effects—add pizzazz to a day of sightseeing, but be prepared to endure long waits and narrow passageways crowded with tourists. (☎821-2544; www.rubyfalls.com. Open daily 8am-8pm. 1hr. tour $13, ages 3-12 $6.) Combination packages for the three attractions are available; inquire at any ticket window.

⬛⬛ ENTERTAINMENT AND NIGHTLIFE. For entertainment listings, check the "Weekend" section of the Friday *Chattanooga Times Free Press* or *The Pulse*, a weekly alternative paper. Most nightlife options are downtown, especially in the area surrounding **Jack's Alley,** from Broad St. to Market St., between 4th and 5th St. There are several bars off the commercialized alley; **Taco Mac's,** 423 Market St., has the best selection with over 50 beers on tap. (☎267-8226. Outdoor seating available. Beer from $2.85. Happy hour M-F 4-7pm. Open M-F 11am-3am, Sa-Su noon-3am.) Nearby, the **Big River Grille and Brewing Works,** 222 Broad St., offers six original beers, plus seasonal ales and lagers. (☎267-2739. Pints $3.25. Happy hour M-F 4-7pm. Pool tables. Live country music Th-Sa. Open Su-Th 11am-12:30am or 1am, F-Sa 11am-2am.) The rooftop bar at the **Tortilla Factory,** 203 W. 2nd St., is a great spot to sip a cold one in nice weather. (☎756-6399. Beer from $3; select beer $2 on Tu. Roof 21+ after 9pm. Bar open nightly 5pm-2:30am; downstairs restaurant open Su-Th 11am-11pm, F-Sa 11am-midnight.) **Rhythm and Brews,** 221 Market St., is the town's best live music venue. (☎267-4644; www.rhythm-brews.com. Beer from $3.25. Open mic W. 21+. Cover $5-20. Usually open W-Sa 8pm-late; music starts around 9:45pm.) **Alan Gold's,** 1100 McCallie Ave., just over the bridge from Central, is a popular gay venue also frequented by straight couples. Only reachable by car, the friendly club includes a couple of bars, a dance floor, lounge areas, and balconies. (☎629-8080. Drag shows Tu-Sa 11:30pm. Cover $5. Open daily 4:30pm-3am.)

The **Chattanooga Lookouts,** a minor league baseball farm team for the Reds, play at the new **BellSouth Park,** at 2nd and Chestnut St. (☎267-2208. Tickets $4-8, seniors and under 12 $2.) For nine nights in June, the riverfront shuts down for live rock, country, blues, jazz, and reggae during the **Riverbend Festival.** (☎756-2211; www.riverbendfestival.com. $24.) The mountains surrounding Chattanooga also offer opportunities for **whitewater rafting;** ask at the visitors center for details.

MEMPHIS   ☎901

Music is the pulse of Memphis, and the reason why most visitors visit the city. However, all the blues, funk, soul, country and rock is entwined with the history of Civil Rights and social change in the United States. Memphis's population swelled in the early 20th century as thousands of cotton workers poured into the city in search of a better life. White farmers brought country music and black workers brought the blues, and their synthesis resulted in a true American melting pot of contemporary musical styles. Beyond this musical phenomenon, however, black and white musicians were playing together and de facto challenging the segregation laws in existence at the time. Today, most visitors make the Memphis pilgrimage to see Graceland, the former home of Elvis Presley and one of the most deliciously tacky spots in the US. There's plenty to do after you've paid your respects to "The King"; unusual museums, fantastic ribs, and live music every night of the week are just some of the reasons you might want to stay a few days.

▇ WHEELS ON MY HEELS

Airport: Memphis International, 2491 Winchester Rd. (☎922-8000; www.mscaa.com), south of the southern loop of I-240. Taxi fare to the city is around $22—negotiate in advance. Operated by MATA, **DASH** runs buses frequently from the airport.

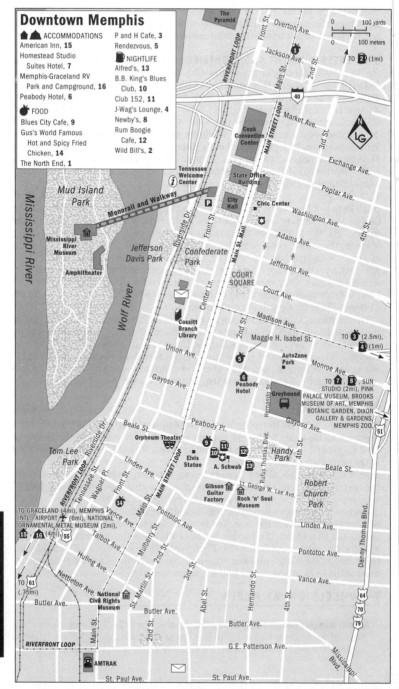

Downtown Memphis

🏠🏠 ACCOMMODATIONS
American Inn, **15**
Homestead Studio
  Suites Hotel, **7**
Memphis-Graceland RV
  Park and Campground, **16**
Peabody Hotel, **6**

🍗 FOOD
Blues City Cafe, **9**
Gus's World Famous
  Hot and Spicy Fried
  Chicken, **14**
The North End, **1**

P and H Cafe, **3**
Rendezvous, **5**

■ NIGHTLIFE
Alfred's, **13**
B.B. King's Blues
  Club, **10**
Club 152, **11**
J-Wag's Lounge, **4**
Newby's, **8**
Rum Boogie
  Cafe, **12**
Wild Bill's, **2**

Trains: Amtrak, 545 S. Main St. (☎526-0052), at G.E. Patterson Ave., on the southern edge of downtown. *The surrounding area can be unsafe.* The Main St. Trolley line runs to the station. Ticket office hours M-F 5am-2:45pm, Sa-Su 5am-6:30am, and daily 9:30pm-midnight. To: **Chicago** (10½hr., 1 per day, $155); **Jackson** (4½hr., 1 per day, $48); **New Orleans** (8½hr., 1 per day, $90).

Buses: Greyhound, 203 Union Ave. (☎523-9253), at 3rd St. downtown. *The area can be unsafe at night.* Open 24hr. To: **Chattanooga** (7-10hr., 4 per day, $41); **Jackson** (4-6hr., 6 per day, $35); **Nashville** (4hr., 13 per day, $32).

Public Transit: Memphis Area Transit Authority, or **MATA** (☎274-6282; www.matatransit.com), corner of Auction Ave. and Main St. Bus routes cover most suburbs but run infrequently (every 30min. at best). Major routes run on Front, 2nd, and 3rd St. Buses run M-F beginning between 4:30 and 6am and stopping between 7 and 11pm, depending on the route. Sa-Su service less frequent. $1.25, transfers $0.10. Refurbished 19th-century **trolley cars** cruise Main St. and the Riverfront. Operate M-Th 6am-11:30pm, F 6am-1am, Sa 9:30am-1am, Su 10am-6pm. Fare $0.60, seniors $0.30, under 5 free. Exact change required. 1-day pass $2.50, 3-day $6. MATA also operates the **Downtown Airport Shuttle (DASH),** which runs between the airport and 9 downtown hotels M-Sa 7:30am-5pm, Su 8:30am-4:30pm. One-way $12, round-trip $20. Info ☎522-1677.

Shuttles: Sun Studio and Graceland both offer free shuttle service between attractions. The Elvis Express, operated by Graceland, runs between Graceland and Beale St. The Sun Studio shuttle transports travelers between Graceland, Sun Studio, and the Rock'n'Soul museum, departing from the Rock'n'Soul Museum every hr. on the ½hr. from 11:30am-6:30pm, 7 days a week. Call attractions for further info. (☎531-0664; www.sunstudio.com.)

Taxi: City Wide ☎722-8294. **Yellow Cab** ☎577-7700. Expect a long wait.

⚓🔒 ON THE SOUTH SIDE, HIGH UP ON THE RIDGE

Downtown, named avenues run east-west and numbered ones run north-south. **Madison Avenue** divides north and south addresses. Two main thoroughfares, **Poplar** and **Union Avenue,** are east-west; **2nd** and **3rd Street** are the major north-south routes downtown. **I-240** and **I-55** encircle the city. **Riverside Drive** takes you to U.S. 61, which becomes **Elvis Presley Boulevard** and leads south straight to Graceland. **Midtown,** east of downtown, is home to the funky music scene and gay venues, and is a break from the tourist attractions (and tourist traps) of **Beale Street.**

Visitor Info: Tennessee Welcome Center, 119 Riverside Dr. (☎543-5333; www.memphistravel.com), at Jefferson St. Open daily 7am-11pm. The **blue suede brigade**—easily identified by their blue-and-white uniforms—roams the city and will happily give directions or answer questions.

Hotlines: Crisis Line, ☎274-7477. **Gay/Lesbian Switchboard,** ☎ 278-4297. Both 24hr.

Internet Access: Cossitt Branch Public Library, 33 S. Front St. (☎526-1712), downtown at Monroe. Open M-F 10am-5pm. Farther away but with longer hours, the **Main Library** is at 3030 Poplar Ave. (☎415-2700). Open M-Th 9am-9pm, F-Sa 9am-6pm, Su 1-5pm. Free. **Empire Coffee,** 2 S. Main at the corner of Madison, downtown, also has access. (☎526-1646. Open M-F 5:30am-10pm, Sa-Su 7am-10pm. $2.50 per 15min.)

Post Office: 1 N. Front St. (☎576-2037) Open M-F 8:30am-5pm. **Postal Code:** 38103. 555 S. 3rd St. (☎521-2559). Open M-F 8:30am-5:30pm, Sa 10am-2pm. **Postal Code:** 38101. **Area Code:** 901.

🏠 HEARTBREAK HOTEL

A few downtown motels have prices in the budget range; more budget lodgings are available near Graceland at **Elvis Presley Boulevard** and **Brooks Road.** For the celebrations of Elvis's historic birth (Jan. 8) and death (Aug. 16), as well as for the Memphis in May festival, book rooms six months to one year in advance.

American Inn, 3265 Elvis Presley Blvd. (☎345-8444), Exit 5B off I-55, close to Graceland. Despite its shabby exterior, you can't help falling in love with the large, clean, comfy rooms and the Elvis-themed mural in the lobby. Cable TV, A/C, pool, and continental breakfast. Singles $35; doubles $46. ❷

Homestead Studio Suites Hotel, 6500 Poplar Ave. (☎767-5522). Though about 16 mi. from downtown, these impeccably clean rooms come with a full kitchen, data ports, and access to laundry facilities–visitors will feel like they are living in their own apartment. The surrounding area also offers plenty of dining options. Rooms $60-85. Weekly rates $50-60 per night. AAA, AARP discounts. ❸

The Peabody Hotel, 149 Union Ave. (☎529-4000 or 800-732-2639; www.peabodymemphis.com). Known as one of the mid-South's grandest hotels since 1869, the Peabody has hosted the likes of William Faulkner, Charles Lindbergh, Presidents Andrew Johnson and William McKinley, and, of course, the famous Peabody Ducks. Singles from $199; doubles from $229. ❺

Memphis-Graceland RV Park and Campground, 3691 Elvis Presley Blvd. (☎396-7125 or 866-571-9236), beside the Heartbreak Hotel, a 2min. walk from Graceland. No privacy, but the location is great. Pool, laundry facilities, and free shuttle to Beale St. Advance reservations recommended. Sites $22, with water and electricity $31, full hookup $34; cabins $33 for 2 people, each additional person $4. ❶

🏰 MEALS FIT FOR THE KING

In Memphis, barbecue is as common as rhinestone-studded jumpsuits; the city even hosts the **World Championship Barbecue Cooking Contest** in May. Don't fret if gnawing on ribs isn't your thing—Memphis has plenty of other Southern restaurants with down-home favorites like fried chicken, catfish, chitlins, and grits.

Rendezvous, 52 S. 2nd St. (☎523-2746; www.hogsfly.com). The entrance is around back on Maggie H. Isabel St., in the alley opposite the Peabody Hotel. A Memphis legend, serving large portions of charcoal-broiled ribs ($16), cheese and sausages ($7.50), Greek salads ($7.25), and cheaper sandwiches ($3-6.50); look for the long line. Open Tu-Th 4:30-11pm, F 11:30am-11:30pm, Sa noon-11:30pm. ❸

The North End, 346 N. Main St. (☎526-0319; www.thenorthendonline.com), at Jackson Ave., downtown on the trolley line. Serves delicious tamales, wild rice, stuffed potatoes, and creole dishes (all $3-11) in a relaxed, friendly atmosphere. The hot fudge pie is known as "sex on a plate" ($3.75), and there are over 270 beers. Sandwiches on home-baked bread $5-9. Happy hour daily 4-7pm. Live music Th-Su 8pm; karaoke Th 10pm. Pool tables. Open daily 11am-3am. ❷

P and H Cafe, 1532 Madison Ave. (☎726-0906; www.pandhcafe.com). The initials stand for Poor and Hungry; this "beer joint of your dreams" grills food for wallet-watchers. The waitresses and kitschy decor are the real draw–Mona Lisa and Elvis look down on you as you feast on fabulous stuffed burgers and drink beer from frosty glasses. During Elvis Week in Aug., P and H hosts the famous "Dead Elvis Ball," with impersonators and live bands. Sandwiches $3-6. M live music; Tu trivia night; W featured artist; Th theater group night; Sa local singer-songwriters. Open M-F 11am-3am, Sa 5pm-3am. ❶

Blues City Cafe, 138 Beale St. (☎526-3637; www.bluescitycafe.com). Chef Bonnie Mack serves cheap tamales ($6) and huge ribs ($15). President Clinton ate here once, but the crowd is usually more modest. All receive friendly service and a great meal in this authentic Beale St. hangout. Open Su-Th 11am-3am, F-Sa 11am-5am. ❷

Gus's World Famous Hot and Spicy Fried Chicken, 310 S. Front St. (☎527-4877), downtown. Wonderfully fresh chicken in an unpretentious atmosphere. The real deal for lunch. Open M-Th 11am-9pm, F-Sa 11am-10:30pm, Su noon-7pm. ❷

👓 GOODNESS, GRACIOUS, GREAT BALLS OF FIRE!

▓ **GRACELAND.** The best strategy for visiting Elvis Presley's home is to know what you want to get out of it before you go, since once you're there it's easy to be subsumed by the crowds. The **Graceland Mansion** itself can be seen in about 2hr.; it takes a whole day to visit the array of secondary shops, museums, and restaurants. The crush of tourists swarms in a delightful orgy of gaudiness around the tackiest mansion in the US. You'll never forget the faux-fur furnishings, mirrored ceilings, green shag carpeting-covered walls, ostrich-feather pillows, and yellow-and-orange decor of Elvis's 1974 renovations. A blinding sheen of hundreds of gold and platinum records illuminates the **Trophy Building,** where exhibits discuss Elvis's stint in the army and his more than 30 movie roles. The King is buried in the adjacent **Meditation Gardens.** Admission includes an audio tour; proceed through the exhibits at your own pace. *(3763 Elvis Presley Blvd. Take I-55 S to Exit 5B or bus #43 "Elvis Presley." ☎ 332-3322 or 800-238-2000. The website www.elvis.com contains info on Graceland as well as all peripheral attractions. Ticket office open Mar.-Oct. M-Sa 9am-5pm, Su 10am-4pm; Nov.-Feb. M and W-Su 10am-4pm Attractions remain open 2hr. after ticket office closes. Mansion closed Tu. $18, students and ages 62 and up $17, children ages 7-12 $7. Parking $2. Trophy Building and Meditation Gardens wheelchair accessible; mansion partially accessible.)*

MORE ELVIS. If you love him tender, love him true, then visit the peripheral Elvis attractions across the street from the mansion. **Walk a Mile in My Shoes,** a free 20min. film screened every 30min., traces Elvis's career from the early (slim) years through the later (fat) ones. The **Elvis Presley Automobile Museum** houses a fleet of Elvis-mobiles including pink and purple Cadillacs and motorized toys aplenty. *($8, students and ages 62 and up $7.20, children 7-12 $4. Wheelchair accessible.)* Visitors to **Elvis's Custom Jets** can walk through the King's private plane, the *Lisa Marie,* complete with a blue suede bed and with a gold-plated seatbelt, and peek into the tiny *Hound Dog II* Jetstar. *($7, seniors $6.30, children $3.50. Not wheelchair accessible.)* The **Sincerely Elvis** exhibit offers a glimpse into Elvis's private side, displaying his wedding announcements, a collection of Lisa Marie's toys, and items from his wild wardrobe, as well as memorabilia and heaps of fan letters. *($6, seniors $5.40, children $3. Wheelchair accessible.)* The **Platinum Tour Package** discounts admission to the mansion and attractions. *($27, students and seniors $25, ages 7-12 $13.)*

Every year during the week of August 16 (the date of Elvis's death), millions of the King's devotees get all shook up for **Elvis Week,** an extended celebration that includes trivia contests, a fashion show, and a candlelight vigil. The festivities attract Elvis impersonators from around the world. The days surrounding his birthday, January 8, are ushered in with speeches by local politicians and birthday cake.

MUSIC: THE MEMPHIS HEARTBEAT. No visit to Memphis is complete without a visit to ▓**Sun Studio,** where rock 'n' roll was conceived. In this legendary one-room recording studio, Elvis was discovered, Johnny Cash walked the line, and Jerry Lee Lewis was consumed by great balls of fire. Tours go through a small museum area and proceed to the studio itself, where visitors listen to the recording sessions that earned the studio its fame. *(706 Union Ave. ☎ 800-441-6249; www.sunstudio.com. Open daily 10am-6pm. 35min. tours every hr. on the ½hr. $9.50, under 12 free; AAA discount.)* Long before Sam Phillips and Sun Studio produced Elvis and Jerry Lee Lewis, historic **Beale Street** saw the invention of the blues and the soul hits of the Stax label. At the must-see ▓**Rock 'n' Soul Museum** the numerous artifacts on display include celebrity stage costumes and B.B. King's famous guitar, "Lucille." Best of all, the audio tour contains a hundred complete songs, from early blues classics to Isaac Hayes's *Shaft* theme song. The museum also provides an account of rock 'n' roll's origins, from the cotton fields to the coming together of black and

THE SOUTH

white music. *(Opposite 145 Lt. George W. Lee Ave., 1 block south of Beale St.* ☎*543-0800; www.memphisrocknsoul.org. Open daily 10am-6pm. $8.50, ages 60 and up $7.50, ages 5-17 $5; audio tour included. Wheelchair accessible.)* The **Gibson Guitar Factory,** in the same building, offers tours detailing the various stages of the guitar-making process, and the loving way the guitars are individually crafted. The factory produces about 35 guitars each day. The tour lasts longer than the advertised 25min.—bank on at least 40min. *(*☎*544-7998, ext. 4080; www.gibsonmemphis.com. Su-W 1 and 2pm, Th-Sa every hr. 11am-2pm. $10; ages 12 and up only.)*

UNIQUE MUSEUMS. On April 4, 1968, Dr. Martin Luther King, Jr. was assassinated at the **Lorraine Motel** in Memphis. Today, the powerful ◪**National Civil Rights Museum** occupies the original building. Relive the courageous struggle of the Civil Rights movement through photographs, videos, and interviews in this moving exhibit, which ends in Dr. King's motel room. *(450 Mulberry St.* ☎*521-9699; www.civilrightsmuseum.org. Open June-Aug. M and W-Sa 9am-6pm, Su 1-6pm; Sept.-May M and W-Sa 9am-5pm, Su 1-5pm. $11, students with ID and ages 55 and up $9, ages 4-17 $7.50. Free M after 3pm. 1hr. audio tours included with admission; children's version available. Audio tapes may be suspended during busy times.)* South of downtown, the ◪**National Ornamental Metal Museum,** the only institution of its kind in the US, displays fine metalwork from international artists. Get a better idea of the artistic process at the working blacksmith shop behind the museum, alongside a sculpture garden overlooking the impressive Mississippi River. Check out the front gate as you walk in. *(374 Metal Museum Dr. Exit 12C from I-55.* ☎*774-6380; www.metalmuseum.org. Open Tu-Sa 10am-5pm, Su noon-5pm. $4, ages 62 and up $3, students $2.)* The **Pink Palace Museum and Planetarium** is a child-oriented science and history museum housed in a grand (and yes, pink) mansion. Visitors are treated to a bit of Memphis history, an IMAX theater, planetarium shows, and some funky exhibits, including a shrunken head display. The mansion was originally built as the dream home of Clarence Saunders, founder of the Piggly-Wiggly supermarket chain, who relinquished the house after losing his fortune on Wall Street. *(3050 Central Ave.* ☎*320-6362; www.memphismuseums.org. Open M-Th 9am-5pm, F-Sa 9am-9pm, Su noon-6pm. $8, ages 60 and up $7.50, children 3-12 $5.50; IMAX film $7.50/$7/$6; planetarium show $4.25/$3.75/$3.75. Combo tickets $17/$16/$13. Wheelchair accessible.)*

OVERTON PARK. The **Brooks Museum of Art,** in the southwest corner of Overton Park east of downtown, showcases a diverse collection of paintings and decorative art and features visiting exhibits. On the first Wednesday of each month, the museum hosts a celebration (6-9pm, $5) with food, films, live music, and drinks. *(1934 Poplar Ave.* ☎*544-6200; www.brooksmuseum.org. Open Tu-F 10am-4pm, Sa 10am-5pm, Su 11:30am-5pm, first W of each month 10am-9pm. $6, ages 65 and up $5, students with ID and ages 7-17 $2; W usually free. Audio tour $3/$2/$2. Wheelchair accessible.)* Also in the park, the small but impressive **Memphis Zoo** is one of four places in the US where you can see giant pandas; however, the cuddly endangered species will cost you an extra $3. Kids will enjoy the sea lion show (daily 10:30am and 2:30pm) or taking a spin on the carousel. *(2000 Prentis Pl.* ☎*276-9453; www.memphiszoo.org. Open daily Mar.-Oct. 9am-6pm, June-Aug. Sa until 9pm; Nov.-Feb. daily 9am-5pm; last admission 1hr. before close. $10, ages 60 and up $9, ages 2-11 $6. Parking $3. Tram tour $1. Wheelchair accessible.)*

MUD ISLAND RIVER PARK. A quick walk or monorail ride over the Mississippi to **Mud Island** allows you to stroll and splash along the **River Walk,** a scale model of the Mississippi River the length of five city blocks that's sure to impress anyone interested in maps. Free tours of the River Walk run several times daily. Also on the island, the **Mississippi River Museum** charts the history and culture of the river over the past 10,000 years with videos, musical recordings, and life-sized replicas of steamboats and ironclads. *(Monorail leaves from 125 N. Front St. every 10min., round-trip $2; pedestrian bridge free.* ☎576-7241 or 800-507-6507; www.mudisland.com. Park open June-Aug. daily 10am-8pm; Mar.-May and Sept.-Oct. Tu-Su 10am-5pm. Last admission 1hr. before close. 3-5 tours daily. Museum $8, ages 60 and up $6, children 5-12 $5. Wheelchair accessible.) Visitors can also paddle around on the Mississippi or pedal through the streets of downtown Memphis. *(1hr. kayak rental $15 for 1 person, for 2 people $20; 1hr. canoe for 2 people $20. Bike rental $10 per hr.)* The newest feature is the **Sleep Out on the Mississippi,** scheduled for the second Friday of each month during the summer. Though it may sound like a form of political protest, it's actually a camping excursion under the stars with dinner, music, kayaks, and breakfast provided. *(Reserve in advance. Info or reservations* ☎576-7241 or 800-507-6507. Bring your own sleeping bag. $40 per person.)

PARKS AND GARDENS. The 96-acre **Memphis Botanic Garden,** with 22 distinct gardens, is the perfect place to take a long stroll. Relish the fantastic 57-variety rose garden, the sensory garden, or the peaceful Japanese garden. *(750 Cherry Rd., in Audubon Park off Park Ave.* ☎685-1566; www.memphisbotanicgarden.com. Open Mar.-Oct. M-Sa 9am-6pm, Su 11am-6pm; Nov.-Feb. M-Sa 9am-4:30pm, Su 11am-4:30pm. $5, ages 62 and up $4, children 3-12 $3, under 2 free. Wheelchair accessible.) Across Park Ave., the **Dixon Gallery and Gardens** flaunts an impeccable garden accented with an impressive range of sculptures, and a collection of European art with works by masters including Renoir, Degas, and Monet. *(4339 Park Ave.* ☎761-2409 or 761-5250; www.dixon.org. Open Tu-F 10am-4pm, Sa 10am-5pm, Su 1-5pm. $5, ages 60 and up $4, students and children free.)

🎵 🎸 SHAKE, RATTLE, AND ROLL

W.C. Handy's 1917 "Beale St. Blues" claims that "You'll find that business never closes 'til somebody gets killed." Today's visitors are more likely to encounter the Hard Rock Cafe and all the mega-commercialism that comes with it than the rough-and-tumble juke joints of old. Despite all the change, the strip between 2nd and 4th St. is still the place visitors come for live music. Few clubs have set closing times. On Friday nights, a $15 wristband lets you wander in and out of any club on the strip, except Alfred's. Save a few bucks by buying a drink at one of the many outdoor stands and soaking up the blues and acrobatics of street performers. The free *Memphis Flyer* and the "Playbook" section of the Friday morning *Memphis Commercial Appeal* can tell you what's goin' down in town.

BEALE STREET BLUES

By week, Beale St. is a great place to enjoy a quiet beer, but come the weekend, you'll find people cartwheeling down the street. While some bars are frequented by a spring-break-style crowd and feature music that is more L.A. than Memphis, older (and pricier) standbys feature the local music that made Beale St. famous.

Rum Boogie Cafe, 182 Beale St. (☎528-0150). One of the first clubs on Beale St., Rum Boogie still rocks with homegrown blues and a friendly ambience. Check out the celebrity guitars hanging from the ceiling and the original Stax Records sign. Live music Su-Th 8pm, F-Sa 9pm. Happy hour M-F 5-7pm. 21+ Su-Th after 9pm, F-Sa after 8pm. Cover M-Th after 8pm $3, F-Sa after 9pm $5. Open daily 11am-2am.

Club 152, 152 Beale St. (☎544-7011). One of the most popular clubs on Beale, offering 3 floors of dancing and drinks. Live music acts range from blues to techno; on weekends DJs spin dance and techno upstairs. Check out the "mood elevator," a wildly painted elevator that takes you to hip-hop (F 2nd fl.), techno (Sa 3rd fl.), and beyond. Beer from $3. 21+. Cover Th $3, F $5-8, Sa $5-10. Open M-W 6pm-3am, Th-Sa 6pm-5am, Su 7pm-2am; in winter closed M-Tu.

B.B. King's Blues Club, 143 Beale St. (☎524-5464; www.bbkingsclub.com). The laid-back atmosphere and live blues bands make this place a popular joint for locals, visitors, and celebrities alike. B.B. himself still shows up for some meals, and occasionally plays a show. If you can't quite make it inside, there's a little bar just outside on the street, a great place to watch Beale St. go by. Entrees $7-19. Cover $5-7, when B.B. plays $50-150. Open Su-Th 10am-1:30am, F-Sa 10am-3am.

Alfred's, 197 Beale St. (☎525-3711; www.alfreds-on-beale.com), is a favorite with locals and offers karoake, live music, and DJs spinning hip-hop into the wee hours. Outdoor patio. 21+ after 10pm. Cover F-Sa $5. Open Su-Th 11am-3am, F-Sa 11am-5am. *Alfred's does not accept the $15 wristbands accepted by the rest of Beale St.*

NIGHTLIFE OFF BEALE STREET

For a collegiate climate, try the **Highland Street** strip near **Memphis State University.** The city's gay bars are in **Midtown;** take the Main St. trolley down Madison to the end of the line by J-Wag's and progress from there. *This area can be unsafe after dark.* Ask any bar to call you a cab to your next place. For info on gay clubs and happenings, *Triangle Journal News* can be found in any gay venue.

Newby's, 539 S. Highland St. (☎452-8408; www.newbysmemphis.com), is a dark, loud, lively college bar with pool tables, comfy red booths, and an outdoor patio. Live bands play everything from rock to reggae almost every night beginning at 10pm. Beer from $3. Happy hour daily 3-10pm daily. 21+. Cover usually $3-5. Open daily 3pm-3am.

Wild Bill's, 1580 Vollintine Ave. (☎726-5473), a neighborhood restaurant and music joint, lies off the beaten track. This small, dark hole-in-the-wall stands in stark contrast to the touristed, trendy places downtown. Live music F-Sa 11pm, Su 10pm. Cover F-Su $5. Open M-Th 7am-11pm, F-Su 7am-late.

J-Wag's Lounge, 1268 Madison (☎725-1909), is a relaxed gay- and straight-friendly bar with pool, darts, and several drink specials including $1.75 long-necks during happy hour daily 10am-7pm. Several years ago, J-Wag's was featured in the movie *The People vs. Larry Flynt* and you can recognize the stage today. Drag shows F-Sa 3am. Cover F-Sa midnight-4am $3. Open 24hr.

ENTERTAINMENT

The majestic **Orpheum Theatre,** 203 S. Main St., hosts Broadway shows and big-name performers. On Fridays during the summer months, the grand old theater shows classic movies with an organ prelude and a cartoon. (☎525-3000; www.orpheum-memphis.com. Box office open M-F 9am-5pm and before shows. Movies 7:15pm; $6, children under 12 and seniors $5. Concerts and shows $15-55; $3 booking fee except on day of show.) Just as things are really beginning to heat up in the South, the legendary **Memphis in May** celebration hits the city, continuing throughout the month with concerts, art exhibits, food contests, and sporting events. (☎525-4611; www.memphisinmay.org.) One such event is the **Beale Street Music Festival,** featuring some of the biggest names from a range of musical genres. There's also the **World Championship Barbecue Cooking Contest** and the **Sunset Symphony,** a concert by the river given by the Memphis Symphony Orchestra.

▶ DAYTRIP FROM MEMPHIS

THE MISSISSIPPI DELTA

South of Memphis, U.S. 61 runs to Vicksburg through the swamps and flatlands of the Mississippi Delta region, where cotton was king and the blues were born. African American farm workers drew strength from a music they created, a blend of African tribal songs, gospel, and work chants. Here, cotton fields are juxtaposed with glittering casinos, a testament to the changing times. The helpful staff of the

Tunica Visitor Center on U.S. 61 S, just across the Mississippi border, provides maps of the region. (☎662-363-3800 or 888-488-6422; www.tunicamiss.com. Open M-F 8:30am-5pm, Sa 10am-5pm, Su 1-5pm.) Tunica is a major center for gambling and casinos, several of which constitute a resort area along the Mississippi shore.

Playwright Tennessee Williams was raised in **Clarksdale, MS,** 70 mi. south of Memphis in the heart of the Delta, and many of his writings are based on his experiences growing up in the area. Housed in an old train depot, the **Delta Blues Museum,** 1 Blues Alley, off 3rd St. at the intersection of John Lee Hooker Ln., displays regional artwork, photographs, and rare Delta artifacts, including harmonicas owned by Sonny Boy Williamson and a guitar fashioned by ZZ Top from a log cabin Muddy Waters once lived in. (☎662-627-6820; www.deltabluesmuseum.org. Call to inquire about special events and exhibits. Open Mar.-Oct. M-Sa 9am-5pm; Nov.-Feb. M-Sa 10am-5pm. $6, ages 6-12 $3.) Take a minute to walk over to ▓**Ground Zero ❶,** 0 Blues Alley, for a plate lunch complete with beverage, cornbread, and dessert for only $7. The vegetables, including okra, turnip greens, and purple peas, are excellent. From Wednesday through Saturday, stay late for local tunes. (☎662-621-9009; www.groundzerobluesclub.com. Open for lunch M-Sa 11am-2pm; for dinner W-F 5pm-1am, Sa 6pm-1am.) For some of the area's best barbecue, try **Abe's ❷,** 616 State St., where a pulled pork sandwich is only $3 and ribs cost $10. (☎662-624-9947. Open M-Th 10am-9pm, F-Sa 10am-10pm, Su 11am-2pm.)

On U.S. 49, across the river in Arkansas, lies **Helena,** the site of a major defeat for the Confederate army on July 4, 1863. Mark Twain called Helena "one of the prettiest situations on the river," and it's hard to argue if you take the boardwalk out to the water's edge in the **Helena Reach River Park.** (☎870-338-9831. Open daily 6am-9pm. Free.) The legendary King Biscuit Time Blues radio show was first broadcast here in 1941. You can relive it every weekday at 12:15pm in the **Delta Cultural Center,** 141 Cherry St., which also displays exhibits on "Delta Sounds" and the history of the Civil War in the region. (☎870-338-4350 or 800-358-0972; www.deltaculturalcenter.com. Open Tu-Sa 9am-5pm. Free.) The first weekend of October, the town hosts the **King Biscuit Blues Festival,** the largest free blues festival in the South.

NORTH CAROLINA

North Carolina conjures images of fields of tobacco, pastel sunsets, and rocking chairs on porches—and these generalizations aren't far from the truth. Travelers, however, won't want to just sit around sipping sweet tea. Outdoorsy types revel in the awesome landscapes and laid-back culture of the western mountains, where thrill-seekers can find snowboarding, mountain-biking, and whitewater-rafting opportunities galore. The central Piedmont region combines the cosmopolitanism of the North with the South's slower pace, and is filled with cultural activities and important historical sights. There's no denying the marked diversity of the state; North Carolina is home to some of the nation's top universities, the country's second-largest financial center, and gorgeous beaches. One thing can be said for the whole of the "Tarheel State"—natural beauty and southern hospitality are the rule.

▟ PRACTICAL INFORMATION

Capital: Raleigh.

Visitor Info: Dept. of Commerce, Travel and Tourism, 301 N. Wilmington St., Raleigh 27601 (☎919-733-8372 or 800-847-4862; www.visitnc.com). **Division of Parks and Recreation,** 512 N. Salisbury St., Archdale Building 7th fl., Room 732 (☎919-733-4181; parkinfo@ncmail.net).

Postal Abbreviation: NC. **Sales Tax:** 7%.

THE TRIANGLE ☎919

Clustered in the northern Piedmont region, The Triangle is comprised of Raleigh, Durham, and Chapel Hill. In the 1950s the three towns were united by the creation of the spectacularly successful Research Triangle Park—a research hub responsible for inventions as inspiring as the AIDS drug AZT and as down-to-earth as Astroturf. **Raleigh,** the state capital and home to North Carolina State University (NC State), is a historic town with recently revamped its tourist attractions. **Durham,** formerly a major tobacco producer, now supports medical research projects devoted to finding cancer cures. It is also the site of Duke University. The University of North Carolina (UNC), chartered in 1789 as the nation's first state university, is located down the road in **Chapel Hill.** College culture infuses all three cities with a hot music scene, popular bars, and interesting stores.

TRANSPORTATION

Airport: Raleigh-Durham International (☎840-2123; www.rdu.com), 10 mi. southeast of Durham and 10 mi. northwest of Raleigh, between U.S. 70 and I-40 on Aviation Blvd. From Durham, take Exit 284B from I-40E or Exit 292 from U.S. 70E. From Raleigh, take Exit 285 from I-40W or Exit 292 from U.S. 70W. A taxi to downtown Raleigh or Durham costs about $30; continuing on to Chapel Hill will cost about $35. Triangle Transit Authority has shuttle service from RDU to surrounding areas; see **Public Transit** below.

Trains: Amtrak, 320 W. Cabarrus St., Raleigh (☎833-7594), 4 blocks west of the Civic Ctr. Open 24hr. To: **Durham** (30min., 2 per day, $4-7); **New York City** (10hr., 2 per day, $84-108); **Richmond** (3½hr., 1 per day, $22-51); **Washington, D.C.** (5½hr., 1 per day, $34-80). In Durham, the station is at 400 W. Chapel Hill St. (☎956-7932). Open daily 7am-9pm. To **Raleigh** (40min., 2 per day, $4-7).

Buses: Greyhound has stations in both Raleigh and Durham. Raleigh: 314 W. Jones St. (☎834-8275). Open 24hr. To: **Chapel Hill** (1¼hr., 4 per day, $13); **Charleston** (7½hr., 3 per day, $49-58); **Durham** (40min., 10 per day, $7). Durham: 820 W. Morgan St. (☎687-4800), 1 block off Chapel Hill St. downtown, 2½ mi. northeast of Duke. Open daily 7:30am-10:30pm. To **Chapel Hill** (25min., 4 per day, $8.50) and **Washington, D.C.** (6hr., 8½hr. during morning rush hour; 6 per day; $49-52).

Public Transit: Triangle Transit Authority (☎549-9999; www.ridetta.org). Buses run approximately M-F 6am-10pm, Sa 7am-6:30pm. $1.50. **Capital Area Transit,** Raleigh (☎828-7228). Buses run M-Sa 5am-10:30pm. $0.75, transfers free. **Durham Area Transit Authority (DATA),** Durham (☎683-3282; www.ci.durham.nc.us/departments/works/data.cfm.) Most routes start downtown at 521 Morgan St. Operates daily; hours vary by route; fewer on Su. $1; seniors, under 18, and disabled $0.50; children under 5 free; transfers free. There is also a free shuttle between Duke's east and west campuses (☎684-2218). **Chapel Hill Transit,** Chapel Hill (☎968-2769; www.townofchapelhill.org/transit). Buses run M-F 6am-7pm, Sa-Su 7am-6pm. Free.

Taxi: Cardinal Cab ☎828-3228. Serves all three cities.

PRACTICAL INFORMATION

Visitor Info: All three of the Triangle cities' visitors centers provide brochures, visitor's guides to the cities, maps, and helpful advice. **Capital Area Visitor Center,** 301 N. Blount St. in Raleigh (☎834-5900 or 800-849-8499; www.visitraleigh.com). Open M-F 8am-5pm,

Sa 10am-5pm, Su 1-4pm. **Durham Convention and Visitors Bureau,** 101 E. Morgan St. (☎687-0288 or 800-446-8604; www.durham-nc.com). Open M-F 8:30am-5pm, Sa 10am-2pm. **Chapel Hill Visitors Bureau,** 501 W. Franklin St., near Carrboro (☎968-2060 or 888-968-2062; www.chocvb.org). Open M-F 8:30am-5pm, Sa 10am-2pm.

Hotlines: Rape Crisis, ☎683-8628. 24hr.

Internet Access: The public libraries in all three cities provide 1hr. free Internet access. Bring identification for a visitor's library card. **North Regional Library,** 200 Horizon Dr. in Raleigh (☎870-4000). Take Exit 8 from the Rt. 440 beltline, head north on Six Forks Rd., then turn left on Horizon Dr. Open M-F 9am-9pm, Sa 10am-5pm, Su 1pm-5pm. **Durham County Public Library,** 300 N. Roxboro St. in Durham, near the visitors center (☎560-0100). Open M-Th 9am-9pm, F 9am-6pm, Sa 9:30am-6pm; also open Aug.-May Su 2-6pm. **Chapel Hill Public Library,** 100 Library Rd. (☎968-2777). From the university, go down Franklin St. toward Durham. Turn left on Estes St.; it's on your right. Open M-Th 10am-9pm, F 10am-6pm, Sa 9am-6pm, Su 1-8pm.

Post Office: 311 New Bern Ave., **Raleigh** (☎832-1604). Open M-F 8am-5:30pm, Sa 8am-noon. **Postal Code:** 27611. **Durham:** 323 E. Chapel Hill St. (☎683-1976). Open M-F 8:30am-5pm. **Postal Code:** 27701. **Chapel Hill:** 125 S. Estes St. (☎967-6297). Open M-F 8:30am-5:30pm, Sa 8:30am-noon. **Postal Code:** 27514. **Area Code:** 919.

▐ ACCOMMODATIONS

Budget lodging in Raleigh surrounds the major exits to the 440 beltline, especially at **Glenwood Ave., Forest Rd.,** and **Capital Blvd.** In Durham, economy motels line **I-85,** especially between Exits 173 and 175, north of the Duke campus. Mid-range motels can be found at the intersection of **I-40** and **U.S. 15/501** in Chapel Hill.

Homestead Suites, 4810 Bluestone Dr. (☎510-8551; www.homesteadhotels.com), off Glenwood Ave. in Raleigh just northwest of Crabtree Valley Mall, has new, comfortable rooms with full kitchens, A/C, cable TV, and free local calls. Free access to local gym. Internet access available for a fee. Laundry facilities and extensive room service available. Queen $46; 2 queen beds or king with pull-out couch $56; for stays of a week or longer, nightly rates drop to $36/$46. ❷

Best Value Carolina Duke Inn, 2517 Guess Rd. (☎286-0771 or 800-438-1158), just off I-85 at Exit 175 in Durham, has clean rooms with laundry facilities, pool, A/C, cable TV. Free local calls and continental breakfast. Doubles have fridges and microwaves. DATA bus access across the street; free shuttle to RDU. Wheelchair accessible. Singles $40-43; doubles $48; family rooms $60. 10% AARP/AAA discount. ❷

Hampton Inn, 1740 U.S. 15/501 (☎968-3000, www.hamptoninn.com/hi/chapelhill), 1 mi. south of I-40 Exit 270 near Chapel Hill, includes free continental breakfast, a pool, and access to town via the 15/501. Singles $59-89; doubles $64-99; with rates highest in summer and during college move-in (mid-Aug.) and move-out (mid-May). ❹

Falls Lake State Recreation Area, 13304 Creedmoor Rd. (☎676-1027; www.ils.unc.edu/parkproject/visit/fala/home.html), about 10 mi. north of Raleigh, off Rte. 98 1 mi. north of NC 50. Falls Lake has 4 campgrounds. The main campground, Holly Point, is adjacent to the lake and has showers, boat ramps, 2 swimming beaches, and a dump station. Max. stay 2 weeks. Gates close June-Aug. 9pm; Apr.-May and Sept. 8pm; Mar. and Oct. 7pm; Nov.-Feb. 6pm. Reservations taken with 2 weeks' notice for stays of more than 7 days. Walk-in sites and non-electric sites $15, ages 62 and up $10. Electric sites $20/$14. Day fee is $5 per car, seniors $3. No credit cards. ❶

🔾 FOOD

The area's universities have spawned a swath of affordable eateries; Raleigh's **Hillsborough Street** and **Capital Boulevard,** Durham's **9th Street,** and Chapel Hill's **Franklin Street** cater to a college (read: budget-oriented) crowd. In Raleigh, travelers can find good dining options in **City Market's** shops, cafes, and bars a few blocks southeast of the capitol. In Durham, **Brightleaf Square,** a mile east of 9th St. on Main St., is a complex of renovated warehouses that holds galleries, shops, and quality restaurants.

RALEIGH

The Rockford, 320½ Glenwood Ave. (☎821-9020), near the intersection with Hillsborough St., is a trendy 2nd fl. restaurant that serves inexpensive, delicious food. A popular choice is the ABC sandwich (Granny Smith apple, bacon, and cheddar on french toast; $6.75). All entrees $7 or less; beer from $1.50 for a PBR. Open M-W 11:30am-2pm and 6-10pm, Th-Sa 11:30am-2pm and 6-10:30pm, Su 6-10pm. ❶

Irregardless Cafe, 901 W. Morgan St. (☎833-8898; www.irregardless.com), after Morgan splits off of Hillsborough St. International gourmet food that leans toward seafood, vegetarian, and vegan dishes. Entrees $14-20. Lunch $6-12. Live jazz, acoustic, or bluegrass most nights. Open for lunch Tu-F 11:30am-2:30pm; for dinner Tu-Th 5:30-9:30pm, F-Sa 5:30-10pm. Su brunch 10am-2pm. F-Sa dancing at 9:30pm until at least 11pm. ❸

Roly Poly Sandwiches, 137 E. Hargett St. (☎834-1135; www.rolypoly.com), downtown, serves over 50 varieties of imaginative wraps. Vegetarians will delight in the "Nut and Honey," while those looking for a grilled wrap should try the "Peachtree Melt" (baked ham, melted brie and swiss, peach and pepper relish served with dill horseradish). Half wraps $3.25-4; full wraps $4.75-6. M-F 10am-5pm, Sa 11am-3pm. ❶

DURHAM

🖾 **The Mad Hatter's Cafe and Bake Shop,** 1802 W. Main St. (☎286-1987; www.madhattersbakeshop.com), 1 block from 9th St., offers a wide selection of delicious dishes in generous portions, including handmade pizza, Asian noodle soups, wraps, and amusingly decorated cookies. The pleasant, modern restaurant has an outdoor patio area and uses only local, organic produce. Sandwiches and wraps $6-8. Occasional live music. Open M-Th 7am-9pm, F-Sa 7am-11pm, Su 8am-4pm. ❷

Pao Lim Asian Bistro and Bar, 2505 Chapel Hill Blvd. (☎419-1771), just off the 15/501 Business Route, prepares some of the area's best Asian cuisine. Dinner entrees start at $7.50, while lunch specials range $5-9. Open M-Th 11:30am-9:30pm, F 11:30am-10pm, Sa noon-10pm, Su noon-9:30pm. ❷

Francesca's, 706 9th St. (☎286-4177), farther down 9th St., serves only coffee and desserts, but their focus pays off. Be sure to sample some of the homemade gelato for just $2.50. Open M-Th 11am-11pm, F-Sa 11am-midnight, Su 11am-10pm. ❶

CHAPEL HILL

Mama Dip's Kitchen, 408 W. Rosemary St. (☎942-5837). This soul food spot feels more like a comfy back-porch picnic than a restaurant. From the sweet potato waffles ($5.75), to the fried okra ($1.75), to the chicken and dumplings ($8.95), Mama Dip's serves some of the best regional delicacies around. Open daily 8am-9pm. ❷

Foster's Market, 750 Airport Rd. (☎967-3663; www.fostersmarket.com). Turn off Franklin St. onto Columbia St., which becomes Airport Rd. This upscale market-restaurant serves pizzas ($8) and sandwiches like the New Wave BLT (bacon, lettuce, tomato, goat cheese, and basil mayo on grilled sourdough; $5.95). Open daily 7:30am-9pm. ❷

Cosmic Cantina, 128 W. Franklin St. (☎960-3955), inside the shopping complex, is a great stop for authentic, cheap, and quick Mexican fare ($3-7). Margaritas $3, pitcher of sangria $12. Also in **Durham,** 1920½ Perry St. (☎286-1875), at the end of the shops on 9th St. Both locations are fairly small and can get busy, so you may need to take your food to go. Su-Th 11am-2am, F-Sa 11am-4am. ❶

📷 SIGHTS

RALEIGH

MUSEUMS. Downtown Raleigh offers a number of engaging, free attractions. Across from the capitol building, in the center of downtown Raleigh, are two first-rate museums. The **Museum of Natural Sciences** has four floors full of exhibits that both adults and children will enjoy. Highlights include a 15 ft. giant ground sloth unearthed near Wilmington and "Willo," a rare dinosaur fossil with an iron concretion within the ribcage—possibly a fossil of the creature's heart. *(11 W. Jones St. ☎ 733-7450 or 877-462-8724; www.naturalsciences.org. Open M-Sa 9am-5pm, Su noon-5pm. Free. Audio tours $4.)* Just down the block, the **North Carolina Museum of History** looks back at North Carolina history through an exhibit on the Civil War, the N.C. Sports Hall of Fame, and a variety of temporary exhibits. Past exhibits have included "Women of Our Time," a photo portrait series of famous American women, and "Pioneers of Aviation," a collection of artifacts from North Carolina inventors, daredevils, and military aces. Program and tour info is available on the website. *(5 E. Edenton St. ☎ 715-0200, www.ncmuseumofhistory.org. Open Tu-Sa 9am-5pm, Su noon-5pm. Free.)*

ARTSPACE. This collection of 46 artists' studios open to the public, in three exhibition galleries, features work by regional, national, and international artists. Come see the process involved in creating art of all types, from watercolor and oil painting to three-dimensional fabric arts. Call ahead or check online for guided tours and special events. *(201 E. Davie St. ☎821-2787; www.artspacenc.org. Open Tu-Sa 10am-6pm, first F of each month 10am-10pm, studio hours vary. Free.)*

OAKWOOD. Stretching east from the visitors center, **Historic Oakwood** is a Victorian neighborhood featuring some of Raleigh's most notable architecture, with attractive homes constructed in the late 19th and early 20th centuries. This neighborhood and the adjacent **Oakwood Cemetery** make a pleasant setting for a walk or drive, a calming escape from the bustle of the city center. *(Historic Oakwood is bordered by Franklin, Watauga, Linden, Jones, and Person St. Cemetery entrance at 701 Oakwood Ave. ☎832-6077. Open daily 8am-6pm; office closes at 4pm. Free self-guided walking tour available at the visitors center. Free maps available in the cemetery office, near the gates.)*

DURHAM

DUKE UNIVERSITY. The Duke family's principal legacy, Duke University, is divided into East and West Campuses. The majestic, neo-Gothic Duke Chapel, completed in the early 1930s, looms grandly at the center of West Campus. Over a million pieces of glass were used to make the 77 stained glass windows depicting 800-900 figures from the Bible and Southern history. *(☎684-2572. Open daily June-Aug. 8am-8pm; Sept.-May 8am-5pm. Free. Self-guided tour available.)* Nearby on Anderson St., the gorgeous **Sarah P. Duke Gardens** has over 55 acres divided into three segments: the Bloomington garden of native plants, the Culberson Asiatic arboretum, and the Terraces. *(☎684-3698. Open daily 8am-dusk. Free. 1½hr. guided tours available by appointment; donations appreciated. 45 min. trolley rides $25, recommended only for disabled visitors.)*

MUSEUM OF LIFE AND SCIENCE. At the other end of Durham, the Museum of Life and Science is a must-see for families with children. Visitors can romp through the musical playground, pet barn animals, ride a train through the Nature Park, and explore hands-on exhibits about everything from bubbles to outer space. In the **Magic Wings Butterfly House,** almost 1000 butterflies flutter among tropical plants. *(433 Murray Ave., off N. Duke St. ☎ 220-5429; www.ncmls.org. Open M-Sa 11am-5pm, Su noon-5pm; late May to early Sept. open Su until 6pm. $8.50, ages 65 and up $7.50, children 3-12 $6, under 3 free; includes butterfly house. Train $1.50; ride 1½ mi.)*

DUKE HOMESTEAD. Visitors can explore the original farm, home, and factories where Washington Duke first planted and processed the tobacco that would become the key to the city's prosperity. Duke's sons founded the American Tobacco Company, which dominated the industry for decades, putting Durham on the map and generating enough profits to found the university. The free historic tour includes an early factory, a curing barn, and a packhouse as well as the restored home. The adjoining **Tobacco Museum** explains the history of the tobacco industry and displays fascinating old cigarette advertisements. *(2828 Duke Homestead Rd., off Guess Rd. ☎ 477-5498. Open Tu-Sa 10am-4pm. Free. Homestead tours depart 15min. after the hr. and last 45min.)*

OTHER SIGHTS. The 1988 movie *Bull Durham* was filmed in the **Durham Bulls' ballpark,** 409 Blackwell St. The AAA farm team for the Tampa Bay Devil Rays plays here, minus Kevin Costner. *(Take "Durham Bulls Stadium" Exit off I-40. ☎ 687-6500, tickets 956-2855; www.durhambulls.com. Games Apr.-Sept.)* Travelers visiting the area during June and July should not miss a modern dance performance at the **American Dance Festival,** hosted annually at Duke. *(☎ 684-6402; www.americandancefestival.org. Tickets $18-36.)*

CHAPEL HILL

UNIVERSITY OF NORTH CAROLINA. Chapel Hill and neighboring Carrboro are virtually inseparable from the beautiful campus of the **University of North Carolina at Chapel Hill.** *(Tour info ☎ 962-1630 or www.unc.edu. Tours Sa 11am or by appointment. Brochures and maps available in the lobby of the Morehead Planetarium.)* The university's Dean Dome hosts sporting events and concerts. *(Tickets available through Ticketmaster, ☎ 834-4000 or www.ticketmaster.com.)* Until 1975, NASA astronauts trained at UNC's **Morehead Planetarium;** of the 12 astronauts who have walked on the moon, 11 worked here. Today, Morehead gives live sky shows and presentations in the 68 ft. domed Star Theater, and houses small exhibits on outer space. *(250 E. Franklin St. ☎ 962-1236; www.moreheadplanetarium.org. Open mid-June to mid-Aug. Su-M 12:30-5pm, Tu-W 10am-5pm, Th-Sa 10am-5pm and 6:30-9:30pm; mid-Aug. to mid-June Su-W 12:30-5pm, Th-Sa 10am-5pm and 6:30-9:30pm. Call for show times. Shows $4.75; students, seniors, and children $3.75. Exhibits free.)* More info about campus attractions, including the Ackland Art Museum and the North Carolina Botanical Garden, can be found in the Campus Visitors Center in Morehead Planetarium.

🎵 🎭 ENTERTAINMENT AND NIGHTLIFE

Pick up a free copy of the weekly *Spectator* and *Independent* magazines, available at many restaurants and bookstores, for listings of Triangle events. Info on happenings in Raleigh can be found at www.raleighnow.com. Chapel Hill offers the Triangle's best nightlife. Popular bars line Franklin St., and several live music clubs congregate near the western end of Franklin St., where it becomes Main St. in the neighboring town of Carrboro. **Cat's Cradle,** 300 E. Main St., in Carrboro, hosts local and national acts. *(☎ 967-9053; www.catscra-*

dle.com. Cover $5-15; doors open between 7:30-9pm and shows begin between 8-9:30pm.) Closer to campus, just off Franklin St., **Go! Room 4,** 100-F Brewer Ln., features local acts. (☎969-1400. Su-Th shows start at 9pm, F-Sa 10pm.) **Local 506,** 506 W. Franklin St., focuses on indie rock. (☎942-5506; www.local506.com. 21+. Cover around $5.)

Nightlife options are also plentiful in Raleigh; the area around Glenwood by Hillsborough St. is home to a number of popular, trendy bars. **Mitch's Tavern,** 2426 Hillsborough St., a second-floor bar across from N.C. State, is a favorite among students and locals for a late-night brew. The dark, smoky charm of the tavern's interior led the producers of *Bull Durham* to select this as the set for two scenes. (☎821-7771; www.mitchs.com. Pints $2.25-3.50, pitchers $8-13. Open daily 11:30am-2am.) **Greenshields,** 214 E. Martin St., at Blount St. in City Market, brews their own beer in a relaxed environment. (☎829-0214, www.greenshields.com. Pints $3.75, liters $7.50. Open Su-Th 11:30am-midnight, F-Sa 11:30am-1am.)

For dancing, head to **Five Star,** 511 W. Hargett St., in downtown Raleigh. This popular Chinese restaurant becomes a nightclub at around 10pm. (☎833-3311. F-Sa 21+. Cover $5 after 10:30pm. Open nightly 5:30pm-2am. Live DJs Th-Sa at 10pm. Dinner menu served all night long.) **Legends,** 330 W. Hargett St., is gay-friendly. (☎831-8888; www.legends-club.com. Tu cabaret night, W brews and cues with $1.50 domestic beer, Th gothic night, Su drag show at 11:30pm and 12:45am. Cover $2-6, under 21 up to $10. Open nightly 9pm-3am, later on F-Sa.)

In Durham, **George's Garage,** 737 9th St., arguably the area's best sushi restaurant, stays open until the wee hours serving drinks. (☎286-4131. M jazz jam sessions. Dancing F-Sa. Bar open Su-Th 4pm until at least 12:30am, sometimes until 2am, F-Sa 4pm-2am.)

WINSTON-SALEM   ☎336

Winston-Salem was, as its name suggests, originally two different towns. Salem was founded in 1766 by the Moravians, a Protestant sect from what is the present-day Czech Republic. One of America's most successful utopian communities, Salem was bolstered by religious fervor, dedication to education, and the production of crafts. Winston, meanwhile, rose to prominence as a center of tobacco production, home to the famous tobacco mogul R.J. Reynolds. When the two towns merged in 1913, a dynamic, bustling city was born. Today, the skyline of Winston-Salem testifies to the towns' continued prominence; visitors can experience the history of the two towns when they visit Old Town Salem or the Reynolda house.

🛈 PRACTICAL INFORMATION. The **Piedmont Triad International Airport** (☎721-0088; www.ptia.org), at Exit 210 off of I-40 where I-85 and I-40 intersect, is the closest airport serving commercial flights. The **Amtrak Connector** van service takes passengers from the Best Western Salem Inn, 127 S. Cherry St. across from the visitors center, to the Amtrak station at 2603 Oakland Ave. in Greensboro. (☎800-298-7246. Departs daily 8:35am. Return trips available at night.) The **Greyhound** station, 250 Greyhound Ct., is downtown at Exit 110A off of Rte. 52N. (☎724-1429. Open daily 7am-1am.) **Winston-Salem Transit Authority** has a main depot at 100 W. 5th St. between Liberty and Trade St. (☎727-2000. $1, transfers free. Buses operate M-F 5:30am-11:30pm, Sa 8am-6:30pm.) **Winston-Salem Visitor Center,** 200 Brookstown Ave., provides brochures and maps. (☎728-4200 or 866-728-4200; www.visitwinstonsalem.com. Open daily 8:30am-5pm.) **Internet Access: Public Library,** 660 W. 5th St., at Spring St. downtown. (☎727-2264. Open M-W 9am-9pm, Th-F 9am-6pm, Sa 9am-5pm; Sept.-May also open Su 1-5pm. Free.) **Post Office:** 1500 Patterson Ave. (☎721-1749. Open M-F 8:30am-5pm.) **Postal Code:** 27101. **Area Code:** 336.

⚐ ACCOMMODATIONS. There are scores of motels that are perfect for the budget traveler at Exit 184 off I-40, on the way into town. On the northern side of the city, budget motels center around Rte. 52, just past Patterson Ave. Most rooms run $39-69, and many hotels off the I-40 Business Route run $59 specials on weekend nights. The **Microtel Inn ❸**, on Hanes Mall Blvd. between I-40 and the Silas Creek Parkway, is a great value with free local calls, cable TV, dataports, an outdoor pool, and an aesthetically pleasing exterior. (☎ 659-1994 or 888-771-7171. Singles $45-52; doubles $55-65.) **Motel 6 ❷**, 3810 Patterson Ave., offers some of the least expensive lodging available in the city. Though a bit far from downtown, the clean rooms are a great value, with A/C, HBO, data ports, a pool, and laundry facilities. However, if the Crazyhorse Saloon and Gentleman's Club next door or the glass pane between the clerk and the lobby at the night check-in counter worry you, you may want to steer clear. (☎ 661-1588. Singles $32; doubles $38; additional adults $3. AARP 10% off.) The **Summit Street Inns ❸**, 434 Summit St., at W. 5th St. a few blocks from downtown, are a two-house B&B that will reward those in the mood for a splurge. The luxurious rooms are outfitted with jacuzzis, stereos, TVs, refrigerators stocked with free goodies, and bathrobes, and amaretto french toast is brought to your door in the morning. (☎ 777-1887 or 800-301-1887; www.bbinn.com. Exercise room and pool table. Reception 4-8pm. Rooms Su-Th $119-159, F-Sa $139-179. Single travelers Su-Th $104, F-Sa $129-169. One room without jacuzzi, Su-Th $89, F-Sa $99. All rooms non-smoking.)

⚏ FOOD. The West End Cafe ❷, 926 W. 4th St., is a laid-back local favorite that makes every kind of sandwich under the sun. Patrons line up for the curry chicken salad sandwich ($5.50) and desserts like the fudge sundae cheesecake sandwich. (☎ 723-4774. Salads $4.75-8. Burgers $4.50-6. Dinner entrees $9-21. Open M-F 11am-10pm, Sa noon-10pm.) Winston-Salem is the birthplace of national doughnut company **Krispy Kreme,** and no visit to the city would be complete without stopping by the **Krispy Kreme Shop ❶**, 259 S. Stratford Rd. You can watch the famous doughnuts being made fresh on-site and feel your heart clog at no extra cost. (☎ 724-2484. Doughnuts $0.69-0.79. Open M-Th 5:30am-11pm, drive-thru open until midnight; F-Sa 5:30am-midnight, drive-thru open until 1am; Su 5:30am-11pm.) In the heart of the Old Salem Village, the romantic **Old Salem Tavern ❸**, 736 Main St., delights the taste buds with dishes served by waiters and waitresses in traditional Moravian garb. Lunch entrees range from quiche and salad ($6.25) to Southern-style catfish ($8.25). Dinner is fancier, with selections such as lobster crab cakes, weinerschnitzel, and venison running $13-21. (☎ 748-8585, www.oldsalemtavern.com. Open for lunch Su-F 11:30am-2pm, Sa 11:30am-2:30pm; dinner M-Th 5-9pm, F-Sa 5-9:30pm.)

◪ SIGHTS. Old Salem Village takes visitors back in time to a working Moravian village. The restored village outlines their fascinating history and traditions. The area stretches south from downtown and includes a visitors center, several museums, and a multitude of traditional Moravian homes and buildings, including shoemaker and gunsmith shops. A ticket into the village includes admission into all of the museums and buildings inside. (☎ 888-653-7253; www.oldsalem.org. Tickets $21, children ages 6-16 $10; mid-Nov. to Dec. adult tickets $22. AAA $2 off adult price; look for other coupons on the website. Visitors center open M-Sa 8:30am-5:30pm, Su 12:30-5:30pm. Most attractions open M-Sa 9am-5pm, Su 1-5pm. Tickets can also be purchased at the Boys School, located at the intersection of Main and Academy St., or at the Horton Museum Center, 924 S. Main St.) Old Salem's **Frank L. Horton Museum Center** features a number of museums, the most extensive of which is the **Museum of Early Southern Decorative Art (MESDA).** The MESDA showcases furnishings from around the Southeast, representing the period from 1690-

1820. Not only are the rooms set up entirely "ropes free," to recreate the full feel of Southern homes, but all of the furnishings are original, right down to the bricks in the fireplace. (1hr. guided tours every 30min.; advance appointment required at the ticketing desk or the visitors center. Open M-Sa 9:30am-3:30pm, Su 1:30-3:30pm.) The **Toy Museum,** in the same building, displays toys spanning 1700 years. Don't be fooled by its name—this museum is geared toward adults and older children. All of the toys are delicate antiques housed in glass cases. For kids, the **Children's Museum**—a period-themed play area in the Horton Museum Center—offers admission separate from these combination passes ($5 for all ages).

Winston-Salem's other premier attraction is the **Reynolda House,** 2250 Reynolda Rd., one of the South's most famous houses. The Reynolda was once home to tobacco tycoon R.J. Reynolds and his visionary wife, Katherine. She is credited with making the household completely self-sufficient, with a working "village" on the grounds. Today the Reynolda is affiliated with Wake Forest University and houses an impressive collection of American art from colonial times up to the present. (☎758-5150 or 888-663-1149; www.reynoldahouse.org. Open Tu-Sa 9:30am-4:30pm, Su 1:30-4:30pm; no admittance after 4pm. $8, seniors and AAA $7, students and children free. Wheelchair accessible.) Don't spend all your time inside; the manor's true allure is the two acres of gardens that surround it. The **Reynolda Garden,** created for the enjoyment of the public as well as the Reynolds family, remains one of the most beautiful spots in Winston-Salem. (☎758-5593. Open dawn-dusk. Free.)

🎭 **ENTERTAINMENT.** Look for listings of local events in the free weekly newspaper *Go Triad* or *Relish,* the Thursday entertainment supplement to the *Winston-Salem Journal.* On weekends from May to August, the city hosts three live music performance series in the downtown area: **Alive After Five** every Thursday evening (Corpening Plaza, 100 W. 2nd St.), **Fourth Street Jazz and Blues** every Friday evening (W. 4th St.), and **Summer on Trade** every Saturday evening (6th and Trade St.). Check out www.winstonsalemevents.com for more info. You'll find quality live rock, roots, and reggae music at **Ziggy's,** 433 Baity St., off University Pkwy. near the Coliseum. (☎748-1064; www.ziggyrock.com. Beer from $2. Cover $5-25. Open Tu-Su 8pm-2am, live music starts around 9pm.) Musicians also rock out at **The Garage,** 110 W. 7th St., at Trade St. Call ahead or check online for the acts of the night, since featured bands play New Grass, pop punk, and everything in between. (☎777-1127; www.the-garage.ws. Beer from $2. Cover around $5-15, $1 extra if under 21. Open Th-Sa, sometimes also W. Acts go on at 9pm; doors open at 8pm.)

CHARLOTTE ☎704

Named in the mid-1700s after the wife of England's King George III, Charlotte is still referred to as the "Queen City" today. Around the turn of the 18th century, settlers flooded the region in the nation's first gold rush after a boy discovered a 17 lb. gold nugget near Charlotte. Shortly thereafter, the first branch of the US Mint was established here in 1837. Now the biggest city in the Carolinas, Charlotte has expanded both outward and upward. For visitors, the city offers top-notch museums, ritzy clubs, and a wide variety of professional sports.

🛈 **PRACTICAL INFORMATION.** The nucleus of Charlotte, the busy uptown area, has numbered streets laid out perpendicular to named streets in a simple grid pattern. **Tryon Street,** running north-south, is the major crossroad. **I-77** crosses the city north-south, providing access to uptown, while **I-85** runs southwest-northeast, connecting the uptown to the UNC campus. Uptown can also be reached from **I-277,** which circles the city, and is called the **John Belk Freeway** to

THE SOUTH

the south of uptown and the **Brookshire Freeway** to the north. The **Charlotte-Douglas International Airport**, about 7 mi. west of the city on Josh Birmingham Pkwy., accessible from the Billy Graham Pkwy. (Rte. 521), is a hub for US Airways (☎359-4910; www.charlotteairport.com). **Amtrak**, 1914 N. Tryon St. (☎376-4416), and **Greyhound**, 601 W. Trade St. (☎372-3332), stop in Charlotte. Both stations are open 24hr. The **Charlotte Area Transit System (CATS)**, operates local buses; the central terminal is at 310 E. Trade St. (☎339-7433; www.ridetransit.org. Most buses operate M-Sa 5:30am-1:30am, Su 6:30am-1:30am. $1.10, $1.55 for express service in outlying areas; most transfers free, local to express transfers $0.45.) Within the uptown area, CATS runs **Gold Rush**, free shuttles that resemble old-fashioned cable cars. There is a **visitors center** at 330 S. Tryon St. (☎800-231-4636. Open 9am-12:30pm and 1:30-4:30pm), and a **Convention and Visitors Bureau** at 500 S. College St., Ste. 300. (☎800-722-1994; www.visitcharlotte.org. Open M-F 8:30am-5pm, Sa 9am-3pm.) **Hotlines: Rape Crisis,** ☎375-9900. **Suicide Line,** ☎358-2800. Both 24hr. **Gay/Lesbian Hotline,** ☎535-6277. Operates Su-Th 6:30-9:30pm. **Internet Access: Public Library of Charlotte and Mecklenburg County,** 310 N. Tryon St., in uptown. (☎336-2572. Open M-Th 9am-9pm, F-Sa 9am-6pm, Su 1-6pm. 1hr. free Internet access per day.) **Post Office:** 201 N. McDowell. (☎800-275-8777. Open M-F 7:30am-6pm, Sa 10am-1pm.) **Postal Code:** 28204. **Area Code:** 704.

▇▇ ACCOMMODATIONS AND FOOD. There are several clusters of budget motels in the Charlotte area: on Independence Blvd. off the John Belk Freeway; off I-85 at Sugar Creek Rd., Exit 41; off I-85 at Exit 33 near the airport; and off I-77 at Clanton St., Exit 7. The **Continental Inn ❷**, 1100 W. Sugar Creek Rd., Exit 41 off I-85, has immaculate, inviting rooms. (☎597-8100. A/C, cable TV with free HBO, continental breakfast. Su-Th singles $36-40, F-Sa $40-45; doubles $46/$52. 10% AAA/AARP discount.) **Homestead Studio Suites Hotel ❸**, 710 Yorkmont Rd., near the airport, provides clean, spacious rooms with full kitchenettes and wireless Internet connections as well as on-site coin-operated laundry facilities and free access to a local Bally's health club. (☎676-0083; www.homesteadhotels.com. Reception M-F 6:30am-9pm, Sa 9am-9pm, Su 10am-8pm. Weekdays $36-46, weekends $60-70. Weekly rates available. 10% AAA/AARP discount and for booking online.)

Two areas outside of uptown offer attractive dining options at reasonable prices. North Davidson **("NoDa")**, around 36th St., is home to a small artistic community inhabiting a set of historic buildings. South from the city center, the **Dilworth** neighborhood, along East and South Blvd., is lined with restaurants serving everything from authentic ethnic meals to pizza and pub fare. For eccentric, tasty cuisine, the hip **Cosmos Cafe ❹**, 300 N. College St., at E. 6th St., has a versatile menu covering everything from tapas and *mezes* ($5.25-10) to sushi and wood-fired pizzas ($8.25-10). The restaurant becomes a popular yuppie bar around 10:30pm; swing by Wednesday nights for superb gourmet martinis at half price. (☎372-3553; www.cosmoscafe.com. Tapas half-price M-F 5-7pm. Th Latin night with free salsa lessons. Open M-F 11am-2am, Sa 5pm-2am.) **Thomas Street Tavern ❷**, 1218 Thomas Ave., is a local favorite with pool, an extensive beer menu, and food that ranges from pub fare to gourmet. For a new twist on an old standby, try the crabcake with citrus aioli on a croissant ($7.50. ☎376-1622. Follow E. 10th St. out of uptown; after E. 10th becomes Central Ave., turn right on Thomas Ave. Grill items $5.25-7.25. Sandwiches $6-7. Pizzas $6-8. Open M-Sa 11am-2am, Su noon-2am.) Find healthful, organic food at **Talley's Green Grocery ❶**, 1408-C E. Blvd. in Dilworth, an upscale market behind the Outback Steakhouse. Cafe Verde, in the back of the store, offers excellent sandwiches and hearty prepared dishes. (☎334-9200; www.talleys.com. Sandwiches $6. Open daily 9am-9pm.) The fun and friendly staff of **Smelly Cat Coffeehouse ❶**, 514 E. 36th St., in NoDa, serves delectable coffee drinks as well as a small selection of pastries. Add a sugar rush to your caffeine high with the "Muddy Kitten" ($4), a combination of ice cream, chocolate, and espresso. (☎374-9656. Ice cream and cinnamon rolls each $2.25. Live music some weekends. Open M-Th 7am-10pm, F-Sa 7am-midnight, Su 9am-5pm.)

◙ **SIGHTS.** Charlotte has a number of museums that give visitors an insider's perspective on the region, most of which are located in the uptown area. The ▧**Levine Museum of the New South,** 200 E. 7th St., is a fantastic new museum that explores the history of the Charlotte and Carolina Piedmont area. From a working cotton gin to a recreation of a soda fountain that was occupied during the civil rights sit-ins, the Levine shows how today's "New South" has developed, from the end of the Civil War to the present. (☎333-1887. Open Tu-Sa 10am-5pm, Su noon-5pm. $6; students, seniors, and ages 6-18 $5; under 6 free.) A single price of admission will grant you access to both the **Mint Museum of Craft and Design,** 220 N. Tryon St., in uptown, and the **Mint Museum of Art,** 2730 Randolph Rd., about 2½ mi. to the southeast. The craft and design museum features contemporary work in glass, wood, metal, and fiber. Even the chandelier in the lobby is an impressive work of craftsmanship, and previous special exhibits have highlighted topics such as goldsmithing and quilting. The art museum, meanwhile, focuses on more traditional painting and ceramics, and displays pieces from local students. Relocated from its original position, the art museum building once functioned as Charlotte's mint; visitors can peruse coins once produced here. (Both museums: ☎337-2000; www.mintmuseum.org. Craft and Design Museum open Tu-Sa 10am-5pm, Su noon-5pm; Museum of Art open Tu 10am-10pm, W-Sa 10am-5pm, Su noon-5pm. $6; college students and ages 62 and over $5, 6-17 $3. Audio tour $2. Free admission to Craft and Design Museum Tu 10am-2pm. Art museum free Tu 5pm-10pm.) Kids will delight at the exhibits in **Discovery Place,** 301 N. Tryon St., a hands-on children's science museum with exhibits about the workings of simple machines, the human body, and environmental ecosystems. (☎372-6261 or 800-935-0553; www.discoveryplace.org. Open June-Aug. M-Sa 10am-6pm, Su 12:30-6pm; Sept.-May Su-F 9am-5pm, Sa 10am-6pm. Museum $8.50, ages 2-13 and 60 and over $6.50. OmniMax Theater $7.50/$6. Museum and OmniMax combo tickets $14/$10.)

◪◩ **ENTERTAINMENT AND NIGHTLIFE.** In addition to having an NFL team, a WNBA team, a Triple-A baseball team, an arena football team, and a hockey team, Charlotte is also a mecca for the fastest-growing sport in national popularity—stock car racing. The **Lowe's Motor Speedway,** Exit 49 off I-85, hosts several major NASCAR events each year. (Tickets and schedule information ☎877-655-0329; www.gospeedway.com.) Charlotte's WNBA team, the **Sting,** shoots hoops in the Coliseum, on Billy Graham Pkwy. southwest of uptown. (Tickets ☎877-962-2849; www.ticketmaster.com or www.charlottesting.com. Coliseum box office open M-F and game days 10am-5pm. Tickets $10-59.) Football fans can catch an NFL game when the **Carolina Panthers** play in Ericsson Stadium, 800 S. Mint St. (Tickets ☎522-6500; www.ticketmaster.com. Stadium tours $4, seniors $3, children 5-15 $2.) Ten miles to the south, the Charlotte **Knights** play AAA minor league baseball at Knights Castle, off I-77 S at Exit 88. (Tickets ☎364-6637; www.charlotteknights.com. Box office open M-F 10am-5pm and 10am until game time on game days. $6-10.)

To check out nightlife, arts, and entertainment listings, grab a free copy of *Creative Loafing* in one of Charlotte's shops or restaurants, visit www.charlotte.creativeloafing.com, or look over the E&T section of the *Charlotte Observer.* Many of Charlotte's hippest clubs can be found uptown, especially on College St. from 5th to 7th St. For live rock bands, pool, and foosball, head to **Amos's Southend,** 1423 S. Tryon St. Live acts are often cover bands of rock's greats, from Led Zeppelin and Pink Floyd to Guns N' Roses and Journey. (☎377-6874; www.amossouthend.com.

THE SOUTH

Beer $3 and up. Usually 18+. Cover $3-35. Open Th-Sa, sometimes W; doors usually open at 9pm.) **The Evening Muse**, 3227 N. Davidson St., in NoDa, is a laid-back venue for a wide variety of musical acts, from acoustic and jazz to rock. Wednesday night is open mic night (no cover), and the third Thursday of every month is rock songwriter's night. (☎376-3737; www.theeveningmuse.com. Beer $1.50 and up. Cover $5. Open Tu-Sa 6pm-midnight.) If you've always wondered what happened to Pauly Shore, you may just find him down the street doing stand-up at **The Comedy Zone**, 516 N. College St. (☎348-4242; www.thecomedyzone.net. Cover W $12, Th Su $15, and F-Sa $19. Open W-Th and Su 8-9:30pm, F-Sa 8-11:30pm.)

CAROLINA MOUNTAINS

The sharp ridges and rolling slopes of the southern Appalachian range create some of the most spectacular scenery in the Southeast. Scholars, ski bums, farmers, and artists all find reasons to call this gorgeous region home. The aptly named High Country stretches between Boone and Asheville, 100 mi. to the southwest. The primary attraction of the mountains is the Blue Ridge Parkway (p. 356), a 469 mi. long road through the mountaintops that connects Virginia's Shenandoah National Park in the north to Tennessee's Great Smoky Mountains National Park in the south. Views from many of the Parkway's scenic overlooks are staggering, particularly on days when the hemlock-, laurel-, and rhododendron-carpeted peaks are wreathed in mist.

ASHEVILLE ☎828

Hazy blue mountains, deep valleys, and spectacular waterfalls form the impressive backdrop to this small, friendly city. Once a popular retreat for the nation's well-to-do, Asheville hosted enough Carnegies, Vanderbilts, and Mellons to fill a 1920s edition of *Who's Who on the Atlantic Seaboard*. The population these days tends more toward dreadlocks, batik, and vegetarianism, providing funky nightlife and festivals all year. The metropolitan feel extends to Asheville's downtown plaza, whose boutique stores and polished office buildings look like they would be more at home in Manhattan than Appalachia.

🔁 **PRACTICAL INFORMATION.** The **Asheville Regional Airport** is at Exit 9 off I-26, 15 mi. south of the city. (☎684-2226; www.flyavl.com.) **Greyhound**, 2 Tunnel Rd. (☎253-8451; open daily 8am-9pm), 2 mi. east of downtown near the Beaucatcher Tunnel, sends buses to: Charlotte (2½-3½hr., 5 per day, $23-31); Knoxville (2-2½hr., 7 per day, $27-29); Raleigh (8-11hr., 5 per day, $39-57). The **Asheville Transit System** handles bus service within city limits. Pick up a copy of bus schedules and routes from the visitors center or visit the **Asheville Transit Center**, 49 Coxe Ave., by the post office. (☎253-5691. Hours vary by route, all M-Sa between 6am and 7pm. $0.75, transfers $0.10; short trips in downtown area free. Discounts for seniors, disabled, and multi-fare tickets.) The **Chamber of Commerce and Visitor Center**, 151 Haywood St., Exit 4C off I-240, on the northwest end of downtown, dispenses a wealth of knowledge about activities and accommodations to visitors. Don't leave without a copy of their accurate and easy-to-read downtown area map. (☎800-257-1300 or 258-6101; www.exploreasheville.com. Open M-F 8:30am-5:30pm, Sa-Su 9am-5pm.) **Internet Access: Pack Memorial Library**, 67 Haywood St. Use your 55min. turn wisely; you only get one per day. (☎255-5203. $2 per turn. Open M-Th 10am-8pm, F 10am-6pm, Sa 10am-5pm; Sept.-May also Su 2-5pm.) **Post Office:** 33 Coxe Ave., off Patton Ave. (☎271-6429. Open M-F 7:30am-5:30pm, Sa 9am-1pm.) **Postal Code:** 28802. **Area Code:** 828.

ACCOMMODATIONS. The cheapest lodgings are on **Tunnel Road,** east of downtown—but be warned, they are not very cheap. If your plans revolve around visiting the Biltmore Estate (see below), the best place to stay is the conveniently located **Plaza Motel ❷** at 111 Hendersonville Rd. in Biltmore Village. (☎274-2050. Reception 8am-11pm. Cable TV and A/C in all rooms. Singles from $45; doubles from $50. AAA and AARP discount.) The **Log Cabin Motor Court ❸,** 330 Weaverville Hwy., 5 mi. north of downtown, provides immaculate, inviting cabins with HBO, wireless Internet, and laundry. Some also have fireplaces, kitchenettes, and A/C. (☎645-6546; www.cabinlodging.com. Reception 10am-8pm. By reservation only Jan.-Mar. Cabins with one bedroom and bath $50, with kitchenette $70; 2 bedrooms and bath $90-115. AAA, military 10% off.) **Days Inn ❸,** 201 Tunnel Rd., has huge rooms with A/C, cable, and coffeemakers, as well as an outdoor pool and a full breakfast. (☎252-4000. Summer singles and doubles start at $53. AAA and AARP discount.) **Powhatan Lake Campground ❶,** 375 Wesley Branch Rd., 12 mi. southwest of Asheville off Rte. 191, is in the **Pisgah National Forest,** offering wooded sites on a 10-acre trout lake open for swimming and fishing. Sites fill up fast in the summer; call ahead to make a reservation. (☎670-5627 or 877-444-6777 for reservations. No hookups, but hot showers and dump station available. Gates close 10pm. Open mid-May to Oct. Sites $15-18.)

FOOD. Downtown Asheville is packed with excellent places to eat. At the **▧Laughing Seed Cafe ❸,** 40 Wall St., the international lineup of vegetarian dishes tastes even better when served on the sunny patio. (☎252-3445. Entrees $9-11. Sandwiches $8-9. Dinner specialties $8-15. Open M-Th 11:30am-9pm, F-Sa 11:30am-10:30pm, Su 9:30am-9pm.) The downtown area is also home to the colorful **Anntony's Caribbean Cafe ❷,** 1 Page Ave. Ste. 129, in the Historic Grove Arcade Building. Before enjoying Jamaican chicken, beef empanadas ($2.79), or the roast pork sandwich ($7.49), start with plantain chips and salsa for $6. (☎255-9620. Restaurant open M-Th 11:30am-9pm, F-Sa 11:30am-10pm, Su 11:30am-3pm. Coffee bar opens M-Sa 7:30am.) The quirky, laid-back **Beanstreets ❶,** 3 Broadway St., serves coffee ($1-4), sandwiches ($3.50-6), and omelettes ($3-5) on cheerfully mismatched tables. (☎255-8180. Open mic Th 9am-11:30pm, live music most F 9pm. Open M-W 7:30am-6pm, Th-F 7:30am-midnight, Sa 9am-midnight, Su 9am-4pm.)

SIGHTS. George Vanderbilt's palatial **Biltmore Estate,** 1 Approach Rd., just north of I-40, was constructed in the 1890s and is the largest private home in America. A self-guided tour of the house and grounds can take all day; try to arrive early. Entrance fee also includes complimentary wine tastings at the on-site winery. (☎225-1333 or 800-624-1575; www.biltmore.com. Estate entrance open daily 8:30am-5pm. Winery open daily Jan.-Mar. 9am-4pm; Apr.-Dec. 8:30am-5pm. $39, ages 6-16 $19.50, ages 5 and under free. Audio guide $6.50. Rooftop tour $14. Trail rides $45. Carriage rides $35. Wheelchair accessible.) If Biltmore is a bit more than your wallet can take, enjoy the free **Botanical Gardens,** 151 W. T. Weaver Blvd. The gardens primarily contain native plants of the Carolina Mountains. The best time to visit is April to mid-May, when the wildflowers are blooming. (☎252-5190; www.ashevillebotanicalgardens.org. Open daily dawn-dusk.) The **Thomas Wolfe Memorial,** 52 N. Market St., between Woodfin and Walnut St., celebrates one of the early 20th century's most influential American authors with a museum and a recreation of his "old Kentucky home." (☎253-8304; www.wolfememorial.com. 30min. tours every hr. on the ½hr. Open Apr.-Oct. Tu-Sa 9am-5pm, Su 1-5pm; Nov.-Mar. Tu-Sa 10am-4pm, Su 1-4pm. $1, students $0.50.) The **Asheville Art Museum** displays 20th-century American artwork. The most prominent ongoing exhibition is "Vantage Points: Perspectives on American Art 1960-1980." (☎253-3227; www.ashevilleart.org. Open Tu-Th and Sa 10am-5pm, F 10am-8pm, Su 1-5pm. $6; students, seniors, and ages 4-15 $5. Wheelchair accessible.) Twenty-five miles southeast of Asheville on U.S. 64/74A, the scenic setting for *Last of the Mohicans* rises up almost ½ mi. in **Chimney Rock Park.** After driving to the base of the Chimney, take the 26-story elevator to the top or walk up for a 75 mi. view. Savor your time on the mountaintop with one of the five hikes that range in length from ½ to 1½ miles, some leading to breathtaking waterfalls. (☎ 625-9611 or 800-277-9611; www.chimneyrockpark.com. Ticket office open daily in summer 8:30am-5:30pm; winter 8:30am-4:30pm. Park open 1½hr. after office closes. $14, ages 4-12 $6.)

🔊📷 **ENTERTAINMENT AND NIGHTLIFE.** Indie and arthouse flicks play at the **Fine Arts Theatre,** 36 Biltmore Ave. (☎ 232-1536; www.fineartstheatre.com. $7, seniors and matinees $5. Ticket sales begin 30min. before showtimes. Box office opens at 12:30pm.) If you are in a literary mood, **Shakespeare in Montford Park,** at the Hazel Robinson Amphitheater, hosts two plays per summer, and all of the performances are free. (☎ 254-4540; www.montfordparkplayers.org. Performances June-July F-Su 7:30pm.) The downtown area, especially the southeast end around the intersection of Broadway and College St., offers music, munchies, and movies. **Jack of the Wood,** 95 Patton Ave., heats up at night with locally brewed ales and live celtic, bluegrass, and old-time mountain music. While you enjoy the soundtrack, fill up with traditional pub fare. (☎ 252-5445; www.jackofthewood.com. Beer $3. M trivia night at 8pm. 21+ after 9pm. Cover F-Sa $5. Open M-F 4pm-2am, Sa noon-2am, Su 3pm-2am.) The free weekly paper, *Mountain Xpress*, and *Community Connections*, a free gay publication, have news, arts, events, and dining listings.

BOONE ☎ 828

Nestled among the breathtaking mountains of the High Country, Boone has a hippie vibe. You'll find tie-dye, unruly beards, vegetarian food, and piercingly of all shapes and sizes everywhere you turn.

🔲 **PRACTICAL INFORMATION.** The **Boone Bowling Center,** 261 Boone Heights Dr., doubles as the **Greyhound** terminal (☎ 264-3167), which sends buses to Charlotte (3hr., 1 per day, from $27). **Boone AppalCart,** 274 Winklers Creek Rd., provides **local bus** service. (☎ 264-2278. Hours vary by route. Fare $0.50.) **Visitor Info: Boone Area Chamber of Commerce,** 208 Howard St. (☎ 800-852-9506; www.boonechamber.com. Open M-F 9am-5pm.) The **North Carolina High Country Host Visitor Center,** 1700 Blowing Rock Rd./U.S. 321, has regional info. (☎ 800-438-7500; www.mountainsofnc.com. Open M-Sa 9am-5pm, Su 9am-3pm.) **Internet Access: Watauga County Public Library,** 140 Queen St., at N. Depot St. one block up from King St. (☎ 264-8784. Open M-Th 9am-7pm, F-Sa 9am-5pm.) **Post Office:** 1544 Blowing Rock Rd. (☎ 262-1171. Open M-F 9am-5pm, Sa 9am-noon.) **Postal Code:** 28607. **Area Code:** 828.

🔲📷 **ACCOMMODATIONS AND FOOD.** The neighboring community of Blowing Rock offers plenty of pricey inns. In Boone, the **Cardinal Motel ❷,** 2135 Blowing Rock Rd./U.S. 321, just south of Boone, features clean, cheap rooms and an outdoor pool. (☎ 264-3630. A/C, HBO. Rooms $29-38.) Along the Parkway near Boone, the **Julian Price Campground ❶,** Mi. 297, has spectacular tent and RV sites. Sites around Loop A are on a lake. (☎ 963-5911. Flush toilets and water; no hookups or showers. Open May-Oct. Sites $14.) King St. offers lots of great little restaurants, most of which have a healthy, earthy feel. The small, hip 📷**Black Cat ❶,** 127 S. Depot St. right off King St., makes humongous and incredibly tasty burritos; vegetarian options are cooked on a separate grill are available. Live acoustic bluegrass music is occasionally played on weeknights, hard rock on weekends. (☎263-9511. Build your own burritos, quesadillas, and nachos from $3.75. Margaritas $3.50. Open Su-Th 11:30am-9pm, F-Sa 11:30am-10pm.) Though vegetarians have plenty of options in Boone, none combines gourmet ingredients with low prices as well as **Angelica's ❷**, 506 W. King St. (☎265-0809. Sandwiches $7.50. Vegetarian sushi $6-9. Smoothies $4. Open Su-Th 11am-9pm, F-Sa 11am-9:30pm.)

🖼 **SIGHTS.** 🖼 **Grandfather Mountain,** near the intersection of U.S. 221 and the Blue Ridge Parkway (Mi. 305), is a great site for families and wildlife enthusiasts. The habitat walk features bald eagles, black bears, mountain lions, and other animals in spacious open-air pens made to mimic the animals' natural habitats. A nature museum, suspension bridge, and a series of hikes round out the park. (☎800-468-7325; www.grandfather.com. Open daily June-Aug. 8am-6pm, Mar.-May and Sept.-Nov. 8am-5pm, Dec.-Feb. 8am-4pm. $12, seniors $11, ages 4-12 $6; ticket sales stop 1hr. before closing. Wheelchair accessible.) Hiking or camping on Grandfather Mtn. requires a permit ($6), available at the park entrance or at several area stores, including the **Mast General Store,** 630 W. King St., downtown. (☎262-0000. Open M-Sa 10am-6pm, Su noon-5pm.) The free *Grandfather Mountain Trail Map and Backcountry Guide,* available anywhere permits are sold, details area hikes. Those without a car can take the AppalCart (see above) up to the mountain. Near Boone, the **Wilson Creek** area offers waterfalls, swimming holes, and trails. **Linville Gorge** is perfect for backcountry camping and rock climbing. For more info, call the ranger's office (☎737-0833).

Didn't think you could ski this far south? Think again—Boone is conveniently located near three ski resorts. **Sugar Mountain,** off Hwy. 184 in Banner Elk (☎898-4521 or 800-784-2768; www.skisugar.com; weekend lift tickets $53, ages 4-11 $39, under 4 and 70+ free), and **Ski Beech,** 1007 Beech Mtn. Pkwy. also off Hwy. 184 (☎800-438-2093; www.skibeech.com; weekend lift tickets $48, ages 5-12 and 60+ $35, under 5 free), are the largest resorts. **Appalachian Ski Mountain,** off U.S. 221/321 in Blowing Rock (☎800-322-2373; www.appskimtn.com; weekend lift tickets $40, ages 5-12 and 60+ $27) is a bit smaller. **Boone AppalCart** (p. 414) runs a free winter shuttle from Boone to Sugar Mountain. Call ☎800-962-2322 for info about daily ski conditions.

ASU's **Appalachian Cultural Museum,** on University Hall Dr. off Blowing Rock Rd. (U.S. 321), seeks to preserve the rich cultural traditions of the region with exhibits on crafts, storytelling, moonshine, and even NASCAR. (☎262-3117. Open Tu-Sa 10am-5pm, Su 1-5pm. $4, seniors $3.50, ages 10-18 $2. Wheelchair accessible.)

🎭🖼 **ENTERTAINMENT AND NIGHTLIFE.** In the town of Todd, 11 mi. north of Boone at the edge of Ashe County, the **Todd General Store** hosts live mountain music concerts on Saturday afternoons during the summer months. From downtown Boone, take U.S. 421S and turn left on Hwy. 194; continue 11 mi. and make a right onto Todd Railroad Grade Rd. It's on the left after half a mile. (☎336-877-1067. Most events free, some concerts up to $10. Times vary; call for schedule.) For a cold beer or a game of pool, head to **Murphy's Pub,** 747 W. King St. (☎264-5117. Beer from $1.75. Live music usually Th-Sa. 21+. Cover $3-5. Open daily 11am-2am.) The **Boone Bowling Center,** at 261 Boone Heights Dr., has a variety of special deals for those tired of skiing. The third Friday of every month is Christian cosmic night (10pm-midnight; $12.50 per person including shoes). The other Fridays are glow bowling (9pm-11pm; $3.25 per game), while Saturdays are supercosmic night (11pm-2am; $4.50 per game). Daytime bowling on weekdays is less flashy, but cheaper. (☎264-3166; www.boonebowling.com. Open M-F 10am-11pm, Sa 10am-2am, Su 2-9pm. M-F before 5pm $2.50 per game, seniors and under 10 $2.25; after 5pm $3.00/$2.50; Sa-Su $3.50.)

NORTH CAROLINA COAST

Lined with barrier islands that shield inlanders from Atlantic squalls, the Carolina Coast has a history as stormy as the hurricanes that pummel its beaches. England's first attempt to colonize North America ended in 1590 with the peculiar disappearance of the Roanoke Island settlement, known today as the "Lost Colony." Later, the coast earned the title "Graveyard of the Atlantic"—over 1000 ships have foundered on the Outer Banks' southern shores, leaving hundreds of wrecks for scuba divers to explore. The same wind that sank ships lifted the world's first flight in 1903, with some assistance from Orville and Wilbur Wright. Flying now forms the basis of much of the area's recreational activities: hang-gliding, parasailing, windsurfing, kiteboarding, and good ol' kite-flying. Those not interested in taking to the sky can take advantage of the abundance of natural sea life and go fishing, crabbing, or aquarium hopping.

OUTER BANKS ☎252

Locals claim that the legendary pirate Blackbeard once roamed the waters off the Outer Banks; some think that his treasures still lie beneath the beaches. But whether or not you dig up Blackbeard's loot, you'll find other gems on the these islands, from historic lighthouses to gorgeous sand dunes. On the northern half of Bodie Island, the three contiguous towns of **Kitty Hawk, Kill Devil Hills,** and **Nags Head** are heavily trafficked commercial areas filled with restaurants, mini golf courses, and souvenir super-stores. However, follow Rte. 12 south to Hatteras Island and you will find largely undeveloped pristine beaches, thanks to protection from the national park system. **Ocracoke Island,** the southernmost of the islands, retains its community charm, despite its growing popularity.

🚍 TRANSPORATION

Ferries: Free ferries run between **Hatteras** and **Ocracoke** (40min., daily 5am-midnight; no reservations accepted). Lines to board and disembark from the ferry may take 10min., so a one-way ferry trip may take up to 1hr. Toll ferries run between **Ocracoke** and **Cedar Island,** east of New Bern on Rte. 12, which becomes U.S. 70 (2¼hr.; $1 per pedestrian, $3 per cyclist, $10 per motorcycle, $15 per car). Toll ferries also travel between Ocracoke and **Swan Quarter,** on U.S. 264 (2½hr., same prices as Cedar Island). Call ahead for schedules and reservations: for ferries from Ocracoke ☎800-345-1665, from Cedar Island 800-856-0343, from Swan Quarter 800-773-1094. General info and reservations at ☎800-293-3779; www.ncferry.org.

Taxi: Beach Cab (☎441-2500 or 800-441-2503), for Bodie Island and Manteo. **Coastal Cab** (☎449-8787), Bodie Island only.

Bike Rental: Ocean Atlantic Rental (☎441-7823), in Nags Head. $35 per week.

🧭 ORIENTATION

The Outer Banks consist of four narrow islands strung along the northern half of the North Carolina coast. The northernmost, **Bodie Island,** is joined to the mainland by the **Wright Memorial Bridge,** which allows U.S. 158 to cross the Currituck Sound and run the length of the island. For much of Bodie Island, Rte. 12 (known as the Beach Road and the Virginia Dare Trail) and U.S. 158 (called the Bypass and the Croatan Hwy.) run parallel. **Roanoke Island** lies between the southern end of Bodie and the mainland and provides the only other point of entry via car. U.S. 64 runs from the mainland to **Manteo** on Roanoke over the Virginia Dare Bridge and then to Bodie just south of Nags Head over the Washington Baum Bridge. From the **Whalebone Junction,** where U.S. 158 ends and U.S. 64 runs into Rte. 12, the **Cape Hatteras National Seashore** stretches south for 70 mi. across the southern end of Bodie Island and almost all of Hatteras Island. Rte. 12 is the only major road running north-south through the Cape Hatteras National Seashore and connects Bodie to Hatteras Island via another bridge. Southernmost **Ocracoke Island** is linked by ferry to Hatteras Island to the north and towns on the mainland to the south. Ocracoke Island is also almost entirely park land, and has only one town, Ocracoke Village. Directions to locations on Bodie Island and Hatteras Island are usually given in terms of distances in miles from the Wright Memorial Bridge. There is **no public transit** on the Outer Banks. Hectic traffic calls for extra caution and travel time.

⑦ PRACTICAL INFORMATION

Visitor Info: Outer Banks Welcome Center on Roanoke Island, 1 Visitors Center Cir., (☎877-629-4386; www.outerbanks.org), at the base of the bridge to the mainland in Manteo; info for all the islands except Ocracoke. Open daily 9am-5:30pm; info by phone M-F 8am-6pm, Sa-Su 10am-4pm. Hotel and ferry reservations. **Aycock Brown Welcome Center** (☎261-4644; www.outerbanks.com/dare/brown.htm), Mi. 1.5 on U.S. 158 in Kitty Hawk, has maps and brochures. Open daily 9am-5:30pm. **Cape Hatteras National Seashore Information Centers: Bodie Island** (☎441-5711), on Rte. 12 at the north entrance to the park at Whalebone Junction. Open daily June-Aug. 9am-6pm; Sept.-May 9am-5pm. **Hatteras Island** (☎995-4474), on Rte. 12 at the Cape Hatteras Lighthouse. Open daily in summer 9am-6pm; in winter 9am-5pm. **Ocracoke Island** (☎928-4531), next to the ferry terminal at the south end of the island. Open daily 9am-5pm. Park info online at www.nps.gov/caha.

Internet Access: Free in the **Dare County Libraries.** On Bodie Island, **Kill Devil Hills Branch,** 400 Mustian St. (☎441-4331), 1 block west of U.S. 158, just south of the Wright Memorial and behind the post office. Open M and Th-Sa 9am-5:30pm, Tu-W 10am-8pm. On Roanoke, **Manteo Branch,** on Rte. 64 at Burnside St. (☎473-2372). Open M 10am-8pm, Tu and F 8:30am-5:30pm, W 10am-5:30pm, Th 8:30am-8pm, Sa 10am-4pm. **Hatteras Branch,** (☎968-2385), on Hwy. 12 in the Community Building in Hatteras. Open Tu and Th-F 9:30am-5:30pm, W 1-7pm, Sa 9:30am-12:30pm.

Post Office: 3841 N. Croatan Hwy./Rte. 158 (☎261-2211), in Kitty Hawk. Open M-F 9am-4:30pm, Sa 10am-noon. **Postal Code:** 27949. **Area Code:** 252.

THE BIG SPLURGE

FLYING HIGH

Visitors to the Outer Banks often experience the islands by land and by sea, but few ever get to see the islands the way the Wright brothers did, by air. If you're in no race to get your pilot's license any time soon, you can still enjoy the rush of flying hundreds of feet above the surf. **Parasail Above Ocracoke** offers exhilarating excursions for less than the price of a night's accommodation in even the cheapest of Outer Banks motels. Expert boat drivers take riders out into the middle of the sound, or, if riders are lucky, to the ocean for coastline-hugging parasailing—just try not to look to smug when you lock eyes with envious landbound tourists. All rides begin and end on the speedboat, so water-shy would-be-parasailers need not fear: unless you ask to be dipped while riding, you'll never get wet. A guide will help you suit up in a harness similar to those used in rock-climbing, hook you up to the parachute, and give you encouraging advice as your line uncoils and you are lifted into the air. Boat trips last 1-1½hr. depending on the number of riders in the boat. Each rider gets 15min. in the air, so enjoy the ride and the rush.

Parasail Above Ocracoke, (☎928-2606). Sign-up stand and boat dock on Silver Lake Rd., next to the Jolly Roger Restaurant. Solo rides $60, tandem rides $50 per person.

🕳🕳 ACCOMMODATIONS AND FOOD

Most motels line **Route 12** on crowded Bodie Island. For more privacy, go farther south; **Ocracoke** is the most secluded. On all three islands, rooming rates are highest from June through August, especially on weekends. Although inter-season rates are good for April, May, September, and October, April can be rainy, October cold, and September hurricane-ridden. To score a good deal without sacrificing good weather, schedule your visit for May. No matter when you visit, it's a good idea to make reservations as far in advance as possible.

CAMPING

While sleeping on public beaches is punishable by fines and oceanview hotel rooms cost an arm and a leg, you can nod off to the sounds of the surf if you camp in one of the National Park Service's four oceanside **campgrounds ❶.** Each of the campgrounds is located in the Cape Hatteras National Seashore and has water, restrooms, picnic tables, grills, and cold-water showers. The northernmost site is **Oregon Inlet,** near the southern tip of Bodie Island. The next two sites, **Cape Point** and **Frisco,** both lie near the elbow of Hatteras Island close to the lighthouse. Finally, the southernmost site, **Ocracoke,** is located on Ocracoke Island, 3 mi. north of Ocracoke Village. Soil in the campgrounds is sandy, so rangers recommend bringing longer-than-usual stakes for tents. (☎473-2111. All sites $20. RVs allowed, no hookups available. Cape Point open late May to early Sept.; all others open mid-Apr. to mid-Oct. Reservations may be made only for Ocracoke Campground.)

BODIE ISLAND

Outer Banks International Hostel (HI) ❶, 1004 W. Kitty Hawk Rd., is the best deal in the northern islands. This friendly, bustling hostel has 60 beds, two kitchens, A/C, volleyball, shuffleboard, and laundry. Late risers, beware: peacocks live on the premises and begin giving loud, shrill calls with the sunrise. (☎261-2294; www.outerbankshostel.com. Linens $2. Reception 8-10am and 5-9pm, but often staff can be found in the office mid-day as well. Dorms $17, nonmembers $20; private rooms $15 plus $17/$20 per person. Camping on the grounds $17 for 2 adults, each additional person $4; tent rental $6. Children under 12 half-price; children under 5 free.) Staying oceanside along Beach Rd. will cost you; one alternative is **Cavalier Motel ❹,** 601 Beach Rd., near Mi. 8.5. This motor court comes with most of the amenities of a large hotel at a fraction of the price: refrigerators, microwaves, free local calls, cable TV, A/C, a pool, a children's play area, horseshoes, shuffleboard, and a volleyball court. (☎441-5585; www.thecavaliermotel.com. Room with twin and double bed June-Aug. $84, Apr.-May and Sept. $52, Oct.-Mar. $31; ocean view and 2 double beds $132/$85/$48; with full bath and kitchenette $160/$94/$54. Multiple-bedroom cottages available.)

The oceanfront deck at **Quagmires ❸,** Mi. 7.5 on Beach Rd., is a popular spot to grab a drink after a day in the sun, and to enjoy fresh seafood and their Mexican specialties. The house specialty is the Bushwacker ($6.50), a huge mug filled with a creamy mixed drink containing almost every type of alcohol known to man. (☎441-9188; www.quags.com. Entrees $10-18. Beer from $2.50. Open daily 11:30am-2am.) **Tortuga's Lie ❸,** Mi. 11 on Beach Rd. in Nags Head, serves Caribbean-influenced seafood, sandwiches, pasta, and grill items in a casual setting. If you like your food spicy, a tasty option is the Pork Antonio rubbed with jerk seasoning and topped with habanero yellow currant glaze for $14. (☎441-7299; www.tortugaslie.com. Sandwiches and burgers $5-6, dinner entrees $13-17. W sushi night after 10pm. Open daily 11:30am-10pm. No reservations, usually a wait for dinner.) **The Outer Banks Brewing Station ❸,** Mi. 8.5 on U.S. 158, offers local micro-brews, a diverse menu, and live music in the evenings. (☎449-2739; www.obbrewing.com. Entrees $6-8. Seafood $10-14. Pints $3.50. $1 off appetizers during 3-5pm happy hour. Open daily 11:30am-2am.)

OCRACOKE

Hatteras Island is almost exclusively park land, so there are few lodging options other than pitching a tent at one of the area's many campgrounds. In Ocracoke, accommodations and restaurants all cluster on the island's southern tip in tiny **Ocracoke Village.** For pleasant, wood-paneled rooms at some of Ocracoke's lowest prices, **Blackbeard's Lodge ❹,** 111 Back Rd., is the place to go. Turn right off Rte. 12 just before the boat filled with seashells. The swing and rocking chairs on the front porch are a perfect spot to relax and watch the world go by. (☎928-3421, reservations 800-892-5314; www.blackbeardslodge.com. Game room, A/C, cable TV, and heated pool. Double beds $75; queen bed $85; lower in winter.) The bright rooms at the **Sand Dollar Motel ❹,** 70 Sand Dollar Rd. in Ocracoke, have a beach-cabin allure. (☎928-5571. Open Apr.-late Nov. Refrigerators, microwaves, A/C, cable TV, pool, and breakfast 8-10am. Queen bed $80; 2 double beds $85; winter rates vary.)

In this tiny town of saltwater taffy counters and catch-of-the-day specials, the **Cat Ridge Deli ❷,** 300 Lighthouse Rd., is an unexpected delight. Occupying a counter along the back wall of Styron's General Store (est. 1920) at the corner of Lighthouse and Creek Rd. in Ocracoke, the deli specializes in Thai-influenced wraps. (☎928-3354. Wraps around $6. Closed Jan.-Mar. Open M-Sa 10:30am-6:30pm; low-season 10:30am-5pm.) Sea lovers can mosey on over to **Jolly Roger ❷,** on Rte. 12 by the harbor in Ocracoke, for waterfront dining and a laid-back atmosphere. Inhale the sea breeze along with locally caught fresh fish specials (market price) and sandwiches for $5-8. (☎928-3703. Beer from $2.50 a pint or $6.50 a pitcher. Open daily mid-Mar. to mid-Nov. 11am-10pm.)

👁 SIGHTS

The **Wright Brothers National Memorial,** Mi. 8 on U.S. 158, marks the spot where Orville and Wilbur Wright took to the skies in history's first powered flight. Exhibits in the visitors center document aerospace technology from the first airplane to the first moon landing. (☎441-7430; www.nps.gov/wrbr. Open daily June-Aug. 9am-6pm; Sept.-May 9am-5pm. $3 per person, under 16 free.) At the nearby **Jockey's Ridge State Park,** Mi. 12 on U.S. 158, **Kitty Hawk Kites** (☎441-4124 or 877-359-8447; www.kittyhawk.com) trains aspiring hang-gliding pilots. Beginner lessons lasting 3hr. and including five solo flights start at $89. Those preferring to explore things at ground level can slide down Jockey Ridge's dunes, the tallest on the East Coast, comprised of some 30 million tons of sand. (Park ☎441-7132. Open daily in summer 8am-9pm; low-season park closes between 6 and 8pm. Free.)

Roanoke Island is a locus of historic and cultural draws. The **Fort Raleigh National Historic Site,** 1409 National Park Rd., just off U.S. 64, marks the place where the British first attempted to settle in the New World. Settlers occupied this area beginning in 1585, but a lack of supplies and tensions with local tribes forced their return to England. A second colony, established in 1587, disappeared without explanation around 1590. The visitors center displays artifacts from the settlement and hosts talks by park interpreters. During the summer, actors perform **The Lost Colony,** a musical version of the settlers' story, in a theater overlooking the sound by the Fort Raleigh site. (☎473-3414 or 866-468-7630. Park: www.nps.gov/fora; Musical: www.thelostcolony.org. Fort Raleigh Visitors Center open daily in summer 9am-6pm; low-season 9am-5pm. Shows June-Aug. M-Sa 8:30pm. $16, ages 62 and up $15, 11 and under $14.)

Just down U.S. 64, **Roanoke Island Festival Park,** staffed largely by actors in 16th-century garb, features *Elizabeth II,* a replica of a 16th-century English merchant ship. (☎475-1500; www.roanokeisland.com. Park and museum open daily in summer 10am-7pm, ship open 10am-6:30pm; Apr.-May and Sept.-Oct. 10am-6pm; Mar. and Dec. 10am-5pm; park closed Jan.-Feb. Two-day tickets $8, students ages 6-17

$5, 5 and under free. At 2pm on Tuesdays in July students from the North Carolina School of the Arts perform classical music at the Park's outdoor pavilion. Nearby, in the romantic **Elizabethan Gardens,** visitors can wander among fountains, antique statues, and beds of flowers changed every season. (☎473-3234; www.elizabe-thangardens.org. Open June-Aug. M-Sa 9am-8pm, Su 9am-7pm; low-season hours vary. $6, ages 62 and up $5, ages 6-18 $2, under 5 free. Wheelchair accessible.)

SCENIC DRIVE: CAPE HATTERAS NATIONAL SEASHORE

The Cape Hatteras National Seashore actually offers two shores for the price of one, because as you drive the 70 mi. of Rte. 12 that run between Whalebone Junction and Ocracoke Village you can see the Atlantic Ocean off to the east and the Pamlico Sound to the west. Traffic may force you to crawl along at 30 mph if you drive south from Hatteras to Ocracoke in the summer, but the leisurely pace is perfect for appreciating the unobstructed bi-coastal view.

Route 12 is a paved two-lane road and the main artery of the park, running from the northern entrance of the park at Nags Head on Bodie Island to the southern tail in the town of Ocracoke Village. A free 40min. ferry shuttles cars from Hatteras to the northern end of Ocracoke Island (see **Transportation,** p. 416). Total transport time from Whalebone to Ocracoke is about 2½hr.

All of the park's major attractions are accessible and clearly marked from Rte. 12. The chief of these are the Outer Banks' three **lighthouses** on Bodie, Hatteras, and Ocracoke Islands. The tallest brick lighthouse in North America is the 196 ft. Cape Hatteras lighthouse, built in 1870. Due to beach erosion, the lighthouse was relocated by 2900 ft. in 1999. To scale the tower for an impressive view, join one of the self-guided tours. (20min. tours every 20min. daily 9am-4:40pm. Ticket sales begin 8am. Open Apr.-Sept. $4; children under 12, disabled, and ages 62 and up $2.) Duck into the visitors center to see a section of the original lens, an inspiring feat of early engineering. (☎995-4474. Open daily in summer 9am-6pm; in winter 9am-5pm.) Another set of attractions along Rte. 12 reminds visitors that lighthouses have a value apart from the picturesque— several **shipwrecks** can be seen from the shore. Turn off Rte. 12 at Coquina Beach to see the wreck of the *Laura A. Barnes*, which was grounded in 1921. Visibility varies over time. For a schedule of the various ranger programs covering history and natural history that run daily at the visitors centers at each lighthouse, pick up a copy of the free paper *In The Park*.

The **Pea Island National Wildlife Refuge** on the northern tip of Hatteras Island can claim over 365 species of birds, including endangered peregrine falcons. The **Charles Kuralt Nature Trail,** next to the visitors center, affords trekkers a chance to glimpse grackles, pelicans, loggerhead turtles, and the Carolina salt marsh snakes. The ½ mi. **North Pond Wildlife Trail,** also beginning at the visitors center, is fully wheelchair accessible. (Visitors center ☎987-2394; www.peaisland.fws.gov. Usually open in summer daily 9am-4pm; in winter Sa-Su only. Beaches in the refuge are open only during daylight.) Farther south, the **Pony Pasture,** on Rte. 12 in Ocracoke, is the stomping ground for a herd of semi-wild horses, said to be descendants of horses left there by shipwrecked explorers in the 16th or 17th century.

WILMINGTON ☎910

Situated on the Carolina coast at the mouth of the Cape Fear River, and only a few miles from the beaches of the Atlantic, Wilmington has long been an important center for shipping and industry. Home to the largest film production facility east of L.A., the city is sometimes referred to as "Wilmywood" and "Hollywood East." Since 1983, over 400 feature films and TV projects have been shot along the picturesque Cape Fear coast, including the hit TV series *Dawson's Creek*. Even if you don't glimpse a celebrity, the historic downtown area has plenty to offer, from historic memorials to excellent restaurants and picturesque views of the waterfront.

⊠ PRACTICAL INFORMATION. Wilmington International Airport, 1740 Airport Blvd., is off 23rd St. about 2 mi. north of Market St. and the downtown area. (☎341-4333; www.flyilm.com). **Greyhound,** 201 Harnett St. (☎762-6073; open daily 8:30-11am, 1-5pm, 8:30-9:15pm), between 3rd and Front St. about a mile north of downtown, departs to Charlotte (9hr., 1 per day, $29-44) and Raleigh (3hr., 2 per day, $29). The Wilmington Transit Authority (☎343-0106; www.wavetransit.com) runs **local buses** (run M-F 6am-7:30pm; $0.75; ages 65 and over, disabled, and students $0.35) and a **free trolley** that travels along Front St. between Ann and Hanover St. (runs M-F 7:30am-7:30pm, Sa 11am-7:30pm). A **river taxi** ferries passengers across the river between downtown Market St. and the *USS North Carolina*. (☎343-1611 or 800-676-0162. Runs daily 10am-5pm. 15min., round-trip $3. Riverboat sightseeing cruises lasting 45min. also available at 11am and 3pm; adults $11, children ages 2-12 $5.) **Taxi: Port City Taxi ☎**762-1165. **Visitor Info: Visitors Center,** 24 N. 3rd St., at the corner of 3rd and Princess. (☎341-4030 or 800-222-4757; www.cape-fear.nc.us. Open M-F 8:30am-5pm, Sa 9am-4pm, Su 1-4pm.) The visitors center also runs an **information kiosk** at the foot of Market St. by the waterfront. (Open daily June-Aug. 9:30am-5pm, Apr.-May and Sept.-Oct. 9am-4:30pm.) **Internet Access: New Hanover County Library,** 201 Chestnut St., at the intersection with 3rd St., one block from the visitors center. (☎798-6302. Open M-W 9am-8pm, Th-Sa 9am-5pm, Su 1-5pm. Free. Internet access limited to 1hr., 30min. if others are waiting.) **Post Office:** 152 N. Front St., at the intersection with Chestnut St. (☎313-3293. Open M-F 9am-5pm, Sa 9am-noon.) **Postal Code:** 28401. **Area Code:** 910.

⋔ ACCOMMODATIONS. Wilmington's best lodging comes in the form of B&Bs; most are conveniently located in the historic downtown area. Though rooms usually cost $100-200 per night, the unique rooms, convenient location, and riverfront views may make Wilmington's B&Bs worth the extra cash. Be sure to reserve as far in advance as your travel plans allow, especially during the summer. **Catherine's Inn ❺,** 410 S. Front St., offers gorgeous rooms, a two-story porch overlooking the Cape Fear River, a sunken garden with a gazebo, a full country breakfast, and warm hospitality. (☎251-0863 or 800-476-0723; www.catherinesinn.com. Private bath, off-street parking, Internet access, free drinks. Check-in 3-5pm. Queen rooms for 1 person $80, for 2 $100-105; kings $85/$115-120.) For less expensive lodging, nearly every budget chain can be found on Market St. between College Rd. and 23rd St. Weekend rates often run $10-20 higher than weekday prices. **Travel Inn ❷,** 4401 Market St., a single-floor motor court, provides basic rooms with tiny showers for some of the lowest rates around. (☎763-8217. Pool, cable TV with free HBO, and A/C. Rooms in summer M-F $35-39, Sa-Su $59-79; in winter from $35. 10% discount for AAA/AARP.) If the B&Bs are full, the **Best Western Coastline Inn ❹,** 503 Nutt St., has large, comfortable rooms overlooking the river. (☎763-2800; www.coastlineinn.com. Data ports, fitness center, free wireless Internet, fax, and continental breakfast included. Rooms Apr.-Oct. singles M-F $79, Sa-Su $119-139; doubles $10 more. Oct.-Apr. $79/$99-109. 10% AAA/AARP discount.) The **Carolina Beach State Park ❶,** about 18 mi. south of the city on U.S. 421, offers campsites as well as hiking, picnic areas, and a marina. (☎458-8206. Restrooms, hot showers, laundry facilities, water, and grills. No RV hookups. Open year-round. Sites $15.)

⧉ FOOD. Quality restaurants are plentiful in historic downtown Wilmington. **▨Rim Wang ❷,** 128 S. Front St., offers authentic Thai cuisine, with options that will please both those looking for something spicy and those who seek their chili-shy counterparts. Lunch specials range from traditional *pad thai* to chicken massaman and include a zesty bowl of coconut soup. (☎763-5552. Lunch specials $6-7.50. Most noodle, rice, and stir-fry dishes $9. Curries $11. Open M-Th 11am-3pm and 5-10:30pm, F 11:30am-3pm and 5-11:30pm, Sa 11:30am-11:30pm, Su 3-10:30pm.) The trendy **Caffé Phoenix ❸**, 9 S. Front St., serves upscale Mediterranean dishes with an emphasis on seafood. Choose between their linen-tableclothed interior or the scenic patio. (☎343-1395. Salads from $7.50. Lunch sandwiches $7.50-9. Seafood $17-21. Open M-Th 11:30am-10pm, F-Sa 11:30am-11pm, Su 10:30am-10pm.) **Nikki's ❶**, 16 S. Front St., is a downtown deli where the atmosphere is casual, the waitresses dreadlocked, and the menu heavily vegetarian. (☎772-9151. Sandwiches $5.25-8. Wraps $5-6.50. Sushi from $3 for 6 pieces or two nigiri. Open Tu-Sa 11am-4pm, also F-Sa 6-10pm.)

◙ **SIGHTS.** No visit to Wilmington would be complete without an afternoon at the relaxing **Wrightsville Beach.** From Market St. downtown, take Eastwood Rd. to the bridge leading over Wrightsville Sound to the beach. Fifteen miles down Rte. 421, **Carolina Beach** has a charming boardwalk and a state park where the carnivorous Venus fly-trap plant flourishes. Five miles farther on Rte. 421 is **Kure Beach,** a state recreation area. The **Fort Fisher Aquarium** in Kure Beach draws visitors from all over the country to the tail end of Cape Fear to see three habitat exhibits: freshwater, coastal marsh, and open ocean. Don't miss the freshwater alligators or the quarter-million gallon Cape Fear Shoals tank, full of eels, sharks, coral reefs, and a variety of fish. (☎458-8257; www.ncaquariums.com. Open 9am-5pm daily. $7, ages 65 and up and active military $6, children ages 6-17 $5, under 6 free.)

For Wilmington's glamorous side, **Screen Gems Studios,** 1223 N. 23rd St., near the airport, is the largest movie and TV production facility east of Hollywood. Guided 1hr. studio tours provide a fascinating behind-the-scenes glimpse of the industry. (☎343-3500; www.screengemsstudios.com. Tours June-Aug. Sa-Su noon and 2pm; Sept.-May Sa noon. Schedules may vary; call for details. $12, children under 12 $5.) Art aficionados shouldn't miss the **Louise Wells Cameron Art Museum,** 3201 S. 17th St., at the intersection of Independence Blvd., which displays the work of American masters, including a major collection of works by artist Mary Cassatt and the work of North Carolinian artists from the 18th to 21st centuries in media as disparate as ceramics and computer-generated art. (☎395-5999; www.cameronartmuseum.com. Open Tu-Sa 10am-5pm, Su 10am-4pm. $7, children 5-18 $4, ages 4 and under free; families $15.)

You can also take a self-guided tour of the massive **Battleship North Carolina,** moored in the Cape Fear River across from downtown, at the junction of Hwys. 17, 74, 76, and 421. This sturdy warship, with a crew of 2339, participated in every major naval offensive in the Pacific during WWII. Highlights of the ship open to visitors include the bridge, soldiers quarters, and galley. (☎251-5797; www.battleshipnc.com. Open daily mid-May to mid-Sept. 8am-8pm; mid-Sept. to mid-May 8am-5pm. Ticket sales end 1hr. before closing. $9, ages 65 and over and military $8, children 6-11 $4.50, 5 and under free.) For a change of pace, take in a jazz or folk concert at the **Airlie Gardens,** 300 Airlie Rd. just off Oleander Dr., or stroll through the **New Hanover County Arboretum,** 6206 Oleander Dr., which includes a Japanese garden with a traditional teahouse. (Airlie Gardens: ☎798-7700; www.airliegardens.org. Open Tu-Th and Sa 9am-5pm, F 9am-7pm, Su 11am-5pm. $8, children under 10 $5, ages 65 and over $7. Concerts first and third F Apr.-Oct. 6pm-8pm, free with admission. Arboretum: ☎452-6393. Open daily dawn-dusk. Free.)

🎭🎪 **ENTERTAINMENT AND NIGHTLIFE.** For local entertainment info, pick up a free copy of *Encore* or *The Outrider*, weekly newspapers with event listings, available in most hotels and cafes. Wilmington's historic **Thalian Hall,** 310 Chestnut

St., offers a wide range of entertainment, from theater, dance, and music to comedy acts. Tours of the hall showcase its history, from the design created by famous architect John Trimble to the famous guests—including Buffalo Bill Cody and John Philip Sousa—hosted during its nearly 150 years of continuous use. (Box office ☎343-3664 or 800-523-2820; www.thalianhall.com. Box office open M-F noon-6pm, Sa-Su 2-6pm. Tours by appointment $6. Tour info ☎343-3660.)

Downtown Wilmington is jumping on Friday and Saturday nights; most bars and clubs cluster around Front St. The **Reel Cafe**, 100 S. Front St., offers three big screen TVs, a dance floor, and live music on the courtyard patio. (☎251-1832; www.thereelcafe.net. Dress code strictly enforced. 21+ after 11pm. Cover F-Sa $5, Sa ladies free. Open daily 3pm-2am. Rooftop bar open Th-Su, dance floor F-Sa.) For low-key chilling with pool tables, classic arcade games, air hockey, over 60 kinds of beer, and a young, casual crowd, head to **Blue Post**, 15 S. Water St., by Dock St. at the back corner of the parking lot. (☎343-1141. Beer from $2.50. 21+. Open M-F 3pm-2am, Sa-Su 2pm-2am.)

Are your socks dirty? Spend an evening at **Soapbox**, 255 N. Front St., a "Laundro-Lounge" where you can do your laundry as you booze. (No, we aren't kidding.) Downstairs, you'll find foosball, pool, occasional live music, a bar, and plenty of washers and dryers. Upstairs you'll find a more conventional nightclub with another bar and a stage for live music ranging from hip-hop and reggae to jazz and good old rock and roll. (☎251-8500; www.soapboxlaundrolounge.com. Downstairs: M heavy-metal bingo, Tu jazz, W "Flat Broke Folk" open mic night, Th "Hard-Core-aoke." No cover downstairs, upstairs $5-10, more for under 21. Open M-F 8am-2am, Sa-Su 10am-2am.) Take in the view from **Level 5**, 21 N. Front St. on the fifth floor, a popular rooftop bar with an elite attitude manifest in the dress code and liberal use of the velvet rope. If you can get in, be sure not to miss the view. (☎342-0272. Beer $2.50 and up. Comedy acts Tu-Th 9pm, live music Th-F, DJ Sa. 21+, shows 18+. Cover Th-Sa $2-5. Open daily 5pm-2am.)

SOUTH CAROLINA

To some, South Carolina's pride in the Palmetto State may seem extreme. Inspired by the state flag, the palmetto tree logo decorates hats, bottles and bumper stickers across the landscape. This pride is justified, though, by the unrivaled beaches of the Grand Strand and the stately elegance of Charleston. Columbia, though less well known, offers an impressive artistic and cultural experience without the smog and traffic that plague other cities of the New South. Tamed for tourists and merchandising, the Confederate legacy of the first state to secede from the Union is groomed as a cash cow. Beyond the commercialized strips, however, South Carolina retains its old-style grace and charm—not to mention its rebellious spirit.

◪ PRACTICAL INFORMATION

Capital: Columbia.

Visitor Info: Department of Parks, Recreation, and Tourism, Edgar A. Brown Bldg., 1205 Pendleton St., Rm. 200, Columbia 29201 (☎803-734-1700; www.discoversouthcarolina.com). **South Carolina Forestry Commission,** 5500 Broad River Rd., Columbia 29212 (☎803-896-8800).

Postal Abbreviation: SC. **Sales Tax:** 5-7%.

CHARLESTON ☎ 843

Built on rice and cotton, Charleston's antebellum plantation system yielded vast riches now seen in its numerous museums, historic homes, and ornate architecture. An accumulated cultural capital of 300 years flows like the natives' long, distinctive drawl. Several of the South's most renowned plantations dot the city, while two venerable educational institutions, the **College of Charleston** and **the Citadel,** add a youthful eccentricity. Horse-drawn carriages, cobblestone streets, pre-Civil War homes, beautiful beaches, and some of the best restaurants in the Southeast explain why Charleston often heads the list of the nation's top destinations.

▐ TRANSPORTATION

Trains: Amtrak, 4565 Gaynor Ave. (☎ 744-8264), 8 mi. west of downtown. Open daily 6am-10pm. To: **Richmond** (7hr., 2 per day, $129); **Savannah** (1¾hr., 2 per day, $20); **Washington, D.C.** (9½hr., 2 per day, $120).

Buses: Greyhound, 3610 Dorchester Rd. (☎ 747-5341 or 800-231-2222 for schedules and fares), in N. Charleston. *Avoid this area at night.* Station open daily 8am-9:30pm. To: **Charlotte** (5hr., 2 per day, $43); **Myrtle Beach** (2½hr., 2 per day, $26); **Savannah** (2¾hr., 2 per day, $26). CARTA's "Dorchester/Waylyn" bus goes into town from the station area; return "Navy Yard: 5 Mile Dorchester Rd." bus.

Downtown Charleston

▲▲▲ ACCOMMODATIONS
1837 Tea Room, **9**
Bed, No Breakfast, **7**
Campground at James
 Island County Park, **2**
Charleston's Historic
 Hostel & Inn, **4**
Motel 6, **1**
Not So Hostel, **3**

🍴 FOOD
East Bay Deli, **8**
Hyman's Seafood
 Company, **13**
Jestine's Kitchen, **11**
Normandy Farm
 Artisan Bakery, **12**
Sticky Fingers, **10**

🍸 NIGHTLIFE
City Bar, **15**
Coast, **6**
Meritage, **14**
Music Farm, **5**

Public Transit: CARTA, 36 John St. (☎724-7420), runs area buses and the **Downtown Area Shuttle (DASH),** trolley routes that circle downtown. $1, seniors $0.50, disabled $0.25; 1-day pass $3, 3-day $7. Runs daily 8am-11pm. Visitors center has schedules.

Taxi: Yellow Cab ☎577-6565.

Bike Rental: The Bicycle Shoppe, 280 Meeting St. (☎722-8168), between George and Society St. Open M-F 9am-7pm, Sa 9am-6pm, Su 1-5pm. $5 per hr., $20 per day.

■✷ 🔽 ORIENTATION AND PRACTICAL INFORMATION

Old Charleston lies at the southernmost point of the mile-wide peninsula below **Calhoun Street.** The major north-south routes through the city are **Meeting, King,** and **East Bay Street.** The area north of the visitors center is run-down and uninviting. **Savannah Highway (U.S. 17)** cuts across the peninsula going south to Savannah and north across two towering bridges to Mt. Pleasant and Myrtle Beach. There are plenty of metered parking spaces, and plenty of police officers giving tickets.

Visitor Info: Charleston Visitors Center, 375 Meeting St. (☎853-8000 or 800-868-8118; www.charlestoncvb.com), across from Charleston Museum. Open daily Apr.-Oct. 8:30am-5:30pm; Nov.-Mar. 8:30am-5pm.

Hotlines: Crisis Line, ☎744-4357 or 800-922-2283. 24hr. general counseling and referral. **People Against Rape,** ☎745-0144 or 800-241-7273. 24hr.

Medical Services: Charleston Memorial Hospital, 326 Calhoun St. (☎577-0600).

Internet Access: Public Library, 68 Calhoun St. (☎805-6801). Open M-Th 9am-9pm, F-Sa 9am-6pm, Su 2-5pm.

Post Office: 83 Broad St. (☎577-0690). Open M-F 8:30am-5:30pm, Sa 9:30am-2pm. Also houses a cute little postal museum. **Postal Code:** 29402. **Area Code:** 843.

🁢 ACCOMMODATIONS

Luckily for budget travelers, Charleston has two fantastic hostels; motel rooms in historic downtown Charleston are expensive. If you have the bucks, opt for one of the charming B&Bs. Cheap motels are just outside the city, around Exits 209-211 on I-26 W in N. Charleston, or across the Ashley River on U.S. 17 S in Mt. Pleasant.

🏠 **Charleston Historic Hostel & Inn,** 194 Saint Philip St. (☎478-1446; www.charlestonhostel.com), is located in an authentic antebellum home and is one of the South's best hostels. With spotless rooms, a great location, and a friendly staff, this hostel truly feels like home. Breakfast, Internet, linens, laundry, kitchen, and call-ahead pick-up—all free! Reservations recommended. Dorms $15-19, private rooms $40. ❶

Charleston's Not So Hostel, 156 Spring St. (☎478-1446; www.notsohostel.com). Friendly, clean, and comfortable, Not So Hostel has 3 more private rooms than its counterpart and even has a platform for campers. Internet, waffle breakfast, and off-street parking included. Dorms $15-19, private rooms $30-38. ❶

Bed, No Breakfast, 16 Halsey St. (☎723-4450). A simple, charming option for lodging, this 2-room inn offers guests a cozy and affordable stay in the historic heart of the city. Shared bathroom. Reservations recommended. Rooms $75-95. No credit cards. ❸

1837 Tea Room, 126 Wentworth St. (☎723-7166 or 877-723-1837; www.1837bb.com). In a wealthy cotton planter's former home, this B&B is in easy walking distance of downtown's main attractions. Each of the 9 rooms is beautifully furnished, and has A/C and microfridge. Reservations recommended. Rooms $79-165. ❹

Motel 6, 2058 Savannah Hwy. (☎556-5144), 5 mi. south of town. Be sure to call ahead and reserve one of these clean rooms; the immensely popular chain motel is often booked solid for days. Rooms Su-Th $45, F-Sa $55; each additional person $6. ❸

THE SOUTH

Campground at James Island County Park (☎795-4386 or 800-743-7275). Take U.S. 17 S to Rte. 171 to Hwy 700 and follow the signs. 125 spacious sites, each with picnic table and access to lakes, bicycle and walking trails, and a small water park. Bike and boat rental. Primitive sites $17, tent sites $22, hookup $28. Seniors 10% discount. ❶

🍴 FOOD

While most restaurants cater to big-spending tourists, there are plenty of budget-friendly opportunities to sample the Southern cooking, barbecue, and fresh seafood that have made the Low Country famous.

Hyman's Seafood Company, 215 Meeting St. (☎723-6000). Since 1890, this casual restaurant has offered 15-25 different kinds of fresh fish daily ($7-15), served in any one of 8 styles. Po' boy sandwich with oyster, calamari, crab, or scallops $7-8. No reservations; expect long waits. Open M-F 11am-11pm, Sa-Su 8am-11pm. ❸

Jestine's Kitchen, 251 Meeting St. (☎722-7224). Serving up some of the best southern food in Charleston, Jestine's has become a local favorite with its daily Southern blue plate specials ($7-10) and "blue collar special" (peanut butter and banana sandwich; $3). Open Tu-Th 11am-9:30pm, F-Sa 11am-10pm, Su 11am-9pm. ❷

East Bay Deli, 334 East Bay Street (☎723-1234). Those who have had enough of Charleston's carnivorous fare should have a look at this veggie-friendly deli. The all-you-can-eat salad bar ($7) is a feast, but there are still plenty of great meaty options; the California chicken is a specialty ($6). Open daily 10:30am-8pm. ❷

Sticky Fingers, 235 Meeting St. (☎853-7427). Rightly voted the best barbecue in town, Sticky Fingers is a Charleston legend for its mouth-watering ribs ($12-15), prepared 5 different ways. The Carolina combo includes meat-falls-off-the-bone ribs, barbecue chicken, and all the sides for a paltry $13. Open M-Sa 11am-11pm, Su 11am-10pm. ❸

Normandy Farm Artisan Bakery, 86 Society St. (☎577-5763), bakes its breads with only the freshest all-natural ingredients, and the result is a collection of fantastic baked goods. They also supply the breads for over 60 area restaurants, so chances are if you're dining in the city you will sample their goods at one point or another. Chocolate croissants $2.50, breads $3. Open Tu-F 7:30am-4pm, Su 7:30am-3pm. ❷

👁 SIGHTS

Charleston's ancient homes, historical monuments, churches, galleries, and gardens can be seen by foot, car, bus, boat, trolley, or horse-drawn carriage—or on one of the nine ghost tours. **City Market,** downtown at Meeting St., stays abuzz in a newly restored 19th-century building. (Open daily from about 9am-5pm.) **Liberty Square** is home to the aquarium and the fantastic Fort Sumter Visitors Center.

PLANTATIONS AND GARDENS. The best value is to be had at **Drayton Hall,** a 265-year-old plantation which has survived both the Revolutionary and Civil Wars, as well as numerous earthquakes and hurricanes. Entrance includes a guided tour of the stately plantation house. Afterwards, stroll on paths along the scenic marsh or bring a picnic lunch to enjoy on tables under moss-draped oak trees. *(On Rte. 61, 9 mi. northwest of downtown. ☎769-2600; www.draytonhall.org. Open daily Mar.-Oct. 9:30am-4pm, Oct.-Feb. 9:30am-3pm. $12, ages 12-18 $8, 6-11 $5, under 5 free. Grounds only $5. AAA discount. Wheelchair accessible.)* The 300-year-old **Magnolia Plantation and Gardens** is by far the most majestic of Charleston's plantations and the oldest major public garden in the country. Visitors can enjoy the staggering wealth of the Drayton family (who used to have relatives living down the road at Drayton Hall) by exploring their 50 acres of gorgeous gardens with 900 varieties of camelia and 250 varieties of azalea. Other attractions include a hedge maze, bike and canoe rental, swamp, and bird sanctuary. *(On Rte. 61, 10 mi. out of town off U.S. 17. ☎ 571-1266 or 800-367-3517; www.magnoliaplantation.com. Open Feb.-Nov. daily 8am-5:30pm; call for winter hours. Gardens and grounds ticket $13, ages 6-12 $7, under 6 free. After purchase of ticket, additional prices as follows: house tour $7 per person, under 6 not allowed; swamp $5, ages 6-12 $4; nature train $7, ages 6-12 $5, under 6 $3; nature boat tour $7/$5/$3; slavery talk free.* Farther out, **Cypress Gardens** lets visitors paddle their own boats out onto the eerie, gator-filled swamps. *(3030 Cypress Gardens Rd. Off Rte. 52. ☎ 553-0515; www.cypressgardens.org. Open daily 9am-5pm. $9, seniors $8, ages 6-12 $3.)*

CHARLESTON MUSEUM AND HISTORIC HOMES.
The **Charleston Museum** and its **Historic Homes** is the nation's oldest museum and a great way to become acquainted with the city's historical offerings. The museum boasts outstanding exhibits on the Revolutionary War and the Civil War, and a thorough look into the history of the Low Country. Across the street, the **Joseph Manigault House** reflects the lifestyle of a wealthy, rice-planting family and the African-American slaves who lived there. Farther downtown, the **Heyward-Washington House** was home to Thomas Heyward, Jr., a signer of the Declaration of Independence. It was rented to George Washington during his 1791 trip through the South. *(Museum: 360 Meeting St. ☎ 722-2996; www.charlestonmuseum.org. Open M-Sa 9am-5pm, Su 1-5pm. Joseph Manigault House: 350 Meeting St. ☎ 723-2926. Heyward-Washington House: 87 Church St. ☎ 722-0354. Both houses open M-Sa 10am-5pm, Su 1-5pm. Museum $9, 1 house $8, 2 sites $14, 3 sites $18. Wheelchair accessible.)* If you're after historic home tours, better bets are the **Nathaniel Russell House** and **Aiken Rhett House.** The Nathaniel Russel House's graceful interior belies the luxurious lifestyle of its former inhabitants. The audio tour of the Aiken Rhett House has a heavy focus on the slave quarters. Each house complements the other, painting a full and vivid picture of antebellum life in Charleston. *(Nathaniel Russell: 51 Meeting St. ☎ 724-8481. Aiken Rhett: 48 Elizabeth St. ☎ 723-1159. Houses open M-Sa 10am-5pm, Su 2-5pm. $8 per house, both for $14.)*

PATRIOT'S POINT AND FORT SUMTER. Climb aboard four Naval ships, including a submarine and a giant aircraft carrier, in **Patriot's Point Naval and Maritime Museum,** the world's largest naval museum. *(40 Patriots Point Rd. Across the Cooper River in Mt. Pleasant. ☎ 884-2727; www.state.sc.us/patpt. Open daily Apr.-Sept. 9am-6pm, ships close 7:30pm; Oct.-Mar. 9am-5pm, ships close 5:30pm. $13, seniors and military $11, ages 6-11 $6.)* From Patriot's Point in Mt. Pleasant, **Fort Sumter Tours** has boat excursions to the National Historic

AFRICA, SOUTH CAROLINA

Every Memorial Day weekend, almost 100,000 people from the world over come to the small, quiet town of Beaufort, SC, to pay homage to the culture and history that emerged when Africans were shipped to America as slaves many generations ago.

Known as the **Gullah Festival,** the gathering is a 5-day celebration of the melding of African and American traditions that has attracted droves of tourists, scholars, and locals since its humble inception in 1986. African storytellers captivate visitors, who also watch seductive African dances, listen to the harmonizing strains of live gospel and jazz music, and enjoy a multitude of authentic African dishes. A former slave market is memorialized in a special ceremony. Basket-weaving and boat-building exhibitions have also made their way into the festival, showcasing the very same techniques that were used centuries ago. Festival organizers have made a point to reach out to a younger audience in recent years, adding to the schedule a Miss Gullah Festival Pageant and a Gullah Golf Tournament.

For more info, call ☎ 843-522-1998.

Site where Confederate soldiers bombarded Union forces in April 1861, turning years of escalating tension into open war. There is a dock at Liberty Square next to the South Carolina Aquarium in Charleston. *(Tours: ☎881-7337. Fort Sumter: ☎883-3123; www.fortsumtertours.com. 2¼hr. tour; 1hr. is at the Fort. 1-3 tours per day from each location. $12, seniors $11, ages 6-11 $6.)*

BEACHES. Folly Beach is popular with students at the Citadel, College of Charleston, and University of South Carolina. *(Over the James Bridge and U.S. 171, about 20 mi. southeast of Charleston. ☎588-2426.)* The more wide open **Isle of Palms** extends for miles toward the less-crowded **Sullivan's Island.** *(Isle of Palms: Across the Cooper Bridge, drive 10 mi. down Hwy. 17 N, turn right onto the Isle of Palms Connector. ☎886-3863.)*

LIBERTY SQUARE. Two of Charleston's finest sights are located in Liberty Square. The ◪**Charleston Aquarium** has quickly become the city's greatest attraction. Although a bit overpriced, its exhibits showcase aquatic life from the region's swamps, marshes, and oceans. Stare down the fishies at the 330,000-gallon Great Ocean Tank, which boasts the nation's tallest viewing window. *(At the end of Calhoun St. on the Cooper River, overlooking the harbor. ☎720-1990; www.scaquarium.org. Open daily mid-June to mid-Aug. 9am-6pm; mid-Aug. to mid-June 9am-5pm. $14, seniors $12, ages 3-11 $7. Wheelchair accessible.)* Next door, the **Fort Sumter Visitor and Education Center** has a fascinating exhibit on the cultural, economical, and political differences between the North and South prior to the Civil War. *(Open daily 8:30am-5pm. Free.)*

BULL ISLAND. To get away from human civilization, take a ferry to Bull Island, a 5000-acre island off the coast of Charleston. The boat is often greeted by dolphins swimming in some of the cleanest water on the planet. Once on the island there are 16 mi. of hiking trails populated by 278 different species of birds. *(☎881-4582. ½hr. ferries depart from Moore's Landing, off Seewee Rd., 16 mi. north of Charleston off U.S. 17. Departs Mar.-Nov. Tu and Th-Sa 9am, 12:30pm; returns Tu and Th-Sa noon, 4pm; departs Dec.-Feb. Sa 10am; returns 3pm. Round-trip $30, under 12 $15.)*

🎵 🍷 ENTERTAINMENT AND NIGHTLIFE

The density of bars and clubs downtown, combined with the high number of 20-somethings working the hotels and services, give Charleston a lively nightlife scene. Free copies of *City Paper*, in stores and restaurants, list concerts and other events. Big-name bands take center stage nightly at the **Music Farm,** 32 Ann St. *(☎853-3276. Tickets $5-25.)* Charleston's trendiest flock to the newly opened **Coast,** 39-D John St. With its high ceilings and beach-themed decor, after a few drinks you'll swear you're on the coast. Sunday nights attract the biggest crowd, when all bottles of wine are half-price and tacos are $2. *(☎722-8838. Dinner 5:30-10pm, bar open 5pm-late.)* **Meritage,** 235 E. Bay St., is popular for its late-night scene. Tasty *tapas* ($6-8) and a wide selection of brews keep the party going strong. *(☎722-8838. Open daily 5pm-2am, food served until 1am.)* For the hottest dance scene in town, **City Bar,** 235 E. Bay St., is the place to go. The college scene keeps the dance floor moving, especially on Thursdays for the "Weekend Warm-Up Party." *(☎577-7383. 21+, except for Th when under 21 "female college co-eds" are allowed. Dress code F-Sa. Open Th-Sa 8:30pm-2am.)* The city explodes with music, theater, dance, and opera, as well as literary and visual arts events when Charleston hosts the annual **Spoleto Festival USA,** the nation's most comprehensive arts festival. Founded in 1977 and dedicated to young artists, it is the American counterpart to the Festival of Two Worlds in Spoleto, Italy. *(☎722-2764; www.spoletousa.org. May 27-June 12, 2005. $10-75.)*

COLUMBIA
☎ **803**

Much ado is made over Columbia's Civil War heritage, and understandably so, as Old South nostalgia brings in big tourist dollars. However, locals point out that more antebellum buildings have been lost to developers in the last century than were burned by Sherman and his rowdy troops. Still, the town is the heart of the nation's "rebel" child, and a defiant spirit is cultivated in Columbia's bars, businesses, and citizens. Southern pride and passion are perpetuated at the **University of South Carolina (USC)**, where "Gamecocks" roam the campus's sprawling green spaces and fascinating museums.

◪ PRACTICAL INFORMATION. The city is laid out in a square, bordered by Huger and Harden St. running north-south and Blossom and Calhoun St. east-west. **Assembly Street** is the main drag, running north-south through the heart of the city, and **Gervais Street** is its east-west equivalent. The Congaree River marks the city's western edge. *The Beltline offers little for tourists and, for safety purposes, is best avoided.*

Columbia Metropolitan Airport, 3000 Aviation Way (☎822-5000; www.columbiaairport.com), is in West Columbia. A taxi to downtown costs about $13-15. **Amtrak,** 850 Pulaski St. (☎252-8246; open daily 10pm-5:30am), sends one train per day to: Miami (15hr., $95); Savannah (2½hr., $35); Washington, D.C. (10hr., $130). **Greyhound,** 2015 Gervais St. (☎256-6465), at Harden St., sends buses to: Atlanta (5hr., 7 per day, $50); Charleston (2½ hr., 2 per day, $27); Charlotte (2hr., 3-4 per day, $18). **Connex TCT** runs transit through Columbia, with most main routes departing from pickup/transfer depots at Sumter and Laurel St. and at Assembly and Taylor St. (☎217-9019. Runs daily 5:30am-midnight; call for schedules. $0.75; seniors and disabled, except 3-6pm, $0.25; under 6 free. Free transfers.) **Taxi: Capital City Cab** ☎233-8294. **Visitor Info: Columbia Metropolitan Convention and Visitors Bureau,** 9000 Assembly St., has maps and info. (☎545-0000; www.columbiacvb.com. Open M-F 9am-5pm, Sa 10am-4pm.) For info on USC, try the **University of South Carolina Visitors Center,** 937 Assembly St. (☎777-0169 or 800-922-9755. Open M-F 8:30am-5pm, Sa 9:30am-12:30pm. Free parking pass.) **Medical Services: Palmetto Richland Memorial Hospital,** 5 Richland Medical Park. (☎434-7000.) **Internet Access: Richland County Public Library,** 1431 Assembly St. (☎799-9084. Open M-Th 9am-9pm, F-Sa 9am-6pm, Su 2-6pm.) **Post office:** 1601 Assembly St. (☎733-4643. Open M-F 7:30am-6pm.) **Postal Code:** 29201. **Area Code:** 803.

◪ ACCOMMODATIONS. Generally, the cheapest digs lie farthest from the city center. A short drive from downtown, the **Masters Inn ❷,** 613 Knox Abbott Dr., offers free local calls, morning coffee, a pool, and cable TV. Take Blossom St. across the Congaree River, where it becomes Knox Abbott Dr. (☎796-4300. Singles $33-36; doubles $35-38.) Inexpensive motels also line the three interstates (I-26, I-77, and I-20) that circle the city. **Knights Inn ❷,** 1987 Airport Blvd., Exit 133 off I-26, has many amenities for a low price. Rooms have refrigerators, microwaves, cable TV, A/C, free local calls, and pool access. (☎794-0222. Singles and doubles Su-Th $35, F-Sa $39. 10% senior discount.) After exploring all that Columbia has to offer, guests at the **Adams Mark Hotel ❹,** 1200 Hampton St., retreat to enormous rooms to take advantage of one of downtown's classiest establishments. This full-service hotel has an indoor pool, fitness center, and three restaurants. (☎771-7000. Rooms from $90.) The 1400 acres of **Sesquicentennial State Park ❶** include swimming and fishing, a nature center, hiking trails, and 87 wooded sites with electricity and water. Public transit does not serve the park; take I-20 to the Two Notch Rd./U.S. 1, Exit 17, and head 3 mi. northeast. (☎788-2706. Open daily Apr.-Oct. 7am-9pm; Nov.-Mar. 8am-6pm. Campsites $16. Entrance $1.50 per person.)

THE SOUTH

⚑ FOOD. It's little wonder that **Maurice's Piggie Park ❶**, 800 Elmwood Ave., 1600 Charleston Hwy., and nine other SC locations, holds the world record for "Most BBQ sold in one day." Maurice's cash "pig" is his exquisite, mustard-based sauce that covers the $5 Big Joe pork barbecue sandwich. (☎256-4377. Open M-Sa 10am-10pm.) Gamecocks past and present give highest marx to **Groucho's ❷**, 611 Harden St., where the famous "dipper" sandwiches ($6) have been delighting patrons for over 60 years. (☎799-5708. Open M-Sa 11am-4pm.) Charge over to the **Rhino Room ❹**, 807 Gervais St., for some of the best and most diverse food in town—from baby lamb ($10) to pepper strip steak ($17). Patrons often glimpse politicians on their lunch or dinner breaks. (☎931-0700. Open M-Sa 11:30am-2pm and 5:30-10pm.) If looking for a quick bite, **El Burrito ❶**, 934 Harden St., serves deliciously fresh and filling Mexican food. The deluxe chipotle chicken burrito ($6) is sure to satisfy, though the deluxe beans and rice ($3) is the best bang for your buck. (☎765-2188. Open M-Sa 11:30am-9:30pm.)

◎ SIGHTS. Bronze stars mark the impact of Sherman's cannonballs on the **State-house**, an Italian Renaissance high-rise. Home to South Carolina's key governmental proceedings, it also holds the state's two most prized symbols—the Senate Sword and a British mace, both of which reflect the rebellious reputation of Carolinians. Survey the surrounding grounds, which have monuments and sculptures scattered throughout the lush and tranquil gardens. (On Sumter, Assembly, and Gervais St. ☎734-2430. Open M-F 9am-5pm, Sa 10am-5pm; first Su each month 1-5pm. Free tours available. Wheelchair accessible.) Across Sumter St. from the Statehouse is the central green of the USC campus—the **Horseshoe.** Here, students play frisbee, sunbathe, study, and nap beneath a canopy of shade trees. At the head of the green, at the intersection of Bull and Pendleton St., **McKissick Museum** explores the folklore of South Carolina and the Southeast through history, art, and science. (☎777-7251; www.cla.sc.edu/mcks. Open May-Aug. M-F 8:30am-5pm, Sa-Su 1-5pm; Sept.-Apr. Tu-W and F 9am-4pm, Th 9am-7pm, Su 1-5pm. Free.) The **South Carolina Confederate Relic Room and Museum,** 301 Gervais St., traces South Carolina's military history and houses an exhaustive collection of Civil War artifacts and displays. (☎737-8095; www.state.sc.us/crr. Open Tu-Sa 10am-5pm. $3, under 21 free. Wheelchair accessible.) Two 19th-century mansions, the **Robert Mills Historic House and Park** and the **Hampton-Preston Mansion,** 1616 Blanding St., two blocks east of Bull St., compete as examples of antebellum opulence and survivors of Sherman's Civil War rampage. Both have been lovingly restored with period fineries. For a broader experience of 19th-century life, stop by the **Manns-Simons Cottage,** once owned by a freed slave, and the **Woodrow Wilson Boyhood Home,** 1705 Hampton St. (☎252-1770; www.historiccolumbia.org. Tours every hr. Su 1-4pm, Tu-Sa 10am-3pm. Tours $5; students, military, and AAA $4; ages 6-17 $3; under 5 free. Combo tickets with tours of all 4 houses $18/$14/$10. Buy all tickets at Mills House Museum Shop.)

One of the top ten zoos in the country, **Riverbanks Zoo and Garden,** on I-126 at Greystone Blvd., northwest of downtown, recreates natural habitats to house over 2000 species. After ogling the adorable koalas and wallabies at the newly added Koala Knockabout, check out the zoo's newest additions—a baby lemur, siamang, and rockhopper penguin. (☎779-8717; www.riverbanks.org. Open M-F 9am-5pm, Sa-Su 9am-6pm. $8.75, students $7.50, seniors $7.25.)

☗ NIGHTLIFE. Columbia's nightlife centers around the collegiate **Five Points District,** at Harden and Devine St., and the blossoming, slightly more mature **Vista area,** on Gervais St. before the Congaree River. In the Vista, the **Art Bar,** 1211 Park St., attracts a funky crowd to match its ambience. Glow paint, Christmas lights, 1950s bar stools, and a troop of life-size plastic robots are complemented by an eclectic music line-up. (☎929-0198. Open M-F 8pm-late, Sa-Su 8pm-2am.) The oldest bar in Columbia, **Group Therapy,** 2107 Greene St., helps locals drown their sorrows the old-fashioned way. Try the Mullet (warm Jack Daniel's with a touch of Budweiser; $7), and you'll never need to see a shrink again. (☎256-1203. Open daily 4:30pm-late.) Across the street, and a bit more uplifting, is **Big Al's**, 749 Saluda Ave., where a suave local crowd shoots pool, smokes stogies, and downs drinks in this dark and smoky den. (☎758-0700. Open M-F 5pm-late, Sa 5pm-2am, Su 9pm-2am.) The weekly publication *Free Times* gives details on Columbia's club and nightlife scene. *In Unison* is a weekly paper listing gay-friendly nightspots.

MYRTLE BEACH AND THE GRAND STRAND ☎843

Each summer, millions of Harley-riding, RV-driving Southerners make Myrtle Beach the second-most-popular summer tourist destination in the country. During spring break and early June, Myrtle Beach is jammed with students on the lookout for a good time. The rest of the year, families, golfers, and shoppers partake in the unapologetic tackiness of the town's theme restaurants, amusement parks, and shops. The pace slows significantly on the rest of the 60 mile Grand Strand. South of Myrtle Beach, Murrell's Inlet is the place to go for good seafood, Pawley's Island is lined with beach cottages and beautiful private homes, and Georgetown showcases white-pillared 18th-century-style rice and indigo plantation homes.

■ ▶ **ORIENTATION AND PRACTICAL INFORMATION.** Most attractions are on **Kings Highway (Route 17)**, which splits into a Business Route and a Bypass 4 mi. south of Myrtle Beach. **Ocean Boulevard** runs along the ocean, flanked on either side by cheap pastel motels. Avenue numbers repeat themselves after reaching 1st Ave. in the middle of town; note whether the Ave. is "north" or "south." Take care not to confuse north **Myrtle Beach** with the town **North Myrtle Beach**, which has an almost identical street layout. **Route 501** runs west toward Conway, **I-95**, and the factory outlet stores. Unless otherwise stated, addresses on the Grand Strand are for Myrtle Beach. **Greyhound**, 511 7th Ave. N (☎448-2471; open daily 9am-1:45pm and 3-6:45pm), runs to Charleston (2½hr., 2 per day, $25). **The Waccamaw Regional Transportation Authority (WRTA)**, 1418 3rd Ave., provides minimal busing; pick up a copy of schedules and routes from the Chamber of Commerce or from area businesses. (☎488-0865. Runs daily 5am-2am. Local fares $0.75-2.) WRTA also operates the **Ocean Boulevard Lymo**, a bus service that shuttles tourists up and down the main drag. (☎488-0865. Runs daily 8am-midnight. Unlimited day pass $2.50.) Rent bikes at **The Bike Shoppe**, 715 Broadway, at Main St. (☎448-5335. Open M-F 8am-6pm, Sa 8am-5pm. Beach cruisers $5 per half-day, $10 per day; mountain bikes $8/$15.) **Visitor Info: Myrtle Beach Chamber of Commerce**, 1200 N. Oak St., parallel to Kings Hwy., at 12th Ave. N. (☎626-7444; www.mbchamber.com. Open daily 8:30am-5pm.) **Mini Golf:** everywhere. **Medical Services: Grand Strand Regional Medical Center**, 809 82nd Pkwy. (☎692-1000). **Internet Access: Chapin Memorial Library**, 400 14th Ave. N. (☎918-1275. Open M and W 9am-6pm, Tu and Th 9am-8pm, F-Sa 9am-5pm; in summer Sa hours 9am-1pm.) **Post Office:** 505 N. Kings Hwy., at 5th Ave. N. (☎626-9533. Open M-F 8:30am-5pm, Sa 9am-1pm.) **Postal Code:** 29577. **Area Code:** 843.

▌ **ACCOMMODATIONS.** Hundreds of motels line Ocean Blvd., with those on the ocean side fetching higher prices than those across the street. Cheap motels also dot Rte. 17. From October to March, prices plummet as low as $20-30 a night for one of the luxurious hotels right on the beach. Call the **Myrtle Beach Lodging Reservation Service**, 1551 21st Ave. N., #20, for free help with reservations. (☎626-9970 or 800-626-7477. Open M-F 8:30am-5pm.) Across the street from the ocean, the family-owned **Sea Banks Motor Inn ❷**, 2200 S. Ocean Blvd., has immaculate rooms with mini-fridges, cable TV, laundry, and pool and beach access. (☎448-2434 or 800-523-0603. Mid-Mar. to mid-Sept. singles $45; doubles $75. Mid-Sept. to mid-Mar. $22/

$28.) The **Hurl Rock Motel ❷**, 2010 S. Ocean Blvd., has big, clean rooms with access to a pool and hot tub. (☎626-3531 or 888-487-5762. 25+. Singles $45; doubles $54-89. Low-season as low as $25/$28.) **Huntington Beach State Park Campground ❶**, 3 mi. south of Murrell's Inlet on U.S. 17, is located in a diverse environment including lagoons, salt marshes, and a beach. (☎237-4440. Open daily Apr.-Oct. 6am-10pm; Nov.-Mar. 6am-6pm. Tent sites Apr.-Oct. $20; water and electricity $25; full hookup $28. Nov.-Mar. $15/$20/$22. Day-use $4.)

❐ FOOD. The Grand Strand offers hungry motorists over 1800 restaurants serving every type of food in every imaginable setting. Massive family-style all-you-can-eat joints beckon from beneath the glow of every traffic light. **Route 17** offers countless steakhouses, seafood buffets, and fast food joints. Seafood, however, is best on **Murrell's Inlet.** With license plates adorning the walls and discarded peanut shells crunching underfoot, the **River City Cafe ❶**, 404 21st Ave. N, celebrates a brand of American informality bordering on delinquency. Peruse the patrons' signatures on tables and walls as you polish off a burger ($3-6) or knock back a $3 beer. (☎448-1990. Open daily 11am-10pm.) While most of the restaurants in Broadway at the Beach seem to sacrifice food quality for elaborate decor, **Benito's ❸**, in the "Caribbean Village" part of the complex, serves delightful stuffed shells ($10) and delectable calzones ($6) that will make you forget the screaming children and blaring lights outside. (☎444-0006. Open daily 11am-10:30pm.) Take a break from Ocean Dr. at **Dagwood's Deli ❷**, 400 11th. Ave. N, where beach bums and businessmen come together to enjoy a "Shag" (ham, turkey, and swiss cheese; $5), reminiscent of the monster sandwiches from the comic strip, or a Philly cheesesteak ($5-7). Be prepared to wait. (☎448-0100. Open M-Sa 11am-9pm.)

◙ ▣ SIGHTS AND NIGHTLIFE. The boulevard and the beach are both "the strand," where fashionable teens strut their stuff, low riders cruise the streets, and beachgoers showcase their sunburns. Never pay full price for any attraction in Myrtle Beach; pick up a copy of the *Monster Coupon Book, Sunny Day Guide, Myrtle Beach Guide,* or *Strand Magazine* at any tourist info center or hotel.

The colossal **Broadway at the Beach,** Rte. 17 Bypass and 21st Ave. N. (☎444-3200 or 800-386-4662), is a sprawling 350-acre complex determined to stimulate and entertain with shops and theaters, a water park, mini golf, 20 restaurants, nightclubs, and other attractions. In Broadway's **Ripley's Aquarium,** guests roam through a 330 ft. underwater tunnel and gaze upward at the ferocious sharks and terrifying piranha swimming above. (☎916-0888 or 800-734-8888; www.ripleysaquarium.com. Open daily 9am-11pm. $17, ages 5-11 $10, ages 2-4 $4. Wheelchair accessible.) The reptile capital of the world is the ▨**Alligator Adventure,** Rte. 17 in North Myrtle Beach at Barefoot Landing, where even the most ardent Animal Planet fans are mesmerized by the exotic collection of snakes, lizards, and frogs and the hourly gator feedings. Don't miss the park's 20 ft., 2000 lb. resident, Utan—the world's largest captive croc. (☎361-0789. Open daily 9am-11pm. $14, seniors $12, ages 4-12 $9. Wheelchair accessible.)

Most visitors to Myrtle Beach putter over to one of the many elaborately themed **mini golf** courses on Kings Hwy. The **NASCAR Speedpark,** across from Broadway at the Beach on the Rte. 17 Bypass, provides 7 different tracks of varying difficulty levels, catering to the need for speed. (☎918-8725. Open daily 10am-11pm. Unlimited rides $25, under 13 $15.) The 9100-acre ▨**Brookgreen Gardens,** Rte. 17 opposite Huntington Beach State Park south of Murrell's Inlet, provide a tranquil respite from the touristy tackiness that dominates Myrtle Beach. Over 500 American sculptures—each more captivating than the last—are scattered throughout the grounds beneath massive oaks. Guided tours of the gardens and wildlife trail are offered in addition to summer drama, music, and food programs. (☎ 235-6000; www.brookgreen.org. Open daily 9:30am-5pm. 7-day pass $12, seniors and ages 13-18 $10, 12 and under free. Wheelchair accessible.)

For a night on the town, the New Orleans-style nightclub district, **Celebrity Square,** at Broadway at the Beach, facilitates stepping out with ten nightclubs, ranging in theme from classic rock to Latin. Elsewhere, **Club Baja,** 1012 S. Kings Hwy. (☎ 445-9630), and **2001,** 920 Lake Arrowhead Rd. (☎ 449-9434), bring clubbers a hot-steppin' odyssey. (21+. Cover varies. Open daily 8pm-2am.)

GEORGIA

Georgia has many faces; the rural southern region contrasts starkly with the sprawling commercialism of the north. Atlanta packs the punch of a booming metropolis, while Savannah fosters a different, distinctively antebellum atmosphere. Collegiate Athens breeds "big" bands, while Macon's compact downtown offers insights into the state's past. Perhaps nowhere are the state's contrasting natures as evident as at Cumberland Island, where deserted beaches and marshes lie just hundreds of yards from the ruins of Gilded Age mansions. In this state of contradictions, only one thing remains constant: enduring Southern hospitality.

🔢 PRACTICAL INFORMATION

Capital: Atlanta.

Visitor Info: Georgia Department of Economic Development, Tourism Division, 75 5th St. NW, Ste. 1220, Atlanta 30308 (☎ 404-656-3590 or 800-847-4842; www.georgia.org). **Department of Natural Resources,** 2 Martin Luther King, Jr. Dr. SE, Ste. 1252 East Tower, Atlanta 30334 (☎ 404-656-3500). **US Forest Service,** 1800 NE Expwy., Atlanta 30329 (☎ 404-248-9142). Open W-Sa 10am-6:30pm, Su 11am-6pm.

Postal Abbreviation: GA. **Sales Tax:** 4-7%, depending on county.

ATLANTA ☎ 404

An increasingly popular destination for recent college graduates weary of more fast-paced cities, Atlanta is cosmopolitan with a smile. Northerners, Californians, the third-largest gay population in the US, and a host of ethnic groups have diversified this unofficial capital of the South, modifying its distinctly Southern feel. A national economic powerhouse, Atlanta holds offices for 400 of the Fortune 500 companies, including the headquarters of Coca-Cola, UPS, and CNN. Nineteen colleges, including Georgia Tech, Morehouse College, Spelman College, and Emory University, also call "Hotlanta" home. The city is equally blessed with hidden gems; touring Atlanta's streets reveals an endless number of trendy restaurants and beautiful old houses.

✈ INTERCITY TRANSPORTATION

Airport: Hartsfield International Airport (☎ 530-2081; www.atlanta-airport.com), south of the city. MARTA (see **Public Transit,** p. 435) is the easiest way to get downtown, with rides departing from the Airport Station (15min., every 8min. daily 5am-1am, $1.75). **Atlanta Airport Shuttle** (☎ 524-3400) runs vans from the airport to over 100 locations in the metropolis and outlying area (every 15min. daily 7am-11pm, shuttle to downtown $14). Taxi to downtown $20.

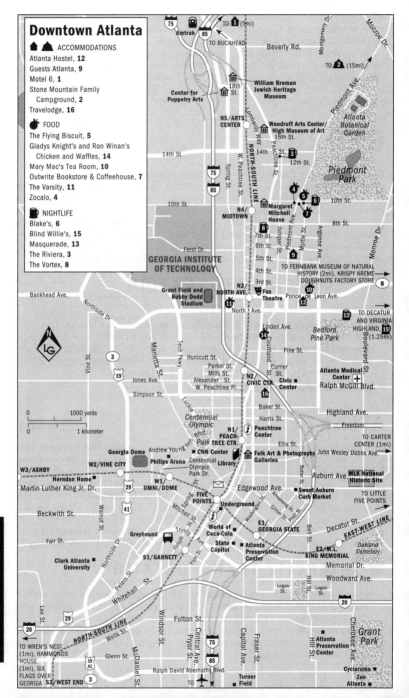

Downtown Atlanta

ACCOMMODATIONS
Atlanta Hostel, **12**
Guests Atlanta, **9**
Motel 6, **1**
Stone Mountain Family
  Campground, **2**
Travelodge, **16**

FOOD
The Flying Biscuit, **5**
Gladys Knight's and Ron Winan's
  Chicken and Waffles, **14**
Mary Mac's Tea Room, **10**
Outwrite Bookstore & Coffeehouse, **7**
The Varsity, **11**
Zocalo, **4**

NIGHTLIFE
Blake's, **6**
Blind Willie's, **15**
Masquerade, **13**
The Riviera, **3**
The Vortex, **8**

Trains: Amtrak, 1688 Peachtree St. NW (☎881-3062), 3 mi. north of downtown at I-85, or 1 mi. north of Ponce de Leon on Peachtree St. Take bus #23 from MARTA: Arts Center. To **New Orleans** (10½hr., 1 per day, $75-120) and **New York City** (19hr., 3 per day, $197). Open daily 7am-9:30pm.

Buses: Greyhound, 232 Forsyth St. SW (☎584-1728), across from MARTA: Garnett. To: **New York City** (18-23hr., 14 per day, $100); **Savannah** (6hr., 6 per day, $45); **Washington, D.C.** (15hr., 12 per day, $95). Open 24hr.

▣ ORIENTATION

Atlanta sprawls across ten counties in the northwest quadrant of the state at the junctures of I-75, I-85 (the city "thruway"), and I-20. **I-285** (the "perimeter") circumscribes the city. Maneuvering around Atlanta's main thoroughfares, which are arranged much like the spokes of a wheel, challenges even the most experienced native. **Peachtree Street** (one of over 100 streets bearing that name in Atlanta), is a major north-south road; **Spring Street** (which runs only south) and **Piedmont Avenue** (which runs only north) are parallel to Peachtree. On the eastern edge, **Moreland Avenue** traverses the length of the city, through Virginia Highland, Little Five Points (L5P), and East Atlanta. **Ponce de Leon Avenue** is the major east-west road, and will take travelers to most major destinations (or intersect with a street that can). To the south of "Ponce" runs **North Avenue,** another major east-west thoroughfare. Navigating Atlanta requires a full arsenal of transportation strategies. Midtown and downtown attractions are best explored using MARTA. The outlying areas of Buckhead, Virginia Highlands and L5P are easiest to get to by car; once you're there, the restaurant and bar-lined streets encourage walking.

NEIGHBORHOODS

Sprouting out of downtown Atlanta, the **Peachtree Center** and **Five Points MARTA** stations deliver hordes of tourists to shopping and dining at **Peachtree Center Mall** and **Underground Atlanta.** Downtown is also home to **Centennial Olympic Park** as well as Atlanta's major sports and concert venues. Directly southwest of downtown, the **West End,** an African-American neighborhood, is the city's oldest historic quarter. From Five Points, head northeast to **Midtown,** from Ponce de Leon Ave. to 17th St., for museums and **Piedmont Park.** East of Five Points at Euclid and Moreland Ave., the **Little Five Points (L5P)** district is a local haven for artists and youth subculture. North of L5P, **Virginia Highland,** a trendy neighborhood east of Midtown and Piedmont Park, attracts yuppies and college kids. The **Buckhead** area, north of Midtown on Peachtree St., greets both Atlanta's professionals and its rappers, and houses designer shops and dance clubs.

▣ LOCAL TRANSPORTATION

Public Transit: Metropolitan Atlanta Rapid Transit Authority, or **MARTA** (☎848-4711; trains run daily 5am-1am, bus hours vary). Clean, uncrowded trains and buses provide hassle-free transportation to Atlanta's major attractions, making MARTA the "SMARTA" way to get around downtown Atlanta. A $1.75 MARTA token is good for both trains and buses, as well as free transfers between either. Exact change or a token from a station machine needed. Unlimited weekly pass $13. Pick up a system map at the **MARTA Ride Store** at Five Points Station downtown, or at the airport, Lindbergh, or Lenox stations. The majority of trains, rail stations, and buses are wheelchair accessible.

Taxi: Atlanta Yellow Cab ☎521-0200. **Checker Cab** ☎351-3179.

Car Rental: Atlanta Rent-a-Car, 3185 Camp Creek Pkwy., ☎763-1110. 2½ mi. east of the airport, just inside I-285. 10 other locations in the area including 2800 Campelton Rd. (☎344-1060) and 3129 Piedmont Rd. (☎231-4898). 21+ with major credit card. $25 per day, $0.24 per mi. over 100 mi.

🔢 PRACTICAL INFORMATION

Visitor Info: Visitors Center, 65 Upper Alabama St. (☎521-6688), on the upper level of Underground Atlanta. MARTA: Five Points. Open M-Sa 10am-6pm, Su noon-6pm. The **Atlanta Convention and Visitors Bureau,** 233 Peachtree St. NE, Peachtree Center #100 (☎521-6600 or 800-285-2682; www.atlanta.net), is geared toward convention planning but operates an automated **information service** (☎222-6688).

GLBT Resources: The Atlanta Gay and Lesbian Center, 170 11th St. (☎874-9890). Gay Yellow Pages (☎892-6454, www.atlantagaypages.com).

Hotlines: Rape Crisis Counseling, ☎616-4861. 24hr.

Medical Services: Piedmont Hospital, 1968 Peachtree Rd. NW (☎605-5000).

Internet Access: Central Library, 1 Margaret Mitchell Sq. (☎730-1700). Open Su 2-6pm, M-Th 9am-9pm, F-Sa 9am-6pm. Internet access available upon registering for a free PC-access card.

Post Office: Phoenix Station (☎524-2960), at the corner of Forsyth and Marietta St., 1 block from MARTA: Five Points. Open M-F 9am-5pm. **Postal Code:** 30303. **Area Code:** 404 inside the I-285 perimeter, 770 outside. In text, 404 unless otherwise noted.

> Safety is no less a concern in Atlanta than it is in any other major city. While recent efforts to beef up police presence in high-risk areas of the city are having an effect, travelers—especially women—should avoid walking alone in much of the city. Exercise special caution in the West End and Midtown areas.

🏠 ACCOMMODATIONS

Atlanta Hostel, 223 Ponce de Leon Ave. (☎875-9449 or 800-473-9449; www.hostel-atlanta.com), in Midtown. From MARTA: North Ave., exit onto Ponce de Leon and walk about 3½ blocks east to Myrtle St., or take bus #2. Look for the sign that reads "Woodruff Inn: Bed and Breakfast." This family-owned and -operated establishment offers immaculate dorm-style rooms in a cozy home that resembles a B&B with a TV, pool table, and kitchen. Internet access $1 per 10min. Enjoy complimentary breakfast on the patio. Free lockers. No sleeping bags allowed, but free blankets are distributed. Linen $1. Laundry available. Dorms $18; private rooms $39-49. ❶

Guests Atlanta, 811 Piedmont Ave. NE (☎872-5846 or 800-724-4381; www.guestsatlanta.com). Nestled in the heart of Midtown, Guests Atlanta is comprised of three gorgeous Victorian mansions. Beautiful rooms with TV, Internet access, and breakfast. Laundry available. Reservations recommended. Singles $70; doubles $90. ❹

Motel 6, 2820 Chamblee Tucker Rd. (☎770-458-6626), Exit 94 off I-85 in Doraville. Spacious, tidy rooms. Free local calls, morning coffee, and A/C. Under 18 stay free with parents. Singles $45. *Be cautious in this area, especially if you are traveling alone.* ❷

The Highland Inn, 644 N. Highland Ave. NE (☎874-5756). Built in 1927 and renovated for the 1996 Olympics, this hotel has over 80 comfortable rooms and is a popular stop for celebrity musicians when playing in town. Reception 24 hours. Singles $70; doubles $96. ❹

Travelodge, 311 Courtland St. NE (☎659-4545), in the heart of downtown Atlanta. Clean rooms in a central location. Free parking and a friendly desk staff. Rates vary in summer; call ahead for reservations. Singles $74, doubles $89. ❹

Stone Mountain Family Campground (☎770-498-5710), on U.S. 78. Far away from the commotion of the city, this expansive campground offers stunning sites (many of which are on the lake), bike rentals, and a free laser show. Internet access available. Max. stay 2 weeks. Sites $20-28. Full hookup $32-37. Entrance fee $7 per car. ❶

◨ FOOD

From Vietnamese to Italian, fried to fricasseed, Atlanta cooks up ample options for any craving. "Soul food" nourishes the city. At legendary "Chicken and Waffles" restaurants, the uncommon combination makes a terrific meal. A depot for soul food's raw materials since 1923, the **Sweet Auburn Curb Market,** 209 Edgewood Ave., has an eye-popping assortment of goodies, from cow's feet to ox tails. (☎659-1665. M-Th 8am-6pm, F-Sa 8am-7pm.) For sweet treats, you can't beat the Atlanta-based **Krispy Kreme Doughnuts** ❶, whose glazed delights ($0.79) are a Southern institution. The factory store, 295 Ponce de Leon Ave. NE (☎876-7307), continuously bakes their wares. (Open Su-Th 5:30am-midnight, F-Sa 24hr.; drive-through daily 24hr.)

BUCKHEAD

Fellini's Pizza, 2809 Peachtree Rd. NE (☎266-0082). 3 watchful gargoyles and an angel welcome hungry customers into this pizzeria, the flagship of 5 Atlanta locations, complete with bright yellow awnings, a spacious deck with fountain and mouth-watering pizza. If Hotlanta has become too warm, enjoy your slice ($1.65, toppings $0.45 each) or pie ($10.50-19) in the brick-walled interior, which combines classic rock with a romantic atmosphere. Open M-Sa 11am-2am, Su 12:30pm-midnight. Cash only. ❷

Ted's Montana Grill, 1874 Peachtree Road. (☎355-3897). Ted's serves a whole slew of western favorites, like nutritious bison, all reasonably priced. Try the fried chicken with gravy ($9) as an alternative to nearly extinct cattle. Open Su-Th 11am-10pm, F-Sa 11am-11pm. ❷

Huey's, 1816 Peachtree Rd. (☎873-2037). Huey's serves the most delicious and most authentic Louisianan cuisine in the city in an unpretentious atmosphere. If your tour doesn't include the bayou (or if you just can't wait to get there), then this is your spot. There's even a patio if you want to chow on your catfish ($12) outside. Tu-F 11am-2pm and 6pm-10pm, Sa 6pm-midnight, Su 9am-3pm. ❷

MIDTOWN

▩ **Gladys Knight's and Ron Winans's Chicken and Waffles,** 529 Peachtree St; MARTA: North Ave. (☎874-9393), screams soul. Situated on the southern border of Midtown, this upscale but reasonably-priced joint serves incredible dishes like the Midnight Train (4 southern-fried chicken wings and a waffle; $8). Among the side dishes ($1-3) are collard greens, cinnamon raisin toast, and corn muffins. Enjoy an Uptown (sweetened iced tea and lemonade; $2) in one of the deep brown leather booths while relaxing to the smooth musical stylings of R&B all-stars. Open M-Th 11am-11pm, F-Sa 11am-4am, Su 11am-8pm. ❷

The Varsity, 61 North Ave. NW (☎881-1707; www.thevarsity.com), at Spring St. MARTA: North Ave. Established in 1928, the Varsity claims to be the world's largest (and some would argue greasiest) drive-in restaurant. Subject of a landmark Supreme Court decision in the 1960s which declared that blacks must be served alongside their white counterparts, The Varsity has since delighted patrons of all colors with its cheap and delicious hamburgers ($1), classic Coke floats ($2), and famous onion rings ($2). Most items around $2. Open Su-Th 10am-11:30pm, F-Sa 10am-12:30am. ❶

Mary Mac's Tea Room, 224 Ponce de Leon Ave. (☎876-1800; www.marymacs.com), at Myrtle. MARTA: North Ave. Whether you're sipping the house specialty tea ($1.25) or enjoying the baked turkey, you'll appreciate the stellar service, charming tea rooms, and elegant dining hall. All entrees come with 2 side dishes and are $9. Open M-Sa 11am-9pm, Su 9am-9pm. ❸

10TH STREET

The Flying Biscuit, 1001 Piedmont Ave. (☎874-8887). Packed with loyal patrons, mostly young professionals and families, the Flying Biscuit serves breakfast feasts. Enjoy the Flying Biscuit Breakfast ($7) and the signature Delio (double espresso mochaccino; $4) on the sun-drenched patio or on the granite-topped bar. Open daily 7am-10pm. ❷

Outwrite Bookstore and Coffeehouse, 991 Piedmont Ave. (☎607-0082). With rainbow streamers gracing the windows, and remarkably friendly service, this unique gay and lesbian establishment has a relaxed and stylish air. Try the espresso specialty drink "Shot in the Dark" ($2) to go along with your bagel ($1), then retreat with your favorite book to the deck where comfy furniture awaits. Open daily 9am-11pm. ❶

Zocalo, 187 10th St. (☎249-7576; www.zocalo.com). Overshadowed by a billboard for Dos Equis beer and with seating exclusively on an outside patio (plastic sheeting traps the warmth in the winter months), Zocalo will make you swear you're on the beach in Zihuatanejo. Boasting some of the best margaritas in Atlanta and a menu loaded with Mexican favorites (chiles rellenos $9.75, taquitos $8.25), Zocalo is a great place to satiate your hunger for a little *comida mexicana.* Open M-Th 11am-11pm, Fr-Sa 11am-12am, Su 10am-10pm. ❸

VIRGINIA HIGHLAND

Doc Chey's, 1424 N. Highland Ave. (☎888-0777), serves heaping mounds of noodles at super prices ($6-8). This pan-Asian restaurant is ultra-popular among young Atlanta locals. Try the delicious Chinese lo mein ($6) or the spicy tomato ginger noodle bowl ($8), one of Doc's originals. Open Su-Th 11:30am-10pm, F-Sa 11:30am-11pm. ❷

Everybody's, 1040 N. Highland Ave. (☎873-4545), receives high accolades for selling Atlanta's best pizza. Their inventive pizza salads, a colossal mound of greens and chicken on a pizza bed ($8), use fresh ingredients. Also try Everybody's pizza sandwiches ($8-9). Open M-Th 11:30am-11pm, F-Sa 11:30am-1am, Su noon-10:30pm. ❸

Highland Tap, 1026 N. Highland Ave. (☎875-3673). Home of the best steaks ($18-25) in the Highlands; springing for the gorgonzola crust ($2.50) is well worth it. Delicious burgers are easier on the wallet ($8.50), as are the $2 beer specials. A happening bar scene on weekends. Lunch Tu-F 11:30am-3pm. Dinner Su-Th 5pm-midnight, F-Sa 5pm-1am. Brunch Sa-Su 11am-3pm. Bar open M-Sa 11:30am-3am, Su 12:30am-2am. ❹

◉ SIGHTS

SWEET AUBURN DISTRICT

MARTIN LUTHER KING, JR. The most powerful sights in the city run along Auburn Ave. in Sweet Auburn. The Reverend Martin Luther King, Jr.'s birthplace, church, and grave are all part of the 23-acre ◪**Martin Luther King, Jr. National Historic Site.** The **visitors center** houses poignant displays of photographs, videos, and quotations oriented around King's life and the struggle for civil rights. *(450 Auburn Ave. NE. MARTA: King Memorial. ☎331-5190; www.nps.gov/malu. Open daily June-Aug. 9am-6pm; Sept.-May 9am-5pm. Free.)* The visitors center administers tours of the **Birthplace of MLK.** *(501 Auburn Ave. Tours every 30 min. June-Aug.; every hr. Sept.-May. Arrive early to sign up; advance reservations not accepted.)* Across the street from the visitors center stands **Ebenezer Baptist Church,** where King gave his first sermon at age 17 and co-pastored with his father from 1960 to 1968. *(407 Auburn Ave. ☎688-7263. Open June-Aug. M-Sa 10am-4pm, Su 2-4pm; Sept.-May M-Sa 9am-5pm, Su 1-5pm.)* Next door at the **Martin Luther King, Jr. Center for Nonviolent Social Exchange** lies a beautiful blue reflecting pool with an island on which King is laid to rest in a white marble tomb. The center's

Freedom Hall holds a collection of King's personal articles (including his Nobel Peace Prize medal), an overview of his role model, Gandhi, and an exhibit on Rosa Parks. *(449 Auburn Ave. NE. ☎ 331-5190. Open daily June-Aug. 9am-6pm; Sept.-May 9am-5pm. Free.)* Plaques lining Sweet Auburn describes the architecture and prominent past residents of this historically black neighborhood.

DOWNTOWN VICINITY

WALKING TOURS. From March to November, the **Atlanta Preservation Center** offers walking tours of seven popular areas, including Druid Hills, the setting of the film *Driving Miss Daisy.* Other popular tour destinations include Inman Park, Atlanta's first trolley suburb, and Historic Downtown, Atlanta's earliest high-rise district. *(327 St. Paul Ave. NE. ☎ 876-2041; www.preserveatlanta.com. $7, students and seniors $5. Call ahead to arrange wheelchair-accessible tours.)*

GRANT PARK CYCLORAMA. The world's largest painting (42 ft. tall and 358 ft. in circumference) is in Grant Park, directly south of Oakland Cemetery and Cherokee Ave. The 117-year-old Cyclorama takes visitors back in time, revolving them on a huge platform in the middle of the "1864 Battle of Atlanta." Far cooler in real life than it sounds on paper, the Cyclorama is an experience no history buff can afford to miss. *(800 Cherokee Ave. SE. Take bus #31 or 97 from Five Points. MARTA: King Memorial. ☎ 624-1071. Open daily June-Sept. 8:30am-4:30pm; Oct.-May 9:30am-4:30pm. $6, seniors and students $5, ages 6-12 $4. Wheelchair accessible.)*

ZOO ATLANTA. Lions and tigers and bears...well, panda bears, anyway. This is one of only four zoos in the nation to exhibit rare giant pandas; when coupled with the East African lion and Sumatran tiger exhibits the Atlanta Zoo will certainly provoke an "Oh My!" *(800 Cherokee Ave. SE. Take bus #31 or 97 from Five Points. ☎ 624-5600; www.zooatlanta.com. Open Apr.-Oct. M-F 9:30am-4:30pm, Sa-Su 9:30am-5:30pm; Nov.-Mar. daily 9:30am-4:30pm. $15, seniors $11, ages 3-11 $10. Wheelchair accessible.)*

STATE CAPITOL. On the corner of Washington and Mitchell St. is the **Georgia State Capitol Building,** a classical structure built in 1889 with Georgia's own natural resources: Cherokee marble, Georgian oak, and gold mined in Lumpkin County, which gilds the dome. The building was completed $118.43 under budget! Exhibits on the 5th floor detail Georgia's often tumultuous history. *(☎ 463-4536; www.sos.state.ga.us. Tours M-F 10, 11am, 1, 2pm. Open M-F 8am-5pm. Free.)*

WORLD OF COCA-COLA (WOCC). Two blocks from the capitol, the World of Coca-Cola educates tourists on the rise of "the real thing" from its humble beginnings in Atlanta to its position of world domination. Uncap the secrets of Coke as you walk through two floors of Coca-Cola history and memorabilia, complete with a "soda jerk" demonstration and TVs that continuously play old Coca-Cola advertisements. The psychological barrage is so intense that even those with the strongest of willpowers will soon be craving a Coke. Luckily, visitors get to sample 46 flavors of Coke from around the world at the tour's end, from the long-lost Tab to Mozambique's "Krest." *(55 Martin Luther King, Jr. Dr. MARTA: Five Points. ☎ 676-5151; www.woccatlanta.com. Open June-Aug. M-Sa 9am-6pm, Su 11am-5pm; Sept.-May M-Sa 9am-5pm, Su noon-5pm. $7, seniors $5, ages 6-11 $4, under 5 free. Wheelchair accessible.)*

UNDERGROUND ATLANTA. Adjacent to the WOCC, this former railroad underpass is now a subterranean mall with over 120 chain restaurants, shops, and nightspots. Once a hotspot for alternative music, the underground now resembles a carnival-like labyrinth of marketing and merchandise. *(Descend at the entrance beside the Five Points subway station. ☎ 523-2311. Shops open June-Sept. M-Sa 10am-9:30pm, Su 11am-7pm; Oct.-May M-Sa 10am-9pm, Su noon-6pm. Bars and restaurants close later.)*

CNN. Overlooking beautiful Centennial Park is the global headquarters of the **Cable News Network (CNN).** Check out the 45min. studio tour, which reveals "the story behind the news." Sit inside a replica control room, learn the secrets of tele-prompter magic, and peer into the renowned CNN newsroom. *(At Centennial Olympic Park Dr. and Marietta St. MARTA: Omni/Dome/GWCC Station at W1. ☎827-2300; www.cnn.com/studiotour. Tours every 10min. daily 9am-5pm. $10, seniors $8, ages 4-12 $7. Elevator tours available for visitors in wheelchairs with 24hr. notice.)*

OLYMPIC PARK. Amidst the commerce and concrete of bustling downtown Atlanta, serenity can be found at the **Centennial Olympic Park,** a 21-acre state park that is both a public recreation area and a lasting monument to the 1996 Olympic Games. Eight enor-mous torches and an array of flags (each representing a nation that has hosted one of the modern Olympic Games) surround the park's central feature, the **Fountain of Rings,** which enthralls (and soaks) children and adults alike. Check out one of the 20min. fountain shows (daily 12:30, 3:30, 6:30, 9pm) in which the water dances to symphonic melodies and dazzling lights. *(265 Park Ave. West NW. MARTA: Peachtree Center. ☎223-4412; www.centennialpark.com. Park open daily 7am-11pm. Wheelchair accessible.)*

CARTER PRESIDENTIAL CENTER. Just north of Little Five Points, a charming gar-den and a circle of state flags surrounding the American flag welcome visitors to this self-guided museum, which relates the works, achievements, and events of Jimmy Carter's life and presidency through films and exhibits. Attached to the museum, the **Jimmy Carter Library,** one of only 11 Presidential libraries in the coun-try, serves as a depository for historic materials from the Carter Administration. *(441 Freedom Pkwy. Take bus #16 to Cleburne Ave. ☎331-0296; www.jimmycarterli-brary.org. Museum open M-Sa 9am-4:45pm, Su noon-4:45pm; grounds open daily 6am-9pm. $7, seniors $5, under 16 free. Wheelchair accessible.)*

WEST END

AFRICAN-AMERICAN HISTORY. Dating from 1835, the West End is Atlanta's old-est neighborhood. A tour of the historic **Wren's Nest** offers a number of twists on the typical "historic home" tour. Home to author Joel Chandler Harris, who popu-larized the African folktale trickster Br'er Rabbit, the Wren's Nest offers a glimpse into middle-class life as it was at the beginning of the 20th century. *(1050 R.D. Aber-nathy Blvd. Take bus #71 from West End Station/S2. ☎753-7735. Open Tu-Sa 10am-2:30pm. Tours every hr. on the ½hr. $7, seniors and ages 13-19 $5, ages 4-12 $4. Wheel-chair accessible.)* The **Hammonds House,** the home-turned-gallery of Dr. Otis Ham-monds, a renowned African-American physician and art lover, displays unique contemporary and historic works in Georgia's only collection dedicated entirely to African-American and Haitian art. *(503 Peeples St. SW. ☎752-8730; www.hammond-shouse.org. Open Tu-F 10am-6pm, Sa-Su 1-5pm. Suggested donation $2, students and seniors $1. Wheelchair accessible.)* Born a slave, Alonzo F. Herndon became a promi-nent barber and founder of Atlanta Life Insurance Co., and eventually attained the status of Atlanta's wealthiest African-American in the early 1900s. A Beaux-Arts Classical mansion, the **Herndon Home** was built in 1910; today it is dedicated to the legacy of Herndon's philanthropy. *(587 University Pl. NW. Take bus #3 from Five Points station to the corner of Martin Luther King, Jr. Dr. and Maple, walk 1 block west, turn right on Walnut, and walk 1 block. ☎581-9813; www.herndonhome.org. Tours every hr. $5, students $3. Open Tu-Sa 10am-4pm. Wheelchair accessible.)*

MIDTOWN

WOODRUFF ARTS CENTER. Cultural connoisseurs, the **Woodruff Arts Center (WAC)** is your place. To the west of Piedmont Park, Richard Meier's award-win-ning buildings of glass, steel, and white porcelain are matched only by the treasures they contain. Within the WAC, the **High Museum of Art** features a rotation of incredible temporary exhibits, which have included the works of Pablo Picasso, Edgar Degas, Edward Hopper, and Ansel Adams. The museum has recently begun construction of three new galleries (expected to be completed in 2005), which will house much of the American collection and showcase the museum's photography section. *(1280 Peachtree St. NE. MARTA: Arts Center; exit Lombardy Way. WAC: ☎ 733-4200. High Museum of Art: ☎ 733-4400; www.high.org. Open Tu-Su 10am-5pm. $13, students with ID and seniors $10, ages 6-17 $8.)* The **Folk Art and Photography Galleries,** part of the High Museum, house additional and more esoteric exhibits. *(30 John Wesley Dobbs Ave. NE. One block south of MARTA: Peachtree Center. ☎ 577-6940. Open M-Sa 10am-5pm, and the first Th of every month 10am-8pm. Free. Wheelchair accessible.)*

MARGARET MITCHELL HOUSE. Located between the 10th St. district and Midtown is the apartment where Mitchell wrote her Pulitzer-Prize-winning novel, *Gone with the Wind.* Tour the house and view her typewriter and autographed copies of the book. Across the street, the **Gone with the Wind Movie Museum,** has memorabilia such as the door to Tara Plantation and the portrait of Scarlett at which Clark Gable hurled a cocktail onscreen—complete with stain. *(990 Peachtree St., at 10th and Peachtree St., adjacent to MARTA: Midtown. ☎ 249-7015; www.gwtw.org. Open daily 9:30am-5pm. 1hr. tours every 45min. $12, students and seniors $9, ages 6-17 $5.)*

WILLIAM BREMAN JEWISH HERITAGE MUSEUM. The largest Jewish museum in the Southeast, featuring a powerful Holocaust exhibit and a gallery tracing the history of the Atlanta Jewish community from 1845 to the present. *(1440 Spring St. NW. From MARTA: N5/Arts Center, walk 3 blocks north to 18th St. and Spring St. ☎ 873-1661; www.thebreman.org. Open M-Th 10am-5pm, F 10am-3pm, Su 1-5pm. $5, students and seniors $3, under 7 free. Wheelchair accessible.)*

CENTER FOR PUPPETRY ARTS. The complexity and sophistication of "puppeteering" will surprise and interest even those who haven't watched "The Muppet Show" in years. As it happens, however, the highlight of the tour is the Jim Henson exhibit, which showcases some of the puppet-master's famous creations. *(1404 Spring St. NW, at 18th St. ☎ 873-3391; www.puppet.org. Open Tu-Sa 9am-5pm, Su 11am-5pm. $8, students and seniors $7. Puppet workshop ages 5 and over $5. Wheelchair accessible.)*

FERNBANK MUSEUM OF NATURAL HISTORY. Sporting outstanding dinosaur and sea-life exhibits, an IMAX theater, and numerous interactive discovery centers, the Fernbank is one of the best science museums in the Southeast. *(767 Clifton Rd. NE. Off Ponce de Leon Ave.; take bus #2 from North Ave. or Avondale Station. ☎ 929-6300; www.fernbank.edu/museum. Open M-Sa 10am-5pm, Su noon-5pm. Museum $12, students and seniors $11, ages 3-12 $10; IMAX film $10/$9/$8; both attractions $17/$15/$13. Wheelchair accessible.)* The adjacent **R.L. Staton Rose Garden** is free for all visitors and blossoms from spring until December. *(Corner of Ponce de Leon Ave. and Clifton Rd.)*

BUCKHEAD

A drive through **Buckhead,** north of Midtown and Piedmont Park, off Peachtree St. near W. Paces Ferry Rd., uncovers Atlanta's Beverly Hills. The majority of these gaudy mansions were built by Coca-Cola bigwigs; the architectural style of this area has been aptly dubbed "Rococo-cola." The main drag along Peachtree Dr. is slowly turning from a hip yuppie hangout to a more underage, and often unruly, crowd. Though this has led a number of locals to refer to the area as "Buckhood," the area remains conducive to wining and dining and is strung with dance clubs and restaurants frequented by Atlanta's twenty-somethings.

BUCKHEAD ATTRACTIONS. One of the most exquisite residences in the Southeast, the Greek Revival **Governor's Mansion** has elaborate gardens and one of the finest collections of furniture from the Federal Period. *(391 W. Paces Ferry Rd. ☎261-1776. Tours Tu-Th 10-11:30am. Free.)* In the same neighborhood, the **Atlanta History Center** traces Atlanta's development from a rural area to an international cityscape. Its Civil War Gallery spotlights the stories of both Confederate and Union soldiers, while the Folklife Gallery expounds on Southern culture from grits to banjos. Also on the grounds are exquisite mansions from the early 20th century, including the **Swan House,** a lavish Anglo-Palladian Revival home built in 1928 (undergoing restoration until 2005), and the **Tullie Smith Farm,** an 1845 Yeoman farmhouse. Abutting the homes, 33 acres of trails and gardens are perfect for an afternoon stroll. *(130 W. Paces Ferry Rd. NW. ☎814-4000; www.atlantahistorycenter.com. Open M-Sa 10am-5:30pm, Su noon-5:30pm. $10, students and seniors $8, ages 6-17 $5; tours of the houses free with museum admission. Wheelchair accessible.)*

◪ ENTERTAINMENT

For hassle-free fun, buy a MARTA pass (see **Local Transportation,** p. 435) and pick up the city's free publications on music and events. *Creative Loafing, Music Atlanta,* the *Hudspeth Report,* and "Leisure" in the Friday edition of the *Atlanta Journal and Constitution* contain the latest info and are available in most coffee shops and on street corners. Check for free summer concerts in Atlanta's parks.

The **Woodruff Arts Center** (see **Midtown,** p. 437) houses the Atlanta Symphony, the Alliance Theater Company, the Atlanta College of Art, and the High Museum of Art. **Atlantix,** 65 Upper Alabama St., MARTA: Five Points, sets you up with same-day, half-price rush tickets to dance, theater, music, and other attractions throughout the city (walk-up service only). Full price advance tickets are also available online. (☎678-318-1400; www.atlantaperforms.com. Open Tu 11am-3pm, W-Sa 11am-6pm, Su noon-3pm.) The **Philips Arena,** 100 Techwood Dr. (☎878-3000 or 800-326-4000), hosts concerts, the **Atlanta Hawks** basketball team, and the **Atlanta Thrashers** hockey team. The pride and joy of Atlanta, the National League's **Atlanta Braves,** play at **Turner Field,** where a Coke bottle over left field erupts with fireworks after home runs. (755 Hank Aaron Dr., MARTA: West End or bus #105. ☎522-7630; Ticketmaster 800-326-4000. $5-50.) 1hr. tours of Turner Field include views of the diamond from the $200,000 skyboxes. (☎614-2311. Open non-game days M-Sa 9:30am-3pm, Su 1-3pm; evening-game days M-Sa 9:30am-noon; no tours afternoon-game days; low-season M-Sa 10am-2pm. $8, under 13 $4.) See the **Atlanta Falcons** play football at the **Georgia Dome,** MARTA: OMNI/Dome/World Congress Center, the world's largest cable-supported dome. Tours are available by appointment. (☎223-8687. Open daily 10am-4pm. $2; students and seniors 3-12 $1.)

Six Flags Over Georgia, 275 Riverside Pkwy., at I-20 W, is one of the largest amusement parks in the nation. Take bus #201 "Six Flags" from Hamilton Homes. Check out the 54 mph "Georgia Scorcher" roller coaster and the "Superman" roller coaster, with a pretzel-shaped inverted loop. (☎770-948-9290. Open mid-May to Aug. M-F 10am-9pm, Sa 10am-10pm; low-season hours vary, so call in advance. $45, seniors and under 4 ft. $25. Parking $10-12.)

◪ NIGHTLIFE

Atlanta's rich nightlife lacks a clear focal point. Fortunately, however, it also lacks limits; young people can be found partying until the wee hours and beyond. Scores of bars and clubs along Peachtree Rd. and Buckhead Ave. in **Buckhead** cater to a younger crowd. Pricier **Midtown** greets the glitzy and the glamorous. Alternative **L5P** plays hosts to bikers and goths, while **Virginia Highland** and up-and-coming **East Atlanta** feature an eclectic mix of all types imaginable.

BARS AND PUBS

▒ **Blind Willie's**, 828 N. Highland Ave. NE (☎873-2583). Blind Willie's is the quintessential blues club: the brick-lined interior is dark and cramped, and the bar serves mostly beer ($3-4) to its ardently loyal patrons. Despite its hole-in-the wall appearance, Blind Willie's is an Atlanta legend. Live blues, zydeco, and folk music starts around 10pm. Cover $5-10. Open Su-Th 8pm-2am, F 8pm-3am, Sa 8pm-2:30am.

The Vortex, 438 Moreland Ave. (☎688-1828), in L5P. An incredible restaurant that doubles as an even cooler bar, Vortex is the no-nonsense spot for serious eaters and drinkers. With burgers named "Coronary Bypass" ($8) and "Italian Stallion" ($7), you'll need a drink like the "Bitch on Wheels" ($8) to make it through the night. Open M-Sa 11am-2am, Su 11am-midnight.

Masquerade, 695 North Ave. NE (☎577-8178, concert info 577-2007), occupies an original turn-of-the-century mill. The bar has 3 levels: "heaven," with live music from touring bands; "purgatory," a more laid-back pub and pool house; and "hell," a dance club with everything from techno to 1940s big band jazz. An outside space provides dancing under the stars, while the 4000-seat amphitheater caters to metal and punk tastes. 18+. Cover $3-8 and up. Open W-Su 8pm-4am.

Eastside Lounge, 485 Flat Shoals Ave. SE (☎522-7841). If the streets of East Atlanta seem empty, it's because everyone is packed into this suave hideout. Couches near the bar and tables in the small upstairs offer rest for the weary, but be prepared to stand with the rest of the trendsetters. DJ spins F-Sa. Open M-Sa 7pm-3am.

Flatiron, 520 Flat Shoals Ave. (☎688-8864). Set on the corner of Glenwood and Flat Shoals, this L5P hotspot is a favorite with locals who are tired of the bohemian scene. Beer $3-4. Open Su-Th 11am-2am, F-Sa 11am-3pm.

Steamhouse, 3041 Bolling Way (☎233-7980). For those who like raw oysters ($8 for a dozen on the half shell) with their beer ($4), Steamhouse has plenty of both. A great place on lazy hot summer evening—the party often spills out onto the patio. Open daily 11:30am-2am.

Fado Fado, 3035 Peachtree Rd. NE (☎841-0066). The interior of this bar was imported from Ireland–right down to the wood of the bar itself. *The* yuppie hang-out in Buckhead. The boxty (rolled Irish pancake; $8) complements a Guinness nicely. Open M-F 11:30am-1am, Sa-Su 10:30am-2am.

DANCE CLUBS

▒ **Tongue and Groove**, 3055 Peachtree Rd. NE (☎261-2325). The club that has been taking Atlanta by storm, Tongue and Groove has been the recipient of praise from both the media and locals alike. Whether you decide to kick back at one of the 2 gorgeous bars or shake it on the dance floor, you're guaranteed to have fun. W Latin night; Th house; F hip-hop; Sa Euro night. Cover for men W and F $5, Sa $10; for women W $5, Sa $10 after midnight. Open Tu, Th, F 10pm-2am, W 9pm-2am, Sa 10pm-2am.

Chaos, 3067 Peachtree Rd. NE (☎995-0064). One of the largest and newest clubs in Buckhead, Chaos manages to avoid the cheesy commercialism of some of its neighbors. M hip-hop; other nights Top 40 and techno. Dress to impress; jeans and baseball caps won't cut it here. 21+. Cover $10 for men. Open M-F 9pm-2am, Sa 9pm-2am.

The Riviera, 1055 Peachtree St. NE (☎607-8050). For some good, old-fashioned Midtown fun, head over to the glitzy "Riv" for a night of athletic dancing, drinking, and pool. Call ahead for a schedule of live local bands. Cover $15. Open daily 8pm-6am.

GLBT NIGHTLIFE

Atlanta is the gay capital of the south, which makes **Midtown** the mecca of southern gay culture. In Atlanta, straight and gay often party together, and some of the city's best all-around joints are rainbow-colored. For information on gay nightlife and events, check out the free *Southern Voice* newspaper, available everywhere.

Blake's, 227 10th St. (☎892-5786). Midtown males flock to this friendly bar, where see-and-be-seen is a way of life. A prime location in gay-friendly Midtown and just steps from Piedmont Park, this popular bar is also a destination for the young lesbian crowd. Open daily 2pm-2:30am. Popular "Drag Races" M nights.

Red Chair, 550-C Amsterdam Ave. (☎870-0532), in Midtown. An expansive menu and 5 huge video screens playing VH-1 jams have quickly vaulted Red Chair to the top of Midtown's gay scene. 21+, Th 18+. Open M-Sa 5:30pm-2am, Su 11:30am-midnight.

The Heretic, 2069 Cheshire Bridge Road NE (☎325-3061), a little outside of the center of Midtown. Many guys head here in search of Mr. Right—or at least Mr. Right Now. If the action on the smoky dance floor gets a little too hot for you, cool off on the outdoor patio. 21+. Cover F-Sa $3. Open M-Sa 9am-3am, Su 12:30pm-midnight.

■ OUTDOOR ACTIVITIES

In the heart of Midtown, **Piedmont Park** is a hotbed of fun, free activities. Look for the **Dogwood Festival** (www.dogwood.org), an art festival in the spring, and the **Jazz Festival** (www.atlantafestivals.com) in May. In June, the park celebrates the **Gay Pride Festival** (www.atlantapride.org), and on July 4th, Atlanta draws 55,000 people to the world's largest 10K race, the famed Peachtree Road Race. Every summer Turner Broadcasting and HBO present **"Screen on the Green,"** a series of free films projected once a week in the meadow behind the visitors center. The **Atlanta Botanical Garden** occupies the northern end of the park and provides a tranquil refuge from the hustle and bustle of everyday life. Stroll through 15 acres of landscaped gardens, a hardwood forest with trails, and an interactive children's garden focusing on health and wellness. The Garden is also home to the Storza Woods and the **Dorothy Chapman Fuqua Conservatory,** which houses some of the world's rarest and endangered plant species. (345 Piedmont Ave. NE. Take bus #36 or MARTA: Arts Center; on Su, bus #31 "Lindburgh: from MARTA: Five Points. ☎876-5859; www.atlantabotanicalgarden.org. Open Apr.-Sept. Tu-Su 9am-7pm; Oct.-Mar. Tu-Su 9am-6pm. $10, seniors $7, students $5; Th free after 3pm.)

Sixteen miles east of the city on U.S. 78, one of Georgia's top natural attractions, **Stone Mountain Park,** provides a respite from the city with beautiful scenery and the remarkable **Confederate Memorial.** Carved into the world's largest mass of granite, the 825 ft. "Mt. Rushmore of the South" profiles Jefferson Davis, Robert E. Lee, and Stonewall Jackson. The hike up the **Confederate Hall Trail** (1½ mi.) provides a spectacular view of Atlanta. The mountain is surrounded by a 3200-acre historic park. On summer nights, be sure to check out the dazzling laser show that illuminates the side of the mountain. (Take bus #120 "Stone Mountain" from MARTA: Avondale. ☎ 770-498-5600 or 800-317-2006; www.stonemountainpark.com. Park open daily 6am-midnight. Attractions open daily in summer 10am-8pm; low-season 10am-5pm. Entrance $7 per car, $7 per attraction; $19 for an all-day pass, ages 3-11 $16. Free laser show daily 9:30pm.)

ATHENS   ☎ 706

In the grand Southern tradition of naming college towns after great classical cultural centers, Athens is perhaps the most successful at living up to its namesake. Of course, the only Greeks around here live in the University of Georgia's (UGA) fraternities and sororities, and the city is better known for its production of rock stars than philosophers or mathematicians—the university and surrounding bars have spawned hundreds of popular bands, including R.E.M. and the B-52s. Strolling around the beautiful campus and downtown, it's easy to see why the nearly 34,000 students who live in Athens choose to spend their college years there.

🔢 PRACTICAL INFORMATION. Situated 70 mi. northeast of Atlanta, Athens can be reached from I-85 via U.S. 316, which runs into U.S. 29. Although there is a commuter airport (☎549-5783), it's easier to fly into Atlanta and take a **commuter shuttle** (☎800-354-7874) to various points in and around Athens ($35). **Southeastern Stages,** 220 W. Broad St., buses to Atlanta and Augusta. (☎549-2255. Call for schedules. Open M-F 7:15am-7:15pm, Sa-Su 7:40am-1pm.) The **Athens Transit System** runs "The Bus" every 30min. on loops around downtown, UGA, and surrounding residential areas. (☎613-3430. Buses M-F 6:15am-7:15pm, Sa 7:30am-7pm. $1, ages 6-18 $0.75, seniors $0.50; transfers free.) UGA's **Campus Transit System** runs everywhere on campus and to some stops downtown. (☎369-6220. Open daily 7am-12:45am. Free.) **Taxi: Alfa Taxi** ☎583-8882. Two blocks north of the UGA campus is the **Athens Welcome Center,** 280 E. Dougherty St., in the Church-Waddel-Brumby House. (☎353-1820. Open M-Sa 10am-6pm, Su noon-6pm.) The **UGA Visitors Center,** at the intersection of College Station and River Rd. on campus, provides info on UGA attractions. (☎542-0842. Open M-F 8am-5pm, Sa 9am-5pm, Su 1-5pm.) **Hotlines: Crisis Line,** ☎353-1912. **Community Connection,** ☎353-1313. **Medical Services: Athens Regional Medical Center,** 1199 Prince Ave. (☎549-9977.) **Post Office:** 575 Olympic Dr. (☎800-275-8777. Open M-F 8:30am-4:30pm.) **Postal Code:** 30601. **Area Code:** 706.

🏠 ACCOMMODATIONS. Accommodations are usually reasonably priced, but rates rise for football weekends. For a luxurious stay, check out **The Foundry Park Inn ❺,** 295 E. Dougherty St. at Thomas, in one of Athens's oldest historic sites. Thoughtfully decorated rooms and suites are available year-round. (☎549-7020; www.foundryparkinn.com. Rooms from $90.) The **Perimeter Inn ❷,** 3791 Atlanta Hwy., 5 mi. from downtown, is a reasonably priced, comfortable, independently-owned motel with a Spanish flair. (☎548-3000 or 800-934-2963. Singles $40; doubles $45.) Within walking distance of the campus and downtown, the **Days Inn ❷,** 230 Finley St., off Broad St., is a more generic option, but the combination of clean rooms, cheap prices, and good location makes the lack of character bearable. (☎543-6511; www.daysinnathens.com. Singles $57; doubles $62.) **Watson Mill Bridge State Park ❶,** 650 Watson Mill Rd., 21 mi. east of Athens, is the best place in the area to camp, with horse and hiking trails, canoe and boat rentals, and plenty of fishing. (☎783-5349 or 800-864-7275. Park open daily 7am-10pm; office 8am-5pm. Sites $15, with water and electricity $17; secluded primitive sites $20.) For camping closer to the city, try **Sandy Creek Park ❶,** 400 Homan Rd., 4 mi. north of Athens Hwy. 441 N, 3 mi. outside of the loop. (☎613-3631. Park open in summer Tu-Su 7am-9pm; call for low-season hours. Primitive sites $10.)

🍴 FOOD. The **Last Resort Grill ❸,** 174 and 184 W. Clayton St., at the corner of Hull St., is an eclectic restaurant with a gourmet atmosphere and reasonable prices. You may never again see a fried green tomato sandwich ($5) presented so elegantly, and the desserts are widely considered the best in Athens. (☎549-0810. Lunch $5-10. Dinner $10-20. Open Su-Th 11am-3pm and 5-10pm, F-Sa 5-11pm; bar until 2am.) R.E.M. fans who wonder what "automatic for the people" means should ask Dexter Weaver, the owner of **Weaver D's Fine Foods ❶,** 1016 E. Broad St., to whom the phrase originally belongs. Located in a small roadside house, Weaver D's offers a true taste of Athens, with pork chop sandwiches ($4.25) and soul-food lunches ($5-6). R.E.M. repaid Weaver for the use of his phrase as their 1992 album

THE TREE THAT OWNS ITSELF

Most trees can only dream of the gift given to the white oak that sits at the corner of Dearing and Finley St. in Athens, Georgia: the gift of self-ownership. That's right, this famed Tree That Owns Itself has the deed to both itself and the land within 8 ft. of its trunk. It is doubly lucky in that, unlike most property holders, it pays no taxes and is beloved by local citizens.

Legend holds that Colonel William H. Jackson, a professor at the University of Georgia, owned the land on which the tree stood and enjoyed its shade and "magnificent proportions" so much that he willed it the land around it. Although the deed has never been tested in the courts, its legitimacy seems irrelevant. Local residents not only acknowledge the tree's ownership of itself, but actually take it as an obligation to see that the oak is protected. In fact, in 1942, when the original oak (estimated to have been around 400 years old) fell in a terrible storm, the Junior Ladies' Garden Club collected acorns from the site in order to grow a successor. They were successful, and in 1946 the sapling that is today's Tree That Owns Itself was planted.

title by inviting him to the Grammy Awards. (☎353-7797. Open M-Sa 11am-6pm.) **The Grill ❷**, 171 College St., is Athens's version of the all-night burger-and-malt joint vital to the life of every college town. In addition to the standard mega-burger platter ($7) and luscious malts ($3.50), the Grill has a mean vegetarian side. (☎543-4770. Open 24hr.) For the best baked goods in town, head to **Big City Bread ❶**, 393 N. Finley St., which serves amazing biscuits ($1.07) and sandwiches ($6) on home-baked bread. (☎543-1187. Open M-Th 7am-8pm, F-Sa 7am-10pm, Su 9am-10pm.)

🟦 **SIGHTS.** The **University of Georgia,** chartered in 1785 as the first land-grant college in the US, is the very reason Athens exists, and it also tops Athens's list of tourist attractions. The campus visitors center, at the corner of College Station and River Rd. in south campus, has self-guided tours, maps, and helpful answers. (☎542-0842. Open M-F 8am-5pm, Sa 9am-5pm, Su 1-5pm.) The campus begins downtown on Broad St., where The Arch guards the official entrance to the institution. **Sanford Stadium** is the home turf of UGA's "Dawgs," the white English bulldogs that serve as the school's mascot. **Butts-Mehre Heritage Hall,** on the corner of Pinecrest Dr. and Rutherford St., houses the school's athletic offices and the Heritage Museum, which celebrates generations of UGA athletes and white English bulldogs. (☎542-9036. Open M-F 8am-5pm, Sa-Su 2-5pm.) The **Georgia Museum of Art,** 90 Carlton St., in the Performing and Visual Arts Complex off East Campus Dr., is an impressive state-funded collection of over 7000 works of art. (☎542-4662. Open Tu and Th-Sa 10am-5pm, W 10am-9pm, Su 1-5pm. Suggested donation $1.)

Beyond the university, Athens boasts a wealth of historic sites, homes, and artifacts chronicling the town's rich history. The many lush gardens and arboretums encourage long walks and picnics. Maps and tours of the city's historic areas and green spaces are available at the Athens Welcome Center (see **Practical Information,** p. 445), the oldest residence in town. The **US Navy Supply Corps School and Museum,** 1425 Prince Ave., was originally a teacher's college, then a Carnegie library, and is now one of only 11 official US Navy Museums. Exhibits of ship models, uniforms, and all manner of Navy flotsam are on display. (☎354-7349. Visitors must call ahead. Open M-F 9am-5:15pm. Free.) The city's most elaborate garden, the **State Botanical Garden of Georgia,** 2450 S. Milledge Ave., houses 313 acres of trails, a tropical conservatory, and a Day Chapel. (☎542-1244. Open daily 8am-8pm; visitors center open Tu-Sa 9am-4:30pm, Su 11:30am-4:30pm. Free.)

If you hesitate to bequeath your property to undeserving offspring, consider making your favorite plant an heir. Professor William H. Jackson set the legal precedent when he willed to a beloved oak tree all the land within 8 ft. of its trunk. Today, **The Tree That Owns Itself** flourishes at the intersection of Finley and Dearing St., near Broad St. downtown. By far Athens's best Civil War relic, the nearby **Double-Barreled Cannon** was a great idea that failed spectacularly. On the grounds of City Hall, at Washington and College St., the two barrels are still ominously pointed north.

⚡📻 ENTERTAINMENT AND NIGHTLIFE. Athens has cradled hundreds of fledging bands in all styles of music over the years. R.E.M. is arguably Athens's most well-known homegrown band, but those plugged into the music world will know that most musicians show up in Athens at one point or another to play in a true-blue music mecca. In late June, **Athfest** takes over the town. (☎548-2516. 1 day $10, both days $15.) Take a look at Athens's free weekly newspaper, *Flagpole Magazine*, available everywhere downtown, to find out which bands are in town. As soon as you're within spitting distance of Athens, tune in to **WUOG 90.5**, one of the nation's last bastions of real college radio. The students who run the station play tons of local music, and liven it up with unscripted, unplanned, and occasionally incoherent commentary. R.E.M. got its start at **The 40 Watt Club**, 285 W. Washington St. Born in 1979 as a raucous Halloween party lit by a single 40-watt bulb, the club has had numerous incarnations and locations, but currently kicks with live music most nights. (☎549-7871. Cover $5-15. Open daily 10pm-3am.) Downtown, bars line the streets between Lumpkin and Thomas streets, and you're sure to find a bar that fits your style, though the **Flicker Theater and Bar**, 263 W. Washington St. (☎546-0039), **The Globe**, 199 N. Lumpkin St. (☎353-4721), and the **Manhattan Cafe**, 337 N. Hull St. (☎369-9767) are current hotspots. If you're looking for something beyond music and booze, Athens lives up to its name academically as well as theatrically. **Jittery Joe's**, 1210 S. Millege Rd., offers a classy coffeeshop atmosphere. (☎208-1979. Open M-Th 6:30am-midnight, F 6:30am-1am, Sa 8:30am-1am, Su 8:30am-midnight.) **The Morton Theater**, 195 W. Washington St., was built in 1910 as a vaudeville theater and was entirely African-American owned and operated. Today it is a fully restored, high-tech performing arts center home to all sorts of theater and music. (☎613-3770. Call for schedules and ticket prices.)

MACON ☎478

The history of Macon is a tale of transition. For over 10,000 years, the forested stretch of the Ocmulgee River where Macon lies has been home to various groups of native peoples, from the ancient mound-builders of the Ocmulgee to the Mississippians and the Creek Indians. The latter was the last group of Native American inhabitants to exist in the area before President Jackson forced them to move to Oklahoma in the "Trail of Tears." The ensuing wave of white settlers then turned the once sacred ground into a port city that became one of Georgia's cultural centers during the antebellum era. During the 20th century, Macon sttracted many of Georgia's top musicians, most of whom performed at the Douglass Theater, one of the greatest venues for black performers in the country. Today, the sleepy town of Macon offer visitors a glimpse of the area's intriguing history.

📋 PRACTICAL INFORMATION. Macon sits at the intersection of I-75 and I-16, about 75 mi. southwest of Atlanta. **I-475** makes a large arc west of downtown, branching off of I-75. Downtown is a grid with numbered streets running east-west and named streets running north-south. **Riverside Drive** is a main artery parallel to I-75 and the river. **Martin Luther King, Jr. Boulevard (MLK)** runs east-west through the heart of downtown. Shops, bars, and restaurants cluster on **Cherry Street,** the main north-south thoroughfare. West of downtown, MLK Blvd. becomes Houston (HOUSE-ton) Ave., which feeds into Eisenhower Pkwy. North of town along Riverside Dr. lie more shopping centers and pricier hotels.

Greyhound, 65 Spring St. (☎743-2868; open daily 4:30am-midnight), runs to: Athens (5hr., 1 per day, $35); Atlanta (1½hr., 11 per day, $18.50); Birmingham (5-6hr., 6 per day, $51). **Macon-Bibb County Transit Authority (MTA-MAC),** 1000 Terminal Dr., operates 20 buses and the **MITSI** trolley throughout the downtown area. (☎746-1387. Operates M-Sa 5:30am-11pm. Buses $0.75, students $0.50, seniors $0.35; transfers $0.25. Trolley $0.25.) For **visitor info,** the **Macon-Bibb Country Convention and Visitors Bureau,** 200 Cherry St., is at the southern tip of downtown. (☎743-3401 or 800-768-3401; www.maconga.org. Open M-Sa 9am-5pm.) **Hotlines: Crisis Line,** ☎745-9292. **Medical Services: Medical Center of Central Georgia,** 777 Hemlock St. (☎633-1000), downtown. **Internet access** is available at the **Washington Memorial Library,** 1180 Washington St., at the corner of College St. (☎744-0800. Open M-Th 9am-9pm, F-Sa 9am-6pm, Su 1:30-5pm.) The **post office** is at 451 College St. (☎752-8432. Open M-F 8am-6pm, Sa 9am-2pm.) **Postal Code:** 31213. **Area Code:** 478.

⚑🛏 ACCOMMODATIONS AND FOOD. While downtown Macon offers limited options, I-75 is lined with cheap motels starting at $25 for a single; look to Riverside Dr. (just off I-75, north of town) and Eisenhower Pkwy. (west of town near I-475). The lowest priced option in downtown Macon is the **Riverview Hotel ❷,** 205 Broadway. (☎738-9030. Singles $31; doubles $35 and up.) A downtown option with a heftier price tag is **The Crowne Plaza ❹,** 108 1st St. Despite it's cookie-cutter feel, the rooms are very clean and come with plenty of amenities. The proximity to downtown is the real value. (☎746-1461 or 800-227-6963. Rooms from $90.) 🅺**Jeneane's Cafe ❶,** 524 Mulberry St., serves lightning-fast lunch to the noontime crowd in the most personal, efficient, sweetie-eat-your-vegetables way imaginable. Desserts are concocted daily by a retired pastry chef, and though the teal plastic seats might remind you of a high school cafeteria, the food won't. (☎743-5267. Meat-and-vegetable lunch plate $5. Open M-F 6:30am-2:30pm.) **Len Berg's Restaurant ❶,** 240 Post Office Alley, south down Walnut St., is a 1908 sit-down lunch counter where all food costs less than $7. (☎742-9255. Open M-F 11am-2:30pm.) Since 1916, **Nu-Way Weiners ❶,** 430 Cotton Ave., has been serving up some of the tastiest dogs ($1.34) in the South. (☎743-1368. Open M-F 6am-7pm, Sa 7am-6pm.)

◪ SIGHTS. Macon is a tour-planner's dream—the entire downtown is compact and walkable, and the major museums are all within one block of each other. The 🅺**Georgia Music Hall of Fame,** 200 MLK Blvd., at the end of Mulberry St., will overwhelm you with its mind-boggling collection of inductees, including Ray Charles, The Allman Brothers, Gladys Knight, James Brown, and the Indigo Girls. From some of Little Richard's wacky suits to Lynyrd Skynyrd's keyboard, the Hall of Fame has priceless treasures and memorabilia. (☎750-0350. Open M-Sa 9am-5pm, Su 1-5pm. $8; students with ID, seniors, and AAA $6; ages 4-16 $3.50.) The **Georgia Sports Hall of Fame,** 301 Cherry St., is another lavish showcase of Georgia talent. It includes relics from the life of Hank Aaron and a basketball court that visitors can play on in between ooh-ing and aah-ing at exhibits. (☎752-1585. Open M-Sa 9am-5pm, Su 1-5pm. $8; students, seniors, and military $6; ages 6-16 $3.50.)

The **Tubman African American Museum,** 340 Walnut Ave., is the South's largest museum exclusively devoted to African-American art, history, and culture. (☎743-8544. Open M-Sa 9am-5pm, Su 2-5pm. $5, under 12 $3.) Enter the 🅺**Ocmulgee National Monument,** 1207 Emery Hwy., across the river from downtown, and stand on some of the most ancient sacred grounds in all of the Americas. The National Park protects gigantic mounds, prehistoric trenches, and village sites of the five distinct Indian groups that inhabited it for over 12,000 years. (☎752-8257. Park and visitors center open daily 9am-5pm. Free.) Macon has many historical houses, including **Cannonball House**, 856 Mulberry St., which was hit by a cannonball in 1864. (☎745-5982. Open M-Sa 10am-5pm. $3, children $2.) **Hay House**, 934 Georgia Ave., near downtown, is the most opulent of all the city's magnificent dwellings. The gigantic Italian Renaissance Revival mansion was built in 1860 and boasts marble hallways, crystal chandeliers, and plenty of pomp to awe visitors. (☎742-8155. Open M-Sa 10am-4:30pm, Su 1-4:30pm. $8, seniors and AAA $7, students $4.)

🔲🔲 **ENTERTAINMENT AND NIGHTLIFE.** The biggest event of Macon's year is the annual **Cherry Blossom Festival**, March 18-27, 2005. The city hosts thousands of visitors, who come to admire the 265,000 Yoshino Cherry trees blooming in every backyard and on every street. Over 500 mostly free events—like concerts, tours, and parades—keep the masses tickled pink.

Macon has as many bars and nightclubs as one might expect from a small southern town where Little Richard grew up. Entertainment clusters along Cherry St. downtown. The free *Synergy Magazine*, available in newsstands downtown, has entertainment listings. Gay-friendly and open to all, **Club Synergy**, 425 Cherry St., has two dance floors, DJs from all over, a full bar, and a willingness to occasionally flood itself for the odd beach party theme. (☎755-9383. Cover $5-7. Open W-Sa 9pm-2am.) **River Front Bluez**, 550 Riverside Dr., in a shack by the side of the road, is a great place to hear gritty, down-and-out blues. (☎741-9970. Happy hour 5-7pm. Live bands W-Sa around 9pm. Open Tu-Sa 5pm-late) If plush clubbing is your thing, go to **Déa**, 420 Martin Luther King Blvd. This swank outfit's dress code is a small price to pay for feeling like a movie star as you strut into the dark interior. (☎755-1620. Cover varies, but can be quite high. Open W-Sa 8pm-3am.)

ANDERSONVILLE   ☎229

Fifty-five miles south of Macon and 10 mi. northeast of Americus on Rte. 49, the **Andersonville National Historic Site** preserves the location where 45,000 Union soldiers were confined in a primitive prison pen without food, water, or shelter in 1864 near the end of the Civil War. Nearly 13,000 men died horrible deaths within the camp's wooden walls due to the barbaric conditions and severe overcrowding—at one point more than 32,000 men were confined in a space intended to hold 10,000. On the grounds, the excellent **National Prisoner of War Museum**, 496 Cemetery Rd., memorializes the experience of American POWs with artifacts, interactive video testimonials, recordings, photographs, and journals. The museum is extraordinarily sobering as you pass actual rations that kept men alive for days, view myriad portrayals of horrible suffering and amazing strength, and finally exit into a small memorial in the sunlight. Also on the grounds, the **Andersonville National Cemetery** is a fitting place to end the visit. (☎924-0343, ext. 201; www.nps.gov/ande/. Park open daily 8am-5pm; museum 8:30am-5pm. Special talks daily 11am and 2pm. Museum audio tours $1.) Directly across Rte. 49 from the park exit is the tiny town of Andersonville. The **Welcome Center**, 114 Main St., doubles as a dusty little museum stuffed with bric-a-brac. To the left of the monument in the middle of town and up the street a quarter mile on the left, the **Andersonville Restaurant ❶** (the only one in town) serves an unpretentious buffet lunch for $6.25 and chatty conversation for free. (☎928-8480. Open M-F 11am-3pm, also F 5-9pm.)

SAVANNAH   ☎912

In February 1733, General James Oglethorpe and his band of 120 vagabonds founded the city of Savannah and the state of Georgia. General Sherman later spared the city during his rampage through the South. Some say he found Savannah too pretty to burn—presenting it instead to President Lincoln as a Christmas gift. Today, that reaction is believable to anyone who sees Savannah's stately trees and Federalist and English Regency houses interwoven with spring blossoms.

◪ PRACTICAL INFORMATION. Savannah rests on the coast of Georgia at the mouth of the **Savannah River,** which runs north of the city along the border with South Carolina. The city stretches south from bluffs overlooking the river. The restored 2½ sq. mi. **downtown historic district,** bordered by East Broad St., Martin Luther King Jr. Blvd., Gwinnett St., and the river, is best explored on foot. *Do not stray south of Gwinnett St.; the historic district quickly deteriorates into an unsafe area.* A parking pass ($8) allows 2-day unlimited use of all metered parking, city lots, and garages. **Savannah/Hilton Head International Airport,** 400 Airways Ave. (☎964-0514; www.savannahairport.com), at Exit 104 off I-95, serves coastal Georgia and the Low Country of South Carolina. **Amtrak,** 2611 Seaboard Coastline Dr. (☎234-2611; open Sa-Th 4:30am-12:15pm and 5pm-12:45am, F 4:30am-12:45am), chugs to Charleston (1½hr., 1 per day, $22). **Greyhound,** 610 W. Oglethorpe Ave. (☎232-2135; open 24hr.), at Fahm St., sends buses to: Atlanta (6hr., 5 per day, $40); Charleston (3hr., 2 per day, $26); Jacksonville (2½hr., 10 per day, $24). **Chatham Area Transit (CAT),** 124 Bull St. (☎233-5767), in the Chatham County Court House, runs buses and a free shuttle through the historic area. (Open daily 7am-11pm. Shuttle M-Sa 7am-9pm, Su 9:40am-5pm. $0.75, seniors $0.37; no transfers. Weekly pass available at Parking Services Office, 100 E. Bryan St., $12.) **Hotline: Rape Hotline,** ☎233-7273, 24hr. **Taxi: Yellow Cab** ☎236-1133. The **Savannah Visitors Center,** 301 Martin Luther King Jr. Blvd., at Liberty St., in a former train station, provides a reservation service for local inns and hostels. (☎944-0455; reservation service 877-728-2662; www.savannahgeorgia.com. Open M-F 8:30am-5pm, Sa-Su 9am-5pm.) **Medical Services: Georgia Regional Hospital,** 1915 Eisenhower Dr. (☎356-2045.) **Internet Access: Public Library,** 2002 Bull St. (☎652-3600. Open M-Th 9am-9pm, F-Sa 9am-6pm, Su 2-6pm.) **Post Office:** 2 N. Fahm St., at Bay St. (☎235-4610. Open M-F 7am-6pm, Sa 9am-3pm.) **Postal Code:** 31402. **Area Code:** 912.

▟ ACCOMMODATIONS. Downtown motels cluster near the historic area, visitors center, and Greyhound station. Venture into the Historic District for a number of very fine B&B options. For those with cars, **Ogeechee Road (U.S. 17)** has several budget options. **The President's Quarters ❺,** 225 E. President St., and its adjoining inns (The Guest House and 17Hundred90) offer it all. Rooms in all three buildings seamlessly combine the classic (antique furnishings) with the modern (high-speed Internet access). If staying with a group, the ground floor in 17Hundred90, with a sitting room and a courtyard featuring 8-foot walls, allows you to feel like a member of Savannah high society, if only for a night. (☎233-1600 or 800-233-1776; www.presidentsquarters.com. Breakfast and daily tea included. Reservations recommended. Ask for daily "walk-in" specials. Rooms $119-225.) The **Eliza Thompson House ❺,** 5 W. Jones St., is the premier bed and breakfast in Savannah, located minutes from the city's beautiful, bustling squares. Built in 1847, this historic inn welcomes guests with complimentary wine, coffee, and dessert hours. (☎236-3620 or 800-348-9378. Reservations recommended. 25 rooms from $140.) **Savannah Hostel ❶,** 304 E. Hall St., is really the only budget option in the historic district, but don't expect too much from this small, bare-bones inn. Though not in the most savory section of downtown, it is only minutes from some of Savannah's greatest sights. (☎236-7744. Linen $1. Bike rental $10. Check-in 7-10am and 5-11pm; call for late-night check-in. Lockout 10am-5pm. 3-night max. stay. Open Mar.-Oct. Dorms $19; private rooms $40-$45.) **Skidaway Island State Park ❶** is 6 mi. southeast of downtown off Diamond Causeway; follow Liberty St. east until it becomes

Wheaton St., turn right on Waters Ave., and follow it to Diamond Causeway. (☎598-2300 or 800-864-7275. Bathrooms, heated showers, electricity, and water. Open daily 7am-10pm. Check-in before 10pm. Sites $20; with hookup $24.)

◪ FOOD. At **Nita's Place ❸**, 129 E. Broughton St., you can read enthusiastic letters from satisfied customers pressed beneath the glass tabletops while you experience the uplifting power of fantastic soul food. The dessert-like squash casserole, a delight beyond description, will make you a believer. (☎238-8233. Entrees $10-13. Open M-Th 11:30am-3pm, F-Sa 11:30am-3pm and 5-8pm.) **Wall's BBQ ❶**, 515 E. York Ln., in an alley between York St. and Oglethorpe Ave., serves mouth-watering barbecue in a hidden hole-in-the-wall location. Don't plan on devouring your delicious barbecue sandwich or ribs ($4.50-12) here; most locals relish their incredible meal in one of the neighboring public squares. (☎232-9754. Baked deviled crabs $3. Open Th-Sa 11am-9pm.) **Mrs. Wilkes Boarding House ❸**, 107 W. Jones St., is a Southern institution where friendly strangers gather around large tables for homestyle atmosphere and soul food. Fried chicken, butter beans, and superb biscuits are favorites. (☎232-5997. All-you-can-eat $12. Open M-F 8-9am and 11am-3pm.) **Clary's Cafe ❶**, 404 Abercorn St., has been serving some of Savannah's best breakfasts since 1903, and was the setting of many scenes in *Midnight in the Garden of Good and Evil*. Weekend brunch features $4 malted waffles. (☎233-0402. Open M-Tu and Th-F 7am-4pm, W 7am-5pm, Sa-Su 8am-4:30pm.)

◩ SIGHTS AND ENTERTAINMENT. Most of Savannah's 21 squares contain some distinctive centerpiece, while elegant antebellum houses and drooping vine-wound trees often cluster around the squares, adding to the classic Southern aura. Bus, van, and horse carriage **tours** leave from the visitors center, but walking can be more rewarding. (Tours daily every 10-15min. $15.) Two of Savannah's best-known historic homes are the **Davenport House**, 324 E. State St., on Columbia Sq., and the **Owens-Thomas House**, 124 Abercom St., one block away on Oglethorpe Sq. Built in 1820, the Davenport House is nearly exactly as Isaiah Davenport left it in the mid-19th century, complete with the original furniture, cantilevered staircase, and exemplary woodwork. The Owens-Thomas House is similar, but the carriage house, holding artifacts and relating stories about slave life, is free. (Davenport: ☎236-8097; www.davenportsavga.com. Open M-Sa 10am-4pm, Su 1-4pm. $7, ages 7-18 $3.50. Owens-Thomas: ☎233-9743. Open M noon-5pm, Tu-Sa 10am-5pm, Su 1-5pm; last tour 4:30pm. $8, seniors $7, students $4, ages 6-12 $2.) The **Green Meldrim House**, 14 W. Macon St., on Madison Sq., is a Gothic Revival mansion that served as General Sherman's Savannah headquarters following his famed "march to the sea." It was from this house that Sherman wrote the famous telegram to President Lincoln, giving him the city as a gift. (☎232-1251. Open Tu and Th-F 10am-4pm, Sa 10am-1pm. Tours every 30min. $5, students $2.)

Savannah's four forts once protected the city's port from Spanish, British, and other invaders. The most intriguing, **Fort Pulaski National Monument**, 15 mi. east of Savannah on U.S. 80 E and Rte. 26, marks the Civil War battle where Union forces first used rifled cannons to decimate the Confederate opposition. (☎786-5787. Partially wheelchair accessible. Open daily 9am-5pm. $3, under 16 free.)

Special events in Savannah include the annual **NOGS Tour of the Hidden Gardens of Historic Savannah** (☎238-0248), in late April, when private walled gardens are opened to the public, who can partake in a special Southern teatime. Green is the theme of the **St. Patrick's Day Celebration on the River**, a five-day, beer- and fun-filled party that packs the streets and warms celebrants up for the annual **St. Patrick's Day Parade**, the second-largest in the US. (Celebration: ☎234-0295. Parade: ☎233-4804. Mar. 17, 2005. Begins 10:15am.) **First Friday for the Arts** (☎232-4903) occurs on the first Friday of every month in City Market, when visitors meet with residents of a local art colony. **First Saturday on the River** (☎234-0295) brings arts, crafts, enter-tainment, and food to historic River St. each month. A free paper, *Connect Savan-nah*, found in restaurants and stores, has the latest in news and entertainment.

■ **NIGHTLIFE.** The waterfront area on **River Street** brims with endless ocean-front dining opportunities, street performers, and a friendly pub ambience. While you're allowed to freely walk the streets with one drink in hand, better not have two or the police will peg you with a $150 ticket. The **Warehouse,** 13 E River St., boasts the "coldest and cheapest beer in town." Happy hour features $1 beer. (☎234-6001. Happy hour M-F 4-7pm. Open daily 11am-late.) At **Kevin Barry's Irish Pub,** 117 W. River St., the Guinness flows and the entire bar jigs with live Irish folk music. (☎233-9626. Music W-Sa after 8:30pm. Cover $2. Open M-F 2pm-3am, Sa 11:30am-3am, Su 12:30pm-2am.) Local college students eat, drink, and shop at the restaurants and stores of **City Market,** the largest historic district in the US. (Jefferson at W. St. Julian St. Live music F-Sa nights.) **Malone's Bar and Grill,** 27 W. Barnard St., serves dancing, drinks, and live music. The lower floor opens up to a game room, while techno and rap beat upstairs Friday and Saturday nights. (☎234-3059. Happy hour daily 4-8pm. F-Sa top level 18+. Open M-Sa 11am-3am, Su noon-2am; kitchen closes 1am.) For the best alternative scene, and a gay- and lesbian-friendly atmosphere, check out **Club One,** 1 Jeffer-son St. near Bay St, where Lady Chablis, a character featured in *Midnight in the Garden of Good and Evil* (see p. 451), performs regularly. (☎232-0200. Cover $3-10. Open M-Sa 5pm-3am, Su 5pm-2am.)

CUMBERLAND ISLAND   ☎912

The prized jewel of Georgia's National Seashore, Cumberland Island was once a playground for the wealthy robber barons of the Gilded Age. Wild horses now out-number the few remaining private homes, loggerhead turtles lay their eggs on the island's beaches, and maritime forests slowly reclaim the ruins of enormous man-sions. The **Ice House Museum,** at Dungeness Dock, displays historical artifacts from the island. (No phone. Restrooms. Open daily 8am-4pm.) Off the main road about 1 mi. south of the dock lie the ruins of **Dungeness,** the abandoned winter home of Andrew Carnegie. Up-island, **Plum Orchard,** the ruins of a Georgian-Revival home built for Carnegie's son and his wife in 1898, is accessible by a short hike from the main road about 5 mi. north of Sea Camp Dock, or by bi-monthly ferry from the dock. (Ferries 2nd and 4th Su of each month, departing Sea Camp Dock at 12:45pm and returning at 4:15pm. $6. Free ranger presentations daily 1:30pm.) The northern and central portions of the island are pine and hardwood forests, while the western side is a tidal marsh, excellent for birdwatching. The ranger-led **Dungeness Trail** runs from Dungeness Dock to the beach, passing the Carn-egie mansion's spooky ruins along the way. The more adventurous can catch the **Parallel Trail** at Sea Camp Beach and follow it 4 mi. through shady oak groves and palmetto stands to the Hickory Hill campsite, where a number of other trails converge for further exploration. Those just wanting to catch some rays can have the beautiful white sand beaches practically to themselves.

Those wishing to spend the night on the island must come prepared—aside from water, all provisions must be carried in and out. The only developed campground, **Sea Camp Beach ❶,** is a 15min. walk from the Sea Camp dock, and has restrooms, cold showers, and drinking water. Sites are under a canopy of beautifully gnarled oaks and just steps from the beach ($4 per person). Those willing to trek farther are rewarded with **backcountry camping ❶,** magnificent in its isolation and scenery. Each of the four areas has a well, but the water should be treated before drinking. Campfires are not permitted in the backcountry, so bring a cook stove. (☎882-4335 or 888-817-3421. All camping requires a reservation and a permit, $4 per person. Backcountry sites $2 per person.) Accommodations on the island are exorbitant; St. Mary's has plenty of overnight options. The **Riverview Hotel ❷**, 105 Osborne St., is located across the street from the ferry docks. (☎882-3242. Continental breakfast. Singles $45; doubles $55.) The **Cumberland Kings Bay Lodges ❷**, 603 Sand Bar Dr. at Charlie Smith Sr. Hwy., is 10min. from the dock and offers mini-suites with kitchenettes and fridge and continental breakfast. (☎882-8900. Singles $43; doubles $47.) As there is no food on the island, either bring your own or have a big meal before you board the ferry. There are a number of restaurants near the ferry dock, though the **Greek Mediterranean Grill ❷**, 122 Osborne St., is noteworthy for both fare and service. The pitas ($5) are served with unusual pizazz. (☎576-2000.)

Georgia's southernmost coastal island, Cumberland Island is 17½ mi. long and nearly 3 mi. wide. The vast majority of the land is owned and operated by the National Parks Service. The **Cumberland Queen**, a ferry operated by the National Parks Service from St. Mary's, GA, is the only transportation to the island. Reservations are strongly recommended. (☎883-4335. $12, ages 65 and over $9, ages 12 and under $7. No pets, bicycles, kayaks, or cars. Departs St. Mary's Mar.-Nov. daily 9 and 11:45am; Dec.-Feb. M and Th-Su 9 and 11:45am. Departs Sea Camp Dock on Cumberland Island Mar.-Nov. daily 10:15am and 4:45pm; Dec.-Feb. M and Th-Su 10:15am and 4:45pm; also Mar.-Sept. W-Sa 2:45pm.) The **Cumberland Island National Seashore Visitors Center** is located near the dock in St. Mary's. (☎888-817-3421; www.nps.gov/cuis. Open daily 8:15am-4:30pm.) On the island, the **Sea Camp Ranger Station** has restrooms, water, exhibits on the island's natural history, trails and general information. (Open daily 8am-4:30pm.) **Area Code:** 912.

ALABAMA

Forty years later, the "Heart of Dixie" is still haunted by its controversial role in the Civil Rights movement of the 1960s, when Governor George Wallace fought a vicious campaign opposing integration. Today, the state has made efforts to broaden its image and has constructed a series of important monuments and homages to the tumult of the Civil Rights movement. While the state's rich colonial past, Native American heritage, and legacy of immigration are on full display, Alabama "the beautiful" offers unique cuisine, nationally acclaimed gardens, and frequent festivals that constantly create an alternative image for the state.

◪ PRACTICAL INFORMATION

Capital: Montgomery.

Visitor Info: Alabama Bureau of Tourism and Travel, 401 Adams Ave., Montgomery 36104 (☎334-242-4169 or 800-252-2262; www.touralabama.org). Open M-F 8am-5pm. **Division of Parks,** 64 N. Union St., Montgomery 36104 (☎800-252-7275). Open daily 8am-5pm.

Postal Abbreviation: AL. **Sales Tax:** 10%.

MONTGOMERY   ☎334

Today, Montgomery stands still and quiet, in sharp contrast to its turbulent past as the first capital of the Confederacy and the birthplace of America's Civil Rights movement. Montgomery's role in the movement began in 1955 with the arrest of Rosa Parks, a black seamstress and activist who refused to give up her seat to a white man on a city bus. The success of the ensuing bus boycott, organized by local minister Dr. Martin Luther King, Jr., encouraged nationwide reform. Montgomery's marketing now relies on its prominent past, proclaiming itself "courageous, visionary, rebellious."

⁊ PRACTICAL INFORMATION. Downtown follows a grid pattern. Major east-west routes are Madison Ave. downtown and Vaughn Rd. south of **I-65;** main north-south roads are Perry St. and Decatur St., which becomes Norman Bridge Rd. farther south. Dexter Ave. is Montgomery's main street, running east-west up an imposing hill to the capitol. West of downtown, **I-65** runs north-south and intersects **I-85,** which forms downtown's southern border. A ring road, varyingly called East, South, West, and North Blvd., encircles both downtown and the outlying neighborhoods. **Greyhound,** 950 W. South Blvd. (☎286-0658 or 800-231-2222; open 24hr.), at Exit 168 on I-65 and a right onto South Blvd., runs to: Atlanta (3-4hr., 10 per day, $31); Birmingham (2hr., 5 per day, $20); Mobile (3-4hr., 8 per day, $32); Selma (55min., 5 per day, $12); Tuskegee (45min., 7-per day, $11). **Montgomery Area Transit System (MATS)** runs local buses. (Operates M-F 6am-6pm. "Fixed route" bus $1.) Call one day in advance to schedule a pick-up and **Demand and Response Transit (DART)** service will send a bus to your exact location if they can accommodate you. (☎262-7321. $2.) **The Lightning Route Trolley** arrives every 25min. at well-marked stops near downtown attractions. Take the Gold route for the State Capitol and Civil Rights Monument. Take the Green route for the Rosa Parks Museum and the Old Town Museum. (Operates M-Sa 9am-6pm. $0.25 per stop, seniors and disabled with MAP card $0.10. Day pass $1, seniors $0.50.) **Taxi: Yellow Cab** ☎262-5225; **New Deal Cab** ☎262-4747. **Visitors Center:** 300 Water St., in Union Station, has a short introductory video to the city and free maps. (☎262-0013; www.visitingmontgomery.com. Open M-Sa 8am-5pm, Su noon-4pm.) **Hotlines: Council Against Rape,** ☎286-5987. Operates 24hr. **Internet Access: Montgomery City-County Public Library,** 245 High St., between McDonough and Lawrence St. (☎584-7144. Open M-Th 9am-9pm, F-Sa 9am-6pm, Su 1-6pm. Free.) **Post Office:** 135 Catoma St. (☎263-4974. Open M-F 7:30am-5:30pm, Sa 8am-noon.) **Postal Code:** 36104. **Area Code:** 334.

⁋ ACCOMMODATIONS. For those with a car, South Blvd., Exit 168 off I-65, overflows with inexpensive beds, while most exits off I-85 lead to standard, more expensive chains. Beware—the cheapest of the cheap can be fairly seedy. If you're looking to stay close to downtown attractions in the historic part of town, the **Red Bluff Cottage ❹,** 551 Clay St., is a B&B worth the price tag. Themed rooms, full baths, free Internet, TV, bathrobes, and flowers add to the cottage's allure. There's a desk in every room and a gazebo out back. (☎264-0056 or 888-551-2529; www.redbluffcottage.com. Rooms from $90.) Travelers with less to spend should check out the **Comfort Inn ❸,** 1035 W. South Blvd., Exit 168 off of I-65 S, which has exceptionally clean rooms, continental breakfast, A/C, microfridge, microwave, free local calls, a pool, and cable TV. (☎281-5090. Singles $64; doubles $69. AAA and AARP discounts.) The site of a 1763 French stronghold, **Fort Toulouse Jackson Park ❶,** 12 mi. north of Montgomery on Ft. Toulouse Rd., off U.S. 231, has 39 sites with water and electricity under hanging Spanish moss in beautiful woods. (☎567-3002. Reception daily 8am-5pm. In spring and fall, reservations are recommended at least 2 weeks in advance. Sites $11, with hookup $14. Seniors $8/$11.)

⟁ FOOD. In a tiny pink house filled with heavenly paintings and posters, ⬛**Martha's Place ❶,** 458 Sayre St., is an authentic Southern family affair. Fried chicken, pork chops, collard greens, and black-eyed peas are all included in Martha's gigantic, authentic soul food lunch. Don't miss the pound cake and sweet tea. (☎263-9135. Traditional lunch $5.50. 4-vegetable plate $4. Open M-F 11am-3pm.) ⬛**Farm-**

ers Market Cafe ❷, 315 N. McDonough St., is a Montgomery institution, founded in 1958 and continuously open ever since. Grab breakfast or lunch canteen style; a two-course meat and vegetable lunch will set you back $7-8. Montgomery's mayor and Supreme Court justices eat here, as do farmers and builders on their way to or from work. (☎202-1970. Open M-F 5:30am-2pm.) The oldest restaurant in town, **Chris's Hot Dogs ❶**, 138 Dexter Ave., has continued to make hot dogs ($1.60) like nobody else since 1917. A stone's throw away from the State House, Chris's draws in the politicos for hamburgers, grilled cheese and other authentic diner fare. (☎265-6850. Open M-Th and Sa 10am-7pm, F 10am-8pm. Cash and local checks only.) **Jimmy's Uptown Grille ❸**, 540 Clay St., offers flavors that are a little more exotic but well worth the extra bucks. Don't be put off by the crummy exterior—it's lavish inside. Take in the old house's ambience at the bar in front, then proceed to dine in the large room overlooking the city. It's a romantic setting and the dishes such as honey-pecan salmon ($22) are superb, as are the $6-12 appetizers. (☎265-8187. Open Tu-Sa 6pm-2am or later. Kitchen closes at 9:30pm. Reservations recommended on weekends.) **Tomatinos ❷**, 1036 E. Fairview Ave., in Old Cloverdale, across the street from the Capri theatre (see **Nightlife**, p. 456), specializes in home-made pizzas and calzones. Whole wheat dough is made fresh daily. Prices at this relaxed, locally-owned Italian spot range from $7 for a small cheese pizza to $25 for their largest. A large selection of beer ($1.75-3.75) and wine (bottle $22) is also available. (☎264-4241. Open M-Sa 11am-10pm, Su 4-10pm.)

◙ **SIGHTS.** The **State Capitol**, at Bainbridge St. and Dexter Ave., is an imposing Greek Revival structure sporting marble floors, cantilevered staircases, and neat echo chambers. On the front steps, a bronze star commemorates the spot where Jefferson Davis took the oath of office as president of the Confederacy. (☎242-3935. Open M-Sa 9am-5pm. Self-guided tours available. Free.) Only two football fields away is the 112-year-old **King Memorial Baptist Church,** 454 Dexter Ave., where Martin Luther King, Jr. was pastor for six years. (☎263-3970. Open Sa 1:30-2pm for walkthrough. 30min.-1hr. guided tours M-Th 10am and 2pm; walkthrough F 10am; Sa 10:30am-1pm by appt.) Maya Lin, the architect who designed the Vietnam Veterans Memorial in Washington, D.C. (p. 332), also designed Montgomery's newest sight—the **Civil Rights Memorial**, 400 Washington Ave., in front of the Southern Poverty Law Center. A circular black granite table over which water continuously flows pays tribute to activists who died fighting for Civil Rights. (Open 24hr. Free. Wheelchair accessible.) The **Alabama Department of Archives and History,** 624 Washington Ave., not only houses important state documents, but is also a museum. Come here to explore Civil War and Civil Rights history or, for younger visitors, to interact with the past in the "Hands-On Gallery." Visit the second-floor exhibit of Spider Martin's **Selma to Montgomery: A March for the Right to Vote** photography exhibit. Twenty-two of Martin's images—from Bloody Sunday to the 54 mi. march from Selma to Montgomery—are housed here, courtesy of the artist. (☎242-4365. Museum open M-F 8:30am-4:30pm, 1st Sa of every month 8:30am-4:30pm. Free. Wheelchair accessible.) The **Rosa Parks Library and Museum,** 252 Montgomery St., was dedicated 45 years after Rosa Parks refused to give up her bus seat on December 1, 1955. The museum uses video, artifacts, audio, and an actual 1955 Montgomery bus to recreate that fateful day and the subsequent events that influenced the nation. (☎241-8661. Open M-F 9am-5pm, Sa 9am-3pm. $5.50, under 12 $3.50.)

The **Hank Williams Museum,** 118 Commerce St., across from the Montgomery Civic Center, features the Montgomery native's outfits, memorabilia, and even the '52 Cadillac in which the songwriter died at the young age of 29. (☎262-3600. Open M-Sa 9am-6pm, Su 1-4pm. $7, under 12 $2.) **Old Alabama Town,** 301 Columbus St., at Hull St., reconstructs 19th-century Alabama with over 40 period buildings, including a pioneer homestead, an 1892 grocery, and an early African-American church. Allow at least 2hr. to wander around the grounds and use the audio tour at your own pace; if you only want to visit a few blocks rather than the whole museum, you can get a reduced entrance fee. (☎240-4500. Tickets sold M-Sa 9am-2pm; grounds open until 4pm. $8, seniors $7.20, ages 6-18 $3.) A modest exterior hides the quirky **F. Scott and Zelda Fitzgerald Museum,** 919 Felder Ave., off Carter Hill Rd. at Dunbar. The curator will be happy to show you photographs, Zelda's paintings, and some of Scott's original manuscripts, not to mention evidence of the couple's stormy marriage and many love letters. (☎264-4222. Open W-F 10am-2pm, Sa-Su 1-5pm. Free.) The **Montgomery Museum of Fine Arts,** 1 Museum Dr., part of the Blount Cultural Park, houses a collection of 19th- and 20th-century American paintings including works by southern painters like Georgia O'Keeffe and Edward Hopper. (☎244-5700. Open Tu-W and F-Sa 10am-5pm, Th 10am-9pm, Su noon-5pm. Free, but donations appreciated.)

🎭 🎟 **ENTERTAINMENT AND NIGHTLIFE.** The nationally acclaimed **Alabama Shakespeare Festival,** considered by many to be Montgomery's leading attraction, is staged at the **Carolyn Blount Theater** on the grounds of the 300-acre private estate, **Wynton M. Blount Cultural Park;** take East Blvd. 15min. southeast of downtown to Vaughn Rd., or Exit 6 off I-85 onto Woodmere Blvd. The theater also hosts contemporary plays; the 2005 season includes *As You Like It, Cat on a Hot Tin Roof,* and *The Taming of the Shrew.* (☎271-5353 or 800-841-4273; www.asf.net. Box office open M-Sa 10am-6pm, Su noon-4pm; performance nights until 9pm. Tickets $15, seniors half-price 1hr. prior to show.) For regional music, head to Montgomery's locally-owned **1048 Bar,** 1104 E. Fairview Ave., to enjoy a beer and listen to the best acts in town. It's jazz and blues every night, and the house jazz band plays every Sunday 5:30-9pm. (☎834-1048. Domestics $2.75, imports $3.75-5, Maker's Mark on the rocks $5.25. Open Su-F 4pm-5am, Sa 4pm-2am.) **Gator's,** 5040 Vaughn Rd., at Vaughn Plaza, does delta, acoustic, blues, and rock in its cafe and nightclub. (☎274-0330. Live music Tu-Sa usually 8pm-late. Kitchen open M-W 11am-2pm and 4-9pm, Th-Sa 4-10pm, Su 11am-2pm.) Montgomery's only independent movie theater, the **Capri Theater,** 1045 E. Fairview (☎262-4858), shows inspired arthouse films. Call for times and current showings. The Thursday *Montgomery Advertiser* ($.50), *The Buzz* (free), and the monthly *King Kudzu* (free) list other entertainment options.

📍 **DAYTRIP FROM MONTGOMERY: TUSKEGEE.** After Reconstruction, "emancipated" blacks in the South remained segregated and disenfranchised. **Booker T. Washington,** a former slave, believed that blacks could best improve their situation through hard work and learning a trade, and the curriculum of the college he founded reflected that philosophy. "What we need we will ourselves create," Washington asserted, a claim made concrete by the fact that virtually the entire school was made through student labor. Today, a more academically-oriented **Tuskegee University** (☎727-8347 for free tours by the Park Service) fills 160 buildings on 5000 acres, while the buildings of Washington's original institute comprise a national historical site. On campus, the **George Washington Carver Museum** has exhibits and films on its namesake. Artist, teacher, scientist, and head of the Tuskegee Agricultural Dept., Carver improved the daily lives of Macon County's poor by discovering hundreds of practical uses for common, inexpensive products like the peanut. (☎727-3200. Open daily 9am-4:30pm. Free.) Across the street from the campus lies **The Oaks,** a restoration of Washington's home. (Tours available daily every 2hr. 10am-4pm; call to schedule.) Grab a wholesome and hearty lunch in the **Kellogg Conference Center ❷** on campus. Burgers go for $8 with all the trimmings, garden salads go for $5, and you can eat outside on the patio. (Menu changes daily. ☎727-3000. Open daily until 2pm.) To get to Tuskegee, take I-85 toward Atlanta, get off at Exit 32, and follow the signs. **Greyhound,** 205 E. MLK, Jr. Blvd./Hwy. 80 (☎727-1290; open M-F 8:30am-5pm, Sa 8:30am-2pm), runs to and from Montgomery (45min., 7 per day, $11). **Area Code:** 334.

SELMA   ☎334

Selma, perhaps more than anywhere else in Alabama, is haunted by the past. The small, historic Southern town was shaped by two momentous events that took place 100 years apart. As a stronghold for the Confederate armies, its fall in 1865 marked a decisive victory for the North. A century later, Selma gained notoriety during the Voting Rights movement. In the Selma of 1964, state-imposed restrictions gave only 1% of eligible blacks the right to vote. In 1965, Civil Rights activists organized an ill-fated march on the state capitol that was quashed by troops using night sticks, cattle prods, and tear gas. Their spirits battered but not destroyed, the marchers kept trying. A third attempt resulted in the 54 mi. trek from Selma to Montgomery that Dr. King declared the "greatest march ever made on a state capitol in the South." Five months later, Congress passed the Voting Rights Act, prohibiting states from using prerequisites to disqualify voters on the basis of color.

These events are remembered in the museums and sights around town. Selma has the largest historical district in Alabama and calls itself home to one of America's most unique festivals, the **Tale Tellin' Festival.** Storytellers and yarn-spinners from across the South converge on Selma during the second Friday and Saturday in October. (☎800-457-3562; www.taletellin.com. $10, children $5.) The **National Voting Rights Museum and Institute,** 1012 Water Ave., houses memorabilia relating to the Voting Rights Act of 1965 and continues to disseminate information about voting rights and responsibilities. (☎418-0800. Open M-F 9am-5pm, Sa 10am-3pm. $5; students, seniors, and children $3.) The **Brown Chapel AME Church and King Monument,** 410 Martin Luther King, Jr. St., served as the headquarters for many Civil Rights meetings during the movement and was the starting point for the march to Montgomery. (☎874-7897. Tours available by appointment M-Sa 10am-4pm, Su 1-4pm.) South of Water Ave., at the end of Broad St., you can walk over the famous **Edmund Pettus Bridge,** where the march left Selma on its way to Montgomery. **The Old Depot Museum,** 4 Martin Luther King Jr. St., explores the history of Selma with artifacts of past and present, some dating back the area's original inhabitants, the Cherokee and Creek Indians. Check out their photography collection by the 19th-century Alabama native Mary Morgan Keipp. (☎874-2197. Open M-Sa 10am-4pm, Su by appointment. $4, seniors $3, students 19-25 $2, students 6-18 $1.)

Budget Inn ❷, 601 Highland Ave. (Hwy. 80 W), opposite McDonald's, is the best of the budget motels along Highland Ave., with basic, clean rooms and a pleasant staff. (☎872-3451. Cable TV, free local calls, pool, fridge and microwave. Singles $38, doubles $45.) ▨**Strongs ❷,** 118 Washington St. off Broad St, offers superb soul food prepared from scratch and worth the wait. Really fresh chicken (boxes $4.25-5.50), fish ($3.50-6), and a choice of 15 vegetable side orders ($1.25) make for a wholesome and filling meal. The owners are proud of their vegetables "raised by the Strong family," the staff is pleasant, and the ambience relaxed and welcoming. (☎875-8800. Open M-F 10am-7pm, Sa 10am-6pm.)

Downtown Selma is bordered by **Jeff Davis Avenue** to the north and the **Alabama River** to the south. **U.S. 80,** which becomes **Broad Street,** runs straight through town. **Greyhound,** 434 Broad St. (☎874-4503; open daily 7am-10pm), runs to: Atlanta (4½-6hr., 5 per day, $38); Dallas (12-13½hr., 4 per day, $102); Montgomery (1hr., 5 per day, $15). **Visitors Center:** 2207 Broad St. (☎875-7485; www.selmashowcase.com. Open daily 8am-8pm.) **Internet Access: Selma/Dallas County Public Library,**

1103 Selma Ave., 2nd fl. (☎874-1727. Open M-Sa 9am-5pm. Free Internet access with library card.) **Post Office:** 1301 Alabama Ave. (☎874-4678. Open M-F 8am-4:30pm, Sa 8am-noon.) **Postal Code:** 36703. **Area Code:** 334.

BIRMINGHAM   ☎205

For many people, Birmingham recalls the struggle for black Civil Rights in the 1960s. Leaders like Martin Luther King, Jr. and Fred Shuttleworth faced some of their toughest fights in what was labeled "Bombingham" after dozens of bombs rocked the city in the early 1960s. Today's Birmingham, Alabama's largest city, has made strides to come to terms with its past, evident in many of the excellent museums, especially the powerful Civil Rights Museum. Birmingham was the first major industrial city of the South, and in recent years, the city has focused on building a substantial medical research community. The city's past looms large, however, in today's residential segregation and the downtown sites in the old black neighborhoods where many of the worst racial crimes took place.

⌐ TRANSPORTATION

Airport: Birmingham International Airport (☎595-0533; www.flybirmingham.com), Exit 129 off I-20/59.

Trains: Amtrak, 1819 Morris Ave. (☎324-3033 or 800-872-7245), south of 1st Ave. N at 19th St. Open daily 9am-5pm. 1 train per day to **Atlanta** (4hr., $20-49) and **New Orleans** (7hr., $23-57). *Be cautious in this area, especially at night.*

Buses: Greyhound, 618 19th St. N (☎252-7190). Open 24hr. To: **Atlanta** (3hr., 5 per day, $22); **Mobile** (5½-8hr., 5 per day, $42); **Montgomery** (2hr., 6 per day, $18); **Nashville** (3½-5½hr., 5 per day, $28).

Public Transit: Metropolitan Area Express (MAX) and **Downtown Area Rapid Transit (DART);** (☎521-0101). MAX: M-F most routes 6am-7pm. $1, students ages 5-11 $0.60; transfers $0.25. DART trolley runs to downtown tourist destinations. Most routes daily 9:30am-10:30pm every 10min. Free.

Taxi: Yellow Cab ☎252-1131.

■ ⁊ ORIENTATION AND PRACTICAL INFORMATION

While most of the city is pancake-flat, the southeastern edge climbs up suddenly into the bluffs, and the streets curl, wind, and become both very confusing and very beautiful. Downtown Birmingham is organized in a grid, with numbered avenues running east-west and numbered streets running north-south. Richard Arrington, Jr. Blvd. is the one exception, that runs along what would have been called 21st St. Downtown is divided by railroad tracks running east-west through the center of the city—thus, avenues and streets are designated "N" or "S." Avenue numbers decrease as they near the railroad tracks (with 1st Ave. N and S running alongside them), while street numbers grow from 11th St. at the western edge of downtown to 26th St. at the east. **Five Points South,** the center of youth nightlife, is at the intersection of 20th St. S and 11th Ave. S, while the **University of Alabama-Birmingham** is just to the northeast, between 6th and 10th Ave.

Visitor Info: Greater Birmingham Convention and Visitors Center, 2200 9th Ave. N, 1st fl. (☎458-8000; www.birminghamal.org), has helpful staff who offer an excellent map. Open M-F 8:30am-5pm.

Hotlines: Crisis Center, ☎323-7777. **Rape Response,** ☎323-7273. Both 24hr.

Internet Access: Birmingham Public Library, 2100 Park Pl. (☎226-3610), at the corner of Richard Arrington, Jr. Blvd near the visitors center. Tell them you're from out-of-town to get a sign-on code. Open M-Tu 9am-8pm, W-Sa 9am-6pm, Su 2-6pm.

Post Office: 351 24th St. N (☎800-275-8777). Open M-F 7am-11pm, Sa-Su 1-7pm. **Postal Code:** 35203. **Area Code:** 205.

▚ ACCOMMODATIONS

Relatively cheap hotels and motels dot the Greater Birmingham area along the various interstates. The closer to downtown, the more expensive the room.

The Hospitality Inn, 2127 7th Ave. S (☎322-0691), 4 blocks north of Five Points South and near the university, is one of the best deals in the city with clean, wood-paneled rooms, a convenient location, and a pleasant staff. Singles or 2 twin beds $39; 2 double beds $46. Wheelchair accessible. ❷

Delux Inn and Suites/Motel Birmingham, 7905 Crestwood Blvd. (☎956-4440). Take Exit 132B from I-20 E. Turn right at Montevallo Ave. and left on Crestwood Blvd. Comfortable rooms with A/C, cable TV, continental breakfast, and a pool make this motel one of the better deals for its price. Rooms for 1-2 people $59. ❸

Oak Mountain State Park (☎620-2527 or 800-252-7275), 15 mi. south, off I-65 in Pelham at Exit 246. Alabama's largest state park, with 10,000 acres of horseback riding, golfing, and hiking, and an 85-acre lake with a beach and fishing. Sites $10.75; with water and electricity $15, full hookup $17. Parking $2. ❶

▐ FOOD

An old streetcar suburb near the University of Alabama-Birmingham, Five Points South, at the intersection of 20th St. S and 11th Ave. S, is the best place to eat with the highest concentration of restaurants.

▨ Bahama Wing World, 321 17th St. N (☎324-9464), in downtown. A hole-in-the-wall that's so local, you'll be the only diner who doesn't live two doors down. *The* place for tasty and cheap wings, from 2 pieces served with a slice of toasted white bread and fries ($1.75) to 15 pieces ($10.50). These aren't your usual wings; they come in dozens of flavors ranging from Spicy Jerk to Bahama Breeze. Catfish dinner $7.25. Open M-Th 11am-7pm, F 11am-11pm, Sa 10am-11pm. ❷

Fish Market Restaurant, 611 Richard Arrington, Jr. Blvd. S (☎322-3330). Birmingham's oldest seafood wholesaler doubles as a no-frills joint with cheap catches. Stand in line, place your order, then wait for your number to be called. Snapper and flounder from the Gulf are very popular ($8-9), but the truly adventurous go for the frog's legs ($6). Fish entrees $8-9. Open M-Th 10am-9pm, F-Sa 10am-10pm. ❷

John's City Diner, 112 Richard Arrington, Jr. Blvd. (☎322-6014), between 1st and 2nd Ave., is a great find for vegetarians and carnivores alike. It feels classy with its stark black decor, yet at the same time incredibly down to earth and unpretentious. Get a vegetarian plate of any 4 sides for $8, or try the macaroni and cheese for $9 (ask for it vegetarian). Appetizers are $6-10 and salads $3.50-8, and there's also a full bar. Open for lunch M-F 11am-3:30pm, for dinner W-F 5pm-9pm. ❸

◉ SIGHTS

CIVIL RIGHTS. Birmingham's efforts to reconcile itself with its past are evident in the **Birmingham Civil Rights District,** nine blocks dedicated to the battles and bombings that took place there. **Kelly Ingram Park,** the site of numerous Civil

Rights protests. Commemorative statues and sculptures now grace the green lawns. *(At 5th and 6th Ave. N between 16th and 17th St. Park open daily 6am-10pm.)* The **Sixteenth Street Baptist Church** served as the center of Birmingham's Civil Rights movement. Four young black girls were killed here in a September 15, 1963 bombing by white segregationists, spurring protests in the nearby park. A small exhibit in the church's basement chronicles its past. *(1530 6th Ave. N.* ☎ *251-9402. Open Tu-F 10am-4pm, Sa by appointment. $3 suggested donation.)* Across the street from the church, the powerful ◪**Birmingham Civil Rights Institute** traces the nation's Civil Rights struggle through the lens of Alabama's segregation battle. Displays and documentary footage balance the imaginative exhibits and disturbing artifacts from the Jim Crow era, like the burnt-out shell of a torched Greyhound bus, and the Birmingham Segregation Ordinances. *(520 16th St. N.* ☎ *328-9696. Audio walking tours of the adjacent park $5 with ID deposit. Open Tu-Sa 10am-5pm, Su 1-5pm. $9, seniors $5, students $4, under 18 free; Su free.)*

4TH AVENUE. In the heart of the old historic black neighborhood, now known as the **4th Avenue District,** is the ◪**Alabama Jazz Hall of Fame.** Jazz greats from Erskine Hawkins to Sun Ra and his Intergalactic Arkestra to the magnificent Ella Fitzgerald each get a small display on their life work. There are free concerts on Sundays 1-3pm and 2-4pm. *(1631 4th Ave. N, in the Carver Theater 1 block south of Kelly Ingram Park.* ☎ *254-2731. Open Tu-Sa 10am-5pm, Su 1-5pm. Free.)* Bama's sports greats, from Willie "The Say Hey Kid" Mays to runner Carl Lewis, are immortalized in the **Alabama Sports Hall of Fame.** *(2150 Civic Center Blvd., at the corner of 22nd St. N.* ☎ *323-6665. Open M-Sa 9am-5pm, Su 1-5pm. $5, students $4, seniors $3, children under 6 free.)* Two blocks away, the **Birmingham Museum of Art** is the largest municipal art museum in the South, containing over 18,000 works and a sculpture garden—and it's free. The gallery also houses the Hanson Library, which features the largest collection of Wedgewood china outside the UK and is one of the most comprehensive art libraries in the South. *(2000 8th Ave. N.* ☎ *254-2565. Self-guided audio tour available. Open Tu-Sa 10am-5pm, Su noon-5pm; closes at 9pm 1st Th every month. Donations appreciated.)*

SMELTING. Birmingham remembers its days as the "Pittsburgh of the South" at the **Sloss Furnaces National Historic Landmark.** Although the blast furnaces closed 20 years ago, they stand as the only preserved example of 20th-century iron-smelting in the world. Plays and concerts are held in a renovated furnace shed by the stacks. *(20 32nd St. N. Adjacent to the 1st Ave. N overpass off 32nd through 34th St. downtown.* ☎ *324-1911; www.slossfurnaces.com. Open Tu-Sa 10am-4pm, Su noon-4pm. Tours Sa-Su 1, 2, 3pm. Free.)* For an insight into the city's history, head to the **Vulcan,** 1701 Valley View Dr., the largest statue ever made in the US and the largest cast-iron statue in the world. At 56 ft. tall upon a 124 ft. pedestal, it rises to a height of 180 ft. on top of a hill to the immediate south of the city. Vulcan, the Roman god of metalwork, was sculpted by Italian artist Giuseppe Moretti to represent Alabama at the 1904 St. Louis World's Fair. From the top you get a 360° view of the region, but you can also get a great view of Birmingham from the base for free. If you do go up the tower, the first thing you see as you emerge from the top of the elevator is the Vulcan's huge iron butt bearing down on you. *(Go south on 20th St. S and follow the signs.* ☎ *933-1409; http://vulcanpark.org. Open M-Sa 10am-6pm, Su 1-6pm. Open till 10pm some nights for great nighttime views. $6, seniors $5, children 5-12 $4, under 5 free. Wheelchair accessible.)*

OTHER SIGHTS. For a breather from the heavy-duty ironworks, revel in the marvelously manicured grounds of the **Birmingham Botanical Gardens.** Spectacular floral displays, an elegant Japanese garden, and an enormous greenhouse occupy a 67-acre site. You can arrange a tour by calling ahead if you want expert advice on flora and fauna. *(2612 Lane Park Rd. Off U.S. 31.* ☎ *414-3900. Garden Center open daily 8am-*

5pm; gardens open dawn to dusk. Free.) If you prefer cogs and grease to petals and pollen, the **Mercedes-Benz U.S. International Visitors Center** is a 24,000 sq. ft. museum that spares no technological expense while celebrating the history of all things Mercedes. After a 1hr. film on the autoplant you get to wander around and see a variety of Mercedes vehicles being produced. *(I-20/59 off Exit 89 on Mercedes Dr. at Vance St. ☎507-2253 or 888-286-8762. Open M-F 9am-5pm, 1st Sa of every month 10am-3pm. $5, seniors and children $4. Under 12 not allowed on factory tour.)*

🎵 🎭 ENTERTAINMENT AND NIGHTLIFE

Opened in 1927, the **Historic Alabama Theater,** 1817 3rd Ave. N, is booked 300 nights of the year with films, concerts, and live performances. Their organ, the "Mighty Wurlitzer," entertains the audience pre-show. (☎251-0418. Order tickets at the box office 1hr. prior to show. Open M-F 9am-4pm. Free. Showtimes generally 7pm, Su 2pm. Films $6, seniors and under 12 $5. Organ plays 15min. before the official show time.) Those visiting Birmingham in the middle of May can hear everything from country to gospel to big-name rock groups at **City Stages.** The 3-day festival, held on multiple stages in the blocked-off streets of downtown, is the biggest event all year and includes food, crafts, and children's activities. (☎251-1272 or 800-277-1700; www.citystages.org. $20, weekend pass $30.)

Nightlife centers around **Five Points South,** at 20th St. S and 11th Ave. S. On spring and summer nights, young adults grab outdoor tables, loiter by the fountain until late, or rock in one of the many lively nightclubs nearby. The hippest people jam at **The Nick,** 2514 10th Ave. S, at the corner of 24th St., opposite "Impact Family Counseling." Locals call it "the place." (☎252-3831. Happy hour M-F 3-9pm. Live rock music most nights. Cover $5-10; usually free M. Open M-F 3pm-late, Sa 8pm-6am.) **The Garage** is a very cool bar tucked out of sight down 23rd St. A former architecture studio turned antique store, all the associated materials are still there—customers just drink around the statues, tools, and artwork. Try a Jubel German beer in the courtyard covered in weeds, munch on a simple sandwich among the nymphs and Greek art, or just soak up the unique atmosphere. (2304 S. 10th Terrace St. at the corner of 10th Ave. and 23rd St. ☎322-3220. Open daily 11am-3am.)

TUSCALOOSA AND MOUNDVILLE ☎205

Moundville is one of the best preserved and most important indigenous sites in North America—yet it is hardly visited. The Mississippian people made this one of their most important settlements, and from AD 1000-1500 their fortified city of 3000 people was the prehistoric metropolis of the South. Based on the rich soil, ample water, and long growing season, the settlement thrived. Its dirt mounds were constructed by the basketful over a 300-year span, and their orderly arrangement suggests some kind of master plan that is still not fully understood. Tuscaloosa, the nearest city, is 13 mi. north of Moundville on Hwy. 69 and 60 mi. southwest of Birmingham along I-59/20. ⬛**Moundville Archaeological Park** is well worth the effort of getting there. The park provides an informative video and you can drive around the earthen mounds and climb the highest one, which, at 60 ft., is thought to be the original chief ceremonial mound and provides a great view over the lesser mounds. (Tours ☎371-2234. $4; seniors, students, and children $2; under 5 free.) Inside the park, the **Jones Archaeological Museum** displays exhibits and artifacts from the mounds, and a model Indian village features reenactments of the daily life of the Mississippian people. Every year during the first full week of October, the **Moundville Native American Festival** is held on the grounds and features Native American dances, crafts, storytelling, and celebration. (☎371-2234. Open M-F 9am-4pm, Sa 9am-5pm.)

THE SOUTH

In Tuscaloosa, home of the University of Alabama, you can take a trip on the **Black Warrior River** aboard the paddle ship Bama Belle. Sunset cruises with live entertainment set sail Tuesdays at 5pm and "Something to do" cruises are on Sundays at 2:30pm (both 1¼hr.; $7.50, seniors $6.50, children $4.50.). The ship also offers dinner cruises on Fridays. (1 Greensboro Ave. ☎339-1108; www.bamabelle.com. Dinner cruise 1½hr. Reservations required.) The **Tuscaloosa Visitors Center** is housed in the basement of the historic **Jemison-Van de Graf House,** 1305 Greensboro Ave., one of the finest remaining examples of Italianate architecture in the South. (☎391-9200. Open M-F 8:30am-5pm, Sa 10am-2pm.) The 1862 antebellum mansion is also open to visitors; inquire at the visitors center.

Accommodations can be found in Tuscaloosa along McFarland Blvd./Hwy 82 near the University of Alabama. **La Quinta Inn ❸,** 4122 McFarland Blvd E, is a clean and comfortable motel with a pool and good breakfast. (☎349-3270. 2-bed room $60-70.) **Camping ❶** is available in Moundville itself in a superb setting among the mounds and under the stars. The 30 sites come with hot showers, electricity, and some with sewage connection for RVs. (☎371-2572. Registration at the Jones Museum daily 9am-5pm. Tent and RV sites $10.) In Tuscaloosa, the **Super China Buffet ❷,** 4127 McFarland Blvd., around the corner from the Foodworld, offers a sensational selection of Chinese food. Partake in the all-you-can-eat dinner buffet for $8. (☎752-8998. Lunch buffet $5.25, children under 2 free. Open Su-Th 11am-10pm, F-Sa 11am-11pm.) In Moundville, **Miss Melissa's Cafe ❶,** 384 Market St., is a local's joint that resembles a small school dining hall—but the cooking you get here is the real deal. There's an all-you-can-eat breakfast ($5), and canteen-style lunch with one meat and three vegetables for $5.70. (☎371-9045. Open M-Sa 6am-2pm.)

In Tuscaloosa, **Greyhound,** at 2520 Stillman Blvd. (☎758-6651; open M-F 7:30am-6pm, Sa 7:30am-5pm, Su 7:30-9am and 1:30-5pm), takes you to: Birmingham (1hr., 7 per day, $12); Jackson (3-8hr., 6 per day, $39); Memphis (7-10hr., 5 per day, $47). **Taxi: A B Taxi Co.** ☎799-0797. **Postal Code:** 35405. **Area Code:** 205.

HUNTSVILLE   ☎256

Huntsville, 80 mi. north of Birmingham, was the first English-speaking settlement in Alabama and the location of the state's Constitutional Convention in 1819. Far more momentous, however, was the 1950 decision to locate the nation's rocket program here. Initially proposed by Wernher von Braun, the city now boasts a museum, visitors center, and Space Camp, as well as one of NASA's ten national research facilities. A 363 ft. replica of a Saturn V rocket at the **US Space and Rocket Center,** Exit 15 off I-565, is easily recognizable for miles around, and the center features space-flight simulators, an IMAX theater, and tours of the Marshall Space Flight Center. You can also see the original Apollo 16 capsule. (☎837-3400. Open daily 9am-5pm. Last admission 4pm; allow 3hr. for museum and film. $17, ages 3-12 $12.) **Huntsville Botanical Garden,** 4747 Bob Wallace Ave., provides a welcome relief from the strip malls. Designed for kids' entertainment as well as adults' appreciation for all things floral, the garden has bonsai trees, a butterfly house, an aquatic garden, and a 110-year-old dogwood tree, plus a shady nature trail and water features. (☎830-4447; www.hsvbg.org. Open daily in summer 9am-8pm, in winter 9am-5pm. $8, seniors $6, children 3-18 $3.)

Miles of budget motels and chain restaurants cluster on **University Drive,** northwest of downtown, and also at the exits near the airport. To peruse possible lodgings, get off I-565 at Exit 19 and head northwest to University Dr. Pick up a copy of "Alabama travel coupons" at various outlets and the visitors center for discount coupons. The **Red Carpet Motel ❷,** 3200 University Dr., has rooms that are standard and clean, if a bit dark, with a pool and free local calls. From I-565, exit Jordan Ln. N and take a right on University Dr. until you see the sign. (☎539-8448. Check-out

11am. Singles $35; doubles $42.) A bit farther down the road, **Knight's Inn ❷**, 4404 University Dr., has 60 clean, well-appointed rooms with fridge and microwave in a two-story complex. (☎864-0388. Free local calls and continental breakfast. Rooms $45-57.) For a bite to eat, the **Wild Rose Cafe ❷**, 121 N. Side Sq., is easy to find in the main square, opposite the courthouse. A traditional lunch counter, it serves quality meat-and-three (vegetables, that is) platters for $7. There are at least 17 vegetable sides to choose from each day and desserts from $1.25. (☎539-3658; www.wildrosecafe.net. Open M-F 7-9:30am and 11am-2:30pm.)

Greyhound, 601 Monroe St. (☎534-1681; open daily 7:30am-11:45pm), runs buses to: Birmingham (2½-7hr., 5 per day, $21); Memphis (7½-8½hr., 3 per day, $77); Nashville (2hr., 4 per day, $20). A **tourist shuttle** runs between downtown, museums, points on University Dr., and the Space and Rocket Center. The trolley can also make hotel pickup stops by reservation. (1 per hr. M-F 6:40am-6:40pm, Sa 8:40am-7:10pm. $1, all-day pass $2. Wheelchair accessible.) **Huntsville Shuttle** runs 11 routes infrequently; the tourist loop is one. (For schedule ☎532-7433. Runs M-F 6am to 6pm. $1; students, seniors, and children under 7 $0.50; transfers free.) **Visitor Info,** 500 Church St., has a very helpful and talkative staff who can provide a variety of local and state maps. (☎551-2230 or 800-772-2348; www.huntsville.org. Open M-Sa 8am-5pm, Su noon-5pm.) **Area Code:** 256.

MOBILE ☎251

Although Bob Dylan lamented being stuck here, Mobile (mo-BEEL) has had plenty of fans in its time—French, Spanish, English, Sovereign Alabama, Confederate, and American flags have each flown over the city since its founding in 1702. This historical diversity is revealed in both the population and local architecture; antebellum mansions, Italianate dwellings, Spanish and French forts, and Victorian homes line azalea-edged streets. The site of the first Mardi Gras, Mobile still hosts a three-week long Fat Tuesday celebration without the hordes that plague its Cajun counterpart, giving the city the feel of an untouristed New Orleans.

🖊 PRACTICAL INFORMATION. The downtown district borders the Mobile River. **Dauphin Street,** which is one-way downtown, and **Government Boulevard (U.S. 90),** which becomes **Government Street** downtown, are the major east-west routes. **Airport Boulevard, Springhill Ave.,** and **Old Shell Road** are secondary east-west roads. **Royal Street** and **Broad Street** are major north-south byways. **Water Street** runs along the river downtown, becoming the **I-10 causeway.** A road variously called **I-65 East/West Access Road, Frontage Road,** and the **Beltline** lies west of downtown. **Amtrak,** 11 Government St. (☎800-321-8684), next to the convention center, uses an unstaffed "station" where passengers can be dropped off or picked up with advance notice; Mobile is on the Jacksonville-New Orleans line. **Greyhound,** 2545 Government Blvd. (☎478-9793 or 478-6089; open 24hr.), at Pinehill St. west of downtown, goes to: Atlanta (6-9hr., 10 per day, $45); Birmingham (5hr., 4 per day, $40); Montgomery (3hr., 7 per day, $32); New Orleans (3hr., 7 per day, $30). **Metro Transit** provides local transportation. (☎344-5656. Every hr. M-F 6am-6pm, reduced service Sa-Su. $1.25, seniors and disabled $0.60; transfers $0.10.) **Moda!** runs free, electric **trolleys** to most of the sights downtown, including the visitors center; the loop route takes about 15min. (☎208-7540. Operates M-F 7am-6pm.) **Taxi: Yellow Cab** ☎476-7711; **Cab Service Inc.** ☎342-0024. **Visitor Info: Fort Condé Info Center,** 150 S. Royal St., in a reconstructed French fort near Government St., is a pleasant place to pick up leaflets. Ask for their great self-guided walking tour of historic houses. (☎208-7304. Open daily 8am-5pm.) **Post Office:** 168 Bay Shore Ave. (☎478-5639. Open M-F 9am-4:30pm.) **Postal Code:** 36607. **Area Code:** 251.

🏠 ACCOMMODATIONS. Few budget lodging options exist in historic Mobile. In lieu of expensive chains, the **Malaga Inn ❹**, 359 Church St., at Claiborne, in front of the Civic Center, offers local charm in a pink-stucco package. Occupying two 1862 townhouses, the hotel has a delightful central courtyard and spacious rooms with private baths, telephones, and cable TV. (☎438-4701; www.malagainn.com. Continental breakfast. Rooms $79-150. Some are wheelchair accessible.) Roughly 7 mi. from downtown, a slew of affordable motels lines I-65 on Beltline, from Spring Hill Rd. to Government Blvd., and U.S. 90. **Olsson's Motel ❷**, 4137 Government Blvd. (U.S. 90 W), Exit 1 off I-65, has quirky perks like recliners and four-poster beds. (☎661-5331. Fridge, free local calls. Singles $35; doubles $39.) **Family Inn ❷**, 900 S. Beltline Hwy., is the best of the chain lodgings. (☎344-5500. Free local calls, continental breakfast, and cable TV. Singles $30; doubles Su-Th $39, F-Sa $49.) **Mobile's I-10 Kampground ❶**, 6430 Theodore Dawes Rd., 7½ mi. west on I-10, south off Exit 13, is a quiet spot in a forest with 173 shady sites. (☎653-9816 or 800-272-1263. Pool and laundry facilities. Sites with hookup $20-24. Each additional person $1.)

🍴🎶 FOOD AND NIGHTLIFE. Mobile's gulf location means fresh seafood and Southern cookin'. **Wintzell's Oyster House ❸**, 605 Dauphin St., is a long-time local favorite that offers oysters "fried, stewed, or nude" in rooms covered with thousands of signs professing Mr. Wintzell's witticisms. (☎432-4605. Entrees $8-14. Lunch special $7. Happy hour M-F 4-7pm with $0.25 raw oysters. Open Su-Th 11am-10pm, F-Sa 11am-11pm.) To taste a bit of the simple American goodness that Mobilians have been enjoying since 1924, head to the **Dew Drop Inn ❶**, 1808 Old Shell Rd., Mobile's oldest restaurant, for a hamburger ($2.25), hot dog ($2.25), or fried chicken ($7). Mull over your options as you sip your Coke from the classic little green bottle. (☎473-7872. Open Tu-F 10am-8pm, Sa 10am-3pm.) For some serious barbecue, follow the cloud of wood smoke to **Dreamland ❷**, 3314 Old Shell Rd. The famous ribs, cooked over the open fire in the large dining room, will stick to yours. Don't expect much flora with your fauna, though; the only vegetarian option is the house salad for $4. (☎479-9898. Half-slab $9. Half-chicken $6.50. Open M-Sa 10am-10pm, Su 11am-9pm.) The **Brick Pit ❷**, 5456 Old Shell Rd. is dedicated to "serious barbecue" and all pulled pork (sandwich $5.50) is smoked for 30 hours. (☎343-0001. Half-slab ribs $9. Open Tu-Th 11am-8:30pm, F-Sa 11am-9:30pm.)

Downtown Mobile's late-night scene is a bit one-dimensional—pool is the name of the game. The **Lower Dauphin Street Entertainment District** is a fancy name for the downtown block of bars, each of which has pool tables, youngish locals, and drinks for under $5. Most places close around 2 or 3am. If you're tired of the downtown scene head to the **Bubble Lounge,** 5546 Old Shell Rd., where you can sip a top-shelf martini ($7) and enjoy the funky, dimly-lit atmosphere. (☎341-5556. Open Su-M 6pm-2am, sometimes later.) Seize the day at **Carpe Diem,** 4072 Old Shell Rd., just slightly west of I-65. Because this locally-beloved coffeehouse has its own roaster, the grounds used to make your coffee ($1.70 and up) are never more than 2 weeks old. (☎304-0448. Open M-F 6:30am-11pm, Sa-Su 6:30am-10pm). Check the free weekly *Lagniappe* in boxes around town for other entertainment options.

🔆 SIGHTS. Mobile's attractions are scattered inland, around downtown, and near the bay. The **Museum of Mobile,** 111 S. Royal St., celebrates and documents Mobilian history in all its glory. Exhibits cover "The Founding of Mobile," the fate of the slave ship *Clotilda*, and the private collections of prominent Mobile families. (☎208-7569. Open M-Sa 9am-5pm, Su 1-5pm. $5, students $3, seniors $4; families $20.) The **MuseuBienville Square,** at the intersection of Dauphin and Conception St., is the locals' main hangout. Eight separate historic districts, all well-marked, display the city's varied architectural and cultural influences. The **Church Street**

East Historic District showcases Federal, Greek Revival, and Victorian architecture, and several spectacular houses have been converted into museums. In the **DeTonti Historical District,** north of downtown, brick townhouses with ornate wrought-iron balconies surround the restored **Richards-DAR House Museum,** 256 North Joachim St. (☎208-7320. Open M-F 11am-3:30pm, Sa 11am-4pm, Su 1-4pm. Tours $5, children $2. Free tea and cookies.) Adjacent to the Historic DeTonti District, the **African-American Archives Museum,** 564 Dr. Martin Luther King, Jr. Ave., is housed in what was the first African-American library. The museum has portraits, biographies, books, carvings, and other artifacts that represent the lives of numerous African-Americans from the Mobile area and abroad. (☎433-8511. Open M-F 8am-4pm, Sa 10am-2pm. Free admission and parking; donations appreciated.) **Oakleigh Historical Complex,** 350 Oakleigh Pl., 2½ blocks south of Government St. at George St., contains the grandiose **Oakleigh House Museum,** the working-class **Cox-Deasy Cottage Museum,** and the **Mardi Gras Cottage Museum** with a 19th- and 20th-century art collection. The houses attempt to portray the lives of various classes of Mobilians in the 1800s. (☎432-1281. Open M-Sa 9am-3pm. Tours every 30min., last tour 2:30pm. $7, seniors and AAA $6.50, ages 6-11 $3.)

The **Bragg-Mitchell Mansion,** 1906 Springhill Ave., complete with tall white columns, is Mobile's grandest antebellum home. The mansion has 7 large bedrooms and was completed in Greek-Italianate style. (☎471-6364. Open for 30-45min. tours Tu-F 10am-3:30pm. $5, children $3.) The **USS Alabama,** moored 2½ mi. east of town at Battleship Park (accessible from I-10 and Government St.'s Bankhead Tunnel), earned nine stars from battles fought in WWII. Open passageways let landlubbers explore the ship's depths. The park also has a collection of airplanes and the *USS Drum,* a submarine that visitors can walk through. (☎433-2703. $10, seniors $9, ages 6-11 $5. Simulated ride $4. Open daily Apr.-Sept. 8am-6pm. Coupon available at Fort Condé Visitors Center; $2 AAA discount. Parking $2.) **Bellingrath Gardens,** 12401 Bellingrath Gardens Rd., Exit 15A off I-10, has lush roses, oriental gardens, and a bayou boardwalk in a 900-acre setting. Admission is expensive but includes a 30min. tour of the home and a 1-2hr. tour of the gardens. (☎800-247-8420. Open daily 8am-dusk; ticket office closes 5pm. Gardens $9, ages 5-11 $5.25.) Early spring is the time to be in Mobile. Beginning at the visitors center, azaleas bloom in a 27 ft. pink line marking **Azalea Trail** which twists through the city. In February, Mobile's **Mardi Gras,** the precursor to New Orleans's debauchery, erupts with parades, costumes, an Out-of-Towners ball, and the crowning of the Mardi Gras King and Queen. Check out the free *Mobile Traveler* and *Mobile Bay Monthly,* available at Fort Condé Visitors Center for more info.

MISSISSIPPI

The pervasive legacy of cotton, a dependence upon slavery, subsequent racial strife, and economic ruin are still visible in Mississippi. Cotton is now machine harvested and mention of slavery is confined to museums, but racial tension persists. You can get a taste of the disparate traditions that make up Mississippi's complex past at Biloxi, home of the only Confederate President, and Tupelo, birthplace of Elvis Presley. Mississippi has had a number of remarkable triumphs, having produced some of the nation's greatest literary giants, among them William Faulkner, Eudora Welty, Tennessee Williams, and Willie Morris. Perhaps most notably, Mississippi is the American home of the blues. The Crossroads State has yielded the likes of Robert Johnson, Bessie Smith, W.C. Handy, Muddy Waters, and B.B. King, whose riffs would eventually spread upriver and throughout the world.

PRACTICAL INFORMATION

Capital: Jackson.

Visitor Info: Division of Tourism, P.O. Box 1705, Ocean Springs 39566 (☎800-927-6378; www.visitmississippi.org). **Department of Parks,** P.O. Box 451, Jackson 39205 (☎800-467-2757).

Postal Abbreviation: MS. **Sales Tax:** 7%.

JACKSON ☎601

Jackson makes a valiant effort to overcome Mississippi's lingering backwater image. Impressive museums and sights line Pascagoula and State St. downtown, and as the state's political and cultural capital, Jackson maintains an international perspective. It is one of only four cities in the world to host the International Ballet Competition, held at the Thalia Mara Center every four years. North Jackson's lush homes and plush country clubs epitomize wealthy Southern living, while cool reservoirs, and national forests invite outdoor exploration. Just don't arrive on a Sunday—true to its deep Southern roots, Jackson will be closed for a rest.

PRACTICAL INFORMATION. West of I-55 and north of I-20, downtown is bordered on the north by **High Street,** on the south by **South Street,** and on the west by **Lamar Street.** North-south **State Street** bisects the city. **Jackson International Airport,** 100 International Dr. (☎939-5631; www.jmaa.com), lies east of downtown off I-20. **Amtrak,** 300 W. Capitol St. in Union Station (☎355-6350; open daily 10:15am-5:45pm), runs to Memphis (4½hr., 7 per week, $33) and New Orleans (4hr., 7 per week, $21). **Greyhound,** also in Union Station (☎353-6342; open 24hr.), goes to: Memphis (5hr., 1 per day, $30-32); Montgomery (5hr., 7 per day, $50-53); New Orleans (4½hr., 4 per day, $27-29). **Jackson Transit System (JATRAN)** provides limited public transit. Maps are posted at most bus stops and are available at JATRAN headquarters, 1025 Terry Rd. (☎948-3840. Open M-F 8am-6pm. Runs at least every 30min. from Union Station M-F 5:30am-6:30pm; every hr. Sa 7am-6pm. $1, transfers free.) **Taxi: City Cab** ☎355-8319. **Visitor Info: Jackson Convention and Visitors Bureau,** 921 N. President St., downtown. (☎960-1891 or 800-354-7695; www.visitjackson.com. Open M-F 8am-5pm.) **Hotlines: Crisis/Rape,** ☎982-7273. 24hr. **Internet:** Jackson Library, 300 State St. (☎968-5801. Open M-Th 9am-9pm, F 9am-6pm, Su 1-5pm. Free.) **Post Office:** 401 E. South St. (☎351-7096. Open M-F 7am-6pm, Sa 8am-noon.) **Postal Code:** 39205. **Area Code:** 601.

ACCOMMODATIONS. The interstate crawls with standard mid-range chains along **I-20** and **I-55**. **Parkside Inn ❷,** 3720 I-55 N, at Exit 98B off the access road, is a cheap and clean motel with pool, cable TV, and free local calls. (☎982-1122. Singles $35; doubles with microwave and fridge $49.) The more pricey but extremely comfortable **Cabot Lodge ❹,** 120 Dyess Rd., in Ridgeland, has cocktails, an extensive breakfast, and a pool, plus free Internet access and local calls. (☎957-0757 or 800-342-2268; www.cabotlodgejacksonnorth.com. Singles $75; doubles $85-95.) For camping, head to **Timberlake Campgrounds ❶.** Take I-55 N to Lakeland East (Exit 98B), turn left after 6 mi. onto Old Fannin Rd., and go 4 mi.; it's inside the Barnett Reservoir. (☎992-9100. Office open daily 8am-11pm. Tent sites $15, seniors $13. Hook-up May-Sept. $19/$16; Oct.-Apr. $13/$10.)

FOOD AND NIGHTLIFE. Downtown, the **George Street Grocery ❷,** 416 George St., off of West St., is packed with state politicians by day and students by night. (☎969-3573. All-you-can-eat Southern lunch buffet $8. Live rock Th-Sa

9pm-2am. Restaurant open M-Th 11am-9pm, F 11am-2am, Sa 5-10pm.) **Mayflower** ❸, 123 W. Capitol St., has been serving gourmet fresh-from-the-Gulf seafood in a relaxed, diner-like atmosphere since 1935. A scene from the movie *Ghosts of Mississippi* was shot right here in the cafe. (☎355-4122. Filet $11. Flounder $16. Open M-F 11am-10pm, Sa 4:30-10pm.) **Two Sisters** ❸, 707 N. Congress St., just around the corner from George St., offers yet another Southern smorgasbord in a delightful old creaky-staired home. Eat all you want for $9.50. (☎353-1180. Open Su-F 11am-2pm.) **Hal & Mal's Restaurant and Brew Bar**, 200 S. Commerce St., near the corner of State and Pascagoula, stages live music in an old, relic-strewn warehouse that can hold 600 people. Acts range from bluegrass on Wednesdays to jazz on Thursdays and country on Fridays. (☎948-0888. Cover F-Sa under $5. Restaurant open M 11am-3pm, Tu-F 11am-11pm, Sa 5-11pm. Bar open Tu-Th until midnight, F-Sa until 2am.) On Thursday, pick up the *Clarion-Ledger* for a list of weekend events. Two other free publications with entertainment and events listings are *Planet Weekly* and *Jackson Free Press* (the city's alternative magazine), available around town.

◙ SIGHTS. The ▨**International Museum of Muslim Cultures (IMMC)**, 117 E. Pascagoula St., was created initially as a temporary satellite to an exhibit at the Mississippi Museum of Art, but became permanent in response to overwhelming community enthusiasm. The museum has extraordinary exhibits on the Muslim diaspora and world mosques. (☎960-0440; www.muslimmuseum.org. Open M-Th and Sa-Su 9:30am-5pm, F 9:30am-12:30pm. $7; students, seniors, children, and disabled $4.) The **Mississippi Museum of Art (MMA)**, 201 E. Pascagoula St., at Lamar St., amazes with its spacious galleries that display over 3100 works of art, from regional and local to rotating national and international exhibits. (☎960-1515; www.msmuseumart.org. Open M-Sa 10am-5pm, Su noon-5pm. $5, seniors $4, students $3, ages 6-17 $2.) Adjacent to the MMA, the **Russell C. Davis Planetarium**, 201 E. Pascagoula, has movies and astronomy shows with music and lasers. (☎960-1550. Shows daily; call ahead. $5.50, seniors and under 12 $4.) The **Old Capitol Museum**, at Capitol and State St., houses a Smithsonian-caliber collection documenting Mississippi history. Exhibits help visitors appreciate the slave's daily life in the 1800s and understand the impact of the great flood of 1979 which devastated the land adjacent to the Mississippi River. (☎359-6920. Open M-F 8am-5pm, Sa 9:30am-4:30pm, Su 12:30-4:30pm. Free.) The **New State Capitol**, 400 High St., between West and President St., was completed in 1903. A recent restoration project preserved the building's Beaux Arts grandeur. (☎359-3114. Self-guided tours M-F 8am-5pm. Free.) Tour the grandiose **Governor's Mansion**, 300 E. Capitol St., one of only two inhabited governor's mansions in the US, with sumptuous bedrooms, including the Pumpkin Bedroom and the Gold Bedroom. (☎359-6421. Tours every 30min. Tu-F 9:30-11am. Free.)

VICKSBURG   ☎601

President Lincoln, referring to Vicksburg, said the Civil War would "never be brought to a close until that key is in our pocket." After a 47-day siege, the Confederacy surrendered to Ulysses S. Grant's army on July 4, 1863. Memorials and combat site markers riddle the grassy 1700-acre **Vicksburg National Military Park**, giving the grounds a sacred air. The park sits on the eastern and northern edges of the city with its visitors center on Clay St., about ½ mi. west of I-20 Exit 4B. Driving along the 16 mi. path, there are three options: taking a self-guided tour with a free map available at the entrance, using an informative audio tour, or hiring a guide to narrate the sights. (☎636-0583; www.nps.gov/vick. Park center open daily 8am-5pm. Grounds open daily in summer 7am-7pm; in winter 7am-5pm. $5 per car. Tape $6, CD

$15, live guide $30.) In the park, the sunk and saved **Union USS Cairo Museum** contains artifacts salvaged in the early 1960s from the old ironclad. (☎ 636-2199. Usually open daily Apr.-Oct. 9:30am-6pm; Nov.-Mar. 8:30am-5pm. Free with park fee.) During the 1863 siege of Vicksburg, Confederate troops used the cupola at the **Old Courthouse Museum,** 1008 Cherry St., as a signal station and held Union prisoners in the courtroom. It now houses Jefferson Davis memorabilia and a restored courtroom. (☎ 636-0741; www.oldcourthouse.org. Open Apr.-Sept. M-Sa 8:30am-5pm, Su 1:30-5pm; Oct.-Mar. M-Sa 8:30am-4:30pm, Su 1:30-5pm. $3, seniors $2.50, under 18 $2.)

Vicksburg has attractions not related to the war; most are along the river on **Washington Street.** One half of the █**Corner Drug Store,** 1123 Washington St., is a fully operating modern pharmacy. On the other half, the owner has created an elaborate 1800s drug store museum, complete with archaic drugs like cocaine, arsenic, opium, and "haschissh." Old implements adorn the walls and old moonshine jugs sit in one corner. (☎ 363-2756. Open M-Sa 8am-6pm, Su 9-11am. Free.) Grab an ice-cream cone at the **Biedenharn Museum of Coca-Cola Memorabilia,** 1107 Washington St. In the 1900 soda fountain you can learn all there is to know about the bottling of "the ideal brain tonic"—Coca-Cola. (☎ 638-6514. Open M-Sa 9am-5pm, Su 1:30-4:30pm. $2.25, age 6-12 $1.75. AAA discount.)

The **Battlefield Inn ❸,** 4137 I-20 N. Frontage Rd., is built on part of the actual battlefield—complete with cannons—right next to the National Military Park. (☎ 800-359-9363. Breakfast included. Pool, laundry, grill, mini golf. Singles $65; doubles $75.) Clean, spacious rooms at the **Beechwood Motel/Inn ❶,** 4449 E. Clay St., have cable TV, and some have microwave and fridge. (☎ 636-2271. Singles $30-35; doubles $33-40.) Close to the military park is **Battlefield Kampground ❶,** 4407 I-20 Frontage Rd., off Exit 4B. (☎ 636-2025. Pool, playground, and laundry. Free shuttle to casinos. Tent sites $12, with water and electricity $15, full hookup $18. Motel rooms $28.) At █**Walnut Hills ❸,** 1214 Adams St., just north of Clay St., noon is "dinnertime." First rate all-you-can-eat round-table dinners of catfish, ribs, okra, snap peas, biscuits, and iced tea cost $12. (☎ 638-4910. Round-table dinners Su-F 11am-2pm. Open M-F 11am-8:30pm, Su 11am-2pm.) Indulge in home-cooked meals at **Burger Village ❶,** 1220 Washington St. Vegetarian options include salads and po' boys for $3-6. (☎ 638-0202. Meals $4.25-6. Open Tu-Sa 9am-4pm.) Wannabe highrollers tired of jamming can get lost in one of the four **casinos** that line the river.

A car is necessary in Vicksburg. The bus station, the visitors center, downtown, and the far end of the sprawling military park mark the city's extremes; no public transit runs between them. **Greyhound,** 1295 S. Frontage Rd. (☎ 638-8389; open daily 7am-8:30pm), goes to Jackson (1hr., 4 per day, $12). The **Tourist Information Center,** on Clay St., across from the military park entrance, west off I-20, has a helpful map of sights, accommodations, and restaurants. (☎ 636-9421 or 800-221-3536; www.visitvicksburg.com. Open in summer daily 8am-5:30pm; in winter M-F 8am-5pm, Sa-Su 8am-4pm.) **Post Office:** 3415 Pemberton Blvd., off U.S. 61 S. (☎ 636-1022. Open M-F 8:30am-5pm, Sa 9am-noon.) **Postal Code:** 39180. **Area Code:** 601.

OXFORD   ☎ 662

When westward explorers first came to this site in northern Mississippi, they decided to name it "Oxford" in hopes of getting the state government to open a university here. The plan worked brilliantly, eventually landing Oxford the **University of Mississippi (Ole Miss).** The school gained notoriety in the early 1960s when James Meredith attempted to be the first black student to enroll. Mississippi Governor Ross Burnett openly defied federal law, banning Meredith until the National Guard arrived. Underneath its rough past, Oxford is the "little postage stamp of native soil" that William Faulkner decided "was worth writing about."

❖❼ ORIENTATION AND PRACTICAL INFORMATION. Oxford is 30 mi. east of I-55 on Rte. 6 (Exit 243), 55 mi. south of Memphis and 140 mi. north of Jackson. The main east-west roads are **Jackson Avenue** and **University Avenue,** while **Lamar Boulevard** runs north-south. The center of town is **Courthouse Square,** at the intersection of Jackson Ave. and Lamar St., bordered by Van Buren Ave. The **Oxford Tourism Info Center,** 107 Courthouse Sq., in the back of the City Hall, offers free audio walking tours and info on Faulkner. (☎234-4680 or 800-758-9177. Open M-F 8am-5pm. The little house next door, Skipwith Cottage, replaces the info center at City Hall on weekends and is open Sa 10am-4pm, Su 1-4pm.) **Internet Access: Public Library,** 401 Bramlett Blvd., at Jackson Ave. (☎234-5751. Open M-Th 9:30am-8pm, F-Sa 9:30am-5:30pm, Su 2-5pm. Free.) **Post Office:** 401 McElroy Dr. (☎234-5615. Open M-F 9am-5pm, Sa 9:30am-12:30pm.) **Postal Code:** 38655. **Area Code:** 662.

▉ ACCOMMODATIONS. Spend a night in Southern comfort at the **Oliver-Britt House Inn ❹,** 512 Van Buren Ave., an unpretentious B&B in a big maroon house. Five small but comfortable rooms fit in this turn-of-the-century house. (☎234-8043. Breakfast on weekends. Rooms Su-Th $70-105, F-Sa $70-115; football weekends $20 more.) Close to town, the best independently-owned budget hotel is **Johnson's Inn ❷,** 2305 W. Jackson Ave., west of town off Hwy. 6, 3 mi. from Courthouse Sq. and only 1½ mi. from Ole Miss. It sports spacious, relatively new rooms with microwaves and fridges, cable TV, and free local calls. (☎234-3611. Singles $35; doubles $38.) **Wall Doxy State Park ❶,** 23 mi. north of town on Rte. 7, is a scenic spot with an expansive lake. (☎252-4231 or 800-467-2757. Sites with water and electricity $9; RV sites with dump stations $13. Cabins $52-58 per night. 3-night min. stay for cabins. Entrance fee $2 per car.)

❏❺ FOOD AND ENTERTAINMENT. Courthouse Square at Jackson Ave. and Lamar Blvd. is the center of it all. **▉Square Books ❶,** 160 Courthouse Sq. is one of the best independent bookstores in the nation. The owner also happens to be the city's mayor. Read upstairs while tasting coffee drinks and pastries ($1-2) or on a balcony overlooking downtown. (☎236-2262. Open M-Th 9am-9pm, F-Sa 9am-10pm, Su 10am-6pm.) **Ajax Diner ❷,** 118 Courthouse Sq., cooks excellent meat-and-vegetable platters ($7) accompanied by jalapeño cornbread. (☎232-8880. Open M-Sa 11:30am-10pm.) The **Bottletree Bakery ❷,** 923 Van Buren Ave., serves large deli sandwiches ($7-8) and fresh pastries in a relaxed atmosphere with brightly painted walls and recycled furniture. (☎236-5000. Open Tu-F 7am-4pm, Sa 9am-4pm, Su 9am-2pm.) At night, live music rolls from **Proud Larry's ❸,** 211 S. Lamar Blvd., where hand-tossed pizzas are served piping hot. Elvis Costello played here last year. (☎236-0050. Pizzas $8-10. Music F-Sa 10pm-1am, also some weeknights 10pm-midnight. Cover $5-7. Kitchen open M-Sa 11am-10pm, Su 11:30am-3pm.) **City Grocery ❺,** 152 Courthouse Sq., serves gourmet fare that will challenge your tastebuds (and your budget). It also runs a less student-heavy bar upstairs from Proud Larry's, with an outdoor balcony overlooking the square. Check out the hangings on the walls by local artist Lamar Serranto. (☎232-8080. Beer $3-4. Lunch entrees $4-12, dinner $19-35. Open M-W 11am-2:30pm and 6-10pm, Th-Sa 11am-2:30pm and 6-10:30pm.) For local entertainment listings, check the free weekly *Oxford Town.*

◪ SIGHTS. Faulkner remains the South's favorite son, and his home, **Rowan Oak,** just south of downtown on Old Taylor Rd, off S. Lamar Blvd., is Oxford's biggest attraction. Entranced by the home's history (it had belonged to a Confederate general), Faulkner bought the place in 1930 and named the property after the Rowan tree, a symbol of peace and security. The plot outline of his 1954 novel *A Fable* is etched in pencil on the walls of the study. (☎234-3284. Grounds open sunrise to sunset. Free self-guided tours.)

THE SOUTH

Aside from Faulkner, Oxford's sights are all affiliated with another symbol of Southern intellectualism—Ole Miss. The town's covered sidewalks and tall cedar trees make it a fitting home for the **Center for the Study of Southern Culture,** a university department in the old Barnard Observatory. The center hosts the ever-popular annual **Faulkner & Yoknapatawpha Conference**—in 2005, the conference will focus on "Faulkner's Inheritance," and is scheduled for July 24-28. Other conferences and festivals sponsored by the center include the **Oxford Conference on the Book,** in April, which celebrates a different author each year, and the **Southern Foodways Symposium,** which brings people together in late October to discuss weighty academic subjects, like barbecue and other Southern food traditions. (☎915-5993; www.olemiss.edu/depts/south. Center open M-F 8am-5pm. Free.) Oxford also hosts a **film festival** during the third week in June (☎236-6429; www.oxfordfilmfest.com). The **Civil Rights Memorial,** next to the library, is scheduled to open in 2005 and will "commemorate equality in education" on the grounds of the Ole Miss campus. Blues buffs will revel in the **Ole Miss Blues Archive,** on the 2nd fl. of the main campus library on University Circle, which has one of the largest collections of blues memorabilia in the world. (☎915-5993. Blues archive open M-F 8am-5pm. Free.) Ask about the new **African-American History Museum,** scheduled to open soon.

TUPELO ☎ 662

This former industrial town was the birthplace of Elvis Aaron Presley and now milks that fact to the maximum extent possible. Tupelo is 1½hr. east of Oxford along Hwy. 6; a prettier drive, however, is along Rte. 30 through the **Holly Springs National Forest** and Rte. 78 into Tulepo from New Albany. The **Elvis Presley Birthplace,** 306 Elvis Presley Blvd., is definitely worth a visit (something that can't be said of the peripheral sights), especially if you've already visited Graceland. There's also an **Elvis Presley Museum** and the **Memorial Chapel** for meditation, alongside features tacked on in recent years, such as a fountain and statue of 13-year-old Elvis and a walk that explores all the years Elvis was alive. You can even take an Elvis driving tour and visit places he went to as a kid, including a hardware store. (☎841-1245; www.elvispresleybirthplace.com. Open M-Sa 9am-5pm, Su 1-5pm; May-Sept. open M-Sa until 5:30pm. House $2.50, children $1.50. Museum $6/$3. Combination ticket $7/$3.50. The **Oren Dunn City Museum,** on Hwy. 6 W at James L. Ballard Park, has a collection of Native American history, a restored "dogtrot" cabin, a recreation of the Battle of Tupelo and, naturally, more Elvis paraphernalia. (☎841-6438. Open Tu-F 9am-4pm, Sa 10am-3pm, Su 1-5pm. Closed Nov.-Feb. $3, seniors $2, children $1.50, under 3 free.) Tupelo is also home to the headquarters of the **Natchez Trace Parkway,** a beautiful, if slow, drive from Natchez, MS, to Nashville, TN. The parkway follows old Native American routes and is free of commercial traffic and advertising. The **Visitors Center,** 2680 Natchez Trace Pkwy., near the 78/45 junction, includes information on early settlers, nature, and history along the route. (☎680-4025 or 800-305-7417; www.nps.gov/natr. Open daily 8am-5pm.)

Accommodations are concentrated around the intersection of McCullough Blvd. and Gloster St. The **Commodore Motel ❷,** 1800 E. Main St., east of downtown, is located close to Elvis's birthplace and provides standard rooms. (☎842-9074. Rooms $30-40.) Six miles to the south of the city, **Tombigbee State Park ❶,** 264 Cabin Dr., offers primitive campsites on a scenic ridge overlooking Lake Lee, and slightly less picturesque developed campsites with water, electricity, and hot showers. (☎842-7669. Parking $2. Reception 8am-5pm. Primitive sites $9; developed sites $13-14.) Grab a bite at Elvis's old haunt, **Johnnie's Drive-In ❶,** 908 E. Main St., where a wonderful barbecue burger and shake can be had for $5. (☎842-6748. Open M-Sa 7am-9pm, closed Su because they've "gone to church.") A more upscale option is **Woody's ❺**, 619 N. Gloster St., which serves certified Angus steaks, wild game, and fresh seafood. There is also bad karaoke in the lounge on an ad hoc basis. (☎840-0460. Entrees around $22. Open M-Sa 5pm-midnight.)

Greyhound is located at 201 Commerce St. (☎842-4557 or 800-231-2222. Open M-F 7am-5pm, Sa-Su 9am-4pm.) Buses run to: Jackson (6-12hr., 4 per day, $43); Memphis (2½hr., 4 per day, $28); Nashville (6-9hr., 2 per day, $51). **Taxi: Brooks Taxi Cab** (☎842-5262) and **Tupelo Cab Company** (☎842-1133). The **Convention and Visitors Bureau** is at 399 E. Main St. (☎841-6521. Open M-F 8am-5pm.) **Internet Access: Lee County Library,** 219 N. Madison St., at the corner of Jefferson and Madison. (☎844-9028. Open M-F 9am-8pm, Sa 9am-5pm.) **Post Office:** 500 W. Main St. (☎841-1286. Open M-F 8.30am-5pm.) **Postal Code:** 33804. **Area Code:** 662.

BILOXI

☎757

When the French arrived in 1699, Biloxi was made capital of French Louisiana. The remains of that municipal grandeur are visible in the town's antebellum homes, including **Beauvoir,** the home of Confederate President Jefferson Davis. The estate is fascinating, giving insight into both the man himself and the entire Confederate cause. The self-guided tour (allow 1½hr.) begins with a 15min. film presented by an actor posing as Davis's lifetime friend, then meanders through the home and grounds, including the **Presidential Library** (unrecognized by the Federal government), a museum, and the **Tomb of the Unknown Confederate Soldier.** (☎388-9074 or 800-570-3818. Open daily 9am-5pm. $7.50, seniors $6.75, children $4.50.) A self-guided historical **walking tour** of Biloxi's buildings, available for free at the visitors center (allow 1-2hr.), sheds light onto the influences that shaped Biloxi's architecture. The tour ends at the **Ohr-O'Keefe Museum of Art,** 136 Ohr St., which boasts the largest assembled collection of George Ohr's work in the US, along with three galleries of contemporary art. Frank Gehry is working on a new building for the museum due to open 2006. (☎374-5547. Open M-F 9am-5pm, in summer until 6pm. $6, seniors $5, students and children free.) From nearby Gulfport, 15 mi. west of Biloxi, catch a ferry to the idyllic **Ship Island,** which played a major role in US colonial and Civil War history. (☎864-1014 or 866-466-7386; http://msshipisland.com. Boat times vary; call ahead to check. $20, seniors $18, ages 3-10 $10.)

Accommodations are expensive during peak season (July-Aug.), and rates can vary wildly; cheaper rooms are easier to find midweek. **Jubilee Inn ❷,** 1678 Beach Blvd., is across from the beach and near the casinos, with rooms as low as $40 during the week. (☎432-1984 or 888-765-1984. Continental breakfast. Free local calls and pool. Rooms $40-100.) **Gulf Beach Resort ❸,** 2428 Beach Blvd., is farther from downtown but very convenient for Beauvoir and quieter beaches. (☎385-5555 or 800-323-9164; www.gulfbeachresort.com. Comfortable, big, clean rooms $40-140.) For cheap camping options, ask at the visitors center about camping to the east in the National Seashore protected area. Good values and family-size portions abound at **Ole Biloxi Schooner's Restaurant ❸,** 159 E Howard Ave. Sandwiches are $6-8, and plentiful platters go for $15-17. (☎374-8071. Open daily 7am-9pm.) **McElroy's Harbor House ❸,** across from McDonald's at 695 Beach Blvd., is the place to go for seafood. (☎435-5001. Appetizers $6-7. Seafood entrees $7-20. Open daily 7am-10pm.) Biloxi's **casinos,** anchored offshore, are a staple of nighttime excitement and usually open 24hr. You can often get into casinos and enjoy the shows for free; pick up a copy of *Jackpot* for the latest on casino offers. For a more sedate evening, take a **schooner cruise** on a replica ship and sail between the beaches and the gulf islands. (☎435-6320. Call for sailing times and reservations. $20, children 3-12 $10.) Boats depart from the Small Craft Harbor, on Hwy. 90 E. ◪**Just Us Lounge,** 906 Division St., at Calliavet, is a friendly gay venue, with cheap beer and free drag shows most nights. (☎374-1007. Open 24hr.)

Biloxi is 1hr. west of Mobile and 2hr. east of New Orleans. The **Visitor Information Center,** 710 Beach Blvd., by Main St., is in an 1895 wooden house. (☎374-3105 or 800-245-6943. Open M-F 8am-4:30pm, Sa 9am-4:30pm, Su 10am-4pm.) **Greyhound,** 166 Main St. (☎436-4335; open daily 7:30am-8:30pm), rolls to: Mobile (1hr., 6 per day, $17); New Orleans (2hr., 3 per day, $21); Pensacola (3hr., 4 per day, $31). **City tours** depart from the lighthouse on Hwy. 90. (☎374-8687. 1hr. Reservations recommended. Tours M-Sa 11am, 1, and 3pm. $13, seniors $12, ages 5-12 $5.) A **city bus** plies the Beach Blvd. every 30min. (☎896-8080; www.coasttransit.com. Runs 5am-10pm. $1, seniors $0.50; day pass $5.) **Taxi: Livery Cab** ☎863-1175. **Internet Access: Biloxi Library,** 139 Lameuse St., around the corner from the visitors center. (☎374-0330. Open M-Th 9am-8pm, F-Sa 9am-5pm. Free.) **Post Office:** 135 Main St. (☎374-0345. Open M-F 8:30am-5pm, Sa 10am-noon.) **Postal Code:** 39530. **Area Code:** 228.

NATCHEZ   ☎601

Natchez lies on the east bank of the Mississippi River, about 1½hr. south of Vicksburg. It's also the start (or end, depending on your direction) of the **Natchez Trace Parkway,** the National Park road that follows the original Natchez, Chickasaw, and Choctaw Indian trading route (p. 470). Visitors flock to the historic antebellum homes and the **Spring Pilgrimage** (March 12-April 16, 2005), when over 30 historic houses open their doors with guides in period dress and various musical performances are held around town. In fall people celebrate the autumnal gardens and Amos Polk's famous Voices of Hope Gospel Choir performs (Oct. 5-22, 2005).

The historic downtown area, full of antique and speciality shops, is bordered by U.S. 84 to the south, Madison St. to the north, Martin Luther King, Jr. St. to the east, and the Mississippi River to the west. The **Museum of African-American History and Culture,** 301 Main St., downtown, has photographs and documentary records of significant African-American leaders and activists who helped secure economic and political advances for African-Americans. (☎445-0728. Open Tu-Sa 1pm-4:30pm.) Farther out of town, two of the antebellum homes in town stand out from the crowd. **Longwood,** 140 Lower Woodville Rd., was built circa 1860-61 and has a beautiful red cupola on top of the white Greek-style tower. (☎442-5193. Open daily 9am-4:30pm. Tours every 30min. $8, children $4.) **Melrose,** 1 Melrose-Montebello Pkwy., was built about 20 years earlier (c. 1841-45), and has four imposing Greco-Roman columns outside and an ornate Italian balcony. (☎446-5790. Open daily 9am-4pm. Tours every hr. on the hr. $6.) **The Grand Village of the Natchez Indians,** 400 Jefferson Davis Blvd., has a recreated Native American village that offers an idea of what life used to be like and inspires an appreciation for the system of residential organization. (☎446-6502. Open M-Sa 9am-5pm, Su 1:30-5pm. Free.) About 20min. west of Natchez, over the Louisiana border, the **Frogmore Plantation** provides an opportunity to reflect on the history of slavery and life in the 1800s. (11054 Hwy. 84. ☎318-757-2453; www.frogmoreplantation.com. Open Mar. to mid-Nov. M-F 9am-3pm, last tour 2pm; Sa 10am-2pm, last tour 1:30pm. Closed June-Aug. Sa $10, ages 6-18 $5, under 5 free.)

The very clean and friendly **Travel Inn,** 271A D'Evereaux Dr., off Hwy. 61 N, has 37 rooms and a good continental breakfast. (☎446-8799 or 800-224-8704. Singles $32; doubles $36.) Listed on the National Register of Historic Places, the **Eola Hotel ❹,** 110 N. Pearl St., is a comfortable downtown splurge with riverside rooms that have beautiful sunset views. (☎445-6000. Rooms $60-110.) Campers should head for **Natchez State Park ❶,** 230B Wickcliff Rd., off Hwy. 61 N. Tent and RV sites are located at a relaxing spot near a lake and the ranger will come around to check you in, so settle in anytime. (☎442-2658. Showers. Sites $13-14.)

For good Southern cookin' try **Cock of the Walk ❸**, 200 N. Broadway, which serves fried catfish ($11) and steaks ($18)—fried or grilled—with all the trimmings. (☎446-8920. Open daily 5-8pm for dinner; lunch hours vary.) Grab a dozen signature tamales ($6.50) and "nock-u-naked" margaritas ($4.50) at **Fat Mama's Tamales ❷**, 500 S. Canal St. (☎442-4548. Beer $2-2.50 Open M-Th 11am-9pm, F-Sa 11am-10pm, Su noon-7pm.)

Greyhound, 103 Lower Woodville Rd. (☎445-5291; open M-Sa 7:15am-5:30pm, Su 9am-12:30pm and 3:30-5:30pm), travels to Jackson (3hr., 1 per day, $28-32) and New Orleans (5hr., 1 per day, $39-44). The **Natchez Convention and Vistors Bureau,** 640 S. Canal St., clearly marked from Hwy. 61, provides information on the area. (☎446-6345; www.natchez.ms.us. Open M-Sa 8:30am-5pm, Su 9am-4pm.) The visitors center also sells tickets for a 50min. trolley tour of downtown, which mainly focuses on the antebellum homes and churches ($15), or 40min. horse-drawn carriage tour ($10). **Internet Access: Judge George W. Armstrong Library,** 220 S. Commerce St., has six computers. (☎445-8862. Open M-Th 9am-6pm, F 9am-5pm, Sa 9am-1pm.) **Area Code:** 601.

LOUISIANA

After exploring the Mississippi River valley in 1682, Frenchman René-Robert Cavalier proclaimed the land "Louisiane," in honor of Louis XIV. The name has endured three centuries, though French ownership of the region has not. The territory was tossed between France, England, and Spain before Thomas Jefferson and the US snagged it in the Louisiana Purchase of 1803. Nine years later, a smaller, redefined Louisiana was admitted to the Union. Each successive government lured a new mix of settlers to the bayous: Spaniards from the Canary Islands, French Acadians from Nova Scotia, Americans from the East, and free blacks from the West Indies. Louisiana's multinational history, Creole culture, Catholic governmental structure (under which counties are called "parishes"), and Napoleonic legal system are unlike anything found in the other 49 states. Here the swamps seep into the towns, beer comes in 10 oz. cans (unlike 12 oz. elsewhere), and the *joie de vivre* is evident in bars and music venues that never close.

🔢 PRACTICAL INFORMATION

Capital: Baton Rouge.

Visitor Info: Office of Tourism, P.O. Box 94291, Baton Rouge 70804 (☎225-342-8100 or 800-261-9144; www.louisianatravel.com). Open M-F 8am-4:30pm.

Office of State Parks, P.O. Box 44426, Baton Rouge 70804 (☎225-342-8111 or 888-677-1400; www.lastateparks.com). Open M-F 8am-4:30pm.

Postal Abbreviation: LA. **Sales Tax:** 8%.

NEW ORLEANS   ☎504

First explored by the French, *La Nouvelle Orléans* was ceded secretly to the Spanish in 1762; the citizens didn't find out until 1766. Spain returned the city to France just in time for the United States to grab it in the Louisiana Purchase of 1803. Centuries of cultural cross-pollination have resulted in a vast melange of Spanish courtyards, Victorian verandas, Cajun jambalaya, Creole gumbo, and French *beignets*. The city's nickname, "The Big Easy," reflects the carefree atti-

THE SOUTH

tude characteristic of this fun-loving place where food and music are the two ruling passions. New Orleans has its own style of cooking, a distinct accent, and a colorful way of making music—come late February, there's no escaping the month-long celebration of Mardi Gras, the peak of the city's already festive mood.

✈ INTERCITY TRANSPORTATION

Airport: Louis Armstrong New Orleans International Airport, 900 Airline Dr. (☎464-0831), 15 mi. west of the city. Cab fare to the Quarter is set at $28 for 1-2 people; $10 each additional person. 24hr. Airport shuttle to and from downtown hotels $12 per person. (☎522-3500; www.flymsy.com.) The **Louisiana Transit Company,** 118 David Dr. (☎818-1077), buses from the airport to Elk St. downtown M-Sa every 15-30min. 5:10am-6:40pm. After 6:40pm, buses go to Tulane Ave. and Carollton Ave. (mid-city) until 11:30pm. Station open M-F 8am-4pm. $1.60; exact change needed. Pick-up on the upper level, near the exit ramp.

Trains: Amtrak, 1001 Loyola Ave. (☎800-872-7245), in the Union Passenger Terminal, a 10min. walk to Canal St. via Elk. Station open daily 6am-10pm. Ticket office open M, W, F-Sa 6:15am-8:30pm; Tu, Th, Su 6:15am-11pm. To: **Atlanta** (12hr., 7 per week, $50-89); **Houston** (9hr., 3 per week, $50-89); **Jackson** (4hr., 7 per week, $18-36).

Buses: Greyhound, 1001 Loyola Ave. (☎524-7571 or 800-231-2222), also in the Union Passenger Terminal. Open 24hr. To: **Atlanta** (10-14hr., 9 per day, $67); **Austin** (12-15hr., 5 per day, $91); **Baton Rouge** (1½-2hr., 7 per day, $13). *Be careful in this area after dark—head into the French Quarter and do not venture northwest.*

■ ORIENTATION

The majority of New Orleans's attractions crowd around the city center. The city's main streets follow the curve of the **Mississippi River,** hence the nickname "the Crescent City." Directions from locals reflect watery influences—"lakeside" means north, referring to **Lake Ponchartrain,** and "riverside" means south. Uptown lies west, up river; downtown is down river. The city is concentrated on the Mississippi's east bank, but **"The East"** refers only to the easternmost part of the city. **Parking** in New Orleans is relatively easy (☎299-3700 for parking info). Throughout the French Quarter (and in most residential areas), signs along the streets designate "2hr. residential parking" areas. Many streets throughout the city have meters, which become free on weekdays after 6pm, on weekends, and on holidays.

NEIGHBORHOODS

Tourists flock to the **French Quarter (Vieux Carré),** bounded by the Mississippi River, **Canal Street, Rampart Street,** and **Esplanade Avenue.** Streets in the Quarter follow a grid pattern. Just northeast, or "downtown/downriver," of the Quarter across Esplanade Ave., **Faubourg Marigny** is a residential neighborhood full of trendy nightclubs, bars, and cafes. Northwest of the Quarter across Rampart St., the little-publicized African-American neighborhood of **Tremé** has a storied history, but has been ruined somewhat by the encroaching highway overpass and the housing projects lining its Canal St. border. *Be extremely careful in Tremé at night.* Uptown, the residential **Garden District,** bordered by **Saint Charles Avenue** to the north and **Magazine Street** to the south, is distinguished by its elegant homes. The scenic **Saint Charles Streetcar route,** easily picked up at Canal St. and Carondelet St., passes through parts of the **Central Business District** ("CBD" or "downtown"), the Garden District via St. Charles Ave., and the **Uptown** and **Carrollton** neighborhoods along **South Carollton Avenue** and past **Tulane** and **Loyola Universities.** *Avoid the area immediately north of Carondelet in the Garden District after dark.* Less populated regions of the city, like **Algiers Point,** are on the **West Bank** across the river. For a detailed guide to all of the city's neighborhoods, pick up *Historic Neighborhoods of New Orleans,* available at the Jackson Sq. Visitors Center.

▐ LOCAL TRANSPORTATION

Public Transit: Regional Transit Authority (RTA), 6700 Plaza Dr. (☎248-3900). Open M-F 9am-5pm. Most buses pass Canal St., at the edge of the French Quarter. Major buses and streetcars run 24hr. but are notoriously irregular and often don't come at all after midnight. Most buses and streetcars $1.25 in exact change. Express buses and the Riverfront Streetcar $1.25, seniors and disabled passengers $0.40; transfers $0.25. 1-day pass $5, 3-day pass $12; passes sold at major hotels in the Canal St. area. Office has bus schedules and maps.

Taxi: United Cabs ☎522-0629 or 522-9771. **Checker Yellow Cabs** ☎943-2411.

Bikes: French Quarter Bicycles, 522 Dumaine St. (☎529-3136), between Decatur and Chartres St. $5 per hr., $20 per day, $15 per day when hiring for a week. Includes lock, helmet, and map. Credit card or $200 cash deposit required. Open M-F 11am-7pm, Sa-Su 10am-6pm. Closed Su during summer.

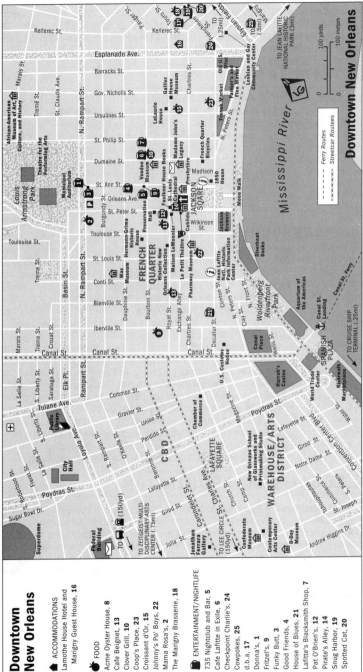

Downtown New Orleans

Downtown New Orleans

▲ ACCOMMODATIONS
Lamothe House Hotel and
Marigny Guest House, **16**

● FOOD
Acme Oyster House, **8**
Cafe Beignet, **13**
Clover Grill, **10**
Coop's Place, **23**
Croissant d'Or, **15**
Johnny's Po' Boys, **22**
Mama Rosa's, **2**
The Marigny Brasserie, **18**

▮ ENTERTAINMENT/NIGHTLIFE
735 Nightclub and Bar, **5**
Cafe Lafitte in Exile, **6**
Checkpoint Charlie's, **24**
Cowpokes, **25**
d.b.a, **17**
Donna's, **1**
Fritzel's, **9**
Funky Butt, **3**
Good Friends, **4**
House of Blues, **21**
Lafitte's Blacksmith Shop, **7**
Pat O'Brien's, **12**
Pirate's Alley, **14**
Snug Harbor, **19**
Spotted Cat, **20**

⚂ PRACTICAL INFORMATION

Visitor Info: Metropolitan Convention and Visitors Bureau, 529 St. Ann St. (☎568-5661; www.neworleanscvb.com), by Jackson Sq. in the French Quarter. Beware of private visitors centers in the Quarter that give less than impartial information, pushing their own services first—the Jackson Sq. center is the only official center in the French Quarter. It is understaffed and often overcrowded but very helpful; grab a good map or a series of walking tour guides. Open daily 9am-5pm.

Hotlines: Cope Line, ☎523-2673. **Domestic Violence Hotline,** ☎486-0377. Both 24hr.

Medical Services: Charity Hospital, 1532 Tulane Ave. (☎903-3000). **LSU Medical Center,** 433 Bolivar St. (☎568-4806).

Internet Access: New Orleans Public Library, 219 Loyola Ave. (☎529-7323), 1½ blocks west of Canal St. Open M-Th 10am-6pm, F-Sa 10am-5pm. If they know you're from out of town, it's $3 per hour. **The Contemporary Arts Center,** 900 Camp Rd., and **Royal Blend,** 621 Royal St., have Internet at much higher rates—see listings for hours.

Post Office: 701 Loyola Ave. (☎589-1775), near the bus station. Open M-F 7am-8pm, Sa 8am-5pm, Su noon-5pm. **Postal Code:** 70113. **Area Code:** 504.

> **⚠ SAFETY IN NEW ORLEANS.** Travelers should be aware of New Orleans's capacity for quick change—safe and decidedly unsafe areas are often separated by a block or less, and usually safe areas can become dangerous in a heartbeat. The tenement areas directly north of the French Quarter and northwest of Lee Circle pose particular threats to personal safety. At night, stick to busy, well-lit roads, never walk alone after dark, and downplay the tourist image.

⌂ ACCOMMODATIONS

Finding inexpensive yet decent rooms in the **French Quarter** can be as difficult as staying sober during Mardi Gras. Luckily, other parts of the city compensate for the absence of cheap lodging downtown. Several **hostels** cater to the young and almost penniless, as do guest houses near the **Garden District.** Accommodations for Mardi Gras and the Jazz Festival get booked up to a year in advance. During peak times, proprietors will rent out any extra space, so be sure you know what you're paying for. However, rates tend to sink in the low season (June to early Sept.) when business is slow, and negotiation can pay off. As for campers, there are oodles of campsites to discover, but even those get pricey during Mardi Gras. The *Louisiana Official Tour Guide,* available at the Jackson Sq. Visitors Center, has the most comprehensive, unbiased campsite listings available.

▨ **India House,** 124 S. Lopez St. (☎821-1904), at Canal St. between N. Broad and Jefferson Davis. What this bohemian haunt lacks in tidiness it makes up for in character. Hand-painted murals and pictures of past guests fight for space on the walls. Communal eating (and, on busier nights, sleeping), comfy couches, and backyard patio. Internet access $3 per 30min. Kitchen, pool, turtle pond out back, A/C, and lounge areas. Linen deposit $5. Coin laundry $1.50. No key deposit—in fact, no keys; the doors don't lock. There's a safe at the front desk which can be used for small items. Reception 24hr. Dorms $15, peak times $18; weekly $90. Private rooms $35, with A/C $45. ❶

▨ **St. Charles Guest House,** 1748 Prytania St. (☎523-6556). A former brothel, the guest house is located in the Garden District, one of New Orleans's most spectacular neighborhoods. Clean and character-filled rooms, a large, leafy courtyard, and continental breakfast. With no phones or TVs, there is plenty of time to contemplate the beauty of New Orleans and chat with the folks that live it and love it. Large, antique signs hang

THE SOUTH

haphazardly in the hallway, and the friendly staff lives out back. Small, single "back-packer" rooms $30-35, with A/C and private bath $55. Rooms with 1 queen-sized bed or 2 twins $55-95. During Jazz Fest and Mardi Gras $100-150. ❷

▨ **House of the Rising Sun Bed and Breakfast,** 335 Pelican Ave. (☎888-842-2747), across the river from the Canal St. ferry dock. Located in historic, residential Algiers Point, minutes from the French Quarter and downtown (via the ferry). The nearby river-front streets are a pleasant contrast to the faster pace of the Quarter. Run by two extraordinarily knowledgeable hosts—one English, one Cajun—the B&B offers "Cajun and Cockney hospitality" out of their charming home. Rooms Sept.-May $95; June-Aug. $75; up to $150 around Mardi Gras. ❹

Marquette House New Orleans International Hostel (HI), 2249 Carondelet St. (☎523-3014), in the Garden District. A very quiet hosteling experience and a pretty safe bet, due to its no-alcohol policy, cleanliness, and slight strictness. Large, semi-rustic private rooms are available. Internet access $0.10 per min. 200 beds, A/C, kitchen (no stove), and study rooms. Linen $2, towel $0.50. Key deposit $5. Dorms $18, nonmembers $20. 2-person private rooms with queen-sized bed and pull-out sofa $50/$53; each additional person $10. Weekly rates available. Wheelchair accessible. ❷

Columns, 3811 St. Charles Ave. (☎899-9308), has a magnificent c. 1893 front porch. Known for its easy-going elegance and classic comfort, this is one of New Orleans's hidden gems. Rates are high, but the atmosphere and full Southern breakfast make it a wonderful base for getting downtown and uptown using the streetcar. If your pockets aren't that deep, simply stop by for a cocktail and a swing. Rooms $85-200. ❺

Lamothe House Hotel, 622 Esplanade Ave. (☎947-1161 or 800-367-5858), is an imposing 1839 pink townhouse across the street from the French Quarter. 20 rooms feature antique furniture, cable TV, phones, A/C, and full bathrooms. Continental breakfast is served in the house's decadent dining room and the large pool is an ideal place to enjoy the complimentary afternoon sherry. Rooms May-Sept. and Dec. $69-79; Oct.-Nov. and Jan.-Apr. $169-229. Behind the big pink building, the **Marigny Guest House,** 621 Esplanade Ave. (☎944-9700), has simpler rooms starting at $59. ❸

CAMPING

Jude Travel Park and Guest House, 7400 Chef Menteur Hwy./U.S. 90 (☎241-0632 or 800-523-2196), just east of the eastern junction of I-10 and U.S. 90, Exit 240B. Bus #98 "Broad" drives past the front gate to #55 "Elysian Fields," which heads downtown. Pool and hot tub, showers, laundry, and 24hr. security. 46 tent/RV sites for 2 people $25. Each additional person $4. 5-room guest house $75-120 per person per night. ❶

St. Bernard State Park, 501 St. Bernard Pkwy. (☎682-2101), 18 mi. southeast of New Orleans; take I-10 Exit 246A, turn left onto Rte. 46, travel for 7 mi., then turn right on Rte. 39 S for 1 mi. 51 sites with water and electricity, as well as swimming pools and walking trails. Office open daily 7am-9pm. Sites $12. ❶

◖ FOOD

If the eats in the Quarter prove too trendy, touristy, or tough on the budget, there are plenty of other options, most notably on **Magazine Street** and in the Tulane area, both of which are accessible via the St. Charles Streetcar.

FRENCH QUARTER

Clover Grill, 900 Bourbon St. (☎598-1010). The Clover has been open 'round the clock since 1950, serving greasy and delicious burgers ($4.50 and up) grilled under an American-made hubcap (makes 'em cook faster), as well as breakfast any time for $3-7. The only place in New Orleans where bacon comes with a side of sexual innuendo—"You can beat our prices, but you can't beat our meat." Open 24hr. ❶

Cafe Beignet, 334B Royal St. (☎524-5530). Call in at this little gem for a dose of the fried, puffed-up doughnut that is a NOLA tradition. You'll find the *beignet* ($1.50) covered in sugar or served any number of other ways. This quiet place has a more relaxing atmosphere than the crowded spots by the river. Open daily 7am-5pm. ❶

Coop's Place, 1109 Decatur St. (☎525-9053), near the corner of Ursuline St., has some of the Quarter's best Southern cooking. The gumbo is thick and spicy ($4.35 per bowl), the beer-battered alligator bits ($8.75) have won awards, and the jambalaya ($9.25) has a flavor found nowhere else. Open Su-Th 11am-3am, F-Sa 11am-4am. ❷

Johnny's Po' Boys, 511 St. Louis St. (☎524-8129), near the corner of Decatur St. This French Quarter institution, with 40 varieties of the famous sandwich, has been the place to grab a po' boy ($4-7.50) since 1950. Decent Creole fare is also on the menu. Jambalaya $4.25. Gumbo $6.25. Open M-F 8am-4:30pm, Sa-Su 9am-4pm. ❷

Acme Oyster House, 724 Iberville St. (☎522-5973). At the bar, patrons slurp fresh oysters (6 for $4, 12 for $7) shucked before their eyes by Hollywood, the senior shucker. Acme is at least partly responsible for Bourbon St. debauchery—their motto is "Eat Louisiana oysters, love longer." Open Su-Th 11am-10pm, F-Sa 11am-11pm. ❶

Croissant d'Or, 617 Ursulines St. (☎524-4663). Fair-priced and delicious French pastries, sandwiches, and quiches are served to the local crowd that comes to this fresh and airy place to read the morning paper. Croissants $1.60. Chocolatey delights $2. Open M and W-Sa 7am-4:30pm. ❶

Mama Rosa's, 616 N. Rampart St. (☎523-5546). Locals adore this casual Italian *ristorante*. Located across from Louis Armstrong Park and down the street from some of the city's best sounds (see Donna's and Funky Butt, p. 486), Mama Rosa serves some of the best pizza you'll ever eat. 14 in. cheese pie $9. The "outrageous *muffuletta*" (deli meats, cheeses, and olive salad on Italian bread) $6.50 for a half. Open daily 11am-9:30pm. ❷

Royal Blend, 621 Royal St. (☎523-2716). The quiet courtyard provides an escape from the hustle of Royal St. and the chain coffee stores in the Quarter. Over 20 hot and iced coffees available, as well as teas and fresh-baked treats. Light meals (croissant sandwiches, quiches, and salads) $5-6. Pastries $1-2. Internet cafe in an adjoining room across the courtyard; $3 per 15min. Open Su-Th 9am-8pm, F-Sa 9am-10pm. ❶

OUTSIDE THE QUARTER

🏶 **Juan's Flying Burrito**, 2018 Magazine St. (☎569-0000; www.juansflyingburrito.com), makes some of the best burritos on the planet. For $5.75, get the "gutter punk" burrito, a meal the size of your head, and wash it down with some Mexican beer ($2.50) from the full-service bar. Open M-Sa 11am-11pm, Su noon-10pm. ❶

The Marigny Brasserie, 640 Frenchmen St. (☎945-4472), at Royal St. in Faubourg Marigny. Experience a slightly more sophisticated side of raucous "N'awlins"—dine surrounded by women in gorgeous dresses and waiters with inscrutable foreign accents. Some of the city's famous favorite dishes are embellished here; mushroom-crusted salmon ($18) is a swanky version of the classic Cajun blackened redfish ($25). Open Su-Th 5:30-10pm, F-Sa 5:30pm-midnight; Su brunch 10:30am-3pm. ❺

Dunbar's, 4927 Freret St. (☎899-0734), on the corner of Robert St. Take St. Charles Ave. west to Jackson St., turn right on Jackson, and then left onto Freret. Residents call it the best place to get mama-just-cooked-it soul food—better, they'll tell you, than any place in the Quarter. Gumbo meal $6.50. Specials, like the seafood platter, $17. Open M-Sa 7am-9pm, Su 10am-6pm. ❸

Camellia Grill, 626 S. Carrollton Ave. (☎866-9573). Take the St. Charles Streetcar to the Tulane area; Camellia is across the tracks. Classic, counter-service diner with talkative cooks. Big drippin' plates, crowds, and excellent service. Chef's special omelette $7. The aptly-named "whole meal" sandwiches $6-7. Open M-Th 9am-1am, F-Sa 8am-3am, Su 8am-1am. ❷

THE LOCAL STORY

CHRISTMAS COME EARLY

2005 will mark the ninth "Christmas in July," when locals at a bar in New Orleans's uptown district get decked out in Father Christmas gear. If you happen to be in the vicinity on the Saturday closest to July 25th, you will see several Santa Clauses boozing it up for charity with hundreds of other partygoers whooping it up alongside them. We interviewed Glen Bove, the bar's manager.

LG: So what is this "Christmas in July" all about?

A: It's an annual fundraiser for the SPCA animal shelter. They take in all the strays. They also act as a shelter for people's animals when they can't take care of them anymore. They've got a full clinic and they help the animals, bring them back to health, and they work through the adoption process to find them good homes. We usually raise $1000 every year.

LG: So why is it July and not June, which is officially halfway to Christmas?

A: Well it is about halfway to Christmas. Well, I've never done the math. I guess they consider it halfway, because of the big car sales and JC Penney with their Santas and stuff—everyone does.

LG: Are there any Santas around I can interview?

A: Oooh, Santa's passed out. He had a bit too much gin.

FRENCH QUARTER

Allow *at least* a full day in the Quarter. The oldest section of the city is famous for its ornate wrought-iron balconies—French, Spanish, and uniquely New Orleans architecture—and raucous atmosphere. Known as the **Vieux Carré** (vyuh ca-RAY), the historic district of New Orleans offers dusty used bookstores, voodoo shops, museums, art galleries, bars, and tourist traps. **Bourbon Street** is packed with touristy bars, strip clubs, and pan-handlers disguised as clowns, but there's a distinct change as you leave the trashy straight end and cross the "Lavender Line" into the more sophisticated gay end, where there's less neon and you can hear yourself speak. **Decatur Street** has mellow cafes and bars, and if you're searching for some bona fide New Orleans tunes, head northeast of the Quarter to **Frenchmen Street,** a block of bars that some locals say is what Bourbon St. was like 20 years ago.

ROYAL STREET. A streetcar named "Desire" once rolled down Royal St., one of the French Quarter's most aesthetically pleasing avenues. Pick up the free *French Quarter Self-Guided Walking Tour* from the visitors center on St. Ann St. to begin an informed jaunt past Louisiana's oldest commercial and government buildings. Don't miss **Maison LeMonnier,** known as the "first skyscraper," towering three stories high, and the **LaLaurie House,** rumored to be haunted by the souls of the slaves abused by the LaLaurie family. *(LeMonnier: 640 Royal St. LaLaurie: 1140 Royal St.)*

JACKSON SQUARE. During the day, much of the activity in the French Quarter centers around Jackson Sq., a park dedicated to Gen. Andrew Jackson, victor of the Battle of New Orleans. The square swarms with artists, mimes, musicians, psychics, magicians, and con artists. Bargain down a horse-drawn tour of the Quarter for $10; wait on the Decatur St. side. The oldest Catholic cathedral in the US, **Saint Louis Cathedral** possesses a simple beauty. Fully operational since 1718, services are still performed. *(615 Père Antoine Alley. ☎ 525-9585. Cathedral open M,W, F-Su 7am-5pm; Tu and Th 7am-6pm. Tours every 15-20min. Free.)* Behind the cathedral lies **Cathedral Garden,** also known as **Saint Anthony's Garden,** bordered by **Pirate's Alley** and **Père Antoine's Alley.** Legend has it that the former was the site of covert meetings between pirate Jean Lafitte and Andrew Jackson as they conspired to plan the Battle of New Orleans. In reality, the alley wasn't even built until 16 years later. Pirate's Alley is also home to **Faulkner House Books,** where the late American author wrote his first novel, *Soldier's Pay.* The small bookshop is a treasure trove of Faulkner's essays and books, alongside an extensive catalogue of other Southern writers. *(624 Pirate's Alley. ☎524-2940. Open daily 10am-6pm.)*

FRENCH MARKET. The historic French Market takes up several city blocks just east of Jackson Sq., toward the water along N. Peters St. *(☎522-2621. Shops open daily 9am-8pm.)* The market begins at the famous **Café du Monde** and for the first block or two is a normal strip mall of touristy shops housed in a historical building. Down by Gov. Nicholls St., it becomes the outdoor **Farmers Market,** which never closes and has been selling "most anything that grows" since 1791. Beyond the Farmers Market is the **Flea Market,** where vendors sell everything from feather boas to woodcarvings. The Jackson Sq. Visitor Center has free maps. *(Flea Market open daily 8:30am-5pm. The other building is open 24hr.)*

OTHER SIGHTS. The **Jean Lafitte National Historical Park and Preserve Visitors Center** conducts free walking tours through the Quarter. *(419 Decatur St. ☎589-2636. 1½hr. tour daily 9:30am. Come early; only the first 25 people are taken. Sometimes there's a second 45min. tour at 11:30am if it's cool enough. Office open daily 9am-5pm.)* It's always a great night to stroll the **Moon Walk,** alongside the Mighty Mississippi. The walk offers a fantastic riverside view and a chance for jokes at Michael Jackson's expense. *Be extremely careful in this area at night.* At the southwest corner of the Quarter, the **Aquarium of the Americas** houses an amazing collection of sea life and birds. Among the 500 species are black-footed penguins, endangered sea turtles, and extremely rare white alligators. Come face to face with sharks as you walk through a 30 ft. acrylic-and-glass tunnel. *(1 Canal St. ☎581-4629. Open daily May-Aug. 9:30am-7pm; Sept.-Apr. 9:30am-6pm. $15, seniors $10, ages 2-12 $8.)* The steamboat **Natchez** breezes down the Mississippi on 2hr. cruises with live jazz and narration on riverside sights. *(Departs near the Aquarium and across from Jackson Brewery. ☎586-8777 or 800-233-2628. Departs 11:30am, 2:30, 7pm. $19 during the day, $26 with lunch, $53 per person at night including live jazz band and buffet dinner.)* The **Zoo Cruise** plies the river between the aquarium and the Audubon Zoo. *(Departs at 10am, 1, 2, 4pm. $17, $23 with zoo entry or $26 with aquarium entry.)*

In spite of 100° heat and near 100% humidity, the Santa Clauses get decked out in full beard, hat, and suit. We managed to track down a Santa to interview outside on Saint Charles St.

LG: You look like you're sweating quite a lot. Are you not hot in there?
A: Well, it's pretty hot, yeah. But I do this every year and I been doing this for eight years.
LG: Do you attract the ladies dressed as Santa like that?
A: The ladies come to me. I have an extra Santa suit and I change halfway through the night. I don't take the streetcar like this but I wouldn't have a problem with it. I like everybody to be part of the atmosphere—and life goes on.

Igor's Lounge, 2133 Saint Charles St., New Orleans (☎522-2145). A full Christmas dinner of roast turkey, ham, potatoes, and all the trimmings is served free of charge at the back of the bar. Drinks range from beer ($2.50) to hurricanes (rum fruit punch; $4.50) and swampades (vodka and raspberry juice). See you there Christmas 2005—July.

OUTSIDE THE QUARTER

WATERFRONT. For an up-close view of the Mississippi River and a unique New Orleans district, take the free **Canal Street Ferry** to Algiers Point. The Algiers of old was home to many of New Orleans's African-Americans and was the birthplace of many of the city's famous jazz musicians. Once called "The Brooklyn of the South," it is now a quiet, beautiful neighborhood to explore by foot. Stop at the **Dry Dock Cafe,** just off the ferry landing, to pick up a free map of the area. At night, the ferry's outdoor observation deck affords a panoramic view of the city's sights. *(Departs daily every 30min. 5:45am-midnight from the end of Canal St. Cars free outward but $1 coming back. For further information contact the Mississippi Bridge Authority ☎ 376-8100.)* The **Riverwalk,** a multimillion-dollar conglomeration of overpriced shops overlooking the port, stretches along the Mississippi. *(☎ 522-1555. Open M-Sa 10am-9pm, Su 11am-7pm.)* Take a chance on the newly opened **Harrah's New Orleans Casino,** at Canal St. and the river. An endless Mardi Gras of slot machines suck down depressingly endless buckets of quarters. *(☎ 800-427-7247. 21+. Open 24hr.)*

WAREHOUSE/ARTS DISTRICT. Relatively new to the downtown area, the **Warehouse/Arts District,** centered roughly at the intersection of Julia and Camp St., contains several revitalized warehouse buildings turned contemporary art galleries and many of the city's museums. The galleries feature widely attended free exhibition openings the first Saturday of every month. On **White Linen Night,** the first Saturday in August, thousands take to the streets in their fanciest white finery. *(☎ 522-1999; www.neworleansartsdistrictassociation.com for Arts District info.)* In an old brick building with a modern glass-and-chrome facade, the **Contemporary Arts Center** mounts exhibits ranging from puzzling to cryptic. The large complex feels like a refuge for all the artists escaping the tourists. *(900 Camp St. ☎ 528-3805; www.cacno.org. Internet access. Open Tu-Su 11am-5pm. Exhibits $5, students and seniors $3, under 12 free. Th free.)* In the rear studio of the **New Orleans School of Glassworks and Printmaking Studio,** observe students and instructors transform blobs of molten glass into vases and sculptures. *(727 Magazine St. ☎ 529-7277. Open in winter M-Sa 11am-5pm; in summer M-F 10am-5:30pm. Free.)* **The Jonathan Ferrara Gallery** hosts local artists and an annual "No Dead Artists: A Juried Exhibition of New Orleans Art Today" every April. Ferrara was nationally recognized for his involvement in "Guns in the Hands of Artists," a 1996 program in which people turned in guns to be made into works of art. *(841 Carondelet St. ☎ 522-5471. Open Tu-Sa noon-6pm. Free.)* Just west of the Warehouse District, the **Zeitgeist Multi-Disciplinary Arts Center** offers films, theatrical and musical performances, and art exhibitions. Alternative, experimental, and provocative, the center states their mission as, "Something for and against everyone!" *(1724 Oretha Castle Haley Blvd., 4 blocks north of St. Charles St. going uptown on O'Keefe. Do not go into this area after dark. ☎ 525-2767.)* A few blocks west on St. Charles St., in **Lee Circle,** a bronze statue of Gen. Robert E. Lee faces due north, continuing to stare down the Yankees.

SAINT CHARLES STREETCAR. Much of the Crescent City's fame derives from the **Vieux Carré,** but areas uptown have their fair share of beauty and action. The **Saint Charles Streetcar** still runs west of the French Quarter, passing some of the city's finest buildings, including the 19th-century homes along **Saint Charles Avenue.** *Gone With the Wind* fans will recognize the whitewashed bricks and elegant doorway of the house on the far right corner of Arabella St.—it's a replica of Tara. But frankly, my dear, it's not open to the public. For more views of fancy living, get off the streetcar in the **Garden District,** an opulent neighborhood around Jackson and Louisiana Ave.

CITY PARK. Brimming with golf courses, ponds, statues, Greek Revival gazebos, softball fields, a stadium, and **Storyland** (a theme park for kids), City Park is a huge green wonderland of non-alcoholic activities. Storyland is the kind of kids' entertainment parents long for, with an antique carousel and fishing from paddle boats in the 11 mi. of lagoons. The **New Orleans Botanical Garden** is also found here, with over 2000 varieties of plants and great Art Deco sculptures throughout the walks. *(1 Palm Dr., at the northern end of Esplanade Ave. ☎ 482-4888; www.neworelanscitypark.com. Maps at Jackson Sq. Visitors Center.)*

HISTORIC HOMES AND PLANTATIONS

Called the "Great Showplace of New Orleans," **Longue Vue House and Gardens** epitomizes the grand Southern estate with lavish furnishings, opulent decor, and sculpted gardens inspired by the Spanish Alhambra. *(7 Bamboo Rd., off Metairie Rd. ☎ 488-5488. Tours every hr. M-Sa 10am-4:30pm, Su 1-5pm. Tours available in English, French, German, Italian, Japanese, and Spanish. $10, seniors $9, students $5, under 5 free.)* On the way to Longue Vue, pause for a peek at the 85 ft. tall monument among the raised tombs in the **Metairie Cemetery**, where country/rock legend Gram Parsons is buried. Across from downtown New Orleans, **River Road** curves along the Mississippi River accessing several plantations preserved from the 19th century. *Great River Road Plantation Parade: A River of Riches*, available at New Orleans or Baton Rouge visitors centers, contains a good map and descriptions of the houses. Pick carefully, since a tour of all the privately owned plantations is expensive. Those below are listed in order from New Orleans to Baton Rouge.

HERMANN-GRIMA HISTORIC HOUSE. Built in 1831, the house exemplifies French style, replete with a large central hall, guillotine windows, a fan-lit entrance, and original parterre beds. On Thursdays from October to May, volunteers demonstrate period cooking in an 1830s Creole kitchen. *(820 St. Louis St. ☎ 525-5661. Tours every hr. M-F 10am-4pm; last tour 3:30pm. $6, ages 8-18 $5.)*

GALLIER HOUSE MUSEUM. The elegantly restored residence of James Gallier, Jr., the city's most famous architect, displays the taste and lifestyle of the wealthy in the 1860s. *(1118-1132 Royal St. ☎ 525-5661. Open M-Sa 10am-4pm; last tour 3:30pm. $6; students, seniors, and ages 8-18 $5; under 8 free.)*

SAN FRANCISCO PLANTATION HOUSE. Beautifully maintained since 1856, the San Francisco is an example of Creole style with a bright blue, peach, and green exterior. *(Rte. 44, 2 mi. northwest of Reserve, 42 mi. from New Orleans on the east bank of the Mississippi. Exit 206 off I-10. ☎ 535-2341 or 888-322-1756. Tours daily Mar.-Oct. 9:40am-4:30pm; Nov.-Feb. 10am-4pm. First tour leaves 9:40am, last tour 4pm. $10, ages 5-17 $5, under 5 free.)*

▨ LAURA: A CREOLE PLANTATION. Laura, unlike the others on the riverbank, was owned and operated by slave-owning Creoles who lived a life apart from that of white antebellum planters. Br'er Rabbit hopped into his first briar patch here, the site of the first recorded "Compair Lapin" West African stories. A valuable, unique look at plantation life in the South. *(2247 Hwy. 18/River Rd., at the intersection of Rte. 20 in Vacherie. ☎ 225-265-7690 or 888-799-7690. Tours based on the "memories" of the old plantation home daily 9:30am-4pm. Maximum 20min. wait. $10, ages 6-17 $5.)*

OAK ALLEY PLANTATION. The name Oak Alley refers to the magnificent lawn-alley bordered by 28 evenly spaced oaks corresponding to the 28 columns surrounding the Greek Revival house. The Greeks wouldn't have approved, though: the mansion is bright pink. *(3645 Rte. 18., between St. James and Vacherie St. ☎ 800-442-5539. Tours daily every 30min. Mar.-Oct. 9am-5:30pm; Nov.-Feb. 9am-5pm. $10, ages 13-18 $5, ages 6-12 $3.)*

NOTTOWAY PLANTATION. The largest plantation home in the South, Nottoway is often called the "White Castle of Louisiana." A 64-room mansion with 22 columns, a large ballroom, and a three-story stairway, it was the first choice for filming

Gone with the Wind, but the owners wouldn't allow it. *(30970 Hwy. Rte. 405., between Bayou Goula and White Castle, 18 mi. south of Baton Rouge on the southern bank of the Mississippi. ☎ 225-545-2730 or 888-323-8314. Open daily 9am-5pm. Lunch served daily 11am-3pm. Admission and 1hr. tour $10, under 12 $4, under 5 free.)*

🏛 MUSEUMS

▨ **New Orleans Pharmacy Museum,** 514 Chartres St. (☎ 565-8027), between St. Louis and Toulouse St. This apothecary shop was built by America's first licensed pharmacist in 1823. In the old house there are 19th-century "miracle drugs" like cocaine and opium, voodoo powders, a collection of old spectacles, the still-fertile botanical garden, and live leeches. Open Tu-Su 10am-5pm. $5, students and seniors $4, under 5 free.

▨ **National D-Day Museum,** 945 Magazine St. (☎ 527-6012), at Andrew Higgins Dr., in the Historic Warehouse District. Founded by historian Stephen Ambrose and dedicated in 2000 by Tom Hanks and Stephen Spielberg, this museum is an engaging study of WWII in its entirety, confronting the lesser-known, gruesome Pacific battles and issues of race and propaganda. Remarkable for its unbiased scrutiny. Open daily 9am-5pm. $14; students, seniors, and military $8; under 12 $6; military in uniform and under 5 free.

▨ **African-American Museum of Art, Culture, and History,** 1418 Gov. Nicholls St. (☎ 565-7497), 4 blocks north of Rampart St. in Tremé. In an 1829 Creole-style villa rescued from blight in 1991, this museum displays a variety of changing and permanent exhibits showcasing African-American artists, along with important historical themes. Slightly off the beaten path, the museum reveals a different New Orleans from the showy one of the French Quarter. Open M-F 10am-5pm, Sa 10am-2pm. $5, seniors $3, ages 4-17 $2.

Louisiana State Museum, P.O. Box 2448, New Orleans 70176 (☎ 800-568-6968; lsm.crt.state.la.us). The "State Museum" really oversees 8 separate museums, 6 of which are in New Orleans. The **Cabildo,** 701 Chartres St., portrays the history of Louisiana and holds Napoleon's death mask. The **Arsenal,** 615 St. Peter (enter through the Cabildo), recounts the history of the Mississippi River and New Orleans as a port city. The **Presbytère,** 751 Chartres St., features an interactive exhibit about Mardi Gras. The **1850 House,** 523 St. Ann St., on Jackson Sq., is—you guessed it—a recreated house from the time period. **Madame John's Legacy,** 632 Dumaine St., showcases Creole architecture as well as contemporary self-taught Louisiana artists. The **Old US Mint,** 400 Esplanade, focuses not only on currency, but on the history of jazz in an exhibit that includes Satchmo's first horn. All open Tu-Su 9am-5pm. Old US Mint, Cabildo, Presbytère: $5; students, seniors, and active military $4. 1850 House, Mme. John's Legacy: $3/$2. Under 12 free for all museums. 20% discount on tickets to 2 or more museums.

New Orleans Museum of Art (**NOMA**); (☎ 488-2631; www.noma.org), in City Park, at the City Park/Metairie exit off I-10. This museum houses art from North and South America, a magnificent glass collection, opulent works by the jeweler Fabergé, a strong collection of French paintings, as well as impressive African and Japanese cultural collections. The impressive new sculpture garden sprawls over acres of walkways. Open Tu-Su 10am-5pm. $8, seniors $7, ages 3-17 $4. Call for tickets to special exhibits.

The Voodoo Museum, 724 Dumaine St. (☎ 581-3824), in the Quarter. At this quirky haunt, learn why dusty shops in the Quarter sell *gris-gris* and alligator parts. A priest or a priestess will do a reading or a ritual for a fee, or visitors can just walk through the rooms full of artifacts for the entrance fee. Open daily 10am-6pm. $7; students, seniors, and military $5.50; high school students $4.50; ages 12 and under $3.50.

Musée Conti Wax Museum, 917 Conti St. (☎ 525-2605 or 800-233-5405), between Burgundy and Dauphine St. A great mix of the historically important, sensationally infamous, and just plain kitschy history of New Orleans in 31 tableaux. Perennial favorites include a voodoo scene and a mock-up of Madame LaLaurie's torture attic. Open M-Sa 10am-5:30pm, Su noon-5:30pm. $6.75, seniors $6.25, under 17 $5.75.

Confederate Museum, 929 Camp St. (☎ 523-4522), in a brownstone building called Memorial Hall, south of Lee Circle at Howard St. and the I-10 Camp St. Exit. The state's oldest museum is a wood-beamed hall with Confederate uniforms, flags, and Jefferson Davis memorabilia. Open M-Sa 10am-4pm. $5, students and seniors $4, under 12 $2.

ENTERTAINMENT

THEATER AND MUSIC

Le Petit Théâtre du Vieux Carré, 616 St. Peter St., is the oldest continuously operating community theater in the US. The 1789 building replicates the early 18th-century abode of Joseph de Pontalba, Louisiana's last Spanish governor. About five musicals and plays go up each year, as well as three fun productions in the "Children's Corner." (☎ 522-9958; www.lepetittheatre.com. Box office open M-Sa 10:30am-5:30pm, Su noon-showtime. $20 for plays, $26 for musicals.)

Uptown tends to house authentic Cajun dance halls and popular university hangouts, while the **Marigny** is home to New Orleans's alternative/local music scene. Check out *Off Beat*, free in many local restaurants; *Where Y'At*, another free entertainment weekly; or the Friday *Times-Picayune* to find out who's playing where. Born at the turn of the century in **Armstrong Park,** traditional New Orleans jazz still wails nightly at the tiny, historic **Preservation Hall,** 726 St. Peter St. With only two small ceiling fans trying to move the air around, the joint heats up in more ways than one. (Daytime ☎ 522-2841 or 800-785-5772, after 8pm 523-8939; www.preservationhall.com. No food or drink allowed. Cover $5. Doors open at 8pm; music 8:30pm-midnight.) Keep your ears open for **Cajun** and **zydeco** bands, which use accordions, washboards, triangles, and drums to perform hot dance tunes and saccharine waltzes. Anyone who thinks couple-dancing went out in the 50s should try a *fais-do-do*, a traditional dance that got its name from the custom parents had of putting their children to sleep before dancing the night away. (*Fais-do-do* is Cajun baby talk for "to make sleep.")

FESTIVALS

New Orleans's **Mardi Gras** celebration is the biggest party of the year, a world-renowned, epic bout of lascivious debauchery that fills the three weeks leading up to Ash Wednesday—the beginning of Lent and a time of penance and deprivation in the Catholic tradition. Mardi Gras, which literally means "Fat Tuesday," is an all-out hedonistic pleasure-fest before 40 days of purity—and tourists pour in by the plane-full (flights into the city and hotel rooms fill up months in advance). In 2005, Mardi Gras falls on February 8th, and the biggest parades and the bulk of the partying will take place the two weeks prior to that. The ever-expanding **New Orleans Jazz and Heritage Festival** (Apr. 22-May 1, 2005) attracts 7000 musicians from around the country to the city's fairgrounds. The likes of Aretha Franklin, Bob Dylan, and Wynton Marsalis have graced this festival. Music plays simultaneously on 12 stages in the midst of a food and crafts festival; the biggest names perform evening riverboat concerts. (☎ 522-4786; www.nojazzfest.com.)

NIGHTLIFE

BARS

FRENCH QUARTER

Lafitte's Blacksmith Shop, 941 Bourbon St. (☎ 522-9377), at Phillip St. Appropriately, one of New Orleans's oldest standing structures is a bar—one of the oldest bars in the US. Built in the 1730s, the building is still lit by candlelight after sunset. Named for the scheming hero of the Battle of New Orleans, it offers shaded relief from the elements of the city and a dim hiding place for celebrities. Beer $4-5. Live piano 8pm-late. Open daily 10 or 11am to 4 or 5am.

🎷 **Funky Butt,** 714 N. Rampart St. (☎558-0872), is an awesome hideout to hear live jazz and marvel at the wonder of the *derrière*. Walk in to face a gigantic, languorous nude painting and hear the strains of a live band 5 ft. from the door. Stay to sip a funkybutt-juice ($6) and sit with a select group in the tiny space alongside the band. House band plays at 7pm. Sets nightly 10pm and midnight. Cover $5-10. Open daily 7pm-2am.

Donna's, 800 N. Rampart St. (☎596-6914). As one fan says about this restaurant-bar, this is "the place where you can sit and watch New Orleans roll by." On the edge of the French Quarter, where the gay bars face the projects, and the extremes of the city swirl together. Brass bands play inside, the smell of ribs and chicken wafts out, and customers sit on the sidewalk and take it all in. Open M and Th-Su 8:30pm-1:30am.

Fritzel's, 733 Bourbon St. (☎561-0432), between Orleans and St. Ann, was opened over 30 years ago by a German proprietor who wanted to give musicians of all abilities the chance to play. It has hosted some of the best traditional and dixie band jazz in the Quarter every night. Although cocktails are still Bourbon St. pricey ($6 for most beers), there's no cover. Open daily 1pm-2am, with entertainment from 8 or 9pm.

Pat O'Brien's, 718 St. Peter St. (☎525-4823). Housed in the first Spanish theater in the US, this busy bar, one of the most famous in the French Quarter, bursts with rosy-cheeked patrons who carouse in a courtyard lined with plants and flowers. Home of the original Hurricane. If you're feeling sentimental, purchase your first in a souvenir glass ($9, without glass $6). Open M-Th 11am-4am, F-Su 10am-5am.

Pirate's Alley, 622 Pirate's Alley (☎524-9332), down the alley on your left when facing the St. Louis Cathedral. Its location on a side street, compounded by the plain wooden walls and awnings, make this bar feel like a safe haven in what can be a sensory-overload city. White Russian $6. Open daily noon till whenever they feel like closing.

OUTSIDE THE QUARTER

The Spotted Cat, 623 Frenchmen St. (☎943-3887), is what you might have imagined most New Orleans bars would be like: cheap beer ($2-4, or $20 bottles of champagne if you're looking to live the high life), a place to sit and chill, and passion-filled trumpets, voices, and piano solos that pour out the front door onto the sidewalk. The wooden walls and floors make for excellent acoustics. "Early" band 6:30pm, "late" band 10pm. Never a cover, just a 1-drink min. (domestics $2 during happy hour). Open M-F 2pm-late, Sa-Su from noon-late.

Snug Harbor, 626 Frenchmen St. (☎949-0696), near Decatur St. Regulars include big names in jazz like Charmaine Neville and Ellis Marsalis. Cover is sometimes steep ($10-25), but the music, played in the beautiful, intimate cypress "jazz room" is incredible. Shows nightly 9, 11pm. All ages. Restaurant open Su-Th 5-11pm, F-Sa 5pm-midnight; bar until 1am. The kitchen closes early some nights; call ahead to find out if they are serving. Advance ticket purchase recommended, especially for weekend events.

Checkpoint Charlie's, 501 Esplanade (☎949-7012), is a combination bar, laundromat, and restaurant that feels like a cozy neighborhood coffeeshop or a wild nightclub, depending on where you're standing. You can drink while you wash your clothes, listen to a poetry slam over jazz, buy a used book, or have a greasy burger while shooting a game of pool. Beer $2-3, pitchers $7.50. Burgers $5-7. Live music nightly, usually starting around 8pm. No cover. Open 24hr.

Carrollton Station, 8140 Willow St. (☎865-9190), at Dublin St. A cozy neighborhood club with live music, antique bar games, and friendly folks. As one regular once said, this is "a place with character full of characters." 12 beers on tap ($2-5) and well-stocked bar. Music F-Sa at 10pm. Cover varies, usually $5-8. Open daily 3pm-6am.

d.b.a., 618 Frenchmen St. (☎942-3731), next to Snug Harbor. Try one of the beers on tap in their wood-paneled bar. It's a twenty-something kind of place and there's live music most nights at 10pm. Monthly beer and tequila tastings. No cover. 1-drink min. Open M-F 4pm-4am, Sa-Su 4pm-5am.

DANCE CLUBS

FRENCH QUARTER

House of Blues, 225 Decatur St. (☎529-2624). A sprawling complex with a large music/ dance hall (capacity over 1000) and a balcony and bar overlooking the action. Check out the gospel brunch on Su. Concerts nightly 9:15pm. 18+. Cover usually $5-10, big names up to $30. Restaurant open Su-Th 11am-11pm, F-Sa 11am-midnight.

735 Nightclub and Bar, 735 Bourbon St. (☎581-6740). Dance music and a hip mixed-age crowd keep this club energized well into the night. Techno, progressive house, and trance play downstairs, with 80s music on the back patio every Th. 18+. Cover $5, under 21 $10 Th-Sa only. Open M-W 2pm-midnight, Th-Su 2pm-4am.

OUTSIDE THE QUARTER

▨ **Tipitina's,** 501 Napoleon Ave. (☎895-8477). The best local bands and some big national names—such as the Neville Brothers and Harry Connick, Jr.—play so close you can almost touch them. Cajun *fais-do-dos* (p. 485) Su 5-9pm. 18+. Cover $7-25. Music usually W-Su 9pm-3am; call ahead for times and prices.

Mid City Lanes Rock 'n' Bowl, 4133 S. Carrollton Ave. (☎482-3133), in the mini-mall at Tulane Ave. Since 1941, this place has attracted multi-tasking partiers to its rockin' lanes. The "home of Rock 'n' Bowl" is a bowling alley by day and traditional dance club by night (you can bowl at night, too). Drinks $2.50-3.50. Lanes $15 per hr. plus $1 for shoes. Live music Tu-W 8:30pm; local zydeco Th 9:30pm, F-Sa 10pm. 18+ at night when the bar gets hopping. Cover $3-10. Open daily noon to around 1 or 2am.

◪ GLBT ACTIVITIES

New Orleans has a long history of sexual diversity, touching on all strands of haute societe, but this never really met with public approval. In spite of the private clubs and mixed bars that have existed for hundreds of years, only today does the city have an open and vibrant gay scene. It is less exclusive than many other urban gay scenes and many straight people visit gay venues because the drinks are cheaper and stronger—and because you are less likely to get into a fight. Someone is keeping track of gay history in New Orleans: Robert Batson, "history laureate," leads the ▨**Gay Heritage Tour**—a walking tour through the French Quarter—leaving from Alternatives, 909 Bourbon St. It lasts for 2½hr. and is perhaps the best possible introduction to New Orleans for anyone, gay or straight. (☎945-6789. W and Sa 2pm. $20 per person. Reservations required.)

You'll find the majority of gay establishments toward the northeast end of Bourbon St. ("downriver"), and along St. Ann St., known to some as the **"Lavender Line."** A good point of reference is where St. Ann St. and Bourbon cross—**Oz** is to the riverside and **Bourbon Pub** is to the lakeside. These are the two biggest gay danceclubs and principal gay institutions in the city. To find the real lowdown on gay nightlife, get a copy of *The Whiz Magazine*, a locally produced guide; there's always a copy on top of the radiator in Cafe Lafitte in Exile. *Ambush* is a more impersonal, mass-produced gay entertainment mag that can be found at many French Quarter businesses. For info and tailored entertainment and community fact sheets, go to the **Lesbian and Gay Community Center of New Orleans,** 2114 Decatur St., in Marigny. (☎945-1103. Open M-F 2-8pm, Sa 11am-6pm. Report hate crimes to ☎944-4325.)

NIGHTLIFE

Cafe Lafitte in Exile, 901 Bourbon St. (☎522-8397). Exiled from Laffite's Blacksmith Shop in 1953 when Lafitte's came under new management, the ousted gay patrons trooped up the street to found the oldest gay bar in America. On the opening night, surrounded by patrons dressed as their favorite exile, Cafe Lafitte in Exile lit an "eternal flame" (it still burns today) that aptly represents the soul of the gay community in New Orleans. Today, though Cafe Lafitte has video screens, occasional live music, pageants, and shows, it's still the same old neighborhood gathering place at heart. Open 24hr.

Good Friends, 740 Dauphine St. (☎566-7191). This is a gay "Cheers" episode. A cozy, friendly neighborhood bar full of locals happy to welcome in a refugee from Bourbon St. Despite the occasional pool tournament, drink specials, and "hot buns" contest, usually things are pretty calm. Don't miss sing-a-long Sundays afternoon. Open 24hr.

Cowpokes, 2240 St. Claude Ave. (☎947-0505), 1 block off Elysian Fields in Marigny. Line dancing, country-western lube wrestling on W, 10-gallon hats, and spurs can be as wholesome as you want to make them. Both cowgirls and pardners are welcome. Tu country line dancing lessons at 8pm, free. Happy hour daily 4-9pm. Open Su-Th 4pm-1am, F-Sa 4pm-2am. Cowpokes also has a great **theater** that puts on drama performances F-Su. There are about 4 productions per year (for info ☎947-0505; www.dramano.org). *Take a cab here as the area can be unsafe at night.*

◪ OUTDOOR ACTIVITIES

The St. Charles Streetcar eventually makes its way to **Audubon Park,** near **Tulane University.** Audubon contains lagoons, statues, stables, and the award-winning ◪**Audubon Zoo,** 6500 Magazine St., where white alligators swim in a recreated Louisiana swamp. Tigers, elephants, rhinos, and sea lions, among others, are grouped into exhibit areas that highlight historical and natural regions of the globe, while peacocks roam the walkways freely. There is a free museum shuttle between the streetcar stop and zoo entrance every 15min. (☎581-4629. Zoo open in summer M-F 9:30am-5pm, Sa-Su 9:30am-6pm; in winter daily 9:30am-5pm. $11, seniors $7, ages 2-12 $6. Combination tickets with the aquarium are $20/$15/$11.)

One of the most unique sights in the New Orleans area, the coastal wetlands along Lake Salvador make up a segment of the **Jean Lafitte National Historical Park** called the **Barataria Preserve,** 7400 Barataria Blvd. South of New Orleans, take Business 90 to Rte. 45. (☎589-2330. Daily park-sponsored foot tour through the swamp 11am. Free maps and trail guides allow you to complete some walks yourself. Open daily 7am-5pm; extended summer hours. **Visitors center** open daily 9am-5pm. Free.) Many commercial boat tours operate in the park; **Cypress Swamp Tours** will pick you up from your hotel. (☎581-4501 or 800-633-0503. 2hr. tours 9:30, 11:30am, 1:30pm. $22, with hotel pick up $39; ages 6-12 $12/$22. Call for reservations.)

BATON ROUGE   ☎225

Once the site of a tall cypress tree marking the boundary between rival Native American tribes, Baton Rouge ("red stick") has blossomed into Louisiana's second largest city. State politics have shaped this town—it was once home to governor, senator, and demagogue "Kingfish" Huey P. Long. The presence of **Louisiana State University (LSU)** adds an element of youth and rabid Tigertown loyalty. Baton Rouge has a simple meat-and-potatoes flavor, albeit spiced with a history of political corruption, that stands in contrast to the sauciness of New Orleans.

◪ **PRACTICAL INFORMATION.** From east to west, the three main streets in Baton Rouge are N. Foster Dr., N. Acadian Thwy., and 22nd St. Baton Rouge Terr. Beginning in the north, Florida Blvd. and Government St. run perpendicular to these.

Close to downtown, **Greyhound,** 1253 Florida Blvd. (☎383-3811 or 800-231-2222; open 24hr.), at 13th St., sends buses to Lafayette (1hr., 8 per day, $15) and New Orleans (2hr., 6 per day, $17). *The area is unsafe at night.* **Public Transit: Capitol Transportation,** ☎389-8282. Runs buses every 30min. 7:15am-7:30pm. $1.25, seniors and children $0.90. **Taxi: Yellow Cab** ☎355-3133. **Visitor Info: State Capitol Visitors Center,** on the first floor of the state capitol, is your best bet for information on the city and region. (☎342-7317. Open daily 8am-4:30pm.) The more corporate **Baton Rouge Convention and Visitors Bureau** is at 730 North Blvd. (☎383-1825; www.bracvb.com. Open M-F 8am-4:30pm.) For community information, including weather, call **Community Connection** (☎267-4221; www.br.com). **Internet Access: State Library of Louisiana,** 701 N. 4th St., a beautiful library with free, fast Internet access—most often without a wait. (☎342-4915. Open M-F 8am-4:30pm.) On weekends access is available at **East Baton Rouge Parish Library,** 7711 Goodwood Blvd. (☎231-3740. Open M-Th 8am-10pm, F-Sa 8am-6pm, Su 2-10pm. Free.) **Post Office:** 750 Florida Blvd., off River Rd. (☎800-275-8777. Open M-F 7:30am-5pm, Sa 8am-12:30pm.) **Postal Code:** 70821. **Area Code:** 225.

⚑ ACCOMMODATIONS. Downtown rooms are pricey, especially during midweek when state capitol business is underway. The university area, however, is home to several motels. For the budget-savvy who need a place to rest their heads before heading out to the swamp, the new and locally-owned **Highland Inn ❷,** 2605 S. Range Ave., at I-12 Exit 10 in Denham Springs, is 15min. from downtown. (☎667-7177. Cable TV, continental breakfast, free local calls, and pool. Singles $45; doubles $90.) To get to the **Motel 6 ❸,** 10445 Rieger Rd., take the Siegen Ln. exit from I-10, a 10min. drive from downtown. Newly renovated, clean rooms make this chain experience a pleasant one. (☎291-4912. Cable TV, complimentary coffee, free local calls, pool, and kids under 18 stay free. Singles $49; doubles $57.) **KOA Kampground ❶,** 7628 Vincent Rd., 1 mi. off I-12 at the Denham Springs exit, keeps 110 well-maintained sites, clean facilities, hot showers and a big pool. (☎664-7281 or 800-562-5673. Sites $19, full RV hookup $28, 50 amp $30. Cabins $35.)

◪⚑ FOOD AND ENTERTAINMENT. Downtown, sandwich shops and cafes line 3rd St.; the **casinos** boast some of the city's best cuisine. For simple, small-town fare, check out the **Frostop ❶,** 402 Government St., downtown, with a giant, gracefully aging root beer can out front. Grilled cheese goes for $1.29, burgers for $3, and seafood platters for $8-10. The Frostop also has an amazing selection of floats, shakes, sundaes, and malts for $2-4. (☎344-1179. Open M-F 10am-7pm, Sa 10am-7pm.) Head to LSU at the intersection of Highland Rd. and Chimes St., off I-10, for cheap chow, bars, and smoothie shops. **Louie's Cafe ❷,** 209 W. State St., grills up fabulous omelettes ($5.25-10) and some great veggie fare in a cross between college hangout and mama's kitchen. Early mornings and late nights are really busy. (☎346-8221. Veggie po' boy $5.50. Open 24hr.) At **The Chimes ❸,** 3357 Highland Rd., at Chimes St., you can sample a beer from almost every country; Chimes stocks 120 brews with 30 on tap. Start with Louisiana alligator (farm-raised, marinated, fried, or blackened, and served with Dijon mustard sauce) for $7.50, then dig into some $8 crawfish *étoufée.* (☎383-1754. Seafood and steak entrees $8-15. Open M-Sa 11am-2am, Su 11am-11:45pm.) Next door is **Varsity,** 5535 Highland Rd., which has hosted some big names in recent years including Tori Amos and They Might Be Giants. (☎383-7018. Beer $2.50. Shots $3.50-4. Cover up to $45, depending on band. Usually open 8pm-2am; hours vary.) Pick up a copy of *Revellie,* LSU's free bi-weekly paper (published daily during school time) for complete listings.

◪ SIGHTS. In a move reminiscent of Ramses II, Huey Long ordered the construction of the **Louisiana State Capitol,** referred to as "the new capitol"—a somewhat startling skyscraper completed over a mere 14 months in 1931 and 1932. "The house that Huey built," was meant to raise Louisiana's prestige and pave Long's path to the presidency. Ironically, Long was assassinated inside it 3 years later; a display marks the spot of the shooting. The **observation deck,** on the 27th floor, provides a panoramic view of the surrounding area. (☎342-5914. Open M-Sa 9am-4pm, Su noon-4pm. Last tour 3pm. Free.) The **Old State Capitol,** 100 North Blvd., resembles a cathedral with a fantastic cast-iron spiral staircase and domed stained glass. Inside, interactive political displays urge voter responsibility alongside exhibits about Huey P. and Louisiana's tumultuous (and often corrupt) political history. (☎800-488-2968. Open Tu-Sa 10am-4pm, Su noon-4pm. $4, seniors $3, students $2.) The **Old Governor's Mansion,** 502 North Blvd., may look familiar—Huey Long insisted that his governor's residence resemble his ultimate goal, the White House. Inside, peruse many of Long's personal belongings, including a book he wrote, somewhat prematurely, called *My First Days in the White House.* (☎387-2464. Open Tu-F 10am-4pm; hours may vary. Last tour 3pm. $5, seniors $4, students $3.)

The **Louisiana Art and Science Museum (LASM),** 100 S. River Rd., is a large, expanding complex and a strange combination of art gallery and hands-on science museum that recently opened a state-of-the-art planetarium. (☎344-5272; www.lasm.org. Open Tu-F 10am-4pm, Sa 10am-5pm, Su 1-5pm. $5; students, seniors, and children $4. First Su of every month free.) At the **USS Kidd and Nautical Center,** 305 S. River Rd., at Government St., you can check out the Destroyer Kidd, which was hit directly by a kamikaze during its career and has been restored to its WWII glory. (☎342-1942. Open daily 9am-5pm. $6, children $3.50, under 5 free.)

The **LSU Rural Life Museum,** 4560 Essen Ln., just off I-10 at Exit 160, depicts the life of 18th- and 19th-century Creoles and working-class Louisianans through their original furnished shops, cabins, and storage houses. Right next door, explore the lakes, winding paths, and flowers of the **Windrush Gardens.** The semi-formal gardens contain native plants used during the time period. (☎765-2437. Both open daily 8:30am-5pm. Joint admission $7, seniors $6, ages 5-11 $4, under 5 free.)

NATCHITOCHES   ☎318

Be careful not to say it how it's spelled; pronounced *NAK-ah-tish*, the oldest city in Louisiana was founded in 1714 by the French to facilitate trade with the Spanish in Mexico. The town was named after the original Native American inhabitants of the region. With its strategic location along the banks of the Red River, Natchitoches should have become a major port city; a big logjam, however, changed the course of the city's history, redirecting the river and leaving the town high and dry, with only a 36 mi. long lake running along historic downtown. Today it makes for a romantic setting as you stroll along the lakefront at night, when jazz seeps out of the bars on one side and a fountain illuminates the lake on the other.

◪ PRACTICAL INFORMATION. Downtown Natchitoches is tiny. **Highway 6** enters town from the west off I-49 and becomes **Front Street,** the main drag, where it follows the **Cane River,** running north until it becomes Hwy. 6 again. **Second Street** runs parallel to Front St., and the town stems out across the lake from those two streets. Historic homes highlight the town, while the plantations lie 7 to 18 mi. south of town, off **Route 1 South.** Both the plantations and Rte. 1 follow the Cane River. **Greyhound,** 331 Cane River Shopping Center (☎352-8341; open M-F 7:30-11am and noon-4pm), sends buses to: Dallas (6hr., 3 per day, $56); Houston (8-10hr., 4 per day, $61); New Orleans (6-8hr., 3 per day, $51). Maps and accommodation info are available at the **Natchitoches Convention and Visitors Bureau,** 781 Front St. (☎352-8072 or 800-259-1714; www.natchitoches.net. Open M-F 8am-6pm, Sa 9am-5pm, Su 10am-4pm.) The **post office** is at

240 St. Denis St. (☎ 352-0378. Open M-F 8am-4:30pm, Sa 9-11am.) **Internet Access: Natchitoches Public Library,** 450 2nd St. (☎ 357-3280. Open M-F 9am-6pm, Sa 9am-5pm. Free.) **Postal Code:** 71457. **Area Code:** 318.

⌂ ACCOMMODATIONS. Natchitoches isn't a cheap town. As the "B&B Capital" of Louisiana, Natchitoches abounds with cozy rooms in historic homes, but during the annual **Christmas Festival of Lights** (p. 492), room rates can triple, and reservations are needed months in advance. An authentic taste of Natchitoches can be had at the elegant and reasonably priced ▨**Chaplin House Bed and Breakfast ❸,** 434 2nd St. The well-travelled proprietors of this exquisitely restored and decorated 1892 home boast a wealth of local knowledge. (☎ 352-2324; www.natchitoches.net/chaplin. Gay friendly. Full continental breakfast, including fresh home-baked bread. Singles $55; doubles $80.) One of the best deals is the **Fleur de Lis Bed and Breakfast ❸,** 336 2nd St., near the southern end of town, an adorable, gingerbready Victorian with a whimsical pastel exterior and quirky flavor all its own. You can relax in rocking chairs out on the balcony alongside plant pots overflowing with herbs. (☎ 352-6621 or 800-489-6621. Rooms Jan.-Nov. $65-85; Dec. $100.)

West of town, you'll find the well-furnished **Microtel Inn ❸,** 5335 Rte. 6 W at University Pkwy. (☎ 214-0700 or 888-771-7171. A/C, cable TV, fridges, pool access, and continental breakfast. Singles $52; doubles $60. 10% AAA discount.) Farther out, the 600,000-acre **Kisatchie National Forest ❶** offers basic outdoor living with trails and scenic overlooks. The park is about 25 mi. south of the Rte. 6 Ranger Station near Natchitoches. Many of its sites, though equipped with bathhouses, are primitive. The **Kisatchie Ranger District,** 106 Rte. 6 W, ¼ mi. past the Microtel Inn, has maps, and park conditions, and provides help finding the well-hidden campsites. (☎ 352-2568; www.r8web.com/kisatchie. Open M-F 8am-4:30pm. Sites $2-3.)

> **TIP**
> Many places in Louisiana have a standard opening time and a closing time that is up for negotiation. If people are having a good time, businesses will often stay open into the small hours or not close at all. If it's slow, however, owners may decide to close up early and go home. Keep in mind that when the hours of an establishment just say "open till," they mean "open till we feel like closing."

◪▧ FOOD AND NIGHTLIFE. ▨**Lasyone's ❷,** 622 2nd St., is the place to go for down-home cooking. Their specialty is meat pie ($3; with salad bar and veggies $8), and travelers can get an eyeful of the 5 ft. meat pie model in the window before enjoying one of more manageable dimensions. (☎ 352-3353. Lunch specials $6. Open M-Sa 7am-till, usually after 6pm.) **Mama's Oyster House ❷,** 606 Front St., is a downtown institution, cooking up lunch gumbo for $9 a bowl and oyster po' boys for $7. For dinner, fried crawfish ($12) complements live jazz and rock on the first and third Friday of each month. (☎ 356-7874. Open M-Sa 11am-10pm.) Next door to Mama's is, of course, **Papa's ❶,** 604 Front St., a great place to get Natchitoches meat pie ($7), a veggie salad ($5), or stuffed potatoes ($4). The atmosphere is casual and relaxed. (☎ 356-5850. Open M-Sa 11am-10pm.) Drink with a friendly, local crowd at **Pioneer Pub,** 812 Washington St., opposite the visitors center. Its blend of neon lighting and musty old-world charm works surprisingly well. (☎ 352-4884. Live music Sa 9pm. Open daily 11am-2am, or until the crowd leaves.)

◪▧ SIGHTS AND ENTERTAINMENT. Much of Natchitoches's charm lies on the Cane River Lake along **Front Street,** where coffeeshops, casual restaurants, and antique stores fill the storefronts of historical buildings that date back to the mid-19th century. To see Natchitoches's landmarks—including many of the sites where *Steel Magnolias* was filmed—from the comfort of a large, green trolley, take a 1hr. ride with the **Natchitoches Transit Company,** 100 Rue Beau Port, next to the visitors center. (☎356-8687. Call for departure times. $8, seniors $7, ages 3-12 $5.)

Many of the popular tourist destinations are in the **Cane River National Heritage Area,** the plantation-dotted countryside around Natchitoches. The visitors center has information about all the plantations and a free tourist guide, *Cane River Heritage Area,* which lists points of interest in the area. To see the next generation of handbags, drive out to **Alligator Park,** 8 mi. north of Natchitoches off Rte. 1 N (look for the school bus in the shape of a gator off Rte. 1). Originally a conservation project, the park now entertains visitors with regular feeding shows (11:30am-4:30pm), a snake house, an aviary, and a nutria (swamp rats the size of small dogs) exhibit. (☎354-0001 or 877-354-7001. Open daily mid-Apr. to Oct. 10am-6pm; call for winter hours, when the alligators are hibernating. $6.50, ages 3-12 $4.75.) A string of plantation homes line the Cane River, south of downtown along Rte. 1. The **Melrose Plantation,** 14 mi. south on Rte. 1, then left on Rte. 493, is unique in origin—its female founder was an ex-slave. The African House, one of the outhouses, is the oldest structure of Congo-like architecture in North America. (☎379-0055. Open daily noon-4pm. $6, ages 13-17 $4, ages 6-12 $3.)

While Natchitoches may not see a white Christmas, she'll most definitely see a bright one. The town's residents spend months putting up some 300,000 Christmas bulbs, only to be greeted in turn by 150,000 camera-toting tourists flocking like moths to the **City of Lights** display, held during the **Christmas Festival of Lights.** After a barge parade down the river on Friday, the month-long exhibition peaks the first Saturday in December when a carnival-like atmosphere—complete with a fair and fireworks—fills the air. (☎800-259-1714; www.christmasfestival.com.) From April to November all can enjoy the **Cane River Green Market,** a wonderful open-air farmers market on the banks of the Cane River downtown. It's big on organic produce, locally grown fruit, and recycling initiatives. (☎352-2746. Open Sa 9am-1pm.)

ACADIANA

Throughout the early 18th century, the English government in Nova Scotia became increasingly jealous of the prosperity of French settlers (Acadians) and deeply offended by their refusal to kneel before the British Crown. During the war with France in 1755, the British rounded up the Acadians and deported them by the shipload in what came to be called *le grand dérangement,* or "the Great Upheaval." The "Cajuns" (as they are known today) of St. Martin, Lafayette, New Iberia, and St. Mary parishes are descendants of these settlers. In the 1920s, Louisiana passed laws forcing Acadian schools to teach in English. Later, during the oil boom of the 1970s and 1980s, oil executives and developers envisioned the Acadian center of Lafayette as the Houston of Louisiana and threatened to flood the area with mass culture. Even so, the proud people of southern Louisiana have resisted such homogenization, and, in fact, the state is officially bilingual.

LAFAYETTE ☎337

The center of Acadiana, Lafayette is ripe for ripping up the dance floors to soul-moving zydeco, getting to know the sweet simple flavor of boiled crawfish, and experiencing the splendor of the magnificent Atchafalaya Basin. Get beyond the highway's chains and into downtown on Jefferson St., and there is no question that Cajuns rule the roost. Dance floors heat up every night of the week, and many locals continue to answer their phones with a proud *bonjour.*

🛈 PRACTICAL INFORMATION. Lafayette stands at a crossroads. **I-10** leads east to New Orleans and west to Lake Charles; **U.S. 90** heads south to New Iberia and the Atchafalaya Basin, and **I-49** heads north to Alexandria and Shreveport. Most of the city is west of the **Evangeline Thruway (I-49/U.S. 90)**, which runs north-south. **Johnston Boulevard** intersects Evangeline Thwy. and is the main street through town. **Jefferson Street** runs north-south through central downtown and is full of fun places to eat and drink. **Amtrak**, 133 E. Grant St. (☎800-872-7245). The "Sunset" calls three times per week en route to: Houston (5½hr., $36); New Orleans (4hr., $21); San Antonio (11hr., $55). Next door, **Greyhound** (☎235-1541; open 24hr.) runs to: Baton Rouge (1hr., 6 per day, $13); New Iberia (40min., 1 per day, $9); New Orleans (3-5hr., 5 per day, $21.) **Public Transit:** The **Lafayette Bus System**, 1515 E. University St., is centered at Lee and Garfield St. (☎291-8570; schedules www.lafayettelinc.net/lts. Infrequent service M-Sa 6:30am-6:30pm; service until 11pm on some routes. Buses approximately every 30min. $0.75, ages 5-12 $0.50, seniors and disabled $0.35.) **Taxi: Yellow/Checker Cab Inc.** ☎234-2111. **Visitor Info: Lafayette Parish Convention and Visitors Commission,** 1400 N. Evangeline Thwy. (☎232-3808; www.lafayettetravel.com. Open M-F 8:30am-5pm, Sa-Su 9am-5pm. Provides free maps and discount coupons.) **Medical Services: Lafayette General Medical Center,** 1214 Coolidge Ave. (☎289-7991). **Internet Access: Lafayette Public Library,** 301 W. Congress St. (☎261-5787. Open M-Th 9am-9pm, F 9am-6pm, Sa 9am-5pm, Su 1-5pm. Free.) **Post Office:** 1105 Moss St. (☎269-7111. Open M-F 8am-5:30pm, Sa 8:30am-noon.) **Postal Code:** 70501. **Area Code:** 337.

🛏 ACCOMMODATIONS. One of the best lodging experiences to be had in the South awaits you at ▧**Blue Moon Guest House ❶**, 215 E. Convent St. As you enter, check out the walkway paved with (fake) doubloons and the local art showcased on the surrounding walls. A large air-conditioned dorm and comfy private rooms are accompanied by a spacious common area, a deck out back, and an attached "saloon" where local and out-of-town bands whoop it up Wednesday through Saturday. Guests get free concert access and a complimentary drink at the bar, as well as Internet access ($3 per day) and use of the kitchen. (☎234-3442 or 877-766-2583. Dorms $18; private rooms $40-80.) Inexpensive hotels line the Evangeline Thwy. **Travel Host Inn South ❷**, 1314 N. Evangeline, rents out large, clean rooms with cable TV, microwaves, fridges, continental breakfast, and an outdoor pool. (☎233-2090. Singles $37; doubles $45.) Close to the center of Lafayette, **Acadiana Park Campground ❶**, 1201 E. Alexander, off Louisiana Ave., has 75 sites with access to tennis courts and a soccer field. (☎291-8388. Office open M-Th and Sa-Su 8am-5pm, F 8am-8pm. Full hookup $9.) The lakeside, but more commercial, **KOA Lafayette ❶**, 5 mi. west of town on I-10 at Exit 97, has over 200 sites and offers a store, mini golf course, and two pools. (☎235-2739. Reception daily 7:30am-9pm. 2-person sites with water and electricity $31, additional persons $3 each.)

🍴 FOOD. It's not hard to find reasonably priced Cajun and Creole cuisine in Lafayette, a city that prides itself on food. Of course, music is also a priority, and can be found live in most of those same restaurants at night. Since 1927, **Dwyer's Cafe ❶**, 323 Jefferson St., a diner with stained glass and murals on the walls, has been the best place in town to get breakfast or lunch. They serve a bang-up breakfast (grits, eggs, ham, biscuits, juice, and coffee) for $4. At lunch locals saunter in from the heat to eat a plate lunch (different every day) of gigantic proportions for $7. (☎235-9364. Open M-F 5am-4pm, Sa-Su 5am-2pm.) In central Lafayette, **Chris's Po' Boys ❷**, 631 Jefferson St., offers seafood platters ($8-12) and—whaddya know—po' boys for under $6. (☎234-1696. F night live Cajun music in the spring and fall. Open M-F 11am-8pm.) For great alternative cuisine on the cheap check out the **Cedar Deli ❶**, 1115 Jefferson St. across the parking lot from Blue Moon Guest House. For 25 years, Syrian owner Nabil Loli has been serving up $5 *muffalatas*, *halloumi*, and falafel. (☎233-5460. Open M-F 9am-5pm, Sa 9am-4pm. Superb ice cream awaits you at **Borden's ❶**, 1103 Jefferson St., which has great malts ($2.50-4.25), sundaes ($2.50-3.50), and a huge banana split ($4). Around since 1940, the joint gets jumping on Sundays after church. The strawberry cheesecake ice cream is to die for. (☎235-9291. Open M-Tu 2-9pm, W-Su 11am-9pm.) **The Filling Station ❶**, 900 Jefferson St., lives up to its name. Occupying the shell of an old gas station, the restaurant serves gigantic burritos and burgers; from March to May you can stock up on shrimp and crawfish ($8). Their full bar will fill your tank nicely, and you can rock out to live music as well—an acoustic group performs on Thursdays and a 70s/80s rock band performs on Fridays. (☎291-9625. Burritos $4-7. Margaritas $5. Kitchen open M-F 11am-9pm; bar open until people empty out.)

🄶 SIGHTS. Driving through south-central Louisiana means driving over America's largest swamp, the **Atchafalaya Basin.** It's a unique environment consisting of hundreds of miles of shallow waterways inhabited by alligators, wildcats, and residential and migratory birds. There's a bizarre **visitors center** at I-10 Exit 112, 1934 Atchafalaya River Hwy., just a few minutes east of Lafayette. The free and spectacularly cheesy introduction to the swamp includes greetings from a talking raccoon who ushers you into a theater for a spectacular light and sound show about the beautiful landscapes of the basin. The show is only 3min. long—leaving plenty of time to fill up on the free coffee and talk to the helpful guides. (☎228-1094. Open daily 8:30am-5pm.) The **Atchafalaya Freeway** (I-10 between Lafayette and Baton Rouge) crosses 32 mi. of swamp and cypress trees. Follow signs to **McGee's Landing**, 1337 Henderson Rd., which sends three 1½hr. **boat tours** into the basin each day. (☎228-2384. Tours daily 10am, 1, 3pm. Spring and fall sunset tours by reservation. $15, seniors $12, under 12 $6, under 2 free.) The **🄼Acadian Cultural Center,** 501 Fisher Rd. (take Johnston St. to Surrey, then follow the signs), is a unit of the **Jean Lafitte National Historical Park and Preserve** that runs throughout the delta region of Louisiana. The Acadian Center has a dramatic 40min. documentary chronicling the arrival of the Acadians in Louisiana, as well as a 16min. film on conservation efforts in the Atchafalaya swamp and terrific bilingual exhibits on Cajun history and culture. (☎232-0789. Open daily 8am-5pm. Shows every hr. 9am-4pm. Free.) Next door, you can take a self-guided tour of a "living museum" that recreates the Acadian settlement of **Vermilionville**, 1600 Surrey St., with Acadian music, crafts, food, actors in costume, and dancing on the Bayou Vermilion banks. (☎233-4077 or 800-992-2968. Live bands Su 1-4pm. Cajun cooking demos daily 10:30am, 12:30, 1:30pm. Open Tu-Su 10am-4pm. Last admission 3pm. $8, seniors $6.50, ages 6-18 $5.) **Acadian Village**, 200 Greenleaf Rd., features authentic 19th-century Cajun homes with an array of artifacts and period displays. While at the village, see the collection of 19th-century medical paraphernalia at the **Doctor's House.** (☎981-2489 or 800-962-9133. Both open daily 10am-5pm. $7, seniors $6, ages 6-14 $4.) Closer to downtown, **Saint John's Cathedral Oak**, 914 St. John St., shades an entire lawn with spidery branches reaching from a trunk 19 ft. in circumference.

🄳🄵 ENTERTAINMENT AND NIGHTLIFE. While in Lafayette, be sure to take advantage of the many local festivals and music performances, starting with **Downtown Alive!**, a 12-week annual concert series held at the 700 block of Jefferson St., playing everything from new wave to Cajun and zydeco. (☎291-5566. Apr.-June and Sept.-Nov. F 5:30pm, music 6-8:30pm.) The **Festival International de Louisiane** is the largest outdoor free francophone festival in the US, transforming Lafayette into a gigantic, French-speaking fairground for one wild weekend in April. Book a hotel or campground well in advance; prices will likely double. (☎232-8086. Apr.

20-24, 2005.) The **Festival de Musique Acadienne et Creole** began with the idea of educating Acadiana youth about their Cajun culture. It now attracts some of the state's best Cajun and zydeco musicians. (☎232-3737. Sept. 16-18, 2005.) The **Breaux Bridge Crawfish Festival** in nearby Breaux Bridge, 10 mi. east on I-10, stages crawfish races, live music, dance contests, cook-offs, and a crawfish-eating contest. (☎332-6655. First weekend of May.) Check out www.festivalinternational.com for further details on the above events.

To find the best zydeco in town, pick up a copy of *The Times*, free at restaurants and gas stations. Most clubs and bars have cover charges around $5-10 when they feel like it or depending on bands playing that night. On Sunday afternoons, the place to be is **Angelle's Whiskey River Landing**, 1365 Henderson Levee Rd., in Breaux Bridge, where live Cajun music heats up the dance floor on the very lip of the levee looking out over the swamp. On weekends you'll see boatmen pulling ashore right outside and coming in to join the party—it sometimes feels like the whole floor could collapse into the swamp with all the stamping. (☎228-8567. Live music Sa 9pm-1am, Su 1-4pm.) **Hamilton's Zydeco Club**, 1808 Verot School Rd., is one of the best places in Louisiana to cut loose at night with live Cajun bands and wild dancing. (☎991-0783. Open sporadically; call or drive by to see the marquee for upcoming events and times.) **Grant Street Dance Hall**, 113 Grant St., features bands playing everything from zydeco to metal. (☎237-8513. 18+. Cover usually $5-10. Only open days of shows; call ahead.) **Randol's**, 2320 Kaliste Saloom Rd., romps with live Cajun and zydeco music nightly and doubles as a restaurant. It's a good place for those unfamiliar with local music varieties to come for a taste and to learn how to dance. (☎981-7080. Open Su-Th 5-10pm, F-Sa 5-11pm.)

NEW IBERIA ☎337

New Iberia is off the beaten track, and though it is only 20 mi. south of Lafayette, you might feel as though you've traveled a long way. Home to the Tabasco Sauce factory, the town proudly calls itself "too hot to pass up" and is also a great place from which to explore the Atchafalaya Swamp. **Shadows on the Teche,** downtown at 316 E. Main St., is a beautiful plantation house surrounded by 2½ acres of gardens and overlooking the Bayou Teche. Guided tours of the house depart on the hr. 9:30am-4:30pm. The garden has a self-guided tour. (☎369-6446. Open daily 9am-5pm. $7, seniors $6.25, ages 6-11 $4, under 6 free.) For more gardens, head to the **Rip Van Winkle House,** 5505 Rip Van Winkle Rd., where dramatic trees cover beautiful floral displays. (☎359-8526. Due to re-open in 2005 after restoration. Call for details of admission prices and hours.)

Seven miles south of New Iberia lies **Avery Island**. It costs $0.50 to cross the bridge, but on the other side you will find the **Tabasco Sauce factory,** where the pepper plants are grown for the following year when they will be turned into the famous sauce. The factory offers an interesting 8min. introductory film followed by a free guided tour. (☎800-834-9599; www.tabasco.com. Open M-Sa 9am-4pm. Free.) Next door on Avery Island is the **Jungle Gardens and Bird City.** This 200-acre park originates from the son of the sauce founder Edmund McIlhenney, a keen naturalist who established the preserve to save the snowy egret from extinction. Today you can enjoy the forest and swamps and, if you are lucky, spot alligators, armadillos, and deer, in addition to the beautiful azaleas and bamboo. (☎369-6243. Open daily 9am-5pm. $6.25, ages 6-12 $4.50, under 6 free.) A 20min. drive to the east (50min. from Lafayette) takes you to the **Marshfield Boat Landing,** where you can take an airboat tour over the swamp to see the flora and fauna up close. Reserve in advance as the seats full up quickly. To get there, take Hwy. 86 to Loreauville and Marshfield Rd. to the landing, or pick up a map from the visitors center. (Reservations ☎229-4457. Tu-Sa 8am-5pm, Su 8am-noon. 1hr. tour $20.)

The most luxurious hotel in town is **The Gougenheim ❺**, 101 W. Main St., in the historic district, situated on the Teche near Bouilgny Plaza. (☎364-3949; www.gougenheim.com. Rooms $200-300.) In a quiet part of town near the bayou, the more affordable **Teche Motel ❷**, 1829 E. Main St., has a series of air-conditioned wooden cabins that can sleep up to four people. (☎369-3756. Cabins $40-45.) You can grab a wonderful po' boy at **Bon Creole Lunch Counter ❶**, 1409 St. Peter St. From outside it looks like a New Age mural, but inside it's a very traditional meat, biscuits, and gravy style canteen. Burgers are $3-5 and phenomenal "overstuffed" sandwiches go for $4-8. (☎367-6181. Open M-Sa 11am-9pm, Su 11am-2pm for barbecue only.) Try the **Farmers Market ❶**, at Bouilgny Plaza on Main St., for great home cooking. Fresh produce is turned into all sorts of wholesome, unpretentious meals in the $5-7 range. (☎369-2330. Open Tu 4-7pm, Sa 7-10:30am.)

Greyhound (☎364-8571), 1103 E. Main St., runs to: Lafayette (1hr., 2 per day, $11); New Orleans (4½hr., 2 per day, $28); Natchitoches (4½hr., 1 per day, $33). **Visitor Info: Iberia Parish Convention and Visitors Bureau**, 2513 Hwy. 14, offers maps and little Tabasco Sauce bottles. (☎365-1540; www.iberiatravel.com. Open daily 9am-5pm.) **Area Code:** 337.

ARKANSAS

Encompassing the Ozark and Ouachita mountains, the clear waters of Hot Springs, and miles of lush pine forests, the "Natural State" lives up to its nickname. Arkansas can be divided into distinct geographies. A more mountainous northwest is home to the University of Arkansas at Fayetteville, and gave birth to Wal-Mart. The flat plains of southeast Arkansas are poorer and support cotton industries where gin farms are found in abundance. The bluesy Mississippi Delta region seeps into east Arkansas, while Hot Springs National Park is an easy daytrip from the capital.

▶ PRACTICAL INFORMATION

Capital: Little Rock.

Visitor Info: Arkansas Department of Parks and Tourism, 1 Capitol Mall, Little Rock 72201 (☎501-682-7777 or 800-628-8725; www.arkansas.com). Open daily in summer 8am-6pm; low-season 8am-5pm.

Postal Abbreviation: AR. **Sales Tax:** 6%.

LITTLE ROCK   ☎501

Located squarely in the middle of the state along the Arkansas River, Little Rock became a major trading city in the 19th century. A small rock just a few feet high served as an important landmark for boats pushing their way upstream. The little rock is still visible today, although it doesn't loom as large in state history as the famous Central High School, where, in 1957, Governor Orval Faubus and local white segregationists violently resisted nine black students who entered the school under the protection of the National Guard. While this made headlines for Little Rock, many other US cities did not desegregate until years later. Today, this and other historical events are remembered in the many museums which can be found in the downtown area. The most recent attraction is the new Clinton Presidential Library, overlooking the Arkansas River.

▶ **PRACTICAL INFORMATION.** Little Rock is at the intersection of **I-40** and **I-30**, 140 mi. west of Memphis. Downtown, numbered streets run east-west, while named streets run north-south. The four major thoroughfares are **I-630, Cantrell**

Road, **University Avenue,** and **Rodney Parham Road.** Near the river, Markham is 1st St. and Capitol is 5th St. The east side of Markham St. is now President Clinton Ave. and moves through the lively **Riverwalk** district. North Little Rock is essentially a separate city across the river from Little Rock proper.

Amtrak, 1400 W. Markham St. (☎372-6841; open daily 11pm-7:45am), at Victory St., runs from Union Station Sq.; take bus #1 or 8. Trains run to: Dallas (6½hr., 1 per day, $60); Malvern, near Hot Springs (1hr., 1 per day, $10); St. Louis (7hr., 1 per day, $53). **Greyhound,** 118 E. Washington St. (☎372-3007; open 24hr.), is in North Little Rock; take bus #7 or 18. Buses run to: Memphis (2½hr., 8 per day, $26); New Orleans (12½hr., 4 per day, $78); St. Louis (8½hr., 1 per day, $52). **Central Arkansas Transit (CAT)** operates an extensive and tourist-friendly bus system through downtown and the surrounding towns. Catch CAT buses and get detailed route info at the **River Cities Travel Center,** 310 E. Capitol St. (☎375-1163. Buses run M-Sa every 30-40min. 6am-6pm, some routes until 10pm; Su 9am-4pm. $1.10, seniors $0.55; transfers $0.10.) CAT is planning to launch a new **trolley** system this year, and the tracks have already been laid. Ask at the Travel Center for info. **Visitor Info: Little Rock Visitor Information Center,** 615 E. Capitol Ave., in the newly renovated Curran Hall. Take the 6th or 9th St. exit off I-30 and follow the signs. (☎370-3290 or 877-220-2568; www.littlerock.com. Open daily 8am-6pm.) **Internet Access: Main Library,** 100 Rock St., near River Market. (☎918-3000. Open M-Th 9am-8pm, F-Sa 9am-6pm, Su 1-5pm. Free.) **Post Office:** 600 E. Capitol St. (☎375-5155. Open M-F 7am-5:30pm.) **Postal Code:** 72701. **Area Code:** 501.

⌐ ACCOMMODATIONS. The historic Capital Hotel ❺, 111 W. Markham St., at Louisiana St., is by far the most sumptuous accommodation in Little Rock. Hailed by the Clintons for its beauty and stellar dining, the hotel is a Little Rock mainstay. (☎800-766-7666. Full buffet breakfast included. Singles M-F $129, Sa-Su from $108.) Budget motels are dense on I-30 southwest of town and at the intersection of I-30 and I-40 in North Little Rock. The Cimarron Motel ❷, 10200 I-30, off Exit 130, has basic rooms and a pool. (☎565-1171. Key deposit $5. Singles $30; doubles $35.) King Motel ❷, 10420 I-30, near the Cimarron, has relatively comfortable, cheap rooms without frills. (☎565-1501. Key deposit $5. Singles $25; doubles $30-40.) Maumell Park ❶, 9009 Pinnacle Valley Rd., on the Arkansas River, has 129 sites near the beautiful Pinnacle Mountain State Park. From I-430, take Rte. 10 (Exit 9) west 3 mi., turn right on Pinnacle Valley Rd., and continue for 3 mi. (☎868-9477 or 753-0086. Sites with water and electricity $20. Boat launch $3; free for campers.)

⌂ FOOD. The city has revamped the downtown area starting with **River Market,** 400 President Clinton Ave. The downtown lunch crowd heads here for a wide selection of food shops, coffee stands, delis, and an outdoor **Farmers Market.** (☎375-2552. Market Hall open M-Sa 7am-6pm; many shops only open for lunch. Farmers Market open May-Oct. Tu and Sa 7am-3pm.) Near Market Hall, ◪**The Flying Fish ❷,** 511 President Clinton Ave., has quickly become downtown's favorite hangout, with an unpretentious atmosphere, walls filled with joke signs, and brusque servers. Hungry patrons clamor for catfish baskets (2 filets $5.79), oyster and catfish po' boy sandwiches ($6.59), and on-tap brews. (☎375-3474. Open daily 11am-10pm.) Just past the Hillcrest area, **Pizza D'Action ❶,** 2919 W. Markham, boasts some of the tastiest pizza and most eclectic crowds in the area, and live music most nights. (☎666-5403. Pizza $5-15. Cheeseburgers and sandwiches $4. Open M-W 11am-10pm, Th-F 11am-10:30pm, Sa noon-10pm, Su noon-9pm.) Chef Nate Townsend cooks up fantastic yet simple feasts at **Grampa's Catfish House ❷,** 1218 Mission Rd., in North Little Rock, a family-run catfish shack on the north shore whose walls are wooden planks. In addition to the popular catfish dinners ($8-10), dine on chicken-fried steak, ribeyes, oysters, and scallops. (☎758-4654; www.grampascatfish.com. Open Tu-Su 4:30-9:30pm.)

A TALE OF TWO LIBRARIES

It is tradition for recent ex-presidents to have libraries built in their honor. Bill Clinton is no exception—but the building is. Designed to blend river and riverbank, to aid Little Rock's revitalization, and to finally put the small city on the map, locals have instead described it as "a cantilevered mobile home on stilts." The problem lies in its box design and its supports—locals say it reminds them of a trailer, the very image the South is trying to shed. Not only the building is controversial. While Clinton is popular here—he was elected Governor six terms in a row—he has his critics. This time they have gone a few step farther and set up camp. A rival Clinton library, only 400 yards down the riverbank, seeks to highlight the impeachment, the sex scandals, and the darker sides of Clinton's presidency. The official library opened with a "globecoming" in November 2004, attended by celebrities, politicians, and citizens. The US's newest Presidential Library is worth a look when you're here. Depending on your own politics, you can always have a quick look next door.

The William J. Clinton Presidential Center, 1200 E. Pres. Clinton Ave. (☎370-8000; www.clintonpresidential-center.com.)
The Counter Clinton Library. (☎866-878-8498; www.counterclintonlibrary.com.)

◐ **SIGHTS.** Tourists can visit **"Le Petite Roche,"** the actual "little rock" of Little Rock, at Riverfront Park at the north end of Rock St. From underneath the railroad bridge at the north end of Louisiana St., look straight down. One blink and you may miss it: the rock is part of the embankment (it's that small), and it's presently covered in graffiti since the plaque was stolen. The aftermath of Little Rock's Civil Rights struggle is manifest at the corner of Daisy L. Gatson Bates Dr. (formerly 14th St.) and Park St., where **Central High School** remains a fully functional (and fully integrated) school. It's therefore closed to visitors, but in a restored Mobil station across the street, a ◪**Visitors Center,** 2125 Daisy L. Gatson Bates Dr., contains an excellent exhibit on the "Little Rock Nine." (☎374-1957; www.nps.gov/chsc. Open M-Sa 9am-4:30pm, Su 1-4:30pm. Free.) The **Arkansas Art Center,** 501 E. 9th St., is a huge complex with out-of-the-ordinary landscapes and still lifes; one of the most prominent sculptures, *Heavy Dog Kiss,* depicts a huge human head kissing a huge dog head. (☎372-4000; www.arkarts.com. Open Tu-Sa 10am-5pm, Su 11am-5pm. Suggested donation $5.)

In the middle of downtown, the **Historic Arkansas Museum,** 200 E. 3rd St., recreates life in 19th-century Little Rock as period actors show off old-time tricks of frontier living. (☎324-9351; www.arkansashistory.com. Open M-Sa 9am-5pm, Su 1-5pm. $2.50, seniors $1.50, under 18 $1.) When the legislature is not in session, visitors are free to explore the **State Capitol,** at the west end of Capitol St. (☎682-5080. Open M-F 7am-5pm, Sa-Su 10am-5pm.) The **Clinton Presidential Library,** 1200 E. President Clinton Ave., opened at the end of 2004 and promises to be a star attraction for the city. The library is located next to the River Market district, and extends to the east. Highlights include the Great Hall, a cafe, classrooms, a theater, replicas of the Oval Office and Cabinet Room, and a pedestrian footbridge over the Arkansas River. (☎370-8000; www.clintonpresidential-center.com. Open M-Sa 9am-5pm, Su 1-5pm.)

Just a 15min. drive to the west of the city is **Pinnacle Mountain State Park,** 11901 Pinnacle Valley Rd., in Roland. The mountain is an easy 1hr. climb which offers stunning views over the greater Little Rock area. Take care on the final part of the climb, however, as the drops are very steep and some scrambling is required. At ground level, interpretive trails and the **Arkansas Arboretum** provide information on the area's flora. (☎868-5806; www.arkansasstateparks.com. Call for hours.)

◪ **NIGHTLIFE.** Vino's, 923 W. 7th St., at Chester St., is Little Rock's original microbrewery-nightclub with tasty Italian fare and a clientele ranging from lunchtime's corporate businessmen to midnight's younger set. (☎375-8466. Cheese pizza slices $1.15. Calzones from $5.50. Live music Th-Sa. ID required. Cover $5-12. Open M-W 11am-10pm, Th 11am-11pm, F 11am-midnight, Sa 11:30am-midnight, Su 1-9pm.) The **Underground Pub,** 500 President Clinton Ave., offers British fare and full bar, with happy hour daily 4-7pm. Enjoy live music, darts, pool, and football (British style) on big-screen TVs. (☎707-2537. Open M-W 11am-midnight, Th-F 11am-2am, Sa 11am-1am.) To the west of downtown, **Discovery,** 1021 Jesse Rd., by Cantrell Rd. and Riverfront, is a gay- and straight-friendly club with three bars. Relax playing pool, kick back a few at the giant video bar, or dance frantically as a DJ spins house, trance, and more. (☎666-2902. Open M and F-Sa 9pm-5am, Su 6pm-5am.)

HOT SPRINGS ☎ 501

Since the region was first settled in 1807, visitors have flocked to the Hot Springs area seeking good health in the waters of the springs. Today, the springs manifest themselves in fountains and water outlets around the town of Hot Springs, all of which are very hot—you have been warned. In the winter, the steam rising from the springs makes for an eerie and beautiful spectacle, and the **Hot Springs Music Festival** brings thousands to the town for classical music concerts during the first two weeks of June. (☎623-4763; www.hotmusic.org.) Year-round people can be seen bottling the water in containers to take home for domestic healing. Al Capone vacationed in Hot Springs in the 1920s and made a deal with his Chicago rivals to refrain from violence while on holiday. The main drag of Hot Springs is known as **Bathhouse Row,** and is lined with spas and baths. A former bathhouse, **Fordyce House Visitors Center,** 369 Central Ave., now hosts exhibitions on the history of the area. (☎624-3383, ext. 640. Open daily June to mid-Aug. 9am-6pm; mid-Aug. to May 9am-5pm.) The **Buckstaff House,** three houses up the road, is the only bathhouse continuously active since 1912. Visitors can rejuvenate with mineral baths ($19) Swedish massage ($20), manicures, pedicures, and facials. (509 Central Ave. ☎623-2308; www.buckstaffbaths.com. Open M-Sa 7-11:45am and 1:30-3pm; closed Sa afternoons Dec.-Feb.) The **hot springs** themselves are in town, along Central Ave. Drinking the bad-tasting water is actually encouraged by the National Park! At the **Hot Springs Mountain Tower,** you can see 70 mi. in every direction on a clear day. From the end of Bathhouse Row, turn right down Fountain St., then continue right up Hot Springs Dr. (☎623-6035; www.hotsprings.org. $6, seniors $5, ages 5-11 $3.)

THIS LITTLE PIGGY DRIVES A CADILLAC

In an age of supposedly sophisticated tourism it is worth remembering that there are exceptions to every rule. Welcome to IQ Zoo. Yes, you can see...wait for it...dancing chickens, a pig that drives a Cadillac, and a bunny rabbit called Harry Lee Lewis, Jr. that plays a mean set of drums. Local resident, and owner of Maggie's Pickle Cafe, Jennifer, took in Harry the musician when he became too old to perform any more. "What do you do with a retired rabbit artist?" she asked. "I built a home for him, bought him loads of toys to play with and prepared a high quality of life for the guy so he could enjoy his retirement." Her husband was none too pleased with Jennifer's efforts, particularly as Harry Lee Lewis, Jr. died six days after he moved in. Now Jennifer is free to focus on her dachshund, Maggie, after whom her cafe is named—as the cafe mission states, "If Maggie won't eat it, we won't serve it." Back at the Zoo, don't miss the grand finale of smart ducks that are taught to escape a sinking Titanic replica while Celine Dion music blares away in the background. In Hot Springs, animal drama goes on.

Clowers Zoo with IQ, 210 Central Ave., Hot Springs. (☎623-9695.) Maggie's Pickle Cafe, 414 Central Ave., Hot Springs. (☎318-1866. Open daily 11am-5pm; closed Jan.)

Heavy tourism has pushed lodging prices sky-high in Hot Springs. One of the best values in town is the **Happy Hollow Motel ❸,** 231 Fountain Ave., on the edge of the park. Built in the late 1940s, it has a funky aluminum patio and clean rooms in a quiet location. (☎321-2230. Free wireless Internet. Singles from $41; doubles from $44.) Just outside of town, the **Alpine Inn ❷,** 741 Park Ave., has clean and spacious themed rooms and a pool. (☎624-9164; www.alpine-inn-hot-springs.com. Rooms $35-80.) For cheap eats, **Maggie's Pickle Cafe ❶,** 414 Central Ave., is a real find. Kosher spears and fried sweet pickles, along with the fabulous reuben sandwiches, are the signature dishes of this modest cafe. (☎318-1866. Open daily 11am-5pm, closed Jan.) **McClard's ❸,** 505 Albert Pike Rd., an old Clinton hangout, has served fabulous Southern fare in large portions for over 75 years. The tamales (2 for $8.35) are great and the selection of ribs is mouth-watering. (☎624-9586; www.mcclards.com. Open Tu-Sa 11am-8pm.) For a fast, cheap meal, **King Kone Drive-In ❶,** 1505 Malvern Ave., is an original burger joint serving pickle juice slushies. (☎321-9766. Open M-Sa 9am-10pm.) To occupy Hot Springs' steamy evenings, the amazing **Poet's Loft,** 514B Central Ave., is a groovy hangout with a variety of poetry readings, music recitals, and jam sessions.

One hour southwest of Little Rock, Hot Springs is easy to reach and navigate. The main drag, Central Ave., contains most of the noteworthy buildings around town, plus the National Park headquarters. Off the main drag the town becomes distinctly less easy on the eyes. Tourist info is available at the **Convention and Visitors Bureau,** 134 Convention Blvd. (☎321-2277. Open M-F 8am-5pm.) **Greyhound,** 229 W. Grand St. (☎623-5574), runs to: Atlanta (12hr., 1 per day, $120); Little Rock (1hr., 2 per day, $14); Memphis (4hr., 2 per day, $40). **Internet access** is available at the cyber cafe in the visitors bureau if you bring your own laptop. (Open M-F 9am-5pm. Free.) **Post Office:** 100 Reserve St., in the Federal Building. (☎623-8217. Open M-F 8am-4.30pm, Sa 9am-1pm.) **Postal Code:** 71901. **Area Code:** 501.

OZARKS ☎870 AND 479

The mountains that encompass the northwest region of Arkansas are accessible from the capital and provide a convenient escape with good roads, good food, and lush green scenery. Although there are no peaks over 2000 ft., the roads are sufficiently winding and the drops sufficiently steep to provide dramatic scenery and interesting drives. Until the last few decades, the region remained isolated. Since, it has grown in leaps and bounds with a booming tourism industry and thousands of retirees settling here. Mountain View and Eureka Springs are two of the most popular towns to visit, although they can get very busy during the summer months.

MOUNTAIN VIEW ☎870

Mountain View is located 123 mi. north of Little Rock, the closest big city. The self-proclaimed "folk music capital of the world" has plenty of music to offer, starting with the free outdoor music that abounds on central **Courthouse Square.** According to the Chamber of Commerce, this starts "anytime two people gather and lasts until they get tired." Locals bring along deck chairs or sit on the grass or walls to listen or even join in. Other venues offer music at a price. The **Jimmy Driftwood Barn,** 2 mi. north of town past the junction of Hwy. 5/9/14 N, is a performance space created by Jimmy Driftwood, called the "Bard of the Ozarks" and most famous for his song "The Battle of New Orleans." Although Jimmy died in 1998, you can still hear folk music there year-round. (☎269-4578. F and Su 7pm. Donations encouraged.) **Cash's White River Hoedown,** at the Hwy 5/9/14 N junction just north of town, has a family-geared comedy and music show. (☎800-759-6474. Apr.-Oct. Th-Sa warm-up 7:30pm, show 8pm. Nov. shows Sa only. $15, under 16 free.) **Brickshy's Backstreet Theater,** on Jefferson St. behind White River Furniture, rotates four bands: Harmony, The Leatherwoods, The River Rat Band, and Homemade Jam. (☎269-6200. Tickets $11, available after 5pm. Shows Apr.-Aug. M and Th-Sa at 8pm; Sept.-Nov. M and Th-Sa 7:30pm.) The **Mountain View Gospel Opry** performs on Thursdays at 7pm in the Folklore Society building, on Franklin St. just off the square.

In the nearby **Ozark National Forest**, the spectacular **Blanchard Springs Caverns** offer fascinating underground tours. There are three levels of caverns; two are accessible to the public, and the Dripstone Trail tour takes visitors through the highlights. The area also has hiking trails, a mountain-bike trail, and a shooting range. (☎757-2211 or 888-757-2246; www.fs.fed.us/oonf/ozark/recreation/caverns.html. Call for directions. Tours $10, children $5, under 5 free. Dripstone Trail Tour is wheelchair accessible with strong assistance.)

Angler's White River Inn ❸, at the junction of Hwy. 5/9/14, offers motel-style accommodations with a fabulous deck overlooking the river. (☎585-2226 or 800-794-2226; www.anglerswhiteriver.com. Singles Su-Th $44, F-Sa $54; doubles $49/$59.) The cheapest place to stay is in one of the **Ozark National Forest Campgrounds ❶**, near the Blanchard Springs Caverns, 15 mi. northwest of Mountain View. The campsites are first come, first served, with toilets, showers, and plenty of local fishing, swimming, and hiking trails. (☎269-3228. Sites $6-10 per night.) Just north of town on Rte. 14, the **Sylamore Creek Campground ❶** offers cabins as well as campsites, with clean bathrooms and hot showers. (☎585-2326 or 877-475-4223; www.sylamorecreek.com. Sites $10, with electricity $15. 2-person cabins $65-90, $5 each additional person over age 12.) Listen to the music from the square at the **Old Bay Cafe and Bakery ❷**, on Courthouse Sq. Try their succulent pork chops and peach cobbler; the chocolate peanut butter pie is to die for. (☎269-2867. Open M-Tu 9am-5pm, W-Th 9am-8pm, F-Sa 9am-9pm, Su 9am-3pm.) At **Jo Jo's Catfish Wharf ❷**, 6 mi. north of town on Hwy. 5 N, enjoy classic Arkansas catfish in a no-nonsense setting by the river. (☎585-2121. Open Su-Th 11am-8pm, F-Sa 11am-9pm.)

Getting to Mountain View is virtually impossible without a car; the town is not accessible by bus and there is no public transit within the town. Your best bet is to drive up from Little Rock. **Visitor Info: Chamber of Commerce and Tourist Information Center**, 199 Peabody St. (☎269-8068; www.mtnviewcc.org. Open M-Sa 9am-5pm; in summer also Su 1-3pm.) **Post Office:** 802 Sylamore Ave. (☎269-3520. Open M-F 8am-4pm.) **Postal Code:** 72560. **Area Code:** 870.

EUREKA SPRINGS   ☎ 479

Achieving an intoxicatingly high quaintness-to-square-foot ratio, Eureka Springs, near the intersection of Hwy. 62 and Rte. 23 in northwest Arkansas, peddles its patent charm, natural scenery, and slow pace to travelers drawn to the wooded mountains of northwestern Arkansas. The biggest tourist attractions are **The Great Passion Play**, 935 Passion Play Rd., off Hwy. 62, and the Bible-inspired sights that surround it. Hundreds of actors depict the final days of Christ on an elaborate outdoor set; while the dialogue is pre-recorded, at least it's not subtitled in Aramaic. (☎253-8559 or 800-882-7529; www.greatpassionplay.com. $24, ages 6-11 $10. May-Aug. M-Tu and Th-Sa 8:30pm; Sept.-Oct. M-Tu and Th-Sa 7:30pm.) The **Bible Museum** has over 6000 copies of the Good Book in over 600 languages and dialects, and the **Sacred Arts Center** features works inspired by Christ. Both are open 10am-8pm on days the passion play is running, and are included in the show's ticket price. (☎253-8559 or 800-882-7529.) Nearby, visitors marvel at the seven-story **Christ of the Ozarks** statue. (Open 24hr. Free.)

Lodging prices fluctuate greatly with the ebb and flow of tourists. The historic **Basin Park Hotel ❹**, 12 Spring St., sits in the center of downtown, but charges high rates for its convenient location. (☎253-7837. Singles and doubles $89-139.) **The Trails Inn ❷**, 2060 E. Van Buren, is one of the better budget motels on Hwy. 62, with clean rooms, continental breakfast, TV, A/C, and swimming pool. (☎ 253-9390 or 800-962-4691. Singles and doubles Su-Th $36-45, F-Sa $49-59.) Campers head to **Kettle Campgrounds and Cabins ❶**, 4119 E. Van Buren St., which offers tent and RV sites as well as a pool, laundry facilities, and showers. (☎ 253-9100 or 800-899-2267. Primitive sites $13, with water and electricity $17, with full hookup $21; cabins $40.) Hwy. 62 offers plenty of all-you-can-eat dinner buffets packed with Southern food staples at reasonable prices. The subterranean **Mud St. Cafe ❷**, 22G S. Main St., serves breakfast ($3-7), sandwiches, burgers, and delicious desserts. Local art-work funkifies the classic timber and stained-glass saloon decor, and the menu provides plenty of tantalizing vegetarian options. (☎ 253-6732. Open M-Tu and Th-Su 8am-3pm, also F-Sa 5-8pm for dessert and drinks only. Closed Jan.) For dinner, **Ermilio's ❸**, 26 White St., lets patrons mix and match a variety of pastas and home-made sauces in a casual dining room. (☎ 253-8806. Open daily 5-9pm. Closed mid-Feb to mid-Mar.) At **Bubba's BBQ ❷**, 166 W. Van Buren St., barbecue sandwiches ($3.50-6) are topped with cole slaw in the traditional Southern fashion and heaping dinner plates run $8.25-10. (☎ 253-7706. Open M-Sa 11am-9pm. Cash or check only.) The **Pine Mountain Jamboree**, 2075 E. Van Buren St., and **Ozark Mountain Hoedown**, 3140 E. Van Buren St., have live, old-fashioned, family-friendly country variety shows, with bluegrass, gospel, and country music, and comedy routines. (Pine Mountain: ☎ 253-9156. Ozark Mountain: ☎ 253-7725. Both Mar.-Dec. M and W-Su 8pm. $19, seniors $18, children $11.) Wash down that wholesome feeling with a cold one at **Chelsea's Corner**, 10 Mountain St., off Center St. (☎ 253-6723. Live music Sa-Su. 21+. Cover $5. Open M-Sa 10am-2am, Su noon-10pm.)

Downtown is steep but pedestrian-friendly; ditch your car at the free lots on Rte. 23 N south of the railroad or on Hwy. 62 W. The **Eureka Springs & North Arkansas Railway**, 299 N. Main St., is an old-fashioned steam engine that chugs through the surrounding countryside. (☎ 253-9623. Tickets $10-15, lunch trains $20-30, dinner trains $30-40. Trains depart 10am-4pm. Office open 9am-5pm.) **Trolleys** run to every conceivable destination around town. (☎ 253-9572; www.eurekatrolley.com. Runs May-Oct. Su-Th 9am-6pm, F-Sa 9am-8pm; Mar.-Apr. and Nov. daily 9am-5pm; Feb. limited service F-Sa 10am-4pm. Day pass $3.50.) The **Eureka Springs Chamber of Commerce Visitors Center** is on Hwy. 62 W, 2 blocks west of Hwy. 23 N. (☎ 253-8737; www.eurekaspringschamber.com. Open daily 9am-5pm.) **Area Code:** 479.

FLORIDA

Ponce de León landed in Florida in 1513, looking for the elusive Fountain of Youth. Although the multitudes who flock to Florida today aren't seeking fountains, many find their youth restored in the Sunshine State, whether they're dazzled by the spectacle of Disney World or bronzed by the sun on the state's seductive beaches. Droves of senior citizens also migrate to Florida—jokingly referred to as heaven's waiting room—where the sun-warmed air is just as therapeutic as de León's fabled magical elixir. Florida's recent population boom has strained the state's natural resources; commercial strips and tremendous development have turned pristine beaches into tourist traps. Still, it is possible to find a deserted spot on the peninsula on which to plop down with a paperback and dig your toes into the sand.

HIGHLIGHTS OF FLORIDA

BEACHES. White sand, lots of sun, clear blue water. Pensacola (p. 550) and St. Petersburg (p. 516) win our thumbs-up for the best of the best.

DISNEY WORLD. Orlando's cash cow...er, mouse (p. 507). What else is there to say?

EVERGLADES. The prime Florida haunt for fishermen, hikers, canoers, bikers, and wildlife watchers (p. 533). Check out the unique mangrove swamps.

KEY LIME PIE. This famous dessert hails from the Florida Keys (p. 538).

⚐ PRACTICAL INFORMATION

Capital: Tallahassee.

Visitor Info: Florida Division of Tourism, 126 W. Van Buren St., Tallahassee 32301 (☎888-735-2872; www.flausa.com). **Division of Recreation and Parks,** 3900 Commonwealth Blvd., #536, Tallahassee 32399 (☎850-488-9872).

Postal Abbreviation: FL. **Sales Tax:** 6%. **Accommodations Tax:** 11%.

CENTRAL FLORIDA

ORLANDO   ☎407

When Walt Disney was flying over the small towns of Central Florida in search of a place to put his Florida operation, he marveled at the endless number of lakes and streams that dominate the Orlando area. Amidst this beautiful setting, he foresaw a world full of thrill-packed amusement rides and life-sized, cartoonish figures. While Orlando is older than Disney World, most of the city's resources are dedicated to supporting the tourism industry that is the lifeblood of the economy. Theme parks, hotels, diners, and other kitschy treats line every major street; even downtown Orlando, 20 mi. from Disney, overflows with tourist attractions.

⬚ TRANSPORTATION

Airport: Orlando International, 1 Airport Blvd. (☎825-2001; www.orlandoairports.net). From the airport take Rte. 436 N, exit to Rte. 528 W/Bee Line Expwy., then head east on I-4 for downtown, and west on I-4 to the attractions, including Disney and Universal.

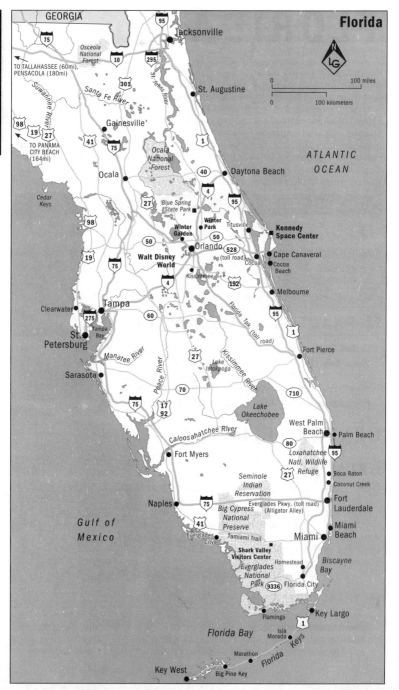

LYNX buses #42 and 51 make the trip for $1. **Mears Motor Shuttle** (☎423-5566) has booths at the airport for transportation to most hotels (about $25 per person). No shuttle reservations are necessary from the airport; for return, call 1 day in advance.

Trains: Amtrak, 1400 Sligh Blvd. (☎843-7611), 3 blocks east of I-4. Take S. Orange Ave., head west on Columbia, then take a right on Sligh. Station open daily 7:30am-7pm. To **Jacksonville** (3-4hr., 2 per day, $20), **Kissimmee** (20min., 2 per day, $5); **Miami** (6hr., 2 per day, $30); **Tampa** (2hr., 2 per day, $30).

Buses: Greyhound, 555 N. John Young Pkwy. (☎292-3440), just south of W. Colonial Dr. (Rte. 50). Open 24hr. To **Jacksonville** (2½-4hr., 8 per day, $30) and **Kissimmee** (40min., 8 per day, $7-8).

Public Transit: LYNX, 445 W. Amelia St., Ste. 800 (☎841-2279 or 800-344-5969). Downtown terminal between Central and Pine St., 1 block west of Orange Ave. and 1 block east of I-4. Buses operate daily 6am-9pm, hours vary with route. $1, seniors and under 18 $0.25; transfers $0.10. Weekly pass $10. Look for signposts with a colored paw. Serves the airport, downtown, and all major parks. The Lynx **Lymmo** is a free downtown transportation service with 11 stations and 8 stops scattered along and around Magnolia Ave. Look for markers with the "Lymmo" name.

Taxi: Yellow Cab ☎699-9999.

✖🛈 ORIENTATION AND PRACTICAL INFORMATION

Orlando lies at the center of hundreds of small lakes, toll highways, and amusement parks. **Orange Blossom Trail (Route 17/92 and 441)** runs north-south and **Colonial Drive (Route 50)** east-west. The **Bee Line Expressway (Route 528)** and the **East-West Expressway (Route 408)** exact several tolls for their convenience. The major artery is **I-4,** which actually runs north-south through the center of town, despite being labeled an east-west highway. The parks—**Disney World, Universal Studios,** and **Sea World**—await 15-20 mi. southwest of downtown; Winter Park is 3-4 mi. northeast.

Visitor Info: Orlando Official Visitor Center, 8723 International Dr., Ste. 101 (☎363-5872; www.orlandoinfo.com), southwest of downtown; take bus #8. Get free "Magic Card" for discounts at sights, restaurants, and hotels. Open daily 8am-7pm. Tickets sold 8am-6pm.

Hotlines: Rape Hotline, ☎740-5408. **Crisis Hotline,** ☎843-4357.

Internet Access: Orlando Public Library, 101 E. Central Blvd. (☎835-7323). Open M-Th 9am-9pm, F-Sa 9am-6pm, Su 1-6pm. Internet access $5 for 7-day unlimited use.

Post Office: 51 E. Jefferson St. (☎425-6464), downtown. Open M-F 7am-5pm. **Postal Code:** 32801. **Area Code:** 407.

🏠 ACCOMMODATIONS

With over 120,000 hotel rooms, there are plenty of options for all tastes and wallet sizes. Prices rise as you approach Disney. **Irlo Bronson Memorial Highway (U.S. 192)** runs from Disney World to downtown Kissimmee, and has cheap motels. Public transit goes from Kissimmee to the major parks. **International Drive (I-Drive),** a north-south road that parallels the interstate, is the center of Orlando's lodging world. Most accommodations have free transportation to Universal and Disney.

The Courtyard at Lake Lucerne, 211 N. Lucerne Circle E (☎648-5188 or 800-444-5289), 30min. from Disney. From I-4, take Exit 82C onto Anderson St., right on Delaney Ave., and right on N. Lucerne Circle. This beautiful B&B offers lavish rooms in 4 houses (of which Wellborn is the best deal). Complimentary wine upon arrival, and a nightly cocktail hour. TV and phone. Rooms $100-250. ⑤

THE HIDDEN DEAL

YACHTING HOME

Trying to get home, but have a fear of flying, driving, biking, and walking? In most cities, this would spell disaster, but not in Fort Lauderdale, the North American yachting capital. With your average yacht running upwards of $20 million, it might be tough for to buy your own to sail home, but that doesn't mean it's impossible to hitch a ride on one.

The uber-rich who own these vessels hire captains to handle the operation of the boat, who in turn hire crews to assist them. As a result of the number of yachts in town Fort Lauderdale has become a destination for young travelers looking to pick up work on a boat crew. The specifics of a crewman's duty can vary from a day swabbing the decks to a month-long voyage to Alaska. And while experience working on boats will certainly help in picking up work, even the unexperienced can usually find work in a week or two if they are persistent.

Begin your search for work at Floyd's Youth Hostel & Crew House (p. 544), or stop by any of the crew agencies along SE 17th St. There they will be able to tell you all the ins and outs of landing a job on a boat, and you might just find one sailing to a port near home.

Disney's All-Star Resorts (☎934-7639), in Disney World, cater to vacationing families looking for full Disney immersion. From I-4, take Exit 64B and follow the signs to Blizzard Beach—the resorts are just behind it. Disney's All-Star Movie, Music, and Sports Resorts, the "value resorts," are a great deal for large groups. Each of the hotels has 2 pools, a food court, a pool bar, and laundry facilities. Get info and tickets at the Guest Services Desk to avoid long lines at park gates. Free parking and Disney transportation. A/C, phone, TV. Rooms $85-150; under 18 free with adult. ❹

Palm Lakefront Resort & Hostel, 4840 W. Irlo Bronson Hwy./U.S. 192 (☎396-6422), is the new hostel on the Orlando scene. Features simple dorm-style rooms, private rooms, and common kitchens. Only 5 mi. from Disney with easy bus access, the hostel is a great crash pad for serious park hoppers. Dorms $15, private rooms $38. ❶

Fort Summit KOA (☎863-424-1880 or 800-424-1800), 7 mi. west of Disney in Baseball City. From I-4, take Exit 55 to U.S. 27, then go south on Frontage Rd. Palm trees and oaks provide shade, while a pool, hot tub, Internet access, horseback riding, bingo games, cookouts, and ice-cream socials provide entertainment. Sites with full hookup in winter $46, in summer $29. Cabins $55/$45. Discounts for KOA, AAA, and AARP. ❶

🍴 FOOD

Most eating in the Orlando area is either fine dining or done on-the-run. Prices are exorbitant inside theme parks; pack food if you have space. Cheap buffets line International Dr., U.S. 192, and Orange Blossom Trail.

Cafe Trastevere, 825 N. Magnolia Ave. (☎839-0235), in downtown Orlando. At this intimate Italian bistro, the too-good-to-be-true Bruschetta Michelangelo ($4.50) and savory Pollo Trastevere ($8.25) will leave you dreaming of Rome. W half-price wine 4-10pm. Tu and Th free wine with dinner 5-7pm. Open M-F 11:30am-10pm, Sa 5-10pm. ❸

Viet Garden, 1237 E. Colonial Dr. (☎896-4154), near Mills Ave. Nestled in a strip of international restaurants, this little gem serves delectable Vietnamese and Thai cuisine. Savor the array of garnished rice dishes, which feature combinations of chicken, beef, and shrimp ($5-9). Open Su-Th 10am-9pm, F-Sa 10am-10pm. ❶

Tijuana Flats, 50 E. Central Blvd. (☎839-0007), serves the biggest burritos in town. The "megajuana burrito" ($7) will satisfy any appetite, while the taquitos ($5.79) are a meal of more mortal proportions. M-Sa 11am-10:30pm, Su noon-9pm. ❶

Beefy King, 424 N. Bumby Ave. (☎894-2241), just south of E. Colonial Dr. Voted "Best Beefy Experience" by *Florida Magazine,* this family eatery has been pleasing residents for 30 years with its fantastic sandwiches ($3-5) served at an old-fashioned lunch counter. Open M-F 10am-5:30pm, Sa 11am-3pm. ❶

Pebbles Restaurant, 12551 State Rd. 535 (☎827-1111), in Lake Buena Vista, in the Crossroads Plaza. Cooks up tasty Florida cuisine in a casual atmosphere. Refreshingly original dishes like seared crab cakes with mango tartar sauce ($10). Open M-Th 11am-10pm, F 11am-11am, Sa 4-11pm, Su 4-10pm. ❷

🎵 🎦 ENTERTAINMENT AND NIGHTLIFE

The best options for one-stop partying in Orlando are Disney's **Pleasure Island** or Universal's **City-Walk** (see park info, below). Downtown Orlando has a lively nightlife scene. Check the Calendar section in Friday's *Orlando Sentinel* for events in town; the free *Orlando Weekly* is also a source for entertainment listings. Relatively inexpensive bars line **North Orange Avenue,** the city's main drag. For more tourist-oriented attractions, head to the bright lights and neon signs of **International Drive,** where mini golf, Ripley's Believe It or Not, the world's largest McDonald's, and Wonderworks (a science funhouse in an upside-down building) await.

◪ SAK Comedy Lab, 380 W. Amelia St. (☎648-0001), at Hughey Ave. downtown. Despite its trademark family-friendly, clean humor, SAK still manages to produce top-notch hilarity that all audiences can enjoy. Shows Tu-W 9pm; Th-F 8 and 10pm; Sa 8, 10pm, midnight. Tickets $5-15.

Tabu, 46 N. Orange Ave. (☎648-8363), downtown, is a South Beach-style haven for 20-somethings. Tu and Th college night, with all-you-can-drink included in the $10 cover. Stylish dress. Usually 18+. Cover $5-10. Open Tu-Sa 10pm-3am.

Jax 5th Ave. Deli and Ale House, 11 S. Court Ave. (☎841-5322), downtown, is a laid-back bar that stocks 250 brands of beer. A friendly and knowledgeable staff will help you choose from the dazzling displays. Deli and pub food $5-10. Live jazz Sa nights. Open M-Tu 11am-1am, W-Sa 11am-2am, Su 5pm-1am.

Back Booth, 37 W. Pine St. (☎999-2570), downtown, keeps the crowds coming with a loaded concert schedule and a bar with 27 beers on tap. Bands range from jazzy funk to ska punk. Cover $5-10. Shows usually 9 or 10pm; call for schedule.

WALT DISNEY WORLD   ☎407

Disney World is the Rome of central Florida: all roads lead to it. Its name is more apt than one might imagine, as Disney indeed creates a "world" of its own, even hosting a full marathon road race run entirely on its grounds. Within this Never-Neverland, theme parks, resorts, theaters, restaurants, and nightclubs all work together to be the embodiment of fun. Of course, the only setback is that magical amusement comes at a price—everything in Walt Disney's World costs almost thrice as much as in the real world. Every attraction is a marketing machine, and all rides end in their own gift shop. In the end, though, the Disney corporate empire leaves no one unhappy or bored.

ⓘ PRACTICAL INFORMATION

Disney dominates **Lake Buena Vista,** 20 mi. west of Orlando via I-4. (☎824-4321 or 939-4636; www.disneyworld.com.) Ticketing options are vast and complex, and the best way to acquaint yourself with them is to visit the Disney World website. The one-day entrance fee ($55, ages 3-9 $44) admits visitors to one of the parks, allowing them to leave and return later in the day. A better value, the **Park-Hopper Pass** buys admission to all four parks. (4-day $219, ages 3-9 $176; 5-day $249/$200.) The **Park Hopper Plus** includes a set number of days of admission plus free access to other Disney attractions. (5-day with 2 extras $282, ages 3-9 $226; 6-day with 3 extras $312/$250; 7-day with 4 extras $342/$274.) The Hopper passes need not be used on consecutive days, never expire, and allow for unlimited transportation between attractions. Attractions that charge separate admissions include **Typhoon Lagoon** ($32, ages 3-9 $26), **Blizzard Beach** ($32/$26), **Disney's Wide World of Sports Complex** ($10/$8), and **Pleasure Island** ($21, 18+ unless with adult). For descriptions, see **Other Disney Attractions** (p. 511). Never pay full fare for a Disney park; official Tourist Info Centers sell Park Hopper passes for about $10-15 less.

Disney World opens its gates 365 days a year, but hours fluctuate by season. Expect the parks to open at 9am and close between 7 and 11pm, but call beforehand—the schedule is set only a month in advance. Prepare for crowds (and afternoon thunderstorms) in summer, but the enormously crowded peak times are Christmas, Thanksgiving, and the month around Easter. The parks are least crowded in January. The free **FASTPASS** option at all of the theme parks allows you to bypass long lines on popular rides. Simply insert your park entrance ticket into a FASTPASS station, and you will receive a ticket telling you when to return, usually 30min.-2hr. later.

⊙ THE PARKS

MAGIC KINGDOM

Seven lands comprise the Magic Kingdom: **Main Street, USA; Tomorrowland; Fantasyland; Liberty Square; Frontierland; Adventureland;** and **Mickey's Toontown Fair.** More than any of the other Disney parks, the Kingdom is geared toward children.

MAIN STREET, USA. As the entrance to the "Most Magical Place on Earth," Main Street captures the spirit and bustle of early 20th-century America, with vendors peddling their wares and a daily parade. The aroma of freshly baked cookies and cakes beckons from **Main Street Bakery,** and the **Emporium** is a one-stop shop for Magic Kingdom souvenirs. A horse-drawn trolley carries visitors up Main St. to **Cinderella's Castle,** Disney World's centerpiece, where there are frequent dancing and singing shows by your favorite Disney characters.

TOMORROWLAND. In the 1990s, Tomorrowland received a neon facelift that skyrocketed it out of the space-race days of the 1960s and into a futuristic intergalactic nation. The indoor roller coaster **Space Mountain** dominates the landscape, providing thrills in the blackness of outer space. **Buzz Lightyear's Space Ranger Spin** equips *Toy Story* fans with laser cannons to fight the Evil Emperor Zurg.

MICKEY'S TOONTOWN FAIR AND FANTASYLAND. Visitors can meet their favorite characters at the **Hall of Fame** and **Mickey's Country House.** To meet Mickey, come equipped with an autograph book and a camera to the **Judge's Tent**, but be ready to wait in line with dozens of expectant children. **Fantasyland** brings some of Disney's all-time favorite animated films to life. Soar above London and Neverland in a pirate ship sprinkled with pixie dust at **Peter Pan's Flight,** then dance with dwarves at **Snow White's Scary Adventures.** Board a honey pot and journey into the Hundred Acre Wood at **The Many Adventures of Winnie the Pooh,** where you will withstand a blustery day, bounce with Tigger, and encounter bizarre Heffalumps. For saccharine but heartwarming melodies, meet mechanical children from around the world on the classic boat ride **"It's a Small World."** RIP, "Mr. Toad's Wild Ride."

FLORIDA

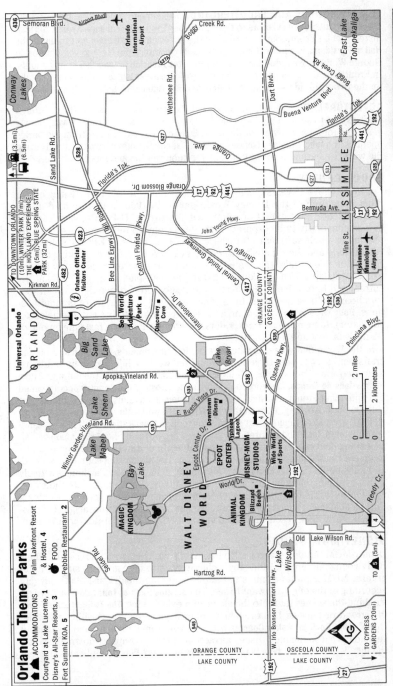

Orlando Theme Parks

▲♦ ACCOMMODATIONS
Courtyard at Lake Lucerne, **1**
Disney's All-Star Resorts, **3**
Fort Summit KOA, **5**
Palm Lakefront Resort
    & Hostel, **4**
■ FOOD
Pebbles Restaurant, **2**

FLORIDA

LIBERTY SQUARE AND FRONTIERLAND. Welcome to Americana, Disney-style. Liberty Sq. introduces visitors to the educational and political aspects of American history, while Frontierland showcases the America of cowboys and Indians. **The Hall of Presidents** is a fun exhibit on US heads of state, from George Washington to George W. Bush. Next door, the spooky **Haunted Mansion** houses 999 happy ghouls. In Frontierland, take a lazy raft ride over to **Tom Sawyer Island** and explore, or take on the two thrill rides—**Splash Mountain** and **Big Thunder Mountain Railroad**.

ADVENTURELAND. The classic **Pirates of the Caribbean** steals the show, though don't expect to see Johnny Depp hidden in the shadows. Fly on the **Magic Carpets of Aladdin** for an aerial view of the park. One of the original rides from the park's opening, **The Jungle Cruise** provides a tongue-in-cheek take on exploration, touring the world's amazing rivers while supplying good wet fun and lots of bad puns.

EPCOT CENTER

For those above 12 years of age or without a Mickey fetish, EPCOT may be the most appealing of the Disney World parks. In 1966, Walt dreamed up an "Experimental Prototype Community Of Tomorrow" (EPCOT), which would evolve constantly to incorporate new ideas from US technology—eventually becoming a self-sufficient, futuristic utopia. At present, EPCOT splits into **Future World** and the expansive **World Showcase**. After a day of walking around EPCOT, it's no wonder that some joke that the true acronym is "Every Person Comes Out Tired." The trademark 180 ft. high geosphere (or "golfball") at the entrance to Future World houses the **Spaceship Earth** attraction, in which visitors board a "time machine" for a tour through the evolution of communications. **Body Wars** takes visitors on a tour of the human body (with the help of a simulator). At nearby **Test Track,** riders experience life in the fast lane on one of Disney's fastest and longest rides.

In the World Showcase, architectural styles, monuments, and typical food and crafts represent 11 countries from around the world, while people in traditional dress perform various forms of cultural entertainment. One of the cultural films, **Impressions de France,** has gorgeous panoramic views of the country accompanied by captivating French classical music. **Maelstrom** is an amusing and thrilling boat ride through Norway, complete with Vikings and trolls. Every night at 9pm, EPCOT presents a magnificent mega-show called **IllumiNations** with music, dancing fountains, laser lights, fireballs, and fireworks. World Showcase also specializes in regional cuisine as each "country" offers both a sit-down restaurant and a more reasonably priced cafeteria-style option. The all-you-can-eat meat, seafood, and salad buffet ($19) at **Restaurant Akershus ❹,** in the Norway Pavilion, is actually a Disney dining bargain. Those with an affinity for brew can create their own around-the-world tour, sampling a beer from each country. Though drinking a Corona in Mexico, then having a Casablanca in Morocco is a truly magical experience, beware: at $4-7 each, they will demolish both your sobriety and your budget.

DISNEY-MGM STUDIOS

Disney-MGM Studios creates a "living movie set." Restaurants resemble their Hollywood counterparts, and movie characters stroll the grounds signing autographs. MGM is built around stunt shows and mini-theatricals; plan your day according to the ones you want to see. The **Studios Backlot Tour** takes visitors on a behind-the-scenes tour into the magic of movie making. **The Twilight Zone Tower Of Terror** drops guests 13 stories in a runaway elevator. The thrilling, twisting, "limo" ride, **Rock 'n' Roller Coaster** will take you from 0 to 60 mph in less than 3 seconds; it's also the only Disney attraction to take you upside down. Based on the hit TV game show, **Who Wants to Be a Millionaire? Play It!** replicates the real show, save affable host Regis Philbin. **The Indiana Jones Epic Stunt Spectacular** shows off some of the greatest scenes from the trilogy in live action. **The Magic of Disney Animation,** a tour that introduces you to actual Disney animators, explains how Disney animated films are created and offers a sneak peak at the sketches of upcoming Disney flicks.

DISNEY'S ANIMAL KINGDOM

If plastic characters and make-believe are getting to be too much, the Animal Kingdom is a dose of reality—in a carefully managed Disney presentation, of course. **Kilimanjaro Safaris** depart for the exotic Harambe preserve where elephants, hippos, giraffes, and other creatures of the African savannah roam. A **Maharajah Jungle Trek** drops riders among tigers, tapirs, and bats, and the **Kali River Rapids** is a white water adventure that exposes riders to the many threats facing our planet. Like any Disney park, though, shows and rides make up a large part of Animal Kingdom (the park's catchphrase is NAHTAZU: "not a zoo"). **DINOSAUR** is the best ride in the park and puts travelers in the middle of the early Cretaceous. Another 3-D spectacular, **It's Tough to be a Bug!,** put on by the cast of the animated flick *A Bug's Life,* is sure to entertain all ages and species.

OTHER DISNEY ATTRACTIONS

Besides the four main parks, Disney offers several other draws with different themes and separate admissions. **Pleasure Island** is hedonistic Disney with an attitude. Party and drink the night away at eight nightclubs, from comedy to jazz to 80s pop. **Mannequins,** with a spinning dance floor and stunning strobes, trumps any South Beach club in terms of venue, though perhaps not "coolness of clientele." (18+ unless accompanied by parent. Cover $21. Open daily 8pm-2am.) **Blizzard Beach** is a water park built on the premise of a melting mountain. Ride a ski lift to the fastest water-slide in the world, plummeting down a 120 ft. descent. **Typhoon Lagoon,** a 50-acre water park, centers on the nation's largest wave pool and its 7 ft. waves. In addition to eight water slides, the lagoon has an inner-tubing creek and a saltwater coral reef stocked with tropical fish and harmless sharks. Water parks fill up early on hot days; late arrivals may be turned away. With venues for over 30 sports, **Disney's Wide World Of Sports Complex** is a hub of athletic activity. Catch the Atlanta Braves in spring training and the Tampa Bay Buccaneers during pre-season camp. The larger-than-life **Downtown Disney** is a neon conglomeration of theme restaurants, nightlife, and shopping encompassing the **Marketplace, Pleasure Island,** and the **West Side.** In the Marketplace at the **LEGO Imagination Center,** take a photo with large LEGO sculptures or create your own. In the West Side, **Cirque Du Soleil** presents La Nouba, a breathtaking blend of circus acrobatics and theater with a price that will also take your breath away. ($82, ages 3-9 $72.) Next door, the high-tech games of **Disney Quest** guarantee a "virtually" exciting time ($31, ages 3-9 $25).

LIFE BEYOND DISNEY ☎407

Believe it or not, it exists. In fact, many visitors will tell you that Universal's **Islands of Adventure** is Orlando's best park. Regardless, Disney has such a domination that the non-Disney parks band together in competition with Mickey: "FlexTickets" combine admission prices to various parks at a discount, though their prices can fluctuate. A four-park ticket ($187, ages 3-9 $152) covers Sea World, both Universal Studios parks, and Wet 'n' Wild, and allows 14 days of visiting with free transportation. The five-park ticket ($223/$187) adds Busch Gardens in Tampa (see p. 515) and also lasts 14 days. Universal City Travel (☎800-224-3838) sells tickets.

FLORIDA

👁 THE PARKS

UNIVERSAL ORLANDO

Swap Mickey and Goofy for Spider-Man and Shrek, and you get a theme park that appeals to those over 12. Universal is a relatively saccharine-free alternative to Disney World, with movie-themed rides that thrill, spin, and make you squeal. With two parks (**Universal Studios Florida** and **Islands of Adventure**), three resort hotels, and an entertainment complex called **CityWalk,** Universal stands toe-to-toe with the "other park." *(I-4 Exit 74B or 75A. ☎ 363-8000. Open daily 9am, closing times vary. City-Walk open until 2am. Each park $58, ages 3-9 $48; 2-park pass $78/$67. CityWalk is ungated and free; club, dinner, and movie packages available. Parking $8, free after 6pm.)*

UNIVERSAL STUDIOS FLORIDA. The first park to "ride the movies" showcases a mix of rides and behind-the-scenes extravaganzas. Live the fairy tale courtesy of "OgreVision" at **Shrek 4-D,** the park's best attraction. **Back to the Future...The Ride,** a staple of any Universal visit, utilizes seven-story OmniMax screens and spectacular special effects. **Men in Black: Alien Attack** puts you through agent training as you navigate your way through an alien infested city armed with your own blaster gun.

ISLANDS OF ADVENTURE. This park encompasses 110 acres of the most technologically sophisticated rides in the world and typically has short wait times. Five islands portray different themes, ranging from cartoons to Jurassic Park to Marvel Superheroes. **The Amazing Adventures of Spider-Man** is the park's crown jewel; new technology and several patents sprung from its conception. A fast-moving car whizzes around a 3-D video system as you and Peter Parker find the stolen Statue of Liberty. The most amusing island is **Seuss Landing,** home of the **Green Eggs & Ham Cafe ❷** (green eggs and ham-wich $5.60). **The Cat in the Hat** turns the classic tale into a ride on a wild couch that loops its way through the story. If that's too tame, the **Dueling Dragons** is the world's first inverted, dueling roller coaster.

CITYWALK. CityWalk greets the eager tourist upon entering Universal Studios. A unique mix of restaurants, bars, clubs, and a cineplex makes it an appealing alternative to Pleasure Island. The **NASCAR Cafe, Jimmy Buffet's Margaritaville,** and **Emeril's** are a few of the pricey theme restaurants that line the main street. Clubs on the walk include **Bob Marley's** and **The Groove.** Packages make it possible to enjoy a meal, a movie, and partying at an affordable price. *(All-club access $10, with a movie $14. Meal and a movie $20. Meal and club access $20.)*

SEA WORLD

One of the largest marine parks in the US, **Sea World Adventure Park** makes a splash with shows, rides, and exhibits. In recent years, it has worked to transform itself into a full-fledged park emphasizing the mystery and dark side of sea creatures. Eels, barracudas, sharks, and other beasties lick their chops in **Terrors of the Deep,** the world's largest collection of dangerous sea creatures. **The Shamu Adventure** thrills with amazing aquatic acrobatics smartly executed by a family of orcas and their trainers. Whale belly flops send waves of salt water into the cheering "soak zone." The park's first thrill ride, **Journey to Atlantis,** gets rave reviews, as does **Kraken,** a floorless roller coaster billed as the highest, fastest, and longest coaster in Orlando. In summer, stick around until 10pm for **Mystify,** a fireworks spectacular. *(12 mi. southwest of Orlando off I-4 at Rte. 528/Bee Line Expwy. Take bus #8. ☎ 351-3600. Open daily 9am-7pm; extended hours in summer. $54, ages 3-9 $45. Parking $8.)* Orlando's newest destination is the adjacent **Dis-**

covery Cove. Swim with dolphins, snorkel among tropical fish, and frolic in an aviary with more than 200 birds. (☎ *877-434-7268; www.discoverycove.com. Open daily 9am-5:30pm. $119-399. Reservations required.)*

THE HOLY LAND EXPERIENCE

Step back in time at this small, controversial park billed as a "living biblical museum." Take in the architecture and sights of ancient Jerusalem and watch costumed performers reenact biblical scenes. The **Scriptorium** is a one-of-a-kind museum displaying Bible-related artifacts. *(4655 Vineland Rd. I-4 Exit 78. ☎ 872-2272. Open M-F 10am-5pm, Sa 9am-6pm, Su noon-6pm. $30, ages 6-12 $20, 5 and under free.)*

CYPRESS GARDENS

Cypress Gardens's botanical gardens feature over 8000 varieties of plants and flowers amidst winding walkways and boat rides, while Southern belles patrol the grounds. Despite the pretty flowers, the **water-ski shows** attract the biggest crowds and the loudest applause. *(Southwest of Orlando in Winter Haven; take I-4 southwest to Rte. 27 S, then Rte. 540 W. ☎ 863-324-2111. Open daily 9:30am-5pm. $37, ages 6-12 $24.)*

BLUE SPRING STATE PARK

Orange City's 3000-acre state park, 32 mi. northeast of Orlando, is home to some of Florida's most pristine flora and fauna. Hike along the **Blue Spring Trail** for a scenic view of the legendary spring itself (a constant 72°F), or come face-to-face with Florida's most endangered mammal, the **manatee,** as you scuba, snorkel, or swim in one of the park's numerous clear lakes and springs. *(2001 W. French Ave., Exit 114 off I-4. ☎ 386-775-3663. Open daily 8am-dusk. $2-4 entrance fee for vehicles, $1 for pedestrians and bicyclists. Partially wheelchair accessible.)*

TAMPA ☎ 813

Even with beautiful weather and ideal beaches, Tampa has managed to avoid the plastic pink flamingos that plague its Atlantic Coast counterparts. While Busch Gardens is Tampa's main theme park and primary tourist attraction, the rest of the bay city provides a less commercial vacation spot. Ybor City (EE-bor), Tampa's Cuban district, is a seething hotbed of energy and activity where sun-bleached tourists can find many of Tampa's best restaurants and spend a late night getting hot and heavy at the dozens of bars and clubs that line 7th Ave.

🖾 🔝 ORIENTATION AND PRACTICAL INFORMATION. Tampa wraps around Hillsborough Bay and sprawls northward. **Nebraska Avenue** and **Dale Mabry Road** parallel **I-275** as the main north-south routes; **Kennedy Boulevard, Columbus Street,** and **Busch Boulevard** go east-west. With some exceptions, numbered streets go north-south and numbered avenues run east-west. **Ybor City** is bounded roughly by Nuccio Pkwy. , 22nd St., Palm St., and 5th St. *Be careful outside these boundaries; the surrounding area can be dangerous.*

Tampa International Airport (☎ 870-8770; www.tampaairport.com) is 5 mi. west of downtown, Exit 39 off I-275. HARTline bus #30 runs between the airport and downtown. **Amtrak,** 601 Nebraska Ave. (☎ 221-7600; open daily 5:45am-7:45pm), at the end of Zack St. two blocks north of Kennedy St., runs to Miami (5½hr., 1 per day, $42). **Greyhound,** 610 Polk St. (☎ 229-2174; open daily 5am-midnight), sends buses to: Atlanta (11-14hr., 9 per day, $66); Miami (7-9hr., 10 per day, $38); Orlando (2-3hr., 7 per day, $20). **Hillsborough Area Regional Transit (HARTline)** provides public transit. Buses #3, 8, and 46 run to Ybor City from downtown. (☎ 254-4278. $1.25, seniors and ages 5-17 $0.60; exact change required.) HARTline also operates Tampa's **Streetcar System** (☎ 254-4278; www.tecolinestreetcar.org;

FLORIDA

$1.50) which runs from Ybor City to downtown Tampa. **Visitor Info: Tampa Bay Convention and Visitors Bureau,** 400 N. Tampa St., Ste. 2800. (☎223-1111 or 800-448-2672; www.visittampabay.com. Open M-F 8:30am-5:30pm.) **Hotlines: Crisis Hotline,** ☎234-1234. **Helpline,** ☎251-4000. **Internet Access: John F. Germany Public Library,** 900 N. Ashley Dr. (☎273-3652), downtown. (Open M-Th 9am-9pm, F 9am-6pm, Sa 9am-5pm, Su 10am-6pm.) **Post Office:** 401 S. Florida Ave. (☎223-4332. Open M-F 8:30am-4:30pm.) **Postal Code:** 33601. **Area Code:** 813.

♠ ACCOMMODATIONS. The only hosteling option in Tampa is **Gram's Place ❶,** 3109 N. Ola Dr., Exit 46B off I-275 N. Music is the theme and tunes are always grooving, whether on the outside deck or over the in-house FM broadcasting signal. Both charming and comfy, this is a great place to spend the night. (☎221-0596. Dorms $19; private rooms $36. Prices higher in winter.) Chain hotels and motels hug I-275 and can be found at most exits. Motels are particularly abundant along bustling Busch Blvd. **Villager Lodge ❷,** 3110 W. Hillsborough Ave., conveniently located 5 mi. from the airport at Exit 30 off I-275, has 33 small rooms with A/C, cable TV, and pool access. (☎876-8673. Singles $40, doubles $55; each additional person $5.) **Motel 6 ❸,** 333 E. Fowler Way, 3 mi. from Busch Gardens in northwest Tampa, has cheap, functional rooms with cable TV. (☎932-4948. Rooms $43.) With spacious, comfortable rooms, the full-service **Baymont Inn ❹,** 9202 N. 30th St., is a great alternative to the motels that line E. Busch Blvd. (☎930-6900 or 877-229-6668. A/C and fridge in every room. Rooms start at $90.)

❏ FOOD. 7th Ave. in Ybor City is lined with a number of fun and funky eateries, many of which stay open late to satiate post-clubbing cravings. Mostly a dinner spot, the swanky **Bernini ❹,** 1702 E. 7th Ave., serves piping hot pizzas ($10-15), savory pasta dishes ($16-24), and the house favorite, Crispy Duck ($22). Hungry customers enjoy their meals under photos and replicas of the eponymous sculptor's works. (☎248-0099. Open M-Th 11:30am-10pm, F 11:30am-11pm, Sa 4-11pm, Su 5-10pm.) Tampa's gulf shore heritage is evident at **Cafe Creole ❸,** 1330 E. 9th Ave., an Ybor City joint known for oysters and jambalaya. (☎247-6283. Entrees $6-18. Live jazz nightly. Happy hour Tu-F 4-7pm. Open Tu-Th 11:30am-10:30pm, F 11:30am-11:30pm, Sa 5-11:30pm.) Those looking for a late-night alternative to pizza should find their way to **Joffery's Coffee Company ❷,** 1616 7th Ave., which offers an array of magnificent sandwiches ($6-8) and coffees ($2-4) perfect for post-clubbin' grubbin'. (☎248-5282. Open M-Tu 7am-6pm, W 7am-10pm, Th 7am-midnight, F 7am-3am, Sa 8:30am-3am, Su 9am-6pm.) Buried in North Tampa lies the legendary **Skipper's Smokehouse ❷,** 910 Skipper Rd., off Nebraska Ave., a tremendous backcountry eatery whose thatched hut restaurant is complemented by an adjacent oyster bar (21+) and the popular backyard "Skipper Dome," which hosts live music nightly with a lawn party vibe. (☎971-0666. Happy hour Th-F 4-8pm. Restaurant and bar open Tu 11am-10pm, W-F 11am-11pm, Sa noon-11pm, Su 1-10pm.)

◨ SIGHTS. Tampa blossomed through the Ybor City, a planned community once known as the cigar capital of the world. Early 20th-century stogie manufacturer Vincent Martínez Ybor employed a wide array of immigrants, and the city soon displayed the influence of intermingled Cuban, Italian, and German heritages. The **Ybor City State Museum,** 1818 9th Ave., details the rise and fall of the tobacco empire and its workers. Exhibits include a detailed look at 19th- and early 20th-century Ybor life, while a display is dedicated to the art of hand-rolled cigars, complete with a viewing of a cigar roller at work. (☎247-6323; www.ybormuseum.org. Open daily 9am-5pm. $3, under 6 free. Neighborhood walking tours Sa 10:30am, $6.)

The **Florida Aquarium,** 701 Channelside Dr., invites you to get up close and personal with fish from Florida's lagoons. Head into the wetlands exhibit to gape at gators, turtles, and fighting river otters, and then check out the coral reef, where menacing sharks and enigmatic jellyfish haunt the waters. Wild dolphins of the gulf stage a meet 'n' greet on Dolphin Quest Eco-Tours of Tampa Bay. (☎273-4000; www.flaquarium.net. Open daily 9:30am-5pm. $18, seniors $15, ages 3-12 $12. 1½hr. Eco-Tours: M-F 2pm; Sa-Su noon, 2, and 4pm. $19/$18/$14. Combo tickets available.) Built in 1891, Henry B. Plant's Tampa Bay Hotel was once considered the most luxurious resort in all the South. A wing of the lavish hotel is open today as the **Henry B. Plant Museum,** 401 W. Kennedy Blvd. View restored bedrooms, card rooms, and authentic artifacts from the opulent mansion, complete with Edison carbon-filament lighting and continuous classical music. (☎254-1891; www.plantmuseum.com. Open Tu-Sa 10am-4pm, Su noon-4pm. Free; suggested donation $5.)

Anheuser-Busch's addition to Florida's theme parks, **Busch Gardens,** 3000 E. Busch Blvd., is the most prized weapon in the arsenal of Tampa tourism. Thrill-seekers head for the park's famous rollercoasters Kumba, Montu, and Gwazi, while others watch 2500 animals roam, fly, slither, and swim through the African-themed zoo areas. The "Edge of Africa" safari experience is among the park's most popular attractions. (☎987-5082 or 888-800-5447; www.buschgardens.com. Hours vary, usually open daily 9:30am-7:30pm. $54, ages 3-9 $45. Parking $7.) Nearby, **Adventure Island,** 10001 Malcolm McKinley Dr., promises a wet and wild experience. (☎987-5660; www.adventureisland.com. Open June-Aug. daily; Sept.-Oct. Sa-Su. Hours vary, usually open M-Th 9am-7pm, F-Su 9am-8pm. $30, ages 3-9 $28. Parking $5. Busch Gardens/Adventure Island combo ticket $60, ages 3-9 $50.)

🎭🎵 **ENTERTAINMENT AND NIGHTLIFE.** Brief yourself on city entertainment with the free *Tampa Weekend* or *Weekly Planet,* in local restaurants and bars and on street corners. Gay travelers should check out the free *Stonewall.*

Every year in the first week of February, the **José Gasparilla,** a 165 ft., fully rigged pirate ship loaded with "buccaneers," invades Hillsborough Bay, kicking off a month of parades and festivals (http://gasparillapiratefest.com). Thousands pack Ybor City every October for **"Guavaween"** (☎621-7121), a Latin-style Halloween celebration.

With over 35 clubs and bars in a small area, Ybor City is teeming with energetic nightlife. Most nighttime hangouts are located on bustling 7th Ave.,

HALLOWEEN FIESTA

Every year during the last week in October, more than 100,000 people flock to Tampa to participate in one of the nation's biggest and baddest street parties. Held in the notoriously festive town of Ybor City, Guavaween is a Halloween celebration infused with Latin love and southern soul.

In the 19th century, Tampa residents tried to cultivate a guava industry on the Gulf Coast. Though the effort was unsuccessful, guavas became synonymous with the region. Columnist Steve Otto noted that if New York City was the "Big Apple," then Tampa could be called the "Big Guava."

The analogy stuck, and for the last 20 years, "Mama Guava" has kicked off the Guavaween bash by leading the legendary "Mama Guava Stumble Parade" through the streets of Ybor. Concerts and costume contests abound during the festival, and winners take home prizes of up to $2000. Guavaween has recently toned down its wild antics and now appeals to partiers and families alike, with the "silly scavenger hunt" entertaining children during the day, but don't be fooled—sin and skin still prevail when the sun goes down, as revelers party early into the morning in search of a trick or a treat. The countdown to the next Guavaween begins on Monday.

For more info, call 813-242-4828 or 888-293-4770, or visit www.cc-events.org/gw. For more info, call ☎813-242-4828 or 888-293-4770.

FLORIDA

though fun can be found on 8th Ave. and 9th Ave. as well. *Use caution when walking down side streets.* During the week, many restaurants close at 8pm, and clubs don't open until 10pm. 7th Ave. is closed to vehicular traffic at night, so though we've listed a few hotspots, don't be afraid to explore the strip in search of a club that fits your fancy. For those first drinks, try **Adobe Gilas**, 1600 E. 8th Ave., a great place to warm up at before hitting the more pounding club scene. (☎241-8588. Open M-Sa 11am-3am, Su 1pm-3am.) **Coyote Ugly Saloon**, 1722 7th Ave., is the hottest club to hit the Ybor strip. Taking its cue from the movie *Coyote Ugly*, the rowdy bar serves mostly single liquor shots with complementary bar dancing and body licking. Their motto? "You will get drunk, you will get ugly." (☎228-8459. Happy hour daily 5-7pm. 21+. Open M-Sa 5pm-3am.) **Green Iguana Bar & Grill**, 1708 E. 7th Ave., turns into a multi-level extravaganza at night. Though there are $1 drinks on Wednesdays, most every night promises a energetic evening. (☎248-9555. Open daily 11am-3am, kitchen closes at midnight.) **The Castle**, 2004 N. 16th St., at 9th Ave., caters to the artsy scene but is open to all who want to enter the sanctum. (☎247-7547. M 80s night. 18+. Cover $3-5. Open M and Th-Sa 9:30pm-3am.)

ST. PETERSBURG AND CLEARWATER ☎727

Across the bay, 22 mi. southwest of Tampa, St. Petersburg is home to a relaxed beach community of retirees and young singles. The town enjoys soft white beaches, emerald water, and about 361 days of sunshine per year. The St. Petersburg-to-Clearwater stretch caters to beach bums and city strollers alike. While the outdoor scenery draws crowds, indoor activities are equally captivating—museum exhibits on Salvador Dalí and John F. Kennedy more than rival the sunset.

█▌ 🛈 ORIENTATION AND PRACTICAL INFORMATION. In St. Petersburg, **Central Avenue** parallels numbered avenues, running east-west in the downtown area. **34th Street (U.S. 19), I-275,** and **4th Street** are major north-south thoroughfares. The beaches line a strip of barrier islands on the far west side of town facing the Gulf. Several causeways, including the **Clearwater Memorial Causeway (Route 60),** access the beaches from St. Pete. Clearwater sits at the far north of the strip. **Gulf Boulevard** runs down the coastline, through Belleair Shores, Indian Rocks Beach, Indian Shores, Redington Shores, Madeira Beach, Treasure Island, and St. Pete Beach. The stretch of beach past the huge pink Don Cesar Hotel, in St. Pete Beach, and Pass-a-Grille Beach have the best sand, and less pedestrian and motor traffic.

St. Petersburg Clearwater International Airport (☎453-7800; www.fly2pie.com), off Roosevelt Blvd., sits across the bay from Tampa. **Airport Super Shuttle** runs shuttles. (☎572-1111; www.supershuttle.com. Approx. $20 to downtown.) **Greyhound,** 180 9th St. N at 2nd Ave. N in St. Pete (☎822-1497; open daily 4:30am-11:30pm), sends buses to Clearwater (30min., 7 per day, $8-9) and Orlando (3-4hr., 5 per day, $18). The Clearwater station is at 2811 Gulf-to-Bay Blvd. (☎796-7315. Open daily 6am-9pm.) **Pinellas Suncoast Transit Authority (PSTA)** handles public transit; most routes depart from Williams Park at 1st Ave. N and 3rd St. N. (☎530-9911. $1.25, students $0.75, seniors $0.60. 1-day unlimited pass $3.) To reach Tampa, take express bus #100X M-F from the Gateway Mall ($1.50). A **beach trolley** runs up and down the shore. (Daily every 20-30min. 5am-10pm, $1.25. 1-day unlimited bus pass $3.) Jump on and off the **Looper Trolley** ($1), which also runs a 1½hr. tour of downtown St. Pete (☎893-7111). **Taxi: Yellow Cab** ☎799-2222. **Visitor Info: St. Petersburg Area Chamber of Commerce,** 100 2nd Ave. N. (☎821-4069; www.stpete.com. Open M-F 8am-5pm, Sa 10am-5pm, Su noon-5pm.) **The Pier Information Center,** 800 2nd Ave. NE, is also in St. Petersburg. (☎821-6443. Open M-Th 10am-9pm, F-Sa 10am-10pm, Su 11am-7pm.) **Hotlines:**

Rape Crisis, ☎ 530-7233. **Medical Services: Bayfront Medical Center,** 701 6th St. S. (☎ 823-1234). **Internet Access: St. Petersburg Main Library,** 3745 9th Ave. N, downtown. (☎ 893-7724. Open M-Th 9am-9pm, F-Sa 9am-6pm, Su 10am-6pm.) **Post Office:** 3135 1st Ave. N, at 31st St. (☎ 322-6696. Open M-F 8am-6pm, Sa 8am-12:30pm.) **Postal Code:** 37370. **Area Code:** 727.

FLORIDA

⚑ ACCOMMODATIONS. St. Petersburg and Clearwater offer two hostels, and many cheap motels line **4th Street N** and **U.S. 19** in St. Pete. Some establishments advertise singles for as little as $25, but these tend to be very worn-down. To avoid the worst neighborhoods, stay on the north end of 4th St. and the south end of U.S. 19. Several inexpensive motels cluster along **Gulf Boulevard.** Tucked away off the sandy Clearwater shore, the **Clearwater Beach International Hostel (HI) ❶,** 606 Bay Esplanade Ave., off Mandalay Ave. at the Sands Motel in Clearwater Beach, is the ultimate beach pad. Sports equipment is available to use at the nearby volleyball, basketball, or tennis courts, and bikes and kayaks are available for cruising the beaches. (☎ 443-1211. Internet access $1 per 8min. Linen and key deposit $5. Reception 9am-noon and 5-9pm. Dorms $13, nonmembers $14; private rooms $40. Surcharge for credit card payments.) The **St. Petersburg International Youth Hostel (HI) ❶,** 711 3rd Ave. S, is an acceptable option if you're in a pinch and can't make it up to Clearwater. Located just blocks from Tropicana Field, the hostel offers very spartan 4-person rooms that occasionally have A/C. (☎ 822-9770. Laundry and kitchen facilities available. Open 24hr. Dorms $16, nonmembers $20.) **Fort De Soto County Park ❶,** 3500 Pinellas Bayway S, composed of five islands, has perhaps the best camping in all of Florida. Though its namesake, Fort De Soto, is available for exploration, with beautiful views and your own picnic bench and grill, you may never leave your campsite. Reservations must be made in person, either at the park office, 501 1st Ave. N, Ste. A116, or at the Parks Dept., 631 Chestnut St. in Clearwater. (☎ 582-2267. Warm showers, electricity, and laundry facilities. Front gate locked 9pm. Curfew 10pm. Sites $28. Cash only. Park office: ☎ 582-7738. Open daily 8am-4:30pm. Parks Dept.: ☎ 464-3347. Open daily 8am-5pm.)

⊡ FOOD. St. Petersburg's cheap, health-conscious restaurants cater to its retired population and generally close by 8 or 9pm. **Dockside Dave's ❷,** 13203 Gulf Blvd. S, in Madeira Beach, is one of the best-kept secrets on the islands. The half-pound grouper sandwich (market price, around $8) is simply sublime. (☎ 392-9399. Open M-Sa 11am-10pm, Su noon-10pm.) Locals rave about **Tangelo's Bar and Grille ❷,** 226 1st Ave. N, a superb Cuban restaurant. Their imported *mole negro* sauce is spicy and accents the grilled chicken mojo sandwich nicely. (☎ 894-1695. Open M 11am-6pm, Tu-Th 11am-8pm, F-Sa 11am-9pm.) Also in St. Pete is the **Fourth Street Shrimp Store ❷,** 1006 4th St. N, a purveyor of all things shrimp. (☎ 822-0325. Filling shrimp taco salad $7. Open Su-Th 11am-9pm, F-Sa 11am-9:30pm.) After a long day of relaxing under the unrelenting Clearwater sun, make your way over to **Frenchy's Cafe ❸,** 41 Baymont St., and cool off with a salted margarita ($3). If beach volleyball has you hungry, have a seat at one of the picnic tables for the boiled shrimp, which comes dusted in secret seasonings for $13. The original grouper burger ($7) is also a fine choice. (☎ 446-3607. Open M-Th 11:30am-11pm, F-Sa 11:30am-midnight, Su noon-11pm.) For something light, the **Computer Port Cafe ❶,** 432 Poinsettia Ave., allows you to surf (the web) while you sip cool smoothies and munch on tasty snacks. (☎ 441-2667. Open daily 8am-11pm.)

⬛ SIGHTS. Grab *See St. Pete* or the *St. Petersburg Official Visitor's Guide* for the lowdown on area events, discounts, and useful maps. Downtown St. Pete is cluttered with museums and galleries. For an incredible history experience, head

FLORIDA

to the ◪**Florida International Museum,** 100 2nd St. N. The "Cuban Missile Crisis: When the Cold War Got Hot" exhibit allows visitors to relive the Cold War era of the 1960s, recounting day-by-day the Cuban Missile Crisis. "John F. Kennedy: The Exhibition" provides a look at JFK's personal and political life. (☎ 822-3693 or 800-777-9882; www.floridamuseum.org. Open M-Sa 10am-5pm, Su noon-5pm; ticket office closes 4pm. $10, seniors $8, students $5. Wheelchair accessible.) The highlight of St. Petersburg is the ◪**Salvador Dalí Museum,** 1000 3rd St. S, the largest private collection of the Surrealist's work in the world. The South's most-visited museum houses 95 of Dalí's oil paintings and provides exceptional guided tours offering fascinating views into the enigmatic artist's life and works. (☎ 823-3767 or 800-442-3254; www.salvadordalimuseum.org. Open M-W and F-Sa 9:30am-5:30pm, Th 9:30am-8pm, Su noon-5:30pm. $13, seniors $11, students $7. Free tours daily 12:15, 1:30, 2:30, 3:45pm. Wheelchair accessible.) The **Florida Holocaust Museum,** 55 5th St. S, traces Jewish life and anti-Semitism from early Europe to the present. (☎ 820-0110 or 800-960-7448; www.flholocaustmuseum.org. Open M-F 10am-5pm, Sa-Su noon-5pm. $8, students and seniors $7, under 19 $3.)

The museum exhibits may impress you with their thorough and informative displays, but for a scene a little more characteristic of eastern Florida, hit the beaches. The nicest beach in the area may be **Pass-a-Grille Beach,** but its parking meters eat quarters by the bucketful. Check out **Clearwater Beach,** at the northern end of the Gulf Blvd. strand, where mainstream beach culture finds a fantastic white sand setting. The **Sunsets at Pier 60 Festival** brings arts and entertainment to Clearwater Beach, but it's the sunsets that draw the crowds. (☎ 449-1036; www.sunsetsatpier60.com. Festival daily 2hr. before sundown until 2hr. after.)

◪ **NIGHTLIFE.** St. Pete caters to those who want to end the night by 9 or 10pm; most visitors looking for nightlife either head to Tampa or to the beach. However, if you're staying in St. Pete and are in the mood for a concert, don't overlook **Jannus Landing,** 200 1st Ave. N, which hosts a number of local and big-name bands throughout the year. The outside courtyard accommodates 1500 and the bar keeps listeners in good spirits. (☎ 896-1244. Call for acts and tickets.) For a more consistent scene infused with the energy of youth, the Clearwater hotels, restaurants, and parks often host free concerts. Free copies of *Weekly Planet* or *Tampa Tonight/Pinellas Tonight* can be found at local restaurants and bars, though an evening stroll through the blocks surrounding the rotary might be all that's needed to sniff out the night's hottest spot. Locals wind down with a beer and a game of pool at the **Beach Bar,** 454 Mandalay Ave. If not in the mood for darts, walk around the corner and find your groove on the dance floor. (☎ 446-8866. Dancing F-Sa 9pm-2am. 21+. Bar open daily 10am-2am.) The younger crowd likes to make a dash for the mainland and party at **Liquid Blue,** 22 N. Ft. Harrison St., Clearwater's premier techno nightspot. (☎ 446-4000. 18+. Open Tu-Sa 9pm-2am.)

ATLANTIC COAST

DAYTONA BEACH   ☎ 386

Though surely not the classiest city in Florida, Daytona has a distinctive surfing-meets-racing character. When locals first started auto-racing on the hard-packed sands of Daytona Beach more than 60 years ago, they combined two aspects of life that would come to define the town's entire mentality: speed and sand. Daytona played an essential role in the founding of the **National Association of Stock Car Auto**

Racing (NASCAR) in 1947, and the mammoth Daytona International Speedway still hosts several big races each year. While races no longer occur on the sand, 23 mi. of Atlantic beaches still pump the lifeblood of the community.

ORIENTATION. Daytona Beach lies 53 mi. northeast of Orlando and 90 mi. south of Jacksonville. **I-95** parallels the coast and the barrier island. **Atlantic Avenue (Route A1A)** is the main drag along the shore, and a scenic drive up A1A goes to St. Augustine and Jacksonville. **International Speedway Boulevard (U.S. 92)** runs east-west, from the ocean, through downtown, and to the racetrack and airport. Daytona Beach is a collection of smaller towns; many street numbers are not consecutive and navigation can be difficult. To avoid the gridlock on the beach, arrive early (8am) and leave early (around 3pm). Visitors must pay $5 to drive onto the beach, and police strictly enforce the 10 mph speed limit. Free parking is plentiful during most of the year but sparse during spring break, Speedweek, Bike Week, Biketoberfest, and the Pepsi 400. See p. 520 for festival dates.

PRACTICAL INFORMATION. Amtrak, 2491 Old New York Ave. (☎734-2322; open daily 8:30am-7pm), in DeLand, 24 mi. west on Rte. 92, runs to Miami (7hr., 2 per day, $37). **Greyhound,** 138 S. Ridgewood Ave. (☎255-7076; open daily 6:30am-10:30pm), 4 mi. west of the beach, goes to Jacksonville (2hr., 11 per day, $20) and Orlando (1½hr., 7 per day, $11). **Volusia County Transit Co. (VOTRAN),** 950 Big Tree Rd., operates local buses and a trolley that covers Rte. A1A between Granada Blvd. and Dunlawton Ave. All buses have bike racks. On beaches where driving is prohibited, free beach trams provide transport. (☎761-7700. Regular service M-Sa 6am-7pm, Su 6am-6pm. Nightly service on select routes. Trolley M-Sa noon-midnight. $1, seniors and ages 6-17 $0.50. Free maps available at hotels.) **Taxi: Yellow Cab** ☎255-5555. **Visitor Info: Daytona Beach Area Convention and Visitors Bureau,** 126 E. Orange Ave., on City Island. (☎255-0415 or 800-544-0415; www.daytonabeachcvb.org. Open M-F 9am-5pm.) **Hotline: Rape Crisis Line,** ☎258-7273. **Medical Services: Halifax Medical Center,** 303 N. Clyde Morris Blvd. (☎254-4000). **Internet Access: Volusia County Library Center,** 105 E. Magnolia Ave. (☎257-6036. Open M and W 9:30am-5:30pm, Tu and Th 9:30am-8pm, F-Sa 9:30am-5pm.) **Post Office:** 220 N. Beach St. (☎226-2618. Open M-F 8am-5pm, Sa 9am-noon.) **Postal Code:** 32115. **Area Code:** 386.

ACCOMMODATIONS. Almost all of Daytona's lodgings front **Atlantic Avenue (Route A1A),** either on the beach or across the street; those off the beach offer the best deals. Spring break and race events drive prices sky high, but low-season rates are more reasonable. Almost all the motels facing the beach cost $35 for a low-season single; on the other side of the street it's $25. The **Camellia Motel ❷,** 1055 N. Atlantic Ave. (Rte. A1A), across the street from the beach, has cozy, bright rooms, free local calls, cable TV, and A/C. (☎252-9963. Reserve early. Singles $30; doubles $35. During spring break, singles $100; each additional person $10.) For a unique experience, try the **Travelers Inn ❷,** 735 N. Atlantic Ave. Each of the 22 rooms has a different theme—find the force in the *Star Wars* room or rock out with Jimi Hendrix or the Beatles in their rooms. (☎253-3501 or 800-417-6466. Singles $29-49; doubles $39-59; each additional person $10. Kitchen additional $10. Prices triple during special events.) The gay-friendly **Streamline Hotel ❷,** 140 S. Atlantic, has some of the cheapest rooms in town. The top floor is the Penthouse Lounge, a sky-roof bar with an expansive view of the beach. (☎258-6937. Singles $25, 3-night special $69. Event prices as high as $150 per room.) **Tomoka State Park ❶,** 2099 N. Beach St., 8 mi. north of Daytona in Ormond Beach, has 100 campsites under a tropical canopy. Enjoy salt-water fishing, nature trails, and a sculpture

FLORIDA

museum. (☎676-4050, reservations 800-326-3521. Open daily 8am-dusk. Sites Nov.-Apr. $23; May-Oct. $13. Seniors 50% discount. $3 per vehicle, $4 with more than 1 occupant. Pedestrians and bicyclists $1.)

🍴 **FOOD.** One of the most famous seafood restaurants in the area is 🖼**Aunt Catfish's ❸**, 4009 Halifax Dr., at Dunlawton Ave. on the mainland side of the Port Orange Bridge. Order any seafood, and you're in for a treat, though the lobster and crab receive the most praise. Most entrees are $9-15; salads are under $9. (☎767-4768. Open M-Sa 11:30am-9:30pm, Su 9am-9:30pm.) At **Maria Bonita ❷**, 1784 S. Ridgewood Ave., don't let the unimpressive exterior mislead you; the food is both authentic and delicious. Though heralded for its Mexican food, the Cuban specials take the prize. The *pechuga de pollo a la plancha* (grilled chicken breast; $10) is a fiesta for your mouth, and during dinnertime can be watered down with a mojito for just 99 cents. (☎767-9512. Open daily 10am-10pm.) From frog legs ($10) to flounder ($10), **B&B Fisheries ❸**, 715 E. International Speedway, serves some of Daytona's best seafood. The B&B is half fish market, half restaurant; if you loved your flounder dinner, you can buy one on your way out to cook at home. Don't worry, landlubbers: B&B also dishes out incredible slabs of steak from $10. (☎252-6542. Open M-F 11am-8:30pm, Sa 4-8:30pm.) The **Dancing Avocado Kitchen ❶**, 110 S. Beach St., is a delicious alternative to the Daytona seafood-and-grill scene, and serves fantastic breakfasts. Enjoy the belly dancer sandwich (avocado, hummus, lettuce, tomato, and olives; $5.50) or the signature symphony salad ($6) in this organically delightful eatery. (☎947-2022. Open M-Sa 8am-4pm.)

🏁 **START YOUR ENGINES.** The center of the racing world, the **Daytona International Speedway** hosts NASCAR's Super Bowl: the Daytona 500 (Feb. 20, 2005). **Speedweek** (Feb. 5-20, 2005) precedes the legendary race, while the **Pepsi 400** (for those who think young) heats up the track July 2, 2005. (NASCAR tickets ☎253-7223.) Next door, **Daytona USA**, 1801 W. International Speedway Blvd., is a must for any NASCAR fan, though the admission price will seem ridiculous if you're not. This interactive experience includes a new simulation ride, an IMAX film on NASCAR, and a fun teaching program on NASCAR commentating. The breathtaking **Speedway Tour** is a unique chance to see the garages, grandstands, and famous 31° banked turns up close. The **Richard Petty Driving Experience** puts fans in a stock car for a ride-along at 150 mph. (☎947-6800. Open daily 9am-7pm. $22, seniors $19, ages 6-12 $16. Tours every 30min. daily 9:30am-5:30pm, $7.50. Richard Petty: ☎800-237-3889. 16+. $106.) **Bike Week** draws biker mamas for various motorcycle duels, and **Biketoberfest** brings them back for more. (Bikeweek: Mar. 4-13 2005; www.bikeweek.com. Biketoberfest: Oct. 20-23, 2004; www.biketoberfest.com.)

🎵 **NIGHTLIFE.** When spring break hits, concerts, hotel-sponsored parties, and other events answer the call of students. News about these events travels fastest by word of mouth, but the *Calendar of Events* and *SEE Daytona Beach* make good starting points. On mellow nights, head to the boardwalk to play volleyball or shake your groove thing at the **Oceanfront Bandshell,** an open-air amphitheater made of *coquina* (crushed sea shells mixed with concrete). Dance clubs line Seabreeze Blvd. just west of N. Atlantic Ave. **Razzle's,** 611 Seabreeze Blvd., caters to the traditionally scandalous spring break crowd with its high energy dance floors, flashy light shows, and nightly drink specials. (☎257-6326. Cover around $5. Open daily 8pm.) **Ocean Deck**, 127 S. Ocean Ave., stands out among the clubs with its live music on the beach and nightly drink specials. Chow down on the "shipwreck" (shrimp, crab, oysters, and clams; $18) while grooving to the nightly reggae, jazz, calypso, and rock. (☎253-5224; www.oceandeck.com. Music nightly 9:30pm-2:30am. 21+ after 9pm. Open daily 11am-3am; kitchen until 2am.)

COCOA BEACH AND CAPE CANAVERAL ☎321

During the Cold War, Cape Canaveral and the surrounding "Space Coast" were the base of operations for major space explorations, from the Apollo moon landings to the current International Space Station effort. Even the local area code (3, 2, 1...liftoff!) reflects the space obsession. The towns of Cocoa Beach and nearby Melbourne are home to Florida's best waves; surfers head to ▧Ron Jon Surf Shop, 4151 N. Atlantic Ave., for two floors of boards, shirts, shorts, and sunscreen. (☎799-8888. Open 24hr.) All NASA's shuttles take off from the Kennedy Space Center, 18 mi. north of Cocoa Beach on Rte. 3; by car via Rte. 405 E off I-95, or Rte. 528 E from the Bee Line Expwy. From Cocoa Beach, take Rte. A1A to Rte. 528, then follow Rte. 3 N. The renovated Kennedy Space Center Visitors Complex (KSC) has two 3-D IMAX theaters, a Rocket Garden, and exhibits on current space exploration. Standard Admission ($29, children $19) will let you into the Visitors Complex; Maximum Access includes the Astronaut Hall of Fame and simulators ($35/$25). NASA Up Close ($22/$16) tours the shuttle launch pads and gets into the International Space Station Center. The tour Cape Canaveral: Then and Now guides visitors through America's first launch sites from the 1960s, the Air Force Space & Missile Museum, and the Cape Canaveral Lighthouse. A closely guarded secret is that after 3:45pm you can pay $10 for museum admission. Check NASA's launch schedule—you may have a chance to watch space shuttles thunder off into the blue yonder. (☎452-2121, launch info 449-4444; www.kennedyspacecenter.com. Open daily 9am-5:30pm.) Nearby, the Merritt Island National Wildlife Refuge teems with sea turtles, manatees, wild hogs, otters, and over 300 bird species. Exit 80 off I-95 and go east on Garden St. to SR 402. (☎861-0667. Open daily dawn-dusk. Visitors center open M-F 8am-4:30pm, Sa 9am-5pm.) On the northeastern shore, ▧Canaveral National Seashore, is an undeveloped beach with gorgeous dunes. Take Rte. 406 E off U.S. 1 in Titusville. (☎267-1110. Open daily Apr.-Oct. 6am-8pm; Nov.-Mar 6am-6pm. Closed 3 days before and 1 day after NASA launches. $5 per car, $1 per pedestrian or bicyclist.)

During summer launch dates, tourists pack the area and hotel prices soar into the stratosphere. Behind the bus station, the Dixie Motel ❷, 301 Forrest Ave., has clean rooms, huge windows, A/C, cable TV, and a pool. (☎632-1600. Laundry. 21+. Rooms $55.) Partying teenagers and vacationing families flock to the Cocoa Beach Comfort Inn ❸, 3901 N. Atlantic Ave., which has giant rooms with A/C, cable TV, free Internet, and, in some rooms, a wet bar. (☎783-2221. Pool and whirlpool. 18+. Rooms Nov.-Apr. from $95; May-Oct. from $85.) Pitch your tent at Jetty Park Campgrounds ❶, 400 E. Jetty Rd., at the northern tip of Cape Canaveral. (☎783-7111. Reserve 3 months ahead. Jan.-Apr. sites $24, with water and electricity $28, with full hookup $31. May-Dec. $18/$22/$24.) Bikini contests, live music, karaoke, drink specials, and tasty seafood make Coconut's on the Beach ❸, 2 Minutemen Causeway at Rte. A1A, a popular hangout. (☎784-1422. Open daily 11am-2am.) New York-style pizza ($2 per slice) can be found at Bizzarro ❶, 4 1st Ave., off Rte. A1A in Indialantic. (☎724-4799. Open M-Th 11am-9pm, F-Sa 11am-11pm, Su noon-9pm.)

The Space Coast, 50 mi. east of Orlando, consists of mainland towns Cocoa and Rockledge, oceanfront Cocoa Beach and Cape Canaveral, and Merritt Island. Greyhound, 302 E. Main St. (☎636-6531; station open daily 7am-5:30pm), in Cocoa, 8 mi. inland, runs to Daytona (1¾hr., 4 per day, $15-16) and Orlando (1hr., 5 per day, $10-11). Space Coast Area Transit (SCAT) has North Beach and South Beach routes and stops at every town in Brevard County. (☎633-1878. Operates M-F 8am-5pm, Sa-Su service on some routes. $1; students, seniors, and disabled $0.50; transfers free.) Visitor Info: Cocoa Beach Chamber of Commerce, 400 Fortenberry Rd., on Merritt Island. (☎459-2200; www.cocoabeachchamber.com. Open M-F 9-5pm.) Space Coast Office of Tourism, 725 Judge Fran Jamieson Way, in Viera. (☎637-5483 or 877-572-3224. Open M-F 8am-5pm.) Medical Services: Cape Canaveral Hospital, 701 W.

Cocoa Beach Cswy. (☎ 799-7111). **Internet Access: Cocoa Beach Public Library,** 550 N. Brevard Ave. (☎ 868-1104. Open M-W 9am-9pm, Th 9am-6pm, F-Sa 9am-5pm, Su 1-5pm.) **Post Office:** 500 N. Brevard Ave., Cocoa Beach. (☎ 783-2544. Open M-F 8:30am-5pm, Sa 8:30am-noon.) **Postal Code:** 32931. **Area Code:** 321.

ST. AUGUSTINE ☎ 904

Spanish adventurer Pedro Menéndez de Áviles founded St. Augustine in 1565, making it the first European colony in North America and the oldest continuous settlement in the United States. Thanks to preservation efforts and a desire to trap as many tourist dollars as possible, much of St. Augustine's Spanish flavor remains intact. This city's pride lies in its provincial cobblestone streets, *coquina* walls, and antique shops rather than in its token beaches. With a little effort the tourist traps can be avoided and the charm, history, and surprisingly lively nights of St. Augustine can be yours.

◤ ▐ ORIENTATION AND PRACTICAL INFORMATION

Most of St. Augustine's sights lie within a 10-15min. walk from the hostel, motels, and bus station, which is convenient as narrow streets and frequent one-ways can make driving unpleasant. The city's major east-west routes, **King Street** and **Cathedral Place,** run through downtown and become the **Bridge of Lions** that leads to the beaches. **San Marco Avenue** and **Avenida Menéndez** run north-south. **Castillo Drive** grows out of San Marco Ave. near the center of town. **Saint George Street,** a charming north-south pedestrian-only route, contains most of the shops and many of the sights in town. **Greyhound,** 1711 Dobbs Rd., about 2 mi. outside of downtown (☎ 829-6401; open daily 7:30am-8:30pm), has service to Daytona Beach (1¼hr., 6 per day, $13-14) and Jacksonville (1hr., 6 per day, $9-10). If the station is closed, drivers accept cash. **Sightseeing Trains,** 170 San Marco Ave., shuttles travelers on a red trolley that hits all the major attractions on their 20 stops. (☎ 829-6545 or 800-226-6545. Runs every 15-20min. 8:30am-5pm. $15, ages 6-12 $4. Ticket good for 3 consecutive days.) **Taxi: Ancient City Taxi** ☎ 824-8161. **Visitor Info: St. Augustine Visitor Information Center,** 10 Castillo Dr., at San Marco Ave. From the bus station, walk three blocks north on Riberia St., then right on Orange St. (☎ 825-1000. Open daily 8:30am-5:30pm. All-day parking $3.) **Post Office:** 99 King St. (☎ 829-8716. Open M-F 8:30am-5pm, Sa 9am-1pm.) **Postal Code:** 32084. **Area Code:** 904.

▐ ACCOMMODATIONS

Pirate Haus Inn and Hostel, 32 Treasury St. (☎ 808-1999 or 877-466-3864), just off Saint George St., is hands-down the best place to stay, with spacious dorms, beautiful private rooms, helpful management, and a great location. From Rte. 16 E, go south on U.S. 1, make a left on King St. and then left on Charlotte St.; parking is available in the metered lot behind the inn. Weary travelers are treated to a lively common room, big free lockers, Internet access, A/C, and a tasty pancake breakfast. Key and linen deposit $5. Reception 8-10am and 6-10pm, no lockout for registered guests. Dorms $16, non-members $17; private rooms $46. Under 13 free. ❶

Casablanca Inn, 24 Avenida Menéndez (☎ 829-0928), in the historic downtown district, stands out among St. Augustine's many B&Bs. Feast on a giant breakfast and unwind on the porch with rocking chairs and a spectacular view of the river. Large rooms boast cable TV, pleasant artwork, and—perhaps inexplicably—fireplaces. Rooms $100-160. ❺

Seabreeze Motel, 208 Anastasia Blvd. (☎ 829-8122), has clean rooms with refrigerators and pool access. A/C, cable TV, kitchenette, and free local calls. Singles Su-Th $40, F-Sa $50, holidays and special events $60; doubles $45/$50/$65. ❷

Anastasia State Recreation Area, (☎461-2033), on Rte. A1A, 4 mi. south of the historic district. From town, cross the Bridge of Lions and turn left past the alligator farm. Nearby, Salt Run and the Atlantic Ocean provide opportunities for great windsurfing, fishing, swimming, and hiking. Office open daily 8am-dusk. Reservations a must in the summer. Sites $18, with electricity $20. Vehicle entrance fee $3-5, pedestrians $1. ❶

🎵🍴 FOOD AND NIGHTLIFE

The bustle of daytime tourists and the abundance of budget eateries make lunch in St. Augustine's historic district a delight, especially among the cafes and bars of **Saint George Street.** The **Bunnery Bakery and Cafe ❶,** 121 Saint George St., is a bakery-diner combo popular with the vacationing crowd. The Bunnery has hearty breakfasts ($2-6), and delectable panini sandwiches ($4-7) at lunch. (☎829-6166. Open 8am-6pm. No credit cards.) Frankly, my dear, you'll get more barbecue than you can handle at **Scarlett O'Hara's ❷,** 70 Hypolita St., at Cordova St. Monster "Big Rhett" burgers ($6) and full slabs of ribs ($15) are consumed by patrons who, after discovering this slat-board house, will never go hungry again. Live music, usually rock or reggae, entertains each night. (☎824-6535. Happy hour M-F 4-7pm. Occasional $2 cover. Open daily 11am-12:30am.) **Pizzalley's ❶,** 117 Saint George St., is the best pizza place in the historic district. Scarf down a piping hot slice ($2) or a tremendous sub ($5-7) in this cramped but worthwhile eatery. (☎825-2627. Open daily 11am-9pm.)

Many of St. Augustine's bars are on Rte. A1A S and Saint George St. *Folio Weekly* has event listings. Local string musicians play on the two stages in the **Milltop,** 19½ Saint George St., a tiny but illustrious bar above an old water mill in the restored district. (☎829-2329. Music daily 1pm-close. Cover varies. Open M-Sa 11am-1am, Su 11am-10pm.) Sample your choice of 24 drafts at the **Oasis Deck and Restaurant,** 4000 Rte. A1A S at Ocean Trace Rd., a family restaurant by day, romping party by night. (☎471-3424. Gator tail $6. Seafood sandwich $3-7. Happy hour 4-7pm. Live rock or reggae M-Sa 8pm-12:30am, Su 7-11:30pm. Open daily 6am-1am.) Throw a few back with Flagler College students at their campus watering hole, the **St. George Tavern,** 116 Saint George St. Happy hours with $2 beer. (☎824-4204. Happy hour M-Th 4-7pm, F 4pm-1am. Open daily 11am-1am.) Dinner and a movie and a beer? You betcha, and all at once at **Pot Belly's,** 36 Granada St., which offers cheap flicks and bargain eats. Screening just-out-of-theaters movies, this combination pub, deli, and cinema serves a range of sandwiches ($3-6), junk food ($1-3), and brew (pitchers $7.50) to the in-house tables. (☎829-3101. Movie tickets $5. Call for showtimes.)

👁 SIGHTS

SPANISH HERITAGE. The oldest masonry fortress in the continental US, **Castillo de San Marcos National Monument** has 14 ft.-thick *coquina* (a mixture of crushed seashells and concrete) walls. The fort, originally built by the Spanish in 1627, is shaped like a four-pointed star complete with drawbridge and moat. It contains a museum, a large courtyard surrounded by quarters for the garrison, a jail, a chapel, and the original cannon brought overseas by the Spanish. *(1 Castillo Dr., off San Marco Ave. ☎829-6506. Open daily 8:45am-5:15pm, last admission 4:45pm. Occasional tours; call ahead. $5, ages 6-16 $2.)* The **La Leche Shrine and Mission of Nombre de Dios** is the birthplace of American Catholicism. The first mass in the US was held here over 400 years ago. A huge steel cross marks the city's religious roots and the shaded lawns offer peaceful strolls. *(27 Ocean St., off San Marco Ave. ☎824-2809. Open M-F 8am-5pm, Sa 9am-5pm, Su 9:30am-5pm. Mass M-F 8:30am, Sa 6pm, Su 8am. Donation suggested.)*

HISTORICAL SIGHTS. Not surprisingly, the oldest continuous settlement in the US holds some of the nation's oldest artifacts. The **González-Álvarez House** is the oldest house on the National Registry of Historic Places. Built in the 17th century, the tiny house now serves as a tourist haven, with exhibits on the area's Spanish, British, and American heritage. *(14 Saint Francis St. ☎824-2872; www.oldcity.com/oldhouse. Open daily 9am-5pm, last admission 4:30pm. $6, seniors $5.50, students $4; families $14. Partially wheelchair accessible.)* For the best view of the city and the water, climb the 219 stairs of the **St. Augustine Lighthouse and Museum,** one of only six lighthouses in the state open to the public. Tour the 19th-century tower and keeper's house to learn about marine archaeological studies in the surrounding waters. *(81 Lighthouse Ave., off Rte. A1A across from the alligator farm. ☎829-0745. Open daily 9am-6pm. Tower, grounds, and house $6.50, seniors $5.50, ages 7-11 $4. House and grounds $4/$3/$2.)* For a view of American history through a shotgun's barrel, check out the **Museum of Weapons and Early American History.** For over 18 years the owner-curator of the museum has collected early American artifacts. *(81C King St. ☎829-3727. Open daily 9:30am-5pm, $4, ages 6-12 $1, under 6 free.)* In the **Colonial Spanish Quarter,** a living history museum, you'll see period craftsmen, soldiers, and housewives as they go about their business in this charming recreation of an 18th-century colonial Spanish town. Lucky for us, 18th-century Spanish colonials were apparently bilingual. *(53 Saint George St. ☎825-6830. Open daily 9am-5:30pm. $6.50, children $4.)*

RESTORATIONS. Flagler College is a small liberal arts institution in the restored Spanish Renaissance-style **Ponce de León Hotel.** Built by railroad and Standard Oil tycoon Henry Flagler in 1888, the hotel was the playground for America's social elite. Celebrity heavyweights like John Rockefeller and Will Rogers once strolled through the gorgeous interior. *(☎823-3378; www.flagler.edu. Tours mid-May to mid-Aug. daily on the hr. 10am-4pm. $4, under 12 $1. Wheelchair accessible.)* The **Memorial Presbyterian Church,** a beautiful model of St. Mark's Cathedral in Venice, was also built by Flagler, but these Tiffany windows are fake. The workmanship is so fine, though, that no one would guess that the church only took 361 days to finish. *(36 Sevilla St. ☎829-6451. Open M-Sa 9am-4pm, Su 12:30-4pm. Free.)* In 1947, Chicago publisher and art lover Otto Lightner converted the Alcazar Hotel into the **Lightner Museum,** holding an impressive collection of cut, blown, and burnished glass, along with old clothing and oddities. Today, the museum's eccentricity is its strongest feature, as it houses everything from a shrunken head to nun's and monk's beer steins. *(75 King St. ☎824-2874; www.lightnermuseum.org. Open daily 9am-5pm. 18th-century musical instruments play daily 11am-2pm. $6, students and ages 12-18 $2. Wheelchair accessible.)*

JUST FOR FUN. Across the Bridge of Lions, the ▨**St. Augustine Alligator Farm** allows visitors to get personal with 'gators. The park, delighting visitors since 1893, is the only place in the world where all 23 known crocodilian species live. *(On Rte. A1A S. ☎824-3337. Open daily 9am-8pm. Presentations every hr. Feeding daily at noon and 3pm. $15, ages 5-11 $9. Discounts for AAA/CAA, military, and seniors.)*

SOUTH FLORIDA

MIAMI ☎305

No longer purely a vacation spot for "snowbirds" (wealthy East Coasters escaping harsh winters), Miami's heart pulses to a beat all its own, fueled by the largest Cuban population this side of Havana. Appearance rules supreme in this city, and

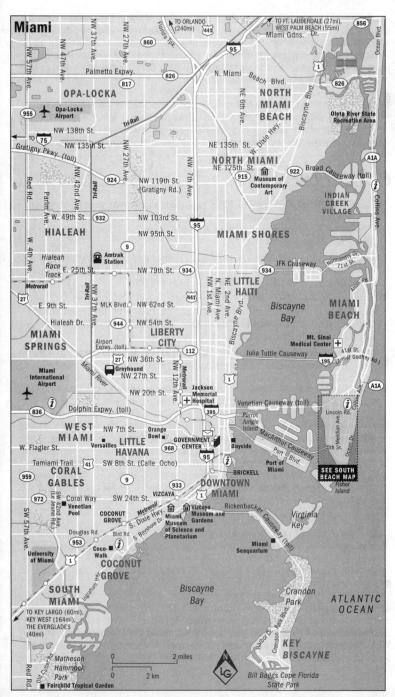

nowhere is this more apparent than on the beaches of South Beach, where visual delights include both the Art Deco hotels and tanned beach bodies. South Beach is also host to a hopping nightclub scene which attracts some of the world's most beautiful (and famous) people. But it's not all bikinis and sand—Miami is the entry point for one of America's greatest natural habitats, the Everglades, as well as the gateway to the Florida Keys and the Caribbean.

> When visiting Miami, it is best to avoid Liberty City, which is considered to be an unsafe area and offers visitors little in the realm of tourism. Also, many residents of SoBe—which has long been considered a gay-friendly area—complain that homosexuals are still verbally berated. It is best to be vigilant at all times.

▐ TRANSPORTATION

Airport: Miami International (☎876-7000; www.miami-airport.com), at Le Jeune Rd. and NW 36th Ave., 7 mi. northwest of downtown. Bus #7 runs downtown; many others make downtown stops. From downtown, take bus "C" or "K" to South Beach. Taxi to/ from Miami Beach $28 flat rate.

Trains: Amtrak, 8303 NW 37th Ave. (☎835-1223), near the Northside Metrorail station. Bus "L" goes directly to Lincoln Rd. Mall in South Beach. Open daily 6:30am-10pm. To: **Charleston, SC** (14hr., 2 per day, $57-125); **Orlando** (5½hr., 2 per day, $29); **Tampa** (5½hr., 1 per day, $32-54); **Washington, D.C.** (24hr., 3 per day, $162-211).

Buses: Greyhound, Miami Station, 4111 NW 27th St. (☎871-1810). To: **Atlanta** (17-19hr., 13 per day, $86); **Fort Lauderdale** (1hr., every hr., $6); **Key West** (5hr., 4 per day, $35); **Orlando** (6hr., 10 per day, $33). Open 24hr.

Public Transit: Metro Dade Transportation (☎770-3131; info M-F 6am-10pm, Sa-Su 9am-5pm). The **Metrobus** network converges downtown, where most long trips transfer. Over 100 routes, but the major, lettered bus routes A, C, D, G, H, J, K, L, R, S, and T serve Miami Beach. After dark, some stops are patrolled (indicated with a sign). Buses run M-F 4am-2:30am. $1.25, transfers $0.25; students, seniors, and disabled $0.60/$0.10. Call for weekend schedule. Exact change only. The **Metrorail** serves downtown's major business and cultural areas. Rail runs daily 5am-midnight. $1.25, rail-to-bus transfers $0.50. The **Metromover** loop downtown is linked to the Metrorail stations. Runs daily 5am-midnight. It glows at night, and is also free. **Tri-Rail** (☎800-874-7245) connects Miami, Fort Lauderdale, and West Palm Beach. Trains run M-Sa 4am-8pm, Su 7am-8pm. M-F $6.75, Sa-Su $4; students, seniors, and ages 5-12 50% off. The **Electrowave** (☎843-9283) offers shuttles along Washington Ave. from S. Pointe to 17th St. Pick up a brochure or just hop on in South Beach. Runs M-Sa 8am-1am, Su 10am-1am. $0.25.

Taxi: Metro ☎888-8888. **Central Cab** ☎532-5555.

Bike Rental: Miami Beach Bicycle Center, 601 5th St. (☎531-4161), at the corner of Washington Ave., Miami Beach. Open M-Sa 10am-7pm, Su 10am-5pm. $8 per hr., $20 per day, $70 per week. Credit card or $200 cash deposit required.

▮ ORIENTATION

Three highways crisscross the Miami area. **I-95,** the most direct north-south route, merges into **U.S. 1 (Dixie Highway)** just south of downtown. U.S. 1 runs to the Everglades entrance at Florida City and then continues as the Overseas Hwy. to Key West. **Route 836 (Dolphin Expressway),** a major east-west artery through town, connects I-95 to **Florida's Turnpike,** passing the airport in between.

When looking for street addresses, pay careful attention to the systematic street layout; it's easy to confuse North Miami Beach, West Miami, Miami Beach, and Miami addresses. Streets in Miami run east-west, avenues north-south; both are numbered. Miami divides into NE, NW, SE, and SW quadrants; the dividing lines downtown are **Flagler Street** (east-west) and **Miami Avenue** (north-south). Some numbered roads also have names; be sure to get a map that lists both.

Several causeways connect Miami to **Miami Beach.** The most useful is **Mac-Arthur Causeway,** which becomes 5th St. Numbered streets run east-west across the island, increasing as you go north. In South Beach, **Collins Avenue (A1A)** is the main north-south drag; parallel are the club-filled **Washington Avenue** and the beachfront **Ocean Drive.** The commercial district sits between 6th and 23rd St. One-way streets, traffic jams, and limited parking make driving around **South Beach (SoBe)** frustrating. Tie on your most stylish sneakers and enjoy the small island at your leisure—it only takes about 20min. to walk up Collins Ave. from 6th to 16th St., not counting all the time you spend checking out the funky fashion stores and restaurants.

Back in Miami, the life of **Little Havana** is on **Calle Ocho**—between SW 12th and SW 27th Ave.; take bus #8, 11, 17, or 37. **Coconut Grove,** south of Little Havana, centers on the shopping and entertainment district on **Grand Avenue** and **Virginia Street. Coral Gables,** an upscale residential area, rests around the intersection of **Coral Way (SW 24th St.)** and **Le Jeune Road,** also known as **SW 42nd Avenue.** Though public transit is reliable and safe, a car can be useful to get around the city and its suburbs.

▐ PRACTICAL INFORMATION

Visitor Info: Miami Beach Visitors Center, 1920 Meridian Ave. (☎672-1270; www.miami-beachchamber.com). Open M-F 9am-6pm, Sa-Su 10am-4pm. In South Beach, **Coconut Grove Chamber of Commerce,** 2820 McFarlane Rd. (☎444-7270). Open M-F 9am-5pm. **Greater Miami Convention and Visitors Bureau,** 701 Brickell Ave. (☎539-3000 or 800-283-2707), 27th fl. of Barnett Bank Bldg., downtown. Open M-F 9am-5pm.

Hotlines: Crisis Line, ☎358-4357. 24hr. **Gay Hotline,** ☎759-5210. **Abuse Hotline,** ☎800-342-9152.

Medical Services: Mt. Sinai Medical Center, 1300 Alton Rd., Miami Beach (☎674-2121). **Rape Treatment Center and Hotline** (☎585-7273), at Jackson Memorial Hospital, 1611 NW 12th Ave. Open 24hr.

Internet Access: Miami Public Library, 101 W. Flagler St. (☎375-2665), across from the Museum of Art. Open M-W and F-Sa 9am-6pm, Th 9am-9pm, Su 1-5pm. 45min. free. There are a number of cheap Internet options in South Beach around Washington Ave. and 15th. An excellent option is **Kafka's Cafe,** 1464 Washington Ave. (☎673-9669), in Miami Beach. Open daily 8am-midnight. $3 per hr., noon-8pm $6 per hr.

Post Office: Downtown: 500 NW 2nd Ave. (☎639-4284). Open M-F 8am-5pm, Sa 9am-1:30pm. Miami Beach: 1300 Washington Ave. (☎672-2447). Open M-F 8am-5pm, Sa 8:30am-2pm. **Postal Code:** 33101; Miami Beach 33119. **Area Code:** 305.

▐ ACCOMMODATIONS

Cheap rooms abound in South Beach, and choosing a place to stay is all about attitude. Hostels in Miami Beach are the cheapest option for people traveling alone. If young bohemian isn't your thing, cruise farther down Collins Ave. to the funky, hot-pink Art Deco hotels. Get a discount when you stay more than two nights in one of the trendy **South Beach Group Hotels,** including Whitelaw, Mercury, Shelly, Chelsea, Chesterfield, and Lily. In general, high season for Miami Beach runs late

December through mid-March; during the low season, hotel clerks are often quick to bargain. The Miami Beach Visitors Center (see **Practical Information,** above) can get you the cheapest rates. Camping is not allowed on Miami Beach.

HOSTELS

The Clay Hotel and International Hostel (HI), 1438 Washington Ave. (☎ 534-2988 or 800-379-2529), located on the charming, pedestrian-only Espanola Way; take bus "C" from downtown. This historic, Mediterranean-style building, once the center of Al Capone's Miami gambling syndicate and often featured on the TV series *Miami Vice*, is now home to the best hostel in SoBe and hosts a largely international crowd. Kitchen, laundry facilities, and A/C. Dorms come with phone and fridges; some have TV. Internet access $6 per hr. Lockers $1 per day. Linen/key deposit $10. 4- to 8-bed dorms $18, nonmembers $20; private rooms $43-79. ❶

The Tropics Hotel/Hostel, 1550 Collins Ave. (☎ 531-0361), across the street from the beach. From the airport, take bus "J" to 41st St., transfer to bus "C" to Lincoln Rd., walk 1 block south on Collins, and it's next to the parking garage. A respite from the intense SoBe scene, this quiet refuge offers large, comfortable rooms with A/C, pool access, and an outdoor kitchen. Internet access $3 per 30min. Lockers at front desk. Free linen. Laundry. Key deposit $10. Dorms $16; singles and doubles $40-55. ISIC discount. ❶

Miami Beach International Travelers Hostel (9th St. Hostel), 236 9th St. (☎ 534-0268 or 800-978-6787), at Washington Ave. From the airport, take bus "J" to 41st and Indian Creek, then transfer to bus "C" or "K." The strength of this establishment lies in its location—right in the heart of SoBe's club scene. Rooms are simple and the prices should appeal to the budget-conscious traveler. Internet access $5 per hr. Laundry and common room with TV and movie library. 4-bed dorms with A/C and bath $14, nonmembers $16. Singles or doubles in winter $60; low-season $40. ❶

Creek Hotel, 2360 Collins Ave. (☎ 538-1951). Though an acceptable and cheap option, the former Banana Bungalow has slipped a bit under new management. A fair distance from the center of the SoBe scene, the Creek Hotel still hosts lively weekend barbecues and offers use of the gym across the street for $5 a visit. Internet access $1 per 5min. Linen/key deposit $20. Parking $5 per night. Dorms $20; private rooms $50-85. ❶

HOTELS

Whitelaw Hotel-Lounge, 808 Collins Ave. (☎ 398-7000). From 7 to 8pm, bright white leather and chrome greet beautiful party people lured into the hotel's lobby by complimentary cocktails. Plush down comforters, continental breakfast, TV, A/C, refrigerator, free Internet access, free airport shuttle, and VIP guest passes to any club in SoBe. Doubles Apr.-Dec. $75; Jan.-Mar. $135. ❹

Chesterfield Hotel, 855 Collins Ave. (☎ 531-5831). Deep house music pumps through this uber-chic retreat, where the motto is "our rooms were made for sharing." Fabulous amenities, great location, and a helpful staff. Continental breakfast, TV, A/C, free Internet access, free airport shuttle, bar, cafe, and free VIP passes to any area club. Doubles Apr.-Nov. $90, third night is free; Dec.-Mar. $125. ❹

Kent Hotel, 1131 Collins Ave. (☎ 604-5068; www.thekenthotel.com). The Kent's tagline, "savvy affordability" is on the mark. With lavender-everything rooms and a dramatic lobby, the vibrant colors energize this hotel. Great location, free Internet access, TV, A/C, and continental breakfast pack in the value. May-Sept. $130; Oct.-Apr. $145. ❺

🍴 FOOD

The food in Miami is like the people: fun, exciting, and very diverse. Four-star restaurants owned by celebrities and celebrity chefs are as prevalent as four-choice sandwich counters known for their affordability. The South Beach strip along

Ocean Drive has an eclectic mix of regulars like **TGI Friday's** and **Johnny Rockets,** star-gazing favorites like **China Grill** and **News Cafe,** and pseudo-clubs like **Mango.** Go at least one block inland from the beach to find more wallet-pleasing prices.

🔲 **Opa,** 36 Ocean Dr. (☎673-6730). On the southern tip of South Beach lies a little piece of Greece. At 8:30pm every night, while you're enjoying a filling *souvlaki* ($6) or the oak-grilled pork loin ($11), the music strikes up and the manager tosses hundreds of napkins in the air while Greek belly dancers gyrate on table tops. Great for groups, Opa is a meal and a Greek festival in one. Open daily from 4pm until the *ouzo* runs out. ❸

🔲 **Flamingo Cafe,** 1454 Washington Ave. (☎673-4302), near the Clay Hostel in Miami Beach. Far and away the biggest bang for your buck, this friendly cafe produces overwhelming amounts of delicious food for staggeringly low prices. Breakfast plate (eggs, toast, and meat) $2.50. Beef tacos and salad $2.75. *Frijoles con queso* $3. Lunch specials $5-7. Open M-Sa 7am-9:30pm. ❶

Versailles, 3555 SW 8th St. (☎444-0240), in the heart of Little Havana. Don't let the name fool you—this place is Miami-Cuban to the core, down to the mirrored interior and Spanish-only menus. Sit in the company of Cuban power-brokers as you enjoy classic Cuban dishes, like the deliciously salty *ropa vieja* with a side of fried sweet plantains ($9). Open M-Th 8am-2am, F 8am-3:30am, Sa 8am-4:30am, Su 9am-2am. ❸

Fairwind Seafood, 1000 Collins Ave. (☎531-0050), across from the Essex House. One of the best-kept secrets in South Beach, Fairwind creates masterful seafood dishes at surprisingly low prices. Try the superb *sashimi* tuna salad with mango salsa ($9.50), seafood pasta ($10.50), and Key Lime Creme Brulée ($4). Happy hour daily 4-7pm. Open daily 7am-6am. ❸

Nexxt Cafe, 700 Lincoln Rd. (☎532-6643). A reputation for serving up the largest portions on South Beach keeps this popular cafe crowded. The menu is extensive and creative, featuring omelettes the size of a human head ($8). The real prize is the chocolate molten cake ($8), baked to order and not to be passed over by any chocolate lover. Open M-Th 11:30am-11pm, F-Sa 11:30am-midnight, Su 11am-11pm. ❸

News Cafe, 800 Ocean Dr. (☎538-6397). Though the food is outstanding, you're really paying for one of the best people-watching locations on Ocean Dr. Go in the evening just for dessert (chocolate fondue for two; $15) to gaze upon the stylish hard-bodies strolling by and perhaps glimpse a celebrity among your fellow diners. Open 24hr. ❸

Macarena, 1334 Washington Ave. (☎531-3440), in Miami Beach. Dance your way to wonderful food in an atmosphere that's intimate and festive. This eatery serves authentic Latin American delights while captivating dancers provide the entertainment. *Paella* big enough for two ($14, lunch $7) and the best rice pudding ever ($5.50) make for perfect Spanish treats. Wine comes from the restaurant's own vineyards. W and F flamenco dancing. Th ladies night. Sa live salsa. Lunch daily 12:30-3:30pm; dinner Su-Tu 7pm-1am, W-Th 7pm-1:30am, F-Sa 7pm-5am. ❸

Taystee Bakery, 1450 Washington Ave. (☎538-4793). A haven for anyone with a South American sweet tooth, Taystee has a large selection of super-cheap baked goods, including no salt/no sugar selections and Latin favorites. Guava pastries $1. *Empanadas* $1.50. *Pan cubano* sandwiches $4. Open M-Sa 6:30am-7:30pm. ❶

👁 **SIGHTS**

SOUTH BEACH. South Beach is the reason to come to Miami. The liberal atmosphere, hot bodies, Art Deco design, and excellent sand make these 17 blocks seem like their own little world. *(Between 6th and 23rd St.)* **Ocean Drive** is where Miami's hottest come to see and be seen. Bars and cafes cram this tiny strip of land, which is part fashion show and part raging party. The **Art Deco Welcome Cen-**

South Beach

ter dispenses free area maps and advice, features a free museum, and hosts walking tours. *(1001 Ocean Dr. ☎531-3484; www.mdpl.org. Open M-F 11am-6pm, Sa 10am-10pm, Su 11am-10pm. Walking tours ☎672-2014. W and Sa-Su 10:30am, Th 6:30pm. 90min. $15, students and seniors $10.)* The **Holocaust Memorial** commemorates the 6 million Jews who fell victim to genocide in WWII. Marvel at the 42 ft. bronze arm protruding from the ground, whose base is supported by dozens of sculpted figures struggling to escape persecution. *(1933-45 Meridian Ave. ☎538-1663. Open daily 9am-9pm. Free. Wheelchair accessible.)* Hidden in the heart of South Beach is the fantastic ◪**Wolfsonian Museum,** located in a former storage center and well worth a visit. The museum's collection of modern art and design projects far outstrips its floor space, so call or check the website for current exhibition info. *(1001 Washington Ave. ☎531-1001; www.wolfsonian.org. Summer hours Th 11am-9pm, F and Sa 11am-6pm, Su 12pm-5pm. In winter also M and Tu 11am-6pm. $5, students and seniors $3.50. Free Th 6-9pm. Wheelchair accessible.)* Since 1936, visitors to **Parrot Jungle Island** have walked among free-flying parrots, strutting flamingos, and swinging orangutans. Also on site are the Parrot Bowl amphitheater, the Serpentarium, the clay cliffs of Manu Encounter, and the Treetop Ballroom. *(1111 Parrot Jungle Tr. From downtown Miami, take the MacArthur Causeway east toward South Beach. Parrot Jungle Tr. is the first exit after the bridge. ☎258-6453; www.parrotjungle.com. Open daily 10am-6pm. $25; seniors, military, and students $23; ages 3-10 $20. Parking $6.)*

COCONUT GROVE. A stroll through the lazy streets of **Coconut Grove** uncovers an unlikely combination of haute boutiques and tacky tourist traps. People-watching abounds at the open-air mall, **CocoWalk,** along Grand Ave. On the bayfront between the Grove and downtown stands the ▨**Vizcaya Museum and Gardens.** Built in 1916 for the affluent James Deering, the 70-room Italianate villa has been the scene of many a rap video shoot. About as bling-bling as it comes, even the free stroll through the garden is magnificent. *(3251 S. Miami Ave.* ☎ *250-9133; www.vizcayamuseum.com. Open daily 9:30am-5pm; last entry 4:30pm. $12, ages 6-12 and seniors $6. $1 off with ISIC. Gardens free. Partially wheelchair accessible.)* Packed with gleeful kiddies during the summer, the **Miami Museum of Science and Planetarium** has enough interactive exhibits to entertain those of all ages, and the laser shows are spectacular. *(3280 S. Miami Ave.* ☎ *646-4200; www.miamisci.org. Open daily 10am-6pm. $10; students and seniors $8; ages 3-12 $6, under 3 free. Wheelchair accessible.)*

BAYSIDE. On the waterfront downtown, Miami's sleek **Bayside** shopping center hops nightly with talented street performers. Stores and restaurants cater mostly to cruise ship guests and tourists with money to burn, though a tour through the center and its surrounding statues makes it a worthwhile trip. *(☎ 577-3344. Open M-Th 10am-10pm, F-Sa 10am-11pm, Su 11am-9pm.)*

CORAL GABLES. In addition to hosting the **University of Miami,** scenic **Coral Gables** boasts one of the most beautiful planned communities in the region. Nearby, the family-friendly **Venetian Pool,** built in 1923, draws tourists and local families alike to its 800,000 gallon oasis. Waterfalls and Spanish architecture dress up this swimming hole, which is always crowded on hot summer weekends. *(2701 DeSoto Blvd.* ☎ *460-5356; www.venetianpool.com. Open Apr.-Oct. M-F 11am-7:30pm, Sa-Su 10am-4:30pm; Nov.-Mar. hours vary. $9, ages 3-12 $5; Nov.-Mar. $6/$3. Partially wheelchair accessible.)*

NORTH MIAMI. The **Museum of Contemporary Art (MOCA)** is known for its often eccentric exhibits and displays. Having played host to Versace dresses and steel drummers alike, MOCA supports uncommon means of artistic expression. *(770 NE 125th St.* ☎ *893-6211; www.mocanomi.org. Open Tu-Sa 11am-5pm, Su noon-5pm. $5, students and seniors $3. Wheelchair accessible.)*

▣ ▣ ENTERTAINMENT AND NIGHTLIFE

For the latest on Miami entertainment, check out the "Living Today," "Lively Arts," and Friday "Weekend" sections of the *Miami Herald.* Weekly *Oceandrive, New Times, Street,* and *Sun Post* list local happenings. *TWN* and *Miamigo,* the major gay papers, are available free along Ocean Dr. Music is an integral part of life in Miami, be it grinding techno in a SoBe nightclub, an impromptu street performance on **Calle Ocho** in little Havana, or the nightly performances at **CoCoWalk** that are particularly well attended on Thursday nights, when University of Miami students flock to this mall. Spring and summer are festival season, which climaxes with **Carnaval Miami,** the nation's largest Hispanic festival, filling 23 blocks of Calle Ocho in early March with salsa dancing and the world's longest conga line.

Nightlife in the Art Deco district of South Miami Beach starts late (after midnight) and continues until well after sunrise. Gawk at models, stars, and beach bunnies while eating at one of Ocean Blvd.'s open cafes or bars, then head down to **Washington Avenue,** between 6th and 18th St., for some serious fun. Miami Beach's club scene is transient; what's there one week may not be there the next. Clubs themselves change character depending on the night, so check beforehand or you may be in for a surprise. Many clubs don't demand covers until after midnight, and often the $20+ door charge includes an open bar. However, even a willingness to pay a steep cover is no guarantee of admission. Difficult doormen can prove impossible after 1am, so it is to your advantage to show up early. Most clubs have dress codes and everyone

BIG MAN ON SOBE

In the Miami sporting world, baseball and football reign supreme. The city's youngsters flock to local baseball diamonds, while in football the Dolphins and UM's Hurricanes are, respectively, professional and collegiate powerhouses. The third of America's "big three" sports, basketball, has traditionally fallen outside the popularity radar.

That was, of course, until the arrival of the Big Diesel himself: Shaquille O'Neal. Following their loss to the Detroit Pistons in the NBA finals, the 2003-2004 L.A. Lakers team was dismantled. Shaq asked to be traded to a city with the same fun-in-the-sun character as L.A., so naturally the 7 ft. tall center ended up in Miami, playing hoops for the Heat.

Shaq immediately became the biggest celebrity in town—no easy feat in a city packed with famous residents. He quickly embraced his role as Public Figure #1, and arrived in Miami with much fanfare, driving a diesel truck and armed with a squirt gun, which he used to spray the assembled crowd. Following this drive-by assault on Miami citizens, the mayor presented him with a key to the city. Though it is clear that Shaq brings a fun-loving attitude, the more important question is whether he will pack enough heat to make his team a contender.

For schedule and ticket info, call ☎ 786-777-4667 or log on to www.nba.com/heat.

dresses to the nines, even on so-called "casual" nights. If discos aren't your thing, check out one of the frat-boy party bars along the beach.

■ **Mansion,** 1235 Washington Ave. (☎532-1525; www.mansionmiami.com). An assault on all the senses, the richly decorated Mansion sets the standard among SoBe clubs. The VIP section is littered with celebrities sipping Cristal and the dance floor is a sea of energy. By midnight lines are around the corner, so arrive early and enjoy the sights and sounds of SoBe's most popular club. 21+. Cover around $20. Open daily 10pm-5am.

Crobar, 1445 Washington Ave. (☎531-8225). Though no longer the clear winner among Washington Ave.'s super-clubs, Crobar is certainly no slouch. Crobar's always-packed dance floor oozes with local chic and out-of-town trendiness. Su gay night. 21+. Reduced cover until 11:30pm. Open daily 10pm-5am.

Mango's Tropical Cafe, 900 Ocean Dr. (☎673-4422). The noise you hear while walking up Ocean Dr. is coming from here. Order a stiff and delicious CoCo-Loco ($7) and stay for a set of live music, concluded by a bar-top dance extraordinaire by thong-wearing waitresses and buff waiters. Not for the faint of heart, the atmosphere here is party, be it 2pm or 2am. No cover during the day, $10-20 at night. Open daily 11am-5am.

Privé, 136 Collins Ave. (☎531-5535). The exclusive upstairs lounge area is home to SoBe's best hip-hop party. If you forgot to bring your white linen Armani suit, you'll have a bit more luck at the door here than at some of the other clubs. The Betty Ford party on Th is legendary. Reduced cover before 11:30pm. Open 10pm-5am.

B.E.D., 929 Washington Ave. (☎532-9070). The acronym stands for Beverage, Entertainment, and Dining, which sums up the attraction of this venue. Patrons lounge on sexy king-sized beds as they enjoy dinner, drinks, and the atmosphere of silky seduction which oozes from every corner of this SoBe favorite. No cover. Open W-Su 8pm-5am.

Wet Willies, 760 Ocean Dr. (☎532-5650), pours a constant stream of strong, cheap daiquiris. Check out the outdoor bar upstairs, a great place to enjoy your "Call-a-Cab" or "Attitude Improvement" while surveying SoBe. 21+. No cover. Open daily noon-2am.

GLBT NIGHTLIFE

South Beach's vibrant gay scene takes to the street at night in search of the new "it club." Gay and mixed clubs in the area have bragging rights as the most trendy, amorphous hot spots, attracting a large crowd of both gay and straight partiers.

Twist, 1057 Washington Ave. (☎538-9478), is a popular 2-story club with an outdoor lounge, rockin' dance floor, and 6 bars. Straight couples welcome. 21+. Cover varies. Open daily 1pm-5am.

Laundry Bar, 721 Lincoln Ln. N. (☎531-7700). Men and women alike flock to the unusual Laundry Bar, where the chic and friendly clientele sips cocktails to the beat of DJ-spun house music and the hum of real laundry machines. A great place for an early drink before dinner or clubbing. 21+ starting at 10pm. No cover. Open 7am-5am.

Score, 727 Lincoln Rd. Mall (☎535-1111). Plenty of style and plenty of attitude. Mostly men frequent this multi-bar hot spot, where a packed dance floor sits under the watchful eye of Adonis himself. 21+. No cover. Open daily M-Sa 3pm-5am, Su 3pm-2am.

THE EVERGLADES ☎305

Encompassing the entire tip of Florida and spearing into Florida Bay, Everglades National Park spans 1.5 million acres, making it the second largest national park and of one of the world's most unique and fragile ecosystems. Vast prairies of sawgrass range through broad expanses of shallow water, creating the famed "river of grass," while tangled mazes of mangrove swamps wind up the western coast. To the south, delicate coral reefs lie below the shimmering blue waters of the bay. A host of species, many of which can be found nowhere else in the world, inhabits these lands and waters: American alligators, dolphins, and sea turtles, as well as the endangered Florida panther, Florida manatee, and American crocodile. Unfortunately, the mosquito is the most prevalent Everglades species.

AT A GLANCE

AREA: 1,508,508 acres.

CLIMATE: Subtropical grassland.

HIGHLIGHTS: Be terrified by the denizens of the Everglades Alligator Farm, be amazed by the flora and fauna of Anhinga Trail, and sleep it off at the amazing Everglades International Hostel.

CAMPING: Reservations must be made in person, at least 1 day in advance, at the Flamingo or Gulf Coast visitors centers. $14. $10 permit plus $2 per person for backcountry camping; free in summer.

FEES: $10 per private automobile, $5 per pedestrian or bike, good for 7 days.

⚡ ORIENTATION AND PRACTICAL INFORMATION

The park's main entrance, the **Ernest Coe Visitors Center,** 40001 Rte. 9366, is just inside the eastern edge of the Everglades. (☎242-7700; www.nps.gov/ever. Open daily 9am-5pm. Hours may be reduced June-Sept.; call if you're considering arriving around opening or closing hours.) Rte. 9366 cuts 40 mi. through the park past campgrounds, trailheads, and canoe waterways to the **Flamingo Visitors Center** (☎239-695-2945; open daily mid-Nov. to Apr. 7:30am-5pm; hours vary in summer.) At the northern end of the park off U.S. 41 (Tamiami Trail), the **Shark Valley Visitors Center** gives access to a 15 mi. loop through a sawgrass swamp by foot, bike, or a 2hr. tram. Shark Valley is an ideal site for those who want a taste of the freshwater ecosystem but aren't inclined to venture too deep into the park. (☎221-8776. Open daily 9am-5pm.) Tram tours are 2hr. round-trip, and worth the time and expense. (Run daily Dec.-Apr. every hr. 9am-4pm; May-Nov. 9:30, 11am, 1, 3pm. $11, seniors $10, under 12 $6.50. Reservations recommended. Wheelchair accessible with reservations. Bike rental daily 8:30am-3pm. $5.50 per hr., including helmet.) The **Gulf Coast Visitors Center,** 800 Copeland Ave. S, in Everglades City in the northwestern end of the park, provides access to the western coastline and the vast river network throughout the park.

(☎239-695-3311. Open daily Nov.-Apr. 7:30am-5pm, May-Sept. 8:30am-5pm.) The **entrance fee** is $10 per car, $5 per pedestrian or bike at the Ernest Coe and Shark Valley entrances. Your receipt will get you into the park for the next seven days. The Gulf Coast entrance is free. For info on lodgings and local discounts, check out the **Tropical Everglades Visitors Association,** on U.S. 1 in Florida City. (☎245-9180 or 800-388-9669; www.tropicaleverglades.com. Open daily 9am-5pm.) **Emergency:** Park headquarters, ☎247-7272. **Area Code:** 305.

Summer visitors can expect mosquitoes aplenty when visiting the Everglades. Stay away from densely vegetated areas, especially around sunrise and sunset. The best time to visit is winter or spring when heat, humidity, storms, and bugs are at a minimum and wildlife congregate in shrinking pools of evaporating water. Wear long-sleeved clothing and bring insect repellent.

⌐▢ ACCOMMODATIONS AND FOOD

Outside the eastern entrance to the park, **Florida City** offers cheap motels along U.S. 1. The ▦**Everglades International Hostel (HI) ❶,** 20 SW 2nd Ave., off Rte. 9336 (Palm Dr.), is a far better option. After venturing into the Everglades on one of the hostel-guided tours ($35-45), hang out with fellow travelers in the gazebo, gardens, or kitchen house, which has a large-screen TV with a free video collection. This amazing hostel also has a fantastic location for daytrips to the Everglades or the Keys. (☎248-1122 or 800-372-3874; www.evergladeshostel.com. Free Internet access. Laundry. Linen $2. Bike rental $10. Canoe rental $20. Dorms $13, with A/C $14; nonmembers $17/$18. Private rooms $33/$35, nonmembers $36/$38.) The only option for lodging inside the park, **Flamingo Lodge ❸,** 1 Flamingo Lodge Hwy., has large rooms with A/C, TV and a great view of Florida Bay. Cottages are also available, and are the only option in the summer. (☎800-600-3813. Reservations recommended. May to mid-Nov. cottages $90; mid-Nov. to Dec. cottages $99, singles $80, doubles $110; Dec.-Apr. $140/$100/$150.) In the park, both **Long Pine** and **Flamingo Campgrounds ❶** offer developed camping. Flamingo is a sun-bleached campground offering beautiful vistas of the bay, while Long Pine provides a bit more shade. (☎800-365-2267. Reservations required Nov.-Apr. Sites in winter $14; in summer free.) There are dozens of **backcountry camping ❶** options in the park, though many are accessible only by boat (see **boating,** p. 535). Required **permits** are available on a first come, first served basis at the Flamingo and Gulf Coast visitors centers. (Applications must be made in person at least 24hr. in advance. Permit Dec.-Apr. $10 plus $2 per person, good for 7 days; May-Nov. free.) By the Gulf Coast Visitors Center, motels, RV parks, and campgrounds encircle Everglades City. The **Barron River Villa, Marina, and RV Park ❶** has 67 RV sites (29 on the river) and tiny motel rooms with TV and A/C. (☎800-535-4961. RV sites May-Sept. full hookup $18, on the river $20; Oct.-Apr. $45. Motel rooms May-Aug. $60; Sept.-Apr. $105.)

Across the street from the hostel, **Rosita's ❶,** 199 Palm Dr., has fabulous Mexican food. *Huevos rancheros* ($4) can get you ready for a long day of exploring the park. Come back to relax with *chiles rellenos* or enchiladas. (☎246-3114. Open daily 8:30am-9pm.) The pinnacle of Homestead eateries, the vegan-friendly **Main St. Cafe ❷,** 128 N. Krome Ave., serves great sandwiches ($4-6) in a charming deli-style restaurant that doubles as a comedy club on the weekends. (☎245-7575. Th teen open mic 8-11pm, F open mic 7pm-midnight, Sa folk and acoustic rock 7pm-midnight. Open M-W 11am-4pm, Th-Sa 11am-midnight.) Just 3 blocks from the hostel, **Farmers Market Restaurant ❸,** 300 N. Krome Ave., is in a farmers wholesale market. Enjoy hearty portions and small-town service at this local favorite. (☎242-0008. Breakfast $4-6; lunch $5-8; dinner $8-13. Open daily 5:30am-9pm.)

⚡ OUTDOOR ACTIVITIES

The park is swamped with fishing, hiking, canoeing, biking, and wildlife-watching opportunities. Forget swimming within the park; alligators, sharks, and barracuda patrol the waters. However, if you're hot for some water sports, the nearby Biscayne National Park is there to satisfy (see **Swimming and Diving**, p. 536). From November through April, the park sponsors amphitheater programs, canoe trips, and ranger-guided Slough Slogs (swamp tours).

HIKING

The Everglades offers excellent hiking opportunities for those who wish to spend a week in the swamp and those who wish to stay within sight of their cars. Even for short hikes, it is advisable to pick up a copy of the **Wilderness Trip Planner** at the station which provides info on trails and conditions. The wheelchair-accessible **Anhinga Trail** yields good results with minimal commitment. Those willing to brave the half-mile stroll down the boardwalk are granted up-close encounters with alligators, anhinga birds, and turtles. Low water from December to March makes for a higher concentration of wildlife, though the walk is a must any time of year. Take the turnoff for the Royal Palms Visitors Center, just 4 mi. inside the park from the main entrance. The **Pa-hay-okee Overlook,** 13 mi. from the main entrance off Rte. 9336, is wheelchair accessible and rewards visitors with a stunning view of the park after a quarter-mile boardwalk hike. For a more difficult trail, head over to Long Pine Key (6 mi. from the main entrance), where the **Long Pine Key Trail** ventures through 10 mi. of slash pine forests. Another arduous hike is the **Mahogany Hammock Trail** (20 mi. from the main entrance, wheelchair accessible). This trail offers incredible routes through freshwater prairie and pineland, but mosquitoes have the run of the land in the summer, making it most enjoyable in the winter.

BOATING

To experience the Everglades, start paddling. The 99 mi. **Wilderness Waterway** winds its way from the northwest entrance to the Flamingo station in the far south. Noteworthy **camping ❶** spots along the way include chickees (wooden platforms elevated above mangrove swamps), beaches, and groundsites. (Permit required. In winter $10 plus $2 per person; in summer free.) **Everglades National Park Boat Tours,** at the **Gulf Coast Visitors Center,** rents canoes ($25) and is the best option for guided boat tours. The **Ten Thousand Island Cruise** ($16) is a 1½hr. tour through the Everglades' tiny islands. Patrons often see bald eagles, dolphins, and manatees. The **Mangrove Wilderness Cruise** ($25) is a 2hr. cruise through the inland swamps that brings its six passengers face-to-face with alligators. (☎239-695-2591 or 800-445-7724. Tours begin at 9am and run every 30min.) For those who would rather do their own paddling, **Hell's Bay Canoe Trail,** located about 29 mi. from the entrance, is the premier spot for canoeing. For more information on navigating the park's waterways, consult the rangers at the **Flamingo Visitor Center**.

BIKING

While the Everglades mostly caters to those with walking sticks and canoeing paddles, it does offer some excellent biking opportunities. The best route can be found at the **Shark Valley Visitors Center,** where a 15 mi. loop awaits the adventurous. The trail peaks at an incredible observation tower that offers great views of the park's rivers of grass, alligators, and the occasional wily fawn. (Bike rentals $5.50 per hr.)

SWIMMING AND DIVING

It can be easy to overlook the nearby **Biscayne National Park,** as 95% of the park is aquatic. Just 15min. from the Everglades International Hostel, Biscayne features amazing diving and snorkeling opportunities as well as remote camping on Boca Chita and Elliott Key, accessible only by boat. (Visitors center: 9700 SW 328th St. ☎230-7275. For information for both the snorkel cruise ($25) and the ferry to the Keys ($25), call 230-1100.) For a lazy swim in a heavenly (and gator-free) lagoon, stop at the **Homestead Bayfront Park,** just south of the Biscayne Visitors Center.

GARDENS AND GATORS

For a truly bizarre time, head up U.S. 1 to the **Coral Castle,** 28655 S. Dixie Hwy., in Homestead. After his fiancée changed her mind the day before the wedding, Latvian immigrant Ed Leedskalnin spent the next 20 years constructing a homage to his lost love. The heartbroken bachelor turned hundreds of tons of dense coral rock into a garden of magnificently odd sculptures. (☎248-6344 or 248-6345; www.coralcastle.com. Open daily 7am-9pm. $9.75, seniors $6.50, ages 7-12 $5. Discounts at visitors center. Guided tours daily. Wheelchair accessible.) View gators, crocs, and snakes at the **Everglades Alligator Farm,** 40351 SW 192 Ave., 4 mi. south of Palm Dr. Though ultra-touristy, this is the best place to see thousands of gators, from little hatchlings clambering for a piece of the sun to 18-footers clambering for a piece of you. (☎247-2628 or 800-644-9711; http://everglades.com. Open May-Sept. daily 9am-6pm. Feedings at noon and 3pm. Wildlife shows—free with admission—11am, 2, 5pm. $12, ages 4-10 $6.50. Wheelchair accessible.)

KEY LARGO   ☎305

Over half a century ago, Hollywood stars Humphrey Bogart and Lauren Bacall immortalized the name "Key Largo" in their hit movie. Quick-thinking locals of Rock Harbor, where some of the scenes were shot, soon changed the name of their town to Key Largo to attract tourists. It worked—Key Largo is now the gateway to the rest of the enchanting Florida Keys. Though laid-back in attitude, the Keys can be aggressive on the budget, especially during the winter high season. Key Largo can be a bit cheaper than the more westward Keys and is renowned for its natural beauty, coral reefs, and incredible fishing. Pennekamp State Park was the country's first underwater park, and divers of all abilities flock to the isle for the chance to glimpse at the reef ecosystem and the numerous shipwrecks.

■■ **ORIENTATION AND PRACTICAL INFORMATION.** The **Overseas Highway (U.S. 1)** bridges the divide between the Keys and the southern tip of Florida, stitching the islands together. Mile markers section the highway and replace street addresses. **Biking** along U.S. 1 is treacherous due to fast cars and narrow shoulders; instead of riding, bring your bike on the bus. Spirits flow freely in the Keys, and drunk driving has become a problem recently—stay alert when on the roads. **Greyhound** (☎871-1810; open daily 8am-6pm), Mi. 102 at the Island Supermarket, runs to Key West (3hr., 4 per day, $28) and Miami (1¾hr., 4 per day, $15). Most bus drivers are willing to stop at mile markers along the side of the road, though you must do all in your power to catch their attention. Tiny Greyhound signs along the highway indicate bus stops (usually hotels), where you can buy tickets or call the **info line** on the red phones provided. **Taxi: Mom's Taxi** ☎852-6000. **Visitor Info: Key Largo Chamber of Commerce/Florida Keys Visitors Center,** 106000 U.S. 1, Mi. 106 (☎451-1414 or 800-822-1088; www.keylargo.org. Open daily 9am-6pm.) **Medical Services: Mariners Hospital,** Mi. 91.5 (☎853-3700). **Post Office:** 100100 U.S. 1, Mi. 100. (☎451-3155. Open M-F 8am-4:30pm, Sa 10am-1pm.) **Postal Code:** 33037. **Area Code:** 305.

FLORIDA

ⁿ ACCOMMODATIONS. Ed and Ellen's Lodgings ❸, 103365 U.S. 1, Mi. 103.4 (on Snapper Ave.), has clean, large rooms with cable TV, A/C, and kitchenettes. Ed, the humorous and ever-present owner, is tremendously helpful with everything from restaurant suggestions to diving and snorkeling reservations. (☎451-9949 or 888-333-5536. Doubles $59-79; low-season $49-59. Each additional person $10. Rates increase on weekends, holidays, and during lobster season.) A few lodgings near downtown Key Largo offer reasonable rates. The **Bay Cove Motel ❹**, 99446 Overseas Hwy., Mi. 99.5, borders a small beach on the bay side of the island. Rooms have cable TV, A/C, and mini-fridges. (☎451-1686. Doubles $75-$150, depending on season.) The waterside **Hungry Pelican ❸**, Mi. 99.5, boasts an explosion of bougainvillea vines, tropical birds in the trees, and cozy rooms with double beds, fridges, and cable TV. (☎451-3576. Free use of paddle boats, canoes, and hammocks. Continental breakfast included. Rooms $50-115; each additional person $10.) The **Sea Trail Motel ❸**, Mi. 99.3, offers an inexpensive (for Key Largo), no-frills place to stay. Rooms are clean and comfortable, and each has a refrigerator. (☎852-8001. Rooms $40-$60.) Reservations are strongly recommended for the popular **John Pennekamp Coral Reef State Park Campground ❶** (see **Sights,** below). The 47 sites are clean, convenient, and well worth the effort required to obtain them. Most sites (90%) are available for reservation online, and the other 10% are reserved for walk-ins on a first come, first served basis. (☎451-1202; www.reserveamerica.com. Bathrooms and showers. No pets allowed. 14-day max. stay. Park open 8am-dusk. Sites $32.)

◖ FOOD. Seafood restaurants of varying price, quality, specialty, and view litter Overseas Hwy. The neighboring island Islamorada boasts one of the best seafood restaurants in all the Keys. The **Islamorada Fish Company ❸**, Mi. 81.5, offers an incredible array of seafood sandwiches ($7-10) and entrees ($13-18), which patrons enjoy under the pristine island sunset. When you finish, be sure to taste the legendary Key Lime Pie for $3. (☎664-9271 or 800-258-2559. Open daily 11am-9pm, sometimes later). Tucked away on a quiet residential street, **Calypso's ❷**, 1 Seagate Dr., at Oceanbay near Mi. 99.5, offers delectable Buffalo shrimp for $7 and an equally delicious dolphin fish sandwich which also goes for $7. (☎451-0600. Open M and W-Th noon-10pm, F-Sa noon-11pm.) For a scrumptious breakfast in Key Largo, head to **The Hideout Restaurant ❷**, concealed on the ocean side of Mi. 103.5 at the end of Transylvania Ave. Plate-size pancakes (2 for $3) and not-soon-forgotten raisin toast ($3) make this the affordable meal you can't afford to miss. Stop by this hidden treasure on Friday nights for an all-you-can-eat fish fest—complete with hush puppies, beans, conch fritters, and free Bud Light—for a paltry $10. (☎451-0128. Open Sa-Th 11:30am-2pm, F 11:30am-2pm and 5-9pm.) **Mary Mac's Kitchen ❶**, Mi. 99 on the bay side, cooks up overwhelming hamburgers ($4) and famous steak sandwiches ($4-5) for eager patrons. (☎451-3722. Open M-Sa 7am-9:30pm.)

◪ SIGHTS. Key Largo is the self-proclaimed "Dive Capital of the World," and many diving instructors offer their services via highway billboards. The best place to go is the nation's first underwater sanctuary, **John Pennekamp Coral Reef State Park,** Mi. 102.5. The park extends 3 mi. into the Atlantic Ocean, safeguarding a part of the coral reef that runs the length of the Keys. (☎451-1202; www.pennecamp-park.com. $3.50 per vehicle with 1 occupant, 2 occupants $6; each additional person $0.50. Walk- or bike-in $1.50.) Stop by the park's **visitors center** for free maps, boat and snorkeling tour info, and films on the park. To see the reefs, visitors must take their own boat or rent one. (☎451-9570, reservations 451-6325. Open daily 8am-5pm. 18 ft. motor boat $125 for 4hr. Canoes $10 per hr. Deposit required.) **Scuba trips** leave from the visitors center. (☎451-6322. 9:30am and 1:30pm. $41 per person for a 2-tank dive. Deposit required.) A **snorkeling tour** also allows you to partake of the underwater quiet. (☎451-6300. 2½hr. total, 1½hr. water time. Tours 9am, noon, 3pm. $33, under 18 $28; equipment $5. Deposit required.) **Glass Bottom Boat Tours** provides a crystal clear view of the reefs without wetting your feet. (☎451-6300. 2½hr. tours 9:15am, 12:15, 3pm. $20, under 12 $12.) Head to any of the local marinas to charter a spot on a **fishing boat.** To avoid paying a commission, hang out on the docks and ask one of the friendly captains yourself. At Mi. 100 on the ocean side, the **Holiday Inn Hotel** also offers a plethora of scuba, snorkel, and boat trips. The best-known is the **Key Largo Princess,** which offers 2hr. glass bottom boat tours ($25). Aside from its active dock, the hotel has become a tourist destination, as it houses the **African Queen,** the original boat on which Humphrey Bogart and Katherine Hepburn sailed in the movie of the same title.

KEY WEST ☎305

The small "last island" of the Florida Keys, Key West has always drawn a cast of colorful characters since its days of pirates, smugglers, and treasure hunters. Henry Flagler, Ernest Hemingway, Tennessee Williams, Truman Capote, and Jimmy Buffett have all called the quasi-independent "Conch Republic" home. Today thousands of tourists hop on the Overseas Hwy. to glimpse the past, visit the over 300 bars, and kick back under the sun. The crowd is as diverse as Key West's past: families spend a week enjoying the water, twenty-somethings come to party and work, and a swinging gay population finds a haven of gay-only clubs and resorts. Key West is as far south as you can get in the continental US. This is the end of the road—enjoy it.

⁙ TRANSPORTATION

Buses: Greyhound, 3535 S. Roosevelt Blvd. (☎296-9072), at the airport. Open daily 8am-6pm. To **Miami** (4½hr., 4 per day, $35).

Public Transit: Key West Port and Transit Authority (☎292-8161). 6 routes service Key west. $1, students with ID $0.50.

Taxi: Keys Taxi ☎296-6666.

Bike Rental: Keys Moped & Scooters, 523 Truman Ave. (☎294-0399), rents wheeled adventures. Open daily 9am-6pm. Bikes $8 per day. Single scooter $30 per day, double scooter $55 per day.

◪ ⁈ ORIENTATION AND PRACTICAL INFORMATION

Key West lies at the end of **Overseas Highway (U.S. 1),** 155 mi. southwest of Miami (3-3½hr.). The island is divided into two sectors; the eastern part, known as **New Town,** harbors tract houses, chain motels, shopping malls, and the airport. Beautiful old conch houses fill **Old Town,** west of White St. **Duval Street** is the main north-south thoroughfare in Old Town; **U.S. 1 (Truman Avenue)** is a major east-west route. A car is the easiest way to get to Key West, though driving in town is neither easy nor necessary. *Do not park overnight on the bridges.*

Visitor Info: Key West Welcome Center, 3840 N. Roosevelt Blvd. (☎296-4444 or 800-284-4482), just north of the intersection of U.S. 1 and Roosevelt Blvd., is a private reservation service. Open M-Sa 9am-7:30pm, Su 9am-6pm. **Key West Chamber of Commerce,** 402 Wall St. (☎294-2587 or 800-527-8539; www.keywestchamber.org), in old Mallory Sq. Open M-F 8:30am-6:30pm, Sa-Su 8:30am-6pm.

GLBT Resources: The Key West Business Guild Gay and Lesbian Information Center, 728 Duval St. (☎294-4603), is helpful for locating exclusively gay guest houses. Open M-F 9am-5pm.

FLORIDA

Hotlines: Help Line, ☎296-4357. 24hr.

Internet Access: Internet Isle Cafe, 118 Duval St. (☎293-1199). $10 per hr. Open daily 8am-11pm.

Post Office: 400 Whitehead St. (☎294-2557), one block west of Duval St. at Eaton St. Open M-F 8:30am-5pm, Sa 9:30am-noon. **Postal Code:** 33040. **Area Code:** 305.

ACCOMMODATIONS

Key West is packed virtually year-round, particularly from January through March, so reserve rooms far in advance. **Pride Week** (www.pridefestkeywest.com) each June is generally a busy time of the year. In Old Town, the multi-colored 19th-century clapboard houses capture the charming flavor of the Keys. B&Bs dominate, and "reasonably priced" means over $50. Some of the guest houses in Old Town are for gay men exclusively.

Casablanca Hotel, 900 Duval St. (☎296-0815), in the center of the main drag. This charming B&B once hosted Humphrey Bogart and James Joyce. Pool, A/C, cable TV, breakfast, and large bathrooms. Call ahead for reservations during Fantasy Fest. Dec.-May $125-450; June-Nov. $99-295. ❺

Key West Youth Hostel and Sea Shell Motel, 718 South St. (☎296-5719). The only hosteling option in Key West is by far the cheapest option in town. Rooms are very simple but the location and price make it a good option. Dorms $23; motel rooms $125, low-season $75. ❶

Eden House, 1015 Fleming St. (☎296-6868 or 800-533-5397), just 5 short blocks from downtown, is a brightly painted hotel with a hostel-like atmosphere. Clean, classy rooms with bath. Pool, jacuzzi, hammock area, and kitchens. Bike rentals $10 per day. Happy hour daily 4-5pm. Summer rooms with shared bath $110; low-season $80. ❺

Wicker Guesthouse, 913 Duval St. (☎296-4275 or 800-880-4275), has a pastel decor, private baths, A/C, and cable TV. Most rooms have kitchenettes. No phones. Kitchen, pool access, and breakfast included. Free parking. Reservations recommended; ask for summer specials. Rooms June-Dec. $89-150; late Dec. to May $130-215. ❹

Caribbean House, 226 Petronia St. (☎296-1600 or 800-543-4518), has festive Caribbean-style rooms with A/C, cable TV, free local calls, fridge, and comfy double beds. Continental breakfast. Reservations not accepted for cottages. Rooms in winter $69; in summer from $49. Cottages $89/69. ❸

Boyd's Campground, 6401 Maloney Ave. (☎294-1465), sprawls over 12 oceanside acres and provides full facilities, including showers. Take a left off U.S. 1 onto Macdonald Ave., which becomes Maloney. Sites for 2 in summer $42-60, with water and electricity $55-70, full hookup $57-75; in winter $65-85; each additional person $10. Waterfront sites additional $15. ❸

FOOD

Expensive and trendy restaurants line festive **Duval Street.** Side streets offer lower prices and fewer crowds. Many visitors appear to skip the fare and jump straight to the bars.

I Love Bagels, 1119 White St. (☎294-2201), is the best breakfast spot in town. Sit down with an soft, warm, fresh-baked bagel ($1) and a cup of coffee, grab a newspaper off the rack, and enjoy the friendly atmosphere of this great bakery. For a real treat, try the Island Sunrise breakfast sandwich ($3.75). Open daily 7am-3pm. ❶

Blue Heaven, 729 Thomas St. (☎296-8666), one block from the Caribbean House. Feast upon the town's best grub: healthy breakfasts with fresh banana bread ($2-9);

Caribbean or Mexican lunches ($2.50-10); and heavenly dinners ($9-19) that include plantains, corn bread, and fresh veggies. Open M-Sa 8am-3pm and 6-10:30pm, Su 8am-1pm and 6-10:30pm. ❸

El Siboney, 900 Catherine St. (☎296-4184). Breaking with the unfortunate Key West tradition of overpriced food, this Cuban establishment serves heaping mounds of beans, rice, and meat—all for around $7. Open M-Sa 11am-9:30pm. ❷

Rooftop Cafe, 308 Fronts Ave. (☎294-2042), at Tifts Ave. This quaint Cuban eatery overlooks the passing tourist trains and scandalous skin shows. The chicken *bella vista* salad ($11) and the steak *largo hueso* ($12), however, seem to keep patrons' minds on their food. Open daily 9am-11pm. ❸

🔘 SIGHTS

ON LAND. Because of limited parking, traversing Key West by bike or moped is more convenient and comfortable than driving. For those inclined toward riding, the **Conch Tour Train** is a fun but pricey 1½hr. narrated ride through Old Town. *(Leaves from Mallory Sq. at 3840 N or from Roosevelt Blvd., next to the Quality Inn. ☎294-5161. Runs daily 9am-5:30pm. $22, ages 4-12 $11.)* **Old Town Trolley** runs a similar narrated tour, but you can get on and off throughout the day at nine stops. *(☎296-6688. Tours 9am-5:30pm. Full tour 1½hr. $22, ages 4-12 $11.)* No one can leave Key West without a visit to the ▨**Ernest Hemingway Home,** where "Papa" wrote *For Whom the Bell Tolls* and *The Snows of Kilimanjaro.* Take a tour with hilarious guides who relate Hemingway and Key West history, then traipse through on your own among 60 descendants of Hemingway's cat, half of which have extra toes. *(907 Whitehead St. ☎294-1136; www.hemingwayhome.com. Open daily 9am-5pm. $10, ages 6-12 $6. Partially wheelchair accessible.)* Tucked into the affluent Truman Annex Gated Community, the **Harry S Truman Little White House Museum** provides an insightful look at the life of President Truman and at his getaway in Key West. *(111 Front St. ☎294-9911; www.trumanlittlewhitehouse.com. Open daily 9am-5pm. $10, children $5; includes tour. Partially wheelchair accessible.)* In addition to its serene garden, the **Audubon House** shelters fine antiques and a collection of original engravings by naturalist John James Audubon. *(205 Whitehead St. ☎294-2116; www.audubonhouse.com. Open daily 9:30am-4:40pm. $10, seniors $9, students $6.50, ages 6-12 $5. Wheelchair accessible.)*

MARITIME MUSEUMS. The ▨**Mel Fisher Maritime Heritage Society Museum** brings to life the amazing discovery and salvage of the Spanish galleon *Atocha*, which sank off the Keys in the 17th century with millions in gold and silver. The museum also has an entire floor dedicated to the study of the harsh 17th- and 18th-century slave trade. *(200 Greene St. ☎294-2633; www.melfisher.org. Open daily 9:30am-5pm; last film 4:30pm. $10, students $8.50, ages 6-12 $6.)* The **Key West Shipwreck Historeum Museum,** located in Mallory Sq., boasts the remains of the *Isaac Allerton*, the 594-ton ship that sunk to the bottom of the Atlantic in 1856. Live demonstrations give a glimpse into the lives of classic adventurers by surveying artifacts and the original cargo that the *Allerton* was carrying. The museum's Lookout Tower, which stands 65 ft. tall, offers a great view of the island. *(1 Whitehead St. ☎292-8990; www.shipwreckhistoreum.com. $9, ages 4-12 $4.50. Open daily 9:45am-4:45pm.)* On Whitehead St. is the 92 ft. **Key West Lighthouse and Museum.** Climb the 88 steps to the top and be rewarded with the best view in town. *(938 Whitehead St. ☎294-0012. Open daily 9:30am-4:30pm. $8, seniors $6, students $4. Partially wheelchair accessible.)*

ON WATER. The **glass-bottomed boat** *Fireball* cruises to the reefs and back. *(☎296-6293. 2hr. cruises daily noon and 2pm; sunset cruise 6pm. $30, sunset cruise $35; ages 5-12 $15.)* Down Whitehead St., past the Hemingway House, you'll come to the southernmost point in the continental US at the fittingly named **Southernmost Beach.** A small, conical monument marks the spot: "90 miles to Cuba." Locals and tourists alike take part in the daily tradition of watching the sun go down. At the **Mallory Square Dock,** street entertainers and kitsch-hawkers work the crowd, while boats parade in revue during the daily **Sunset Celebration.**

NIGHTLIFE

The free *Island News,* found in local restaurants and bars, lists dining spots, music, and clubs. Nightlife in Key West revs up at 11pm and winds down in the wee daylight hours. The action centers around upper **Duval Street.** Key West nightlife reaches its annual exultant high the third week of October during **Fantasy Fest** (☎296-1817; www.fantasyfest.net), when decadent floats filled with drag queens, pirates, and wild locals take over Duval St.

The Green Parrot, 601 Whitehead St. (☎294-6133). Though off the beaten path of Duval St., this bar has enough of a reputation to have warranted a nod from *Playboy* as Key West's best bar. A real local hangout; stop by and meet a crowd of local characters. Open daily 11am-late.

Capt. Tony's Saloon, 428 Greene St. (☎294-1838), the oldest bar in Key West and reputedly one of Tennessee Williams's preferred watering holes, this saloon has been serving since the early 1930s. Bras and business cards festoon the ceiling. Live entertainment daily. Open M-Sa 10am-2am, Su noon-2am.

Rick's, 202 Duval St. (☎296-4890). An unabashed meat market, Rick's boasts well-placed body shots and a hot clientele. Happy hour, with $2 longneck Buds, daily 3-6pm. W-Th all-you-can-drink $7. Open M-Sa 11am-4am, Su noon-4am.

Sloppy Joe's, 201 Duval St. (☎294-5717). For the best party you'll most likely forget, stop by Hemingway's favorite hangout and be blown away by the house specialty, the Hurricane ($7). Grab the *Sloppy Joe's News* to learn the latest on upcoming entertainment. 21+. Open M-Sa 9am-4am, Su noon-4am.

GAY AND LESBIAN NIGHTLIFE

Known for its wild, outspoken gay community, Key West hosts more than a dozen fabulous drag lounges, night clubs, and private bars for the gay man's enjoyment. Most clubs also welcome straight couples and lesbians, but check with the bouncer before entering. Most gay clubs line Duval St. south of Fleming Ave. Check out *Celebrate!* for coverage of the Key West gay and lesbian community.

Aqua, 711 Duval St. (☎294-0555), has become the hottest drag club in Key West. You're likely to see many wide-eyed tourists checking out the singing beauties. Next door, **KWEST MEN,** 705 Duval St. (☎292-8500), is a sweaty, scandalous dance club where boys in G-strings gyrate on the dance floor. Drag show nightly 10pm. Tu amateur night. 21+. No cover. Open 4pm-4am.

The Bourbon Street Pub, 724 Duval St. (☎296-1992; www.bourbonstreetpub.com). A good alternative to the Duval St. bars' jock-strap clad waiters, this is a more traditional bar, though antics still get wild. No cover. Open 4pm-4am. Its sister club, **801 Bourbon,** 801 Duval St. (☎294-4737), is also very popular. Open daily 11am-4am.

FORT LAUDERDALE ☎954

During the past two decades, Fort Lauderdale has transformed itself from a city known as a beer-stained spring break mecca to the largest yachting center in North America. City streets and highways may be fine for the commoner's transportation needs, but Fort Lauderdale adds another option: canals. Intricate water-

Fort Lauderdale

ACCOMMODATIONS
Floyd's Hostel/Crew House, **11**
Fort Lauderdale Beach Hostel, **1**
Tropic-Cay Beach Hotel, **10**
Tropi-Rock Resort, **9**

FOOD
The Floridian, **8**
Squiggy's NY Style Pizza, **2**
Tokyo Bowl, **12**

NIGHTLIFE
Beach Bums, **13**

Dicey O'Riley's Irish Pub, **3**
Elbo Room, **14**
Ramrod, **4**
Saint, **15**
Tarpon Bend, **5**
The Voodoo Lounge, **6**

ways connect ritzy homes with the intracoastal river, and while the elite cruise these waterways in multi-million dollar vessels, even mere mortals can cruise the canals via the WaterTaxi, an on-the-water bus system. "The Venice of America" also boasts 23 mi. of beach where spring break mayhem still reigns supreme, making Fort Lauderdale fun even for those who can't afford a yacht. For the aquaphobic, trendy Las Olas Blvd. has some of the best shopping in south Florida.

■ TRANSPORTATION

Airport: Fort Lauderdale/Hollywood International, 1400 Lee Wagoner Blvd. (☎359-6100; www.fort-lauderdale-fll.com), 3½ mi. south of downtown on U.S. 1. Or take I-595 E from I-95 to Exit 12B. Buses to and from the airport go through Broward Transit Central Terminal (☎367-8400). Take bus #11 south to the airport, and #1 from the airport.

Trains: Amtrak, 200 SW 21st Terr. (☎587-6692), just west of I-95, ¼ mi. south of Broward Blvd. Take bus #22 from downtown. Open daily 7:30am-9pm. To **Orlando** (4¾hr., 2 per day, $29-56).

Buses: Greyhound, 515 NE 3rd St. (☎764-6551), 3 blocks north of Broward Blvd. downtown. *Be careful in this area, especially at night.* Open 24hr. To: **Daytona Beach** (7hr., 8 per day, $40); **Miami** (1hr., 26 per day, $6); **Orlando** (5½hr., 12 per day, $40).

Public Transit: Broward County Transit (BCT), ☎ 357-8400. Central Terminal located at NW 1st Ave. and Broward Ave. downtown. Buses #11 and 36 run north-south on A1A through the beaches. Operates daily 6am-11pm. $1; seniors, under 18, and disabled $0.50; transfer $0.15. 1-day passes $2.50, 7-day passes $9, 10-ride passes $8. Schedules available at hotels, libraries, and the central terminal. **City Cruiser** (☎ 761-3543) loops through downtown and the beach strip between Sunrise Blvd. and Las Olas Blvd. F-Sa every 30min. 6pm-1am. Free. **Tri-Rail** (☎ 728-8445 or 800-874-7245) connects West Palm Beach, Fort Lauderdale, and Miami. Trains run M-F 4am-10pm, Sa-Su 7am-5pm. Schedules available at airport, motels, or Tri-Rail stops. $2-6; children, disabled, students, and seniors with Tri-Rail ID 50% discount.

Taxi: Yellow Cab ☎ 777-7777. **Public Service Taxi** ☎ 587-9090.

Bike Rental: Mike's Cyclery, 5429 N. Federal Hwy. (☎ 493-5277). Open M-F 10am-7pm, Sa 10am-5pm. A variety of bicycles $20 per day, $50 per week; racing bikes slightly more. Credit card deposit required.

ORIENTATION

North-south **I-95** connects West Palm Beach, Fort Lauderdale, and Miami. **Rte. 84/I-75 (Alligator Alley)** slithers 100 mi. west from Fort Lauderdale across the Everglades to Florida's Gulf Coast. Florida's Turnpike runs parallel to I-95. Fort Lauderdale is bigger than it looks, extending westward from its 23 mi. of beach to encompass nearly 450 sq. mi. Streets and boulevards are east-west and avenues are north-south, and all are labeled NW, NE, SW, or SE. The two major roads in Fort Lauderdale are **Broward Boulevard,** running east-west, and **Andrews Avenue,** running north-south. The brick-and-mortar downtown centers around **U.S. 1 (Federal Highway)** and **Las Olas Boulevard,** about 2 mi. west of the oceanfront. Between downtown and the waterfront, yachts fill the ritzy inlets of the **Intracoastal Waterway. The Strip** (a.k.a. Rte. A1A, Fort Lauderdale Beach Blvd., 17th St. Causeway, Ocean Blvd., or Seabreeze Blvd.) runs 4 mi. along the beach between Oakland Park Blvd. to the north and Las Olas Blvd. to the south.

PRACTICAL INFORMATION

Visitor Info: Greater Fort Lauderdale Convention and Visitors Bureau, 1850 Eller Dr. #303 (☎ 765-4466, 800-227-8669, or 527-5600 for 24hr. travel directions and hotel info; www.sunny.org), in the Port Everglades, has the useful *Superior Small Lodgings,* a comprehensive and detailed list of low-priced accommodations. Open M-F 8:30am-5pm. **Chamber of Commerce,** 512 NE 3rd Ave. (☎ 462-6000), 3 blocks off Federal Hwy. at 5th St. Open M-F 8am-5pm.

Hotlines: First Call for Help, ☎ 537-0211. **Sexual Assault and Treatment Center,** ☎ 761-7273. Both 24hr.

Medical Services: Fort Lauderdale Hospital, 1601 E. Las Olas Blvd., at SE 16th Ave. (☎ 463-4321).

Internet Access: Broward County Library, 100 S. Andrews Ave. (☎ 357-7444). Open M-Th 9am-9pm, F-Sa 9am-5pm, Su noon-5:30pm.

Post Office: 1900 W. Oakland Park Blvd. (☎ 527-2028). Open M-F 7:30am-7pm, Sa 8:30am-2pm. **Postal Code:** 33310. **Area Code:** 954.

ACCOMMODATIONS

Thank decades of spring breakers for the abundance of hotels lining the beachfront. Generally, it is easy to find an available room at any time of the year, depending on how much you are willing to pay. High season runs from mid-February to early April. Motels just north of the strip and a block west of A1A are the cheapest. Many hotels offer low-season deals for under $35. The **Greater Fort Lauderdale Lodging and Hospitality Association,** 1412 E. Broward Blvd., provides a free directory of area hotels. (☎567-0766. Open M-F 9am-5pm.) The *Fort Lauderdale News* and the *Miami Herald* occasionally publish listings by local residents who rent rooms to tourists in spring. Sleeping on the well-patrolled beaches is illegal. Instead, check out one of the outstanding hostels in the area.

■ **Fort Lauderdale Beach Hostel,** 2115 N. Ocean Blvd./A1A (☎567-7275), between Sunrise and Oakland Park Blvd. Take bus #11 from the central terminal. After a long day of tanning and swimming at the adjacent beach, backpackers mingle in the tropical courtyard, TV-equipped common room, and well-stocked kitchen. Internet access. A/C, grill, and local phone calls. Call ahead for free daytime pickup from anywhere in Fort Lauderdale. Breakfast included. Free lockers. Linen deposit $10. Reservations suggested Dec.-June. Dorms $16-18. ❶

■ **Floyd's Hostel/Crew House,** 445 SE 16th St. (☎462-0631). From downtown take bus #1 or 40 and get off at 17th St. Call ahead for free pickup in the Fort Lauderdale area. Floyd's is a homey hostel catering to international travelers and boat crews. The owners, who also own the Beach Hostel, got engaged thanks to *Let's Go: USA 1995.* We're just that good. Internet access, free food, cable TV, lockers, linen, and laundry. Check-in midnight or call for special arrangement. Passport or American driver's license required. 4-bed dorms $19, $115 per week. Private rooms $35 for one person, $42 for 2. ❶

Tropic-Cay Beach Hotel, 529 N. Ft. Lauderdale Beach Blvd./A1A (☎564-5900 or 800-463-2333), directly across from the beach; take bus #11 or 44. Don't be fooled by the lackluster exterior; Tropic-Cay is the best deal on the beach. Before heading back to the super-clean, extremely large rooms, guests return from late-night partying to the outdoor patio bar and central pool, where fun continues long into the night. Tropic-Cay is one of the most crowded party spots on the beach, so be sure to call ahead. Kitchens available. During spring break, you must be 21+ to rent. Key deposit $10. Doubles June-Nov. $35-59, Dec.-May $59-99. Mar.-Apr. all rooms $99; $10 per extra person. ❸

Tropi-Rock Resort, 2900 Belmar St. (☎564-0523 or 800-987-9385), 2 blocks west of A1A at Birch Rd.; take bus #11 or 44. A few blocks inland from the beach, this yellow-and-orange hotel provides a resort atmosphere at affordable prices. The lush hibiscus garden, caged birds, and tile pool with fountain make the Tropi-Rock feel more like a glitzy mansion than a beach motel. Internet access. Gym, tennis courts, free local calls, refrigerators. Kitchens available. Rooms mid-Dec. to mid-May $91-104; mid-May to mid-Dec. $68-84. AAA discount. ❹

⬛ FOOD

Though clubs along the strip offer massive quantities of free happy hour grub—wieners, chips, and hors d'oeuvres come on surfboard-sized platters—most bars have hefty cover charges (from $5) and drink minimums (from $3).

■ **The Floridian,** 1410 E. Las Olas Blvd. (☎463-4041), is a local favorite, serving up heaping portions of french toast ($5), cheeseburgers ($5), and veggie burger platters ($7). Try the house specialty—the Floridian (grilled tuna salad sandwich; $7)—with one of the to-die-for milkshakes ($4), and you might never want to leave. Open 24hr. ❷

Squiggy's N.Y. Style Pizza, 207 SW 2nd St. (☎522-6655), in Old Town. Whether you're between bars or looking for a bite before bed, Squiggy's is the place for those late-night munchies. Gooey slices of Sicilian pie ($2, after 8pm $2.50) satisfy the cravings of the post-club hordes. Open M 11am-11:30pm, Tu-W 11am-3am, Th-Su 11am-4am. ❶

Tokyo Bowl, 1720 S. Federal Hwy. (☎524-8200). Think McDonald's meets sushi, with the exception that this fast-food Japanese restaurant serves far higher-quality fare than the Golden Arches. The best deal is the teriyaki chicken bowl ($4), though the all-you-can-eat sushi ($13) is also fantastic. Located just blocks from the Crew House Hostel, they'll even deliver. M-F 11am-2pm and 5-10pm, Sa-Su 5pm-10pm. ❶

◉ SIGHTS

Most visitors flock to Fort Lauderdale to lounge on the sunny beaches. When floating in the crystal-clear waves of the Atlantic, it's easy to forget the city's other notable attractions. Cruising down the palm-lined shore of Beachfront Ave. (A1A), biking through a nature preserve, or boating through the winding intracoastal canals reveal the less sandy side of Fort Lauderdale.

ON THE BEACH. Spring break lasts 365 days a year on Fort Lauderdale Beach, and after a Corona or two in any of the big bars along Rte. A1A, you'll swear you're in Cancún. If extreme inebriation isn't your thing, have no fear; the beach area offers plenty of booze-free activities. For a family-friendly overview of Fort Lauderdale, take a tour aboard the tourist-targeted **Jungle Queen.** The captain's commentary acquaints you with the changing scenery as the riverboat cruises up the New River. *(801 Seabreeze Blvd. At the Bahía Mar Yacht Center, on Rte. A1A, 3 blocks south of Las Olas Blvd. ☎462-5596; www.junglequeen.com. 3½hr. tours daily 10am, 2, 7pm. $14, ages 2-10 $9.25; 7pm tour $30/$17, dinner included.)* If you'd like to hit the water in more active style, **Water Sports Unlimited** has water sport rentals and trips. Sail the ocean on a boat ($95 for 2hr.) or enjoy its serene blue water from above on a parasailing trip ($65). Speed boats and wave runners also available. *(301 Seabreeze Blvd./A1A. ☎467-1316. Open daily 9am-5pm.)* For a different kind of high-seas adventure, doggy-paddle on over to the **International Swimming Hall of Fame and Museum** for exhibits on the sport and some of its greatest athletes. *(1 Hall of Fame Dr. ☎462-6536; www.ishof.org. Open daily 9am-5pm. $3; students, seniors, and military $1. Wheelchair accessible.)* Get lost in an oasis of subtropical trees and animals in the middle of urban Fort Lauderdale at **Hugh Taylor Birch State Park.** Bike, jog, canoe, or drive through mangroves and royal palms, or relax in the freshwater lagoon area with herons, gophers, tortoises, and marsh rabbits. *(3109 E. Sunrise Blvd., west off A1A. ☎564-4521. Open daily 8am-dusk. $3.25 per vehicle, $1 per person. Canoes $5.30 per hr. Cabins and primitive sites available by reservation; call ahead.)*

IN TOWN. The landscape of downtown Fort Lauderdale is still dominated by water, though in river form. The **Riverwalk** provides a shaded stroll along the banks of the New River, which cuts through downtown. Beginning at U.S. 1, the brick-lined, oak-shaded path meanders along the river, passing numerous sights and enormous mega-yachts. *(☎468-1541, www.goriverwalk.com.)* First along the route is Fort Lauderdale's **Museum of Art,** 1 E. Las Olas Blvd., home to an extensive collection of American painter William Glacken's work and remarkable temporary exhibits, which have included everything from Surrealism to photojournalism. *(☎468-3283; www.museumofart.org. Open M, W, F-Su 11am-7pm, Th 11am-9pm. $6, seniors $5, students $3. Wheelchair accessible.)* The next stop is the **Las Olas Waterfront,** the latest on-the-beach mall, boasting a bevy of clubs, restaurants, and bars. *(2 SW 2nd St.)* Two hundred yards farther, the Riverwalk cuts through **Old Town,** a district loaded with bars and cheap eateries. If you'd rather ride than walk, the **Water Taxi** offers a relaxing way to beat the rush-hour traffic and maneuver through town. The friendly captains will drive right up to any Las Olas restaurant or drop you off anywhere along the Intracoastal Waterway of New River. Alternatively, ride through the entire route for an intimate viewing of the fabulous, colossal houses along the canal. Special packages include a canal pub crawl to Fort Lauderdale's best bars. *(651 Seabreeze Blvd./A1A.* ☎ *467-6677; www.watertaxi.com. Call 30min. before pick-up. Open 9am-midnight. $4, seniors and under 12 $2; 1-day unlimited pass $5, 3-day pass $7; pub crawl $15.)* A bit farther from the heart of downtown are a number of intriguing attractions. Anointed by Guinness as the "fastest game in the world," Jai-Alai still remains mostly unknown to Americans outside the state of Florida. Take a break from the beach heat and watch a match at **Dania Jai-Alai,** which sports one of the largest frontons (courts) in the state. *(301 E. Dania Beach Blvd. Off U.S. 1, 10min. south of Fort Lauderdale.* ☎ *927-2841. Games Tu and Sa noon and 7pm, W-F 7pm, Su 1pm. General admission $1.50, reserved seats from $2.50.)* Cast your line at the **International Game Fishing Association's Fishing Hall of Fame and Museum,** where a gallery of odd-looking fish, the inside scoop on fishing hot spots, and an interactive reeling exercise amaze even the most avid fisherman. For the true fish fetishist, check out the large wooden replicas of world-record catches adorning the museum's ceiling and the film *Journeys* in the big screen theater. *(300 Gulf Stream Way. Off I-95 at Griffin Rd., Exit 23.* ☎ *922-4212; www.igfa.org/museum. Open daily 10am-6pm. $6, seniors $5, ages 3-16 $5. IGFA members free. Wheelchair accessible.)*

◼ NIGHTLIFE

Ask any local and they'll tell you that the real nightlife action is in **Old Town.** Two blocks northwest of Las Olas on 2nd St. near the **Riverwalk** district, the 100 yards of Old Town are packed with raucous bars, steamy clubs, cheap eats, and a stylish crowd. More expensive and geared specifically toward spring break seeking youngsters, the **Strip** houses several popular nightspots across from the beach.

Tarpon Bend, 200 SW 2nd St. (☎ 523-3233). Always the busiest place on the block. Starched shirts from the office converge with flirty black tube tops around the icy beer tubs of "the Bends." Bottled beer $3-4; "draft of the month" $1. W ladies drink free until 11pm. Open daily 11:30am-1am, sometimes later.

Dicey O'Riley's Irish Pub, 217 SW 2nd St. (☎ 522-1908). Under new (and Irish) ownership, this establishment has undergone beautiful renovations to its interior, which on Friday nights is packed to the rafters. Cheap happy hour pints (domestic $2, imported $3), a free buffet on F afternoons, live music M-Sa 10pm-2am, and cheap and delicious fare (NY strip steak $8). Open M-F 5pm-4am, Sa-Su 4pm-4am.

Elbo Room, 207 S. Atlantic Blvd. (☎ 463-4615), on prime real estate at the corner of A1A and Las Olas Blvd. The booming sidewalk bar, chock full of scantily clad beach beauties, is one of the most visible and packed scenes on the Strip. Live local rock music nightly. Open M-Th 11am-2am, F-Sa 11am-3am, Su noon-2am.

Beach Bums, 219 S. Ft. Lauderdale Beach Blvd. (☎ 779-2544). Are we in Cancún? May as well be at this club, a popular hangout for sin-seeking teens. "Hard Body" contest on the upper deck and scandalous grinding on the dance floors. 18+. Cover varies. Open daily 9pm-4am.

The Voodoo Lounge, 111 SW 2nd St. (☎ 522-0733). A well-dressed and well-known party in lush red VIP rooms, this upscale club offers a more refined approach to fun. Su drag shows, W ladies night. F-Sa 21+. Cover F-Sa $10. Open M, W, F-Su 10pm-4am.

The Saint, 1000 State Rd. 84 (☎ 779-2544, www.thesaintnightclub.net). A large dance club which attracts the crowds, The Saint is a gay-friendly club that draws straight partygoers as well. Cover $4-5. Open daily 2pm-2am.

Ramrod, 1508 NE 4th Ave, Wilton Manners. (☎ 763-8219; www.ramrodbar.com). Gay club with nightly happy hour 3-9pm. F leather. Cover varies. Open daily noon-2am.

PALM BEACH/WEST PALM BEACH ☎561

Nowhere else in Florida is the line between the "haves" and the "have-nots" as visible as at the intracoastal waterway dividing aristocratic vacationers on Palm Beach Island from blue-collar residents of West Palm Beach. Five-star resorts and guarded mansions reign over the "Gold Coast" island, while auto repair shops and fast-food restaurants characterize the mainland. Budget travel may be difficult here, but the region still offers some unique museums and stunning houses.

■ ■ **ORIENTATION AND PRACTICAL INFORMATION.** Palm Beach is located approximately 60 mi. north of Miami and 150 mi. southeast of Orlando. **I-95** runs north-south through the center of West Palm Beach, then continues south to Fort Lauderdale and Miami. The more scenic coastal highway, **A1A**, also travels north-south, crossing over Lake Worth at the Flagler Memorial Bridge to Palm Beach. Large highways cut through urban areas and residential neighborhoods; finding your way around can be a bit confusing. Stick to the major roads like north-south **Highway 1** (which turns into S. Dixie Hwy.), A1A, east-west **Palm Beach Lakes Boulevard,** and **Belvedere Road.** The heart of downtown West Palm Beach is **Clematis Street,** across from the Flagler Memorial Bridge, which offers both affordable restaurants and wild nightclubs.

Palm Beach International Airport (☎471-7420; www.pbia.org), at Belvedere and Australian Ave., Exit 51 from I-95 N, is 2½ mi. east of downtown West Palm Beach. The Tri-Rail stops at the airport, as does bus #44 from the downtown West Palm Beach Quadrille. **Amtrak,** 201 S. Tamarind Ave., east of I-95 in the downtown West Palm Beach Quadrille (☎832-6169; open daily 7:30am-8:45pm.) runs to Orlando (4hr., 2 per day, $22) and Charleston (12hr., 3 per day, $54). **Greyhound** leaves from the same station (open daily 5am-11:30pm) for Orlando (4hr., 8 per day, $36) and Miami (2hr., 15 per day, $21). **Public Transit: Palm Tran,** 3201 Electronics Way, has 35 routes from North Palm Beach Gardens to Boca Raton, with #41 and 42 traveling through the Palm Beach area. The major hub is at the intersection of Quadrille Blvd. and Clematis St. in downtown West Palm Beach. Schedules are available on all buses, at the main office, or at any public library. (☎841-4200 or 877-870-9489. $1.25; seniors, under 21, and disabled $0.60; 1-day pass $3/$2.) **Tri-Rail** connects West Palm Beach to Fort Lauderdale and Miami and leaves from the train station on Tamarind. (☎954-788-7936 or 800-874-7245. Hours vary by route: generally M-F 4am-10pm, Sa-Su 7am-5pm. $2-6; students, seniors, and disabled half-price; under 4 free.) **Taxi: Yellow Cab** ☎689-2222. **Visitor Info: Palm Beach County Convention and Visitors Bureau,** 1555 Palm Beach Lakes Blvd. (☎471-3995; www.palmbeachfl.com. Open M-F 8:30-5:30.) **Medical Services: Columbia Hospital,** 2201 45th St. (☎842-6141). **Hotlines: Helpline,** ☎615-4029. (24hr.); **Teenline,** ☎930-1234 (24hr.). **Internet Access: Clematis St. News Stand,** 206 Clematis St. (☎832-2302. Open Su-W 7:30am-10pm, Th-Sa 7:30am-midnight. $4 per ½hr.) **Post Office:** 640 Clematis St., in West Palm Beach. (☎833-0929. Open M-F 8:30am-5pm.) **Postal Code:** 33401. **Area Code:** 561.

▐ **ACCOMMODATIONS.** Catering to the rich and famous who flock to Palm Beach during the winter months, extravagant resorts and hotels are arguably the most notable attraction lining the Gold Coast. While the idea of mingling with royalty might sound like a fairy tale come true, the words "budget" and "hostel" will only receive blank stares from receptionists. Many reasonably priced B&Bs are booked far in advance; reserve a room before you arrive. West Palm Beach is the best bet for an affordable room near the action, but the absolute cheapest options are the chain hotels near the highway. **Hotel Biba ❹,** 320 Belvedere Rd., in West Palm Beach, bus #44, is fun, funky, and eclectic. Hidden within an unassuming exterior is a hip hotel that has become a haven for those budget-conscious travelers with a sense of style. Rooms are painted in shagadelic tones and beautiful bodies lounge on the pool deck and gather in the garden bar for drinks in the evening. Wednesday nights feature live jazz, with a cool scene that burns until 2am. (☎832-0094. Continental breakfast included. Rooms Dec.-Mar. $109-129; Apr.-Nov. $79-109.) Built in 1922 by a former Palm Beach mayor and elegantly restored in 1990, **Hibiscus House Bed & Breakfast ❹**, 501 30th St., in West Palm Beach at the corner of Spruce St. west of Flagler Dr., is affordable without sacrificing luxury. Sleep in one of nine antique-decorated bedrooms and wake up to a two-course gourmet breakfast served on Waterford crystal. Each room has a terrace, TV, phone, and A/C. (☎863-5633 or 800-203-4927. Rooms Dec.-Mar. $100-270; Apr.-Nov. $75-135.) Budget options on the island of Palm Beach are nonexistent. The closest it comes is **Heart of Palm Beach Hotel ❺**, 160 Royal Palm Way, in Palm Beach, bus #41, which welcomes visitors with cool pinks and greens. Palm Beach's most inexpensive hotel still manages to embody the prestige of the nearby beaches and ritzy Worth Ave. (☎655-5600. Internet access, refrigerators, TV, heated pool, free parking. Rooms Dec.-Mar. $199-399; Apr.-Nov. $89-169; under 18 stay free with parents.)

🛱🎭 **FOOD AND NIGHTLIFE.** Clematis St. in downtown West Palm Beach offers a lively option for travelers on the cheap, and a Wednesday to Saturday nightlife scene that rivals any college town. A mixture of pool hall, sports bar, concert venue, and meat market, 🏠**Spanky's ❷**, 500 Clematis St., is West Palm Beach's notoriously fun night spot. Enjoy cold beer (pitchers $5) and tasty bar food in this enormous venue, whose closing time is marked only by a question mark, but usually comes around 4am. Every night is a different theme and drink special, like Island Tuesdays with $0.75 Coronas and $2 Rum Runners. Spanky's is also a concert venue which has featured the likes of Blink-182 and Sugar Ray in their early days. (☎659-5669; check www.downtownspankys.com for concert schedules. Beer-battered onion rings $4. Hot wings $12. Open M-F at 11:30am, Sa noon, Su 1pm; closes when the place empties out.) Voted "Best Burger" and "People's Choice" in a recent cook-off, **O'Shea's Irish Pub and Restaurant ❷**, 531½ Clematis St., at Rosemary St., will modify any dish to fit vegetarian needs. Locals and those nostalgic for Dublin flock here for the live nightly music, usually Irish rock or folk, and Mrs. O'Shea's $7.50 savory chicken pie. (☎833-3865. Open Su-Tu 11am-10pm, W-Th 11am-midnight, F-Sa 11am-1am.) **Sushi Jo ❷**, 318 Belvedere Road #12, is just across the street from the swanky Hotel Biba and stays open on Wednesday until 2am when the hotel's jazz scene winds down. Try the *naruto maki* ($8), a refreshing plate of crab, salmon, and scallion sushi. (☎868-7893. Open M-F 11:30am-2pm and 5-10pm, W until 2am; Sa-Su 5-11pm.) Known for exclusive dinner parties and black-tie galas, nightlife on Palm Beach is an invitation-only affair. You won't find a disco or "local bar" anywhere along the ritzy downtown area. You will, however, find **Sprinkles Ice Cream & Sandwich Shop ❶**, 279 Royal Poinciana Way, the best bargain for a hungry stomach. Customers line up for a scoop of homemade ice cream ($3.75) in a hand-dipped cone. (☎659-1140. French bread pizza $5.50. Open Su-Th 10am-10pm, F-Sa 10am-11pm.)

🔆 **SIGHTS.** The prize of blue-collar West Palm Beach is 🏠**Ragtops**, 2119 S. Dixie Hwy., as fine a collection of Americana as you'll find. It just so happens that all the items have four wheels and some muscle under the hood. First opened in 1925 as a Cadillac dealership, the five show floors are now home to over 70 beautiful classic automobiles, and should you fall in love with one you need not leave broken-hearted—most are for sale. (☎655-2836; www.ragtopsmotorcars.com. Open M-Sa 10am-5pm. $5, seniors $4, ages 12 and under $3. Wheelchair accessible.) Though the net value of the art in the mansions of Palm Beach is probably greater, the **Norton Museum of Art,** 1451 S. Olive Ave., is well-known for its collection of European, American, contemporary, and Chinese art. Be sure to stop by the central garden, which features its own fountain of youth. (☎832-5196; www.norton.org. Open May-Sept. Tu-Sa 10am-5pm, Su 1-5pm; Nov.-Apr. M-Sa 10am-5pm, Su 1-5pm. $6, ages 13-21 $2, under 13 free. Tours daily 2-3pm; lectures M-F 12:30-1pm. Free. Self-guided audio tour $4. Wheelchair accessible.) If you're visiting in early spring, catch the training seasons of the **Montréal Expos** and **St. Louis Cardinals,** who make their winter home at **Municipal Stadium,** 1610 Palm Beach Lakes Blvd. (☎683-6012. Call for times and schedules.) In Palm Beach, just walking around can be one of the most enjoyable (and affordable) activities. Known as the "Rodeo Drive of the South," **Worth Avenue,** between S. Ocean Blvd. and Coconut Row, outfits Palm Beach's rich and famous in the threads of fashion heavyweights like Gucci, Polo, and Armani. Walk or drive along **Ocean Boulevard** to gawk at the spectacular, enormous mansions owned by celebrities and millionaires. One particularly remarkable complex is **The Breakers,** 1 S. County Rd., a sizable Italian Renaissance resort. Even if you can't afford the bare-minimum $270 price tag for a night of luxury, live vicariously and stroll the grounds, or get more up close and personal though a guided tour. (☎659-8440 or 888-273-2537. Tour W 2pm. $15 for non-guests.) Of course, a trip to Palm Beach County is incomplete without relaxing on one of its picturesque beaches. Although you'll see few residents swimming (they all go to the country clubs or their own private beaches), the sand is beautiful and the water serene. Good options on Palm Beach include the popular **Mid-town Beach,** 400 S. Ocean Blvd., and **Phipps Ocean Park,** 2185 S. Ocean Blvd. (☎585-9203).

NORTH FLORIDA

PANAMA CITY BEACH   ☎850

Panama City Beach, a 27 mi. long strip along the Gulf of Mexico, is the place for everything touristy, beachy, and kitschy. Regardless of whether you're in college or not, the "PCB" experience is the essence of spring-break. There is no pretense or high culture here—just miles of parties and loud, thumping bass. Over 1000 acres of gators, nature trails, and beaches make up the **Saint Andrews State Recreation Area** (Open daily 8am-sunset; $4 per car). **The Glass Bottom Boat** takes visitors on a dolphin-watching excursion and sails to Shell Island from **Treasure Island Marina,** 3605 Thomas Dr. (☎234-8944. 3hr. trips 9am, 1, 4:30pm. $15, seniors $14, under 12 $8. $3 discount coupon available at the visitor center.) The **Sea Dragon** takes swashbucklers on Pirate Cruises. (5325 N. Lagoon Rd. ☎234-7400. 2hr. cruises; call ahead for times. $17, seniors $15, ages 3-14 $15, under 2 $5.) **Gulf World Marine Park,** 15412 Front Beach Rd. has shows that feature dolphins, sea lions, and parrots, as well as exhibits on coastal creatures like sharks and turtles. Take it a step further and swim with dolphins or learn how to be a trainer. (☎234-5271; www.gulfworldmarinepark.com. $22, children $15.)

Depending on the location and time of year, lodging rates range from outrageous to extremely outrageous. The family-owned ⬛**South Pacific Motel** ❷, 16701 Front Beach Rd., is definitely one of the best deals on the beach, thanks to a secret treasure: two motel rooms that go for $45 in peak season. The rest of the rooms are also relatively cheap. (☎234-2703 or 800-966-9439. Pool, private beach, and cable TV. In summer 2 rooms $45; doubles $70; 2-bedroom apartments $98.) **The Palmetto** ❸, 17255 Front Beach Rd. right on the beach, is safe and sunny. (☎234-2121. Indoor/outdoor pool, shuffleboard, TV, on-site laundry, and A/C. Rooms $98;

low-season from \$55.) Camp on the beach at **Saint Andrews State Recreation Area ❶**, 4607 State Park Ln., at the east end of Thomas Dr. All 176 sites are beneath the pines and near the water. (☎233-5140, reservations 800-326-3521. Reserve far in advance. Sites with electricity or waterside, for up to 8 people and 2 cars, \$24.)

Buffets stuff the Strip and Thomas Dr. "Early bird" specials (usually 4-6pm) get you the same food at about half the price. **Scampy's ❸**, 4933 Thomas Dr., is a notable exception to the strip's often low-quality food, offering delicious seafare in a smaller, less harried atmosphere than the mega-troughs. (☎235-4209. 18 lunch specials \$4-8. Seafood salad \$9. Dinner entrees \$11-20. Open Su-Th 11am-10pm, F-Sa 11am-11pm.) At night, many of the restaurants on the Strip turn into bars and clubs, and most have live bands. Cool off at **Sharky's ❷**, 15201 Front Beach Rd., with a Hurricane or a Sharkbite specialty drink (\$5.25). More adventurous spirits will savor their signature appetizer, "shark bites" (fried shark cubes; \$7). Live music on the beach deck most nights generally runs to country, 80s, and the Eagles. (☎235-2420. Cover \$8; free if you eat there. Kitchen open daily 11:30am-11pm; club open until 2am.) The back patio bar at **Harpoon Harry's**, 12627 Front Beach Rd., overlooks the beach. Build a midnight sandcastle after having a drink. (☎234-6060. Pitchers \$6. Open daily 11am-2am.) The largest club in the US (capacity 8000), **Club LaVela**, 8813 Thomas Dr., has eight clubs and 48 bar stations under one jammin' roof. Live bands work the Rock Pavilion every night. Wet T-shirt, bikini, and male hard body contests fill the weekends and are every night during Spring Break. (☎234-3866. 18+. Nightly cover \$10-25. Open daily 10am-4am.)

After crossing Hathaway Bridge from the east, **Thomas Drive** and **Front Beach Road** (marked as Alt. U.S. 98) fork off from U.S. 98 and run along the gulf. This becomes the **"Miracle Strip,"** the main drag of PCB. **Greyhound,** 917 Harrison Ave. (☎785-6111; open M-F 7am-9pm, Sa-Su 7-11am, 1:15-4:15pm and 6:45-8:30pm), stops at the junction of U.S. 98 and 79 and continues on to Atlanta (9hr., 4 per day, \$48-52) and Orlando (8-11hr., 3 per day, \$63-70). **Bay Town Trolley,** 1021 Massalina Dr., shuttles along the beach. (☎769-0557. M-F 6am-5pm. \$1, students and seniors \$0.50; \$1 to cross bridge. One-use transfers \$0.25. Day pass \$3.) **Panama City Beach Convention and Visitors Bureau,** 17001 Panama City Beach Pkwy., at U.S. 98 and 79, has info and a free **Internet** kiosk. (☎233-6503 or 800-722-3224; www.thebeachloversbeach.com. Open daily 8am-5pm.) **Post Office:** 420 Churchwell Dr., (☎236-0589. Open M-F 8am-5pm, Sa 9am-noon.) **Postal Code:** 32407. **Area Code:** 850.

PENSACOLA ☎850

A military population and conservative reputation have characterized Pensacola since before the Civil War, when three forts on the shores of Pensacola guarded its deep-water ports. One of the forts, Fort Pickens, remains and can be easily visited. Most visitors, however, are drawn the **Gulf Island National Seashore's** sugar-white beaches and secluded, emerald waters. The **National Museum of US Naval Aviation** in the Naval Air Station at Exit 2 off I-10, is the home of the Blue Angels US Air Force Display Team and has over 130 planes and an IMAX theater. (☎452-3604. 5 mi. southwest from downtown. Open daily 9am-5pm. 1½hr. tours daily 9:30, 11am, 1, and 2:30pm. Films 9am-4pm. Free; films \$6.) At the **Naval Live Oaks Area,** 1801 Gulf Breeze Pkwy., paths meander through a forest that John Quincy Adams established as the US's first and only naval tree reservation. (☎934-2600. Open daily 8am-5:30pm. Free.) The Pensacola Beach Bridge leads to **Santa Rosa Island** for some of the best beaches (\$1); the island's coast feels cleaner, gets more waves, and is less crowded than the inland beaches. ◪**Fort Pickens,** where Apache leader Geronimo was imprisoned in the late 1800s, commands the western part of Santa

Rosa. Visitors can explore the ruins and sunbathe on the secluded seashore. (Park open daily 8am-sunset. Visitors center open daily 8:30am-4pm. Self-guided tours available; guided tours daily at 2pm. Entrance fee $8 per car.)

Hotels along the beach cost at least $65 and get more expensive in summer. The **Five Flags Inn ❹**, 299 Fort Pickens Rd., is a good beachfront deal, offering free local calls, gulfside rooms, and a beach patio and pool. (☎932-3586. May-Aug. $109; Sept.-Oct. $89; Nov.-Dec. $59; Feb.-May $89.) Also offering good beachside rates is the **Sandpiper Gulf Aire Inn ❸**, 21 Via De Luna. The inn offers motel rooms and villas for prices that will help you sleep. Private beach, pool, and cable TV. (☎800-301-5925; www.gulfairemotel.com. Rooms $69-105; low-season from $39.) Cheaper options lie north of downtown at the exits of I-10 and I-110, a 15min. drive from the beach. Clean and well-furnished, the **Harbor Inn ❷**, 200 N. Palafox St., is by downtown and budget friendly. (☎432-3441. Continental breakfast, A/C, TV. Key deposit $5. Local calls $0.50. Singles Su-Th $43, F-Sa $53; doubles $53/$60.) At the western edge of Santa Rosa Island, the **Fort Pickens Campground ❶** on the Gulf Islands National Seashore offers sites in walking distance of gorgeous beaches. (☎934-2621 for camping info, reservations 800-365-2267. Electricity and water. Sites $20.)

◪**Jerry's ❶**, 2815 E. Cervantes, has been serving fabulous diner fare since 1939. (☎433-9910. $5 pitchers of beer. Open M-F 10am-10pm, Sa 7am-10pm. Cash only.) **Tre Fratelli ❸**, 304 Alcaniz St., a Sicilian restaurant and pizzeria, makes fantastic pasta sauces. (☎438-3663. Pasta $9-15. Pizza $10-18. Open M-Sa 11am-3pm and 5-10pm.) All are welcome at the **End of the Line Coffee Shop**, 610 E. Wright St., which serves fair trade coffee ($1.50) and a mean slice of quiche ($6). It also doubles as an Internet cafe ($0.10 per minute) and features punk music and poetry readings; call for details. (☎429-0336. Open daily 11am-10pm.) **Emerald City**, 406 E. Wright St., hosts guys and gals, young and old, straight and gay, for dancing, with its two main bars, several rooms and a rooftop terrace. (☎433-9491. Shows some nights—call ahead. Cover $2-3. Open daily 5pm-3am.)

The city buttresses Pensacola Bay. **Palafox Street**, which becomes one-way near the bay, and **I-110** are the main north-south roads. The **Pensacola Beach Road** leads to Santa Rosa Island and Pensacola Beach, while **Gulf Breeze Parkway** trails along the coast. **Amtrak**, 980 E. Heinburg St. (☎433-4966 or 800-872-7245; open M-F 12am-7:30am), runs to New Orleans (7hr., 3 per week, $30-65) and Orlando (13hr., 3 per week, $50-108). **Greyhound**, 505 W. Burgess Rd. (☎476-4800; open daily 4:30am-10:45pm), goes to: Atlanta (8-12hr., 4 per day, $51); New Orleans (4-7hr., 4 per day, $44); Orlando (10-11hr., 5 per day, $63). A **trolley** runs from the tourist information center on a 1hr. tour of the major sights and beaches. (Tour $10. Departs at 10:30, 11:30am, 12:30 and 1:30pm. $0.25 for general trolley token.) In summer, two free **Tiki Trolley** shuttles run along the beach. (☎494-2270. F-Sa 10am-3am, Su 10am-10pm.) **Visitor Info: Pensacola Convention and Visitors Bureau**, 1401 E. Gregory St., near the Pensacola Bay Bridge., has coupons for otherwise expensive lodgings. (☎800-874-1234; www.visitpensacola.com. Open M-F 8am-5pm, Sa 9am-4pm and Su 11am-4pm.) **Post Office:** 101 S. Palafox St. (☎439-0169. Open M-F 8:30am-5pm.) **Postal Code:** 32501. **Area Code:** 850.

FLORIDA

GREAT LAKES

Though the region's alternate name—the Midwest—evokes a bland image of corn-fields and small-town, white-picket-fence America, the states that hug the five Great Lakes encompass a variety of personalities. The world's largest freshwater lake, Lake Superior, and its unpopulated, scenic coast cradle some of the most stunning natural features in the region—from the dense forests in northern Wisconsin to the waterfalls of the Upper Peninsula in Michigan. Meanwhile, the Lake Michigan coast hosts sand dunes, swimming, sailing, and deep-water fishing. Minneapolis and St. Paul form a bonafide coastal metropolis, while Chicago dazzles with a stunning skyline, incredible culinary offerings, and world-class museums.

HIGHLIGHTS OF THE GREAT LAKES

FOOD. Chicago pizza (p. 596), "pasties" in Michigan's Upper Peninsula (p. 586), and Door County's fish boils (p. 619) are some regional specialties.

RECREATIONAL ACTIVITIES. Canoeing and kayaking are popular in the northern reaches of the Great Lakes; Grand Traverse Bay, MI (p. 582), is a recreation hot spot.

SCENIC DRIVES. In MI, see the Lake Michigan shore on U.S. 31 and Rte. 119 (p. 585), Brockway Mountain Dr. (p. 589), or the dirt roads of Pictured Rocks State Park (p. 588). In MN, drive Rte. 61 N from Duluth along the Lake Superior shore (p. 638).

OHIO

Of all the Great Lakes states, Ohio best reflects the traditional definition of "Middle America." The state's farmland is a patchwork of cornfields and soybean plants, and three cities—Cincinnati, Cleveland, and Columbus—are home to millions of Ohioans. Away from the big cities, small towns cultivate a friendly atmosphere while liberal colleges challenge a practical, traditional Midwestern identity.

🔲 PRACTICAL INFORMATION

Capital: Columbus.

Visitor Info: State Office of Travel and Tourism, 77 S. High St., 29th fl., Columbus 43215 (☎614-466-8844; www.ohiotourism.com). Open M-F 8am-5pm. **Ohio Tourism Line** (☎800-282-5393).

Postal Abbreviation: OH. **Sales Tax:** 6%.

CLEVELAND   ☎216

Ridiculed for having a river so polluted it caught fire (twice) and branded "Mistake on the Lake," Cleveland has tried hard to correct its beleaguered image. In the early 90s, new football and baseball stadiums catalyzed the downtown makeover, which reached its zenith in 1995 with the arrival of the Rock and Roll Hall of Fame. The lake and river were cleaned, the city skyline was redefined, and the deserted warehouses of the Flats were transformed into bustling bars and nightclubs. Modern sculptures and flower-lined streets now give the downtown a sense of vitality, while colorful neighborhoods and fine museums complement the city center.

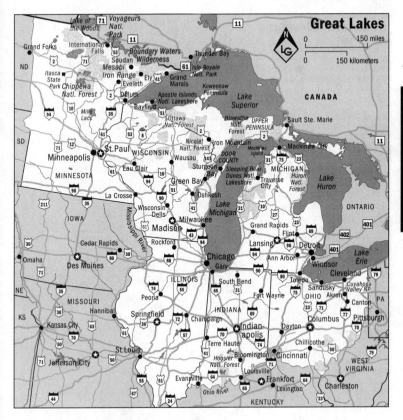

Great Lakes

0 — 150 miles

0 — 150 kilometers

TRANSPORTATION

Airport: Cleveland Hopkins International (☎265-6030; www.clevelandairport.com), 10 mi. southwest of downtown in Brook Park. RTA line #66X "Red Line" to Terminal Tower. Taxi to downtown $20.

Trains: Amtrak, 200 Cleveland Memorial Shoreway NE (☎696-5115), across from Brown Stadium east of City Hall. Open Su-F 9:30pm-1pm, Sa 9:30pm-8:30am. To **Chicago** (6½-7½hr., 3 per day, $40-50) and Pittsburgh (3hr., 12 per day, $19-24).

Buses: Greyhound, 1465 Chester Ave. (☎781-1841), at E. 14th St., 7 blocks from Terminal Tower. Near RTA bus lines. Open daily 24hr. To: **Chicago** (6½-7½hr., 12 per day, $43-47); **Cincinnati** (4½-6½hr., 12 per day, $38-42); **New York City** (9hr., 11 per day, $60-65); **Pittsburgh** (2½-4½hr., 10 per day, $22-25).

Public Transit: Regional Transit Authority (RTA), 315 Euclid Ave. (☎621-9500; www.riderRTA.com). Open M-F 7am-6pm. Bus lines, connecting with Rapid Transit trains, travel from downtown to most of the metropolitan area. Service daily 5am-midnight; call for info on "owl" (after midnight) service. Train $1.50. Bus $1.25, express $1.50, downtown loop $0.75. 1-day pass $3, seniors $1; family $5. Travelers with cars staying out-

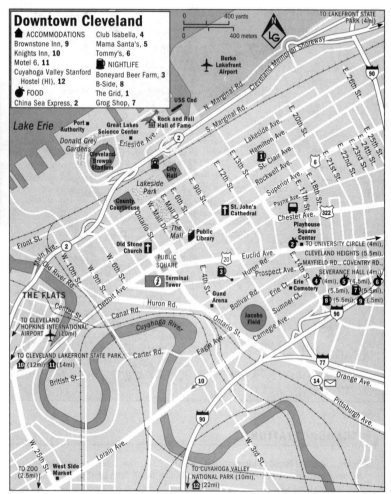

Downtown Cleveland

🏠 **ACCOMMODATIONS**
Brownstone Inn, **9**
Knights Inn, **10**
Motel 6, **11**
Cuyahoga Valley Stanford
 Hostel (HI), **12**

🍴 **FOOD**
China Sea Express, **2**

Club Isabella, **4**
Mama Santa's, **5**
Tommy's, **6**

🍸 **NIGHTLIFE**
Boneyard Beer Farm, **3**
B-Side, **8**
The Grid, **1**
Grog Shop, **7**

side the downtown area can park for free at one of the many park-and-rides and take the train to Terminal Square for $1.50. The **Waterfront Line** serves the Science Center, Rock and Roll Hall of Fame, and the Flats.

Taxi: Americab ☎ 881-1111.

⚡🚹 ORIENTATION AND PRACTICAL INFORMATION

Terminal Tower, in **Public Square,** at the intersection of Detroit Ave. and Ontario St., forms the center of downtown and splits the city into east and west. Many street numbers correspond to the distance of the street from Terminal Tower; e.g., E. 18th St. is 18 blocks east of the Tower. To reach Public Sq. from **I-90** or **I-71,** take the Ontario St./Broadway exit. From **I-77,** take the 9th St. exit to Euclid Ave., which runs into Public Sq. While downtown and University Circle are relatively safe, the area between the two around 55th St. can be rough. **The Flats,** along both banks of the Cuyahoga River, and **Coventry Road,** in Cleveland Heights, are the happening spots for food and nightlife.

Visitor Info: Cleveland Convention and Visitors Bureau, 3100 Tower City Ctr. (☎621-4110 or 888-323-2787; www.travelcleveland.com), in Terminal Tower. Open daily 9am-4pm.

Hotline: Rape Crisis Line, ☎619-6192 or 619-6194. Operates 24hr.

Internet Access: Cleveland Public Library, 525 Superior Ave. (☎623-2800). 15min. limit if crowded. Open M-Sa 9am-6pm, Su 1-5pm; closed Su in summer.

Post Office: 2400 Orange Ave. (☎443-4494, after 5pm 443-4096.) Open M-F 7am-8pm, Sa 8:30am-4pm. **Postal Code:** 44101. **Area Code:** 216; 440 or 330 in suburbs. In text, 216 unless otherwise noted.

ACCOMMODATIONS

With hotel taxes (not included in the prices listed below) as high as 14.5%, cheap lodging is hard to find in Cleveland. **Cleveland Private Lodgings,** P.O. Box 18557, Cleveland 44118, will place you in a home around the city for as little as $45. (☎291-1209; http://my.en.com/~privlodg/. Call M-F 9am-noon or 3-5pm. Allow 2-3 weeks for a letter of confirmation; for faster response, correspond by e-mail.) Those with cars might consider staying in the suburbs or near the airport, where prices tend to be lower. Most accommodations will not rent to those under 21.

▨ **Cuyahoga Valley Stanford Hostel (HI),** 6093 Stanford Rd. (☎330-467-8711), in Peninsula, 22 mi. south of Cleveland in the Cuyahoga Valley National Park. Housed in a 19th-century farmhouse, this idyllic hostel offers clean, cozy dorms with the comforts of country living. Kitchen, living room, and access to miles of trails. Linens $3. Lockout 10am-5pm. Reservations recommended. Dorms $16, under 18 with guardian half price. ❶

▨ **Brownstone Inn Bed and Breakfast,** 3649 Prospect Ave. (☎426-1753). Located a short drive from downtown or nightlife in University Circle and Cleveland Heights, the ivy-covered inn offers soft beds in a historic 19th-century home with restored original decor. Full breakfast and kitchenette. Most rooms with private baths. $65-95. ❹

Motel 6, 7219 Engle Rd. (☎440-234-0990), off Exit 235 on I-71, 15 mi. southwest of the city, has comfy rooms with cable TV and A/C. Located near restaurants, stores, and a park-and-ride lot. 21+. Singles Su-Th $43, F-Sa $50; doubles $49/$56. ❸

Knights Inn, 22115 Brookpark Rd. (☎440-734-4500), at Exit 9 off I-480; take the first 2 rights after the freeway. Standard motel rooms, free local phone calls, continental breakfast, free shuttle to airport. 21+. Singles Su-Th $45, F-Sa $49; doubles $50/$55. Weekly rate $242. ❷

FOOD

The delis downtown satiate most hot corned beef cravings, but Cleveland has more to offer elsewhere. Cafes and colorful shops grace **Coventry Road,** in **Cleveland Heights** between Mayfield Rd. and Euclid Heights Blvd. The sounds of Italian crooners fill the sidewalks of **Little Italy,** around **Mayfield Road,** where visitors can shop in the tiny stores before enjoying a delicious Italian meal. Over 100 vendors hawk produce, meat, and cheese at the old-world-style **West Side Market,** 1979 W. 25th St., at Lorain Ave. (☎781-3663. Open M and W 7am-4pm, F-Sa 7am-6pm.)

Mama Santa's, 12305 Mayfield Rd. (☎231-9567), in Little Italy, just east of University Circle, has kept hordes of college students and courting couples happy for over 40 years with its sumptuous Sicilian pizzas, authentic pasta dishes, and welcoming atmo-

EXTRA VALUE MEAL

When it comes to lunch on the go, $3 will barely get you a meal at most fast food chains, and forget about super-sizing that order. But at **Massimo da Milano,** a tony Italian bistro just across the Cuyahoga River from downtown, $3 buys you the mother of all extra value meals: a scrumptious lunch buffet that puts all quarter-pounders to shame.

After paying the cashier, grab a plastic box and soup container and get to work. The menu varies, but generally includes a soup and two pastas, as well as freshly baked pizza, meat dishes, salad, bread, and gorgeous desserts. There are no seconds in this buffet, so choose wisely; however, the containers are large enough that savvy patrons won't have enough room in their stomachs for an encore. Once your carton is full, head for the door: $3 covers the food but not a seat in the restaurant.

Customers with bigger appetites, thicker wallets, and more time can grab a seat in the main dining room. In addition to the sit-down buffet ($6.75), choose from traditional fare such as veal parmesan ($17) and *pollo alla Milanese* ($12).

Massimo da Milano, 1400 W. 25th St. (☎696-2323), just across the Detroit Ave. bridge. Open for lunch M-F 11:30am-2:30pm; dinner M-Sa by reservation only. The lunch buffet is served M-F 11am-2:30pm.

sphere. Lasagna and *cavatelli* with meatballs both $6.25. Pizzas $4.75-13. Open M-Th 11am-10:30pm, F-Sa 11am-11pm; closed most of Aug. ❷

Club Isabella, 2025 University Hospital Dr. (☎229-1177), in the shadow of a hospital complex off Euclid Ave., is an upscale bistro with a gourmet menu and substantial wine list guaranteed to fit any prescription. Live jazz Tu-Sa. Entrees $13-31. Open M 11:30am-9pm, Tu-W 11:30am-10pm, Th-F 11:30am-11pm, Sa 5:30-10pm. ❹

Tommy's, 1824 Coventry Rd. (☎321-7757), in Cleveland Heights. Take bus #9X east to Mayfield and Coventry Rd. Tommy's whips up tantalizing veggie cuisine, including a variety of falafels ($4.35-6). The epic menu also offers non-vegetarian options. Entrees from $4. Open M-Th 7:30am-10pm, F-Sa 7:30am-11pm, Su 9am-10pm. ❶

China Sea Express, 1507 Euclid Ave. (☎861-0188), downtown, has Chinese food worth more than its price. A delicious all-you-can-eat lunch buffet (11am-3pm) is $5.75 and includes wonton soup, lo mein, General Tso's chicken, crab rangoon, and all of the expected Chinese staples. Open Su-Th 11am-9pm, F-Sa 11am-10pm. ❷

◉ SIGHTS

DOWNTOWN. The aspirations of a new Cleveland are revealed in the new downtown—a self-declared "Remake on the Lake." One of the city's centerpieces is I.M. Pei's glass pyramid that houses the ◪**Rock and Roll Hall of Fame,** where blaring music invites visitors into a dizzying retrospective of rock music. Take a tour through rock history on the "Mystery Train," listen to the "500 Songs that Shaped Rock and Roll," and ogle memorabilia—from Elvis's jumpsuits to Jimi Hendrix's guitar—sure to wow fans of any era. (*1 Key Plaza.* ☎781-7625; www.rockhall.com. Open M-Tu and Th-Su 10am-5:30pm, W 10am-9pm; June-Aug. Sa until 9pm. $20, students $18, seniors $14, ages 9-11 $11, under 9 free. Wheelchair accessible.*) Next door, the **Great Lakes Science Center** educates with interactive exhibits. Hang-glide over the Grand Canyon, deliver a weather forecast, and step inside a giant steel cauldron. (*601 Erieside Ave.* ☎694-2000; www.greatscience.com. Open daily 9:30am-5:30pm. Science center or OMNIMAX $9, seniors $8, ages 3-17 $7; both $13/$11/$9. Wheelchair accessible. Parking for Hall of Fame and Science Center $7.*)

THE WILD SIDE. Escape the urban jungle at the **Cleveland Metroparks,** which extend into the Cuyahoga Valley. The **Cleveland Metroparks Zoo,** 5 mi.

south of downtown on I-71 at the Fulton Rd. exit, allows visitors to walk through the African Savannah and the Northern Trek, catching glimpses of red pandas and Madagascar hissing cockroaches. One of the zoo's highlights is the Australian Adventure, where kangaroos frolic and cuddly koalas cling to eucalyptus trees. (☎661-6500; www.clemetzoo.com. Open daily 10am-5pm. $9, children 2-11 $4, under 2 free.)

UNIVERSITY CIRCLE. While much has been made of Cleveland's revitalized downtown, the city's cultural nucleus still lies in **University Circle,** 4 mi. east of the city. The **Cleveland Museum of Art** boasts a grand hall of armor—part Medieval, part Asian—along with a survey of art from the Renaissance to the present. An exceptional collection of Impressionist and modern works is highlighted by nine Picasso pieces. (11150 East Blvd. ☎421-7340; www.clevelandart.org. Open Tu, Th, Sa-Su 10am-5pm, W and F 10am-9pm. Free.) Nearby, the **Cleveland Museum of Natural History** sends visitors to the stars in the planetarium, while those dreaming of a different kind of sparkle can explore the new gallery of gems. The outdoor Wildlife Center and Woods Gardens display plants and wildlife indigenous to Ohio, from barn owls to bobcats. The museum will feature a special exhibit on feathered dinosaurs from February to May 2005. (1 Wade Oval Dr. ☎231-4600 or 800-317-9155; www.cmnh.org. Open M-Tu and Th-Sa 10am-5pm, W 10am-10pm, Su noon-5pm. $7; students, seniors, and ages 7-18 $5; ages 3-6 $4. Planetarium $3.) Reopened in the summer of 2003 after a $40 million renovation, the **Cleveland Botanical Garden** provides a peaceful respite from urban life with traditional Victorian and Japanese gardens. (11030 East Blvd. ☎721-1600; www.cbgarden.org. Open Apr.-Oct. daily 10am-5pm. $7, ages 3-12 $3.)

🎵 🎭 ENTERTAINMENT AND NIGHTLIFE

Football reigns supreme in Cleveland, where the **Browns** grind it out on the gridiron at **Cleveland Browns Stadium** during the winter. (☎241-5555. Tickets from $25.) Baseball's **Indians** hammer the hardball at **Jacobs Field,** 2401 Ontario St. (☎420-4200. Tickets from $5.) If you can't catch a game, the best way to see the field is on a 1hr. **stadium tour.** (☎420-4385. Tours May-June and Sept. M-F 10am-2pm every hr., and Sa when the Indians are away. $6.50, seniors and under 15 $4.50.) The NBA's **Cavaliers** play shoot hoops at **Gund Arena,** 1 Center Ct. (☎420-2000.)

The **Cleveland Orchestra** performs at impressive **Severance Hall,** 11001 Euclid Ave. (☎231-7300; www.clevelandorch.com. Box office open M-F 9am-5pm. From $25.) **Playhouse Square Center,** 1519 Euclid Ave. (☎771-4444), a 10min. walk east of Terminal Tower, is the second-largest performing arts center in the US. Inside, the **State Theater** hosts the **Cleveland Opera** (☎575-0900; www.clevelandopera.org. Box office open daily 11am-6pm or until intermission on show nights.)

Most of Cleveland's nightlife is centered in **the Flats,** which has recently been transformed into a haven of beer and debauchery. For info on clubs and concerts, pick up a copy of *Scene* or the *Free Times*. The *Gay People's Chronicle* and *OUTlines* are available at gay clubs, cafes, and bookstores.

Grog Shop, 2785 Euclid Heights Blvd. (☎321-5588), at Coventry Rd., in Cleveland Heights, is a mainstay of Cleveland's alternative music scene. A move to a larger, less dingy location in the summer of 2003 had some purists waxing nostalgic about an era lost, but the Grog still hosts the best in underground rock and hip-hop night after night. Cover varies. All ages, additional $2 cover for under 21. Open daily 8pm-2:30am.

B-Side, 2785 Euclid Heights Blvd. (☎932-1966), at Coventry Rd. downstairs from the Grog Shop, is an upscale bar mixing up over 30 brands of martinis (from $7) for patrons reclining on leather couches. DJ nightly. Open Su-Th 8pm-2:30am, F-Sa 7pm-2:30am.

The Grid, 1437 St. Claire Ave. (☎623-0113), entertains a predominantly gay crowd with a space-aged dance floor and four bars. Su karaoke, Th male strippers. Free parking. 18+. Cover F-Sa after 11pm $5. Open daily 8pm-2:30am; dance floor open F until 3am, Sa until 4am.

Boneyard Beer Farm, 748 Prospect Ave. (☎575-0226), in the Gateway District, rears over 150 beers from around the world for a clientele of brew lovers. Skull and cross-bones decor, faux cow-skin chairs, and barrels of peanuts make this a great hangout. Beer $3-7. Happy hour M-F 4-8pm. Open M-Sa 4pm-2:30am, Su 7pm-2:30am.

▨ DAYTRIPS FROM CLEVELAND

CUYAHOGA VALLEY NATIONAL PARK

Just 10 mi. south of Cleveland lies the northern edge of the scenic **Cuyahoga Valley National Park.** The park's lifeline is the **Cuyahoga River,** which winds 30 mi. through dense forests and open farmland, passing stables, aqueducts, and mills along the way. The best way to see the natural beauty of the park is by hiking or biking its long trails. The **Ohio & Erie Canal Towpath Trail** runs through shaded forests and past the numerous locks used during the canal's heyday, when it served as a vital link between Cleveland and the Ohio River. The park's **visitors center,** 7104 Canal Rd., just inside the park, has information on the canal and hands out park maps. (☎216-524-1497. From Cleveland, take I-77 south to Rockside Rd., take a left after the exit, continue to Canal Rd., and make a right into the park. Open daily 10am-4pm.)

For wheels, go to **Century Cycles,** 1621 Main St., in Peninsula. (☎330-657-2209. Open M-Th 10am-8pm, F-Sa 10am-6pm, Su 10am-5pm. $6 per hr.) To see the park by rail, hop on the **Cuyahoga Valley Scenic Railroad,** which runs along the river's banks from Peninsula, Independence, and Akron. (☎330-657-2000 or 800-468-4070; www.cvsr.com. Open Feb.-Dec. $11-25, seniors $10-23, children $7-17. Call ahead for reservations.) In the summer, the **Cleveland Orchestra** performs outdoor evening concerts at the **Blossom Music Center,** 1145 W. Steels Corners Rd., in Cuyahoga Falls. (☎330-920-8040. Lawn seating $22-70.)

CEDAR POINT AMUSEMENT PARK

Consistently ranked the "best amusement park in the world" by *Amusement Today,* ▨**Cedar Point Amusement Park,** off U.S. 6, 65 mi. west of Cleveland in Sandusky, earns its superlatives. Many of the world's highest and fastest roller coasters reside here. The towering **Top Thrill Dragster** takes the cake in both categories, launching thrill-seekers 420 ft. before plummeting down at 120 mph, while the enormous **Millennium Force** (310 ft., 90 mph) gives it a run for its money. (☎419-627-2350 or 800-237-8386; www.cedarpoint.com. Laser light shows in summer nightly at 10pm. Open late June to Aug. daily 10am-11pm; Sept. to early Oct. hours vary. Parking $8. $44, children 3 and older or shorter than 4 ft. $25.)

PRO FOOTBALL HALL OF FAME

The **Pro Football Hall of Fame,** 2121 George Halas Dr. NW, in Canton, 60 mi. south of Cleveland, Exit 107A from I-77, honors the pigskin greats. Bronze busts of football greats line the Hall of Heroes, while interactive exhibits test fans' knowledge of the game. O.J. Simpson's jersey and helmet are displayed, but not his glove. (☎330-456-8207; www.profootballhof.com. Open daily June-Aug. 9am-8pm; Sept.-May 9am-5pm. $13, seniors $8, ages 6-14 $6; families $32. Wheelchair accessible.)

COLUMBUS ☎ 614

Rapid growth, huge suburban sprawl, and some gerrymandering have nudged Columbus's population beyond that of Cincinnati or Cleveland. Columbus has refused to let its size affect its character, and the city is still a showcase of America without glitz, fame, pretentiousness, or smog. Friendly neighborhoods, down-to-earth people, and impressive museums make Columbus a worthwhile stop.

■ 7 ORIENTATION AND PRACTICAL INFORMATION. Columbus is laid out in a simple grid. **High Street,** running north-south, and **Broad Street,** running east-west, are the main thoroughfares, dividing the city into quadrants. Most of the city's activity is centered around High St., which heads north from the office complexes of downtown to the lively galleries in the Short North. It ends in the collegiate cool of **Ohio State University (OSU),** America's largest university, with nearly 60,000 students. South of downtown, schnitzel is king at the historic **German Village.**

Port Columbus International Airport, 4000 International Gateway (☎239-4000; www.port-columbus.com), is 8 mi. east of downtown. Taxi to downtown is about $18. **Greyhound,** 111 E. Town St. (☎221-2389 or 800-231-2222), offers service from downtown to: Chicago (7-11hr., 6 per day, $52); Cincinnati (2-3½hr., 8 per day, $17); Cleveland (2-4½hr., 9-10 per day, $21). The **Central Ohio Transit Authority (COTA),** 60 E. Broad St., runs local transportation until 11pm or midnight, depending on the route. (☎228-1776. $1.25, express $1.75; transfers $0.10.) **Taxi: Yellow Cab** ☎444-4444. **Visitor Info: Experience Columbus** maintains an administrative office downtown at 90 N. High St., and a visitors center on the 1st floor of the Easton Town Mall. (☎221-6623 or 800-345-2657; www.experiencecolumbus.com. Visitors center open M-Sa 10am-9pm, Su noon-6pm; administrative office open M-F 8am-5pm.) **Internet Access: Columbus Metropolitan Library,** 96 S. Grant St. (☎645-2275. Open M-Th 9am-9pm, F-Sa 9am-6pm, Su 1-5pm.) **Post Office:** 850 Twin Rivers Dr. (☎469-4226. Open M-F 7am-8pm, Sa 8am-2pm.) **Postal Code:** 43215. **Area Code:** 614.

n C ACCOMMODATIONS AND FOOD. Those under 21 should be aware that a city ordinance prevents hotels from renting to underaged visitors. Budget options can be found at almost any exit off I-270. In the summer, **OSU ❷** offers cheap, clean dorm rooms with A/C, free local calls, private bathroom, microwave, and a fridge, within walking distance of High St.'s nightlife and restaurants. (☎292-9725. Open mid-June to mid-Aug. Singles and doubles $50.) Northwest of downtown, the **Westerville Inn Bed and Breakfast ❸,** 5 S. West St., maintains 3 homey rooms on a quiet suburban street, a 15 min. drive from downtown. Take I-270 to Exit 27. Take Cleveland Ave. north, turn right on Main St., and right on West St. (☎882-3910. All rooms with private baths. Full breakfast included. $55-95.) The remodeled **German Village Inn ❸,** 920 S. High St., close to downtown, offers clean, well-appointed rooms with cable TV, A/C, fridges, and free local calls. (☎443-6506. 21+. Singles Su-Th $48, F-Sa $54; doubles $54/$59; each additional person $6.)

For great budget eats, there's no beating the **North Market,** 59 Spruce St., in the Short North Arts District, which is packed with fresh produce and food vendors selling everything from falafel to gourmet chocolate. (☎463-9664. Meals around $5. Open Tu-F 9am-7pm, Sa 8am-5pm, Su noon-5pm, some vendors open M 9am-5pm; hours of individual vendors may vary.) **High Street** features a variety of tasty budget options. **Bernie's Bagels and Deli ❶,** 1896 N. High St., serves healthy sandwiches ($2-5) and all-day breakfast in a subterranean dive, with live music every night. (☎291-3448. Open daily 11am-2:30am. Music 10pm. Cover $2-4.) **Dragonfly ❹,** 247 King Ave., offers pricey, but absolutely fantastic, gourmet vegetarian dishes in an upscale setting not far from the OSU campus and High St.

GREAT LAKES

bars. (☎298-9981. Entrees $13-25. Open Tu-Th 5-10pm, F-Sa 11:30am-3pm and 5-11pm.) The **Elements Grille ❷**, 733 N. High St., in the Short North District, serves delightful breakfasts like cinnamon pecan pancakes ($5) and the martini breakfast ($6), a combination of fruit, yogurt, and granola brought to the table in a martini-glass-shaped dish. (☎294-1850. Open Tu-F 7am-10pm, Sa 8am-10pm, Su 8am-2pm.) **Mozart's ❶**, 2885 N. High St., is a neighborhood coffee shop that plays in a different key altogether—classical music wafts through the air, mingling with the smell of gourmet desserts. (☎268-3687. Pastries $1-3. Sandwiches $4.75-7. Live music F-Sa 7:30-10:30pm, Su 10:30am-1:30pm. Open Su-M 8am-5:50pm, Tu-Th 7am-10pm, F-Sa 7am-11pm.)

◗ SIGHTS. OSU rests 2 mi. north of downtown. **The Wexner Center for the Arts,** 1871 N. High St., by 15th Ave., was the first public building by controversial modernist architect Peter Eisenman. The museum galleries are under renovation and are scheduled to reopen in summer 2005, but until then much of its avant-garde collection is scattered throughout various venues around the city. Performance spaces host dance, music, and theater productions. (☎292-3535; www.wexarts.org. Exhibits open Tu-W 11am-6pm, Th-F 11am-9pm, Sa-Su noon-6pm. Galleries free. Films $6, students and seniors $4, under 12 $2. Call for info on satellite locations. Wheelchair accessible.) The **Columbus Museum of Art,** 480 E. Broad St., hosts a growing collection of contemporary American art and one of the most renowned collections of early Modern art in the country. Other highlights include a collection of local folk art and a great children's exhibit that allows kids to walk into a Dutch studio. (☎221-6801; www.columbusmuseum.org. Open Tu-W and F-Su 10am-5:30pm, Th 10am-8:30pm. $6; students, seniors, and ages 6-18 $4. Th free. Parking $3. Wheelchair accessible.) The submarine-shaped **Center of Science and Industry (COSI),** 333 W. Broad St., allows visitors to explore space from the safety of an armchair, create their own short stop-animation film, and bring it back to the old school with arcade games like Pong, Centipede, and Space Invaders. A seven-story Extreme Screen shows action-packed films. (☎228-2674; www.cosi.org. Open W-Sa 10am-5pm, Su noon-6pm. $12, seniors $10, ages 2-12 $7. Extreme Screen $6. Combo $17/$15/$12. Wheelchair accessible.) Nearby, James Thurber's childhood home, the **Thurber House,** 77 Jefferson Ave., off E. Broad St., guides visitors through the major events of the famous *New Yorker* writer's life. It also serves as a literary center, hosting seminars with authors like John Updike. (☎464-1032. Open daily noon-4pm. Free. Tours Su $2.50, students and seniors $2.)

For some good Germanica, march down to the **German Village,** south of Capitol Sq. This area, first settled in 1843, is now the largest privately funded historical restoration in the US, full of stately homes and beer halls. At **Schmidt's Sausage Haus ❸**, 240 E. Kossuth St., lederhosen-clad waitresses serve Bavarian specialties like huge sausage platters ($9.25-11) while traditional oompah bands (Schnickel-Fritz, Schnapps, and Squeezin' 'n' Wheezin') lead polkas. (☎444-6808. Polkas in summer W-Th 7-10pm, F-Sa 8-11pm; in winter no W show. Open Su-M 11am-9pm, Tu-Th 11am-10pm, F-Sa 11am-11pm.) One block west, **Schmidt's Fudge Haus,** 220 E. Kossuth St., makes savory fudge and chocolate concoctions. (☎638-1187. Open M and W-Th noon-7pm, Tu noon-4pm, F-Sa noon-9pm.) The **German Village Society Meeting Haus,** 588 S. 3rd St., provides info on happenings. (☎221-8888. Open M-F 9am-4pm, Sa 10am-2pm; shorter hours in winter.)

▣ ▧ ENTERTAINMENT AND NIGHTLIFE. Four free weekly papers available in shops and restaurants—*The Other Paper, Columbus Alive, The Guardian,* and *Moo*—list entertainment options. The **Ohio State Buckeyes** play football in the historic **Ohio Stadium.** Major League Soccer's **Columbus Crew** (☎447-2739; tickets $20-

GREAT LAKES

22) kicks off at **Crew Stadium.** Columbus's NHL hockey team, the **Blue Jackets** (☎246-3350; tickets $17-93), plays in **Nationwide Arena.** In early August, the **Ohio State Fair** rolls into town, as it has for more than 150 years, with livestock competitions, rides, and concerts. (☎888-646-3976; www.ohiostatefair.com. On 17th Ave., Exit 111 off I-71. $8, seniors and ages 5-12 $7. Ride wristbands $17. Parking $5.)

Columbus's nightlife scene is driven by rock 'n' roll. Bar bands are a Columbus mainstay, and it's hard to find a bar that doesn't have live music on the weekend. Bigger national acts stop at the **Newport,** 1722 N. High St. (☎294-1659; www.newportmusichall.com. Tickets $5-40.) To see smaller alternative and local bands before they hit the big time, head to **Little Brothers,** 1100 N. High St. (☎421-2025. 18+. Cover $5-20. Open daily 8pm-2am.) As Ohio State's iconic college bar, the **Varsity Club,** 278 W. Lane Ave., at the upper edge of North Campus near the intersection of High St., is where alums return and current students crowd on Columbus's many cold nights. (☎299-6269. Open daily 11am-2am, 9am for home football games.) South from Union Station is the **Brewery District,** where barley and hops have replaced coal and iron in the once-industrial area.

◾ DAYTRIP FROM COLUMBUS: HOPEWELL CULTURE PARK. One   hour south of Columbus, the area around Chillicothe (CHILL-i-caw-thy) features several American Indian cultural sites. The **Hopewell Culture National Historical Park,** 16062 Rte. 104, swells with 23 Hopewell burial mounds spread over 13 acres. A museum provides theories about the mounds and the 2000-year-old Hopewell culture. (☎740-774-1126; www.nps.gov/hocu. Museum open daily Sept.-May 8:30am-5pm; June-Aug. extended hrs. Grounds open dawn-dusk. $5 per car, $3 per pedestrian.) Learn about Hopewell life at the **Sugarloaf Mountain Amphitheater,** on the north end of Chillicothe off Rte. 23. Between mid-June and late August the theater presents *Tecumseh,* a reenactment of the life of the Shawnee leader. A tour explains how the stuntmen dive off a 21 ft. cliff. (☎740-775-0700 or 866-775-0700. Shows M-Sa 8pm. M-Th $16, under 10 $8; F-Sa $18/$9. Tour $3.50/$2.50.) After seeing the sights, travelers can enjoy **Scioto Trail State Park ❶,** 12 mi. south of Chillicothe off U.S. 23, with walk-in camping. (☎740-663-2125. Sites $14, with electricity $18.)

CINCINNATI   ☎513

Founded in 1788 as a frontier outpost on the Ohio River, Cincinnati quickly emerged as a vital gateway between the South and the West. Industry thrived as major trade routes passed through the city, and a profusion of meat-packing plants earned Cincinnati the nickname "Porkopolis,"—slightly less flattering than Longfellow's more regal title, "Queen City of the West." Cincinnati straddles its dualistic past: in many ways it is an archetypical Northern industrial city, but it has the feel of a Southern city. Nevertheless, its stellar ballet, brand-new baseball stadium, and world-famous chili make Cincinnati a highlight of the region.

▐ TRANSPORTATION

Airport: Greater Cincinnati International (☎859-767-3151; www.cvgairport.com), in Kentucky, 12 mi. south of Cincinnati and accessible by I-71, I-74, and I-75. **Jetport Express** shuttles to downtown. (☎859-767-3702. $12.) The **Transit Authority of Northern Kentucky,** or **TANK** (☎859-331-8265), also offers shuttle services.

Trains: Amtrak, 1301 Western Ave. (☎651-3337), in Union Terminal. Open Tu-Su 11pm-6:30am. To **Chicago** (12hr., 1 per day, $19-36) and **Indianapolis** (3hr., 1 per day, $17). *Avoid the area to the north of the train station, especially Liberty St.*

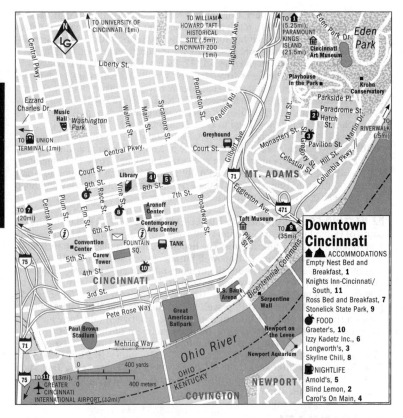

Downtown Cincinnati

▲▲ ACCOMMODATIONS
Empty Nest Bed and
  Breakfast, **1**
Knights Inn-Cincinnati/
  South, **11**
Ross Bed and Breakfast, **7**
Stonelick State Park, **9**
♦ FOOD
Graeter's, **10**
Izzy Kadetz Inc., **6**
Longworth's, **3**
Skyline Chili, **8**
◼ NIGHTLIFE
Arnold's, **5**
Blind Lemon, **2**
Carol's On Main, **4**

Buses: Greyhound, 1005 Gilbert Ave. (☎352-6012), past the intersection of E. Court and Broadway. Open 24hr. To: **Cleveland** (4-6hr., 14 per day, $36); **Columbus** (2-3hr., 14 per day, $17); **Louisville** (2hr., 8 per day, $20).

Public Transit: Cincinnati Metro and **TANK,** both in the bus stop in the Mercantile Center, 115 E. 5th St. (☎621-9450). Open M-F 8:30am-5pm. Most buses run out of Government Sq., at 5th and Main St., to outlying communities. $0.65; rush-hour $0.80; transfers $0.15; extra to suburbs. Office has schedules and info.

Taxi: Yellow Cab ☎241-2100.

⚑ 🛈 ORIENTATION AND PRACTICAL INFORMATION

The downtown business district is an easy grid centered around **Fountain Square,** at **5th** and **Vine Street.** Numbered cross streets are designated E. or W. by their relation to Vine St. **Downtown** is bounded by Central Pkwy. on the north, Broadway on the east, 3rd on the south, and Central Ave. on the west. The **University of Cincinnati** spreads out from the Clifton area north of the city. To the south, the **Great American Ballpark,** the **Serpentine Wall,** and the **Riverwalk** border the Ohio River. *Be careful outside of the downtown area at night, especially north of Central Pkwy.*

Visitor Info: Cincinnati Convention and Visitors Bureau, 300 W. 6th St. (☎621-2142 or 800-246-2987; www.cincyusa.com). Open M-F 8:30am-5:30pm. **Visitor Center at Fifth Third Center,** 511 Walnut St., on Fountain Sq., offers brochures on sights all over the area. Staff can also help find discounted tickets to shows and sights. Free Internet access. Open M-Sa 10am-5pm, Su noon-5pm.

Hotlines: Rape Crisis Center, 216 E. 9th St., downtown (☎872-9259). **Gay/Lesbian Community Switchboard,** ☎591-0222. Both 24hr.

Internet Access: Cincinnati Public Library, 800 Vine St. (☎369-6900). Open M-W 9am-9pm, Th-Sa 9am-6pm, Su 1-5pm.

Post Office: 525 Vine St., on the Skywalk. (☎684-5667. Open M-F 8am-5pm.) **Postal Code:** 45201. **Area Codes:** 513; Kentucky suburbs 859. In text, 513 unless otherwise noted.

⚑ ACCOMMODATIONS

Cheap hotels are scarce in downtown Cincinnati. About 30 mi. north of Cincinnati, in **Sharonville,** budget motels cluster along **Chester Road.** Twelve miles south of the city, inexpensive accommodations line I-75 in **Florence, KY.** Closer to downtown, the motels at **Central Parkway** and **Hopple Street** offer good, mid-priced lodging.

Knights Inn-Cincinnati/South, 8048 Dream St. (☎859-371-9711), in Florence, just off I-75 at Exit 180, has homey rooms, cable TV, A/C, and outdoor pool. 21+. Singles $35-40; doubles $40-45. ❷

Empty Nest Bed and Breakfast, 2707 Ida Ave. (☎631-9498), offers well-appointed rooms in a beautiful gingerbread-style home. Take Exit 6 from I-71, head north on Rte. 561, and turn right onto Ida Ave. Rooms from $75. ❹

Ross Bed and Breakfast, 88 Silverwood Circle (☎671-2645), just off I-275 at Princeton Pike, near the intersection of I-75, provides a suburban rest stop north of downtown. Private bath and full breakfast. Singles $49. ❸

Stonelick State Park (☎625-6593, reservations 866-644-6727), 35 mi. east of the city, outside the I-275 loop, has 115 campsites at the edge of a lake and provides relief from Cincinnati's pricey lodgings. Sites $16, with electricity $20; lakeside $22. ❶

◨ FOOD

Cincinnati's greatest culinary innovation is its chili, which consists of noodles topped with meat, cheese, onions, and kidney beans—and a distinctive secret ingredient. The city has also given rise to a number of noteworthy fast-food chains. Fine restaurants and bars can be found in **Mount Adams,** while moderately priced chains cluster at **Newport on the Levee** and **Covington Landing** across the river.

Skyline Chili, 643 Vine St. (☎241-2020; www.skylinechili.com), at 7th St., and locations all over Cincinnati, dishes up the best beans in town. The secret ingredient has been debated for years—some say chocolate, but curry is more likely. 5-way large chili from $3.69. Cheese "Coney dog" $1.35. Open M-F 10:30am-8pm, Sa 11am-4pm. ❶

Graeter's, 41 E. 4th St. (☎381-0653), between Walnut and Vine St. downtown, as well as 14 other locations. Since 1870, Graeter's has blended their specialty giant chocolate chips into dozens of different ice cream flavors. Sandwiches ($3-5) and baked goods also served. Single cone $1.95. Open M-F 7am-6pm, Sa 7am-3pm. ❶

Izzy Kadetz Inc., 800 Elm St. (☎721-4241), downtown. At lunchtime, locals flock to "Izzy's" for great reubens ($6.30) and corned beef sandwiches ($5.35), served with a big, fluffy potato pancake. Open M-F 8am-8pm, Sa 10am-5pm. ❷

Longworth's, 1108 St. Gregory St. (☎651-2253), in Mt. Adams. A mainstay of the laid-back Mt. Adams neighborhood, Longworth's packs a restaurant, bar, and nightclub into one building. The simple, hearty fare includes satisfying burgers (from $5.50), pizzas (from $8), and pastas ($8.75-12). Live bands jam on the first floor W-Su while DJs spin 80s pop on the upstairs dance floor F-Sa. Cover $5-10. Open M-Sa 11am-late, Su noon-2am. Kitchen closes M-Th 10pm, F-Sa 11pm, Su 9pm. ❷

🗺 SIGHTS

DOWNTOWN. Downtown Cincinnati orbits around the **Tyler Davidson Fountain,** at 5th and Vine St., a florid 19th-century masterpiece. To the east, the expansive garden at **Procter and Gamble Plaza** is just one mark that the giant company left on its hometown. Around **Fountain Square,** business complexes and shops are connected by a series of skywalks. The observation deck atop **Carew Tower,** Cincinnati's tallest building, provides the best view in the city. *(441 Vine St. ☎ 579-9735. Open M-Th 9am-5:30pm, F 9am-8pm, Sa-Su 10am-8pm. $2, children 5-11 $1.)* Close to Fountain Sq., the 🖼**Contemporary Arts Center** has a new, ultra-modern structure, and boasts six floors of avant-garde art. The fantastic "UnMuseum" on the sixth floor displays contemporary art for children, including a giant, robotic metal tree that responds to visitors. *(44 E. 6th St. ☎ 345-8420; www.contemporaryarts-center.org. Open M and Th 11am-9pm; Tu-W, F, and Su 11am-6pm; Sa noon-6pm. $6.50, seniors $5.50, students $4.50, children 3-13 $3.50. M 5-9pm free. Audio tour $3. Wheelchair accessible.)* At the eastern edge of downtown, the **Taft Museum of Art** has a modest, traditional collection of Western art in a renovated 19th-century mansion. *(316 Pike St. ☎ 241-0343; www.taftmuseum.org. Open Tu-W and F 11am-5pm, Th 11am-8pm, Sa 10am-5pm, Su noon-5pm. $7, seniors and students $5, under 18 free. Free W and F. Wheelchair accessible.)*

EDEN PARK. Eden Park provides a nearby respite from the city with rolling hills, a pond, and cultural centers. *(Northeast of downtown and Mt. Adams. Take bus #49 to Eden Park Dr. Open daily 6am-10pm.)* The collection at the elegant **Cincinnati Art Museum,** inside the park, spans 5000 years and includes Near Eastern artifacts, Chagall's Expressionist works, and Andy Warhol's rendition of infamous Cincinnati baseball great Pete Rose. The "Cincinnati Wing" explores the city's own artistic legacy. *(953 Eden Park Dr. ☎ 721-5204; www.cincinnatiartmuseum.org. Open Tu and Th-Su 11am-5pm, W 11am-9pm. Tours M-F 1pm; Sa 1, 2pm; Su 1, 2, 3pm. Free. Special exhibits extra. Wheelchair accessible.)* The nearby **Krohn Conservatory** is one of the largest public greenhouses in the world, boasting a lush rainforest and a butterfly garden. *(950 Eden Park Dr. ☎ 421-5707; www.cinci-parks.org. Open daily 10am-5pm. Donations accepted. Wheelchair accessible.)* For more outdoor fun, head to the **Cincinnati Zoo,** where standard inhabitants like elephants and gorillas are neighbors to rare manatees, as well as the zoo's newest resident: a baby rhinoceros. *(3400 Vine St. ☎ 475-6124; www.cincinnatizoo.org. Call for seasonal schedules. $12, seniors $9, children 2-12 $6. Parking $6.50.)*

MUSEUM CENTER. Built in 1933, the enormous Art Deco **Union Terminal** is now Cincinnati's cultural center, housing three major museums and an Omnimax theater. The **Cincinnati History Museum** begins with huge scale models of the city before leading visitors through exhibits charting Cincinnati's past, from its beginnings as a trading post to its emergence as the "Queen City" and beyond. A giant mastodon skeleton welcomes visitors into the **Museum of Natural History and Science,** where intrepid explorers can uncover the secrets of the Ice Age and descend into a cave's damp, dark depths to see bats, cave beetles, and other subterranean creatures. Kids are in control at the **Cinergy Children's Museum,** where they can clamber through caves and across bridges in a giant playspace or frolic in the waterworks, complete with splash zone. *(1301 Western Ave. ☎ 287-7000;*

www.cincymuseum.org. Open M-Sa 10am-5pm, Su 11am-6pm. Admission to 1 museum or Omnimax $6.75, ages 3-12 $4.75; 2 attractions $9.75/$6.75; 3 attractions $13/$8.75; 4 attractions $16/$11.)

OTHER SIGHTS. Just across the river from downtown in Kentucky, the spectacular **Newport Aquarium** offers full immersion in a water world with glass tunnels that blur the separation between visitors and toothy sharks. The baby American Alligators are about as cute as carnivorous reptiles get, while the stunning Jellyfish Gallery—featuring blue-lit aquariums in a chandeliered room with classical music—is living art. *(Located at Newport on the Levee. ☎ 859-261-7444; www.newportaquarium.com. Open in summer daily 9am-7pm; in winter hours vary. $18, seniors $16, children 3-12 $11.)* One mile north of downtown, the **William Howard Taft National Historic Site** is the birthplace and childhood home of the ex-President and Supreme Court Justice. A tour guides visitors through three fully restored rooms in the house. *(2038 Auburn Ave. ☎ 684-3262; www.nps.gov/wiho. Tours daily 8am-4pm. Free. Wheelchair accessible.)*

🎵 ENTERTAINMENT

The free newspapers *City Beat, Everybody's News*, and *Downtowner* list happenings around town. **Mount Adams** supports a thriving arts and entertainment district; perched on its own wooded hill in Eden Park, the **Playhouse in the Park,** 962 Mt. Adams Circle, performs theater in the round. (☎ 421-3888. Performances mid-Sept. to June Tu-Su. $34-48. Senior and student rush tickets 2hr. before show, $15.)

The **Music Hall,** 1241 Elm St. (☎ 721-8222), hosts the **Cincinnati Symphony Orchestra** and the **Cincinnati Pops Orchestra** from September through May. (☎ 381-3300. $17-91; call for additional information on discounted tickets.) The **Cincinnati Opera** also sings here. (☎ 241-2742. $25-90.) The symphony's summer season (June-July) tunes up at **Riverbend,** near Coney Island. The **Cincinnati Ballet Company** (☎ 621-5219) performs at the **Aronoff Center for the Arts,** 650 Walnut St., which also hosts a Broadway series. (☎ 241-7469. Ballet performances Nov.-Mar. $12-47, matinees $9-40; musicals $15-65. Broadway Oct.-May. $25-65. Wheelchair accessible.)

In Mason, off I-71 at Exit 24, **Paramount's King Island** cages **The Beast,** the world's longest wooden roller coaster. In spring 2005, the brand-new **Italian Job coaster** will simulate the film's car chase scenes. (☎ 573-5800 or 800-288-0808; www.pki.com. Open late May to late Aug. Su-F 10am-10pm, Sa 10am-11pm; call for low-season hours. $43, seniors and ages 3-6 $26. Parking $9.) Baseball's **Reds** (☎ 381-7337; $5-50) take the field at the **Great American Ball Park,** 100 Main St., and football's long-suffering **Bengals** (☎ 621-8383; $40-60) play at **Paul Brown Stadium** five blocks west.

📻 NIGHTLIFE

Overlooking downtown from the east, the winding streets of **Mount Adams** have spawned some offbeat bars and music venues, creating a relaxed environment removed from the bustling city below. On the Kentucky side of the river, a more commercialized, but still vibrant, nightlife scene has emerged in **Newport.**

Blind Lemon, 936 Hatch St. (☎ 241-3885), at St. Gregory St. Live blues and rock fill the cavernous tavern where Jimmy Buffet got started. During the colder months, bonfires light up the outdoor courtyard from Oct.-May. Th-Sa. Drafts $2. Live music daily 8:30pm. 21+. Open M-Tu 5:30pm-1am, W-F 5pm-2am, Sa-Su 3pm-2:30am.

Arnold's, 210 E. 8th St. (☎ 421-6234), between Main and Sycamore St. This wood-paneled mainstay provides good domestic beer ($2.50-3.75). After 9pm, Arnold's offers music in the courtyard. Pasta and sandwiches $6.75-11. Music F-Sa 9pm-midnight. Kitchen open M-Tu 11am-9pm, W-Sa 11am-10pm; bar open M-Sa until 1am.

Carol's On Main, 825 Main St. (☎651-2667). Drawing theater groups and 30-something yuppies, this trendy restaurant/bar is known for great food and late hours. **Crush,** a cabaret upstairs, thumps to hip-hop and indie rock on weekends. Entrees $6.50-15. 18+. Cover $5. Kitchen open M 11:30am-3pm, Tu-Th 11:30am-11pm, F 11am-1am, Sa-Su 5-11pm; bar closes Sa-Th 1am, F 2:30am. Crush open F-Sa 9pm-late.

INDIANA

The cornfields of southern Indiana's Appalachian foothills give way to expansive plains in the industrialized north, where Gary's smokestacks spew black clouds over the waters of Lake Michigan, and urban travel hubs string along the interstates. Despite its official motto—"The Crossroads of America"—Indiana is a modest, slow-paced state, where farms roll on and on, big cities are a rarity, and countless Hoosier school kids grow up dreaming of becoming the next Larry Bird.

◪ PRACTICAL INFORMATION

Capital: Indianapolis.

Visitor Info: Indiana Division of Tourism, 1 N. Capitol Ave., #700, Indianapolis 46204 (☎888-365-6946 or 317-232-8860; www.state.in.us/tourism). **Division of State Parks,** 402 W. Washington St., #W-298, Indianapolis 46204 (☎317-232-4125; www.in.gov/dnr/parklake).

State Bird: Larry. **Postal Abbreviation:** IN. **Sales Tax:** 5%.

Time Zone: Eastern Standard Time. However, with the exception of a few counties in the northwest and southwest corners, Indiana does not observe Daylight Savings Time.

INDIANAPOLIS   ☎317

Surrounded by flat farmland, Indianapolis feels like a model Midwestern city. Folks shop and work all day among downtown's skyscrapers before returning to sprawling suburbs. Life ambles here—until May, that is, when 400,000 spectators overrun the city and the road warriors of the Indianapolis 500 claim the spotlight.

█◪ DRIVER'S MANUAL. The city is laid out in concentric circles, with a dense central cluster of skyscrapers and low-lying outskirts. The very center of Indianapolis is just south of **Monument Circle,** at the intersection of **Washington Street (U.S. 40)** and **Meridian Street.** Washington St. divides the city north-south; Meridian St. divides it east-west. **I-465** circles the city and provides access to downtown. **I-70** cuts through the city east-west. Meter parking is abundant along the edge of the downtown area and near the Circle Centre Mall.

Indianapolis International Airport (☎487-7243; www.indianapolisairport.com) is located 7 mi. southwest of downtown off I-465, Exit 11B; take bus #8 "West Washington." Taxi to downtown costs around $17. **Amtrak,** 350 S. Illinois St. (☎263-0550; open daily 7am-2:30pm and 11pm-6:30am), behind Union Station, runs to Chicago (5hr., 1 per day, $16-31). **Greyhound,** 350 S. Illinois St. (☎267-3071; open 24hr.), buses to: Bloomington (1hr., 2 per day, $15); Chicago (3-4hr., 12 per day, $29); Cincinnati (2-5hr., 6 per day, $20). **Indygo,** 209 N. Delaware St., runs routes throughout the city, as well as shuttles to special events. (☎635-3344; www.indygo.net. Office open M-F 8am-6pm, Sa 9am-noon. $1.25, under 6 free.) **Taxi: Yellow Cab** ☎487-7777. **Visitor Info: Indianapolis City Center (Visit Indy),** on the first floor of Circle Centre Mall, dispenses info and maps. (☎ 639-4282 or 800-323-4639; www.indy.org.) **Hotline: Rape Crisis Line,** ☎ 800-221-6311; 24hr. **Post Office:** 125 W. South St., across from Amtrak. (☎ 464-6874. Open M-F 7am-5:30pm.) **Postal Code:** 46204. **Area Code:** 317.

ⓕ PIT STOP. Budget motels line the I-465 beltway, 5 mi. from downtown. Make reservations a year in advance for the Indy 500, which drives rates up drastically in May. Though hard to come by, the rooms at the **Methodist Tower Inn ❸,** 1633 N. Capitol Ave., are the cheapest ones close to downtown. The inn provides large rooms with TV and A/C, but the helicopters that land at the hospital across the street may interrupt restful slumber. (☎ 925-9831. Singles $63; doubles $68.) Head to **Motel 6 ❷,** 6330 Debonair Ln., at Exit 16A off I-465, for clean, pleasant rooms with A/C and cable TV. (☎ 293-3220. Singles $35; doubles $40. Each additional person $5.) The **Renaissance Tower Historic Inn ❹,** 230 E. 9th St., offers reasonable overnight rates for rooms with cable TV, A/C, kitchenette, and stately canopy beds. (☎ 261-2652 or 800-676-7786. Rooms $75 per night, $431 per week; call for availability.) The **Indiana State Fairgrounds Campgrounds ❶,** 1202 E. 38th St., bus #4 or 39 from downtown, have 170 sod-and-gravel sites packed by RVs. (☎ 927-7520. Sites with hookup $19.)

ⓗ HIGH-OCTANE FUEL. Ethnic food stands, produce markets, and knick-knack vendors fill the spacious **City Market,** 222 E. Market St., a renovated 19th-century building. Meals start around $5. (☎ 630-4107. Open M-F 6am-6pm, Sa 8am-2pm.) Moderately priced restaurants cluster in Indianapolis's newly constructed **Circle Centre,** 49 W. Maryland St. (☎ 681-8000). Massachusetts Ave. houses some of the liveliest restaurants and bars in the city; in the summer, crowded outdoor patios seat diners every night. **Bazbeaux Pizza ❷,** 334 Massachusetts Ave. (☎ 636-7662) and 832 E. Westfields Blvd. (☎ 255-5711), serves Indianapolis's favorite pizza. The Tchoupitoulas pizza, topped with a concoction of shrimp, is a Cajun masterpiece (from $12). Construct your own pie (from $6.50) from a choice of 53 toppings. (Both locations open Su-Th 11am-10pm, F-Sa 11am-11pm.) **The Abbey ❷,** 771 Massachusetts Ave. (☎ 269-8426), is a popular coffee shop with wireless Internet, offering wraps, sandwiches ($6-7), and vegetarian options. Sip cappuccinos in velvet chairs for $2.50. (Open M-Th 7am-midnight, F 7am-1am, Sa 8am-1am, Su 8am-midnight.) For the best Mexican food in town, head to **Don Victor's ❷,** 1032 S. East St., which offers heaping platters of authentic cuisine (entrees $7.75-13). The Fiesta Platter ($21; serves 2) is a good way to sample various dishes. (☎ 637-4397. Live Mariachi F and Su. Open M and W 11am-10pm, Th-Su 11am-11pm.)

ⓖ SUNDAY DRIVE. The newly restored canal at **White River State Park,** near downtown, entices locals to stroll, bike, or nap on the banks. Bikes can be rented at **Wheel Fun,** 801 W. Washington St., next to the State Museum (☎ 435-1675; www.wheelfunrental.com. Open June-Aug. daily 10am-10pm; Sept.-Oct. Sa-Su 10am-10pm; May Sa-Su 10am-8pm. $7 per hr., $20 full-day.) Near the park entrance, the **Eiteljorg Museum of American Indians and Western Art,** 500 W. Washington St., is in the midst of a major expansion and is scheduled to reopen in June 2005. The museum features an impressive collection of art depicting the Old West, as well as a collection of Native American artifacts from across the United States. (☎ 636-9378; www.eiteljorg.org. Open Tu-Sa 10am-5pm, Su noon-5pm; May-Sept. also M 10am-5pm. Tours daily 1pm. $7, seniors $6, students and ages 5-17 $4. Wheelchair accessible.) Next door, the **Indiana State Museum,** 650 W. Washington St., allows visitors to follow the "Hoosier Heritage Trail" through in-depth exhibits on Indiana history, starting off with the beginning of the earth itself and wrapping up with profiles of Indiana's most famous citizens, from Larry Bird to Axl Rose. (☎ 232-1637; www.indianamuseum.org. Open M-Sa 9am-5pm, Su 11am-5pm. $7, seniors $6.50, children $4. IMAX $8.75/$7.50/$6. Combo $13/$11/$8. Wheelchair accessible.)

No sports fan should miss the **NCAA Hall of Champions,** 700 W. Washington St., which pays homage to the best in American college sports. Relive the passion of the Final Four in the March Madness Theater and try your hand at hitting a clutch shot in the 1930s-style gymnasium, marked out with famous game-winners. (☎916-4255; www.ncaahallofchampions.org. Open M-Sa 10am-5pm, Su noon-5pm. $7, seniors $6, students $4, under 6 free. Wheelchair accessible.) Though far from downtown, the **Indianapolis Museum of Art,** 1200 W. 38th St., is worth a visit for its beautiful 52 acres with nature trails, a historic home, botanical gardens, a greenhouse, and a theater. The museum's collection includes extensive collections of American, African, and Neo-Impressionist works. The museum will close from January to April 2005 for renovations, but the grounds will remain open. Some exhibits will remain closed as late as 2006. (☎923-1331; www.ima-art.org. Open Tu-W and F-Sa 10am-5pm, Th 10am-8:30pm, Su noon-5pm. Free; special exhibits $5. Wheelchair accessible.) A majestic stained-glass dome graces the marbled interior of the **State House,** 200 W. Washington St., between Capitol and Senate St. (☎233-5293. Open M-F 8am-4pm. 2-5 1hr. guided tours per day. Free.) Animal lovers should check out the seemingly cageless **Indianapolis Zoo,** 1200 W. Washington St., which holds large whale and dolphin pavilions. Adjacent to the zoo, frolic with fluttering butterflies and exotic flora at **White River Gardens.** (☎630-2001; www.indyzoo.com. Open June-Aug. M-Th 9am-5pm, F-Su 9am-6pm; Sept.-May M-Th 9am-4pm, F-Su 9am-5pm. Zoo $11, seniors and ages 2-12 $7; gardens $7/$6; combo $13/$8.50. Parking $3.) Kids will get a kick out of the fun-filled **Indianapolis Children's Museum,** 3000 N. Meridian St., the largest children's museum in the world. Explore an Egyptian tomb, ride a carousel, or explore the museum's newest exhibit, Dinosphere, where you can find the world's largest display of juvenile dino fossils. (☎334-3322; www.childrensmuseum.org. Open Mar.-Aug. daily 10am-5pm; Sept.-Feb. Tu-Su 10am-5pm. $12, seniors $11, children $6.50.)

■ **DAYS OF THUNDER.** The country's passion for fast cars reaches fever pitch during the **500 Festival** (☎927-3378; www.500festival.com), an entire month of parades and hoopla leading up to race day at the **Indianapolis Motor Speedway,** 4790 W. 16th St., off I-465 at the Speedway exit. (Bus #25.) The festivities begin with time trials in mid-May and culminate with the "Gentlemen, start your engines" of the **Indianapolis 500** the Sunday before Memorial Day. In quieter times for the track, buses full of tourists drive around the 2½ mi. track at slightly tamer speeds. (☎481-8500; www.indy500.com. Track tours daily 9am-4:40pm. $3, ages 6-15 $1.) The **Speedway Museum,** at the south end of the infield, houses **Indy's Hall of Fame** and a large collection of cars that have tested their mettle on the storied track over the years. (☎492-6784. Open daily 9am-5pm. $3, ages 6-15 $1.) Tickets for the race go on sale the day after the previous year's race and usually sell out within a week.

■ **IN THE FAST LANE.** The **Walker Theatre,** 617 Indiana Ave., a 15min. walk northwest of downtown, used to house the headquarters of African-American entrepreneur Madame C.J. Walker's beauty enterprise. Today the national historic landmark hosts arts programs, including the biweekly **Jazz on the Avenue.** (☎236-2099. Tours M-F 9am-3:30pm. Jazz every other F 6-10pm. $10.) The **Indianapolis Symphony Orchestra** performs from late June to August in the **Hilbert Circle Theater** on Monument Circle. (☎639-4300; www.indyorch.org. Box office open M-F 9am-5pm, Sa 10am-2pm.) The city's theater scene centers on the **Indiana Repertory Theatre,** 140 W. Washington St. (☎635-5252. Box office open M-F noon-6pm, or until 30min. before showtime on performance days.) Sports fans can be thankful for more than just the speedway. Basketball fans watch the **Pacers** (☎917-2500) take the court from November to April at the **Conseco Fieldhouse**, 125 S. Pennsylvania St. (Tickets $10-96.) The WNBA's **Indiana Fever** (☎239-5151) take over in the summer. (Tickets $10-75.) The NFL's **Colts** (☎239-5151) toss the pigskin at the **RCA Dome**, 100 S. Capital Ave. (Tickets $15-65.)

Somewhat bland by day, the **Broad Ripple** area, 6 mi. north of downtown at College Ave. and 62nd St., transforms into a center for nightlife after dark. Downtown, the **Slippery Noodle**, 372 S. Meridian St., is the oldest bar in Indiana, as well as one of the country's best venues for live blues every night. (☎631-6974. 21+. Cover Th-Sa $5. Open M-Sa 11am-3am, Su 4pm-12:30am.) The **Jazz Cooker**, 925 E. Westfield Blvd., heats up Broad Ripple with hot jazz. Attached to the Jazz Cooker, **Monkey's Tale** is a relaxed bar with a great jukebox. (☎253-2883. Music W-Sa 7-10pm. 21+ after 9pm. Bar open M-Sa until 3am, Su until midnight.) **Vogue**, 6259 N. College Ave., is the hottest club in town and hosts national acts. (☎255-2828. Shows 8pm; call for schedule. 21+. Cover $1-5; ladies free F till 11:30pm. Open W 9pm-3am, F-Sa 10pm-3am.) For local and alternative acts, head to the nearby **Patio**, 6308 N. Guildford, which offers live music every night on a small stage. (☎253-0799. 21+. Cover around $5. Open M-W 8pm-late, Th-Sa 9pm-late.) **Metro**, 707 Massachusetts Ave., is a lively gay bar that features pool, darts, and daily drink specials, and draws a diverse crowd. (☎639-6022. Karaoke Tu and Th 10pm. No cover. Open M-Sa 4pm-3am, Su noon-12:30am.)

BLOOMINGTON ☎812

The region's rolling hills create an exquisite backdrop for Bloomington's most prominent institution, Indiana University (IU). The college town atmosphere, nightlife hot spots, die-hard fans of Hoosier basketball, and a strong Tibetan influence help Bloomington compete with its northern neighbor, Indianapolis.

Designed by I.M. Pei, IU's architecturally striking **Art Museum**, E. 7th St., on campus, maintains an excellent collection of Oriental and African artwork, along with impressive collections of Greek pottery and German Expressionist art. (☎855-5445; www.indiana.edu/~iuam. Open Tu-Sa 10am-5pm, Su noon-5pm.) Nearby, the **Mathers Museum of World Cultures**, 416 N. Indiana St., near E. 8th St., has a vast collection of artifacts from around the world that serves as the foundation for changing exhibits on the technologies and dress of various cultures. (☎855-6873; www.indiana.edu/~mathers. Open Tu-F 9am-4:30pm, Sa-Su 1-4:30pm. Tours every 30min. F-Sa noon-4:30pm, Su 1-4:30pm. Free.) The **Tibetan Cultural Center**, 3655 Snoddy Rd., offers meditation. (☎334-7046; www.tibetancc.com. Grounds open daily 10am-5pm. Center open Su noon-3pm.)

Though rooms are often in short supply, the recently renovated **College Motor Inn** ❸, 509 N. College Ave., has an elegant exterior and pleasant rooms with cable TV and free local calls. (☎336-6881. Reservations recommended. Singles Su-Th $56, F-Sa $61; doubles $61/$67. Prices rise for special events.) Usually rooms at the **Scholar's Bed & Breakfast** ❹, 801 N. College Ave., go for over $100, but on weekdays, the comfortable rooms with TV/VCR, A/C, and private baths drop in price. (☎332-1892. Gourmet breakfast included. Check-in 4-6pm. Call for room availability. Rooms from $79.) **Paynetown "Peyton" State Recreation Area** ❶, 10 mi. southeast of downtown on Rte. 446, has open campsites on Lake Monroe with access to trails, a beach, boat rentals, and a wheelchair-accessible fishing dock. (☎837-9546. Primitive sites Su-W $13, Th-Sa $16; with electricity $19/$23. Vehicle registration $5, IN residents $3. For boats, call ☎837-9909. Kayaks and canoes $9 per hr., $25 per 8hr. with $25 deposit; fishing boats $60-70 per 8hr. with $50 deposit.) **☒Snow Lion** ❷, 113 S. Grant St., owned by the Dalai Lama's nephew, is one of only a few Tibetan restaurants in the country. Spicy dishes and authentic decor transport diners. An extensive Pan-Asian menu is also available. (☎336-0835. Entrees $7-13.

Tibetan Butter Tea $1.50. Open M-Sa 11am-3pm and 5-10pm, Su 5-10pm.) **The Laughing Planet Cafe ❶**, 322 E. Kirkwood Ave., in the Kenwood Manor Building, serves bean-heavy burritos ($3.60-6) and other organic delights made from local produce in a cafe setting. (☎323-2233. Open daily 11am-9pm.) **Nick's**, 423 E. Kirkwood Ave., looks like a quaint English pub, but is full of IU students guzzling beer and watching sports. (☎332-4040. Beer from $2.25. 21+ after 8pm. 18+ must have ID and be with parent or guardian. Open M-Sa 11am-2am, Su noon-midnight. Open Th-Sa until 3am during school year.)

Bloomington lies south of Indianapolis on Rte. 37. **North Walnut** and **College Street** are the main north-south thoroughfares. The town centers on **Courthouse Square**, which is surrounded by restaurants, bookshops, and bars. **Greyhound,** 219 W. 6th St. in the Yellow Cab office (☎332-1522; station open daily 9am-3pm and 5-6pm), connects Bloomington to Chicago (5hr., 2 per day, $50) and Indianapolis (1hr., 2 per day, $15). **Bloomington Transit** sends buses on eight routes through both the town and the IU campus. Service is infrequent; call ahead. (☎336-7433. $0.75, seniors and ages 5-17 $0.35.) The campus also has a shuttle ($0.75). The **visitors center,** 2855 N. Walnut St., offers free local calls and a helpful staff. (☎334-8900 or 800-800-0037. Open Apr.-Oct. M-F 8:30am-5pm, Sa 9am-4pm; Nov.-Mar. M-F 8:30am-5pm, Sa 10am-3pm. Brochure area open 24hr.)

MICHIGAN

Pressing up against four of the Great Lakes, two peninsulas present visitors with two distinct Michigans. The sparsely populated Upper Peninsula hangs over Lake Michigan, housing moose, wolves, and the stunning waterfalls of the Hiawatha National Forest. Campers and hikers have recently begun discovering the U.P., and the resplendent forests now entertain backpackers and families alike. In the Lower Peninsula, beach bums hang out in the many quaint communities along the western coast of the state, sunning and boating along some of Michigan's 3000 miles of coastline. Those craving an urban environment head to Ann Arbor, the intellectual center of the state, or to industrial Detroit for world-class museums.

🚩 PRACTICAL INFORMATION

Capital: Lansing.

Visitor Info: Michigan Travel Bureau, 333 S. Capitol St., Ste. F, Lansing 48909 (☎888-784-7328; www.michigan.org). **Department of Parks and Recreation,** Information Services Ctr., P.O. Box 30257, Lansing 48909 (☎517-373-9900). State parks require a motor vehicle permit; $4 per day, $20 per year. Call ☎800-447-2757 for reservations.

Postal Abbreviation: MI. **Sales Tax:** 6%.

DETROIT   ☎313

Long the ugly step-sister of America's big cities, Detroit has nowhere to go but up. Violent race riots in the 1960s caused a massive flight to the suburbs, turning much of the city into a post-industrial urban wasteland. The unmistakable sound of Motown kept Detroit funky through the 60s, but the decline of the auto industry in the late 1970s added unemployment to the city's ills. Despite the poverty and violence that plague Detroit, the tourism industry focuses on the city's jewels. Top-notch museums cluster in the cultural center of the city,

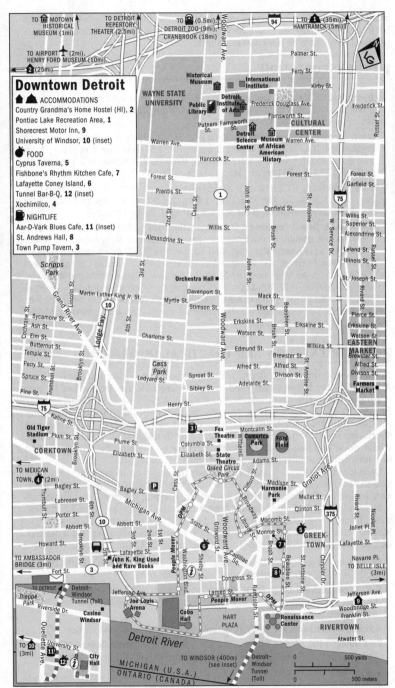

GREAT LAKES

Downtown Detroit

▲▲ ACCOMMODATIONS
Country Grandma's Home Hostel (HI), 2
Pontiac Lake Recreation Area, 1
Shorecrest Motor Inn, 9
University of Windsor, 10 (inset)

🍖 FOOD
Cyprus Taverna, 5
Fishbone's Rhythm Kitchen Cafe, 7
Lafayette Coney Island, 6
Tunnel Bar-B-Q, 12 (inset)
Xochimilco, 4

🍷 NIGHTLIFE
Aar-D-Vark Blues Cafe, 11 (inset)
St. Andrews Hall, 8
Town Pump Tavern, 3

while professional sports and a music scene inherited from Motown entertain both locals and travelers. Across the river, Windsor, Ontario exudes a cosmopolitan flavor from its bars and restaurants.

⌐ TRANSPORTATION

Airport: Detroit Metropolitan (☎ 734-247-7678; www.metroairport.com), 2 mi. west of downtown, off I-94 at Merriman Rd. in Romulus. **Metro Cabs** (☎ 800-745-5191) offers taxi service to downtown for $32.

Trains: Amtrak, 11 W. Baltimore St. (☎ 873-3442). Open daily 6:45am-3pm and 3:45pm-midnight. To **Chicago** (6hr., 3 per day, $23-57) and **New York** (16hr., 1 per day, $64-125). For Canadian destinations, **VIA Rail,** 298 Walker Rd., Windsor, ON (☎ 888-842-7245). To **Toronto** (4hr.; 4 per day; CDN$85, 35% off with ISIC).

Buses: Greyhound, 1001 Howard St. (☎ 961-8011). Station open 24hr.; ticket office open daily 5am-11:30pm. To: **Ann Arbor** (1½hr., 4 per day, $7.50); **Chicago** (5½-7½hr., 7 per day, $30); **Cleveland** (4-6hr., 8 per day, $24). *At night, the area is unsafe.*

Public Transit: Detroit Department of Transportation (DOT), 1301 E. Warren St. (☎ 933-1300). Serves downtown, with limited service to the suburbs. Many buses stop service at midnight. $1.50, some short routes $0.50; transfers $0.25. An ultramodern elevated tramway, **People Mover,** 150 Michigan Ave. (☎ 962-7245), circles the Central Business District on a 2¾ mi. loop; worth a ride just for the view of the riverfront and downtown architecture. Runs M-Th 7am-11pm, F 7am-midnight, Sa 9am-midnight, Su noon-8pm. $0.50. **Southeastern Michigan Area Regional Transit (SMART),** 600 Woodward Ave. (☎ 962-5515), runs bus service to the suburbs 4am-midnight. $1.50, transfers $0.25.

Taxi: Checker Cab ☎ 963-5000.

■*■ ORIENTATION AND PRACTICAL INFORMATION

Detroit lies on the Detroit River, which connects Lake Erie and Lake St. Clair. Across the river to the south, the town of **Windsor, ON,** can be reached by tunnel just west of the Renaissance Center (toll $2.50), or by the Ambassador Bridge (free). Detroit can be a dangerous town, but it is typically safe during the day. The **People Mover** surrounds the downtown area where businesses and sports venues cluster. Driving is the best way to negotiate this sprawling city, where good and bad neighborhoods alternate on a whim. Parking is easy to find and driving avoids less safe public transit options.

Detroit's streets form a grid. **The Mile Roads** run east-west as major arteries. **Eight Mile Road** is the city's northern boundary and the beginning of the suburbs. **Woodward Avenue** heads northwest from downtown, dividing the city and suburbs into "east side" and "west side." **Gratiot Avenue** flares out northeast from downtown, while **Grand River Avenue** shoots west. **I-94** and **I-75** pass through downtown. Streets tend to end suddenly and reappear several blocks later; for a particularly helpful map, check *Visit Detroit,* available at the Visitors Bureau.

Visitor Info: Convention and Visitors Bureau, 211 W. Fort St., 10th fl. (☎ 202-1800 or 800-338-7648; www.visitdetroit.com). Open M-F 9am-5pm.

GLBT Organizations: Triangle Foundation of Detroit, ☎ 537-3323. **Affirmations,** 195 W. 9 Mile Rd. (☎ 248-398-7105; www.goaffirmations.com), in Ferndale, has a large library and nightlife info.

Hotlines: Crisis Hotline, ☎ 224-7000. **Sexual Abuse Helpline,** ☎ 876-4180. Both 24hr.

Post Office: 1401 W. Fort St. (☎ 226-8304.) Open 24hr. **Postal Code:** 48233. **Area Codes:** 313 (Detroit); 810, 248, and 734 (suburbs). In text, 313 unless noted.

ACCOMMODATIONS

Detroit's suburbs harbor loads of chain motels. Those near the airport in **Romulus** tend to be pricey, and others along **East Jefferson Avenue**, near downtown, can be of questionable quality. For a mix of convenience and affordability, look along **Telegraph Road** off I-94, west of the city. If the exchange rate is favorable, good deals can be found across the border in **Windsor**. *Visit Detroit* lists accommodations by area and includes price ranges.

Country Grandma's Home Hostel (HI), 22330 Bell Rd. (☎734-753-4901), in New Boston, 6 mi. south of I-94 off I-275. Take Exit 11B, turn right, and then make an immediate right onto Bell Rd. Though inaccessible by public transit, Grandma's is worth the trip for the hospitality and respite from urban Detroit. 6 beds, kitchen, free parking. Bring your own linen. Reservations required; call ahead. Open Apr.-Sept. Dorms $15, non-members $18. Cash only. Wheelchair accessible. ❶

Shorecrest Motor Inn, 1316 E. Jefferson Ave. (☎568-3000 or 800-992-9616), is ideally located 3 blocks east of the Renaissance Center. Rooms include A/C, fridges, and data ports. Key deposit $20 when paying cash. Free parking. Reservations recommended. 21+. Clean, comfortable singles $69; doubles $89. Wheelchair accessible. ❸

University of Windsor, 401 Sunset Ave. (☎519-973-7074), in Windsor, rents pleasant dorm rooms with refrigerators, A/C, and shared bathrooms early May to late Aug. Free Internet access and use of university facilities. Parking CDN$5-8. Singles CDN$69; doubles CDN$79. Wheelchair accessible. ❸

Pontiac Lake Recreation Area, 7800 Gale Rd. (☎248-666-1020), in Waterford, 45min. northwest of downtown; take I-75 to Rte. 59 W, turn right on Williams Lake northbound, and left onto Gale Rd. Huge wooded sites in rolling hills, just 4 mi. from the lake. Vehicle permit $6 per day for Michigan residents, $8 non-residents; $24/$29 per year. 176 sites with electricity $14. ❶

FOOD

Although many restaurants have migrated to the suburbs, there are still some budget dining options in town. The downtown area doesn't offer much after 5pm, but ethnic neighborhoods provide interesting choices. At the **Greektown** People Mover stop, Greek restaurants and excellent bakeries line one block of Monroe St., near Beaubien St. To snag a *pierogi*, cruise Joseph Campau Ave. in **Hamtramck** (Ham-TRAM-eck), a Polish neighborhood northeast of Detroit. **Mexican Town,** just west of downtown, is packed with Mexican restaurants, markets, and nightspots. No traveler should miss the **Eastern Market,** at Gratiot Ave. and Russell St., an 11-acre produce-and-goodies festival. (☎533-393-8800. Open Sa 7am-5pm.)

Cyprus Taverna, 579 Monroe St. (☎961-1550), serves *moussaka* ($9) and other Greek specialties in the heart of Greektown. If you're tired of the flaming cheese routine, try *haloumi*, a fried Cypriot cheese delivered warm to the table ($6). Lunch specials from $5.25. Dinner entrees $8-12. Open Su-Th 11am-2am, F-Sa 11am-4am. ❸

Lafayette Coney Island, 118 W. Lafayette St. (☎964-8198). Detroit's most famous culinary establishment, Lafayette doles out its Coney dogs ($2.25) and chili cheese fries ($3) to loyal customers. Brusque service is worth it for a perfect dog. Open M-Th 7:30am-4am, F-Sa 7:30am-5am, Su 9:30am-4am. ❶

Xochimilco, 3409 Bagley St. (☎843-0179), draws the biggest crowds in Mexican Town with cheap, delicious enchiladas and burrito platters ($5-8.75). Muraled walls, great service, and warm chips with your salsa are just a few of the details that separate Xochimilco (so-she-MO-ko) from its competition. Open daily 11am-2am. ❷

Fishbone's Rhythm Kitchen Cafe, 400 Monroe St. (☎965-9600), in Greektown, brings Mardi Gras to the Motor City, with zydeco music, an oyster bar, and Cajun specialties like deep-fried alligator ($10), jambalaya ($15), and seafood gumbo ($4). 21+ after 10pm. Open daily 10am-midnight, Su brunch 10am-2pm. Bar open F-Sa until 2am. ❸

◉ SIGHTS

Sections of Detroit and the surrounding area allow visitors a chance to explore everything from books to wildlife while enjoying the city's public parks. For wandering book lovers, **John K. King Used and Rare Books,** 901 W. Lafayette St., is a four-floor maze of over a half million books on every topic imaginable. Friendly and knowledgeable staff help guide new customers through the impressive warehouse. (☎961-0622. Open M-Sa 9:30am-5:30pm. Wheelchair accessible.)

DETROIT ZOO. You'll find exotic animals like tigers and red pandas roaming the suburban grounds of the **Detroit Zoological Park.** The park features the National Amphibian Conservation Center, where visitors can get up close and personal with live critters, while the Arctic Ring of Life exhibit features polar bears and a trek through the Tundra. (8450 W. Ten Mile Rd., just off the Woodward exit of Rte. 696 in Royal Oak. ☎248-398-0900; www.detroitzoo.org. Open July-Aug. M-Tu and Th-Su 10am-5pm, W 10am-8pm; May-June and Sept.-Oct. daily 10am-5pm; Nov.-Mar. W-Su 10am-4pm. $11, seniors $8.50, and ages 2-12 $6.50. Parking $5.)

ONE HELL OF A PREP SCHOOL. In posh Bloomfield Hills, 15 mi. north of Detroit, **Cranbrook's** scholarly campus holds public gardens, several museums, and an art academy. Far and away the best of the lot is the **Cranbrook Institute of Science,** 39221 N. Woodward Ave., with a planetarium and rotating exhibits emphasizing educational fun. The new Bat Zone houses bats, owls, and other nocturnal creatures. (☎248-645-3209 or 877-462-7262; www.cranbrook.edu. Open M-Th and Sa-Su 10am-5pm, F 10am-10pm. $7, seniors and ages 2-12 $5. Planetarium shows $3, under 2 $1. Bat Zone $3/$1; free with general admission. Wheelchair accessible.)

BELLE ISLE. The best escape from Detroit's urban wasteland is the 1000-acre **Belle Isle,** where a conservatory, nature center, aquarium, and maritime museum allow animal lovers to drift from sight to sight. (3 mi. from downtown via the MacArthur Bridge at the foot of E. Grand Blvd. ☎852-4075. Isle accessible daily 6am-10pm; attractions 10am-5pm. $4 per sight, seniors and ages 2-12 $3.)

🏛 MUSEUMS

Motown Historical Museum, 2648 W. Grand Blvd. (☎875-2264; www.motownmuseum.org). "Dexter Avenue" bus. Housed in the apartment where entrepreneur and producer Berry Gordy founded Hitsville, USA, and created the unmistakable Motown sound. Upstairs, an impressive collection of memorabilia includes the piano used by the legendary Motown artists and the hat and gloves donned by Michael Jackson in "Thriller." Downstairs, Studio A—where the Jackson 5, Marvin Gaye, and Smokey Robinson recorded—has been meticulously preserved, right down to the holes worn in the floor by toe-tapping recording engineers. Open Tu-Sa 10am-6pm. $8, under 13 $5. Wheelchair accessible.

Detroit Institute of Arts, 5200 Woodward Ave. (☎833-7900; www.dia.org). The majority of the museum's extensive collection of American art is on tour while renovations continue for the new American Wing, set to open in 2006. However, there is an extensive collection of traditional Dutch and Flemish art in an elaborate setting, as well as a modern collection boasting works by Picasso, Van Gogh, and Matisse. Highlights include Diego Rivera's monumental mural "Detroit Industry," which fills an entire room and pays homage to the city and its industrial past. Open W-Th 10am-4pm, F 10am-9pm, Sa-Su 10am-5pm; first F of each month 11am-9pm. Suggested donation $4, students and children $1. Wheelchair accessible.

Henry Ford Museum, 20900 Oakwood Blvd. (☎271-1620; www.hfmgv.org), off I-94 in Dearborn. Take SMART bus #200 or 250. Housing full-scale planes, trains, and automobiles, the museum's enormous exhibit hall explores "100 Years of the Automobile in American Life," detailing the major cultural changes that cars have brought about in American history. The premises hold the convertible in which President Kennedy was assassinated, the bus in which Rosa Parks sat up front, and the chair in which Lincoln was shot. Next door, experience a microcosm of America at **Greenfield Village,** where over 80 historic edifices salute American ingenuity. Museum and village open daily 9:30am-5pm; June-Aug. village open F-Sa until 9pm. Museum $14, seniors $13, ages 5-12 $10. Village $20/$19/$14. Combination pass $26/$24/$20. IMAX $10/$9/$8.50. Museum wheelchair accessible; limited accessibility in village.

Museum of African American History, 315 E. Warren Ave. (☎494-5800; www.maah-detroit.org), features a poignant core exhibit that begins with the slave trade and then moves through African-American history, ending in a bittersweet display of modern African-American culture. Open Tu 9:30am-8pm, W-Sa 9:30am-5pm, Su 1-5pm. $8, seniors $5, ages 3-12 $5. Wheelchair accessible.

Detroit Science Center, 5020 John R St. (☎577-8400; www.detroitscience.org). Children can learn about waves while strumming a stringless harp or take virtual trips through the rings of Saturn in the planetarium. Open mid-June to early Sept. M-F 9am-5pm, Sa-Su 10:30am-6pm; mid-Sept. to early June M-F 9:30am-3pm, Sa-Su 10:30am-6pm. $7, seniors and ages 2-12 $6; IMAX additional $4. Wheelchair accessible.

Detroit Historical Museum, 5401 Woodward Ave. (☎833-1805; www.detroithistorical.org), explores the region's transformation from "frontiers to factories"—visitors can tour a streetscape of old town Detroit and gawk at a working piece of the real Cadillac automobile assembly line. Open Tu-F 9:30am-5pm, Sa 10am-5pm, Su 11am-5pm. $5, college students $3.50, seniors $3, children 5-18 $3. Wheelchair accessible.

🎵 ENTERTAINMENT

Music has always filled the streets of Detroit, with the city's sidewalk performers carrying on the Motown legacy. Though the era of Motown has come and gone, a vibrant music scene still dominates the Motor City. The **Detroit Symphony Orchestra** performs at **Orchestra Hall,** 3711 Woodward Ave., at Parsons St. (☎576-5100, box office 576-5111; www.detroitsymphony.com. Open M-F 10am-6pm. Tickets $15-105. Half-price student and senior rush tickets 1½hr. prior to show.)

Celebrated dramatic works are performed in the newly restored **theater district,** clustered around Woodward Ave. and Columbia St. The 4800-seat **Fox Theatre,** 2211 Woodward Ave., near Grand Circus Park, features high-profile dramas, comedies, and musicals. (☎983-6611. Box office open M-F 10am-6pm. $25-100.) The **State Theater,** 2115 Woodward Ave. (☎961-5450, tickets 248-645-6666), hosts a variety of popular concerts. Beyond the theater district, the acclaimed **Detroit Repertory Theater,** 13103 Woodrow Wilson Ave., puts on four productions a year. (☎868-1347. Shows Th-F 8:30pm, Sa 3 and 8:30pm, Su 2 and 7:30pm. Tickets from $17.)

Sports fans won't be disappointed in Detroit. During the dog days of summer, baseball's **Tigers** round the bases in the newly built **Comerica Park,** 2100 Woodward Ave. (☎471-2255. $5-60.) Football's **Lions** hit the gridiron next door at **Ford Field,** 200 Brush St. (☎262-2003. $40.) Inside the **Joe Louis Arena,** 600 Civic Center Dr., the 2002 Stanley Cup champion **Red Wings** play hockey. (☎396-7575. $20-40.) Thirty minutes outside Detroit in Auburn Hills, basketball's 2004 NBA Champion **Pistons** play at **The Palace at Auburn Hills,** 2 Championship Dr. (☎248-377-0100. $10-80.)

🐾 🔲 FESTIVALS AND NIGHTLIFE

Detroit's numerous **festivals** draw millions of visitors. Most outdoor events take place at **Hart Plaza,** a downtown oasis that hugs a scenic expanse of the Detroit River. A new and rousingly successful downtown tradition, the ▨**Detroit Electronic Music Festival** (☎567-0080) has lured over one million ravers to Hart Plaza on Memorial Day weekend. Jazz fans jet to the riverbank during Labor Day weekend for the four-day **Ford Detroit International Jazz Festival** (☎963-2366; www.detroit-jazzfest.com), which features more than 100 acts on three stages and mountains of international food at the World Food Court. A week-long extravaganza in late June, the international **Freedom Festival** (☎923-7400) celebrates the friendship between the US and Canada. The continent's largest fireworks display ignites the festivities with over 10,000 colorful explosions. On the Detroit side, food and a bandstand dominate the festival, while Windsor hosts a carnival. Detroit's **African World Festival** (☎494-5860; www.africanworldfestival.com) brings over a million people to Hart Plaza on the third weekend in August for free reggae, jazz, and gospel concerts. The nation's oldest state fair, the **Michigan State Fair** (☎369-8250), at Eight Mile Rd. and Woodward Ave., beckons with bake-offs, art, and livestock birth exhibits during the two weeks before Labor Day.

For info on nightlife, pick up a free copy of *Orbit,* in record stores and restaurants, or the *Metro Times. Between the Lines,* also free, has GLBT entertainment info. Head to **Harmonie Park,** near Orchestra Hall, for some of Detroit's best jazz. Alternative fans should check out **Saint Andrews Hall,** 431 E. Congress St., Detroit's mainstay for local and national alternative acts. **Shelter,** the dance club downstairs in St. Andrews Hall, draws young, hip crowds on non-concert nights. (☎961-6358. Shows F-Su. St. Andrews 18+; Shelter 21+. Advance tickets through Ticketmaster $7-15.) On Saturdays, the State Theater (see **Entertainment,** p. 575) houses **Altered State,** a giant party that enlists DJs from a local radio station to play alternative dance music. (☎961-5450. 2115 Woodward Ave. 18+. Cover starts at $5. Sa 10pm-2am.) If all you want is a good pint, try the **Town Pump Tavern,** 100 W. Montcalm St., behind the State Theater. Good beer abounds at this watering hole, which is cloaked in ivy and features a mock study with comfy leather chairs. (☎961-1929. Live music Th-Sa. Open daily 11am-2am; kitchen closes at 10pm.) The bars and clubs along **Ouellette Avenue** in Windsor (see below) attract young party kids looking to take advantage of Ontario's lower drinking age.

🔳 DAYTRIP FROM DETROIT

WINDSOR, ON   ☎519

Combining cultural highlights, natural attractions, and a vibrant nightlife, Windsor offers tourists an alternative to the grittier city across the river. Outdoor cafes, tree-lined streets, and lively shopping give Windsor a pleasant European feel. Its many bars, favorable exchange rates, and drinking age (19) lure Detroiters of all ages across the river, creating a cosmopolitan mix on the crowded streets.

For a small industrial city, Windsor scores big with its collection of contemporary art. Stroll through the "museum without walls" at the **Odette Sculpture Garden,** part of a 6 mi. long riverfront green area between the Ambassador Bridge and Curry Ave. Visitors are enchanted by native totem poles next to unusual modern sculptures. (☎253-2300. Open daily dawn-dusk. Free.) The city's other major exhibit space, **The Art Gallery of Windsor,** 401 Riverside Dr. W, provides a showcase for a rotating cast of Canada's best modern artists. (☎977-0013; www.artgalleryofwindsor.com. Open Th noon-5pm, F noon-8pm,

Sa-Su 11am-5pm. CDN$2.) Beauty of the natural type is on display at **Point Pelee National Park of Canada,** 407 Monarch Ln., Leamington, ON, 45 mi. southeast of downtown. Visitors look for the butterflies flying through the park's tall grass. (☎322-2365. Open daily Apr. and June to mid-Oct. 6am-9:30pm; mid-Oct. to Mar. 7am-6:30pm; May 5am-9:30pm. CDN$5, seniors CDN$4.25, students CDN$2.50; families CDN$13. Rates are lower in winter. Guided butterfly tours in Sept. W-Su CDN$10.)

Locals come from miles around to eat finger-lickin' good barbecue at the ▓**Tunnel Bar-B-Q ❸,** 58 Park St. E, across from the tunnel exit. The terrific half-strip rib dinner (CDN$16) is particularly recommended. (☎258-3663. Open Su-Th 8am-2am, F-Sa 8am-4am.) The rest of Windsor's culinary and nightlife activity is centered along Ouellette (OH-let) Ave. downtown. Family-run **Aar-D-Vark Blues Cafe,** 89 University Ave. W, offers a Canadian take on a traditional Chicago blues joint. Pink aardvarks lead customers into the graffitied bar. (☎977-6422. Live music Th-Sa 9:30pm. Open M-F noon-2am, Sa 4pm-2am, Su 7pm-2am.) For the traveler who prefers the clank of quarters to the beat of drums, the **Casino Windsor,** 377 Riverside Dr., offers three floors of gambling in a glimmering new building and draws thousands of American gamers looking to cash in on good exchange rates. Test Lady Luck 24hr. a day. (Reservations ☎800-991-8888, info 800-991-7777. 19+.)

Canada's national rail service, **VIA Rail,** 298 Walker Rd. (☎888-842-7245; www.viarail.com; ticket window open M-Sa 5:10am-9pm), provides service to Toronto (4hr.; 4 per day; CDN$85, 35% discount with ISIC). **Transit Windsor,** 3700 N. Service Rd. E, sends buses throughout the city. (☎944-4111. CDN$2.35, seniors and students CDN$1.60.) **Taxi: Veteran's Cab** ☎256-2621. **Visitor Info: The Convention and Visitors Bureau of Windsor, Essex County, and Pelee Island,** 333 Riverside Dr. W, #103. (☎255-6530 or 800-265-3633; www.visitwindsor.com. Open M-F 8:30am-4:30pm.) The **Ontario Travel Center,** 110 Park St., offers maps, currency exchange, and help from a knowledgeable staff. (☎973-1338 or 800-668-2746; www.ontariotravel.net). Open daily 8am-8pm.) **Post Office:** City Centre, corner of Park St. and Ouellette Ave. (☎253-1252. Open M-F 8am-5pm.) **Postal Code:** N9A 4K0. **Area Code:** 519.

ANN ARBOR ☎734

Ann Arbor's namesakes, Ann Rumsey and Ann Allen—the wives of two of the area's early pioneers—supposedly enjoyed sitting under grape arbors. Now known to locals as "A2," the town has managed to prosper without losing its relaxed charm, despite being tucked between several major industrial hubs. Meanwhile, the huge and well-respected University of Michigan adds a hip collage of young, liberal Middle Americans. Ann Arbor is the prototype for a great college town, and is well worth a visit for anyone traveling in the area.

▓▓ **ORIENTATION AND PRACTICAL INFORMATION.** Ann Arbor's streets lie in a grid, but watch out for the slant of Packard St. and Detroit St. **Main Street** divides the town east-west, and **Huron Street** cuts it north-south. The central campus of the **University of Michigan (U of M)** lies east of Main St. and south of E. Huron, a 5min. walk from downtown. In spite of plentiful meter parking, authorities ticket ruthlessly, and one-way streets and frequent dead-ends can make driving stressful. Luckily, downtown Ann Arbor is walkable, and a car is generally unnecessary.

Amtrak, 325 Depot St. (☎994-4906; ticket window open daily 7:15am-11:30pm), sends trains to Chicago (4hr., 3 per day, $23-57) and Detroit (1hr., 3 per day, $9-21). **Greyhound,** 116 W. Huron St. (☎662-5511; open daily 8am-6pm), sends buses to: Chi-

Downtown Ann Arbor

🏠 ACCOMMODATIONS
1st St. Garden Inn, **10**
Motel 6, **12**

🍴 FOOD
Casey's Tavern, **1**
Krazy Jim's Blimpy Burger, **11**
Seva, **7**
Zingerman's Deli, **2**

🍷 NIGHTLIFE
Ashley's, **9**
Áut Bar, **3**
Blind Pig, **5**
Conor O'Neill's, **8**
Firefly Club, **4**
Oz, **6**

cago (5-7hr., 4 per day, $33); Detroit (1-1½hr., 3 per day, $8.50); Grand Rapids (4-5hr., 2 per day, $22). **Ann Arbor Transportation Authority (AATA),** 331 S. 4th Ave., provides public transit in Ann Arbor and a few neighboring towns. (☎ 996-0400; www.theride.org. Station open M-F 7:30am-9:30pm, Sa noon-6:15pm. Buses run M-F 6:45am-11pm, Sa-Su 8am-5:45pm. $1, ages 6-18 $0.50; seniors can obtain card for $0.25-0.50 fares.) AATA's **Nightride** provides safe door-to-door transportation. (☎ 663-3888 to reserve; the wait is 15-40min. Runs M-F 11pm-6am, Sa-Su 7pm-7:30am. $3.) **Checker Sedan** runs between Ann Arbor and the Detroit Metro Airport. (☎ 800-351-5466. $48. Reserve in advance.) **Visitor Info: Ann Arbor Area Convention and Visitors Bureau,** 120 W. Huron St., at Ashley. (☎ 995-7281 or 800-888-9487; www.annarbor.org. Open M-F 8:30am-5pm.) **Hotlines: Sexual Assault Crisis Line,** ☎ 483-7273. **University of Michigan Sexual Assault Line,** ☎ 936-3333. **S.O.S. Crisis Line,** ☎ 302-4225. All 24hr. **University of Michigan Gay/Lesbian Referrals,** ☎ 763-4186. Operates M-F 9am-5pm. **Internet Access: Ann Arbor Public Library,** 343 S. 5th Ave. (☎ 324-4200. Open M 10am-9pm, Tu-F 9am-9pm, Sa 9am-6pm, Su noon-6pm.) **Post Office:** 2075 W. Stadium Blvd. (☎ 665-1100. Open M-F 7:30am-5pm, Sa 10am-1pm.) **Postal Code:** 48103. **Area Code:** 734.

🏠 ACCOMMODATIONS. Expensive hotels, motels, and B&Bs cater to the many business travelers and college sports fans who flock to Ann Arbor throughout the year. Reservations are always advisable, especially during the school year. Reasonable rates exist at discount chains farther out of town or in Ypsilanti, 5 mi. southeast along I-94. On the outskirts of Ann Arbor, good ol' **Motel 6 ❸**, 3764 S. State St., rents well-kept, standard rooms equipped with cable TV and A/C, a 10min. drive from campus and downtown. (☎665-9900. Singles Su-Th $43, F-Sa $49; doubles $50/$56.) For accommodations with a touch of home— and a few added creature comforts—try the **First Street Garden Inn ❹**, 549 1st St., a 5min. walk from downtown and 10min. to campus. Lovely rooms are comple-mented by gourmet breakfasts, a beautiful garden, and wireless Internet. (☎741-9786. Call in advance for reservations. Rooms $90-120.) Seven **campgrounds ❶** lie within a 20 mi. radius of Ann Arbor, including the **Pinckney Recreation Area**, 8555 Silver Hill, in Pinckney, and the **Waterloo Recreation Area**, 16345 McClure Rd., in Chelsea. (Pinckney ☎426-4913. Waterloo ☎475-8307. Both: primitive sites $9, with water and electricity $19. Vehicle permit $6 per day for Michigan residents, $8 for non-residents; $24/$29 per year.)

� FOOD. Where there are students, there are cheap eats. The cheapest cram the sidewalks of **State** and **South University Street,** while the more upscale line **Main Street.** ▨**Zingerman's Deli ❸**, 422 Detroit St., is an institution in Ann Arbor and is famous for its gourmet breads, cheeses, and huge deli sandwiches, which come in over 40 varieties ($7-10). Expect a line out the door during the lunch-time rush. Try **Zingerman's Next Door** for baked goods, desserts, homemade gelato, and espresso drinks. (☎663-3354. Open daily 7am-10pm.) **Krazy Jim's Blimpy Burger ❶**, 551 S. Division St., near campus, caters to the college crowd with gorgeously greasy "cheaper than food" burgers, from a single patty all the way up to the monstrous half-pound "Quint" ($1.90-4.10). Krazy Jim does not take kindly to poor ordering technique, so make sure to acquaint yourself with the color-coded "Helpful Hints for Blimpy Virgins" before stepping to the counter. (☎663-4590. Open M-Sa 11am-10pm, Su noon-8pm.) Enjoy meatless delights at Ann Arbor's long-established veggie haven **Seva ❸**, 314 E. Liberty St. Its earthy decor complements a menu that offers Mexican entrees, stir-fry dishes, goat cheese ravioli, and all points in between. (☎662-1111. Entrees $9-14. Open June-Aug. M-F 11am-10pm, Sa 10am-10pm, Su 10am-9pm; low-season closes M-F 9pm.) The truly hungry should head to **Casey's Tavern ❷**, 304 Depot St., across from the train station, for gigantic portions. The Caesar Steak Sand-wich ($8.25) has locals and travelers alike raving. (☎665-6775. Sandwiches $4-8.25. Open M-Th 11am-11pm, F-Sa 11am-midnight.)

◪ ◪ SIGHTS AND ENTERTAINMENT. Most of Ann Arbor's cultural attrac-tions are provided by the university. The **University of Michigan Museum of Art (UMMA)**, 525 S. State St., packs a collection of African and Chinese artifacts, early European paintings, and pieces of American interior design into a small but stately building. Works by Picasso and Monet highlight the museum's cache. (☎763-8662; www.umich.edu/~umma. Open Tu-W and F-Sa 10am-5pm, Th 10am-9pm, Su noon-5pm. Free.) The **University of Michigan Exhibit Museum of Natural His-tory**, 1109 Geddes Ave., displays *T. rex* and mastodon skeletons (Michigan's offi-cial state fossil) along with other exhibits on everything from anthropology to zoology. The planetarium offers indoor star-gazing on weekends. (☎764-0478; www.exhibits.lsa.umich/edu. Open M-Sa 9am-5pm, Su noon-5pm. Museum free; planetarium $3.75.) Security won't escort you to the door for touching the exhib-its at the **Ann Arbor Hands-On Museum**, 220 E. Ann St., which houses four floors of exhibits designed to be touched, twisted, and turned. Let your inner child loose as you test the mechanics of a car, explore the technology behind the Internet, and make your way up a climbing wall. (☎995-5439; www.aahom.org. Open M-Sa

10am-5pm, Su noon-5pm. $7.50; students, seniors, and ages 2-17 $6.) Artists and chefs peddle homemade paper, unique clothing, and gourmet food in a trio of historic brick buildings at the **Kerrytown shops,** on Detroit St. Prices are a little steep, but browsing never hurts. (☎662-5008. Open M-F 8am-7pm, Sa 7am-6pm, Su 9am-5pm.) In front of the shops, growers haul their crops, baked goods, and perennials to the popular **Farmers Market,** 315 Detroit St. (☎994-3276. Open May-Dec. W and Sa 7am-3pm; Jan.-Apr. Sa 8am-3pm.) Paintings and pottery take over the market space on Sundays, when local artists display their creations at the **Artisans Market.** (Open May-Dec. Su 11am-4pm.) Book lovers should scour the many **bookshops** along S. Main St. for unusual or inexpensive finds. It's near impossible to get tickets for a **Wolverine football game** at U of M's 115,000 capacity stadium, but fans can give it a shot by calling the athletics office (☎764-0247). As tens of thousands of students depart for the summer, locals indulge in a little celebration. The **Ann Arbor Summer Festival** (☎647-2278; www.annarborsummerfestival.org) draws crowds from mid-June to early July for comedy, dance, and theater productions from national and local acts, as well as musical performances including jazz, country, and classical. Nightly outdoor performances are followed by popular movies at **Top of the Park,** on top of the Fletcher St. parking structure, next to the Health Services Building. In late July, thousands pack the city to view the work of 200 artists at the **Ann Arbor Summer Art Fair** (☎994-5260; www.artfair.org). Classical music lovers should contact the **University Musical Society,** in the Burton Memorial Clock Tower at N. University and Thouper, for info on area performances. (☎764-2538 or 800-221-1229; www.ums.org. Open M-F 9am-5pm, Sa 10am-1pm. $10-90.)

🎵 **NIGHTLIFE.** Free in restaurants and music stores, the monthly *Current, Agenda, Weekender Entertainment,* and the weekly *Metrotimes* print up-to-date nightlife and entertainment listings. For GLBT info pick up a copy of *Between the Lines.* The hottest spot in town for live music, the **Blind Pig,** 208 S. 1st St., feels its way through the night with rock 'n' roll, hip-hop, blues, and swing. (☎996-8555; www.blindpigmusic.com. Shows Sa-Su 9:30pm. 19+. Cover $3-10, under 21 $2 extra. Open daily 3pm-2am.) The **Firefly Club,** 207 S. Ashley St., offers an intimate setting for all varieties of jazz from traditional big band to modern avant garde. (☎665-9090; www.fireflyclub.com. Latin jazz every Th. 21+. Cover $3-10. Open M-W 7pm-2am, Th-F and Su 5pm-2am, Sa 8pm-2am.) **Oz,** 210 S. 5th Ave., transports guests from the Midwest to the Mid East. Near Eastern decor, hookahs ($10-18), and a belly dancer supplement traditional club offerings. (☎222-4770; www.ozan-narbor.com. DJ Tu-Su. Belly dancer F 12:30am. Cover varies. Open Tu-W 8pm-2am, Th-Sa 8pm-4am, Su 6pm-midnight.) Mingle with locals and students at **Conor O'Neill's,** 318 S. Main St., Ann Arbor's "Best Pick-Up Joint," where the food and beer are as authentically Celtic as the bartenders. (☎665-2968. Open daily 11:30am-2am. Kitchen closes M-Th 11pm, F-Su midnight.) **Áut Bar,** 315 Braun Ct., near the intersection of 4th Ave. and Catherine St., pours strong drinks for a primarily gay clientele. (☎994-3677. Open daily 4pm-2am. Su brunch 10am-3pm.) **Ashley's,** 338 S. State St., is a beer drinker's heaven with over 70 brews on tap and another 70 bottled, all described in detail in the encyclopedic drink menu. (☎996-9191; www.ashleys.com. Pints $4.25-6. Open M-Sa 11:30-2am, Su noon-midnight.)

LAKE MICHIGAN SHORE

The freighters that once powered the rise of Chicago still steam along the coast of Lake Michigan, but these days they are greatly outnumbered by pleasure boats cruising along the coast. Valleys of sand beckon sunbathers, while hikers trek through the virgin forests of Michigan's state parks. When autumn comes, the weather forbids swimming, but inland, festivals celebrate local fruits and blossoms—from cherries in July to apples in September. Snow covers much of the coast in winter, drawing snowmobile, skiing, and ice-skating enthusiasts. The coastline stretches 350 miles north from the Indiana border to the Mackinac Bridge; its southern end is a scant two hours from downtown Chicago.

⑦ PRACTICAL INFORMATION

Many of the region's attractions lie in the small coastal towns that cluster around **Grand Traverse Bay** in the north. **Traverse City,** at the southern tip of the bay, is the famous "cherry capital of the world." Fishing is best in the Au Sable and Manistee Rivers. The main north-south route along the coast is U.S. 31. Numerous green "Lake Michigan Circle Tour" signs lead closer to the shoreline, providing an excellent view of the coast. Coastal accommodations can be quite expensive; head inland for cheaper lodging. Determined travelers can occasionally find a good deal lakeside, and numerous camping options exist in the summer months. Based in Grand Rapids, the **West Michigan Tourist Association,** 950 28th St. SE, Ste. E-200, hands out info on the area. (☎616-245-2217 or 800-442-2084; www.wmta.org. Open M-Th 8:30am-5pm, F 8:30am-6pm, Sa 9am-1pm.) **Area Codes:** 616 and 231.

CENTRAL MICHIGAN SHORE

SLEEPING BEAR DUNES   ☎231

The Sleeping Bear Dunes lie along the western shores of the Leelanau Peninsula, 20 mi. west of Traverse City on Rte. 72. **Sleeping Bear Dunes National Lakeshore** includes 25 mi. of lakeshore and both the Manitou Islands, located a few miles off the mainland coast. Near the historic Fishtown shops at the end of River St., **Manitou Island Transit,** in **Leland,** makes daily trips to South Manitou from June to August. (☎256-9061. Check-in 9:15am. Daily trips to North Manitou July to mid-Aug. June 1-15 3 per week, June 15-30 5 per week. May and Sept.-Oct. service M, W, F-Su. Call ahead for May and Sept.-Nov. schedule. Round-trip $25, under 12 $14. Reservations recommended.) Hardcore **backpackers** looking for an adventure can **camp** on both islands with the purchase of a **permit** ($5), though there is an entrance fee ($10 per 7 days; available at the visitors center). The Manitou Islands do not allow wheeled vehicles, including cars and bikes. On South Manitou, a small village near the dock provides a rest area for day-hikers. North Manitou Island travelers should take note—once the boat leaves for the day, hikers are cut off from the modern world until the next morning. In bad weather, the ferry won't venture to the island until the weather clears, even if that is several days later.

Willing climbers can be king of the sandhill at **Dune Climb,** 5 mi. north of Empire on Rte. 109. From there, a 2½ mi. hike over sandy hills leads to Lake Michigan ($5 in addition to park entrance fee. Allow 3-4½hr. for the hike and bring lots of water). If you'd rather let your car do the climbing, drive to an overlook along the 7 mi. **Pierce Stocking Scenic Drive,** off Rte. 109 just north of Empire, where a 450 ft. sand cliff descends to the cool water below. ($5; open mid-May to mid-Oct. daily 9am-10pm). For maps and info on the cross-country skiing, hiking, and mountain biking trails in the lakeshore area, stop by the **National Parks Service Visitors Center,** 9922 Front St., in Empire. (☎326-5134, reservations 800-365-2267. Open daily June-Aug. 8am-6pm; Sept.-May 9am-4pm.)

The Sleeping Bear Dunes have four **campgrounds: DH Day ❶** (☎334-4634), 1 mi. west of Glen Arbor on Rte. 109, with 88 primitive sites ($12); **Platte River ❶** (☎325-5881 or 800-365-2267), off the southern shore, with 179 sites and showers ($16, with electricity $21); and two backcountry campsites, **Whitepine ❶** and **Valley View ❶**, accessible by 1½-2½ mi. trails (no reservations; $5 permit required, available at visitors center or at any campground). The Platte River, at the southern end of the lakeshore, and the Crystal River, at the northern end, are ideal for canoeing or lazy floating. **Riverside Canoes,** 5042 Scenic Hwy. (Rte. 22), at Platte River Bridge, also organizes 2½hr. canoe and kayak excursions, as well as relaxed tubing trips. (☎325-5622; www.canoemichigan.com. Open May to early Oct. daily 8am-10pm. Inner tubes $6 per hr., canoes $31 per hr., kayaks $23 per hr. Includes shuttle to river. Prices higher for trips on more advanced Upper Rapids.)

TRAVERSE CITY   ☎231

Traverse City offers the summer vacationer sandy beaches and picturesque orchards—half of the nation's cherries are produced in the surrounding area. Swimming, boating, and scuba diving interests focus on Grand Traverse Bay, and the scenic waterfront makes for excellent biking. The **TART** bike trail runs 8 mi. along E. and W. Grand Traverse Bay, while the 30 mi. loop around Old Mission Peninsula, north of the city, provides great views of the bay. **McLain Cycle and Fitness,** 750 E. 8th St. and 2786 Garfield Rd. N, has bikes and trail info. (☎941-8855. Open in summer M-F 9am-6pm, Sa 9am-5pm, Su 11am-4pm; low-season closed Su. $10 per 2hr. M-Th $15 per day, F-Su $30.) The annual **National Cherry Festival** (☎947-4230; www.cherryfestival.org), held the first full week in July, is a rousing tribute to the annual cherry harvest. In early to mid-July, many orchards near Traverse City let visitors pick their own cherries, including **Elzer Farms,** 9 mi. north of Traverse City on Rte. 37. (☎223-9292. Open May-Sept. M-Sa 9am-6pm, Su 9am-4pm. $2.50 per quart. Pies $6-15.) Sophisticated fruit connoisseurs can indulge their taste buds at one of the area's many well-respected **wineries.**

East Front St. (U.S. 31) is lined with motels, and during the summer rates generally start at $50. The **Old Mission Inn ❺**, 18 mi. north of town on Rte. 37 in the hamlet of Old Mission, once hosted Babe Ruth and boxing great Joe Louis on the same night in 1936, and has the guest register to prove it. The B&B is a veritable museum, with impressive antiques recalling the inn's 145-year history. (☎223-7770; www.oldmissioninn.com. Full breakfast. Rooms May-Oct. $80-175, rates drop Nov.-Apr.) **Northwestern Michigan College ❷**, 1701 E. Front St., West and East Halls, has rooms that offer all the comforts of college life, including laundry, a common room, and access to outdoor basketball courts, volleyball nets, and a track. (☎995-1409. Linen service $12 per week. Reserve several weeks in advance. Open June-Aug. Singles $32; doubles $44.) For those who prefer to commune with nature, **Traverse City State Park ❶**, 1132 U.S. 31 N, 2 mi. east of town, has 344 wooded sites crowded along U.S. 31, adjacent to the beach. (☎922-5270 or 800-447-2757. Toilet and shower facilities. Sites with hookup $20; cabins $37. Vehicle permit fee $6 per day for Michigan residents, $8 for non-residents; $24/$29 per year.) Downtown Front St. offers a range of appealing food options. **Poppycock's ❷**, 128 E. Front St., is a vegetarian-friendly bistro that doles out gourmet sandwiches ($6.50-9) and pastas ($8-14). From Wednesday to Saturday, the restaurant dims the lights and brings in live music. (☎941-7632. Open in summer M-W 11am-10pm, Th-Sa 11am-1am, Su 11am-9pm; low season Su-Tu and Th 11am-10pm, W and F-Sa 11am-midnight.) The smell of freshly baked goods tempts the hungry into **The Omelette Shoppe ❷**, 124 Cass St. This bustling bakery and breakfast joint specializes in gooey cinnamon buns and 18 varieties of omelettes for $6.50. (☎946-0590. Pancakes $4-5. Open M-F 6:30am-3pm, Sa-Su 7:30am-3pm. Another location at 1209 E. Front St., ☎946-0590, in the Campus Plaza complex. Open M-Sa 7am-3pm, Su 10am-3pm.) Those with a sweet tooth will find nirvana at **Grand Traverse Pie Company ❶**, 525 W.

Front St., where mouthwatering pies are sold by the slice ($2.75-3.25) and by the pan. (☎922-7437; www.gtpie.com. Open M-F 9am-6pm, Sa 9am-5pm.) No Anglophile should miss **Cousin Jenny's ❶**, 129 S. Union St., a purveyor of pasties that takes the portable meat pies back to their Cornish roots. Try the breakfast bobby, a 6 oz. pastie stuffed with eggs, hash browns, and other goodies. (☎941-7281. Pasties $4.59 for 10 oz., $5.59 for 16 oz. Open M-F 7:30am-6pm, Sa 7:30am-6pm. Breakfast pasties served 7:30-10:30am.) The **U & I Lounge**, 214 E. Front St., is the hottest bar in town, thanks in part to local brews. (☎946-8932. Sandwiches $5.25-6.50. Hot dogs $2.50. Happy hour daily 4-7pm. 21+ after 9pm. Open M-Sa 11am-2am, kitchen closes 1:30am; Su noon-2am, kitchen closes 1:15am.) For more entertainment info, pick up the weekly *Northern Express* at corner kiosks in the city.

Indian Trails and **Greyhound**, 3233 Cass Rd. (☎946-5180 or 800-231-2222), run to Detroit (8hr., 1 per day, $48-55) and the Upper Peninsula via St. Ignace (3hr., 1 per day, $19). Call the **Bay Area Transportation Authority** and they'll pick you up in the Traverse City area; a 24hr. notice is preferred. (☎941-2324. Available M-Sa 6am-midnight, Su 8am-1pm. $2, seniors and under 12 $1.) **Traverse City Convention and Visitors Bureau:** 101 West Grandview Pkwy./U.S. 31 N. (☎947-1120 or 800-872-8377; www.mytraversecity.com. Open M-F 9am-6pm, Sa 9am-5pm, Su 11am-3pm.) **Post Office:** 202 S. Union St. (☎946-9616. Open M-Sa 8am-5pm.) **Postal Code:** 49684. **Area Code:** 231.

NORTHERN MICHIGAN SHORE

STRAITS OF MACKINAC ☎ 231

Mackinac is pronounced "MACK-i-naw"; only fur'ners say "MACK-i-nack." The **Mackinac Bridge** ("Mighty Mac") soars over the intersection of Lake Michigan and Lake Huron, connecting **Mackinaw City** to St. Ignace in the Upper Peninsula. The five-mile span is the third-longest suspension bridge in the US and the tenth-longest in the world. A local tradition not to be missed is the annual **Labor Day Bridge Walk,** where Michigan's governor leads thousands north across the bridge to St. Ignace. Just to the west of the bridge's southern landfall in Mackinaw City, **Colonial Fort Michilimackinac's** log palisade still guards the straits. (☎436-4100; www.mackinac-parks.com. Open daily early May to mid-Oct. 9am-5pm; mid-July to late Aug. until 6pm. $9, ages 6-17 $5.75.) **Historic Mill Creek,** which includes a working

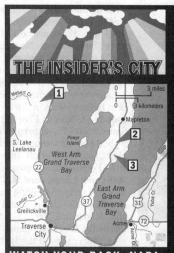

WATCH YOUR BACK, NAPA.

France. California. Traverse City? Michigan resort towns are not usually named among the world's great wine producers, but a handful of wineries are quietly bottling a revolution in the hills to increasing acclaim—and we're not just talking about blue ribbons at the county fair.

1 **L. Mawby,** 4519 S. Elm Valley Rd., south of Sutton's Bay, makes only sparkling wines, including a vintage known simply as Sex. (☎271-3522; www.lmawby.com.)

2 **Chateau Grand Traverse,** 12239 Center Rd., makes a mean Dry Johannisberg Riesling ($10). Free tastings and tours. (☎223-7355; www.cgtwines.com.)

3 **Peninsula Cellars,** 11480 Center Rd., off Rte. 37 north of Traverse City, offers free tastings in an 1895 schoolhouse. Don't miss the world-class Gewurtztraminer, $15. (☎933-9787; www.peninsulacellars.com.)

sawmill and nature trails, is located 3½ mi. south of Mackinaw City on Rte. 23. (☎436-4226. Open daily early May to mid-Oct. 9am-5pm; mid-July to late Aug. until 6pm. $7.50, ages 6-17 $4.50.) Historic Mill Creek, Fort Michilimackinac, and Fort Mackinac (on Mackinac Island, see below) form a trio of State Historic Parks in the area. Colonial enthusiasts should buy a **Combination Pack,** good for seven days from date of purchase, for unlimited daily admission to all three. ($19, ages 6-17 $11. Available at all 3 sights.)

Lakeshore accommodation options abound on Rte. 23, south of the city. The best lodging deals in the area lie across the Mackinac Bridge on the **I-75 Business Loop** in St. Ignace. Five minutes from the docks, the **Harbor Light Motel ❷,** 1449 State St. on I-75, rents sparkling rooms with cable TV, A/C, and refrigerators. A volleyball net and the occasional bonfire on the beach make this a good bet for travelers. (☎906-643-9439. In summer singles $35; doubles $40-45. Low-season $30/$32.) For an outdoor escape, campers can crash at one of the 600 sites of **Mackinac Mill Creek Campground ❶,** 3 mi. south of town on Rte. 23. The grounds provide beach access and biking trails. (☎436-5584; www.campmackinaw.com. Internet access, public showers, and pool. Sites $20, with full hookup $26. Cabins $55. Free shuttle to island ferry.) For the best pasties in town, head to the **Mackinaw Pastie & Cookie Co. ❶,** 117 W. Jamet St., two blocks south of Colonial Michilimackinac, for seven variations of the U.P.'s favorite meat pie, including a low-carb nod to the health conscious. (☎231-436-8202; www.mackinawpastie.com. Pasties $5-6.65. Open daily 9am-9pm. Other location at 516 S. Huron.)

For transportation outside the city, **Indian Trails** (☎800-292-3831 or 800-231-2222) has a flag stop at City Hall, 102 S. Huron. One bus runs north and one south each day; buy tickets at the next station. The **Michigan Department of Transportation Welcome and Travel Information Center,** on Nicolet St. off I-75 at Exit 338, has loads of helpful info on lodging, food, and area attractions. (☎436-5566. Open daily mid-June to Aug. 8am-6pm; Sept. to mid-June 9am-5pm. Free reservation service.)

MACKINAC ISLAND   ☎231

Mackinac Island, a 16min. ferry ride from the mainland, has long been considered one of Michigan's greatest treasures. Victorian homes and the prohibition of cars on the heavily touristed island—and the resulting proliferation of horse-drawn carriages—give Mackinac an aristocratic air with a decidedly equine aroma. Travelers flock to the island for its stunning parks, museums, and coastal, old-world charm. Escape touristy Main St. for a quiet look at what made the island popular in the first place: its beautiful fauna and rolling hills.

Resting atop the island's limestone bluffs, **Fort Mackinac** was a key piece in the War of 1812. Today the fort's restored buildings and daily reenactments are among the island's main draws. (☎436-4100. Open daily mid-July to late Aug. 9am-7pm; May to mid-July and Sept. to mid-Oct. 9:30am-6pm. $9, ages 6-17 $5.75, under 6 free.) Tickets to the fort also grant access to four museums of island history that are housed in refurbished period buildings. Travelers with a sweet tooth flock to the birthplace of Mackinac Fudge (½ lb. $6), though the tantalizing aroma wafts out of storefronts all over the island and along the entire Michigan coastline. **Mackinac Island Carriage Tours,** Main St., cart guests on tours all over the island in horse-drawn buggies, showcasing architectural wonders such as the ritzy Grand Hotel. (☎906-847-3307; www.mict.com. Open daily 9am-5pm. $17, ages 4-11 $7.50.) For those who would rather take the reins in their own hands, **Jack's Livery Stable,** off Grande Ave. on Mahoney Ave., rents saddle horses and horses with buggies. (☎847-3391. Saddle horses $30 first hr., $25 each additional hr. 2-person horse and buggie $45 per hr.; 4-person $55 per hr.) Bicycles are the best way to see the island's beaches and forests. Rental shops line Main St. by the ferry docks and generally offer identical rates ($4 per hr., $25 per day). Encompassing 80% of the island, **Mackinac Island State Park** features a circular 8¼ mi. shoreline road for biking and hiking that takes about an hour by bike, or two by foot.

Hotel rates on the island generally reach into the stratosphere, but ▨**McNally Cottage ❹**, on Main Street, offers a haven for thrifty travelers. Situated in the heart of downtown, this B&B has been owned and operated by the same family every summer since its construction in the 1880s. (☎847-3565; www.mcnallycottage.net. Shared baths. Call well in advance for reservations. Single room $50; doubles $70-95.) For food, **Mighty Mac ❶**, Main St., cooks it cheap, with ¼ lb. burgers for $4. (☎847-8039. Open daily 8am-9pm.) The **3 Brothers Sarducci Pizzeria ❶**, on Main St., serves "good food fast," and lots of it. One delicious slice of their Sicilian-style pizza ($4.25) is a meal in itself. (☎847-3880. Open daily 11am-9pm.)

Transportation to the island via ferry is quick and pleasant, providing terrific views of the Mackinac Bridge. Three ferry lines, **Shepler's** (☎800-828-6157), **Arnold Transit Co.** (☎800-542-8528), and **Star** (☎800-638-9892) leave Mackinaw City (in summer every 30min. Su-Th 8am-10pm, F-Sa 8am-11pm) and St. Ignace with overlapping schedules, though service from St. Ignace is slightly less frequent. (Round-trip $17, children 5-12 $8, bikes and strollers $6.50. All lines charge identical rates.) An invaluable and free visitors guide can be found at the **Mackinac Island Tourism Bureau,** on Main St. (☎800-454-5227; www.mackinacisland.org. Open May-Oct. Su-W 9am-5pm, Th-Sa 9am-9pm; Nov.-April daily 9am-5pm.)

SCENIC DRIVE: NORTHERN MICHIGAN SHORE

Cherry trees, tranquil lake shores, and intimate resort villages dot the Northern Michigan Shore. Once used by Native Americans and French traders to peddle goods, the route now guides visitors through diverse aspects of Michigan's natural beauty. It takes about 3hr. to do the drive justice, stopping along the way to admire both the natural and fabricated wonders that line the route.

Heading north, the drive begins in Michigan's coastal beach communities before moving through lush forest. U.S. 31 winds its way 65 mi. north from Traverse City, skirting the opulent vacation homes and resorts that line the Lake Michigan waterfront. Upon reaching Petoskey, the tortuously slow Rte. 119 completes the 31 mi. journey to Cross Village. Although the roads are generally well maintained, drivers should be careful on the 27 mi. stretch of Rte. 119 between Cross Village and Harbor Springs, known as the **Tunnel of Trees.** This patch of road is very narrow and twists through many sharp curves, necessitating slow speeds and care in passing.

North of Traverse City, tiny towns form the center of picturesque cherry orchard communities. Twelve miles outside of the city, orchards line the road around **Acme.** Twenty miles north of Acme, and west on Barnes Park Rd., the village of **Torch Lake** harbors pristine, isolated beaches on **Grand Traverse Bay** at **Barnes County Park.** More cherry trees line the route north of **Atwood,** one of the most prolific areas of the cherry harvest. Though the small towns that line the route are easily missed, they are worth the stop; many have antique and unique clothing shops.

Rolling hills and elaborate homes mark the entrance into **Charlevoix** (SHAR-le-voy), a resort village set in the narrow strip of land between Lake Michigan and Lake Charlevoix. The community that once was the setting for Ernest Hemingway's Nick Adams stories now inspires yachting and sunbathing. The **Charlevoix Area Chamber of Commerce,** 408 Bridge St., dispenses info on golfing, boating, and shopping in the area. (☎547-2101; www.charlevoix.org. Open in summer M-Sa 9am-5pm; low-season M-F 9am-5pm, Sa 10am-4pm.) Lodging rarely comes cheap in this coastal resort town, but the **Colonial Motel ❷**, 6822 U.S. 31 S, is a good option, with cable TV, a grill and picnic area, and easy access to the state park. (☎547-6637. Reservations recommended. Open May-Oct. Singles Su-Th from $35, F-Sa from $65; low-season rates lower. Special rates for longer stays.) Campers who don't mind going without showers and electricity can bask in 81 rustic sites on the shores of Lake Michigan at **Fisherman's Island State Park ❶,** on Bells Bay Rd., 5 mi. south of Charlevoix on U.S. 31. The park offers 5 mi. of undeveloped shoreline, although a section of the beautiful reserve was recently closed after a rare bird was sighted. (☎547-6641 or 800-447-2757. Rustic sites $9. Vehicle permit required, $8 for nonresidents.)

Charlevoix also serves as the gateway to **Beaver Island,** one of the Great Lakes's best-kept secrets. Hiking, boating, biking, and swimming abound on the 53 sq. mi. island, a 2hr. ferry trip from shore. **Ferries** depart from 102 Bridge St., in Charlevoix. (☎547-2311 or 888-446-4095; www.bibco.com. 1-4 per day. Round-trip $35, ages 5-12 $17; bikes $16.) The **Beaver Island Chamber of Commerce** can be found just north of the ferry dock. (☎448-2505; www.beaverisland.org. Open in summer M-F 8am-4pm, Sa 10:30am-2:30pm; low-season M-F 8am-noon.)

PETOSKEY   ☎231

Eighteen miles north of Charlevoix, the slightly larger resort town of Petoskey is best known for its Petoskey Stones: fossilized coral from an ancient sea that remains strewn about the area's beaches. Another vacation haunt of Hemingway, the town honors him with a small collection of memorabilia, including signed first editions, childhood photos, and a typewriter, at the **Little Traverse History Museum,** 100 Depot Ct. (☎347-2620. Open in summer M-F 10am-4pm, Sa-Su 1-4pm. $1, students and children free.) Nearby, off U.S. 31, the gazebo and grassy areas of **Sunset Park Scenic Overlook** are unbeatable places to watch the sunset.

Budget accommodations are hard to come by, but major chains clump at the junction of U.S. 31 and U.S. 131. If you don't mind roughing it, the **Petoskey State Park ❶,** 5 mi. north of downtown off Rte. 119, has 170 sites along Little Traverse Bay. (☎347-2311 or 800-447-2757. Showers and toilets available. Open Apr. to early Nov. Sites with electrical hookup $20. Cabins $37.) Petoskey's **Gaslight District,** just off U.S. 31 downtown, features local crafts and foods in period shops. In the heart of the district, an outdoor collage of coffee cups lures droves of famished passers-by into the **Roast and Toast Cafe ❶,** 309 E. Lake St. Large sandwiches ($4.25-6), a huge array of coffee concoctions, and wickedly delicious smoothies (from $3) ensure that everyone leaves satisfied. (☎347-7767. Open mic Su 6-8pm. Open M-Th 7am-7pm, F-Su 7am-8pm.) The **City Park Grill ❷,** 432 E. Lake St., sells sandwiches ($6-8) in an elegant setting befitting the quaint town. (☎347-0101. Live music W-Sa 10pm. Cover Th-Sa $3. Kitchen open Su-Th 11:30am-10pm, F-Sa 11:30am-11pm; bar closes Su-Tu midnight, W 1am, Th-Sa 2am.) Although it lies 20 mi. east of Petoskey in a remote woodland just outside Indian River, the **Cross in the Woods,** 7078 Rte. 68 (☎238-8973), a 31 ft. bronze Jesus cleaved onto a 55 ft. tall wooden cross, forms a monument to both the religious fervor of Middle America and the country's obsession with size.

UPPER PENINSULA

A multi-million-acre forestland bordered by three of the world's largest lakes, Michigan's Upper Peninsula (U.P.) is among the most scenic, unspoiled stretches of land in the world. Vacationers in the Upper Peninsula escape urban life in a region where cell phones don't work and locals laugh if you ask about the nearest Internet access. Dominated by the **Hiawatha National Forest,** the U.P. is a wonderland of hiking, biking, hunting, and kayaking. Those who are less adventurous can enjoy the many scenic outlooks in the region's parks. Deposits of copper have colored the cliffs with a tapestry of colors that draws visitors from all over the state.

Only 24,000 people live in the U.P.'s largest town, **Marquette.** Here hikers enjoy numerous treks, including Michigan's section of the **North Country Trail,** a scenic trail extending from New York to North Dakota. The **North Country Trail Association,** 229 E. Main Street, Lowell 49331 (☎ 616-897-5987; www.northcountrytrail.org), provides details on the path. A vibrant spectrum of foliage makes autumn a beautiful time to hike; in the winter, skiers and snowmobilers replace hikers as layers of snow blanket the trails. After the ice thaws, dozens of pristine rivers beckon canoers. Those who heed the call of the water should contact the **Michigan Association of Paddlesport Providers,** P.O. Box 522, Cadillac, MI 49601 (☎ 231-862-3227; www.michigancanoe.com), for canoeing tips.

Lodging is fairly inexpensive throughout the U.P., and outside the major tourist spots motel rooms start at around $30. The peninsula is littered with **campgrounds.** (Reservations at National Forest sites: ☎ 877-444-6777; www.reserveusa.com. Reservations at state parks: ☎ 800-447-2757; www.michigan.gov/dnr.) Bring extra blankets—temperatures in these parts drop to 50°F or lower, even in July. For regional cuisine, indulge in the Friday night **fish-fry**—all-you-can-eat whitefish, perch, or walleye buffets served in most restaurants. The local ethnic specialty is a **pastie** *(PASS-tee)*, a meat pie imported by Cornish miners in the 19th century.

▐ PRACTICAL INFORMATION

Helpful **Welcome Centers** surround the U.P. at its six main entry points: **Ironwood,** 801 W. Cloverland Dr. (☎ 932-3330; open daily June-Sept. 8am-6pm; Oct.-May 8am-4pm); **Iron Mountain,** 618 S. Stephenson Ave. (☎ 774-4201; open daily 8am-4pm); **Marquette,** 2201 U.S. 41 S (☎ 249-9066; open daily 9am-5pm); **Menominee,** 1343 10th Ave. (☎ 863-6496; open daily 8am-4pm); and **Saint Ignace,** on I-75 N north of the Mackinac Bridge (☎ 643-6979; open daily June-Aug. 8am-6pm; Sept.-May 9am-5pm); **Sault Sainte Marie,** 943 Portage Ave. W (☎ 632-8242; open daily 9am-5pm). The **Upper Peninsula Travel and Recreation Association** (☎ 800-562-7134; info line staffed M-F 8am-4:30pm) publishes the invaluable *Upper Peninsula Travel Planner.* For additional help planning a trip, write or call the **US Forestry Service** at the **Hiawatha National Forest,** 2727 N. Lincoln Rd., Escanaba 49829 (☎ 786-4062). **Area Code:** 906.

SAULT SAINTE MARIE AND THE EASTERN U.P.   ☎ 906

The shipping industry rules in gritty Sault ("Soo") Ste. Marie, where "the locks" are the primary attraction for both tourists and prospective residents. Back in the day, St. Mary's River, the only waterway linking Lake Superior to the other Great Lakes, dropped 21 vertical feet over one mile in this area, rendering the river impassable by boat. In 1855, entrepreneurs built the first modern locks, an advancement that opened up industrial opportunities that led the region to relative economic prosperity. Now the busiest in the world, the city's four locks float over 12,000 ships annually, lowering them through successive, emptying chambers. Raging rapids still exist on the Canadian side of the river, juxtaposing the tamed water of the locks, but a plan is currently underway to build two new locks there.

On the American side of the bridge, a 2hr. **Soo Locks Boat Tour** leaves from both 1157 and 515 E. Portage Ave., and introduces travelers to the mechanics of the locks' operation. (☎ 632-6301 or 800-432-6301; www.soolocks.com. Call for departure times. Open mid-May to mid-Oct. $18, ages 13-18 $16, ages 4-12 $8.50, under 4 free. Call ahead for specific dock.) The **Soo Locks Park,** accessed from Portage

Ave., gives visitors a close-up view of the 1000 ft. supertankers that use the locks (open daily 6am-midnight). For a panoramic view of the locks, visitors can ascend the **Tower of History,** 326 E. Portage Ave., which has three levels of observation decks and exhibits tracing the city's history. (☎632-3658. Open daily mid-May to mid-Oct. 10am-6pm. $4, ages 13-18 $2.) On the waterfront, at the end of Johnston St., lies the **Museum Ship Valley Camp,** a 1917 steam-powered freighter turned tribute to the sailing industry. A theater and the **Marine Hall of Fame** highlight the museum. (☎632-3658. Open daily July-Aug. 10am-8pm; mid-May to June and Sept. to mid-Oct. 10am-6pm. $8, ages 6-16 $4.) The **Soo Locks Visitor Center,** 300 W. Portage Ave. in the park, dispenses info. (☎253-9101. Open May-Nov. daily 7am-11pm).

MIDDLE OF THE PENINSULA   ☎906

The western branch of the **Hiawatha National Forest** straddles the middle of the peninsula, offering limitless wilderness activities for outdoors enthusiasts. The **visitors center,** at the junction of M-28 and County Rte. H-58 in **Munising,** serves as the primary gateway to the forest and helps administer over a dozen rustic **campsites ❶.** (☎387-3700, or 877-444-6777 for reservations at all National Forest Service sites. Pit toilets, running water, no showers. Hours vary, usually open daily mid-May to mid-Oct. 8am-6pm; mid-Oct. to mid-May M-Sa 9am-4:30pm. Campsites open Apr.-Nov. Sites $7-15.) The Munising Visitors Center also administers the not-to-be-missed **Pictured Rocks National Lakeshore,** where **Lake Superior's** waters—saturated with copper, manganese, and iron oxide—paint the cliffs with multicolored bands. Various overlooks within the park offer spectacular glimpses of the rocks, but the **Pictured Rocks Boat Cruise,** at the city dock in Munising, gives the best view. (☎387-2379; www.pictured-rocks.com. Tours leave July to mid-Aug. daily every hr. 9am-5pm. 3hr. tour $27, ages 6-13 $12, under 6 free.) The forest and lakeshore share a **visitors center** at the intersection of M-28 and Rte. 58 in Munising. (☎387-3700. Open mid-May to mid-Oct. daily 8am-6pm; mid-Oct. to mid-May M-Sa 9am-4:30pm.) Heading east from Munising, County Rte. 58—a bumpy, partially unpaved gem of a road—weaves along the lakeshore, eventually ending up in Grand Marais. Ask about road conditions at the visitors center. For a paved (but less scenic) alternative from Munising to Grand Marais, go east on Rte. 28, then north on Rte. 77. At **Miner's Falls,** 10 mi. east of Munising off Rte. 58, a 1½ mi. round-trip hike rewards visitors with a staggering, rocky waterfall, where torrents of water empty into the rocky, bubbling cauldron below. Two miles farther up the road, **Miner's Castle Overlook** allows trekkers to walk up to the edge of the cliffs and see the colorful rocks across the deep blue water of the lake. Twenty miles east of Miner's Castle off Rte. 58, visitors can stroll, birdwatch, or collect smooth stones along the shore at **Twelve Mile Beach ❶.** (Running water, pit toilets. Open May-Oct. Self-registered rustic campsites $10.) From atop the sandy ▧**Log Slide,** 5 mi. west of Grand Marais on Rte. 58, hikers are rewarded with a magnificent view of Lake Superior. Campers should check at the Munising Visitors Center to ascertain road conditions before entering the lakeshore, as some portions of Rte. 58 may be hazardous. Twelve Mile Beach and the Log Slide are most easily accessed from Grand Marais. Go east from Munising on Rte. 28, then north on Rte. 77.

As an alternative to the campsites at Twelve Mile Beach, **backcountry camping permits ❶** are available from the **Munising** or **Grand Sable Visitors Center,** 3 mi. west of Grand Marais on Rte. 58. (☎494-2660. Open mid-May to early Oct. daily 9am-7pm. 2-week permits $8 for 1 person, 2-6 people $15, 7-20 people $30.) For non-campers, the **Poplar Bluff Cabins ❸,** 12 mi. east of Munising on Rte. 28, then 6 mi. south from Shingleton on Rte. 94, have small, functional lakeview cottages with kitchens and hot showers. (☎452-6271. Free use of boats on lake. Cabins $60 per night, $250-350 per week.) Those looking for comic relief should stop by **Da Yooper's Tourist Trap,** 490 N. Steel St., 12 mi. west of Marquette on U.S. 41. This little theme park is the ultimate collection of tacky Americana. The lawn holds the world's largest operational chainsaw and biggest rifle, while the backyard pays homage to Yoopers (U.P. residents) of the past. (☎800-628-9978. Open M-F 9am-9pm, Sa 9am-8pm, Su 9am-7pm. Free.)

KEWEENAW PENINSULA ☎906

Located at Michigan's northern-most point, the Keweenaw (KEE-wa-naw) Peninsula—with its lush forests, low mountains, and smooth stone beaches—doesn't seem like part of the Midwest. The peninsula once basked in the glory of a copper mining boom, but when mining petered out, the land was left barren. Now, Keweenaw has become a haven for outdoor enthusiasts. Towering pines shade hiking trails while state parks provide beaches and camping grounds. In the winter, visitors don skis and snowshoes to trek across the mountains.

The **Porcupine Mountain Wilderness State Park ❶,** affectionately known as "The Porkies," hugs Lake Superior at the base of the peninsula, 18 mi. west of **Ontonagon** on S.R. 107. (☎800-447-2757; www.michigan.gov/dnr. Primitive sites $9; with toilets, showers, and electricity at the Union $19. Call the park directly at ☎885-5275 for 2- to 8-person cabins, $45-55.) The **visitors center** on S. Boundary Rd. near the junction of Rte. 107, provides required vehicle **permits** good for all Michigan state parks. (☎885-5208. Open mid-May to mid-Oct. daily 10am-8pm. Permits $6 per day for Michigan residents, $8 for non-residents; $24/$29 per year.) Eight miles inside the park on S.R. 107, **Lake of the Clouds** outlook leads visitors to a ledge, where woods give way to a view of the lake etching out a path between rugged cliffs and mountains in the Big Carp River valley. **Summit Peak,** off Boundary Rd., allows visitors to ascend a lookout tower offering stunning vistas of Lake Superior and the untouched forests of the park. Farther east, at the end of Boundary Rd., the **Presque Isle Falls** are a great place to relax and listen to the water rushing past. From the park, paths lead into the **Old Growth Forest,** the largest tract of uncut forest between the Rockies and the Adirondacks. The park has 95 mi. of hiking trails, with circuits ranging in length from 12 to 26 mi. The **Pinkerton Trail** winds 2½ mi. from S. Boundary Rd. to lakefront beaches and campsites.

The twin towns of **Houghton** and **Hancock** link the Porkies to the rest of Keweenaw. The towns are home to an ethnic enclave of fiercely proud Finns, and locals head to **Suomi ❶,** 54 Huron St. in downtown Houghton, for authentic dishes like *pannukakku* with *nisu* toast ($4. ☎482-3220. Entrees $3-7. Open M-F 6am-6pm, Sa 6am-4pm, Su 7am-2pm.) Eight miles north of Hancock on Rte. 203, **McLain State Park ❶** is home to some of the area's best camping. The campground rests along a 2 mi. agate beach and harbors an impressive lighthouse. (Reservations ☎482-0278 or 800-447-2757. 103 sites with electricity $19; cabins $50-65. 15 walk-in sites. Vehicle permit required.) From the state park, U.S. 41 winds north through Keweenaw. Drivers and bikers can take Rte. 26, off Rte. 41, to access the most scenic path to the tip of the peninsula, winding through small lakeside villages and desolate ghost towns where copper miners once toiled. Rising over 1300 ft. above sea level, the breathtaking ◪**Brockway Mountain Drive** (6 mi.), between Eagle Harbor and Copper Harbor, offers a panoramic view of the pine-covered peaks and lake-filled valleys of the Upper Peninsula. In **Copper Harbor,** the northernmost town in Michigan, the **Keweenaw Adventure Company,** 155 Gratiot St., provides kayaks and bikes to those who wish to explore the wild side of Keweenaw. (☎289-4303. 2½hr. intro paddle $29; bike rentals $30 per half-day, $40 per day.)

GREAT LAKES

ILLINOIS

At first glance, Illinois is a state with dual personalities. In the northern part of the state, Chicago gleams as a Midwestern metropolis with top-notch museums, stunning architecture, and suburban sprawl stretching into two neighboring states. Once removed from suburbia, a second Illinois—the "Land of Lincoln"—reaches outward with endless corn fields and small towns. In its politics and its culture, Illinois is a compromise between these contrasting landscapes, and can claim a mix of urban chic and rural values as perhaps no other state can.

⚡ PRACTICAL INFORMATION

Capital: Springfield.

Visitor Info: Chicago Cultural Center, 77 E. Randolph St., Chicago 60607 (☎800-226-6632; www.enjoyillinois.com). **Springfield Convention and Visitors Bureau,** 109 N. 7th St. (☎789-2360 or 800-545-7300; www.visit-springfieldillinois.com. Open M-F 8am-5pm.)

Postal Abbreviation: IL. **Sales Tax:** 6.25-9.25%, depending on the city.

CHICAGO ☎312

From the renowned museums and shops that dot the downtown lakefront to the varied and vibrant music and comedy scenes, Chicago blends big-city fun with Midwestern charm. Retaining some of the flavor of its industrial legacy, Chicago is both a contemporary city and a place acutely aware of its historical roots. A symbol of industrialized city life in middle America since the late 1800s, Chicago continues to wear the mantle admirably—travelers can expect to find a city of many voices, diverse neighborhoods, and spectacular food and entertainment options.

⌨ INTERCITY TRANSPORTATION

Airports: O'Hare International (☎773-686-3700; www.ohare.com), off I-90. Although O'Hare is only 18 mi. away, the drive from downtown can take up to 2hr., depending on traffic. The Blue Line **Rapid Train** runs between the Airport El station and downtown (40min.-1hr.; M-F 5am-8pm, Sa-Su 5am-11pm; $1.75). **Midway Airport** (☎773-839-2500), on the western edge of the South Side, often offers less expensive flights. To get downtown, take the El Orange Line from the Midway stop. **Airport Express** (☎888-284-3826; www.airportexpress.com) connects to downtown hotels from O'Hare (45min.-1hr., daily every 10-15min. 4am-11:30pm, $21) and Midway (30-45min., daily every 15min. 4am-10:30pm, $16).

Trains: Amtrak, Union Station, 225 S. Canal St. (☎655-2101), at Adams St. just west of the Loop. Amtrak's nationwide hub. Getting there by bus is easiest; buses #1, 60, 125, 151, and 156 all stop at the station. Otherwise, take the El to State and Adams St., then walk 7 blocks west on Adams. Station open 5:30am-midnight; tickets sold daily 7am-10:30pm. To: **Detroit** (6½-7hr., 3 per day, $23-57); **Milwaukee** (1½hr., 6 per day, $20); **New York** (22hr., 2 per day, $81-85).

Buses: Greyhound, 630 W. Harrison St. (☎408-5980), at Jefferson and Desplaines Ave. Take the El to Linton, or buses #60, 125, 156, or 157 to the terminal. Station open 24hr.; tickets sold 5am-2am. To: **Detroit** (6-7hr., 6 per day, $30-33); **Indianapolis** (3½-4½hr., 9 per day, $29); **Milwaukee** (2hr., 9 per day, $15). **Van Galder** in Union Station (☎608-752-5407 or 800-747-0994; www.vangalderbus.com) runs to **Madison** (3-4hr., 4 per day, $22).

GREAT LAKES

Chicago

🏠 ACCOMMODATIONS
Arlington House, **2**
International House, **3**

🍖 FOOD
Army and Lou's, **4**

🎷 NIGHTLIFE
The Green Mill, **1**

0 ——— 2 miles
0 ——— 2 kilometers

MORTON GROVE
NILES
SKOKIE
TO BAHA'I HOUSE OF WORSHIP (2mi)
Northwestern University
EVANSTON
Harlem Ave.
Skokie Blvd.
Crawford Ave.
N. Shore Channel
N. Shore Channel
Chicago Ave.
Sheridan Rd.
Rogers Park
Milwaukee Ave.
TO O'HARE INT'L. AIRPORT (4mi)
Forest Preserve
LINCOLNWOOD
Western Ave.
Lincoln Ave.
Loyola University of Chicago
HARWOOD HEIGHTS
Lawrence Ave.
Andersonville
Ashland Ave.
Lake Shore Dr.
Broadway
Irving Park
Uptown
Milwaukee Ave.
Belmont Ave.
Wrigleyville
Wrigley Field
Fullerton St.
N. Br. Chicago River
Lakeview
Lincoln Park
Lake Michigan
North Ave.
Bucktown
Lincoln Park
Lincoln Park Zoo
Chicago Historical Society
Grand Ave.
Humboldt Park
Wicker Park
Near North
SEE DOWNTOWN CHICAGO MAP
Frank Lloyd Wright Home & Studio
OAK PARK
Austin
Garfield Park
United Center
Greektown
Chicago River
Madison St.
Congress Pkwy.
Cook County Hospital
Hull House
U. of Illinois at Chicago
Grant Park
Soldier Field
Roosevelt Rd.
CICERO
Douglas Park
Near South Side
Cermak Rd.
BERWYN
Pilsen
Chinatown
Des Plaines River
Chicago Sanitary and Ship Canal
Bridgeport
Comiskey Park
Back of the Yards
Damen Ave.
Burnham Park
55th St.
Garfield Blvd.
Roble House
Museum of Science and Industry
Chicago Midway Airport
Englewood
University of Chicago
Hyde Park
Jackson Park
S. Chicago Ave.
S. Shore Dr.
BEDFORD PARK
Marquette Park
79th St.
BURBANK
Cicero Ave.
Pulaski Rd.
Kedzie Ave.
Western Ave.
Dan Ryan Woods
Ashland Ave.
Halsted St.
Michigan Ave.
EVERGREEN PARK
95th St.
OAK LAWN
111th St.
Crawford Ave.
WORTH
Calumet Sag Channel
ALSIP
Morgan Park
Pullman
Lake Calumet
TO INDIANA DUNES STATE PARK (38mi)
William W. Powers State Conservation Area
Calumet River
Mackinaw Ave.
Ewing Ave.

ORIENTATION

Chicago dominates the entire northeastern corner of Illinois, running along 29 mi. of the southwest Lake Michigan shorefront. Almost all roads lead to Chicago; the city sits at the center of a web of interstates, rail lines, and airplane routes, so most cross-country traffic swings through the city. A good map is essential for navigating Chicago; pick up a free one at the tourist office or any CTA station.

The flat, sprawling city's grids usually make sense. Navigation is pretty straightforward, whether by car or by public transit. At the city's center is the **Loop** (p. 598), Chicago's downtown business district and the public transit system's hub. The block numbering system starts from the intersection of State and Madison, increasing by about 800 per mi. The Loop is bounded loosely by the Chicago River to the north and west, Wabash Ave. to the east, and Congress Pkwy. to the south. Directions in *Let's Go* are usually from downtown. South of the Loop, east-west street numbers increase toward the south. Many ethnic neighborhoods lie in this area (see **Neighborhoods,** p. 592), but farther south, avoid the struggling South Side. Most of the city's best spots for food and nightlife jam into the first few miles north of the Loop. Beware the 45mph speed limit on **Lake Shore Drive,** a scenic freeway hugging Lake Michigan that offers express north-south connections.

To avoid driving and parking in the city, daytrippers can leave their cars in one of the suburban park-and-ride lots ($1.50-1.75); call CTA (see below) for info. Parking downtown costs around $8-15 per day. Check out the lots west of the South Loop and across the canal from the **Sears Tower** (p. 599) for the best deals.

It is a good idea to stay within the boundaries made apparent by tourist maps. Aside from small pockets such as Hyde Park and the University of Chicago, areas south of the loop and west of the little ethnic enclaves are mostly industrial or residential and pose a safety threat to the unwary tourist. **Cabrini Green** (bounded by W. Armitage Ave. on the north, W. Chicago Ave. on the south, Sedgwick St. on the east, and Halsted St. on the west) was once the site of an infamously dangerous public housing development and sits within tourist map borders. (The neighborhood is now part of a city experiment in mixed-income housing and is surrounded by redeveloped areas.)

NEIGHBORHOODS

The diverse array of communities that composes the Windy City justifies its title as a "city of neighborhoods." North of the Loop, LaSalle Dr. loosely defines the west edge of the posh **Near North** area; here, most activity is centered along the **Magnificent Mile** of Michigan Ave. between the Chicago River and Oak St. A trendy restaurant and nightlife district, **River North** lines N. Clark St., just north of the Loop and west of Michigan Ave. The primarily residential **Gold Coast** shimmers on N. Lakeshore Dr. between Oak St. and North Ave. The **Bucktown/ Wicker Park** area, at the intersection of North, Damen, and Milwaukee Ave., is the place to be for artsy, cutting-edge cafes and nightlife. **Lincoln Park** revolves around the junction of N. Clark St., Lincoln Ave., and Halsted St. To the north, near the 3000 block of N. Clark St. and N. Halsted St., sits **Lakeview,** a gay-friendly area teeming with food and nightlife that becomes **Wrigleyville** in the 4000 block. **Andersonville,** 5 mi. farther up N. Clark St. north of Foster Ave., is the center of the Swedish community, though immigrants from Asia and the Middle East have recently settled here.

The near south and west sides are filled with other vibrant ethnic districts. While much of the German community has scattered, the beer halls and restaurants in the 3000 and 4000 blocks of N. Lincoln Ave. keep the torch of German cul-

GREAT LAKES

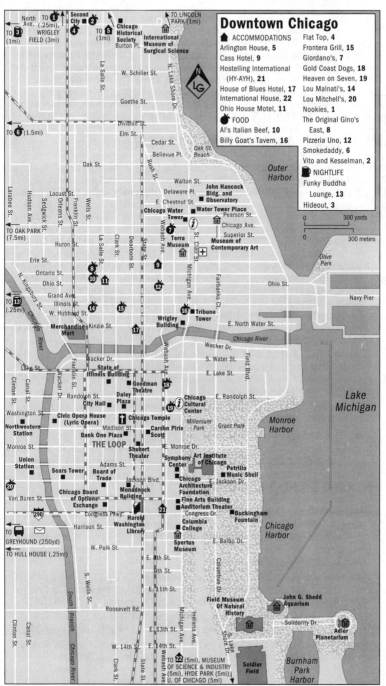

Downtown Chicago

⌂ ACCOMMODATIONS
Arlington House, **5**
Cass Hotel, **9**
Hostelling International (HY-AYH), **21**
House of Blues Hotel, **17**
International House, **22**
Ohio House Motel, **11**

🍎 FOOD
Al's Italian Beef, **10**
Billy Goat's Tavern, **16**

Flat Top, **4**
Frontera Grill, **15**
Giordano's, **7**
Gold Coast Dogs, **18**
Heaven on Seven, **19**
Lou Malnati's, **14**
Lou Mitchell's, **20**
Nookies, **1**
The Original Gino's East, **8**
Pizzeria Uno, **12**
Smokedaddy, **6**
Vito and Kesselman, **2**

🎵 NIGHTLIFE
Funky Buddha Lounge, **13**
Hideout, **3**

ture burning. The former residents of **Greektown** have also moved, but S. Halsted St. still houses authentic Greek restaurants. *The area is bustling and safe until the restaurants close, at which point tourists wisely clear out.* Although nearby **Little Italy** has fallen prey to the encroachments of **University of Illinois at Chicago (UIC),** good dining options remain. Jewish and Indian enclaves center on Devon Ave., from Western Ave. to the Chicago River. The **Pilsen** neighborhood, around 18th St., offers a slice of Mexico and a developing art community. Chicago's Polish population is the largest of any city outside of Warsaw; those seeking Polish cuisine should go to N. Milwaukee Ave. between blocks 2800 and 3100.

ⴹ LOCAL TRANSPORTATION

Public Transit: The **Chicago Transit Authority (CTA),** 350 N. Wells, on the 7th fl. of the Mart (☎836-7000 or 888-968-7282; www.transitchicago.com), runs efficient trains, subways, and buses. The **elevated rapid transit train system,** called the **El,** encircles the Loop. The El operates 24hr., but check ahead for schedules, as *late-night service is infrequent and unsafe in many areas.* Some buses do not run all night; call the CTA for schedules and routes. Many routes are "express," and different routes may run along the same track. Helpful CTA maps are available at many stations and at the Chicago Visitor Information Center. Train and bus fare $1.75; add $0.25 for express routes. Transfers ($0.25) allow for up to 2 more rides on different routes during the following 2hr. Buy **transit cards** (min. $1.75) for fares and transfers at all CTA stations on the Internet and at some museums. CTA also offers a variety of consecutive-day passes for tourists, available at airports and Amtrak stations, ranging $5-18, depending on length of pass. On Sa from early May to late Oct., a **Loop Tour Train** departs on a free 40min. elevated tour of the downtown area (tickets must be picked up at the **Chicago Cultural Center;** see p. 594. Tours start at 11:35am, 12:15, 12:55, 1:35pm).

Commuter Rail: METRA, 547 W. Jackson St. (M-F ☎322-6777, Sa-Su 836-7000; www.metrarail.com), distributes free maps and schedules for its extensive commuter rail network of 11 rail lines and 4 downtown stations. Open M-F 8am-5pm. Fare $2-6.60, depending on distance.

Suburban Bus: PACE (☎836-7000; www.pacebus.com) runs the suburban bus system. Many free or cheap shuttle services run throughout the Loop.

Taxi: Yellow Cab ☎829-4222. **Flash Cab** ☎773-561-4444.

Car Rental: Dollar Rent-a-Car, (☎800-800-3665; www.dollar.com), at O'Hare and Midway St. Must be 21 with major credit card to rent; under-25 surcharge $18 per day.

ⴷ PRACTICAL INFORMATION

Visitor Info: Chicago has 2 visitors centers located at well-known landmarks. **Chicago Cultural Center,** 77 E. Randolph St., at Michigan Ave., has maps and tour info. Open M-F 10am-6pm, Sa 10am-5pm, Su 11am-5pm. **Water Works Visitors Center,** 163 E. Pearson St. at Michigan Ave., is located in the Water Tower Pumping Station. Open daily 7:30am-7pm. **Visitor hotline,** ☎877-244-2246; open 24hr.

Bi-Gay-Lesbian Resources: Gay and Lesbian Hotline, ☎773-929-4357. Operates Su-W and F 6-10pm. For current info on events and nightlife, pick up the *Windy City Times* or *Gay Chicago* at Lakeview's **Unabridged Books,** 3251 N. Broadway (☎773-883-9119).

Medical Services: Northwestern Memorial Hospital, 251 E. Huron St. (☎926-2000), near Michigan Ave.; **emergency division** at 250 E. Erie St. (☎926-5188). Open 24hr.

Internet Access: Free at the **Chicago Public Library.** Main branch at 400 S. State St. (☎747-4300), at Congress. Open M-Th 9am-7pm, F-Sa 9am-5pm, Su 1-5pm.

Post Office: 433 W. Harrison St. (☎983-8183 or 800-275-8777), at the Chicago River. Open 24hr. **Postal Code:** 60607. **Area Code:** 312 (downtown) or 773 (elsewhere in Chicago); 708, 630, or 847 (outside the city limits). In text, 312 unless noted.

⚡ ACCOMMODATIONS

Find a cheap place to rest your head at one of Chicago's many hostels. The motels on **Lincoln Avenue** in Lincoln Park are moderately priced. **At Home Inn Chicago** (☎800-375-7084) offers a reservation and referral service for many downtown B&Bs. Most have a two-night minimum stay, and rooms average $120. Travelers should be aware of Chicago's 15% tax on most accommodation rates.

Hostelling International—Chicago (HI), 24 E. Congress Pkwy. (☎360-0300; www.hichicago.org), off Wabash Ave. in the Loop. Easy access to Loop attractions, organized activities, and a student center guarantee a memorable experience. Internet access, laundry, and an amazing kitchen. All rooms with A/C. Check-out 11am. Reservations recommended. Dorms $35, nonmembers $38. ❷

Arlington House, 616 W. Arlington Pl. (☎773-929-5380 or 800-467-8355), off Clark St. Located on a quiet, safe residential street near food and nightlife, this hostel in Lincoln Park features tidy dorms and a friendly atmosphere. Kitchen, TV room, laundry. Linen and deposit $10. Dorms $25; singles with shared bath $55, with private bath $70. ❶

House of Blues Hotel, 330 N. Dearborn St. (☎245-0333; www.loewshotels.com). This unique hotel, with its eclectic mix of Gothic, Moroccan, Indian, and American folk art influences, is hard to beat. The colorful fusion of architectural and decorative styles is complemented by excellent service and prime location near entertainment and food. Spacious, vibrant rooms come with big bathrooms, TV, VCR, CD player, in-room Internet access, and video games. Music F-Sa in lobby bar. Access to Crunch gym $15. Rooms from $119, but prices increase during peak season; check the web for lowest rates. ❺

Cass Hotel, 640 N. Wabash Ave. (☎787-4030 or 800-227-7850; www.casshotel.com), just north of the Loop. Take the El to State St. Reasonable rates, a convenient location near the Magnificent Mile, and $2 breakfasts at the coffeeshop make this hotel a favorite find of the budget-conscious. Small but clean rooms with TV, A/C, and private bath. Coin laundry. Key deposit $5 if paying cash. Parking $19 per day. Reservations recommended. Rooms from $69; check website for lowest rates. Wheelchair accessible. ❹

Ohio House Motel, 600 N. LaSalle St. (☎943-6000), at Ohio St. This 2-story inn looks out of place among its skyscraping neighbors, but it puts guests within easy walking distance of Near North and Loop attractions. TV, A/C, and private baths. Reservations recommended. Queen or 2 twin beds $85; 2 doubles $115. ❹

International House, 1414 E. 59th St. (☎773-753-2270), in Hyde Park, off Lake Shore Dr. Take the Illinois Central Railroad from the Michigan Ave. station (20min.) or METRA South Shore Line to 59th St. and walk ½ block west. On the grounds of the University of Chicago; *avoid walking off-campus at night*. Common areas and an outdoor courtyard filled with the activity of a diverse group of students augment neat, spacious singles with shared bath at this newly renovated hostel. Linen provided. Laundry, game room, exercise room, and coffee shop. Reservations with credit card required. Rooms $52. ❸

🍴 FOOD

Chicago's many culinary delights, from pizza to po' boy sandwiches, are among its main attractions. One of the best guides to city dining is the monthly *Chicago* magazine, which includes an extensive restaurant section, indexed by price, cuisine, and quality. It can be found at tourist offices and newsstands everywhere.

PIZZA

No trip to Chicago would be complete without sampling deep-dish pizza. Over the years, several deep-dish empires have competed to conquer the Windy City. Each local has a preference, but these samplings should provide a good overview.

■ **Giordano's,** 730 N. Rush St. (☎951-0747), is the home of the famous stuffed crust. An absurdly overfilled pizza, with heaps of cheese and other toppings sizzling inside it, is $11-24. The "not less famous" thin crust pie ($7-24) is also satisfying. Lines can be long, but customers can pre-order while they wait. Open M-Th 11am-11pm, F-Sa 11am-midnight, Su noon-11pm. Call for other locations throughout the city. ❸

Lou Malnati's, 439 N. Wells St. (☎828-9800), at Hubbard downtown. A Chicago mainstay for over 30 years, Lou's is a sports-themed chain offering deep-dish masterpieces. Pizzas take 30min. There are more than 20 branches throughout the Chicago area. Pizzas $4.50-20. Open M-Th 11am-11pm, F-Sa 11am-midnight, Su noon-10pm. ❷

The Original Gino's East, 633 N. Wells St. (☎988-4200), at Ontario. Life-sized tributes to the Blues Brothers overlook customer-decorated walls at this legendary deep-dish joint. Open M-Th 11am-9:30pm, F-Sa 11am-11pm, Su noon-9:30pm. ❹

Pizzeria Uno, 29 E. Ohio St. (☎321-1000), at Wabash. It may look like any other Uno's, but rest assured the original is of a different order than its offspring. Lines are long, but the world-famous pies have a made-from-scratch taste. Individual-sized pies ($5.50) take 25min. Open M-F 11:30am-1am, Sa 11:30am-2am, Su 11:30am-11:30pm. ❷

'ROUND THE LOOP

Many of Chicago's best restaurants, from ragin' Cajun to tried-and-true German, inhabit the streets of the Loop.

■ **Lou Mitchell's,** 565 W. Jackson Blvd. (☎939-3111), 2 blocks west of the Sears Tower. Situated at the jumping-off point of historic Route 66, this retro diner has been stuffing faithful customers for almost 80 years. Start the day with "meltaway pancakes" that take up the whole plate ($5.25) or hearty omelettes served simmering in the skillet ($6.50-8.50). Cash only. Open M-Sa 5:30am-3pm, Su 7am-3pm. ❷

Heaven on Seven, 111 N. Wabash Ave. (☎263-6443), 7th fl. of the Garland Bldg. This is paradise—Cajun-style. Mardi Gras and voodoo decor compliment the endless hot sauce and spicy cuisine perfectly. Lunchtime lines are long, but the jambalaya is fantastic. Open M-F 8:30am-5pm, Sa 10am-3pm. Cash only. Other locations at 600 N. Michigan Ave. (☎280-7774) and 3478 N. Clark St. (☎773-477-7818). ❸

Gold Coast Dogs, 159 N. Wabash Ave. (☎527-1222), between Randolph and Lake St. Hot dogs are sacred in Chicago, but only when topped Second City-style with a veritable salad of relish, onions, pickles, and tomatoes. Locals rank Gold Coast as the best. "One Magnificent Dog" will set you back $2.19. Open M-F 7am-10pm, Sa-Su 11am-8pm. ❶

RIVER NORTH

River North houses some of the trendiest eateries in town, as well as Chicago's famous pizzerias (see **Pizza**, p. 596).

■ **Al's Italian Beef,** 169 W. Ontario (☎943-3222), at Wells. Featuring layers of beef on top of a huge sausage, an Italian beef sandwich ($4.69) is a Chicago institution guaranteed to expand your waistline. Open M-Th 10am-midnight, F-Sa 10am-3am, Su 11am-10pm.

Frontera Grill, 445 N. Clark St. (☎661-1434), between Illinois and Hubbard St. Take El Red Line to Grand/State. Frontera delivers what many claim is the best authentic Mexican cuisine in the region, changing their menu frequently in order to use the freshest seasonal ingredients in their superb entrees ($15-20). The usual 1-1½hr. wait is bearable if you snag a bar seat and order appetizers (from $5). Lunch Tu-F 11:30am-2:30pm, Sa 10:30am-2:30pm. Dinner Tu 5:20-10pm, W-Th 5-10pm, F-Sa 5-11pm. ❹

Billy Goat's Tavern, 430 N. Michigan Ave. (☎222-1525). Buried deep below the Magnificent Mile on lower Michigan Ave., locals and professional types gather at this no-frills joint to grab a burger fresh off the grill, down a cocktail, and watch the ball game. Delicious "cheezeborgers" $2.85. Open daily 6:30am-2am. ❶

SOUL FOOD

Head to the **South Side** for good, cheap soul food, like ribs, fried chicken, and collard greens. *Be very careful south of the Loop,* though, especially after dark. **Wicker Park,** to the north, is another option for satisfying soul food.

☒ **Army & Lou's,** 422 E. 75th St. (☎773-483-3100), on the South Side. Locals come here for some of the best southern fare around, served in an upscale setting. Fried chicken and 2 sides $9; mixed greens and ham $9. Open M and W-Su 9am-10pm. ❷

Dixie Kitchen & Bait Shop, 5225A S. Harper St. (☎773-363-4943). Tucked in a shopping center near 52nd St. in Hyde Park, this place is a local hot spot. Fried green tomatoes ($5) and oyster po' boy sandwiches ($8) are among Dixie's southern highlights. Blackened Voodoo beer $2. Open Su-Th 11am-10pm, F-Sa 11am-11pm. ❷

The Smokedaddy, 1804 W. Division St. (☎773-772-6656; www.thesmokedaddy.com), north of the Loop in Wicker Park. Fantastic rib platters ($9.50-20) and pulled pork sandwiches ($7) merit the neon "WOW" sign out front. Live blues nightly. Open Su-W 11:30am-midnight, Th-Sa 11:30am-1am. ❷

GREEKTOWN

☒ **The Parthenon,** 314 S. Halsted St. (☎726-2407). The staff converses in Greek, the murals transport you to the Mediterranean, and the food wins top awards. The tasty Greek Feast family-style dinner ($17 per person) includes everything from *saganaki* (flaming goat cheese) to baklava. Open M-Su 11am-1am. ❸

Rodity's, 222 S. Halsted St. (☎454-0800), between Adams St. and Jackson Blvd. With slightly cheaper fare than the other Greektown options (daily specials around $10), Rodity's prepares more than generous portions of spinach and cheese-filled *spanakopita* ($8) and other Greek treats. Open Su-Th 11am-midnight, F-Sa 11am-1am. ❷

LINCOLN PARK

Cafe Ba-Ba-Reeba!, 2024 N. Halsted St. (☎773-935-5000), just north of Armitage. Hard to miss with its colorful facade and bustling interior, the sprawling Ba-Ba-Reeba pleases an upbeat crowd with unbeatable tapas ($4-8) and hearty Spanish *paellas* ($9-15 per person). During the summer, sip sangria ($4-5) on the outdoor terrace. Lunch Sa-Su noon-5pm. Dinner Su-Th 5-10pm, F-Sa 5pm-midnight. Reservations recommended. ❸

Potbelly Sandwich Works, 2264 N. Lincoln Ave. (☎773-528-1405), between Belden and Webster. Originally an antique shop whose owners also made sandwiches for customers, this laid-back deli offers delicious subs ($4), smoothies and thick shakes ($3), and cozy booths. Open daily 11am-11pm. Call for additional locations. ❶

Penny's Noodle Shop, 950 W. Diversey Ave. (☎773-281-8448), at Sheffield Ave. One of the best budget options in town, Penny's delivers generous portions of Asian noodles (all under $6) in a hip setting to scores of locals who pack the place at all hours. Open Su-Th 11am-11pm, F-Sa 11am-10:30pm. Call for additional locations. ❷

ANDERSONVILLE

Kopi, A Traveler's Cafe, 5317 N. Clark St. (☎773-989-5674), near Foster St., a 10min. walk from the Berwyn El. Kopi provides a friendly refuge and caffeine fix for travelers. Sip on espresso ($1.35) while browsing the extensive travel library. Music M nights. Open Su-Th 8am-11pm, F-Sa 8am-midnight. ❶

GREAT LAKES

Ann Sather, 5207 N. Clark St. (☎773-271-6677). One of the last remaining authentic Swedish diners left in the neighborhood delights locals with their wildly popular and addictively gooey cinnamon rolls ($4). Open M and W-F 7am-2:30pm, Sa-Su 7am-4pm. Call for other locations. ❶

BUCKTOWN/WICKER PARK

Kitsch'n on Roscoe, 2005 W. Roscoe St. (☎773-248-7372), at Damen Ave. in nearby Roscoe Village. The joint's title is a good indication of the campy experience this breakfast and lunch spot has to offer. Try the "Kitsch'n Sink Omelette" ($7) or enjoy "Jonny's Lunch Box" (soup, sandwich, fruit, and a snack cake served in a lunch box, $6.50) on kitschy theme tables. Meals $3-12. Open Tu-Sa 9am-10pm, Su 9am-3pm. ❷

OLD TOWN

Vito and Kesselman, 1617 N. Wells St. (☎664-0460), across the street from Second City. Patrons scarf down meatball sandwiches alongside matzo ball soup at this superb Italian-Jewish deli. Sandwiches $7-9. Open Su-Th 11am-10pm, F-Sa 11am-11pm. ❷

Flat Top Grill, 312 W. North Ave. (☎787-7676). You're the chef at this do-it-yourself stir-fry joint. Start with noodles or rice and then produce your own culinary masterpiece from a selection of fresh vegetables, meats, and sauces. Don't worry, though—there are a host of suggested recipes for clueless cooks. One bowl $8. Open Su-Th 11:30am-10pm, F-Sa 11:30am-11pm. Call for other locations. ❸

Nookies, 1746 N. Wells St. (☎337-2454). Start with the most important meal of the day at this neighborhood diner, where breakfast is served all day. Pancakes $5-7; cornflake-crusted french toast $5. Open M-Sa 6:30am-10pm, Su 6:30am-9pm. Cash only. Other locations at 2114 (☎773-327-1400) and 3334 N. Halsted (☎773-248-9888). ❷

WRIGLEYVILLE

▓ **Mia Francesca,** 3311 N. Clark St. (☎773-281-3310), is a bustling urban trattoria serving Northern Italian cuisine in an upscale, romantic atmosphere. Entrees $10-25, pizzas $7-8. Open Su-Th 5-10pm, F-Sa 5-11pm. Reservations recommended. ❹

◉ SIGHTS

Only a fraction of Chicago's eclectic sights are revealed by tourist brochures, bus tours, and strolls through the downtown area. Sights range from well-publicized museums to undiscovered back streets, from beaches and parks to towering skyscrapers. To see it all requires some off-the-beaten path exploration.

THE LOOP

When the **Great Fire of 1871** razed Chicago's downtown, the burgeoning metropolis had an opportunity to start anew. Bounded by the river on one side and **Lake Michigan** on the other, the city was forced to build up rather than out. The result was both functional and fabulous, and the Windy City's famous skyline is today one of the world's great architectural treasures.

TOURS. Visitors can view the architecture via **walking tours** organized by the **Chicago Architecture Foundation.** One tour of early skyscrapers and another of modern architecture starts at the foundation's gift shop and last 2hr. Highlights include Louis Sullivan's arch, classic Chicago windows, and Mies van der Rohe's revolutionary skyscrapers. *(224 S. Michigan Ave. ☎922-3432, ext. 240; www.architecture.org. Historic Skyscrapers May-Oct. M-Tu and Th-Su 10am and 3pm, W 10am. Modern skyscrapers May-Oct. daily 11am and 1pm. $12, students and seniors $9. Both tours for $20/$15. Call for info on special tours.)*

SEARS TOWER. A few blocks west on Jackson, the Sears Tower is undoubtedly Chicago's most immediately recognizable landmark. The Tower is the second-tallest building in the world (although it still has the tallest antenna), standing 1454 ft. tall, and the ear-popping elevator ride to the 103rd fl. Skydeck earns visitors a view of three states on a clear day. *(233 S. Wacker Dr.; enter on Jackson. ☎875-9696; www.the-skydeck.com. Open daily May-Sept. 10am-10pm; Oct.-Apr. 10am-8pm. $10, seniors $8, youth $7. Lines are long, usually at least 1hr.)*

THE PLAZA. The **Bank One Building and Plaza** is one of the world's largest bank buildings. It leads gazes skyward with its diamond-shaped, diagonal slope. Back on the ground, Marc Chagall's vivid mural *The Four Seasons* lines the block and defines a public space used for concerts and lunchtime entertainment. The mosaic is a fabulous sight at night, when it is lit by various colored bulbs. Two blocks north, the Methodist **Chicago Temple,** the world's tallest church, sends its towering steeples heavenward. *(77 W. Washington St., at the corner of Clark and Washington St. ☎236-4548. Tours M-F 2pm, Su after services. Free.)*

STATE STREET. State and Madison St., the most famous intersection of "State Street, that great street," forms the focal point of the Chicago street grid. Louis Sullivan's beloved **Carson Pirie Scott** store is adorned with exquisite ironwork and an extra-large Chicago window. Sullivan's other masterpiece, the **Auditorium Building,** sits several blocks south at the corner of Congress St. and Michigan Ave. Once Chicago's tallest building, it typifies Sullivan's obsession with form and function, housing a hotel and an opera house with some of the world's finest acoustics.

OTHER ARCHITECTURAL WONDERS. Burnham and Root's **Monadnock Building** deserves a glance for its alternating bays of purple and brown rock. *(53 W. Jackson Blvd.)* Just to the southeast, the **Sony Fine Arts Theatre** screens current arthouse and foreign films in the grandeur of the **Fine Arts Building.** *(410 S. Michigan Ave. ☎427-7602. Open M-Th. $8.25; students $6; seniors, children, and matinees $5.)* The $144 million **Harold Washington Library Center** is a researcher's dream, as well as a postmodern architectural delight. *(400 S. State St. ☎747-4300. Open M-Th 9am-7pm, F-Sa 9am-5pm, Su 1-5pm.)* On the north side of the Loop, at Clark and Randolph, the glass **State of Illinois Building** offers an elevator ride to the top that gives a thrilling (and free) view of a sloping atrium, circular floors, and hundreds of employees.

SCULPTURE. In addition to its architectural masterpieces, Chicago is decorated with a fantastic collection of outdoor sculpture. The Chicago Cultural Center (p. 594) sells the *Loop Sculpture Guide* for $4. The piece known simply as "The Picasso," at the foot of the **Daley Center Plaza,** was the first monumental modern statue to be placed in the Loop, eventually becoming an unofficial symbol of the city. *(Intersection of Washington and Dearborn St.)* Directly across Washington St. rests Surrealist Joan Miró's *Chicago,* the artist's gift to the city. *(69 W. Washington St.)* Two blocks north on Clark St., Jean Dubuffet's *Monument with Standing Beast* stands guard in front of the State of Illinois Building (see above). Three blocks south on Dearborn at Adams, Alexander Calder's *Flamingo,* a stark red structure, stands in front of the Federal Center Plaza. Calder's other Chicago masterpiece, *The Universe,* swirls in the lobby of the Sears Tower.

NEAR NORTH

MAGNIFICENT MILE. Chicago's row of glitzy shops along N. Michigan Ave. between the Chicago River and Oak St. can magnificently drain the wallet. Several of these retail stores were designed by the country's foremost architects and merit a look. The plain **Chicago Water Tower** and **Pumping Station** stick out among the ritzy stores at the corner of Michigan and Pearson Ave. Built in 1867, these were the sole structures in the vicinity to survive the Great Chicago Fire. *(Open daily 10am-*

6:30pm.) The Pumping Station houses a visitors center (p. 594). One block north, the **John Hancock Building**'s exoskeleton of black steel girders and glass casts a stunning figure on the skyline. *(Observation deck open daily 9am-11pm; adults $9.50, seniors $7.50, children 5-12 $6.)*

TRIBUNE TOWER. North of the Loop along the lake, just past the Michigan Ave. Bridge, lies the city's ritziest district. The Tribune Tower, a Gothic skyscraper just north of the bridge, overlooks this stretch. The result of an international design competition in the 1920s, the tower is now home to Chicago's largest newspaper, *The Chicago Tribune. (435 N. Michigan Ave.)*

THE MART. Over 8 mi. of corridors fill the nearby Merchandise Mart. As one of the largest commercial buildings in the world (25 stories high and 2 blocks long), it even has its own postal code. The first two floors house a public mall, while the remainder contain private showrooms. **Tours at the Mart** guides visitors through the building. *(Entrance on N. Wells or Kinzie St., north of the river. Bus #114.* ☎*644-4664. 2hr. tours Th-F 1:30pm. $12, seniors $10, students $9.)*

NAVY PIER. With a concert pavilion, dining options, nightspots, sightseeing boats, a spectacular Ferris wheel, a crystal garden with palm trees, and an IMAX theater, the mile-long pier is like Las Vegas, Mardi Gras, and the state fair rolled into one. Now *that's* America. From here, explorers can rent bicycles to navigate the Windy City's streets or book a seat on a boat tour of Chicago's skyline. *(600 E. Grand Ave. Take El Red Line to Grand/State and transfer to a free pier trolley bus. Pier is wheelchair accessible. Bike rental open daily Apr.-May 9am-7pm; June-Aug. 8am-10pm; Sept.-Oct. 9am-7pm. $8.75 per hr., $34 per day. Boat tours at 2 pier locations daily June-Aug. 10am-11pm; May and Sept. 11am-5pm. 30min. cruises $10, seniors $9, children under 12 $5.)*

OLD TOWN. The bells of the pre-fire **Saint Michael's Church** ring 1 mi. north of the Magnificent Mile in **Old Town**, a neighborhood where eclectic shops and nightspots fill revitalized streets. Architecture buffs should explore the W. Menomonee and W. Eugenie St. area. In early June, the **Old Town Art Fair** attracts artists and craftsmen nationwide. *(Take bus #151 to Lincoln Park and walk south down Clark or Wells St.)*

NORTH SIDE

LINCOLN PARK. Urban renewal has made **Lincoln Park** a popular choice for wealthy residents. Bounded by Armitage to the south and Diversey Ave. to the north, Lincoln Park offers a lakeside community of harbors and parks. Cafes and nightspots pack its tree-lined streets. For some of Chicago's liveliest clubs and restaurants, check out the area around N. Clark St., Lincoln Ave., and N. Halsted St.

LAKEVIEW. North of Diversey Ave. on N. Clark St., the streets of Lincoln Park become increasingly diverse as they melt into the community of Lakeview around the 3000 block. In this self-proclaimed "gay capital of Chicago," shopping plazas alternate with tiny markets and vintage clothing stores, while apartment towers and hotels spring up between aging two-story houses. Lakeview dance clubs form a center of Chicago nightlife. Polish diners share blocks with Korean restaurants, and Mongolian eateries face Mexican bars in this ethnic enclave.

WRIGLEYVILLE. Around the 4000 block of N. Clark, Lakeview shifts into **Wrigleyville**. Even though the **Cubs** (p. 605) haven't won a World Series since 1908, Wrigleyville residents remain fiercely loyal to their hometown team. Tiny, ivy-covered **Wrigley Field** is the North Side's most famous institution, and tours of the historic park are available during summer weekends when the Cubs are away. *(1060 W. Addison St., just east of the junction of Waveland Ave. and N. Clark St. Take bus #22 "Clark" or #152 "Addison."* ☎*773-404-2827. Tours $15.)*

NEAR WEST SIDE

The Near West Side, bounded by the Chicago River to the east and Ogden Ave. to the west, assembles a cornucopia of vibrant ethnic enclaves.

JANE ADDAMS'S HULL-HOUSE MUSEUM. Aside from great food options, the primary attraction on the Near West Side lies a few blocks south of Greektown on Halsted, where activists Jane Addams and Ellen Gates Starr devoted their lives to the historic Hull House and the immigrants who inhabited the surrounding neighborhoods at the turn of the century. *(800 S. Halsted St. Take El Blue Line to Halsted/U of I or bus #8 "Halsted."* ☎ *413-5353; www.uic.edu/jaddams/hull/hull_house.html. Open Tu-F 10am-4pm, Su noon-4pm. Free.)*

SOUTH OF THE LOOP

HYDE PARK AND THE UNIVERSITY OF CHICAGO. Seven miles south of the Loop along the lake, the scenic campus of the ivy-clad **University of Chicago** dominates the **Hyde Park** neighborhood. The university's efforts at revitalizing the area have resulted in a community of scholars and a lively campus life amidst the degenerating neighborhoods surrounding it. University police patrol the area bounded by 51st St. to the north, Lakeshore Dr. to the east, 61st St. to the south, and Cottage Grove to the west—but *don't test these boundaries, even during the day.* Lakeside Burnham Park, east of campus, is *fairly safe during the day, but not at night.* The impressive **Oriental Institute, Museum of Science and Industry** (see **Museums,** p. 602), and **DuSable Museum of African-American History** are all in or near Hyde Park. On the first weekend in June, the **Arts Fest** *(http://artsfest.uchicago.edu)* showcases the diverse cultural offerings of the area. *(From the Loop, take bus #6 "Jefferson Express" or the METRA Electric Line from the Randolph St. Station south to 59th St.)*

ROBIE HOUSE. On campus, Frank Lloyd Wright's famous **Robie House,** designed to resemble a hanging flower basket, is the seminal example of his Prairie-style house. Now in the midst of a 10-year restoration project to return Robie House to its original 1910 state, the house will remain open to visitors during all stages of renovation. *(5757 S. Woodlawn, at the corner of 58th St.* ☎ *773-834-1847. Tours M-F 11am, 1, 3pm, Sa-Su 11am and 3:30pm. $9, seniors and ages 7-18 $7. Not wheelchair accessible.)*

WEST OF THE LOOP

OAK PARK. Gunning for the title of the most fantastic suburb in the US, Oak Park sprouts off of Harlem St. *(10 mi. west of downtown, I-290 W to Harlem St.)* Frank Lloyd Wright endowed the downtown area with 25 of his spectacular homes and buildings, all of which dot the Oak Park Historic District. His one-time home and workplace, the ⬛**Frank Lloyd Wright House and Studio,** offers an unbeatable look at his interior and exterior stylings. *(951 Chicago Ave.* ☎ *708-848-1976; www.wrightplus.org. Bookshop open daily 10am-5pm. 45min. tours of the house M-F 11am, 1, 3pm; Sa-Su every 20min. 11am-3:30pm. 1hr. self-guided tours of Wright's other Oak Park homes, with a map and audio cassette, available daily 10am-3:30pm. Guided tours Mar.-Nov. Sa-Su every hr. 11am-4pm; Dec.-Feb. Sa-Su every hr. noon-2pm. $9, seniors and under 18 $7; combination interior/exterior tour tickets $16/$14. Limited wheelchair access.)* Visitors should also stop by the former home of Ernest Hemingway. Throughout the year, fans flock to the **Ernest Hemingway Birthplace and Museum** to take part in the many events honoring an architect of the modern American novel. The museum features rare photos of Hemingway, his letters, and other memorabilia. *(Birthplace: 339 N. Oak Ave. Museum: 200 N. Oak Park Ave.* ☎ *708-848-2222. House and museum open Th-F and Su 1-5pm, Sa 10am-5pm. Combined ticket $7, seniors and under 18 $5.50.)* Swing by the **visitors center** for maps, guidebooks, tours, and local history. *(1118 Westgate.* ☎ *708-524-7800; www.visitoakpark.com.)*

🏛 MUSEUMS

Chicago's museums range from some of the largest collections in the world to one-room galleries. The first five listings (known as the **Big Five**) provide a diverse array of exhibits, while a handful of smaller collections target specific interests. Lake Shore Dr. has been diverted around Grant Park, linking the Field Museum, Adler, and Shedd. This compound, known as **Museum Campus,** offers a free shuttle between museums. Visitors who plan on seeing the Big Five, plus the Hancock Observatory, can save money by purchasing a **CityPass** that grants admission to the sights and provides discount coupons for food and shopping. ($49, ages 3-11 $39; available at each attraction and good for 9 days.) All museums are wheelchair accessible unless otherwise noted.

🖼 **Art Institute of Chicago,** 111 S. Michigan Ave. (☎443-3600; www.artic.edu/aic), at Adams St. in Grant Park; take the El Green, Brown, Purple, or Orange Line to Adams, or the Red or Blue Line to Monroe. It's easy to feel overwhelmed in this expansive museum, whose collections span 4 millennia of art from around the world. Make sure to see Chagall's stunning *America Windows*—the artist's blue-stained glass tribute to the country's bicentennial—between visits to Wood's *American Gothic*, Hopper's *Nighthawks*, and Monet's *Haystacks*. Visiting exhibitions in 2005 include a Toulouse-Lautrec collection (July 16-Oct. 10, $12-15). Open M-W and F 10:30am-4:30pm, Th 10:30am-8pm, Sa-Su 10am-5pm. $12, students and children $7, under 6 free. Free Th.

🖼 **Field Museum of Natural History,** 1400 S. Lake Shore Dr. (☎922-9410; www.fieldmuseum.org), at Roosevelt Rd. in Grant Park; take bus #146 from State St. Sue, who at 42 feet from tooth to tail is the largest *Tyrannosaurus rex* skeleton ever unearthed, shares space with a 5500-year-old mummy, as well as excellent geology, anthropology, botany, and zoology exhibits. Open daily 9am-5pm. Tours M-F 11am and 2pm, Sa-Su 11am and 1pm. $17, students and seniors $14, ages 3-11 $8, under 3 free.

🖼 **Shedd Aquarium,** 1200 S. Lake Shore Dr. (☎939-2438; www.sheddaquarium.org), in Grant Park. The world's largest indoor aquarium has 650 species of fish and marine life. The Oceanarium features beluga whales, dolphins, seals, and other marine mammals in a giant pool that appears to flow into Lake Michigan. See piranhas and tropical fish of the rainforest in the *Amazon Rising* exhibit or get a rare glimpse of seahorses in the oceanarium exhibit *Seahorse Symphony*. Also, check out the sharks at the new Wild Reef exhibit. Open June-Aug. M-W and F-Su 9am-6pm, Th 9am-10pm (Oceanarium and *Seahorse Symphony* 9am-8pm); Sept.-May M-F 9am-5pm, Sa-Su 9am-6pm. Feedings M-F 11am, 2, 3pm. All-access pass $23, seniors and ages 3-11 $16.

Museum of Science and Industry, 5700 S. Lake Shore Dr. (☎773-684-1414; www.msichicago.org), at 57th St. in Hyde Park. Take bus #6 "Jeffrey Express," the #10 "Museum of Science and Industry" bus (runs in summer daily, rest of the year Sa-Su and holidays), or METRA South Shore line to 57th St. The crown jewel of the Museum's collection is a newly renovated exhibit featuring the World War II-era German submarine used as the basis for the hit movie *U-571*. Other highlights include the Apollo 8 command module and a full-sized replica of a coal mine. Omnimax shows completely immerse you in another world. Open June-Aug. daily 9:30am-5:30pm; Sept.-May M-Sa 9:30am-4pm, Su 11am-4pm. Call for a schedule of Omnimax shows. Admission $9, seniors $7.50, ages 3-11 $5; with Omnimax $15/$12.50/$10. Parking $12.

Chicago Historical Society, 1601 Clark St. (☎642-4600; www.chicagohs.org), at the south end of Lincoln Park. Hands-on exhibits with a contemporary feel link Chicago's rich history to the present day. Among an impressive list of artifacts are Lincoln's death bed, pieces of the Haymarket bomb, and a copy of the first *Playboy*. Open M-Sa 9:30am-4:30pm, Su noon-5pm. Live jazz Th 6-9pm. Suggested donation $5, seniors and students ages 13-22 $3, children 6-12 $1. Free M. Call for tour information.

Adler Planetarium, 1300 S. Lake Shore Dr. (☎922-7827; www.adlerplanetarium.org), on Museum Campus in Grant Park. Aspiring astronauts can discover their weight on Mars, read the news from space, and explore a medieval observatory. Open daily 9:30am-4:30pm. Admission and choice of sky show $13, seniors $12, ages 4-17 $11. Some exhibits $5 extra. Sky show daily on the hr. $5.

Museum of Contemporary Art, 220 E. Chicago Ave. (☎280-2660; www.mcachicago.org), 1 block east of Michigan Ave.; take #66 "Chicago Ave." bus. The beautiful view of Lake Michigan is the only unchanging feature in the MCA's ultra-modern exhibition space. Pieces from the outstanding permanent collection rotate periodically. Call to see what is on display—their extensive collection includes works by Calder, Warhol, Javer, and Nauman. Open Tu 10am-8pm, W-Su 10am-5pm. $10, students and seniors $6, under 12 free. Free Tu.

Terra Museum of American Art, 623 N. Michigan Ave. (☎664-3939; www.terramuseum.org), between Huron and Erie St. Wedged between the posh shops on N. Michigan, this is one of only a few galleries to showcase exclusively American art from colonial times to the present. Includes works from the celebrated Hudson River School and the provocative Thomas Hart Benton. Open Tu 10am-8pm, W-Sa 10am-6pm, Su noon-5pm. Suggested donation for adults $5. Tours Tu-F noon and 6pm, Sa-Su noon and 2pm.

Spertus Museum, 618 S. Michigan Ave. (☎322-1747; www.spertus.edu/museum.html), near Harrison St. downtown; take El Red Line to Harrison. A moving Holocaust Memorial is the only permanent exhibit at this small museum that features Jewish art and history. Open Mar.-Dec. Su-W 10am-5pm, Th 10am-7pm, F 10am-3pm. Artifact center open Su-Th 1-4:30pm. $5, students, seniors, and children $3. Free F.

🎭 ENTERTAINMENT

The free weeklies *Chicago Reader* and *New City*, available in many bars, record stores, and restaurants, list the latest events. The *Reader* reviews all major shows with times and ticket prices. *Chicago* magazine includes theater reviews alongside exhaustive club, music, dance, and opera listings. *The Chicago Tribune* includes an entertainment section every Friday. *Gay Chicago* provides info on social activities as well as other news for the area's gay community.

THEATER

One of the foremost theater centers of North America, Chicago's more than 150 theaters feature everything from blockbuster musicals to off-color parodies. Downtown, the recently formed Theater District centers around State St. and Randolph, and includes the larger venues in the city. Smaller theaters are scattered throughout Chicago. Most tickets are expensive. Half-price tickets are sold on the day of performance at **Hot Tix Booths,** 78 W. Randolph (open Tu-F 8:30am-6pm, Sa 10am-6pm, Su noon-5pm), and 163 E. Pearson in the Water Works Visitors Center (open Tu-Sa 10am-6pm, Su noon-5pm). Purchases must be made in person. (☎977-1755.) **Ticketmaster** (☎559-1212) supplies tickets for many theaters; ask about discounts at all Chicago shows. The "Off-Loop" theaters on the North Side put on original productions, with tickets usually under $18.

Steppenwolf Theater, 1650 N. Halsted St. (☎335-1888; www.steppenwolf.org), where Gary Sinise and the eerie John Malkovich got their start and still stop by. Tickets $10-60, rush tickets available. Box office open M 11am-5pm, Tu-Su 11am-7:30pm.

Goodman Theatre, 170 N. Dearborn (☎443-3800; www.goodman-theatre.org), presents consistently solid original works. Tickets around $40-60; half-price after 6pm or after noon for matinees; $12 for students after 6pm or after noon for matinees. Box office open M-F 10am-5pm; 10am-8pm show nights, usually W-Su.

Bailiwick Repertory, 1229 W. Belmont Ave. (☎773-883-1090; www.bailiwick.org), in the Theatre Bldg. A mainstage and experimental studio space. Tickets from $10. Box office open M-W 10am-6pm, Th-Su noon-showtime.

COMEDY

Chicago boasts a plethora of comedy clubs. The most famous, **◪Second City,** 1616 N. Wells St. (☎664-4032; www.secondcity.com), at North Ave., spoofs Chicago life and politics. Alums include Bill Murray, Chris Farley, and John Belushi. Most nights a free improv session follows the show. At next door **Second City Etc.,** 1608 N. Wells St. (☎642-8189), a group of up-and-coming comics offers more laughs. (Tickets $10-19. Shows for Second City Tu-Th 8:30pm, F-Sa 8 and 11pm, Su 8pm, touring company M at 8:30pm; free improv sessions M-Th 10:30pm, Sa 1am, Su 10pm; Second City Etc. shows Su 8pm, Th 8:30pm, F-Sa 8 and 11pm. Box office opens M-Sa 10:30am, Su noon. Reservations recommended for weekend shows.) Watch improv actors compete at **Comedy Sportz,** 2851 N. Halsted. Two teams of comedians create sketches based on audience suggestions, all in the spirit of competition. (☎773-549-8080. Tickets $17. Shows Th 8pm, F-Sa 8 and 10:30pm.)

DANCE, CLASSICAL MUSIC, AND OPERA

Ballet, comedy, live theater, and musicals are performed at **Auditorium Theatre,** 50 E. Congress Pkwy. (☎922-2110; www.auditoriumtheatre.org. Box office open M-F noon-6pm.) From October through May, the sounds of the **Chicago Symphony Orchestra** resonate throughout **Symphony Center,** 220 S. Michigan Ave. (☎294-3000; www.cso.org.) **Ballet Chicago,** 218 S. Wabash Ave., 3rd fl., pirouettes throughout theaters in Chicago. (☎251-8838; www.balletchicago.org. Tickets $12-45.) The acclaimed **Lyric Opera of Chicago** performs from September through March at the **Civic Opera House,** 20 N. Wacker Dr. (☎332-2244; www.lyricopera.org.) The **Grant Park Music Festival** affords a taste of classical music for free. From mid-June through late August, the acclaimed **Grant Park Symphony Orchestra** plays a few free evening concerts per week at the new **Jay Pritzker Pavilion** in **Millennium Park.** (☎742-4763; www.grantparkmusicfestival.com.)

FESTIVALS

The city celebrates summer on a grand scale. The **Taste of Chicago** festival cooks for eight days in late June and early July. Seventy restaurants set up booths with endless samples in Grant Park, while crowds chomp to the blast of big name bands. The Taste's fireworks are the city's biggest. (Free entry; food tickets $0.50 each.) In mid-June, the **Blues Festival** celebrates the city's soulful music along with the **Chicago Gospel Festival,** and Nashville moves north for the **Country Music Festival** at the end of the month. The **¡Viva Chicago!** Latin music festival steams up in late August, while the **Chicago Jazz Festival** scats over Labor Day weekend. All festivals center at the Grant Park Petrillo Music Shell. The Mayor's Office's **Special Events Hotline** (☎744-3370; www.ci.chi.il.us/SpecialEvents/Festivals.htm) has more info.

The **Ravinia Festival** (☎847-266-5100; www.ravinia.org), in the northern suburb of Highland Park, runs from late June to early September. During the festival's 14-week season, the Chicago Symphony Orchestra, ballet troupes, folk and jazz musicians, and comedians perform. On certain nights, the orchestra allows students free lawn admission with student ID. (Shows 8pm, occasionally 11am, 4:30, and 7pm—call ahead. Round-trip on the METRA costs about $7; the festival runs 1½hr. every night. Charter buses $12. Lawn seats $10-15, other $20-75.)

SPORTS

The National League's **Cubs** step up to bat at **Wrigley Field,** 1060 W. Addison St., at N. Clark St., one of the few ballparks in America to retain the early grace and intimate feel of the game. (☎773-404-2827; www.cubs.com. $6-50.) The **White Sox,** Chicago's American League team, swing on the South Side at new **Comiskey Park,** 333 W. 35th St. (☎866-769-4263. $12-45.) The **Bears** of the NFL play at the newly renovated **Soldier Field,** 425 E. McFetridge Dr. (☎847-617-2327; www.chicagobears.com. $45-315.) The **Bulls** have won three NBA championships at the **United Center,** 1901 W. Madison, just west of the Loop. (☎455-4000; www.nba.com/bulls. $30-450.) Hockey's **Blackhawks** skate onto United Center ice when the Bulls aren't hooping it up. (☎455-4500; www.chicagblackhawks.com. $25-100.) **Sports Information** (☎976-1313) has up-to-the-minute info on local sports events.

◢ NIGHTLIFE

"Sweet home Chicago" takes pride in the innumerable blues performers who have played here. Jazz, folk, reggae, and punk clubs throb all over the **North Side.** The **Bucktown/Wicker Park** area stays open late with bars and clubs. Aspiring pickup artists swing over to **Rush Street** and **Division Street.** Full of bars, cafes, and bistros, **Lincoln Park** is frequented by singles and young couples, both gay and straight. The bustling center of gay culture is between 3000 and 4500 **North Halsted Street.** Many of the more colorful clubs and bars line this area. For more upscale raving and discoing, there are plenty of clubs near **River North,** in Riverwest, and on Fulton St.

BARS AND BLUES JOINTS

▩ **The Green Mill,** 4802 N. Broadway Ave. (☎773-878-5552). El Red Line: Lawrence. Founded as a Prohibition-era speakeasy, Mafiosi-to-be can sit in Al Capone's old seat. This authentic jazz club draws late-night crowds after other clubs shut down. The cover-free jam sessions on weekends after main acts finish are reason enough to chill until the wee hours. Cover $3-15. Open M-Th noon-4am, Sa noon-5am, Su 11am-4am.

▩ **Lakeview Lounge,** 5110 N. Broadway Ave. (☎773-769-0994). This joint is as small as a shoebox, but if you can wedge yourself inside you'll be treated to the Night Watch, the best cover band in the known universe, playing everything from jazz to rock to surf music. Music Th-F 10pm. Open Su-F 2pm-4am, Sa 2pm-5am.

Kingston Mines, 2548 N. Halsted St. (☎773-477-4646; www.kingstonmines.com), just up the street from B.L.U.E.S. Celebrities like Mick Jagger and Led Zeppelin have been known to drop in for a jam session at this venerable club, which features dueling blues acts alternating on 2 stages. Live blues Su-F starting at 9:30pm, Sa 8pm. Cover Su-Th $12-15, F-Sa $15 or more. Open Su-F 8pm-4am, Sa 8pm-5am.

Hydrate, 3458 N. Halsted (☎773-575-5244; www.hydratechicago.com), in Lakeview. Cool off with a frozen cocktail ($6) after grooving on this trendy gay bar's red-hot dance floor. Cover Th-Sa $3-10. Open M-Tu 8pm-4am, W-F and Su 4pm-4am, Sa 4pm-5am.

The Hideout, 1354 W. Wabansia Ave. (☎773-227-4433). El Brown Line: Clybourn and North. Nestled in a municipal truck parking lot, this is the insider's club for everything from alt country to jazz. Some weekends, the lot fills with "kid's shows" for families still able to rock, and their block party in late Sept. draws thousands. Cover Tu-F $5-10. Open M 7:30pm-2am, Tu-F 4pm-2am, Sa 7:30pm-3am.

B.L.U.E.S., 2519 N. Halsted St. (☎773-528-1012; www.chicagobluesbar.com). Fullerton El: Howard, Dan Ryan. Crowded and intimate with unbeatable music. Albert King, Bo Diddley, Wolfman Washington, and Dr. John have played here. Live music every night 9:30pm-close. 21+. Cover $7-10. Dual cover for Kingston Mines and B.L.U.E.S. on Su. Open Su-F 8pm-2am, Sa 8pm-3am.

DANCE CLUBS

▨ **Berlin,** 954 W. Belmont Ave. (☎773-348-4975; www.berlinchicago.com). El Red or Brown Line: Belmont, in Lakeview. Anything goes at Berlin, a gay-friendly mainstay of Chicago's nightlife. Crowds pulsate to house/dance music as go-go girls, go-go boys, and divas rock out on raised stages. Tu-Th gay-oriented, W women's night. 21+. Cover Th $3, F-Sa $5. Open Tu-F 5pm-4am, Sa 5pm-5am, Su-M 8pm-4am.

Funky Buddha Lounge, 728 W. Grand Ave. (☎666-1695; www.funkybuddha.com). El Blue Line: Chicago. Trendy, eclectic dance club where hip-hop and funk blend with leopard and velvet decor. W and Su soul. Cover for women $10, for men $20. Free before 10pm. Open M-W 10pm-2am, Th-F 9pm-2am, Sa 9pm-3am, Su 6pm-2am.

Smart Bar, 3730 N. Clark St. (☎773-549-4140). Resident DJ spins punk, techno, hip-hop, and house just up the street from Wrigley Field. 21+. Cover $2-12. Open Su and Tu-F 10pm-4am, Sa 10pm-5am.

🅝 OUTDOOR ACTIVITIES

A string of lakefront parks fill the area between Chicago proper and Lake Michigan. On sunny afternoons dog walkers, in-line skaters, and skateboarders storm the shore. Close to downtown, the two major parks are Lincoln and Grant. ▨**Lincoln Park** extends across 5 mi. of lakefront on the north side with winding paths, groves of trees, and asymmetrical open spaces. The **Lincoln Park Zoo** features some of humankind's distant cousins in its new Great Apes exhibit. (☎742-2000; www.lpzoo.com. Open in summer M-F 10am-5pm, Sa-Su 10am-6:30pm; low-season daily 10am-5pm. Free.) Next door, the **Lincoln Park Conservatory** provides a glass palace of plants from varied ecosystems. (☎742-7736. Open daily 9am-5pm. Free.)

Grant Park, covering 14 lakefront blocks east of Michigan Ave., follows the 19th-century French park style: symmetrical and ordered with corners, a fountain, and wide promenades. The Grant Park Concert Society hosts free summer concerts in the **Petrillo Music Shell,** 520 S. Michigan Ave. (☎742-4763). Colored lights illuminate **Buckingham Fountain** from 9 to 11pm. On the north side, Lake Michigan lures swimmers and sun-bathers to **Lincoln Park Beach** and **Oak Street Beach.** Beware, though: the rock ledges are restricted areas, and swimming from them is illegal. Although the beaches are patrolled 9am-9:30pm, they can be unsafe after dark. The **Chicago Parks District** (☎742-7529) has further info.

Starting from Hyde Park in the south, **Lake Shore Drive** offers sparkling views of Lake Michigan all the way past the city and one of the best views of the downtown skyline. At its end, Lake Shore becomes **Sheridan Road,** which twists and turns its way through the picturesque northern suburbs. Just north of Chicago is **Evanston,** a lively, affluent college town (home to **Northwestern University**) with an array of parks and nightclubs. Ten minutes north is upscale **Wilmette,** home to the ornate **Baha'i House of Worship,** 100 Linden Ave., at Sheridan Rd. This architectural wonder is topped by a stunning nine-sided dome. (☎847-853-2300. Open daily June-Sept. 10am-8pm; Oct.-May 10am-5pm. Services M-Sa 12:15pm, Su 1:15pm).

The ▨**Indiana Dunes State Park** and **National Lakeshore** lie simultaneously 45min. southeast of Chicago on I-90 and in a different world. The State Park's gorgeous dune beaches on Lake Michigan provide hikes through dunes, woods, and marshes. Info about the State Park is available at their office, 1600 N. 25 E in Chesterton, IN (☎219-926-1952). Obtain Lakeshore details at their **visitors center,** 1100 N. Mineral Springs Rd., in Porter, IN (☎219-926-7561).

SPRINGFIELD   ☎ **217**

Springfield, "the town that Lincoln loved," was a hotbed of political activity during the antebellum years, and today the sleepy state capital plays curator to the 16th president's legacy. Luckily, many Lincoln sights are free. (Info line ☎ 800-545-7300.) The **Lincoln Home Visitors Center,** 426 S. 7th St., shows a film and doles out free tickets to tour the **Lincoln Home,** at 8th and Jackson St. (☎ 492-4241. Open daily 8:30am-5pm. 15min. tours every 5-10min. starting at the front of the house. Arrive early in summer months to avoid crowds.) Lincoln served in the legislature in the **Old State Capitol,** where he gave his prophetic "House Divided" speech in 1858. (☎ 785-9363. Open Tu-Sa Mar.-Oct. 9am-5pm; Nov.-Feb. 9am-4pm. Last tour 1hr. before closing. $2 donation suggested.) Lincoln, his wife Mary Todd, and three of their sons rest in the towering **Lincoln Tomb,** 1500 Monument Ave., at Oak Ridge Cemetery. (☎ 782-2717. Open daily Mar.-Oct. 9am-5pm; Nov.-Feb. 9am-4pm.)

The **◪Dana-Thomas House,** 301 E. Lawrence Ave., was one of Frank Lloyd Wright's early experiments in the Prairie Style and still features Wright's original fixtures. (☎ 782-6776. Open W-Su 9am-4pm. 1hr. tours every 15-20min. Suggested donation $3, under 18 $1. Limited wheelchair accessibility.)

Bus service to the cheap lodgings off I-55 and U.S. 36 on Dirksen Pkwy. is limited. Rooms downtown should be reserved early for holiday weekends and the **Illinois State Fair** in mid-August. For a comfortable stay without a hefty price, head to the **Stevenson Inn ❸,** 2860 Stevenson Dr. just west of I-55, which offers rooms with cable TV and A/C. (☎ 585-4002. Rooms from $50.) The colorful **Cafe Brio ❹,** 524 E. Monroe, adds a creative twist to flavorful Latin dishes. (☎ 544-0574. Entrees $7-22. Open M-Th 11am-10pm, F-Sa 11am-11pm, Su 11am-3pm.) **Cozy Drive-In ❶,** 2935 S. 6th St., is a landmark on historic Rte. 66 and the birthplace of the "Cozy Dog," or corndog ($1.60). Today, it's a family-owned diner devoted to roadside memorabilia and deep-fried food. (☎ 525-1992. Burger $1.70. Open M-Sa 8am-8pm.)

Amtrak, (☎ 753-2013; station open daily 6am-8:30pm), at 3rd and Washington St., near downtown, runs trains to Chicago (3½hr., 3 per day, $16-45) and St. Louis (2hr., 3 per day, $11-20). **Greyhound,** 2351 S. Dirksen Pkwy., (☎ 800-231-2222; depot open M-F 9am-1pm and 2-8pm, Sa-Su 9am-noon and 2-4pm), on the eastern edge of town, goes to: Chicago (4-6hr., 5 per day, $36); Indianapolis (8-10hr., 2 per day, $46); St. Louis (2hr., 4 per day, $20). The **downtown trolley** system is designed for tourists moving between the downtown sights. (☎ 528-4100. Trolleys run W-Su 9am-4pm; call ahead to confirm hours. Hop-on/off $10, seniors $9, ages 5-12 $5; full circuit $5.) **Taxi: Lincoln Yellow Cab** ☎ 523-4545. **Visitor Info: Springfield Convention and Visitors Bureau,** 109 N. 7th St. (☎ 789-2360 or 800-545-7300; www.visit-springfieldillinois.com. Open M-F 8am-5pm.) **Internet Access: Lincoln Library,** 326 S. 7th St. (☎ 753-4900. Open June-Aug. M-Th 9am-9pm, F 9am-6pm, Sa 9am-5pm; Sept.-May also open Su 12:30pm-4pm.) **Post Office:** 411 E. Monroe, at Wheeler. (☎ 753-3432. Open M-F 7:45am-5pm.) **Postal Code:** 62701. **Area Code:** 217.

WISCONSIN

Hospitality is served up with every beer and every piece of Wisconsin cheddar sold in the Great Lakes's most wholesome party state. A wide variety of wily creatures make themselves at home in the thick woods of Wisconsin's extensive park system, while the state's favorite animal—the cow—grazes near highways. Along the shoreline, fishermen haul in fresh perch, and on rolling hills farmers grow barley for beer. Visitors to "America's Dairyland" encounter cheese-filled country stores en route to the ocean-like vistas of Door County, as well as the ethnic *fêtes* (not to mention other, less refined beer bashes) of Madison and Milwaukee.

🔼 PRACTICAL INFORMATION

Capital: Madison.

Visitor Info: Department of Tourism, 201 W. Washington Ave., P.O. Box 8690, Madison 53708 (☎608-266-2161 or 800-432-8747; www.tourism.state.wi.us).

Postal Abbreviation: WI **Sales Tax:** 5%.

MILWAUKEE ☎414

Home to beer and countless festivals, Milwaukee is a city with a reputation for *gemütlichkeit* (hospitality). Ethnic communities throw rolling, city-wide parties each summer weekend, from the traditional Oktoberfest to the Asian Moon festival. When the weather turns cold, the city celebrates with the International Arts Festival Milwaukee, during which galleries and museums extend their hours. Milwaukee's countless bars and taverns fuel the revelry with as much beer as anyone could ever need. In addition to merrymaking, the city boasts top-notch museums, German-inspired architecture, and a long expanse of scenic lakeshore.

🚃 TRANSPORTATION

Airport: General Mitchell International Airport, 5300 S. Howell Ave. (☎747-5300; www.mitchellairport.com). Take bus #80 from 6th St. downtown (30min.). **Airport Connection,** ☎769-2444 or 800-236-5450. 24hr. pickup and dropoff from most downtown hotels. $10, round-trip $18. Reservations required.

Trains: Amtrak, 433 W. St. Paul Ave. (☎271-9037), at 5th St. downtown. In a fairly safe area, but less so at night. To **Chicago** (1½hr., 7 per day, $20) and **St. Paul** (6½hr., 1 per day, $50-100). Open M-Sa 5:15am-9:30pm, Su 7am-9:30pm.

Buses: Greyhound, 606 N. James Lovell (☎272-9301), off W. Michigan St., 3 blocks from the train station. To **Chicago** (2-3hr., 11 per day, $15) and **Minneapolis** (7-9hr., 5 per day, $50). Station open 24hr.; office open daily 6:30am-11:30pm. **Coach USA Milwaukee** (☎262-542-8861), in the same terminal, covers southeastern Wisconsin. **Badger Bus,** 635 N. James Lovell St. (☎276-7490 or 608-255-1511; www.badgerbus.com), across the street, burrows to **Madison** (1½hr., 6 per day, $15). Open M-Sa 6:30am-8pm, Su 9:30am-8pm. *Be cautious at night.*

Public Transit: Milwaukee County Transit System, 1942 N. 17th St. (☎344-6711; www.ridemcts.com). Efficient metro area service. Most lines run 5am-12:30am. $1.75, seniors and children $0.85; weekly pass $13. Fare includes transfer that can be used for 1hr. after first ride. Free maps at the library or at Grand Ave. Mall. Call for schedules. The **Trolley** (☎344-6711) runs in a loop through downtown. All-day ride $1, seniors $0.50. Runs May-Sept. W-Th 11am-10pm, F-Sa 11am-midnight, Su 11am-6pm.

Taxi: Veteran ☎220-5000. **Yellow Taxi** ☎271-1800.

✈️🔼 ORIENTATION AND PRACTICAL INFORMATION

Most of Milwaukee's action is downtown, which lies between **Lake Michigan** and **10th Street.** Address numbers increase north and south from **Wisconsin Avenue,** the center of east-west travel. Most north-south streets are numbered, increasing from Lake Michigan toward the west. The **interstate system** forms a loop around Milwaukee: **I-43 S** runs to Beloit; **I-43 N** runs to Green Bay; **I-94 E** is a straight shot to Chicago; **I-94 W** goes to Madison and then Minneapolis/St. Paul; **I-794** cuts through the heart of downtown Milwaukee; and **I-894** connects with the airport.

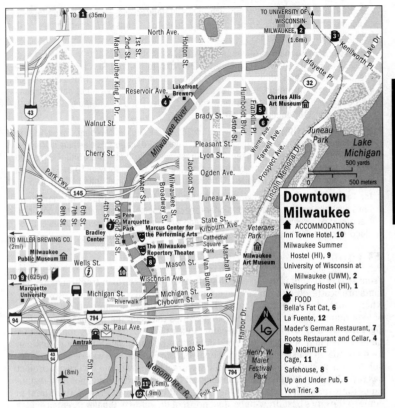

Downtown Milwaukee

🏠 ACCOMMODATIONS
Inn Towne Hotel, **10**
Milwaukee Summer Hostel (HI), **9**
University of Wisconsin at Milwaukee (UWM), **2**
Wellspring Hostel (HI), **1**

🍎 FOOD
Bella's Fat Cat, **6**
La Fuente, **12**
Mader's German Restaurant, **7**
Roots Restaurant and Cellar, **4**

🍸 NIGHTLIFE
Cage, **11**
Safehouse, **8**
Up and Under Pub, **5**
Von Trier, **3**

GREAT LAKES

Visitor Info: Greater Milwaukee Convention and Visitors Bureau, 400 W. Wisconsin Ave. (☎908-6205 or 800-554-1448; www.milwaukee.org), in the Midwest Airlines Center lobby. Open M-F 9am-1pm and 2-5pm; in summer also Sa 9am-2pm, Su 11am-3pm.

Hotlines: Crisis Intervention, ☎257-7222. **Women's Center Hotline,** ☎933-2722. Both operate 24hr. **Gay People's Union Hotline,** ☎645-0585. Operates daily 7-10pm.

Internet Access: $2 per week at the **Milwaukee Public Library.** Main branch at 814 W. Wisconsin Ave. (☎286-3000). Open M-Sa 9am-8:30pm.

Post Office: 345 W. St. Paul Ave. (☎270-2308), south along 4th Ave. from downtown, by the Amtrak station. Open M-F 7:30am-8pm. **Postal Code:** 53201. **Area Code:** 414.

🏠 ACCOMMODATIONS

Downtown lodging options tend to be expensive; travelers with cars should head out to the city's two hostels. **Bed and Breakfast of Milwaukee** (☎277-8066) finds rooms from $55 in picturesque B&Bs around the area.

Milwaukee Summer Hostel (HI), 525 N. 17th St. (☎244-4737; www.hostellingwisconsin.org), on the Marquette University campus. Take bus #10 or 30 down Wisconsin to 16th St. Fully furnished dorm rooms and super location make this hostel the best place in town to rest your head for the night. Free Internet access. Free linen, laundry, and kitchen facilities. Parking $5 per day. Open June-Aug. Dorms $17, nonmembers $20. Private rooms $36/$40. ❶

University of Wisconsin at Milwaukee (UWM), Sandburg Hall, 3400 N. Maryland Ave. (☎229-4065 or 299-6123). Take bus #30 north to Hartford St. Close to East Side restaurants and bars, the UWM sports spotless, dorm-style suites, divided into singles and doubles. No linens available. Laundry facilities and free local calls. Parking $8.50. 24hr. advance reservations required. Open June to mid-Aug. Singles with shared bath $36; doubles $60. ❷

Wellspring Hostel (HI), 4382 Hickory Rd. (☎262-675-6755), in Newburg. Take I-43 N to Rte. 33 W to Newburg and exit on Main St.; Hickory Rd. intersects Newburg's Main St. just northwest of the Milwaukee River. Those willing to make the 45min. drive find respite from the pace of the city on this riverside farm. Well-kept with 10 beds, kitchen, and nature trails. Linens included. Office open daily 8am-8pm. Dorms $17-20. ❶

Inn Towne Hotel, 710 N. Old World 3rd St. (☎224-8400 or 800-469-6130), downtown. This centrally located Best Western offers spacious rooms with complimentary continental breakfast, exercise facilities, cable TV, and A/C. Proximity to Water St. offers endless food and nightlife options. Parking $10 per day. Rooms from $79. ❹

🍴 FOOD

From *wurst* to *bier*, Milwaukee is best known for its German traditions. Restaurants are scattered along nearly every street in the city, particularly downtown, where most adopt continental attitudes and hefty prices to match their 100 years of experience. Nearby Lake Michigan provides the main ingredient for the **Friday night fish fry,** a gluttonous all-you-can-eat extravaganza offered by many restaurants. Polish and Serbian influences dominate the **South Side,** and good Mexican food prevails in **Walker's Point,** at National and 5th St. **East Side** eateries are cosmopolitan and quirky, with a mix of ethnic flavors. Downtown, the Riverwalk project has revitalized the **Water Street Entertainment District,** which boasts hot new restaurants for a range of palates. On the north end of the Riverwalk, **Water Street** is home to the city's best brew-pubs. Just north of downtown, **Bradley Street** provides upscale, trendy dining options.

Mader's German Restaurant, 1037 N. Old World Third St. (☎271-3377). Suits of armor and steins conjure up images of a Bavarian hunting lodge, while frauleins dish out plates of *schnitzel* and *sauerbraten*. Entrees $7.50-14. Open M-Th 11:30am-9pm, F-Sa 11:30am-10pm, Su 11am-9pm. Reservations recommended. ❸

Roots Restaurant and Cellar, 1818 N. Hubbard St. (☎374-8480). The flavorful cuisine and hip atmosphere are punctuated by panoramic views of downtown and the river. In the more casual cellar, tasty lunch entrees and sandwiches are only $7-15. The fancier and mostly organic Roots Restaurant upstairs is heavy on fusion, with dishes like Jerk Mahi Mahi ($18) and Soy Grilled Tilapia ($17). Dinner entrees run $15-27. Open M-Sa 11am-2pm and 5-10pm, Su brunch 11am-2pm. ❸/❹

La Fuente, 625 S. 5th St. (☎271-8595), on the South Side. Locals flock here for authentic Mexican food and the best margaritas in town ($6.50-7.50). Murals, mariachi music, and a patio add to the laid-back atmosphere. Lunches from $4. Dinner entrees $6-11. Open Su-Th 10am-10:30pm, F-Sa 10am-11:30pm. ❷

Bella's Fat Cat, 1233 E. Brady St. (☎273-2113), grills up tasty sandwiches and burgers for under $5. Wash them down with a frozen custard, offered in creative daily flavors like Blue Moon and Jamaican Mango. Open M-Sa 11am-11pm, Su 11am-10pm. ❶

⊙ SIGHTS

BREWERIES. Although many of Milwaukee's breweries have left, beer is still a tried-and-true staple of the city. The ⊠**Miller Brewery,** a corporate giant that produces 43 million barrels of beer annually, offers a free 1hr. tour with three generous samples. *(4251 W. State St. ☎931-2337; www.millerbrewery.com. Under 18 must be accompanied by an adult. ID required. Open M-Sa 10am-5:30pm; 2 tours per hr., 3 during busy days; in winter M-Sa 10am-5pm. Call for tour schedule.)* For a taste of Milwaukee's microbreweries, take a 3hr. **Riverwalk Boat Tour.** The tour's pontoon boat travels to the Milwaukee Alehouse, the Lakefront Brewery, and the Rock Bottom Brewery. *(Tours start from Père Marquette Park on Old World 3rd St. between State and Kilbourn. ☎283-9999. Tours Sa-Su, call for times. $18.)* Some microbreweries offer their own tours as well. The **Lakefront Brewery** produces seven popular year-round beers and several seasonal specials. Sip samples while watching the beer being made before your eyes. *(1872 N. Commerce St. ☎372-8800; www.lakefrontbrewery.com. Tours F 3, 6, 7pm; Sa 1, 2, 3pm. $5 with souvenir mug, $2 non-beer drinkers. ID required without legal guardian.)* One of the state's most renowned microbreweries, **Sprecher Brewing** still believes in Old World brewing techniques. The 1hr. tour, which includes a visit to an old lager cellar and the Rathskellar museum of beer memorabilia, is followed by four beer samples. *(701 W. Glendale, 5 mi. north of the city on I-43, then east on Port Washington St. ☎964-2739; www.sprecherbrewery.com. Tours F 4pm, Sa 1, 2, 3pm; June-Aug. additional tours M-Th. Call for tour times. $2, under 21 $1. Reservations required.)*

MUSEUMS. Several excellent museums dot the shores of Milwaukee. The ⊠**Milwaukee Art Museum** is a sculpture in and of itself with its cylindrical elevators and windows that frame a spectacular view of Lake Michigan. Moveable, sail-like wings jut out from the building, which houses a wide spectrum of works, including Haitian folk art and 19th-century German paintings. *(700 N. Art Museum Dr., on the lakefront downtown. ☎224-3200; www.mam.org. Free audio tour available. Open Su-W and F-Sa 10am-5pm, Th 10am-8pm. $8, seniors $6, students $4, under 12 free.)* Visitors can wander through the cobbled streets of Old Milwaukee and venture into a replica of a Costa Rican rainforest at the **Milwaukee Public Museum.** The museum's Discovery World also has kid-oriented exhibits like Area 51 and the TechnoJungle. *(800 W. Wells St., at N. 8th St. ☎278-2700; www.mpm.edu. Open daily 9am-5pm. Free tours M-Sa noon, Su 1pm. $7, seniors $6, children $4.75, under 3 free. Free M. Discovery World $6/$5/$4.25. Combo tickets $10.50/$9/$7.50. Parking available. Wheelchair accessible.)* The intimate **Charles Allis Art Museum,** a refurbished 1911 mansion, holds an eclectic collection of pieces gathered by a globetrotting industrialist. *(1801 N. Prospect Ave. at E. Royal Pl., 1 block north of Brady. Take bus #30, 31, or River Rte. Trolley. ☎278-8295; www.cavtmuseums.org. Open W 1-5pm and 7-9pm, Th-Su 1-5pm. $5, students and seniors $3, children free.)*

PARKS. Better known as "The Domes," the **Mitchell Park Horticultural Conservatory** recreates a desert and a rainforest and mounts seasonal floral displays in three seven-story, conical glass greenhouses. *(524 S. Layton Ave., at 27th St. Take bus #10 west to 27th St., then #27 south to Layton. ☎649-9830. Open daily 9am-5pm. $4.50, seniors and ages 6-17 $3, under 6 free.)* The **Boerner Botanical Gardens** cultivate gorgeous blossoms and host open-air concerts on Thursday nights. *(9400 Boerner Dr., exit I-894 at S. 92nd St. ☎525-5601. Open May-Sept. daily 8am-sunset. $4, seniors $3, age 6-17 $2.)* For an escape from the city, visit one of the many parks along the waterfront.

OTHER SIGHTS. A road warrior's nirvana, locally headquartered **Harley-Davidson** gives 45min. tours of its engine plant that will enthrall any aficionado. *(11700 W. Capitol Dr. ☎342-4680. Tours June-Aug. M-F 9:30, 11am, 1pm; Sept.-Dec. M, W, F 9:30-1pm. Call ahead; the plant sometimes shuts down in summer. Reservations required for*

A MIDWESTERN FOURTH

There was the local Little League baseball team on a flat-bed truck. Then came a fire truck, lights flashing and sirens blaring. There was even a man on his John Deere tractor. This was the 4th of July parade in the small town of Wausaukee, WI, a celebration that will never be nationally televised or written up in newspapers, except perhaps by the local gazette. There was no grand fireworks display, no symphony assembled to play Sousa's *Stars and Stripes Forever*. But in a town of 656 people, it seemed that 250 were in the parade and the rest were lined up along the town's main street to watch. They cheered for every entry—even the man on his tractor—as participants in classic cars threw candy to children watching from the curb. In its own way, this small display was more impressive than the expensive spectacles put on by big cities, because the Wausaukee parade represented an idyllic image of small-town USA that metropolises and suburbs can only attempt to recreate. Of course, this image of the Midwest is just that, and the region has its troubles just like any other part of the country. Yet it was still somehow comforting for this traveler when, for one afternoon at least, an idealized image of America's heartland translated into reality.

- Chris Loomis

groups larger than 5. Closed-toe shoes must be worn. No children under 18. Photo ID required for over 18.) For a brush with Olympic glory, amateur ice skaters should head to daily open skates at the **Pettit National Ice Center.** (500 S. 84th St., at I-94, next to the state fairgrounds. ☎ 266-0100. Call for open skating schedules. $6, seniors and children $5. Skate rental $2.50.)

🎵 ENTERTAINMENT

Music comes in almost as many varieties as beer in Milwaukee. The modern **Marcus Center for the Performing Arts,** 929 N. Water St., across the Milwaukee River from Père Marquette Park, is the area's major arts venue. Throughout the summer, the center's Peck Pavilion hosts **Live at the Center,** a series of free lunchtime concerts performed by both professional and local bands. (☎ 273-2787 or 888-612-3500; www.marcuscenter.org. Concerts Tu noon and 7:30pm.) The music moves indoors during the winter with the **Milwaukee Symphony Orchestra,** the **Milwaukee Ballet,** and the **Florentine Opera Company.** (☎ 273-7206. Symphony $15-81, ballet and opera $17-82. Ballet and symphony offer half-price student and senior rush tickets. Box office open M-F 11:30am-9pm, Sa-Su noon-9pm.) From September through May the **Milwaukee Repertory Theater,** 108 E. Wells St., opens its three stages, offering a mix of innovative shows and classics. (☎ 224-9490; www.milwaukeerep.com. $8.50-49; students and seniors $2 discount, as well as half-price rush 30min. before shows. Box office open M-Sa 10am-6pm, Su noon-6pm.)

Baseball's **Brewers** step up to bat at **Miller Park,** at the interchange of I-94 and Rte. 41. (☎ 902-4000 or 800-933-7890; www.milwaukeebrewers.com. Tickets $5-75. Tours Apr.-Sept. Tu-F 10:30am-1:30pm every hr., Sa 10:30am-1:30pm and Su 11:30am-1:30pm every ½hr. $6, seniors and children under 14 $3.) The NBA's **Bucks** shoot hoops at the **Bradley Center,** 1001 N. 4th St. (☎ 227-0500. Tickets $10-100.)

🌸 FESTIVALS

Summertime livens up Milwaukee's scene with countless free festivals and live music events. On any given night, a free concert is happening; call the **Visitors Bureau** (☎ 908-6205) to find out where. On Thursdays in summer, **Cathedral Park Jazz** (☎ 271-1416) jams for free in **Cathedral Square Park,** at N. Jackson St. between Wells and Kilbourn St. In Père Marquette Park, at 3rd and Kilbourn St., **River Flicks** (☎ 276-6696) screens free movies at dusk Fridays in August.

Locals line the streets in July for ▨**The Great Circus Parade** (☎608-356-8341), a recreation of turn-of-the-century processions, complete with trained animals, daredevils, and 65 original wagons. During the 11 days of **Summerfest,** the largest of Milwaukee's festivals, daily life comes to a halt as musical acts, culinary specialties, and a crafts bazaar take over the city. (☎273-3378 or 800-273-3378; www.summerfest.com. Late June to early July. Tickets $12, seniors and children 3-10 $3; 3-day pass $30.) In early August, the **Wisconsin State Fair** rolls into the fairgrounds, next to the Pettit National Ice Center, toting 12 stages along with exhibits, rides, cream puffs, fireworks, and a pie-baking contest. (☎266-7000 or 800-884-3247; www.wsfp.state.wi.us. $8, seniors $5, ages 7-11 $3.) Ethnic festivals also abound during festival season and are held in the **Henry W. Maier Festival Park,** on the lakefront downtown. The most popular are: **Polish Fest** (☎529-2140; www.polishfest.org) and **Asian Moon** (☎483-8530; www.asianmoon.org), both in mid-June; **Festa Italiana** (☎223-2808; www.festaitaliana.com) in mid-July; **Bastille Days** (☎271-1416; http://bastille.easttown.com) around Bastille Day (July 14); and **German Fest** (☎464-9444; www.germanfest.com) in late July. (The Milwaukee County Transit Trolley runs a Lakefront extension to the festivals. Most festivals $7-10, under 12 free; some free plus price of food.) Pick up a copy of the free weekly *Downtown Edition* or call ☎800-554-1448 for more information.

◪ NIGHTLIFE

Milwaukee never lacks something to do after sundown. The downtown business district becomes desolate at night, but the area along **Water Street** between Juneau and Highland Ave. offers hip, lively bars and clubs. Nightspots that draw a college crowd cluster around the intersection of **North Avenue** and **North Farwell Street,** near the UW campus. Running east-west between Farwell St. and the Milwaukee River, **Brady Street** is lined with the hottest bars and coffeehouses. **South 2nd Street** is a fairgrounds for eclectic, trendy nightclubs and lounges.

▨ **Safehouse,** 779 N. Front St. (☎271-2007; www.safe-house.com), across from the Pabst Theater downtown. A wooden sign labeled "International Exports, Ltd." welcomes guests to this bizarre world of spy hideouts and secret passwords. A briefing with "Moneypenny" in the foyer is just the beginning of the intrigue. The "Ultimate Martini" is propelled through a maze of plastic tubes before it is served just how Mr. Bond likes it ($13 with souvenir shaker and glass). Draft beer $2.75; 24oz. specialty drinks $7.50. Cover $1-4. Open M-Th 11:30am-1:30am, F-Sa 11:30am-2am, Su 4pm-1am.

Von Trier, 2235 N. Farwell Ave. (☎272-1775), at North Ave., features a German-style *biergarten*, big oak bar, and stein-lined walls that combine to create a laid-back atmosphere for enjoying some serious beer. The bar boasts a vast selection of imports, but the house special is German *weiss* ($5). Open Su-Th 4pm-2am, F-Sa 4pm-2:30am.

Up and Under Pub, 1216 E. Brady St. (☎276-2677; www.upandunderpub.com). Mostly local rock, jazz, and blues bands groove at this friendly neighborhood bar 4 nights a week. Live music Th-Su. Tu free pool. Cover $3-5. Open Tu-Th and Su 5pm-2am, F-Sa 5pm-2:30am.

Cage, 801 S. 2nd Ave. (☎383-8330; www.cagenightclub.com). Newly renovated, the largest nightspot in town boasts 5 bars and a loyal 20- to 30-something gay clientele. Cage considers itself "straight-friendly," and crowds are often mixed. Downstairs, the upscale bistro **E.T.C.** serves tapas ($8-12) and hosts live jazz. Drag shows F and Su. Cover W $2, Th $3, F-Sa $5. Open Su-Th 9pm-2am, F-Sa 9pm-2:30am.

MADISON
☎ **608**

Locals in Madison refer to their city as "The Isthmus." For those who have forgotten their geography, that's a narrow strip of land that connects two larger landmasses. In other words, it's a rather awkward place to build a city. As a result, the capitol and the University of Wisconsin-Madison share very close living quarters. The odd coupling, though, has proven fruitful, as Madison's peculiar flavor is a fine blend of mature stateliness and youthful vigor.

TRANSPORTATION

Airport: Dane County Regional Airport, 4000 International Ln. (☎246-3380). Cabs to downtown run $8.50-12.

Buses: Greyhound, 2 S. Bedford St. (☎257-3050), has buses to **Chicago** (3-4hr.; 6 per day; M-Th $24, F-Su $26) and **Minneapolis** (5-6hr.; 4-6 per day; M-Th $40, F-Su $42.50). **Badger Bus** (☎255-6771; www.badgerbus.com) is located at the same address and offers service to **Milwaukee** (1½hr., 8 per day, $15). **Van Galder** (☎752-5407 or 800-747-0994; www.vangalderbus.com) departs from the UW Memorial Union, 800 Langdon St., to **Chicago** (3-4hr., 4 per day, $22).

Public Transit: Madison Metro Transit System, 1101 E. Washington Ave. (☎266-4466; www.ci.madison.wi.us/metro), serves downtown, campus, and environs ($1.50).

Taxi: Union Cab ☎242-2000.

ORIENTATION AND PRACTICAL INFORMATION

Madison's main attractions are centered around the capitol and the University of Wisconsin-Madison. **State Street,** which is reserved for pedestrians, bikers, and buses, connects the two and serves as the city's hub for eclectic food, shops, and nightlife. **Lake Monona** to the southeast and **Lake Mendota** to the northwest lap at Madison's shores. The northeast and southwest ends of the isthmus are joined by **Washington Avenue (U.S. 151),** the city's main thoroughfare. **I-90** and **I-94** are joined

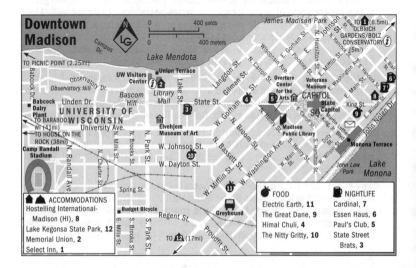

Downtown Madison

FOOD
Electric Earth, 11
The Great Dane, 9
Himal Chuli, 4
The Nitty Gritty, 10

NIGHTLIFE
Cardinal, 7
Essen Haus, 6
Paul's Club, 5
State Street Brats, 3

ACCOMMODATIONS
Hostelling International-Madison (HI), 8
Lake Kegonsa State Park, 12
Memorial Union, 2
Select Inn, 1

through the city, but separate on either side of it. I-94 E goes to Milwaukee, then Chicago; I-94 W goes to Minneapolis/St. Paul; I-90 E goes direct to Chicago through Rockford, IL; I-90 W goes to Albert Lea, MN.

Visitor Info: Greater Madison Convention and Visitors Bureau, 615 E. Washington Ave. (☎255-2537 or 800-373-6376; www.visitmadison.com. Open M-F 8am-5pm.)

Internet Access: Madison Public Library, 201 W. Mifflin St. (☎266-6300. Open M-W 8:30am-9pm, Th-F 8:30am-6pm, Sa 9am-5pm; Oct.-Apr. also open Su 1-5pm.)

Post Office: 3902 Milwaukee St., at Rte. 51. (☎245-6091. Open M-F 8am-6pm, Sa 9am-2pm.) **Postal Code:** 53714. **Area Code:** 608.

ACCOMMODATIONS

Motels stretch along Washington Ave. (U.S. 151) west of its intersection with I-90, with rooms starting at $40 per weeknight and rising dramatically on weekends. From the capitol, bus routes #6 and 7 drive the 5 mi. between the Washington Ave. motels and downtown. Prices get steeper downtown, starting around $60.

Hostelling International–Madison (HI), 141 S. Butler St. (☎441-0144; www.madison-hostel.org), at King St. This well-located hostel is a good bet for social travelers, and its no-shoe policy helps keep the rooms clean and comfortable. Internet access $1 per 10min. Kitchen, laundry. Reception 8am-10pm; in winter 8-11am and 5-9pm. Dorms $17, nonmembers $20; private rooms $41/$44. ❶

Memorial Union, 800 Langdon St. (☎262-1583), on the UW campus next to Union Terrace. Spacious rooms with excellent lake and city views. Cable TV, A/C, and free parking. Call ahead; the 6 rooms fill up—especially on football weekends—up to a year in advance. No-frills **college cafeterias** here dole out the quickest, cheapest food in town, with meals $5-8. Rooms from $65. Discounts for Union members. ❸

Select Inn, 4845 Hayes Rd. (☎249-1815), west of the junction of I-94 and U.S. 151. Large rooms with cable TV, A/C, whirlpool, and laundry. Free wireless Internet. Continental breakfast included or 10% off at Perkins next door. In summer singles from $46; doubles from $57. In winter $39/$46. ❸

Lake Kegonsa State Park, 2405 Door Creek Rd. (☎873-9695, reservations 888-947-2757), 20min. south on I-90 in Stoughton. Pleasant single, family, and large group sites in a wooded area near the beach. Showers, flush toilets. Parking permits $10/$5 per day. Park open 6am-11pm; campground open May-Oct. Sites M-F $10, WI residents $8; Sa-Su $12/$10. ❶

FOOD

Fine dining establishments pepper Madison, spicing up the university and capitol areas. **State Street** hosts a variety of cheap restaurants, including chains and Madison originals; at the Library Mall on its west end, vendors peddle international delicacies, including Thai, Indonesian, and East African treats.

The Great Dane, 123 E. Doty St. (☎284-0000), near the capitol. This popular, spacious brewpub serves hearty sandwiches, burgers, and other pub favorites ($7-18) along with a host of hand-crafted beers. Outdoor garden patio in summer. Open Su-Th 11am-2am, F-Sa 11am-2:30am. ❷

Himal Chuli, 318 State St. (☎251-9225). This storefront stirs up Nepalese favorites such as *tarkari, dal,* and *bhat.* In English, that means terrific veggie meals and lentil soup ($3). Flavorful meat dishes also available. Entrees $6-13. Open Su-Th 11am-9pm, F-Sa 11am-9:30pm.

The Nitty Gritty, 223 N. Frances St. (☎251-2521), at Johnston St. Burgers, beer, and birthdays abound at this grill, which celebrates a gazillion birthdays each day with loud-speaker announcements, balloons, and free beer (for the birthday person only). Just don't wear your birthday suit; they will totally throw you out. "Gritty Burger" $6.60. Entrees $5-10. Open M-Th 11am-2am, F-Sa 11am-2:30am, Su 5pm-midnight. ❷

Electric Earth, 546 W. Washington Ave. (☎255-2310), across from the bus station. Known affectionately as "EE," this funky juice bar keeps regulars satisfied with rich smoothies ($4) and sandwiches with homemade side salads ($5-7). Open M-F 7am-10pm, Sa 8am-8pm, Su 8am-10pm. ❶

👁 SIGHTS

INSIDE MADISON

With its two faces as a seat of government and home to a thriving college scene, the isthmus has an eclectic mix of sights. The imposing **State Capitol,** at the center of downtown, boasts beautiful ceiling frescoes and mosaics. (☎266-0382. Open M-F 8am-6pm, Sa-Su 8am-4pm. Free tours every hr. from the ground floor info desk M-F 9-11am and 1-4pm, Sa 9-11am and 1-3pm, Su 1-3pm.) Facing the capitol is the **Veterans Museum,** 30 W. Mifflin St., which contains exhibits tracing US military history from the Civil War to WWII with a focus on Wisconsin-born soldiers and infantry units. (☎267-1799; http://museum.dva.state.wi.us. Open Mar.-Sept. M-Sa 9am-4:30pm, Apr.-Sept. also Su noon-4pm. Free.) Close to the capitol at the end of Martin Luther King, Jr. Blvd. is the **Monona Terrace Community and Convention Center,** 1 John Nolen Dr., Frank Lloyd Wright's impressive 352,610 sq. ft. structure overlooking the lake. The rooftop gardens offer the city's best views of the capitol and Lake Monona. (☎261-4000; www.mononaterrace.com. Open daily 8am-5pm. 1hr. guided tours available daily 1pm. $3, students $2.) Every Wednesday and Saturday morning from late April to early November, visitors swarm the capitol grounds for the **Dane County Farmers Market,** where farmers sell fresh-picked crops. (☎800-373-6376; www.madfarmmkt.org. Open W 8:30am-2pm, Sa 6am-2pm.)

The **University of Wisconsin-Madison (UW)** itself has a few noteworthy museums. One of the state's most acclaimed art museums, the **Elvehjem Museum of Art** (EL-vee-hem), boasts an astounding collection of ancient Greek vases and several galleries of American and European painting. (800 University Ave. ☎263-2246; www.lvm.wisc.edu. Open Tu-F 9am-5pm, Sa-Su 11am-5pm. Tours Th 12:30pm permanent galleries, Su 2pm temporary galleries. Self-guided audio tours also available. Free.) In the mornings before 11am, visitors can watch their favorite ice-cream flavors being made at UW's own **Babcock Dairy Plant,** 1605 Linden Dr., at Babcock Dr. (☎262-3045. Store open M-F 9:30am-5:30pm, Sa 10am-1:30pm.)

Also part of UW, the outdoor **Olbrich Botanical Gardens** and indoor **Bolz Conservatory,** 3330 Atwood Ave., showcase dynamic exhibits, from butterfly-attracting plants to the exquisite Thai Pavilion—unique in the continental US—constructed entirely without nails and painted in gold leaf. (☎246-4550; www.olbrich.org. Gardens open daily Apr.-Sept. 8am-8pm; Oct.-Mar. 9am-4pm. Free. Conservatory open M-Sa 10am-4pm, Su 10am-5pm. $1, under 5 free; free W and Sa 10am-noon.) Aspiring botanists can trek along the 20 mi. of trails among the 1260 acres of the **University Arboretum,** 1207 Seminole Hwy., off Beltline Hwy. (☎263-7760. Grounds open daily 7am-10pm; Visitors center open M-F 9:30am-4pm, Sa-Su 12:30-4pm.) For more info visit the **UW Visitors Center,** 716 Langdon St., adjacent to the Memorial Union (☎263-2400).

OUTSIDE MADISON

Some of Madison's most unique sights are far from the town proper. The **House on the Rock,** 5754 Rte. 23, 1hr. west of Madison off U.S. 14 in Spring Green, is an unparalleled multilevel house built into a chimney of rock and contains kitschy collections ranging from dollhouses to airplanes. The 40-acre complex also features a 200 ft. fiberglass whale engaged in an epic struggle with a squid and the world's largest carousel—of its 269 animals, not one is a horse. (☎935-3639; www.thehouseontherock.com. Open daily July-Aug. 9am-7pm; June and late Aug. to early Sept. 9am-6pm; mid-Mar. to May and Sept. to early Nov. 9am-5pm. $19.50, ages 7-12 $11.50, ages 4-6 $5.50, under 3 free.) Nine miles north of the House on the Rock, Frank Lloyd Wright's famed **Taliesin** home and school hugs the hills and valley that inspired his style of organic architecture. (On Rte. 23 at Rte. C in Spring Green. ☎877-588-7900; www.taliesinpreservation.org. Open May-Oct. daily 9am-6pm. Call ahead for low-season tours. 5 walking tours examine various aspects of the estate. $16-75. Call for exact rates and schedules.) Twenty miles northwest of Madison, the **Circus World Museum**—once the winter home of the world-famous Ringling Brothers Circus—pays homage to the Greatest Show on Earth with a full lineup of events from big-top performances to street parades. (426 Water St. ☎356-8341; www.circusworldmuseum.com. Open in summer daily 9am-6pm. Bigtop shows 11am and 3:30pm. $15, seniors $13, ages 5-11 $8.)

🎵 ENTERTAINMENT

Twenty thousand music-lovers flood Capitol Sq. for six Wednesday nights in June and July when the Wisconsin Chamber Orchestra performs free **Concerts on the Square.** (☎257-0638. 7pm.) Leading out from the capitol, **State Street** exudes a lively college atmosphere, sporting many offbeat clothing stores and record shops, as well as a host of bars and restaurants. Replacing the Madison Civic Center in 2006, the **Overture Center for the Arts,** 201 State St. (258-4141; www.overture-center.com), will serve as an umbrella for theater, music, visual art, and dance. The former Oscar Mayer Theatre will be restored to its original name, the Capitol Theater, and will continue to host the **Madison Symphony Orchestra.** (☎258-4141; www.madisonsymphony.org. Tickets $24-68. Hours vary due to renovations. Season runs late Aug. to May.) During renovations, the **Madison Art Center** (☎257-0158; www.madisonartcenter.org) will sponsor off-site exhibits. The **Madison Repertory Theatre,** also located in the Overture Center in Promenade Hall, performs classic and contemporary works. (☎258-4141; www.madisonrep.org. Tickets $6.50-22. Showtimes vary.) Students and locals pass their days and nights on the signature chairs of UW's gorgeous, lakeside **Union Terrace.** (800 Langdon St. ☎265-3000.) The terrace is home to free weekend concerts year-round, which take place on the lakeshore in the summer, and move indoors in the winter.

🎶 NIGHTLIFE

Fueled by the 40,000-plus students who pack an aptly labeled party school, Madison's nightlife scene is active, with crowded bars scattered throughout the isthmus, particularly along **State Street** and **U.S. 151.**

Essen Haus, 514 E. Wilson St. (☎255-4674), off U.S. 151. This lively German bar and restaurant is the only place in town where college girls dance the polka with octogenarians. Round up a crew and pass around the infamous "beer boot" (from $15). On the menu, traditional German fare (bratwurst $6) rubs shoulders with American cuisine. Incredible beer selection (from $1.50). Open Tu-Sa 4-11pm, Su 3-11pm.

Cardinal, 418 E. Wilson St. (☎251-0080). A benchmark of Madison's gay scene, Cardinal also attracts straight clubbers who come for its wide array of themed dance nights every day of the week, from goth industrial and electronic underground to Latin jazz and 80s hits. Cover $3-5. Open M-Th 8pm-2am, F-Sa 8pm-2:30am.

State Street Brats, 603 State St. (☎255-5544). Head to "Brats" for the true wild and crazy college bar experience. 2 floors of frat-house fun with a wide list of Wisconsin microbrews. Brats and burgers ($3-8) anchor the menu. Open daily 11am-2am.

Paul's Club, 212 State St. (☎257-5250). Mingle under the branches of the full-size oak tree that adorns the bar at Paul's Club, a laid-back lounge that offers refuge from the drunken hijinks of State St. Enticing leather couches provide a great place to chat with the trendy crowd. Open M-Th 4pm-2am, F 4pm-2:30am, Sa noon-2:30am, Su 5pm-2am.

⚠ OUTDOOR ACTIVITIES

Madison's many parks and lakeshores offer endless recreational activities. There are 10 gorgeous public **beaches** along the two lakes for swimming or strolling (☎266-4711 for info). Back on dry land, **bicycling** is possibly the best way to explore the city and surrounding parklands. Madison is, in fact, the bike capital of the Midwest, with more bikes than cars traversing the landscape. **Budget Bicycle Center,** 1230 Regent St. (☎251-8413), loans out all types of two-wheeled transportation ($10 per day, $30 per week, tandems $15-30 per day). Hikers and picnickers can enjoy great views of the college at **Picnic Point** on Lake Mendota, a bit of a hike off University Bay Dr. For other city parks, the **Parks Department,** 215 Martin Luther King, Jr. Blvd., in the Madison Municipal Building, can help with specific park info. (☎266-4711. Office open M-F 8am-4:15pm; parks open daily 4am-dusk. Admission to Madison parks is free.) Wisconsin Union guests can rent canoes and equipment for croquet and horseshoes through **Outdoor Rentals** in the Memorial Union boathouse. (☎262-7351. Call ahead for rates and seasonal hours.) At nearby Lake Wingra, the **Wingra Canoe and Sailing Center,** 824 Knickerbocker Pl., rents canoes, kayaks, and other boats. (☎233-5332; www.wingraboats.com. $20 per half-day).

DOOR COUNTY ☎920

Jutting out like a thumb from the Wisconsin mainland between Green Bay and Lake Michigan, the Door Peninsula exudes a coastal spirit unlike any other in the nation's heartland. The rocky coastline, azure waters, and towering pines resemble a northeastern fishing village more than a Midwestern getaway. Door County beckons to both campers and vacationers with miles of bike paths, national and state parks, beaches, and quaint country inns. Despite its undeniable popularity as a tourist destination, the Door has largely managed to avoid commercialism and maintain its unique flavor. Its 12 villages swing open on a summer-oriented schedule; visitors are advised to make reservations for accommodations and campsites if they plan to be on the peninsula during a weekend in either July or August.

■ ⚡ **ORIENTATION AND PRACTICAL INFORMATION.** Door County begins at **Sturgeon Bay,** where Rte. 42 and 57 converge and then split again. Rte. 57 hugs the eastern coast; Rte. 42 runs up the west. The peninsula's west coast tends to be more expensive and touristy, while the eastern side contains sleepy villages and lakeside parks. From south to north along Rte. 42, **Egg Harbor, Fish Creek, Ephraim, Sister Bay,** and **Ellison Bay** are the largest towns. During the summer, the days are warm, but temperatures can dip to 40°F at night, even in July. Public transit only comes as close as **Green Bay,** 50 mi. southwest of Sturgeon Bay, where **Greyhound** has a station at 800 Cedar St. (☎ 432-4883; open M-F 6:30am-5pm; Sa-Su 10:30am-noon and 3:30-5pm) and runs to **Milwaukee** (2½hr., 4 per day, $25). Reserve tickets at least a day in advance. **Door County Chamber of Commerce:** 1015 Green Bay Rd., on Rte. 42/57 entering Sturgeon Bay. (☎ 743-4456 or 800-527-3529; www.doorcounty.com. Open Apr.-Oct. M-F 8:30am-5pm, Sa-Su 10am-4pm; Nov.-Mar. M-F 8:30am-4:30pm.) **Post Office:** 359 Louisiana, at 4th St. in Sturgeon Bay. (☎ 743-2681. Open M-F 8:30am-5pm, Sa 9:30am-noon.) **Postal Code:** 54235. **Area Code:** 920.

⌗ ACCOMMODATIONS. Unique, country-style lodgings crowd Rte. 42 and 57; reservations for July and August should be made far in advance. The ▨**Century Farm Motel ❸**, 10068 Rte. 57, 3 mi. south of Sister Bay on Rte. 57, rents cozy two-room cottages hand-built in the 1920s. The motel, situated on a chicken and buffalo farm, is removed from the tourist activity of the Door's towns and offers fantastic peak season prices. (☎ 854-4069. A/C, TV, and fridge. Open mid-May to mid-Oct. $45-65. Cash only.) Relaxed and convenient, the **Lull-Abi Motel ❸**, 7928 Egg Harbor Rd./Rte. 42 in Egg Harbor, soothes visitors with spacious rooms, a patio, an indoor whirlpool, free coffee, and some suites with wet bars and refrigerator. (☎ 868-3135. Open May to late Oct. Rooms $59-159.)

✴ CAMPING. Except for the restricted **Whitefish Dunes**, the area's **state parks ❶** offer outstanding camping. (Reservations for all parks ☎ 888-947-2757; www.wiparks.net. $10, WI residents $8; F-Sa $12/$10.) All state parks require a **motor vehicle permit** ($3 per hr.; $10/$5 per day; $30/$20 per yr.). **Peninsula State Park,** just past Fish Creek village on Rte. 42, contains 20 mi. of shoreline and 17 mi. of trails, and puts campers within easy reach of western shore attractions. (☎ 868-3258. 469 sites with showers and toilets. Make reservations far in advance, or try your luck with one of 25 walk-in sites.) The relatively uncrowded **Potawatomi State Park,** 3740 Park Dr., sits just south of Sturgeon Bay off Rte. 42/57. (☎ 746-2890. 123 campsites, 19 open to walk-ins. 25 sites have electricity.) Highlighted by hidden coves, **Newport State Park,** 7 mi. from Ellison Bay off Rte. 42, is a wildlife preserve at the tip of the peninsula. Sites are accessible by hiking only. (☎ 854-2500. 16 sites, 3 open to walk-ins. No showers.) The untamed **Rock Island State Park** offers 40 remote sites off Washington Island's northern shore. (☎ 847-2235. Open late May to mid-Oct. 15min. ferry ride $8, children 5-10 $4, campers $9.)

◻ FOOD. Food from the lake and traditional Scandinavian dishes dominate Door County fare. Many people visit the region just for ▨**fish boils,** a Scandinavian tradition in which cooks toss potatoes, spices, and whitefish into a large kettle over a wood fire. To remove the fish oil from the top of the water, the boilmaster throws kerosene into the fire, producing a massive fireball; the cauldron boils over, signaling chow time. The local favorite on the peninsula is the ▨ **Coyote Roadhouse ❹**, on County Rte. E, west of Baileys Harbor, which dishes out a mean jambalaya ($15) and a Friday night fish-fry ($12) that is not to be missed. (☎ 839-9192. Open daily 11am-10pm.) Patrons crowd into the **Bayside Tavern ❶**, on Rte. 42 in Fish Creek, sidling up to the bar for spicy, Cincinnati-style chili ($4) and specialty burgers for $4.25-7. (☎ 868-3441; www.baysidetavern.com. Live music M and Sa. Open mic Th. Sa cover $5. Open Su-Th 11am-2am, F-Sa 11am-2:30am.) Door County's best-known fish boils bubble up at **The Viking Grill ❹**, in Ellison Bay. (☎ 854-2998. Open daily 6am-8pm, fish boils mid-May to Oct. 4:30-8pm. $14, under 12 $11.) Drop in on **Al Johnson's Swedish Restaurant ❹**, 700-710 Bayshore Dr., in the middle of Sister Bay on Rte. 42, for Swedish pancakes ($6.75), served with lingonberries. The restaurant is hard to miss; just look for the goats grazing atop the sod-covered roof. (☎ 854-2626. Entrees $14-18. Open daily 6am-9pm; low-season 7am-8pm.)

GREAT LAKES

GREAT LAKES

◨ **SIGHTS.** Most of Door County's sights are located on the more populated west side. At the base of the peninsula, the historic Great Lakes shipbuilding center of Sturgeon Bay houses the intriguing **Door County Maritime Museum,** 120 N. Madison St., downtown. The museum offers insight into the area's maritime history, and features a working periscope that offers visitors a 360° view of the bay. (☎743-5958; www.dcmm.org. Open May-Oct. daily 9am-6pm. $6.50, ages 5-17 $3.) The museum also operates an exhibit at **Gill's Rock,** where visitors can explore a 1930 fishing boat. (☎854-1844. Open mid-May to mid-Oct. daily 10am-5pm. $4, children 5-17 $1.) The ◨**Skyway Drive-In,** on Rte. 42 between Fish Creek and Ephraim, screens double features at great prices. (☎854-9938. Current release double feature $6, ages 6-11 $3. Call for schedules.) Just south of the Skyway, Peninsula State Park houses the outdoor **American Folklore Theatre,** where a local troupe performs original, Wisconsin-themed shows. (☎854-6117; www.americanfolktheatre.com. $14, ages 13-19 $7.50, ages 6-12 $4.50.)

In the quiet shipping town of **Green Bay,** 50 mi. south of Sturgeon Bay at the foot of the Door peninsula, fanatical Green Bay Packers fans swarm **Lambeau Field** to witness bone-crushing gridiron action in the house that Vince Lombardi built. (☎965-3709. Tours daily 10am-4pm. $8, seniors $7, children 6-11 $5.)

◨ OUTDOOR ACTIVITIES. Biking is the best way to take in the largely untouched lighthouses, rocks, and white-sand beaches of the Door's rugged eastern coastline. Village tourist offices have free bike maps. **Whitefish Dunes State Park,** off Rte. 57, glimmers with extensive sand dunes, hiking/biking/skiing trails, and a well-kept wildlife preserve. (Open daily 8am-8pm. Vehicle permit required.) Just north of the Dunes off Rte. 57 on Cave Point Rd., the rugged **Cave Point County Park** has some of the best views on the peninsula. (Open daily 6am-9pm. Free.) In **Baileys Harbor,** 3 mi. north of Lakeside, waves and wind have carved miles of sand ridges along the coastline. **Ridges Sanctuary,** north of Baileys Harbor off Rte. Q, has trails meandering through the 30 ridges, which are separated by wetlands called swales. The unique ecosystem is home to a thriving population of plants and fauna, including a number of endangered species. Also offered are birdwatching opportunities and a boreal forest at **Toft's Point.** (☎839-2802. Nature center open daily 9am-4pm. $2.) **Baileys Harbor Ridges Beach,** an uncrowded stretch of sand that allows for secluded swimming, adjoins the sanctuary on Ridges Rd.

Accessed via Cana Island Rd. off Rte. Q, **Cana Island Lighthouse** juts out from the lake, compelling visitors to cross the rocky path (at low tide) or wade through the frigid waters (at high tide) to reach its oft-photographed shores. There is no access to the lighthouse itself, but the island provides an expansive view of the bay. (No phone. No facilities. Open daily 10am-5pm. $3, ages 5-17 $1.)

The west side's recreational offerings are fewer than the east side's, but they are no less exciting. **Peninsula State Park,** in Fish Creek, is a popular spot for tourists. Visitors rent boats and ride bicycles along 20 mi. of shoreline road. More crowded than east coast beach options, **Nicolet Beach** (inside the park) attracts sunbathers from all over the peninsula. One mile and 110 steps up from the beach, **Eagle Tower** offers the highest view of the shore. On a clear day, the tower allows a glimpse of Michigan's shores across the waters of Green Bay. (Open daily 6am-11pm. Vehicle permit required.) Across from the Fish Creek entrance to Peninsula State Park, **Nor Door Sport and Cyclery,** 4007 Rte. 42, rents out bikes and winter equipment. (☎868-2275; www.nordoorsports.com. Open June-Oct. M-Sa 9am-6pm, Su 9am-5pm; Nov.-May M and F-Sa 9am-5pm, Su 9am-3pm. Bikes $5 per hr., $20 per day. Cross-country skis $10 per day.)

Situated at the northern tip of the peninsula, **Washington Island** is separated from the mainland by **Death's Door,** a treacherous channel that brought about the demise of hundreds of vessels in the 19th century. Today, modern ferries deposit daytrippers safely on the island's shores, allowing them to experience a unique ethnic enclave built by Icelandic settlers, pedal over 75 mi. of quiet country roads, and relax on peaceful beaches. (Two ferry companies, Washington Island Ferry and Island Clipper, depart frequently from Gill's Rock. Ferry $9, children 6-11 $5. Washington Island Ferry shuttles automobiles for $22 and bikes for $4; bike transport is free on the Island Clipper. One-speed bikes can be rented at the island dock for $3.50 per hr.)

APOSTLE ISLANDS   ☎ 715

The National Lakeshore protects 22 of the breathtaking islands off the coast of northern Wisconsin, as well as a 12 mi. stretch of mainland shore. Bayfield, a tiny mainland town, serves as the access point to the islands. Tourism is focused on the mainland and Madeline Island, where coastal inns draw families looking for a back-to-nature weekend. Backpackers pour into town on their way to and from hikes, kayakers explore island caves, and sailors delight in the clear waters. Adventure companies allow summer tourists with all levels of outdoor experience to enjoy kayaking, hiking, and camping among the unspoiled sandstone bluffs.

⑦ PRACTICAL INFORMATION. Most excursions begin in the sleepy mainland town of **Bayfield** (pop. 686), in northwest Wisconsin on the Lake Superior coast. The **Bay Area Rural Transit (BART),** 300 Industrial Park Rd., 21 mi. south on Rte. 13 in Ashland, offers a shuttle to Bayfield. (☎ 682-9664. 4 per day M-F 7am-5pm. $2.10, students $1.75, seniors $1.35.) **Visitor Info: Bayfield Chamber of Commerce,** 42 S. Broad St. (☎ 779-3335 or 800-447-4094; www.bayfield.org. Open M-F 8:30am-5pm, Sa-Su 9am-4:30pm. Lobby with free local phone open 24hr.) **National Lakeshore Headquarters Visitors Center,** 415 Washington Ave., distributes hiking info and **camping permits,** and screens a short film on the islands. (☎ 779-3398. Open mid-May to mid-Sept. daily 8am-4:30pm; mid-Sept. to mid-May W-Su 8am-4:30pm. Permits for up to 14 consecutive days $15.) For **short-term work** picking apples and raspberries, contact the **Bayfield Apple Company,** on County J Rd. near the intersection of Betzold Rd. (☎ 779-5700 or 800-363-4526. Open May-Jan. daily 9am-6pm.) **Post Office:** 22 S. Broad St., Bayfield. (☎ 779-5636. Open M-F 9am-4:30pm, Sa 9am-11am.) **Postal Code:** 54814. **Area Code:** 715.

⑥ ACCOMMODATIONS. In summer months, the budget pickings are slim for Bayfield, and rooms should be booked weeks in advance for trips during

THE LOCAL STORY

DEATH'S DOOR

Today ferries and pleasure craft happily ply the waters between Washington Island and the mainland peninsula. With the recent arrival of a double-hulled ferry capable of breaking through layers of ice, even Lake Michigan's stormy winter waters seem less menacing. However, according to local lore, the 6-mile-wide strait wasn't always so inviting. Legend has it that long ago, a war party of Potawatomi Indians—Washington Island's first settlers—set out in canoes for the mainland, only to be drowned when the weather turned foul. Their bodies washed up on a narrow spit of land in the channel known as Detroit Island, and skeletons were said to dot the landscape there until the mid-19th century. Thus, the Potawatomi named this strait "door to death."

Another tale is that French explorer Robert La Salle rests somewhere at the bottom of the strait. In 1679, La Salle sailed his ship from Mackinac to Washington Island to trade furs with the Native Americans. After completing his business, he weighed anchor and was never seen again. Translated into French, the strait became known as *Porte des Mortes.* The strait took its Anglicized name in the 19th century. Even with a lighthouse to aid mariners in navigating the tricky currents, over 100 ships were lost in 1872, and in 1895 the authorities finally installed a second lighthouse.

July and August. For cheaper lodgings, try Ashland, an easy 30min. drive south of Bayfield. The **Seagull Bay Motel ❸**, off Rte. 13 at S. 7th St., offers spacious, smoke-free rooms with cable TV and a lake view. (☎779-5558; www.seagull-bay.com. Mid-May to mid-Oct. $70-90; mid-Oct. to mid-May $40-70.) **Greunke's First Street Inn ❹**, 17 Rittenhouse Ave., has been accommodating guests for 139 years. Quaint country rooms and a homey atmosphere make this a great place to experience Bayfield hospitality. (☎779-5480 or 800-245-3072. Open May-Oct. Rooms $55-130.) **Dalrymple Park ❶**, ¼ mi. north of town on Rte. 13, has 30 campsites and a sweeping view of Madeline Island. (Open mid-May to mid-Oct. No showers; self-regulated; no reservations. Sites $15.) **Apostle Islands Area Campground ❶**, ½ mi. south of Bayfield on County Rd. J off Rte. 13, has 55 campsites buried in the woods of Bayfield. (☎779-5524. Open early May to early Oct. Reservations recommended 1 month in advance for July-Aug. Sites $15, with hookup $20, with full sewer and cable $27. Primitive cabins $40.) The Chamber of Commerce has info on **guesthouses** (from $35).

⬢ FOOD. The bright pink exterior is just the beginning at **Maggie's ❷**, 257 Manypenny Ave., where satisfying burgers ($6-7) and zesty fajitas ($10) complement the Mardi Gras and flamingo decor. (☎779-5641; www.maggiesbayfield.com. Open M-F 11:30am-9pm, Sa-Su 11:30am-10pm.) One of the oldest establishments in Bayfield, **Greunke's Restaurant ❸**, 17 Rittenhouse Ave., at 1st St., has been serving hungry fisherman for over a century. These days, it specializes in huge breakfasts by day ($3.25-7) and famous fish boils by night. Check out the shrine to the late John F. Kennedy, Jr., located next to the still-working 1946 Wurlitzer jukebox. (☎779-5480. Fish boils W-Su 6:30-8pm. $11, children $6. Open M-Sa 6am-10pm, F-Su 7am-9:30pm.) **Egg Toss Cafe ❷**, 41 Manypenny Ave., specializes in the first meal of the day, serving up Eggs Benedict with smoked trout or crabcakes ($8.75), as well as more traditional breakfasts for $5.50-10. (☎779-5181; www.eggtoss-bayfield.com. Open daily 7am-2pm.)

⬢ ⬤ SIGHTS AND OUTDOOR ACTIVITIES. Though often overshadowed by Bayfield and Madeline Island (see below), the other 21 islands have their own subtle charms. The **sandstone quarries** of Basswood and the Hermit Islands and the abandoned logging and fishing camps on some of the other islands serve as silent reminders of a more prosperous era. The restored **lighthouses** on Sand, Raspberry, Long, Michigan, Outer, and Devil's Islands offer spectacular views. **Sea caves**, carved out by thousands of years of wind and water, create a spectacular sight on several islands. The **Apostle Islands Cruise Service** runs narrated 3hr. tours that provide a brief look at these sights and a sampling of the history and lore of the islands. From late June to early September, the cruise service runs an inter-island shuttle. (☎779-3925 or 800-323-7619. Tours of the archipelago depart the Bayfield City Dock mid-May to mid-Oct. daily 10am. Call for additional tours and departure times. $26, children $15. Reservations recommended.)

The best beach on the mainland is **Bayview Beach**, just south of Bayfield along Rte. 13, near Sioux Flats. Look carefully for the dirt road marked Bayview Park Rd. to enter this serene beach. **Trek and Trail**, at 1st and Washington St., rents bikes and kayaks and runs various kayaking tours of the islands. (☎800-354-8735. Bikes $5 per hr., $20 per day. 4hr. kayak rental from $20, all equipment included, but renters must complete a $50 kayaking safety course. Tours from $50.)

Bayfield's apples attract visitors after the summer hikers leave. The population swells to 40,000 during the **Apple Festival** in the first full weekend of October, when natives and tourists alike gather for the street fairs. The **Bayfield Apple Company** offers fresh-picked fruit and tasty jam. Locals flock to **Big Top Chautauqua**, 3 mi.

south of Bayfield off Hwy. 13 on Ski Hill Rd., to see national acts such as Willie Nelson and the ever-popular "house shows," original musicals about life in northern Wisconsin. (☎373-5552 or 888-244-8386; www.bigtop.org. Open June-Sept. Call for showtimes. Tickets can be purchased at the Bayfield Branch Box Office, Rittenhouse Ave. and 1st St., next to Greunke's. Reserved seating $18, children 12 and under $8; general admission $12/$4.)

MADELINE ISLAND   ☎ 715

Several hundred years ago, the Ojibwe tribe came to Madeline Island from the Atlantic in search of the megis shell, a light in the sky purported to bring prosperity and health. Today, the island maintains its allure, housing a colony of artists alongside relaxing beaches frequented by thousands of summer visitors.

The **Madeline Island Motel ❹**, on Col. Woods Ave. across from the ferry landing, has private patios as well as clean rooms named for local historical figures. (☎747-3000. TV, A/C, fridges, microwaves. Continental breakfast included. July to early Sept. doubles $95; low-season $60-70.) **Cadotte's Cottages ❺**, on Col. Woods Ave. across from the ferry landing, has well-kept cottages with two bedrooms, TV, and a kitchen for some of the lowest rates on the island. (☎747-3075. Open May-Oct. Linens and towels provided. 2-night min. stay. $100-120.) Rooms in the area fill during the summer; call ahead for reservations. Madeline Island has two campgrounds. **Big Bay Town Park ❶**, 6½ mi. from La Pointe off Big Bay Rd., sits next to tranquil Big Bay Lagoon. (☎747-6913. No reservations. Open mid-May to mid-Oct. Sites $15, with electricity $20.) Across the lagoon, **Big Bay State Park ❶** rents 60 primitive sites and five sites with electricity. (☎747-6425, reservations 888-947-2757; www.wiparks.net. Reservations $8.50. Sites $10-12, with electricity $45. Daily vehicle permit $10, WI residents $5.)

Tom's Burned Down Cafe ❷, 1 Middle Rd., may look like a garage sale with bizarre sculptures out front, but the lively bar serves healthy food, including many vegan options, and hosts the islands' artist community. (☎747-6100. Wraps and sandwiches $5.50-7, pizzas $9. Open mic Th; live music Sa-Su. Cover $3-5. Open daily Su-Th 10am-2am, F-Sa 10am-2:30am.) **Ella's Island Cafe ❷**, to the left of the ferry landing, is a crowded breakfast joint by morning, pie shop and bar by night. Breakfast $3-9. (☎747-2400. Open daily 7:30am-1pm, most evenings also 5-10pm.)

With roughly five streets, Madeline Island is easy to navigate. **Visitor Info: Madeline Island Chamber of Commerce,** on Main St. to the right of the ferry landing. (☎747-2801 or 888-475-3386; www.madelineisland.com. Open M-F 9am-5pm, Sa 10am-3pm.) For pamphlets about the island, visit the chamber's booth near the ferry landing in Bayfield. **Madeline Island Ferry Line** shuttles between Bayfield and La Pointe on Madeline Island. (☎747-2051; www.madferry.com. June-Aug. daily every 30min. 9:30am-6pm, every hr. 6:30-9:30am and 6-11pm. $4.25, ages 6-11 $2; bikes $2; cars $9.25. Mar.-May and Sept.-Dec. ferries run less frequently and prices drop.) In winter, the state highway department builds an ice road. During transition periods, the ferry service runs **windsleds** between the island and the mainland. **Motion to Go,** 102 Lake View Pl., on Middle Rd. about one block from the ferry, rents scooters and bikes. (☎747-6585. Open daily May to mid-June 9am-6pm; mid-June to July 8:30am-7pm; July-Aug. 8am-8pm; Sept. to mid-Oct. 9am-7pm. Mopeds $20 per hr.; mountain bikes $7 per hr., $26 per day.) Housed in a 19th-century fur trader's warehouse, the **Madeline Island Historical Museum** keeps alive the island's rich history, from Indians and missionaries to fishermen and loggers. (☎747-2415. Open June-Sept. daily 10am-5pm. $5.50, seniors $5, children 5-12 $2.75.) The **Post Office** is just off the dock on Madeline Island in La Pointe. (☎747-3712. Open M-F 9am-4:20pm, Sa 9:30am-12:50pm.) **Postal Code:** 54850. **Area Code:** 715.

MINNESOTA

In the 19th century, floods of German and Scandinavian settlers edged native tribes out of the rich lands now known as Minnesota, a name derived from a Dakota word meaning "sky-tinted waters." More than 15,000 lakes cover the state, from the northern wilderness and Boundary Waters to the more settled south and Twin Cities. From farmers to city dwellers, Minnesotans persevere through harsh winters and cultivate close-knit communities. Attempts at preserving the state's rugged northern frontier have helped raise awareness about Minnesota's natural resources and the culture of the Ojibwe, the area's Native American antecedents.

◪ PRACTICAL INFORMATION

Capital: St. Paul.

Visitor Info: Minnesota Office of Tourism, 100 Metro Sq., 121 7th Pl. E, St. Paul 55101 (☎800-657-3700; www.exploreminnesota.com). Open M-F 8am-4:30pm.

Postal Abbreviation: MN. **Sales Tax:** 6.5%.

MINNEAPOLIS AND ST. PAUL ☎612

Native Garrison Keillor wrote that the "difference between St. Paul and Minneapolis is the difference between pumpernickel and Wonder bread." Indeed, the story of the Twin Cities is one of contrast: St. Paul is accurately described as a conservative, Irish-Catholic town, while Minneapolis deserves its distinction as a rising young metropolis. Minneapolis's theaters and clubs rival those of New York City, while stately sights such as the traditional capitol and cathedral reside in St. Paul.

▬ TRANSPORTATION

Airport: Minneapolis-St. Paul International (☎726-5555; www.mspairport.com), 15min. south of the cities on Rte. 5, off I-494 in Bloomington. From the airport, take the Hiawatha light rail line to Minneapolis or bus #54 to St. Paul. **Super Shuttle** (☎827-7777; www.supershuttle.com) shuttles to both downtowns and to some hotels roughly every 30min. Desk open 8am-11pm. To **Minneapolis** ($13) and **St. Paul** ($11).

Trains: Amtrak, 730 Transfer Rd. (☎651-644-6012 or 800-872-7245), on the east bank off University Ave. SE, between the Twin Cities. City bus #16 connects to both downtowns. Open daily 6:30am-11:30pm. To **Chicago** (8hr., 5 per day, $44-97) and **Milwaukee** (6hr., 3 per day, $41-90).

Buses: Greyhound, 950 Hawthorne Ave. (☎371-3325; open daily 5:30am-1am), in downtown Minneapolis. In St. Paul, 950 University Ave. (☎651-222-0507; open daily 6:15am-9pm), 2 blocks west of the capitol. To **Chicago** (9-12hr., 10 or more per day, $61-68) and **Milwaukee** (7-9 hr., 7 or more per day, $50-55). Both routes depart from Minneapolis and St. Paul stations.

Public Transit: MetroTransit, 560 6th Ave. N (☎373-3333; www.metrotransit.org), serves both cities. Most major lines end service by 12:45am; some buses operate 24hr. $1.25; seniors, ages 6-12, and disabled $0.50. Peak fare (M-F 6-9am and 3-6:30pm) $1.75. Express lines $2.50/$1.75. Bus #16 connects the 2 downtowns and operates 24hr. (45min.); bus # 94 (B, C, or D) takes 30min.; bus #50 runs limited rush hour service (20min.).

Taxi: Yellow Taxi ☎824-4444 in Minneapolis, 651-222-4433 in St. Paul.

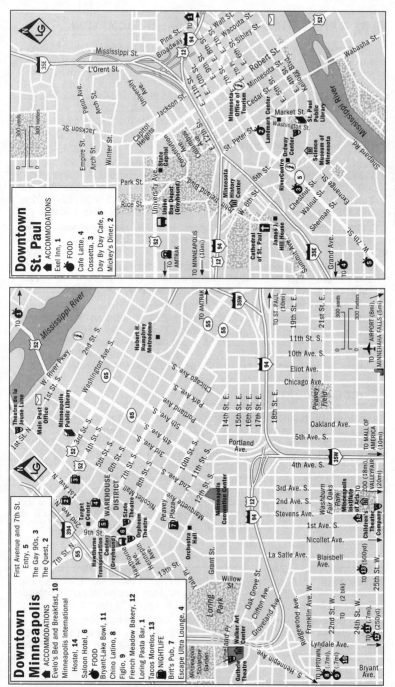

GREAT LAKES

Downtown St. Paul

▲ ACCOMMODATIONS
Exel Inn, **1**

◆ FOOD
Cafe Latte, **4**
Cossetta, **3**
Day By Day Cafe, **5**
Mickey's Diner, **2**

Downtown Minneapolis

▲ ACCOMMODATIONS
Evelo's Bed and Breakfast, **10**
Minneapolis International Hostel, **14**

◆ FOOD
Saloon Hotel, **6**
Bryant-Lake Bowl, **11**
Chino Latino, **8**
Figlio, **9**
French Meadow Bakery, **12**
Loring Pasta Bar, **1**
Tacos Morelos, **13**

◆ NIGHTLIFE
Brit's Pub, **7**
Escape Ultra Lounge, **4**
First Avenue and 7th St. Entry, **5**
The Gay 90s, **3**
The Quest, **2**

✳ ⁊ ORIENTATION AND PRACTICAL INFORMATION

Public transit is improving in the Twin Cities with the addition of the Hiawatha light rail line. Despite one-way streets and skewed numbered grids, the streets are not congested and parking garages are reasonably priced, making driving in the city manageable. Downtown Minneapolis lies about 10 mi. west of downtown St. Paul via **I-94**. **I-35** splits in the Twin Cities, with **I-35 W** serving Minneapolis and **I-35 E** serving St. Paul. **I-494** runs to the airport and the Mall of America, while **I-394** heads to downtown Minneapolis from the western suburbs. **Hennepin Avenue** and the pedestrian **Nicollet Mall** are the two main roads in Minneapolis; **Kellogg Avenue** and **7th Street** are the primary thoroughfares in St. Paul.

Visitor Info: Minneapolis Convention and Visitors Association, 250 Marquette Ave., in a kiosk at the Convention Center (☎335-6000; www.minneapolis.org). Publications available M-Sa 6am-10pm, Su 7am-8pm; desk open M-Sa 8am-4:30pm, Su noon-5pm. **St. Paul Convention and Visitors Bureau,** 175 W. Kellogg Blvd., #502 (☎800-627-6101 or 651-265-4900; www.visitstpaul.com), in the River Centre. Open M-F 8am-4:30pm.

Hotlines: Crime Victim Center Crisis Line, ☎340-5400. **Rape/Sexual Assault Line,** ☎825-4357. Both open 24hr. **Gay-Lesbian Helpline,** ☎822-8661. Open M-F noon-midnight, Sa 4pm-midnight.

Internet Access: Minneapolis Public Library, 250 Marquette Ave. (☎630-6200; www.mplib.org). Open M, W, F 10am-5pm, Tu and Th noon-7pm, Sa 10am-5pm. **St. Paul Public Library,** 90 W. 4th St. (☎651-266-7000; www.sppl.org). Open M 11:30am-8pm, Tu-W and F 9am-5:30pm, Th 9am-8pm, Sa 11am-4pm.

Post Office: In Minneapolis, 100 S. 1st St. (☎349-4713), at Marquette Ave. on the river. Open M-F 7am-8pm, Sa 9am-1pm. In St. Paul, 180 E. Kellogg Blvd. (☎651-293-3268). Open M-F 8:30am-5:30pm, Sa 9am-noon. **Postal Codes:** Minneapolis 55401, St. Paul 55101. **Area Codes:** Minneapolis 612, St. Paul and eastern suburbs 651, southwestern suburbs 952, northwestern suburbs 763. In text, 612 unless otherwise noted.

⌂ ACCOMMODATIONS

The Twin Cities are filled with unpretentious, inexpensive accommodations. Minneapolis caters to a younger crowd and consequently has cheaper hotels; St. Paul offers finer establishments for those with thicker wallets. The visitors centers have lists of **B&Bs,** while the **University of Minnesota Housing Office** (☎624-2994; www.umn.edu/housing/offcampus.htm) keeps a list of local rooms ($15-60) that can be rented on a daily or weekly basis. The section of I-494 at Rte. 77, near the Mall of America, is lined with chain motels from $40. The nearest private campgrounds are about 15 mi. outside the city; the closest state park camping is in the **Hennepin Park** system, 25 mi. away. Call **Minnesota State Parks** (☎651-296-6157 or 888-646-6367) or the **Minnesota Alliance of Campground Operators** (☎651-778-2400).

Minneapolis International Hostel, 2400 Stevens Ave. S (☎522-5000; www.minneapolishostel.com), south of downtown Minneapolis by the Institute of Arts. Take bus #17 from Nicollet Mall to 24th St. and walk 2 blocks east to Stevens. Visitors from around the world give this clean hostel a strong community feel. Internet access, kitchen, living room, porch, and patio. Check-in 1pm. Check-out 11am. Reservations recommended. Beds with linen $20, with student ID or HI membership $19; singles $49. ❶

Evelo's Bed and Breakfast, 2301 Bryant Ave. (☎374-9656), in south Minneapolis, just off Hennepin Ave. Take bus #17 from downtown to Bryant Ave. Owners rent out 3 lovingly tended rooms in this 1897 Victorian home. Fresh flowers in each room, continental breakfast, and shared bathroom. Reservations and deposit required. Singles $55; doubles $70. ❸

Saloon Hotel, 828 Hennepin Ave. (☎288-0459; www.gaympls.com), in downtown Minneapolis, between 8th and 9th St. Located above the Saloon nightclub, this hotel offers visitors food, lodging, and entertainment in a venue geared toward the BGLT community, though all are welcome. "The inn that's out" has a colorful lounge with TV and free Internet access. Private rooms with communal bathrooms. Reservations recommended. Singles $44; doubles $50-65. ❷

Exel Inn, 1739 Old Hudson Rd. (☎651-771-5566; www.exelinns.com), in St. Paul off 94E, exit #245. Clean rooms, cable TV, and easy access to St. Paul and the Mall of America (15min.). Reservations recommended. Singles $45-55; doubles $60-65. ❷

◧ FOOD

The Twin Cities' cosmopolitan, cultured vibe is reflected in its many culinary choices. Posh restaurants share the streets with intimate cafes. **Uptown** Minneapolis, near Lake St. and Hennepin Ave., offers plenty of funky restaurants and bars where the Twin Cities' young socialites meet after work. In downtown Minneapolis, the **Warehouse District,** on 1st Ave. N between 8th St. and Washington Ave., and **Nicollet Mall,** a 12-block pedestrian stretch of Nicollet Ave., attract locals and tourists with shops and simple food options ranging from burgers to Tex-Mex. While grabbing a bite to eat, check out the statue of **Mary Tyler Moore,** famous for turning the world on with her smile, at Nicollet and 7th St. South of downtown, Nicollet turns into **Eat Street,** a 17-block stretch of international cuisine. In St. Paul, the upscale **Grand Avenue,** between Lexington and Dale, is lined with laid-back restaurants and bars, while **Lowertown,** along Sibley St. near 6th St. downtown, is a popular nighttime hangout. Near the University of Minnesota (U of M) campus between the downtowns, **Dinkytown,** on the East Bank of the river, and the **Seven Corners** area of the West Bank, on Cedar Ave., cater to student appetites—including late night cravings. In the Twin Cities, many forgo restaurants for area **cafes** (p. 628). The **Minneapolis Farmers Market** off 94W at E. Lyndale Ave. and 3rd Ave. N, offers an array of fruits, vegetables, and crafts in over 450 booths that comprise the "largest open-air market in the Upper Midwest." (☎333-1737. Open Sa-Su 6am-1pm.)

MINNEAPOLIS

▩ Chino Latino, 2916 Hennepin Ave. (☎824-7878), at Lake St., Uptown. Drinks like the signature watermelon *mojito* ($8.50) characterize this trendy Latin-Asian fusion. Offering entrees for two ($13-40), a chic *satay* bar ($7-9), and unusual dishes that often require instruction from the waitstaff, Chino Latino is a destination for the hip. Call ahead to order guinea pig. Open daily 4:30pm-1am. Reservations recommended. ❸

Bryant-Lake Bowl, 810 W. Lake St. (☎825-3737), at Bryant St. near Uptown. Built in the 1930s, this funky bowling alley/bar/cabaret serves quality food at friendly prices—the "BLB Scramble" (a breakfast dish of eggs and vegetables; $5.50), ravioli, soups, and sandwiches ensure that the stylish patrons throw strikes with pleasantly full stomachs. Bowling $3.75. Entrees $8-15. Open daily 8am-1am. ❷

Loring Pasta Bar, 327 14th Ave. SE (☎378-4849; www.loringpastabar.com), in Dinkytown near the U of M campus. The meticulously decorated restaurant is simultaneously whimsical and sophisticated, with an eclectic menu ranging from potstickers ($7) to pastas ($13-15). Musicians play nightly, with a Su night tango DJ. Open M-Sa 11:30am-1am, Su 5:30pm-1am (kitchen closes earlier). ❷

Figlio, 3001 Hennepin Ave. (☎822-1688), at W. Lake St. in the Calhoun Square complex, Uptown. Figlio has been awarded the honor of "Best Late Night Dining" by Twin City residents for many years for its scrumptious sandwiches (from $9) and delicious pastas and pizzas (from $11). You haven't lived until you've indulged in "Death By Chocolate" ($6.50), which packs layers of chocolate and amaretto underneath two delightful scoops of ice cream. Open Su-Th 11:30am-1am, F-Sa 11:30am-2am. ❸

Tacos Morelos, 14 26th St. W (☎870-5050), at Nicollet Ave. Hispanophiles can practice their Spanish at this award-winning, authentic Mexican establishment. Try the "3 Amigos" enchiladas (3 enchiladas, each with a different sauce; $11.50), or gorge on their famous tacos ($2.25 each). Entrees from $8. Open daily 10am-10pm. ❷

French Meadow Bakery, 2901 Lyndale Ave. S (☎870-4740, www.organicbread.com), on "Breakfast Row," serves sit-down meals that include organic bread made with "healthy hemp." Breakfast entrees from $4, lunch and dinner from $7. 9 sq. in. cinnamon rolls $3.50. Open Su-Th 6:30am-10pm, F-Sa 6:30am-11pm. ❷

ST. PAUL

Cossetta, 211 W. 7th St. (☎651-222-3476). What began as an Italian market in 1911 now serves quality eat-in or take-out specialties. Try the veal parmigiana ($9) or Cossetta's famous pizza ($11-21). Open Su-Th 11am-9pm, F-Sa 11am-10pm; in winter Su 11am-8pm, M-Th 11am-9pm, F-Sa 11am-10pm. ❷

Mickey's Diner, 36 W. 7th St. (☎651-222-5633), at St. Peter St. A 1937 diner on the National Register of Historic Places, Mickey's offers food that outshines its bright history and chrome-and-vinyl decor. Take a spin at a counter stool, or groove to some oldies on the juke box at each booth (30min. limit). Steak and eggs from $6. Pancakes $3.75. 2 eggs $2.25. Omelette $6. Open 24hr. ❶

Day By Day Cafe, 477 W. 7th St. (☎227-0654; www.daybyday.com). Started in 1975 by an alcoholism treatment center, Day By Day now serves the community at large, with breakfast all day ($4.50-8), as well as lunch and dinner specials ($7.50-9), in its library-like dining room and spacious outdoor patio. Live music F 7-10pm. Open M-Th 6am-8pm, F 6am-10pm, Sa 6am-3pm, Su 7am-3pm. Cash only. ❷

Cafe Latte, 850 Grand Ave. (☎651-224-5687), at Victoria St. More substantial than a cafe, and more gourmet than its prices and cafeteria-style setup would suggest, this cafe/bakery/pizzeria/wine bar is also famous for its wonderful desserts. Chicken-salsa chili ($5), turtle cake ($4), and daily specials fill the 2 spacious and smoke-free floors with hungry locals. Open M-Th 9am-11pm, F-Sa 9am-midnight, Su 9am-10pm. ❶

⚑ CAFES

Cafes are an integral part of the Twin Cities' nightlife. Particularly in Uptown Minneapolis, quirky coffeehouses caffeinate the masses and draw crowds as large as those at any bar. Most of these creatively decorated coffeehouses complement their java with some of the cheapest food in town.

▨ **Uncommon Grounds,** 2809 Hennepin Ave. S (☎872-4811), at 28th St., Uptown. The self-described "BMW of coffeeshops" uses secret ingredients to make the tastiest coffees ($2-5) and teas around. With velour booths and relaxing music in a smoke-free interior, this coffeeshop lives up to its name. Open M-F 5pm-1am, Sa-Su 10am-1am.

Pandora's Cup and Gallery, 2516 Hennepin Ave. (☎381-0700), at 25th St., Uptown. This 2-story coffeehouse offers great coffee, tasty sandwiches (portobello and swiss $5.25) and Internet access ($1 per 6min.). Hip patrons vie for spots on the retro furniture or on the 2 outdoor patios ($1 minimum per person to hang out), sipping espresso ($1.35-2) and munching on peanut butter and jelly "sammiches" ($2). Open daily 7am-1am.

GREAT LAKES

Vera's Cafe, 2901 Lyndale Ave. (☎872-1419), between 29th and Lake St., Uptown, serves the gay community with its signature "White Zombie" ($4.40), free wireless Internet, and breakfast all day ($5). Regulars return daily for the great java and for the strong community feel. Occasional events on the back patio. Open daily 7am-midnight.

Plan B Coffeehouse, 2717 Hennepin Ave. (☎872-1419), between 27th and 28th St., Uptown, has an intellectual bent, as evidenced by its sign—the periodic table. Animated conversation, artwork, and mismatched furniture surround serious readers and game players. Try the "tripper's revenge" ($3.75). Internet access. Open Su-Th 9am-midnight, F-Sa 9am-1am.

◉ SIGHTS

MINNEAPOLIS

LAKES AND RIVERS. In the land of 10,000 lakes, Minneapolis boasts many of its own; the city contains 22 lakes, 150 parks, and 100 golf courses. **Lake Calhoun,** on the west end of Lake St., Uptown, is the largest of the bunch, and a recreational paradise. Scores of inline skaters, bicyclists, and runners loop the lake on all but the coldest days. Ringed by stately mansions, the serene **Lake of the Isles** is an excellent place to commune with Canada geese. Just southeast of Lake Calhoun on Sheridan St., **Lake Harriet** lures the locals with tiny paddleboats and a bandshell with nightly free concerts in summer. The city maintains 28 mi. of lakeside trails around the three lakes for strolling and biking. **Calhoun Cycle Center,** three blocks east of Lake Calhoun, rents out bikes for exploring the paths. *(1622 W. Lake St. ☎827-8231. Open M-Th 10am-8pm, F-Sa 9am-9pm, Su 9am-8pm. Half-day $15-25, full-day $25-40. Credit card and driver's license required.)* At the northeast corner of Lake Calhoun, **The Tin Fish** offers canoe, kayak, and paddleboat rentals on the side of the restaurant. *(3000 E. Calhoun Pkwy. ☎555-1234; www.thetinfish.com. Open M-Sa 11am-9pm, Su 11am-7pm. All boats $10 per hr. $20 deposit, driver's license, or credit card required.)* **Minnehaha Park** offers striking views of the impressive **Minnehaha Falls,** immortalized in Longfellow's *Song of Hiawatha.* *(Park is near the airport; take bus #7 from Hennepin Ave. downtown. Falls are off Minnehaha Ave. at Minnehaha Pkwy.)*

MUSEUMS. Lakes are only the beginning of Minneapolis's appeal—locals and visitors have plenty to do during the (at least) six months of frigid winter. The **Minneapolis Institute of Arts,** south of downtown,

OUT OF THE WAY

MALLIN' OUTTA CONTROL

Visitors to the Twin Cities cruise Minneapolis's vibrant streets and admire St. Paul's stately grandeur, but when the sass and class become too much, a sure cure awaits 10 mi. south at the Mall of America, where consumer culture is celebrated in an unrestrained, all-American fashion. With over 525 specialty stores and 60 restaurants and nightclubs extending over 2 mi., the nation's largest shopping mall is the ultimate articulation of America's obsession with all things obscenely large. A gaudy, gleaming beacon of buying power in the country's cold northern climes, the mega-mall truly lives up to its name, hosting an entire metropolis in one big, climate-controlled environment. What this city lacks in culture and class it makes up for with perfect weather, safe streets (yes, the mall has streets), and attractions including a movie-megaplex, an aquarium, and the world's largest indoor amusement park. The mall even has a medical clinic and nearby motels, turning the 13-year-old girl's dream of living in the mall into a reality.

The Mall of America is in Bloomington. From St. Paul, take I-35 south to I-494 W then to 24th Ave. exit. Metro Transit express buses depart every 30min. from the mall. ☎952-833-8800; www.mallofamerica.com. Open M-Sa 10am-9:30pm, Su 11am-7pm.

showcases more than 100,000 art objects spanning 5000 years, including Rembrandt's *Lucretia* and the world-famous *Doryphoros*, Polykleitos's perfectly proportioned man. *(2400 3rd Ave. S.* ☎ *870-3131; www.artsmia.org. Open Tu-W and Sa 10am-5pm, Th-F 10am-9pm, Su noon-5pm. Free.)* A few blocks southwest of downtown, the world-renowned, not-to-be-missed ◪**Walker Art Center** counts daring exhibits by Lichtenstein, Rothko, and Warhol among its amazing galleries of contemporary art. Currently closed for a major renovation project that will double its size, the Walker Center will re-open in Spring 2005. *(725 Vineland Pl. at Lyndale Ave.* ☎ *375-7622; www.walkerart.org. Call ahead for new information or visit http://expansion.walkerart.org.)* Next to the Walker lies the **Minneapolis Sculpture Garden,** the largest urban sculpture garden in the US. The iconic, postcard-friendly **Spoonbridge and Cherry** sculpture joins rotating exhibits in the impressive gardens. The adjacent **Cowles Conservatory** houses an array of plants and an impressive Frank Gehry fish sculpture. *(Gardens open daily 6am-midnight; conservatory open Tu-Sa 10am-8pm, Su 10am-5pm. Both free.)* Gehry also holds the honor of having designed the Cities' most unique and controversial structure: the **Weisman Art Museum,** on the East Bank of the U of M campus. The undulating metallic pseudo-building was the rough draft for his famous Guggenheim in Bilbao, and hosts an inspired collection of modern art, including works by O'Keeffe, Warhol, and Kandinsky. The thought-provoking walk-through apartment replica, by Edward and Nancy Reddin Kienholz, engages all the senses by asking viewers to eavesdrop at each door. *(333 E. River Rd.* ☎ *625-9494. Open Tu-W and F 10am-5pm, Th 10am-8pm, Sa-Su 11am-5pm. Free.)*

ST. PAUL

ARCHITECTURE. History and architecture define sedate and stately St. Paul. Mark Twain once said that the city "is put together in solid blocks of honest bricks and stone and has the air of intending to stay." Nowhere is this more evident than along ◪**Summit Avenue,** the nation's longest continuous stretch of Victorian houses, including the childhood home of novelist **F. Scott Fitzgerald** and the Minnesota **Governor's Mansion.** *(Fitzgerald: 599 Summit Ave. Currently a private residence. Governor's Mansion: 1006 Summit Ave.* ☎ *651-297-8177. Tours May-Oct. F 1-3pm. Reservations required. Free.)* Also on Summit, the magnificent home of railroad magnate **James J. Hill**—the largest and most expensive home in the state when it was completed in 1891—offers 1¼hr. tours. *(240 Summit Ave.* ☎ *651-297-2555. Open W-Sa 10am-4pm, Su noon-4pm. Reservations preferred. $8, seniors $7, ages 6-12 $4. Wheelchair accessible.)* **Walking Tours of Summit Avenue,** lasting 1½hr., depart from the Hill House and explore the architectural and social history of the area. *(☎ 651-297-2555. Sa 11am and 2pm, Su 2pm. $4-6.)* Golden horses top the ornate **State Capitol,** the world's largest unsupported marble dome. *(75 Constitution Ave.* ☎ *651-296-3962. Open M-F 9am-5pm, Sa 10am-3pm, Su 1-4pm. Tours on the hr. M-F 9am-3pm, Sa 10am-2pm, Su 1-3pm. Free.)* A scaled-down version of St. Peter's in Rome, the **Cathedral of St. Paul,** at the end of Summit Ave., overlooks the capitol. *(239 Selby Ave.* ☎ *651-228-1766. Mass M-Th 7:30am and 5:15pm; F 7:30am; Sa 8am and 7pm; Su 8, 10am, noon, 5pm. Tours M, W, F 1pm. Open M-Th 7am-5:30pm, F 7am-4pm, Sa 7am-7pm, Su 7am-5pm.)*

HISTORY AND SCIENCE. Along the river, the innovative and exciting ◪**Minnesota History Center** houses nine interactive, hands-on exhibit galleries on Minnesota history that entertain young and old alike. Learn how Minnesotans cope with their extreme seasons in "Weather Permitting," or admire Prince's "Purple Rain" attire in "Sounds Good to Me: Music in Minnesota." Children can participate in the grain-storing process, climbing through a model of a grain elevator. *(345 Kellogg Blvd. W.* ☎ *651-296-6126; www.mnhs.org. Open Tu 10am-8pm, W-F 10am-*

3pm, Sa 10am-5pm, Su noon-5pm. Free, with a pay parking lot. Wheelchair accessible.) Downtown's **Landmark Center** is a grandly restored 1894 Federal Court building replete with towers and turrets, a collection of pianos, a concert hall, and four courtrooms. *(75 W. 5th St. ☎651-292-3230. Open M-W and F 8am-5pm, Th 8am-8pm, Sa 10am-5pm, Su noon-5pm. Free tours Th 11am, Su 1pm.)* Out front, **Rice Park,** the oldest park in Minnesota, is an ideal place for a stroll or a picnic. The **Science Museum of Minnesota** includes a beautiful atrium, an exhibit on the human body, and an expanded Paleontology Hall. The "Virtual River Pilot" allows visitors to take a ride on the Mississippi River. *(120 W. Kellogg Blvd. ☎651-221-9444; www.smm.org. Open mid-June to early Sept. M-Sa 9:30am-9pm; low-season M-W 9:30am-5pm, Th-Sa 9:30am-9pm, Su noon-5pm. $7.50, seniors and ages 4-12 $5.50; combo with omnitheater $13/$10.)*

AMUSEMENTS. Located on 500 wooded acres out in suburban Apple Valley, the **Minnesota Zoo** houses local and exotic animals in their natural habitats, including 15 endangered and threatened species, a Tiger Lair exhibit, and native beavers, lynx, and wolverines. *(13000 Zoo Blvd. Take Rte. 77 S to Zoo exit and follow signs. ☎952-431-9500 or 800-366-7811; www.mnzoo.org. Open daily June-Aug. 9am-6pm; Sept. and May M-F 9am-4pm, Sa-Su 9am-6pm; Oct.-Apr. daily 9am-4pm. $12, seniors $8.25, children 3-12 $7. Parking $5.)* In Shakopee, even the most daring thrill-seekers can get their jollies at **Valleyfair,** a quality amusement park with five coasters and the heart-stopping Power Tower, which drops over 10 stories, as well as a waterpark. *(1 Valleyfair Dr. Take 35W south to Rte. 13 W. ☎800-386-7433; www.valleyfair.com. Open daily June-Aug.; May and Sept. select days. Call for hours, usually 10am-10pm, waterpark closes earlier. $32, ages over 60 and under 48 in. tall $16, under 3 free. Parking $7.)*

🎵 ENTERTAINMENT

Second only to New York City in number of theaters per capita, the Twin Cities are alive with drama and music. Most parks offer free concerts and shows on summer weekends, while theaters present a wide variety of classical and modern plays during the winter. Music is an important part of the cities—the thriving alternative, pop, and classical music scenes fill out the wide range of cultural options. For more info, read the free *City Pages* (www.citypages.com), available at libraries, most cafes, and newsstands around town.

THEATER

The renowned repertory **⬛Guthrie Theater,** 725 Vineland Pl., Minneapolis, adjacent to the Walker Art Center just off Hennepin Ave., draws praise for its mix of daring and classical productions. *(☎377-2224; www.guthrietheater.org. Season Aug.-June. Box office open M-F 9am-8pm, Sa 10am-8pm, Su hours vary. $16-44, students and seniors $5 discount. Rush tickets 15min. before show $12.50; line starts 1-1½hr. before show.)* The historic **State Theatre,** 805 Hennepin Ave., the **Orpheum Theatre,** 910 Hennepin Ave. N, and the **Pantages Theatre,** 710 Hennepin Ave., comprise the Hennepin Theater District in downtown Minneapolis, with touring Broadway shows and musical events. *(Box office ☎339-7007; www.hennepintheaterdistrict.com. Tickets from $15.)* For family-oriented productions, the **Children's Theater Company,** 2400 3rd Ave. S, next to the Minneapolis Institute of Arts, comes through with first-rate plays. *(☎874-0400. Season Sept.-June. Box office open in season M-Sa 9am-5pm; in summer M-F 9am-4pm. $15-28; students, seniors, and children $9-22. Rush tickets 15min. before show $11.)* The ingenious **Théâtre de la Jeune Lune,** 105 1st St. N, stages critically acclaimed, off-the-beaten-path productions in an old warehouse. *(☎332-3968; box office 333-6200. Open M-F 10am-6pm. $10-26.)* **Brave New Workshop,** 3001 Hennepin Ave., in Uptown, stages satirical comedy shows and improv in an intimate club. (☎332-6620; www.bravenewworkshop.com. Box office open M-W 9:30am-5pm, Th-F 9:30am-9pm, Sa 10am-11pm. $15-22.)

MUSIC

The Twin Cities' vibrant music scene offers everything from opera and polka to hip-hop and alternative. **Sommerfest,** a month-long celebration of Viennese music put on by the **Minnesota Orchestra,** is the best of the cities' classical options during July. **Orchestra Hall,** 1111 Nicollet Mall, in downtown Minneapolis, hosts the event. (☎371-5656 or 800-292-4141; www.minnesotaorchestra.org. Box office open M-Sa 10am-6pm. $15-65. Student rush tickets 30min. before show $10.) Nearby, **Peavey Plaza,** on Nicollet Mall, holds free nightly concerts and occasional film screenings. The **Saint Paul Chamber Orchestra,** the **Schubert Club,** and the **Minnesota Opera Company** all perform at St. Paul's glass-and-brick **Ordway Center For The Performing Arts,** 345 Washington St., which also hosts touring Broadway productions. (☎651-224-4222; www.ordway.org. Box office open M-F 9am-6pm, Sa 11am-5pm, Su 11am-4pm. $15-85.) Bands gravitate to the artist Prince's studio complex, formerly and currently known as **Paisley Park,** just outside the city in Chanhassen.

SPORTS

The puffy **Hubert H. Humphrey Metrodome,** 900 S. 5th St., in downtown Minneapolis, houses baseball's **Minnesota Twins** (☎375-7454; www.twinsbaseball.com) and football's **Minnesota Vikings** (☎338-4537; www.vikings.com). The NBA's **Timberwolves** (☎337-3865; www.timberwolves.com) and WNBA's **Lynx** (☎673-8400; www.wnba.com/lynx) howl at the **Target Center,** 601 1st Ave. (☎673-0900), between 6th and 7th St. in downtown Minneapolis. The NHL team, the **Wild,** takes to the ice at St. Paul's **Xcel Energy Center** (☎651-222-9453; www.wild.com). The soccer craze hits the Midwest with the minor-league **Thunder,** at the **National Sports Center** (☎763-785-5600) in suburban Blaine.

FESTIVALS

Both to liven up the dreary cold days and to celebrate the coming of summer, the Twin Cities celebrate countless festivals. In late January and early February, the **St. Paul Winter Carnival,** near the state capitol, cures cabin fever with ice sculptures, ice fishing, skating, and an ice palace. On the 4th of July, St. Paul celebrates the **Taste of Minnesota** with fireworks, concerts, and regional and ethnic cuisine from hordes of local vendors. The **Minneapolis Riverfront Fourth of July Celebration and Fireworks** is a family affair with trolley rides, concerts, food, and fireworks. (☎378-1226; www.mississippimile.com.) On its coattails rides the 10-day **Minneapolis Aquatennial,** with concerts and art exhibits glorifying the lakes. (☎518-3486.) In the two weeks prior to Labor Day, everyone heads to the nation's largest state fair, the **Minnesota State Fair,** at Snelling and Como St. in St. Paul. With cheese curds and walleye-on-a-stick, the fair provides a sampling of the area's flavor. (☎651-642-2200; www.mnstatefair.org. $8, seniors and ages 5-12 $7, under 5 free.)

■ NIGHTLIFE

Minneapolis's vibrant youth culture feeds the Twin Cities' nightlife. Anchored by strong post-punk influences, the area's music scene remains localized until bands such as Soul Asylum, Hüsker Dü, and The Replacements make it big. A cross-section of the diverse nightlife options can be found in the downtown **Warehouse District** on Hennepin Ave.; in **Dinkytown,** by U of M, and across the river on the **West Bank** (bounded on the west by I-35 W and to the south by I-94), especially on **Cedar Avenue.** The top floor of the **Mall of America** invites bar-hopping until the wee hours.

The Quest, 110 5th St. (☎338-3383; www.thequestclub.com), between 1st Ave. N and 2nd Ave. N in the Warehouse District. Once owned by Prince, this upper-class poppin' dance club pays homage to His Purple Highness with purple windows and lots of funk. Live salsa on M and house music draw in a young, cosmopolitan crowd. Cover $5-10. Hours vary, so call ahead.

Escape Ultra Lounge, 6000 Hennepin Ave. (☎333-8850; www.escapeultral-ounge.com), between 6th St. and 7th St. on Hennepin Ave. in the Warehouse District, casts itself as an "ultra lounge" where you can go to dress "to inspire." Changing themes and occasional live music draw new crowds each night. 21+, but call ahead for varying age restrictions. Cover M-F $5-10, Sa-Su $10-15. Open Tu-Su 9pm-2am.

Brit's Pub, 1110 Nicollet Mall (☎332-3908; www.britspub.com), between 11th St. and 12th St., allows patrons to play a game of "lawnboy" ($5 per person per hr.) on the rooftop garden. 18 different beers ($5.50), the stilton burger ($9), and fish and chips ($13) add to the English flavor. Open daily 11am-1am.

First Avenue and 7th St. Entry, 701 1st Ave. N (☎338-8388; www.first-avenue.com), downtown Minneapolis, rocks with the area's best live music several nights a week, including concerts with the hottest rock bands in the nation. Music from grunge to hip-hop to world beat. Cover $6-10, for concerts $6-30. Usually open M-Th 8pm-2am, F-Sa 9pm-3am, Su 7pm-2am.

The Gay 90s, 408 Hennepin Ave. (☎333-7755; www.gay90s.com), at 4th St., claims the seventh-highest liquor consumption rate of all clubs in the nation. This gigantic complex hosts thousands of gay and lesbian partiers in its 8 bars and showrooms, though the straight crowd is sizeable. Drag shows upstairs Tu-Su 9:30pm. W-Th and Su 18+, M-Tu and F-Sa 21+. Cover after 9pm $3-5. Open M-Sa 8am-2am, Su 10am-2am.

DULUTH   ☎218

Originating as an industrial town built on timber and mining, Duluth today has tremendous appeal outside its continuing role as a major freshwater port, harboring huge ships from over 60 different countries. The popularity of Canal Park and the Aerial Lift Bridge have enticed microbreweries, restaurants, theaters, and museums to occupy the old factories down on the wharf, creating a sparkling haven on beautiful Lake Superior.

⌨ TRANSPORTATION AND PRACTICAL INFORMATION. Greyhound, 4426 Grand Ave. (☎722-5591; ticket office open daily 6:30am-5:30pm), stops 3 mi. west of downtown; take bus #1 "Grand Ave. Zoo" from downtown. Buses run to Minneapolis (3½hr., 3 per day, $24) and St. Ignace (9hr., 1 per day, $80). The **Duluth Transit Authority,** 2402 W. Michigan St., runs buses within the city. (☎722-7283. Peak fare M-F 7-9am and 2:30-6pm $1; off-peak $0.50.) The **Port Town Trolley** moves tourists around. (☎722-7283. Runs June-Aug. daily 11:30am-6:30pm. $0.25.) **Convention and Visitors Bureau:** 100 Lake Place Dr., at Endion Station in Canal Park. (☎722-4011 or 800-438-5884; www.visitduluth.com. Open M-F 8:30am-5pm.) **Hotlines: Crisis Line,** ☎723-0099. **Internet Access: Duluth Public Library,** 520 W. Superior St. (☎723-3836. Open M-Tu 10am-8:30pm, W-F 10am-5:30pm. 1hr. free per day.) **Post Office:** 2800 W. Michigan St. (☎723-2555. Open M-F 8am-5pm, Sa 9am-1pm.) **Postal Code:** 55806. **Area Code:** 218.

⌂ ACCOMMODATIONS. Motel rates rise and rooms fill during the summer months. The **Chalet Motel ❸,** 1801 London Rd., 2 mi. west of downtown, offers comfortably furnished and well-decorated rooms with A/C near scenic Leif Erickson Park, which overlooks Lake Superior. (☎728-4238 or 800-235-2957. Apr.-Sept. singles Su-Th $45, F-Sa $55. Doubles $58/$68. Prices lower in winter.)

GREAT LAKES

Voyageur Lakewalk Inn ❸, 333 East Superior St., lies off the Lakewalk with rooms overlooking Lake Superior. (☎722-3911. Rooms in summer Su-Th $48, F-Sa $63; in winter $35/$45.) A few miles south of town, the **Duluth Motel ❷,** 4415 Grand Ave., houses visitors in affordable, well-kept rooms right across from the Greyhound station. (☎628-1008. In summer $35-50; in winter from $25.) With a decidedly less urban feel, the rocky **Jay Cooke State Park ❶,** southwest of Duluth on I-35 Exit 242, draws in travelers with hiking, snowmobiling, cross-country skiing, and 83 campsites among the tall trees of the St. Louis River Valley. (☎384-4610 or 800-246-2267. Office open daily 9am-9pm. Reservations recommended; $8.50 reservation fee. Backcountry sites $7, sites with showers $15, with electricity $18; vehicle permit $7 per day.)

⌂ ▤ FOOD AND NIGHTLIFE. Fitger's Brewery Complex, 600 E. Superior St., and the **Canal Park** region, south from downtown along Lake Ave., feature plenty of pleasant eateries. **The Brewhouse ❷,** located in Fitger's Brewery Complex, has home-brewed beer like Big Boat Oatmeal Stout ($2.75), root beer on tap (float $4.25), specialty burgers, sandwiches, and plentiful vegetarian options for $6-8. (☎726-1392. Live entertainment F-Sa. Open daily 11am-1am; grill closes 10pm.) **Blue Note Cafe ❷,** 357 Canal Park Dr., serves sandwiches ($5-8) and desserts ($2-4) in a coffeehouse setting that picks up with live music on the weekends. (☎727-6549. Live music F-Sa. Open May-Sept. M-Th 9:30am-9pm, F-Sa 9:30am-10pm, Su 9:30am-8pm; call for winter hours.) Located in an old pipe-fitting factory in Canal Park, **Grandma's Sports Garden ❷,** 425 S. Lake Ave., is the most popular place in town, especially among the college crowd. Casual dining, an upstairs patio and a half-price happy hour (M-F 3-6pm) keep people coming over the river and through the woods to Grandma's. (☎722-4724. DJs W and F-Sa. Bar open daily 11am-2am. Restaurant open daily June-Aug. 11am-10pm; Sept.-May W-Th 5-10pm, F-Su 11:30am-10pm.)

◐ ♫ SIGHTS AND ENTERTAINMENT. Duluth's proximity to majestic **Lake Superior** is its biggest draw. Nearly 400 mi. across, it is the largest body of fresh water in the world—indeed, it is so massive that when frozen, each person in the world could lay out their own 12' x 12' picnic blanket on its surface (it's true—we checked twice). Many visitors head down to **Canal Park** to watch the big ships go by at the ▨**Aerial Lift Bridge.** Accompanied by deafening horn blasts, this unique bridge climbs 138 ft. in 1min. to allow vessels to pass. Traffic is generally heavier in the late afternoon, but check the **Boatwatcher's Hotline** (☎722-6489; www.lsmma.com) and the **Duluth Shipping News** (☎722-3119; www.duluthshipping-news.com), published daily and usually available by 3pm at the **Lake Superior Maritime Visitors Center,** by the Aerial Lift Bridge at Canal Park. The visitors center prepares extensive displays on commercial shipping in Lake Superior. (☎727-2497. Open daily 10am-9pm.) Canal Park also serves as the beginning and end of the **Duluth Lakewalk,** a beautiful 4.3 mi. promenade which remains cleared in the winter. In West Duluth, onlookers can watch ships loading at the **Ore Docks Observation Platform,** located at 35th Ave. W and Superior St.

A 39-room neo-Jacobian mansion built on iron-shipping wealth, **Glensheen Historical Sites,** 3300 London Rd., lies on the eastern outskirts of town and provides visitors with a glimpse of Duluth's most prosperous period. (☎726-8910 or 888-454-4536; www.glensheen.org. Open daily May-Oct. 9:30am-4pm; Nov.-Apr. F-Su 11am-2pm. $11, seniors $9, ages 6-12 $6.) Waterfront tours aboard the giant steamer **William A. Irvin,** and her companion tugboat *Lake Superior,* reveal more of Duluth's shipping past. The *Irvin,* docked at Duluth's Downtown Waterfront, is longer than two football fields and was the "Queen of the Lakes" in her prime. (☎722-7876; www.williamirvin.com. Open June-Aug. Su-Th 9am-6pm, F-Sa 9am-8pm; May and

Sept. to mid-Oct. Su-Th 10am-4pm, F-Sa 10am-6pm. 1hr. tours every 20min. $7, students and seniors $6, ages 3-12 $5.) Across the road from the *Irvin* is the **Duluth OMNIMAX Theatre.** (☎727-0022. $7, students and seniors $6, children 12 and under $5.) Across the Aerial Lift Bridge, **Park Point** has excellent but cold swimming areas (Lake Superior's water averages 39°F), parks, and sandy beaches. The scenic **Willard Munger State Trail** links West Duluth to Jay Cooke State Park and continues to Hinckley, providing 80 mi. of paved path perfect for bikes; the **Willard Munger Inn**, 7408 Grand Ave., takes care of rentals. (☎624-4814 or 800-982-2453. $15 per 2hr.; $20 per 4hr.)

Great Lakes Aquarium and Freshwater Discovery Center, 353 Harbor Dr., is America's first and only all-freshwater aquarium. The Isle Royale exhibit holds over 85,000 gallons of water and is just one of over 50 fascinating displays. (☎740-3474; www.glaquarium.org. Open daily 10am-6pm. $11, seniors $9, children 3-11 $6. Parking $3.) **The Depot,** 506 W. Michigan St., a former railroad station, houses four museums including the **Lake Superior Railroad Museum,** which allows visitors to enjoy the North Shore Scenic Railroad trip. (☎727-8025; www.duluthdepot.org. Open June-Aug. daily 9:30am-6pm; Sept.-May M-Sa 10am-5pm, Su 1-5pm. Depot: $8, children 3-13 $4.50. Railroad trip: $10/$5. Combination tickets $16/$8.50.)

CHIPPEWA NATIONAL FOREST ☎218

Gleaming white strands of birch lace the pine forests of the Chippewa National Forest, home to the highest density of breeding bald eagles in the continental US. The national forest shares territory with the **Leech Lake Indian Reservation,** home of 3725 Ojibwe tribespeople. The Ojibwe, mistakenly called Chippewa, migrated from the Atlantic coast in the 18th century and, in the mid-19th century, were forced by the US government onto reservations such as Leech Lake.

The National Forest has a wide variety of cheap **camping ❶** options. The **Forest Office** (☎547-1044; www.fs.fed.us/r9/chippewa; open M-F 7:30am-4:30pm), just east of town on Rte. 200/371, has info on 23 campgrounds and more than 400 free primitive recreation sites, as well as the **National Forest Campground ❶** in Stony Point. (☎877-444-6777; www.reserveusa.com. Check-out 2pm. Self-regulated sites $18.) Billboards for private campgrounds line the edges of Rte. 71 along the western border of the forest.

For the northbound traveler, the small town of **Walker,** in the southwest corner of the park and reservation, serves as an ideal gateway to the forest. Known as the "Fishing Capital of Minnesota" for its famous muskies, it draws thousands of tourists each summer. The **Leech Lake Area Chamber of Commerce** is on Rte. 200/371 downtown, at 205 Minnesota Ave. (☎547-1313 or 800-833-1118; www.leech-lake.com. Open M-F 8:30am-4:30pm; May-Sept. also Sa 10am-1pm.) **Paul Bunyan's Trail Sports,** in Hackensack, 10 mi. south of Walker on Rte. 371 (☎275-5590), rents bikes and in-line skates (open Tu-Sa 10am-6pm; call for winter hours). In **Cass Lake,** 20 mi. north of Walker, **Adventure Tours and Rentals,** 32326 Wolf Lake Rd. (☎800-635-8858), rents canoes and kayaks ($10 per hr.) to explore the lakes; reservations are strongly recommended. **Post Office:** 515 Michigan Ave. at 6th St. (☎547-1123. Open M-F 9am-4pm, Sa 9-11:30am.) **Postal code:** 56484. **Area code:** 218.

ITASCA STATE PARK ☎218

Among Itasca State Park's claims to fame is the **Beginning of the Mississippi,** which Henry Rowe Schoolcraft and his Native American guide Ozawinib discovered in 1832. Here people gather to cross over the Mississippi on the rock bridge where water flows both to the north and 2552 mi. south toward the Gulf of Mexico. Thirty mi. west of Chippewa National Forest on Rte. 200, Minnesota's most visited state park has the oldest and largest tree in the state, representative of the large pine forests through which visitors can walk or bike on the 17 incredible miles of paved trail around the lake. A vacation spot in itself, the ◪**Mississippi Headwaters Hostel (HI)** stays open in the winter to facilitate access to the park's excellent cross-country skiing. (☎266-3415; www.himinnesota.org. Linen $2-4. Laundry, kitchen, multiple bathrooms. $7 per day vehicle permit. 2-night min. stay some weekends. Check-in Su-Th 5-10pm, F-Sa 5-11pm. Check-out M-F 10am, Sa-Su noon. Dorms $15-17, nonmembers $18-20. Private rooms available.) Next door, **Itasca Sports Rental** rents bikes ($3.50 per hr.) and motorized and non-motorized boats (from $4.50 per hr.), as well as fishing supplies. (☎218-266-2150. Open in summer daily 7am-9pm; call for low-season hours). The **park office,** through the north entrance down County Rd. 122, has camping info. (☎266-2100. Office open May to mid-Oct. M-F 8am-4:30pm, Sa-Su 8am-4pm; mid-Oct. to Apr. M-F 8am-4:30pm. Ranger on call after hours.)

IRON RANGE   ☎218

Lured by the cry of "Gold!", the miners that rushed to join loggers and trappers in the Vermillion and Mesabi ranges soon set their sights on iron. Today, the 120 mi. of wilderness and over 500 majestic lakes along the Iron Trail serve as a corridor to the Boundary Waters, the Mississippi Headwaters, and the north shores of Lake Superior. Although these days the closest one can get to the mining techniques of old is on a tour of the Soudan Underground Mine, Iron Rangers continue to celebrate their heritage with exhibitions of past industrial glory. The industry continues to have great relevance, since taconite is used in the production of steel automobiles, especially in the US.

EVELETH

The town of Eveleth, 20 mi. east of Chisolm on Rte. 53, has produced more elite hockey players than any other city of its size in the country. As such, it is the home of the **US Hockey Hall of Fame,** 801 Hat Trick Ave. Focusing on collegiate and Olympic success, the Hall honors American-born players of the hardest hitting sport. (☎744-5167 or 800-443-7825; www.ushockeyhall.com. Open M-Sa 9am-5pm, Su 10am-3pm. $8, seniors and ages 13-17 $7, ages 6-12 $6, under 6 free.) Further proof that they take their hockey seriously in Eveleth is the new 110 ft., 10,000 lb. **World's Largest Hockey Stick,** which replaced the slightly less imposing 107 ft., 7,000 lb. stick built in 1995. Just follow the signs marked "Big Stick."

SOUDAN

For those who feel the need to dig deeper, the town of Soudan, 50 mi. northeast of Chisolm on Rte. 169, features an unforgettable journey ½ mi. underground in a high-speed elevator (or "cage") at the ◪**Soudan Underground Mine State Park,** off Rte. 1. The oldest and deepest iron ore mine in the state, the "Cadillac of Underground Mines" offers fascinating tours. Within the underground world, visitors experience the complete dark of the mine, the noise of the drills, and chilly 50°F temperatures while learning the history of the dark, difficult lives of ore workers in the Iron Range. (☎753-2245. Park open daily June-Sept. 9:30am-6pm; tours every hr. on the hr. 10am-4pm. $7, ages 5-12 $5, 4 and under free; $7 state park vehicle permit required.) Two miles down the road, the **McKinley Park Campground ❶,** overlooking Lake Vermilion, has semiprivate campsites with restrooms, showers, laundry facilities, bait and tackle, firewood, and a sandy swimming beach. (☎753-5921; www.mckinleypark.net. Open May-Sept. Sites $15, with electricity $20.)

ELY

The charming town of Ely serves as a launching pad into the **Boundary Waters Canoe Area Wilderness** (**BWCAW;** see **Boundary Waters,** p. 640), and thus supports an extensive range of wilderness outfitters who provide gear and guidance. The main attraction within town is the **International Wolf Center,** just north of downtown at 1396 Rte. 169, which houses eight gray wolves, offers BWCAW permits, and has displays on *canis lupus.* (☎365-4695 or 800-359-9653; www.wolf.org. Open July-Aug. daily 9am-7pm; mid-May to June and Sept. to mid-Oct. daily 9am-5pm; mid-Oct. to mid-May Sa-Su 10am-5pm. $7, seniors $6, ages 6-12 $3.25. Call for wolf presentation times.) **Stony Ridge Resort ❶,** 60 W. Lakeview Pl., off Shagawa Rd., has RV and tent campsites, cabins, and a boatload of personality. (☎365-6757. RV and tent sites with water, electricity, and showers $15; 1-bedroom cabins from $80. Canoe rental $20 per day.)

VOYAGEURS NATIONAL PARK ☎218

Named for the French-Canadian fur traders who once traversed the area, Voyageurs is one of Minnesota's best-kept secrets, providing an undeniably unique experience as a water-based park with fewer than 10 mi. of roads. The waterways that connect Minnesota's boundary with Ontario provide ample opportunities for fishing, camping, kayaking, canoeing, hiking, and birdwatching—all of which are accessible almost solely by boat. Today's voyagers are invited to leave the auto-dominated world and push off into the serene waters of the longest inland lake waterway on the continent. Summer visitors explore the hiking trails and camp on the islands, while winter visitors bundle up to cross-country ski and snowmobile. The dangers of undeveloped wilderness, however, still remain. Water should be boiled for at least 10min.; some fish contain mercury. Ticks bearing Lyme disease have been found as well.

For hikers, the **Oberholtzer Trail** at Rainy Lake leads to two overlooks that showcase the range of flora found in the park. A wheelchair-accessible trail at Ash River leads to a nice view of Kabetogama Lake and serves as the starting point for the **Blind Ash Bay Trail.** The new 24 mi. **Kab-Ash Trail** has multiple entrances for extensive hiking and skiing. The 9½ mi. **Cruiser Lake Trail system,** accessible from either Rainy Lake or Kabetogama Lake, offers hiking on the cliffs and canoeing and is known for great possibilities of seeing wildlife, though the only guaranteed moose sighting is the taxidermy at the Rainy Lake Visitors Center. The popular **Vince Shute Wildlife Sanctuary** in Orr offers a guaranteed opportunity to see wild black bears who return daily for their feeding, a tradition started by a logger who used to put garbage out for the bears. (☎800-357-9255; www.americanbear.org. Open June-Sept. Tu-Su 5pm-dusk, except during heavy rain.)

Although many people bring their own gear, outfitting is available in the park. Most outfitters can be found at Kabetogama Lake, including the reputable **Voyageurs Adventures,** which provides a wide variety of boat rentals (from $15), mandatory lessons ($10), guided trips (from $30), and accommodations (from $45) as well as a water taxi service. (☎877-465-2925; www.voyageursadventures.com. Open in summer daily 7:30am-7pm; call ahead for winter hours.) **Woody's Fairly Reliable Guide Service** at Rainy Lake offers guided snowmobiling from $275 per day for two people. (☎866-410-5001; www.fairlyreliable.com.) The park service itself offers cruises, canoe trips, ranger-led hikes, and talks about the park; call any visitors center or log onto www.nps.gov/voya for more info.

The best way to experience the park is to camp at the free campsites accessible only by water. The closest sites are only about ¼ mi. from the mainland, allowing those with little experience to camp without straying too far from assistance. Several car-accessible sites lie outside Voyageurs in the state forest, including the beautiful private sites at **Woodenfrog ❶**, about 4 mi. from Kabetogama Lake Visitors Center on Rte. 122, and 10 other sites at **Ash River ❶**, 3 mi. from the visitors center on Rte. 129. (☎753-2245. Primitive sites $10.) The **Ash Trail Lodge ❺**, 10 mi. east of Rte. 53 on Rte. 129, has 10 luxurious, roomy cabins, a few lodge rooms, a restaurant and bar, and year-round socializing in a wooded environment. (☎374-3131 or 800-777-4513; www.ashtraillodge.com. 3-night min. stay for cabins. Lodge rooms $85; cabins from $390 for 3 nights.) Just south of International Falls, which inspired the fictional Frostbite Falls of Rocky and Bullwinkle fame, Rte. 53 is loaded with motels, including the darling **Hilltop Motel and Cabins ❸**, 2002 2nd Ave. W at Rte. 53, which offers immaculate rooms and friendly service. (☎283-2505 or 800-322-6671. Open mid-Apr. to mid-Oct. Singles $46; doubles $49.) **International Voyageurs RV Campground ❶**, 5min. south of town on Rte. 53 at City Rd. 24, offers RV sites with showers and laundry. (☎283-4679. Tent sites for 1-2 people $14, with hookup $18-20; additional person $2.)

On the way into Voyageurs from the south, visitors can stop at the **Voyageurs National Park and Orr Area Info Center**, 4429 Hwy. 53 in Orr, which has information on navigating Voyageurs. (☎757-3932 or 800-357-9255. Open June-Sept. daily 9am-6pm; Oct.-May Th-Sa 9am-4pm.) The **International Falls Convention and Visitors Bureau**, 301 2nd Ave., downtown, hands out travel info on the area. (☎283-9400 or 800-325-5766; www.rainylake.org. Open M-F 8am-5pm.) Visitors can access the park through International Falls at the northern tip of Rte. 53, just below Ft. Frances, ON., or through **Crane Lake, Rainy Lake, Ash River,** or **Kabetogama Lake** (all east of Rte. 53). There are three visitors centers in the park: **Rainy Lake,** at the end of Rte. 11, 12 mi. east of International Falls (☎286-5258; open mid-May to Sept. daily 9am-5pm, Oct. to mid-May W-Su 9am-4:30pm), which has a large museum; **Ash River,** 8 mi. east of Rte. 53 on Rte. 129, then 3 mi. north (☎374-3221; open mid-May to Sept. daily 9am-5pm); and **Kabetogama Lake,** 5 mi. east of Rte. 53 (☎875-2111; open mid-May to Sept. daily 9am-5pm). *Rendezvous*, the visitors guide to the park, is available at visitors centers and provides information on outdoor recreation, outfitting, and lodging.

SCENIC DRIVE: NORTH SHORE DRIVE

The Lake Superior North Shore extends 646 mi. from Duluth to Sault Ste. Marie, ON, but Minnesota's **Route 61** glides through the trees from Duluth to Grand Portage and the Canadian border, offering a condensed 150 mi. version packed with beautiful shoreline and mesmerizing views of the vast lake. With jagged, glacier-carved edges and a seemingly limitless surface, the lake is a sharp contrast to the **Sawtooth Mountains,** which hover over the lake with stunning rock formations and tall, sweeping birch trees.

Though thriving fishing and logging industries once defined this area, tourism now plays a key role in the North Shore's vitality. Whether enjoying the serenity of the lake or hiking and camping on the **Superior Hiking Trail,** visitors flock to the area year-round to enjoy its outdoor opportunities. Most of the small fishing towns along the shore maintain visitors centers; in picturesque **Two Harbors,** the knowledgeable staff at the **R.J. Houle Visitor Information Center**, 1330 Hwy. 61, 21 mi. from Duluth, offers stellar advice and personal anecdotes about each town on the Minnesota stretch of the North Shore. (☎834-4005 or 800-554-2116; www.lakecnty.com. Open June to mid-Oct. M-Sa 9am-5pm, Su 9am-3pm; mid-Oct. to May W-Sa 9am-1pm.) On summer weekends, Rte. 61 is often congested with boat-towing pickup trucks and family-filled campers. Accommodations flanking the roadside fill up fast in summer; make reservations early. Bring warm clothes—temperatures can drop as low as 40°F, even during the summer.

While state parks along Rte. 61 boast striking views of the mirror-like lake, they also offer their own unique attractions. With 26 gorgeous stone structures created by the Civilian Conservation Corps, camping at **Gooseberry Falls State Park ❶** is an appealing lodging option. (☎ 834-3855. Park open daily 8am-10pm; visitors center open daily June-Sept. 9am-7pm; Oct.-May 9am-4pm. Sites with shower $15; vehicle permit $7 per day.) Gooseberry Falls offers 18 mi. of trails and five waterfalls, as well as a beautiful ½ mi. walk to the rocky shore. Three of the falls are located near the visitors center and are wheelchair accessible.

Eight miles down the road, the **Split Rock Lighthouse** hearkens back to the lake's industrial heyday and offers a spectacular view atop a 130 ft. cliff. Visitors can enter the lighthouse, light keeper's home, and fog-signal building, all restored to look as they did during operation in the 1920s. (☎ 226-6372 or 888-727-8386; www.mnhs.org. Open mid-May to mid-Oct. daily 10am-6pm. $8, seniors $7, ages 6-17 $4. 45min. tours every hr. on the hr.) Since Canada technically holds the upper half of a larger waterfall farther north, the **Tettegouche State Park** can call itself home to the tallest waterfall in Minnesota. An easy ¾ mi. hike leads to the falls. (☎ 226-6365. Park open daily 8am-10pm; visitors center open 9am-4pm.) Rte. 61 then winds its way through the **Lake Superior National Forest,** passing over countless winding rivers and creeks toward Tofte, where the 1526 ft. **Carlton Peak** dominates the landscape. In Tofte, outdoors enthusiasts can pick up gear for canoeing, kayaking, and cycling at the **Sawtooth Outfitters,** 7213 Hwy. 61. (☎ 663-7643; www.sawtoothoutfitters.com. Open daily mid-May to Aug. daily 8am-6pm; in winter M and Th-Su 8am-6pm.) The **Coho Cafe ❷,** in Tofte on Rte. 61, serves delicious pastries, pastas ($11-18), and pizzas (from $5) as well as strong coffee ($1.50) for the weary traveler. (☎ 663-8032. Sandwiches $8. Open May-Oct. daily 7am-9pm.) The pine-paneled **Cobblestone Cabins ❸,** off Rte. 61, 2 mi. north of Tofte, provides guests with eight cabins and access to a cobblestone beach, canoes, a wood-burning sauna on the beach, and kitchens. (☎ 633-7957. Open year-round; no running water in winter. Cabins $60-105. Cash or check only.)

GRAND MARAIS ☎ 218

Near the north end of the 150 mi. scenic drive lies the fishing resort village and former artists' colony of Grand Marais, overlooking a large harbor with a lighthouse and marina. This popular tourist spot is a great place to sleep, eat, and enjoy the scenery. **The Grand Marais Visitor Information Center,** 13 N. Broadway, is one block south of the town's one stoplight on Hwy. 61. (☎ 387-2524 or 888-922-5000; www.grandmarais.com. Open M-Sa 9am-5pm; in winter 10am-4pm.) The family-owned **Nelson's Traveler's Rest ❷,** on Rte. 61, ½ mi. west of town, provides fully-equipped cabins with fireplaces and lake views, as well as one cabin split into two cheaper motel rooms. (☎ 387-1464 or 800-249-1285; www.travelersrest.com. Open mid-May to mid-Oct. Call in advance. Singles from $38; cabins from $53.) **Grand Marais Recreation Area RV Park-Campground ❶,** off Rte. 61 on 8th Ave W, has 300 wooded sites by the lake. (☎ 387-1712 or 800-998-0959. Office open daily 8am-8pm. Reservations recommended. Open May to mid-Oct. $19; with water and electricity $23. July-Aug. $24/$28. Rates apply for parties of 2; $3 per each additional person per day. Discounted use of municipal pool.)

Cheap and popular with locals and fishermen, **South of the Border Cafe ❶,** 4 W. Rte. 61, specializes in huge breakfasts and satisfying diner food. The bluefin herring sandwich costs $3.75. (☎ 387-1505. Breakfast under $7. Open daily 5am-2pm.) Though equally popular, the **Angry Trout Cafe ❺** is a bit more expensive, serving only organic dishes ranging from Alaskan cod ($18) to Shiitake mushroom and vegetable skewers ($18). The Angry Trout is environmentally conscious and generates its electricity from windpower. (☎387-1265. Open seasonally Su-Th 11am-8:30pm, F-Sa 11am-9pm.)

BOUNDARY WATERS. Grand Marais also serves as a gateway to the **Boundary Waters Canoe Area Wilderness (BWCAW),** a designated wilderness area comprising 1.2 million acres of lakes, streams, and forests. The BWCAW is strict about when, where, and how many people it will allow to enter in order to preserve this pristine environment; phoning ahead is essential. One mile south of Grand Marais, the **Gunflint Ranger Station** distributes permits and has tourist information. (☎387-1750. Open May-Sept. daily 6am-6pm; Oct.-Apr. M-F 8am-4:30pm.) Make reservations with National Recreation Reservation Service. (☎877-444-6777 for camping, 877-550-6777 for BWCAW permits; www.reserveusa.com. Reservation fee $12. Self-issue permits for day use free. Camping permits $10 per adult per trip, children $5. Seasonal passes $40.) The **Gunflint Trail (County Road 12)** runs northwest from town for 65 mi. to Lake Saganaga, on the border of Canada. This developed road offers access to amazing trails and lakes for nature enthusiasts and serves as the eastern entrance into the BWCAW. **The Gunflint Trail Association** has hosts spread throughout the trail. (☎800-338-6932; www.gunflint-trail.org.) At Rte. 61 and Wisconsin St. is the **Gunflint Trail Information Center,** which offers information about the trail and the BWCAW, as well as guidance finding available sites among the many private (from $20) and forest service **campgrounds** ($12) on the trail. (☎387-3191. Open daily 9am-5pm.) A variety of outfitters are stationed along the Gunflint Trail. One of the best is the family-run **Bear Track Outfitting Company,** 2011 W. Hwy. 61, right across from the Ranger Station, whose knowledgeable staff supplies rentals and leads short and extended guided trips for canoeing ($25 per day), kayaking ($38 per day, 6hr. guided trip $80), backpacking, fly-fishing, skiing, and snowshoeing. (☎387-1162 or 800-795-8068; www.bear-track.com. Open in summer daily 8am-6pm, call ahead for winter hours.)

Many people believe that regional variation in the US is disappearing, thanks to the insidious and pervasive influence of television and mainstream American culture. There is hope for those of us who relish linguistic and cultural diversity, though: recent research by William Labov at the University of Pennsylvania and by Scott Golder and myself at Harvard University has found that regional variation is alive and well, and along some dimensions is even increasing between the major urban centers.

Consider, for instance, the preferred cover term for sweetened carbonated beverages. As can be seen in the map below, Southerners generally refer to them as coke, regardless of whether the beverages in question are actually made by the Coca-Cola Company; West and East coasters (including coastal Florida, which consists largely of transplanted New Yorkers) and individuals in Hawaii and the St. Louis, Milwaukee, and Green Bay spheres of influence predominantly employ soda. The remainder of the country prefers pop.

National television advertisements and shows generally employ soda, presumably due to the concentration of media outlets in soda areas New York City and California, but this has had no effect on the robust regional patterns. (The three primary terms do appear, however, to be undermining traditional local expressions such as tonic in Boston and cocola in the South.)

Another deeply entrenched, regionally conditioned food product is the long sandwich made with cold cuts. Its unmarked form in the US is submarine sandwich or just sub. Pennsylvanians (and New Jerseyites in the Philadelphia sphere of influence) call it a hoagie, New Yorkers call it a hero, western New Englanders call it a grinder, Mainers call it an Italian sandwich, and people in the New Orleans area call it a po' boy.

Confrontation between traditional regional terms and newer interlopers has created subtle variations in meaning in some areas. In the Boston sphere of influence, for instance, grinder is commonly relegated to hot subs, whereas sub is used for cold ones. Similarly, in stores in northern Vermont grinder refers to large (12 in.) subs, whereas hoagie is used for their small (6 in.) counterpart. Many in the Philadelphia area divide up the sub domain in the same manner as Boston, but hoagie is used for the cold version and steak sandwich for the hot one.

In other cases, the dialectal picture is so evenly distributed that there is no clear national standard, as with the terms for the machine out of which one drinks water in schools and other public spaces.

The preferred term in the southeastern half of the US is water fountain, whereas in the northwestern half it's drinking fountain. If you're in eastern Wisconsin or the Boston area, be sure to elicit bubbler from the locals.

These examples should suffice to show that regional variation is alive and well in the US. But where did these differences come from, and how have they resisted the influence of the American media juggernaut? The second question has a relatively straightforward answer: humans are generally unaware of the properties of their language, and normally assume that the way they behave and speak is the way everyone else does and should behave and speak. You, for example, were probably unaware before reading this that a large swathe of the US doesn't share your term for water fountains. Since humans are generally unaware of the idiosyncrasies of their own speech, it is to be expected that they would typically fail to notice that what is said on TV differs from their own forms.

The maps employed in this chapter were designed by Prof. Vaux on the basis of previously published materials (primarily William Labov's forthcoming *Atlas of North American English* and Frederick Cassidy's *Dictionary of American Regional English*) and his online survey of English dialects. Specific references are available on request by emailing the author at vaux@post.harvard.edu. Please note that all generalizations made here reflect statistical predominance, not absolute invariance. One can find individuals who say *soda* in the South, for example, but these are in the minority.

The examples adduced in this chapter are primarily lexical, due to the difficulty of conveying subtleties of pronunciation in a publication intended for non-linguists.

SETTLEMENT PATTERNS AND THE ORIGINS OF THE AMERICAN DIALECTS

The other question, involving the origins of linguistic variation, can be answered in part by considering the history of US settlement by speakers of English.

The continental US was settled by three main waves of English speakers: Walter Raleigh brought settlers primarily from the southwest of England to form the Chesapeake Bay Colony in 1607; Puritans from East Anglia came to the Massachusetts Bay Colony in 1620; and Scots-Irish, Northern English, and Germans came to America through Philadelphia in large numbers beginning in the 18th century. Settlers then moved horizontally westward across the country from these three hearths, giving rise to the three main dialect areas in the US: the South, the North, and the Midlands. The fourth area on the map, the West, contains a mixture of features imported from the other three.

The particular linguistic variables on which these dialect divisions are based in many cases can be connected to dialect differences in the areas of England from which the various settlers came. The original English-speaking settlers in New England, for example, came from East Anglia in the southeast of England. There, in the 17th century (and still today), "r"s were only pronounced before vowels, and "r"s were (and still are) inserted inside certain vowel sequences, as in draw[r]ing and John F. Kennedy's famous Cuba[r] and China[r]. The New England lengthening of "a" in words like aunt ("ahnt") and bath ("bahth") was also imported from the British dialect of East Anglia.

Other features cannot be connected to British antecedents so transparently, but nicely demonstrate the North/South/Midlands boundary. One of my favorite examples is the large wasplike critter that is usually seen when it stops by puddles to collect mud, which it then rolls into a ball and carries off to construct a nest. Northerners call this a mud wasp, midlanders and westerners call it a mud dauber, and southerners call it a dirt

dauber. Another such example is the small freshwater lobster-like critter, which is a crayfish in the North, a crawdad in the Midlands, and a crawfish or mudbug in the South.

The North breaks into two main areas, the Northeast and the Inland North. The Northeast and its crony, southeast coastal Florida, are roughly the home of sneakers; the rest of the country uses tennis shoes or gym shoes as the generic term for athletic shoes. The Inland North is most famous for pop and for the so-called "Rust Belt Vowel Shift." This is a change in the pronunciation of most of the American vowels that produces what is perceived by most Americans as "Midwestern," even though it is also found in eastern Rust Belt cities such as Rochester, Syracuse, and Utica, New York.

The Midlands region is home not only to mud dauber, but also to the oft-noted regionalisms warsh and the needs X-ed construction, as in the car needs warshed. The Midlands and the South together are home to catty-corner (diagonally across from), which in the North is normally kitty-corner. (My personal favorite expression for this concept is kitty wampus, which is used by a handful of individuals in the Upper Midwest.)

The South is home to the "pin-pen merger" ("i" and "e" are pronounced identically before "m," "n," and "ng"), preservation of the contrast in pronunciation between "w" and "wh" (as in witch and which respectively), use of y'all to address a group of individuals, multiple modal constructions (as in I might could do that), nekkid for "naked," and commode for "toilet."

The inland part of the South features gems such as rolling for the act of covering a house and/or its front yard in toilet paper. In the rest of country, this is generally called tp'ing or toilet papering. (It's wrapping in the Houston area.)

AMERICAN DIALECTS YOU HAVE TO HEAR

Since, as we have just seen, regional variation is alive and well in the US, where should one go to hear the most satisfying range of dialects? Here are some of my favorites, which also provide a representative sample of the main dialect groups in the country. (If you get to one of these locales and have trouble finding a really juicy local accent, try a police station, working-class bar, or farm.)

THE NORTHEAST

No linguistic tour of the Northeast would be complete without visiting the two main linguistic spheres of influence in the area, Boston and New York City. Though locals would probably die rather than admitting it, the two actually share a large number of linguistic features, such as pronouncing can (is able) differently than can (container), wearing sneakers and drinking soda, having no word for the roly poly/potato bug/sow bug/doodlebug (though the critter itself is just as rampant in the Northeast as anywhere else in the country), and pronouncing route to rhyme with moot and never with out.

Perhaps the most striking feature shared by these two areas is the behavior of "r": it disappears when not followed by a vowel (drawer is pronounced draw), and conversely gets inserted when between certain vowels (drawing comes out as drawring). Because these dialects don't allow "r" to follow a vowel within a syllable, they end up preserving vowel contrasts that were neutralized before "r" in other dialects. This is heard in the "3 Maries": Mary, marry, and merry are each pronounced differently, whereas in most of the country all three are homophonous. Similarly mirror and nearer have the same first vowel in most of the US, but not in Boston and New York City. Bostonians and New Yorkers pronounce words like hurry, Murray, furrow, and thorough with the vowel of hut, whereas most other Americans use the vowel in bird. And of course there's the first vowel in words like orange and horrible, which in most of the US is the same as in pore, but in Boston and New York City is closer to the vowel in dog.

New York City

Though New York City shares many important features with Boston and other parts of the Northeast, it is also in many ways a linguistic island, undergoing little influence from the rest of the country and—despite the ubiquity of New York accents on TV and in movies—propagating almost none of its peculiarities to the outside world. Its lack of linguistic influence can be connected to its stigmatization: two surveys in 1950 and the 1990s found that Americans considered New York City to have the worst speech in the country.

When you visit the New York City area (including neighboring parts of New Jersey and Long Island), be sure to listen for classic New Yorkisms. This includes the deletion of "h" before "u" (e.g. huge is pronounced yuge, and Houston becomes Youston), and the rounding of "a" to an "o"-like vowel before "l" in words like ball and call (the same vowel also shows up in words like water, talk, and dog). New Yorkers who don't have a thick local accent may not have these particular features, but they are sure to have other shibboleths like stoop (small front porch or steps in front of a house), on line instead of in line (e.g. We stood on line outside the movie theater for three hours), hero for sub, pie for pizza, and egg cream for a special soft drink made with seltzer water, chocolate syrup, and milk. You can also tell New Yorkers by their pronunciation of Manhattan and forward: they reduce the first vowel in the former (it comes out as Mn-hattan), and delete the first "r" in the latter (so it sounds like foe-ward). Believe it or not, it is also common in the New York City area to pronounce donkey to rhyme with monkey (which makes sense if you consider the spelling), even though they typically aren't aware that they are doing so.

New England

Moving up the coast to New England, we find that most people don't actually sound like John F. Kennedy, but they do all use cellar for basement (at least if it's unfinished), bulkhead for the external doors leading out of the cellar, and rotary for what others call a roundabout or traffic circle. New England itself is divided by the Connecticut River into two linguistically distinct areas, Eastern and Western.

Eastern New England: Boston

You can hear great Eastern New England speech almost anywhere in Maine, New Hampshire, Rhode Island, or Massachusetts, especially if you stay away from more affluent areas in the bigger cities, but I'll focus here on the Boston area. (Revere, South Boston, Somerville, and Dorchester are traditionally considered to harbor especially thick local accents.) Thanks to park your car in Harvard Yard and Nomar Garciaparra many Americans are familiar with the Boston pronunciation of -ar-, which generally comes out as something very similar to the Southern pronunciation of -ay- (Boston park sounds like Southern pike). The sequence -or- also has an interesting outcome in many words, being pronounced like the vowel in off. For instance, the Boston pop group LFO, in their 1999 song "Summer Girls," rhymed hornet with sonnet.

In the domain of vocabulary, be sure to get a frappe (or if you're in Rhode Island, a cabinet), a grinder, harlequin ice cream with jimmies or shots on it, and of course a tonic. (Frappes are milkshakes, harlequin is Neapolitan ice cream, and jimmies and shots are sprinkles.) You might also want to visit a package store (or packie for short) to buy some alcohol, or a spa to buy cigarettes and lottery tickets. There aren't many spas (small independent convenience stores, equivalent to party stores in Michigan, as used in the movie True Romance) left in the area at this point, but you can still find a few that haven't been replaced by 7-11 in Boston, Cambridge, Somerville, Allston, and Watertown.

The towns where you'll hear the best Boston accents (and classic local terms like wicked and pissa) also feature many triple deckers, three-family houses with three front porches stacked on top of one another. These seem to be less common in Connecticut, but if you happen to pass through that area, be sure to look out for tag sales (yard sales). Connecticut is also home to the term sleepy seed for the gunk that collects in the corner of your eye after you've been sleeping; not all Connecticutians have this expression, but your trip will have been worthwhile if you find someone who does.

Western New England: Vermont

West of the Connecticut River, I recommend you head up to the Northeast Kingdom in Vermont. Here you'll find the best Canadian features south of the border, thanks to the heavy French Canadian representation in the area, including toque ("tuke") for a woolen winter hat (known as a toboggan in some other parts of the country); poutin (put-SIN) for french fries coated with gravy and cheese curds, and sugar pie. This is also the land of the skidoo (snowmobile), the skidder (giant machine with jaws used to haul logs), and the camp (summer cabin, typically on a body of water). If you're wise enough to visit the Northeast Kingdom, be sure to check out how they pronounce the "a" and the "t" in the name of the local town Barton.

THE MIDLANDS

Pennsylvania

As you head out of the Northeast, you should try to stop through Pennsylvania, which is unique among the fifty states for having a significant number of dialect features peculiar to it. Some of these are due to the Pennsylvania Dutch presence in the region (redd up "clean up," gumband "rubber band" (cf. German Gummi "rubber"; now limited to parts of western Pennsylvania), toot "bag," rootch "scootch up (in a bed)"); the reasons for the restriction of other terms to Pennsylvania are less clear. To this category belongs hoagie, which as we already saw is limited to Pennsylvania plus the parts of New Jersey in Philadelphia's sphere of influence. Pennsylvania also shows extreme internal diversity: Philadelphia groups with the Northeastern dialects (e.g., in preferring soda), whereas Pittsburgh is tied to the Inland North (pop), the Midlands (many of my relatives there use the needs warshed construction), and the Appalachian region, of which it is the northernmost extremity.

Philadelphia and its satellites in southern New Jersey are perhaps best known for their pronunciation of water, which comes out as something like wooder. This conveniently shows up in the local term water ice, which refers to something between Italian ice and a snow cone. Residents of the Philly sphere of influence are also more likely than other Americans to bag school rather

than skip school or play hooky. When you make your trip to Philly to hear these choice linguistic tidbits and you run short of money, be sure to ask where the MAC machine is, not the ATM or cash machine.

You should also make a special effort to visit the opposite end of the state, anchored by the beautiful city of Pittsburgh, which (unknown to most Americans) has its own distinctive dialect. Here the "aw" sound is replaced by something approaching "ah," as in dahntahn for downtown; "ay" similarly loses its "y" in certain situations, as in Pahrts for Pirates and Ahrn City for Iron City. The "o" in this region is very rounded in words like shot, and comes out sounding a lot like the New York vowel in ball. It is also popular to delete the "th-" at the beginning of unstressed words in certain collocations, such as up 'ere (for up there), like 'at, and 'n 'at (for and that, which western Pennsylvanians are fond of ending sentences with).

In terms of vocabulary, Pittsburgh and environs have some real whoppers, such as yins or you 'uns, used to address a group of two or more people; jagoff meaning "a jerk or loser" (shared with Chicagoland); jumbo "bologna sandwich"; and slippy "slippery."

These days many Pittsburgh residents don't have the traditional dialect, but you're sure to come across at least a few of the items just discussed. You'll have even better luck if you visit some of the unknown small towns in western Pennsylvania such as Franklin, Emlenton, and Oil City, which have satisfying variants of the Pittsburgh speech patterns and also happen to be unusually scenic.

Cincinnati

From Pittsburgh you're in striking distance of Cincinnati, one of the better representatives of the Midlands dialect region. Here, instead of inserting "r," as we saw in Boston and New York City, they insert "l": saw comes out as sawl, drawing as drawling, and so on. In the Cincinnati area one can also find drive-through liquor stores (and for some people, regular liquor stores) referred to as pony kegs. (Elsewhere in the US, on the other hand, pony keg usually refers to a small keg.)

THE RUST BELT

Milwaukee

Moving westward, the next interesting dialect zone is the Inland North or Rust Belt, within which I recommend Milwaukee, WI (not to be confused with Zilwaukee, MI.) Here, in the land so eloquently etymologized by Alice Cooper in *Wayne's World*, you will find—especially if you visit an area where there hasn't been much immigration, such as West Allis—not only the classic speech features identified with the Midwest (as canonized for example in the Da Bears skit on "Saturday Night Live"), but also features characteristic of areas other than the Midwest (freeway, otherwise associated with the West Coast; bubbler, most familiar from the Boston area; soda, otherwise characteristic of the West and East coasts). Milwaukeeans share some features with the rest of Wisconsin: they pronounce Milwaukee as Mwaukee and Wisconsin as W-scon-sin rather than Wis-con-sin; they refer to annoying Illinoisans as FIB's or fibbers (the full form of which is too saucy to explain here), and they eat frozen custard and butter burgers. They also share some features with the Upper Midwest, notably pronouncing bag as baig and using ramp or parking ramp for "parking garage" (the same forms surface in Minnesota and Buffalo). Milwaukee is also known for the cannibal sandwich, raw ground sirloin served on dark rye bread and covered with thin-sliced raw onions.

Milwaukee is only an hour and a half drive north of Chicago, yet it lacks many of the classic Chicagoisms, such as jagoff, gaper's block (a traffic jam caused by drivers slowing down to look at an accident or other diversion on the side of the road), black cow (root beer with vanilla ice cream, known elsewhere as a root beer float), expressway, and pop. It also differs from the more northern reaches of Wisconsin with respect to many of the classic Upper Midwestern features so cleverly reproduced in the movie Fargo, such as the monophthongal "e" and "o" in words like Minnesota and hey there. You can find the occasional inhabitant of Wisconsin's northern border with Minnesota who has Upper Midwest terms like pasties, whipping shitties (driving a car in tight circles, known elsewhere as doing donuts), hotdish (elsewhere called a casserole), and farmer matches (long wooden matches that light on any surface), but for the most part these are less commonly used than in Minnesota and the Dakotas (and the Upper Peninsula of Michigan in the case of pasties).

THE WEST

The San Fernando Valley

Moving ever westward, we come next to the West Coast. Here it is more difficult to find hardcore traditional dialects, largely because the West was settled relatively recently, and by individuals from a wide variety of different locales; one is hard-pressed to find any Californian (or other Westerner) whose family has been there for more than two generations. Perhaps the best place to start is the San Fernando Valley of California, home of the Valley Girl. Many of the Valley Girl quirks immortalized in Frank Zappa's 1982 song "Valley Girl" and the 1995 film Clueless are now profoundly out of favor, such as gnarly, barf out, grodie (to the max), gag me with a spoon, rad, for sure, as if, and bitchin'. Others are now ubiquitous throughout the US, such as totally, whatever, sooo X (as in, That's so like 5 years ago), and the use of like to report indirect speech or state of mind (as in, I was like, "No way!"). Others are still used in the area but have yet to infiltrate the rest of the country, such as flip a bitch or bust a bitch (make a U-turn) and bag on (make fun of, diss).

And if you're interested in figuring out whether someone's from northern or southern California, I recommend seeing if they use hella or hecka to mean "very" (e.g. that party was hella cool; characteristic of northern California), and if they refer to freeway numbers with or without "the" before them (Southern Californians refer to "the 5", "the 405", and so on, whereas northern Californians just use "5" and "405").

THE SOUTH

Looping back around the country we come to the South, which is perhaps the most linguistically distinct and coherent area in the US. This is not only more to obvious cases like y'all, initial stress on Thanksgiving, insurance, police, and cement, and the other features mentioned above, but also showcases feeder road (small road that runs parallel to a highway), wrapping (tp'ing), doodlebug (the crustacean that rolls into a ball when you touch it) in the Houston area, and party barns (drive-through liquor stores) in Texas (bootlegger, brew thru, and beer barn are also common terms for this in the South). The South as a whole differs from the rest of the country in pronouncing lawyer as law-yer, using tea to refer to cold sweet tea, and saying the devil's beating his wife when it rains while the sun is shining (elsewhere referred to as a sunshower, or by no name at all). The South is so different from the rest of the country that almost anywhere you go you will hear a range of great accents, but I especially recommend the Deep South (start with Mississippi or Alabama) and New Orleans.

New Orleans

Louisiana is famous for the Cajuns, a local group descended from the Acadians, French people who were exiled from Nova Scotia and settled in southern Louisiana in the 1760s. Some Cajuns still speak their own special creole, Cajun French, and this in turn has influenced the English dialect of the region. This can be seen in local expressions such as: by my house for "in/at my place" (e.g., he slept by my house last night), which is claimed to be based on the French expression chez moi; make dodo meaning "to sleep," based on Cajun French fais do do; make groceries meaning "do grocery shopping," cf. French faire le marché; and lagniappe, French for "a little something extra," e.g., when your butcher gives you a pound and two ounces of hot sausage but only charges you for a pound.

Some of the creole elements that have made their way into the local English dialect may be of African rather than French origin, such as where ya stay (at)? meaning "where do you live?", and gumbo, referring to a traditional southern soup-like dish, made with a rich roux (flour and butter) and usually including either sea food or sausage. The word gumbo is used in Gullah (an English-based creole spoken on the Sea Islands off the Carolina coast) to mean okra, and appears to have descended from a West African word meaning okra.

The New Orleans dialect of English also includes words drawn from other sources, such as yat (a typical neighborhood New Orleanian), neutral ground (the grassy or cement strip in the middle of the road), po' boy (basically a sub sandwich, though it can include fried oysters and other seafood and may be dressed, i.e., include lettuce, tomatoes, pickles, and mayonnaise), hickey (a knot or bump you get on your head when you bump or injure it), and alligator pear (an avocado).

HAWAII

Last but not least we come to Hawaii, which in many ways is the most interesting of the fifty states linguistically. Many Americans are aware of Hawaiian, the Austronesian language spoken by the indigenous residents of the Hawaiian Islands before the arrival of colonizers from Europe and Japan. Fewer, however, know of the English-based creole that has arisen since that time, known as Hawaiian Pidgin English, Hawaiian Creole English, or just Pidgin. This variety of English is spoken by a fairly large percentage of Hawaiians today, though they tend not to use it around haole (Caucasian) tourists.

Pidgin combines elements of all of the languages originally spoken by settlers, including Portuguese (cf. where you stay go? meaning "where are you going?", or I called you up and you weren't there already meaning "I called you up and you weren't there yet"), Hawaiian (haole, makapeapea "sleepy seed," lanai "porch," pau "finished"), Japanese (shoyu "soy sauce"), and even Californian/surfer (dude, sweet, awesome, freeway). They also have some English expressions all their own, such as shave ice (snowcone) and cockaroach (cockroach).

The syntax (word order) of Pidgin differs significantly from that of mainland English varieties, but resembles the English creoles of the Caribbean in important ways. This includes deletion of the verb be in certain contexts (e.g., if you one girl, no read dis meaning "if you're a girl, don't read this"), lack of inversion of the subject and finite verb in questions and subordinate clauses (e.g. doctah , you can pound my baby? Meaning "doctor, can you weigh my baby?", or how dey came up wid dat? meaning "how did they come up with that?"), null subjects (e.g. cannot! meaning "I can't!", or get shtrawberry? meaning "do you have strawberry [flavor]?"), and the use of "get" to express existential conditions ("there is," "there are"), as in get sharks? meaning "are there sharks [in there]?".

IN CONCLUSION

This tour only begins to scratch the surface of the range of English varieties to be found in the US, but it should provide enough fodder to keep you busy for a while on your travels, and with any luck will enable you to provide some entertainment for your hosts as well. And if the info I've provided here isn't enough to sate your thirst for American dialects, I urge you to visit the Sea Islands, where Gullah is still spoken, Tangier Island in Chesapeake Bay, and Ocracoke Island, off the coast of North Carolina. Each of these islands features a variety of English that will shock and titillate you; I'll leave the details for you to discover.

Bert Vaux is Ph.D. in Linguistics and currently teaches at the University of Wisconsin-Milwaukee. He has written extensively, and taught popular classes on linguistics and dialects at Harvard University.

GREAT PLAINS

In 1803, the Louisiana Purchase doubled America's size, adding French territory
west of the Mississippi at the bargain price of $0.04 per acre. Over time, the plains
spawned legends of pioneers and cowboys and of Native Americans struggling to
defend their homelands. The arrival of railroads and liberal land policies spurred
an economic boom, until a drought during the Great Depression transformed the
region into a dust bowl. Modern agriculture has reclaimed the soil, and the heartland of the US now thrives on the trade of farm commodities. The Plains are also a
vast land of prairies, where open sky stretches from horizon to horizon, broken
only by long, thin lines of trees. The land rules here, as its inhabitants know. While
signs of humanity are unmistakable—checkerboard farms, Army posts, and railroad corridors—the region's most staggering sights are the works of nature, from
the Badlands and the Black Hills to the mighty Missouri and Mississippi Rivers.

HIGHLIGHTS OF THE GREAT PLAINS

NATIONAL PARKS AND MONUMENTS. Discover the rugged, uncrowded Theodore
Roosevelt National Park, ND (p. 650), and the Badlands, SD (p. 655), or join the
crowds in the Black Hills around Mt. Rushmore (p. 658).

HISTORICAL SITES. Scotts Bluff National Monument, NE (p. 676), and Chimney
Rock, NE (p. 676), will fascinate anyone interested in the pioneers.

NORTH DAKOTA

Vast open spaces usher visitors to North Dakota, where two-thirds of the state's
small population lives in the Fargo area. An early visitor to Fargo declared, "It's a
beautiful land, but I doubt that human beings will ever live here." Posterity begs to
differ. The stark, haunting lands that intimidated settlers eventually found willing
tenants, and the territory became a state along with South Dakota on Nov. 2, 1889.
The event was not without confusion—President Benjamin Harrison concealed
the names when he signed the two bills, so both Dakotas claim to be the 39th state.

⚅ PRACTICAL INFORMATION

Capital: Bismarck.

Visitor Info: Tourism Department, 1600 E. Century Ave., Bismarck 58501 (☎800-435-
5663; www.ndtourism.com). **Parks and Recreation Department,** 1600 E. Century Ave.,
Bismarck 58501 (☎328-5357; www.ndparks.com). **Game and Fish Department,** 100
N. Bismarck Expwy., Bismarck 58501 (☎328-6300). State offices open M-F 8am-5pm.

Postal Abbreviation: ND. **Sales Tax:** 7%.

BISMARCK   ☎701

In Bismarck, the people are friendly, the streets are clean, and the scenery is spectacular. Seas of yellow wildflowers, grids of green farmland, and fields of golden
wheat blend with surprising harmony. Located at the center of the Lewis and
Clark Trail, it is an excellent city in which to learn about the state's rich pioneering
history and relax before embarking on outdoors excursions.

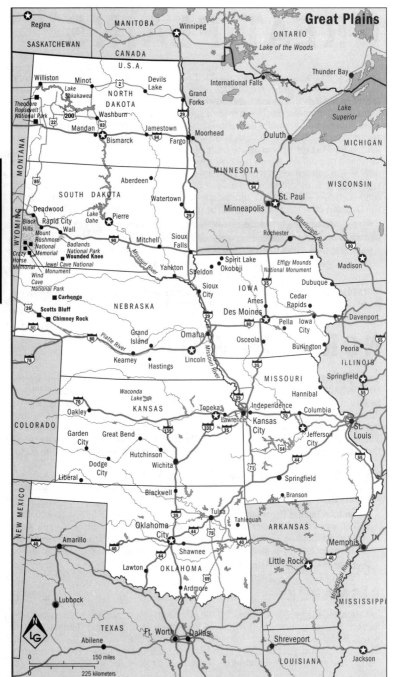

Great Plains

◼◼ ORIENTATION AND PRACTICAL INFORMATION.

Bismarck is on I-94, halfway between Fargo and Theodore Roosevelt National Park. The **Missouri River** separates Bismarck from Mandan, its neighbor to the west. **Washington** and **9th Street** are the main north-south thoroughfares and are intersected by **Main, Divide,** and **Interstate Avenue.** The **Bismarck Municipal Airport** (☎222-6502) is on Airport Rd., 2 mi. southeast of the city. Take the Bismarck Expwy. east from downtown and turn right on Airport Rd. **Taxi: Taxi 9000** ☎223-9000. The **Bismarck-Mandan Visitors Center,** 1600 Burnt Boat Dr., Exit 157 off I-94, distributes the *Bismarck-Mandan Visitors Guide,* which often has discount coupons for lodging. (☎800-767-3555; www.bismarckmandancvb.com. Open June-Oct. M-F 7:30am-7pm, Sa 8am-6pm, Su 10am-5pm; Nov.-May M-F 8am-5pm.) **Medical Services: St. Alexius Medical Center,** 900 E. Broadway Ave. (☎530-7000; Emergency and Trauma Center 530-7001.) **Internet Access: Bismarck Public Library,** 515 N. 5th St. (☎222-6410. $0.25 per 15min.; 1hr. limit. Open M-Th 9am-9pm, F 9am-6pm, Sa 9am-5pm, Su 1-6pm.) **Post Office:** 220 E. Rosser Ave. (☎221-6512. Open M-F 7:45am-5:30pm, Sa 9am-noon.) **Postal Code:** 58501. **Area Code:** 701.

◼◻ ACCOMMODATIONS AND FOOD.

Budget motels abound off I-94 at Exit 159. The **Select Inn ❷,** 1505 Interchange Ave., Exit 159 off I-94, provides clean rooms, laundry access, and continental breakfast. (☎223-8060 or 800-641-1000. Singles $45; doubles $55. AAA discount.) The **Expressway Inn ❷,** 200 E. Bismarck Expwy., offers rooms with refrigerators and microwaves on the south side of town. (☎222-2900 or 800-456-6388. Singles $48; doubles $58. Weekends $63.) The beautiful **Fort Abraham Lincoln State Park ❶,** 7 mi. south on Rte. 1806 in Mandan (see **Sights,** below), offers tent sites on the banks of the Missouri River with amazing views of the surrounding prairie. (☎667-6342 or 800-807-4723. Reservations recommended. Primitive sites $8, with electricity $14; vehicle fee $5.)

With an enormous menu of pasta ($10), meat ($10-18), seafood ($10-13), and sandwiches ($5-10), the Italian restaurant **Walrus ❷,** 1136 N. 3rd St., in Arrowhead Plaza, is a local favorite. The Italian sausage pizziola ($9.50) is a house specialty. (☎250-0020. Open M-Sa 10:30am-1am.) **Peacock Alley Bar and Grill ❸,** 422 E. Main Ave., delivers scrumptious salads ($7), sandwiches ($6-8), and dinner entrees ($14-20) in the historic Patterson Hotel. (☎255-7917. Open for brunch Su 9am-1pm; lunch M-Sa 11am-2pm; dinner M 5:30-9pm, Tu-Sa 5:30-10pm. Bar open until 1am.) Housed

IN RECENT NEWS

GOODBYE, GREYHOUND

Widening the gulf between the small towns and big cities in the US, Greyhound has made significant schedule and route changes, decreasing and eliminating service in the Great Plains and Pacific Northwest.

In August 2004, Greyhound canceled bus service on its northern route between Chicago and Seattle, dropping service to 260 communities and leaving just 99 stops in the 13-state region. This down-size marked the beginning of a three-year "network transformation," in which Greyhound will seek to streamline into a "smaller, simpler network of routes that is short- and medium-haul focused." The new local hub focus has made efficient cross-country travel incredibly difficult and busing around the Great Plains almost impossible. Indeed, the company even closed all of its routes in North Dakota except for those east of Fargo, as well as the entire Minneapolis-to-Seattle line.

In the wake of Greyhound's impending exit from the region, smaller bus lines are cropping up or extending their services. Travelers should be very aware of the lack of dependability of bus service in the region and the possibility of increased prices and inconvenient schedules. With stations changing their carriers, be sure to call ahead for the depot hours and other important information.

in the old Northern Pacific train depot, **Fiesta Villa ❷**, 411 E. Main Ave., serves quesadillas, tacos, and other Mexican fare. The authentic homemade sauces and margaritas shake things up while the nearby railroad tracks rattle the foundation. (☎222-8075. Entrees $8-12. Patio and bar 21+. Open M-Th 11am-10:30pm, F-Sa 11am-11pm. Bar open until 1am on busy evenings.)

◪ SIGHTS. In the heart of downtown is the **North Dakota Heritage Center,** 612 E. Boulevard Ave., an excellent museum with exhibits ranging from triceratops to tractors and a fabulous children's display. (☎328-2666; www.state.nd.us/hist. Open M-F 8am-5pm, Sa 9am-5pm, Su 11am-5pm. Free.) Across from the Heritage Center is the **North Dakota State Capitol,** 600 E. Boulevard Ave, a 19-story office-style building that was built between 1932 and 1934 for only $2 million and reflects the state's inclination toward the practical and economical. The observation deck on the 18th floor is a perfect place to see the prairie and the capitol's 130 acres of well-manicured grounds. (☎328-2000. Open M-F 7am-5:30pm. 30min. tours leave every hr. June-Aug. M-F 8-11am and 1-4pm, Sa 9-11am and 1-4pm, Su 1-4pm; Sept.-May M-F 8-11am and 1-4pm. Free.) North Dakota's oldest state park, **Fort Abraham Lincoln State Park,** lies on Rte. 1806 in Mandan, along the Missouri River, in an area which was occupied by the Mandan Indians until they succumbed to smallpox in 1837. Lewis and Clark came through in 1804, and General George Armstrong Custer, commanding the 7th Cavalry, took up residence here. Now, Fort Lincoln houses the **"On-a-Slant" Mandan Indian Village,** with several reconstructed earth lodges, as well as replicas of the cavalry post and Custer's Victorian-style home. (☎667-6380. Open June-Aug. Buildings open daily 9am-7pm; tours on the ½hr. 9am-6:30pm; park open daily 9am-9:30pm. $5, students $3; vehicle fee $5.)

North Dakota's obsession with Lewis and Clark's Corps of Discovery continues 38 mi. north of Bismarck at the **Lewis and Clark Interpretive Center,** which presents an overview of the explorers' wilderness journey. Visitors can don bison robes and a cradle board, just like those Sacagawea once wore, or simulate trading with Native Americans using an interactive computer program. Two miles away at **Fort Mandan,** modern-day trailblazers can enter a replica of the rugged riverside lodgings that sheltered the expedition during the winter of 1804. (☎462-8535 or 877-462-8535; www.fortmandan.com. Center and fort open daily June-Aug. 9am-7pm; Sept.-May 9am-5pm. Admission to both $7.50, students $5.)

◪◪ ENTERTAINMENT AND NIGHTLIFE. The **Bismarck Symphony** (☎258-8345) plays in the magnificent **Belle Mehus Auditorium,** 201 N. 6th St. The symphony celebrates holidays in style—8000 people turn up for their Fourth of July concert on the capitol steps. (Concert series Sept.-Apr. $10-35.) **Borrowed Buck's Roadhouse,** 118 S. 3rd St., has a full dance floor and a live DJ every night. Rock music and themed nights fuel the frat-house fun, while live bands take the stage once or twice a month. (☎224-1545. 21+. Open M-Sa 4pm-1am.) For a true country experience, try **Lonesome Dove,** 3929 Memorial Hwy. on the border of Mandan, a real country joint with a large dance floor and live, toe-tappin' country music Wednesday through Sunday. (☎663-2793. 21+. Cover F-Sa $2. Open daily noon-1am.)

THEODORE ROOSEVELT NATIONAL PARK ☎701

After his mother and wife died on the same day, pre-White House Theodore ("Teddy") Roosevelt moved to his ranch in the Badlands for spiritual renewal. He was so influenced by this "place of grim beauty," with its buttes and gorges, horseback riding, big-game hunting, and cattle ranching, that he later claimed, "I never

I-94, ROAD OF CONCRETE WONDERS

Two gargantuan concrete monuments separated by 131 mi. of interstate symbolize North Dakota's past and present. Looming on the horizon in Jamestown, ND, at Exit 258, is the **world's largest buffalo**—a towering 24 ft. monument to the animals that once freely roamed the plains. Across the highway, a herd of real buffalo regards their concrete brother apathetically from behind a protective fence. In New Salem, ND, 33 mi. west of Bismarck, at Exit 127, Salem Sue, the **world's largest Holstein cow** (38 ft. tall and 50 ft. long), keeps an eye on the interstate and the spectacular patchwork fields of the plains. ($1 suggested donation.)

would have been President if it weren't for my experiences in North Dakota." Roosevelt National Park was created in 1947 as a monument to his conservation efforts, and its vast open spaces and rugged outdoors opportunities preserve the spirit of the land that so profoundly inspired the rising president.

■ ◪ **ORIENTATION AND PRACTICAL INFORMATION.** The park is split into the **North Unit** and **South Unit.** On the radio, AM 1610 offers information about both parts of the park. The North Unit is located off of I-85 and the entrance to the more developed South Unit is just north of I-94 in **Medora,** a revamped tourist haven where you can see wildlife just minutes away from immaculate public restrooms, old-fashioned ice-cream parlors, and gift "shoppes." The park entrance fee ($5 per person, under 17 free; $10 max. per vehicle) covers admission to both the North and South units for 7 days. The **South Unit Visitors Center,** in Medora, maintains a mini-museum displaying Roosevelt's guns, spurs, and old letters, and shows a 13min. film detailing his relationship with the land. (☎623-4466. Open daily late June to Sept. 8am-8pm; Sept. to mid-June 8am-4:30pm.) The **North Unit Visitors Center,** located next to the park entrance, has an interesting exhibit on the nature and wildlife in the park. (☎842-2333. Open daily 9am-5:30pm. Call ahead in winter.) For more info, write to **Theodore Roosevelt National Park,** P.O. Box 7, Medora 58645, call one of the visitors centers or visit www.nps.gov/thro.

Dakota Cyclery, 275 3rd Ave., rents bikes. (☎623-4808 or 888-321-1218; www.dakotacyclery.com; open in summer daily 9am-6pm; half-day $20-30; full-day $30-45) and leads bike tours of the plains and badlands by reservation and has a **shuttle service.** Off-road biking is not allowed in either unit of the park.

Medora lacks a real pharmacy and grocery store. However, both the **Ferris Store,** 251 Main St. (☎623-4447; open daily 8am-8pm), and **Medora Convenience and Liquor,** on Pacific Ave. at Main St. (☎623-4479; open daily 7am-11pm), sell basic pharmaceutical goods, food, and cooking items. There is a 24hr. **Wal-Mart** (☎225-8504; closed midnight Sa to noon Su) in Dickinson, 30 mi. east on I-94. **South Unit Time Zone:** Mountain (2hr. behind Eastern). **North Unit Time Zone:** Central (1hr. behind Eastern). **Post Office:** 355 3rd Ave., in Medora. (☎623-4385. Open M-Sa 8am-7pm. Window service M-F 8am-11:45am and 12:30-4:30pm, Sa 8:15-9:45am.) **Postal Code:** 58645. **Area Code:** 701.

◪ ◪ **ACCOMMODATIONS AND FOOD.** Free backcountry camping permits are available from the visitors centers. **Cottonwood Campground ❶** lies 5 mi. past the South Unit Visitors Center on Scenic Loop Dr. In the north, **Juniper Campground ❶,** 5 mi. west of the North Unit entrance, is in a beautiful valley. Be cautious: the campground is frequented by buffalo year-round. Both campgrounds have toilets and running water in the summer, but only pit toilets in the winter, and no hook-ups. (Sites $10; in winter $5.) It is difficult to find cheap lodging other than camping in Medora and most places are closed during the winter

GREAT PLAINS

months. The **Bunkhouse** ❸, 400 E. River Rd. S, offers some of the cheapest rates around and has A/C, cable TV, and a heated outdoor swimming pool. (☎800-633-6721. Register at the Badlands Motel at 500 Pacific Ave. Open late May to early Sept. Doubles $66; family units $95). For a bit more luxury, the historic **Rough Riders Hotel** ❹, 301 3rd Ave., offers rooms with original furniture and a restaurant serving reasonably-priced breakfasts ($4-8), lunches ($6-10), and dinners ($14-20) in upscale surroundings. Teddy himself addresses the public every day at 3:30pm on the Rough Riders' balcony. (☎623-4444, ext. 497. Restaurant open daily 7am-2pm and 5-9pm. In summer singles $80, doubles $93; low-season $42/$49.) If homey comfort has more appeal than historic charm, try **Custer's Cottage** ❷, 156 E. River Rd. S, which has two comfortably furnished condo units with full kitchens, laundry facilities, A/C, and cable TV. (☎623-4378 or 888-383-2574; www.custerscottage.com. 1-bedroom unit $50-60 for one night, $40-50 per night for longer stays. Larger units available.)

The **Iron Horse Saloon** ❸, 160 Pacific Ave., offers a variety of burgers and deep-fried food year-round, served at the bar or on the patio. (☎623-9894. Breakfast and lunch $4-7. Dinner $7-15. Open daily June-Sept. 6am-1am; Oct.-May 10:30am-1am.) For cheap meals, **Lunch and Munch More** ❶, 314 Pacific Ave., has sandwiches with a range of fillings ($3.25) and sides for under $3. (☎623-2805. Open in summer daily 7am-8:30pm; call for winter hours.) On the corner of Main St. and Broadway, Medora's **Fudge & Ice Cream Depot** ❶ offers a sweet retreat from the heat. (☎800-633-6721. One scoop $2, two scoops $2.50. Open summer daily 11am-7:30pm.)

⛳ ENTERTAINMENT. The popular **Medora Musical** is a comical singing, dancing, and theatrical experience celebrating the glory of the West, America, and Teddy Roosevelt himself. The patriotic show, held in the open-air **Burning Hills Amphitheatre** west of town, incorporates pyrotechnics, magicians, horses, and Argentine *Gauchos*. (Show runs early June to late Aug. daily 8:30-10:30pm. $21-23, students $13-14.) Before the show, at the Tjaden Terrace, cast members from the musical serenade the audience as feast at a rowdy Western cookout. At the **Pitchfork Steak Fondue** ❺, the "chef" puts ten steaks on a pitchfork and dips them into a vat of boiling oil for 5min. (Daily at 6:30pm. Reservations required. $20, half steak $16. Buffet only $12, pre-schoolers $4.) Tickets for both the musical and the fondue are available at the Burning Hills Amphitheatre, 335 4th St., at the **Harold Schafer Heritage Center**. (☎800-633-6721; www.medora.com. Open daily 10am-6pm.)

The seclusion of Theodore Roosevelt National Park provides ample opportunity for wildlife contact, but be careful not to surprise the bison; you may wish to sing while hiking so they can hear you coming. Do not approach any wild animal, and beware of rattlesnakes and black widow spiders living in prairie dog burrows. Even if you avoid the creepy-crawlies, stay on guard; prairie dogs have bites more menacing than their barks. The park also has ticks and poison ivy. Stay aware of changing weather; severe and violent weather changes often catch people by surprise. There are no approved drinking water sources in the park.

⛰ OUTDOOR ACTIVITIES. The South Unit is busier and more crowded than the North Unit and includes the 36 mi. **Scenic Loop Drive,** from which all sights and trails are accessible. **Painted Canyon Overlook,** 7 mi. east of Medora off I-94, has its own **visitors center** with picnic tables, public phones, restrooms, and a breathtaking panoramic view of the Badlands. The occasional bison roams through the parking lot. (☎575-4020. Open Apr.-Nov. daily 8:30am-4:30pm; call ahead for extended summer hours.) The **Painted Canyon Trail** is a worthwhile 1 mi. hiking loop that winds gently into the valley through shady wooded areas and scorching buttes. **Peaceful Valley Ranch**, 7 mi. into the park, offers horseback excursions. (☎623-4568. Open Sept.-May. 1½hr. trail rides leave in summer daily 8:30am-2pm;evening ride 6pm. 6 per day. $24.) The **Ridgeline Trail** begins with a steep climb but is a relatively flat half-mile hiking trail. Signs along the way describe the ecology and geology of the terrain. For a little more exercise, try the **Coal Vein Trail.** This three-quarter mile trail traces a seam of lignite coal that ignited and burned from 1951 to 1977; the searing heat of the blaze served as a natural kiln, baking the adjacent clay and sand. The beautiful **Buck Hill** is accessible by car, but a short climb up a steep paved path to an elevation of 2855 ft. yields an unforgettable 360° view of the Badlands landscape that should not be missed. Constant winds morph the soft sands of **Wind Canyon,** while a short dirt path leading along the bluffs gives a closer look at the canyon walls and the river below. The third largest **petrified forest** in the US is a day's hike into the park; if you prefer to drive, ask a ranger for directions and expect to walk about 3 mi. Tours leave intermittently in the summer between 8:45am and 4:15pm from the South Unit Visitors Center for Teddy's **Maltese Cross Cabin,** built circa 1883. For more info on hiking, pick up *Frontier Fragments* and the *Backcountry Guide* (both free) at one of the visitors centers.

The state historic site **Chateau de Mores,** 3448 Chateau Rd. on the west side of town, details Medora's history even before Roosevelt arrived on the scene, with guides in each room of the town founder's gentrified hunting cabin. (☎623-4355. Open May 16-Sept. 15 8:30am-6:30pm; in winter by appointment. $6, children $3.)

The newly developed, 120 mi. **Maah Daah Hey Trail** connects the North and South Units through the scenic Little Missouri Badlands. Bikes are not allowed within the park boundaries, but many mountain bikers, horseback riders, and backpackers take a re-routed trail around the parks, following what was once a principal trade route for the Native Americans. Most would probably prefer to drive between the units; the North Unit is 70 mi. from the South Unit on U.S. 85. The North Unit is known for more dramatic scenery and greater opportunities for hiking and exploring. Most of the land is designated wilderness, resulting in unlimited backcountry hiking possibilities. For those eager to escape the crowds, but reluctant to leave the car, the North Unit's 14 mi. **Scenic Drive** connects the entrance and visitors center to **Oxbow Overlook** and is relatively unspoiled. The 1 mi. **Little Mo Trail** weaves through woodlands and badlands, and three-quarters of the 1 mi. trail is paved and wheelchair accessible. The 4½ mi. looped **Caprock Coulee Trail** winds its way through a variety of habitats, climbing to an outlook over the Little Missouri River. The 11 mi. **Buckhorn Trail** is moderately strenuous and passes two prairie dog towns. Seasoned hikers and adventurers thrive on the challenging 18 mi. **Achenbach Trail,** which features vertical drops, uphill climbs, and two river crossings as it winds around the Little Missouri River, visible from the **River Bend Overlook.**

SOUTH DAKOTA

With fewer than ten people per square mile, South Dakota has the highest ratio of sights to people in all of the Great Plains. Colossal carvings such as Mt. Rushmore and the Crazy Horse Memorial and stunning natural spectacles like the Black Hills and the Badlands draw adventure-seeking summer crowds.

◪ PRACTICAL INFORMATION

Capital: Pierre.

GREAT PLAINS

Visitor Info: Department of Tourism, 711 E. Wells Ave., Pierre 57501 (☎605-773-3301 or 800-732-5682; www.travelsd.com). Open M-F 8am-5pm. **US Forest Service,** 330 Mt. Rushmore Rd., Custer 57730 (☎605-673-4853). Open M-F 7:30am-4:30pm. **Game, Fish, and Parks Department,** 523 E. Capitol Ave., Foss Bldg., Pierre 57501 (☎605-773-3391, campground reservations 800-710-2267; www.campsd.com), has info on state parks and campgrounds. Open M-F 8am-5pm.

Postal Abbreviation: SD. **Sales Tax:** 4% (1-2% added by towns).

SIOUX FALLS   ☎605

As South Dakota's eastern gateway and largest city, Sioux Falls is a classic "family town": friendly, clean, and a little boring. For many travelers, this makes it a good place to take a breather rather than a destination in itself. The city's namesake rapids are at **Falls Park,** north of downtown. Five miles west of Sioux Falls at Exit 390 off I-90, the ghost town of **Buffalo Ridge** has over 50 exhibits portraying life in the Old West. Glimpse the ghost of Comanche, Custer's horse, and witness a mechanized reenactment of Bill Hickock's murder in the saloon. A herd of bison makes periodic appearances near the town. (☎528-3931. Open early Apr. to Oct. sunrise-sunset. $4, ages 5-12 $3.) The **Corn Palace,** 604 N. Main St., in Mitchell, 70 mi. west of Sioux Falls on I-90, was specifically designed to put the town on the map and now poses as a regal testament to the "a-maize-ing" power of corn. Dating back to 1892, the structure is refurbished with a new mural every year using 275,000 ears of corn in nine colors and 3000 bushels of grains and grasses. (☎996-5031 or 866-273-2676; www.cornpalace.com. Open June-Aug. daily 8am-9pm; May and Sept.-Oct. daily 8am-5pm; Nov.-Apr. M-F 8am-5pm. Free.)

Budget motels flank 41st St. at Exit 77 off I-29. The **Red Roof Inn ❷,** 3500 Gateway Blvd., is a good value with large TVs, continental breakfast, and laundry. (☎361-1864 or 800-733-7663. Singles $44; doubles $55. AAA discount.) Of the many nearby state parks, **Split Rock City Park ❶,** 20 mi. northeast in Garretson, has the cheapest camping. From I-90 E, take Exit 406 to Rte. 11 N (Corson), and drive 10 mi. to Garretson; turn right at the sign for Devil's Gulch, and the park will be on your left before the tracks. (☎594-6721. Pit toilets and drinking water. Sites $6.) Phillips Ave., between 9th and 12th St., is lined with coffeehouses and restaurants, and leads to the falls on its northern end. **Soda Falls ❶,** 209 S. Phillips Ave., at the back of Zandbroz Variety Store, has fantastic sandwiches ($2-4) and sundaes ($3-4). The 1920s lunch counter was built from some of the first marble used in the Dakotas. (☎331-5137. Open M-Sa 9am-8pm, Su noon-5pm.) An oasis of flavor amidst the bland strip malls of Sioux Falls, **Shalom Ethiopian Cafe ❸,** 1701 E. 10th St., east of downtown, serves spicy meat and vegetable dishes with *injera* bread for utensil-free eating. (☎339-2919. Entrees $7-10. Open daily 9am-10pm.) **Nitwits Comedy Club,** 431 N. Phillips Ave., showcases local talent along with Hollywood imports. (☎274-9656 or 888-798-0277; www.nitwitscomedy.com. Cover $10. Box office opens W-F 6pm, Sa 3pm. Club office open Tu-F 10am-6pm. Shows W-Sa 7:30pm, F-Sa 10pm.) Dance the night away at the **ACME DRINK COMPANY,** 305 N. Main Ave. (☎339-1131. W 18+, Th-Sa 21+. Cover W $5. Open W 9pm-2am, Th-Sa 8pm-2am.)

Jefferson Lines, 301 N. Dakota Ave. (☎336-0885 or 800-678-6543; open M-Sa 8am-9pm, Su 8-11:30am and 2-9pm), runs buses to: Minneapolis (6hr., 1 per day, $52); Omaha (3½hr., 2 per day, $38); Rapid City (6hr., 1 per day, $84). **Sioux Falls Transit** buses run throughout the city. (☎367-7183. Buses operate M-F 5:40am-6:50pm, Sa 8am-6:50pm. $1; transfers free.) The **Sioux Falls Trolley** offers free rides around downtown. (☎367-7183. Runs Apr.-Sept. M-Sa 8am-10pm.) **Taxi: Yellow Cab** ☎336-1616. **Visitor Info: Sioux Falls Convention and Visitors Bureau,** on Falls Park Dr. between Main Ave. and Weber Ave. The observation tower has aerial views of the falls. (☎367-7430; www.siouxfallscvb.com. Open mid-Apr. to Sept. daily 9am-9pm; Oct. to mid-Apr. Sa-Su 9am-5pm; mid-Nov. to early Jan. also M-F 5-9pm, Sa-Su 9am-9pm for Christmas lights in the park.) **Medical Services: Avera McKennan Hospital and University Health Center,** 800 E. 21st St. (☎322-8000.) **Internet Access: Sioux Falls Public Library,** 201 N. Main Ave., at 8th St. (☎367-8740. 1hr. limit. Open June-Aug. M-Th 9:30am-9pm, F 9:30am-6pm, Sa 9:30am-5pm; Sept.-May M-Th 9:30am-9pm, F 9:30am-6pm, Sa 9:30am-5pm, Su 1-5pm.) **Post Office:** 320 S. 2nd Ave. (☎357-5001. Open M-F 8am-5:30pm, Sa 10am-1pm.) **Postal Code:** 57104. **Area Code:** 605.

BADLANDS ☎605

When faced with the mountainous rock formations suddenly appearing out of the prairie, early explorers were less than enthusiastic. General Alfred Sully called these arid and treacherous formations "Hell with the fires out," and the French translated the Sioux name for the area, *mako sica,* as *les mauvaises terres:* "bad lands." Late spring and fall in the Badlands offer pleasant weather that can be a relief from the extreme temperatures of mid-summer and winter; however, even at their worst, the Badlands are worth a visit. Deposits of iron oxide lend layers of marvelous red and brown hues to the present land, and the colorful moods of the Badlands change with the time, season, and weather.

🛂 **PRACTICAL INFORMATION. Badlands National Park** lies about 50 mi. east of Rapid City on I-90. The **entrance fee** comes with a free copy of *The Prairie Preamble* with trail map. ($10 per car, $5 per person on bike, foot, or motorcycle.) **Driving tours** of the park can start at either end of Rte. 240, which winds through wilderness in a 32 mi. detour off I-90 Exit 110 or 131. The **Ben Reifel Visitors Center,** 5 mi. inside the park's northeastern entrance, serves as the park headquarters. (☎433-5361. Open daily 9am-4pm; extended hours vary.) A drive along **Route 240/Loop Road** is an excellent introduction to the entire northern portion of the park. This scenic byway makes its way through rainbow-colored bluffs and around hairpin turns, with numerous turnoffs for views of the Badlands. The gravel **Sage Creek Rim Road,** west of Rte. 240, has fewer people and more animals. Highlights are the Roberts Prairie Dog Town and the park's herds of bison and antelope; across the river from the Sage Creek campground lies another prairie dog town and some popular bison territory. The more remote **White River Visitors Center,** is located 55 mi. to the southwest, off Rte. 27, in the park's less-visited southern section. (☎455-2878. Open June-Aug. daily 10am-4pm.) Both visitors centers have potable water and restrooms. The **National Grasslands Visitors Center (Buffalo Gap),** 708 Main St., in Wall, has films and exhibits on the complex ecosystem of the surrounding area. (☎279-2125. Open daily June-Aug. 8am-5pm; Sept.-May 8am-4:30pm.) For info, write to Badlands National Park, P.O. Box 6, Interior, SD 57750 (www.nps.gov/badl). **Area Code:** 605. **Time Zone:** Mountain (2hr. behind Eastern).

🏠 **ACCOMMODATIONS.** In addition to standard lodging and camping, **backcountry camping** (½ mi. from the road and out of sight) offers close contact with this austere landscape, but be sure to bring water. Campers are strongly urged to contact one of the rangers at the visitors center before heading out and to be extra careful of bison, which are extremely dangerous. Within the park, the **Cedar Pass Lodge ❸,** 1 Cedar St., next to the Ben Reifel Visitors Center, rents cabins with A/C and showers. (☎433-5460; www.cedarpasslodge.com. Open mid-Apr. to mid-Oct. Reservations recommended. 1 person $58, additional person $5.) The slightly cheaper **Badlands Inn ❷,** at Exit 131 off I-90, south of the Ben Reifel Visitors Center in Interior on Rte. 44, sits outside the park but all rooms have a wide view of the Badlands and access to an outdoor pool. (☎433-5401 or 800-341-8000; www.badlandsinn.com. Open mid-May to mid-Sept. Singles $65, additional person $5.) If you'd rather sleep under the stars, the **Sage Creek Campground ❶,** 13 mi. from the Pinnacles entrance south of Wall, is on an open field in the prairie with pit toilets and no water. (Take Sage Creek Rim Rd. off Rte. 240. Free.) You pay for view at the **Cedar Pass Campground ❶,** south of the Ben Reifel Visitors Center, which has more organized sites with water and flush toilets, but no showers. It's best to get there before 6pm in summer. (For info, contact Ben Reifel Visitors Center. Sites $10.)

❏ FOOD. A true South Dakota experience, the **Cuny Table Cafe ❶,** 8 mi. west of the White River Visitor Center on Rte. 2, doesn't advertise because it doesn't need to—the food does all the talking. The restaurant is packed at lunchtime; try the Indian Tacos (home-cooked fry bread piled with veggies, beans, and beef) for $5. (☎455-2957. Open daily 5:30am-5:30pm. Cash only.) About 60mi. north, by the main visitors center, the **Cedar Pass Lodge Restaurant ❷** has buffalo burgers ($5.50), fry bread ($2.25), and fantastic views to the north of the Badlands. (☎433-5460. Open daily mid-May to Aug. 7am-8:30pm; Sept. 7:30am-7pm; Oct.-May 8am-4:30pm.) The **A&M Cafe ❷,** just 2 mi. south of the Ben Reifel Visitors Center on Rte. 44, outside the park in Interior, is a small but hectic cafe with generous breakfasts ($4-8) and ample sandwich platters for $4-7. (☎433-5340. Open daily 6:30am-9pm.)

⚠ OUTDOOR ACTIVITIES. The 244,000-acre park protects large tracts of prairie and stark rock formations. The Ben Reifel Visitors Center has an 18min. video on the Badlands as well as a wealth of info on nearby activities and camping. Park rangers offer free talks daily at 2pm and a prairie walk daily at 5:30pm from June to August. Check the handy *Prairie Preamble* for other events. **Hiking** is permitted throughout the entire park, although officials discourage climbing on the formations and request sticking to high-use trails. The south unit is mostly uncharted territory, and the occasional found path is most likely the tracks of wildlife. For backcountry hikers, it's a good idea to bring a compass, a map, and lots of water. Despite the burning heat in summer, long pants are advisable to protect hikers from poison ivy, stinging and biting insects, and the park's one venomous snake—the prairie rattlesnake. Five hiking trails begin off Loop Rd. near the Ben Reifel Visitor Center. The **Notch Trail** (1½ mi., 1½-2hr.) demands surefootedness through a canyon and a willingness to climb a shaky ladder at a 45° angle. Not for the faint of heart, the trail blazes around narrow ledges before making its way to the grand finale: an unbelievable view of the Cliff Shelf and White River Valley. The moderate **Cliff Shelf Nature Trail** (½ mi., 30min.) consists of stairs, a boardwalk, and unpaved paths. It is the best bet for coming face-to-face with wildlife. **Door Trail** (¾ mi., 20min.) is wheelchair accessible for the first 100m. The rest of the trail cuts through buttes and crevices for spectacular views of the surrounding countryside. **Window Trail** (¼ mi., 10min.), more of a scenic overlook than an actual hike, consists of a wheelchair-accessible ramp with a splendid view.

Those interested exploring the area on horseback rather than on foot can check out **Badlands Trail Rides,** 1½ mi. south of the Ben Reifel Visitors Center on Rte. 377. While the trails do not lead into the park, they do cover territory on the park's immediate outskirts. All levels are welcome, and a full introduction is given before the ride. (☎309-2028. Open summer daily 8am-7pm. $15 for 30min. ride; $20 for 1hr. ride.)

RAPID CITY
☎ 605

Rapid City's location makes it a convenient base from which to explore Mount Rushmore, Crazy Horse, the Black Hills, and the Badlands, all within an hour's drive of downtown. The area welcomes three million tourists each summer, over 60 times the city's permanent population. The Civic Center supplies a brochure and map of the **Rapid City Star Tour,** which leads to 12 free attractions, including a jaunt up Skyline Drive for a view of the city and the seven concrete dinosaurs of **Dinosaur Park,** as well as a trip to **Storybook Island,** an amusement park inhabited by the Gingerbread Man, the Three Little Pigs, and other childhood pals. In Memorial Park, America's largest **Berlin Wall exhibit** features two pieces of the wall. The **Journey Museum,** 222 New York St., traces the history of the region, detailing its geology, archaeology, and people, with life-size skull castings of a *T. rex* and a holographic story tent. (☎394-6923; www.journeymuseum.org. Open late May to early Sept. daily 9am-5pm; in winter, M-Sa 10am-5pm, Su 1-5pm. $6, seniors $5, students $4.) The 8 mi. **Rapid City Recreational Path** runs along Rapid Creek.

Rapid City accommodations are more expensive during the summer, and motels often fill weeks in advance. Needless to say, reservations are a good idea. Winter travelers benefit from an abundance of low-season bargains. Budget motels surround the junction of I-90 and Rte. 59 by the Rushmore Mall. Large billboards guide the way to **Big Sky Motel ❸,** 4080 Tower Rd., 5min. south of town on a service road off Mt. Rushmore Rd. The rooms are very clean and the doubles have great views of Rapid City and the surrounding valley. (☎348-3200 or 800-318-3208. Open May-Oct. No phones. Mid-June to mid-Aug. singles $50; doubles $65. Low-season $35-40/$45-55. AAA discount.) **Camping ❶** is available at **Badlands National Park** (p. 655), **Black Hills National Forest** (p. 658), and **Custer State Park** (p. 661). The **Millstone Family Restaurant ❸,** 2010 W. Main St., at Mountain View Rd., cooks up large portions of chicken ($5.65-8), spaghetti and meatballs ($7.35), and pork ribs ($9). Try the steak and salad bar combo for $8. (☎343-5824. Open daily 6am-11pm.) **Pauly's Sub Co. ❶,** 2060 W. Main St. west of downtown, shares space with **Java Junkie,** creating a one-stop spot for cheap coffee ($1) and a selection of subs from $2.30. (☎348-2669. Open M-Sa 10am-9pm, Su 11am-8pm. Java Junkie open M-F 6:30am-7pm, Sa 8am-6pm, Su 8am-4pm.) For a beer as black as the Hills, throw back a Smokejumper Stout ($3) at the **Firehouse Brewing Company,** 610 Main St. The company brews five beers and serves sandwiches, burgers, and salads for $6-10 in the restored 1915 firehouse or outside on their heated patio. (☎348-1915; www.firehousebrewing.com. Live music on weekends. Open M-Th 11am-10pm, F-Sa 11am-11pm, Su 4-9pm. Open 1hr. later and Su 11am-10pm in summer.)

Downtown Rapid City is located off Exit 57 on I-90. Rapid City's roads form a sensible grid pattern, making driving along its wide streets easy. **Saint Joseph Street** and **Main Street** are the main east-west thoroughfares and **Omaha Street** is two-way. **Mount Rushmore Road (Route 16)** is the main north-south route. Many north-south roads are numbered, and numbers increase from east to west, beginning at **East Boulevard.** The Airport Express Shuttle (☎399-9999; $13) can get you quickly to the **Rapid City Regional Airport** (☎393-9924), off Rte. 44, 8½ mi. east of the city. **Rapid Taxi Inc.** (☎348-8080) will take you around town. **Jefferson Lines** travels east from the **Milo Barber Transportation Center,** 333 6th St. (☎348-3300), downtown, with one bus daily to: Omaha (12hr., $106); Pierre (4hr., $34-36); Sioux Falls (10hr., $96). **Powder River Lines,** also in the Transportation Center, runs once daily to Billings (7hr., $67) and Cheyenne (9hr., $79). Station open M-F 8am-5:30pm, Sa-Su 8am-10am and 3-5:30pm. **Rapid Ride** runs city buses. Pick up a schedule at the terminal in the Transportation Center. (☎394-6631. Operates M-F 6:25am-5:30pm. $1, seniors $0.50.) **Visitor Info: Rapid City**

GREAT PLAINS

Chamber of Commerce and Visitors Information Center, 444 Mt. Rushmore Rd. N, in the Civic Center. (☎343-1744 or 800-487-3223; www.rapidcitycvb.com. Open M-F 8am-5pm.) **The Rapid City Regional Hospital** (☎719-8100) is located at 353 Fairmont Blvd. **Internet Access: Rapid City Public Library,** 610 Quincy St., at 6th St. (☎394-4171. Open Labor Day-Memorial Day M-Th 9am-9pm, F-Sa 9am-5:30pm; Sept.-May M-Th 9am-9pm, F-Sa 9am-5:30pm, Su 1-5pm. 1hr. per day. Free.) **Post Office:** 500 East Blvd., east of downtown. (☎394-8600. Open M-F 8am-5:30pm, Sa 8:30am-12:30pm.) **Postal Code:** 57701. **Area Code:** 605.

BLACK HILLS REGION

The Lakota called this region Paha Sapa, meaning Black Hills, for the hue that the Ponderosa pines take on when seen from a distance, and they thought the region so sacred that they would only visit, but not settle. The Treaty of 1868 gave the Black Hills and the rest of South Dakota west of the Missouri River to the tribe, but when gold was discovered in the 1870s, the US government snatched back 6000 square miles. Today, the area attracts millions of visitors annually with a trove of natural treasures, including Custer State Park, Wind Cave National Park, and Jewel Cave National Monument. Meanwhile, Mt. Rushmore and Crazy Horse stand as larger-than-life symbols of the cultural clash that defines the region's history.

BLACK HILLS NATIONAL FOREST   ☎ 605

The Black Hills region holds over 130 attractions—including a reptile farm, a Flintstones theme park, and a Passion play—but the greatest sights are the natural ones. Most of the land in the Black Hills is part of the Black Hills National Forest and exercises the "multiple use" principle—mining, logging, ranching, and recreation all take place in close proximity. The forest itself provides opportunities for backcountry hiking, swimming, biking, and camping, as do park-run campgrounds and private tent sites. In the hills, the **visitors center,** on I-385 at Pactola Lake, offers a great view of the lake, a wildlife exhibit with a bald eagle, maps of the area, and details on backcountry camping. (☎343-8755. Open late May to early Sept. daily 8:30am-6pm.) There is also a **Black Hills Visitor Information Center** at Exit 61 off I-90 in Rapid City. (☎355-3700. Open daily June-Aug. 8am-8pm; Sept.-May 8am-5pm.) **Backcountry camping** in the national forest is free. Camping is allowed 1 mi. away from any campground or visitors center and at least 200 ft. off the side of the road (leave your car in a parking lot or pull off). Open fires are prohibited, but controlled fires in provided grates are allowed. Good **campgrounds ❶** include: **Pactola,** on the Pactola Reservoir just south of the junction of Rte. 44 and U.S. 385; **Sheridan Lake,** 5 mi. northeast of Hill City on U.S. 385 (north entrance for group sites, south entrance for individuals); and **Roubaix Lake,** 14 mi. south of Lead on U.S. 385. (Sites at all 3 campgrounds $17-20.) All three have some sites open in the winter. All national forest campgrounds are quiet and wooded, offering fishing, swimming, and pit toilets. No hookups are provided. (Reservations ☎877-444-6777; www.reserveusa.com.) The national forest extends into Wyoming, and the **Bearlodge Ranger Station** in Sundance directs visitors to the west. (☎307-283-1361. Open M-F 7:30am-5pm, Sa 9am-3pm.) The Wyoming side of the forest permits campfires (sometimes) and horses, and draws fewer visitors. The hostel in **Deadwood** (p. 662) is the cheapest and best indoor accommodation in these parts.

I-90 skirts the northern border of the Black Hills from Spearfish in the west to Rapid City in the east. **U.S. 385** twists from Hot Springs in the south to Deadwood in the north. The beautiful winding routes and dirt Forest Service roads hold driv-

TIP
HOG HEAVEN. Unless you've got a Harley underneath you, the Black Hills are best avoided during the first two weeks in August, when the **Sturgis Rally** takes over the area. Nearly 500,000 motorcyclists roar through the Hills, filling up campsites and motels and bringing traffic to a standstill.

ers to half the speed of the interstate. Winter in the northern area of the Black Hills offers stellar skiing and snowmobiling. Unfortunately, many attractions close or have limited hours, and most resorts and campgrounds are closed in winter.

MOUNT RUSHMORE   ☎ 605

Mount Rushmore National Memorial boasts the faces that launched a thousand minivans. Historian Doane Robinson originally conceived of this "shrine of democracy" in 1923 as a memorial for frontier heroes, carved among the spectacular Needles; sculptor Gutzon Borglum chose four presidents instead. Borglum initially encountered opposition from those who felt the work of God could not be improved, but the sculptor defended the project's size, insisting that "there is not a monument in this country as big as a snuff box." In 1941, the 60 ft. heads of Washington, Jefferson, Roosevelt, and Lincoln were finished. The 465 ft. tall bodies were never completed—work ceased when US funds were diverted to WWII.

From Rapid City, take U.S. 16 and 16A to Keystone, and Rte. 244 up to the mountain. The memorial is 2 mi. from downtown Keystone. There is an $8 per car "annual parking permit" for the lot adjacent to the entrance. The **Info Center** details the monument's history and has ranger tours every hour on the half hour. A state-of-the-art **visitors center** chronicles the monument's history and the lives of the featured presidents in addition to showing a film that explains how the carving was accomplished—about 90% of the "sculpting" was done with dynamite. (Info center ☎574-3198. Visitors center ☎574-3165. Both open daily in summer 8am-10pm; low-season 8am-5pm. Wheelchair accessible.)

From the visitors center, it is half a mile along the planked wooden **Presidential Trail** to **Borglum's Studio.** Visitors can stare at Borglum's full-bodied plaster model of the carving as well as tools and designs for Mt. Rushmore. (Open in summer daily 9am-6pm. Ranger talks every hr. on the ½hr.) During the summer, the **Mount Rushmore Memorial Amphitheater** hosts an evening program. (☎574-2523; www.nps.gov/moru. Patriotic speech and film 9pm, light floods the monument 9:30-10:30pm. Trail lights extinguished 11pm.) With historical scenes rendered in minute detail and engaging audio tours, the **National Presidential Wax Museum,** Hwy. 16A in downtown Keystone, offers a glimpse of figures from American history in a different medium. (☎666-4455; www.presidentialwaxmuseum.com. Open May-Sept. daily 9am-9pm; last selfguided tours leave 8pm. $9, seniors $7, ages 6-12 $6.)

Horsethief Campground ❶ lies 2 mi. west of Mt. Rushmore on Rte. 244 in the Black Hills National Forest. Former President George Bush fished here in 1993; rumor has it that the lake was overstocked with fish to guarantee his success. (☎877-444-6777; www.reserveusa.com. Water and flush toilets. Reservations recommended on weekends. Sites $22. Wheelchair accessible sites available.) The commercial **Mt. Rushmore KOA/Palmer Gulch Lodge ❷,** 7 mi. west of Mt. Rushmore on Rte. 244, has campsites for two and cabins with showers, two pools, spa, laundry, nightly movies, a small strip mall, car rental, and free shuttle service to Mt. Rushmore. (☎574-2525 or 800-562-8503; www.palmergulch.com. Make reservations early, up to 2 months in advance for cabins. Open May-Oct. Sites June-Aug. $28, with water and electricity $35; cabins $52-60. May and Sept.-Oct. $24/$32/$44-52.)

CRAZY HORSE MEMORIAL ☎ 605

In 1947, Lakota Chief Henry Standing Bear commissioned sculptor Korczak Ziolkowski to sculpt a memorial to Crazy Horse as a reminder that Native Americans have their own heroes. A famed warrior who gained respect by refusing to sign treaties or live on a government reservations, Crazy Horse was stabbed in the back by a treacherous white soldier in 1877. The **Crazy Horse Memorial,** which at its completion will be the world's largest sculpture, stands in the Black Hills the Lakota hold sacred as a spectacular tribute to the revered Native American leader.

The first blast rocked the hills on June 3, 1948, and on the memorial's 50th anniversary, the completed face (all four of the Rushmore heads could fit inside it) was unveiled. Believing that Crazy Horse should be a project funded by those who truly cared about the memorial, Ziolkowski twice refused offers of $10 million in federal funding. With admission prices funding 85% of the cost, Ziolkowski's wife Ruth and seven of their 10 children carry on his work, currently concentrating on the horse's head, which will be 219 ft. high. Eventually, Crazy Horse's entire torso and head, as well as part of his horse, will be carved into the mountain.

The memorial, 4 mi. north of Custer on U.S. 385/U.S. 16, includes the **Indian Museum of North America,** the **Sculptor's Studio-Home,** and the **Native American Educational and Cultural Center,** where native crafts are displayed and sold. During the first full weekend of June, visitors have the opportunity to trek 6¼ mi. up to the face in the annual Volksmarch. Otherwise, expect to pay $3 to take a bus. (☎ 673-4681; www.crazyhorse.org. Open daily May-Sept. 7am-dark; Oct.-Apr. 8am-dark. Monument lit nightly about 10min. after sunset for 1hr. $9, under 6 free; $20 per carload.)

WIND CAVE AND JEWEL CAVE ☎ 605

In the cavern-riddled Black Hills, the subterranean scenery often rivals the above-ground sites. After the Black Hills formed from shifting plates of granite, warm water filled the cracked layers of limestone. Since then, intricate and unusual structures have formed in the area's prime underground real estate: **Wind Cave National Park** (☎ 745-4600; www.nps.gov/wica), adjacent to Custer State Park (p. 661) on U.S. 385, and **Jewel Cave National Monument** (☎ 673-2288, tour reservations 800-967-2283; www.nps.gov/jeca), 13 mi. west of the U.S. 385/U.S. 16 junction, in Custer. There is no public transit to the caves. Bring a sweater on all tours—Wind Cave remains a constant 53°F, while Jewel Cave is 49°F.

WIND CAVE. Wind Cave was discovered by Tom Bingham in 1881 when he heard the sound of air rushing out of the cave's only natural entrance. The wind was so strong that it knocked his hat off; when Tom returned to show his friends, his hat got sucked in. Air forcefully gusts in and out of the cave due to changes in outside pressure, informally called "breathing." Scientists estimate that only 5% of the volume of the cave has been discovered. Within the 100 mi. that have been explored, geologists have found a lake over 200 ft. long in the cave's depths. Instead of the typical crystal formations of stalagmites and stalactites, Wind Cave is known for housing over 95% of the world's "boxwork"—a honeycomb-like lattice of calcite covering its walls. Five **tours** cover a range of caving experience. (☎ 745-4600. Tours June-Aug. daily 8:40am-6pm; less frequently in winter.) The **Garden of Eden Tour** (1hr., ¼ mi., 5 per day, 150 stairs) is the least strenuous. ($7, seniors and ages 6-16 $3.50, under 6 free.) The **Natural Entrance Tour** (1¼hr., ½ mi., 11 per day, 300 stairs) and the **Fairgrounds Tour** (1½hr., ½ mi., 8 per day, 450 stairs) are both moderately strenuous, and one of the two leaves about every 30min. ($9, seniors and ages 6-16 $4.50, under 6 free.) Light your own way on the more rigorous **Candlelight Tour.** (Limited to 10 people. 2hr. June-Aug. 10:30am and 1:30pm. $9, seniors and children $4.50. 8+.

"Non-slip" soles on shoes required.) The rather difficult **Wild Cave Tour,** an intro to basic caving, is limited to 10 people ages 16 and over who can fit through a 10 in. high passageway. (Parental consent required for under 18. 4hr. tour daily 1pm. $23, seniors $12. Reservations required.) In the afternoon, all tours fill up about 1hr. ahead of time, so buy tickets in advance. **Wind Cave National Park Visitors Center** at RR1, P.O. Box 190, Hot Springs, can provide more info. (☎ 745-4600. Open June to mid-Aug. daily 8am-7pm; winter hours vary. Parts of some tours are wheelchair accessible.) The **Elk Mountain Campground ❶,** 1 mi. north of the visitors center, is an excellent site in the woods that rarely fills up. (Potable water and restrooms. Sites mid-May to mid-Sept. $12; mid-Sept. to mid-May $6.) Backcountry camping is allowed in the northwestern sector of the park. Campers must have a permit, which is free at the visitors center.

JEWEL CAVE. Distinguishing itself from nearby Wind Cave's boxwork, the walls of Jewel Cave are covered with a layer of calcite crystal. These walls enticed the cave's discoverers to file a mining claim for the "jewels," only to realize that giving tours would be more profitable. Today the park service continues this tradition. The **Scenic Tour** (1¼hr., ½ mi., 723 stairs) highlights chambers with the most interesting crystal formations. (Leaves in summer roughly every 20min. 8:20am-6pm; in winter call ahead. $8, ages 6-16 $4, under 6 free.) The **Lantern Tour** is an illuminating journey lasting 1¾hr. Walk, duck, and stoop by lantern through the many tunnels. (In summer every hour 9am-5pm; in winter call ahead. $8, ages 6-16 $4.) Reservations, pants, a long-sleeve shirt, kneepads, sturdy boots, and a willingness to get down and dirty are required for the 3-4hr. **Spelunking Tour,** limited to five people over age 16. (June-Aug. daily at 12:30pm. $27. Must be able to fit through an 8½ in. by 2 ft. opening.) The **visitors center** has more info. (☎ 673-2288. Open daily June to mid-Aug. 8am-7:30pm; Oct. to mid-May 8am-4:30pm.) The **Roof Trail** behind the visitors center is short, but provides a memorable introduction to the Black Hills' beauty while trekking across the "roof" of Jewel Cave.

CUSTER STATE PARK   ☎ 605

Peter Norbeck, governor of South Dakota in the late 1910s, loved to hike among the thin, towering rock formations that haunt the area south of Sylvan Lake and Mt. Rushmore. In order to preserve the land, he created Custer State Park. The spectacular **Needles Highway (Route 87)** follows his favorite hiking route—Norbeck designed this road to be especially narrow and winding so that newcomers could experience the pleasures of discovery. **Iron Mountain Road (U.S. 16A)** from Mt. Rushmore to near the Norbeck Visitors Center (see below) takes drivers through a series of tunnels, "pigtail" curves, and switchbacks. The park's **Wildlife Loop Road** twists past prairie dog towns, bison wallows and corrals, and wilderness areas near prime hiking and camping territory. Pronghorns, elk, deer, and ponies also hang out by the side of the road, and often cars will stop for one of Custer's 1500 **bison** crossings; don't get out—bison are dangerous.

The park requires an **entrance fee.** (7-day pass May-Oct. $5 per person, $12 per carload; Nov.-Apr. $2.50/$6.) The **Peter Norbeck Visitors Center,** on U.S. 16A, ½ mi. west of the State Game Lodge (where Eisenhower and Coolidge stayed), serves as the park's info center. Learn to date a tree (only then will you understand the heartbreak of being dumped by a sycamore), explore the park's history, and gather information on bison. (☎ 255-4464; www.custerstatepark.info. Open daily Apr.-May and mid-Oct. to Nov. 9am-5pm; June-Aug. 8am-8pm; Sept. to mid.-Oct. 8am-6pm.) The visitors center also has information on **primitive camping,** which is available for $2 per person per night in the **French Creek Natural Area ❶.** Eight **campgrounds ❶** have sites with showers and restrooms. No

GREAT PLAINS

hookups are provided; only the Game Lodge Campground offers two electricity-accessible sites. (☎800-710-2267; daily 7am-9pm. Over 200 of the 400+ sites can be reserved; the entire park fills in summer by 3pm. Sites $13-18. $5 non-resident user fee or $12 per vehicle.)

Slightly less touristy than Rapid City, the town of Custer also serves as a convenient base for exploring the Black Hills region. An anomaly among campgrounds, the visionary **Fort Welikit** ❶, 24992 Sylvan Lake Rd., has private bathrooms and large sites. (☎673-3600 or 888-946-2267; www.blackhillsrv.com. Tent sites $9 per person. RV sites $23, with hook-up $27.) The **Shady Rest Motel** ❸, 238 Gordon Rd., sits on the hill overlooking Custer and has homey cabins with linens, towels, a free whirlpool, and friendly owners. (☎673-4478 or 800-567-8259. Closed in winter. Singles $60; doubles $65.) **The Wrangler** ❷, 302 Mt. Rushmore Rd., is a local family restaurant, serving up dependable breakfasts ($3-5), buffalo burgers ($5.25), and dinners ($8-10) on the early side. (☎673-4271. Open M-Sa 5am-8pm, Su 6am-8pm). **Sage Creek Grille** ❷, 607 Mt. Rushmore Rd., downtown, serves upscale food at reasonable prices. Try their delicious salads ($4-8), sandwiches ($7-9), and buffalo and elk burgers for $9. (☎673-2424. Open Tu-F 11am-2pm, Th-Sa 5-8pm, 9pm in summer.) The **Custer Visitors Center,** 615 Washington St., can help visitors get situated in the area. (☎673-2244 or 800-992-9819; www.custersd.com. Open mid-May to Aug. M-F 8am-7pm, Sa-Su 9am-6pm; in winter M-F 8am-5pm.)

At 7242 ft., **Harney Peak** is the highest point east of the Rockies and west of the Pyrenees. Waiting at the top are a few mountain goats and a great view of the Black Hills. The hike is a strenuous 6 mi. round-trip, so bring water and food, wear good shoes, and check the weather beforehand. The 3mi. **Sunday Gulch Trail** offers the most amazing scenery of all the park's trails—rivers, boulders, and creatures await the adventurous. At popular **Sylvan Lake,** on Needles Hwy., you can also hike, fish, paddleboat, or canoe. (☎575-2561. Paddleboats $4 per person per 30min.) Fishing is allowed anywhere in the park, but a South Dakota fishing license is required. ($7, non-residents $12, plus $2 license fee.) One hour horse rides are available at **Blue Bell Lodge,** on Rte. 87 about 1 mi. from the south entrance. (☎255-4571. Reservations recommended. $21, under 12 $18.) Mountain bikes can be rented at the **Legion Lake Resort,** on U.S. 16A, 6 mi. west of the visitors center. (☎255-4521. $10 per hr., $25 per half-day, $40 per day.) The strong granite of the Needles makes for great rock climbing. For more info contact **Sylvan Rocks,** 208 Main St. in Hill City, 20 mi. north of Custer City, which leads guided expeditions. (☎574-2425. Open in summer M-Tu and Th-Su 8am-10am.)

DEADWOOD   ☎605

Gunslingers **Wild Bill Hickok** and **Calamity Jane** sauntered into Deadwood during the height of the Gold Rush in the summer of 1876. Bill stayed just long enough—three weeks—to spend eternity here. Jane and Bill now lie side-by-side in the Mount Moriah Cemetery, just south of downtown. ($1, ages 5-12 $0.50.) **Saloon #10,** 657 Main St., was forever immortalized by Wild Bill's murder. Hickok was shot holding black aces and eights, now known to poker players as a "dead man's hand." The chair in which he died is on display, and every summer the shooting is reenacted on location. (☎578-3346 or 800-952-9398; www.saloon10.com. Saloon open daily 8am-2am. Reenactments in summer daily at 1, 3, 5, 7pm.) Onlookers follow the scene as assassin Jack McCall is apprehended by authorities outside of Saloon #10 (in summer Tu-Su 7:45pm) and tried at the Deadwood Theatre (Su-F 8pm). More **shootouts** happen daily along Main St. at 2, 3, 4, and 6pm—listen for gunshots and the sound of Calamity Jane's whip. **Trolleys** ($0.50) circle downtown and provide a good overview of sights that the town has to offer.

Gambling takes center stage in this authentic western town—casinos line **Main Street,** and many innocent-looking establishments have slot machines and poker tables waiting in the wings. There's live music outside the **Stockade** at the **Buffalo-Bodega Complex,** 658 Main St. (☎578-1300), which is packed with throngs of 24hr. gambling spots. For the fun of gambling without the high stakes, many casinos offer nickel slot machines. Even those who lose most of their money at the gambling tables can afford to stay at ⧉**Hostelling International Black Hills at the Penny Motel (HI) ❶,** 818 Upper Main St. (Look for the Penny Motel sign.) A great kitchen with free pasta and rice, comfortable beds with linen provided, super-clean rooms, and a friendly owner await visitors. Free Internet, a book swap, a video club, and private bathrooms seal the deal. (☎578-1842 or 877-565-8140; www.pennymotel.com. Dorms $13, nonmembers $16; 1 private room $39. Motel rooms $46-68; in winter $29-56.) The Penny Motel also rents **bikes.** ($5 per hr.; half-day $14; full-day $18. 50% discount for guests.) The **Whistlers Gulch Campground ❶,** off U.S. 85, has a pool, laundry facilities, and showers. (☎578-2092 or 800-704-7139. Sites $22, full hookup $33.) The **Deadwood History and Information Center,** 3 Siever St., behind Main Street's Silverado, can help with any questions. (☎578-2507 or 800-999-1876; www.deadwood.org. Open daily in summer 8am-7pm; in winter 9am-5pm.)

Right outside Deadwood is Kevin Costner's new museum **Tatanka: Story of the Bison,** 1 mi. north on Rte. 85, an educational center with a spectacular outdoor sculpture of three riders pursuing bison over a cliff. The cafe serves dishes with bison meat for $4-8. (☎584-5678; www.storyofthebison.com. Open May 15-Oct. 15 daily 9am-6pm. $6.50, seniors $5.50, children $4.50.) **Post Office:** 68 Sherman St., in the Federal Building. (☎578-1505. Open M-F 8:15am-4:15pm, Sa 10am-noon.) **Postal Code:** 57732. **Area Code:** 605.

IOWA

Named for the Ioway Native Americans who lived along the state's many riverbanks, Iowa contains one-fourth of all US Grade A farmland and prides itself on being the "heartland of the heartland." Farming is a way of life in Iowa, a land where men are measured by the size of their John Deere tractors. The state ripples with gentle hills between the two great rivers that sculpt its boundaries: the "Great Muddy" to the west and the "Mighty Miss" to the east. Despite its distinctly American landscape, Iowa preserves its European heritage in small towns.

⚆ PRACTICAL INFORMATION

Capital: Des Moines.

Visitor Info: Iowa Tourism Office, 200 E. Grand Ave., Des Moines 50309 (☎515-242-4705 or 800-345-4692; www.traveliowa.com).

Postal Abbreviation: IA. **Sales Tax:** 6%; some towns add an additional 1-2%.

DES MOINES   ☎515

Des Moines hums with the activity of its affable residents. The Skywalk, a second-floor maze of passageways connecting buildings downtown, is without equal in the Midwest. A beautiful system of parks traces the area's rivers and presents a welcome contrast to the now-bustling downtown area. From the "BarbeQlossal" at the **World Pork Expo** (June 9-11, 2005; ☎847-838-6772; www.worldpork.org) to world-class art, Des Moines's offerings run the gamut from kitsch to cosmopolitan.

Des Moines

🍎 FOOD

▲ ACCOMMODATIONS

The Carter House Inn, **2**
Iowa State Fairgrounds
  Campgrounds, **1**
Motel 6, **9**

Bauder's Pharmacy and
  Fountain, **3**
Cafe Su, **8**
Raccoon River Brewery
  Co., **6**

🍸 NIGHTLIFE
The Garden, **4**
Java Joe's, **7**
The Lift, **5**

⬛ TRANSPORTATION

Airport: Des Moines International, 5800 Fleur Dr. (☎256-5100; www.dsmairport.com), at Army Post Rd., 5 mi. southwest of downtown. (M-F take bus #8 "Havens." Taxi to downtown $11-15.) **Buses: Greyhound and Burlington Trailways,** 1107 Keo Way (☎243-1773 or 800-231-2222), at 12th St., just northwest of downtown; take bus #3, 5, or 6. To: Chicago (8hr., 10 per day, $38-40); Iowa City (2hr., 7 per day, $22); Omaha (2hr., 8 per day, $23-25); St. Louis (10hr., 5 per day, $67-71). Station open 4am-midnight. **Public Transit: Metropolitan Transit Authority (MTA),** 1100 MTA Ln. (☎283-8111; www.dmmta.com), south of the 9th St. viaduct. (Open M-F 8am-5pm. Buses run M-F approximately 6am-11pm, Sa 6:45am-5:50pm. $1, seniors (except M-F 3-6pm) and disabled persons $0.50 with MTA ID card; transfers $0.10.) Routes serve Clive, Des Moines, Urbandale, West Des Moines, and Windsor Heights. Maps are at the MTA office and website, the public library, and supermarkets. **Taxi: Yellow Cab**☎243-1111. **Car Rental: Enterprise,** 5601 Fleur Dr. (☎285-2525), just outside the airport, with speedy airport pickup.

⬛ ORIENTATION AND PRACTICAL INFORMATION

I-80 and U.S. 65 encircle Des Moines; I-235 bisects the circle from east to west. Numbered streets run north-south, named streets east-west. Addresses begin with zero downtown at the **Des Moines River** and increase as you move east or west;

Grand Avenue divides addresses north-south. Other east-west thoroughfares are **Locust Street, University Avenue** (home to Drake University), and **Hickman Road.** Note that numbered streets in Des Moines and West Des Moines are not the same.

Visitor Info: Greater Des Moines Convention and Visitors Bureau, 405 6th Ave., Ste. 201 (☎286-4960 or 800-451-2625; www.seedesmoines.com), along Locust in the Skywalk. Open M-F 8:30am-5pm. Up a few blocks is the **Chamber of Commerce,** 700 Locust St. (☎286-4950). Open M 9am-5pm, Tu-Th 8am-5pm, F 8am-4pm.

Medical Services: Mercy Medical Center, 111 6th Ave. (☎243-2584), downtown.

Internet Access: Des Moines Public Library, 100 Locust St. (☎283-4152; www.desmoineslibrary.com). Free 1hr. per day. Open M 9am-8pm, Tu-Su 9am-6pm.

Post Office: 1165 2nd Ave. (☎283-7585), downtown just north of I-235. Open M-F 7:30am-5:30pm. **Postal Code:** 50318. **Area Code:** 515.

ACCOMMODATIONS

Downtown Des Moines is cluttered with high-end hotels, but numerous cheap accommodations are sprinkled along Fleur Dr. by the airport, off I-80, and on Merle Hay Rd., 5 mi. northwest of downtown. Campgrounds are located west of the city off I-80. Remember the 7% hotel tax, and be sure to make reservations a few months in advance for visits during the **Iowa State Fair** in August and at least one month in advance during the high school sports tournament season in March.

The Carter House Inn, 640 20th St. (☎288-7850; www.carter-house.com), at Woodland St. in historic Sherman Hill. This beautifully reconstructed 19th-century Victorian home houses 4 elegant rooms. Breakfast is served by candlelight with classical music playing in the background. Rooms $70-100. Ask about 15% student discount. ❹

Motel 6, 4817 Fleur Dr. (☎287-6364), 10min. south of downtown at the airport. Simple, clean, secure rooms with free local calls, coffee, and HBO. 20+. Singles Su-Th $34; doubles $40; F-Sa $44/$50. AARP discount. 2 wheelchair accessible rooms. ❷

Iowa State Fairgrounds Campgrounds, E. 30th St. (☎262-3111), at Grand Ave. After the main entrance, make a right on Hoover, then a left into the campground, or take bus #1 "Fairgrounds" to the Grand Ave. gate and follow East Grand Ave. 1800 campsites on 160 acres. No fires. Reservations accepted only during the State Fair in Aug. Open mid-Apr. to mid-Oct. Tent sites $15, with water and electricity $18, with full hookup $20. ❶

FOOD

Restaurants cluster on **Court Avenue** downtown. Warm weather lures street venders peddling gyros, hot dogs, and pizza to **Nollen Plaza,** on Locust St. between 3rd and 4th Ave. West Des Moines boasts budget eateries along Grand Ave. and in the antique-filled **Historic Valley Junction.** The **Farmers Market** (☎243-6625) sells fresh fruit and vegetables, baked goods, and ethnic food on Saturday mornings (mid-May to Oct. 7am-noon); Court Ave. between 1st and 4th St., is blocked off for the extravaganza. The Skywalk houses many joints that serve cafeteria-style cuisine.

Cafe Su, 225 5th. St. (☎274-5102), in West Des Moines, serves delicious Chinese food, with healthy and vegetarian options among the usual suspects ($11-13). Meals in the chic and jazzy restaurant finish with chocolate-covered fortune cookies. Reservations recommended on weekends. Open Tu-Th 4:30-10pm, F-Sa 4:30-11pm. ❷

Raccoon River Brewery Co., 200 10th St. (☎362-5222), at Mulberry St. Enjoy a freshly brewed beer with barbecue chicken pizza ($10) or yellowfin tuna ($17). Live music on weekends at 10:30pm. Open M-Th 11am-midnight, F 11am-2am, Sa noon-2am. ❹

Bauder's Pharmacy and Fountain, 3802 Ingersoll Ave. (☎255-1124), at 38th St. A throwback to the good old days, serving old-fashioned ice-cream ($1.50 per scoop). Wax nostalgic while enjoying simple sandwiches ($2-4) at the authentic lunch counter or drinks from the soda fountain. Shakes, floats, and malts $2.75. Open M-F 8:30am-7pm, Sa 9am-4pm, Su 10am-2pm. ❶

🏛 SIGHTS

The newly renovated **State Capitol,** E. 9th St. and Grand Ave., combines elegance with politics. Its impressive interior includes a grand stairway and mosaic artwork. The gold-domed building also offers a clear view of the Des Moines skyline. (☎281-5591. Call ahead to arrange a free tour. Open M-F 8am-4:30pm, Sa 9am-4pm.) Located at the base of the capitol complex parking lot, the **State of Iowa Historical Building,** 600 E. Locust St., addresses the history of Iowa, Native American culture, and conservation through interactive exhibits. In addition to the wonderful "A Few of Our Favorite Things," which showcases 100 creations from the past century that have changed the way Iowans live, the newest exhibit, "Witness To Change," traces the story of a full mammoth skeleton. The building also houses the state historical library and archives and a rooftop restaurant with a panoramic view. (☎281-5111; www.iowahistory.org. Open Sept.-May Tu-Sa 9am-4:30pm, Su noon-4:30pm; June-Aug. also M 9am-4:30pm. Free.)

The phenomenal ◪**Des Moines Art Center,** 4700 Grand Ave., is composed of three unique contemporary buildings designed by world-renowned architects Eliel Saarinen, I.M. Pei, and Richard Meier. In addition to a collection of African tribal art, the museum houses modern masterpieces by Monet, Matisse, and Picasso, along with an expansive collection of Pop, Minimalist, and contemporary paintings and sculptures by Andy Warhol, Eva Hesse, and Jeff Koons. (☎277-4405; www.desmoinesartcenter.org. Open Tu-W and F-Sa 11am-4pm, Th and 1st F of the month 11am-9pm, Su noon-4pm. Free.) Behind the Art Center lie the immaculately groomed **Rose Garden** and **Greenwood Pond,** a small, stillwater lagoon where you can relax in the sun (or ice skate in the winter). **Salisbury House,** 4025 Tonawanda Dr., off 42nd St., lets visitors explore an early 20th-century mansion in its original condition. With an incredible collection of art and rare books, this 42-room home shows how the upper class lived over 80 years ago and is packed with such oddball items as a chair designed specifically for cockfighting. (☎274-1777; www.salisburyhouse.org. Open for tours Mar.-Apr. and Oct.-Nov. Tu-Sa 11am and 2pm; May Tu-F 11am and 2pm; June-Sept. M-F 11am, 1, 2pm, Su 1, 2 and 3pm; Dec. Tu-F 2pm. $7, seniors $6, ages 6-12 $3.) Built on urban renewal land east of the Des Moines River, the geodesic greenhouse and outdoor gardens of the **Botanical Center,** 909 E. Robert D. Ray Dr. (E. 1st St.), house exotic flora and fauna. (☎323-8900. Open M-Th 10am-6pm, F 10am-9pm, Sa-Su 10am-5pm. $4, seniors and children 6-17 $2.)

🎵 🎭 ENTERTAINMENT AND NIGHTLIFE

On Thursday, the Des Moines Register publishes *The Datebook* (www.desmoines-register.com/entertainment), a listing of concerts, sporting events, and movies that is distributed throughout town. *Cityview,* a free local weekly, lists free events and is available at the Civic Center box office and most supermarkets. The **Iowa State Fair,** one of the nation's largest, captivates Des Moines for 11 days in mid-August with prize cows, crafts, cakes, and corn. (☎800-545-3247; www.iow-astatefair.org. Runs Aug. 11-21, 2005. Call for prices and to purchase tickets in advance.) Tickets for **Iowa Cubs** baseball games, Chicago's farm team, are a steal; they play at **Sec Taylor Stadium,** 1 Line Dr. Call for game dates and times. (☎243-

6111 or 800-464-2827; www.iowacubs.com. General admission $6, children $4; reserved grandstand $8/$6.) The **Civic Center,** 221 Walnut St. (☎246-2328; www.civ-iccenter.org), sponsors concerts and theater; call for info. **Jazz in July** (☎280-3222; www.metroarts.org) presents free concerts throughout the city every day of the month; grab a schedule at restaurants, Wells Fargo banks, or the visitors bureau. **Music Under the Stars** has free concerts on the steps of the state capitol (☎283-4294; June-July Su 7-9pm). In June and July, **Nitefall on the River** brings music to the Simon Estes Amphitheater on the riverbank at E. 1st and Locust St. (☎237-1386; www.dmparks.org. Concerts begin at 7pm. $8, children under 12 free with adult.)

Court Avenue and 4th Street, in the southeast corner of downtown, serves as the focal point for much of Des Moines's nightlife scene. ◙**Java Joe's,** 214 4th St., is the place to hear Des Moines's best up-and-coming bands. This hip, mellow coffeehouse with Internet access ($1 per 10min., free wireless), sells exotic coffee blends and beer ($3). Vegetarians will delight in the creative array of sandwiches, all for $3-7. (☎288-5282; www.javajoescoffeehouse.com. Open M-Th 7am-11pm, F-Sa 7am-midnight, Su 9am-10pm.) Inspired by its art-covered walls, **The Lift,** 222 4th St., serves creative martinis ($5-6) in almost every flavor imaginable. (☎288-3777. Open Su-Th 5pm-late, F 4:30pm-2am, Sa 7pm-2am.) Billing itself as "Iowa's Gay Nightclub," **The Garden,** 112 SE 4th St., has a video bar, dance floor, and performances every weekend. (☎243-3965; www.grdn.com. Open W-Su 8pm-2am.)

▶ DAYTRIPS FROM DES MOINES

PELLA
Forty-one miles east of Des Moines on Hwy. 163, Pella blooms in May with its annual **Tulip Time Festival,** featuring Dutch dancing, a parade, concerts, and glockenspiel performances. (☎641-628-4311; www.pellatuliptime.com. May 5-7, 2005.) For Dutch culinary culture, visit the **Jaarsma Bakery,** 727 Franklin St. (☎641-628-2940. Pecan rolls 2 for $1.70. Almond poppyseed cakes 4 for $1.49. Open M-Sa 6am-6pm.) The bakery uses wheat ground in America's tallest working windmill, found at the **Pella Historical Village,** 507 Franklin St., along with other relics and recreations of Dutch culture. (☎641-628-4311. Guided tours available. Open Jan.-Mar. M-F 9am-5pm, Sa 10am-3pm; Apr.-Dec. M-Sa 9am-5pm. $8, ages 18 and under $2.)

PRAIRIE CITY
Twenty miles east of Des Moines on Hwy. 163 at Hwy. 117, the **Neal Smith National Wildlife Refuge** transports visitors back 150 years to Iowa's prairie days, when nearly 31 million acres of tallgrass prairie graced the Iowa plains. Today, only one-tenth of one percent remains. The wildlife refuge has restored 8600 acres of this endangered landscape, opening the largest tallgrass prairie ecosystem in the US for exploration through 5 mi. of walking trails (½ mi. wheelchair accessible) and an auto tour. The refuge is home to bison, elk, and an exceptional learning center, with particularly kid-friendly exhibits and a great 15min. movie. In August, the big bluestem grass grows up to 6 ft. tall. (☎515-994-3400. Learning center open M-Sa 9am-4pm, Su noon-5pm. Trails and auto tour open daily sunrise-sunset. Free.)

IOWA CITY   ☎319

Home to the University of Iowa and its beloved Hawkeyes, Iowa City is full of collegiate flavor and youthful vitality. The downtown area hosts tons of cheap restaurants, trendy shops, and coffeehouses, while an active nightlife scene and college football fanaticism keep students happy. In the summer, cultural activities blossom, from the Iowa Arts Festival in June (☎337-7944; www.iowaartsfestival.com) to the Iowa City Jazz Festival in July (☎358-9346; www.iowacityjazzfestival.com).

◗◗ ORIENTATION AND PRACTICAL INFORMATION. Iowa City is off I-80, 114 mi. east of Des Moines. North-south **Madison** and **Johnson Street** and east-west **Market** and **Burlington Street** mark the boundaries of downtown. **Greyhound** and **Burlington Trailways,** both located at 404 E. College St. (☎337-2127; station open M-F 6:30am-6pm, Sa-Su 10am-6pm) travel to: Chicago (6hr., 6 per day, $42); Des Moines (2-4hr., 7 per day, $22); Minneapolis (8-12hr., 3 per day, $60-69); St. Louis (10-11hr., 1 per day, $81). **Iowa City Transit** runs a free downtown shuttle 7:30am-6:30pm and additional routes when school is in session. (☎356-5151. Operates M-F 6:30am-10:30pm, Sa 6:30am-7pm. $0.75; children 5-12 $0.50; seniors with pass $0.35 9am-3:30pm, after 6:30pm, and Sa.) The **Cambus** runs daily all over campus and downtown and is free. (☎335-8633. Operates M-F 6:30am-midnight; in winter also Sa-Su noon-midnight, in summer also Sa-Su noon-6pm.) **Taxi: Old Capitol Cab** ☎354-7662.

Visitor Info: The **Convention and Visitors Bureau,** 408 1st Ave., sits across the river in Coralville off U.S. 6. (☎337-6592 or 800-283-6592; www.icccvb.org; open M-F 8am-5pm) and also runs an **information kiosk** at the Coral Ridge Mall (open M-Sa 10am-9pm, Su noon-6pm). More info is available at the University of Iowa's **Campus Information Center,** in the Iowa Memorial Union at Madison and Jefferson St. (☎335-3055. Open Sept.-May M-F 8am-8pm, Sa 10am-8pm, Su noon-4pm; June-Aug. M-F 8am-5pm.) **Medical Services: Mercy Iowa City,** on Market St. at Van Buren St. Mercy On Call (☎358-2767 or 800-358-2767, operator 800-637-2942) is staffed daily 7am-midnight with registered nurses. **Internet Access: Iowa City Public Library,** 123 S. Linn St., allows 30min. of free Internet per day. (☎356-5200; www.icpl.org. Open M-Th 10am-9pm, F-Sa 10am-6pm, Su 1-5pm.) **Post Office:** 400 S. Clinton St. (☎354-1560; open M-F 8:30am-5pm, Sa 9:30am-1pm). **Postal Code:** 52240. **Area Code:** 319.

◗◗ ACCOMMODATIONS AND FOOD. One mile from Exit 244 on I-80 and six blocks from downtown is **Haverkamp's Linn Street Homestay ❷,** 619 N. Linn St., a 1908 bed and breakfast offering three reasonably priced rooms filled with classic antiques. Hot breakfast is served on weekends. (☎337-4363; www.bbhost.com/haverkampslinnstbb. Rooms $35-50.) Cheap motels line U.S. 6 in **Coralville,** 2 mi. west of downtown, and **1st Avenue** at Exit 242 off I-80. The cheapest of the bunch is the **Big Ten Inn ❷,** 707 1st Ave., off U.S. 6, which provides comfortable rooms with HBO. (☎351-6131. Singles $29; doubles $42; prices increase significantly on football weekends.) **Kent Park Campgrounds ❶,** 15 mi. west on U.S. 6, has 86 secluded sites near a lake with fishing, boating, and swimming. (☎645-2315. Check-in by 10:30pm. $10, with electricity $15.)

The lively downtown centers around the open-air **Pedestrian Mall,** on College and Dubuque St., where musicians serenade passersby and vendors man their food carts, sometimes until 3am. The city's oldest family-owned restaurant, **Hamburg Inn #2 Inc. ❷,** 214 N. Linn St., affectionately called "The Burg," serves breakfast all day alongside decadent pie shakes (milkshakes with a slice of pie blended in, $4.95) and chicken-fried steaks for $6.50. (☎337-5512. Open daily 6am-11pm.) **The Pita Pit ❶,** 113 Iowa Ave., offers a refreshing combination of colorful walls and generously filled pitas. (☎351-7482; www.pitapit.com. Open M-W 11am-3am, Th-Sa 11am-4am, Su noon-midnight.) **Masala ❷,** 9 S. Dubuque St., Iowa City's award-winning vegetarian Indian restaurant, may offer the best deals in town with its $6.25 lunch buffet and $6 Monday dinner special. (☎338-6199. Open daily 11am-2:30pm and 5-9:30pm.) Next door, **Z'Mariks Noodle Cafe ❷,** 19 S. Dubuque St., is packed for lunch and dinner. Customize "bowlz" of noodles, rice, or soup, and wait for friendly servers to bring them steaming hot to your table. (338-5500. Most dishes $6-8. Open M-Sa 11am-9pm, Su 11am-8pm.)

◪ **SIGHTS.** The University of Iowa's **Museum of Natural History,** at Jefferson and Clinton St., details the ecology, geology, and Native American culture of Iowa through dioramas and a large collection of stuffed mammals and birds. (☎335-0480; www.uiowa.edu/~nathist. Open M-Sa 9:30am-4:30pm, Su 12:30-4:30pm. Free.) A short drive from downtown is **Plum Grove Historic Home,** 1030 Carroll St., off Kirkwood Ave., the 1844 home and garden of Robert Lucas, the first governor of the Iowa Territory. (☎351-5738; www.iowahistory.org. Open June-Oct. W-Su 1-5pm. Free.) In West Branch, 15min. northeast of the city (Exit 254 on I-80; follow signs), lies the **Herbert Hoover National Historic Site,** where an 1870s American town is beautifully recreated. Take a walking tour of the cottage where the 31st President was born, his father's blacksmith shop, and the schoolhouse and Quaker meetinghouse he attended. A ½ mi. prairie trail includes the graves of President and Mrs. Hoover, while the fascinating **Herbert Hoover Presidential Library-Museum** chronicles his life and presidency. (☎643-2541; www.nps.gov/heho. Open daily 9am-5pm. $4, under 17 free. Wheelchair accessible.)

◪ **NIGHTLIFE.** With hordes of college students bar-hopping on the **Pedestrian Mall** ("Ped Mall") and loud music escaping from bars that double as dance clubs, Iowa City's weekends are four nights long. For many students, the weekend begins with the "Thursday Night Special" (mug for $4 and unlimited refills for $1) at **Brother's Bar and Grill,** 125 S. Dubuque St. in the Ped Mall, where loyal patrons return with their mugs week after week. (☎338-6373. Open daily 11am-1:30am.) Local musicians play Th-Sa at 9:30pm (in summer, F-Sa only) at **The Sanctuary,** 405 S. Gilbert St., a casual restaurant and bar with 120 beers and comfortable sofas. (☎351-5692; www.sanctuarypub.com. Food $5-18. Cover varies. Bar open M-Sa 4pm-2am; restaurant open M-Tu 4-11pm, W-Sa 4pm-midnight.) **The Sports Column,** 12 S. Dubuque St., draws a crowd every night with their laid-back attitude, swingin' music, and nightly specials. (☎356-6902. Th $1 draft night, Sa 2-for-1. Cover varies. Open until 2am.) In summer, the **Friday Night Concert Series** (☎354-0863; 6:30-9:30pm) offers everything from jazz to salsa to blues on the Pedestrian Mall.

EFFIGY MOUNDS

Native Americans built the mysterious and striking Effigy Mounds as early as 1000 BC. The enigmatic mounds are low-lying piles of earth formed into distinct geometric and animal shapes for burial and ceremonial purposes. Though they once covered much of the Midwest, farmers' plows have ensured that only some remain, mostly in western Wisconsin and eastern Iowa. One of the largest concentrations of intact mounds composes the **Effigy Mounds National Monument,** 151 Rte. 76, in Marquette, IA, 106 mi. west of Madison, WI, located on more than 2500 acres along the Mississippi River. Offering striking views of the river from high, rocky bluffs, 15 mi. of winding trails explore the lives of the indigenous Woodland People and the social and spiritual meanings the mounds had for them. Take Rte. 18 W from Madison. (☎563-873-3491; www.nps.gov/efmo. Visitors center open June to early Sept. daily 8am-6pm; closes earlier in fall and winter. Guided tours available twice a day; call ahead for times and events.) Seven miles south on Rte. 76 in McGregor is **Pike's Peak State Park ❶.** Follow Hwy. X56 from the south end of Main St. in McGregor up the twisty road 1½ mi. The park boasts amazing views and over 70 campsites. (☎563-873-2341. Check-out 4pm. Reservations not accepted. Sites July-Aug. $11, with electricity $16; Sept.-June $8/$13.) **Wyalusing State Park ❶,** just across the Mississippi and 10 mi. south of Prairie du Chien in Wisconsin, offers

THE MYTH OF HIGHER LEARNING

Visitors often ask for the registrar's office when they come to Okoboji, Iowa, enticed by the prospect of going to college within the beautiful setting of Iowa's "Great Lakes." But there's a catch: although the University of Okoboji hosts annual marathons, softball leagues, and a homecoming in July, it is a complete myth. "The only piece missing is the classes," say the founders—the hotels and resorts are the dorms, bars and clubs stand in for Greek life, and every restaurant serves as the dining hall. Besides, the motto of this university is, "Where fun in life is your degree."

Befuddled out-of-towners easily get confused, since the fictional institution has on-campus radio at KUOO, a hefty endowment of $3.5 million, and campus-wide social events every weekend during the academic year (i.e. summer). Indeed, the university has achieved a reputation as a one of the best "party schools" in the nation, while loyal "alumni" who never seem to graduate display their school pride with t-shirts, flags, and car decals bearing the university's crest.

With a rich history, the university celebrated its centennial in 1978 as a fundraising effort for the town's fire department—the theme of the centennial was "1878 to 1978: Seven Years of Progress."

more than 110 campsites overlooking the stunning confluence of the Wisconsin and the Mississippi Rivers. (☎608-996-2261 or 888-947-2757; www.wyalusing.org. Campsites $10; summer weekends $12. Electricity $3 extra per night.)

SPIRIT LAKE AND OKOBOJI ☎712

In attempts to rival its neighbors, Iowa boasts its own "Great Lakes." **Spirit Lake, West Okoboji Lake,** and **East Okoboji Lake** are all popular vacation destinations. The 10,000-year-old, glacier-carved West Okoboji Lake ranks with Switzerland's Lake Geneva and Canada's Lake Louise as one of the world's beautiful blue-water lakes.

It's hard to miss the **amusement park** in **Arnolds Park,** off Rte. 71, with its 1927 wooden roller coaster, kiddie rides, and ice cream shops. (☎332-2183 or 800-599-6995; www.arnoldspark.com. Open Memorial Day-Labor Day Su-Th 11am-10pm, F-Sa 11am-11pm. $17, children 3-4 ft. tall and seniors $13, under 3 ft. free. Individual ride tickets $1.50-4.50.) During summer, the park's **Roof Garden** hosts concerts on Thursdays; the action shifts to the **Green Space** on Saturdays and some Fridays (call the park for info). The **Abbie Gardner Historic Log Cabin,** 34 Monument Dr., one block west of the amusement park, has artifacts, paintings, and a 13min. video explaining the origins of the dispute between encroaching settlers and members of the Sioux that eventually led to the Spirit Lake Massacre of March 1857. (☎332-7248. Open June-Sept. M-F noon-4pm, Sa-Su 9am-4pm. Free, but donation suggested.) Theater buffs can catch productions by the **Stephens College Okoboji Summer Theater.** (☎332-7773. Box office open M 10am-6pm, Tu-Sa 10am-9pm, Su 1-7pm. $12, musicals $14; student and senior discounts some nights.) For a dose of the outdoors, hike, skate, or bike **The Spine,** a 22 mi. trail that runs through the area and connects with multiple loops. Rent bikes at **Okoboji Expedition Co.,** 1021 Rte. 71 in Okoboji before the bridge. (☎332-9001. Open M-Sa 9am-6pm, Su 10am-4pm. Half-day $20-30, full day $25-40.) **Orleans Beach,** on Hwy. 327, half a mile east of the Hwy. 276 junction, offers a long stretch of sand on Spirit Lake, while Sunset Beach is by the "boardwalk" in Arnolds Park. Beaches line the lakes; maps available around town. For aquatic fun, rent kayaks, boats, and jetskis at **Funtime Rentals,** in Arnold's Park, south of the bridge on U.S. 71. (☎332-2540. Open daily 9am-9pm.)

Budget accommodations in the immediate lake area are scarce, especially in summer. Cheap motels line U.S. 71 in Spencer, about 15 mi. south of

Okoboji. **The Northland Inn ❸**, at the junction of Rte. 9 and Rte. 86, just north of West Okoboji Lake, offers wood-paneled rooms with refrigerators. (☎336-1450. May-Sept. Singles $50; doubles $60; add $15 on weekends; Oct.-Apr. $23-28/$38.) Pitch your tent year-round at tranquil **Marble Beach Campground ❶** (☎336-4437, winter ☎337-3211), in the state park on the shores of Spirit Lake. Other camping options include **Emerson Bay ❶** (☎332-3805) and **Gull's Point ❶** (☎332-3870), both off Rte. 86 on the more beautiful West Okoboji Lake. (Sites at all 3 campgrounds $11; with electricity $16; cable only at Emerson Bay $18.) The **Koffee Kup Kafe ❶**, off U.S. 71 at Broadway in Arnolds Park, serves an all-day power breakfast (eggs, bacon, pancakes, hash browns, and juice) for $5.95 and a variety of tasty pancakes for $1-3. (☎332-7657. Open daily 6am-2pm.) Away from the amusement park, **Tweeter's ❷**, off U.S. 71 in Okoboji, grills burgers ($7), tosses salads ($5-7), and melts sandwiches ($7-9) in a family-dining atmosphere. (☎332-9421. Open daily June-Aug. 11am-midnight; Sept.-May 11am-11pm.) **Okoboji Spirit Center,** 243 W. Broadway Ave., houses an informative welcome center and maritime museum, despite the fact that Iowa is landlocked. (☎322-2209 or 800-270-2574; www.vacationokoboji.com. Open May-Sept. daily 9am-9pm; Oct.-Apr. M-F.) In Spirit Lake, **Post Office:** 1513 Hill Ave. (☎336-16383. Open M-F 8:30am-4:30pm, Sa 9-10am.) **Postal Code:** 51360. **Area Code:** 712.

NEBRASKA

Nebraska suffers from accusations of being "boring," "endless," or "the Great American Desert," but in reality, the landscape is the state's greatest attraction. Central Nebraska features the Sandhills, an immense windblown dune region with cattle, windmills, and tiny towns. The Panhandle offers Western-style mountains and canyons, historical trails, and national monuments. For the more urbane traveler, Omaha and Lincoln feature quality sports, fine music, and some of the best darn meat in America. While the urge might be to speed through the Cornhusker State, patient travelers will be rewarded with a true Great Plains experience.

⌕ PRACTICAL INFORMATION

Capital: Lincoln.

Visitor Info: Nebraska Tourism Office, 301 Centennial Mall S., Lincoln 68509 (☎402-471-3796 or 800-426-6505; www.visitnebraska.org). Open M-F 8am-5pm. **Nebraska Game and Parks Commission,** 1212 Bob Gibson Blvd., Omaha 68108 (☎402-595-2144). Open M-F 8am-5pm.

State Soft Drink: Kool-Aid. **Postal Abbreviation:** NE. **Sales Tax:** 7%.

OMAHA   ☎402

Omaha is a city of seemingly endless sprawl, stretched out over miles and miles of the Nebraska prairie. The heart of the city, however, is refreshingly compact. Omaha's museums, world-renowned zoo, and sports complex are the envy of other medium-sized cities. The Old Market in downtown lures visitors with a large concentration of quiet cafes, breweries, and nightclubs. Recently, a burgeoning indie rock scene has put Omaha musicians in the national spotlight. The town settles comfortably into its role as a gateway to the West, while its down-to-earth residents still embody that small-town spirit common to Midwestern America.

⬛🄷 ORIENTATION AND PRACTICAL INFORMATION. Omaha rests on the west bank of the **Missouri River,** next to the Iowa border. Though the city has numbered streets (north-south) and named streets (east-west), neighborhoods and campuses interfere, making maps a necessity. **Dodge Street** (Rte. 6) divides the city east-west. **I-480/Rte. 75** (the Kennedy Expwy.) intersects with **I-80,** which runs across the southern half of town. *At night, avoid N. 24th St., Ames Ave., and the area north of I-480.* **Eppley Airfield,** 4501 Abbott Dr., only 5min. from downtown, has domestic flights. (☎422-6817; www.eppleyairfield.com.) **Amtrak,** 1003 S. 9th St. (☎342-1501; open 10pm-8am), at Pacific St., chugs to Chicago (9hr., 1 per day, $133) and Denver (9hr., 1 per day, $109). **Greyhound,** 1601 Jackson St. (☎341-1906; open 24hr.), runs to: Des Moines (2-2½hr.; 7 per day; M-Th $26, F-Su $31); Lincoln (1hr., 6 per day, $11/$14); St. Louis (9hr., 3 per day, $78/$89). **Metro Area Transit (MAT),** 2222 Cumming St., handles local transportation. Get schedules at 16th and Douglas St. near the library. (☎341-0800. Open M-F 8am-4:30pm. $1.25, transfers $0.05.) **Taxi: Happy Cab** ☎339-8294. **Visitor Info: Greater Omaha Convention and Visitors Bureau,** 1001 Farnam St. (☎444-4187 or 866-937-6624; www.visitomaha.com. Open June-Aug. M-Sa 9am-4:30pm, Su 1-4:30pm; Sept.-May M-Sa 9am-4:30pm.) The **Nebraska Travel Information Center,** 1212 Bob Gibson Blvd., is right off I-80 by the zoo. (☎595-3990. Open Apr.-Oct. daily 9am-5pm; Nov.-Mar. M-F 9am-5pm.) **Hotlines: Rape Crisis,** ☎345-7273. 24hr. **First Call for Help,** ☎444-6666. Operates daily 7am-7pm. **Internet Access: Omaha Library,** 215 S. 15th St., between Douglas and Farnham. (☎444-4800. 30min. limit if crowded. Open M-Th 10am-8pm, F-Sa 10am-6pm.) **Post Office:** 1124 Pacific St. (☎348-2698. Open M-F 7:30am-6pm, Sa 7:30am-noon.) **Postal Code:** 68108. **Area Code:** 402.

🄷 ACCOMMODATIONS. Motels in downtown Omaha are not particularly budget-friendly. The usual chain motels are located just 5min. from downtown near the airport. For better deals, start around L St. and 60th and head west from there. The **Satellite Motel ❷,** 6006 L St., south of I-80 at Exit 450 (60th St.), is a round two-story building with clean, wedge-shaped rooms equipped with fridge, microwave, coffeemaker, and cable TV. (☎733-7373. Singles $42; doubles $50.) For a taste of the countryside and good cooking in a homey farmhouse, go to the first B&B in Nebraska (since 1984), **Bundy's Bed and Breakfast ❶,** 16906 S. 255th St., 20 mi. southwest of Omaha in Gretna. Take Exit 432 off I-80, follow Hwy. 6 west for 4 mi., and take a right on 255th St. before the Linoma Lighthouse. (☎332-3616. No smoking, drinking, or children. 4 rooms with shared bath. Singles $25; doubles $45.) Camping is available at the **Haworth Park Campground ❶,** in Bellevue on Payne St. at the end of Mission Ave., south of downtown. Take the exit for Rte. 370 E off Rte. 75 (Kennedy Expwy.), turn right onto Galvin Rd., left onto Mission Ave., and right onto Payne St. before the toll bridge. (☎291-3379 or 293-3098. Showers, toilets, and shelters. Office open daily 6am-10pm, but stragglers can enter after hours. Check-out 3pm. Reservations recommended. Tent sites $7; RV sites $15.)

🄲 FOOD. It's no fun being a chicken, cow, or vegetarian in Omaha, where there is a fried chicken joint on every block and a steakhouse in every district. Once a warehouse area, the brick streets of the **Old Market,** on Jackson, Howard, and Harney St. between 10th and 13th, now feature popular shops, restaurants, and bars. The **Farmers Market** (☎345-5401; www.omahafarmersmarket.org) is located at 11th and Jackson St. (Open June-Sept. W 3-7pm, Sa 8am-12:30pm; May Sa 8am-12:30pm.) To find out what all the beeftastic hubbub's about, sink your teeth into some prime-grade USDA beef at **Omaha Prime ❺,** 415 S. 11th St., in the Old Market. Their steak and chops will cost you $25-44, but keep in mind that only five percent of all beef holds the coveted honor of being "prime." (☎341-7040. Open M-Sa 5-

9pm.) **M's Pub ❷**, 422 S. 11th St., in the Old Market, cooks up both traditional American fare and international delights (try the *lahvosh*, $7-11), while the trendy bar crowd sips beer for $4.50. (☎342-2550; www.mspubomaha.com. Open M-Sa 11am-1am, Su 5-11pm; kitchen closes M-Sa at midnight.) Vegetarians and vegans can find their fix at **McFoster's Natural Kind Cafe ❷**, 302 S. 38th St. in midtown, which serves a large variety of tempeh and free range chicken dishes ($7-14), along with milks of cow, soy, and rice origins. (☎345-7477; www.mcfosters.com. Open M-Th 11am-10pm, F-Sa 11am-11pm, Su 10am-3pm.)

◙ **SIGHTS.** With the world's largest desert dome, indoor rainforest, and nocturnal exhibit, the ever-evolving ▧**Henry Doorly Zoo**, 3701 S. 10th St., has recently added the Hubbard Gorilla Valley, where great apes roam free and gawk at visitors. The zoo's reproductive ecology team produced the world's first test tube gorilla, and other newborn animals grow up in the nursery, which is open to the public. (☎733-8401; www.omahazoo.com. Take Exit 454 from I-80 and turn left at the sign for the stadium and zoo; continue until the road turns north onto 10th St. Open daily 9:30am-5pm. $9.75, over 62 $8.25, ages 5-11 $6.) About 30min. west on I-80, the **Wildlife Safari Park** lets visitors drive 4½ mi. through a nature preserve inhabited by bison, pronghorns, moose, wolves, and other beasts. (☎944-9453. Open Apr.-Oct. daily 9:30am-5pm. $4, children 5-11 $2.)

The **Durham Western Heritage Museum**, 801 S. 10th St., occupies the former Union Train Station, an impressive Art Deco structure. Visitors can tour a Pullman car, climb aboard an old steam engine on the Track Level, and learn about Omaha's neighborhoods in the historical galleries to gain a complete picture of the railroad's influence before indulging in a malted milkshake at the authentic 1931 soda fountain. (☎444-5071; www.dwhm.org. Open Tu-Sa 10am-5pm, Su 1-5pm. $6, seniors $5, ages 3-12 $4.) Across the river in Council Bluffs, the **Union Pacific Railroad Museum**, 200 Pearl St., off Rte. 6, includes furniture from a train car intended for Lincoln before he was shot, a locomotive simulator, and a fascinating exhibit detailing the future of the railroad. (☎712-329-8307; www.up.com. Open Tu-Sa 10am-4pm. Free.) The **Joslyn Art Museum**, 2200 Dodge St., displays 19th- and 20th-century American and European art, including the original plaster cast of Degas's famous sculpture *Little Dancer* and colorful glasswork by Dale Chihuly. (☎342-3300; www.joslyn.org. "Jazz on the Green" mid-July to mid-Aug. Th 7-9pm. Open Tu-Sa 10am-4pm, Su noon-4pm. $6, students and seniors $4, ages 5-17 $3.50; free Sa 10am-noon.) See the gargantuan remnants of US airpower from the past half-century in the equally enormous **Strategic Air and Space Museum**, at Exit 426 off I-80 in Ashland. The museum displays military aircraft, including a B-52 bomber and an SR-71—still the world's fastest plane—as well as exhibits on military history. Bunker down in a 1950s bomb shelter, or practice your duck-and-cover technique in a 1960s classroom. (☎827-3100 or 800-358-5029; www.strategicairandspace.com. Open daily 9am-5pm. $7, seniors and military $6, ages 5-12 $3. AAA discount.)

◪▧ **ENTERTAINMENT AND NIGHTLIFE.** The brand-new **Qwest Center Omaha**, 455 N. 10th St., hosts major concerts and sporting events. (☎341-1500; www.omahameca.com. Box office open M-F 10am-6pm.) At **Rosenblatt Stadium**, across from the zoo on 13th St., you can watch the **Omaha Royals** round the bases from April to early September. (☎738-5100; www.oroyals.com. General admission $5, reserved seats $7, box seats $9. Wheelchair accessible.) The stadium has also hosted the NCAA College Baseball World Series every June since 1950. From June 23 to July 10, 2005, **Shakespeare on the Green** will stage free performances in Elmwood Park, on 60th and Dodge St. (☎280-2391. Shows Th-Su 8pm.)

GREAT PLAINS

Punk and progressive folk have found a niche near several area universities; check the windows of the **Antiquarian Bookstore,** 1215 Harney St., and **Homers,** 114 Howard St., both in the Old Market, for the scoop on shows. Nearby, the subterranean **Dubliner,** 1205 Harney St., stages live Irish music on Friday and Saturday evenings. (☎342-5887. Cover $2-5. Open daily noon-1am.) The **13th Street Coffee Company,** 519 S. 13th St., keeps more than 20 types of beans on hand and brews three different varieties daily. (☎345-2883. Open mic Tu. Live music most weekends. Open M-Th 6:30am-11pm, F 6:30am-midnight, Sa 8am-midnight, Su 9am-11pm.) **The Max,** 1417 Jackson St., is one of the most popular gay bars in the state. With five bars, a dance floor, DJs, fountains, and a patio, The Max also attracts a straight crowd on Saturday nights. (☎346-4110; www.themaxomaha.com. Happy hour daily 4-9pm. 21+. Cover F $3, Sa $5, Su varies. Open daily 4pm-1am.)

LINCOLN   ☎402

The spirit of Lincoln rises and falls with the success of its world-famous college football team, the Nebraska Cornhuskers. Many a youngster has spent his childhood running wind sprints, lifting weights, and practicing, all for the dream of stepping onto the celebrated field at Memorial Stadium. Off the field, Lincoln mixes stateliness with a distinctly collegiate atmosphere, hosting both the Nebraska state legislature and rows of bars heaving with frat-style hijinks.

█▆ ORIENTATION AND PRACTICAL INFORMATION. Lincoln's grid makes sense—numbered streets increase as you go east, and lettered streets progress through the alphabet as you go north. **O Street** is the main east-west drag, becoming Hwy. 6 west of the city and Rte. 34 to the east. **R Street** runs along the south side of the **University of Nebraska-Lincoln (UNL).** Most downtown sights lie between 7th and 16th St. and M and R St. Here, parking options abound, with metered, on-street, and garage parking available. **Lincoln Municipal Airport,** 2400 W. Adams St. (☎458-2480; www.lincolnairport.com), is located 5 mi. northwest of downtown off Cornhusker Hwy.; take Exit 399 off I-80. **Amtrak,** 201 N. 7th St. (☎476-1295; open daily 11:30pm-7am), runs once daily to: Chicago (11hr., $113); Denver (7hr., $107); and Omaha (1hr., $18). Prices vary with availability. **Greyhound,** 940 P St. (☎474-1071; ticket window open M-F 7:30am-6pm, Sa 9:30am-3pm), sends buses to: Chicago (12hr.; 5 per day; M-Th $57, F-Su $66); Denver (10-17hr., 5 per day, $70/$81); Kansas City (6-10hr., 3 per day, $55/$64); Omaha (1hr., 3 per day, $11/$14). **StarTran,** 710 J St., handles public transit. Schedules are available on buses, at the office on J St., and at many locations downtown. All downtown buses connect at 11th and O St., two blocks east of Historic Haymarket. (☎476-1234. Buses run M-F 6am-6pm, Sa 6:30am-6pm. $1, seniors $0.50.) Taxi: **Yellow Cab** ☎477-4111. **Visitor Info: Lincoln Visitors Center,** 201 N. 7th St., at P St. in Lincoln Station. (☎434-5348 or 800-423-8212; www.lincoln.org. Open May-Sept. M-F 9am-8pm, Sa 8am-4pm, Su noon-4pm; Oct.-Apr. M-F 9am-6pm, Sa 10am-4pm, Su noon-4pm.) **Medical Services: Bryan LGH Medical Center East,** 1600 S. 48th St. (☎489-0200 or 481-3142.) **Internet Access: Lincoln Public Library,** 136 S. 14th St., at N St. (☎441-8500. Open M-Th 10am-9pm, F-Sa 10am-6pm, Su 1:30-5:30pm.) **Post Office:** 700 R St. (☎473-1728. Open M-F 7:30am-6pm, Sa 9am-1pm.) **Postal Code:** 68501. **Area Code:** 402.

▐ ACCOMMODATIONS. There are few inexpensive motels downtown. Cheaper places are farther east, around the 5600 block of Cornhusker Hwy. (U.S. 6). The **Cornerstone Hostel (HI) ❶,** 640 N. 16th St., at U St. just south of Vine St. on frat row, is conveniently located in a church basement on the university's downtown campus. It rarely fills up, and while the basement can get stuffy in summer, the organ music drifting from upstairs will take your mind off the heat. (☎476-0926. 9 beds in 2 single-sex rooms. Full kitchen and laundry facilities. Linen included. Curfew 11pm. Dorms $10, nonmembers $13.) **The Great Plains Budget Host Inn ❷,** 2732 O St., at 27th St., has large rooms with fridges and coffeemakers. Take bus #9 "O St. Shuttle." (☎476-3253 or 800-288-8499. Free parking and kitchenettes available. Singles $47; doubles $53. 10% AAA discount.) The elegant **Atwood House Bed and Breakfast ❺,** 740 S. 17th St., at G St., two blocks from the capitol, dazzles guests with antiques nestled in every corner and whirlpool baths in most suites. A stay in this 1894 mansion allows weary travelers to relax in the lap of luxury. (☎438-4567 or 800-884-6554; www.atwoodhouse.com. Suites $115-179.) To reach the pleasant **Camp-A-Way ❶,** 200 Ogden Rd., near 1st and Superior St., take Exit 401 or 401a from I-80, then Exit 1 from I-180/Rte. 34. Though next to a highway, the 87 sites are peaceful and shaded. (☎476-2282 or 866-719-2267; www.camp-a-way.com. Showers, laundry, heated pool, and convenience store. Reservations recommended in Aug. Sites $15, with water and electricity $22, full hookup $25. AAA discount.)

🍴🎵 **FOOD AND NIGHTLIFE. Historic Haymarket,** 7th to 9th St. and O to R St., is a renovated warehouse district near the train tracks with cafes, bars, restaurants, and a **farmers market.** (☎435-7496. Open mid-May to mid-Oct. Sa 8am-noon.) **Lazlo's Brewery and Grill ❹,** 710 P St., prides itself on freshly brewed beer ($4), fresh fish ($10-20), and ground beef. (☎434-5636. Burgers $5-7. Steak and chops $15-21. Open Su-Th 11am-10pm, F-Sa 11am-11pm.) **Kuhl's ❶,** 1038 O St., at 11th St., serves classic diner meals including the $5.75 "Lincoln special"—two eggs, toast, hash browns, and ham, bacon, or sausage. (☎476-1311. Breakfasts $3-6. Open M-F 6am-7pm, Sa 6am-4pm, Su 7am-3pm.) **Maggie's Vegetarian Wraps ❶,** 311 N. 8th St., sustains Lincoln's vegetarians and vegans with $2 pastries, $4-6 wraps, and $6 lunch specials. (☎477-3959. Open M-F 8am-3pm.) Spot legislators on their lunch break at **Billy's ❸,** 1301 H St., which offers fresh fish and meat ($14-24) in a historic setting. (☎474-0084. Lunch $7-9. Open M-F 11am-2pm and 5-10pm, Sa 5-10pm.)

With as many as ten bars per block, it's clear that Lincoln is a college town. For the biggest names in Lincoln's live music scene, try the suitably dark and smoky **Zoo Bar,** 136 N. 14th St., where blues is king. (☎435-8754; www.zoobar.com. Live music Tu-Sa. Cover $4-8. Open M 3-7pm, Tu-Sa 3pm-1am.) Those more interested in the college sports bar scene should head to **Iguana's,** 1426 O St. (☎476-8850. Open M-Sa 7pm-1am.) **Duffy's Tavern,** 1412 O St., showcases up-and-coming local rock bands as well as national acts. (☎474-3543. Nightly drink specials. Open M-Sa 4pm-1am, Su 6pm-1am.) **The Bricktop,** 1427 O St., delivers a pulsating techno scene (Th-Sa) with 80s night, reggae, and "down tempo house" rounding out the week. (☎202-8780. 21+. Open M-Sa 5pm-1am, Su 8pm-1am.) When the bars and clubs start to close at 12:45am, **O'Rourke's,** 1329 O St., keeps serving up until the last minute. (☎435-8052. Open M-F, Su noon-1am, Sa 11am-1am.)

🏛 **SIGHTS.** Intricate mosaics covering the walls, floors, and ceilings inside the sophisticated "Tower on the Plains," the 400 ft. **Nebraska State Capitol,** at 15th and K St., contrast with the streamlined exterior. Although outside renovations continue, the inside remains untouched and remarkable. A 19 ft. statue, *The Sower,* sits atop the building as a reminder of Nebraska's agricultural roots. (☎471-0448. Open M-F 8am-5pm, Sa 10am-5pm, Su 1-5pm. Free 30min. tours every hr. except noon.) On **Centennial Mall,** a renamed portion of 15th St., the **Museum of Nebraska History** has a phenomenal collection of headdresses, moccasins, jewelry, and other artifacts in its permanent exhibit on Plains Indians, as well as an impressive colonial dollhouse on the third floor. (At P St. ☎471-4754. Open Tu-F 9am-4:30pm, Sa-Su 1-4:30pm. Free; $2 donation recommended.) The **University of Nebraska State Museum,** 14th and U St., in Morrill Hall, boasts a fossil collection that includes Archie, the largest mounted mammoth in any American museum. (☎472-2642; www.museum.unl.edu. Open M-Sa 9:30am-4:30pm, Su 1:30-4:30pm. $4, ages 5-18 $2, under 5 free.) For a wheel-y good time, coast to the **National Museum of Roller Skating,** 4730 South St., at 48th St., to learn the history of the sport. (☎483-7551, ext. 16; www.rollerskatingmuseum.com. Open M-F 9am-5pm. Free.)

In August, the **Nebraska State Fair** offers car races, tractor pulls, and plenty of rides, as well as a birthing pavilion and "Nebraska Idol." (☎474-5371; www.statefair.org. $7, ages 6-12 $2.) **Pioneers Park,** 3201 S. Coddington Ave., a quarter of a mile south of W. Van Dorn, is a perfect spot for a prairie picnic. In winter there is a sled run with lights open until 11pm. The **Pioneers Park Nature Center** has bison and elk within its sanctuary and is the starting point for 6 mi. of trails. (☎441-7895. Park open sunrise-sunset. Nature Center open June-Aug. M-Sa 8:30am-8:30pm, Su noon-8:30pm; Sept.-May M-Sa 8:30am-5pm, Su noon-5pm. Free. Wheelchair accessible.)

SCOTTS BLUFF AND CHIMNEY ROCK ☎308

Known to the Plains Indians as *Me-a-pa-te* ("hill that is hard to go around"), the imposing clay and sandstone highlands of **Scotts Bluff National Monument** were landmarks for people traveling the Mormon and Oregon Trails in the 1840s. For some time the bluff was too dangerous to cross, but in the 1850s a single-file wagon trail was opened just south of the bluff through narrow **Mitchell's Pass,** where traffic wore deep marks in the sandstone. Today, visitors can see remnants of a half-mile stretch of the original **Oregon Trail** at the pass, complete with a pair of covered wagons. The **visitors center,** at the entrance on Rte. 92, relates the multiple and contradictory accounts of the mysterious death of Hiram Scott, the fur trader who gave the bluffs their name. (☎436-4340; www.nps.gov/scbl. Open daily in summer 8am-7pm; in winter 8am-5pm. $5 per carload, $3 per motorcycle.) To get to the top of the bluffs, hike the challenging **Saddle Rock Trail** (1½ mi. one-way) or motor up **Summit Drive.** (Shuttle available at visitors center; Summit Dr. closes at 6:30pm.) At the top, you'll find two short **nature trails.** Guidebooks ($0.50) are available at the trailheads and at the visitors center. The **North Overlook** is a ½ mi. paved walk with a view of the North Platte River Valley. The short and easy **South Overlook** (¼ mi.) provides a spectacular view of Scotts Bluff and the Oregon Trail route.

Take U.S. 26 to Rte. 71 to Rte. 92; the monument is on Rte. 92 about 2 mi. west of **Gering** (not in the town of Scottsbluff). A 1¼ mi. bike trail links Gering with the visitors center at the base of the bluffs. July 7-10, 2005, expect festive folk to pack the towns near Gering for the carnival, concerts, and chili cook-off of the 84th annual **Oregon Trail Days** festival. (☎436-4457; www.oregontrail-days.com.) Twenty miles east on Rte. 92, south of Bayard, the 475 ft. spire of **Chimney Rock,** visible from more than 30 mi. away, served as another landmark that inspired travelers on the Oregon Trail. There is no path up to the base of the rock due to the rough terrain and rattlesnakes. The Nebraska State Historical Society operates a **visitors center.** (☎586-2581; www.nps.gov/chro. Open daily in summer 9am-5pm; in winter Tu-Su 9am-5pm. $3, under 18 free.) For an extra historical delight, continue down the road past the visitors center, take a right onto Chimney Rock Rd., and follow the gravel road ½ mi. to its end. Here you will find a graveyard of Oregon Trail settlers and a closer view of the rock itself. **Area Code:** 308. **Time Zone:** Mountain.

GREAT PLAINS

KANSAS

Boasting America's largest tallgrass prairie, as well as junctures of the Anne Chisolm, Santa Fe, and Oregon Trails, Kansas epitomizes rural America. Vast stretches of farmland dotted with cattle make up the majority of the landscape, while several small cities offer more urban amenities. Steeped in Civil War and Wild West history, Kansas provides myriad opportunities for the history buff and antique collector. As highway signs remind travelers, this heartland has plenty of heart to go around because "every Kansas farmer feeds 101 people—and you."

⚑ PRACTICAL INFORMATION

Capital: Topeka.

Visitor Info: Division of Travel and Tourism: 350 Speedway Blvd., Kansas City 66111 (☎913-299-2253 or 800-252-6727; www.travelks.com). Open daily 8am-6pm.

Kansas Department of Wildlife and Parks, 512 SE 25th Ave., Pratt 67124 (☎620-672-5911; www.kdwp.state.ks.us). Open M-F 8am-5pm.

Postal Abbreviation: KS. **Sales Tax:** 5.3% or higher, depending on city.

WICHITA ☎316

Wichita made a name for itself in the early 19th century as home to the Wild West's long arm of the law. In the 20th century, its economy took off as the town became a center of aviation manufacturing and an agricultural commodities hub for the Southern and Central Plains. Today's Wichita is the cultural center of Kansas, with renowned museums and performing arts companies. Downtown emits a suburban vibe, while Old Town has become the nightlife mecca for party-seeking yuppies.

⚑ **ORIENTATION AND PRACTICAL INFORMATION.** Wichita lies on I-35, 170 mi. north of Oklahoma City and 200 mi. southwest of Kansas City. A small, quiet downtown makes for easy walking and parking. **Broadway Street** is the major north-south artery. **Douglas Avenue** separates the numbered east-west streets to the north from the named east-west streets to the south. Running east-west, **Kellogg Avenue (U.S. 54)** serves as an expressway through downtown and as a main commercial strip. The closest **Amtrak** station, 414 N. Main St. (☎283-7533; open M-F midnight-8am), 30 mi. north of Wichita in Newton, sends trains to Dodge City (2½hr., 1 per day, $26-51) and Kansas City (4½hr., 1 per day, $33-64). **Greyhound,** 308 S. Broadway St., two blocks east of Main St. (☎265-7711; open daily 3am-6pm), runs to: Denver (13-14hr., 2 per day, $72); Kansas City (3-5hr., 3 per day, $33); Oklahoma City (4hr., 3 per day, $32). **Wichita Transit,** 214 S. Topeka St., runs 18 bus routes in town. (☎265-7221. Open M-F 6am-6pm, Sa 7am-5pm. Buses run M-F 5:45am-6:45pm, Sa 6:45am-5:45pm. $1, ages 6-17 $0.75, seniors and disabled $0.50; transfers $0.10.) **Visitor Info: Convention and Visitors Bureau,** 100 S. Main St., at Douglas Ave. (☎265-2800 or 800-288-9424; www.visitwichita.com. Open M-F 8am-5pm.) **Internet Access: Public Library,** 223 S. Main St. (☎261-8500. Open M-Th 10am-9pm, F-Sa 10am-5:30pm, Su 1-5pm.) **Post Office:** 330 W. 2nd St. N, at N. Waco St. (☎267-7710. Open M-F 7:30am-5pm, Sa 9am-noon.) **Postal Code:** 67202. **Area Code:** 316.

⚑☐ **ACCOMMODATIONS AND FOOD.** Wichita offers a bounty of cheap hotels. S. Broadway St. has plenty of mom-and-pop places, *but be wary of the surrounding areas.* Chains line **East and West Kellogg Avenue,** 5-8 mi. from downtown. Only 10 blocks from downtown, the **Mark 8 Inn ❷**, 1130 N. Broadway St., has small, comfortable rooms with free local calls, cable TV, A/C, fridge, free coffee in the front office, and laundry facilities. (☎265-4679 or 888-830-7268. Singles $34; doubles $37.) **Wichita Inn ❷**, 8220 E. Kellogg Ave., is your next best bet, offering cable, continental breakfast, TV/VCR, and microfridges. (☎685-8291. Singles $42; doubles $46.) **USI RV Park ❶**, 2920 E. 33rd St. N, right off Hillside Rd., is the most convenient of Wichita's hitchin' posts, with laundry, showers, and a storm shelter—in case there's a twister a-comin'. (☎838-0435. No tents. RV sites $23-27.) Beef is what's for dinner in Wichita. If you eat only one slab here, get it from **Doc's Steakhouse ❸**, 1515 N. Broadway St., bus #13 "N. Broadway," where the most expensive entree, a 17 oz. T-bone with salad, potato, and bread, is only $11. (☎264-4735. Open M-Th 11:30am-9:30pm, F 11:30am-10pm, Sa 4-10pm.) The Old Town area is a good choice for $5 lunch buffets and other specials. **Hog Wild Pit Bar-B-Q ❶**, 1200 S. Rock Rd. (also at 233 S. West St. and 662 E. 47th St.), has dine-in, drive-thru, and carry-out lip-smackin' Kansas goodness. Six-dollar dinners include choice of meat, two sides, and bread. (☎618-7227. Sandwiches $4. Open daily 11am-8pm.) N. Broadway St., around 10th St., offers authentic Asian food. **Saigon ❷**, 1103 N. Broadway St., creates good, greasy Vietnamese fare with plenty of dishes to choose from. (☎262-8134. Noodles with chicken $6. Open daily 10am-9pm.)

🎬 **SIGHTS.** Wichita's five **Museums on the River** are within a few blocks of each other; take the trolley or bus #12 to "Riverside." Walk through the rough-and-tumble cattle days of the 1870s in the **Old Cowtown** museum, 1871 Sim Park Dr., which is lined with many original buildings. (☎264-6398; www.old-cowtown.org. Open Apr.-Oct. M-Sa 10am-5pm, Su noon-5pm; Nov.-Mar. Sa 10am-5pm, Su noon-5pm. $7, seniors $6.50, ages 12-17 $5, ages 4-11 $3.50, under 3 free; Tu-W seniors 2-for-1.) The **Mid-America All-Indian Center and Museum,** 650 N. Seneca St., boasts Native American artifacts, the outdoor **Indian Village,** and the **Gallery of Nations,** which includes a regal display of Native American tribal flags. The late Blackbear Bosin's awe-inspiring sculpture *Keeper of the Plains* stands guard over the confluence of the Arkansas and Little Arkansas Rivers. The center hosts the annual **Mid-America All-Indian Intertribal Powwow**, featuring dancing, food, arts, and crafts. Call for dates. (☎262-5221. Open Tu-Sa 10am-5pm, Su 1-5pm. $7, seniors $6, ages 6-12 $5, ages 3-5 $1.) The **Wichita Art Museum,** 1400 W. Museum Blvd., displays collections of mostly American paintings, glass, furnishings, and rotating exhibits of both international and local artists. (☎268-4921. Open Tu-W and F-Sa 10am-5pm, Th 11am-8pm, Su noon-5pm. $5, seniors and students with ID $4, children 5-17 $2; Sa Free.)

Exploration Place, 300 N. McLean Blvd., Wichita's newest and most impressive piece of riverfront architecture, houses the city's interactive museum. Excavate area fossils, touch a 20 ft. tornado, or examine the miniature display of early 1950s Kansas landmarks. The museum also houses the Cyberdome Theater and a full-motion simulation theater. (☎263-3373 or 877-904-1444; www.exploration.org. Open Tu-F 9am-5pm, Sa 10am-8pm, Su noon-6pm; in summer also M noon-6pm. $8, seniors $7.50, ages 5-15 $6, ages 2-4 $3. Theater admission $5/$4.50/$4/N/A. Combo tickets available.) **Botanica**, 701 N. Amindon St., the Wichita botanical gardens, contains a wide collection of flora from the Americas and Asia. Though Kansas may be completely landlocked, Botanica hosts an amazing array of aquatic plants in the Jaynew Milburn Aquatic Collection. (☎264-0448; www.botanica.org. Open M-Sa 9am-5pm, Su 1-5pm. $6, seniors $5, students and under 21 $3.)

DODGE CITY ☎ 620

In its heyday in the 1870s, Dodge City ("the wickedest little city in America") was a haven for gunfighters, prostitutes, and other lawless types. At one time, the main drag had one saloon for every 50 citizens, and today, downtown Dodge recreates the Old-West-style boardwalk with shops and watering holes along **Front Street**. Legendary lawmen Wyatt Earp and Bat Masterson earned their fame cleaning up the streets of Dodge. Disputes were settled man-to-man with a duel, and the slower draw ended up in **Boot Hill Cemetery**, so named for the boot-clad corpses buried there. The **Boot Hill Museum** on Front St. admits visitors to the old cemetery site with wooden grave markers based on real period newspaper articles and obituaries. They also have a "People of the Plains Exhibit" with a talking animatronic bison. (☎ 227-8188. www.boothill.org. Open June-Sept. daily 8am-8pm; low-season M-Sa 9am-5pm, Su 1-5pm. $8, students and seniors $7.50, children 6 and under free.) The town's most conspicuous residents, about 50,000 cows, reside on the feedlots in the eastern part of town, but one, the bronze longhorn **El Capitán,** rests at 2nd and Front St. The statue is based on an actual steer that made the cattle drive several times. The **Home of Stone,** 112 E. Vine St., built in 1881 by German pioneer John Mueller and his wife Karoline, is the oldest building in town still on its original site, furnished with period artifacts, much of them original. (Free.) Nine miles west of town on Hwy. 50, 19th-century **Sante Fe Trail wagon tracks** traverse the rolling Kansas grasslands near remnants of the Eureka Irrigation Canal. In the opposite direction, just east of Dodge City on Hwy. 400, lies **Fort Dodge,** which was established in 1865 to defend the region from Indian assaults. Decommissioned in 1890, the site is now the Kansas Soldiers Home for retired military personnel and retains some of its historic buildings. (☎ 227-2121.) The **Fort Dodge Museum** displays a mix of antiques and artifacts, military and otherwise, and also gives tours of a house in which General Custer spent a night. (☎ 227-2121, ext. 152. Open May-Sept. M-Sa 10am-4pm, Su 1-4pm; Oct.-Apr. daily 1-4pm.)

Motels line Wyatt Earp Blvd., and one of the best places among them to hang your (cowboy) hat is the **Thunderbird Motel ❷,** 2300 W. Wyatt Earp Blvd., which offers very clean and well-furnished rooms with microfridges and HBO. (☎ 225-4143. Singles $35; doubles $43.) Campers looking for an oasis on the dusty Dodge plain should head to **Water Sports Campground & RV Park ❶,** 500 E. Cherry St., which has tent and RV sites around a swimming-only lake. (☎ 225-8044. Laun-

OUT OF THE WAY

HEY COOL, THAT'S OZ-SOME!

There's no place like home—especially if home is Liberal, Kansas. Proud of their state's fame as the cinematic home to Dorothy Gale, the bright-eyed heroine of *The Wizard of Oz,* citizens of Liberal found a house that resembled Dorothy's and, in 1981, had it relocated to Liberal's Coronado Museum. They furnished the home with antiques and artifacts to make it like its black-and-white counterpart, constructed characters from the movie around the grounds, and laid a yellow brick road around the whole thing. Dorothy's House was born and subsequently recognized by the governor as the official home of the little girl from Kansas.

The Land of Oz, a 5000 sq. ft. multimedia walkthrough tour of the movie, reconstructs the movie's plot with near life-size figures, sound clips, and video. It also houses film memorabilia, including artifacts donated by some of the actors who played munchkins in the film. The main office in the Coronado Museum has everything you'd ever want to know about the film, and tours are led by girls in ruby red slippers and gingham dresses.

567 Yellow Brick Rd., just north of the Oklahoma border on Hwy. 54, 85 mi. south of Dodge City. 316-624-7624. Tours $3.50. Open in summer M-Sa 9am-6pm, Su 1-5pm; low-season Tu-Sa 9am-5pm, Su 1-5pm.

dry, hot showers. 2-person tent sites $17, full hookup $19. $1.50 per extra person.) **Peppercorn's Bar & Grill ❸**, 1301 W. Wyatt Earp Blvd., serves some of the 20,000 head of cattle that are slaughtered around Dodge City each day (steaks $10-15), as well as cheaper burgers and sandwiches, in a casual setting. (☎225-1396. Open M-Sa 11am-2am.) Among Dodge's many Mexican eateries, **Casa Alvarez ❷**, 1701 W. Wyatt Earp Blvd., has one of the largest and cheapest menus. (☎225-7164. Burritos $4.75-$7.75. Open M-Th 10:30am-2pm and 5-9pm, F-Sa 11am-9:30pm, Su 10am-8pm.)

Amtrak's unmanned station, at Central Ave. and Wyatt Earp Blvd., goes to Albuquerque (10hr., 1 per day, $88-98) and Kansas City (7hr., 1 per day, $68-81). **Greyhound,** at T&T Convenience Store, 2305 Wyatt Earp Blvd. (☎227-9547), goes to: Amarillo (8hr., 1 per day, $55); Kansas City (8½hr., 1 per day, $67); Wichita (3hr., 1 per day, $33). **Dodge City Convention and Visitors Bureau** is at 400 W. Wyatt Earp Blvd. (☎225-8186 or 800-653-9378; www.visitdodgecity.org. Open daily June-Sept. 8:30am-6:30pm; low-season M-F 8:30am-5pm.) **Postal Code: 67801. Area Code: 620.**

LAWRENCE ☎785

Lawrence was founded in 1854 by anti-slavery advocates to ensure that Kansas became a free state. Now home to the flagship **University of Kansas (KU),** Lawrence offers numerous first-rate artistic, architectural, historical, cultural, and social activities. KU's **Watkins Community Museum of History,** 1047 Massachusetts St., whets the appetites of Kansas history buffs with rotating exhibits displayed in an 1888 bank building. (☎841-4109; www.watkinsmuseum.org. Open Tu-W 10am-6pm, Th 10am-9pm, F 10am-5pm, Sa 10am-4pm. Suggested donation $3, children $2.) The main attractions, however, are two tours through downtown Lawrence. A 1½hr. driving tour beginning at 1111 E. 19th St., **Quantrill's Raid: The Lawrence Massacre** traces the events leading up to the murder of over 200 men by pro-slavery vigilantes on August 21, 1863. The second tour, **House Styles of Old West Lawrence,** provides a look at gorgeous 19th-century homes, via a walking (45min.) or a driving (25min.) tour. Maps are at the visitors center and Chamber of Commerce.

Inexpensive motels are hard to find in Lawrence; look around Iowa and 6th St., just west of campus. Three blocks from downtown, the **Halcyon House Bed and Breakfast ❸**, 1000 Ohio St., is close to local attractions and good parking. (☎841-0314. Breakfast included. Rooms $49.) The traditional **Westminster Inn and Suites ❸**, 2525 W. 6th St., offers many amenities to make stays more comfortable. (☎841-8410. Pool. Continental breakfast included. Singles M-Th $48, F-Su $55; doubles $52/$65. 2 wheelchair-accessible rooms.)

Downtown Lawrence features traditional barbecue joints and ethnic eateries. The **Wheatfields Bakery and Cafe ❷**, 904 Vermont St., serves large sandwiches ($6.50) on home-baked breads and delicious breakfasts. Vegetarians will enjoy the Pan Bagnet sandwich ($5.50), with hard-boiled eggs, zucchini, sprouts, and roasted red peppers, slathered in herb cream cheese. (☎841-5553. Open M-Sa 6:30am-8pm, Su 7:30am-4pm.) **Captain Ribman's Meat Market ❷**, 881 New Hampshire St., is a downtown barbecue joint and sports bar with 14 televisions and its own patron superhero. A ½ lb. burger and fries ($5.50) or barbecue sandwich ($6-7.50) goes great with a fried Twinkie ($3.50), but be sure to keep the defibrillators handy. (☎856-6328. Open daily 11am-2am.) The popular **La Parilla ❷**, 814 Massachusetts St., offers Latin American dishes and daily drink specials. (☎841-1100. Open Su-M 11am-9pm, Tu-Th 11am-10pm, F-Sa 11am-3am.) **The Free State Brewing Company ❷**, 636 Massachusetts St., the first legal brewery in Kansas and a popular local hangout, brews over 50 beers yearly and has at least five on tap. (☎843-4555. Beer $2.75; M beer $1.25. Sandwiches $6. Open M-Sa 11am-midnight, Su noon-11pm.) For live music and a neighborhood bar feel, **Jazzhaus,** 926½ Massachusetts St., features local groups and the occasional regional act. (☎749-3320. Cover after 9pm $2-8; Tu $1.50, but no live music. Open daily 4pm-2am; music begins at 10pm.)

Lawrence lies just south of I-70 in northeastern Kansas. Massachusetts St. is the town's main drag, lined with restaurants and shops. There is an unstaffed **Amtrak** station at 413 E. 7th St.; trains chug to Chicago (10hr., 1 per day, $86-107). **Greyhound,** 2447 W. 6th St. (☎843-5622; ticket window open M-F 7:30am-4pm, Sa 7:30am-noon), runs buses to: Dallas (13-15hr., 5 per day, $59-82); Denver (12-13hr., 3 per day, $74-79); Kansas City, MO (1hr., 3 per day, $12-14). The **Lawrence Transit System (the "T"),** 930 E. 30th St., has schedules in local businesses, in the library, and on every bus. (☎832-3465. Open M-F 6am-8pm, Sa 7am-8pm. $0.50, seniors and disabled $0.25.) **Visitors Center:** 402 N. 2nd St., at Locust St. (☎865-4499 or 888-529-5267. Open Apr.-Sept. M-F 8:30am-5:30pm, Su 1-5pm; Oct.-Mar. M-Sa 9am-5pm, Su 1-5pm.) **Lawrence Chamber of Commerce:** 734 Vermont St. #101. (☎865-4411; www.lawrencechamber.com. Open M-F 8am-5pm.) **Internet Access: Public Library,** 707 Vermont Ave. (☎843-3833. Open M-F 9am-9pm, Sa 9am-6pm, Su 2-6pm.) **Post Office:** 645 Vermont St. (☎843-1681. Open M-F 8am-5:30pm, Sa 9am-noon.) **Postal Code:** 66045. **Area Code:** 785.

MISSOURI

Nestled in the middle of the country, Missouri serves as the gateway to the west while hugging the Midwest and South, blending the three identities into a state that defies regional stereotyping. Its large cities are defined by wide avenues, lazy rivers, humid summers, and blues and jazz wailing into the night. In the countryside, Bible factory outlets stand amid fireworks stands and barbecue pits. Missouri's patchwork geography further complicates its characterization. In the north, near Iowa, amber waves of grain undulate. Along the Mississippi, towering bluffs inscribed with Native American pictographs evoke western canyonlands, while in Hannibal, cavers enjoy the limestone caverns that inspired Mark Twain.

⁊ PRACTICAL INFORMATION

Capital: Jefferson City.

Visitor Info: Missouri Division of Tourism, P.O. Box 1055, Jefferson City 65102 (☎573-751-4133 or 800-877-1234 for a free travel guide; www.missouritourism.org). Open M-F 8am-5pm; toll-free number operates 24hr. **Dept. of Natural Resources,** Division of State Parks, P.O. Box 176, Jefferson City 65102 (☎573-751-3443 or 800-361-4827). Open M-F 8am-5pm.

Postal Abbreviation: MO. **Sales Tax:** 5-7.5%, depending on county.

ST. LOUIS ☎314

Directly south of the junction of three rivers—the Mississippi, Missouri, and Illinois—St. Louis marks the transition between Midwest and West. The silvery Gateway Arch rises above the sprawling and diverse city, framing it against the mighty river that nurtured its growth. Combining Southern hospitality, Midwestern pragmatism, and Western optimism, St. Louis offers visitors both fast-paced urban life and lazy days spent floating on the Mississippi.

▮ TRANSPORTATION

Airport: Lambert-St. Louis International (☎426-8000; www.lambert-stlouis.com), 12 mi. northwest of the city on I-70. MetroLink and Bi-State bus #66 "Clayton Airport" provides easy access to downtown ($3). Taxis to downtown $30.

Downtown St. Louis

🏠 ACCOMMODATIONS
Huckleberry Finn Youth
  Hostel (HI-AYH), **3**
The Roberts Mayfair, **5**
Royal Budget Inn, **8**

🍎 FOOD
Imo's, **1**

🌙 NIGHTLIFE
The Big Bang, **6**
Clementine's, **4**
Mississippi
  Nights, **7**
The Pageant, **2**

Trains: Amtrak, 550 S. 16th St. (☎621-5386). Office open daily 6am-1am. To **Chicago** (6hr., 4 per day, $21-59) and **Kansas City** (5½hr., 2 per day, $25-41).

Buses: Greyhound, 1450 N. 13th St. (☎231-4485), at Cass Ave. From downtown, take Bi-State bus #30, less than 10min. away. *Use caution in this area at night.* To **Chicago** (6-8hr., 7 per day, $36) and **Kansas City** (4½-5hr., 4 per day, $33).

Public Transit: Bi-State (☎231-2345; www.metrostlouis.org), also known as MetroBus, runs local buses. Info and schedules available at the **Metroride Service Center,** in the St. Louis Center. (☎982-1485. Open M-F 6am-8pm, Sa-Su 8am-5pm.) **MetroLink,** the light-rail system, runs from Lambert Airport through downtown and on to Shiloh, IL. Operates M-F 4:30am-12:15am and Sa-Su 5am-midnight. Travel for free in the "Ride Free Zone" (from Laclede's Landing to Union Station) M-F 11:30am-1pm. Bi-State or MetroLink $1.25, seniors and ages 5-12 $0.60; transfers $0.25/$0.15. Day pass $4, available at MetroLink stations. **Shuttle Bugs** cruise around Forest Park and the Central

West End. Operates M-F 6:45am-6pm, Sa-Su 10am-6pm. $1 buys an all-day ride. The **Shuttle Bee** buzzes around Forest Park, Clayton, Brentwood, and the Galleria. Operates M-F 5:40am-11:15pm, limited service Sa-Su 7:30am-10:00pm.

Taxi: Yellow Cab ☎ 361-2345.

✈ 🛈 ORIENTATION AND PRACTICAL INFORMATION

I-64 (U.S. 40) and **I-44** run east-west through the entire metropolitan area. Downtown is defined as the area east of Tucker between **Martin Luther King** and **Market Street,** which run north-south and divide the city. Numbered streets run parallel to the Mississippi River, increasing to the west. The historic **Soulard** district borders the river south of downtown. **Forest Park** and the **University City Loop,** home to **Washington University** and old, stately homes, lie west of downtown; the Italian neighborhood called **The Hill** rests south of these neighborhoods. St. Louis is a driving town: parking comes easily, wide streets offer lots of metered street parking, and private lots are often cheap (from $2 per day).

> **!** While the safety situation in St. Louis has shown improvement of late, visitors are still well advised to be alert; areas in North County can be dangerous at night, and East St. Louis—across the river in Illinois—is generally to be avoided.

Visitor Info: St. Louis Visitors Center, 308 Washington Ave. (☎241-1764). Open daily 9:30am-4:30pm. The *Official St. Louis Visitors Guide* and the monthly *Where: St. Louis,* both free, contain helpful info and good maps. A second **information center** (☎342-5160) is inside America's Convention Center. Open M-F 9am-5pm, Sa 9am-2pm.

Hotlines: Rape Hotline, ☎531-2003. **Suicide Hotline,** ☎647-4357. **Kids Under 21 Crisis,** ☎644-5886. All 24hr. **Gay and Lesbian Hotline,** ☎367-0084. Operates M-Sa 6-10pm.

Medical Services: Barnes-Jewish Hospital, 1 Barnes-Jewish Hospital Plaza, in the Central West End (☎ 747-3000).

Post Office: 1720 Market St. (☎436-4114. Open M-F 8am-8pm, Sa 8am-1pm.) **Postal Code:** 63101. **Area Code:** 314 (in St. Louis), 636 (in St. Charles), 618 (in IL); in text, 314 unless noted otherwise.

🛏 ACCOMMODATIONS

Most budget lodging is far from downtown. For chain motels, try Lindbergh Blvd. (Rte. 67) near the airport, or the area north of the I-70/I-270 junction in Bridgeton, 5 mi. beyond the airport.

Huckleberry Finn Youth Hostel (HI), 1908 S. 12th St. (☎241-0076), at Tucker Blvd. in the Soulard District. Take bus #73 "Carondelet." Weathered but comfortable dorms with full kitchen located close to Soulard attractions. Linen $2. Key deposit $5. Reception daily 8-10am and 6-10pm. Check-out 9:30am. Dorms $18, nonmembers $21. ❶

The Roberts Mayfair, 806 St. Charles St. (☎421-2500). Chocolates on pillows originated at this elegant Jazz Age hotel, which has played host to celebrities like Cary Grant and Harry Truman. Standard rooms are spacious with marble-topped sinks and soft queen-sized beds. Rooms $109-179, web specials from $69 at www.wyndham.com. ❺

Congress Airport Inn, 3433 N. Lindbergh Blvd. (☎ 739-5100), 1 mi. south of I-70, west of the airport. Clean accommodations just a 20min. drive from the Loop and close to the airport. Singles $45; doubles $50. ❸

Royal Budget Inn, 6061 Collinsville Rd., Fairmont City, IL (☎618-874-4451), 15min. east of the city off I-55/I-70, Exit 6 (left on Collinsville Rd. off the exit). Adequate, 1-bed rooms across the river from downtown. Limit 2 people per room. $2 key deposit. Rooms $40. Cash only. ❷

GREAT PLAINS

Dr. Edmund A. Babler Memorial State Park, 800 Guy Park (☎636-458-3813; reservations 877-422-6766 or www.mostateparks.com.) in Wildwood. 10 mi. north of I-44 off Hwy. 109. Well-maintained facilities and hot showers nestled in an arboresque setting. Tent sites Apr.-Oct. $8, Nov.-Mar. $7. RV sites with electric hookup $14/$12. ●

🍴 FOOD

In St. Louis, the difference of a few blocks can mean vastly different cuisine. The area surrounding **Union Station,** at 18th and Market St. downtown, has recently been revamped with hip restaurants and bars. The **Central West End** offers trendy cafes and upscale bars centered on **Euclid Avenue,** just north of Lindell Blvd.; take the MetroLink to "Central West End" and walk north, or catch the Shuttle Bug. St. Louis's historic Italian neighborhood, **The Hill,** southwest of downtown and just northwest of Tower Grove Park, produces plenty of inexpensive pasta; take bus #99 "Shaw-Russell." Ethnic restaurants, ranging from Vietnamese to Middle Eastern cuisine, spice up the **South Grand** area, at Grand Blvd. just south of Tower Grove Park; board bus #70 "Grand." Coffee shops and unique restaurants cluster on **University City Loop,** on Delmar Blvd. between Des Peres and Big Bend Blvd.

🏅 **Blueberry Hill,** 6504 Delmar Blvd. (☎727-0880; www.blueberryhill.com), on the Loop. Eclectic rock 'n' roll restaurant with 9 different rooms including the "Elvis Room." Walls decked with record covers, Howdy Doody toys, a Simpsons collection, and giant baseball cards. Call ahead to find out if Chuck Berry is playing; he usually jams in the "Duck Room" once a month. Burgers $5-7. Call ahead for entertainment schedule. 21+. Cover $4-15. Limited menu after 9pm. Open M-Sa 11am-1:30am, Su 11am-midnight. ❷

🏅 **In Soo,** 8423 Olive Blvd. (☎997-7473), is home to some delectable Asian cuisine, including a formidable moo-shu ($16) and several authentically prepared Korean dishes. The chef's wife meticulously manages every aspect of the restaurant, personally wrapping customers' moo-shoo pancakes. Open M and W-F 11:30am-10pm, Sa 5-10pm, Su 11:30am-9pm. ❸

Mangia Italiano, 3145 S. Grand Blvd. (☎664-8585), offers savory cuisine and a trendy atmosphere popular with the younger crowd. Entrees $7-14. Lunch buffet $6 M-F 11:30am-2:30pm. Kitchen open M-Th 11:30am-10pm, F-Sa 11:30am-10:30pm, Su 5pm-10pm. Bar open until 3am. ❸

Imo's, 1000 Hampton at I-64 (☎644-5480), makes razor-thin crust St. Louis-style pizza using the locally revered provel cheese and receives numerous shout-outs from native rap superstar Nelly. Over 80 locations throughout the city. Pizzas from $4.25. Open M-Th 10am-midnight, F-Sa 10am-1am, Su 10am-11pm. ❷

Ted Drewes Frozen Custard, 4224 S. Grand Blvd. (☎352-7376; www.teddrewes.com) and 6726 Chippewa St. (☎481-2652) at Rte. 66. Take refuge from the summer heat in a thick "concrete" shake ($1.80-3.90) at this St. Louis institution, established in 1929. Both locations open daily May-Aug. 11am-11pm; Chippewa St. site also Sept.-Dec. and Feb.-May 11am-11pm. ●

Cha Yoon Elixir Bar, 4 N. Euclid Ave. (☎367-2209), is a chic sushi joint offering fresh fish and an encyclopedic tea menu. Lounge on leather couches and sip tieguanyin oolong ($6 per pot), which is said to be hand-picked by monkeys who are trained to reach the most inaccessible tea trees. Open M-Th 11am-10pm, F-Sa 11am-11pm, Su 5-9pm. ❸

South Grand Coffee House, 3183 S. Grand Blvd. (☎865-2326). Wireless Internet and desktop terminals set against a backdrop of groovy murals and arcade games, including the original Ms. Pac-Man. Weeknight pool and chess tournaments and open mic Su. Open M-Th 4pm-3am, F 4pm-4am, Sa 2pm-4am, Su 2pm-3am. ●

Kabob International, 3200 S. Grand Blvd. (☎771-3411). This Persian bistro cooks up sizzling kabobs (beef $10, chicken $9) and a mean falafel, in addition to offering a sprawling vegetarian menu. Dinner entrees $7-16. Open daily 11:30am-9pm. ❸

🔍 SIGHTS

JEFFERSON EXPANSION MEMORIAL. At 630 ft., the 🔳**Gateway Arch**—the nation's tallest monument—towers gracefully over all of St. Louis and southern Illinois, serving as a testament to the city's historical role as the "Gateway to the West." The ground-level view is impressive, but the 4min. ride to the top in quasi-futuristic elevator modules is jaw-dropping. Waits are shorter on weekday mornings, but are uniformly long on weekends. Beneath the arch, the underground **Museum of Westward Expansion** adds to the appeal of the grassy park complex known as the **Jefferson Expansion Memorial.** The museum radiates in a semi-circle from a statue of a surveying Jefferson, and features talking robotic figures such as Red Cloud and William Clark, who narrate their own part in the settlement of the West. *(☎ 982-1410; www.gatewayarch.com. Museum and arch open daily summer 8am-10pm; winter 9am-6pm. Tram $8, ages 13-16 $5, ages 3-12 $3. Museum free. Tram not wheelchair accessible.)* Scope out the city from the water with **Gateway Riverboat Cruises;** tours leave from the docks in front of the arch. *(☎ 877-982-1410. 1hr. riverboat tours daily; call for departure times. $10, ages 3-12 $4. Limited wheelchair access.)* Across the street but still part of the Memorial, the magnificently ornate **Old Courthouse,** where the Dred Scott case began, has been restored as a museum detailing the case as well as the story of St. Louis's growth. *(11 N. 4th St. ☎ 655-1600. Open daily 8am-4:30pm. Call ahead for tour schedules. Free. Limited wheelchair access.)*

ST. LOUIS HISTORY. It's a strike either way at the **International Bowling Museum and Hall of Fame** and the **St. Louis Cardinals Hall of Fame Museum,** which share a home across from Busch Stadium. The mildly amusing bowling museum provides a light-hearted and largely speculative account of the sport's history and allows visitors to bowl. The baseball museum exhibits memorabilia from the glory days of St. Louis hardball, as well as paraphernalia belonging to present-day slugger Mark McGwire. The museum also offers stadium tours. *(111 Stadium Plaza. ☎ 231-6340. Open Apr.-Sept. daily 9am-5pm, game days until 6:30pm; Oct.-Mar. Tu-Su 11am-4pm. Museums or stadium tour $7.50, ages 66 and up $7, under 16 $6; both $12/$11/$10. Wheelchair accessible.)* Historic **Union Station,** ½ mi. west of downtown, houses a shopping mall, food court, and entertainment center beneath the iron girders and soaring roof that once housed the nation's busiest railroad terminal. *(At 18th and Market St. MetroLink to Union Station. ☎ 421-6655; www.stlouisunionstation.com. Open M-Sa 10am-9pm, Su 10am-6pm.)* "The Entertainer" lives on at the **Scott Joplin House,** just west of downtown near Jefferson St., where the ragtime legend tickled the ivories and penned classic tunes from 1900 to 1903. The 45min. tour delves into Joplin's long-lasting influence on American music. *(2658 Delmar Blvd. ☎ 557-2333. Tours Apr.-Oct. M-F every hr. Open Apr.-Oct. M-Sa 10am-4pm, Su noon-4pm.; Nov.-Mar. Tu-Sa 10am-4pm. $2.50, ages 6-12 $1.50. Wheelchair accessible.)*

SOUTH OF DOWNTOWN. Soulard is bounded by I-55 and 7th St. In the early 1970s, the city proclaimed this area a historic district because it once housed German and Eastern European immigrants, many of whom worked in the breweries. Today, it is a gentrified, tree-lined neighborhood packed with 19th-century brick townhouses. The district surrounds the bustling **Soulard Farmers Market,** where fresh, inexpensive produce abounds. *(730 Carroll St. From downtown, travel south on Broadway or 7th St. to Lafayette. Take bus #40 "Soulard." ☎ 622-4180. Open W-Sa 6am-7pm; hours vary among merchants.)* At the end of 12th St., the **Anheuser-Busch Brewery,** the largest brewery in the world, pumps out 16.5 million 12 oz. servings of beer each day. The 1½hr. tour includes a glimpse of the famous Clydesdales and two beer samples. *(1127 Pestalozzi St. at 12th and Lynch St. Take bus #40 "Broadway" south from downtown. ☎ 557-2333; www.budweisertours.com. Tours June-Aug. M-Sa 9am-5pm, Su 11:30am-5pm; Sept.-May M-Sa 9am-4pm, Su 11:30am-4pm. Wheelchair accessible.)*

The internationally acclaimed 79-acre **Missouri Botanical Garden** thrives north of Tower Grove Park on grounds left by entrepreneur Henry Shaw. The Japanese Garden is guaranteed to soothe the weary traveler. *(4344 Shaw Blvd. From downtown, take I-44 west, or ride MetroLink to "Central West End" and take bus #14 "Garden Express."* ☎ *800-642-8842; www.mobot.org. Open daily 9am-5pm; June-Aug. M until 8pm. $7, seniors $5, under 12 free. Guided tours daily 1pm. Wheelchair accessible.)* Family-friendly **Grant's Farm**, set on land once owned by President Ulysses S. Grant, is now a zoo operated by Anheuser-Busch. The tram-ride tour crosses terrain inhabited by over 1000 free-roaming animals, including elephants, zebras, and more Clydesdales. Arrive early to avoid lines. *(3400 Grant St. Take I-55 west to Reavis Barracks Rd. and turn left onto Gravois.* ☎ *843-1700; www.grantsfarm.com. Open mid-May to Aug. Tu-F 9am-3:30pm, Sa 9am-4pm, Su 9:30am-4pm; Sept.-Oct. W-F 9:30am-2:30pm, Sa-Su 9:30am-3:30pm; Apr. to early May W-F 9am-3pm, Sa 9am-3:30pm, Su 9:30am-3:30pm. Free. Parking $6.)*

FOREST PARK. At almost 1400 acres, **Forest Park** dwarfs its New York City cousin by 500 acres, easily absorbing an array of museums and recreational areas amid its pastoral lawns and serene canals. *(Take MetroLink to Forest Park and catch the Shuttle Bug. All Forest Park sites are wheelchair accessible.)* Take a break from the heat and step into the chilly penguin habitat at the **St. Louis Zoo**, where the birds will obligingly splash you if you get close enough. *(*☎ *781-0900; www.stlzoo.com. Open daily late May to early Sept. 8am-7pm; Sept.-May 9am-5pm. Free.)* Atop **Art Hill**, the palatial **St. Louis Art Museum** conjures up images of Versailles and commands an impressive view of the park. The museum contains masterpieces of Asian, Renaissance, and American art, as well as impressive Impressionist exhibit. *(*☎ *721-0072; www.slam.org. Open Tu-Th and Sa-Su 10am-5pm, F 10am-9pm. Main museum free; special exhibits usually $10, seniors and students $8, ages 6-12 $6; F free. Free tours Tu-Su 2pm.)* The **Missouri History Museum** focuses on the city's cultural heritage and has a full-scale replica of Lindbergh's Spirit of St. Louis. *(At Lindell and DeBaliviere.* ☎ *454-3150; www.mohistory.org. Open June-Aug. M-Th 10am-8pm, F-Su 10am-6pm; Sept.-May M and W-Su 10am-6pm, Tu 10am-8pm. Main museum free. Special exhibits usually $5, seniors and students $4, Tu 4-8pm free.)* The family-oriented **St. Louis Science Center** features an Omnimax theater, a planetarium, and over 700 interactive exhibits. Build your own arch or gape at the life-size *T. rex* model. *(5050 Oakland Ave.* ☎ *289-4444; www.slcs.org. Main museum free. Omnimax $7, seniors and ages 2-12 $6. Planetarium $6/$5. Open June-Aug. M-Th and Sa 9:30am-5:30pm, F 9:30am-9:30pm, Su 11:30am-5:30pm; Sept.-May M-Th and Sa 9:30am-4:30pm, F 9:30am-9:30pm, Su 11:30am-4:30pm.)*

CENTRAL WEST END. From Forest Park, head a few blocks east to gawk at the Tudor homes of the **Central West End**. The vast **Cathedral Basilica of St. Louis** features intricate ceilings and glittering tile mosaics depicting Missouri church history. *(4431 Lindell Blvd. MetroLink stop "Central West End" or bus #93 "Lindell" from downtown.* ☎ *533-0544. Open daily summer 7am-7pm; low-season 7am-dusk. Tours M-F 10am-3pm. Mass Su afternoon. Call to confirm hours. Wheelchair accessible.)* Northwest of the Central West End, the sidewalks of the **Loop** are studded with gold stars on the **St. Louis Walk of Fame**, which features local luminaries from Maya Angelou to Ike and Tina Turner. *(6504 Delmar Blvd.* ☎ *727-7827; www.stlouiswalkoffame.org.)*

OTHER SIGHTS. The slightly surreal ◙**City Museum** is constructed from salvaged parts of area buildings and is one of the few places in town where "all ages" means big people can join in the fun. The world's coolest playground includes "enchanted caves," a train ride, the world's largest pair of underwear, and a gigantic outdoor jungle gym known as "Monstrocity." Made entirely of recycled parts, this playscape includes two planes, a firetruck, a ferris wheel, sky tunnels, and a gothic tower with gargoyles. Geared toward the young but accessible and entertaining to all ages, the "Monstrocity" is an amalgamation of all things weird and wonderful. *(701 N. 15th St., downtown.* ☎ *231-2489; www.citymuseum.org. Open June-Aug. M-Th 9am-5pm, F 9am-1am, Sa 10am-1am, Su 11am-5pm; Sept.-May W-Th 9am-5pm, F 9am-1am, Sa 10am-1am, Su 11am-5pm. Main museum*

$7.50, museum and "Monstrocity" $10, museum and caves $12.50. Wheelchair accessible.) Monster truck enthusiasts pay homage to **Bigfoot,** the "Original Monster Truck," whose descendants live near the airport. *(6311 N. Lindbergh St.* ☎ *731-2822; www.bigfoot4x4.com. Open M-F 9am-5pm, Sa 9am-3pm. Free.)*

🎵 ENTERTAINMENT

Powell Hall, 718 N. Grand Blvd., holds the renowned **St. Louis Symphony Orchestra** in acoustic and visual splendor. (☎ 534-1700. Performances late Sept. to early May Th-Sa 8pm, Su 3pm. Box office open late May to mid-Aug. M-F 9am-5pm; mid-Aug. to late May M-Sa 9am-5pm; and before performances. Tickets $12-99, students half-price for most shows.)

St. Louis offers theatergoers many choices. The outdoor **Municipal Opera,** known as the "Muny," presents hit musicals on summer nights in Forest Park. (☎ 361-1900; www.muny.com. Box office open June to mid-Aug. M-F 9am-5pm, Sa 9am-1pm. Tickets $8-54.) Productions are also regularly staged by the **St. Louis Black Repertory,** 634 N. Grand Blvd., Ste. 10F (☎ 534-3807; tickets $10-37), and by the **Repertory Theatre of St. Louis,** 130 Edgar Rd. (☎ 968-4925). The **Fox Theatre,** 527 N. Grand Blvd., was originally a 1930s movie palace, but now hosts Broadway shows, classic films, and Las Vegas, country, and rock stars. (☎ 534-1111. Open M-Sa 10am-6pm, Su noon-4pm. Tours Tu, Th, Sa 10:30am. Tu $5, Th and Sa $8; under 12 $3.) **Metrotix** has tickets to most area events. (☎ 534-1111. Open daily 9am-9pm.)

St. Louis ordinances permit gambling on the river for those over 21. The **President Casino on the Admiral** floats below the Arch on the Missouri side. (☎ 622-1111 or 800-772-3647; www.presidentcasino.com. Open M-Th 8am-4am, F-Su 24hr. Entry tax $2.) On the Illinois side, the **Casino Queen** claims "the loosest slots in town." (☎ 618-874-5000 or 800-777-0777; www.casinoqueen.com. Open daily 9am-7am.) Parking for both is free, and both are wheelchair accessible. **Six Flags St. Louis,** 30min. southwest of St. Louis on I-44 at Exit 261, reigns supreme in the kingdom of amusement parks. "Xcalibur" catapults thrill-seekers 113 ft. into the air while spinning in circles, and the vaunted "Boss" wooden roller coaster features a 570° helix. (☎ 636-938-4800. Hours vary by season. $39, seniors and under 48 in. $24.) The **St. Louis Cardinals** play ball at **Busch Stadium.** (☎ 421-2400. Tickets $9-59.) The **Rams,** Super Bowl XXXIV champions, take to the field at the **Edward Jones Dome.** (☎ 425-8830. Tickets $42-51.) The **Blues** hockey team slices ice at the **Savvis Center** at 14th St. and Clark Ave. (☎ 622-2500. Tickets from $15.)

◾ NIGHTLIFE

Music rules the night in St. Louis. The *Riverfront Times* (free at many bars and clubs) and the *Get Out* section of the *Post-Dispatch* list weekly entertainment. *St. Louis Magazine*, published annually, lists seasonal events. For beer and live music, often without a cover charge, St. Louis offers **Laclede's Landing**, a collection of restaurants, bars, and dance clubs housed in 19th-century industrial buildings north of the Arch on the riverfront. In the summer, bars take turns sponsoring "block parties" with food, drink, music, and dancing in the streets. (☎241-5875. 21+. Generally open 9pm-3am, with some places open for lunch and dinner.) Other nightlife hot spots include the bohemian **Loop** along Delmar Blvd., **Union Station** and its environs, and the less touristy **Soulard** district.

◾ **Pin-Up Bowl,** 6191 Delmar Blvd. (☎727-5555; www.pinupbowl.com), allows Loop-goers to knock down pins while knocking back a cocktail ($7-8). Eight lanes available by the game ($3.50-5) or by the hour ($30-50). Shoes $3. 21+ after 9pm. Open M-Th 3pm-3am, F-Su noon-3am.

Mississippi Nights, 914 N. 1st St. (☎421-3853), at Laclede's Landing. St. Louis's favorite place for music since 1979 hosts the best national acts of all genres. Call ahead for performance schedule and cover info. Open F-Sa 7pm-midnight.

The Pageant, 6161 Delmar Blvd. (☎726-6161; www.thepageant.com). Patrons sometimes camp out overnight for a spot in this fantastic 33,000 sq. ft. nightclub, which hosts national acts like Alice Cooper, Reel Big Fish, and Dave Chappelle. Age restrictions vary. Call for ticket and cover prices. Doors usually open 7pm. The swanky Halo Bar (☎726-1414) is open daily 5pm-3am.

Absolutli Goosed, 3196 S. Grand (☎772-0400), is the city's premier martini bar, serving up over 120 double-shot variations on the classic cocktail. Open W-Th 4pm-midnight, F 4pm-1am, Sa 5pm-1am, Su noon-11pm.

The Big Bang, 807 N. 2nd St. (☎241-2264), at Laclede's Landing. Dueling pianists lead the crowd in an all-request rock 'n' roll sing-along show, and if you hang around long enough the staff will stand on the bar and sing. Beer from $3.25. Cover Tu-Th $3, F-Sa $6. Open Tu-Th 7pm-3am, F-Sa 5pm-3am.

Clementine's, 2001 Menard St. (☎664-7869), in Soulard, has a crowded restaurant and St. Louis's oldest gay bar (established in 1978). Open M-Sa 10am-1:30am, Su 11am-midnight.

Graffiti Global Grill & Bar, 313 N. Euclid (☎361-1701), in the Central West End, hosts a terrific happy hour M-F 4-7pm, serving shrimp, oysters, and sushi tacos ($1 each) with sangria and margaritas ($3). Patrons can also leave messages on the bar's blackboard-like columns. Chalk provided. Open M-Su 11am-1am.

HANNIBAL   ☎573

Mark Twain's boyhood home is anchored on the Mississippi River, 100 mi. west of Springfield and 100 mi. northwest of St. Louis. Founded in 1819, Hannibal slept in obscurity until Twain used it as the setting of *The Adventures of Tom Sawyer*. Tourists now flock to this small, charming town to imagine Tom, Huck, and Becky romping around its old-fashioned streets and spooky caves. Despite its tourist traps, Hannibal is an irresistible stop for a traveler with a Mark Twain fixation.

With massive renovations scheduled for completion in spring 2005, the **Mark Twain Boyhood Home and Museum,** 208 Hill St., will feature an interpretive center with interactive exhibits commemorating the events of the witty wordsmith's life, updated displays in the Clemens' residence, as well as a newly-constructed replica of Huck Finn's house. The museum also includes the **Pilaster House/Grant's Drug Store** and **Clemens Law Office,** where a young Twain crawled into bed one night, only to awake to the sight of a murdered man lying on the floor next to him. Farther down Main St., the

New Mark Twain Museum takes visitors through the author's novels. Upstairs, the highlight of the museum is the collection of Norman Rockwell illustrations entitled *Tom and Huck*. (☎221-9010. Open June-Aug. daily 8am-6pm; Sept.-Oct. and Apr. daily 9am-5pm; Nov.-Feb. M-Sa 10am-4pm, Su noon-4pm; Mar. M-Sa 9am-4pm, Su noon-4pm; May daily 8am-5pm. Single ticket covers all sites; $6, ages 6-12 $3.) On the riverfront landing, the **Mark Twain Riverboat** steams down the Mississippi for a 1hr. sightseeing cruise that is part history, part folklore, and part advertisement for the land attractions. (☎221-3222. Late May to early Sept. 3 per day; May and Sept.-Oct. 1 per day. $10, ages 5-12 $7; dinner cruises 6:30pm $29/$20.) The **Mark Twain Cave,** 1 mi. south of Hannibal on Rte. 79, winds through the complex series of caverns Twain explored as a boy. A 1hr. tour guides visitors to the author's favorite spots and details the myths and legends associated with the cave. Graffiti from as early as the 1830s, including Jesse James's signature, still marks the walls. The cave tour includes the only section of the cave christened by Twain: **Aladdin's Castle,** the picturesque spot where Tom and Becky were "married." (☎221-1656. Open June-Aug. daily 8am-8pm; Apr.-May and Sept.-Oct. daily 9am-6pm; Nov.-Mar. M-F 10am-4pm, Sa-Su 9am-4pm. 1hr. tour $12, ages 5-12 $6.) From June to August, nearby **Cameron Cave,** Hwy. 79 S, provides a slightly longer and far spookier lantern tour. (Tickets available at Mark Twain Cave. $14, ages 5-12 $7. Discount tickets available for both caves.) Every 4th of July weekend, 100,000 fans converge on Hannibal for the fence-painting, frog-jumping fun of the **Tom Sawyer Days** festival (☎221-2477).

Hannibal's historic district is dotted with beautiful 19th-century homes, one of which houses ▧**The Gilded Age Bed & Breakfast ❸,** 215 N. 6th St., an 1871 mansion built by one of Twain's close friends and the site where an exorcism was once performed. A restored cupola offers riverfront views, but the home isn't haunted—at least not anymore. (☎248-1218; www.thegildedage.net. Spacious rooms $60-98. Call ahead for reservations.) As befits a state bordering the Deep South, Hannibal is also home to some tasty barbecue establishments. Even though catfish ($10) is the specialty at ▧**Bubba's ❷,** 101 Church St. on the riverfront, a former warehouse that dishes out good food and Southern hospitality, the pit-smoked barbecue pork and beef sandwiches (from $4.50) are not to be missed. (☎221-5552. M-Sa 11am-9pm, Su 11am-3pm.) Cool down with a hand-dipped ice-cream cone (from $1.50) at the 100-year-old **Main Street Soda Fountain ❶,** 207 S. Main St., which still sells old-fashioned phosphates. (☎248-1295. Open Tu-Su 11am-around 7pm.)

The **Hannibal Convention and Visitors Bureau,** 505 N. 3rd St., offers free local calls and information. (☎221-2477; www.visithannibal.com. Open M-F 8am-5pm, Sa 9am-6pm, Su 9am-5pm.) **Post Office:** 801 Broadway. (☎221-0957. Open M-F 8:30am-5pm, Sa 8:30am-noon.) **Postal Code:** 63401. **Area Code:** 573.

INDEPENDENCE   ☎ 816

Independence is a city defined by its heritage as an American starting point, both for the thousands of pioneers venturing westward on the frontier trails in the 1800s, and for President Harry S Truman's political career. Truman was known in town for his brisk walks; here, historic sites are marked by large blue signs with a white, cane-in-hand silhouette of the strolling 33rd president. Grab a map of the 43-stop **Truman Historic Walking Trail** at the visitors center. Most attractions lie in or near **Independence Square,** which is lined with shops and restaurants. In the middle of the square, the **Jackson County Courthouse** houses the **Harry S Truman Office and Courtroom,** 112 W. Lexington St., where Truman began his political life as a county judge. (☎252-7454. Open M-F 9am-3:30pm. Tours and presentations M-F 9am-3:30pm. $2, seniors and children 5-13 $1.) The painstakingly preserved interior of the Victorian **Harry S Truman Home,** 219 N. Delaware St., is furnished with artifacts from the Trumans' elegant but unpretentious lifestyle. (☎254-9929. Purchase tickets at the visitors center, 5 blocks west in the square on Truman Rd. Tours daily Tu-Su 8:30am-5pm; Sept.-May closed M. $3, 16 and under free.) The candid **Truman Presidential Museum and Library,** 500 W. Hwy. 24, recounts Truman's life and administration, following the chain of difficult decisions that constituted Truman's presidency, often annotating exhibits of Truman's correspondences or actual pages from his diary. The remains of the president and his wife are interred in the courtyard. (☎ 800-833-1225. Open M-W and F-Sa 9am-5pm, Th 9am-9pm, Su noon-5pm. $7, seniors $5, ages 6-10 $3.) The **National Frontier Trails, Center** 318 W. Pacific St., follows the routes taken by wagon trains embarking from Independence in the 19th century and has interactive exhibits that simulate the critical decisions facing pioneers. (☎ 325-7575; www.frontiertrailscenter.org. Open M-Sa 9am-4:30pm, Su 12:30-4:30pm. $4, seniors $3.50, students 6-17 $2.50, under 5 free.)

Chain motels congregate around the intersection of I-70 and Noland Rd. A good alternative is the ▨**Serendipity Bed and Breakfast ❷,** 116 S. Pleasant St., a three-story 1887 building replete with Victorian decor which offers a full breakfast, historic home tours, and pickup from the train station in a 1928 Buick, weather and time permitting. (☎ 833-4719 or 800-203-4299. Singles $45-70; doubles $80-85.) Of the chain motels, the **American Inn ❷,** 4141 S. Noland Rd., stands out both for its gaudy red, white, and blue exterior and its moderate price. (☎ 373-8300. Singles $40-45; doubles $49-54.) Most cheap eats in Independence come fast and fried, though a few cafes around Independence Sq. are generally open for lunch. Harry Truman held his first job at the **Clinton's Soda Fountain & Coffee Shop ❶,** 100 W. Maple St., which still serves old-fashioned phosphate sodas, ice cream, hot dogs, and sandwiches for around $2.50-3.50. (☎ 833-2046. Open M-F 8:30am-6pm, Sa 10am-6pm.) For hearty, authentic German fare, head to **The Rheinland Restaurant ❸,** 208 N. Main St. While dinner can be pricey, lunch features sandwiches for $6.25-8.50. (☎ 461-5383. Open Tu-Sa 11am-9pm, Su-M 11am-2:30pm.) **Ophelia's ❹,** 201 N. Main St., serves contemporary American cuisine in a classy setting. (☎ 461-4525. Open daily 11am-2:30pm, Tu-Th also 5:30pm-9pm, F-Sa also 5:30-10pm.)

Independence is 10 mi. east of downtown Kansas City, bound by Hwy. 24 and I-70. Noland Rd. is the town's main drag, running north-south; most attractions lie on the western side of Noland Rd. Well-placed signs direct travelers to sights. Free parking is abundant throughout town. The unmanned **Amtrak** station at 600 S. Grand Ave. goes to: Jefferson City (2½-3hr., 2 per day, $19); Kansas City (30min., 2 per day, $7); St. Louis (5½hr., 2 per day, $25). **Kansas City Metro** transports people within Independence for $1.10, with six routes that all start or stop in Independence Sq., and run 5:30am-6pm. Bus #24 runs between Kansas City and Independence Sq. for $1.20. **Visitors Center: Harry S. Truman National Historic Site Visitor Center** houses Truman and Independence information. (☎ 816-254-9929; www.visitindependence.com. Open daily 8:30am-5pm.) **Postal Code:** 64050. **Area Code:** 816.

KANSAS CITY   ☎ 816

With more miles of boulevard than Paris and more working fountains than Rome, Kansas City looks and acts more European than one might expect from the "Barbecue Capital of the World." Nonetheless, it still maintains its big bad blues-and-jazz reputation in a city spanning two states: the highly suburbanized town in Kansas (KCKS) and the quicker-paced commercial metropolis in Missouri (KCMO).

▣ TRANSPORTATION

Airport: Kansas City International (☎ 243-5237; www.flykci.com), 18 mi. northwest of KC off I-29. Take bus #129. **KCI Shuttle** (☎ 243-5000 or 800-243-6383) serves downtown, Westport, Crown Center, and Plaza in KCMO and Overland Park, Mission, and Lenexa in KCKS. Daily every 30min. 4:30am-midnight. $14. Taxi to downtown $42-46.

Trains: Amtrak, 30 W. Pershing Rd. (☎ 421-3622), in the newly renovated Union Station. Take bus #27. Open daily 6:30am-midnight. To **Chicago** (7-12hr., 2 per day, $50-100) and **St. Louis** (5-6hr., 2 per day, $25-58).

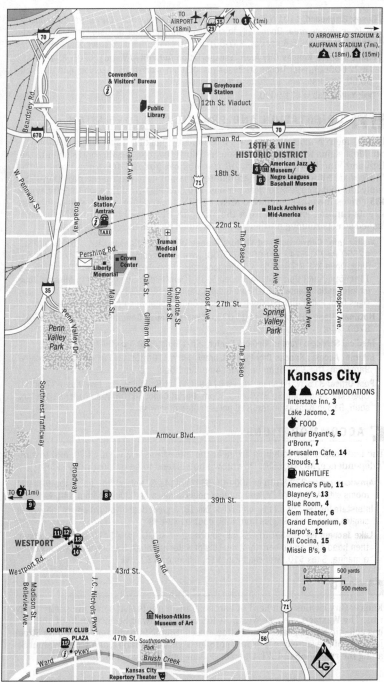

Kansas City

🏠🏠 ACCOMMODATIONS

Interstate Inn, **3**
Lake Jacomo, **2**

🍎 FOOD

Arthur Bryant's, **5**
d'Bronx, **7**
Jerusalem Cafe, **14**
Strouds, **1**

🍺 NIGHTLIFE

America's Pub, **11**
Blayney's, **13**
Blue Room, **4**
Gem Theater, **6**
Grand Emporium, **8**
Harpo's, **12**
Mi Cocina, **15**
Missie B's, **9**

Buses: Greyhound, 1101 N. Troost (☎221-2835). Take bus #25. *Stay alert—the terminal is in an unsafe area.* Open daily in summer 24hr.; in winter 5:30am-midnight. To **Chicago** (10-12½hr., 5-6 per day, $47-55) and **St. Louis** (4-5hr., 3-5 per day, $29-33).

Public Transit: Kansas City Area Transportation Authority (Metro), 1200 E. 18th St. (☎221-0660), near Troost St. Buses run 4:30am-midnight. $1, seniors and disabled $0.50; free transfers. $1.20 to Independence, MO.

Taxi: Yellow Cab ☎471-5000.

⚑ 🛈 ORIENTATION AND PRACTICAL INFORMATION

The KC metropolitan area sprawls interminably, making travel difficult without a car. Most sights worth visiting lie south of downtown on the Missouri side or in the 18th and Vine Historic District. *All listings are for KCMO, unless otherwise indicated.* Although parking around town is not easy during the day, there are many lots that charge $5 or less per day. **I-70** cuts east-west through the city, and **I-435** circles the two-state metro area. KCMO is laid out on a grid with numbered streets running east-west from the Missouri River well out into suburbs, and named streets running north-south. **Main Street** divides the city east-west.

Visitor Info: Convention and Visitors Bureau of Greater Kansas City, 1100 Main St., #2550 (☎221-5242 or 800-767-7700; www.visitkc.com), 25th fl. of City Center Sq. Bldg. Open M-F 8:30am-5pm. Other locations in the Plaza (open M-Sa 10am-6pm, Su 11am-5pm) and Union Station (open M-Sa 10am-10pm, Su noon-5pm). **Missouri Tourist Information Center,** 4010 Blue Ridge Cutoff (☎889-3330 or 800-877-1234); follow signs from Exit 9 off I-70. Open daily 8am-5pm, except when the Chiefs are at home.

Hotlines: Rape Crisis Line, ☎531-0233. **Synergy House General Crisis Hotline,** ☎741-8700. 24hr.

Medical Services: Truman Medical Center, 2301 Holmes St. (☎404-1000).

Internet Access: Kansas City Public Library, 14 W. 10th St. (☎701-3400). Open M-W 9am-9pm, Th-F 9am-6pm, Sa 10am-4pm, Su 1-5pm.

Post Office: 315 W. Pershing Rd. (☎374-9101), at Broadway St.; take bus #27 or 51. Open M-F 8am-8pm, Sa 8:30am-3:30pm. **Postal Code:** 64108. **Area Code:** 816 in Missouri, 913 in Kansas; in text 816 unless noted otherwise.

▐ ACCOMMODATIONS

The least expensive lodgings are near the interstates, especially I-70, and toward Independence, MO (p. 689). Downtown hotels tend to be on the pricey side.

American Inn (☎373-8300 or 800-905-6343), 4141 S. Noland Rd., has large, pleasant rooms with A/C, cable TV, and outdoor pools. Singles and doubles from $40. ❷

Interstate Inn (☎229-6311), off I-70 at Exit 18. A great deal if you get one of the walk-in singles or doubles. Singles from $29; doubles $34. ❷

Lake Jacomo (☎795-8200), 22 mi. southeast of KCMO. Take I-470 south to Colbern, then head east on Colbern for 2 mi. Lots of water activities, 33 forested campsites, and a marina. Sites $10, with electricity $15, full hookup $22. ❶

▐ FOOD

Kansas City rustles up a herd of barbecue restaurants that serve unusually tangy ribs. The **Westport** area, at Westport Rd. and Broadway St. just south of 40th St., has eclectic menus, cafes, and coffeehouses. Ethnic fare clusters along **39th Street** just east of the state line. For fresh produce, visit **City Market,** at 5th and Walnut St. along the river. (☎842-1271. Open Su-F 9am-4pm, Sa 6am-4pm.)

▓ **Arthur Bryant's,** 1727 Brooklyn Ave. (☎231-1123). Take the Brooklyn Exit off I-70 or bus #110 from downtown. The grand-daddy of KC barbecue and a perennial candidate for best barbecue in the country. Bryant's "sandwiches" are a carnivore's delight—wimpy triangles of bread drown in pork perfection ($9). Open M-Th 10am-9:30pm, F-Sa 10am-10pm, Su 11am-8pm. ❷

▓ **d'Bronx,** 3904 Bell St. (☎531-0550), on the 39th St. restaurant row. A New York deli transplanted to Middle America, d'Bronx has over 35 kinds of subs (half sub $4-6, whole $8-12) and powdered sugar brownies ($1.50). Open M-W 10:30am-9pm, Th 10:30am-10pm, F-Sa 10:30am-11pm. ❷

Strouds, 1015 E. 85th St. (☎333-2132), at Troost Ave., 2 mi. north of the Holmes Exit off I-435. Belt-bustin' fried chicken, steak, and catfish served with homemade cinnamon rolls. Open M-Th 4-10pm, F 11am-11pm, Sa 2-11pm, Su 11am-10pm. ❸

Jerusalem Cafe, 431 Westport Rd. (☎756-2770; www.jerusalembakery.com). A Middle Eastern restaurant that skewers the usual kebab but is also a great refuge for vegetarians in a bovine-centric city. Sandwiches with rice and salad $5-7. Try the popular falafel for $5. Open M-Sa 11am-10pm, Su noon-8pm. ❷

◉ SIGHTS

18TH AND VINE. Jazz once flourished in the recently designated **18th and Vine Historic District.** The **American Jazz Museum** brings back the era with classy displays, music listening stations, neon dance-hall signs, and everything from Ella Fitzgerald's eyeglasses to Louis Armstrong's lip salve. In the same building, the **Negro Leagues Baseball Museum** recalls the American pastime's segregated era with photographs, interactive exhibits, and bittersweet nostalgia. At the end of the exhibits, visitors can take the field with 12 bronze statues of NLB players and hall-of-famers. *(1616 E. 18th St. Take bus #108 "Indiana." Jazz museum: ☎474-8463; www.americanjazzmuseum.com. Baseball museum: ☎221-1920; www.nlbm.com. Both open Tu-Sa 9am-6pm, Su noon-6pm. Each museum $6, under 12 $2.50; both museums $8/$4.)* Nearby, the **Black Archives of Mid-America** holds a large collection of paintings and sculpture by African-American artists and focuses on local black history. *(2033 Vine St. ☎483-1300; www.blackarchives.org. Open M-F 9am-4:30pm. Tours 10am. $2, under 17 $0.50.)*

OTHER MUSEUMS. The **Nelson-Atkins Museum of Art** contains one of the best East Asian art collections in the world, and a sculpture park with 13 pieces by Henry Moore. The museum is under renovation; call ahead for exhibit closings. *(4525 Oak St., 3 blocks northeast of Country Club Plaza. Take bus #147, 155, 156, or 157. ☎561-4000; www.nelson-atkins.org. Open Tu-Th 10am-4pm, F 10am-9pm, Sa 10am-5pm, Su noon-5pm. Live jazz in the museum's Rozzelle Court Restaurant F 5:30-8:30pm. Free walking tours Sa 11am-2pm, Su 1:30-3pm. Admission is free during construction, except for special exhibits.)* When the *Arabia* sank in the Missouri River, it was buried in the silt-filled banks. When the river shifted over a century later, excavations yielded bottles of bourbon, plates, stationery, and other treasures now displayed at the **Arabia Steamboat Museum.** *(400 Grand Blvd. ☎471-1856; www.1856.com. Open M-Sa 10am-6pm, Su noon-5pm. $9.75, seniors $9.25, ages 4-12 $4.75.)*

THE PLAZA AND CROWN CENTER. A few blocks to the west of the Nelson-Atkins Museum, at 47th St. and Southwest Trafficway, **Country Club Plaza,** known as "the Plaza," is the oldest and perhaps most picturesque shopping center in the US. Modeled after buildings in Seville, Spain, the Plaza boasts fountains, sculptures, hand-painted tiles, grinning gargoyles, and latte-sipping yuppies. *(☎753-0100. Take bus #39, 51, 56, 57, or 155. Free outdoor concerts June-Aug. Th 5pm-8pm, F-Sa 2pm-5pm.)* **Crown Center,** headquarters of Hallmark Cards, houses a maze of restaurants and shops and the children's **Coterie Theatre.** In the winter, the **Ice Terrace** is KC's only

GREAT PLAINS

public outdoor ice-skating rink. On the third floor, see how cards and accessories are made at the **Hallmark Visitors Center.** *(2405 Grand Ave., 2 mi. north of the Plaza near Pershing Rd. Take bus #27, 28, 51, 55, 56, 57, 142, 173, or any trolley. Crown Center: ☎274-8444. Coterie: ☎474-6552. $10; children, students, and seniors $8. Ice Terrace: ☎274-8411. Rink open Nov.-Dec. Su-Th 10am-9pm, F-Sa 10am-11pm; Jan.-Mar. daily 10am-9pm. $5, under 13 $4; rentals $1.50. Visitors center: ☎274-3613, recording 274-5672; http://hallmarkvisitorscenter.com. Open Tu-F 9am-5pm, Sa 9:30am-4:30pm. Free.)*

🎵 ENTERTAINMENT

From September to June, the **Kansas City Repertory Theatre,** 4949 Cherry St., stages American classics. (☎235-2700; www.kcrep.org. Box office open M-F 10am-5pm; call for weekend hours. Tickets $10-52, students with ID $6-8, seniors $3 off.) **Quality Hill Playhouse,** 303 W. 10th St., produces off-Broadway plays and revues from September to June. (☎421-1700. Tickets available by phone or at the theater 1hr. before showtime. $23, students and seniors $21.) From late June to mid-July, the **Heart of America Shakespeare Festival** in Southmoreland Park, 47th and Oak St., puts on free shows. (☎531-7728; www.kcshakes.org. Most nights 8pm.) In Shawnee Mission, KS, the **New Theatre Restaurant,** 9229 Foster St., stages dinner theater productions of classic comedies and romances and attracts nationally recognized actors. Take Metcalf Ave. and turn into the Regency Park Center between 91st and 95th St. (☎913-649-7469; www.newtheatre.com. Box office open M-Sa 9am-6pm, Su 11am-3pm. Tickets $31-45, buffet meal included.)

Sports fans stampede to **Arrowhead Stadium,** at I-70 and Blue Ridge Cutoff, home to football's **Chiefs** (☎920-9400 or 800-676-5488; tickets $59-80) and soccer's **Wizards** (☎920-9300; tickets $13-22). Next door, the water-fountained **Kauffman Stadium** houses baseball's **Royals.** (☎921-8000 or 800-676-9257. Tickets $5-22. A stadium express bus runs from downtown and Country Club Plaza on game days.)

🎤 NIGHTLIFE

In the 1920s, jazz musician Count Basie and his "Kansas City Sound" reigned at the River City bars. Twenty years later, saxophonist Charlie "Bird" Parker spread his wings and soared, asserting Kansas City's prominence as a tried-and-true jazz music roost. KC's modern-day jazz hot spots draw a diverse crowd of both locals and tourists of all ages. Look for current weekly entertainment in *The Pitch*, free and widely available. The restored **Gem Theater,** 1615 E. 18th St., stages old-time blues and jazz. (☎474-6262. Tickets and info in the American Jazz Museum across the street.) Across the street, the **Blue Room,** 1600 E. 18th St., heats up four nights a week with some of the smoothest acts in town. (☎474-2929. Cover F-Sa from $5. Bar open M and Th 5-11pm, F 5pm-1am, Sa 7pm-1am.) The **Grand Emporium,** 3832 Main St., twice voted the best blues club in the US, has live music five nights a week. (☎531-1504. Cover and hours vary depending on act; call for info.)

Blayney's, 415 Westport Rd. (☎561-3747). An earthy blues joint where the bar is festooned with bras and covered in stickers with the obvious puns off the owner's name (it's short for Richard). Live music every night, and back patio open Sa-Su. Cover $2-6. Open Tu-Th 8pm-3am, F 6pm-3am, Sa 5pm-3am.

America's Pub, 510 Westport Rd. (☎531-1313). A lively crowd lights up this dark, popular Westport spot. While the dance floor is usually packed, the elevated barstools provide a chance to relax. Th $1 drinks. Cover $6. Open W-Sa 8pm-3am.

Harpo's, 4109 Pennsylvania Ave. (☎753-3434). The keystone of Westport's young nightlife. The live music and $0.25 beer on Tu attract collegiates and co-eds ready to party. Cover Tu and Sa $2-4. Open daily 11am-3am.

Mi Cocina, 620 W. 48th St. (☎960-6426). A place to see and be seen in Kansas City. Latin music accompanies couture-clad fashionistas. Forgo the pricey Mexican food and swill their infamous margaritas ($8.50). Open Su-W 11am-10pm, Th-Sa 11am-3am.

Missie B's, 805 W. 39th St. (☎561-0625; www.missiebs.com). A large, hopping two-story gay bar with DJs, dance floors, and drag shows M, W, F-Sa 10pm-2am. Cover Su-Th $1, F $3, Sa $5. Open daily noon-3am.

BRANSON ☎417

Back in 1967, the Presley family had no idea the impact the tiny theater they opened on **West Route 76** would have. Now, over 30 years later, millions of tourists clog Branson's strip to visit the "live music show capital of the world." Billboards, motels, and giant showplaces call the masses to embrace all things plastic, franchised, and "wholesome." Branson boasts over 30 indoor theaters and a few outdoor ones as well, housing family variety shows, magic acts, comedians, plays, and music. Box office prices for most shows run $20-50, depending on who's playing. Never pay full price for a show or attraction in Branson—coupon books, including the *Sunny Day Guide* and the *Best Read Guide*, offer dozens of discounts.

To see a live battle between the North and the South, head to Dolly Parton's **Dixie Stampede,** 1525 W. Hwy. 76, where "a friendly competition" between Yankees and Rebs is staged on the backs of ostriches, horses, and other animals that lend themselves to trick riding. Ticket prices include a four-course "feast." (☎800-520-5101. Shows daily 5:30, also 8pm in Aug. and some weekends. $38, ages 4-11 $20. AAA discounts available.) Big-name country acts, such as Loretta Lynn and Billy Ray Cyrus, play the **Grand Palace,** 2700 W. Rte. 76. (☎334-7263 or 800-572-5223. Tickets vary by performance; call ahead for more info.) One of Branson's more unique shows is **The Shepherd of the Hills,** 5586 Rte. 76 W, an outdoor drama/dinner that tells the story of a preacher stranded in the Ozark mountains and his growing relationship with the people of the area. (☎334-4191 or 800-653-6288. Shows May Tu-W and F-Sa, June-Aug. M-Sa. Tickets $28, seniors $26, ages 4-16 $13.)

Motels along Rte. 76 generally start around $25, but prices often increase from July to September. Less tacky motels line Rte. 265, 4 mi. west of the strip, and Gretna Rd. at the west end of the strip. **Budget Inn ❶,** 325 N. Gretna Rd., has slightly dim but spacious rooms close to the action. (☎334-0292. A/C, free local calls, cable TV, and pool access. Rooms $29-48.) For a more colorful option, **JR's Motor Inn ❷,** 1944 W. 76 Country Blvd., has an on-site coffeeshop, free continental breakfast, and pool. (☎800-837-8531. Rates from $48-59.) For affordable eats, head downtown to the **Branson Cafe ❶,** 120 Main St. Burger and fries are only $4.45, and breakfast and lunch will set you back about $6. (☎334-3021. Open M-Sa 6am-8:00pm, Su 7am-3pm.) **Uncle Joe's Barbeque ❷,** 2819 W. Rte. 76, next to **Uncle Joe's Jazz,** serves barbecue sandwiches for $6 and tenderloin for $7. (☎334-4548. Jazz nightly in lounge. Open M-Su 11am-10pm. Lounge open Tu-Sa 5pm-1am.)

Branson is impossible without a car, but infuriating with one. Especially on weekends, endless traffic jams clog Hwy. 76, the two-lane road that runs by all the attractions. Avoid peak tourist times, like Saturday nights. **Gray Line Shuttle,** (☎339-2550), picks up from the Springfield airport and drops off in Branson area hotels. (Call to reserve. $36, 2-person minimum.) Branson's low-season runs from January to March, when many attractions close. Beware of fake "tourist information centers"—they are trying to sell you something. The real info center is the **Branson Chamber of Commerce and Convention and Visitors Bureau Welcome Center,** 269 Rte. 248, west of the Rte. 248/65 junction. (☎800-961-1221; www.explorebranson.com. Open M-Sa 8am-5pm, Su 10am-4pm; in summer M-Sa 8am-6pm.) **Area Code:** 417.

GREAT PLAINS

OKLAHOMA

Oklahoma is a state that remembers its distinctive, though not always glamorous, history. Originally dubbed "Indian Territory," Oklahoma was the designated relocation area for the "Five Civilized Tribes" traveling the Trail of Tears. In 1889, the tribes were forced onto reservations even farther west when Oklahoma was opened up to white settlers known as Sooners. Today, the state celebrates its native heritage through museums, artwork, and cultural events. Also a state rich in African-American heritage, Oklahoma played a substantial role in the Civil War. Present-day Oklahoma City mourns its losses from the second-worst terrorist attack on American soil and honors the victims with a striking national memorial.

◪ PRACTICAL INFORMATION

Capital: Oklahoma City.

Visitor Info: Oklahoma Tourism and Recreation Department, 15 N. Robinson Ave., #801, Oklahoma City 73152 (☎521-2406 or 800-652-6552; www.travelok.com), in the Concord Bldg. at Sheridan St. Open M-F 8am-5pm.

Postal Abbreviation: OK. **Sales Tax:** 4.5%. **Tolls:** Oklahoma is fond of toll booths, so keep a wad of bills (and a roll of coins for unattended booths) handy.

TULSA ☎918

Tulsa was first settled by Creek Native Americans arriving on the Trail of Tears, and its location on the banks of the Arkansas River made it a logical trading outpost. Contemporary Tulsa's Art Deco skyscrapers, French villas, Georgian mansions, and substantial Native American population reflect its varied heritage. Rough-riding motorcyclists and slick oilmen, seeking the good life on the Great Plains, have recently joined the city's cultural melange.

◪◪ ORIENTATION AND PRACTICAL INFORMATION. Tulsa is divided neatly into 1 sq. mi. quadrants. Downtown surrounds the intersection of **Main Street** (north-south) and **Admiral Boulevard** (east-west). Numbered streets lie in ascending order parallel to Admiral. Named streets run north-south in alphabetical order; those named after western cities are west of Main St., while eastern cities lie to the east. **Tulsa International Airport** (☎838-5000; www.tulsaairports.com), just northeast of downtown, is accessible by I-244 or U.S. 169. **Greyhound,** 317 S. Detroit Ave. (☎584-4428; open 24hr.), departs to: Dallas (6½-7½hr., 8 per day, $48-56); Oklahoma City (2hr., 4 per day, $18); St. Louis (9½hr., 6 per day, $76-87). **Metropolitan Tulsa Transit Authority,** 510 S. Rockford Ave., runs local buses. (☎582-2100. Call center open M-F 4:30am-9pm, Sa 5:30am-9pm, Su 9am-5pm. Buses operate daily 5am-12:30am. $1.25, seniors and disabled $0.60, under 5 and over 74 free; transfers $0.05.) **Taxi: Yellow Checker Cab** ☎582-6161. **Visitor Info: Tulsa Convention and Visitors Bureau,** Williams Center Tower Two, 2 W. 2nd St., #150. (☎585-1201 or 800-558-3311; www.visittulsa.com. Open M-F 8am-5pm.) **Medical Services: Hillcrest Medical Center,** 1120 S. Utica Ave. (☎579-1000). The **Center for Women's Health** (☎749-4444) is located in Hillcrest. **Internet Access: Tulsa Public Library,** 400 Civic Center, at 4th and Denver. (☎596-7977. Open June-Aug. M-Th 9am-9pm, F-Sa 9am-5pm; Sept.-May. also Su 1-5pm.) **Post Office:** 333 W. 4th St. (☎732-6651. Open M-F 7:30am-5pm.) **Postal Code:** 74103. **Area Code:** 918.

⌐ ACCOMMODATIONS. Decent budget accommodations are scarce downtown. The **Victorian Inn ❷**, 114 E. Skelly Dr., off I-44, offers comfortable rooms that are more motel-style than Victorian, with free local calls, cable TV, fridge, and whirlpool. (☎743-2009. Check-out 11am. Singles $25-38; doubles $42-52.) The best deal in town is the **male-only YMCA ❶**, 515 S. Denver Ave. (☎583-9622. Pool, track, weight rooms, and racquetball courts. Key deposit $20. Rooms $20.) Visitors can also try the budget motels around the junction of **I-44** and **I-244** (Exit 222 off I-44); take bus #17 "Southwest Blvd." **Georgetown Plaza Motel ❶**, 8502 E. 27th St., off I-44 at 31st and Memorial St., rents clean rooms with free local calls and cable TV. (☎622-6616. Singles $28-31; doubles $30-34.) The **Gateway Motor Hotel ❷**, 5600 W. Skelly Dr., at Exit 222C, may have a dated, pea-green decor, but it also has a warm personality, DVD players in some rooms, and, best of all, extremely cheap rates. (☎446-6611. Singles $28-35; doubles $34-37.) The 250-site **Mingo RV Park ❶**, 801 N. Mingo Rd., at I-244 and Mingo Rd., provides laundry and showers in a semi-urban setting. (☎832-8824 or 800-932-8824. Reception 8am-7pm. Sites with hookup $25.)

◖▌◗ FOOD AND NIGHTLIFE. Most downtown restaurants cater to lunching businesspeople, closing at 2pm on weekdays and altogether on weekends. On the 1st fl. of the historic Atlas Life Building, **The Atlas Grill ❶**, 415 S. Boston Ave., prepares a variety of specialty sandwiches ($4.50-6) along with daily blue plate specials. (☎583-3111. Open M-F 11am-2:30pm.) Located in a converted Art Deco movie theater, **The Brook Restaurant ❷**, 3401 S. Peoria, has chicken, burgers, and salads ($6-8), along with a list of signature martinis for $4.50-6.25. (☎748-9977. Open M-Sa 11am-1am, Su 11am-11pm.) For 24hr. eats, try **Mama Lou's Restaurant ❶**, 5688 W. Skelly Dr. All-day breakfasts include the ever-popular #1—2 eggs, 4 bacon strips or 4 sausage links, 2 biscuits, and fruit for $4.35. (☎445-1700.)

The free *Urban Tulsa*, at local restaurants, and *The Spot* in the Friday *Tulsa World* have up-to-date entertainment info. Good bars line an area known as **Brookside**, along the 3000 block of S. Peoria Ave. and 15th St. east of Peoria. At the **Suede Lounge**, 3340 S. Peoria Ave., a martini lounge and champagne bar, imbibe your lip-smacking libation while watching beautiful people dance to live music Tuesday through Friday and canned tunes Saturday nights. (☎744-0896. 21+. Cover up to $5. Open Tu-Sa 7pm-2am.) A true Tulsan sports bar, **Boston's,** 1738 Boston Ave., serves everything from chips and salsa ($3) to chicken fried steak ($8), accompanied by eclectic tunes. On Wednesdays, enjoy "Red Dirt" music, a distinctively Oklahoman sound. (☎583-9520. Cover $5. Open M-Sa 11am-2am.) Across the street, **The Venue,** 1212 E. 18th St., hosts live music of all genres. (☎734-0574; www.tulsavenue.com. Live music Th-Sa. Cover $5-10. Shows generally 8pm-2am.)

◖◉⬗ SIGHTS AND ENTERTAINMENT. Perched atop an Osage foothill 2 mi. northwest of downtown, the **Thomas Gilcrease Museum,** 1400 Gilcrease Museum Rd., houses the world's largest collection of Western American art, as well as 250,000 Native American artifacts. The new **Kravis Discovery Center** downstairs displays 5000 of those artifacts, all indexed and searchable at public computer stations. Take the "Gilcrease" exit off Rte. 412 or bus #114. (☎596-2700 or 888-655-2278; www.gilcrease.org. Open Tu-Su 10am-4pm. Requested donation $3.) The **Philbrook Museum of Art,** 2727 S. Rockford Rd., displays international art alongside artifacts from the oil-rich Oklahoma of the 1920s in a renovated 23-acre Italian Renaissance-style villa. (☎749-7941 or 800-324-7941; www.philbrook.org. Take bus #105 "Peoria." Open Tu-W and F-Su 10am-5pm, Th 10am-8pm. $7.50, students and seniors $5.50, under 13 free.) A 60 ft. tall, solid-bronze pair of praying hands greets visitors at **Oral Roberts University,** 7777 S. Lewis Ave., about 6 mi. south of downtown between Lewis and Harvard Ave.; take bus #870. In 1964, Roberts had a

GREAT PLAINS

dream in which God commanded, "Build me a university," and Tulsa's biggest tourist attraction was born. The **visitors center,** in the Prayer Tower, has free tours. (☎495-6807; www.oru.edu. Open M-Sa 10am-4:30pm, Su 1-4:30pm.)

Tulsa thrives during the **International Mayfest** (☎582-6435) in mid-May. August brings both **Jazz on Greenwood,** which includes ceremonies and concerts at Greenwood Park, 300 N. Greenwood Dr., as well as the **Intertribal Powwow,** at the Tulsa State Fairgrounds Expo Building, which attracts Native Americans and thousands of onlookers for a 3-day festival of food, crafts, and nightly dance contests. (☎744-1113. $5; 4-person family $16, 5-person family $20.)

⟩⟩ DAYTRIP FROM TULSA: TAHLEQUAH. The Cherokee, suffering from the loss of nearly one-quarter of their population along the Trail of Tears, began anew by placing their capital in Tahlequah, 66 mi. southeast of Tulsa on Rte. 51. In the center of town, on Cherokee Sq., stands the old capitol building of the Cherokee Nation, 101 S. Muskogee Ave. (Rte. 51/62/82). Built in 1870, the building, along with other tribal government buildings like the Supreme Court building and the Cherokee National Prison, formed the highest authority in Oklahoma until the state was admitted to the Union in 1907. The **Cherokee Heritage Center,** 4 mi. south of town on Rte. 82, reminds visitors of the injustices perpetrated against Native Americans, and provides a look into their old way of life. In the center's **Ancient Village,** local Cherokees recreate a 16th-century settlement with ongoing demonstrations of skills like bow-making and basket-weaving, and the **Trail of Tears Drama,** a play which tells the saga of a Native American family from before the relocation to modern times. Next door, the well-executed **Cherokee National Museum** presents a wealth of information on the Trail of Tears using artifacts and personal histories. (☎456-6007 or 888-999-6007; www.cherokeeheritage.org. Village and museum open M-Sa 10am-5pm, Su 1-5pm; closed Jan. $8.50, seniors and students $7.50, under 13 $5. 10% AAA discount.) Across from the northeast corner of Cherokee Sq., the **visitors center,** 123 E. Delaware St., offers free maps of the major sites downtown. (☎456-3742 or 800-456-4860. Open M-F 9am-5pm.)

OKLAHOMA CITY ☎405

In the late 1800s, Oklahoma's capital was a major transit point on cattle drives from Texas to the north, and today its stockyards are still packed. Lying along the Santa Fe Railroad, the city was swarmed by over 100,000 homesteaders when Oklahoma was opened to settlement in 1889. The city continues to celebrate westward expansion at one of the nation's largest museums devoted to the American West, but the memory of the 1995 Federal Building bombing remains vivid.

▣⟩ ORIENTATION AND PRACTICAL INFORMATION. Oklahoma City is constructed as a nearly perfect grid. **Santa Fe Avenue** divides the city from east to west, and **Reno Avenue** slices it north to south. Cheap and plentiful parking makes driving the best way to go. **Will Rogers World Airport** (☎680-3200; www.flyokc.com) is on I-44 southwest of downtown, Exit 116B. **Amtrak** has an unattended station at 100 S. E.K. Gaylord Blvd., and rumbles to Fort Worth (4hr., 1 per day, $23-32). To get to the **Greyhound** station, 427 W. Sheridan Ave. (☎235-4083; open 24hr.), at Walker St., take bus #4, 5, 6, 8, or 10. *Be careful at night; the area is unsafe.* Buses run to: Fort Worth (6-8hr., 6 per day, $39-48); Kansas City, MO (6-10hr., 7 per day, $49-84); Tulsa (2hr., 7 per day, $20-23). **Oklahoma Metro Transit** has local bus service. Their office, 300 SW 7th St., distributes schedules. (☎235-7433; www.gometro.org. Buses run M-F 5:30am-7:30pm, Sa 6:30am-5:30pm. $1.25, seniors and ages 6-17 $0.60.)

Look for the **Oklahoma Spirit** trolley ($0.25, ages 60 and up and disabled $0.10) downtown and in Bricktown. **Taxi: Yellow Cab** ☎ 232-6161. The **Oklahoma City Convention and Visitors Bureau**, 189 W. Sheridan Ave., at Robinson St., has city info. (☎ 297-8912 or 800-225-5652; www.okccvb.org. Open M-F 8:30am-5pm.) **Internet Access: Oklahoma City Public Library**, 300 Park Ave. (☎ 231-8650. Open M and W-Th 9am-6pm, Tu 9am-9pm, F-Sa 9am-5pm.) **Post Office:** 305 NW 5th St. (☎ 232-2176. Open M-F 7am-9pm, Sa 8am-5pm.) **Postal Code:** 73102. **Area Code:** 405.

⌂ ACCOMMODATIONS. Ten minutes from downtown, **Flora's B&B ❸**, 2312 NW 46th St., has one old-fashioned room with a private bath. (☎ 840-3157. Double $70.) Other cheap lodging lies along the interstate highways, particularly on I-35 north of the I-44 junction. **The Royal Inn ❷**, 2800 S. I-35, south of the junction with I-40, treats you to modest rooms and free local calls. (☎ 672-0899. Singles $30; doubles $40.) A more scenic option, **Lake Thunderbird State Park ❶** offers campsites near a beautiful lake. Take I-40 east to Choctaw Rd. (Exit 166), go south 10 mi. until the road ends, then make a left and drive another mile. (☎ 360-3572. Showers. Reception M-F 8am-5pm. Sites $8-10, with water and electricity $16-23; huts $45.)

◖▣ FOOD AND NIGHTLIFE. Oklahoma City contains the largest cattle market in the US, and beef tops most menus. Most downtown eateries close in the afternoon after they've served businesspeople. Restaurants with longer hours lie east of town on Sheridan Ave. in Bricktown and north of town along Classen Blvd. and Western Ave. Asian restaurants congregate around the intersection of Classen and NW 23rd St. **Pho 89 Café ❷**, 2800 N. Classen Blvd., #108, has satisfying Vietnamese dishes, including a large selection of beef, pork, and $5 chicken soups and noodles. (☎ 524-2233. Open daily 9am-9pm.) The late Leo's recipes live on at **Leo's Original BBQ ❶**, 3631 N. Kelley St., a hickory-smoking outfit in the northwest reaches of town that also bakes a popular strawberry banana cake for $2.50 per slice. (☎ 424-5367. Beef sandwich and baked potato $4.20. Open M-Sa 11am-9pm.)

OKC nightlife is growing by leaps and bounds—head to Bricktown to get into the thick of it all. **The Bricktown Brewery**, 1 N. Oklahoma St., at Sheridan Ave., brews five beers daily and serves traditional sandwiches and burgers downstairs. (☎ 232-2739. Live music F-Sa 9pm. Upstairs 21+. Cover $5-15 during live music. Open Su-M 11am-10pm, Tu-Th 11am-midnight, F-Sa 11am-2am.) **City Walk**, 70 N. Oklahoma, houses seven clubs under one roof. Enjoy the tropical Tequila Park, line dance inside the City Limits, or sing along at Stooge's piano bar. (☎ 232-9255. 21+. Cover $5-8. Open Th-Sa 8pm-2am.)

◙⤬ SIGHTS AND ENTERTAINMENT. Monday morning is the time to visit the **Oklahoma City Stockyards**, 2500 Exchange Ave. (☎ 235-8675), the busiest in the world. Take bus #12 from the terminal to Agnew and Exchange Ave. Cattle auctions (M-Tu) begin at 8am and may last into the night. Visitors enter for free via a catwalk that soars over cattle herds from the parking lot northeast of the auction house. The auction is as Old West as it gets; beware of tight jeans and big hair. The **National Cowboy and Western Heritage Museum**, 1700 NE 63rd St., the city's most popular tourist attraction, features an extensive collection of Western art and exhibits on rodeos, Native Americans, and frontier towns. In the entrance hall, James Earle Fraser's large and poignant sculpture, *The End of the Trail*, symbolizes the fate of Native Americans in the West. (☎ 478-2250; www.nationalcowboy-museum.org. Open daily 9am-5pm. $8.50, seniors $7, ages 6-12 $4, under 6 free.)

Plant lovers should head to **Myriad Gardens**, 301 W. Reno Ave., with 17 acres of vegetation ranging from desert to rainforest. The **Crystal Bridge** is an impressive glass cylinder 70 ft. in diameter that houses a tropical conservatory. (☎ 297-3995. Gardens: Open daily 7am-11pm. Free. Crystal Bridge: Open M-Sa 9am-6pm, Su

GREAT PLAINS

noon-6pm. $6, students and seniors $5, ages 4-12 $3.) The **Oklahoma City Museum of Art,** 415 Couch Dr., has a solid collection of European, American, and Asian works, as well as the world's largest exhibition of Dale Chihuly's dazzling and colorful glass *objets d'art.* The 55 ft. tall glass sculpture in the museum's entrance uses 2400 separate pieces. (☎236-3100. Open Tu-W and F-Sa 10am-5pm, Th 10am-9pm, Su noon-5pm. $7; seniors, students, and children $5; children under 4 free.) Military buffs can march over to the **45th Infantry Division Museum,** 2145 NE 36th St., which displays a sizable collection of American military artifacts from the Civil War to the Persian Gulf War, including items from three of Hitler's German residences liberated by the 45th Division in WWII. Military trucks, tanks, planes, and helicopters adorn the 12-acre Thunderbird Military Park surrounding the museum. (☎424-5313. Open Tu-F 9am-4:15pm, Sa 10am-4:15pm, Su 1-4:15pm. Free.)

The **Oklahoma City National Memorial,** at 5th and Harvey St., downtown, is a haunting testimonial to the victims of the 1995 bombing of the Murrah Federal Building. Outside lies the Field of Empty Chairs (one for each of the 169 victims), a stone gate, and a reflecting pool. It is especially powerful at night when each chair is lit. Indoors, a museum tells the story of the bombing through photographs, videos, and testimonials. (☎235-3313. Open M-Sa 9am-6pm, Su 1-6pm. $7, seniors $6, students $5, under 6 free.) Oklahoma City hosts the **Red Earth Festival** (☎427-5228; June 2005), the country's largest celebration of Native American culture. In early summer 2005, the 20th annual **Charlie Christian Jazz Festival** will entertain music lovers (☎424-3800). The **Cox Business Convention Center** (☎602-8500) hosts art fairs, conventions, and scrapbooking shows. Fall visitors should check out the **World Championship Quarter Horse Show** in mid-November.

◪ **DAYTRIP FROM OKLAHOMA CITY: NORMAN.** Lying on a plain about 20 mi. south of Oklahoma City, Norman is the third-largest city in Oklahoma. Old-fashioned brick buildings house shops and businesses along Main St., though much of the city's culture and population is defined by the **University of Oklahoma** and its more than 30,000 students. The **OU Visitor Center** runs campus tours and lies at 550 Parrington Oval, the campus loop off Boyd St. between Elm Ave. and Asp Ave. (☎325-2151 or 800-234-6868. Open M-F 8am-5pm.) The **Sam Noble Oklahoma Museum of Natural History,** 2401 Chautauqua Ave., at the corner of Timberdell Rd., has exhibits on prehistoric creatures, ancient civilizations, and Oklahoman ecology. Ride the "dinovator" 26 ft. up to stare down the world's largest Apatosaurus skeleton, which is depicted struggling with the world's largest Saurophanganax. (☎325-4712; www.snomnh.ou.edu. Open Tu-Sa 10am-5pm, Su 1-5pm.) The **Fred Jones, Jr. Museum of Art,** 555 Elm Ave., spotlights one of the Plains's best collections of French Impressionist art, from Degas to Van Gogh, along with American, Native American, Asian, and European art. After construction that will nearly double the building's size, it is scheduled to reopen on January 21, 2005. (☎325-3272. www.ou.edu/fjjma. Open Tu-W and F 10am-4pm, Th 10am-9pm, Sa 10am-4:30pm, Su noon-4:30pm. $5, seniors and children 6-17 $3, under 6 free.) Football fans shouldn't leave without checking out OU's hallowed **Oklahoma Memorial Stadium.**

Metro Transit Norman runs seven bus routes that serve most of Norman, and one that goes on to Oklahoma City. (☎325-2278. Buses run M-F 7am-9pm. $0.50; to Oklahoma City $2.25. Open 8am-5pm.) **Visitor Info: Norman Convention and Visitors Bureau,** 224 W. Gray St., Ste. 104. (☎366-8095 or 800-767-7260; www.visitnorman.com. Open M-F 8am-5pm.) **Area Code:** 405.

TEXAS

Covering an area as long as the stretch from North Carolina to Key West, Texas has more the brawn of a country than a state. The fervently proud, independent citizens of the "Lone Star State" seem to prefer it that way, with their official road signs that proclaim "Don't Mess With Texas." After revolting against the Spanish in 1821 and splitting from Mexico in 1836, the Republic of Texas stood alone until 1845, when it entered the Union as the 28th state. The state's unofficial motto proclaims that "everything is bigger in Texas." This truth is evident in prolific wide-brimmed hats, boat-sized American autos, giant ranch spreads, countless steel skyscrapers, and oil refineries the size of small towns.

HIGHLIGHTS OF TEXAS

FOOD. Drippin' barbecue and colossal steaks reign supreme in the state where beef is king and vegetables are for the cows. Some of the best beef awaits in Dallas (p. 716) and Amarillo (p. 733).

SAN ANTONIO. Remember the Alamo! This city is rich with Spanish heritage (p. 701).

RODEOS/COWBOYS. The ol' West lives on in Fort Worth (p. 722) and at the Mesquite Rodeo in Dallas (p. 721), with the finest rope-riders in the land.

▐ PRACTICAL INFORMATION

Capital: Austin.

Visitor Info: Texas Transportation Information Centers, ☎800-452-9292. For a free guidebook, call **Texas Tourism,** ☎800-888-8839; www.traveltex.com. **Texas Parks and Wildlife Department,** Austin Headquarters Complex, 4200 Smith School Rd., Austin, TX 78744 (☎512-389-4800 or 800-792-1112).

Postal Abbreviation: TX. **Sales Tax:** 6-8.25%.

SAN ANTONIO   ☎210

Though best known as the home of the Alamo—the symbol of Texas's break from Mexico—San Antonio today is more defined by its integration of Anglo and Hispanic cultures. Using this cultural amalgamation to its economic advantage, San Antonio annually attracts 8 million tourists with a variety of sights and offerings. The region's early Spanish influence can be seen in missions originally built to convert Indians to Catholicism and in La Villita, a village for the city's original settlers and now a workshop for local artisans. Mexican culture is on display in Market Sq., where mariachi bands entertain weekend revelers. Visit one of San Antonio's galleries for exquisite displays of Southwestern art. The blend of diverse cultures comes together in the eateries and shops of the vibrant Riverwalk.

▐ TRANSPORTATION

Airport: San Antonio International Airport, 9800 Airport Blvd. (☎207-3411; www.sanantonio.gov/airport), north of town. Accessible by I-410 and U.S. 281. Bus #2 ("Airport") connects the airport to downtown at Market and Alamo. Taxi to downtown $14-16.

Trains: Amtrak, 350 Hoefgen St. (☎223-3226), facing the northern side of the Alamo-dome. To: **Dallas** (9hr., 1 per day, $20-49); **Houston** (5hr., 3 per week, $21-51); **Los Angeles** (29hr., 3 per week, $110-215). Open daily 11am-10:30pm.

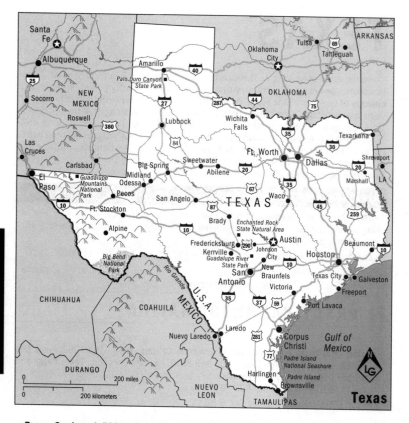

Buses: Greyhound, 500 N. Saint Mary's St. (☎270-5824). To **Dallas** (5-7hr., 15 per day, $34) and **Houston** (3-4hr., 10 per day, $24). Open 24hr.

Public Transit: VIA Metropolitan Transit, 1021 San Pedro (☎362-2020). Buses operate daily 5am-midnight; many routes stop at 6pm. Infrequent service to outlying areas. $0.80, transfers $0.15. 1-day passes $3, available at 260 E. Houston St.

Taxi: Yellow Checker Cab ☎226-4242.

🚩 PRACTICAL INFORMATION

Visitor Info: San Antonio Visitor Information Center, 317 Alamo Pl. (☎207-6748; www.sanantoniocvb.com), downtown across from the Alamo. Open daily 8:30am-6pm. Free maps and brochures.

Hotlines: Rape Crisis, ☎349-7273. Operates 24hr. **Supportive Services for the Elderly and Disabled,** ☎337-3550. Referrals and transportation.

Medical Services: Metropolitan Methodist Hospital, 1310 McCullough Ave. (☎208-2200).

Internet Access: San Antonio Public Library, 600 Soledad St. (☎207-2534). Open M-Th 9am-9pm, F-Sa 9am-5pm, Su 11am-5pm.

Post Office: 615 E. Houston St. (☎800-275-8777), 1 block from the Alamo. Open M-F 9am-5pm. **Postal Code:** 78205. **Area Code:** 210.

▗ ACCOMMODATIONS

For cheap motels, try **Roosevelt Avenue**, a southern extension of Saint Mary's St., and **Fredericksburg Road**. Inexpensive motels also line **Broadway** between downtown and Brackenridge Park. Drivers should follow **I-35 North** or the **Austin Highway** to find cheaper and often safer lodging within a 15 mi. radius of town.

■ **Bullis House Inn San Antonio International Hostel (HI)**, 621 Pierce St. (☎223-9426), 2 mi. north of downtown on Broadway, right on Grayson. From the bus station, go south 6 blocks down Navarro St. to Commerce St. Take bus #20 to the corner of Carson and Palemeadow, then walk north 1 block up Carson to Pierce. Next door to Fort Sam Houston on Government Hill, this spacious, ranch-style hostel has 42 dorm beds, a pool, and a kitchen. Fills quickly in summer. Breakfast $5. Linen $2. Key deposit $10 cash. Reception daily 8am-10pm. Dorms $20, nonmembers $23. For a more upscale option, Bullis's main house has been renovated into a B&B; each room includes cable and most have a queen bed or larger. Rooms range $51-91; with breakfast $59-99. ❶/❸

La Villita Inn, 736 S. Saint Mary's (☎798-1121), just south of downtown's main attractions. Most of the clean, comfortable rooms have a computer with Internet access. Singles $40; doubles $49; rates sometimes higher on weekends and holidays. ❷

Alamo KOA, 602 Gembler Rd. (☎224-9296 or 800-562-7783), 6 mi. from downtown. Take bus #24 "Industrial Park." From I-10 E, take Exit 580/W.W. White Rd., drive 2 blocks north, then turn left onto Gembler Rd. Well-kept grounds with grill, patio, and lots of shade. Showers, laundry facilities, pool, hot tub, rec room, and free movies. Reception daily 8am-9pm. Sites $22, full hookup $30; each additional person $3. ❶

▗ FOOD

Expensive cafes and restaurants surround the **Riverwalk.** North of town, Asian restaurants open onto **Broadway** across from Brackenridge Park. On weekends, hundreds of carnival food booths crowd the walkways of **Market Square.** If you come late in the day, prices drop and vendors are willing to haggle. (☎207-8600. Open daily June-Aug. 10am-8pm; Sept.-May 10am-6pm.) The Texas original, **Pig Stand** (☎222-2794) restaurants offer cheap, decent diner fare, including their signature Pig Sandwich ($4.50), in multiple locations; the branches at 801 S. Presa (off S. Alamo) and 1508 Broadway (both near downtown) stay open 24hr.

■ **Mi Tierra**, 218 Produce Row (☎225-1262), in Market Sq. Perpetually smiling mariachi musicians serenade patrons under a ceiling plastered with piñatas and streamers. Try the Puebla plate, which includes a quarter of a chicken smothered in *mole poblano*, with rice and beans ($10). Lunch specials $6. Grab dessert on the run from the bakery. Jumbo pineapple biscuits $0.75. Open 24hr. ❷

■ **Madhatters**, 320 Beauregard St. (☎212-4832). Located in the lovely King William area of downtown, Madhatters provides the best tea this side of the rabbit hole. Serving 60 exotic hot teas, $4 breakfasts, and $5 lunches on cleverly shabby-chic china, there's no need to ask Alice—this place is an adventure everyone can enjoy. Open M-F 7am-9pm, Sa 9am-9pm, Su 9am-4pm. ❶

Rosario's, 910 S. Alamo St. (☎223-1806), at S. Saint Mary's St., is a cafe and cantina offering classic Tex-Mex cuisine with several vegetarian options. Lunch draws a business crowd with the specials (around $6), but evenings are more laid-back with live music F-Sa. Open M 11am-3pm, Tu-Th 11am-10pm, F 11am-1:30am, Sa 11am-11pm. ❷

Josephine St. Steaks/Whiskey, 400 Josephine St. (☎224-6169). At Hwy. 281 and Josephine St., rough-hewn home cookin' is the daily special. Try the chicken fried steak sandwich ($9), or the bacon-wrapped filet steak ($12). Lunch specials ($6.50-8.50). Open M-Th 11am-10pm, F-Sa 11am-11pm. ❸

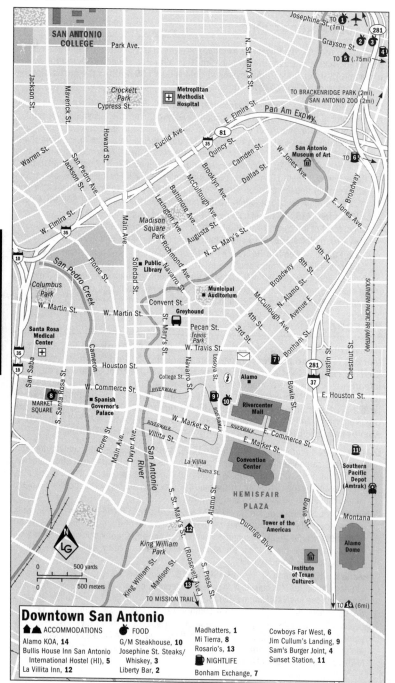

Downtown San Antonio

🏠🏠 ACCOMMODATIONS

Alamo KOA, **14**
Bullis House Inn San Antonio
    International Hostel (HI), **5**
La Villita Inn, **12**

🍽 FOOD

G/M Steakhouse, **10**
Josephine St. Steaks/
    Whiskey, **3**
Liberty Bar, **2**

Madhatters, **1**
Mi Tierra, **8**
Rosario's, **13**

🎷 NIGHTLIFE

Bonham Exchange, **7**

Cowboys Far West, **6**
Jim Cullum's Landing, **9**
Sam's Burger Joint, **4**
Sunset Station, **11**

Liberty Bar, 328 E. Josephine St. (☎227-1187). A friendly local hangout with daily specials and a large selection of sandwiches ($6-9). Try the Karkade (iced hibiscus and mint tea with fresh ginger and white grape juice). Open M-Th 11am-10:30pm, F-Sa 11am-midnight, Su 10:30am-10:30pm. ❷

G/M Steakhouse, 211 Alamo Pl. (☎223-1523). Grab a cheap 'n' greasy breakfast (2 eggs with bacon and a biscuit; $3), or drop in for a bite later (chop steak dinner with potato and salad; $5). Open M-F 7am-10:30pm, Sa-Su 7am-11pm. ❶

ⓒ SIGHTS

Much of historic San Antonio lies in the present-day downtown and surrounding areas. The city may seem diffuse, but almost every major sight or park is within a few miles of downtown and accessible by public transit.

DOWNTOWN

THE ALAMO. Built as a Spanish mission during the colonization of the New World, The Alamo has come to signify the bravery of those who fought for Texas's independence and serves as a touchstone of Lone Star pride. For 12 days in 1836, Texan defenders of the Alamo, outnumbered 20 to 1, held their ground against Mexican attackers. The morning of the 13th day saw the end of the defiant stand with the strains of the infamous *deguello.* (Literally "throat-cutting" in Spanish, the *deguello* is military music that signified annihilation of the enemy in Mexican history.) All 189 men were killed. The massacre united Texans behind the independence movement, and "Remember the Alamo!" was the rallying cry for Sam Houston's ultimately victorious forces. After languishing for decades (including being used as an arms depot during the Civil War), the site is presently under the care of the Daughters of the Republic of Texas and is the locus of the city's downtown. The Alamo's interior now features a collection of historic weapons and artifacts on display, including Jim Bowie's famous knife. Historical talks are available every every 30min. from the north wall—the weak point of the compound where the Mexican army broke through Alamo defenses. *(At the center of Alamo Pl. near Houston and Alamo St. ☎225-1391; www.thealamo.org. Open M-Sa 9am-5:30pm, Su 10am-5pm. Free.)*

OTHER MISSIONS. The **San Antonio Missions National Historical Park** preserves the four missions along the river that once formed the soul of San Antonio. To reach the missions, follow the brown-and-white "Mission Trail" signs that begin on S. Saint Mary's St. downtown. **Mission San José** (the "Queen of the Missions") has remnants of its own original irrigation system, a gorgeous sculpted rose window, and a number of restored buildings. **Mission Concepción** is the oldest unrestored stone church in North America, and traces of the once-colorful frescoes are still visible. **Mission San Juan Capistrano** and **Mission San Francisco de la Espada,** smaller and simpler than the others, evoke the isolation of such outposts. Between them lies the **Espada Aqueduct,** the only remaining waterway built by the Spanish. *(Bus #42 stops within walking distance of Mission Concepción and right in front of Mission San José. The main visitors center is located at Mission San José. ☎534-8833 or www.nps.gov/saan for info on all missions. San José: 6701 San José Dr., off Roosevelt Ave. ☎932-1001. Four Catholic masses held each Su 7:30 (in Spanish), 9, 10:30am, and a noon "Mariachi Mass." Concepción: 807 Mission Rd., 4 mi. south of the Alamo off E. Mitchell St. ☎534-1540. San Juan: 9101 Graf St. ☎534-0749. San Francisco: 10040 Espada Rd. ☎627-2021. All missions open daily 9am-5pm. Free.)*

TEXAS

SECULAR SAN ANTONIO

DISTRICTS. Southwest of the Alamo, black signs indicate access points to the 2½ mi. **Riverwalk (Paseo del Río),** a series of shaded stone pathways that follow a winding canal built by the WPA in the 1930s. Lined with picturesque gardens, shops, and cafes, the Riverwalk connects most of the major downtown sights and is the hub of San Antonio's nightlife. To ride the river, try **Río San Antonio Cruises.** Buy tickets at the Rivercenter Mall or at any of the hotels along the walk; board at either Rivercenter, near the Holiday Inn Riverwalk, or across from the Hilton Palacio Del Río. Evening dinner cruises are also available, and reservations should be made through one of the 20 participating restaurants on the Riverwalk. *(315 E. Commerce St. ☎244-5700 or 800-417-4139; www.sarivercruise.com. Open daily May-Aug. and Dec. 9am-10:30pm; Jan.-Apr. and Sept.-Nov. 10am-8pm. Narrated tours $6.50, seniors $4.50; shuttle service to any point on Riverwalk $3.50.)* A few blocks south, the recreated artisans' village, **La Villita,** has restaurants, craft shops, and art studios. *(418 Villita. ☎207-8610. Shops open daily 10am-6pm; restaurant hours vary.)* On weekends, **Market Square** features the upbeat tunes of Tejano bands with a backbeat of buzzing frozen margarita machines. *(Between San Saba and Santa Rosa St. ☎207-8600. Shops open daily June to mid-Sept. 10am-8pm; mid-Sept. to May 10am-6pm.)*

HEMISFAIR PLAZA. Created for the 1968 World's Fair, **HemisFair Plaza,** on S. Alamo, draws tourists with restaurants, museums, and historic houses. The observation deck of the **Tower of the Americas** rises 750 ft. above the Texas Hill Country—the view is best at night. *(600 HemisFair Park. ☎207-8617. Open Su-Th 9am-10pm, F-Sa 9am-11pm. $4, seniors $2.50, ages 4-11 $1.50.)* Inside the park, the **Institute of Texan Cultures** showcases 25 ethnic and cultural groups and their contributions to the history of Texas. *(801 S. Bowie St. ☎458-2300; www.the-museum.org. Open Tu-Sa 9am-5pm, Su noon-5pm. $6.50, seniors $4, ages 3-12 $4.)*

OTHER ATTRACTIONS. Former home of the San Antonio Spurs, the **Alamodome,** modeled after a Mississippi riverboat, hosts special events and shows. *(100 Montana St., at Hoefgen St. Take bus #24 or 26. ☎207-3600.)* For info on Spurs games, call the SBC Center *(☎444-5000).* The **San Antonio Museum of Art,** in the former Lone Star Brewery just north of the city center, contains the Nelson A. Rockefeller Center for Latin American art, the first center in the United States devoted exclusively to Latin American art. The rest of the museum houses impressive collections of Texan furniture and pre-Columbian, Egyptian, Oceanic, Asian, and Islamic art. *(200 W. Jones Ave. ☎978-8100; www.samuseum.org. Open early Sept. to mid-June Su noon-5pm, Tu 10am-9pm, W-Sa 10am-5pm; mid-June to early Sept. Su noon-6pm, Tu and Th 10am-8pm, W, and F-Sa 10am-5pm. $6, seniors $5, students $4, ages 4-11 $1.75; Tu 4-8pm free.)*

OUTSIDE CITY CENTER

BRACKENRIDGE PARK. To escape the commercialism of downtown San Antonio, amble up to Brackenridge Park. The 343-acre show ground includes a miniature train, extensive bike trails, and a driving range. The main attraction of the park is a lush Japanese tea garden with pathways that weave in and out of a pagoda and around a goldfish pond. *(3910 N. Saint Mary's St., 5 mi. north of the Alamo. Take bus #8. ☎207-3022. Open 5am-11pm. Train runs daily 9:30am-6:30pm. $2.50, children $2.)* Directly across the street, the **San Antonio Zoo** exhibits 3800 creatures, utilizing the area's varied climate to create natural-seeming habitats for the animals. The zoo also engages in numerous wildlife preservation, field conservation, and educational programs. *(3903 N. Saint Mary's St. ☎734-7184; www.sa-zoo.org. Open daily late May to early Sept. 9am-6pm; early Sept. to late May 9am-5pm. $8, seniors and ages 3-11 $6.)*

🎵 🎮 ENTERTAINMENT AND NIGHTLIFE

In late April, the 10-day **Fiesta San Antonio** (☎227-5191; www.fiesta-sa.org) ushers in spring with concerts, carnivals, and plenty of Tex-Mex celebrations to commemorate the Battle of San Jacinto and Texas's heroes, as well as the state's diverse cultural landscape. The huge Battle of Flowers parade is a longstanding San Antonio tradition that began as a reenactment of the Battle of San Jacinto, using ammunition of a more floral (and less dangerous) variety.

The first Friday of every month is a fiesta in San Antonio: the art galleries along S. Alamo St. put on **Artswalk** (☎207-6748), with free food and drink. For excitement after dark any time, any season, stroll down the Riverwalk. The **Theatre District,** just north of the Riverwalk downtown, puts on concerts, opera, and theater in three restored 1950s movie houses. *The Friday Express* or weekly *Current* (available at the tourist office and many businesses in town) are guides to concerts and entertainment. **Sam's Burger Joint,** 330 E. Grayson St. (☎223-2830), hosts the **Puro Poetry Slam** every Tuesday night at 10pm ($2 cover) and swing dancing every Monday night at 7pm ($5). Sam's also features live music Thursday to Saturday and the "Big Monster Burger," a pound of beef for $7. Around the corner from the Alamo, San Antonio's biggest gay dance club, the **Bonham Exchange,** 411 Bonham St., plays high-energy music with house and techno on the side. Strut your stuff on the sunken dance floor, boogie to top 40 in the video bar, or hustle over to the retro pumping gameroom. (☎271-3811. 3 dance floors, 7 bars. W college night. Cover up to $5. Open W-Th 4pm-2:30am, F 4pm-3am, Sa 8pm-3am.) Traditional jazz goes down at **Jim Cullum's Landing,** 123 Losoya St., in the Hyatt downtown, including the legendary Cullum and his jazz band. Stop by for a drink during the *al fresco* performances by the improv jazz quintet Small World on Sunday nights. (☎223-7266. All ages. Cover $5; Su no cover. Open M-F 4pm-midnight, Sa-Su noon-1am; Cullum's band starts playing at 8pm.) **Cowboys Far West,** 3030 Rte. 410 NE, plays two types of music—country and Western. With a mechanical bull and two dance floors, you best bring your cowboy hat. Can't two-step? Don't worry—every Thursday evening begins with dance lessons. (☎646-9378. 18+. Cover $3-15. Open Tu-Sa 5pm-2am.) **Sunset Station,** 1174 E. Commerce St. (☎222-9481), across from the Amtrak Station, houses concerts and clubs in a restored train depot.

AUSTIN   ☎512

Austin shatters the classic Texas stereotype of rough-and-tumble cattle ranchers riding horses across the plains. Exhibiting the trendiness of Soho and the funk of Seattle, Austin is its own star deep in the Lone Star State. Proud of their panache, Austinites sport a bumper sticker campaign to "Keep Austin Weird." As the "Live Music Capital of the World," and home to 50,000 University of Texas college students (and many an aging hippie), Austin's vibrance radiates from its eclectic offerings. From food co-ops to boundless supplies of live music, Austin is a liberal, alternative oasis in a traditional state.

▗ TRANSPORTATION

Airport: Austin Bergstrom International, 3600 Presidential Blvd. (☎530-2242; www.ci.austin.tx.us/austinairport). Head east on Cesar Chávez, which ends at Hwy. 183, 8 mi. from downtown. Take bus #100 (the Airport Flyer) or 350. Taxi to downtown $25.

Trains: Amtrak, 250 N. Lamar Blvd. (☎476-5684 or 800-872-7245); take bus #38. Office open M-F 8am-10:30pm. To: **Dallas** (8hr., 1 per day, $21-41); **El Paso** (20hr., 3 per week, $65-127); **San Antonio** (2½hr., 1 per day, $10-21).

TEXAS

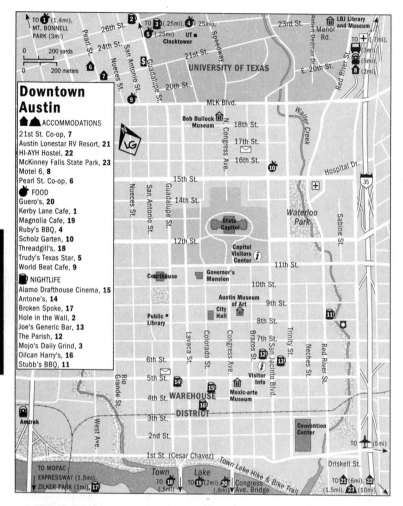

Downtown Austin

▲▲ **ACCOMMODATIONS**
21st St. Co-op, **7**
Austin Lonestar RV Resort, **21**
HI-AYH Hostel, **22**
McKinney Falls State Park, **23**
Motel 6, **8**
Pearl St. Co-op, **6**

🍎 **FOOD**
Guero's, **20**
Kerby Lane Cafe, **1**
Magnolia Cafe, **19**
Ruby's BBQ, **4**
Scholz Garten, **10**
Threadgill's, **18**
Trudy's Texas Star, **5**
World Beat Cafe, **9**

🍸 **NIGHTLIFE**
Alamo Drafthouse Cinema, **15**
Antone's, **14**
Broken Spoke, **17**
Hole in the Wall, **2**
Joe's Generic Bar, **13**
The Parish, **12**
Mojo's Daily Grind, **3**
Oilcan Harry's, **16**
Stubb's BBQ, **11**

Buses: Greyhound, 916 E. Koenig Ln. (☎458-4463 or 800-231-2222), several miles north of downtown off I-35. Easily accessible by public transit; bus #7 and 15 stop across the street and run downtown. Schedules and prices vary. Station open 24hr. To: **Dallas** (3hr., 8 per day, $29); **Houston** (3½hr., 5 per day, $21-26); **San Antonio** (2hr., 10 per day, $15.)

Public Transit: Capitol Metro, 323 Congress Ave. (☎474-1200 or 800-474-1201; call M-F 6am-10pm). Office has maps and schedules. Buses run 4am-midnight, but most start later and end earlier. Office open M-F 7:30am-5:30pm. $0.50; students $0.25; seniors, children, and disabled free. The **'Dillo Bus Service** (☎474-1200) runs downtown on Congress, Lavaca, San Jacinto, and 6th St. Most buses operate M-F every 10-15min.; service varies in off-peak times. Red and Silver service daily. The 'Dillos, which look like trollies on wheels, are always free. Free parking at Bouldin and Barton Springs.

Taxi: American Yellow Checker Cab ☎ 452-9999.

Bike Rental: Yellow bicycles are "free to ride but not to keep" as part of a community effort to refurbish donated bikes for public use. If used, make sure to leave the bike in a conspicuous spot for the next person. **Waterloo Cycles,** 2815 Fruth St. (☎ 472-9253), offers rentals. Open M-Sa 10am-7pm, Th 10am-8pm, Su noon-5pm. $10-15 per day, Sa-Su $15-20; fee includes helmet. Lock rental $5 ($1.50 each additional day).

🔲🔁 ORIENTATION AND PRACTICAL INFORMATION

Divided north-south by the Colorado River, the majority of Austin lies between **Mopac Expressway/Route 1** and **I-35,** both running north-south and parallel to one another. UT students inhabit central **Guadalupe Street ("The Drag"),** where plentiful music stores and cheap restaurants thrive. The state capitol governs the area a few blocks to the southeast. **Congress Avenue** has upscale eateries and classy shops downtown, while funkier **South Congress (SoCo)** offers a mix of antique and thrift stores across the river. The many bars and clubs of **6th Street** hop and clop at night, though some nightlife has moved to the growing **Warehouse District,** around 4th St., west of Congress. Away from the urban gridiron, **Town Lake** is a haven for the town's joggers, rowers, and cyclists.

Visitor Info: Austin Convention and Visitors Bureau/Visitors Information Center, 209 E. 6th St. (☎ 478-0098 or 800-926-2282; www.austintexas.org). Open Su-Th 9am-6pm, F-Sa 9am-7pm.

Medical Services: St. David's Medical Center, 919 E. 32nd St. (☎ 476-7111). Off I-35, close to downtown. Open 24hr.

Hotlines: Crisis Intervention Hotline, ☎ 472-4357. **Austin Rape Crisis Center Hotline,** ☎ 440-7273. Both operate 24hr. **Outyouth Gay/Lesbian Helpline,** ☎ 800-969-6884. Operates M-Sa 6:30-9pm.

Internet Access: Austin Public Library, 800 Guadalupe St. (☎ 974-7300). Open M-Th 10am-9pm, F-Sa 10am-6pm, Su noon-6pm.

Post Office: 510 Guadalupe (☎ 494-2210), at 6th St. Open M-F 8:30am-6:30pm. **Postal Code:** 78701. **Area Code:** 512.

🔳 ACCOMMODATIONS

Chain motels lie along **I-35,** running north and south of Austin. This funkified city, however, has plenty of cheap accommodations with character. In town, **co-ops** run by College Houses at UT, such as the 21st St. Co-op and the Pearl St. Co-op (see below), peddle rooms and meals to hostelers. Guests have access to all co-op facilities, including fully stocked kitchens. (☎ 476-5678, or check www.college-houses.coop to find the contact representative for individual houses. Reservations recommended; walk-ins welcome when space permits. Open May-Aug.) For campers, a 10-20min. drive separates Austin and the nearest campgrounds.

🔲 **Hostelling International-Austin (HI),** 2200 S. Lakeshore Blvd. (☎ 444-2294 or 800-725-2331), about 3 mi. from downtown. Take bus #7 "Duval" to Burton, then walk 3 blocks north. From I-35, exit at Riverside, head east, and turn left at Lakeshore Blvd. A beautiful, environmentally conscious hostel with a 24hr. common room overlooking Town Lake. 39 beds, single-sex rooms. Rents bikes, kayaks, and canoes ($10). Linen provided. Laundry and kitchen. No alcohol. Reception 8-11am and 5-10pm; arrivals after 10pm must call ahead to check in. Dorms $17, nonmembers $20. ❶

TEXAS HILL COUNTRY DRIVE

Parts of the **Texas Hill Country** are as country as they come. Long-horns graze on grassy plains between rolling wooded hills, while rusty pickup trucks driven by big men in big hats dominate the roads. But the Texas Hill Country is more than ranches and cattle: the limestone-rich soil is well-suited for the pastoral pursuits of wine-making and peach-growing. There is a noticeable German influence in the area, dating back to 1846 and the founding of **Fredericksburg**—stop off at a biergarten to sample some German cuisine. Finally, a series of well-maintained parks links San Antonio and Austin while offering campers and day visitors alike the chance to experience the natural beauty of Texas firsthand. Although not the most direct route between these two cities, unique diversions and beautiful scenery make up for the extra miles.

TIME: 6hr

DISTANCE: 190mi.

1 NEW BRAUNFELS. The entire economy of New Braunfels, TX, depends on the inner tube. Almost 2 million visitors per year come to this town hoping to spend a day floating along the spring-fed Comal River. **Rockin' "R" River Rides** will send you off with a life jacket and tube before picking you up downstream 2½hr. later. (193 S. Liberty. ☎830-620-6262. Open May-Sept. daily 9am-7pm. Tube rentals and bottomless floats $10, $12 with bottom.) Car keys, proper ID, or $25 deposit required for rental.) If the Comal doesn't float your boat, head for the chlorinated waters of **Schlitterbahn**, a 65-acre waterpark extravaganza with 17 waterslides, nine tube chutes, three uphill watercoasters, and three miles of tubing. Take I-35 to Exit 189, turn left, and follow the signs for Schlitterbahn. (400 N. Liberty. ☎830-625-2351. Call for hours; generally around 10am-8pm. Open May-Sept. Full-day passes $28.50, ages 3-11 $24. Mid-day pass $20) From New Braunfels, take Rte. 46 west for 6½ mi., then turn left on Herbelin Rd. Here you'll find **Dry Comal Creek Vineyards**, 1741 Herbelin Rd., beckoning with tastings ($2-5) and tours ($2) of the small vineyard. (☎830-885-4121. Open W-Su noon-5pm.) Yes, Texas makes wine—in fact, the state is currently fifth in the nation in wine production.

2 GUADALUPE RIVER STATE PARK. You can swim in the cliff-lined river, or camp in the nearby sites of **Guadalupe River State Park ❶**, 25 mi. west of Dry Comal Creek along Rte. 46. (☎830-438-2656, for reservations 512-389-8900. Open M-F 8am-8pm, Sa 8am-10pm. Day entrance $5 per person, under 12 free; $17 for water and electricity, $13 for water only.)

3 BOERNE. Farther down Rte. 46 is Boerne (pronounced BUR-nee), a jewelry lover's paradise where a string of converted barns and old farmhouses sell a wide array of odds and ends.

4 BANDERA. After 12 mi. of twists through a series of low hills along the way to Bandera, Rte. 46 intersects with Rte. 16; take Rte. 16 north. Bandera's central street passes through a row of ramshackle buildings that look like backdrops to old cowboy movies. Consistent with the image, Bandera is home to the 🎬**Frontier Times Museum**, 510 13th St., a haven for cowboy memorabilia, odd knick-knacks, and relics of the Old West. (☎830-796-3864. Open M-Sa 10am-4:30pm, Su 1pm-4:30pm. $2, under 18 $0.25.)

5 MEDINA. Continuing down 15 mi. of zig-zag roads through dramatic countryside, Rte. 16 brings you to the town of Medina, the "apple capital of Texas." Stop off at **Love Creek Orchards** (☎800-449-0882), on Rte. 16 in the heart of town, to buy a homemade apple pie ($18, $3 per slice). Leaving Medina on Rte. 16 N, the next 35 miles wind through some of the most breathtaking Texas country. *Be cautious driving this leg of the trip; hairpin turns and steep inclines can be treacherous.* Safety aside, the real reason to proceed slowly is to enjoy the scenery.

6 KERRVILLE. The center of a region known for its abundance of local art, Kerrville is home to many artists and craftspeople. Check the Kerrville Visitor Information Center, 2108 Sidney Baker, downtown of Rte. 16, for guides to nearby galleries. (☎830-792-3535, www.kerrville-texas.cc. Open M-F 8:30am-5pm, Sa 9am-3pm, Su 10am-3pm.) The **Museum of Western Art**, 1550 Bandera Hwy., take Rte. 173 S from Rte. 16 N, showcases action-packed scenes of the Wild West and America's gun-toting heroes. (☎830-896-2553. Open June-Aug. M-Sa 9am-5pm, Su 1-5pm; Sept.-May Tu-Sa 9am-5pm, Su 1-5pm. $5, seniors $3.50, ages 6-18 $1.)

7 FREDERICKSBURG. Twenty-five miles along Rte. 16 from Kerrville sits historic Fredericksburg, a German-rooted town of biergartens, wineries, and sausage, and the heart of the Hill Country. **The Fredericksburg Convention and Visitors Bureau**, 302 E. Austin St., behind the Nimitz Museum (☎888-997-3600), has maps and information. (Open M-F 8:30am-5pm, Sa-Su 9am-noon and 1pm-5pm.) The **Admiral Nimitz Museum**, 340 E. Main St., honors the Fre-

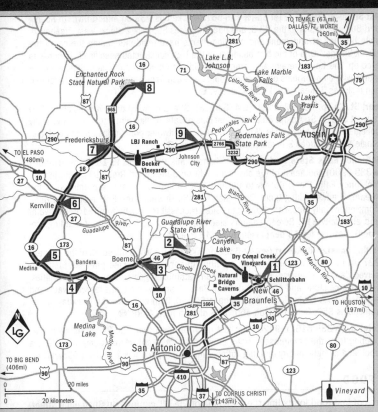

dricksburg-born general and contains an excellent exhibit on the Pacific theater of World War II. (☎830-997-4379. Open daily 10am-5pm. $5, students $3.)

8 ENCHANTED ROCK STATE NATURAL PARK. With the double allure of being both a natural wonder (a tree-less, 440 ft. dome of pink granite) as well as a place to pitch a tent, **Enchanted Rock State Natural Park ❶,** 18 miles north of Fredericksburg on Rte. 965, offers hiking—a relatively easy scramble to the top—and rock-climbing for the experienced. (☎800-792-1112 or 325-247-3903. Open daily 8am-5pm. Entrance fee $5, under 12 free. 46 regular tent sites available with shower, water, and grill $10; 60 hike-in primitive sites $8. No RVs or trailers permitted. Reservations strongly recommended.)

9 JOHNSON CITY. Ten miles east of Fredericksburg on U.S. 290, **Becker Vineyards,** on Jenschke Ln., offers free tastings as well as free tours of the winery. (☎830-644-2681. Open M-Th 10am-5pm, F-Sa 10am-6pm, Su noon-6pm). Farther down U.S. 290, is Johnson City, near the birthplace of 36th President **Lyndon Baines Johnson** (the city was named for his grandfather). The LBJ National Historic Park (☎830-644-2252) consists of two different sites: the house where Johnson was born (tours 9am-4:30pm every ½hr.), and his ranch 14 miles west (tours 10am-4pm on no set schedule, $3). Nine miles east of Johnson City off Rte. 2766 is **Pedernales Falls State Park ❶.** Waterfalls, hiking trails, tent sites, and swimming/tubing areas make the park a favorite getaway from Austin. (☎800-792-1112. Park open daily 8am-10pm; office open daily 8am-5pm. Entrance fee $4 per person, under 12 free. Sites with water and electricity $18, primitive sites $8.) For more info, check out the **Hill Country Visitor's Center,** 803 H.W. 281 S., in Johnson City. (☎830-868-5700. Open M-Sa 9am-5pm.)

21st St. Co-op, 707 W. 21st St. (☎476-5678). Take bus #39 on Airport Blvd. to Koenig and Burnet, transfer to the #3 S, and ride to Nueces St.; walk 2 blocks west. Treehouse-style building arrangement and hanging plants have residents calling the co-op the "Ewok Village." One of the first buildings in the U.S. constructed specifically to serve as a co-op, the house retains its communal spirit and colorful character. Suite arrangements with all bedrooms off common rooms on each floor. Linen and A/C. $15 per person includes 3 meals and kitchen access. ❶

Pearl St. Co-op, 2000 Pearl St. (☎476-5678). Straightforward dorm rooms, about 100 ft. west of 21st St. Co-op. Relatively spacious private singles with A/C in the classically collegiate cinder block style. Wooden deck and saltwater pool in back. Linen included Single $20; includes 3 meals and kitchen access. ❶

McKinney Falls State Park, 5808 McKinney Falls Pkwy. (☎243-1643, reservations ☎389-8900) southeast of the city. Turn right on Burleson off Rte. 71 E, then right on McKinney Falls Pkwy. Caters to RV and tent campers. Swimming permitted in the stream; 6 mi. of hiking trails. Open Mar.-Nov. Su-Th 8am-5pm, F 8am-8pm, Sa 8am-7pm; open daily Dec.-Feb. 8am-5pm. Sites (accessible only by foot) $10; with water and electricity $14. Screen shelters sleep up to 8 for $32 (no cots or bedding provided). Day-use fee $3 per person, under 13 free. ❶

Austin Lonestar RV Resort (☎444-6322 or 800-284-0206), 6 mi. south of the city; exit 227 off I-35 and continue on the northbound service road. Free pancake breakfast served daily to all guests. Has a pool, clean bathrooms, game room, laundry facilities, convenience store, and playground. Open 8am-10pm. RV and tent sites with water and electricity $37, full hook-up with telephone $45-50, third night free if a weekday. 4-person cabins $50; 6- to 8-person $60; 10% off with AAA, AARP. ❷

Motel 6, (☎339-6161), 9420 I-35; just north of downtown; Exit 241. This exemplary offering from the omnipresent motel chain offers well-kept, clean rooms with HBO, a pool, and complimentary morning coffee. Singles $30; doubles $36. F-Sa $35/41. ❷

◘ FOOD

Scores of fast-food joints line the west side of the UT campus on **Guadalupe Street.** Patrons can often enjoy drink specials and free hors d'oeuvres around **6th Street,** south of the capitol, where the battle for happy hour business rages with unique intensity. Farther down the road, **Barton Springs Road** offers a range of inexpensive restaurants, including Mexican and Texas-style barbecue joints. The **Warehouse District** has swankier options. Get your groceries at the **Wheatsville Food Co-op,** 3101 Guadalupe. The only food co-op in Texas, Wheatsville features organic foods and is a community gathering place and information resource. Grab a smoothie ($3) in the deli and enjoy it on the patio. (☎478-2667. Open daily 9am-11pm.)

▨ **Ruby's BBQ,** 512 W. 29th St. (☎477-1651). Ruby's barbecue is good enough to be served on silver platters, but that wouldn't seem right in this cow-skulls and butcher-paper establishment. The owners order naturally lean beef, farm-raised without the use of hormones, and invite patrons to check out their slow-cooking brick and mortar barbecue pits. Try a brisket sandwich ($4.75) and rosemary, mozzarella-infused homefries ($3). Plates with meat, bread, and side items $7-11. Open daily 11am-midnight. ❷

▨ **World Beat Cafe,** 600 W. Martin Luther King Jr. Blvd. (☎236-0197). This contemporary African eatery dishes up specialties like okra vegetable soup ($5) and *yam fu fu* with *egusi* (African porridge), as well as chicken, beef, and goat over rice and covered in traditional or eye-wateringly spicy sauce ($7-11). The Cafe also grills a terrific burger and fries ($4). Open M-Sa 11am-10pm, Su noon- 8pm. ❶

Threadgill's, 301 W. Riverside Dr. (☎472-9304); another location at 6416 N. Lamar Blvd. (☎451-5440). A legend in Austin since 1933, Threadgill's serves terrific Southern soul food, including the obligatory fried chicken ($9) and chicken fried steak ($9), among creaky wooden floors, slow-moving ceiling fans, and antique beer signs. A variety of vegetarian and non-dairy sides can be combined to make a full meal. Live music Th-Sa 7pm. Open M-Th 11am-10pm, F-Sa 10am-10:30pm, Su 11am-9pm. ❷

The Kerbey Lane Cafe, 3704 Kerbey Ln. (☎451-1436); An Austin institution with other locations at 2700 Lamar, 2606 Guadalupe and 12602 Research Blvd. Their pancakes ($3.50-5) are renowned, and the steak and avocado *arepas* (corn griddlecake; $9) is excellent. Many vegetarian options include savory tomato pie. Open 24 hr. ❷

Magnolia Cafe, 1920 S. Congress Ave. (☎445-0000); another location at 2304 Lake Austin Blvd. (☎478-8645). A lively place with healthy, tasty dishes. Try the tropical turkey tacos, with turkey, cheese, pico de gallo, and pineapple ($6.25 for 2). Open 24hr. ❷

Guero's, 1412 S. Congress Ave. (☎447-7688), across the river from downtown. This Mexican restaurant is very popular with locals and is the locus of South Congress activity. Live music at their adjacent outdoor patio and bar on summer weekends. Lunch specials $6-8. Combo plates $8-12. Open M-F 11am-11pm, Sa-Su 8am-11pm. ❸

Scholz Garten, 1607 San Jacinto Blvd. (☎474-1958), near the capitol. Both students and politicians gather at this restaurant, recognized by the legislature for "epitomizing the finest traditions of the German heritage of our state." It serves the best *wurst* in Austin along with general fried dishes and barbecue. Sausage and bratwurst po' boys ($6), and Reuben sandwich ($6). Open M-W 11am-10pm, Th-Sa 11am-11pm. ❷

Trudy's Texas Star, 409 W. 30th St. (☎477-2935); other locations at 8800 Burnet Rd. (☎454-1474), and 4141 Capital of Texas Hwy. S. (☎326-9899). Tex-Mex entrees ($7-9) and fantastic margaritas. Famous *migas* ($6) are a delicious mix of eggs, cheese, and salsa on a tortilla. Happy hour all-day M. 409 W. 30th St. location open M-F 7am-2am, Sa 8am-2am, Su 8am-midnight; bar open M-Th 2pm-2am, F-Su noon-2am. ❷

🔘 SIGHTS

GOVERNMENT. Not to be outdone, Texans built their **state capitol** 7 ft. taller than the national one. *(At Congress Ave. and 11th St. ☎463-0063. Open M-F 8:30am-4:30pm, Sa 9:30am-3:30pm, Su noon-3:30pm. 45min. tours every 15-30 min. Free.)* The **Capitol Visitors Center** is located in the southeast corner of the capitol grounds. *(112 E. 11th St. ☎305-8400. Open daily 9am-5pm. Free 2hr. parking at 12th and San Jacinto St. garage.)* Near the capitol, the **Governor's Mansion** is open for tours. *(1010 Colorado St. ☎463-5516. Free tours M-Th every 20min. 10am-11:40am.)* The **Austin Convention and Visitors Bureau** sponsors free walking tours of the area from March to November. *(☎454-1545. Tours Th-F 9am and Sa-Su 9am, 11am, and 2pm. Tour starts at the capitol steps.)*

MUSEUMS. The **Lyndon B. Johnson Library and Museum** sets the public and personal life of the Texas native against the background of a broader history of the American Presidency. A life-size animatronic LBJ tells jokes and anecdotes on the second floor, while the eighth floor features a model of the Oval Office from Johnson's era. *(2313 Red River St. Take bus #20. ☎916-5136; www.lbjlib.utexas.edu. Open daily 9am-5pm. Free.).* If you've ever wondered about "The Story of Texas," the **Bob Bullock Texas State History Museum** is waiting to tell it to you with three floors of exhibits, an IMAX theater, and the special effects-equipped Texas Free Spirit Theater. The museum traces the history of the state from its Native American legacy and Spanish colonization to statehood and the 20th-century oil boom. *(1800 N. Con-*

TEXAS

gress Ave. ☎ 936-8746; www.thestoryoftexas.com. Open M-Sa 9am-6pm, Su noon-6pm. Exhibits $5.50, seniors $4.50, under 18 free; IMAX $7, seniors $6, under 19 $5; Texas Free Spirit Theater $5, seniors $4, under 18 $3.50; discounted combination tickets available.)

The downtown **Austin Museum of Art** features mostly traveling exhibits of contemporary art. *(At the corner of Congress Ave. and 9th St. ☎ 495-9224; www.amoa.org. Open Tu, W, F-Sa 10am-5pm, Th 10am-8pm, Su noon-5pm. $5, seniors and students $4, 12 and under free. $1 entrance on Tu.)* A second branch, at 3809 W. 35th St., is housed in a Mediterranean-style villa in a beautiful country setting with an exquisite sculpture garden. The **Mexic-Arte Museum** features a permanent collection of Mexican masks and photos. *(419 Congress Ave. ☎ 480-9373; www.mexic-artemuseum.org. Open M-Th 10am-6pm, F-Sa 10am-5pm, Su noon-5pm. $5, students and seniors $3, children free)*

PARKS. **Mount Bonnell Park** offers a sweeping view of Lake Austin and Westlake Hills from the highest point in the city. *(3800 Mt. Bonnell Rd., off W. 35th St.)* On hot afternoons, Austinites flock to **Zilker Park,** just south of the Colorado River. Relax in the serene Japanese garden or natural butterfly habitat in Zilker Botanical Gardens. *(2100 Barton Springs Rd. Take bus #30. ☎ 477-7273. Open daily. Free.)* Nearby, the outdoor **Umlauf Sculpture Garden** showcases the work of the late Charles Umlauf, longtime UT professor and prolific artist. *(605 Robert E. Lee Rd. off Barton Springs Rd. ☎ 445-5582. $3.50, seniors $2.50, students $1.)* Flanked by walnut and pecan trees, ◙**Barton Springs Pool,** a spring-fed swimming hole in the park, is 1000 ft. long and 200 ft. wide. The pool's temperature hovers around 68°F year-round, and women occasionally go topless. *(☎ 974-6700. Open M-W and F-Su 5am-10pm, Th 5-9am and 7-10pm. $3, 12-17 $1, under 12 $0.50. Parking $3. Free daily 5am-8am and 9-10pm.)* The **Barton Springs Greenbelt** offers tough hiking and biking trails. Free spirits go au natural in Lake Travis at **Hippie Hollow,** Texas's only public nude swimming and sunbathing haven, 15 mi. northeast of downtown. Take Mopac (Rte. 1) north to the F.M. 2222 exit. Follow 2222 west and turn left at I-620; Comanche Tr. will be on the right. *(7000 Comanche Tr. ☎ 854-7275. 18+. Open daily May-Aug. 8am-9pm, Sept.-Oct. and Mar.-Apr. 9am-7:30pm, Nov.-Feb. 9am-6pm; no entry after 8:30pm. $10 per car, pedestrians $5.)*

OTHER SIGHTS. The **University of Texas at Austin (UT)** is the wealthiest public university in the country, with an annual budget of over a billion dollars, and, with its over 50,000 students, the backbone of city's cultural life. Just before dusk, head underneath the south side of the **Congress Avenue Bridge,** near the Austin American-Statesman parking lot, and watch the massive swarm of ◙**Mexican free-tail bats** emerge from their roosts to feed on the night's mosquitoes. When the bridge was reconstructed in 1980, the engineers unintentionally created crevices which formed ideal homes for the migrating bat colony. The city began exterminating the night-flying creatures until **Bat Conservation International** moved to Austin to educate people about the benefits of their presence—the bats eat up to 3000 lb. of insects each night. The colony, seen from mid-March to November, peaks in August, when a fresh crop of pups increases the population to around 1.5 million. *(For flight times, call the bat hotline ☎ 416-5700, ext. 3636)*

🎵 📷 ENTERTAINMENT AND NIGHTLIFE

Beverly Sheffield Zilker Hillside Theater (☎ 477-5335 for schedule), across from the Barton Springs pool, hosts free outdoor bands, ballets, plays, musicals, and symphony concerts most weekends from May to October. In mid-March, entertainment industry giants and eager fans descend upon Austin for the 10-day **South by Southwest Music, Media, and Film Festival.** Nearly 1300 musical acts fill 50 stages, while movie screens show 180 film screenings, making this festival the premier entertainment industry event in the Southwest (☎ 467-7979; www.sxsw.com). In early April, the Austin Fine Arts Guild sponsors **The Fine**

Arts Festival, attracting 200 national artists, local eateries, live music, and art activities. Austin's smaller events calendar is a mixed bag. Each spring, **Spamarama** (www.spamarama.com) gathers Spam fans from all walks of life to pay homage to the often misunderstood meat. A cookoff, samplings, sports, and live music at the **Spam Jam** are all in store.

Austin has replaced Seattle as the nation's underground musical mecca, so look out for rising indie stars, as well as old blues, folk, country, and rock favorites. Collegiate revelers and swingers seek out dancing and drinks on **6th Street,** an area filled with warehouse nightclubs and theme bars. Mellow night owls gather at the cocktail-lounges in the **4th Street Warehouse District.** Along **Red River Street,** bars and hard-rocking clubs have less of the glamour but all of the grit of 6th St. If you aren't in the mood to face club crowds, try Austin's regionally unparalleled coffeehouse scene. The weekly *Austin Chronicle* (www.austinchronicle.com) and *XLent* provide details on current music performances, shows, and movies.

■ **Mojo's Daily Grind,** 2714 Guadalupe St. (☎477-6656), fuels Austin's students, artists, hipsters, and other colorful constituents with coffee and beer. DJs spin every M, and poets wax eloquent on the first F of the month. Try the Iced Mojo ($2.50). Open 24hr.

■ **Antone's,** 213 W. 5th St. (☎ 320-8424; www.antones.net). This legendary blues paradise has attracted the likes of B.B. King and Muddy Waters and was the starting point for Stevie Ray Vaughn. Now offering a variety of music to all ages. Times vary. Cover $5-25. Open daily 9pm-2am. Visit website for specific daily times and covers.

■ **The Parish,** 214 E. 6th St. (☎478-6372; www.theparishroom.com) has the latest in funk, hip-hop, indie rock, and electronica. 2 bars, pool table, and art-adorned walls create one of the hippest spaces on 6th St. Mood depends on the musical act—check the website for schedules. Cover from $9 ages 18-20, 21+ from $6. Open W-Sa 9pm-2am.

Stubb's BBQ, 801 Red River St. (☎480-8341). Stubb's serves a fabulous Sunday gospel brunch—all-you-can-eat buffet plus live gospel for $15 (reservations recommended). The 18+ club downstairs hosts nightly live music, and the amphitheater receives headlining bands. Swing by earlier for scrumptious, inexpensive grub, like the chopped beef sandwich ($4.25). Amphitheater all ages. Cover $5-25. Shows at 10:30pm. Open Tu-Th 11am-10pm, F-Sa 11am-11pm, Su 11am-9pm; nightclub open Tu-Sa 11am-2am.

Joe's Generic Bar, 315 E. 6th St. (☎480-0171; www.joebates.com/joes.htm). Enter the door marked with Joe's generic barcode on any night and you'll be greeted with good-humored, raunchy Texas-style blue. 21+. No cover. Open daily 7pm-2am.

Hole in the Wall, 2538 Guadalupe St. (☎477-4747), at 26th St. Its self-effacing name belies the popularity of this renowned music spot, which features a mix of "Austin music"—punk/alternative and country-western bands. Music most nights. 21+. No cover. Open M-F 11am-2am, Sa-Su noon-2am.

Broken Spoke, 3201 S. Lamar Blvd. (☎442-6189; www.brokenspokeaustintx.com). One of the top honky-tonks in the land, the Broken Spoke is real country, with wagon wheel decor and Texan hospitality. The "tourist trap" room is full of country music memorabilia, but the otherwise inconspicuous place has rare artifacts and photos, including LBJ's hat. Chicken-fried steak dinner for $8.25. All ages. Cover $5-8. Music nightly at 9pm. Open Su-Th 11am-10:30pm, F-Sa 11am-11:30pm.

Oilcan Harry's, 211 W. 4th St. (☎320-8823). One of the biggest and best gay bars in Austin, with three bars, a pool table, dancefloor, and outdoor patio. Strip shows bare all on Th, Sa, and Su 10:30pm and midnight. 21+. No cover. Open daily 2pm-2am.

Alamo Drafthouse Cinema, 409 Colorado St. (☎476-1320; www.drafthouse.com), screens second-runs, cult classics, and offbeat films while serving food, beer, and wine. See how great the Karate Kid is on the big screen or watch the Turkish Wizard of Oz. Admission $5-10, $1 on M and free W at midnight. Website has movie schedules.

DALLAS
☎ **214**

Denim and diamonds define the Dallas decor, skyline, and attitude. Rugged western virility coupled with cosmopolitan offerings create the city's truly Texan aura. Big Tex, an enormous cowboy float in Fair Park, welcomes visitors to one of the country's finest Asian art collections and a slew of restaurants. While the intrigue surrounding the assassination of President Kennedy haunts the city to this day, Dallas describes itself as a city imbued with a maverick's spirit where—even though an urban landscape has replaced the sprawling plains—"the people still swagger and the frontier still calls."

▐ TRANSPORTATION

Airport: Dallas-Fort Worth International (☎972-574-8888; www.dfwairport.com), 17 mi. northwest of downtown; take bus #202 ($2). For door-to-gate service, take the **Super Shuttle,** 3010 N. Airfield Dr. (☎800-258-3826). 24hr. service. First passenger $23; each additional passenger $8. $16 to downtown hotels. Taxi to downtown $38.

Trains: Amtrak, 400 S. Houston St. (☎653-1101), in Union Station. Open daily 10:30am-6pm. To: **Austin** (6½hr., 1 per day, $17-41); **Little Rock** (7½hr., 1 per day, $56-88); **Los Angeles** (41hr., 3 per week, $138-215).

Buses: Greyhound, 205 S. Lamar St. (☎655-7727), 3 blocks east of Union Station. Open 24hr. To: **Austin** (3hr., 15 per day, $26-28); **Houston** (4hr., 8 per day, $32); **New Orleans** (13hr., 12 per day, $75).

Public Transit: Dallas Area Rapid Transit (DART), 1401 Pacific Ave. (☎979-1111; www.dart.org). Open M-F 6am-8pm, Sa-Su 8am-5pm. Buses dispatch from 2 downtown transfer centers, East and West, and serve most suburbs. Downtown daily 5:30am-9:30pm, to suburbs 5:30am-8pm. Confirm schedules before riding, however, as times are subject to change depending on the route. Local fares $1.25, all-day pass $2.50; Express buses and longer trips $2.25/$4.50. Maps at 1401 Pacific office. **DART Light Rail** runs north-south through downtown. Operates daily generally 5:30am-12:30am.

Taxi: Yellow Cab Co. ☎426-6262.

◢✲ ❼ ORIENTATION AND PRACTICAL INFORMATION

Most of Dallas lies within the **I-635** loop, bisected north-south by **I-35 E (Stemmons Freeway)** and **U.S. 75 (Central Expressway)** and east-west by **I-30.** The suburban areas lie along the northern reaches of Central Expwy. and the **Dallas North Toll Road.** Driving and parking in downtown Dallas can be tricky. Beware of ravenous downtown parking meters which demand feeding until 10pm, and later in Deep Ellum. Ross Ave. has cheaper parking rates, which tend to go down after 5pm.

Visitor Info: Dallas Convention and Visitors Bureau, 100 S. Houston St. (☎571-1300 or 800-232-5527; 24hr. events hotline 571-1301; www.dallascvb.com), at Main St., in the Old Red Courthouse. Open daily 8am-5pm.

GLBT Organizations: Dallas Gay and Lesbian Community Center, 2701 Reagan St. (☎528-9254). Open 9am-9pm.

Hotlines: Contact Counseling Crisis Line, ☎972-233-2233. Operates 24hr.

Internet Access: Dallas Public Library, 1515 Young St. at Ervay St. (☎670-1400). Open M-Th 9am-9pm, F-Sa 9am-5pm, Su 1-5pm. *Be careful around this area at night.*

Post Office: 401 Dallas-Ft. Worth Tpk. (☎760-4545). Take Sylvan exit. Open 24hr. **General Delivery** mail should be addressed to the **downtown branch,** located at 400 N. Ervay St. Open M-F 8:30am-5pm. **Postal Code:** 75201; for General Delivery 75221. **Area Codes:** 214, 972, and 817. In text, 214 unless otherwise noted.

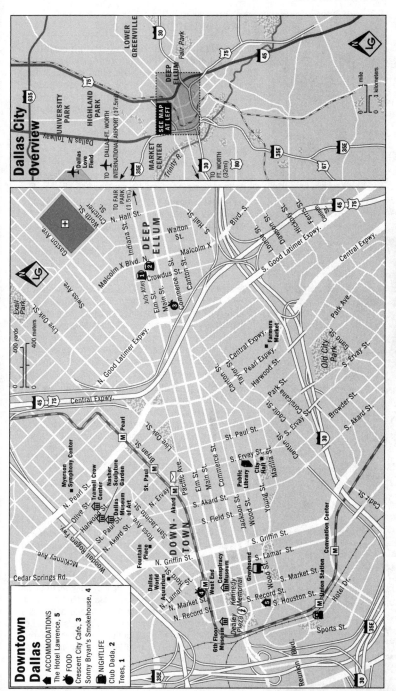

Downtown Dallas

▲ ACCOMMODATIONS
The Hotel Lawrence, **5**

● FOOD
Crescent City Cafe, **3**
Sonny Bryan's Smokehouse, **4**

◗ NIGHTLIFE
Club Dada, **2**
Trees, **1**

Dallas City Overview

SEE MAP AT LEFT

DEEP ELLUM

LOWER GREENVILLE

Fair Park

UNIVERSITY PARK

HIGHLAND PARK

Dallas N. Tollway

Dallas Love Field

TO DALLAS–FT. WORTH
INTERNATIONAL AIRPORT (17.5mi)

MARKET CENTER

Trinity R.

TO FT. WORTH (32mi)

TEXAS

OUT OF THE WAY

DAMN, THAT'S SMOKIN'

While good barbecue is plentiful in cattle-driven Texas, truly great barbecue is harder to find. Clark's Outpost, in Tioga, TX, about 1½hr. north of Dallas, is one of the best, most authentic barbecue restaurants around. The restaurant has catapulted Tioga, a town that used to be marked only as the birthplace of Gene Autry, country-music legend of "Rudolph the Red Nose Reindeer" fame, into the barbecue limelight. The food is ecstasy-inducing, with brisket treated with a delectably spicy rub and slow-cooked for three days, giving it the smoky-sweet tang and tender, succulent texture that define great barbecue. The unique "French fried corn-on-the-cob," corn has been fried just long enough to make each kernel crispy and buttery. Sauce is served in old beer bottles (a hallmark of authentic Texas barbecue), and black-and-white photos of Wild West heroes, wagon wheels, cow skulls, and old boots adorn the walls, making it clear that at Clark's, barbecue isn't just a way of cooking, but a way of life.

101 Hwy. 377 at Gene Autry Dr., Tioga, Texas. Take I-35 N past Denton, go east on Hwy. 922 at Exit 487, then south on Hwy. 377. After about 1 mi., Clark's will be on your left. ☎904-437-2414 *or* 800-932-5051. *Sliced beef sandwich $4.50, beef and ribs combo plate $16. Open M-Th 11am-9pm, F-Sa 11am-9:30pm, Su 11am-8:30pm.* ❷

ACCOMMODATIONS

Cheap lodgings in Dallas are nearly impossible to come by; big events like college football's Cotton Bowl (Jan. 1) and the state fair in October exacerbate the problem. Look within 10 mi. of downtown along three of the major roads for inexpensive motels: north of downtown on **U.S. 75**, north along **I-35**, and east on **I-30**. Hotels with a primarily business clientele often have lower rates on weekends.

Welcome Inn, 3243 Merrifield Ave (☎826-3510). Exit Dolphin Rd. (exit 49A) off I-30, a few minutes southeast of downtown near Fair Park. HBO and free local calls in rooms. Singles $40; doubles $46 plus tax. ❷

The Hotel Lawrence, 302 S. Houston St. (☎761-9090), downtown near Dealey Plaza and the West End. 2½ blocks from the Light Rail and CBD West transfer center—your cheapest bet in the city center. Fitness center. Internet access $10 per day. Breakfast included. Singles $69-89; doubles $79-99, but can be higher during conventions. ❹

Cedar Hill State Park (☎972-291-3900, reservations 972-291-6641), 20-30min. from the city. Take I-35 E to Rte. 67 and turn right onto FM 1382; the park is on the left. Swimming, jet-skis, mountain-bike and walking trails. Reserve at least 2 weeks in advance. Reception Su-Th 7am-5pm, F-Sa 7am-10pm. 24hr. gate access with reservations. Primitive sites $7, with water and electricity $18. Park entry $5 per person. ❶

Sandy Lake RV Park, 1915 Sandy Lake Rd. (☎972-242-6808). Take I-35 E north of the city to Exit 444, then go left under the highway about 1 mi. No tent sites. Wireless Internet, pool, laundry, showers, pool table, and convenience store. Reception M-F 7:30am-7:30pm, Sa 8am-7pm, Su 1-6pm. Sites $25. ❶

FOOD

Dallas offers eclectic dining options, coupling urban delights with tried and true Texan fare. For the lowdown on dining options, pick up the "Friday Guide" of the *Dallas Morning News*. Stock up on produce at the **Farmers Market,** 1010 S. Pearl, next to International Marketplace. (☎939-2808. Open daily 7am-6pm.)

EatZi's, 3403 Oaklawn Ave. (☎526-1515), in Turtle Creek, at Lemmon Ave., 1 mi. east of Oaklawn exit from I-35 E, north of downtown. A paradise for the frugal gourmet, this grocery store, cafe, kitchen, and bakery is a culinary delight. Fabulous focaccia ($3), sandwiches ($4-9), and tons of other delicacies. Fresh chef-prepared dinners ($5-11) sold 2-for-1 after 9pm. Open daily 7am-10pm. ❷

▓ **Bubba's,** 6617 Hillcrest Dr. (☎373-6527). For the best no-frills grub in the swankiest part of town, head to Highland Park for Bubba's famous fried chicken. Dine-in, drive-thru, or take-out. Grab 2 pieces of chicken, 2 veggies, and a roll for $6-7. Banana pudding $2. Delicious breakfasts. Open daily 6:30am-10pm. ❷

▓ **Hererra's,** 4001 Maple Ave. (☎528-9644), serves the best, cheapest Mexican food in Dallas. Their long menu has over 40 heaping combination plates ($7-9) that all come with fabulous, free bean soup. Try "Nora's Dinner," which is a guacamole *tostado,* a sour cream chicken enchilada, a beef taco, and rice and beans ($8.35). Open M and W-Th 11am-9pm, F 11am-10pm, Sa 9am-10pm, Su 9am-9pm. ❷

Crescent City Cafe, 2615 Commerce St. (☎745-1900). One of the city's most popular lunch spots, the cafe serves New Orleans cooking in the heart of Deep Ellum. Enjoy 3 fresh, warm beignets ($1.50) and cafe au lait ($1.35), or an Italian muffaletta (an Italian bun filled with ham, salami, mozzarella, provolone, swiss cheese, and olive salad dressing; $6.25 for a half). Open M-Th 8am-9pm, F-Sa 8am-midnight. ❶

Sonny Bryan's Smokehouse, 302 N. Market St. (☎744-1610), in the West End. Other locations at 2202 Inwood Rd. and 5519 W. Lover's Lane. The most famous barbecue joint in town. Try a brisket sandwich with two veggies ($6.59), their huge onion rings ($5 for 10). Vegetarian options available. Open Su-Th 11am-9pm, F-Sa 11am-10pm. ❸

Wild About Harry's, 3113 Knox St. (☎520-3113), purveyor of gourmet hot dogs and frozen custard, because, as Harry explains, "real cowboys never ate yogurt." Try a Knox St. Dog with Thousand Island dressing, sauerkraut, and swiss cheese (regular $3.45, jumbo $4.24). Single scoop custard $2.25, sundaes $3.25-5.25. Open Su-Th 11am-10pm, F-Sa 11am-11pm. ❶

⊙ SIGHTS

Downtown Dallas's architecture reflects the Art-Deco period of the city's glory days during the initial burst of oil. "Historic Dallas" can easily be seen via downtown walking tours. Dallas, however, is more notorious for its recent history—JFK's assassination during a campaign parade in 1963 is permanently preserved in various museums and landmarks.

JFK SIGHTS. At the **6th Floor Museum,** look out the window through which Lee Harvey Oswald allegedly fired the shot that killed President John F. Kennedy on Nov. 22, 1963. Immaculately preserved (the gunman's lunch sack remains underneath the windowsill), the museum traces the dramatic and macabre moments of the assassination through various media. *(411 Elm St., at Houston St., in the former Texas School Book Depository building. ☎747-6660; www.jfk.org. Open daily 9am-6pm. $10; seniors, students, and ages 6-18 $9. Audio cassette rental $3.)* To the south of the depository, Elm St. runs through **Dealy Plaza,** a national landmark beside the infamous grassy knoll. **Philip Johnson's Memorial** to Kennedy looms nearby at Market and Main. The cenotaph (open tomb), a symbol of the freedom of JFK's spirit, is most striking when viewed at night. To find out what they *didn't* tell you, investigate the **Conspiracy Museum,** which delves into the mysteries and inconsistencies of the accepted explanation of JFK's assassination with an *X-Files*-like paranoia and skepticism. The museum also hosts exhibits about other historical American assassinations, including those of four U.S. Presidents and Martin Luther King, Jr., as well as a mural downstairs depicting alien encounters. *(110 Market St., across the street from the Memorial. ☎741-3040. Open daily 10am-6pm. $10, students and seniors $6, children $3.)*

ART AND ARCHITECTURE. The architecture of the **Dallas Museum of Art** is as graceful and beautiful as its impressive collections of Egyptian, African, Early American, Impressionist, modern, and decorative art. *(1717 N. Harwood St. ☎922-*

1200; www.dm-art.org. Open Tu-W and F-Su 11am-5pm, Th 11am-9pm. $10, seniors and ages 12-17 $7, students with ID $5, children under 12 free. Admission includes audio tour of permanent collection. Free Th after 5pm and the first Tu of each month. Special exhibit admission varies.) Wrought bronze, steel, and stone grace the urban landscape in the contemporary and 20th-century sculptures at the new **☒Nasher Sculpture Center.** The center has a gallery inside, but the bulk of the collection lies in the beautiful, well-manicured garden. *(2001 Flora St. ☎ 242-5100. Open Tu-W and F-Su 11am-6pm, Th 11am-9pm. $10, seniors $7, students $5, under 12 free.)* Just across Harwood St., the **☒Trammell Crow Center** has a must-see collection of Asian art, and its sculpture garden displays works by Rodin, Maillol, and Bourdelle alongside famous American pieces. *(2010 Flora St., at Hardwood and Olive St. ☎ 979-6430. Open Tu-W and F-Su 10am-5pm, Th 10am-9pm. Free. Sculpture garden always open.)* The ubiquitous **I.M. Pei** designed many downtown Dallas buildings. Pei's **Fountain Place** at the Wells Fargo Bldg., on Ross St. just past Field St., creates an indelible mark on the city's skyline, and cools weary travelers with a two-acre water garden. The **Morton H. Meyerson Symphony Center,** 2301 Flora St., a few blocks east, and the imposing **Dallas City Hall** were also designed by Pei. Free tours of the Symphony Center are sometimes available. *(100 Marilla St., off Young St. ☎ 670-3600. Tours on selected M and Th-Sa 1pm.)*

OTHER ATTRACTIONS. The multilevel rainforest, giant river otters, and Japanese fighting crabs at the **Dallas World Aquarium** make this spot worth a plunge. Check out the new Mayan-themed "Mundo Maya" exhibit, with a jaguar and 400,000 gallon shark tunnel. *(1801 N. Griffin St., northeast of the West End, 1 block north of Ross Ave. ☎ 720-2224; www.dwazoo.com. Open daily 10am-5pm. $16, seniors $14, children $9.70.)* In bloom year-round, the 66-acre **Dallas Arboretum,** on the southeastern shore of White Rock Lake, provides a haven for pedestrian horticulture fans. *(8617 Garland Rd. Take bus #19 from downtown. ☎ 515-6500. Open daily 10am-9pm. $7, seniors $6, ages 3-12 $4, under 2 and members free. Parking $4.)*

FAIR PARK. Home to the state fair since 1886, **Fair Park** has earned national landmark status for its Art Deco architecture. During the fair, **Big Tex**—a 52 ft. smiling cowboy float—towers over the land, and only the **Texas Star,** a huge Ferris wheel, looms taller. The 277-acre park also hosts the **Cotton Bowl** on January 1. In association with the Smithsonian Institute, **The Women's Museum: An Institute for the Future** features a timeline of US women's history from 1500 to the present along with exhibits on famous American women. *(3800 Parry Ave. ☎ 915-0860; www.thewomensmuseum.org. Open Tu-Su noon-5pm. $5, seniors $4, and students $3.)*

HISTORIC DALLAS. The city's oldest park, aptly named **Old City Park,** hosts 35 renovated and restored 19th-century edifices. Locals enjoy lunching al fresco in the antiqued ambience. *(1717 Gano St., 9 blocks south of City Hall at Ervay St. ☎ 421-5141; www.oldcitypark.org. Open daily 9am-6pm. Exhibit buildings open Tu-Sa 10am-3pm, Su noon-4pm. $7, seniors $5, children $4.)* The **West End Historic District and Marketplace,** full of broad sidewalks, shops, and restaurants, lies north of Union Station. *(Most stores open M-Sa 11am-10pm, Su noon-6pm.)* Dallas's **mansions** are in the **Swiss Avenue Historic District,** and along the ritzy, boutique-lined streets of **Highland Park,** between Preston Rd. and Hillcrest Rd. south of Mockingbird Ln.

🎵 ENTERTAINMENT

The Observer, a free weekly found in stands across the city, has unrivaled entertainment coverage. For the scoop on Dallas's **gay scene,** pick up copies of the *Dallas Voice* and *Texas Triangle* in **Oaklawn** shops and restaurants.

Prospero works his magic at the **Shakespeare in the Park** festival, in Samuel-Grand Park just northeast of Fair Park. During June and July (no performances the last week of June), two free plays run six nights per week. (☎559-2778. Performances Tu-Su 8:15pm. Gates open 7:30; arrive early. $7 optional donation.) At Fair Park, the **Music Hall** hosts Broadway national tours in the **Dallas Summer Musicals** series. (☎691-7200 for tickets; www.dallassummermusicals.org. Shows run June-Oct. $11-75.) The **Dallas Symphony Orchestra** plays in the Symphony Center, 2301 Flora St. at Pearl St. in the arts district. (☎692-0203; www.dallassymphony.com. Box office open M-Sa 10am-6pm. $12-100.) In the summer, free outdoor jazz concerts are held every Thursday night at 9pm in front of the Museum of Art.

If you come to Dallas looking for cowboys, the **Mesquite Championship Rodeo,** 1818 Rodeo Dr., is the place to find them. Take I-30 east to I-635 S to Exit 4 and stay on the service road. Nationally televised, the rodeo is one of the most competitive in the country. (☎972-285-8777 or 800-833-9339; www.mesquiterodeo.com. Shows Apr. to early Oct. F-Sa 8pm. Gates open 6:30pm. $10, seniors $5, children 3-12 $5. Barbecue dinner $9.50, children $6.50. Pony rides $3. Parking $3.)

Six Flags Over Texas, 20 mi. from downtown off I-30 at Rte. 360 in Arlington, between Dallas and Fort Worth, boasts 38 rides, including the speedy, looping roller coasters "Batman: The Ride" and "Mr. Freeze." (☎817-530-6000. Open June to early Aug. daily from 10am; late Aug. to Dec. and Mar.-May Sa-Su from 10am. Park sometimes opens at 11am and closing times vary from 7 to 10pm. $41, over 55 or under 4ft. $25, under 2 free. Parking $9.) Across the highway lies the 47-acre waterpark, **Hurricane Harbor.** Open late May to early June most days 10:30am-6pm; June to early Aug. Su-Th 10:30am-8pm, F-Sa 10:30-9pm; mid-Aug. to early Sept. most days 10:30am-6pm. $30, over 55 or under 4 ft. $20, under 2 free. Parking $7.) Find coupons for both parks on soda cans and at Dallas or Ft. Worth tourist info offices.

In Dallas, the moral order is God, Texas, country, and the **Cowboys.** See "The Boys" in action from September to January at **Cowboys Stadium** at the junction of Rte. 12 and 183, west of Dallas in Irving. (☎972-785-5000. Ticket office open M-F 9am-5pm. From $37.) The **Ballpark in Arlington,** 1000 Ballpark Way, hosts the **Texas Rangers** from April to September. (☎817-273-5100. Ticket office open M-F 9am-6pm, Sa 10am-4pm, Su noon-4pm; on game days 9am until 2hr. before the start of the game. $5-55.) Experience the mystique of the game with a 1hr. tour of the locker room, dugout,

RIDE 'EM COWBOY

Don Gay is an eight-time world bull-riding champion, a celebrity in the rodeo world. His father was also a bullrider and founded the Mesquite Rodeo in Dallas, TX.

On becoming a bullrider: My Dad and Jim Shoulders, who was like the Babe Ruth of rodeo, 16-time world champion, began the Mesquite Rodeo when I was just five years old...With the rodeo every Friday and Saturday night it was kind of a natural progression for me to start riding the calves when I was little...I wanted to be the world champion bullrider, and that was my focus from childhood on. As soon as I got out of high school I set out on the quest.

On riding: It's just a reaction...A bull weighs an average of 1800 pounds, some of them are over 2000, so every time they jump, you make a countermove to stay in the middle. Pretty hard to do, actually.

On the best part of the rodeo: Being 5'6", 150 lb., I wasn't going to be able to play NBA, I wasn't going to be able to play any professional baseball. But the bull doesn't care how big you are. If you can enter the competition and ride the bulls, when you win, you've earned it. That's the best part of rodeo: this is not only a sport, it's a lifestyle. I think it has a lot to do with our heritage here in America. It's pretty wholesome; you don't blow the whistle and stop the action once the gate opens, you've got to ride her out.

and the press box on the **ballpark tour.** (☎817-273-5098. Non-game days tours every hr. M-Sa 9am-4pm, Su 11am-4pm; hours vary for game days, usually 9am-1pm. $10, students with ID and seniors $8, ages 4-18 $6.)

🎵 NIGHTLIFE

Head to **Deep Ellum,** east of downtown, an area that, in the 1920s, was a blues haven for legends Blind Lemon Jefferson, Lightnin' Hopkins, and Robert Johnson. In the 1980s, Bohemians revitalized the area. The first Friday of every month is Deep Friday (www.deepfriday.com), when an $8 wrist band gets you into eight Deep Ellum clubs featuring local rock acts. Other nightlife epicenters include **Lower Greenville Avenue** and **Yale Boulevard,** near Southern Methodist University's fraternity row. Many gay clubs rock a bit north of downtown in **Oaklawn.**

Trees, 2709 Elm St. (☎248-5902), rated the best live music venue in the city by the *Dallas Morning News,* occupies a converted warehouse with a loft full of pool tables and tree trunks in the middle of the club. Bands tend to play alternative rock music. 17+. Cover $2-20. Generally open W-Su 7pm-2am.

Club Dada, 2720 Elm St. (☎744-3232). A former haunt of Edie Brickell and the New Bohemians, this hoppin' club boasts diverse clientele, eclectic decor, and a spacious outdoor patio. Live acts every night range from rock to classical to jazz to the occasional stand-up comic. Open mic night Su. 21+. Cover W-Sa $5. Open Tu-Su 6pm-2am.

The Beagle, 1806 Lower Greenville Ave. (☎824-8767). Dallas's college hot spot. Enjoy the view from the third story rooftop deck, shoot pool, or boogie down to a wide variety of musical options—everything from country to top 40. Open daily W-M 5pm-2am.

Al Amir, 7402 Greenville Ave. (☎739-2647). A Lebanese restaurant and large multi-level club complete with hookah ($10-15) and belly dancers. Dine traditionally, seated on cushions at the low-to-the-ground tables (falafel $7), then hit the dance floor to the latest in Middle Eastern, Latin, and other international dance music. (Bar and club 21+, restaurant all ages. Open W-Su 6pm-2am. F-Sa business casual dress minimum. F-Sa $5 cover; free entry for females over 21 or parties with a food reservation on Sa.)

Roundup, 3912 Cedar Springs Rd. (☎522-9611), at Throckmorton St. A huge, cover-free country-western gay bar that packs a large crowd on weekends. Free dance lessons M-Th 8:30pm. Open M-F 3pm-2am, Sa-Su noon-2am.

FORT WORTH ☎817

If Dallas is the last Eastern city, Fort Worth is undoubtedly the first Western one. Less than 40min. west on I-30 from Dallas, Fort Worth boasts raw Texan flair with cultural refinement. The city has three districts: the **Stockyards Historic District, Sundance Square,** and the **Cultural District.** The Stockyards Historic District, along E. Exchange Ave., is the stompin' ground for both cowboys and Western wannabes. Exchange Ave., the main drag, is a window into the Wild West, with saloons, restaurants, shows, and prize-only gambling parlors. Catch the **cattle drive** down Exchange Ave. daily at 11:30am and 4pm. For more info, visit www.fortworth-stockyards.org. Uncover the mystery of cattle raising at the **Cattle Raisers Museum,** 1301 7th St., between Sundance Sq. and the Cultural District. (☎332-8551; www.cattleraisersmuseum.org. Open M-Sa 10am-5pm. $3, seniors and ages 13-18 $2, ages 4-12 $1.) With country music and a collection of cowboy hats, the **White Elephant Saloon,** 106 Exchange Ave., is a favorite. (☎624-1887. Cover F-Sa $8-10. Open Su-Th noon-midnight, F-Sa noon-2am.) At 121 Exchange Ave., the **Cowtown Coliseum** (☎625-1025 or 888-269-8696; www.cowtowncoliseum.com) hosts **rodeos** (F-Sa 8pm; $9, seniors $7.50, children $5.50) and **Pawnee Bill's Wild West Show.** (In summer Sa-Su 8pm; in winter, sporadically. $8, seniors $6.50, ages 3-12 $4.50.) The world's largest honky-tonk, **Billy Bob's Texas,** 2520 Rodeo Pl., ropes in crowds with country music's big names. The 126,000 sq. ft. club has a restaurant, pool tables, casino games, and 25 bar stations. (☎624-7117. Free dance lessons Th 7pm. Bull-riding F-Sa 9 and 10pm. Under 18 must be with parent. Cover before 6pm $1; after 6pm Su-M $3, Tu-Th $4, F-Sa $6.50-11. Open M-Sa 11am-2am, Su noon-2am.)

Sundance Sq. offers quality shops, museums, and restaurants. In the square, the **Sid Richardson Collection,** 309 Main St., displays paintings primarily by Western artists Remington and Russell. (☎332-6554. Open Tu-W 10am-5pm, Th-F 10am-8pm, Sa 11am-8pm, Su 1-5pm. Free.) West of downtown along 7th St., the Cultural District boasts a trio of high-caliber art museums. ◪**The National Cowgirl Museum and Hall of Fame,** 1720 Gendy St., has rhinestone-encrusted saddles, cowgirl apparel, and Andy Warhol's rendering of Annie Oakley. (☎336-4475; www.cowgirl.net. Open Tu-Sa 10am-5pm, Su noon-5pm. $6, seniors $5, under 18 $4.) The **Kimbell Art Museum,** 3333 Camp Bowie Blvd., touted as "America's best small museum," has masterpieces in a building that's a work of art in itself. (☎332-8451; www.kimbellart.org. Open Tu-Th and Sa 10am-5pm, F noon-8pm, Su noon-5pm. Free; special exhibits $10, students and seniors $8, ages 3-18 $6.) The excellent concrete and glass **Modern Art Museum,** 3200 Darnell, is just across the street. (☎738-9215 or 866-824-5566; www.themodern.org. Open Tu-Th 10am-5pm, F 10am-8pm, Sa 11am-5pm, Su noon-5pm. $6, seniors and students $4, ages 12 and under free.) The **Amon Carter Museum,** 3501 Camp Bowie Blvd., has a large collection of mostly Western art. Photos from their collection of over 30,000 prints rotate regularly on the 2nd fl. (☎738-1933; www.cartermuseum.org. Open Tu-W and F-Sa 10am-5pm, Th 10am-8pm, Su noon-5pm. Free.) After a day in cowtown, enjoy Mexican food at ◪**Joe T. Garcia's ❸,** 2201 N. Commerce St., which has a sprawling patio (with a swimming pool) and lush gardens. Joe T's only offers a choice between fajitas ($10-12) and cheese enchiladas with two tacos for $9.25. (☎626-8571. Open M-Th 11am-2:30pm and 5-10pm, F-Sa 11am-11pm, Su 11am-10pm.)

The **Trinity Railway Express,** 1600 Throckmorton St. and the corner of 9th and Jones St. (☎215-8600), runs from Fort Worth to Dallas, with stops at **Dallas-Fort Worth Airport.** (Trains run 5:30am-9pm.) **Visitor Info: Fort Worth Convention and Visitors Bureau,** 415 Throckmorton St., in Sundance Sq. (☎336-8791 or 800-433-5747; www.fortworth.com. Open M-F 8:30am-5pm, Sa 10am-4pm.) Other locations in Stockyards and Cultural District. **Post Office:** 251 W. Lancaster Ave. (☎870-8104. Open M-F 8:30am-6pm.) **Postal Code:** 76102. **Area Code:** 817.

HOUSTON ☎713

Though often overshadowed by its more famous counterparts, Houston is America's fourth-largest city. Coupling classy cosmopolitan amenities with a distinctive Texan attitude, Houston is home to an $88-million-dollar performing arts center as well as two new sports arenas. Once a city fueled by maritime commerce, Houston's economy is now reliant upon oil; the headquarters of energy conglomerates dominate the city's skyline. Yet beyond the glass-and-steel skyscrapers, culture abounds with an impressive array of world-class restaurants, museums, and cultural organizations that call Houston home. With her many resources (both natural and achieved), Houston has the potential to be America's next great city.

▐▆ TRANSPORTATION

Airport: George Bush Intercontinental Airport (☎281-230-3000), 25 mi. north of downtown. Get to city center via **Express Shuttle** (☎523-8888); buses depart daily from Astrodome, Downtown, Galleria, Greenway Plaza, and Westside area hotels every

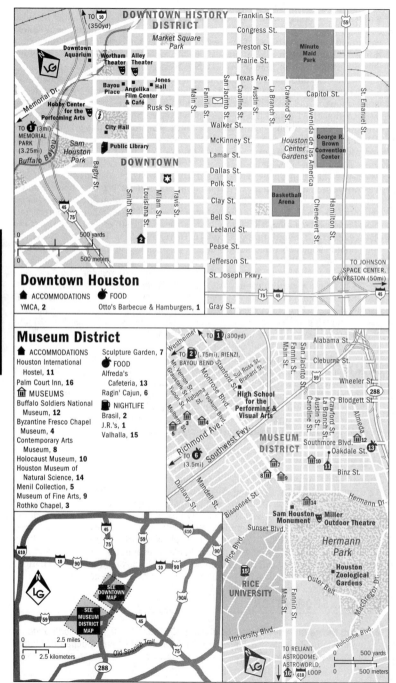

DOWNTOWN HISTORY DISTRICT

Downtown Aquarium

Wortham Theater

Alley Theater

Bayou Place

Angelika Film Center & Café

Jones Hall

Hobby Center for the Performing Arts

City Hall

Public Library

Sam Houston Park

Buffalo Bayou

TO MEMORIAL PARK (3mi) (3.25mi)

TO (10) (350yd)

Market Square Park

DOWNTOWN

Franklin St.

Congress St.

Preston St.

Prairie St.

Texas Ave.

Capitol St.

Rusk St.

Walker St.

McKinney St.

Lamar St.

Dallas St.

Polk St.

Clay St.

Bell St.

Leeland St.

Pease St.

Jefferson St.

St. Joseph Pkwy.

Gray St.

Minute Maid Park

Houston Center Gardens

George R. Brown Convention Center

Basketball Arena

TO JOHNSON SPACE CENTER, GALVESTON (50mi)

Main St.

Fannin St.

San Jacinto St.

Caroline St.

Austin St.

La Branch St.

Crawford St.

Avenida de las America

St. Emanuel St.

Hamilton St.

Chenevert St.

Memorial Dr.

Bagby St.

Smith St.

Louisiana St.

Milam St.

Travis St.

0   500 yards

0   500 meters

Downtown Houston

♦ ACCOMMODATIONS   🍗 FOOD

YMCA, 2   Otto's Barbecue & Hamburgers, 1

Museum District

♦ ACCOMMODATIONS

Houston International Hostel, 11

Palm Court Inn, 16

🏛 MUSEUMS

Buffalo Soldiers National Museum, 12

Byzantine Fresco Chapel Museum, 4

Contemporary Arts Museum, 8

Holocaust Museum, 10

Houston Museum of Natural Science, 14

Menil Collection, 5

Museum of Fine Arts, 9

Rothko Chapel, 3

Sculpture Garden, 7

🍗 FOOD

Alfreda's Cafeteria, 13

Ragin' Cajun, 6

🍸 NIGHTLIFE

Brasil, 2

J.R.'s, 1

Valhalla, 15

TO (300yd)

TO (.75mi), RIENZI, BAYOU BEND

Westheimer

High School for the Performing & Visual Arts

Richmond Ave.

TO (3.5mi) Southwest Frwy.

Dunlavy St.

Bissonnet St.

Mandell St.

MUSEUM DISTRICT

Sam Houston Monument

Miller Outdoor Theatre

Sunset Blvd.

Hermann Park

Houston Zoological Gardens

Rice Blvd.

RICE UNIVERSITY

University Blvd.

TO RELIANT ASTRODOME, ASTROWORLD, LOOP

Alabama St.

Cleburne St.

Wheeler St.

Blodgett St.

Southmore Blvd.

Oakdale St.

Binz St.

Hermann Dr.

Montrose Blvd.

Stanford St.

Mt. Vernon St.

Greeley St.

Yoakum Blvd.

Alabama St.

Yupon St.

Mulberry St.

Sul Ross St.

Branard St.

Fannin St.

Main St.

San Jacinto St.

Crawford St.

Austin St.

Caroline St.

La Branch St.

Almeda

Fannin St.

Main St.

MacGregor Dr.

Outer Belt

Holcombe Blvd.

0   2.5 miles

0   2.5 kilometers

Old Spanish Trail

SEE DOWNTOWN MAP

SEE MUSEUM DISTRICT MAP

0   500 yards

0   500 meters

30min.-1hr., depending on the destination. Runs 5:30am-11:30pm. $19-20, ages 5-12 $6, under 5 free. From downtown, allow 1hr. to get to the airport. **William P. Hobby Airport,** 7800 Airport Blvd. (☎640-3000; www.hou.houstonairportsystem.org), lies about 10 mi. south of downtown and specializes in regional travel.

Trains: Amtrak, 902 Washington Ave. (☎224-1577). From downtown, during the day, catch a bus west on Washington Ave. to Houston Ave.; at night, call a cab. To **San Antonio** (5hr., 1 per day, $33-59) and **New Orleans** (9hr., 1 per day, $50-93). Open M-F 9am-midnight, Su 9am-4:30pm. *Be careful entering and exiting station; the surrounding area can be unsafe, especially at night.*

Buses: Greyhound, 2121 Main St. (☎759-6565). *Be careful at night; this area can be unsafe.* Open 24hr. To: **Dallas** (4-6hr., 9 per day, $30); **San Antonio** (3½hr., 11 per day, $22); **Santa Fe** (24hr., 5 per day, $130).

Public Transit: Metropolitan Transit Authority (☎635-4000; www.ridemetro.org). Offers reliable service anywhere between NASA (15 mi. southeast of town) and Katy (25 mi. west of town). Operates M-F 6am-9pm, less often Sa-Su 8am-8pm. $1, seniors $0.40, ages 5-11 $0.25; day pass $2. The new light rail has 16 stops, running north-south from the University of Houston to Reliant Park. The METRO runs a free trolley throughout downtown. Free maps available at the **Houston Public Library** (see **Internet Access,** below) or at METRO stores. (720 Main or 1001 Travis. Open M-F 7:30am-5:30pm.)

Taxi: United Cab ☎699-0000.

▚ ▟ ORIENTATION AND PRACTICAL INFORMATION

Though Houston is sprawled out over a large expanse of flat Texan terrain that supports several mini-downtowns, the true downtown Houston, a squarish grid of interlocking one-way streets, borders the **Buffalo Bayou** at the intersection of I-10 and I-45. Much of downtown's foot traffic goes subterranean in the network of underground **tunnels** that connect most major skyscrapers and buildings. **The Loop (I-610)** encircles the city center with a radius of 6 mi. Anything inside the Loop is easily accessible by car or bus. *Be careful in some areas of south and east Houston, as they may be unsafe.* **Westheimer,** the main drag of the ritzy "Uptown" district, can be found west of downtown. Restaurants and shops line the nearby mansion-infested **Kirby Drive** and **Richmond Avenue,** but look out for detours, as these up-and-coming areas are perpetually under construction.

Visitor Info: Greater Houston Convention and Visitors Bureau (☎437-5200 or 800-446-8786; www.houston-spacecityusa.com), in City Hall, at the corner of Walker and Bagby St. Open M-Sa 9am-4pm, Su noon-4pm.

Hotlines: Crisis Center, ☎468-5463. **Rape Crisis,** ☎528-7273. **Women's Center,** ☎528-2121. **Gay and Lesbian Switchboard of Houston,** ☎529-9615. All operate 24hr.

Medical Services: Bellaire Medical Center, 5314 Dashwood (☎512-1200). **Woman's Hospital of Texas,** 7600 Fannin (☎790-1234).

Internet Access: Houston Public Library, 500 McKinney (☎236-1313), at Bagby St. Open M-Th 9am-9pm, F-Sa 9am-6pm, Su 2-6pm.

Post Office: 701 San Jacinto St. (☎800-275-8777). Open M-F 8am-5pm. **Postal Code:** 77052. **Area Codes:** 713, 281, and 832; in text, 713 unless indicated.

▛ ACCOMMODATIONS

A few cheap motels dot the **Katy Freeway (I-10W)** and **South 59th Street.** Budget accommodations along **South Main Street** are more convenient (located on bus route #8), but *not all are safe.* Most campgrounds in the Houston area lie a considerable distance from the city center.

Houston International Hostel, 5302 Crawford St. (☎523-1009; resv@houstonhostel.com), at Oakdale St., in the museum district near Hermann Park. Take the METRO rail south from the Downtown Transit Center and get off at the Museum District Station. Walk northeast ½ block to Binz St. Turn right, walk 5 blocks east to Crawford St., then left 2½ blocks to the hostel. 33 beds in 7 well-kept rooms. Internet access ($10 unlimited access, members free), kitchen, and common area. Reception 8-10am and 5-11pm. No dorm access 10am-5pm, but common area stays open all day. No curfew, but ask for a front door key if you expect to return after 11pm. Dorms $13 for Hostels Americas members, nonmembers $15. Private rooms $8 extra. Cash only. ●

YMCA, 1600 Louisiana St. (☎758-9250), between Pease and Bell St. Downtown location features small, bright rooms—all singles with daily maid service. Some have private baths. Towel deposit $2.50. Key deposit $10. Singles $27-38. Another **branch** is located at 7903 South Loop East (☎643-2804), off the Broadway exit from I-610, near I-45. Take bus #50 to Broadway. Key deposit $15. Singles $28. ●

Palm Court Inn, 8200 South Main St. (☎668-8000 or 800-255-8904; www.palmcourtinn.com). Plain, clean rooms. HBO, outdoor pool and spa, and continental breakfast. Reception 24hr. Singles $41; doubles $49. ❷

Traders Village, 7979 N. Eldridge Rd. (☎281-890-5500). Off I-10, take Eldridge Pkwy. exit, head north. This RV park provides shower, pool, and laundry facilities, and hosts an area-wide flea-market on weekends. Sites $20-26; RVs $24-26. Hookup included. ●

🍴 FOOD

A city by the sea, Houston has harbored many immigrants, and their cultures are well represented in the city's cuisine. Along with indigenous barbecue and southern soul food, Mexican, Greek, Cajun, and Asian fare supply travelers with many options. Bust your belt, not your budget, in the **tunnels** connecting downtown's skyscrapers, or along the chain-laden streets of Westheimer and Richmond Ave. Cheap Mexican food can be found almost anywhere, but the **East End** has authentic fare. Check out **Chinatown, DiHo,** or **Little Vietnam,** on S. Main, for tasty, budget eats.

🍽 **Otto's Barbecue and Hamburgers,** 5502 Memorial Dr. (☎864-2573 or 864-8526). A Houston institution, Otto's, in the corner of an old strip mall, has excellent burgers ($3-4) and great barbecue with all the fixins. The Bush Plate (sliced beef, links, ribs, potato salad, and beans; $9.50) is a favorite among both customers and a certain former President, who has been known to drop in. Open M-F 11am-7pm, Sa 11am-6pm. ❷

🍽 **Ragin' Cajun,** 4302 Richmond Ave. (☎623-6321). A local favorite for Cajun-style seafood. Indoor picnic tables, creole music, a full-service oyster bar, and a casual atmosphere. For an authentic taste of bayou home-cooking, try a bucket of Atchafalaya fresh boiled crawfish. Po' boys $6-9. Gumbo $4. Longneck beer $2.75. Open M-Th 11am-10pm, F-Sa 11am-11pm. ❷

One's A Meal: The Greek Village Restaurant, 607 W. Gray St. (☎523-0425), at Stanford St. This family-owned, Greek-American establishment serves everything from chili 'n' eggs ($7) to a gyro with fries ($6). Try the Greek pizza (6 in. $6) or the crowd-pleasing *dolmades* (stuffed grape leaves; $6). Other entrees range $8-20. Open 24hr. ❷

Alfreda's Cafeteria, 5101 Almeda Rd. (☎523-6462), close to Perry House. Alfreda's serves soul food for cheap; the special of the day includes meat, 2 vegetables, and bread for only $5. Open daily 6:30am-7:30pm. ●

House of Pies, 3112 Kirby Dr. Another location at 6142 Westheimer Rd. (☎782-1290). Cakes and pies of 40 varieties grace the formica countertops of this diner, which draws a diverse crowd of sweet-toothed clientele who can't resist the signature Bayoo Goo pie. In addition to its diverse desserts, House of Pies serves breakfast all day ($5-6.50), as well as the usual short-order sandwiches and entrees. Open 24hr. ●

👁 SIGHTS

JOHNSON SPACE CENTER. The city's most popular attraction, **Space Center Houston,** is outside Houston city limits in Clear Lake, TX. Admission includes tours of the center's historic mission control, an abandoned prototype hangar, and the astronaut training facility, as well as educational film-showings in Texas's largest Giant Screen theater. The complex also houses models of Gemini, Apollo, and Mercury crafts. No visit is complete without taking a moment to touch the moon rock on public display. (1601 NASA Rd. 1. Take I-45 south to NASA Rd. exit, then head east 3 mi.; or take bus #246. ☎281-244-2100; www.spacecenter.org. Open June-Aug. daily 9am-7pm; Sept.-May M-F 10am-5pm, Sa-Su 10am-7pm. $17, seniors $16, ages 4-11 $13. Parking $4.) You can get closest to the stars on the **Level 9 Tour,** which takes visitors to areas of the Space Center not usually open to tourists, including the New Mission Control Center, the Robotics Lab, the Space Environment Simulation Lab, and the Neutral Buoyancy Lab. The tour has a steep price, but for the wannabe rocketman (or woman), it's the only way to see the sights. (☎244-2115. 1 tour per day, M-F 11:50am-4pm. Limited to 12 people, reservations recommended.)

THE SAN JACINTO BATTLEGROUND STATE HISTORICAL PARK. This 570 ft. monument built in honor of those who fought for Texas's independence is the world's largest memorial tower. Riding to the top gives a stunning view of the battleground upon which Sam Houston's hugely outnumbered Texan Army defeated Santa Anna's Mexican troops, sealing Texas's independence. The monument's base houses a Texas history museum with remnants like the Battleship Texas—the last surviving Dreadnought and the only surviving battleship to have served in both World Wars. (Take loop 610 to Hwy. 225 E. Take the Battleground Road (Hwy. 134) exit, head north, and exit onto Juan Seguin Blvd. ☎281-479-2421. Open daily Apr.-Sept. 8am-9pm; Oct.-Mar. 8am-7pm. Free. Museum: ☎281-479-2431. Open daily 9am-6pm. Free. Elevator to observation deck $4, seniors $3.50, children $3. 40min. multimedia slide show daily every hr. 10am-5pm. $4.50/$4/$3.50. Combo tickets with elevator ride $7.50/$6.50/$5.50. Battleship: ☎281-479-2431. Open daily 10am-5pm. $5, seniors $4, ages 6-18 $3, under 6 free.)

HERMANN PARK. Made up of 445 acres of carefully preserved urban green space near Rice University, the Texas Medical Center, and Miller Outdoor The-

THE LOCAL STORY

HE'S A ROCKETMAN

Steve Swanson is an astronaut currently training at the Johnson Space Center in Houston, TX. He has worked at NASA for 11 years, was selected to be an astronaut in 1998, and is waiting to be assigned a mission.

LG: Why did you decide to become an astronaut?
A: It had adventure in it. It combined aspects of both mental and physical capabilities.

LG: What does the training involve?
A: Once you get selected, the first thing you go through is basic shuttle training, followed by basic space station trainings. Each one is about a year. Then there are multiple advanced training you can start to do. By the end of it, everyone...is well-trained. That's what makes the missions go well.

LG: What would you look forward to most in a flight mission?
A: The launch would be exciting, and it would be fun to float around and work in a zero-G environment, do a spacewalk, use a robotic arm...I'm looking forward to everything. I'll be able to tell you what was the most fun once I get back.

LG: What, in your view, is the future of man in space?
A: I do hope we start doing more exploration and going back to the moon, and going to planets. I think it's going to happen, it's just a matter of when it's going to happen. We will explore, and...keep going as far as we can.

atre (see p. 729), **Hermann Park** hosts a children's zoo, golf course, sports facilities, kiddie train, and Japanese garden. Near the northern entrance of the park, the **Houston Museum of Natural Science** has a planetarium, IMAX theater, six-story butterfly center, and hands-on learning gallery. Walk through the new Weiss Energy Hall, funded by Houston's biggest oil companies, which illustrates through sleeve guns and interactive computer stations how an urban cowboy can strike it rich. The **Houston Zoological Gardens,** at the southern end of the park, entertains crowds with 3500 exotic animals representing over 700 species. *(Museum of Natural Science: 1 Hermann Circle Dr. ☎639-4629; www.hmns.org. Exhibits open M-Sa 9am-6pm, Su 11am-6pm. Museum $6, seniors and under 12 $3.50; IMAX $7/ $4.50; planetarium $5/$3.50; butterfly center $5/$3.50. Japanese tea garden: Open daily 10am-6pm. Free. Zoo: 1513 N. MacGregor. ☎533-6500; www.houstonzoo.org. Open daily 10am-6pm. $7, seniors $5, ages 3-12 $3.)*

DOWNTOWN AQUARIUM. Located on the western border of downtown, this underwater adventure isn't your average fishtank. With valet parking and upscale drinking and dining, the **Downtown Aquarium** caters to a varied clientele. Kids enjoy the intricately choreographed dancing fountains and Ferris wheel, while grownups flock to the Dive Lounge for after dinner drinks. *(410 Bagby St. ☎223-3473. Aquarium exhibits open Su-Th 10am-10pm, F-Sa 10am-11pm. $7.50, seniors $6.50, ages 2-12 $5.50. Restaurants and lounge operate on different hours—call to check.)*

ART ATTRACTIONS. At Houston's **Museum of Fine Arts,** the Caroline Weiss Law building showcases contemporary and modern collections, while the Audrey Jones Beck building displays everything from ancient European art to Impressionist pieces. Be sure to see Bouguereau's famous painting, "The Elder Sister," and the Glassell Collection of African Gold, considered one of the best of its kind in the world. *(1001 Bissonet. ☎639-7300; www.mfah.org. Open Tu-W 10am-5pm, Th 10am-9pm, F-Sa 10am-7pm, Su 12:15-7pm. $7, students and seniors $3.50. Audio tour $10/$5. Th free. Garden: 5101 Montrose Blvd. Open daily 9am-10pm. Free.)* Across the street, the **Contemporary Arts Museum** frequently rotates exhibits of all different media. *(5216 Montrose St. ☎284-8250; www.camh.org. Open Tu-W and F-Sa 10am-5pm, Th 10am-9pm, Su noon-5pm.)*

The **Menil Foundation** consists of five buildings within a block of each other, housing everything from ancient antiquities to contemporary neon light sculptures. Showcasing Surrealist paintings and sculptures, Byzantine and medieval artifacts, and European, American, and African art, the **Menil Collection** also features touring installments. *(1515 Sul Ross. ☎525-9400; www.menil.org. Open W-Su 11am-7pm. Free.)* A block away, the **Rothko Chapel** houses 14 of Mark Rothko's famous monochromatic paintings in a non-denominational sanctuary. The Broken Obelisk sculpture out front provides a backdrop for area religious festivals staged on the chapel's grounds. *(3900 Yupon. Open daily 10am-6pm. Free.)* The **Byzantine Fresco Chapel Museum** displays the carefully restored ornate dome and apse from a 13th-century Byzantine chapel in Cyprus that was rescued in 1983 from antiquity thieves. *(4011 Yupon. ☎521-3990. Open F-Su 11am-6pm. Free.)*

OTHER MUSEUMS. Between the end of the Civil War in 1865 and the integration of the armed forces in 1944, the US Army had several all-black units. During the Indian Wars of the late 1800s, Cheyenne soldiers nicknamed these troops "Buffalo Soldiers," both because of their naturally curly hair and as a sign of respect for their fighting spirit. The history of African-Americans in the military from the Revolutionary War to the present is on display at the ☒**Buffalo Soldiers National Museum.** *(1834 Southmore. ☎942-8920; www.buffalosoldiermuseum.com. Open M-F 10am-5pm, Sa 10am-4pm. Free.)* The **Holocaust Museum,**

built in a chilling architectural style, has a rotating art gallery and two films about the Holocaust. *(5401 Caroline St. ☎942-8000; www.hmh.org. Open M-F 9am-5pm, Sa-Su noon-5pm. Free.)*

BAYOU BEND. The Hogg collection of American decorative art found in the **Bayou Bend Collection and Gardens** in **Memorial Park** is an antique-lover's dream. This mecca of Americana includes John Singleton Copley portraits and Paul Revere silver pieces, all preserved in the Hogg mansion. *(1 Westcott St. ☎639-7750, ext. 7750; www.mfah.org/bayoubend. Collection open Tu-Sa 10am-5pm, Su 1-5pm. Audio tours Sa-Su. $10, seniors and students $8.50, ages 10-18 $5, under 10 free. Guided tours for ages 10 and over every 90min. M-F $10/$8.50/$5. Gardens open Tu-Sa 10am-5pm, Su 1-5pm. 1½hr. garden tours by reservation. $3, under 10 free.)* For the European counterpart to Bayou Bend, visit Rienzi, located along the same ravine. Formerly the residence of Houstonian Harris Masterson III, the **Rienzi Mansion** exhibits Georgian English decorative art including gilded footstools made for Spencer House, once the London home of Princess Diana. *(1406 Kirby Dr. ☎639-7800. M and Th-Sa 10am-4pm, Su 1-5pm. $4. Viewing of the house is only available via tour, so call ahead to reserve your spot.)*

🎵 ENTERTAINMENT

From March to October, symphony, opera, ballet companies, and various professional theaters stage free performances at the **Miller Outdoor Theatre** (☎284-8352), in Hermann Park. The annual **Shakespeare Festival** struts and frets upon the stage in August. The downtown **Alley Theatre**, 615 Texas Ave., puts on Broadway-caliber productions at moderate prices. (☎228-8421; www.alleytheatre.org. Tickets $37-54; Su-Th $12 student rush tickets 1hr. before the show.) For downtown entertainment, **Bayou Place**, 500 Texas Ave., holds several restaurants and live music venues. The **Angelika Film Center and Café**, 510 Texas Ave., plays foreign, independent, and classic American films. (☎333-3456. $8, students $6.) The new **Hobby Center for the Performing Arts**, 800 Bagby St. (☎315-2400; www.thehobbycenter.org), features a dome ceiling with a fiber optic display of the Texas night sky and hosts **Theatre Under the Stars** as well as the **Broadway in Houston Series. Jones Hall**, 615 Louisiana St. (☎227-3974), stages more of Houston's highbrow entertainment. The **Houston Symphony Orchestra** performs in Jones Hall from September to May. (☎227-2787. Tickets $5-95.) Between October and May, the **Houston Grand Opera** (www.houstongrandopera.org) produces eight operas in the nearby Wortham Center, 500 Texas Ave. (☎546-0200. Tickets $30-275; student rush tickets available day of show $15-30, call ahead to reserve.) The **Houston Astros** play at Minute Maid Park (☎295-8000), located at the intersections of Texas, Crawford, and Congress St. near Union Station downtown. From February to mid-March, there's plenty of space in both the Reliant Center and Reliant Arena to house the **Houston Livestock Show and Rodeo** (☎832-667-1000; www.hlsr.com). It's nothin' but net in the new downtown Toyota Center, at Polk and Crawford St., home of the **Houston Rockets,** while the **Houston Texans** pass the pigskin at **Reliant Stadium**, 8400 Kirby Dr. (☎336-7700).

🍸 NIGHTLIFE

The 2004 Super Bowl spawned clubs in Houston's skyscraper district, but most of Houston's nightlife is west of downtown around Richmond and Westheimer Ave. Montrose hosts several gay bars and clubs, while warehouse-style dance halls line Richmond's upper reaches. For a swanky evening, head to the Galleria district.

TEXAS

Brasil, 2604 Dunlavy St. (☎528-1993). This hip coffeehouse is a popular Westheimer Ave. hangout with live music most nights. Sip coffee, beer, or wine amid walls adorned by local artists' work, or head to the foliage-enclosed patio for a small but lush oasis in the city. Serves breakfast in the morning and sandwiches, pizzas and desserts into the night; plenty of vegetarian options. Open M-Sa 8am-2am, Su 8am-midnight.

Valhalla, Keck Hall, Rice University (☎348-3258). For "gods, heroes, mythical beings, and cheap beer," students, locals, and travelers alike descend to the depths of Keck Hall located on the Rice campus. Beer on tap from $0.85. Lunch ($3-4) served M-F 11:30am-1pm. Open M-F 4pm-2am, Su 7pm-2am.

J.R.'s, 808 Pacific St. (☎521-2519). This upbeat gay bar and nightclub plays techno and dance. Drinks $3-5. Strip contests Tu-W 11pm. No cover. Open daily noon-2am.

▶ DAYTRIP FROM HOUSTON

GALVESTON ISLAND

When cotton was king, Galveston was "Queen of the Gulf." The glamorous port that played a large role in the expansion of Western trade, however, was dethroned on September 8, 1900, when a devastating hurricane ripped through the city and claimed 6000 lives. Yet with over 32 mi. of sand and a wealth of history, it's no wonder today's tides bring in scores of visitors. A popular spring break destination, the southern end of the island, **Seawall Boulevard,** is full of cheap eats and rentals, while the northern end, the historic **Strand District,** attracts antique collectors and history buffs. Found along Strand St. between 20th and 25th St., the Strand District is a national landmark with restored gas lights and brick-paved walkways, with many Victorian buildings, cafes, and shops. The elegant **Moody Mansion,** 2618 Broadway, features handcarved wood and stunning stained glass. (☎762-7668. Open M-Sa 10am-4pm, Su noon-4pm. $6, seniors $5, ages 6-18 $3.) On the west side of the island lies an amusement park by the same name. The **Moody Gardens** consist of three glass pyramids housing a tropical rainforest, an aquarium with viewing areas both above and below the tanks, and interactive science exhibits. The park also features an IMAX 3D theater, over 25 acres of garden, and an artificial white sand beach with lagoons and palm trees. (1 Hope Blvd. From Seawall Blvd., take a right on 81st St. ☎683-4200 or 800-582-4673; www.moodygardens.com. Open daily in summer 10am-9pm; in winter 9am-6pm. Aquarium $14, seniors $10, ages 4-12 $7. Rainforest $9/$7/$6. IMAX $9/$7/$6. Ridefilm $8/$7/$6. Day pass to all attractions $30. Adult admission discounted after 6pm.)

The only beach in Galveston which permits alcoholic beverages is **R.A. Apffel Park,** on the far eastern edge of the island (known as East Beach). On the west end of the island, east of Pirates Beach, **#3 Beach Pocket Park** has bathrooms, showers, playgrounds, and a concession stand. (Open daily 10am-6pm; some open later. Car entry for beaches generally $7.) At Ferry Rd. (off the far eastern end of Seawall, across from the Sandpiper Motel), catch a free ferry to **Port Bolivar,** fondly dubbed "The Zoo" by spring breakers. The oldest restaurant on the island, **The Original Mexican Cafe ❷,** 1401 Market St., dishes up tasty enchilada plates starting at $4.50. (☎762-6001. Open M-Th 11am-9pm, F 11am-10pm, Sa 8am-10pm, Su 8am-9pm.)

CORPUS CHRISTI ☎361

Corpus Christi's shoreside location makes it a multi-faceted money-maker. The warm gulf waters produce Corpus's copious amounts of tourists and crude oil. Summer vacationers are replaced in the cooler months by "winter Texans," a breed of northern mobile-home owners who head south to enjoy coastal warmth. Defined by its pricey knick-knacks, natural stretches of sand, and offshore oil derricks on the horizon, Corpus Christi is a unique Texas stopover.

TRANSPORTATION. Greyhound, 702 N. Chaparral (☎882-9206; open daily 7am-2am) runs to: Austin (6hr., 3-4 per day, $31); Dallas (10-11hr., 6 per day, $50); Houston (5hr., 7 per day, $24). **Regional Transit Authority** (☎289-2600), also known as the "B," buses within Corpus Christi. Get maps and schedules at the visitors center or at **The B Headquarters,** 1806 S. Alameda (☎883-2287; open M-F 8am-5pm). City Hall, Port Ayers, Six Points, Padre Staples Mall, and the Staples St. stations are central transfer points. (Runs M-Sa 5:30am-9:30pm, Su 11am-6:30pm. $0.50; students, seniors, and children $0.25; Sa $0.25; transfers free.) The **Harbor Ferry** follows the shoreline and stops at the aquarium (runs daily 10:30am-6:30pm; $3). On the north side of Harbor Bridge, the free **Beach Shuttle** also travels to the beach, aquarium, and other attractions (runs May-Sept. 10:30am-6:30pm). **Taxi: Yellow Cab** ☎884-3211.

PRACTICAL INFORMATION. Corpus Christi's tourist district follows **Shoreline Drive,** which borders the Gulf Coast, 1 mi. east of the downtown business district. **Convention and Visitors Bureau,** 1823 Chaparral, 6 blocks north of I-37 and 1 block from the water. (☎561-2000 or 800-766-2322; www.corpuschristi-tx-cvb.org. Open daily 9am-5pm.) **Medical Services: Spohn Hospital Shoreline,** 600 Elizabeth St. (☎881-3000). **Hotlines: Battered Women and Rape Victims Shelter** (☎884-2900 or 800-580-4878), operates 24hr. **Internet Access: Corpus Christi Public Library,** 805 Comanche. (☎880-7000. Open M-Th 9am-9pm, F-Sa 9am-6pm, Su 2-6pm.) **Post Office:** 809 Nueces Bay Blvd. (☎800-275-8777. Open M-F 7:30am-5:30pm, Sa 8am-1pm.) **Postal Code:** 78469. **Area Code:** 361.

ACCOMMODATIONS. Cheap accommodations are scarce downtown, and posh hotels and motels take up much of the shoreline. The island-like strip off U.S. 181 north of the Harbor Bridge houses cheaper motels, though prices skyrocket on holiday weekends. Most are within walking distance of the aquarium, the *USS Lexington,* and the Harbor Ferry. One of the cheapest among them is the clean, comfortable **Budget Inn ❷,** 231 Stewart Pl., which has rooms with HBO and microfridges. (☎883-1155. Key deposit $5. Singles $40; doubles from $49.) When holiday-weekending tourists drive prices up near the shore, consider the cheaper motel bargains that lie several miles south on Leopard St. (take bus #27) or at the Port Ave. exit off I-37. Campers should head to **Padre Island National Seashore** (p. 732). **Nueces River City Park ❶** (☎241-1464), off I-37 N from Exit 16, approximately 18 mi. from downtown Corpus, has free tent sites but only pit toilets and no showers. Camping permits are available from the tourist info center at 14333 IH-37 S.

FOOD AND NIGHTLIFE. Corpus Christi manages to bring the Gulf Coast into its otherwise chain-laden cuisine, with several inexpensive seafood shacks along the shore. **Pier 99 ❷,** 2822 N. Shoreline Dr., specializes in fried fresh fish, with $7 shrimp or oyster baskets, and "Macho Gumbo". (☎887-0764. Open M-F 11am-10pm, Sa-Su 11am-11pm.) **Blackbeard's ❷,** 3117 N. Surfside Blvd., serves true Texan cuisine—both Mexican platters and country fried goodness—as well as seafood. The lunch specials are inexpensive and great after a morning on beach. Try either the enchiladas or the chicken fried steak for $5. (☎884-1030. Full bar. Open daily 11am-10pm.) In the evening, boot-scoot to top 40 country at **Dead Eye Dick's,** then bump and grind to top 40 dance at **Stinger's,** both located at 301 N. Chaparral St. (☎882-2192. 21+. Cover $3-8. Open W-Sa 11pm-2am.)

TEXAS

◙ **SIGHTS.** Although obstructed by monolithic seaside motels and overrun by ravenous gulls, Corpus Christi's endless shoreline provides quite a sight. The best beach is **Port Aransas,** reachable by ferry (on Rte. 361). To find beaches that allow swimming (some lie along Ocean Dr. and north of Harbor Bridge), just follow the signs. On the north side of Harbor Bridge, the **Texas State Aquarium,** 2710 N. Shoreline Blvd., has a popular dolphin show four times each day, and one that exhibit showcases sharks and rays roaming, in true Texas fashion, beneath an oil platform (☎881-1200 or 800-477-4853; www.texasstateaquarium.org. Open June-Aug. M-Sa 9am-6pm, Su 10am-6pm; Sept.-May M-Sa 9am-5pm, Su 10am-5pm. $13, seniors $11, ages 4-12 $7.50.) Just offshore floats the aircraft carrier **USS Lexington,** a WWII relic which made a cameo in the Hollywood blockbuster *Pearl Harbor.* Today's Lexington features self-guided tours of the ship and an aircraft on the flight deck. (☎888-4873 or 800-523-9539. Open daily June-Aug. 9am-6pm; Sept.-May 9am-5pm. $10, seniors $8, ages 4-12 $5.) Pick up $1-off coupons to the aquarium and ship at the visitors center.

PADRE ISLAND   ☎ 361

With over 80 mi. of painstakingly preserved beaches, dunes, and wildlife refuge land, the **Padre Island National Seashore (PINS)** is the longest stretch of undeveloped barrier island in the world, sandwiched between the North Padre Island's prolific condos and resort-laden South Padre Island's seasonal and scandalous springbreakers. The seashore provides excellent opportunities for windsurfing, swimming, or surf fishing. Driving is allowed at most places on the beach, but 4WD is recommended. Padre Island is divided into several areas; gain entrance to each through the access roads. Access 1A is at the far northern tip of the island near Port Aransas, while Access 6 is closest to PINS. Motorists enter PINS via the JFK Causeway, from the Flour Bluff area of Corpus Christi. PINS can only be reached by car. For up-to-date info on prices and activities, as well as maps and exhibits about the island, call or visit the **Malaquite Visitors Center,** 20402 Park Rd. 22, 10 mi. south from the Causeway and bridge to the island. (☎949-8068; www.nps.gov/pais. Open daily in summer 8:30am-6pm; in winter 8:30am-4:30pm.) Garbage from nearby ships litters the sands, but a lucky few may spot one of the endangered Kemp's Ridley sea turtles nurtured by PINS. A yearly entrance pass into PINS costs $20, or buy a weekly pass ($10). Windsurfing or boat-launching from the **Bird Island Basin** is $10 for a yearly pass or $5 for a day. **Worldwinds Windsurfing** (☎949-7472 or 800-793-7471) rents a large range of windsurfing equipment (beginner's rig and lesson $50) as well as sea kayaks (single $20 per 2hr., $40 per day). Many avoid these higher fees by going to **North Beach,** the 3 mi. stretch between Bob Hall Pier and the Malaquite Beach vehicle barrier that is accessible by Access Road 6. **Bob Hall Pier,** Access 4, is the main fishing pier. (☎949-0999. Open 24hr. $1.)

Five miles south of the entrance station, **Malaquite Beach** has all the amenities for a day at the beach. In summer, a rental station is set up on the beachfront (inner tubes $2 per hr., chairs $2 per hr., body boards $2.50 per hr.) Loose sand stops most vehicles from venturing far onto the beach, but the first 5 mi. of **South Beach,** just south of Malaquite Beach, are accessible by two-wheel drive vehicles. Visitors with 4WD and a taste for solitude should make the 60 mi. trek to the **Mansfield Cut,** the most remote and untraveled area of the seashore. Call the **PINS Headquarters** (☎949-8173, ext. 0), 3½ mi. south of the park entrance, for emergency assistance. No wheels? Hike the **Grasslands Nature Trail,** a ¾ mi. paved loop through sand dunes and grasslands. Guide pamphlets are available at the trailhead. The **PINS Campground ❶,** 1 mi. north of the visitors center, has an asphalt area for RVs, restrooms, and cold-rinse showers. (Sites $8.) Outside of this area—with the exception of the 5 mi. pedestrian-only beach—camping is free. **Area Code:** 361.

WEST TEXAS

AMARILLO   ☎ 806

Named for the yellow clay of nearby Lake Meredith (*amarillo* is Spanish for "yellow"), Amarillo began as a railroad construction camp in 1887 and ultimately evolved into a Texas-size truck stop. After years of cattle and oil, Amarillo is now the prime overnight stop for motorists en route from Dallas, Houston, or Oklahoma City to Denver and other Western destinations. For travelers, it's little more than a one-day city, but what a grand, shiny stop it is.

The largest history museum in Texas, the **Panhandle-Plains Historical Museum,** 2401 4th Ave., I-27 S to Rte. 87 in nearby Canyon, tells the region's story from dinosaurs to oil drillers, and includes "cowboy" art, a replicated life-size pioneer town, and working oil derrick. (☎651-2244. Open in summer M-Sa 9am-6pm, Su 1-6pm; low-season M-Sa 9am-5pm, Su 1-6pm. $4, seniors $3, ages 4-13 $1.) The **American Quarter Horse Heritage Center and Museum,** 2601 I-40 E, at Exit 72B, tells the heroic story of "America's horse." Try your hand at the mechanical horse ride. (☎376-5181 or 888-209-8322; www.aqha.com. Open M-Sa 9am-5pm, Su noon-5pm. $4, seniors $3.50, ages 6-18 $2.50.) At ⬛**Cadillac Ranch,** eccentric millionaire Stanley Marsh III planted 10 Cadillacs—model years 1948 to 1963—at the same angle as the Great Pyramids, and as one local noted, "they didn't take root, neither." Take the Hope Rd. exit off I-40, 9 mi. west of Amarillo, cross to the south side of I-40, turn right at the end of the bridge, and drive ½ mi. down the highway access road.

Amarillo provides over 4000 beds for travelers to leave their boots by. Budget motels proliferate along I-40, I-27, and U.S. 287/87 near town. Prices rise near downtown. One of the most popular options is the **Big Texan Motel ❸,** 7701 I-40 E, with an 1860s Texas-style facade and a horse hotel in case you rode in on your trusty steed. (☎372-5000. Restaurant and swimming pool. Singles $45-51; doubles $60-65. $5 AAA/AARP discount.) **KOA Kampground ❶,** 1100 Folsom Rd., has a pool in summer. Take I-40 to Exit 75, go north to Rte. 60, then east 1 mi. (☎335-1792. Laundry and coffee. Reception daily June-Aug. 8am-10pm; Sept.-May 8am-8pm. Tent sites $20, water and electricity $27-29, full hookup $28-31.)

At I-40 and Georgia north of the interstate, heaping portions and a friendly vibe make **Dyer's BBQ ❷** a favorite. The rib plate includes three finger-lickin'-good ribs, potato salad, cole slaw, baked beans, apricots, and onion rings for $8. (☎358-7104. Open M-Sa 11am-10pm, Su 11am-9pm.) The **Big Texan Steak Ranch ❸,** 7701 I-40 E, next to the Big Texan Motel, with its sign proclaiming "yes, everything's bigger in Texas," offers a simple challenge: eat a 72 oz. steak dinner in under an hour, and receive the meal for free. Note, though, that an unfinished steak will set you back $50. (☎372-6000. Open daily 7am-10:30pm.) For West Texas Mexican eats, head to **Tacos García ❷,** 1100 S. Ross. Try the Laredo platter (3 roast beef *flautas* with rice, beans, and guacamole; $7.75), and delicious *sopapillas* for $3. (☎371-0411. Open M 10:30am-9:30pm, Tu-Sa 10:30am-10pm, Su 10:30am-3:30pm.)

Amarillo sprawls at the intersection of I-27, I-40, and U.S. 287/87. To explore, you need a car. Rte. 335 (the Loop) encircles the city. Amarillo Blvd. (historic Rte. 66) runs east-west, parallel to I-40. **Greyhound,** 700 S. Tyler (☎374-5371; open 24hr.), buses to Dallas (8hr., 4 per day, $60-66) and Santa Fe (9-10hr., 4 per day, $58-64). **Amarillo City Transit,** 801 SE 23rd, operates eight bus routes departing from 3rd and Fillmore St. Maps are at the office. (☎378-3095. Buses run every 15-30min. M-Sa 6:30am-6:30pm. $0.75.) The **Texas Travel Info Center,** 9700 I-

40 E, at Exit 76, has state info. (☎335-1441. Open daily 8am-6pm.) The **Amarillo Convention and Visitors Bureau**, 401 S. Buchanan St., Ste. 101, dishes the local scoop. (☎374-8474 or 800-692-1338; www.amarillo-cvb.org. Open M-F 9am-6pm, Sa-Su 10am-4pm.) **Internet Access: Public Library**, 413 E. 4th Ave., at Buchanan and Pierce across from the Civic Center. (Open M-Th 9am-9pm, Sa 9am-6pm, Su 2-6pm.) **Post Office:** 505 E. 9th Ave., at Buchanan St. (☎468-2148. Open M-F 8am-5pm.) **Postal Code:** 79105. **Area Code:** 806.

▐ DAYTRIP FROM AMARILLO: PALO DURO CANYON STATE PARK.

Twenty-three miles south of Amarillo, Palo Duro Canyon, the "Grand Canyon of Texas," covers 20,000 acres. Take I-27 to Exit 106 and head east on Rte. 217. The breathtaking 16 mi. **scenic drive** begins at the park headquarters. Backcountry **hiking** is permitted, but most visitors stick to the marked trails. Most hikers can manage the **Sunflower Trail** (3 mi.), the **Juniper Trail** (2 mi.), or the **Paseo del Río Trail** (2 mi.), but only experienced hikers should consider the rugged **Running Trail** (9 mi.). Avid bikers enjoy the **Capitol Peak Mountain Bike Trail** (4 mi.). The **Lighthouse Trail** (5 mi.) leads to amazing geological formations. (Park open daily in summer 7am-10pm; in winter 8am-10pm. $3, under 12 free.) Canyon temperatures often climb to 100°F; bring plenty of water. The headquarters, just inside the park, has trail maps and info on park activities. (☎488-2227. Open daily in summer 7am-10pm; in winter 8am-5pm.) The official play of Texas, the musical █**Texas Legacies,** is performed in Pioneer Amphitheater, 1514 5th Ave. The epic drama (with plenty of pyrotechnics) tells the tale of a Texas ranch family through the Civil War and other turbulent times. (☎655-2181. June-Aug. M-Sa 8:30pm. $11-27, under 12 $5-23.) **Old West Stables**, ¼ mi. farther along, runs 1- and 4-hour guided horse tours through the canyon. (☎488-2180. Rides offered Mar.-Nov. 10am, noon, 2, 4, 6pm; 1hr. rides $21, 4hr. $75. Wagon rides for groups of 10 or more $5 per person, children $3 per person. Reservations required for 4hr. rides.) A ½ mi. past the headquarters, the **visitors center** has exhibits on the canyon's history. (Open M-Sa 9am-5pm, Su 1-5pm.)

GUADALUPE MOUNTAINS NATIONAL PARK   ☎915

Rising austerely above the parched West Texas desert, these peaks are the highest, most remote of the West Texas ranges. Mescalero Apaches hunted and camped on these lands until they were driven out by the USA army. Today, Guadalupe Mountains National Park encompasses 86,000 acres of desert, caves, canyons, and highlands. From U.S. 62/180 drivers can see the park's most dramatic sights: **El Capitán,** a 2000 ft. limestone cliff, and **Guadalupe Peak,** which at 8749 ft. is the highest point in Texas. The mountains provide over 80 mi. of challenging desert trails. Park entrance is free. Hiking and backcountry access is $3 per person.

The major park trailhead is at Pine Springs Campground, near the **main visitors center** (see below). It's a strenuous full-day hike to the summit of the imposing **Guadalupe Peak** (8½ mi., 5-8hr.). A shorter trek (4¼ mi., 3-4hr.) traces the sheltered streambed of **Devil's Hall.** Accessible from a trailhead at its own visitors center, **McKittrick Canyon** attracts travelers with its brilliant foliage in fall.(4½-6¾ mi. round-trip). The **Smith Spring Trail** (2¼ mi., 1-2hr.) leads from the **Frijole Ranch,** 1 mi. north of the visitors center, to a spring frequented by deer and pig-like *javelinas*.

The park's lack of development is attractive to backpackers, but it creates some inconveniences. The nearest gas and food spot is the **Nickel Creek Cafe ❶,** 5 mi. north of Pine Springs. (☎828-3295. Burgers $4. Open M-Sa 7am-2pm and 6-9pm. Cash only.) The park's two campgrounds, **Pine Springs ❶,** just past park headquarters, and **Dog Canyon ❶,** south of the New Mexico border at the north end of the park, have water and restrooms but no hookups or showers. (☎828-3251. No wood or charcoal fires. Reservations for groups only. Sites $8.) Dog Canyon is accessible only via Rte. 137 from Carlsbad, NM (72 mi.), or by a full-day hike from the main visitors center at Pine Springs, off U.S. 62/180. (☎828-3251. Open daily June-Aug. 8am-6pm; Sept.-May 8am-4:30pm. After hours, info is posted on the outside bulletin board.) Free **backcountry camping** permits are available at the visitors center.

Carlsbad, NM (see p. 902), 55 mi. northeast, and **El Paso** (see p. 735), 110 mi. west, both make good bases for visiting the park. **TNM&O Coaches** (☎505-887-1108) runs along U.S. 62/180 between them and will stop at the main visitors center if you call ahead (from Carlsbad 2½hr., $26). For additional info about the park, check the website (www.nps.gov/gumo), call the visitors center, or write to **Guadalupe Mountains National Park**, HC 60, Box 400, Salt Flat, TX 79847. **Area code:** 915.

EL PASO   ☎915

El Paso, the largest US border town, boomed in the 17th century as a stopover on an east-west wagon route that followed the Río Grande through "the pass" (*el paso*) between the Rocky Mountains and the Sierra Madre. Today, the El Paso-Ciudad Juárez metropolitan area has nearly three million inhabitants. Nearly everyone speaks Spanish, and the majority are of Mexican descent. Downtown bustles during the day, but the action moves across the border after dark. *Stay on El Paso St. if walking between San Antonio Ave. and the border late at night.*

Historic **San Jacinto Plaza** houses shaded benches and a fiberglass alligator sculpture honoring the three reptiles the city once kept there. For a view of the Río Grande Valley, head northwest of downtown along Stanton and make a right turn on Rim Rd. (which becomes Scenic Dr.) to reach **Murchison Park**, at the base of the ridge. The park offers a sweeping vista of El Paso, Ciudad Juárez, and the Sierra Madre Mountains. The **El Paso Museum of Art**, 1 Arts Festival Plaza, is one of the largest art museums in the Southwest, with over 5000 works. The collections of 19th- to 20th-century Southwestern art and 18th- to 19th-century Latin American colonial art are particularly extensive. (☎532-1707. Open Tu-Sa 9am-5pm, Su noon-5pm. Free.) **Hueco Tanks State Historical Park,** 32 mi. east of town off U.S. 62, has nationally-recognized rock climbing, bouldering, and hiking in cliffs adorned by ancient pictographs. Call ahead: only 70 people are allowed in the park at once. (☎849-6684, reservations ☎512-389-8900. Open Oct.-Apr. daily 8am-6pm; May-Sept. M-Th 8am-6pm, F-Su 7am-7pm. Park admission $4, children 12 and under free.)

El Paso offers safer, more appealing places to stay than Ciudad Juárez. The town center, by Main St. and San Jacinto Sq., has several good budget hotels. The best place in town is the ▨**El Paso International Hostel** ❶, 311 E. Franklin, between Stanton and Kansas in the Gardner Hotel. Staff are happy to assist in arranging any tourist or travel plans. From the airport, take bus #33 to San Jacinto Park, walk ½ block east to Mesa, then two blocks north to Franklin, turn right, and head east 1½ blocks. (☎532-3661; www.elpasohostel.com. Sheets $2, towels $0.50. Dorms $15.) Operated in tandem by the same friendly staff, the **Gardner Hotel** ❷, 311 E. Franklin, is the oldest operating hotel in El Paso. John Dillinger stayed here in 1934. All rooms have A/C and cable TV. (☎532-3661; www.gardnerhotel.com. Singles with shared bath $21.60, doubles with shared bath $33, private baths from $40.) Camp at **Hueco Tanks State Historical Park** ❶ (see below), 32 mi. east of town. (☎849-6684. Water and showers. Entrance $4, sites $10, water and electricity $12.)

At the **Tap Bar and Restaurant** ❶, 408 E. San Antonio enjoy the tasty $2.00-3.75 burritos, $4.25-5.00 enchiladas, and $9 grilled shrimp in garlic. (☎532-1848. Open M-Sa 7am-2am, Su noon-2am.) **Ay! Chihuahua Restaurant** ❶, 122 S. Mesa, between

Overland and San Antonio, serves burritos ($1.50-2.25) and entrees for $3-5.50 with rice and beans. (☎532-7661. Open M-Sa 7am-5pm, Su 7:30am-3pm.) **Club 101,** 500 San Francisco, is a casual but lively scene where a diverse crowd lets loose on the dance floor to music with a rock/alternative bent. (☎544-2101. Live music F, DJ Sa. F-Sa, 9pm-3am. 18+. Cover $5-20). The more upscale **Club Xcape,** 209 S. El Paso St., downtown in a restored theater, caters to a chic crowd, and plays top 40, latin, and hip-hop. The club also has an upstairs lounge. (☎542-3800. Open F-Sa 9pm-2am. 21+.) Both clubs occasionally host major bands.

El Paso International Airport (☎780-4749; take Sun Metro bus #33 to the city center) has major airline service. **Amtrak** runs trains from **Union Train Depot,** 700 San Francisco St., to **Tucson** (6hr., 3 per week, $67) and **San Antonio** (12½hr., 3 per week, $65-127). **Greyhound,** 200 W. San Antonio (☎532-2365) near the Civic Center, has daily service to: **Albuquerque** (5½hr., 3 per day, $38); **Tucson** (6hr., 12 per day, $37); **Dallas** (12hr., 11 per day, $54). **El Paso-LA Bus Lines,** 720 Oregon St. (☎532-4061), on the corner of 6th Ave., is significantly cheaper than Greyhound and offers service to major destinations in the Southwest. (Tickets $15-90.) **Visitor Info: Visitors Center,** 1 Civic Center Plaza, at Santa Fe and San Francisco. (☎534-0601 or 800-351-6024; www.visitelpaso.com. Open daily 8am-5pm.) **Area Code:** 915.

BIG BEND ☎432

The arid Chihuahuan Desert, lofty Chisos Mountains, and muddy Río Grande unite in a marriage of land, air, and water to form one of Texas's most remote and wild natural areas. Roadrunners, coyotes, wild pigs, mountain lions, and a few black bears make their home in Big Bend National Park, an 800,000-acre tract (about the size of Rhode Island) cradled by the mighty Río Grande.

☰ TRANSPORTATION. There is no transportation service into or around the park. **Amtrak** offers trains to Alpine, 103 mi. north of the park entrance where **Car rentals** are also available. Three roads lead south from U.S. 90 into the park: from Marfa, U.S. 67 to Rte. 170; from Alpine, Rte. 118; from Marathon, U.S. 385 (the fastest route). There are two **gas stations** within the park, one at **Panther Junction** (☎477-2294; open daily Sept.-Mar. 7am-7pm, Apr.-Aug. 8am-6pm; 24hr. credit card service), next to the park headquarters, and one at **Río Grande Village** (☎477-2293; open daily Mar.-May 9am-8pm; June-Feb. 9am-6pm). On Rte. 118, about 1 mi. from the western park entrance, the **Study Butte Store** also sells gas. (Open 24hr. Credit cards only.)

◼◪ ORIENTATION AND PRACTICAL INFORMATION. Park headquarters is at **Panther Junction,** 26 mi. south of the northern park boundary. (☎477-2251, visitor center 477-1158; www.nps.gov/bibe. Open daily 8am-6pm. Vehicle pass $15 per week, pedestrians and bikers $5.) **Visitor centers** are located at Río Grande Village (☎477-2271; usually closed June-Oct.), Persimmon Gap (☎477-2393; open daily 8am-5pm), and Chisos Basin (☎477-2264; open daily 9am-4:30pm). The Río Grande Village Store has showers ($0.75). **Post Office:** Main office in Panther Junction, next to Park Headquarters. (☎477-2238. Open M-F 8am-4pm.) Chisos Basin office is inside the grocery store. (Open M-Sa 9am-5pm.) Accepts general delivery. **Postal Code:** 79834. **Area Code:** 432.

◪◖ ACCOMMODATIONS AND FOOD. The expensive **Chisos Mountains Lodge ❹,** in the Chisos Basin, 10 mi. from park headquarters, provides the only roof over non-campers' heads within the park. Reservations are a must for high season (winter)—the lodge is often booked a year in advance. (☎477-2291. Singles $78; doubles $88. Additional person $10.) The lodge contains the only **restaurant ❷** in the park, serving three meals a day. (Breakfast buffet $6.75. Sandwiches $5-8. Dinner $6-15. Open daily 7-10:30am, 11:30am-4pm, and 5:30-8pm.) The closest budget motel to the park, the **Chisos Mining Company Motel ❷**, on Rte. 170, ¾ mi. west of the junction with Rte. 118, has clean rooms with A/C. (☎371-2254. Singles $45; doubles $56-66; 5-6 person cabins with kitchenettes $61-85.)

The three developed campsites within the park do not take reservations and are run on a first come, first served basis. During Thanksgiving, Christmas, March, and April the campgrounds fill early; call park headquarters (☎477-2251) to inquire about availability. The **Chisos Basin Campground ❶**, at 5400 ft., has 65 sites with running water and flush toilets and stays cooler than the other campgrounds in the summer. (Sites $10.) The **Río Grande Village Campground ❶**, at 1850 ft., has 100 sites near the only showers in the park. Flush toilets and water are also available. (Sites $10.) The **RV park ❶** at Río Grande Village has 25 full hookups. (Sites $18.50 for up to 2 people; $1 per additional person.) **Backcountry camping ❶** in the park is free but requires a permit from one of the visitors centers.

Restaurants are scarce around Big Bend, but there are some options near Terlingua and Lajitas. Travelers can stop at **Ms. Tracy's Cafe ❷**, Rte. 170 in Terlingua Ghost Town, 7 mi. from the park entrance. Ms. Tracy, exhibiting the famed Texas hospitality, chats with visitors while serving eggs ($3.50-6), hamburgers ($5-7), burritos ($3.50-5), and vegetarian entrees. (☎371-2888. Entrees $8-15. Open daily Oct.-May 7am-10pm; June 7am-2pm; July-Sept. 7am-5pm.) About one-quarter of a mile farther past Tracy's, the lively **Starlight Theater Bar and Grill ❸** opens for dinner and has steaks ($16-25), burgers ($7-10), and entrees ($10-20) like the spicy chicken in avocado sauce ($11). Live music plays on weekends. (☎371-2326. Open daily 5:30-10pm; bar open Su-F 5pm-midnight, Sa 5pm-1am.)

⚠ OUTDOOR ACTIVITIES. Big Bend spans over 200 miles of hiking trails, ranging from 30min. nature walks to multi-day backpacking trips. *Always carry at least one gallon of water per person per day in the desert.* For those short on time, the best sight-seeing is along the **Ross Maxwell Scenic Drive**, a 30 mi. paved route from the western edge of the Chisos Mountains leading down to the Río Grande and Santa Eleña Canyon. Call ahead for road conditions.

Park rangers are happy to suggest hikes and sights. Pick up the *Hiker's Guide to Big Bend* pamphlet ($2), available at Panther Junction. The **Window Trail** (5¼ mi., 2-3hr.) departs the Chisos Basin lot and leads to the U-shaped Window rock formation, passing a variety of other formations and flora along the way. Just one-quarter of a mile from the same parking lot, **Window View** is an excellent location to enjoy vivid desert sunsets. The **Lost Mine Trail** (4¾ mi., 3-4hr.) rewards hikers with a breathtaking view of the desert and the Sierra de Carmen in Mexico. Also in the Chisos, the **Emory Peak Trail** (4½ mi. one-way, 5-8hr.) is a more intense hike. An easier walk ambles through the **Santa Eleña Canyon** (1¾ mi., 1½hr.) along the Río Grande. Canyon walls rise as high as 1000 ft. over the riverbank. Visitors can relax in the 104°F **hot springs** near Río Grande Village (¾ mi. walk from parking).

Though upstream damming has markedly decreased the river's flow, rafting on the Río Grande is still highly enjoyable. Free permits and info are available at the visitors center. Several companies rent kayaks and offer river trips down the 118 mi. of designated Río Grande Wild and Scenic River within park boundaries. **Far-Flung Adventures,** on Hwy. 170, half a mile west of Rte. 118, organizes half- to 10-day trips. They also offer jeep rentals and expeditions. (☎371-2633 or 800-839-7238; www.texasriver.com.) In Terlingua off Hwy. 170, **Big Bend River Tours** (☎371-3033 or 800-545-4240; www.bigbendrivertours.com) rents canoes ($45 per day) and inflatable kayaks ($35 per day). Guided trips available. (Half-day $62, full day $130.) Both offer shuttle services to pick people up downriver.

ROCKY MOUNTAINS

Created by immense tectonic forces some 65 million years ago, the Rockies mark a vast wrinkle in the North American continent. Sculpted by wind, water, and glaciers over eons, their weathered peaks extend 3000 miles from northern Alberta to New Mexico and soar to altitudes exceeding two vertical miles.

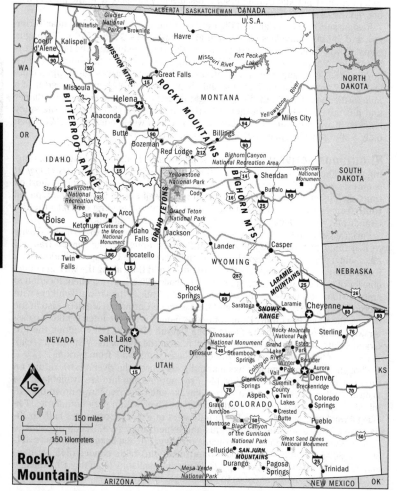

Rocky Mountains

Cars overheat and humans gulp thin alpine air as they ascend into bear country. The highest peaks of the Rockies are accessible only to veteran mountain climbers and wildlife adapted for scant air and deep snow. Although the Rocky Mountain area supports less than 5% of the US population, each year millions flock to its spectacular parks, forests, and ski resorts, while hikers follow the Continental Divide along the spine of the Rockies. Nestled in valleys or springing from the surrounding plains, the region's mountain villages and cowboy towns welcome travelers year-round.

HIGHLIGHTS OF THE ROCKY MOUNTAINS

HIKING. Memorable trails include the Gunnison Rte. in the Black Canyon, CO (p. 763); lake, geyser and canyon trails in Yellowstone National park (p. 772); and just about anything in the Grand Tetons (p. 783).

SKIING. The Rockies are filled with hot spots, but try Sawtooth, ID (p. 817); Vail, CO (p. 755); or Jackson Hole, WY (p. 789).

SCENIC DRIVES. Going-to-the-Sun Rd. in Glacier National Park (p. 807) is unforgettable, as is the phenomenally high San Juan Skyway in Colorado (p. 767). The Chief Joseph Scenic Hwy. (p. 783) explores the rugged Wyoming wilderness.

ALPINE TOWNS. Aspen, CO (p. 757), and Stanley, ID (p. 817): two of the loveliest.

COLORADO

In the high, thin air of Colorado, golf balls fly farther, eggs take longer to cook, and visitors tend to lose their breath just getting out of bed. Hikers, skiers, and climbers worship Colorado's peaks and mountain enclaves. Denver, the country's highest capital, has long since shed its cow-town image and matured into the cultural center of the Rocky Mountains. Colorado's extraordinary heights are matched by its equally spectacular depths, like the Black Canyon of the Gunnison, etched over millions of years by the Gunnison River. Silver and gold attracted early settlers to Colorado, but it is Mother Nature that has continued to appeal to travelers.

⁊ PRACTICAL INFORMATION

Capital: Denver.

Visitor Info: Colorado Travel and Tourism Authority (CTTA), 1620 Broadway, Ste. 1700 Denver 80202 (☎303-893-3885, vacation guide 800-COLORADO/265-6723; www.colorado.com). **US Forest Service,** Rocky Mountain Region, 740 Sims St., Golden, 80401 or P.O. Box 25127, Lakewood 80225 (☎303-275-5350). Open M-F 7:30am-4:30pm. **Ski Country USA,** 1507 Blake St., Denver 80202 provides info on all Colorado ski resorts. (☎303-837-0793.) Open M-F 9am-5pm. **Colorado State Parks,** 1313 Sherman St., #618, Denver 80203 (☎303-866-3437; state park reservations ☎800-678-2267). Open M-F 7am-4:45pm. $8 reservation fee; make reservations at least 3 days in advance.

Postal Abbreviation: CO. **Sales Tax:** 7.4%.

DENVER   ☎303

In 1858, the discovery of gold in the Rockies brought a rush of eager miners to northern Colorado. After an excruciating trek through the plains, the desperados set up camp before heading west into the "hills," and Denver became a flourishing

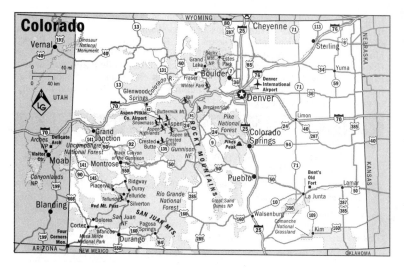

frontier town. Denver combines urban sophistication and western grit and boasts the nation's largest city park system, brews the most beer of any metropolitan area and has the highest number of high school and college graduates per capita.

TRANSPORTATION

Airport: Denver International (☎342-2000; www.flydenver.com), 23 mi. northeast of downtown off I-70. Shuttles run from the airport to downtown and ski resorts. The **RTD Sky Ride** (☎299-6000) runs buses every hr. from the Market St. station to the airport. Office open M-F 6am-8pm, Sa-Su 9am-6pm. Buses operate daily 5am-10:30pm. $8, seniors and disabled $4, under 15 free. From the main terminal, **Supershuttle** (☎370-1300 or 800-525-3177) runs to downtown hotels (1hr., $19). Taxi downtown $50.

Trains: Amtrak, Union Station, 1701 Wynkoop St. (☎534-2812 for arrivals/departures, 825-2583 or 800-872-7245 for ticket office), at 17th St. Office open daily 6am-9pm. To: **Chicago** (20hr., 1 per day, from $196); **Salt Lake City** (15hr., 1 per day, from $131); **San Francisco** (35hr., 1 per day, from $194). **Winter Park Ski Train** (☎296-4754), in the same building, chugs 2¼hr. through the Rockies, stopping in **Winter Park.** Free ground transport to town. Reservations required. Runs Jan. Sa-Su; Feb. to late Mar. F-Su; mid-June to mid-Aug. Sa. Round-trip $45, over 61 $35, under 14 $25.

Buses: Greyhound, 1055 19th St. (☎293-6555). Office open daily 6am-midnight. To: **Chicago** (20-22hr., 6 per day, $95); **Colorado Springs** (1½hr., 7 per day, $14); **Salt Lake City** (10-13hr., 5 per day, $61); **Santa Fe** (7½-9hr., 4 per day, $59). **Estes Park Shuttle** (reservations ☎970-586-5151) provides access to Rocky Mountain National Park from the airport and downtown ($39).

Public Transit: Regional Transportation District (RTD), 1600 Blake St. (☎299-6000 or 800-366-7433). Serves Denver, Longmont, Evergreen, Golden, and suburbs. Hours vary; many lines shut down by 9pm. $0.75, seniors and disabled $0.25; peak hours $1.25. Exact change. Regional routes go to Boulder, Nederland, and the national forests to the west for $3.50. Main terminals are at Market and 16th St. and Colfax and Broadway. A free 16th St. **mall shuttle** covers much of downtown. Runs daily 5am-1am.

Taxi: **Yellow Cab** ☎ 777-7777. **Zone Cab** ☎ 444-8888.
Car Rental: Enterprise, 7720 Calawaba Ct. (☎ 800-720-7222), at the airport.

▓ ▒ ORIENTATION AND PRACTICAL INFORMATION

Running north-south, **Broadway** slices Denver in half. East of Broadway, **Colorado Boulevard** is also a major north-south thoroughfare. Immediately west of Downtown, **I-25** winds its way north-south along the Platte River, intersecting with east-west **I-70** just north of downtown, providing the quickest access to the city center. **Colfax Avenue,** running east-west, is the main north-south dividing line. Travel complications most often result from confusing the numbered streets and the numbered avenues: both **named** and **numbered streets** run diagonally in the downtown area, at a 45° angle to the city's perpendicular grid. In the rest of the city, **numbered avenues** run east-west and increase as you head north. Named streets run north-south. Many of the avenues on the eastern side of the city become numbered streets downtown. The pedestrian-only **16th Street Mall** is the hub of Denver's downtown, and the social, dining, and entertainment center of the city. *At night, avoid traveling south of W. Colfax and west of Speer Blvd. Extra care should be taken after dark in LoDo (Lower Downtown), especially if alone.*

Visitor Info: Denver Visitors Bureau, 918 16th St. (☎ 892-1505: www.denver.org), in the 16th St. Mall. Open June-Aug. M-F 9am-5pm, Sa 9am-1pm; Sept.-May M-F 9am-5pm.

GLBT Resources: The Gay, Lesbian, and Bisexual Community Services Center of Colorado, ☎ 733-7743. Open M-F 9am-5pm.

Hotlines: Rape Crisis Hotline, ☎ 322-7273.

Internet Access: Public Library, 10 W. 14th Ave. (☎ 865-1351). Open M-Tu 10am-9pm, Th-Sa 10am-5:30pm, Su 1-5pm.

Post Office: 951 20th St. (☎ 296-4692). Open M-F 7am-10:30pm, Sa 8:30am-10:30pm. **Postal Code:** 80202. **Area Code:** 303.

▐ ACCOMMODATIONS

Inexpensive hotels line E. Colfax Ave., as well as Broadway and Colorado Blvd. Denver hotels tend to be less vacation- and more commerce-oriented, and generally have better rates on weekends than during the week.

Broadway Plaza Motel, 1111 Broadway (☎ 893-0303), 3 blocks south of the capitol building, is a spotless, well-preserved example of 1950s architecture. Spacious, clean rooms within a 5min. walk of downtown. Singles $45-55; doubles $55-65. ❸

Hostel of the Rocky Mountains (HI), 1530 Downing St. (☎ 861-7777), just off E. Colfax Ave. The most inexpensive lodging in Denver, though the facilities show their age. Internet access $1 per 10min. Library, kitchens, and breakfast included. Linen ($2) and laundry facilities. Key deposit $5. Call about free pickup from the bus and train depots. Reception 7-10am and 5-10pm. Reservations recommended. Dorms $19; private rooms $40. ❶ The **B&B of the Rocky Mountains,** next door to the hostel, shares its phone number. Classy and quiet, the rooms are well-kept with shared baths. Guests can enjoy free breakfast at the hostel or use the kitchen facilities. Rooms $40-55. ❷

Cherry Creek State Park, 4201 S. Parker Rd. (☎ 699-3860), in Aurora, is conveniently located in an urban area anchored around Cherry Creek Lake. Take I-25 to Exit 200, then head north for about 3 mi. on I-225 and take the Parker Rd. exit. Pine trees provide limited shade. Boating, fishing, swimming, hiking, and horseback riding available. Arrive early. Open May-Dec. Sites $12, with electricity $20. Additional day-use fee $7. ❶

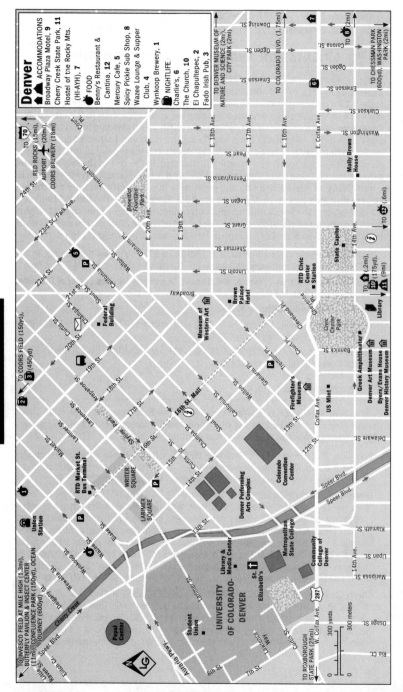

Denver

⌂ ACCOMMODATIONS
Broadway Plaza Motel, **9**
Cherry Creek State Park, **11**
Hostel of the Rocky Mts.
(HI-AYH), **7**

● FOOD
Benny's Restaurant &
Cantina, **12**
Mercury Cafe, **5**
Spicy Pickle Sub Shop, **8**
Wazee Lounge & Supper
Club, **4**
Wynkoop Brewery, **1**

■ NIGHTLIFE
Charlie's, **6**
The Church, **10**
El Chapultepec, **2**
Fado Irish Pub, **3**

◘ FOOD

Downtown Denver offers a full range of cuisines, from Russian to traditional Southwestern. The **16th Street Mall** is a great place for *al fresco* dining in warm weather. Gourmet eateries are located southwest of the mall on Larimer St., in **Larimer Square.** Sports bars and trendy restaurants occupy historic **LoDo,** the neighborhood extending from Wynkoop St. to Larimer Sq., between Speer Blvd. and 20th St. Outside downtown, **Colorado Boulevard** and **6th Avenue** also have their share of posh restaurants. **East Colfax Avenue** offers a number of reasonably priced ethnic restaurants, including Greek and Ethiopian cuisine. You may wonder what sort of delicacies **"Rocky Mountain oysters"** are, especially given Denver's distance from the ocean—these salty-sweet bison testicles, sold at the **Buckhorn Exchange,** 1000 Osage St. (☎534-9505), do not hail from the sea.

▒ Wazee Lounge & Supper Club, 1600 15th St. (☎623-9518), in LoDo. The black-and-white tile floor, Depression-era wood paneling, gas lights, and mahogany bar give this laid-back diner a bohemian ambience. This LoDo favorite's award-winning pizza ($6-8) and strombolis ($8-9) are always popular. Happy hour M-F 4-6pm. Kitchen open M-Sa 11am-1am, Su noon-11pm. Bar open M-Sa until 2am, Su until midnight. ❷

Benny's Restaurant and Cantina, 301 E. 7th Ave. (☎894-0788), remains a local favorite for cheap, tasty Mexican food, including trademark breakfast burritos ($4.75), fish tacos ($7.35), and spicy *huevos con chorizo* ($6.25). If you can, snag a seat out on the patio, which is either open-air or enclosed, depending on whether a sequence of 8 snazzy garage doors are open. Open M-F 8am-10pm, Sa-Su 9am-11pm. ❷

Wynkoop Brewery, 1634 18th St. (☎297-2700), at Wynkoop St. across from Union Station in LoDo. Colorado's first brewpub serves beer (20 oz. $4), homemade root beer, and a full menu including buffalo burgers and catfish tacos ($7-9). An improv comedy troupe performs downstairs Th-Sa (reservations ☎297-2111). Pool tables, darts, and shuffleboard. Pints $2. Happy hour M-F 3-6pm and M-Th 10-midnight, Su 9-midnight. Free brewery tour Sa 1-5pm. Kitchen open M-Th 11am-11pm, F-Sa 11am-midnight, Su 11am-10pm. Bar open M-Sa until 2am, Su until midnight. ❷

Mercury Cafe, 2199 California St. (☎294-9281), at 22nd St. Decorated with a new-age flair, "the Merc" specializes in home-baked wheat bread and reasonably priced soups ($2-3), salads ($6-9), enchiladas ($5.50-7), and vegetarian dishes. Live bands provide jazz, salsa, and reggae music in the dining room, while the upstairs dance area hosts free swing and tango lessons Su and Th. Open Tu-F 5:30-11pm, Sa-Su 9am-3pm and 5:30-11pm; dancing F-Sa until 2am, Tu-Th and Su 1am. Cash only. ❷

Spicy Pickle Sub Shop, 745 Colorado Blvd. (☎321-8353), and 988 Lincoln St., at 10th and Lincoln (☎860-0730), serves fresh grilled panini (pressed focaccia bread sandwiches; $6-7) and a host of sub sandwiches ($5-7) with—what else—a spicy pickle. Gourmet meats, including Salsalito turkey and Cajun roast beef, are available on the sandwiches and in bulk to take home. Open daily 10:30am-8pm. ❷

◎ SIGHTS

AROUND DOWNTOWN. Many of the best sights in Denver center on downtown. At E. Colfax Ave. and Grant St., the gold-domed **Capitol Building,** built of Colorado-mined granite, marble, and limestone, is a sensible place to start a visit to the Mile High City. A small engraving on the 15th step leading to the building's entrance sits exactly 1 mi. above sea level. (☎866-2604. 45min. tours every 30min. M-F 9:15am-2:30pm. Open M-F 7am-5:30pm. Wheelchair accessible.) Near the capitol is the **Denver Art Museum (DAM),** a "vertical" museum housing a world-class collection of Native American art and pre-Columbian artifacts and works by local artists. *(100 W. 14th Ave. Pkwy. ☎ 720-865-5000; www.denverartmuseum.org. Open Tu and Th-Sa 10am-5pm, W 10am-9pm, Su noon-5pm. Daily tours of special exhibits; call for times. $6; students, ages 13-18, and over 65 $4.50. Sa free to Colorado residents. Wheelchair accessible.)* The **city tour bus** provides a 2hr. whirlwind introduction to Denver's major attractions with knowledgeable local guides. *(☎ 289-2841. Departs daily 11:30 from 16th St. Mall. $25.)*

OCEAN JOURNEY. The new ▨**Denver Aquarium** offers two spectacular underwater exhibitions: the Colorado River Journey, descending from the Continental Divide to the Sea of Cortez in Mexico, and the Indonesian River Journey, emptying from the volcanic Barisan Mountains in Sumatra into the South China Sea. The aquarium also houses over 15,000 exotic marine creatures, including several species of sharks, sea otters, and the magnificent Napoleon wrasse. *(700 Water St. Exit 211 off I-25. RTD bus 10. ☎ 561-4450 or 888-561-4450; www.oceanjourney.org. Open daily June-Aug. 10am-6pm; Sept.-May 10am-5pm. $15, over 65 and ages 13-17 $13, ages 4-12 $7.)*

CITY PARK AREA. This gigantic **Denver Museum of Nature and Science** hosts a variety of interesting exhibits, including the Hall of Life, the Prehistoric Journey room, and a superb exhibit on Egyptian mummies. Ride the skies in the museum's digital **Gates Planetarium,** one of the first of its kind in the country. *(2001 Colorado Blvd., at Colorado and Montview Blvd. ☎ 322-7009 or 800-925-2250; www.dmns.org. Open daily 9am-5pm. $9; students, over 60, and ages 3-18 $6. IMAX and museum $13/$9, planetarium and museum $13/$9. Call for show times. Wheelchair accessible.)*

COORS BREWERY. Located in nearby Golden, this is the world's largest one-site brewery. Interestingly, the brewery also has one of the nicest wellness centers in the corporate world. All 42,000 workers are allowed two free beers after every shift, and can work them off in the company workout center. Free tours take visitors through the Coors brewing process and finish with free samples for those 21 and over. *(Take I-70 W to Exit 264; head west on 32nd Ave. for 4½ mi., then turn left on East St. and follow the signs. A shuttle bus runs from the parking lot to the brewery, but not before a very short historical tour of Golden. ☎ 277-2337. 1½hr. tours every 30min. M-Sa 10am-4pm.)*

BUTTERFLY PAVILION AND INSECT CENTER. Stand in a tropical rainforest and let exotic butterflies land on your shoulders at this unusual butterfly conservatory, shielded from the Front Range's aridity by glass walls and misted water. In addition to the pavilion, a hands-on aquatic and insect center will thrill both young and old. *(6252 W. 104th Ave., in Westminster, just off U.S. 36 on the way to Boulder. ☎ 467-5441. Open daily 9am-5pm. $8, seniors $6, children 4-12 $5. Wheelchair accessible.)*

▣ ▨ ENTERTAINMENT AND OUTDOOR ACTIVITIES

Life in Denver is never boring for sports fans. Denver's baseball team, the **Colorado Rockies,** plays at **Coors Field,** 2201 Blake St. *(☎ 762-5437 or 800-388-7625. Tickets $4-41. $4 "Rockpile" bleacher tickets available day of game. 75min. tours M-Sa at 10am, noon, and 2pm. $6, children and seniors $4.)* As reward for their back-to-back Super Bowl victories in the late 90s, football's **Denver Broncos** got a new and larger **Mile High Stadium** (officially renamed Invesco Field at Mile High, but virtually never called such by locals), 1701 Bryant St. *(☎ 720-258-3888. 70min. tours every 30min. Th-Sa 10am-2pm. $6, children and seniors $4.)* The stadium is used by soccer's **Colorado Rapids** *(☎ 299-1599)* in spring and summer. The NBA's **Denver Nuggets** and the NHL's **Colorado Avalanche** share the state-of-the-art **Pepsi Center,** 1000 Chopper Cir. *(☎ 405-8556 for info on both teams. 75min. tours M and W at 10am, noon, and 2pm; Sa at 10:15am and 12:15pm. $5, children and seniors $4).*

Denver has more public parks per square mile than any other city, providing prime space for bicycling, walking, or lolling. **Cheesman Park,** 8th Ave. and Humboldt St., offers picnic areas, manicured flower gardens, and a view of snow-capped peaks from endless green lawns. **Confluence Park,** at Cherry Creek and the South Platte River, lures bikers and runners with paved riverside paths and kayakers with rapids. Diverse, free live music defines **Confluence Concerts,** along the banks of the South Platte. (☎455-7192. July to early Aug. Th 6:30-8pm.) One of the best parks for sporting events, **Washington Park,** at Louisiana Ave. and Downing St., hosts impromptu volleyball and soccer games almost every summer weekend. Paths for biking, jogging, and in-line skating encircle the park, and the two lakes in the middle are popular fishing spots. **City Park** (☎697-4545) houses the **Museum of Nature and Science** and the **Denver Zoo** on its east end, and a golf course on the west end. **Colorado State Parks** has the low-down on nearby state parks. (☎866-3437. Open M-F 8am-5pm.) At **Roxborough State Park** (☎973-3959), visitors can hike and ski among rock formations in the **Dakota Hogback** ridge. Take U.S. 85 S, turn right on Titan Rd., and follow it 3½ mi. (Open dawn-dusk.) The mammoth **Red Rocks Amphitheater and Park** (☎697-4939), 12 mi. southwest of Denver, on I-70 at the Morrison exit, is carved into sandstone, and performers like R.E.M. and the Denver Symphony Orchestra compete with the view. The actual Red Rocks Park contains over 800 acres. (Park open daily 5am-11pm. Visitors center open daily 8am-7pm.) Forty miles west of Denver, the road to the top of **Mount Evans** (14,264 ft.) is the highest paved road in North America. Take I-70 W to Rte. 103 in Idaho Springs. (☎567-2901. Open late May to early Sept. Daily vehicle fee $10.)

The **Denver Performing Arts Complex** (DPAC), at Speer Blvd. and Arapahoe St., is the largest arts complex in the nation and is home to the Denver Center for the Performing Arts, the Colorado Symphony, the Colorado Ballet, and Opera Colorado. (☎893-4100 or 800-641-1222 for tickets M-Sa 10am-6pm.) The **Denver Center Theater Company** offers one free Saturday matinee per play. (☎893-4000. Tickets distributed day of performance; call for schedule.) Small theaters in the metro area stage fantastic productions at bargain prices. At the intimate **Geminal Stage Denver,** 2450 W. 44th Ave., every seat is a good one. Plays range from traditional to more experimental. (☎455-7108. Shows F-Su $14-18.) **The Bluebird Theater,** 3317 E. Colfax Ave., hosts local and national acts. (☎322-2308. W-Sa live music including rock, blues, folk, reggae, Latin, and jazz. Su movie nights.)

❋ FESTIVALS

Every January, Denver hosts the **National Western Stock Show & Rodeo,** 4655 Humboldt St., the nation's largest livestock show and one of the biggest rodeos. Cowboys compete for prize money while over 10,000 head of cattle, horses, sheep, and rabbits compete for "Best of Breed." Between big events, all sorts of oddball fun takes place, including western battle recreations, monkey sheep herders, and rodeo clowns. (☎295-1660; www.nationalwestern.com. Tickets $10-20.) The whole area vibrates with ancient rhythms during the **Denver March Pow-Wow,** at the Denver Coliseum, 4600 Humboldt St., when over 1000 Native Americans from tribes all over North America dance simultaneously in full costume to the beat of drums. (☎934-8045; www.denvermarchpowwow.org. Mid-March. $6 for a 1-day pass, $12 for a 3-day pass, under 6 and over 60 free.) **Cinco de Mayo** (☎534-8342, ext. 106), held at Civic Center Park between Colfax Ave. and 14th St., attracts 250,000 visitors per year in celebration of Mexico's victory over the French in 1862. In the same location during the first full week of June, the **Capitol Hill People's Fair** (☎830-1651; www.peoplesfair.com) is an arts and crafts festival. Along with over 500 exhibitors, this large outdoor free celebration includes food, dance, and local bands. **The Festival of Mountain and Plain: A Taste of Colorado** (☎295-6330; www.atasteofcolorado.com), originally named to celebrate Denver's dual personality as the "Queen City of the Plains" and the "Monarch Metropolis of the Mountains," packs Civic Center Park on Labor Day weekend. Food, crafts, entertainment, and carnival rides create the family-oriented fun.

☕ NIGHTLIFE

Downtown Denver, in and around the 16th St. Mall, is an attraction in itself. With ample shopping, dining, and people-watching opportunities, there's something for everyone. A copy of the weekly *Westword* gives the lowdown on LoDo, where much of the action is found after dark.

The Church, 1160 Lincoln St. (☎832-3528). In a remodeled chapel complete with stained-glass windows and an elevated altar area, the Church offers 4 full bars, a cigar lounge, and a weekend sushi bar. On weekends, the congregation swells with 3 floors of dancing to a variety of musical styles. Th 18+, F-Su 21+. Cover after 10pm $5-15. Open Th and Su 9pm-2am, F-Sa 8pm-2am.

Fado Irish Pub, 1735 19th St. (☎297-0066). Built in Ireland and brought to Denver piece by piece, Fado is a truly authentic Irish pub. With a perfect pint of Guinness in hand, relax in a cozy nook or stop at the intricate wrought-iron bar. At the southwest gate of Coors Field, this is the place to be before and after Rockies games. Live traditional Irish music Su-M, W, Sa. Open daily 11:30am-2am, food served until midnight.

El Chapultepec, 1962 Market St. (☎295-9126), at 20th St., is a be-boppin' jazz holdover from Denver's 1950s Beat era. Live music nightly starting at 9pm. No cover. 1-drink min. per set. Open daily 8am-2am. Food until 1am. No credit cards.

Charlie's, 900 E. Colfax Ave. (☎839-8890), at Emerson, is a well-known bar frequented largely by gay men, but all are welcome. A dance floor with a Western-style atmosphere is complemented by a separate disco floor. No cover. Open daily 11am-2am.

MOUNTAIN RESORTS ON I-70   ☎970

WINTER PARK AND THE FRASER VALLEY

Hwy. 40 connects Winter Park with Fraser just 2 mi. north, and together the towns thrive as a unique mountain community with genuine small-town charm. Nestled among mountain pines in the upper Fraser River Valley, the popular **Winter Park Resort** is the closest ski and summer resort to Denver, a mere 67 mi. from downtown. Named after a local lady of pleasure, the **Winter Park Mary Jane Ski Area** (☎726-5514 or 800-453-2525) is home to the first man-made ski trail in the western US; the trail was laid on land Mary Jane received for providing favors to local railroad workers and miners. The ski area boasts the most snow in Colorado, a 3060 ft. vertical drop, 22 lifts, and two mountains: Winter Park caters to families and beginners, while Mary Jane challenges experts with mogul-riddled trails. (Single-day lift ticket $61, multiday tickets $47-49 per day. Passes apply to both mountains.) **Fraser Tubing Hill,** ½ mi. off Hwy. 40 in Fraser, offers another popular winter escape. (☎726-5954. $12 per hr., ages 12 and under $10 per hr.) The resort also hosts a variety of summer activities, including a scenic chairlift, climbing walls, bungee jumps, the longest alpine slide in the country, and a zip-line. (Open mid-June to early Sept. daily 10am-5:30pm. Half-day park pass $38, full-day $44.) Over 600 mi. of biking and hiking trails climb the mountains of the Continental Divide, and the **Zephyr Express** chairlift blows to the summit of Winter Park Mountain, allowing bikers and hikers to start at the top and then make their way down. (☎726-1564. Open mid-June to early Sept.

daily 10am-5pm. Full-day chair pass $22, includes bike haul; single ride $16. Mountain bike rentals from $14 per hr., $33 per day. 2hr. clinic $35; groups of 4 or more $25.) **Viking Ski Shop,** on Hwy. 40, under the Viking Lodge, rents ski

 MUDSLIDES. During mud season—typically May, October, and November— many places close or shorten their hours, and lodging prices are generally lower. For those traveling during mud season, be sure to call ahead.

packages in winter and bikes in summer. (☎ 800-421-4013. Open daily June-Sept. 9am-5pm; Oct.-May 8am-9pm. Ski packages $14 per day for basic skis, $21 per day for performance skis; multi-day discounts available. Kids 13 and under rent skis free with adult rental. Bikes $18 per day for 2 road bikes, $24-36 for 2 mountain bikes. Helmets included.) **Mad Adventures** is a popular **whitewater rafting** company that offers guided treks on wild Clear Creek and the Colorado River, which is more suitable for novices. (☎ 726-5290 or 800-451-4844. Open 8am-5pm. Half-day $40, full-day $57; ages 4-11 $33/$47.) The **High Country Stampede Rodeo** bucks at the John Work Arena, west of Fraser on County Rd. 73, with competitions in calf roping, ladies' barrel racing, and bareback bronc and bull riding. (☎ 726-4118 or 800-903-7275. Open July-Aug. Sa nights. Western barbecue 5pm; $8, ages 6-13 $4. Rodeo 7:30pm. $10, ages 62 and over $8, ages 6-13 $6.)

▓The **Rocky Mountain Inn and Hostel ❶,** on Hwy. 40, 2 mi. north of Winter Park in Fraser, offers immaculate, newly renovated rooms with a Julia Child-caliber kitchen, hot tub, and outdoor patio and grill, as well as DVDs, discounts for lift tickets, ski and mountain bike rentals, raft trips, and horseback rides. (☎ 726-8256 or 866-467-8351. Internet access $3 per hr. Linen $3. Reception 8am-10pm. Dorms $19-22; private rooms from $79 in winter, $53 in summer.) The **Viking Lodge ❷,** on Hwy. 40 in Winter Park, next to the shuttle stop for the lifts, offers rooms with phones and TVs. Lodgings include access to the hot tub, sauna, and game room, and a 10% discount on rentals at the adjacent store. (☎ 726-8885 or 800-421-4013. Reception 8am-9pm. Winter singles $55-70; doubles $60-75. Summer singles $45; doubles $50.) The Fraser River Valley Lions Club offers campgrounds in the Arapaho National Forest from mid-May to early Sept. The closest site to town, **Idlewild ❶,** just 1½ mi. south of Winter Park on Hwy. 40, offers 24 sites right along the Fraser River. (No hookups. Max. stay 14 days. Sites with water $12.)

Located right off Hwy. 40 in downtown Fraser, **Crooked Creek Saloon and Eatery ❷,** 401 Zerex Ave., is a local landmark with wise advice: "Enjoy a few laughs, eat 'til it hurts, and drink 'til it feels better." Locals elbow up to the bar alongside mountain bikers and skiers in a lively atmosphere year-round. (☎ 726-9250. Breakfast from $3; burgers, pasta, and Mexican fare $6-9. Happy hour M-F 3-7pm; $1.75 domestic bottles, $0.15 hot wings. Open daily 7am-1am, kitchen closes at 10pm.) Deliciously healthy breakfasts ($3-10) and lunches ($4-10), including an excellent Highland Pudding, are served on the patio at **Carver's Bakery Cafe ❷,** at the end of the Cooper Creek Mall off U.S. 40. (☎ 726-8202. Massive cinnamon rolls $2.25. Open daily in summer 7am-2pm; in winter 7am-3pm.)

The **Lift Resort Shuttle** provides free bus service between Winter Park and Fraser. (☎ 726-4163. Runs July-Sept. and late Nov. to mid-Apr.) To reach Winter Park from Denver, take I-70 W to Hwy. 40. The Chamber of Commerce (see below) also serves as the **Greyhound** depot with service to Denver (1¾hr., 1 per day, $15-16). **Home James Transportation Services** runs door-to-door shuttles to and from Fraser, Winter Park, and the Denver airport. (☎ 726-5060 or 800-359-7536. Office open daily 8am-6pm. Reservations required. $43 to airport.) The **Río Grande Ski Train** (☎ 303-296-4754; Dec.-Mar. Sa-Su; mid-June to Aug. Sa) leaves Denver's Union Station (p. 740) for Winter Park. **Visitor Info: Winter Park-Fraser Valley Chamber of Commerce,**

78841 Hwy. 40. (☎726-4118 or 800-903-7275; www.winterpark-info.com. Open daily 8am-5pm.) **Snow Conditions:** ☎303-572-7669 or 800-729-5813. **Internet Access: Fraser Valley Library,** 421 Norgren Rd., (☎726-5689. Open M-W 10am-6pm, Th noon-8pm, F 10am-6pm, Sa 10am-4pm.) **Post Office:** 520 Hwy. 40 (☎726-5578. Open M-F 8am-5pm, Sa 10am-noon.) **Postal Code:** 80442. **Area Code:** 970.

BRECKENRIDGE

Fashionable Breckenridge lies east of Vail on I-70, 9 mi. south of Frisco on Rte 9. One of the most popular ski resorts in the country, **Breckenridge** has a 3400 ft. vertical drop, 139 trails, the best halfpipe in North America, and 2043 acres of skiable terrain accessed by 25 lifts. (☎453-5000 or 800-789-7669; www.breckenridge.com. Snow conditions ☎453-6118.) Most of the summer action takes place at the **Breckenridge Peak and Fun Park** on Peak 8, 3 mi. west on Ski Hill Rd., including a scenic **chairlift** ride (single ride $5), a superslide ($10, ages 7-12 and seniors 65-69 $8), Colorado's largest human maze ($6, ages 5-12 $5), and a climbing wall ($7 per climb; half-day $48, full-day $60). The **Breckenridge Mountain Bike Park** at the same location offers a variety of biking trails. (Chairlift with bike haul $12, ages 7-12 $10. Bike rentals $12 for 2hr., half-day $20, full-day $28.) "Super-passes" for unlimited use of the Fun Park and Mountain Bike Park are also available (half-day $48, all-day $60). Beautiful music surrounds Breckenridge in the summer. The **Breckenridge Music Festival** provides a wide selection of musical acts from jazz and pop to Broadway and blues, including performances from the Breckenridge Music Institute Orchestra and the National Repertory Orchestra. (☎453-9142; www.breckenridgemusicfestival.com. Late May to late Sept. Box office open Tu-Su 10am-5pm. Many shows free, classical concerts $17-27, ages 18 and under $7.)

Despite the many expensive restaurants and stores in town, you can still find well-priced, smoke-free accommodations at the █**Fireside Inn (HI) ❷,** 114 N. French St., two blocks east of Main St. on the corner of Wellington Rd. The indoor hot tub is great for après-ski and the "Afternoon Tea" offers a taste of charming British hospitality. (☎453-6456; www.firesideinn.com. Breakfast $3-6. Reception daily 8am-9:30pm. Dorms in summer $25; in winter $38. Private rooms $65/$180.) A few miles north of town on Hwy. 9, right next to the Breckenridge Golf Course, **Wayside Inn ❸,** 165 Tiger Rd., offers tidy rooms with a nice soak in the hot tub, a warm fire in the lounge, and a pretty hot price. (☎453-5540 or 800-927-7669. Mid-Apr. to late Nov. singles $45, doubles $55; Dec. $65/$75; Jan. to mid-Apr. $88/$98.)

Taste the difference of high altitude slow-roasted coffee beans at **Clint's Bakery and Coffeehouse ❶,** 131 S. Main St., where you'll also find breakfast croissant sandwiches ($3.50), homemade quiche ($2.50), and soups made daily from scratch. The hot portobello mushroom and turkey pepperjack sandwich ($5) is a lunch favorite, as are the blackberry smoothies for $4.50. (☎453-2990. Open daily 7am-8pm, sandwiches made until 3pm.) With a name like **Fatty's ❷,** 106 S. Ridge St., you know the burgers are gonna be big ($5-7). With 10 TVs and $1.75 drafts during happy hour (daily 4-7pm), Fatty's knows how to keep the locals satisfied. (☎453-9802. Open daily 11am-12:30am; kitchen closes at 10pm.) Spiced up with colorful murals and a straw-covered bar, **Rasta Pasta ❷,** 411 S. Main St., serves creative pasta entrees with garlic bread, salad, and Jamaican flair. Outside dining is available alongside the creek. (☎453-7467. Lunch entrees $4-7, dinner $8-11. Open daily 11am-9pm.)

Free Ride Breckenridge shuttles skiers and bikers around town and to the mountains for free. (☎547-3140. Operates daily 6:30am-midnight.) **Summit Stage** provides free shuttle service from Breckenridge to surrounding areas in Summit County. (☎668-0999. Operates daily 6:30am-1:30am.) **Breckenridge Activities Center:** 137 S. Main St., at Washington St. (☎453-5579 or 877-864-0868. Open daily 9am-5pm.) **Ski Conditions and Weather:** ☎453-6118. **Breckenridge Medical Center:** 555 S. Park Ave.

ROCKY MOUNTAINS

(☎453-1010.) **Internet Access: Summit County Library,** 504 Airport Rd. (☎453-6098. Open M-Th 9am-7pm, F-Sa 9am-5pm, Su 1-5pm.) **Post Office:** 305 S. Ridge Rd. (☎453-5467. Open M-F 8am-5pm, Sa 10am-1pm.) **Postal Code:** 80424. **Area Code:** 970.

BOULDER ☎303

The 1960s have been slow to fade in Boulder; the town is known by leftists as a "little liberal haven in a vast conservative wasteland" and by right-wingers as "The People's Republic of Boulder." Brimming with coffeeshops, teahouses, and juice bars, Boulder is also home to both the central branch of the University of Colorado (CU) and Naropa University, the only accredited Buddhist university in the US. Seek spiritual enlightenment through meditation and healing workshops at Naropa, or pursue a physical awakening through Boulder's incredible local outdoor activities, including biking, hiking, and rafting along Boulder Creek.

⚎ 🖪 ORIENTATION AND PRACTICAL INFORMATION. Boulder is a small, manageable city, easily accessible from Estes Park and Denver by Hwy. 36. The most developed area lies between **Broadway (Highway 7/93)** and **28th Street (Highway 36),** two busy north-south streets. Broadway, 28th St., **Arapahoe Avenue** and **Baseline Road** border the **University of Colorado (CU)** campus. The area immediately west of the school, across Broadway, is known as **the Hill** and features a number of restaurants, bars, and student-oriented shopping and entertainment. The pedestrian-only **Pearl Street Mall,** between 9th and 15th St., is lined with cafes, restaurants, and posh shops. **Greyhound,** at 30th St. and Diagonal Hwy. (☎800-231-2222; open 24hr.), goes to: Denver (1hr., 2 per day, $5); Glenwood Springs (6-7hr., 2 per day, $40); Vail (5-5½hr., 2 per day, $33). Boulder's extensive **public transit** system is run by **RTD,** at 14th and Walnut St., in the center of town. (☎299-6000 or 800-366-7433. Open M-F 6am-8pm, Sa-Su 9am-6pm. Call for schedules and fares.) **Taxi: Boulder Yellow Cab** ☎442-2277. **Bike Rental: University Bicycles,** 839 Pearl St., downtown, rents mountain bikes with helmet and lock. (☎444-4196. Open M-F 10am-7pm, Sa 10am-6pm, Su 10am-5pm. Bikes $25 per day, snowshoes $10 per day.) **Visitor Info: Boulder Chamber of Commerce/Visitors Service,** 2440 Pearl St., has info and free **Internet access.** (☎442-1044; www.boulderchamber.com. Open M-Th 8:30am-5pm, F 8:30am-4pm.) **University of Colorado Information,** on the second floor of the University Memorial Center (UMC) student union, on the corner of Broadway and Euclid, has **Internet access** downstairs and free local calls upstairs. (☎492-6161. Open in summer M-F 7am-10pm, Sa 9am-11pm, Su noon-10pm; term-time M-F 7am-11pm, Sa 9am-midnight, Su noon-11pm.) **Post Office:** 1905 15th St., at Walnut St. (☎938-3704. Open M-F 7:30am-5:30pm, Sa 10am-2pm.) **Postal Code:** 80302. **Area Code:** 303.

🏠 ACCOMMODATIONS. Right on the Hill next to the CU campus, **Boulder International Hostel ❶,** 1107 12th St., at College Ave., is the best deal in town. Youthful travelers fill the spacious downstairs lobby, surf the Internet ($2 per 30min.), and watch cable TV. The front door is locked after 11pm, but guests are given a code to enter after hours. (☎442-0522. Kitchen, laundry. Linen $5. Key deposit $10. 3-night max. stay in dorms during the summer. Reception 8am-midnight. Lockout 10am-5pm. Dorms in summer $19, in winter $17; singles $39/$35; doubles $45/$39.) Located 2 mi. west of Boulder off Canyon Blvd./Hwy. 119, **Boulder Mountain Lodge ❸,** 91 Four Mile Canyon Dr., is in the mountains, yet just 5min. from downtown. Guests are treated to clean rooms (many with full kitchens) at great rates, as well as a hot tub by Four Mile Creek. Campsites are also available on a first come, first served basis. (☎444-0882 or 800-458-0882. In summer singles $68; doubles $88. In winter $53/$68. Sites $14.) **The Hotel Boulderado ❺,** 2115 13th St., was built in high Victorian style and opened in 1905. Today the Boulderado is one of the city's most popular hotels, in spite of (or perhaps because of) the rumored presence of a ghost on the fifth floor. (☎442-4344 or 800-433-4344. Standard queen in summer $125, in winter $169; with 2 queens $145/$199.) **Chautauqua Association ❸**, off Baseline Rd. at the foot of the Flatirons, has lodge rooms and private cottages. Turn at the Chautauqua Park sign and take Kinnikinic to Morning Glory Dr., or take RTD bus #203. (☎442-3282, ext. 11. Reception June to early Sept. M-F 8:30am-7pm, Sa-Su 9am-5pm; Sept.-May M-F 8:30am-5pm, Sa-Su 9am-3pm. Small additional charge for stays fewer than 4 nights. Reserve months in advance. In summer lodge rooms $63; 1-bedroom suites $99-119; 2-bedroom cottages $124-209; 3-bedroom cottages $149-164. In winter, limited number of cottages $94-139.) **Camping** info for **Arapahoe/Roosevelt National Forest ❶** is available from the **Boulder Ranger District**, 2140 Yarmouth Ave., just off of Rte. 36 to the north of town. (☎541-2500, reservations 877-444-6777. Open mid-May to early Sept. M-Th 8am-4:30pm, F 8am-5:30pm, Sa 9am-3pm; Sept. to mid-May M-F 8am-5pm. Campsites open mid-May to Oct. Most sites have water; none have electric hookups.) **Kelly Dahl ❶**, 26 mi. southwest of Boulder on Hwy. 119, via Nederland, is the closest National Forest campground to Boulder. The 46 sites are situated among pine trees and picnic tables with views of the Continental Divide. (Sites $13.) For a quieter camping experience, **Rainbow Lakes ❶** lies 6½ mi. north of Nederland off Hwy. 72; turn at the Mountain Research Station (CR 116) and follow the gravel road for 5 mi. *Drive slowly and carefully on the access road.* The 16 primitive sites are first come, first served. (No water. $7 per night.)

◖◗ FOOD AND NIGHTLIFE. The streets on **the Hill**, along the **Pearl Street Mall**, burst with eateries, natural food markets, and colorful bars. 🔲**Half Fast Subs ❶**, 1215 13th St., makes over 90 oven-baked subs, listed in colored chalk on the walls. Seven-inch cheesesteak, meat specialty, and vegetarian subs galore are deliriously inexpensive ($3.50-5). All 7 in. subs are $3.75 during happy hour, M-F 5-7pm, when domestic pitchers are only $4.50. (☎449-0404. Open Su-W 11am-10pm, Th-Sa 11am-1:30am.) **Buchanan's Coffee Pub ❶**, 1301 Pennsylvania, is the home of university professors and neo-hippies alike as they sip 20 oz. iced blonde mochas ($3.90), hot chai ($3.65), and fruit smoothies ($4.25) at all hours of the day. (☎440-0222. Open M-F 7am-11pm, Sa-Su 8am-11pm.) **Illegal Pete's ❶**, 1320 College Ave., on the Hill, and at 1447 Pearl St., on the Mall, creates scrumptious burritos for $4.85. (☎444-3055. Open daily Sept.-May 11am-8pm; June-Aug. 11am-3:30pm.) At **Moshi Moshi Bowl ❶**, 1628 Pearl St., fill up on tasty noodle and rice bowls, salads, and sushi, all for under $6. (☎720-565-9787. Open M-Th 11am-8pm, F 11am-9pm, Sa noon-8pm.) A Boulder classic, **The Sink ❷**, 1165 13th St., still awaits the return of its one-time janitor, Robert Redford, who quit his job and headed to Hollywood. The Sink serves surprisingly upscale cuisine and great pizzas amid wild graffiti and low ceilings. Students fill the place for late-night drinking. (☎444-7465. Burgers $6.50-9. Open M-Sa 11am-2am, Su noon-2am; kitchen closes at 10pm.)

Boulder overflows with unique nightlife hot spots. For bluegrass, funk, and the best brews in Boulder (try the "Annapurna Amber"), head to the wildly popular 🔲**Mountain Sun Pub and Brewery**, 1535 Pearl St. (☎546-0886. Acoustic performances Su 10pm-1am. $2 pints during happy hour, daily 4-6pm and 10pm-1am. Open M-Sa 11:30am-1am, Su noon-1am.) **The West End Tavern**, 926 Pearl St., has a rooftop bar where views of downtown, the cool evening breeze, and a classic film screenings make for an enchanting atmosphere. (☎444-3535. Draft beer $3-4. Open M-Sa 11am-11:30am, Su 11:30am-1:30am; kitchen closes at 11pm.) **The Library Pub**, 1718 Broadway, boasts the largest outdoor patio in Boulder, right along the creek. Punk, hard rock, and reggae fans flood the floors for live music Thursday through Saturday. (☎443-2330. Happy hour daily 4-6pm, 9-11pm. Open daily noon-2am.)

◎ 〽. **SIGHTS AND OUTDOOR ACTIVITIES.** The 🏛**Dushanbe Teahouse ❸**, 1770 13th St., the only one of its kind in the Western hemisphere, was built by artists in Tajikistan, then piece-mailed from Boulder's sister city of Dushanbe. The building is owned by the city and leased to a private restauranteur, who lays out scrumptious global cuisine. (☎442-4993. Tea $2-4. Lunch $7-9. Dinner $9-12. Open M-Th 8am-3pm, F 8am-10pm, Sa 3-10pm, Su 3-9pm. Tea time 3-5pm.) The intimate **Leanin' Tree Museum,** 6055 Longbow Dr., presents an acclaimed collection of over 200 paintings and 80 bronze sculptures depicting Western themes from cattlemen to Native Americans. (☎530-1442, ext. 299; www.leanintreemuseum.com. Open M-F 8am-4:30pm, Sa-Su 10am-4pm. Free.) Minutes away, the **Celestial Seasonings Tea Company,** 4600 Sleepytime Dr., lures visitors with tea samples and free tours of the factory and herb garden, including the infamous Mint Room, featuring the "mind-clearing power" of peppermint and spearmint. (☎581-1202. Open M-Sa 9am-6pm, Su 11am-5pm. Tours daily every hr.)

Boulder's location supports many outdoor activities. Starting at **Scott Carpenter Park,** trails follow **Boulder Creek** to the foot of the mountains. **Chautauqua Park** has trails varying in difficulty that climb up and around the **Flatirons.** Starting at the auditorium, the **Enchanted Mesa/McClintock Trail** is an easy 2 mi. loop through meadows and ponderosa pine forests. The challenging **Greg Canyon Trail** starts at the Baird Park parking lot and rises through pines above Saddle Rock, winding back down past Amphitheater Rocks. Before heading into the wilderness, grab a trail map at the entrance to Chautauqua Park. *Beware of mountain lions.*

🎭 **ENTERTAINMENT.** An exciting street scene pounds through both the Mall and the Hill; the university's kiosks have the lowdown on downtown happenings. From June to August, find live music and street performances on Pearl St. Mall. (Tu and Th-F noon-1:30pm.) The **University Memorial Center,** 1609 Euclid St. (16th St. becomes Euclid St. on campus), hosts many events. (☎492-6161.) From late June to mid-August, the **Colorado Shakespeare Festival** draws over 50,000 people. Performances occur in a red sandstone amphitheater on the CU campus. (☎492-0554; www.coloradoshakes.org. Tickets $10-50, previews $5-25. $5 student and senior discount.) The **Colorado Music Festival** hosts performances July through August. (☎449-1397; www.coloradomusicfest.org. Lawn seats $5; other tickets $10-40.) The local indie music scene is on display at the popular and retro-styled **Fox Theater and Cafe,** 1135 13th St. (☎447-0095; www.foxtheater.com.) Twice a week from April through October, Boulder shuts down 13th St. between Canyon and Arapahoe for a **Farmers Market.** (Open Apr.-Oct. W 5-8pm, Sa 8am-2pm.)

ROCKY MOUNTAIN NATIONAL PARK ☎970

Of all the US national parks, Rocky Mountain National Park is closest to heaven, with over 60 peaks surpassing 12,000 ft. Here among the clouds, the alpine tundra ecosystem supports bighorn sheep, dwarf wildflowers, and arctic shrubs among granite boulders and crystal lakes. The city of **Estes Park,** immediately east of the park, hosts the vast majority of would-be mountaineers. West of the park, the town of **Grand Lake,** on the edges of two glacial lakes, is a more tranquil base from which to explore the park's less traversed but equally stunning western side.

◢◣ 🔢 ORIENTATION AND PRACTICAL INFORMATION

The park is accessible from Boulder via U.S. 36 or scenic Rte. 7. From the northeast, the park can be accessed up the Big Thompson Canyon via U.S. 34, but beware of flash floods. **Trail Ridge Road (Highway 34)** runs 48 mi. through the park.

Visitor Info: Park Headquarters and Visitors Center (☎586-1206), 2½ mi. west of Estes Park on Rte. 36, at the Beaver Meadows entrance to the park. Open daily mid-June to Aug. 8am-6pm; Sept. to mid-June 8am-5pm.

Kawuneeche Visitors Center (☎627-3471), just outside the park's western entrance, 1¼ mi. north of Grand Lake, offers similar info. Open daily mid-May to Aug. 8am-6pm; Sept. 8am-5pm; Oct. to mid-May 8am-4:30pm. Evening programs in summer Sa 7pm; call for winter program.

Alpine Visitors Center, at the crest of Trail Ridge Rd., has a great view of the tundra. Open daily mid-June to late Aug. 9am-5pm; late May to mid-June and late Aug. to mid-Oct. 10am-4:30pm.

Lily Lake Visitors Center, 6 mi. south of Headquarters on Rte. 7. Open June-Oct. daily 9am-4:30pm.

Fall River Visitors Center, 5 mi. west of downtown Estes Park on Rte. 34 at the northern entrance to the park, is the newest center. Open May-Oct. daily 8:30am-6pm.

Entrance Fee: $15 per car, $5 per motorcycle, bicyclist, or pedestrian; valid for 7 days.

Weather Conditions: Park Weather and Road Conditions, ☎586-1333.

Medical Services: Estes Park Medical Center, ☎586-2317. **Park Emergency,** ☎586-1399.

Internet Access: Estes Park Public Library, 335 E. Elkhorn (☎586-8116). Open in summer M-Th 9am-9pm, F-Sa 9am-5pm, Su 1-5pm; in winter M-Th 10am-9pm, F-Sa 10am-5pm, Su 1-5pm.

Post Office: Grand Lake, 520 Center Dr. (☎627-3340). Open M-F 8:30am-5pm. **Postal Code:** 80447. **Estes Park,** 215 W. Riverside Dr. (☎586-0170). Open M-F 9am-5pm, Sa 10am-2:30pm. **Postal Code:** 80517. **Area Code:** 970.

▗ ACCOMMODATIONS

ESTES PARK

Although Estes Park has an abundance of expensive lodges, there are deals on indoor beds in the winter, when temperatures drop and tourists leave.

YMCA of the Rockies, 2515 Tunnel Rd. (☎586-3341, ext. 1010), 2 mi. from the park entrance. Follow Rte. 36 to Rte. 66. Guests have access to extensive facilities, including mini golf, gym, and a pool, as well as horseback rides, fly fishing, and daily hikes. Fireplaces, kitchens, dishwashers, multiple baths, and cribs available. Call ahead; reservations for summer accepted starting May 1st. 4-person lodges $47; 4-person cabins with kitchen and bath from $74; 5-person cabins $133; 7-person cabins $179. 1-day "guest membership" required: $3; families $5. ❹

The Colorado Mountain School, 341 Moraine Ave. (☎586-5758). Tidy, dorm-style accommodations are open to travelers unless booked by mountain-climbing students. Wood bunks with mattresses, linen, and showers. 16 beds. Reservations recommended. Reception June-Sept. daily 8am-5pm. Winter hours vary. Dorms $25. ❶

Saddle & Surrey Motel, 1341 S. Saint Vrain/Hwy. 7 (☎586-3326 or 800-204-6226). Clean and comfy rooms. Heated outdoor pool and spa on site. Microwave, fridge, A/C, breakfast, and cable TV. Singles $80; doubles $110. ❸

GRAND LAKE

Grand Lake is the "snowmobile capital of Colorado" and offers spectacular cross-country routes. Boating and fishing are popular summertime activities.

Shadowcliff Hostel (HI), 405 Summerland Park Rd. (☎627-9220). From the western entrance, go left to Grand Lake, then take the left fork into town on W. Portal Rd. The hand-built pine lodge perches on a cliff, affording excellent daytime views; at night, a wood-burning stove and piano make for pleasant evenings. Kitchen and showers. Internet $3 per 30min. Linen $2. 7-day min. stay for cabins. Cabin reservations as far as 1 year in advance. Open June-Sept. Dorms $15, non-members $18. Private singles or doubles with shared bath $45; additional person $11. 6-8 person cabins $100. ❶

Sunset Motel, 505 Grand Ave. (☎627-3318), stands out against the mountains with its yellow front and baby-blue trim. Friendly owners eager to advise on local activities complement cozy rooms with gas fireplaces, cable TV, large bathrooms, and the only heated indoor pool in Grand Lake. Summer singles $65; doubles $80. Winter $50/$65. ❸

Bluebird Motel, 30 River Dr. (☎627-9314), on Rte. 34 west of Grand Lake, overlooks Shadow Mountain Lake and the mountains. Some rooms have couches or kitchenettes. No phones; swimming pool access at the Sunset Motel. Singles $45; doubles $65. ❷

🏕 CAMPING

Visitors can camp a total of seven days within the park. In the backcountry, the maximum stay increases to 14 days from October to May. Campgrounds are open throughout the winter, though would-be campers are responsible for clearing their own snow. All five **national park campgrounds ❶** are $20 in the summer, while winter sites are $12 unless otherwise noted. A backcountry camping **permit** ($20) is required in summer for stays in the over 120 backcountry areas in the park. Backcountry sites become less crowded the farther one hikes from the trailhead. **Sprague Lake** has a wheelchair accessible backcountry site. On eastern slopes, permits are available from the **Backcountry Permits and Trip Planning** building, 2min. from the park headquarters. (☎586-1242. Open daily mid-May to Oct. 7am-7pm; Nov. to mid-May 8am-5pm.) In the west, go to the **Kawuneeche Visitors Center.**

GRAND LAKE

The only national park campground on the western side of the park is **Timber Creek,** 10 mi. north of Grand Lake. Open year-round, it offers 100 sites available on a first come, first served basis. Campsites can also be found in the surrounding **Arapaho National Forest.** (☎887-4100.) **Stillwater Campground,** west of Grand Lake on the shores of Lake Granby, has 148 tranquil sites, a boat ramp, flush toilets, and wheelchair accessible sites. (Open year-round. Sites $16, with water $19, with hookup $21.) **Green Ridge Campground,** on the south end of Shadow Mountain Lake, has 81 sites in close proximity to good fishing and hiking. (Open mid-May to mid-Nov. Sites $13.) For both campgrounds, reservations, which should be made at least 5 days in advance, can be made at ☎877-444-6777 or www.reserveusa.com.

EAST SIDE OF THE PARK

Moraine Park, 3 mi. west of Beaver Meadows Park Headquarters on Bear Lake Rd., is open year-round and has 247 sunny sites as well as nightly campfires and evening programs from mid-June to mid-August. The open meadows can afford great wildlife viewing. In summer, **Glacier Basin,** 9 mi. from Estes Park, south of Moraine Park, provides 150 secluded sites near popular hiking trails; the Bear Lake shuttle buses also stop here. Both Moraine and Glacier Basin require summer reservations. (☎800-365-2267; http://reservations.nps.gov.) **Longs Peak,** 8 mi. south on Hwy. 7, has 26 year-round tent sites, but also has a 3-night maximum stay.

🍴 FOOD

ESTES PARK

Sweet Basilico Cafe, 401 E. Elkhorn Ave. (☎586-3899). The intimate seating area overflows with patrons seeking authentic Italian cuisine. Focaccia bread sandwiches $6. Freshly made pastas $7-10. Open June-Sept. M-F 11am-10pm, Sa-Su 11:30am-10pm; Oct.-May Tu-Su 11am-2:30pm and 4:30-9pm. ❷

The Notchtop Bakery & Cafe, 459 E. Wonderview, #44 (☎586-0272), in the upper Stanley Village Shopping Plaza, east of downtown off Rte. 34. Breads, pastries, and pies baked fresh every morning, breakfast burritos and frittatas. Wireless Internet. Soups $4-5. Salads $5-8. Sandwiches and wraps $6-7. Open daily 7am-5pm. ❷

Local's Grill, 153 E. Elkhorn Ave. (☎586-6900), downtown, is a self-proclaimed "world-famous gathering place." Customers crowd the front patio for gourmet sandwiches, wraps ($5-8), and pizza ($5-22). Open M-Th 11am-9pm, F-Su 11am-10pm. ❷

GRAND LAKE

Chuck Hole Cafe, 1119 Grand Ave. (☎627-3509). A popular breakfast and lunch spot, this Grand Lake tradition has been doling out its homemade cinnamon rolls, famous reuben sandwiches ($7-9), and spicy red chili since 1938. Open daily 7am-2pm. ❷

Pancho and Lefty's, 1120 Grand Ave. (☎627-8773). With an outdoor patio overlooking Grand Lake and a bar large enough to fit most of its residents, Pancho and Lefty's is an understandably popular hangout. Try the *rellenos fritos* ($11) or crunchy *chimichangas* ($11), and wash it all down with a margarita ($4.50). Live music W 8pm, Sa 9pm. Open daily June-Sept. 11am-11pm, kitchen closes at 9pm; Sept.-June 11am-8pm. ❷

Mountain Inn, 612 Grand Ave. (☎627-3385). Serving up the best dinner deals in town, including mouth-watering chicken-fried steak ($10-11). Live blues and rock in summer Sa 12:30-4pm. Open M-F 5-10pm, Sa-Su 11:30am-2:30pm and 5-10pm. ❸

🏔 OUTDOOR ACTIVITIES

SCENIC DRIVES

The star of the park is **Trail Ridge Road** (U.S. 34), a 48 mi. stretch that rises 12,183 ft. above sea level into frigid tundra, where snow patches can be found through much of the summer. The round-trip drive takes roughly 3hr. by car. *Beware of slow-moving tour buses and people stopping to ogle wildlife.* The road is sometimes closed or inaccessible (especially from October to May) due to bad weather. Many sights within the park are accessible from Trail Ridge Rd. Heading west, find an open view of the park from the boardwalk along the highway at **Many Parks Curve** (9,260 ft.). **Rainbow Curve** (10,829 ft.) and the **Forest Canyon Overlook** (11,716 ft.) offer impressive views of the vast tree-carpeted landscape, formed by glacial action. The 30min. **Tundra Communities Trail** provides a once-in-a-lifetime look at the fragile alpine tundra. Signposts along the paved trail explain local geology and wildlife. The **Lava Cliffs** attract crowds, but are worth the hassle. After peaking at **Gore Range,** a mighty 12,183 ft. above sea level, Trail Ridge Rd. runs north to the **Alpine Visitors Center.** Entering the west side of the park past the Alpine Visitors Center, congestion becomes noticeably less.

A wilder alternative to Trail Ridge Rd. is **Old Fall River Road.** Entering Rocky Mountain National Park from the east side on Rte. 34, you'll pass **Sheep Lakes,** a popular crossing for bighorn sheep. After Sheep Lakes, veer right toward the **Alluvial Fan** and Old Fall River Rd. Open only in the summer, Old Fall River Rd. starts at **Endovalley** picnic area and is a 9 mi., gravel, one-way uphill road that features spectacular mountain views and a sense of the rigors of pre-asphalt travel. (Sharp switchbacks. No trailers; max. vehicle length 25 ft.) The road intersects Trail Ridge Rd. behind the Alpine Visitors Center. **Bear Lake Road,** south of Trail Ridge Rd., leads to the most popular hiking trails within the park. **Moraine Park Museum,** off Bear Lake Rd. 1½ mi. from the Beaver Meadows entrance, has exhibits on the park's geology and ecosystem, as well as comfortable rocking chairs with a view of the mountains. (☎586-1206. Open in summer daily 9am-5pm.)

SCENIC HIKES

Numerous trailheads lie in the western half of the park, including the Continental Divide and its accompanying hiking trail. Trail Ridge Rd. ends in **Grand Lake,** a small town with ample outdoor opportunities. An overnight trek from Grand Lake into the scenic and remote **North** or **East Inlets** leaves the crowds behind.

Lake Nanita (11 mi., 5½hr.), is one of the most photogenic destinations in the park, a quality enhanced by the effort it takes to get there. Starts at North Inlet trailhead just north of Grand Lake. Don't let the easy and well-shaded first 6½ mi. fool you. After reaching **Cascade Falls,** the last half of the trail is a steep grade that ascends 2240 ft. through pristine wilderness to a fantastic view of the lake.

Lake Verna (7 mi., 3½hr.), starts at East Inlet trailhead at the far east end of Grand Lake. This moderate hike gains a total of 1800 ft. in elevation as it passes **Adams Falls** and **Lone Pine Lake** and rewards hikers with open views of **Mount Craig** before re-entering the forest. The culmination of the hike is an overlook of the fjord-like lake.

Mill Creek (1½ mi., 40min.), beginning at Hollowell Park off Bear Lake Rd. This easy and pleasant trail (elevation gain 600 ft.) crosses an open meadow and then empties out into a serene field of aspen, providing a look at the significant beaver activity along the creek and the soaring hawks in the sky.

Bear Lake Hikes. The park's most popular trails are all accessible from the Bear Lake Trailhead at the south end of Bear Lake Rd. Bear Lake serves as the hub for snowshoeing and cross-country skiing.

Flattop Mountain (4½ mi., 3hr.), the most challenging and picturesque of the Bear Lake hikes, climbs 2800 ft. to a vantage point along the Continental Divide.

Nymph (½ mi., 15min.); **Dream** (1 mi., 30min.); and **Emerald Lakes** (1¾ mi., 1hr.) are a series of 3 glacial pools offering inspiring glimpses of the surrounding peaks. Although the first 2 legs of the hike are relatively easy, the Emerald Lake portion is steep and rocky at points.

Lake Haiyaha (2¼ mi., 1¼hr.), forking left from the trail, is more intimate, with switchbacks through dense sub-alpine forests and superb views of the mountains. A scramble over the rocks at the end of the trail earns you a peek at the hidden (and sometimes difficult to find) Lake Haiyaha, arguably the most astounding of the 4 lakes.

VAIL ☎970

The largest one-mountain ski resort in all of North America, Vail has its fair share of ritzy hotels and boutiques, but it's the mountain that wows skiers with its prime snow and famed back bowls. Discovered by Lord Gore in 1854, the Vail area was invaded during the 1870s Rockies gold rush. According to local lore, the Ute Indians adored the area's rich supply of game, but became so upset with the white settlers that they set fire to the forest, creating the resort's open terrain.

🛈 PRACTICAL INFORMATION. The communities of Vail consist of **East Vail, Vail Village, Lionshead Village, Cascade Village,** and **West Vail.** Vail Village and Lionshead Village, which are the main centers of action, are pedestrian-only; visitors must park in garages off **South Frontage Road,** but parking is free during the summer. Free **Vail Buses** take visitors within and between each of the villages year-round. (Schedule info ☎477-3456.) **Vail Resort Express** runs bus routes between Vail and its surrounding areas, including Eagle, Edwards, and Beaver Creek. (☎328-3520 for schedule info. Office open daily 6:30am-10pm. $2-3.) **Greyhound,** in the Transportation Building next to the main visitors center (☎476-5137; ticket office open daily 7:30am-6pm), buses eager skiers to: Denver (2hr., 5 per day, $22); Glenwood Springs (1½hr., 4 per day, $17); Grand Junction (3½hr., 4 per day, $17). Vail's two **visitors centers** are both on S. Frontage Rd. The larger one is in Vail Village, at the **Vail Transportation Center** (☎479-1394 or

(side tab) ROCKY MOUNTAINS

800-525-3875; open daily in summer 8am-7pm, in winter 8am-6pm), and the smaller is at the parking structure in Lionshead Village (☎800-525-3875; open daily in summer 8:30am-7pm; in winter 8am-5pm). **Weather Conditions: Road report,** ☎476-2226. **Snow report,** ☎476-8888. **Internet Access: Vail Public Library,** 292 W. Meadow Dr. (☎479-2184. Open M-Th 10am-8pm, F 11am-6pm, Sa-Su 11am-6pm.) **Post Office:** 1300 N. Frontage Rd. (☎476-5217. Open M-F 8:30am-5pm, Sa 8:30am-noon.) **Postal Code:** 81657. **Area Code:** 970.

Ⓝ ACCOMMODATIONS. The phrase "cheap lodging" is not part of Vail's vocabulary. Rooms in the resort town rarely dip below $175 per night in winter, and summer lodging is often equally pricey. Call the visitors centers for info on special rates; hotels and lodges often offer big discounts during the summer and slower seasons. **Lionshead Inn ❸,** 705 W. Lionshead Cir., has great deals on luxury accommodations. With an exercise room, game room, hot tub, fireplace lounge, Internet access, and continental breakfast included, the inn also offers plush robes, down comforters on every bed, and balconies in every room. Call for lower walk-in rates or book online for 50% off rooms during the summer. (☎476-2050 or 800-283-8245; www.lionsheadinn.com. Singles with valley view from $59; mountain view from $79.) The **Roost Lodge ❹,** 1783 N. Frontage Rd., in West Vail, provides affordable lodging right on the free bus route. The impressively clean rooms come with breakfast, cable TV, fridge, microwave, and access to a jacuzzi, sauna, and heated indoor pool. (☎476-5451 or 800-873-3065. Continental breakfast in winter. Singles in summer from $59; in winter $109-129.) Located in Eagle, about 30 mi. west of Vail, **The Prairie Moon ❷,** 738 Grand Ave., offers some of the cheapest lodging near the resort. EcoTransit shuttles visitors daily between Eagle and Vail. The large, clean rooms have A/C, fridges, and microwaves. (☎328-6680. Singles $34-50; doubles $40-$63.) The **Holy Cross Ranger District,** right off I-70 at Exit 171 (follow signs), provides info on the six summer campgrounds near Vail. (☎827-5715. Open M-F 8am-5pm.) With 25 sites, **Gore Creek ❶** is the closest and most popular campground. Well-situated among aspen trees, wildflowers, and mountains just outside East Vail, Gore Creek is within hiking distance of the free East Vail Express bus route. (Drinking water available by hand pump. Max. stay 10 days. Sites $12.)

Ⓕ FOOD AND NIGHTLIFE. You'll never need to cook breakfast in Vail as long as the griddle is hot at **DJ's Classic Diner ❶,** 616 W. Lionshead Plaza, on the west end of Lionshead Village. In winter, locals ski in 'round the clock to warm up on DJ's crepes ($4-6), omelettes ($4-5), and pasta frittatas from $7.50. (☎476-2336. Open in summer M-Th and Sa-Su 7am-1pm, F 10pm-3am; in winter M 7am-1pm and 24hr. from Tu 7am to Su 1pm.) Right in the heart of Vail Village, **The Red Lion ❹,** Hanson Ranch Rd. and Bridge St., was built by its owners over 60 years ago as a hotel, but they had so many children that there were no rooms left for guests. Today it's a hot spot for succulent barbecue brisket ($13) or ribs ($19) over drinks. (☎476-7676. Nightly drink specials. Open 11am-late.) **Moe's Original BBQ ❷,** 675 W. Lionshead Cir., offers an Alabama-style "Southern Soulfood revival." Their box lunches ($8-9) with pulled pork or smoked chicken and two choices of sides (baked beans and homemade banana puddin' are favorites) might be the best deal in town. (☎479-7888. Open M-Sa 11am-sellout.) Stuffing burritos and chiles chock-full, **La Cantina ❶,** in the Transportation Center, serves a fine selection of Mexican food ($3-6) for an even finer price. (☎476-7661. Open daily 11:30am-10pm.)

With two clubs, three floors, four bars, and seven decks, **The Tap Room & Sanctuary,** 333 Bridge St. in Vail Village, attracts all types of crowds. While the Tap Room caters to those looking for good rowdy fun, the Sanctuary upstairs is for those in search of a more sleek and classy nightclub. (☎479-0500. $0.50 Coors F 5-8pm. Tap Room open daily 10am-2am, Sanctuary open Tu-Sa 8pm-2am). **Garfinkel's,** 536 E. Lionshead Cir., a hidden hangout accessible by foot in Vail's Lionshead Village (directly across from the gondola) calls out "Ski hard, party harder." Enjoy your meal on a slope-side porch. (☎476-3789. Meals $8-11. Restaurant open June-Sept. and Nov.-Apr. daily 11am-2am, kitchen closes at 10pm.)

◙ **SIGHTS.** The **Ski Hall of Fame** is housed in The **Colorado Ski Museum,** on the 3rd level of the Vail Transportation Center, and captures the history of the sport and of Vail and includes a fascinating section on the 10th Mountain Division and its training in the mountains around Vail for the rigors of fighting in the mountains of Italy during WWII. (☎476-1876 or 800-950-7410. Open June-Sept. and Nov.-Apr. Tu-Su 10am-5pm. $1, under 12 free.) In the summer, the **Gerald R. Ford Amphitheater,** right at the east edge of Vail Village, presents a number of outdoor concerts, dance festivals, and theater productions on its grounds. (☎476-2918. Box office open M-Sa noon-6pm. Lawn seats $15-40; Tu free.) Next door in the lovely **Betty Ford Alpine Gardens,** view the peaceful meditation and rock gardens. (☎476-0103. Guided tours M, Th, and Sa 10:30am. Open May-Sept dawn-dusk. Free.) The **Vilar Center for the Arts,** in Beaver Creek, hosts world-renowned performers and shows from Shakespeare to Broadway. (☎845-8497 or 888-920-2787. Box office open M-Sa 11am-5pm.)

◪ **OUTDOOR ACTIVITIES.** Before hitting the slopes, the unequipped visit **Ski Base,** 610 W. Lionshead Cir., for equipment. (☎476-5799. Open in winter daily 8am-7pm. Skis, poles, and boots from $14 per day. Snowboard and boots from $20 per day.) The store transforms into the **Wheel Base Bike Shop** in the summer. (Open in summer daily 9am-6pm. Path bikes $15 per 8hr.; mountain bikes from $27 per 8hr.) Vail caters to sun worshippers in the summer, when the ski runs turn into hiking and biking trails. The **Eagle Bahn Gondola** in Lionshead and the **Vista Bahn Chairlift,** part of the Vail Resort, whisk hikers, bikers, and sightseers to the top of the mountains for breathtaking views. (☎476-9090. Office open daily 8:30am-4:30pm. Eagle Bahn open in summer Su-W 10am-4pm, Th-Sa 10am-9pm; in winter F-Su 10am-4pm. Vista Bahn open mid-July to early Sept. F-Su 10am-4pm. All-day pass on either Bahn $17, ages 65-69 and 5-12 $10, 70 and over $5; $29 for bike haul.) During the summer months, enjoy the **Eagle Bahn Gondola Twilight Ride.** (Th-Sa 5-9pm. Free.) The Holy Cross Ranger District (see above) provides maps and information on the many snowmobile, cross-country skiing, and hiking routes near Vail Pass. The **Gore Creek Fly Fisherman,** 183-7 Gore Creek Dr., reels in the daily catch and has river info. (☎476-3296. Rod rentals $15 per half-day, with boots and waders $30.)

ASPEN
☎970

Aspen was founded in 1879 as a silver mining camp, but the silver ran out quickly and by 1940 the town was almost gone. Wealthy visionaries took one look at the location of the foundering village and transformed it into a winter playground. Today, Aspen's skiing, scenery, and festivals are matched only by the prices in the exclusive boutiques downtown. To catch Aspen on the semi-cheap, stay in Glenwood Springs, 40 mi. north on Rte. 82.

▟ **PRACTICAL INFORMATION. Aspen Shuttles** and the **RFTA** provide year-round free service around town and in the Roaring Fork Valley for a small fare. (☎925-8484. Fare $1-9 depending on destination). **Visitors Centers:** 320 E. Hyman Ave., in the Wheeler Opera House (☎920-7148; open daily 10am-6pm); 425 Río Grand Pl.

(☎925-1940 or 888-290-1324; open M-F 8am-5pm). **The Aspen Ranger District,** 806 W. Hallam, provides info on hikes and camping within 15 mi. of Aspen. (☎925-3445. Open June-Aug. M-Sa 8am-5pm; Sept.-May M-F 8am-4:30pm. Topographic maps $4.) **Roads and Weather:** ☎877-315-7623. **Snow Report:** ☎925-1221 or 888-277-3676. **Internet Access: Pitkin County Library,** 120 N. Mill St. (☎925-4025. Open M-Th 10am-9pm, F-Sa 10am-6pm, Su noon-6pm.) **Post Office:** 235 Puppy Smith Rd. (☎925-7523. Open M-F 8:30am-5pm, Sa 9am-noon.) **Postal Code:** 81611. **Area Code:** 970.

ⱪ ACCOMMODATIONS. Staying in Aspen means biting the bullet and reaching deep into your pockets. The last sound deal in town, **St. Moritz Lodge ❷,** 344 W. Hyman Ave., charms ski bums with continental breakfast, a pool, steam room, and hot tub. (☎925-3220 or 800-817-2069; www.stmoritzlodge.com. Reception hours 7am-7pm. Dorms $36-44, depending on season. Hotel rooms $79-200.) For all the pampering of an Aspen resort without the heavy price tag, **Limelite Lodge ❹,** 228 E. Cooper St., is outfitted with two outdoor pools, two jacuzzis, a fireplace lounge, and allows pets. (☎925-3025 or 800-433-0832; www.limelite-lodge.com. Singles $59-$250 depending on season.) Unless more than 6 ft. of snow covers the ground, **camping ❶** is available in one of the nine National Forest campgrounds that lie within 10 mi. of Aspen. **Silver Bar, Silver Bell,** and **Silver Queen** campgrounds lie 5 mi. southwest of town on Maroon Creek Rd. and fill quickly. Five miles southeast on Rte. 82, **Difficult** campground usually has more openings. (☎877-444-6777. Water, but no hookups. 5-day max. stay throughout the district. Open June to mid-Sept. Reservations recommended. Sites $12-15.)

◨◪ FOOD AND ENTERTAINMENT. Always packed, the **Hickory House ❸,** 730 W. Main St., smokes up award-winning barbecue favorites. (☎925-2313. Lunch specials $7-10. Dinner $10-20. Open daily 6am-2:30pm and 5-10pm.) Try the famed beef stew at **Little Annie's Eating House ❸,** 517 E. Hyman Ave., a longtime Aspen staple. Everyday, all day long, throw back a beer and a shot for $2.75. (☎925-1098. Burgers $8.25. Veggie lasagna $10. Open daily 11:30am-1:30am; kitchen closes at 10pm.) With jukeboxes and TVs blaring, the **Cooper Street Pier ❷,** 508 E. Cooper St., is the local hot spot. Feast on the hamburger special (burger with fries and a soda or beer; $7.50) and $5.75 Coors pitchers during happy hour. (☎925-7758. Happy hour 3-6pm. Open daily 11am- 2am; kitchen closes at 10pm. Cash only.) With an espresso bar and freshly squeezed juices, **Main Street Bakery ❷,** 201 E. Main St., also serves gourmet soups ($5), vegetarian sandwiches ($7), and "naked" smoothies ($3.75). Their patio offers *al fresco* dining and a prime people-watching spot. (☎925-6446. Open M-Sa 7am-9:30pm, Su 7am-4pm.) Fast, cheap, and easy, **The Big Wrap ❷,** 520 E. Durant Ave., rolls up gourmet wraps ($6), like the tasty "To Thai For." (☎544-1700. Fresh salads $5. Smoothies $4. Open M-Sa 10am-6pm.)

Entering its 55th year, the acclaimed **Aspen Music Festival** features jazz, opera, and classical music from late June through August. Shows are held every night in venues around town, and a free Music Shuttle bus takes listeners from Rubey Park to the music tent 30min. prior to each concert. (☎925-9042; www.aspenmusicfestival.com. Many concerts free.) Take the Silver Queen Gondola (see **Outdoor Activities,** p. 759) up to Aspen Mountain for open-air free **Saturday Classic Music Concerts** (late June to mid-Aug. Sa 1pm) and **Bluegrass Sundays** (mid-June to late Aug. Su noon-3pm). **Aspen Theatre in the Park,** 110 E. Hallam St., performs from mid-June to late August. (☎925-9313, box office 920-5770; www.aspentip.org. $25-30.)

◮ SKIING. Skiing is the main attraction in Aspen. The surrounding hills contain four ski areas: Aspen Mountain, Aspen Highlands, Buttermilk Mountain, and Snowmass, known collectively as **Aspen/Snowmass.** A free **Skier Shuttle Service**

runs between the four mountains 8am-4:30pm. Interchangeable lift tickets enable the four areas to operate as a single extended resort; for the best deal, buy multi-day passes at least 2 weeks in advance. (☎925-1220 or 800-525-6200. Day passes from $72, college students 24 and under, ages 13-17, and ages 65-69 $64, 7-12 $43, over 70 and under 7 free; prices vary by season.) **Incline Ski Shop,** 555 E. Durant, one of the oldest and most experienced retailers around, rents boots and skis. (☎925-7748.) Each of the mountains offers unique skiing opportunities of varying difficulty. **Buttermilk's** gentle slopes are perfect for beginners interested in lessons (and snowplowing down the mountain). The **Highlands** now includes the steep cliffs of Highland Bowl and offers a diverse selection for advanced and expert skiers. **Aspen Mountain,** though smaller than the Highlands, also caters to experts; there are no easy trails. The granddaddy of the Aspen ski areas, **Snowmass,** with its 20 lifts and countless runs, remains the most family-friendly of the mountains, and with half-pipes and terrain parks, it's popular among snowboarders. All but the most timid will find something to enjoy here.

⚠ OUTDOOR ACTIVITIES. The **Silver Queen Gondola** heads to the 11,212 ft. summit of Aspen Mountain, providing an unparalleled panorama. (☎920-0719 or 800-525-6200. Open daily mid-June to early Sept. 10am-4pm, late Nov. to mid-April 9am-4pm. $17 per day, ages 4-12 $10; $30/$20 per week.) At Snowmass Mountain, you can take a chairlift to the top and ride your mountain bike down. (Open in summer daily 9:30am-4pm. $8, children $4.) **Rick's Adventure Cafe,** at the corner of Durant and Hunter St., has great deals on mountain bike rentals. (☎925-8200. Open late May to Oct. 8am-5pm. Full suspension bikes half-day $35, full-day $45.) Hikers can explore the **Maroon Bells** on the unforgettable 1½ mi. trek to Crater Lake. Maroon Creek Rd. is closed to traffic daily 9am-5pm in an effort to preserve the wilderness. RFTA tour buses to the Bells operate during these times and leave from Aspen Highlands Village every 20min. (☎925-8484. $5.50 per person.) If you're planning a hike outside these times, there is a $10 fee per car to drive into the area. The steep but short **Ute Trail** (2½ mi.) departs from Ute Ave. and weaves its way to the top of Aspen Mountain, a spectacular sunset-watching spot. The gentler **Hunter Trail** wanders through town and is popular for jogging and biking. Multi-day backpacking or mountain-biking treks throughout the White River Forest between Aspen, Vail, and Leadville can be complemented by night stays at the **10th Mountain Division Huts ❷,** built in WWII and carefully maintained ever since. The huts sleep 3-20 people and have heating stoves, propane burners, lighting, and mattresses. (☎925-5775; www.huts.org. Call for reservations. Open year-round. $25-39 per person.) For an adrenaline rush and a bird's-eye view of the region, **Aspen Paragliding,** 426 S. Spring St. does tandem jumps for $175. (☎925-7625.)

COLORADO SPRINGS ☎719

Once a resort town frequented only by America's elite, Colorado Springs is now the second-most visited city in Colorado. Early explorers found stunning red rock formations here and proceeded to name the region Garden of the Gods, partly because of a Ute legend that the rocks were petrified bodies of enemies hurled down by the gods. Today, the formations remain a popular attraction, joined by the US Olympic Complex and the US Air Force Academy.

▨ 🛈 ORIENTATION AND PRACTICAL INFORMATION. Colorado Springs is laid out in a grid of broad thoroughfares. **Nevada Avenue** is the main north-south strip, just east of **I-25.** Starting at Nevada Ave., numbered streets ascend moving westward. I-25 from Denver bisects downtown, separating Old Colorado City from the eastern sector of the town, which remains largely residential. **Colorado Avenue** and **Pikes Peak Avenue** run east-west across the city. Just west of Old Colorado City lies Manitou Springs and the Pikes Peak Area. Colorado Ave., which becomes **Manitou Avenue** as it extends into Manitou Springs, serves as the main street through town. **Greyhound,** 120 S. Weber St. (☎635-1505; tickets sold daily 5:15am-10pm), runs buses to: Albuquerque (8hr., 4 per day, $61); Denver (1½-2hr., 6 per day, $14); Pueblo (1hr., 6 per day, $10). **City Bus Service,** 127 E. Kiowa St. (☎385-7423), at Nevada Ave., serves the local area as well as the surrounding Garden of the Gods, Manitou Springs, and Widefield. Pick up a schedule at the Kiowa bus terminal. ($1.25, seniors and ages 6-11 $0.60, under 6 free; to Ft. Carson, Widefield, Fountain, Manitou Springs, and Peterson AFB $0.95 extra.) **Gray Line Tours,** 3704 W. Colorado Ave. (☎633-1181 or 800-345-8197; open daily 8am-5pm), offers whitewater rafting trips on the Arkansas River (7hr.; $75, under 12 $40; includes lunch), as well as a combo tour of the US Air Force Academy and the Garden of the Gods (4hr.; $30, under 12 $15). **Taxi: Yellow Cab** ☎634-5000. **Visitor Info: Visitors Bureau,** 515 S. Cascade Ave. (☎635-7506 or 800-888-4748; www.coloradosprings-travel.com. Open M-F 8:30am-5pm, Sa-Su 9am-5pm.) **Internet Access: Penrose Public Library,** 20 N. Cascade Ave. (☎531-6333. Open M-Th 10am-9pm, F-Sa 10am-6pm, Su 1-5pm.) **Post Office:** 201 E. Pikes Peak Ave., at Nevada Ave. (☎570-5336. Open M-F 7:30am-5:30pm, Sa 8am-1pm.) **Postal Code:** 80903. **Area Code:** 719.

ACCOMMODATIONS. Motels can be found all along Nevada Ave. near downtown, although the best options are farther west in and around Manitou Springs. **Ute Pass Motel ❸,** 1123 Manitou Ave., is a bit pricey, but a soak in the indoor hot tub will soothe the damage on your wallet. Settle on the hammock in the upper deck, and enjoy barbecue and picnic facilities on the lower deck next to Fountain Creek. (☎685-5171. Rooms with kitchens available. Laundry facilities on site. In summer, singles $65, doubles $85; in winter $35/$50.) At the south entrance of the Garden of the Gods, **Beckers Lane Lodge ❸,** 115 Beckers Ln., supplies clean rooms with microwave, fridge, and cable TV, along with an outdoor swimming pool and barbecue area. (☎685-1866. Rooms $42-50.) The **Apache Court Motel ❷,** 3401 W. Pikes Peak Ave., at 34th St., has pink adobe rooms with A/C, cable TV, microwave and refrigerator; some have kitchens. (☎471-9440. Rooms $26-65.) Located conveniently on the main bus line, the **Maverick Motel ❷,** 3620 W. Colorado Ave., is an explosion of pastels. Rooms come fully equipped with cable TV, fridge, and microwave. (☎634-2852 or 866-520-1977. Singles $25; 2-room unit $37.)

Several **Pike National Forest Campgrounds ❶** lie in the mountains flanking Pikes Peak, about 30min. from Colorado Springs. No local transportation serves this area. Campgrounds clutter Rte. 67, 5-10 mi. north of **Woodland Park,** 18 mi. northwest of the Springs on U.S. 24. **Colorado, Painted Rocks,** and **South Meadows** are near Manitou Park; others border U.S. 24 near the town of Lake George, 50 mi. west of the Springs. (Generally open May-Sept. Sites $12-14.) Farther afield, visitors may camp by Lake George Reservoir, at the **Eleven Mile State Recreation Area ❶,** off County Rd. 90 from U.S. 24. (☎748-3401, reservations 800-678-2267. Pay showers and laundry. Reception M-F 7:30am-4:30pm. Sites $13, with electricity $17; vehicle fee $5.) Unless otherwise posted, you can camp on national forest property for free if you are at least 500 ft. from a road or stream. The **Pikes Peak Ranger District Office,** 601 S. Weber St., has maps. (☎636-1602. Open M-F 8am-4:30pm.)

FOOD AND NIGHTLIFE. Students and locals perch among outdoor tables in front of the cafes and restaurants lining **Tejon Avenue. Old Colorado City** is home to a number of fine eateries. During the summer months, there are several **Farm-**

ers **Markets** scattered throughout the city. **Henri's ❷**, 2427 W. Colorado Ave., has served up chimichangas ($7.50) and a wide variety of *cerveza* on the cheap for over 50 years. Drop in for a margarita during happy hour (M-Th 4-8pm, F 3-8pm) or check out the strolling mariachi singers Friday and Saturday nights. (☎ 634-9031. Open Su-Th 11am-9pm, F-Sa 11am-10pm.) **Meadow Muffins ❷**, 2432 W. Colorado Ave., is a virtual museum of old movie props. The two buckboard wagons hanging from the ceiling were used in the filming of *Gone With The Wind*, and the windmill-style fan installed above the bar was originally cast in *Casablanca*. (☎ 633-0583. Drafts $3.50, happy hour $2.50. Burgers $6-7. Tu-Sa live music; Tu all-day happy hour. 21+ after 8pm. Open daily 11am-2am.) **Poor Richard's Restaurant ❷**, 324½ N. Tejon Ave., is a popular local hangout with great New York-style pizza (cheese slices $3.25; pies $12), sandwiches ($6), and salads for $5-7. (☎ 632-7721. W live bluegrass, Th Celtic. Open Su-Tu 11am-9pm, W-Sa 11am-10pm.) Vegans and carnivores alike find heaven at **Organic Earth Cafe ❷**, 1124 Manitou Ave. An amazing list of smoothies and plant shakes ($4-5) sets apart this establishment, consisting of a 1904 Victorian Tea Room, the Future Earth Room, and Fairy Tale Rose Gardens bordering Fountain Creek. (☎ 685-0986. Su 8pm-2am open mic, M 8-10pm drum circle, Tu and Th guest speakers and films, W 8pm-midnight spoken word, F 8pm-2am live funk/jazz. Open M-Th 9am-midnight, F-Su 9am-2am.) If an unbeatable breakfast is what you're looking for, **The Olive Branch ❷**, 23 S. Tejon Ave., is famous for their omelettes ($5-7) and country-style skillets ($7-8), and is outfitted with a smoothie, juice, and espresso bar ($2-5). Lunch and dinner menus also feature the hearty pot pie for $10. (☎ 475-1199. Open daily 6:30am-9pm.) **Rum Bay Bourbon Street**, 20 N. Tejon St., is a multi-level complex with six clubs included under one cover charge ($5). Besides the main Rum Bay club, the crowds swell into Masquerade (a disco club), Copy Cats (a karaoke bar), Fat City (a martini lounge with live blues), and Sam's—the world's smallest bar as noted in the *Guinness Book of World Records*. (☎ 634-3522. Specialty rum drinks $6-7. Th ladies night. 21+ after 8pm. Rum Bay open Tu-Sa 11am-2am. All other clubs open Th-Sa 6pm-2am.)

🄶 **SIGHTS.** Olympic hopefuls train with some of the world's most high-tech sports equipment at the **US Olympic Complex**, 1750 E. Boulder St., on the corner of Union St. The complex has free 1hr. tours. The best times to get a glimpse of athletes in training are 10-11am and 3-4pm. (☎ 866-4618 or 888-659-8687; www.usolympicteam.com. Open M-Sa 9am-5pm, Su 10am-5pm. Tours M-Sa every 30min.) Earlier quests for gold are recorded at the **Pioneers' Museum**, 215 S. Tejon Ave., which recounts the settling of Colorado Springs. (☎ 385-5990. Open in summer Tu-Sa 10am-5pm, Su 1-5pm; in winter closed Su. Free.) The **World Figure Skating Museum and Hall of Fame**, 20 1st St., just north of Lake St., traces the history, art, and science of skating and boasts an extensive collection of rare medals and skating outfits. The only institution of its kind in the world, the museum pays homage to the great American and international skaters that have etched their mark on ice. (☎ 635-5200; www.worldskatingmuseum.org. $3, ages 6-12 and over 59 $2. Open M-Sa 10am-4pm.) Chronicling the exploits of the rough-riding American cowboy, the **Pro Rodeo Hall of Fame and Museum**, Exit 145 immediately off I-25, is at once monument and memorial to the rigors and triumphs of the quintessential Western lifestyle and its two centuries of history. (☎ 528-4764. Open daily 9am-5pm. $6, children $3.) Adding life to earth with fire and water for over 100 years, potters at **Van Briggle Pottery**, Hwy. 24 and 21st St., display their skills during free tours through the studio and showroom. Witness the spinning, casting, and etching process that has produced pieces displayed in the world's most famous museums. (☎ 800-847-6341. Open M-Sa 8:30am-5pm, Su 1-5pm. Free tours M-Sa.) Among the old vehicles, saddles, and riding accessories found at **El Pomar Foundation Carriage Museum**, 16 Lake Cir., travelers can take a closer look at two presidential inaugural coaches and a Conestoga wagon, the colors of which supposedly inspired the design of the American flag. (☎634-7711. Open M-Sa 10am-5pm, Su 1-5pm. Free.)

▲ OUTDOOR ACTIVITIES. Between Rte. 24 (Colorado Ave.) and 30th St. in northwest Colorado Springs, the red rock towers and spires of the **Garden of the Gods Park** rise strikingly against a mountainous backdrop. (Open daily May-Oct. 5am-11pm; Nov.-Apr. 5am-9pm.) **Climbers** are lured by the large red faces and over 400 permanent routes. Climbers must register at the visitors center; $500 fines await those who climb without permit or proper gear. A number of exciting **mountain biking** trails cross the Garden as well. The park's hiking trails, many of which are paved wheelchair-accessible routes, have great views of the rock formations and can easily be completed in one day. A map is available from the park's **visitors center**, 1805 N. 30th St., at Gateway Rd. (☎634-6666; http://gardenofgods.com. Open daily June-Aug. 8am-8pm; Sept.-May 9am-5pm. Daily walking tours depart in summer 10, 11am, 1, 2pm; in winter 10am and 2pm.)

Looming on the horizon, the 14,110 ft. **Pikes Peak** is visible from almost any part of town. Ambitious hikers can ascend the peak along the strenuous, well-maintained **Barr Trail** (26 mi. round-trip, 7500 ft. altitude gain, 16hr. round-trip). Overnight shelter is available at Barr Camp (7 mi. from the trailhead) and the Timberline Shelter (8½ mi.). The trailhead is in Manitou Springs by the "Manitou Incline" sign on Ruxton Ave. Just down the street from the trailhead, visitors can hop on the **Pikes Peak Cog Railway**, 515 Ruxton Ave., operating since 1891, which takes visitors to the summit every 80min. From the summit, the Sangre de Cristo Mountains, the Continental Divide, and the state of Kansas unfold in a lofty view that inspired Kathy Lee Bates to write "America the Beautiful." (☎685-5401; www.cograilway.com. Open mid-Apr. to late Dec.; 6-8 trips per day, call for hours. Round-trip $27, ages 3-11 $15. Reservations recommended.) Avoid crowded parking lots at both the Railway and Barr Trailhead by using the free Manitou Springs Trolley ("SMART" Shuttle) which runs along Manitou and Ruxton Ave. late May to early Sept. For a fee, visitors can drive up the gorgeous 10 mi. **Pikes Peak Highway**—it's worth every penny. (☎385-7325 or 800-318-9505. Open daily May to mid-Sept. 7am-7pm; mid-Sept. to Apr. 9am-3pm. $10, ages 6-15 $5; $35 max. per vehicle.)

For adventurous hiking through subterranean passages, head to the contorted caverns of the **Cave of the Winds,** on Rte. 24, 6 mi. west of Exit 141 off I-25. Discovery and lantern tours go into the more untamed areas of the cave. (☎685-5444; www.caveofthewinds.com. Guided tours daily every 15min. late May to Aug. 9am-9pm; Sept. to late May 10am-5pm. 45min. Discovery tour $15, ages 6-15 $8. 1-1½hr. Lantern Tour $18/$9. Laser light show in summer daily 9pm $10/$5.) Just above Manitou Springs on Rte. 24, the **Cliff Dwellings Museum** contains replicas of ancestral Puebloan dwellings dating from AD 1100-1300 and actual ruins which serve as backdrop for Indian dancers in colorful traditional dress performing from June to August. (☎685-5242 or 800-354-9971; www.cliffdwellingsmuseum.com. Open daily May-Sept. 9am-6pm; Oct.-Apr. 10am-5pm. $8, seniors $7, ages 7-11 $6.) The only waterfall in Colorado to make it on *National Geographic*'s list of international waterfalls, **Seven Falls**, 10min. west of downtown on Cheyenne Blvd., cascades 181 ft. in seven distinct steps down Pikes Peak and is lit up on summer nights. (☎632-0765; www.sevenfalls.com. Open daily in summer 8:30am-10:30pm, in winter 9am-4:15pm. Before 5pm $8.25, ages 6-15 $5.25; after 5pm $9.75/$6.25.

SAN JUAN MOUNTAINS

Ask Coloradoans their favorite mountain retreats, and they're likely to name a peak, lake, stream, or town in the San Juan Range of southwestern Colorado. Four **national forests**—the **Uncompahgre** (un-cum-PAH-gray), the **Gunnison**, the **San Juan**, and the **Río Grande**—encircle this sprawling range. **Durango** is an ideal base camp for forays into these mountains. Northeast of Durango, the **Weminuche Wilderness** tempts the hardy backpacker with a vast expanse of rugged terrain. Get maps and hiking info from the **USFS headquarters** at 15 Burnett Ct., Durango. (☎247-4874. Open Apr. to mid-Dec. M-F 8am-5pm; mid-Dec. to Mar. M-F 8am-4:30pm.)

The San Juan Mountains are easily accessible via U.S. 50, which is traveled by hundreds of thousands of tourists each summer. **Greyhound** serves the area, but very poorly; traveling by car is the best option in this region. The San Juans are loaded with superb campgrounds, making them one of the most economical places to visit in Colorado.

BLACK CANYON OF THE GUNNISON NATIONAL PARK ☎970

Native American parents used to tell their children that the light-colored strands of rock streaking through the walls of the Black Canyon were the hair of a blonde woman—and that if they got too close to the edge they would get tangled in it and fall. The edge of **Black Canyon of the Gunnison National Park** is a staggering place, literally—watch for those trembling knees. The Gunnison River slowly gouged out the 53 mi. long canyon, crafting a steep 2500 ft. gorge that is, in some places, deeper than it is wide. The Empire State Building, if placed at the bottom of the river, would reach barely halfway up its canyon walls.

The Black Canyon lies 15 mi. east of the town of **Montrose.** The **South Rim** is easily accessible year-round via a 6 mi. drive off U.S. 50 ($8 per car, $4 walk-in or motorcycle); the wilder **North Rim** can only be reached by an 80 mi., 2-3 hr. detour around the canyon followed by a gravel road from Crawford off Rte. 92. The road is closed in winter. The spectacular 8 mi. South Rim Drive traces the edge of the canyon, and boasts jaw-dropping vistas, including the spectacular **Chasm View,** where you can peer 2300 ft. down the highest cliff in Colorado at the Gunnison River and the "painted" wall. *Don't throw stones;* you might kill a defenseless hiker in the canyon. On the South Rim, the moderate 2 mi. round-trip **Oak Flat Loop Trail** gives a good sense of the terrain below, while the North Rim's 7 mi. round-trip **North Vista Trail** provides a spectacular view. From the South Rim, you can scramble down the **Gunnison Route,** which drops 1800 ft. over a 1 mi. span, or tackle the more difficult **Tomichi** or **Warner Routes,** which make good overnight hikes. Not surprisingly, the sheer walls of the Black Canyon are a climber's paradise; register at the South Rim Visitors Center. Between the **Painted Wall** and **Cedar Point Overlooks,** a well-worn path leads to **Marmot Rocks,** which offer great bouldering for those not ready for the big walls. On the South Rim, Chasm View, Sunset View, and Tomichi overlooks are all wheelchair accessible. Balanced Rock overlook, on the North Rim, is also wheelchair accessible.

At the canyon, the **South Rim Campground ❶** has 102 well-designed sites with pit toilets, charcoal grills, and water. Some sites are wheelchair accessible. (Sites $10, full hookup $15.) The **North Rim Campground ❶** offers 13 sites, rarely fills, and is popular with climbers. (Sites with water and toilets $10.) In Montrose, inexpensive motels line Main St./U.S. 50 east of downtown, including the **Western Motel ❷,** 1200 E. Main St. (☎249-3481 or 800-445-7301; pool, hot tub, winter sauna, continental breakfast; singles in summer from $52, in winter from $42), and **Canyon Trails Inn ❷,** 1225 E. Main St. (☎249-3426. Hot tub, continental breakfast. Singles $32-45.) **◪Starvin' Arvin's ❸,** 1320 S. Townsend, is wildly popular with locals and visitors alike; it's been serving up cowboy-sized portions for as long as most can remember. Don't miss the 16 oz. steak and eggs breakfast for $14. (☎249-7787. Entrees $4-18. Open 6am-10pm.) **Nav-Mex Tacos ❶**, 475 W. Main St., cooks up the best Mexican food around. (Tacos $1.25; tostadas $3. Open M-F 11am-9pm, Sa-Su 9am-9pm.) For tasty cold or grilled sandwiches ($6) and skillet breakfasts ($7), head for the **Daily Bread Bakery and Cafe ❶**, 346 Main St. (☎249-8444. Open M-Sa 6am-3pm.)

Greyhound (☎249-6673; tickets sold Su-Tu 7:30-8:30am nd 7-8pm, W-Sa 7:30am-12:30pm and 7-8pm) shuttles once a day between Montrose and the **Gunnison County Airport,** 711 Río Grande (☎641-0060), and will drop you off on U.S. 50, 6 mi. from the canyon ($15). A **visitors center** sits on the South Rim. (☎249-1914, ext. 423; www.nps.gov/blca. Open daily May-Oct. 8am-6pm; Nov.-Apr. 8:30am-4pm.) **Post Office:** 321 S. 1st St. (☎249-6654. Open M-F 8am-5pm, Sa 10am-noon.) **Postal Code:** 81401. **Area Code:** 970.

CRESTED BUTTE   ☎970

Crested Butte, 27 mi. north of Gunnison on Rte. 135, was first settled by miners in the 1870s. The coal was exhausted in the 1950s, but a few years later the powder fields on the Butte began to attract skiers. Thanks to strict zoning rules, the downtown is a throwback to the early mining days. Just north of town, **Crested Butte Mountain Resort,** 12 Snowmass Rd., takes skiers to "the extreme limits," offering over 800 acres of bowl skiing. With 14 lifts, a longest run of 2½ miles, and a drop of 3000 ft., the mountain aims to impress, and the views aren't bad either. (☎800-544-8448; www.cmbr.com. Open mid-Dec. to mid-Apr. Prices vary. Day passes around $60, ages 65-74 half-price, children 5-12 pay the numerical value of their age, over 75 free.) In the summer, Crested Butte becomes the mountain biking capital of Colorado. The last week of June is the **Fat Tire Bike Festival** (www.ftbw.com), four days of mountain biking, racing, and fraternizing. In 1976, a group of cyclists rode from Crested Butte to Aspen, starting the oldest mountain biking event in the world. Every September, bikers repeat the trek over the 12,705 ft. pass to Aspen and back during the **Pearl Pass Tour,** organized by the **Mountain Biking Hall of Fame,** 331 Elk Ave. (☎349-1880.) Trail maps are available at bike shops and **The Alpineer,** 419 6th St. (☎349-5210. Open daily June to mid-Sept. and Dec. to mid-Apr. 9am-6pm; otherwise 10am-5pm.) Trails begin at the base of Mt. Crested Butte and extend into the Gothic area. **Trail 401** is a demanding and famous 24 mi. round-trip loop with an excellent view. The trek to **Green Lake** (3 mi.) is also a favorite.

Finding budget accommodations in the winter is about as easy as striking a vein of gold, but there are a few possibilities. ◼**Crested Butte International Hostel and Lodge (HI) ❶**, 615 Teocalli Ave., two blocks north of the four-way stop, treats travelers to gorgeous, modern facilities. Its huge kitchen and bright common area make it an ideal base for exploring the area. (☎349-0588 or 888-389-0588; www.crestedbuttehostel.com. Showers for non-guests $5. Coin-op laundry. 4- to 6-bed dorms $20-32; doubles $50-89. Spacious 3rd-floor apartment sleeps up to 6; $125-210. Rates vary depending on season; call in advance for prices and reservations. Group discounts available.) The US Forest Service operates a number of campgrounds in the area. **Cement Creek Campground ❶**, 10 mi. south of town off Hwy. 135, is near several hiking and motorbike trails and its namesake creek, in which the adventurous can find several hot springs. Located 7 mi. west of Crested Butte on Country Rd. 12, **Lake Irwin Campground ❶** provides delightfully secluded camping on the shores of a clear alpine lake. (Reservations ☎877-444-6777; www.reserveusa.com. Open mid-June to Sept. Sites $12.) Contact **Gunnison National Forest Office,** 216 N. Colorado, 30 mi. south in Gunnison., for more info on area camping. (☎641-0471. Open M-F 7:30am-4:30pm.)

Pitas in Paradise ❶, 214 Elk Ave., a self-proclaimed "Mediterranean Cafe with Soul," wows diners with its delicious $5 gyros, $3-5 salads, and $3 smoothies. Watch your meal being made at the counter or sit down to wait for it in the backyard. (☎349-0897. Open daily 11am-10pm.) **The Secret Stash ❷**, 21 Elk Ave., at the west end of town, has one of the highest-altitude coffee roasters in the world and a menu that ranges from eclectic pizzas ($8-17) to wraps ($3.50-8) to grilled wings (10 for $7). Sip a soy latte in the garden or upstairs, where the cushy couches, mood lighting, and acoustic guitar recall a hippie's living room. (☎349-6245. Open M-Sa 5-10pm with additional lunch hours during summer and winter seasons.)

The **Crested Butte Chamber of Commerce** is at 601 Elk Ave. (☎800-545-4505; www.crestedbuttechamber.com. Open daily 9am-5pm.) A free shuttle to the mountain leaves from the chamber. (☎349-5616. Every 40min. 7:20-10:20am and 8pm-midnight, every 20min. 10:20am-8pm.) **Internet Access: The Old Rock Community Library**, 507 Maroon Ave. (☎349-6535. Open M, W, F 10am-6pm, Tu and Th 10am-7pm, Sa 10am-2pm.) **Post Office:** 215 Elk Ave. (☎349-5568. Open M-F 7:30am-4:30pm.) **Postal Code:** 81224. **Area Code:** 970.

TELLURIDE   ☎970

Site of the first bank Butch Cassidy ever robbed (the San Miguel), Telluride was very much a town of the Old West. Locals believe that their city's name derives from a contraction of "to hell you ride," likely a warning given to travelers. In the last few decades, outlaws have been replaced with film stars, and six-shooters with cinnamon buns. Skiers, hikers, and vacationers come to Telluride to pump gold and silver into the mountains, and the town also claims the most festivals per capita of any postal code in the US. Still, a small-town feeling prevails—rocking chairs sit outside brightly painted houses, and dogs lounge on storefront porches.

🛈 **PRACTICAL INFORMATION.** Telluride sits on Rte. 145, 125 mi. northwest of Durango in the San Juan Mountains. Most of the action lies on Colorado Ave./Rte. 145. The public bus line, **Galloping Goose,** runs through town on a regular basis. (☎728-5700. May-Nov. M-F every 20min. 7:30am-6pm; Dec.-Apr. M-F every 10min. 7am-midnight. Town loop free, outlying towns $1-2.) A free gondola runs continuously between downtown and Mountain Village, with spectacular view of the surrounding mountains. The station is at the corner of Oak St. and San Juan Ave. (☎728-8888. 15min. each way. Runs late May to early Apr. daily 7am-midnight.) **Taxi** service from **Mountain Limo** serves the western slope. (☎728-9606 or 888-546-6894. Airport fare $8.) The **visitors center** is at the corner of Davis St. and W. Colorado Ave. near the entrance to town. (☎800-525-3455; www.telluride.com. Open in summer daily 9am-8pm.) **Police:** ☎728-3818. **Hotlines: Rape Crisis,** ☎728-5660. **Medical Services: Telluride Medical Center,** 500 W. Pacific (☎728-3848). **Internet Access: Wilkinson Public Library,** 100 W. Pacific St. (☎728-6613. Open M-Th 10am-8pm, F-Sa 10am-6pm, Su noon-5pm.) **Post Office:** 150 S. Willow St. (☎728-3900. Open M-F 9am-5pm, Sa 10am-noon.) **Postal Code:** 81435. **Area Code:** 970.

🛌 **ACCOMMODATIONS.** If you're visiting Telluride during a festival, bring a sleeping bag; the cost of a bed is outrageous. The **Oak Street Inn ❸**, 134 N. Oak St., offers cozy rooms at the cheapest price in town. (☎728-3383. Singles with shared bath $42, with private bath $60; doubles $58/$72; rooms around $20 more during festivals.) William Jennings Bryan delivered his "Cross of Gold" speech from the front balcony of the **New Sheridan Hotel ❹**, 231 W. Colorado Ave. If you can afford it, the luxurious rooms, full breakfast, and free Internet access justify the splurge. (☎728-4351 or 800-200-1891. Rooms with shared bath from $95.) 🏕**Sunshine Campground**, 8 mi. south on Rte. 145, is situated

ROCKY MOUNTAINS

among the aspens on a hillside with 360° views of all the surrounding peaks. (☎327-4261. No electricity or showers. No reservations. Open May-Sept. Sites $14.) The **Telluride Town Park Campground ❶**, east of downtown, offers 29 nice, if closely spaced, sites along the San Miguel River. (☎728-2173. Water, full bathrooms, no hookups. 7-night max. stay. Open Mid-May to mid-Oct. $15 per vehicle. Primitive sites $12. Office open M-W 8am-5pm, Th-F 8am-7pm, Sa-Su 8am-4pm.) During festivals in the town park, ticket holders can crash anywhere in the campground; hot showers ($2) are available at the high school.

⬛ FOOD. La Cocina de Luz ❷, 123 E. Colorado Ave., serves authentic and affordable *taquería*-style Mexican cuisine. Featuring fresh handmade tortillas and fire-roasted chiles, La Cocina's cooking methods add flavor to their quesadillas, tamales ($6-10), and large selection of vegetarian options. (☎728-9355. Open M-Sa 9am-9pm.) The subterranean **Deli Downstairs ❶**, 217 W. Colorado St., is usually packed with locals and visitors alike; the sandwiches ($5-8) will keep you boogying for hours. Finish off with a scoop of ice cream ($1-2); unique flavors include vanilla with peanut butter cups. (☎728-4004. Open daily 10am-midnight. Cash only.) The wooden benches and long tables at **Fat Alley Barbeque ❸**, 122 S. Oak St., are reminiscent of the sawdust saloons of yore, but Telluride's miners never ate barbecue ($5-17) like this. (☎728-3985. Open daily 11:30am-10pm.) **Baked in Telluride ❷**, 127 S. Fir St., has enough rich coffee, delicious pastries, pizza, sandwiches, and bagels to get you through a festival weekend. The apple fritters ($2) and enormous calzones ($7-10) are justifiably popular. (☎728-4775. Open daily 5:30am-10pm.)

🎭🎵 FESTIVALS AND NIGHTLIFE. Given that only 2000 people live in Telluride, the sheer number of festivals in the town seems staggering. For general festival info, contact the **Telluride Visitors Center** (☎800-525-3455). Gala events occur throughout the summer and fall, from the quirky **Mushroom Festival** (☎303-296-9359; www.shroomfestival.com; late Aug.) to the renowned **Bluegrass Festival.** (☎800-624-2422; www.planetbluegrass.com. 3rd weekend in June. $55 per day, 4-day pass $155.) One weekend in July is actually designated "Nothing Festival" to give locals a break from the onslaught of visitors and special events. The **Telluride International Film Festival** premiers some of the hippest independent flicks; *The Crying Game* and *The Piano* were both unveiled here. (☎728-4640; www.telluridefilmfestival.com. 1st weekend in Sept.) Telluride also hosts a **Jazz Celebration** during the first weekend of August (☎728-7009; www.telluridejazz.com) and a **Blues & Brews Festival** (☎728-8037; www.tellurideblues.com) during the third weekend in September. For most festivals (including the more expensive Bluegrass Fest and Jazz Celebration), volunteering to usher or perform other tasks can result in free admission. Call the contact number of the specific event for more info. Throughout the year a number of concerts and performances go on at the **Sheridan Opera House**, 110 N. Oak St. (☎728-6363.) Tickets for all these events, and others, can also be purchased in advance at **Telluride Ticket**, located at Gondola Station Plaza. (☎728-8199; www.tellurideticket.com.)

Telluride may have a new-age air by day, but its bars still rollick with old-fashioned fun by night. The lively **Last Dollar Saloon**, 100 E. Colorado Ave., affectionately referred to as "the buck," is a favorite among locals. With the jukebox blaring and darts flying, it's easy to see why. (☎728-4800. Beer $3-4.50. Open daily 11am-2am. Cash only.) Telluride's freshest musical talent jives at **Fly Me to the Moon Saloon**, 136 E. Colorado Ave., which thrills groovers with its spring-loaded dance floor. (☎728-6666. Cover $2-5. Open daily 3pm-late. Cash only.) The historic **New Sheridan Bar**, 231 W. Colorado Ave., inspires hubbub around town with $3.50 drinks during happy hour (daily 5-7pm), Tuesday pool tournaments, and Wednesday open poker nights. (☎728-9100. 21+ after 8pm. Open daily 3pm-2am.)

⚡ OUTDOOR ACTIVITIES. Biking, hiking, and backpacking opportunities are endless; ghost towns and lakes are tucked behind almost every mountain crag. The tourist office has a list of suggestions for hikes in the area. The most popular trek (about 2hr.) is up the 4WD road to **Bridal Veil Falls,** the waterfall visible from almost anywhere in Telluride. The trailhead is at the end of Rte. 145. Continuing another 2½ mi. from the top of the falls will lead to **Silver Lake,** a steep but rewarding climb. Starting from the north end of Aspen St., the **Jud Wiebe Trail** takes you on a 2¾ mi. loop with panoramas of the entire valley. For more Rocky Mountain highs, ride the free gondola to St. Sophia station at the top of the mountain, where a number of hiking and biking trails run.

In winter, even avowed atheists can be spied praying before hitting the "Spiral Stairs" and the "Plunge," two of the Rockies's most gut-wrenching ski runs. For more info, contact the **Telluride Ski Resort,** P.O. Box 11155, Telluride 81435. (☎728-3856. Regular season lift tickets: full-day $65, children $36; half-day $58/$28.) **Paragon Ski and Sport,** 213 W. Colorado Ave., rents bikes in summer and skis in winter. (☎728-4525. Open daily in ski season 8:30am-9pm; in summer 9am-7pm. Bikes from $18 per half-day, $35 per day; skis and boots $28 per day.)

SCENIC DRIVE: SAN JUAN SKYWAY

More a runway to the mountains and clouds than a terrestrial highway, the San Juan Skyway soars across the rooftop of the Rockies. Winding its way through San Juan and Uncompahgre National Forests, Old West mountain towns, and Native American ruins, the byway passes a remarkably wide range of southwestern Colorado's splendors. Reaching altitudes up to 11,000 feet, with breathtaking views of snowy peaks and verdant valleys, the San Juan Skyway is widely considered one of America's most beautiful drives. Travelers in this area inevitably drive at least parts of it as they head to destinations like Telluride, Durango, and Mesa Verde. Call the San Juan (☎970-247-4874) or Uncompahgre (☎970-874-6600) National Forests to check road conditions or to inquire about driving the skyway.

A loop road, consisting of Rte. 550, 62, 145, and 160, the skyway voyage can be started from anywhere along the loop. Beginning in Durango, the skyway heads north along **Route 550 N (Million Dollar Highway),** climbing into the San Juan Mountains parallel to the Animas River. Twenty-seven miles north of Durango, the road passes **Durango Mountain Resort** as it ascends. (☎800-979-9742. Annual snowfall 260 in. Open late Nov. to early Apr. 9am-4pm. Full-day lift ticket $55, under 12 $29.) At Mi. 64 on Rte. 550, the road reaches Molas Point, a whopping 10,910 ft. above sea level. Less than 1 mi. farther north, **Molas Lake Public Park Campground ❶** offers visitors an oasis with both tent and RV sites ($15) near a breathtaking little lake. (☎970-387-5848. Drinking water available, no hookups.)

Descending to a mere 9318 ft., the skyway arrives in easy-going **Silverton.** A mining town until the early 1990s, Silverton is a subdued mountain village with a permanent population of just 500, but the town hosts over 250,000 visitors a year. One of the most exciting times is the last weekend in July, when the **Silverton Jubilee** transforms the town into a three-day musical extravaganza featuring everything from bluegrass to funk. (☎800-752-4494; www.silvertonfestival.org. 3-day pass $80, 2-day $65; if purchased before June 1 $70/$60.) The **visitors center** sits close to the entrance to town on Rte. 550. (☎387-5654 or 800-752-4494; www.silverton.org. Open daily June-Sept. 9am-6pm; Oct.-May 10am-4pm.) Hiking, mountain biking, and skiing at **Kendall Mountain** (lift tickets $7) await those who can still catch their breath. Southeast of Silverton, 5 mi. up Rte. 2, **One Hundred Gold Mine** features tours down 1500 ft. into the depths of one of the richest mines in Colorado. A chance to try your hand at panning gold is included. (☎970-387-5444. Tours depart daily early May to mid-Oct. every hr. on the hr., 10am-4pm. $15, children $7.95.)

ROCKY MOUNTAINS

From Silverton, the San Juan Skyway climbs higher until it reaches 11,018 ft. at Mi. 80 on Rte. 550. Known as **Red Mountain Pass,** this scenic point has some hiking and more than a few Kodak moments. In the winter, this is the most dangerous part of the route; several snowplows (and their drivers) have gone off the steep cliffs here. Continuing north, the drive from Silverton to Ouray showcases stellar 14,000 ft. mountain peaks and defunct mines. In 1991, the Reclamation Act shut down most of the mines, leaving only remnants of the past. The skyway next arrives in **Ouray;** the **visitors center** is at the north end of town on Rte. 550. (☎325-4746; www.ouraycolorado.com. Open M-F 9am-5pm, Sa 10am-4pm, Su noon-4pm.) With fabulous mountain views, well-preserved historic buildings, and hedonistic hot springs, this heavily Swiss-influenced town known as "America's Switzerland" is a relaxing stop for the weary. Be certain not to miss the **Ouray Hot Springs Pool,** next to the visitors center; several pools of varying temperature offer a chance to unwind beneath the soaring peaks in winter or summer. (☎325-7073. Open June-Aug. 10am-10pm, Sept.-May noon-9pm. $8, students and seniors $6, ages 3-6 $3.) Beyond Ouray, the skyway returns to Earth. Traversing mesas, Rte. 550 junctions with Rte. 62 in Ridgeway. Rte. 62 assumes the reins of the skyway and leads travelers to Placerville, where the skyway connects with Rte. 145.

Telluride next awaits travelers along Rte. 145. Past the Mountain Village, the dubiously named **Lizard's Pass** offers a tranquil 6 mi. hike reaching over 12,000 ft. From the pass, the skyway glides down along the Taylor Mesa through the quiet towns of Rico, Stoner, and Dolores. Rte. 145 connects with Rte. 160 just east of Cortez and west of **Mesa Verde National Park,** home of the world-famous cliff-dwellings of the ancient Puebloan people. Moving east along Rte. 160, the skyway cuts through **Mancos** and finally returns to Durango.

DURANGO ☎970

In its heyday, Durango was one of the main railroad junctions in the Southwest. Walking down the town's main thoroughfare today, it is easy to see that Durango remains a crossroads. Dreadlocked, hemp-clad youths share the sidewalks with weathered ranchers in ten-gallon hats and stiff Wranglers; toned, brazen mountain bikers rub shoulders in the bars with camera-toting tourists.

🛈 PRACTICAL INFORMATION. Durango is at the intersection of U.S. 160 and 550. Streets run east-west and avenues run north-south, but everyone calls Main Ave., the principal road through town, "Main St." **Greyhound,** 275 E. 8th Ave. (☎259-2755; open M-F 7:30am-noon and 3:30-5pm, Sa 6:30am-noon, Su and holidays 6:30-10am), runs once per day to: **Albuquerque** (5hr., $43-48); **Denver** (11½hr., $64-68); **Grand Junction** (5hr., $33-35). The **Durango Lift** provides trolley service in and around town. (☎259-5438. Runs Memorial Day-Labor Day M-F 6:30am-7:30pm, Sa 9:30am-7:30pm. $1, seniors $0.50.) **Taxi: Durango Transportation** ☎259-4818. The **Durango Area Chamber Resort Association,** 111 S. Camino del Río, on the southeast side of town, offers info on sights and hiking. (☎247-0312 or 800-525-8855; www.durango.org. Open M-Sa 8am-5:30pm, Su 10am-4pm.) **Road Conditions:** ☎264-5555. **Police:** 990 E. 2nd Ave. (☎385-2910). **Internet Access: Durango Public Library,** 1188 E. 2nd Ave. (☎385-2970. Open M-W 9am-9pm, Th-Su 9am-5:30pm, closed Su in the summer.) **Post Office:** 222 W. 8th St. (☎247-3434. Open M-F 8am-5:30pm; Sa 9am-1pm.) **Postal Code:** 81301. **Area Code:** 970.

🛏🍴 ACCOMMODATIONS AND FOOD. If you don't mind staying 20 mi. north of Durango, you'll be pampered at **Silverpick Lodge ❸,** 48475 U.S. 550, with luxurious rooms, goose-down comforters, on-site hot tub, huge game room, laundromat, and library. Call within 48hr. of check-in for their year-round "Last Second Special" and get any available room for only $48, about half the price of what they usually run for. (☎259-6600.) The reasonably priced **Budget Inn ❷**, 3077 Main Ave., offers clean rooms with on-site hot tub, outdoor pool, and laundry facility. (☎247-5222 or 800-257-5222; www.budgetinndurango.com. Cable TV, telephone, some with microwave and fridge. June-Aug. singles $43, doubles $61; Sept.-May $28/$36.) Find great camping at **Junction Creek Campground ❶**, on Forest Rd. 171. From Main Ave., turn west on 25th St., which becomes Forest Rd. 171 after 4 mi.; the turn-off is 1 mi. past the national forest entrance. As the southern terminus of the Colorado Trail, hikers and bikers make this a popular spot in summer. (☎247-4874. 14-night max. stay. $6 per person, $13 per vehicle.)

Decked out with Texan and local paraphernalia, **Serious Texas BBQ ❶**, 3535 N. Main Ave., doles out generous ½ lb. portions of smoked meat ($6.50), Texas tacos ($3.50) and "cheezy potatoes" for $1.25. (☎946-1149. Open daily 11am-9pm.) **Skinny's Grill ❷**, 1017 Main Ave., offers great Southwestern food, as well as vegetarian options, in a low-key atmosphere. Thai chicken tacos ($8) and deep-dish spinach enchiladas ($8) are local favorites. (☎382-2500. Open Su-Th 11:30am-9pm, F-Sa 11:30am-10pm.) At **Carver's Restaurant and Brewpub ❷**, 1022 Main Ave., locals enjoy pitchers of home-brewed beer ($8.75), lobster tacos ($14) and bison bratwurst ($12) on the outdoor patio. (☎259-2545. Open M-F 6:30am-10pm, Su 6:30am-1pm.) Right at the south end of town, **Kachina Kitchen ❶**, in Centennial Center at the junction of Hwy. 550 and 160, serves huge burrito and tamale platters ($5). Check out the over-stuffed *sopapillas* ($5.15) and piping hot Indian fried bread. (☎247-3536. Open M-Sa 10am-8pm.)

◨ ◪ SIGHTS AND NIGHTLIFE. More a tourist attraction than a means of transportation, the **Durango and Silverton Narrow Gauge Train,** 479 Main St., runs up the Animas River Valley to the historic mining town of Silverton. In continuous operation since 1881, the old-fashioned, 100% coal-fed locomotives wheeze through the San Juans, making a 2hr. stop in Silverton before returning to Durango. The train also offers access to the Weminuche Wilderness, dropping off and picking up backpackers at various scenic points; call for more info. While waiting for the train, step into some of the very first iron horses to operate at the **Railroad Museum** across the tracks. (☎247-2733; www.durangotrain.com. Office open daily June to mid-Aug. 6am-8pm; May

OUT OF THE WAY

ROCKY MOUNTAIN HIGH

Durango, CO, and Moab, UT have long been hotspots for mountain-biking aficionados. In the summer of 2004, a wilderness trail between the two was at last opened to mountain bikers. The 215 mi. trail, operated by San Juan Hut Systems under permit from the Forest Service, traverses some of the most scenic regions of the two states, including the San Juan Wilderness, the Dolores River basin, and the La Sal Mountains. The trail features mountain passes 14,000 feet in elevation, scorching sunshine, thin air, freezing nights, and unforgettable Rocky Mountain wilderness, with everything from columbines to elk. The trek is designed to take seven days, with nights spent at a system of six huts along the way. The huts are spaced roughly 35 miles apart and are each equipped with bunks, propane stoves and lights, firewood, sleeping bags, outhouses, kitchen facilities, drinking water, and food. The trek between them is more challenging than the company's sister route between Telluride and Moab, and demands some route-finding abilities, a good degree of physical fitness, mountain-biking experience, and an eagerness for adventure.

For information and reservations, contact San Juan Hut Systems, ☎970-626-3033; *www.sanjuanhuts.com. $475, including food and maps.*

and mid-Aug. to Oct. 7am-7pm; Nov.-Apr. 8am-5pm. Morning trains from Durango and afternoon trains from Silverton; 9hr. including stop, layover day optional. Summer $60, ages 5-11 $30. Trains to Cascade Canyon in winter $45/$22. Museum free with train fare.) The **Durango Pro Rodeo Series,** at the LaPlata County Fairgrounds at 25th St. and Main Ave., moseys into town in summer. Saddling up on Friday and Saturday nights and sometimes Wednesday, the action starts at 7pm after a barbecue at 6pm. (☎909-2346; www.durangoprorodeo.com. Open mid-June to Aug. $12, under 12 $5; barbecue $7.) On U.S. 550, 7 mi. north of Durango, **Trimble Hot Springs** treats visitors to a soak in three hot pools and an Olympic-sized swimming pool—and you can't beat the great view of Missionary Ridge. During the summer on Sunday afternoons 1-4pm, lie out on their huge lawn and picnic area and enjoy live jazz music. (☎247-0111; www.trimble-hotsprings.com. Open in summer daily 8am-11pm; in winter Su-Th 9am-10pm, F-Sa 9am-11pm. $9, ages 3-12 $6.50.) The ski-lodge atmosphere and frequent live music at **The Summit,** 600 Main Ave., near the train station, attract the college crowd for good, rowdy fun. (☎247-2324. Happy hour M-F 4-7pm with nightly drink specials (Tu $1 drafts) and free pool. Open M-F 4pm-2am, Sa 8pm-2am.)

🏔 **OUTDOOR ACTIVITIES.** Unlike most Colorado towns that thrive on tourism, Durango's busiest season is summer, though winter is no stranger to strangers. **Durango Mountain Resort,** 27 mi. north on U.S. 550, hosts skiers of all levels (p. 767). Bikes are available at **Hassle Free Sports,** 2615 Main St. (☎259-3874 or 800-835-3800. Open in winter daily 7:30am-7pm; otherwise M-Sa 8:30am-6pm. Half-day $16, full-day $25. Full suspension $24/$35. Ski rental packages $16-27 per day.) **Southwest Adventures,** 1205 Camino del Río, offers mountain bikes, climbing gear, and backpacking gear. (☎259-0370. Open daily 8am-6pm.) The Durango area is engulfed by the **San Juan National Forest.** Call the Forest Headquarters for info on hiking and camping, especially if you're planning a trip into the massive Weminuche Wilderness, northeast of Durango. (☎247-4874. Open daily Apr. to mid-Dec. 8am-5pm; mid-Dec. to Mar. 8am-4:30pm.) The **Animas River** offers rapids from placid Class II splashes to intense Class V battles. Keep in mind that the river is more powerful and wilder earlier in the summer, when runoff is strongest. The largest area outfitter is **Mild to Wild Rafting,** 701 Main Ave. (☎247-4789 or 800-567-6745. Open Apr.-Sept. daily 9am-9pm. Half-day mild trips $41, children $32; full-day mild trips $65/$55. Full-day intense trips $215, including wetsuit and narrow gauge train ticket to the jump-off point at Upper Animas River. Reservations recommended.) **Durango Rivertrippers,** 720 Main Ave., also leads whitewater rafting jaunts on the river and rents inflatable kayaks. (☎259-0289 or 800-292-2885; www.durangorivertrippers.com. Open late May to mid-Aug. daily 8:30am-9pm. 2hr. rafting trip $25, children $17; half-day trip with lunch $35/$25; kayaks $30 per 2hr.)

PAGOSA SPRINGS   ☎970

The Ute people—the first to discover the waters of Pagosa—believed that the springs were a gift of the Great Spirit, and the Chamber of Commerce would be hard-pressed not to think so, too. From the Ute Indian word "Pag-Osah," meaning "healing waters," Pagosa contains some of the world's hottest and largest springs, which bubble from the San Juan Mountains 60 mi. east of Durango on Rte. 160 and draw visitors from around the globe. Follow the sulfur smell to **The Springs,** 165 Hot Springs Blvd., where 17 naturally hot, therapeutic mineral baths ranging from 83° to 114°F are terraced above the San Juan River. The brave can escape the hot pools by taking a dip in the snow-fed river, polar bear-style. (☎264-2284 or 800-225-0934. Open Su-Th 7am-11pm, F-Sa 7am-1am. Admission

Su-Th $13, F-Sa $15; seniors $12, ages 2-7 $5.) **Chimney Rock Archaeological Area,** 17 mi. west of Pagosa Springs on U.S. 160 and Rte. 151 S, is a National Historical Site overlooked by two towering stone pinnacles. The site protects the ruins of a high-mesa ancestral Puebloan village, where over 200 undisturbed structures have been found in a 6 sq. mi. area. (☎883-5359 or 264-2268; www.chimney-rockco.org. Open mid-May to late Sept. daily 9am-4:30pm. 2½hr. tours leave at 9:30, 10:30am, 1, 2pm. $6, ages 5-11 $2.) **Wolf Creek Ski Area,** 20 mi. east of Pagosa, claims to have the most snow in Colorado, and offers access to many glades and bowls. Six lifts service over 1500 acres and 1600 ft. of vertical drop. (☎264-5639 or 800-754-9653; www.wolfcreekski.com. Open mid-Nov. to early Apr. daily 8:30am-4pm. Full-day lift ticket $43, half-day $31; ski rental $13. In Pagosa, the **Pioneer Museum,** 1st St. and Hwy. 160, features photographs and historical items documenting the region's colorful Native American and settler past. (☎264-4424. Open late May to early Sept. 9am-4pm. Free.) Learn to ride a horse at **Rocky Mountain Wildlife Park,** 5 mi. south on Hwy 84., or take a full-day ride into the South San Juan Wilderness. (☎264-5546. Rides 8am-4pm. 1hr. lesson $30, full-day $95. Park admission $6, children $4.)

Pinewood Inn ❸, 157 Pagosa St. (Hwy. 160), downtown, rents 25 wood-paneled rooms with cable TV and phones, including several with kitchens. (☎264-5715 or 888-655-7463. Reception 7:30am-11pm. Check-in 1pm. Check-out 11am. Singles $45-52; doubles $58-62.) **East Fork Campground ❶,** on East Fork Rd., 10 mi. east of Pagosa Springs, offers 26 shaded, rarely crowded sites. (☎264-2268. 14-night max. stay. Open May-Sept. $8 per vehicle.) **Bear Creek Saloon & Grill ❷,** 473 Lewis, right off Hwy. 160, is the best place for burgers in town. You'll barely get your mouth around their jalapeño cream cheese or Pagosa bacon green chili burgers ($5-7). Along with pool tables, arcades, and a big screen TV, Bear Creek features live classic rock and blues Friday and Saturday nights and karaoke Wednesday. (☎264-5611. Drafts $3.50. Bar open daily 11am-2am. Food served in summer M-Sa 11am-10pm, Su 11am-9pm; in winter M-Sa 11am-9pm, Su 11am-7am.) At **Daylight Donuts & Cafe ❶,** 2151 W Hwy. 160, enjoy big portions of classic breakfast and lunch fare ($2.50-5) while the farmers in the booth next to you discuss tractor repair. (☎731-4050. Open M-F 6am-1:30pm, Sa-Su 6am-1:30pm.) **Harmony Works ❶,** 145 Hot Springs Blvd., sells organic food and a large selection of vegetarian and vegan options ($3-5), including veggie wraps, breakfast burritos, and smoothies. (☎264-6633. Open May-Sept. M-Th 8am-9pm, F-Sa 8am-10pm, Su 8am-8pm; Oct.-Apr. M-Th 8am-8pm, F-Sa 8am-9pm, Su 8am-7pm.)

The **Mountain Express** bus line provides transportation in and around town. (☎264-2250. M-F about every 1½hr. 6am-8pm, $0.50.) The **Pagosa Springs Chamber of Commerce,** 402 San Juan St., offers info on accommodations, food, and sights. (☎264-2360 or 800-252-2204; www.pagosaspringschamber.com. Open May-Oct. M-F 8am-5pm, Sa-Su 9am-5pm; Nov.-Apr. Sa-Su 10am-2pm.) **Post Office:** 250 Hot Springs Blvd. (☎731-6245. Open M-F 7:30am-5:30pm, Sa 9am-2pm.) **Postal Code:** 81147. **Area Code:** 970.

WYOMING

The ninth-largest state in the Union, Wyoming is also the least populated. This is a place where men don cowboy hats and boots, and livestock outnumbers citizens. It is also a land of unique firsts: it was the first state to grant women the right to vote without later repealing it, and was the first to have a national monument

(Devils Tower) and national park (Yellowstone) within its borders. Those expecting true cowboy culture will not be disappointed; Cheyenne's Frontier Days festival, held every July, is a celebration of all things Western.

⛏ PRACTICAL INFORMATION

Capital: Cheyenne.

Visitor Info: Wyoming Business Council Tourism Office, I-25 at College Dr., Cheyenne 82002 (☎307-777-7777 or 800-225-5996; www.wyomingtourism.org). Open daily 8am-5pm. **Dept. of Commerce, State Parks, and Historic Sites Division,** 122 W. 25th St., Herschler Bldg., 1st fl. E, Cheyenne 82002 (☎307-777-6323; http://wyoparks.state.wy.us). Open M-F 8am-5pm. **Game and Fish Dept.,** 5400 Bishop Blvd., Cheyenne 82006 (☎307-777-4600; http://gf.state.wy.us). Open M-F 8am-5pm. **Wyoming Road Conditions:** 888-WYO-ROAD/996-7623.

Postal Abbreviation: WY. **Sales Tax:** 4%.

YELLOWSTONE NATIONAL PARK ☎307

Yellowstone National Park holds the distinctions of being the largest park in the contiguous US and the first national park in the world. Yellowstone also happens to be one of the largest active volcanoes in the world, with over 300 geysers and 10,000 geothermal features spewing steam and boiling water from beneath the earth's crust. Much of Yellowstone is in fact a giant, 45-by-30-mile caldera (volcanic crater), one of the largest in the world. The park's hot springs are popular with local wildlife; bison and elk gather around them for warmth and easier grazing during the winter months. Today, Yellowstone is still recovering from fires that burned over a third of the park in 1988. The destruction is especially evident in the western half of the park, where charred tree stumps line the roads. Despite the fires, Yellowstone retains its rugged beauty. Park roads are clogged tourists eagerly snapping photos of geysers and wildlife. With the reintroduction of wolves in 1995, all of the animals that lived in the Yellowstone area before the arrival of Europeans still roam the landscape, with the exception of the black-footed ferret.

ROCKY MOUNTAINS

AT A GLANCE	
AREA: 2,219,791 acres.	**CLIMATE:** Extremely varied.
VISITORS: Almost 3 million annually.	**"ROUGHING" IT:** Embrace corporate behemoth Xanterra's borg-like camping options ($18), or arrive early for the Park Service's first come, first served sites.
HIGHLIGHTS: Be astonished by the 140-foot eruptions of Old Faithful, frolic with bighorn sheep in Yellowstone's very own Grand Canyon, and relax alongside North America's largest high-altitude lake.	
	FEES: Entrance fee $20 per car, $10 per pedestrian. Backcountry permit free.

▐ TRANSPORTATION

The bulk of Yellowstone lies in the northwest corner of Wyoming, with slivers in Montana and Idaho. There are five entrances to the park. **West Yellowstone, MT,** and **Gardiner, MT,** are the most developed entrance points. **Cooke City, MT,** the northeast entrance to the park, is a rustic town nestled in the mountains. East of Cooke City, the **Beartooth Highway (U.S. 212),** open only in summer, ascends the surrounding slopes for a breathtaking view of eastern Yellowstone. **Cody** lies 53 mi. east of the East Entrance to the park along U.S. 14/16/20. The southern entrance to the park is bordered by **Grand Teton National Park** (see p.

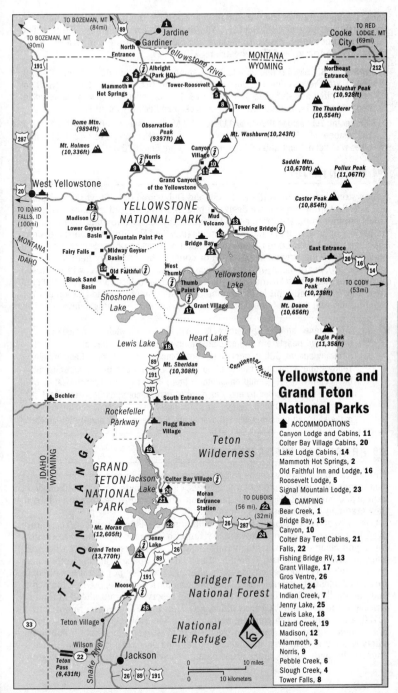

Yellowstone and Grand Teton National Parks

▲ ACCOMMODATIONS

Canyon Lodge and Cabins, 11
Colter Bay Village Cabins, 20
Lake Lodge Cabins, 14
Mammoth Hot Springs, 2
Old Faithful Inn and Lodge, 16
Roosevelt Lodge, 5
Signal Mountain Lodge, 23

▲ CAMPING

Bear Creek, 1
Bridge Bay, 15
Canyon, 10
Colter Bay Tent Cabins, 21
Falls, 22
Fishing Bridge RV, 13
Grant Village, 17
Gros Ventre, 26
Hatchet, 24
Indian Creek, 7
Jenny Lake, 25
Lewis Lake, 18
Lizard Creek, 19
Madison, 12
Mammoth, 3
Norris, 9
Pebble Creek, 6
Slough Creek, 4
Tower Falls, 8

783). The only road in the park open year-round is the northern strip between the North Entrance and Cooke City. All other roads are open May-October. The park's **entrance fee** is good for 7 days at both Yellowstone and Grand Teton. (Cars $20, motorcycles $15, pedestrians $10.)

Car Rental: Big Sky Car Rental, 415 Yellowstone Ave. (☎406-646-9564 or 800-426-7669), West Yellowstone, MT. Open daily May to mid-Oct. 8am-5pm. Compact $49 per day, mid-sized $54, full-sized $59, vans $99, 10% discount for 7 days or more. Unlimited mileage. 21+ with a credit card. Free pickup and delivery within 10 mi.

Bike Rental: Yellowstone Bicycle and Video, 132 Madison Ave. (☎406-646-7815), West Yellowstone, MT. Open May-Oct. daily 8:30am-9pm; Nov.-Apr. 11am-7pm. Mountain bikes with helmet and water $3.50 per hr., $13 per 5hr., $20 per day.

■ ORIENTATION

Yellowstone is huge; both Rhode Island and Delaware could fit within its boundaries. Yellowstone's roads are designed in a figure-eight configuration, with side roads leading to park entrances and some of the lesser-known attractions. The natural wonders that make the park famous (e.g., Old Faithful) are scattered along the Upper and Lower Loops. Construction and renovation of roads is ongoing; call ahead (☎344-7381; www.nps.gov/yell) or consult the extremely helpful *Yellowstone Today*, available at the entrance, to find out which sections will be closed during your visit. Travel through the park can be arduously slow regardless of construction. The speed limit is 45 mph and is closely radar-patrolled; steep grades, tight curves, and frequent animal crossings can also cause driving delays.

> Yellowstone can be a dangerous place. While roadside wildlife may look tame, these large beasts are unpredictable and easily startled. Stay at least 75 ft. from any animal, 300 ft. from bears. Both black bears and grizzly bears inhabit Yellowstone; consult a ranger about proper precautions before entering the backcountry. If you should encounter a bear, inform a ranger for the safety of others. Bison, regarded by many as mere overgrown cows, can actually travel at speeds of up to 30 mph; visitors are gored every year. Finally, watch for "widow makers"—dead trees that can fall over at any time, especially during high winds.

■ PRACTICAL INFORMATION

The park's high season extends roughly from mid-June to mid-September. If you visit during this period, expect large crowds, clogged roads, and filled-to-capacity motels and campsites. Most of the park shuts down from November to mid-April, then gradually reopens as the snow melts.

Over 95% of Yellowstone—almost 2 million acres—is backcountry. To venture overnight into the wilds of Yellowstone requires a **backcountry permit.** The permit is free if you reserve in person at any ranger station or visitors center no earlier than 48hr. in advance of the trip. There is almost always space available in the backcountry, with over 300 designated sites, although the more popular areas fill up in July and August. In general, the deeper into the park you hike, the less likely it is that sites will be taken. For a $20 fee, you can reserve a permit ahead of time by writing to the **Central Backcountry Office,** P.O. Box 168, Yellowstone National Park 82190, and receive a **trip planning worksheet.** (☎344-2160. Open daily 8am-5pm.) Before heading into the backcountry, visitors must watch a short film outlining safety regulations. No firearms, pets, or mountain bikes are permitted in the backcountry. In many backcountry areas campfires are not permitted; bring a stove and related cooking gear. Food, cooking utensils, and any items that might attract bears or wildlife should be stored 10 ft. off the ground and 4 ft. from the nearest tree. Camps are equipped with food poles between trees at this height: *use them.* Consult a ranger before embarking on a trail for tips on how to avoid bears, ice, and other natural hindrances, or check out the free *Backcountry Trip Planner.*

Fishing and **boating** are both allowed within the park, provided visitors follow a number of regulations. Permits, available at any ranger station or visitors center, are required for fishing. Some areas may be closed due to feeding patterns of bears. The park's three native species are catch-and-release only. (Fishing permits $15 per 3 days, $20 per 10 days, $35 per year; ages 12-15 require a non-fee permit. Wyoming state licenses not valid in Yellowstone.) In addition to Yellowstone Lake, popular fishing spots include the Madison and Firehole rivers; the Firehole is available for fly fishing only. To go boating or even floating on the lake, you'll need a **boating permit,** available at backcountry offices (check *Yellowstone Today*), Bridge Bay Marina, and the South, West, and Northeast entrances to the park. (Motorized vessels $10 for 10-day pass, season pass $20; motor-free boats $5/$10.) **Xanterra** rents rowboats, outboards, and dockslips at Bridge Bay Marina. (☎344-7311. Open mid-June to early Sept. Rowboats $8 per hr., $36 per 8hr.; outboards $37 per hr.; dockslips $15-20 per night.) Parts of Yellowstone Lake and some other lakes are limited to non-motorized boating; inquire at the Lake Village or Grant Village ranger stations for more advice.

Visitor Info: Most regions of the park have their own central visitors center. All centers offer general info and backcountry permits, but each has distinct hiking and camping regulations and features special **regional exhibits.** All stations are usually open late May to early Sept. daily 8am-7pm. Albright and Old Faithful are open year-round.

Albright Visitors Center (☎344-2263), at Mammoth Hot Springs, features exhibits on the history of Yellowstone Park, along with stuffed examples of natural wildlife and a gallery of Thomas Moran's artwork. Open daily late May to early Sept. 8am-7pm; early Sept. to May 9am-5pm.

Canyon (☎242-2550) features an exhibit on bison. Open late May to Aug. daily 8am-7pm.

Fishing Bridge (☎242-2450). Exhibits describe local wildlife and Yellowstone Lake. Open daily late May to Aug. 8am-7pm; Sept. 9am-6pm.

Grant Village (☎242-2650) has details on the 1988 fire and park wildlife. Open daily late May to Aug. 8am-7pm, Sept. 9am-6pm.

Madison (☎344-2821) has a bookstore. Open daily early June to Sept. 9am-5pm.

Norris (☎344-2812). Major exhibit depicts "Geothermic Features of the Park." Open late May to mid-Oct. daily 10am-5pm.

Old Faithful (☎545-2750). Learn about geysers and eruption predictions. Open daily late May to early Sept. 8am-7pm; early Sept. to May 9am-5pm.

West Thumb (☎242-2652), on the southern edge of the lake, has a bookstore. Open late May to late Sept. 9am-5pm.

West Yellowstone Chamber of Commerce, 30 Yellowstone Ave. (☎406-646-4403; www.westyellowstonechamber.com), West Yellowstone, MT, 2 blocks west of the park entrance. Open late May to early Sept. daily 8am-8pm; early Sept. to early Nov. and mid-Apr. to late May M-F 8am-4pm.

General Park Information: ☎344-7381. **Weather:** ☎344-2113. **Road Report:** ☎344-2117. **Radio Information:** 1610AM.

Medical Services: Lake Clinic, Pharmacy, and Hospital (☎242-7241), across the road from the Lake Yellowstone Hotel. Clinic open late May to mid-Sept. daily 8:30am-8:30pm. Emergency room open May-Sept. 24hr. **Old Faithful Clinic** (☎545-7325), near the Old Faithful Inn. Open early May to mid-Sept. daily 7am-7pm. **Mammoth Hot Springs Clinic** (☎344-7965). Open in summer daily 8:30am-5pm.

Disabled Services: All entrances, visitors centers, and ranger stations offer the *Visitor Guide to Accessible Features*. Fishing Bridge RV Park, Madison, Bridge Bay, Canyon, and Grant campgrounds have accessible sites and restrooms; Lewis Lake and Slough Creek have accessible sites. Write the **Park Accessibility Coordinator,** P.O. Box 168, Yellowstone National Park, WY 82190. For more info visit www.nps.gov/yell.

Internet Access: West Yellowstone Public Library, 220 Yellowstone Ave. (☎406-646-9017), West Yellowstone, MT. Open Tu and Th 10am-6pm, W 10am-8pm, F 10am-5pm, Sa 10am-3pm. Free.

Post Office: There are 5 post offices in the park: at **Lake, Old Faithful, Canyon, Grant,** and **Mammoth Hot Springs** (☎344-7764). All open M-F 8:30am-5pm. Specify which station at Yellowstone National Park when addressing mail. **Postal Code:** 82190. In **West Yellowstone, MT:** 209 Grizzly Ave. (☎406-646-7704). Open M-F 8:30am-5pm, Sa 8-10am. **Postal Code:** 59758.

Area Codes: 307 (in the park), 406 (in West Yellowstone, Cooke City, and Gardiner, MT). In text, 307 unless noted otherwise.

ACCOMMODATIONS

Camping is cheap, but affordable indoor lodging can be found with preparation. Lodging within the park can be hard to come by on short notice but is sometimes a better deal than the motels along the outskirts of the park. During peak months, the cost of a motel room can skyrocket to $100, while in-park lodging remains relatively inexpensive.

IN THE PARK

Xanterra (☎344-7311; www.travelyellowstone.com) controls all accommodations within the park, employing a unique code to distinguish between cabins: "Roughrider" means no bath, no facilities; "Budget" offers a sink; "Pioneer" offers a shower, toilet, and sink; "Frontier" is bigger and more plush; and "Western" is the biggest and swankiest. Facilities are located close to cabins without private bath. Rates are based on two adults; $10 for each additional adult; under 12 free. Reserve cabins well in advance of the June-September tourist season.

■ **Old Faithful Inn and Lodge,** 30 mi. southeast of the West Yellowstone entrance, between Madison and Grant on the lower loop, is not only conveniently located in the heart of key attractions, it is also a masterpiece unto itself. Admire the cavernous 6-story central lobby and massive stone fireplace from the birds-eye vantage of numerous balconies and stairways, all built from solid tree trunks. Constructed in 1904 by architect Robert Reamer as an embodiment of the natural surroundings, it is the quintessential example of "parkitecture," which emerged in America's national parks in the early 20th century. Open mid-May to mid-Sept. Budget cabins $55; Frontier cabins $81; well-appointed hotel rooms from $78, with private bath $99-136. ❷

Roosevelt Lodge, in the northeast portion of the upper loop, 19 mi. north of Canyon Village. A favorite of Teddy Roosevelt, who seems to have frequented every motel and saloon west of the Mississippi. The lodge provides cheap and scenic accommodations, and it is located in a relatively isolated section of the park. Open June to early Sept. Roughrider cabins with wood-burning stoves $56; Frontier cabins $91. ❸

Canyon Lodge and Cabins, in Canyon Village at the middle of the figure-eight, overlooks the "Grand Canyon" of Yellowstone. Less authentic than Roosevelt Lodge, but centrally located and more popular among tourists. Open early June to mid-Sept. Budget cabins with bath $44; Pioneer cabins $59; Frontier cabins $82; Western cabins $119. ❸

Mammoth Hot Springs, on the northwest portion of the upper loop near the north entrance, is a good base for early-morning wildlife-viewing excursions in the Lamar Valley to the east. Open early May to mid-Oct. Lattice-sided Budget cabins $64; Frontier cabins (some with porches) from $91; hotel rooms $73, with bath $96. ❸

Lake Lodge Cabins, 4 mi. south of Fishing Bridge, at the southeast corner of the lower loop, is a cluster of cabins from the 1920s and 50s, all just a stone's throw from Yellowstone Lake. Open mid-June to late Sept. Pioneer cabins $59; larger Western cabins $119. Next door, **Lake Yellowstone Hotel and Cabins** has yellow Frontier cabins with no lake view for $80. ❸

WEST YELLOWSTONE, MT

Guarding the west entrance of the park, West Yellowstone (pop. 1020) capitalizes on the hordes of tourists who pass through en route to the park. The closest of the border towns to popular park attractions, West Yellowstone has numerous budget motels, while nearby Gardiner presents a more limited, and somewhat more expensive, selection of accommodation options.

West Yellowstone International Hostel, 139 Yellowstone Ave. (☎406-7745 or 800-838-7745), at the **Madison Hotel,** provides the best indoor budget accommodations around the park. The friendly staff and welcoming lobby make travelers feel right at home. Kitchen has microwave and hot water only. Internet access $5 per hr. Open late May to mid-Oct. Dorms $20, nonmembers $23; singles and doubles $27-39, with private bath $49-53. ❶

Lazy G Motel, 123 Hayden St. (☎406-646-7586), has an affable staff and 15 spacious 1970s-style rooms with queen beds, refrigerators, and cable TV. Reservations recommended. Open May-Mar. Singles $32-48; doubles $40-59, with kitchenette $42-68. ❷

GARDINER, MT

Hillcrest Cottages (☎406-848-7353 or 800-970-7353), on U.S. 89 across from the Exxon station, rents out tidy, whitewashed deluxe cabins with kitchenettes on a hillside overlooking town. Open May to early Sept. Singles $64; doubles $68; 5-person rooms $80, $6 per additional adult, $2 per additional child under 18. ❸

The Town Cafe and Motel (☎406-848-7322), on Park St. across from the park's northern entrance. Compact, wood-paneled, carpeted rooms are among the best deals in town. Cable TV. No phones. June-Sept. singles $45; doubles $55. Oct.-May $25/$30-35. ❷

Bear Creek Camp, on Jardine Rd. 8 mi. northeast of Gardiner, has rugged backcountry sites on the edge of the roaring Bear Creek, deep in the midst of Gallatin National Forest. The unpaved gravel road leading to the sites offers stunning views of Mammoth's terraces, inside Yellowstone. Pit toilets, no water. Free. ❶

COOKE CITY, MT

Cooke City (pop. 90) is located 3 mi. east of the northeast entrance to the park. The Nez Percé slipped right by the US cavalry here, Lewis and Clark deemed the area impassable, and few people visit this rugged little town. Nonetheless, Cooke City is a great location for exploring the remote backcountry of Yellowstone and is conveniently situated between the park and the junction of two scenic drives: the **Chief Joseph Scenic Highway (Route 296)** and the **Beartooth Highway (Route 212).**

Antler's Lodge (☎406-838-2432). Built in 1936, each cabin has its own personality and a great mountain view. Hemingway spent several nights editing *For Whom the Bell Tolls* here. Open in summer and fall. 2-person cabins $60, some with kitchenettes. ❸

Range Rider's Lodge (☎406-838-2359), in Silver Gate on Rte. 212, 1 mi. east of the park on the way to Cooke City. As the second-largest all-wood structure in the US, this lodge was originally a brothel commissioned by Teddy Roosevelt to keep the miners in good spirits.

ROCKY MOUNTAINS

WOLVES ARE BITEY

For many years, the only wolves in Yellowstone were the pair stuffed and on display in the Albright Visitors Center. These two, along with all the other wolves in Yellowstone, were killed in 1922 when these predators were considered a menace to Yellowstone's other wildlife.

When gray wolves were declared endangered in 1973, talk of bringing back the wolf population started up. After more than 20 years of public debate, 14 wolves from Canada were released into the park in 1995. Today, over 300 wolves roam the area. Although every effort has been made to reduce the concerns of opponents, the reintroduction of wolves has undoubtedly meant that some livestock and domestic animals have become prey. A wolf compensation trust, brainchild of the Bailey Wildlife Foundation, was established to pay ranchers for losses due to wolves, and this shift in the economic responsibility from ranchers to wolf supporters has created broader acceptance. Wolves seem to be a hit with the ecosystem as well; other animals and scavengers have benefited from the food remaining after wolf kills, and studies indicate that biodiversity in the ecosystem has increased now that wolves have returned.

For more information on the Bailey Wildlife Foundation, check out www.defenders.org.

Remnants of the previous business still exist, and wooden tags on the room doors are still carved with Lucy, Mae, Sweet Sue, and 20 other girls' names. Clean, refurbished rooms with shared bath. Open June-Sept. Singles $40; doubles $52. Cash or check only. ❸

🏕 CAMPING

Campsites fill quickly during the summer months; be prepared to make alternate arrangements. Call **Park Headquarters** (☎ 344-7381) for info on campsite vacancies. The seven **National Park Service campgrounds ❶** do not accept advance reservations. During the summer, these smaller campgrounds generally fill by 10am, and finding a site can be frustrating. Check-out time is 10am, and the best window for claiming a campsite is 8-10am. Their popularity arises from their often stunning locations; most are well worth the effort to secure a spot. Two of the most beautiful campgrounds are **Slough Creek Campground**, 10 mi. northeast of Tower Jct. (29 sites; vault toilets; open June-Oct.; $12) and **Pebble Creek Campground** (32 sites; vault toilets; no RVs; open early June to late Sept.; $12). Both are located in the northeast corner of the park, between Tower Falls and the Northeast Entrance (generally the least congested area), and offer relatively isolated sites and good fishing. Travelers in the southern end of the park might try **Lewis Lake** (85 sites; vault toilets; open mid-June to early Nov.; $12), halfway between West Thumb and the South Entrance, a rugged campground with several walk-in tent sites that tend to fill up late in the day, if at all. **Tower Falls** (32 sites; vault toilets; open mid-May to late Sept.; $12) between the Northeast Entrance and Mammoth Hot Springs, has sites situated atop a hill, with fine views over mountain meadows. **Norris** (116 sites; water and flush toilets; open late May to late Sept.; $14); **Indian Creek,** between the Norris Geyser Basin and Mammoth Hot Springs (75 sites; vault toilets; open mid-June to mid-Sept.; $12); and **Mammoth** (85 sites; water and flush toilets; $14) are less scenic but still great places to camp. The lodges at Mammoth and Old Faithful have showers for $3 (towels and shampoo included), but no laundry facilities.

Xanterra ❶, P.O. Box 165, Yellowstone National Park 82190, runs five of the 12 developed campgrounds (all $18, except Fishing Bridge RV) within the park: **Canyon,** with 272 spacious sites on forested hillsides, is the most pleasant, while **Madison,** 277 sites on the banks of the Firehole River, has the advantage of being in the heart of the park's western attractions. **Grant Village** (425 sites) and **Bridge Bay**

(432 sites), both near the shores of Yellowstone Lake, have little vegetation to provide privacy. Finally, **Fishing Bridge RV ❷** ($32; RVs only) provides closely-packed parking spots for larger motor homes and those desiring full hookups. All five sites have flush toilets, water, and dump stations. Canyon, Grant Village, and Fishing Bridge RV also have showers ($3, towel rental $0.75) and coin laundry facilities (open 7am-9pm). Campgrounds are usually open mid-May to early October, though Canyon has the shortest season: mid-June to mid-September Xanterra accepts advance (☎344-7311) and same-day reservations (☎344-7901). Reservations are accepted up to two years in advance. During peak summer months (especially on weekends and holidays) it is best to make reservations at least a day ahead, especially for the more popular campgrounds listed first. The two largest Xanterra campgrounds, Grant Village and Bridge Bay, are the best bet for last-minute reservations. Group camping is available at Madison, Grant, and Bridge Bay for $47-77 per night; reservations required (☎344-7311).

█ FOOD

Buying food at the restaurants, snack bars, and cafeterias in the park can be expensive; stick to the **general stores** at each lodging location. The stores at Fishing Bridge, Lake, Grant Village, and Canyon sell lunch-counter-style food. (Open daily 7:30am-9pm, but times may vary.) Stock up at the **Food Round-Up Grocery Store,** 107 Dunraven St., in West Yellowstone. (☎406-646-7501. Open daily in summer 7am-10pm; in winter 7am-9pm.) At the original entrance to the park, Gardiner is less touristy than West Yellowstone; it is also moderately pricier. **Food Farm,** on U.S. 89 in Gardiner, has cheap food. (☎406-848-7524. Open M-Sa 7am-9pm, Su 8am-8pm.)

▨ Running Bear Pancake House, 538 Madison Ave. (☎406-646-7703), at Hayden in West Yellowstone, has inexpensive breakfasts and sandwiches in a friendly home-town atmosphere. Breakfast served all day; don't miss the special walnut and peach pancakes ($3-5). Burgers, salads, and sandwiches $5-7. Open daily 7am-2pm. ❶

Grizzly Pad Grill and Cabins (☎406-838-2161), 315 Main St., on Rte. 212 on the eastern side of Cooke City, serves the Grizzly Pad Special—a milkshake, fries, and large cheeseburger ($8). Alternatively, pick up a sack lunch ($6.50) or fried chicken (8 pc. $7.75) to go. Open late May to mid-Oct. daily 7am-9pm; Jan. to mid-Apr. hours vary. ❷

Ka-Bar Restaurant (☎406-848-9995), on U.S. 89 just as it enters Gardiner, fixes up a fiery Mexican chipotle steak ($8) and meat-laden pizzas (8 in. $6.75). Don't let the rustic exterior fool you: this is one of the tastiest and most filling places to enjoy dinner after a trip in the park. Open daily 11am-10pm. ❷

Timberline Cafe, 135 Yellowstone Ave. (☎406-646-9349), in West Yellowstone, prepares travelers for a day in the park with a large salad-and-potato bar and homemade pies. Burgers, sandwiches, and omelettes $6-8. Open daily 6:30am-10pm. ❷

Helen's Corral Drive-In (☎406-848-7627), a few blocks west on U.S. 89 in Gardiner, rounds up super ½ lb. buffalo burgers and pork chop sandwiches ($5-8) in a lively street-side atmosphere. Open in summer daily 11am-10pm. ❷

The Gusher Pizza & Sandwich Shoppe (☎406-646-9050), at the corner of Madison and Dunraven in West Yellowstone, boldly declares "pizza is always eaten with the fingers," so abandon any pretentious predilections for tableware. Red, white, or pesto sauce pizzas (10 in. $7-13, 15 in. $13-22), ½ lb. burgers, and hot sandwiches ($6-7) keep those fingers busy. Food is only half their specialty—partake of the full video game room, pool tables, and casino (21+). Open daily 11:30am-10:30pm. ❷

The Miner's Saloon (☎406-838-2214), 108 Main St., on Rte. 212 in downtown Cooke City, is the best place to go for a frosty Moose Drool beer ($3). Tasty burgers and fish tacos $6-7. Live music F-Sa. Open daily noon-10pm, bar until 2am. ❷

ROCKY MOUNTAINS

🔘 SIGHTS

Xanterra (☎ 344-7311) organizes tours, horseback rides, and chuckwagon dinners. These outdoor activities are expensive, however, and Yellowstone is best explored on foot. Visitors centers give out informative self-guided tour pamphlets with maps for each of the park's main attractions ($0.50). Trails to these sights are accessible from the road via walkways, usually extending ¼-1½ mi. into the various natural environments. Before you depart on a wilderness adventure, the **Museum of the Yellowstone,** on the corner of Canyon St. and Yellowstone Ave. in West Yellowstone, has extensive exhibits on park flora and fauna, earthquakes, fires, and historical development. (☎ 406-646-1100. Open mid-May to mid-Oct. daily 9am-8pm. $6, children $4.)

Yellowstone is set apart from other national parks and forests in the Rockies by its **geothermal features**—the park protects the largest geothermic area in the world. The bulk of these geothermal wonders can be found on the western side of the park between Mammoth Hot Springs in the north and Old Faithful in the south. The most dramatic thermal fissures are the **geysers.** Hot liquid magma close to the surface of the earth superheats water from snow and rain until it boils and bubbles, eventually building up enough pressure to burst through the cracks with steamy force. The extremely volatile nature of this area means that attractions may change, appear, or disappear due to forces beyond human control.

While bison-jams and bear-gridlock may make wildlife seem more of a nuisance than an attraction, they afford a unique opportunity to see a number of native species co-existing in their natural environment. The best times for viewing are early morning and just before dark, as most animals nap in the shade during the hot midday. The road between Tower-Roosevelt and the Northeast Entrance, in the untamed Lamar River Valley, often called the "Serengeti of Yellowstone," is one of the best places to see wolves, grizzlies, and herds of bison (among other species). Some species take to the higher elevations in the heat of summer, so travel earlier or later in the season (or hike to higher regions) to find the best viewing opportunities. Consult a ranger for more specific advice.

> ⚠ Beware: the crust around many of Yellowstone's thermal basins, geysers, and hot springs is thin, and boiling, acidic water lies just beneath the surface. Stay on the marked paths and boardwalks at all times. In the backcountry, keep a good distance from hot springs and fumaroles.

OLD FAITHFUL AREA

Yellowstone's trademark attraction, 🔖**Old Faithful,** is the most predictable of the large geysers and has consistently pleased audiences since its discovery in 1870. Eruptions usually shoot 100-190 ft. in the air, typically occur every 45min.-2hr. (average 90min.) and last about 1½-5min. Predictions for the next eruption, usually accurate to within 10min., are posted at the Old Faithful Visitors Center. Old Faithful lies in the **Upper Geyser Basin,** 16 mi. south of the Madison area and 20 mi. west of Grant Village. This area has the largest concentration of geysers in the world and boardwalks connect them all. The spectacular rainbow spectrum of **Morning Glory Pool** is an easy 1½ mi. from Old Faithful, and provides up-close-and-personal views of hundreds of hydrothermal features along the way, including the tallest predictable geyser in the world, **Grand Geyser,** and the graceful **Riverside Geyser,** which spews at a 60° angle across the Firehole River. Between Old Faithful and Madison, along the Firehole River, lie the **Midway Geyser Basin** and the **Lower Geyser Basin.** Many of these geysers are visible from the side of the road, and stopping for a closer look is highly recommended. The

Excelsior Geyser Crater, a large, steaming lake created by a powerful geyser blast, and the **Grand Prismatic Spring,** the largest hot spring in the park, located in the Midway Geyser Basin, sit about 5 mi. north of Old Faithful and are well worth the trip. Two miles north is the less developed but still thrilling **Firehole Lake Drive,** a 2 mi. side loop through hot lakes, springs, and dome geysers. Eight miles north of Old Faithful gurgles the **Fountain Paint Pot,** a bubbling pool of hot, milky white, brown, and grey mud. Four types of geothermal activity present in Yellowstone (geysers, mudpots, hot springs, and fumaroles) are found along the trails of the Firehole River. There is a strong temptation to wash off the grime of camping in the hot water, but swimming in the hot springs is prohibited. You can swim in the **Firehole River,** near Firehole Canyon Dr., just south of Madison Jct. Prepare for a chill; the name of the river is quite deceiving. Call park info (☎344-7381) to make sure the river is open.

NORRIS GEYSER BASIN

Fourteen miles north of Madison and 21 mi. south of Mammoth, the colorful **Norris Geyser Basin** is the oldest and the hottest active thermal zone in the park. The geyser has been erupting at temperatures of up to 459°F for over 115,000 years. The area has a ½ mi. northern **Porcelain Basin** loop and a 1½ mi. southern **Back Basin** loop. **Echinus,** in the Back Basin, is the largest known acid-water geyser, erupting 40-60 ft. every 1-4hr. Its neighbor, **Steamboat,** is the tallest active geyser in the world, erupting over 300 ft. for 3 to 40min. Steamboat's eruptions, however, are unpredictable; major eruptions often occur months or even years apart.

MAMMOTH HOT SPRINGS

Shifting water sources, malleable travertine limestone deposits, and temperature-sensitive, multicolored bacterial growth create the most rapidly changing natural structure in the park. The hot spring terraces resemble huge wedding cakes at **Mammoth Hot Springs,** 21 mi. north of the Norris Basin and 19 mi. west of Tower in the northwest corner of the upper loop. The **Upper Terrace Drive,** 2 mi. south of Mammoth Visitors Center, winds for 1½ mi. through colorful springs and rugged travertine limestone ridges and terraces. When visiting, ask a local ranger where to find the most active springs, as they vary in intensity from year to year. Some go dormant for decades, their structures gradually crumbling, only to revive unexpectedly to build new domes and cascades. In recent years, **Canary Spring,** on the south side of the main terrace, has been extremely active as it expands into virgin forest, killing trees and bushes. Also ask about area trails that provide some of the park's best wildlife viewing. Xanterra offers **horseback rides** just south of the hot springs. (☎344-7311; call at least 1 day ahead. Open late May to early Sept. 5-7 trail rides per day 7am-6pm. $29 per hr., $48 per 2hr.) **Swimming** is permitted in the **Boiling River,** 2½ mi. north. Check with a ranger to make sure that this area is open.

GRAND CANYON

The east side's featured attraction, the ◪**Grand Canyon of the Yellowstone,** wears rusty red and orange hues created by hot water acting on the rock. The canyon is 800-1200 ft. deep and 1500-4000 ft. wide. For a close-up view of the mighty **Lower Falls** (308 ft.), hike down the short, steep **Uncle Tom's Trail** (over 300 steps). **Artist Point,** on the southern rim, and **Lookout Point,** on the northern rim, offer broader canyon vistas and are accessible from the road between Canyon and Fishing Bridge. Keep an eye out for bighorn sheep along the canyon's rim. Xanterra also runs **horseback rides** at Canyon and in the Tower-Roosevelt area 19 mi. north. (☎344-7311; reservations required. Open June-Aug. 6-8 rides per day 7am-6pm. $29 per hr., $48 per 2hr.) **Stagecoach rides** ($8.25, ages 2-11 $7) along the canyon in yellow wagons are available early June to early September at Roosevelt Lodge.

YELLOWSTONE LAKE AREA

In the southeast corner of the park, **Yellowstone Lake** is the largest high-altitude lake in North America and serves as a protective area for the cutthroat trout. While the surface of the lake may appear calm, geologists have found evidence of geothermal features at the bottom. **AmFac** offers lake cruises that leave from the marina at Bridge Bay. (☎ 344-7311. 5-7 per day early June to mid-Sept. $9.75, ages 2-11 $5.) Geysers and hot springs in **West Thumb** dump an average of 3100 gallons of water into the lake per day. Notwithstanding this thermal boost, the temperature of the lake remains quite cold, averaging 45°F during the summer. Visitors to the park once cooked freshly-caught trout in the boiling water of the **Fishing Cone** in the West Thumb central basin, but this is no longer permitted. Along this same loop on the west side of the lake, check out the **Thumb Paint Pots,** a field of puffing miniature mud volcanoes and chimneys. On the northern edge of the lake is **Fishing Bridge,** where fishing is now prohibited due to efforts to help the endangered trout population. The sulfurous odors of **Mud Volcano,** 6 mi. north of Fishing Bridge, can be distinguished from miles away, but the turbulent mudpots are worth the assault on your nose, caused by the creation of hydrogen sulfide gas by bacteria working on the naturally-occurring sulfur in the spring water. The unusual mudpots—with their rhythmic belching, acidic waters, and cavernous openings—have appropriate names such as **Dragon's Mouth, Sour Lake,** and **Black Dragon's Cauldron.**

OFF THE (EXTREMELY WELL) BEATEN PATH

Most visitors to Yellowstone never get out of their cars, and therefore miss out on over 1200 mi. of trails in the park. Options for exploring Yellowstone's more pristine areas range from short day-hikes to long backcountry trips. When planning a hike, pick up a topographical trail map ($9-10 at any visitors center) and ask a ranger to describe the network of trails. Some trails are poorly marked, so be sure of your route-finding abilities and skill with a map and compass before setting off on more obscure paths. The 1988 fires scarred over a third of the park; hikers should consult rangers and maps on which areas are burned. Burned areas have less shade, so hikers should pack hats, extra water, and sunscreen.

In addition to the self-guided trails at major attractions, many worthwhile sights are only a few miles off the main road. The **Fairy Falls Trail** (5¼ mi. round-trip, 2½hr.), 3 mi. north of Old Faithful, provides a unique perspective on the Midway Geyser Basin and up-close views of 200 ft. high Fairy Falls. This easy round-trip trail begins in the parking lot marked "Fairy Falls" just south of Midway Geyser Basin. A more strenuous option is to follow the trail beyond the falls up Twin Buttes, a 650 ft. elevation gain, which turns this trail into a moderate, 4hr. round-trip hike. The trail to the top of **Mount Washburn** (5½ mi. round-trip, 4hr., 1380 ft. elevation gain) is enhanced by an enclosed observation area with sweeping views of the park's central environs, including the patchwork of old and new forests caused by the 1988 fires. This trail begins at the Chittenden Rd. parking area, 10 mi. north of Canyon Village, or Dunraven Pass, 6 mi. north of Canyon Village. A more challenging climb to the top of **Avalanche Peak** (4 mi., 4hr., final elevation 10,568 ft.) starts 8 mi. west of the East Entrance on East Entrance Rd. A steep ascent up several switchbacks opens to stunning panoramas out over Yellowstone Lake and the southern regions of the park, west to the Continental Divide and east to Shoshone National Forest. The trail along **Pebble Creek** (12 mi. one-way) makes a great trip though some of Yellowstone's most pristine backcountry. Beginning 1½ mi. west of the Northeast Entrance, the trail climbs steeply up a 1000 ft. ridge the first 1½ mi. before descending to the Pebble Creek Valley, following it mostly downhill for the remaining 10½ mi., exiting below Pebble Creek campground. Wildlife-viewing opportunities in this area are superb. This route is ideal with a second vehicle or bicycle, negating a return along the same route. There are dozens of extended backcountry trips in the park, including treks to the Black Canyon of the Yellowstone, in the north-central region, and to isolated Heart Lake in the south. Rangers can provide more detailed maps and information on these routes.

Nearly all of Yellowstone shuts down in winter. For those intrepid souls who wish to see the geothermal features at their most spectacular, in cold and snow, **Jackson Hole Snowmobile Tours,** 515 N. Cache St. in Jackson, leads the way, with guided treks to Old Faithful and the Grand Canyon. (☎733-6850 or 800-633-1733. $210-230 for snowmobile driver, $80 per adult passenger.)

SCENIC DRIVE: NORTH FORK DRIVE

Linking Yellowstone National Park with Cody, WY, the **Buffalo Bill Cody Scenic Byway (U.S. 14/16/20)** bridges the majestic peaks of the Absaroka Mountains (ab-SOR-ka) with the sagebrush lands of the Wyoming plains. This 52 mi. drive winds through the canyon created by the North Fork of the Shoshone River; the high granite walls and sedimentary formations of the **Shoshone Canyon** are noticeable from the road, as is the smell of sulfur from the DeMaris springs in the Shoshone River. Once the world's tallest dam, the **Buffalo Bill Dam Visitors Center and Reservoir,** 6 mi. west of Cody, celebrates man's ability to control the flow of water to fit human needs. Built between 1904 and 1910, the Buffalo Bill Dam measures 350 ft. in height. (☎527-6076. Visitors center open daily June-Aug. 8am-8pm; May and Sept. 8am-6pm.) West of the dam, strange rock formations, created millions of years ago by volcanic eruptions in the Absarokas, dot the dusty hillsides. Continuing west to Yellowstone, sagebrush and small juniper trees gradually lead into the thick pine cover of the **Shoshone National Forest,** the country's first national forest. This area, known as the **Wapiti Valley,** is home to over 20 dude ranches. The **East Entrance** to Yellowstone National Park guards the west end of the scenic byway and is closed in winter. The **Chief Joseph Scenic Highway (Route 296)** connects Cooke City, MT, to Cody, WY, and passes through rugged, sagebrush-covered mountains across **Dead Indian Summit.** This scenic byway traces the route traveled by the Nez Percé Indians as they skillfully evaded the USA army in the summer of 1877. From Cody, follow the Buffalo Bill Cody Scenic Byway back into eastern Yellowstone, completing a spectacular drive through the western half of Wyoming.

GRAND TETON NATIONAL PARK ☎307

The Grand Tetons are the youngest mountains in the entire Rocky Mountain system, their jagged peaks (12 over 12,000 feet), sculpted by glaciers more than 3000 ft. thick, carving U-shaped valleys and gouging out Jackson and Jenny lakes. Though the Shoshone Indians called them the "hoary-headed fathers," when French trappers first observed the three most prominent peaks—South Teton, Grand Teton, and Mt. Teewinot—they dubbed the mountains *"Les trois tetons,"* meaning "the three breasts." Upon discovering that these were surrounded by numerous smaller peaks, the Frenchmen renamed the range *"Les grands tetons."* Grand Teton National Park, officially established in 1929, delights hikers with miles of strenuous trails and steep rock cliffs along the range's eastern face.

✦ ⁊ ORIENTATION AND PRACTICAL INFORMATION

Grand Teton's roads consist of a main loop through the park with side roads coming from Jackson in the south, Dubois in the east, and Yellowstone in the north. There are two entrances to the park, at Moose and Moran Jct. The east side of the main loop, **U.S. 89,** from Jackson to Yellowstone, does not pass through either entrance and offers excellent, free views of the Tetons. All roads in the park are open year-round. Those who elect to enter the park pay an **entrance fee.** ($20 per car, $15 per motorcycle, $10 per pedestrian or bicycle; annual pass $40. Passes good for 7 days in Tetons and Yellowstone.)

Permits are required for all **backcountry camping** and are free if reserved in person within 24hr. of the trip. Reservations made more than 24hr. in advance require a $15 service fee. Requests are accepted by mail from January 1 to May 15; write to Grand Teton National Park, Permits Office, P.O. Drawer 170, Moose 83012. (For more info, contact the **Moose Visitor Center, ☎** 739-3309.) Advance reservations are recommended for sites in a mountain canyon or near lakes. After May 15, two-thirds of all backcountry spots are available first come, first served; the staff can help plan routes and find campsites. Wood fires are only permitted in existing fire grates. At high elevations, snow often remains into July, and the weather can become severe or even deadly any time of the year. Severe weather gear is strongly advised.

Public Transit: Grand Teton Lodge Co. (☎ 800-628-9988) runs in summer from Colter Bay to Jackson Lake Lodge. (7 per day, round-trip $7.) Shuttles also run to **Jackson** (3 per day, $40) and the **Jackson Hole** airport (by reservation only, $30).

Visitor Info: Visitors centers and campgrounds have free copies of the *Teewinot*, the park's newspaper containing info on special programs, hiking, camping, and news. For general info and a visitor's packet, or to make backcountry camping reservations, contact **Park Headquarters** (☎ 739-3600; www.nps.gov/grte) or write the **Superintendent,** Grand Teton National Park, P.O. Drawer 170, Moose 83012.

Moose Visitors Center and Park Headquarters (☎ 739-3399), Teton Park Rd., at the southern tip of the park, ½ mi. west of Moose Jct. Open daily early June to early Sept. 8am-7pm; early Sept. to mid-May 8am-5pm.

Jenny Lake Visitors Center (☎ 739-3392), next to the Jenny Lake Campground in South Jenny Lake. Open daily early June to mid-Sept. 8am-7pm; late Sept. 8am-5pm.

Colter Bay Visitors Center (☎ 739-3594), on Jackson Lake in the northern part of the park. Houses the Indian Arts Museum. Open daily June to early Sept. 8am-8pm; May and Sept. 8am-5pm.

Info Lines: Weather, ☎ 739-3611. **Wyoming Highway Info Center, ☎** 733-1731. **Wyoming Department of Transportation, ☎** 888-996-7623. **Road Report, ☎** 739-3614.

Emergency: Sheriff's Office, ☎ 733-2331. **Park Dispatch, ☎** 739-3300.

Medical Services: Grand Teton Medical Clinic, Jackson Lake Lodge (☎ 543-2514, after hours 733-8002). Open daily late May to early Oct. 10am-6pm. **St. John's Medical Center,** 625 E. Broadway (☎ 733-3636), in Jackson.

Post Office: In Moose (☎ 733-3336), across from the Park Headquarters. Open M-F 9am-1pm and 1:30-5pm, Sa 10:30-11:30am. **Postal Code:** 83012. **Area Code:** 307.

▐ ▟ ACCOMMODATIONS AND FOOD

The Grand Teton Lodge Company runs most indoor accommodations in the park. (Reservations ☎ 800-628-9988; or write to the **Reservations Manager,** Grand Teton Lodge Co., P.O. Box 240, Moran 83013. Deposit required.) Lodges are pricey, but there are two options for affordable cabins at Colter Bay. **Signal Mountain Lodge ❹** (☎ 543-2831) has scenic lodging options on the shores of Jackson Lake and the closest rooms to the hiking trails near Jenny Lake. Options include rustic log cabins with private bath (doubles $98), lodge-style rooms (quads $127), and lakefront retreats with living areas and kitchenettes (6 people $189). **Colter Bay Village Cabins ❷** maintains 208 log cabins near Jackson Lake. The cabins with shared baths are probably the best deal in the entire

Jackson Hole area; book early. (☎543-2828. Open late May to late Sept. Reception 24hr. 2-person cabins with shared bath from $35. 1 room with private bath $70-109; 2 rooms with private bath $115-134.) **Colter Bay Tent Cabins ❷** offers primitive log and canvas shelters with dusty floors, tables, wood-burning stoves, and bunks. Sleeping bags, cots, and blankets are available for rent. (☎800-628-9988. Open early June to early Sept. Restrooms and $3 showers. Tent cabins for 2 $36; each additional person $5.)

The best way to eat in the Tetons is to bring your own food. Non-perishables are available at the **Trading Post Grocery,** in the Dornan's complex in Moose, and the deli makes thick subs for $5-6. (☎733-2415, ext. 201. Open daily May-Sept. 8am-8pm, deli open 8am-7pm; Oct.-Apr. 8am-6pm, deli open 8am-5pm.) Jackson has an **Albertson's** supermarket, 105 Buffalo Way, at the intersection of W. Broadway and Rte. 22. (☎733-5950. Open daily 6am-midnight.) Gather 'round pots of ribs, stew, and mashed potatoes at **Dornan's Chuckwagon ❷,** across from the Trading Post Grocery in Moose, for an authentic Old West dinner. (☎733-2415, ext. 203. Breakfast $5-7. Lunch $6-9. Chuckwagon dinner $14, ages 6-11 $7.) The **Trapper Grill ❸,** inside Signal Mountain Lodge, tops off a day of hiking with a heaping mound of nachos ($7-12), a meal unto itself. If you've still got room, the elk chili burgers ($8) are unbeatable. (☎543-2831. Breakfast omelettes and skillets $8. Open early May to mid-Oct. 7am-10pm. **John Colter Cafe Court ❷,** in Colter Bay, serves pizza ($7), burgers, and sandwiches. (☎543-2811. Open daily 11am-10pm.)

📷 CAMPING

To stay in the Tetons without emptying your wallet, find a tent and pitch it. The park service maintains five campgrounds, all first come, first served. (☎739-3603 for info. Sites generally open mid-May to late Sept.) All sites have restrooms, cold water, fire rings, dump stations, and picnic tables. The maximum length of stay is 14 days, except for Jenny Lake sites, where it is 7 days. There is a maximum of six people and one vehicle per site; Colter Bay and Gros Ventre accept larger groups for $3 per person plus a $15 reservation fee.

Signal Mountain, along the southern shore of Jackson Lake. The 86 sites are roomier and more secluded than at Colter Bay and have the best views and lake access of any of the campgrounds, situated on hillsides overlooking the water. The campground is usually full by 10am. Open early May to late Oct. Sites $12. ❶

Jenny Lake has 51 closely-spaced sites in the shadow of the towering Mt. Teewinot, within walking distance of Jenny Lake. Sites usually fill before 8am; get there early. Some have success with politely approaching campers planning to depart that morning to inquire if they can occupy their vacated spot. No RVs. Open mid-May to late Sept. Vehicle sites $12, bicycle sites $5 per person. ❶

Lizard Creek, closer to Yellowstone than to the Tetons, has 60 spacious, secluded sites along the northern shore of Jackson Lake. The campsites fill up by about 2pm. Open June to early Sept. Vehicle sites $12. ❶

Colter Bay is not exactly a wilderness experience—with 350 crowded sites, a grocery store, laundromat, and two restaurants, it's more accurately described as a suburb. Sites usually fill by noon. Showers open 7:30am-9pm; $3. Open late May to late Sept. Vehicle sites $12, with full hookup $31. ❶

Gros Ventre (☎739-3603), along the edge of the Gros Ventre River, close to Jackson, is the biggest campground with 360 sites and 5 group sites. The Tetons, however, are hidden from view by Blacktail Butte. The campsite rarely fills and is the best bet for late arrivals. Open early May to mid-Oct. Sites $12. ❶

◢ OUTDOOR ACTIVITIES

While Yellowstone wows visitors with geysers and mudpots, the Grand Tetons boast some of the most scenic mountains in the US, if not the world. Only 2-3 million years old, the Tetons range between 10,000 and 13,770 ft. in elevation. The absence of foothills creates spectacular mountain vistas that accentuate the range's steep rock faces. These dramatic rocks draw scores of climbers, but even less seasoned hikers can still experience the beauty of the Tetons' backcountry.

HIKING

All visitors centers provide pamphlets about day-hikes and sell guides and maps ($3-10). Rangers also lead informative hikes; check the *Teewinot* or the visitors centers for more info. Before hitting the trail or planning extended hikes, be sure to check in at the ranger station; trails at higher elevations may still be snow-covered *and thus require ice axes and experience with icy conditions*. During years with heavy snowfall, prime hiking season does not begin until well into July.

The Cascade Canyon Trail to Lake Solitude (round-trip with boat ride 14½ mi., 9hr.; without boat ride 18½ mi., 10hr.) begins on the far side of tranquil Jenny Lake and follows Cascade Creek through U-shaped valleys carved by glaciers. The **Hidden Falls Waterfall** is located ½ mi. up; views of Teewinot, Mt. Owen, and Grand Teton are to the south. Hikers with more stamina can continue another ½ mi. upward toward **Inspiration Point** (elevation 7200 ft.), with stunning views eastward across Jackson Hole and the Wind River Range, but only the lonely will trek 6¾ mi. farther to **Lake Solitude** (9035 ft.). Ranger-led trips to Inspiration Point depart from Jenny Lake Visitors Center every morning June-Aug. 8:30am. Hikers can reach the Cascade Canyon Trail by way of the 2 mi. trail around the south side of Jenny Lake or by taking one of the shuttles offered by **Jenny Lake Boating.** (☎733-2703. Boats leave Jenny Lake Visitors Center every 20min. daily 8am-6pm. $5, ages 7-12 $4; round-trip $7/$5.) Most hikers, including many families, choose one of these options. An alternative route begins at String Lake trailhead and traverses the isolated north side of Jenny Lake though lush forest for 1¾ mi. Trail begins easy to moderate, but becomes more difficult as you progress.

Taggart Lake (3¼ mi. round-trip, 2hr., 277 ft. elevation change) passes through the 1000-acre remains of the 1985 Beaver Creek fire, which opportunely removed most of the tree cover for an open view of the Tetons and Taggart lakeshore. This moderate trail also winds through the broad spectrum of plant and wildlife that has developed since the fire; keep a lookout for marmots sunning themselves.

Bradley Lake (4 mi. round-trip, 3hr., 397 ft. elevation change), beginning at Taggart Lake trailhead, passes Taggart Lake and then proceeds up a glacial moraine to the more secluded Bradley Lake. For a longer trek, follow the trail another 1½ mi. along the eastern shore, over another moraine, and along a meadow for an elevation gain of 397 ft. before joining Amphitheater Lake Trail 1¾ mi. above the Lupine Meadows trailhead.

The Amphitheater Lake Trail (9¾ mi. round-trip, 8hr., 2958 ft. elevation change), originating just south of Jenny Lake at the Lupine Meadows parking lot, is a strenuous trek with a significant elevation change along several switchbacks. 3 mi. along the trail, a fork directs hikers either to **Garnet Canyon** to the left or **Surprise Lake** and **Amphitheater Lake** to the right. Garnet Canyon is 1¼ mi. from the fork and provides access to several mountain-climbing routes up South, Middle, and Grand Teton. Camping at the trail's end requires a permit and all climbing endeavors should be registered with park officials. The lakes are another 1¾ mi. from the fork; both are stunning examples of high alpine tarns gouged out by glaciers long since melted. Lupines, the purple flowers visible all along the roads in the park, bloom June-July along the trail.

Hermitage Point (8¾ mi. round-trip, 4hr., 100 ft. elevation change), beginning at Colter Bay, is an easy hike along gently rolling meadows and streams and past Swan Lake and Heron Pond. The trail provides a unique perspective on Jackson Lake, which it approaches at several points, and is a prime spot for observing wildlife.

Static Peak Divide (15½ mi. round-trip, 10hr., 4000 ft. elevation change), one of the most challenging trails in the park, begins at the Death Canyon trailhead, 4½ mi. south of Moose Visitors Center. The trail loops through whitebark pine forest and up numerous switchbacks over loose talus. With some of the best vistas in the park, the area is perfect for longer 2- to 3-day hikes. Prepare for ice in this area, even into August.

The Cunningham Cabin Trail (¾ mi. round-trip, 1hr., 20 ft. elevation change) relives the history of cattle ranching and early homesteading in the valley. Trailhead lies 6 mi. south of Moran Jct.

CLIMBING

Two companies offer more extreme backcountry adventures, including 4-day packages that let beginners work their way up the famed Grand Teton. **Jackson Hole Mountain Guides and Climbing School,** 165 N. Glenwood St., in Jackson, has a one-day beginner course for $100 and a one-day guided climbing course for $125. More advanced programs are also available: one-day guided climbs that do not require training start at $175 and four-day Grand Teton ascents at $995. (☎733-4979 or 800-239-7642. Open 8:30am-5:30pm. Reservations necessary.) **Exum Mountain Guides** offer similar classes and rates. (☎733-2297. 1-day beginner rock-climbing course $105. Guided 1- to 2-day climbs $110-385. Reservations necessary.)

BOATING, FISHING, AND BIKING

Getting out onto the water provides an entirely different perspective on the surrounding landscape. Non-motorized **boating** and hand-powered crafts are permitted on a number of lakes; motorboats are allowed only on Jackson, Jenny, and Phelps Lakes. Boating permits can be obtained at the Moose or Colter Bay Visitors Centers and are good in Yellowstone National Park as well. (Motorized boats $10 per 7 days, annual pass $20; non-motorized craft $5/$10. Jet-skis prohibited on all park waterways.) **Grand Tetons Lodge Company** rents boats at Colter Bay and has scenic cruises of Jackson Lake leaving from Colter Bay. (Colter Bay Marina ☎543-2811, Jenny Lake ☎733-2703. 1½hr. cruises $17, ages 3-11 $8. Canoes $10 per hr., motor boats $23 per hr.; 2hr. min. and $50 deposit. Rentals available May-Aug. daily 8am-4pm.) **Signal Mountain Lodge** rents boats and kayaks at Signal Mountain on Jackson Lake. (☎543-2831. Large pontoon boats $59 per hr., motorboats $23 per hr., canoes $11 per hr., sea kayaks $10 per hr. Rentals available May-Aug.)

Fishing is permitted within the park with a Wyoming license, available at Moose Village Store, Signal Mountain Lodge, Colter Bay Marina, and Flagg Ranch Village. ($10 Wyoming Conservation stamp required with all annual fishing licenses. WY residents $3 per day; $18 per season, ages 14-18 $3 per season. Non-residents $10 per day; $75/$15 per season.) Ladies interested in learning how to fly fish can learn with **Reel Women Fly Fishing Adventures,** an Idaho-based company developed to introduce women to this traditionally male-dominated sport. (☎208-787-2657. Full-day Wyoming float trips $395, 2-day basic fly fishing school $450. Reservations required.) Couples can fly fish with **Jack Dennis Fishing Trips,** which has float fishing trips on the Snake River and wading fishing trips in Grand Teton for two. (☎733-3270 or 800-570-3270. Both $375.) **Solitude Float Trips** sends raft floats down scenic Snake River. (☎733-2871. 10 mi. trip $42, ages13 and under $27; 5 mi. trip $25/$18.)

Mountain biking is a popular activity on roads in the park, but is strictly forbidden on hiking trails. Outdoor equipment rentals are in the Dornan's complex. **Adventure Sports** rents bikes and provides advice on the best trails. (☎733-3307.

ROCKY MOUNTAINS

Open May-Oct. daily 8am-8pm. Front suspension $8 per hr., $25 per day; full suspension $9/$28; kayaks and canoes $40 per 24hr. Credit card or deposit required.) **Snake River Angler** has fishing advice and rents rods. (☎ 733-3699. Open May-Oct. daily 8am-8pm. Rods $15-25 per day.) **Moosely Seconds** rents mountaineering and camping equipment. (☎ 739-1801. Open in summer daily 8am-8pm. Climbing shoes $5 per day, $25 per week; crampons $10/$50; ice axes $6/$30; trekking poles $4/$20.)

WINTER ACTIVITIES

In the winter, all hiking trails and the unplowed sections of Teton Park Rd. are open to **cross-country skiers.** Pick up winter info at the Moose Visitors Center. Guides lead free **snowshoe hikes** from the Moose Visitors Center. (☎ 739-3399. Jan.-Mar. Tu-Th 1pm.) **Snowmobiling** is only allowed on the Continental Divide Snowmobile Trail; pick up a $15 permit at the Moose Visitors Center and a map and guide at the Jackson Chamber of Commerce. **Grand Teton Park Snowmobile Rental,** in Moran Jct. at G.T.P. RV Resort, rents snowmobiles. (☎ 733-1980 or 800-563-6469. $89 per half day, $129 per day; includes clothing, helmet, and boots. Trail and snowmobile instruction included.) The Colter Bay and Moose parking lots are available for parking in the winter. All **campgrounds** close in winter, but **backcountry snow camping** (only for those who know what they're doing) is allowed with a permit obtained from the Moose Visitors Center. Before making plans, consider that temperatures regularly drop below -25°F. Be sure to carry extreme weather clothing and check with a ranger station for current weather and avalanche info.

SCENIC DRIVE: CENTENNIAL SCENIC DRIVE

Weaving through some of the most breathtaking expanses of uninhabited wilderness on earth, this all-day drive is a vacation unto itself. For 162 mi., the Centennial Scenic Byway passes by the high peaks, roaring whitewater rivers, and broad windswept plains of western Wyoming. The drive is open year-round but occasionally closes due to snow. The drive begins in the small frontier town of **Dubois,** home of the **National Bighorn Sheep Interpretive Center,** 907 W. Ramshorn St., a fascinating museum that educates visitors about the majestic creatures as they exist (many in endangered states) around the globe, from Alaska to Afghanistan. (☎ 455-3429 or 888-209-2795. Open daily late May to early Sept. 9am-8pm; in winter 8am-5pm. $2, under 12 $0.75; families $5.) Leaving town on Rte. 26, the crumbly breccia of the volcanic Absaroka Mountains becomes visible to the north; the 11,920 ft. jagged pinnacles are those of **Ramshorn Peak.** Gently rising through a conifer forest, the road eventually reaches **Togwotee Pass,** elevation 9544 ft., 30 mi. west of Dubois. Before the pass, 24 mi. west of Dubois, **Falls Camp ❶** is one of the region's best campgrounds, situated next to a massive waterfall concealed in the forest to the south of the highway. Even if you don't intend to enjoy this camp overnight, stop to be awed by this extraordinary canyon. (Toilets, no water. Sites $8.)

As the road begins to descend, the famed panorama of the Teton mountain range becomes visible. The highest peak is Grand Teton (13,770 ft.); the exhibit at the **Teton Range Overlook** labels each visible peak in the skyline. After entering **Grand Teton National Park** (p. 783), the road winds through the flat plain of the **Buffalo Fork River.** This floodplain is the beginning of the wide, long valley known as Jackson Hole (early trappers referred to any high mountain valley as a hole). The road follows the **Snake River,** renowned for its whitewater rafting and kayaking. Nearing Jackson (p. 789), the 24,000-acre **National Elk Refuge,** winter home to thousands of elk, is visible to the east. To bypass Jackson, take U.S. 189/191 south. As the route turns east at Hoback Jct., one of the West's most popular whitewater rafting segments, the **Grand Canyon of the Snake,** is just downstream. The road winds through the deep and narrow Hoback Canyon with the boiling Hoback River cutting through. As the Tetons fade out of sight, the Wind River Range, home to several active glaciers, appears on the horizon, and soon the highest peak in Wyoming, **Gannet Peak** (13,804 ft.), rises majestically in the distance. The drive ends in the tiny, authentically Western town of Pinedale. In Pinedale, the **Museum of the Mountain Man** chronicles the history of the Plains Indians, the fur trade, and the white settlement of western Wyoming. (☎877-686-6266. Open early May to late Sept. daily 10am-5pm; Oct. M-F 10am-noon and 1-3pm. $4, seniors $3, children $2.)

JACKSON ☎307

Jackson Hole, the valley that separates the Teton and Gros Ventre mountain ranges, is renowned for its world-class skiing. In recent years, however, the town of Jackson (pop. 5000) has exploded into a cosmopolitan epicenter, lined with chic restaurants, faux-Western bars, and expensive lodgings. To appreciate the area's true beauty, explore the nearby Tetons or navigate the winding Snake River.

▨ 🛈 ORIENTATION AND PRACTICAL INFORMATION. Downtown Jackson is centered around the intersection of Broadway (east-west) and Cache St. (north-south) and marked by **Town Square Park.** Most shops and restaurants are within a four-block radius of this intersection. South of town, at the intersection with Rte. 22, W. Broadway becomes U.S. 191/89/26. To get to **Teton Village,** take Rte. 22 to Rte. 390 (Teton Village Rd.) just before the town of Wilson. Winding backroads, unpaved at times, with close underbrush and frequent wildlife, connect Teton Village to Moose and the southern entrance of the national park. North of Jackson, Cache St. turns into Rte. 89, leading directly into the park. **Jackson Hole Airport** is located between Moose and Jackson (☎733-7682). **Jackson Hole Express** (☎733-1719 or 800-652-9510) provides bus service to the Salt Lake City airport (5½hr., 2 per day, $56) and the Idaho Falls airport (2hr., 2 per day, $35). Reservations are required. **Jackson START** runs buses all around town and between Jackson and Teton Village. (☎733-4521. Runs mid-May to late Sept. daily 6am-10:30pm; early Dec. to early Apr. 6am-11pm. In town free, on village roads $1, to Teton Village $2; under 9 free.) **Leisure Sports,** 1075 Rte. 89, has boating and fishing equipment and the best deals on camping and backpacking rentals. (☎733-3040. Open daily in summer and winter 8am-6pm; in fall and spring 8am-5pm. Tents for 2 $7.50, for 6 $25; sleeping bags $5-8; backpacks $3.50-7.50. Canoes and kayaks $35-45 per day, rafts $65-110 per day.) **Visitor Info: Jackson Hole and Greater Yellowstone Information Center,** 532 N. Cache St., has an interesting grass-covered roof. It lists the times at which park campgrounds filled the previous day. (Open early June to early Sept. daily 8am-7pm; early Sept. to early June M-F 8am-5pm.) **Internet Access: Jackson Library,** 125 Virginian Ln. (☎733-2164. Open M-Th 10am-9pm, F 10am-5:30pm, Sa 10am-5pm, Su 1-5pm.) **Post Office:** 1070 Maple Way, at Powderhorn Ln. (☎733-3650. Open M-F 8:30am-5pm, Sa 10am-1pm.) **Postal Code:** 83002. **Area Code:** 307.

🛏 ACCOMMODATIONS. Jackson draws hordes of visitors year-round, making rooms outrageously expensive and hard to find without reservations. ▨**The Hostel X (HI) ❸,** 12 mi. northwest of Jackson in Teton Village, lets skiers and others stay close to the slopes for cheap. The hostel has free Internet access, a lounge with TVs, ping-pong, and pool tables, as well as shelves of puzzles and games. Perks include laundry facilities, a ski-waxing room, and a convenient location just a close stumble from The Mangy Moose (see **Festivals and Nightlife,** below).

All rooms are private with either four twin beds or one king-size bed, private bath, and maid service. (☎733-3415. Open in summer and winter. Singles and doubles $52; triples and quads $65.) Jackson's own hostel, **The Bunkhouse ❶**, 215 N. Cache St., in the basement of the Anvil Motel, has the most affordable beds in town, a lounge with HBO, and a kitchen. (☎733-3668. Showers, coin laundry, and ski storage. Showers for non-residents $5, including towel. Bunks $25.) One of the few lodgings in Jackson with rooms under $100 during peak season, **Alpine Motel ❹**, 70 S. Jean, two blocks from the town square, provides clean basic rooms with cable TV, free local calls, and an outdoor pool. (☎739-3200. June-Sept. singles $68; doubles $80. Oct.-May $56/$64.) For those willing to rough it, the primitive campgrounds in Grand Teton National Park and the 4.4 million acre **Bridger-Teton National Forest** offer the area's cheapest accommodations. **Gros Ventre** campground (p. 786) is only a 15min. drive north of Jackson on Rte. 89. There are 45 **developed campgrounds ❶** in the Bridger-Teton National Forest, including several along U.S. 26 east of Jackson. **Hatchet Camp,** 9 mi. east of Moran Junction on U.S. 26, can provide a fitting base for a Grand Teton trip, especially if camps within the park are full. (☎739-5500. Most have no water due to freezing, no showers. Sites $5-15.) The publication *The Bridge* is available at the visitors center in Jackson; the national forest offices have additional info. Dispersed **backcountry camping ❶** is free within the national forest; campers must stay at least 200 ft. from water and 100 ft. from roads or trails. Consult with a ranger beforehand; some areas may be restricted. Showers including towels are available at the Anvil Motel, 215 N. Cache St., for $5.

◖ FOOD. Jackson has dozens of restaurants, but few are suited to the budget traveler. For a real Western dinner, join Clyde, a giant stuffed bison, at **The Gun Barrel Steak & Game House ❺**, 862 W. Broadway, for cowboy-sized helpings of Rocky Mountain rainbow trout ($18), elk tenderloin ($26), and buffalo prime rib ($28) in a giant lodge of rough-hewn hardwood beams. (☎733-3287. Open daily 5-10pm.) **The Bunnery ❷**, 130 N. Cache St., attracts both locals and tourists to their spacious outdoor patio for delicious breakfasts and baked goods, including classic and southwest omelettes and the special O.S.M. (oats, sunflower, and millet) bread. (☎733-5474 or 800-349-0492. Breakfast $3-6. Omelettes $8. Sandwiches $7-8. Desserts $4. Open daily in summer 7am-9pm; in winter 7am-2pm.) The always-busy **Mountain High Pizza Pie ❸**, 120 W. Broadway, lets you create your own pizza or choose from a large selection of pies. (☎733-3646. 10 in. pizza $7.25, 15 in. $14. Subs $6-7. Calzones $7.25. Open daily in summer 11am-midnight; in winter 11am-10pm.) Locals flock to the chic retro styling of **Betty Rock Cafe ❷**, 325 W. Pearl Ave., which cooks up fresh panini on homemade focaccia bread ($7-8) and pot pies ($10) chock full of goodies. (☎733-0747. Open M-Sa 11am-10pm.) For a homeopathic remedy, or a healthy bite to eat, the **Harvest Bakery and Cafe ❷**, 130 W. Broadway, is a New Age jack-of-all-trades with natural foods, teas, coffees, sorbet, books on yoga and wicca, and an in-house cafe. (☎733-5418. Smoothies $3-4.60. Fresh pastries $2. Soup and salad $6-7. Breakfast $5-8. Open M-Sa 7am-7:30pm, Su 8:30am-4:30pm; in winter M-Sa 8:30am-6pm, Su 9am-4pm.) A popular family restaurant, **Bubba's Bar-B-Que ❸**, 515 W. Broadway, serves generous portions of ribs and sides in a rustic environment. (☎733-2288. Lunch specials $6.50-8. Spare ribs $11. 10 oz. sirloin $13. Open daily in summer 7am-10pm; in winter 7am-9pm.)

▦ ◪ FESTIVALS AND NIGHTLIFE. When the sun goes down on a long day of skiing, hiking, or rafting, Jackson has bars, concerts, and festivals to suit all tastes. Frontier justice is served at the **Town Square Shootout.** Live reenactments take place Monday through Saturday at 6:15pm during the summer in Jackson's town square. (☎733-3316. Free.) Catch cowboy fever at the **JH Rodeo**, held at the fairgrounds, at Snow King Ave. and Flat Creek Dr., which features men riding bucking colts and bulls, ladies racing 'round barrels, and lots of antics for the kids. (☎733-2805. June to early Sept. W and Sa 8pm. $10, ages 4-12 $8; reserved tickets $13; families $32.) Over Memorial Day weekend, tourists, locals, and nearby Native American tribes pour in for the free dances and parades of **Old West Days**; for info, call the Chamber of Commerce (☎733-3316; www.jackson-holechamber.com). World-class musicians roll into Teton Village each summer during the **Grand Teton Music Festival** for shows like "Moosely Mozart and a Little Wolf." (☎733-3050, ticket office 733-1128; www.gtmf.org. Early July to late Aug. Festival orchestra concerts F-Sa 8pm $18-60. Spotlight concerts Th 8pm $13-60. Chamber music concerts Tu-W 8pm. $16, ages 6-18 $5. Adult half-price seats Th-F.) In mid-September, the **Jackson Hole Fall Arts Festival** (☎733-3316) showcases artists, musicians, and dancers in a week-long party that features everything from "Cowboy Jubilee Music" to a "Poetry Roundup." **The National Museum of Wildlife Art**, 2820 Rungius Rd., features 12 galleries recounting the history of wildlife in art from the 19th-century explorers to recent artists. (☎733-5771. Open daily 9am-5pm. Free.) **Jackson Hole Museum**, Glenwood and Mercill, has an extensive introduction to the area's human and natural history, including Native American stone tools and mountain man gear. (☎733-2414. Open Memorial Day-Sept. M-Sa 9:30am-6pm, Su 10am-5pm. $3, children $1.)

For nighttime fun, head to **The Mangy Moose**, in Teton Village at the base of Jackson Hole Ski Resort, a quintessential après-ski bar. (☎733-4913, entertainment hotline 733-9779. Cover $7-15, big names $20-25. Shows at 10pm. Kitchen open daily 5:30-10pm; food served 11:30am-2am.) Slither on down to the **Snake River Brewery**, 265 S. Millward St., for the award-winning "Zonkers Stout." Pub favorite burgers and brats are $6-9. (☎SEX-BEER/739-2337. Pints $3.50, pitchers $11. Open M-F 11:30-midnight, F-Sa 11:30am-1am; food served until 11pm.) Live music and good beer make the **Stagecoach Bar**, 7 mi. west of Jackson on Rte. 22 in Wilson, a popular nightspot, especially on Thursday Disco Night. (☎733-4407. Live music Su-M. Open M-Sa 11am-2am, Su 11am-1am.)

◪ OUTDOOR ACTIVITIES. World-class skiing and climbing lie within minutes of Jackson, and **whitewater rafting** the legendary Snake River is an adrenaline rush. **Barker-Ewing**, 45 W. Broadway, provides tours of varying lengths and difficulty levels, led by a highly-experienced staff. (☎733-1000 or 800-448-4202. 8 mi. tour 14-person raft $42, ages 6-12 $34; more agile 8-person raft $48/$40. Gentle 13 mi. scenic trip $40/$25; overnight 16 mi. adventure $140/$110; 16 mi. tour with breakfast: 14-person $73/$56, 8-person $79/$62.) **Mad River**, 1255 S. Rte. 89, 2 mi. south of Town Sq., offers similar trips with a promise of "smaller boats, bigger action." (☎733-6203 or 800-458-7238. 8 mi. trip $45, under 13 $40; with barbecue $50/$45.) During winter months, skiing enthusiasts flock to Jackson to experience pure Wyoming powder. **Jackson Hole Mountain Resort**, 12 mi. north of Jackson in Teton Village, has some of the best runs in the US, including the jaw-droppingly steep Corbet's Couloir. (☎733-2292. Open early Dec. to Apr. Lift tickets $62, ages 15-21 $48, seniors and under 14 $31.) Even after the snow melts, the **aerial tram** whisks tourists to the top of **Rendezvous Mountain** (elevation 10,450 ft.) for a view of the valley. (☎739-2753. Open late May to late Sept. daily 9am-5pm. $18, over 65 $14, ages 6-12 $6.) Mountain bike rentals are available atop Rendezvous. (☎739-2626. Front suspension $19 per half day, $29 per day; full suspension $25/$39.) Located in the town of Jackson, **Snow King** presents a less expensive and less extreme skiing option. (☎733-5200. Open daily 10am-4pm, night skiing Th-Sa 4-8pm. Lift tickets: half-day $25, full-day $35, 2hr. $17, night $15; under 15 and over 60 $15/$25/$12/$10.) Snow King also has sum-

ROCKY MOUNTAINS

mer rides to the summit for views of the Tetons ($8 round-trip). Jackson Hole is a prime locale for **cross-country skiing. Skinny Skis,** 65 W. Delorney, in downtown Jackson, points nordics in the right direction. (☎733-6094. Open 9am-8pm. Rentals with skis, boots, and poles half-day $12; full-day $18.)

CHEYENNE ☎307

"Cheyenne," the name of the Native American tribe that originally inhabited the region, was considered a prime candidate for the name of the whole Wyoming Territory. The moniker was struck down by notoriously priggish Senator Sherman, who pointed out that the pronunciation of Cheyenne closely resembled that of the French word *chienne*, meaning "bitch." Once one of the fastest-growing frontier towns, Cheyenne may have slowed down a bit, but its historical downtown area still exhibits traditional Western charm, complete with simulated gunfights.

◪ **PRACTICAL INFORMATION. Greyhound,** 222 Deming Dr. (☎634-7744; open 24hr.), off I-80, makes trips to: Chicago (19hr., 3 per day, $135); Denver (3-5hr., 5 per day, $19); Laramie (1hr., 3 per day, $13); Rock Springs (5hr., 3 per day, $55); Salt Lake City (8hr., 3 per day, $74). **Powder River Transportation** (☎634-7744), in the Greyhound terminal, honors Greyhound passes and sends buses daily to: Billings (11½hr., 2 per day, $79); Casper (4hr., 2 per day, $37); Rapid City (10hr., 1 per day, $74). For local travel, flag down one of the shuttle buses provided by the **Cheyenne Transit Program.** (☎637-6253. Buses run M-F 6am-7pm. $1, students $0.75, 4-6pm $0.50.) **Shamrock Airport Express** runs six shuttles daily to and from the Denver airport and Cheyenne; call for times and reservations. (☎866-482-0505. $32, children 12 and under $8.) **Visitor Info: Cheyenne Area Convention and Visitors Bureau,** 15th and Capitol Ave., in the Cheyenne Depot. (☎778-3133 or 800-426-5009; www.cheyenne.org. Open May-Sept. M-F 8am-6pm, Sa-Su 9am-5pm; Oct.-Apr. M-F 8am-5pm.) **Hotlines: Domestic Violence and Sexual Assault Line,** ☎637-7233. 24hr. **Internet Access: Laramie County Public Library,** 2800 Central Ave., has 30min. first come, first served slots available. (☎634-3561. Open mid-May to mid-Sept. M-Th 10am-9pm, F-Sa 10am-6pm; mid-Sept. to mid-May also Su 1-5pm.) **Post Office:** 4800 Converse Ave. (☎800-275-8777. Open M-F 7:30am-5:30pm, Sa 7am-1pm.) **Postal Code:** 82009. **Area Code:** 307.

⌂ **ACCOMMODATIONS.** As long as your visit doesn't coincide with Frontier Days (the last full week of July), during which rates skyrocket, it's easy to land a cheap room in Cheyenne. Budget motels line Lincolnway (16th St./U.S. 30). The **Ranger Motel ❷,** 909 W. 16th St., has rooms with cable TV, microwave, and fridge. (☎634-7995. Singles in summer from $30; in winter from $21. The aging **Pioneer Hotel ❶,** 208 W. 17th St., provides the cheapest lodgings in town. (☎634-3010. Cable TV. Singles with shared bath $18.) Sleep among the bison, horses, and singing cowboys in the original bunkhouses at the **Terry Bison Ranch ❷,** 51 I-25 Service Rd. E, 5 mi. south of Cheyenne. A fishing lake and Wyoming's first cellar are also on site. The ranch offers bison tours, horseback riding, and even stables to board your own horse. (☎634-4171. Private rooms with shared bath $38; cabins $79.) **Curt Gowdy State Park ❶,** 1319 Hynds Lodge Rd., 24 mi. west of Cheyenne on Happy Jack Rd. (Rte. 210), provides 150 year-round campsites centered around two lakes with excellent fishing. The park also offers horseback riding (bring your own horse) and archery in a beautiful location once frequented by the Comanche, Pawnee, Crow, and Shoshone tribes. (☎632-7946; reservations 877-996-7275 or www.wyo-park.com. Drinking water, dump station, boat dock. Sites $12, day use $4. Federal Bay and Sherman Hills areas are wheelchair accessible.)

🔃 **FOOD.** Cheyenne has only a smattering of reasonably-priced, non-chain restaurants. The walls at the popular 🈳**Sanford's Grub and Pub ❷**, 115 E. 17th St., are littered with every type of kitsch imaginable, including hub caps and coyote skulls. The extensive menu includes everything from Cajun burgers topped with crab meat ($5-7) and pasta ($9-12) to gizzards ($5) and crawfish jambalaya ($13). Check out the game room downstairs. (☎634-3381. 55 beers on tap, 99 bottles of beer on the wall, and 132 different liquors. Open M-Sa 11am-midnight, Su 11am-10pm.) A favorite with local politicians and businessmen, **The Albany ❹**, 1506 Capitol Ave., just across from the Depot, is the place to go for great sit-down lunches and dinners. The locally-raised prime rib ($16) and catfish ($11) can't be beat. (☎638-3507. Open daily 11am-2pm and 5-9pm.) For a dirt-cheap breakfast or lunch, the **Driftwood Cafe ❶**, 200 E. 18th St., at Warren St., complements its homestyle cooking with the feel of a quintessential mom-and-pop diner; it doesn't get more authentic than this. (☎634-5304. Burgers $3-6. Cinnamon rolls $1.45. Slice of pie $2. Open M-F 7am-3pm.) Psychedelic mobiles hang from the ceiling and glitter glue quotes mark the pastel walls at **Zen's Bistro ❷**, 2606 E. Lincolnway, where you'll find a healthy selection of salads ($6-8) and sandwiches ($6), as well as a full espresso and smoothie bar ($3-5) and an Internet room ($2 per 30min.). Sip your tea in the garden room, or take it to the back where live music, poetry readings, and local art exhibits are staged. (☎635-1889. Open M-F 7am-10pm, Sa 8am-10pm, Su 11am-5pm.) The **Luxury Diner ❶**, 1401A W. Lincolnway, an operating trolley car from 1896 to 1912, serves hearty classic breakfast platters all day ($4-9), with names like the "Engineer" and "Boxcar." (☎638-8971. Open daily 6am-4pm.)

🔆🗺 **SIGHTS AND NIGHTLIFE.** During the last week of July, make every effort to attend the one-of-a-kind 🈳**Cheyenne Frontier Days,** a 10-day festival of non-stop Western hoopla appropriately dubbed the "Daddy of 'Em All." The town doubles in size to see the world's largest outdoor rodeo competition and partake of the free pancake breakfasts, parades, big-name country music performances, square dancing, steer wrestling, and chuckwagon racing. (☎778-7222 or 800-227-6336. July 22-31, 2005. Rodeo $11-23. Concerts $18-42.) During June and July, a "gunfight is always possible," as the **Cheyenne Gunslingers,** W. 16th and Carey, shoot each other in a not altogether convincing display of undead rancor. (☎653-1028. M-F 6pm, Sa high noon.) Take a free **S&V Carriage Ride** through historic downtown Cheyenne, boarding at 16th and Capitol Ave. (☎634-0167. Rides daily noon-6pm.) The downtown has a number of well-maintained historic buildings; pick up a free walking tour guide at the visitors center. The **Wyoming State Capitol,** at the base of Capitol Ave. on 24th St., has beautiful stained-glass windows and a gorgeous rotunda under the gold-leaf dome; self-guided tours are available. A giant stuffed bison on the first level is often all alone in the building: the Wyoming legislature meets only 60 days over every two year period. (☎777-7220. Open M-F 8:30am-4:30pm. Free.) The **Old West Museum,** 4610 N. Carey Ave., in Frontier Park, houses a collection of Western memorabilia, including the third-largest carriage collection in the nation. (☎778-7290; www.oldwestmuseum.org. Open June-Aug. M-F 8am-6pm, Sa-Su 9am-5pm; Sept.-May M-F 9am-5pm, Sa-Su 10am-5pm. $5, under 12 free.) To get to **Vedauwoo Recreation Area,** 28 mi. west of Cheyenne, take Happy Jack Rd. (Rte. 210), then turn south on Vedauwoo Rd., or take Exit 329 north off I-80. Vedauwoo consists of a collection of oddly jumbled rocks eroded into seemingly impossible shapes by wind and weather. From the Arapaho word meaning "earthborn spirits," Vedauwoo was once considered a sacred place where men went on vision quests; today, rock climbers worship the towering formations, which provide an excellent backdrop for hiking, picnics, and biking (☎745-2300).

ROCKY MOUNTAINS

At **The Outlaw Saloon,** 3839 E. Lincolnway, live country music pours onto the dance floor and leaks out to the patio, where there's always a good game of sand volleyball to be played, even at night under stars and stadium lights. (☎ 635-7552. Live music M-Sa 8:30pm-1:45am. Free dance lessons Tu and Th 7:30-8:30pm. Happy hour with free food M-F 5-7pm. Cover W-Sa $2. Open M-Sa 2pm-2am, Su noon-10pm.) Shoot pool upstairs at the **Crown Bar,** or descend below for hip-hop, Top 40, and alternative dance at the **Crown Underground,** 222 W. 16th St., at the corner of Carey St. (☎ 778-9202. Nightly drink specials $1.75. Dancing Th-Sa 9pm-2am. Live music Sa 9pm-1:30am. Th ladies night and all drinks $1.75. Downstairs open W 9pm-midnight, F-Su 9pm-2am. Bar open M-Sa 11am-2am, Su 11am-10pm; food served until 1am.) Twang with the locals at the **Cowboy Restaurant and Bar,** 312 S. Greeley Hwy., and test your skill as a cowboy on the mechanical bull ($5 per ride). The live music and large dance floor always draw a crowd. (☎ 637-3800. Live music Tu-Sa 9pm-1:30am. Open M-Sa 11am-2am, Su noon-2am.)

THE SNOWY RANGE ☎ 307

Local residents call the forested granite mountains to the east of the Platte Valley the Snowy Mountain Range. Snow falls nearly year-round on the higher peaks, and when the snow melts, quartzite outcroppings reflect the sun, creating the illusion of a snowy peak. The Snowy Range, 40 mi. west of Laramie, is part of **Medicine Bow National Forest.** Cross-country skiing is popular in the winter; campsites and trails usually don't open until May or June due to heavy snowfall. On the west side of the Snowy Range along Rte. 130, chase the cold away with the geothermal stylings of **Saratoga's hot springs,** running between 104° and 120°F, at the end of E. Walnut St. behind the public pool. (Free. Open 24hr.) Nearby, the **North Platte River** offers fishing and a chance to enjoy snowmelt mixed with the runoff of the hot springs. Fishing permits ($10) are available at **Hack's Tackle Outfitters,** 407 N. 1st St., which also sells hunting licenses and offers both fishing advice and guided trips. (☎ 326-9823. Scenic tours $40 per half-day, $90 per day. Fishing trips for 2 $235 per half-day, $350 per day. Canoes $35/$95; $100 per boat deposit required. Shuttles to any location on the river can be hired for a $25 flat fee, regardless of number of canoes or rafts onboard.) At **Snowy Range Ski and Recreation Area,** enjoy 25 moderately challenging downhill trails, cross-country trails, and a snowboard halfpipe. Take Exit 311 off I-80 to Rte. 130 W. (☎ 745-5750 or 800-462-7669. Open mid-Dec. to Easter. Lift ticket full-day $32, half-day $25; ages 6-12 and over 60 $18/$14.)

From late May to November, cars can drive 27 mi. through seas of pine and aspen trees, around treeless mountains and picture-perfect lakes at high elevations on the **Snowy Range Scenic Byway (Route 130).** From the east, exit I-80 in Laramie; from the west exit at Walcott Jct., 22 mi. east of Rawlins. Early along the byway from the east, Barber Lake Rd. branches off along noisy Libby Creek, bypassing the entrance to the Snowy Range Ski Area before returning to Rte. 130. At the summit, the **Libby Flats Observation Point,** at the top of Snowy Range Pass (elevation 10,847 ft.), has a wildflower nature walk and an inspiring view of the surrounding alpine landscape. On bright days, delicate alpine sunflowers turn their faces to the sun. Before the road descends, don't miss the Silver Lake outlook, with a gorgeous view of the waters and surrounding area. Keep an eye out for bighorn sheep, pine martens, and yellow-bellied marmots. The challenging **Medicine Bow Trail** (4½ mi., 1600 ft. elevation change) has trailheads at both **Lake Marie** and **Lewis Lake** and climbs through rocky alpine terrain to **Medicine Bow Peak** (12,013 ft.), the highest point in the forest. All 16 of the park's developed **campgrounds** ❶ are only open in summer and have toilets and water, but no hookups or showers. **Sugarloaf** ❶ (16 sites) and **Brooklyn**

Lake ❶ (19 sites) are open July to September and are reservable through the National Recreation Reservation Service. (☎877-444-6777; www.reserve-usa.com. Pit toilets, water provided. Max 14-night stay. Sites $10. Reservation fee $9.) A drive up **Kennaday Peak** (10,810 ft.), Rte. 130 to Rte. 100 and 215, at the end of Rte. 215, grants an impressive view.

Biking and driving are permitted only on designated trails in the high country and on trails below 10,000 ft. The 7 mi. **Corner Mountain Loop,** just west of Centennial Visitors Center, is a roller coaster ride through forests and meadows. In winter, the trails are used for cross-country skiing and snowmobiling. **Brush Creek Visitors Center,** at the west entrance, provides hiking, biking, camping, and bear safety info. (☎326-5562. Open daily mid-May to Oct. 8am-5pm.) **Centennial Visitors Center,** 1 mi. west of Centennial, is at the east entrance. (☎742-6023. Open daily 9am-4pm.) Get cross-country skiing equipment and trail info at the **Cross Country Connection,** 222 S. 2nd St., in Laramie. (☎721-2851. Open M-F 10am-6pm, Sa 9am-5pm, Su noon-4pm. $12 per day.) Downhill ski and snowboard rentals are available at **The Fine Edge,** 1660E N. 4th St. (☎745-4499. Open in winter M-Th 8am-6pm, F-Sa 7am-6:30pm, Su 7:30am-5pm; in summer M-Th 8am-6pm, F-Sa 8am-6:30pm, Su 10am-5pm. Skis $16 per full day, children $12. Snowboards $22/$17; boots $9. $300 credit card or check deposit required for snowboards.) **Area Code:** 307.

MONTANA

If any part of the scenery dominates the Montana landscape more than the pristine mountain peaks and shimmering glacial lakes, it's the sky—welcome to Big Sky country. With 25 million acres of national forest and public lands, Montana's grizzly bears, mountain lions, and pronghorn antelope outnumber the people. Small towns, set against unadulterated mountain vistas, offer a true taste of the Old West. Copious fishing lakes, 500 species of wildlife (not including millions of insect species), and beautiful rivers combine with hot springs and thousands of ski trails to make Montana an American paradise.

🛈 PRACTICAL INFORMATION

Capital: Helena.

Visitor Info: Travel Montana, P.O. Box 200533, Helena 59620 (☎800-847-4868; www.visitmt.com). **National Forest Information,** Northern Region, Federal Bldg., 200 E. Broadway, Box 7669, Missoula 59807 (☎406-329-3511). **Road Conditions:** ☎800-226-ROAD/226-7623. Statewide.

Postal Abbreviation: MT. **Sales Tax:** None.

BILLINGS ☎406

Situated along the Yellowstone River and surrounded by six mountain ranges, including the distinctive sandstone rimrock cliffs to the north, Billings is the largest city in Montana. In 1806, William Clark carved his name on Pompey's Pillar, the only permanent physical evidence of Lewis and Clark's expedition. Following its humble beginnings as a railhead for the Northern Pacific, the city earned the nickname "Magic" due to its instantaneous and phenomenal growth in the 1880s. Today, Billings is the region's undisputed hub of commerce and trade, but the metropolitan flavor doesn't take away from its rich history, ready to be rediscovered.

ROCKY MOUNTAINS

⚡ PRACTICAL INFORMATION. Billings lies on I-90 just west of the I-90/94 junction. Downtown centers around the intersection of N. 27th St. and Montana/Minnesota Ave. **Billings Logan International Airport,** 1901 Terminal Cir., 5 mi. north of downtown, serves the area (☎238-3420; www.flybillings.com). **Greyhound,** 2502 1st Ave. N (☎245-5116; open 24hr.), makes trips to: Bozeman (3hr., 3 per day, $25); Butte (5hr., 3 per day, $37); Helena (7hr., 2 per day, $37). The **MET Transit System** city buses get you around town. (☎657-8218. Buses run M-F 6am-7pm, Sa-Su 8am-5pm. $0.75, seniors $0.25, under 6 free.) **Assistance for Travelers with Disabilities:** Living Independently for Today and Tomorrow (LIFT), ☎800-669-6319 or 259-5181. **Taxi: City Cab** ☎252-8700. **Visitors Info: Billings Area Chamber of Commerce Convention and Visitors Council,** 815 S. 27th St. (☎252-4016 or 800-735-2635; www.billingschamber.com. Open June-Sept. M-Sa 8:30am-6pm, Su 10am-4pm; Oct.-May M-F 8:30am-5pm.) **Internet Access: Parmly Billings Library,** 510 N. Broadway, at 28th St. (☎657-8257. Open M-Th 10am-9pm, F 10am-6pm, Sa 10am-5pm, Su 1-5pm; June-Aug. closed Su.) **Post Office:** 841 S. 26th St. (☎657-5700. Open M-F 8am-5:30pm.) **Postal Code:** 59101. **Area Code:** 406.

⚡ ACCOMMODATIONS. Rooms with reasonable rates line 1st Ave. N and N. 27th St. For a taste of luxury at an unbeatable price, **The Cherry Tree Inn ❷,** 823 N. Broadway, provides an exercise room and sauna, continental breakfast, and HBO. Some rooms have kitchenettes. (☎252-5603 or 800-237-5882. Reservations recommended. Singles $43; doubles $54.) Escape the city for a night at the **Sanderson Inn Bed & Breakfast ❷,** 2038 S. 56th W, 15min. west of downtown on King Ave. W. The delightful Margaret Sanderson maintains a charming country home and cooks up homemade breakfast with fresh fruit. (☎656-3388. 1-2 person rooms $40-50. Cash or check only.) **Big 5 Motel ❷,** 2601 4th Ave. N, has 34 clean, modern rooms with cable TV and some of the lowest rates in town. (☎245-6646 or 888-544-9358. Pets allowed. Singles $33; doubles $44.) Commercial campgrounds and RV parks in Billings are almost as expensive as the indoor lodgings. For a slightly more natural and significantly cheaper camping experience, **Riverside Park ❶,** in Laurel, 13 mi. west on I-90 at Exit 434, lies along the Yellowstone River and has grills, picnic areas, showers, and flush toilets. (Open June-Sept. Sites $10, full RV hookup $15.)

⚡⚡ FOOD AND NIGHTLIFE. A number of budget eateries lies along N. 27th St. and west of downtown on Kings Ave W. The chic **McCormick Cafe ❷,** 2419 Montana Ave., is filled to its copper-coffered ceilings with the lunchtime chatter of Billings's big-wigs and average Joes alike. Along with a sizable selection of heart-healthy salads and sandwiches ($5-6), McCormick prepares delectable Parisian crepes ($2) and works a full espresso and juice bar. (☎255-9555. Open M-F 7am-4pm, Sa 8am-3pm.) Wake up to freshly baked breads, cakes, and muffins at **Stella's Kitchen & Bakery ❷,** 110 N. 29th St. The breakfast combos ($5-6), corned beef hash ($6), and warm white or wheat cinnamon rolls ($1.50) have been saying a cheery good morning to Billings for decades. (☎248-3060. Open M-F 5:30am-5:30pm, Sa 5:30am-4pm, Su 7am-1pm.) People travel for miles across the dusty plains to sink their teeth into their famous $8 pork chop sandwich and ribbon fries at the friendly **Pug Mahon's ❷,** 3011 1st Ave N, where authentic Irish cuisine is the order of the day. (☎259-4190. Open M-Th 11am-10pm, F-Sa 11am-10:30pm, Su 8am-2pm. Bar open M-Sa until 2am.) The **Pickle Barrel ❶,** 1503 13th St. W, piles up hefty 9 in. sandwiches ($5) with names like "Dragon Slayer" and "Bobcat Special," all served with a free pickle from the barrel. (☎248-3222. Open M-Sa 7am-10pm, Su 8am-9pm.)

Vintage record albums cover every inch of the walls at the award-winning **Casey's Golden Pheasant,** 222 N. 28th St. (N. Broadway), where the stage rocks six nights a week with live blues, jazz, rock, and reggae. There is free pool—on blue

ROCKY MOUNTAINS

pool tables—during happy hour. (☎256-5200. Drafts $2-3. Happy hour M-F 5-7pm. Cover $5-20 for weekend bands.) **Scoops Tavern,** 2329 River Woods Dr., along the Sunshine River, was originally built in 1903 in honor of the six Kjev sisters who nurtured injured railroad workers back to health. In keeping with tradition, six $1 drink specials every night draw a rowdy crowd of cowboys, oilmen, and everyday folk. (☎355-8826. Open daily 2pm-2am.)

◙ SIGHTS. The largest event in the state, **MontanaFair,** at MetraPark just east of downtown, is a full-fledged one-week western state fair experience in August. Country-western's top musical performers grace the stage along with buckin' bull rodeos, "Bump-N-Run" demolition derby racing, and Arenacross motorcycling. (☎256-2400; www.montanafair.com. Admission $7, children and seniors $4. Concert tickets $15-25. Rodeo: $12, reserved seating $14, children $8. Bump-N-Run: $14/$20/$8. Arenacross: $14, children $8.) **Little Bighorn Days and Custer's Last Stand Reenactment,** in downtown Hardin, 45 mi. east of Billings on I-90, honors the anniversary of the Battle of Little Bighorn with western-style street dancing, period costume balls, carnivals, and chuckwagon feeds. (☎665-1672; www.custerslaststand.org. Weekend of June 25-26.) The history of the untamed Yellowstone River Valley is preserved at the **Western Heritage Center,** 2822 Montana Ave. Interactive exhibits, from a full-sized teepee to an irrigation head-gate, and over 17,000 artifacts and photos retell the often tragic story of the development of the West. (☎256-6809; www.ywhc.org. Open June-Aug. Tu-Sa 10am-5pm, Su 1-5pm; Sept.-May Tu-Sa 10am-5pm. Free.) Once the living quarters of prehistoric hunters, **Pictograph Cave State Park,** east of Billings at Exit 452 on I-90, then 6 mi. south on Coburn Rd., explores some of the relics, pictographs, and stories they left behind. Bring binoculars for the best views along the ½ mi. trail and don't be scared to enter the spooky "Ghost Cave." A self-guiding trail booklet explains local flora and fauna, many of which can be seen along the trail, along with the cultural aspect of the park. (☎247-2940. Open daily June-Aug. 8am-8pm; May-Sept. 10am-7pm. $5 per vehicle.) On Coburn Rd. along the way to Pictograph Cave, notice **Sacrifice Cliff,** the site of an old Crow Indian village. Legend has it that when a war party returned to find the village here decimated by smallpox, warriors blindfolded their horses and rode them over the cliff to appease the gods and halt the epidemic.

🔁 DAYTRIP FROM BILLINGS: LITTLE BIG HORN. Little Big Horn National Monument, 60 mi. southeast of Billings, off I-90 on the Crow Reservation, marks the site of one of the most dramatic episodes in the conflict between Native Americans and the US government. Here, on June 25, 1876, Sioux and Cheyenne warriors, led by Sioux chiefs Sitting Bull and Crazy Horse, annihilated five companies of the US Seventh Cavalry under the command of Lt. Colonel George Armstrong Custer. White stone graves mark where the US soldiers fell. The exact number of Native American casualties is unknown, since their families and fellow warriors removed the bodies from the battlefield almost immediately. Formerly known as the Custer Battlefield Monument, its renaming signifies the government's admission that Custer's brutal acts against Native Americans merit no glorification. Congress also prescribed that a memorial be built in honor of the Native Americans killed at the battle. This memorial, which the Cheyenne had been working toward since 1925, was finished in September 2002. The **visitors center** has a small movie theater and an electronic map of the battlefield. (☎638-3224; www.nps.gov/libi. Monument and visitors center open daily June-Aug. 8am-9pm; Sept. 8am-6pm; Oct.-May 8am-4:30pm. Entrance $10 per car, $5 per pedestrian.) Rangers offer talks daily in the summer (every hr. 9am-6pm). **Audio tours** ($15) narrating the battle are available. A 1hr. bus tour leaves from the visitors center in the summer. (Daily June-Aug. 9,

ROCKY MOUNTAINS

THE LOCAL STORY

FIRE IN THE SKY

While most people run from wildfires, Mark Wright is part of the elite group of aerial firefighters who jump right on in.

LG: How did you start jumping?

A: I started working for the Helena National Forest as a summer job. Among other things like cleaning picnic tables, cutting brush, and patrolling, one of the things they train you to do is put out fires. So I started out as a young firefighter putting my way through college. The "problem" is that it gets in your blood and you become addicted to it. After 4 years of firefighting through college, I got a teaching degree and ended up continuing to fight fires in my summers off. I've been doing it for the past 27 years.

LG: What does smokejumper training involve?

A: To be a smokejumper, you need recommendations and a minimum of 2 years firefighting experience. Many people apply and only a limited number get selected to go through rookie training, which is over a month long. I would compare it to boot camp. They start their morning with calisthenics, go through daily training, and have to pass physical fitness tests. People wash out at any time, and they need to make a minimum of 15 jumps before they're even allowed in a fire.

LG: What happens in a typical fire?

A: Smokejumpers are initial attack, so we get calls right when

10:30am, noon, 2, 3:30pm. $10, seniors $8, under 12 $5.)

HELENA ☎406

Helena, Montana's capital city, is a successful example of a modern city that has retained its Old West feel. A product of the 1864 gold rush at Last Chance Gulch, Helena has transformed itself from a humble mining camp into a sophisticated city equipped with a symphony, several theaters, and an outdoor pedestrian mall. Halfway between Glacier and Yellowstone National Parks, Helena provides a pleasant stopover for travelers tackling the two, but is an outdoors destination in its own right with hiking, boating, and fishing opportunities.

∏ ACCOMMODATIONS. There aren't many cheap places in Helena to hang your hat, but **Budget Inn Express ❷**, 524 N. Last Chance Gulch, has an attractive downtown location and large, tidy rooms. (☎442-0600 or 800-862-1334. Laundry, cable TV, and kitchenettes. In summer singles $37; doubles $47. In winter $34/$44.) The best deal in town for women, **Helena YWCA ❶**, 501 N. Park Ave., rents private singles with shared bath and use of the full kitchen and laundry facilities. (☎442-8774. Women only. Free Internet access. Key deposit $12. Singles $18.)

The **Helena Campground and RV Park ❶**, 5820 N. Montana Ave., north of Helena just west of I-15, has grassy, shaded tent sites and an outdoor pool and recreation room. (☎458-4714. Laundry and showers. Sites $23, full hookup $26. Cabins $39.) Escape the summer heat at **Moose Creek Campground ❶**, 10 mi. west of Helena on U.S. 12, then 4 mi. southwest on Rimini Rd., which has pleasantly cool, high-elevation forested camping alongside a stream. (Vault toilets, water. Open mid-May to mid-Sept. Sites $6.) Fifteen miles east of Helena, 13 public campgrounds line **Canyon Ferry Reservoir ❶**, popular for both fishing and boating; take either Canyon Ferry Rd. or Rte. 284 from U.S. 12. The campgrounds are open year-round, but can be prohibitively warm for tent campers in the summer months. (7 campgrounds $8 per site. 6 campgrounds free.) The free **Fish Hawk Campground ❶**, on W. Shore Dr., has tent sites and toilets, but no drinking water. The **BOR Canyon Ferry Office**, 7661 Canyon Ferry Rd., has more info. (☎475-3310 or 475-3921.)

⬛⬛ FOOD AND NIGHTLIFE. Local paintings and a forest of records dangling from a graffiti ceiling decorate the ⬛**Staggering Ox ❷**, 400 Euclid Ave., in the Lundy Center. Their patented, award-winning bread is baked in a soup can and constructed into sandwiches with names like "Yo' Momma Osama" ($7) and "Headbanger Hoagie" ($6). The very popular "bread guts" are sold with such sauces as "Camel Spit." (☎ 443-1729. Open M-F 9am-8pm, Sa 10am-8pm, Su 11am-7pm.) Enjoy an authentic taste of southern Europe at ▧**Mediterranean Grill ❹,** 42 S. Park Ave., enhanced by the friendly conversation of the Turkish-born chef and owner. Follow your appetizer of stuffed grape leaves ($6) with an eggplant dish ($12) or the salmon *amaretti* for $16. (☎ 495-1212. Open M-F 11am-2pm and 5-9:30pm, Su 10am-2pm.) In a building that housed "one of the cleanest, most respected bordellos in all Montana" until 1973, the **Windbag Saloon & Grill ❹,** 19 S. Last Chance Gulch, has a long history of hospitality. Today, the locals rave about their excellent service and superb dinners. (☎ 443-9669. Burgers and salads $7-9. Filet mignon $21. Open for M-Th 11am-2pm and 5:30-9:30pm, F 11am-2pm and 5-10pm, Sa 5:30-9:30pm, Su 11:30am-2:30pm.) All the meats, grains, and produce are organic and locally-grown at **No Sweat Cafe ❶,** 427 N. Last Chance Gulch, a popular hangout where whole-wheat pancakes ($4) and delightful egg dishes ($5-6) are the specialties. (☎ 442-6954. Open Tu-F 7am-2pm, Sa-Su 8am-2pm.) **Miller's Crossing,** 52 S. Park Ave., has pool tables, a large dance floor, and live music some nights, including rock, funk, and blues. A special $2.50 brew is always on tap. (☎ 442-3290. Cover $2-5. Open daily 11am-2am.) Drinking starts early at **O'Tooles,** 330 N. Last Chance Gulch, a quintessential Western bar. (☎ 443-9759. Drafts $1. Open daily 8am-2am.)

◨ ⚠ SIGHTS AND OUTDOOR ACTIVITIES. A strategic point from which to begin an exploration of Helena, the **Montana Historical Society Museum,** 225 N. Roberts St., has chronological displays recounting the region's development from pre-history to the present through artifacts, maps, and clothing. Don't miss a stuffed rare white buffalo, and the displays of military gear, including Nazi clothing and medals brought back from WWII by returning American GIs. (☎ 444-2694; www.his.st.mt.us. Open June-Aug. M-W and F-Sa 9am-5pm, Th 9am-8pm; Sept.-May M-F 8am-5pm, Sa 9am-5pm. $3, ages 5-18 $1.) The historical society's popular 1hr. **Last Chance Tour Train** departs in front of the museum and features commentary on the city's historical buildings and sights. (☎ 442-1023. Tours M-Sa May and Sept. 3 per day; June 5 per day; July-Aug. 7 per day. $6, seniors $5.50, ages 4-12 $5.) The **State Capitol** building, 1301 6th Ave., at Montana Ave., has several pieces of notable artwork, including a giant mural by Charles M. Russell depicting the Salish Indians welcoming Lewis and Clark in 1804. Also

the fire is detected and still fairly small. One of the great advantages smokejumpers have is that we are on an airplane above the fire with the door off. We take a good look at the terrain and see what the fire behavior is. People coming from the ground can only see smoke and don't know what they're getting into. Before we even jump out of the plane, we check for safety zones to see which ways we can approach the fire, pinpoint safe jump spots that are close to the fire but not endangering ourselves, and look for routes out of the fire. After we land in parachutes, we pack it up to put in a safe spot. The plane flies over and drops our cargo, which contains chainsaws, tools, water, freeze-dried food, everything we'll need to fight the fire and camp overnight.

LG: What is one of your most memorable smokejumping experiences?

A: This was about 21 years ago. I had just jumped a fire and we had it pretty well whipped. Smoke was coming off the last dying embers and the sun was coming up. As I was wiping the soot off my face, the dispatcher came on the radio and asked, "Is there a smokejumper there named Mark Wright?" I knew immediately what he was going to tell me. I started hooting and hollering as he announced, "Congratulations. You have a healthy baby girl."

note a statue of Jeannette Rankin, the first woman elected to Congress, who voted against entry into both WWI and WWII. (☎444-4789. Tours on the hr. May-Sept. M-Sa 9am-3pm, Su noon-4pm; Oct.-Apr. in even years Sa 10am-2pm, self-guided tours available; Jan.-Apr. in odd years M-Sa 9am-3pm. Free.) The towering spires of the **Cathedral of Saint Helena,** at Lawrence and Warren St., are visible throughout downtown. The marble furnishings and stained glass windows of this neo-Gothic structure emulate Vienna's Votive Church of the Sacred Heart. (☎442-5825. Open June-Aug. M-Sa 7am-9pm; Sept.-May M-Sa 7am-7pm. Guided tours Tu-Th 1pm.) The gold vanished from **Last Chance Gulch** long ago, but today this pedestrian mall offers restaurants, shops, and public artwork. The **Myrna Loy Center,** 15 S. Ewing St., presents foreign films, dance, music, and performance art in the historic former county jail. (☎443-0287.) Take in all of Helena and the surrounding area from the top of **Mount Helena** (5460 ft.); the trail begins from the Adams St. Trailhead, just west of Reeders Alley. Observe the Missouri River as Lewis and Clark did on a 2hr. boat tour of the ⚓**Gates of the Mountains,** 18 mi. north of Helena, off I-15 at Exit 209. Extensive commentary on local plants and birds makes for an educating journey. The boat stops near Mann Gulch, where a 1949 forest fire killed 13 smokejumpers. (☎458-5241. June-Sept. 2-7 tours per day; call for times. $10, seniors $9, ages 4-17 $6.)

BOZEMAN ☎406

Surrounded by world-class hiking, skiing, and fishing, Bozeman has recently become a magnet for outdoor enthusiasts. To Montanans, however, Bozeman remains "that boisterous college town." Cowboy hats and pickup trucks are still popular among students at Montana State University (MSU), but the increasing diversity of the student body reflects the cultural vigor of this thriving community.

🛈 PRACTICAL INFORMATION. I-90 forms the northeast boundary of the city center. Main St. is the primary east-west road, intersecting I-90 at Exit 309. Wilson Ave. and 19th Ave. are the primary north-south routes, with the latter intersecting I-90 at Exit 305. Named streets run east-west; north-south avenues east of Wilson are also named. North-south avenues are numbered west of Wilson. **Greyhound** and **Rimrock Stages,** 1205 E. Main St. (☎587-3110; open M-F 7:30am-5:30pm and 7pm-midnight; Sa-Su 7:30am-noon, 3:30-5:30pm, and 7pm-midnight), both send buses to: Billings (3hr., 3 per day, $25); Butte (2hr., 3 per day, $18); Helena (4hr., 2 per day, $18); Missoula (5hr., 3 per day, $34). **Car Rental: Budget,** 850 Gallatin Field Rd., Ste. 2, at the airport. (☎388-4091 or 800-952-8343. Open daily 7:30am-11pm, or until last flight. Rentals with unlimited mileage from $40 per day. Ages 21-24 $15 per day surcharge. Credit card required.) **Visitor Info: Bozeman Area Chamber of Commerce,** 2000 Commerce Way, at the corner of 19th Ave. and Baxter Ln. (☎586-5421 or 800-228-4224; www.bozemanchamber.com. Open M 9am-5pm, Tu-F 8am-5pm.) **Summer Visitors Center,** 1003 N. 7th Ave. (Open June-Sept. daily 9am-6pm.) **Internet Access: Bozeman Public Library,** 220 E. Lamme St. (☎582-2400. Open in winter M-Th 10am-8pm, F-Sa 10am-5pm, Su 1-5pm; in summer closed Su.) **Post Office:** 32 E. Babcock St. (☎586-2373. Open M-F 9am-5pm.) **Postal Code:** 59715. **Area Code:** 406.

🛏 ACCOMMODATIONS. Budget motels line Main St. and 7th Ave. north of Main. **Bozeman Backpacker's Hostel ❶,** 405 W. Olive St., has a kitchen, living room, three dogs, a lovely porch, co-ed rooms, and the cheapest beds in town. (☎586-4659. Linens included. Laundry facilities. Dorms $15; private rooms with shared bath $34.) The **Blue Sky Motel ❸,** 1010 E. Main St., has comfortable rooms with microwave, fridge, and cable TV. (☎587-2311 or 800-845-9032. Hot tub. Continental breakfast included. Singles $52; doubles $61.) **Langhor Campground ❶**, 11 mi. south of Bozeman on Hyalite Canyon Rd., has shaded sites along Hyalite Creek. For good fishing, **Hood Creek ❶** and **Chisholm ❶** campgrounds, located 6 and 7 mi. farther up the canyon, respectively, are situated on the shores of the stunning Hyalite Reservoir, beneath the high forested peaks of Gallatin National Forest. (Reservations ☎877-444-6777. Open mid-May to mid-Sept. Sites $8.) The **Bear Canyon Campground ❶**, 4000 Bozeman Trail Rd., 4 mi. east of Bozeman at Exit 313 off I-90, has great views of the countryside from the heated outdoor pool. (☎587-1575 or 800-438-1575. Laundry and showers. Open May to mid-Oct. Sites $16, with water and electricity $21, full hookup $26. Each additional person $2.) The **Bozeman Ranger Station**, 3710 Fallon, Ste. C, has more info on camping in the **Gallatin National Forest** (☎522-2520).

❐❚ FOOD AND NIGHTLIFE. Thrifty eateries aimed at the college crowd line W. College near the university. **MacKenzie River Pizza Co. ❸**, 232 E. Main St., is pure Montana, with rough-hewn tree-trunk pillars and murals of cattle herds. The selection of gourmet pizzas includes the "Sequoia," topped with basil pesto, sun-dried tomatoes, artichokes, and almonds. (☎587-0055. 12 in. pizzas $14-17. Open M-Th 11am-10pm, F-Sa 11am-11pm, Su noon-10pm.) **Sweet Pea Bakery and Cafe ❷**, 19 S. Wilson St., cooks healthy gourmet lunch and brunch with artistic flair; dishes like mango chicken salad are around $8. (☎586-8200. Open Tu 7am-3pm, W-Sa 7am-9pm.) **The Cateye Cafe ❷**, 23 N. Tracy Ave., is a downtown diner with a colorful paint job and a menu with a sense of humor, delighting in cats and all who love them. Banana bread french toast ($6.75), sandwiches on "fogatcha" bread ($6-7), and meatloaf and egg breakfasts ($7.50) feed any craving. (☎587-8844. Open M and W-F 7am-2:30pm, Sa-Su 7am-2pm.) **La Parrilla ❷**, 1533 W. Babcock, wraps up just about everything in their giant 1 ft. tortillas ($5-6), including homemade barbecue, fiery jambalaya, organic bison, and fresh seafood. (☎582-9511. Open daily 11am-9pm.) **Montana Harvest**, 31 S. Wilson, has a supply of granola, soy nuts, and other natural and organic foods. (☎585-3777. Open M-Sa 8am-8pm, Su 10am-6pm.)

Get the lowdown on music and nightlife from the weekly *Tributary* or *The BoZone*, found at cafes, bars, and bookstores around town. Locals and travelers thirsty for good beer and great live music head over to the **Zebra Cocktail Lounge**, in the basement at Rouse Ave. and Main St. The large selection of beers and hipster atmosphere draw a young, cool crowd. (☎585-8851. W-Sa DJ or bands. Open daily 8pm-2am.) One of only two non-smoking bars in Bozeman, the **Rocking R Bar**, 211 E. Main St., lives up to its name with hot drink specials every night in a classy atmosphere. (☎587-9355. Free food W-F 5-9pm. Live music W and Sa. Karaoke Th. Open daily 11am-2am.) Sample some of Montana's best brews from a selection of the over 40 on tap at **Montana Ale Works**, 611 E. Main St. This former storage facility for the Northern Pacific Railway Co. now houses six pool tables for serious sharks. (☎587-7700. Open Su-Th 4pm-midnight, F-Sa 4pm-1am.)

◪◪ SIGHTS AND OUTDOOR ACTIVITIES. Get up close and personal with dinosaurs at the **Museum of the Rockies**, 600 West Kagy Blvd., near the university. Dr. Jack Horner (the basis for *Jurassic Park's* Alan Grant) and other paleontologists make this their base for excavating prehistoric remains throughout the West. An exhibit on Lewis and Clark is complemented by outdoor exhibits, including recreations of Mandan and settler villages. (☎994-2251; www.museumoftherockies.org. Open in summer daily 8am-8pm; low-season M-Sa 9am-5pm, Su 12:30-5pm. $9.50, ages 5-18 $6.50.) In an old county jail, **The Gallatin Pioneer Museum**, 317 W.

Main St., offers a look at the gallows and jail cells along with a reconstructed pioneer cabin. (☎522-8122; www.pioneermuseum.org. Open mid-May to mid-Sept. M-Sa 10am-4:30pm; mid-Sept. to mid-May Tu-F 11am-4pm, Sa 1-4pm. Free.)

Surrounded by three renowned trout fishing rivers—Yellowstone, Madison, and Gardiner—the small town of **Livingston,** about 25 mi. east of Bozeman off I-90, is an angler's heaven; the film *A River Runs Through It* was shot here and in Bozeman. Livingston's Main St. features early 20th-century buildings, including bars (with gambling), restaurants, fishing outfitters, and a few modern businesses. **The Bozeman Angler,** 23 E. Main St., leads float and wade trips with expert instruction in fly fishing on the Yellowstone, Gallatin, Madison, and Missouri rivers. (☎800-886-9111; www.bozemanangler.com. 3hr. group lesson $40 per person; full-day lesson $110 per person.) **Dan Bailey's,** 209 W. Park St., sells licenses and rents gear. (☎222-1673 or 800-356-4052. Open in summer M-Sa 8am-7pm; in winter M-Sa 8am-6pm. 2-day fishing license $22, season $67. Rod and reel $10; waders and boots $10.)

The world-class ski area **Big Sky,** 45 mi. south of town on U.S. 191, has over 150 trails and short lift lines. The Lone Peak trams reach an altitude of 11,166 ft. for extreme skiing options. (☎995-5000 or 800-548-4486. Open mid-Nov. to mid-Apr. Full-day ticket $59, college students and ages 11-17 $47, seniors $30. Ski rentals $27-39, juniors $19. Snowboards $33.) More intimate and less expensive than Big Sky, **Bridger Bowl Ski Area,** 15795 Bridger Canyon Rd., 16 mi. northeast of town on Hwy. 86, has trails for a variety of abilities. (☎587-2111 or 800-223-9609. Open early Dec. to early Apr. Full-day ticket $35, seniors $29, ages 6-12 $13. Ski rentals $20, juniors $10. Snowboards $30.) In summer, scenic **lift rides** soar up Big Sky. (Open June to early Oct. daily 9:45am-5pm. $14, seniors $9, under 10 free.) Full suspension mountain bike rentals are also available up top. ($23 per hr., $46 per 8hr.)

Equestrian types gallop at nearby **Big Sky Stables,** on the spur road off U.S. 191, about 2 mi. before Big Sky's entrance. (☎995-2972. Open mid-May to early Oct. $32 per hr., $52 per 2hr. 1-day notice required.) Floating in the warm and shallow **Madison River** is a relaxing and cheap way to pass long summer days. Rent inner tubes ($3 per day) at **Big Boys Toys,** 28670 Norris Rd., west on Main St. 7 mi. from downtown. (☎587-4747. Open daily 8am-6pm. Canoes $25 per day; windgliders $25 per day.) **Yellowstone Raft Co.** shoots the rapids of the Gallatin River, 7 mi. north of the Big Sky area on U.S. 191. Trips meet at the office, between mileposts 55 and 56 on U.S. 191. (☎995-4613 or 800-348-4376. Half-day $39, children $30; full-day $79/$63.)

MISSOULA ☎406

A liberal haven in a largely conservative state, Missoula attracts new residents every day with its revitalized downtown and bountiful outdoors opportunities. Home to the University of Montana, downtown Missoula is lined with bars and coffeehouses spawned by the large student population. Twelve thousand years ago, the town was located at the bottom of a glacial lake; today, four different mountain ranges and five major rivers surround Missoula, supporting skiing during the winter and fly fishing, hiking, and biking during the summer.

⚐ PRACTICAL INFORMATION. Flights stream into the **Missoula International Airport,** 5225 Hwy. 10 W (☎728-4381; www.msoairport.org), 6 mi. west of town. Follow Broadway, which turns into Hwy. 10/200. **Greyhound,** 1660 W. Broadway (☎549-2339; ticket office open M-F 6:15am-4pm and 8pm-midnight, Sa noon-4pm and 9-10pm, Su 1-4pm and 9-10pm), has buses to Bozeman (4½-5½hr., 4 per day, $34) and Spokane (4hr., 3 per day, $37). From the same terminal, **Rimrock Stages** serves Whitefish via St. Ignatius and Kalispell (3½hr., 1 per day, $25) and Helena (4hr., 2 per day, $21). Catch a ride on **Mountain Line City Buses** from the Transfer

Center, at Ryman and Pine St., or at a curbside around town. (☎721-3333. Buses operate M-F 6:45am-8:15pm, Sa 9:45am-5:15pm. $0.85, seniors $0.35, under 18 $0.25.) **Taxi: Yellow Cab** ☎543-6644. **Car Rental: Rent-A-Wreck,** 1905 W. Broadway, provides free transportation to and from the airport and great prices. (☎721-3838 or 800-552-1138. 21+. $29-45 per day; 150 free mi., $0.25 each additional mi.) **Visitor Info: Missoula Chamber of Commerce,** 825 E. Front St. at Van Buren. (☎543-6623; www.missoulachamber.com. Open M-Th 8am-7pm, F 8am-6:30pm, Sa 9am-1pm.) **Internet Access: Missoula Public Library,** 301 E. Main St. (☎721-2665. Open M-Th 10am-9pm, F-Sa 10am-6pm.) **Post Office:** 200 E. Broadway St. (☎329-2222. Open M-F 8am-5:30pm.) **Postal Code:** 59801. **Area Code:** 406.

🏠 **ACCOMMODATIONS.** There are no hostels in Missoula, but there are plenty of inexpensive alternatives along **Broadway.** Rooms at the **City Center Motel ❷,** 338 E. Broadway, have cable TV, fridges, and microwaves. (☎543-3193. May-Sept. singles $45; doubles $48-52. Oct.-Dec. $35/$42.) Downtown, but still in a quiet setting, the **Royal Motel ❷,** 338 Washington, has clean rooms with cable TV, fridges, and microwaves. (☎542-2184. June-Sept. singles $40; doubles $42-46. Oct.-May $32/ $36.) The **Missoula/El-Mar KOA Kampground ❶,** 3450 Tina Ave., just south of Broadway off Reserve St., has everything: a petting zoo, nightly ice-cream socials, a pool, hot tub, mini golf, and laundry facilities. Shaded tent sites are set apart from RVs. It(☎549-0881 or 800-562-5366. 2-person sites $23, with water and electricity $25, full hookup $33. Cabins $40-48. Each additional person $3.)

🍴 **FOOD.** Missoula, the culinary capital of Montana, boasts a number of innovative, delicious, and thrifty eateries. Restaurants and coffeehouses line Higgins Ave., north of the Clark Fork River, downtown. Snag one of the cozy redleather "lovers" nooks upstairs at **The Bridge ❹,** 515 S. Higgins Ave. Enjoy the fresh halibut ($21) or wild salmon ($19), or go for the white or red sauce thincrust pizzas. (☎542-0638. 12 in. pizzas $11-14. Open daily 5-10pm.) Boasting fine espresso and billiards, the hip **Raven Cafe ❷,** 130 E. Broadway, handles heavenly slices of quiche ($3) and black bird pizza pies (10 in. $7-8), as well as delicious breakfasts and decadent desserts. With free Internet access, a fresh jukebox, and plenty of books and magazines, the cafe keeps people sipping coffee for hours. (☎829-8188. Open M-Sa 8am-11pm, Su 8am-3pm.) **Worden's ❶,** 451 N. Higgins Ave., serves sandwiches in three sizes: 4 in. roll ($4.50), 7 in. ($7.50), and 14 in. ($14); alternatively, chow down on the "frito pie" ($4). You can also pick up groceries while munching. (☎549-1293. Open in summer M-Th 8am-10pm, F-Sa 8am-11pm, Su 9am-10pm; in winter M-Th 8am-9pm, F-Sa 8am-10pm, Su 9am-10pm.) **Tipu's ❷,** 115½ S. 4th St. W in the alley, is one of the only all-veggie establishments and the lone Indian restaurant in Montana, serving *samosas* and its own "*curritos.*" (☎542-0622. Lunch buffet $7. Open daily 11:30am-9:30pm.) **Tacos del Sol ❶,** 422 N. Higgins Ave., is the place for cheap eats; get $2 fish tacos or a hefty 14 in. Mission Burrito for under $4. (☎327-8929. Open M-F 11am-7pm.) The **Good Food Store,** 1600 S. 3rd St. W, is home to natural and organic products and produce, including meats, specialty cheeses, wines, and bulk items. (☎541-3663. Open daily 7am-10pm.)

📷🎭 **SIGHTS AND ENTERTAINMENT.** Missoula's hottest sight is the **Aerial Fire Depot and Smokejumper Center,** 5756 W. Broadway, just past the airport, 7 mi. west of town. It's the nation's largest training base for smokejumpers—aerial firefighters who parachute into remote forests and serve as an initial attack against wildfires. Displays and videos recount their heroism and skill. (☎329-4934. Open May-Sept. daily 8:30am-5pm. Tours every hr. 10-11am and 2-4pm, lasting 45-60min.

ROCKY MOUNTAINS

Free; donations accepted.) The **Carousel,** 101 Carousel Dr., in Caras Riverfront Park, is one of the oldest hand-carved carousels in America. (☎549-8382. Open daily June-Aug. 11am-7pm; Sept.-May 11am-5:30pm. $1, seniors and under 19 $0.50, disabled free.) **Out to Lunch,** also in Caras Riverfront Park, offers free performances in the summer along with plenty of food vendors; call the Missoula Downtown Association for more info. (☎543-4238. June-Aug. W 11am-1:30pm.) If you miss "Out to Lunch," the food vendors return Thursday nights for **Downtown Tonight,** which features live music, food, and a beer garden. (☎543-4238. July-Sept. Th 5:30-8:30pm.) Free concerts are also available Wednesday nights with **Bonner Park Concerts,** in Bonner Park. (☎728-2400, ext. 7041. June-Aug. W 8pm.) Stock up on fresh local produce, flowers, and breads at the **Farmers Market,** in Circle Sq. (☎543-4238. Mid-May to mid-Oct. Sa 9am-noon.) The **Western Montana Fair and Rodeo,** held in August, has live music by big names like Brad Paisley and Chris LeDoux, plus a carnival, fireworks, a rodeo, arenacross, and concession booths. (☎256-2422 or 800-366-8538; www.montanafair.com. Open 10am-10pm.)

⬛ NIGHTLIFE. The **Iron Horse Brew Pub,** 501 N. Higgins Ave., always packs a crowd on its large patios, and is popular with fraternity-types. (☎728-8866. Drafts $2. Open daily 11am-2am.) Follow the advice of the "beer coaches" at **The Kettle House Brewing Co.,** 602 Myrtle, one block west of Higgins between 4th and 5th, and "support your local brewery." The Kettle House serves a delectable assortment of beers, including hemp beer—Bongwater Stout. (☎728-1660. Open M-Th 3-9pm, F-Sa noon-9pm; no beer served after 8pm. 2 free samples; then $3-3.25 per pint.) College students swarm the downtown bar area around Front St. and Higgins Ave. during the school year. **Charlie B's,** 420 N. Higgins Ave., draws bikers, farmers, students, and hippies alike. Framed photos of longtime regulars cover the walls. (☎549-3589. Drafts $1.75. Wells $2-3. Open daily 8am-2am.) The *Independent* and *Lively Times,* free at newsstands and cafes, have the lowdown on Missoula's music scene. The *Entertainer,* in the Friday *Missoulian,* has event schedules.

🏔 OUTDOOR ACTIVITIES. Soak your weary feet at the **Lolo Hot Springs,** 35 mi. southwest of Missoula on Hwy 12. The 103-105°F springs were an ancient meeting place for local Native Americans and were frequented by Lewis and Clark in 1805. (☎273-2290 or 800-273-2290. Open daily June-Sept. 10am-10pm; Oct.-May 10am-8pm. $7, under 13 $5.) Farther along Rte. 12 into Idaho are two free natural **hot springs,** Jerry Johnson and Weir. Indulge your sense of history at **Garnet Ghost Town,** Montana's most intact ghost town—well-preserved, but not commercialized. During mining's heyday at the turn of the century, the population reached several thousand. Today it is an eerie reminder of the transience of civilization. (☎329-3914. Take I-90 to Exit 109; follow Hwy. 200 to Mile 22, and turn right on Garnet Range Rd. for 11 miles. Open to most vehicular traffic mid-May to Sept. Snowmobiles are the only form of transportation Jan.-March. Free.)

Parks, recreation areas, and nearby wilderness areas make Missoula an outdoor enthusiast's dream. The bicycle-friendly city is located along both the Trans-America and Great Parks bicycle routes, and all major streets have designated bike lanes. **Open Road Bicycles and Nordic Equipment,** 517 S. Orange St., has bike rentals. (☎549-2453. Open M-F 9am-6pm, Sa 10am-5pm, Su 11am-3pm. Front suspension $3.50 per hr., $18 per day; full suspension $7.50/$35.) **Adventure Cycling,** 150 E. Pine St., is the place to go for info about Trans-America and Great Parks routes. (☎721-1776 or 800-755-2453. Open M-F 8am-5pm.) The **Rattlesnake Wilderness National Recreation Area,** named after the shape of the river (there are no rattlers for miles), 11 mi. northeast of town off Exit 104 on I-90, and the **Pattee Canyon Recreation Area,** 3½ mi. east of Higgins on Pattee Canyon Dr., have excellent biking trails. Contact the **Missoula Ranger District,** Building 24-A at Fort Missoula, for trail info. (☎329-3814. Open M-F 7:30am-4:30pm.) **Missoulians on Bicycle** (www.missoulabike.org) hosts rides and events for cyclists in a fun collegiate atmosphere.

Alpine and Nordic **skiing** keep Missoulians busy during winter. To indulge the Nordic craving, **Pattee Canyon Recreation Area** has groomed trails close to town. **Marshall Mountain** is a great place to learn how to downhill ski, with 480 acres, night skiing, and free shuttles from downtown; take the East Missoula exit from I-90. (☎258-6000. $24 per day, ages 6-12 $19.) Experienced skiers should check out the **Montana Snowbowl,** 12 mi. northwest of Missoula, with a vertical drop of 2600 ft. and over 35 trails. Take the Reserve St. exit off I-90 and follow Grant Creek Rd., then turn left onto Snowbowl Rd. (☎549-9777 or 800-728-2695. Open Nov.-Apr. daily 10am-4:30pm. Full-day $31, seniors and students $18, ages 6-12 $14.)

Floating on rafts and tubes is a favorite local weekend activity. The Blackfoot River, along Rte. 200 east of Bonner, makes a good afternoon float; take I-90 to Exit 109. Call the **Montana State Regional Parks and Wildlife Office,** 3201 Spurgin Rd., for more information about rafting locations. (☎542-5500. Open M-F 8am-5pm.) Rent tubes or rafts from the **Army and Navy Economy Store,** 322 N. Higgins. (☎721-1315. Open M-F 9am-7:30pm, Sa 9am-5:30pm, Su 10am-5:30pm. Tubes $4 per day. Rafts $40 per day, $20 deposit. Credit card required.)

Hiking opportunities abound in the Missoula area. The relatively easy 30min. hike to the "M" (for the U of M, not Missoula) on Mount Sentinel has a tremendous view of Missoula and the surrounding mountains; continue another mile to the top of the mountain (elevation gain 620 ft.). The **Rattlesnake Wilderness National Recreation Area** makes for a great day of hiking; follow Van Buren St. and then Rattlesnake Dr. 4 mi. north from Missoula to the area entrance. Other popular areas include **Pattee Canyon** and **Blue Mountain,** south of town; for Blue Mountain, travel 2 mi. southwest on U.S. 93 and turn right on Blue Mountain Rd. *For* maps ($6) and hiking info, try The **US Forest Service Information Office,** 200 E. Broadway; the entrance is at 200 Pine St. (☎329-3511. Open M-F 7am-4pm.) For equipment rentals, stop by **The Trail Head,** 229 E. Front St. (☎543-6966. Open M-F 9:30am-8pm, Sa 9am-6pm, Su 11am-6pm. Tents $10-14 per day; backpacks $9; sleeping bags $5.)

Missoula is at the heart of Western Montana's **fly fishing** country. The Bitterroot River is the place to catch brown trout, while the Blackfoot River is known for its bull trout. **Fishing licenses** are required and can be purchased from the **Department of Fish, Wildlife, and Parks,** 3201 Spurgin Rd. (☎542-5500), or from local sporting goods stores. (Non-resident license $11 for the first day, each additional day $4.) **Kingfisher,** 926 E. Broadway, offers licenses and pricey guided fishing trips. Their free weekly fishing reports are printed in the *Missoula Independent.* (☎721-6141 or 888-542-4911. Open daily June-Aug. 6am-8pm; Sept.-May 9am-5pm.)

FROM MISSOULA TO GLACIER

St. Ignatius Campground and Hostel ❶, off U.S. 93 at Airport Rd. in **Saint Ignatius** (look for the camping sign), is an eco-friendly structure built into a hillside, made from recycled tires and aluminum cans. The hostel rents ski equipment and mountain bikes ($11 per day) and is a good blasting-off point for exploring the backcountry. (☎745-3959. Showers, laundry, and kitchenette. Co-ed rooms. Sites for 1 $10; for 2 $12. Cots under a teepee $10. Dorms $15.) **RimRock Stages** (☎745-3501) buses stop ½ mi. away in St. Ignatius, at the Malt Shop on Blaine St.

Beneath the towering peaks of Mission Mountain Range, **St. Ignatius Mission,** in St. Ignatius, is home to the first Jesuit mission in the northwest, built in 1854 by Native Americans. The original log dormitories are still intact, as is the mission church. Inside, 58 bold murals by Joseph Carignano depict holy scenes and images of St. Ignatius Loyola, the mission's namesake. (☎745-2768. Open daily

8am-8pm. Free.) The **National Bison Range** was established in 1908 in an effort to save the dwindling bison population from extinction. At one time 30-70 million roamed the plains, but the population dropped to less than 1000 due to over-hunting. The 19,000-acre range is home to 350-500 bison as well as deer, prong-horn, elk, bighorn sheep, and mountain goats. The 2hr. **Red Sleep Mountain** self-guided tour is a 19 mi. drive on steep gravel roads and offers a spectacular view of the Flathead Valley and glimpses of wildlife, though binoculars are helpful. Not to be missed is the annual October roundup. To access the range, travel 40 mi. north of Missoula on U.S. 93, then 5 mi. west on Rte. 200, and 5 mi. north on Rte. 212. (☎ 644-2211. Visitors center open mid-May to Oct. M-F 8am-7pm, Sa-Su 9am-6pm; Nov. to mid-May M-F 8am-4:30pm. Red Sleep Mountain drive open mid-May to mid-Oct. daily 7am-7pm. $4 per vehicle.) With displays of old post-ers, uniforms, vintage cars, and motorcycles, the ▨**Miracle of America Museum,** 58176 U.S. 93, at the southern end of Polson, houses one of the country's great-est collections of Americana. A general store, saddlery, barber shop, soda foun-tain, and gas station sit among the memorabilia. (☎ 883-6804. Open June-Sept. daily 8am-8pm; Oct.-May M-Sa 8am-5pm, Su 2-6pm. $3, ages 3-12 $1.) Fresh fruit and fish stands line **Flathead Lake,** on U.S. 93 between Polson and Kalispell, the largest natural lake west of the Mississippi.

WATERTON-GLACIER PEACE PARK

Waterton-Glacier transcends international boundaries to encompass one of the most strikingly beautiful portions of the Rockies. The massive Rocky Mountain peaks span both parks, providing sanctuary for many endangered bears, bighorn sheep, moose, mountain goats, and gray wolves. Perched high in the northern Rockies, Glacier is sometimes called the "Crown of the Continent," and the high alpine lakes and glaciers shine like jewels.

▨ PRACTICAL INFORMATION

Technically one park, Waterton-Glacier is actually two distinct areas: the small **Waterton Lakes National Park** in Alberta, and the enormous **Glacier National Park** in Montana. There are several **border crossings** nearby: **Piegan/Carway,** at U.S. 89 (open daily 7am-11pm); **Roosville,** on U.S. 93 (open 24hr.); and **Chief Mountain,** at Rte. 17 (open daily June-Aug. 7am-10pm; mid- to late May and Sept. 9am-6pm). The fastest way to Waterton is to head north along the east side of Glacier, entering Canada through Chief Mountain. Since snow can be unpredictable, the parks are usually in full operation only from late May to early September—check conditions in advance. The *Waterton-Glacier Guide,* provided at any park entrance, has dates and times of trail, campground, and border crossing openings. To find out which park areas, hotels, and campsites will be open when you visit, contact the **Park Headquarters,** Waterton Lakes National Park, Waterton Park, AB T0K 2M0 (☎ 403-859-2224), or **Glacier National Park,** West Glacier, MT 59936 (☎ 406-888-7800). Mace and firewood are not allowed into Canada.

GLACIER NATIONAL PARK ☎406

⌐ TRANSPORTATION

Amtrak (☎226-4452) traces a dramatic route along the southern edge of the park. The station in West Glacier is staffed mid-May to September, but the train still stops there in the winter. Trains chug daily to: East Glacier (1½hr., $14); Seattle (14hr., $117); Spokane (6hr., $46-59); Whitefish (30min., $7-8). Amtrak also runs from East Glacier to Chicago (32hr., $152-198). **Rimrock Stages** (☎800-255-7655; www.rimrocktrailways.com), the only bus line that nears the park, stops in Kalispell at the Kalispell Bus Terminal, 3794 U.S. 2 E, and goes to Billings (8hr., 1 per day, $59-82) and Missoula (3hr., 1-2 per day, $21-23). A car is the most convenient mode of transport, particularly within the park. **Glacier Park, Inc.'s** (☎892-2525; www.glacierparkinc.com) famous red jammer buses run tours on Going-to-the-Sun Rd. (4hr. tours $25, 6hr. $45; children half-price.) **Sun Tours** offers tours from East Glacier and St. Mary. (☎226-9220 or 800-786-9220. All-day tour from East Glacier $55, from St. Mary $40.) Shuttles for hikers ($8 per segment, under 12 $4) roam the length of Going-to-the-Sun Rd. from early July to early September; schedules are available at visitors centers or at www.nps.gov/glac/shuttles.htm.

▟ ORIENTATION

There are few roads in Glacier, and the locals like it that way. Glacier's main thoroughfare is the **Going-to-the-Sun Road,** which connects the two primary points of entry, West Glacier and St. Mary. **U.S. 2** skirts the southern border of the park and is the fastest route from Browning and East Glacier to West Glacier. At the "Goat Lick," about halfway between East and West Glacier, mountain goats traverse steep cliffs to lap up the natural salt deposits. **Route 89** heads north along the eastern edge of the park past St. Mary. Those interested in visiting the northwestern section of the park can either take the unpaved **Outside North Fork Road** and enter through Polebridge or brave the rough, pothole-ridden **Inside North Fork Road,** which takes an hour longer. While most of Glacier is primitive backcountry, a number of villages provide lodging, gas, and food: St. Mary, Many Glacier, and East Glacier in the east, and West Glacier, Apgar, and Polebridge in the west.

▟ PRACTICAL INFORMATION

The park's **admission fee** is $20 per car per week, $10 for pedestrians and cyclists; yearly passes $25. Knowledgeable rangers at each of the three **visitors centers** give the inside scoop on campsites, day-hikes, weather, flora, and fauna. **Saint Mary** guards the east entrance of the park. (☎732-7750. Open daily July 9am-9pm; May-June and Sept. 8am-5pm.) **Apgar** is located at the west entrance. (☎888-7939. Open daily late June to Aug. 8am-7pm; May-June and Sept. 9am-5pm.) A third visitors center graces **Logan Pass,** on the Going-to-the-Sun Rd. (Open daily July-Aug. 9am-7pm; Sept. 9am-4:30pm; June 9:30am-4:30pm.) The **Many Glacier** ranger station can also answer important questions. (Open daily mid-May to mid-Sept. 8am-5pm.)

Visitors planning overnight backpacking trips must obtain the necessary **backcountry permit.** With the exception of the **Nyack/Coal Creek** camping zone, all backcountry camping must be at designated campsites equipped with pit toilets, tent sites, food preparation areas, and food hanging devices. (June-Sept. camping $4 per person per night, ages 9-16 $2; Oct.-May free. For an additional $20, reservations are accepted beginning in mid-Apr. for trips between June 15 and Oct. 31.) Reservations can be made in person at the Apgar Permit Center, St. Mary Visitors

ROCKY MOUNTAINS

Center, Many Glacier Ranger Station, and Polebridge, or by writing to Backcountry Reservation Office, Glacier National Park, West Glacier, MT 59936. Pick up a free *Backcountry Camping Guide* from visitors centers or the **Backcountry Permit Center,** next to the visitors center in Apgar, which also has valuable info for those seeking to explore Glacier's less-traveled areas. (☎888-7857. Open daily July 7am-4pm; May-June and Sept. 8am-4pm.) **Medical Services: Kalispell Regional Medical Center,** 310 Sunny View Ln. (☎752-5111), north of Kalispell off Rte. 93. **Post Office:** 110 Going-to-the-Sun Rd., in West Glacier. (☎888-5591. Open M-F 8:30am-12:30pm and 1:30-4:45pm.) **Postal Code:** 59936. **Area Code:** 406.

ACCOMMODATIONS

Staying indoors within Glacier is expensive, but several affordable options lie just outside the park boundaries. On the west side of the park, the small, electricity-less town of ◪**Polebridge** provides access to Glacier's remote and pristine northwest corner. From Apgar, take Camas Rd. north, then a right onto the poorly-marked gravel Outside North Fork Rd., just past a bridge over the North Fork of the Flathead River. (Avoid Inside North Fork Rd.—your shocks will thank you.) From Columbia Falls, take Rte. 486 N. To the east, inexpensive lodging is just across the park border in **East Glacier. Glacier Park, Inc.** (☎756-2444; www.glacierparkinc.com) handles reservations for all in-park lodging.

◪ **North Fork Hostel,** 80 Beaver Dr. (☎888-5241; www.nfhostel.com), in Polebridge; follow the signs through town. Wooden walls and kerosene lamps are reminiscent of a hunting retreat. Hot showers and fully-equipped kitchen, but no flush toilets. During the winter, wood-burning stoves warm frozen fingers after skiing or snowshoeing, and thick quilts keep guests warm at night. Internet access $2 per 20min. Call ahead for pickup from the West Glacier Amtrak station ($30-35). Canoes $20 per day; mountain bikes $15 per day; snowshoes $5 per day; nordic skis $5 per day. Showers $4 for non-lodgers. Linen $2. Check-in by 10pm. Check-out noon. Call ahead, especially in winter. Teepees $10 per person; dorms $15, $12 after 2 nights; cabins $30; log homes $65. ❶

Brownies Grocery (HI), 1020 Rte. 49 (☎226-4426), in East Glacier Park. Reception is in the grocery store; the hostel occupies the 2nd fl. Internet access $1.75 per 15min. Kitchen, showers, linens, laundry, and a stunning view. Key deposit $5. Check-in by 9pm; late arrivals call ahead. Check-out 10am. Reservations recommended; credit card required. Open May-Sept., weather permitting. Tent sites $10. Dorms $13, nonmembers $16; doubles $26/$29; room for 4-6 $38/$41. Extra bed $5. ❶

Backpacker's Inn Hostel, 29 Dawson Ave. (☎226-9392), just east of the East Glacier Amtrak station and behind Serrano's Mexican Restaurant, has 14 clean but narrow beds. Hot showers. No kitchen. Sleeping bags $1. Open May-Sept. Rooms $10; private room with queen-sized bed and full linen $20 for 1 person, $30 for 2. ❶

Swiftcurrent Motor Inn (☎732-5531), in Many Glacier Valley, is one of the few budget motels in the area. All cabins are shared bath. Open early June to early Sept. 1-bedroom cabins $43, 2-bedroom $53. ❸

FOOD

Polebridge Mercantile Store (☎888-5105), on Polebridge Loop Rd. ¼ mi. east of N. Fork Rd., has homemade pastries ($1-3) as splendid as the surrounding peaks. Gas, gifts, groceries, and pay phones available. Open daily June-Sept. 8am-9pm; Oct.-May 8am-6pm. ❶

Northern Lights Saloon (☎888-5669), right next to the Polebridge Mercantile. The friendly staff and patrons make this saloon an excellent place to order cheeseburgers ($5-6) and Montana-brewed pints ($3) while sitting on a tree trunk bar stool. Kitchen open June-Sept. M-Sa 4-9pm, Su 9am-noon and 4-9pm; bar open until midnight. ❶

Whistle Stop Restaurant (☎226-9292), in East Glacier next to Brownies Grocery. Sample homemade delicacies at this restaurant best known for unbelievable deep-fried, huckleberry-injected french toast ($7). Open daily mid-May to mid-Sept. 7am-9pm. ❷

Park Cafe (☎732-4482), in St. Mary on Rte. 89, just north of the park entrance, provides sustenance to those who dare to cross the Going-to-the-Sun Road. Incredible homemade pies $2.75 per slice. "Hungry Hiker" special (2 eggs with hash browns and toast) $5. Vegetarian Caribbean burrito $6. Open daily May-Sept. 7am-10pm. ❶

🎿 HIKING

Most of Glacier's spectacular scenery lies off the main roads and is accessible only by foot. An extensive trail system has something for everyone, from short, easy day-hikes to rigorous backcountry expeditions. Stop by one of the visitors centers for maps with day-hikes. *Beware of bears and mountain lions, and ask the rangers about wildlife activity in the area in which you plan to hike.*

Avalanche Lake (4 mi. round-trip, 3hr.) is a breathtaking trail and by far the most popular day-hike in the park. Starting north of Lake McDonald on Going-to-the-Sun Rd., this moderate hike climbs 500 ft. to picture-perfect panoramas.

Trail of the Cedars (¾ mi. loop, 20min.) begins at the same trailhead as Avalanche Lake and is an easy nature walk that also has a shorter, wheelchair-accessible hike.

Numa Ridge Lookout (12 mi. round-trip, 9hr.) starts from the Bowman Lake Campground, northeast of Polebridge. After climbing 2930 ft., this challenging hike ends with sweeping vistas of Glacier's rugged northwest corner.

Grinnell Glacier Trail (11 mi. round-trip, 7hr.) passes within close proximity of several glaciers and follows along Grinnell Point and Mt. Grinnell, gaining a steady and moderate 1600 ft. Trailhead at the Many Glacier Picnic Area.

Hidden Lake Nature Trail (3 mi. round-trip, 2hr.), beginning at the Logan Pass Visitors Center, is a short and modest 460 ft. climb to a lookout of Hidden Lake and a chance to stretch your legs while winding along the Going-to-the-Sun Rd.

🏞 OUTDOOR ACTIVITIES

BIKING AND HORSEBACK RIDING

Opportunities for bicycling are limited and confined to roadways and designated bike paths; cycling on trails is strictly prohibited. Although the Going-to-the-Sun Rd. is a popular **bike route,** only experienced cyclists with appropriate gear and legs of titanium should attempt this grueling ride; the sometimes nonexistent shoulder of the road can create hazardous situations. From mid-June to August, bike traffic is prohibited 11am-4pm from the Apgar campground to Sprague Creek and eastbound (uphill) from Logan Creek to Logan Pass. The Inside North Fork Rd., which runs from Kintla Lake to Fish Creek on the west side of the park, is good for **mountain biking,** as are the old logging roads in the Flathead National Forest. Ask at a visitors center for more details. **Equestrian** explorers should check to make sure trails are open; there are steep fines for riding on closed trails. **Trail rides** from **Mule Shoe Outfitters** (www.mule-shoe.com; open May to early Sept.; $47) are available at Many Glacier (☎732-4203) and Lake McDonald (☎888-5121).

BOATING

The **Glacier Park Boat Co.** (☎257-2426; www.glacierparkboats.com) provides **boat tours** that explore all of Glacier's large lakes and surrounding peaks. Tours leave from: **Lake McDonald** (☎888-5727; 1hr., 4 per day, $10); **Many Glacier** (☎732-4480; 1¼hr., $12); **Rising Sun**, at St. Mary Lake (☎732-4430; 1½hr., 5 per day, $11); **Two Medicine** (☎226-4467; 45min., 5 per day, $9.50). Children ages 4-12 ride for half price. The tours from Two Medicine, Rising Sun, and Many Glacier provide access to Glacier's backcountry, and there are sunset cruises from Rising Sun and Lake McDonald. You can rent **rowboats** ($10 per hr.) at Lake McDonald, Many Glacier, Two Medicine, and Apgar; **canoes** ($10 per hr.) at Many Glacier, Two Medicine, and Apgar; **kayaks** ($10 per hr.) at Apgar and Many Glacier; and **outboards** ($17 per hr.) at Lake McDonald and Two Medicine. **Glacier Raft Co.**, in West Glacier, leads trips down the middle fork of the Flathead River. (☎888-5454 or 800-235-6781. Half-day $40, under 13 $30; full-day trip with lunch $65/$48.)

FISHING

No permit is needed to **fish** in the park, and limits are generally high, but some areas are restricted, and certain species may be catch-and-release. Pick up *Fishing Regulations*, available at visitors centers. Ellen Wilson Lake, Gunsight Lake, and Lake Elizabeth are good places to sink a line. On Blackfoot land a special permit is needed, and everywhere else in Montana a state permit is required.

BROWNING

The center of the **Blackfeet Indian Reservation,** Browning, 13 mi. east of East Glacier, provides a glimpse into the past and present of Native American life. The **Museum of the Plains Indian,** at the junction of U.S. 2 and 89 W, displays traditional clothing, artifacts, and crafts. (☎338-2230. Open daily June-Sept. 9am-4:45pm; Oct.-May M-F 10am-4:30pm. $4, ages 6-12 $1; Oct.-May free.) During **North American Indian Days** (during the second week in July), Native Americans from the surrounding area gather for a celebration that includes tribal dancing, a rodeo, and a parade. Call **Blackfeet Planning** (☎338-7406) for details.

WATERTON LAKES NATIONAL PARK, ALBERTA ☎403

Only a fraction of the size of its Montana neighbor, Waterton Lakes offers spectacular scenery and activities without the summer crowds that plague Glacier. The town of Waterton is a genuine alpine town; bighorn sheep and mule deer frequently wander down the surrounding slopes, causing unexpected traffic delays.

◪ PRACTICAL INFORMATION. Admission to the park in summer is CDN$5 per day, seniors CDN$4.25, ages 6-12 CDN$2.50, groups of up to seven people CDN$13. The only road from Waterton's park entrance leads 5½ mi. south to **Waterton Park.** En route, stop at the **Waterton Lakes Visitors Center,** 5 mi. inside the park on Rte. 5, for a schedule of events and hikes. (☎859-5133. Open daily mid-May to Oct. 8am-7pm.) In winter, pick up info at **Park Administration,** 215 Mt. View Rd. (☎859-2224. Open M-F 8am-4pm.) Although businesses in the park accept US dollars, each has its own currency exchange rate. To get the most Canadian for the US dollar, exchange money at **Waterton Visitor Services** on Mt. View Rd. in Tamarack Sq., which often has the best rate. (☎859-2378; www.watertonvisitorservices.com. Open daily July-Aug. 8am-6:30pm; May-June and Sept.-Oct. usually 8am-6pm.) **Pat's Gas and Cycle Rental,** Mt. View Rd., Waterton, rents bikes. (☎859-2266. Path bikes CDN$7 for 1st hr., CDN$5 each additional hr., CDN$34

ROCKY MOUNTAINS

per day; full suspension mountain bikes CDN$11/$45.) **Post Office:** In Waterton on Windflower Ave. at Fountain. (☎859-2294. Open M-F 8:30am-4:30pm.) **Postal Code:** T0K 2M0. **Area Code:** 403.

EMERGENCY INFORMATION
Waterton Lakes lacks ☎911 service. In a park emergency, call the warden, ☎589-2636. For town emergencies, call the police, ☎859-2244. The nearest hospitals are in Cardston (☎653-4411) or Pincher Creek (☎627-3333).

ACCOMMODATIONS AND FOOD. Camping in the park is very affordable. **Belly River ❶,** outside the park entrance on Chief Mountain Hwy. 3 mi. north of the border, has scenic, uncrowded primitive sites with pit toilets and water. (☎859-2224. Open mid-May to mid-Sept. Sites CDN$10.) **Crandell ❶,** in a forest area on the road to Red Rock Canyon, has flush toilets and running water but no showers. (Open mid-May to late Sept. Sites CDN$13.) Camp with 100 of your best RV pals at **Townsite ❶** in Waterton Park, which has showers and a lakeside vista, but no privacy. The satisfactory walk-in sites are usually the last to fill. (Open mid-Apr. to late Oct. Walk-in sites CDN$19; sites CDN$22, full hookup CDN$30.) **Backcountry camping** requires a permit from the visitors center. Campsites are rarely full, and several, including **Crandell Lake ❶,** are less than an hour's hike from the trailhead. (☎859-5133. Permit CDN$6 per person per night. Reserve up to 90 days in advance for an additional CDN$10.) For indoor lodging, reserve one of the 21 comfy beds at the **Waterton Alpine Hostel (HI) ❶,** in the Waterton Lakes Lodge. (☎859-2150 or 888-985-634. Discounted rate to fitness room and pool next door. Laundry and kitchen. CDN$31, nonmembers CDN$35.) **Peace Park Pitas ❷,** on the corner of Cameron Falls Dr. and Windflower Ave., rolls up sandwiches (CDN$7) and bakes pita pizzas for CDN$7. (☎859-2259. Internet access $0.30 per min. Open daily 10am-10pm. Cash only.) The the 9 in. subs at **The Big Scoop ❶,** on Waterton Ave., are a steal at CDN$5. (☎859-2346. Open May-Oct. M-Sa 10am-10pm, Su 1:30-10pm.)

OUTDOOR ACTIVITIES. Waterton Lakes has 120 mi. of trails of varying difficulty. In addition to exploring the snow-capped peaks, many of these trails link up with the trail network of Glacier National Park. The **Hiker Shuttle** runs from Tamarack Village Sq., in town, to many trailheads. (☎859-2378. Reservations strongly recommended. Around CDN$10.) **Waterton Lakeshore Trail** (8 mi., 4hr.) extends the length of the western shore of Upper Waterton Lake, from Waterton townsite to Goat Haunt, MT, and affords great views of the surrounding peaks. At the trail's end, the **Waterton Inter-Nation Shoreline Cruise Co.** will shuttle hikers back to Waterton (CDN$13 one-way). The cruise company will also ferry visitors to the trailhead for the popular **Crypt Lake Trail** (10½ mi. round-trip, 2297 ft. elevation gain, 5-6hr.), which trickles past waterfalls in a narrow canyon, through a 65 ft. natural tunnel, and, after 3¾ mi., arrives at the icy green Crypt Lake, straddling the international border. The Waterton Marina also runs a 2hr. boat tour of Upper Waterton Lake. (☎859-2362. Open mid-May to mid-Sept. Crypt Lake water taxi: departs Waterton 9 and 10am; returns from Crypt Landing 4 and 5:30pm. Round-trip CDN$13, ages 4-12 CDN$6.50. Tour: CDN$26, ages 13-17 CDN$13, ages 4-12 CDN$9.) Gear is available at **Waterton Visitor Services** (see **Practical Information,** above). Horses are allowed on many trails. **Alpine Stables,** ¾ mi. north of the townsite, conducts trail rides. (☎859-2462; www.alpinestables.com. Open May-Sept. 9am-5pm. CDN$25.)

Fishing in Waterton requires a **license,** available from area park offices, campgrounds, warden stations, and service stations (CDN$7 per day, CDN$24 per year, good in all Canadian national parks). Lake trout cruise the depths of Cameron and

Waterton Lakes, while pike prowl the weedy channels of Maskinonge. Most of the backcountry lakes and creeks support rainbow and brook trout. There are many fish in the creeks that spill from Cameron Lake, just east of the parking lot, and Crandell Lake, a 1 mi. hike. Rent rowboats, paddleboats, kayaks, or canoes at **Cameron Lake Boat Rentals.** (☎859-2396. Open daily June 15-Sept. 15 7:30am-7:30pm. CDN$22 first hr. for 2 people, CDN$17 each additional hr. Cash only.)

IDAHO

The Rocky Mountains divide the state of Idaho into three distinct regions, each with its own natural aesthetic. Northern Idaho possesses the greatest concentration of lakes in the western US, interspersed with lush green valleys and rugged mountain peaks. In central Idaho, ski slopes, hiking trails, and hot springs span across the semi-arid landscape. To the southeast, world-famous potatoes are cultivated in valleys rich with volcanic sediment. With miles of untouched national forest and wilderness, Idaho has seen little change since 1805, when Lewis and Clark first laid eyes on the state as they crossed the Continental Divide at Lemhi Pass.

◪ PRACTICAL INFORMATION

Capital: Boise.

Visitor Info: Idaho Department of Commerce, 700 W. State St., P.O. Box 83720, Boise 83720 (☎208-334-2470 or 800-842-5858; www.visitid.org). **State Parks and Recreation Dept.,** 5657 Warm Springs Ave., Boise 83712 (☎334-4199). **Idaho Outfitters and Guide Association,** P.O. Box 95, Boise 83702 (☎800-494-3246; www.ioga.org). Open in summer M-F 6am-5pm.

Postal Abbreviation: ID. **Sales Tax:** 6%. **Area Code:** 208.

BOISE   ☎208

Built along the banks of the Boise River, Idaho's surprisingly cosmopolitan capital straddles the boundary between desert and mountains. A network of parks protects the natural landscape of the river banks, creating a greenbelt perfect for walking, biking, or skating. Most of the city's sights cluster in the ten-block area between the capitol and the river, making Boise supremely navigable. A revitalized downtown offers a vast array of ethnic cuisine and has a thriving nightlife.

◪ **ORIENTATION AND PRACTICAL INFORMATION.** The pedestrian-friendly **Grove** is Boise's town plaza. Its brick walkway extends along 8th St. between Main and Front St., the two primary downtown thoroughfares. Front St. becomes Hwy. 184 at its west end. **Greyhound,** 1212 W. Bannock (☎343-3681; open daily 5:30am-9pm and 11pm-2:30am), a few blocks west of downtown, runs to: Portland (11hr., 4 per day, $48); Salt Lake City (7hr., 4 per day, $47); Seattle (14hr., 5 per day, $47). **Boise Urban Stages** (the **BUS**) has several routes throughout the city. (☎336-1010. Maps available at the visitors center. Buses operate M-F 5:15am-7:40pm, Sa 7:45am-6:10pm. M-F $0.75, ages 6-18 $0.50, over 59 $0.35; Sa all fares $0.35.) **McU's Sports,** 822 W. Jefferson St., rents outdoor gear and offers hiking tips. (☎342-7734. Open M-Th and Sa 9:30am-6pm, F 9:30am-7pm, Su 11am-5pm. In-line skates $11 for 3hr., $16 for 8hr. Mountain bikes $17 per half-day, $27 per day.) McU's also has a **ski shop** at 2314 Bogus Basin Rd. (☎336-2300. Ski equipment $16 per day, children $13.) **Visitor Info:**

Downtown Boise Visitors Center, 245 8th St., at Boise Centre on the Grove. (☎344-5338. Open M-F 10am-4pm, Sa 10am-2pm.) **Internet Access: Boise Public Library,** 715 S. Capitol Blvd. (☎384-4076. Open M-Th 10am-9pm, F 10am-6pm, Sa 10am-5pm; June-Sept. also open Su noon-5pm.) **Post Office:** 750 W. Bannock St. (☎331-0037. Open M-F 8:30am-5pm.) **Postal Code:** 83702. **Area Code:** 208.

⌂ ACCOMMODATIONS. Inexpensive motels bunch around Exit 53 of I-84, near the airport. A recent addition to the town of Nampa, **▩Hostel Boise (HI) ❶,** 17322 Can-Ada Rd., is 15-20min. from downtown Boise. Take Exit 38 off I-84 W and turn right onto Garrity Blvd., which turns into Can-Ada Rd. This country-style home has mountain views and evening campfires. (☎467-6858. Airport pick-up or drop-off $10. Internet access $1 per 20min. Linen $1.50. 3-night max. stay. Check-in 5-10:30pm. Dorms $14, nonmembers $17; private rooms $31-35.) For all the comforts of home at an unbeatable price, **▩Bond Street Motel Apartments ❷,** 1680 N. Phillippi St., right off Fairview Ave., rents out beautiful, fully furnished studios and two-story one-bedroom apartments with full kitchens stocked with everything you need—even the kitchen sink. (☎322-4407 or 800-545-5345. Office open M-F 8am-5pm. Reservations recommended. Studio $44; 1-bedroom $50. Lower weekly rates available.) The newly renovated **University Inn ❸,** 2360 University Dr., next to Boise State University, has cable TV, continental breakfast, and a free airport shuttle. The lovely courtyard holds an outdoor pool and jacuzzi. (☎345-7170 or 800-345-7170. Singles $50-58; doubles $55-65.) The **Boise National Forest Office/Bureau of Land Management,** 1387 S. Vinnell Way, provides info on Boise's RV-oriented campgrounds. (☎373-4007. Open M-F 7:45am-4:30pm.) To escape the city heat, head to the mountains to **Willow Creek Campground ❶,** 16 mi. east on Hwy. 21, then 23 mi. on Forest Rd. 268, which has good fishing. (Water, vault toilets. Sites $12.) Farther up Hwy. 21, 2½ mi. south of Idaho City, **Grayback Gulch Campground ❶** has higher-elevation forested sites. (Water, vault toilets. Open May-Oct. Sites $10.)

◪▤ FOOD AND NIGHTLIFE. Boise offers much more than spuds for hungry budget travelers. The downtown area, centered around **8th** and **Main Street,** bustles with lunchtime delis, coffeeshops, ethnic cuisine, and several stylish bistros. **▩ Moon's Kitchen ❶,** 815 W. Bannock St., a hopping vintage diner that has blended malts ($4) and heaping chili burgers. (☎385-0472. Breakfast $4.50-7. Burgers $6-8. Open M-F 7am-3pm, Sa 8am-3:30pm, Su 9am-2pm.) **Gernika Basque Pub & Eatery ❷,** 202 S. Capitol Blvd., is the place to taste the unique local Basque cuisine. Down a glass of *sagardoa,* a hard, natural Basque cider, while enjoying sandwiches of pork loin ($7.50), lamb ($7.75), or *chorizo* ($6.25). Finish off with Basque-style rice pudding for $2. (☎344-2175. Open M 11am-11pm, Tu-Th 11am-midnight, F-Sa 11am-1am.) For fresh and creative vegetarian food, juice, and smoothies, try **Kulture Klatsch ❷,** 409 S. 8th St. (☎345-0452. Breakfasts $4-8. Lunch specials $6-8. Dinners $8-11. Live music Tu-Th 8-10pm, F-Sa 9-11pm, Su 11am-1pm including jazz, classical guitar, folk, and rock. Open M 7am-3pm, Tu-Th 7am-10pm, F 7am-11pm, Sa 8am-11pm, Su 8am-3pm.) **Zeppole Baking Company ❶,** 217 N. 8th St., puts together gourmet sandwiches ($2-3) on fresh-baked bread, including a great walnut michette. (☎345-2149. Lunch combos $4-5. Open M-Sa 7am-5pm, Su 7am-4pm.)

Upstairs at **The Balcony Club,** 150 N. 8th St., #226, one block from the Grove, DJs spin nightly with 10 TVs surrounding the dance floor. All kinds of people gather at this gay-friendly bar to dance, relax on the outdoor terrace, and play pool. (☎336-1313. Happy hour daily 2-7pm. 21+. Cover F-Sa $3. Open daily 2pm-2am.) Musicians regularly perform on Main St., while vendors from nearby restaurants hawk food and beer. Cheap drinks and nightly live music draws locals to the classy **Blues Bouquet,** 1010 Main St. (☎345-6605. Free swing lessons M 8pm. $1-2 drink specials every night. 21+. Cover F-Sa nights $5. Open M-F 1pm-2am, Sa-Su 8pm-2am.)

◙ **SIGHTS.** The logical starting point for exploring Boise is the beautiful **Julia Davis Park** (☎384-4240), at Myrtle and Capitol Blvd., with paddleboating, a bandshell featuring free summer entertainment, extensive rose gardens, and several of Boise's most popular museums. The **Boise Tour Train and River Float** begins and ends in the parking lot at the park, covering about 75 city sights in 1¼hr. Train tours can be followed by relaxing raft floats down the Boise River, with guides focusing on wildlife and plant lore. (☎342-4796. Tours Apr.-May Sa-Su 1 and 2:30pm; late May to early Sept. M-Sa 10, 11:15am, 12:30, 1:45, 3pm; Su noon, 1:15, 2:30, 3:45pm; fall W-Su noon, 1:30, 3pm. $7.50, ages 64 and up $7, ages 3-12 $5. With river float $30, seniors $28, ages 2-12 $17.) Learn about Idaho and the Old West at the **Idaho Historical Museum,** 610 Julia Davis Dr., in the park, which showcases a replica 19th-century bar, high-class Idahoan parlors, and working-class homesteads, as well as Native American artifacts and displays on Idaho's Basque and Chinese populations. (☎334-2120. Open M-Sa 9am-5pm; in summer also Su 1-5pm. $2, students and ages 6-18 $1.) Nearby, the **Boise Art Museum,** 670 Julia Davis Dr., displays contemporary international and local works, including extensive collections from the northwest US. (☎345-8330; www.boiseartmuseum.org. Open M-W and F-Sa 10am-5pm, Th 10am-8pm, Su noon-5pm; Sept.-May closed M. $5, college students and ages 61 and up $3, ages 6-18 $1. First Th of every month free.)

Standing on the old Idaho State Penitentiary grounds, the **Idaho Botanical Garden,** 2355 N. Penitentiary Rd., has extensive horticultural displays on its 33 acres, including rose, herb, alpine, English, and water gardens. (☎343-8649 or 877-527-8233. Open M-F 9am-5pm, Sa-Su 10am-6pm. $4, seniors $3, ages 6-18 $2.) Raptors perch and dive at the **World Center for Birds of Prey,** 566 W. Flying Hawk Ln. From I-84, take Exit 50 and go south 6 mi. on S. Cole; turn right onto W. Flying Hawk Ln. Tiptoe through their actual breeding chambers and observe the rare and striking birds, including California Condors and Harpy Eagles, up close. (☎362-8687. Open daily Mar.-Oct. 9am-5pm; Nov.-Feb. 10am-4pm. $4, ages 61 and up $3, ages 4-16 $2, under 4 free.) Basque culture, imported to Idaho settlements by emigrants from northeast Spain, remains a vibrant part of the contemporary society. The fascinating **Basque Museum and Cultural Center,** 611 Grove St. at the corner of Grove St. and Capitol Blvd., includes a gallery of Basque art and the 1864 Cyrus Jacobs-Uberuaga House, the city's oldest brick building. (☎343-2671. Open Tu-F 10am-4pm, Sa 11am-3pm. Free.) The **Museum of Mining and Geology,** 2455 N. Penitentiary Rd., has great displays on mining, geology, gems, and minerals from early mining days to the present. (☎368-9876. Open Apr.-Oct. W-Su noon-5pm. Free.) The **State Capitol,** Capitol Blvd. and Jefferson, is the only geothermally heated capitol building in the nation. (☎334-2470. Open M-F 8am-5pm, Sa 9am-5pm. Free self-guided tours.)

◙ **ENTERTAINMENT.** In the **Alive After Five** series, live music infuses the Grove every Wednesday from May to September, 4:30-7:30pm. (☎472-5200; www.downtownboise.org.) The **Capital City Public Market** takes over N. 8th St. between Main and Bannock St. every Saturday 9:30am-1:30pm from mid-April to October, vending local produce and crafts. The **Boise River Greenbelt** provides over 20 mi. of paved paths that extend along the Boise River. Fishing and tubing along the Greenbelt are popular summer pursuits. The ever-growing **Idaho Shakespeare Festival** hits town from June to September (☎429-9908;

www.idahoshakespeare.org; tickets $18-26). In late June, Boise hosts a **River Festival,** featuring hot-air balloons, a carnival, live music, and fireworks. (☎338-8887. Free.) Upcoming events are listed in Thursday's *Boise Weekly.*

KETCHUM AND SUN VALLEY ☎208

In 1935, Union Pacific chairman Averill Harriman sent Austrian Count Felix Schaffgotsch to scour the western US for a site to develop into a ski resort that would rival Europe's best. After traveling for months, the Count stumbled onto the small mining and sheep-herding town of Ketchum in Idaho's Wood River Valley and was awestruck. Harriman immediately purchased the land and built the world's first chairlift. Sun Valley was quickly recognized as a world-class ski resort, fulfilling Harriman's dream. The permanent population is only 5600, but traffic extends for miles in each direction in peak months. Skiing reigns supreme in winter, while biking, hiking, and fishing draw thrill-seekers in the summer.

⚇ PRACTICAL INFORMATION. The best times for fun in the Sun are winter and summer. The town does its best to shut down in "slack" times (Oct.-Nov., May to early June), but during these periods accommodations offer lower rates and the natural beauty stays the same. Most of the food and nightlife centers around Main St. (Rte. 75) in Ketchum, while Sun Valley, just 3 mi. northeast on Sun Valley Rd., governs the ski slopes. **Sun Valley Express** picks up door-to-door in the Sun Valley/Ketchum area and runs daily to the Boise airport. (☎877-622-8267; www.sunvalleyexpress.com. 3hr. Leaves Sun Valley 8:30am; Dec.-Mar. also 6:30am and 12:30pm. Leaves Boise 2:45pm; Dec.-Mar. also 12:45 and 5:45pm. Closed late Oct. to late Nov. Standard rates $59, under 12 $49; Aug. and Dec.-Mar. $69/$59. All vans TV/VCR equipped. Reservations required.) **KART,** Ketchum's bus service, tours the city and its surrounding areas including Sun Valley, Warm Springs, and Elkhorn. (☎726-7576. Runs daily 7:30am-midnight. Door-to-door service for disabled and elderly upon request. Free.) **Visitor Info: Chamber of Commerce,** 4th and Main St. in Ketchum. (☎726-3423 or 800-634-3347; www.visitsunvalley.com. Open Nov.-Apr. and July-Sept. daily 9am-6pm; May-June and Oct. M-Sa 9am-5:30pm.) **Internet Access: Community Library,** 415 Spruce Ave. (☎726-3493. Open M and Sa 9am-6pm, Tu and Th noon-9pm, W 9am-9pm, F 1-6pm. Free.) **Post Office:** 151 W. 4th St. (☎726-5161. Open M-F 8:30am-5:30pm, Sa 11am-2pm.) **Postal Code:** 83340. **Area Code:** 208.

❔ ACCOMMODATIONS. From early June to mid-October, camping is the best option for cheap sleep in the Sun Valley area. Check with the **Ketchum Ranger Station,** 206 Sun Valley Rd., just outside of Ketchum on the way to Sun Valley. (☎622-5371. Open M-F 8:30am-5pm.) **Boundary Campground ❶,** 3 mi. northeast of town on Trail Creek Rd. past the Sun Valley resort, is closest to town and has nine wooded sites near a creek. (Restrooms, picnic area and water. 7-night max stay. Sites $10.) **Federal Gulch ❶** and **Sawmill Campground ❶,** both 15 mi. southeast of Ketchum on E. Fork Rd. off Hwy. 75, each have three free sites amid groves of aspen trees with restrooms, grills, and picnic areas, and a 16-day max. stay. Up Rte. 75 in the SNRA lie several scenic camping spots; **Murdock ❶** (11 sites with water; $10) and **Caribou ❶** (7 sites, no water; $8) are cheapest. They are, respectively, 2 and 3 mi. up the unpaved, but 2WD-suitable, N. Fork Rd., which begins as a paved road to the right of the visitors center. **North Fork ❶** (28 sites; $11) and **Wood River ❶** (29 sites; $11) are 8 and 10 mi. north of Ketchum, respectively, along Rte. 75, and are popular fishing spots along Big Wood River. For North Fork, take the first campground road north of SNRA headquarters. Both have water and restrooms. For comfortable rooms, refrigerators, an outdoor jacuzzi, and continental breakfast, try the **Lift Tower Lodge ④**, 703 S. Main St. (☎726-5163 or 800-462-8646. Rooms $66-90. Each additional adult $10.) **Bald Mountain Lodge ❸**, 151 S. Main St., rents basic rooms with cable TV for some of the best rates in Ketchum. (☎726-9963. Rooms $65-70.)

🏠🍴 FOOD AND NIGHTLIFE. Ketchum's small confines bulge with over 80 restaurants catering to resort-goers' gourmet tastes, but relatively cheap food can be found. Beer cans of all shapes and sizes grace the walls of **Grumpy's ❶**, 860 Warm Springs Rd., a flavorful hangout with an always-crowded porch featuring views of Baldy. (Burger specials $3-5. Goblet of beer $3.25. Open daily 11am-10pm.) Build your own burrito at **KB's Ketchum Burritos ❷**, on the corner of 6th and Washington, or choose from their selection of favorites "just like mom used to never make" ($8). Locals rave about their fish tacos and quesadillas, a steal at $4-6. (☎726-2232. Open daily 11:30am-9pm.) Chase back some stiff drinks for $1 on Sunday and Tuesday at **Whiskey Jacques**, 251 N. Main St., which has nine televisions for sports junkies. (☎726-5297. Live music most nights 9:30pm-2am. Happy hour daily 4-7pm. 21+ after 9pm. Cover $5. Open daily 4pm-2am. Food served 5-9pm.) Head downstairs to the **Cellar Pub,** 400 Sun Valley Rd., near Leadville Ave., for a young crowd, excellent burgers ($8-9) and bangers sausages, and inventive pints like the "straight jacket." (☎622-3832. Open daily 5pm-2am. Food served until 10pm.)

🏔 OUTDOOR ACTIVITIES. The **Wood River and Sun Valley trail system** consists of over 20 mi. of paved trails for bikers, skiers, skaters, joggers, and horseback riders. The trail starts in Bellevue and parallels Hwy. 75 north through Ketchum and east around Dollar Mountain to Sun Valley, passing ski slopes and historic sites. The *Wood River Trails* pamphlet, available at the visitors center, has more info. Visible for miles, **Bald Mountain,** or "Baldy," is a beacon for serious skiers. Two plazas serve Baldy—River Run on the north side of town and Warm Springs on the south. Whereas mostly advanced skiers go to Bald Mountain, the gentle slopes of **Dollar Mountain** are perfect for beginners. (☎622-6136, ski conditions 800-635-4150. Full-day lift ticket $67, under 13 $38; half-day $50/$32.) For those seeking the rigors of Nordic skiing, the **Nordic & Snowshoe Center,** behind Sun Valley Lodge, has 25 mi. of marked trails for cross-country skiing and snowshoe trekking. (☎800-786-8259. Full-day trail pass $13, ages 6-12 $7. Ski rental $16, snowshoe rental $15.)

The Sawtooth area is nationally renowned for its stunning mountain bike trails, which traverse the gorgeous canyons and mountain passes of the Sawtooth National Recreation Area (SNRA). *Trails may be snowbound or flooded well into July.* Take a high-speed quad to the top of Bald Mountain and ride down on a mountain bike during the summer. (☎622-2231. Open in summer daily 9am-3:45pm. $15 per ride, $20 per day; ages 3-12 $7/$10.) Ask about trail conditions and rent gear at **Formula Sports,** 460 N. Main St. (☎726-3194. Bikes from $14 per 4hr., $18 per day; full suspension and tandems $25/$35. Skis $18-40. Discounts for multiday rentals. Open daily 9am-6pm.) **The Elephant's Perch,** 280 East Ave., at Sun Valley Rd., has a complete stock of outdoor gear. (☎726-3497. Open daily 9am-6pm. Bikes $15 per 4hr., $20 per day. Backpacks $15 per day, sleeping bags $25 per day, tents $20 per day. Nordic and telemark ski packages $15-25 per day.) Inquire about biking trails at the Chamber of Commerce or the SNRA Headquarters.

The **Sun Valley Summer Symphony,** behind the Sun Valley Lodge on the Esplanade, offers free open-air chamber and orchestral concerts from late July to early August. (☎622-5607 for exact dates. Concerts 6:30-7:30pm.) Rock, Latin, and bluegrass bands gather at the public park on 1st St. and Washington Ave. every Wednesday in summer for a free show starting at 7:30pm. After a hard day on the trails, locals soak their weary legs in hot springs hidden in Ketchum's hills and canyons. Melting snow and rain can render the springs inaccessible in spring and early summer, but they are safe for swimming once the current subsides in July. The Chamber of Commerce has suggestions on which pools are safe and accessible. One of the more accessible, non-commercial springs is **Warfield Hot Springs,** on Warm Springs Rd., 11 mi. west of Ketchum, which lingers right around 100°F. Just west on FS 227, **Worswick Hot Springs** bubbles at a steamy 150°F. The commercial **Easley Hot Springs** is12 mi. north of Ketchum on Rte. 75. (☎726-7522. Open in summer Tu and Th-Sa 11am-7pm, W 11am-5pm, Su noon-5pm; in winter Sa 11am-5pm, Su noon-5pm. $6, under 15 $5, seniors $4.50.) For info on **fishing,** including equipment rentals, stop by **Silver Creek Outfitters,** 500 N. Main St. (☎726-5282 or 800 732-5687. Open M-Sa 9am-6pm, Su noon-5pm; hours vary in peak season. Fly rods $20 per day; waders and boots $20 per day. Full-day guided trip $390.)

SAWTOOTH RECREATION AREA ☎208

Established by Congress in 1972, the Sawtooth National Recreation Area (SNRA) sprawls over 756,000 acres of National Forest, nearly the size of Rhode Island, including 217,000 acres of untouched wilderness and the headwaters of the Boise and Payette Rivers. The park is home to four mountain ranges with more than 40 peaks over 10,000 ft. The glacier-scoured Sawtooth and White Cloud Mountains tower above surrounding landscapes in the north, while the Smoky and Boulder Mountains dominate the southern horizon. Over 300 alpine lakes and the headwaters of four of Idaho's major rivers are situated in the park's dense forest.

🛈 **PRACTICAL INFORMATION.** The tiny, frontier-style town of **Stanley** (pop. 100), located 60 mi. north of Ketchum at the intersection of Rte. 21 and 75, serves as a northern base for exploring Sawtooth. The diminutive business district is located one block south of Rte. 21, along Ace of Diamonds St., the town's main (and really only) drag. **Lower Stanley** is a small continuation of the business region and lies on Hwy. 75 just 1 mi. north of Stanley. The **Stanley Ranger Station,** 3 mi. south of Stanley on Rte. 75, offers maps, SNRA passes, and sage outdoor advice. (☎774-3000. Open in summer M-F 8:30am-5pm; in winter M-F 8:30am-4:30pm.) The **Redfish Lake Visitors Center** provides additional info, including educational programs about wildlife and geology. The center also has a small museum with exhibits detailing the diversity of flora and fauna in the Redfish Lake area. (☎774-3376. Open mid-June to early Sept. daily 9am-5pm; late May to mid-June Sa-Su 9am-5pm. Ranger programs nightly at 9pm.) **Sawtooth National Recreation Area (SNRA) Headquarters,** 9 mi. north of Ketchum off Rte. 75, stocks detailed info on the hot springs and area forests and trails. SNRA maps are $6-7 and local hiker Margaret Fuller's excellent trail guides are $15. (☎727-5013 or 800-260-5970. Open daily in summer 8:30am-5pm; in winter 9am-3:30pm.) **Chamber of Commerce:** Located on Rte. 75 between Stanley and Lower Stanley. (☎774-3411 or 800-878-7950. Open in summer daily 9am-5pm; reduced hours in winter.) **Internet Access: Stanley Community Library,** Ace of Diamonds St. (☎774-2470. Open M noon-8pm, Tu-W and Sa noon-4pm, Th noon-6pm. Unlimited use $3.) **Post Office:** Ace of Diamonds St., Stanley. (☎774-2230. Open M-F 8-11am and noon-5pm.) **Postal Code:** 83278. **Area Code:** 208.

🛌 **ACCOMMODATIONS.** For a real bed to end a day in the wilderness, Stanley provides reasonably-priced lodging options. At **Danner's Log Cabin Motel ❸,** on Rte. 21, ex-mayor and Stanley history buff Bunny Danner rents historic cabins built by gold miners in 1939. The office, built in 1906, is the oldest building in town and originally served as the ranger station. (☎774-3539. Cabins in summer $55-75; in spring and fall $45-60.) **Redfish Lake Lodge ❸**, on the shores of the lake with convenient access to kayaking and fishing, has comfy, historic lodge rooms and cabins with refrigerators and kitchen areas. (☎774-3536. Lodge rooms $62; cabins $120-170.) **Redwood Cabins ❸**, on Hwy. 75 at the east end of Lower Stanley, has cottages along the Salmon River with cable TV. (☎774-3531. Open May-Sept. Singles $58; doubles $64.) The SNRA also boasts 33 campgrounds throughout the park; consult a ranger for help in selecting (and locating) a campsite. **Alturas Lake ❶**, 21 mi. south of Stanley on Rte. 75 (the Alturas Lake Rd. turnoff is marked about 10 mi. north of Galena Pass), has three first come, first served campgrounds with fishing and swimming. These sites offer greater privacy and are more scenic than some other area campgrounds. (Vault toilets and water. 55 sites, $10.) The area around **Redfish Lake ❶**, 5 mi. south of Stanley off Rte. 75, is a sometimes overcrowded spot with lightly forested sites. Several Forest Service campgrounds in the area are close to Stanley and trailheads. (☎877-444-6777; www.reserveusa.com for **Glacier View, Outlet, and Point.** Sites $13 with 6- to 10-day max. stay.) East on Rte. 75, past the town of Stanley, numerous campgrounds are available along the wild **Salmon River ❶**. (Water available; no hookup. First come, first served. 10-day max. stay. Sites $11.) One of the best of these is Mormon Bend, 8 mi. east of Stanley on Rte. 75, with 15 sites close to whitewater rafting. Other inviting spots right along the Salmon River are **Casino Creek,** 6 mi east of Stanley on Rte. 75; the **Salmon River Campground,** 5 mi east of Stanley on Rte. 75; and **Upper** and **Lower O'Brien,** 2 mi. past Sunbeam Dam. Showers are $3 at the laundromat on Ace of Diamonds St. in Stanley.

🖸🖺 **FOOD AND NIGHTLIFE.** Dining options are limited in Stanley, but locals rave about the $5 deli sandwiches at **Papa Brunee's ❷**, on Ace of Diamonds St. downtown, which also serves meat-laden calzones and pizzas with names like "The Bullfighter." (☎774-2536. 12 in. pizzas $11-14. Open daily 11am-10pm.) Stock up on food, gas, and fishing licenses at **Jerry's Country Store and Motel,** on Rte. 75 in Lower Stanley. (☎774-3566 or 800-972-4627. Open May-Sept. M-Sa 9am-9pm, Su 9am-5pm; winter hours vary.) The local watering hole is the **Rod and Gun Club Bar,** on Ace of Diamonds St. This Western bar has pool tables, a dance floor, and live music on the weekends. (☎774-9920. 21+. Open daily 6pm-1:30am.)

🏞 **OUTDOOR ACTIVITIES.** The Sawtooth Scenic Byway (Rte. 75) spans 60 mi. of National Forest land between Ketchum and Stanley, following the Big Wood River and crossing the Galena Pass at 8701 ft. Pause at ▨**Galena Overlook,** 31 mi. north of Ketchum, which rises 2000 ft. above the plain below and provides one of the finest views in the Rockies, where the headwaters of the Salmon River rise beneath the jagged Sawtooth Range in the distance. The SNRA's backcountry is perfect for hiking, boating, fishing, and mountain biking. Parking at most trailheads in the park requires a **trailhead pass** ($5 for 3 days, $15 annual pass), obtained at the SNRA Headquarters or the Stanley Ranger Station (see **Practical Information,** above). Pick up a free map and inquire about trail conditions at SNRA Headquarters before heading into the park, particularly in early summer, when trails may be flooded; much of the backcountry stays buried in snow well into the warm weather. Watch out for black bears; ranger stations have info about necessary precautions.

Redfish Lake is the source of many trails. Some popular, leisurely hikes include those to **Fishhook Creek** (4½ mi. roundtrip, elevation gain 250 ft., excellent for children), **Bench Lakes** (8 mi. round-trip, elevation gain 1225 ft.), and the **Marshall Lake trail** (10 mi. round-trip, elevation gain 1500 ft.). Keep an eye out for native ospreys, Lincoln's sparrows, and ruby-crowned kinglets. The long, gentle loop around **Yel-**

low **Belly, Toxaway,** and **Petit Lakes** (16 mi. round-trip, elevation gain 1680 ft.) is a moderate overnight trip suitable for novices. Starting at the Inlet Trailhead on the southern end of Redfish Lake, the challenging 10½ mi. round-trip hike to **Alpine Lake** (elevation gain 1800 ft.) rewards with stunning views and exposure to the diverse land that the Sawtooths have to offer. Redfish Lake Lodge operates ferries to and from the south end of the lake to access the trailhead (one-way $5).

The Sawtooths have miles of mountain biking, but check a map; biking is allowed in National Forest areas, but prohibited in the Sawtooth Wilderness. **Riverwear,** on Rte. 21 in Stanley, rents bikes. (☎774-3592. Open daily 7am-10pm. Front suspension $17 per day, full suspension $25.) The 18 mi. **Fischer/Williams Creek Loop,** starting at the Williams Creek trailhead 10 mi. south of Stanley, is the most popular trail, ascending from 6800 ft. to an elevation of 8280 ft. Beginners will enjoy the dirt road that accesses the North Fork campgrounds from SNRA Headquarters. This gorgeous passage parallels the North Fork of the Wood River for 5 mi. before branching off into narrow, steep trails for more experienced riders. The trails can be combined into loops; consult a trail map or the ranger station. Advanced bikers will love the challenge of the **Stanley Basin Trail** (20 mi. round-trip, elevation gain 2500 ft.), ascending to the summit of Basin Butte. (Access at Stanley Creek turnoff.) The steep **Boulder Basin Road,** 5 mi. from the SNRA Headquarters, leads to pristine Boulder Lake and an old mining camp.

Topographical maps ($6) and detailed trail books ($6-12) are available at **McCoy's Tackle and Gift Shop,** on Ace of Diamonds St. McCoy's also sells sporting goods, fishing tackle, and licenses. (☎774-3377. Licenses $11 for the first day, $4 each additional day. Open June-Sept. daily 8am-8pm; low-season hours vary.) **Sawtooth Adventure Company,** on Rte. 75 in Lower Stanley, rents kayaks and rafts and leads guided kayak, Class IV whitewater rafting, and fly fishing trips along the Salmon River. (☎866-774-4644. Open May-Sept. Kayaks $25-50 per 24hr. Rafts for 8 people $75 per day. Half-day kayak trips $30-65. Full-day fly-fishing trips $225.) For boat tours of the lake, head for **Redfish Lake Lodge Marina.** (☎774-3536. Open in summer daily 7am-8:30pm. 1hr. tours $8, ages 6-12 $5; min. $32. Paddleboats $5 per 30min. Canoes $10 per hr., $32 per half-day, $50 per day. Single-person kayaks $7/ $20/$35, doubles $10/$32/$50. Aquacycles $15 per hr. Outboards $15/$50/$80.) The most inexpensive way to enjoy the SNRA waters is to visit the **hot springs** just east of Stanley. **Sunbeam Hot Springs,** 10 mi. northeast of Stanley on Rte. 75, triumphs over the rest at a scalding 150°F, though pools allow for the water to be mixed with river water for a more pleasant soaking experience. The natural rock pools of **Kem Hot Springs,** 6 mi. northeast of Stanley on Rte. 75, in the Salmon River, are less commonly visited soaking spots. Both are free and open 24hr.

CRATERS OF THE MOON NATIONAL MONUMENT   ☎208

The otherworldly landscape of **Craters of the Moon National Monument** first drew national attention in the 1920s. An early visitor claimed it was "the strangest 75 square miles on the North American continent." The same geological hot spot responsible for the thermal activity in Yellowstone National Park created the monument's twisted lava formations. Eruptions ended only 2000 years ago, and are expected to resume within the next 1000. Located 70 mi. southeast of Sun Valley at the junction of Rte. 20 and 26/93 (the visitors center is between Arco and Carey), the park's unusual craters, cinder cones, and twisted rock formations make for a fascinating visit. ($5 per car, $3 per person, $3 per bike.) The visitors center has videos, displays, and inexpensive printed guides outlining the area's geological past. A 7 mi. drive winds through the monument, guiding tourists to the major sights, while several short trails lead to more unusual rock formations and a variety of caves; bring a flashlight. The 2 mi. **Broken Top Loop,** starting at Tree Molds parking lot, goes through Buffalo Caves and is a quick but comprehensive survey of the surrounding land. Don't forget sturdy shoes, water, sunscreen, and hats; the black rocks absorb heat and there are no trees for miles. The town of **Arco,** the closest source of services and lodging, is 18 mi. east of the Craters of the Moon on Rte. 20. Arco claims to have become the "first city in the world lighted by atomic energy" on July 17, 1955, when a local reactor fed energy to the town for two hours—an anniversary still celebrated.

There are 51 campsites scattered throughout the monument's single **campground ❶,** located just past the entrance station. (Water and restrooms. No hookups. Open year-round. $10.) Wood fires are prohibited, but charcoal fires are permitted in the grills. Camping at unmarked sites in the dry lava wilderness of the park is permitted with a free **backcountry permit,** available at the **visitors center,** right before the entrance to the monument. (☎527-3257. Open daily in summer 8am-6pm; low-season 8am-4:30pm.) **Echo Crater,** a flat and easy 4 mi. hike (1½hr.) from the Tree Molds parking lot, is one of the most popular backcountry camping areas. Comfy, modern rooms with telephones and cable TV are available at the **D-K Motel ❷,** 316 S. Front St., situated beneath towering cliffs. (☎527-8282 or 800-231-0134. Laundry facilities. Singles $32; doubles $40-47.) Barbecue chicken and ribs beckon from the backyard at **Grandpa's Southern Bar-B-Q ❷,** 434 W. Grand Ave. Grab a seat on the front porch for a great pork sandwich ($5) and some small-town hospitality. (☎527-3362. Full dinners $7-13. Open in summer daily 11am-8pm; in winter Th-Sa 11am-8pm.) With a big green rocking chair in front, **Pickle's Place ❶,** 440 S. Front St., is an easy diner to identify. Home of the atomic burger ($5-6) and the Black Russian sandwich ($5), Pickle's also dishes out breakfasts ($4-5) in plentiful portions. (☎527-9944. Dinners $6-11. Open daily June-Aug. 6am-11pm; Sept.-May 6am-10pm.) The **Arco Deli Sandwich Shop ❷,** on Rte. 20/26/93, at Grand Ave. and Idaho St., serves fresh deli sandwiches. (☎527-3757. 6 in. sandwiches $4, 12 in. $7. Open M-F 8am-8pm, Sa 8am-7pm.)

The **Chamber of Commerce,** 159 N. Idaho St., has info on local attractions (☎527-8977; open M-F 8am-5pm). If traveling from Arco to Sun Valley (see p. 817), you can also pick up a free cassette tour of the Central Idaho Rockies which recounts the geological and anthropological history of the region.

THE SOUTHWEST

The Ancestral Puebloans of the 10th and 11th centuries were the first to discover the Southwest's arid lands could support an agrarian civilization. Years later, in 1803, the US bought parts of the Southwest in the Louisiana Purchase, and claimed the rest of it in 1848 with the treaty that ended the US-Mexican War. The hope for a Western "empire of liberty," where Americans could live a virtuous farm life, motivated further expansion and inspired the region's individualist mentality. Today, the Southwest's vastness—from the dramatically colored canvas of Arizona's red rock, scrub brush, and pale sky, to the breathtaking vistas of Utah's mountains—invites contemplation and awe, and the area's potential for outdoor adventures is as unparalleled as its kaleidoscopic mix of cultures. For more on the region, check out ⬛*Let's Go Adventure Guide: Southwest USA*.

HIGHLIGHTS OF THE SOUTHWEST

NATIONAL PARKS. Experiencing Utah's "Fab Five" (p. 839) and Arizona's Grand Canyon (p. 849) is nothing short of a spiritual revelation.

SKIING. In a region famous for its blistering sun, the sublime slopes (p. 834) near Salt Lake City, UT, boast some of the plushest powder in the world.

MEXICAN FOOD. You can't get away from it, and in the colorful eateries of New Mexico's Albuquerque (p. 891) and Santa Fe (p. 881), you won't want to.

NEVADA

Nevada's Great Basin stretches for hundreds of miles across land that rejects all but the most hardy forms of life. At the few outposts of human habitation, prostitution and gambling mark the state as a purveyor of loose, Wild West morality. Beyond patches of shimmering lights, sin, and showtunes, Nevada is barren and dusty, but this hasn't kept it from becoming the US's fastest growing state. Nevada exemplifies America at its most excessive and contradictory.

🔃 PRACTICAL INFORMATION

Capital: Carson City.

Visitor Info: Nevada Commission on Tourism, Capitol Complex, Carson City 89701 (☎800-638-2328; 24hr.). **Nevada Division of State Parks,** 1300 S. Curry St., Carson City 89703 (☎702-687-4384). Open M-F 8am-5pm.

Postal Abbreviation: NV. **Sales Tax:** 6.75-7%; 9% room tax in some counties.

LAS VEGAS   ☎702

Rising out of the Nevada desert, Las Vegas is a shimmering tribute to excess. Those who embrace it find an oasis of vice and greed, and one very, very good time. Sleeping (and decision-making) can be nearly impossible with sparkling casinos, cheap gourmet food, free drinks, and spectacular attractions. Nowhere else do so many shed inhibitions and indulge with abandon. Know

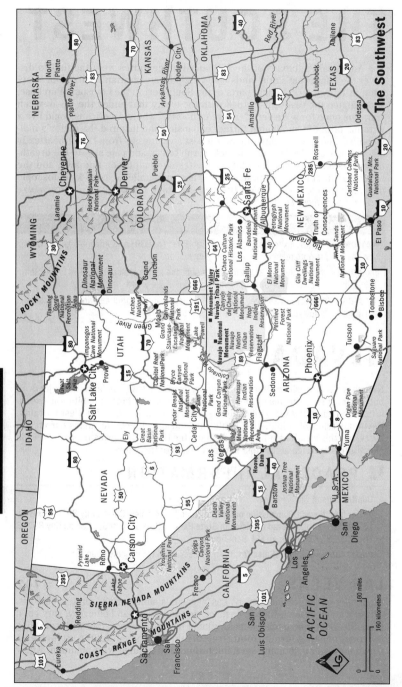

thy tax bracket; walk in knowing what you want to spend and get the hell out when you've spent it. In Las Vegas, there's a busted wallet and a broken heart for every garish neon light.

TRANSPORTATION

Airport: McCarran International (☎261-5743), at the southwest end of the Strip. Shuttles run to the Strip ($4.75) and downtown ($7); taxis $10-15/$16-20.

Buses: Greyhound, 200 S. Main St. (☎384-9561 or 800-231-2222), downtown at Carson Ave., near the Plaza Hotel/Casino. To **L.A.** (5-7hr., 22 per day, $38) and **San Francisco** (13-16hr., 6 per day, $69).

Public Transportation: Citizens Area Transit (CAT; ☎228-7433). Bus #301 serves downtown and the Strip. Buses #108 and 109 serve the airport. Wheelchair accessible. Buses run daily 5:30am-1:30am (24hr. on the Strip). Strip routes $2, residential routes $1.25; seniors and ages 6-17 $1/$0.60. Tourist office or the **Downtown Transportation Center,** 300 N. Casino Center Blvd., has schedules and maps (☎228-7433). **Las Vegas Strip Trolleys** (☎382-1404) cruise the Strip every 20min. daily 9:30am-1:30am. Trolley fare $1.75; day pass $5. The new **Monorail** (www.lvmonorail.com) runs along the Strip, connecting major casinos daily 8am-midnight. $3; day pass $15.

Taxi: Yellow, Checker, and **Star** ☎873-2000.

Car Rental: Sav-Mor Rent-A-Car, 5101 Rent-A-Car Rd. (☎736-1234 or 800-634-6779).

ORIENTATION AND PRACTICAL INFORMATION

Driving to Vegas from L.A. is a straight, 300 mi. shot on I-15 N (4½hr.). From Arizona, take I-40 W to Kingman and then U.S. 93 N. Las Vegas has two major casino areas. The **downtown** area, around 2nd and Fremont St., has been converted into a pedestrian promenade. The **Strip,** a collection of mammoth hotel-casinos, lies along **Las Vegas Boulevard.** Parallel to the east side of the Strip and in its shadow is **Paradise Road,** also strewn with casinos. Some areas of Las Vegas should be avoided, especially downtown areas far from the casino district. Despite (or because of) its debauchery, Las Vegas has a **curfew.** Those under 18 aren't allowed in most public places late at night (Su-Th 10pm-5am, F-Sa midnight-5am), unless accompanied by an adult. Laws are even harsher on the Strip, where no one under 18 is allowed unaccompanied 9pm-5am—ever. **The drinking and gambling age is 21.**

Visitor Info: Las Vegas Convention and Visitors Authority, 3150 Paradise Rd. (☎892-0711), 4 blocks from the Strip in the big pink convention center by the Hilton. Up-to-date info on headliners, shows, hotel bargains, and buffets. Open M-F 8am-5pm.

Marriage: Marriage License Bureau, 200 S. 3rd St. (☎455-4415), in the courthouse. 18+ or parental consent. Licenses $55; cash only. Witness required. Open Su-Th 8am-midnight, F-Sa 24hr. **Little White Wedding Chapel,** 1301 Las Vegas Blvd. (☎382-5943; www.alittlewhitechapel.com). Frank Sinatra, Michael Jordan, and Britney Spears have been hitched here. Basic drive-through packages begin at $40 and end at the limits of imagination. All necessities included, like photographer, tux and gown, flowers, and, for honeymooners, a pink Caddy. Grab your marriage license first. Open 24hr.

Hotlines: Compulsive Gamblers Hotline, ☎800-LOST-BET/567-8238. **Gamblers Anonymous,** ☎385-7732. **Rape Crisis Center Hotline,** ☎366-1640. **Suicide Prevention,** ☎731-2990 or 800-885-4673.

Post Office: 4975 Swenson St. (☎736-7649), near the Strip. Open M-F 8:30am-5pm. **Postal Code:** 89119. **Area Code:** 702.

ACCOMMODATIONS

Room rates in Las Vegas fluctuate greatly; a room that costs $30 can cost hundreds during a convention weekend. **Vegas.com** (www.vegas.com) or **casino websites** often have the best prices. Free publications like *What's On In Las Vegas*, *Today in Las Vegas*, *24/7*, and *Vegas Visitor* list discounts, coupons, info, and event schedules. If you get stuck, call the **Room Reservations Hotline** (☎ 800-332-5333).

Strip hotels are the center of the action and within walking distance of each other, but their rooms sell out quickly. A number of motels cluster around **Sahara Road** and **South Las Vegas Boulevard.** If you stay downtown, it is best to stay in one of the casinos in the **Fremont Street Experience** (p. 827). Budget motels also stretch along the southern end of the **Strip,** across from Mandalay Bay. In the rooms listed below, the **hotel taxes of 9%** (11% for downtown Fremont St.) are not included.

Barbary Coast, 3595 S. Las Vegas Blvd. (☎ 737-7111), at Flamingo Rd. With the best location on the Strip, mere minutes from Bally's, Caesar's Palace, and Paris, Barbary Coast is perfect for those looking to be in the middle of everything. Large rooms and low table limits make this popular with a young crowd. Restaurants, bars, and casino floor always buzzing. Rooms Su-Th $49-79, F-Sa $69-129. ❸

Excalibur, 3850 S. Las Vegas Blvd. (☎ 597-7777), at Tropicana Ave. The best value of all of the major resort casinos. This King Arthur-themed castle features a moat and drawbridge, 2 pools, a modern spa and fitness center, a large casino and poker room, and a monorail station to Luxor and Mandalay Bay. Many of the 4000 rooms have been recently renovated. Rooms Su-Th $49-79, F-Sa $79-129. ❸

San Remo, 115 E. Tropicana Ave. (☎ 800-522-7366). Just off the Strip, this is a smaller, quieter version of the major players. Delicious prime rib draws an older crowd. Live entertainment every night, featuring the "Showgirls of Magic" ($39). Rooms may go as low as $32 during slow periods, but are usually Su-Th $45, F-Sa $70. ❸

USAHostels Las Vegas, 1322 Fremont St. (☎ 800-550-8958 or 385-1150; www.usahostels.com). Though it's far from the Strip's action in a dreary section of town, this hostel's staff keeps guests comfy and entertained. Free trips including a champagne limo tour of the Strip. Pool, hot tub, laundry, and billiard room. Free pickup from Greyhound station 10am-10pm. International passport, proof of international travel, or out-of-state college ID required. Dorms Su-Th $15-19, F-Sa $17-21; suites Su-Th $40-42, F-Sa $40-49. Prices about $3 higher in the summer and peak times. ISIC discount. ❷

FOOD

From swanky eateries run by celebrity chefs to gourmet buffets, culinary surprises abound in Las Vegas, and usually at a great price.

Le Village Buffet, 3655 Las Vegas Blvd. (☎ 946-7000), in the Paris. French cuisine at 5 stations, each representing a different region. Begin with fresh shellfish and cheeses, then order fresh fruit crepes. Get beef and veal at carving stations, while a pastry chef makes *gateaux*. Breakfast $14. Lunch $18. Dinner $24. Open daily 7am-10pm. ❺

Victorian Room, 3595 S. Las Vegas Blvd. (☎ 737-7111), in Barbary Coast. Home to the best night-owl breakfast special (full breakfast $3; midnight-7am) and excellent Chinese food. Also serves pasta, steak, and seafood. Entrees $7-20. Open 24hr. ❷

Battista's Hole in the Wall, 4041 Audrie St. (☎ 732-1424), behind the Flamingo. 33 years' worth of celebrity photos, novelties from area brothels, and the head of "Moosolini" (the fascist moose) adorn the walls. Generous portions; many diners share. An accordion player adds to the charm. Dinner ($18-34) includes all-you-can-drink wine. Open Su-Th 4:30-10:30pm, F-Sa 4:30-11pm. Reservations recommended. ❹

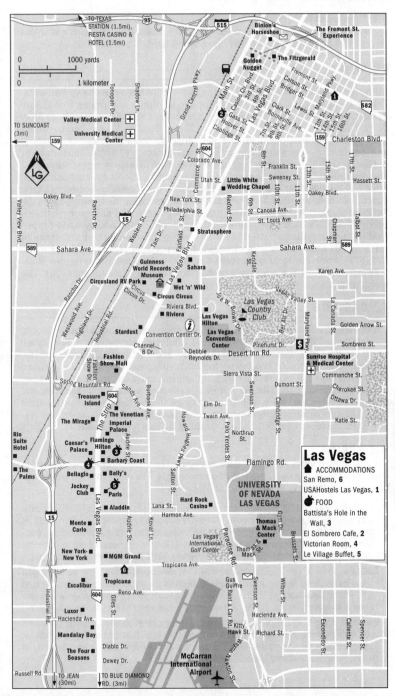

Las Vegas

⌂ ACCOMMODATIONS
San Remo, **6**
USAHostels Las Vegas, **1**

🍗 FOOD
Battista's Hole in the Wall, **3**
El Sombrero Cafe, **2**
Victorian Room, **4**
Le Village Buffet, **5**

El Sombrero Cafe, 807 S. Main St. (☎382-9234). Where locals go for authentic Mexican food. Small room, huge portions, friendly staff. Their combination plates offer a lot of food for a little money ($9-11). Lunch $7. Open M-Sa 11am-9:30pm. ❷

🎵 ENTERTAINMENT

All hotels have city-wide ticket booths in their lobbies. Check out *Showbiz, Today in Las Vegas,* or *What's On* for shows, times, and prices. For a more opinionated perspective, try one of the independent weeklies—*Las Vegas Mercury, City Life, Las Vegas Weekly,* or *Neon,* the *Las Vegas Review-Journal's* weekly entertainment supplement. **Cirque du Soleil's** shows—*O, Mystère,* and *Zumanity*—are awe-inspiring but bank-busting ($94-150). Performed at the Bellagio, ▨*O* is easily the best of the three, with agile performers suspended above a moving pool. **Mystère,** at Treasure Island, is almost as impressive, and often has $60 discount seats. At New York-New York, **Zumanity,** hosted by a drag queen, caters to an adult audience. ▨**Blue Man Group,** at the Luxor, pushes the limits of stage entertainment with unique percussion and audience participation ($75-85). Those looking for an illusionist will be thrilled by **David Copperfield** (appearing often at MGM; $90-100), while those who think the genre of magic needs a few new tricks will enjoy the irreverent ▨**Penn and Teller** at the Río ($70). For a cheap laugh, **Second City,** at the Flamingo, is an improv show featuring some of the country's best up-and-coming comedians ($20). The group inspired the show *Saturday Night Live.*

🎰 CASINOS

Casinos spend millions of dollars attracting big spenders, and they do this by fooling guests into thinking they are somewhere else. Efforts to bring families to Sin City are evident everywhere, with arcades and thrill rides at every turn. Still, Vegas is no Disneyland. With the steamy nightclubs, topless revues, and scantily clad waitresses serving free liquor, it's clear that casinos' priorities center on the mature, moneyed crowd. Casinos are open 24hr. Almost every casino resort has a full casino, several restaurants, a club or two, a buffet, and a feature show. There is valuable art, thrill rides, and startling architecture at every corner. Look for casino "funbooks" that feature deals on chips and entertainment. **Gambling is illegal for those under 21.**

THE STRIP

The undisputed locus of Vegas's surging regeneration, the Strip is a neon fantasyland, teeming with people, casinos, and restaurants. The nation's 10 largest hotels line the legendary 3½ mi. stretch of Las Vegas Blvd.

Mandalay Bay, 3950 S. Las Vegas Blvd. (☎632-7777; www.mandalaybay.com). Undoubtedly Vegas's hippest casino, Mandalay Bay tries to convince New York and L.A. fashionistas they haven't left home. With the swank restaurants and chichi clubs, gambling seems an afterthought. Shark Reef has 100 aquatic beasts from all over the globe, including 15 shark species. House of Blues hosts some of Vegas's best music.

Bellagio, 3600 S. Las Vegas Blvd. (☎693-7444; www.bellagio.com). The world's largest 5-star hotel, made famous in the remake of *Ocean's Eleven.* Houses a gallery of fine art and a floral conservatory that changes with the seasons. Check out the fountains, where water is propelled several stories high during daily free water ballet shows set to opera.

Venetian, 3355 S. Las Vegas Blvd. (☎414-1000; www.venetian.com). Singing gondoliers serenade passengers on the 3 ft. deep chlorinated "canal" that runs through this palatial casino. The Guggenheim Hermitage Museum presents modern artwork from around the world, alongside Madame Tussaud's wax museum.

Caesar's Palace, 3570 S. Las Vegas Blvd. (☎ 731-7110; www.caesars.com). At Caesar's, busts abound; some are plaster and others are barely covered by the cocktail waitresses' low-cut outfits. The Forum Shops lead the Strip's high-end shopping craze.

Luxor, 3900 S. Las Vegas Blvd. (☎ 262-4000; www.luxor.com). This architectural marvel recreates the majestic pyramids of ancient Egypt in opaque glass and steel. Luxor has all sorts of diversions for when gambling loses its appeal; there's an IMAX Theater, a full-scale replica of King Tut's Tomb, Club Ra, and the Blue Man theater.

Paris, 3655 S. Las Vegas Blvd. (☎ 946-7000; www.parislasvegas.com). From restaurants that resemble French cafes to replicas of the Arc de Triomphe, the French Opera House, and the Eiffel Tower, this resort adds a Parisian *je ne sais quois* to Las Vegas.

The Mirage, 3400 S. Las Vegas Blvd. (☎ 791-7111; www.mirage.com). Shelters 8 bottle-nose dolphins and a garden of white tigers and lions. A volcano that puts science fair projects to shame erupts every 15min.

MGM Grand, 3799 S. Las Vegas Blvd. (☎ 891-1111; www.mgmgrand.com). A huge bronze lion guards Las Vegas's largest hotel (5000 rooms), which echoes the green glam-our of the Emerald City from *The Wizard of Oz.* Cowardly and brave felines dwell in the Lion Habitat. The MGM often hosts world-class sporting events and concerts.

New York-New York, 3790 S. Las Vegas Blvd. (☎ 740-6969; www.nynyhotelcasino). Tow-ers mimic the Manhattan skyline, recreating the Big Apple. Walk under Brooklyn Bridge or ride the Manhattan Express (open daily 11am-11pm, $12), the wildest ride on the Strip.

Treasure Island (TI), 3300 S. Las Vegas Blvd. (☎ 894-7111; www.treasureisland.com). Refurbished and fully embracing the wave of pirate chic. See the *Sirens of TI* for a sea bat-tle in one of Vegas's most scantily-clad shows, daily at 7, 8:30, 10pm, 1:30am.

Circus Circus, 2880 S. Las Vegas Blvd. (☎ 734-0410; www.circuscircus.com). While par-ents run to card tables and slot machines, children watch free circus acts and spend their quarters in the enormous video game arcade upstairs. Adventuredome, in the hotel com-plex, is the one of the world's largest indoor theme parks.

DOWNTOWN AND OFF-STRIP

🟦TIP **CASINO TIPPING.** While gambling, players are served free cocktails, and $1 is the standard tip for servers. Leave at least $1 per person for the drink server and busers at a buffet. Many players reward a good table-game dealer with a $1 tip next to their main bet.

The frenzy of the Strip is less noticeable in "old" Downtown Vegas. **Glitter Gulch** has smaller hotels, cheaper alcohol and food, and gambling with table game limits as low as $1. Years of decline were reversed with Las Vegas's rebound and the 1995 opening of the **Fremont Street Experience.** Now, a protective canopy of neon and construction of a pedestrian promenade have aided the area's renaissance.

Golden Nugget, 129 Fremont St. (☎ 385-7111; www.goldennugget.com). An outpost of Strip-like class downtown, this 4-star hotel charms gamblers with marble floors, elegant chandeliers, and high-end gambling.

Binion's Horseshoe, 128 Fremont St. (☎ 382-1600). A place to learn the tricks of the trade by observation, this casino has been the site of the World Series of Poker. Come at night to watch the large poker room in full swing. High craps odds, single-deck blackjack, and a willingness to honor almost any bet are Horseshoe hallmarks.

Palms, 4321 W. Flamingo Rd. (☎ 942-7777; www.palms.com). The ultimate venue to spot celebrities and party with the young and beautiful. The Skin Pool Lounge has swings and cabanas to enjoy before you hit the bars and clubs on the property.

HOOVER DAM

Built to subdue the flood-prone Colorado River and give vital water and energy to the southwest, this ivory monolith, also known (by New-Deal Democrats) as the Boulder Dam, took 5000 men five years to construct. By the time the dam was finished in 1935, 96 men had died. Their labor rendered a 726 ft. colossus that now shelters agricultural land, pumps more than 4 billion kilowatt-hours of power to Las Vegas and L.A., and furnishes Lake Mead. Though the dam has altered the local environment, it is a spectacular engineering feat, weighing 6,600,000 tons and measuring 660 ft. thick at its base and 1244 ft. across the canyon at its crest. It is a lasting tribute to America's "think-big" era. Tours and an interpretive center explore the dam's history and future. (From Las Vegas, take U.S. 93/95 26 mi. to Boulder City. From Boulder City, head east 5 mi. on U.S. 93. ☎866-291-8687. Open daily 9am-5pm. Self-guided tours with short presentations $10, seniors $8, ages 7-16 $4. Parking on the Nevada side $5; free on the Arizona side.)

LAKE MEAD

From Las Vegas, take Lake Mead Blvd./Hwy. 147 off I-15 east 16 mi. to North-shore Rd. The largest reservoir in the US and the country's first national recreation area, Lake Mead was built by the construction of the Hoover Dam across the Colorado River in the 1930s. First-time visitors will benefit from a trip to the **Alan Bible Visitors Center**, 4 mi. east of Boulder City on Hwy. 93, where the helpful staff has brochures, maps, and the *Desert Lake View*, the lake's newspaper and guide. (☎293-8990; www.nps.gov/lame. Open daily 8:30am-4:30pm. Entrance $3 per pedestrian, $5 per vehicle.) Falling water levels has left Lake Mead at roughly half its usual depth. This effect of the southwestern drought has closed boat ramps and exposed previously submerged hazards, making it extremely important to be aware of the terrain. For the most recent information on lake conditions, check the visitors center's website. Despite its water levels, Lake Mead is a water recreation haven. Park service-approved outfitters rent boats and more on the shores; www.funonthelake.com has more info. Popular **Boulder Beach**, the departure point for many water-based activities and home to one of the area's many campgrounds, is accessible from Lakeshore Dr. at the south end of the lake. (Restrooms, water. Sites $10.) Beware of oppressively hot summer temperatures, which can make it too uncomfortable to sleep. It may be a better idea to head for the higher (and cooler) elevations west of Las Vegas or in western Arizona, or on a houseboat on the lake itself.

RENO ☎775

Reno, with its decadent casinos cradled by snowcapped mountains, captures both the natural splendor and opportunist frenzy of the West. Acting as the hub of northern Nevada's tourist cluster, including nearby Lake Tahoe and Pyramid Lake, the self-proclaimed "biggest little city in the world" does a decent job of compressing Las Vegas-style gambling, entertainment, and dining into a few city blocks.

◪ **PRACTICAL INFORMATION. Amtrak** is at 135 E. Commercial Row. (☎800-872-7245. Open daily 8:30am-5pm.) **Greyhound,** 155 Stevenson St. (☎800-231-2222), rolls to: Las Vegas (1 per day, $72); Salt Lake City (4 per day, $57-61); San Francisco (12 per day, $30-32). **Visitor Info: Reno-Sparks Convention and Visitors Authority,** 1 E. 1st St., is on the second floor of the Cal-Neva Building. (☎800-367-7366; www.renolaketahoe.com. Open M-F 8am-5pm.) **Post Office:** 50 S. Virginia St., at Mill St. (Open M-F 8:30am-5pm.) **Postal Code:** 89501.

◪ **ACCOMMODATIONS.** While weekend prices at casino resorts are usually high, weekday rates and low-season discounts can be very affordable. Prices fluctuate, so call ahead. In some cases, low rates may reflect a lack of wholesomeness—heterosexual prostitution is legal in most of Nevada (though not in Reno itself). The rates below don't include Reno's **12% hotel tax**. **Harrah's Reno ❸**, 219 N. Center St., has a central location, seven restaurants, pool, health club, and a 65,000 sq. ft. casino. (☎800-427-7247. Rooms M-Th from $49, F-Su from $89.) Off Hwy. 395 at the Glendale exit, the **Reno Hilton ❸**, 2500 E. 2nd St., has elegant rooms, an amphitheater, driving range, bowling alley, health club, and shopping mall. If Harrah's isn't big enough, the Hilton's casino is 115,000 sq. ft. (☎800-648-5080. Rooms $35-149.) The **Sundowner ❷**, 450 N. Arlington Ave., is a working man's casino. No frills here, but the rooms are clean and come with A/C and telephones, and there's a pool and jacuzzi. (☎800-648-5490. Rooms Su-Th from $26, F $50, Sa $70.)

◖ FOOD. Casinos offer a range of all-you-can-eat buffets and next-to-free breakfasts, but you can escape the clutches of these giants to find inexpensive eateries. The large Basque population cooks up spicy, hearty cuisine. ▨ **The Pneumatic Diner ❷**, 501 W. 1st St., in Truckee River Lodge, is a funky, cramped diner that creates Italian, Mexican, French, and Middle Eastern food from all-natural ingredients. (☎786-8888, ext. 106. Open M-F 11am-11pm, Sa 9am-11pm, Su 8am-11pm.) Those who seek refuge from the seemingly inescapable steak and burritos will enjoy the Thai flavors of **Bangkok Cuisine ❷**, 55 Mt. Rose St. (☎322-0299. Open M-Sa 11am-10pm.) In the Eldorado Hotel at 345 N. Virginia St., **La Strada ❷** has won numerous accolades for its northern Italian cuisine. (☎348-9297. Open daily 5-10pm.)

▨ ENTERTAINMENT. Almost all casinos offer live nighttime entertainment, but most shows are not worth the steep admission prices. **Harrah's**, 219 N. Center St. (☎786-3232), offers a particularly good deal with its **Night on the Town** packages, which cost slightly more than the price of a show ticket, but include dinner and a show. At **Circus Circus**, 500 N. Sierra St., a small circus on the midway above the casino floor performs "big top" shows approximately every 30min. (☎329-0711. Shows M-Th 11:30am-11:30pm, F-Su 11:15am-11:45pm.) For more entertainment listings and info on casino happenings, check out the free *This Week* or *Best Bets* magazines. *The Reno News & Review*, published every Thursday, provides an alternative look at weekly happenings and events off the beaten casino path.

▶ DAYTRIP FROM RENO: PYRAMID LAKE. Thirty miles north of Reno on Rte. 445, on the Paiute Indian Reservation, lies emerald green Pyramid Lake, one of the most heart-achingly beautiful bodies of water in the US. The lake's pristine tides are set against the barren desert, making it a soothing respite from Reno's neon and a fantastic spot for fishing and boating. **Camping ❶** is allowed anywhere on the lake shore, but only designated areas have toilet facilities. Permits are required for day-use ($6), camping ($9), and fishing ($7) and are available at the **Ranger Station** and **Marina**, housed in the same building, 2500 Lakeview Dr. (☎476-1156), on the western side of the lake. The Marina handles **boat rental**; call for reservations.

UTAH

In 1848, persecuted members of the Church of Jesus Christ of Latter-Day Saints (colloquially called Mormons) settled on the land that is now Utah, intending to establish their own theocratic state. President James Buchanan struggled to quash their efforts in 1858, and the Mormons eventually gave up their dreams of theocracy and their rights to polygamy, and statehood was granted on January 4, 1896.

Today the state's population is 70% Mormon—a religious presence that creates a haven for family values. Utah's citizens dwell primarily in the 100 mi. corridor along I-15, from Ogden to Provo. Outside this area, Utah's natural beauty dominates, intoxicating visitors in a way that Utah's watered-down 3.2% beer cannot.

⓰ PRACTICAL INFORMATION

Capital: Salt Lake City.

Visitor Info: Utah Travel Council, 300 N. State St., Salt Lake City 84114 (☎801-538-1030 or 800-200-1160; www.utah.com), across from the capitol building. Has the *Utah Vacation Planner*'s lists of motels, national parks, and campgrounds, and brochures on biking, rafting, and skiing. **Utah Parks and Recreation,** 1594 W. North Temple, Salt Lake City 84116 (☎801-538-7220). Open M-F 8am-5pm.

Controlled Substances: Mormons abstain from alcohol (along with other "strong drinks" like coffee and tea). State liquor stores are sparse, and grocery and convenience stores only sell beer. Restaurants serve wine, but licensing laws can split a room—you may have to move to the bar for a mixed drink. Waiters may not offer drink menus; diners must request one. Places that sell hard alcohol must be "members only"; tourists can find a "sponsor"—i.e., an entering patron—or get a short-term membership.

Postal Abbreviation: UT. **Sales Tax:** 5.75-7.75%.

SALT LAKE CITY   ☎801

Tired from five months of travel, Brigham Young looked out across the Great Salt Lake and said: "This is the place." He believed that in this desolate valley his band of Mormon pioneers had finally found a haven where they could practice their religion freely. To this day, Salt Lake City is dominated by Mormon influence. The Church of Jesus Christ of Latter-Day Saints (LDS) owns the tallest office building downtown and welcomes visitors to Temple Square. Despite its commitment to tradition, Salt Lake is rapidly attracting high-tech firms and outdoor enthusiasts. The city, in all its homogeneity, has a surprisingly diverse set of communities.

⧉ TRANSPORTATION

Airport: Salt Lake City International, 776 N. Terminal Dr. (☎575-2400), 6 mi. west of Temple Sq. UTA buses #50 and 150 run between the terminal and downtown ($1.25). Buses leave every hr. M-Sa 7am-11pm, Su 7am-6pm. Taxi to Temple Sq. about $15.

Trains: Amtrak, 340 S 600 W (☎322-3510). *This area can be dangerous at night.* To **Denver** (15hr., 1 per day, $75-112) and **San Francisco** (19hr., 1 per day, $77-115). Open daily 10:30pm-6am.

Buses: Greyhound, 160 W. South Temple (☎355-9579), near Temple Sq. To **Denver** (7-10hr., 5 per day, $54) and **Las Vegas** (12-13hr., 2 per day, $49). Open daily in summer 6:30am-2:30am; in winter 6:30am-11:30pm, ticket window until 10:30pm.

Public Transit: Utah Transit Authority (UTA; ☎743-3882). Frequent service to University of Utah campus, buses to suburbs, airport, mountain canyons. The #11 express runs to Provo ($2.25). New TRAX light rail follows Main St. from downtown to Sandy and to the University of Utah. Buses every 20min.-1hr. M-Sa 6am-11pm. Fare $1-2, under 5 free. Senior discounts. Maps available at libraries and the visitors center. UTA buses and TRAX trains traveling downtown near the major sites are free.

Taxi: Ute Cab ☎359-7788. **Yellow Cab** ☎521-2100. **City Cab** ☎363-5550.

Salt Lake City

⚑ ACCOMMODATIONS
The Avenues Hostel (HI), **2**
Base Camp Park City, **12**
City Creek Inn, **1**
Ute Hostel, **14**

🍴 FOOD
Orbit, **7**
Rio Grande Cafe, **9**
Ruth's Diner, **3**
Sage's Cafe, **10**

NIGHTLIFE
Bricks, **6**
Club Naked, **11**
Club Splash, **13**
DV8, **5**
Utopia, **4**
Zipperz, **8**

TRAX Light Rail

⚡🔧 ORIENTATION AND PRACTICAL INFORMATION

Temple Square is the heart of downtown. Street names increase in increments of 100, indicating how many blocks east, west, north, or south they lie from Temple Sq.; the "0" points are **Main Street** (north-south) and **South Temple** (east-west). State St., West Temple, and North Temple are 100-level streets. Occasionally, streets are called 13th S or 17th N, which are the same as 1300 S or 1700 N. Local addresses often include two cross streets. For example, a building on 13th S (1300 S) might be listed as 825 E 1300 S, meaning the cross street is 800 E (8th E). Smaller streets and those that do not fit the grid pattern sometimes have non-numeric names.

Visitor Info: Salt Palace Convention Center and Salt Lake City Visitors Bureau, 90 S. West Temple (☎ 534-4902). Located in Salt Palace Convention Center. Open daily 9am-5pm.

GLBT Resources: The **Little Lavender Book** (☎ 323-0727; www.lavenderbook.com), a directory of gay-friendly Salt Lake City services, is distributed twice yearly. The **Salt Lake Metro,** a newspaper with articles and ads on GLBT issues and events, is published bi-weekly. (☎ 323-9500. Free.)

Hotlines: Rape Crisis, ☎ 467-7273. **Suicide Prevention,** ☎ 483-5444. Both 24hr.

Internet Access: Salt Lake Public Library, 210 E 400 S (☎524-8200), a new high-tech, space-age facility. Open M-Th 9am-9pm, F-Sa 9am-6pm, Su 1-5pm.

Post Office: 230 W 200 S, 1 block south and 1 block west of visitors center. Open M-F 8am-5pm, Sa 9am-2pm. **Postal Code:** 84101. **Area Code:** 801.

ACCOMMODATIONS

Affordable motels cluster at the southern end of downtown, around 200 W and 600 S, and on North Temple. Most prices will rise during the Sundance Festival.

Base Camp Park City, 268 Historic Main St. (☎655-7244, 888-980-7244; www.parkcitybasecamp.com), 30 mi. east of Salt Lake City on I-80, Exit 145, and south on Rte. 224. Free Internet and parking, restaurant discounts, movie/DVD theater, and free transportation to Deer Valley, The Canyons, and Park City ski areas. Park City Transportation (☎649-8567 or 800-637-3803; $27) runs from airport. Reserve in advance in winter. In summer dorms $25; in winter $35. Private room (for up to 4) $80/$120. ❷

City Creek Inn, 230 W. North Temple (☎533-9100 or 866-533-4898; http://citycreekinn.com), by Temple Sq, has clean ranch-style rooms. HBO, free local calls. Singles $54; doubles $66. AAA discount. 2 wheelchair-accessible rooms. ❸

The Avenues Hostel (HI), 107 F St. (☎359-3855). 15min. walk from Temple Sq. in a residential area. Free parking, a new entertainment system, 2 kitchens, and mountain bike rentals ($10 per day, $100 deposit). Key deposit $5. Reception 7:30am-noon and 4-10:30pm. Reservations recommended July-Aug. and Jan.-Mar. Dorms $14, nonmembers $17. Private rooms with shared baths $25/$31. ❶

Ute Hostel (AAIH/Rucksackers), 21 E. Kelsey Ave. (☎595-1645 or 888-255-1192), near the intersection of 1300 S and Main St. Free pickup can be arranged from airport, Amtrak, Greyhound, or the visitors center. Kitchen, free tea and coffee, linen, parking. Check-in 24hr. Reservations accepted only with pre-payment, recommended July-Sept. and Jan.-Mar. Dorms $15. Singles $25; doubles $35. Cash only. ❶

FOOD

Good, cheap, and surprisingly varied restaurants pepper the city. For a quick bite, **ZCMI Mall** and **Crossroads Mall,** both across from Temple Sq., have food courts.

Ruth's Diner, 2100 Emigration Canyon Rd. (☎582-5807; www.ruthsdiner.com). The best breakfasts in the city and a full bar with live music at night. Ruth's, 70-years-old, is the second-oldest restaurant in Utah and is a Salt Lake City landmark for its huge portions (all with Ruth's Mile High biscuit), delicious omelettes ($6-8), and brownie sundaes ($6). For lunch, the pan-seared fresh salmon ($11) is unbeatable. Open daily 8am-10pm. ❶

Orbit, 540 W 200 S (☎322-3808), is casual but elegant, famed for its weekend brunch (smoked salmon Benedict and crabcakes Benedict), in a space-age interior. It also serves wraps ($7-8) and salads ($6-11), and has a full smoothie bar. Open M-W 11am-3pm, Th-F 11am-10pm, Sa 9am-10pm, Su 9am-3pm. Brunch Sa-Su 9am-3pm. ❸

Rio Grande Cafe, 270 S. Rio Grande St. (☎364-3302), in the northern wing of the historic train station, is the place to go for tons of great Mexican fare and margaritas. $7-8 enchiladas, and $7.25 *flautas* and *chimichangas*. Open M-Th 11am-2:30pm and 5-9pm, F 11am-2:30pm and 5-10pm, Sa 11:30am-2:30pm and 5-10pm, Su 4-9pm. ❸

Sage's Cafe, 473 E 300 S (☎322-3790). This organic vegan cafe is a hotbed of culinary innovation. Calling themselves as "culinary astronauts," chefs produce delectable dishes. Try the basil and macadamia nut pesto pasta dish for $13. Sugar- and oil-free meals available. Weekday lunch buffet $7-8. Sandwiches $6-9. Open W-Th 5-9:30pm, F 5-10pm, Sa 9am-10pm, Su 9am-9pm. ❷

👁 SIGHTS

LATTER-DAY SIGHTS. Most of Salt Lake City's sights are sacred to the Church of Jesus Christ of Latter-Day Saints, and free. The seat of the highest Mormon authority and the central temple, **Temple Square** is the symbolic center of the Mormon religion. The square has two **visitors centers,** north and south. Visitors can wander around the 10-acre square, but the temple is off-limits to non-Mormons. The North Visitors Center has two films, both free: *Legacy*, a 55min. depiction of the Mormon's trek to Utah, and *First Vision*, a 20min. film recounting the visions of 14-year-old Joseph Smith. *(Legacy every 90min. 10:30am-7:30pm; First Vision every 90min. 10am-8:30pm.)* A visitor info line *(☎800-537-9703)* provides up-to-date hours and tour info. Guided 45min. tours leave from the flagpole every 10min., showing the highlights of Temple Sq. *The Testaments*, a 65min. film detailing the coming of Christ to the Americas (as told by the Book of Mormon), is screened at the **Joseph Smith Memorial Building.** *(☎ 240-4383 for films, 240-1266 for tours. Open M-Sa 9am-9pm. Film shown at 10:30am, noon, 1:30, 3, 4:30, 6, 7:30pm; in summer also 9pm. Free.)* Temple Sq. is also home to the **Mormon Tabernacle** and its famed choir. Rehearsals and performances are free. *(Organ recitals M-Sa noon-12:30pm, Su 2-2:30pm; in summer also M-Sa 2-2:30pm. Choir rehearsals Th 8-9:30pm; choir broadcasts Su 9:30-10am, must be seated by 9:15am.)* In summer, free concerts play at **Assembly Hall** next door. *(☎800-537-9703.)*

The **Church of Jesus Christ of Latter Day Saints Office Building** is the tallest building in town. The elevator to the 26th floor grants a view of the Great Salt Lake in the west opposite the Wasatch Range. *(40 E. North Temple. ☎240-3789. Observation deck open M-F 9am-4:30pm, but accessible only by guided tour.)* The LDS church's collection of genealogical materials is free at the **Family Search Center,** 15 E. South Temple St., in the Joseph Smith Memorial Building. The actual collection is housed in the **Family History Library.** *(35 N. West Temple. ☎240-2331. Search Center open M-F 9am-9pm, Sa 9am-5pm. Library open M 8am-5pm, Tu-Sa 8am-9pm.)* Early Mormon history is recounted at the **Museum of Church History and Art,** 45 N. West Temple St., with an original 1830 Book of Mormon, a rare portrait of Joseph Smith, and Brigham Young's famous prayer bell. *(☎240-3310. Open M-F 9am-9pm, Sa-Su 10am-7pm.)*

THE GATEWAY. The city's newest mall, The Gateway, between North Temple and 200 South, along 400 West, is open-air and chic, incorporating the restored 1908 Union Pacific Depot. The Clark Planetarium has free exhibits and IMAX. *(☎456-7827. www.clarkplanetarium.org. Star shows $6, children $3; IMAX $7, children $4; combo tickets $10/$5. Open M-Th 10:30am-9:15pm, F-Sa 10:30am-11:15pm, Su 10:30am-8pm.)*

MUSEUMS. Visiting exhibits and a permanent collection of world art wow enthusiasts at the hyper-modern **Utah Museum of Fine Arts,** on the University of Utah campus, just off S. Campus Dr. *(☎581-7332. Open Tu and Th-F 10am-5pm, W 10am-8pm, Sa-Su 11am-5pm. $4; students, ages 65 and up and 6-18 $2.)* Also on campus, the **Museum of Natural History** has displays on the history of the Wasatch Front, with an emphasis on anthropology, biology, and paleontology. *(☎581-6927. M-Sa 9:30am-5:30pm, Su noon-5pm. $6, ages 3-12 $3.50, under 3 free.)* The **Salt Lake Art Center** shows an impressive array of contemporary art and documentary films. *(20 S. West Temple. ☎328-4201. Open Tu-Th and Sa 10am-5pm, F 10am-9pm, Su 1-5pm. Suggested donation $2.)*

THE GREAT SALT LAKE. The Great Salt Lake, administered by Great Salt Lake State Marina, is a remnant of primordial Lake Bonneville and is so salty that only blue-green algae and brine shrimp can survive in it. The salt content varies from 5 to 27%, providing the buoyancy credited with keeping the lake free of drownings. Decaying organic material on the lake shore gives the lake its pungent odor. **Antelope Island State Park**, in the middle of the lake, separated from the city by Farmington Bay, is a favorite for visitors. *(Bus #37 "Magna" will take you within 4 mi. For the lake's south shore, take I-80 17 mi. west of Salt Lake City to Exit 104. To the island, take Exit 335 from I-15 and follow signs to the causeway.* ☎625-1630. *Open in summer daily 7am-10pm; in winter dawn-dusk. Day use: vehicles $8, bicycles and pedestrians $4.)*

🎷 🎧 ENTERTAINMENT AND NIGHTLIFE

Salt Lake City's summer months are jammed with evening concerts. Every Tuesday and Friday at 7:30pm, the **Temple Square Concert Series** presents a free outdoor concert in Brigham Young Historic Park, with music ranging from string quartet to unplugged guitar (☎240-2534; call for schedule). The **Utah Symphony Orchestra** performs in gold-leafed **Abravanel Hall,** 123 W. South Temple. (☎533-6683. Office open M-F 10am-6pm. Tickets Sept. to early May $15-40. Limited summer season; call 1 week in advance.) The University of Utah's **Red Butte Garden,** 300 Wakara Way (☎587-9939; www.redbuttegarden.org), has a summer concert series with national acts in an immaculate garden with stunning views of the entire Salt Lake basin.

The free *City Weekly* and *Salt Lake Metro* list events and are available at bars, clubs, and restaurants. Early Mormon theocrats instated laws making it illegal to serve alcohol in a public place. Hence, all liquor-serving institutions are "private clubs," serving only members and their "sponsored" guests. In order to get around this barrier, most bars and clubs charge a "temporary membership fee"—a cover charge. Despite the Mormons' contempt for the bottle, Salt Lake City has an active nightlife scene, centering on S. West Temple and the blocks near the railroad tracks. **Utopia,** 108 S 500 W, has VIP lounges, a jungle-themed bar, outdoor patios, and multiple dance floors. (☎519-2947; www.utopiaslc.com. F gay night, W and Sa dress to impress. Separate 18+ and 21+ areas. Cover $5-7. Open W-Sa 10pm-2am.) Salt Lake's trendy and fashionable dig the retro styling of **Club Naked,** 326 S. West Temple, with both a relaxing bamboo-accented patio, and pounding dance floor. (☎521-9292. W ladies night, Th house groove, Sa alternative lifestyle. Cover $5. Open W-Sa 9:30pm-2am.) **Club Splash,** 404 S. West Temple, has pool tables, a martini bar, and a 2000 sq. ft. dance floor. (☎363-2828 Open Tu 8pm-3am, F-Sa 9pm-2am.) **Bricks,** 200 S 600 W, is the city's oldest and largest dance club, with arguably its best sound system. (☎238-0255; www.bricksclub.com. Separate 18+ and 21+ areas. Cover $5-7. Open daily 9:30pm-2am.) At six stories, **DV8,** 115 S. West Temple, is the city's second largest club and features live acts Monday to Thursday for all ages. (☎539-8400. F-Sa club nights 9pm-2am, 21+. Cover $5-7.) Salt Lake City's gay and lesbian crowd flocks to the classy **Zipperz,** 155 W 200 S, to sip martinis ($5) and groove on the tiered dance floor. (☎521-8300. 21+. Cover $5-6. Open Su-Th 2pm-2am, F-Sa 5pm-2am. Kitchen open until 11pm.)

🎿 PARK CITY AND SKI RESORTS

Utah sells itself with pictures of intrepid skiers on pristine powder, hailed by many as "the greatest snow on earth." Seven major ski areas lie within 45min. of downtown Salt Lake, making Utah's capital a good base camp for the winter vacation paradise of the Wasatch Mountains. Nearby **Park City** is the quintessential ski town with the 🏠**Base Camp Park City** (p. 832) as its only budget option. Call or check ski area websites for deals before purchasing lift tickets. Besides being fun, the Utah ski hills are also an excellent source of employment. If you are interested in working while you ski, check the employment section on each mountain's website or call Snowbird's job hotline (☎947-8240). Most slopes are open in the summer for hiking, mountain biking, and horseback riding. The area code for some resorts is ☎435. Unless noted, all other numbers share SLC's ☎801 area code.

Alta (☎359-1078; www.alta.com), 25 mi. southeast of Salt Lake City in Little Cotton-wood Canyon. Cheap tickets; magnificent skiing. No-frills resort continues to eschew opulence and reject snowboarders. 500 in. of champagne powder annually. Open mid-Nov. to mid-Apr. daily 9:15am-4:30pm. Lift tickets: full-day $47, half-day $37-42; day pass for beginner lifts $25; joint ticket with nearby Snowbird $66.

Brighton (☎800-873-5512; www.skibrighton.com), south of Salt Lake in Big Cottonwood Canyon. Bargain skiing and snowboarding in a down-to-earth atmosphere. Especially family- and beginner-friendly. Open early Nov. to late Apr. M-Sa 9am-9pm, Su 9am-4pm. Lift tickets: full-day $41, half-day $35, night $25, ages 10 and under free. Rentals: ski/board packages $26-32 per day, children $18.

Deer Valley (☎435-649-1000; www.deervalley.com), in Park City. Host of several Winter Olympics events in 2002 and a world-class ski area, if expensive. No snowboards. Open Dec.-Apr. daily 9am-4:15pm. Lift tickets: full-day $69, half-day $48; seniors $48/$32; children $38/$30. Ski rentals: adult package $40-50 per day, children $30.

Solitude (☎800-748-4754; www.skisolitude.com), in Big Cottonwood Canyon 30min. south of Salt Lake. Uncrowded slopes and 20km of nordic trails at Silver Lake (8700 ft.). Open Nov. to late Apr. daily 9am-4pm. Lift tickets: full-day $44, half-day $37; seniors (60-69) $37, children $24, over 70 $10. Nordic Center full-day $11, half-day $8. Rentals: $25 per day, snowboards $28, high-performance ski package $38.

The Canyons (☎435-649-5400; www.thecanyons.com), in Park City. Lodges, shops, and restaurants, and a ton of territory. 146 trails, 16 lifts. Open Nov.-Apr. M-F 9am-4pm, Sa-Su 8:30am-4pm. Lift tickets: full-day $62, half-day $45; children and seniors $31/$24. Rentals: adult ski or board package $34-45 per day, child ski or board package $25. Free season pass in exchange for 1 day of work at the resort per week.

▶ DAYTRIP FROM SALT LAKE CITY

TIMPANOGOS CAVE

Legend has it that a set of mountain lion tracks first led Martin Hansen to the cave that bears his name. **Hansen's Cave** is only one-third of the cave system of American Fork Canyon, collectively called **Timpanogos Cave**. n a rich alpine environment, Timpanogos is a gem for both speleologists (cave nuts) and tourists. Though early miners shipped boxcars of stalactites and other mineral wonders back east to sell to universities and museums, plenty remain to bedazzle guests along the 1hr. walk through the depths. The cave is open to visitors only through ranger-led tours.

Timpanogos Cave National Monument is only accessible via Rte. 92 (20 mi. south of Salt Lake City off I-15, Exit 287; Rte. 92 also connects with Rte. 189 northeast of Provo). The **visitors center** has tour tickets and info on the caves. Reservations for summer weekends should be made far in advance. Bring water and warm layers: the rigorous hike to the cave climbs 1065 ft. over 1½ mi., but the temperature inside stays at 45°F. (☎756-5238. Open mid-May to late Oct. daily 7am-5:30pm. 3hr. hikes depart daily every 15min. 7am-4:15pm. $6, ages 6-15 $5, Golden Age Passport and ages 3-5 $3, ages 2 and under free.)

The National Monument is dwarfed by the **Uinta National Forest,** which blankets the mountains of the Wasatch Range. The **Alpine Scenic Drive (Route 92)** provides great views of Mt. Timpanogos and other snowcapped peaks. The 20 mi. trip takes almost 1hr. one-way. (Open late May to late Oct.; not recommended for vehicles over 30 ft. long. 3-day Forest Service pass $3 per vehicle; 14-day pass $10; annual pass $25.) The **Timpooneke Trail** (16¼ mi. round-trip) is a hiking trek leading to the sheer summit of **Mt. Timpanogos** (11,749 ft.), beginning at the Aspen Grove Trailhead (6860 ft.) and meeting the summit trail at Emerald Lake.

SOUTHWEST

The **Pleasant Grove Ranger District** has info on area **campgrounds ❶**. (Reservations ☎800-280-2267. Sites $11-13.) **Backcountry camping ❶** in the forest requires no permit or fee as long as you respect minimum-impact guidelines. While the National Park Service forbids camping within the national monument, **Little Mill Campground ❶**, on Rte. 92 past the monument, is a good jumping-off point from which to beat the Cave crowds. (Water, vault toilets. Open early May to late Sept. Sites $11.) **Timpanooke Campground ❶**, 2 mi. farther up the Alpine Loop, has more forested and private sites. (Water, vault toilets. Open mid-June to late Sept. Sites $10.)

DINOSAUR NATIONAL MONUMENT AND VERNAL ☎435

Dinosaur National Monument was created in 1915, seven years after paleontologist Earl Douglass found fossilized dinosaur bones here while working for the Carnegie Museum. Since then, some 350 million tons of dinosaur remains have been carted away from this Jurassic cemetery. The **Dinosaur Quarry Visitors Center**, a remarkable Bauhaus building, houses the park's crown jewel: an exposed river bank, brimming with 1600 fossils—the only place in the park to see dinosaur bones. The town of Vernal, west of Dinosaur on U.S. 40, is a popular base for exploring the monument, Flaming Gorge, and the Uinta Mountains. Stop by the visitors center in Vernal for free auto tour guides that direct motorists to historical sights and beautiful vistas; **Harper's Corner**, at the confluence of the Green and Yampa Rivers (take the Harper's Corner Rd. from the Monument Headquarters) has one of the best views around. At the end of the road, an easy 2 mi. round-trip hike (allow 1½-2hr.) leads to the view. The less-explored parts of the over 200,000-acre monument boast incredible rock-climbing. **Don Hatch River Expeditions**, 221 N 400 E in Vernal, is descended from one of the nation's earliest commercial rafting enterprises, and sends expeditions through the monument and the nearby Flaming Gorge along Class II and III rapids. Request a paddle trip if you want to help steer the raft. (☎789-4316 or 800-342-8243; www.hatchriver.com. Open M-F 9am-5pm. 1-day trip $66, age 6-12 $56. Seniors 10% off. Reservations recommended.) In Vernal, the new **Utah Field House of Natural History**, 496 E. Main St., is a high-tech facility with geological timelines and full-size dinosaur replicas. (☎789-3799. Open daily in summer 8am-7pm; in winter 9am-5pm. $5, children and seniors $3.)

The most accessible camping spot, **Green River ❶**, lies along Cub Creek Rd. about 5 mi. from the entrance fee station. (88 sites. Flush toilets and water. Closed in winter. Sites $12.) **Echo Park ❶**, 13 mi. along Echo Park Rd. from Harper's Corner Dr. (4WD road impassable when wet), is the perfect location for an evening under the stars. (9 sites. Pit toilets and water in summer. Sites $6; free in winter.) Free **backcountry camping ❶** permits are available from Monument Headquarters or the Quarry Visitors Center. Those less inclined to rough it should head to the **Sage Motel ❸**, 54 W. Main St., in Vernal, which has standard rooms, A/C, satellite TV, and free local calls. (☎789-1442 or 800-760-1442. Singles $52, in winter $46. Doubles $61/$56.) **Betty's Cafe ❶**, 416 W. Main St. in Vernal, has breakfast favorites ($5-7) and cinnamon rolls for $1.50. (☎781-2728. Open M-Sa 6am-4pm, Su 6am-noon. Cash only.) **Stockman's ❸**, 1684 W. U.S. 40, lures hungry Vernalians with burgers ($6-8), all-you-can-eat sirloin steak ($13), and gargantuan desserts ($5-6). (☎781-3030. Open Tu-F 10am-11pm, Sa 11:30am-11pm.)

The monument's western entrance lies 20 mi. east of Vernal on Rte. 149, which splits from U.S. 40 southwest of the park in Jenson, UT. In summer, a shuttle whisks passengers ½ mi. to the **visitors center;** between September and late May cars can drive directly to the center. (☎781-7700. Open June-Aug. daily 8am-7pm, Sept.-May M-F 8am-4:30pm. Entrance fee $10 per car; $5 per cyclist, pedestrian, or tour-bus passenger.) **Monument Headquarters** is 2 mi. east of Dinosaur, CO, on U.S. 40. (☎970-374-3000. Open June-Aug. daily 8am-4:30pm, Sept.-May M-F 8am-

4:30pm.) **Gas** is available in Vernal, Jenson, and Dinosaur, CO. The **Northeast Utah Visitors Center,** 235 E. Main St., in Vernal, provides info on regional recreational activities. (☎789-7894. Open daily 8am-7pm.) **The Ashley National Forest Service Office,** 355 N. Vernal Ave., has info about outdoors activities in the Ashley and Uinta National Forests. (☎789-1181. Open M-F 8am-5pm.) Mail kitschy dino postcards from the **post office,** 67 N 800 W. **Postal Code:** 84078. **Area Code:** 435.

FLAMING GORGE NATIONAL RECREATION AREA ☎435

Seen at sunset, the contrast between the red canyons and the Green River's aquamarine water makes the landscape glow. Not everyone was satisfied with this natural beauty; legislation was passed in 1963 to dam the Green River. The resulting reservoir, 91 mi. long with over 350 mi. of scenic shoreline, is the centerpiece of the Flaming Gorge National Recreation Area. Boating and fishing enthusiasts descend into the gorge every summer to take advantage of the water.

The Green River below the dam teems with trout, allowing for top-notch **fishing.** To fish, get a **permit,** available at Flaming Gorge Lodge (see below) and Flaming Gorge Recreation Services. (☎885-3191. Open Mar.-Oct. daily 7am-10pm.) For more info, call the **Utah Division of Wildlife Resources,** 1594 W. North Temple, in Salt Lake City. (☎800-538-4700. Open M-F 7:30am-6pm.) Several establishments rent gear for reservoir recreation. **Cedar Springs Marina,** 2 mi. south of the dam, rents boats and offers guided fishing trips. (☎889-3795. Open daily 8am-6pm. 10-person pontoon boats from $120 for 3hr., $200 per day. 6-person fishing boats $50/$90.) Nearby, **Flaming Gorge Lodge,** 4 mi. south of the dam, rents fishing rods and rafts. (☎889-3773; www.fglodge.com. Open daily 6:30am-10pm. Rods $10 per day. 7-person raft $59 per day.) Hikers and bikers will love the area's trails, some of which snake along dangerous cliff edges. All trails allow bikes. The flat **Canyon Rim Trail** (7 mi.) has access points at Red Canyon Visitors Center and several campgrounds, and offers spectacular views of Flaming Gorge. Another popular hike begins at **Dowd Mountain** (5 mi. one-way, 3hr., 1600 ft. descent). Turn off Rte. 44 east of Manila, take Forest Rd. 94, and go down Hideout Canyon to reach the trailhead. The strenuous **Elk Park Loop** (20 mi. round-trip) is perfect for mountain biking and departs from Rte. 44 at Deep Creek Rd., follows it to Forest Rd. 221 and Forest Rd. 105, skirts Browne Lake, and runs along **Old Carter and South Elk Park Trails.**

Camping is scenic and accessible with over 30 campgrounds around the lake. The **visitors center** offers advice for reserving sites. (☎888-444-6777; call 5 days ahead.) **Canyon Rim ❶,** on the road to Red Canyon Visitors Center, offers views of the red-walled gorge. (Vault toilets. Sites $14; late Oct. to late Apr. free.) The 19 sunny sites at **Dripping Springs ❶,** just past Dutch John on Rte. 191, are a prime fishing location. (Vault toilets. Reservations accepted. Sites $14.) For a roof and four walls, the **Red Canyon Lodge ❸,** 2 mi. south of the visitors center on Rte. 44, 24 mi. south of Manila, offers a great location, views, and luxury-resort activities at good prices. (☎889-3759. Private lake, restaurant. 2-person cabins with restrooms $95; 4-person $105; each additional adult $6, under 12 $2; rollaway beds $6 per night.) In **Manila,** the **Steinnaker Motel ❷,** at Rte. 43 and 44, has cramped but clean rooms. (☎784-3104. Check-in at the Chevron station. Singles $36; doubles $44.)

From Vernal, follow U.S. 191 north to the recreation area on the **Flaming Gorge Scenic Byway.** The reservoir extends as far north as Green River, WY, and is also accessible from I-80 by way of Rte. 414 and Rte. 530 on the west side of the reservoir, as well as from U.S. 191, which continues along the eastern side. A recreation pass ($2 per day, $5 per 16 days, $20 per season) can be obtained at the **Flaming Gorge Visitors Center,** on U.S. 191 on the Flaming Gorge Dam, or at most stores surrounding the gorge, but is not needed in developed campgrounds, the dam, and businesses. The visitors center also offers free tours of the dam. (☎885-3135. Open daily 8am-6pm; low-season 10am-4pm.) A few miles off U.S. 191 and 3 mi. off Rte. 44 to Manila, the **Red Canyon Visitors Center** hangs 1360 ft. above the reservoir, offering staggering views into the canyon and stuffed examples of local wildlife. (☎889-3713. Open late May to Aug. daily 10am-5pm.) **Post Office:** 4 South Blvd., in Dutch John. (☎885-3351. Open M-F 7:30am-3:30pm, Sa 8:30am-11am and 1:45-3:15pm.) **Postal Code:** 84023. **Area Code:** 435.

MOAB   ☎435

Moab first flourished in the 1950s when uranium miners rushed to the area, transforming the town from a quiet hamlet into a gritty desert outpost. Today, mountain bikes and whitewater rafts have replaced the Geiger counter, and tourists flock to Moab, eager to bike the red slickrock, raft the rapids, and explore the surrounding Arches and Canyonlands National Parks. The town has adapted to its onslaught of visitors and adventure-seekers—microbreweries and t-shirt shops now fill the rooms of the old uranium mine headquarters on Main St.

◪ ◪ ORIENTATION AND PRACTICAL INFORMATION. Moab is 30 mi. south of I-70 on U.S. 191, just south of the junction with Rte. 128. The town center is 5 mi. south of the entrance to Arches National Park and 38 mi. north of the turnoff to the Needles section of Canyonlands National Park. U.S. 191 becomes Main St. for 5 mi. through downtown. The closest Amtrak (☎800-872-7245) and Greyhound (☎800-454-2487) stations are in Green River, some 52 mi. northwest of town. Some hotels and hostels will pick guests up from the train or bus station for a fee. Bighorn Express (☎888-655-7433) runs daily to and from the Salt Lake City airport, stopping in Green River and Price. Shuttles leave from the Ramada Inn, 182 S. Main St. (Departs Salt Lake City airport at 2pm, departs Moab at 7:30am; 4½hr.; $54. Reservations recommended.) Roadrunner Shuttle (☎259-9402) and Coyote Shuttle (☎259-8656) take you where you want to go on- or off-road in the Moab area. The Moab Information Center, 3 Center St., at the intersection of Center and Main, has copious information on the city and surrounding parks. (☎259-8825 or 800-635-6622. Open daily May-Sept. 8am-9pm; Oct. 8am-8pm; Nov.-Apr. 8am-5pm.) Internet Access: Free at the Grand County Library, 100 E. 25 S. (☎259-5421. Open M-W 9am-9pm, Th-F 9am-7pm, Sa 9am-5pm.) Post Office: 50 E. 100 N. (☎259-7427. Open M-F 8am-5pm, Sa 9am-1pm.) Postal Code: 84532. Area Code: 435.

◪ ACCOMMODATIONS. Chain motels line Main St., but Moab isn't cheap and rooms fill up fast from April to October, especially on weekends. **◪Lazy Lizard International Hostel ❶,** 1213 S. U.S. 191, is 1 mi. south of Moab on U.S. 191. The staff of this clean and comfortable hostel will tell you about the area, while the kitchen, TV/VCR lounge, laundry, showers, and hot tub draw a friendly mix of students, backpackers, and aging hippies. (☎259-6057. Reception 8am-11pm, but late arrivals can be arranged. Check-out 11am. Reservations recommended for weekends in spring and fall. Tent sites $6; dorms $9. Private rooms for up to 4 $22-36; cabins for up to 6 $27-47.) The **Center Street Hotel ❷,** 96 E. Center St., a block off Main, is a mix between a high-class hostel and a bargain hotel. Nine private theme rooms will transport you to the beach or the middle of a movie set. Shared bathrooms, common kitchen, and lounge area. Check in at the Kokopelli Lodge, 72 S, 100 E. (☎259-7615 or 888-530-3134. Rooms Nov.-Aug. $35; Sept.-Oct. $45. Each additional person $5.)

One thousand campsites blanket the Moab area, so finding a place to sleep under the stars shouldn't be a problem, even if hotels are booked. **Goose Island, Hal Canyon, Oak Grove, Negro Bill,** and **Big Bend Campgrounds ❶,** all on Rte. 128, sit on the banks of the Colorado River three to nine mi. northeast of Moab. (☎259-2100.

Fire pits. Water is available at Negro Bill at the intersection of U.S. 191 and Rte. 128. Sites $5 at Negro Bill, $10 at all other campgrounds.) The shady, secluded **Up the Creek Campground ❶**, 210 E. 300 S, is close to downtown and caters solely to tent camping. (☎259-6995. 20 sites. Showers. Open Mar.-Oct. $10 per person.)

◘ FOOD. ▧EklectiCafé ❶, 352 N. Main St., dishes out delicious pastries, coffee drinks, breakfast ($3-7), and lunch ($4-8), with great organic and vegetarian options. Check out the giant mosaic coffee cup in front, grab a seat on the shady, patio, and be ready to chat with the welcoming locals. Area musicians perform on Sunday mornings in the summer. (☎259-6896. Open M-Sa 7:30am-2:30pm, Su 7:30am-1pm.) **Milt's Stop & Eat ❶**, 356 Mill Creek Dr., grills up tasty diner fare at low prices. The eight stools at the worn counter make for a personal dining experience; you can watch your food being prepared while talking to the cook. Cheeseburgers $1.80, great malts $2. (☎259-7424. Open Tu-Sa 6am-8pm, breakfast until 11:30am.) Adding a little Fifth Ave. flair to an otherwise Western town, **Breakfast at Tiffany's ❷**, 90 E. Center St., defies the bacon-and-eggs breakfast standard. The amaretto french toast ($5.25) and catfish and eggs ($7) are favorites. (☎259-2553. Open M-F 7am-2pm, Sa-Su 7am-11:30am. Cash only.) The **Peace Tree Juice Cafe ❶**, 20 S. Main St., will cool you off with a smoothie or fresh juice ($2.50-5), the perfect antidote to a hot day in the desert. (☎259-8503 Open daily 8am-6:30pm.)

◰ OUTDOOR ACTIVITIES. Mountain biking is the big draw in Moab and attracts thousands each year. The **Slickrock Trail** (10 mi.) is one of the most popular choices. Rolling up and down the slickrock outside Moab, the trail lacks big vertical gain, but is technically difficult. Novices may enjoy the Bar M Loop (7 mi.) or Gemini Bridges (14 mi.), while those looking for a challenge can check out the new, single-track Sovereign Trail. **Rim Cyclery,** 94 W. 100 N, rents both basic and mountain bikes, and provides information on the trails. (☎259-5333 or 888-304-8219. Open daily 9am-6pm. Full suspension $32-50 per day; town bikes $2 per hr.)

Countless rafting companies help outdoor enthusiasts explore the Colorado and Green Rivers. **▧Canyon Voyages Adventure Co.,** 211 N. Main St., has friendly, knowledgeable guides and will personalize their services to meet customer requests and all skill levels. (☎800-733-6007. Half-day $36, ages 4-15 $26; full day $49/$39. Some trips include lunch, with vegetarian options. Hiking tours also available.) Numerous outfitters arrange horseback, motorboat, canoe, jeep, and helicopter rides.

UTAH'S NATURAL WONDERS

Arches, Canyonlands, Capitol Reef, Bryce Canyon, and Zion National Parks comprise Utah's Grand Circle of national parks. In a line running through southern Utah, they are connected by a series of scenic highways. In their midst lies the mammoth Grand Staircase-Escalante National Monument, sprawling south and east of Bryce Canyon and west of Capitol Reef. The spectacular arches, canyons, amphitheaters, plateaus, and redrock of these public lands put them among the densest collection of geological and panoramic brilliance the nation has to offer.

From Moab, take U.S. 191 north 5 mi. to **Arches.** Continue 60 mi. north on U.S. 191 to Rte. 313 S and the Island in the Sky area of **Canyonlands.** Or, to reach the Needles area of Canyonlands (87 mi.), take U.S. 191 south from Moab to Rte. 211 W. To get to **Capitol Reef,** continue south on U.S. 191, then take Rte. 95 northwest to Rte. 24. Continue west on Rte. 24 to Torrey, where scenic Rte. 12 heads south past **Grand Staircase-Escalante National Monument** and Dixie National Forest to **Bryce Canyon.** For **Zion,** follow Rte. 12 W to U.S. 89 S through Mt. Carmel Jct. and take Rte. 9 W. Routes 12 and 95 are among the most scenic highways in the US.

SOUTHWEST

Southern Utah's two national forests are divided into districts, some of which lie near the national parks and serve as excellent places to stay on a cross-country jaunt. **Manti-La Sal National Forest** has two sections near Arches and the Needles area of Canyonlands. **Dixie National Forest** stretches from Capitol Reef through Bryce all the way to the western side of Zion.

ARCHES   ☎ 435

Edward Abbey wrote of Arches National Park: "This is the most beautiful place on earth." Arches, spires, pinnacles, and fins tower above the desert with overwhelming grandeur, some which are so perfect that explorers compared them to the architectural feats of lost civilizations. Deep red sandstone blends with a strikingly blue sky, and green piñon pines in an unforgettable palette of colors.

■ ⁊ **ORIENTATION AND PRACTICAL INFORMATION.** The park entrance is on U.S. 191, 5 mi. north of Moab. Although no public transit serves the park, shuttle bus companies go to both Arches and Moab from surrounding towns and cities. Construction on U.S. 191 and near the park's entrance is scheduled through the summer of 2005 and may create traffic difficulties, but the park will continue to operate as usual. Many visitors come in the summer, but 100°F temperatures make hiking difficult—make sure to bring plenty of water. The weather is best in the spring and fall, when temperate days and nights make for a comfortable stay. In winter, white snow brilliantly contrasts with the red arches. An entrance pass ($10 per car, $5 for pedestrians, bicycles, and motorcycles) covers admission for seven days and comes with a map of the park, its hiking trails, and the locations of the largest, most well-known arches. More detailed maps are available at the **visitors center** just inside the park entrance. (☎ 719-2299. Open daily 8am-4:30pm; extended hours Mar.-Sept.) Write the Superintendent, Arches National Park, P.O. Box 907, Moab 84532, or see www.nps.gov/arch for more info.

⁊ **CAMPING.** The park's only campground, **Devil's Garden ❶,** has 52 excellent campsites amid piñons and giant sandstone formations. The campground is within walking distance of the Devil's Garden and Broken Arch trailheads, but is a winding 18 mi. from the visitors center. Reservations are available for 30 of the sites between March 1 and October 31 for an additional $9 (www.reserveusa.com). The remaining sites are available on a first come, first served basis at the visitors center beginning at 7:30am and can fill up very quickly in the high season. (☎ 719-2299. Bathrooms, water, no showers or wood-gathering. 1-week max. stay. Sites $10.) If the heat is too much at Arches, the **Manti-La Sal National Forest** offers a respite. Take Rte. 128 along the Colorado River and turn right at Castle Valley, or go south 6 mi. from Moab on U.S. 191 and turn left onto Loop Rd. There are many campgrounds in the forest, including **Warner Lake ❶,** where hillside sites sit 4000 ft. above Arches, and are far cooler. ($10. Reserve at www.reserveusa.com.) **Oowah Lake,** a 3 mi. hike from the Geyser Pass Rd., is a rainbow trout haven. Fishing permits are available at stores in Moab and at the Forest Service Office, 62 E. 100 N ($5 per day). Contact the Manti-La Sal National Forest (☎ 259-7155) for more info.

◳ **HIKING.** While the roads that snake through Arches offer exceptional scenery, the real points of interest are only accessible by foot. In addition to the free map distributed on entering, more detailed hiking maps and info, especially desert precautions, are available at the visitors center. Those hiking in the summer will want to load up on water and sunscreen, and start early to avoid the midday heat. Stay on trails; the land may look barren, but the soil crust is home to biological life forms that are easily destroyed by footsteps. Pets are not allowed on trails.

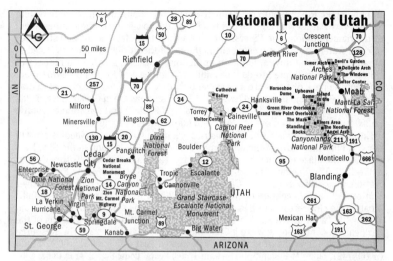

National Parks of Utah

The most popular hike in the park leads to the oft-photographed **Delicate Arch.** The trail (3 mi., 2½hr. round-trip) begins at the Wolfe Ranch parking area and climbs 480 ft. To view the spectacular Delicate Arch without the arduous hike, take the **Delicate Arch Viewpoint Trail** which begins in the Viewpoint parking area. This trail, really a 300 ft. pathway, takes around 15min. and is wheelchair accessible. **Devil's Garden** (7¼ mi., 3-5hr. round-trip) is a challenging hike and requires some scrambling over rocks, but hardy travelers will be rewarded by the eight arches visible along the trail. An optional primitive loop for experienced hikers adds both time and difficulty to the trek but provides access to another arch away from the crowds. The trek is not recommended in wet or snowy conditions. **Tower Arch** (3½ mi., 2-3hr. round-trip) can be accessed from the trailhead at the Klondike Bluffs parking area via Salt Valley Rd. This moderate hike explores one of the park's more remote regions. The trail ascends a steep, short rock wall before meandering through sandstone fins and sand dunes. Salt Valley Rd. is occasionally washed out—check at the visitors center before departing.

CANYONLANDS ☎ 435

"Cliffs of rock, tables of rock, plateaus of rock, terraces of rock, crags of rock...with the heavens for a ceiling." This description of Canyonlands, penned by explorer John Wesley Powell, is as true today as it was when he wrote it in 1875. The colorful high desert of Canyonlands's canyons, mesas, buttes, fins, and spires are set into sharp relief against the brilliant blue of the Utah sky in a rugged, yet artful example of one of Mother Nature's finest creations.

■ ⋒ ORIENTATION AND PRACTICAL INFORMATION. In southeastern Utah, Canyonlands, is divided into four districts by the Green and Colorado Rivers: **Island in the Sky,** the **Needles,** the **Maze,** and the **Rivers** themselves. The park also includes the detached **Horseshoe Canyon** district. Island in the Sky is the most popular and accessible region. Take U.S. 191 to Rte. 313, 10 mi. north of Moab and 22 mi. south of I-70. Follow Rte. 313 22 mi. to the southwest. The Needles, geared more toward backcountry adventure, is on Rte. 211, 40 mi. south of Moab and 14 mi. north of Monticello. To reach the Maze, the most remote portion of the park,

SOUTHWEST

from I-70 take Rte. 24 south for 29 mi. to a turnoff just past the entrance to Goblin Valley State Park. From there, a dirt road will take you 46 mi. to the southeast and to the ranger station. The Rivers, known for their first-class rapids and stretches of calm water, are best accessed through one of the rafting companies based in Moab. Horseshoe Canyon, home to prehistoric cultures, and later a hideout of Butch Cassidy, is limited to day use, and is 32 mi. east of Rte. 24 on a dirt road. None of the park districts are accessible by public transit, but the closest **Amtrak** (☎ 800-872-7245) and **Greyhound** (☎ 800-454-2487) stations are in Green River, 52 mi. northwest of Moab on I-70. **Coyote Shuttle** (☎ 259-8656) and **Roadrunner Shuttle** (☎ 259-9402), both based out of Moab, will take visitors to Canyonlands.

Entrance fees vary according to district: Island in the Sky and Needles are $10 per car, but other parts of the park have no entrance fees. Island in the Sky, Needles, and the Maze each have a visitors center. (Island in the Sky Visitors Center: ☎ 259-4712. The Needles Visitors Center: ☎ 259-4711. The Maze Hans Flat Ranger Station: ☎ 259-2652. Horseshoe Canyon also operates out of the Hans Flat Ranger Station. All visitors centers open daily 8am-4:30pm; extended hours spring-fall.) Moab is the closest town to Island in the Sky and Needles, while Green River and Hanksville (west of the part on Rte. 24) are closest to the Maze. All areas of the park can be contacted by writing Canyonlands National Park, 2282 SW Resource Blvd., Moab, UT 84532 or at www.nps.gov/cany. **Post Office:** 50 E. 100 N. Moab (☎ 259-7427. Open M-F 8am-5pm, Sa 9am-1pm.) **Postal Code:** 84532. **Area Code:** 435.

> **!** No gas, food, water, or other services are available within the park, so bring everything you need; the National Park Service recommends one gallon of water per person per day. Much of the park is composed of slickrock. Trails on or near slickrock are extremely treacherous in wet or icy conditions.

▊▊ ACCOMMODATIONS AND FOOD. Indoor accommodations can only be found in Moab, Green River, or Hanksville, but campers are treated to well-maintained campgrounds. Island in the Sky has one campground, **Willow Flat ❶**, 7 mi. southeast of the visitors center, with 12 first come, first served sites. (Pit toilets, no water. $5.) There are also 20 backcountry campsites along the White Rim which require a $30 backcountry permit; reservations for permits are accepted and recommended in spring and fall. Backcountry permits go quickly, but a few walk-up permits are usually available in the summer and winter. (☎ 259-4351.) Nearby **Dead Horse Point State Park ❶**, on Rte. 313, has 21 campsites. Nine sites are held on a first come, first served basis, and are usually filled by early afternoon. (☎ 800-322-3770. Reservations recommended. Water, hookups, covered picnic tables, and grills. $14, including admission to the park. Wheelchair accessible.) Free **primitive camping** is available in designated areas of the Bureau of Land Management (BLM) lands along Rte. 313 east of the park. The **Needles Outpost**, just before the entrance booth, offers showers and limited, expensive groceries. (☎ 979-4007. Open daily 9am-6pm.) The Maze has no developed campsites but primitive campgrounds dot the terrain and are first come, first served. A variety of restaurants are located in Moab, Green River, and Hanksville, but there is no food available in the park.

◙ ▨ SIGHTS AND OUTDOOR ACTIVITIES. Each part of Canyonlands offers a unique view of the same area. Island in the Sky, named for the peninsula surrounded by deep canyons (except for a 40 ft. neck), offers the most options for car touring. The **Grand View Point Overlook** and **Green River Overlook**, both clearly marked, offer awe-inspiring views of the mighty rivers that carved the canyons. Those wishing to stretch their legs can enjoy the easy **Mesa Arch Trail** (½ mi. round-trip) or the **Syncline Loop**, a challenging 8.3 mi. loop around the Upheaval

Dome area. For the most spectacular views of the Colorado River, ◪**Dead Horse Point State Park** is a few miles north of the Island entrance on Rte. 313. (Park open daily 6am-10pm, visitors center open daily 8am-5pm. Entrance fee $7.) For more information, write Box 609, Moab, UT 84532, or call ☎259-2614 or 800-322-3770. The eerie spires of the wilder Needles district is best explored on foot. **Roadside Ruin** (0.3 mi.), an easy trail to a Puebloan granary, is a quick introduction to the area's history. The **Slickrock Trail** (2.4 mi. loop) is an intermediate hike with good views down into the canyons. The Needles is also home to an array of four wheel-drive roads, like **Elephant Hill**, a highly technical route. The Maze contains only very challenging and technical backcountry hiking and climbing. Horseshoe Canyon's **Great Gallery** (6.5 mi. round-trip) grants access to a vast collection of prehistoric rock art.

CAPITOL REEF ☎435

The hundred-mile Waterpocket Fold is a geologist's fantasy and Capitol Reef's feature attraction. With its rocky peaks and pinnacles, the fold, created 65 million years ago in the land that Native Americans declared the "Land of the Sleeping Rainbow," bisects the park's 378 square miles. Yet the cliffs and domes of this wrinkle in the earth's crust, are not the only attraction. Ancient Native Americans' petroglyphs and the early Mormon settlers' orchards and buildings are found throughout the park, making Capitol Reef a blend of natural and cultural history.

■🖪 **ORIENTATION AND PRACTICAL INFORMATION.** The middle link in the Fab Five chain, east of Zion and Bryce, and west of Arches and Canyonlands, Capitol Reef is on Rte. 24, flanked by the small towns of Hanksville to the east and Torrey on the west. Unreachable by major bus lines, the closest **Greyhound** and **Amtrak** stops are in Green River. **Entrance** to the park is free except for the scenic drive, which is $5 per vehicle. The **visitors center**, on Rte. 24, supplies travelers with free maps, trail brochures, and info on daily activities. (☎425-3791. Open daily June-Aug. 8am-6pm, Sept.-May 8am-4:30pm.) *Summer temperatures average 95°F. After rain, beware of flash floods.* For more info, contact the Superintendent, Capitol Reef National Park, HC 70 Box 15, Torrey 84775 (☎425-3791; www.nps.gov/care). **Post Office:** 75 W. Main St., in Torrey. (☎425-3716. Open M-F 7:30am-1:30pm, Sa 7:30-11:00am.) **Postal Code:** 87175. **Area Code:** 435.

🏠🍴 **ACCOMMODATIONS AND FOOD.** The park's campgrounds offer sites on a first come, first served basis. The main campground, **Fruita ❶**, 1¼ mi. south of the visitors center off Rte. 24, sits in the orchards and has 71 sites with water and toilets. (Sites $10; limit 8 people per site.) **Cedar Mesa Campground ❶** on Notom-Bullfrog Rd. and **Cathedral Valley ❶**, in the north (accessible by 4WD or on foot), have five sites each; neither has water, but they're free. Both areas, and all backcountry camping, require a free **backcountry permit**, available at the visitors center.

Torrey, a sleepy town 11 mi. west of the visitors center on Rte. 24, has the closest lodging and restaurants. The **Sandcreek RV Park, Campground, and Hostel ❶**, 540 W. Main St., offers an espresso bar, organic produce, local jewelry and crafts, and restful lodgings. One dorm room houses eight beds, a minifridge, and a microwave. There are also 12 tent sites, 12 hookups, and two rustic cabins that sleep up to four people. (☎425-3577 or 877-425-3577. Showers for non-guests $4. Linens $2. Laundry $5. Reception 7:30am-7pm. Check-out 11am. Open Apr. to mid-Oct. Dorms $10; tent sites $11; hookups $16-19; cabins $28-34.) The **Capitol Reef Inn ❷**, 360 W. Main St., is simple and comfortable with a Southwestern touch. (☎425-3271. Jacuzzi, minifridge. Connected to the **Capitol Reef Cafe ❷**, open daily 7am-10pm. Reception 7am-10pm. Check-out 11am.

Open Apr.-Oct. Rooms $44, each additional person $4.) Specializing in innovative Southwestern cuisine, **Cafe Diablo ❾,** 599 W. Main St., is an upscale dining experience. Those with wallets up to the task are rewarded with Rattlesnake Cake appetizers ($9), entrees like Glazed Ribs and Pecan Chicken ($17-25), and sinfully rich desserts. (☎ 425-3070. Open Apr. 15-Oct. 15 daily 5pm-10pm.) More affordable food awaits at **Brink's Burgers ❶,** 163 E. Main St. Their basic burger, a quarter-pound of deliciousness, is only $2.60. Even the SuperBurger, with two kinds of cheese, bacon, and ham, is under $5. (☎ 425-3710. Take-out available. Open daily 11am-9pm. Cash only.)

■ ◪ **SIGHTS AND OUTDOOR ACTIVITIES.** You can see the Reef's haunting landforms from the seat of your car on the 25 mi. **scenic drive,** a 1hr. round-trip that wiggles along the cliffs, washes, and canyon floors on paved and improved dirt roads. Along Rte. 24, you can view the bathroom-sized **Fruita Schoolhouse** built by Mormon settlers, 1000-year-old **petroglyphs** etched on the stone walls, and **Panorama Point. Chimney Rock** and the **Castle** are two striking sandstone formations along the route. The **Fruita orchards** line the roads throughout the park. You're welcome to eat as much free fruit as you desire while in the park (usually cherries and apricots), but there is a nominal fee to take fruit out of the orchards.

Wild Hare Expeditions, 2600 E. Rte. 24, in the Best Western Capitol Reef Resort, embarks on a variety of backpacking and hiking tours. (☎ 425-3999 or 888-304-4273. Half-day $40-50, children $35; full-day $60-75/$50.) If you want to strike out on your own, most trailheads lie along Rte. 24 or the scenic drive. The easy **Capitol Gorge Trail** (2 mi. round-trip, 2-3hr.) runs off the scenic drive. The **Rim Overlook and Navajo Knobs Trail** (9 mi. round-trip, 4-8hr.), one of the more challenging routes in the park, departs from the Hickman Bridge parking area and climbs to the canyon rim above the river to offer breathtaking vistas. **Cassidy Arch** (3½ mi. round-trip), starting on Grand Wash Rd., has a steep, challenging climb that will take you above the arch, but is a shorter alternative to other hikes if you're pressed for time. In the northern and southern sections of the park, all hikes are considered backcountry travel and require a **free backcountry permit** for overnight trips.

BRYCE CANYON   ☎ 435

If Nature enjoys painting with a big brush in the Southwest, she discarded her coarse tool when creating Bryce Canyon. The canyon brims with slender, fantastically shaped rock spires called hoodoos. What it lacks in Grand Canyon-esque magnitude, Bryce makes up for in intricate beauty. Early in the morning or late in the evening the sun's rays bring the hoodoos to life, transforming them into color-changing stone chameleons, melting from fiery orange to muted peach and near-translucent, glowing white. The first sight of the canyon can be breathtaking: as Ebenezer Bryce, a Mormon carpenter with a gift for understatement, put it, the canyon is "one hell of a place to lose a cow."

■ ◪ **ORIENTATION AND PRACTICAL INFORMATION.** Approaching from the west, Bryce lies 1½hr. east of Cedar City; take Rte. 14 or Rte. 20 to U.S. 89. From the east, take I-70 to U.S. 89, turn east on Rte. 12 at Bryce Jct. (7 mi. south of Panguitch), and drive 14 mi. to the Rte. 63 junction; head south 4 mi. to the park entrance. To assuage the park's traffic problem, the Park Service has implemented a free shuttle system that takes visitors to the visitors center, lodge, and prime scenic overlooks in air-conditioned comfort. Private vehicles can travel park roads, but the Park Service urges visitors to leave their cars outside the park. The entrance fee is $20 per car and $10 per pedestrian. The **visitors center** is just inside the park. (☎ 834-5322. Open daily June-Aug. 8am-8pm; Apr.-May and Sept.-Oct. 8am-6pm; Nov.-Mar. 8am-4:30pm.) Write Bryce National Park, P.O. Box 170001, Bryce Canyon, UT 84717 or see www.nps.gov/brca. **Post Office:** In Ruby's Inn Store (☎834-8088), just north of the park entrance. (Open M-F 8:30am-noon and 12:30-4:30pm, Sa 8:30am-12:30pm. No credit cards.) **Postal Code:** 84717. **Area Code:** 435.

▮▯ ACCOMMODATIONS AND FOOD. North and **Sunset Campgrounds ❶**, both within 3 mi. of the visitors center, offer toilets, picnic tables, water, and 209 sites. North is open year-round and sites can be reserved May 15-Sept. 30 for an additional $9 by calling ☎877-444-6777. Sunset is open from late spring to early fall and is first come, first served. (Sites $10; arrive early to claim the best spots.) Two campgrounds lie just west of Bryce on scenic Rte. 12, in Dixie National Forest. At 7400 ft., the **Red Canyon Campground ❶** has 36 sites on a first come, first served basis amid the red rocks' awesome glory. (Sites $11.) Obtain **backcountry camping permits** ($5) from the ranger at the visitors center. The **King Creek Campground ❶**, 11 mi. from Bryce on Forest Service Road 087 off Rte. 12 (look for signs to Tropic Reservoir), features lakeside sites. (☎800-280-2267. Sites $10.)

Sleeping inside the park requires either a tent and sleeping bag or a fat wallet, but good deals line Rte. 12 in Tropic. Panguitch, 23 mi. west of the park on U.S. 89, has over 15 inexpensive, independent motels. Winter rates are much lower, and in slow summers, bargain walk-in rates abound. ▧**Bybee's Steppingstone Motel ❷**, 21 S. Main St., in Tropic, offers clean, spacious and comfortable rooms minutes from the park entrance, but far from the tourist bustle. (☎679-8998. Microwave, fridge, satellite TV. Singles in summer $44; doubles $48.) The **Country Inn Motel ❷**, 121 N. Main St. in Tropic, has basic, recently furnished rooms at good prices. (☎679-8600. $45 up to two people, $5 for each additional person, children free.)

Inside and immediately surrounding the national park, food options are scarce. A slice of pizza, microwave-burrito, or prepackaged sandwich ($2-3) await at the **Bryce Canyon Camper Store ❶**. For a sit-down lunch in the park, try the $7-8 burgers and sandwiches at **Bryce Canyon Lodge Dining Room ❸**. Dinner is more expensive (entrees $15-22) and reservations are recommended. (☎834-5361. Open Apr.-Oct. 6:30-10:30am, 11am-3:30pm, 5:30-9:30pm.) With a little driving, you can find more options. All-you-can-eat golden pancakes ($3) beckon starving passersby at the **Hungry Coyote ❷**, 2 N. Main St. in Tropic, which also serves $10-15 dinners. (☎679-8811. Open daily Apr.-Oct. 6:30-10:30am and 5-10pm.) Several miles west of the park on Rte. 12, the **Bryce Pines Restaurant ❸** serves delicious meals. (☎834-5441. Sandwiches $5-8; dinner entrees $13-19. Open daily in summer 6:30am-9:30pm.)

◼▨ SIGHTS AND OUTDOOR ACTIVITIES. Bryce's 18 mi. main road winds past spectacular lookouts, with Bryce and Inspiration Points providing quintessential postcard-worthy views of the canyon. One oft-missed viewpoint is **Fairlyland Point,** at the north end of the park, 1 mi. off the main road, which has the best sights in the canyon. A range of hiking trails lure visitors from their cars. The **Rim Trail** can be accessed anywhere along the rim and has very little elevation change (11 mi., 4-6hr.). The moderate ▧**Navajo/Queen's Garden Loop** (3 mi., 2-3hr., some very steep grades) is an excellent way to experience the canyon and see some of the park's most famous vistas. More challenging options include the **Peek-A-Boo Loop** (3½ mi., 3-4hr.), which winds in and out of hoodoos. A word to the wise: the air is thin—if you start to feel giddy or short of breath, take a rest. Very sturdy shoes or hiking boots are a must for hiking into the canyon. **Canyon Trail Rides** arranges guided horseback rides. (☎679-8665. 2hr. rides $40, half-day $55.)

SOUTHWEST

GRAND STAIRCASE-ESCALANTE NAT'L MONUMENT ☎435

The last corner of American wilderness to be captured by a cartographer, Grand Staircase-Escalante National Monument remains remote, rugged, pristine, and beautiful. Stretching along scenic Rte. 12 between Capitol Reef and Bryce Canyon, the 1.9 million acres of painted sandstones, high alpine plateaus, treacherous canyons, and raging rivers encompass diverse areas of geological, biological, and historical interest. The mammoth expanse of the monument necessitates a visitors center in each gateway community: Kanab, Big Water, Cannonville, Boulder, and Escalante. Hours vary slightly by location, and Big Water, Cannonville, and Boulder are only open mid-March to October. The main source of visitor information is the **Escalante Interagency Visitors Center,** 755 W. Main in Escalante. (☎826-5499. Open daily Mar.-Oct. 7:30am-5:30pm, Nov.-Feb. 8am-4:30pm.) The official **monument headquarters** is at **Kanab Field Office,** 190 E. Center St., in Kanab. (☎644-4300; www.ut.blm.gov/monument. Open daily late Mar. to mid-Nov. 7:30am-5:30pm.)

The Staircase is big and wild, best suited to backcountry adventure. Only one developed trail, the moderate **Calf Creek Falls Trail** (6 mi. round-trip, 3-5 hr.), accessible from Calf Creek Recreation Area 15 mi. east of Escalante on Rte. 12, exists in the entire monument. Leading to the 126 ft. lower falls, the trail follows the creek bed. Sections of deep sand may slow you down, but the falls are worth it. All other excursions are considered backcountry, with perhaps the most popular destination being the Canyons of Escalante, in the eastern portion of the monument. **Hole-in-the-Rock Road,** heading south from Rte. 12 east of Escalante, is a primary access road for the area (4WD). **Death Hollow Wilderness,** a 30 mi. trek requiring technical climbing and stretches of swimming, is one of the most challenging routes. A **free backcountry permit** is required for all stays in the monument and can be obtained at any visitors center. Most routes require technical climbing or canyoneering skills, and the slot canyons and terrain are susceptible to extremely dangerous flash floods. Unless you are a seasoned backpacker and well prepared for your adventure, it may be a wise idea to hire a guide to show you the area. ◪**Excursions of Escalante,** 125 E. Main in Escalante, crafts backcountry outings to meet your personal desires and provides helpful expert advice. (☎800-839-7567; www.excursions-escalante.com. $75 per day, students and seniors $50; $150 overnight trips.)

Escalante, along Rte. 12, is an easy place to find accommodations and food. The aroma of delicious burgers ($5) wafts from ◪**The Trailhead Cafe ❶,** 125 E. Main, which also offers refreshing smoothies and shakes ($3), coffee drinks, breakfasts ($2-4), and pick-up volleyball games.(☎826-4714. Open Apr.-Nov. Su-M and W-Sa 8am-6pm.) **Escalante Outfitters ❷,** 320 W. Main, (☎826-4266; www.escalanteoutfitters.com), is a gear store, espresso bar, and cafe, and even has private cabins ($30) and tent sites ($15). Their pizza is amazing, and the cafe has free wireless Internet. There are many options if you're looking for campgrounds. The 13 shaded sites at **Calf Creek Campground ❶,** 15 mi. east of Escalante, offer easy access to the Calf Creek Trail but fill up fast. (Toilets and water. Sites $7.) Six miles north of Boulder on Rte. 12, there are seven primitive sites at **Deer Creek ❶.** (Toilets. Sites $4.) Two miles west of Escalante on Rte. 12, the **Escalante Petrified Forest State Park ❶** has 22 sites along the banks of the reservoir; swimming is allowed. (☎826-4466. Showers, modern restrooms, 1 handicapped-accessible site. Sites $14.)

ZION NATIONAL PARK ☎435

Russet sandstone mountains loom over the puny cars and hikers that flock to Zion National Park in search of the promised land, and rarely does Zion disappoint. In the 1860s, Mormon settlers came to the area and enthusiastically proclaimed that they had found Zion, the promised land representing freedom from persecution. Brigham Young disagreed, however, and declared that the place was awfully nice, but "not Zion." The name "not Zion" stuck for years until a new wave of explorers dropped the "not," giving the park its present name. The park might very well be the fulfillment of Biblical prophecy for outdoor recreationalists. With unparalleled hiking trails and challenging and mysterious slot canyons set against a tableau of sublime sandstone, a visit to Zion can be a spiritual experience.

▓▓ ORIENTATION AND PRACTICAL INFORMATION. Zion's main entrance is in **Springdale**, on Rte. 9, which borders the park to the south along the Virgin River. Approaching Zion from the west, take Rte. 9 from I-15 at Hurricane. From the east, pick up Rte. 9 from U.S. 89 at Mt. Carmel Jct. **Greyhound** (☎800-231-2222), has service as far as Hurricane, while Zion Canyon Transportation (☎877-635-5993) has shuttle service from St. George to Zion (round-trip $27.) The highway, campgrounds, visitors center, and museum are all accessible by car, but to enter the heart of the canyon, you'll need to park and take the **free shuttle bus,** which stops at all major trailheads and sites, and is an excellent way to get an overview of the park in just under 1½hr. Another free shuttle connects the park to food and lodgings in town, making a car unnecessary once you arrive in Springdale.

The ecologically harmonious **Zion Canyon Visitors Center,** just inside the south entrance, has an info center, bookstore, and backcountry permit station. (☎772-7616; www.nps.gov/zion. Open daily late May to early Sept. 8am-7pm; mid-Apr. to late May and early Sept. to Oct. 8am-6pm; Oct. to mid-Apr. 8am-5pm.) At the northwest entrance to the park, the **Kolob Canyons Visitors Center** offers info on the Kolob Canyon Scenic Drive and the surrounding trails, and has books and maps. (☎586-9548; www.nps.gov/zion. Open daily June-Aug. 8am-4:30pm; Apr.-May and Sept.-Oct. 7am-4:30pm. For more info, write Zion National Park, Springdale, UT 84767.) The park's entrance fee is $10 for pedestrians, bikes, and motorcycles; $20 per car. **Emergency:** ☎911 or 772-3322. **Post Office:** Stamps and mail drop in the visitors center, full service in Springdale on Zion Park Blvd. **Postal Code:** 84767. **Area Code:** 435.

▓▓ ACCOMMODATIONS AND CAMPING. The **USAHostels Grand Canyon ❶**, 143 E. 100 S, in Kanab, 50 mi. southeast of Zion is the closest hostel. It has $15 dorms and $32 private rooms that fill quickly. (☎644-5554. Free pancake breakfast.) In Springdale, the **El Río Lodge ❸**, 995 Zion Park Blvd., welcomes guests with clean rooms, friendly service, and dazzling views. (☎772-3205 or 888-772-3205. Queen bed $48, two double beds $53; winter rates slightly lower.) Across the street, the **Terrace Brook Lodge ❸**, 990 Zion Park Blvd., offers clean rooms. (☎800-342-6779. Singles $55; doubles $71. $10 less in winter. AAA discount.) More than 300 sites are available at the **South** and **Watchman Campgrounds ❶**, near the brand-new visitors center. Campgrounds fill quickly in summer; arrive before noon to ensure a spot. Watchman Campground takes reservations, but South is first come, first served. (☎800-365-2267 for Watchman reservations. Water, toilets, and sanitary disposal station. Sites $14.)

❑ FOOD. The Zion Canyon Lodge houses the only in-park concessions: the **Castle Dome Cafe ❶** feeds hungry families and hikers (burgers, salads, and subs $3-7; open Apr.-Oct. daily 10am-7pm; cash only), while the **Red Rock Grill ❸** caters to a less rambunctious and sweaty group. (☎772-3213. Open daily 6-10am, 11:30am-2:30pm, and 5-10pm; reservations recommended.) Nearby Springdale has more options. With cheap breakfasts ($5 and under), creative, filling wraps ($6), gigantic smoothies ($4), coffee drinks, and ice cream, **Tsunami Juice & Java ❶**, 180 Zion Park Blvd, a block from the south park entrance, draws Zion tourists all day. (☎772-

3818. Showers $4. Open daily Mar.-Nov. 8am-dusk.) The funky **Oscar's Cafe ❸**, 948 Zion Park Blvd., has burgers ($8-13) and breakfasts ($4-8), along with innovative, homemade Mexican entrees for $12-17. (☎ 772-3232. Open daily 7:30am-11pm.)

🏔 **OUTDOOR ACTIVITIES.** Zion seems to have been made for hiking; unlike in the surrounding canyons, most trails won't have you praying for a stray mule. However, many trails spiral around cliffs with narrow ledges and long drop-offs, so those with a fear of heights may want to choose carefully. The trails are serviced by a shuttle bus that delivers hikers to and from trailheads (runs 5:45am-11pm). Shuttle maps are available at the visitors center. The **Riverside Walk** (2 mi., 1-2hr.), paved and wheelchair accessible with assistance, is Zion's easiest, most popular trail. It begins at the Temple of Sinawava at the north end of the shuttle route, and runs along the Virgin River, passing beautiful wildflowers. The **Emerald Pools Trail** (1-3.1 mi., 1-3hr.) is wheelchair accessible along the lower loop, but the middle and upper loops are steep and narrow. Although it may seem inviting, swimming is not allowed in the pools. The **Hidden Canyon Trail** (2 mi., 2-3hr.), is short but harrowing, and grants impressive valley views. The tough **Observation Point Trail** (8 mi., 5hr.) leads through **Echo Canyon,** a spectacular kaleidoscope of sandstone. Overnight hikers can spend days on the 13 mi. **West Rim Trail,** while **The Narrows** is one of the most popular backcountry hikes. The route, up to 16 mi. one-way, follows the riverbed through the neck of Zion Canyon above the end of the Riverwalk Trail. The trail is beautiful and remote, but be careful—*the canyon's high walls make flash floods deadly.* **Kolob Canyons,** the northwest region of the park, has its own impressive vistas and hiking trails. The **⛰Zion-Mt. Carmel Highway,** connecting the park's south and east entrances, winds through the canyon, offering excellent views of the valley and a ride through a 1920s, 1¼ mi. long tunnel. The area also has a loyal **mountain biking** following. **Gooseberry Mesa,** about 15 mi. from Springdale, has great singletrack and novice trails. **Springdale Cycles,** 1458 Zion Park Blvd., has bike rentals, single and multi-day tours, and advice. (☎ 772-0575 or 800-776-2099; www.springdalecycles.com. Open daily 9am-1pm and 3-7:30pm. Front suspension half-day $25, full-day $35; full suspension $35/$45; kids $7/$10.)

CEDAR BREAKS NATIONAL MONUMENT ☎ 435

Shaped like a giant amphitheater, the semicircle of canyons that compose Cedar Breaks National Monument are over 3 mi. wide and 2000 ft. deep. Sandstone spires decorate the bowl's vibrant red, orange, and yellow surface. To reach this geological marvel, take Rte. 14 east from Cedar City and turn north on Rte. 148. A 29-site **campground ❶** on the edge of an alpine meadow (water, toilets; open June to mid-Sept.; sites $12) and the **visitors center** (☎ 586-0787; open daily June to mid-Sept. 8am-6pm) await at **Point Supreme.** Tourists travel to the Monument nearly exclusively for the view, most easily seen by parking at the visitors center and walking to Point Supreme, or by stopping at one of the vistas along scenic Rte. 143. The Monument has two established hiking trails. Starting at the **Chessman Ridge Overlook** (10,467 ft., about 2 mi. from the visitors center), the 2 mi. round-trip **Alpine Pond Trail** follows the rim to a spring-fed alpine lake whose waters trickle into the breaks, winding toward slow evaporation in the Great Basin. The hike takes 1-2hr. and can be accompanied by a trail guide available at the visitors center or trailhead ($1). The 4 mi. round-trip **Ramparts Trail** departs from the visitors center at 10,300 ft. and traces the amphitheater's edge through a Bristlecone grove to a 9950 ft. point, granting spectacular views of the terrain below. Though reaching the monument in the winter is difficult on snowy roads, winter recreationalists cherish the rolling meadows and serene winter scenery. There are no services inside the monument; the nearest gas, food, and lodging are in Cedar City or Brian Head. (☎586-9451; www.nps.gov/cebr. Entrance $3 per person per week, under 17 free.)

ARIZONA

Home to the Grand Canyon, most of the Navajo Reservation, seven national forests, and two big cities, Arizona defies its image as a land of endless desert highway. The Sonoran desert's dry scrub, spotted with cacti and the occasional dusty town, makes for a starkly beautiful landscape, while Arizona's cities, sky-island forests, and mountain biking and hiking country provide enough variety for hours, days, or weeks of exploration. Populated primarily by Native Americans until the end of the 19th century, Arizona has been hit by waves of settlers—from the speculators and miners of the late 1800s, to the soldiers who trained here during World War II and returned afterwards, to more recent immigrants from Mexico. Traces of lost Native American civilizations remain at Canyon de Chelly, Navajo National Monument, and Wupatki and Walnut Canyons, and these ancient tribes' descendants now occupy reservations on one-half of the state's land, making up one-seventh of the US Native American population. Ghost towns, relics of mining booms and busts, are scattered throughout the state, while Phoenix defines urban sprawl.

◪ PRACTICAL INFORMATION

Capital: Phoenix.

Visitor Info: Arizona Tourism, 1110 W. Washington St., Phoenix 85007 (☎888-520-3434; www.arizonaguide.com). Open M-F 8am-5pm. **Arizona State Parks,** 1300 W. Washington St., Phoenix 85007 (☎602-542-4174 or 800-285-3703). Open M-F 8am-5pm.

Postal Abbreviation: AZ. **Sales Tax:** variable, around 5%.

Time Zone: Mountain Standard Time. *With the exception of the Navajo Reservation, Arizona does not observe Daylight Savings Time.*

GRAND CANYON

Millions of visitors travel from across the globe to witness the Grand Canyon, the natural wonder which captures the themes that make the Southwest so awe-inspiring. First, there's the space: 277 mi. long and over one mile deep, the Canyon overwhelms the human capacity for perception. Then, there's the color: the shifts in hue translate to millions of years of geologic history. Finally, there's the river: the chaotic, creative force behind most of the area's landforms is on full display.

The Grand Canyon extends from Lee's Ferry, AZ, to Lake Mead, NV. In the north, the Glen Canyon Dam backs up the Colorado into mammoth Lake Powell. To the west, Hoover Dam traps the remaining outflow from Glen Canyon to form Lake Mead. Grand Canyon National Park is divided into three sections: the popular South Rim, the more serene North Rim, and the canyon gorge itself. Traveling between rims takes approximately 5½hr. via the long drive to the Lee's Ferry bridge or a grueling, inconvenient 13 mi. hike. Sandwiched between the national park and Lake Mead, the Hualapai and Havasupai Reservations abut the river.

SOUTH RIM ☎928

In the summer, everything on two legs or four wheels comes to this side of the Grand Canyon. If you plan to visit at this time, make reservations for everything far in advance, and prepare to battle crowds. A friendly Park Service staff, well-run facilities, and beautiful scenery ease crowd anxiety. Fewer tourists brave the canyon in the winter; many hotels and facilities close then. Leading to the park, Rte. 64 is surrounded by Kaibab National Forest and traces the North Rim.

TRANSPORTATION

There are two park entrances: the main **south entrance** is about 6 mi. from the visitors center, while the eastern **Desert View** entrance is 27 mi. away. Both are accessible via Rte. 64. From Las Vegas, the fastest route to the South Rim is U.S. 93 S to I-40 E, and then Rte. 64 N. From Flagstaff, head north on U.S. 180 to Rte. 64.

Trains: The **Grand Canyon Railway** (☎800-843-8724) runs an authentically restored train from Williams, AZ, to the Grand Canyon (2¼hr.; leaves 10am, returns 3:30pm; $58, children $25). Guided tours of the rim are $21-36.

Buses: Open Road Tours & Transportation (☎226-8060 or 877-226-8060) departs from the Flagstaff Amtrak station (1 E. Rte. 66) daily at 8:30am and 3pm for the Grand Canyon with return trips departing from Maswik Lodge at 11:45am and 5:45pm. (1¾hr.; $20, reservations recommended).

Public Transit: Free shuttle buses run along the West Rim to Hermits Rest (1¼hr. roundtrip; operates daily May-Sept. 1hr. before sunrise to 1hr. after sunset) and the Village Loop (1hr. round-trip. Operates daily 1hr. before sunrise to 10pm) every 10-30min. May-Sept., the Hermits Rest shuttle is the only way to access the West Rim area. A free **hiker's shuttle** runs between the info center and the South Kaibab Trailhead, on the East Rim near Yaki Point. Early buses run June-Aug. 4, 5, and 6am.

Taxi: ☎638-2822.

ORIENTATION AND PRACTICAL INFORMATION

Posted maps and signs in the park make orientation easy. Lodges and services concentrate in **Grand Canyon Village**, at the west end of Park Entrance Rd. To the east, lie the visitors center, campground, and general store, while most of the lodges and the **Bright Angel Trail** are in the west section. The **South Kaibab Trail** is off **Desert View Drive** east of the village. Free shuttle buses to eight rim overlooks run along **Hermit Road** in the west (closed to private vehicles in summer). Avoid walking on the drive; the rim trails are safer and more scenic. An **entrance pass** is $20 per car and $10 for travelers using other modes of transportation; the pass lasts one week. For most services in the park, call the main switchboard at ☎638-2631.

Visitor Info: The **Canyon View Information Plaza,** across from Mather Point by the park entrance, is the one-stop center for info, stocking *The Guide* (an essential), pamphlets, and info on hiking. To get there, park at Mather Pt., then walk ½ mi. to the info plaza. The Park Service, through the Grand Canyon Association, sells a variety of books and packets. (☎800-858-2808; www.grandcanyon.com, or www.nps.gov/grca.) The **transportation info desks** in the **Bright Angel Lodge** and the **Maswik Lodge** (☎638-2631) take reservations for mule rides, bus tours, plane tours, Phantom Ranch, taxis, and more. Open daily 6am-8pm.

Equipment Rental: At the gear counter in Canyon Village Marketplace in Market Plaza. Hiking boots and socks ($8), sleeping bags ($9), tents (2-person $15, 4-person $16), day packs (large $6, small $4), and more (stoves $5). Deposit required. Open daily 7am-8:30pm.

Weather and Road Conditions: ☎638-7888.

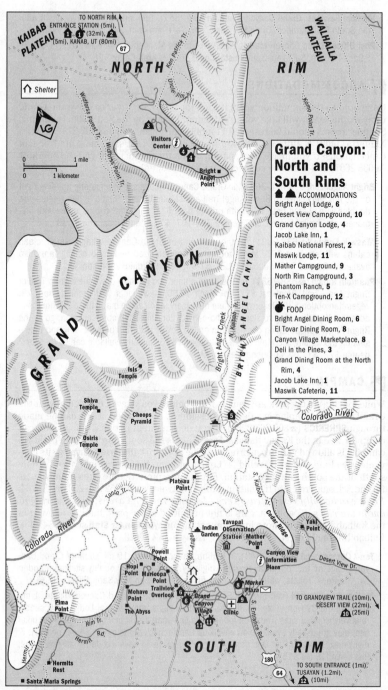

Grand Canyon: North and South Rims

🛏️ ▲ ACCOMMODATIONS

Bright Angel Lodge, **6**
Desert View Campground, **10**
Grand Canyon Lodge, **4**
Jacob Lake Inn, **1**
Kaibab National Forest, **2**
Maswik Lodge, **11**
Mather Campground, **9**
North Rim Campground, **3**
Phantom Ranch, **5**
Ten-X Campground, **12**

🍴 FOOD

Bright Angel Dining Room, **6**
El Tovar Dining Room, **8**
Canyon Village Marketplace, **8**
Deli in the Pines, **3**
Grand Dining Room at the North Rim, **4**
Jacob Lake Inn, **1**
Maswik Cafeteria, **11**

Medical Services: Grand Canyon Clinic (☎638-2551). Turn left at the first stoplight after the South Rim entrance. Open M-F 7am-7pm, Sa 10am-4pm. 24hr. emergency aid.

Post Office: Grand Canyon Market Plaza, next to the Marketplace (☎638-2512.) Open M-F 9am-4:30pm, Sa 11am-3pm. **Postal Code:** 86023. **Area Code:** 928.

ACCOMMODATIONS

Compared to the six million years it took the Colorado River to carve the Grand Canyon, the year it will take you to get indoor lodging by the South Rim is nothing. Summer rooms should be reserved 11 months in advance (☎888-297-2757 or write Xanterra, 14001 E. Iliff, Ste. 600, Aurora, CO 80014). That said, there are frequent cancellations; if you arrive unprepared, check for vacancies or call the operator (☎638-2631) and ask to be connected with the proper lodge.

Bright Angel Lodge (☎638-2631), in Grand Canyon Village sits in a historic building right on the rim. Very close to Bright Angel Trail and shuttle buses. "Rustic" lodge singles and doubles with shared bath $55, with private bath $71. "Historic" cabins, some with fireplaces, are available for 1 or 2 people $84-107. $7 per additional person. ❸

Maswik Lodge (☎638-2631), at the west end of Grand Canyon Village. Small, clean cabins with showers $77. Motel rooms with queen-sized beds and ceiling fans also available. Singles $79; doubles $121. $7-9 for each additional person. ❹

Phantom Ranch (☎638-2631), on the canyon floor, a day's hike down the Kaibab Trail or Bright Angel Trail. Breakfast $17; box lunch $8.50; stew dinner $20; steak dinner $28; vegetarian option $20. Reservations are necessary, and can be made up to 23 months in advance. If you're dying to sleep on the canyon floor but have no reservation, go to the Bright Angel transportation desk at 6am on the day prior to your planned stay and take a shot on the waiting list. Male and female dorms $26; seldom-available cabins for 1 or 2 people $72, $11 per additional person. ❷

CAMPING

While lodgings in the park are usually filled before you've even decided to visit the Grand Canyon, camping is a definite possibility. Some reservations can be made through **SPHERICS** (☎800-365-2267). If you do run out of options, though, you can camp for free in the **Kaibab National Forest,** along the south border of the park. No camping is allowed within a quarter of a mile of U.S. 64. **Dispersed camping** sits conveniently along the oft-traveled N. Long Jim Loop Rd.—turn right about a mile south of the south entrance station. For quieter, more remote sites, follow signs for the Arizona Trail into the national forest between miles 252 and 253 on U.S. 64. *Fires are heavily restricted or even banned in some areas; make sure you know the rules.* Sleeping in cars is not permitted in the park, but it is allowed in the Kaibab Forest. For more info, contact the **Tusayan Ranger Station** (☎638-2443), Kaibab National Forest, P.O. Box 3088, Tusayan, AZ 86023.

Ten-X Campground (☎638-2443), in Kaibab National Forest, 10 mi. south of Grand Canyon Village off Rte. 64. Away from the highway, Ten-X offers 70 quality sites surrounded by pine trees. Toilets, water. First come, first served. Open May-Sept. Sites $10. ❶

Mather Campground (call SPHERICS, ☎800-365-2267), in Grand Canyon Village, 1 mi. south of the Canyon Village Marketplace; follow signs from Yavapai Lodge. 320 shady, relatively isolated sites. Those on foot or bike can snag a spot in a communal hiker/biker site; they are usually available on a walk-up basis (check at the office, $4 per person). 7-night max. stay. For Apr.-Dec. reserve up to 5 months in advance; Jan.-Mar. first come, first served. Sites $15. ❶

Desert View Campground (☎638-7888), 25 mi. east of Grand Canyon Village. Short on shade and far from the South Rim, but a perfect place to avoid crowds. Sites with toilets; no hookups, campfires, or reservations. Open mid-May to Oct. Sites $10. ❶

▐ FOOD

Fast food has yet to spawn in the South Rim (the closest McDonald's is 7 mi. south in Tusayan), but you can find slightly better quality meals at fast-food prices. The **Canyon Village Marketplace** ❶, at Market Plaza 1 mi. west of Mather Point on the main road, has a deli counter with the cheapest eats in the park, groceries, camping supplies, and enough Grand Canyon apparel to clothe your entire extended family. (☎638-2262. Sandwiches $2-4. Open daily 7:30am-8:30pm.) **Maswik Cafeteria** ❶, in Maswik Lodge, serves a variety of food focusing on grilled entrees, country favorites, and Mexican specialties. (Hot entrees $6-7, sandwiches $3-5. Open daily 6am-10pm.) **Bright Angel Dining Room** ❷, in Bright Angel Lodge, is popular with families and serves hot sandwiches ($7-9) and breakfasts ($6-7), and pricey dinner entrees ranging $10-15. (☎638-2631. Open daily 6:30am-10pm.) Just outside the dining room, the **Soda Fountain** ❶ at Bright Angel Lodge has eight flavors of ice cream and stocks a variety of snack-bar sandwiches. (Open seasonally, hours vary. 1 scoop $2.) The classiest dining in the park can be found at **El Tovar Dining Room** ❹, in the El Tovar Hotel in the Village. The grandly appointed dining room has a great view of the canyon and the food lives up to its surroundings. (☎638-2631, ext. 6432. Open 6:30am-10pm, dinner reservations recommended.)

▐ HIKING

Hikes in and around the Grand Canyon can be broken down into two categories: day-hikes and overnight hikes. Confusing an overnight hike for a day-hike can lead to disaster, and permanent residency in the canyon. Hiking to the Colorado River is reserved for overnight trips. All overnight trips require permits obtained through the Backcountry Office. In determining what is an appropriate day-hike, remember that the Canyon has no loop hikes. Be ready to retrace every footstep uphill on the way back. An enjoyable hike usually means beginning before 7am for day-hikes and consulting a ranger and the Canyon View Information Plaza before leaving. Park Service rangers also present a variety of free talks and guided hikes; times and details are listed in *The Guide.*

Seeing the canyon from the inside is harder than it looks. Even the young at body and heart should remember that there are no easy trails below the rim, and what starts as a downhill stroll can become a nightmarish 50° incline on the way back. Also, note that the lower you go, the hotter it gets; when it's 85°F on the rim, it's around 100°F at Indian Gardens and around 110°F at Phantom Ranch. Heat stroke, the greatest threat to a hiker, is marked by a monstrous headache and red, sweatless skin. *For a day-hike, take at least a gallon of water per person; drink at least a quart per hour hiking uphill under the hot sun.* Footwear with excellent tread is also necessary; the trails are steep, and every year careless hikers take what locals morbidly call "the 12-second tour." Safety tips can be found in *The Guide,* but it's probably a good idea to speak with a ranger before embarking on a hike. Parents should think twice about bringing children more than 1 mi. down any trail.

The **Rim, Bright Angel, South Kaibab,** and **River** trails are the only South Rim trails regularly maintained and patrolled by the Park Service. While other trails do exist, they are only for experienced hikers, and may contain steep chutes and technical terrain. Consult a ranger and *The Guide* before heading out

Rim Trail (12 mi. one way, 4-6hr.). With only a mild elevation change (about 200 ft.) and the security of the nearby shuttle, the Rim Trail is excellent for hikers seeking a tame way to see the Canyon. The trail is handicapped accessible to Maricopa Point in the west, and has 8 viewpoints along Hermit Rd. and 3 east of it. Near the Grand Canyon Village, the Rim Trail resembles a crowded city street, but toward the eastern and western ends, hikers have a bit more room. Hopi Point is a great place to watch the sun set with its panoramic canyon views—*The Guide* lists sunset and sunrise times.

Bright Angel Trail (up to 18 mi. round-trip, 1-2 days). Bright Angel's many switchbacks and water stations make it the into-the-canyon choice of moderate hikers. Depending on distance, the trail can be either a day or overnight hike. Departing from the Rim Trail near the western edge of the Grand Canyon Village, the first 1-2 mi. attract droves of day-hikers looking for a taste of canyon descent. Rest houses are strategically stationed 1½ and 3 mi. from the rim, each with water May-Sept. **Indian Gardens,** 4½ mi. down, offers restrooms, picnic tables, 15 backcountry campsites open year-round, and blessed shade. From rim to river, the trail drops 4460 ft. The round-trip is too strenuous for a day-hike—do not attempt to make it one. With a permit, overnighters can camp at Indian Gardens or on the canyon floor at Bright Angel Campground, while day-hikers are advised to go no farther than Plateau Point (12¼ mi. round-trip) or Indian Gardens (9¼ mi. round-trip). The **River Trail** (1¾ mi.) links the Bright Angel with South Kaibab.

South Kaibab Trail (7 mi. to Phantom Ranch, 4-5hr. descent) is for those seeking a more challenging descent. Beginning at Yaki Pt. (7260 ft.), Kaibab is trickier, steeper, and lacks shade or water, but it rewards the intrepid with a better view of the canyon. The South Kaibab avoids the safety and obstructed views of a side-canyon route, as it winds directly down the ridge, offering panoramic views across the canyon. Day-hikes to Cedar Ridge (3 mi. round-trip) and Skeleton Point (6 mi. round-trip) are reasonable only for experienced hikers due to the trail's steep grade. Kaibab meets up with Bright Angel at the Colorado River. Fewer switchbacks and a more rapid descent make the South Kaibab Trail 1¾ mi. shorter than the Bright Angel to this point—guests staying at the Phantom Ranch or Bright Angel Campground can use either trail to reach the ranch.

◪ OUTDOOR ACTIVITIES

Beyond using your feet, there are other ways to conquer the canyon. **Mule trips** from the South Rim are an option, but they're expensive and often booked up to one year in advance. (☎303-297-2757. Daytrip to Plateau Point 6 mi. down the Bright Angel Trail $120, lunch included; overnight including lodging at Phantom Ranch and all meals at $325 per person.) Looking up at the Grand Canyon from a **whitewater raft** is also both popular and pricey. Trips into the Grand Canyon vary in length from a week to 18 days and are booked far in advance. The *Trip Planner* (available by request at the info center) lists several guides licensed to offer trips in the canyon; check the park website for info well in advance of your visit. **Smoothwater rafting** trips are also available for those not quite ready for a wet and wild time in the heart of the canyon. Drifting from Glen Canyon Dam to Lee's Ferry generally takes a half-day. **Wilderness River Adventures** arranges such trips. (☎800-528-6154. $62, kids $52.) If the views from the rim fail to dazzle and astound you, try the higher vantages provided by one of the park's many **flightseeing** companies, located at the Grand Canyon Airport outside of Tuyasan. **Grand Canyon Airlines** flies 45min. tours hourly in the summer. (☎866-235-9422. $79, children $49. Reservations recommended, but walk-ins generally available. Discount for lunchtime tours, 11am-2pm.) For a list of flight companies, write the Grand Canyon Chamber of Commerce, P.O. Box 3007, Grand Canyon, AZ 86023.

NORTH RIM ☎928

If you're coming from Utah or Nevada, or are looking to avoid the crowds and development of the South Rim, the park's North Rim is rugged and serene, with a view almost as spectacular as that from the South Rim. Unfortunately, it's hard to reach by public transit, and is a long drive by car. From October 15 to December 1, the North Rim is open for day use only; from December 1 to May 15, it is closed entirely. Any visit to the North Rim centers around the North Rim Lodge, an elegant structure overlooking the canyon.

▣ ⁊ ORIENTATION AND PRACTICAL INFORMATION

To reach the North Rim from the South Rim, take Rte. 64 E to U.S. 89 N, which runs into Alt. 89; from Alt. 89, follow Rte. 67 S to the edge. Altogether, the beautiful drive is over 220 mi. From Utah, take Alt. 89 S from Fredonia. From Page, take U.S. 89 S to Alt. 89 to Rte. 67 S. Snow closes Rte. 67 from early December to mid-May and park facilities (including the lodge) close mid-October through mid-May. The visitor **parking** lot is near the end of Rte. 67, close to both the visitors center and North Rim Lodge, about 13 mi. south of the park entrance. Trailhead parking is also available at the North Kaibab and Widforss trails and at scenic points along the road to Cape Royal.

Buses: Transcanyon, P.O. Box 348, Grand Canyon 86023 (☎638-2820). Buses run to the South Rim (5hr.; late May to Oct. leaving 7am from North Rim Lodge, 1:30pm from Bright Angel Lodge at the South Rim; $65). Reservations required.

Public Transit: A **hikers' shuttle** runs from the North Rim Lodge to the North Kaibab Trailhead. (Late May to Oct. 5:20, 7:20am; $6, $3 per additional person.) Tickets must be purchased in advance at the North Rim Lodge.

Visitor Info: North Rim Visitors Center (☎638-2611), on Rte. 67 just before the Lodge. Open May-Oct. daily 8am-6pm. **Kaibab Plateau Visitors Center** (☎643-7298), at Jacob Lake, next to the Inn. Displays provide details on the creation of the canyon and its ecosystem, and backcountry permits are issued here. Open daily 8am-5pm.

Weather Conditions: ☎638-7888. Updated daily 7am.

Post Office: Grand Canyon Lodge (☎638-2611). Open M-F 8-11am and 11:30am-4pm, Sa 8am-1pm. **Postal Code:** 86052. **Area Code:** 928.

⌂ ACCOMMODATIONS

Staying inside on the North Rim is pricey and requires advance planning, but there are still many lodging options. If you can't get in-park lodgings, many less expensive accommodations can be found 80 mi. north in Kanab, UT.

Grand Canyon Lodge (☎638-2611, reservations 888-297-2757), on the edge of the rim. This swank but rustic lodge is the only indoor rim lodging in the park. The overlook near the reception area is open to all. Reception 24hr. Reserve as early as 6 months in advance, or 2 years in advance for 1 of the 4 rim-view cabins. Open mid-May to Oct. Cabins $92-121; motel rooms for up to 3 people $91. ❺

North Rim Campground (call SPHERICS ☎800-365-2267), on Rte. 67 near the rim, is the only park campground on this side of the chasm with spacious sites among the ponderosas. Generally fills entirely by reservation in summer. Groceries, showers, and laundry nearby. 83 campsites. 7-night max. stay. Open mid-May to mid-Oct. Sites $15. ❶

Jacob Lake Inn (☎643-7232), 32 mi. north of the North Rim entrance at Jacob Lake. Western lodge, gift shop, cafe (see below), and bakery. Reception daily 6am-9pm. Furnished cabins for 2 $72-83; triples $86-88; quads $90-92; motel units $91-106. ❸

Kaibab National Forest runs from north of Jacob Lake to the park entrance. You can camp for free, as long as you're ¼ mi. from the road, water, or official campgrounds, and 1 mi. from any commercial facility. A strict fire ban is in effect. ●

⬛ FOOD

Grand Dining Room at the North Rim (☎ 638-2612, ext. 160). On the edge of the canyon, the North Rim Lodge's dining room treats guests to sweeping views. The breakfast buffet ($8) and the lunch options (salads and burgers $6-10), while generic, are affordable. Gourmet dinners (from $13) do justice to the grand atmosphere. Open daily 6:30-10am, 11:30am-2:30pm, and 5-9:30pm. Reservations required for dinner. ●

Deli in the Pines, at the North Rim Lodge, specializes in no-frills dining on the go. Standard salads, sandwiches, and burgers $4-6; cheese pizza by the slice $2.50. Breakfasts $3-5. Open daily 7am-9pm. ●

Jacob Lake Inn, 30 mi. north of the park entrance, is a good alternative to North Rim establishments. The old-fashioned diner counter, full restaurant, and tempting bakery offer a variety of options. Pick up a gravity-defying milkshake ($4) to make the remaining drive more enjoyable. Sandwiches $8. Breakfasts $5-6. Dinners $12-15. ●

⬛ OUTDOORS

Hiking in the leafy North Rim seems like a trip to the mountains—the mountain just happens to be upside-down. While the temptation to plunge down into the canyon is strong, it would be an extraordinarily bad idea. The North Rim is at a surprisingly high elevation, so the air is very thin, and there are absolutely no easy trails down into the canyon. *You should never attempt to hike to the river and back in a single day.* Info on trails can be found in the North Rim's version of *The Guide.* Day-hikes of various lengths beckon the active North Rim visitor. The **Bright Angel Point Trail** (½ mi. round-trip, 30min.) departs from the lodge area, and the **Cape Royal Trail** (¾ mi. round-trip, 30min.; handicapped accessible) departs from the Cape Royal parking area. Both offer impressive views of the canyon with little effort. The **Widforss Trail** (up to 10 mi. round-trip, 6hr.) is a more challenging day-hike. The **North Kaibab Trail** (28 mi. round-trip) is the only maintained trail into the canyon on the North Rim and is for only the most experienced hikers. *Consult rangers before beginning this hike.* Pick up the invaluable *Official Guide to Hiking the Grand Canyon,* available in all visitors centers and gift shops. Overnight hikers must get permits from the **Backcountry Office** in the ranger station. ($10 permit plus $5 per person per night. Open daily 8am-noon and 1-5pm.) Park Rangers run nature walks, lectures, and evening programs at the North Rim Campground and Lodge. The info desk or campground bulletin boards have schedules. One-hour ($30), half-day ($55), and full-day ($105) **mule trips** through **Canyon Trail Rides** circle the rim or descend into the canyon. (☎ 435-679-8665. In the lodge lobby. Open May-Oct. daily 7am-5pm. No credit cards.) Reservations are recommended, but walk-ins can be accommodated more often than on the South Rim.

HAVASUPAI RESERVATION ☎ 928

To the west of the bustle of the South Rim lies the tranquil Havasupai Reservation. Meaning "people of the blue-green water," the Havasupai live in a protected enclave, bordered by the national park. Ringed by dramatic sandstone faces, their village, Supai, rests on the shores of the Havasu River. Just beyond town, rushing crystal-clear water cascades over a series of spectacular falls. Such beauty attracts thousands each year, but a grueling 10 mi. hike separates the falls from any vehicle-accessible surface and prevents over-exposure of the reservation. For most, blistered feet or a saddle-sore rump make bathing in the cool waters even sweeter.

Supai and the campground can only be reached by a trail starting at the Hualapai Hilltop. To reach the trailhead, take I-40 E to Rte. 66 at Seligman; follow Rte. 66
for 30 mi. until it meets Indian Rd. 18, which ends at the Hilltop after 60 mi. No
roads lead to Supai, but mules and helicopters can be hired to carry bags or people. For mule reservations, contact **Havasupai Tourist Enterprise.** (☎448-2141. One-
way $70, half of which is required as a deposit. Includes 4 pieces of luggage not
exceeding 130 lb. total. Groups leave at 10am.) **Skydance Helicopter** flies between
the hilltop and village. (☎800-882-1651. Flights every 15-20min. on Su-M and Th-F
9am-3pm. One-way $70; first come, first-served.) The hike, a grueling, exposed 8
mi. to Supai and then an additional 2 mi. to the campground, is not to be under-
estimated. *Do not hike down without a reservation*—you may have to go right
back to the trailhead. Reservations for the campground, lodge, and mules can be
made by calling the Havasupai Tourist Enterprise. Visitors must check in at the
tourist office in Supai before heading on to the campground. The village has a post
office, general store, and cafe. Prices are high because everything must be brought
in by mule or helicopter; bringing your own food is advised. All trash must be
packed out. No **gas** or **water** is available past Rte. 66, so stock up beforehand.

The Havasupai tribe operates the ◙**Havasupai Campground** and the Havasupai
Lodge, both on the canyon floor. The campground, 2 mi. past Supai, lies between
Havasu and Mooney Falls, bordering the Havasu River's blue-green water and
swimmer-friendly lagoons. The tribe charges a one-time entry fee ($20 per visitor,
$10 per night) at the campground. There are no showers or flush toilets. A spring
provides fresh water, and the falls are close by. The **Havasupai Lodge ❹,** in Supai,
offers basic accommodations ($75-96 for up to 4 people, plus the entrance fee; low
season $45-66). The trail from Supai to the campground extends to **Mooney Falls** (1
mi. from campground), **Beaver Falls** (3 mi.), and the **Colorado** (8 mi.). The hike down
to Mooney Falls is steep; extreme caution should be exercised—shoes with good
tread are a must. Swimming and frolicking are both permitted and encouraged in
the lush lagoons at the bottom of the falls.

FLAGSTAFF ☎928

Born on the 4th of July, 1876, Flagstaff was a rest stop along the transcontinen-
tal railroad; its mountain springs provided precious refreshment on the way to
the Pacific. These days, Flagstaff is still a major stop on the way to Southwestern sights. Travelers pass through en route to the Grand Canyon, Sedona, and
the Petrified Forest, all of which are in close proximity. The citizens welcome
travelers to their rock formations by day and their breweries by night. Many
have wandered into town and ended up settling down; retired cowboys, earthy
Volvo owners, New Agers, and adventurers comprise much of the population.

▐ TRANSPORTATION

Flagstaff sits 138 mi. north of Phoenix (take I-17), 26 mi. north of Sedona (take
U.S. 89A), and 81 mi. south of the Grand Canyon's south rim (take U.S. 180).

Trains: Amtrak, 1 E. Rte. 66 (☎774-8679), runs to: **Albuquerque** (7hr., $63-110); **Gal-
lup, NM** (3½hr., $35-61); **Kansas City** (26hr., $173); **Chicago** (34hr., $177); **Los
Angeles** (12hr., $68-119). Station open daily 4:15am-11:45pm.

Buses: Two bus lines provide service to regional destinations. Check at the DuBeau and
Grand Canyon International Hostels for their Grand Canyon and Sedona shuttles.

Greyhound: 399 S. Malpais Ln. (☎774-4573), across from Northern Arizona University (NAU) campus, 3 blocks southwest of the train station on U.S. 89A. Turn off 89A by Dairy Queen. To: **Albu-**

querque (6½hr., 4 per day, $45); **Las Vegas** (5-6hr., 3 per day, $48*)*; **Los Angeles** (10-12hr., 11 per day, $52); **Phoenix,** including airport (3hr., 3 per day, $24). Terminal open 24hr.

Open Road Tours & Transportation (☎226-8060 or 877-226-8060) offers daily trips to and from the Phoenix airport. (3hr., departs Flagstaff at 4:30, 7:30, 9:45am, 12:30, 3:30pm. $30. Departs Phoenix Sky Harbor Airport at 8:30, 11:30am, 2:30, 4:30, 7:30pm. $31.)

Public Transit: Mountain Line (☎779-6624). Routes cover most of town. Buses run every 30min.-1hr.; route map and schedule available at visitors center in the Amtrak station. $1, seniors and children $0.50. Day pass $3/$1.50. Book of 20 passes $18/$9.

Taxi: Friendly Cab ☎774-4444.

Car Rental: Enterprise Rent-A-Car (☎774-9407), 100 N. Humphreys.

■♦ ? ORIENTATION AND PRACTICAL INFORMATION

Downtown revolves around the intersection of **Leroux Street** and **Aspen Street,** a block north of **Route 66** (formerly Santa Fe Ave.); the visitors center, bus station, hostels, and inexpensive restaurants and bars all lie within a half-mile of this spot. **South San Francisco Street,** a block east of Leroux St., has many outdoor shops. Split by Rte. 66, the more visited northern area is also the center of downtown. The area south of the tracks is less developed, but houses hostels and several eateries.

Visitor Info: Flagstaff Visitors Center, 1 E. Rte. 66 (☎774-9541 or 800-842-7293), in the Amtrak station. Open late May to early Sept. M-Sa 8am-7pm, Su 9am-5pm; in winter M-Sa 8am-6pm, Su 9am-4pm.

Equipment Rental and Outfitting:

Peace Surplus, 14 W. Rte. 66 (☎779-4521), 1 block from either of Flagstaff's hostels, is a one-stop shop for any of your gear needs. Rents tents ($7-9 per day), packs ($5-6 per day), sleeping bags ($3-6 per day), and stoves ($3 per day), as well as alpine, nordic, and snowshoe packages in winter ($10-20). 3-day min. rental; hefty $100-300 credit card or cash deposit required. Open M-F 8am-9pm, Sa 8am-8pm, Su 8am-6pm.

Summit Divers and Watersports, 103 S. Milton (☎556-8780; the western part of Rte. 66 in town), rents kayaks for $35 per day, $65 per weekend, $100 per week. Open M-Sa 10am-5pm.

Four Season Outfitters and Guides, 107 W. Phoenix Ave. (☎226-8798; www.fsoutfitters.com), has guided backcountry hikes and canyoneering in the Grand Canyon and Escalante.

Police: 911 E. Sawmill Rd. (☎911, non-emergencies 774-1414).

Medical Services: Flagstaff Medical Center, 1200 N. Beaver St. (☎779-3366). 24hr.

Internet Access: Free at NAU's **Cline Library** (☎523-2171). Take Riordan Rd. east from Rte. 66 and turn left on Knoles. Open May-Aug. M-Th 7:30am-10pm, F 7:30am-6pm, Sa 10:30am-5pm, Su noon-10pm; Sept.-Apr. M-Th 7:30am-11:30pm, F 7:30am-6pm, Sa 10:30am-6pm, Su 10:30am-11:30pm.

Post Office: 2400 N. Postal Blvd. (☎714-9302), on Rte. 66. General delivery accepted. Open M-F 9am-5pm, Sa 9am-noon. **Postal Code:** 86004. **Area Code:** 928.

⌐ ACCOMMODATIONS

▓ **The DuBeau International Hostel,** 19 W. Phoenix Ave. (☎774-6731). A block south of the visitors center and train station, the DuBeau lives up to its ritzy name. The common room, game room, and kitchen create a lively and friendly atmosphere. Each 6-bed dorm and private room has its own bathroom, and all have access to the courtyard. Internet, laundry, and Grand Canyon and Sedona tours available. Free breakfast, linens, and pick-up at the bus station. Reception 7am-midnight, but late arrivals can be accommodated. In summer dorms $16, in winter $14; private single $35/$28.) ❶

▓ **The Grand Canyon International Hostel,** 19 S. San Francisco St. (☎ 779-9421), just east of the DuBeau. Managed with the DuBeau, it offers the same great value and friendly atmosphere. The 44 beds are often filled with backpackers and globe-trotters resting up before heading to the next stop, so travel-tales flow like water and the hostel stays lively. 4-bed dorms in summer $17, in winter $15; private singles $30-37. ●

The Weatherford Hotel, 23 N. Leroux St. (☎ 779-1919), at Aspen and Leroux. Flagstaff's oldest hotel, dating to 1898, the Weatherford has 8 cozy rooms with historic furnishings on the 3rd floor of one of the oldest brick buildings in town. No TVs or in-room phones, but it has a lively atmosphere and is in a handy downtown location. Reservations recommended. Rooms M-F $60, Sa-Su $65; some rooms have shared baths. ●

▓ CAMPING

Free backcountry camping is available around Flagstaff in designated wilderness areas. Pick up a map from the **Peaks Ranger Station,** 5075 N. 89A (☎ 526-0866) to see where. All backcountry sites must be at least 200 ft. from trails, waterways, wet meadows, and lakes. There is a 14-night max stay in the **Coconino National Forest**; fire restrictions apply. For info on camping, call the **Coconino National Forest Line.** (☎ 527-3600. Open M-F 7:30am-4:30pm.) The following campgrounds are all just south of Flagstaff on Lake Mary Rd., which is accessible off of I-17 N, but must be reached by following Milton Rd. to Beulah Dr. when coming from the north.

Lakeview Campground, on the east side of Upper Lake Mary, 11½ mi. south on Lake Mary Rd., is surrounded by a pine forest that supports an alpine ecosystem. Drinking water, pit toilets. No reservations. Open May-Oct. $12 per vehicle per night. ●

Pinegrove Campground (reservations ☎ 877-444-6777; www.reserveamerica.com), sits 5 mi. south of Lakeview at the other end of Upper Lake Mary. In a charming location, Pinegrove offers drinking water and flush toilets. Showers $3. $15 per vehicle. ●

Canyon View Campground, 6 mi. south on Mary Lake Rd. 10 spacious sites with a few trees scattered about. Pit toilets, water. First come, first served. $12 per vehicle. ●

▓ FOOD

▓ **Cafe Espress,** 16 N. San Francisco St. (☎ 774-0541), has inventive, delicious entrees made with fresh ingredients. Breakfast ($4-8) includes everything from hearty biscuits and gravy to decadent champagne and strawberry crepes. Lunch ($5-10) and dinner ($12-20) are just as good. Open M 7am-5pm, Tu-Su 7am-5pm and 6-9am. ●

Mountain Oasis Global Cuisine and Juice Bar, 11 E. Aspen St. (☎ 214-9270). This downtown oasis is a haven for hungry travelers, complete with lush plants and a fountain. Offering cuisine from around the world, ranging from vegan to seafood and steak (lunch $5-7, dinner $8-16), they also serve up smoothies, coffee drinks, and cocktails. Open Su-Th 11am-9pm, F-Sa 11am-10pm; may close early if business is slow.

Macy's European Coffee House and Bakery, 14 S. Beaver St. (☎ 774-2243), behind DuBeau hostel. This cheery hangout serves only vegetarian and vegan food. $4-7 specials change daily. Try some granola ($4) with fresh-roasted coffee ($1-3.50). Open Su-Th 6am-8pm, F-Sa 6am-10pm. Food served until 1hr. before close. No credit cards. ●

▓ SIGHTS

In 1894, Percival Lowell chose Flagstaff as the site for an astronomical observatory, and spent the rest of his life here. The **Lowell Observatory,** 1400 W. Mars Hill Rd., 1 mi. west of downtown off Rte. 66, where he discovered Pluto, is still a functioning laboratory, but also has a visitors center with astronomy exhibits and daily tours (10am, 1, 3pm) of Lowell's telescopes. There is also an excellent evening program about constellations and the night sky. (☎774-3358; www.lowell.edu. Open daily Mar.-Oct. 9am-5pm; Nov.-Feb. noon-5pm. Evening programs June-Aug. M-Sa 8pm; Mar.-May and Sept.-Oct. W and F-Sa 7:30pm; Nov.-Feb. F-Sa 7:30pm. $5, students and seniors $4, ages 5-17 $2.) The **Museum of Northern Arizona,** 3 mi. north of downtown on U.S. 180, details anything and everything about the land and peoples of the Colorado Plateau. The museum has a geology gallery but dedicates most of its space to the area's diverse cultures, traditions, and artistic works. It also hosts the annual Zuni (last weekend in May), Hopi (4th of July weekend), Navajo (first weekend in Aug.), and Hispanic (last weekend in Oct.) heritage marketplaces, celebrating each group's traditional arts and way of life. (☎774-5213; www.musnaz.org. Open daily 9am-5pm. $5, seniors $4, students $3, ages 7-17 $2.)

ENTERTAINMENT AND NIGHTLIFE

North of town by the museum, the **Coconino Center for the Arts** houses exhibits, festivals, performers, and a children's museum (☎779-2300). The second weekend in June, the annual **Flagstaff Rodeo** brings competitions, barn dances, a carnival, and a cocktail waitress race. Events run from Friday to Sunday at the Coconino County Fair Grounds. (On Hwy. 89A just south of town, the Flagstaff Visitors Center has details.) On the 4th of July, the town celebrates its birthday with street fairs, live music, barbecues, a parade, and, of course, fireworks. At the end of the summer (Labor Day), the **Coconino County Fair** arrives with rides, animal competitions, and carnival games. **Theatrikos,** a local theater group, performs in town. (11 W. Cherry Ave. ☎774-1662; www.theatrikos.com.)

Two nifty nightspots reside in the Hotel Weatherford, 23 N. Leroux St. **Charly's,** on the main floor, has nightly live music and a friendly, relaxed atmosphere, while **Zane Grey,** upstairs, has similar low drink prices in a classy setting. (☎779-1919. Happy hour daily 5-7pm, free taco bar F. Charly's open daily 11am-2am. Zane Grey open daily 5pm-2am.) **Joe's Place,** on the corner of S. San Francisco and Rte. 66, hosts indie bands on weekend nights and is frequented by both locals and out-of-towners. (☎774-6281. Happy hour 4-7pm. Open 11am-2am.) If you feel the urge to two-step, the **Museum Club,** 3404 E. Rte. 66, a roadhouse dating back to the Prohibition, is the spot for honky-tonk action. Dime beers on Wednesday 8pm-midnight bring in masses of local college students and other beer lovers. (☎526-9434. Cover $3-5. Open daily 11am-4am.)

OUTDOOR ACTIVITIES

With the northern **San Francisco Peaks** and the surrounding **Coconino National Forest,** Flagstaff offers numerous options like skiing, hiking, biking, and breathtaking landscapes, for either the rugged outdoorsman or those just interested in walking off last night's fun. Due to altitudes of over 7000 ft., bring plenty of water, regardless of the season or activity. In late spring and summer, national and state park rangers may close trails if the potential for fire gets too high. **Backcountry camping ❶** is free, as the mountains are on National Forest Land.

SKIING

The **Arizona Snowbowl** operates four chairlifts and a tow rope and maintains 32 trails. The majestic **Humphrey's Peak** (12,633 ft.) is the backdrop, though the skiing takes place on **Agassiz Peak** (11,500 ft.). With an average snowfall of 260 in.

and 2300 ft. of vertical drop, the Snowbowl rivals some of the ski resorts of the Rockies and easily outclasses its Arizona competition. To reach the Snowbowl, take U.S. 180 about 7 mi. north to the Fairfield Snowbowl turnoff.

The Snowbowl caters to a wide range of skiers and snowboarders and is evenly divided among beginner, intermediate, and advanced runs. (☎ 779-1951; www.arizonasnowbowl.com. Open daily 9am-4pm. Lift tickets M-F half-day $27, full-day $42; Sa-Su $34/$42; ages 8-12 $19/$24. Free for under 7, over 70, and on your birthday.) **Equipment rental** is available on the mountain. (Half-day ski package $16, full-day $22; extreme performance package $22/$32; snowboards $21/$29.)

HIKING

In the summer, these peaks attract hikers and bikers aplenty. The Coconino National Forest has trails for hikers of all abilities. Consult the **Peaks Ranger Station,** 5075 N. 89A (☎ 526-0866), for trail descriptions and possible closures. For the energetic hiker, the **Elden Lookout Trail** (6 mi. round-trip, 5hr., 2400 ft.) is ideal for jaw-dropping mountaintop views, and is demanding, but worthwhile. The trailhead is at the Peaks Ranger Station. The most popular trail in the area is the strenuous hike to **Humphrey's Peak,** Arizona's highest mountain (4½ mi. one-way, 3hr.). The trail begins in the first parking lot at the Snowbowl ski area (7 mi. north of Flagstaff on U.S. 180) and climbs nearly 3400 ft. A more moderate hiking option is the **Kachina Trail** (5 mi. one-way, 2½hr.). Also leaving from the Snowbowl, it parallels the road before winding through quiet aspen groves and lush ferns.

MOUNTAIN BIKING

Flagstaff has excellent mountain biking. **Schultz Creek Trailhead,** on Schultz Pass Rd. off U.S. 180 N, is the starting point for many interconnected trails in the San Francisco Mountains, including the popular **Schultz Creek Trail.** The trail gradually climbs north along the bottom of a ravine, and after almost 4 mi. splits into the difficult **Sunset Trail** which heads south, and the eastbound **Little Elden Trail.** Sunset Trail climbs through the woods before cresting and descending along **Brookbank Trail,** down singletrack dropoffs and switchbacks. This 2 mi. stretch spits out riders with satisfied grins onto Forest Service Road 557, which can be used to ride back to the trailhead, or to access the renowned, more technical **Rocky Ridge Trail,** which leads to the same trailhead. Bikes can be rented throughout Flagstaff. **Flagstaff Adventure Sports,** 612 N. Humphreys, rents full-suspension bikes ($25 per day, $35 overnight) and has great advice. (☎ 877-572-2300. Open M-Sa 10am-5pm.)

◪ DAYTRIPS FROM FLAGSTAFF

WALNUT CANYON NATIONAL MONUMENT

The remnants of over 300 rooms in 13th-century Sinaguan dwellings make up Walnut Canyon National Monument. A glassed-in observation deck in the **visitors center,** 10 mi. east of Flagstaff, at Exit 204 off I-40, overlooks the canyon. (☎ 526-3367. Open daily 8am-6pm; low-season 8am-5pm. $5, under 17 free.) The steep **Island Trail** (1 mi. loop, 240 stairs) snakes down from the visitors center past 25 cliff dwellings. The **Rim Trail** (¾ mi.) offers views of the canyon and passes rim-top sites. Saturdays at 10am, rangers lead groups of five on 2 mi. hikes into Walnut Canyon to remote cliff dwellings. There is a similar hike to the original Ranger Cabin (Th and Su 10am). Reservations are required for these challenging 2½hr. hikes.

SUNSET CRATER VOLCANO NATIONAL MONUMENT

The 1000 ft. tall cinder cone of Sunset Crater Volcano National Monument is the result of nearly 200 years of periodic volcanic eruptions beginning in AD 1065. The easy **Lava Flow Nature Trail,** 1½ mi. east of the visitors center, wanders 1 mi. through the rocky black terrain that glows with tinges of yellow and red, inspiring the formation's name. Hiking up Sunset Crater itself is not allowed, but the **Lenox Crater Trail** is a tough ¼ mi. scramble up the loose cinders of a neighboring cone, followed by a quick slide back down. The new **visitors center,** 12 mi. north of Flagstaff on U.S. 89, explores the area's history. (☎ 526-0502. Open daily in summer 8am-6pm; in winter 8am-5pm. $5, under 16 free; includes admission to Wupatki, below.)

WUPATKI NATIONAL MONUMENT

Located 18 mi. northeast of Sunset Crater along a scenic loop with views of the Painted Desert, Wupatki has fascinating Pueblo sites. The Sinagua moved here in the 11th century, after a Sunset Crater eruption forced them to evacuate. Archaeologists speculate that in less than 200 years, droughts, disease, and over-farming led the Sinagua to abandon these stone houses. The remnants of five pueblos form a loop off U.S. 89. The largest and most accessible, **Wupatki,** on a ½ mi. round-trip loop trail from the visitors center, is three stories high. The spectacular **Doney Mountain Trail** rises ½ mi. from the picnic area to the summit. Get info and trail guide brochures at the **visitors center.** Backcountry hiking is not permitted. (☎ 679-2365. Monument and visitors center open daily 8am-5pm.)

SEDONA ☎ 928

The Martians said to make frequent visits to Sedona may simply be mistaking its deep red rock towers for home. The scores of tourists who descend upon the town (Sedona rivals the Grand Canyon for tourist volume) certainly aren't; they come for sights that put others in the area to shame. Dramatic copper-toned behemoths dotted with pines tower over Sedona, rising from the earth with such flair and crowd appeal that they seem like manufactured tourist attractions—they aren't. Though downtown is overrun with overpriced shops, the rocks are worth a visit.

⌖ PRACTICAL INFORMATION. Sedona is 120 mi. north of Phoenix (take I-17 north to Rte. 179) and 30 mi. south of Flagstaff (take I-17 south to Rte. 179). The **Sedona-Phoenix Shuttle** (☎ 282-2066) runs eight trips daily ($40). The **Sedona Chamber of Commerce,** at Forest Rd. and U.S. 89A, has info on accommodations and local attractions. (☎ 282-7722. Open M-Sa 8:30am-5pm, Su 9am-3pm.) **Post Office:** 190 W. U.S. 89A. (☎ 282-3511. Open M-F 8:45am-5pm.) **Postal Code:** 86336. **Area Code:** 928.

⌂ ACCOMMODATIONS. Lodging in town is pricey, but deals can be found. Still, it's not a bad idea to make Sedona a daytrip from Flagstaff or Cottonwood. The **White House Inn ❸,** 2986 W. U.S. 89A (☎ 282-6680), is the cheapest option, with unremarkable singles and doubles, some with kitchenettes, from $47. An alternative to commercial lodging is renting a room in a private residence; look in papers or on bulletin boards at New Age shops for opportunities. Cheaper options can be found in Cottonwood, 15 mi. south, where budget motels line U.S. 89.

Most campsites in the area cluster around U.S. 89A as it heads north along Oak Creek Canyon on the way to Flagstaff. There are plenty of private campgrounds, but most cater to the RV crowd rather than to backpackers. The **US Forest Service campsites ❶** along 89A are the best, cheapest option for tent-toters. North of Sedona, between nine and 20 mi. from town, four separate campgrounds—**Manzanita, Bootlegger, Cave Springs, and Pine Flat (east and west) ❶**—maintain over 150 campsites along the forested canyon floor. They all have similar facilities, with picnic tables and toilets. All but Bootlegger have drinking water. (Info ☎ 527-3600; reservations 877-444-6777. 7-night max. stay. Tent sites $16.) **Dead Horse Ranch State Park ❶**, just off Hwy. 89 in Cottonwood and minutes from Tuzigoot National Monument, has over 200 sites, many of which are surrounded by willows and cottonwoods growing in the wetlands of the nearby Verde River. (☎ 634-5283. Modern restrooms, showers, tent sites. First come, first served. $12, with hookup $19.)

❍ FOOD. **Casa Rincón ❷**, 2620 U.S. 89A, attracts patrons with a daily happy hour (3-6pm; $3 margaritas), mouth-watering combination platters ($10-13), and live entertainment. (☎ 282-4849. Open daily 11:30am-9pm, cantina open until 1am.) **The Coffee Pot Restaurant ❷**, 2050 W. U.S. 89A, a local favorite, serves 101 varieties of omelettes ($4-9) all day and a full Mexican and diner-style lunch menu. (☎ 282-6626. Lunch $5-9. Open daily 6am-2:30pm.) **Pizza Picazzo ❷**, 1855 W. U.S. 89A, turns pizza-making into an artistic endeavor with creative, delicious specialty pizzas and salads. A daily lunch combo gets you a slice of gourmet pizza, soup or salad, and drink for $6. (☎ 282-4140. Open Su-Th 11am-10pm, F-Sa 11am-11pm.)

◎ SIGHTS. The formations at **Red Rock State Park** (☎ 282-6907) beckon visitors for a contemplative stroll. Located 15 mi. southwest of Sedona, the park entrance is on the Red Rock Loop Road off U.S. 89A. Rangers lead nature hikes (10am and 2pm) into the formations and are happy to give trail advice. ($5 entrance fee.) The **Chapel of the Holy Cross**, on Chapel Rd., lies at the base of a 1000 ft. rock wall and is wedged into the red sandstone. The view from the church's parking lot is a religious experience in itself. (☎ 282-4069. Open M-Sa 9am-5pm, Su 10am-5pm.)

Tlaquepaque (Tlah-key-pockey), off U.S. 179, just southeast of the intersection of 179 and 89, is an upscale shopping and art colony done in the style of a historic Hispanic plaza. You may not have the cash to get one of the life-sized bronze wildlife statues (prices start around $5000 and soar to a bank-shattering $70,000), but you can stroll the gardens, admire the profusion of Spanish tile, artwork, and fountains scattered around the plaza, or shop and dine at one of the village's establishments. Tlaquepaque is also home to **Shakespeare Sedona**, a theater troupe that presents two productions each July. (☎ 203-9381 for more info. $20, students $10.)

Montezuma Castle National Monument, 10 mi. south of Sedona on I-17, isn't a castle and Montezuma didn't live there, but it is a remarkable 45-room cliff dwelling built by the Sinagua in the 12th century. You can't get very close to the ruins, but the view from the path below is excellent and wheelchair accessible. (☎ 567-3322. Open daily in summer 8am-6pm, in winter 8am-5pm. $3, under 17 free.) A beautiful lake, **Montezuma Well**, was formed by the collapse of an underground cavern. The well, off I-17 11 mi. north of the castle, was once a source of water for the Sinagua. (Open daily 8am-6pm. Free.) Take U.S. 89A to Rte. 279 and continue through Cottonwood to reach **Tuzigoot National Monument**, 20 mi. from Sedona, a Sinaguan ruin in the Verde Valley. (☎ 634-5564. Open daily 8am-6pm. $3, under 17 free.)

◤ OUTDOOR ACTIVITIES. The U.S. Forest Service publishes a free guide to recreation in Sedona (available at any visitors center) that lists options for hiking, biking, and driving in "Red Rock Country." It's hard to go wrong with any of the well-maintained hiking trails in and around Sedona. Most trailheads are on the forest service roads that snake from the highways and into the hills and canyons around Sedona. The **Red Rock Pass**, a parking permit, is required to park at most recreation areas. The passes are $5 per day or $15 per week and are available from vending machines at most visitors centers and trailheads. Hiking highlights include the difficult **Wilson Mountain Loop** (5 mi.), which ascends Wilson Mountain, and the more moderate **Huckaby Trail** (6 mi.), which traverses fantastic red rocks. **Boynton Canyon Trail** (5 mi.) is an easy to moderate trail along the floor of Boynton

Canyon, the site of one of Sedona's legendary vortices. Biking offers similar wonders. Considered a rival to Moab by those in the mountain-biking know, Sedona has over 100 mi. of interconnected trails. **Broken Arrow,** an intermediate trail of adjustable distance, is a very popular trail. Tamer trails can be found along the **Bell Rock Pathway,** south of town. Bike rentals (from $7.50 per hr. or $25 per day) and trail information can be found at **Mountain Bike Heaven,** 1695 W. U.S. 89A. They also offer guided bike trips and do repairs. (☎282-1312. Open M-F 9am-6pm, Sa 8am-5pm, Su 9am-5pm.) Scenic drives are almost as plentiful as the rocks. The **Red Rock Loop** (20 mi., 1hr., off U.S. 89 west of town) is mostly paved, but provides some dirt road adventure and mind-blowing views of rock formations. **Dry Creek Road** and **Airport Road** are also good drives. For those hoping to see Sedona's wild side, many companies offer 4WD tours. **Adventure Company,** 336 Hwy. 179 at Tlaquepaque, has knowledgeable guides and great prices for some of Sedona's most famous 4x4 trails. (☎877-281-6622. Tours at your convenience daily 8:30am-5:30pm. Call to reserve times at least 24hr. in advance. From $30, children from $15.)

NAVAJO RESERVATION

Anthropologists think the Navajo are descended from groups of Athabascan people who migrated to the Southwest from Canada in the 14th and 15th centuries, but the Navajo see their existence as the culmination of a journey through three other worlds to this life, the "Glittering World." Four sacred mountains watch over Navajo land—Mt. Blanca to the east, Mt. Taylor to the south, San Francisco Peak to the west, and Mt. Hesperus to the north. In the second half of the 19th century, reservations evolved out of the US government's *ad hoc* attempts to end fighting between Native Americans and Anglos while facilitating white settlement on native lands. The reservation system imposed a kind of wardship over the Native Americans, which lasted for over a century, until Supreme Court decisions starting in the 1960s reasserted the tribes' standing as semi-sovereign nations. Today, the **Navajo Nation** is the largest reservation in the US, covering over 27,000 sq. mi. of northeastern Arizona, southeastern Utah, and northwestern New Mexico.

Cultural sensitivity is very important on the reservation; despite the many state and interstate roads that traverse it, the land is both legally and culturally distinct. Driving or hiking off designated trails and established routes is considered trespassing unless you are with a guide. Possession and consumption of alcohol are prohibited on the reservation. The Navajo people have their own language and social norms. While many cultures find eye contact, firm handshakes, and cheerful conversation desirable, among the Navajo these behaviors are generally impolite. General photography is allowed unless otherwise stated, but photographing the Navajo people requires their permission (a gratuity is usually expected). As always, the best remedy for cultural friction is simple respect.

For a taste of the Navajo language and ritual songs, tune your radio to 660AM, "The Voice of the Navajo." Remember to advance your watch 1hr. during the summer; the Navajo Nation runs on **Mountain Daylight Time,** while the rest of Arizona, including the Hopi Reservation, does not observe daylight savings, operating on Pacific Standard Time in the summer and Mountain Standard Time in the winter. The reservation's **area code** is ☎928 in Arizona, 505 in New Mexico, 435 in Utah.

Monument Valley, Canyon de Chelly, Navajo National Monument, Rainbow Bridge, Antelope Canyon, and all their roads and trails are on Navajo land. Those planning to hike through Navajo territory should get a backcountry permit at one of the **parks and recreation departments** or mail a request with a money order or certified check to P.O. Box 9000, Window Rock, AZ 86515 ($5 per person). **Gallup, NM** (p. 898) and **Flagstaff, AZ** (p. 857) are good gateways to the reservation, with car rental agencies, inexpensive accommodations, and Greyhound service on I-40. Budget travelers can camp at the National Monuments or Navajo campgrounds, or stay in a student-run motel in high schools around the reservation.

MONUMENT VALLEY ☏ 435

The red sandstone mesas, buttes, and towers of Monument Valley Navajo Tribal Park have provided the backdrop for many Hollywood westerns, but long before John Wayne, ancestral Puebloans sustained small communities here despite the arid climate. The park's 17 mi. **Valley Drive** winds around 11 of the most spectacular formations, including the famous pair of **Mittens** and the slender **Totem Pole.** The gaping ditches, large rocks, and mudholes on this dirt road, however, can be jarring to both you and your car—observe the 15 mph speed limit. The drive takes at least 1½hr. Less-touristed parts of the valley can be reached only by 4WD vehicle, horse, or foot, usually with the assistance of a guide. The visitors center parking lot is crowded with booths selling Jeep, horseback, and hiking tours. (1½hr. jeep tour about $35 per person, full-day $100; horseback tours $40/ $120.) In winter, snow laces the rocky towers. Call the visitors center for road conditions. The park entrance is on U.S. 163 just south of the Utah border, 24 mi. north of **Kayenta,** at the intersection of U.S. 163 and U.S. 160. The **visitors center** has info, a gift shop, and restaurant. (☏ 727-3353. Park and visitors center open daily May-Sept. 6am-8pm, Oct.-Apr. 8am-5pm. $5, under 9 free; National Passes not accepted.) **Mitten View Campground ❶,** a ¼ mi. from the visitors center, has a view and showers, but no hookups and little shade. (Register at the visitors center, first come, first served. Sites $10; winter $5.) Cheap motels can be found in **Mexican Hat, UT,** and **Bluff, UT.**

CANYON DE CHELLY ☏ 928

The colorful and subtly crafted sheer walls of Canyon de Chelly (da-SHAY), just north of Chinle on Navajo Rte. 7, are a welcome surprise in the scrub desert of northeastern Arizona. From the rim, you can stare down into 4000 years of inhabited history; the remains of ancient Puebloan homes are still nestled into alcoves and perched precariously on ledges, and Navajo farmers still work the land of the canyon floor using traditional agricultural practices.

FROM THE ROAD

WHY DID THE HORSE CROSS THE ROAD?

As I cruised into Chinle, AZ, I stopped at a light, scoping out the town. My glancing turned into bewildered scrutiny as I saw two men casually riding their horses down the highway. They stopped at the intersection, checked for traffic, and turned onto Rte. 7. I turned into a gas station, giggling at what I perceived to be a very bizarre situation. As the tank filled, I watched a middle-aged man on horseback trot up the highway, stop at the light, and trot through the intersection when the light turned green. I dissolved into laughter. As I headed toward Canyon de Chelly, I nearly put my car in a ditch when I saw cattle grazing outside the local high school. I'd heard of free-range animals and seen the roadsigns warning of their presence, but that was only in the middle of nowhere, right? Oh, no. As I learned in Chinle, traditional grazing practices and transportation methods commingle with the Navajo Reservation's relatively new cities and towns. Before I left, I even saw cattle nibbling the grass in a Burger King parking lot, and yielded to a group of sheep crossing the road. And the horses on the four-lane highway? A legitimate form of transportation for Navajo farmers and ranchers, provided they adhere to road regulations. So if you're driving across northeastern Arizona, keep your eyes open, yield to livestock, and share the road.

-Katy Bartelma

The canyon is best viewed from one of two scenic drives. The **North Rim Drive** (15¼ mi., 1½-2hr.) gives four vistas of Canyon del Muerto, including one of Massacre Cave, the site of the slaying of 115 women and children by Spanish soldiers in 1805. The **South Rim Drive** (16 mi., 1½-2hr.) has seven views of the Canyon de Chelly, including one at the start of the **White House Trail.** This moderately difficult hike (2½ mi. round-trip, 2hr.) leads down to the canyon floor and the White House ruin. The drives and White House Trail are the only self-guided activities in the park; everything else must be under the supervision of an authorized Navajo guide.

The **visitor center** houses archaeological and cultural displays detailing the lives of the canyon's many inhabitants, and has helpful advice and *Canyon Overlook*, the park's newspaper with info and a listing of guided tours. (☎ 674-5500, ext. 270. Open daily Mar.-Sept. 8am-6pm, Oct.-Feb. 8am-5pm. Free.) Visitors are cautioned to lock their doors at all overlooks as thefts can occur. Watch your wallet as well—hoards of people illegally sell jewelry at the overlooks. Visitors must stay on established roads and trails—to deviate from them is considered trespassing.

Thunderbird Lodge ❹ is the park's only indoor accommodation. Behind the visitors center in a historic trading post, it provides modern, comfortable rooms. (☎ 674-5841. Showers, TV. Reservations recommended in summer. Rooms from $70.) The same complex also houses a gift shop (open daily 8am-7pm), guide service (full-day tours $65, half-day $40), and a cafeteria (sandwiches $5, steaks $12-18; open daily 6:30am-8:30pm). Free camping is available in the 93 spacious, shady sites at **Cottonwood Campgrounds ❶**, just southwest of the visitors center. (Toilets, no showers. First come, first served. Free.)

NAVAJO NATIONAL MONUMENT   ☎ 520

Ancestors of today's Hopi occupied the cliffs of Tsegi Canyon from the late 1200s until hard times left the villages vacant by 1300. Today, the site contains three remarkable cliff dwellings. **Inscription House** has been closed to visitors since the 1960s due to its fragile condition, and the other two admit a very limited number of visitors. The stunning **Keet Seel** (open late May to early Sept.) can be reached only by a challenging 17 mi. round-trip hike. Hikers can stay overnight in a **free campground ❶** nearby (no facilities or drinking water). Reservations for permits to visit Keet Seel can be made up to five months in advance through the visitors center (see below). Ranger-led tours to **Betatakin**, a 135-room complex, are limited to 25 people. (5 mi. round-trip, 3-5hr. May to late Sept. 8:30 and 11am; first come, first served.) The paved (but not wheelchair accessible) 1 mi. round-trip **Sandal Trail** lets you gaze down on Betatakin from the top of the canyon. The **Aspen Forest Overlook Trail,** another 1 mi. hike, overlooks aspens and firs that are the remnants of an ancient forest. To get to the monument, take Rte. 564 from U.S. 160, 20 mi. southwest of Kayenta. The **visitors center** is 9 mi. down Rte. 564 and has artifact displays, and local artisans demonstrate traditional crafts. (☎ 672-2700. Open daily 8am-5pm. Entrance free, but donations accepted.) Two free campgrounds reside in the park. **Sunset View ❶** has 31 sites wedged among the pygmy conifer forest. (Water, toilets. Free) **Canyon View ❶** provides a nifty view of the canyon, but the 11 sites are quite primitive. (Dirt road, no water, portable toilets. Free.)

HOPI RESERVATION   ☎ 928

The Hopi people have called the desolate beauty of Black Mesa's arid valleys and prominent finger mesas home for well over a millennium. Landlocked by the Navajo Reservation, the Hopi Reservation is divided into three regions known, from east to west, as First, Second, and Third Mesas. While roadside stands brimming with Hopi pottery, baskets, and jewelry line the only paved highway, Hwy. 264, **First Mesa** is the only region intended to accommodate visitors. To reach First

Mesa, drive to Polacca and follow the signs to the **Ponsi Hall Community Center,** a general info center and starting point for **guided tours.** (☎ 737-2262. Open daily June-Aug. 9:30am-5pm, Sept.-May 10am-5pm. Tours last 1hr. and begin at opening time; the last tour departs 1hr. prior to closing. $8, children $5.) The villages on the **Second** and **Third Mesas** are less developed for tourism. *Photography and recording are strictly forbidden.* On Second Mesa, though, the **Hopi Cultural Center,** 5 mi. west of the intersection of Rte. 264 and 87, serves as a visitors center and has the reservation's only museum, which focuses on the tribe's history and arts and crafts. (☎ 734-6650. Open M-F 9am-5pm, Sa-Su 9am-3pm. $3, under 14 $1.) The **Hopi Cultural Center Restaurant ❷** and the **Hopi Cultural Center Motel ❹,** one of the only accommodations on the reservation, are in the same complex. (☎ 734-2401. Restaurant: Open daily Apr.-Sept. 6am-9pm, Oct.-Mar. 7am-8pm. Hotel: open daily. Reservations recommended. Apr.-Sept. $90, Oct.-Mar. $60; $5 per additional person.) **Free camping ❶** is allowed at 10 primitive sites next to the Cultural Center.

Visitors can attend a few Hopi **village dances** during the year. Often announced only a few days in advance, these religious ceremonies usually occur on weekends and last from sunrise to sundown. The dances are formal; do not wear shorts, tank tops, or other casual wear. Photos, recordings, and sketches are strictly forbidden. Often several villages will hold dances on the same day, allowing tourists to village-hop. The **Harvest Dance,** in mid-September at Second Mesa, is spectacular with tribes from all over the US. Ask at the cultural center or the **Hopi Cultural Preservation Office** (☎ 734-3613), P.O. Box 123, Kykotsmovi 86039, for more info.

PETRIFIED FOREST NATIONAL PARK ☎ 520

Spreading over 60,000 acres, the Petrified Forest National Park looks like the aftermath of a prehistoric Grateful Dead concert—an enormous tie-dyed desert littered with rainbow-colored trees. Some 225 million years ago, when Arizona's desert was swampland, volcanic ash covered the logs, slowing their decay. Silica-infused water seeped through the wood, and the silica crystallized into quartz, combining with iron-rich minerals to produce rainbow hues. Colorful sediment was also laid down in this floodplain, creating the stunning colors that stripe the rock formations of the park's badlands.

■ ▌ **ORIENTATION AND PRACTICAL INFORMATION.** The park can be split into two parts separated by I-40: the northern Painted Desert and the southern Petrified Forest. At each end of the 28 mi. road connecting the two is an entrance station and a visitors center. With lookout points and trails along the road, driving from one end of the park to the other is a good way to take in the full spectrum of colors and landscapes. The park can be entered from either the north or the south. (Open daily June-Aug. 7am-7pm; Sept.-May 8am-5pm, but hours can vary in the spring and fall. Entrance $10 per vehicle, $5 per pedestrian, $5 per motorcycle.) There is no public transit to the park. To reach the northern Painted Desert, take I-40 to Exit 311, 107 mi. east of Flagstaff and 65 mi. west of Gallup, NM. The **Painted Desert Visitors Center** shows a 20min. orientation video and has displays on the origins of the multi-colored desert. (☎ 524-6228. Open in summer daily 7am-7pm; call for low-season hours.) To reach the park's southern section, take U.S. 180 west 36 mi. from St. Johns, AZ, or east 19 mi. from Holbrook. Inside the south entrance, the **Rainbow Forest Museum and Visitors Center** gives a look at petrified logs and has info on local geology and paleontology. (☎ 524-6822. Open June-Aug. daily 7am-7pm, reduced hours in the low-season. Free.) Water and restrooms are available at both visitors centers and at the **Painted Desert Inn,** a historic adobe structure in the northern portion that houses cultural history exhibits. The Painted Desert Visitors Center has gas and a convenience store. In case of **emergency,** call the ranger dispatch (☎ 524-9726). There are no campgrounds in the park, but **back-**

SOUTHWEST

country camping ❶ is allowed in the Painted Desert Wilderness with a free permit. Backpackers must park at Kachina Point and enter the wilderness via the 1 mi. access trail. No fires are allowed. Budget motels and diners line Rte. 66, but there are none right around the park. **Gallup** and **Holbrook** offer more lodging and eating options.

◙ **SIGHTS.** Most travelers opt to drive the 27 mi. park road from north to south. From the north, the first stop is **Tiponi Point.** From the next stop, **Tawa Point,** the **Painted Desert Rim Trail** (½ mi. one-way) skirts the mesa edge above the Lithodendron Wash and the Black Forest before ending at ▨**Kachina Point** where the panoramic views are among the best in the park. The point provides access for travel into the **Painted Desert Wilderness,** the park's region for backcountry hiking and camping. As the road crosses I-40, it enters the Petrified Forest part of the park. The next stop is the 100-room **Puerco Pueblo,** believed to have housed nearly 1200 people. A short trail through the pueblo offers views of nearby petroglyphs. Many more petroglyphs can be seen at **Newspaper Rock,** but only at a distance. The road then wanders through the **The Tepees's** eerie moonscape before arriving at the 3 mi. **Blue Mesa** vehicle loop. At the loop's fourth overlook, you can hike the **Blue Mesa Trail** (1 mi. round-trip, 45min.), a steep descent into the heart of the park's desolate and beautiful formations. The **Giant Logs Trail** starts at the south visitors center and winds ½ mi. past the largest logs in the park, including one 10 ft. across at the base. The **Long Logs Trail** (1¾ mi. loop) travels through the world's densest concentration of petrified wood. The **Agate House Trail** (2 mi. round trip) leads to a partially restored pueblo of petrified wood. Although both trails start ¼ mi. to the east, the only parking is at the visitors center. Don't pick up the petrified wood—it's already scared enough. Also, taking fragments is illegal and traditionally unlucky.

PHOENIX ☎ 602

The name Phoenix was chosen for a small farming community in the Sonoran Desert by settlers who thought their oasis had risen from the ashes of ancient Native American settlements like the phoenix of Greek mythology. The 20th century has seen this unlikely metropolis live up to its name; the expansion of water resources, the proliferation of railroad transportation, and the marvel of air conditioning have fueled Phoenix's ascent to be one of America's leading cities.

> Because of its explosive growth, the city has three area codes. 602 is limited to Phoenix proper, 623 is western greater Phoenix, and 480 is the East Valley (including Scottsdale, Tempe, and Mesa). Unless otherwise noted, all listings in the text are within the 602 area code.

▛ TRANSPORTATION

Airport: Sky Harbor International Airport (☎273-3300; www.phxskyharbor.com), just southeast of downtown. Take the Valley Metro red line bus into the city (3:15am-11:45pm, $1.25). The largest city in the Southwest, Phoenix is a major airline hub and tends to be an affordable and convenient destination. **SuperShuttle** offers transportation to and from the airport; approx. $6 to downtown Phoenix (☎244-9000 or 800-258-3826).

Buses: Greyhound, 2115 E. Buckeye Rd. (☎389-4200). To: **El Paso** (8hr., 13 per day, $39); **Los Angeles** (7hr., 11 per day, $39); **San Diego** (8hr., 6 per day, $62); **Tucson** (2hr., 10 per day, $17). Open 24hr. There is no direct service to Phoenix, but **Amtrak** (☎800-USA-RAIL; www.amtrak.com) operates connector buses to and from rail stations in Tucson and Flagstaff. The Greyhound bus station is their busiest connecting Thruway motorcoach service location.

Downtown Phoenix

🏠 ACCOMMODATIONS
Metcalf Hostel (HI), **8**
Super 8 Motel, **4**
YMCA Downtown
 Phoenix, **9**

🍴 FOOD
Cherry Blossom Noodle
 Cafe, **2**
Dos Gringos Trailer Park, **6**
Los Dos Molinos, **10**

🍸 NIGHTLIFE
Ain't Nobody's Bizness, **3**
Char's Has the Blues, **1**
Graham Central Station, **7**
The Willow House, **5**

TO ① (2mi)
W. Cypress St.
TO ② (2.5mi)
TO ③ (4mi)
Heard Museum
E. Monte Vista Rd.
W. Monte Vista Rd.
TO ④ (4mi)
N. 3rd St.
Palm Ln.
1st St.
E. Coronado Rd.
Phoenix Art Museum
McDowell Rd.
TO SCOTTSDALE (15mi)
Central Ave.
⑤
E. Brill St.
E. Willetta St.
W. Willetta St.
Burton Barr Central Library
N. 3rd St.
7th Ave.
5th Ave.
3rd Ave.
W. Culver St.
10
Papago Fwy.
10
TO ⑥ (9mi), ⑦ (12mi),
TEMPE (5mi), PAPAGO
PARK (5mi), MESA (12mi),
SALT RIVER (7mi)
Portland St.
1st St.
Portland St.
⑧
Roosevelt St.
Roosevelt St.
7th Ave.
5th Ave.
3rd Ave.
1st Ave.
Central Ave.
Garfield St.
5th St.
7th St.
9th St.
McKinley St.
McKinley St.
Pierce St.
S. 3rd St.
W. Fillmore St.
E. Fillmore St.
W. Taylor St.
E. Taylor St.
2nd St.
Polk St.
⑨
Central Station
Arizona Center
Phoenix Union Municipal Center
TO ✚ (1.5mi)
Van Buren St.
Van Buren St.
9th St.
Monroe St.
Herberger Theater Center
Adams St.
Museum of History
HERITAGE SQUARE
Orpheum Theater
Renaissance Square
Visitor Information ⓘ
Phoenix Civic Plaza
Arizona Science Center
Washington St.
CÉSAR CHÁVEZ PLAZA
PATRIOT'S SQUARE
Symphony Hall
Washington St.
Jefferson St.
Jefferson St.
6th Ave.
5th Ave.
4th Ave.
3rd Ave.
Madison St.
2nd Ave.
1st Ave.
1st St.
America West Arena
Jefferson St.
9th St.
TO SKY HARBOR INTERNATIONAL AIRPORT (3mi)
7th Ave.
Union Station Amtrak
Jackson St.
Bank One Ballpark
3rd St.
7th St.
E. Jackson St.
TO GREYHOUND (3mi)
TO ⑩ (5mi)
Buchanan St.
N
0   600 yards
0   600 meters

SOUTHWEST

Public Transit: Downtown, **Valley Metro** (☎ 253-5000; www.valleymetro.org). Most lines run out of Central Station, at Central and Van Buren St. Most routes operate M-F 5am-8pm with reduced service Sa. $1.25; disabled, seniors, and children $0.60. All-day pass $3.60, 10-ride pass $12. Bus passes and system maps at the terminal or the downtown visitors center. In Tempe, the **City of Tempe Transit Store**, 502 S. College Ave., Ste. 101, is the public transit headquarters. The red line runs to and from Phoenix, and the last few stops of the yellow line are in Tempe. The red line also services Mesa. Bus passes and system maps at the terminal. Loloma Station, just south of Indian School and Scottsdale Rd., is Scottsdale's main hub for local traffic. The green line runs along Thomas St. to Phoenix.

Taxi: Yellow Cab ☎ 252-5252. **Discount Taxi** ☎ 200-2000.

Car Rental: Enterprise Rent-A-Car, 1402 N. Central Ave. (☎ 257-4177; www.enterprise.com), with other offices throughout the city. Compact cars around $30 per day, with lower weekly and monthly rates. Surcharge for drivers under 21. A valid credit card and driver's license are required. N. Central St. office open M-F 8am-6pm, Sa 9am-noon; other offices' hours vary.

◼◼ ORIENTATION AND PRACTICAL INFORMATION

The intersection of **Central Avenue** and **Washington Street** marks the heart of downtown. Central Ave. runs north-south, Washington St. east-west. Numbered avenues and streets both run north-south; avenues are numbered sequentially west from Central, while streets are numbered east. Greater Phoenix includes many smaller municipalities. **Tempe,** east of Phoenix, is dominated by students from Arizona State University. **Mesa,** east of Tempe, has much of Tempe's overflow. **Scottsdale,** north of Tempe, is a swanky district with adobe palaces, shopping centers, and sights. These areas combine to form what is referred to as "The Valley."

Visitor Info: Phoenix and Valley of the Sun Convention and Visitors Center (☎ 254-6500 or 877-225-5749, info and calendar 252-5588; www.phoenixcvb.com). Downtown at S. 2nd St. and Adams St. Open M-F 8am-5pm. Free **Internet access** (15min. limit). Camping and outdoors info at the **Bureau of Land Management Office,** 222 N. Central Ave. (☎ 417-9200).

Hotlines: Crisis Hotline, ☎ 800-631-1314. 24hr. **Gay Hotline,** ☎ 234-2752, daily 10am-10pm. **Sexual Assault Hotline,** ☎ 254-9000. **Suicide Prevention,** ☎ 480-784-1500.

Internet Access: Free (15min. limit) at **Burton Barr Central Library,** 1221 N. Central Ave. (☎ 262-4636). Open M-Th 10am-9pm, F-Sa 9am-6pm, Su noon-6pm.

Post Office: 522 N. Central Ave. (☎ 800-275-8777). Open M-F 8:30am-5pm. General delivery: 1441 E. Buckeye Rd. Open M-F 8:30am-5pm. **Postal Code:** 85034.

◣ ACCOMMODATIONS

Budget travelers should consider visiting Phoenix during July and August, when motels slash their prices by as much as 70%. In the winter, temperatures drop, the number of vacationers rises, vacancies are few, and prices go up; make reservations if possible. Although they are distant, the areas around Papago Fwy. and Black Canyon Hwy. are loaded with motels. **Mi Casa Su Casa/Old Pueblo Homestays Bed and Breakfast,** P.O. Box 950, Tempe 85280, arranges stays at B&Bs throughout Arizona, New Mexico, southern Utah, southern Nevada, and southern California. (☎ 800-456-0682. Open M-F 9am-5pm, Sa 9am-noon. Rooms $45 and up.) The reservationless should cruise the rows of motels on **Van Buren Street** east of downtown, toward the airport, but beware: *parts of this area can be unsafe, and guests should examine a motel thoroughly before checking in.*

Metcalf Hostel (HI), 1026 N. 9th St. (☎258-9830), between Roosevelt and Portland a few blocks north-east of downtown. Look for the house with lots of foliage out front. The cheery owner fosters a lively community in this renovated, spotless house. Kitchen, common room. Bikes for rent, and discounts to some city sights included in the price. Check-in 7-10am and 5-10pm. Light cleaning or other chores required. Dorms $15. ❶

Super 8 Motel, 4021 N. 27th Ave. (☎248-8880; www.super8.com), west on Indian School Rd. from the 17 Fwy. just north of downtown. Safe, well-lit, and close enough to a freeway and downtown to serve as a base for the Phoenix area. In winter $49; low-season $39. ❸

YMCA Downtown Phoenix, 350 N. 1st Ave. (☎253-6181). Another option in the downtown area, the YMCA provides small, single-occupancy rooms and shared bathrooms. Various athletic facilities and a few women's rooms available. Ask at the desk about storing valuables. 18+. Reception 9am-10pm. $20 per day; $99 per week. ❷

🍴 FOOD

Downtowners eat at small coffeehouses, most of which close on weekends. **McDowell** and **Camelback Road** offer Asian restaurants. The **Arizona Center,** an open-air shopping gallery at 3rd St. and Van Buren, has food, fountains, and palm trees. Sports bars and grilles sit around the America West Arena and Bank One Ballpark.

Los Dos Molinos, 8646 S. Central Ave. (☎243-9113). From downtown, go south on Central Ave. and keep going. Once you leave the *barrio,* it comes up on your right, between S. Mountain and Euclid. Lively, colorful, and fun, it's worth the trip. The food is authentic and delicious, and they "don't know mild," so be ready to swallow fire. No reservations, so come early or try its sister establishment on 260 S. Alma School Dr. in Mesa. Enchiladas $3.50, burritos $3-7. Open Tu-F 11am-2:30pm and 5-9pm, Sa 11am-9pm. ❶

Dos Gringos Trailer Park, 216 E. University (☎480-968-7879). Dos, as it's affectionately known, skirts the line between restaurant and nightspot with its laid-back, day-drinking mentality and inexpensive but tasty Mexican food ($6 meals). Contribute to the tally that makes Dos the #1 national consumer of Corona. After dark there's a more rowdy atmosphere. Open M-Sa 10am-1am, Su 11am-1am. ❶

THE HIDDEN DEAL

ORGANIC PIZZA

It isn't often that you get to both eat pizza and listen to the world's largest theater pipe organ, but such is possible at **Organ Stop Pizza.** The food is good, and the music is fabulous. Locals line up to order pizzas, then head to the cavernous dining-room-turned-performance-hall to sit at one of the long common tables and enjoy the show. The master organist's fingers fly across the mammoth 6-ft.-tall organ, jauntily playing soundtrack staples from Disney movie classics (with cascading bubbles), then smoothly transitioning into the haunting melodies of symphony masterpieces. The organ, an antique Wurlitzer, has since been restored and customized to its current 5500 pipes with turbines, visible from outside the building, providing the air needed to operate the instrument. Pizza is ready in two or three songs, and requests and dedications are accepted in a box at the edge of the stage. Don't be surprised when, at the organist's command, curtains rise, puppets dance, oowgah horns blow, and rows of lightbulbs flash in whimsical accompaniment.

Organ Stop Pizza, 1149 E. Southern Ave., Mesa (☎480-813-5700). Take the Stapley exit north off I-10. Turn left onto Southern Ave.; it's on your left. Open Su-Th 5-9pm, F-Sa 5-10pm; music starts 30min. after opening and continues until close.

Cherry Blossom Noodle Cafe, 914 E. Camelback Rd. Hiding behind the strip-mall facade is a chic interior and noodle-lover's heaven. The wide variety of Asian and Italian noodle dishes and sushi are well-prepared and sure to satisfy your carb-craving. (☎248-9090. Entrees $12-14. Open Su-Th 11am-9pm, F-Sa 11am-10pm.) ❸

🔍 SIGHTS

DOWNTOWN. The center of Phoenix, often called Copper Park, is divided into downtown (south of I-10) with cultural and sports attractions, and uptown (north of I-10), an artistic quarter with many museums. The price of most attractions is about $7; most are worth the price. The **Heard Museum** is renowned for its ancient Native American art. A new exhibition, HOME, will open in spring 2005, focusing on the experiences and lives of contemporary Native Americans. *(2301 N. Central Ave., 4 blocks north of McDowell Rd. ☎252-8840, recorded info 252-8848. Open daily 9:30am-5pm. Free tours at noon, 1:30, 3pm. $7, seniors $6, ages 4-12 $3; Native Americans with status cards free.)* Three blocks south, at Central and McDowell, the **Phoenix Art Museum** displays art of the American West, 19th-century European and American works, and special exhibits. *(1625 N. Central Ave., at McDowell Rd. ☎257-1880. Open Tu-Su 10am-5pm, Th 10am-9pm. $7, students and seniors $5, ages 6-17 $2. Free after 4:15pm and on Th.)*

PAPAGO PARK AND FARTHER EAST. The **Desert Botanical Garden,** in Papago Park, 5 mi. east of downtown, showcases a colorful collection of cacti and other, often rare, desert plants. The park's trails are pleasant in cooler weather but can be too hot for comfort in the summer. Guided tours are given daily at 11am and 1pm October through April.*(1201 N. Galvin Pkwy. ☎941-1225. Open daily May-Sept. 7am-8pm; Oct.-Apr. 8am-8pm. $9, seniors $8, students $5.)* Take bus #3 east to **Papago Park,** on the eastern outskirts of the city for spectacular views of the desert, and hiking, biking, and driving trails. The **Phoenix Zoo,** in the park has a formidable collection of tropical, African, and Southwestern critters. *(455 N. Galvin Pkwy. ☎273-1341. Open daily Sept.-May 9am-5pm; June-Aug. 7am-4pm. Sept.-Aug. $12, seniors $9, children $5; June-Aug. $9/$7/$5.)* Farther east of the city, in Mesa, flows the **Salt River,** one of the last remaining desert rivers in the US. **Salt River Recreation** arranges tubing trips. *(☎480-984-3305. Open May-Sept. daily 9am-4pm. Tube rental $12 per day, includes shuttle service.)*

SCOTTSDALE SIGHTS. Taliesin West was originally built as the winter camp of Frank Lloyd Wright's Taliesin architectural collective; in his later years he lived there full-time. It is now a campus for an architectural college run by his foundation, which also gives guided tours. *(12621 Frank Lloyd Wright Blvd. Head east off the Cactus St. exit from Rte. 101. ☎480-860-2700. Open Sept.-June daily 9am-4pm, closed Tu-W during July-Aug. 1hr.-1½hr. guided tours required. See www.franklloydwright.org for specific tour info. In summer $14, in winter $18, students and seniors $12/$16; ages 4-12 $4.50.)* Wright also designed the impressively posh **Arizona Biltmore** hotel. *(24th St. and Missouri. ☎955-6600.)* One of the last buildings designed by Wright, the **Gammage Memorial Auditorium** wears the pink-and-beige earth tones of the surrounding environment. *(Mill Ave. and Apache Blvd., on the Arizona State University campus in Tempe. Take bus #60, or #22 on weekends. ☎965-3434. 20min. tours daily in winter.)* **Cosanti** is a working studio and bell foundry designed by the architect and sculptor Paolo Soleri, one of Wright's students. The buildings fuse with the natural landscape even more strikingly than those at Taliesin West, and morning visitors may have the chance to watch the craftsmen work. *(6433 Doubletree Rd., in Scottsdale. With I-10 behind you, turn right off of Scottsdale Rd. ☎480-948-6145. Open M-Sa 9am-5pm, Su 11am-5pm. Suggested donation $1.)*

🎵 🎭 ENTERTAINMENT AND NIGHTLIFE

Phoenix offers many options for the sports lover. NBA basketball action rises with the **Phoenix Suns** (☎ 379-7867) at the **America West Arena**, while the **Arizona Cardinals** (☎ 379-0101) play NFL football. The **Arizona Diamondbacks** (☎ 514-8400) use the fabulous **Bank One Ballpark,** complete with a retractable roof, an outfield swimming pool, and "beer gardens." (☎ 462-6799. Tickets start at $7. $1 tickets available 2hr. before games; first come, first served. Tours of the stadium $6.)

The Willow House, 149 W. McDowell Rd., is a self-proclaimed "artist's cove," combining a coffeehouse, deli, and musicians' hangout. (☎ 252-0272. No alcohol. 2-for-1 coffee happy hour M-F 4-7pm. Live music Sa 8pm. Open M-Th 7am-midnight, F 7am-1am, Sa 8am-1am, Su 8am-midnight.) **Char's Has the Blues,** 4631 N. 7th Ave., houses local blues acts. On Friday nights, come early for the barbecue. (☎ 230-0205; www.charshastheblues.com. For shows, doors open 7pm. Cover usually $2, F-Sa $7, women free on Tu. Hours vary.) **Graham Central Station,** 7850 S. Priest Dr., Tempe, has four venues under one roof. The smaller Top 40, retro, and karaoke venues supplement the good times of the Rockin' Rodeo, a western-themed club, complete with mechanical bull. (☎ 480-496-0799. Open W-Su 6pm-2am. Cover up to $7.) A large, predominantly lesbian but straight-friendly bar, **Ain't Nobody's Bizness,** 3031 E. Indian School Rd. #7, has more space devoted to pool tables than to the dance floor, but dance and hip-hop music get people moving. (☎ 224-9977. Th $2 pitchers. Occasional cover during guest vocalist appearances. Open M-F 4pm-2am, Sa-Su 2pm-2am.) The free *New Times Weekly,* available on local magazine racks, lists schedules for Phoenix's after-hours scene. The *Cultural Calendar of Events* covers area entertainment in three-month intervals. The *Western Front* and *Echo,* both found in bars and clubs, cover GLBT nightlife.

SCENIC DRIVE: APACHE TRAIL

Steep, gray, and haunting, the **Superstition Mountains** derive their name from Pima Native American legends, but their rugged, forbidding outlines have long appealed to the area's settlers. Stories of gold led to mining bonanzas, but Apache warriors limited such advances. It wasn't until the early 20th century that **Route 88** was carved through the mountains to move supplies for the construction of Roosevelt Dam. The road, loosely following ancestral Indian paths, became known as the **Apache Trail** to the early motorists who raced around the road's harrowing turns and along its 10% grades in their primitive cars, hoping for new records. Though the days of the Model T are gone, motorists still hug the turns and climb the same steep roadbed as they travel to one of the three artificial lakes along the Salt River or ogle the Superstition Mountain Wilderness's wild crags and canyons.

The drive winds from **Apache Junction,** a small mining town 40 mi. east of Phoenix, through the mountains. Although the road is only about 50 mi. one-way, trips require at least 3hr. because of the partially unpaved, narrow roadbed. Info about the drive can be found at the **Apache Junction Chamber of Commerce,** 112 E. 2nd Ave. (☎ 480-982-3141. Open M-F 8am-5pm, in summer 8am-4:30pm.) The **Superstition Mountain Museum,** 3½ mi. northeast of Apache Junction along the Apache Trail, doles out free info and has an impressive collection of mining equipment, artifacts, and memorabilia. (☎ 480-983-4888. $4, students $2. Open daily 9am-4pm.) The carless can drive with **Apache Trail Tours,** which offers on- and off-road Jeep tours. (☎ 480-982-7661. 2-4hr. tours from $70 per person. Reserve at least 1 day ahead.)

The trail's views of the arid landscape make it one of the most beautiful driving routes in the nation. The deep blue waters of **Lake Canyon, Lake Apache,** and **Lake Roosevelt** contrast with the surrounding red and beige rock formations. **Goldfield Ghost Town Mine Tours,** on Rte. 88, 5 mi. north of the U.S. 60 junction, offers humorous but informative tours of the nearby mines and gold-panning in a resurrected ghost town. (☎480-983-0333. Open daily 10am-5pm. Mine tours $5, ages 6-12 $3; gold-panning $4.) "Where the hell am I?" asked Jacob Waltz when he came upon **Lost Dutchman State Park ❶,** 1 mi. farther north on Rte. 88. At the base of the Superstitions, the park has nature trails, picnic sites, and campsites with showers. (☎480-982-4485. Entrance $5 per vehicle. Sites $12, with electricity $20.)

Grab a saddle for a bar stool at **Tortilla Flat,** another refurbished ghost town 18 mi. farther on Rte. 88. The town, once a stagecoach stop, keeps its spirits up and tourists fed with a restaurant, ice-cream shop, and saloon. (☎480-984-1776. Restaurant open M-F 9am-6pm, Sa-Su 8am-7pm.) **Tonto National Monument,** on Rte. 88, 5 mi. east of Lake Roosevelt, preserves 800-year-old masonry and Pueblo ruins. A short but steep trail (½ mi., 350 ft.) leads from the visitors center up to the ruins. You can then climb inside and walk through the pueblo. (☎928-467-2241. Open daily 8am-5pm, trail closes at 4pm. $4 per car.) **Tonto National Forest ❶** has nearby camping. (☎602-225-5200. Sites $4-11.) The trail ends at the **Theodore Roosevelt Dam** (finished in 1911), the last dam built by hand in the US. At the end of the trail, Rte. 60 is a scenic trip back to Phoenix; the higher elevations' increased moisture and decreased temperature give rise to lush greenery (by Arizona standards).

TUCSON
☎520

"A little bit country, a little bit rock 'n' roll," Tucson carries its own, often contradictory, tune. Mexican property until 1854, the city retains many of its south-of-the-border influences and juxtaposes its Mexican heritage with such disparate elements as the University of Arizona and the Davis-Monthan Air Force Base. Boasting mountain flora beside desert cacti, and art museums next to the war machines of the Pima Air and Space Museum, the city nearly defies categorization.

▐ TRANSPORTATION

Airport: Tucson International Airport (☎573-8000; www.tucsonairport.org), on Valencia Rd., south of downtown. Bus #6 goes downtown from the terminal drop-off area. **Arizona Stagecoach** (☎889-1000; http://azstagecoach.com) goes downtown for around $16-18 for the first adult plus $2-3 per each additional family member.

Trains: Amtrak, 400 E. Toole Ave. (☎623-4442), at 5th Ave., 1 block north of the Greyhound station. To: **Albuquerque** (4 per week, $99) via **El Paso; Los Angeles** (9hr., 3 per week, $32); **San Francisco** (18hr., 3 per week, $88) via **Los Angeles.** Book 2 weeks ahead or rates are substantially higher. Open M and Sa-Su 6:15am-1:45pm and 4:15-11:30pm, Tu-W 6:15am-1:45pm, Th-F 4:15-11:30pm.

Buses: Greyhound, 2 S. 4th Ave. (☎792-3475), between Congress St. and Broadway. To: **Albuquerque** (12-14hr., 5 per day, $88); **El Paso** (6hr., 11 per day, $39); **Los Angeles** (10-12hr., 9 per day, $53); **Phoenix** (2hr., 10 per day, $17). Station open 24hr.

Public Transit: Sun-Tran, (☎792-9222). Buses run from the Ronstadt terminal downtown at Congress and 6th St. $1; seniors, disabled, and students $0.40; day pass $2. Most routes M-F 5:30am-10pm, Sa-Su 8am-7pm; times vary by route.

Taxi: Yellow Cab ☎624-6611.

Bike Rental: Fair Wheel Bikes, 1110 E. 6th St. (☎884-9018), at Fremont. $10 per day; $60 per week; $500 credit card deposit required. Open M-F 9am-6pm, Sa 9am-5:30pm, Su noon-4pm.

◀✳ ▐ ORIENTATION AND PRACTICAL INFORMATION

Just east of I-10, Tucson's downtown area surrounds the intersection of **Broadway Boulevard** and **Stone Avenue,** two blocks from the train and bus terminals. The **University of Arizona** is 1 mi. northeast of downtown at the intersection of **North Park**

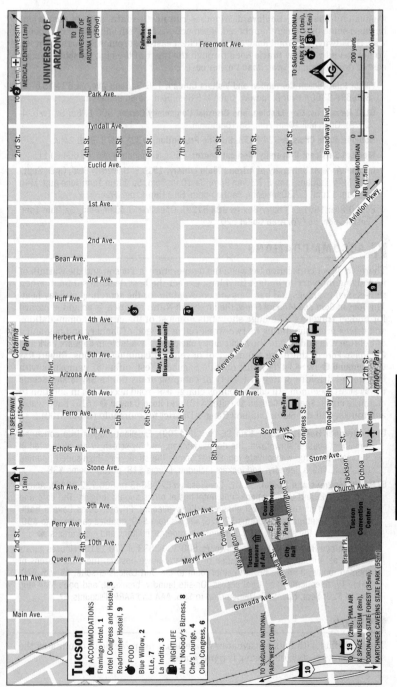

SOUTHWEST

Avenue and **Speedway Boulevard.** Avenues run north-south, streets east-west; because some of each are numbered, intersections like "6th and 6th" exist. Speedway, Broadway, and **Grant Road** are the quickest east-west routes through town. To go north-south, follow **Oracle Road** through the heart of the city, **Campbell Avenue** east of downtown, or **Swan Road** farther east.

Visitor Info: Tucson Convention and Visitors Bureau, 130 S. Scott Ave. (☎624-1817 or 800-638-8350), near Broadway. Open M-F 8am-5pm, Sa-Su 9am-4pm.

GLBT Resources: Gay, Lesbian, and Bisexual Community Center, 300 E. 6th St. (☎624-1779). Open M-F 10am-7pm, Sa 10am-5pm.

Hotlines: Rape Crisis, ☎624-7273. **Suicide Prevention,** ☎323-9373. Both 24hr.

Medical Services: University Medical Center, 1501 N. Campbell Ave. (☎694-0111).

Internet Access: University of Arizona Main Library, 1510 E. University Blvd. Open Sept.-May M-Th 7:30am-1am, F 7:30am-9pm, Sa 10am-9pm, Su 11am-1am; June-Aug. M-Th 7:30am-11pm, F 7:30am-6pm, Sa 9am-6pm, Su 11am-11pm. Free.

Post Office: 1501 S. Cherry Bell (☎388-5129). Open M-F 8:30am-8pm, Sa 9am-1pm. **Postal Code:** 85726. **Area Code:** 520.

ACCOMMODATIONS

There's a direct correlation between the temperature in Tucson and the warmth of its lodging industry to budget travelers: expect the best deals in summer, when rain-cooled evenings and bargains are consolation for the scorching midday heat. The **Tucson Gem and Mineral Show,** the largest in North America, is an added hazard for budget travelers. The huge show fills up most of the city's accommodations and drives prices up during its two-week run at the end of January and beginning of February. In addition to the **backcountry camping** ❶ available in **Saguaro Park** and **Coronado Forest,** there are a number of developed camping options. **Gilbert Ray Campground** ❶ (☎883-4200), just outside Saguaro West, offers $7 campsites with toilets and drinking water. A variety of camping areas flanks **Sky Island Scenic Byway** at Mt. Lemmon. All campgrounds charge a $5 road access fee in addition to camping costs. **Spencer Canyon** ❶ (sites $12) and **Rose Canyon** ❶ ($15) have water and toilets. Call the Santa Catalina Ranger District for more info (☎749-8700).

▨ **Roadrunner Hostel,** 346 E. 12th St. (☎628-4709). Excellent lodging in a converted home just south of downtown. The dorms, kitchen, and big-screen TV are all located in the main building, with private rooms just across the street. Free high-speed Internet. Breakfast, linens, laundry, and lockers included. Dorms $18; private rooms $38.

▨ **Hotel Congress and Hostel,** 311 E. Congress (☎622-8848 or 800-722-8848). Across from the bus and train stations, this hotel-hostel offers superb lodging. The cafe and club located on the first level ensures a lively evening. Private rooms have a bath, phone, and vintage radio. Dorms $20-25; singles from $49; doubles can be up to $90, depending on the season. 10% discount for students, military, and local artists. ❶

The Flamingo Hotel, 1300 N. Stone Ave. (☎800-300-3533 or 770-1910). Houses guests as well as Arizona's largest collection of Western movie posters. There are dozens of themed rooms, from the Kevin Costner room to the Burt Lancaster suite, all with A/C, cable TV, telephones, and pool access. On-site laundry, breakfast, and pool. May-Aug. rooms $29; Sept.-Nov. $49; Dec.-Apr. up to $85. AAA and AARP discounts. ❸

FOOD

Tucson brims with inexpensive, tasty eateries. Cheap Mexican dominates the scene, but every style of cooking is represented.

▨ **The Blue Willow,** 2616 N. Campbell Ave. (☎327-7577), serves absolutely delicious, reasonably priced comfort food. The relaxing enclosed patio fills with locals lured by the wholesome entrees (whole wheat pancakes $4, quiche and crepes $7, meatloaf $8, rice and vegetables $5) and outstanding homemade pastries and desserts (chocolate *du jour* $5). Open M-Th 7am-9pm, F 7am-10pm, Sa 8am-10pm, Su 8am-9pm.

▨ **eLLe,** 3048 E. Broadway Blvd. (☎327-0500), has a carefully crafted menu of mouth-watering pastas, risottos, and grilled meats ($12-22). Cool jazz resonates through this stylish eatery, and the airy bar is open until 1am, providing an elegant option for a late-night drink or an amazing dessert. Open M-F 11:30am-1am, Sa 4:30pm-1am. ❹

La Indita, 622 N. 4th Ave. (☎792-0523), delights customers with traditional Mexican cuisine ($3-9) and welcoming service. Behind the faded storefront, the unique, flavorful food is still prepared by *la indita* herself using family recipes and the freshest ingredients. Open M-Th 11am-9pm, F 11am-6pm, Sa 6-9pm, Su 9am-9pm. ❶

◎ SIGHTS

UNIVERSITY OF ARIZONA. Lined with cafes, restaurants, galleries, and vintage clothing shops, **4th Avenue** is an alternative magnet and a great place to stroll. Between Speedway and Broadway Blvd., the street is a historical shopping district with increasingly touristy shops. **University Boulevard** leads into the university grounds from the west, and is edged with shops, breweries, and cafes that appeal to the younger crowd. With lovely and varied vegetation, the University of Arizona's mall sits where E. 3rd St. should be, just east of 4th Ave. The **Center for Creative Photography,** on the UA campus, houses changing exhibits, including the archives of Ansel Adams and Richard Avedon. (☎621-7968. Open M-F 9am-5pm, Sa-Su noon-5pm. Archives available to the public through print-viewing appointments. Free.) The **Flandrau Science Center,** on Cherry Ave. at the campus mall, dazzles visitors with a public observatory and a laser show. (☎621-7827. Open M-Tu 9am-5pm, W-Sa 9am-5pm and 7-9pm, Su noon-5pm. $3, under 14 $2. Shows $5/$4, seniors and students $4.50.) The **University of Arizona Museum of Art** offers visitors a glimpse of modern American and 18th-century Latin American art and sculpture, along with student art. (1031 N. Olive. ☎621-7567. Open mid-Sept. to mid-May M-F 9am-5pm, Su noon-4pm; May-Sept. M-F 10am-3:30pm, Su noon-4pm. Free.)

TUCSON MUSEUM OF ART. This museum has impressive exhibits in all media, in addition to its permanent collection of American, Mexican, and European art. Historic houses in the surrounding and affiliated Presidio Historic Block boast an impressive collection of Pre-Columbian and Mexican folk art, and art of the American West. (140 N. Main Ave. ☎624-2333. Open M-Sa 10am-4pm, Su noon-4pm. Closed M late May to early Sept. $5, seniors $4, students $3, under 13 free. Su free.)

WEST SPEEDWAY. As Speedway Blvd. winds its way west from Tucson's city center, it passes a variety of attractions. The left fork leads to **Old Tucson Studios,** an elaborate Old West-style town constructed for the 1938 movie *Arizona* and used as a backdrop for Westerns ever since, including many John Wayne films and the 1999 Will Smith movie, *Wild Wild West.* Now more of a theme park than anything out of the olden days, it's open year-round to tourists, who can stroll around in the Old West mock-up and view gunfight reenactments and other tourist shows. (☎883-0100. Open early Sept. to late May daily 10am-6pm; fewer attractions late May to early Sept. Su-F 10am-3pm, all attractions Sa 10am-4pm. Sometimes closed on M in winter. Call ahead, since occasionally Old Tucson is closed for group functions. $15, seniors $14, ages 4-11 $9.45; in summer Su-F $10, children $7.) Those opting to take the right fork will eschew the Wild Wild West for the merely wild, more natural, West; less than

2 mi. from the fork lies the ⧉**Arizona-Sonora Desert Museum,** a first-rate zoo and nature preserve. The living museum recreates a range of desert habitats and features over 300 kinds of animals. Park employees are stationed throughout the park, eager to answer any questions or to offer the venomous reptile presentation (daily 12:15pm) and the raptor free flight program (Nov.-Apr.). A visit requires at least 2hr., preferably in the morning before the animals take their afternoon siestas. *(2021 N. Kinney Rd.* ☎ *883-2702. Follow Speedway Blvd. west of the city as it becomes Gates Pass Rd., then Kinney Rd. Open daily Mar.-Sept. 7:30am-5pm, June-Sept. Sa until 10pm; Oct.-Feb. 8:30am-5pm. $9, Oct.-May. $12; ages 6-12 $2.)*

CAVES. The recently opened **Kartchner Caverns State Park** is enormously popular, filled with magnificent rock formations and home to over 1000 bats. This is a "living" cave which contains water and is still experiencing the growth of its formations; the damp conditions cause the formations to shine and glisten in the light. Two separate, 1½hr. tours are offered of the cave: one exploring the Rotunda and Throne Rooms (offered year-round) and another through the Big Room (Sept.-Apr.). Taking a tour is the only way to enter the cave, and only 500 people are allowed in the cave each day. Most tickets are reserved far in advance, but approximately 100 tickets are held for walk-ups and dispensed starting at 7:30am. *(Located 8 mi. off I-10 at Exit 302.* ☎ *586-4100. Open daily 7:30am-6pm. Tours run every 30min. 8:30am-4:30pm. Entrance fee $10 per vehicle, tour $14, ages 7-13 $6. Reservations strongly recommended.)* In contrast to the recent discovery and exploration of Kartchner Caverns, **Colossal Cave** has been known to humans for over a thousand years. The Hohokam Indians were the first to utilize this dormant cave (no water or new formations), and it was later a hideout for train robbers. Today, a variety of tours are offered; in addition to 1hr. walking tours occurring throughout the day, a special ladder tour through otherwise sealed-off tunnels, crawlspaces, and corridors can be arranged. *(*☎ *647-7275. Open mid-Mar. to mid-Sept. M-Sa 8am-6pm, Su 8am-7pm; mid-Sept. to mid-Mar. M-Sa 9am-5pm, Su 9am-6pm. $7.50, ages 6-12 $4. Ladder tour: Sept.-Mar. Sa 5:30-8pm, Mar.-Sept. Sa 6:30-9pm; $35, including meal and equipment rental. Reservations required.)*

PIMA AIR AND SPACE MUSEUM. This impressive museum follows aviation history from the days of the Wright brothers to its modern military incarnations. Exhibits on female and African-American aviators are interesting, but the museum's main draw is a fleet of decommissioned war planes. *(*☎ *574-0462. Open in summer daily 9am-5pm; in winter M-F 7am-3pm, Sa-Su 7am-5pm. $9.75, seniors $8.75.)* Tours of the **Davis-Monthan Air Force Base** are also offered, but be prepared for rigorous security checks and possible cancellations. *(5 tours per day M-F. $6, ages 6-12 $3.)*

🎵 NIGHTLIFE

The free *Tucson Weekly* is the local authority on nightlife, while the weekend sections of the *Star* or the *Citizen* also provide good coverage. UA students kick back on **University Boulevard,** and rock 'n' roll on **Speedway Boulevard,** while others do the two-step along **North Oracle.** Young locals hang out on **4th Avenue,** where most bars have live music and low cover charges.

Club Congress, 311 E. Congress St. (☎ 622-8848), alternates DJs with live indie and rock concerts to keep the dance crowd happy. Its warehouse-like interior fills with hipster regulars and anyone looking to add a bit of rock 'n' roll to their time in Tucson. M 80s night with $0.80 vodkas. Cover $3-5. Open daily 9pm-1am.

Che's Lounge, 350 4th Ave. (☎ 623-2088), houses an eclectic crowd so busy chatting, they sometimes forget to groove to the music. Show up early; there are lines early in the night on weekends, and crowds during the week. Live music Sa. Open daily 4pm-1am.

Ain't Nobody's Bizness, 2900 E. Broadway Blvd. (☎318-4838), in a shopping plaza, is the big mama of the Tucson lesbian scene. With a large bar, themed contests, and pool tournaments, "Biz" attracts crowds of all backgrounds and has some of the best dancing in Tucson. W 18+. Open daily 2pm-2am.

🔹 DAYTRIPS FROM TUCSON

SAGUARO NATIONAL PARK. Saguaro National Park is split into two districts flanking Tucson to the west and east. The western half (Tucson Mountain District) is accessed by following Speedway Blvd. out of town and taking Kinney Rd. beyond the Arizona-Sonora Desert Museum. The **Red Hills Visitors Center** has exhibits on desert flora and fauna, as well as *The Saguaro Sentinel*, the park's free newspaper guide. *(☎733-5158. Visitors center open daily 9am-5pm; park and auto loop 7am-sunset. Free.)* The **Bajada Loop Drive** runs only 6 mi. on a graded dirt road, but passes through some of the most striking desert scenery the park has to offer. The Tucson Mountain District has over 40 mi. of trails. The wheelchair-accessible **Desert Discovery Nature Trail** (½ mi., 20min.), 1 mi. NW of the visitors center, is a good introduction to the desert environment. **Valley View Overlook** (1 mi., 30min.) has a moderate climb to the top of a ridge and, as the name suggests, gives a spectacular vista of the valley below. The eastern portion of the park (Rincón Mountain District) is larger, with even more trails, but the scenery is largely the same. The **Rincón Visitors Center** offers natural history exhibits and guides to the park's activities. The **Cactus Forest Loop Drive** winds 8 mi. through impressive stands of saguaros, many of them well over 100 years old. *(☎733-5158. Visitors center open daily 9am-5pm. Park and auto loop open 7am-sunset; $6 per vehicle.)* Mountain biking is permitted only around the **Cactus Forest Loop Drive** and **Cactus Forest Trail,** at the western end of the park near the visitors center.

BIOSPHERE 2. Ninety-one feet high, with an area of more than three acres, Biosphere 2 is sealed off from Earth—"Biosphere 1"—by 500 tons of stainless steel. In 1991, eight research scientists locked themselves inside this giant greenhouse to cultivate their own food and knit their own socks as they monitored the behavior of five man-made ecosystems: savanna, rainforest, marsh, ocean, and desert. After two years, they began having oxygen problems and difficulty with food production. No one lives in Biosphere 2 now, but it is still used as a research facility and is open to the public by guided tour. *(30min. north of Tucson; follow Oracle Rd. north until it becomes Rte. 77 N. From Phoenix, take I-10 to exit 185, follow Rte. 387 to Rte. 79 (Florence Hwy.), and proceed to Oracle Jct. and Rte. 77. ☎800-838-2462. Call for daily tour info. Open daily 8:30am-5:30pm, last admission 5pm. $20, ages 6-12 $13.)*

MISSION SAN XAVIER DE BAC. Built by the Franciscan brothers in the late 1700s, the "white dove of the desert" is the northernmost Spanish Baroque church in the Americas, and the only such church in the US. *(South of Tucson off of I-19 to Nogales, take the San Xavier exit and follow the signs. ☎294-2624. Open for viewing 7am-5pm; mass held daily. Free, but donations are appreciated.)*

TOMBSTONE
☎520

Long past the glory days when it was the largest city between the Pacific and the Mississippi, Tombstone is now a veritable Cowboy Disneyland. The storefronts and saloons of Allen St., once the site of countless gun battles and the stomping grounds of western legends, are now the territory of tourists hoping to experience a little slice of the town "too tough to die." Cowboys swagger down the streets, promising gunfight reenactments and western fun. The **Shoot-**

out at the O.K. Corral is one of the most popular attractions with a gunfight at 2pm daily, staged at the supposed fight site. The voice of Vincent Price narrates the town's history next door to the O.K. Corral in the **Tombstone Historama,** while a plastic mountain revolves onstage and a dramatization of the gunfight is shown on a movie screen. (☎457-3456. Shootout open daily 9am-5pm, arrive before 2pm reenactment. Historama shows daily every hr. 9am-4pm. $7.50 for admission to both attractions.) Site of the longest poker game in Western history (8 years, 5 months, and 3 days), the **Bird Cage Theater,** at 6th and Allen, was named for the suspended cages that once housed prostitutes. It is now a museum that features the original fixtures and the Black Myriah, the gold-plated hearse that transported Boothill Cemetery's new residents to their final resting places. (☎457-3421. Open daily 8am-6pm. Self-guided tour. $6, seniors $5.50.) The tombstones of Tombstone, largely the result of all that gunplay, stand in **Boothill Cemetery,** on Rte. 80 just north of town. (☎457-3421 or 800-457-3423. Open daily 7:30am-6pm. Free.)

Staying in Benson and commuting out for a day in Tombstone is a good idea. If you want to stay in town, though, the **Trail Riders Inn ❷,** on the corner of 7th and Fremont, has clean rooms with a homey, comfortable feel. (☎457-3573. Singles from $30; doubles from $35.) **Six Gun City Crazy Horse Saloon ❷,** 5th and Toughnut, serves hearty, meaty entrees in a welcoming, rustic interior. Mingle with the locals as you listen to live country music at night or join the tourists at the outdoor Wild West shows. (☎457-3827. Shows at 11:30am, 1, 3pm. Open W-Su 11am-10pm.) **Nellie Cashman's Restaurant ❶,** named after the "angel of the mining camps" who devoted her life to clean living and public service, is less Old West and a bit more down-home. Delicious half-pound burgers start at $5.50. (☎457-2212. Open daily 7:30am-9pm.) For moonshine and country music, head to **Big Nose Kate's Saloon,** on Allen St., named for "the girl who loved Doc Holliday and everyone else too." (☎457-3107. Live music. Open daily 10am-midnight; closes early if business is slow.)

To get to Tombstone, head to the Benson exit off I-10, then go south on Rte. 80. The nearest **Greyhound** station is in Benson. The **Tombstone Visitors Center,** a large, white building on 4th St. and Allen, provides brochures and maps, although Tombstone is so small that nothing takes long to find. (☎457-3929. Open M-F 9am-4pm, Sa-Su 10am-4pm.) The Tombstone **Marshal's office** (☎457-2244) is just behind City Hall. **Internet access** is available at **Gitt Wired,** 5th and Fremont. (☎457-3250. Open 7am-5pm. $0.15 per min.) The **post office** is at 100 N. Haskell Ave. **Postal Code:** 85638.

BISBEE   ☎520

Located 100 mi. southeast of Tucson and 20 mi. south of Tombstone, Bisbee, a former mining town, is now a laid-back artists' colony. Visitors revel in the town's proximity to Mexico, picture-perfect weather, and excellent accommodations. **Queen Mines,** on the Rte. 80 interchange entering Old Bisbee, ceased mining in 1943 but now gives 1¼hr. subterranean tours. (☎432-2071. Tours at 9, 10:30am, noon, 2, 3:30pm. $12, ages 4-15 $5.) The Smithsonian-affiliated **Mining and Historical Museum,** 5 Copper Queen, highlights the discovery of Bisbee's copper surplus and the lives of the fortune-seekers who extracted it. (☎432-7071. Open daily 10am-4pm. $4, seniors $3.50, under 3 free.) About 18 mi. west of Bisbee on Rte. 92, along Mexico's border, **Coronado National Memorial** marks the place where Francisco Coronado and his expedition first entered American territory. **Coronado Cave,** a small, relatively dry cave, is ¾ mi. from the visitors center along a short, steep path. A free permit is required to explore the cave, and can be picked up at the visitors center; each caver must have two flashlights. (☎366-5515. Park open daily dawn-dusk. Visitors center open daily 8am-5pm.)

Ramsey Canyon Preserve, 5 mi. farther down the road, attracts nearly as many bird-watchers as birds. In the middle of major migratory routes, thousands of hummingbirds throng here in late summer. (Open daily 8am-5pm. $5, under 16 free. First Sa of every month free.)

On Tombstone Canyon Rd., at the south end of town, the **School House Inn ❸** houses guests in a remodeled 1918 school house. Rooms are themed and vary in size; the principal's office is palatial, while the classrooms, each devoted to a school subject, have a cozier charm. (☎ 432-2966 or 800-537-4333. All rooms have private bath. TV in common room. Ironically, no children under 14 allowed. Full breakfast included. Single bed $60; double/queen/king $75-85; 2-bed suite $95.) A 10min. walk from downtown, the **Jonquil Inn ❷,** 317 Tombstone Canyon, has clean rooms. (☎ 432-7371. In summer singles $40-45; doubles $55-65. In winter about $10 more.) **Old Tymers ❷** has steak ($11) and hamburgers ($5) any way you like, along with other homestyle favorites. (☎ 432-7364. Open M-Th 11am-9pm, F-Sa 11am-10pm, Su 11am-8pm.) The **Chamber of Commerce,** 31 Subway St., has maps that will help you navigate Bisbee's labyrinthine streets. (☎ 432-5421. Open M-F 9am-5pm, Sa-Su 10am-4pm.) The **post office,** on Main St., is one block south of the highway exit. (☎ 432-2052. Open M-F 8:30am-4:30pm.) **Postal Code:** 85603. **Area Code:** 520.

NEW MEXICO

New Mexico is a dreamscape of varied terrains and peoples. Going back to the days when Spaniards arrived with delusions of golden riches, this expansive land of high deserts, mountain vistas, and roadrunners has always been a place where people come to fulfill their fantasies. Today, most explorers arrive in search of natural beauty, adobe architecture, and cultural treasures instead of gold, and the mountains of New Mexico are a haven for hikers, backpackers, cyclists, mountain-climbers, and skiers. And with its mix of Spanish, Mexican, Native American, and Anglo heritage, the state is as culturally varied as it is geographically diverse.

🛈 PRACTICAL INFORMATION

Capital: Santa Fe.

Visitor Info: New Mexico Dept. of Tourism, 491 Old Santa Fe Trail, Santa Fe 87501 (☎ 800-545-2040; www.newmexico.org). Open M-F 8am-5pm. **Park and Recreation Division,** 2040 S. Pacheco, Santa Fe 87505 (☎ 505-827-7173). Open M-F 8am-5pm. **US Forest Service,** 517 Gold Ave. SW, Albuquerque 87102 (☎ 505-842-3292). Open M-F 8am-4:30pm.

Postal Abbreviation: NM. **Sales Tax:** 7%.

SANTA FE   ☎ 505

Nestled in dramatic red mesas and forests of piñon pine trees, Santa Fe is the soul of the Southwest's pueblo country. The city evokes a primitive sense of earth, sky, and mountain, but it is also a renowned cosmopolitan center of food and culture. Built in 1607 by Spanish explorers, the Plaza is home to street vendors selling local art, the historic Palace of the Governors (the oldest public building in the US), a seemingly endless assemblage of tourists, and restaurants offering distinctive Northern New Mexican cuisine. Santa Fe's flavors are not limited to food—the plentiful museums and galleries will make any art connois-

Santa Fe

▲■ ACCOMMODATIONS
Hyde State Park, **1**
Pueblo Bonito Bed
and Breakfast, **13**
Santa Fe International
Hostel, **14**
Silver Saddle Motel, **15**

🍎 FOOD
Cafe Oasis, **12**
Cafe Pasqual's, **7**
Tía Sophia's, **6**

🎵 NIGHTLIFE
Bar B, **11**
Cowgirl Hall of Fame, **9**
La Casa Sena Cantina, **5**
Paramount, **10**

🏛 MUSEUMS
Georgia O'Keeffe
Museum, **2**
Institute of American
Indian Arts, **8**
Museum of Fine Arts, **3**
Museum of Indian Arts &
Culture Laboratory of
Anthropology, **17**
Museum of International
Folk Art, **16**
Museum of Spanish
Colonial Art, **18**
Palace of the Governors, **4**
Wheelwright Museum of
the American Indian, **19**

seur's mouth water. The city can be expensive, but the renowned artistic and culinary accomplishments combined with its pristine, awe-inspiring natural environment, make Santa Fe a sophisticated city, fragrant with the smoky aroma of hatch chiles and piñon-scented mountain air.

▣ TRANSPORTATION

Trains: Amtrak's nearest station is in Lamy (☎ 466-4511), 18 mi. south on U.S. 285. 1 train daily to: **Albuquerque** (1½hr., $36); **Flagstaff** (7hr., $116); **Kansas City** (17hr., $148); **Los Angeles** (18½hr., $127). Call ☎ 982-8829 in advance for a shuttle to Santa Fe ($18). Open daily 8am-5pm.

Buses: Greyhound, 858 St. Michael's Dr. (☎ 471-0008), goes to: **Albuquerque** (1¼hr., 4 per day, $10); **Denver** (8-9hr., 4 per day, $59); **Taos** (1½hr., 2 per day, $16). Open M-F 7am-5:30pm and 7:30-9:35pm, Sa-Su 7-9am, 12:30-1:30pm, 3:30-5pm, and 7:30-9:35pm.

Public Transit: Santa Fe Trails, 2931 Rufina St. (☎ 955-2001). Schedules at the visitors center or the public transit office. Runs 9 downtown bus routes M-F 6am-11pm, Sa 8am-8pm, Su (routes 1, 2, 4, and M only) 10am-7pm. Most routes start at the downtown Sheridan Transit Center, 1 block from the plaza between Marcy St. and Palace Ave. Buses

#21 and 24 go down Cerrillos Rd., the M goes to the museums on Camino Lejo, and #5 passes the Greyhound station between St. Vincent Hospital and the W. Alameda Commons. $1; under 17, students, and seniors $0.50; day pass $2.

Sandía Shuttle Express (☎474-5696 or 888-775-5696) runs from downtown hotels to the Albuquerque airport (the main airport that services Santa Fe) every hr. on the hr. 5am-5pm. From Albuquerque to Santa Fe hourly 8:45am-10:45pm (one-way $23, round-trip $40). Reserve at least 4 days in advance. Open M-F 6am-6pm, Sa-Su 6am-5pm.

Car Rental: Enterprise Rent-a-Car, 2641 Cerrillos Rd. (☎473-3600). Must be 21+ with driver's license and major credit card. Open M-F 8am-6pm, Sa 9am-noon.

⭐ ORIENTATION

Abutting the **Sangre de Cristo Mountains,** Sante Fe stands at an elevation of 7000 ft., 58 mi. northeast of Albuquerque on I-25. The streets of downtown Santa Fe seem to wind without rhyme or reason; locals say the roads were built on old burro paths. It may be helpful to think of the city as a wagon wheel, with the **Plaza** in the center and roads leading outward like spokes. **Paseo de Peralta** forms a loop around the downtown area, and the main roads leading out toward I-25 are **Cerrillos Road, Saint Francis Drive,** and **Old Santa Fe Trail.** Except for the museums southeast of the city center, most upscale restaurants and sights in Santa Fe cluster within a few blocks of the downtown Plaza, inside the loop formed by the Paseo de Peralta. Narrow streets make driving troublesome; park your car and pound the pavement. Several public **parking lots** are within walking distance of the plaza, charging $8-14 for a full day. Most convenient is the municipal parking lot, one block south of the plaza on Water St. between Don Gaspar Ave. and Shelby St. Though you'll be a slave to the bus schedule, look into the free parking at Museum Hill or the Villa Linda Mall and ride the bus to and from downtown.

🛈 PRACTICAL INFORMATION

Visitor Info: Visitors Information Center, 491 Old Santa Fe Trail (☎875-7400 or 800-545-2040). Open daily 8am-6:30pm; low-season 8am-5pm. **Santa Fe Convention and Visitors Bureau,** 201 W. Marcy St. (☎800-777-2489 or 955-6200). Open M-F 8am-5pm. **Info booth** at the northwest corner of the plaza, next to the First National Bank. Open mid-May to Aug. daily 9:30am-4:30pm.

Hotlines: Rape Abuse, ☎986-9111. 24hr. **Gay and Lesbian Information Line,** ☎891-3647.

Medical Services: St. Vincent Hospital, 455 St. Michael's Dr. (☎983-3361).

Internet Access: Santa Fe Public Library, 145 Washington Ave. (☎955-6781), 1 block northeast of the Plaza. Open M-Th 10am-9pm, F-Sa 10am-6pm, Su 1-5pm.

Post Office: 120 S. Federal Pl. (☎988-6351), next to the courthouse. Open M-F 7:30am-5:45pm, Sa 9am-1pm. **Postal Code:** 87501. **Area Code:** 505.

🏠 ACCOMMODATIONS

Hotels in Santa Fe tend to be on the expensive side. As early as May they become swamped with requests for rooms during **Indian Market** and **Fiesta de Santa Fe.** Make reservations early or plan to sleep in your car. In general, the motels along **Cerrillos Road** have the best prices, but even these places run $50-70 per night. For budget travelers, nearby camping is pleasant during the summer, not to mention easier on the wallet. Two popular sites for **free primitive camping** are **Big Tesuque ❶** and **Ski Basin Campgrounds ❶** on national forest land. These campgrounds are both off Rte. 475 toward the Ski Basin and have pit toilets.

FOOD FIESTA

Eating in New Mexico is a confusing jumble of New Mexican, Mexican, and Southwestern food. The main difference between Mexican and New Mexican cuisine is the type of chile used. Each features the chiles that grow most readily in the respective regions. New Mexican food is flavored with Hatch and Chimayo chiles. Chimayo (red) chiles are sun-dried on the vine and have an earthier flavor, while Hatch chiles are picked while still green, before they develop a more complex flavor, resulting in a hotter chile. Mexican food uses Ancho and Poblano chiles, is less spicy than New Mexican cuisine, and includes more seafood. In the Santa Fe area, most "Mexican" restaurants offer pricier contemporary Southwestern or traditional New Mexican cuisine. Contemporary Southwestern uses some indigenous ingredients and traditional techniques, but also brings in ingredients not generally served in the region, resulting in dishes such as red chile duck tamales. Traditional New Mexican, however, is not expensive or fancy (but just as tasty), and can often be found in hole-in-the-wall family restaurants, where they will likely ask if you want your meal with red or green chile. So if you check what type of chiles are used, what other ingredients are included, and what the price is, you'll be distinguishing between Mexican, New Mexican, and Southwestern in no time.

🏨 **Pueblo Bonito Bed and Breakfast,** 138 W. Manhattan at Galisteo (☎984-8001). This quiet, century-old adobe compound houses 18 cozily charming private rooms less than a 5min. walk from the downtown plaza. Each room has cable TV, phones, and a fireplace. Luxury perks include a hot tub, a lavish breakfast buffet, and afternoon "tea" with delicious margaritas, wine, and cheese. Reception 8am-10pm. May-Oct. $130-165, Mar.-Apr. and Nov.-Dec. $95-125, Jan.-Feb. $85-115. ❺

Santa Fe International Hostel, 1412 Cerrillos Rd. (☎988-1153). Conveniently located on one of the city's main streets, this hostel provides affordable, comfortable rooms to a diverse and accepting crowd of travelers. A gigantic kitchen, free linens, and parking make up for the lack of a television. Dorms $15; private rooms from $35. ❷

Silver Saddle Motel, 2810 Cerrillos Rd. (☎471-7663). Comfortable adobe rooms decorated with cowboy paraphernalia have A/C and cable TV. Reception 7am-11:30pm. In summer singles $67; doubles $72. In winter $45/$50. ❸

Hyde State Park Campground (☎983-7175), 8 mi. from Santa Fe on Rte. 475. Over 50 sites in the forest with water, pit toilets, and shelters. Sites $10, hookups $14. ❶

🍴 FOOD

The **Santa Fe Farmers Market,** near the intersection of Guadalupe St. and Paseo de Peralta, has fresh fruits and vegetables. (☎983-4098. Open late Apr. to early Nov. Tu and Sa 7am-noon. Call to ask about indoor winter location and hours.)

🍴 **Cafe Pasqual's,** 121 Don Gaspar (☎983-9340). The chefs at this small restaurant named for the patron saint of cooking dish up deliciously inventive Southwestern cuisine. Long lines of those eager to savor the best brunch in town—fantastic omelettes ($10), smoked trout hash ($13), and salmon, black bean, and blue cheese burritos ($16)—form daily, but the food and great service are worth the wait. Breakfast and lunch can be enjoyed around the friendly communal table, but dinner reservations are recommended. Open M-Sa 7am-3pm, Su 8am-2pm, and daily 5:30-10:30pm. ❹

🍴 **Cafe Oasis,** 526 Galisteo St. (☎983-9599), at Paseo de Peralta, is a perfect earthy, hippie hangout where you can take refuge from the bustle of the city. Each themed seating area caters to customers' comfort; the Womb Room envelops you in plush pillows, while the Tahitian Tearoom is painted like a garden. The creative, organic dishes range from veggie enchiladas ($11) to Samari stir-fry ($14). Breakfast and coffee drinks served all the time. Live music nightly. Open Su-Th 9:30am-midnight, Sa 9am-2am. ❸

Tía Sophia's, 210 W. San Francisco St. (☎983-9880). This unassuming diner near the plaza serves traditional New Mexican favorites with little pretense and plenty of taste. The most popular item is the Atrisco plate ($7)—chile stew, cheese enchilada, beans, *posole*, and a *sopapilla*. Open M-Sa 7am-2pm. ❷

◎ ♫ SIGHTS AND ENTERTAINMENT

The grassy **Plaza de Santa Fe** is a good starting point for exploring the city's museums, sanctuaries, and galleries. Since 1609, the plaza has been the site of religious ceremonies, military gatherings, markets, cockfights, and public punishments. Today, it shelters ritzy shops, stalls of Native American artisans, and packs of loitering tourists. Historic **walking tours** leave from the blue doors of the Palace of the Governors on Lincoln Ave. (Apr.-Oct. M-Sa 10:15am. $10, under 17 free with adult.)

MNM MUSEUMS. Sante Fe is home to world-class museums. Five are run by **The Museum of New Mexico,** and all keep the same hours and charge the same admission. A 4-day pass ($15) includes admission to all five museums and can be bought at any of them. (☎827-6463; www.museumofnewmexico.org. Open Tu-Su 10am-5pm. $7, under 16 free. The 2 downtown museums—Fine Arts and Palace of the Governors—are both free F 5-8pm.) In a large adobe building on the northwest corner of the plaza, the **Museum of Fine Arts** dazzles visitors with the works of major Southwestern artists, as well as galleries for special exhibitions of new acquisitions. (107 W. Palace Ave. ☎476-5072. Open daily 10am-5pm.) The **Palace of the Governors,** on the north side of the plaza, is the oldest public building in the US and was the seat of seven successive governments after its construction in 1610. The *hacienda* palace is now a museum with exhibits on Native American, Southwestern, and New Mexican history. (☎476-5100.) The most distinctive museums in town are 2½ mi. south of the Plaza on Old Santa Fe Trail at **Museum Hill.** The fascinating ▨**Museum of International Folk Art** explores the beauty of everyday objects through its vibrant and varied collection of handmade toys, furniture, clothing, costumes, and jewelry from around the world. (706 Camino Lejo. ☎476-1200.) Next door, the **Museum of Indian Arts and Culture Laboratory of Anthropology** displays Native American artwork, photos, and artifacts. (710 Camino Lejo. ☎476-1250.) The new **Museum of Spanish Colonial Art** houses an extensive collection of artifacts representing the rich artistic traditions of territories that were once part of the Spanish Empire, spanning four continents and 500 years. (750 Camino Lejo. ☎982-2226.) Although not directly affiliated with the Museum of New Mexico, the **Wheelwright Museum of the American Indian** is also located at Museum Hill. Constructed in 1937 in the shape and style of hogan, the free museum features a small but outstanding collection of Native American artwork and pottery. (704 Camino Lejo. ☎982-4636. Open M-Sa 10am-5pm, Su 1-5pm.)

OTHER PLAZA MUSEUMS. The popular **Georgia O'Keeffe Museum** pays tribute to the famous New Mexican artist, and attracts the masses with up-close views of her famous flower paintings and some of her more abstract works. The collection spans O'Keeffe's entire life and accents her versatility. This year's exhibitions will include Flowers of Distinction, a display of O'Keeffe's flowers along with selected works of Andy Warhol. (217 Johnson St. ☎946-1017. Open daily 10am-5pm. $8, under 17 and students with ID free. F 5-8pm free. Audio tour $5.) Downtown's **Institute of American Indian Arts Museum** houses a large collection of contemporary Indian art with an intense political edge. (108 Cathedral Pl. ☎983-8900. Open June-Sept. M-Sa 9am-5pm, Su 10am-5pm; Oct.-May M-Sa 10am-5pm, Su noon-5pm. $4, students and seniors $2, under 16 free.) The **New Mexico State Capitol** was built in 1966 in the form of the Zia sun symbol. The House and Senate galleries are open to the public, and the building also contains an impressive art collection. (☎986-4589. *5 blocks south of the Plaza on Old Santa Fe Trail. Open M-F 7am-7pm; June-Aug. also Sa 8am-5pm. Free tours M-F 10am and 2pm.)*

CHURCHES. Santa Fe's Catholic roots are evident in the Romanesque **St. Francis Cathedral,** built from 1869 to 1886 under the direction of Archbishop Lamy (the central figure of Willa Cather's book *Death Comes to the Archbishop*) to help convert westerners to Catholicism. *(213 Cathedral Pl. ☎982-5619. 1 block east of the Plaza on San Francisco St. Open daily 7:30am-5:30pm.)* The **Loretto Chapel** was the first Gothic building west of the Mississippi River. The church is famous for its "miraculous" spiral staircase—both its builder and the details of its construction are a mystery. *(207 Old Santa Fe Trail. ☎982-0092. 2 blocks south of the cathedral. Open M-Sa 9am-5pm, Su 10:30am-5pm. $2.50, seniors and children $2.)* About five blocks southeast of the plaza lies the **San Miguel Mission,** at DeVargas St. and the Old Santa Fe Trail. Built in 1610 by the Tlaxcalan Indians, the mission is the oldest functioning church in the US. Also in the church is the San Jose Bell, the oldest bell in the US, which was made in Spain in 1356. (☎988-9504. *Open M-Sa 9am-5pm, Su 10am-4pm; may close earlier in winter. Mass Su 5pm. $1.)*

GALLERIES. Santa Fe's most successful artists live and sell their work along Canyon Rd. To reach the galleries, leave the Plaza on San Francisco Dr., take a left on Alameda St., a right on Paseo de Peralta, and a left on Canyon Rd. For about 1 mi., the road is lined with galleries and many indoor/outdoor cafes. Most galleries are open from 10am until 5pm and house interesting and fantastically expensive collections ranging from western landscapes to vibrant abstract works and mammoth bronze statues. **Off the Wall** has affordable, creative, and functional art and a small cafe and patio behind the gallery. *(616 Canyon Rd. ☎983-8337. Open daily 10am-5pm.)*

A BIT OF CLASS. Old verse and distinguished acting invade the city each summer when **Shakespeare in Sante Fe** raises its curtain. The shows play in an open-air theater on the St. John's College campus from late June to late August. *(Shows run F-Su 7:30pm. Number of shows per week varies; call to check schedule. Reserved seating tickets $15-32; lawn seating is free, but a $5 donation is requested. Tickets available at show or call ☎982-2910.)* The **Santa Fe Opera,** on Opera Dr., performs outdoors against a mountain backdrop. Nights are cool; bring a blanket, and formal attire is definitely not required. *(7 mi. north of Santa Fe on Rte. 84/285. ☎800-280-4654 or 986-5900; www.santafeopera.org. July W and F-Sa at 9pm; Aug. M-Sa at 8 or 8:30pm. Tickets $20-130, rush standing-room tickets $8-15; 50% student discount on same-day reserved seats. Box office is at opera house; call or drop by the day of the show for prices and availability.)* The **Santa Fe Chamber Music Festival** celebrates the works of Baroque, Classical, Romantic, and 20th-century composers in the **St. Francis Auditorium of the Museum of Fine Arts** and the **Lensic Theater.** *(☎983-2075, tickets 982-1890; www.sfcmf.org. Mid-July to mid-Aug. $16-40, students $10.)*

FESTIVALS. The **Santa Fe Jazz and International Music Festival** runs through the month of July, showcasing the talent of some of the world's finest musicians. *(☎988-1234; www.santafejazzfestival.com. Tickets $20-40 per show, 7-show pass $119-238. 2 free shows take place at noon in the Plaza in mid-July. All other shows at Lensic Theater, 7:30pm.)* The Santa Fe Plaza is home to three of the US's largest festivals. The **Spanish Market,** a combination celebration and sale of Hispanic-influenced artwork, comes to town the third week in July. In the third week of August, **Indian Market,** the nation's largest and most impressive showcase of Native American culture and art floods the plaza. The **Southwestern Association for Indian Arts** (☎983-5220) has more info. Don Diego de Vargas's reconquest of New Mexico in 1692 marked the end of the 12-year Pueblo Rebellion, now celebrated in the three-day **Fiesta de Santa Fe** *(☎988-7575; www.santafefiesta.org).* Held in mid-September, festivities begin with the burning of the *Zozobra* (a 50 ft. marionette) and include street dancing, processions, and political satires. The *New Mexican* publishes a guide and a schedule of the fiesta's events.

⚡ NIGHTLIFE

The diverse citizens of Santa Fe—from retired Wall Street investment bankers to world-famous or starving artists—ensure a variety of nightlife. The town's laid-back demeanor, however, doesn't disappear when the sun goes down. The entertaining and talented waitstaff of **█La Casa Sena Cantina,** 125 E. Palace Ave., serenades customers with jazz standards and Broadway showtunes. The rustic, classy interior is a relaxing place to sip a drink, sample a wildly decadent dessert, and enjoy the show. (☎ 988-9232. Open Su-Th 5:30-10pm, F-Sa 5:30-11pm.) The **Cowgirl Hall of Fame,** 319 S. Guadalupe St., has live music hoe downs that range from bluegrass to rock 9pm-1am each night. Barbecue, Mexican food, and burgers are served all evening, with midnight food specials and 12 microbrews on tap. (☎ 982-2565. Cowgirl margaritas $3.50. Sa-Su ranch breakfast. Happy hour 4-6pm. 21+ after midnight. Cover varies but is rarely more than $5. Open M-F 11am-2am, Sa 8:30am-2am, Su 8:30am-midnight.) **Paramount,** 331 Sandoval St., is the only dance club in Santa Fe, and does an admirable job of keeping the scene pumping. Groove and jazz on Mondays are replaced with Latin on Tuesdays, and crowds pour in for Friday night hip-hop. (☎ 982-8999. 21+. Cover $3-10, Sa $5-20. Open M-Sa 9pm-2am, Su 9pm-midnight.) **Bar B,** a smaller annex of Paramount, has a laid-back feel despite its futuristic decor, and focuses on live rock and punk music. (☎ 982-8999. Cover up to $7. Open M-Sa 5pm-2am, Su 5pm-midnight.)

🏔 OUTDOOR ACTIVITIES

The nearby **Sangre de Cristo Mountains** reach heights of over 12,000 ft. and offer countless opportunities for hikers, bikers, skiers, and snowboarders. The **Pecos** and **Río Grande** rivers make great playgrounds for kayakers, rafters, and canoers. Before heading into the wilderness, stop by the **Public Lands Information Center,** 1474 Rodeo Rd., near the intersection of St. Francis Rd. and I-25, to pick up maps, guides, and friendly advice. (☎ 438-7542 or 877-276-9404; www.publiclands.org. Open M-F 8:30am-4:30pm.) The Sierra Club guide, *Day Hikes in the Santa Fe Area* and the Falcon guide, *Best Easy Day Hikes in Santa Fe* are good purchases for those planning to spend a few days hiking in the area.

The closest **hiking** trails to Santa Fe are along Rte. 475 on the way to the Santa Fe Ski Area. On this road, 10 mi. northeast of town, the easy **Tesuque Creek Trail** (2hr., 4 mi.) leads through the forest to a flowing stream. Near the end of Rte. 475 and the Santa Fe Ski Area, trailheads venture into the 223,000 acre **Pecos Wilderness.** A variety of extended backpacking trips can be had throughout this swath of pristine alpine forests. For a rewarding day-hike 14 mi. northeast of Santa Fe on Rte. 475, the strenuous climb to the top of 12,622 ft. **Santa Fe Baldy** (8-9hr., 14 mi.) affords an amazing vista of the Pecos Wilderness to the north and east. Forty miles southwest of Santa Fe, **Kasha-Katuwe Tent Rocks National Monument** provides a surreal landscape that will remind you of Bryce Canyon in grayscale. The national monument has beautiful hiking trails but is largely undeveloped. (☎ 761-8704. Take I-25 S from Santa Fe, Exit 259 and follow the signs. Open Apr.-Oct. 7am-7pm; Nov.-Mar. 8am-5pm; day use only. $5 per vehicle.)

The best skiing is 16 mi. northeast of downtown, at **Ski Santa Fe.** Located in the Sangre de Cristo Mountains on Rte. 475, the ski area has six lifts including four chairs and two surface lifts, servicing 43 trails (20% beginner, 40% intermediate,

40% advanced) on 600 acres with a 1650 ft. vertical drop. (☎982-4429; www.skisan-tafe.com. Open late Nov. to early Apr. 9am-4pm. Lift tickets: full-day $47, teens $38, children and seniors $34; ½ day $34. Rental packages start at $18.)

◼ DAYTRIPS FROM SANTA FE

BANDELIER NATIONAL MONUMENT

Bandelier, 40 mi. northwest of Santa Fe (take U.S. 285 to 502 W, then follow the signs), features the remnants of over 2400 cliff dwellings and pueblos amidst 50 sq. mi. of mesas and ruggedly eroded canyons. The park centers around Frijoles Canyon, the site of many natural caves and settlements along the canyon floor that were occupied for roughly 500 years. The **visitors center,** 3 mi. into the park at the bottom of Frijoles Canyon, has an archaeological museum and shows a short video. There are few placards along the pathways, but trail guides for the most popular hikes are available to purchase for $1 or borrow with a $1 deposit. (☎672-3861, ext. 517. Open daily June-Aug. 8am-6pm; Sept. to late Oct. 9am-5:30pm; late Oct. to late Mar. 8am-4:30pm; late Mar. to May 9am-5:30pm.) The 1½ mi. **Main Loop Trail** begins at the back porch of the visitors center and passes the ruins of **Tyuonyi Pueblo** and the aptly named **Long House,** an 800 ft. section of adjoining, multi-storied stone homes. Sections of the trail are wheelchair accessible, but at other points ladders provide a chance to climb up into the caves. Those with more time should go ½ mi. farther to **Ceremonial Cave,** a *kiva* carved into a natural alcove, high above the canyon floor and accessible only by climbing four ladders. Free permits are required for backcountry hiking and camping; topographical maps ($10) are sold at the visitors center. Just past the main entrance, **Juniper Campground ❶** offers the only developed camping in the park, with water and toilets (first come, first served sites $10). The park entrance fee is $10 per vehicle and $5 per pedestrian; National Park passes are accepted.

LOS ALAMOS

Known only as the mysterious P.O. Box 1663 during the heyday of the Manhattan Project, Los Alamos is no longer the nation's biggest secret. Overlooking the Río Grande Valley, Los Alamos hovers above the Pueblo and Bayo Canyons on thin finger-like mesas, 35 mi. northeast of Sante Fe. The birthplace of the atomic bomb, Los Alamos attracts visitors with its natural beauty, outdoor activities, and the allure of its secret past. In town, the **Bradbury Science Museum,** at 15th St. and Central, explains the history of the Los Alamos National Laboratory and its endeavors with videos and hands-on exhibits. (☎667-4444. Open M and Sa-Su 1-5pm, Tu-F 9am-5pm. Free.) The ◼**Black Hole,** 4015 Arkansas Ave., sells all the junk the laboratory doesn't want anymore, including 50-year-old calculators, fiber-optic cables, flow gauges, time-mark generators, optical comparators, and other technological flotsam. Leave with your very own $2 atomic bomb detonator cable. (☎662-5053. Open M-Sa 10am-5pm.) Outdoors, the town brims with activity. The **Sante Fe National Forest** has countless trails for hiking and biking in and along the town's many canyons. The 89,000 acres of the **Valles Caldera,** a lush volcanic crater, have recently become a National Preserve. Fifteen miles west on Rte. 4, the pristine meadow valley is open to a limited number of visitors each day for hiking, fishing, and horse-drawn wagon or van tours (☎877-851-8946; www.vallescaldera.gov. Permits $10, ages 15 and under $5; other fees apply for fishing licenses and touring.) **Los Alamos Visitors Center** is at 109 Central Park Sq., at Central Ave. just west of 15th St. (☎662-8105. Open M-F 9am-5pm, Sa 9am-4pm, Su 10am-3pm.)

SOUTHWEST

TAOS
☎505

Before 1955, Taos was a remote artist colony in the Sangre de Cristo Mountains. When the ski valley opened and the thrill-seekers trickled in, they soon realized that the area had the best whitewater rafting in New Mexico, and excellent hiking, mountain biking, and rock climbing. By the 1970s, Taos had become a paradise for New-Age hippies, artists, and extreme athletes. Tourists weren't far behind. Today, Taos balances an active lifestyle with a bohemian pace and culture, making it an ideal locale for both outdoor adventure and hardcore relaxation.

■♨ 🏂 **ORIENTATION AND PRACTICAL INFORMATION.** Taos is 79 mi. north of Santa Fe (p. 881), between the dramatic Río Grande Gorge and Wheeler Peak. **Paseo del Pueblo** (Rte. 68) is the town's main north-south thoroughfare, called **"Paseo del Pueblo Norte"** north of Kit Carson Rd. and **"Paseo del Pueblo Sur"** to the south. Traffic on Paseo del Pueblo can move in inches during the summer and ski season—use Rte. 240 and Upper Ranchitos Rd. as a bypass if possible. Drivers should park at the metered **Camino de la Placita**, a block west of the plaza, in any of the free municipal parking lots, or at meters on side streets. The **Chamber of Commerce**, 1139 Paseo del Pueblo Sur, 2 mi. south of town at the junction of Rte. 68 and Paseo del Cañón, has visitor info. (☎758-3873 or 800-732-8267. Open daily 9am-5pm.) The **Carson National Forest Office**, 208 Cruz Alta Rd., has free info on camping and hiking. (☎758-6200. Open M-F 8am-4:30pm.) **Police**, 107 Civic Plaza Dr. (☎758-2216). **Holy Cross Hospital**, 1397 Weimer Rd. (☎758-8883). **Internet Access** ($1 per 30min.) at the **public library**, 402 Camino de la Placita (☎758-3063; open M noon-6pm, Tu-F 10am-6pm, Sa 10am-5pm). **Post Office**, 318 Paseo del Pueblo Norte. (☎758-2081. Open M-F 8:30am-5pm.) **Postal Code:** 87571. **Area Code:** 505.

🏠 **ACCOMMODATIONS.** The **Abominable Snowmansion Hostel (HI) ❶**, 9 mi. north of Taos in the village of Arroyo Seco, has spacious dorm rooms and a pool table adorning the common room. A hostel by summer and ski lodge by winter, the Snowmansion is only 9 mi. west of the ski valley. Teepees and camping are available in the warmer months, but it's accessible by public transit only during the ski season. (☎776-8298. Breakfast included. Reception 8am-noon and 4-10pm. Reservations recommended. Dec. to mid-Apr. dorms, tent sites, and dorm teepees $22, mid-Apr. to Nov. $19; private rooms $40-54/$32-44.) The **Budget Host Motel ❷**, 1798 Paseo del Pueblo Sur, 3¼ mi. south of the plaza, has clean, fairly spacious rooms. (☎758-2524 or 800-323-6009. Singles $44-50; doubles $49-61. 10% AAA discount.)

Camping around Taos is easy with a car, and considering the area's natural beauty, sleeping under the stars is an appealing option. The **Orilla Verde Recreation Area ❶**, 15 mi. south of Taos on Rte. 68, has five campgrounds in the scenic **Río Grande Gorge**. (☎751-4899 or 758-8851. Water and toilets. Sites $7.) The **Carson National Forest ❶** has four campgrounds to the east of Taos on Rte. 64. Tent sites are by a stream and surrounded by tall pines on one side and a piñon forest on the other. The closest two, **El Nogal** and **Las Petacas**, are 2 and 4 mi. east of Taos, with vault toilets but no drinking water. For more info, contact the **Carson National Forest Office** in Taos (☎758-6200; sites $8). Campgrounds on the road to Taos Ski Valley are free, but have no facilities. **Backcountry camping** doesn't require a permit. Dispersed camping is popular along Rte. 518 south of Taos and Forest Rd. 437; park on the side of the road and pitch your tent a few hundred feet inside.

🍴 **FOOD.** Restaurants cluster around Taos Plaza and Bent St. but cheaper options can be found north of town along Paseo del Pueblo. **Taos Pizza Out Back ❷**, 712 Paseo del Pueblo Norte, serves giant slices of gourmet pizza ($4-7).

Entertain yourself by helping to cover the restaurant's exterior with crayon graffiti, but when your food comes, be ready to dip your pizza-pie in the ambrosial basil-pesto sauce. (☎758-3112. Open daily 11am-10pm.) **Michael's Kitchen ❷**, 304 Paseo del Pueblo Norte, specializes in hearty family-style dining, with traditional Mexican dishes, fresh baked goods, and the best breakfast in town available all day long. (☎758-4178. Open daily 7am-8:30pm.) **Abe's Cantina y Cocina ❶**, 6 mi. north of Taos on the road to Taos Ski Valley in the village of Arroyo Seco and a block up from the Abominable Snowmansion Hostel, has cheap, homestyle New Mexican food. The somewhat limited options include excellent breakfast burritos for $3.50. (☎776-8516. Open M-F 7am-5:30pm, Sa 7am-1:30pm, bar open until around 10pm.) **Taos Wrappers ❶**, 616 Paseo del Pueblo Sur, caters to the lighter side of luncheon dining with delicious wraps, inventive soups, and lots of veggie options. (☎751-9727. Open in summer M-F 11am-4pm, Sa-Su 8am-4pm; in winter M-F 11am-1pm, Sa 11am-2pm.)

◪ **SIGHTS.** For a small town, Taos has a surprising number of high-quality art museums. The ◪**Millicent Rogers Museum**, 1504 Millicent Rogers Rd., 4 mi. north of the plaza on Rte. 64, has an extravagant collection of Indian jewelry, Navajo textiles, Pueblo pottery, and Apache baskets that belonged to Millicent Rogers, a fashion maven and socialite. There is also a gallery dedicated to the ceramic works of the María Martínez family, known for their black-on-black pottery. (☎758-2462. Open Apr.-Oct. daily 10am-5pm; Nov.-Mar. Tu-Su 10am-5pm. $7, students and seniors $6, under 16 $2.) The **Harwood Museum**, 238 Ledoux St., houses a large collection of Hispanic art, works by 20th-century local artists, a gallery of minimalist painter Agnes Martin, and a visiting exhibit of Asian art. (☎758-9826. Parking on Ranchitos Rd. Open Tu-Sa 10am-5pm, Su noon-5pm. $5.) The **Taos Art Museum** at Fechin House, 227 Paseo del Pueblo Norte, exhibits the oil paintings, watercolors, and sketches of the Taos Society of Artists, originally formed in 1915. The collection is housed inside the Spanish Mission-style home of Russian immigrant, Taos resident, and portrait painter Nicolai Fechin. (☎758-2690. Open June-Sept. Tu-Su 10am-5pm, Oct.-May W-Su 10am-4pm. $6.)

The ◪**Martínez Hacienda,** 2 mi. southwest of the plaza on Ranchitos Rd., is one of few surviving Spanish Colonial mansions in the United States. Built in 1804, this fortress-like structure housed the prosperous Martínez family and the headquarters of a farming, ranching, and trading operation. The restored 21-room *hacienda* has exhibits on life in the northern reaches of the former Spanish Empire. (☎758-1000. Open daily Apr.-Oct. 9am-5pm; Nov.-Mar. 10am-4pm. $5, children $3.)

Taos ranks second only to Santa Fe as a center of Southwestern art galleries. Local artists' shows cluster around the plaza and Kit Carson Rd., but the **Lumina Gallery and Sculpture Garden** is more captivating than any art museum in town. North of Taos and nestled under trees by a gurgling stream, the beautiful gardens, fountains, cutting-edge contemporary paintings, and sculptures create an idyllic escape. On the way to Arroyo Seco, turn onto Hwy. 230. Lumina will be immediately to your right. (☎758-7282. Sculpture garden open 24hr., gallery hours vary.)

The five-story adobe homes of the **Taos Pueblo** are between 700 and 1000 years old, making the pueblo the oldest continuously inhabited settlement in the US. Taos Pueblo was named a UNESCO World Heritage Site in 1992, and is the only pueblo in Northern New Mexico where the inhabitants still live traditionally. The pueblo includes the **St. Jerome Church,** built in 1850, ruins of the old church and cemetery, adobe houses, and *kivas.* (☎758-1028. Guided tours daily May-Sept.; self-guided tours available. Open daily May-Sept. 8am-4:30pm; Oct.-Apr. 8am-4pm. $10, students $5, 12 and under free. Camera permit $5.)

SOUTHWEST

⚡ OUTDOOR ACTIVITIES. Hailed as one of the best ski resorts in the country, **Taos Ski Valley**, about 15 mi. northeast of town on Rte. 150, has 72 trails and 12 lifts. Ski Valley boasts over 2500 ft. of vertical drop and over 300 in. of annual snowfall. (☎776-2291, lodging info 800-992-7669, ski conditions 776-2916. Lift tickets $31-51.) Reserve a room in advance if you plan to come in the winter holiday season. There are also two smaller, family-oriented ski areas near Taos: **Angel Fire** (☎377-6401; lift tickets $48, ages 7-12 $31) and **Red River** (☎800-494-9117; lift tickets $49, teen $43, ages 4-12 and seniors $34). Multi-day passes are available for use at all three resorts (from $36 per day). In summer, the nearly deserted ski valley and the nearby **Wheeler Peak Wilderness** become a hiker's paradise (most trails begin off Rte. 150).The ascent of **Wheeler Peak**, the highest point in New Mexico at 13,161 ft., is a strenuous 16 mi. round-trip trek that begins at the Twining Campground in Taos Ski Valley. Due to the town's prime location near New Mexico's wildest stretch of the Río Grande, **river rafting** is very popular in Taos. **Los Ríos River Runners** (☎776-8854 or 800-544-1181), **Far Flung Adventures** (☎758-2628 or 800-359-2627), and **Native Sons Adventures** (☎758-9342 or 800-753-7559) all offer a range of guided half-day ($45-50) and full-day ($85-110) rafting trips. For bike rentals, visit **Gearing Up**, 129 Paseo del Pueblo Sur. (☎751-0365. Open daily 9:30am-6pm. Bikes $35 per day, $90 per 5 days.)

ALBUQUERQUE ☎505

Albuquerque, full of history and culture, also has ethnic restaurants, offbeat cafes, and raging nightclubs. Most residents still refer to Central Ave. as Route 66, and energy seems to flow from this mythic highway. The University of New Mexico creates the town's young demographic, while Hispanic, Native American, and gay and lesbian communities add to the cultural vibrancy and diversity. From historic Old Town to modern museums, ancient petroglyphs to towering mountains, travelers will learn how much there is to see and do in New Mexico's largest city.

⌷ TRANSPORTATION

Airport: Albuquerque International, 2200 Sunport Blvd. SE (☎244-7700), south of downtown. Take bus #50 from 5th St. and Central Ave., or pick it up along Yale Blvd. **Airport Shuttle** (☎765-1234) runs to the city ($12, 2nd person $5). Open 24hr.

Trains: Amtrak, 214 1st St. SW (☎842-9650). 1 train per day to: **Flagstaff** (4hr., $73); **Kansas City** (17hr., $110); **Los Angeles** (16hr., $83); **Santa Fe** (1hr. to Lamy, 20min. shuttle to Santa Fe; $36). Reservations required. Station open daily 10am-6pm.

Buses: Greyhound (☎243-4435) and **TNM&O Coaches,** 300 2nd St. Both run buses from 3 blocks south of Central Ave. To: **Denver** (10hr., 4 per day, $64); **Los Angeles** (18hr., 6 per day, $78); **Santa Fe** (1½hr., 4 per day, $10). Station open 24hr.

Public Transit: Sun-Tran Transit, 601 Yale Blvd. SE (☎843-9200). Open M-F 8am-6pm, Sa 8am-noon. Maps at visitors centers, the transit office, and the main library. Most buses run M-Sa 6:30am-8:30pm and leave from Central Ave. and 5th St. Bus #66 runs down Central Ave. $1, seniors and ages 5-18 $0.25. Request free transfers from driver.

Taxi: Albuquerque Cab ☎883-4888.

◧▣ ORIENTATION AND PRACTICAL INFORMATION

Central Avenue (Route 66), is still the main thoroughfare of Albuquerque, running through all the city's major neighborhoods. Central Ave. (east-west) and **I-25** (north-south) divide Albuquerque into four quadrants. All downtown addresses

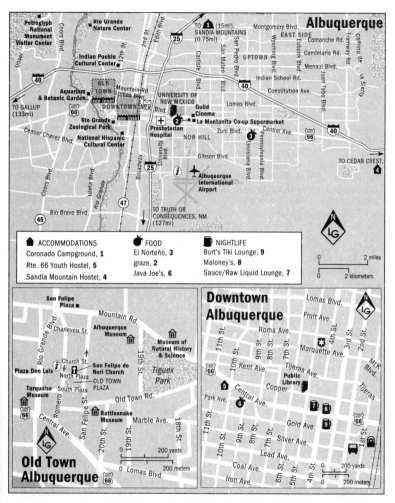

Albuquerque

TO ① (15mi), SANDIA MOUNTAINS (6.75mi)

ACCOMMODATIONS
Coronado Campground, **1**
Rte. 66 Youth Hostel, **5**
Sandía Mountain Hostel, **4**

FOOD
El Norteño, **3**
graze, **2**
Java Joe's, **6**

NIGHTLIFE
Burt's Tiki Lounge, **9**
Maloney's, **8**
Sauce/Raw Liquid Lounge, **7**

0   2 miles
0   2 kilometers

Downtown Albuquerque

Old Town Albuquerque

come with a quadrant designation: NE, NW, SE, or SW. The **University of New Mexico (UNM)'s** adobe campus spreads along Central Ave. from University Ave. to Carlisle St. **Nob Hill,** the area of Central Ave. around Carlisle St., features offbeat shopping, coffee shops, and art galleries. The revitalized **downtown** lies on Central Ave. between 10th St. and Broadway. Historic **Old Town Plaza** sits between San Felipe, North Plaza, South Plaza, and Romero, a block north of Central Ave.

Visitor Info: Old Town Visitors Center, 303 Romero St. NW (☎243-3215), in the shopping plaza west of the church. Open daily Apr.-Oct. 9am-5pm; Nov.-Mar. 9:30am-4:30pm. Airport **info booth** open Su-F 9:30am-8pm, Sa 9:30am-4:30pm.

Hotlines: Rape Crisis Center, 1025 Hermosa SE (☎266-7711). Center open M-F 8am-noon and 1-5pm. 24hr. **Gay and Lesbian Information Line,** ☎891-3647. 24hr.

Medical Services: Presbyterian Hospital, 1100 Central Ave. SE (☎841-1234).

Post Office: 1135 Broadway NE, (☎346-8044) at Mountain St. Open M-F 8am-5:30pm. **Postal Code:** 87101. **Area Code:** 505.

ACCOMMODATIONS

Cheap motels line **Central Avenue,** but be sure to evaluate the quality before paying. During the **balloon festival,** rooms are scarce; call ahead for reservations.

- **Route 66 Youth Hostel,** 1012 Central Ave. SW (☎247-1813), at 10th St. Get your kicks at this inviting hostel, conveniently placed between downtown and Old Town. Simple but clean dorms and private rooms. 1 of 10 easy chores required. Linen $1. Key deposit $5. Reception daily 7:30-10:30am and 4-11pm. Check-out 10:30am. Dorms $15; singles with shared bath $20; doubles $25; twin double with private bath $30. ●

- **Sandía Mountain Hostel,** 12234 Rte. 14 N (☎281-4117), in nearby Cedar Crest. Take I-40 E to Exit 175 and go 4 mi. north on Rte. 14. Call ahead for pickup in Albuquerque. Only 10 mi. from the Sandía Ski Area, this large wooden building makes a great ski chateau or just a nice place to relax. Living room with fireplace and kitchen, plus a family of donkeys out back. Hiking and biking trails are across the street. Linen $1. Coin-op laundry. Camping $7. Dorms $14; private cabin $32. Wheelchair accessible. ●

- **Coronado Campground** (☎980-8256). About 15 mi. north of Albuquerque. Take I-25 to Exit 242 and follow the signs. A pleasant campground on the banks of the Río Grande. Adobe shelters offer a respite from the heat. Toilets, showers, and water available. Open M and W-Su 8:30am-5pm, self-service pay station after hours. Tent sites $8, with shelters and picnic tables $11, full hookup $18-20. ●

FOOD

A diverse ethnic community, hordes of hungry interstate travelers, and a lot of green chiles make Albuquerque a surprisingly tasty destination. The area around **UNM** is the best bet for inexpensive eateries. A bit farther east, the hip neighborhood of **Nob Hill** is a haven for yuppie fare—avocado sandwiches and iced cappuccinos abound. Groceries, including an excellent selection of organic and specialty items, are available at **La Montanita Co-op Supermarket,** 3500 Central Ave SE. (Open M-Sa 7am-10pm, Su 8am-10pm.)

- **graze,** 3128 Central Ave. SE (☎268-4729). Inside the classy but casual interior, patrons are encouraged to peruse the eclectic menu and eat what they like with-

THE BIG SPLURGE

"HAUTE" CUISINE

A restaurant called High Finance sounds a scary to a budget traveler, but it is worth every penny. Perched atop Sandia Peak, nearly 2 mi. high, High Finance is the highest full-service restaurant in the United States. From its wide windows, Albuquerque and the beautiful New Mexico landscape stretch out before you. The restaurant and amazing view are accessible only by the 2.7-mi.-long Sandia Peak Tramway, the world's longest aerial tramway, so you'll have already had a bit of a chance to *ooh* and *aah* before you settle down to eat— and you'll eat well. High Finance serves superb steaks and seafood, a few carefully prepared vegetarian entrees, and fabulous desserts. At dinnertime, twilight spreads across the scenery and Albuquerque twinkles. Lunch holds its own appeal, as it costs $7-9, instead of the $17-30 for dinner. Delicious food, a ride on the longest tramway in the world, and the stunning view stretching all the way to Taos, make the entire experience a a treat.

High Finance Restaurant and Tavern, ☎*505-243-9742. Reservations recommended. Open daily 11am-3pm and 4:30pm-late.* ***Sandia Peak Tramway,*** *10 Tramway Loop NE.* ☎*505-856-7325. Open daily late May to early Sept. 9am-9pm; early Sept. to late May 9am-8pm, except W open 5-8pm. $15, seniors $12, ages 5-12 $10; with dinner reservations $10.*

out the limits of conventional courses. The menu is highly seasonal to take advantage of fresh ingredients, but is always inventive, artfully prepared, and delicious ($8-12). Chic but friendly; smallish servings. Open Tu-Sa 11am-11pm. ❸

El Norteño, 6416 Zuni Rd. SE (☎256-1431), at California St. A family-run joint renowned for the most authentic and varied Mexican food in town. Extensive menu ranging from chicken *mole* ($8) to *cabrito* (young goat) to beef tongue ($7-9). The garlic-roasted shrimp is a treat. Lunch buffet 11am-2pm $6. Open daily 8:30am-9pm. ❷

Java Joe's, 906 Park Ave. SW (☎765-1514), 1 block south of Central Ave. and 2 blocks from the Rte. 66 Hostel. This lively coffeehouse and restaurant with an artsy atmosphere has hearty wraps ($5), sandwiches ($5.50), salads ($4-5), and great breakfast burritos ($3). Lots of vegetarian dishes. Open daily 6:30am-3:30pm. ❶

👁 SIGHTS

OLD TOWN. When the railroad cut through Albuquerque in the 19th century, it missed Old Town by almost 2 mi. As downtown grew around the railroad, Old Town remained untouched until the 1950s, when the city realized that it had a tourist magnet right under its nose. Just north of Central Ave. and east of Río Grande Blvd., the adobe plaza today looks much like it did over 100 years ago, save the ubiquitous restaurants, gift shops, and jewelry vendors. Though a tourist trap, Old Town is an architectural marvel, and a stroll through it is worthwhile. **Walking tours** of Old Town meet at the Albuquerque Museum. *(1hr. Tours mid-Mar. to mid-Dec. Tu–Su 11am. Free with museum admission.)* On the north side of the plaza, the quaint **San Felipe de Neri Church,** dating back to 1706, has stood the test of time. *(Open daily 9am-5pm, accompanying museum open M-Sa 10am-4pm; Su mass in English 7 and 10:15am, in Spanish 8:30am.)* A host of museums and attractions surrounds the plaza. To the northeast, the **Albuquerque Museum** showcases four centuries of New Mexican art and history. The comprehensive exhibit on the Conquistadors and Spanish colonial rule is a must-see for anyone interested in history. *(2000 Mountain Rd. NW. ☎243-7255. Open Tu-Su 9am-5pm. $4, seniors $2, children $1. First W of each month free. Wheelchair accessible. Tours of sculpture garden Apr.-Nov. Tu-Sa at 10am; free with admission.)* No visit to Old Town is complete without seeing the **Rattlesnake Museum,** lying just south of the plaza. Earn a "Certificate of Bravery" by visiting the largest collection of live rattlesnakes in the world, with over 30 species ranging from the deadly Mojave to the tiny Pygmy. *(202 San Felipe NW. ☎242-6569. Open M-Sa 10am-6pm, Su 1-5pm. $2.50, seniors $2, under 18 $1.50.)* A block off the plaza, the **Turquoise Museum** has fine examples of turquoise and provides an interesting overview of the associated mineralogy, geology, and mining, and a tutorial on what to look for in high-quality turquoise stones and jewelry. *(2107 Central Ave. NW. ☎247-8650. Open M-Sa 10am-4pm. $4; seniors, children, and AAA $3.)* Spike and Alberta, two statuesque dinosaurs, greet tourists outside the kid-friendly **New Mexico Museum of Natural History and Science.** Interactive exhibits take visitors through the history of life on earth. The museum features a five-story movie theater, planetarium, and simulated ride through the world of the dinosaurs. *(1801 Mountain Rd. NW. ☎841-2802. Open daily 9am-5pm, closed M in Sept. $5, seniors $4, children $2; admission and theater ticket $10/$8/$4.)*

UNIVERSITY MUSEUMS. The University of New Mexico campus has a couple of delightfully free museums worth a quick visit. **The Maxwell Museum of Anthropology** has excellent exhibits on the culture and history of Native American settlement in the Southwest. *(☎277-5963. On University Blvd., just north of MLK Blvd. Open Tu-F 9am-4pm,*

Sa 10am-4pm. Free.) The **University Art Museum** features changing exhibits focusing on 20th-century New Mexican painting and photography. *(Near the corner of Central Ave. and Cornel St. ☎ 277-4001. Open Tu-F 9am-4pm. Free.)*

BIOPARKS. Albuquerque is home to one of the top zoos in the nation. Visitors can see over 250 animal species at the **Río Grande Zoological Park** and watch caretakers feed the seals and sea lions (10:30am and 3:30pm daily) or present programs on animals from around the world. The **Albuquerque Aquarium** features a 285,000 gallon mini-ocean, complete with sharks and a coral reef. Connected to the aquarium is the **Río Grande Botanic Garden** with paths lined with desert plants. *(Zoo: 903 10th St. SW. Aquarium and garden: 2601 Central Ave. NW. ☎ 764-6200. Open daily 9am-5pm. Admission to zoo or aquarium and botanic gardens $7, seniors and children $3. All 3 parks $10/$5.)*

CULTURAL ATTRACTIONS. The **Indian Pueblo Cultural Center** has a commercial edge but still provides a good introduction to the history, culture, traditions, and art of the 19 American Indian pueblos of New Mexico. You're welcome to wander the museum at your leisure, but it's worth it to see if any guided tours are planned. The center includes a museum, store, and restaurant. *(2401 12th St. NW. ☎ 843-7270. Take bus #36 from downtown. Museum open daily 9am-4:30pm. Art demonstrations Sa-Su 11am-2pm, Native American dances Sa-Su 11am and 2pm. $4, seniors $3, students $1.)* The **National Hispanic Cultural Center** has an excellent art museum with exhibits that explore folk art and representations of Hispanic social and cultural life in America. New Mexican and Chicano artists will figure prominently in *Inspirados* and *¡Arte Caliente!*, two exhibitions planned for 2005. *(1701 4th St. SW, on the corner of Bridge St. ☎ 246-2261. Open Tu-Su 10am-5pm. $3, seniors $2, under 16 free.)*

🎎🎏 FESTIVALS AND NIGHTLIFE

If you're looking for a change from honky-tonk, Albuquerque is an oasis of interesting bars, jamming nightclubs, art film houses, and college life. Check flyers posted around the university area for live music shows or pick up a copy of *Alibi*, the free local weekly. During the first week of October, hundreds of aeronauts take flight in colorful hot-air balloons during the **Albuquerque International Balloon Fiesta.** Even the most grounded of souls will enjoy the week's barbecues, musical events, and the sublime spectacle of a sky full of hot air balloons. (☎ 888-422-7277; www.balloonfiesta.com. Admission $5.)

Most nightlife huddles on and near Central Ave., downtown and near the university. Nob Hill establishments tend to be the most gay-friendly. The offbeat **Guild Cinema**, 3405 Central Ave. NE, runs independent and foreign films. (☎ 255-1848. $7; students, seniors, and all shows before 6pm $5.)

Sauce/Raw Liquid Lounge, 405 Central Ave. NW (☎ 242-5839), is a magnet for trendy 20-somethings looking for a place to drink and dance the night away. The dim interior of Sauce throbs with house music on weekends and a shadow dancer sets the semi-scandalous mood, while the adjoining Raw pumps hip-hop and also boasts an outdoor patio. W Latin/salsa. Open Tu-Sa 4pm-2am.

Maloney's, 325 Central Ave. NE (☎ 242-7422), packs in college kids and young professionals with a comfortable brewpub interior and extremely popular outdoor patio. Burgers and standard pub fare are available throughout the evening, but the focus shifts to the 15 beers on tap as the night wears on. Open M-Sa 11am-2am, Su 11am-midnight.

Burt's Tiki Lounge, 313 Gold St. SW (☎ 247-2878). Situated a block south of the Central Ave. club strip, the difference shows in its more laid-back atmosphere. Surf and tiki paraphernalia cover the walls, while anything from funk to punk to live hip-hop takes the stage. Live music Tu-Sa and occasionally Su-M. Usually open Tu-Sa 9pm-2am.

▲\ OUTDOOR ACTIVITIES

Rising a mile above Albuquerque, the sunset-pink crest of the **Sandía Mountains** gives them their name, which means "watermelon" in Spanish. The crest beckons to New Mexicans, drawing thousands to hike and explore. One of the most popular trails in New Mexico, **La Luz Trail** (7½ mi. one-way) climbs the Sandía Crest, beginning at the Juan Tabo Picnic Area. From Exit 167 on I-40, drive north on Tramway Blvd. 10 mi. to Forest Rd. 333. Follow Trail 137 for 7 mi. and take Trail 84 to the top. To eliminate one leg of the journey, hikers can drive or take the tram. The Sandía Mountains have excellent mountain biking trails. Try the moderately easy **Foothills Trail** (7 mi.), which skirts the bottom of the mountains, just east of the city. The trail starts at the Elena Gallegos Picnic Area, off Tramway Blvd. The most popular place for biking is the **Sandía Peak Ski Area,** 6 mi. up Rte. 536 on the way to Sandía Crest. Bikers can take their bikes up the chairlift and then ride down on 35 mi. of mountain trails and rollers covering all skill levels. (☎242-9133. Chairlifts run June-Sept. Th-Su 10am-4pm. Full-day lift ticket $14, single ride $8. Bike rentals at the summit $38 per day. Helmets required.)

Sandía Peak Ski Area, only 30min. from downtown, is also a serviceable ski area for those who can't escape north to Taos or south to Ruidoso. Six lifts service 25 short trails (35% beginner; 55% intermediate; 10% advanced) on 200 skiable acres. The summit (10,378 ft.) tops a vertical drop of 1700 ft. (☎242-9133. Snowboards allowed. Annual snowfall 125 in. Open mid-Dec. to mid-Mar. M-F 9am-4pm, Sa-Su 8:30am-4pm. Full-day $38, half-day $29; ages 13-20 $32, ages 13 and under and seniors $29/$20.) There are also excellent cross-country skiing trails in the **Cibola National Forest.** The North Crest and 10-K trails are particularly popular.

▶️ DAYTRIPS FROM ALBUQUERQUE

PETROGLYPH NATIONAL MONUMENT   ☎505

Located on Albuquerque's west side, this national monument features more than 20,000 images etched into lava rocks between AD 1300 and 1680 by Pueblo Indians and Spanish settlers. The park encompasses much of the 17 mi. West Mesa, a ridge of black basalt boulders that formed as a result of volcanic activity 130,000 years ago. The most easily accessible petroglyphs can be found via three short trails at **Boca Negra Canyon,** 2 mi. north of the visitors center (hiking times 5-30min.). The **Rinconada Canyon Trail,** 1 mi. south of the visitors center, has more intricate rock art and is a sandy, but fairly easy, 2½ mi. desert hike along the base of the West Mesa. To see the nearby volcanoes, take Exit 149 off I-40 and follow Paseo del Volcán to a dirt road. The volcanoes are 4¼ mi. north of the exit. To reach the park itself, take I-40 to Unser Blvd. (Exit 154) and follow signs for the park. (☎899-0205. Park open daily 8am-5pm. Admission to Boca Negra Canyon M-F $1, Sa-Su $2; National Parks Pass accepted. Rinconada Canyon, volcanoes, and visitors center free.)

CHACO CULTURE NATIONAL HISTORICAL PARK   ☎505

Sun-scorched Chaco Canyon served as the first great settlement of the Ancestral Puebloans and the center of a civilization that began around AD 800 and lasted nearly 400 years. The ruins of nine Great Houses, massive and intricate multi-story dwellings, stretch along the 10-mile-long canyon. A complex system of roads, irrigation canals, and astronomical markers in the canyon hint at the central role Chaco played in their remarkably sophisticated society. Each Great House is aligned according to solar, lunar, and directional axes, and walking amongst the ruins inspires awe at the knowledge, engineering, and organization it took to construct such perfectly oriented structures. Chaco is also revered by the Pueblos as a spiritual and powerful place central to their heritage. Many of today's visitors to the park believe a mysterious presence lingers in this birthplace of Pueblo culture.

Chaco Canyon is 92 mi. northeast of Gallup. From the north, take U.S. 550 (formerly Rte. 44) to County Rd. 7900 (3 mi. east of **Nageezi** and 50 mi. west of **Cuba**), follow the road for 21 mi., then take the unpaved 16 mi. County Rd. 7950 into the park. From the south, take Rte. 9 from **Crownpoint** (home of the nearest ATM and grocery stores to the park) 36 mi. east to the marked park turnoff in Pueblo Pintado; turn north onto unpaved Rte. 46 for 10 mi., then left on County Rd. 7900 for 7 mi. and finally left onto County Rd. 7950. There is no gas in the park, and gas stations en route are few and far between. County Rd. 7900 is a rough ride; settle in for a slow, bone-shaking drive. Call the park in advance (☎988-6727) to ask about road conditions, which may deteriorate in bad weather, necessitating 4WD or leading to road closures.

The **Chaco Visitors Center,** at the east end of the park, has an excellent museum exhibiting Ancestral Puebloan art and architecture, and showing films that detail the knowns and unknowns of the ruins. The Chaco Night Sky Program—an astronomy program and solar observation—is held Tuesday, Friday, and Saturday at 9pm. All the ruins have brochures at their sites that can be bought for $0.50-0.75, and, during the summer, rangers lead guided tours of Pueblo Bonito (10am and 2pm) and Hungo Pavi (4pm) that meet in the respective Great House parking lots. (☎786-7014. Open daily 8am-5pm. $8 per vehicle.) The largest sites, such as **Pueblo Bonito** and **Chetro Ketl,** are accessible by short, paved paths from the main road, but **backcountry hiking trails** lead to many others; get a free **backcountry permit** from the visitors center before leaving. One of the best backcountry hikes is the moderately strenuous **Pueblo Alto Trail** (5½ mi. round-trip, 3-4hr.). After a fun scramble to the mesa top along a Chacoan path, the trail loops around the mesa and canyon rims, providing access to Pueblo Alto and New Alto, as well as impressive overlook views of Pueblo Bonito, Chetro Ketl, and the San Juan Basin.

An accessible, inexpensive lodging option is the ⬛**Circle A Hostel ❶,** just northwest of Cuba, which offers friendly, homey lodging. Circle A is a converted 1920s hacienda with a shady veranda, the perfect place to relax. The ranch is 5 mi. east of U.S. 550 on Los Piños Rd. Turn at the cattle guard and follow the signs along Los Piños. (Reservations recommended. Dorms $20; private room $40, with bath $45; tent sites $20, including use of facilities. Group use available.) **The Gallo Campground ❶,** a little more than 1 mi. from the visitors center, offers serene desert camping for $10 per site; register at the campground. The 48 sites are by a small ruin and have access to tables, fireplaces, and toilets. As there is no food in the park, **Presciliano's Cafe ❷,** 6478 Hwy. 550 in Cuba, is a good place to silence your growling stomach. The giant cinnamon rolls ($2) and breakfast menu are incredible, and the burgers ($6) and variety of Mexican entrees ($6-8) aren't bad themselves. (☎289-3177. Open daily in summer 8:30am-10pm; in winter 8:30am-9pm.)

EL MORRO NATIONAL MONUMENT ☎505

With signatures of Spanish and English explorers and settlers dating back to 1605, **Inscription Rock** has been the centerpiece of El Morro National Monument since its founding in 1906. The monument offers two hiking options. The half-mile, wheelchair-accessible **Inscription Trail** winds past the rock, providing excellent views of the signatures and neighboring petroglyphs and of the rainwater pool that attracted travelers in centuries past. The **Mesa Top Trail** (2 mi.) climbs 200 ft. to the top of the rock before skirting the edge of an ancient pueblo. The trail is well-marked and affords impressive panoramas of the region. A trail guide that details the most famous engravings and provides translations of those in foreign script is available for loan or purchase at the visitors center ($1). The trails close 1hr. before the visitors center does. The monument is located west of the Continental Divide on Rte. 53, 125 mi. west of Albuquerque, 42 mi. west of the I-40 exit at Grants, and 56 mi. southeast of Gallup. The **visitors center** includes a small museum and warnings against adding your own graffiti. (☎783-4226. Open daily June-Aug. 9am-7pm; Sept.-May 9am-5pm. $3, under 17 free.) The small, tranquil **El Morro Campground ❶** has running water and primitive toilets, and rarely fills. (9 sites, 1 wheelchair accessible. Sites $5.)

GALLUP   ☎ 505

Gallup's proximity to the Petrified Forest National Park (p. 867), Navajo Reservation (p. 864), Chaco Culture National Historic Park (p. 896), and El Morro National Monument (p. 897) makes it a good base for exploring the region, even if the town itself has few attractions. **Old Route 66,** which runs parallel to I-40 through downtown, is lined with dirt-cheap motels (often with emphasis on the dirt), while the chains cluster on the western edge of town. The best place to stay in town is **El Rancho Hotel and Motel ❸,** 1000 E. Rte. 66—it's a step up in price from other options, but a leap up in quality. A who's who of the silver screen (John Wayne, Jack Benny, Kirk Douglas) have stayed in this posh, western-style hotel and have rooms named after them. Just across the parking lot, the motel offers slightly less fancy, but perfectly serviceable and clean, accommodations. (☎863-9311. Hotel singles $48; doubles $68. Motel singles $40.) One of the best spots for those willing to brave train noise in order to protect their bottom line is the **Blue Spruce Lodge ❷,** 119 E. Rte. 66. Most of the rooms are adequate, but you may want to scope your room out before you check in. (☎863-5211. Singles $26; doubles $30.) You can pitch a tent in the shadow of sandstone cliffs at **Red Rock State Park Campground ❶,** Rte. 566, which offers access to hiking 5 mi. east of town off Rte. 66. During the warmer months Red Rock is the site of concerts, rodeos, and motorcycle races—call to make sure the park is open for regular camping. (☎863-1329. 142 sites with showers and hookups. Tent sites $10, with hookup $14.) In addition to the fast food joints located primarily on 491 N, diners and cafes line both sides of I-40. **Oasis Mediterranean Restaurant ❷,** 100 E. Rte. 66, has a full array of tasty Mediterranean fare, some with a slight Southwestern kick, and a hookah bar upstairs. (Entrees $4-11. Open M-Sa 10am-9pm.) **The Ranch Kitchen ❸,** 3001 W. Rte. 66, has filling breakfasts ($4-6) and meaty, traditional meals ($9-12). The barbecue, bluecorn trout, and Navajo tacos are local favorites. (Open daily in summer 7am-10pm; in winter 7am-9pm.)

You can visit the **Gallup Visitors Center,** 701 Montoya Blvd. (☎863-4909 or 800-242-4282; www.gallupnm.org), just off Rte. 66, for info on all of New Mexico. Upstairs is a free museum detailing the changes to Pueblo life over the last four centuries, complete with audio recordings that explain Native American traditions and artwork. (Open daily June-Aug. 8am-6pm., Sept.-May 8am-5pm.) **Greyhound,** 201 E. Rte. 66 (☎863-3761), runs buses to Albuquerque (2½hr., 4 per day, $21) and Flagstaff (4hr., 4 per day, $41). **Post Office:** 950 W. Aztec Ave. (☎722-5265. Open M-F 8:30am-5pm, Sa 10am-1:30pm.) **Postal Code:** 87301. **Area Code:** 505.

TRUTH OR CONSEQUENCES   ☎ 505

In 1950, the popular radio game show *Truth or Consequences* celebrated its 10th anniversary by seeking a town to rename in its honor. Cities from all over the US volunteered, and Hot Springs, NM, was selected. Once known only for its mineral baths, the dusty little town became the focus of national attention when its residents formally agreed to rename their town Truth or Consequences. While the name has changed, the mineral baths still infuse the town with fountain-of-youth effects and a funky down-home spirit. Maybe there's something in the water.

⚡🏠 ORIENTATION AND PRACTICAL INFORMATION.

"T or C" sits about 150 mi. south of Albuquerque on I-25. **Greyhound,** 8 Date St. (☎894-3649), runs to Albuquerque (3hr., 1 per day, $30-40). The **Chamber of Commerce,** 400 W. 4th St., has free maps and brochures about area accommodations and attractions. (☎894-3536. Open M-F 9am-5:30pm, Sa 9am-1pm.) There are two **post offices:** 300 Main St., in the middle of town (open M-F 9am-3pm), and 1507 N. Date St. (open M-F 8:30am-5pm). **Postal Code:** 87901. **Area Code:** 505.

🏠 ACCOMMODATIONS.

Riverbend Hot Springs Hostel ❶, 100 Austin St. (☎894-6183; www.nmhotsprings.com), may not be the cleanest place, but the friendly, atmosphere and on-site hot springs make it a nice place to soak your cares away; take Exit 79 off I-25, turn toward town, and continue 1½ mi. to a traffic light. Turn left at the light, then immediately turn right onto Cedar St. and follow it to the river and the blue building at the road's bend. (Kitchen, and laundry. Reception 8am-10pm; call ahead for late-night arrivals. Teepees or tent sites $17; dorms $20, students $18; private rooms $36-55.) Budget hotels line N. Date St., just off I-25 at Exit 70. Most offer standard lodging at reasonable rates. Downtown, the **Charles Motel and Spa ❷,** 601 Broadway, has simple and clean rooms, with mineral baths on the premises. The rooms are spacious, and the largest have kitchenettes. (☎894-7154 or 800-317-4518; www.charlesspa.com. Singles $39; doubles $45.) **Campsites** at the nearby **Elephant Butte Lake State Park ❶** have access to restrooms and cold showers. (Primitive sites $8, developed sites with showers $10, with electricity $14.)

🍴 FOOD.

Nearly all of T or C's restaurants are as easy on the wallet as the baths are on the body. **La Hacienda ❷,** 1615 S. Broadway, the best Mexican food around, is well worth the short drive out of the center of town. They have excellent *arroz con pollo* (rice with chicken; $7) and breakfast *chorizo con huevos*—sausage with eggs for $5. (Open Tu-Su 11am-9pm.) The popular **La Cocina ❷,** 1 Lake Way Dr. (look for the "Hot Stuff" sign above N. Date St.), pleases with huge portions of Mexican and New Mexican food, including chimichangas ($7). A Carrizozo cherry cider ($1.50) will slake your thirst. (☎894-6499. Open daily 10:30am-10pm.) **Bar-B-Que on Broadway ❷,** 308 Broadway, is a local staple, quickly dishing up plentiful breakfast specials that start at $2.50 and hearty lunch entrees running $5-8. (☎894-7047.

DON'T COUNT YOUR CHILES BEFORE THEY HATCH

Early each September, 30,000 crazed chile fanatics descend upon the town of Hatch, NM, for the Hatch Chile Festival, a celebration of the harvest of the state's official vegetable (the town's 2000 permanent residents don't care that the Hatch chile is actually a fruit) and staple meal ingredient. The land surrounding Hatch, the self-proclaimed Chile Capital of the world, is ideally suited to growing the green chile—the hotter climate is said to create a hotter chile. The chiles are renowned for their unique flavor, and the town is the namesake for New Mexican green chiles and natural host for a chile festival. The festival's revelers participate in a chile cookoff and chile roasting. A parade Saturday morning includes the proud procession of the newly crowned Chile Queen. Carnival rides, musical performances, and food booths featuring chile-laced goodies take place all weekend long. Few visitors are content to leave emptyhanded. Most stock up on Hatch chiles for the coming year, carrying 30- to 40-lb. burlap bags of the fragrant, roasted Hatch chiles home with them.

Can't get your burritos covered with enough green chile? Head for Hatch, 40 mi. south of Las Cruces and 40 mi. north of Truth or Consequences, on Labor Day weekend. www.hatchnm.biz.

Open M-Sa 7am-4pm.) **White Coyote Cafe,** 113 Main St, offers a simple but tasty vegetarian menu that changes weekly in order to take advantage of seasonal organic produce. (☎894-5160. Open M 8am-3pm, Th-Sa 11am-8pm, Su 9am-3pm.)

◨ ⚠ SIGHTS AND OUTDOOR ACTIVITIES. The town's main attractions are its **mineral baths;** locals claim that the baths heal virtually everything. The only outdoor tubs are located at the **Riverbend Hot Springs Hostel** (see above), where four co-ed tubs sit alongside the Río Grande. You can even head for the chilly river itself if you feel the urge to take the plunge after cleansing your pores in the hot water. Access to the baths is $10 per hr. for the public with a $25 minimum (10am-7pm), but complementary for hostel guests (7-10am and 7-10pm).

Five miles north of T or C, **Elephant Butte Lake State Park** features New Mexico's largest lake (take Date St. north to a sign for Elephant Butte; turn right onto Hwy. 181 and follow the signs). A public works project dammed up the Río Grande in 1916 after the resolution of a major water rights dispute between the US and Mexico. The resulting lake is named after the elephantine rock formation at its southern end. The park has sandy beaches and a marina. (Day use $5.) **Marina del Sur,** just inside the park, rents all kinds of boats. (☎744-5567. Must be 18+ with a valid driver's license to rent. Jet skis $129 per 3hr., pontoon boats $99 per 3hr., ski boats $139 per 3hr., kayaks $19 per 3hr., houseboats $259 per day. 2-day min. for houseboats, 3hr. min for all other rentals.) **Sports Adventure,** on the lake at the end of Long Point Rd. and also at Rock Canyon Rd., both north of the town of Elephant Butte, rents jet skis. (☎744-5557 or 888-736-8420. Rentals start at $35 per 30min.) There is a **visitors center** at the entrance to the park with a small museum on the area's natural history. (☎877-664-7787. Open M-F 7:30am-4pm, Sa-Su 7:30am-10pm.) An easy 1½ mi. trail begins in the parking lot just past the visitors center.

GILA CLIFF DWELLINGS NATIONAL MONUMENT ☎505

The mysterious Gila Cliff Dwellings National Monument preserves over 40 stone and timber rooms carved into the cliff's caves by the Mogollon tribe during the late AD 1200s. About a dozen families lived here for about 20 years, farming on the mesa top and along the river. During the early 1300s, however, the Mogollon abandoned their homes leaving the ruins as their only trace. The cliff dwellings are 44 mi. north of Silver City on Rte. 15. The road is narrow, winding, and requires 2hr. for safe passage. Road conditions can be impassable in winter, so pay close attention to the weather and the road surface. The **visitors center,** at the end of Rte. 15, shows a film and sells maps of the Gila National Forest. (☎536-9461. Open daily in summer 8am-5pm; in winter 8am-4:30pm.) The picturesque 1 mi. round-trip hike to the dwellings begins with a steep ascent up the canyon walls, but the rest of the hike is fairly level or downhill and offers opportunities to go inside the ruins. A trail guide ($0.50) can be purchased at the trailhead or at the visitors center. Those who want more info about the ruins can go on one of the free, ranger-guided tours (11am and 2pm) that meet at the first overhang. (Dwellings open daily late May to early Sept. 8am-6pm; late Sept. to early May 9am-4pm. $3, under 12 free.) The park has two campgrounds: **Upper** and **Lower Scorpion ❶.** Both are located along the road on the way to the trailhead. Water and pit toilets are available in the summer, but there is no water in winter. There is no fee for either campground. The nearest indoor accommodations can be found at the comfy **Grey Feathers Bed & Breakfast ❸,** 20 mi. south at the intersection of Forest Rd. 15 and Rte. 35. Drawing as many as 4000 hummingbirds on some summer weekends, the lodge is a perfect place to relax and bird-watch. (☎536-3206. Singles $40-45; doubles $45-50; suites $65-75.) The adjoining **cafe ❶** offers sandwiches ($3-7) and ice cream ($1.25 per scoop).

WHITE SANDS NAT'L MONUMENT ☎ 505

In the Tularosa Basin between the Sacramento and San Andres Mountains, the world's largest gypsum dune field formed as rainwater flushed the mineral from the nearby peaks and into Lake Lucero. As desert heat evaporated the lake, the gypsum crystals were left behind and now form the blindingly white sand dunes. These drifts of fine sand create the look of arctic tundra, but don't be fooled: the midday sun assaults the shadeless with potentially unbearable light and heat—be prepared with protective clothing and eyewear, heavy-duty sunscreen, and plenty of water. Trekking or rolling through the dunes can provide hours of mindless fun or mindful soul-searching; the sand is particularly awe-inspiring at sunset.

■■ ▨ **ORIENTATION AND PRACTICAL INFORMATION.** White Sands is on Rte. 70, 15 mi. southwest of Alamogordo, 52 mi. northeast of Las Cruces. Rte. 70 is prone to closures due to missile testing at the nearby military base. Delays can run up to 1hr.; call the **visitors center** to check Rte. 70's status. The visitors center itself has a small museum with an introductory video and a gift shop. (☎479-6124. Park open daily June-Aug. 7am-10pm, last entrance 9pm; Sept.-May 7am-sunset. Visitors center open daily June-Aug. 8am-7pm; Sept.-May 8am-5pm. The entrance booth distributes a park map. Park admission $3, under 16 free.) The nearest **ATM, grocery store, hospital, Internet access,** and **post office** are in Alamogordo. No public transit serves the park. For more info, see the park website www.nps.gov/whsa.

▛ **CAMPING.** The only way to sleep in the park is to camp at one of the **backcountry campsites ❶.** Ten daily permits for the sites ($3 per person plus the park entry fee) are first come, first served. The sites have no water or toilets, and are not accessible by road, requiring up to a 2 mi. hike through the sand dunes. Campers must register in person at the visitors center and be at their sites before dark. Campfires are prohibited, but stoves are allowed. Sleeping amid the white dunes can be an extraordinary experience, but plan ahead because sites fill up early on full-moon nights. Occasionally, the sites are closed due to missile range launches.

◨ ▨ **SIGHTS AND OUTDOOR ACTIVITIES.** The 8 mi. **Dunes Drive** is a good way see White Sands. However, really experiencing the monument means getting out and walking across the dunes. Off-trail hiking is allowed anywhere in the eastern section of the park. Anyone considering a backcountry hike should bring a compass and map—it's easy to get lost in the sea of seemingly uniform gypsum dunes. The only wheelchair accessible trail in the park is the **Interdune Boardwalk,** expected to be renovated by 2005, an easy ¼ mi. walk above the sand. The best hike is the **Alkali Flat Trail,** a moderately strenuous loop through the heart of the dunes to the parched, salty lakebed of Lake Otero. The entire trail is 4½ mi., but it isn't necessary to hike the whole thing in order to obtain spectacular vistas. The trail is marked by white posts with orange reflective tape, but do not attempt this hike in strong winds, when blowing sand reduces visibility and makes it easy to lose the trail. Bring lots of water and protect yourself from the intense sun. There is a free, guided **sunset stroll** every evening (call ahead to the visitors center), and on summer nights, park rangers give **evening talks** on various topics (June-Aug. 8:30pm). On **full-moon nights** in the summer, the park stays open late (until 11pm, last entrance 10pm), and a guest speaker presents a program on a topic relating to the Southwest at 8:30pm. A **star talk** takes place most Fridays during the summer at 8:30pm. During the **Perseid Meteor Shower** (around the second week of August), the park stays open until midnight. Once a month, a ranger-guided expedition heads for the dry bed of **Lake Lucero.** These special tours last about 3hr. and include 1½ mi. of hiking. Reservations and a fee of $3 per person are required.

ROSWELL ☎505

With giant inflatable Martians advertising used cars, streetlights donning painted-on pointy eyes, and flying saucers adorning fast-food signs, one thing is certain: aliens *have* invaded Roswell. The fascination began in July 1947, when an alien spacecraft reportedly crashed near the dusty town. The official press release reported that the military had recovered pieces of a "flying saucer," but a retraction followed next day—the wreckage, the government claimed, was actually a weather balloon. Many people weren't convinced, and Roswell is a hotbed of alien-related hype and study. Both believers and skeptics will find the alien side of Roswell entertaining, if not enlightening. During the first week of July, the **UFO Festival** celebrates the anniversary of the alleged encounter, drawing thousands for live music, an alien costume contest, and a 5km "Alien Chase" race. With a plastic flying saucer above its storefront, the popular **International UFO Museum and Research Center,** 114 N. Main St., recounts the events near Roswell in 1947. Exhibits testimonials and newspaper clippings about the incident, as well as features on alien sightings worldwide. (☎625-9495. Open daily 9am-5pm. Free. Audio tour $1.)

Fast-food restaurants are as prevalent in Roswell as allusions to alien life, and they are concentrated along N. Main St. and W. 2nd St. Side streets are home to less commercial budget eateries. **Nuthin' Fancy Cafe ❶,** 2103 N. Main, takes pride in its simple, well-prepared, and delicious menu, promising guests "home cooking without the mess." Indeed, the daily blue plate specials ($5-7), wide array of vegetables and healthy options, and fresh homemade pies ($2) are just like Mom would make, if she were a really, really good cook. (☎623-4098. Open daily 6am-9pm.) **Tía Juana's ❸,** 3601 N. Main St., is the kind of funky Tex-Mex restaurant that the big chains try to imitate. Try the chili-rubbed ribeye for $15, or refresh yourself with something from the huge margarita menu for $5-8. (☎624-6113. Dining room open M-Th 11am-9:30pm, F-Sa 11am-10pm, Su 11am-9pm; bar open daily 11am-10pm.)

Aside from its extraterrestrial peculiarities, Roswell is a normal town. The intersection of **2nd Street** (Rte. 70/380) and **Main Street** (Rte. 285) is the center of the Roswell galaxy. To reach Roswell from Albuquerque, head 89 mi. south on I-25 to San Antonio, then 153 mi. east on U.S. 380. **Greyhound,** 1100 N. Virginia Ave. (☎622-2510), in conjunction with TNM&O, runs buses to Albuquerque (4hr.; Th-Sa 2 per day, Su 1 per day; Tu-Th $36, F-Su $38) and El Paso (4½hr.; 3 per day; M-Th $41, F-Su $44). **Pecos Trails Transit,** 515 N. Main St., runs buses all over town. (☎624-6766. Open M-F 6am-10:30pm, Sa 7:10am-10pm, Su 10:30am-7pm. $0.75, students $0.50, seniors $0.35.) The **visitors center** is at 426 N. Main St. (☎624-0889 or 623-5695. Open M-F 8:30am-5:30pm, Sa-Su 10am-3pm.) Free **Internet access** is available at the **Roswell Public Library,** 301 N. Pennsylvania Ave. (☎622-7101. Open M-Tu 9am-9pm, W-Sa 9am-6pm, Su 2pm-6pm.) **Post Office:** 415 N. Pennsylvania Ave. (☎623-7232. Open M-F 7:30am-5:30pm, Sa 8am-noon.) **Postal Code:** 88202. **Area Code:** 505.

CARLSBAD CAVERNS NATIONAL PARK ☎505

Imagine the surprise of European wanderers in southeastern New Mexico at the turn of the century when 250,000 bats appeared seemingly out of nowhere. This swarm led to the discovery of the Carlsbad Caverns. By 1923, colonies of tourists clung to the walls of this desolate attraction. Carlsbad Caverns National Park marks one of the world's largest and oldest cave systems; even the most jaded caver will be struck by its unusual geological formations. The aptly-named **Big Room** is the park's central and most accessible attraction. A 1¼ mi. self-guided tour circumscribes the 14-acre chamber, highlighting subterranean wonders like the Hall of Giants, the Rock of Ages, and the Bottomless Pit. (Natural entrance open daily June to mid-Aug. 8:30am-3:30pm; mid-Aug. to May 8:30am-2pm. Elevators open daily June to mid-Aug. 8:30am-5pm; mid-Aug. to May 8:30am-3:30pm. $6, ages

6-15 $3. Audio tour $3. Segments of trail wheelchair accessible.) The **King's Palace Tour,** guided by a ranger, goes through four of the cave's lowest rooms. (May-Aug. 1½hr. tours leave every hr. 10-11am and 1-3pm; Sept.-Apr. 10am and 2pm only. $8, Golden Age Passport holders and ages 6-15 $4. Advance reservations recommended.) Other guided tours in the Big Room include a tour though the **Left Hand Tunnel** lit only by the lanterns given to each participant (2hr., daily 9am; $7), and a moderately strenuous tour of the **Lower Cave** that descends 50ft. on ladders. (3hr., M-F 1pm; $20. Bring gloves and 4 AA batteries.) Plan your visit for late afternoon to catch the **bat flight.** The ritual, during which hungry bats storm out of the cave at a rate of 6000 per min., is preceded by a ranger talk. (May-Oct. daily just before sunset.) **Backcountry hiking** is permitted above ground, but a permit, map, and at least a gallon of water per person per day are strongly recommended. **Caverns Visitors Center** has trail maps and tour info. (☎785-2232. Open daily June to late Aug. 8am-7pm; late Aug. to May 8am-5:30pm.) Make reservations through the Guided Tour Reservation Hotline (☎800-967-2283) or at http://reservations.nps.gov.

Tours of the undeveloped **Slaughter Canyon Cave** are a rugged caving experience. A car is required to get there; there's no public transit, and the parking lot is 23 mi. down unpaved Rte. 418, several miles south of the main entrance to the park on U.S. 62/180. The cave entrance is a steep, strenuous ½ mi. from the lot. Ranger-led tours (bring a flashlight) traverse difficult and slippery terrain; there are no paved trails or handrails. (2hr. tours June-Aug. Sa-Su 10am and 1pm, Sept.-May 10am only. $15, Golden Age Passport holders and ages 6-15 $7.50. Call the visitors center as least 2 days ahead for reservations.) Tours of the **Hall of the White Giant** and **Spider Cave** require crawling and climbing through tight passages. (☎800-967-2283. Tours 4hr., 1 per week. $20. Call at least a month in advance for reservations.)

A slew of budget motels line U.S. 62/180 south of downtown Carlsbad. The **Stage Coach Inn ❷,** 1819 S. Canal St., offers the best value of the lot with an outdoor pool, indoor jacuzzi, and laundry. Comfortable, clean rooms have A/C, cable, and refrigerators. (☎887-1148. Singles $34-40; doubles $36-47. 15% AAA and AARP discount.) The **Carlsbad RV Park and Campground ❶,** 4301 National Parks Hwy. 4 mi. south of town, has two wooden cabins with a full-size bed, two bunk beds, A/C, cable, DVD player, microwave, and refrigerator. Tent camping is also available. All guests have access to showers, swimming pool, and game room. (☎888-885-6333. Breakfast included Sa-Su. Cabin $32; linen not provided. Tent sites $14.50.)

The closest town to the park is **White's City,** on U.S. 62/180, 20 mi. southwest of the larger Carlsbad and 6 mi. from the visitors center. Flash floods occasionally close the roads; call the park for road conditions. El Paso, TX (p. 735) is the nearest big city, 150 mi. west past Guadalupe Mountains National Park (p. 734). **Greyhound,** in cooperation with TNM&O Coaches, runs three buses per day between El Paso and Carlsbad ($38.50) and will stop at White's City. The **Post Office,** 23 Carlsbad Caverns Hwy., is by the Best Western gift shop. (☎785-2220. Open M-F 8am-noon and 12:30-4:30pm, Sa 8am-noon.) **Postal Code:** 88268. **Area Code:** 505.

CALIFORNIA

California, and its iconic Hwy. 1, offer a wild ride—exhilaration doesn't begin to describe the feeling of being poised upon the very western edge of the country, with better times and wilder sights in the cliff-hugging turns ahead, and the past receding in your rearview mirror. Glaring movie spotlights, clanging San Francisco trolleys, vanilla-scented Jeffrey pines, alpine lakes, and ghostly desert landscapes all thrive in California. Indeed, there's so much going on you'd need a whole book (like ✳*Let's Go: California*) to describe it.

HIGHLIGHTS OF CALIFORNIA

LOS ANGELES. Follow your star to the place where media legends carouse, Ice Age fossils calcify, and boardwalk freaks commune (p. 941).

SAN FRANCISCO. Drive through the Golden Gate Bridge to the City by the Bay, where bluesmen, iconoclasts, students, and old hippies all congregate (p. 904).

SCENIC DRIVES. Along the coast, Hwy. 1 and U.S. 101 breeze past earthy beach towns and along soaring cliffs, passing Santa Barbara (p. 938), Hearst Castle (p. 938), and Redwood National Park (p. 986).

NATIONAL PARKS. Hike among the granite peaks of Yosemite (p. 980), or climb a boulder and view the sunset at Joshua Tree (p. 975).

🞂 PRACTICAL INFORMATION

Capital: Sacramento.

Visitor Info: California Office of Tourism, P.O. Box 1499, Sacramento 95812 (☎800-862-2543; www.visitcalifornia.com). **California State Parks Department,** P.O. Box 942896, Sacramento 94296 (☎800-777-0369; www.parks.ca.gov).

Postal Abbreviation: CA. **Sales Tax:** 7-8%, depending on county.

SAN FRANCISCO ☎415

If California is a state of mind, San Francisco is euphoria. This city will take you to new highs, leaving your mind spinning, your taste buds tingling, and your calves aching. Though it's smaller than most "big" cities, the City by the Bay more than compensates for its size with personality that simply won't quit. The dazzling views, daunting hills, one-of-a-kind neighborhoods, and laid-back people have a unique charisma. The city packs an incredible amount of vitality into its 47 square miles of thriving art communities, bustling shops, and wild nightlife.

By California standards, San Francisco is steeped in history. The lineage of free spirits and troublemakers started in the 19th century, with smugglers, pirates, and Gold Rush '49ers. In the 1950s came the brilliant, angry, young Beats, and the late 60s ushered in the most famous of SF rabble rousers—hippies and flower children, who turned on one generation and freaked out another by making love, not war. The queer community became undeniably visible in the 70s as one of the city's most vocal groups. Anti-establishment rallies and movements continue to fill the streets and newspapers. In addition, Mexican, Central American, and Asian immigrants have made SF one of the most racially diverse cities in the United States. For more coverage of the City by the Bay, see ✳*Let's Go: San Francisco*.

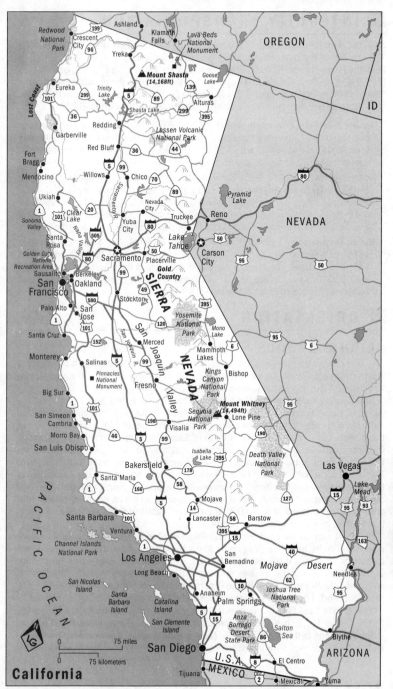

California

✗ INTERCITY TRANSPORTATION

San Francisco is 403 mi. north of Los Angeles and 390 mi. south of the Oregon border. The city lies at the northern tip of the peninsula separating the San Francisco Bay from the Pacific Ocean. The city is 6hr. from L.A. via I-5, 8hr. via U.S. 101, or 9½hr. via Hwy. 1. From inland California, **I-5** approaches the city from the north and south via **I-580** and **I-80**, which runs across the **Bay Bridge** (westbound toll $2). From the north, U.S. 101 and Hwy. 1 come over the **Golden Gate Bridge** (southbound toll $3).

> **Airport: San Francisco International** (SFO; ☎650-821-8211; ground transportation info 650-821-2732; www.flysfo.com), 15 mi. south of downtown via U.S. 101. **Bay Area Rapid Transit** (BART; ☎989-2278; www.bart.gov), runs M-F 4am-midnight, Sa 6am-midnight, Su 8am-midnight. $5 to downtown.

> **Trains: Amtrak** (☎800-872-7245). Connects from both Oakland and Emeryville to downtown SF ($3.50-7). To **Los Angeles** (8-12hr., 5 per day, $50). **Caltrain** (☎800-660-4287; www.caltrain.org), at 4th and King St. in SoMa (operates M-F 5am-midnight, Sa-Su unreliable due to construction), is a regional commuter train that runs south to Palo Alto ($4.50, seniors and under 12 $2.25) and San Jose ($5.25/$2.50), making many stops along the way.

> **Buses: Greyhound** runs buses from the **Transbay Terminal,** 425 Mission St. (☎495-1575), between Fremont and 1st St. downtown. To **Los Angeles** (8-12hr., 25 per day, $45) and **Portland** (14-20hr., 8 per day, $66). **Golden Gate Transit** (Marin County, ☎923-2000; www.goldengate.org), **AC Transit** (East Bay, ☎510-817-1717), and **SamTrans** (San Mateo County) also stop at the terminal.

✗ ORIENTATION

NEIGHBORHOODS

San Francisco's diverse neighborhoods are loosely organized along a few central arteries. **Market Street** runs on a diagonal from the Ferry Building through downtown and all the way to the Castro.

Retail-heavy **Union Square,** the center of downtown, is just north of Market St. North of Union Square, **North Beach,** a historically Italian area, overflows with restaurants and cafes in the northeastern corner of the peninsula, while **Chinatown** is the largest Chinese community outside of Asia. The skyscrapers of the **Financial District** crowd east toward the **Embarcadero** and west to the high-culture **Civic Center,** which lines Market St. and is bounded on the west by wide Van Ness Ave. Between Union Sq. and Civic Center is the **Tenderloin,** where—despite attempts at urban renewal—drugs, crime, and homelessness prevail. Northwest of Union Sq., old money presides on ritzy **Nob Hill,** newer money walks its dogs on **Russian Hill,** and Fillmore St. leads north to the Victorians of **Pacific Heights,** as well as the few *udon*-filled blocks of **Japantown.**

South of Market St. to the east, the **South of Market Area (SoMa)** holds museums near 3rd St. and thumping clubs scattered among industrial buildings down to 14th St. To the southwest of SoMa, the trendy **Mission,** largely populated by Latino residents during the day and super-hip barhoppers by night, takes over south of 14th St., merging into the diners and cafes of the **Castro,** a legendary gay neighborhood. To the south, **Bernal Heights** and **Noe Valley** are largely residential.

Vast **Golden Gate Park** dominates the western half of the peninsula, surrounded by the former hippie haven of the **Haight** to the east and the residential and largely Asian **Richmond District** to the north. **Lincoln Park** reaches westward to the ocean, connecting to Ocean Beach at the foot of Golden Gate Park. The majestic **Golden**

Gate Bridge stretches over the bay from the **Presidio** in the city's northwest corner. The posh stucco of the **Marina**, cultural **Fort Mason**, and touristy **Fisherman's Wharf** line the north shore of the peninsula. **Alcatraz** sits isolated in the bay.

⬛ LOCAL TRANSPORTATION

San Francisco Municipal Railway (MUNI; ☎673-6864; www.sfmuni.com) is a system of buses, cable cars, subways, and streetcars and is the most efficient way to get around the city. Runs daily 6am-1am. $1.25, seniors and ages 5-17 $0.35. **MUNI passports** are valid on all MUNI vehicles (1-day $9, 3-day $15, 7-day $20). Weekly pass ($12) is valid for a single work week but requires an additional $1 to ride the cable cars. Wheelchair access varies among routes; all below-ground stations, but not all above-ground sites, are accessible.

Cable cars: Noisy, slow, and usually crammed full, but charming relics. To avoid mobs, ride in the early morning. The **Powell-Mason (PM)** line, which runs to the wharf, is the most popular. The **California (C)** line, from the Financial District up through Nob Hill, is usually the least crowded, but the **Powell-Hyde (PH)** line, with the steepest hills and the sharpest turns, may be the most fun. $3, under 6 free; $1 before 7am and after 9pm. No transfers.

Bay Area Rapid Transit (BART; ☎989-2278; www.bart.org) operates trains along 5 lines connecting San Francisco with the **East Bay,** including Oakland, Berkeley, Concord, and Fremont. All stations provide maps and schedules. There are 8 BART stops in San Francisco proper. Runs M-F 4am-midnight, Sa 6am-midnight, Su 8am-midnight. $1.25-5. Wheelchair accessible.

Car Rental: City, 1748 Folsom St. (☎877-861-1312; www.cityrentacar.com), between Duboce and 14th St. Compacts $32-40 per day, $170 per week. Small fee for unlimited mileage. 21+; under 25 $8 per day surcharge. Open M-F 7:30am-6pm, Sa 9am-4pm. Additional location: 1433 Bush St. (☎866-359-1331).

Taxi: National Cab ☎648-4444. **Yellow Cab** ☎626-2345.

TIP **PREVENT RUNAWAYS.** When parking facing uphill, turn front wheels away from the curb, and, if driving a standard transmission, leave the car in first gear. If your car starts to roll, it will stop (hopefully) when the tires hit the curb. When facing downhill, turn the wheels toward the curb and leave the car in reverse. *Always* set the emergency brake.

🔢 PRACTICAL INFORMATION

Visitor Information: Visitor Information Center (☎391-2000, 24hr. info 391-2001; www.sfvisitor.org), in Hallidie Plaza, at Powell St. Open M-F 9am-5pm, Sa-Su 9am-3pm; Nov.-June closed Su.

Hotlines: AIDS Hotline, ☎863-2437. **Crisis Line for the Handicapped,** ☎800-426-4263. **Drug Crisis Line,** ☎362-3400. **Rape Crisis Center,** ☎647-7273.

Internet Access: San Francisco Public Library Main Branch, 100 Larkin St. (☎557-4400; http://sfpl.lib.ca.us), at Grove St. Open M and Sa 10am-6pm, Tu-Th 9am-8pm, F noon-6pm, Su noon-5pm. Free. Check www.cheesebikini.com for free wireless locations in SF and the Bay Area.

Post Office: Pine Station, 1400 Pine St. (☎351-2435), at Larkin. Open M-F 8am-5:30pm, Sa 8am-3pm.

Area Code: ☎415, unless otherwise noted.

CALIFORNIA

TO ALCATRAZ & ANGEL ISLAND

45 U.S.S. Pampanito

San Francisco Bay

Balcutha   Eureka   43   41   Sea Lions
47   43 1/2   Pier 39
C.A. Thayer   Hyde St. Pier   California Welcome Center   35
Aquatic Park   Ferry Terminal

Maritime Museum   The Cannery   33
FISHERMAN'S WHARF   Jefferson St.   31
Beach St.   Beach St.
North Point St.   29
Bay St.   27

TO FORT MASON & 2 (275yd)   Francisco St.   23
Chestnut St.   19
17
Lombard St.   **RUSSIAN HILL**   Lombard St.   **TELEGRAPH HILL**   15
Greenwich St.   6 Greenwich Steps   9
Filbert St.   Filbert Steps   7
Union St.   **NORTH BEACH**   Public Fishing Pier
Green St.   Green St.
Vallejo St.   Vallejo St.   9 10
Broadway   Broadway   11
Broadway Tunnel   13
Pacific Ave.   Pacific Ave.   14 Jackson St.
Jackson St.   15
Washington St.   16   17   **MARITIME PLAZA**   **EMBARCADERO PLAZA**   **Ferry Building**
Clay St.   Clay St.
Sacramento St.   **CHINATOWN**   Sacramento St.   **Embarcadero Center**
CALIFORNIA ST. LINE   **NOB HILL**   18   California St.

Pine St.   **FINANCIAL DISTRICT**   Pine St.   **EMBARCADERO**
Bush St.   19
Sutter St.   21   20
Post St.   24   25   **UNION SQUARE**   32   33   **MONTGOMERY**   **Transbay Terminal**
Geary St.   26   **POWELL-HYDE LINE**
O'Farrell St.   29 30 31   34
Ellis St.   **TENDERLOIN**   37
Eddy St.   **POWELL**   38
Turk St.   San Francisco Centre   **Sony Metreon**   40   **Moscone Center**
Golden Gate Ave.   39   **Old Mint**   42
McAllister St.   41   **South Park**   48
CIVIC CENTER   U.N. PLAZA   45
Grove St.   43   **CIVIC CENTER**   **SOUTH OF MARKET**   49
Hayes St.
Fell St.   50   **SBC Park**
51
CalTrain Depot

TO 52 (1mi)   TO SAN FRANCISCO INTERNATIONAL AIRPORT (12mi)
Downtown San Francisco

0 250 yards
0 250 meters

⌐ ACCOMMODATIONS

For those who don't mind sharing a room with strangers, many San Francisco **hostels** are homier and cheaper than most budget **hotels**. B&Bs are often the most comfortable and friendly, albeit expensive, option.

HOSTELS

San Francisco International Guesthouse, 2976 23rd St. (☎641-1411), in the Mission. No sign; look for the blue Victorian with yellow trim near the corner of Harrison St. Hardwood floors, wall tapestries, and comfortable common areas. Caters primarily to international visitors; passport "required." Free coffee and magazines. TV area, 2 kitchens, guest phones, and free Internet. 5-night min. stay. No reservations, but chronically filled to capacity. Try calling a few days ahead. Dorms $16; doubles $32. ❶

Adelaide Hostel and Hotel, 5 Isadora Duncan (☎359-1915 or 877-359-1915; www.adelaidehostel.com), at the end of a little alley off Taylor St. between Geary and Post St. in Union Sq. The bottom 2 floors, recently renovated with fresh paint and new furniture, entice an international crowd. Try to avoid the top 2 floors until they undergo the same renovations. TV and wash basin in each room. Free safe deposit. Laundry (wash $1.50, dry $1.50). 4-day max. stay. Check-out 11am. Reserve online or by phone. Dorms $22; singles and doubles from $65. ❶

Green Tortoise Hostel, 494 Broadway (☎834-1000; www.greentortoise.com), off Columbus Ave. at Kearny St. in North Beach. Fun-seeking travelers hang out amid abandoned finery in the spacious common room. Free sauna. Free Internet access. Open mic with free keg Tu. Breakfast and dinner (M, W, F) included. Lockers $1 per day; smaller free lockers under every bed. Laundry (wash $1.25, dry $0.75). Key deposit $20. 10-day max. stay. Reception 24hr. Check-in noon. Check-out 11am. Reservations recommended. 3-, 4-, 5- and 8-bed dorms $19-22; private rooms $48-60. No credit cards. ❶

Fort Mason Hostel (HI), Bldg. #240 (☎771-7277; sfhostel@norcalhostels.org), in Fort Mason. Once you enter the complex at the corner of Bay and Franklin St., the hostel is at the corner of Funston and Pope St. past the administrative buildings. Beautiful surrounding forest and wooden bunks give this 160-bed hostel a campground feel. Strictly enforced quiet hours (11pm) and no smoking or alcohol. Huge, clean kitchen, and cute cafe with vegetarian dinner. Movies, walking tours, kitchen, dining room, bike storage, lockers, and parking. Laundry (wash $1, dry $1). Check-in 2:30pm. Check-out 11am. Reserve weeks in advance. Dorms $23-29, under 13 $15-17. ❶

Interclub Globe Hostel, 10 Hallam Pl. (☎431-0540), off Folsom St. between 7th and 8th St. in SoMa. A cool hostel primarily for young international travelers. Happening common room has pool table, TV, microwave, and fridge. All rooms have private bath. Passport or out-of-state ID required. Linen $2.50. Key deposit $10. 14-day max. stay. Check-out noon. 5-bed dorms $18; doubles $45. Weekly dorms $100. No credit cards. ❶

Hostel at Union Square (HI), 312 Mason St. (☎788-5604; www.norcalhostels.org), between Geary and O'Farrell St. in Union Sq. A converted hotel, these tidy, unadorned dorm-style triples and quads are quieter than the typical hostel. Internet. $5 deposit for locker or key. Laundry (wash $1.25, dry $0.75). Reception 24hr. Check-in 2pm. Check-out 11am. Reservations recommended. 3- and 4-bed dorms $22, nonmembers $25; private rooms $60/$66. Under 13 half-price with parent. ❶

HOTELS

▨ **The San Remo Hotel,** 2237 Mason St. (☎776-8688; www.sanremohotel.com), between Chestnut and Francisco St. in Russian Hill. Small but elegantly furnished rooms with antique armoires, bedposts, lamps, and complimentary (if random) backscratchers. The hotel's penthouse offers a private garden, bathroom, and windowed rooftop room with an amazing view of the city and Coit Tower. Friendly staff. Laundry (wash $1.50, dry $1). Check-in 2pm. Check-out 11am. Reservations recommended. Singles and doubles $50-70; triples $70. Penthouse $155; reserve 2-3 months in advance. ❸

San Francisco Zen Center, 300 Page St. (☎863-3136; www.sfzc.org), near Laguna St. in the Lower Haight. Even if rigorous soul-searching is not for you, the Zen Center offers breezy, unadorned rooms whose courtyard views instill a meditative peace of mind. Breakfast included in daily rates; all meals included in the discounted weekly (10% off) or monthly (25% off) rates. Singles and doubles $66-120. ❸

Phoenix Hotel, 601 Eddy St. (☎776-1380 or 800-248-9466; www.jdvhospitality.com), at Larkin St. in the Tenderloin. Delightful cabanas-by-the-pool setup, complete with breezy courtyard and wide-leafed palm trees. Freshly painted rooms and somewhat garish comforters lovingly hearken back to the 70s. Parking included. Singles and doubles from $99, in low-season from $89. Suites $179-265. ❹

BED & BREAKFASTS

▨ **Hayes Valley Inn,** 417 Gough St. (☎431-9131, reservations 800-930-7999; www.hayesvalleyinn.com), just north of Hayes St. in Hayes Valley. European-style B&B with small rooms, shared bath, and lace curtains. All rooms have cable TV, phone, and private sink. Some smoking rooms. Breakfast of cereal, cheeses, and ham. Check-in 3pm. Check-out 11am. Reservations recommended. Singles $47; doubles $53-71. ❸

▨ **The Red Victorian Bed, Breakfast, and Art,** 1665 Haight St. (☎864-1978; www.red-vic.com), west of Belvedere St. in the Upper Haight. Inspired by the "Summer of Love," the proprietress nurtures guests with themed rooms. Breakfast included. Reception 8am-9pm. Check-in 2-5pm or by appointment. Check-out 11am. Reservations strongly recommended. Rooms $86-200. Discounts for stays longer than 3 days. ❹

The Parker House, 520 Church St. (☎621-3222 or 888-520-7275; www.parkerguesthouse.com), near 17th St. in the Castro. Extravagant and stylish, the Parker House is regularly voted best GLBT B&B in the city. Beautiful parlor, with dark wood paneling, grand piano, and flowers galore. Spa and steam room downstairs. Breakfast is served in a sunny enclosed porch overlooking rose gardens. Parking $15 per day. 2-night min. stay on weekends; 4-night min. stay some holiday weekends. Check-in 3pm. Check-out noon. Reservations recommended. Rooms from $119, with private bath from $149. ❺

◖◗ FOOD

UNION SQUARE

▨ **Millennium,** 580 Geary St. (☎345-3900), in the Savoy Hotel at Jones St. Though the award-winning menu is entirely vegan, Millennium is patchouli-free. The dark wood interior, complete with spare detailing and high ceilings, fits the high-class dining. The first restaurant in the US to feature an all-organic wine list. Elaborate entrees, such as Truffled Flageolet Gratin, average $20 and draw upon global influences. Open M-F 5:30-9:30pm, Sa-Su 5:30-10pm. Reservations recommended. ❺

Le Colonial, 20 Cosmo Pl. (☎931-3600; www.lecolonialsf.com), off Post St. between Taylor and Jones St. Le Colonial presents exquisite French-Vietnamese cuisine in a stunning French-inspired building. The veranda, with its high white adobe walls, ivy-clad lattice, and overhead heating lamps, is a perfect spot to sip signature mojitos artfully garnished with lime and kumquat ($8). Entrees $20-33. F-Sa no athletic wear or torn jeans. Open Su-W 5:30-10pm, Th-Sa 5:30-11pm; lounge open from 4:30pm. ❺

Café Bean, 800 Sutter St. (☎346-9527). A crazy cosmopolitan atmosphere and the restorative powers of Dutch pancakes ($4-7) offer jet-setting diners much-needed respite. Parisian posters, maps of Amsterdam, and German road signs hang above makeshift couches. Creative sandwiches $5-8. Internet $3 per 20min. Open M 6am-8pm, Tu-Sa 6am-7pm, Su 6am-5pm; kitchen closes M-F 2pm, Sa 4pm, Su 3pm. ❷

NORTH BEACH AND CHINATOWN

▨ **Chef Jia,** 925 Kearny St. (☎398-1626), at Pacific St. Insanely cheap and delicious food draws a local crowd. Known for lunch and dinner specials ($4.80), and the celebrated signature dishes, such as rolling lettuce chicken with pine nuts ($9). Entrees $6-10. Open M-F 11:30am-10pm, Sa-Su 5-10pm. No credit cards. ❷

▨ **L'Osteria del Forno,** 519 Columbus Ave. (☎982-1124), between Green and Union St. This picture-perfect Italian eatery features acclaimed Italian meats. Enthusiastic and devoted staff serves up terrific thin-crust pizzas (slices $2.50-3.75, whole pizzas $10-17), and focaccia sandwiches ($5-7). Salads and antipasti $5-9. Entrees $8-13. Open Su-M and W-Th 11:30am-10pm, F-Sa 11:30am-10:30pm. No credit cards. ❸

House of Nanking, 919 Kearny St. (☎421-1429), near Columbus Ave. Big portions of excellent food compensate for off-putting white tile decor and brusque service in this famous, tourist-laden Chinatown institution. Some regulars trust their server to select their meal. Entrees $8-12. Open M-F 11am-10pm, Sa noon-10pm, Su noon-9:30pm. ❸

CIVIC CENTER AND THE TENDERLOIN

▨ **The California Culinary Academy,** 625 Polk St. (☎216-4329), between Turk and Eddy St. Academy students cook behind a window visible from the high-ceilinged Carême dining room. The Tu-W *prix-fixe* 3-course lunch ($16) or dinner ($24) indulges patrons with ambitious and extremely successful culinary combinations. Wine pairings with each course are a steal at $5 total. The Th-F grand buffet lunch ($22) or dinner ($38) draws large crowds; reserve 1 week ahead. Open Tu-F 11:30am-1pm and 6-8pm. ❺

Lalita Thai Restaurant and Bar, 96 McAllister St. (☎552-5744), at Leavenworth St. Mood lighting, a beautifully elaborate water-lily mural, and a touch of plastic foliage complement the daring yet understated flavors of the menu. The $20 4-course *prix-fixe* dinner special (available before 9pm) is a favorite of theater-goers; allow 1½hr. for the entire meal. Most dinner entrees $11 (specialty entrees $15-29), with veggie options. Open M-Sa 11am-10pm. Reservations recommended, especially for weekend nights. ❸

SOMA, THE MISSION, AND THE CASTRO

▨ **Taquería Cancún,** 2288 Mission St. (☎252-9560), at 19th St. Additional locations: 3211 Mission St. (☎550-1414), at Cesar Chavez Ave.; open daily 10am-12:45am. 1003 Market (☎864-6773), at 6th St.; open daily 9am-11:45pm. So good they need three branches to meet customer demand. Delicious burritos ($4; grilled chicken upon request) and scrumptious egg dishes served with chips and salsa, small tortillas, and choice of sausage, ham, or salsa ($5). Open Su-Th 9am-1:45am, F-Sa 9am-3am. ❶

◪ **The Butler and the Chef Cafe,** 155A S. Park Ave. (☎896-2075; www.thebutlerandth-echef.com), between Bryant, Brannan, 2nd, and 3rd St. Advertising itself as San Francisco's only authentic French bistro, this stellar reproduction of a Parisian street cafe serves breakfast crepes ($4-10) and baguette sandwiches ($7). The scrumptious *Croque Mademoiselle* ($8) will have you reeling in bliss. Open Tu-Sa 8am-4:30pm. ❷

Welcome Home, 464 Castro St. (☎626-3600), near the Castro Theatre. Whether placing a doily under your milkshake ($3.75) or playfully reminding you that shakes and burgers ($8-9) were made for each other, Welcome Home's friendly waitstaff always makes sure patrons feel at home. Open M-F 8am-3pm, Sa-Su 8am-4pm. No credit cards. ❸

Nirvana, 544 Castro St. (☎861-2226), between 18th and 19th St. Greeted by a metal sculpture of Buddha and a flirty host, patrons come for Burmese cuisine with a twist. Playfully concocted cocktails such as "nirvana colada" ($8-9) complement more traditional dishes (from $8) that the gorgeous waitstaff serves up to a young crowd of local scenesters. Open M-Th 4:30-9:30pm, F-Sa noon-10:30pm, Su noon-9:30pm. ❸

Mitchell's Ice Cream, 688 San Jose Ave. (☎648-2300), at 29th St. This take-out parlor gets so busy that you have to take a number at the door. With a list of awards almost as long as the list of flavors (from caramel praline to Thai iced tea), Mitchell's will chocolate dip any scoop. Cones $2.10, pints $5.10. Open daily 11am-11pm. ❶

THE HAIGHT AND THE RICHMOND DISTRICT

◪ **Lee Hou Restaurant,** 332 Clement St. (☎668-8070), at 5th Ave. Some of the best dim sum San Francisco has to offer. The service and decor may seem basic, but Lee Hou is the rare restaurant that indulges patrons with dim sum ($1.30-3.20) so fresh that it must be made-to-order. Entrees $3-8. Open Su-Th 8am-1am, F-Sa 8am-2am. ❷

Pork Store Cafe, 1451 Haight St. (☎864-6981), between Masonic Ave. and Ashbury St. in the Upper Haight. A breakfast place that charges itself very seriously with the mission to fatten you up. The two delicious healthy options ("Tim's Healthy Thursdays" and "Mike's Low Carb Special"; each $7) pack enough spinach, avocado, and salsa to hold their own against the Piggy Special ($7). Open M-F 7am-3:30pm, Sa-Su 8am-4pm. ❷

PACIFIC HEIGHTS AND THE MARINA

◪ **La Boulangerie,** 2325 Pine St. (☎440-0356; www.baybread.com), at Fillmore St. Homesick Parisians and Francophiles migrate to this French countryside bakery for freshly baked baguettes, loaves, and rounds ($2-7) in brown wicker baskets. Friendly management serves Parisian-style *macarons* ($1.50), richly textured *cannelès* ($1.75), and the most delicious almond croissants ($2.25) this side of the Seine. Small selection of savory tarts and sandwiches ($4.25). Check the website for additional SF locations. Open Tu-Sa 8am-6pm, Su 8am-4pm. ❶

Home Plate, 2274 Lombard St. (☎922-4663), off Pierce St. in the Marina. While diners eagerly await apple buckwheat pancakes ($5.50) or homemade apricot-pistachio granola ($4.25), this inventive breakfast and lunch joint wins them over with complimentary warm scones with homemade mango or mixed fruit jam. Open daily 7am-4pm. ❶

La Méditerranée, 2210 Fillmore St. (☎921-2956; www.cafelamed.com), between Sacramento and Clay St. Additional locations: 288 Noe St. (☎431-7210), at 16th and Market St. in the Castro; 2936 College Ave. (☎510-540-7773) in Berkeley. Narrow, colorful, and bustling, La Méditerranée hearkens back to modest Greek and Lebanese traditions but adds a chic twist. Lunch specials (served until 5pm; $6-8.50) and entrees ($8-10) are light and Mediterranean-inspired. Locals gravitate toward the Middle Eastern platter ($9.75), but the filled phyllo dough ($9.25) and quiche of the day ($8.25) are also delectable. Open Su-Th 11am-10pm, F-Sa 11am-11pm. ❸

◙ SIGHTS

UNION SQUARE

When the Barbary Coast (now the Financial District) was down and dirty, Union Square's Morton Alley was dirtier. Around 1900, murders on the Alley averaged one per week and prostitutes waved to their favorite customers from second-story windows. After the 1906 earthquake and fires destroyed most of the brothels, merchants moved in and renamed the area **Maiden Lane** in hopes of changing the street's image. Today, the pedestrian-only street that extends two blocks from Union Square's eastern side is packed with big-name designer shops. Architecture enthusiasts will love the artful swirling brick design of **Xanadu Gallery,** 140 Maiden Ln., the only Frank Lloyd Wright building in SF. (☎392-9999; www.xanadugallery.us. Open M-Sa 10am-6pm.)

NORTH BEACH

WASHINGTON SQUARE. North Beach's piazza, a pretty, tree-lined lawn, fills every morning with practitioners of *tai chi*. By noon, sunbathers and picnickers take over. This was the site of Joe DiMaggio's wedding to his first wife, Dorothy Arnold (and not, as you may hear, to his second wife, Marilyn Monroe). The **St. Peter and St. Paul Catholic Church** invites tired sightseers to take refuge in its dark, wooden nave. *(666 Filbert St.)* Turn-of-the-century San Francisco philanthropist Lillie Hitchcock Coit donated the **Volunteer Firemen Memorial** after being rescued from a fire as a young girl. *(Washington Sq. is bordered by Union, Filbert, Stockton, and Powell St.)*

COIT TOWER. The Coit Tower (est. 1933) stands 210 ft. high and commands a spectacular view of the city and the bay. During the Depression, the government's Works Progress Administration employed artists to paint the inside of the dome with colorful and surprisingly subversive murals that depict laborers at work. *(MUNI bus #39. By car, follow Lombard St. to the top, where there is free 30min. parking daily 10am-6:30pm. Tower: ☎362-0808. Open daily 10am-6:30pm. Free guided tour of the murals Sa 11am. Elevator $3.75, ages 6-12 $1.50, seniors $2.50, under 6 free.)*

▧CITY LIGHTS BOOKSTORE. Beat writers came to national attention when Lawrence Ferlinghetti's City Lights Bookstore (est. 1953) published Allen Ginsberg's *Howl,* which was banned in 1956 and then subjected to an extended trial at the end of which a judge found the poem "not obscene." A glance around the store confirms the obvious radical leanings of a bookstore rooted in the subversive potential of intellectual countermovements. City Lights has expanded since its Beat days and now stocks wide selection of fiction and poetry, but remains committed to publishing young poets and writers under its own label. *(2261 Columbus Ave. ☎362-8193. Open daily 10am-midnight.)*

CHINATOWN

WAVERLY PLACE. This little alley offers offbeat architecture without the garishness of Grant Ave. The fire escapes are painted in pinks and greens and held together by railings made of intricate Chinese patterns. The alley is also home to **Tien Hou Temple,** the oldest Chinese temple in the US. *(Between Sacramento and Washington St. and between Stockton St. and Grant Ave. Tien Hou Temple at 125 Waverly Pl.)*

ROSS ALLEY. Ross Alley was once lined with brothels and gambling houses; today, it epitomizes the cramped look of old Chinatown. The narrow street has starred in such films as *Big Trouble in Little China, Karate Kid II,* and *Indiana Jones and the Temple of Doom. (Ross Alley is located off Washington St., between Stockton and*

Grant St.) Squeeze into a tiny doorway to watch fortune cookies being shaped by hand at the ■**Golden Gate Cookie Factory.** All cookies that don't meet the baker's high standards are put in big tins for free taste-testing. *(56 Ross Alley.* ☎*781-3956. Open daily 9am-8pm. Bag of cookies $3, with "funny," "sexy," or "lucky" fortunes $5.)*

CIVIC CENTER

The palatial **San Francisco City Hall,** modeled after Rome's St. Peter's Basilica, is the centerpiece of the largest US gathering of Beaux Arts architecture. *(1 Dr. Carlton B. Goodlett Pl., at Van Ness Ave.* ☎*554-4000. Open M-F 8am-8pm, Sa-Su noon-4pm.)* The **United Nations Plaza** hosts the city's **Farmers Market.** *(On Polk St. Market open in summer W and Su 5:30am-5:30pm.)* The seating in the glass-and-brass **Louise M. Davies Symphony Hall** was designed to give most audience members a close-up view of performers. Visually, the building is a smashing success, as is the **San Francisco Symphony.** *(201 Van Ness Ave.* ☎*552-8000.)* The highly regarded **San Francisco Opera Company** and the **San Francisco Ballet** perform at the recently renovated **War Memorial Opera House.** *(301 Van Ness Ave., between Grove and McAllister St.)*

NOB HILL AND RUSSIAN HILL

THE CROOKEDEST STREET IN THE WORLD. The famous curves of **Lombard Street** were installed in the 1920s so that horse-drawn carriages could negotiate the extremely steep hill. From the top, both pedestrians and passengers enjoy the view of city and harbor. *(Between Hyde and Leavenworth St., running down Russian Hill.)*

GRACE CATHEDRAL AND HUNTINGTON PARK. The largest Gothic edifice west of the Mississippi, **Grace Cathedral** is Nob Hill's stained-glass studded crown. The castings of its portals are such exact imitations of the Baptistry in Florence that they were used to restore the originals. Inside, modern murals mix San Franciscan and national historical events with saintly scenes. The altar of the AIDS Interfaith Memorial Chapel celebrates the church's "inclusive community of love." *(1100 California St., between Jones and Taylor St.* ☎*749-6300; www.gracecathedral.org. Open Su-F 7am-6pm, Sa 8am-6pm. Services: M-F 7:30, 9am, 12:10pm; Sa 9am and 3pm; Su 7:30, 8:15, 11am, 6pm. Additional services Th 5:15pm and mid-Sept. to mid-June Su 3pm. Tours M-F 1-3pm, Sa 11:30am-1:30pm, Su 12:30-2pm. Suggested donation $3.)* Outside, the neatly manicured turf and trees of **Huntington Park** are equipped with a park and playground.

PACIFIC HEIGHTS AND JAPANTOWN

Along Union and Sacramento St., Pacific Heights has the greatest number of Victorian buildings in the city. Pierce and Clay St., in particular, have an abundance of grand homes. The public library offers free tours of Pacific Heights mansions. *(www.sfcityguides.com. Tours meet in Alta Plaza atop the stairs at Pierce and Clay St. every Sa and 3rd Tu at 11am.)* **St. Dominic's Cathedral** wows visitors with its towering altar, featuring an elaborate sculpture of Jesus and the 12 apostles, and its imposing gray stone and Gothic-style facade. *(2390 Bush St., at Steiner St. Open M-Sa 6:30am-5:30pm, Su 7:30am-9pm. Mass M-F 6:30, 8am, 5:30pm; Sa 8am and 5:30pm; Su 7:30am quiet mass, 9:30am family mass, 11:30am solemn choral, 1:30pm Spanish, 5:30pm contemporary music, 9pm candlelight service.)* The **Kabuki Springs and Spa** treats its patrons to communal baths, a dry sauna, steam room, cold pool, and hot pool. *(1750 Geary Blvd., at Fillmore St.* ☎*922-6000; www.kabukisprings.com. Women Su, W, F; men M, Th, Sa; co-ed Tu. Photo ID required. Open daily 10am-9:45pm. $16, after 5pm and on weekends $20. Massages $55-130. Body treatments $50-150. Facials $75-125.)*

THE MISSION

The Mission is slowly outgrowing its reputation as one of the most underappreciated neighborhoods in the city. **16th Street** is perhaps the most pulsing, pluralistic, personality-filled boulevard in all of San Francisco, where shops cater to various vegetarian diets, political radicals, and literary dissenters. Founded in 1776 in the old heart of San Francisco, the **Mission Dolores** is thought to be the city's oldest building. Due to its proximity to the Laguna de Nuestra Señora de los Dolores (Lagoon of Our Lady of Sorrows), the mission became universally known as *Misión de los Dolores*. Bougainvillea, poppies, and birds of paradise bloom in its cemetery, featured in Alfred Hitchcock's 1958 film *Vertigo*. *(3321 16th St., at Dolores St. ☎ 621-8203. Open May-Oct. Su-F 9am-4:30pm; Nov.-Apr. daily 9am-4pm. $3, ages 5-12 $2. Mass in English M-F 7:30 and 9am, Sa 5pm, Su 8 and 10am; in Spanish Su noon.)* The magnificent **murals** scattered throughout the mission certainly warrant straying from the main thoroughfare. Standouts include the political murals of **Balmy Alley** off 24th St. between Harrison and Folsom St., a three-building tribute to guitar god Carlos Santana at 22nd St. and Van Ness Ave., the face of **St. Peter's Church** at 24th and Florida St., and the latest addition to the mural scene, **Mona Caron's mural** at 300 Church St., at the corner of 15th St. one block south of Market St. The mural shows the evolution of Market St. since the 1920s.

THE CASTRO

The concept, as well as the reality, of an all-queer neighborhood draws GLBT tourists and their friends to the Castro. Beyond the glitz of shimmering bodies and the gyms where they are sculpted, the Castro harbors a more playful side. A slew of kitschy stores and a contingent of rebellious youth add flair to the picture-perfect streets, where couples make a full-time job out of seeing and being seen. Trevor Hailey, a resident since 1972, leads a 4hr. **walking tour** of Castro life and history. *(☎ 550-8110; trvrhailey@aol.com. Tours Tu-Sa 10am. $45; lunch included. Reservations required.)* For architecture without the walk, head to the **Castro Theatre,** an Art Deco appropriation of a Mexican cathedral design. *(429 Castro St.)*

TWIN PEAKS

Tourist hub by day, lovebird locale by night—the lookout-turned-make-out point atop Twin Peaks offers the best views of the city. From Alcatraz to the Transamerica Pyramid to a big rainbow flag at the foot of Market St. in the Castro, all major San Francisco landmarks are on display. The peaks are located between Portola Dr., Clarendon Ave., and Upper Market St. From Noe Valley, take MUNI bus #48 to Diamond Heights. From elsewhere in the city, take MUNI bus K, L, or M to Forest Hills, then MUNI bus #36. For a scenic route by car, bike, or foot, take 17th St. to Clayton St. to Clarendon Ave. and head up Twin Peaks Blvd. to the top.

THE HAIGHT

All around Haight and Ashbury St., vestiges of the 60s exist in inexpensive bars and ethnic restaurants. Action-packed street life, anarchist literature, and shops selling pipes for, um, tobacco carry on the legacy of the free-love era. The former homes of several countercultural legends continue to attract visitors. From the corner of Haight and Ashbury St., walk up Ashbury St. to #710, just south of Waller St., to check out the house occupied by the **Grateful Dead** when they were still the Warlocks. Look across the street for the **Hell's Angels'** house. If you walk back to Haight St., go right three blocks and make a left on Lyon St. to check out **Janis Joplin's** old abode. *(122 Lyon St., between Page and Oak St.)* Cross the Panhandle, continue three blocks to Fulton St., turn right, and wander seven blocks toward the park to see where the Manson "family" planned murder and mayhem at the **Charles Manson** man-

CALIFORNIA

sion. *(2400 Fulton St., at Willard St.)* Several parks dot the Haight. You may see police lurking in the bushes, as the parks are rumored to be popular places to buy marijuana. **Buena Vista Park,** which runs along Haight St. between Central and Baker St. and continues south, resembles a jungle complete with a dense canopy. Across **Alamo Squares'** gentle grassy slope, a string of beautiful and brightly colored Victorian homes known as the **Painted Ladies** glow against the backdrop of the skyline.

GOLDEN GATE PARK

In-line skaters, neo-flower children, and sunbathers converge in this lush city oasis. The park has a municipal golf course, equestrian center, sports fields, tennis courts, and stadium. On Sundays, traffic is banned from park roads, and bicycles and in-line skates come out in full force. The **visitors center** is located in the Beach Chalet on the western edge of the park. *(☎ 751-2766. Open daily 9am-7pm.)*

GARDENS. The soil of Golden Gate Park is rich enough to support a wealth of flowers. The **Strybing Arboretum** is home to over 7000 varieties of plants, including collections from Chile, New Zealand, and the tropical, high-altitude New World Cloud Forests. The **Garden of Fragrance** is designed especially for the visually impaired; all labels are in Braille and the plants are chosen specifically for their textures and scents. Near the Music Concourse off South Dr., the **Shakespeare Garden** contains almost every flower and plant ever mentioned by the Bard. Plaques with the relevant quotations are displayed, and maps help you find your favorite hyacinths and rue. *(Open daily dawn-dusk.)* The **Japanese Cherry Orchard,** at Lincoln Way and South Dr., blooms the first week in April. Created for the 1894 Mid-Winter Exposition, the elegant **Japanese Tea Garden** is a serene collection of wooden buildings, small pools, graceful footbridges, carefully pruned trees, and lush plants. *(☎ 752-4227. Open daily in summer 8:30am-6pm; in winter 8:30am-5pm. $3.50, seniors and ages 6-12 $1.25. Free in summer 8:30-9:30am and 5-6pm; in winter 8:30-9:30am and 4-5pm.)*

LINCOLN PARK AND OCEAN BEACH

At the northwest end of San Francisco, **Lincoln Park** has spectacular views of the Pacific and the Golden Gate Bridge. The bulky patch of meandering paths and historical sights is ideal for an afternoon hike or summertime picnic. **Ocean Beach,** the largest and most popular of San Francisco's beaches, begins south of Point Lobos and extends down the northwestern edge of the city's coastline. The strong undertow along the point is very dangerous, but die-hard surfers brave the treacherous currents and the ice-cold water anyway.

GOLDEN GATE BRIDGE AND THE PRESIDIO

When John Fremont coined the term "Golden Gate" in 1846, he meant to name the harbor entrance to the San Francisco Bay. In 1937, however, the colorful name became permanently associated with Joseph Strauss's engineering masterpiece—the **Golden Gate Bridge.** Built for only $35 million, the bridge stretches across 1¼ mi. of ocean, its towers looming 65 stories above the bay. It can sway up to 27 ft. in each direction during high winds. On sunny days, hundreds of people take the 30min. walk across the bridge. The views from the bridge are amazing, especially from the Vista Point at the Marin end of the bridge. To see the bridge itself, it's best to get a bit farther away. Fort Point and Fort Baker in the Presidio, Land's End in Lincoln Park, Mt. Livermore on Angel Island, and Hawk Hill off Conzelman Rd. in the Marin Headlands all offer spectacular views of the bridge on clear days. *(MUNI #28 and 29 buses take passengers to the bridge. By car, take Lincoln Blvd.)*

When Spanish settlers forged their way up the San Francisco peninsula from Baja California in 1769, they established *presidios,* or military outposts, as they went. San Francisco's **Presidio,** the northernmost point of Spanish territory in

Appearances can be deceiving: take the state of sexuality in America. Take a nation founded by Puritans whose descendents now find themselves possessed of the right to receive unsolicited pornographic e-mail of every persuasion while sex between men and oral sex (of any kind) is still illegal in a number of states. The 1960s may have encouraged us to assume that the freedoms for which America was founded must extend fully into the realms of gender, sex, and sexuality. But the whole world has yet gone queer, especially not in America. Still, a widening range of sexual practices and identities continue to fascinate American audiences of an ever-widening variety of media. How can we tell progress from mere publicity?

The new millennium has seen changes in thinking about gender and sexuality, changes improbable—even unimaginable—a decade ago. Sodomy laws are being struck down all over the country as gay marriage and domestic partnership struggle into law in Massachusetts, Vermont, and elsewhere. Gay, lesbian, and other queer sexualities are no longer just cool but a new form of salvation. Queer has gone from edgy to mainstream, from risqué to right around the corner in record time. From *Will and Grace* to *The L Word, Queer as Folk,* and *Boy Meets Boy,* television is scrambling to stay ahead of the queer curve. MTV, it is reported, is already developing a queer television network. In such a climate, the transgender fistfights and bisexual recriminations of the *Jerry Springer* show seem ever less provocative.

If queer sexualities become increasingly *de rigueur*, heterosexuality increasingly seeks its image in bent lenses. A growing tolerance—even desire—for contact with the sexual fringe may explain the birth of new identities such as the "metrosexual," a term reserved for heterosexual men with good grooming and a sense of style. It may not be new to seek style somewhere over the rainbow but queer style advice has been powerfully codified by the insipid if influential *Queer Eye for the Straight Guy,* which seems to exist for the sole purpose of satisfying the desires of women across the United States who long for boyfriends that dress well, clean up their own messes, and tinker with interior decorating. The popular HBO series *Sex and the City* has, however frivolously, exemplified another variety of metrosexuality by making its subject women's experience of sexu-

ality and urbanity. Decades after Luis Buñuel's *Belle de Jour*, sadomasochism is witnessing a heterosexual renaissance in films like *Secretary*, as the language of bondage and discipline becomes even more acceptably sexy. If anything, heterosexuality, forced to question itself in the light of queer chic, has remade itself in the image of previously subaltern sexualities.

When supermodels play lesbian serial killers (see Charlize Theron's Oscar-winning performance in *Monster*), when Oscars are won for gender ambiguity (see Hilary Swank in *Boys Don't Cry*), and when prominent heterosexual actors clamber for a good, meaty gay role (see Ang Lee's upcoming *Brokeback Mountain*), one wonders where the radical energy of sexuality has gone. That is, this "re-invention" of heterosexuality may be more posture than politics, bringing increased sexual freedom to neither queer nor straight sexuality. Visibility and media exposure may reap benefits for those of all sexual orientations and persuasions. But with the proliferation of a candy store full of acts and identities also comes intense commodification. Sex still sells, of course, but we notice an ever-increasing demand for an expanding smorgasbord of sexualities, as femmes, fetishists, and even furbies, march through our living rooms on network news and nightly dramas. And let's not forget the almost unlimited resources available online—from information to community, from pop-up porn to chat rooms, web cruising, and virtual sex.

Where then are the promises of sexual revolution? San Francisco and New York City are still, to some extent, sexual playgrounds while the murder of Matthew Shepherd—crucified on a fence in Laramie, WY for being gay—is not so distant a memory. Gender ambiguity can be chic but it can also be deadly, as the murders of Brandon Teena in Falls City, NE and, more recently, Eddie "Gwen" Araujo, just 30 miles from San Francisco, make clear. Gay marriage may bring "equal rights" but the desire for its legitimacy may also hamper efforts to redefine—for everyone—what partnerships can be. AIDS continues to spread alarmingly both globally and nationally, in both straight and queer populations. It appears that sexuality in America is defined only by its irresolvable tensions: is America a sexual backwater and lingering Puritan enclave or a virtual playground of endless pleasures?

Joseph A. Campana, Jr. is Ph.D. in Renaissance English Literature and currently teaches at Kenyon College in Ohio.

North America, was dedicated in 1776. The settlement was passed to the US as part of the 1848 Treaty of Guadalupe Hidalgo. It is now part of the **Golden Gate National Recreation Area (GGNRA),** run by the National Park Service.

MARINA AND FORT MASON

PALACE OF FINE ARTS. With its open-air domed structure and curving colonnades, the ▨**Palace of Fine Arts** is one of the best picnic spots in the city. It was originally built to commemorate the opening of the Panama Canal and testify to San Francisco's recovery from the 1906 earthquake. Shakespearean plays are often performed here during the summer. *(On Baker St., between Jefferson and Bay St. next to the Exploratorium. Open daily 6am-9pm. Free.)* The **Palace of Fine Arts Theater,** located behind the rotunda, also hosts various dance and theater performances and film festivals. *(☎ 563-6504; www.palaceoffinearts.com. Call for shows, times, and ticket prices.)*

FORT MASON. Fort Mason Center is home to some of the most innovative and impressive cultural museums and resources in San Francisco. The outstanding attractions seem to remain unknown to most travelers, making it a quiet waterfront counterpart to the tourist blitz of Fisherman's Wharf. On the first Wednesday of every month all museums are free and open until 7pm. The grounds are also the headquarters of the Golden Gate National Recreation Area. *(The park is at the eastern portion of Fort Mason, near Gashouse Cove. ☎ 441-3400, ext. 3; www.fortmason.org.)*

FISHERMAN'S WHARF AND THE BAY

Piers 39 through 45 provide access to San Francisco's most famous and touristy attractions. Easily visible from boats and the waterfront is Alcatraz Island.

ALCATRAZ. In its 29 years as a maximum-security federal penitentiary, **Alcatraz** harbored a menacing cast of characters, including Al "Scarface" Capone, George "Machine Gun" Kelly, and Robert "The Birdman" Stroud. There were 14 separate escape attempts—some desperate, defiant bolts for freedom, others carefully calculated and innovative. Only one man is known to have survived crossing the bay; he was recaptured. On the Rock, the cell-house audio tour takes you back to the infamous days of Alcatraz. A **Park Ranger guided tour** can take you around the island and through its 200 years of occupation, from a hunting and fishing ground for Native Americans to a Civil War outpost to a military prison, a federal prison, and finally a birthplace of the Native American civil rights movement. Now part of the Golden Gate National Recreation Area, Alcatraz is home to diverse plants and birdlife. *(The Blue and Gold Fleet (☎ 705-8200, tickets 705-5555; www.blueandgoldfleet.com) runs to Alcatraz (14 per day; $11 round-trip, with audio tour $16; over 62 $9.75/ $15, ages 5-11 $8.25/$11). Ticket lines can be painfully long. Often sells out in summer. Reserve at least a day and preferably a week in advance.)*

GHIRARDELLI SQUARE. Chocolate-lovers' heaven, Ghirardelli Sq. houses a mall in what used to be a chocolate factory. Everyone's got a golden ticket to the **Ghirardelli Chocolate Manufactory,** with its vast selection of chocolatey goodies, and the **Ghirardelli Chocolate Shop and Caffe,** which sells drinks, frozen yogurt, and a smaller selection of chocolates. Both hand out **free samples** of chocolate, but the Caffe is often less crowded. *(Mall: 900 N. Point St. ☎ 775-5500; www.ghirardellisq.com. Stores open in summer M-Sa 10am-9pm, Su 10am-6pm. Manufactory: ☎ 771-4903. Open Su-Th 9am-11pm, F-Sa 9am-midnight. Soda fountain: Open Su-Th 10am-11pm, F-Sa 10am-midnight. Chocolate Shop and Caffe: ☎ 474-1414. Open daily May-Dec. 7am-8pm; Jan.-Apr. 7am-7pm.)*

🏛 MUSEUMS

🔳 **San Francisco Museum of Modern Art (SFMOMA),** 151 3rd St. (☎357-4000; www.sfmoma.org), between Mission and Howard St. This black-and-gray marble-trimmed museum houses 5 spacious floors of art, with an emphasis on design. It houses the largest selection of 20th-century American and European art this side of New York City. 4 free gallery tours per day. Open June-Aug. M-Tu and F-Su 10am-6pm, Th 10am-9pm; Sept.-May M-Tu and F-Su 11am-5:45pm, Th 11am-8:45pm. $10, seniors $7, students $6, under 13 free. Th 6-9pm half-price. Free 1st Tu of each month.

🔳 **Exploratorium,** 3601 Lyon St. (☎563-7337 or 561-0360; www.exploratorium.edu), in the Marina. The Exploratorium can hold over 4000 people, and when admission is free, it usually does. Over 650 interactive displays—including miniature tornadoes, computer planet-managing, and giant bubble-makers—explain the wonders of the world. The **Tactile Dome**—a dark maze of tunnels, slides, nooks, and crannies—refines your sense of touch. Open Tu-Su 10am-5pm. $12; students, seniors, disabled, and ages 13-17 $9.50; ages 12-17 $8; under 4 free. Free first W of each month. Tactile Dome $15, reservations recommended.

California Palace of the Legion of Honor (☎863-3330; www.legionofhonor.org), in the middle of Lincoln Park. A copy of Rodin's *Thinker* beckons visitors into the courtyard, where a little glass pyramid recalls the Louvre. A thorough catalogue of great masters, from the medieval to the modern, hangs inside. Other draws include a pneumatically operated 4500-pipe organ, played in free recitals weekly (Sa-Su 4pm). Outside the Palace, a **Holocaust memorial** depicts a mass of emaciated victims with a single survivor looking out through a barbed-wire fence to the Pacific. Open Tu-Su 9:30am-5pm. $8, seniors $6, under 17 $5, under 12 free. $2 discount with MUNI transfer; Tu free.

California Academy of Sciences, 875 Howard St. (☎750-7145; www.calacademy.org), between 4th and 5th St. in SoMa. Temporary location (+until 2008) of the Golden Gate Park museums. The **Steinhart Aquarium,** home to over 600 aquatic species, is more lively than the **Natural History Museum.** Open daily 10am-5pm. $7; seniors, students, and ages 12-17 $4.50; ages 4-11 $2. Free 1st W of each month.

Yerba Buena Center for the Arts, 701 Mission St. (☎978-2787; www.yerba-buenaarts.org). The center runs an excellent theater and gallery space, with programs emphasizing performance, film, viewer involvement, and local multicultural work. It is surrounded by the **Yerba Buena Rooftop Gardens,** a vast expanse of concrete, fountains, and foliage. Open Su and Tu-W noon-5pm, Th-Sa noon-8pm. Free tours 1st Th of each month 6pm. $6, seniors and students $3. Free 1st Tu of each month, students and seniors free every Th.

ZEUM, 221 4th St. (☎777-2800; www.zeum.org), at Howard St. Within the Yerba Buena gardens, this "art and technology center" is aimed at children and teenagers. The best draw is the 1906 carousel. Open in summer Tu-Su 11am-5pm; low-season W-Su 11am-5pm. $7, seniors and students $6, ages 5-18 $5. Carousel open daily 11am-6pm. $2 for 2 rides.

Museum of Craft and Folk Art, Fort Mason Bldg. A, 1st fl. (☎775-0991; www.mocfa.org). The MOCFA brings together a fascinating collection of crafts and functional art (vessels, clothing, furniture, and jewelry) from past and present, near and far, showcasing everything from 19th-century Chinese children's hats to war-time commentary made through light bulbs. Open Su and W-F noon-5pm, Sa 10am-5pm. $4, seniors and ages 12-17 $3, under 12 free. Free 1st W of each month.

African-American Historical and Cultural Society Museum, Fort Mason Bldg. C, #165 (☎441-0640). Displays historic artifacts and artwork, modern works, and a permanent collection by local artists. Open W-Su noon-5pm. $3, seniors and ages 12-17 $1, under 12 free. Free 1st W of each month.

CALIFORNIA

San Francisco Art Institute, 800 Chestnut St. (☎771-7020 or 800-345-7324; www.sfai.edu), in North Beach. The oldest art school west of the Mississippi, the Institute is lodged in a converted mission and has produced a number of American greats including Mark Rothko, Ansel Adams, Imogen Cunningham, Dorothea Lange, and James Weeks. To the left as you enter is the **Diego Rivera Gallery,** 1 wall of which is covered by a huge 1931 Rivera mural. The gallery hosts weekly student exhibits with receptions Tu 5-7pm. Open daily June-Aug. 9am-8pm; Sept.-May 9am-9pm. Professional exhibits are housed in the **Walter and McBean Galleries.** Open Tu-Sa 11am-6pm.

🎭 ENTERTAINMENT

MUSIC

Look for the latest live music listings in *S.F. Weekly* and *The Guardian.* Hardcore audiophiles might snag a copy of *Bay Area Music (BAM).*

▩ **Bottom of the Hill,** 1233 17th St. (☎626-4455, 24hr. info 621-4455; www.bottomofthehill.com), between Missouri and Texas St., in Potrero Hill. Intimate rock club with tiny stage is the best place to see up-and-comers; The White Stripes, Incubus, and Kid Rock all passed through here. Most Su afternoons feature local bands and all-you-can-eat barbecue for $5-10 (from 4pm, music from 5pm). Usually 21+, with occasional all-ages shows. Cover $6-25. Shows typically start around 8:30 or 9pm.

The Independent, 628 Divisadero St. (☎771-1421), at Hayes St., in the Lower Haight. Known for live hip-hop and everything from indie rock and punk to funk, jazz, and reggae. Cover $10-25. Box office open M-F 11am-6pm and 1hr. before the show.

Boom Boom Room, 1601 Fillmore St. (☎673-8000, bar 673-8040; www.boomboomblues.com), at Geary St., near Japantown. Once owned by John Lee Hooker, Boom Boom is known as the city's home to "blues and boogie, funk and bumpin' jazz" and features live music, often big-name acts, daily at 9pm. Beer $2.50, mixed drinks $4. Happy hour 4-7:30pm. Cover $4-10. Open M-F 4pm-2am, Sa-Su 3pm-2am.

Biscuits & Blues, 401 Mason St. (☎292-2583; www.biscuitsandbluessf.com), at Geary St., in Union Sq. This basement joint serves up Southern fare such as a spicy jambalaya, but it's the nightly live blues acts that really make things simmer. Entrees $11-16. Drinks $3-7. Happy hour until 7:30pm; $2 drafts, $4 specialty drinks. All ages. Tickets $5-20. Dinner served M-Sa 6pm, Su 5pm. Open M-Sa 6pm-1am, Su 5-10pm.

THEATER

Downtown, **Mason Street** and **Geary Street** constitute **"Theater Row,"** the city's prime place for theatrical entertainment. **TIX Bay Area,** located in a kiosk in Union Sq. on the corner of Geary and Powell St., is a Ticketmaster outlet with tickets for almost all shows and concerts in the city. Buy a seat in advance, or try for cash-only, half-price tickets on the day of the show. (☎433-7827; www.theaterbayarea.org. Open Tu-Th 11am-6pm, F-Sa 11am-7pm, Su 11am-3pm.)

▩ **Theatre Rhinoceros,** 2926 16th St. (☎861-5079; www.therhino.org), at S. Van Ness Ave., in the Mission. From the drag queen starlet to the audacious onstage lesbian lovers, the mural in the foyer says it all: queer, fabulous, diverse. The oldest queer theater in the world. $15-30; $5 off for students, seniors, and groups of 10+. Box office open W-Su 1-6pm. Call in advance for wheelchair access.

Magic Theatre, Bldg. D, 3rd fl. (☎441-8822; www.magictheatre.org), in Fort Mason. Use Fort Mason Center entrance. This daring theater stages both international and American premieres. Tickets Tu-Th $24-37; F-Su $29-41; previews $20-29. Senior and student rush tickets available 30min. before the show ($10). Shows at 8 or 8:30pm. Box office open Tu-Sa noon-5pm.

Geary Theater, 405 Geary St. (☎749-2228; www.act-sfbay.org), at Mason St., in Union Sq. Home to the renowned American Conservatory Theater, the jewel in SF's theatrical crown. The elegant theater is a show-stealer in its own right. Tickets $11-73 (cheaper for previews and on weekdays). Half-price student, teacher, and senior tickets available 2hr. before showtime. Box office open Su-M noon-6pm, Tu-Sa noon-8pm.

The Orpheum, 1192 Market St. (☎512-7770; www.bestofbroadway-sf.com), at Hyde St., near the Civic Center. Hosts the big Broadway shows. The Orpheum box office also serves two sister theaters in the area: **Golden Gate Theatre,** 1 Taylor St., at Market St.; and **Curran Theatre,** 445 Geary St. Box office open M 10am-6pm, Tu-Sa 10am-8:30pm; on show days also Su 11am-7pm.

DANCE

▨ **Alonzo King's Lines Contemporary Ballet,** 26 7th St. (☎863-3040; www.linesballet.org), at Market St., in Civic Center. One of San Francisco's premier dance companies, specializing in modern and contemporary ballet. Dancers combine elegant classical moves with athletic flair to the music of great living jazz and world music composers. 2-week fall season and 1-week spring season are performed at the Yerba Buena Center for the Arts. Tickets $20-50.

San Francisco Ballet (☎865-2000; www.sfballet.org), in the Opera House in Civic Center. Season runs Feb.-May. Tickets from $30; available online or by phone M-F noon-4pm. Box office open from noon on performance days only. Discounted standing-room-only tickets at the Opera House 2hr. before performances.

SPORTS

The **San Francisco Giants** (☎800-734-4268, tickets 510-762-2277; www.sfgiants.com) play baseball at the newly opened ▨**SBC Park** (formerly Pac Bell Park) in SoMa, near the water off Townsend St. Most games sell out before the season starts, except for 500 seats reserved for day-of-game sale. (Tickets $10-42. Tours of the park $10.) The NFL's **49ers** (☎468-2249; www.49ers.com) still play at the windy **Candlestick Park** (☎467-1994). Now officially called **3COM Park,** the stadium is 8 mi. south of the city with its own exit off U.S. 101. MUNI offers express roundtrip service to the park via the 9x, 28x, and 47x buses (www.sfmuni.com; $6; seniors, disabled, and youth $4; with a MUNI pass $3; under 5 free).

❀ FESTIVALS

Cultural, ethnic, and queer festivals take place year-round in San Francisco. The High Holy Day of the queer calendar, ▨**Pride Day** celebrates with a parade and events downtown starting at 10:30am. (☎864-3733; www.sfpride.org; last week of June.) The leather-and-chains gang lets it all hang out at the **Folsom Street Fair,** Pride Day's ruder, raunchier, rowdier little brother. (On Folsom St. between 7th and 11th St. ☎861-3247; www.folsomstreetfair.com; last week of Sept.) In fall, the **San Francisco Fringe Festival** (☎931-1094; www.sffringe.org), beginning the first Thursday after Labor Day, is experimental theater at its finest, with over 60 international companies presenting short shows, all for less than $8. **Ghirardelli Square Chocolate Festival** (☎775-5500; www.ghirardellisq.com), in Ghirardelli Sq., makes the beginning of September chocolate heaven. Follow the drummers and dancing skeletons to **Día de los Muertos** (Day of the Dead; ☎821-1155), the festive Mexican celebration of the dead. The party starts in the evening of November 2 at the Mission Cultural Center, 2868 Mission St. at 25th St.

⚑ NIGHTLIFE

Nightlife in San Francisco is as varied as the city's personal ads. Everyone from the "shy first-timer" to the "bearded strap daddy" can find places to go on a Saturday (or Tuesday) night. The spots listed below are divided into bars and clubs, but the lines get pretty blurred in SF after dark, and even cafes hop at night. For additional information, check out the nightlife listings in the *S.F. Weekly*, *S.F. Bay Guardian*, and *Metropolitan*. **All clubs listed are 21+ only.**

BARS AND LOUNGES

▨ **Noc Noc,** 5574 Haight St. (☎861-5811), between Steiner and Fillmore St., in the Lower Haight. This lounge is the only happening place before 10pm—neo-hippies and other inheritors of the Haight aesthetic mingle at high-backed bar stools, relax cross-legged on the padded floor cushions, or otherwise ensconce themselves in dimly lit nooks and crannies. Happy hour daily 5-7pm; pints $2.50. Open daily 5pm-2am.

▨ **111 Minna St.** (☎974-1719; www.111minnagallery.com), at 2nd St., in SoMa. A funky gallery by day, hipster groove-spot by night. The bar turns club W 5-10pm for a crowded night of progressive house music. Check for openings and receptions. Cocktails and beer $4. Cover $5-15 for bands and progressive house DJs. Gallery open M-F noon-5pm. Bar open Tu 5pm-9pm, W 5pm-11pm, Th-F 5pm-2am, Sa 10pm-2am.

Lush Lounge, 1092 Post St. (☎771-2022; www.thelushlounge.com), at Polk St., in Nob Hill. Ample vegetation, sassy classic Hollywood throwback decor, and frozen margaritas ($3). Kick back as the best in 80s nostalgia, from ABBA to Madonna, streams through the speakers. Open daily 4pm-2am; in summer M-Tu from 5pm. No credit cards.

Swig, 561 Geary St. (☎931-7292; www.swig-bar.com), between Taylor and Jones St., in Union Sq. Outfitted with an intimate back room and an upstairs smoking lounge, this hip new bar has already entertained Eminem, D12, and the Wallflowers. Caters to a fashionable semi-professional crowd. Open daily 5pm-2am.

The Dubliner, 3838 24th St. (☎826-2279) between Sanchez and Church St., in Noe Valley. A grand pub and sports bar that devotes its 11 TVs to broadcasting every NFL game playing on a given day. Domestic beer $3.50, imported $4. Toasted sandwiches $4. Open M-Th 2pm-2am, F 1pm-2am, Sa noon-2am, Su 9:30am-2am (NFL season) and noon-2am (off-season); opens earlier during college football season.

CLUBS

▨ **El Río,** 3158 Mission St. (☎282-3325), between César Chavez and Valencia St., in the Mission. This club sprawls in all directions, from the chill lounge with pool table to the dance floor. The patio is center stage for young, stylin' urbanites who play cards and smoke cigars. Diverse queer and straight crowd. M $1 drinks. Tu $2 margaritas, free pool. W and Sa live Bay Area bands. Th "Arabian Nights." F world music. Su live salsa (mainly GLBT) 3-8pm; salsa lessons 3-4pm. Cover M $2, Th after 10pm $5, Su $7. Open M 5pm-1am, Tu-Sa 5pm-2am, Su 3pm-midnight. No credit cards.

Pink, 2925 16th St. (☎431-8889), at S. Van Ness Ave., in the Mission. With a new set of French owners, this venue plays it chic. Pink satin and gossamer draperies lend a lounge feel during the week but expect clubbers F-Sa. DJs spin a mix of world music, soulful house, Cuban jazz, and Afro beats. Cover $5, F-Sa $10. Open Su and Tu-Th 9:30pm-2am, F-Sa 9:30pm-3am.

The EndUp, 401 6th St. (☎646-0999; www.theendup.com), at Harrison St. in SoMa. Beautiful people inevitably end up here for euphoric after-hours fun. DJs spin progressive house for mostly straight Th KitKat, F pretty-boy Fag, and a blissful mix during popular all-day Sa-Su parties. Sa morning "Otherwhirled" party 6am. Infamous Su "T" Dance (27 years strong) 6am-8pm. Cover $10-15. Open Th 10:30pm-4am, F 10pm-6am, Sa 6am-noon and 10pm-4am, Su 6am-8pm. No credit cards.

GLBT NIGHTLIFE

■ **Divas,** 1081 Post St. (☎928-6006; www.divassf.com), at Polk St., in the Tenderloin. With a posh starlet collecting covers at the door and a savvy pin-striped madam working the bar, this full-time transgender nightclub is simply fabulous. 1st level bar, 2nd level dance floor, 3rd level TV lounge. Tu Talent (singing, comedy, lip synching); $50 prize. W-Th pole dancers. F-Sa midnight drag show. Happy hour M-F 5-7pm; $2.75 well drinks, wine, domestic beer. Cover W-Th $7, F-Sa $10. Open daily 6am-2am. No credit cards.

The Bar on Castro, 456 Castro St. (☎626-7220), between Market and 18th St. An urbane Castro staple with padded walls and dark plush couches perfect for eyeing the stylish young crowd, scoping the techno-raging dance floor, or watching *Queer as Folk* on Su. Happy hour M-F 3-8pm; beer $2.25. Su beer $1.75. Open M-F 4pm-2am, Sa-Su noon-2am. No credit cards.

Wild Side West, 424 Cortland Ave. (☎647-3099), at Wool St., in Bernal Heights. The oldest lesbian bar in SF is a friendly neighborhood favorite for women and men alike. The hidden highlight is a backyard jungle with benches, fountains, and scrap-art statues contributed by patrons. Open daily 1pm-2am. No credit cards.

THE BAY AREA

BERKELEY
☎510

Berkeley implanted itself in the nation's consciousness as a progressive leader and haven for iconoclasts in 1964, when activist Mario Savio led the UC Berkeley student body in a series of highly visible protests. While the town remains staunchly liberal, true radicals may chuckle at the irony of today's yuppified Berkeley, where polished storefronts sell organic goods to a niche market of Marxists with bourgeois incomes. Hirsute hippies stalk down Telegraph Ave., which teems with stylishly dressed down students, while the posh boutiques and pricey eateries of Shattuck Ave. and 4th St. avoid such ambiguity with an unapologetic embrace of upscale living. Berkeley's restaurants range from high California cuisine to family-run Asian takeout, and its bookstores provide the perfect material for an afternoon spent sunning in the park, making the city an ideal trip from San Francisco.

■ ∄ **ORIENTATION AND PRACTICAL INFORMATION.** Berkeley lies across the Bay Bridge northeast of San Francisco, just north of Oakland. If you're driving from SF, cross the Bay Bridge on **I-80** and take one of the four Berkeley exits. The **University Avenue Exit** leads most directly to UC Berkeley and downtown. The magnetic heart of town, **Telegraph Avenue,** runs south from the UC Berkeley Student Union, while the **Gourmet Ghetto,** on Shattuck Ave., just north of campus, has some of California's finest dining. **Bay Area Rapid Transit (BART)** has three Berkeley stops. The Downtown Berkeley station, 2160 Shattuck Ave., at Center St., is close to the western edge of campus, while the North Berkeley station, at Delaware and Sacramento St., lies four blocks north of University Ave. To get to Southern Berkeley, take the BART to the Ashby stop at the corner of Ashby and Adeline St. (☎465-2278; www.bart.gov. 20-30min. to downtown SF, $3.50.) **Alameda County Transit** city buses #15, 40, 43, and 51 run from the Berkeley BART station to downtown Oakland on Martin Luther King, Jr. Way, Telegraph Ave., Shattuck Ave., and Broadway, respectively ($1.50; seniors, disabled, and ages 5-12 $0.75; under 5 free; 1hr. transfers $0.25). **Visitor Info: Berkeley Convention and Visitor Bureau,** 2015 Center St., at Milvia St., has area maps, accommodation resources, and tons of brochures. (☎549-8710. Open M-F 9am-1pm and 2-5pm.) **UC Berkeley Visitors Center,** 101 University Hall (☎642-5215; www.berkeley.edu), at the corner of University

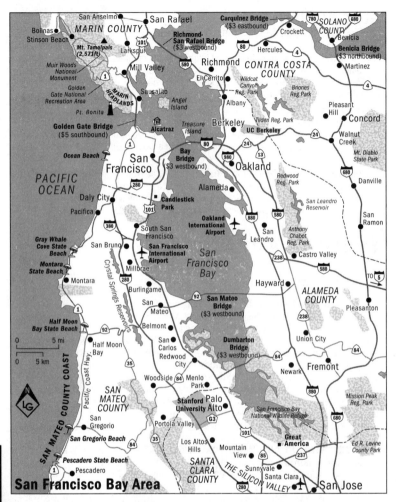

San Francisco Bay Area

Ave. and Oxford St., offers detailed maps and campus info. (Campus tours depart from the center M-F 10am, from Sather Tower Sa 10pm, Su 1pm. Open M-F 8:30am-4:30pm.) **Internet Access: Berkeley Public Library,** 2090 Kittredge St. (☎981-6100. Open M-Tu noon-8pm, W-Sa 10am-6pm.) **Post Office:** 2000 Allston Way, at Milvia St. (☎649-3155. Open M-F 9am-5pm, Sa 9am-3pm.) **Postal Code:** 94704.

⌐ ACCOMMODATIONS. There are surprisingly few cheap accommodations in Berkeley. The **Berkeley-Oakland Bed and Breakfast Network** (☎547-6380; www.bbonline.com/ca/berkeley-oakland) coordinates some great East Bay B&Bs with a range of rates (singles $85-175). No-frills motels line University Ave. between Shattuck and Sacramento St.; ritzier joints are downtown, especially on Durant Ave. **UC Berkeley Summer Visitor Housing ❸** has simple college dorms, a great location, shared baths, and free Internet access. (☎642-4108. Open June to mid-Aug. Singles $54; doubles $68; 7th night free.) The **YMCA ❷**, 2001 Allston Way, has a communal kitchen, shared bath, computer room, and TV lounge. Use of the pool and fitness facilities is included. (☎848-6800. 10-night max. stay. Reception 7am-9:30pm. 18+. Singles $39; doubles $50; triples $65.)

⬛ FOOD. Berkeley's **Gourmet Ghetto**, at Shattuck Ave. and Cedar St., is where California Cuisine began. The north end of **Telegraph Avenue** caters to student appetites and wallets, with late-night offerings of all varieties along **Durant Avenue**. If you'd rather talk to a cow than eat one, you're in luck; Berkeley does greens like nowhere else. A growing number of international establishments are helping to diversify the area. **Solano Avenue** to the north is great for Asian cuisine, while 4th Street is home to trendy upscale eats. **◪Chez Panisse ❺**, 1517 Shattuck Ave., is the birthplace of California Cuisine, opened by chef Alice Waters in 1971. Alice still prepares the nightly fixed menu (4 courses; $50-75) in the downstairs restaurant. Upstairs, the more casual cafe serves similar, but less expensive, fare. (☎548-5525, cafe 548-5049; www.chezpanisse.com. Starters $7-13. Entrees $15-20. Reservations for restaurant or cafe strongly recommended; available up to 1 month in advance. Cafe open M-Th 11:30am-3pm and 5-10:30pm, F-Sa 11:30am-3:30pm and 5-11:30pm.) **Cheese Board Pizza ❸**, 1512 Shattuck Ave., between Cedar and Vine St., prepares only one type of pizza per day (always vegetarian), and customers line up halfway down the block for a slice. (☎549-3055. Whole pizza $18, half $9, slice $2.25. Open Tu-F 11:30am-2pm and 4:30-7pm, Sa noon-3pm and 4:30-7pm.) **Café Intermezzo ❶**, 2442 Telegraph Ave., at Haste St., serves heaping salads ($3.50-7) with homemade dressing, huge sandwiches on freshly baked bread, and hot soups. (☎849-4592. Sandwiches $5. Open daily 10am-10pm. No credit cards.)

◪ SIGHTS. In 1868, the private College of California and the public Agricultural, Mining, and Mechanical Arts College united as the **University of California.** The 178-acre university in Berkeley was the first of nine University of California campuses, so by seniority it has sole right to the nickname "Cal." Campus is bounded on the south by Bancroft Way, on the west by Oxford St., on the north by Hearst Ave., and on the east by Tilden Park. Enter through **Sather Gate** into **Sproul Plaza**, both sites of celebrated student sit-ins and bloody confrontations with police. Tours leave from **Sather Tower**, the tallest building on campus; you can ride to its observation level for a great view. (Open M-F 10am-4pm, $2; tip-top is not wheelchair accessible.) **◪Berkeley Art Museum**, 2626 Bancroft Way, is most respected for its collection of 20th-century American and Asian art. BAM is also associated with the **Pacific Film Archive.** (☎642-0808; www.bampfa.berkeley.edu. Open W and F-Su 11am-5pm, Th 11am-7pm. $8; students, seniors, disabled, and ages 12-17 $5. First Th of each month free.) You haven't really visited Berkeley until you've been on **Telegraph Avenue**, lined with a motley assortment of cafes, bookstores, and used clothing and record stores. In the pine and eucalyptus forests east of the city lies beautiful **Tilden Regional Park.** By car or bike, take Spruce St. to Grizzly Peak Blvd. to Canon Ave. Hiking, biking, running, and riding trails criss-cross the park and provide impressive views of the Bay Area. Inside the park, the small, sandy beach at **Lake Anza** is a popular swimming spot during the hottest summer days. (☎843-2137. Open in summer daily 11am-10pm. $3.50, seniors and children $2.50.)

◪ NIGHTLIFE. ◪Jupiter, 2181 Shattuck Ave., near the BART station, houses a huge beer garden and offers live music and terrific pizza for $8. (☎843-8277. Open M-Th 11:30am-1am, F 11:30am-2am, Sa noon-2am, Su noon-midnight.) **Blakes**, 2367 Telegraph Ave., near Durant Ave., is a jam-packed and unabashed meat market.

CALIFORNIA

(☎848-0886. Local bands W-Sa. Happy hour M-F 4-7pm; $0.75 off pints and cocktails. Drink specials 9pm-midnight; W $1 PBR, Th $2.75 well drinks. Cover $2-12. Open M-Sa 11:30am-2am, Su noon-1am.) The boisterous and friendly **Triple Rock Brewery**, 1920 Shattuck Ave., north of Berkeley Way, was the first of Berkeley's many brewpubs. (☎843-2739. Award-winning Red Rock Ale $3.75. Open Su-W 11:30am-midnight, Th-Sa 11:30am-1am. Rooftop garden closes 10pm, kitchen closes Su-W 10pm, Th-Sa 11:30pm.)

MARIN COUNTY ☎415

Just across the Golden Gate Bridge, the jacuzzi of the bay—Marin (muh-RIN) County—bubbles over with enthusiastic residents who casually blend the chic and the radical. Marin is strikingly beautiful, politically liberal, and visibly wealthy. On the county's west side, the cathedral stillness of ancient redwoods, sweet smell of eucalyptus (though not a native species), brilliant wildflowers, high bluffs, and crashing surf converge along Hwy. 1.

█ TRANSPORTATION

Buses: Golden Gate Transit (☎455-2000, in SF 923-2000; www.goldengate.org), provides bus service between San Francisco and Marin County via the Golden Gate Bridge, as well as local service in Marin ($2). **West Marin Stagecoach** (☎526-3239; www.marin-stagecoach.org) provides weekday service connecting West Marin communities to the rest of the county. Stops include: Muir Beach, Pt. Reyes Station, Samuel P. Taylor Park, and Stinson Beach. Call for schedules and routes. $1.50.

Ferries: Golden Gate Ferry (☎455-2000) runs from San Francisco to the Sausalito terminal at the end of Market St. ($5.60, under 18 $4.20, seniors and disabled $2.80), and to the Larkspur terminal (M-F $3.10/$2.35/$1.55; Sa-Su $5.30/$4/$2.65). **Blue and Gold Fleet** (☎773-1188) runs ferries from Pier 41 at Fisherman's Wharf to Sausalito and Tiburon ($6.75, under 5 free). Offices open M-F 6am-8pm, Sa-Su 7am-8pm.

Taxi: Belaire Cab Co. ☎388-1234.

Bike Rental: Cycle Analysis (☎663-9164; www.cyclepointreyes.com), a trailer in the empty, grassy lot at 4th and Main St. off Hwy. 1 in **Point Reyes Station.** Rents unsuspended bikes ($10 per hr., $32 per day), front-suspension mountain bikes ($12/$35), and child trailers ($30 per day). Helmets included. Emergency repairs and advice for self-guided tours. Open M-Th by appointment, F-Su 10am-5pm.

█ ORIENTATION AND PRACTICAL INFORMATION

The Marin peninsula lies at the northern end of the San Francisco Bay and is connected to the city by **U.S. 101** via the **Golden Gate Bridge.** U.S. 101 extends north inland to Santa Rosa and Sonoma County, while **Route 1** winds north along the Pacific coast. The **Richmond-San Rafael Bridge** connects Marin to the East Bay via **I-580.** Gas is scarce and expensive in West Marin, so fill up in town before you head out for the coast. Drivers should exercise caution in West Marin, where roads are narrow, sinuous, and perched on the edges of cliffs.

Visitor Information: Marin County Visitors Bureau, 1013 Larkspur Landing Cr. (☎925-2060; www.marincvb.org), near the Sir Francis Drake Blvd. exit off U.S. 101, by the ferry terminal. Open M-F 9am-5pm.

Park Visitor Information:

Point Reyes National Seashore Headquarters (also referred to as Bear Valley Visitor Center; ☎464-5100; www.nps.gov/pore), on Bear Valley Rd., ½ mi. west of Olema. Open M-F 9am-5pm, Sa-Su and holidays 8am-5pm.

Pan Toll Ranger's Station, 801 Panoramic Hwy. (☎388-2070), in Mt. Tamalpais State Park, about 2½ mi. inland from Stinson Beach. Bus #63 stops on the weekends (about 5 per day). Open daily June-Aug. 9am-6pm; Sept.-May intermittently.

Muir Woods National Monument Visitors Center (☎388-2596; www.nps.gov/muwo), near the entrance to Muir Woods. Muir Woods trail map $2 (free download on website). Open daily Sept.-May 9am-6pm; June-Aug. 8am-8pm.

Marin Headlands Visitors Center, Bldg. 948, Fort Barry (☎331-1540), at Bunker and Field Rd. The center is also a museum. Open daily 9:30am-4:30pm. Wheelchair accessible.

Post Office: 15 Calle del Mar (☎868-1504), at Shoreline Hwy. in Stinson Beach. Open M-F 8:30am-5pm. **Postal Code:** 94970.

▐ ACCOMMODATIONS

▨ **West Point Inn** (info ☎388-9955, reservations 646-0702), on Mt. Tamalpais, 2 mi. up Stage Rd. Park at the Pan Toll Ranger Station ($6, seniors $5) and hike or bike up. Not the lap of luxury, but one hell of an experience. Propane-generated heat, light, and refrigeration; no other electricity. Bring your own linens, sleeping bags, food, and flashlight. 7 private rooms, 5 private cabins, and a well-equipped shared kitchen. Reservations required. Sa vacancies are rare. Closed Su-M nights. $35, under 18 $18, under 5 free. ❷

Point Reyes Hostel (HI; ☎663-8811; norcalhostels.org), just off Limatour Rd. 2 mi. from Limatour beach in the Point Reyes National Seashore. Miles from civilization, this excellent hostel provides shelter and solace in the wilderness. Linen $1; sleeping bags encouraged. Towels $1. Check-in 4:30-9:30pm. Check-out 10am. Lockout 10am-4:30pm. Dorms $16, under 17 $10. ❶

The Headlands (☎331-1540; www.nps.gov/goga/camping/index.htm) offers 3 small walk-in campgrounds with 11 primitive campsites for individual backpackers and small groups. No water. No fires or pets allowed. Showers and kitchen ($2 each) at Headlands Hostel. Free cold showers at Rodeo Beach. 3-day max. stay per site; 9-day max. stay per year. Reserve up to 90 days in advance. All individual sites free with a permit from the Marin Headlands Visitors Center (see above). ❶

▐ FOOD

Marinites take their fruit juices, tofu, and double-shot cappuccinos very seriously; restaurateurs know this, and raise both alfalfa sprouts and prices.

▨ **Venice Gourmet Delicatessen,** 625 Bridgeway (☎332-3544; www.venicegourmet.com), in Sausalito. Serves a wide variety of sandwiches ($3.75-6.50) and side dishes ($1.50-5) in a Mediterranean-style marketplace. Waterside seating with a stunning view of the San Francisco skyline across the bay. Open daily 9am-6pm; summer weekends until 7pm. ❷

Avatar's Punjabi Burrito, 15 Madrona St. (☎381-8293), in Mill Valley. Take chickpeas, rice, chutney, yogurt, and spice; add tofu and meats; and wrap in yummy Indian flatbread, for an inspired and filling meal. Burritos $5.50-8.50. Rice plates, salads, and mango *lassi* also available. Open M-Sa 11am-8pm. ❷

Bubba's Diner, 566 San Anselmo Ave. (☎459-6862), in San Anselmo. A local favorite that serves all the essentials. All-day breakfast menu, including "chocoholic" pancakes ($8). Open M and W-F 9am-9pm, Sa-Su 8am-9pm. ❸

◐ SIGHTS

Marin's proximity to San Francisco makes it a popular daytrip destination. Almost everything worth seeing or doing in Marin is outdoors. An efficient visitor can hop between parks and enjoy several short hikes along the coast and through the redwood forests in the same day, topping it off with dinner in one of the small cities.

CALIFORNIA

POINT REYES NATIONAL SEASHORE

Surrounded by nearly 100 mi. of isolated coastline, Point Reyes National Seashore is a wilderness of pine forests, chaparral ridges, and grassy flatlands. (Hwy. 1 provides direct access to the park from the north or south; Sir Francis Drake Blvd. comes west from U.S. 101 at San Rafael.) Swimming is safest at **Heart's Desire Beach,** in separate Tomales Bay State Park north of the visitors center on sheltered **Tomales Bay.** To reach the dramatic **Point Reyes Lighthouse** at the very tip of the point, follow Sir Francis Drake Blvd. to its end (20 mi. from the visitors center). From December to February, migrating gray whales can be spotted from the overlook. (Lighthouse Visitors Center ☎669-1534. Open M and Th-Su 10am-4:30pm.)

MOUNT TAMALPAIS AND MUIR WOODS

Between the upscale towns of eastern Marin and the rocky bluffs of western Marin rests beautiful **Mount Tamalpais State Park** (tam-ull-PIE-us). The park has miles of hilly, challenging trails on and around Mt. Tamalpais (2571 ft.). The bubbling waterfall on Cataract Trail (off Hwy. 1, follow signs) and the Gardner Lookout on Mt. Tam's east peak are worthy destinations. (☎388-2070. Free. Parking $6, seniors $5.) Visit the Pan Toll Ranger Station, on Panoramic Hwy., for trail suggestions and biking restrictions. On weekends and holidays, bus #63 stops at the ranger station between the Golden Gate Bridge and Stinson Beach. At the center of the state park is **Muir Woods National Monument,** a 560-acre grove of old coastal redwoods. Spared from logging by the steep sides of Redwood Canyon, these massive, centuries-old redwoods are shrouded in silence. (5 mi. west of U.S. 101 on Hwy. 1. ☎388-2595. Open 8am-sunset. $3 9am-6pm, under 17 free.)

BEACHES

Sheltered **Muir Beach** is scenic and popular with families. The crowds thin out significantly after a 5min. climb on the shore rocks to the left. (Open dawn-9pm.) Six miles to the north, ◪**Stinson Beach** attracts a younger, rowdier surfer crowd, although cold and windy conditions often leave them languishing on dry land. (Bus #63 runs from Sausalito to Stinson Beach on weekends and holidays. Open 9am-1hr. after sunset.) The Bard visits Stinson Beach from July to October during **Shakespeare at Stinson.** (☎868-1115; www.shakespeareatstinson.org.) Between Muir and Stinson Beaches lies Red Rocks Beach, where many beachgoers do without their swimsuits. The beach is a secluded spot reached by a steep hike from a parking area 1 mi. south of Stinson Beach.

MARIN HEADLANDS

Fog-shrouded hills just west of the Golden Gate Bridge constitute the Marin Headlands. These windswept ridges, precipitous cliffs, and hidden sandy beaches offer superb hiking and biking within minutes of downtown SF. For instant gratification, drive up to any of the several look-out spots and pose for your own postcard-perfect shot of the Golden Gate Bridge and the city skyline.

PALO ALTO   ☎650

Palo Alto is home to **Stanford University,** founded in 1885 by Jane and Leland Stanford to honor their son who died of typhoid. The Stanfords loved Spanish colonial mission architecture and collaborated with Frederick Law Olmsted to create a Spanish-tiled sandstone campus of uncompromising beauty. Often called "a hotbed of social rest," the school has produced such eminent conservatives as Chief Justice William Rehnquist. An information booth is across from Hoover Tower (☎723-2560; open daily 9am-5pm). Free student-led tours daily 11am and 3pm.

Close to Stanford, **Coronet Motel ❸,** 2455 El Camino Real, at California St., has rather generic rooms, cable TV, pool, telephone, private baths, and kitchenettes. (☎326-1081. Check-out 11am. Singles $55; doubles $60. $5 per additional person.

Weekly rates available.) **Café Borrone ❷**, 1010 El Camino Real, offers great salads and entrees. (☎327-0830. Open M-Th 7am-11pm, F-Sa 7am-midnight, Su 8am-5pm.) Every day is a fiesta at **Nola ❸**, 535 Ramona St., thanks to the late-night menu and cocktails. (☎328-2722. Open M-F 11:30am-2am, Sa-Su 5:30pm-2am.)

Palo Alto is 35 mi. southeast of San Francisco; from the north, take **U.S. 101 S** to the University Ave. exit. Alternatively, motorists from SF can split off onto **I-280 (Junípero Serra Highway)** for a longer but more scenic route. From I-280, exit at Sand Hill Rd. and follow it to the northwest corner of Stanford University. The **Palo Alto Transit Center**, 95 University Ave., serves local and regional buses and trains. (☎323-6105. Open daily 5am-12:30am.) The transit center connects to points north via **San Mateo County buses** and to Stanford via the free **Marguerite Shuttle.**

WINE COUNTRY

NAPA VALLEY   ☎707

Napa catapulted American wine into the big leagues in 1976, when a bottle of red from the area's Stag's Leap Vineyards beat a bottle of critically acclaimed (and unfailingly French) Château Lafitte-Rothschild in a blind taste test in Paris. Napa Valley is certainly the best-known of America's wine-growing regions. Its golden hills, natural hot springs, and consistently gorgeous weather attract everyone from the well-to-do urbanite staying in a high-priced B&B to the group of tourists cruising in a rental limousine. Expect insufferable traffic congestion, especially at the south end of Napa where all the major highways meet. Regardless of tourist traffic, Napa's dense collection of vineyards promise winery after winery of intoxicating pleasure and vistas that are equally disarming.

■ ⏹ 🔁 ORIENTATION AND PRACTICAL INFORMATION

Scenic **Route 29 (Saint Helena Highway)** runs north from **Napa** through Napa Valley and the well-groomed villages of **Yountville** and **Saint Helena** (where it's called Main St.) to **Calistoga's** soothing spas. The relatively short distances between wineries can take unpleasantly long to cover on weekends when the roads crawl with visitors. The **Silverado Trail,** parallel to Rte. 29, is less crowded, but watch out for cyclists. Napa is 14 mi. east of Sonoma on **Route 12.** From San Francisco, take U.S. 101 over the Golden Gate Bridge, then follow Rte. 37 east to catch Rte. 29, which runs north to Napa.

Public Transit: Napa City Bus, or **Valley Intercity Neighborhood Express (VINE),** 1151 Pearl St. (☎800-696-6443 or 255-7631, TDD 226-9722), has a few bus services that cover the entire stretch of Napa Valley from Vallejo to Calistoga M-F 5:20am-9:20pm, Sa 6am-8:10pm, Su 8:15am-6pm. $1-2.50, students $0.75-1.80, seniors $0.50-1.25. Ask for a free transfer as you board the bus. The nearest **Greyhound** station is in Vallejo at 1500 Lemon St. (☎643-7661 or 800-231-2222).

Bike Rental: 🚲 **St. Helena Cyclery,** 1156 Main St. (☎963-7736; www.sthelenacyclery.com). Hybrid bikes $10 per hr., $30 per day; road bikes $50 per day; tandem bikes $70 per day. All bikes come with maps, helmet, and lock; hybrid and tandem with picnic bag. Reservations recommended. Open M-Sa 9:30am-5:30pm, Su 10am-5pm.

Visitor Info:

Napa Conference & Visitors Bureau, 1310 Town Ctr. (☎226-7459; www.napavalley.com/nvcvb.html). Provides free maps, info, and the useful *Napa Valley Guidebook* ($6). Ask about any specials from local businesses. Open daily 9am-5pm.

St. Helena Chamber of Commerce, 1010A Main St. (☎963-4456; www.sthelena.com). Eager to help. Open M-F 10am-5pm, Sa 11am-3pm.

Calistoga Chamber of Commerce, 1458 Lincoln Ave. (☎942-6333; www.calistogafun.com). Open M-F 10am-5pm, Sa 10am-4pm, Su 11am-3pm.

Winery Tours:

Napa Valley Holidays (☎255-1050; www.napavalleyholidays.com). Afternoon tours $75 per person, with round-trip transportation from San Francisco $85.

Napa Valley Wine Train, 1275 McKinstry St. (☎253-2111 or 800-427-4124; www.winetrain.com), offers dining and drinking on board in the style of the early 1900s, traveling from Napa to St. Helena and back. Train ride 3hr. M-F 11am and 6pm; Sa-Su 8:30am, 12:10, 5:30pm. Ticket and meal plans $35-90. Advance reservations and payments required.

Police: 1539 1st St. (☎253-4451), in Napa; 1235 Washington St. (☎942-2810), in Calistoga.

Medical Services: Queen of the Valley Hospital, 1000 Trancas St. (☎252-4411), in Napa.

Post Office: 1625 Trancas St. (☎255-0190), in Napa. Open M-F 9am-5pm. **Postal Code:** 94558.

▚ ACCOMMODATIONS

Rooms in Napa Valley go quickly despite high prices and varying quality; reserving ahead is best. Though Napa is close to the Bay Area and has the advantages of a city, smaller towns will prove more wallet-friendly. Calistoga is a good first choice; the quaint town is a short drive from many wineries and is close to Old Faithful Geyser, Petrified Forest, and Bothe-Napa State Park. It is also home to natural hot-spring spas. Campers should be prepared for intense summer heat.

▨ Golden Haven Hot Springs Spa and Resort, 1713 Lake St. (☎942-6793; www.golden-haven.com), a few blocks from Lincoln Ave., in Calistoga. Well-sized and tastefully decorated rooms. TV and private bath in all rooms. Mineral swimming pool and hot tub access. No children under 16 F-Sa. 2-night min. stay on weekends. Room with queen-size bed $89, with private sauna $149; king-size bed $99, with kitchenette $139, with private hot tub $189. Nov.-Mar. M-Th $10-40 less. ❹

Calistoga Inn and Brewery, 1250 Lincoln Ave. (☎942-4101; www.calistogainn.com), at the corner of Rte. 29, in Calistoga. 18 clean, simple, country inn rooms that barely accommodate a queen-sized bed. Shared bathrooms. Microbrewery and restaurant downstairs; open M-Th 11:30am-9:30pm, F 11:30am-10pm, Sa-Su 10am-10pm. Rooms Su-Th $75, F $110, Sa $125. ❹

Bothe-Napa Valley State Park, 3801 Rte. 29 (☎942-4575, reservations 800-444-7275; www.napanet.net/~bothe), north of St. Helena. 50 rustic sites near Ritchey Creek Canyon. Toilets, fire pits, and picnic tables at each site. Pool $3, under 17 $1. Hot showers $0.25 per 3min. Check-in 2pm. Park open daily 8am-dusk. Sites for up to 8 people and 1 vehicle $20. Picnic area day use $4. ❷

◖ FOOD

Extremely cheap eats aren't an option in Wine Country. Picnics are an inexpensive and romantic alternative—many wineries have shaded picnic grounds, but most require patronage. The **Napa Farmers Market,** 500 1st St., at Soscol Ave., offers a sampling of the valley's produce. (☎252-7142. Open Tu and Sa 7:30am-noon.)

Taylor's Automatic Refresher, 933 Main St. (☎963-3486), on Rte. 29 across from the Merryvale Winery, in St. Helena. Roadside stand dishes up burgers ($5.50-10) and super-thick milkshakes ($4.60). Outdoor seating. Open daily 11am-9pm. ❷

First Squeeze Cafe and Juice Bar, 1126 1st St. (☎224-6762), in Napa. A friendly staff serves up healthy favorites such as the Vanessa (grilled tofu with avocado on health nut bread), *huevos rancheros* ($8), or fresh fruit smoothies ($4). Beer and wine $2.50-3.50. Breakfast served until 2pm. Open M-F 7am-3pm, Sa-Su 8am-3pm. ❷

Pinot Blanc, 641 Main St. (☎963-6191), on Rte. 29, in St. Helena. All the charm of a French country inn. Dinner entrees around $17. Lunch $9-20. W "Local night" 3-course dinner $28. Free corkage. Open M-Th 5:30-9pm, F-Sa noon-5pm and 5:30-9:30pm, Su noon-3pm and 5:30-9pm. Reservations recommended W and F-Sa. ❺

🔏 WINERIES

There are more than 250 wineries in Napa County, nearly two-thirds of which line Rte. 29 and the Silverado Trail in Napa Valley. Some wineries have free tastings and some have free tours; all have large selections of bottled wine available for purchase at prices cheaper than in stores. A good way to begin your Napa Valley experience is with a tour such as the ones offered at **Domaine Carneros,** or a free tastings class, like the one on Saturday mornings at **Goosecross Cellars,** 1119 State Ln. (☎944-1986; open daily 11am-4pm; classes Sa 11am-12:30pm), in Yountville. **⬛Clos Du Val Wine Company, Ltd.,** stakes its claim with wines that age with balance and subtlety. Small, elegant grounds and plenty of name recognition attract lots of tourists. (5330 Silverado Trail, north of Oak Knoll Rd., in Yountville. ☎259-2225; www.closduval.com. Tastings $5. Free tours by appointment. Open daily 10am-5pm.) **⬛V. Sattui,** named "Best Winery in California" at the 2004 California State Fair, is one of the few wineries in the valley that only sells at its winery, which means great prices. The family-owned operation has a gourmet cheese counter, meat shop, and bakery. (1111 White Ln., at Rte. 29, in St. Helena. ☎963-7774 or 800-799-2337; www.vsattui.com. Picnic area for customers. Very popular and crowded free tastings. Open daily Mar.-Oct. 9am-6pm; Nov.-Feb. 9am-5pm.) **Robert Mondavi Winery** is massive and touristy, with a beautiful mission-style visitors complex, three tasting rooms selling by the glass ($4-15), and the atmosphere of a luxury resort. (7801 Rte. 29 , 8 mi. north of Napa. ☎963-9611 or 888-766-6328; www.robertmondaviwinery.com. Vineyard and Winery tour daily every hr. 10am-4pm $15; includes 3 tastes and hors d'oeuvres. Reserve 1hr. in advance. Open daily 9am-5pm.) **Kirkland Ranch** is a family-operated winery with windows overlooking the production facilities. True to its country-western style, the winery's walls are adorned with family pictures of cattle-herding cowboys. (1 Kirkland Ranch Rd., south of Napa off Rte. 29. ☎254-9100; www.kirklandranchwinery.com. Tours by appointment. Tastings $5. Open daily 10am-4pm.) **Niebaum-Coppola Estate Winery** was purchased by famed director Francis Ford Coppola and his wife in 1975. Restoring the historic 1880 Inglenook Chateau and Niebaum vineyards to production capacity, Coppola also added a free family history museum upstairs that contains film memorabilia, including the desk from *The Godfather* and his Oscar and Golden Globe statues. (1991 St. Helena Hwy. ☎968-1100, tours 968-1161. 4 tastes and commemorative glass $12-30. Vineyard tours daily 11am, $25; rubicon tours by reservation Th and Sa-Su 1pm, $50. Open daily 10am-6pm.)

👁 🏔 SIGHTS AND OUTDOOR ACTIVITIES

Napa's gentle terrain makes for an excellent bike tour. The area is fairly flat, although small bike lanes, speeding cars, and blistering heat can make routes more challenging, especially after a few samples of wine. The 26 mi. **Silverado Trail** has a wider bike path than Rte. 29.

CALIFORNIA

Calistoga is known as the "Hot Springs of the West." Its luxuriant mud baths, massages, and mineral showers will feel even more welcome after a hard day of wine-tasting. Be sure to hydrate beforehand; alcohol-thinned blood and intense heat do not mix. A basic package consisting of a mud bath, mineral bath, eucalyptus steam, and blanket wrap costs around $50. Salt scrubs and facials are each about $50. **The Calistoga Village Inn and Spa** gives friendly service. (☎942-0991. Mud bath $50. 50min. massage $75. Body wrap $80.) **Golden Haven** also offers full spa services. (☎942-6793. Mud bath $64. 30min. massage $48. 30min. facial $48. Prices lower in winter.)

SONOMA VALLEY   ☎707

Sprawling Sonoma Valley is a quieter alternative to Napa. Many wineries are on winding side roads rather than a freeway strip, creating a more intimate wine-tasting experience. Sonoma Plaza is surrounded by art galleries, novelty shops, clothing stores, and Italian restaurants. Petaluma, west of the Sonoma Valley, has more budget-friendly lodgings than the expensive wine country.

■ TRANSPORTATION

From San Francisco, take **U.S. 101 N** over the Golden Gate Bridge; then follow Rte. 37 E to Rte. 116 N, which turns into Rte. 121 N and crosses Rte. 12 N to Sonoma. Alternatively, follow U.S. 101 N to Petaluma and cross over to Sonoma by Rte. 116. Driving time from San Francisco is about 1-1½hr. **Route 12** traverses the length of Sonoma Valley, from **Sonoma** through **Glen Ellen** to **Kenwood** in the north. The center of downtown Sonoma is **Sonoma Plaza,** which contains City Hall and the visitors center. **Broadway** dead-ends at Napa St. in front of City Hall. Numbered streets run north-south. **Petaluma** lies to the west and is connected to Sonoma by **Route 116,** which becomes **Lakeville Street** in Petaluma.

Buses: Sonoma County Transit (☎576-7433 or 800-345-7433; www.sctransit.com) serves the entire county. Bus #30 runs from **Sonoma** to **Santa Rosa** (daily every 1-1½hr. 6am-7pm; $2.25, students $1.90, seniors and disabled $1.05, under 6 free); #44 and 48 go from **Santa Rosa** to **Petaluma** (daily; $1.90, students $1.60, seniors and disabled $0.90). Within Sonoma, county buses must be flagged down at bus stops (daily 8am-4:25pm; $1, students $0.80, seniors and disabled $0.50). **Golden Gate Transit** (from Sonoma County ☎541-2000, from SF 415-923-2000) runs buses frequently between **San Francisco** and **Santa Rosa. Volunteer Wheels** (☎800-992-1006) offers door-to-door service for people with disabilities. Open daily 8am-5pm.

Bike Rental: Sonoma Valley Cyclery, 20093 Broadway (☎935-3377). $6 per hr., $20 per day; includes helmet, lock, and bags. Open M-Sa 10am-6pm, Su 10am-4pm.

■ PRACTICAL INFORMATION

Visitor Info: Sonoma Valley Visitors Bureau, 453 1st St. E (☎996-1090; www.sonomavalley.com), in Sonoma Plaza. Maps $2. Open daily 9am-5pm. **Petaluma Visitors Program,** 800 Baywood Dr. (☎762-2785), at Lakeville St. The free visitor's guide has listings of restaurants and activities. Open daily 9am-5pm.

Police: In Sonoma ☎996-3602, in Petaluma ☎778-4372.

Medical Services: Petaluma Valley Hospital, 400 N. McDowell Blvd. (☎778-1111).

Post Office: Sonoma, 617 Broadway (☎996-9311), at Patten St. Open M-F 8:30am-5pm. **Postal Code:** 95476. **Petaluma,** 120 4th St. (☎769-5352). Open M-F 8:30am-5pm, Sa 10am-2pm. **Postal Code:** 94952.

ACCOMMODATIONS

Pickings are pretty slim for lodging; rooms are scarce even on weekdays and generally start at $85. Less expensive motels cluster along **U.S. 101** in Santa Rosa and Petaluma. Campers with cars should try the **Russian River Valley** to the west.

Sonoma Creek Inn, 239 Boyes Blvd. (☎939-9463 or 888-712-1289), west off Hwy. 12, in Sonoma. Just 10min. from the Sonoma Plaza. Bold and colorful rooms with fridge, cable TV, phone, and full bath. Rooms Su-Th $79, with patio $89; F-Sa $149/$159. ❹

Redwood Inn, 1670 Santa Rosa Ave. (☎545-0474), in Santa Rosa. At least 30min. drive from Sonoma. Comfortable, motel-style rooms with cable TV, phone, and bath. Some with kitchenette. Rooms with 1 bed $55-75, 2 beds $65-85. $5 less in winter. ❸

Sugarloaf Ridge State Park, 2605 Adobe Canyon Rd. (☎833-5712), off Rte. 12, north of Kenwood in the Mayacamas mountains. 49 sites with tables and fire rings. Arranged around a central meadow with flush toilets and running water (but no showers). In summer and fall, take advantage of Ferguson Observatory inside the park; see www.rfo.org for details. Reserve sites through ReserveAmerica (☎800-444-7275; www.reserveamerica.com). Sites $12-19. ❶

FOOD

Seasonal produce is available directly from area farms or at roadside stands and farmers markets. Those in the area toward the end of the summer should ask about the ambrosial **crane melon,** a tasty hybrid of fruits grown only on the Crane Farm north of Petaluma. The **Sonoma Market,** 520 W. Napa St., in the Sonoma Valley Center, is an old-fashioned grocery store with deli sandwiches ($5-7) and produce. (☎996-0563. Open daily 6am-9pm.) The **Fruit Basket,** 18474 Sonoma Hwy., sells inexpensive fruit. (☎996-7433. Open daily 7am-7pm.)

Maya, 101 E. Napa St. (☎935-3500; www.mayarestaurant.com), at the corner of 1st St. E in Sonoma's Town Sq. Mouthwatering Yucatan food and extensive wine and tequila menu. Margaritas $5. Entrees $10-23. Occasional live music in summer. Open M-Th 11:45am-9:30pm, F-Sa 11:45am-10:30pm, Su 4-9pm. ❹

Murphy's Irish Pub, 464 1st St. E (☎935-0660; www.sonomapub.com), tucked in an alleyway off Sonoma Plaza. Good-natured Irish staff welcomes newcomers with a perfectly pulled pint. Favorites include fish 'n' chips ($12) and any of the beers and ales. Popular open mic night on the 2nd and 4th M of each month at 8pm. Live music Th-Su 8pm. Open Su-Th 11am-11pm, F-Sa 11am-midnight. ❸

Meritage Martini Oyster Bar and Grill, 165 W. Napa St. (☎938-9430; www.sonomameritage.com), in Sonoma. This bistro serves equally well as an indulgent breakfast joint (orange brandy french toast with mascarpone $7, decadent gelato getaway $5) or trendy lounge. Lunch specials $7-10. Oyster bar $1.75-2.50 per piece; 2-person sampling platter $15. Pastas and entrees $9-20. Brunch served Sa-Su until 3pm. Open M-Th 11am-9pm, F 11am-10pm, Sa-Su 10am-10pm. ❹

WINERIES

Sonoma Valley's wineries, near Sonoma and Kenwood, are less touristy but just as elegant as Napa's. As an added bonus, there are more complimentary tastings of current vintages. **Gundlach-Bundschu,** established in 1858, is the 2nd-oldest winery in Sonoma and the oldest family-owned and run winery in the country. Delightfully fragrant wines (e.g., Tempranillo Rosé), German offerings (e.g, Gewürztraminer), and Zinfandels draw people from across the country. (2000

Denmark St., off 8th St. E. ☎938-5277; www.gunbun.com. Free wine storage cave tours Sa-Su every 30min. noon-3:30pm. Tastings $5 for 4-6 samples with the extremely personable staff. Open daily 11am-4:30pm.) ◼**Benziger,** certified as biodynamic, brings a great deal of care to the winemaking process in order to preserve the natural character of its grapes. (1883 London Ranch Rd. ☎888-490-2739 or 935-4014; www.benziger.com. Acclaimed 45min. tram ride tour through the vineyards runs in summer daily every 30min. 11am-3:30pm and includes reserve tasting and 20% off purchases; $10, under 21 $5. Self-guided tours lead from the parking lot through the vineyards and peacock aviary. Tastings of current vintage $5, estate and reserves $10. Open daily 10am-5pm. **Ledson Winery and Vineyards,** a relatively new Merlot estate, does not market its wines. The stunning French-Normandy "castle" houses a lavish parlor and an equally impressive gourmet marketplace featuring fine cheeses, chocolate wine sauces, and exclusive fruit spreads. (7335 Sonoma Hwy. ☎833-2330; www.ledson.com. Monthly events themed around holidays. Tastings $5-10. Open daily 10am-5pm.) **Buena Vista** is the oldest premium winery in the valley. Famous stone buildings are preserved just as Mr. Haraszthy built them in 1857 when he founded the California wine industry. (18000 Old Winery Rd.; take E. Napa St. from Sonoma Plaza and turn left on Old Winery Rd. ☎938-1266; www.buenavistawinery.com. Historical presentation and guided tour daily at 11am and 2pm; $15. Tastings $5; includes glass. Open daily 10am-5pm.)

◎ SIGHTS

SONOMA STATE HISTORIC PARK. Within the park, an adobe church stands on the site of the **Mission San Francisco-Solano,** the northernmost and last of the 21 Franciscan missions. Built in 1826 by Padre Jose Altimira, the mission contains a fragment of the original California Republic flag, the rest of which was burned in the 1906 San Francisco earthquake fires. *(E. Spain and 1st St., in the northeast corner of Sonoma. ☎938-1519. Open daily 10am-5pm. $2, children under 17 free. Includes admission to Vallejo's Home, Sonoma Barracks, and Petaluma Adobe.)*

JACK LONDON STATE PARK. Around the turn of the 20th century, hard-drinking and hard-living Jack London, author of *The Call of the Wild* and *White Fang,* bought 1400 acres here, determined to create his dream home. London's hopes were frustrated when the estate's main building, the Wolf House, was destroyed by arsonists in 1913. London died three years after the fire and is buried in the park, his grave marked by a volcanic boulder intended for the construction of his house. The nearby **House of Happy Walls,** built by London's widow in fond remembrance of him, is now a two-story museum devoted to the writer. Scenic trails in this area abound. *(Take Hwy. 12 4 mi. north from Sonoma to Arnold Ln. and follow signs. ☎938-5216. Park open daily 10am-7pm; in winter 10am-5pm. Museum open daily 10am-5pm.)*

THE CENTRAL COAST

The 400 mi. stretch of coastline between L.A. and San Francisco embodies all that is purely Californian—rolling surf, a seaside highway built for cruising, dramatic bluffs topped by weathered pines, self-actualizing New-Age adherents, and always a hint of the offbeat. This is the solitary magnificence that inspired John Steinbeck's novels and Jack Kerouac's musings. The landmarks along the way—Hearst Castle, the Monterey Bay Aquarium, the historic missions—are well worth visiting, but the real highlight of the Central Coast is the journey itself.

SANTA CRUZ   ☎ 831

Negotiating the liminal space between NorCal and SoCal, Santa Cruz (pop. 56,000) embraces sculpted surfers, aging hippies, freethinking students, and same-sex couples. The atmosphere here is fun-loving but far from hedonistic, intellectual but nowhere near stuffy. This small city exudes fun, whether you find it gobbling cotton candy on the Boardwalk or sipping wheatgrass at poetry readings.

▊▮ ORIENTATION AND PRACTICAL INFORMATION.

Santa Cruz is on the north tip of Monterey Bay, 65 mi. south of San Francisco. Through west Santa Cruz, Hwy. 1 becomes **Mission Street.** The **University of California at Santa Cruz (UCSC)** blankets the hills inland from Mission St. Southeast of Mission St. lies the waterfront and downtown. By the ocean, **Beach Street** runs roughly east-west. **Greyhound,** 425 Front St. (☎ 423-1800 or 800-231-2222; open daily 8:30-11:30am and 1-6:45pm), runs to: L.A. (6 per day, $44); San Francisco (4-5 per day, $11); San Jose (4-5 per day M-Th, $6). **Santa Cruz Metropolitan Transit District (SCMTD),** 920 Pacific Ave. (☎ 425-8600; www.scmtd.com; open M-F 8am-4pm), handles local transportation. (Buses run daily 6am-11pm. $1.50, seniors and disabled $0.75, under 46 in. free; day pass $4.50/$2.25/free.) Pick up the *Santa Cruz County Traveler's Guide* at **Santa Cruz County Conference and Visitor Council,** 1211 Ocean St. (☎ 425-1234 or 800-833-3494; www.santacruzca.org; open M-Sa 9am-5pm, Su 10am-4pm.) **Post Office:** 850 Front St. (☎ 426-8184. Open M-F 8:30am-5pm.) **Postal Code:** 95060.

▟▛ ACCOMMODATIONS AND CAMPING.

Santa Cruz gets jam-packed in summer, especially on weekends; room rates skyrocket and availability plummets. Always make reservations. Camping may be the best budget option. **Carmelita Cottage Santa Cruz Hostel (HI) ❶,** 321 Main St., is a 40-bed Victorian hostel. (☎ 423-8304. Chores requested. Towels $0.50. Overnight parking free, day permits $1.25. July-Aug. 3-night max. stay. Reception 8-10am and 5-10pm. Lockout 10am-5pm. Strict curfew 11pm. Call for reservations. Dorms $18; non-members $21, ages 12-17 $14, ages 4-11 $10, under 4 free.) The **Harbor Inn ❸,** 645 7th Ave., is a beautiful 19-room hotel well off the main drag. In late June, pick plums from the trees out back. (☎ 479-9731. Check-in 2-7pm. Check-out 11am. Rooms Su-Th $50-115, F-Sa $70-135.) Sleeping on the beach is strictly forbidden. ▨**Big Basin Redwoods State Park ❶,** (☎ 338-8860; www.bigbasin.org), offers great camping and breezy trails.

THE LOCAL STORY

HANGING 10 AND OTHER SURFER FAUX PAS

Brian, a 19-year-old surfer dude from San Jose, was spotted with his longboard and wetsuit at Carmel City Beach.

LG: How long have you been surfing?

A: 'Bout 12 years.

LG: And exactly how long did it take you to actually stand up on the board and "catch a wave"—is that the proper terminology nowadays?

A: No that's fine, some people still say that....And it took me a good year until I could ride a wave.

LG: But how long did it take you to even stand up on the board? [It took our researcher 2hr.]

A: I think just about anyone could do it in a day with some instruction.

LG: [Feeling validated—he said *day*] What are the big rules of surfing?

A: The biggest one is that up-wave surfers have the right of way. So, like, if someone is on a wave before you then it is his and you can't get in his way.

LG: Now getting back to the issue of jargon or slang, you said that some people will say "catch a wave." What are some other examples of contemporary surfing parlance?

A: Um, like, what do you mean?

LG: I mean, what words would you use to describe a fantastic surfing expedition? "Gnarly," "rad," "wicked"? And does anyone say "hang ten"?

A: [Pensive] I guess I say "killer" a lot and call going out to surf a "sesh" [short for session]. "Hang ten" is not something I hear.

◘ FOOD. Santa Cruz offers an astounding number of budget eateries. Fresh local produce is sold at the **farmers market** (W 2:30-6:30pm) at Lincoln and Cedar St. downtown. **Zoccoli's ❸,** 1534 Pacific Ave., is a phenomenal deli that uses only the freshest ingredients. (☎ 423-1711. Open in summer M-Sa 9am-7pm, Su 10am-6pm; low-season daily 9am-6pm.) Healthy, vegetarian Sri Lankan cuisine and incredible flatbread can be found at **Malabar ❸,** 1116 Soquel Ave. (☎ 423-7906. Open M-Th 11am-2:30pm and 5:30-9pm, F 11am-2:30pm and 5:30-10pm, Sa 5:30-9pm.)

◙ SIGHTS. Santa Cruz has a great beach, but the water is frigid. Many casual beachgoers catch their thrills on the **Boardwalk,** a three-block strip of over 25 amusement park rides, guess-your-weight booths, shooting galleries, and corn-dog vendors. It's a gloriously tacky throwback to 50s-era beach culture. Highly recommended is the **Giant Dipper,** the 1924 wooden roller coaster where Dirty Harry met his enemy in 1983's *Sudden Impact.* (Boardwalk open daily June to Sept. 6, plus many low-season weekends and holidays. $30 per 60 tickets, with most rides 4 or 5 tickets; all-day pass $26. Mini golf $5.) The **Santa Cruz Wharf,** off Beach St., is the longest car-accessible pier on the West Coast. Seafood restaurants and souvenir shops will try to distract you from expansive views of the ocean. Munch on candy from local favorite **Marini's** (☎ 423-7258) while watching sea lions hang out on rafters beneath the end of the pier.

◪ Ⓚ BEACHES AND OUTDOOR ACTIVITIES. The **Santa Cruz Beach** (Cowell Beach) is broad, reasonably clean, and packed with volleyball players. More secluded beaches line Hwy. 1. The best vantage points for **watching surfers** are along W. Cliff Dr. To learn more about surfing, stop at **Steamer's Lane,** the deep water where Hawaiian "Duke" Kahanamoku kick-started California's surf culture 100 years ago. For surfing lessons, contact the **Richard Schmidt Surf School** or ask around for him at the beach. (☎ 423-0928; www.richardschmidt.com. 1hr. private lesson $80, 2hr. group lesson $80. Lessons include equipment.)

Around the point at the end of W. Cliff Dr. is **Natural Bridges State Beach.** Only one natural bridge remains standing, but the park offers a pristine beach, awe-inspiring tidepools, and tours during **monarch butterfly** season (Oct.-Mar.). In November and December, thousands of the stunning *lepidoptera* swarm along the beach and cover the nearby groves with their orange hues. (☎ 423-4609. Open daily 8am-dusk. Parking $6, seniors $5, disabled $3.) Parasailing and other pricey pastimes are popular on the wharf. **Kayak Connection,** 413 Lake Ave., offers tours ($40-45), and rents ocean-going **kayaks** at decent rates. (☎ 479-1121. Open-deck singles $30 per day, closed-deck singles $33. Paddle, life jacket, brief instruction, and wetsuit included. Open M-F 10am-5pm, Sa-Su 9am-6pm.)

◪ NIGHTLIFE. There are comprehensive events listings in the free *Good Times* and *Metro Santa Cruz,* and in *Spotlight* in Friday's *Sentinel.* The Boardwalk bandstand offers free summertime Friday concerts around 6:30 and 8:30pm. Make it onto the Wall of Fame at **99 Bottles Restaurant and Pub,** 110 Walnut Ave., in the heart of downtown, by making it through all 99 beers. (☎ 459-9999. Happy hour M and F 4-6pm, Tu and Th 4-6pm and 10pm-1:30am; beers $3, pitchers $8.75. 21+ and appetizers only after 10pm. Open M-Th 11:30am-1:30am, F-Sa 11:30am-2am, Su 11:30am-midnight.) The mega-popular gay-straight club **Blue Lagoon,** 923 Pacific Ave., has won many awards, including "best place you can't take your parents." (☎ 423-7117. Stronger-than-the-bouncer drinks $3-4. Happy hour daily 4-9pm; $2.75 drinks. Cover $1-3. Open daily 4pm-1:30am.)

CALIFORNIA

MONTEREY   ☎ 831

Monterey (pop. 33,000) makes good on its claim to have preserved more of its heritage than any other Californian city. Although luxury hotels and tourist shops abound and the Cannery Row of Steinbeck fame has all but vanished, a number of important sites testify to the city's colorful past.

🛈 PRACTICAL INFORMATION. Monterey-Salinas Transit (MST; ☎ 899-2555; call M-F 7:45am-5:15pm, Sa 10am-2:30pm) is the public transit system. The free *Rider's Guide*, available on buses, at motels, and at the visitors center, has route info. **Visitor Info: Monterey Peninsula Visitor and Convention Bureau,** 150 Olivier St. (☎ 657-6400 or 888-221-1010; www.montereyinfo.org). **Post Office:** 565 Hartnell St. (☎ 372-3021. Open M-F 8:30am-5pm, Sa 10am-2pm.) **Postal Code:** 93940.

🛏🍴 ACCOMMODATIONS AND FOOD. Inexpensive hotels line the 2000 block of **Fremont Street** in Monterey (bus #9 or 10). Others cluster along **Munras Avenue** between downtown Monterey and Hwy. 1. The **Monterey Carpenter's Hall Hostel (HI) ❷,** 778 Hawthorne St., one block west of Lighthouse Ave., is a clean, modern, 45-bed hostel. (☎ 649-0375. Towels $0.50. Linens provided. Free parking. Lockout 11am-5pm. Curfew 11pm. Reservations essential June-Sept. Dorms $22, non-members $25, ages 7-17 $17; private rooms for 2-5 people $60-74.) **Del Monte Beach Inn ❹,** 1110 Del Monte Blvd., near downtown and across from the beach, is a Victorian-style inn with pleasant rooms. (☎ 649-4410. Check-in 2-8pm. Reserve ahead. Rooms $55-88; with private bath and 1 with kitchenette $88-99.) Call the **Monterey Parks** line (☎ 755-4895 or 888-588-2267) for camping info.

Once a hot spot for the canned sardine industry, Monterey Bay now yields crab, red snapper, and salmon. Seafood is bountiful but expensive—early-bird specials (usually 4-6:30pm) are easier on the wallet. **Fisherman's Wharf** has smoked salmon sandwiches ($7) and free chowder samples. Get free samples of fruit, cheese, and seafood at the **Old Monterey Market Place**, on Alvarado St. (☎ 655-2607. Open Tu 4-8pm.) **🍽Thai Bistro II ❸,** 159 Central Ave., in Pacific Grove, offers quality Thai cuisine in a flower-encircled patio. (☎ 372-8700. Lunch combos $7-9. Open daily 11:30am-3pm and 5-9:30pm.) At vegetarian **Tillie Gort's ❷,** 111 Central Ave., large portions will please even the most devout carnivore. (☎ 373-0335. Open daily June-Oct. 10am-10pm; Nov.-May M-F 11am-10pm.)

◳ SIGHTS. The extraordinary **🐠Monterey Bay Aquarium,** 886 Cannery Row, has the **world's largest window;** gaze at an enormous marine habitat with sea turtles, giant sunfish, large sharks, and yellow- and blue-fin tuna. There's a new, provocative exhibit connecting the shape, movement, and beauty of jellyfish to various art forms. Watch the **sea otters** at feeding time. The lines are unbelievable; pick up tickets the day before and save 20-40min. (☎ 648-4888 or 800-756-3737; www.montereybayaquarium.org. Open daily June to early Sept. and holidays 9:30am-6pm; early Sept. to May 10am-6pm. $18, students and ages 13-17 $16, disabled and ages 3-12 $9.) **Cannery Row** was once a dilapidated street of languishing sardine-packing plants. Now, the **Great Cannery Row Mural** covers 400 ft. of a construction-site barrier on the 700 block with depictions of 1930s Monterey. The best time to go **whale-watching** is during gray whale migration season (Nov.-Mar.), but the trips are hit-or-miss year-round. **Chris' Fishing Trips,** 48 Fisherman's Wharf, offers tours and charters. (☎ 375-5951. 2-3hr. tours May-Nov. 11am and 1pm. $28, under 13 $18. 2hr. gray whale migration tours Dec.-Apr. $18, under 13 $12.)

CALIFORNIA

In nearby Carmel, the amazing 550-acre, state-run wildlife sanctuary of ⊠**Point Lobos Reserve** is popular with skindivers and day-hikers. From the cliffs, watch otters, sea lions, seals, brown pelicans, and gulls. There are also tidepools, scuba access, and marvelous vantage points for watching the winter whale migration. (☎624-4909. Open daily Apr.-Oct. 9am-7pm; Nov.-Mar. 9am-5pm. $8 per car, seniors $4, free for campers registered with one of the state parks. Required diving reservations ☎624-8413; ptlobos@mbay.net. Dive fee $7.)

BIG SUR   ☎831

Big Sur offers everything from redwood forests with freshwater rivers to rocky shores with surf crashing on golden beaches. More of a region than a precise destination, a fair amount of driving is required to get around, but all parks and camping lie on Hwy. 1. Big Sur's state parks and **Los Padres National Forest** beckon to outdoor enthusiasts of all types. Their **hiking** trails penetrate red-wood forests offering grand views. Within **Pfeiffer Big Sur State Park** are seven trails of varying lengths ($1 map available at park entrance). Big Sur's most fiercely guarded treasure is the USFS-operated **Pfeiffer Beach** ($5). An offshore rock formation protects sea caves and seagulls from the pounding ocean waves. Roughly at the midpoint of the Big Sur coast, about 10 mi. south of Big Sur Station, lies **Julia Pfeiffer Burns State Park,** where picnickers find refuge in the red-wood forest and sea otters in **McWay Cove.** At the point where McWay Creek flows into the ocean is a spectacular 80 ft. waterfall, visible from a semi-paved path ¼ mi. from the park entrance.

Camping in Big Sur is heavenly, but neglecting to bring equipment is a big mistake; what little equipment is available is expensive. Low site availability reflects the high demand for camping in the area, so reserve well in advance by calling ReserveAmerica (☎800-444-7275; $7.50 fee). Grocery stores are at Big Sur Lodge (in Pfeiffer Big Sur State Park), Pacific Valley, and Gorda, and some packaged food is sold in Lucia and at Ragged Point, but it's better to arrive prepared because prices in Big Sur are generally high.

SAN SIMEON   ☎805

Newspaper magnate and multi-millionaire owner William Randolph Hearst casually referred to it as "the ranch," or, in his more romantic moments, "La Cuesta Encantada" (Spanish for "the Enchanted Hill"). Today, officially referred to as the Hearst San Simeon State Historic Monument, and popularly known as **Hearst Castle,** this fabulous estate stands as a monument to Hearst's unfathomable wealth and Julia Morgan's architectural genius. An indescribably decadent dreamland of limestone castle, shaded cottages, exquisite pools, fragrant gardens, and Mediterranean *esprit*, the complex rests high on grassy hills sloping down to the Pacific. Hearst Castle sits on Hwy. 1, 3 mi. north of San Simeon and 9 mi. north of Cambria. (Info ☎927-2010, reservations 800-444-4445, wheelchair-accessible reservations 927-2070 or 866-712-2286. Visitors center open 8am-6pm. Call in advance, as tours often sell out. Each tour involves climbing 150-370 staircase steps. 1¾hr. tours $24, ages 6-12 $12, under 6 free.)

SANTA BARBARA   ☎805

Santa Barbara (pop. 92,500) epitomizes worry-free living. Spanish Revival architecture predominates on State St., a lively pedestrian-only, palm-lined promenade of cafes, thrift stores, boutiques, and galleries. The city's golden beaches, museums, historic missions, and scenic drives make it a frequent weekend escape for the wealthy, and an attractive destination for surfers, artists, and backpackers.

▗ TRANSPORTATION

Many downtown lots and streets offer 1¼hr. of **free parking**, including two underground lots at Pasco Nuevo, accessible on the 700 block of Chapala St. All parking is free on Sundays. **Biking** is a nice alternative. The **Cabrillo Bikeway** runs east-west along the beach from the Bird Refuge to the City College campus.

Trains: Amtrak, 209 State St. (☎963-1015 or 800-USA-RAIL/872-7245). Be careful around the station after dark. Reserve in advance. Open daily 5:45am-9pm. To **L.A.** (5-6hr., 4-5 per day, $20-25) and **San Francisco** (7hr., 3 per day, $48-68).

Buses: Greyhound, 34 W. Carrillo St. (☎965-7551), at Chapala St. Open M-F 5:30am-8pm, Sa-Su 7am-8pm. To **L.A.** (2-3hr., 9 per day, $12) and **San Francisco** (9-10hr., 5 per day, $34). **Santa Barbara Metropolitan Transit District (MTD),** 1020 Chapala St. (☎683-3702), at Cabrillo Blvd. behind the Greyhound station, provides bus schedules and serves as a transfer point. Open M-F 6am-7pm, Sa 8am-6pm, Su 9am-6pm. The MTD runs a purple electric **crosstown shuttle** from Franklin Center on Montecito St. to Mountain and Valerio, running through the transit center. $1.25, seniors and disabled $0.60, under 45 in. free; transfers free. Runs M-F 7am-6pm. The **downtown-waterfront shuttle** along State St. and Cabrillo Blvd. runs every 15min. Su-Th 10am-6pm, F-Sa 10am-10pm. Stops designated by circular blue signs. $0.25.

▰ ▰ ORIENTATION AND PRACTICAL INFORMATION

Santa Barbara is 92 mi. northwest of L.A. and 27 mi. from Ventura on **U.S. 101.** Since the town is built along an east-west stretch of shoreline, its street grid is slightly skewed. The beach lies at the south end of the city, and **State Street,** the main drag, runs northwest from the waterfront. All streets are designated east and west from State St. The major east-west arteries are **Cabrillo Boulevard** and **U.S. 101,** which runs east-west between Castillo St. and Hot Springs Rd.

Visitor Info: Tourist Office, 1 Garden St. (☎965-3021 or 800-676-1266), at Cabrillo Blvd. across from the beach. Open July-Aug. M-Sa 9am-6pm, Su 10am-5pm; Sept.-Nov. and Feb.-June M-Sa 9am-5pm, Su 10am-5pm; Dec.-Jan. M-Sa 9am-4pm, Su 10am-4pm. Outdoor 24hr. computer kiosk with information on services, dining, shopping, hotels, and entertainment.

Police: 215 E. Figueroa St. (☎897-2300.)

Medical Services: Cottage Hospital, Pueblo St. (☎682-7111), at Bath St.

Post Office: 836 Anacapa St. (☎564-2226), 1 block east of State St. Open M-F 8am-6pm, Sa 9am-5pm. **Postal Code:** 93102.

▰ ACCOMMODATIONS

A 10min. drive north or south on U.S. 101 will reward you with cheaper lodging than that in Santa Barbara proper. **Motel 6 ❸** is always an option—this chain of budget-friendly motels originated in Santa Barbara. Welcoming, comfortable, and meticulously clean, ▨**Hotel State Street ❷,** 121 State St., is located 1 block from the beach and next to the train station. (☎966-6586. Rooms have sinks and cable TV. Reservations recommended. Rooms July-Aug. $60-80; Sept.-June $50-70.) **Santa Barbara International Tourist Hostel ❶,** 134 Chapala St., near the beach and bustling State St., draws a young staff and clientele. (☎963-0154; sbres@bananabungalow.com. Internet $1 per 10min. Laundry. Key deposit $5. 6- to 8- person dorms $21-23. Doubles July-Aug. $59-65; May-June and Sept. $55-59; Oct.-Apr. $49-55.) Campsites can be reserved through ReserveAmerica (☎800-444-7275).

⚓ FOOD

Santa Barbara may well have more restaurants per capita than anywhere else in America; finding a place to eat is easy on hip State St. and cheaper Milpas St. Ice cream lovers flock to award-winning **McConnel's ❶**, 201 W. Mission St. (☎ 569-2323. Scoops $2.90. Open Su-Th 11am-10:30pm, F-Sa 11am-11pm.) The reproduction of the Sistine Chapel ceiling at **Palazzio ❹**, 1026 State St., is nearly as impressive as the enormous pasta dishes ($17-20, half-portion $12-15), amazing garlic rolls, and serve-yourself wine. (☎ 564-1985. Lunch pasta dishes $7.75-10. Open Su-Th 11:30am-3pm and 5:30-11pm, F-Sa 11:30am-3pm and 5:30pm-midnight.) Bourbon St. spice meets Santa Barbara class at **The Palace Grill ❺**, 8 E. Cota St., a vibrant Cajun-Creole-Caribbean restaurant. (☎ 963-5000. Fish and grill selections $14-26. Open Su-Th 11:30am-3pm and 5:30-10pm, F-Sa 11:30am-3pm and 5:30-11pm.)

👁 SIGHTS

One of the best sights in Santa Barbara is seasonal. Starting in October, and assembling most densely from November to February, hordes of **monarch butterflies** cling to the eucalyptus trees in Ellwood Grove, just west of UCSB, and at the end of Coronado St. off Hollister Ave.; take the Glen Annie/Storke Rd. exit off U.S. 101. Pick up *Santa Barbara's Red Tile Tour*, a walking tour guide (free at the visitors center; $0.25 inside the courthouse).

SANTA BARBARA ZOO. This delightfully leafy habitat has such an open feel that the animals seem kept in captivity only by sheer lethargy. A mini-train provides a tour of the exhibits, including a miniaturized African plain where giraffes stroll lazily, silhouetted against the Pacific. *(500 Niños Dr., off Cabrillo Blvd. from U.S. 101. Take bus #14 or the downtown-waterfront shuttle. ☎ 962-5339. Open daily 10am-5pm. $9, seniors and ages 2-12 $7, under 2 free. Train $1.50, children $1. Parking $3.)*

BEACHES AND ACTIVITIES. Santa Barbara's beaches are breathtaking, lined on one side by flourishing palm trees and on the other by sailboats around the harbor. **East** and **Leadbetter Beaches** flank the wharf on either side. **Skater's Point Park,** along the waterfront on Cabrillo Blvd., south of Stearns Wharf, is a free park for skateboarders. **Beach Rentals** will rent beachgoers a covered, Flintstone-esque bicycle seating up nine. *(22 State St. ☎ 966-6733. Open daily 8am-8pm. Surreys $15-28 per 2hr., depending on number of riders.)* **Beach House** rents surfboards and body boards plus all the necessary equipment. *(10 State St. ☎ 963-1281. Surfboards $7 per hr., $35 per day; body boards $4/$16; wet suits $3/$16. Credit card required.)*

STATE STREET. State St., Santa Barbara's monument to city planning, runs a straight, tree-lined 2 mi. through the center of the city. Among the countless shops and restaurants are cultural and historical landmarks. Everything that doesn't move has been slathered in Spanish tile. The **Santa Barbara Museum of Art** owns an impressive collection of classical Greek, Asian, and European works, mostly donated by wealthy local residents. *(1130 State St. ☎ 963-4364. Open Tu-Su 11am-5pm. $7, seniors $5, students ages 6-17 $4, under 6 free. Free Su.)*

MISSION SANTA BARBARA. Praised as the "Queen of Missions" when built in 1786, the mission was restored after the 1812 earthquake and assumed its present incarnation in 1820. Towers with Moorish windows stand around a Greco-Roman temple and facade and a Moorish fountain bubbles outside. *(At the end of Las Olivas St. Take bus #22. ☎ 682-4149. Open daily 9am-5pm. Self-guided museum tour starts at the gift shop. Mass M-F 7:30am, Sa 4pm, Su 7:30, 9, 10:30am, noon. $4, under 12 free.)*

HIKING. Very popular **Inspiration Point** is a 3½ mi. round-trip hike that climbs 800 ft. Half of the hike is an easy walk on a paved road; the other half consists of a series of mountainside switchbacks. The reward on a clear day is an extensive view of the city, the ocean, and the Channel Islands. Following the creek upstream will lead to **Seven Falls.** *(From Mission Santa Barbara, drive toward the mountains and turn right onto Foothill Rd. Turn left onto Mission Canyon Rd. and continue 1 mi. Bear left onto Tunnel Rd. and drive 1¼ mi. to its end.)* **Rattlesnake Canyon Trail** is a moderate 3½ mi. round-trip hike to the Tunnel Trail junction with a 1000 ft. gain. It passes many waterfalls, pools, and secluded spots, but is highly popular—expect company. *(From Mission Santa Barbara, drive toward the mountains and turn right onto Foothill Rd. Turn left onto Mission Canyon Rd. and continue for ½ mi. Make a sharp right onto Las Conas Rd. and travel 1¼ mi. Look for a large sign on the left side of the road.)*

UNIVERSITY OF CALIFORNIA AT SANTA BARBARA (UCSB). This beautiful out-post of the UC system is stuck in Goleta, a shapeless mass of suburbs and coffee shops, but the beachside dorms and gorgeous student body more than make up for the lackluster town. The excellent **art museum** houses the Sedgwick Collection of 15th- to 17th-century European paintings. *(From Santa Barbara, take U.S. 101 N to Ward Memorial Hwy., or take bus #11. ☎893-7564. Open W-Su noon-5pm. Free.)*

🔊 NIGHTLIFE

Every night of the week, the clubs on **State Street,** mostly between Haley and Cañon Perdido St., are packed. Consult the *Independent* to see who's playing on any given night. ■**Sharkeez,** 416 State St., is a wild college hangout, with live mermaids swimming in the tank behind the bar Thursday to Saturday from 11pm on. (☎963-9680; www.sharkeez.net. Nightly drink deals like Tu 2-for-1 margaritas or mai tais and 4 Coronas for $8. F $2 martinis. Sa 9:30-11pm 2-for-1 beers, shots, cocktails, and pitchers. M international night. Open M-F 11am-2am, Sa-Su 10am-2am. Kitchen closes 10pm.) **Q's Sushi A-Go-Go,** 409 State St., boasts a three-level bar, eight pool tables, and dancing. (☎966-9177. Sushi $3-14. *Sake* $3-5. Happy hour M-Sa 4-7pm; 20% off sushi rolls, 50% off drinks and selected appetizers. M Brazilian night. Tu 80s night. W karaoke. Th college night; $1 hot dogs. $16 all-you-can-eat sushi M-Sa 7-9:30pm. Cover Sa $5 after 9pm. Open M-Sa 4pm-2am.)

LOS ANGELES

There's a reason 17 million people choose to live in the spawling collection of neighborhoods and freeways they call the City of Angels. Yes, the traffic is terrible, the smog is worse, the socio-economic divisions are tense, and the plastic surgery rate is high. However, L.A. also has the nicest beaches, freshest clubs, hottest art-ists, best ethnic food, and balmiest weather of any city in the country. In this movie-making town, everyone works in the industry or is related to someone who does, and Angelenos take their movie-going very seriously.

✖ INTERCITY TRANSPORTATION

Three major freeways connect L.A. to the rest of the state. **I-5,** which travels the length of California, bisects L.A. on a north-south axis; it continues north to Sacra-mento and south to San Diego. **U.S. 101** links L.A. to other coastal cities, heading west from Pasadena before turning north toward San Francisco and running paral-lel to I-5. **I-10** comes in from the east, providing access to Las Vegas and Arizona.

Los Angeles & Vicinity
SEE COLOR INSERTS FOR MORE LOS ANGELES AREA MAPS

Airport: Los Angeles International Airport (LAX) is in Westchester, about 15 mi. south-west of downtown. LAX information (☎310-646-5252) aids Spanish- and English-speakers. Airport police (☎310-646-7911) patrol 24hr. Travelers Aid, a service for air-port info, transportation, accommodations, and major transit emergencies, is in all ter-minals. (☎310-646-2270. Open M-F 9am-5pm.)

Trains: Amtrak, Union Station, 800 N. Alameda St. (☎213-683-6729 or 800-USA-RAIL/872-7245), at the northeastern edge of downtown.

Buses: Greyhound (☎800-231-2222 or 213-629-8401). The downtown station, 1716 E. 7th St. (☎213-629-8536), at Alameda St., is in an extremely rough neighborhood. If you must get off in downtown, *be very careful near 7th and Alameda St.*, one block southwest of the station, where you can catch MTA bus #60 traveling north to Union Station. The new terminal in Hollywood, 1715 N. Cahuenga Blvd. (☎323-466-1249), is at a great location. From Union Station buses run to: **Las Vegas** (19 per day, $38); **San Diego** (every hr., $15); **San Francisco** (15 per day, $48); **Santa Barbara** (9 per day, $12); **Tijuana** (4-5 per day, $20).

ORIENTATION

I-5 (Golden State Freeway), I-405 (San Diego Freeway), I-110 (Harbor Freeway), U.S. 101 (Hollywood Freeway), and Pacific Coast Highway (PCH or Highway 1) all run north-south. **I-10 (Santa Monica Freeway)** runs east-west, connecting Santa Monica to downtown and beyond. I-5 intersects I-10 just east of downtown and serves as one of the two major north-south thruways. I-405, which stretches from Orange County in the south all the way through L.A., parallels I-5 on a route closer to the coast, separating Santa Monica and Malibu from the inland Westside. The best way to orient yourself is by learning a couple of important freeways and remaining aware of L.A.'s natural landmarks; the ocean is west and the mountains are east.

THE COAST. Santa Monica reigns over the coast with its superior shopping and well-kept houses. Its wealthier neighbor to the north, **Malibu,** is purely focused on the beach, and its seaside cliffs are home to many incognito celebrities. **Venice** and **Marina del Rey** extend south along Santa Monica's ocean beach path and into crazier territory. Drum circles and in-line skaters characterize Venice, while Marina del Rey caters to the yachting set. Even farther down the coast, the **South Bay** beaches are relaxed and fun.

THE WESTSIDE. East of I-405, the Westside sits comfortably along Santa Monica Boulevard. This is the cleanest, most happening part of the city. UCLA brings students to **Westwood** and **West L.A.,** while the neighboring hills of **Bel Air, Brentwood,** and **Pacific Palisades** accommodate stellar homes and the impressive Getty Center. **Beverly Hills** is, as always, the land of luxury shopping and gaudy mansions. Still on the Westside, but inching toward eastern messiness, predominantly gay **West Hollywood** is the center of much of the city's best nightlife and shopping.

HOLLYWOOD. Hollywood, in all its faded glamour and neon excitement, lies just up Sunset Blvd. from West Hollywood. It's a good place for late-night eats and celebrity stalking, and holds many of the city's most famous landmarks. Lodging here is among the cheapest available. South of Hollywood, the **Wilshire District** houses Museum Mile.

EAST OF HOLLYWOOD. East of Hollywood are the bohemian neighborhoods **Los Feliz** and **Silver Lake,** and the greenery of Griffith Park. Southeast, **downtown L.A.** *does* exist and is undergoing a minor rejuvenation with the recent construction of Frank Gehry's Walt Disney Concert Hall. Farther east, at the foot of the San Gabriel Mountains, **Pasadena** has old-time charm and hosts the Rose Bowl. Movies are made and theme parks reign in the **San Fernando Valley,** north of downtown on I-5.

LOCAL TRANSPORTATION

Whether they're driving pimped-out low-riders or sparkling luxury sedans, Angelenos love their cars with a fervor that comes from constant contact with the road. L.A.'s roadways are often jammed, and heavy traffic moves toward downtown from 7 to 10am on weekdays and streams outbound from 4 to 7pm. However, since L.A. has a huge population that doesn't work 9-to-5, traffic can occasionally be as bad at 1pm as it is at 6pm. No matter how crowded the freeway is, it's almost always quicker and safer than taking surface streets to your

C A L I F O R N I A

destination. The **Automobile Club of Southern California,** 2601 S. Figueroa St., at Adams Blvd., has additional driving info and maps. Club privileges are free for AAA members and cost $2-3 for nonmembers. (☎213-741-3686, emergency assistance 800-400-4222. Open M-F 9am-5pm.)

As a result of this obsession with driving, public transportation systems are limited and inconvenient. Though renting a car is expensive, your own set of wheels is the best way to navigate the sprawling city. If you must forgo the rental, use the subway and the bus to get around. Walking or biking around the city is simply not feasible—distances are just too great. However, some colorful areas such as Melrose, Third St. Promenade in Santa Monica, Venice Beach, Hollywood, and Old Town Pasadena are best explored by foot. At night, those on foot, especially outside the Westside, should exercise caution. *If you hitch-hike, you will probably die.* It is exceptionally dangerous, not to mention illegal. Don't even consider it.

Local Buses: Metropolitan Transit Authority (MTA) Metro Customer Center, Arco Plaza, 515 S. Flower St., Level "C" (open M-F 7:30am-3:30pm), in downtown and Gateway Transit Center, Union Station E. Portal (open M-F 6am-6:30pm) in downtown. Bus fare $1.25 (transfer $0.25), seniors and disabled $0.45 (transfer $0.10); exact change is required. Weekly passes ($14) available at customer service centers and grocery stores. Transfers can be made between MTA lines or to other transit authorities. Unless otherwise noted, all route numbers are MTA; BBBus stands for **Big Blue Bus** and indicates Santa Monica buses. (☎800-COMMUTE/266-6883; www.mta.net. Open M-F 6am-8:30pm, Sa-Su 8am-6pm.) The local **DASH shuttle** ($0.25), designed for short distance neighborhood hops, serves major tourist destinations in many communities. (☎213-808-2273; www.ladottransit.com. Open M-F 9am-5pm, Sa 10am-2pm.)

Subway: The **Blue Line** runs from downtown to the southern L.A. communities and Long Beach. The **Green Line** goes along I-105 from Norwalk to Redondo Beach, with shuttle service to LAX at Aviation/I-105. The **Red Line** runs from downtown through Hollywood to the San Fernando Valley. The new **Beige Line** (Pasadena line) runs from Union Station to Sierra Madre Villa in Pasadena. Other lines go west to Wilshire and east to Union Station. $1.25, bus and rail transfers $1.60; seniors and disabled $0.45/$0.55. All lines run daily 5am-12:30am.

Taxi: Independent ☎213-385-8294 or 800-521-8294. **L.A. Taxi/Yellow Cab Co.** ☎800-711-8294 or 800-200-1085. **Bell Cab** ☎888-235-5222.

Car Rental: Universal Rent A Car, 920 S. La Brea Ave. (☎323-954-1186). Cars from $20 per day with 150 mi. free, $140 per week with 1050 mi. free. No under-25 surcharge. Open M-F 8am-6pm, Sa-Su 9am-5pm.

⁊ PRACTICAL INFORMATION

Visitor Info: L.A. Convention and Visitor Bureau, 685 S. Figueroa St. (☎213-689-8822; www.visitlanow.com), between Wilshire Blvd. and 7th St. in the Financial District. Staff speaks English, French, German, and Japanese. Detailed bus map of L.A. available and *L.A. Now,* a free booklet with tourist and lodging info. Open M-F 8:30am-5pm.

Hotline: Rape Crisis, ☎310-392-8381.

Medical Services: Cedars-Sinai Medical Center, 8700 Beverly Blvd. (☎310-423-3277, emergency 423-8605). **Good Samaritan Hospital,** 616 S. Witmer St. (☎213-977-2121, emergency 977-2420). **UCLA Medical Center,** 10833 Le Conte Ave. (☎310-825-9111, emergency 825-2111).

Post Office: Central branch at 7001 S. Central Ave. (☎800-275-8777). Open M-F 7am-7pm, Sa 7am-3pm. **Postal Code:** 90052.

> **AREA CODES.** L.A. is big. Really big. **213** covers Downtown L.A. **323** covers Hollywood, Huntington Park, Montebello, and West Hollywood. Prestigious **310** covers Beverly Hills, Santa Monica, and the Westside. **562** covers Long Beach and the South Bay. **626** covers Pasadena. **818** covers Burbank, Glendale, and the San Fernando Valley. **909** covers San Bernardino and Riverside.

ACCOMMODATIONS

In choosing where to stay, the first consideration should be location. Those visiting for beach culture should choose lodgings in Venice or Santa Monica. Avid sightseers will be better off in Hollywood or the more expensive (but cleaner and nicer) Westside. One campground fairly close to L.A. is **Leo Carrillo State Beach ❶** (☎805-488-5223), on Hwy. 1 20 mi. north of Malibu. It has 135 sites with flush toilets and showers (sites $13). Listed prices do not include L.A.'s 14% hotel tax.

THE COAST

Los Angeles Surf City Hostel, 26 Pier Ave. (☎798-2323), in Pier Plaza in Hermosa Beach. Right in the center of the local scene. A relaxed atmosphere with a young, mostly international clientele enjoying the nightlife. The bottom floor of the building is a popular bar and nightclub. Discount car rentals, showers, and Internet access. Boogie boards, breakfast, and linen included. Passport or driver's license required. Key deposit $10. 28-night max. stay; 3-day max. stay for US citizens. Reservations recommended. 4- to 6- bunk dorms $19; private rooms $48. ❶

Seaview Motel, 1760 Ocean Ave. (☎310-393-6711), in Santa Monica. Tastefully decorated rooms, a patio ideal for sunbathing, and a path straight to the beach. Prime location at a reasonable price. Singles to quads $65-80. ❸

Venice Beach Cotel, 25 Windward Ave. (☎310-399-7649; www.venicebeachcotel.com). Easily identifiable with its international flag display. International staff and guests enliven the cramped quarters. Aqua Lounge features big-screen TV and a BYOB bar where guests chill at night (open 7pm-midnight). Free tea and coffee. Tennis rackets, table tennis, and boogie boards ($20 deposit). Passport required. Key deposit $5. Reservations always recommended. 3-, 4-, and 6-bed dorms with ocean view and bath $15-19; doubles $36-52; triples with bath and view $66. ❶

THE WESTSIDE

Orbit Hotel and Hostel, 7950 Melrose Ave. (☎323-655-1510 or 877-672-4887; www.orbithotel.com), a block west of Fairfax Ave., in West Hollywood. Orbit sets new standards for swank budget living. With a spacious retro kitchen, big-screen TV lounge, small courtyard, and late-night party room. Bright, fashion-conscious furniture. Centrally located. Dorms accept only international students with passport. Internet access. Breakfast included. 6-bed dorms $21; private rooms for up to 4 $70-90. ❶

Hotel Claremont, 1044 Tiverton Ave. (☎310-208-5957 or 800-266-5957), near UCLA in Westwood Village. A house-like hotel in a beautiful area, still owned by the same family that built it 60 years ago. All rooms with ceiling fans and private baths. Fridge and microwave next to a Victorian-style TV lounge. Reservations recommended. Singles $56; doubles $62; 2 beds (sleep up to 4) $71. ❸

The Beverly Hills Reeves Hotel, 120 S. Reeves Dr. (☎310-271-3006; www.bhreeves.com). This recently renovated mansion near Rodeo Dr. offers both affordability and location. Rooms with A/C and TV. Continental breakfast included. Parking $6. Rooms $50, with bath $69. Weekly rooms $315/$450. ❸

CALIFORNIA

HOLLYWOOD

▩ Hollywood Bungalows International Youth Hostel, 2775 W. Cahuenga Blvd. (☎888-259-9990; www.hollywoodbungalows.com), just north of the Hollywood Bowl in the Hollywood Hills. A wacky summer-camp atmosphere, with spacious rooms and nightly jam sessions. Outdoor pool, billiards, weight room, big-screen TV, and mini-diner. On-site Universal Rent A Car (p. 944). Internet $2 per 10min. Breakfast $3.50. Dinner $10. Lockers $0.25. Free parking. Check-in 24hr. 6- to 10-bed dorms with bath $15-19; private rooms for up to 4 $59. ❶

USA Hostels Hollywood, 1624 Schrader Blvd. (☎323-462-3777 or 800-524-6783; www.usahostels.com), south of Hollywood Blvd., west of Cahuenga Blvd. Buzzing with young travelers, this lime-green edifice is filled with energy and organized fun. Special events nightly, including free comedy W and Su. Passport or proof of travel required. Stay for 4 days and get free pickup from airport. Free beach shuttles run Tu, Th, Sa. All-you-can-eat pancakes included. To use lockers, bring your own lock or buy one for $0.50. Free street parking; parking lot $4.50 per day. 6- to 8-bed dorms with private bath $17-25; private rooms for 2-4 people $55-65. Prices $1-2 less in winter. ❶

Orange Drive Manor, 1764 N. Orange Dr. (☎323-850-0350). A pleasant, converted mini-mansion in a residential neighborhood. Grandeur (and lack of sign) disguises this hostel. Spacious rooms with antique furniture. Cable TV lounge, limited kitchen. Internet $1 per 10min. Lockers $0.75. Parking $5. Reservations recommended. 4- to 6-bed dorms (some with private baths) $19-24; private rooms $40-52. $2 discount with ISIC. Cash or traveler's checks only. ❷

◘ FOOD

From celebrity eateries to taco wagons, there's never a shortage of great food in L.A. This expansive range of culinary options is a direct result of the city's ethnic diversity. If you're looking to cook, **Trader Joe's** specializes in budget gourmet food. They save by doing their own packaging, and, as a result, amazing deals like $3 bottles of good Napa wines abound. There are 74 locations in SoCal; call ☎800-SHOP-TJS/746-7857 to find the nearest one. (Most open daily 9am-9pm.) ▩**Farmers Market,** 6333 W. 3rd St., at Fairfax Ave., attracts about 3 million people every year and has over 160 produce stalls, as well as international food booths, handicraft shops, and a phenomenal juice bar. A cheaper and less touristy source of produce is the **Grand Central Public Market,** 317 S. Broadway, between 3rd and 4th St. in downtown. Entrances are on both Broadway and Hill St. between 3rd and 4th St. (☎213-624-2378. Open daily 9am-6pm.)

THE COAST

▩ Rose Cafe and Market, 220 Rose Ave. (☎310-399-0711), at Main St., in Venice. A rose-lined entrance leads to a bright, floral-themed facade. The cafe features local art, industrial architecture, and healthy deli specials, including sandwiches ($6-8) and salads ($6-8) available from 11:30am. Limited menu after 3pm. Open M-F 7am-5:30pm, Sa 8am-6pm, Su 8am-5pm. ❷

Fritto Misto, 601 Colorado Ave. (☎310-458-2829), at 6th St., in Santa Monica. "Neighborhood Italian Cafe" with cheery waitstaff lets you create your own pasta (from $6). Vegetarian entrees $8-12. Daily pasta specials $8. Weekend lunch special of all-you-can-eat calamari and salad $12. Omelettes Su 11:30am-4pm ($7-8). Open M-Th 11:30am-10pm, F-Sa 11:30am-10:30pm, Su 11:30am-9:30pm. ❸

Wahoo's Fish Tacos, 1129 Manhattan Ave. (☎562-796-1044), in Manhattan Beach. Famous for cheap, flavorful Mexican-inspired grub such as beer-battered Maui onion rings. Try the signature Wahoo bowl (flame-broiled, blackened, or teriyaki Polynesian shrimp on rice with either black or white beans and salsa; $4.25). Mug of Ono Ale $2. Open daily 10:30am-9:30pm. ❶

Neptune's Net Seafood, 42505 Hwy. 1 (☎310-457-3095), in Malibu. It's worth the drive north for this friendly, lively restaurant known for some of the best (and most affordable) seafood in Malibu ($8-10). It's Hell's Angels' heaven on Su. Open M-Th 10:30am-8pm, F 10:30am-9pm, Sa-Su 10am-8:30pm. ❸

The Spot, 110 2nd St. (☎562-376-2355; www.worldfamousspot.com), in Hermosa Beach. Opened in 1977, this is one of the oldest vegetarian restaurants in the L.A. area and a favorite with local hippies. Tempeh, tofu, and tahini entrees. Homemade bread and desserts $3.50. Trademarked "Inflation Buster" combos such as the "Dear George" include veggies served on pasta or rice with tofu ($5-7). Open daily 11am-10pm. ❷

THE WESTSIDE

▨ **The Apple Pan,** 10801 W. Pico Blvd. (☎310-475-3585), 1 block east of Westwood Blvd. across from the Westside Pavilion, in West L.A. Legend has it that *Beverly Hills 90210's* Peach Pit was modeled after The Apple Pan, so lean on the white counter and make like it's 1992. Famous original apple pies $4. Hickory-smoked burgers $6. Fries $2. Open Su and Tu-Th 11am-midnight, F-Sa 11am-1am. No credit cards. ❷

▨ **Asahi Ramen,** 2027 Sawtelle Blvd. (☎310-479-2231). A tiny, simple Japanese restaurant that serves huge bowls of ramen soup ($5) and the freshest *gyoza* ($3.50) ever. Well worth the frequent wait. Open M-W and F-Su 11:30pm-9pm. Cash only. ❶

Bossa Nova, 685 N. Robertson Blvd. (☎310-657-5070), in West Hollywood. At lunchtime the patio of this laid-back Brazilian/Italian restaurant fills up with stars in shades, who come for the incredible plantains. By the end of the night, everyone's here. Entrees $10-18. Open daily 11am-4am. Reservations recommended. ❹

Al Gelato, 806 S. Robertson Blvd. (☎310-659-8069), between Wilshire and Olympic Blvd., in Beverly Hills. Though known for its homemade gelato, Al Gelato also serves large portions of pasta with a delicious basil tomato sauce. Popular with the theater crowd. Giant meatball $5.25. Rigatoni $12. For dessert, stick to the famous gelato ($4-6) and made-to-order cannoli ($4.50). Open Tu-Su 10am-midnight. No credit cards. ❸

Diddie Riese Cookies, 926 Broxton Ave. (☎310-208-0448), in Westwood Village. Cookies baked from scratch every day. Lines stretch down the block (but move fairly quickly) for a $1 ice-cream-and-cookie sandwich (any two cookies with your choice of ice cream). $1 also buys you 2 cookies and milk, juice, or coffee. Popular late-night spot. Open M-Th 10am-midnight, F 10am-1am, Sa noon-1am, Su noon-midnight. ❶

HOLLYWOOD

▨ **Canter's,** 419 N. Fairfax Ave. (☎323-651-2030), north of Beverly Blvd. An L.A. institution and the heart and soul of historically Jewish Fairfax since 1931. Grapefruit-sized matzoh ball in chicken broth $4.50. Giant sandwiches $8-9. Cheap beer ($2.50). Visit the Kibbitz Room for nightly free rock, blues, jazz, and cabaret-pop (from 10pm). Lenny Kravitz is known to make appearances in the audience. Open 24hr. ❷

Roscoe's House of Chicken and Waffles, 1514 Gower St. (☎323-466-7453), at the corner of Sunset Blvd. Additional location at 5006 W. Pico Blvd, in West L.A. The downhome feel and menu make this a popular spot for regular folk and celebs. Try "1 succulent chicken breast and 1 delicious waffle" ($7.40). Expect a 30min.-1hr. wait on weekends. Open Su-Th 8:30am-midnight, F-Sa 8:30am-4am. ❷

Nyala Ethiopian Cuisine, 1076 S. Fairfax Ave. (☎323-936-5918), 2 blocks south of Olympic Blvd. The Fairfax area may be known for its kosher delis, but it's also the backbone of L.A.'s Ethiopian community. Nyala's decor combines traditional African influences with Western table settings, but there's no fusion with the food—just large plates of spongy flatbread *(injera)* topped with spicy stews (lunch $8; dinner $11). The vegetarian lunch buffet (M-F 11:30am-3pm) is a steal at $6. Open daily 11:30am-11pm. ❸

Pink's Hot Dog Stand, 709 N. La Brea Ave. (☎323-931-4223; www.pinksholly-wood.com), at Melrose Ave. An institution since 1939, Pink's serves up chili-slathered goodness in a bun, attracting droves of tourists and Angelenos. Rumor has it that Sean Penn proposed to Madonna here. Try the special "Ozzy Osbourne Spicy Dog" for $5. Chili dogs $2.40. Open Su-Th 9:30am-2am, F-Sa 9:30am-3am. Cash only. ❶

Carlitos Gardel, 7963 Melrose Ave. (☎655-0891; www.carlitosgardel.com), 1½ blocks west of Fairfax Ave. Argentine restaurant with Italian influences. Bread comes accompanied by chimichurri sauce so addictive, you'll want to hunt down a bottle to bring home. Try the signature "Papas Fritas Provenzal" ($6) or "Ojo de Costilla a la Criolla," a rib-eye steak marinated in chimichurri ($34). Entrees $12-38. Open M-F 11:30am-2:30pm and 6-11pm, Sa 6-11pm, Su 5-10pm. Reservations recommended. ❺

EAST OF HOLLYWOOD

▨ **Fair Oaks Pharmacy and Soda Fountain,** 1516 Mission St. (☎626-799-1414), at Fair Oaks Ave. in South Pasadena. From Colorado Blvd., go south 1 mi. on Fair Oaks Ave. to Mission St. This old-fashioned drug store with soda fountain and lunch counter has been serving travelers on Rte. 66 since 1915; now, a bit of Pasadena's upscale boutique flavor has crept in. An infamous phosphate drink made of flavored syrup splashed with water and secret "potion" is a fountain favorite ($2). Hand-dipped shakes and malts $4.25. Deli sandwiches $5.50. Soda fountain open M-F 11am-9pm, Sa 11am-10pm, Su 11am-8pm. Lunch counter open Su-F until 5pm, Sa until 8pm. ❶

▨ **Philippe, The Original,** 1001 N. Alameda St. (☎213-628-3781; www.philippes.com), 2 blocks north of Union Station, downtown. A longtime fixture, Philippe is one of downtown's most popular lunch eateries. The invention of the French Dip sandwich occurred here in 1918 when Philippe allegedly dropped a sliced French roll into a roasting pan filled with juice still hot from the oven. The policeman Philippe served loved the dipped sandwich so much, he showed up the next day with a dozen cop buddies requesting the same. Choose from pork, beef, ham, turkey ($4.40), or lamb ($4.70). Top it off with apple pie ($2.75) and $0.09 coffee. Free parking. Open daily 6am-10pm. ❶

The Pantry, 877 S. Figueroa St. (☎213-972-9279), in downtown. Since 1924, it hasn't closed once—not for the earthquakes, not for the 1992 riots (when it served as a National Guard outpost), and not even when a taxicab drove through the front wall. There aren't even locks on the doors. Owned by former L.A. mayor Richard Riordan, this diner is known for its large portions, free cole slaw, and fresh sourdough bread. Giant breakfast specials $6. Lunch sandwiches $8. Open 24hr. No credit cards. ❷

La Luz del Día, 1 W. Olvera St. (☎213-628-7495), tucked inside El Pueblo Historic Park along the circular walking path. Family-run and completely authentic Mexican restaurant. The park's trees and performance artists are a nice complement to the great food. Specialties are the homemade tortillas ($0.20), tacos, and rice and beans ($5-6). Open Tu-Th 11am-9pm, F 11am-10pm, Sa 10am-10pm, Su 8:30am-10pm. ❶

◎ SIGHTS

SANTA MONICA

Santa Monica is known more for its lively shoreside scene than for its surf, and the area on and around the carnival pier is filled with hawkers and local tourist activity. The fun spills over onto the pedestrian-only Third St. Promenade, where street performers and a farmers market add a bit of spice to the outdoor mall-ish ambience. Farther inland, along Main St. and beyond, a smattering of galleries, design shops, and museums testify to the city's love for art and culture.

SANTA MONICA PIER, PACIFIC PARK, AND THE BEACH. The famed pier is the heart of Santa Monica Beach and home to the rollercoasters, arcades, and Ferris wheels of carnivalesque Pacific Park. Along the pier, amidst pizza joints and souvenir shops, look for free TV show tickets near the north entrance. *(Off Hwy. 1 on the way to Venice Beach from Santa Monica Beach. ☎458-8900; http://santamonicapier.org. Pier open 24hr. Park open in summer Su-Th 11am-11pm, F-Sa 11am-12:30am; winter hours vary. Ticket window closes 30min. before the park closes. Tickets $2 each; most rides 2-3 tickets. Day pass $20, children under 42 in. $11.)* The paved **Ocean Front Walk** is a mini-freeway of cyclists, skaters, and runners, stretching 20¼ mi. along the beach between Santa Monica and Torrance. Immediately south of the pier on Ocean Front Walk, skilled players match wits at the public chess tables at the **International Chess Park.** Opposite the chess masters is the original location of **Muscle Beach** (now in Venice Beach), where bodybuilders and athletes used to show off chiseled physical perfection in the 1930s, 40s, and 50s.

THIRD STREET PROMENADE. Angelenos always claim that nobody walks in L.A., but the rules change on the Third St. Promenade, an ultra-popular pedestrianized three blocks of mosaic art tiles, chain clothing stores, movie theaters, and patio restaurants. The trendy shopping runs from overpriced bikini shops to some of L.A.'s best bookstores. On Wednesday and Saturday mornings, the area transforms into a popular **Farmers Market** selling fresh California-grown flowers and produce, with Saturdays featuring exclusively organic products. *(Between Broadway and Wilshire in downtown Santa Monica. Exit off 4th St. from I-10.)*

MALIBU, VENICE, AND SOUTH BAY

North of Santa Monica along the Pacific Coast Highway (PCH; Hwy. 1), the cityscape gives way to appealing stretches of sandy, sewage-free shoreline. **Malibu's** beaches are clean and relatively uncrowded, easily the best in L.A. County for surfers, sunbathers, and swimmers alike. Along the 30000 block of PCH, 30min. west of Santa Monica, stretches ☒**Zuma Beach,** L.A. County's northernmost, largest, most popular, and happiest sandbox. You can jet through the wave tubes at **Surfrider Beach,** a section of Malibu Lagoon State Beach north of the pier at 23000 PCH. Walk there via the Zonker Harris Access Way at 22700 PCH.

Venice is a carnivalesque beach town where guitar-toting, wild-eyed, tie-dyed residents sculpt masterpieces in sand or compose them in graffiti, all before hitting the waves. Grab a corn dog and head to **Ocean Front Walk,** where street people converge on shaded clusters of benches, evangelists drown out off-color comedians, and bodybuilders of both sexes pump iron in skimpy spandex outfits at **Muscle Beach,** 1800 Ocean Front Walk, closest to 18th St. and Pacific Ave. Fire-juggling cyclists, master sand sculptors, bards in Birkenstocks, and **"skateboard grandmas"** define the bohemian spirit of this playground population.

About 20 mi. southwest of downtown L.A. are the South Bay beaches of **Manhattan Beach, Hermosa Beach,** and **Redondo Beach.** Manhattan Beach is favored for surfing; Hermosa Beach, L.A. County's most popular urban beach, is also one of the cleanest. Both host elite beach volleyball and surf competitions (☎426-8000; www.avp.com or www.surffestival.org). Most visit Redondo Beach for its harbor, pier, and seafood-rich boardwalk. **The Strand** is a concrete bike path that runs from Santa Monica (where it's called Ocean Front Walk) to Hermosa Beach.

WESTWOOD

Westwood is home to **University of California at Los Angeles (UCLA),** a prototypical California university, with grassy open spaces, dazzling sunshine, massive brick buildings, and deeply tanned bodies on 400 acres in the foothills of the Santa Monica

Mountains. Once voted the #1 jock school in the country by *Sports Illustrated*, UCLA also boasts an illustrious film school whose graduates include James Dean, Jim Morrison, Oliver Stone, Francis Ford Coppola, and Tim Robbins. Outdoor highlights include the **Murphy Sculpture Garden,** in the northeast corner of campus, which contains over 70 pieces by major artists such as Auguste Rodin and Henri Matisse, and the UCLA **Botanical Gardens,** in the eastern part of campus, at the intersection of Le Conte and Hilgard Ave. By car, take I-405 to the Wilshire Blvd./ Westwood exit and head east into Westwood. A parking pass ($6) is valid all day at 14 different parking structures. Just south of UCLA, **Westwood Village** is a walkable student area with trendy stores and affordable restaurants.

BEVERLY HILLS

Beverly Hills glows in the televised mystique of expensive hotels, ritzy boutiques, and movie stars galore. You can live it up on a budget here simply by throwing on your trendiest jeans, slipping on the shades, and making clerks work for the money they think you have. Pick up a star map, available at the Santa Monica Pier, local newsstands, or from vendors along Sunset Blvd. just outside Beverly Hills, to take a drive by the houses of celebrities past and present.

RODEO DRIVE. The heart of designer shopping beats in the **Golden Triangle,** a wedge formed by Beverly Dr., Wilshire Blvd., and Santa Monica Blvd. Built like an old English manor house, Polo Ralph Lauren *(444 N. Rodeo Dr.)* stands out from the white marble of the other stores. The divine triple-whammy of Cartier *(370 N. Rodeo Dr.),* Gucci *(347 N. Rodeo Dr.),* and Chanel *(400 N. Rodeo Dr.)* sits on prime real estate, where rents approach $40,000 per month. At the south end of Rodeo Dr. (the end closest to Wilshire Blvd.) is pedestrian-only **2 Rodeo Drive,** a.k.a. **Via Rodeo,** which contains Dior, Tiffany, and numerous salons frequented by the stars. Across the way is the venerable **Beverly Wilshire Hotel,** where Julia Roberts went from Hollywood hooker to Richard Gere's queen in *Pretty Woman. (9500 Wilshire Blvd.)*

BEVERLY HILLS HOTEL. A ludicrously extravagant retreat as famous as the starlets who romanced here, the pink Beverly Hills Hotel sits among 12 acres of tropical gardens and pools. Marilyn Monroe reportedly had trysts with both JFK and RFK in one of the 22 "bungalows." In case you were wondering, rooms run $380-470, bungalows $430-4590, and suites $820-5000. *(9641 Sunset Blvd. ☎ 276-2251.)*

WEST HOLLYWOOD

Bring your walking shoes and spend a day on the 3 mi. strip of **Melrose Avenue** from Highland Ave. west to the intersection of Doheny Dr. and Santa Monica Blvd. This strip began to develop its funky flair in the late 1980s when art galleries, designer stores, lounge-like coffee shops, used clothing and music stores, and restaurants began to take over. Now the hippest stretch lies between La Brea and Fairfax Ave. North of the **Beverly Center** is the **Pacific Design Center,** 8687 Melrose Ave. (☎ 310-657-0800; www.pacificdesigncenter.com), a sea-green glass complex nicknamed the Blue Whale and constructed in the shape of a rippin' wave.

HOLLYWOOD

Exploring the Hollywood area takes a pair of sunglasses, a camera, some cash, and a whole lot of fortitude. **Hollywood Boulevard** is the center of L.A.'s tourist madness, home to the Walk of Fame, famous movie theaters, and souvenir shops.

HOLLYWOOD SIGN. Those 50 ft. high, 30 ft. wide, slightly crooked letters perched on Mt. Lee in Griffith Park stand as a universal symbol of the city. The original 1923 sign read HOLLYWOODLAND as an advertisement for a new subdivision in the Hollywood Hills. The sign has been a target of many college pranks, which have made it read everything from "Holly-weird" to "Ollywood" (after the infamous Lt. Col. Oliver North). A fence keeps you at a distance of 40 ft. *(Getting as close to the sign as possible requires a strenuous 2½ mi. hike. Take the Bronson Canyon entrance to Griffith Park and follow Canyon Dr. to its end, where parking is free. The Brush Canyon Trail starts where Canyon Dr. becomes unpaved. At the top of the hill, follow the road to your left; the sign looms just below. For those satisfied with driving, go north on Vine St., take a right on Franklin Ave. and a left on Beachwood, and drive up until you are forced to drive down.)*

GRAUMAN'S CHINESE THEATRE. Loosely modeled on a Chinese temple, this monumental theater is a Hollywood icon and still rolls out the red carpet for movie premieres. The exterior columns, known as "Heaven Dogs," were imported from China, where they once supported a Ming Dynasty temple. It houses a collection of over 200 celebrity footprints as well as other star trademarks—Whoopi Gold-berg's dreadlocks, R2D2's wheels, and George Burns's cigar. *(6925 Hollywood Blvd., between Highland and Orange St. ☎323-461-3331. 4-5 tours per day; call ahead. $7.50, under 6 free.)*

WALK OF FAME. Pedestrian traffic along Hollywood Blvd. mimics L.A.'s congested freeways as tourists stop mid-stride to gawk at the sidewalk's over 2000 bronze-inlaid stars, which are inscribed with the names of the famous, the infamous, and the down-right obscure. Stars are awarded for achievements in one of five categories—movies, radio, TV, recording, and live performance; only Gene Autry has all five stars. The stars have no particular order, so don't try to find a method to the madness. Recent inductees include Mary Kate and Ashley Olsen (one star, two girls, half the calories) in front of Hollywood and Highland Mall. To catch today's (or yesterday's) stars in person, call the Chamber of Commerce for info on star-unveiling ceremonies. *(☎323-469-8311; www.holly-woodchamber.net. Free.)*

OTHER SIGHTS. The hillside **Hollywood Bowl** is perfect for picnic dining and classy summer entertain-ment. All are welcome to listen to the L.A. Philharmonic at rehearsals on Mondays, Tuesdays, Thursdays, and Fridays. *(2301 N. Highland Ave. ☎323-850-2058, concert line 850-2000; www.hollywoodbowl.org. Open July-Sept. Tu-Sa 10am-8pm; Oct.-June Tu-Sa 10am-4:30pm. Free.)* The **Hollywood and Highland Mall** con-tains ritzy brand-name stores, restaurants, and the $94 million **Kodak Theater,** built specifically for the Academy Awards. *(6801 Hollywood Blvd. Box office ☎323-308-6363. Open daily 10am-6pm; on performance days until*

THE LOCAL STORY

PRICELESS POOLS

Scattered throughout L.A. are some of the country's most exclu-sive hotels, catering to pop stars, trust-fund kids, and anyone with a platinum card. For most budget travelers, the $300 per night prices and $20 valet tips make these hotels off-limits, and the hope of hobnobbing with the rich and famous is but a pipe dream.

However, if you dress appropri-ately, act cool, and buy a couple of expensive drinks at the bar, you may very well be able to claim a chaise lounge by the side of the pool and people-watch without being chal-lenged. If you do get caught, though, you're on your own!

Mondrian, 8440 Sunset Blvd. (☎323-650-8999), in West Holly-wood, is an Ian Schrager-owned, Philippe Starck-designed beacon of trendiness. The lounge is perfectly designed for preening and posing. **Hollywood Standard,** 8300 Sunset Blvd. (☎323-650-9090), in Holly-wood, has mod styling and an incredible view of the Los Angeles basin. **W Hotel,** 930 Hilgard Ave. (☎310-208-8765), in Westwood, is part of a posh chain, and features two exquisite pools.

9pm. Tours in summer every 30min. 10:30am-4pm; in winter 10:30am-2:30pm. $15, seniors and children under 12 $10.) **Capitol Records Tower** was designed to look like a stack of records with a needle on top blinking H-O-L-L-Y-W-O-O-D in Morse code. *(1750 Vine St., ¾ block north of Hollywood Blvd.)*

GRIFFITH PARK AREA

GRIFFITH PARK. For a breath of fresh air and a respite from city life, take to the rugged, dry slopes of Griffith Park, the nation's largest municipal park, nestled in the hills between U.S. 101, I-5, and Rte. 134. A stark contrast to the concrete heights of downtown and the star-studded streets of Hollywood, the park is a refuge from the city and the site of many outdoor diversions. Fifty-two miles of hiking and horseback trails, three golf courses, a planetarium, an enormous zoo, several museums, and the 6000-person Greek Theatre are contained within its rolling 4107 acres. *(Nestled in the hills between U.S. 101, I-5, and Rte. 134. Visitors center and Ranger Headquarters: 4730 Crystal Spring Dr. ☎ 323-913-4688, emergency 913-7390. Park open daily 5am-10pm.)* The park has numerous equestrian trails and places to saddle up, such as **J.P. Stables.** *(914 S. Mariposa St., in Burbank. ☎ 818-843-9890. Open daily 7:30-6pm. 1st hr. $20, $12 each additional hr. Cash only.)*

PLANETARIUM AND OBSERVATORY. The world-famous white stucco and copper domes of the castle-like mountaintop observatory would be visible from nearly any point in the L.A. basin were it not for the smog. The observatory parking lot affords a terrific view of the Hollywood sign. You may remember the planetarium from the James Dean film *Rebel Without A Cause.* The observatory and planetarium are closed until early to mid-2006. *(Drive to the top of Mt. Hollywood on Vermont Ave. or Hillhurst St. from Los Feliz Blvd., or take MTA #180 or 181 from Hollywood Blvd. ☎ 323-664-1181, recording 664-1191; www.griffithobs.org. Grounds open Tu-F 1-10pm, Sa-Su 10am-10pm.)*

L.A. ZOO. The park's northern end furnishes habitats for rare animals from around the world. The Komodo dragon and Red Ape Rain Forest exhibits, along with the elephants and the chimps, are among the most popular spots in the zoo's well-kept 113 acres. *(5333 Zoo Dr. From Los Feliz Blvd., take Crystal Springs Dr. into the park; the zoo will be on your left. ☎ 644-4200; www.lazoo.org. Open daily July-Aug. 10am-6pm; Sept.-June 10am-5pm. Animals are put away for the night starting 1hr. before closing. $10, seniors $7, ages 2-12 $5.)*

FOREST LAWN CEMETERY. A rather twisted sense of celebrity sightseeing may lead some travelers to Glendale, where they can gaze upon stars who can't run away when asked for an autograph. Among the illustrious dead are Clark Gable, George Burns, and Jimmy Stewart. The cemetery has a 30 ft. by 15 ft. reproduction of Leonardo da Vinci's *The Last Supper (every 30min. 9:30am-4pm).* If you're still obsessed with oversized art, swing by the Forest Lawn in Hollywood Hills (only a 10min. drive) to see "Birth of Liberty," America's largest historical mosaic composed of 10 million pieces of Venetian glass. *(1712 S. Glendale Ave. ☎ 800-204-3131. Open daily 8am-6pm. Mausoleum open 9am-4:30pm.)*

DOWNTOWN

The **DASH Shuttle** runs six lines downtown that cover most of the major tourist destinations. *($0.25; p. 944.)* If driving, park in a secure lot, rather than on the street. Due to expensive short-term lot parking ($3 per 20min.) and exorbitant meter prices ($0.25 per 10min.), it's best to park in a public lot ($5-10 per day) and hit the pavement on foot. The **L.A. Visitors Center,** 685 S. Figueroa St., between Wilshire and 7th St., should have pamphlets and answers to your travel queries. *(☎ 213-689-8822. Open M-F 8am-4pm, Sa 8:30am-5pm.)*

EL PUEBLO HISTORIC PARK. The historic birthplace of L.A. is now known as **El Pueblo de Los Angeles Historical Monument,** bordered by Cesar Chávez Ave., Alameda St., Hollywood Fwy., and Spring St. (DASH B). In 1781, 44 settlers established a pueblo and farming community here; today, 27 buildings from the eras of Spanish and Mexican rule are preserved. Established in 1825, the **Plaza** is the center of El Pueblo, and hosts several festivals including the Mexican Independence celebration (Sept. 16), *Día de los Muertos* celebrations (Nov. 1-2), and *Cinco de Mayo* (May 5). Treat yourself to the cheapest churros around (2 for $1). Walk down one of L.A.'s historic streets, **Olvera Street,** which resembles a colorful Mexican marketplace, and bargain at *puestos* (vendor stalls) selling everything from Mexican handicrafts and food to personalized t-shirts. The **Avila Adobe** (circa 1818), 10 E. Olvera St., is the "oldest" house in the city. *(Open daily 9am-3pm.)*

MUSIC CENTER. The Music Center is an enormous, beautiful complex that includes **The Dorothy Chandler Pavilion,** home of the L.A. Opera *(☎213-972-8001; www.laopera.org),* former site of the Academy Awards. Across the street rise the radical silver slices of the Frank Gehry-designed 🏛**Walt Disney Concert Hall.** This gleaming 2265-seat structure is the brand-new home of the L.A. Philharmonic and the L.A. Master Chorale. *(151 S. Grand Ave. ☎213-972-7211; www.disneyhall.org.)* Also part of the Music Center are the **Mark Taper Forum** and the **Ahmanson Theatre,** known for their world-class shows. *(☎213-628-2772; www.taperahmanson.com. Tours of the 3-theater complex offered weekdays at 11:30am, 12:30, and 1:30pm as performance schedules permit. Go to the information booth in the large outdoor courtyard between the theaters.)*

OTHER SIGHTS. One of the best-known buildings in SoCal, **City Hall** "has starred in more movies than most actors." *(200 N. Spring St.)* Bargain hounds can haggle to their hearts' delight in the **Fashion District,** which is bordered by 6th and 9th St. along Los Angeles St. At 1017 ft., the tallest building between Chicago and Hong Kong, called the **Library Tower,** punctuates the L.A. skyline with its distinctive glass crown. *(633 W. 5th St.)* The **Westin Bonaventure Hotel** is composed of five sleek cylinders sheathed in black glass, and has appeared in *Rain Man, In the Line of Fire,* and *Heat. (404 S. Figueroa St.)* Slightly southeast of the Bonaventure is the historic **Biltmore Hotel,** a $10 million, 683-room hotel designed by Schultze and Weaver, best known for designing New York's Waldorf-Astoria. *(506 S. Grand Ave.)* The **Japanese American Cultural and Community Center** in Little Tokyo is the largest Asian-American cultural center in the country. Make sure to visit the serene **James Irvine Garden,** better known as *Seiryu-en* or "Garden of the Pure Stream." *(244 S. San Pedro St. ☎213-628-2725. www.jaccc.org. Gallery open Tu-F noon-5pm, Sa-Su 11am-4pm. Small donation may be requested.)* North of Exposition Park, the **University of Southern California (USC)** brings a youthful character to the streets of downtown. *(☎213-740-2311; www.usc.edu. Campus tours offered M-F every hr. 10am-3pm.)*

PASADENA AREA

Famous as home of the Rose Bowl, Pasadena's other main draw is **Old Town Pasadena,** bound approximately by Walnut St. and Del Mar Ave., between Pasadena Ave. and Arroyo Pkwy. This vibrant and trendy shopping and dining arena has reinvigorated buildings dating back to the 1880s and 1890s.

ROSE BOWL. In the gorge that forms the city's western boundary stands Pasadena's most famous landmark. The sand-colored, 90,000-seat stadium is home to "the granddaddy of them all," the annual college football clash on New Year's Day between the champions of the Big Ten and Pac 10 conferences. The Bowl Championship Series comes every four years, and the UCLA Bruins play regular-season home games here as well. *(1001 Rose Bowl Dr. ☎577-3100; www.rosebowlstadium.com.*

Bruins info: ☎ *310-825-29469; www.cto.ucla.edu.*) The Bowl also hosts an enormous monthly flea market that attracts upwards of 2000 vendors, selling nearly one million items. (☎ *323-560-7469. Held the 2nd Su of each month 9am-4:30pm. Admission 5-7am $20, 7-8am $15, 8-9am $10, 9am-3pm $7.)*

TECHNOLOGY. Some of the world's greatest scientific minds do their work at the **California Institute of Technology (Caltech).** Founded in 1891, Caltech has amassed a faculty that includes several Nobel laureates and a student body that prides itself both on its staggering collective intellect and its loony practical jokes, which range from unscrewing all the chairs in a lecture hall and bolting them in backwards to a nationally televised message added to the Rose Bowl scoreboard during the January 1 game. *(1201 E. California Blvd., about 2½ mi. southeast of Old Town. ☎ 626-395-6327. Tours M-F 2pm.)* **NASA's Jet Propulsion Laboratory,** about 5 mi. north of Old Town, executed the journey of the Mars Pathfinder. Ask to see pictures of the face of Mars. *(4800 Oak Grove Dr. ☎ 818-354-9314. Free tours by appointment.)*

■ **HUNTINGTON LIBRARY, ART GALLERY, AND BOTANICAL GARDENS.** Founded in 1919 and opened to the public in 1928, its stunning 150 acres of gardens are broken into thematic areas including the Rose Garden, the Shakespeare and herb gardens, and the Japanese Garden. (Picnicking and sunbathing among the greens is strictly forbidden.) The library holds one of the world's most important collections of rare books and British and American manuscripts, including a Gutenberg Bible, Benjamin Franklin's handwritten autobiography, a 1410 manuscript of Chaucer's *Canterbury Tales*, and a number of Shakespeare's first folios. The art gallery is known for its 18th- and 19th-century British paintings. No visit is complete without taking tea in the Rose Garden Tea Room. *(1151 Oxford Rd., between Huntington Dr. and California Blvd. in San Marino, south of Pasadena, about 2 mi. south of the I-210 Allen Ave. exit. Take bus #79 or 379 from Union Station to San Marino Ave. and walk 1½ mi. ☎ 405-2100; www.huntington.org. Open Memorial Day-Labor Day Tu-Su 10:30am-4:30pm; Labor Day-Memorial Day Tu-F noon-4:30pm, Sa-Su 10:30am-4:30pm. $13, seniors $10, students $8.50, ages 5-11 $5, under 5 free. Free 1st Th of each month. Rose Garden set tea $15; reservations required.)*

DESCANSO GARDENS. The 165-acre garden includes one of the world's largest camellia forests, a historic rose collection, and man-made waterfalls. Events include tutorials on home gardening, bug displays, and cool night walks. Blooming peaks in early spring. *(1418 Descanso Dr., by the intersection of Rte. 2 and Rte. 210. ☎ 818-949-4290. Open daily 9am-5pm. $6, students and seniors $4, ages 5-12 $1.50. Events $7-10.)*

SAN FERNANDO VALLEY

The Valley can't seem to shake the infamy it gained for breeding the Valley Girl, who started a worldwide trend in the 1980s with her huge hair, and, ohmigod, like, totally far-out mall adventures. But the Valley deserves some respect; all of the major movie studios (and many pornographers) make their blockbusters here. Passing Burbank on Rte. 134, you may catch glimpses of the Valley's most lucrative studios: **Universal, Warner Bros., NBC,** and **Disney.** To best experience the industry, attend a **free TV show taping** or take a studio tour.

■ **UNIVERSAL STUDIOS.** A movie and television studio that happens to have the world's first and largest movie-themed amusement park attached, Universal Studios Hollywood is the most popular tourist spot in Tinseltown. The signature Studio Tour tram brings riders face-to-face with King Kong and Jaws, rattles through a massive earthquake, and wanders past blockbuster sets from America's movie tradition, including *Apollo 13, Jurassic Park,* and *Psycho.* But for some, the tour plays second fiddle to the park's interactive attractions.

While the movie may have bombed, the live stunts and pyrotechnics at the *Waterworld* spectacular are impressive. (*Take U.S. 101 to the Universal Center Dr. or Landershim Blvd. exits. By MTA rail: exit North Hollywood Red Line at Universal Station. ☎ 800-UNIVERSAL; www.universalstudios.com. Open July-Aug. M-F 9am-9pm, Sa-Su 9am-10pm; Sept.-June M-F 10am-6pm, Sa-Su 10am-7pm. $50, under 48 in. $40, under 3 free. Parking $8.*)

UNIVERSAL CITY WALK. This neon-heavy, open-air strip of shopping, dining, movie theaters, and nightlife is the Valley's more colorful but less charming answer to Santa Monica's Third St. Promenade. The mammoth green guitar outside the Hard Rock Cafe, lurid King Kong sign, and the towering IMAX screen at the Cineplex Odeon set the tone for the vivid, larger-than-life complex. (*At Universal Studios. ☎ 818-622-4455; www.citywalkhollywood.com. City Walk parking $8; $2 rebate with purchase of 2 or more movie tickets.*)

MISSION SAN FERNANDO REY DE ESPAÑA. Founded in 1797, the **San Fernando Mission** is rich with history and is the largest adobe structure in California. The grounds, with museum and gift shop, are beautifully kept and definitely worth a visit. (*15101 San Fernando Mission Blvd. ☎ 361-0186. Open daily 9am-4:30pm. Mass M-Tu and Th-Sa 7:25am, Su 9 and 10:30am. $4, seniors and ages 7-15 $3, under 7 free.*)

MAGIC MOUNTAIN. At the opposite end of the Valley, 40min. north of L.A. in Valencia, is thrill-ride heaven **Six Flags Magic Mountain**, boasting the most roller coasters in the world. Its newest addition, **Scream!,** is Southern California's first floorless mega-coaster where your feet dangle in the air as you scream through 4000 ft. of twists, plunges, and loops. Next door, Six Flags's waterpark **Hurricane Harbor** features the world's tallest enclosed speed slide. (*Take U.S. 101 N to Rte. 170 N to I-5 N to Magic Mountain Pkwy. ☎ 661-255-4100; www.sixflags.com. Open Apr.-Aug. 6 daily; Sept.-Mar. weekends and holidays. Hours vary. $47, seniors and under 48 in. tall $30, under 2 free. Parking $8. Hurricane Harbor: ☎ 661-255-4527. Open May-Sept.; hours vary. $24, seniors and under 48 in. $17, under 2 free. Combined admission to both parks $57.*)

🏛 MUSEUMS

▨ **J. Paul Getty Center & Museum,** 1200 Getty Center Dr. (☎ 310-440-7300; www.getty.edu), Getty Center Dr. exit off I-405, in Bel Air. High in the Santa Monica Mountains shines a modern masterpiece, "The Getty." Wedding classical materials to modernist form, renowned architect Richard Meier designed the stunning $1 billion complex, which opened to the public in 1997. The museum consists of five pavilions overlooking the Robert Irwin-designed Central Garden, a living work of art that changes with the seasons. The pavilions contain the impressive Getty painting collection. Audio guides $3. Open Su and Tu-Th 10am-6pm, F-Sa 10am-9pm. Parking $5. Free.

▨ **Los Angeles County Museum of Art (LACMA),** 5905 Wilshire Blvd. (☎ 323-857-6000; www.lacma.org), in the Wilshire District. Opened in 1965, LACMA is the largest museum on the West Coast. The Steve Martin Gallery, in the Anderson Building, holds the famed comedian's collection of Dadaist and Surrealist works. Open M-Tu and Th noon-8pm, F noon-9pm, Sa-Su 11am-8pm. $9, students and seniors $5, under 18 free. Free 2nd Tu of each month and daily from 5pm. Free jazz F 5:30-8:30pm, chamber music Su 6-7pm. Film tickets $8, seniors and students $6. Parking $5, free after 7pm.

▨ **Norton Simon Museum of Art,** 411 W. Colorado Blvd. (☎ 626-449-6840; www.nortonsimon.org), in Pasadena. Rivaling the Getty Museum in quality, this world-class private collection chronicles Western art from Italian Gothic to 20th-century abstract. Paintings by Raphael, Van Gogh, Monet, and Picasso are featured, as well as rare print etchings by Rembrandt and Goya. The Impressionist and Post-Impressionist hall, the Southeast

Asian sculptures, and the 79,000 sq. ft. sculpture garden by California landscape artist Nancy Goslee Power, are particularly impressive. Open M, W-Th, and Sa-Su noon-6pm, F noon-9pm. $6, seniors $3, students and children under 18 free. Free parking.

UCLA Hammer Museum of Art, 10899 Wilshire Blvd. (☎310-443-7000; www.hammer.ucla.edu), in Westwood, houses the world's largest collection of works by 19th-century French satirist Honoré Daumier, as well as Van Gogh's *Hospital at Saint Rémy.* Open Tu and Sa-Su noon-7pm, W-F noon-9pm. Summer jazz concerts F 6:30-8pm. $5, seniors $3, under 17 free. Free Th. Tours of permanent collection Su 2pm, of traveling exhibits Th 6pm, Sa-Su 1pm. 3hr. parking $2.75, $1.50 each additional 20min.

Autry Museum of Western Heritage, 4700 Western Heritage Way (☎323-667-2000), in Griffith Park. City slickers and lone rangers may discover that the American West is not what they thought—the museum insists that the real should not be confused with the reel, drawing the line between Old West fact and fiction. Open Tu-W and F-Su 10am-5pm, Th 10am-8pm. $7.50, students and seniors $5, ages 2-12 $3. Free Th after 4pm.

Petersen Automotive Museum (PAM), 6060 Wilshire Blvd. (☎323-930-2277; www.petersen.org), at Fairfax Ave., in the Wilshire District. This slice of Americana showcases one of L.A.'s enduring symbols—the automobile. PAM is the world's largest car museum, with over 150 classic cars, hot rods, motorcycles, and movie and celebrity cars, not to mention the 1920s service station, 50s body shop, and 60s suburban garage. Call to set up a guided tour. Open Tu-Su 10am-6pm; Discovery Center closes 4pm. $10, students and seniors $5, ages 5-12 $3, under 5 free. Parking $6.

George C. Page Museum of La Brea Discoveries, 5801 Wilshire Blvd. (☎323-934-7243). The smelly **La Brea Tar Pits** fill the area with an acrid petroleum stench and provides bones for this natural history museum. Thirsty prehistoric mammals became stuck and perished in these oozing tar pools; their bones are arranged in interesting displays and depicted in murals of primeval L.A. A viewing station exists at Pit 91 where archaeologists continue to dig. Open M-F 9:30am-5pm, Sa-Su 10am-5pm. Tours of grounds Tu-Su 1pm, museum tours Tu-Su 2:15pm. $7, students and seniors $4.50, ages 5-12 $2. Free 1st Tu of each month. Parking $6 with validation.

Museum of Contemporary Art (MOCA), 50 S. Grand Ave. (☎213-626-6222; www.moca.org). Architect Arata Isozaki found inspiration for the facade's celebrated curve in L.A.'s favorite daughter, Marilyn Monroe; inside is a compelling collection of Western modern visual art. The Frank Gehry-renovated **MOCA at The Geffen Contemporary,** 152 N. Central Ave. (☎213-626-6222; www.moca.org), was once the garage for the LAPD fleet. The "Temporary Contemporary" and its highly-acclaimed installation art exhibitions eventually became permanent to the delight of its adoring public. Both locations open M and F 11am-5pm, Th 11am-8pm, Sa-Su 11am-6pm. $8, students and seniors $5, under 12 free. Free Th 5-8pm. Admission good for both MOCA locations. Shuttle transportation between the 2 locations offered.

◪ ENTERTAINMENT

FILM AND TELEVISION STUDIOS

A visit to the world's entertainment capital isn't complete without some exposure to the actual business of making a movie or TV show. Fortunately, most production companies oblige. **Paramount** (☎323-956-5000), **NBC** (☎818-840-3537), and **Warner Bros.** (☎818-954-1744) offer 2hr. guided tours that take you onto sets and through backlots. The best way to get a feel for the industry is to land yourself tickets to a taping. Tickets are free, but studios tend to overbook, so holding a ticket does not always guarantee you'll get in; show up early. **NBC,** 3000 W. Alameda Ave., at W. Olive Ave. in Burbank, is your best bet. Arrive at the ticket office on a weekday at 8am for passes to Jay Leno's **Tonight Show,** filmed at 5pm the same evening (2 tickets per person, must be 16+). Studio tours run on the hour. (☎818-840-3537. Tours M-F 9am-3pm. $7.50, ages 5-12 $4.) Many of NBC's "Must-See TV" shows are taped at **Warner Bros.**, 4000 Warner Blvd. (☎818-954-6000), in Burbank—call the studio at least five business days in advance to secure tickets.

A **CBS box office**, 7800 Beverly Blvd., next to the Farmers Market (p. 949) in West Hollywood, hands out free tickets to Bob Barker's game-show masterpiece *The Price is Right* (taped M-Th) up to one week in advance. Audience members must be over 18. (☎323-575-2458. Open M-F 9am-5pm.) You can request up to ten tickets on a specific date by sending a self-addressed, stamped envelope to *The Price is Right* Tickets, 7800 Beverly Blvd., Los Angeles, CA 90036, about four to six weeks in advance. If all else fails, **Audiences Unlimited, Inc.**, 100 Universal City Plaza, Building 4250, Universal City, CA 91608 (☎818-506-0067; www.tvtickets.com), is a great resource.

MOVIES

L.A.'s movie palaces show films the way they were meant to be seen—on a big screen, in plush seats, and with top-quality sound. The huge theaters at **Universal City,** as well as those in **Westwood Village** near UCLA, are incredibly popular, especially on weekends; expect long lines. **Santa Monica** has 22 screens within the three blocks between Santa Monica Pl. and Wilshire Blvd. along Third St. Promenade.

To ogle the stars as they walk the red carpet into the theater for a **premiere,** check the four main premiere venues: **Grauman's Chinese** (about 2 per month), **El Capitán** (Disney films only), and **Mann's Village** and **Bruin**, in Westwood. For info on what's playing, call ☎323-777-3456 or read the daily Calendar section of the *L.A. Times*. Devotees of second-run, foreign-language, and experimental films are rewarded by the Santa Monica theaters away from the Promenade. Foreign films play consistently at the eight **Laemmle Theaters** in Beverly Hills (☎310-274-6869), West Hollywood (☎323-848-3500), Santa Monica (☎310-394-9741), Pasadena (☎626-844-6500), and downtown (☎213-617-0268).

▧ **Grauman's Chinese Theatre**, 6925 Hollywood Blvd. (☎323-464-8111), between Highland and La Brea Ave., in Hollywood. Hype to the hilt. For more information, see **Sights: Hollywood**, p. 950. Tickets $10, ages 3-12 and over 65 $7; 1st show of the day $7.50.

▧ **Archlight Hollywood Cinerama Dome**, 6360 Sunset Blvd. (☎323-466-3401), near Vine St., in Hollywood. 14 movie screens surround a gigantic dome that seats 820 people and displays a screen that expands from 80 to 180 ft. A spectacular, rumbling sound system. Don't be late—doors close 7min. after movies begin. Tickets $7.75-14.

Nuart Theatre, 11272 Santa Monica Blvd. (☎310-478-6379), just west of I-405 at Sawtelle Ave., in West L.A. Perhaps the best-known revival house. The playbill changes nightly. Classics, documentaries, animation festivals, and foreign and modern films. *The Rocky Horror Picture Show* screens Sa at midnight with a stellar live cast. Tickets $9.50, seniors and under 12 $7.25. Discount card (5 tickets for $35).

Mann's Village Theatre, 961 Broxton Ave. (☎310-208-0018), in Westwood. Vibrant neons illuminate the Art Deco facade. One huge auditorium, one big screen, and one great THX sound system. Watch the balcony for late-arriving celebrities. Frequent premieres. Tickets $10, students $7.50, seniors $7, under 12 $6.50; M-F before 6pm $7.

LIVE THEATER AND MUSIC

L.A.'s live theater scene does not hold the weight of New York's Broadway, but its 115 "equity waiver theaters" (under 100 seats) offer dizzying, eclectic choices for theatergoers, who can also view small productions in art galleries, universities, parks, and even garages. Browse listings in the *L.A. Weekly* to find out what's hot.

CALIFORNIA

L.A.'s music venues range from small clubs to massive amphitheaters. The **Wiltern** (☎213-380-5005) shows alterna-rock/folk acts. The **Hollywood Palladium** (☎323-962-7600) is of comparable size with 3500 seats. Midsized acts head for the **Universal Amphitheater** (☎818-622-4440). Huge indoor sports arenas, such as the **Great Western Forum** (☎310-330-7300) and the newer **Staples Center** (☎213-742-7100), double as concert halls for big acts. Few dare to play at the 100,000-seat **Los Angeles Memorial Coliseum and Sports Arena**; only U2, Depeche Mode, Guns 'n' Roses, and the Warped Tour have filled the stands in recent years. Call Ticketmaster (☎213-480-3232) to purchase tickets for any of these venues.

🏛 **Hollywood Bowl,** 2301 N. Highland Ave. (☎323-850-2000), in Hollywood. The premier outdoor music venue in L.A., the Bowl hosts a summer music festival from early July to mid-Sept. Free open house rehearsals by the Philharmonic and visiting performers usually Tu and Th at 10:30am. Parking at the Bowl is limited and pricey ($11-12). It's better to park at one of the lots away from the Bowl and take a shuttle (parking $5, shuttle $2.50; departs every 10-20min. starting 1½hr. before showtime). Lots at 10601 and 10801 Ventura Blvd., near Universal City; at the Kodak Theatre at 6801 Hollywood Blvd.; and at the L.A. Zoo, 5333 Zoo Dr., in Griffith Park. Call Ticketmaster (☎213-480-3232) to purchase tickets.

Geffen Playhouse, 10886 LeConte Ave. (☎310-208-5454), in Westwood. Currently undergoing a $17 million renovation. Home to Off-Broadway and Tony-Award-winning shows. Tickets $34-46; $10 student rush tickets available 1hr. before the show.

Pasadena Playhouse, 39 S. El Molino Ave. (☎626-356-7529 or 800-233-3123; www.pasadenaplayhouse.org), in Pasadena. California's premier theater and historical landmark has spawned Broadway careers and productions. Tickets $35-60. Call for rush tickets. Shows Tu-F 8pm, Sa 5 and 9pm, Su 2 and 7pm.

SPORTS

Exposition Park and the often dangerous city of **Inglewood,** southwest of the park, are home to many sports teams. The **USC Trojans** play football at the **L.A. Memorial Coliseum,** 3911 S. Figueroa St. (☎213-740-4672), which seats over 100,000 spectators. The NBA's **L.A. Clippers** (☎213-742-7500) seek a revival while the **L.A. Lakers** (☎310-426-6000) cope with the post-dynasty blues at the new **Staples Center,** 1111 S. Figueroa St. (☎213-742-7100, box office 213-742-7340), along with the **L.A. Kings** hockey team (☎888-546-4752) and the WNBA's **L.A. Sparks** (☎310-330-3939). Call Ticketmaster (☎213-480-3232) for tickets. About 3 mi. northeast of downtown, **Elysian Park** curves around the northern portion of Chávez Ravine, home of **Dodger Stadium** and the popular **L.A. Dodgers** baseball team. Single-game tickets ($6-21) are a hot commodity during the April to October season, especially if the Dodgers are playing well. (Call ☎323-224-1448 for info and advance tickets.)

🎵 NIGHTLIFE

L.A.'s nightlife scene is constantly shifting. Pick up a copy of *L.A. Weekly* or the *L.A. Times*'s Calendar section for the latest entertainment news.

COFFEEHOUSES AND LATE-NIGHT RESTAURANTS

Given the extremely short shelf life and unpredictability of the L.A. club scene, late-night restaurants have become the reliable fallback option of L.A. nightlife, popular with underage club kids and celebs in rehab. Many coffeehouses stay open late and have open-mic nights or live music.

◪ **The Kettle,** 1138 N. Highland Ave. (☎562-545-8511), at the corner of Manhattan Beach Blvd., in Manhattan Beach. Come nightfall, surfers take over the carved-wood tables for heaping platefuls of home-style cooking. The menu is only a guide—creativity is encouraged. Salads and sandwiches $7-9. "Hangover" omelette with green chiles and jack cheese $7. Beer and wine served until midnight. Open 24hr.

◪ **Highland Grounds,** 742 N. Highland Ave. (466-1507; www.highlandgrounds.com). Intimate, laid-back coffeehouse and restaurant. Great breakfasts (served until 4pm; $5-9) and a fire pit. Live music every night. Lunch and late-night entrees $7-9. Beer and wine $0.50-6.50. Open M 9am-5pm, Tu-Th 9am-midnight, F-Sa 9am-1am, Su 9am-4pm.

The Rainbow Bar and Grill, 9015 Sunset Blvd. (☎310-278-4232; http://rainbowbarandgrill.com), next to the Roxy. Dark red vinyl booths, dim lighting, loud music, and colorful characters set the scene. Marilyn Monroe met Joe DiMaggio on a blind date here. Brooklyn-quality pizza $6; calamari $8; grandma's chicken soup $3.50. Open M-F 11am-2am, Sa-Su 5pm-2am.

Jerry's Famous Deli, 8701 Beverly Blvd. (☎310-289-1811), at San Vicente Ave. Additional locations: 10925 Weyburn Ave. (☎310-208-3354), in Westwood, and 12655 Ventura Blvd. (☎818-980-4245), in Studio City in the Valley. An L.A. deli with sleek red leather and sky-high prices. Note the menu's height—Jerry is rumored to have wanted "the longest menu possible while still maintaining structural integrity." Something on it is bound to be perfect for your 4am snack. Known for its jumbo triple-deckers ($13-14) and salads served in a pizza crust ($10-13). Open 24hr.

Elixer, 8612 Melrose Ave. (☎310-657-9300), just east of San Vicente Blvd., in Hollywood. Outdoor garden imitates a tranquil tropical paradise inspired by celebrities' spiritual trends—look for red Kabbalah bracelets. Tonics ($4-5) based on Chinese herbal traditions and international teas. Free live music most Tu nights; chess, checkers, Chinese checkers, and other board games are always ready for takers. Licensed herbalists are on duty daily 11am-6pm for spontaneous consultations (call ahead for a comprehensive one-on-one session). Open M-Sa 9am-midnight, Su 10am-10pm.

COMEDY CLUBS

L.A.'s comedy clubs are among the best in the world. Catch the newest comedians or watch skilled veterans hone new material.

Comedy Store, 8433 Sunset Blvd. (☎323-650-6268), in West Hollywood. 3 rooms each feature a different type of comedy. The Main Room and Original Room host headliner comics (cover M-F $15, Sa-Su $20; Main Room only open Sa). Belly Room provides a testing ground for up-and-comers (no cover). Drinks $5-9; 2-drink min. 21+. Showtimes vary; call a week ahead to reserve tickets. Open daily until 2am.

Groundling Theater, 7307 Melrose Ave. (☎323-934-4747; www.groundlings.com), in Hollywood. One of the most popular improv and comedy clubs in town. The Groundling's alums include Pee Wee Herman and many current and former *Saturday Night Live* regulars like Will Ferrell, Julia Sweeney, and Chris Kattan. Don't be surprised to see *SNL* producer Lorne Michaels sitting in the back. Lisa Kudrow of *Friends* also got her start here. Polished skits. Tickets $13-20. Shows W-Th 8pm, F-Sa 8 and 10pm, Su 7:30pm.

BARS

Though it's hard to barhop when the best places are a 30min. drive away from each other (don't forget your designated driver), L.A.'s **bars** run the gamut from casual beach hangouts to swanky hotel lounges. Unless otherwise specified, **bars in California are 21+.**

▨**Temple Bar,** 1026 Wilshire Blvd. (☎393-6611). Dark "eastern" decor and cool live music give Temple Bar a smooth vibe. Food and drink complete the eclectic mix with house favorites such as jerk chicken enchiladas with plantains ($8.50) and mojitos ($10). Live music nightly. Open daily 8pm-2am.

▨**Standard Lounge,** 8300 Sunset Blvd. (☎323-822-3111), in the Standard Hotel in Hollywood. No dress code, no cover, no guest list, but you'd never know it. Insanely chic— Carrie Bradshaw drank here in the "Sex and Another City" episode of *Sex and the City*. Drinks $9. Nightly DJ. Open daily 10pm-2am.

3 of Clubs, 1123 N. Vine St. (☎323-462-6441), at the corner of Santa Monica Blvd., in Hollywood, hidden in a strip mall. Simple, classy, and spacious hardwood bar famous for appearing in *Swingers*. Live bands Th. DJ F-Sa. Open daily 6pm-2am.

Miyagi's, 8225 Sunset Blvd. (☎323-650-3524), on the Sunset Strip, in West Hollywood. With 3 levels, 7 sushi bars (rolls $5-7), 6 liquor bars, and indoor waterfalls, this Japanese-themed restaurant, bar, lounge, and hip-hop dance club is a Strip hot spot. "*Sake* bomb, *sake* bomb, *sake* bomb" $4.50. Open daily 5:30pm-2am.

Beauty Bar, 1638 Cahuenga Blvd. (☎323-464-7676), in Hollywood. Get a manicure while sipping a cocktail. Martinis are *so* much headier when sitting under an old-school hair dryer. Beautify while boozing on drinks like the "perm" or the "platinum blonde" ($8, with manicure $10). DJ nightly 10pm. Open Su-W 9pm-2am, Th-Sa 6pm-2am.

CLUBS

With the highest number of bands per capita in the world and more streaming in every day, L.A. is famous for its club scene. The Sunset Strip holds many of the city's best clubs. L.A. clubs are often expensive, but many are still feasible on a limited budget. Coupons in *L.A. Weekly* and those handed out inside clubs can save you a bundle. To enter the club scene, it's best to be at least 21 (although it also helps to be a beautiful woman). Nevertheless, if you're over 18, you can still find a space to dance, though it may mean a hefty cover charge in a less desirable venue. **All clubs are 21+ unless otherwise noted.**

▨**Largo,** 432 N. Fairfax Ave. (☎323-852-1073), between Melrose Ave. and Beverly Blvd., in West Hollywood. Intimate sit-down (or, if you get there late, lean-back) club. Rock, pop, folk, and comedy acts. Cover $2-12. Open Su-Th 8pm-2am, F-Sa 8:30pm-2am.

The Shelter, 8117 Sunset Blvd. (☎310-654-0030), just west of Crescent Heights Ave., in West Hollywood. Hot lounge and dance club spins different beats in each of its 7 rooms. Hip-hop thumps on the main dance floor. Cover $20. Open F-Sa 10pm-2am.

The Derby, 4500 Los Feliz Blvd. (☎323-663-8979; www.the-derby.com), at the corner of Hillhurst Ave. in Los Feliz. Still jumpin' and jivin' with the kings of swing. Ladies, grab your snoods; many dress the 40s part. Full bar. Free swing lessons Su 6:30pm. Cover F-Sa $5-12. Open daily 7:30pm-2am. Back bar open daily 5pm-2am (no cover).

Whisky A Go-Go, 8901 Sunset Blvd. (☎310-652-4205), in West Hollywood. Historically, this was the great prophet of L.A.'s music scene. It hosted progressive bands in the late 70s and early 80s and was big in the punk explosion. The Doors, Janis Joplin, and Led Zeppelin played here. All ages. Cover M-Th $10, F-Su $13. Shows begin 7pm.

GLBT NIGHTLIFE

The slice of Santa Monica Blvd. in West Hollywood is the Sunset Strip of GLBT nightlife. All of the clubs listed below are in West Hollywood. Still, many "straight" clubs have gay nights; check *L.A. Weekly* or contact the Gay and Lesbian Community Services Center. Free weekly magazine *fab!* lists happenings in the GLBT community. **All clubs are 21+ unless otherwise noted.**

▓ **Abbey Cafe,** 692 N. Robertson Blvd. (☎310-289-8410), at Santa Monica Blvd. 6 candlelit rooms, 2 huge bars, a large outdoor patio, and a hall of private booths make this beautiful lounge and dance club the best gay nightspot in town. The comfy couches cry out for some lovin'. Open daily 8am-2am.

Micky's, 8857 Santa Monica Blvd. (☎310-657-1176). Huge dance floor filled with delectable men. On a Sa night when bars close, head to Micky's for another 2hr. of grooving. Music is mostly electronica and techno, although hip-hop is sometimes sprinkled into the mix. M drag shows. Happy hour M-F 5-9pm. Cover $3-10. Open Th-F 4pm-2am, Sa 11pm-4am, Su 11pm-2am.

Here, 696 N. Robertson St. (☎310-360-8455), at the corner of Santa Monica Blvd. Known for Su nights when the bartenders dress up in scandalous surfer shorts, this sleek gay bar and dance club caters to the well dressed and trendy. DJs spin a mix of house and hip-hop. Don't miss the frozen cosmopolitans ($8). Th lesbian night. Happy hour daily 4-8pm; drinks $2-3 off. Open daily 4pm-2am.

Trunks, 8809 Santa Monica Blvd. (☎310-652-1015), a friendly and popular neighborhood gay and lesbian bar. Open daily 1pm-2am.

ORANGE COUNTY

Directly south of L.A. County lies Orange County (pop. 2.9 million). Composed of 34 cities, it is a microcosm of Southern California: dazzling sandy shoreline, bronzed beach bums, oversized shopping malls, homogenous suburban neighborhoods, and frustrating traffic snarls. As one of California's staunchest Republican enclaves, Orange County (and no, they don't actually call it "The O.C.") supports big business, and has the economy and the multimillion-dollar hillside mansions oozing luxury cars and disaffected teens to prove it. Disneyland, the stronghold of the Walt Disney Company's ever-expanding empire, is the premier inland attraction. The coast runs the gamut from the budget- and party-friendly surf burg of Huntington Beach to the opulent excess of Newport Beach and the artistic vibe of Laguna. Farther south lies the quiet mission of San Juan Capistrano, set amid rolling hills that spill onto the laid-back beaches of Dana Point and San Clemente.

▐ TRANSPORTATION

Airport: John Wayne Airport, 18601 Airport Way (☎949-252-5200), in Santa Ana. 20min. from Anaheim. Domestic flights only.

Trains: Amtrak (☎800-USA-RAIL/872-7245; www.amtrakcalifornia.com) stations, from north to south: **Fullerton,** 120 E. Santa Fe Ave. (☎714-992-0530); **Santa Ana,** 1000 E. Santa Ana Blvd. (☎714-547-8389); **Irvine,** 15215 Barranca Pkwy. (☎949-753-9713); **San Juan Capistrano,** 26701 Verdugo St. (☎949-240-2972).

Buses: Greyhound (☎800-231-2222). 3 stations in the area. **Anaheim,** 100 W. Winston Rd. (☎714-999-1256), 3 blocks south of Disneyland. Open daily 6:30am-9:15pm. **Santa Ana,** 1000 E. Santa Ana Blvd. (☎714-542-2215). Open daily 6:15am-8:30pm. **San Clemente,** 2421 S. El Camino Real (☎949-366-2646). Open daily 7am-9pm.

Public Transit: Orange County Transportation Authority (OCTA; ☎714-636-7433; www.octa.net), 550 S. Main St., in Orange. Thorough service is useful for getting from Santa Ana and Fullerton Amtrak stations to Disneyland and for beach-hopping along the coast. Long Beach, in L.A. County, serves as the terminus for several OCTA lines. Bus #1 travels the coast from Long Beach to San Clemente (every hr. until 8pm); #25, 33, and 35 travel from Fullerton to Huntington Beach; #91 goes from Laguna Hills to

San Clemente. $1, day pass $2.50.) **Info center** open M-F 6am-8pm, Sa-Su 8am-5pm. **MTA Info** (☎213-626-4455 or 800-266-6883) available by phone daily 5am-10:45pm. MTA buses run from L.A. to Disneyland and Knott's Berry Farm.

Visitor Info: Anaheim Area Visitors and Convention Bureau, 800 W. Katella Ave. (☎714-765-8888; www.anaheimoc.org), in Anaheim Convention Ctr. Lodging and dining guides. Open M-F 8am-5pm. **Newport Visitors Bureau,** 110 Newport Center Dr., #120 (☎949-719-6100 or 800-942-6278), in Newport Beach. Eager-to-help staff, maps of area attractions, and events brochures. Open M-F 8am-5pm. **Laguna Beach Visitors Bureau,** 252 Broadway (☎949-497-9229). Open M-F 9am-5pm, Sa 10am-4pm, Su noon-4pm.

Police: Anaheim, 425 S. Harbor Blvd. (☎714-765-1900). **Huntington Beach,** 2000 Main St. (☎714-960-8811).

Hotlines: Sexual Assault Hotline, ☎714-957-2737. **Orange County Referral Hotline,** ☎714-894-4242. **Surf and Weather Conditions,** ☎213-554-1212.

Medical Services: St. Jude Medical Center, 101 E. Valencia Mesa Dr. (☎714-871-3280), Fullerton. **Lestonnac Free Clinic,** 1215 E. Chapman Ave. (☎714-633-4600). Hours vary; call for an appointment.

Post Office: 701 N. Loara St. (☎714-520-2639 or 800-275-8777), 1 block north of Anaheim Plaza, in Anaheim. Open M-F 8:30am-5pm, Sa 9am-3pm. **Postal Code:** 92803. **Area Codes:** 714 (Anaheim, Santa Ana, Orange, Garden Grove), 949 (Newport, Laguna, Irvine, Mission Viejo, San Juan Capistrano).

▐ ACCOMMODATIONS

Countless budget chain motels and garden-variety rooms flank Disneyland on all sides. Keep watch for family and group rates posted on marquees, and seek out establishments offering the **3-for-2 passport** (3 days of Disney for the price of 2).

▦ **Huntington Beach Colonial Inn Youth Hostel,** 421 8th St. (☎714-536-3315), 4 blocks inland at Pecan Ave. in Huntington Beach. Take OCTA #29 (which also goes to Knott's Berry Farm) or #50. From PCH, turn onto 8th St. This large, early 20th-century yellow and blue house was once a brothel. Common bath, large kitchen, reading/TV room, coin-op laundry, Internet access, deck, and shed with surfboards, boogie boards, and bikes. Breakfast and linen included. Key deposit $5. Check-in 8am-11pm. Reserve 2 days in advance for summer weekends. 3- to 4-person dorms $23; doubles $55. ❶

Fullerton Hostel (HI), 1700 N. Harbor Blvd. (☎714-738-3721), in Fullerton, 10min. north of Disneyland. Shuttle from L.A. Airport $21. OCTA bus #43 runs along Harbor Blvd. to Disneyland. In the woods and away from the thematic craziness of nearby Anaheim, this hostel has an international feel. The enthusiastic staff invites questions but forbids drinking. Kitchen, relaxing living room, communal bathrooms. Linen $2. Laundry (wash $0.75, dry $0.75). 7-night max. stay. Check-in 8am-11pm. Reservations encouraged. Open June-Sept. Dorms $19, nonmembers $22. ❶

Balboa Inn, 105 Main St. (☎949-675-3412; www.balboainn.com), on the sand in Newport. From PCH, follow signs to Balboa Peninsula and turn onto Main St. This recently renovated historical landmark offers rooms with ocean or bay views and is close to area attractions. Relax in the pool or hot tub. Room service available. Continental breakfast, fans, cable TV, and fridge included. Rooms from $139. Overnight parking $8. ❺

◖ FOOD

Orange County thrives on light California Cuisine and exquisitely fresh seafood.

▓ **Rutabegorz,** 211 N. Pomona Blvd. (☎714-738-9339; www.rutabegorz.com), in Fullerton. Also at 264 N. Glassell St. (☎714-633-3260), in Orange; and 158 W. Main St. (☎731-9807), in Tustin. With a name derived from the often unloved rutabaga, this hippie-cum-hipster joint has a 20-page recycled newsprint menu. Crepes, curries, quesadillas, and club sandwiches are all fresh and veggie-heavy. Heaping salads with homemade dressings $4-9. Mexican casserole $7. Smoothies, veggie juices, and coffee drinks $2-4. Open M-Th 11am-10pm, F-Sa 11am-11pm, Su 4-9pm. ❷

Laguna Village Market and Cafe, 577 S. Coast Hwy. (☎949-494-6344), 5 blocks south of Broadway in Laguna Beach. Located on top of a cliff, the restaurant is housed in an open-air gazebo selling art and jewelry by local artists and designers. Its oceanfront terrace is the main draw. Lap up the view along with some seafood or the house specialty, Village Huevos ($9.50). Calamari plate $9. Open daily 8:30am-dark. ❷

Ruby's (☎714-969-7829), at the end of the Huntington Beach Pier. A 5-7min. trek down the pier. With windows on all sides, this flashy white and neon-red 50s-style diner has great burgers ($8) and a fabulous ocean view. ❷

◉ ☌ SIGHTS AND BEACHES

DISNEYLAND. Disneyland calls itself the "Happiest Place on Earth," and a part of everyone agrees. After a full day there, your precious wallet, of course, may not. Weekday and low-season visitors will undoubtedly be the happiest, but the clever can wait for parades to distract children from the epic lines or utilize the line-busting FastPass program. Recently, Disneyland introduced its new kid brother, "California Adventure," to the theme park family. The park features ambitious attractions divided into four districts. **Sunshine Plaza,** the gateway to the park, is anchored by a 50 ft. tall sun enlivened by a flood of red, orange, and yellow lights at night. **Golden State** offers an eight-acre mini-wilderness, a citrus grove, a winery, and even a replica of San Francisco. **Paradise Pier** is dedicated to the so-called "Golden Age" of amusement parks—with rides such as **California Screamin'** and **Mulholland Madness.** Finally, the **Hollywood Pictures Backlot** realizes your aspirations to stardom without those embarrassing before-you-were-famous nude photos hanging over your head. (*Main entrance on Harbor Blvd., and a smaller one on Katella Ave. Parking $8. ☎714-781-4565; www.disneyland.com. Disneyland open Su-Th 8am-11pm, F-Sa 8am-midnight; hours may vary. California Adventure open Su-Th 9am-10pm, F-Sa 9am-10:30pm. Disneyland passport $50, ages 3-9 $40, under 3 free; allows repeated single-day entrance. 2- and 3-day passes also available. California Adventure passport prices are the same as Disneyland's. Combination ticket $70, ages 3-9 $60.*)

(K)NOT(T) DISNEYLAND. Knott's is a local favorite and aims at being "the friendliest place in the West"—it has long since given up on being the happiest place on Earth. The park's highlights include roller coasters like **Montezooma's Revenge, Boomerang,** and **Ghostrider,** the largest wooden roller coasters in the West. The latest addition is **Xcelerator,** bringing you from 0 to 80 mph in three seconds. (*8039 Beach Blvd., at La Palma Ave., 5 mi. northeast of Disneyland. From downtown L.A., take MTA bus #460 from 4th and Flower St.; 1¼hr. If driving from L.A., take I-5 south to Beach Blvd., turn right at the end of the exit ramp, and proceed south 2 mi. Recorded info ☎714-220-5200. Open Su-Th 9am-10pm, F-Sa 9am-midnight; hours may vary. $43, ages 3-11 $13, under 3 free; after 4pm all tickets half-price. Parking under 3hr. free, each additional hr. $2; all-day parking $8.*) **Soak City USA** is Knott's 13-acre effort to make a splash in the already drenched water park scene. (*Next to Knott's. ☎220-5200. Open Su-Th 10am-6pm, F-Sa 10am-8pm; hours may vary. $25, ages 3-11 $13, under 3 free.*)

SPORTS. For more evidence of Disney's world domination, catch a game by one of the teams they own. The major league **Anaheim Angels** play baseball from early April to October at **Edison Field.** (☎ 940-2000 or 800-626-4357. General tickets $9-30.) To check out some NHL action, catch a **Mighty Ducks** hockey game at **Arrowhead Pond.**

ORANGE COUNTY BEACH COMMUNITIES. Orange County's various beach communities have cleaner sand, better surf, and less madness than their L.A. County counterparts; it is here that L.A. residents seek refuge. The prototypical Surf City, **Huntington Beach** is a perfect beach bum playground. This town has surf lore galore, and the proof is on the **Surfing Walk of Fame** and in the **International Surfing Museum.** (Walk of Fame: the sidewalk along PCH at Main St. Museum: 411 Olive St. ☎ 714-960-3483. Open daily noon-5pm. $2, students $1.) Multimillion-dollar summer homes, the world's largest leisure-craft harbor, and Balboa Peninsula are all packed closely enough on the Newport Beach oceanfront to make even New Yorkers feel claustrophobic. Surfing and beach volleyball are popular, as is strolling on residential Balboa Peninsula. Punctuated by rocky cliffs, shady coves, and lush hillside vegetation, lovely, artsy **Laguna Beach's** character is decidedly Mediterranean. **Ocean Avenue,** at the Pacific Coast Hwy., and **Main Beach** are the prime parading areas. The latest incarnation of the original 1914 Laguna Beach art association is the **Laguna Art Museum.** The collection showcases local and state art, including some excellent early 20th-century Impressionist works. (307 Cliff Dr. ☎ 949-494-8971; www.lagunaartmuseum.com. Open daily 11am-5pm. Tours daily 2pm. $9, students and seniors $7, under 12 free. Free 1st Th of each month 5-9pm.) The evocative **Mission San Juan Capistrano,** 30min. south of Anaheim on I-5, was established by Father Junípero Serra and is considered the "jewel of the missions."

BIG BEAR ☎ 909

Big Bear is easily Southern California's most popular mountain and lake resort. In the summer, the central lake provides ample opportunities for fishing, sailing, and watersports, while the nearby mountains and forest offer enjoyable hikes and well-preserved campgrounds.

Hiking the trails in the surrounding mountains is a superb way of exploring the San Bernardino wilderness. Maps, trail descriptions, and the *Visitor's Guide to the San Bernardino National Forest* are available at the **Big Bear Discovery Center (BBDC).** The 3½ mi. **Alpine Pedal Path** runs its gentle, paved course from the Stanfield Cutoff on the lake's north shore to the BBDC. The moderately difficult 2½ mi. **Castle Rock Trail,** starting 1 mi. east of the dam on Hwy. 18, is a steep haul to stupendous views of Big Bear Lake. In summer, **mountain biking** takes over the Big Bear slopes. Grab a *Ride and Trail Guide* at the BBDC or at **Snow Summit,** 1 mi. west of Big Bear Lake, which runs lifts in summer so armored adrenaline monsters can grind serious downhill terrain. (☎ 866-4621. $10, ages 7-12 $5; day pass $20/$10. Helmet required. Open Su-F 9am-4pm, Sa 8am-5pm.) **Team Big Bear,** 476 Concklin Rd., operating out of the Mountain Bike Shop at the base of Snow Summit, rents bikes and sponsors organized bike races each summer. (☎ 866-4565. $9 per hr., $27 for 4hr., $50 per day; helmet included.) Big Bear Lake is well stocked with rainbow trout and catfish. State **fishing** licenses are available at sporting goods stores (day $10, season $28). Boats can be rented at **Holloway's Marina,** 398 Edgemor Rd., on the south shore. (☎ 866-5706 or 800-448-5335; www.bigbearboating.com. $50-175 per day.)

When snow conditions are favorable, ski areas quickly run out of lift tickets, which may be purchased through Ticketmaster (☎ 714-740-2000). **Big Bear Mountain Resorts** (www.bigbearmountainresorts.com) splits 55 runs between two ski resorts. The huge vertical drops and adventure skiing terrain at **Bear Mountain,** 43101 Goldmine Dr., are geared toward freestyle skiing and snowboarding. (☎ 585-

2519; www.bearmtn.com.) **Snow Summit,** 880 Summit Blvd., is a more family-oriented resort with snowmaking, night skiing, and a well-rounded assortment of beginner runs. (☎866-5766; www.snowsummit.com. Lift tickets are interchangeable, and a shuttle runs between the 2 parks. Lift tickets $43, ages 13-19 $35, ages 7-12 $14; holidays $50/$50/$21. Skis $25 per day; snowboards $30 per day. Deposit required.) **Snow Valley,** 35100 Highway 18, near Running Springs, is the most family-oriented resort in Big Bear. (☎867-2751. Lift ticket $37, ages 6-13 $23. Ski rental $17, snowboard $30.) **Renting** ski and snowboard equipment from the ski stores along Big Bear Blvd. can save you up to half the price of renting at the mountains. **Cross-country skiing** is very popular in Big Bear. The Rim Nordic Ski Area, across the highway from Snow Valley, is a network of cross-country ski trails. An Adventure Passport ($5) is required (p. 963).

As Big Bear is a year-round destination, rooms below $50 a night are often only found down the mountain in San Bernardino. **Big Bear Boulevard** is lined with lodging possibilities. ▧**Robinhood Inn ❹,** 40797 Lakeview Dr., has a courtyard complete with spa and barbecue, and fireplaces and kitchenettes in many rooms. (☎866-4643. Singles and doubles from $59; suites for up to 6 people under $100.) **Serrano ❶,** 40650 N. Shore Ln., off Hwy. 38, in Fawnskin, is the most popular campground in Big Bear, with the highest occupancy of any national forest campground. (☎866-8021, reservations 877-444-6777. Flush toilets and showers. Sites $23.) Food can get pricey, so those with kitchens should forage at **Stater Bros.,** 42171 Big Bear Blvd. (☎866-5211. Open daily 7am-11pm.) **Peppercorn Grille ❷,** 553 Pine Knot Ave., has $7 lunch specials of mainly American and California cuisine. (☎866-5405. Open daily 11am-3pm and 5-9pm.)

To reach Big Bear, take **I-10** to **Route 30** in San Bernardino and follow Rte. 30 north to **Route 330** (Mountain Rd.), which turns into **Route 18,** a winding 30-45min. ascent. Rte. 18 hits the west end of Big Bear Lake and splits into a continuing Rte. 18 branch along the south shore, where it is called Big Bear Blvd., and **Route 38** along the north shore. Driving time from L.A. is about 2½hr., barring serious weekend traffic or road closures. Driving to Big Bear should not be attempted during the winter without checking road conditions with **CalTrans** (☎427-7623; www.dot.ca.gov). **Mountain Area Regional Transit Authority (MARTA)** runs two **buses** per day from the Greyhound station in San Bernardino to Big Bear. (☎584-1111. $5, seniors and disabled $3.75.) The **Big Bear Chamber of Commerce,** 630 Bartlett Rd., in Big Bear Village, is helpful. (☎866-4608; www.big-bearchamber.com. Open M-F 8am-5pm, Sa-Su 9am-5pm.) Other services include: the ranger station (☎383-5651); **Big Bear Public Library,** 41930 Garstin Dr. (☎866-5571; Internet access; open M-Tu noon-8pm, W-F 10am-6pm, Sa 9am-5pm); and the **post office,** 472 Pine Knot Blvd. (☎866-7481; open M-F 8:30am-5pm, Sa 10am-noon). **Postal Code:** 92315.

SAN DIEGO ☎619

The locals call it "America's Finest City," and visitors pulling into this picturesque port will soon understand why. In a state where every town stakes a claim on paradise, San Diego may be Southern California's best return on the promises of a golden state, offering perfectly sunny weather almost every day of the year.

▣ TRANSPORTATION

San Diego is in the extreme southwest corner of California, 127 mi. south of L.A. and 15 mi. north of the Mexican border. **I-5** runs south from L.A. through the North County cities of Oceanside and Carlsbad, skirting the eastern edge of downtown

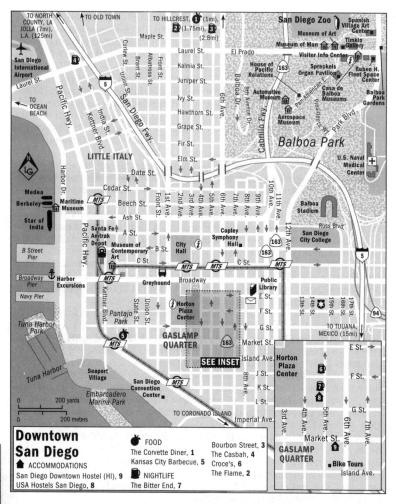

Downtown San Diego

⌂ ACCOMMODATIONS
San Diego Downtown Hostel (HI), **9**
USA Hostels San Diego, **8**

🍴 FOOD
The Corvette Diner, **1**
Kansas City Barbecue, **5**

🍸 NIGHTLIFE
The Bitter End, **7**

Bourbon Street, **3**
The Casbah, **4**
Croce's, **6**
The Flame, **2**

on its way to the Mexican border; **I-15** runs northeast through the desert to Las Vegas; and **I-8** runs east-west along downtown's northern boundary, connecting the desert with Ocean Beach. The downtown core is laid out in a grid.

Airport: San Diego International (Lindbergh Field), at the northwest edge of downtown. Call the Travelers Aid Society (☎231-7361) for info. Society open daily 8am-11pm. Bus #992 goes downtown ($2.25), as do cabs ($8-10). **Cloud 9 Shuttle** (☎800-974-8853) offers affordable shared van transportation throughout the region.

Trains: Amtrak, 1050 Kettner Blvd. (☎800-872-7245), just north of Broadway in the Santa Fe Depot. Station has info on bus, trolley, car, and boat transportation. Ticket office open daily 5:15am-10pm. To **L.A.** (11 per day 6am-8:30pm, $25-28).

Buses: Greyhound, 120 W. Broadway (☎239-8082 or 800-231-2222), at 1st St. Ticket office open 24hr. To **L.A.** (30 per day 5am-11:35pm; $15) and **Tijuana** (16 per day 5am-11:35pm, $5).

Public Transit: San Diego Metropolitan Transit System (MTS). MTS's automated 24hr. information line, **Info Express** (☎685-4900), has info on San Diego's buses, trains, and trolleys. The **Transit Store** at 1st Ave. and Broadway has info. Get a 1- to 4-day **Day Tripper Pass** if you plan to use public transit of any kind more than once. Open M-F 8:30am-5:30pm, Sa-Su noon-4pm. 1-day pass $5, 2-day $9, 3-day $12, 4-day $15.

Car Rental: @West Rent a Car, 3045 Rosecrans St., #215, (☎619-223-2343; www.atwestrentacar.com), just north of downtown San Diego. Cars from $20 per day. Under-25 surcharge $5-25 per day. Insurance $17 per day if driving to Mexico. Open daily 8am-8pm.

Bike Rental: Action Sports, 4000 Coronado Bay Rd. (☎424-4466), at the Marina Dock of the Loews Coronado Bay Resort on Coronado Island. Beach cruisers and mountain bikes $10 per hr., $30 per 4hr. Open M-F 9am-6pm, Sa-Su 8:30am-6:30pm.

⚡🛈 ORIENTATION AND PRACTICAL INFORMATION

The epicenter of **inland** San Diego tourism is historic **Balboa Park.** Northwest of the park is the stylish **Hillcrest** neighborhood, the city's gay enclave, which has great shopping and restaurants. San Diego's **downtown** attractions are concentrated in the corridor that includes its business and **waterfront** districts. The **Gaslamp Quarter,** the nexus of San Diego nightlife, sits in the southern section of downtown between 4th and 6th St. and contains many of San Diego's signature theaters, nightclubs, and restaurants. Farther to the north and near the water, **Little Italy** is its own tiny international epicenter of food and entertainment. Just north of downtown in the southeast corner of the I-5 and I-8 junction lies a little slice of old Mexico known as **Old Town.** Along the **coast,** San Diego Bay opens up south of downtown, bounded by classy **Coronado Island.** Northwest of town sits the collection of shiny beaches and man-made inlets known as **Mission Bay.** A jaunt up the coast leads to the swanky tourist haven of **La Jolla.** Up the coast beyond La Jolla are the laid-back, sun-soaked beach communities of the **North County.**

Visitor Info: San Diego Convention and Visitors Bureau, 401 B St., #1400, Dept. 700, 92101 (☎236-1212; www.sandiego.org), provides info. **Just Call** (☎615-6111) is an information line operated by the city of San Diego.

Library: San Diego Public Library, 820 E St. (☎236-5800), offers **Internet access,** foreign newspapers, borrowing privileges for visitors, and more. Open M-Th 10am-9pm, F-Sa 9:30am-5:30pm, Su 1-5pm.

Police: ☎531-2000.

Medical Services: Kaiser Foundation, 4647 Zion Ave. (☎528-5000).

Hotlines: GLBT Crisis Line, ☎800-479-3339. **Rape Hotline,** ☎233-3088.

Post Office: Hillcrest Station, 3911 Cleveland Ave. (☎295-5091). Open M 7:30am-5pm, Tu-F 8:30am-5pm, Sa 8:30am-2pm. **Postal Code: 92103.**

Area Code: Most of San Diego, including downtown, Coronado, and Ocean Beach: **619.** Northern San Diego area codes (including Del Mar, La Jolla, parts of North County, and Pacific Beach): **858** and **760.** In text, 619 unless otherwise noted.

▌ ACCOMMODATIONS

Rates predictably rise on weekends and in summer. Reserve ahead. Beyond the hostel and residential hotel scene, San Diego is littered with generic chain motels, generally clean and safe. There is a popular cluster known as **Hotel Circle** (2-3 mi. east of I-5 along I-8), where summer prices begin at $60 for a single and $70 for a double during the week ($70 and $80, respectively, on weekends). Several beaches in North County, as well as one on Coronado, are state parks and allow camping.

▓ **USA Hostels San Diego,** 726 5th Ave. (☎232-3100 or 800-438-8622; www.usahostels.com), between F and G St. in the Gaslamp Quarter. This colorful Euro-style funhouse is right in the middle of a popular clubbing street. Festive common areas. Hosts frequent parties and organizes Tijuana tours ($11) and Gaslamp pub crawls ($4). Pancake breakfast included. Free linen and lockers. Coin-op laundry with free detergent. Reserve private rooms in advance. International passport or out-of-state student ID required. Dorms $21; private rooms $46-50. $1 off for ISIC, VIP, and BUNAC cardholders. $3 off with brochures available at other USA hostels. ❶

▓ **San Diego Downtown Hostel (HI),** 521 Market St. (☎525-1531 or 800-909-4776, ext. 156; www.sandiegohostels.org), at 5th Ave., in the heart of the Gaslamp Quarter. Clean and quiet almost to the point of sterility, this hostel caters to the calm traveler. Airy common room. No alcohol. Breakfast included. Lockers (bring a lock) and laundry available. Reception 6:30am-12:30am. Groups welcome. 4- to 6-bed dorms $18-25, nonmembers $21-28; doubles $45-56. ❶

International House, 4502 Cass St. (☎858-274-4325), in Pacific Beach, and 3204 Mission Bay Dr. (☎858-539-0043), in Mission Beach. Sister hostels that offer excellent service, clean and airy rooms, Internet access, breakfast, free surfboard and boogie board use, and beach locations. Out-of-state student ID or international passport required. 28-day max. stay. Dorm rooms $20, students $18. Weekly dorms $110. ❶

Old Town Inn, 4444 Pacific Hwy. (☎800-643-3025), near I-5 and I-8, a 10min. walk from Old Town. Clean rooms with standard amenities. Across the street from the trolley station; perfect for those without cars. Some rooms have kitchenettes. Pool access. Large continental breakfast included. Standard rooms $56-80. ❸

🍴 FOOD

With its large Hispanic population and proximity to Mexico, San Diego is renowned for exemplary Mexican cuisine. Old Town serves up some of the best authentic Mexican food in the state. San Diego also offers a spectacular assortment of ethnic and more traditional eateries, concentrated in both the Hillcrest neighborhood and the trendy Gaslamp Quarter.

▓ **Casa de Bandini,** 2754 Calhoun St. (☎297-8211), in the Bazaar del Mundo in Old Town. Repeatedly voted best Mexican restaurant in San Diego. Set in a Spanish-style architectural landmark (built in 1829), Bandini dishes out superb food and boisterous *mariachi* music. The combo plates ($5-9) are fantastic, but the heavyweight margarita ($4-7) is what's truly responsible for Bandini's iconic status. Many outdoor tables on a beautiful tiled patio with fountain. Open Su-Th 11am-9:30pm, F-Sa 11am-10pm. ❷

▓ **The Corvette Diner,** 3946 5th Ave. (☎542-1001), in Hillcrest. The ultimate flashback to the days of nickel milkshakes, this 50s-style diner has more chrome than Detroit and more neon than Las Vegas. Extraordinary greasy-spoon classics and a number of unique creations like the Rory Burger (peanut butter and bacon burger; $7). Costumed waitresses give as much lip as service. Open Su-Th 11am-10pm, F-Sa 11am-midnight. ❷

Kono's Surf Club, 704 Garnet Ave. (☎483-1669), across from the Crystal Pier in Pacific Beach. Identifiable by the line stretching down the block, Kono's is a surfer's shrine. Breakfast served all day ($3-5). Try the huge Egg Burrito #3, which includes bacon, cheese, potatoes, and sauce ($4). Open M-F 7am-3pm, Sa-Su 7am-4pm. ❶

Kansas City Barbecue, 610 W. Market St. (☎231-9680), near Seaport Village. The setting for *Top Gun*'s "Great Balls of Fire" scene. While the wooden piano remains, all that's left of Goose, Maverick, and Charlie is an abundance of autographed posters and neon signs. Vegetarians will find themselves in the Danger Zone in this barbecue-slathered meatfest. Entrees $9-16. Open daily 11am-1am. ❸

⊙ SIGHTS

San Diego's world-famous attractions are varied enough to keep any traveler engaged. Pick up the free weekly *Reader* for local event listings. The **San Diego 3-for-1 Pass** ($92, ages 3-9 $67) offers unlimited admission for five consecutive days at a discounted price to three of the city's premier sights—Sea World, the San Diego Zoo, and the San Diego Wild Animal Park. Visit www.sandiegozoo.org or the websites of the other two parks for information and online ticketing.

DOWNTOWN. Petco Park, the new home of the San Diego Padres, offers fans a close-up view of the action, with excellent views from almost every seat. *(Games Mar.-Oct. Check www.padres.com for schedule and tickets.)* The **Gaslamp Quarter** houses antique shops, Victorian buildings, trendy restaurants, and nightclubs (see **Nightlife,** p. 971). The steel-and-glass structure of the **San Diego Museum of Contemporary Art** encases 20th-century works of art from the museum's permanent collection, as well as visiting exhibits. Works include those of Andy Warhol and a wall that looks as though it breathes. *(1001 Kettner Blvd. ☎ 234-1001. Open Su-Tu and Th-Sa 11am-5pm. Free.)* Housed within some of San Diego's oldest ships, the **San Diego Maritime Museum** showcases San Diego's rich maritime history and maintains three ships. *(1492 N. Harbor Dr. ☎ 234-9153; www.sdmaritime.org. Open daily 9am-8pm. $8; seniors, military, and ages 13-17 $6; ages 6-12 $5.)* Spanish for "dock," the Embarcadero has boardwalk shops and museums that face moored windjammers, cruise ships, and the occasional naval destroyer. *(Most afternoon tours of naval craft free.)* The jewel of San Diego's redevelopment efforts is Horton Plaza, at Broadway and 4th, a pastel, open-air, multi-level shopping center.

⊠ SAN DIEGO ZOO. With over 100 acres of exquisite habitats, this zoo well deserves its reputation as one of the finest in the world. Its unique "bioclimatic" exhibits group animals and plants together by habitat. The legendary **panda** exhibit is the most timeless feature of the park. The educational 40min. **double-decker bus tour** covers about 75% of the zoo. The non-narrated express bus will take you to any of five stops throughout the park anytime during the day. The **Skyfari Aerial Tramway** rises 170 ft. above the park and lasts about two minutes but can save on walking time. Don't expect to see anything but a pleasant view of the tops of trees and the skyline. *(One-way $2.)* If the bus and tramway appeal to you, purchase your tickets when you buy zoo admission. *(2920 Zoo Dr., Balboa Park. ☎ 234-3153; www.sandiegozoo.org. Open daily late June to early Sept. 9am-10pm; early Sept. to late June 9am-dusk. $21, $32 with 35min. bus tour and 2 tickets for the aerial tramway; ages 3-11 $14/$20; military in uniform free. Free on Founder's Day, the 1st M in Oct.)*

BALBOA PARK AND THE EL PRADO MUSEUMS. Most of the museums reside within the resplendent Spanish colonial-style buildings that line **El Prado Street,** which runs east-west through the park's central **Plaza de Panama.** The Passport to Balboa Park *($30)* provides admission to (and is available for purchase) at all park museums. The Best of Balboa Park passport *($55)* also includes admission to all ticketed options at the zoo. The **Balboa Visitors Center,** 1549 El Prado, is in the House of Hospitality at the Plaza de Panama. It sells park maps *($0.50)* and the Passport to Balboa Park. *(☎ 239-0512. www.balboapark.org. Open daily in summer 9am-4:30pm; in winter 9am-4pm.)* Creationists beware: the **Museum of Man** dedicates an entire floor to the 98.4% of DNA we share with chimpanzees. *(On the west end of the park. ☎ 239-2001; www.museumofman.org. Open daily 10am-4:30pm. $6, seniors $5, ages 6-17 $3; free 3rd Tu of each month.)* The **Aerospace Museum** displays 24 full-scale replicas and 44 original planes, as well as exhibits on aviation history and the International Space Station project. *(2001 Pan American Plaza. ☎ 234-8291; www.aerospacemuseum.org. Open daily 10am-4:30pm; extended summer hours. $9, seniors $7, ages 6-17 $4, under 6 and military* *free; free 4th Tu of each month.)* The **Reuben H. Fleet Space Theater and Science Center** houses interactive exhibits and the world's first hemispheric Omnimax theater. *(1875 El Prado Way. ☎ 238-1233; www.rhfleet.org. Open daily 9:30am-8pm. $6.75, with Omnimax show $12; seniors $6/$9.75; ages 3-12 $5.50/$8.75. Free 1st Tu of each month.)* The small, ultra-modern **Museum of Photographic Arts (MOPA)** features contemporary photography in 8 to 10 exhibits per year. Its film program ranges from cult classic film festivals to technical and thematic examination of more serious cinematic works. *(☎ 238-7559; www.mopa.org. Open M-W and F-Su 10am-5pm, Th 10am-9pm. $6; students, seniors, and military $4; free 2nd Tu of each month. Films $10.)* The **San Diego Museum of Art** has a collection ranging from ancient Asian to contemporary Californian works. At the adjoining outdoor **Sculpture Garden Court,** a sensuous Henry Moore piece presides over other large abstract blocks. *(☎ 232-7931; www.sdmart.org. Open Tu-W and F-Su 10am-6pm, Th 10am-9pm. $9; seniors, students, and ages 18-24 $7; ages 6-17 $4. Special exhibits $2-20.)* The fragrant **Botanical Building** may look like a giant wooden cage, but it's filled with plants, not birds. The **orchid collection** is particularly striking, set among murmuring fountains. The **Desert Garden** and **Rose Garden** prove a salient floral contrast. The Desert Garden is in full bloom from January to March, while the roses are best admired between April and December. *(2200 Park Blvd. ☎ 235-1100. Botanical Building open M-W and F-Su 10am-4pm. Free.)*

OLD TOWN. In 1769, Father Serra, supported by a brigade of Spanish infantry, established the first of 21 missions that would eventually line the California coast in the area now known as Old Town. The remnants of this early settlement have become one of San Diego's tourist mainstays. The most popular of the area's attractions, the **State Park's** early 19th-century buildings contain museums, shops, and restaurants. **Seely Stable** houses a huge museum devoted to the 19th century's primary mode of transportation: the horse and carriage. *(☎ 220-5427. Open daily 10am-5pm. Tours every hr. 11am-2pm.)* Take a tour of the **Whaley House,** which stands on the site of San Diego's first gallows. It is one of two **official haunted houses** recognized by the State of California. *(2482 San Diego Ave. ☎ 298-2482, tours 293-0117. Open daily 10am-4:30pm; last entry 4pm. $5, seniors $4, ages 3-12 $2.)* The stout adobe walls of the **Serra Museum** were raised at the site of the original fort and mission in 1929. *(2727 Presidio Dr., in Presidio Park. ☎ 297-3258. Open F-Su 10am-4:30pm. $5; seniors, students, and military $4; ages 6-17 $2.)*

CORONADO ISLAND. Lovely Coronado Island is now actually a peninsula: a slender 7 mi. strip of hauled sand known as the "Silver Strand" tethers it to the mainland down near Imperial Beach. Coronado's most famed sight is its Victorian-style **Hotel Del Coronado,** one of America's largest wooden buildings. *(1500 Orange Ave. ☎ 435-6611. Tours depart from the lobby of the Glorietta Bay Inn, 1630 Glorietta Bay Blvd. ☎ 435-5993. Tours Tu, Th, Sa 11am. $8.)* Coronado also has a huge military presence, and its entire northern chunk comprises the **North Island Naval Air Station,** the birthplace of American naval aviation. In fact, it was a group of navy men who carted sand to connect the island to the rest of Coronado in 1947.

OCEAN, MISSION, AND PACIFIC BEACHES. Much of San Diego's younger population flocks to these communities for the surf and hopping nightlife; unsurprisingly, noisy bars and grills crowd these shores (see **Food,** p. 968, and **Entertainment Nightlife,** p. 971). The three beaches line up consecutively, but each has its own flavor. **Ocean Beach (O.B.)** cultivates a homegrown, earthy atmosphere. With local hippies lounging in the gentle surf, O.B. is the most laid-back of the beaches and the best place to learn the art of wave-riding. Farther north, **Mission Beach,** at the corner of W. Mission Bay Dr. and Mission Blvd., is a people-watcher's paradise. **Belmont Park,** a combination amusement park and shopping center, draws a youthful crowd. **Pacific Beach** and its boisterous Garnet Ave. is home to the best nightlife. **Ocean Front Walk** is packed with joggers, cyclists, and beachfront shops.

SEA WORLD. Take Disneyland, subtract most of the rides, add a whole lot of fish and marine life, and you've got Sea World. Though critics have condemned the practice of training highly intelligent marine mammals to perform unnatural circus acts, the goofy shows are surprisingly charming. The A-list star and poster-whale is the orca **Shamu,** whose signature move is a cannonball splash that soaks anyone in the first 20 rows. Those looking to cool down who don't want a face full of salt water should head to the free **Budweiser's Beer School** and brewery. The 30min. class, 🍺**free beer,** and general merriment come courtesy of Anheuser-Busch, the proud owners of Sea World. The best show in the park is **Fools with Tools,** a delightful spoof of Tool Time from *Home Improvement. (☎800-380-3203; www.seaworld.com. Open in summer daily 9am-11pm. The park opens at 10am in winter, but closing hours vary. $50, ages 3-9 $38; 2 consecutive days $54, ages 3-9 $44 Parking $7, RVs $9.)*

LA JOLLA. This affluent seaside locality houses few budget options, but offers some of the finest public beaches in the San Diego area. *(Take the Ardath Exit west from I-5 or bus #30 or 34 from downtown.)* The **La Jolla Cove** is popular with scuba divers, snorkelers, and brilliantly colored Garibaldi goldfish. Wander south along the cliffs to a striking semi-circular inlet known as **The Children's Pool,** home to a thriving community of sea lions. Some of the best breaks in the county can be found in La Jolla at **Tourmaline Beach** and **Wind 'n' Sea Beach.** However, these are notoriously territorial spots, so outsiders might be advised to surf elsewhere. **La Jolla Shores** has gentle swells ideal for new surfers, boogie boarders, and swimmers. 🏖**Black's Beach** is not officially a nude beach, but that doesn't seem to stop sunbathers from going *au natural.* The north end generally attracts gay sunbathers.

Next to La Jolla Shores, the 🐠**Birch Aquarium at the Scripps Institute of Oceanography** has great educational exhibits including a tank of oozing jellyfish, a large collection of seahorses, and a 70,000-gallon kelp and shark tank. *(2300 Expedition Way. ☎858-534-3474; http://aquarium.ucsd.edu. Open daily 9am-5pm. $10, seniors $8.50, students with ID $7, ages 3-17 $6.50.)* The **San Diego Museum of Contemporary Art** houses a rotating exhibition of Pop, Minimalist, and Conceptualist art from the 1950s onward. It shares its collection with the downtown branch. The museum is as visually stunning as the art it contains, with gorgeous ocean views, high ceilings, and light-filled spaces. *(700 Prospect St. ☎858-454-3541; www.mcasd.org. Open M-Tu and F-Su 11am-5pm, Th 11am-7pm. $6; students, seniors, military, and ages 12-18 $2. 3rd Tu and 1st Su of every month free.)* Be sure to check out the terraces and buttresses of **Geisel Library** at the **University of California San Diego (UCSD),** a space-age structure endowed by La Jolla resident Theodore Geisel, better known as Dr. Seuss, the late children's books author. *(☎858-534-2208. Open M-F 7am-9pm, Sa-Su 7am-5:30pm.)*

🎵 📺 ENTERTAINMENT AND NIGHTLIFE

Nightlife in San Diego is concentrated in several distinct pockets of action. Posh locals and party-seeking tourists flock to the **Gaslamp Quarter,** where numerous restaurants and bars feature live music. The **Hillcrest** area, next to Balboa Park, draws a young, largely gay crowd to its clubs and dining spots. Away from downtown, the **beach areas** (especially Garnet Ave. in Pacific Beach) are loaded with clubs, bars, and cheap eateries that attract college-age revelers. The city's definitive source of entertainment info is the free *Reader,* available in shops, coffeehouses, and visitors centers. Listings can also be found in the *San Diego Union-Tribune*'s Thursday "Night and Day" section. If boozin' isn't your idea of nightlife, you can spend a more sedate evening at one of San Diego's excellent theaters, such as the **Balboa Theatre,** 225 Broadway Ave. (☎544-1000), and the **Horton Grand Theatre,** 444 4th Ave. (☎234-9583), both downtown. The **La Jolla Playhouse,** 2910 La Jolla Village Dr., presents shows on the UCSD campus. (☎858-550-1010; www.lajollaplayhouse.com.)

CALIFORNIA

▨ **Croce's Top Hat Bar and Grille** and **Croce's Jazz Bar,** 802 5th Ave. (☎233-4355), at F St. in the Gaslamp Quarter. A combo rock/blues bar and jazz bar opened by Ingrid Croce, widow of singer Jim Croce. Live music nightly from 8:30pm. Cover $5-10 (includes 2 live shows). Top Hat open F-Sa 7pm-1:30am. Jazz Bar open daily 5:30pm-12:30am.

The Bitter End, 770 5th Ave. (☎338-9300), in the Gaslamp Quarter. This 3-level dance club is always packed with those dressed to impress, so leave the torn Levi's and sandals at home. DJs spin everything from hip-hop to Top 40 to trance on the upper floors, while live music pounds below. Happy hour Th-F 3-7pm; free buffet. 21+. Cover $10 after 9pm. Open daily 5pm-2am.

The Casbah, 2501 Kettner Blvd. (☎232-4355), at Laurel St., near the airport. Eddie Vedder of the alternative rock legend Pearl Jam owns this intimate nightspot, one of the best live music venues in the city. Call ahead for a schedule, as tickets sometimes sell out. Cover varies. 21+. Hours vary; usually 5pm-2am.

The Flame, 3780 Park Blvd. (☎295-4163), in Hillcrest. One of the most popular lesbian dance clubs in the nation. 21+. Open daily 5pm-2am.

Bourbon Street, 4612 Park Blvd. (☎291-0173), in University Heights. A perennially popular piano bar with a gay following. 21+. Open M-F 2pm-2am, Sa-Su 11am-2pm.

TIJUANA ☎664

Just minutes from San Diego lies the most notorious specimen of border subculture: Tijuana (often referred to as "TJ"; pop. 2 million). The city's cheap booze, haggling vendors, and kitschy, unapologetic hedonism attract 30 million US visitors each year. But Tijuana is more than just another Sin City. As one of Mexico's wealthiest cities, it teems with megastores, museums, and monstrous industrial activity. Most travelers stick to Revolución, the city's main strip, which reverberates with *mariachi* bands, thumping dance beats from the packed nightclubs, and the sounds of eager tourists unloading wads of cash on everything from *jai alai* gambling to slimy strip shows. As an introduction to Mexican culture, flashy, trashy TJ is about as unrepresentative and unrepentant as they come.

◼▟ **ORIENTATION AND PRACTICAL INFORMATION.** For the vast majority of visitors, Tijuana simply *is* **Avenida Revolución,** in the middle of **Zona Centro,** the tourist hot spot. *Calles* run east-west and are named and numbered; *avenidas* run parallel to Revolución and perpendicular to the *calles.* The **Tourist Office** is located in the small booth on the corner of Revolución and Calle 3. English-speaking staff offer good maps and advice. (☎685-2210. Open M-Th 10am-4pm, F-Su 10am-7pm. Other branches at the Mexicoach station and at the border crossing.) The **Customs Office** is at the border on the Mexican side after crossing the San Ysidro bridge. (☎683-1390. Open 24hr.) **Consulates: Canada,** Germán Gedovius 10411-101, in the Zona Río. (☎684-0461, after-hours emergency 800-706-2900. Open M-F 9am-1pm.) **UK,** Salinas 1500, in Col. Aviación, La Mesa. (☎681-8402, after-hours emergency 681-5320. Open M-F 9am-5pm.) **US,** Tapachula Sur 96, in Col. Hipódromo, next to the racetrack southeast of town. In an **emergency,** call the San Diego office at ☎619-692-2154 and leave a message; an officer will respond. (☎622-7400 or 681-8016. Open M-F 8am-4pm.) Banks along Constitución **exchange money.** Banamex, Constitución at Calle 4, has shorter lines (☎688-0021; open M-F 8:30am-4:30pm) than the more central **HSBC,** Revolución 129, at Calle 2. (☎688-1914. Open M-F 8am-7pm, Sa 8am-3pm.) Both have 24hr. **ATMs.** *Casas de cambio* offer better rates but may charge commission and refuse to exchange traveler's checks. **Police:** (☎685-6557, specialized tourist assistance 688-0555), Constitución at Calle 8. English spoken. **Hospital General,** Centenario 10851 (☎684-0237 or 684-0922), in the Zona Río. **Post Office:** on Negrete at Calle 1. (☎684-7950. Open M-F 8am-5pm, Sa 9am-1pm.) **Postal Code:** 22000. **Area Code:** 664.

⌐⌐ ACCOMMODATIONS AND FOOD. As a general rule, hotels in Tijuana become less reputable the farther north you go. Avoid any in the area downhill from Calle 1 (the Zona Norte). Rooms at some motels may not fit the standards of cleanliness expected by US travelers. **Hotel Colonial ❶,** Calle 6 1812, between Constitución and Niños Héroes, has large, very clean rooms with A/C and private baths in a quieter, residential neighborhood. (☎688-1620. Singles and doubles 260 pesos.) **Hotel Lafayette ❶,** Revolución 325, between Calle 3 and 4, is quiet considering its location in the middle of Revolución's chaos. Large rooms have color TV, phone, fans, and private bath. (☎685-3940 or 685-3339. Singles 245 pesos; doubles 320 pesos.) For those too squeamish for Tijuana's truly budget offerings, **Hotel La Villa de Zaragoza ❷,** Madero 1120, between Calle 7 and 8, has semi-affordable luxury in the form of spacious rooms with TV, phone, and king-size beds. Laundry, room service, and 24hr. security keep you and your car very safe. (☎685-1832. Singles from 393 pesos; doubles 474 pesos. Reservations accepted.)

As with most things in Tijuana, loud, in-your-face promoters try to herd tourists into the overpriced restaurants lining **Revolución.** For ultra-cheap food, **taco stands ❶** all over the *centro* sell several tacos or a *torta* for 10 pesos. The supermarket **Calimax** is at Calle 2 at Constitución. (☎633-7988. Open 6am-midnight.) ▨**La Cantina de los Remedios ❷,** Diego Rivera 19, in the Zona Río, has competing *mariachis,* lots of tequilas, and a big crowd. Authentic Mexican cuisine starts at 80 pesos and extends well beyond the usual options. (☎634-3065. Open M-Th 1pm-midnight, F-Sa 1pm-2am, Su 1-10pm.) **Restaurante Ricardo's Tortas ❶,** at Madero and Calle 7, serves the best *tortas* in town (25-40 pesos). Try the *super especial,* with ham, *carne asada,* cheese, avocado, tomato, and mayo. (☎685-4031. Open 24hr.)

◗ SIGHTS AND FIGHTS. Many of the most entertaining sights in town are right on Revolución. While the so-called "attractions" of the main tourist drag tend toward mind-numbing predictability, Tijuana's cultural assets and parks counter its one-dimensional image. The huge sphere and plaza of Tijuana's cultural center, ▨**Centro Cultural Tijuana (CECUT),** is the most visually striking feature of Paseo de los Héroes. The superb **Museo de las Californias** traces the history of the peninsula from its earliest inhabitants through the Spanish conquest and the Mexican-American War to the 20th century. (☎687-9633. Museum open daily 10am-7pm. 20 pesos, students and children 12 pesos.) Pleasant walks, rides, an open-air theater, and a small zoo await at the sprawling state-run park of **Parque Morelos,** Blvd. de los Insurgentes 26000. (Take an orange and grey communal cab for 5 pesos on Calle 4 and Madero. ☎625-2470. Open Tu-Su 9am-5pm. 5 pesos, children 2 pesos; parking 10 pesos.) If you're in town on the right Sunday, you can watch the graceful and savage battle of *toreador* versus bull in one of Tijuana's two bullrings. **El Toreo de Tijuana,** southeast of town just off Agua Caliente, hosts the first round of fights. (Catch a bus on Calle 2a west of Revolución. May-Aug. every other Su at 4pm.) The seaside **Plaza Monumental** hosts the second round (Aug.-Oct.). Mexicoach sends buses (round-trip US$4) to Plaza Monumental on fight days. Alternatively, take the blue-and-white local buses (5 pesos) on Calle 3 at Constitución all the way down Calle 2. Tickets to both rings go on sale at the gate (☎685-1510 or 685-1219) or at the Mexicoach office (☎685-1470) on Revolución between Calle 6 and 7 the Wednesday before a fight. (Tickets 95-400 pesos.)

◖ NIGHTLIFE. In the 1920s, Prohibition drove US citizens south of the border to revel in the forbidden nectars of cacti, grapes, and hops. The flow of *gringos* thirsty for booze remains unquenched, with many taking advantage of Mexico's drinking age (18) to circumvent US laws. Stroll down Revolución after dusk and you'll be bombarded with thumping music, neon lights, and abrasive club promoters hawking "two-for-one" margaritas at the not-so-low price of US$5.

CALIFORNIA

Those who prefer laid-back nights of good conversation are in the wrong place. **Animale,** Revolución at Calle 3, is the biggest, glitziest, and loudest hedonistic haven in Tijuana. (Open daily 10am-4am.) A sublimely wacky world of life-sized plaster clowns and an authentic yellow school bus can be found at **Iguanas-Ranas,** Revolución at Calle 3a. (☎685-1422. Open M-Th 10am-2am, F-Su 10am-5am.) At **People's,** Revolución and Calle 2, fluorescent constellations and crudely painted sportsmen decorate the terrace, and revelers guzzle 10 beers for US$15. (☎688-2706. Open M-Th 10am-2am, F-Su 10am-4am.)

THE CALIFORNIA DESERT

California's desert is one of the most beautiful places in the world; it's also one of the loneliest. Roads cut through endless expanses of barren earth and landscapes that seem untouched by human existence. Exploration turns up elusive treasures: diverse flora and fauna, staggering topographical variation, and scattered relics of the American frontier. Throughout the year, the desert switches from a pleasantly warm refuge to an unbearable wasteland and back again.

PALM SPRINGS   ☎760

From its first known inhabitants, the Cahuilla, to today's geriatric fun-lovers, the restorative oasis of Palm Springs (pop. 43,520) has attracted an odd menagerie of old and young people. With warm winter temperatures, celebrity residents, and a casino, this city is a sunny break from everyday life.

Mt. San Jacinto State Park, Palm Springs's primary landmark, offers outdoor recreation like hiking and cross-country skiing. If the 10,804 ft. peak seems too strenuous, the world-famous **Palm Springs Aerial Tramway** can whisk you to the top in 10min. (☎325-1449 or 888-515-8726. Trams run at least every 30min. M-F 10am-8pm, Sa-Su 8am-8pm. Round-trip $21, over 60 $19, ages 3-12 $14, under 3 free.) Palm Springs's namesake, the **Desert Hot Springs Spa,** 10805 Palm Dr., features eight naturally heated mineral pools, saunas, massages, and body wraps. (☎800-808-7727. Open daily 8am-10pm. $3-7; includes admission to pools, dry sauna, and locker rooms.) Prep for nearby Joshua Tree at **Uprising Rockclimbing Center,** 1500 Gene Autry Trail, a gigantic outdoor structure, the only one of its kind in the US. (☎888-254-6266. Open Sept.-June M-F 10am-8pm, Sa-Su 10am-6pm; July-Aug. Tu-F 4-8pm, Sa-Su 10am-6pm. Day pass $15. Equipment rental $7. Lessons from $45 per day.)

Despite Palm Springs's reputation as a luxury getaway, affordable lodgings do exist. **Orchid Tree Inn ❺,** 251 S. Belardo Rd., has large rooms with tasteful Spanish decor overlooking a lush courtyard. (☎325-2791. Singles and doubles in winter from $145; in summer $99-119. Studios, suites, and bungalows also available.) Palm Springs offers an array of culinary treats, from standard burger joints to ultra-trendy fusion cuisine. Satisfying and inexpensive Thai cuisine is served at ▧**Thai Smile ❷,** 651 N. Palm Canyon Dr. Don't miss the $5 lunch specials. (☎320-5503. Open daily 11am-10pm.) **Cedar Creek Inn ❸,** 1555 S. Palm Canyon Dr., is a charming eatery with an outdoor patio, fresh flowers, and an extensive wine list. (☎325-7000. Open daily 11am-10pm.) To experience Palm Springs's heralded nightlife, head to **Village Pub,** 266 S. Palm Canyon Dr., to relive your college days by swilling beer and grooving to folksy live rock. (☎323-3265. Open daily 11am-2am.)

Greyhound, 311 N. Indian Canyon Dr. (☎325-2053), runs buses to Las Vegas, L.A., and San Diego; rates and times vary widely. **SunBus** covers Coachella Valley cities. (☎343-3451. $1.) The **Visitor Center,** 2781 N. Palm Canyon Dr. (☎778-8415 or 800-347-7746; www.palm-springs.org), offers friendly advice. **Post Office:** 333 E. Amado Rd. (☎322-4111. Open M-F 9am-5pm, Sa 9am-1pm.) **Postal Code:** 92262; General Delivery 92263. **Area Code:** 760.

JOSHUA TREE NATIONAL PARK ☎ 760

When devout Mormon pioneers crossed this faith-testing desert in the 19th century, they named the enigmatic tree they encountered after the Biblical prophet Joshua. The tree's crooked limbs resembled the Hebrew general, and, with arms upraised, seemed to beckon these Latter-Day pioneers to the Promised Land. Even today, Joshua Tree National Park inspires reverent awe in those who witness it.

■▊ **ORIENTATION AND PRACTICAL INFORMATION.** The park is ringed by three highways: **I-10** to the south, **Route 62 (Twentynine Palms Highway)** to the west and north, and **Route 177** to the east. The north entrances to the park are off Rte. 62 at the towns of **Joshua Tree** and **Twentynine Palms.** The south entrance is at **Cottonwood Spring,** off I-10 at Rte. 195, southeast of Palm Springs. The **park entrance fee,** valid for a week, is $5 per person, $10 per car. **Visitor Info: Headquarters and Oasis Visitor Center,** 74485 National Park Dr. (☎367-5500; www.nps.gov/jotr. Open daily 8am-5pm.) **Post Office:** 73839 Gorgonio Dr., in Twentynine Palms. (☎800-275-8777. Open M-F 8:30am-5pm.) **Postal Code:** 92277. **Area Code:** 760.

▐ **ACCOMMODATIONS.** Most campgrounds in the park don't accept reservations, but group reservations can be made at Cottonwood, Sheep Pass, Indian Cove, and Black Rock Canyon online at www.nps.gov/jotr. All established sites have tables, firepits, and pit toilets, but no hookups. ▨**Indian Cove ❶,** 3200 ft., on the north edge of Wonderland of Rocks, is a popular spot for climbers. (Sites $10; group sites $20-35.) ▨**Jumbo Rocks ❶,** 4400 ft., near Skull Rock Trail on the eastern edge of Queen Valley, is the highest and coolest campground. (Sites $5.) Experienced campers can register for a **backcountry permit** at the visitors center or at self-service boards throughout the park. Those who can't stomach desert campgrounds will find inexpensive motels in Twentynine Palms. The **29 Palms Inn ❹,** 73950 Inn Dr., is an attraction in its own right, with 23 rooms facing the Mara Oasis. Robert Plant composed "29 Palms" here. (☎367-3505; www.29palmsinn.com. Reservations required Feb.-Apr. Doubles Oct.-May Su-Th $60-95, F-Sa $85-135; June-Sept. Su-Th $50-75, F-Sa $75-115.)

▟ **OUTDOOR ACTIVITIES.** Over 80% of Joshua Tree is designated wilderness, safeguarding it against development and paved roads. Hikers eager to enter this primitive territory should pack plenty of water and keep alert for flash floods and changing weather conditions. A **driving tour** is an easy way to explore the park and linger until **sunset.** All roads are well marked, and signs labeled "Exhibit Ahead" lead to unique floral and geological formations. One of these tours, a 34 mi. stretch winding through the park from Twentynine Palms to the town of Joshua Tree on **Park Boulevard,** provides access to the park's most outstanding sights and hikes. An especially spectacular leg of the road is **Keys View** (5185 ft.), 6 mi. off Park Blvd. and just west of Ryan Campground. On a clear day, you can see to Palm Springs and the Salton Sea. The sunrise from here is renowned. The **Cholla Cactus Garden** lies just off the road. Those with **4WD** vehicles have even more options, including the 18 mi. **Geology Tour Road,** west of Jumbo Rocks off Park Blvd., which climbs through striking rock formations and ends in the Little San Bernardino Mountains.

Hiking is perhaps the best way to experience Joshua Tree. On foot, visitors can tread through sand, scramble over boulders, and walk among the park's namesakes. Anticipate slow progress even on short walks; the oppressive heat and the scarcity of shade can strain even the hardiest hikers. Although the 1 mi. **Barker Dam Trail,** next to Hidden Valley Campground, is often packed with tourists, its petroglyphs (though sadly vandalized) and eerie tranquility make it a worthwhile stroll, especially at twilight. From the top of **Ryan Mountain** (3 mi. round-trip), off Park Blvd., the boulders in the encircling valley share an uncanny resemblance to

CALIFORNIA

enormous beasts of burden slouching toward Bethlehem. Bring lots of water for the strenuous, unshaded climb to the summit. Visitors centers have info on the park's other hikes, which range from a 15min. stroll to the **Oasis of Mara** to a three-day trek along the 35 mi. **California Riding and Hiking Trail.** The ranger-led **Desert Queen Ranch Walking Tour** covers a restored ranch ($5; call for reservations).

The crack-split granite of Joshua provides some of the best rock climbing and bouldering in the world for experts and novices alike. The renowned boulders at **Wonderland of Rocks** and **Hidden Valley** are always swarming with hard-bodied climbers, making Joshua Tree the most climbed area in America. Adventurous novices will find thrills at the **Skull Rock Interpretive Walk,** which runs between Jumbo Rocks and Skull Rock. The walk offers info on local plants and animals, and exciting yet non-technical scrambles to the tops of monstrous boulders.

 You have made it through our entire Joshua Tree coverage without being subjected to a U2 joke. You're welcome.

DEATH VALLEY NATIONAL PARK ☎ 760

The devil owns a lot of real estate in Death Valley: he grows crops at Devil's Cornfield and hits the links at Devil's Golf Course, and the park is home to Hell's Gate itself. The area's extreme heat and surreal landscape explain this identification with the dark side. Winter temperatures dip well below freezing in the mountains, and summer readings in the valley average 115°F. The second-highest temperature ever recorded in the world (134°F in the shade) was measured at the valley's Furnace Creek Ranch on July 10, 1913.

⛽ TRANSPORTATION. Cars are virtually the only way to get to and around Death Valley, but conditions are notoriously hard on vehicles. **Radiator water** (*not* for drinking) is available at critical points on Rte. 178 and 190 and Nevada Rte. 374. There are only four **gas stations** in the park, and though prices are hefty, be sure to keep the tank at least half full at all times. Always travel with 2 gallons of water per person per day. In the case of a breakdown, stay in the shade of your vehicle. Of the seven **park entrances,** most visitors choose Rte. 190 from the east. The road is well maintained and the visitors center is relatively close. However, since most of the major sights adjoin **Badwater Road,** the north-south road, the daytripper can see more of the park by entering from the southeast (Rte. 178 W from Rte. 127 at Shoshone) or the north (direct to Scotty's Castle via Nevada Rte. 267). Unskilled mountain drivers in passenger cars should not attempt to enter on the smaller Titus Canyon or Emigrant Canyon Dr. No regular public transportation runs in the Valley. *It goes without saying that attempting to hitchhike through Death Valley is suicide. Don't try to hitchhike through Death Valley. It's suicide.*

▮ PRACTICAL INFORMATION. Visitor Info: Furnace Creek Visitors Center, on Rte. 190 in the Valley's east-central section. (☎ 786-3244; www.nps.gov/deva. Open daily 8am-6pm.) Contact stations are at **Grapevine** (☎ 786-2313), at Rte. 190 and 267 near Scotty's Castle, **Shoshone** (☎ 832-4308), at Rte. 127 and 178 outside the Valley's southeast border, and **Beatty, NV** (☎ 702-553-2200), on Nevada Rte. 374. Fill up outside Death Valley at Lone Pine, Olancha, Shoshine, or Beatty, NV. **Post Office: Furnace Creek Ranch** (☎ 786-2223). Open Oct. to mid-May M-F 8:30am-5pm; mid-May to Sept. M, W, F 8:30am-3pm, Tu and Th 8:30am-5pm. **Postal Code:** 92328. **Area Code:** 760.

▮ ACCOMMODATIONS. Motel rooms in surrounding towns are cheaper than those in Death Valley, but can be over an hour away from top sights. Never assume that rooms will be available, but your chances (and the prices) will be better in the summer. In winter, camping with a stock of groceries saves money and driving time. In summer, camping can get quite uncomfortable. **Furnace Creek Ranch ❹,** in Furnace Creek, has a supremely convenient location next to the visitors center. (☎ 786-2345; www.furnacecreekresort.com. Singles and doubles in summer from $85; in winter from $105.) The National Park Service maintains nine **campgrounds** in Death Valley. All have toilets but no showers, and limit stays to 30 days (except Furnace Creek, with a 14-day limit). **Backcountry camping** is free and legal, provided you check in at the visitors center and pitch tents at least 2 mi. from your car and any road and a ¼ mi. from any backcountry water source.

◪ HIKING. Death Valley has hiking to occupy the gentlest wanderer and hardiest adventurer. Camera-toters should keep in mind that the best photo opportunities are at sunrise and sunset. Astronomy buffs should speak to the rangers, who often set up telescopes at **Zabriskie Point** to capitalize on the Valley's clear skies. Perhaps the most spectacular sight in the park is the light-hued vista at **Dante's View,** reached by a 13 mi. paved road from Rte. 190. **Badwater,** a briny pool four times saltier than the ocean, is in the lowest point (282 ft. below sea level) in the Western Hemisphere. The boardwalk provides a closer look at the strange orange floor. **Artist's Drive,** 10 mi. south of the visitors center, is a one-way loop that contorts its way through brightly colored rock formations. The loop's early ochres and burnt siennas give way at **Artist's Palette** to vivid green, yellow, periwinkle, and pink mineral deposits in the hillside. About 5 mi. south is **Devil's Golf Course,** a vast expanse of gnarled salt pillars formed by flooding and evaporation where Death Valley is at its most surreal; jagged crystalline deposits, some quite delicate and beautiful, stretch as far as the eye can see.

THE SIERRA NEVADA

The Sierra Nevada Mountain Range is known as California's backbone. It runs 450 mi. along the line where two gigantic tectonic plates, the Pacific and North American, collided 400 million years ago. Stretching from stifling Death Valley to just below the Oregon border, the range is a living record of the tireless work of the elements—a product of Mt. Lassen's volcanic activity hundreds of millions of years ago and granite-smoothing glaciation a mere few thousand years ago. It also nurtures some of the most breathtaking scenery in the country, including Lake Tahoe's crystalline waters, Mono Lake's giant tufa formations, Sequoia National Park's towering redwoods, and Yosemite's incredible waterfalls.

LAKE TAHOE   ☎ 530/775

Shimmering blue water, pristine beaches, immense mountains, and an unobtrusive but ubiquitous commercial presence make Tahoe an ideal destination for boating, fishing, sunning, skiing, hiking, and spending money. Each season brings wonders of its own to Tahoe; accordingly, tourist season is yearlong.

▐ TRANSPORTATION

Trains: Amtrak (☎ 800-USA-RAIL/872-7245). Trains running between Chicago and San Francisco stop at the Truckee Depot in downtown Truckee. 1 westbound train daily to **Sacramento** (4½hr., $22-40) and **Oakland/San Francisco** (6½hr., $45-93), and 1 eastbound train to **Reno** (1hr., $10-21).

Buses: Greyhound (☎ 800-231-2222), at the Truckee Depot. To: **Sacramento** (3hr., 4 per day, $21-24); **San Francisco** (5½hr., 4 per day, $31-35); **Reno** (1hr., 3 per day, $11-13).

Tahoe Casino Express (☎ 775-785-2424 or 800-446-6128). Provides shuttle service between the Reno airport and South Shore Tahoe casinos. (Daily 6:15am-12:30am; $20, under 12 free.)

Tahoe Area Regional Transport (TART; ☎550-1212 or 800-736-6365; www.laketahoetransit.com). Connects the western and northern shores from Incline Village through Tahoe City to Meeks Bay, where it joins with South Lake Tahoe (STAGE) buses in the summer at a transfer station. Stops daily every 30min.-1hr., depending on the route. Buses also run from Tahoe City to Truckee and Squaw Valley and back (5 per day 7:30am-4:45pm). $1.25, day pass $3. Exact fare required.

South Tahoe Area Ground Express (STAGE; ☎541-7149). Operates in both NV and CA on the South Shore. It runs several routes between the Stateline, NV, casinos, and the Hwy. 89/50 intersection. Runs 6:40am-12:40pm. $1.25, day pass $2, 10-ride pass $10.

Bus Plus (☎541-7149) runs door-to-door service within city limits (24hr., $3) and within El Dorado County (7am-7pm, $5).

■*■ ☎ ORIENTATION AND PRACTICAL INFORMATION

Located in the northern Sierra Nevadas on the California-Nevada border, Lake Tahoe is a 3hr. drive from San Francisco. The lake rests 100 mi. northeast of Sacramento (via **Highway 50**) and 35 mi. southwest of Reno (via **Highway 395** and **431**). Highway 395 runs 20 mi. east. Lake Tahoe is divided into two main regions, **North Shore** and **South Shore**. The North Shore includes **Tahoe City** in California and **Incline Village** in Nevada; the South Shore includes **South Lake Tahoe** in California and **Stateline** in Nevada.

Visitor Info: N. Lake Tahoe North Visitors Bureau, 380 N. Lake Blvd. (☎583-3494; www.mytahoevacation.com). A helpful office with tons of info on the area. Open M-F 9am-5pm, Sa-Su 9am-4pm. Taylor Creek Visitors Center (USFS; ☎543-2674; www.fs.fed.us/r5/ltbmu), 3 mi. north of S. Lake Tahoe on Hwy. 89. Permits for Desolation Wilderness. Camping fee $5 per person per night, $10 per person for 2 or more nights, $20 for yearly pass. Under 12 free. Reservations (☎644-6048, $5) are available for overnight permits mid-June to Sept. 6. Open daily May 31 to mid-June and Oct. 8am-4pm; mid-June to Sept. 8am-5:30pm.

Medical Services: Incline Village Community Hospital, 880 Alder Ave. (☎775-833-4100), off Hwy. 28 in Incline Village. **Barton Memorial Hospital,** 2170 South Ave. (☎541-3420), at 3rd St. and South Ave. off Lake Tahoe Blvd. in South Lake.

Post Office: Tahoe City, 950 N. Lake Blvd. (☎800-275-8777). Open M-F 8:30am-5pm. **Postal Code: 96145. South Lake Tahoe,** 1046 Al Tahoe Blvd. (☎800-275-8777). Open M-F 8:30am-5pm, Sa noon-2pm. **Postal Code:** 96151. **Area Code:** 530 in CA, 775 in NV; in text, 530 unless otherwise noted.

☎ ACCOMMODATIONS

The South Shore hosts many of the cheapest motels, which usually have just basic amenities. Accommodations in the North Shore, while pricier and fewer in number, are generally more polished and refined. In Tahoe City and Incline Village, the priciest lodgings tend to be booked solid for weekends and holidays; reserve well in advance. Fall and spring are the most economical times to visit Tahoe. Whatever your budget, the area's campgrounds are great options in warmer months.

■ **Tahoe Valley Lodge,** 2214 Lake Tahoe Blvd. (☎800-669-7544 or 541-0353; www.tahoevalleylodge.com), in South Lake. Decorative detail and exquisite comfort (and comforters) in spacious rooms with a simple log-cabin theme. All rooms have queen-size beds, cable TV, and coffeemakers; many have microwaves, refrigerators, and in-room spas. Reception 24hr. Singles $95; doubles $125. ❹

■ **Firelite Lodge,** 7035 N. Lake Blvd. (☎800-934-7222 or 546-7222), in Tahoe Vista 8 mi. east of Tahoe City. Right across from a sandy beach, this hotel has understated, relaxing rooms with microwaves, refrigerators, coffeemakers, and cable TV. Some rooms with balconies overlooking the pool. Laundry service available. Reception 8am-11pm. Singles and doubles summer and winter from $59; spring and fall from $49. ❸

Royal Inn, 3520 Lake Tahoe Blvd. (☎544-1177), in South Lake. Generic, well-maintained rooms with cable TV. Heated pool and laundry facilities. Singles Su-Th $28-35; doubles $39-49. Rates inflate greatly on weekends and holidays. Mention *Let's Go* for a possible discount. ❷

Tahoe State Recreation Area (☎583-3074), on the eastern edge of Tahoe City off Hwy. 28. In these 39 compact sites within walking distance of downtown Tahoe City (and adjacent a shopping center), you may not feel like you're camping. Water, flush toilets, and showers ($0.50). Open May-Nov. Sites $15; $4 per additional vehicle. ❶

🍴 FOOD

In the south, casinos offer low-priced buffets, but grilles and burger joints around the lake promise superior food at reasonable prices.

Jakes on the Lake, 780 N. Lake Blvd. (☎583-0188), in Boatworks Shopping Mall in Tahoe City. A taste of the South Seas in a relaxed wood-paneled dining room. Hawaiian-inspired creations alongside options like the New Rack of Lamb ($22). Open M-F 11:30am-2:30pm and 5:30-9:30pm, Sa-Su 11:30am-2:30pm and 5-9:30pm. ❺

Sprouts Natural Foods Cafe, 3123 Harrison Ave. (☎541-6969), at the intersection of Lake Tahoe Blvd. and Alameda Ave. in South Lake. Young, hip waiters dish out creative natural foods to an intelligent and healthy crowd. Try a breakfast burrito with avocados ($5), a smoothie ($3-3.75), or a shot of wheatgrass ($2). Open daily 8am-10pm. ❶

The Red Hut Cafe, 2723 Lake Tahoe Blvd. (☎541-9024), in South Lake, and another location at 22 Kingsbury Grade (☎588-7488). A Tahoe original since 1959. Friendly staff serves homestyle cooking. Waffles piled with fruit and whipped cream $5.75, avocado burgers $6.50. Open daily 6am-2pm. No credit cards. ❶

🏔 OUTDOOR ACTIVITIES

BEACHES

Many beaches dot Lake Tahoe, providing the perfect setting for sunning and people-watching. Parking costs $3-7; bargain hunters should leave cars in turn-outs on the main road and walk. On the North Shore, **Sand Harbor Beach,** 2 mi. south of Incline Village on Hwy. 28, has gorgeous granite boulders and clear waters that attract swimmers, snorkelers, and boaters to its marina. **Tahoe City Commons Beach,** in the heart of Tahoe City, has a playground, sandy beach, and pristine lake waters. **Baldwin Beach,** on the South Shore, and neighboring **Pope Beach,** near the southernmost point of the lake off Hwy. 89, are popular, shaded expanses of shoreline. Quiet spots on both can be found on the edges. **Nevada Beach,** on the east shore, 3 mi. north of South Lake Tahoe off Hwy. 50, is close to casinos but offers sanctuary from jangling slot machines. Recently renovated **Zephyr Cove Beach,** 5 mi. north of S. Lake Tahoe, hosts a youthful crowd keen on beer and bikinis. The West Shore offers **Meeks Bay,** 10 mi. south of Tahoe City, a family-oriented beach with picnic tables and volleyball courts. The minimal **D.L. Bliss State Park,** 17 mi. south of Tahoe City on Hwy. 89, is home to **Lester** and **Calawee Cove Beaches** on striking Rubicon Bay and is the trailhead for the Rubicon Trail.

HIKING

After decades of work, the 165 mi. **Tahoe Rim Trail** has finally been completed. The route encircles the lake, following the ridge tops of the basin, and welcomes hikers, equestrians, and, in most areas, **mountain bikers.** On the western shore, the route is part of the Pacific Crest Trail. In the north, **Mount Rose,** at 10,778 ft., is one of the tallest mountains in the region as well as one of the best climbs. The panoramic view from the summit includes views of the lake, Reno, and the surrounding Sierra Nevadas. Take Hwy. 431 north from Incline Village to the trailhead. The rugged trails and mountain streams of **Granite Chief Wilderness,** west of Squaw Valley, wind through forests in 5000 ft. valleys up to the summits of 9000 ft. peaks. The **Alpine Meadows Trailhead,** at the end of Alpine Meadows Rd. off Hwy. 89 between Truckee and Tahoe City, and the **Pacific Crest Trailhead,** at the end of Barker Pass Rd. (Blackwood Canyon Rd.), provide convenient access into the wilderness. The picturesque **Emerald Bay,** on Hwy. 89 between S. Lake Tahoe and Tahoe City, is best explored on foot. Waterfalls cascade down the mountains above this partially enclosed bay, which contains Lake Tahoe's only island, Fannette. ▨**Emerald Bay State Park,** which abuts Desolation Wilderness, offers hiking and biking trails of varying difficulty. One of the best hikes in Tahoe is **Rubicon Trail,** which wraps 6 mi. around the beach and granite cliffs.

ROCK CLIMBING

Alpenglow Sports, 415 N. Lake Blvd., in Tahoe City, provides rock and ice climbing literature and know-how. (☎583-6917. Shoe rental $8 per day. Open M-F 10am-6pm, Sa-Su 9am-6pm.) Pleasant climbs abound in Lake Tahoe, but safety precautions and equipment are a must. The inexperienced can try bouldering in **D.L. Bliss State Park.** The South Shore has many popular climbing spots, including the celebrated **Ninety-Foot Wall** at Emerald Bay, Twin Crags at Tahoe City, and Big Chief near Squaw Valley. **Lover's Leap,** in S. Lake Tahoe, is an incredible, albeit crowded, route spanning two giant cliffs.

SKIING

With world-class alpine slopes, 15 ski resorts, knee-deep powder, and California sun, Tahoe is the stuff of skiers' dreams. Skiing conditions range from winter storms to t-shirt weather; snow covers the slopes into early summer. Rates listed are for peak season. ▨**Squaw Valley,** 5 mi. north of Tahoe City off Hwy. 89, site of the 1960 Winter Olympics, has 4000 acres of terrain across six Sierra peaks. The 33 ski lifts, including the 110-passenger cable car and high speed gondola, access high-elevation runs for all levels. (☎583-6985 or 888-766-9321. Open late Nov. to May. Full-day lift ticket $59; half-day $43, ages 13-15 and 65-75 $29, under 12 $5, over 76 free. Night skiing mid-Dec. to mid-Apr. daily 4-9pm; $20.) The largest and most popular resort is **Heavenly,** on Ski Run Blvd. off S. Lake Tahoe Blvd., with over 4800 acres, 29 lifts, and 84 trails. Its vertical drop is 3500 ft., Tahoe's biggest. (☎775-586-7000. Full-day lift ticket $57, ages 13-18 $47, seniors and ages 6-12 $29.)

One of the best ways to enjoy the solitude of Tahoe's pristine snow-covered forests is to **cross-country ski** along the thick braid of trails around the lake. **Spooner Lake,** at the junction of Hwy. 50 and 28, offers 57 mi. of machine-groomed trails and incredible views. (☎775-749-5349. $19, children $3.) **Tahoe X-C,** 2 mi. northeast of Tahoe City on Dollar Hill off Hwy. 28, maintains 40 mi. of trails for all abilities. (☎583-5475. $18, midweek $13; children $6.) Snowshoeing is easier to pick up. Follow hiking or cross-country trails, or trudge off into the woods. Equipment rentals are available at sporting goods stores for about $15 per day.

YOSEMITE NATIONAL PARK ☎209

Yosemite became a national park over 100 years ago, but geologic work on the park began eons before that. About 50 million years ago, the flat floor and granite walls of Yosemite Valley, the park's most spectacular and popular area, were no more than a slow-moving river and rolling hills. Then the Sierra Nevadas rose, the Merced River deepened the terrain 3000 ft., and glaciers carved out the valley's trademark "U" shape. Today, Yosemite is the most famous of the national parks and for good reason; world-class sightseeing, outdoor activities, and an unimaginable geologic history are just a few of its offerings. Yosemite Valley, at the bustling, awe-inspiring heart of the park, still lives up to its old name: "The Incomparable Valley."

AT A GLANCE

AREA: 1189 sq. mi.

CLIMATE: Temperate forest.

FEATURES: Tuolumne (tah-WALL-um-ee) Meadows, Mariposa Grove, Hetch Hetchy Reservoir, Yosemite Valley.

HIGHLIGHTS: Swimming in Tenya Lake, climbing El Capitán, getting sprayed at Bridalveil Falls.

GATEWAYS: Fresno, Merced, Manteca, and Lee Vining.

CAMPING: Reservations necessary. 7-night max. stay in the valley and Wawona; 14-night max. stay elsewhere. Free wilderness permit is required for backcountry camping in the high country; backcountry camping is not permitted in Yosemite Valley.

FEES AND RESERVATIONS: Entrance fee $20 per car; $10 per pedestrian, cyclist, or bus passenger. Valid for 7 days. Annual pass $40.

TRANSPORTATION. Yosemite runs public **buses** that connect the park with Fresno, Merced, and Mariposa. **Yosemite VIA** runs buses from the Merced bus station at 16th and N St. (☎384-1315 or 800-VIA-LINE/842-5463. 4 trips per day. $10.) VIA

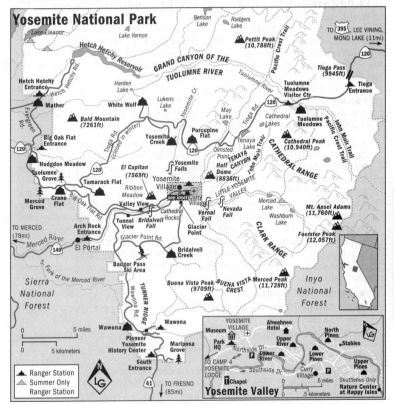

CALIFORNIA

meets Amtrak trains at the Merced train station. Tickets can be purchased from the driver. (☎384-1315. Buses run M-F 8am-5pm. Fares include Yosemite entry.) **Yosemite Gray Line (YGL)** runs buses to and from **Fresno Yosemite International Airport (FYI)**, Fresno hotels, and Yosemite Valley ($20). **YARTS** provides four daily trips to Yosemite from Merced, making stops along the way, and sends one bus a day along Rte. 120 and 395, hitting Mammoth and June Lakes, Lee Vining, and Tuolumne Meadows. (☎877-989-2787 or 388-9589. Buses depart Merced 7, 8:45, 10:30am, 5:25pm. Round-trip $20. Fares include Yosemite entry.) **Amtrak** runs a **bus** from Merced to Yosemite (4 per day, $22) and **trains** (☎800-USA-RAIL/872-7245) from L.A. (5½hr, 4 per day, $28-51) and San Francisco (3½hr., 5 per day, $22-29) to Merced. Despite traffic and congestion, the best way to see Yosemite is by **car.** Be sure to fill the tank before heading out, as there is no gas in Yosemite Valley except for emergency gas at the Village Garage ($15 for 5 gallons). There are overpriced 24hr. gas stations at Crane Flat, Tuolumne Meadows, and Wawona. Within the Valley, there is no reason to drive since the shuttle system is free and very convenient. If you do need **auto repairs,** however, call **Village Garage.** (☎372-8320. Open daily 8am-noon and 1-5pm. Cars towed 24hr. Emergency gasoline available. AAA and National Auto Club accepted.) **Bikes** can be rented from **Yosemite Lodge** (☎372-1208) and **Curry Village.** (☎372-8319. Bikes $5.50 per hr., $21 per day. Driver's license or credit card required as deposit. Both open daily 8:30am-7pm, weather permitting; open on a limited basis after Sept. 6.)

■╋⟷ ORIENTATION AND PRACTICAL INFORMATION. Yosemite covers 1170 sq. mi. of mountainous terrain, 95% of which is officially designated as wilderness. The center of activity, **Yosemite Valley** contains the area's most enduring monuments, including **El Capitán, Half Dome,** and **Yosemite Falls. Yosemite Village,** the Valley's service and info center, is perhaps the least natural part of the park. Facing the sheer southern wall of the valley and boasting incomparable 360° views, **Glacier Point** brims all summer with tourists. **Tuolumne Meadows,** in the northeast, is a rock-strewn alpine meadow surrounded by streams and snow-capped peaks. **Mariposa Grove** is a forest of giant sequoia trees in the south. **Wawona,** just north of Mariposa, is a historic, upscale development that features museums and a golf course. The vast majority of the park, however, is wild.

General Park Information (☎372-0200; www.yosemite.org). **Yosemite Valley Visitors Center** (☎372-0299), in Yosemite Village. Open daily 8am-6pm; in winter 9am-5pm. **Wilderness Center** (☎372-0745; www.nps.gov/yose/wilderness), in Yosemite Village. Wilderness permit reservations up to 24 weeks in advance (☎372-0740; $5 per person per reservation; M-F 8:30am-4:30pm), or first come, first served (free). 40% of backcountry quota is held for first come, first camp. Open daily 7:30am-6pm; low-season 8am-5pm. **Tuolumne Meadows Visitors Center** (☎372-0263). The high-country headquarters. Open in summer daily 9am-7pm.

Equipment Rental: Yosemite Mountaineering School (☎372-8344 or 372-8436), in Tuolumne Meadows. Sleeping bags $10.50 per day, backpacks $8.50; 3rd day half-price. Driver's license or credit card required as deposit. Rock climbing classes daily. Open daily 8:30am-noon and 1-5pm.

Weather and Road Conditions: ☎372-0200. 24hr.

Medical Services: Yosemite Medical Clinic (☎372-4637). 24hr. emergency room. Open M-Sa 8am-5pm.

Post Office: Yosemite Village, next to the visitors center. Open M-F 8:30am-5pm, Sa 10am-noon. **Postal Code:** 95389. **Area Code:** 209.

▐ ACCOMMODATIONS. When American Transcendentalist Ralph Waldo Emerson visited Yosemite in 1884, the park's accommodations were so simple that he was awakened in the morning by the clucking of a hen climbing over his bed.

These days, Yosemite's lodgings have become much more comfortable. Reservations are necessary and can be made up to one year in advance at ☎559-252-4848. All park lodgings provide access to dining, laundry, showers, and supplies. █Curry Village ➍, 2 mi. southeast of Yosemite Village, has a pool, outdoor amphitheater, store, and ice rink from November to February. (☎252-4848. Canvas tent cabins $60; cabins $77, with bath $92; standard motel rooms $112.) The army barracks-style Housekeeping Camp ➌ feels slightly less developed. "Camping shelters" for up to four include two bunk beds, a double bed, a picnic table, and a fire pit. (☎372-8338. Camping equipment rental. Shelters $64.) Tuolumne Meadows Lodge ➌, on Tioga Pass Rd., in the park's northeastern corner, has rustic cabins. (☎372-8413. Canvas-sided cabins, wood stoves, no electricity. Cabins $67; additional adult $9, child $4.) Outside the park, the █Yosemite Bug Hostel ➋, on Rte. 140 in Midpines, 25 mi. west of Yosemite, is a woodsy, spirited spot where backpackers lounge in hammocks. (☎966-6666; www.yosemitebug.com. Swimming hole with waterfall. Dorms $16; tent sites $17; private rooms $40-70, with bath $55-115.)

▐ ACCOMMODATIONS. One of the first views of Yosemite a visitor gets during the summer may be of the endless "tent cities" in the valley. Make reservations as far in advance as possible, especially in summer. (☎800-436-7275; http://reservations.nps.gov. Reserve by phone or online daily 7am-7pm.) All Valley campgrounds fill completely every summer night. Natural stream water must be boiled, filtered, or treated. Backcountry camping is prohibited in the Valley but encouraged outside it. Catering to seasoned climbers, Camp 4 ➊, 4000 ft., at the western end of the valley, past Yosemite Lodge, has 35 walk-in sites that fill up before 9am. Meet new friends; every site is filled with 6 random people. (Water, flush toilets, and tables. First come, first served. Limited parking. Sites $5 per person.) Drive in or escape the RVs in the 25 sites saved for walk-in hikers at Tuolumne Meadows ➊, 8600 ft., on Rte. 120, 55 mi. east of the Valley. (152 sites require advance reservations, 152 saved for same-day reservations. Open July-Sept., depending on snow. Drive-in sites $18; backpacker sites $3 per person.)

▐ FOOD. The Village Store is your best bet for groceries. (Open daily June-Sept. 8am-10pm; Oct.-May 8am-9pm.) With views of Yosemite Falls from nearly every seat, Mountain Room Restaurant ➎, in Yosemite Lodge, is ideal for a post-hike meal. (☎372-9033. Hearty fare $17-28. Open daily 5:30-9pm.) Degnan's Delicatessen ➋, in Yosemite Village, is inside a convenience store and adjacent to an ice-cream parlor and pizza place. (☎372-8454. Sandwiches $5.75. Open daily 7am-7pm.)

▐ OUTDOOR ACTIVITIES. Although the view is better if you get out of the car, you can see a large portion of Yosemite from the bucket seat, and if you only have one day in the park, scenic drives are the way to see the sights. The Yosemite Road Guide ($3.50 at every visitors center) is keyed to roadside markers and outlines a superb tour of the park. Spectacular panoramas and beautiful glades abound along Rte. 120 (Tioga Road) from Crane Flat to Tuolumne Meadows. This stretch of road is the highest highway strip in the country; as it winds down from Tioga Pass through the park's eastern exit, it plunges a mile down to reach the lunar landscape of Mono Lake. The drive west from the pass brings you past Tuolumne Meadows, with its colorful grasses and rippling creeks, to shimmering Tenaya Lake. No less incredible are the views afforded by the southern approach to Yosemite, Rte. 41. Most recognizable is the Wawona Tunnel turn-out (also known as Inspiration Point), which gives views many visitors will recognize from Ansel Adams photographs. From here, Yosemite Valley unfurls its humbling beauty. El Capitán, a gigantic granite monolith (7569 ft.), looms over awestruck crowds. Opposite El Capitán, Bridalveil Falls drops 620 ft. A drive into the valley's heart leads to the staggering Yosemite Falls (the highest waterfall in North America at 2425 ft.). Incredible views of the falls are available at many parking lots and turn-outs, making it possible to avoid areas with shoulder-to-shoulder tourists photographing the sight. In the valley's eastern end stands **Half Dome,** a monolithic rock formation that can be seen from virtually everywhere in the valley.

Glacier Point Rd., off Rte. 41 in the southern part of the park, meanders past lush meadows and rounded domes to the southeast. At its end, **Glacier Point** gives a bird's-eye view of the Valley floor, which is considered one of the most spectacular views on earth. Half Dome arcs majestically from the Valley's east side and water seems to tumble down Nevada Falls in slow motion. When the moon is full, this is an extraordinary (and very popular) place to visit. Arrive at sunset and watch the fiery colors fade over the valley as the stars and moon appear.

With two or more days in Yosemite, it's worthwhile to explore some of its trails. World-class **hiking** abounds for anyone willing to lace up a pair of boots, though sneakers will suffice for a few trails. Daytrip trails are well populated—at nearly any point in the day, you may find yourself stuck behind groups of other tourists. Hiking just after sunrise is the best and sometimes the only way to beat the crowds, but even then, trails like Half Dome are busy. A colorful trail map of short day-hikes from the Valley is available at the visitors center ($0.50). The popular Mist Trail (6 mi.) starts at Happy Isles trailhead (shuttle bus stop #16) at the valley's eastern end. The trail runs parallel to the Merced River to the base of Vernal Falls. From there, steep and slippery steps carved out of the granite put you next to the falls, which sprays hikers with its mist. The trail ends at the top of the falls. The strenuous hike to the top of **Half Dome** is a popular option. This hike, which starts at the Happy Isles trailhead, affords the thrill of conquering Yosemite's most recognizable monument. The 16 mi. hike is recommended for those in good condition and comfortable with heights. Half Dome attracts lightning, and midsummer thunderstorms make early- morning departures advisable.

The **Mirror Lake Loop** is a flat 3 mi. walk past Mirror Lake (½ mi.), up Tenaya Creek, and back. The **Lower Yosemite Falls Trail** is a favorite, starting across from Yosemite Lodge. On moonlit nights, mysterious moonbows (nighttime rainbows) can often be spotted off the water. **Upper Yosemite Falls Trail,** a backbreaking 3½ mi. trek to the summit, climbs 2700 ft. but rewards the intrepid hiker with an overview of the vertiginous 2425 ft. drop. Those with energy to spare can trudge on to **Yosemite Point** or **Eagle Peak,** where views of the Valley below rival those from Glacier Point. The trail begins with an extremely steep, unshaded ascent. Leaving the marked trail is not wise—a sign warns, "If you go over the waterfall, you will die." From **Glacier Point,** the steep **Four Mile Trail** (actually 4½ mi. long) is a switchbacked descent to the Valley floor. Walk through forests of white firs and sugar pines with sporadic Valley views as you gain a sense of the valley's 3000 ft. depth.

In Yosemite's quietest season, the landscape undergoes a facelift as the waterfalls freeze and the meadows frost over. Unlike much of the mountain range, Yosemite Valley remains accessible year-round. **Route 140** from Merced, a designated all-weather entrance, is usually open and clear. Although Tioga Pass and Glacier Point Rd. close at the first sign of snowfall, **Route 41** from the south and **Route 120** from the west typically remain traversable. Verify road conditions before traveling (☎372-0200) and carry tire chains.

Well-marked trails for **cross-country skiing** and **snowshoeing** cut into the backcountry of the Valley's South Rim at Badger Pass and Crane Flat. Rangers host snowshoe walks from mid-December to March, but the forests are perhaps best explored without guidance. Guided cross-country skiing trips (☎327-8444) with meals and hut lodgings are available. The state's oldest ski resort, **Badger Pass Ski Area,** on Glacier Point Rd. south of Yosemite Valley, is the park's only downhill ski area, and has a family atmosphere. **Ice skating** at Curry Village is beautiful, with

Half Dome towering above a groomed outdoor rink encircled by snow-covered pines. (☎372-8319. Open in winter M-F noon-9:30pm, Sa-Su 8:30am-9:30pm. $5; skate rental $2.) **Sledding** and **tobogganing** are allowed at Crane Flat off Rte. 120.

MAMMOTH LAKES   ☎760

Home to one of the most popular ski resorts in the U.S., the town of Mammoth Lakes (pop. 5305) is a giant year-round playground. The snowfall averages over 350 in. per year, creating 3500 acres of skiable terrain. When the snow melts, mountain bikers invade to take on Mammoth Mountain, skateboarders come to test their skills in competitions, and fisherfolk come to the magma-warmed creeks. A **free shuttle bus (MAS)** transports skiers between lifts and the ski lodge.

Devil's Postpile National Monument is a stunning 60 ft. wall made of eerily uniform hexagonal rock columns. The **Inyo Craters** are open pits 600 ft. across with blue-green water at the bottom. The ¼ mi. jaunt to the craters can be reached from Mammoth Scenic Loop Rd. The climbing wall at **Mammoth Mountain High Adventure** beckons both the inexperienced and the professional. (☎924-5683. Open daily 10am-6pm. $6 per climb, $13 per hr., $22 per day; discount for groups of 3 or more.) The **Map and Compass Course** simulates an escape from the jungle. ($15 round-trip for 2hr. course; includes compass rental, map, and intro lesson.) The **Mammoth Mountain Gondola** affords mile-high views. (☎934-2571. Open daily 9am-4:30pm. Round-trip $16, children $8; day pass for gondola and trail use $25. Chair-lift round-trip $10, children $5.) Exit the gondola at the top to tackle more than 80 mi. of twisted trails in **Mammoth Mountain Bike Park;** the ride starts at 11,053 ft. and heads straight down on rocky ski trails. (☎934-0706. Helmets required. Open 9am-6pm. Day pass $29, children $15. Unlimited day pass and bike rental $62/31.)

As in most ski resort towns, lodging is much more expensive in winter. Condo rentals are good for groups of three or more and start at $100 per night. **Mammoth Reservation Bureau** (☎800-462-5571; www.mammothvacations.com) can make arrangements. For lone travelers, dorm-style motels are cheapest. Reservations are highly recommended. **Davison St. Guest House ❶**, 19 Davison Rd., at Lake Mary Rd., is the best value in town. (☎924-2188. Dorms $21-25; private rooms $45-75.) There are nearly 20 Inyo Forest public **campgrounds ❶** (sites $13-16) in the area. All sites have piped water and most are near fishing and hiking. Contact the **Mammoth Ranger District** (☎924-5500) for info. **Paul Schat's Bakery and Cafe ❶**, 3305 Main St., is the best in town. (☎934-6055. Open Su-Th 5:30am-6pm, F-Sa 5:30am-8pm.)

THE NORTH COAST

Windswept and larger than life, the North Coast winds from the San Francisco Bay Area to the Oregon border. Redwoods tower over undiscovered black-sand beaches, and otters frolic next to jutting rock formations—the North Coast's untouched wilderness is simply stunning. U.S. 101 snakes along cliffs between pounding surf and humbling redwoods.

MENDOCINO   ☎707

Teetering on bluffs over the ocean, isolated Mendocino (pop. 1107) is a charming coastal community of art galleries, craft shops, bakeries, and B&Bs. The town's greatest feature lies 900 ft. to its west, where the earth falls into the Pacific at the impressive **◪Mendocino Headlands.** The windy ¼ mi. meadow of tall grass and wildflowers separates the town from the rocky shore. Poor drainage, thin acidic soil, and ocean winds have created unusually stunted vegetation 3 mi. south of town at the **Pygmy Forest** in **Van Damme State Park ❶.** (Sites $20; day use $6.)

Jug Handle Creek Nature Center ❶, about 3 mi. north of Mendocino off Hwy. 1, across the street from the Jug Handle State Reserve, is a beautiful 134-year-old house sitting on 39 acres of gardens, campsites, and small rustic cabins. Trails from the property lead to coastal access. (☎964-4630. Reservations recommended in summer; walk-ins welcome. Rooms $27, students $21; cabins $35 per person; sites $11; $5 off for 1hr. of chores.) **MacKerricher State Park campground ❶**, 2½ mi. north of Fort Bragg, has excellent views of tide pool life, passing seals, sea lions, and migratory whales, as well as 9 mi. of beaches and a murky lake for trout fishing. (☎937-5804. Showers, bathrooms, and drinkable water. Sites $20.) For picnic fare head to **Mendosa's Market**, 10501 Lansing St. Like most things in Mendocino, it's pricey, but most items are fresh and delicious. (☎937-5879. Open daily 8am-9pm.) Mendocino restaurants often close early. **Lu's Kitchen ❷**, 45013 Ukiah St., west of Lansing St., serves vegetarian cuisine in an informal, outdoor atmosphere. (☎937-4939. Entrees $5-9. Open daily Apr.-Sept. and Dec.-Jan. 11:30am-5pm.)

Tiny Mendocino sits on **Highway 1**, right on the Pacific coast, 30 mi. west of U.S. 101 and 12 mi. south of Fort Bragg. Like all northern coast areas, Mendocino can be very chilly, even in summer. Travelers should prepare for 40-70°F temperatures. The nearest **Greyhound** station (☎800-231-2222) is two hours away in Ukiah. **Mendocino Transit Authority**, 241 Plant Rd., in Ukiah, makes one round-trip daily between Mendocino and Santa Rosa ($16), stopping at Willits ($2.75) and Ukiah ($4.25) on the way. The bus leaves from the Cookie Company at Lansing and Ukiah St. (☎800-696-4682.) **Visitor Info: Fort Bragg-Mendocino Coast Chamber of Commerce**, 332 N. Main St., in Fort Bragg. (☎961-6300 or 800-726-2780. Open M-F 9am-noon and 12:30-5pm, Sa 9am-3pm.) **Park Info:** ☎937-5804 or the **MacKerricher State Park Visitors Center**, 2½ mi. north of Fort Bragg. (☎964-8898. Open in summer Su-M, W, F-Sa 10:30am-4:30pm; limited hours in winter.) **Internet Access:** The **Fort Bragg Library**, 499 Laurel St., in Fort Bragg (open Tu and Th 10am-6pm, W noon-8pm, F-Sa 10am-5pm). **Police:** (☎961-0200), stationed in Fort Bragg. **Medical Services: Mendocino Coast District Hospital**, 700 River Dr. (☎961-1234), in Ft. Bragg. **Post Office:** 10500 Ford St. (☎937-5282; open M-F 7:30am-4:30pm). **Postal Code:** 95460.

AVENUE OF THE GIANTS ☎707

About 10 mi. north of Garberville on U.S. 101 in Humboldt Redwoods State Park, the Avenue of the Giants splits off the highway and winds its way through 31 mi. of redwoods, the world's largest living organisms above ground level. The staff at **Humboldt Redwoods State Park Visitors Center** can highlight the avenue's groves, facilities, great trails, and bike routes. (☎946-2263. Open daily Apr.-Oct. 9am-5pm; Nov.-Mar. 10am-4pm.) The plentiful **campsites ❶** in the park offer coin showers, flush toilets, and fire rings. (☎946-2409. Sites $15.) The very worthwhile ½ mi. loop at **Founder's Grove** features the 1300- to 1500-year-old **Founder's Tree**, and the former tallest tree in Humboldt Redwoods State Park, the fallen 362 ft. **Dyerville Giant**, whose massive, three-story root-ball looks like a mythic entanglement of evil. Uncrowded trails wind through **Rockefeller Forest** in the park's northern section, which contains the largest grove of continuous old-growth redwoods in the world.

REDWOOD NAT'L AND STATE PARKS ☎707

The redwoods are the last remaining stretch of the old-growth forest that used to blanket two million acres of Northern California and Oregon. Within the parks, black bears and mountain lions roam the backwoods and elk graze the meadows.

CALIFORNIA

🏛 PRACTICAL INFORMATION

Redwood National and State Parks is an umbrella term for four contiguous parks. From south to north, they are: **Redwood National Park, Prairie Creek Redwoods State Park, Del Norte Coast Redwoods State Park,** and **Jedediah Smith Redwoods State Park.**

Entrance Fees: Charges vary by park and are different for camping, parking, and hiking. While there is usually no charge to enter, a day-use fee ($4 per car) for parking and picnic areas is typical.

Buses: Greyhound, 500 E. Harding St. (☎ 464-2807), in Crescent City, runs 1 or 2 buses daily, 1 in the morning and 1 in the evening, to Portland ($61-71) and San Francisco ($61-71). Call for exact rates and departure times.

Auto Repairs: AAA Emergency Road Service (☎ 800-222-4357). 24hr.

Visitor Info: Redwood National Park Headquarters and Information Center, 1111 2nd St. (☎ 464-6101, ext. 5826), in Crescent City. Headquarters of the entire national park, but ranger stations are also well informed. Open daily 9am-5pm; Nov.-Mar. closed Su.

Medical Services: Sutter Coast Hospital, 800 E. Washington Blvd. (☎ 464-8511), in Crescent City.

Internet Access: Del Norte County Library, 190 Price Mall (☎ 464-9793), at the corner of K and Front St., in Crescent City. $1 per 30min. Open M and W-Th 10am-6pm, Tu 10am-8pm.

Post Office: Crescent City: 751 2nd St. (☎ 464-2151), at H St. Open M-F 8:30am-5pm, Sa noon-2pm. **Postal Code:** 95531.

🏠 ACCOMMODATIONS

🏠 **Redwood Youth Hostel (HI),** 14480 U.S. 101 (☎ 482-8265; www.redwoodhostel.com), at Wilson Creek Rd., 7 mi. north of Klamath. The family that runs this hostel welcomes travelers of all ages. Breathtaking sunsets from 2 ocean-view decks—the beach is just across the street. Simple chores and rules (no shoes inside) keep the house immaculate. Check-in 5-10pm. Check-out 10am. Lockout 10am-5pm. Curfew 10pm. Reservations recommended in summer. Dorms $18-19, under 18 half-price; doubles $45. ❶

Historic Requa Inn, 451 Requa Rd. (☎ 482-1425 or 866-800-8777), west off U.S. 101, about 1 mi. from the Klamath overlook. Lace-curtained windows look out over the picturesque Klamath River. Breakfast (included) served in the Victorian parlor. Elegant evening dining M-Sa (entrees $12-22). Reservations recommended June-Sept. Rooms May-Sept. $85-135, Oct.-Apr. $79-120. ❹

Jedediah Smith Redwoods State Park, north of Crescent City on U.S. 199. Picnic tables, water, restrooms, and showers. Campfire programs and nature walks offered during the summer. Sites $20; day-use $5; hike/bike $2. ❶

🍴 FOOD

There are more picnic tables than restaurants in the area, so the best option for food is probably the supermarket. In Crescent City, head to the 24hr. **Safeway,** 475 M St. (☎ 465-3353), on U.S. 101 between 2nd and 5th St. The **Palm Cafe ❷,** on U.S. 101 in Orick, bakes delicious fruit, coconut, and chocolate pies. (☎ 488-3381. Pie slices $2.25. Open daily 5am-8pm.) The dedicated regulars at **Glen's Bakery and Restaurant ❶,** at 3rd and G St., love the huge pancakes ($4) and sandwiches ($4-6.50). Breakfast is served all day. (☎ 464-2914. Open Tu-Sa 5am-6:30pm.)

🔲 🔲 SIGHTS AND HIKING

All plants and animals in the park are protected—even feathers dropped by birds of prey are off-limits. California **fishing licenses** (1 day $10) are required for fresh and saltwater fishing off any natural formation, but fishing is free from any man-made structure. There are minimum-weight and maximum-catch requirements specific to both fresh and saltwater fishing. Call the **Fish and Game Department** (☎ 445-6493; www.dfg.ca.gov) for more information on how to obtain a permit.

The **Orick Area** covers the southernmost section of Redwood National and State Parks. The **visitors center** lies on U.S. 101, just 1 mi. south of Orick and ½ mi. south of the Shoreline Deli (the Greyhound bus stop). A popular sight is the **Tall Trees Grove,** accessible by car to those with permits (free from the visitors center) when the road is open. Allow at least 3-4hr. for the trip. The criss-crossing 70 mi. of trails in the **Prairie Creek Area** can be confusing; be sure to pick up a trail map ($1). The **James Irvine Trail** (4½ mi. one-way) snakes through a prehistoric garden of towering old-growth redwoods. The less ambitious can cruise part of the **Foothill Trail** (¾ mi. one-way) to a 1500-year-old behemoth, the 306 ft. high **Big Tree.**

The northern **Klamath Area** connects Prairie Creek with Del Norte State Park; the main attraction is the spectacular coastline. The **Klamath Overlook,** where Requa Rd. meets the steep **Coastal Trail** (8 mi.), is an excellent **whale-watching** site. An outstanding location from which to explore the parks, **Crescent City** is the city "where the redwoods meet the sea." The **Battery Point Lighthouse** is on a causeway jutting out from Front St. and houses a museum open only during low tide. (☎ 464-3089. Open Apr.-Sept. W-Su 10am-4pm, tide permitting; Nov.-Mar. F-Sa at low tide. $3, children $1.) From June to August, **tidepool walks** leave from Enderts Beach. (At the turnoff 4 mi. south of Crescent City; call ☎ 464-6101, ext. 5064, for schedules.)

HAWAII

A state unlike any other, Hawaii has been billed as the American tropical paradise since the 1950s. Half a century later, millions of people have discovered Hawaii— they've sunbathed on its spectacular white-, black-, golden-, green-, and red-sand beaches; become infatuated with Hawaiian culture and the forgivably tacky *aloha* shirts; felt the sublime allure of powerful Pacific waves and the inexplicable awesomeness of flowing lava and active volcanoes; and succumbed to the indelible charm of a laid-back Hawaiian lifestyle. Hawaii's six major islands—Oahu, the Big Island, Maui, Molokai, Lanai, and Kauai—have so many facets that it is impossible to uncover them all in one trip. Along every coast there is a more secluded stretch of sand, and beyond each stunning vista an even more breathtaking view. For complete coverage of this diverse and wonderful state, see 🔖 *Let's Go: Hawaii 2005*.

HIGHLIGHTS OF HAWAII

OAHU. Relax on miles of sand or at world-class resorts in Waikiki (p. 993).

THE BIG ISLAND. Take a sunset hike at Hawaii Volcanoes National Park and watch lava flows illuminate the night sky (p. 996).

MAUI. Catch a spectacular sunrise or similarly stunning sunset from the summit of Haleakala (p. 1000).

KAUAI. Get back to the basics on one of Hawaii's most pristine islands (p. 1001).

🔁 PRACTICAL INFORMATION

Oahu is the major hub for transportation to all the Hawaiian islands. International flights, flights between Hawaii and the mainland, and interisland flights depart from Honolulu International Airport in Honolulu (p. 990).

Capital: Honolulu.

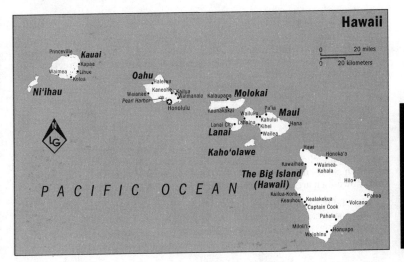

Visitor Info: Hawaii Visitors and Convention Bureau, 2270 Kalakaua Ave., Ste. 801, Honolulu 96815 (☎923-1811; www.gohawaii.com).
Postal Abbreviation: HI. **Sales Tax:** 4%. **Accommodations Tax:** 11.42%.
Area Code: ☎808.

OAHU ☎808

Visitors can discover the multifaceted appeal of Hawaii on Oahu, which seems to contain distilled versions of the best her sister islands have to offer. There is a trace of the Big Island's hippie culture on the sands of the North Shore, some of Maui's beauty and opulence in the Windward Coast's resorts, a dash of Kauai's natural splendor in the lush interior valleys, and a little bit of rustic Molokai in the streets of Waimanalo. Meanwhile, the bustling metropolis of Honolulu, Hawaii's state capital and premier city, is the island's nexus, with all the glamorous trappings of a major urban center and tourist capital. Waikiki, the southeastern quarter of the city, is one of the most famous destinations in the world: a magical mile of beachfront hotels, shops, restaurants, and endless entertainment.

▐ OAHU TRANSPORTATION

Airport: Honolulu International Airport (☎836-6413; www.honoluluairport.com) is off the Airport exit from H-1, 9 mi. west of Waikiki. Most domestic and international flights fly through here, with carriers such as **Aloha Airlines** (☎484-1111; www.alohaairlines.com) and **Hawaiian Airlines** (☎838-1555; www.hawaiianair.com).

Buses: TheBus (☎848-4500; www.thebus.org) offers safe and clean service across the island. You may have to wait for quite a while, since buses are often stuck in traffic. One-way $2; seniors 65 and over, disabled, and ages 6-17 $1. Free transfers are good for 2hr. and available upon request from bus driver.

Car Rental: Driving is the easiest way to get around Oahu, despite traffic and limited parking. The major national chains have branches by the airport. Waikiki has some excellent smaller car and moped rental companies.

HONOLULU ☎808

Hawaii's capital and largest city, Honolulu is a commercial center, college town, and living landmark of Hawaiian history. Businesspeople in their finest *aloha*-wear bustle through downtown on palm-tree-lined, skyscraper-filled streets, while Chinatown is crammed with shoppers in search of a deal among its markets and restaurants. The mellow residential areas of Kaimuki and Manoa escape a fast pace of life on the outskirts of Honolulu, while the sights in downtown's Civic Center illuminate the complex history of Hawaii's Western modernization.

▐✦▐ ORIENTATION AND PRACTICAL INFORMATION

Depending on whom you ask, Honolulu can include the suburban sprawl across the south shore of Oahu, from Koko Head to the airport, or the comparatively small downtown area surrounded by **Ala Moana, Chinatown, Kaimuki,** and **Manoa.**

Visitor Info: Hawaii Visitors and Convention Bureau Information Office, 2270 Kalakaua Ave., Ste. 801 (☎923-1811 or 800-464-2924; www.gohawaii.com), at Waikiki Business Plaza. Open M-F 8am-4:30pm.

Police: Honolulu Police Department, 801 S. Beretania St. (☎529-3111).

Medical Services: Queen's Medical Center, 1301 Punchbowl St. (☎538-9011). An **Emergency Services Dept.** (☎547-4311) provides pre-hospital emergency care and ambulance services. Their referral line (☎537-7117) can help visitors find a doctor.

Internet Access: etopia, 1363 S. Beretania St. (☎593-0226; www.theetopia.com). Nonmembers $3 per hr. Under 18 not allowed during school hours. 30 computers. Open daily 9am-4am. Cash only.

Post Office: Airport, 3600 Aolele St., Rm. 209 (☎423-6029), offers the only General Delivery service in Honolulu. Open M-F 7:30am-8pm, Sa 8am-4pm. **Postal Code:** 96819. **Downtown,** 335 Merchant St. (☎532-1987), in the Civic Center. Open M-F 8am-4:30pm. **Postal Code:** 96813.

▐ ACCOMMODATIONS

▥ **Manoa Valley Inn,** 2001 Vancouver Dr. (☎947-6019; manoavalleyinn@aloha.net). 2 mi. from rainforest hiking and Waikiki, this cozy inn is a perfect hideaway from the hurried pace of Honolulu. On the National Register of Historic Places, with classic Victorian-style rooms. Breakfast is served each morning on the breezy veranda with a sweeping view of the city and Diamond Head. Hot tub in the garden. 2-night min. Check-in 3pm. Check-out 11am. Doubles with shared bath $89-100, private bath $140-160; cottage with A/C and fridge $140-150. ❹

Hostelling International Honolulu (HI), 2323A Seaview Ave. (☎946-0591). The best-kept hostel in Honolulu welcomes international travelers with tidy rooms and a calm atmosphere in a residential area within walking distance of university nightlife and a short bus ride to Waikiki or Ala Moana. Communal bath, full kitchen, coin-op laundry, and TV lounge. Free lockers (bring padlock). Linen deposit $2. Key deposit $5. Maid service daily. 3-day max. for nonmembers, 7-day max. for members. Reception 8am-noon and 4pm-midnight. Reserve 2 weeks in advance. Single-sex 6- or 7-bed dorms $16, nonmembers $19; basic 2-person studio (bunk bed, no amenities) $42/$48. ❶

Ala Moana Hotel, 410 Atkinson Dr. (☎955-4811 or 800-367-6025; www.alamoanahotel.com), 2 blocks from Kapiolani Blvd. A great location within walking distance of the Ala Moana Shopping Center, TheBus routes, Ala Moana Beach Park, and Waikiki, but still far enough away to duck the crowds. It also tops all but the best of Waikiki's hotels, with a business center, fitness room, heated pool (and pool bar), sundeck, 4 restaurants, and Rumours nightclub. Parking $10 per day. Check-in 3pm. Check-out noon. Doubles $135-215; floors 29-35 (which have slightly better views and hot tubs) $235. The frequent "super saver" rate can get you a room for $99. ❺

▐ FOOD

▥ **Indigo,** 1121 Nuuanu Ave. (☎521-2900; www.indigo-hawaii.com), next to the Hawaii Theater Center, amid fountains and trees. Indigo cooks dishes and desserts in a delicious fusion of European and Asian flavors (grilled shrimp and Thai macadamia nut pesto $22; Sumatran coffee bread pudding with *crème anglaise* sauce $6). Its 2 bar/lounges are decked with distinctive, chic Zen decor. Reservations recommended. Lunch Tu-F 11:30am-2pm. Dinner Tu-Sa 6-9:30pm. ❺

▥ **Little Village,** 1113 Smith St. (☎545-3008). Step into this soothing little bamboo village for exquisite, healthy Chinese food (no MSG). Signature dishes include the Szechuan spicy chicken ($8), sizzling scallops ($13), and eggplant with garlic sauce ($8). Open Su-Th 10:30am-10:30pm, F-Sa 10:30am-midnight. ❸

Auntie Pasto's, 1099 S. Beretania St. (☎523-8855), on the corner of Beretania and Pensacola St. Auntie's pasta ($7.25-9.25) is big enough to fill a hungry *braddah* and authentic enough for any Italian. Eggplant parmesan $9. Wine $3.25-9. Open M-Th 11am-10:30pm, F 11am-11pm, Sa 4-11pm, Su 4-10:30pm. ❷

Andy's Sandwiches and Smoothies, 2904 E. Manoa Rd. (☎988-6161), across the street from Manoa Marketplace. This walk-up deli cooks healthy food—a rarity in Honolulu. Known and loved for big sandwiches on fresh homemade bread (fresh-roasted turkey sandwich $4), vegetarian options (mushroom medley $5), and fruit smoothies ($3.25-5). Open M-Th 7am-5:30pm, F 7am-4pm, Su 7am-2pm. ❶

👁 SIGHTS

PEARL HARBOR. During Japan's swift and devastating attack on Pearl Harbor, 40min. outside Honolulu, over 2400 military personnel and civilians were killed, 188 planes demolished, and eight battleships either damaged or destroyed. Solemn and graceful, the ▧**USS Arizona Memorial** is a fitting tribute to the 1177 crewmen who died aboard the ship. The 184 ft. memorial affords visitors a poignant view of the ship that still entombs 1100 men. There are three main sections: an entry room; a central area where visitors can observe the ship; and the shrine room, which has a marble wall engraved with the names of those who died on the *Arizona*. The on-shore visitors center has a museum and a somber and moving tour that includes a documentary film and boat ride to the memorial itself. Come early, as wait times can reach 2hr. and on busy summer days most tickets are gone by noon. *(From Honolulu, take H-1 west to the Arizona Memorial/Stadium exit and follow the signs. ☎422-0561. Open daily 7:30am-5pm. 1¼hr. tours every 15min. 7:45am-3pm. No bags, purses, backpacks, or strollers with pockets or compartments. Baggage storage available in the parking lot for $2; cash only. Admission free.)*

IOLANI PALACE. Hawaii's latter monarchs resided in the "American-Florentine" style ▧ **Iolani Palace,** situated amidst lovely, coral-fenced grounds. Iolani was the official residence of King Kalakaua and Queen Liliuokalani, the last king and queen to rule Hawaii before a *coup d'état* abolished the monarchy in 1893. It was here that Liliuokalani was tried, convicted, and imprisoned for treason after a failed loyalist retaliation in 1895. The Palace Galleries hold the royal crown jewels and replicas of the chamberlain's office and palace kitchen. The imprisonment room is especially moving. Still on the grounds is an ancient burial site, *Pohukaina*, which holds the sacred remains of *alii* (royalty). The **Royal Hawaiian Band** plays free concerts Fridays at noon. *(364 King St. ☎538-1471. Open Tu-Sa 9am-2:15pm. 1½hr. tours every 30min. 9am-2pm. $20, ages 5-17 $5; no children under 5. Self-guided gallery tour $6, children under 17 $3, children under 5 $2. Gallery open Tu-Sa 8:30am-4pm, last admission 3:30pm.)*

BISHOP MUSEUM. Founded in 1889, the **Bishop Museum** is the best place to learn about the history and culture of Hawaii. The museum has almost 25 million works of art and artifacts, including publications, photographs, films, audio recordings, manuscripts, and millions of animal and plant species, many of which are extinct. One must-see exhibit is the Kahili Room, which showcases the *kahili* (feather standards of Hawaiian royalty) and portraits of 19th-century Hawaiian monarchs. A program of museum tours, garden tours, planetarium shows, and music, dance, and dramatic performances is included with admission. *(1525 Bernice St. ☎847-3511; www.bishopmuseum.org. 1 free return is allowed within 1 week of ticket purchase. $15, seniors and ages 4-12 $12.)*

HAWAII STATE ART MUSEUM. The **Hawaii State Art Museum**'s ongoing exhibit, "Enriched by Diversity: The Art of Hawaii," houses 360 pieces by Hawaiian artists, most of which date from the 1960s to the present and combine Western aesthetics with traditional Hawaiian and Pacific art forms. The unique focus of the museum and its beautiful setting in an old Spanish mission-style YMCA building make it a must-see for all those interested in Hawaiian culture, tradition, and art. *(No. 1 Capitol District Building, 250 S. Hotel St., 2nd fl. ☎586-0900. Open Tu-Sa 10am-4pm. Tours Tu-Sa 1pm. Call to arrange group tours. Large bags checked at the door. Free.)*

◤ NIGHTLIFE

■ **Anna Banana's**, 2440 S. Beretania St. (☎946-5190). This hole-in-the-wall bar is a love-worn Manoa and UH institution, with a 35-year history of live music. Excellent happy hour (daily 3-6pm) and nightly drink specials. The biggest nights are M (open mic 9pm) and F-Sa (live bands 10pm). 21+. Cover M and F-Sa $5. Open daily 3pm-2am.

The Green Room and Opium Den at Indigo's, 1121 Nuuanu Ave. (☎521-2900). The party starts during Martini Madness (Tu-F 4-7pm; $2.75 martinis, and free mini-buffet of *pupus* at 5pm). Its 2 bar/lounges—the French-themed Green Room and the Chinese-inspired Opium Den, with floor cushions—are popular hangouts. Tu wine tasting 6-8pm in the Opium Den ($20). W "Vintage" (old-school hip-hop, soul, and R&B); F "Get Fresh!" with visiting DJs. Lounges open nightly 4pm-2am.

Mai Tai Bar, 1450 Ala Moana Blvd. (☎947-2900), in the Ala Moana Shopping Center. Mai Tai brings in droves of young, energetic bar-goers with a late-night happy hour daily 8-11pm; pitchers $5-7, wine $2, and Icy Mai Tais $3. Live Hawaiian music daily 4-7pm and 9:30pm-12:30am. 21+. Open daily 11am-1am.

WAIKIKI   ☎808

The center of tourism in Hawaii's biggest city, Waikiki is a thoroughly commercial destination, but the area has an electrifying allure nonetheless. An international mélange of travelers and tourists and a smaller contingent of natives crowd the area's streets, shops, sights, sands, and dance floors—if Oahu is "the gathering place," Waikiki is where the party's at.

◪ PRACTICAL INFORMATION

Police: Waikiki Substation, 2425 Kalakaua Ave. (☎529-3801), in the Duke Paoa Kahanamoku Building on Waikiki Beach, opposite the Hyatt Regency. Open 24hr.

Medical Services: Urgent Care Clinic of Waikiki, 2155 Kalakaua Ave., Ste. 308 (☎924-3399), at Beachwalk above Planet Hollywood. Accepts walk-ins. Free rides to clinic. Open daily 8:30am-7pm. **Straub Doctors on Call**, ☎971-6000.

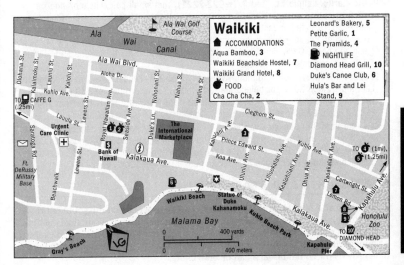

Internet Access: Hawaii Digital, 2301 Kuhio Ave., Ste. 2 (☎923-9797). High-speed Internet access $1 per 10min., $5 per hr. Open daily 9am-10pm.

Post Office: Waikiki Post Office, 330 Saratoga Rd. (☎973-7515). Open M-F 8am-4:30pm, Sa 9am-1pm. **Postal Code:** 96815.

ACCOMMODATIONS

⊠ **Waikiki Grand Hotel,** 134 Kapahulu Ave. (☎923-1814), rents out bright, minimalist, and refreshing luxury vacation units; many have great views of Diamond Head and the ocean. Given the room quality and beach proximity, a room at the Waikiki Grand is a steal. Amenities include a swimming pool and coin-op laundry. Hula's gay bar is on the 2nd fl. Reserve 1 month in advance. 1-bed studios $80-130; suites with kitchenette $105-150. ❹

⊠ **Aqua Bamboo,** 2425 Kuhio Ave. (☎922-7777). The units in this hotel are accented with cool beige-and-black decor and a calm bamboo-and-Buddha motif. The small pool is surrounded by a beautiful garden area, spa, and sauna. Complimentary cocktail reception every W at 5pm. Doubles $155; studios (sleep 1-2) with kitchenette $175-195; 1-bedroom (sleeps 1-4) with full kitchen $215. ❺

Waikiki Beachside Hostel, 2556 Lemon Rd. (☎923-9566; www.hokondo.com). Young international travelers share animated nighttime conversations on patios overlooking a parking-lot-turned-courtyard (with big-screen TV), just a block from the beach. All rooms have full kitchen and cable TV, most have safe, and some have A/C. The hostel rents surfboards ($20), boogie boards ($8), and snorkel equipment ($10). Breakfast included. Lockers $3. 2-week advance reservations recommended. 8-bed dorms $18; 4-bed dorms $23-27; semi-private rooms $49-58; private rooms $109-280. ❶

FOOD

⊠ **The Pyramids,** 758B Kapahulu Ave. (☎737-2900). Egypt isn't *exactly* at the crossroads of the Pacific, but this place still mixes up excellent Egyptian and Mediterranean cuisine. Hieroglyph-inscribed walls and Egyptian music enhance your Saharan dining experience. Live belly dancer nightly at 7:30 and 8:30pm. *Tabouleh* salad $5. Shawarma with beef, lamb, chicken, and rice $16. All-you-can-eat lunch buffet $10. Lunch daily 11am-2pm; dinner M-Sa 5:30-10pm, Su 5-9pm. ❸

⊠ **Petite Garlic,** Lauula St., 2nd fl. (☎922-2221). This small cafe/kitchen/wine bar is classy, chic, and always chill, with a warm and intimate atmosphere (even without the wine buzz). Despite the central location, Petite Garlic has that special hole-in-the-wall *je ne sais quoi* and an exquisite, experimental blend of Eurasian cuisine using the freshest garlic and herbs. Garlic rice $9. Kona lobster $24. Salads $8-14. Desserts $5.50. Wine $6.25-8. Open daily 6pm-2am. ❸

Leonard's Bakery, 933 Kapahulu Ave. (☎737-5591). Locals have been coming to Leonard's since 1952 for delectable tarts ($1-1.25) and danishes ($0.67). Mouthwatering *malasadas* (Portuguese doughnuts) are worth the short trip from Waikiki ($0.66 each, $7.90 per dozen). Open Su-Th 6am-9pm, F-Sa 6am-10pm. ❶

Cha Cha Cha, 342 Seaside Ave. (☎923-7797). Cha Cha Cha shakes it up right with two 2hr. happy hours (daily 4-6pm and 9-11pm; lime margaritas $2.50) and a fun Caribbean-Mexican menu (rice, bean, and cheese El Cheapo burrito $7; roasted jerk chicken Jamaica-Me-Crazy enchiladas $12). Open daily 11:30am-11pm. ❷

SIGHTS AND BEACHES

WAIKIKI BEACH. "Waikiki Beach" refers to all the beaches on the south shore of Oahu. It begins at the Hilton Lagoon in the west and continues along the coastline of Waikiki's premier beach hotels all the way to the edge of Diamond Head Crater. Although the beach reaches moments of absolute saturation, the perpetual daytime crowds on Waikiki Beach can be enlivening.

DIAMOND HEAD. The 350-acre Diamond Head crater was created 300,000 years ago during a single, brief eruption that flung ash and fine particles into the air. At the park entrance, you'll find picnic tables, restrooms, a pay phone, and drinking water. The 30min. hike to the 560 ft. summit is fairly easy, but challenging enough to give hikers a sense of accomplishment once they've reached the top. A flashlight is unnecessary—lights have been added to the once poorly lit tunnels. If claustrophobia still holds you back, rest assured that the journey becomes worthwhile—the view at the top is enchanting. *(By car, take Monsarrat Ave. to Diamond Head Rd. The park comes up quickly on the right and has an easy-to-spot sign. Open 6am-6pm. Go before 8am or after noon to beat the morning rush. $1, vehicles $5.)*

FREE OUTDOOR FILMS AND HULA. In Waikiki, watching beautiful island girls shake their hips and surf-chiseled men flex in nothing but sarongs is not only civilized, it's free. The Kuhio Beach Torch Lighting and Hula Show is followed by **Sunset on the Beach** on weekends. The mayor's office sets up a movie screen on the beach for a double feature of recent or classic family films. Before the show, area restaurants set up portable booths on the east side of Kapahulu Pier, selling overpriced concessions to the first come, first seated beach-blanket crowd. *(Kuhio Beach Park. ☎ 523-2489. Hula daily 6:30-7:30pm. Movies most Sa-Su at sunset, around 7pm.)*

⚡ NIGHTLIFE

Diamond Head Grill, 2885 Kalakaua Ave. (☎ 922-3734), in the W. Honolulu Hotel. The poshest place to see and be seen, the Diamond Head Grill offers the socially suave 1 dance and 1 hip-hop room. F night is most popular. Beer $5. Cocktails $7-8. Dress to impress. No flip-flops, shorts, hats, or tank tops (for men). Cover $10, special events $20. Open F-Sa 9pm-2am.

Duke's Canoe Club, 2335 Kalakaua Ave. (☎ 922-2268), inside the Outrigger Waikiki, on the beach. A Waikiki institution, Duke's is the ultimate beachside bar, mixing drinks to live contemporary Hawaiian music (nightly 10pm-midnight and F-Su 4-6pm) under palm-thatched umbrellas at the inside-outside barefoot bar. Beer $3.25-4.25. Tropical drinks $6. Food served daily 7am-midnight. Bar open 5pm-1am.

Hula's Bar and Lei Stand, 134 Kapahulu Ave. (☎ 923-0669). Crowds gather in this famous gay bar to watch the sunset and stay for the fun, social atmosphere. Sophisticated black-lit interior with pool table, and a view of the beach. Pitchers $5 daily 3pm-2am, $4.50 10am-3pm. F free *pupus* 3-9pm. Su beach party "Beerblast." Cover $3, on promotional nights $5. Open daily 10am-2am.

THE BIG ISLAND   ☎ 808

While Hawaii evokes images of palm trees, white-sand beaches, and curling surf, the state's namesake island does everything but fit that stereotype. The youngest Hawaiian island, the Big Island is nonetheless the largest (hence the name) and the most naturally diverse. Within the island, 11 climate ecosystems are represented, from the subarctic summits of Mauna Loa and Mauna Kea to the rainforests along the Hamakua Coast and the desert lava fields of the Kau. A journey through the Big Island is a brush with the rawest forces of nature. Here, you can almost reach the stars at the observatories on Saddle Rd., witness land as it is born at the lava flows of Kilauea, and ride the waves of the mighty Pacific Ocean. As awe-inspiring as the island's elements are, it is their close proximity that is the most incredible part of the Big Island experience. A day of hiking will take visitors through a natural display more diverse than a roadtrip across the continental US.

▊ BIG ISLAND TRANSPORTATION

Flights between the Big Island and neighboring islands start at around $90 each way. **Keahole-Kona International Airport** sees the majority of international traffic, while **Hilo International Airport** sees mostly interisland flights. The **Hele-On Bus** (☎ 961-8744; www.co.hawaii.hi.us) is the Big Island's system of public transport; it is easiest to get around by renting a car.

HAWAII VOLCANOES NATIONAL PARK

Home to the world's most active oceanic hot spot, Hawaii Volcanoes National Park is never the same place twice. Along the park's coast, 2000°F lava enters the Pacific Ocean, in a constant redefinition of the island's coastline. Whereas the Western imagination has been obsessed with volcanoes for their hellfire destructive powers, Hawaiians worship Pele, the goddess of fire, as goddess of both creation and destruction. Hiking through desolate lava fields, visitors witness the slow rebirth of life firsthand. Once the sun sets, a trek across the most recent lava flows to watch the lava river meet the ocean is a once-in-a-lifetime chance to view an indescribable battle between the natural elements.

AT A GLANCE: HAWAII VOLCANOES NATIONAL PARK

AREA: 333,000 acres.

FEATURES: Kilauea, Mauna Loa, Kau Desert, Puna Coast, Puu Loa Petroglyphs.

QUICK FACT: NASA astronauts have trained for lunar landings in the Kau Desert and Kilauea Iki Crater, because of their similarity to the moon's surface.

FEES: 7-day permit $10 per vehicle; $5 per bicyclist, pedestrian, or motorcyclist.

HIGHLIGHTS: Hiking over aa and pahoehoe lava rocks, steam vents, cinder cones, pit craters, ancient petroglyphs, and (if lucky) active lava flows along the East Rift Zone of the Kilauea Caldera.

▊ TRANSPORTATION

Volcano is the nearest gateway town and can satisfy all visitors' basic needs. While a car isn't essential, it is significantly more difficult to see everything without one. If renting a car is impossible, the **Hele-On Bus** runs between the park's visitors center and the Mooheau Bus Terminal in Hilo. Parking is plentiful.

▊ ▊ ORIENTATION AND PRACTICAL INFORMATION

The only entrance to the park is from **Route 11 (Hawaii Belt Road),** 30 mi. southwest of Hilo and 96 mi. southeast of Kona. Within the park the 11 mi. **Crater Rim Drive** circles Kilauea Caldera, and the 20 mi. **Chain of Craters Road** descends toward the coast and ends where the road meets an active flow. This area, known as the "End of Chain of Craters Rd.," is the trailhead for the night hike to the lava flow. **Hilina Pali Road** accesses the remote western portion of the park and **Mauna Loa Road** ascends Mauna Loa and ends at the trailhead to the summit. Volcanoes National Park is hospitable at any time of year, but visitors should come prepared for extremes of hot, cold, wet, and dry, often within the same day.

> **Visitor Info: Hawaii Volcanoes National Park,** P.O. Box 52, Hawaii National Park, 96718 (☎ 985-6000; www.nps.gov/havo). **Kilauea Visitor Center** and **Park Headquarters,** a couple hundred yards beyond the entrance station along the northern arc of Crater Rim Dr., should be everyone's 1st stop in the park for maps and eruption updates. Visitors center open daily 7:45am-5pm. For **weather** conditions, eruption information, and general questions, call ☎ 985-6000. The park also broadcasts on AM 530.

HAWAII

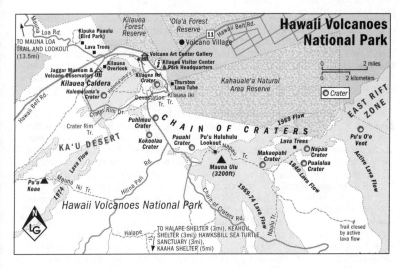

Guided Hikes and Events: The visitors center shows a 25min. introductory film about the park daily 9am-4pm on the hr. Ranger-led lectures and walks also offer a good introduction to the natural history and geology of the region. Daily schedule for lectures and walks varies; consult the Ranger Activity bulletin board at the visitors center.

IN THE PARK

Many of the park's major attractions can be accessed by car along **Crater Rim Drive, Chain of Craters Road,** and **Mauna Loa Road.** Crater Rim Dr. circles Kilauea Caldera and is the busiest. In the evening, Chain of Craters Rd. sees a decent amount of traffic as park visitors head to the end of the road for the night hike. For some background on the geological phenomena that make up the island, head to the **Jaggar Museum,** on Crater Rim Dr., where exhibits combine information on geologic research and the park's natural history with traditional Hawaiian myth and legend. (☎ 985-6049. Open daily 8:30am-5pm. Admission included in park entrance fee.)

Don't be fooled—the barren summit crater of **Kilauea Caldera** is one of the most active volcanoes in the world. From the 1800s until 1954, the caldera was the site of Kilauea's most dramatic eruptions, which included fountains of lava up to 2000 ft. high and a boiling lava lake. However, after 1955, most of the action has shifted to Kilauea's Southwest and East Rift Zones (a rift zone describes a weak spot in the mountainside where underground magma breaks to the surface). Nonetheless, evidence of volcanic activity, past and present, is still visible around the caldera.

Until 1924, **Halemaumau Crater** was the site of a dramatic lake of lava that captivated the world. The crater visible today was formed in 1924 when the lava suddenly drained and the ground dropped several hundred feet. In Hawaiian, the name "Halemaumau" means "house surrounded by the *amaumau* fern," referring to a longstanding battle between Pele and Kamapuaa, the god of cloud, rain, and forest. Eventually, Kamapuaa protected himself from Pele's rage by surrounding Kilauea with the rugged *amaumau* fern. Although Pele's home is visible from all of Crater Rim Dr., it is best seen from the Jaggar Museum or the Steaming Bluff Lookout. *Take caution: due to strong sulfur fumes, children, pregnant women, and those with heart and/or respiratory problems should avoid the crater.*

HAWAII

Lava tubes are formed when a river of hot lava cools enough that the outer edges of the flow form a crust while the molten interior continues to move, leaving a tunnel behind. In 1913, Lorrin Thurston was the first non-native to discover the tube, and it has been a popular attraction ever since. The first portion of the ☒**Thurston Lava Tube** is lit up, and you can walk down and investigate. Although stairs lead back to the surface after a couple hundred yards, the tube extends another 300 ft. Damp and dark, this extra stretch is far more exciting than the short, guided part. You will, of course, need a flashlight.

Since **Puu Oo** first blew her top on January 3, 1983, the **Puu Oo-Kupaianaha Rift Zone** has been erupting continuously, though things have calmed down since the dynamic early years, when lava fountains blasted 1500 ft. high. Today, the eruption is characterized by gentler *pahoehoe* flows and lava tubes. With tubes insulating the lava from heat loss, these flows are able to travel across the long *palis* (cliffs) all the way to the ocean, where they continue to add substantial landmass to Hawaii's youngest island. The volcano's power is viscerally apparent; if you hike northeast along the coastal lava rocks from the end of the road, you'll come upon a series of road signs ("reduce speed ahead," "stop") buried by lava that make for ironic pictures. Although sea arches are common on the coasts of Hawaii, where large waves provide the raw power for erosion, the **Holei Sea Arch,** at more than 90 ft., is exceptional. This is the site where, according to Hawaiian legend, a great battle took place between Pele and her sister Namakaokahai, goddess of the sea.

Mauna Loa is the world's most massive mountain. Rising 18,000 ft. from the ocean floor below the surface of the Pacific and climbing another 13,677 ft. above sea level, Mauna Loa towers over Mt. Everest. The scenic drive of **Mauna Kea Road** starts about 2 mi. west of the park entrance off Rte. 11. The road climbs 3000 ft. through rainforest to the ☒**Mauna Loa Lookout** (13½ mi. from Rte. 11), a secluded spot great for a quiet moment of reflection. Near the start of the road there is a turnoff to see the **lava trees**. These phantoms of the old forest were formed when *pahoehoe* lava flows engulfed an especially moist tree (usually *'ohi'a*) and hardened around it before the tree burned away. On Mauna Loa Rd., just over 1 mi. after the turnoff from Hwy. 11, is **Kipuka Puaulu,** an enclave of native forest that has managed to avoid the torrents of lava that have ravaged Mauna Loa over the centuries. An easy 1¼ mi. trail offers a good view of this treasure.

There are many fantastic hikes in the park. If you only have time for one, try the moderate ☒**Kilauea Iki Trail** (4 mi., 2-3hr. round-trip). Just over 40 years ago, the surface of Kilauea Iki Crater was a boiling lake of molten lava. Today, hikers revel in the experience of walking on what might be called hell frozen over. The first part of the hike descends 400 ft. through *'ohi'a* and *hamuu* (tree fern) rainforest. Once in the crater, the desolate moon-like landscape provides a rare chance to see the first stages of ecological succession after an eruption. For a more challenging hike, try the **Napau Trail** (14 mi., 6-9hr. round-trip). Picking up where the Puu Huluhulu Trail leaves off and going beyond the Puu Huluhulu summit, the Napau Trail is the only day-hike that requires hikers to register at the visitors center. Napau is also the only trail that brings you face-to-face with the heart of the current eruption. If you were able to walk to the rim of Puu Oo, you'd see a giant, bubbling lava lake. Unfortunately, the land around Puu Oo is too unstable, so you can only go as far as Napau Crater to watch the billowing clouds of volcanic gas.

MAUI ☎ **808**

Not as developed as Oahu, but with more sights than Kauai and much of the same natural beauty, Maui stakes a solid claim that *Maui no ka oi!* (Maui is the best!). Families delight in the activities on buzzing beaches of Kaanapali and Kihei, and honeymooning couples romance on secluded coasts and waterfall hikes. This is only the beginning—travelers will find themselves breathless at the end of their vacation, as much by the things they did as the things that remain undone until a future trip. Most visitors first become familiar with the dry leeward side, where the resorts have turned deserts into golf courses; many go on to the dense rainforest of the windward side of the West Maui mountains; and a trip to Maui isn't complete without watching the sun rise from the heights of Haleakala.

🛈 PRACTICAL INFORMATION

Flights to Maui from the neighboring islands start at around $100 round-trip and most go through Maui's major airport, **Kahului International (OGG)**.

Visitor Info: Maui Visitors Bureau, 1727 Wili Pa Loop (☎244-3530; www.visit-maui.com), in Wailuku. Open M-F 8am-4:30pm. **Maui Information and Visitors Center** (☎874-4919) will make reservations for car rental, accommodations, activities, etc., free of charge. **Lahaina Visitor Center,** 648 Wharf St. (☎667-9193; www.visitla-haina.com), in Lahaina. Open daily 9am-5pm.

Medical Services: Maui Memorial Medical Center, 221 Mahalani St. (☎244-9056), has 24hr. emergency service and serves both sides of the island.

Internet Access: A $10 3-month visitor's card grants Internet access at all state librar-ies, including: **Kahului Public Library,** 90 School St. (☎873-3097); **Wailuku Public Library,** 251 High St. (☎243-5766); **Kihei Public Library,** 35 Waimahaihai St. (☎875-6833); **Lahaina Public Library,** 680 Wharf St. (☎662-3950).

🏠 ACCOMMODATIONS

▩ **Peace of Maui,** 1290 Haliimaile Rd. (☎572-5045), in Haliimaile. Surrounded by pine-apple fields and great views of Haleakala, Peace of Maui's 6 hostel-style rooms share 3 toilets, 3 showers, a common living room, and a kitchen. All have TV and access to coin-op laundry and free Internet. A 2-bedroom cottage sleeps 2-4 people, with full bath, kitchen, and lanai. Full payment due 30 days in advance. Singles $50; doubles $55; cottages $100 for 2 people, $120 for 4 or more people. ❷

▩ **Rainbow's End Surf Hostel,** 221 Baldwin Ave. (☎579-9057), in Paia. Well-maintained, friendly, and only a walk from Paia and the beach. Free Internet, a safe, board and bike storage, and parking. Coin-op laundry. Linens included. 4 dorms and 3 private doubles share a living room with TV/VCR, 2 kitchens, and 3 bathrooms. Quiet hours after 10pm. Reserve in advance with $50 deposit. Dorms $25, $135 per week, $375 per month; doubles $55/$300/$750. Cash and traveler's checks only. ❶

Kai's Bed and Breakfast, 80 E. Welakahao Rd. (☎874-6431), in Kihei. Each of the 3 differently themed rooms features stone floors, cable TV, microwave, and refrigerator. Continental breakfast every morning in a basket on your porch. Beach towels, boogie boards, snorkel gear, bicycles, garden hot tub, and washer/dryer are available. Usually 3- to 5-night min. Check-in 2pm. Check-out 10am. Reserve with 50% deposit at least 2 months ahead; balance due 30 days before arrival. Rooms $60-80, $400-550 per week; less in low-season. Also rents 5 studios, cottages, and condos $90-155. ❸

🍴 FOOD

▩ **Paia Fishmarket,** 100 Hana Hwy. (☎579-8030), in Paia. A standby, filled with familiar people at long wooden tables eating good food and sipping choice beers. The mahi mahi burgers ($7) are the best on the island. Fries, fish tacos, salads, seafood entrees ($12-16), and a *sashimi* appetizer ($13). Open daily 11am-9:30pm. ❸

▩ **Cafe O'Lei Lahaina,** 839 Front St. (☎661-9491), in Lahaina. Cafe O'Lei is a real find: the ocean breeze and sunset view from the restaurant's 2-tiered dining room are delight-ful. The food emphasizes fresh local ingredients: taro salad with Okinawan sweet potatoes ($9), sautéed mahi mahi with ginger butter and papaya salsa ($16). Lunch features salads and foccacia sandwiches ($7-13). Music downstairs Tu-F 6-9pm. Lunch daily 10:30am-5pm; dinner 5-9:30pm. ❸

Cafe des Amis, 42 Baldwin Ave. (☎579-6323), in Paia. The scrumptious crepes at this funky and intimate cafe are equally popular with the morning latte crowd and Merlot-toting diners. Savory crepes ($6.50-8.50) are substantial enough for a full meal, while sweet crepes ($2-4) finish things off nicely (try the sugar and lime juice). The curries pack a tasty punch. BYOB. Open daily 8:30am-8:30pm. ❷

🏄🏖 BEACHES AND ACTIVITIES

ONELOA BEACH. 🏖**Oneloa Beach** is usually nearly empty and perfect for secluded sunbathing. It's better suited for boogie boarding than swimming, though, as the sand gives way to reef and the waves are rather large. To reach public parking and beach access, take Office Rd. (the main road leading from the highway into Kapalua), turn left at the end, and then right on Ironwood Ln. Parking is before the gate, and the unlabeled access path is opposite the parking lot.

HALEAKALA NATIONAL PARK. The gradually sloping **Haleakala Volcano** ("house of the sun") dominates the island of Maui. Haleakala National Park protects the fragile ecosystems and rare native species of the Haleakala summit. There are three **visitors centers** in the park. **Park Headquarters** (7000 ft.) issues camping and cabin permits and has information on the park. (Open daily 8am-4pm.) The **Haleakala Visitor Center** (9740 ft.) has restrooms, geological displays, a glassed-in overlook of the crater, and a knowledgeable staff. *(Open daily in summer 6am-3pm; in winter 6:30am-3pm.)* **Kipahulu** also has a visitors center and public phones. *(Open daily 9am-5pm.)* To see the **sunrise,** check sunrise times and weather conditions by calling ☎877-5111 before driving up, and note that the first light (as impressive as the sunrise itself) is about 45min. before the sun actually rises. Weather conditions at the summit are extreme and can change rapidly. Be prepared for cold (30-50°F). Talks on natural and cultural history are held at the Summit Building daily at 9:30, 10:30, 11:30am. Park rangers lead two guided hikes. Dozens of independent companies offer activities in the park, including biking down the volcano and horseback-riding in the crater. There are also two main trails that traverse the park: the **Halemauu Trail** and **Sliding Sands Trail.** *(P.O. Box 369, Makawao 96768. ☎572-4400; www.nps.gov/hale. Park open 24hr. Entrance fee $10 per vehicle, good for 7 days.)*

THE ROAD TO HANA. The 52 mi. trip from Kahului to Hana is one of the world's most impressive coastal drives, with over 50 single-lane bridges, incredible views of rainforests and waterfalls, and more curves than a Hula dancer. While it takes about 2hr. to drive the route, the experience is much more rewarding if you stop along the way. Fill up on gas in Paia (there are no gas stations along the way), pack a cooler with snacks, and go! Stop along the way at Hookipa Lookout, Twin Falls (go early—like 7am early), the Waikamoi Ridge Nature Walk, Kaenae Arboretum, Wailua, the freshwater pools of Puaa Kaa, and the small fishing village of Nahiku.

WHALE-WATCHING. From December to April, anywhere you can see the ocean in south Maui, you can see whales. To learn more about these creatures, stop by the **Hawaiian Islands Humpback Whale National Marine Sanctuary,** 726 S. Kihei Rd., where you'll find friendly volunteers, colorful displays about whales from scientific and cultural perspectives, and free brochures. *(726 S. Kihei Rd. ☎879-2818. Open M-F 10am-3pm. Free.)* To see the real thing, contact the 🏖**Pacific Whale Foundation**, a non-profit organization known for eco-friendly tours. *(☎249-8811; www.pacificwhale.org.)*

KAUAI   ☎808

The oldest and northernmost major island, Kauai is at the lonely end of the chain, next to only Niiahu and the tiny Northwestern Islands. Hawaiian spirit burns brightly in the island's residents—locals are fiercely proud of their heritage and Kauai's lack of development (law prohibits any buildings taller than a palm tree). Kauai's plentiful rain nurses the verdant land and local agriculture, including coffee, sugar, and taro root. Its rainforest is best described as primordial, and evidence of the island's six million years of weathering is seen in cliffs of the Na Pali Coast and the jagged Waimea Canyon, both carved by millennia of rainfall.

⚡ PRACTICAL INFORMATION

All commercial flights fly into **Lihue Airport (LIH).** Most flights to Kauai from the mainland connect in Honolulu. Interisland flights begin at around $100 round-trip.

Visitor Info: Kauai Visitors Bureau, 4334 Rice St., Ste. 101 (☎245-3971; www.kauaivisitorsbureau.com), in Lihue. Open M-F 8am-4:30pm.

Police: Kauai Police Department, 3060 Umi St. (☎241-6715).

Medical Services: Wilcox Memorial Hospital, 3420 Kuhio Hwy. (☎245-1100).

Internet Access: Internet access is available at all state libraries with the purchase of a $10 3-month visitor's card, including: **Lihue Public Library,** 4344 Hardy St. (☎241-3222); **Kapaa Public Library,** 1464 Kuhio Hwy. (☎821-4422); **Princeville Public Library,** 4343 Emmalani Dr. (☎826-4310).

⛏ ACCOMMODATIONS

▨ **The Kauai Inn,** 2430 Hulemalu Rd. (☎245-9000), in Lihue. Beautifully landscaped grounds, tropical flowers, and lush palm trees surround a small swimming pool and courtyard. The deluxe rooms—with soft carpeting, private lanai, king-size bed, refrigerator, microwave, and cable TV—are arguably the best deal in Lihue. 48 units. Continental breakfast included. Basic rooms $69, with A/C $89; deluxe suites $109. ❸

▨ **Kapaa Beach House,** 1552 Kuhio Hwy. (☎822-3313), in Kapaa. A relaxed, family-run hostel. Guests of the rambling, 3-story building share an outdoor kitchen, comfortable patio-style common area with TV/VCR, stereo, couches, and a fantastic view of the Pacific from the rooftop shower. Spacious dorms with extra-long full bunks, curtains, and mirrored walls open to oceanfront patios. Very friendly and accommodating management. Reserve in advance. Single bunks $23; doubles $35; private rooms with 4 beds and shared bath $50 for 2 people; each additional person $5. Cash only. ❶

Koloa Landing Cottages, 2704B Hoonani Rd. (☎742-1470), in Koloa. 4 colorful cottages all have full kitchens and lanais. The cottages are cheerful, airy, and clean, and the hospitable owners do their best to make you feel at home. Units $85-200. ❹

🍴 FOOD

▨ **Deli and Bread Connection** (☎245-7115), in Lihue. The Oriental sweet bread, endless variety, and reasonable prices make the wait worthwhile. Vegetarian selections and daily soups complement the standard and unique sandwiches (BLT $4.25; crab and shrimp $5). Open M-Th and Sa 9:30am-7pm, F 9:30am-9pm, Su 10am-6pm. ❶

▨ **Lighthouse Bistro** (☎828-0480), in Kilauea. This open-air bistro serves gourmet food including mango cherry chicken ($17), cannelloni *quatro formaggio* ($16), and fresh fish ($20) with a long wine list and mixed drinks (Mai Tai $7). Nightly all-you-can-eat pasta $14. Lunch M-F 11am-2pm, Sa noon-2pm. Dinner daily 5:30-9pm. ❺

Mother of All Juice Bars, 1586 Kuhio Hwy. (☎821-1905), in Kapaa. This stand sells cold coconuts ($1.50), fresh organic bread, and creative sandwich combos (*chèvre* cucumber *nori* wrap $5), fresh juice, frozen fruit frosties, smoothies, and cookies the size of your face ($1.50). Open daily 8:30am-6pm. Credit card min. $20. ❶

Jo-Jo's Shave Ice, 9374 Kaumualii Hwy. (☎338-9729), in Waimea. Jo-Jo's has been crowned the best shave ice on Kauai. Choose from a whopping 60 flavors for your ultra-fine ice ($2). Open daily 11am-6pm. ❶

◪ ⚑ BEACHES AND SIGHTS

SECRET BEACH. This formerly hidden spot has outgrown its mysterious nickname and the parking area can barely hold the lines of shiny rental cars. ◪**Secret Beach's** magnetic appeal is in its irresistible scenery: a vast expanse of superfine golden sand sprinkled with lava rocks surrounded by bluffs and a fetching view of Kilauea Point. The beach, one of the widest on the island, also features big surfing waves. From the base of the trail, the sands stretch far to the right, where a sheltered cove and gently sloping shore provide safer swimming.

LUMAHAI BEACH. A picture of the beautiful ◪**Lumahai Beach** sits in every postcard rack on the island. *Devastating surf and powerful currents make swimming here unsafe year-round.* Sunbathers and fans of *South Pacific* frequent the captivating beach. The east half of Lumahai, also known as Kahalahala Beach, is an exquisite place to swim, though swimmers should still be careful.

TUNNELS BEACH. A wide horseshoe reef encloses the fine, and often hot, sand of the North Shore's premier snorkel and shore dive locale. On calm summer days, Tunnels's crystalline waters and intricate reef are a sight to behold. Despite its famously complex underwater topography, the beach's name actually describes the hollowness of its winter surf. With the perfect wind and swell direction, the right-breaking Tunnels is arguably the best surf location on the island.

POIPU BEACH PARK. Extensive facilities, including picnic tables, showers, restrooms, playgrounds, a large lawn, and a lifeguard station attract a diverse crowd to Poipu's—and probably Kauai's—most popular beach. At low tide, sunbathers can walk all the way out to the point along a thin sandy peninsula, but high tide submerges the path and turns the tip of the point into an island. Swimming is safe on both sides of the isthmus, but snorkelers prefer the shallow protected area west of the point. Poipu Beach is also home to one of the South Shore's better surf breaks, especially for beginner- and intermediate-level surfers. Sand space is at a premium, and late arrivals will probably be relegated to the western end.

NA PALI COAST. Comprised of 15 rugged miles of nearly inaccessible jagged cliffs and pristine coastline, the Na Pali Coast stretches from Kee Beach in the north to Polihale State Park in the south. Those who do gain access to the coast's hidden treasures will encounter steep lava rock walls, lush green valleys, secluded sandy beaches, and cascading waterfalls. Adventurers from around the globe come to travel 11 mi. along the ◪**Kalalau Trail** (22 mi. round-trip), which alternates between exposed oceanside cliffs and ridges with outstanding views of the coastline, and sheltered, quiet stretches through shady valleys.

KOKEE STATE PARK. Drive past Waimea Canyon State Park for the cool forests of Kokee State Park, with temperatures often 10-15°F cooler than at sea level. For trail information, maps, and advice, head to the **Kokee Natural History Museum,** on the left after mile marker 15. (☎335-9975. *Open daily 10am-4pm. Donations appreciated.*) The main attraction of Kokee State Park is its network of over 40 mi. of trails, from short forest walks through groves of Methley plums to heart-pounding, narrow rocky ridges. The trails cover four types of terrain: the Na Pali Coast, Waimea Canyon, the forests of Kokee, and Alakai Swamp. Our favorites are the moderate ◪**Canyon Trail** and the hard-core ◪**Nualolo-Nualolo Cliff-Awaawapuhi Loop.**

PACIFIC NORTHWEST

The Pacific Northwest became the center of national attention when gold rushes and the Oregon Trail ushered masses into the region. In the 1840s, Senator Stephen Douglas argued, sensibly, that the Cascade Range would make a good natural border between Oregon and Washington, but sense is often ignored in politics, and the Columbia River, perpendicular to the Cascades, became the border instead. Yet even today, the range and not the river is the region's most important cultural divide: west of the rain-trapping Cascades lie the microchip, mocha, and music meccas of Portland and Seattle; to the east sprawl farmland and an arid plateau. For more, see ◪*Let's Go: Pacific Northwest Adventure Guide.*

HIGHLIGHTS OF THE PACIFIC NORTHWEST

SEATTLE. Offbeat neighborhoods, fine museums, ample green space, and pioneering cafes make this thriving city a fabulous place to visit (p. 1003).

NATIONAL PARKS. Crater Lake National Park (p. 1033) displays a volcanic past, Olympic National Park (p. 1018) has mossy grandeur and deserted beaches, and life beautifully blankets the dormant Mt. Rainier (p. 1022).

WASHINGTON

On Washington's western shores, Pacific storms feed one of the world's only temperate rainforests in Olympic National Park. To the east, clouds linger over Seattle, hiding the Emerald City. Visitors to Puget Sound, an ecologically staggering inlet, can experience everything from isolation in the San Juan Islands to cosmopolitan entertainment on the mainland. Past the Cascades, the state's eastern half spreads out into fertile farmlands and grassy plains as inland fruit bowls run over.

◪ PRACTICAL INFORMATION

Capital: Olympia.

Visitor info: Washington State Tourism, Dept. of Community, Trade, and Economic Development, P.O. Box 42500, Olympia 98504 (☎800-544-1800; www.experiencewashington.com). **Washington State Parks and Recreation Commission,** P.O. Box 42650, Olympia 98504 (☎360-902-8844 or 888-226-7688; www.parks.wa.gov).

Postal Abbreviation: WA. **Sales Tax:** 7-9.1%, depending on the county.

SEATTLE   ☎206

Seattle's mix of mountain views, clean streets, espresso stands, and rainy weather was the magic formula of the 90s, attracting transplants from across the US. The droves of newcomers provide an interesting contrast to the older residents who remember Seattle as a city-town, not a thriving metropolis bubbling over with

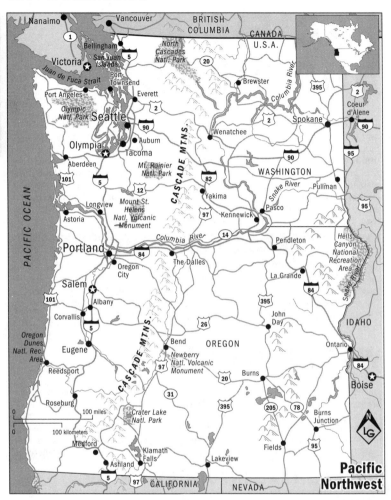

young millionaires. Computer and coffee money have helped drive rents sky-high in some areas, but the grungy, punk-loving street culture still prevails in others. Every hilltop offers an impressive view of Mt. Olympus, Mt. Baker, and Mt. Rainier. The city is shrouded in cloud cover 200 days a year, but when the skies clear, Seattleites rejoice that "the mountain is out" and head for the country.

⊏ TRANSPORTATION

Airport: Seattle-Tacoma International (Sea-Tac; ☎433-5388; www.portseattle.org), on Federal Way, 15 mi. south of Seattle, exit right off I-5 to Rte. 518 (signs are clear).

Trains: Amtrak, King St. Station, 303 S. Jackson St. (☎382-4125, reservations 800-872-7245), 1 block east of Pioneer Square. Open daily 6:15am-10pm. To: **Portland** (4 per day, $26-37); **San Francisco** (1 per day, $100-167); **Spokane** (4 per day, $41-85); **Tacoma** (4 per day, $9-15); **Vancouver** (1 per day, $23-36).

Buses: Greyhound (☎628-5526 or 800-231-2222), at 8th Ave. and Stewart St. Try to avoid night buses, since the station can get seedy after dark. Ticket office open daily 6:30am-2:30am, station open 24hr. To: **Portland** (11 per day, $25); **Spokane** (3 per day, $28); **Tacoma** (8 per day, $6); **Vancouver** (8 per day, $24).

Ferries: Washington State Ferries (☎464-6400 or 888-808-7977; www.wsdot.wa.gov/ferries) has 2 terminals in Seattle. The main terminal is downtown, at Colman Dock, Pier 52. Service departs to **Bainbridge Island** (35min.; $5.70, with car $13), **Bremerton** on the Kitsap Peninsula (50min.; $5.70, with car $13), and **Vashon Island** (25min., passengers only, $7.70). From the waterfront, passenger-only ferries leave from Pier 50. Schedules are tricky, so it's worth spending a few minutes perusing the schedule or calling the toll-free info line. Ferries leave frequently 6am-2am. The **Victoria Clipper** (☎800-888-2535, reservations 448-5000; www.victoriaclipper.com) goes from Seattle to **Victoria.** Departs from Pier 69. (3hr.; 4 per day May to mid-Sept., 2 per day mid-Sept. to Apr.; $60-79, under 12 half-price; bikes $10, no cars.)

Public Transit: Metro Transit, Customer Service Offices, King St. Center, 2nd Ave S and S. Jackson St. and Westlake Station in Downtown Metro Bus Tunnel. (☎553-3000, or 24hr. 800-542-7876; http://transit.metrokc.gov). King St. Center open M-F 8am-5pm; Westlake Station open M-F 9am-5pm. Fares are based on a 2-zone system. **Zone 1** is everything within the city limits (peak hours $1.50, off-peak $1.25). **Zone 2** is everything else (peak $2, off-peak $1.25). Ages 5-17 always $0.50. **Peak hours** in both zones are M-F 6-9am and 3-6pm. Weekend day passes $2.50. Ride free daily 6am-7pm in the downtown **ride free area,** bordered by S. Jackson St. on the south, 6th Ave. and I-5 on the east, Blanchard St. on the north, and the waterfront on the west. Free **transfers.** Most buses **wheelchair accessible** (info ☎684-2046).

Taxi: Farwest Taxi ☎622-1717. **Orange Cab Co.** ☎522-8800.

Car Rental: Enterprise, 11342 Lake City Way NE (☎364-3127).

ORIENTATION

Seattle stretches from north to south on an isthmus between **Puget Sound** to the west and **Lake Washington** to the east. The city is easily accessible by car via **I-5,** which runs north-south through the city, and by **I-90** from the east, which ends at I-5 southeast of downtown. Get to **downtown** (including **Pioneer Square, Pike Place Market,** and the **waterfront**) from I-5 by taking any of the exits from James St. to Stewart St. Take the Mercer St./Fairview Ave. exit to the **Seattle Center;** follow signs from there. The Denny Way exit leads to **Capitol Hill,** and, farther north, the 45th St. exit heads toward the **University District.** The less crowded **Route 99,** also called Aurora, runs parallel to I-5 and skirts the western side of downtown.

PRACTICAL INFORMATION

Tourist Information: Seattle's **Convention and Visitors Bureau** (☎461-5840; www.seeseattle.org), at 7th and Pike St., is on the 1st floor of the convention center; look for the signs to the "City Concierge." Helpful staff doles out maps, brochures, newspapers, and Metro schedules. Open late May to early Sept. M-F 9am-6pm, Sa-Su 10am-4pm; early Sept. to late May M-F 9am-5pm.

Outdoor Information: Seattle Parks and Recreation Department, 100 Dexter Ave. N (☎684-4075; www.co.seattle.wa.us/parks). Open M-F 8am-5pm. **Outdoor Recreation Information Center,** 222 Yale Ave. (☎470-4060; www.nps.gov/ccso/oric.htm), in REI. Does not sell permits. Free brochures on hiking trails. Open Su-F 10:30am-8pm, Sa 10am-8pm. Closed M late Sept. to late spring.

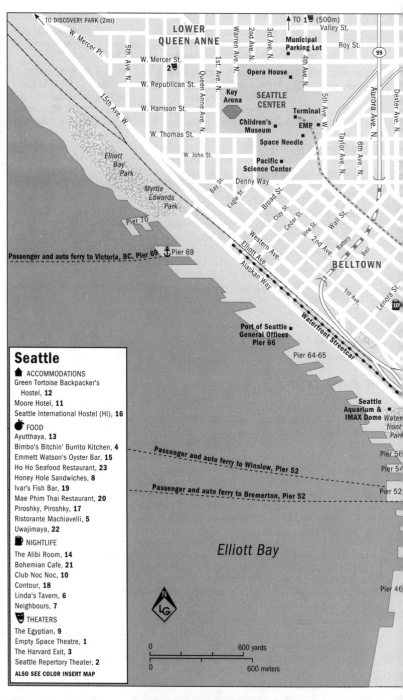

PACIFIC NORTHWEST

TO DISCOVERY PARK (2mi)

TO 1 (500m)

LOWER QUEEN ANNE

Valley St.

Roy St.

W. Mercer Pl.

W. Mercer St.

Municipal Parking Lot

W. Republican St.

Opera House

W. Harrison St.

Key Arena

SEATTLE CENTER

Terminal

W. Thomas St.

Children's Museum

EMP

Space Needle

W. John St.

Pacific Science Center

Elliott Bay Park

Denny Way

Myrtle Edwards Park

Bay St.

Eagle St.

Broad St.

Clay St.

Cedar St.

Vine St.

Wall St.

Battery

Bell

Pier 70

Western Ave.

Elliott Ave.

BELLTOWN

Passenger and auto ferry to Victoria, BC, Pier 69   Pier 69

Alaskan Way

1st Ave.

Lenora St.

Waterfront Streetcar

Port of Seattle General Offices Pier 66

Pier 64-65

Seattle Aquarium & IMAX Dome

Waterfront Park

Passenger and auto ferry to Winslow, Pier 52

Pier 56

Pier 54

Passenger and auto ferry to Bremerton, Pier 52

Pier 52

Pier 46

Elliott Bay

Seattle

♠ ACCOMMODATIONS
Green Tortoise Backpacker's
  Hostel, **12**
Moore Hotel, **11**
Seattle International Hostel (HI), **16**

🍴 FOOD
Ayutthaya, **13**
Bimbo's Bitchin' Burrito Kitchen, **4**
Emmett Watson's Oyster Bar, **15**
Ho Ho Seafood Restaurant, **23**
Honey Hole Sandwiches, **8**
Ivar's Fish Bar, **19**
Mae Phim Thai Restaurant, **20**
Piroshky, Piroshky, **17**
Ristorante Machiavelli, **5**
Uwajimaya, **22**

🍸 NIGHTLIFE
The Alibi Room, **14**
Bohemian Cafe, **21**
Club Noc Noc, **10**
Contour, **18**
Linda's Tavern, **6**
Neighbours, **7**

🎭 THEATERS
The Egyptian, **9**
Empty Space Theatre, **1**
The Harvard Exit, **3**
Seattle Repertory Theater, **2**
ALSO SEE COLOR INSERT MAP

0   600 yards

0   600 meters

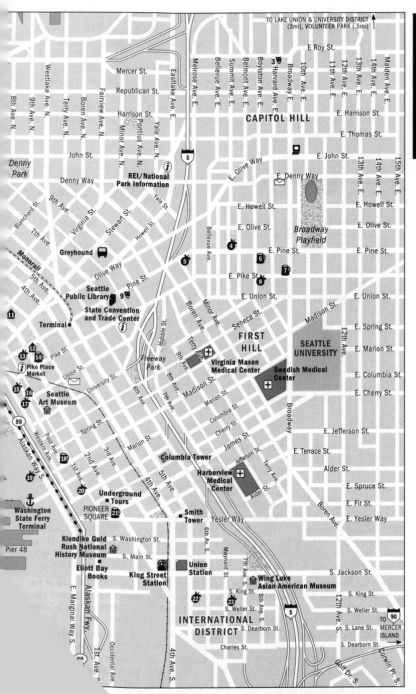

Medical Services: International District Emergency Center, 720 8th Ave. S, Ste. 100 (☎461-3235). Medics with multilingual assistance available. Clinic open M-F 9am-6pm, Sa 9am-5pm; phone 24hr. **Swedish Medical Center, Providence Campus,** 500 17th Ave. (☎320-2111), for urgent care and cardiac. 24hr.

Internet Access: Seattle Public Library, 1000 4th Ave. (☎386-4636; www.spl.org), at Madison. Internet free with photo ID for 15min.; free unlimited wireless Internet. Open M-Tu 1-8pm, W 10am-8pm, Th-Sa 10am-6pm, Su 1-5pm.

Post Office: 301 Union St. (☎748-5417 or 800-275-8777), at 3rd Ave. downtown. Open M-F 8am-5:30pm, Sa 8am-noon. General delivery window open M-F 9-11:20am and noon-3pm. **Postal Code:** 98101.

ACCOMMODATIONS

Pacific Reservation Service (☎800-684-2932) can arrange B&B singles for $50-65. For inexpensive motels farther from downtown, drive north on Aurora Ave. or take bus #26 to Fremont.

Seattle International Hostel (HI), 84 Union St. (☎622-5443 or 888-622-5443; www.hiseattle.org), at Western Ave. by the waterfront. Take Union St. from downtown; follow signs down the stairs under the Pike Pub & Brewery. Great location, but can sometimes feel cramped. Continental breakfast included. Laundry. 7-night max. stay in summer. Reception 24hr. Check-out 11am. Reservations recommended. Dorms $21, nonmembers $24. $2 extra for private bathroom. 2- to 4-person rooms; $54/$60. ❶

Green Tortoise Backpacker's Hostel, 1525 2nd Ave. (☎340-1222; www.greentortoise.net), between Pike and Pine St. on the #174 or 194 bus route. A party hostel with free beer on F, dinner on M, daily breakfast (7-9:30am), and Internet. Kitchen, library, laundry. Key deposit $20 cash. Reception 24hr. Dorms $22; private rooms $50. ❶

Moore Hotel, 1926 2nd Ave. (☎448-4851 or 800-421-5508; www.moorehotel.com), at Virginia, 1 block east from Pike Place Market, next to the Moore Theater. Built in 1905, the Moore has a swanky lobby, cavernous halls, and great service. "European-style"—smaller beds and shared bathrooms—singles from $39; doubles $49. Standard singles $59; doubles $68. Large suites, some with kitchen, $150. ❷

FOOD

When Seattleites are not drinking coffee, they seek out healthy cuisine, especially seafood. **Puget Sound Consumer Coops (PCCs)** are local health-food markets at 7504 Aurora Ave. N (☎525-3586), in Green Lake. Capitol Hill, the U District, and Fremont close main streets on summer Saturdays for **farmers markets.**

PIKE PLACE MARKET AND DOWNTOWN

In 1907, angry citizens demanded the elimination of the middle-man and local farmers began selling produce by the waterfront, creating the Pike Place Market. Today thousands of tourists mob the market to watch flying fish. (Open M-Sa 9am-6pm, Su 11am-5pm. Produce and fish open earlier; restaurants and lounges close later.) In the **Main Arcade,** on the west side of Pike St., fishmongers hurl fish from shelves to scales.

Piroshky, Piroshky, 1908 Pike St. (☎441-6068), across from the fr___
market building. The Russian *piroshky* is a croissant-like doug
sages, mushrooms, cheeses, salmon, or apples doused in cin
$5.50 soup and *piroshky* combo is a steal. Open daily 6am-6:30

Emmett Watson's Oyster Bar, 1916 Pike Pl. (☎448-7721). Intima
checkered pattern and trinkets from the sea highlight the Oyster B
3 shrimp, bread, and a heaping bowl of chowder ($7.25). Shelv
their brews. Open M-Th 11:30am-7pm, F-Sa 11:30am-8pm, Su 11

Ayutthaya, 727 E. Pike St. (☎324-8833), on a side alley a block up from the main market building. Thai infused with Caribbean spices in a quiet mint-green nook. All lunch entrees are $5.95 and well-sized; go for those with spice if you can handle the kick. The deep-fried banana dessert ($2.50) is worth saving room for. Open M-Sa 11am-7pm. ❷

THE WATERFRONT

Budget eaters, steer clear of Pioneer Sq. Instead, take a picnic to **Waterfall Garden,** on the corner of S. Main St. and 2nd Ave. S. The garden sports tables and chairs and a man-made waterfall that masks traffic outside. (Open daily dawn-dusk.)

Mae Phim Thai Restaurant, 94 Columbia St. (☎624-2979), a few blocks north of the waterfront between 1st Ave. and Alaskan Way. *Pad thai* junkies crowd in for cheap, delicious Thai cuisine. All dishes $6. Open M-Sa 11am-7pm. ❷

Ivar's Fish Bar, Pier 54 (☎467-8063; www.ivars.net). A fast-food window that serves the definitive Seattle clam chowder ($2) amid flocks of aggressive seagulls. Clam and chips ($5). Open Su-Th 10am-midnight, F-Sa 10am-2am. For a slightly more upscale seafood meal, check out **Ivar's Restaurant** next door (same hours). ❶/❸

INTERNATIONAL DISTRICT

Along King and Jackson St., between 5th and 8th Ave. east of the Kingdome, Seattle's International District is packed with great eateries.

🗺 **Uwajimaya,** 600 5th Ave. S (☎624-6248; www.uwajimaya.com). The Uwajimaya Center is a full city block of groceries and gifts; it's the largest Japanese department store in the region. Don't miss the food court's panorama of delicacies, particularly the Korean barbecue and Taiwanese-style baked goods. Open M-Sa 9am-11pm, Su 9am-10pm. ❷

Ho Ho Seafood Restaurant, 653 S. Weller St. (☎382-9671). Generous portions of Cantonese-prepared tank-fresh seafood, including specialty steamed rock cod ($8.25). Stuffed fish hang from the ceiling in an otherwise sparse but clean locale. Lunch $5-7 (until 4pm), dinner $7-12. Open Su-Th 11am-1am, F-Sa 11am-3am. ❷

CAPITOL HILL

With bronze dance-steps on the sidewalks and neon storefronts, **Broadway Avenue** is a land of espresso houses, imaginative shops, elegant clubs, and good eats.

🗺 **Bimbo's Bitchin' Burrito Kitchen,** 506 E. Pine St. (☎329-9978). The name explains it, and the decorations (plastic palm trees) prove it. Walk through the door to the bar, **Cha Cha** (tequila shots $3.50). Spicy Bimbo's burrito $4.25. Tacos $2.50. Happy hour daily 4-7pm; bar open until 2am. Open M-Th noon-11pm, F-Sa noon-2am, Su 2-10pm. ❶

Ristorante Machiavelli, 1215 Pine St. (☎621-7941). A small Italian place with deep Seattle roots whose simplicity in decor and food proves it has nothing to prove. The gnocchi are widely considered the best in town ($8.25). Pasta $7-10. Open M-Sa 5-11pm; bar open until 2am. ❸

Honey Hole Sandwiches, 703 E. Pike St. (☎709-1399). Red walls and a skeleton hanging from a swing compliment the many vegetarian, cold, and hot options, like the Texas Tease (shredded barbecue chicken on fresh bread; $5.95). Open daily 10am-2am. ❷

UNIVERSITY DISTRICT

The neighborhood around the immense **University of Washington** ("U-Dub"), north of downtown between Union and Portage Bay, supports funky shops, international restaurants, and coffeehouses. The best of each lies within a few blocks of University Way, known as "the Ave."

🗺 **Araya's Vegetarian Place,** 4732 University Way NE (☎524-4332). Consistently rated among the top vegan restaurants in Seattle, Araya's will satisfy any appetite, vegan or not. Lunch buffet has all the classics—*pad thai* and curries—as well as some more unconventional offerings ($6.50). Be sure to try the rice pudding. Buffet 11:30am-3:30pm. Open M-Th 11:30am-9pm, F-Sa 11:30am-9:30pm, Su 5-9pm. ❷

Flowers Bar & Restaurant, 4247 University Way NE (☎633-1903). This 1920s landmark was a flower shop; now, the mirrored ceiling reflects an all-you-can-eat vegetarian Mediterranean buffet ($7.50), plus sandwiches filled with everything from steak to falafel to Thai chicken ($5). Daily drink specials like $2 tequila shots W and $3 margaritas Sa. Open M-Sa 11am-2am, Su 11am-midnight. Bar open Th-Sa 6pm-2am. ❷

CAFES

The coffee bean is Seattle's first love; you can't walk a single block without passing an institution of caffeination. The city's obsession with Italian-style espresso drinks even has gas stations pumping out thick, dark, soupy java.

■ **Victrola Coffee & Art,** 411 15th Ave. E (☎325-6520; www.victrolacoffee.com). On mellow 15th Ave., this cafe possesses atmosphere in abundance; avoiding the table clutter that plagues other cafes, it balances private sitting space with an inviting, conversational sofa area. Signature espresso roasts ($2.15) are complimented by sandwiches and top-notch pastries. It's not uncommon to hear live music every night of the week. Open M-Th 5:30am-11pm, F 5:30am-midnight, Sa 6am-midnight, Su 6am-11pm.

■ **Still Life,** 705 N. 35th St. (☎547-9850). Displaying local art and offering quality coffee, homemade soups ($2.75-4), and irresistible desserts to locals and tourists alike, Still Life proves there is still energy in the funky community. Open daily 7:30am-5pm.

Cafe Besalu, 5909 24th Ave. NW (☎789-1463). The coffee is nice, but the real draw is Cafe Besalu's delectable pastries—from artisan bread to croissants and brioches ($0.95-3.25)—being made in the open kitchen. Open W-Su 7am-3pm.

SIGHTS

Most of the city's major sights are within walking distance of one another or the Metro's ride free zone. Seattle has unparalleled public art installations in the city (self-guided tours begin at the visitors center), and plentiful galleries. While dotcom success drove Seattle's collective worth up and some of the art out, the money has begun to pay off; the investments of Seattle-based millionaires have brought new architecture in the Experience Music Project (EMP), the new Seattle Central Library, and the upcoming Olympic Sculpture Park. Outside cosmopolitan downtown, Seattle boasts over 300 areas of well-watered greenery.

DOWNTOWN AND THE WATERFRONT

The ■**Seattle Central Library,** 1000 4th Ave., at Madison St., opened in May 2004. The transparent new library, designed by Rem Koolhaas, with jagged angles and floating floors, hovers above the downtown streets. The Book Spiral allows for four floors of constant walking through shelves, while the living room and 10th-floor reading room are comfortable spaces to relax. (☎386-4636; www.spl.org. Free 1hr. general tours M-W 12:30, 2:30, 4:30pm; Th-Sa 10:30am, 12:30, 2:30, 4:30pm; Su 2 and 4pm. Free 1hr. architectural tours M-W 5:30 and 6:45pm, Sa-Su 1:30 and 3:30pm. Open M-W 10am-8pm, Th-Sa 10am-6pm, Su 1-5pm.) The ■**Pike Place Market,** 1531 Western Ave., is worth a look, even if food is not on your mind. Tours start at the Market Heritage Center. (☎682-7453; www.pikeplacemarket.com. $7, ages 60 and up and under 18 $5. W-Sa 11am and 2pm, Su 2pm.) The **Pike Place Hillclimb** descends from the south end of Pike Place Market past chic shops and restaurants to the Alaskan Way and waterfront. (Wheelchair accessible.) The **Seattle Art Museum (SAM),** 100 University St., near 1st Ave., is in a grandiose building designed by father of postmodernism Robert Venturi. The SAM balances special exhibits with the region's largest collection of African, Native American, and Asian art, and contemporary western painting and sculpture. Call for info on special musical shows, films, and lectures. Just up the hill is the museum's **Rental/Sales Gallery,** with local art for perusal or purchase. *(☎ 654-3100; www.seattleartmuseum.org. Open Tu-W and F-Su 10am-5pm, Th 10am-9pm. $15; students, ages 62 and up and 7-17 $12; under 6 free; first Th of the month free. Special exhibits $5-15. Rental/Sales Gallery: 1220 3rd Ave. ☎ 343-1101; www.seattleartmuseum.org/artrentals. Open M-Sa 11am-5pm.)*

THE SEATTLE CENTER

The 1962 World's Fair demanded a Seattle Center to herald the city of the future. Now the Center houses everything from carnival rides to ballet. It is bordered by Denny Way, W. Mercer St., 1st Ave., and 5th Ave., and has eight gates, each with a map of its facilities; it's also accessible by a short **monorail** departing from downtown's **Westlake Center.** *(400 Pine St. ☎ 625-0280; www.seattlemonorail.com.)* The Center's anchor point is the **Center House,** holding a food court, stage, and info desk. The **International Fountain** squirts water 20 ft. in the air from all angles off its silver, hemispherical base. The grass around it is a wonderful place to relax. *(Info desk open daily 11am-6pm. For info about special events and attractions, call ☎ 684-8582 for recorded info or 684-7200 for a live person; www.seattlecenter.com. Monorail every 15min. M-F 7:30am-11pm, Sa-Su 9am-11pm. $1.50, seniors $0.75, ages 5-12 $0.50.)*

The ⊠**Experience Music Project (EMP),** 325 5th Ave., at the Seattle Center. Take Exit 167 from I-15 or bus #3, 4, or 15. EMP is the brainchild of Seattle billionaire Paul Allen, whose pet project of a shrine to his music idol Jimi Hendrix ballooned to include the technological sophistication of Microsoft, dozens of ethnomusicologists and multimedia specialists, a collection of over 80,000 musical artifacts, the world-renowned architect Frank Gehry, and $350 million. The result? The rock 'n' roll museum of the future. The building alone—sheet metal molded into abstract curves and acid-dyed gold, silver, purple, light blue, and red—will make you gasp. Inside, check out the guitar Hendrix smashed on a London stage; the Sound Lab's state-of-the art computer teaching devices that let you try your own hand at music making; and On Stage, a first-class karaoke stage gone haywire. *(☎ 367-5483 or 877-367-5483, ticket office 770-2702; www.emplive.com. Open late May to early Sept. M-Th and Su 9am-6pm, F-Sa 9am-9pm; early Sept. to late May Su-Th 10am-5pm, F-Sa 10am-9pm. $20; military with ID, seniors, and ages 13-17 $16; ages 7-12 $15. Free live music Tu-Sa in the lounge; national acts perform almost every F-Sa in the Sky Church.)*

The **Space Needle** was built in 1962 for the World's Fair. When this 607-ft. rotating building was constructed, it was hailed as futuristic and daring. Today, the Space Needle is the symbol of Seattle. It has a great view and is an invaluable landmark for the disoriented. The needle houses an observation tower and a high-end rotating restaurant, and its top changes colors and accessories to celebrate local events. *(400 Broad St. ☎ 905-2100; www.spaceneedle.com. $13, seniors $11, ages 4-13 $6.)*

THE INTERNATIONAL DISTRICT/CHINATOWN

What do you do when you have too much good art to exhibit all at once? Open a second museum, which is what SAM did, creating the ⊠**Seattle Asian Art Museum (SAAM),** 1400 E Prospect St., in Volunteer Park, just past the water tower. The collection is particularly strong in Chinese art, but most of East Asia is well represented, with exhibits on Buddhist art and daily life in Japan. *(☎ 654-3100; www.seattleartmuseum.org. Open Tu-W and F-Su 10am-5pm, Th 10am-9pm. Suggested donation $3, under 12 free; free with SAM ticket from the previous 7 days; SAAM ticket good for $3 discount at SAM. First Th and Sa of every month free.)* The ⊠**Wing Luke Asian Museum,** 407 7th Ave. S, gives a description of life in an Asian-American community, investigating different Asian nationalities in Seattle and showing work by local Asian artists. One permanent exhibit is Camp Harmony, a replica of barracks from a Japanese internment camp in WWII. *(☎ 623-5124; www.wingluke.org. Open Tu-F 11am-4:30pm, Sa-Su noon-4pm. $4, students and seniors $3, ages 5-12 $2. First Th of every month free.)* The **University of Washing-**

ton Arboretum, 10 blocks east of Volunteer Park, has over 4000 species of trees, shrubs, and flowers, and superb trails. Take bus #11, 43, or 48 from downtown. There's space to wander wooded areas, stroll along a waterfront pathway, or explore the carefully crafted gardens, including a serene Japanese Garden, Rhododendron Glen, and Azalea Way. Tours depart the **Graham Visitor Center,** at the southern end of the arboretum on Lake Washington Blvd. *(☎543-8800; http:// depts.washington.edu/wpa. Open daily dawn-dusk, visitors center 10am-4pm. Japanese Garden: open Apr.-Nov. 10am-dusk. $2.50, students and ages 60 and up $1.50. Free tours 1st Su of each month or by appointment.)*

🎵 ENTERTAINMENT

Seattle has one of the world's most famous underground music scenes and a bustling theater community. The free **Out to Lunch** series (☎623-0340; schedules at www.downtownseattle.com) brings everything from reggae to folk dancing to parks, squares, and buildings (June-Sept. M-F noon-1:30pm).

MUSIC

The **Seattle Opera** performs from October to August in **McCaw Hall.** The culmination of a 10-year renovation project, the new Opera House reopened in 2003, with a glass facade, decked-out lobbies, a modernized auditorium, and a new cafe. Opera buffs should reserve in advance, but rush tickets are sometimes available. (☎389-7676; www.seattleopera.com. Ticket office is at 1020 John St., 1 level below the 13 Coins Restaurant parking lot. Students and seniors can get half-price tickets 1½hr. before performances at the ticket office. Open M-F 9am-5pm. Tickets from $35.) The **Seattle Symphony** performs in the beautiful **Benaroya Hall,** 200 University St., at 3rd Ave., from September to June. (☎212-4700, tickets 215-4747; www.seattlesymphony.org. Ticket office open M-F 10am-6pm, Sa 1-6pm. Tickets from $15, most $25-39; seniors half-price; students $10 day of show. Call ahead; ticket availability varies by season.) (☎215-4895. Tours Tu and F noon and 1pm. Free.) Free organ concerts attract crowds on the first Monday of every month at 12:30pm.

THEATER AND CINEMA

The city has exciting plays and alternative works, particularly by talented amateur groups. Rush tickets are often available at nearly half-price on the day of the show from **Ticket/Ticket.** (☎324-2744. Cash only.) **The Empty Space Theatre,** 3509 Fremont Ave. N, one and a half blocks north of the Fremont Bridge, has comedies from October to early July. (☎547-7500. Tickets $20-40. Half-price tickets 30min. before curtain.) **Seattle Repertory Theater,** 155 Mercer St., at the Bagley Wright Theater in the Seattle Center, presents winter productions. (☎443-2222; www.seattlerep.org. $15-45, ages 65 and up $32, under 25 $10. Rush tickets 30min. before curtain.)

   Seattle is a cinephile's paradise. Most of the theaters screening non-Hollywood films are on Capitol Hill and in the University District. On summer Saturdays, **outdoor cinema** in Fremont begins at dusk at 670 N. 34th St., in the U-Park lot, behind the Red Door Alehouse. (☎781-4230. Entrance 7pm; live music 8pm. $5.) **TCI Outdoor Cinema** shows films from classics to cartoons at the Gasworks Park. (☎694-7000. Live music 7pm-dusk. Free.) **The Egyptian,** 801 E. Pine St., at Harvard Ave. on Capitol Hill, hosts the **Seattle International Film Festival** (☎324-9997; www.seattlefilm.com) at the end of May and the first week of June. (☎323-4978. $9, seniors $6.)

SPORTS

The Mariners, or "M's," play baseball in the half-billion-dollar, hangar-like **Safeco Field,** at First Ave. S and Royal Brougham Way S, under a giant retractable roof. (☎622-4487; www.mariners.org. From $7.) Seattle's football team, the **Seahawks,** play in a new stadium, the recently dubbed **Qwest Field,** one of the most modern in the world. (☎ 628-0888; www.seahawks.com. From $20.) On the other side of town, the sleek **Key Arena,** in the Seattle Center, hosts Seattle's NBA basketball team, the **Supersonics.** (☎ 628-0888; www.supersonics.com. From $9.)

🌿 FESTIVALS

Pick up the visitors center's *Calendar of Events* (www.seeseattle.org/events) for coupons and listings. The first Thursday of each month, the art community sponsors **First Thursday,** a free gallery walk where galleries and art cafes open to the city. The **Fremont Fair** (☎ 694-6706; www.fremontfair.com), in honor of the summer solstice, is in mid-June, with the **Fremont Solstice Parade,** led by dozens of bicyclists wearing only brightly colored body paint. The International District holds an annual two-day bash in mid-July, with arts and crafts booths, East Asian and Pacific food booths, and presentations by groups from the Radical Women/Freedom Socialist Party to cultural dance groups. For more info, call **Chinatown Discovery** (☎ 382-1197; www.seattlechinatowntour.com). **Bumbershoot,** a giant four-day festival, caps off the summer Labor Day weekend with major rock bands, street musicians, and a young, exuberant crowd. (☎ 281-7788; www.bumbershoot.org. 4 days $48-55; 2 days $26-28; 1 day $15-25. Some events require additional tickets.)

Puget Sound's yachting season starts in May. **Maritime Week,** in the third week of May, and the **Shilshole Boats Afloat Show** (☎ 634-0911; www.boatsafloatshow.com), in August, let boaters show off their crafts. Over the 4th of July weekend, the Center for Wooden Boats sponsors the free **Wooden Boat Festival** (☎ 382-2628; www.cwb.org) on Lake Union, which includes a demonstration of boat-building skills. The finale is the **Quick and Daring Boatbuilding Contest,** when people build and sail wooden boats of their own design using limited tools and materials.

🐟 NIGHTLIFE

DOWNTOWN

🌊 **The Alibi Room,** 85 Pike St. (☎ 623-3180; www.alibiroom.com), across from Market Cinema, in Post Alley in Pike Place. A friendly indie filmmaker hangout, with a bookshelf of scripts at the entrance. Bar with music. Downstairs dance floor open F-Sa. Mediterranean-style cuisine; brunch Sa-Su. Open daily 11am-3pm and 5pm-2am.

Club Noc Noc, 1516 2nd Ave. (☎ 223-1333; www.clubnocnoc.com). Casual and spacious, with exposed brick walls, lots of red lighting, and a real dance floor, Club Noc Noc embraces patrons from goths to frat boys. Drink specials feature Pabst Blue Ribbon (M $0.50, Su $0.25) and an outstanding 5-9pm happy hour ($1 for well drinks and more PBR). Cover varies from free to $5. Open M-F 5pm-2am, Sa-Su 5pm-5am.

PIONEER SQUARE

Pioneer Square is hopping with twenty-somethings and cover bands. A number of the bars have a joint cover (Su-Th $5, F-Sa $10) that lets you bar hop. **Larry's Blues Cafe,** 209 1st Ave. S (☎ 624-7665; www.larrysbluescafe.com), features great blues and jazz nightly (no cover weekdays). **J & M Cafe and Cardroom,** 201 1st Ave. (☎ 292-0663; www.jandmcafeandcardroom.com), is in the center of Pioneer Sq.

🌊 **Bohemian Cafe,** 111 Yesler Way (☎ 447-1514), adorned with Jamaican art, pumps reggae every night. Live shows 6 nights per week; often national acts on weekends. Happy hour 4-7pm. Part of the joint cover. Open M-Th and Sa 4pm-2am, F 3pm-2am.

Contour, 807 1st Ave. (☎447-7704; www.clubcontour.com). Intimate and elegant, the paintings, swanky statues, and wide windows make a decadent dance spot. Happy hour M-F 4-8pm, Sa-Su 2-8pm, with $2 food, $2 beer, and $3.50 cocktails. Cover free-$12. Open M 3pm-2am, Tu-Th 11:30am-2am, F 11:30am-5am, Sa 2pm-5am, Su 2pm-2am.

CAPITOL HILL

East off Broadway, Pine St. is filled with cool lounges. West off Broadway, Pike St. clubs push the limits (industrial, punk, fetish) and the sound barrier.

■ **Linda's Tavern,** 707 E. Pine St. (☎325-1220). A quirky post-gig local scene, with pool tables, a buffalo head, and Southern comfort foods. DJ spins jazz, alternative, and rock M and Th. Happy hour 7-9pm. Open daily 4pm-2am.

Neighbours, 1509 Broadway (☎324-5358; www.neighboursonline.com). Enter from the alley on Pike. A fixture in Seattle's gay scene, Neighbours is a techno-slick dance club. Frequent drag nights. Open Tu-W and Su 4pm-2am, Th 4pm-3am, F-Sa 4pm-4am.

▲ OUTDOOR ACTIVITIES

Biking is very popular in Seattle. The city prides itself on 30 mi. of bike-pedestrian trails, 90 mi. of signed bike routes, and 16 mi. of bike lanes on city streets. Almost 10,000 **cyclists** compete in the 190 mi. **Seattle to Portland Classic (STP)** race in late June or early July. Call the **bike hotline** (☎522-2453; www.cascade.org) for info. On **Bicycle Saturdays/Sundays** from May to September, Lake Washington Blvd. is open only to cyclists 10am-6pm; the schedule can change, but it is usually the second Saturday and third Sunday of each month. Call the **Seattle Parks and Recreation Activities Office** (☎684-4075; www.cityofseattle.net/parks) for info. The closest, most crowded area for hiking surrounds 4167 ft. **Mount Si.** An hour from downtown, hikers can reach the **Tiger Mountain State Forest,** home to both Mt. Si and **Tiger Mountain.** The difficult 8 mi. round-trip **Mount Si Trail** brings you to **Haystack Basin,** the false summit, but don't try climbing higher unless you have rock-climbing gear. (Take I-90 east to SE Mt. Si Rd., 2 mi. from Middle Fork.)

▶ DAYTRIP FROM SEATTLE

VASHON ISLAND

Only a 25min. ferry ride from Seattle, Vashon Island is inexplicably invisible to most Seattleites. With its forested hills and expansive sea views, this artists' colony feels like the San Juan Islands without the tourists. Most of the island is covered in Douglas fir, rolling cherry orchards, wildflowers, and strawberry fields, and all roads lead to rocky beaches. **Point Robinson Park** is a gorgeous spot for a picnic; free tours (☎217-6123) of the 1885 **Coast Guard lighthouse** are available. **Vashon Island Kayak Co.,** at Burton Acres Park, Jensen Point Boat Launch, runs guided tours and rents sea kayaks. (☎463-9257. Open F-Su 10am-5pm. Singles $18 per hr., $58 per day; doubles $28/$80.) Over 500 acres of woods in the middle of the island are interlaced with mildly difficult hiking trails. The **Vashon Park District** has more info. (☎463-9602; www.vashonparkdistrict.com. Open daily 8am-4pm.) The ■**Vashon Island AYH Ranch Hostel (HI) ❶,** at 12119 SW Cove Rd., west of Vashon Hwy., is sometimes called the "Seattle B." Resembling an Old Western town, the hostel offers bunks, open-air teepees, and covered wagons. (☎463-2592; www.vashonhostel.com. Free pancake breakfast and 1-gear bikes. Mountain bikes $6 per day. Check-in 24hr. Full hostel open May-Oct.; private double open year-round. $13, nonmembers $16. Private double $45/$55; $10 per extra person; children half-price. Shuttle to morning ferry $1.25.) Vashon Island stretches between Seattle and Tacoma on its east side and between Southworth and Gig Harbor in the west. **Washington State Ferries** (☎464-6400 or 800-843-3779; www.wsdot.wa.gov/ferries) runs to Vashon Island from Seattle (see **Transportation,** p. 1004). The local **Thriftway,** 9740 SW Bank Rd. (☎463-2100), has maps, as does the **Chamber of Commerce,** 17232 SW Vashon Hwy. (☎463-6217; www.vashonchamber.com. Open Tu-Sa 10am-3pm.)

OLYMPIA ☎360

Inside Olympia's seemingly interminable network of suburbs lies a festive downtown area known for its art, antiques, liberalism, and irresistible microbrews. Evergreen State College is a few miles from the city center, and its highly pierced, tree-hugging student body spills into town in a kind of chemistry experiment that only gets weirder when Olympia politicians join in. The product of this grouping resists definition, but it is worth experiencing.

🛈 **PRACTICAL INFORMATION.** Olympia is at the junction of I-5 and U.S. 101. **Amtrak,** 6600 Yelm Hwy. (☎923-4602; open daily 8:15am-noon, 1:45-3:30pm, and 5:30-8:30pm), runs to Portland (2½hr., 4 per day, $22-27) and Seattle (1¾hr., 4 per day, $24-27). **Greyhound,** 107 7th Ave. SE (☎357-5541), at Capitol Way, goes to Portland (2¾hr., 6-7 per day, $23) and Seattle (1¾hr., 4-6 per day, $8.50). **Intercity Transit (IT)** provides service almost anywhere in Thurston County. (☎786-1881 or 800-287-6348; www.intercitytransit.com. $0.75; day passes $1.50.) **Washington State Capitol Visitors Center** is on Capitol Way at 14th Ave., next to the state capitol; follow the signs on I-5. (☎586-3460; www.ga.wa.gov/visitor. Open M-F 8am-5pm; May-Sept. also Sa-Su 10am-3pm.) The **Olympic National Forest Headquarters,** 1835 Black Lake Blvd. SW, has info. (☎956-2400; www.fs.fed.us/r6/olympic. Open M-F 8am-4:30pm.) **Post Office:** 900 Jefferson St. SE (☎357-2289. Open M-F 7:30am-6pm, Sa 9am-4pm.) **Postal Code:** 98501. **Area Code:** 360.

🛏🍴 **ACCOMMODATIONS AND FOOD.** Motels in Olympia cater to policymakers ($60-80); chains in nearby Tumwater are more affordable. **Millersylvania State Park ❶,** 12245 Tilly Rd. S, 10 mi. south of Olympia, has 168 sites. Take Exit 95 off I-5 S or Exit 95 off I-5 N, then take Rte. 121 N and follow signs to trails and Deep Lake. (☎753-1519, reservations 888-226-7688. Showers $0.25 per 3min. Hiker/biker sites $6; drive-in sites $16, with hookup $21. Wheelchair accessible.) Diners, veggie eateries, and Asian quickstops line 4th Ave. east of Columbia. The **Olympia Farmers Market,** 700 N. Capital Way, sells produce and fantastic fare. (☎352-9096; www.farmers-market.org. Open Apr.-Oct. Th-Su 10am-4pm; Nov.-Dec. Sa-Su 10am-3pm.) The **Spar Cafe & Bar ❷,** 114 E. 4th Ave., is a local icon for beer, burgers, and cigars with live jazz Saturday nights. (☎357-6444. Cafe open M-Th 6am-9pm, F-Sa 6am-11pm, Su 6am-8pm. Bar open M-Th 11am-midnight, F-Sa 11am-2am.)

🎦 **SIGHTS.** Olympia's crowning glory is **State Capitol Campus,** a complex of government buildings, fountains, manicured gardens, and veterans' monuments. Tours depart from just inside the front steps, at 4th and Capitol. (☎586-3460. Tours daily on the hr. 10am-3pm. Building open M-F 8am-5pm, Sa-Su 10am-4pm.) **Wolf Haven International,** 3111 Offut Lake Rd., 10 mi. south of the capitol, is a permanent home for captive-born gray wolves reclaimed from zoos or illegal owners. (☎264-4695 or 800-448-9653; www.wolfhaven.org. Open M and W-Su May-Sept. 10am-5pm; Oct.-Apr. 10am-4pm. 45min. tours on the hr.; last tour leaves 1hr. before closing. $7, seniors $6, ages 3-12 $5.)

■ **NIGHTLIFE.** Olympia's ferocious nightlife seems to have outgrown its daylife. The *Olympian* (www.theolympian.com) lists live music. ■**Fishbowl Brewpub & Cafe,** 515 Jefferson St. SE, captures Olympia's love for the sea, art, and beer. The British ales ($3.50) are named after fish. (☎943-3650; www.fishbrewing.com. Open M-Sa 11am-midnight, Su noon-10pm. Kitchen open M-Sa until 11pm.) At **Eastside Club and Tavern,** 410 E. 4th St., old men play pool, college students slam micro pints, and local bands play. (☎357-9985; www.olywa.net/dwight/eastside-club. Open M-F noon-2am, Sa-Su 3pm-2am.)

SAN JUAN ISLANDS   ☎360

With hundreds of tiny islands and endless parks and coastline, the San Juan Islands are an explorer's dream. The islands are filled with great horned owls, puffins, sea lions, and pods of orcas patrolling the waters. Over 1½ million visitors come ashore each year during the peak of summer. To avoid the rush and enjoy good weather, visit in late spring or early fall.

■ PRACTICAL INFORMATION

Washington State Ferries (☎206-464-6400 or 800-843-3779), in Anacortes, serves Lopez (40min.), Orcas (1½hr.), San Juan Island (2hr.), and Shaw (1hr.); check the schedule at the visitors centers in Puget Sound. In summer, arrive 1hr. before departure. (For peak/non-peak travel $9/$12; vehicle $30/$44; bike $2/$4. Cash only. Eastbound traffic free.) The **Bellingham Airporter** (☎380-8800 or 866-235-5247; www.airporter.com) shuttles between Sea-Tac and Anacortes (10 per day, $31). **Victoria Clipper** (☎800-888-2535; www.victoriaclipper.com) departs **Seattle's** Pier 69 daily for San Juan Island, arriving at Spring St., landing in **Friday Harbor** (2½hr.; 2 per day; round-trip $43-53, ages 11 and under $27-32). Short hops and good roads make the islands great for biking. **Area Code:** 360.

SAN JUAN ISLAND

The biggest and most popular of the islands, San Juan is easy to explore, with ferry docks in town, flat roads, and a shuttle bus. Seattle weekenders flood the island in summer. A drive around the island's 35 mi. perimeter takes about 2hr., and the route is good for a day's cycle. The **West Side Road** traverses gorgeous scenery and provides the best chance for seeing orcas. Mullis Rd. merges with Cattle Point Rd. and goes straight into **American Camp,** on the south side of the island. Volunteers in period dress re-enact daily life from the time of the Pig War, a mid-19th-century squabble between the US and Britain over control of the islands. (☎378-2240. Open June-Aug. daily dawn-11pm; Sept.-May Th-Su. Visitors center open June-Aug. daily 8:30am-5pm; Sept.-May Th-Su 8:30am-4:30pm. Walks June-Sept. Sa 11:30am.) **English Camp,** the second half of the **San Juan National Historical Park,** lies on West Valley Rd. in **Garrison Bay.** (Buildings open June-Aug. daily 9am-5pm.) In June and July, the two camps alternate performing re-enactments on Saturday afternoons 12:30-3:30pm. **Lime Kiln Point State Park,** along West Side Rd., is the best whale-watching spot in the area. The **San Juan Island Jazz Festival** swings in late July.

■**Wayfarer's Rest ❶,** 35 Malcolm St., is a 10min. walk from the ferry up Spring onto Argyle St.; turn left at the church. This house-turned-hostel has driftwood bunks, TV, a patio and garden, full kitchen, two cats, showers, and laundry. (☎378-6428; www.rockisland.com/~wayfarersrest. Bike rental $15 per day. Check-in 2-9pm. Dorms $22; private room and cabins from $55.) **Hungry Clam Fish and Chips ❷,** 130 1st St., serves excellent fresh beer-battered Alaskan cod. (☎378-3474. Open daily late May to early Sept. 11am-9pm; early Sept. to late May 11am-7pm.)

San Juan Transit (☎378-8887 or 800-887-8387; www.sanjuantransit.com) travels from Friday Harbor to Roche Harbor on the hour and will stop upon request. ($5, return trip $8; day pass $10, 2-day pass $17. Tours depart Friday Harbor at 11am and 1pm. $17.) **Island Bicycles,** 380 Argyle Ave. (☎378-4941; www.islandbicycles.com), rents bikes from $7 per hr. or $35 per day. The **Chamber of Commerce,** 1 Front St. 2A, is at Front and Spring St. (☎378-5240 or 888-468-3701; www.sanjuanisland.org or www.guidetosanjuans.com. Open Apr.-Nov. M-F 9:30am-4:30pm, Sa 10am-2pm. Call for low-season hours.)

ORCAS ISLAND

Retirees, artists, and farmers live on Orcas Island in understated homes surrounded by green shrubs and red madrona trees. The trail to **Obstruction Pass Beach** is the best way to clamber down to the rocky shores. **Moran State Park** is unquestionably Orcas's star attraction. Over 30 mi. of hiking trails range from a 1hr. jaunt around **Mountain Lake** to a day-long trek up the south face of **Mount Constitution** (2407 ft.), the highest peak on the islands. Partway down, **Cascade Falls** is spectacular in the spring and early summer. **Orcas Tortas** makes a slow drive on a green bus from Eastsound to the peak. **Shearwater Adventures** runs an intense sea kayak tour of north Puget Sound. (☎376-4699. 3hr. tour with 30min. of dry-land training $49.) **Crescent Beach Kayak,** on the highway 1 mi. east of Eastsound, rents kayaks. (☎376-2464. $18 per hr., $50 per half-day. Open daily 9am-7pm.)

Doe Bay Resort ❶ is off Horseshoe Hwy. (Olga Rd.) on Pt. Lawrence Rd., 5 mi. east of Moran State Park. A former commune, this retreat has a treehouse, vegetarian **cafe ❷,** and co-ed clothing-optional hot tub and sauna. (☎376-2291. Sauna $10 per day. Cafe open M 8am-noon, Th 5-9pm, F-Su 8am-noon and 5-9pm. Reception 11am-9pm. Dorms $25; camping $35; private rooms from $55; yurts $75.) **Moran State Park ❶,** on Horseshoe Hwy. (Olga Rd.), is 15 mi. from the ferry landing. Follow Horseshoe Hwy. into the park, 14 mi. from the ferry on the east side of the island. The park has the islands' most popular camping, but sites are often reserved months in advance. (☎376-2326, reservations 888-226-7688. 151 sites. 12 sites open year-round. Showers $0.50 per 3min. Hiker/biker sites $10; vehicle sites $16.) The ferry lands on the southwest tip of Orcas; the main town of **Eastsound** is 9 mi. northeast. **Olga** and **Doe Bay** are an additional 8 and 11 mi., respectively, down the island's eastern side. **San Juan Transit** (☎378-8887 or 800-887-8387; www.sanjuantransit.com) runs ferries to most of the island. **Dolphin Bay Bicycles** (☎376-4157; www.rockisland.com/~dolphin), near the ferry, rents bikes for $30 per day.

LOPEZ ISLAND

Smaller than either Orcas or San Juan, "Slow-pez" lacks some of the tourist facilities of the larger islands. The small **Shark Reef** and **Agate Beach County Parks,** on the southwest end of the island, have tranquil, well-maintained hiking trails, and Agate has calm, deserted beaches. Roads on the island are ideal for biking. **Lopez Village** is 4½ mi. from the ferry dock off Fisherman Bay Rd. To rent a bike or kayak, go to **Lopez Bicycle Works** or **Lopez Kayak,** south of the village. (☎468-2847; www.lopezbicycleworks.com, www.lopezkayak.com. Bicycle Works open Apr.-Oct. daily 10am-6pm. Kayak open May-Oct. daily 10am-5pm. Bikes $5 per hr., $25 per day. Kayaks $12-25 per hr.) **Spencer Spit State Park ❶,** on the northeast corner of the island about 3½ mi. from the ferry terminal, has seven beach sites and 30 wooded sites up the hill. (☎468-2251, reservations 888-226-7688. Reservations necessary for summer weekends. Open Apr.-Oct. until 10pm. Sites $16; bunkhouse $22.)

OLYMPIC PENINSULA

West of Seattle and its busy neighbors, the Olympic Peninsula is a backpacking paradise. Olympic National Park dominates much of the peninsula, preventing the timber industry from threatening the glacier-capped mountains and temperate rainforests. The Pacific Ocean stretches to the west; to the north, the Strait of Juan de Fuca separates the peninsula from Vancouver Island; and to the east, Hood Canal and the Kitsap Peninsula isolate the sparse wilderness from Seattle.

PORT TOWNSEND   ☎360

Port Townsend's Victorian splendor has survived the progression of time and weather. Cafes, galleries, and bookstores line somewhat drippy streets, cheering the urbanites who move there. The **Ann Starrett Mansion,** 744 Clay St., has nationally renowned Victorian architecture, frescoed ceilings, and a three-tiered spiral staircase. (☎385-3205 or 800-321-0644; www.starrettmansion.com. Tours daily noon-3pm. $2.) The ✪**Olympic Hostel (HI) ❶,** in Fort Worden State Park, 1½ mi. from town, has bright rooms. (☎385-0655; www.olympichostel.org. Check-in 5-10pm, check-out 9:30am. $14, nonmembers $17.) To reach **Fort Flagler Hostel (HI) ❶,** in Fort Flagler State Park on gorgeous Marrowstone Island, 20 mi. from Port Townsend, go south on Rte. 19, which connects to Rte. 116 E, leading into the park. (☎385-1288. Check-in 5-10pm. Lockout 10am-5pm. Dorms $14, nonmembers $17.) Camp on the beach at the 116-site **Fort Flagler State Park ❶.** (☎385-1259. Sites $6; tents $16; RVs $22.) Reservations are recommended at all accommodations.

Port Townsend sits at the terminus of Rte. 20 on the northeastern corner of the Olympic Peninsula. It can be reached by U.S. 101 on the peninsula or from the Kitsap Peninsula across the Hood Canal Bridge. **Washington State Ferries** (☎206-464-6400 or 800-843-3779; www.wsdot.wa.gov/ferries) go from Seattle to Winslow on Bainbridge Island, where a **Kitsap County Transit** bus goes to Poulsbo. From Poulsbo, **Jefferson County Transit** runs to Port Townsend. A free shuttle goes to downtown from the Park 'n' Ride lot. (☎385-4777; www.jeffersontransit.com. Most buses M-Sa, some Su. $0.50.) **P.T. Cyclery,** 232 Tyler St., rents mountain bikes. (☎385-6470; www.olympus.net/ptcyclery. Open M-Sa 9am-6pm. $7 per hr., $25 per day. Ages 100 and over free.) **Visitor Info: Chamber of Commerce,** 2437 E. Sims Way, southwest of town on Rte. 20. (☎385-2722 or 888-365-6978; www.ptchamber.org. Open M-F 9am-5pm, Sa 10am-4pm, Su 11am-4pm.) **Post Office:** 1322 Washington St. (☎385-1600. Open M-F 9am-5pm, Sa 10am-2pm.) **Postal Code:** 98368. **Area Code:** 360.

OLYMPIC NATIONAL PARK   ☎360

With glacier-encrusted peaks, river valley rainforests, and jagged shores, Olympic National Park has something for everyone. Roads lead to many corners of the park, but a dive into the backcountry leaves tourists behind and reveals the richness and diversity of the park's many faces.

■✳🛈 ORIENTATION AND PRACTICAL INFORMATION

Olympic National Park's wilderness is best reached by car. U.S. 101 encircles the park in the shape of an upside-down U with Port Angeles at the top. The park's **eastern rim** runs up to Port Angeles, from which the **northern rim** extends westward. The tiny town **Neah Bay** and stunning **Cape Flattery** perch at the peninsula's northwest tip. Farther south on U.S. 101, the slightly larger town of **Forks** is a gateway to the park's rainforested **western rim.** Separate from the rest of the park, much of the Pacific coastline is a gorgeous **coastal zone.** The **entrance fee,** good for seven days, is charged at ranger stations and entrances such as Hoh, Heart o' the Hills, Sol Duc, Staircase, and Elwha. ($10 per car; $5 per hiker/biker; backcountry $2 extra per night. Parking $1.) **Olympic National Park Visitors Center,** 3002 Mt. Angeles Rd., is off Race St. in Port Angeles. (☎565-3130; www.nps.gov/olym/home.htm. Open daily May to early Sept. 9am-5:30pm; late Sept. to Apr. 9am-4pm.) Staff at the **Olympic National Park Wilderness Information Center** (☎565-3100; www.nps.gov/olym/wic), just behind the visitors center, help design trips within the park.

ACCOMMODATIONS

The closest budget accommodations are at the **Rainforest Hostel ❶,** 169312 U.S. 101, 20 mi. south of Forks. Follow the signs from U.S. 101. Two family rooms, a men's dorm, and rooms for couples require deposits. (☎374-2270; http://fp1.centurytel.net/rainforesthostel. Morning chore required. Internet and laundry. Hiker/biker sites $6; dorms $12.) Olympic National Park maintains many **campgrounds ❶,** some of which can be reserved (☎800-280-2267; www.reserveusa.com). Most camping is first come, first served. Olympic National Forest requires a trailhead pass to park at sites off main trails. The Washington Department of Natural Resources allows free **backcountry camping ❶** 300 ft. off any state road on DNR land, mostly by the western shore along the Hoh and Clearwater Rivers. From July to September, most spaces are taken by 2pm, while very popular sites fill by noon.

OUTDOOR ACTIVITIES

EASTERN RIM

The eastern rim stuns visitors with its canals and grandiose views. Canyon walls rise treacherously, their jagged edges leading to mountaintops offering glimpses of the whole peninsula and Puget Sound. Steep trails lead up **Mt. Ellinor,** 5 mi. past Staircase on Rte. 119. Hikers can choose the 3 mi. path or an equally steep but shorter journey to the summit; look for signs on the Upper Trailhead along Forest Road #2419-04. Adventurers who hit the mountain before late July should bring snow clothes to "mach" (as in Mach 1) down a ¼ mi. snow chute. A 3¼ mi. hike goes to **Lena Lake,** 14 mi. north of Hoodsport off U.S. 101; follow Forest Service Rd. 25 off U.S. 101 for 8 mi. to the trailhead. The Park Service charges $3 per trailhead pass. The **West Forks Dosewallip Trail,** a 10½ mi. trek to **Mount Anderson Glacier,** is the shortest route to any glacier in the park. The road to **Mount Walker Viewpoint,** 5 mi. south of Quilcene on U.S. 101, is steep with sheer dropoffs, and shouldn't be attempted in bad weather or a temperamental car. A view of Hood Canal, Puget Sound, Mt. Rainier, and Seattle awaits travelers on top. Ask about base camps and trails at **Hood Canal Ranger Station,** southeast of reserve lands on U.S. 101 in Hoodsport. (☎877-5254. Open in summer daily 8am-4:30pm; in winter M-F 8am-4:30pm.)

NORTHERN RIM

The most developed section of Olympic National Park lies along its northern rim, near Port Angeles, where glaciers, rainforests, and sunsets over the Pacific are only a drive away. Farthest east off U.S. 101 lies **Deer Park,** where trails tend to be uncrowded. Past Deer Park, the **Royal Basin Trail** meanders 6¼ mi. to the **Royal Basin Waterfall.** The road up **Hurricane Ridge** is an easy but curvy drive. Before July, walking on the ridge usually involves some snow-stepping. Clear days provide splendid views of Mt. Olympus and Vancouver Island set against a foreground of snow and indigo lupine. From here, the uphill **High Ridge Trail** is a short walk from Sunset Point. On weekends from late December to late March, the Park Service organizes free snowshoe walks atop the ridge. Farther west on U.S. 101, 13 mi. of paved road penetrates the popular **Sol Duc Hot Springs Resort,** where retirees de-wrinkle in the springs and eat in the lodge. (☎327-3583; www.northolympic.com/solduc. Open daily late May to Sept. 9am-9pm; late Mar. to mid-May 9am-7pm. Suit, locker, and towel rental available.) The **Sol Duc trailhead** is a starting point for those heading up; crowds thin dramatically above **Sol Duc Falls.** The **Eagle Ranger Station** has info and permits. (☎327-3534. Open in summer daily 8am-4:30pm.)

NEAH BAY AND CAPE FLATTERY

At the westernmost point on the Juan de Fuca Strait and north of the park's west-ern rim is **Neah Bay.** The only town in the **Makah Reservation,** Neah Bay, known as the "Pompeii of the Pacific," is a 500-year-old village that was buried in a landslide at Cape Alava. You can reach Neah Bay and Cape Flattery by a 1hr. detour from U.S. 101. From Port Angeles, Rte. 112 leads west to Neah Bay; Rte. 113 runs north from Sappho to Rte. 112. The Makah Nation, whose recorded history goes back 2000 years, still lives, fishes, and produces artwork here. Just inside the reserva-tion, the **Makah Cultural and Research Center,** in Neah Bay on Rte. 112, has artifacts from the archaeological site. (☎645-2711; www.makah.com/mcrchome.htm. Open June to mid-Sept. daily 10am-5pm; mid-Sept. to May W-Su 10am-5pm. Free tours W-Su 11am. $5, students and seniors $4.) During **Makah Days,** the last weekend of August, Native Americans from the region come for canoe races, dances, and bone games. Visitors are welcome; call the center for details. **Clallam Transit System** runs bus #14 from Oak St. in Port Angeles to Sappho, then #16 to Neah Bay. (☎452-4511; www.clallamtransit.com. $1, ages 6-19 $0.85, seniors $0.50; day pass $2.) **Cape Flat-tery,** the northwesternmost point in the contiguous US, is gorgeous. Take the road through town until it turns to dirt, past the "Marine Viewing Area" sign to a parking area where a trailhead leads toward the cape.

WESTERN RIM

In the rainforests of ONP's western rim, ferns, mosses, and giant old-growth trees blanket the earth. The drive along the **Hoh River Valley,** actively logged land, is alter-nately overgrown and barren. **Hoh Rainforest Visitors Center** is a 45min. drive from U.S. 101 on the western rim. (☎374-6925; www.nps.gov/olym. Open mid-June to early Sept. daily 9am-5pm.) From the visitors center, take the ¾ mi. **Hall of Mosses Trail** for a tour of the rainforest. With a smattering of educational panels explaining natural quirks, the **Spruce Nature Trail** leads 1¼ mi. through the forest and along the Hoh River. The **Hoh Rainforest Trail** is the area's most heavily traveled path, starting at the visitors center and edging the Hoh River for 18 mi. to **Blue Glacier** on the shoulder of Mt. Olympus. The 4 mi. **Quinault Lake Loop** and ½ mi. **Maple Glade Trail** leave from the **Quinault Ranger Station,** 353 S. Shore Rd. (☎288-2525. Open May-Sept. M-F 8am-4:30pm, Sa-Su 9am-4pm; Oct.-Apr. M-F 9am-4:30pm.) Snow-seekers go to **Three Lakes Point,** which is snowy until July. **Quinault Lake** lures anglers, row-ers, and canoers. The **Lake Quinault Lodge,** by the ranger station, rents boats. (☎288-2900 or 800-562-6672; www.visitlakequinault.com. Rentals from $12 per hr.)

COASTAL ZONE

Pristine coastline traces the park's far western region for 57 mi., separated from the rest of ONP by U.S. 101 and non-park timber land. Eerie fields of driftwood, sculptured arches, and dripping caves frame flaming sunsets, while the waves are punctuated by rugged sea stacks. Between the Quinault and Hoh Reservations, U.S. 101 hugs the coast for 15 mi., with parking lots a short walk from the sand. North of where the highway meets the coast, **Beach #4** has abundant tide pools, plastered with sea stars. **Beach #6,** 3 mi. north at Mi. 160, is a favorite whale-watch-ing spot. Near Mi. 165, sea otters and eagles hang amid tide pools and sea stacks at **Ruby Beach.** Beach camping is permitted north of the Hoh Reservation between **Oil**

City and **Third Beach** and north of the Quileute Reservation between **Hole-in-the-Wall** and **Shi-Shi Beach.** Day-hikers and backpackers adore the 9 mi. loop that begins at **Ozette Lake.** The trail has two 3 mi. legs leading along boardwalks through the rainforest. One heads toward sea stacks at **Cape Alava,** and the other goes to a sublime beach at **Sand Point.** A 3 mi. hike down the coast links the two legs, passing ancient petroglyphs. The **Ozette Ranger Station** has more info (☎963-2725). Campers should reserve permits (☎565-3100) in advance; spaces fill quickly in summer.

CASCADE RANGE

Intercepting the moist Pacific air, the Cascades divide Washington into the lush, wet green of the west and the low, dry plains of the east. The Cascades are most accessible in July, August, and September. Many high mountain passes are snowed in during the rest of the year. Mt. Baker, Vernon, Glacier, Rainier, Adams, and St. Helens are accessible by four major roads. The North Cascades Hwy. (Rte. 20) is the most breathtaking and provides access to North Cascades National Park. Scenic U.S. 2 leaves Everett for Stevens Pass and descends along the Wenatchee River. Rte. 20 and U.S. 2 can be traveled in sequence as the Cascade Loop. U.S. 12 approaches Mt. Rainier through White Pass and passes north of Mt. St. Helens. I-90 sends four lanes from Seattle past the ski resorts of Snoqualmie Pass.

MOUNT SAINT HELENS   ☎360

In one cataclysmic blast on May 18, 1980, Mt. St. Helens erupted, transforming what had been a perfect cone into a crater. The force of the ash-filled blast robbed the mountain of 1300 ft. and razed forests, strewing trees like matchsticks. Ash from the crater rocketed 17 mi. upward, blackening the sky. The explosion was 27,000 times the force of the atomic bomb dropped on Hiroshima. Today, Mt. St. Helens forms the middle third of the **Gifford Pinchot National Forest** and the **Mount Saint Helens National Volcanic Monument.** The monument is part national park, part laboratory, and encompasses most of the area affected by the explosion.

■ **ORIENTATION.** Vigorous winter rains often spoil access roads; check at a ranger station for road closures before heading out. From the west, take Exit 49 off **I-5** and use the **Spirit Lake Memorial Highway (Route 504).** For most, this is the quickest and easiest daytrip to the mountain, and the main visitors centers line the way to the volcano. **Route 503** skirts the south side of the volcano until it connects with **Forest Service Road 90.** Though views from this side don't highlight recent destruction, green glens and remnants of age-old explosions make this the best side for hiking and camping. From the north, the towns of **Mossyrock, Morton,** and **Randle** line **U.S. 12,** offering the closest major services to the monument.

■ **PRACTICAL INFORMATION.** The monument charges entrance fees at almost every visitors center, viewpoint, and cave. (1-day all access $6, ages 5-15 $2. Individual monument fees $3/$1.) With displays and interactive exhibits, **Mount Saint Helens Visitors Center,** across from Seaquest State Park on Rte. 504, is most visitors' first stop. (☎274-2100. Open daily 9am-6pm.) **Coldwater Ridge Visitors Center,** 38 mi. farther on Rte. 504, emphasizes the area's recolonization by living things through exhibits, a short film, and a ¼ mi. trail. (☎274-2131. Open daily 10am-6pm.) Overlooking the crater, **Johnston Ridge Observatory,** at the end of Rte. 504, focuses on geological exhibits and offers the best roadside view of the steaming dome and crater. (☎274-2140. Open May-Oct. daily 10am-6pm.) **Pine Creek Information Station,** 17 mi. east of Cougar on Rd. 90, shows an interpretive film of the eruption. (☎449-7800. Open mid-June to Sept. daily 9am-6pm.) **Apes Headquarters,** at Ape Cave on Rd. 8303 on the south side of the volcano, answers all your lava tube questions. (Open late May to Sept. daily 10am-5:30pm. Tours daily 10:30am-4:30pm, every hr. on the half-hour.) From mid-May to October, the Forest Service allows 100 people per day to hike to the crater rim. (Applications accepted from Feb. 1; $15. See www.fs.fed.us/gpnf/recreation/mount-st-helens/permit-application.shtml for reservation forms.) Procrastinators should head for **Jack's Restaurant and Country Store,** 13411 Louis River Rd., 5 mi. west of Cougar (I-5 Exit 21) on Rte. 503, where a lottery is held at 6pm each day to distribute the next day's 50 unreserved permits. (☎231-4276. Open Su-Th 6am-8pm, F-Sa 6am-9pm.)

⚑ CAMPING. Although the monument itself has no campgrounds, a number are scattered throughout the surrounding national forest. Free dispersed camping is allowed within the monument, but finding a site takes luck. **Iron Creek Campground ❶** is the closest campsite to Mt. St. Helens and has good hiking and a beautiful forest. All 98 sites can fill up on busy weekends. (☎877-444-6777. Reservations strongly recommended in summer. Sites $14-28.) **Swift Campground ❶,** 30min. east of Cougar on Rd. 90, just west of the Pine Creek Information Station, has spacious sites on Swift Reservoir. It is one of the most popular campgrounds in the area. The 93 sites are first come, first served. (☎503-813-6666. Sites $12.) Along Yale Lake are **Cougar Campground ❶** and **Beaver Bay ❶,** 2 and 4 mi. east of Cougar, respectively. Cougar Lake has 60 sites that are more spread out and private than Beaver Bay's 78 sites ($12-26).

⚑ OUTDOOR ACTIVITIES. Along each approach, short interpretive trails loop into the landscape. The 1hr. drive from the Mt. St. Helens Visitors Center to Johnston Ridge offers spectacular views of the crater and its resurgence of life. Another 10 mi. east, the hike along **Johnston Ridge** gets incredibly close to the crater where geologist David Johnston died studying the eruption. On the way west along Rd. 99, **Bear Meadow** provides the first interpretive stop, an excellent view of Mt. St. Helens, and the last restrooms before Rd. 99 ends at **Windy Ridge.** The monument begins just west of Bear Meadow, where Rd. 26 and 99 meet. Rangers lead ½ mi. walks around emerald **Meta Lake;** meet at Miner's Car at the junction of Rd. 26 and 99. (Late June to Sept. daily 12:45 and 3pm.) Farther west on Rd. 99, **Independence Pass Trail #227** is a difficult 3½ mi. hike with overlooks of Spirit Lake and superb views of the crater and dome. For a serious hike, continue along this trail to its intersection with the spectacular **Norway Pass Trail,** which runs 8 mi. through the blast zone to the newly reopened **Mt. Margaret peak.** Farther west, the 2 mi. **Harmony Trail #224** provides access to Spirit Lake. From Windy Ridge, a steep ash hill grants a magnificent view of the crater from 3½ mi. away. The **Truman Trail** leaves from Windy Ridge and meanders 7 mi. through the **Pumice Plain,** where hot flows sterilized the land.

Cavers should head to **Ape Cave,** 5 mi. east of Cougar just off Rd. 83. The cave is a broken 2½ mi. lava tube formed by an ancient eruption. When exploring the cave, wear a jacket and sturdy shoes, and take at least two flashlights or lanterns. Rangers lead 10 free 30min. guided cave explorations per day.

MOUNT RAINIER NATIONAL PARK ☎360

At 14,411 ft., Mt. Rainier presides regally over the Cascades. The Klickitat native people called it Tahoma, "Mountain of God," but Rainier is simply "the Mountain" to most Washington residents. Perpetually snowcapped, this dormant volcano draws thousands of visitors from around the globe. Clouds mask the mountain 200 days each year, frustrating visitors who come solely to see its distinctive summit. Over 305 mi. of trails weave peacefully through old-growth forests, alpine meadows, rivers, and bubbling hot springs.

ORIENTATION. To reach Mt. Rainier from the west, take **I-5** to Tacoma, then go east on **Route 512**, south on **Route 7**, and east on **Route 706**. Rte. 706 meanders through the town of Ashford and into the park by the **Nisqually** entrance, leading to the visitors centers of **Paradise** and **Longmire**. Snow usually closes all other park roads from November to May. **Stevens Canyon Road** connects the southeast corner of the national park with Paradise, Longmire, and the Nisqually entrance, unfolding superb vistas of Rainier and the Tatoosh Range along the way.

PRACTICAL INFORMATION. Gray Line Bus Service, 4500 W. Marginal Way SW, runs buses from the Convention Center, at 8th and Pike in Seattle, to Mt. Rainier (depart 8am, return 6pm), allowing about 3½hr. at the mountain. (☎206-624-5208 or 800-426-7532. Runs May to mid-Sept. daily. Round-trip $54, under 12 $27.) **Rainier Shuttle** (☎569-2331) runs daily from Sea-Tac to: Ashford (2hr., 2 per day, $37); Paradise (3hr., 1 per day, $46).

The best place to plan a backcountry trip is at the **Longmire Wilderness Information Center** (☎569-4453; open late May to early Oct. daily 7:30am-4pm), east of the Nisqually entrance; or the **White River Wilderness Information Center** (☎663-2273; open late May-Sept. W 7:30am-4:30pm, Th 7:30am-7pm, F 7am-7pm, Sa 7am-5pm), off Rte. 410 on the park's east side. Both distribute **backcountry permits.** Permits are good for seven days; an **entrance fee** is required. ($10 per car, $5 per hiker. Gates open 24hr.) **Rainier Mountaineering, Inc. (RMI),** in Paradise (☎253-627-6242 or 888-892-5462), rents gear and leads summit climbs. (Open May-Sept. daily 7am-8pm; Oct.-Apr. M-F 9am-5pm.) **Post Office:** National Park Inn, Longmire. (Open M-F 8:30am-noon and 1-5pm.) **Postal Code:** 98397. **Area Code:** 360.

ACCOMMODATIONS AND FOOD. Hotel Packwood ❷, 104 Main St., in Packwood, is a charming reminder of the Old West with a sprawled-out grizzly gracing the parlor. (☎494-5431; www.packwoodwa.com. Shared or private bath. Singles and doubles $29-49.) **Whittaker's Bunkhouse ❶,** 6 mi. west of the Nisqually entrance, offers spiffy rooms with sparkling clean showers, and a homey espresso bar, but no kitchen or linens. (☎569-2439; whittakersbunkhouse.com. Reservations strongly recommended. Bunks $30; private rooms $75-100.)

Camping ❶ in the park is first come, first served from mid-June to late September. (Low-season reservations ☎800-365-2267 or http://reservations.nps.gov. Prices range from free to $15.) National park campgrounds all have wheelchair-accessible facilities, but no hookups or showers. Coin-operated showers are available at Jackson Memorial Visitors Center, in Paradise. **Sunshine Point ❶** (18 sites, $10), near the Nisqually entrance, and **Cougar Rock ❶** (200 sites, $15), 2¼ mi. north of Longmire, are in the southwest. The serene high canopy of **Ohanapecosh ❶** (205 sites, $15) is 11 mi. north of Packwood on Rte. 123, in the southeast. **White River ❶** (112 sites, $10) is 5 mi. west of White River on the way to Sunrise, in the northeast. **Backcountry camping** requires a **permit,** free from ranger stations and visitors centers. Fires are prohibited in the backcountry. Hikers with a valid permit can camp at trailside, alpine, and snowfield sites (most with toilets and water). **Blanton's Market,** 13040 U.S. 12, in Packwood, is the closest decent supermarket and has an ATM. (☎494-6101. Open M-Th and Sa-Su 7am-8pm, F 7am-9pm.) **Highlander ❷,** in Ashford, serves standard pub fare in a dimly lit room with a pool table. (☎569-2953; www.the-highlander.com. Burgers $6-7. Open daily 7am-9pm.)

⚠ OUTDOOR ACTIVITIES. Ranger-led interpretive hikes delve into everything from area history to local wildflowers. Each visitors center conducts hikes on its own schedule and most campgrounds have evening talks and campfire programs. Mt. Adams and Mt. St. Helens can be seen from mountain trails like **Paradise** (1½ mi.), **Pinnacle Peak** (2½ mi.), **Eagle Peak** (7 mi.), and **Van Trump Park** (5½ mi.). One of the oldest stands of trees in Washington, the **Grove of Patriarchs** grows near the Ohanapecosh Visitors Center. An easy 1½ mi. walk leads to these 500- to 1000-year-old Douglas firs, cedars, and hemlocks. The **Summerland** and **Indian Bar Trails** are excellent for serious backpacking—this is where rangers go on their days off. **Carbon River Valley,** in the park's northwest corner, is one of the only inland rainforests in the US and has access to the Wonderland Trail. Winter storms keep the road beyond the Carbon River entrance in constant disrepair. The most popular staging ground for a summit attempt, **⊠Camp Muir** (9 mi. round-trip) is also a challenging day-hike. It begins on Skyline Trail, another popular day-hiking option, and heads north on Pebble Creek Trail. The latter half of the hike is covered in snow for most of the year. A segment of the **Pacific Crest Trail,** which runs from Mexico to the Canadian border, dodges in and out of the park's southeast corner. A trip to the summit requires substantial preparation and expense. The ascent involves a vertical rise of more than 9000 ft. over a distance of 9 or more mi., usually taking two days and an overnight stay at Camp Muir on the south side (10,000 ft.) or **Camp Schurman** on the east side (9500 ft.). Permits for summit climbs are $30.

OREGON

Over a century ago, families liquidated their possessions, sank their life savings into covered wagons, corn meal, and oxen, and high-tailed it to Oregon in search of prosperity and a new way of life. Today, Oregon remains a popular destination for backpackers, cyclists, anglers, beach crawlers, and families. The caves and cliffs of the coastline are still a siren call to tourists. Inland attractions include Crater Lake National Park and Ashland's Shakespeare Festival. From microbrews to snowcapped peaks, Oregon is worth crossing the Continental Divide.

ⓘ PRACTICAL INFORMATION

Capital: Salem.

Visitor info: Oregon Tourism Commission, 775 Summer St. NE, Salem 97310 (☎800-547-7842; www.traveloregon.com). **Oregon State Parks and Recreation Dept.,** 725 Summer St. NE, Ste. C, Salem 97301 (☎800-551-6949; www.prd.state.or.us).

Postal Abbreviation: OR. **Sales Tax:** 0%.

PORTLAND   ☎503

With over 200 parks, the pristine Willamette River, and snowcapped Mt. Hood in the background, Portland is an oasis of natural beauty. An award-winning transit system and pedestrian-friendly streets make it feel like a pleasantly overgrown town. In the rainy season, Portlanders flood pubs and clubs, where musicians often strum, sing, or spin for free. Improv theaters are in constant production, and the brave can chime in at open-mic nights all over town. Throughout it all, America's best beer pours from the taps of the microbrewery capital of the US.

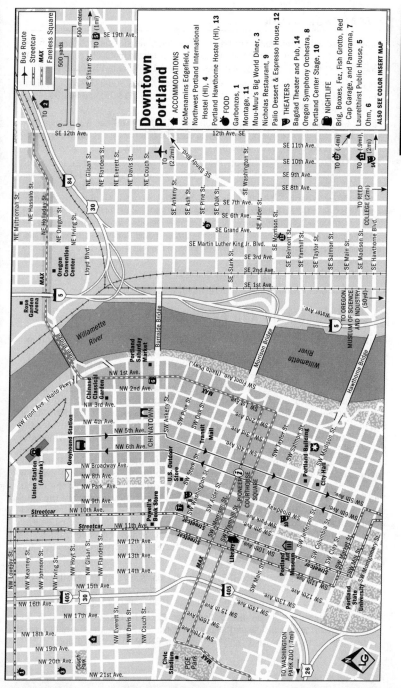

Downtown Portland

♦ ACCOMMODATIONS
McMenamins Edgefield, **2**
Northwest Portland International Hostel (HI), **4**
Portland Hawthorne Hostel (HI), **13**

🍴 FOOD
Garbonzos, **1**
Montage, **11**
Muu-Muu's Big World Diner, **3**
Nicholas Restaurant, **9**
Palio Dessert & Espresso House, **12**

🎭 THEATERS
Bagdad Theater and Pub, **14**
Oregon Symphony Orchestra, **8**
Portland Center Stage, **10**

🌙 NIGHTLIFE
Brig, Boxxes, Fez, Fish Grotto, Red Cap Garage, and Panorama, **7**
Laurelthirst Public House, **5**
Ohm, **6**

ALSO SEE COLOR INSERT MAP

PACIFIC NORTHWEST

▣ TRANSPORTATION

Airport: Portland International Airport (☎460-4234; www.portlandairportpdx.com) is served by almost every major airline. The airport is connected to the city center by **MAX Red Line,** an efficient light rail system (38min.; every 15min. 5am-11:30pm; $1.55).

Trains: Amtrak, 800 NW 6th Ave. (☎273-4866; reservations 800-872-7245), at Hoyt St. Open daily 7:45am-9pm. To **Eugene** (2½hr., 5 per day, $18-30) and **Seattle** (4hr., 4 per day, $24-38).

Buses: Greyhound, 550 NW 6th Ave. (☎800-229-9424), at NW Glisan St. by Union Station. Ticket counter open daily 5am-1am. To: **Eugene** (2½-4hr., 9 per day, $15); **Seattle** (3-4½hr., 8 per day, $21); **Spokane** (7½-11hr., 4 per day, $40).

Public Transit: Tri-Met, 701 SW 6th Ave. (☎238-7433; www.tri-met.org), in Pioneer Courthouse Sq. Open M-F 8:30am-5:30pm. **Call-A-Bus** info system ☎231-3199. Buses generally run 5am-midnight, with reduced hours on weekends. $1.30-1.60; disabled, ages 65 and older or 7-18 $0.60; under 7 free. Day pass $4. All of the city's public transit is free in the **No-Fare Zone:** North and east of 405, west of the river and south of Hoyt St. **MAX** (☎228-7246), based at the Customer Service Center, is Tri-Met's light rail train running between downtown, Hillsboro in the west, and Gresham in the east. Transfers from buses can be used to ride MAX. Runs M-F about 4:30am-1:30am, Sa 5am-12:30am, Su 5am-11:30pm.

Taxi: Radio Cab ☎227-1212. **Broadway Cab** ☎227-1234.

Car Rental: Crown Auto Rental, 1315 NE Sandy Blvd. (☎230-1103).

▨ ▤ ORIENTATION AND PRACTICAL INFORMATION

Portland lies in the northwest corner of Oregon, where the Willamette River flows into the Columbia River. **I-5** connects Portland with San Francisco and Seattle, while **I-84** follows the route of the Oregon Trail through the Columbia River Gorge, heading along the Oregon-Washington border toward Boise, ID. West of Portland, **U.S. 30** follows the Columbia downstream to Astoria, but **U.S. 26** is the fastest path to the coast. **I-405** runs just west of downtown, linking I-5 with U.S. 26 and 30.

Every street name in Portland carries one of five prefixes: **N, NE, NW, SE,** or **SW,** indicating where in the city the address is found. **Burnside Street** divides the city into north and south, while east and west are separated by the **Willamette River.** SW Portland is known as **downtown** but also includes the southern end of Old Town and a slice of the wealthier **West Hills. Old Town,** in NW Portland, encompasses most of the city's historic sector. *Some areas in the NW and SW around W. Burnside St. are best not walked alone at night.* To the north, **Nob Hill** and **Pearl District** hold recently revitalized homes and many of the chicest shops in the city. **Southeast** Portland contains parks, factories, local businesses, and residential areas of all income brackets. A rich array of cafes, theaters, and restaurants lines **Hawthorne Boulevard. Williams Avenue** frames "the North." **North** and **Northeast** Portland are chiefly residential, punctuated by a few parks and the **University of Portland.**

Visitor Info: Visitors Association (POVA), 701 SW Morrison St. (☎275-9750; www.travelportland.com), in Pioneer Courthouse Sq. Free *Portland Book* has maps and info on local attractions. Open M-F 8:30am-5:30pm, Sa 10am-4pm.

Internet Access: The elegant and distinguished **Central Library,** 801 SW 10th Ave. (☎988-5123; www.multcolib.org), between Yamhill and Taylor. 1hr. free with a guest pass from customer service. Open M-Th 9am-9pm, F-Sa 9am-6pm, Su 1-5pm.

Post Office: 715 NW Hoyt St. (☎800-275-8777). Open M-F 7am-6:30pm, Sa 8:30am-5pm. General delivery open M-F 8am-5:30pm, Sa 8:30am-noon. **Postal Code:** 97208.

ACCOMMODATIONS

Although chain hotels dominate downtown and smaller motels steadily raise prices, Portland still welcomes the budget traveler. Prices drop as you leave the city center, and inexpensive motels can be found on SE Powell Blvd. and the southern end of SW 4th Ave. Accommodations in Portland fill up during the summer months, especially during the Rose Festival, so make your reservations early.

Portland Hawthorne Hostel (HI), 3031 SE Hawthorne Blvd. (☎236-3380; www.portlandhostel.org), at 31st Ave. across from Artichoke Music. Take bus #14 to SE 30th Ave. This laid-back hostel has a common space and porch. Kitchen, laundry. Free wireless Internet; "conventional" Internet is $1 per 10min. $1 all-you-can-eat pancakes. 34 beds and a tent yard for overflow. Fills early in summer. Reception 8am-10pm. Checkout 11am. Dorms $18, nonmembers $21; private rooms $41-46. ❶

Northwest Portland International Hostel (HI), 1818 NW Glisan St. (☎241-2783; www.2oregonhostels.com), at 18th Ave. Centrally located between Nob Hill and the Pearl District. Take bus #17 down Glisan to the corner of 19th Ave. This snug Victorian building has a kitchen, Internet access, lockers, laundry, and a small espresso bar. 34 dorm beds and private doubles starting at $55. Reception 8am-11pm. Reservations at least 2 weeks ahead are recommended June-Sept. $19, nonmembers $22. ❶

McMenamins Edgefield, 2126 SW Halsey St. (☎669-8610 or 800-669-8610; www.mcmenamins.com), in Troutdale. Take MAX east to the Gateway Station, then Tri-Met bus #24 (Halsey) east to the main entrance. This 38-acre former farm is a posh escape that keeps 2 hostel rooms. On-site brewery and vineyards, plus 18-hole golf course ($8-9, club rental $1), and restaurants and pubs. Offers many activities, including 2-day rafting trips ($140). Breakfast included with private rooms. Lockers included. Reception 24hr. Call ahead in summer (but no reservations for the hostel). 2 12-bed dorms ($20) are a budget option. Singles $50; doubles $85-100. ❶

FOOD

Portland ranks high nationwide in restaurants per capita, and dining experiences are seldom dull. Downtown can be expensive, but restaurants and quirky cafes in the NW and SE quadrants have great food at reasonable prices.

Muu-Muu's Big World Diner, 612 NW 21st Ave. (☎223-8169), at Hoyt St. Bus #17. Where high and low culture meet. Artful goofiness—the name of the restaurant was drawn from a hat—amidst red velvet curtains and gold upholstery. Brutus salad, "the one that kills a caesar" $6. 'Shroom-wich $7.50. Many vegetarian options. Open M-F 11:30am-1am, Sa-Su 10am-1am. ❷

Montage, 301 SE Morrison St. (☎234-1324; www.montage.citysearch.com). Take bus #15 to the east end of the Morrison Bridge and walk under it. Straight-laced, mainstream Portlanders enter a surreal land of dining while seated Last-Supper-style under a macaroni-framed mural of that famous meal. Try oyster shooters ($1.75) or huge portions of jambalaya (chicken $11, gator $15). Veggie gumbo ($5.50). Open Su-Th 6pm-2am, F-Sa 6pm-4am. No credit cards. ❷

Garbonzos, 922 NW 21st Ave. (☎227-4196), at Hoyt St. Bus #17. This quiet eatery offers delicious falafel and shish kebabs in a relaxed atmosphere. The falafel plate, 6 balls and 6 sides ($7), offers a taste of the menu's variety. Open daily 11am-11pm. ❷

Nicholas Restaurant, 318 SE Grand Ave. (☎235-5123; www.nicholasrestaurant.com), between Oak and Pine, opposite Miller Paint. Bus #6 to the Andy and Bax stop. Phenomenal Mediterranean food in an authentic and relaxed atmosphere. The meat, vegetarian, or vegan *mezzas* ($8) are fantastic deals for both quality and quantity. Sandwiches $5-6. Open M-Sa 10am-9pm, Su noon-9pm. ❶

Palio Dessert and Espresso House, 1996 SE Ladd St. (☎232-9214), on Ladd Circle. Bus #10 stops right in front of the cafe, or walk south 3 blocks on SE 16th Ave. from Hawthorne. This tranquil cafe offers Mexican mochas ($2.50), espresso mousse ($4), and sandwiches (half $3.50-7). Open M-F 8am-11pm, Sa-Su 10am-11pm. ❶

◉ SIGHTS

PARKS AND GARDENS. Portland has more park acreage than any other American city, thanks in good measure to **Forest Park,** a 5000-acre tract of wilderness in NW Portland with a web of trails that leads through lush forests, scenic overviews, and idyllic picnic areas. Less than 2 mi. west of downtown, in the middle of the posh neighborhoods of **West Hills,** is mammoth **Washington Park,** with miles of beautiful trails and serene gardens. From there, take the MAX to the **Rose Garden,** the pride of Portland. In summer months, a sea of blooms arrests the eye, showing visitors exactly why Portland is the City of Roses. *(400 SW Kingston St. ☎823-3636. Open daily 5am-10pm. Free.)* Across from the Rose Garden, the scenic **Japanese Gardens** are said to be the most authentic this side of the Pacific. *(611 SW Kingston Ave. ☎223-1321; www.japanesegarden.com. Open Apr.-Sept. M noon-7pm, Tu-Su 10am-7pm; Oct.-Mar. M noon-4pm, Tu-Su 10am-4pm. Tours daily mid-Apr. to Oct. at 10:45am and 2:30pm. $6.50, seniors $5, students $4, under 6 free.)* The **Hoyt Arboretum,** at the crest of the hill above the other gardens, features 200 acres of trees and trails. *(44000 SW Fairview Blvd. ☎823-8733. Visitors center open M-F 9am-4pm, Sa 9am-3:30pm. Free guided tours leave from the visitors center Sa-Su 2pm.)* The largest Ming-style gardens outside of China, the **Classical Chinese Gardens** occupy a city block with a large pond and ornate decorations. *(NW 3rd and Everett. ☎228-8131; www.portlandchinesegarden.org. Open daily Apr.-Oct. 9am-6pm.; Nov.-Mar. 10am-5pm. $7; seniors, students, and ages 6-18 $6; under 6 free.)*

MUSEUMS. The **Portland Art Museum (PAM)** sets itself apart from the rest of Portland's burgeoning arts scene with the strength of its collections, especially in Asian and Native American art. *(1219 SW Park, at Jefferson St. on the west side of S. Block Park. Bus #6, 58, 63. ☎226-2811, ext. 4245 for info on new exhibits. Open Tu-W and Sa 10am-5pm, Th-F 10am-8pm, Su noon-5pm. Th-F closes at 5pm in winter. $15, students and seniors $13, ages 6-19 $6, under 5 free.)* The **Oregon Museum of Science and Industry (OMSI)** keeps visitors mesmerized with exhibits like an earthquake simulator chamber, an Omnimax theater, and the Murdock Planetarium. *(1945 SE Water Ave., 2 blocks south of Hawthorne Blvd., next to the river. Bus #63. ☎797-4000; www.omsi.edu. Open early June to early Sept. daily 9:30am-7pm; early Sept. to early June Tu-Su 9:30am-5:30pm. Museum and Omnimax admission $8.50, seniors and 3-13 $6.50, under 3 free. Omnimax ☎797-4640. Shows on the hr. Su-Tu 11am-7pm, F-Sa 11am-9pm. Planetarium ☎797-4646. Shows every 30min. 11am-3:30pm. $5. Combo ticket for museum, Omnimax, and either the planetarium or the submarine $18, seniors or ages 3-13 $14.)*

OTHER SIGHTS. The still-operational **Pioneer Courthouse,** at 5th Ave. and Morrison St., is the centerpiece of the **Square.** Since opening in 1983, it has become "Portland's Living Room." Tourists and urbanites of every ilk hang out in the brick quadrangle. *(701 SW 6th Ave. Along the Vintage Trolley line and the MAX light rail. Events hotline ☎223-1613. Music W noon-1pm.)* Downtown on the edge of the NW district is ◪**Powell's City of Books,** a cavernous establishment with almost a million new and used volumes, more than any other bookstore in the US. *(1005 W. Burnside St. Bus #20.*

☎ *228-4651 or 800-878-7323; www.powells.com. Open daily 9am-11pm.)* **The Grotto,** a 62-acre Catholic sanctuary, houses magnificent religious sculptures and gardens. *(Sandy Blvd. at NE 85th.* ☎ *254-7371; www.thegrotto.org. Open daily late May to early Sept. 9am-7:30pm; early Sept. to mid-Nov. 9am-5pm; mid-Nov. to late May 9am-4pm.)* The **Oregon Zoo** has gained fame for its successful efforts at elephant breeding. Exhibits include a goat habitat and a marine pool as part of the zoo's "Great Northwest: A Crest to Coast Adventure" program. *(4001 SW Canyon Rd.* ☎ *226-1561; www.oregonzoo.com. Open daily Apr.-Sept. 9am-7pm; Oct.-Mar. 9am-4pm. $9, ages 65 and up $7.50, ages 3-11 $6, under 3 free; 2nd Tu of each month free after 1pm.)*

🎵 ENTERTAINMENT

Portland's daily newspaper, the *Oregonian*, lists upcoming events in its Friday edition, and the free cultural reader, the Wednesday *Willamette Week*, is a reliable guide to local music, plays, and art. **Oregon Symphony Orchestra,** 923 SW Washington St., plays classics from September to June. On Sundays and Mondays, students can buy $5 tickets one week before showtime. (☎ 228-1353 or 800-228-7343. Box office open M-F 9am-5pm, in Symphony Season also Sa 9am-5pm. $17-76; "Symphony Sunday" afternoon concerts $10-15.) **High Noon Tunes,** at Pioneer Courthouse Sq., hosts rock, jazz, folk, and world music. (☎223-1613. July-Aug. W noon-1pm.)

Portland Center Stage, in the Newmark Theater at SW Broadway and SW Main St., puts on classics, modern adaptations, and world premiers. (☎274-6588; www.pcs.org. Late Sept. to Apr. $27-55. $15 youth matinee seats sometimes available for ages 30 and under.) The **Bagdad Theater and Pub,** 3702 SE Hawthorne Blvd., puts out second-run films and has an excellent beer menu. (☎225-5555, ext. 8831; www.mcmenamins.com. 21+.) Basketball fans can watch the **Portland Trailblazers** at the **Rose Garden Arena,** 1 Center Ct. (☎321-321; www.nba.com/blazers).

Northwest Film Center, 1219 SW Park Ave., hosts the **Portland International Film Festival** in the last two weeks of February, with 100 films from 30 nations. (☎221-1156. Box office opens 30min. before each show. $7, students and seniors $6.) Portland's premier summer event is the **Rose Festival** (☎227-2681; www.rosefestival.org), during the first three weeks of June. In early July, the outrageously good three-day ☒**Waterfront Blues Festival** draws some of the world's finest blues artists. (☎800-973-3378; www.waterfrontbluesfest.com. Admission $5 and 2 cans of food to benefit the Oregon Food Bank.) The **Oregon Brewers Festival,** on the last full weekend in July, is the continent's largest gathering of independent brewers, making for an incredible party at Waterfront Park. (☎778-5917; www.oregonbrewfest.com. Mug $3 (required to taste); tastings $2 each. Under 21 must be accompanied by parent.)

🅟 NIGHTLIFE

Once a rowdy frontier town, always a rowdy frontier town. Portland's clubs cater to everyone from the college athlete to the neo-goth aesthete.

▨ **Ohm,** 31 NW 1st Ave. (☎796-0909; www.ohmnightclub.com), at Couch under the Burnside Bridge, dedicated to electronic music and unclassifiable beats. Achieve oneness dancing in the cool brick interior or mingle outside. Tu Dahlia, W breakbeat and trance, Th spoken word, F-Sa often big-name live DJs. 21+. Cover $3-15. Open M-W 9pm-2:30am, Th-F 9pm-3:30am, Sa 9pm-4am, Su 9pm-3am. Kitchen open until 2am.

Laurelthirst Public House, 2958 NE Glisan St. (☎232-1504), at 30th Ave. Bus #19. Local talent makes a name for itself in 2 intimate rooms of groovin', boozin', and schmoozin'. Burgers and sandwiches $5-8. Free pool Su-Th before 7pm. Cover $3-6 after 8pm. Open daily 9am-1am.

HAIR OF THE DOG

Hidden among factories and behind one of the least pretentious facades of any brewery around, █ Hair of the Dog Brewing Company produces what might just be the best beer in a city known for its microbreweries. Let's Go took a tour of the small-scale brewery from co-owner Alan Sprints and got the skinny on the brewing process. These brews are superlative, and the experience is an essential notch on any microbrewery fan's belt. (4509 SE 23rd Ave. ☎ 232-6585; www.hairofthedog.com. Tours by appointment weekdays only. 12 oz. bottles $3, 1.5L "magnums" $10.)

LG: Do your beers ferment in bottles?
A: They do ferment in the bottles, but it's a very small refermentation, just enough to get bubbles... if you do any more than that the bottles will explode.
LG: But they mature like wine?
A: Yeah.
LG: What's the reason for that?
A: Higher alcohol content, more hops, and the bottle conditioning process...it's like champagne, where the product is naturally fermented. That's a better environment for the product to age.
LG: Does that prevent contamination?
A: Refermentation scavenges oxygen out of the liquid, and that helps stop failing and off-flavors that might occur in beer if it ages.

Brig, Fish Grotto, Fez, Red Cap Garage, Panorama, and **Boxxes,** 341 SW 10th Ave. (☎221-7262; www.boxxes.com), form a network of clubs along Stark St. between 10th and 11th. On weekdays the clubs are connected, but on weekends they are often sealed off—check at the door to see what's going on. Magic happens at the 23-screen video and karaoke bar. Brig (the dance floor extension of Red Cap) and Boxxes are gay clubs, while Panorama hosts the straight scene. Fez, a music venue, caters to a diverse crowd, and Fish Grotto, more a restaurant than club, serves seafood (entrees $15-18). Cover $2-5. Open daily 9pm-2:30am; Panorama stays open F-Sa until 4 or 4:30am.

EUGENE ☎541

Epicenter of the organic foods movement and a haven for hippies, Eugene has a well-deserved liberal reputation. Home to the University of Oregon, the city is packed with college students during the school year before mellowing out considerably during summer. The town's Saturday market, nearby outdoor activities, and sunny disposition make Oregon's second-largest city one of its most attractive.

⬛ 🛈 ORIENTATION AND PRACTICAL INFORMATION. Eugene lies 111 mi. south of Portland on I-5. The main north-south arteries are, from west to east, **Willamette Street, Oak Street,** and **Pearl Street. High Street Highway 99** also runs east-west and splits in town—**6th Avenue** goes west, and **7th Avenue** goes east. The **pedestrian mall** is downtown, on Broadway between Charnelton and Oak St. The numbered avenues run east-west and increase toward the south. Eugene's main student drag, **13th Avenue,** leads to the **University of Oregon (U of O)** in the southeast of town. Walking the city is very time-consuming—the most convenient way to get around is by bike. Every street has at least one bike lane, and the city is quite flat. *The Whitaker area, around Blair Blvd. near 6th Ave., can be unsafe at night.* **Amtrak,** 433 Willamette St. (☎687-1383; open daily 5:15am-9pm), at 4th Ave., treks to Portland (2½-3hr., 3 per day, $17-29) and Seattle (6-8hr., 3 per day, $37-62). Don't count on taking the third train at 12:44pm—it is regularly 5-10hr. late. **Greyhound,** 987 Pearl St. (☎344-6265; open M-Sa 6:15am-9:30pm, Su 6:15-10:45am and 12:30-9:30pm), at 10th Ave., runs to Portland (2-4hr., 9 per day, $18) and Seattle (6-9hr., 4 per day, $35). **Lane Transit District (LTD)** handles public transit. Map and timetables are at the LTD Service Center, at 11th Ave. and Willamette St. (☎687-5555; www.ltd.org. Runs M-F 6am-10:40pm, Sa 7:30am-10:40pm, Su 8:30am-7:30pm. $1.25, seniors and

under 18 $0.60. Wheelchair accessible.) **Taxi: E-Z Taxi**
☎341-1550. **Visitor Info:** 754 Olive St. (☎484-5307 or
800-547-5445; www.visitlanecounty.org. Courtesy
phone. Free maps. Open late May to early Sept. M-F
8am-5pm, Sa-Su 10am-4pm; closed Su early Sept to
late May.) **University of Oregon Switchboard,** 1244 Walnut St., in the Rainier Bldg., is a referral service for
everything from rides to housing. (☎346-3111. Open
M-F 7am-6pm.) **Ranger Station,** about 60 mi. east of
Eugene on Rte. 126, sells maps and $5-per-day park-
ing passes for the National Forest. (☎822-3381.
Open late May to mid-Oct. daily 8am-4:30pm; closed
Sa-Su mid-Oct. to late May.) There's **free Internet
access** at **Oregon Public Networking,** 43 W. Broadway.
(☎484-9637. Open M-F 1am-5pm, Sa noon-4pm.)
Post Office: 520 Willamette St., at 5th Ave. (☎800-
275-8777. Open M-F 8:30am-5:30pm, Sa 10am-2pm.)
Postal Code: 97401. **Area Code:** 541.

⌂⌂ ACCOMMODATIONS AND FOOD. The
cheapest motels are on E. Broadway and W. 7th Ave.
and tend toward seediness. Make reservations early;
motels are packed on big football weekends. The
◨**Eugene Hummingbird Hostel ❶,** 2352 Willamette St.,
is a graceful neighborhood home and a wonderful
escape from the city, with a book-lined living room,
vegetarian kitchen, and mellow atmosphere. Take
bus #24 or 25 south from downtown to 24th Ave. and
Willamette, or park in back on Portland St. (☎349-
0589. Check-in 5-10pm. Lockout 11am-5pm. Dorms
$16 with any hosteling membership, non-members
$19; private rooms from $30. Cash or traveler's
checks only.) Tenters have been known to camp by
the river, especially in the wild, woolly northeastern
side near Springfield. Farther east on Rte. 58 and
126, the immense **Willamette National Forest ❶** is full
of campsites ($6-16).

Eugene's downtown area specializes in gourmet
food; the university hangout zone at 13th Ave. and
Kincaid St. has grab-and-go options, and natural food
stores are everywhere. *Everything* is organic. ◨**Keystone Cafe ❶,** 395 W. 5th St., serves creative dinners
with organic ingredients. (☎342-2075. Famous pancakes $3.25. Open daily 7am-5pm.) ◨**Cozmic Pizza ❶,**
199 W. 8th Ave., has vegetarian, organic pizzas with
gourmet toppings and crust, and free wireless Internet access. (☎338-9333; www.cozmicpizza.com.
Open M-F 11am-11pm, Sa-Su 4-11pm.)

◙ SIGHTS. Every Saturday the area around 8th
Ave. and Willamette St. fills for the **Saturday Market,**
with live music and stalls hawking everything from
hemp shopping bags to tarot readings. The food
stalls serve delicious, cheap local fare. Next to the

LG: Are you more interested in
product consistency, or do you
prefer experimenting with different brews?

A: I enjoy when people like using
our beer for celebrating special
events and special occasions...it
makes me feel good. If it wasn't
for people that enjoyed drinking
the beer, brewing it wouldn't be
so much fun.

LG: What about the name of the
brewery, Hair of the Dog?

A: Originally, the term literally
referred to using the hair of a dog
that bit you to help heal the bite.
They'd chase a dog down, cut off
some of its hair, [then] wrap it
around the wound. And that
helped chase away the evil spirit.

LG: And that's also for a hangover?

A: Yes, the term later became
used in reference to curing a
hangover—drinking some of the
"hair of the dog" you had the
night before (more beer).

LG: Do these beers, having a
higher alcohol content, give drinkers a stronger hangover the next
morning?

A: All I know is we've generated
quite a few hangovers.

LG: Oh yeah...? [Feels forehead
and eyes the empty glass warily.]

A: Whether the hangovers are
worse or not, I don't know. It
depends on what you are used to
drinking. We only use quality
ingredients, so you should have a
quality hangover.

shopping stalls is the **farmers market,** where you can buy organic, locally-grown produce. (Open Apr. to mid-Nov. Sa 9am-5pm; June-Oct. also Tu 10am-3pm.) Take time to see the ivy-covered halls that set the scene for National Lampoon's *Animal House* at the **University of Oregon.** The visitor parking and info booth are on 13th Ave., the first right after the entrance off Franklin. Tours begin at the reception desk at **Oregon Hall.** (At E. 13th Ave. and Agate St. ☎346-3014; www.uoregon.edu. Tours M-F 10am and 2pm, Sa 10am.) A few blocks away, the **Museum of Natural History,** 1680 E. 15th Ave., at Agate St., shows relics from native cultures, including the world's oldest pair of shoes. (☎346-3024; http://natural-history.uoregon.edu. Open W-Su noon-5pm. Suggested donation $2.)

The *Eugene Weekly* (www.eugeneweekly.com) lists concerts and local events, and features the greater Eugene community. From June 24 to July 10, 2005, during the **Oregon Bach Festival,** Baroque authority Helmut Rilling will conduct performances of Bach's concertos. (☎346-5666 or 800-457-1486; http://bachfest.uoregon.edu. Concert and lecture series $16; main events $23-55.) The vast ◙**Oregon Country Fair,** the most exciting event of the summer, takes place in **Veneta,** 13 mi. west of town on Rte. 126. During the festival, 50,000 people enjoy 10 stages' worth of shows and 300 booths of art, clothing, crafts, herbal remedies, furniture, food, and free hugs. Most people park for free at Civic Stadium, at 19th and Willamette in Eugene. From there, free, wheelchair-accessible buses run every 10-15min. 10am-7pm. (☎343-4298; www.oregoncountryfair.org. Every year on the weekend after the 4th of July. Tickets F and Su $13, Sa $16.)

◪ OUTDOOR ACTIVITIES. Within a 1½hr. drive from Eugene, the McKenzie River has several stretches of class II-III whitewater, best enjoyed in June, when warm weather and high water conspire for a thrilling but comfortable ride. The Upper McKenzie is continuous for 14 mi. and can be paddled in 2-2½hr. **High Country Expeditions** (☎888-461-7233), on Belknap Springs Road about 5 mi. east of McKenzie Bridge, is one of the few rafting companies that floats the Upper McKenzie. (Half-day $50, full-day $75. Student and senior discounts.) The large, popular Cougar Lake features the Terwilliger Hot Springs, known by all as **Cougar Hot Springs.** Drive through the town of Blue River, 60 mi. east of Eugene on Rte. 126, and then turn right onto Aufderheide Dr. (Forest Service Rd. 19), and follow the road 7¼ mi. as it winds on the right side of Cougar Reservoir. (Open dawn-dusk. $3 per person. Clothing optional.)

East of Eugene, Rte. 126 runs adjacent to the beautiful McKenzie River, and on a clear day, the Three Sisters of the Cascades are visible. Just east of the town of McKenzie Bridge, about 70 mi. east of Eugene, the road splits into a scenic byway loop; Rte. 242 climbs east to the vast lava fields of McKenzie Pass, while Rte. 126 turns north over Santiam Pass and meets back with Rte. 242 in Sisters. Often blocked by snow until the end of June, Rte. 242 tunnels its narrow, tortuous way between **Mount Washington** and the **Three Sisters Wilderness** before rising to McKenzie Pass. The 26 mi. **McKenzie River Trail** starts 1½ mi. west of the ranger station (trail map $1). Parallel to Rte. 126, it winds through mossy forests and leads to two of Oregon's most spectacular waterfalls—**Koosah Falls** and **Sahalie Falls.** They flank Clear Lake, a volcanic crater now filled with clear waters. The entire trail is also open to mountain bikers and considered fairly difficult because of the volcanic rocks. A number of Forest Service campgrounds cluster along this stretch of Rte. 126. Ambitious hikers can sign up for overnight permits at the ranger station and head for the high country, where the hiking opportunities are endless.

▣ NIGHTLIFE. Come nightfall, bearded hippies mingle with pierced anarchists and muscle-bound frat boys in Eugene's eclectic nightlife scene. In the *Animal House* tradition, the row by the university along 13th Ave. is often dominated by fraternity-style beer bashes. ▓**Sam Bond's Garage,** 407 Blair Blvd., is a laid-back hangout in the Whitaker neighborhood. Live entertainment every night complements an always-evolving selection of local microbrews ($3 per pint). Take bus #50 or 52. (☎431-6603; www.sambonds.com. 21+ after 8:30pm. Open daily 3pm-1am.) **The Downtown Lounge/Diablo's,** 959 Pearl St., is a casual scene with pool tables upstairs and Eugene's most beautiful people shaking their thangs amid flame-covered walls downstairs. (☎343-2346; www.diablosdowntown.com. Cover $2-3. Open M-F 11am-2:30pm, Sa-Su 4pm-2:30am.) **John Henry's,** 77 W. Broadway, is Eugene's prime site for punk, reggae, and virtually any other kind of live music. Call or check the website for schedule and covers. (☎342-3358; www.johnhenrysclub.com. Open daily 5pm-2:30am.)

CRATER LAKE NATIONAL PARK   ☎541

The deepest lake in the US, the seventh-deepest in the world, and one of the most beautiful anywhere, Crater Lake is well worth a visit. Formed 7700 years ago in an eruption of Mt. Mazama, it began as a deep caldera and filled itself with centuries worth of melted snow. The circular lake plunges to a depth of 1936 ft.

From the visitors center at the rim to the **Sinnott Memorial Overlook** it is an easy 300 ft. walk to the park's most panoramic and accessible view. Above the lake, **Rim Drive,** which does not open entirely until mid-July, is a 33 mi. loop around the rim of the caldera. Trails to **Watchman Peak** (¾ mi., 1hr.), on the lake's west side, are the most spectacular. The strenuous 2½ mi. hike up **Mount Scott,** the park's highest peak (almost 9000 ft.), begins from by the lake's eastern edge. The steep **Cleetwood Cove Trail** (2¼ mi., 2hr.) leaves from the north edge of the lake and is the only route to the water. All trails give spectacular views of **Wizard Island,** a cinder cone rising 760 ft. from the lake, and **Phantom Ship Rock.** In addition to trails around the lake, the park has over 140 mi. of wilderness trails for hiking and cross-country skiing. Picnics, fishing (with artificial lures only), and swimming are allowed, but surface temperatures only reach 50°F. Park rangers lead free tours daily in the summer and periodically in the winter (on snowshoes).

A convenient base for forays to Crater Lake, **Klamath Falls** has several affordable hotels. The **Townhouse Motel ❶,** 5323 6th St., 3 mi. south of Main St., offers clean, comfy rooms. (☎882-0924. Cable TV, A/C. Singles $30; doubles $35.) Campgrounds abound near the lake. **Williamson River Campground ❶,** run by the National Forest Service, is 30 mi. north of Klamath Falls on U.S. 97 N. On the river, it offers secluded sites with one toilet and water. (Tents only, $6.) Where's **Waldo's Mongolian Grill and Tavern ❷?** Behind the samurai, next to the space ship! Actually, it's at 610 Main St., and will grill your choice of veggies and meats. (☎884-6863. Medium bowl $8.50. All-you-can-eat $10. Open M-Th 11am-11:30pm, F-Sa 11am-1am.)

Crater Lake averages over 44 ft. of snow per year, and snowbound roads can keep the northern entrance closed as late as July. Before then, enter the park from the south. The park entrance fee is $10 for cars, $5 for hikers and cyclists. **Amtrak** (☎884-2822; open daily 7:30-11am and 8:30-10:15pm) and **Greyhound** are both in Klamath Falls; from Main St., turn right onto Spring St. and immediately left onto Oak St. One train per day runs to Redding (4½hr., $26), while one bus per day rolls to Eugene (4½hr., $19) and then on to Portland ($42-48). **Visitor Info: Chamber of Commerce,** 507 Main St. (☎884-0666 or 800-445-6728; www.klamath.org. Open M-F 8am-5pm.) The **William G. Steel Center** issues free backcountry camping permits. (☎594-2211, ext. 402; www.nps.gov/crla. Open daily 9am-5pm.) **Post Office:** 317 S. 7th St. in Klamath Falls. (☎800-275-8777. Open M-F 7:30am-5:30pm, Sa 9am-noon.) **Postal Code:** 97604. **Area Code:** 541.

ASHLAND ☎ 541

Near the California border, Ashland mixes hip youth and British literary history, setting an unlikely but intriguing stage for the world-famous ▓Oregon Shakespeare Festival, P.O. Box 158, Ashland 97520 (☎482-4331; www.osfashland.org). From mid-February to October, drama devotees can choose from 11 Shakespearean and newer works performed in Ashland's three elegant theaters: the outdoor Elizabethan Stage, the Angus Bowmer Theater, and the intimate Black Swan. The 2005 schedule includes *Twelfth Night, Richard III, Love's Labours Lost,* and *The Tragical History of Doctor Faustus,* as well as several contemporary plays. Ticket purchases are recommended six months in advance. (In spring and fall $23-44; in summer $29-55. $5 fee per order for phone, fax, or mail orders. Children under 6 not admitted. Those under 18 receive 25% discounts in the summer and 50% in the spring and fall.) At 9:30am, the box office, 15 S. Pioneer St., releases any unsold tickets for the day's performances and sells 20 standing room tickets for sold-out shows on the Elizabethan Stage ($13). Half-price rush tickets are sometimes available 1hr. before performances. Backstage tours provide a glimpse of the festival from behind the curtain. (Tu-Sa 10am. $11, ages 6-17 $8.25, under 6 not admitted.)

In winter, Ashland is a budget paradise; in summer, hotel and B&B rates double, while the hostel bulges. Only rogues and peasant slaves arrive without reservations. ▓Ashland Hostel ❶, 150 N. Main St., is well-kept and cheery with an elegant air. (☎482-9217; www.ashlandhostel.com. Laundry and kitchen. Check-in 5-10pm. Lockout 10am-5pm. Dorms $21; private rooms $50. Cash only.) Campers should check out the free Mount Ashland Campground ❶, 20 mi. south of Ashland off I-5 at Exit 6. Follow signs for Mt. Ashland Ski Area through the parking lot. (7 sites with pit toilets and no drinking water. Can be snowy in June.)

The incredible food selection on N. and E. Main St. has earned the plaza a strong culinary reputation. The Ashland Food Cooperative, 237 1st St., stocks cheap and mostly organic groceries in bulk. (☎482-2237; www.asfs.org. Open M-Sa 8am-9pm, Su 9am-9pm.) If you're sick of the Man keeping you down, fight back at ▓Evo's Java House and Revolutionary Cafe ❶, 376 E. Main St., where the politics are as radical as the vegetarian burritos and sandwiches ($3.50-$5) are tasty. (☎774-6980. Open M-Sa 7am-5pm, Su 7am-2pm.) Morning Glory ❸, 1149 Siskiyou Blvd., deserves a medal for "most pleasant dining environment," earned either by the fireplace and bookcases or by the rose-covered porticos. (☎488-8636; www.morninggloryrestaurant.com. Sandwiches around $9. Open daily 7am-2pm.) Ashland's renowned nightlife concentrates around N. and E. Main St. Try the excellent microbrews at Siskiyou Brew Pub, 31 Water St., just off N. Main St. by the hostel. (☎482-7718. Occasional live music. 21+ after 9pm. Open M-Th 4-11pm, F-Su 3-11pm.)

Ashland is in the foothills of the Siskiyou and Cascade Ranges, 285 mi. south of Portland and 15 mi. north of the California border, near the junction of I-5 and Route 66. Visitor Info: Chamber of Commerce, 110 E. Main St. (☎482-3486; www.ashlandchamber.com. Open M-Sa 10am-6pm, Su 11am-4pm.) Ashland District Ranger Station, 645 Washington St., off Rte. 66 by Exit 14 on I-5, has info on hiking, biking, and the Pacific Crest Trail. (☎482-3333; www.fs.fed.us/r6/rogue. Open M-F 8am-1pm and 2-4:30pm.) Post Office: 120 N. 1st St., at Lithia Way. (☎800-275-8777. Open M-F 9am-5pm.) Postal Code: 97520. Area Code: 541.

WESTERN CANADA

> ⚠ All prices in this chapter are listed in Canadian dollars unless otherwise noted.

For every urban metropolis like Vancouver in Western Canada, there's a stunning national park or outdoor area, like Banff, Jasper, or Pacific Rim. Hikers, mountaineers, and ice climbers find a recreational paradise in the Canadian Rockies; the parks represent Western Canada's most consistent draw—and for good reason. They pack enough scenic punch, exhilarating thrills, and luxurious hostels to stun travelers of all ages. The region boasts prime fishing holes, renowned fossil fields, and centers of indigenous Canadian culture.

HIGHLIGHTS OF WESTERN CANADA

NATIONAL PARKS. Banff (p. 1051) and **Jasper** (p. 1053) in Alberta are two of the region's most beautiful parks. Pacific Rim National Park, BC, contains the **West Coast Trail** (p. 1043), with its isolated beaches and old-growth rainforest.

VANCOUVER. With its beautiful surroundings and Asian influences, Vancouver is a treat, but with everything at incredibly low prices, it is a budget traveler's playground.

BRITISH COLUMBIA

With stunning parks and vibrant cities, British Columbia (BC) is home to the world's third-largest movie production center and a huge tourism industry. This province has room for it all, though. At over $900,000km^2$ BC is over twice as large as California, and it borders four US states (Washington, Idaho, Montana, and Alaska), two territories (the Yukon and Northwest), and a province (Alberta).

🛈 PRACTICAL INFORMATION

Capital: Victoria.

Visitor Info: Tourism British Columbia, 1166 Alberni St., Vancouver V6E 3Z3 (☎800-435-5622; www.hellobc.com). **British Columbia Parks Headquarters,** www.bcparks.ca.

Drinking Age: 19. **Postal Abbreviation:** BC. **Sales Tax:** 7% PST, plus 7% GST.

VANCOUVER ☎604

Like any self-respecting city in North America, Vancouver boasts a thriving multicultural populace; the Cantonese influence is so strong that it is often referred to by its nickname, "Hongcouver." With the third-largest Chinatown in North America and strong showings by many other major cultures, visitors are never hard-pressed to find food or entertainment. Vancouver matches its cultural splendor with a lush, gorgeous setting and quick, easy access to outdoor adventures.

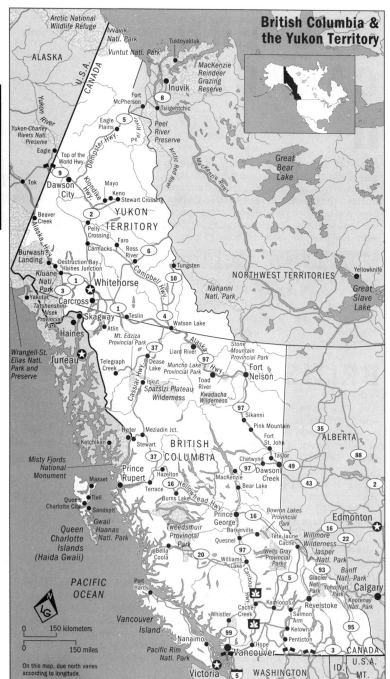

British Columbia & the Yukon Territory

⌐ TRANSPORTATION

Airport: Vancouver International Airport (☎207-7077; www.yvr.ca), on Sea Island, 23km south of the city center. **Visitors center** (☎207-1598). Open daily 8:30am-11:30pm. For downtown, take bus #424 and transfer to the 98 B-line. An **Airporter** bus (☎946-8866 or 800-668-3141) leaves from the airport to downtown hotels and the bus station. (4 per hr.; runs 6:30am-midnight; $12, seniors $9, ages 5-12 $5.)

Trains: VIA Rail, 1150 Station St. (☎888-842-7245, US 800-561-3949; www.viarail.com), runs eastbound trains. Open M, W-Th, Sa 8:30am-6pm; Tu, F, Su 9am-7pm. 3 trains per week to **Edmonton** (23hr., $288) and **Jasper** (17hr., $215).

Buses: Greyhound Canada, 1150 Station St. (☎683-8133 or 800-661-8747; www.greyhound.ca), in the VIA Rail station. Open daily 5am-12:15am. To: **Banff** (14hr., 5 per day, $116); **Calgary** (15hr., 5 per day, $133); **Jasper** (2 per day, $116). **Pacific Coach Lines,** 1150 Station St. (☎604-662-8074; www.pacificcoach.com), runs to **Victoria** every time a ferry sails (3½hr.; $30, includes ferry). **Quick Shuttle** (☎940-4428 or 800-665-2122; www.quickcoach.com) makes 8 trips per day from the Holiday Inn on Howe St. via the airport to: **Bellingham** (2½hr.; $22, students with ID $17); **Seattle** (4hr.; $33, students with ID $22); **Sea-Tac (Seattle-Tacoma) Airport** (4½hr.; $41, students with ID $29). **Greyhound USA** (☎800-229-9424 or 402-330-8552; www.greyhound.com) goes to **Seattle** (3-4½hr., $25).

Ferries: BC Ferries (☎888-BC-FERRY/223-3779; www.bcferries.com) connects Vancouver to the **Gulf Islands,** the **Sechelt Peninsula,** and **Vancouver Island.** Ferries to the **Gulf Islands, Nanaimo** (3hr.; 4-8 per day; $10, low-season $8.25; cars $38; reservations required), and **Victoria** (1½hr.; 8-16 per day; $11; bikes $2.50, cars $36) leave from the **Tsawwassen Terminal,** 25km south of the city center (take Hwy. 99 to Hwy. 17). To reach downtown from Tsawwassen by bus (1hr.), take #640 "Scott Rd. Station," or take #404 "Airport" to the Ladner Exchange, then transfer to bus #601.

Public Transit: Coast Mountain Buslink (☎953-3333; www.translink.bc.ca) covers most of the city and suburbs, with easy access to the airport and the ferry terminals. The city is divided into 3 fare zones. Riding in the **central zone,** which encompasses most of Vancouver, costs $2. During peak hours (M-F before 6:30pm), it costs $3 to travel between 2 zones and $4 for 3 zones. During off-peak hours, all zones are $2. Ask for a **free transfer** (good for 1½hr.) when you board buses. **Day passes** $8/$6.

Taxis: Vancouver Taxi ☎871-1111. **Black Top Cabs** ☎731-1111. 24hr.

▓ 🛈 ORIENTATION AND PRACTICAL INFORMATION

Vancouver is in the southwestern corner of mainland BC. South of the city flows the **Fraser River,** and the **Georgia Strait** is to the west, separating the mainland from Vancouver Island. **Downtown** juts into the Burrard Inlet from the city's core; **Stanley Park** goes farther north. The **Lions Gate Bridge** over Burrard Inlet links Stanley Park with North and West Vancouver, known as **West Van.** The two are known as the **North Shore.** The bridges over False Creek south of downtown link it with **Kitsilano ("Kits")** and the rest of the city. West of Burrard St. is the **West Side** or **West End.** **Gastown** and **Chinatown** are east of downtown. The **University of British Columbia (UBC)** lies on the west end of Kits on Point Grey. The **Trans-Canada Highway** (Hwy. 1) enters town from the east, and **Highway 99** runs north-south.

Visitor Info: 200 Burrard St., plaza level (☎683-2000; www.tourismvancouver.com). BC-wide info on hotels and activities. Open daily 8:30am-6pm.

GLBT Resources: The Centre, 1170 Bute St. (☎684-5307; www.lgtbcentrevancouver.com), has info and counseling M-F 9am-5pm. *Xtra West* is a gay/lesbian biweekly.

Hotlines: Crisis Center, ☎872-3311. **Rape Crisis Center,** ☎255-6344. Both 24hr.

Medical Services: Vancouver General Hospital, 855 W. 12th Ave. (☎875-4111). **UBC Hospital,** 2211 Westbrook Mall (☎822-7121), on the UBC campus.

Internet Access: At the library, 350 W. Georgia St. (☎331-3600; www.vpl.vancouver.bc.ca). Free Internet access. Open M-Th 10am-9pm, F-Sa 10am-6pm, Su 1-5pm.

Post Office: 349 W. Georgia St. (☎662-5725). Open M-F 8am-5:30pm. **Postal Code:** V6B 3P7. **Area Code:** 604.

ACCOMMODATIONS

■ **Vancouver Hostel Downtown (HI),** 1114 Burnaby St. (☎684-4565 or 888-203-4302), in the West End. A sleek 225-bed facility between downtown, the beach, and Stanley Park. Internet ($4 per hr.), library, kitchen. Pub crawls W and F. Reception 24hr. Reservations recommended June-Sept. Dorms June-Sept. $26; nonmembers $29; Oct.-May $20/$24. Private doubles June-Sept. $63, nonmembers $72; Oct.-May $59/$68. ●

■ **SameSun Hostel** 1018 Granville St. (☎682-8226 or 888-844-7875; www.samesun.com), on the corner of Nelson. They give $5 refunds on taxis from the train station. Laid-back, technicolor hangout by great nightlife. Internet, pool table, free lockers, laundry ($2 per load). $23, nonmembers $27; doubles $53/$60, with bath $60/$65. ●

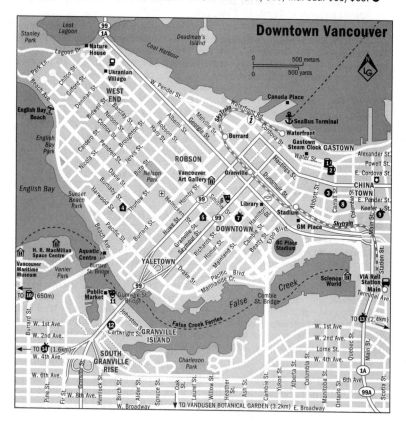

Downtown Vancouver

Vancouver Hostel Jericho Beach (HI), 1515 Discovery St. (☎224-3208 or 888-203-4303), in Jericho Beach Park. Follow 4th Ave. west past Alma and go right at the fork. Bus #4 from Granville St. Free linen, kitchen, TV room, laundry, and cafe (breakfast $6; dinner $7-8). Open May-Sept. $19, nonmembers $23; family rooms $50-60. ❶

🍴 FOOD

🌿 **The Naam,** 2724 W. 4th Ave. (☎738-7151; www.thenaam.com), at MacDonald St. Bus #4 or 7 from Granville Mall. Diverse vegetarian menu with great prices. Crying Tiger Thai stir-fry $9; dairy-free ice cream $3.50. Live music nightly 7-10pm. Open 24hr. ❷

🌿 **Subeez Cafe,** 891 Homer St. (☎687-6107), at Smithe, downtown. Serves hipster kids in a cavernous setting. Eclectic menu, from vegetarian *gyoza* ($8) to organic beef burgers ($10), complements a hefty wine list and home-spun beats (DJs W and F-Sa 9pm-midnight). Entrees $7-15. Open M-F 11:30am-1am, Sa 11am-1am, Su 11am-midnight. ❷

Hon's Wun-Tun House, 268 Keefer St. (☎604-688-0871). Over 300 options make reading the menu last as long as dinner at this award-winning Cantonese noodle house (bowls $4-8). Open Su-Th 8:30am-9pm, F-Sa 8:30am-10pm. Cash only. ❶

Mongolian Teriyaki, 1918 Commercial Dr. (☎253-5607). Diners fill a bowl with meats, veggies, sauces, and noodles, and the chefs fry everything and serve it with miso soup, rice, and salad for $4 (large bowl $6). Take-out menu. Open daily 11am-9:30pm.

👁 SIGHTS

DOWNTOWN. The 🎨**Vancouver Art Gallery** has fabulous exhibitions and a varied collection of contemporary art. *(750 Hornby St., in Robson Sq. ☎662-4700; www.vanartgallery.bc.ca. Open Apr.-Oct. M-W and F-Su 10am-5:30pm, Th 10am-9pm; call for hours Nov.-Mar. $15, seniors $11, students $10, under 12 free; Th 5-9pm pay-what-you-can; 2-for-1 HI discount.)*

GARDENS. The city's temperate climate, which includes ample rain, allows flora to flourish. Locals take great pride in their private gardens and public parks, and green spaces showcase plant life. Some 55 acres of former golf course have been converted into the immense 🌳**VanDusen Botanical Garden,** showcasing 7500 taxa from six continents. An international **sculpture** collection is interspersed among the plants, while over 60 species of birds can be seen in areas like the Fragrance Garden, Bonsai House, or Elizabethan Maze, which is planted with 3000 pyramidal cedars. The **Flower and Garden Show** is the first weekend of June. *(5251 Oak St., at W. 37th. Take #17 "Oak" bus to W. 37th and Oak. ☎257-8665. Free parking. Open daily June-Aug. 10am-9pm; Sept. 10am-8pm; Oct.-Mar. 10am-4pm; Apr. 10am-6pm. Apr.-Aug. $7.50, ages 65 and older $5.20, ages 13-18 $6, ages 6-12 $4; families $17. Call for Sept.-Mar. rates. Wheelchair accessible.)* Journey from tropics to desert in 100 paces inside the **Bloedel Floral and Bird Conservatory,** a triodetic geodesic dome, made of plexiglass and aluminum tubing. The conservatory, a constant 18°C (65°F), is home to 500 types of plants and 150 types of birds, and provides great views of downtown. *(Center of Queen*

Downtown Vancouver

🏠 **ACCOMMODATIONS**
SameSun Hostel, **5**
Vancouver Hostel
  Downtown, **4**

🍴 **FOOD**
Mongolian Teriyaki, **13**
The Naam, **14**
Subeez Cafe, **7**
Hon's Wun-Tun House, **9**

🎭 **THEATRES**
Arts Club Theatre, **11**
Orpheum Theatre, **6**

🍸 **NIGHTLIFE**
The Irish Heather, **2**
The King's Head, **10**
Sonar, **1**

● **SIGHTS**
Dr. Sun Yat-Sen Classical
  Chinese Garden, **8**
Granville Island Brewing
  Co., **12**
World's Skinniest
  Building, **3**

ALSO SEE COLOR INSERT MAP

WESTERN CANADA

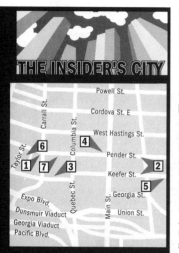

THE INSIDER'S CITY

VANCOUVER CHINATOWN

Savvy tourists should take a break from downtown's hotspots and experience the bustling urban scene of Chinatown, Vancouver.

1 Gawk at the impossibly narrow **Sam Kee Building,** said to be the narrowest in the world.

2 Barter, bicker, and haggle at the **Chinatown Night Market.** Open June-Sept. F-Su 6:30-11:30pm.

3 Let the tranquil **Dr. Sun Yat-Sen Classical Chinese Garden** (☎604-689-7133) ease your stress.

4 Recognize the history of Chinese Canadians at the **Winds of Change Mural.**

5 Choose from hundreds of meals at **Hon's Wun-Tun House** (☎604-688-0871). Open Su-Th 8:30am-9pm; F-Sa 8:30am-10pm. Cash only.

6 Visit the huge **Western Han Dynasty Bell.**

7 Explore the exhibitions at the **Chinese Cultural Center** (☎604-658-8865).

Elizabeth Park on Cambie and 37th Ave., a few blocks east of VanDusen. ☎257-8584. Open Apr.-Sept. M-F 9am-8pm, Sa-Su 10am-9pm; Feb.-Mar. daily 10am-5:30pm; Nov.-Jan. daily 10am-5pm. $4.10, ages 13-18 $3.10, seniors $2.90, ages 6-12 $2, under 6 free.)

UNIVERSITY OF BRITISH COLUMBIA (UBC). The high point of a visit to UBC is the breathtaking 🖾**Museum of Anthropology.** The high-ceilinged glass and concrete building houses totems and other giant carvings, highlighted by Bill Reid's depiction of Raven discovering the first human beings in a giant clam shell. (6393 NW Marine Dr. Bus #4 or 10 from Granville St. Museum. ☎822-5087; www.moa.ubc.ca. Open June-Sept. M and W-Su 10am-5pm, Tu 10am-9pm. $9, students and ages 65 and over $7, under 6 free; families $25; Tu after 5pm free.) Across the street, caretakers tend to **Nitobe Memorial Garden,** the finest classical Shinto garden outside of Japan. (☎822-9666; www.nitobe.org. Open daily mid-May to Aug. 10am-6pm; mid-Mar. to mid-May and Sept.-Oct. 10am-5pm. $3, ages 65 and older $1.75, students $1.50.) The **Botanical Gardens** encompass eight gardens in the central campus, including the largest collection of rhododendrons in North America. (6804 SW Marine Dr. ☎822-9666; www.ubcbotanicalgarden.org. Same hours as Nitobe Garden. $5, ages 65 and older $3, students $2. Dual ticket for both Nitobe and the Botanical Gardens, $6.)

STANLEY PARK. Established in 1889 at the tip of the downtown peninsula, the 1000-acre **Stanley Park** is a testament to the foresight of Vancouver's urban planners. The thickly wooded park is laced with cycling and hiking trails and surrounded by a popular 10km **seawall** promenade. (☎257-8400. To get to the park, take the #19 bus. A free shuttle runs throughout the park on the ½hr., late June to Sept. 10am-6:30pm.) The 🖾**Vancouver Aquarium,** on the park's eastern side, features exotic aquatic animals and skillfully replicates BC, Amazonian, and other ecosystems. Dolphin and beluga whales demonstrate their training and intelligence by drenching gleeful visitors. The new Wild Coast exhibit allows visitors to get a close-up view of marine life. (☎659-3474. Open daily July-Aug. 9:30am-7pm; Sept.-June 10am-5:30pm. $17; students, seniors and 13-18 $13; ages 4-12 $9.50; under 3 free.) The **Lost Lagoon,** brimming with fish, birds, and the odd trumpeter swan, provides a utopian escape from the skyscrapers. Nature walks start from the **Nature House,** underneath the Lost Lagoon bus loop. (☎257-8544. 2hr. Su 1-3pm. $5, under 12 free. Nature House open June-Aug. F-Su 11am-7pm.) The park's edges boast a few restaurants, tennis courts, a cinder running track with hot showers and a changing room, swimming beaches, and an outdoor theater, the **Malkin Bowl** (☎687-0174).

🎭🎵 ENTERTAINMENT AND NIGHTLIFE

The **Vancouver Symphony Orchestra** (☎876-3434; www.vancouversymphony.ca) plays September to May in the **Orpheum Theatre**, at the corner of Smithe and Seymour; you can tour the theater in summer. (☎665-3050. $5.) The VSO often joins other groups like the **Vancouver Bach Choir** (☎921-8012; www.vancouverbachchoir.com). The **Vancouver Playhouse Theatre Co.** (☎873-3311), on Dunsmuir and Georgia St., and the **Arts Club Theatre** (☎687-1644), on Granville Island, stage low-key shows. The **Ridge Theatre**, 3131 Arbutus, shows arthouse, European, and vintage film double features. (☎738-6311; www.ridgetheatre.com. $5.)

🍺 **The Irish Heather,** 217 Carrall St. (☎688-9779; www.irishheather.com). This 2nd-highest seller of Guinness in BC serves 20 oz. drafts ($6.10), and bangers and mash ($14). Live music Tu-Th. Open M-Th noon-11pm, F-Sa noon-midnight.

Sonar, 66 Water St. (☎683-6695; www.sonar.bc.ca). A popular beat factory. Pints $3.75-5. W house, F techno, and Sa hip-hop. Open W 9pm-2am, F-Sa 9pm-3am

The King's Head, 1618 Yew St. (☎738-6966), at 1st St., in Kitsilano. Cheap food and drinks, chill atmosphere, and a great location. Daily specials, $3.50 pints. Bands play nightly acoustic sets. Open M-F 9am-1am, Sa 8am-1am, Su 8am-midnight.

WHISTLER   ☎604

Thirty-three lifts (15 of them high-speed), three glaciers, over 200 marked trails, a mile (1609m) of vertical drop, and unreal scenery make **Whistler Blackcomb** a top destination for skiers and boarders. Whistler Creekside offers shorter lines and the closest access for those coming from Vancouver. (☎800-766-0449; www.whistlerblackcomb.com. Lift tickets $45-71 per day. Multi-day packages available.) A **Fresh Tracks** upgrade ($15), available daily at 7am, offers breakfast in Blackcomb's mountaintop lodge and the opportunity to begin skiing as soon as the ski patrol has finished avalanche control. Most **snowboarders** prefer the younger Blackcomb for its natural quarter-pipes and 16-acre terrain park. Endless **backcountry skiing** is accessible from resort lifts and in Garibaldi Park's **Diamond Head** area.

The gorgeous lakeside 🏠**Whistler Hostel (HI)** ❶, 5678 Alta Lake Rd., lies 5km south of Whistler Village on Hwy. 99. (☎932-5492. Dorms $20; nonmembers $24.) The **Fireside Lodge** ❶, 2117 Nordic Dr., 3km south of the village, offers funky bedrooms with a mammoth kitchen, lounge, sauna, and game room. (☎932-4545; www.firesidelodge.org. Dorms $21; private rooms from $80.)

Whistler Sky to Ski (☎932-5031 or 800-661-8747; www.whistlerbus.com) runs to Vancouver from the **Village Bus Loop** (2½hr., 6 per day, $18). You can find **visitor info** in the heart of the village, (☎931-3977; www.mywhistler.com; open daily 9am-6pm), and the **post office** in the Market Place Mall. (☎932-5012. Open M-F 8:30am-5:30pm, Sa 8:30am-12:30pm.) **Postal Code:** V0N 1B4. **Area Code:** 604.

VICTORIA   ☎250

Clean, polite, and tourist-friendly, Victoria is a homier alternative to cosmopolitan Vancouver. Although many tourist operations would have you believe that Victoria fell off Great Britain in a neat little chunk, its High Tea tradition began in the 1950s to draw tourists. Double-decker buses motor past native art galleries, New-Age bookstores, and countless English pubs. Victoria also lies within easy striking distance of the rest of Vancouver Island's "outdoor paradise."

⚑ PRACTICAL INFORMATION. Victoria surrounds the **Inner Harbour;** the main north-south streets are **Government** and **Douglas Street.** To the north, Douglas St. becomes Hwy. 1, which runs north to Nanaimo. **Blanshard Street,** one block to the east, becomes Hwy. 17. The **E&N Railway,** 450 Pandora St. (☎800-561-8630), near the Inner Harbour at the Johnson St. Bridge, runs daily to Nanaimo (2½hr.; $23, students with ISIC $15). **Gray Line,** 700 Douglas St. (☎800-318-0818), at Belleville St., and its affiliates, **Pacific** and **Island Coach Lines,** run buses to: Nanaimo (2½hr., 6 per day, $19); Port Hardy (9hr., 1-2 per day, $95); Vancouver (3½hr., 8-14 per day, $31). **BC Ferries** (☎888-223-3779; www.bcferries.com) depart Swartz Bay to Vancouver's Tsawwassen terminal (1½hr.; 8-16 per day; $9-11, bikes $2.50, car and driver $26-36), and to the Gulf Islands. **Victoria Clipper's** (☎800-888-2535; www.victoriaclipper.com) ferries travel to Seattle (2-3hr.; May-Sept. 2-4 per day, Oct.-Apr. 1 per day; US$64-79). **Victoria Taxi** (☎383-7111; www.victoriataxi.com) serves the city. **Tourism Victoria,** 812 Wharf St., at Government St, has info. (☎953-2033. Open daily July-Aug. 8:30am-6:30pm; Sept.-June 9am-5pm.) The **post office** is at 621 Discovery St. (☎963-1350. Open M-F 8am-6pm.) **Postal Code:** V8W 2L9. **Area Code:** 250.

⚐ ACCOMMODATIONS. The colorful ⬛**Ocean Island Backpackers Inn ❶,** 791 Pandora St., downtown, boasts a better lounge than most clubs, tastier food than most restaurants, and accommodations comparable to most hotels. This is undoubtedly one of the finest urban hostels in Canada. (☎385-1788 or 888-888-4180; www.oceanisland.com. Laundry, Internet access. Parking $5. Depending on the time of year, dorms $18-23, students and HI members $18-20; singles $25-36.) To reach the **The Cat's Meow ❶,** 1316 Grant St., take bus #22 to Fernwood and Grant St. A mini-hostel three blocks from downtown, it offers free parking, discounts on kayaking and whale watching, and complimentary breakfast. (☎595-8878. $20; private rooms $44-48.) **Goldstream Provincial Park ❶,** 2930 Trans-Canada Hwy., 20km northwest of Victoria, offers a forested riverside area with great hiking trails and swimming. (☎391-2300 or 800-689-9025. Toilets and firewood. $20.)

⚎⚏ FOOD AND NIGHTLIFE. Diverse food options exist in Victoria, if you know where to go; ask locals, or wander through downtown. **Chinatown** extends from Fisgard and Government St. to the northwest. Cook St. Village, between McKenzie and Park St., offers an eclectic mix of creative restaurants. ⬛**John's Place ❷,** 723 Pandora St., is a hopping joint serving wholesome Canadian fare with Thai and Mediterranean influences. (☎389-0711. Entrees $10-15. Open M-Th 7am-9pm, F 7am-10pm, Sa 8am-4pm and 5-10pm, Su 8am-4pm and 5-9pm.) A trip to Victoria is just not done without a spot of tea. The Sunday High Tea ($11) at the **James Bay Tea Room & Restaurant ❷,** 332 Menzies St., behind the Parliament Buildings, is lower-key and significantly less expensive than the famous High Tea at the Empress Hotel. (☎382-8282. Open M-Sa 7am-5pm, Su 8am-5pm.) The free weekly *Monday Magazine* lists venues and performers. At night, **Steamers Public House,** 570 Yates St., attracts a young dancing crowd. (☎381-4340. Open stage M, jazz night Tu. Open M-Tu 11:30am-1am, W-Su 11:30am-2am.)

⚏⚒ SIGHTS AND OUTDOOR ACTIVITIES. For excellent exhibits on the province's biological, geological, and cultural history, check out the ⬛**Royal British Columbia Museum,** 675 Belleville St. (☎356-7226; www.royalmuseum.bc.ca. Open daily 9am-5pm. $11; students, ages 65 and older, or 6-18 $7.70; under 6 free. IMAX 9am-9pm. With museum entrance $19, students $18, ages 65 and older or 6-18 $16, 6 and under $5.) Unwind with an educational, alcoholic tour of the **Vancouver Island Brewery,** 2330 Government St. (☎361-0007; www.vanis-landbrewery.com. 1hr. tours F-Sa 3pm. $6 for four 4-oz. samples and souvenir pint glass. 19+ to taste.) The elaborate landscaping of the ☒**Butchart Gardens** includes gardens, fountains, and wheelchair-accessible paths. (☎652-4422; www.butchartgardens.com. Bus #75 "Central Saanich" runs from downtown. Open daily mid-June to Aug. 9am-10:30pm. $21, ages 13-17 $11, ages 5-12 $2, under 5 free. The **Gray Line** (☎388-6539) runs a package from downtown that includes round-trip transportation and admission to gardens. $55, youth $44, children $20.) Mountain bikers can tackle the **Galloping Goose,** a 100km trail beginning downtown and continuing to the west coast of the island through towns, rainforests, and canyons. **Ocean River Sports** offers kayak rentals, tours, and lessons. (☎381-4233 or 800-909-4233; www.oceanriver.com. Open M-Th and Sa 9am-5:30pm, F 9:30am-8pm, Su 11am-5pm. Single kayak $42 per day, double $50.) Many whale-watching outfits give 10% discounts for hostel guests. **Ocean Explorations,** 602 Broughton St., runs 3hr. expeditions. (☎383-6722. Apr.-Oct. $70, students $60, children $49; less during low-season.)

PACIFIC RIM NATIONAL PARK RESERVE   ☎250

The Pacific Rim National Park stretches along a 150km sliver of Vancouver Island's Pacific coast. The region's frequent downpours create a lush landscape rich in both marine and terrestrial life. Hikers trek through enormous red cedar trees while beaches on the open ocean draw bathers, kayakers, and surfers.

A winding, 1½hr. drive up Hwy. 14 from Hwy. 1 near Victoria lands you in **Port Renfrew.** Spread out in the trees along a peaceful ocean inlet, this isolated coastal community of 400 is the southern gateway to the world-famous ☒**West Coast Trail.** The other end of the trail lies 75km north, in Bamfield. The route weaves through primeval forests of giant red cedars and spruce, waterfalls, rocky slopes, and rugged beach. Exciting challenges lie at every bend, but wet weather and slippery terrain can make the trail dangerous. Hikers pay about $140 per person for access to the trail (reservation fee $25, backcountry camping $90 in summer, two ferry-crossings $14 each). If you only want to spend the afternoon roughing it, visit the gorgeous **Botanical Beach Provincial Park,** but be sure to go at low tide or you won't see much (info centers have tide charts).

☒**Whalers on the Point Guesthouse (HI) ❶,** 81 West St., in Tofino, was voted the best hostel in Canada by HI, and has a sauna, billiards, and harborside views. (☎725-3443; www.tofinohostel.com. Internet $1 per 10min. Check-in 7am-2pm and 4-11pm. $22, nonmembers $24.) Near Port Renfrew, adjacent to the West Coast Trail registration office, lies the **Pacheedaht Campground ❶.** (☎647-0090. First come, first served. Tent sites $15; RV sites $20.) The **Lighthouse Pub & Restaurant ❷,** on Parkinson Rd., serves tasty fish and chips. (☎647-5505. Open daily 11am-9pm.)

Seek out maps and info on the area and registration at one of the two **Trail Information Centers,** one in **Port Renfrew** (☎647-5434), at the first right off Parkinson Rd. (Hwy. 14) once in "town;" and one at **Pachena Bay** (☎728-3234), 5km south of Bamfield. Both are open May-Sept. daily 9am-5pm. **West Coast Trail Express** (☎888-999-2288; www.trailbus.com) goes daily from Victoria to Port Renfrew via the Juan de Fuca trailhead (2¼hr., May-Sept., $35); Nanaimo to Bamfield (3½hr., $55); Bamfield to Port Renfrew (3¼hr., $50); and from Port Renfrew or Bamfield to Nitinat (2hr., $35). Reservations are recommended, and can be made for beaches and trailheads. The **Juan de Fuca Express** runs a water taxi between Port Renfrew and Bamfield. (☎888-755-6578; www.islandnet.com/~jberry/juanfuca.htm. 4½hr., $85.)

ALBERTA

With its gaping prairie, oil-fired economy, and conservatism, Alberta is the Texas of Canada. Petrol dollars have given birth to gleaming cities on the plains, while the natural landscape swings from the towering Canadian Rockies down to beautifully stark badlands. With its legendary national parks, Banff and Jasper, Alberta is a year-round playground for outdoor adventurers.

PRACTICAL INFORMATION

Capital: Edmonton.

Visitor Info: Travel Alberta, P.O. Box 2500, Edmonton T5J 2Z4 (☎780-427-4321 or 800-252-3782; www.travelalberta.com). **Parks Canada** (☎888-773-8888; www.pc.gc.ca).

Drinking Age: 18. **Postal Abbreviation:** AB. **Sales Tax:** 7% GST.

EDMONTON ☎780

This popular destination hosts the Canadian Finals Rodeo, and is home to the world's largest shopping mall. Museums attract children and art lovers, while the Saskatchewan River valley draws hikers and bikers. A perpetual stream of music, art, and performers brings summer crowds to the self-proclaimed "City of Festivals." A happening strip on Whyte Ave. transforms Edmonton into an urban oasis near the overpowering splendor of the neighboring Rockies.

TRANSPORTATION

The city lies 294km north of Calgary, an easy but tedious 3hr. drive on the **Calgary Trail** (Hwy. 2). Jasper is 362km to the west, a 4hr. drive on Hwy. 16. Edmonton's streets run north-south, and avenues run east-west. Street numbers increase to the west, and avenues increase to the north. The first three digits of an address indicate the nearest cross street: 10141 88 Ave. is on 88 Ave. near 101 St. The **city center** is actually off-center at 105 St. and 101 Ave.

Airport: Edmonton International Airport (☎890-8382; www.edmontonairports.com) sits 29km south of town, a $35 cab fare away. The **Sky Shuttle Airport Service** (☎465-8515 or 888-438-2342) shuttles downtown, to the university, or to the mall for $13.

Trains: VIA Rail, 12360 121 St. (☎800-842-7245), is a 10min. drive NW of downtown in the CN Tower. 3 per week to **Jasper** (5hr., $145) and **Vancouver** (24hr., $270).

Buses: Greyhound, 10324 103 St. (☎420-2400). Open daily 5:30am-12:30am. To: **Calgary** (3½hr., 11 per day, $46); **Jasper** (5hr., 4 per day, $57); **Vancouver, BC** (16-21hr., 6 per day, $152); **Yellowknife** (22-28hr.; 1 per day M-F, fewer in winter; $210). Locker storage $2 per day. **Red Arrow,** 10010 104 St. (☎800-232-1958; www.redarrow.pwt.ca), at the Holiday Inn. Open daily 7:30am-10pm. 10% HI discount. To **Calgary** (3hr., 4-7 per day, $53) and **Fort McMurray** (5hr., 2 per day, $61).

Public Transit: Edmonton Transit (schedules ☎496-1611, info 496-1600; www.takeets.com). Buses and **Light Rail Transit (LRT)** run frequently. LRT is **free downtown** between Grandin Station at 110 St. and 98 Ave. and Churchill Station at 99 St. and 102 Ave. Runs M-Sa 5:30am-1:30am, Su 5:30am-12:30am. $2, ages 65 and older or 6-15 $1.75, under 6 free. Info booth open M-F 8:30am-4:30pm.

Taxi: Yellow Cab ☎462-3456. **Alberta Co-op Taxi** ☎425-0954.

Car Rental: Budget, 5905 104 St. (☎448-2000 or 800-661-7027).

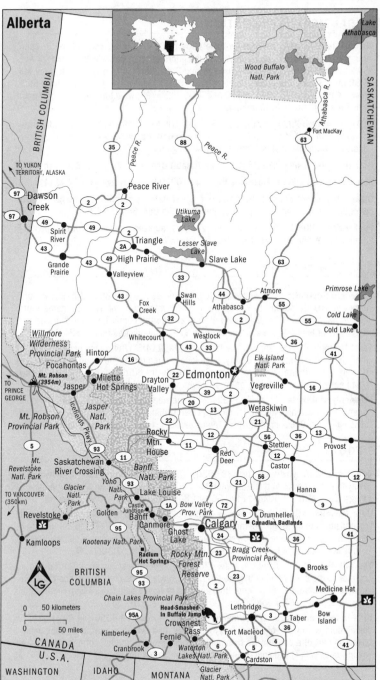

⚡ PRACTICAL INFORMATION

Visitor Info: Edmonton Tourism (☎ 496-8400 or 800-463-4667; www.edmonton.com/tourism), at **Gateway Park** on Hwy. 2, at the intersection of Gateway Blvd. and 24 Ave. SW, south of town. Open daily June to mid-Sept. 8am-8pm; mid-Sept. to May M-F 8:30am-4:30pm, Sa-Su 9am-5pm. Also at 9990 Jasper Ave. Open M-F 9am-5pm. **Travel Alberta** (☎ 427-4321 or 800-ALBERTA/252-3782; www.travelalberta.com) open M-F 7am-7pm, Sa-Su 8:30am-5pm.

GLBT Resources: Pride Centre, Ste. 45, 9912 106 St. (☎ 488-3234; www.pridecentreofedmonton.org). Open M-F 7-10pm. **Womonspace** (☎ 482-1794; www.gaycanada.com/womonspace) is Edmonton's lesbian group.

Hotlines: Crisis Line ☎ 482-4357. **Sexual Assault Centre** ☎ 423-4121. Both 24hr.

Medical Services: Royal Alexandra Hospital, 10240 Kingsway Ave. (☎ 477-4111).

Internet Access: Free at the library, 7 Sir Winston Churchill Sq. (☎ 496-7000; www.epl.ca); 1hr. per day. Open M-F 9am-9pm, Sa 9am-6pm, Su 1-5pm.

Post Office: 9808 103A Ave. (☎ 800-267-1177), adjacent to the CN Tower. Open M-F 8am-5:45pm. **Postal Code:** T5J 2G8.

🏠 ACCOMMODATIONS

🏨 **Edmonton International Youth Hostel (HI),** 10647 81 Ave. (☎ 988-6836). Bus #7 or 9 from the 101 St. station to Whyte Ave in a renovated convent. Kitchen, game room, lounge, laundry, and a small backyard. Just around the corner from the clubs, shops, and cafes of Whyte Ave. $22, nonmembers $25; semi-private doubles $24/$27. ❶

Saint Joseph's College, 89 Ave. (☎ 492-7681), at 114 St. The rooms here are smaller than those at the university. Library, huge lounges, rec room, and laundry, and close to University of Alberta sports facilities. Call ahead; the 60 dorms often fill up quickly. Open early May to late Aug. Singles $33, with full board $43. ❷

University of Alberta, 87 Ave. (☎ 492-4281), between 116 and 117 St. Generic dorm rooms. Dry cleaning, kitchen, Internet ($1 per 10min.), convenience store, and buffet-style cafeteria. Check-in after 4pm. Rooms available late May to Aug. Singles $36. ❷

🍴 FOOD

🍽 **Dadeo's,** 10548 Whyte Ave. (☎ 433-0930). Get spicy Cajun and Louisiana-style food away from the bayou at this 50s diner. M-Tu $7 po' boys. Su $4 for a pint or a plate of wings. Open M-Th 11:30am-11pm, F-Sa 11:30am-midnight, Su 10am-10pm. ❷

Cafe Mosaics, 10844 Whyte Ave. (☎ 433-9702), offers socially and environmentally responsible dining. Breakfast ranges from eggs and hash browns ($5) to the fresh fruit, granola, and yogurt bowl ($6). Vegetarian and vegan options available all day, and the coffee is fair trade ($1.25). Open M-Sa 9am-9pm, Su 11am-2:30pm. ❶

The Silk Hat, 10251 Jasper Ave. (☎ 425-1920). The oldest restaurant in Edmonton maintains the smoky feel of bygone days. This greasy spoon diner in the heart of downtown serves a huge array of food, from seafood to veggie burgers ($6.25). Breakfast all day. Happy hour M-F 4-6pm. Open M-F 7am-8pm, Sa 10am-8pm. ❶

Kids in the Hall Bistro, 1 Sir Winston Churchill Sq. (☎ 413-8060), in City Hall. This lunchroom is truly one-of-a-kind. Every employee, from waiter to chef, is a young person hired as part of a cooperative community service project. Various entrees ($5-10) and sandwiches ($5-7). Takeout available. Open M-F 8am-4pm. ❷

◉ SIGHTS

Another blow against Mother Nature in the battle for tourists, the world's biggest mall, the $1.3 billion **West Edmonton Mall,** engulfs the general area between 170 St. and 87 Ave. It has water slides, the world's largest indoor wave pool, an amusement park, mini golf, exotic animals, over 800 stores, an ice-skating rink, 110 eateries, a full-scale replica of Columbus's *Santa Maria,* an indoor bungee-jumping facility, a casino, a luxury hotel, a dolphin show, swarms of teenagers, and twice as many submarines as the navy. Just remember where you park. (☎444-5200 or 800-661-8890; www.westedmall.com. Bus# 1, 2, 100, or 111. Open M-F 10am-9pm, Sa 10am-6pm, Su 11am-6pm. Amusement park open later.) At the far end of **Fort Edmonton Park,** on Whitemud Dr. at Fox Dr., sits the fort proper: a 19th-century office building for Alberta's first capitalists, the fur traders of the Hudson Bay Company. Between the fort and the park entrance are three streets—1885, 1905, and 1920 St.—each with period buildings from apothecaries to blacksmith shops, decorated to match the streets' respective eras. (☎496-8787; www.gov.edmonton.ab.ca/fort. Buses #4, 30, 32, 104, 105, and 106 stop near the park. Open mid-May to late June M-F 10am-4pm, Sa-Su 10am-6pm; late June to early Sept. daily 10am-6pm; rest of Sept. wagon tours only M-Sa 11am-3pm, Su 10am-6pm. $9, ages 65 and older and 13-17 $6.75, ages 2-12 $4.50; families $29.) In the **Odyssium,** 11211 142 St., the Space and Science Centre appeals to all ages with exhibits like the bodily-function-themed **Gallery of the Gross** and a hands-on **Crime Lab.** In a building shaped like an alien spacecraft, the largest **planetarium dome** in Canada uses a booming 23,000 watts of audio during its laser shows. Canada's first **IMAX theater** makes the planetarium seem like a child's toy. (☎451-3344; www.odyssium.com. Open Su-Th 10am-5pm, F-Sa 10am-9pm. Day pass includes planetarium shows and exhibits: $10, students and ages 65 and older $8, ages 3-12 $7, families $39. General admission and IMAX show $16, students and ages 65 and older $13, ages 3-12 $11; families $60.)

❄ ♫ FESTIVALS AND ENTERTAINMENT

"Canada's Festival City" (www.festivalcity.ca) hosts some kind of celebration at any point in the year. The **Jazz City International Music Festival** offers club dates and free performances by international and Canadian jazz musicians. (☎432-7166; www.jazzcity.ca. June 25 to July 3, 2005. Concerts $15-90, most around $25.) **The Works,** a visual arts fest, is about the same time. (☎426-2122; www.theworks.ab.ca. Most events free, some $5-10.) In August, the **Folk Music Festival,** considered one of the best in North America, takes over Gallagher Park. (☎429-1899; www.edmontonfolkfest.org.) At the **Fringe Theater Festival,** top alternative music and theater pours from parks, stages, and streets. The high point of Edmonton's festival schedule, 500,000 travelers come to the city for the Fringe. (☎448-9000; www.fringetheatreadventures.ca. Mid-Aug.) The **Edmonton Oilers,** the local NHL franchise, are in an extended rebuilding period after their glorious Stanley Cup runs of the 1980s. But this is Canada, and even a rebuilding hockey team has a fierce following. The Oilers play at 11230 110th St. (☎451-8000; www.edmontonoilers.com. $35-147.)

◉ NIGHTLIFE

▨ **Blues on Whyte,** 10329 Whyte Ave. (☎439-5058). Cheap beer (pints $2.50-3) and live blues and R&B each night make this gritty bar an excellent hangout. 8 oz. beer $1. Sa jam 3-8:30pm. Cover $3 F-Sa from 8pm. Open daily 10am-3am.

Squires, 10505 Whyte Ave. (☎439-8594), lower level by Chianti. Popular with the college crowd. Specials include M $3 shots, W $0.17 ribs, Th $2.25 beer and highballs, F $4 Molson Coldshots. Open daily 5pm-3am.

The Armory, 10310 85 Ave. (☎432-7300). This well-known dance club shows Edmonton's younger crowd how to party. M is Ladies Night, with male strippers. Th $0.50 highballs until 10pm. Open M and Th-Sa 9pm-3am.

CALGARY ☎403

Mounties founded Calgary in the 1870s to control Canada's flow of illegal whiskey, but oil made the city what it is today. Petroleum fuels Calgary's economy and explains why the city hosts the most corporate headquarters in Canada outside of Toronto. As the host of the 1988 Winter Olympics, the city's dot on the map grew larger, and Calgary is now the second-fastest-growing city in all of Canada.

⌐ TRANSPORTATION

Flights: The **Calgary International Airport** (☎735-1200; www.calgaryairport.com) is 17km northeast of the city center. Take Bus #57. Taxi to downtown $30-40, but an Airport Shuttle (☎509-4799; www.airportshuttleexpress.com) runs from downtown for $14. Call or reserve at least 1½hr. ahead.

Buses: Greyhound, 877 Greyhound Way SW (☎260-0877 or 800-661-8747). To: **Banff** (1¾hr., 4 per day, $24); **Drumheller** (2hr., 2 per day, $26); **Edmonton** (3½-5hr., 10-11 per day, $46). Free shuttle from Calgary Transit C-Train at 7th Ave. and 10th St. to bus depot (1 per hr. 6:30am-7:30pm). **Red Arrow,** 205 9th Ave. SE (☎531-0350; www.redarrow.pwt.ca), goes to **Edmonton** (3hr., 4-7 per day, $53) and other northern spots. 10% HI discount; student and senior rates. **Brewster Tours** (☎221-8242), from the airport to **Banff** (2hr., 2 per day, $42) and **Jasper** (8hr., 1 per day, $80). 10% HI discount.

Public Transit: Calgary Transit, 224 7th Ave. SW (☎262-1000; www.calgarytransit.com). Open M-F 6am-9pm, Sa-Su 8am-6pm. C-Trains free in downtown zone on 7th Ave. S from 3rd St. E to 10th St. W. Buses and C-Trains outside downtown $2, ages 6-14 $1.25, under 6 free. Day pass $5.60, ages 6-14 $3.60. Runs M-F 6am-12:30am, Sa-Su 6am-11:30pm. Tickets at stops, the transit office, or Safeway stores.

Taxi: Checker Cab ☎299-9999. **Yellow Cab** ☎ 974-1111.

Car Rental: Rent-A-Wreck, 113 42nd Ave. SW (☎287-1444).

⚐ PRACTICAL INFORMATION

Visitor Info: 220 8th Ave. SW (☎800-661-1678; www.tourismcalgary.com). Open daily June-Sept. 9am-5pm; Oct.-May 9:30am-5:30pm.

GLBT Resources: Gay and Lesbian Community Services Association (events and clubs ☎234-9752, counseling 234-8973; www.glcsa.org).

Equipment Rental: Outdoor Program Centre, 2500 University Dr. (☎220-5038; www.ucalgary.ca/opc), at U of Calgary, rents tents (from $11), canoes ($23), and skis ($21). Open daily 8am-8pm. **Mountain Equipment Co-op,** 830 10th Ave. (☎269-2420; www.mec.ca), has watercraft ($20-55 per day, including all safety equipment and paddles), camping gear ($8-20), rock- and ice-climbing gear ($4-22), and snow sports equipment ($8-35). Both have weekend specials and required deposits.

Weather: ☎299-7878.

Medical Services: Peter Lougheed Centre, 3500 26th Ave. NE (☎943-4555).

Internet Access: At the library, 616 Macleod Trail SE (☎260-2600; www.calgarypubliclibrary.com). $2 per hr. Open June-Aug M-Th 10am-9pm, F-Sa 10am-5pm; Sept.-May also Su 1:30-5pm.

Post Office: 207 9th Ave. SW (☎974-2078). Open M-F 8am-5:45pm. **Postal Code:** T2P 2G8.

ACCOMMODATIONS

Calgary International Hostel (HI), 520 7th Ave. SE (☎269-8239), near downtown. Walk east along 7th Ave. from the 3rd St. SE C-Train station; the hostel is on the left just past 4th St. SE. This urban hostel has some nice accessories; the clean kitchen, lounge areas, laundry, and backyard with barbecue are pluses. Info desk, occasional guest activities. 120 beds. May to mid-Oct. $29, nonmembers $34; mid-Oct. to Apr. $20/$24. Private rooms $75/$83. Wheelchair accessible. ❶

Auberge Chez Nous, 149 5th Ave. SE (☎866-651-3387; www.auberge-cheznous.com). This distinctly French-Canadian hostel has large dorm rooms divided into cubicles, offering more privacy than a standard dorm. Kitchen, TV room, Internet access ($3 per hr.), laundry ($2). Reception 8am-3am. Dorms $25. ❶

University of Calgary, in the ex-Olympic Village in the NW quadrant, far from downtown if you're walking. Accessible by bus #9 or a 12min. walk from the University C-Train stop. Popular with conventioneers and often booked solid. Coordinated through **Cascade Hall,** 3456 24th Ave. NW (☎220-3203). Open May-Aug. Singles $36-56. ❷

FOOD

▨**Thi-Thi Submarine,** 209 1st St. SE (☎265-5452). Some people have closets larger than Thi-Thi, but this place manages to pack in 2 plastic seats, a bank of toaster ovens, and the finest Vietnamese subs in Calgary. Most meaty subs are sub-$5; the veggie sub is an unreal $2.25. Open M-F 10am-7pm, Sa-Su 10:30am-5pm. ❶

Elisabelle Resto-Bar, 137 5th Ave. SE (☎232-5499). Elisabelle serves breakfast ($4-6) until 11am and an American bistro-style menu afterward (entrees $6-8). Nightly drink specials include $3.50 pints and highballs. Open M-F 8am-10pm, Sa 9am-10pm. ❷

Lido Cafe, 144 10th St. NW (☎283-0131). Lido feels like a bit of an anomaly—a truck-stop-style restaurant in the trendy Kensington area. Breakfast special $3.88. Burgers $5. Open M-Sa 8am-9pm, Su 9am-8pm. ❶

SIGHTS

For two weeks in 1988, the world's eyes were on Calgary for the Winter Olympics. Almost 15 years later, the world has moved on, but the city still has its exciting facilities, and memory of Olympic stardom. Visit the **Canada Olympic Park,** a 10min. drive northwest of downtown on Hwy. 1, or on the #408 bus route from the Brentwood C-Train, and its looming ski jumps and twisted bobsled and luge tracks. The **Olympic Hall of Fame,** also at Olympic Park, honors Olympic achievements with displays and films. In summer, the park opens its hills, terrain park, and lift to **mountain bikers.** (☎247-5452; www.canadaolympicpark.ca. Open in summer daily 8am-9pm; in winter M-F 9am-9pm, Sa-Su 9am-5pm. $10 ticket includes chairlift and entrance to ski-jump buildings, Hall of Fame, and icehouse. Tour $15; families $45. Mountain biking open May-Oct. daily 9am-9pm. Roadway pass $9 for cyclists. Front-suspension bike rental $15 per hr., $35 per day.) Keep an eye out for ski-jumpers, who practice at the facility year-round. The miniature mountain (113m vertical) also opens up for recreational **downhill skiing** in winter. (Snow report ☎289-3700. $30.)

Footbridges stretch from either side of the Bow River to **Prince's Island Park,** a natural refuge only blocks from the city center. In July and August, Mount Royal College performs **Shakespeare in the Park.** (☎ 240-6908; www.mtroyal.ab.ca/shakespeare-in-the-park. Various matinees and evening shows; call for shows and times.) Calgary's other island park, **Saint George's Island,** is accessible by the river walkway to the east or by car, with parking off Memorial Dr. on the north side of the river. It houses the **Calgary Zoo,** including a botanical garden and children's zoo. For those who missed the wildlife in Banff and Jasper, the **Canadian Wilds** exhibit has recreated animal habitats. Life-sized plastic dinosaurs are also on display. (☎ 232-9300; www.calgaryzoo.ab.ca. Open daily 9am-5pm. $15, seniors $13, ages 13-17 $9, ages 3-12 $7.50.)

The more cosmopolitan Calgary becomes, the more tenaciously it clings to its frontier roots. The **Stampede** draws 1.1 million cowboys and tourists in the first couple weeks in July, when the grounds, just southeast of downtown, bordering the east side of Macleod Trail between 14th Ave. SE and the Elbow River, are packed for world-class steer wrestling, bareback and bull-riding, and pig and chuck wagon races. Check out the livestock shows, cruise the midway and casino, ride the roller coaster, or hear live country music and marching bands. The festival spills into the streets from first thing in the morning (free pancake breakfasts) through the night. (☎ 269-9822 or 800-661-1767; www.calgarystampede.com. $11, ages 65 and older and 7-12 $6. Rodeo and evening shows $23-67, rush tickets sold at the grandstand 1½hr. before showtime.)

▶ NIGHTLIFE

▨ **Cowboys,** 826 5th St. SW (☎ 265-0699; www.cowboysniteclub.com) is Calgary's premier country-western bar. The drink specials are unreal, including the famous Th $0.25 drafts. Cover $7. Open W-Sa 7:30pm-2:30am.

▨ **Ship & Anchor,** 534 17th Ave. SW (☎ 245-3333; www.shipandanchor.com). A popular soccer-oriented pub (during the World Cup, they open at 5am to catch the live action) that has more beers on tap (29) than any other bar in the city. Pints run $4.25-5.25. The pub grub is satisfying and cheap (burgers $4-6). Live music W night, open jam session Sa 2-6pm. Open daily 11am-3am.

Vicious Circle, 1011 1st St. SW (☎ 269-3951). A relaxing bar, "The Vish" offers a solid menu of health-conscious bar fare, colored mood lights, and a disco ball, plus pool tables, couches, a constantly changing gallery of eclectic local art, and TV. All kinds of coffee, a full bar, and 140 martinis ($7.60). Summer patio. Happy hour daily 4-7pm and all night Su. Live music W. Open M-Th 11:30am-1am, F-Su noon-2am.

▶ DAYTRIP FROM CALGARY

ALBERTA BADLANDS   ☎ 403

Once the fertile shallows of a huge ocean, the Badlands are now one of the richest dinosaur fossil sites in the world. After the sea dried up, wind, water, and ice molded twisting canyons into sandstone and shale bedrock, creating the desolate splendor of the Alberta Badlands. The **Royal Tyrrell Museum of Paleontology** (TEER-ull), with its remarkable array of dinosaur exhibits and hands-on paleontological opportunities, is the region's main attraction. **Greyhound** runs from Calgary to Drumheller (1¾hr., 2 per day, $26), which is 6km southeast of the museum.

The ▨**Royal Tyrrell Museum of Paleontology,** Hwy. 838 in Midland Provincial Park, has the world's largest display of dinosaur specimens. Head east on Hwy. 1 from Calgary then northeast on Hwy. 9. From the Big Bang to the present, the museum celebrates evolution with quality displays, videos, computer activities, and towering skeletons, including one of only 12 reconstructed *T. rex* skeletons in existence. (☎823-7707 or 888-440-4240; www.tyrrellmuseum.com. Open late May to early Sept. daily 9am-9pm; early Sept. to 2nd M in Oct. daily 10am-5pm; 2nd M in Oct. to late May Tu-Su 10am-5pm. $10, seniors $8, ages 7-17 $6, under 7 free; families $30.) The museum's hugely popular 12-person **Day Digs** include instruction in paleontology and excavation techniques, and a chance to dig in a fossil quarry. The fee includes lunch and transportation; participants must also agree that all finds go to the museum. (July-Aug. daily; June Sa-Su. Digs depart 8:30am, return 4pm. $90, ages 10-15 $60. Reservations required; call the museum.)

The Badlands, a UNESCO World Heritage Site, are the source of many finds on display at the Tyrrell Museum; more fossil species—over 300, including 35 species of dinosaurs—were discovered here than anywhere else in the world. The museum's **Field Station**, 48km east of the town of **Brooks** in **Dinosaur Provincial Park**, contains a small museum, but the main attraction is the **Badlands Bus Tour.** The bus chauffeurs visitors into a restricted hot spot of dinosaur finds. Many fossils still lie within the eroding rock. The park's **campground ❶** is shaded from summer heat, and grassy plots cushion most sites. Although it is open year-round, the campground only has electricity and running water in summer. (Field Station ☎378-4342. Follow Hwy. 56 south for 65km, then take Hwy. 1 about 70km to Brooks; once in Brooks, go north along Hwy. 873 and east along Hwy. 544. Field Station Visitor Centre exhibits $3, seniors $2.50, ages 7-17 $2. Open mid-May to Aug. daily 8:30am-9pm; Sept. to mid-Oct. daily 9am-5pm; mid-Oct. to mid-May M-F 9am-4pm. Tours $6.50, ages 7-17 $4.25. Campground ☎378-3700. Sites $15, with electricity $18.)

THE ROCKIES

Every year, some five million visitors make it within sight of the Rockies' majestic peaks and stunning glacial lakes. Thankfully, much of this traffic is confined to highwayside gawkers, and only a tiny fraction of these visitors make it far into the forest. Of the two big national parks—Banff and Jasper—Jasper feels a little farther removed from the crowds and offers great wildlife viewing from the road. Without a car, guided bus rides may be the easiest way to see some of the park's main attractions. **Brewster Tours** has an express bus from Banff to Jasper and offers tours at an additional cost. (☎403-762-6767; www.brewster.ca. 9½hr.; $98.) **Bigfoot Tours** does the trip in two days. (☎888-244-6673; www.bigfoottours.com. $175.)

BANFF AND LAKE LOUISE   ☎403

Banff is Canada's best-loved and best-known national park, with 6641km². of peaks, forests, glaciers, and alpine valleys. Itinerant 20-somethings arrive with mountain bikes, climbing gear, and skis, but a trusty pair of hiking boots remains the park's most popular outdoor equipment.

■❼ ORIENTATION AND PRACTICAL INFORMATION.

Hugging Alberta's border with BC, 129km west of Calgary, civilization in the park centers around the towns of **Banff** and **Lake Louise,** 58km apart on Hwy. 1. All of the following info applies to Banff Townsite, unless otherwise specified. **Greyhound,** 100 Gopher St. (☎800-661-8747; depot open daily 7:45am-9pm), runs to Calgary (1½hr., 5 per day, $24) and Vancouver (12½-15hr., 4 per day, $118). **Brewster Transportation,** 101 Gopher St. (☎762-6767), runs buses to: Calgary (2hr., $42); Jasper (5hr., $57); Lake Louise (1hr., $14). The **Banff Visitor Centre,** 224 Banff Ave., includes the **Banff/Lake Louise Tourism Bureau** and the **Canadian Parks Service.** (Tourism Bureau: ☎762-8421;

www.banfflakelouise.com. Parks Service: ☎ 762-1550. Open daily June-Sept. 8am-8pm; Oct.-May 9am-5pm.) The **Lake Louise Visitor Centre** is at Samson Mall in Lake Louise. (☎ 522-3833. Open daily June-Sept. 9am-7pm; Oct.-May 9am-4pm.) **Post Office:** 204 Buffalo St. (☎ 762-2586. Open M-W 8:30am-5:30pm, Th-F 8:30am-7pm, Sa 8:30am-5pm.) **Postal Code:** T0L 0C0. **Area Code:** 403.

▐▌ ACCOMMODATIONS AND FOOD. HI runs a **shuttle service** connecting all the Rocky Mountain hostels and Calgary ($8-90). Beds on the wait-list become available at 6pm, and the larger hostels save some standby beds. ▨**Castle Mountain Hostel (HI) ❶,** on Hwy. 1A, 1.5km east of the junction of Hwy. 1 and Hwy. 93, between Banff and Lake Louise, is a quiet hostel with running water, electricity, a general store, a library, and a fireplace. (☎ 670-7580 or 866-762-4122. Dorms $21, nonmembers $25; more on weekends). **Lake Louise Alpine Centre (HI) ❶,** 500m west of the visitors center in Lake Louise Townsite, on Village Rd., is more like a resort with a reference library, common rooms with beamed ceilings, a stone fireplace, two full kitchens, and a cafe. (☎ 670-7580. Dorms $27-34, nonmembers $31-38.) Two rustic hostels—**Rampart Creek ❶** and **Mosquito Creek ❶**—can be booked by calling Banff International Hostel. At Banff's park **campgrounds,** sites are first come, first served ($13-24). The only winter campsite is Village 2 of **Tunnel Mountain Village ❶,** 4km from Banff Townsite, on Tunnel Mountain Rd.

The Banff and Lake Louise Hostels serve affordable meals ($3-8), but **Laggan's Mountain Bakery and Deli ❶** (☎ 522-2017; www.samsonmall.com/lagganswin.htm), in Samson Mall in Lake Louise, is the best thing going. A thick sandwich on whole wheat costs $5-6; a fresh-baked loaf runs $3. **Aardvark's ❷,** 304A Caribou St., picks up after the bars close. The place is short on seating but serves thick slices of pizza. (☎ 762-5500. Slices $3; small pizza $7-10, large $15-22. Open daily 11am-4am.)

▞▌ OUTDOOR ACTIVITIES. A visitor on the paved byways will see only a tiny bit of the park and most of the park's visitors. Those interested in the endless outdoor options can hike or bike on over 1600km of trails; grab the free *Mountain Biking and Cycling Guide* or *Dayhikes in Banff* and peruse park and trail maps at info centers. The summit of **Tunnel Mountain** (2.3km, 2hr.) gives a dramatic view of the **Bow Valley** and **Mount Rundle.** Follow Wolf St. east from Banff Ave. and turn right on St. Julien Rd. to reach the head of the steep trail. At 2949m, Mt. Rundle is a more demanding hike (5.5km, 7-8hr., 1600m elevation gain). **Johnston Canyon,** about 25km from Banff toward Lake Louise along the Bow Valley Pkwy. (Hwy. 1A), is a popular half-day hike that runs past waterfalls to blue-green springs known as the **Inkpots.** The park might not exist if not for the **Cave and Basin Hot Springs,** southwest of town on Cave Ave., once said to have miraculous healing properties. The **Cave and Basin National Historic Site,** a resort built circa 1914, is now a museum. (☎ 762-1566. Open mid-May to Sept. daily 9am-6pm; Oct. to mid-May M-F 11am-4pm, Sa-Su 9:30am-5pm. Tours daily mid-May to Sept. 11am; Oct. to mid-May Sa-Su. $4, ages 65 and older $3.50, ages 6-18 $3.) For a dip in the hot springs, follow the sulfur smell to the 40°C (104°F) pools on Mountain Ave. (☎ 762-1515.)

The highest community in Canada, at 1530m (5018 ft.), Lake Louise and its surrounding glaciers have often passed for Swiss scenery in movies. Once at the lake, the hardest task is escaping fellow gawkers at the posh, though aesthetically misplaced, **Château Lake Louise.** Several hiking trails begin at the water, like the 3.6km **Lake Agnes Trail** and the 5.5km **Plain of Six Glaciers Trail,** both ending at teahouses.

Winter activities range from world-class ice climbing to ice fishing. Those 1600km of hiking trails make for exceptional **cross-country skiing,** and three allied resorts offer a range of **skiing** and **snowboarding** opportunities from early November to mid-May. **Sunshine Mountain** has the largest snowfall (☎762-6500 or 760-7669; www.skibanff.com; lift tickets $60), while **Lake Louise** has the most expert terrain (☎522-3555, snow report 762-4766; www.skilouise.com; $58).

SCENIC DRIVE: ICEFIELDS PARKWAY (HWY. 93)   ☎780

The 230km Icefields Parkway is one of the most beautiful routes in North America, heading north from Lake Louise to Jasper Townsite. Get free maps of the parkway at visitors centers in Jasper and Banff, or at the **Icefield Centre,** at the boundary between the two parks, 132km north of Lake Louise and 103km south of Jasper Townsite. (☎852-6288. Open daily July-Aug. 9am-6pm; May-June and Sept. to mid-Oct. 9am-5pm.) Although the center is closed in winter, the parkway only closes for plowing after heavy snowfalls. An extensive campground and hostel network along the parkway makes longer trips convenient and affordable. **Biking** the highway is a very popular option; rent bikes in Banff or Jasper for a one-way trip. Make sure to set aside time for hikes and vistas. At **Bow Summit,** the parkway's highest point (2135m), a 10min. walk leads to a view of the fluorescent aqua **Peyto Lake,** especially vivid toward the end of June. The **Athabasca Glacier,** a whale of an ice flow, spreads from the 200 sq. km **Columbia Icefield,** the largest accumulation of ice and snow between the Arctic and Antarctic Circles. **Columbia Icefield Snocoach Tours** carries visitors onto the glacier in bizarre monster buses for 1¼hr. trip. (☎877-423-7433; www.columbiaicefield.com. Open mid-Apr. to mid-Oct. daily 9am-5pm. $30, ages 6-15 $15.)

JASPER NATIONAL PARK   ☎780

Northward expansion of the Canadian railway system led to the exploration of the Canadian Rockies and the creation of Jasper National Park in 1907. The largest of the national parks in the region, Jasper encompasses herculean peaks and plummeting valleys that dwarf the battalion of motorhomes and charter buses parading through the region. In the winter, the crowds melt away, and a blanket of snow descends, and a ski resort welcomes visitors to a slower, more relaxed town.

⁊ PRACTICAL INFORMATION. All of the addresses below are in **Jasper Townsite,** near the center of the park. **VIA Rail,** 607 Connaught Dr. (☎888-842-7245), sends three trains per week to Edmonton (5hr., $155) and Vancouver (17hr., $215). **Greyhound** (☎852-3926), in the train station, runs to Edmonton (4½hr., 3 per day, $57) and Vancouver (10½hr., 2 per day, $116). **Brewster Transportation Tours** (☎852-3332), across from the station, runs daily to Calgary (8hr., $80) via Banff (6hr., $57). The **Park Information Centre,** 500 Connaught Dr., has trail maps. (☎852-6176. Open daily mid-June to early Sept. 8:30am-7:30pm; early Sept. to late Oct. and late Dec. to mid-June 9am-5pm.) **Post Office:** 502 Patricia St. (☎852-3041. Open M-F 9am-5pm.) **Postal Code:** T0E 1E0. **Area Code:** 780.

⁊⁊ ACCOMMODATIONS AND FOOD. HI runs a shuttle service connecting all the Rocky Mountain hostels and Calgary; call the Jasper International Hostel for reservations. The modern **Jasper International Hostel (HI) ❶,** 3km up Whistlers Rd. from Hwy. 93, also known as **Whistlers Hostel,** anchors the chain of HI hostels stretching from Jasper to Calgary. Jasper International attracts gregarious backpackers and cyclists, but a "leave-your-hiking-boots-outside" rule keeps the hardwood floors and dorm rooms clean. (☎852-3215 or 877-852-0781 for all HI hostels. Curfew 2am. Dorms $20, nonmembers $25.) **Maligne Canyon Hostel (HI) ❶,** 11km east of town on Hwy. 16, has small cabins on the bank of the Maligne River. (Check-in 5-11pm. Open Oct.-Apr. $13, nonmembers $18.) **Mount Edith Cavell Hostel (HI) ❶,** 12km up Edith Cavell Rd., off Hwy. 93, offers cozy quarters with wood-burning stoves. In winter, the road is closed, but pick up keys at Jasper International Hostel and ski there. (Propane, pump water, solar shower. Dorms $13, nonmembers $18.)

Most of Jasper's campgrounds have primitive sites with few facilities ($13-22). They are first come, first served, and none are open in winter. Call the park visitors center (☎852-6176) for details. Fire permits are $4. A 781-site behemoth, **Whistlers ❶**, on Whistlers Rd. off Hwy. 93, is closest to the townsite. (Open early May to mid-Oct. $22, full hookup $30.) The highlight of the Icefields Pkwy. campgrounds is **Columbia Icefield ❶**, 109km south of the townsite, which lies close enough to the Athabasca Glacier to intercept an icy breeze and even a rare summer night's snowfall. (Open mid-May to mid-Oct. $13.) ◪**Coco's Cafe ❶**, 608 Patricia St., is a small vegetarian-friendly cafe downtown. Homemade items include tasty soups, baked goods, smoothies ($3.50), and hearty breakfast wraps made with free-range eggs, served all day ($5.25). (☎852-4550. A variety of tasty sandwiches from $5. Open daily June-Oct. 7am-8:30pm; Nov.-Apr. 7:30am-5pm.)

⚠ OUTDOOR ACTIVITIES. The visitors center distributes *Day Hikes in Jasper National Park.* **Cavell Meadows Loop,** featuring views of the glacier-laden peak of **Mount Edith Cavell,** is a rewarding half-day hike. The trailhead is 30km south of the townsite; take Hwy. 93 to 93A to the end of the bumpy 15km Mt. Edith Cavell Rd. (Open June-Oct.) Or tackle the **Sulpher Skyline Trail,** a challenging 4-6hr. hike with views of the limestone Miette Range and Ashlar Ridge (9.6km round-trip, 700m elevation gain). The trail leaves from the **Miette Hot Springs,** 42km north of the townsite on Hwy. 16. (☎866-3939; www.hotspring.ca. Open daily mid-June to early Sept. 8:30am-10:30pm; May to mid-June and early Sept. to mid-Oct. 10:30am-9pm. $6.25, seniors and children $5.25. Swimsuit $1.50; towel $1.25.)

The spectacular, if overcrowded, **Maligne Canyon** is 11km east of the townsite on Maligne Lake Rd. From the trailhead, a 4km path follows the Maligne River as it plunges through the narrow limestone gorge, across footbridges, and eventually into Medicine Lake. Brilliant turquoise **Maligne Lake,** the longest (22km) and deepest lake in the park, sprawls at the end of Maligne Lake Rd. The **Opal Hills Trail** (8.2km loop) winds through subalpine meadows and ascends 460m to views of the lake. **Maligne Tours,** 627 Patricia St., rents kayaks and leads fishing, canoeing, rabbiting, horseback-riding, hiking, and whitewater rafting tours. (☎852-3370; www.malignelake.com. Kayaks $85 per day.) **Fishing permits** are available at fishing shops and the Parks Canada Visitors Center ($7 per day, $20 per year).

The **Jasper Tramway,** 4km up Whistlers Rd., climbs 1200m up Whistlers Mtn., leading to a panoramic view of the park and, on a clear day, very far beyond. (☎852-3093; www.jaspertramway.com. Open daily mid-June to July 8:30am-10pm; mid-May to mid-June and Sept. 9:30am-9pm; mid-Apr. to mid-May and Oct. 9:30am-4:30pm. $24, ages 5-14 $10, under 5 free.) The demanding 9km **Whistlers Trail** covers the same ground.

ALASKA

Alaska is a land of superlatives. The largest state in the US, and northernmost outpost of US civilization, it spans 591,004 sq. mi. on the edges of the world. It encompasses the tallest mountains, the most active glaciers, the highest concentration of grizzlies, the most punishing highways, the deepest temperate rainforests, the largest nonpolar icefields, rivers and streams churning with the most salmon, the longest hours of sunlight, the biggest vegetables, and the tastiest sourdough. Its population desnity averages only one person per square mile, the lowest in the US.

Disillusioned with the region's dwindling fur trade, Russia sold the region to the US for a piddling two cents per acre in 1867. Critics mocked "Seward's Folly," named after the Secretary of State who negotiated the deal, but just 15 years after the purchase, huge deposits of gold were unearthed in the Gastineau Channel.

Many say the Klondike gold rush of 1898 was only the first in the discovery of Alaska's precious commodities, from the "black gold" of the oil pipeline boom to the "ocean gold" pulled up in the form of king crab pots in the Bering Sea. Boom and bust has always been the state's reality, but travelers looking for adventure never fail to find it here. Alaska's natural beauty unfurls a mighty backdrop, calling pioneers to the "last wilderness" on earth. For more on Alaska and its wonders, check out ◼ *Let's Go: Alaska Adventure Guide 2004.*

> ### HIGHLIGHTS OF ALASKA
>
> **NATURAL WONDERS.** Denali National Park (p. 1059) is the state's crown jewel, while Glacier Bay National Park (p. 1066) basks in a symphony of sea and ice.
>
> **WILDLIFE.** Cruises in the Kenai Fjords National Park (p. 1058) give ample opportunity to view marine life. Grizzlies and black bears amble all over the state. Beware.
>
> **RECREATION.** Kayaking in Misty Fjords Monument (p. 1065) is an adventurer's dream come true.

⁊ PRACTICAL INFORMATION

Capital: I don't know...Juneau?
Visitor Info: State of Alaska Travel and Vacation Information, P.O. Box 110804, Juneau 99811 (☎907-465-5478; www.travelalaska.com). **Alaska Department of Fish & Game,** P.O. Box 25526, Juneau 99802 (☎907-465-4100; www.state.ak.us/adfg/adfghome.htm).
Postal Abbreviation: AK. **Sales Tax:** None.

◼ TRANSPORTATION

The **Alaska Marine Highway** remains the most practical and enjoyable way to explore much of the Panhandle, Prince William Sound, and the Kenai Peninsula. (☎907-465-3955; www.dot.state.ak.us/amhs). The **Alaska Railroad** covers 470 mi. from Seward to Fairbanks, with stops in Anchorage and Whittier (☎907-265-2300; www.akrr.com). Most of the state's major **highways** are known by their name as often as their number (e.g., George Parks Hwy. is the same as Rte. 3, which is the same as The Parks). Highways reward drivers with stunning views, but they barely scratch the surface of the massive state. For Alaska's most remote destinations, **air travel** is an expensive necessity. The state's major airline, **Alaska Airlines** (☎800-252-7522; www.alaskaair.com), links up major cities and towns in the state and connects Alaska with destinations all over North America.

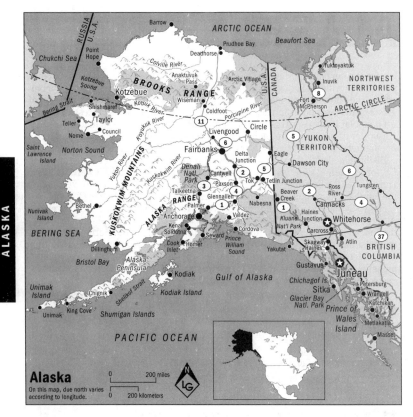

Alaska
On this map, due north varies
according to longitude.

0   200 miles
0   200 kilometers

ANCHORAGE

☎907

Anchorage, Alaska's foremost urban center, is home to 270,000 citizens—two-fifths of the state's population. As far north as Helsinki and almost as far west as Honolulu, the city achieved its large size (2000 sq. mi.) by hosting three major economic projects: the Alaska Railroad, WWII military developments, and the Trans-Alaska Pipeline. Anchorage serves as a good place to get oriented and stock up on supplies before journeying into the breathtaking wilderness outside.

TRANSPORTATION. Most Alaskan airstrips can be reached from **Anchorage International Airport** (☎266-2526); take International Airport Rd. to Minnesota Dr., then head north to downtown. **Alaska Railroad**, 411 W. 1st Ave., runs to: Denali (7½hr., $125); Fairbanks (12hr., $175); Seward (4½hr., summer only, $59). The low-season (Sept.-May) Aurora and Hurricane trains offer flagstop service; to flag a train, stand 25 ft. back from the rail and wave a white cloth. (☎265-2494 or 800-544-0552; www.akrr.com. Ticket window open M-F 5:30am-5pm, Sa-Su 5:30am-1pm.) Though the **Alaska Marine Highway** does not service Anchorage, their office at 605 W. 4th Ave. sells tickets and makes reservations. (☎272-7116, Juneau central reservations office 800-642-0066. Open in summer daily 9am-5pm; in winter M-F 10am-5pm.) **People Mover Bus,** headquartered in the Transit Center on 6th Ave. between

G and H St., runs public transit throughout the city. (☎343-6543. M-F 6am-11pm, Sa 8am-8pm, restricted service Su 9:30am-6:30pm. $1.50, ages 5-18 $0.75, seniors $0.35; day passes $3, monthly passes available.) **Taxi: Yellow Cab** ☎272-2422. **Affordable New Car Rental**, 4707 Spenard Rd., has rates from $39 per day with unlimited mileage. (☎800-248-3765; www.ancr.com. Open daily June-Aug. 6am-1am, Sept.-May 7am-10pm. Must be 22+, 25+ for SUV rentals.)

🛈 PRACTICAL INFORMATION. The **Log Cabin Visitor Information Center**, 524 W. 4th Ave., at F St., sells a guide to hiking and biking trails for $4. (☎274-3531. Open daily June-Aug. 7:30am-7pm; May and Sept. 8am-6pm; Oct.-Apr. 9am-4pm.) The **Alaska Public Lands Information Center**, Old Federal Building, 605 W. 4th Ave., Ste. 105, between F and G St., combines the NPS, USFS, State Parks, and Fish and Wildlife under one roof. (☎271-2737. Open in summer daily 9am-5pm; in winter M-F 10am-5pm.) **Internet Access: Loussac Library**, at Denali St. and 36th Ave., is a real architectural oddity. Buses #2, 36, and 60 stop out front; bus #75 stops at C St. and 36th is half a block away. (☎343-2975. Open in winter M-Th 10am-8pm, F-Sa 10am-6pm, Su 1-5pm; in summer closed Su. Free.) **Post Office:** 344 W. 3rd Ave. (☎800-275-8777. Open M-F 10am-5:30pm.) **Postal Code:** 99510. **Area Code:** 907.

🛏 ACCOMMODATIONS. Visitors can call **Alaska Private Lodgings** (☎888-235-2148; www.alaskabandb.com) for itinerary planning and B&B reservations, or the **Anchorage Reservation Service** (☎272-5909; www.anchorage-bnb.com) for B&Bs from $80. Guests take pride in the elegant kitchen and common area at the 🏠**Anchorage Guesthouse ❶**, 2001 Hillcrest Dr., and gladly earn their keep with a chore. Take bus #3, 4, 6, 36, or 60 from downtown or bus #7 from the airport; get off at West High School and go west on Hillcrest. (☎274-0408; www.akhouse.com. Bikes $2.50 per hr., $20 per day. Key deposit $5. Bunks $28; private rooms $78.) Originally a commune, the **Spenard Hostel ❶**, 2845 W. 42nd Pl., still retains its original character without sacrificing cleanliness. On Spenard, turn west on Turnagain Blvd., then left onto 42nd Pl., or take bus #7 or 36. (☎248-5036. Reception 9am-1pm and 7-11pm. Chores requested; free stay for 3hr. work. $18.) The clean and modern **Puffin Inn ❺**, 4400 Spenard Ave., has a range of rooms, continental breakfast, laundry services, and a 24hr. airport shuttle. (☎243-4044. Economy rooms with queen bed, phone, TV, shower mid-June to mid-July $129; mid-July to mid-Sept. $99; low-season $59. Larger moderate rooms $169/$139/$79; deluxe rooms with A/C $189/$159/$99. $10 AAA discount.) The Public Lands info center has information on camping; the **Eagle River Campground ❶** at Chugach State Park is 12 mi. north off of the Glenn Highway (☎694-7982; open May-Sept.; sites $15).

📇🍴 FOOD AND NIGHTLIFE. 🏔**Moose's Tooth ❷**, 3300 Old Seward, bus #2 or 36, serves pizza and beer as hearty as the climbers who tackle the nearby peak. Try the chicken ranch pizza. In summer, on the first Thursday of the month, Moose's Tooth introduces a new brew and celebrates with a live band. (☎258-2537. Open mic M 9-11pm. Open M-Th 11am-midnight, F-Sa noon-1am, Su noon-midnight.) **Sweet Basil Cafe ❶**, 335 E St., makes fresh-baked treats, juices and smoothies, and sandwiches on homemade bread. (☎274-0070. Open M-F 8am-3pm, Sa 9am-4pm.) Art-bedecked **Snow City Cafe ❷**, 1034 W. 4th St., at L St., is famous for the best breakfast in town and reindeer sausage. (☎272-2489. Live acoustic music W evenings. Open daily 7am-4pm, W also 7-11pm.) The Historic Alaska Art Tile Building, 817 W. 6th Ave., crafts solid sandwiches ($5-9), salads ($9-10), and veggie options ($5-8) at **Café 817/Muffin Man ❸**. Muffins and scones ($2) are baked daily. (☎279-6836. Open in summer M-F 7am-3pm, Sa-Su 7am-2pm; in winter M-F 7am-3pm.)

ALASKA

The brewpub revolution has hit Anchorage, and microbrews gush from taps like oil through the pipeline. Catch a flick with brew in hand at the **Bear Tooth Grill,** 1230 W. 27th Ave. (☎276-4200. Pints $3.75. Cover for movie $3. Call for showtimes.) The young and retro at **Bernie's Bungalow Lounge,** 626 D St., relax in one of many wing-back chairs as they sip $5 lemon drop martinis. (☎276-8808. Open daily in summer noon-2am; in winter 3pm-2am.) **Chilkoot Charlie's,** 2435 Spenard Rd., has cavernous dance floors and 10 differently themed bars. (☎272-1010. $1 drink specials M-F until 10pm. Cover $3-6. Open daily 10:30am-2:30am.)

◙ ♫ **SIGHTS AND OUTDOOR ACTIVITIES.** █Cyrano's Off Center Playhouse, 413 D St., between 4th and 5th, contains a cafe, bookshop, the **Eccentric Theatre Company,** and a cinema screening foreign and art films. (☎274-2599. Shows in summer M-Tu and F-Su 7pm; in winter Th-Su 7pm. Tickets $15, students $10.) With a huge collection of native, national, and international artwork and a gallery on Alaska's rough-and-tumble history, █Anchorage Museum of History and Art, 121 W. 7th Ave., tops all the others in the state. (☎343-4326. Open mid-May to mid-Sept. daily 9am-6pm, Sept. 16-May 14 Tu-Sa 10am-6pm, Su 1-5pm. $6.50, seniors and military $6, under 18 $2.) The █Alaska Native Heritage Center, 8800 Heritage Ctr. Dr., has amazing cultural shows, storytelling, and dancing from Alaska's 11 Native American traditions, and can be reached via buses #4 and 75. (☎330-8000. First right off the North Muldoon exit from the Glenn Hwy. Open daily 9am-6pm. $21, seniors and military $19, ages 7-16 $16, under 7 free.) At **Resolution Park,** off L St., take in views of Cook Inlet, Mt. Sustina, beluga whales, and Denali. Near town off Northern Lights Blvd., **Earthquake Park** recalls the 1964 Good Friday quake, which at 9.2 on the Richter scale was the biggest ever recorded in North America.

In town, hikers and bikers crowd the 11 mi. **Tony Knowles Coastal Trail,** one of the best urban bike paths in the country; in the winter, it's groomed for cross-country skiing. The serene **Chugach State Park,** surrounding the city to the north, east, and south, has roughly 30 established day-hiking trails, including the difficult **Flattop Mountain** (4500 ft.), the most frequently climbed mountain in Alaska. A bit farther from Anchorage along the Seward Hwy., the bohemian ski town of Girdwood and the **Alyeska Ski Resort** (☎800-880-3880) offer world-class terrain. **Nancy Lake State Recreation Area,** just west of the Parks Hwy. (Rte. 3) near Mile 67.3, contains the **Lynx Lake Loop,** at the Tanaina Lake Canoe Trailhead, Mile 4½ of the Nancy Lake Pkwy. Canoeing the entire loop takes 1-2 days and weaves through 8 mi. of lakes and portages with designated campsites along the way. (Boil water before drinking). Nancy Lake also has **cabins ❷** for $35-50 per night (☎269-8400). For **canoe rental,** call **Tippecanoe.** (☎495-6688; www.paddle-alaska.com. Open mid-May to mid-Sept. Call for hours.) **Lifetime Adventures** leads guided float and whitewater trips down **Eagle River,** 10min. from Anchorage in the Chugach State Park. (☎800-952-8624; www.lifetimeadventures.net. Class III trip $30, float and wildlife trip $55.)

SEWARD AND KENAI FJORDS   ☎907

Seward serves as a gateway to the hulking tidewater glaciers and yawning ice fields of **Kenai Fjords National Park** and the alpine trails of **Chugach National Forest. Exit Glacier,** the only road-accessible glacier in the park, lies 9 mi. west of Mile 3¾ of the Seward Hwy. (Rte. 9). **Kenai Fjords Tours** leads a variety of informative boat tours to different locations in the park. (☎224-8068 or 800-478-8068. 3-9½hr. $59-149, children $30-75.) **Major Marine Tours** brings along a ranger to narrate natural history. (☎800-764-7300. 3-6hr. $54-117, children $27-58.) **Sunny Cove Sea Kayaking** offers a joint trip with Kenai Fjords Tours, including a wildlife cruise, a salmon bake, kayaking lessons, and a 2½hr. wilderness paddle. (☎224-8810. 8hr. Joint trips $149-169, daytrips $59-129.) Though pricey, **Scenic Mountain Air's** flight tours provide the best views of **Harding Ice Field's** vastness. (☎288-3646. 45min. tours from $89 per person, 1hr. tours from $159.)

The rustic **Snow River Hostel ❷**, Mile 16 of the Seward Hwy., lures travelers with a peaceful atmosphere under the eaves of the surrounding Chugach National Forest. (☎440-1907. Dorms $15. Cozy cabin for 2 $40. Office open daily 6-10pm.) Gaze at the peaks across the bay while fishing from the front deck of the **Alaska Saltwater Lodge ❹**, 3 mi. south of town in Lowell Point on Beach Rd. (☎224-5271. Rooms with full bath and continental breakfast $85; view rooms with 2 double beds $139.) ▓**Exit Glacier Campground ❶**, at the end of the road to Exit Glacier, creates the idyllic illusion of roughing it alone on the glacier outwash, complete with food storage, pit toilets, and a cooking shelter. (Max. stay 14 days. Walk-in, tents-only campsites. Free.) Four public-use cabins are available, but three of the four are only accessible by boat or plane. The fourth is only open in winter when the roads are closed. (☎271-2737. Open for reservations after Jan. 2. $35.) Rejoice in Seward's fresh fish and relaxed atmosphere at the ▓**Railway Cantina ❷**, 1401 4th Ave., where the Cantina's flagship meal, halibut burritos ($8), arrive with chips, Mexican slaw, and a choice of salsas. (☎224-8226. Open June to mid-Sept. daily 11am-8pm; Jan.-May M-F 11am-6pm.) Mountainous portions of reindeer sausage and salmon and a thoroughly Alaskan feel grace the **Exit Glacier Salmon Bake ❹**, Mile ¼ Exit Glacier Rd. The salmon bake dinner ($19) includes a hefty portion of salmon with an array of sides. (☎224-2204. Open mid-May to Sept. daily 4:30-10pm; Oct.-Apr. M and Th-Sa 6-10pm.)

Seward is 127 mi. south of Anchorage on the scenic **Seward Highway (Route 9).** Most services cluster in the small boat harbor on Resurrection Bay. The **Alaska Marine Highway** (☎800-642-0066) docks at Port Ave., just before Seward, with connections to: Homer (25hr., $121) via Kodiak (12hr., $70); Valdez (12hr., $74). At the **Alaska Railroad** depot (☎265-2300), trains leave for Anchorage in summer at 6pm. (Round-trip $98, ages 2-11 $49.) **Park Connection** (☎800-266-8625), located at the small boat harbor, has two buses daily to Anchorage at 10:30am and 6:30pm. (3hr., $49.) The **Kenai Fjords National Park Visitors Center** is at the small boat harbor. (☎224-7500. Open in summer daily 9am-6pm.) **Post Office:** 507 Madison Ave. (☎224-3001. Open M-F 9:30am-4:30pm, Sa 10am-2pm.) **Postal Code:** 99664.

DENALI NATIONAL PARK   ☎907

Only a solitary ribbon of gravel less than 100 mi. long dares to interrupt Denali's six million acres of snowcapped peaks, braided streams, and glacier-carved valleys. Visitors to the park are guests of the countless grizzly bears, moose, caribou, wolves, and Dall sheep that thrive here. With 18,000 of its 20,320 ft. towering over the surrounding lands, the park's centerpiece, Denali (Mt. McKinley), is the tallest mountain in North America. August is an excellent time to visit—fall colors peak, mosquito season has virtually ended, and September's snows have not yet arrived. Be sure to check out the park's newspaper, *Alpenglow*.

▊ TRANSPORTATION. The **George Parks Highway (Route 3)** is a smooth road to the park, 240 mi. north from Anchorage or 125 mi. south from Fairbanks. The dirt **Denali Highway (Route 8)** meets the Parks Hwy. 27 mi. south of the park entrance at Cantwell and extends 140 mi. east to Paxson, but is closed in winter. The **Alaska Railroad** (☎265-2494 or 800-544-0552; open daily 10am-5pm) stops at Denali Station, 1½ mi. from the park entrance, and runs to Anchorage (7½hr., $125) and Fairbanks (4½hr., $50). **Parks Highway Express** (☎888-600-6001) runs motor coaches daily from Anchorage (5½hr., $119 round-trip) and Fairbanks (3½hr., $74).

Only the first 15 mi. of the park road are accessible by private vehicle; the remaining 75 mi. of dirt road can be reached only by shuttle bus, camper bus, or bicycle. **Shuttle buses** leave from the visitors center daily 5am-6pm, pause at the sighting of any major mammal, and turn back at various points along the park road. Most buses are wheelchair accessible. **Camper buses** transport only those with campground or backcountry permits, and move faster than the shuttle buses. (☎272-7275 or 800-622-7275. $18-35, ages 13-16 half-price. Call for schedule.) Avoid sold-out shuttles by booking ahead by phone or online at www.nps.gov/dena.

7 PRACTICAL INFORMATION. All travelers must stop at the **Denali Visitors Center,** ½ mi. from the Parks Hwy. (Rte. 3), for orientation. Most park privileges are first come, first served; conduct business at the visitors center as early as possible. (☎683-1266. Open daily Memorial Day-Labor Day 7am-8pm; late Apr. to Memorial Day and Labor Day to late Sept. 10am-4pm. 7-day entrance fee $5; families $10.) **Denali Outdoor Center,** at Parks Hwy. Mile 238.5, north of the park entrance, rents bikes. (☎683-1925. Half-day $25, full-day $40.) **Medical Services: Healy Clinic,** 13 mi. north of the park entrance. (☎683-2211. On call 24hr.) **Post Office:** ¼ mi. inside the park entrance. (☎683-2291. Open May-Sept. M-F 8:30am-5pm, Sa 10am-1pm; Oct.-Apr. M-Sa 10am-1pm.) **Postal Code:** 99755. **Area Code:** 907.

☎◨ ACCOMMODATIONS AND FOOD. The rustic ▩**Denali Mountain Morning Hostel ❶,** 13 mi. south of the park entrance, has showers, Internet, groceries, four free park shuttles per day, helpful advice, and outdoor gear rental. (☎683-7503; www.hostelalaska.com. Backpacker kit $40 first day, $10 each additional day. 4- to 6-bed bunks $25, ages 5-13 $19. Private rooms from $65. 2-bed cabins $50. Reservations recommended.) **Campers** must obtain a permit from the visitors center and may stay for up to 14 nights per year in the six **campgrounds ❶** lining the park road. (☎272-7275 or 800-622-7275 for reservations. Sites $9-18, large-group campsites $40. First come, first served sites are distributed rapidly at the visitors center.) Most campgrounds are open May-September and have running water and toilets. All except Sanctuary River are wheelchair accessible. Backcountry campers must watch a 30min. video and attend a safety talk to obtain a free backcountry permit.

Once you board that park bus, there is no food available anywhere. **Riley Creek Mercantile** provides groceries from its convenient location next to Riley Creek Campground. (☎683-9246. Open daily 5am-10pm.) At **Black Bear Coffee House ❶,** 1 mi. north of the park entrance, the coffee is hot and strong, the muffins are fresh, and the staff is all smiles. (☎683-1656. Sandwiches $8. Internet access $5 per 30min. Open May-Sept. daily 6:30am-10pm.)

◪ FLIGHTSEEING. Oddly, the best services for flightseeing around Denali are actually in Talkeetna, 60 mi. to the south, where the same flights come at cheaper prices. If the weather cooperates, these flights are worth every penny and will leave you itching for more. Flights come in two standard flavors: a 1hr. flight approaching the mountain from the south (from $135 per person), and a 1½hr. tour that circumnavigates the peak ($190-200). The 15-30min. glacier stop-off costs an extra $55-60 per person but is definitely worthwhile. All flights are weather-dependent; most companies fly over the rugged Talkeetna Mountains to the south if Denali weather is uncooperative. Discounts to groups of four or five may be available. In Talkeetna, **K2 Aviation** (☎733-2291 or 800-764-2291), **McKinley Air Service** (☎733-1765 or 800-564-1765), **Doug Geeting Aviation** (☎733-2366 or 800-770-2366), and **Talkeetna Air Taxi** (☎733-2218 or 800-533-2219) offer standard services, plus a variety of other specialized trips. All flight services suspend glacier landings in mid-July due to unpredictable snow conditions. In Denali, try **Denali Air** (☎683-2261) or **ERA Helicopters Flightseeing Tours** (☎683-2574; www.eraaviation.com).

⚑ OUTDOOR ACTIVITIES. The best way to experience Denali is to get off the bus and explore the land. Beyond Mile 15 (the point which only shuttle and camper buses can cross), there are no trails. As long as you don't plan on staying overnight, no permits are required, although you will need a shuttle ticket. You can begin day-hiking from anywhere along the park road by riding the shuttle bus to a suitable starting point and asking the driver to let you off. It's rare to wait more than 30min. to flag a ride back. **Primrose Ridge,** beginning at Mile 16, is bespangled with wildflowers and has spectacular views of the Alaska Range and the carpeted emerald valley below. A walk north from Mile 14 along the **Savage River** provides a colorful, scenic stroll through this valley. **Polychrome Overlook** at Mile 47 offers a spectacular 360° view of the park and grants easy ridge access. The more challenging **Mt. Healy Overlook Trail** affords the best views, climbing from the hotel parking lot to an impressive 3400 ft. view. (5 mi. round-trip; 1700 ft. elevation gain; 3-4hr.) **Discovery hikes** are guided 3-5hr. hikes departing on special buses from the visitors center. The $23 cost includes bus fare; 1-2 day advance reservations required.

There are no trails in the backcountry. The park's backcountry philosophy rests on the idea that independent wandering creates more rewards and less impact than would a network of trails or routes. Only two to 12 backpackers can camp at a time in each of the park's 43 units. Overnight stays in the backcountry require a free permit, available 24hr. in advance at the backcountry desk in the visitors center. Hikers line up outside as early as 6:30am to grab permits for popular units. Talk to rangers and research your choices with the handy *Backcountry Unit Description Guides* and *Denali Backcountry Companion*, available at the visitors center, which also sells essential topo maps ($6.50). Most zones in Denali require that food be carried in bear-resistant food containers, available for free at the backcountry desk. With the park's cool, drizzly weather and many rivers and streams, your feet will get wet. Hypothermia can set in quickly and quietly; talk with rangers about prevention and warning signs. Mosquito repellent is a must.

FAIRBANKS ☎ 907

Fairbanks stands unchallenged as North American civilization's northernmost hub. Things have changed since the free-wheeling, gold-mining days—which lasted well into the 1960s—when prospectors ruled the city. Even so, Fairbanks remains a frontier town, where men outnumber women, four-wheel-drive pickups choke the streets, and beer flows more freely than the Chena River's waters. From here, adventurers can drive, float, or fly to experience the true Arctic wilderness.

⛏ PRACTICAL INFORMATION. Most attractions lie in the square of Airport Way, College Rd., Cushman Blvd., and University Way. Fairbanks is bicycle-friendly, with wide shoulders and multi-use paths. **Fairbanks International Airport,** 2½ mi. southwest of the city, is on Airport Way. **Alaska Railroad,** 280 N. Cushman St. (☎ 458-6025 or 800-544-0552; open daily 6:30am-3pm and for evening arrivals), runs one train daily to Anchorage ($175) via Denali ($50), with less service during the winter. **Parks Highway Express** (☎ 888-600-6001) runs buses daily to Anchorage ($84) and Denali ($44). **Municipal Area Commuter Service (MACS)** runs buses through downtown. (☎ 459-1011. $1.50; students, seniors, and disabled $0.75; children under 5 free. Day pass $3. Operates M-F 6:15am-7:45pm, limited service Sa; in winter M-F 9am-6:15pm.) **Taxi: King Alaska Taxi** ☎ 455-7777. **Visitor Info:** 550 1st Ave. (☎ 456-5774 or 800-327-5774. Open daily in summer 8am-8pm; in winter 8am-5pm.) The **Alaska Public Lands Info Center,** 250 Cushman St., #1A, is in the basement of the Federal Building, at Courthouse Sq. (☎ 456-0527. Open in summer daily 9am-6pm; in winter Tu-Sa 10am-6pm.) **Post Office:** 315 Barnette St. (☎ 452-3223. Open M-F 9am-6pm, Sa 10am-2pm.) **Postal Code:** 99709, **General Delivery** 99701. **Area Code:** 907.

ACCOMMODATIONS AND FOOD. ⬛**Boyle's Hostel ❶**, 310 18th Ave., has a TV in every room and a full kitchen. (☎456-4944. Showers and laundry. Dorms $17; private doubles $30; cabins $15 per person.) ⬛**Billie's Backpackers Hostel ❶**, 2895 Mack Rd., is a cluttered but welcoming place to meet outdoorsy international travelers. (☎479-2034. Common room, laundry, and free Internet access. 10 bunks in coed rooms. Tent sites $15, dorms $22. Private rooms available.) The **Fairbanks Hotel ❸**, 517 3rd Ave., has spacious Art Deco rooms with cable TV and wireless Internet. (☎456-6411. Complimentary airport/train shuttle and bike rental. Singles with shared bath $55, with private bath $89; doubles $65/$110.) **Chena River State Campground ❶**, off Airport Way on University Ave., has a boat launch and camping on a quiet stretch of the river. (73 sites. $10-15.) An artery-blocking good time fills Airport Way and College Rd. ⬛**Bun on the Run ❶**, located in a trailer in the parking lot between Beaver Sports and the Marlin on College Rd., whips up scrumptious pastries. (Hours vary.) ⬛**Second Story Cafe ❷**, 3525 College Rd., above Gulliver's, has the best and freshest wraps in town, plus salads, sandwiches, and veggie-friendly soups. All wraps and sandwiches cost $6.50. (☎474-9574. Open M-F 9am-9pm, Sa 9am-7pm, Su 10am-5pm.) A chic addition to the Fairbanks culinary scene, **Cafe Alex ❸**, 310 1st Ave., serves contemporary fusion cuisine. (☎452-2539. Entrees $7-12. Open M-Th 11:30am-2pm and 5-10pm, F 11:30-2pm and 5-11pm, Sa 5-11pm.)

SIGHTS AND SKIING. The ⬛**University of Alaska Museum,** a 10min. walk up Yukon Dr. from the Wood Center, features a thorough look at the Aleut/Japanese evacuation during WWII, Native culture, and Blue Babe, a 36,000-year-old steppe bison recovered from the permafrost. (☎474-7505. Open mid-May to mid-Sept. daily 9am-7pm; mid-Sept. to mid-May M-F 9am-5pm, Sa-Su noon-5pm. $5, ages 7-17 $3, seniors $0.50, under 6 free.) Stand upwind of the **Large Animal Research Station,** which offers a rare chance to see baby musk oxen and other Arctic animals up close. Take Farmer's Loop to Ballaine Rd. and turn left on Yankovich; the farm is 1 mi. up on the right. (☎474-7207. Full tours Memorial Day-Labor Day daily 1:30 and 3:30pm; 30min. tours daily 10:45am and 2:25pm; night tours Tu-Sa 6:30pm. $5, seniors $4, students $2.)

Moose Mountain, 20min. from Fairbanks, has over 30 ski trails. Take the Parks Hwy. to the Sheep Creek Rd. exit. (☎479-4732; www.shredthemoose.com. Open F-Su 10am-5pm, or dusk. Lift tickets $27, students with ID $22, ages 7-12 $17. Snowboard or ski rentals $20.) **Mt. Aurora SkiLand,** 2315 SkiLand Rd., holds over 20 trails. Take a right onto Fairbanks Creek Rd. off the Steese Hwy. (Rte. 6) at Mile 20½ and then turn left. (☎389-2314. Open Nov.-Apr. on weekends, holidays, and spring break 10am-6pm or dusk. Lift tickets $25, students with ID $20, ages 6-11 and seniors $15. Rentals $20/$15/$10.)

ENTERTAINMENT AND NIGHTLIFE. The **Blue Loon Saloon,** 2999 Parks Hwy., screens a range of movies most nights ($5), and has music some nights with higher covers. The grille serves a bar menu ranging $2-14. (☎457-5666. Open in summer Tu-Sa 5pm-late; in winter M-Sa 5pm-late.) In mid-July, Fairbanks citizens don old-time duds and whoop it up for **Golden Days,** a celebration of Felix Pedro's 1902 discovery that sparked the Fairbanks gold rush. A sports spectacular, the **World Eskimo-Indian Olympics,** July 20-23, 2005, gathers Native Alaskans from all over the state in tests of strength and survival. Witness the ear pull, but be warned: ears have been pulled off in this event. (☎452-6646; www.weio.org.)

BARROW   ☎907

Barrow (pop. 4500) holds a distinctive position as the northernmost point of the US. Polar bears prowl the pack ice on the edges of this town of mostly Inupiat (Eskimo) descent. With no roads leading out of town, lonely Barrow must fly in all of its supplies, and most visitors arrive on one- or two-day **"A Day At The Top"** package tours via Alaska Airlines (☎800-468-2248). But don't be fazed by the remoteness or the frosty temperatures—Barrow offers a challenging exploration of the Arctic at its wildest and most desolate.

The **Inupiat Heritage Center,** on Ahkovak St. and North Star St., has exhibits on the indigenous people, natural history, native whaling, and more. Performances, games, art shows, and the annual spring whale hunt blend the border between archaic relics and living culture. (Open M-F 8:30am-5pm. $5, students $2, ages 7-14 $1, under 6 and seniors free.) A **hike** above the Arctic Circle to **Point Barrow,** the northernmost tip of the US, is reward enough for those who come for the latitude. Take Stevenson St. north out of town, past the **Naval Arctic Research Laboratory (NARL)** to a beachy area. The road ends in front of a sign warning of polar bears, and a strenuous walk along a sandy spit leads to Pt. Barrow. **Alaskan Arctic Adventures** runs polar bear tours and trips to Pt. Barrow. (☎852-3800. 2-2½hr. polar bear tours $60 per person, 2-person min.)

Out of town in the NARL complex, **NARL Hotel ❸,** Beach Rd., Bldg. 360, caters mainly to visiting scientists with warm, comfortable rooms. (☎852-7800. Shared bath. Singles $75; doubles $90. Cash or check only.) With immaculate pine furnishings, **King Eider Inn ❺,** 1752 Ahkovak St., has become a lodging of choice for those with money to spend. (☎852-4700. $170; in winter $150.) 🔳**Arctic Pizza ❷,** 125 Apayuak St., cranks out the best pizzas north of the Arctic Circle ($18), Mexican dishes, and—go figure—Indian food. (☎852-4222. Open daily 11:30am-11:30pm.)

Air transportation provides the only year-round access to Barrow. The **airport** is on Ahkovak St., on the south edge of town. The **bus** system ($1) runs two routes in town and one to the NARL complex. (☎852-2611, ext. 689.) The **police** (☎852-6111) provide 24hr. dispatch services for the **North Slope Borough Search and Rescue** (☎852-2822), which also lends emergency beacons to hikers. Beacons may also be obtained from the **Barrow Volunteer Search and Rescue.** (☎852-2808.) The **post office** sits at Eben Hopson St. and Tahak St. (☎852-6800. Open M-F 9am-5pm, Sa 10am-1pm.) **Postal Code:** 99723. **Area Code:** 907.

THE PANHANDLE

Southeast Alaska, sometimes called "the Panhandle," spans 500 miles from the Misty Fjords National Monument to Skagway and the foot of the Chilkoot Trail. Countless straits weaving through the Panhandle, collectively known as the **Inside Passage,** divide up thousands of islands, inlets, and fjords. The absence of roads in the steep coastal mountains has helped most Panhandle towns maintain their small size and hospitable personalities.

KETCHIKAN   ☎907

Ketchikan may be Alaska's fourth-largest city, but its island location enlaces the town's fringes with dense wilderness, stunting sprawl and attracting an array of eclectic residents. Surrounded by the Tongass National Forest and Misty Fjords National Monument, Ketchikan provides a vital base for some of the most outstanding hiking, kayaking, fishing, and flightseeing in southeast Alaska.

🔳 **PRACTICAL INFORMATION.** Ketchikan clings to Revillagigedo Island (ruh-VIL-ya-GIG-a-doe). Renting a bike may be the most economic way to see the sights out of town. The **airport** is across from Ketchikan on Gravina Island, connected to town by a small **ferry.** (Every 30min., more during peak times. $4, ages 6-12 $2, under 6 free; cars $6.) **Alaska Marine Highway** (☎800-642-0066) docks at the far end of town on N. Tongass Hwy. and goes to: Juneau ($99); Sitka ($77); Wrangell ($35). **The Bus** blue line route loops between the airport parking lot near the ferry terminal, the dock, and Saxman Village. (☎225-8726. M-Sa every 30min. 5:30am-11pm, Su every hr. 9am-3pm. $2.25; seniors, students, and children $2.) **Taxi: Sourdough Cab** ☎225-5544. **Visitor Info: Ketchikan Visitors Bureau,** 131 Front St., on the cruise ship docks downtown. (☎225-6166 or 800-770-3300; www.visit-ketchikan.com. Open daily 8am-5pm.) **Southeast Alaska Discovery Center (SEADC),** 50 Main St., helps plan outdoor adventures in the Tongass. (☎228-6220. Open early May-late Sept. M-Sa 8am-5pm, Su 8am-4pm; late Sept.-early May Tu-Sa 10am-4:30pm.) **Post Office:** 3609 Tongass Ave. (☎225-9601. Open M-F 8:30am-5pm.) **Postal Code:** 99901. **Area Code:** 907.

◪◱ ACCOMMODATIONS AND FOOD. The **Ketchikan Reservation Service** specializes in B&Bs. (☎800-987-5337. Singles from $75.) The **Ketchikan Youth Hostel (HI) ❶,** at Main and Grant St. in the First Methodist Church, has clean and functional dorm rooms. (☎225-3319. Common area, kitchen. 4-night max. stay. Lockout 9am-6pm. Curfew 11pm. Call ahead if arriving on a late ferry. Open June-Aug. $12, nonmembers $15. No credit cards.) Rooms and furnishings are elegant and individual at the **New York Hotel ❹,** 207 Stedman St. (☎225-0246. Singles $99. Less for multiple nights. Prices drop by as much as 60% in the winter.)

Campgrounds are a refuge from expensive beds. **Signal Creek ❶** sits on Ward Lake Rd. in the temperate rainforest. Drive 5 mi. north of the ferry terminal on Tongass Hwy. and go right at the sign for Ward Lake. Bring your fishing gear. (☎877-444-6777. Water, pit toilets. Open June-Sept. Sites $10.) Ten miles north of Ketchikan on Revilla Rd., the **Last Chance** campground has 19 campsites, 17 of which are wheelchair accessible. Most sites are first come, first served, but some can be reserved. (☎877-444-6777. Toilets, water, garbage cans. Sites $10.)

The freshest seafood swims in **Ketchikan Creek;** in summer, anglers frequently hook king salmon from the docks by Stedman St.) ◪**Ocean View Restaurante ❷,** 1831 Tongass Ave., serves enchiladas and pizza with equal gusto. The fried ice cream is a winner for dessert. (☎225-7566. Entrees $8-10. Open daily 11am-11pm.) Come to the **New York Cafe ❷,** 207 Stedman St., for soup, healthful lunch specials (around $8), and veggie options. (☎225-2645. Open M-Sa 7am-3pm, Su 8am-2pm.

◪◪ SIGHTS AND NIGHTLIFE. Saxman Totem Park, south of town on the Tongass Hwy., has brightly colored carvings collected and restored from ancestral villages in southeast Alaska—the state's largest collection of totems. The **Totem Heritage Center,** 601 Deermount St., up Park St., houses 33 19th-century totem poles from Tlingit, Haida, and Tsimshian villages in their raw, unrestored state. (☎225-5900. Open May-Sept. daily 8am-5pm; Oct.-Apr. M-F 1-5pm. $5.) A $11 combination ticket also provides admission to the **Deer Mountain Fish Hatchery and Eagle Center,** across the creek. (☎225-6760. Open May-Sept. daily 8am-4:30pm. $8.) **First City Saloon,** ¼ mi. north of the tunnel on Water St., is the most festive hangout in town and liberally distributes Guinness and a variety of microbrews. (☎225-1494. Live local music in summer Tu-Sa; varies in winter. Open M-Sa noon-2am, Su 4pm-2am.) **Arctic Bar,** 509 Water St., is a hop, skip, and stagger north of the downtown tunnel. Distinguished by its copulating bears logo, this popular bar sports a deck with a harbor view. (☎225-4709. Open in summer daily 9am-2am; winter hours vary but usually opens at 9am.)

◪ OUTDOOR ACTIVITIES. A hike up the 3001 ft. **Deer Mountain** provides inexpensive access into the wilderness. Walk up the hill past the city park on Fair St.; at the crossroads, follow the signs, and veer right to the trailhead. A steep climb yields sparkling views of the sea and surrounding islands. While most hikers stop at the peak after 2½ mi., the trail continues for another 8 mi., past Blue Lake and over John Mountain to Silvas Lake. This portion of the trail is poorly marked, and snow and ice are common on the peaks into summer; arrange transportation at the far trailhead, bring raingear, and inform someone in town of your planned return date. Ketchikan offers sumptuous **kayaking** in nearby Tongass Narrows, Naha Bay, George Inlet, and the Tatoosh Islands. Only experienced kayakers should tackle the waters alone; beginners can join **Southeast Sea Kayaks** for small-group guided tours with personal attention. (☎225-1258. 2½hr. Pennock Paddling $76; 4hr. Orca Cove $139.) They also rent kayaks. (Singles $40 per day; doubles $65.)

◪ DAYTRIP FROM KETCHIKAN: MISTY FJORDS NATIONAL MONUMENT.
The sawtooth peaks, ravine abysses, and dripping vegetation of Misty Fjords National Monument, 22 mi. east of Ketchikan, make biologists swoon and outdoors enthusiasts drool. Only accessible by boat or float plane, the 2.3 million-acre park offers superlative camping, kayaking, hiking, and wildlife viewing. **Camping ❶** is permitted throughout the park, and is best on the sandy beaches, though there are no established campsites or facilities. The Forest Service maintains four first come, first served three-sided **shelters** (free) and 14 **cabins** ($25; max. stay 7 nights). Cabins may be reserved in advance. Contact the **Misty Fjords Ranger Station**, 3031 Tongass Ave. (☎225-2148), in Ketchikan, or ask the SEADC (p. 1064) for advice. Misty Fjords is one of North America's most popular destinations for proficient sea kayakers. **Southeast Sea Kayaks** charges $200 per person for drop-off and pick-up at the entrance to the fjords. For independent trip planning, contact SEADC for helpful suggestions and advice. **Flightseeing** is one of the best ways to see the park; most flights are based out of Ketchikan. Check out **Taquan Air** (☎225-8800) and **Island Wings** (☎888-854-2444), who both run a similar 1½hr. trip for $199.

JUNEAU ☎907

Springing up during the gold rush, Juneau went from hard-rock mining capital to Alaska's state capital. Built upon the fortunes of its mines, the city now has the most diverse economy, cultural sights, and population of any city in southeast Alaska. Accessible only by water and air, Juneau is still swamped by hordes of travelers heading for the Mendenhall Glacier, numerous hiking trails, and access to Glacier Bay, so be prepared to share the beauty.

◪ PRACTICAL INFORMATION. Franklin Street is the main drag downtown. **Glacier Highway (Egan Drive)** connects downtown, the airport, the Mendenhall Valley, and the ferry terminal. **Juneau International Airport** is 9 mi. north on Glacier Hwy. **Alaska Marine Highway** (☎465-3940; www.ferryalaska.com) docks at the Auke Bay terminal, 14 mi. north of the city on the Glacier Hwy., and runs to: Haines (4½hr., $32); Ketchikan (18-36hr., $90); Sitka (9hr., $37). **Capital Transit** runs buses from Main St. downtown to within 1½ mi. of the Mendenhall Glacier every 30min., with express service to the airport every hour. (☎789-6901. Runs M-Sa 7am-11:30pm, Su 9am-6:30pm; express bus M-F 8:10am-5pm. $1.50.) **Juneau Taxi** (☎586-2121) runs to the airport ($20). The **visitors center** is at 101 Egan Dr. in Centennial Hall. (☎586-2201 or 888-581-2201. Open June-Sept. M-F 8:30am-5pm, Sa-Su 9am-5pm; Oct.-May M-F 9am-4pm.) The **Forest Service**, 8465 Old Dairy Rd., has trail maps and hiking information. (☎586-8800. Open M-F 8am-5pm.) **Trail Hotline,** ☎856-5330. **Post Office:** 709 W. 9th St. (☎586-7987. Open M-F 9am-5pm.) **Postal Code:** 99801. **Area Code:** 907.

◪◪ ACCOMMODATIONS AND FOOD. On a steep hill, the spacious ▨**Juneau International Hostel (HI) ❶**, 614 Harris St., at 6th St., exudes a relaxed atmosphere and provides Internet access, kitchen, and laundry facilities. (☎586-

9559; www.juneauhostel.org. Reception May to mid-Sept. 7-9am and 5pm-midnight; mid-Sept. to Apr. 8-9am and 5-10:30pm. Lockout 9am-6pm. Reservations available by phone. Beds $10, ages 6-17 with parent $5, under 5 free.) **Alaskan Hotel ❸**, 167 S. Franklin St., downtown, has been restored to its original 1913 decor. (☎800-327-9347. Laundry, baggage storage. Singles and doubles with shared bath $60, with private bath $80. 1-4 person studios $90, $10 each additional person.) **Mendenhall Lake Campground ❶** has stunning views of the glacier and trail access. Take Glacier Hwy. north 10 mi. to Mendenhall Loop Rd. and turn left on Montana Creek Rd. (Open June-Sept. Firepits, water, toilets, and firewood. First come, first served. Sites $10, full hookup $26.) Local favorite **Fiddlehead Restaurant ❸**, 429 Willoughby Ave., has the best gourmet vegetarian options in town. (☎586-3150. Open June-Aug. daily 7am-9:30pm; Sept.-May M-F 7am-9pm, Sa-Su 8am-9pm.)

▨ OUTDOOR ACTIVITIES. The steep ▨**Mt. Roberts Trail** winds 5 mi. round-trip through old-growth forest and alpine meadows, past gorgeous views to the summit of Mt. Roberts. The trail begins at the end of 6th St., up a stairway. The ▨**West Glacier Trail** begins off Montana Creek Rd., by the Mendenhall Lake Campground. The strenuous 3½ mi. walk yields stunning views of **Mendenhall Glacier** from the first step in the western hemlock forest to the final outlook at the peak of 4226 ft. **Mt. McGinnis.** At the end of Basin Rd., the easy **Perseverance Trail** (3 mi. one-way) leads to the ruins of the Silverbowl Basin Mine and booming waterfalls. **Tracy Arm,** a mini-fjord near Juneau, is known as "the poor man's Glacier Bay," for it offers the same spectacular beauty as the national park at under half the cost. **Auk Nu Tours,** 76 Egan Dr., has a naturalist on board for its iceberg-studded cruise through Tracy Arm. (☎800-478-3610. 8hr. tour $119, under 18 $70; includes lunch, snacks, and binoculars.) **Above and Beyond Alaska** (☎364-2333) offers customized kayak trips from Juneau, as well as **glacier treks,** including overnight trips and ice climbing.

GLACIER BAY NATIONAL PARK ☎907

Explorer Jean François de Galaup de la Perouse called Glacier Bay "perhaps the most extraordinary place in the world." Crystal monoliths, broken off of glaciers, float peacefully in fjords, while wildlife maneuver through the icy blue depths. The landscape of this roadless, trailless park changes daily as about a dozen of its glaciers advance and retreat at geologically rapid speeds, opening new land for colonization by plants and wildlife. Only two centuries ago, the **Grand Pacific Glacier** covered the entire region under a sheet of ancient ice. Charter flights, tours, and cruise ships all probe Glacier Bay, providing encounters with glaciers, rookeries, whales, and seals. The bay is divided into two major arms: the **West Arm** reaches north to the termini of the Grand Pacific and Margerie Glaciers, which advance 6 ft. every year, while the **East Arm,** closed to most motorized boat traffic, is a solitude-filled haven for kayakers. **Mt. Fairweather,** part of the highest coastal range in the world, reigns over it all.

Getting to **Bartlett Cove,** the principle access point to the bay, is relatively easy. A plane takes visitors to **Gustavus,** and from there a taxi or shuttle (about $20) goes to **Glacier Bay Lodge** and the **Visitor Information Station** (☎697-2230; open daily June-Aug. 7am-9pm; May and Sept. 8am-5pm), both close to the campground in the immediate Bartlett Cove area. The ferry from Juneau docks directly at Bartlett Cove. All visitors must attend an orientation at the Visitors Information Center to receive a first come, first served permit. Wilderness camping (pick up a bear-resistant food container at the info station) and hiking are permitted throughout the park, though there are no trails except the two near the lodge. Backcountry hiking and kayaking are possible in the Dry Bay area, as is **rafting** down the Alsek River. For info, contact the **Yakutat District Office** of the National Park Service (☎784-3295). The Glacier Bay Lodge operates a daily **Glacier Cruise** popular with both sightseers and paddlers optimizing their time in the upper bay. The boat delivers (and picks up) kayakers, hikers, and their gear at rotating locations within the bay. (☎264-4600 or 888-229-8687. $95, round-trip $190, tour alone $160.)

 THE END. Congratulations! You've made it across the North American continent, conceivably from Key West (p. 538) to Barrow (p. 1062), meaning you've earned your stripes (and stars). Take a deep breath, get your film developed, and get some sleep. Thanks for taking us along for the ride.

ALASKA

DISTANCES (MI.) AND TRAVEL TIMES (BY BUS)

	Atlanta	Boston	Chic.	Dallas	D.C.	Denver	L.A.	Miami	N. Orl.	NYC	Phila.	Phnx.	St. Lou.	Sa. Fran.	Seattle	Trnto.	Vanc.	Mont.
Atlanta		1108	717	783	632	1406	2366	653	474	886	778	1863	560	2492	2699	959	2825	1240
Boston	22hr.		996	1794	442	1990	3017	1533	1542	194	333	2697	1190	3111	3105	555	3242	326
Chicago	14hr.	20hr.		937	715	1023	2047	1237	928	807	767	1791	302	2145	2108	537	2245	537
Dallas	15hr.	35hr.	18hr.		1326	794	1450	1322	507	1576	1459	906	629	1740	2112	1457	2255	1763
D.C.	12hr.	8hr.	14hr.	24hr.		1700	2689	1043	1085	225	139	2350	845	2840	2788	526	3292	665
Denver	27hr.	38hr.	20hr.	15hr.	29hr.		1026	2046	1341	1785	1759	790	860	1267	1313	1508	1458	1864
L.A.	45hr.	57hr.	39hr.	28hr.	55hr.	20hr.		2780	2005	2787	2723	371	1837	384	1141	2404	1285	2888
Miami	13hr.	30hr.	24hr.	26hr.	20hr.	39hr.	53hr.		856	1346	1214	2368	1197	3086	3368	1564	3505	1676
New O.	9hr.	31hr.	18hr.	10hr.	21hr.	26hr.	38hr.	17hr.		1332	1247	1535	677	2331	2639	1320	2561	1654
NYC	18hr.	4hr.	16hr.	31hr.	5hr.	35hr.	53hr.	26hr.	27hr.		104	2592	999	2923	2912	496	3085	386
Phila.	18hr.	6hr.	16hr.	19hr.	3hr.	33hr.	50hr.	23hr.	23hr.	2hr.		2511	904	2883	2872	503	3009	465
Phoenix	40hr.	49hr.	39hr.	19hr.	43hr.	17hr.	8hr.	47hr.	30hr.	45hr.	44hr.		1503	753	1510	2069	1654	2638
St. Louis	11hr.	23hr.	6hr.	13hr.	15hr.	17hr.	35hr.	23hr.	13hr.	19hr.	16hr.	32hr.		2113	2139	810	2276	1128
San Fran.	47hr.	60hr.	41hr.	47hr.	60hr.	33hr.	7hr.	59hr.	43hr.	56hr.	54hr.	15hr.	45hr.		807	2630	951	2985
Seattle	52hr.	59hr.	40hr.	40hr.	54hr.	25hr.	22hr.	65hr.	50hr.	55hr.	54hr.	28hr.	36hr.	16hr.		2623	146	2964
Toronto	21hr.	11hr.	10hr.	26hr.	11hr.	26hr.	48hr.	29hr.	13hr.	11hr.	13hr.	48hr.	14hr.	49hr.	48hr.		4563	655
Vancvr.	54hr.	61hr.	42hr.	43hr.	60hr.	27hr.	24hr.	67hr.	54hr.	57hr.	56hr.	30hr.	38hr.	18hr.	2hr.	53hr.		4861
Montreal	23hr.	6hr.	17hr.	28hr.	12hr.	39hr.	53hr.	32hr.	31hr.	7hr.	9hr.	53hr.	23hr.	56hr.	55hr.	7hr.	55hr.	

INDEX

INDEX

MAP INDEX

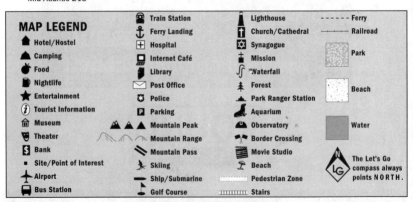

MAP LEGEND

- 🏨 Hotel/Hostel
- ⛺ Camping
- 🍴 Food
- 🍷 Nightlife
- ★ Entertainment
- ℹ️ Tourist Information
- 🏛 Museum
- 🎭 Theater
- $ Bank
- ▪ Site/Point of Interest
- ✈ Airport
- 🚌 Bus Station

- 🚆 Train Station
- ⚓ Ferry Landing
- ✚ Hospital
- 💻 Internet Café
- 📗 Library
- ✉ Post Office
- ✪ Police
- P Parking
- ▲▲▲ Mountain Peak
- 〰 Mountain Range
- ⬎ Mountain Pass
- 🎿 Skiing
- ➖ Ship/Submarine
- ⛳ Golf Course

- 🗼 Lighthouse
- ✝ Church/Cathedral
- ✡ Synagogue
- ✝ Mission
- ∫ Waterfall
- 🌲 Forest
- 🔺 Park Ranger Station
- 🦭 Aquarium
- 🔭 Observatory
- 🚩 Border Crossing
- 🎬 Movie Studio
- 🏖 Beach
- ⬛ Pedestrian Zone
- ▥ Stairs

- ----- Ferry
- ———— Railroad
- ▨ Park
- ⬚ Beach
- ⬛ Water

LG The Let's Go compass always points NORTH.